Contents

ON THE ROAD

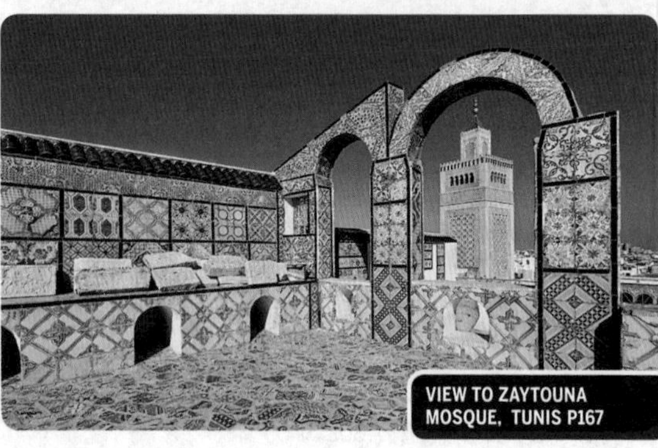
YOSHIO TOMII / GETTY IMAGES ©

VIEW TO ZAYTOUNA MOSQUE, TUNIS P167

Contents

UNDERSTAND

SURVIVAL GUIDE

SPECIAL FEATURES

Welcome to Africa

Something special about Africa touches the soul; it is a continent of 54 immensely diverse countries that is both deeply troubled and profoundly uplifting.

Natural Beauty

Whether you're a wide-eyed first-timer or a frequent visitor, Africa cannot fail to get under your skin. The canvas upon which the continent's epic story is written is itself astonishing, and reason enough to visit. From the tropical rain forests of Central Africa to the endless rippling dunes and waterless tracts of the Sahara, from the signature savannah of the east to jagged mountains and green-tinged highlands all across the continent, Africa has few peers when it comes to natural beauty.

Wildlife Bonanza

A Noah's Ark of wildlife brings these landscapes to life, with a tangible and sometimes profoundly mysterious presence that adds so much personality to the African wild. So many of the great beasts, including elephants, hippos and lions, call Africa home. Going on safari may be something of a travel cliché, but we're yet to find a traveller who has watched the wildlife world in motion in the Masai Mara, stumbled upon the paradise that is the Ngorongoro Crater, or communed with gorillas in Uganda's Bwindi Impenetrable National Park, and has not been reduced to an ecstatic state of childlike wonder.

Ancient Africa

But there's so much more to Africa than nature's considerable bounty. On this continent where human beings first came into existence, customs, traditions and ancient rites tie Africans to generations past and to the collective memory of myriad people. In many rural areas, it can feel as though the modern world might never have happened, and old ways of doing things – with a certain grace and civility, hospitality and a community spirit – survive. Welcome to Old Africa.

New Africa

Even as the past retains its hold over the lives of many Africans, just as many have embraced the future, bringing creativity and sophistication to the continent's cities and urban centres. Sometimes this New Africa is expressed in a restless search for solutions to the continent's problems, or in an eagerness to break free of the restrictive chains of the past. But just as often, modern Africans are taking all that is new and fusing it onto the best of the old. The continent is still prone to all the ills of humanity, but if you come with an open mind it's easy to see how amazing Africa can be.

Why I Love Africa

By Simon Richmond, Author

Some of my most evocative travel memories of Africa – amazing live concerts in the shadow of Table Mountain, the mad circus of Marrakesh's Djemaa el-Fna – are musical ones. Boy, can this continent bang out a beat! Africa's enormously talented musicians pay homage to the traditions of the past at the same time as they push the boundaries of contemporary music. The fruits of their labours provide a constantly evolving playlist to the continent's diversity and an unforgettable soundtrack to your African journey. The results can be stunning and are always unmistakeably African.

For more about our authors, see page 1128

Above: Elephant in front of Mount Kilimanjaro

Africa

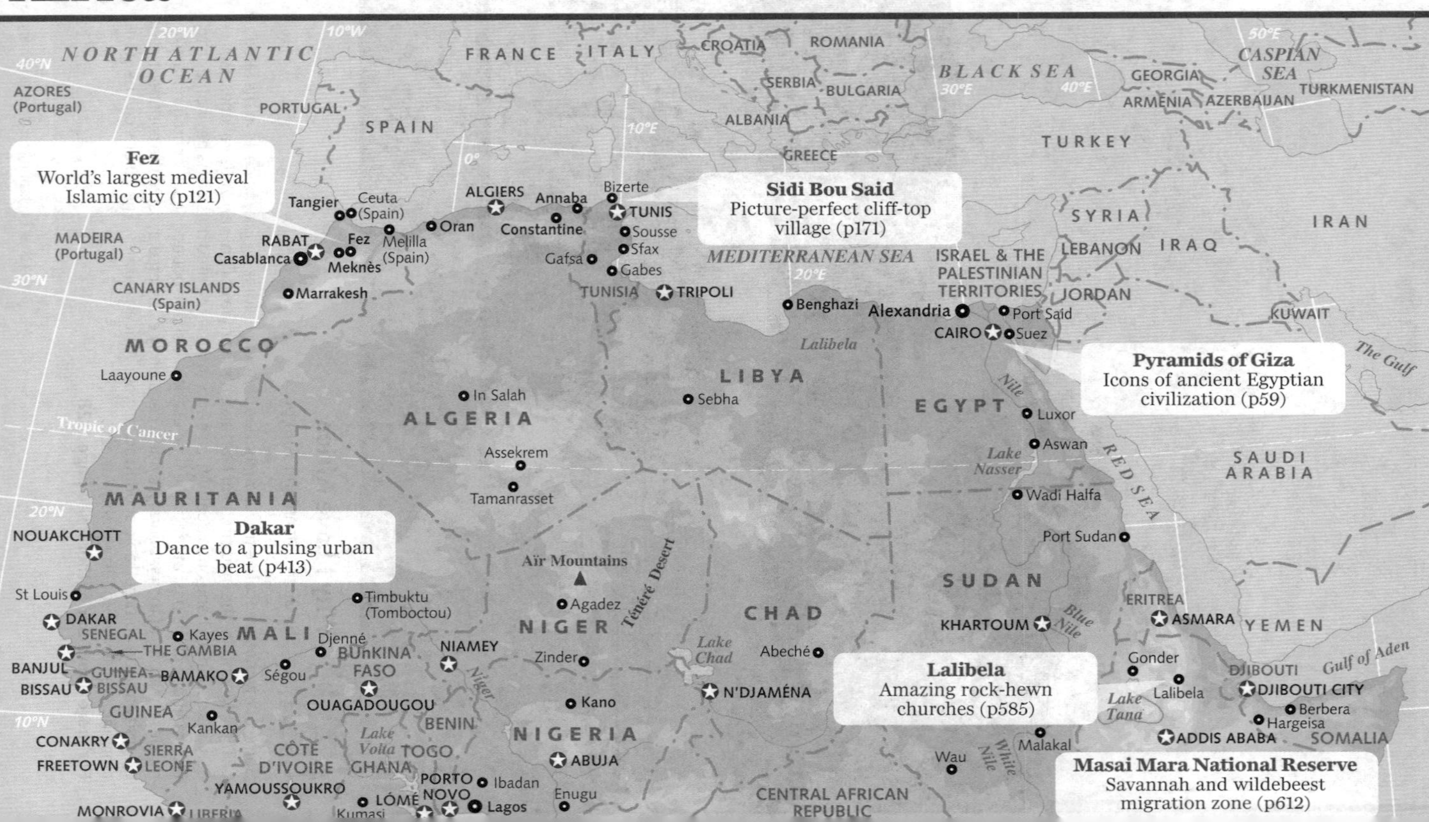

Fez
World's largest medieval Islamic city (p121)
Sidi Bou Said
Picture-perfect cliff-top village (p171)
Pyramids of Giza
Icons of ancient Egyptian civilization (p59)
Dakar
Dance to a pulsing urban beat (p413)
Lalibela
Amazing rock-hewn churches (p585)
Masai Mara National Reserve
Savannah and wildebeest migration zone (p612)
NORTH ATLANTIC OCEAN
AZORES (Portugal)
MADEIRA (Portugal)
CANARY ISLANDS (Spain)
PORTUGAL
SPAIN
FRANCE
ITALY
CROATIA
ROMANIA
SERBIA
BULGARIA
ALBANIA
GREECE
BLACK SEA
GEORGIA
ARMENIA
AZERBAIJAN
CASPIAN SEA
TURKMENISTAN
TURKEY
SYRIA
LEBANON
IRAQ
IRAN
ISRAEL & THE PALESTINIAN TERRITORIES
JORDAN
KUWAIT
The Gulf
SAUDI ARABIA
YEMEN
Gulf of Aden
MEDITERRANEAN SEA
RED SEA
Tangier
Ceuta (Spain)
Melilla (Spain)
RABAT
Casablanca
Fez
Meknès
Marrakesh
Oran
ALGIERS
Constantine
Annaba
Bizerte
TUNIS
Sousse
Sfax
Gafsa
Gabes
TUNISIA
TRIPOLI
Benghazi
Alexandria
Port Said
CAIRO
Suez
MOROCCO
Laayoune
Tropic of Cancer
ALGERIA
In Salah
Assekrem
Tamanrasset
LIBYA
Sebha
Lalibela
EGYPT
Nile
Luxor
Aswan
Lake Nasser
Wadi Halfa
Port Sudan
MAURITANIA
NOUAKCHOTT
St Louis
DAKAR
SENEGAL
THE GAMBIA
BANJUL
GUINEA-BISSAU
BISSAU
GUINEA
CONAKRY
SIERRA LEONE
FREETOWN
MONROVIA
LIBERIA
MALI
Kayes
BAMAKO
Ségou
Kankan
Djenné
Timbuktu (Tombouctou)
BURKINA FASO
OUAGADOUGOU
CÔTE D'IVOIRE
YAMOUSSOUKRO
Lake Volta
GHANA
Kumasi
TOGO
LOMÉ
BENIN
PORTO NOVO
NIAMEY
Niger
NIGER
Aïr Mountains
Agadez
Ténéré Desert
Zinder
Kano
NIGERIA
ABUJA
Ibadan
Lagos
Enugu
CHAD
Lake Chad
Abeché
N'DJAMÉNA
CENTRAL AFRICAN REPUBLIC
SUDAN
KHARTOUM
Blue Nile
White Nile
Malakal
Wau
ERITREA
ASMARA
Gonder
Lalibela
Lake Tana
ADDIS ABABA
DJIBOUTI
DJIBOUTI CITY
Berbera
Hargeisa
SOMALIA
40°N
30°N
20°N
10°N
20°W
10°W
0°
10°E
20°E
30°E
40°E
50°E

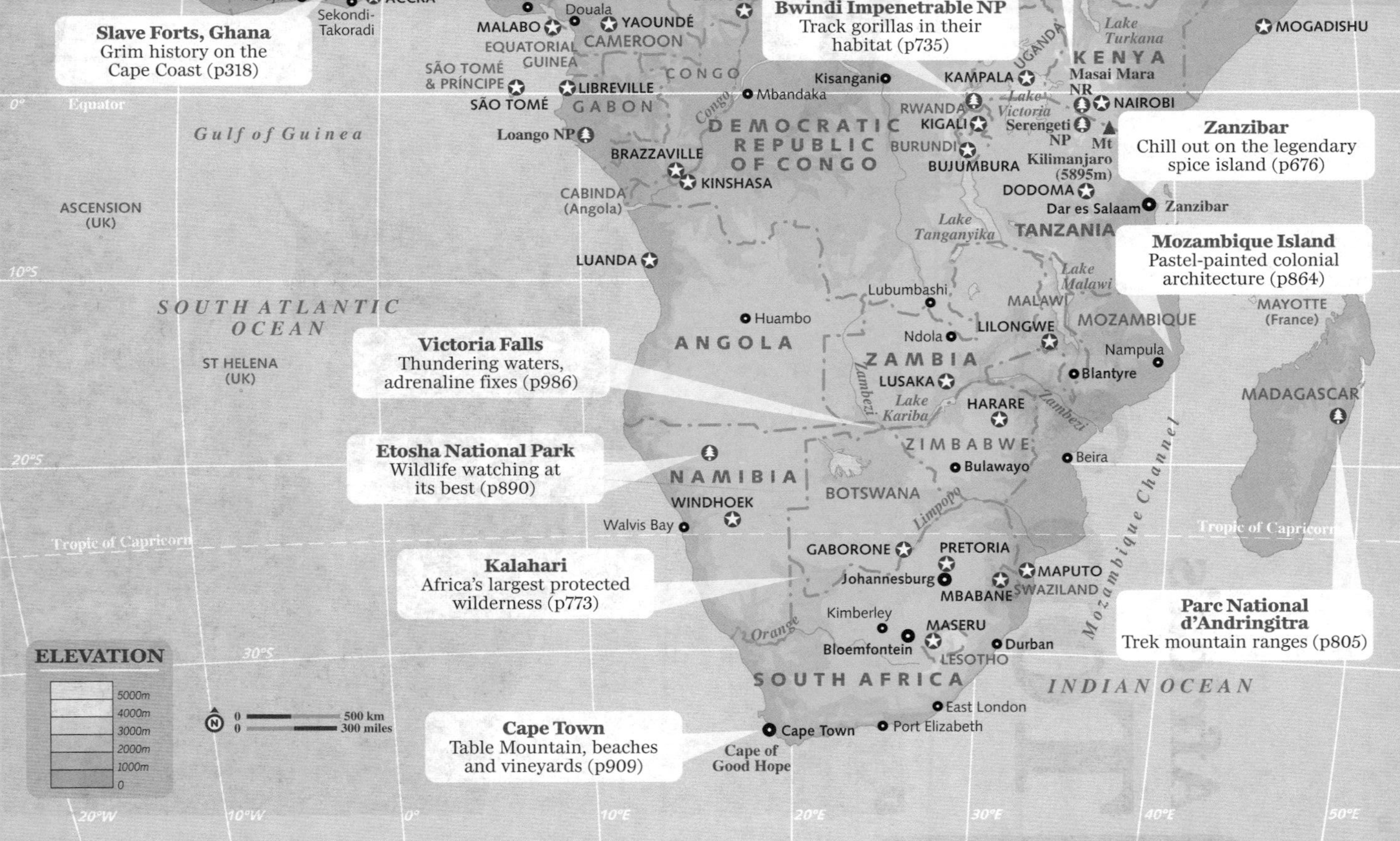
Slave Forts, Ghana
Grim history on the Cape Coast (p318)
Bwindi Impenetrable NP
Track gorillas in their habitat (p735)
Zanzibar
Chill out on the legendary spice island (p676)
Mozambique Island
Pastel-painted colonial architecture (p864)
Victoria Falls
Thundering waters, adrenaline fixes (p986)
Etosha National Park
Wildlife watching at its best (p890)
Kalahari
Africa's largest protected wilderness (p773)
Parc National d'Andringitra
Trek mountain ranges (p805)
Cape Town
Table Mountain, beaches and vineyards (p909)
Abidjan
Sekondi-Takoradi
ACCRA
Port Harcourt
Douala
MALABO
YAOUNDÉ
BANGUI
MOGADISHU
EQUATORIAL GUINEA
CAMEROON
SÃO TOMÉ & PRÍNCIPE
SÃO TOMÉ
LIBREVILLE
GABON
CONGO
Loango NP
Equator
Gulf of Guinea
Kisangani
Mbandaka
Congo
DEMOCRATIC REPUBLIC OF CONGO
BRAZZAVILLE
KINSHASA
CABINDA (Angola)
ASCENSION (UK)
LUANDA
UGANDA
KAMPALA
Lake Turkana
KENYA
Masai Mara NR
NAIROBI
RWANDA
KIGALI
Lake Victoria
Serengeti NP
Mt Kilimanjaro (5895m)
BURUNDI
BUJUMBURA
DODOMA
Dar es Salaam
Zanzibar
Lake Tanganyika
TANZANIA
Lake Malawi
MALAWI
LILONGWE
MOZAMBIQUE
Nampula
Blantyre
MAYOTTE (France)
MADAGASCAR
Lubumbashi
Huambo
ANGOLA
Ndola
ZAMBIA
LUSAKA
Zambezi
Lake Kariba
HARARE
ZIMBABWE
Bulawayo
Beira
Mozambique Channel
NAMIBIA
WINDHOEK
Walvis Bay
BOTSWANA
Limpopo
GABORONE
PRETORIA
Johannesburg
MBABANE
MAPUTO
SWAZILAND
Kimberley
Bloemfontein
MASERU
LESOTHO
Durban
Orange
SOUTH AFRICA
East London
Port Elizabeth
Cape Town
Cape of Good Hope
SOUTH ATLANTIC OCEAN
ST HELENA (UK)
INDIAN OCEAN
Tropic of Capricorn
ELEVATION
5000m
4000m
3000m
2000m
1000m
0
0 500 km
0 300 miles
0°
10°S
20°S
30°S
20°W
10°W
10°E
20°E
30°E
40°E
50°E

Africa's Top 21

1

Bathing in Devil's Pool, Victoria Falls, Zambia

1 The mighty Victoria Falls offers many viewpoints but none so gut-wrenching as from the aptly named Devil's Pool (p986). Adrenaline fiends can take the precarious walk, literally out across the top of the falls, to this natural infinity pool. Test your nerve by leaping in where the water will carry you to the edge, only to be stopped by the natural barrier on the lip of this massive sheer curtain of water. Lap it up while peeking over the edge for the ultimate bird's-eye view.

Pyramids of Giza, Egypt

2 The last of the seven wonders of the ancient world stands right on the edge of Cairo, as if guarding the desert from the city's creeping urban sprawl. You may have seen the images a thousand times beforehand but nothing beats your first face-to-face meeting with the impeccable geometry and sheer bulk of this mammoth funerary complex (p59). Battered by the passing of time, from the Sphinx's chipped nose to the graffiti of past explorers, these age-old structures have not lost their ability to awe.

YVETTE CARDOZO / GETTY IMAGES ©

2

DOMINIK PABIS / GETTY IMAGES ©

Medinas of Fez & Marrakesh, Morocco

3 Ancient meets modern in the medinas of Morocco, and those of Fez (p121) and Marrakesh (p128) sit at the top of any travel list. Narrow alleyways hide centuries-old riads restored into guesthouses, while the deliveryman outside unloads his donkeys while chatting on his mobile phone. Fez is the older city, with mosques and the longest and most-winding streets, while in Marrakesh all paths seem to converge on the Djemaa el-Fna square, which springs to life daily with 1001 nights' worth of attractions. Medina, Marrakesh

Mozambique Island, Mozambique

4 There are no crowds and few vehicles, but Mozambique Island (p864) is hardly silent. Echoes of its past mix with the squawking of chickens, the sounds of children playing and the calls of the muezzin to remind you that the island is still very much alive. Wander along cobbled streets, past graceful squares rimmed with once-grand churches and colonial-era buildings. This Unesco World Heritage Site, with its time-warp atmosphere and backdrop of turquoise seas, is a highlight and not to be missed.

3

4

ANDREW BURKE / GETTY IMAGES ©

NIGEL PAVITT / GETTY IMAGES ©

ART DIRECTORS & TRIP / ALAMY ©

Lalibela, Ethiopia

5 Follow a white-robed pilgrim down a dark passageway, hear the hypnotic thud of a muffled drumbeat, smell the sweet aroma of incense and emerge into a sliver of daylight just in time to see a priest in royal robes, holding a cross of gold, enter a church carved into and out of the rust red rock. Lalibela (p585) is a place of pilgrimage where the buildings are frozen in stone and the soul is alive with the rites and awe of Christianity at its most ancient and unbending.

Rock-hewn church, Lalibela

Stone Town in Zanzibar, Tanzania

6 Whether it's your first visit or 50th, Zanzibar's Stone Town (p676) never loses its touch of the exotic. You'll see the skyline, with the spires of St Joseph's Cathedral and the Old Fort. Wander through alleys that reveal surprises at every turn. Linger at dusty shops scented with cloves, watch as kanzu-clad men play the board game *bao*. Admire intricate henna designs on the hands of women in their *bui-bui* (a black cloak like a burka that devout muslim women use to cover up in public).

Dakar, Senegal

7 Hit West Africa's trendiest nightlife venues and swing your hips to *mbalax*, the mix of Cuban beats and traditional drumming that forms the heart and soul of the Senegalese music scene. Relax with a lazy day at the beach and feast on fresh-off-the-boat seafood, or explore the workshops of Senegal's most promising artists at the Village des Arts. Finally, climb up one of Dakar's 'breasts' to contemplate the controversial, socialist-style African Renaissance Monument and take in sweeping views across the city (p417).

Drummers and dancer, Dakar

DARYL BALFOUR / GETTY IMAGES ©

Walking Safari in South Luangwa National Park, Zambia

8 Strolling through the bush single file with a rifle-carrying scout in the lead, there's no Land Rover, no obstructed sight lines and no barrier between you and the wildlife, both predator and prey. Animals scurry in the underbrush on approach, so the focus is on the little things, including a *CSI*-like investigation of animal dung. Even simply sitting under a tree looking over a plain filled with munching grazers is an opportunity for a quasi-meditative immersion in the park (p983).

Sidi Bou Said, Tunisia

9 Mediterranean Africa doesn't get more enchanting than Sidi Bou Saïd (p171). These days, the clifftop village of blue shuttered houses is a suburb of Tunis, but it remains a world apart. Winding streets reveal spectacular bay views at every turn and cliffs of bougainvillea, eucalypt, pine and palm tumble down to a bijou beach. Its beauty has long drawn European artists and writers, most notably Paul Klee; now devotees descend by the tour-bus load. Come sunset, though, it's you and the locals: stroll, sip tea and take in the salty breeze.

Etosha National Park, Namibia

10 There are few places in Southern Africa that can compete with the wildlife prospects in extraordinary Etosha National Park (p890). A network of waterholes dispersed among the bush and grasslands surrounding the pan – a blindingly white, flat, saline desert that stretches into the horizon – attracts enormous congregations of animals. A single waterhole can render thousands of sightings over the course of a day – Etosha is simply one of the best places on the planet for watching wildlife.

Crossing the Sahara

11 The Sahara (p120) is a place of haunting beauty and crossing it is likely to be one of the most memorable journeys of your life. The classic west-coast route takes you through the wonders of Morocco and down into little-known Mauratania. On the opposite side of the continent you can roll back the pages of history as you amble lazily down the Nile from Egypt through Sudan and on up into Ethiopia. For the explorer there are a thousand other possibilities.

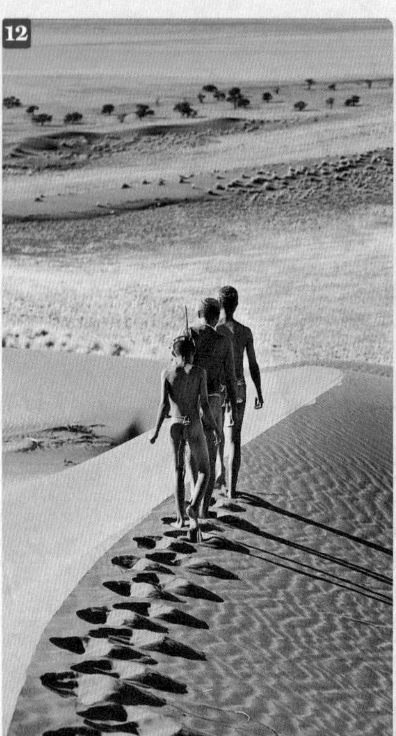

MARTIN HARVEY / GETTY IMAGES ©

JONATHAN AND ANGELA SCOTT / GETTY IMAGES ©

ANDREW MCCONNELL / GETTY IMAGES ©

Kalahari Landscape & People, Botswana

12 There's something about the Kalahari (p773). Perhaps it owes its unmistakable gravitas to its vastness; Africa's largest protected wilderness area is a place where the San inhabitants once roamed free and still guide travellers onto their ancestral lands. The presence of black-maned Kalahari lions doesn't hurt either. Whatever the reason, this is not your average desert; it's home to ancient river valleys, light woodland and surprising concentrations of wildlife around its extensive network of salt pans.

Wildlife on the Masai Mara, Kenya

13 The sweeping savannah of the Masai Mara (p612), studded with acacia trees and cut through by the occasional red-dirt road, is the perfect theatre for the world's most spectacular display of wildlife. Giraffes, elephant herds and zebras are just some of the sights you're pretty much guaranteed to see. The drama is at its most intense in August, the start of the tragi-comic wildebeest migration, when vast numbers of the hapless animals fall prey to rushing rivers, pacing lions and scavenging hyenas.

Congo Boat Adventure, Democratic Republic of Congo

14 You came to Africa for adventure right? Well this is adventure with a capital A. The slow boat ride between the DRC cities of Kisangani and Kinshasa down the Congo River (p507) can take anywhere from two to six weeks; you'll sleep on the deck of a creaky old barge, exposed to the elements alongside hundreds of others. Markets are held onboard, villagers paddle out selling bush meat and there's always a beer or two to be had. Bangui (CAR) to Brazzaville (Congo) is a shorter version.

Gorilla Tracking in Bwindi Impenetrable National Park, Uganda

15 It's one of the most thrilling wildlife encounters on the planet and nothing can prepare you for the moment you stand just metres from a family of mountain gorillas. It's a humbling experience, particularly that first glimpse of the silverback, whose size and presence will leave you in awe. The term 'once in a lifetime' is one that's bandied about a lot, but gorilla tracking in Bwindi (p735) is a genuine one that you'll cherish forever.

Cape Town, South Africa

16 Sitting in the continent's southwest corner, Cape Town (p909) is one of those places that travellers don't want to leave. The city is heavily peppered with fine restaurants, theatres, museums and galleries; the suburbs boast encounters with penguins, seals and baboons. The coast caters to beach babes, surfers and photographers with its white-sand beaches and craggy ocean-sprayed cliffs. And sitting amid it all is the ever-visible form of Table Mountain, a hub for adventure activities including hiking, climbing, mountain biking and abseiling.

15

16

Trekking in Parc National d'Andringitra, Madagascar

17 With more than 100km of trails, a majestic mountain range, three challenging peaks and epic landscapes, this national park (p805) is a trekker's paradise. Walkers will be rewarded with a dip in natural swimming pools and wonderful accommodation. You could also spend a couple of nights under the stars: the park office rents out everything you need to mount your very own expedition, from guides to cooks, porters and even camping equipment. Just don't forget a warm sleeping bag.

Las Geel Rock Art Site, Somaliland

18 Nothing brings you back to the roots of humanity like gaping at the rock paintings at Las Geel (p660). This enigmatic archaeological site feels like a time capsule into the prehistoric past. It was known only to locals until late 2002, when a team of French archaeologists undertook a field mission in Somaliland, finding rock paintings that are striking both for their rich complexity and incredible state of preservation. If that wasn't enough, the site is easily accessible from Hargeisa, the capital.

17

18

MAX MILLIGAN / GETTY IMAGES ©

ROBIN SMITH/ GETTY IMAGES ©

Lake Malawi, Malawi

19 This jewel in Malawi's crown is fringed by golden beaches and offers travellers an underwater palace to swim among brilliantly coloured chichlid fish. On this 'interior sea' (p835) are hidden idylls straight from a Bond movie like Mumbo Island and Likoma Island. Think turquoise coves, scuba diving, kayaking, candlelit beach dinners and rock-carved rooms…and you're halfway there.

Slave Forts, Ghana

20 No matter how well versed you are with the history of the slave trade, nothing can prepare you for the experience of visiting Ghana's slave forts (p318). Standing in the damp dungeons or being shut in the pitch-black punishment cells will chill your blood, and the wreaths and messages left by those whose forebears went through the ordeal are poignant. Cape Coast Castle and St George's Castle are the two largest and best-preserved forts, but there are also many smaller ones along the coast, that tell the same sorry tale.

Loango National Park, Gabon

21 Of Gabon's myriad spectacular national parks, Loango (p531) is the most impressive. Heaving with elephants, hippos, gorillas, monkeys and crocodiles, it offers long journeys through island-studded lagoons, nature hikes through virgin rainforest and walks along empty beaches. Whether you visit the luxuriously appointed north of the park, with its eye-wateringly expensive safari lodges, or choose a DIY approach in the charming hamlet of Setté Cama in the south, the impressive wildlife, the vast, Eden-like spaces and the charming locals will be the same.

Need to Know

For more information, see Survival Guide (p1063)

Currency
US dollar ($) is most readily recognised international currency; euros (€) and UK pounds (£) also accepted.

Languages
Locals may speak English, French, Portuguese or German depending on colonial history.

Money
ATMs increasingly common but don't rely on them or being able to pay by credit card; always carry sufficient cash.

Visas
For short trips sort out before leaving home; for longer ones, arrange as you go.

Mobile Phones
Buy local SIM cards to access local mobile networks cheaply.

Time
Four times zones from UTC (fomer GMT) in the west to UTC+3 in the east.

When to Go

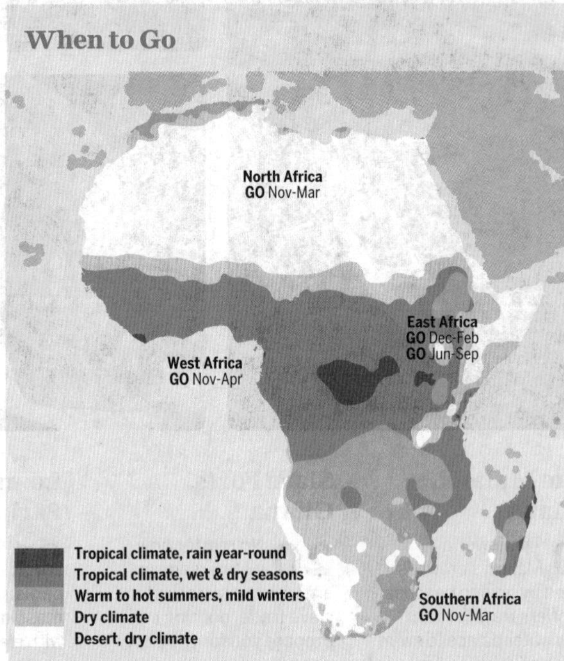

High Season

➡ **North Africa** Nov–Mar is the coolest period.

➡ **Central Africa** Jun–Sep is the dry time.

➡ **East Africa** Dec–Feb and Jun–Sep are the two main dry seasons.

➡ **West Africa** Nov–Apr is the dry season.

➡ **Southern Africa** Nov–Mar, but rain can continue until Dec in South Africa.

Shoulder

➡ **North Africa** Apr, May, Sep and Oct.

➡ **Central, West & Southern Africa** Oct and May.

➡ **East Africa** Mar and Oct.

Low Season

➡ **North & West Africa** Jun–Aug.

➡ **Central Africa** Nov–Apr.

➡ **East Africa** Apr, May and Nov.

➡ **Southern Africa** Jun–Sep.

Websites

- **Lonely Planet** (www.lonelyplanet.com) Good for pre-planning.
- **Sahara Overland** (www.sahara-overland.com) Best practical guide for travellers to the Sahara.
- **Ranger Diaries** (www.rangerdiaries.com) Lowdown from safari guides mainly covering Southern Africa.
- **Travel Africa** (www.travelafricamag.com) Features articles on every corner of the continent and a useful 'safari planner'.
- **Open Africa** (www.openafrica.org) Sustainable travel tool for Southern Africa.
- **African Studies Centre** (www.africa.upenn.edu/Home_Page/Country.html) Extensive links from the University of Pennsylvania's Africa program.

Daily Costs

Budget: less than US$50

- Guesthouse or basic hotel: US$10
- Eat at cafes and street stalls; shop in markets
- Travel on buses and 'bush' (shared) taxis

Midrange: US$50 to US$200

- Double room in midrange hotel: US$50 to US$70
- Lunch and dinner in restaurants
- Car hire: from US$30 per day

Top End: more than US$200

- safari-lodge room: US$200
- guided safari:from US$100 per day
- meal in top restaurant with wine: US$50 to US$100

Arriving in Africa

Cairo International Airport Buses E£2, every 20 minutes 7am to midnight, one hour to central Cairo; taxi around E£75.

Léopold Sédar Senghor International Airport Official taxi rates for trips to Dakar are put up outside the airport. Don't pay more.

Jomo Kenyatta International Airport Recommended to take taxi (KSh1200 to KSh1500, but bargain hard) to centre of Nairobi.

OR Tambo International Airport Taxi R9 to central Jo'burg; buses R7.90 to R19.80.

Getting Around

Travelling around much of Africa often requires time, patience and stamina. African public transport sometimes leaves and arrives roughly on time (off-the-beaten-track transport is more unreliable), but there are few interesting places that you cannot reach without your own car, even if you have to wait for a few days. If you can fly, this will save you considerable time and hardship on roads. However, flights can also be subject to delays, cancellations and bureaucratic pantomimes.

It's also worth remembering that some of your most memorable and enjoyable travel experiences will take place en route between places – in Africa, the journey is the destination.

Safety & Country Coverage

Eleven countries out of the 50 African nations covered in this guide have shorter chapters covering only the basics and background information; this approach has been adopted either because of security issues relating to travel in the territory or because the country is not on the general travel radar. Things change fast in Africa – places we list as dangerous might become safe and vice versa. Keep yourself up to date with what's happening on the ground by checking out reliable news websites such as bbc.co.uk.

For much more on **getting around**, see p1078

If You Like

Beaches & Islands

Many visitors looking for a break from life on the African road end up on a beach or island. And what beaches and islands!

Zanzibar The very name of this Tanzanian island conjures up a spicy heaven of perfume plantations, endless white beaches and whispering palm trees. (p676)

Lake Malawi Soft sand fringes the shore of this turquoise lake, where you can swim in fresh water and mingle with laid-back locals in reggae bars. (p835)

Tofo On Mozambique's southern coast, Tofo is legendary for its azure waters, sweeping white sands, rolling breakers and party atmosphere. (p859)

Limbe Blissful beach destination surrounded by banana plantations in the shade of Mt Cameroon. (p249)

Jerba This Tunisian island has an intoxicating mix of soft sandy beaches and idiosyncratic architecture. (p186)

Music

In Africa music is more than a way of life. It is a force. Get ready to feel it at these rhythmic destinations.

Harare Zimbabwe's capital has a rockin' music scene including major festivals such as the Harare International Festival of Arts. (p1001)

Cape Town Music is the lifeblood of the Mother City; groove at scores of musical events from November through March, including an international jazz festival. (p909)

Stone Town Hit the spice island of Zanzibar for its five-day Sauti za Busara Swahili Music Festival in February. (p676)

Essaouira Visit this laid-back Moroccan seaside resort in June for its Gnaoua and World Music Festival. (p115)

Abidjan Hit the bars and dance floors of Côte d'Ivoire's principal city and experience the crazy upbeat sound of *coupé-décalé*. (p270)

Saint-Louis This charming French colonial settlement in northern Senegal hosts an international jazz festival in May. (p429)

Markets & Bazaars

Mingle with locals in the continent's many colourful markets and bazaars. Hone your bargaining skills and support local enterprises by buying food and souvenirs.

Tunis Navigate the mazelike alleys of the medina and discover busy souqs, gorgeous ancient doorways and tiled cafes.(p166)

Fez and Marrakesh The medinas of both these star Moroccan destinations are marvelous places to soak up an exotic commercial atmosphere. (p121 & p128)

Addis Ababa The Merkato is possibly the largest open-air market on the continent; watch out for shady characters.(p574)

Kumasi The huge Kejetia market feels like it has colonised every corner of Ghana's second city; it's a great place to buy beautiful kente cloth and Ashanti crafts. (p321)

Banjul Join the frenzy of buying, bartering and bargaining for everything from fabric to false plaits at the mid-19th-century Albert Market. (p286)

World Heritage Sites

Among the 129 Unesco-designated World Heritage Sites of Africa, well over half are cultural or mixed, representing both natural and cultural factors.

Pyramids of Giza So iconic as to defy description, this trio of mausoleums plus a Sphinx are the last remaining wonder of the ancient world. (p59)

Lalibela A mind-blowing maze of rock-hewn churches: one of nine

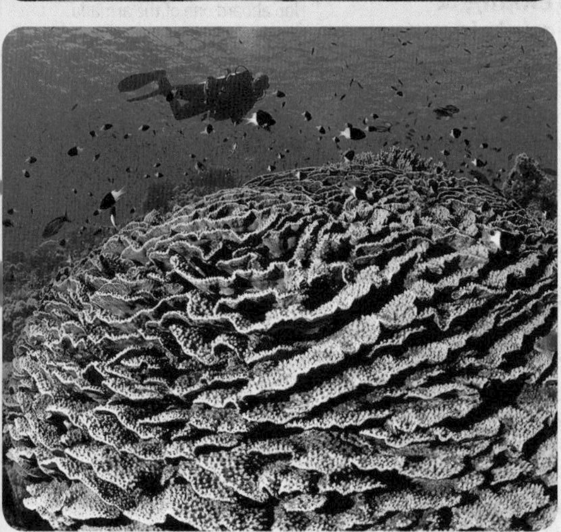

(Above) Marimba players, Harare International Festival of the Arts (p1001), Zimbabwe
(Below) Diver examining marine life in the Red Sea (p81), Egypt

World Heritage Sites in Ethiopia, the most in a single African country. (p585)

Elmina The 15th-century St George's Castle in this Ghanaian coastal town is one of the oldest European structures in sub-Saharan Africa. (p318)

Aksum Ponder the mysteries of the stelae in an Ethiopian town that may have been home to the Queen of Sheba. (p583)

Leptis Magma One of the best-preserved Roman cities in the Mediterranean includes the ornately carved Arch of Septimius Severus. (p99)

Adrenaline Activities

Many travellers are drawn to Africa by the lure of high-adrenaline thrills. If you're among them, you'll want to make a beeline for these locations.

Victoria Falls White-water rafting and a host of other adrenaline activities are on offer at both the Zambian and Zimbabwean sides of the 'smoke that thunders'. (p1015)

Swakopmund This Namibian town is becoming world famous for its chances to get sweaty and breathless on everything from sand-dune surfing to skydiving. (p883)

Jinja Ugandan base that combines the source of the Nile with white-water rafting, kayaking, mountain biking and quad bikes. (p727)

Storms River Take a dive from the world's highest bungee jump at Bloukrans River Bridge; the South African hamlet also has a tree-canopy slide. (p923)

Dahab A smooth fusion of hippie mellowness and resort chic rules at this Egyptian resort that's a prime base for diving and snorkelling in the Red Sea. (p78)

Inspiring Landscapes

Africa has few peers when it comes to natural beauty, encompassing everything from the shifting dunes of the Sahara to the steamy rain forests of the Congo.

Masai Mara National Reserve The northern extension of the equally famous Serengeti Plains is backed by the spectacular Siria Escarpment and is breathtaking any time of year. (p612)

Sani Pass Leading to the kingdom of Lesotho, this 2865m road pass is the highest in South Africa and affords spectacular views across the southern Drakensberg wilderness area. (p935)

Mt Kilimanjaro Its summit icecaps may be melting but the continent's highest peak remains a magnificent site. Hiking up it is an experience never forgotten. (p690)

Okavango Delta Take in the lush, watery scenery from a *mokoro*, a traditional dugout canoe. (p765)

Lac Abbé Sensational scenery of limestone chimneys across this moonscape in Djibouti. (p561)

Urban Adventures

Africans are leaving the countryside and flocking to cities in their legion. Sample the dynamic urban vibe in these booming metropolises.

Harare Join a meet-the-sculptors tour; enjoy top arts festivals and a lively music scene. (p1001)

Johannesburg South Africa's corporate capital, with a thriving black middle class and the famous township of Soweto. (p937)

Lagos The pluses of Africa's largest city include a superb live-music scene and West Africa's most inimitable street life. (p394)

Nairobi Kenya's crime capital is also a extremely dynamic and cosmopolitan city with a superb national park just a few miles from the city centre. (p598)

Maputo Easily one of the continent's most attractive capitals, this waterside city features Mediterranean-style architecture. (p851)

Antananarivo Climb cobbled streets up rocky hills past houses with painted shutters and soaring church spires. (p796)

Trekking & Mountaineering

As befitting a continent where humankind first walked out of the jungle, there are world-class hiking trails all across Africa, plus mountains so high they are capped by glaciers.

Mt Meru If you're not up to tackling Kilimanjaro, this nearby peak in Arusha National Park offers some lovely (and much cheaper) hiking. (p698)

Mt Kenya Africa's second-highest mountain crowns some wonderful hiking country and provides superb views. (p609)

Rwenzori Mountains National Park Uganda's fabled Mountains of the Moon feature snow and glaciers and a lack of other climbers. (p733)

High Atlas Tread steep paths past flat-roofed, earthen Berber villages, terraced gardens and walnut groves in this beautiful part of Morocco. (p132)

Otter Trail This glorious 42km hike along the South African coast from Storms River to Nature's Valley takes five day and four nights. (p924)

Overland Travel

It's the journey that matters in Africa – they are always memorable, be they on a rattling train or gliding down rivers or across lakes.

Cape Town to Jo'burg Cross the Karoo on the overnight Shosholoza Meyl trains. (p920)

Nampula to Cuamba A Southern African classic train journey through northern Mozambique. (p864)

Esna (for Luxor) and Aswan Hop aboard one of the armada of cruise boats that travel the Nile; alternatively sail in a felucca upriver from Luxor to Banana Island. (p89)

Yaoundé to N'Gaoundéré Riding the rails from Cameroon's lush capital is like crossing a continent with rain forests en route. (p245)

Kigoma and Mpulungu The venerable *MV Liemba*, a former WWI German battleship turned ferry, crosses Lake Tanganyika connecting Tanzania and Zambia. (p704)

Wadif Halfa to Dongola Hundreds of historic sites plus striking desert and river scenery line this 400km stretch of the Nile in Sudan. (p152)

Month by Month

TOP EVENTS

Cape Town Minstrel Carnival, January

Fespaco, February/March

La Cure Salée, September

Festival of the Dhow Countries, July

AfrikaBurn, April

January

High season across most of the continent, particularly sub-Saharan Africa. The northern hemisphere winter is also a cooler time to visit North and West Africa; one downside can be the early arrival of the dust-laden harmattan winds late in the month.

Cape Town Minstrel Carnival

Called the Kaapse Klopse in Afrikaans, the Mother City's equivalent of Mardis Gras (www.capetown-minstrels.co.za) runs throughout the month. The big parade on 2 January sees thousands take to the street in satin- and sequin-bedecked costumes.

Voodoo Festival

Held on 10 January across Benin; the celebrations in the voodoo heartland around Ouidah are the largest and most exuberant.

Timkat

Ethiopa's most important Christian festival is this celebration of Epiphany (19 January) involving elaborate costumed processions and ritual.

Mt Cameroon Race of Hope

In late January/early February Cameroonian and international athletes gather for the Race of Hope to the summit of Mt Cameroon, West Africa's highest peak.

February

Relatively cool, dry weather in North and West Africa makes for good hiking and it's the last month where you would sensibly head into the Sahel and Sahara. Southern Africa is still enjoying summer.

Hands on Harvest

The wine-producing region of Robertson, South Africa, celebrates the first of its five annual festivals (www.handsonharvest.com). Budding vintners can help with the harvest and sample the results.

Buganu (Marula) Festival

One of Swaziland's most popular 'first fruits' harvest festivals, Buganu celebrates the marvelous marula. Throughout this month and March women make *buganu* (marula wine), men drink the results and everyone celebrates. Swazi royals attend the three-day ceremony.

Sauti za Busara

The island of Zanzibar is the location of this Swahili music and dance festival (www.busaramusic.org) held in the middle of the month.

Festival au Désert

The troubles in Mali have sent this Tuareg culture-meets-rock-music festival (www.festival-au-desert.

ISLAMIC HOLIDAYS

The Hejira (Islamic calendar) is 11 days shorter than the Gregorian (Western) calendar, so Islamic holidays tend to fall 11 days earlier each Western year.

org) into exile; in 2013 it was staged in Kobenni in Mauritania. Check the website for future venues.

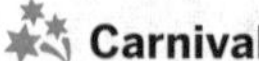

Carnival

West Africa's former Portuguese colonies celebrate Carnival (sometimes spelled Carnaval) with infectious zeal. Bissau – with its Latin-style street festival of masks, parties and parades – and Cape Verde are the places to be, while Porto Novo in Benin also gets into the spirit. Sometimes in January, sometimes March.

Mask Festivals

Held in the villages around Man in western Côte d'Ivoire, the region's most significant mask festival (Fêtes des Masques) brings together a great variety of masks and dances from the area.

Fespaco

Africa's premier film festival (www.fespaco-bf.net) is held in February/March in Ouagadougou in Burkina Faso in odd years. Cinemas across the city screen African films with a prestigious awards ceremony.

Argungu Fishing Festival

This fantastic fishing and culture festival takes place on the banks of the Sokoto River in Nigeria's north. It's celebrated with traditional music performances, sports and a massive regional market.

March

While temperatures are warming up in North and West Africa, the harmattan winds are blowing in Southern and some of East Africa. It's beginning to cool down as the season moves to autumn.

Infecting the City

Cape Town's squares, fountains, museums and theatres are the venues for this innovative performing arts festival (www.infectingthecity.com) featuring artists from across the continent.

Cape Argus Pick n Pay Cycle Tour

Held in mid-March, this spin around the Cape Peninsula is the world's largest timed cycling event (www.cycletour.co.za) attracting more than 30,000 contestants from serious racers to costumed Capetonians.

Kilimanjaro Marathon

Runners can take part in the full marathon, half marathon or fun runs around the base of the great Tanzanian mountain. The entire race (www.kilimanjaromarathon.com) is held between 830m and 1150m above sea level, on good tarred roads.

Maulid Festival

A huge celebration in Lamu, Kenya, this annual four-day celebration of the Prophet Mohammed's birthday falls in March/April.

Mardis Gras

Cape Verde can feel like Rio during the Mardi Gras, held 40 days before Easter. It's a sexy, spectacular carnival-type celebration with street parades, especially in Mindelo.

April

By now, much of the Sahel and Sahara are too hot for comfort and the harmattan is a staple throughout the month. The humidity along the West African coast and hinterland is starting to get uncomfortable. Meanwhile temperatures continue to drop in Southern Africa.

AfrikaBurn

Inspired by the USA's Burning Man event, this is both a subcultural blow-out and a survivalist challenge (www.afrikaburn.com). Art installations and themed camps turn a corner of South Africa's Karoo into a surreal experience even without mind-altering substances.

Jazz à Ouaga

An established fixture on West Africa's musical circuit, this fine festival (www.jazz-ouaga.org) traverses jazz, Afrobeat, soul and blues with some respected regional names in attendance.

May

Avoid the northern and western desert and coastal areas unless you favour extreme heat and humidity. Rains are also coming down in East and Southern Africa.

Harare International Festival of Arts (HIFA)

This six-day festival and workshop program (www.hifa.co.zw) showcases a range of arts and culture both local and international in scope.

Art Bienale

In even years in May/June, Dakar hosts the Dak'Art Biennale (http://www.biennaledakar.org), which is easily West Africa's premier arts festival. In addition to the main exhibitions, there's some fabulous fringe stuff happening.

June

The rains are well and truly underway in West Africa. Morocco and other North African countries start to see the annual influx of summer visitors from Europe. The month-long Islamic festival of Ramadan will start in June from 2014 to 2016.

National Arts Festival

Feel South Africa's creative pulse at the country's premier arts festival (www.nationalartsfestival.co.za), held in Grahamstown from late June to early July.

Gnaoua & World Music Festival

Held on the third weekend in June in Essaouira, this four-day musical extravaganza (www.festival-gnaoua.net/en) features international, national and local performers as well as a series of art exhibitions.

Festival of World Sacred Music

This world-renowned festival (www.fesfestival.com) based on the pluralism of Moroccan Sufism has in recent years attracted international stars such as Patti Smith, Youssou N'Dour and Salif Keita. Sometimes spills over into July.

July

Rain is heavy south of the Sahara – it's a good time for a travel bargain in South Africa, for example. In Morocco, Europeans flood the country; accommodation can be pricey and scarce.

Lesotho Ski Season

That's right, skiing in Southern Africa. Lesotho's peaks and passes receive snow in winter – particularly around Oxbow where a ski slope makes the most of snowfall. See Afri Ski resort (www.afriski.net).

Oyster Festival

There's no 'r' in the month which means it's the best time to travel to the South African Garden Route resort of Knysna to indulge in a 10-day oyster orgy (www.oysterfestival.co.za). Events include the Knysna Forest Marathon.

Festival of the Dhow Countries

The Zanzibar International Film Festival (www.ziff.or.tz) is the centrepiece of this two-week jamboree of arts and culture that can sometimes kick off at the end of June.

Harvest Festival

On the first Tuesday in July, Elmina (Ghana) hosts the colourful Bakatue Festival, a joyous harvest thanksgiving feast. One of its highlights is watching the priest in the harbour waters casting a net to lift a ban on fishing in the lagoon.

Fire Festival

In the heat of Tamale in Ghana, the Dagomba Fire Festival commemorates the local legend whereby a chief was overjoyed to find his missing son asleep under a tree. Angry that the tree had hidden his son, he punished it by having it burnt.

August

Rains and humidity make travel difficult in West and East Africa.

Panafest

Ghana's Cape Coast hosts the biennial Pan-African Historical Theatre Festival (Panafest; www.panafest-ghana.org) with a focus on African contemporary and traditional arts, including music, dance, fashion and theatre. Its centrepiece is a moving candlelit emancipation ceremony to honour African slaves.

Osun Festival

With nary a tourist in sight, the Osun Festival takes place in Oshogbo, 86km northeast of Ibadan in Nigeria, on the last Friday in August. It has music, dancing and sacrifices, and is a highlight of the Yoruba cultural and spiritual year.

September

The wet weather is beginning to ease in East and West Africa while Southern Africa moves out of winter towards spring,

look out for brilliant displays of wildflowers in South Africa's Northern and Western Cape regions. This is a good time to hit North African Mediterranean-facing countries minus the European crowds.

Hermanus Whale Festival

One of the world's best land-based whale-watching destinations is the town of Hermanus, 122km east of Cape Town – visit during this annual September/October 'enviro-arts festival' (www.whalefestival.co.za).

La Cure Salée

Niger's world-famous annual celebration by Fula herders features a male beauty contest and camel races, near In-Gall. It's in the first half of September but, like most Saharan festivals, it depends on the prevailing security situation.

Kano Durbar & Tabaski

West Africa's most colourful Tabaski celebrations are those in Kano where there are cavalry processions and high ceremony. Tabaski, which takes place 69 days after Ramadan, is widely celebrated in Muslim areas, especially Niger and Cameroon.

Ashanti Festivals

Coinciding with the yam harvest season, the Adae Kese Festival in Ghana celebrates the glorious Ashanti past and involves ritual purifications of the ancestral burial shrines.

October

Clear, post-rain skies make for good visibility and the high-season crowds have yet to arrive across much of the continent. Temperatures can be decidedly chilly in Morocco, especially in the High Atlas.

Artisans in Ouagadougou

In even-numbered years Ouagadougou hosts the Salon International de l'Artisanat de Ouagadougou (www.siao.bf), which attracts artisans and vendors from all over Africa.

November

The beginning of the month can be a quiet time to travel across the continent. Night-time temperatures in desert regions drop close to zero.

Grand Bassam Carnival

Close to Abidjan in Côte d'Ivoire, Grand Bassam hosts the Fête de l'Abissa (www.abissafestivale.com) in October/November. Over the course of a week, the N'Zima people honour their dead and exorcise evil spirits with big street parties and men in drag.

Mombasa Carnival

The Kenyan port city celebrates Rio-style with this street celebration of dance and music involving two converging parades.

International Sahara Festival

Held in Douz, Tunisia's oldest festival (going since 1910) is a showcase of Bedouin culture including camel and horse races, dancing and a marriage ceremony.

Old Mutual Kirstenbosch Summer Sunset Concerts

Sunday-afternoon concerts (www.dogreatthings.co.za/music/kirstenbosch) in Cape Town's gorgeous Kirstenbosch Botanical Gardens run from the end of November through early April with shows by top South African performers.

December

High season is very much underway south of the Sahara, and accommodation should be booked months in advance; beach areas are particularly busy with sun-starved Europeans. Weather is mild and dry.

East African Safari Rally

Participants in this classic car rally (www.eastafricansafarirally.com) covering Kenya, Tanzania and Uganda can only use pre-1971 vehicles.

Igue Festival

Also called the Ewere Festival, this colourful seven-day festival in Benin City, Nigeria, in the first half of the month, showcases traditional dances, mock battles and a procession to the palace to reaffirm local loyalty to the *oba* (king).

Itineraries

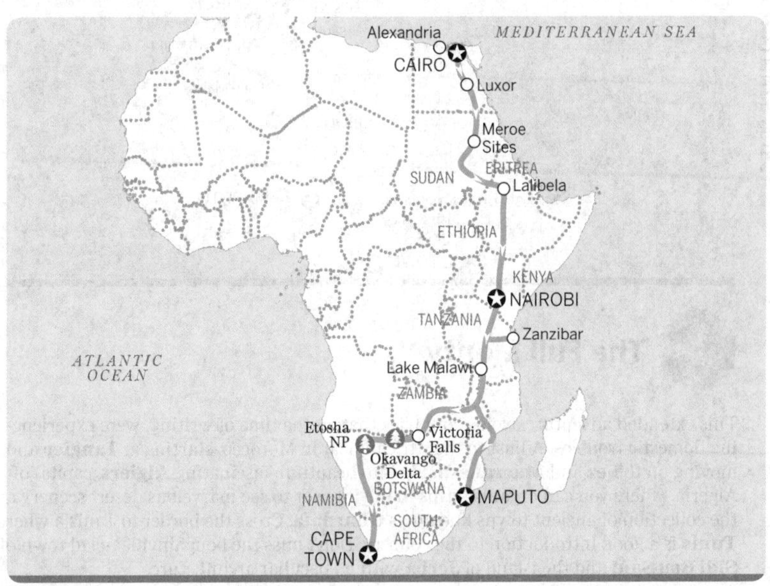

Top To Bottom

Who says you need a year to travel the length of Africa? The Cairo to Cape Town route can easily be tailored to a shorter time frame. Start off with a visual bang at the pyramids in **Cairo**, then head to the Mediterrenean coast to sample the colonial grandeur and period cafes of **Alexandria**. Return to Cairo and take the overnight train to **Luxor**, where you can explore the temples and tombs of ancient Egypt.

Continue south across Lake Nasser into Sudan where the glorious **Meroe Sites** and the rest of northern Sudan are the highlights. Ethiopia has some exceptional sites, especially **Lalibela**, before you journey down to **Nairobi**.

The wildlife-sprinkled plains of Kenya and Tanzania form the centrepiece of many classic African journeys; afterwards recharge your batteries by chilling out on **Zanzibar** or on the shores of beautiful **Lake Malawi**. Detour into Mozambique where you shouldn't miss dynamic **Maputo**.

Head to Zambia to experience breathtaking **Victoria Falls**, then on to the spectacular wildlife in Botswana's **Okavango Delta** and Namibia's **Etosha National Park**, before reaching stunning **Cape Town**, South Africa, on the continent's southern tip.

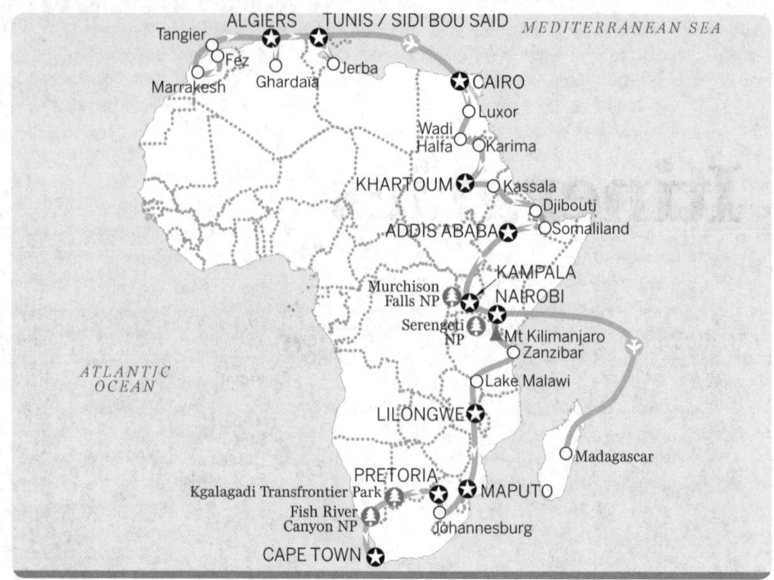

The Full Monty

This extended adventure avoids countries that, at the time of writing, were experiencing domestic troubles. Adjust to the African beat in Morocco, starting at **Tangier** and moving on to **Fez** and **Marrakesh**. Fly into beautiful, fascinating **Algiers**, capital of Algeria, where you can organise trips to the interior to see marvelous desert scenery and the collection of ancient towns known as **Ghardaïa**. Cross the border to Tunisia where **Tunis** is a good introduction to the country. Don't miss the bougainvillea-clad town of **Sidi Bou Saïd** and the island of **Jerba** with its peculiar architecture.

Fly over Libya to Egypt; experience the ancient sites of **Cairo** and a felucca trip down the Nile to **Luxor**. Follow the Nile to Aswan, where you can take the ferry to **Wadi Halfa** in Sudan. Continue along the river to **Karima** for Pharaonic ruins and see more of the same at the Meroe Sites closer to Khartoum. From **Kassala** you could go rock climbing on the sheer peaks of the Taka Mountains.

Detour across Ethiopia to Djibouti to view **Lac Assal**, the lowest point on the continent, and the amazing moonscape of **Lac Abbé**. The intrepid will want to nip across to Somaliland to see the extraordinary rock art of **Las Geel**. Cross over into Ethiopia and fly from Addis Ababa to Kampala from where you can catch a bus to **Murchison Falls National Park** via Masindi. Continue to **Jinja**, the adrenaline centre of East Africa, then **Nairobi**; spend time exploring Kenya's wonderful attractions but also consider taking a flight from here to Madagascar to experience its extraordinary natural environment.

Resume your mainland travels in Tanzania; **Mt Kilimanjaro**, **Serengeti National Park** and the **Zanzibar Archipelago** should be on the itinerary. Hop around **Lake Malawi**, working your way to **Maputo**. Pop into Swaziland en route to **Johannesburg** and **Pretoria**. Make your way west across South Africa to the **Kgalagadi Transfrontier Park**, a magical environment that spreads into Botswana.

Cross into Namibia where you can trek through the spectacular **Fish River Canyon**. Make your final run down along South Africa's Atlantic Coast to **Cape Town** and celebrate the conclusion of your African odyssey atop Table Mountain.

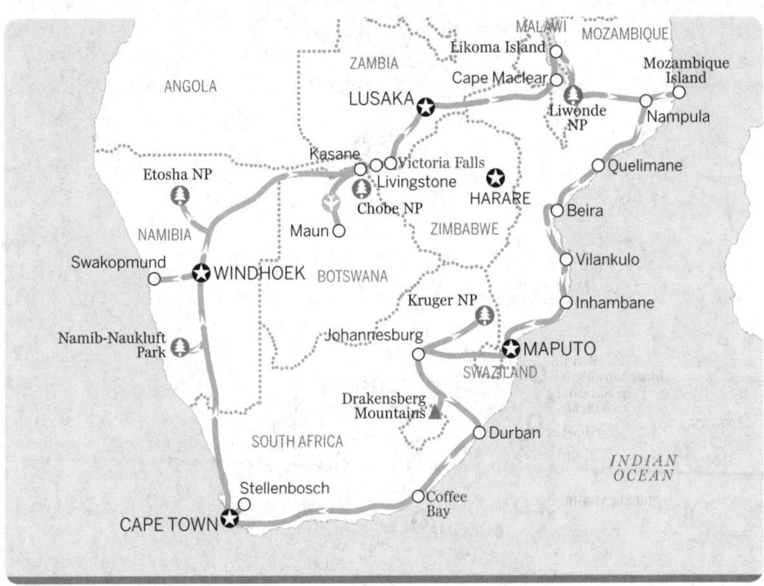

Southern Africa Smorgasbord

This itinerary – ideal for Africa novices – takes in nine countries and the best Southern Africa has to offer. Most places are easily accessible, English is widely spoken and the countries are well set up for foreign visitors.

Start in South Africa's mother city, vibrant **Cape Town**, where you can stand on top of Table Mountain, sleep off your jet lag on stunning beaches and party into the night on Long St. Squeeze in a trip to the Winelands: **Stellenbosch** is a good choice. Head north into Namibia for the endless sand dunes of **Namib-Naukluft Park**, well-heeled **Windhoek** with its German colonial heritage and the adrenaline activities of **Swakopmund**.

Continue north to **Etosha National Park**, then east along the Caprivi strip to **Kasane**, gateway to Botswana's **Chobe National Park** and its elephants. Fly to **Maun** for a few days in the swampy maze of the **Okavango Delta**. Back in Kasane, it's a hop to Zambia's **Livingstone** for some high-speed thrills and the spectacular **Victoria Falls**.

Zambia's capital **Lusaka** might not be a looker but its bar and clubbing scene is lively as you pass through en route to Malawi. From **Lilongwe** head first south to **Liwonde National Park** for elephant and hippo spotting. The white beaches and clear waters of Lake Malawi beckon – experience them at **Cape Maclear** and blissful **Likoma Island**.

Once across the border in Mozambique, take the train from Cuamba to **Nampula**, the jumping-off point for trips to the unforgettable **Mozambique Island**. Take a trip to the lost-in-time **Quirimbas Archipelago** then head south via the sleepy towns of **Quelimane**, **Beira**, **Vilankulo**, for the **Bazaruto Archipelago**, and **Inhambane**. Next stop is beguiling **Maputo** for a fiesta of seafood and caipirinhas.

Drop into Swaziland en route to **Johannesburg**, South Africa's bustling commercial capital. From here head to **Kruger National Park** or venture south to the **Drakensberg Mountains** for great hiking – even across the border into Lesotho. Drop back down to tropical **Durban**, a good base for exploring Zululand. On the Wild Coast pause at beautiful **Coffee Bay** before making your way back to Cape Town.

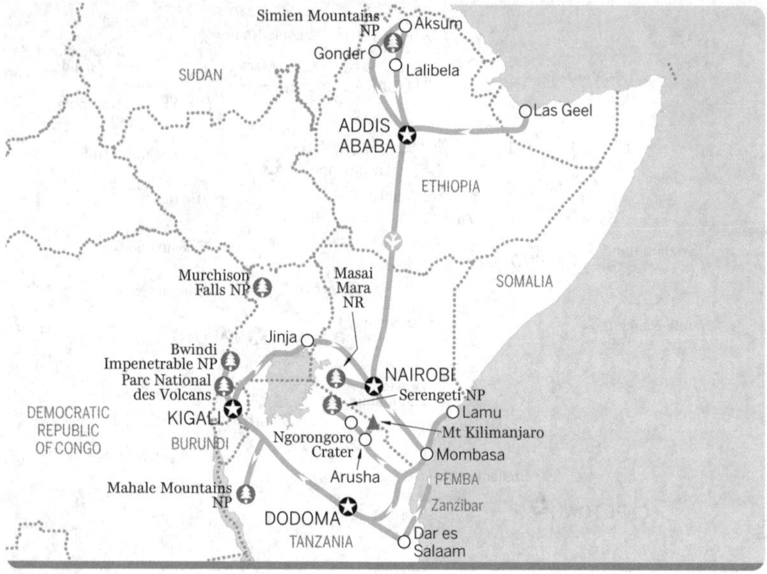

East African Extravanganza

The wildlife of Kenya and Tanzania and the island of Zanzibar are well known but there's so much more to East Africa, including gorillas in Rwanda and Uganda, and the other-worldly natural and cultural attractions of Ethiopia and Somaliland.

Fly into Kenya's **Nairobi** and explore the **Masai Mara National Reserve** and Central Highlands around **Mt Kenya**. Head east via **Mombasa** to the palm-fringed beaches and coral reefs of the **Lamu archipelago** to experience the ultimate in Swahili culture.

Cross the border to Tanzania, where your first stop is **Arusha**, to arrange a 4WD safari to the **Ngorongoro crater** or **Serengeti National Park**, and trekking trips up **Mt Kilimanjaro**. From **Dar es Salaam** head to the Spice Island of **Zanzibar**, then on to **Pemba**, an intriguing island further north. Return to Dar es Salaam and head directly west to spend time with the wild chimpanzees in **Mahale Mountains National Park**.

Walk across the Kagera River Bridge to Rusumu, Rwanda, to catch a minibus to **Kigali**. This attractive city is worth seeing before striking out for **Parc National des Volcans**, to hike in search of silverback gorillas. Cross into western Uganda, stopping at stunning **Lake Bunyonyi**, before visiting to **Bwindi Impenetrable National Park**. Also possible is the chance to kick back at the **Crater Lakes** or **Ssese Islands** or go white-water rafting at **Jinja**; in the north, **Murchison Falls National Park** is a gem.

From Uganda travel east back into Kenya to remote **Loyangalani**, home to unforgettable tribes and the jade-coloured Lake Turkana. Cross the border north into Ethiopia; in the south, the **Lower Omo Valley** is one of East Africa's most underrated wilderness areas, while the north is home to the castles of **Gonder**, the rock churches of **Lalibela**, the ancient city of **Aksum** and hiking in the **Simien Mountains National Park**.

Possible detours include the fascinating walled city of **Harar** and, for the more intrepid, the incredible prehistoric rock art galleries of **Las Geel**, across the border in Somaliland. Realign yourself to the contradictions and pleasures of contemporary Africa in **Addis Ababa** for your flight back to Nairobi.

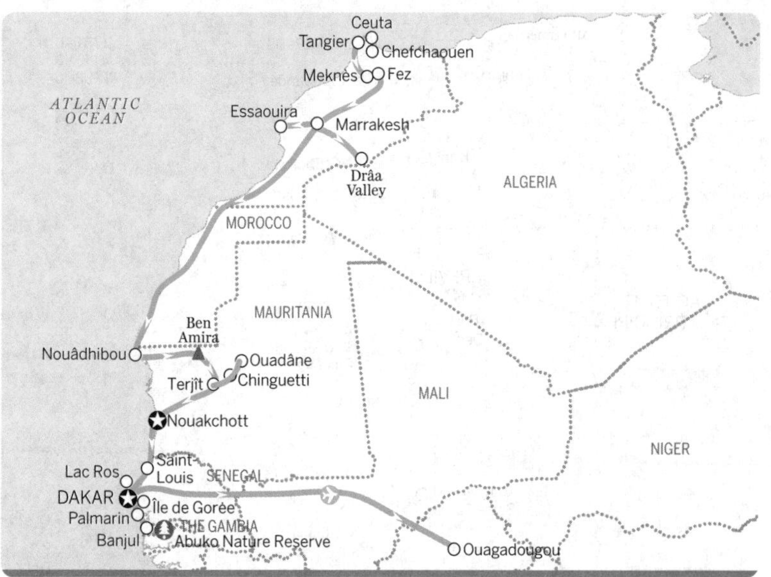

Colonial Footsteps

When the dust settled from the colonial scrabble for Africa in the 19th century, the French held sway in large parts of the north and west of the country. The language and culture of France's legacy provides a fascinating counterpoint to the indigenous cultures of Islam and animism. There are also elements of Spanish and British culture embedded in this part of the continent.

Before France took control in 1912, Spain had had its African foothold in Morocco. From **Tangier** make your way to **Ceuta**, a Spanish enclave since 1640. Another Andalucían-flavoured medina lies in charming **Chefchaouen**, at the base of the Rif Mountains.

Islam comes to the fore in the Imperial cities of **Meknès** and **Fez** in the Middle Atlas; from the former you can visit **Volubilis**, the best-preserved Roman ruins in Morocco. **Marrakesh** shouldn't be missed and from here you can make excursions to **Essaouira** on the coast, the **High Atlas Mountains** and the **Drâa Valley** on the edge of the Sahara.

The long journey south through the Western Sahara, via Dakhla, takes you to **Nouâdhibou** in Mauritania. After detours to see Africa's biggest monolith, **Ben Amira**, and the Sahara caravan towns, **Chinguetti** and **Ouadâne**, head back to the coast, via the oasis **Terjît**, to the capital **Nouakchott**, then across the border to charming **Saint-Louis** in Senegal.

Dakar is one of West Africa's cultural capitals, with great live music and nightlife. Visit nearby **Île de Gorée** and the pink-coloured **Lac Rose**. At bird-rich **Siné-Saloum Delta** drift in a *pirogue* (traditional canoe) through the mangroves and chill out in palmy **Palmarin**.

Africa's smallest mainland country, The Gambia, was once a sliver of the British empire within French colonial Africa. Bounce from the capital **Banjul** to the lively **Atlantic Coast resorts** and the easy-to-reach and well-managed **Abuko Nature Reserve**.

At the time of writing, the overland route to Burkina Faso via Mali was inadvisable due to conflict in the country. So backtrack to Dakar to fly to the wonderfully named capital, **Ouagadougou**. Move on to languid, semitropical **Bobo-Dioulasso** and the spectacular **Sindou Peaks**, both highlights of this friendly country.

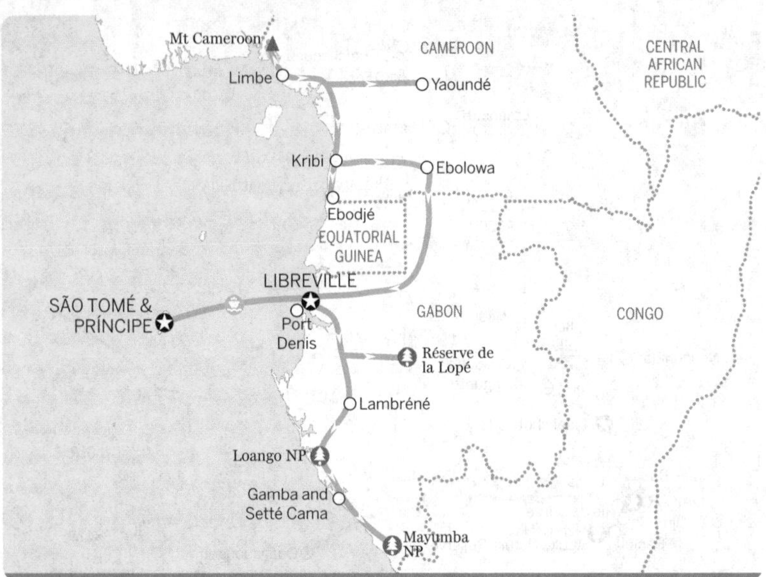

Wildlife Galore

From Cameroon's capital, **Yaoundé**, head west to the lazy, chocolate-coloured beaches around **Limbe**, where the Limbe Wildlife Centre is home to rescued gorillas, chimps and drills. After exploring **Mt Cameroon** head south to the lovely white-sand beaches of **Kribi**. Even better for wildlife enthusiasts, continue down the coast to **Ebodjé**, with its nesting turtles and impressive ecotourism project.

From **Ebolowa** venture across the Gabon border. The capital **Libreville** is organised, clean and expensive. From here you can make road trips to **Lambréné**, the site of Albert Schweitzer's famous hospital, and the superb beaches of **Port Denis**, or a train trip to see elephants and spectacular scenery at **Réserve de la Lopé**.

If you don't have the cash for the luxury resort in **Loango National Park**, enter this incredible wildlife haven from the southern towns of **Gamba** and **Setté Cama**. From here you can continue to **Mayumba National Park** to view humpback whales and go body surfing.

Finish the trip with a jaunt to one of Africa's smallest countries, **São Tomé & Príncipe**, where the highlights include watching nesting turtles at Praia Jalé and the deserted and generally perfect Banana Beach.

Plan Your Trip

Planning Safaris

Africa's multitude of national parks, reserves and conservation areas are some of the most beautiful places on the planet, and home to a bewildering variety of wild animals – watch lions stalk their prey, see wildebeest and zebras migrating, or track gorillas through rainforest. Wherever you go, a wildlife safari (from the Swahili meaning 'long journey') will undoubtedly be a major highlight of your trip. However, they can be expensive. This chapter provides an overview of the factors to consider when planning a safari, particularly whether to opt for an organised affair or go DIY.

Organised Safaris

Vast distances – some parks are bigger than small nations – and the unpredictable nature of large animals usually mean you need a vehicle to visit the national parks, often a 4WD, and a knowledgable guide. The obvious solution is to join an organised safari. There are options to suit all budgets, starting from around US$100 per day for a basic all-inclusive experience.

If you want to team up and share the costs of a safari, companies in Nairobi (Kenya), Arusha (Tanzania) and Kampala (Uganda) will help you find other travellers. Some have regular departures where you can just rock up, pay, and head for the wilds the next day. Many safari companies also take bookings in advance via email.

One factor that can make or break a safari is the driver. A good driver is a guide too, and can turn even the most mundane trip into a fascinating one; a driver's experience in spotting animals and understanding their behaviour is paramount. A bad driver does just that – drive. Always try to meet your driver-guide before booking a safari, to gauge their level of knowledge and enthusiasm.

If you're offered a ridiculously cheap deal by a safari company, think again.

Safari Bests

West Africa

Parc National de la Pendjari (Benin; p213)

Mole National Park (Ghana; p327)

Parc National du Waza (Cameroon; p261)

Central Africa

Loango National Park (Gabon; p531)

Réserve de la Lopé (Gabon; p532)

Parc National Nouabalé-Ndoki (Congo; p491)

East Africa

Masai Mara National Reserve (Kenya; p116)

Serengeti National Park (Tanzania; p700)

Bwindi Impenetrable National Park (Uganda; p735)

Parc National des Volcans (Rwanda; p642)

Simien Mountains National Park (Ethiopia; p583)

Southern Africa

Chobe National Park (Botswana; p762)

Etosha National Park (Namibia; p890)

South Luangwa National Park (Zambia; p983)

Kruger National Park (South Africa; p948)

Anything less than the norm may compromise quality – vehicles break down, food is substandard, park fees are dodged or fuel is skimped on, meaning your driver won't take detours in search of animals. At the higher end of the price spectrum, ambience, safari style and the operator's overall focus are important considerations.

The best way to avoid the sharks and find good guides is to get advice from other travellers who've recently returned from a safari, so do your research online beforehand and ask around once you arrive in Africa. Also check to see if an operator is a member of a professional association or regulatory body such as the Kenyan Association of Tour Operators (KATO; www.katokenya.org) or the Tanzanian Association of Tour Operators (TATO; www.tatotz.org).

Types of Safari

Most of the time your safari will be in a vehicle – either a 4WD or minibus. Four to six days is often ideal. At least one full day will normally be taken up with travel, and after six you may well feel like a rest. Also check carefully the number of passengers; most price quotes are based on groups of three to four passengers, which is about the maximum number of people most vehicles can hold comfortably. Some companies put five or six passengers in a standard 4WD, but the minimal savings don't compensate for the extra discomfort.

In many places throughout East and Southern Africa, including Tanzania and Mozambique, it's possible to organise multiday bushwalking safaris or multiday canoe safaris in wildlife areas, usually also with community and/or cultural components. Such safaris are widely considered the future of safari tourism. Balloon safaris are also possible over Kenya's Masai Mara National Reserve and Tanzania's Serengeti National Park, while Kenya also has opportunities for safari by bicycle (Hell's Gate National Park) and camel safaris.

TIPPING

Tips are an important part of the income of safari employees, so if your driver-guide and cook have given good service, tip them around 10% of the total cost of your safari (about 5% for the driver, 5% for the cook). If the service has been poor, tip less, and explain why.

DIY Safaris

When it comes to safaris, doing things yourself (taking the bus, using your own tent, carrying your own food) is rarely cheaper, and is a lot more complicated. Public transport rarely goes into parks, and even if it does, you still need to rent a vehicle or arrange lifts to tour the park itself. And the main expense – park entry fees – has to be paid however you get there.

However, in some countries there's less of an organised safari set-up, and the usual way of doing things is to get to the park under your own steam, stay at a lodge or campsite (either inside the park, or just outside, to save on park fees), then arrange activities on the spot to suit your budget and interest. You can join walking safaris, wildlife-viewing drives, boat trips or visits to nearby villages – all normally for a half or full day, although longer options may also be available. National parks where this is possible include Liwonde (Malawi), Kruger (South Africa), Gorongosa (Mozambique) and South Luangwa (Zambia). Doing things this way can cost more than fully organised trips, but generally you're paying for a more exclusive experience.

Where & When to Go

North Africa is the one part of the continent where you won't be planning a safari as most of the large animals are long gone.

Much of East and Southern Africa offers exceptional wildlife-viewing year-round. That said, wildlife is generally easier to spot during the dry season when waterholes become a focus for activity. This is also when visitor numbers and prices will be highest – something to bear in mind when weighing up costs and scheduling.

Wildlife usually disperses during the wet season and denser vegetation can make observation more difficult, but you may be rewarded with viewings of behaviour such as breeding activity without the tourist crowds.

West Africa

West Africa is an underrated wildlife destination and its little-known national parks host more African megafauna than they do tourists.

Cameroon has some of West Africa's best national parks. In the north, the Parc National de Waza is home to elephants, giraffes and lions, while the southern Parc National de Campo-Ma'an hosts buffaloes, elephants, mandrills and a nascent ecotourism project.

Benin's Parc National de la Pendjari is one of the region's best parks with lions, leopards, elephants and hippos. The same can be said for the Benin-Niger cross-border Parc Regional du W. Ghana's Mole National Park, with 94 mammal species, including elephants, baboons and antelopes, is that country's conservation showpiece.

The Gambia offers the compact Abuko Nature Reserve, home to crocodiles and hundreds of bird species. Senegal's Parc National des Oiseaux du Djoudj and Mauritania's Parc National du Banc d'Arguin are among the best birding sites in the world for migratory species.

SANGHA TRINATIONAL PARK

National Geographic magazine once described it as 'the World's Last Eden', but maybe that was selling it short. Listed as a Unesco World Heritage Site in 2012, Sangha Trinational Park (http://whc.unesco.org/en/list/1380) is a giant slab of the Congo rainforest. Divided between the national parks of Dzanga-Sangha (Central African Republic; see boxed text, p477), Nouabalé-Ndoki (Congo; p491) and Lobéké (Cameroon), this is a place where elephants gather in forest clearings by their hundred, chimpanzees swing through the trees, chest thumping gorillas crash through the undergrowth, pygmies 'fish' for antelope with nets and the occasional lucky tourist stares in amazement at Africa at her raw and wild best.

Central Africa

Gabon is the region's star ecotourism destination with 10% of its territory locked away in national parks. Habituated gorillas live in the national parks of the Central African Republic, Congo and the Democratic Republic of Congo's far east, but these areas will be off the travel agendas of all but the most intrepid.

East Africa

From the spectacular wildebeest migrations across the Masai Mara to the millions of flamingos gathered at Lake Nakuru National Park and the gorillas of Bwindi Impenetrable National Park, East Africa offers an amazing range of safari opportunities. However, don't be tempted to fit too much into your itinerary. Distances between parks in East Africa are great, and moving too quickly from park to park is likely to leave you tired and unsatisfied. Instead, try to stay at just one or two parks, exploring them in depth and taking advantage of nearby cultural and walking opportunities.

Southern Africa

If you thought that East Africa was safari wonderland, prepare yourself for an equally enticing sweetie shop in Southern Africa. South Africa alone has close to 600 national parks and reserves, many featuring wildlife, although others are primarily wilderness sanctuaries or hiking areas. Throughout South Africa, park infrastructure is of a high quality, You can drive your own car (a 2WD is adequate in most parks) and can often get by without a guide, although you'll almost certainly see and learn more with one. Major parks, including Kruger, offer guided wilderness walks accompanied by rangers.

Elsewhere both Bostwana's Chobe National Park and Namibia's Etosha National Park have good populations of iconic species plus excellent birdwatching. If you make it across to Madagascar, look for the endangered lemur, the indri, in Parc National d'Andasibe.

Regions at a Glance

Split from the rest of Africa by the Sahara, North Africa is the continent's bridge between Europe and the Middle East. West Africa is home to signature African landscapes and is inhabited by an astonishing diversity of people who hold fast to their traditions.

Hot, steamy and precarious, Central Africa is the continent's proverbial 'dark heart' but also a land rich in virgin jungle, fabled rivers and amazing wildlife. East Africa plays host to profound cultural riches and overwhelming natural splendour, as well as people who have remained resilient to tragic conflict.

Southern Africa has some of the continent's most accessible wilderness and dynamic cities, the playgrounds in which to experience a multitude of adventures.

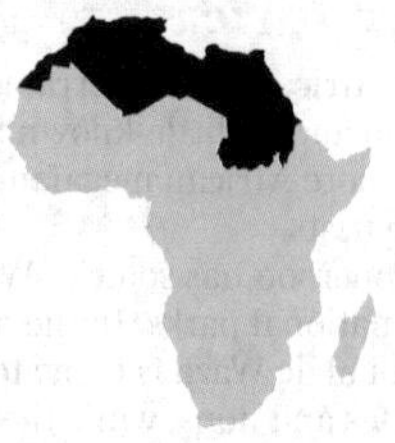

North Africa

Cities
Landscapes
Islamic Culture

Ancient Cities

The glories of ancient Egypt are the most famous, but extraordinary Roman and Greek cities are found all along the North African coast and its hinterland, while remote pyramids peer out from beneath the sand in Sudan.

Amazing Landscapes

The Sahara in Algeria and Libya is the stuff of dreams, while more accessible desert expeditions are possible in Egypt, Tunisia and Morocco. In the last, you can drop down from the epic Atlas Mountains, with their fortress-studded valleys, into the dunes that stretch deep into Africa.

Islamic Culture

Whether in Marrakesh, Fez, Algiers, Tripoli or Cairo, you'll find yourself surrounded by the best of Arab-Islamic culture, from the soaring mosques and exquisite architecture to the warm hospitality for which the region is famous.

p43

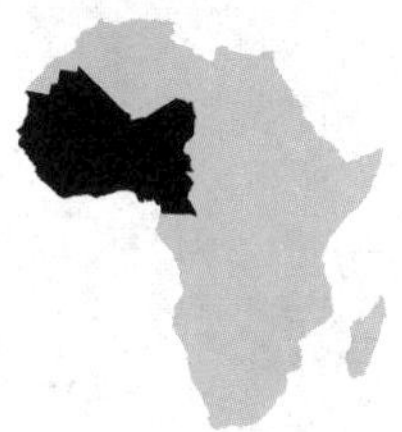

West Africa

Landscapes
Music
Diversity

Contrasting Vistas

West Africa's allure will take hold amid the verdant rainforests of Cameroon (a country that is home to 280 distinct cultural groups); while contemplating an Atlantic sunset alongside swaying palm trees; or with the red Sahel dust beneath your feet.

Feel the Beat

Extraordinarily rich musical traditions animate this epic landscape, from the live-music scene in Bamako and Dakar to the masks and stilt dancing of the Dans in Côte d'Ivoire.

Diverse Countries

Another big part of West Africa's appeal resides in its isolation in one of the least-known corners of the continent. Emerging destinations such as Sierra Leone, Benin and Togo sit easily alongside the better-known attractions of the Dogon Country, and the beaches of The Gambia.

p197

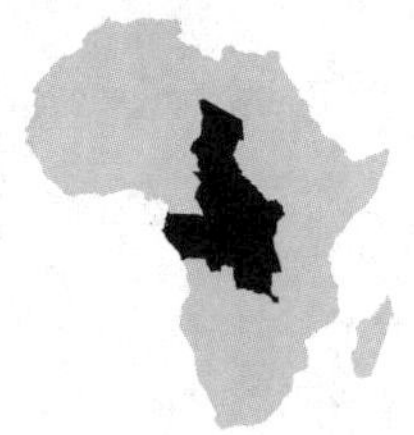

Central Africa

Adventure
Wildlife
Islands

Off the Beaten Track

Until recently instability and appalling infrastructure across a swath of Central Africa kept it off limits to all but seriously hard-core adventurers. While it would be wrong to paint a picture of Central Africa as an oasis of peace, much of the region can now be visited and destinations such as Congo are opening up to intrepid travellers.

Wonderous Wildlife

Wildlife wedded to extraordinary natural beauty is the region's trump card. Gabon is an ecotourism destination par excellence, and Congo is also shaping up to be a worthy rival. In the DRC there are national parks where you can see gorillas and a sanctuary for rare bonobo primates.

Island Life

Off the coast, São Tomé and Príncipe offers the chance to watch whales, snorkel with dolphins, dive in azure waters, laze on unspoiled beaches and soak up the languid equatorial air.

p473

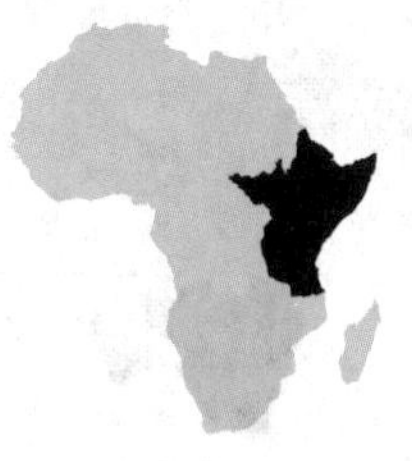

East Africa

Architecture
Landscapes
Wildlife

Amazing Architecture

On the islands of Zanzibar and Lamu, cities of hewn coral pay tribute to once vast trading empires that stretched along the coastline and deep into the interior. Ethiopia's rock churches and ruined palaces are poignant reminders of treasures won and lost.

Beautiful Landscapes

Home to Africa's largest lake, deepest point, swaths of primate-rich equatorial rainforest and some of the world's greatest wildlife parks. Up in the heavens the summits of Mt Kilimanjaro and Mt Kenya beckon to be conquered by hardened shoe leather.

Superb Safaris

Witness the annual wildebeest migration between the Serengeti and Masai Mara. Penetrate Uganda's Bwindi Impenetrable National Park to encounter mountain gorillas or the Mahale Mountains National Park to hang with chimpanzees.

p543

Southern Africa

Wildlife & Landscapes
Adventure Activities
Relaxation

Accessible Africa

This corner has some of Africa's most accessible wilderness – an astonishing variety and density of wildlife, dreamy landscapes and world-class natural features like thundering Victoria Falls. Botswana offers the wildlife-rich, water-soaked Okavango Delta, Zambia majestic national parks – the list goes on and on.

Adrenaline Activities

Southern Africa will fill the part of your heart that yearns for adventure. Want to bungee jump? No problem. Fly over mighty Victoria Falls? Absolutely. White-water raft raging rapids? Of course!

Chilling Out

The region's ambient rhythm swoons visitors into a blissful stupor. Change down a gear and relax on Mozambique's uncrowded beaches and romantic offshore islands, or join locals for a drink at a South African *shebeen* (an informal drinking establishment).

p749

On the Road

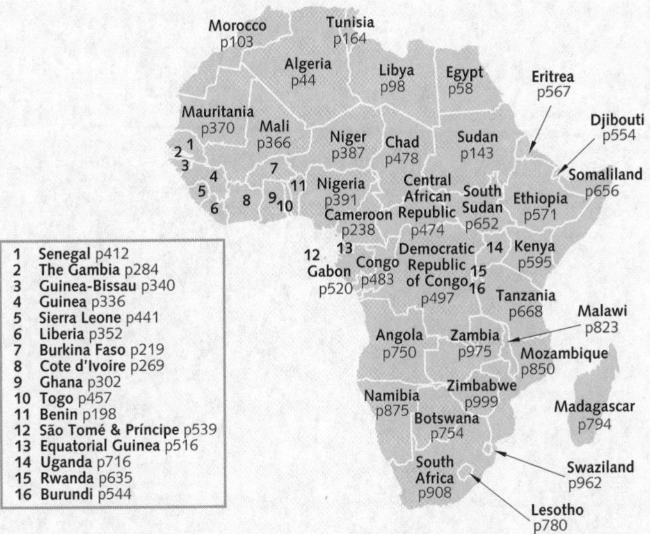

Morocco p103
Tunisia p164
Algeria p44
Libya p98
Egypt p58
Eritrea p567
Djibouti p554
Mauritania p370
Mali p366
Niger p387
Chad p478
Sudan p143
Somaliland p656
Nigeria p391
Central African Republic p474
South Sudan p652
Ethiopia p571
Cameroon p238
Democratic Republic of Congo p497
Kenya p595
Gabon p520
Congo p483
Tanzania p668
Malawi p823
Angola p750
Zambia p975
Mozambique p850
Zimbabwe p999
Namibia p875
Botswana p754
Madagascar p794
South Africa p908
Swaziland p962
Lesotho p780
1 Senegal p412
2 The Gambia p284
3 Guinea-Bissau p340
4 Guinea p336
5 Sierra Leone p441
6 Liberia p352
7 Burkina Faso p219
8 Cote d'Ivoire p269
9 Ghana p302
10 Togo p457
11 Benin p198
12 São Tomé & Príncipe p539
13 Equatorial Guinea p516
14 Uganda p716
15 Rwanda p635
16 Burundi p544

North Africa

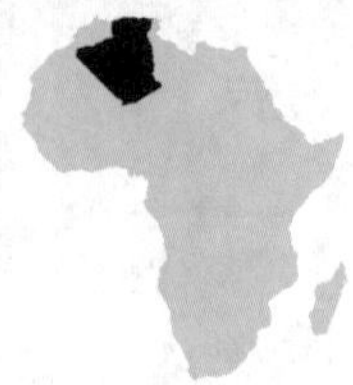

Algeria

POP 37.4 MILLION

Includes ➡

Best Places for History

- Algier's Casbah (p47)
- Beni Isguen (p50)
- Tipaza (p49)
- Djanet (p51)

Best Places to Stay

- Residence des Deux Tours (p50)
- Hotel Ksar Massine (p51)
- Royal Hotel (p49)

Why Go?

Africa's largest country lies just a short hop from Europe and, with tourists still a novelty, offers attractions as unpeopled as they are varied. The capital, Algiers, is one of the Maghreb's most urbane and charismatic cities, with a heady, nostalgic mix of colonial and modernist architecture, and a traditional medina at its vertiginous heart. Across the north are stunning coastlines, lush rural hinterland and a number of well-preserved Roman cities.

Algeria's trump card is, though, its extraordinary Saharan region. Whether it's a glimpse of the sand seas that surround Timimoun, or a plunge headlong into the far south from Tamanrasset, these are the desert landscapes of dream and legend.

Perhaps best of all, Algerians welcome visitors with warmth and a genuine curiosity. For accessible adventure and a complex, enthralling cultural odyssey, head for Algeria now.

When to Go

Algiers

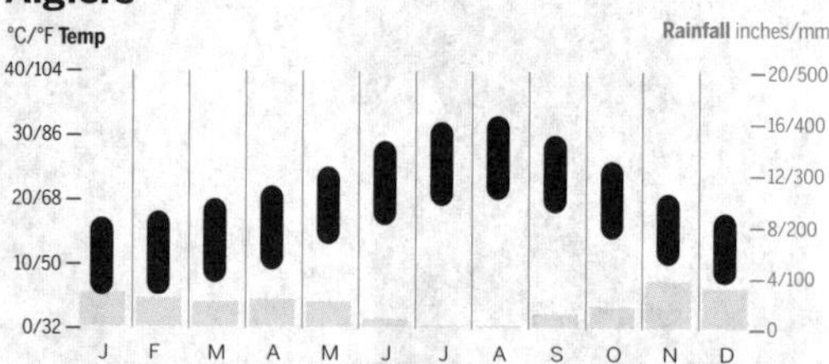

Nov–Apr Less fierce temperatures = high season in the Sahara (the autumn date harvest a bonus).

Mar–Jul The north literally blooms in spring; warm, dry days for exploring sprawling Roman sites.

Aug Oran's annual Raï festival and Ramadan.

ALGIERS

☎021 / POP 5 MILLION

Algiers (Al-Jazaïr) never fails to make an impression. This is a city of rare beauty and of thrilling, disorientating, and sometimes brutal, contrast. The country's turbulent history is writ large in the city's richly textured architecture: wide French-built boulevards and elegant apartments and villas, Socialist-era monuments and public buildings, and an enduring Islamic heart secreted in the steep, hillside Casbah. Labyrinthine streets spill down to the big blue of the Bay of Algiers, sea and sky and green ravines glimpsed at every step. Though people often spend just enough time in Algiers to organise an onward journey, it's a fascinating place well worth at least a couple of days' exploration.

Sights

Much of the enjoyment to be had in Algiers comes from clambering up its steep streets, strolling in the parks and taking in

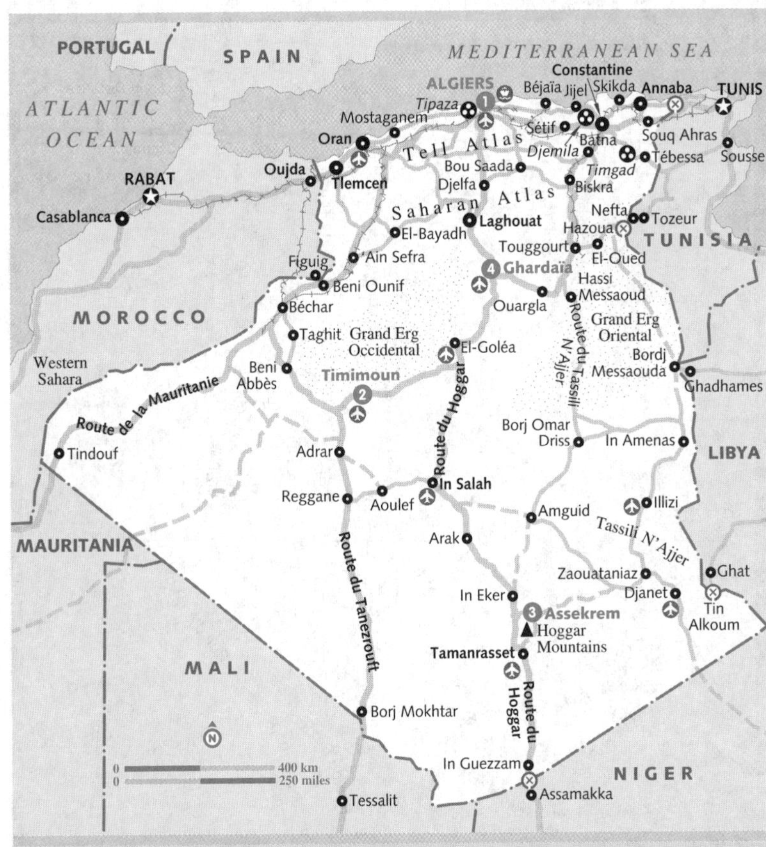

Algeria Highlights

1. Experience 'la Blanche', the country's fascinating capital, **Algiers** (p45), where modern, traditional and colonial Algeria meet.
2. Strike out into the dunes of the Grand Erg Occidental from the red oasis of **Timimoun** (p50).
3. Watch the sun set beyond a sea of mountains and sleep under the stars in **Assekrem** (p51).
4. Bargain for a boldly patterned carpet in the main square of **Ghardaïa** (p50), peek at a pristine medieval town then swimming in the shade of date palms.

Algiers

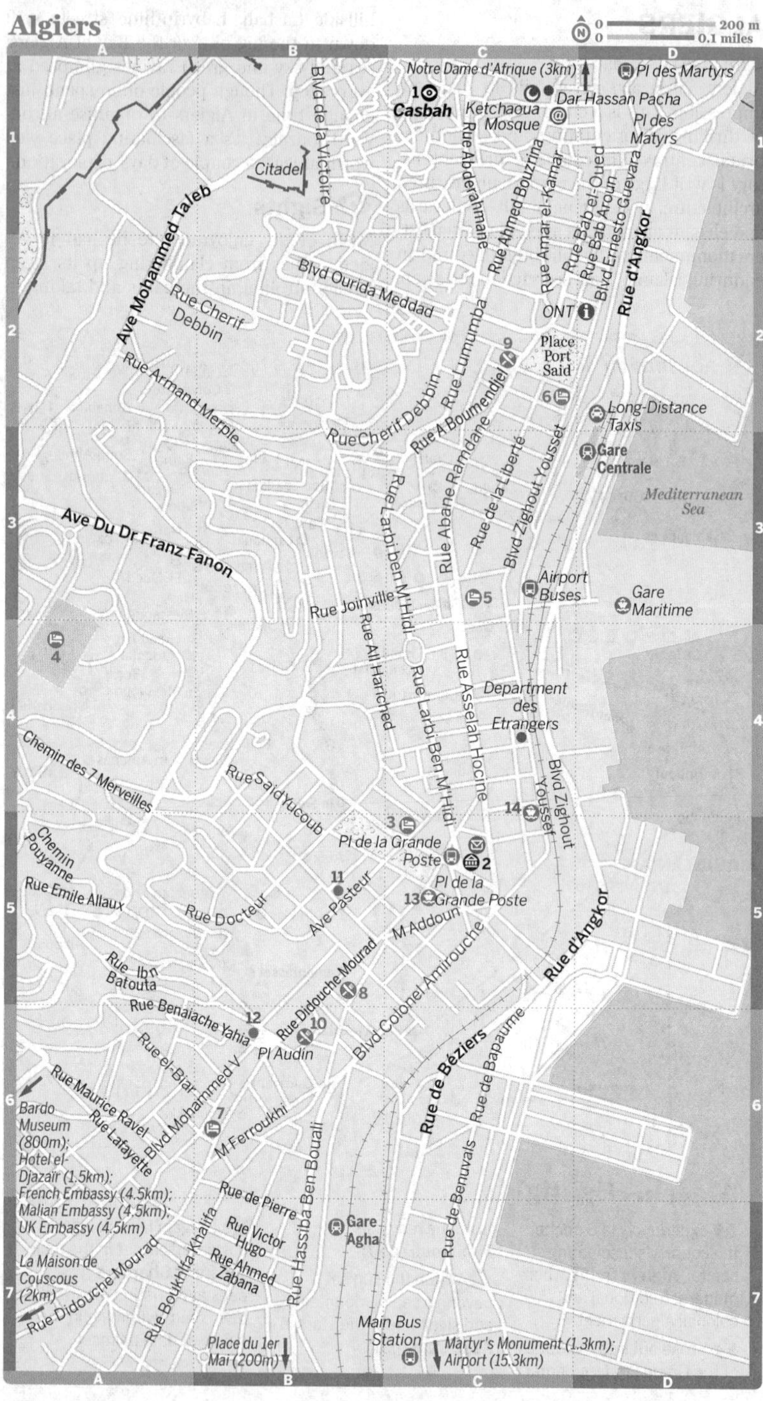
0 200 m
0 0.1 miles
Notre Dame d'Afrique (3km)
Pl des Martyrs
Casbah
Dar Hassan Pacha
Ketchaoua Mosque
Pl des Matyrs
Citadel
Blvd de la Victoire
Rue Abderahmane
Rue Ahmed Bouzrina
Rue Amar el-Kamar
Rue Bab el-Oued
Rue Bab Aroun
Blvd Ernesto Guevara
Rue d'Angkor
Ave Mohammed Taleb
Blvd Ourida Meddad
ONT
Rue Cherif Debbin
Place Port Said
Rue Lumumba
Rue Armand Merple
Rue Cherif Debbin
Rue A Boumendjel
Long-Distance Taxis
Gare Centrale
Mediterranean Sea
Rue Abane Ramdane
Rue de la Liberté
Blvd Zighout Youssef
Rue Larbi Ben M'Hidi
Ave Du Dr Franz Fanon
Rue Joinville
Airport Buses
Gare Maritime
Rue Ali Hariched
Rue Larbi Ben M'Hidi
Rue Asselah Hocine
Department des Etrangers
Blvd Zighout Youssef
Chemin des 7 Merveilles
Rue Said Yucoub
Pl de la Grande Poste
Chemin Pouyanne
Rue Emile Allaux
Rue Docteur
Ave Pasteur
Pl de la Grande Poste
M Addoun
Rue d'Angkor
Rue Ibn Batouta
Rue Didouche Mourad
Rue Benaiache Yahia
Rue Didouche Mourad
Pl Audin
Blvd Colonel Amirouche
Rue de Béziers
Rue de Bapaume
Rue el-Biar
Blvd Mohammed V
Rue Maurice Ravel
Rue Lafayette
Bardo Museum (800m); Hotel el-Djazair (1.5km); French Embassy (4.5km); Malian Embassy (4.5km); UK Embassy (4.5km)
M Ferroukhi
Rue Hassiba Ben Bouali
Rue de Benuvals
Rue de Pierre
Rue Victor Hugo
Gare Agha
Rue Ahmed Zabana
Rue Boukhlifa Khalifa
La Maison de Couscous (2km)
Rue Didouche Mourad
Main Bus Station
Place du 1er Mai (200m)
Martyr's Monument (1.3km); Airport (15.3km)

Algiers

Top Sights

1 Casbah C1

Sights

2 Grande Poste C5

Sleeping

3 Hôtel Albert Premier C5
4 Hôtel el-Aurassi A4
5 Hôtel Safir C3
6 Hôtel Terminus C2
7 ST Hotel B6

Eating

8 Brasserie des Facultés B5
9 Café Tontonville C2
10 Club 54 .... B6

Transport

11 Aigle Azur B5
12 Air Algérie B6
13 Algérie Ferries C5
14 SNCM C4

those views. That said, there are a number of sights and interesting museums to easily fill a few days.

★Casbah NEIGHBOURHOOD

The heart of the city is its ancient Casbah, a steep and narrow maze of streets just west of the Pl des Martyrs. There are several magnificent **Ottoman palaces** to explore, most concentrated around the **Ketchaoua Mosque** at the end of Rue Ahmed Bouzrina; the finest is the **Dar Hassan Pacha**. Above the medina is the city's Citadel. It's been closed while undergoing major renovation for several years, though it's still possible to skirt its rambling exterior.

This fiercely traditional neighborhood saw some of the bitterest fighting during the Battle of Algiers (Gillo Pontecorvo's extraordinary film of the same name was shot in situ shortly after the war's end). The Casbah is fine to walk around today, but exercise extreme caution with personal belongings and avoid going there at night. Hiring a guide (ask at your hotel) is not a bad idea.

Martyrs' Monument MONUMENT

The distinctive abstract monolith that dominates the skyline south of the centre is the Martyrs' Monument, opened in 1982 on the 20th anniversary of Algeria's independence. Locals scoff at its bombast, but there are some great views over the city from here.

Bardo Museum of Prehistory & Ethnography MUSEUM

(☎74 76 41; www.musee-bardo.art.dz; 3 Ave FD Roosevelt; ⏰9am-noon & 2-5pm Sun-Thu) Closed for renovation at the time of writing (as was the website), this has always been the city's best museum, where the collection runs from a superb display of fossils to neolithic pottery, rock carvings and paintings from the Sahara.

Notre Dame d'Afrique CHURCH

(⏰11am-12.30pm & 3-5.30pm) One of the city's most famous buildings, this Catholic basilica still celebrates mass at 6pm daily, despite its dwindling flock. Its striking neo-Byzantine architecture and freshly restored more-is-more interior are matched by amazing views out to sea and across the capital. Take a taxi from the centre.

Grande Poste HISTORIC BUILDING

(☎72 60 72; Pl de la Grande Poste) Algier's beloved main post office is an unmissable piece of living history, a fine example of French-designed early-20th-century Moorish architecture. Look out for what is possibly the world's most exquisitely decorated post box near the entrance.

Jardin d'Essai GARDENS

(www.jardindessai.com; Rue Belouizdid, El-Hamma; adult/child DA60/30; ⏰10am-7pm Jun-Sep, 10am-5pm Oct-May) This bayside botanical garden dates to the first years of French occupation and today is a sprawling natural hothouse. It's a place of outstanding beauty; escape from the city among the avenues of palms and stands of exotic trees.

WARNING

While Algeria is now generally a safe country, check the latest situation when finalising your itinerary. All travellers to the Sahara beyond In Salah must, by law, be accompanied by an official guide and need to show a copy of an authorised invitation upon arrival. This can also extend to western towns such as Timimoun and Taghit. Currently all borders apart from those with Tunisia are either closed or considered dangerous. All non-Maghreb passport holders require visas and these must be applied for well in advance from your country of residence, and you'll need invitations and itineraries from a hotel or travel agency/tour operator.

SET YOUR BUDGET

Budget

- Hotel room US$45
- Kebab US$5
- Mint tea US$1
- Algiers metro ticket US$0.6

Midrange

- Hotel room US$100
- Two-course dinner US$20
- Beer in bar US$3
- Short taxi ride US$5

Top End

- Hotel room US$300
- Two-course dinner US$50
- Glass of wine US$7
- Driver and car US$70

Sleeping

City accommodation can be hard to find (book well ahead) and is seldom good value. If you've got a morning flight, the airport chain hotels are a good option. Budget hotels cluster around Pl Port Said on the edge of the Casbah, though they're not for the faint-hearted.

Hôtel Terminus HOTEL $

(☎73 78 17; 2 Rue Rachid Ksentini; s/d DA1800/3500) Excellently located in the heart of the city, the Terminus is just moments from the train station. Rooms vary enormously from windowless boxes with grim shared facilities to rooms with good views and private bathrooms.

ST Hotel HOTEL $$

(☎63 80 65; www.tourisme-hotel.dz; 4 Rue Mikideche Mouloud; s/d DA6200/8500; ❄📶) A great find in the centre of town: a well-run, bright and friendly midrange hotel. Rooms, some with small balconies, are generous in size and smart enough. A good breakfast is served in a sun-filled top-floor room.

Hôtel Albert Premier HOTEL $$

(☎73 65 06, 73 74 41; hotelalbert@yahoo.fr; 5 Ave Pasteur; r DA7500; P❄📶) This white colonial building oozes history and charm – from the outside at least. The rooms are a big disappointment, but its location can't be beaten (plus there's a bar).

Hôtel Safir HOTEL $$

(☎73 50 40; safirhot@yahoo.fr; 2 Rue Asselah Hocine; s/d DA7200/9000; P❄📶) This historic hotel has grand public spaces and harbour views. But the rooms are tatty, service nonexistent and its popularity with local powerbrokers can make solo female travellers uncomfortable.

Hôtel el-Djazaïr HISTORIC HOTEL $$$

(☎69 21 21, 23 09 33; www.hoteleldjazair.dz; 24 Ave Souidani Boudjemma; s/d DA20,000/24,000; ❄@🏊) Kipling, Gide, Churchill and Eisenhower stayed in this gracious five-star hotel, once known as the St George. While the rooms and service these days are wanting, especially so for the price, the location, lavish public areas and heritage gardens are hugely atmospheric. There are four restaurants, a bar, a nightclub and a pool.

Hôtel el-Aurassi LUXURY HOTEL $$$

(☎74 82 52; www.el-aurassi.com; 2 Blvd Frantz Fanon; s/d DA22,000/27,000; P❄@🏊) This landmark modernist white box overlooks the city centre. A recent renovation saw its retro decor shipped off to auction and it's now courting the business market big time, with ultracomfortable, if bland, rooms. The bar, open to nonguests, has sensational views.

Eating & Drinking

There's no shortage of cheap fast food on every corner and excellent bread and pastries from ubiquitous bakeries. Good-value seafood restaurants can be found along the Rampe de la Pêcherie near the port, as well as in the beach suburbs to the west. Most of city's more upmarket eating options are in leafy Hydra.

Algiers is not a hard place to find a drink, although bars are hardly a pleasant experience. Brasserie des Facultés serves alcohol, as does the bar at the Hôtel el-Djazaïr, along with most of the business-oriented hotels.

Café Tontonville CAFE $

(7 Pl Port Said; mains DA200-400) This Algiers institution is a great place for breakfast and coffee on the terrace. Inside they also serve full meals and thin-crust pizza.

Club 54 FAST FOOD $

(11 Rue Didouche Mourad; mains DA200-650; ⏰7am-9pm Sun-Thu) A bustling place for lunch or dinner with a loyal following of students. Pizzas, grills, omelettes, salads and soups are served up in a modern two-floor venue with cosy booths.

La Maison de Couscous ALGERIAN **$$**
(5 Rue Ernest Zeys, Debussy; mains DA700-1400) Up by the concrete Sacré Coeur Cathedral, high up Rue Didouche Mourad, this local no-frills place serves what its name says: couscous, along with *chorba* (soup) and *bourek* (filled pastry). Algerians don't often go out to eat couscous – it's the sort of dish your wife or mother cooks best – but they come here in numbers.

Brasserie des Facultés ALGERIAN, FRENCH **$$**
(☎64 40 53; 1 Rue Didouche Mourad; mains DA650-1200; ⊙10am-midnight) This venerable spot on Algiers' main drag offers hearty, pubby standards in a dark and atmospheric dining room. Good service and a reasonable selection of Algerian wine make this a long-time favourite of well-to-do Algerians and expats. It's also one of the few restaurants that opens on Fridays.

Orientation

Use the harbour to get your bearings, along with Hotel el-Aurassi and the Matyr's Monument. Four main streets run parallel to the waterfront, changing names every 500m or so. The medina lies between Blvd de la Victoire and Rue Ahmed Bouzrina.

Information

There are banks all over the city centre, but international ATMs are rare: try the airport or the lobby of one of the five-star hotels. For medical emergencies, call ☎115 (good French and/or Arabic will be useful), or ask your hotel to call a private ambulance.

Cyber Casbah (Rue Aoua Abdelkader; internet per hr DA60; ⊙10am-midnight)

Fire (☎14)

Main post oOffice (Pl de la Grande Poste)

Office National du Tourisme (ONT; ☎021-71 29 81; www.ont.dz; 2 Rue Kerrar; ⊙8am-4.30pm Sat-Wed)

Police (☎17)

Getting There & Away

AIR

Air Algerie, Aigle Azur, Tunisair, Royal Maroc and major European airlines have regular flights to Algiers. Air Algerie's domestic network is extensive, as is its connections into Africa.

Houari Boumediene airport is located a very congested 20km southeast of the city. There are infrequent buses into town (DA70); it's simpler to take a private taxi (DA1000). The domestic and international terminals are a short walk apart.

BUS

The main intercity bus station is south of Pl de la Grande Poste on Rue de Compiègne.

TRAIN

The Algerian state rail company SNTF (p57) no longer has any international lines. East-bound national trains run out of **Gare Centrale** (☎64 73 80/81; Rue d'Angkor), beside the Gare Maritime, and west-bound services are from **Gare de l'Agha** (☎63 65 25; off Rue Hassiba ben Bouali).

Getting Around

The four major city bus stations are at Pl des Martyrs, Pl de la Grande Poste, Pl Audin and Pl du 1er Mai.

Taxis can be hired by you alone, or shared. Drivers can be found outside the larger central hotels. If you want to book a taxi pick-up, ask for recommended drivers at your hotel, or try **Radio Taxi El Feth** (☎68 90 90). Private **Taxi Mustapha** (☎771 18 86 16) also comes recommended. Short trips across town should not cost more than DA500. Note prices are higher between 9pm and 5am.

NORTHERN ALGERIA

Northern Algeria's various urban hubs make fascinating destinations for adventurous city lovers. **Oran**, a port city with extraordinary 20th-century architecture, is the home of rai and still known for its music scene. Quietly booming, it also has some outstanding accommodation and eating options, including the glamorous **Royal Hotel** (☎041-29 17 17; www.royalhoteloran.com; 3 Blvd de la Soummam; rooms from DA18,500; ❄📶). Inland, there's former Islamic capital, medieval **Tlemcen**. On the east coast, **Annaba** possesses a pretty, seaside melancholy, and has a significant Roman site, **Hippo Regius**, the home of Christian church father St Augustine. **Constantine**, a bustling inland city, is known for its spectacularly spanned gorges.

Two stand-out attractions are the Roman cities of Tipaza, a short day trip from Algiers, and Djemila, a much larger and even more impressive site set in the rolling hills around Sétif.

The enchanting cliffside position and leafy surrounds of **Tipaza** (admission DA20; ⊙9am-6pm), a city that was at its height in the 2nd century AD, attracts scores of young Algerian couples, and in spring and summer the sprawling ruins have a festive feel. The beaches that can be seen to the west feature largely in the work of Albert Camus; a commemorative stele was placed at the end of the necropolis that overlooks them. To get to Tipaza, take a direct bus, or one bound for Cherchell (1½ hours, DA120), from the Gare Routière at the Agha train station. A regular taxi one way will cost you DA1500, or return chauffeured trips can be organised at any travel agent or hotel for around DA6000 to DA10,000. It's a 45-minute drive on the freeway.

The spectacular ruins of **Djemila** (☎036-94 51 01; adult/student DA20/10; ⏱8am-5pm) will demand several hours of your time. This sight is best reached by car or with a guide, due to the region's occasional instability, and it's usually necessary to stay overnight. Local accommodation is poor, but nearby Sétif has several reasonable options. You can also arrange a private taxi from there to the site if you do chose to come by train.

CENTRAL ALGERIA

In the mysterious, picturesque **M'Zab Valley**, life goes on much as it has for centuries (give or take the odd game of football). Southwest, deep into the sand seas of the Grand Erg Occidental, is **Timimoun**, an oasis town with evocative red architecture, a unique ethnic mix and easy access to gob-smacking desert scenery.

Ghardaïa

☎029 / POP 356,000

In the river valley of the Oued M'Zab, in a long valley on the edge of the Sahara, is a cluster of five towns: Ghardaïa, Melika, Beni Isguen, Bou Noura and El-Ateuf. Often referred to collectively as Ghardaïa, the capital, the once distinct villages are gradually sprawling together, but retain separate identities.

The M'Zab is home to a conservative Muslim sect known as the Ibadites, who broke from mainstream Islam some 900 years ago. This is, some say, a country unto itself, with ancient, unchanging social codes. The traditional white *haik*, a head to toe wool wrap, is worn by most women, who cover their entire face, exposing only one eye. Men sport extravagantly pleated baggy trousers, called *saroual loubia*. While locals here can be deeply reserved, it's a friendly and surprisingly laid-back place. The area is justifiably famous for its carpets – head for Ghardaïa's market square for a good selection.

To enter Ghardaïa's old upper town or neighbouring **Beni Isguen**, you'll need to be accompanied and dress modestly; official guides can be found at the respective old gates. Don't overlook little **El-Ateuf**: the 12th-century **mosque of Sidi Brahim** is a must-see. This wonderfully austere, profoundly spiritual building inspired French architect Le Corbusier. Meet guides at the tourist office on the main square – these guys are born entertainers.

The most charming accommodation options can be found on the edge of Beni Isguen's palmeraie. **Maison Traditionnele Akham** (☎87 31 27, 071-77 48 20; takbout_said@yahoo.fr; s/d DA3000/4000) has simple rooms set around shady multilevelled terraces. **Residence des Deux Tours** (☎88 86 69; www.residencedesdeuxtours.com; s/d/quad DA4200/6400/12000; ❄📶🏊) is a sprawling, excellently run place with a huge modern pool shaded by trees. Free breakfast and wi-fi make it good value. In the centre of Ghardaïa, **Hotel Izorane** (☎/fax 88 92 38; carrefour Wilaya de Ghardaïa; s/d DA2000/3000; ❄) has a cosy 1950s feel, clean and comfortable rooms and a small terrace that surveys the main street.

Smart, affable and endearingly eccentric **Restaurant Palmier** (☎83 92 89; Ave du 1er Novembre; set meals DA1500; ⏱noon-2pm & 7.30pm-midnight Sat-Thu) serves tasty local dishes, steaks and French standards (not to mention beer and wine). Otherwise, most guesthouses provide dinner, and there's fast food and excellent fresh juice shops aplenty in downtown Ghardaïa. Almond *lait de poule* (eggnog) and date smoothies are a speciality.

Air Algérie flies here from Algiers (one hour, five weekly) and Tamanrasset (2½ hours, four weekly). Regular buses run from Ghardaïa to Algiers (DA800, eight hours, 10 daily) and to Tamanrasset (DA2400, 20 hours, four daily).

Timimoun

☎049 / POP 33,000

The largest oasis in the Grand Erg Occidental, this dusty desert city is an enchanting place. Its characteristic architecture, red mud buildings studded with spikes, hints at sub-Saharan Africa. Its location, at the edge of an escarpment, makes for breathtaking views across a salt lake and out to the dunes beyond. The main street bustles in the morning and evening; the locals are a diverse mix that includes Haratines, Berbers and the descendants of Malian merchants and slaves.

Town highlights are the beautiful colonial-era **Hotel de l'Oasis Rouge** (av du 1er Novembre; admission free; ⌚8am-noon & 3-7pm, closed Fri) and watching the gurgling *fougara* (irrigation) at work in the shady palmeraie. Authentic craftwork can be found at **Artisanat Timimoun** (Rue Emir AEK; ⌚Sun-Thu Nov-Apr) and at **Trait d'Union Solidarité Alsace** (☎778 07 81 50; http://tusalsace.free.fr/Index.html), a rug-making workshop (call to visit). The latter has revived traditional designs and trains and employs local women as weavers.

Base yourself here to do the **Sebkha Circuit**, a 75km-to-90km loop that takes in the Saharan dunes of popular imagination, as well as the salt lake, crumbling hilltop *ksars* (fortofoed strongholds or castles) and deep red caves. You can arrange a car and driver with the tourist office in the commune office near the market, or ask your hotel.

There are a few notable places to stay (although the legendary Hotel Gourara was closed for renovations at time of writing). **Hotel Ksar Massine** (☎408 720 44; www.hotelksarmassine.com; s/d DA6500/8000; P❄🛜≋), out towards the airport, has good facilities and comfortable rooms. It functions as the area's business hotel, but don't be put off by that; fellow guests are most likely engineers, archaeologists and geologists – the mix makes for a wonderful desert bonhomie, and the Algerian-Dutch-Swiss family who own the place are delightful. Also out of town is **Camping Roses de Sable** (☎049-90 25 95; www.agence-merdesable.com; huts per person DA2500, r with/without bathroom per person DA3000/2800; ⌚closed May-Oct), a lovely place set in a large garden where you can sleep in a *zeriba* under the shade of a palm tree or in the pretty bungalow at the back. Beyond the walls lie an ocean of dunes as far as the eye can see. **Gite Djenane Malek** (☎90 04 88; djenanemalek@gmail.com; rooms from DA4000; P❄), in between the old town and the palmeraie, has cute rooms and a terrace with spectacular views, although service and facilities are lacking, and the caged animals might distress some travellers.

SOUTHERN ALGERIA

The far south's vast and stunning Saharan expanses are by far the country's most compelling attraction, a remote and often harsh place of extraordinary beauty, and the heartland of the Tuareg. The 'capital' Tamanrasset is a well-serviced frontier town and gateway to the area's many treasures. Northwest lies **Djanet**, home to some of the best prehistoric rock art in the world.

Tamanrasset

☎029 / POP 84,550

As the last major town on the road south to Niger, Tam (as it's affectionately known) is a surprisingly busy place with plenty of modern amenities, including banks, Air Algérie offices, innumerable travel agencies and an ONT branch. Almost everything can be found on the main street, Ave Emir Abdelkader, and the main square, Pl du 1er Novembre.

Around 80km northeast lies the fantastical landscape of **Assekrem**, part of the **Hoggar** range. Watching the sun set and rise across the sea of mountains from here is a bucket list experience of every serious traveller. There is a basic *refuge* (DA1800 half board per person), where you can rest up, stay warm and join in a game of checkers with the Tuaregs. The owners, Tim Missaw Tours (p56), can arrange transport and a guide.

At the time of writing, although considered safe by most Algerians and receiving reasonably good numbers of travellers, it is only possible to visit this region as part of a fully escorted tour, official proof of which is needed on arrival. This can be done as part of a tour, or prebooked directly with guides in Tamanrasset. All offer a range of 4WD and camel-trekking circuits to Assekrem, the Hoggar and on to Djanet. Expect to pay from around €90 to €200 per person per night (this will include all meals, accommodation and transport), with a minimum of three nights suggested for Assekrem alone.

Air Algérie flies between Tamanrasset and the major northern towns – Algiers, Oran, Constantine, Djanet and Ghardaïa. The French company Aigle Azur also has weekly flights to Paris and Marseille.

The bus station is on the road to the north of town. By bus it takes around 20 hours to Ghardaïa, or 30 hours to Algiers.

UNDERSTAND ALGERIA

Algeria Today

In July 2012 Algeria celebrated the 50th anniversary of its independence, and the end of what is considered one of the most brutal of the 20th century's wars of decolonisation. Apart from the usual official pomp, Algerians didn't appear to be much in a party mood. Elections held earlier in May of the same year had replicated the results of 2004 and 2009, with the 75-year-old (and increasingly frail) President Abdelazziz Bouteflika returned to power, along with a majority Front de Libération Nationale (FLN; National Liberation Front) government. International observers reported that it was one of the fairest elections the country had held, but many Algerians doubted the official turnout estimate of 43%, citing figures of half that as being more realistic.

Since the horrors of the *décennie noir*, the civil war of the 1990s, the country has enjoyed a period of peace, but oil- and gas-fuelled prosperity has failed to trickle down. People did take to the streets during January 2011, protesting, like their Tunisian neighbours, about painfully high unemployment, housing shortages and the spiraling cost of living. But this dissent was soon becalmed; many Algerians suggest they are just too haunted by their blood-spattered past to stomach the possibility of a return to violence.

While this can be read as cynical resignation or stoic pragmatism, Algerians *are* slowly rebuilding their country, often in the face of crushing bureaucratic inertia. Cultural festivals are springing up and chic shops and restaurants are common on the bustling streets of Algiers, Oran and Constantine. The government has loosened restrictions on private ownership of hotels, something that would have been unthinkable 20 years ago. And, despite not entirely unfounded fears about who might be listening, and exactly what their government is capable of, Algerians talk of past trauma and future aspiration with a surprising, and hopeful, candor.

History

While the region's documented history reaches far back into the Neolithic period, the modern state of Algeria is a relatively recent creation, a name coined by the Ottoman Turks in the 16th century for the territory controlled by the regency of Algiers, then a Turkish colony.

The Barbary Coast

By the late 1600s, Algeria was a military republic, ruled by locally appointed officers, with Istanbul-anointed pashas (governors) retaining only a symbolic role. Coffers brimmed with the proceeds of piracy, and although assignation was the favoured form of regime change, this was a period of stability.

The country was, of course, better known to Europeans as the Barbary (a corruption of Berber) Coast, an anarchic place where fearsome pirates preyed on Christian – and in particular, Catholic – shipping. Mediterranean piracy took off during the Holy Wars, and a few centuries later it had become the mainstay of North Africa's economy. Khayr al-Din, also known as Barbarossa, the first regent of Algiers, at one point held no fewer than 25,000 Christians captive in the city. Algiers drew a steady flow of Protestant English and Dutch privateers and adventurers, who often 'took the turban', converting to Islam while amassing great fortunes.

The power vacuums created by the French Revolution and Napoleonic Wars gave the pirate trade a lucrative second wind, and Algerian attacks on US shipping led to the two Barbary Wars, and the eventual defeat of the Algerian fleet off Algiers in 1815.

French Rule

France's second, and greatest, colonial empire was ostensibly spawned by a diplomatic crisis, involving unpaid French debts, a slap-happy *dey* (Ottoman governor) and a slighted French consul. In truth, France's economic troubles played a large part, as well as it being an act of desperate popularism by the failing Bourbon monarch Charles X. A naval blockade became an invasion in 1830, Algiers was looted by the French forces, and a land grab ensued.

Northern Algeria was mostly under French control by 1834 but resistance continued, led by Emir Abdelkader, ruler of western and central Algeria and the great hero of Algeria's nationalist movement. His armies held off the French for almost six years before they were defeated near Oujda in 1844. Abdelkader himself finally surrendered in 1846 and spent the rest of his life in exile. He died in Damascus in 1883, but not before being honoured by Queen Victoria for saving British citizens from a massacre there. Later, a rebellion in the Kabylie region spread throughout the country in 1871. The French only tightened their grip, responding with great force and confiscating more land from native Algerians.

French Algeria was not a colony, rather its three *departements* were constitutionally part of France. The French rebuilt Algeria in France's image and distributed large parts of prime farming land to European settlers (known as *colons* and later *pied-noirs*) who arrived from Italy, Malta, Spain and Portugal, as well as France. Algerians could become citizens if they renounced Islam and Islamic law, something very few did, otherwise they remained 'subjects' with severely limited rights. By 1960, the population consisted of around nine million 'Muslims' and a million 'Algerians' – Europeans.

Revolution & Independence

Algeria's war of independence, led by the newly formed FLN, began on 31 October 1954 in Batna, east of Algiers. The French military, the FLN and the *pied-noirs* all committed atrocities, with the use of torture routine. It's estimated that between 700,000 and 1.5 million lives were lost over seven years. President Charles de Gaulle, convinced of the impossibility of continued French rule, agreed to a referendum on independence in March 1962. The result was nearly unanimous, with most *pied-noirs* either abstaining or long departed. Independence was declared on 5 July 1962. By August, around 900,000 *pied-noirs* and *harkis* (Algerians who worked with the French) had left for France.

FLN candidate Ahmed ben Bella became Algeria's first president. He pledged to create a 'revolutionary Arab-Islamic state based on the principles of socialism and collective leadership at home and anti-imperialism abroad'. He was soon overthrown by former colleague Colonel Houari Boumédienne, who effectively returned the country to military rule in 1965.

Boumédienne died in December 1978 and the FLN replaced him with the slightly more moderate Colonel Chadli Benjedid, who was re-elected in 1984 and 1989. There was very little political change. The FLN continued to be the sole political party, pursuing secular, socialist policies. Any opposition was well underground, but in October 1988, thousands of people took to the streets in protest against austerity measures and food shortages. The army was called in to restore order, and between 100 and 600 people were killed.

The government reacted by pledging to relax the FLN monopoly on political power and work towards a multiparty system. The extent of the opposition became clear at local government elections held in early 1990, with landslide victories for the previously outlawed fundamentalist group Front Islamique du Salut (FIS; Islamic Salvation Front).

The initial round of Algeria's first multiparty parliamentary elections, held in December 1991, produced another landslide win for the FIS. Chadli's apparent acceptance of this prompted the army to step in, replacing him with a five-person Haut Conseil d'Etat (HCE; High Council of State) headed by Mohammed Boudiaf, a hero of the Algerian revolution. The second round of elections was cancelled, and FIS leaders Abbas Madani and Ali Belhadj were arrested, while others fled into exile.

Civil War

Boudiaf lasted six months before he was assassinated amid signs of a growing guerrilla offensive led by the Groupe Islamique Armé (GIA; Armed Islamic Group). He was replaced by former FLN hardliner Ali Kafi, who oversaw the country's rapid descent into civil war before he was replaced by a retired general, Liamine Zéroual. Zéroual attempted to defuse the situation by holding fresh elections in 1995, but Islamic parties were barred from the poll and Zéroual's sweeping victory came amid widespread claims of fraud.

Hopes for peace went unfulfilled; the war became even more remorseless, with Amnesty International accusing both sides of massacres. The GIA, angered by French aid to the government, extended the war to French soil with a series of bombings and hijackings.

Eventually, government security forces began to gain the upper hand, and at the beginning of 1999 Zéroual announced that he would be stepping down. New elections held in April that year resulted in a controversial victory for the establishment candidate Abdelaziz Bouteflika, a former foreign minister, who was elected unopposed after the rest of the candidates in the field claimed fraud and withdrew.

Bouteflika moved quickly to establish his legitimacy by calling a referendum on a plan to offer amnesty to the rebels. War-weary Algerians responded overwhelmingly with a

98% 'yes' vote, and by the end of 1999 many groups had responded and laid down their weapons.

The People of Algeria

The majority of Algerians are ethnically Arab-Berber and live in the north of the country. Berber traditions are best preserved in the Kabylie, east of Algiers, where people speak the Berber toungue, Tamazight, as their first language. The Tuareg people of the Sahara are also Berbers, and speak Tamashek. An estimated 99% of Algeria's population are Sunni Muslims, along with the Ibadis of the Mzeb Valley, and small numbers of Christians and Jews. While Islam is part of everyday life in Algeria, alcohol is available in bars and upmarket restaurants and not all women wear hijab.

Music

Algeria's most well-known cultural export is rai, a musical hybrid that was spawned in the clubs of colonial Oran and flourished as protest pop fusion in the 1970s and '80s. Initially suppressed by the Boumédienne government, it was, ironically, the popularity of rai in France that ended its censorship. Early greats include the Algerian James Brown, Boutaïba S'ghir, sweet, soulful Belkacem Bouteldja and the lyrical and sensual Chiekha Remiti. The celebrity status of Khaled, Rachid Taha and Faudel was cemented in a legendary concert *1, 2, 3 Soleils* in Paris in 1998; the live album is a good place to start for rai neophytes.

The country's ethnic diversity and turbulent history is reflected in its broader musical heritage. The Andalusian-Arabic vocal work of Mahieddine Bachtarzi helped forge a new national identity for Algerians during the early days of independence, as did Hadj M'Hamed El Anka with the Casbah's own Chaabi style. More recently the potent acoustic Amazigh folk of Kabylie singer Idir has championed the Berber cause, while the pan-Saharan sounds of Gwana give voice to Tuareg and black African Algerians.

Environment

After the succession of South Sudan, Algeria became Africa's largest nation. About 85% of the country is taken up by the Sahara, and the mountainous Tell region in the north makes up the balance. The Tell consists of two main mountain ranges: the Tell Atlas, which runs right along the north coast into Tunisia, and the Saharan Atlas, about 100km to the south. The area between the two ranges is known as the High Plateaus. The Sahara covers a great range of landscapes, from the classic seif dunes of the great *ergs* (sand seas) to the rock-strewn peaks of the Hoggar Mountains in the far south.

SURVIVAL GUIDE

ℹ Directory A–Z

ACCOMMODATION

Algerian hotels have long fallen into two camps: business-oriented four- to five-star hotels or grim budget places aimed squarely at travelling workers. Facilities in the former are improving with a new breed of private operators challenging the state-run (and often chronically run-down) monoliths. There are now also some good midrange newcomers in the northern cities, and pleasant guesthouses and campsites in the south.

BUSINESS HOURS

Most businesses in Algeria work from 8am or 9am until 4pm or 5pm, Sunday to Thursday. Friday's day of rest is almost universally observed. Some businesses and most shops are open half day on Saturday. In the south, expect long afternoon siestas.

EMBASSIES & CONSULATES

Diplomatic missions in Algiers:

British Embassy (☎0770 08 50 00; ukinalgeria.fco.gov.uk/en/; 3 Chemin Slimane, Hydra)

Canadian Embassy (☎0770 08 30 00; www.voyage.gc.ca; 18 Rue Mustapha Khalef, Ben Aknoun; ⏰Sat-Wed 8.30am-4pm) Also provides consular assistance to Australians.

French Embassy (☎021-98 15 05; www.ambafrance-dz.org; 25 Chemin Gadouche, Hydra)

German Embassy (☎021-74 19 41; www.algi.diplo.de; 165 Chemin Sfindja)

Italian Embassy (☎021-92 25 50; 18 Rue Ouidir Amellal, El-Biar)

Libyan Embassy (☎021-92 52 93; 15 Chemin Cheikh Bachir el-Ibrahimi, El-Biar)

Malian Embassy (☎021-54 72 14; Cité DNC, Villa No 15, Chemin Kara, Hydra)

Mauritanian Embassy (☎021-93 71 08; 30 Rue du Vercors, Bouzaréah)

Moroccan Embassy (☎021-60 50 60; 8 Rue Azil, El-Mouradia)

Nigerien Embassy (☎021-93 71 89; 54 Rue du Vercors, Bouzaréah)

Spanish Embassy (☎021-92 27 13; 46bis Rue Mohamed Chabane, El-Biar)

Tunisian Embassy (☎021-69 13 88; 11 Rue du Bois de Boulogne, Hydra)

US Embassy (☎0770 08 20 00; algiers.usembassy.gov; 5 Chemin Cheikh Ibrahimi, El-Biar)

GAY & LESBIAN TRAVELLERS

Homosexual sex is illegal for both men and women in Algeria, and incurs a maximum penalty of three years in jail and a stiff fine. You're unlikely to have any problems as a tourist, but discretion is advised.

INTERNET ACCESS

Wi-fi is common in the north. Cybercafe prices are reasonable (no more than DA150 per hour).

MONEY

Credit cards can be used only in big hotels and at car-hire companies. You'll need dinars for day-to-day expenses, although tourist-oriented businesses (hotels, airlines, tour companies etc) will often accept euros.

The black-market exchange rate is significantly better than that you'll get at banks. Ask locals where you can change money (it's considered routine, if not strictly legal). You can only change dinars back to euros or dollars unofficially.

Some Algerians, especially in rural areas, might give prices in centimes rather than dinars (there are 100 centimes in a dinar). To confuse matters further, they might also drop the thousands, so a quote of '130' means 130,000 centimes (ie DA1300).

POST & TELEPHONE

The postal system in Algeria is very slow. International delivery services such as Chronopost, DHL and Fedex are more reliable. International phone calls can be made from any of the public Taxiphone offices found in most towns. SIM cards from local carriers – Nedjma, Djezzy and Mobilis – are readily available.

PUBLIC HOLIDAYS

Algeria observes Islamic holidays as well as the following national holidays:

Labour Day 1 May

Revolutionary Readjustment (1965) 19 June

Independence Day 5 July

National Day (Revolution Day) 1 November

SAFE TRAVEL

Algeria has improved in safety immensely in recent years, and while foreigners were never usually the targets of violence, there's still every reason to exercise caution.

Check for the current local advisories when travelling to the northwest Kabylie region and the region about Batna. Driving here without a guide is not advised, as is driving anywhere in the countryside after dark.

Since the kidnapping of tourists in the southern Sahara in 2003, it's illegal to visit this region without an officially accredited guide. This includes any trips south of In Salah, including Tamanrasset. Many *pistes* (sandy tracks) around Tamanrasset and Djanet remain closed. Be ready to show your passport and agency invitation along the way.

TOURIST INFORMATION

Tourist offices can be found in many southern towns and are generally pretty helpful. The Algiers office of the state-run travel agency, ONT (p49), organises excursions.

TRAVEL AGENCIES

Anyone wanting to visit the Sahara will need to organise a trip through a travel agency, either as part of a tour, or directly with an agency in the south. The following are well-established local operators, but we advise soliciting feedback from various forums for other traveller's experiences (try Lonely Planet's Thorntree, Horizons Unlimited and Chris Scott's Sahara Overland).

Akar Akar (☎029-34 60 09; http://akar-akar.net) One of the oldest and biggest agencies in Tamanrasset. It accommodates guests in red-walled bungalows or authentic Tuareg tents at its own *gîte*.

Bachir Hafach (☎Skype touareg.bachir; www.touaregbachir.blogspot.com)

PRACTICALITIES

City listings *Guide Nomad* (in French) has comprehensive coverage of restaurants, cafes, shops and activities in Algiers and surrounds.

Electricity 220V, European-style two-pin plugs

Languages Algerian Arabic, Berber, French

Newspapers Arabic-language *El Khabar* (www.elkhabar.com) and *El Watan* (www.elwatan.com), *Liberté* (www.liberte-algerie.com) and *Quotidien d'Oran* (www.lequotidien-oran.com) in French.

Radio Algerian Radio is operated by state-run Radio-Television Algerienne, and runs national Arabic, Berber and French networks.

TV Enterprise Nationale de Television (ENTV) is the often derided state TV station, broadcasting on four channels, including one in Tamazight.

This English-speaking Toureg guide is based in Djanet but can also organise circuits from Tamanrasset.

Tim Missaw Tours (☎029-34 75 16; http://timmissawtours.e-monsite.com/) This company also owns and operates the Asekrem *refuge*. It is happy to organise simple packages with transport and a stay at the *refuge* (€90 per night, all inclusive) or full circuit tours.

Waléne Voyages (www.walene-voyages.com) Organises 4WD and camel trekking to Askrem and the Hoggar, including a footsteps of Foucauld circuit.

VISAS

Everyone except Moroccan, Tunisian and Malaysian nationals needs a visa to enter Algeria. Nationals of Israel, Malawi and Taiwan are not allowed into the country, and if you have a stamp in your passport from any of these countries your application might be rejected.

Visa applications must include at least an 'invitation' to visit the country from an Algerian contact or tourist agency – some embassies also require proof of flight bookings, travel insurance and a full itinerary. Visas are not available at Algiers airport, or at any of the country's border posts. Currently applications can only be made from your own country of residence.

A 30-day visa costs anywhere between US$40 and US$90, depending on the embassy. Allow plenty of time for your application to be issued. Waits of up to eight weeks are not unknown, but there are promising signs that the process is being streamlined.

Visa Extensions

Visa extensions can be applied for in Algiers from the **Department des Etrangers** (19A Blvd Zighout Youssef, Algiers) but are not easy to obtain.

Getting There & Away

AIR

Algeria is well serviced by local, European and African carriers.

Air Algérie (☎021-74 24 28, 65 33 40; www.airalgerie.dz; 1 Pl Maurice Audin, Algiers) Flies to destinations throughout North and West Africa, including Tripoli (Libya), Casablanca (Morocco), Dakar (Senegal) and Bamako (Mali). It flies five times daily to Paris and several times a week to London, Frankfurt, Istanbul and Dubai.

Aigle Azur (☎021-64 20 20; www.aigle-azur.com; 11 Ave Pasteur, Algiers) This French airline has four daily flights to Algiers from Paris Orly and services from eight regional cities including Marseille, Lyon and Lille. There are two daily Orly–Oran flights and less frequent services to Annaba, Batna, Bejaia, Biskra, Chlef, Constantine, Djanet, Hassi Messaoud, Setif, Tamanrasset and Tlemcen.

LAND

Libya

The Libyan–Algerian border is closed.

Mali & Mauritania

Algeria's southwestern borders with Mali and Mauritania are currently closed to all traffic.

Morocco

The border with Morocco has been closed for some time, although there are numerous flights between the two countries.

Niger

Travelling south into Niger via Guezzam (Algeria) and Assamakka (Niger) has loads of romantic trans-Saharan cachet, but is a bureaucratic and time-consuming route. In the current climate, it's even more difficult, if not impossible.

Tunisia

There are numerous border-crossing points between Tunisia and Algeria, and these are currently the only way for overlanders to enter Algeria. The main one is just outside Hazoua on the route between El-Oued and Nefta/Tozeur. North coast crossings include those from El Kala to Tabarka or inland, to Babouch near Ain Draham.

SEA

It's possible to arrive in Algiers by ferry from Europe, though it's far from the cheapest option. The ferry terminal is near the main train station. French **SNCM** (☎021-71 81 15; www.sncm.fr; 28 Blvd Zighout Youssef, Algiers) operates ferry services between Marseille and Algiers or Oran once a week, and less frequently to Alicante (Spain). **Algérie Ferries** (☎021-42 46 50; www.algerieferries.com; 37 Rue Didouche Mourad) connects Algiers or Oran to Marseille (twice a week) and Alicante (approximately twice a month). Tickets between Algiers and Marseille cost between DA8500 for a seat, and DA21,050 for cabins. The voyage to Marseille takes about 20 hours, and to Alicante 10 hours. Expect long waits on disembarkation if travelling with a car.

Getting Around

AIR

Air Algérie offers extensive and reasonably priced domestic services, including flights to Tamanrasset and Ghardaïa.

BUS

Long-distance buses are run by various regional companies and are usually reasonably comfortable. Routes go as far south as Tamanrasset. Try to buy your ticket at least a day ahead: less-frequently-serviced Saharan routes sell out.

CAR & MOTORCYCLE

Driving yourself anywhere in the country theoretically requires an agency escort, but it's not strictly enforced in the north, even with numerous police checks. The Kabylie region in Algeria's northwest is currently settled, but can be dangerous for unescorted nonresidents.

The main route across the Sahara is the Route du Hoggar, from Ghardaïa via El-Goléa and In Salah to Tamanrasset and on to the border and Arlit in Niger. The road is tar all the way to Tamanrasset. Other less-used roads include the eastern Route du Tassili N'Ajjer, from Hassi Messaoud to Tamanrasset across the Grand Erg Oriental, and the Route du Tanezrouft, from Adrar to Borj Mokhtar near the Malian border. The latter two routes include sections of *piste*.

LOCAL TRANSPORT

Louages only operate in the north of the country. They are often more expensive than buses.

TRAIN

Société Nationale des Transports Ferroviaires (SNTF; www.sntf.dz) trains run from Algiers along the eastern line to Bejaia, Constantine and Annaba (seven to 10 hours) and along the western line to Oran (four to six hours) and from there to Tlemcen (2½ hours). Additional lines run south from Oran to Béchar and from Constantine to Touggourt. International services to Morocco and Tunisia have long been suspended.

Egypt

POP 83 MILLION

Includes ➡

Best Places to Eat

- ➡ Sofra (p87)
- ➡ Zööba (p65)
- ➡ Farag (p74)
- ➡ Seabride (p79)
- ➡ Abou El Sid (p68)

Best Places to Stay

- ➡ Shali Lodge (p75)
- ➡ Beit Sabée (p86)
- ➡ Pension Roma (p63)
- ➡ Hotel Longchamps (p64)
- ➡ Sinai Old Spices (p77)

Why Go?

Herodotus let the cat out of the bag in the 5th century BC, leaving the door open for over a millennium of conquerors and adventurers to gawp, graffiti and pilfer Egypt's mammoth racks of pharaonic rubble. Today it may be 'gawping-only' allowed but these ancient monuments still inspire the same reverence in travellers as they have for centuries.

Walk away from the click of a million camera-shutters for a minute though and you'll discover Egypt isn't just mummies and colossal columns. Sink into a meditative stupor of *shisha* (hookah) smoking in a cafe. Bed down on a desert dune. Watch the sun rise over the palm-tree-fringed Nile banks. Stand streetside when the call to prayer wafts over the nightmare symphony of car horns. Modern Egypt can frustrate and confound but it enchants in equal measures. The temples, tombs and pyramids will still be there when you get back to them; basking in their sheer awesomeness as they have done since time immemorial.

When to Go

Cairo

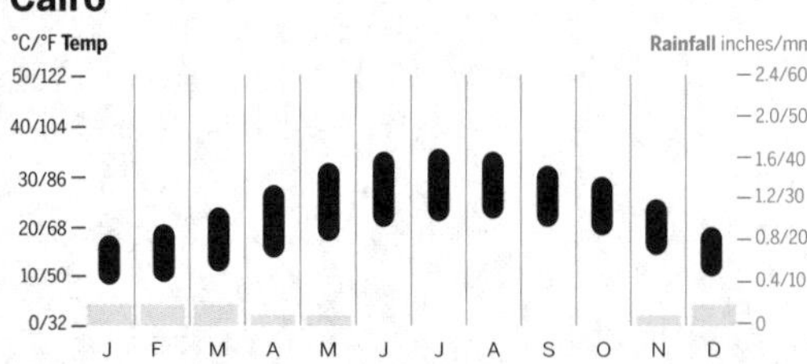

Mar–Apr Dust off your explorer hat and head into the Western Desert while temperatures stay mild.

Jul–Sep Summer's furnace sizzles but underwater conditions are perfect for Red Sea diving.

Oct–Nov In Upper Egypt, the gorgeous painterly light makes a Nile journey a photographer's dream.

CAIRO

02 / POP 20 MILLION

Let's address the drawbacks first. The crowds on a Cairo footpath make Manhattan look like a ghost town. You will be hounded by papyrus sellers at every turn. Your life will flash before your eyes each time you venture across a street. And your snot will run black from the smog.

But it's a small price to pay to visit the city Cairenes call Umm ad-Dunya – the Mother of the World. One taxi ride can span millenniums, from the resplendent mosques and mausoleums built at the pinnacle of the Islamic empire, to the 19th-century palaces and grand avenues (which earned the city the nickname 'Paris on the Nile'), to the brutal concrete blocks of the Nasser years – then all the way back to the days of the pharaohs, as the Pyramids of Giza hulk on the western edge of the city.

So blow your nose, crack a joke, and learn to look through the dirt to see the city's true colours. If you love Cairo, she will love you back.

Sights

★ Pyramids & Sphinx at Giza ARCHAEOLOGICAL SITE

(Sharia al-Haram, Giza; adult/student E£60/30; 8am-4pm) Built on a desert plateau, encroached upon by the modern city of Cairo, the Giza pyramids are the last remaining wonder of the ancient world. They were built as the mausoleums of pharaohs to help their souls on the path to heaven.

Completed around 2600 BC, the **Great Pyramid of Khufu** (Pyramid of Cheops; adult/student E£100/50; 8am-noon & 1-6pm) is the oldest pyramid at Giza, and the largest (146.5m high). Climbing the steep, narrow passage to the heart of the pyramid is an unforgettable, if claustrophobic, experience.

Immediately south of the Great Pyramid is the **Solar Barque Museum** (Cheops Boat Museum; adult/student E£50/25; 9am-4pm), displaying one of the pharaoh's funerary barques (boats) unearthed in 1954.

The neighbouring **Pyramid of Khafre** (Pyramid of Chephren; adult/student E£30/15; 8am-4pm) was built by Khufu's son. In deference to his father, he built a slightly smaller pyramid but located it on higher ground, giving the impression of greater size.

At a height of 62m, the **Pyramid of Menkaure** (Pyramid of Mycerinus; adult/student E£30/15; 8am-4pm) is the smallest of the three pyramids; it was built by Khafre's son, Menkaure.

Known in Arabic as Abu al-Hol (Father of Terror), the **Sphinx** (8am-4pm) is carved from a single piece of wind-eroded limestone. With the face of a man and the body of a lion, it remains one of the most evocative monuments of the ancient world.

★ Egyptian Museum MUSEUM

(2579 6948; www.egyptianmuseum.gov.eg; Midan Tahrir, Downtown; adult/student E£60/30; 9am-6pm Sat-Thu, to 4pm Fri) Home to one of the world's most important collections of ancient artefacts, to walk around the Egyptian Museum is to embark on an adventure through time itself.

On the ground floor some highlights not to miss include the black **statue of Khafre** (Room 42), the builder of the second pyramid at Giza, and the **Amarna Room** (Room 3), which displays many of the artistic achievements of Akhenaten's reign (1352–1336 BC).

The 1st floor's eastern side hosts the famed **Tutankhamun Galleries** with about 1700 items unearthed from the young New Kingdom pharaoh's tomb spread throughout a series of rooms. The **Royal Mummies Halls** (1st fl, Rooms 56 & 46; adult/student E£100/60) houses the remains of some of Egypt's most illustrious pharaohs and queens.

The entire caboodle is planned to be moved to the new state-of-the-art Grand Egyptian Museum being built at the Giza Plateau. The opening is slated for 2015 but construction progress has been painfully slow, so don't hold your breath.

Islamic Cairo

The medieval heart of Cairo, this area was one of the power centres of the Islamic empire and its monuments are some of the most resplendent architecture inspired by Islam.

★ Mosque-Madrassa of Sultan Hassan MOSQUE

(Midan Salah ad-Din; admission E£25; 8am-5pm) The square courtyard of this elegant complex, regarded as the finest piece of early Mamluk architecture in Cairo, boasts soaring walls punctured by four majestic *iwans* (vaulted halls).

★ Al-Azhar Mosque MOSQUE

(Gami' al-Azhar; Sharia al-Azhar; 24hr) FREE Founded in AD 970 as the centrepiece of the newly created Fatimid city, Al-Azhar is one of

Egypt Highlights

1. Tip your head back and gape at the **pyramids of Giza** (p59).
2. Stroll through the spiderweb souqs and medieval streets of **Islamic Cairo** (p59).
3. Wander through the gigantic papyrus-shaped stone columns in the hypostyle hall at **Karnak** (p83).
4. Follow in the footsteps of prophets and pilgrims on the time-worn Steps of Repentance at **Mt Sinai's** (p80).
5. Dive at **Ras Mohammed National Park** (p77), an underwater fantasia of coral mountains and ghostly shipwrecks.
6. Soak up the tranquil vibes and unique culture of breathtaking **Siwa Oasis** (p74).
7. Explore the geological wonder of the **White Desert** (p75).
8. Soak up the last drops of 19th-century grandeur at **Alexandria** (p71) with a walk along the corniche.
9. Experience Egypt's lifeblood, the Nile, on a felucca ride from **Aswan** (p88) to Kom Ombo.
10. Sense the vanity of Ramses II in the awe-inspiring **Great Temple of Abu Simbel** (p91).

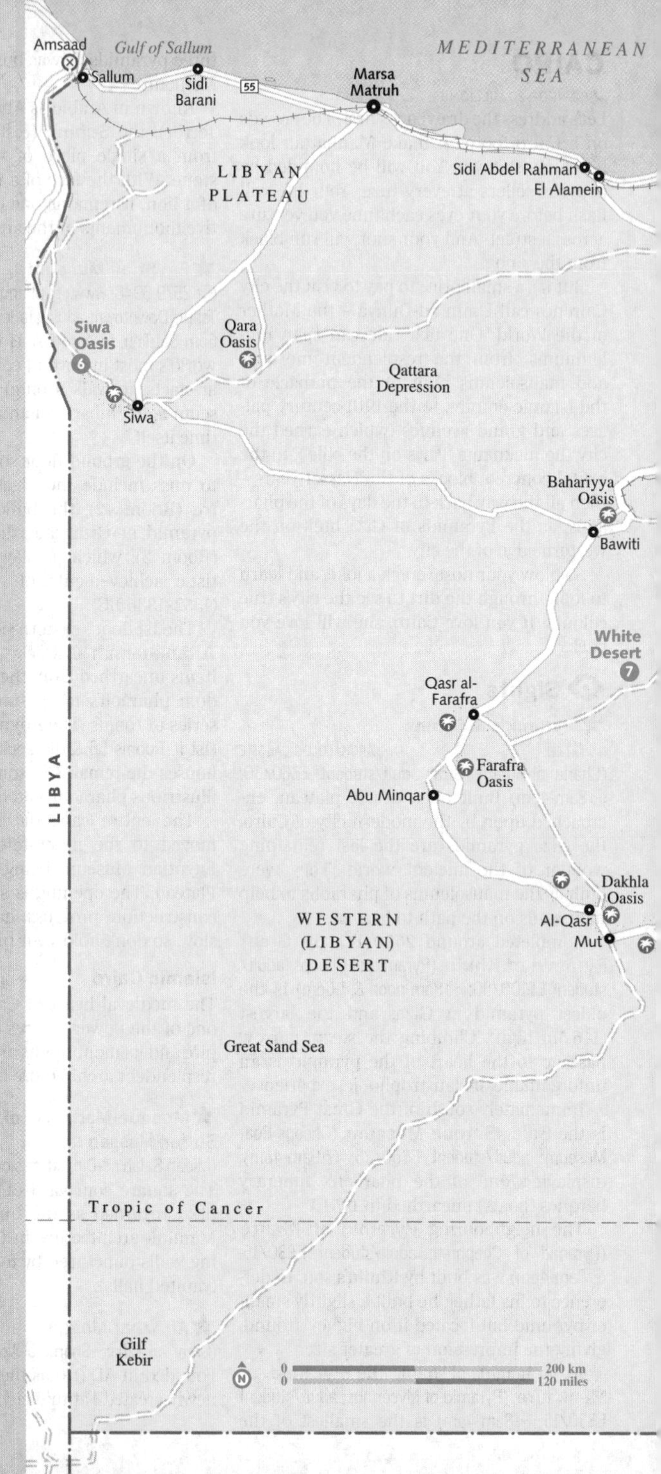

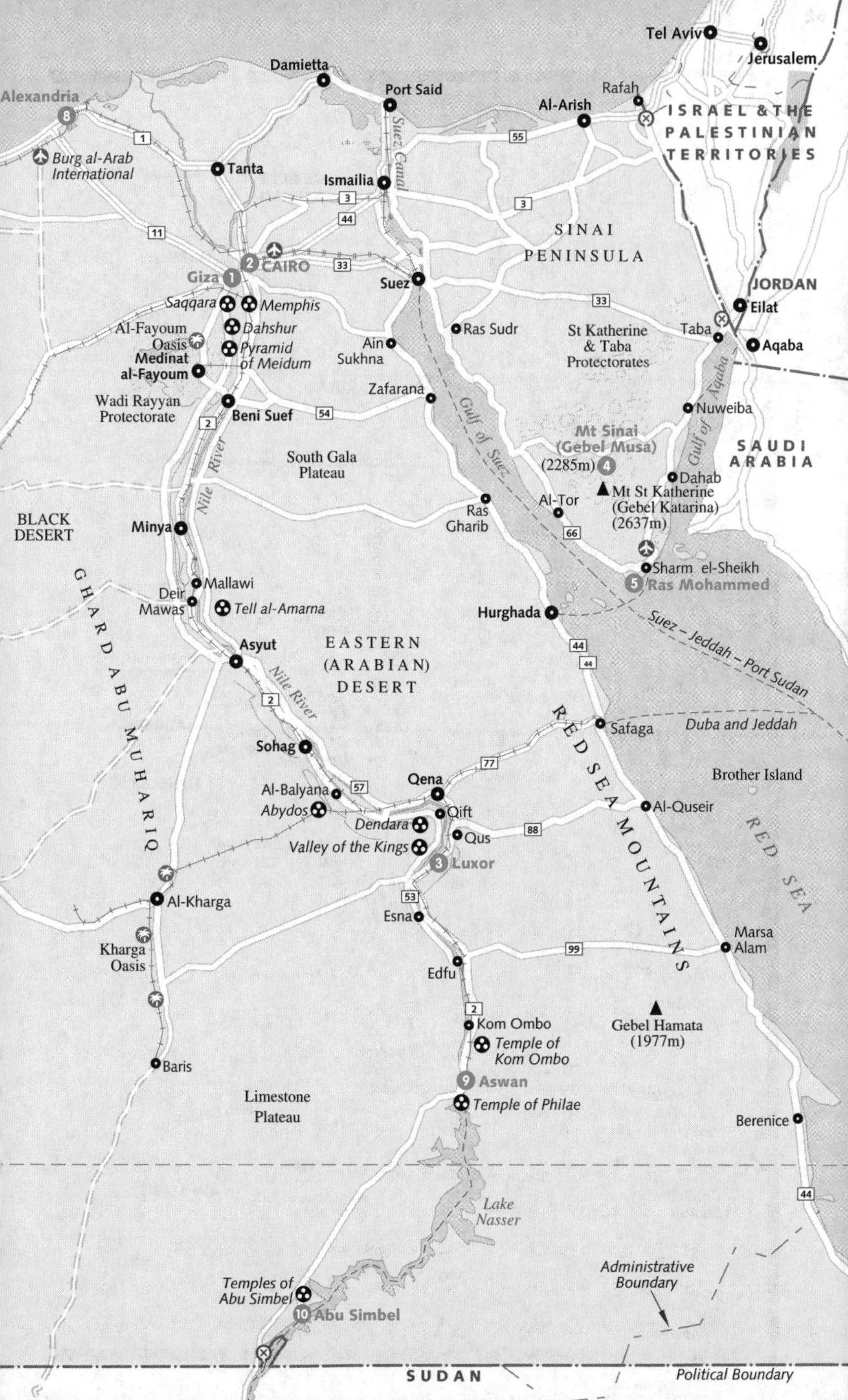

Tel Aviv
Jerusalem
Damietta
Port Said
Rafah
Al-Arish
ISRAEL & THE PALESTINIAN TERRITORIES
Alexandria
8
Burg al-Arab International
Tanta
Ismailia
Suez Canal
SINAI PENINSULA
CAIRO
2
Giza
1
Suez
JORDAN
Saqqara
Memphis
Dahshur
Al-Fayoum Oasis
Pyramid of Meidum
Medinat al-Fayoum
Eilat
Taba
Aqaba
Ras Sudr
Ain Sukhna
St Katherine & Taba Protectorates
Zafarana
Wadi Rayyan Protectorate
Beni Suef
Nuweiba
Gulf of Aqaba
Gulf of Suez
Mt Sinai (Gebel Musa)
(2285m)
4
SAUDI ARABIA
South Gala Plateau
Nile River
Dahab
Mt St Katherine (Gebel Katarina) (2637m)
Ras Gharib
Al-Tor
BLACK DESERT
Minya
Sharm el-Sheikh
5
Ras Mohammed
Mallawi
Deir Mawas
Tell al-Amarna
Hurghada
GHARD ABU MUHARIQ
Asyut
EASTERN (ARABIAN) DESERT
Suez – Jeddah – Port Sudan
RED SEA MOUNTAINS
Safaga
Duba and Jeddah
Sohag
Brother Island
Al-Balyana
Qena
Abydos
Qift
Al-Quseir
Dendara
Qus
Valley of the Kings
3
Luxor
RED SEA
Al-Kharga
Esna
Kharga Oasis
Marsa Alam
Edfu
Kom Ombo
Gebel Hamata (1977m)
Temple of Kom Ombo
Baris
9
Aswan
Limestone Plateau
Temple of Philae
Berenice
Lake Nasser
Administrative Boundary
Temples of Abu Simbel
10
Abu Simbel
SUDAN
Political Boundary
1
55
3
44
11
33
54
2
66
57
77
88
53
99

Cairo

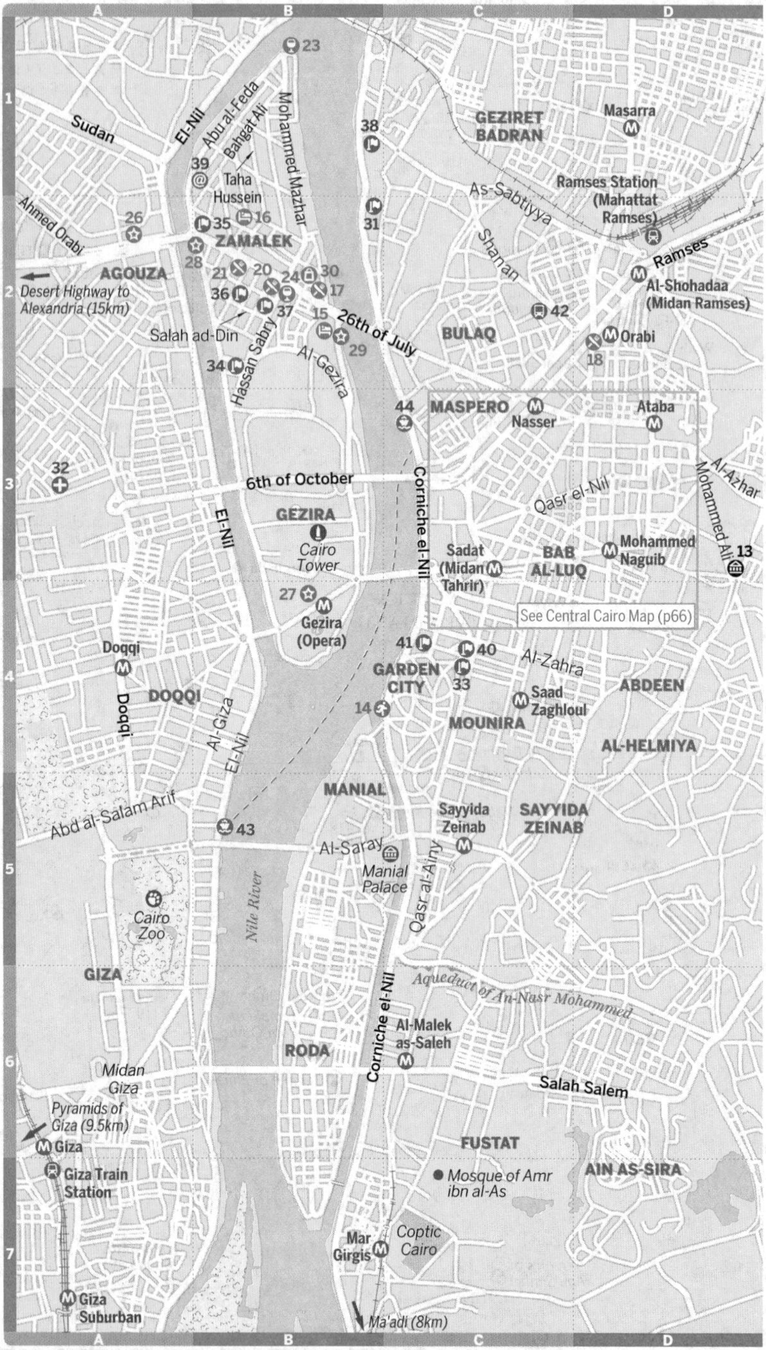

A B C D

1 2 3 4 5 6 7

23
Sudan
El-Nil
Abu al-Feda
Bahgat Ali
Mohammed Mazhar
38
GEZIRET BADRAN
Masarra
39
Taha Hussein
31
As-Sabtiyya
Ramses Station (Mahattat Ramses)
Ahmed Orabi
26
35
16
ZAMALEK
28
Shanan
AGOUZA
21
20
24
30
17
Ramses
Al-Shohadaa (Midan Ramses)
Desert Highway to Alexandria (15km)
36
37
15
26th of July
42
Salah ad-Din
Hassan Sabry
29
BULAQ
Orabi
18
34
Al-Gezira
44
MASPERO
Nasser
Ataba
32
6th of October
Corniche el-Nil
Qasr el-Nil
Al-Azhar
Mohammed Ali
GEZIRA
Cairo Tower
El-Nil
Sadat (Midan Tahrir)
BAB AL-LUQ
Mohammed Naguib
13
27
Gezira (Opera)
See Central Cairo Map (p66)
Doqqi
41
40
Al-Zahra
GARDEN CITY
33
ABDEEN
DOQQI
Doqqi
14
Saad Zaghloul
MOUNIRA
Al-Giza
El-Nil
AL-HELMIYA
MANIAL
Abd al-Salam Arif
43
Sayyida Zeinab
SAYYIDA ZEINAB
Al-Saray
Manial Palace
Qasr al-Ainy
Nile River
Cairo Zoo
GIZA
Aqueduct of An-Nasr Mohammed
Al-Malek as-Saleh
RODA
Corniche el-Nil
Midan Giza
Salah Salem
Pyramids of Giza (9.5km)
FUSTAT
Giza
Giza Train Station
Mosque of Amr ibn al-As
AIN AS-SIRA
Mar Girgis
Coptic Cairo
Giza Suburban
Ma'adi (8km)

A B C D

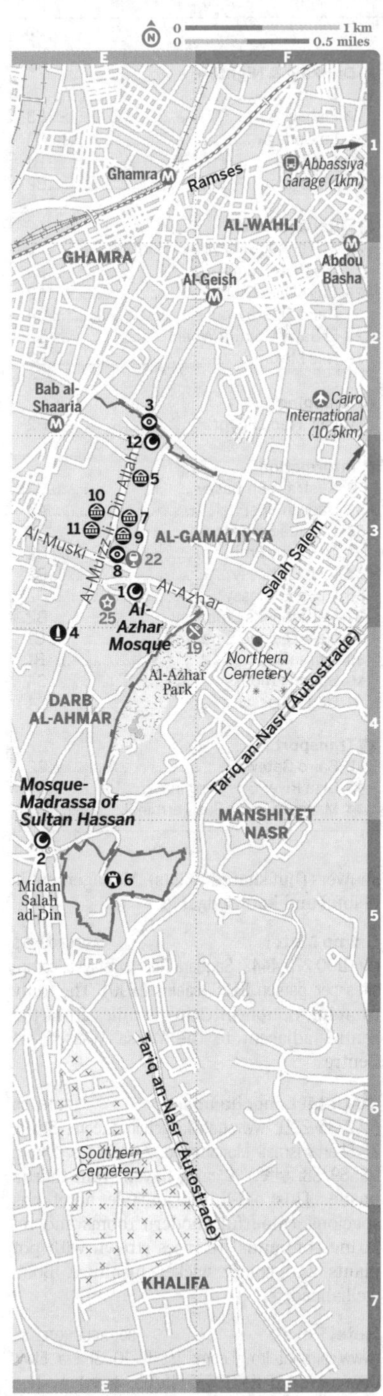

Cairo's earliest mosques and its madrassa (AD 988) is the world's second-oldest university.

Khan al-Khalili MARKET

Opposite Al-Azhar Mosque, this labyrinthine bazaar was built in the 14th century, and the merchants of its twisting, atmospheric alleyways stock everything from copperware and antiques to gaudy toy camels and alabaster pyramids.

Bab Zuweila MONUMENT

(Sharia al-Muizz li-Din Allah; adult/student E£15/8; ⏲8.30am-5pm) Bab Zuweila is the only surviving southern gate of medieval Cairo. Visitors may climb up to the two minarets on top for one of the best available views of the area.

Museum of Islamic Art MUSEUM

(☎2390 1520; Sharia Bur Said; admission £E50; ⏲9am-5pm Sat-Thu, 9am-noon & 2-5pm Fri) Recently renovated, this museum holds one of the world's finest collections of Islamic art. Only a sliver of the 80,000 objects the museum owns are on display but the selected items are stunning.

Citadel FORTRESS

(Al-Qala'a; ☎2512 1735; Sharia Salah Salem; adult/student E£50/25; ⏲8am-4pm, mosques closed during prayers Fri) Commenced by Saladin in the 12th century, the Citadel houses an assortment of mosques and underwhelming museums but a visit is worthwhile for the panoramic city views.

Activities

A lovely way to enjoy sunset is to take a ride on a felucca (traditional Nile sailing vessel). It costs between E£50 and E£70 per hour. The best felucca mooring point is the **Dok Dok landing stage** (Corniche el-Nil), opposite the Four Seasons Hotel.

Sleeping

★**Pension Roma** PENSION $

(☎2391 1088; www.pensionroma.com.eg; 4th fl, 169 Sharia Mohammed Farid, Downtown; s/d with fan E£80/125, with air-con E£165/253; ❄📶) Filled with old-fashioned charm, the Roma brings a touch of elegance to the budget-travel scene. Staff here are friendly, and the lack of tour-touting is a welcome relief. A few newer rooms have private facilities but most share bathrooms.

Hotel Luna HOSTEL $

(☎2396 1020; www.hotellunacairo.com; 5th fl, 27 Sharia Talaat Harb, Downtown; s/d/tr from E£150/

Cairo

Top Sights
1 Al-Azhar Mosque ... E3
2 Mosque-Madrassa of Sultan Hassan ... E5

Sights
3 Bab al-Futuh ... E2
4 Bab Zuweila ... E4
5 Beit el-Suhaymi ... E3
6 Citadel ... E5
7 Egyptian Textile Museum ... E3
8 Khan al-Khalili ... E3
9 Madrassa & Mausoleum of as-Salih Ayyub ... E3
10 Madrassa & Mausoleum of Barquq ... E3
11 Madrassa & Mausoleum of Qalaun ... E3
12 Mosque of Al-Hakim ... E3
13 Museum of Islamic Art ... D3

Activities, Courses & Tours
14 Dok Dok Landing Stage ... B4

Sleeping
15 Cairo Marriott Hotel ... B2
16 Hotel Longchamps ... B2

Eating
17 Abou El Sid ... B2
18 At-Tabei Ad-Dumyati ... D2
19 Citadel View ... E4
La Bodega ... (see 17)
20 La Mezzaluna ... B2
21 Zööba ... B2

Drinking & Nightlife
Deals ... (see 17)
22 Fishawi's ... E3
La Bodega ... (see 17)
23 Sequoia ... B1
24 Simonds ... B2

Entertainment
25 Al-Tannoura Egyptian Heritage Dance Troupe ... E3
26 Cairo Jazz Club ... A2
27 Cairo Opera House ... B4
28 El Sawy Culture Wheel ... B2
29 Nile Maxim ... B2

Shopping
30 Fair Trade Egypt ... B2

Information
31 Australia Embassy ... B2
32 Badran Hospital ... A3
33 Canada Embassy ... C4
34 Germany Embassy ... B2
35 Irish Embassy ... B2
36 Libya Embassy ... B2
37 Netherlands Embassy ... B2
38 New Zealand Embassy ... B1
39 Sigma Net ... B1
40 Sudan Embassy ... C4
41 UK Embassy ... C4

Transport
42 Cairo Gateway ... C2
43 Giza River Bus Terminal ... B5
44 Maspero River Bus Terminal ... C3

200/250, without bathroom E£100/140/180; ❄📶) Backpacker-friendly Luna has a range of rooms, all with air-con, overseen by a fastidious owner who makes sure everything is clean and surprisingly colour-coordinated. The 'Bella Luna' rooms are spacious and quiet.

Dina's Hostel HOSTEL $
(☎2396 3902; www.dinashostel.com; 5th fl, 42 Sharia Abdel Khalek Sarwat, Downtown; dm/s/d without bathroom E£50/110/140, d E£200; ❄📶) With a female owner, and low on pressure tactics, Dina's has tidy rooms with lots of homely touches, and the shared kitchen is an added bonus.

Berlin Hotel HOSTEL $
(☎2395 7502; berlinhotelcairo@hotmail.com; 4th fl, 2 Sharia Shawarby, Downtown; s/d with fan 100/130, with air-con 147/177; ❄📶) This budget-traveller stalwart has colourful rooms with showers (but shared toilets). Management is helpful and knowledgable.

Salma Motel CAMPGROUND $
(☎0100 270 4442; Saqqara Rd, Harraniyya; campsites per person E£25, cabins E£90) The only camping option in Cairo is miles from the centre, adjacent to the Wissa Wassef Art Centre.

★ **Hotel Longchamps** HOTEL $$
(☎2735 2311; www.hotellongchamps.com; 5th fl, 21 Sharia Ismail Mohammed, Zamalek; s/d from US$69/88; ❄📶) A calm haven from Cairo's bustle. This old-European-style hotel has spacious, colourful, modern rooms and relaxing communal terraces strewn with pot plants and comfy wicker furniture. Book well ahead.

Hotel Royal BOUTIQUE HOTEL $$
(www.cairohotelroyal.com; 1st fl, 10 Sharia Elwy, Downtown; s/d/ste US$35/45/65; ❄📶) A slice

of Scandinavian-minimalist styling in the middle of Cairo? We never thought we'd see the day. Comfortable, streamlined rooms boast crisp white bed linen and fresh flowers on bedside tables.

Windsor Hotel HOTEL $$
(2591 5277; www.windsorcairo.com; 19 Sharia Alfy, Downtown; s/d from US$46/59, with shower & hand basin US$37/47;) Despite the dim rooms with noisy air-conditioners, the beautifully maintained elevator and a restaurant interior that fell out of a 1950s time capsule make this place hard for nostalgia buffs to resist.

Grand Hotel HOTEL $$
(2575 7700; www.grandhotelcairo.com; 17 Sharia 26th of July, Downtown; s/d from E£275/385;) This seven-storey dame's 100 rooms still cling to some art-deco style despite a modern conversion. The balcony views onto the street bedlam below are fantastic.

Cairo Marriott Hotel LUXURY HOTEL $$$
(2728 3000; www.marriott.com/caieg; 16 Sharia Saray al-Gezira, Zamalek; r from US$205; P) Historic atmosphere is thick in the lobby and other public areas, which occupy a 19th-century palace. The rooms (in two modern towers) have plush beds and plasma-screen TVs. The beautiful garden and pool are a relaxing retreat from the city streets.

Eating & Drinking

In Zamalek, trendsetters prop up the bar at the stylish **La Bodega** (2735 6761; 157 Sharia 26th of July; noon-2am) and lounge Nile-side at swanky fashionista-haunt **Sequoia** (2576 8086; 3 Sharia Abu al-Feda; beer E£28, cocktails E£50-60, mezze E£20-40, minimum charge Sun-Wed E£125, Thu-Sat E£150; 1pm-1am). For something less sedate, try the rowdy **Deals** (2 Sharia Sayed al-Bakry; 6pm-2am), off Sharia 26th of July.

★ **Zööba** EGYPTIAN $
(Sharia 26th of July, Zamalek; sandwiches E£5-14; 7am-late;) New-kid-on-the-block Zööba is giving Egyptian fast-food favourites a reboot and making it hip to eat *baladi* (local) style. Modern interpretations of Egyptian classics *fuul* (fava-bean paste), *ta'amiyya* (Egyptian variant of felafel) and *shwarma* (kebab) sandwiches feature fresh flavours and quirky ingredient combinations.

Abu Tarek EGYPTIAN $
(40 Sharia Champollion, Downtown; dishes E£3-10; 8am-midnight;) This veritable *kushari* (a blend of pasta, rice, lentils and fried onions smothered in a tomato sauce) palace has expanded, decade by decade, into the upper storeys of its building, and held on to the unofficial Best Kushari in Cairo title.

At-Tabei Ad-Dumyati EGYPTIAN $
(2575 4211; 31 Sharia Orabi, Downtown; dishes E£3-15 ; 7am-1am;) Cheap, tasty Egyptian

LOCAL KNOWLEDGE

WALKING THROUGH HISTORY ON SHARIA AL-MUIZZ LI-DIN ALLAH

A walk through this former grand thoroughfare of medieval Cairo evokes a sense of once-imposing might. A combined ticket for most monuments (E£100) can be bought from the Madrassa & Mausoleum of as-Salih Ayyub, though some sites have separate entry tickets.

Head north from the intersection with Sharia Al-Azhar. The imposing **Madrassa & Mausoleum of as-Salih-Ayyub** (9am-4.30pm) was built in 1247 at the end of the Ayyubid era. Across the road the **Madrassa & Mausoleum of Qalaun** (9am-4.30pm), completed in 1279, includes a *maristan* (hospital) and a dazzling mausoleum. A few steps north brings you to the 14th-century **Madrassa & Mausoleum of Barquq** (9am-4.30pm), with its lavish inner court decorated with a blue-and-gold ceiling. Nearly directly opposite is the small but interesting **Egyptian Textile Museum** (adult/student E£20/10; 9am-4.30pm).

Further along, down the narrow lane Darb al-Asfar, which runs to the east, **Beit el-Suhaymi** (Darb al-Asfar; adult/student E£30/15; 9am-4.30pm) is a restored mansion with a peaceful inner courtyard surrounded by tiled reception halls.

At the end of Sharia al-Muizz li-Din Allah you'll reach the imposing northern gate of **Bab al-Futuh** (Gate of Conquests), built in 1087. On its eastern side is the giant **Mosque of Al-Hakim** (Sharia al-Galal), completed in 1013 by notorious Fatimid ruler Al-Hakim.

Central Cairo

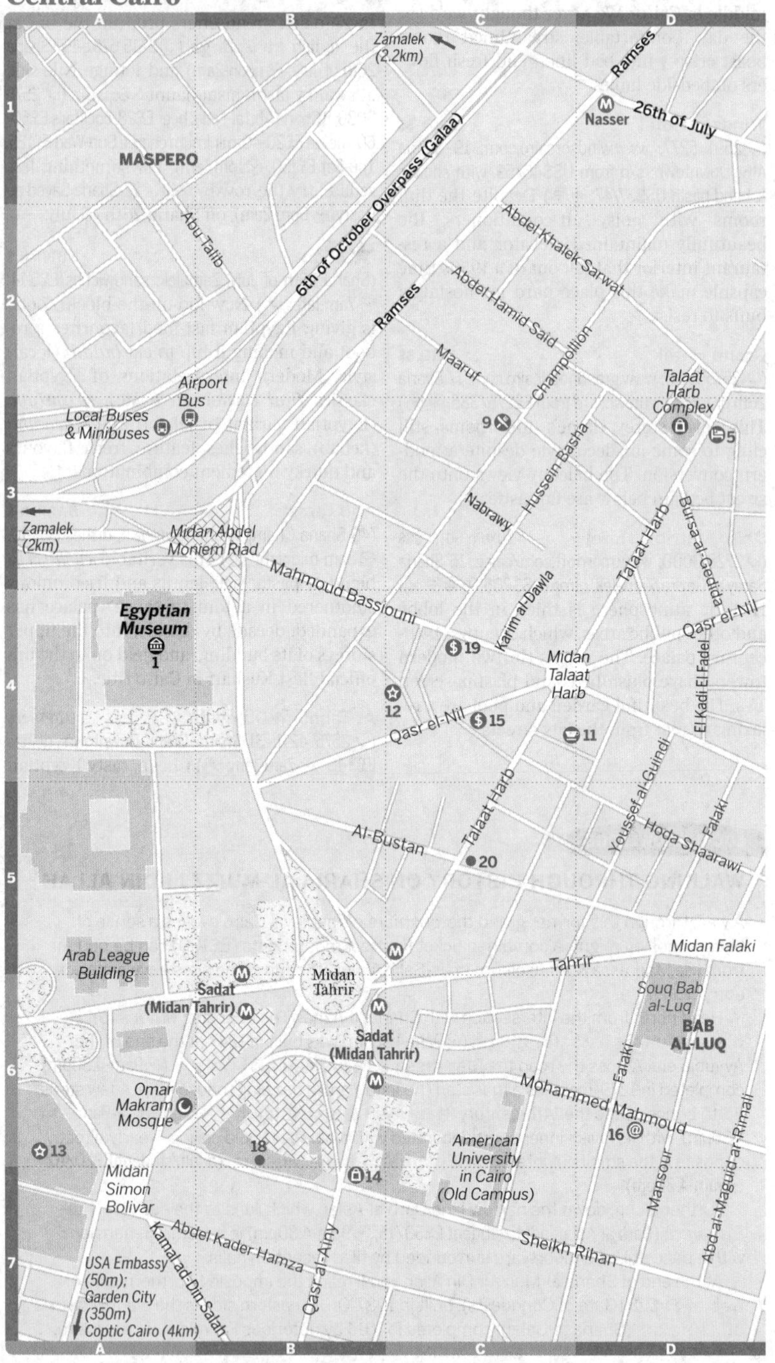

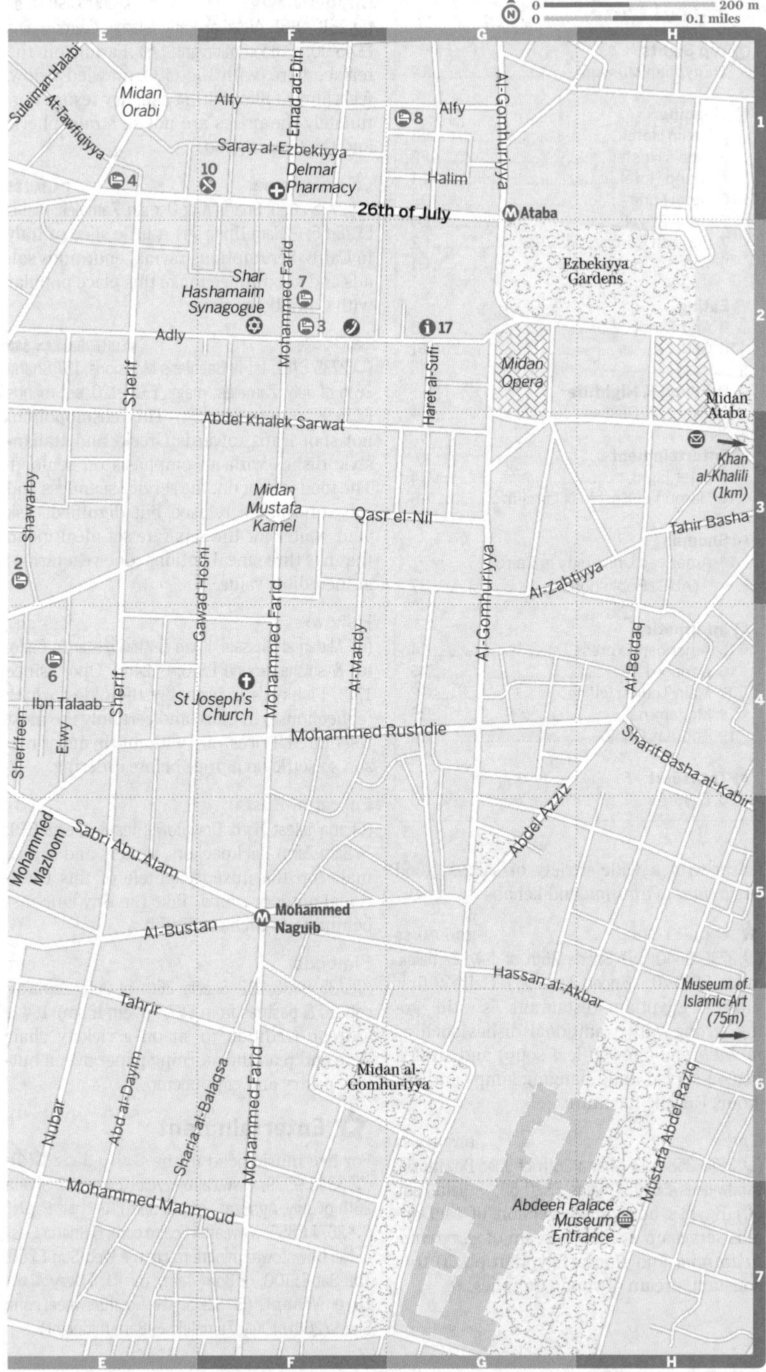
0 200 m
0 0.1 miles
Midan Orabi
Suleiman Halabi
At-Tawfiqiyya
Alfy
Emad ad-Din
8
Saray al-Ezbekiyya
10
4
Delmar Pharmacy
Halim
Al-Gomhuriyya
26th of July
Ataba
Ezbekiyya Gardens
Shar Hashamaim Synagogue
7
3
17
Adly
Mohammed Farid
Sherif
Haret al-Sufi
Midan Opera
Midan Ataba
Abdel Khalek Sarwat
Khan al-Khalili (1km)
Shawarby
Midan Mustafa Kamel
Qasr el-Nil
Tahir Basha
2
Gawad Hosni
Al-Zabtiyya
Al-Gomhuriyya
Al-Mahdy
Al-Beidaq
6
Ibn Talaab
St Joseph's Church
Sheriffeen
Elwy
Mohammed Rushdie
Sharif Basha al-Kabir
Abdel Azziz
Mohammed Mazloom
Sabri Abu Alam
Mohammed Naguib
Al-Bustan
Hassan al-Akbar
Museum of Islamic Art (75m)
Tahrir
Midan al-Gomhuriyya
Nubar
Abd al-Dayim
Sharia al-Balaqsa
Mustafa Abdel Raziq
Abdeen Palace Museum Entrance
Mohammed Mahmoud

Central Cairo

Top Sights

1 Egyptian Museum........A4

Sleeping

2 Berlin Hotel........E3
3 Dina's Hostel........F2
4 Grand Hotel........E1
5 Hotel Luna........D3
6 Hotel Royal........E4
7 Pension Roma........F2
8 Windsor Hotel........G1

Eating

9 Abu Tarek........C3
10 Gad........F1

Drinking & Nightlife

11 Zahret al-Bustan........C4

Entertainment

12 After Eight........C4
13 Haroun El-Rashid Nightclub........A6

Shopping

14 American University in Cairo (AUC) Bookshop........B7

Information

15 American Express........C4
16 Concord........D6
17 Main Tourist Office........G2
18 Mogamma........B6
19 Thomas Cook........C4

Transport

20 EgyptAir........C5

feasts with a wide variety of salads, good *shwarma*, *ta'amiyya* and kebabs.

★ **Abou El Sid** EGYPTIAN $$

(☎2735 9640; 157 Sharia 26th of July, Zamalek; mains E£25-70; ⊙noon-2am;) Cairo's first hipster Egyptian restaurant is still going strong with traditional dishes such as *molokhiyya* (stewed leaf soup) and stuffed pigeon served amid hanging lamps and gilt 'Louis Farouk' furniture.

Gad EGYPTIAN $$

(☎2576 3583; 13 Sharia 26th of July, Downtown; sandwiches E£2-15, mains E£20-50; ⊙9am-2am;) Egypt's homemade version of McDonalds serves up a steady stream of *shwarma*, *ta'amiyya* and *fiteer* (Egyptian pizza) to a constant stream of young Cairenes.

Citadel View MIDDLE EASTERN $$

(☎2510 9151; Al-Azhar Park, Islamic Cairo; mains E£45-90; ⊙noon-midnight;) Eating on the terrace here, with the city sprawled below, feels almost like visiting a luxury resort. Fortunately the prices are not so stratospheric and the food is good.

La Mezzaluna ITALIAN $$

(☎2735 2655; Sharia Aziz Osman, Zamalek; mains E£28-66; ⊙8am-11pm;) A little slice of Italy in Cairo. Scrumptious ravioli, enormous salads and good coffee make this place popular with Cairo bohemians.

La Bodega MEDITERRANEAN $$$

(☎2735 6761; 1st fl, Baehler's Mansions, 157 Sharia 26th of July, Zamalek; mains E£75-120, set menus E£75-95; ⊙noon-2am;) This cosmopolitan hot spot leans towards Greek- and Italian-style dishes with an emphasis on seafood. The food is spot on, the service seamless and the atmosphere relaxed but dignified. Ask your waiter for the separate set-meal menu that has three meal options (one vegetarian) at incredible value.

Fishawi's CAFE

(off Midan al-Hussein, Khan el-Khalili, Islamic Cairo; tea & shisha around E£10; ⊙24hr) Open since 1773, Fishawi's is probably the oldest *ahwa* (coffeehouse) in Cairo and certainly the most celebrated. Prices vary without rhyme or reason so settle on a price before ordering.

Zahret al-Bustan CAFE

(Sharia Talaat Harb, Downtown; tea & shisha E£9; ⊙8am-2am) Backpackers, writers and artists make up the mixed clientele of this traditional outdoor *ahwa*. Take the tiny lane just behind Café Riche to find it.

Simonds CAFE

(☎735 9436; 112 Sharia 26th of July, Zamalek; coffees & pastries from E£7; ⊙7am-10pm) It's a Cairene tradition to sit on a rickety chair here and read the morning paper over a buttery pastry and cappuccino.

☆ Entertainment

For live music head to the **Cairo Jazz Club** (☎3345 9939; www.cairojazzclub.com; 197 Sharia 26th of July, Agouza; ⊙5pm-3am), **After Eight** (☎2574 0855; www.after8cairo.com; 6 Sharia Qasr el-Nil, Downtown; minimum charge Wed-Sun E£60, Thu-Sat E£100; ⊙8pm-4am) or **El Sawy Culture Wheel** (El Sakia; www.culturewheel.com; Sharia 26th of July, Zamalek; ⊙8am-midnight).

The **Cairo Opera House** (☎2739 8144; www.operahouse.gov.eg; Gezira Exhibition Grounds, Gezira) hosts regular performances of classical music and opera.

Catch Cairo's best belly dancers at **Haroun El-Rashid Nightclub** (☎3795 7171; Semiramis InterContinental, Corniche el-Nil, Garden City, Downtown; ⏲11pm-4am Tue-Thu & Sun). Performances generally begin late (around 1pm) and expect to pay from E£250 for admission, including food.

A Nile dinner cruise (which includes a belly-dancing performance) is a less expensive option. **Nile Maxim** (☎2728 3000; Sharia Saray al-Gezira, Zamalek, opposite Cairo Marriott Hotel; minimum charge E£180; ⏲sailings at 7.30pm & 10.45pm) runs some of the better ones.

Al-Tannoura Egyptian Heritage Dance Troupe TRADITIONAL DANCE
(☎2512 1735; Wikala of Al-Ghouri, Sharia Mohammed Abduh, Islamic Cairo, off Sharia al-Azhar; ⏲performances at 8pm Mon, Wed & Sat) FREE Arrive at least one hour ahead to secure your seat for this mesmerising Sufi dancing performance.

Shopping

Brass plates, boxes inlaid with mother-of-pearl, leather slippers, and copperware are just some of the many crafts you will find in the labyrinthine passages of Khan al-Khalili (p63).

American University in Cairo (AUC) Bookshop BOOKS
(☎2797 5370; Sharia Sheikh Rihan, Downtown; ⏲9am-6pm Sat-Thu) This is the best English-language bookshop in Egypt.

Fair Trade Egypt HANDICRAFTS
(☎2736 5123; www.fairtradeegypt.org; 1st fl, 27 Sharia Yehia Ibrahim, Zamalek; ⏲9am-8pm Sat-Thu, 10am-6pm Fri) Textiles, pottery and jewellery here are produced in income-generating projects throughout the country.

Information

EMERGENCY

Ambulance (☎123)
Fire Department (☎180)
Police (☎122)
Tourist Police (☎126)

INTERNET ACCESS

Wi-fi is available at most hotels and many cafes and restaurants.

Concord (28 Sharia Mohammed Mahmoud, Downtown; per hr E£5; ⏲10am-2am)
Sigma Net (Sharia Gezirat al-Wusta, Zamalek; per hr E£8; ⏲24hr)

MEDICAL SERVICES

Al-Salam International Hospital (☎2524 0250, emergency 19885; www.assih.com; Corniche el-Nil, Ma'adi)
Badran Hospital (☎3337 8823; www.badranhospital.com; 3 Sharia al-Ahrar, Doqqi)

MONEY

There are banks, foreign-exchange bureaus and ATMs all over town.

American Express (☎2574 7991; 15 Sharia Qasr el-Nil, Downtown; ⏲9am-3pm Sat-Thu)
Thomas Cook (☎2574 3955; 17 Sharia Mahmoud Bassiouni, Downtown; ⏲8am-4.30pm Sat-Thu)

POST

Main post office (☎2391 2615; Midan Ataba, Downtown; ⏲8am-6pm Sat-Thu)

PYRAMIDS PRACTICALITIES

➡ **Getting there** To beat the traffic go via metro to Giza station and then by taxi (about E£15), microbus (E£3) or bus (E£1). Microbuses cluster at the bottom of the west-side metro stairs (drivers yell 'Haram'). Buses 355 and 357 can be hailed on the north side of Sharia al-Haram, just west of the metro underpass.

➡ **Entry** The main entrance is on Sharia al-Haram (Pyramids Rd) but you can also enter/exit through a gate below the Sphinx in the village of Nazlet as-Samaan.

➡ **Additional entry tickets** Great Pyramid interior tickets (300 available in summer, 500 in winter) are sold at the main entrance at 8am and 1pm. Interior tickets for other pyramids and for the Solar Barque Museum are sold all day at their entrance booths

➡ **Sound and Light Show** (☎3385 2880; www.soundandlight.com.eg; Sphinx Entrance; admission E£75, translation headset E£10; ⏲shows at 7pm & 8pm) Although it's neat to see the pyramids so dramatically lit, the show is a rather dated spectacular. The first show is typically in English; the second varies.

SET YOUR BUDGET

Budget

- Dorm bed E£70
- *Ta'amiyya* (Egyptian felafel) sandwich E£1.50
- Beer from alcohol shop E£5
- Day train to Luxor E£90

Midrange

- Hotel room with air-con E£180
- Two-course dinner E£80
- Beer in bar E£20
- Sleeper to Luxor E£368

Top End

- Luxury hotel room US$150
- Two-course dinner E£140
- European-style coffee E£15
- Flight to Luxor US$120

TELEPHONE

Telephone Centrale (8 Sharia Adly, Downtown; ⏲24hr)

TOURIST INFORMATION

Main tourist office (☎2391 3454; 5 Sharia Adly, Downtown; ⏲8.30am-7pm) Staff are notoriously unhelpful.

Getting There & Away

AIR

Cairo International Airport (☎flight info 0900 77777; www.cairo-airport.com) is 20km northeast of Cairo.

Buses 27 and 356 run every 20 minutes from 7am to midnight between the terminals and Midan Abdel Moniem Riad, behind the Egyptian Museum in central Cairo (E£2, plus E£1 per large luggage item, one hour).

A taxi to central Cairo costs around E£75. You'll need to negotiate the fare. A taxi to the airport costs about E£60.

The main **EgyptAir** (☎2393 0381; Sharia Talaat Harb) office is Downtown.

BOAT

In early 2013, after a 20-year hiatus, cruise itineraries beginning in Cairo and heading all the way to Aswan became a reality once more.

BUS

Cairo's main bus station is **Cairo Gateway** (Turgoman Garage; Sharia al-Gisr, Bulaq; M Orabi), 1km northwest of the intersection of Sharia Galaa and Sharia 26th of July. It's 400m west from the Orabi metro stop, or pay E£5 or so for a taxi from Tahrir or Talaat Harb.

Abbassiyya Garage (Sinai Station; Sharia Ramses, Abbasiyya; M Abbassiyya) is where all of the services from Sinai usually terminate – it's about E£15 in a taxi to the centre.

TRAIN

Ramses Train Station (Mahattat Ramses; ☎2575 3555; Midan Ramses, Downtown; M Al-Shohadaa) is Cairo's main terminus.

The **Watania Sleeping Train** (☎3748 9488; www.wataniasleepingtrains.com) to Luxor (9½ hours) and Aswan (13 hours) is something of a travel classic. Tickets to either destination cost US$60/80 per person one way in a double/single cabin. Tickets can be paid for in dollars, Egyptian pounds or euros and the price includes dinner and breakfast.

The sleeping train departs from **Giza Train Station** (Mahattat Giza ; Pyramids Road, Giza; M Giza) at 8pm. Buy tickets in advance from either Ramses Station's sleeping train ticket office on platform 11 or from Giza Train Station in the trailer to the right of the entrance.

Restrictions on foreigners travelling to Upper Egypt on other trains have now been lifted. Seating-only trains travel to Luxor (E£90, 10½ hours) and Aswan (E£109, 14 hours) from Ramses Station at 8am, noon, 7pm, 8pm and 1am.

There are nine direct services (E£50/35 in 1st/2nd class, 2½ hours) and eight slow (E£35/15 in 1st/2nd class, four hours) from Ramses Station to Alexandria daily.

Getting Around

BUS & MINIBUS

Cairo's main local bus and minibus stations, serving all parts of the city, are at Midan Abdel Moniem Riad (behind the Egyptian Museum) and Midan Ataba.

FERRY

On the corniche in front of the Radio & TV Building you'll find the Maspero river bus terminal. From here boats depart every 15 minutes for Giza (near the Giza Zoo). The trip takes 30 minutes and the fare is E£1.

METRO

The Metro system is startlingly efficient with trains running every five minutes between 6am and 11.30pm. A one-way ticket costs E£1. The two middle carriages are reserved for women only.

TAXI

New white taxis have working meters. Riding in the old black-and-white taxis necessitates bargaining. Both can be hailed off the street.

AROUND CAIRO

If you're looking to escape Cairo for the day, organised tours can be easily arranged through your accommodation, and it's not hard to find a cab driver willing to offer their services for the day. A private car should cost about E£300 for the day (around seven hours), excluding entry fees and the obligatory baksheesh (tip).

Saqqara ARCHAEOLOGICAL SITE
(adult/student E£50/25; ⌚8am-4pm) Here you'll find a massive necropolis strewn with pyramids, temples and tombs where pharaohs, generals and sacred animals were interred. The star attraction is the **Step Pyramid of Zoser**, the world's oldest stone monument.

Dahshur ARCHAEOLOGICAL SITE
(adult/student E£25/15; ⌚8am-4pm) Ten kilometres south of Saqqara is a 3.5km-long field of pyramids, including the **Bent Pyramid** (unfortunately closed) and the mystical **Red Pyramid**.

ALEXANDRIA

☎03 / POP 4.1 MILLION

The city of Alexandria (Al-Iskendariyya) is the stuff that legends are made of: the city was founded by none other than Alexander the Great, and sassy queen Cleopatra made this the seat of her throne. During the 19th century, a cosmopolitan renaissance had Alexandria flirting with European-style decadence; however, this was cut short in the 1950s by Gamal Abdel Nasser's wave of change.

Despite the fact that much of its grand old architecture is now teetering into decay, Alexandria has an old-world elegance that can't be beaten. This is an ideal place to spend a few days sipping coffee in cafes dripping with faded grandeur after pondering the city's glorious past at its museums and monuments.

Sights

★**Bibliotheca Alexandrina** LIBRARY, MUSEUM
(☎483 9999; www.bibalex.org; Al-Corniche, Shatby; adult/student main library E£10/5, antiquities museum E£20/10, manuscript collection E£20/10; ⌚11am-6pm Sat-Thu) Opened in 2002, inspired by Alexandria's original 3rd-century-BC library, this complex has become one of Egypt's major cultural venues. As well as viewing the main reading room, there is an array of art exhibitions and museums to explore.

Alexandria National Museum MUSEUM
(110 Sharia Tariq al-Horreyya; adult/student E£35/20; ⌚9am-4.30pm) The small, thoughtfully selected and well-labelled collection here does a sterling job of relating the city's history from antiquity until the modern period.

Roman Amphitheatre ARCHAEOLOGICAL SITE
(Kom al-Dikka; Sharia Yousri, off Midan Gomhuriyya; adult/student amphitheatre E£20/15, Villa of the Birds E£15/8; ⌚9am-5pm) The marble terraces of the only Roman amphitheatre in Egypt were discovered in 1964. Also here, and worth seeing, is the 'Villa of the Birds' mosaic.

Catacombs of Kom ash-Suqqafa ARCHAEOLOGICAL SITE
(Carmous; adult/student E£35/20; ⌚9am-5pm) Dating from the 2nd century AD, this honeycomb burial chamber once housed 300 corpses.

Fort Qaitbey FORTRESS
(Eastern Harbour; adult/student E£25/15; ⌚9am-4pm) This fort was built on the foundations of the destroyed Pharos lighthouse in 1480.

Pompey's Pillar ARCHAEOLOGICAL SITE
(Carmous; adult/student E£20/15; ⌚8am-4.30pm) This famed and misnamed pillar is the only ancient monument remaining whole and standing today in Alexandria.

Graeco-Roman Museum MUSEUM
(☎483 6434; 5 Sharia Al-Mathaf ar-Romani) Unfortunately, this wonderful museum is currently closed for renovations.

Sleeping

Hotel Union HOTEL $
(☎480 7312; 5th fl, 164 Al-Corniche; s E£80-140, d E£120-160; ❄) The best budget choice on Alexandria's corniche. Rooms are simple but relatively well-maintained and come in a bewildering mix of bathroom, view and air-con options and rates.

Swiss Canal Hotel HOTEL $
(☎480 8373; 14 Sharia al-Bursa al-Qadima; s/d E£80/100, with air-con E£100/120) Sunglasses are needed to view the iridescent pink walls but the rooms are clean, with towering ceilings and spongy beds, overlooking a reasonably quiet souq area.

Hotel Crillon HOTEL $
(☎480 0330; 3rd fl, 5 Sharia Adib Ishaq; s without bathroom E£110-120, d without bathroom 150-180) This place has oodles of historic character

Alexandria

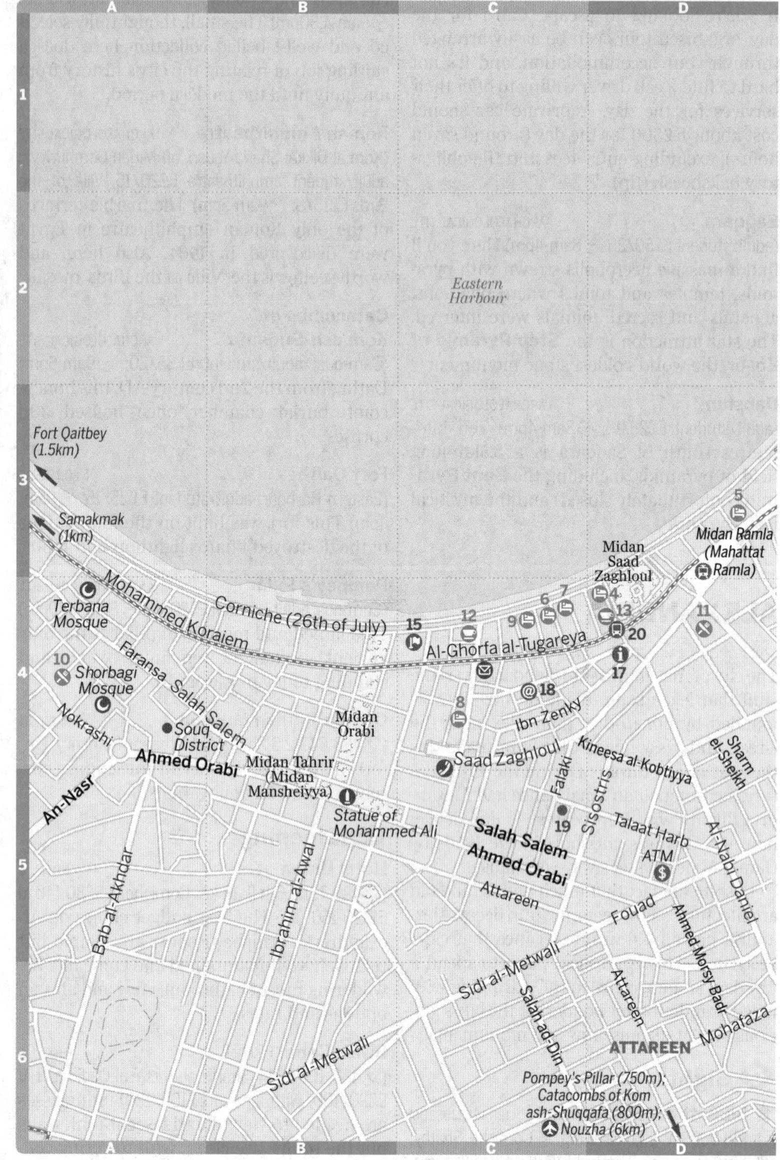

but unfortunately some of the rooms could do with a power-hose and a bottle of bleach.

★ **Egypt Hotel** HOTEL $$
(☎ 481 4483; 1 Sharia Degla; s US$50-60, d US$60-70) Set in a 100-year-old Italian building, the Egypt single-handedly fills a desperate need for decent midrange Alexandria digs. The lobby is turgid cream and brown but the rooms boast lush beds, wood floors and teensy balconies.

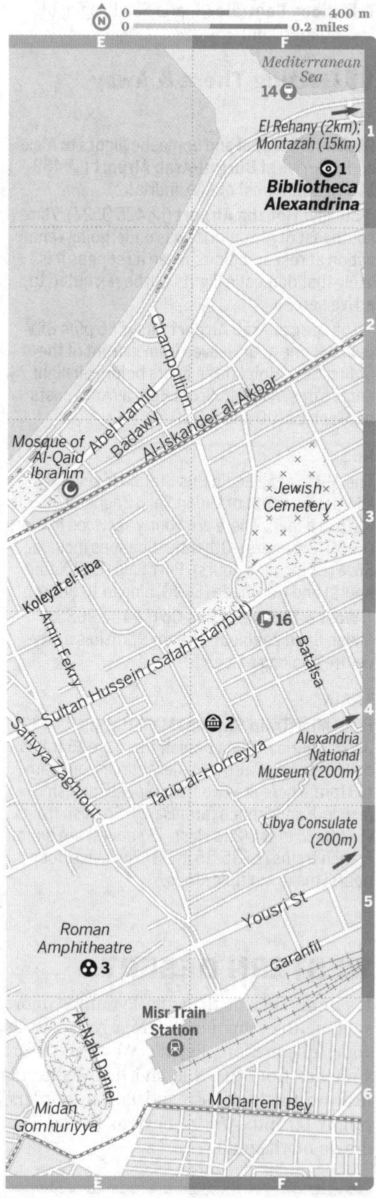

Alexandria

Top Sights
1 Bibliotheca Alexandrina....F1

Sights
2 Graeco-Roman Museum....F4
3 Roman Amphitheatre....E5

Sleeping
4 Cecil Hotel....D4
5 Egypt Hotel....D3
6 Hotel Crillon....C4
7 Hotel Union....C4
8 Swiss Canal Hotel....C4
9 Windsor Palace Hotel....C4

Eating
China House....(see 4)
10 Farag....A4
11 Mohammed Ahmed....D4

Drinking & Nightlife
12 El Tugareya....C4
13 Imperial Cafe & Restaurant....D4
14 Selsela Cafe....F1

Information
15 France Consulate....C4
16 Germany Consulate....F4
17 Main Tourist Office....D4
18 MG@Net....C4
19 Passport Office....C5

Transport
Airport Bus Departures....(see 4)
20 West & Mid Delta Bus Co....D4

★ **Windsor Palace Hotel** HISTORIC HOTEL $$$
(☎480 8123; www.paradiseinnegypt.com; 17 Sharia ash-Shohada; r US$150) This bejewelled Edwardian gem is an institution unto itself, keeping a watchful eye on the Med since 1907. Despite a thorough modernisation, the wonderful old elevators and grand lobby have been retained and the rooms have an old-world green-and-gold pizzazz.

Cecil Hotel HISTORIC HOTEL $$$
(☎487 7173; www.sofitel.com; 16 Midan Saad Zaghloul; s/d US$130/165, with sea view US$145/185) The latest refit of this Alexandrian legend sees its rooms modernised and fully equipped though the grand lobby and famous bar (now relocated to the 1st floor) have retained only a fraction of the lustre they had when Durrell and Churchill came to visit.

Eating

★ **Mohammed Ahmed** EGYPTIAN $
(☎483 3576; 17 Sharia Shakor Pasha; dishes E£2-5; ⏰24hr) The undisputed king of *fuul* and *ta'amiyya,* Mohammed Ahmed is filled day and night with locals downing small plates of spectacularly good and cheap Egyptian standards.

★**Farag** SEAFOOD **$$**
(☎481 1047; 7 Souq al-Tabakheen, Anfushi; mains E£35-75; ⏲noon-3am & 6pm-late) Deep in the heart of the souq, this highly recommended and very local joint is where to go for seafood feasting. The sign is high above street level, so look up to find it or just ask around; everyone knows it.

Samakmak EGYPTIAN **$$**
(☎481 1560; 42 Qasr Ras at-Tin, Anfushi; mains E£50-120; ⏲1-4pm & 6pm-2am) Owned by Zizi Salem, the retired queen of the Alexandrian belly-dancing scene, Samakmak is known for its delicious seafood specials.

China House CHINESE **$$**
(☎487 7173; top fl, Cecil Hotel, 16 Midan Saad Zaghloul; mains E£30-50; ⏲11am-11.30pm) Great views over Alexandria's harbour and decent Chinese, Thai and Japanese food.

Drinking

Alexandria is famous for its cafes and coffeehouses, where an accompanying pastry is de rigueur.

★**Selsela Cafe** CAFE
(Chatby Beach, Al-Corniche) Directly on the water, this fantastic *ahwa* has rustic open-air tables and palm trees with cheerful coloured lights, set around a small curving beach where you can hardly hear the traffic. It's across from the Bibliotheca Alexandrina

Imperial Cafe & Restaurant CAFE
(Midan Saad Zaghloul) This recently renovated classic cafe is now a chic space with comfortable sofas, wi-fi and a full menu of espresso-based coffees.

El Tugareya CAFE
(Al-Corniche; ⏲9am-late) This 90-year-old institution is one of the most important *ahwas* in town.

Information

There are dozens of banks with ATMs in central Alexandria, particularly on and around Sharia Salah Salem and Sharia Talaat Harb.

Main post office (Sharia al-Bursa al-Qadima; ⏲9am-9pm Sat-Thu)

Main tourist office (☎485 1556; Midan Saad Zaghloul; ⏲8.30am-6pm) Closed for renovation at time of research. There is another branch at the train Station.

MG@Net (10 Sharia el-Shohada; per hr E£3; ⏲7am-2am)

Telephone Centrale (Sharia Saad Zaghloul; ⏲8.30am-10pm)

Getting There & Away

AIR

Both international and domestic flights to Alexandria arrive at **Burg al-Arab Airport** (☎459 1483), 40km west of Alexandria.

Smaller **Nouzha Airport** (☎425 0527), 7km southeast of Alexandria, was undergoing renovation at research time. When it reopens it is likely that domestic flights will be re-routed to arrive here.

The Burg al-Arab **Airport bus** (E£6 plus E£1 per bag, one hour) leaves from in front of the Sofitel Cecil Hotel three hours before all flight departures. A taxi to/from Burg al-Arab costs between E£100 and E£150.

BUS

The Al-Mo'af al-Gedid Bus Station is several kilometres south of Midan Saad Zaghloul (about E£15 in a taxi). There are hourly services to Cairo (E£30, 2½ hours). Other destinations include Siwa (E£38, nine hours), Port Said (E£30, four hours) and Hurghada (E£90, nine to 10 hours).

West & Mid Delta Bus Co (☎480 9685; Midan Saad Zaghloul; ⏲9am-9pm) has a city-centre booking office.

TRAIN

From **Misr Train Station** (Mahattat Misr; ☎426 3207; Sharia Al-Nabi Daniel) there are 15 trains daily between Cairo and Alexandria, from 6am to 11pm. There are two train types: Spanish *(espani)*, and French *(faransawi)*. Spanish trains (E£50/35 in 1st/2nd class, 2½ hours) are direct. French trains (E£35/15 in 1st/2nd class, four hours) make multiple stops.

WESTERN DESERT

It's more ancient than the Pyramids, more sublime than any temple. Nearly as vast as your imagination, Egypt's Western Desert stretches from the Nile and the Mediterranean to the Sudanese and Libyan borders, rolling far into Africa oblivious to any lines drawn on the map.

Siwa Oasis

☎046

Ringed by salt lakes, dunes and desert escarpment, Siwa is a haven of date plantations and olive groves. It has a distinctive Berber culture, preserved due to its relative isolation – an asphalt road to the coast was

WORTH A TRIP

FARAFRA OASIS

Remote Farafra is the best place from which to visit the spectacular **White Desert** – an outstanding area of wind-blown rock formations.

Budget travellers can bed down at spartan **Al-Waha Hotel** (0122 720 0387; waha-farafra@yahoo.com; Qasr al-Farafra; r with/without bathroom E£75/60). For a significant step up in comfort, with a traditional Bedouin theme, **Al-Badawiya Safari & Hotel** (092-751 0060; www.badawiya.com; Sharia al-Mishtafa Nakhas, Qasr al-Farafra; s/d r US$36/32, ste with air-con US$45/65) is a highly recommended choice.

Buses travel to Cairo (E£45, eight to 10 hours) via Bahariya (E£25, three hours) daily at 10am and 10pm. Buses coming from Cairo go on to Dakhla (E£25, four hours) and leave from outside the petrol station and across from Al-Abeyt Restaurant.

only constructed in the 1980s. With the 13th-century *shali* (fortress) at its core, there's plenty to potter around while relaxing into the rhythm of life in the slow lane.

Sights & Activities

Siwa's attractions include swimming **springs**, the mudbrick **Fortress of Shali** in the town centre, the Graeco-Roman tombs of **Gebel al-Mawta** (adult/student E£25/15; 9am-5pm) and the **Temple of the Oracle** (adult/student E£25/15; 9am-5pm), where Alexander came to confirm his divinity. At the edge of town are the towering dunes of the **Great Sand Sea**.

Desert Trips

All desert trips require permits, which cost US$5 plus E£11 and are usually obtained by your guide from the tourist office. Prices and itineraries vary; one of the most popular trips takes you to the desert hot spring at Bir Wahed, on the edge of the Great Sand Sea, a half-day trip costing about E£120 per person.

Overnight trips vary in length according to destination. Most trips are done by 4WD so ensure that the vehicle is roadworthy before you set out and that you have enough water.

Sleeping & Eating

Kelany Hotel HOTEL $

(460 1052, 0122 403 9218; zaitsafari@yahoo.com; Sharia Azmi Kilani; s with/without air-con E£120/70, d E£150/100) This friendly budget option has decent, if ageing, rooms with reliable hot water. The rooftop restaurant features views of Shali Fortress, Gebel Dakrur and everything in between.

★**Shali Lodge** BOUTIQUE HOTEL $$

(460 1299; www.siwa.com/accommodations.html; Sharia Subukha; s/d/tr E£285/365/450) This beautiful mudbrick hotel, owned by environmentalist Mounir Neamatalla, nestles in a lush palm grove about 100m from Siwa main square. The extremely comfortable rooms have rock-walled bathrooms and cushioned sitting nooks. Tasteful and quiet, this is how small hotels should be.

★**Adrère Amellal** BOUTIQUE HOTEL $$$

(02-2736 7879; www.adrereamellal.net; Sidi Jaafar, White Mountain; s/d full board incl desert excursions US$460/605, ste from US$800) This impeccable desert retreat lies in its own oasis. It is a truly unique place, built from *kershef* (large chunks of salt mixed with rock), and using revived traditional building techniques.

Abdu's Restaurant INTERNATIONAL $

(460 1243; Central Market Sq; dishes E£5-30; 8.30am-midnight) The longest-running restaurant in Siwa remains the best eating option with a huge menu of breakfast, pasta, traditional dishes, vegetable stews, couscous, roasted chickens and fantastic pizza whipped to your table by efficient service.

Information

Internet cafes are found in the town centre. Most charge E£10 per hour.

Banque du Caire (Siwa Town; 8.30am-2pm & 5-8pm) Has an ATM.

Post office (Siwa Town; 8am-2pm Sat-Thu)

Tourist office (046 460 1338; mahdi_hweiti@yahoo.com; Siwa Town; 9am-2pm & 5-8pm Sat-Thu Oct-Apr, 9am-2pm Sat-Thu May-Sep) Helpful.

Getting There & Around

There are three daily buses to (and from) Alexandria (E£37, eight hours). Buses are often full, so buy a ticket in advance from the bus stop opposite the tourist police station.

Bicycles can be hired from most hotels and shops in the main square for about E£20 per day. Donkey carts within town cost about E£30 for two to three hours.

RESPECTING LOCAL TRADITION

Siwans are very proud of their traditions, which are part of what makes the place so unique. They are particularly sensitive where female modesty is concerned. The least visitors can do to help preserve Siwa's culture is to respect local sensibilities and act accordingly. Modest dress is appreciated and women travellers in particular should make sure they cover their upper arms and their legs, and wear baggy T-shirts over bathing suits when taking a dip in any of the numerous springs.

Bahariya Oasis

☎011

Bahariya is one of the more fetching desert-circuit oases, and at just 365km from Cairo is also the most accessible. Surrounded by towering ridges, much of the oasis floor is covered by plantations of date palms and pockmarked with refreshing springs.

Attractions include the **Temple of Ain el-Muftella**, the **Temple of Alexander** and the **Golden Mummies Museum** (al-Mathaf; Sharia al-Mathaf, Bawiti; ⊙8am-2pm) with 10 of the 10,000 famous Graeco-Roman Bahariya mummies on display. You have to buy a combined ticket covering five of the oasis' ancient sites from the **ticket office** (Sharia al-Mathaf, Bawiti; adult/student E£45/25; ⊙8am-4pm) beside Golden Mummies Museum before visiting.

Sleeping & Eating

The restaurant scene is feeble at best. **Popular Restaurant** (☎847 2239; Sharia Safaya, Bawiti; set meals E£25) offers good set meals.

New Oasis Hotel HOTEL $
(☎0122 847 4171; max_rfs@hotmail.com; s/d with air-con E£70/120, without air-con E£50/100; ❄) This homely hotel next to El-Beshmo spring has several teardrop-shaped rooms, some with balconies overlooking the expansive palm groves nearby.

Old Oasis Hotel HOTEL $$
(☎3847 3028; www.oldoasissafari.com; by El-Beshmo spring; s/d/tr with air-con E£120/180/220, without air-con E£90/120/180; ❄@📶🏊) The Old Oasis Hotel sits above a pretty, shaded garden of palm and olive trees, and has a dozen or so simple but impeccable fan rooms, as well as a few fancier stone-wall air-con rooms.

Western Desert Hotel HOTEL $$
(☎0122 301 2155; www.westerndeserthotel.com; off Sharia Misr; s/d E£140/240; ❄@📶) The clean, tiled rooms here are well-kept and good value. Back rooms have views of the gardens and desert in the distance.

Information

National Bank of Development (off Sharia Misr, Bawiti; ⊙9am-2pm Sun-Thu) Has an ATM.

Tourist office (☎3847 3039; Sharia Misr, Bawiti; ⊙8am-2pm & 7-9pm Sat-Thu) Main road.

Getting There & Away

Buses run to Cairo (E£30, four to five hours) at 6.30am, 10am and 3pm from the kiosk near the post office. These are often full, so it's strongly advised to buy tickets the day before travelling.

If you're heading to Farafra (E£20, two hours) or Dakhla (E£40, four to five hours), you can hop on one of the buses headed that way from Cairo. They leave Bahariya around noon and 11.30pm from the Upper Egypt kiosk and Hilal Coffeehouse.

Dakhla Oasis

☎092

With more than a dozen fertile hamlets sprinkled along the Western Desert circuit road, Dakhla lives up to most visitors' romantic expectations of oasis life. Lush palm groves and orchards support traditional villages, where imposing, ancient mudbrick forts still stand guard over the townships and allude to their less tranquil past. The oasis of Dakhla contains two small towns **Mut** and **Al-Qasr**; Mut has the most facilities.

There are 600 **hot springs** in the vicinity. The atmospheric mudbrick citadel at Al-Qasr with its medieval architecture is one of the Western Desert's must-see sights.

Sleeping

Al-Qasr Hotel HOSTEL $
(☎787 6013; Main Highway, Al-Qasr; r without bathroom E£30) Simple and friendly, this is the best backpacker option in Al-Qasr.

Bedouin Camp & El-Dohous Village HOTEL $$
(☎785 0480; www.dakhlabedouins.com; Al-Dohous; s/d half board E£125/150; @📶) El-Dohous has a huge variety of domed, curvy rooms, decorated with local crafts, and a wonderful

hilltop restaurant with outstanding views. It's 3km from Mut centre.

Desert Lodge BOUTIQUE HOTEL $$$
(☎772 7061; www.desertlodge.net; Al-Qasr; s/d/tr half board US$98/156/228; ❄@≋) This thoughtfully designed, ecofriendly mud-brick fortress of a lodge crowns a hilltop overlooking the old town of Al-Qasr. There is also a bar and a private hot spring.

Eating

In Mut **Said Shihad** (Sharia as-Sawra al-Khadra; meals E£20-35), long-established **Abu Mohamed Restaurant** (☎782 1431; Sharia as-Sawra al-Khadra; meals E£20-40) and **Ahmed Hamdy's Restaurant** (☎782 0767; Sharia as-Sawra al-Khadra; meals E£20-30) keep the hungry happy.

Information

Bank Misr (Sharia Al-Wadi, Mut; ⏲8.30am-2pm Sun-Thu) Money changing, ATM.

Internet Cafe (Sharia Basateen, Mut; per hr E£2; ⏲11am-midnight)

Tourist office (☎782 1685, 0122 179 6467; Sharia as-Sawra al-Khadra, Mut; ⏲8am-3pm) Extremely helpful.

Getting There & Around

Buses leave from Mut **bus station** (☎782 4366; Sharia al-Wadi) at 6am, 5pm, 7pm and 8pm to Cairo (E£75, 10 hours). The 6am and 5pm services go via Farafra Oasis (E£25, four hours) and Bahariya Oasis (E£50, seven hours).

Local pick-ups depart from Sharia as-Sawra al-Khadra, near Midan al-Tahrir, in Mut for transport to Al-Qasr for E£1.50. Abu Mohamed Restaurant hires out bikes for E£20 per day.

SINAI

Sinai, a region of stark beauty, has been a place of refuge, conflict and curiosity for thousands of years. Wedged between Africa and Asia, it is an intercontinental crossroads par excellence – prophets, nomads, exiles and conquerors have all left their footprints here.

Sharm El-Sheikh & Na'ama Bay

☎069 / POP 38,478

Commonly described as Egypt's answer to Las Vegas, what was once a small village that attracted hard-core divers has now spawned into Sinai's most popular package-holiday destination. Over the past decade the march of concrete sprawl along the coastline to cater for these crowds has been relentless. However, despite the brash development, Sharm remains a scuba-diving paradise. Just offshore is some of the world's most amazing underwater scenery with rare and lovely reefs, stunning wreck diving and an incredible variety of exotic fish all awaiting those who dive on in.

Sights & Activities

★**Ras Mohammed National Park** PARK
(admission per person €5; ⏲8am-5pm) Home to spectacular coral reefs and world-famous Shark and Jolanda Reefs dive sites, the waters surrounding this peninsula 20km west of Sharm el-Sheikh teem with most of the Red Sea's 1000 fish species.

Diving

Diving is the area's star attraction. The following clubs in Na'ama Bay are recommended.

Sinai Divers DIVING
(☎360 0697; www.sinaidivers.com; Ghazala Beach Hotel, Na'ama Bay Promenade)

Camel Dive Club DIVING
(☎360 0700; www.cameldive.com; Camel Hotel, King of Bahrain St)

Sleeping

★**Sinai Old Spices** B&B $$
(☎0122 680 3130; www.sinaioldspices.com; Roissat area; s/d E£150/240; P❄📶) This dinky B&B serves up bundles of quirky style using locally inspired architecture. Individually decorated rooms all come with kitchenette and fabulous modern bathrooms. It's a E£30 taxi ride from Sharm itself. Phone beforehand to arrange a pick-up, or get directions – it's tricky to find.

Camel Hotel HOTEL $$
(☎360 0700; www.cameldive.com; King of Bahrain St, Na'ama Bay; r from US$50; ❄📶≋) One of the best places to stay right in the centre of Na'ama Bay if diving is your main Sharm agenda. The spacious, modern rooms here are gloriously quiet (thanks to soundproof windows) so you're guaranteed a good night's sleep.

Shark's Bay Umbi Diving Village HOTEL $$
(☎360 0942; www.sharksbay.com; Shark's Bay; s/d US$45/58, huts s/d without bathroom US$22/26, beach cabins s/d US$31/45; P❄📶) The tumble of cute chalets flows down towards the beach. Pine beach cabins are spick and span and there are larger air-con rooms built into

the cliff above. A taxi from Na'ama Bay to here is about E£25.

Sofitel Sharm el-Sheikh Coralia Hotel LUXURY HOTEL $$$
(☎360 0081; www.sofitel.com; Na'ama Bay; s/d from US$128/167; P❄📶🏊) Dominating Na'ama Bay's northern cliffs, this whitewashed hotel terraces majestically down towards the sea like a sultan's palace from a children's fairy tale. The distinctly Middle Eastern–style rooms are decked out in exotic wooden furniture, and boast stunning views over the bay.

Eating

El-Masrien EGYPTIAN $$
(Sharm Old Market, Sharm al-Maya; dishes E£25-40) El-Masrien's continued success is due to the fact that it delivers succulent kebabs and kofta (minced meat and spices grilled on a skewer) that perfectly hit the spot, without hiking its prices to try and compete with fancier Sharm restaurants.

Tam Tam EGYPTIAN $$
(Na'ama Bay Promenade, Na'ama Bay; dishes E£20-60; 🖉) This laid-back waterfront restaurant is great for those who want to sample a range of Egyptian fare and while away a few hours puffing on a *shisha*.

★**Fairuz** MIDDLE EASTERN $$$
(King of Bahrain St, Na'ama Bay; mezze dishes E£18, mains E£80-100; 🖉) This Levantine restaurant will lead you on a mouth-watering journey through the subtle flavours of the Middle East. Forgo the main-course menu completely and concentrate on the mezze (starter-sized dishes), which are the heart of any Middle Eastern meal.

Drinking & Nightlife

Popular party spots are **Bus Stop Lounge** (King of Bahrain St, Na'ama Bay; ⏲4pm-3am) and **Pacha** (Sanafir Hotel, King of Bahrain St).

For a more relaxed evening check out the diver-centric **Camel Roof Bar** (Camel Hotel, King of Bahrain St, Na'ama Bay; ⏲3pm-2.30am) and the cosy **Pirates' Bar** (☎360 0137; Hilton Fayrouz Village, Na'ama Bay Promenade, Na'ama Bay).

Information

There are numerous ATMs and banks in Na'ama Bay.

Internet outlets can be found in **Sharm Old Market** (Sharm-Na'ama Bay Rd, Sharm al-Maya) and inside the **Na'ama Centre** (Sharia Sultan Qabos, Na'ama Bay).

The **post office** (Bank St, Hadaba; ⏲8am-3pm Sat-Thu) and **telephone centrale** (Bank St, Hadaba; ⏲24hr) are next door to each other on the Hadaba hill.

Getting There & Away

AIR

From **Sharm el-Sheikh Airport** (☎360 1140; www.sharm-el-sheikh.airport-authority.com; Sharm-Na'ama Bay Rd) there are domestic flights to Cairo and Luxor with **EgyptAir** (☎366 1056; www.egyptair.com; Sharm al-Maya, opposite Sharm Old Market; ⏲9am-9pm).

EasyJet (www.easyjet.com) operates daily direct flights to the UK.

BOAT

The ferry service between Sharm el-Sheikh and Hurghada is currently not operating. Enquire at any of Sharm's hotels and travel agencies to see if it has started services again.

BUS

The bus station is along the Sharm-Na'ama Bay Rd. There are frequent services to Cairo (E£60 to E£85, six to seven hours) and Dahab (E£15 to E£20, one to two hours).

Getting Around

From the airport prepare to pay at least E£25 in a taxi. Microbuses charge E£2 between Na'ama Bay and Sharm Old Market; taxis charge a minimum of E£10.

Dahab

☎069

Low-key, laid-back and low-rise, Dahab is the Middle East's prime beach resort for independent travellers and the perfect base from which to explore some of Egypt's most spectacular diving and snorkelling. Reeled in by a fusion of hippy mellowness and resort chic (where good cappuccino and sushi are as much a part of the action as cheap rooms and herds of goats fossicking in the back alleys), many travellers plan a few nights here and instead stay for weeks.

If Dahab is in your sights be forewarned that after a few days of diving, desert trekking, oceanside dinners and countless *shisha* sessions, you're probably going to want to cancel the rest of your itinerary.

Activities

Snorkelling & Diving

Other than lounging around, snorkelling and diving are the most popular activities in Dahab. The best reefs for snorkelling are Eel Garden and Lighthouse Reef, in Assalah. These dive centres are recommended.

Red Sea Relax Dive Centre DIVING
(☎364 1309; www.red-sea-relax.com; Red Sea Relax Hotel, Masbat)

Poseidon Divers DIVING
(☎364 1309; www.poseidondivers.com; Crazy Camel Camp, Mashraba)

Nesima Dive Centre DIVING
(☎364 0320; www.nesima-resort.com; Nesima Resort, Mashraba)

Camel & Jeep Safaris

Dahab is one of the best places in Sinai to arrange camel safaris into the dramatic desert mountains, especially the spectacular Ras Abu Gallum Protectorate. Expect to pay E£200 per person for an evening trip with dinner at a Bedouin camp, and from about E£300 to E£400 per person per day for a safari, including all food and water.

One of the most popular jeep safaris is to the Coloured Canyon, northwest of Nuweiba.

All tour operators in Dahab can organise overnight tours to Mt Sinai and St Katherine's Monastery.

Sleeping

★Sunrise Lodge GUESTHOUSE $
(☎0109 057 4242; www.sunrisedahab.com; Masbat; r E£120;) Tucked down a sandy alley just off the promenade, this welcoming home-from-home has just five spotless rooms set around a sandy courtyard shaded by palm trees. It's a more peaceful scene than many of the other budget hotels in Dahab and very family friendly.

Alaska Camp & Hotel HOTEL $
(☎364 1004; www.dahabescape.com; Masbat; r with/without air-con E£200/100;) Easy on the wallet without sacrificing the small comforts, Alaska has a variety of spacious rooms with comfortable beds. Air-con rooms with balcony are worth paying the extra for. The central location means you're just a stone's throw from the promenade bustle.

Bishbishi Garden Village HOSTEL $
(☎364 0727; www.bishbishi.com; Sharia al-Mashraba, Mashraba; s/d without bathroom US$6.50/10.50;) This classic backpacker spot continues to offer a winning mix of basic rooms and cushion-strewn, palm-shaded communal spaces for socialising.

★Red Sea Relax HOTEL $$
(☎364 1309; www.red-sea-relax.com; Masbat; dm/s/d US$10.50/48/60;) With rooms wrapped around a glistening pool, Red Sea Relax dishes up a winning formula of resortlike facilities for bargain prices. Large rooms come with nice added extras such as tea- and coffee-making facilities while cheap dormitory accommodation means you get the resort feel on a backpacker budget.

Alf Leila BOUTIQUE HOTEL $$
(☎364 0595; www.alfleila.com; cnr Peace Rd & Sharia al-Fanar, Masbat; s/d US$39/47;) Alf Leila's seven rooms pay tribute to the distinct architectural design elements that have emerged over the centuries from the Arab world with lots of gorgeous tilework and traditional textiles. Unfortunately the location (on the main road) isn't the best.

Nesima Resort RESORT $$
(☎364 0320; www.nesima-resort.com; Mashraba; s/d/ste US$60/80/110;) This modest resort with cosy cottages set amid mature gardens is a great compromise for those who want resort living without feeling as if they're isolated from the town.

Eating & Drinking

King Chicken FAST FOOD $
(Sharia al-Mashraba, Mashraba; dishes E£15-25) Budget chicken-dinner heaven at this cheap and cheerful little place, always crowded with locals.

★Seabride Restaurant SEAFOOD $$
(Mashraba; meals E£40-60) This is the locals' favourite seafood haunt, serving up startling good value. All meals come loaded down with fish soup, rice, salad, tahini and bread. Choose your fish fresh from the display or opt for a menu dish, such as spicy Bedouin calamari, to sample some seafood Dahab-style.

Blue House THAI $$
(Masbat; mains E£35-60;) An inspiring selection of flavour-filled and authentic Thai cuisine keeps this breezy upstairs terrace packed with diners.

Kitchen INTERNATIONAL $$
(Masbat; mains E£60-95;) With a menu offering a choice of Chinese, Indian, Thai and Japanese, plus superb service, this is the closest Dahab gets to fine dining.

DON'T MISS

ST KATHERINE PROTECTORATE

A place of pilgrimage since the Middle Ages, the 4350-sq-km St Katherine Protectorate incorporates Mt Sinai and the 6th-century monastery of St Katherine's at the foot of the mountain.

One of the world's oldest continually functioning monastic communities, **St Katherine's Monastery** (in Cairo 02-2482 8513; 9am-noon Mon-Thu & Sat, except religious holidays) FREE traces its founding to about AD 330 when the Roman empress Helena ordered a chapel built beside what was believed to be the burning bush from which God spoke to Moses. In the 6th century Emperor Justinian extended the building, creating a fortified refuge for the monks. Today about two-dozen Greek Orthodox monks are in residence here.

The friendly **El-Malga Bedouin Camp** (0100 641 3575; www.sheikmousa.com; Al-Milga; dm/s/d E£25/100/150) is a 500m walk from the bus station and has spacious private rooms and dormitory accommodation. For those wishing to savour the sanctity of St Katherine's Monastery once the tour parties have departed, the attached **Monastery Guesthouse** (347 0353; St Katherine's Monastery; s/d US$35/60) offers well-kept rooms.

In the village of Al-Milga, 3.5km from the monastery, there's a post office, a **Banque Misr** (beside petrol station; 10am-1pm & 5-8pm Sat-Thu) with ATM, shops and cafes.

The bus station is just off the main road in Al-Milga, behind the mosque. There is a daily bus to Cairo (E£50, seven hours). Bedouin Bus (p81) run a minibus to Dahab at 11am every Tuesday and Friday and to Nuweiba at 8am every Wednesday and Sunday (both services E£50, two hours). They leave from opposite the mosque on Al-Milga's main road.

Taxis charge E£10 between Al-Milga and the monastery and E£250 to either Dahab or Sharm el-Sheikh.

Climbing Mt Sinai

There are two well-defined routes up **Mt Sinai** (Gebel Musa; compulsary guide E£125, camel rides 1 way E£125) that meet about 300m below the summit at a plateau known as Elijah's Basin. Here, everyone must take a steep series of 750 rocky and uneven steps to the top, where there is a small chapel and mosque (usually kept locked). Most people make the climb in the pre-dawn hours to see the magnificence of the sun rising over the surrounding peaks, and then arrive back at the base before 9am, when the monastery opens for visitors.

The **camel trail** is the easier route, and takes about two hours to ascend, moving at a steady pace. The trail is wide, clear and gently sloping as it moves up a series of switchbacks, with the only potential difficulty being gravelly patches that can be slippery on the descent. It's also possible to hire a camel for a negotiable price at the base, just behind the monastery, to take you all or part of the way to where the camel trail meets the steps.

The alternative path to the summit, the taxing **Steps of Repentance**, was laid by one monk as a form of penance. The steps – 3000 up to Elijah's basin and then the final 750 to the summit – are made of roughly hewn rock, and are steep and uneven in many places, requiring strong knees and concentration in placing your feet.

If you want to try both routes, it's best to take the path on the way up and the steps – which afford impressive views of the monastery – on the way back down.

Ralph's German Bakery CAFE
(Sharia al-Fanar, Masbat; coffee E£12-15, pastries E£4-15, sandwiches E£18-25; 7am-6pm) Single-handedly raising the bar for coffee in Dahab, this place is caffeine heaven and also serves up a range of tempting, calorific pastry treats.

Information

There are banks with ATMs along the waterfront pedestrian promenade throughout Masbat. The post office and *telephone centrale* are both in Dahab City.

Wi-fi is widely available in most hotels and nearly all the shore-side restaurants. **Seven Heaven Internet** (Seven Heaven Camp, Masbat; per hr E£5; 24hr) is an efficient internet outlet.

Getting There & Away

From the **bus station** (364 1808; Peace Rd, Dahab City) there are four daily services to Cairo (E£90, nine hours), which all stop in Sharm el-Sheikh (E£15 to E£20, one to two hours).

There is no public bus service to St Katherine but private company **Bedouin Bus** (☎0101 668 4274; www.bedouinbus.com) runs a twice-weekly service between Dahab and St Katherine leaving at 5pm every Tuesday and Friday (E£50, two hours). Check the website for pick-up point details.

SUEZ CANAL

The Suez Canal severs Africa from Asia and links the Mediterranean with the Red Sea. A triumph of modern engineering, the canal opened in 1869 and remains one of the world's busiest shipping lanes.

Port Said

☎066 / POP 570,600

At Port Said, watching enormous supertankers lining up to pass through the canal's northern entrance is an impressive sight to behold. Away from the waterway, the historic waterfront quarter is a muddle of once grand architecture slowly going to seed, evoking this port town's raffish 19th-century heyday.

Sights & Activities

Waterfront Quarter NEIGHBOURHOOD

The heart of Port Said is located along the edge of the canal, on and around Sharia Palestine. Here, the streets are lined with belle époque period buildings complete with rickety wooden balconies and louvred doors.

Port Fuad NEIGHBOURHOOD

Across the canal from Port Said is the genteel suburb of Port Fuad, founded in 1925. The streets near its quay invite a stroll, with sprawling French-inspired villas and lush gardens that recall the one-time European presence in the area. Free ferries from Port Said to Port Fuad offer impressive views of the canal, and leave about every 10 minutes throughout the day from the terminal at the southwestern end of Sharia Palestine.

Sleeping & Eating

★**Hotel de la Poste** HISTORIC HOTEL $

(☎322 4048; 42 Sharia al-Gomhuriyya; s/d E£75/95; ❄) This faded classic still manages to maintain a hint of its original charm and boasts clean, comfortable rooms with a decent on-site restaurant. Rooms with balcony cost an extra E£15.

New Continental HOTEL $$

(☎322 5024; 30 Sharia al-Gomhuriyya; s/d E£110/183; ❄) Efficient and friendly with light-filled rooms in a range of shapes and sizes.

Resta Port Said Hotel HOTEL $$$

(☎332 5511; www.restahotels.com; off Sharia Palestine; s/d US$160/295; P❄📶≋) Not as luxurious as it likes to think it is but about as snazzy as Port Said gets.

El Borg SEAFOOD $$

(☎332 3442; Beach Plaza, off Sharia Atef as-Sadat; mains E£20-50; ⊙10am-3am) A local favourite with good-value, fresh seafood.

Information

Most important services including banks and ATMs and the are strung along, or just off, Sharia al-Gomhuriyya, two blocks inland from the canal.

Main post office (Sharia al-Geish; ⊙8.30am-2pm Sat-Thu)

Mody Net (Sharia Salah Salem; internet per hr E£3; ⊙9am-midnight).

Tourist office (☎323 5289; 8 Sharia Palestine; ⊙10am-7pm Sat-Thu) Enthusiastic staff and good maps of town.

Getting There & Away

The bus station is about 3km from the town centre (about E£5 in a taxi). There are hourly buses to Cairo (E£25, four hours) and buses to Alexandria (E£25, four to five hours) at 7am, 11am, 2pm, 4pm, 6pm and 8pm.

For Africa-overlanders with vehicles there is a ferry to Turkey (p97).

RED SEA COAST

Arguably the world's most famous stretch of coast, it was here that Moses allegedly parted a great sea and set free the Hebrew slaves. For independent travellers weary of package tourism, the Red Sea Coast can be a frustrating place to visit, though it remains a decent destination for families and divers in search of a cheap holiday.

Hurghada

☎065 / POP 160,900

Put on the map because of its superb diving, Hurghada has long since morphed into today's dense band of coastline concrete. Despite its immense popularity as a package-holiday destination, many travellers now tend to shun Hurghada because of the rampant construction. To be fair, there are still some incredible diving sites that remain in good health and Hurghada is a decent stop if you want to combine a diving holiday with a visit to Upper Egypt without going all the way to the Sinai.

Activities

Although there is some easily accessible coral at the southern end of the resort strip, the best reefs are offshore, and the only way to see them is to take a boat and/or join a snorkelling or diving excursion. The following is a list of recommended operators:

Jasmin Diving Centre DIVING
(346 0334; www.jasmin-diving.com; Grand Seas Resort Hostmark, Resort Strip)

Subex DIVING
(354 7593; www.subex.org; off the Corniche, Ad-Dahar)

Emperor Divers DIVING
(0122 234 0995; www.emperordivers.com; Hilton Plaza Hotel, Resort Strip)

Sleeping

4 Seasons Hotel BACKPACKERS $
(0122 704 3917; fourseasonshurghada@hotmail.com; off Sharia Sayyed al-Qorayem, Ad-Dahar; s/d E£60/80;) Simple, clean rooms and helpful management make this old-school hostel every budgeteer's first port of call in Hurghada.

White Albatross HOTEL $$
(344 2519; walbatros53@hotmail.com; Sharia Sheraton, Sigala; s/d/tr US$25/30/35;) The spick-and-span rooms at the White Albatross are a good choice if you want to be right in the centre of the Hurghada bustle.

Dana Beach Resort RESORT $$
(346 0401; www.pickalbatros.com; Resort Strip; s/d full board US$75/105; P) This mega-resort serves up masses of amenities at good-value prices making it a winner for families on a budget.

Oberoi Sahl Hasheesh LUXURY HOTEL $$$
(344 0777; www.oberoihotels.com; Sahl Hasheesh; ste from US$260; P) Peaceful, exclusive and opulent beyond your imagination, the Oberoi features palatial suites decorated in minimalist Moorish style.

Eating & Drinking

Kastan SEAFOOD $$
(Arena Mall, Sharia Sheraton, Sigala; meals E£40-100) We like Kastan's hearty seafood soup and good-value shrimp curry. For fresh seafood with an Egyptian twist this is one of Hurghada's top choices.

Shade Bar & Grill INTERNATIONAL $$
(Marina Rd, Sigala; mains E£50-95) If you're pining for a steak look no further. Sprawl out on the terrace beanbags and order your red-meat fix.

Al-Araby EGYPTIAN $$
(Sharia Sheraton, Sigala; mains E£25-50) This busy place has streetside seating and serves up a satisfying menu of Egyptian classics.

Papas Bar BAR
(www.papasbar.com; New Marina Rd, Sigala) This Dutch-run bar is the centre of nightlife in Hurghada, and popular with diving instructors and foreign residents.

Information

There are banks with ATMs all over town.

Main post office (Sharia an-Nasr, Ad-Dahar; 8.30am-2.30pm Sat-Thu)

Telephone centrale (Sharia an-Nasr, Ad-Dahar; 24hr)

Estenv Internet (Sharia Sheikh Sabak, Ad-Dahar; internet per hr £E5; 24hr)

02 Internet (Sharia Sheraton, Sigala; internet per hr E£10; 10.15am-11.15pm).

Tourist office (344 4420; 8am-8pm Sat-Thu, 2-10pm Fri) On the resort strip.

Getting There & Around

EgyptAir (344 3592/93; www.egyptair.com; Resort Strip) has daily flights to Cairo from **Hurghada Airport** (346 2722; Main Hwy), near the Resort Strip.

There are frequent buses to Cairo (E£45 to E£60, six to seven hours) and Luxor (E£30 to E£45, four hours) from both the **Upper Egypt Bus Co** (354 7582; off Sharia an-Nasr, Ad-Dahar) and **Super Jet** (354 4722; Sharia an-Nasr, Ad-Dahar) bus stations.

The Hurghada–Sharm el-Sheikh ferry service is currently not operating.

NILE VALLEY

Measuring 6680km in length, the Nile is the world's longest river. It brought the nation of Egypt into being and its banks are clustered with the temples and tombs of the country's illustrious past. Luxor and Aswan are the jewels in the crown and few can resist time spent on the water itself.

Luxor

095 / POP 451,300

Built around the 4000-year-old site of Thebes, the ancient capital of the New Kingdom, contemporary Luxor is an eccentric combination of provincial town and staggering ancient splendour.

Although the modern East Bank city has grown rapidly in recent years, the setting is still breathtakingly beautiful, the Nile flowing between the modern town and the West Bank necropolis, backed by the enigmatic Theban escarpment. Scattered across the landscape is an embarrassment of riches, from the temples of Karnak and Luxor on its East Bank to the temples of Hatshepsut and Medinat Habu, the Colossi of Memnon and the Valley of the Kings on the West Bank.

Sights

East Bank

★Karnak TEMPLE

(238 0270; Sharia Maabad al-Karnak; adult/student E£65/40; 6am-6pm) Much more than a temple, Karnak is a spectacular complex of sanctuaries, pylons and obelisks. Its crowning glory is the **Great Hippostyle Hall**, constructed around 134 lotus-blossom pillars. Begun in the Middle Kingdom, the complex was added to, dismantled, restored, enlarged and decorated over 1500 years.

The site covers over 2 sq km and its main structure, the Temple of Amun, is one of the world's largest religious complexes.

If you can tolerate the kitsch, the **sound-and-light show** (238 6000, 238 2777; www.soundandlight.com.eg; adult/student E£100/60, video camera E£35; shows 6.30pm, 7.45pm & 9pm winter, 8pm, 9.15pm & 10.30pm summer) offers a nonetheless atmospheric introduction to Karnak.

Luxor Temple TEMPLE

(237 2408; Corniche an-Nil; adult/student E£50/30; 6am-9pm) Largely built by the New Kingdom Pharaoh Amenhotep III, this temple is a strikingly graceful monument in the heart of modern Luxor.

Visit early, before the crowds, or later at sunset when the stones glow.

Luxor Museum MUSEUM

(Corniche an-Nil; adult/student E£80/40; 8.30am-2pm) This museum has a beautifully displayed collection, from the end of the Old Kingdom right through to the Mamluk period.

Mummification Museum MUSEUM

(Corniche an-Nil; adult/student E£50/25; 9am-2pm) The well-presented exhibits here explain the art of mummification.

West Bank

The West Bank of Luxor was the necropolis of ancient Thebes, a vast city of the dead where magnificent temples were raised to honour the cults of pharaohs entombed in nearby cliffs, and where queens, nobles, priests and artisans built tombs with spectacular decor.

The first monuments you'll see are the 18m-high **Colossi of Memnon**. These statues are all that remain of a temple built by Amenhotep III.

★Valley of the Kings TOMBS

(Wadi Biban al-Muluk; www.thebanmappingproject.com; adult/student for 3 tombs excl Ramses VI, Ay & Tutankhamun E£80/40, Tomb of Ramses VI E£50/25, Tomb of Tutankhamun E£100/50, Tomb of Ay tickets available from the Antiquities Inspectorate office near Medinat Habu E£25/15; 6am-4pm) Couched in a sun-ravaged ravine of Al-Qurn (Horn) escarpment, this celebrated valley is the last resting place of the pharaohs. Many of them weren't allowed much rest, however, as the pillage of tombs began before the last pharaohs were buried.

The tombs of **Ramses IX**, **Tuthmosis III** and **Horemheb** have some of the most interesting designs and wall paintings while the **tomb of Amenhotep II**, hidden in the escarpment, is the most exciting to visit.

The famed **tomb of Tutankhamen**, found in 1922 by Howard Carter, is the only tomb that has, so far, been discovered intact. The fabulous treasure it contained, displayed in the Cairo Museum, far outshines its actual appearance and it is one of the least impressive tombs in the valley.

Due to preservation issues, replicas of the tombs of **Seti I** (currently closed) and Tutankhamen are planned in the near future.

★Memorial Temple of Hatshepsut TEMPLE

(Deir al-Bahri; adult/student E£30/15; 6am-5pm) This dazzling temple blends in beautifully with the rugged limestone cliffs from which it was cut. It was vandalised by Hatshepsut's

Luxor – East Bank

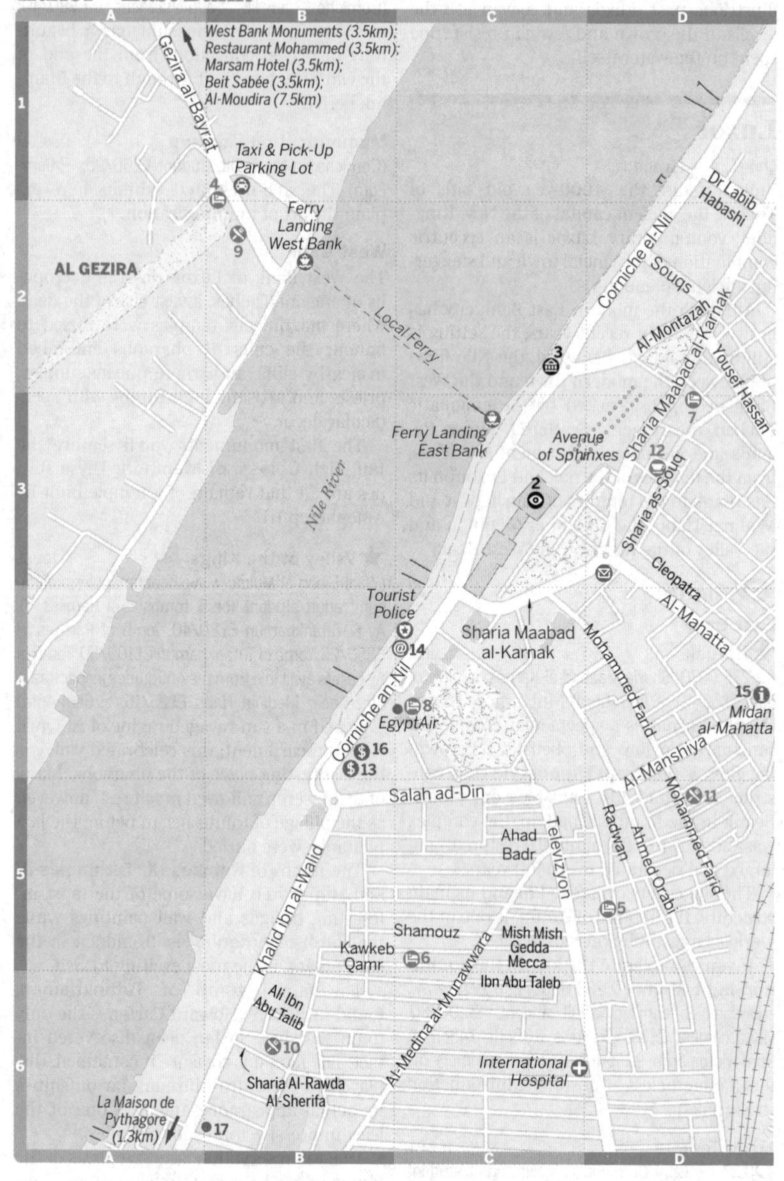

bitter successor, Tuthmosis III, but retains much of its original magnificence, including elaborate friezes.

★ **Medinat Habu** TEMPLE

(adult/student E£30/15; 6am-5pm) The superbly preserved reliefs and golden stones of Ramses III's magnificent memorial temple of Medinat Habu are perhaps one of the

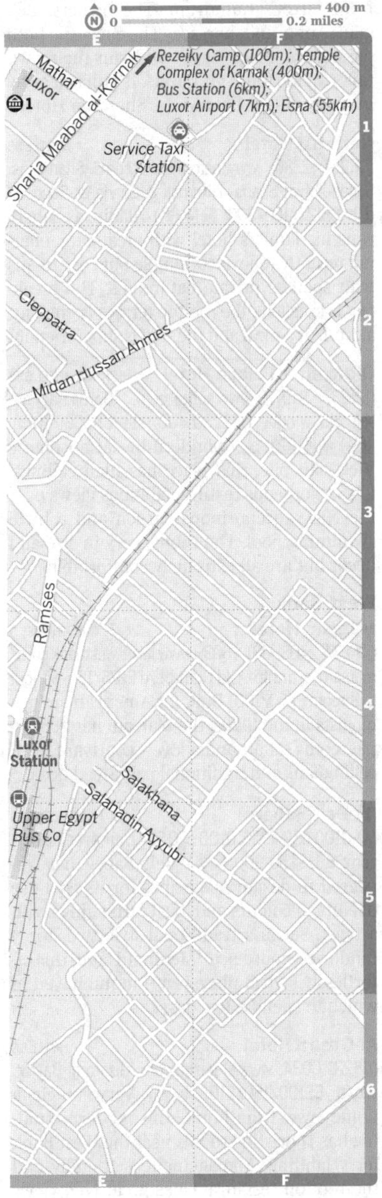

most underrated sites on the West Bank. It's especially magical at sunset.

Valley of the Queens TOMBS
(Biban al-Harim; adult/student E£35/20; 6am-5pm) There are at least 75 tombs in the Valley of the Queens but only a couple are open. The **Tomb of Amunherkhepshef** has beautiful, well-preserved reliefs. The crowning glory of the site, the **Tomb of Nefertari**, remains closed but a replica is being built.

Luxor – East Bank

Sights
1 Luxor Museum....E1
2 Luxor Temple....C3
3 Mummification Museum....C2

Sleeping
4 Al-Gezira Hotel....B1
5 Fontana Hotel....D5
6 Happy Land Hotel....C5
7 Nefertiti Hotel....D3
8 Old Winter Palace Hotel....C4

Eating
As-Sahaby Lane....(see 7)
9 Nile Valley Hotel....B2
10 Oasis Café....B6
11 Sofra Restaurant & Café....D5

Drinking & Nightlife
12 New Oum Koulsoum Coffee Shop....D3

Information
American Express....(see 8)
13 Banque du Caire....B4
14 Gamil Centre....C4
15 Main Tourist Office....D4
16 National Bank of Egypt....B4
17 Passport Office....B6
Telephone Centrale....(see 8)
Thomas Cook....(see 8)

Activities

Felucca Rides

The nicest place to be in the late afternoon is on the Nile. Take a felucca from either bank and sail for a few hours to catch the soft afternoon light and the sunset; cool down in the afternoon breeze and calm down after sightseeing. Prices range from E£30 to E£50 per boat per hour, depending on your bargaining skills.

Sleeping

East Bank

Fontana Hotel HOSTEL $
(228 0663, 010 733 3238; www.fontanaluxorhotel.com; Sharia Radwan, off Sharia Televizyon; s/d/tr E£40/60/75, without bathroom E£30/50/65;) An old stalwart of the budget hotel scene, this 25-room hotel has clean rooms,

WEST BANK PRACTICALITIES

A private taxi to visit sites on the West Bank costs between E£150 and E£250 for the day. Bicycles can be hired for E£15 to E£20 per day.

The local ferry costs E£1 for foreigners and leaves from a dock in front of Luxor Temple. For an idea of the distances involved: from the local ferry landing on the west bank it is 3km straight ahead to the ticket office, 4km to the Valley of the Queens, and 8km to the Valley of the Kings.

The **Antiquities Inspectorate ticket office** (6am-5pm) on the main road, 3km inland from the ferry landing, 500m west of the Colossi of Memnon, near Medinat Habu, sells tickets to all monument except the Valley of the Kings, Valley of the Queens and the Memorial Temple of Hatshepsut, which have their own ticket offices on site.

Photography is not allowed inside any of the tombs.

Don't forget to bring plenty of water, small change to tip site guardians and a torch (flashlight).

a washing machine for guest use, a rooftop terrace and a kitchen. Owner Magdi Soliman is always ready to help.

Happy Land Hotel HOSTEL **$**
(227 1828; www.luxorhappyland.com; Sharia Qamr; s/d E£85/90, without bathroom E£75/80;) A backpackers favourite, Happy Land offers clean rooms and spotless bathrooms, as well as very friendly service, a copious breakfast with fruit and cereal, and a rooftop terrace.

Rezeiky Camp CAMPGROUND **$**
(238 1334; www.rezeikycamp.com.eg; Sharia Maabad al-Karnak; campsites per person E£25, vehicles E£20, s/d with fan E£55/110, with air-con E£65/120;) The only place to pitch a tent. Rezeiky has a large garden, pool and restaurant.

★ **La Maison de Pythagore** GUESTHOUSE **$$**
(0100 535 0532; www.lamaisondepythagore.com; Al-Awamiya; s/d/tr US$45/58/77;) This small guesthouse with its traditional Egyptian architecture and garden full of tumbling bougainvillea is a world away from Luxor's humdrum. The owners, Belgian Anne and her son Thomas, are both passionate about Egypt and run their own tailor-made tours for guests. It's tucked away in a tiny village behind the Sheraton Hotel.

Nefertiti Hotel HOTEL **$$**
(237 2386; www.nefertitihotel.com; Sharia as-Sahabi, btwn Sharia al-Karnak & Sharia as-Souq; s/d/tr E£120/160/200;) Aladin as-Sahabi runs his family's hotel with great care, offering recently renovated, simple but cosy rooms with spotless private bathrooms. The breakfast is excellent, the rooftop terrace is great for a drink or a meal and the staff is super friendly.

Old Winter Palace Hotel HISTORIC HOTEL **$$$**
(237 1197; www.sofitel.com; Corniche an-Nil; old wing r US$230-400, ste US$580-1000; P) A wonderfully atmospheric Victorian pile, this place has high ceilings, lots of gorgeous textiles, fabulous views over the Nile, an enormous garden and a huge swimming pool. The rooms vary in size and decor but are all extremely comfortable.

West Bank

Marsam Hotel GUESTHOUSE **$**
(237 2403, 231 1603; www.luxor-westbank.com/marsam_e_az.htm; Old Gurna; s/d E£75/150, without bathroom E£50/100) Built for American archaeologists in the 1920s, the Marsam has 30 simple rooms set around a lovely courtyard, with ceiling fans and traditional palm-reed beds.

★ **Beit Sabée** BOUTIQUE HOTEL **$$**
(0100 632 4926, 0100 570 5341; info@beitsabee.com; d US$50-90;) Beit Sabée has appeared in design magazines for its cool use of Nubian colours and local furnishings with a twist. Set in a traditional-style two-storey mudbrick house near Medinat Habu, this effortlessly stylish place is a tranquil haven in which to spend a few days.

Al-Gezira Hotel HOTEL **$$**
(231 0034; www.el-gezira.com; Gizera al-Bayrat; s/d/tr E£100/150/210;) Very much a home away from home, this modern building has 11 pristine rooms near the West Bank ferry landing. Management is friendly and the rooftop restaurant has great Nile views as well as cold beer (E£12) and good food.

Al-Moudira LUXURY HOTEL **$$$**
(0122 325 1307; www.moudira.com; Daba'iyya; r/ste US$285/355;) A Moorish fantasy of soaring vaults, pointed arches and enormous domes. Each room is different in shape, size and colour, and decorated with

antiques found throughout Egypt, while the public spaces are even more spectacular.

Eating & Drinking

East Bank

★Sofra Restaurant & Café EGYPTIAN $$
(235 9752; www.sofra.co.eg; 90 Sharia Mohamed Farid; mains E£20-60; 11am-midnight) Sofra remains our favourite restaurant in Luxor. Located in a 1930s house, it is as Egyptian as can be, both in menu and decor – and even in price.

Oasis Café INTERNATIONAL $$
(336 7121; Sharia St Joseph, off Sharia Khalid Ibn Walid; mains E£15-60; 10am-10pm;) The perfect place for lunch or to linger over a latte, Oasis has a menu of pasta, grills and sandwiches as well as a wide selection of pastries.

As-Sahaby Lane EGYPTIAN $$
(236 5509; www.nefertitihotel.com/sahabi.htm; Sharia as-Sahaby, off Sharia as-Souq; mains E£35-60; 9am-11.30pm) This easygoing alfresco restaurant in the souq serves up fresh and well-prepared Egyptian dishes.

New Oum Koulsoum Coffee Shop CAFE
(Sharia as-Souq; 24hr) Pleasant *ahwa* right at the heart of the souq, on a large terrace where you can recover from haggling and watch the crowds without any hassle.

West Bank

Restaurant Mohammed EGYPTIAN $$
(0120 325 1307; Kom Lolah; set meals E£25-60) Mohammed Abdel Lahi's wife cooks up tasty, wholesome local meals on the laid-back terrace of their mudbrick house. The perfect place to relax after a day of temple and tomb exploring.

Nile Valley Hotel INTERNATIONAL $$
(Al-Gezira; meals E£35-60; 8am-11pm) A popular rooftop restaurant with a bird's-eye view along the West Bank's waterfront and a wide-ranging menu.

Information

There are banks with ATMs all over town.

American Express (237 8333; Old Winter Palace Hotel, Corniche el-Nil; 9am-4.30pm)

Banque du Caire (Corniche an-Nil; 8:30am-2pm & 5-6pm Sun-Thu)

Gamil Centre (lower level, Corniche an-Nil; 24hr) In front of Winter Palace Hotel.

Main post office (Sharia al-Mahatta; 8.30am-2.30pm Sat-Thu)

Main tourist office (237 2215; Midan al-Mahatta; 8am-8pm) Very helpful and well-informed.

National Bank of Egypt (Corniche an-Nil; 8:30am-2pm & 5-6pm Sun-Thu)

Telephone Centrale (Corniche an-Nil; 8am-8pm) Below entrance to Winter Palace Hotel.

Thomas Cook (237 2196; Old Winter Palace Hotel, Corniche an-Nil; 8am-2pm & 3-8pm)

Getting There & Away

AIR

EgyptAir (238 0581; Old Winter Palace Hotel, Corniche an-Nil; 8am-8pm) operates daily flights to Cairo from Luxor Airport 7km east of town.

A taxi from the airport to Luxor costs between E£70 and E£100.

BOAT

An armada of cruise boats travels the most famous stretch of the Nile between Luxor and Aswan, stopping at Edfu and Kom Ombo en route. Prices vary wildly as can facilities and standards. Reservations are best made through official travel agencies.

BUS

Zanakta bus station (237 2118) is out of town on the road to the airport. A taxi from town costs from around E£25 to E£35.

Tickets for **Upper Egypt Bus Co** (232 3218, 237 2118; Midan, al-Mahatta) buses can be bought at its office in town, south of the train station. Some buses leave from there as well.

Buses heading to Cairo leave at 6.30pm from the office and 7pm from the bus station (E£100, 10 to 11 hours), but booking ahead is essential. Five daily buses head from the bus station to Hurghada (E£35 to E£40, five hours) from 6.30am to 8pm.

The bus to Sharm el-Sheikh (E£130, 14 hours) and Dahab (E£140, 16 hours) leaves at 4.30pm from the town office.

TRAIN

From **Luxor Train Station** (237 2018; Midan al-Mahatta) the **Watania Sleeping Train** (237 2015, 02-2574 9474; www.wataniasleepingtrains.com) goes daily to Cairo at 7.15pm and 10.30pm. Tickets cost US$60/80 per person in a double/single cabin and can be paid for in dollars, Egyptian pounds or euros.

The 981, which leaves at 8.25am, is the best day train to Cairo (E£90/46 in 1st/2nd class). The slower 983 leaves at 10.30am, and the 935 at noon.

To Aswan (E£41/25 in 1st/2nd class, three hours) catch the 996 at 7.30am, the 1902 at 9.30am, or the 980 at 6pm.

Getting Around

The ferry between the East Bank and the West Bank runs about every 20 minutes.

Short taxi rides around town cost between E£10 and E£15.

South of Luxor

Edfu

Temple of Horus TEMPLE
(adult/student E£50/25; 7am-7pm) The attraction in Edfu town is the most completely preserved temple in Egypt. Built by the Ptolemies over a period of 200 years, it was dedicated to the falcon-headed son of Osiris.

Kom Ombo

Temple of Kom Ombo TEMPLE
(adult/student E£30/20; 7am-7pm) Spectacularly perched on the Nile near the village of Kom Ombo, this temple is dedicated to the crocodile god and falcon-headed sky god.

Getting There & Around

Trains running between Luxor and Aswan stop at Edfu; the station is approximately 4km from the temple and taxis to the site cost E£20.

If you're travelling from Luxor you can stop at Kom Ombo on the train but be aware that the station is some way from the temple. A taxi from Kom Ombo centre to the temple should cost about E£20 return.

A return taxi from Luxor to Edfu and Kom Ombo costs about E£450.

Aswan

097 / POP 265,004

Egypt's southernmost city sits on the banks of a particularly beautiful stretch of the Nile, decorated with palm-fringed islands and flotillas of white-sailed feluccas. Associated with the Nubian people, a distinct ethnic group with their own language and customs, the town is more African in character than the cities of the north.

Sights & Activities

★ **Nubia Museum** MUSEUM
(Sharia Abtal at-Tahrir; adult/student E£50/25; 9am-5pm) This excellent museum is a showcase of the history, art and culture of the Nubian people and is a reminder of the history that was lost when the building of Lake Nasser flooded the Nubian lands. Exhibits are beautifully displayed with clearly written explanations that take you from 4500 BC through to the present day.

★ **Aswan Museum & the Ruins of Abu** ARCHAEOLOGICAL SITE
(Elephantine Island; adult/student E£30/15; 8am-5pm) At the southern end of Elephantine Island, the fascinating Aswan Museum houses antiquities discovered in Aswan. A path leads through the garden behind the museum to the evocative ruins of ancient Abu, which marks the island's long history from around 3000 BC to the 14th century AD.

Unfinished Obelisk ARCHAEOLOGICAL SITE
(adult/student E£30/20; 8am-5pm) This discarded obelisk lies in the quarries that supplied the ancient Egyptians with granite. Three sides of the shaft, which is nearly 42m long, were excavated before it was abandoned due to a flaw in the rock. Taxis charge E£15 from the centre of Aswan.

Feluccas

Felucca trips (from E£25 per hour) can be organised to Kitchener's Island's verdant **botanical garden** (admission E£20; 8am-6pm) and the 6th-century Coptic **Monastery of St Simeon** (Deir Amba Samaan; adult/student E£25/15; 8am-4pm). To reach the monastery, take a camel from the dock (from E£30). You can also get a boat to the Old and Middle Kingdom **Tombs of the Nobles** (adult/student E£25/15; 8am-4pm) on the West Bank.

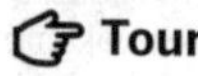

Tours

All travel agencies and most hotels in Aswan offer trips to Abu Simbel, but watch out for huge price differences, and check that the bus is comfortable and has air-con. Thomas Cook charges about E£1000 per person, including a seat in an air-con minibus, admission fees and guide, and E£1400 by air, including transfers, fees and guide. By contrast, budget hotels offer tours for between E£200 and E£300 in a smaller bus, often not including the entrance fee or guide.

Sleeping

Baaba Dool GUESTHOUSE $
(0100 497 2608; Siou, Elephantine Island; r without bathroom E£80) A great place to unwind for a few days. The basic rooms (bring a sleeping bag) in this beautiful mudbrick house are painted in Nubian style, and have

superb views over the Nile and the botanical gardens. Book ahead.

Hathor Hotel HOTEL $
(☎231 4580; www.hathorhotel.com; Corniche an-Nil; s/d E£85/120; ❄📶≋) The 36 spotless rooms vary in size and some are gloomy, but all have a private bathroom and most have air-con (which is controlled at reception) – all in all offering good value for money.

Adam's Home CAMPGROUND $
(☎0100 640 4302; www.adamsnubyana.com; Sheikh Mohammed, Gharb Aswan; r E£50) Overlanders have long known of this place, which provides camping facilities 7km north of Aswan as well as little mudbrick rooms; bring your sleeping bag.

★ **Philae Hotel** HOTEL $$
(☎231 2090; philaehotel@gmail.com; Corniche an-Nil; s/d US$80/100; ❄📶) A serious revamp has resulted in comfortable rooms, decorated with fabrics full of Arabic calligraphy and elegant local furnishings. The hotel restaurant serves very reasonably priced organic vegetarian meals sourced from its own garden.

Keylany Hotel HOTEL $$
(☎231 7332; www.keylanyhotel.com; 25 Sharia Keylany; s/d/tr US$23/34/45; ❄@📶≋) Keylany's spotless rooms are furnished with pine furniture and its endlessly helpful staff have guaranteed this hotel's continual popularity. Breakfast here, on the lovely roof terrace, is superb.

Bet al-Kerem GUESTHOUSE $$
(☎0109 239 9443, 0122 384 2218; www.betelkerem.com; Gharb Aswan, West Bank; s/d US$45/58; ❄) The peaceful nine rooms (some share bathrooms) overlooking the desert here are a great find. There's a wonderful rooftop terrace with Nile and Nubian village views and a good restaurant.

Sofitel Old Cataract Hotel & Spa HISTORIC HOTEL $$$
(☎231 6000; www.sofitel-legend.com; Sharia Abtal at-Tahrir; r/ste from US$495/730; ❄≋) Completely refitted in 2011, the grande dame of hotels on the Nile takes you back to the days of Agatha Christie, who is said to have written part of her novel *Death on the Nile* here.

Eating & Drinking

Salah Ad-Din INTERNATIONAL $$
(☎231 0361; Corniche an-Nil; mains E£40-70; ⏲noon-late) The best of Aswan's Nile-side restaurants, with several terraces and a menu of Egyptian, Nubian and international dishes. Service is efficient and the beers (E£18) are cold.

Panorama EGYPTIAN
(☎231 6169; Corniche an-Nil; dishes E£8-20) With its pleasant Nile-side terrace, this is a great place to tuck into simple Egyptian stews.

Sunset PIZZERIA $$
(☎233 0601; Sharia Abtal at-Tahrir, Nasr City; set menus E£40-50; ⏲9am-3am) Spectacular views over the First Cataract make this cafe's terrace the place to be at sunset.

Nubian Beach EGYPTIAN $$
(West Bank; set menu per person E£55) This wonderful Nubian cafe-restaurant on Aswan's West Bank has a backdrop of towering sand dunes.

Information

The main banks have branches, all with ATMs, on the corniche.

American Express (☎230 6983; Corniche an-Nil; ⏲9am-5pm)

Aswanet (☎231 7332; Sharia Keylany; per hr E£10; ⏲9am-11pm)

Main post office (Corniche an-Nil; ⏲8am-8pm Sat-Thu, 1-5pm Fri)

Main tourist office (☎231 2811; Midan al-Mahatta; ⏲8am-3pm & 7-9pm Sat-Thu)

Telephone Centrale (Corniche an-Nil; ⏲24hr)

Thomas Cook (☎230 4011; Corniche an-Nil; ⏲8am-2pm & 5-9pm)

Getting There & Away

AIR

EgyptAir (☎231 5000; Corniche an-Nil; ⏲8am-3pm & 7-9pm Sat-Thu) has daily flights to Cairo, Luxor and Abu Simbel from **Aswan Airport** (☎248 0333), 25km southwest of town.

BOAT

Most overnight or longer felucca trips begin in Aswan as the strong northward current means boats are not marooned if the wind dies.

Trips go to Kom Ombo (one night), Edfu (two nights) or Esna (three nights). Expect to pay around E£100 per person to Kom Ombo, E£130 to Edfu, and E£160 to Esna, including food.

Cruise boats also sail from Aswan to Luxor and reservations can be made through any travel agent.

BUS

The bus station is 3.5km north of the train station. At the time of research there were no buses

Aswan

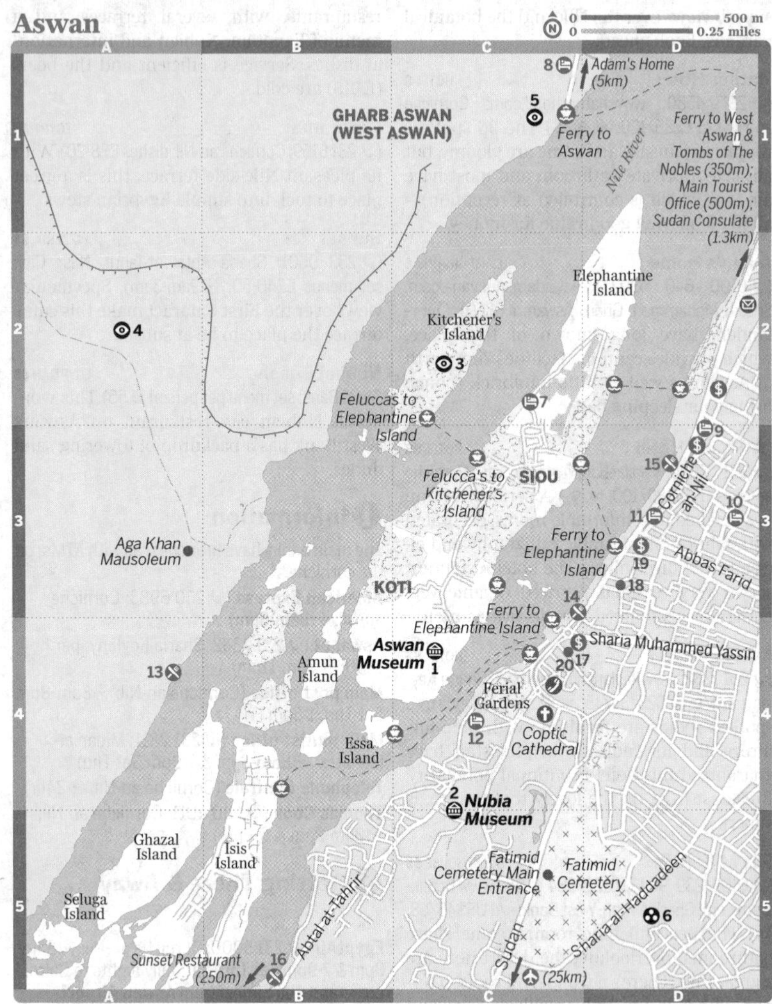

to Luxor. A direct bus to Cairo (E£150, 14 hours) leaves at 6am and 3pm daily.

Travelling by public bus to Abu Simbel is restricted to four foreigners per bus. From the station, Upper Egypt Bus Co has two daily buses to Abu Simbel (E£35, four hours, departing 8am and 5pm).

TRAIN

From **Aswan Train Station** (☎231 4754; Midan al-Mahatta) a number of daily trains run north to Cairo between 5am and 9.10pm (E£175, 14 hours). All stop at Kom Ombo (E£24/17 in 1st/2nd class, one hour), Edfu (E£28/19, two hours) and Luxor (E£45/29, three hours).

The **Watania Sleeping Train** (☎230 2124; www.wataniasleepingtrains.com) has two daily services to Cairo at 5pm and 7pm. Tickets cost US$60/80 per person in a double/single cabin, including dinner and breakfast.

Getting Around

A taxi to/from the airport costs between E£50 and E£80.

Aswan

Two public ferries link Aswan with Elephantine Island (E£1) and a third ferry goes to the Tombs of the Nobles on the West Bank.

A taxi anywhere in town costs between E£5 and E£10.

Around Aswan

High Dam

The construction of the controversial **Aswan High Dam** (as-Sadd al-Ali; adult/child E£20/10) created Lake Nasser, the world's largest artificial lake. The dam, completed in 1971, doubled the country's power supply and has brought great benefits to Egypt's farmers, increasing cultivable land by at least 30%. On the downside the dam stopped the flow of silt essential to the land's fertility and much of ancient Nubia disappeared under the waters of Lake Nasser.

Most people visit the dam as part of an Abu Simbel tour. A taxi to the dam from Aswan costs about E£25.

Philae (Aglikia Island)

Dedicated to the goddess Isis, the beautiful **Temple of Isis** (adult/child E£50/25; 7am-4pm Oct-May, to 5pm Jun-Sep) was disassembled stone by stone and reconstructed on Aglikia Island to be saved from the High Dam's rising waters.

The **Sound-and-Light show** (230 5376; www.soundandlight.com.eg; adult/child E£70/50; shows 6.30pm, 7.45pm & 9pm Oct-May, 7pm, 8.15pm & 9.30pm May-Sep) is worthwhile for the opportunity to wander through the temple at night.

A return taxi from Aswan costs around E£60. The return boat trip from the landing to Aglikia Island should not cost more than E£10 per person.

Abu Simbel

097

Few tourists linger more than the couple of hours necessary to view the giant temples for which Abu Simbel is famous. But anyone interested in seeing the temples without the crowds and experiencing the peaceful beauty of Lake Nasser's shore will enjoy choosing to hang around for a few days.

The **Temples of Abu Simbel** (adult/student incl guide fee E£90/48.50; 6am-5pm Oct-Apr, to 6pm May-Sep) Overlooking Lake Nasser, the two temples of Abu Simbel are perhaps the most striking in Egypt.

The imposing Great Temple of Ramses II was cut from the hillside to honour the gods Ra-Harakhty, Amun and Ptah. The four colossal sttatues of Ramses II are like giant sentinels watching over incoming traffic from the south. Next door the smaller Temple of Hathor has a rock-cut facade fronted by a further six 10m-high statues of Ramses and Nefertari.

Submerged in desert sand, the temples were rediscovered in 1813 by Jean-Louis Burckhardt and in the 1960s both temples were winched to higher ground to avoid the rising waters of Lake Nasser in an ingenious feat of engineering.

SECURITY AFTER THE REVOLUTION

The 2011 revolution that ousted long-term president Hosni Mubarak also disrupted security. At first it appeared that Egypt's first democratic elections, and the appointment of Mohammed Morsi to the presidency, had done much to normalise the situation. But security remained a problem in the Northern Sinai and in the major cities occasional violent protests – such as the November 2012 demonstrations and 2013's June and July demonstrations, which resulted in the military toppling Morsi – can still break out at short notice.

It is however important to note that these are extremely localised activities. For example, even when a protest is ongoing at Cairo's Midan Tahrir, the rest of the city (even as close as two blocks away) is generally calm.

The nightly **Sound-and-Light show** (www.soundandlight.com.eg; adult/child E£80/45; ⏲ shows 7pm, 8pm & 9pm Oct-Apr, 8pm, 9pm & 10pm May-Sep) has a stunning laser display although the commentary is predictably cheesy.

Eskaleh (Beit an-Nubi; ☎ 0122 368 0521; www.eskaleh.net; d US$75-90; ❄ @) is a Nubian culture centre and ecolodge with simple rooms, furnished with local furniture. It's a destination in its own right, if a bit pricey. **Abu Simbel Village** (☎ 340 0092; s/d E£90/120) has basic, vaulted rooms.

Buses from Abu Simbel to Aswan (E£35, four hours) leave at 8am, 9.30am, 1pm and 4pm from the Wadi el-Nil Restaurant on the main road. There are no advance bookings and tickets are purchased on board. Note that the official limit is four foreign passengers per bus, although they will generally turn a blind eye to one or two extra.

UNDERSTAND EGYPT

Egypt Today

After 30 years in power, on 11 February 2011 President Hosni Mubarak resigned after an 18-day uprising that saw Cairo's Midan Tahrir occupied by hundreds of thousands of protesters. Power was initially handed over to the Supreme Council of the Armed Forces (SCAF) under the command of Field Marshal Tantawi. Although there was initial euphoria over Mubarak's departure, the slow pace of democratic change led to further demonstrations throughout the year while a spate of tourist kidnappings and attacks on military installations in the Sinai prompted security fears.

Egypt's decades-long state of emergency was repealed in May 2012. By June the Islamist Muslim Brotherhood candidate, Mohammed Morsi, became Egypt's first democratically elected president. In the same month ex-president Mubarak was sentenced to life in prison for his role in trying to quell the 2011 uprising.

However, it was just a year into his term when President Morsi was ousted by the military in response to widespread dissatisfaction with his government among the population. Egypt's future political stability will depend on whether the aspirations of an increasingly young population are able to be met; and how Egypt's continuing economic challenges are tackled.

History

Old, Middle & New Kingdoms

Ancient Egyptian history comprises three principal kingdoms. The pyramids date from the Old Kingdom (2670–2150 BC), when lively trade made ambitious building projects possible. Ruling from the nearby capital of Memphis, Pharaoh Zoser and his chief architect, Imhotep, built the pyramid at Saqqara. Subsequent pharaohs constructed ever larger temples and pyramids, which eventually culminated in the mighty pyramids of Giza, built for Cheops, Chephren and Mycerinus.

The Middle Kingdom (2056–1650 BC) was marked by the rise of a new and illustrious capital at Thebes (Luxor). It was during the period of the New Kingdom (1550–1076 BC), however, that ancient Egyptian culture blossomed. Wonders such as the Temple of Karnak and the West Bank tombs were the visible expression of a rich culture that established Egypt, under the great dynasties of Tuthmosis and Ramses, as the greatest regional power.

From Alexander to Sadat

From the year 1184 BC, Egypt disintegrated into local principalities, and it wasn't until Alexander the Great arrived in the 4th century BC that the country was reunited. For the next 300 years, Egypt was ruled from Alexandria by the descendants of his general, Ptolemy. The Romans arrived in 31 BC, leaving behind little to show for their occupation except the introduction of Christianity in AD 2.

In AD 640, Arab armies brought Islam to Egypt. With it came a cultural revival and the foundation of Cairo in AD 969 by the Fatimid dynasty. The arts and sciences flourished, and trade brought much wealth into the country. Bu the Turks found the prize irresistible, and in the early 16th century, Egypt became part of the Ottoman Empire. The French followed suit during the 19th century under Napoleon, and then the British made Egypt a protectorate during WWI.

After nearly 2000 years of colonisation, revolution resulted in self-rule in 1952. Gamal Abdel Nasser became Egypt's first president in 1956, and established his authority by buying out French and British claims to the Suez Canal. He did, however, lose the 1967 war with Israel. His successor, Anwar Sadat, who came to power in 1970, concluded the second war with Israel with the controversial 1978 Camp David Accords. Widely blamed for betraying pan-Arabist principles, Sadat was assassinated by a member of the extremist organisation Islamic Jihad in 1981.

The Mubarak Era

Sadat's successor, Hosni Mubarak, retaliated against the extremists, declaring a state of emergency that continued throughout his presidency. Although Mubarak was canny in rehabilitating Egypt's relations with Arab states, harsh socio-economic domestic conditions, continual government crackdowns on legitimate opposition and abuses by Mubarak's security forces meant his rule was marked by violence.

During the 1990s Egyptian Islamist extremist groups began to target tourism, the state's most valuable source of income, in their campaign to overthrow the government. This culminated in the massacre of 58 holidaymakers at the Funerary Temple of Hatshepsut in 1997. The following decade saw further bombings in the Sinai holiday centres of Taba, Sharm el-Sheikh and Dahab, resulting in multiple deaths and a serious decline in tourism.

Mubarak introduced some minor democratic measures in 2005, but with Egypt's economy in turmoil and with an ever-growing population and rising unemployment, this wasn't enough to stop the tide of disenchantment with his regime.

People of Egypt

Egypt has the third-highest population in Africa. Growing at a rate of 2% annually, it places enormous strain on infrastructure and the national economy. Unemployment is officially 12%; unofficially, it's much higher.

About 90% of Egypt's population is Muslim, with Coptic Christians being the largest minority.

Culture

One characteristic that links the majority of Egyptians, from the university professor in Alexandria to the shoeshine boy in Luxor, is an immense pride in simply being Egyptian. It's hard sometimes for outsiders to see where that pride could come from, given the pervasive poverty, infrastructure failings and myriad other pitfalls that face the country. But aiding each Egyptian in the daily struggle are large extended families and close-knit neighbourhoods that act as social support groups – whatever goes wrong, somebody always knows someone who can help fix it.

Religion also cushions life's blows and permeates Egyptian life. Islam is manifested not in a strictly authoritarian manner – Egyptians love enjoying themselves too much for that – but it's there in the background. And when all else fails – and it so often fails – there's humour. Egyptians are renowned for it. Jokes and wisecracks are the parlance of life and one of the most enjoyable aspects of travelling in Egypt is how much can be negotiated with a smile.

Environment

Egypt's central feature is the Nile Valley, either side of which are barren plateaus punctuated by occasional escarpments and oases. The highest mountains are Mt Sinai (Gebel Musa; 2285m) and Mt St Katherine (Gebel Katarina; 2637m), in the Sinai Peninsula.

Environmental awareness is not a top priority in Egypt: Cairo is thick with smog, the Red Sea coast is threatened by opportunistic development, and freshwater lakes are blighted by agricultural toxins.

On a positive note, there are now 20-plus protected areas throughout Egypt, with another 20-plus more in various planning stages, and the government is beginning to encourage responsible tourism within its borders.

Food & Drink

A combination of Arabic and Mediterranean influences, Egypt's cuisine is focused on minced, seasoned meat, locally made cheese and fresh vegetables such as tomatoes and aubergines. Staples include *fuul* (fava beans cooked with oil and lemon), *ta'amiyya* (felafel), *kushari* (a mixture of noodles, rice and lentils) and unleavened bread.

Birds (as you'll note from the dovecotes) form an integral part of Egyptian culture, and pigeon, stuffed with rice and raisins, is a popular delicacy.

Although beer and *arak* are produced locally, fresh fruit juices are the favoured drink. Sweet mint tea and Turkish coffee are indispensable punctuations to any social interaction.

SURVIVAL GUIDE

Directory A–Z

CUSTOMS REGULATIONS

Duty-free allowances on arrival: 2L alcohol, 200 cigarettes.

DISCOUNT CARDS

Discounts to museums and sites are available for students with an International Student Identity Card (ISIC).

EMBASSIES & CONSULATES

Australian Embassy (02-2575 0444; www.egypt.embassy.gov.au; 11th fl, World Trade Centre, 1191 Corniche el-Nil, Cairo; 8am-4.15pm Sun-Wed, 8am-1.30pm Thu)

British Consulate (03-546 7001; Sharia Mena, Rushdy, Alexandria; 10am-1pm Sun-Thu)

British Embassy (02-2791 6000; www.ukinegypt.fco.gov.uk; 7 Sharia Ahmed Ragheb, Garden City, Cairo; 8am-3.30pm Sun-Wed, 8am-2pm Thu)

Canadian Embassy (02-2791 8700; www.egypt.gc.ca; Sharia Ahmed Raghab, Garden City, Cairo; 8am-4pm Sun-Wed, 8am-1.30pm Thu)

Dutch Embassy (02-2739 5500; http://egypt.nlembassy.org; 18 Sharia Hassan Sabry, Zamalek, Cairo; 8am-4pm Sun-Thu)

French Consulate (03-484 7950; 2 Midan Orabi, Alexandria)

French Embassy (02-3567 3200; www.ambafrance-eg.org; 29 Sharia Charles de Gaulle, Giza)

German Consulate (03-486 7503; 9 Sharia el-Fawatem, Alexandria)

German Embassy (02-2728 2000; www.kairo.diplo.de; 2 Sharia Berlin, Zamalek, Cairo)

Irish Embassy (02-2735 8264; www.embassyofireland.org.eg; 22 Hassan Assem, Zamalek, Cairo; 9am-noon Sun-Thu)

Libyan Consulate (03-494 0877; 4 Sharia Batris Lumomba, Alexandria)

Libyan Embassy (02-735 1269; 7 Sharia el-Saleh Ayoub, Zamalek, Cairo)

New Zealand Embassy (02-2461 6000; www.nzembassy.com; Level 8, North Tower, Nile City Towers, 2005 Corniche el-Nil, Cairo; 9am-3pm Sun-Thu)

Sudanese Consulate (097-230 7231; Bldg 20, Atlas, Aswan)

Sudanese Embassy (02-2794 9661; 3 Sharia al-Ibrahimy. Garden City, Cairo)

US Embassy (02-2797 3300; www.egypt.usembassy.gov; 5 Sharia Tawfiq Diab, Garden City, Cairo; 9am-4pm Sun-Thu)

GAY & LESBIAN TRAVELLERS

Egypt is a conservative society that condemns homosexuality and although not strictly criminalised, statutes against obscenity and public indecency have been used in the past to prosecute gay men. The scene is strictly underground and tapping into it can be tricky. The main gay and lesbian Egypt site is www.gayegypt.com.

INTERNET ACCESS

Internet cafes are common; rates are usually between E£5 and E£10 per hour. Most hotels offer wi-fi. In budget and midrange hotels it is usually free.

MONEY

ATMs are common except in the Western Desert. Banque Misr, the National Bank of Egypt and HSBC usually have reliable machines.

Small change is in short supply. Try to break big bills at fancier establishments.

Money can be changed at Amex and Thomas Cook offices (also where travellers cheques are cashed) , banks, foreign-exchange bureaus and some hotels. Rates don't vary much. US dollars, euros and British pounds are the easiest to change.

The local currency is the Egyptian pound (E£), guinay in Arabic, divided into 100 piastres (pt).

Coins of 5pt, 10pt and 25pt are nearly extinct. Common coins are 50pt and E£1 (notes for these are still in circulation but are becoming rarer). Notes come in denominations of E£5, E£10, E£20, E£50, E£100 and E£200.

Baksheesh (tipping) is part of life in Egypt and is relied upon to supplement low salaries.

OPENING HOURS

The weekend is Friday and Saturday. During Ramadan, offices, museums and tourist sites keep shorter hours.

Banks 8.30am to 2.30pm Sunday to Thursday

Post offices 8.30am to 2pm Saturday to Thursday

Private offices 10am to 2pm and 4 to 9pm Saturday to Thursday

Restaurants and cafes Noon to midnight

Shops 9am to 1pm and 5pm to 10pm June to September, 10am to 6pm October to May

POST

The main post offices handle parcels. Bring them unsealed so customs can inspect the contents. Egypt Post's service is reasonably reliable. The express service (EMS) is downright speedy.

PUBLIC HOLIDAYS

New Year's Day 1 January; official national holiday but many businesses stay open.

Coptic Christmas 7 January; most government offices and all Coptic businesses close.

January 25 Revolution Day 25 January

Sham an-Nessim March/April; first Monday after Coptic Easter. Few businesses close.

Sinai Liberation Day 25 April; celebrating Israel's 1982 return of the peninsula.

May Day 1 May; Labour Day.

Revolution Day 23 July; date of the 1952 coup.

Armed Forces Day 6 October

SAFE TRAVEL

The incidence of crime, violent or otherwise, in Egypt is negligible compared with most Western countries. Following the 2011 revolution, after which police activity was severely curtailed, there has been a spike in petty crimes such as wallet and bag snatchings but statistically it is still quite rare.

The biggest hindrance to unwary visitors are tourist scams, including bogus guides who use remarkable ingenuity to steer you into 'no-hassle, government emporiums' (usually their friend's papyrus/perfume store), and touts and hustlers who lie to divert travellers to hotels for which they get a commission. This is a particular problem in Cairo and Luxor and in some places it can be difficult to walk more than a few metres without being accosted. A smile and a quick stride short-circuits most sales pitches.

PRACTICALITIES

Electricity 220V/50Hz

Languages Arabic, English (widely used)

Newspapers The best English newspaper is the *Daily News Egypt* (E£14).

Smoking Nonsmoking facilities are rare in hotels and restaurants.

Time Two hours ahead of GMT.

TV CNN and BBC World can be accessed in hotel rooms across Egypt.

Water With the exception of Cairo, tap water is not considered safe to drink.

SHOPPING

Egypt has a long lineage in arts and crafts, as a glimpse of Tutankhamen's treasure amply shows. Handmade beadwork from Sinai, basketry from the Western Oases, glass from Alexandria and alabaster pots from Luxor form part of that ancient tradition.

TELEPHONE

The country code for Egypt is ☎20, and the international access code from Egypt is ☎00.

Pay-as-you-go SIM cards from any of the three carriers (Vodafone; Mobinil; Etisalat), and top-up cards, can be purchased from most kiosks

Pay phones (from yellow-and-green Menatel and red-and-blue Nile Tel) are card-operated. Cards are sold at shops and kiosks.

Alternatively a Telephone Centrale is an office where you book your call at the desk and then take your phone call in a booth.

TIME

Egypt is two hours ahead of GMT. In 2012 Egypt did not observe Daylight Saving Time in order to cut the day short for Ramadan observers. This is expected to continue at least through 2014.

VISAS

Visas are required for most foreigners, and are vailable for most nationalities at airports on arrival.

Airport-arrival single-entry tourist visas are valid for 30 days and cost US$15, payable in US dollars, British pounds or euros. Multiple-entry visas are applied for in advance or issued at visa extension offices within Egypt.

South Sinai free 15-day visas are issued at Sharm el-Sheikh Airport, and are valid for travel between Sharm el-Sheikh and Taba, including St

Katherine's Monastery but not Ras Mohammed National Park. If you plan to travel to other parts of Egypt, buy a normal single-entry tourist visa upon arrival at the airport instead.

Travelling by ferry from Jordan, visas are available at Nuweiba Port on arrival.

From Israel, a South Sinai free 15-day visa can be issued at Taba border. Single-entry tourist visa at the border are only available if guaranteed by an Egyptian travel agency; otherwise, apply in advance in Tel Aviv or at the consulate in Eilat.

At the time of research it was not possible to get an Egyptian visa at the Lbyan border: apply in advance. Overland from Sudan, visas are available on the Wadi Halfa ferry for most nationalities, though check before departure.

Visa Extensions

You'll need one photo and two photocopies each of your passport's data page and the visa page. The fee depends on where you apply but is about E£50. Multiple-entry visas can be applied for at the same time and cost an extra E£60.

Alexandria (☎03-482 7873; 2nd fl, 25 Sharia Talaat Harb; ⏰8.30am-2pm Mon-Thu, 10am-2pm Fri, 9am-11am Sat & Sun)

Aswan (☎097-231 2238; 1st fl, Police Bldg, Corniche an-Nil; ⏰8.30am-1pm Sat-Thu)

Cairo (Mogamma Bldg, Midan Tahrir, Downtown; ⏰8am-1.30pm Sat-Wed) Get form from window 12, on the 1st floor, then pay for stamps at window 43. File all back at window 12; pick-up is at window 38.

Luxor (☎095-238 0885; Sharia Khalid ibn al-Walid; ⏰8am-2pm Sat-Thu)

WOMEN TRAVELLERS

Street harrassment is a major problem in Egypt. Solo women will certainly receive comments in the street – some polite, others less so – and possible groping. As a small consolation, street harrassment is a major problem for Egyptian women as well.

Wear conservative clothing; long sleeves and pants or skirts. Sunglasses also deflect attention. Outside of Red Sea resorts, swim in shorts and a T-shirt at the least. On public transport sit next to a woman if possible. Ignore obnoxious comments – if you respond to every one, you'll wear yourself out.

POLICE CONVOYS

Driving between Aswan and Luxor no longer needs to be done in a convoy.

There is still a twice-daily (4.30am and 11am) convoy from Aswan to Abu Simbel, compulsary for foreigners travelling there. Armed convoys congregate at the beginning of Sharia Sadat in Aswan, near the Coptic Cathedral. Be there at least 15 minutes in advance.

Getting There & Away

AIR

Most air travellers enter Egypt through Cairo or Sharm el-Sheikh. Egypt's international and national carrier is EgyptAir (p97), which has its hub at Cairo International Airport.

LAND

Egypt has land borders with Israel and the Palestinian Territories, Libya and Sudan.

Israel & the Palestinian Territories

The Rafah border crossing to the Gaza Strip is officially open Saturday to Thursday but can be closed for weeks at a time due to ongoing security issues. Foreigners can only cross here if they have special permission from the Palestinian Affairs division of the Ministry of Foreign Affairs in Cairo (rarely granted).

The Taba border is open 24 hours. Only Israeli-registered cars can cross here.

Israeli visas are not required for most nationalities. Egyptian departure tax is E£75.

Libya

The border is at Amsaad, and officially open 24 hours. The nearest town on the Egyptian side is Sallum, 12km away.

Officially Libyan tourist visas are only arranged in advance and only granted if you have an invitation from a Libyan tour agency. There was no Egyptian exit tax at the time of research.

Sudan

The new road between Abu Simbel and Wadi Halfa has been completed and was scheduled to open in 2013. Don't hold your breath though as its opening has already been delayed several times. For now the only way to travel between the two countries is to fly or take the Wadi Halfa ferry.

SEA

Jordan

ABMaritime (☎Nuweiba ticket office 069-352 0427; www.abmaritime.com.jo; Ticket Office, opposite Nuweiba Port, Nuweiba) operates two daily ferries between Nuweiba in Egypt and Aqaba in Jordan. Both the fast ferry (US$95/75 in 1st/2nd class, motorbike/car US$50/190, two hours) and slow ferry (US$70/65 in 1st/2nd class, motorbike/car US$45/175, five hours) leave Nuweiba at 5pm. From Aqaba, the fast ferry departs at 1pm and the slow ferry at 11pm. Delays are common on both services.

PORT TAX

Egyptian international ferries charge E£50 port departure tax per person on top of the ticket price.

Tickets are purchased on the day of departure at the ferry ticket office in Nuweiba port.

Jordanian visas are free of charge for anyone entering at Aqaba.

Sudan

The **Nile River Valley Transport Corporation** Aswan (☎0118 316 0926; shopping arcade behind tourist police office; ⏰8am-2pm Sat-Thu); Cairo (☎02-2575 9058; Ramses Train Station, Downtown, Cairo) runs a passenger ferry on Monday from Aswan to Wadi Halfa in Sudan. One-way tickets cost E£500 for 1st class with a bed in a cabin, and E£322 for deck class. From Wadi Halfa to Aswan the ferry leaves on Wednesday. The trip takes 18 to 24 hours.

You must show a valid Sudanese visa in your passport before you can purchase a ferry ticket.

Turkey

Sisa Shipping (☎09 326-613 4374; www.sisa-shipping.com) has a new service operating four sailings per week from Port Said to Iskenderun in Turkey (US$130/275 for pullman seat/2-bed berth, motorbike/car US$230/460). The journey takes 15 to 20 hours. Its agent in Port Said, **Kadmar** (☎066-334 4016; for reservations in Egypt medhat@kadmar.com; El Mahrousa Bldg, Sharia Mahmoud Sedkey, Port Said), organises reservations for Egypt departures.

From Iskanderun to Port Said, contact Sisa Shipping directly.

GETTING AROUND

Air

EgyptAir (MS; ☎national call centre 0900 70000; www.egyptair.com.eg; ⏰8am-8pm) is the only domestic carrier, and flights can be surprisingly cheap, though fares vary considerably depending on season and availability. Domestic one-way fares can be less than US$100.

Boat

No trip to Egypt is complete without a trip down the Nile. You can take the trip on a felucca or opt for a modern cruise ship. Plenty of cruise ships ply the river between Luxor or Aswan. Felucca trips begin from Aswan.

Bus

Bus services cover almost every destination in Egypt. Deluxe buses, with decent seats, air-con and loud Arabic videos, travel between main cities. Keep your ticket until you disembark, as inspectors board the bus to check fares. There are no student discounts on bus fares.

Car & Motorcycle

Driving in Cairo is a crazy affair, so think seriously before you decide to hire a car there. Driving in other parts of the country isn't so bad, though you should avoid intercity driving at night.

Fill up when you can, as many stations run out of petrol. The speed limit outside towns is usually 70km/h to 90km/h, and 100km/h on major highways. Checkpoints are frequent. Be ready with identity papers and licence.

If you're bringing your own vehicle, registration papers, liability insurance and an international driving permit, in addition to your domestic driving licence, are required. Cars in Egypt are required to carry a fire extinguisher.

At the Egyptian border you'll be issued with a licence of the same duration as your visa. The customs charge is approximately US$200, plus another US$50 for number-plate insurance.

Local Transport

Travelling by *servees* (usually microbuses or Peugeot 504 cars) is a quick way of travelling between cities. A driver won't leave until all the seats are paid for.

Train

Egypt's British-built rail system is antiquated, and the cars are often battered and grubby. Aside from two main routes that are in good condition (Cairo–Alexandria, Cairo–Aswan), you have to be fond of trains to prefer them to a deluxe bus.

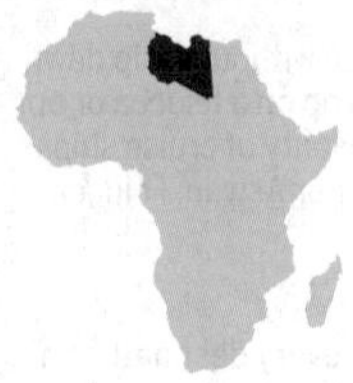

Libya

Includes ➡

Fast Facts

- **Capital** Tripoli
- **Population** 5.6 million
- **Languages** Arabic, Berber
- **Area** 1.759 million sq km
- **Currency** Libyan dinar (LD)
- **Visa requirements** Arranged as part of organised tour; current requirements in a state of flux

Roman Ruins & Saharan Sand

Libya is a classic North African destination and its primary appeal derives from its position as an ancient crossroads of civilisations – these civilisations bequeathed to the Libyan coast some of the finest Roman and Greek ruins in existence, among them Leptis Magna, Cyrene and Sabratha. This is also one of the best places in Africa to experience the Sahara Desert, from seas of sand the size of Switzerland and sheltering palm-fringed lakes (the Ubari Sand Sea) to remote massifs adorned with prehistoric rock art (the Jebel Acacus), labyrinthine caravan towns (Ghadames) and an isolated black-as-black volcano (Wawa al-Namus) in the desert's heart.

The upheaval caused by Libya's democratic revolution in 2011–12 continues, but Libya's tourism and transport infrastructure are excellent. As such, once peace returns fully to the country, expect it to be one of the hottest travel destinations on the continent.

Libya Top Sights

- **Leptis Magna** One of the world's best-preserved Roman cities looking out across the Mediterranean
- **Tripoli** Atmospheric whitewashed medina and a world-class museum that largely survived the war
- **Ghadames** The Sahara's most enchanting oasis town with a labyrinth of covered passageways shadowed by palm gardens
- **Cyrene** Extraordinary ancient city in the country's east with some of the finest monuments to ancient Greece in North Africa
- **Jebel Acacus** Jagged Saharan massif with 12,000-year-old rock art, Tuareg inhabitants and extraordinary scenery
- **Ubari Lakes** Idyllic lakes surrounded by exquisite sand dunes in one of the world's largest and most beautiful sand seas
- **Waw al Namus** Black-sand volcano sheltering multicoloured lakes and otherworldly scenery

UNDERSTAND LIBYA

Libya Today

Libya is a country awakening from a nightmare. In February 2011, at the beginning of the so-called Arab Spring and with neighbouring Tunisia and Egypt in turmoil, a protest in the eastern Libyan city of Benghazi quickly spread. Most of northeastern Libya soon feel to the rebels. The rebels, backed by NATO air strikes, battled government forces loyal to the old regime, with fighting particularly heavy along the coast road and in the Jebel Nafusa in the country's northwest. The government's failure to take the cities of Misrata and Zintan in particular enabled the rebels to close in on Tripoli, which finally fell to the rebels in August 2011. Most of Libya soon fell into rebel hands, and the capture and killing of Colonel Qaddafi in October 2011 marked the end of a brutal civil war in which as many as 10,000 people died.

Despite reports of score settling, the ongoing power of armed militias and the difficulties in building national, democratic institutions, the aftermath of the war in Libya has been largely peaceful. Elections for a General People's Congress in July 2012 saw liberals outnumber Islamists, although neither secured absolute majority. After several false starts, a new government was formed in November of the same year. A month later, insecurity in the south prompted the government to close its southern borders and declare vast swathes of the country's south to be closed military zones. The move highlighted what remains the greatest threat to a peaceful future in Libya – the ongoing power of armed militias and the government's difficulties in asserting effective control over the country.

COUNTRY COVERAGE

At the time of research very few travellers were heading to Libya so we're providing historical and cultural information rather than reviews and listings. A good source of information for on-the-ground travel in Libya is Lonely Planet's Thorn Tree online travel forum www.lonelyplanet.com/thorntree. Another good source of internet-based information is www.sahara-overland.com. For the latest security information, check out the travel advisories from Western governments.

History

The Great Civilisations of Antiquity

From 700 BC, Lebdah (Leptis Magna), Oea (Tripoli) and Sabratha formed some of the links in a chain of safe Phoenician (Punic) ports stretching from the Levant around to Spain. Traces of the Phoenician presence in Libya remain at Sabratha and Leptis Magna.

On the advice of the Oracle of Delphi, in 631 BC Greek settlers established the city of Cyrene in the east of Libya. Within 200 years the Greeks had built four more cities of splendour as part of the Pentapolis (Five Cities), which included Apollonia. But with Greek influence on the wane, the last Greek ruler, Ptolemy Apion, finally bequeathed the region of Cyrenaica to Rome in 75 BC.

Meanwhile, the fall of the Punic capital at Carthage (in Tunisia) prompted Julius Caesar to formally annex Tripolitania in 46BC. The Pax Romana saw Tripolitania and

LEPTIS MAGNA

If Leptis Magna was the only place you saw in Libya, you wouldn't leave disappointed. Leptis (originally spelled Lepcis and known locally in Arabic as Lebdah) was once the largest and greatest Roman city in Africa; it enjoyed its golden age in the 1st and 2nd centuries AD. Because no modern city was later built on the site and because it was constructed of sturdy limestone, Leptis is that rare ancient city where sufficient traces remain to imagine the city in its heyday. Among its numerous monumental highlights, the triumphal arches (particularly the Arch of Septimius Severus), Hadrianic Baths, Severan Forum, theatre and amphitheatre all stand out. Adjacent to the site entrance is the splendid Leptis Museum, one of Africa's premier collections of Roman statuary.

Leptis Magna is 3km east of Al-Khoms and 123km east of Tripoli. Although you *could* visit as a day trip from Tripoli, Al-Khoms is a better choice as it means you can be here early morning or late afternoon when the Mediterranean light is at its most magical.

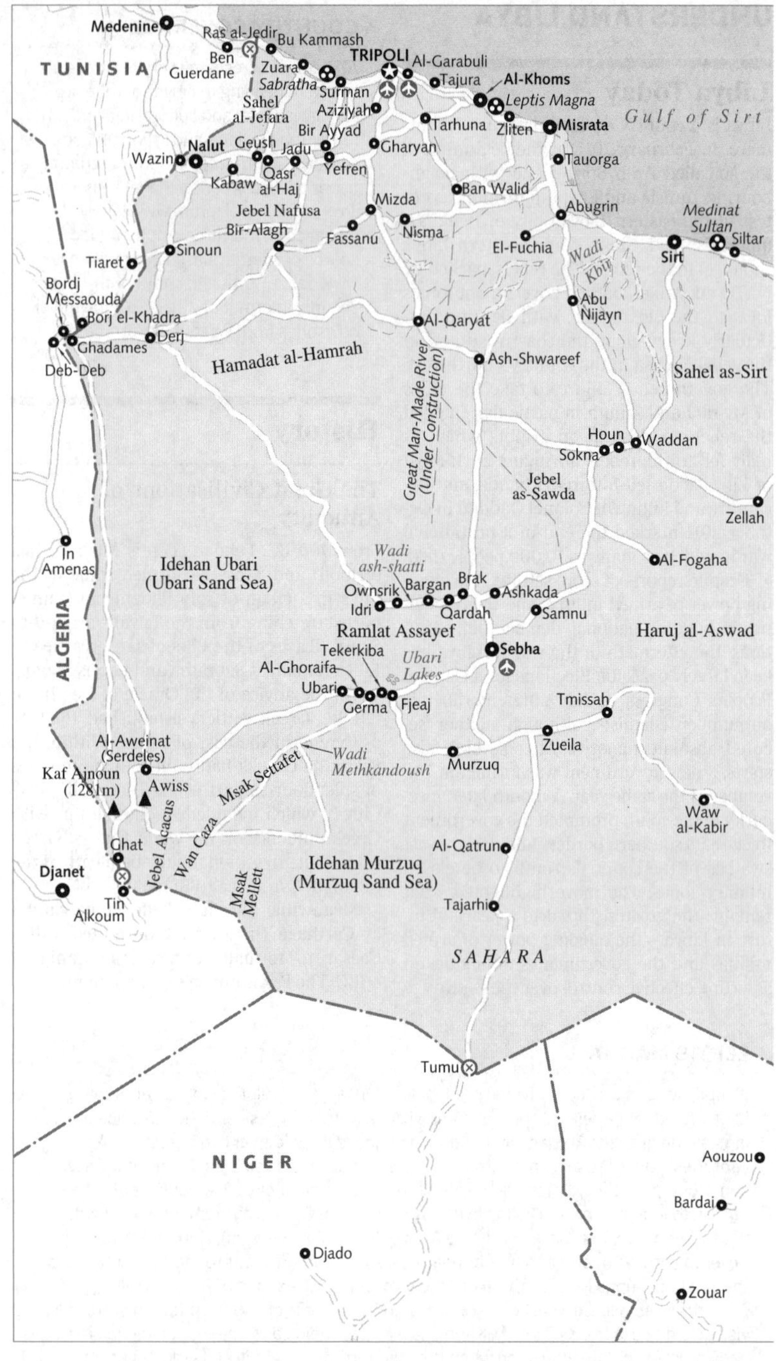
Medenine
TUNISIA
Ras al-Jedir
Ben Guerdane
Bu Kammash
Zuara
Sabratha
Surman
TRIPOLI
Al-Garabuli
Tajura
Al-Khoms
Leptis Magna
Gulf of Sirt
Sahel al-Jefara
Aziziyah
Tarhuna
Zliten
Misrata
Bir Ayyad
Wazin
Nalut
Geush
Jadu
Gharyan
Tauorga
Kabaw
Qasr al-Haj
Yefren
Ban Walid
Jebel Nafusa
Mizda
Abugrin
Medinat Sultan
Bir-Alagh
Fassanu
Nisma
El-Fuchia
Sirt
Siltar
Tiaret
Sinoun
Wadi Kbir
Bordj Messaouda
Borj el-Khadra
Abu Nijayn
Al-Qaryat
Deb-Deb
Ghadames
Derj
Hamadat al-Hamrah
Ash-Shwareef
Sahel as-Sirt
Great Man-Made River (Under Construction)
Houn
Waddan
Sokna
Jebel as-Sawda
Zellah
In Amenas
Idehan Ubari (Ubari Sand Sea)
Wadi ash-shatti
Al-Fogaha
Ownsrik
Bargan
Brak
Ashkada
Idri
Qardah
Samnu
ALGERIA
Ramlat Assayef
Haruj al-Aswad
Sebha
Tekerkiba
Ubari Lakes
Al-Ghoraifa
Ubari
Germa
Fjeaj
Tmissah
Zueila
Al-Aweinat (Serdeles)
Wadi Methkandoush
Murzuq
Kaf Ajnoun (1281m)
Awiss
Msak Settafet
Waw al-Kabir
Jebel Acacus
Wan Caza
Ghat
Al-Qatrun
Djanet
Idehan Murzuq (Murzuq Sand Sea)
Msak Mellett
Tin Alkoum
Tajarhi
SAHARA
Tumu
NIGER
Aouzou
Bardai
Djado
Zouar

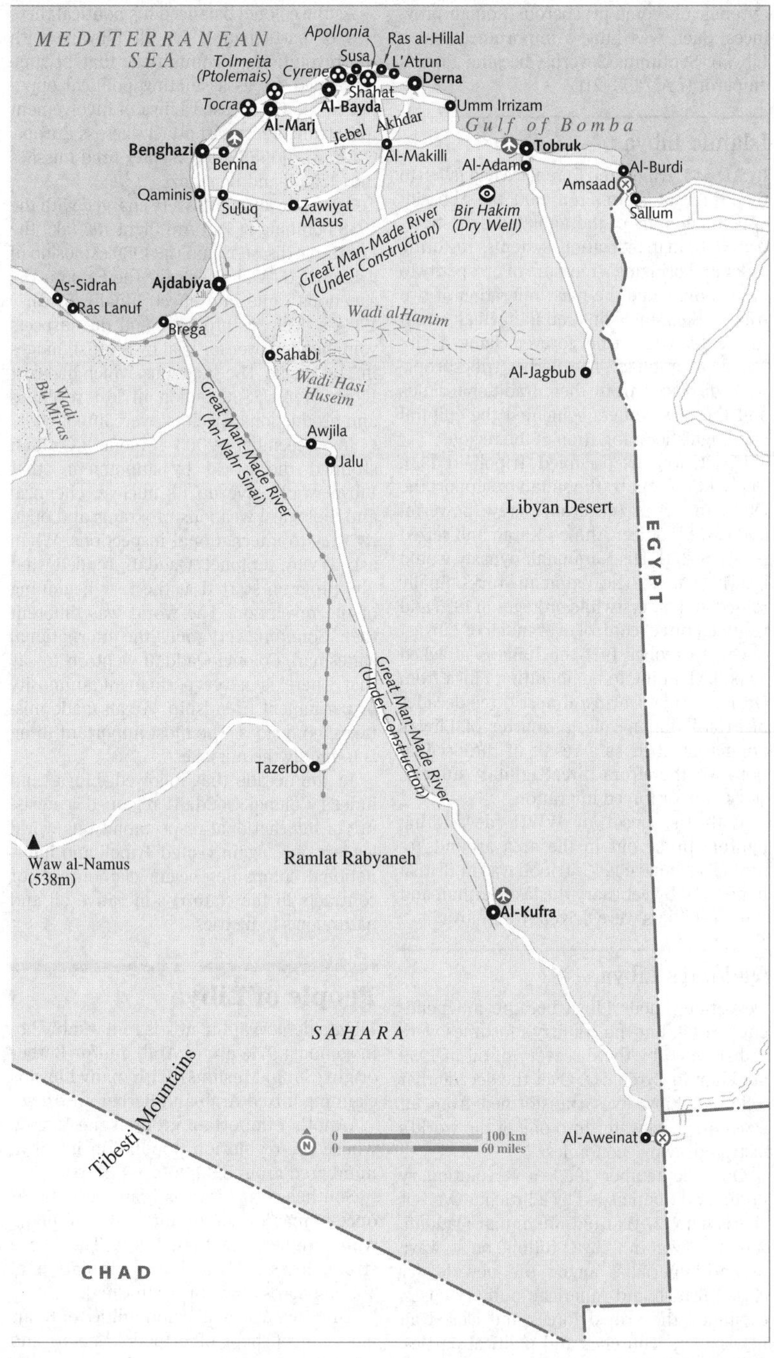
MEDITERRANEAN SEA
Apollonia
Ras al-Hillal
Susa
L'Atrun
Tolmeita (Ptolemais)
Cyrene
Derna
Shahat
Tocra
Al-Bayda
Umm Irrizam
Al-Marj
Jebel Akhdar
Gulf of Bomba
Benghazi
Tobruk
Benina
Al-Makilli
Al-Adam
Al-Burdi
Amsaad
Qaminis
Sallum
Suluq
Zawiyat Masus
Bir Hakim (Dry Well)
Great Man-Made River (Under Construction)
As-Sidrah
Ajdabiya
Ras Lanuf
Wadi al-Hamim
Brega
Sahabi
Al-Jagbub
Wadi Bu Miras
Wadi Hasi Huseim
Great Man-Made River (An-Nahr Sinai)
Awjila
Jalu
Libyan Desert
EGYPT
Great Man-Made River (Under Construction)
Tazerbo
Waw al-Namus (538m)
Ramlat Rabyaneh
Al-Kufra
SAHARA
Tibesti Mountains
0 100 km
0 60 miles
Al-Aweinat
CHAD

Cyrenaica become prosperous Roman provinces. Such was Libya's importance that a Libyan, Septimius Severus, became Rome's emperor (r AD 193–211).

Islamic Libya

By AD 643, Tripoli and Cyrenaica had fallen to the armies of Islam. From 800, the Abbasid-appointed emirs of the Aghlabid dynasty repaired Roman irrigation systems, restoring order and bringing a measure of prosperity to the region, while the mass migration of two tribes – the Bani Salim and Bani Hilal – from the Arabian Peninsula forever changed Libya's demographics. The Berber tribespeople were displaced from their traditional lands and the new settlers cemented the cultural and linguistic Arabisation of the region.

The Ottomans occupied Tripoli in 1551. The soldiers sent by the sultan to support the Ottoman pasha (governor) grew powerful and cavalry officer Ahmed Karamanli seized power in 1711. His Karamanli dynasty would last 124 years. The Ottoman Turks finally reined in their erstwhile protégés in 1835 and resumed direct control over much of Libya.

On 3 October 1911 the Italians attacked Tripoli, claiming to be liberating Libya from Ottoman rule. During almost three decades of brutal Italian rule, a quarter of Libya's population died as a result of the occupation, whether from direct military attacks, starvation or forced migration.

With the onset of WWII, devastating fighting broke out in the area around Tobruk. By January 1943, Tripoli was in British hands and by February the last German and Italian soldiers were driven from Libya.

Qaddafi's Libya

Desperately poor Libya became independent in 1951, but the country's fortunes were transformed by the discovery of oil in 1959 at Zelten in Cyrenaica. Over the decade that followed, Libya was transformed from an economic backwater into one of the world's fastest-growing economies.

On 1 September 1969, a Revolutionary Command Council, led by a little-known but charismatic 27-year-old Muammar Qaddafi, seized power in Libya. Riding on a wave of anti-imperialist anger, the new leader closed British and American military bases, expanded the armed forces and closed all newspapers, churches and political parties. Some 30,000 Italian settlers were deported.

As the colonel balanced his political theories of participation for all Libyans with the revolutionary committees that became renowned for assassinating political opponents, the US accused Libya of involvement in a string of terrorist attacks across Europe. On 15 April 1986, the US Navy fired missiles into Tripoli and Benghazi.

After Libyan agents were charged with the 1988 bombing of Pan Am flight 103 (aka the Lockerbie disaster) and the 1989 explosion of a French UTA airliner over the Sahara, UN sanctions came into effect. Finally, in early 1999, a deal was brokered and the suspects were handed over for trial by Scottish judges in The Hague. The sanctions, which had cost Libya over US$30 billion in lost revenues and production capacities, were lifted.

In December 2003 Colonel Qaddafi stunned the world by announcing that Libya would give up its nuclear, chemical and biological weapons programs and open its sites to international inspections. When asked why, Colonel Qaddafi replied that 'the program started at the very beginning of the revolution. The world was different then.' Sounding very much the international statesman, Colonel Qaddafi went on to say that 'there is never permanent animosity or permanent friendship. We all made mistakes, both sides. The most important thing is to rectify the mistakes.'

In the decade that followed, Libya (and indeed Colonel Qaddafi) regained a measure of international respectability, as world leaders once again visited Tripoli and international companies began clamouring for contracts in the country's lucrative oil and natural-gas industries.

People of Libya

Libya's demographic mix is remarkably homogenous: 97% are of Arab and/or Berber origin (Sunni Muslims), with many Libyans claiming mixed Arab and Berber ancestry.

\Another important group is the Tuareg, whose pre-revolution population in Libya numbered around 50,000.

Southeastern Libya is home to another once-nomadic community: the Toubou, who number less than 3000. They have strong links with a larger population of Toubou across the border in Chad.

There are also mall communities of Kharijites (an offshoot of orthodox Islam) and Christians.

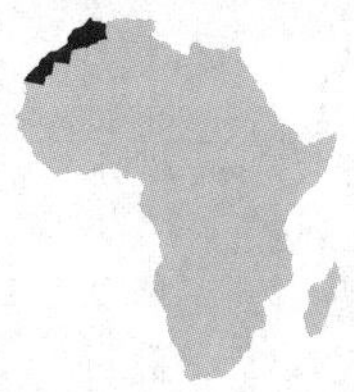

Morocco

☎ 212 / POP 33.3 MILLION

Includes ➡

Best Places to Eat

- ➡ Le Salama (p129)
- ➡ Outdoor Fish Grill Stands (p117)
- ➡ Ty Potes (p111)
- ➡ Café Clock (p123)
- ➡ Rick's Café (p115)

Best Places to Stay

- ➡ Dar Finn (p121)
- ➡ Le Pietri Urban Hotel (p111)
- ➡ Dar el Janoub (p135)
- ➡ Dar Baraka (p109)
- ➡ La Tangerina (p107)

Why Go?

For many travellers Morocco might be just a short hop by budget airline, or by ferry from Spain, but culturally it's a much further distance to travel. On arrival, the regular certainties of Europe are swept away by the full technicolour arrival of Africa and Islam. It's a complete sensory overload.

Tangier – that faded libertine on the coast – has traditionally been a first port of call, but the winds quickly blow you along the coast to cosmopolitan, movie-star-famous Casablanca and the whitewashed fishing-port gem Essaouira. Inland the great imperial cities of Marrakesh and Fez attract visitors in droves; the winding streets of their ancient medinas hold enough surprises to fill a dozen repeat trips.

If you really want to escape from everything, Morocco still has a couple of trump cards. The High Atlas Mountains seem custom-made for hiking, with endless trails between Berber villages, and North Africa's highest peak to conquer.

Morocco can feel like another world, but you don't need a magic carpet to get there.

When to Go

Marrakesh

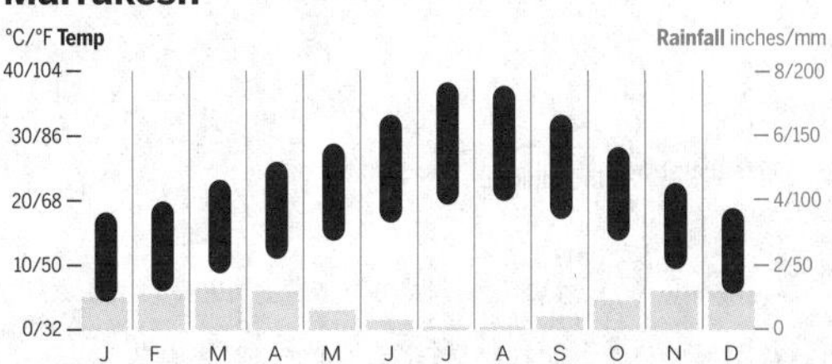

Mid-Mar–May Morocco is at its best in spring, when the country is lush and green.

Sep–Nov Autumn is also good, when the heat of summer has eased.

Nov–Jul In winter, head for the south – but be prepared for bitterly cold nights.

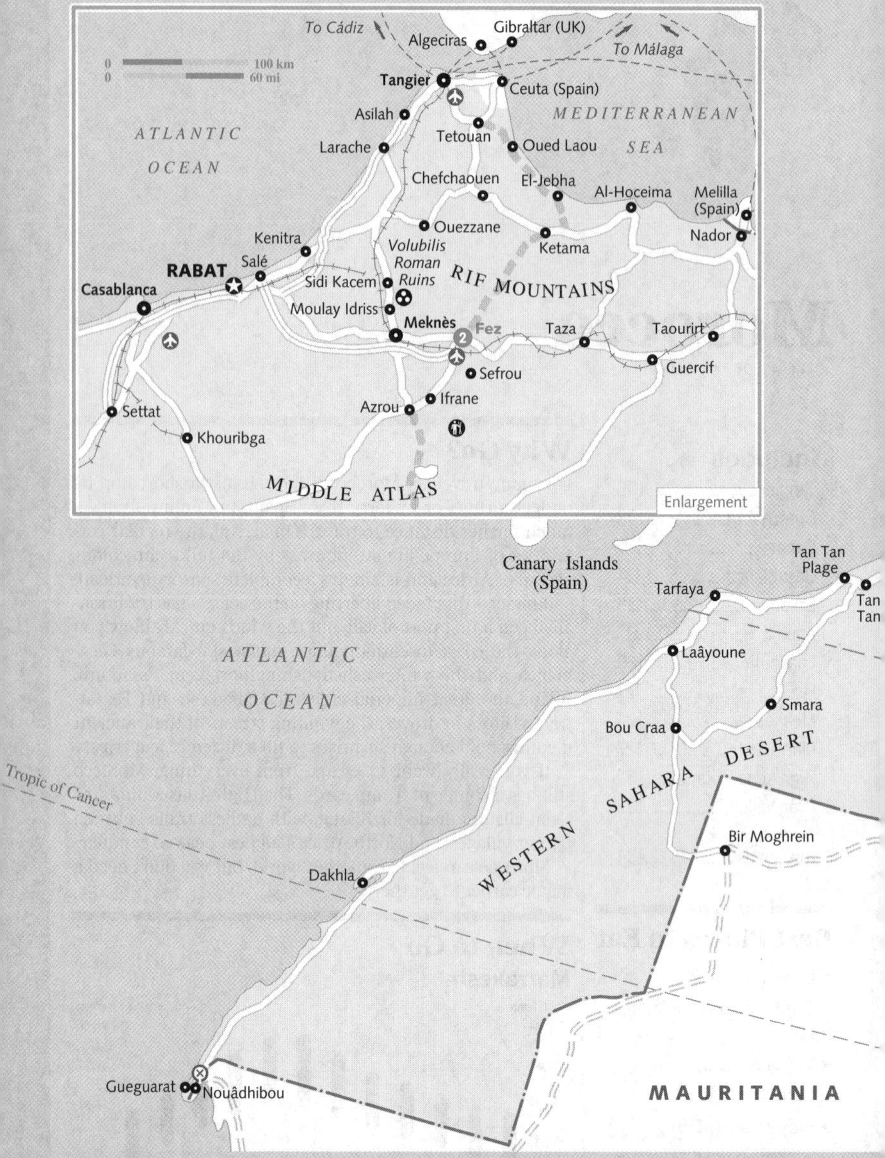

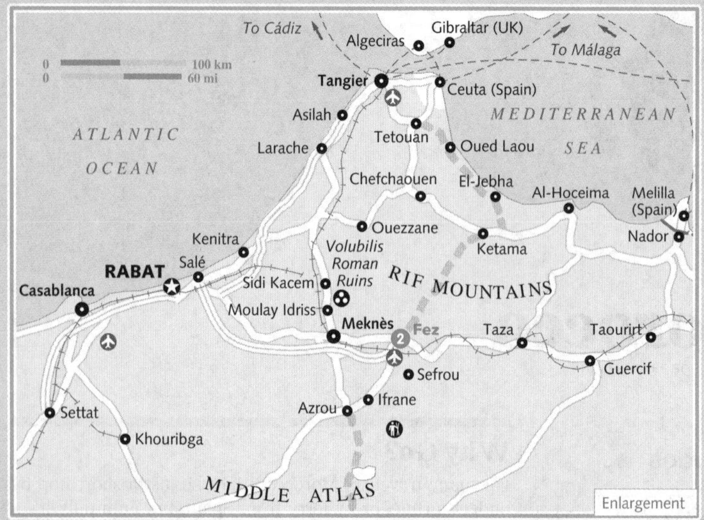

Morocco Highlights

1 Dive into the clamour and endless spectacle of Morocco's most dynamic city, **Marrakesh** (p127).

2 Lose yourself in the exotic charms of a medieval city replete with sights, sounds and smells in **Fez** (p121).

3 Laze by the sea in Morocco's coolest and most evocative resort at **Essaouira** (p115).

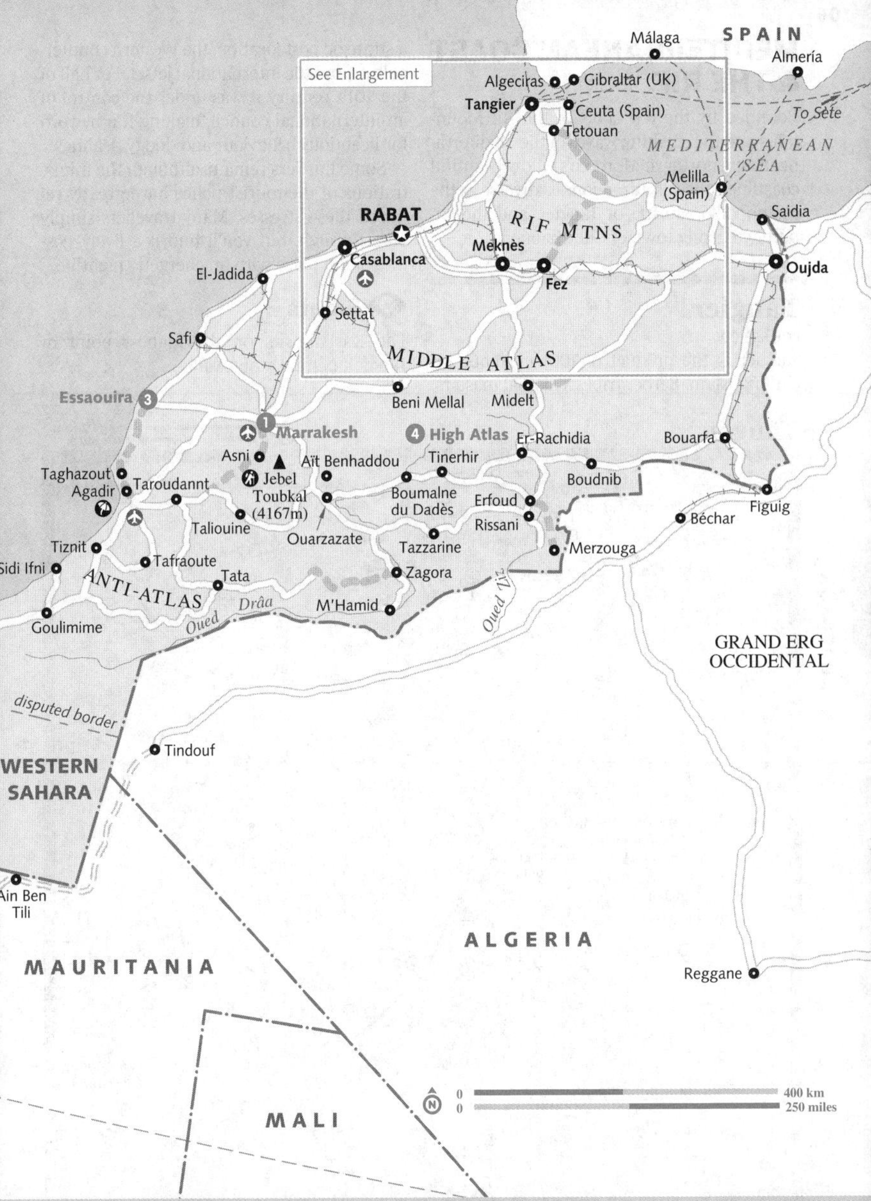

4 Trek deep into a world of stunning scenery and isolated Berber villages in the **High Atlas** (p132).

MEDITERRANEAN COAST & THE RIF

Bounded by the red crags of the Rif Mountains and the crashing waves of the Mediterranean Sea, northern Morocco's wildly beautiful coastline conceals attractions as diverse as the cosmopolitan hustle of Tangier, and the superbly relaxing town of Chefchaouen.

Tangier

POP 688,000

Tangier is the product of 1001 currents, including Islam, Berber tribes, colonial masters, a strategic port location, the Western counterculture and the international jetset. For half of the 20th century it was under the control of an international council, making it a byword for licentious behaviour and dodgy dealings.

Some hustlers remain, although the ministrations of the tourist police have greatly reduced these stresses. Many travellers simply pass through, but you'll find it a lively, cosmopolitan place with an energetic nightlife.

Sights

The Kasbah sits on the highest point of Tangier, behind stout walls.

Tangier

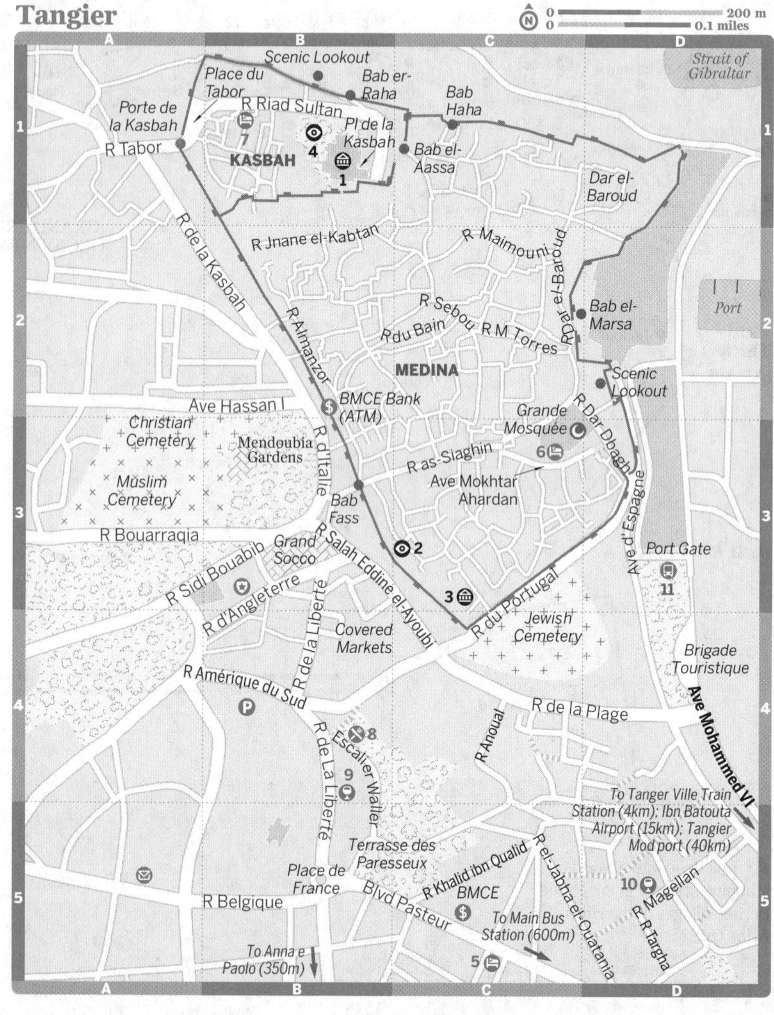

Kasbah Museum MUSEUM
(☎0539 932097; admission Dh10; ⏲9am-12.30pm & 3-5.30pm Wed, Thu & Sat-Mon, 9am-12.30pm Fri) Enter the medina through Bab el-Aassa, the southeastern gate, to find the Kasbah Museum. Housed in the 17th-century palace of Dar el-Makhzen, this is a worthwhile museum devoted to Moroccan arts. Before leaving, take a stroll around the Andalucían-style **Sultan's Gardens.**

Old American Legation Museum MUSEUM
(☎0539 935317; www.legation.org; 8 Rue d'Amerique; donations appreciated; ⏲10am-1pm & 3-5pm Mon-Fri) The Old American Legation Museum is an intriguing relic of the international zone, with a fascinating collection of memorabilia from the international writers and artists who passed through Tangier.

Festivals & Events

Le Festival International de Théâtre Amateur THEATRE
(☎039 930306; fondationlorin@gmail.com; 44 Rue Touahine, Fondation Lorin; ⏲11am-1pm & 3.30-7.30pm Sun-Fri) A week of Arabic- and French-speaking theatre, traditionally held every May, run by Fondation Lorin.

Sleeping

Hôtel Mamora HOTEL $
(☎0539 934105; www.hotelmamora.site.voila.fr; 19 Rue des Postes; low season s/d with toilet Dh100/150, with shower Dh200/230) With a variety of rooms at different rates, this is a good bet. It's a bit institutional, but clean, well run and strong value for money. The rooms overlooking the green-tiled roof of the Grande Mosquée are the most picturesque, if you don't mind the muezzin's call.

Hotel de Paris HOTEL $
(☎0539 9931877; 42 Blvd Pasteur; s/d with bathroom & breakfast Dh350/450) This reliable choice in the heart of the Ville Nouvelle has a variety of room types and prices depending on bathroom arrangements and balconies. All are clean and modern, but those overlooking Blvd Pasteur can get noisy. The helpful front desk makes for a pleasant stay.

La Tangerina HOTEL $$
(☎0539 947733; www.latangerina.com; Rue Riad Sultan, Kasbah; d incl breakfast Dh 600-1620) A perfectly renovated riad (traditional courtyard house) at the very top of the Kasbah, La Tangerina has 10 rooms of different personality. Bathed in light and lined with rope banisters, it feels like an elegant, Berber-carpeted steamship cresting the medina, with the roof terrace overlooking the ancient crenellated walls of the Kasbah. Dinner is available on request.

Eating

In the medina there's a host of cheap eating possibilities around the Petit Socco and the adjacent Ave Mokhtar Ahardan, with rotisserie chicken, sandwiches and *brochettes* (kebabs) on offer. In the Ville Nouvelle, try the streets immediately south of Place de France, which are flush with fast-food outlets and sandwich bars.

Anna e Paolo ITALIAN $
(☎0539 944617; 77 Ave Prince Heretier; mains from Dh60) This is the top Italian bistro in the city: a family-run restaurant with Venetian owners who make you feel like you've been invited for Sunday dinner. Expect a highly

WHEN TO VISIT

The timing of Ramadan (the traditional Muslim month of fasting and purification, which is likely to occur during June or July when you are reading this) is an important consideration when planning your trip to Morocco, as many restaurants and cafes close during the day and general business hours are reduced.

Tangier

Sights
1 Kasbah Museum ... B1
2 Le Festival International de Théâtre Amateur ... C3
3 Old American Legation Museum ... C3
4 Sultan's Gardens ... B1

Sleeping
5 Hotel de Paris ... C5
6 Hôtel Mamora ... C3
7 La Tangerina ... B1

Eating
8 Populaire Saveur de Poisson ... B4

Drinking & Nightlife
9 Caid's Bar ... B4
10 Tanger Inn ... D5

Transport
11 CTM Bus Station ... D3

SET YOUR BUDGET

Budget

- Hotel room Dh130
- Street food Dh30
- Glass of mint tea Dh10
- Petit taxi ride Dh9

Midrange

- Hotel room Dh350
- Tajine Dh70
- Drink in a bar Dh50
- Intercity train ticket (2nd class, four hours) Dh80

Top End

- Hotel room Dh1500
- Two-course meal Dh200

international crowd, lots of cross-table conversations about the events of the day, wholesome food and a shot of grappa on your way out the door.

Populaire Saveur de Poisson SEAFOOD **$$$**
(0539 336326; 2 Escalier Waller; set menu Dh150; 12.30-4pm & 7-10pm Sat-Thu) This charming little seafood restaurant offers excellent, filling set menus in rustic surroundings. The owner serves inventive plates of fresh catch, with sticky *seffa* (sweet couscous) for dessert, all of it washed down with a homemade 15-fruit juice cocktail. Not just a meal, but a whole experience.

Drinking & Entertainment

Tangier's nightlife picks up in the summer, and nightclubs cluster near Place de France and line the beach. Tangier's gay scene has long since departed for Marrakesh, but the **Tanger Inn** (1 Rue Magellan, Hotel el-Muniria; beer Dh10; 10.30pm-1am, to 3am Fri & Sat) and some of the bars along the beach attract gay clientele, particularly late on weekends.

Caid's Bar BAR
(El-Minzah; 85 Rue de la Liberté; wine from Dh20; 10am-midnight) Long the establishment's drinking hole of choice, this el-Minzah landmark is a relic of the grand days of international Tangier, and photos of the famous and infamous adorn the walls.

Information

Blvd Pasteur and Ave Mohammed V are lined with numerous banks with ATMs and bureau-de-change counters. Blvd Pasteur also has plenty of internet places.

BMCE (Banque Marocaine du Commerce Extérieur; Blvd Pasteur; 9am-1pm & 3-7pm Mon-Fri, 10am-1pm & 4-7pm Sat & Sun) One of several in this area.

Clinique du Croissant Rouge (Red Cross Clinic; 0539 946976; 6 Rue al-Mansour Dahabi) Medical service.

Main Post Office (Blvd Mohammed V)

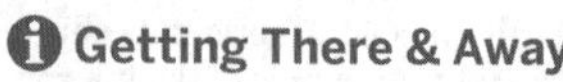

Getting There & Away

FERRY

Ferries go to and from Tarifa (Spain) from Tanger Port, in the city; all other destinations (including Algeciras) sail from Tanger Med. There's a free shuttle bus to Tanger Med from the CTM bus station. For more information, see p140.

BUS

The **CTM bus station** (0539 931172) is beside the port gate. Destinations include Casablanca (Dh130, six hours), Rabat (Dh100, 4½ hours), Fez (Dh110, six hours), Meknès (Dh90, five hours) and Chefchaouen (Dh40, three hours). Cheaper bus companies operate from the **main bus station** (gare routière; 0539 946928; Place Jamia el-Arabia), 2km south of the city centre.

TAXI

Grands taxis (shared taxis) leave from a lot next to the main bus station. Destinations include Tetouan (Dh25, one hour; change for Chefchaouen) and, for Ceuta, Fnideq (Dh40, one hour).

TRAIN

Five trains depart daily from Tanger Ville, 3km southeast of the city centre, to Casablanca (Dh125, five hours), Rabat (Dh95, 3½ hours), Fez (Dh80, 4½ hours) and Marrakesh. Some services involve changing at Sidi Kacem. A night service goes all the way to Marrakesh (seat/couchette Dh205/350, 12 hours).

Getting Around

Petits taxis (blue with yellow stripes) journey around town for Dh7 to Dh10. From **Ibn Batouta airport** (0539 393720), 15km southeast of the city, take a cream-coloured *grand taxi* (Dh150).

Chefchaouen

POP 50,000

Set beneath the striking peaks of the Rif Mountains, Chefchaouen has long been charming travellers. One of the prettiest towns in Morocco, its old medina is a delight of Moroccan and Andalucían influences, with red-tiled roofs, bright-blue buildings and narrow lanes converging on a delightful square.

Sights

Chefchaouen's medina is one of the loveliest in the country, with blinding blue-white hues and a strong Andalucían flavour. At its heart is the cobbled **Plaza Uta el-Hammam**, which is dominated by the red-hued walls of the **kasbah** (☎039 986343; admission incl museum & gallery Dh10; ⌚9am-1pm & 3-6.30pm Wed-Mon, 9-11.30am & 3-4.30pm Fri) and the **Grande Mosquée** (Plaza Uta el-Hammam), noteworthy for its octagonal minaret. Inside the kasbah's gardens is a modest **ethnographic museum**, where the photos of old Chefchaouen are the highlights.

Sleeping

Hostal Guernika GUESTHOUSE $
(☎0539 987434; hostalguernika@hotmail.com; 49 Onssar; d/tr Dh200/300) This is a warm and charming place, not too far from Plaza Uta el-Hammam. There are several great, street-side rooms – large and bright, facing the mountains – but others are dark. All have showers.

Dar Baraka GUESTHOUSE $
(☎0614 682480; www.riad-baraka.com; Derb Ben Yacoub; d Dh240-280, q per person Dh120; 📶) Friendly and bright guesthouse, with comfortable, spotless facilities. The terrace is great, with a chill-out room with DVDs. A few rooms share bathrooms.

Casa Hassan HOTEL $$
(☎0539 986153; www.casahassan.com; 22 Rue Targui; s/d/tr incl half board from Dh500/650/800; ❄) Large hotel with a boutique feel, this long-established choice has sizeable rooms with creative layouts, plus in-house *hammam* (traditional bathhouse). The terrace provides an elegant lounge, and the cosy Restaurant Tissemlal a warm hearth.

Eating

A popular eating option is to choose one of about a dozen **plaza cafe-restaurants** (Plaza Uta el-Hammam; breakfast from Dh15, mains from Dh25; ⌚8am-11pm) on the main square. Menus are virtually identical – Continental breakfasts, soups and salads, tajines and seafood – but the food is generally decent and the ambience lively.

Assaada MOROCCAN $
(☎0666 317316; Bab el-Ain; set menu Dh40) Located on both sides of the alley just prior to Bab el-Ain, it offers the usual *menu complet*, but also great fruit shakes and a funky graffiti rooftop terrace that exudes an urban charm. The staircase is not for the faint-hearted.

Restaurant Les Raisins MOROCCAN $$
(☎0667 982878; 7 Rue Sidi Sifri; tajines Dh20, set menu from Dh40; ⌚7am-9pm) A bit out of the way, this family-run place is a perennial favourite with locals and tourists alike, and known for its couscous royal. Late,

CEUTA

Jutting out east into the Mediterranean, this 20-sq-km peninsula has been a Spanish enclave since 1640. Its relaxed, well-kept city centre, with bars, cafes and Andalucían atmosphere, provides a sharp contrast to the other side of the border. Nonetheless, Ceuta is still recognisably African. Between a quarter and a third of the population are of Rif Berber origin, giving the enclave a fascinating Iberian-African mix.

Ceuta makes a good alternative entry point by ferry from Spain to Morocco. Its ferry port *(estación marítima)* is west of the town centre, and has several daily high-speed ferries to Algeciras (around €28, 35 minutes). Bus 7 runs up to the Moroccan border *(frontera)* every 10 minutes from Plaza de la Constitución (€0.60). For Tangier, take a *grand taxi* to Fnideq (Dh5, 10 minutes), just south of the border, and change there.

Ceuta's main attraction is its **Royal City Walls** (☎956 511770; Ave González Tabla; ⌚10am-2pm & 5-8pm) FREE, and there's a helpful **tourist office** (☎956 200560; Baluarte de los Mallorquines; ⌚8.30am-8.30pm Mon-Fri, 9am-8pm Sat & Sun). If you get stuck for the night, try the **Pensión La Bohemia** (☎956 510615; 16 Paseo de Revellín; s/d €25/35); you'll find good restaurants around the harbour. Remember that Ceuta is on Spanish time and uses the euro.

Chefchaouen

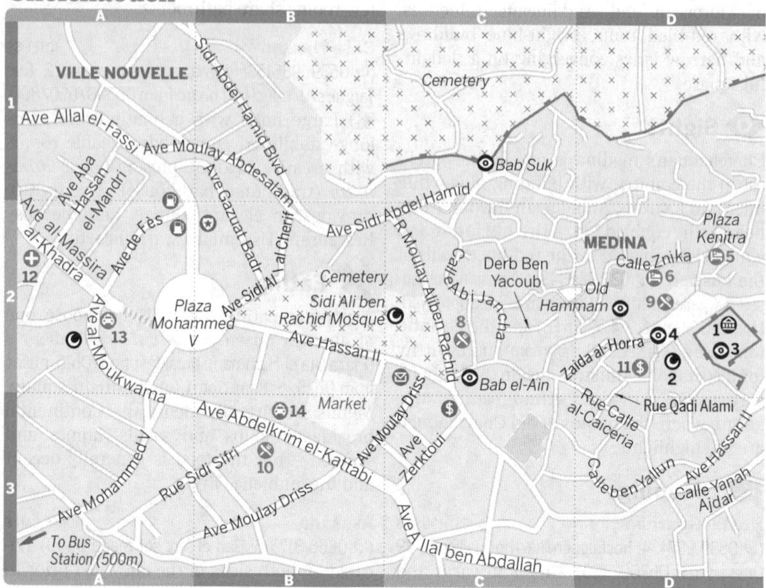

lazy lunches are best, with the front terrace catching the afternoon sun.

Information

Banque Populaire (Plaza Uta el-Hammam; 9.30am-1pm & 3.30-9pm Mon-Fri) Has an ATM.

Hospital Mohammed V (0539 986228; Ave al-Massira al-Khadra) Medical service.

Post Office (Ave Hassan II; 8am-4.30pm Mon-Fri, to noon Sat & Sun)

Getting There & Away

Many bus services from Chefchaouen originate elsewhere, so book in advance if possible. **CTM** (039 987669) services include Casablanca (Dh115, eight hours), Rabat (Dh85, six hours), Fez (Dh70, four hours) and Tangier (Dh40, three hours).

Grands taxis heading to Tetouan (Dh30, one hour) leave from just below Plaza Mohammed V – change for Tangier or Ceuta.

THE ATLANTIC COAST

Morocco's Atlantic shoreline is surprisingly varied, with sweeping beaches and lagoons, the economic motor of the urban sprawl around the political and economic capitals of Rabat and Casablanca, respectively, and the pretty fishing ports/tourist drawcards of Essaouira and Asilah.

Rabat

POP 1.7 MILLION

Relaxed, well kept and very European, flag-waving capital Rabat is just as cosmopolitan as Casablanca down the coast but lacks the frantic pace and grimy feel of its economic big brother. Its elegant, tree-lined boulevards and imposing administrative buildings exude an unhurried, diplomatic and hassle-free charm that many travellers grow to like.

Sights

Barely 400 years old, Rabat's medina is tiny compared to that of Fez or Marrakesh, although it still piques the senses with its rich mixture of spices, carpets, crafts, cheap shoes and bootlegged DVDs.

The Kasbah des Oudaias sits high up on the bluff overlooking the Oued Bou Regreg and contains within its walls a 12th-century **mosque**. The southern corner of the kasbah is home to the **Andalucían Gardens** (sunrise-sunset), laid out by the French during the colonial period. The centrepiece

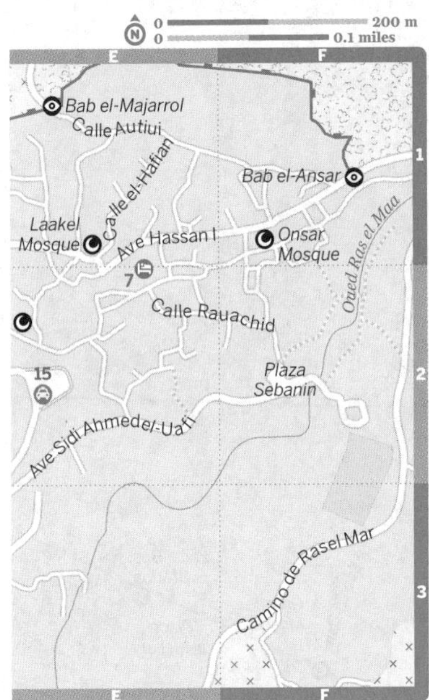

Chefchaouen

Sights
1 Ethnographic Museum....D2
2 Grande Mosquée....D2
3 Kasbah....D2
4 Plaza Uta el-Hammam....D2

Sleeping
5 Casa Hassan....D2
6 Dar Baraka....D2
7 Hostal Guernika....E2

Eating
8 Assaada....C2
9 Plaza Cafe-Restaurants....D2
10 Restaurant Les Raisins....B3

Information
11 Banque Populaire....D2
12 Hospital Mohammed V....A2

Transport
13 Grands Taxis to Tetouan....A2
14 Petits Taxis....B3
15 Petits Taxis....E2

is the grand 17th-century palace containing the **Musée des Oudaia** (0537 731537; admission Dh10; 9am-noon & 3-5pm Oct-Apr, to 6pm May-Sep).

Le Tour Hassan TOWER
(Hassan Tower; off Blvd Abi Radraq) Towering above the Oued Bou Regreg is Rabat's most famous landmark. This 44m unfinished minaret was begun in 1195; the beautifully designed and intricately carved tower still lords over the remains of the adjacent mosque.

Mausoleum of Mohammed V MAUSOLEUM
(sunrise-sunset) FREE The cool, marble Mausoleum of Mohammed V (and since 1999 Hassan II), built in traditional Moroccan style with intense *zellij* (mosaic tiles), lies opposite the tower.

Sleeping

Hôtel Splendid HOTEL $
(0537 723283; 8 Rue Ghazza; s/d Dh128/187, without bathroom Dh104/159) In the heart of town, this hotel has spacious, bright rooms with high ceilings, big windows, cheerful colours and simple wooden furniture. Bathrooms are new, and even rooms without bathrooms have a hot-water washbasin. The hotel is set around a pleasant courtyard.

Hôtel Balima HOTEL $$
(0537 707755; www.hotel-balima.com; Ave Mohammed V; s/d Dh453/716;) The grand dame of Rabat hotels isn't as grand as she used to be but still offers comfortable rooms with views over the city. The hotel has a glorious shady terrace facing Ave Mohammed V, a great place for lazy coffees.

Le Pietri Urban Hotel HOTEL $$
(0537 707820; www.lepietri.com; 4 Rue Tobrouk; s/d Dh720/790; @) This is a good-value boutique hotel in a quiet side street. The spacious, bright rooms, with wooden floors, are well equipped and decorated in warm colours and a contemporary style. The hotel has an excellent, trendy restaurant with a small garden for elegant alfresco dining.

Eating

For quick eating, go to Ave Mohammed V just inside the medina gate, where you'll find a slew of hole-in-the-wall joints dishing out tajines, *brochettes,* salads and chips.

Ty Potes CAFE $
(0537 07965; 11 Rue Ghafsa; set menu Dh70-105; closed Mon & dinner Tue/Wed) A pleasant and welcoming lunch spot, serving sweet and savoury crepes and salads. It's popular with well-heeled locals. The atmosphere is more

Central Rabat

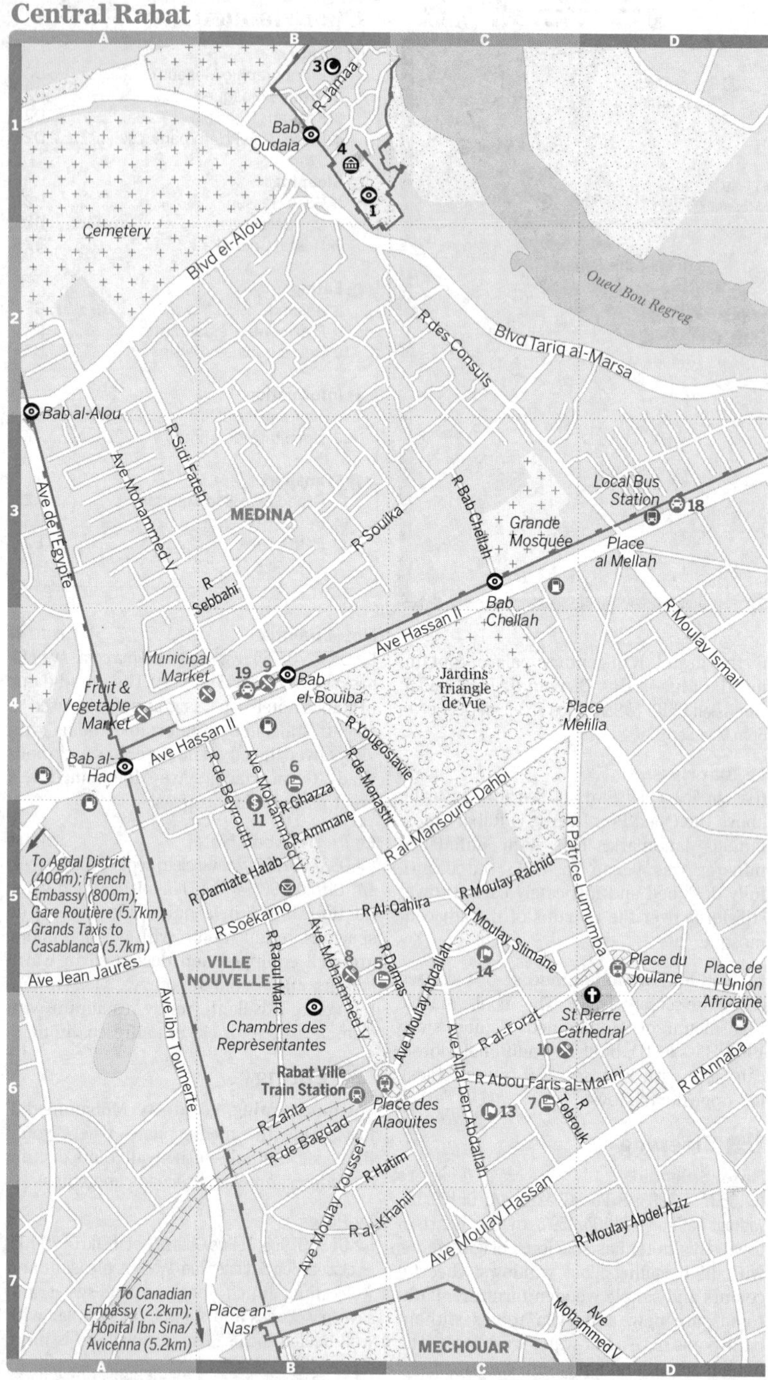

A
B
C
D
1
2
3
4
5
6
7
R Jamaa
Bab Oudaia
Cemetery
Blvd el-Alou
Oued Bou Regreg
R des Consuls
Blvd Tariq al-Marsa
Bab al-Alou
R Sidi Fateh
Ave Mohammed V
Ave de l'Egypte
MEDINA
R Souika
R Bab Chellah
Grande Mosquée
Local Bus Station
Place al Mellah
R Sebbahi
Bab Chellah
Ave Hassan II
R Moulay Ismail
Municipal Market
Fruit & Vegetable Market
Bab el-Bouiba
Jardins Triangle de Vue
Place Melilia
Bab al-Had
R de Beyrouth
R Ghazza
R Yougoslavie
R de Monastir
R Ammane
R al-Mansour-Dahbi
R Patrice Lumumba
To Agdal District (400m); French Embassy (800m); Gare Routière (5.7km); Grands Taxis to Casablanca (5.7km)
R Damiate Halab
R Moulay Rachid
R Soékarno
R Al-Qahira
R Moulay Slimane
Ave Jean Jaurès
VILLE NOUVELLE
R Raoul Marc
R Damas
Ave Moulay Abdallah
Place du Joulane
Place de l'Union Africaine
Ave Ibn Toumerte
Chambres des Reprèsentantes
St Pierre Cathedral
R al-Forat
Ave Allal ben Abdallah
R Abou Faris al-Marini
R d'Annaba
Rabat Ville Train Station
Place des Alaouites
R Tobrouk
R Zahla
R de Bagdad
R Hatim
Ave Moulay Youssef
R al-Khahil
Ave Moulay Hassan
R Moulay Abdel Aziz
To Canadian Embassy (2.2km); Hôpital Ibn Sina/ Avicenna (5.2km)
Place an-Nasr
MECHOUAR
Ave Mohammed V
1
3
4
5
6
7
8
9
10
11
13
14
18
19

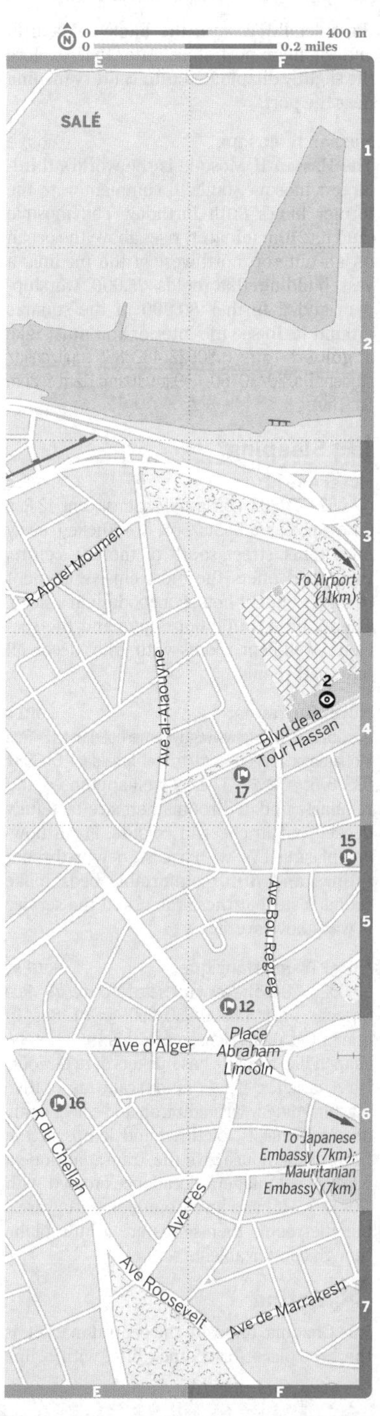

Central Rabat

Sights

1 Andalucían Gardens B1
Le Tour Hassan (see 2)
2 Mausoleum of Mohammed V F4
3 Mosque B1
4 Musée des Oudaia B1

Sleeping

5 Hôtel Balima B5
6 Hôtel Splendid B4
7 Le Pietri Urban Hotel C6

Eating

8 Le Grand Comptoir B5
9 Restaurant el-Bahia B4
10 Ty Potes C6

Information

11 BMCE B5
12 Dutch Embassy F5
13 French Consulate-General C6
14 German Embassy C5
15 Italian Embassy F5
16 Spanish Consulate E6
17 UK Embassy F4

Transport

18 Grands Taxis for Fez, Meknès & Salé D3
19 Petits Taxi Stand B4

European, with a little garden at the back, and alcohol is served.

Restaurant el-Bahia MOROCCAN $
(0537 734504; Ave Hassan II; mains Dh50; 6am-midnight, closes 10.30pm winter) Built into the outside of the medina walls, and a good spot for people-watching, this laid-back restaurant has the locals lapping up hearty Moroccan fare. Choose to sit on the pavement terrace, in the shaded courtyard or upstairs in the traditional salon.

Le Grand Comptoir FRENCH $$
(0537 201514; www.legrandcomptoir.ma; 279 Ave Mohammed V; mains Dh95-175) Oozing the charms of an old-world Parisienne *brasserie,* this suave restaurant and lounge bar woos customers with its chic surroundings and classic French menu. Go for the succulent steaks or be brave and try the *andouillette* (tripe sausage) or veal kidneys.

Information

Numerous banks (with ATMs) are concentrated along Ave Mohammed V.

BMCE (Ave Mohammed V; ⏲8am-8pm Mon-Fri) Bank with ATM.

Hopital Ibn Sina/Avicenna (☎0537 674450, for emergencies 0537 672871; Place Ibn Sina, Agdal) Medical service.

Main Post Office (cnr Rue Soékarno & Ave Mohammed V)

Getting There & Away

Rabat Ville train station (☎0537 736060) is in the centre of the city. Trains run twice hourly to either Casa-Port or Casa Voyageurs in Casablanca (Dh35, one hour), with services to Fez (Dh80, 3½ hours, eight daily) via Meknès (Dh65, 2½ hours), Tangier (Dh95, 4½ hours, seven daily) and Marrakesh (Dh120, 4½ hours, eight daily).

Rabat has two bus stations: the main **gare routière** (☎0537 795816) and the less-chaotic **CTM station** (☎0537 281488), both on the outskirts of the city. CTM has daily services to Casablanca (Dh35, 1½ hours), as well as Essaouira (Dh120, three hours), Fez (Dh70, 3½ hours), Marrakesh (Dh130, five hours) and Tangier (Dh100, 4½ hours).

Grands taxis leave for Casablanca (Dh35) from just outside the intercity bus station. Other *grands taxis* leave for Fez (Dh65), Meknès (Dh50) and Salé (Dh4) from a lot off Ave Hassan II behind the Hôtel Bouregreg.

Getting Around

Rabat's blue *petits taxis* are plentiful, cheap and quick. Short rides will cost about Dh10. Trams run by Rabat's **Tramway** (www.tram-way.ma) link the city to Salé. Tickets cost Dh6 and are sold at kiosks.

Casablanca

POP 4 MILLION

Many travellers stay in 'Casa' just long enough to change planes or catch a train, but Morocco's economic heart offers a unique insight into the country. This sprawling, European-style city is home to racing traffic, simmering social problems, wide boulevards and parks. The facades of imposing Hispano-Moorish and art deco buildings stand in sharp contrast to Casablanca's modernist landmark: the enormous, incredibly ornate Hassan II mosque.

Sights

Central Casablanca is full of great **art deco** and **Hispano-Moorish buildings**. Get the best taste by strolling the area around the Marché Central and Place Mohammed V. This grand square includes the law courts, the splendid Wilaya, the Bank al-Maghrib and the main post office. After that, explore the slightly dilapidated 19th-century medina near the port.

Hassan II Mosque MOSQUE

The Hassan II Mosque is the world's third-largest mosque, built to commemorate the former king's 60th birthday. The mosque (and its 210m minaret) rises above the ocean on an outcrop northwest of the medina, a vast building that holds 25,000 worshippers and a further 80,000 in the squares around it. To see the interior you must take a **guided tour** (☎0522 482886; adult/child/student Dh120/30/60; ⏲9am, 10am, 11am & 2pm Sat-Thu).

Sleeping

Hôtel Astrid HOTEL $

(☎0522 277803; hotelastrid@hotmail.com; 12 Rue 6 Novembre; s/d Dh315/368; 📶) Tucked away on a quiet street south of the city centre, the Astrid offers the most elusive element of Casa's budget hotels: a good night's sleep. There's little traffic noise here and the spacious, well-kept rooms with frilly decor all have bathrooms.

Hôtel Guynemer HOTEL $

(☎0522 275764; www.guynemerhotel.net; 2 Rue Mohammed Belloul; s/d/tr incl breakfast Dh398/538/676; ❄@📶) The 29 well-appointed and regularly updated rooms here are tastefully decked out in cheerful colours. Fresh flowers, plasma TVs, wi-fi access, new bathroom fittings and firm, comfortable beds make rooms a steal at these rates, and the service is way above average.

Hôtel Transatlantique HOTEL $$

(☎0522 294551; www.transatcasa.com; 79 Rue Chaouia; s/d/tr Dh600/750/950; ❄📶) Set in one of Casa's art deco gems, this 1922 hotel – shaped like a boat – has buckets of neo-Moorish character. The grand scale, decorative plaster, spidery wrought iron and eclectic mix of knick-knacks, pictures and lamps at the front of the house give the Transatlantique a whiff of colonial-era decadence crossed with '70s retro. It has a lovely outdoor seating area, but the rooms themselves are a little plain, though comfortable.

Eating

Rue Chaouia, opposite the central market, is the best place for a quick bite, with a line of rotisseries, stalls and restaurants serving roast chicken, *brochettes* and sandwiches

Taverne du Dauphin FRENCH $
(☎0522 221200; 115 Blvd Houphouët Boigny; mains Dh70-90, set menu Dh110; ⊙Mon-Sat) A Casablanca institution, this traditional Provençal restaurant and bar has been serving up *fruits de mer* (seafood) since it opened in 1958. A humble, family-run place with food that leaves you smitten.

Sqala Café Maure & Restaurant MOROCCAN $$
(☎0522 260960; Blvd des Almohades; mains Dh70-160; ⊙8am-10.30pm Tue-Sun, daily in summer) Nestled in the walls of the *sqala* (an 18th-century fortified bastion), this lovely restaurant has a rustic interior and a delightful garden surrounded by flower-draped trellises – a lovely spot for a Moroccan breakfast or a selection of salads for lunch. Tajines are a speciality.

Rick's Café INTERNATIONAL $$
(☎0522 274207; 248 Blvd Sour Jdid; mains Dh130-160; ⊙noon-3.30pm & 6pm-midnight) This bar, lounge and restaurant has furniture, fittings and nostalgia inspired by the film *Casablanca*. Lamb chops, chilli, hamburgers and American breakfasts – as well as a few French and Moroccan specialities – are all on the menu. It also boasts an in-house pianist and Sunday jazz session.

Drinking & Entertainment

The beachfront suburb of Aïn Diab is the place for late-night drinking and dancing in Casa. Expect to pay at least Dh100 to get into a club and as much again for drinks.

Café Alba CAFE
(☎0522 227154; 59-61 Rue Indriss Lahrizi; ⊙8am-1am) High ceilings, swish, modern furniture, subtle lighting and a hint of elegant colonial times mark this cafe out from the more traditional smoky joints around town. It's hassle-free downtime for women and a great place for watching Casa's up-and-coming.

La Bodéga BAR
(☎0522 541842; 129 Rue Allah ben Abdellah; ⊙12.30-3pm & 7pm-midnight) Hip, happening and loved by a mixed-ages group of Casablanca's finest, La Bodega is essentially a tapas bar where the music (everything from salsa to Arabic pop) is loud and the Rioja flows freely. It's a fun place with a lively atmosphere and a packed dance floor after 10pm.

Information

There are banks – most with ATMS and bureaus de change – on almost every street corner in the centre of Casablanca.

Crédit du Maroc (☎0522 477255; 48 Blvd Mohammed V) Central bureau de change.

Gig@net (☎0522 484810; 140 Blvd Mohammed Zerktouni; per hr Dh10; ⊙24hr) Internet.

Main Post Office (cnr Blvd de Paris & Ave Hassan II)

Getting There & Away

All long-distance trains depart from **Casa-Voyageurs train station** (☎0522 243818). Destinations include Marrakesh (Dh90, three hours), Fez (Dh110, 4½ hours) via Meknès (Dh90, 3½ hours), and Tangier (Dh125, 5¾ hours). **Casa Port station** (☎0522 223011) has commuter services to Rabat (Dh35, one hour).

There are two bus stations – the **CTM bus station** (☎0522 541010; 23 Rue Léon L'Africain) and the **Gare Routière Ouled Ziane** (☎0522 444470), 4km southeast of the centre.

CTM services from Casablanca include:

- Essaouira (Dh145, seven hours, two daily)
- Fez (Dh100, five hours, 10 daily)
- Marrakesh (Dh90, four hours, nine daily)
- Meknès (Dh90, four hours, 11 daily)
- Rabat (Dh35, one hour, hourly)
- Tangier (Dh145, six hours, six daily)

Getting Around

Trains run hourly from 6am to midnight from Casa Voyageurs to Blvd Mohammed V international airport (Dh35, 35 minutes); a *grand taxi* between the airport and the city centre will cost you Dh250.

Casablanca's red *petits taxis* are notorious for arguing about using their meters. Trams run by the city's new **Tramway** (www.casatramway.ma) network were due to start in 2013; stops will include Casa Voyageurs, along Blvd Mohammed V and out towards Aïn Diab.

Essaouira

POP 70,000

The port town of Essaouira has long been a favourite of the travellers trail: laid-back and artsy, with sea breezes and picture-postcard ramparts. Although it can appear swamped with visitors in summer, once the day-trippers get back on the buses there's more than enough space to sigh deeply and just soak up the atmosphere.

Central Casablanca

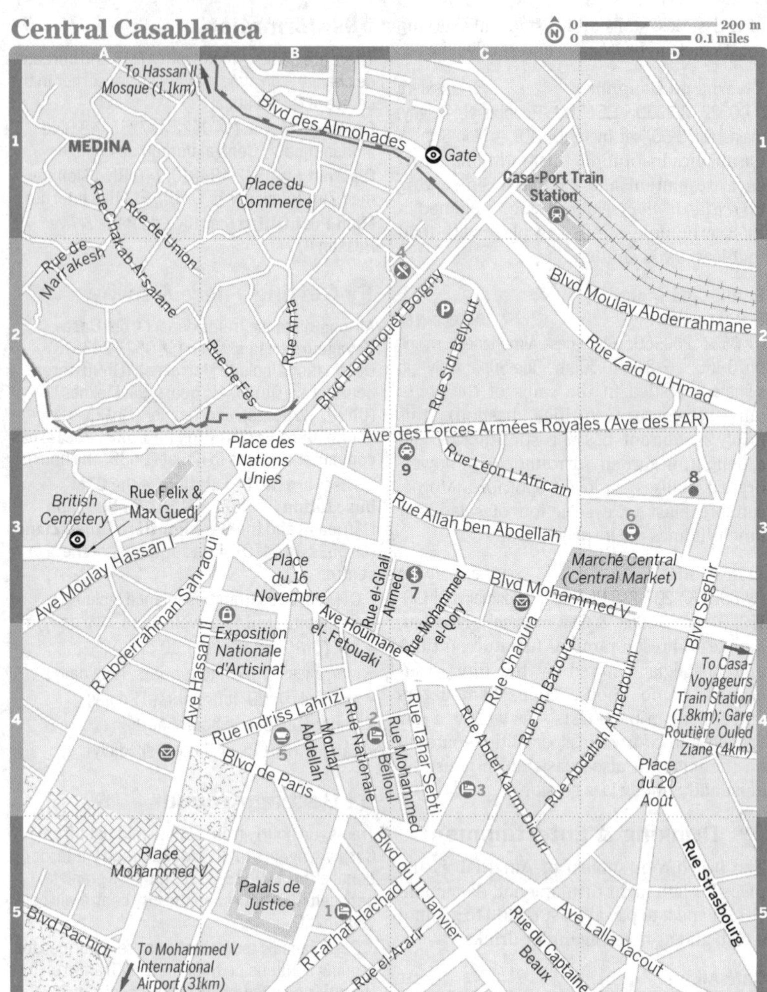

Sights & Activities

The narrow winding streets of Essaouira's walled medina are a great place to stroll. Its late-18th-century fortified layout is a prime example of European military architecture in North Africa. The easiest place from which visitors can access the ramparts is the impressive sea bastion **Skala de la Ville**. By the harbour, the **Skala du Port** (adult/child Dh10/3; 8.30am-noon & 2.30-6pm) offers picturesque views over both the fishing port and the **Île de Mogador** (boats from Port du Peche).

It's possible to rent water-sports equipment to Essaouira's wide sandy beach. **Océan Vagabond** (0524 783934; www.oceanvagabond.com; 9am-6pm daily) has surfboards (Dh750 for three days' rental) plus lessons in surfing (two hours, Dh440), kitesurfing (six hours, D2310) and windsurfing (two/six hours Dh825/1750). Beware the strong Atlantic currents.

Festivals & Events

Gnaoua & World Music Festival MUSIC

The Gnaoua & World Music Festival (the third weekend of June) is a four-day extravaganza with concerts on Place Moulay Hassan.

Central Casablanca

Sleeping

1 Hôtel Astrid B5
2 Hôtel Guynemer B4
3 Hôtel Transatlantique C4

Eating

4 Taverne du Dauphin C2

Drinking & Nightlife

5 Café Alba B4
6 La Bodéga D3

Information

7 Crédit du Maroc C3

Transport

8 CTM Bus Station D3
9 Petits Taxis C3

Sleeping

Hotel Beau Rivage HOTEL $
(☎0524 475925; beaurivage@menara.ma; 14 Place Moulay Hassan; s/d/tr Dh250/350/450, d without bathroom Dh200, breakfast Dh20) A longtime backpackers' favourite, this cheery hotel on the central square could hardly be better located. Rooms are clean, comfortable and airy.

Riad Nakhla HOTEL $
(☎tel/fax 0524 474940; www.essaouiranet.com/riad-nakhla; 2 Rue d'Agadir; s/d Dh225/325, ste Dh400-500) Riad Nakhla greets weary travellers with a friendly reception in a beautiful courtyard with elegant stone columns and a trickling fountain. The well-appointed bedrooms are simple but comfortable. Breakfast on the roof terrace with views over the ocean and town is another treat.

Lalla Mira HOTEL $$
(☎0524 475046; www.lallamira.net; 14 Rue d'Algerie; s/d/ste Dh436/692/920; @) This gorgeous little place has simple rooms with wrought-iron furniture, natural fabrics and solar-powered underfloor heating. The hotel also has a *hammam* and a restaurant serving a decent selection of vegetarian food.

Eating & Drinking

Outdoor Fish Grill Stands SEAFOOD $
(port end of Place Moulay Hassan; around Dh40) These unpretentious stands offer a definitive Essaouira experience. Just choose what you want to eat from the colourful displays of freshly caught fish and shellfish at each grill, cooked on the spot and served with a pile of bread and salad.

Restaurant Ferdaous MOROCCAN $$
(☎0524 473655; 27 Rue Abdesslam Lebadi; mains Dh60-80, set menu Dh105; ⊗closed Mon) Delightful Moroccan restaurant, and one of the few places in town that serves real (as in home-cooked) traditional Moroccan food. The seasonal menu offers an innovative take on traditional recipes, the service is good, and the low tables and padded seating make it feel like the real McCoy.

Taros Café MEDITERRANEAN $$
(☎5247 476407; 2 Rue du Skala; mains Dh70-120; ⊗8am-11pm Mon-Sat) At this rooftop restaurant and bar, you can sip your drink under giant lamps and huddle round your table to fend off the wind whipping up from the sea. The restaurant is heavy on fish.

Information

There are several banks with ATMs around Place Moulay Hassan. There are also plentiful internet cafes, most opening from 9am to 11pm and charging Dh8 to Dh10 per hour.

Délégation du Tourisme (☎0524 783532; www.essaouira.com; 10 Rue du Caire; ⊗9am-noon & 3-6.30pm Mon-Fri) Very helpful staff.

Hôpital Sidi Mohammed ben Abdallah (☎0524 475716; Blvd de l'Hôpital) For emergencies.

Main Post Office (Ave el-Mouqawama)

Getting There & Away

CTM (☎0524 784764) has buses daily to Casablanca (Dh135, six hours), Marrakesh (Dh75, 2½ hours) and Agadir (Dh60, three hours). Other companies run cheaper and more frequent buses to the same destinations, as well as to Taroudannt (Dh70, six hours).

Supratours (☎0524 475317) runs buses to Marrakesh train station (Dh70, 2½ hours), connecting with trains to Casablanca. Book in advance.

Agadir

POP 680,000

Levelled by an earthquake in 1960, Agadir rose from its ruins to become Morocco's main beach resort, with a glitzy marina. Rebuilt into a neat grid of residential suburbs and wide boulevards, the town feels strangely bereft of the sort of bustling life often associated with Moroccan cities. Its lure, however, lies in its huge sandy bay, which is more sheltered than many other Atlantic beaches.

Essaouira

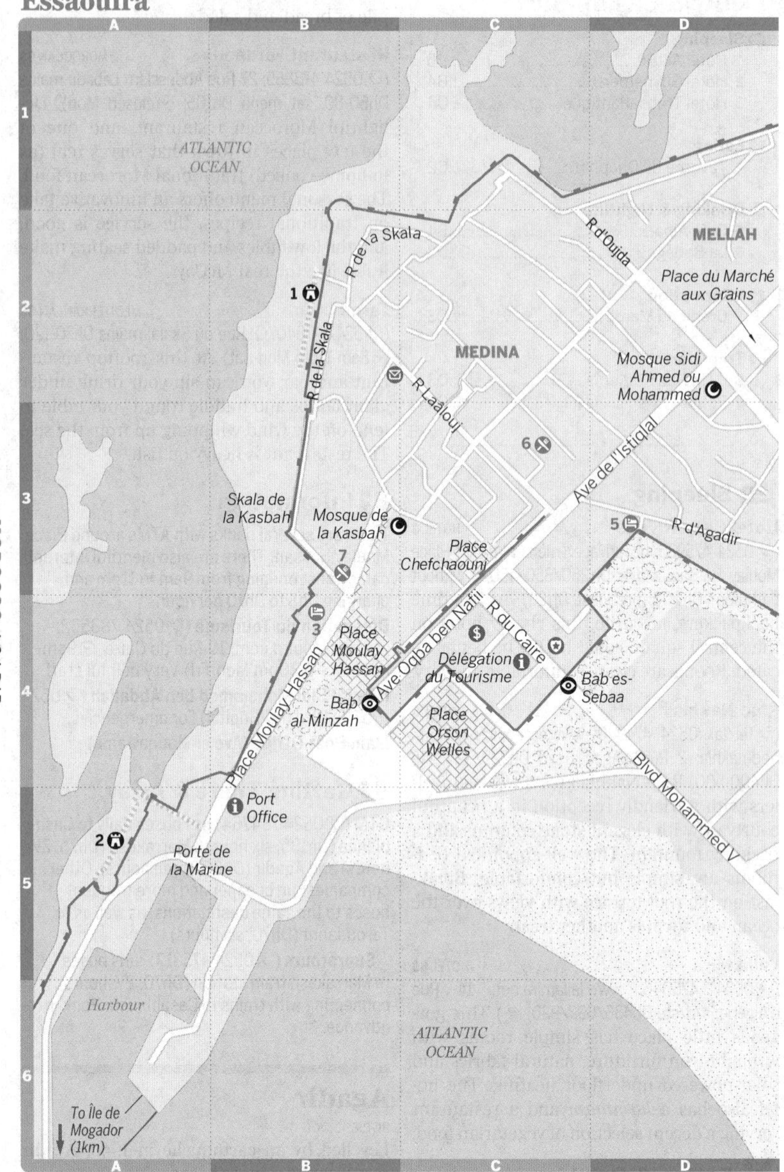

Sleeping

Hôtel Tiznine HOTEL $
(☎0528 843925; 3 Rue Drarga; s/d Dh100/150, with shower Dh120/150) One of Agadir's best budget places, with a dozen good-sized rooms around a green-and-white tiled flowering courtyard. Some rooms have bathrooms, but even the communal facilities are spotless.

Hôtel Kamal HOTEL $$
(☎0528 842817; www.hotel-kamal.com; Ave Hassan II; s/d Dh405/462) A popular and well-run

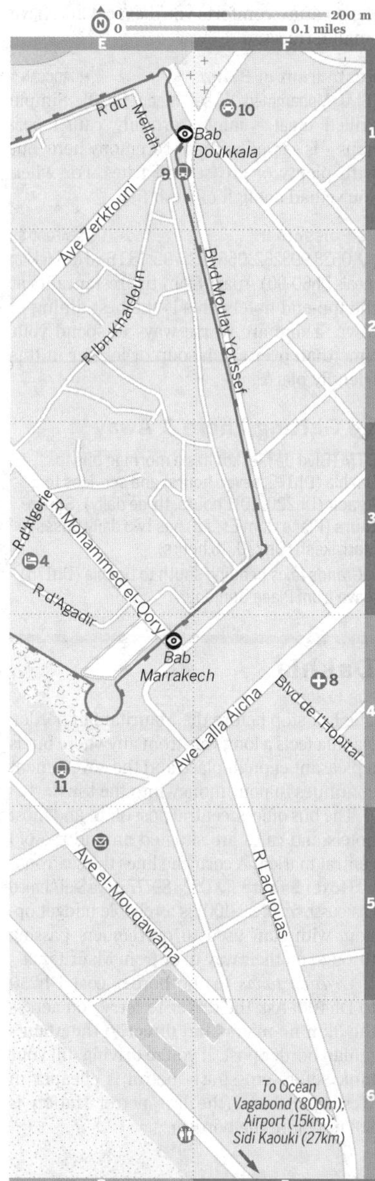

hotel in a modernist white block near the town hall, the Kamal manages to appeal to a wide range of clients, including package-tour groups and travelling Moroccans. Rooms are bright and clean, and there's a pool large enough to swim laps in.

Essaouira

Sights

1 Skala de la Ville....B2
2 Skala du Port....A5

Sleeping

3 Hotel Beau Rivage....B4
4 Lalla Mira....E3
5 Riad Nakhla....D3

Eating

6 Restaurant Ferdaous....C3
7 Taros Café....B3

Information

8 Hôpital Sidi Mohammed ben Abdallah....F4

Transport

9 Local Buses....E1
10 Petits Taxis....F1
11 Supratours....E4

Eating

The cheap snack bars in Nouveau Talborjt and around the bus stations are open after hours. The **fish stalls** (meals around Dh50) at the entrance to the commercial port are excellent. There are plenty of places along the beach to chill at midday or toast the sunset. Some places along Palm Beach stay open till 1am in summer.

Bab Marrakesh MOROCCAN $

(☎0528 826144; Rue de Massa; sandwiches Dh25-35, couscous Dh70, tajine for 2 Dh100) Near Souq al-Had, this is the real thing – far removed from the tourist traps near the beach. Highly regarded by locals, it serves authentic Moroccan food at authentic prices.

La Scala MOROCCAN $$$

(☎0528 846773; Rue du Oued Souss; meal incl wine Dh350) An excellent Moroccan restaurant, La Scala has a pleasantly cosmopolitan atmosphere. The food is elegant and fresh, and beautifully presented.

Information

Banks with ATMs and internet places proliferate along Blvd Hassan II.

Getting There & Away

Although a good number of buses serve Agadir, it is quite possible you'll end up in the regional transport hub of Inezgane, 13km south – check before you buy your ticket. Plenty of *grands taxis*

(Dh8) and local buses shuttle between there and Agadir.

CTM has buses to Casablanca (Dh180, eight hours, six daily), Marrakesh (Dh80, four hours, seven daily) and Essaouira (Dh60, two hours, one daily). There are more bus options at the regional transport hub of Inezgane, 13km to the south.

The main *grand taxi* rank is at the south end of Rue de Fès. Destinations include Inezgane (Dh8), Taroudannt (Dh35) and Essaouira (Dh70).

WESTERN SAHARA

Ask any Moroccan about the status of the Western Sahara and they'll insist it's sovereign soil, yet international law is clear that this is still under dispute. For travellers, it's mainly an empty windswept stretch of country for transiting to or from Mauritania.

There's no officially designated border between Morocco and the Western Sahara. Although the region is peaceful you'll be more aware of military and police checkpoints.

Laâyoune

POP 200,000

The former Spanish phosphate-mining outpost of Laâyoune has been turned into the principal city of the Western Sahara. Now neither Sahrawi nor Spanish, its population is mostly Moroccan, lured from the north by the promise of healthy wages and tax-free goods.

The town's showpiece is the vast Place du Méchouar, but there's no obvious centre. The post office, banks and most hotels are along either Blvd Hassan II or Blvd de Mekka.

Sleeping & Eating

There are many cafes and simple restaurants around Place Dchira. Lively food stalls can be found at the Souq Djemal.

Hôtel Jodesa HOTEL **$**
(☎0528 992064; 223 Blvd de Mekka; s/d Dh100/144, with shower Dh144/155) North of Place Dchira, this modern hotel is a good budget option. Rooms are basic but reasonably spacious.

Hôtel Parador HOTEL **$$$**
(☎0528 892814; Ave de l'Islam; s/d Dh1100/1400; ❄ 🏊) Built in Spanish hacienda style around gardens, the Parador has a faintly colonial bar and a good, if expensive, restaurant (set menu Dh200). Rooms are equipped with all the creature comforts you'd expect and have small terraces.

Restaurant el-Bahja MOROCCAN **$**
(Blvd Mohammed V; set menu Dh20) Simple grilled meat – lamb, certainly, camel perhaps – is served without ceremony here, but with plenty of grease and frites. For when you've had enough of fresh fish.

Le Poissonier SEAFOOD **$$**
(☎0528 993262, 0661 235795; 183 Blvd de Mekka; meals Dh60-90) Apart from the restaurants at the top-end hotels, this is the best dining in town. There are worse ways to spend your time than over a fish soup or lobster in this friendly place.

Getting There & Away

CTM (Blvd de Mekka) has a morning bus to Dakhla (Dh175, seven hours) and services to Agadir (Dh220, 10½ hours, three daily). **Supratours** (Place Oum Essad) has two daily buses to Marrakesh (Dh270, 16 hours).

Grands taxis heading south to Dakhla (Dh175) leave from Place Boujdour.

Dakhla

POP 40,000

The last stop before the Mauritanian border, Dakhla feels a long way from anywhere but is a pleasant enough place and the government continues to pour money into the town.

The bus offices, central post office and most hotels and cafes are situated around the old central market. A corniche lines the seafront.

Hôtel Sahara (☎0528 897773; Ave Sidi Ahmed Laaroussi; s/d Dh80/100) is a reliable budget option, with staff used to overlanders passing through on their way to or from Mauritania.

Grands taxis to the border cost Dh250 to Dh400. Ask the driver to ferry you across the 3km no-man's-land direct to the Mauritanian border post. If you're driving, fill your tank before crossing – petrol is cheaper in Western Sahara (the last petrol station is 80km before the border).

IMPERIAL CITIES & THE MIDDLE ATLAS

The rolling plains that sweep along the base of the Middle Atlas are Morocco's breadbasket, dotted with olive groves and wheat fields. Several important cities have also taken root here, including ancient Fez, Meknès and the Roman city of Volubilis – Morocco's most interesting archaeological site.

Fez

POP 1 MILLION

At 1200 years old Fez is Morocco's spiritual heart. Its medina (Fez el-Bali) is the largest living medieval Islamic city in the world. A first visit can be overwhelming: an assault on the senses through bazaars, winding alleys, mosques, workshops, people and pack animals that seem to take you out of the 21st century and back to imagined *Arabian Nights*.

Sights

The Medina (Fez el-Bali)

Within the old walls of Fez el-Bali lies an incredible maze of twisting alleys, blind turns and hidden souqs. Navigation can be confusing and getting lost is a certainty, but this is part of the medina's charm: you never quite know what discovery lies around the next corner.

Kairaouine Mosque MOSQUE
(Map p124) The Kairaouine Mosque is Fez's true heart. Built in 859 by refugees from Tunisia, and rebuilt in the 12th century, it can accommodate up to 20,000 people at prayer. Non-Muslims have to be content with glimpses of its seemingly endless columns from the gates on Talaa Kebira and Place as-Seffarine.

Medersa Bou Inania NOTABLE BUILDING
(Map p124; admission Dh10; ⏲9am-6pm, closed during prayers) Located 150m east of Bab Bou Jeloud, the 14th-century Medersa Bou Inania is the finest of Fez's theological colleges. The *zellij, muqarna* (plasterwork) and woodcarving are amazingly elaborate.

Nejjarine Museum of Wooden Arts & Crafts MUSEUM
(Map p124; ☎0535 740580; Place an-Nejjarin; admission Dh20; ⏲10am-7pm) Located in a wonderfully restored *funduq* (caravanserai for travelling merchants), with a host of fascinating exhibits. Photography is forbidden. The rooftop cafe has great views over the medina.

Tanneries NEIGHBOURHOOD
(Map p124) The tanneries are one of the city's most iconic sights (and smells). Head northeast of Place as-Seffarine and take the left fork after about 50m; you'll soon pick up the unmistakeable waft of skin and dye that will guide you into the heart of the leather district.

Fez el-Jdid (New Fez)

Only in a city as old as Fez could you find a district dubbed 'new' because it's only 700 years old. It's home to the Royal Palace, whose entrance at **Dar el-Makhzen** (Royal Palace; Map p122; Place des Alaouites) is a stunning example of modern restoration; palace grounds are closed to the public.

In the 14th century, Fez el-Jdid became a refuge for Jews, thus creating a *mellah* (Jewish quarter). The *mellah's* southwest corner is home to the fascinating **Jewish Cemetery & Habarim Synagogue** (Map p122; donations appreciated; ⏲7am-7pm).

Festivals & Events

Fez Festival of World Sacred Music MUSIC
(☎0535 740691; www.fesfestival.com) Every June the Fez Festival of World Sacred Music brings together musicians from all corners of the globe. It's an established favourite on the 'world music' festival circuit.

Sleeping

Medina

Hôtel Cascade HOTEL $
(Map p124; ☎0535 638442; 26 Rue Serrajine, Bab Bou Jeloud; dm/r Dh80/160, breakfast Dh20) One of the grandaddies of the Morocco budget-hotel scene. You shouldn't expect much for the price, but if you're up for meeting plenty of like-minded travellers, then this might be the place for you.

Funky Fes HOSTEL $
(Map p124; ☎0535 633196; www.funkyfes.com; Arset Lamdisi, Bab Jdid; dm Dh130-170) Fez's first proper hostel, offering up good, cheap backpacker accommodation, with activities, tours, cooking and more.

Dar Finn GUESTHOUSE $$
(Map p124; ☎0535 740004; www.darfinn.com; r Dh850-1200; P wi-fi) A lovingly restored guesthouse, with high-Fassi style in the front and a sunny back courtyard with plunge pool. Very welcoming, with delicious breakfasts.

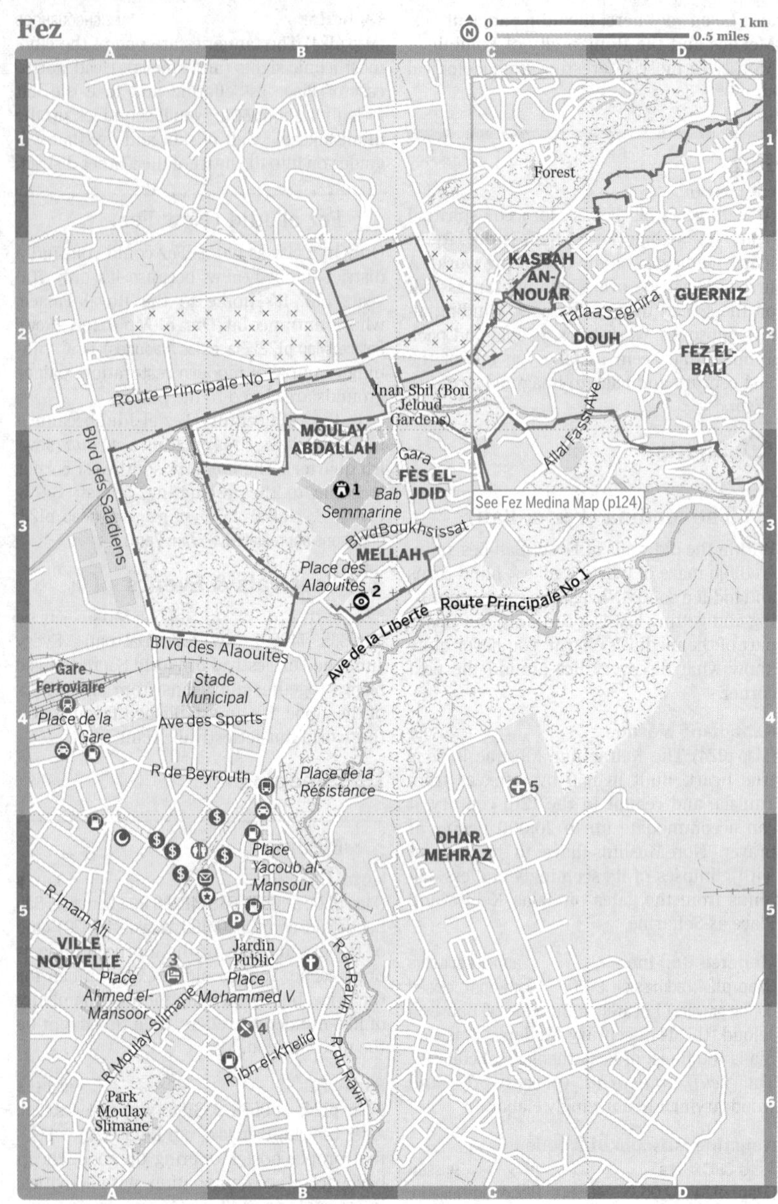

MOROCCO FEZ

Ville Nouvelle

Hôtel Splendid HOTEL $
(Map p122; ☎0535 622148; splendid@iam.net.ma; 9 Rue Abdelkarim el-Khattabi; s/d Dh318/412; ❄ 🏊) This hotel makes a good claim for three stars. It's all modern and tidy, plus there's a pool for the heat and a bar for the evenings.

Fez

Sights

1 Dar el-Makhzen ... B3
2 Jewish Cemetery & Habarim Synagogue ... B3

Sleeping

3 Hôtel Splendid ... A5

Eating

4 Restaurant Marrakech ... B6

Information

5 Hôpital Ghassani ... C4

Eating & Drinking

Medina

In the medina, you won't have to walk far to find someone selling food – tiny cell-like places grilling *brochettes*, cooking up cauldrons of soup or just a guy with a pushcart selling peanut cookies. Bab Bou Jeloud has quite a cluster of options, with streetside tables for people-watching.

Café Clock CAFE $$
(Map p124; 0535 637855; www.cafeclock.com; 7 Derb el-Mergana, Talaa Kebira; mains Dh55-80; 9am-10pm;) In a restored townhouse, this funky place has a refreshing menu with offerings such as falafel, some interesting vegetarian options and a monstrously large camel burger. Its 'Clock Culture' program includes sunset concerts every Sunday (cover charge around Dh20), attracting a good mix of locals, expats and curious tourists.

Médina Café MOROCCAN $$
(0535 633430; 6 Derb Mernissi, Bab Bou Jeloud; mains Dh70-100; 8am-10pm) Just outside Bab Bou Jeloud, this small restaurant is good for a quick bite or a fruit juice; in the evening better Moroccan fare is on offer.

Mezzanine CAFE
(Map p124; 5356 633430; 17 Kasbah Chams; tapas selection from Dh100 or per dish around Dh30; noon-1am) Scoring highly on the fashion meter, this new bar is the hippest thing in the medina – more Ibiza than Moulay Idriss. The terrace overlooking Jnan Sbil gardens is a good place to chill with a beer or cocktail, and there's tapas too if you want some finger food.

Ville Nouvelle

Restaurant Marrakech MOROCCAN $$
(Map p122; 0535 930876; 11 Rue Omar el-Mokhtar; mains from Dh55;) A charming restaurant with red walls and dark furniture, plus a cushion-strewn salon at the back. The menu's variety refreshes the palate, with dishes like chicken tajine with apple and olive, or lamb with aubergine and peppers (there's also a set three-course menu).

Information

There are plenty of banks (with ATMs) in the Ville Nouvelle along Blvd Mohammed V.

Cyber Batha (Derb Douh; per hr Dh10; 9am-10pm) Internet; has English as well as French keyboards.

Hôpital Ghassani (Map p122; 0535 622777) One of the city's biggest hospitals; located east of the Ville Nouvelle in the Dhar Mehraz district.

Main Post Office (cnr Ave Hassan II & Blvd Mohammed V) Poste restante is at the far left; the parcels office is through a separate door.

Post Office (Place Batha) In the medina.

Getting There & Away

BUS

The main station for **CTM buses** (0535 732992) is near Place Atlas in the southern Ville Nouvelle.

Non-CTM buses depart from the **main bus station** (Map p124; 0535 636032) outside Bab el-Mahrouk.

CTM services from Fez include:

- Casablanca (Dh105, five hours, seven daily)
- Chefchaouen (Dh45, four hours, three daily)
- Marrakesh (Dh150, nine hours, two daily)
- Meknès (Dh25, 1½ hours, six daily)
- Rabat (Dh70, 3½ hours, seven daily)
- Tangier (Dh115, six hours, three daily)
- Tetouan (Dh100, five hours, two daily)

TAXI

There are several *grand taxi* ranks dotted around town. Taxis for Meknès (Dh20) and Rabat (Dh60) leave from in front of the main bus station (outside Bab el-Mahrouk) and from near the train station.

TRAIN

The **train station** (0535 930333) is in the Ville Nouvelle. Trains depart every two hours to Casablanca (Dh110, 4½ hours), via Rabat (Dh80, 3½ hours) and Meknès (Dh20, one hour); there are also services to Marrakesh (Dh195, eight hours) and Tangier (Dh105, five hours).

Getting Around

Drivers of the red *petits taxis* generally use their meters without any fuss. Expect to pay about Dh9 from the train or CTM stations to Bab Bou Jeloud.

Meknès

POP 690,000

Morocco's third imperial city is often overlooked by tourists, but Meknès (Map p127) is worth getting to know. Quieter and smaller than nearby Fez, it's more laid-back and less

Fez Medina

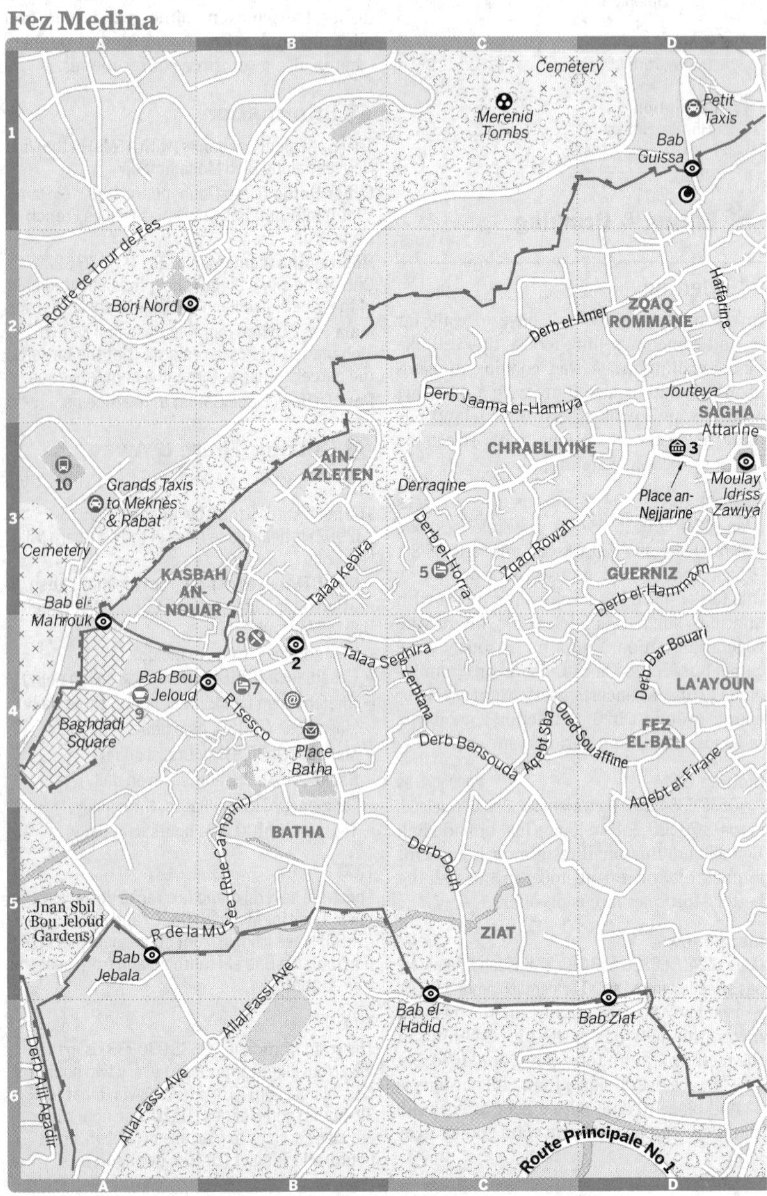

hassle, but still awash with the winding, narrow medina streets and grand buildings befitting a one-time capital of the sultanate.

Meknès is also the ideal base from which to explore the Roman ruins at Volubilis and the hilltop holy town of Moulay Idriss, two of the country's most significant historical sites.

Sights

The heart of Meknès' medina lies to the north of the main square, Place el-Hedim, with the *mellah* to the west. To the south, Moulay Ismail's imperial city opens up through one of the most impressive monumental gateways

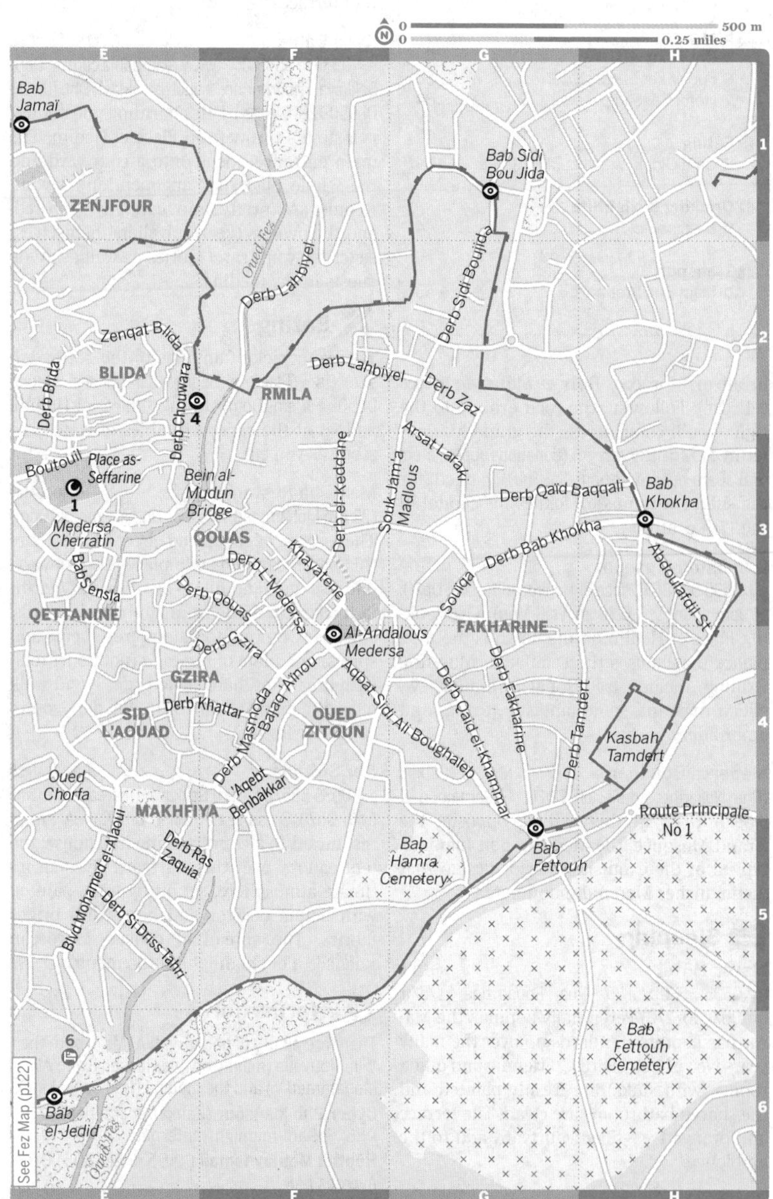

Fez Medina

Sights
1 Kairaouine Mosque E3
2 Medersa Bou Inania B4
3 Nejjarine Museum of Wooden Arts & Crafts D3
4 Tanneries E2

Sleeping
5 Dar Finn C3
6 Funky Fes E6
7 Hôtel Cascade B4

Eating
8 Café Clock B4

Drinking & Nightlife
9 Mezzanine A4

Transport
10 Main Bus Station A3

in all of Morocco, **Bab el-Mansour** (Place el-Hedim). Following the road around to the right, you'll come across the grand **Mausoleum of Moulay Ismail** (donations appreciated; 8.30am-noon & 2-6pm Sat-Thu), named for the sultan who made Meknès his capital in the 17th century.

Dar Jamaï Museum MUSEUM
(0535 530863; Place el-Hedim; admission Dh20; 9am-noon & 3-6.30pm Wed-Mon) Overlooking Place el-Hedim on the north is the 1882 palace that houses the Dar Jamaï Museum. Exhibits include traditional ceramics, jewellery, rugs and some fantastic textiles and embroidery.

Medersa Bou Inania NOTABLE BUILDING
(Rue Najjarine; admission Dh20; 9am-noon & 3-6pm) Deep in the medina, opposite the Grand Mosquée, the Medersa Bou Inania is typical of the exquisite interior design that distinguishes Merenid monuments.

Sleeping

Maroc Hôtel HOTEL $
(0535 530075; 7 Rue Rouamzine; s/d/tr Dh100/200/270) Perennially popular, the Maroc has kept its standards up over the many years we've been visiting. Friendly and quiet, rooms (with sinks) are freshly painted and the shared bathrooms are clean. The terrace and orange tree–filled courtyard add to the ambience.

Hôtel Majestic HOTEL $
(0535 522035; 19 Ave Mohammed V; s/d Dh159/210, with shower Dh231/322) Built in the 1930s, this grand old lady carries her age well. There's a good mix of rooms (all have sinks) and there's plenty of character to go around, plus a peaceful patio and panoramic roof terrace.

Ryad Bahia GUESTHOUSE $$
(0535 554541; www.ryad-bahia.com; Derb Sekkaya, Tiberbarine; r incl breakfast Dh670, ste Dh950-1200;) This charming guesthouse is a stone's throw from Place el-Hedim. The main entrance opens onto a courtyard and the whole place has an open, airy layout. Rooms are pretty and carefully restored, and the owners (keen travellers themselves) eager to swap travel stories as well as guide guests in the medina.

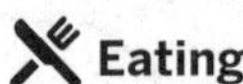

Eating

Take your pick of any one of the **sandwich stands** (Place el-Hedim; sandwiches around Dh30; 7am-10pm) lining Place el-Hedim, and sit at the canopied tables to watch the scene as you eat.

Marhaba Restaurant MOROCCAN $
(23 Ave Mohammed V; tajines Dh25; noon-10pm) The essence of cheap and cheerful; we adore this basic, canteen-style place. Do as everyone else does and fill up on a bowl of *harira* (a thick soup made from lamb stock, lentils, chickpeas, onions, tomatoes, fresh herbs and spices) or a plate of *makoda* (potato fritters) with bread and hard-boiled eggs – and walk out with change from Dh15. We defy you to eat better for less.

Dar Sultana MOROCCAN $$
(0535 535720; Derb Sekkaya, Tiberbarine; mains from Dh70, 3-course set menu Dh150) A small restaurant in a converted medina house, the tent canopy over the courtyard gives an intimate atmosphere, set off by walls painted with henna designs and hung with bright fabrics. The spread of cooked Moroccan salads is a big highlight of the menu.

Information

There are plenty of banks with ATMs in both the Ville Nouvelle (mainly on Ave Hassan II and Ave Mohammed V) and the medina (Rue Sekkakine).

Cyber Bab Mansour (Zankat Accra; per hr Dh6; 9am-midnight) Internet.

Hôpital Moulay Ismail (0535 522805) Off Ave des FAR.

Meknès

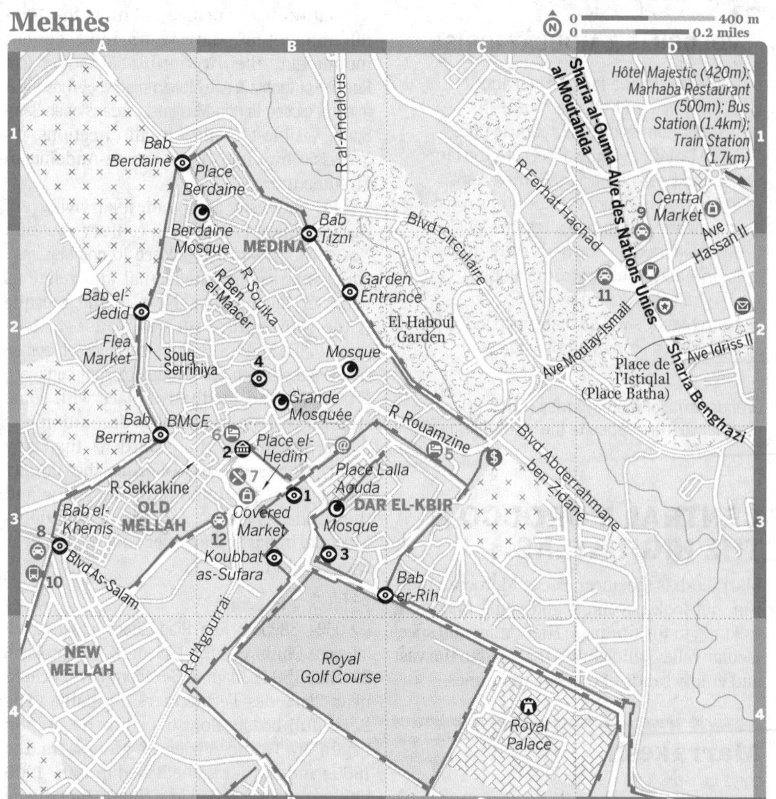

Main Post Office (Place de l'Istiqlal) The parcel office is in the same building, around the corner on Rue Tetouan.

Getting There & Away

Meknès has two train stations; use the more central **El-Amir Abdelkader** (☎ 0535 522763). There are plentiful trains to Fez (Dh20, one hour), and Casablanca (Dh90, 3½ hours) via Rabat (Dh65, 2¼ hours), five for Marrakesh (Dh174, seven hours) and one for Tangier (Dh85, four hours) – or take a westbound train and change at Sidi Kacem.

CTM bus departures include Casablanca (Dh90, four hours, six daily) via Rabat (Dh55, 2½ hours), Marrakesh (Dh160, eight hours, daily) and Tangier (Dh100, five hours, three daily). The main bus station lies just outside Bab el-Khemis, west of the medina.

The principal *grand taxi* rank is at Bab el-Khemis. There are regular departures to Fez (Dh16, one hour) and Rabat (Dh44, 90 minutes).

Meknès

Sights
- 1 Bab el-Mansour ... B3
- 2 Dar Jamaï Museum ... B3
- 3 Mausoleum of Moulay Ismail ... B3
- 4 Medersa Bou Inania ... B2

Sleeping
- 5 Maroc Hôtel ... C3
- 6 Ryad Bahia ... B3

Eating
- Dar Sultana ... (see 6)
- 7 Sandwich Stands ... B3

Transport
- 8 Grands Taxis ... A3
- 9 Grands Taxis for Moulay Idriss ... D1
- 10 Main Bus Station ... A3
- 11 Petits Taxis ... D2
- 12 Petits Taxis ... B3

WORTH A TRIP

VOLUBILIS & MOULAY IDRISS

In the midst of a fertile plain about 33km north of Meknès, **Volubilis** (Ouailili; admission Dh20, parking Dh5, guide Dh140; ⌚8am-sunset) are the largest and best-preserved Roman ruins in Morocco. One of the country's most important pilgrimage sites, the lovely whitewashed hill town **Moulay Idriss**, is only about 4.5km from Volubilis.

A half-day outing by *grand taxi* from Meknès will cost around Dh350, including a stop at Moulay Idriss.

Grands taxis for Moulay Idriss (Dh12, 20 minutes) leave from opposite the Institut Français.

CENTRAL MOROCCO & THE HIGH ATLAS

Marrakesh is the queen bee of Moroccan tourism, but look beyond it and you'll find great trekking in the dramatic High Atlas, and spectacular valleys and gorges that lead to the vast and empty sands of the Saharan dunes.

Marrakesh

POP 2 MILLION

Marrakesh grew rich on the camel caravans threading their way across the desert, although these days it's cheap flights from Europe bringing tourists to spend their money in the souqs that fatten the city's coffers. But Marrakesh's old heart still beats strongly enough, from the time-worn ramparts that ring the city to the nightly spectacle of the Djemaa el-Fna that leaps from the pages of the *1001 Nights* on the edge of the labyrinthine medina.

Sights

The focal point of Marrakesh is **Djemaa el-Fna** (⌚approx 9am-1pm, later during Ramadan), a huge square in the medina and the backdrop for one of the world's greatest spectacles. Djemaa el-Fna comes into its own at dusk, when the curtain goes up on rows of open-air food stalls smoking the immediate area with mouth-watering aromas. Jugglers, storytellers, snake charmers, musicians, acrobats and spectators fill the remaining space.

Southwest of Djemaa el-Fna is the 70m-tall minaret of Marrakesh's most famous monument, the **Koutoubia Mosque** (cnr Rue el-Koutoubia & Ave Mohammed V; ⌚mosque & minaret closed to non-Muslims, gardens open 8am-8pm). Visible for miles in all directions, it's a classic example of Moroccan-Andalucían architecture.

The largest and oldest-surviving of the mosques is the 12th-century **Ali ben Youssef Mosque** (⌚closed to non-Muslims), which marks the intellectual and religious heart of the medina. Next to the mosque is the 14th-century **Ali ben Youssef Medersa** (☎0524 441893; Place ben Youssef; admission Dh40; ⌚9am-6pm winter, to 7pm summer), a peaceful and meditative place with some stunning examples of stucco decoration.

Marrakesh has more gardens than any other Moroccan city, offering the perfect escape from the hubbub of the souqs and the traffic. The rose gardens of Koutoubia Mosque, in particular, offer cool respite near Djemaa el-Fna.

Palais de la Bahia PALACE
(☎0524 389564; Rue Riad Zitoun el-Jedid; admission Dh10; ⌚8.30-11.45am & 2.30-5.45pm Sat-Thu, 8.30-11.30am & 3-5.45pm Fri) Located near Place des Ferblantiers, La Bahia (The Beautiful) boasts floor-to-ceiling decoration begun by Grand Vizier Si Moussa in the 1860s and further embellished in 1894–1900 by slave-turned-vizier Abu 'Bou' Ahmed. The painted, gilded, inlaid woodwork ceilings still have the intended effect of subduing crowds, while the carved stucco is cleverly slanted downward to meet the gaze.

Saadian Tombs TOMBS
(Rue de la Kasbah; admission Dh10; ⌚8.30-11.45am & 2.30-5.45pm) Long hidden from intrusive eyes, the area of the Saadian Tombs, alongside the Kasbah Mosque, is home to ornate tombs that are the resting places of Saadian princes.

Jardin Majorelle GARDENS
(☎0524 301852; www.jardinmajorelle.com; cnr Ave Yacoub el-Mansour & Ave Moulay Abdullah; garden Dh30, museum Dh15; ⌚8am-6pm summer, to 5pm winter) In the Ville Nouvelle, the Jardin Majorelle is a sublime mix of art deco buildings and psychedelic desert mirage.

Sleeping

Hôtel Central Palace HOTEL **$**
(☎0524 440235; hotelcentralpalace@hotmail.com; 59 Derb Sidi Bouloukat; d Dh305, with shower

Dh205, without bathroom Dh155) Sure it's central, but palatial? Actually, yes! With 40 clean rooms on four floors arranged around a burbling courtyard fountain, and a roof terrace lording it over the Djemaa el-Fna, this is a rare example of a stately budget hotel.

Jnane Mogador GUESTHOUSE **$**
(☎0524 426323; www.jnanemogador.com; 116 Riad Zitoun el-Kedim, Derb Sidi Bouloukat; s/d/tr/q Dh360/480/580/660; @) An authentic 19th-century riad with all the 21st-century guesthouse fixings: prime location, in-house *hammam,* double-decker roof terraces and owner Mohammed's laid-back hospitality. Perennially popular; book in advance.

Riad Nejma Lounge GUESTHOUSE **$$**
(☎0524 382341; www.riad-nejmalounge.com; 45 Derb Sidi M'Hamed el-Haj, Bab Doukkala; d incl breakfast Dh495-795; ❄@≋) Lounge lizards chill on hot-pink cushions in the whitewashed courtyard, and graphic splashes of colour make wood-beamed guest rooms totally mod, though the rustic showers can be temperamental. Handy for Ville Nouvelle restaurants and shops.

Dar Soukaina GUESTHOUSE **$$$**
(☎0661 245238; www.darsoukaina.com; 19 Derb el-Ferrane, Riad Laârouss; s/tr incl breakfast Dh790/1150, d incl breakfast Dh970-1400; ❄≋) Sister riads: the original is all soaring ceilings, cosy nooks and graceful archways, while the newer extension across the street is about sprawling beds, the grand patio and handsome woodwork. A 20-minute walk from the Djemaa, but worth the discovery.

Eating

The cheapest and most exotic place in town to eat remains the **food stalls** (⊙sunset-1am) on Djemaa el-Fna, piled high with fresh meats and salads, goats' heads and steaming snails.

Just before noon, the vendors at a row of stalls in **Mechoui Alley** (250g lamb with bread Dh30-50; ⊙11am-2pm), on the east side of Souq Ablueh (Olive Souq), start carving up steaming sides of *mechoui* (slow-roasted lamb), with bread and spices.

Earth Café VEGETARIAN **$$**
(2 Derb Zouak, Riad Zitoun el-Kedim; mains around Dh60; ⊙9am-11pm; ✎) Run by an enthusiastic Moroccan-Australian, Earth Café claims to be Morocco's first vegetarian/vegan restaurant. The atmosphere is laid-back hippy-chic, and the food fresh and fabulous (we fell in love with the ricotta-and-squash *bastilla,* a multilayer pastry). Produce comes from the owner's nearby farm, to which visits can be arranged.

Le Salama MOROCCAN **$$**
(☎0524 391300; www.lesalama.com; 40 Rue des Banques) Low lighting and dark Moroccan decor lend atmosphere to this upscale dining experience – more than just traditional tajines, and with a rooftop bar that's the closest place to Djemma el-Fna where you can get a drink.

Terrasse des Épices MOROCCAN **$$**
(☎0524 375904; 15 Souq Cherifia; set meals Dh100-150) Head to the roof for lunch on top of the world in a mudbrick *bhou* (booth). Check the chalkboard for the Dh100 fixed-price special: Moroccan salads followed by chicken-leg tajine with fries, then strawberries and mint. Reservations handy in the high season.

Drinking

Dar Cherifa CAFE
(☎0524 426463; 8 Derb Cherifa Lakbir; tea/coffee Dh15-25; ⊙noon-7pm) Revive souq-sore eyes at this serene late-15th-century Saadian riad, near Rue Mouassine, where tea and saffron coffee is served with contemporary art and literature downstairs or terrace views upstairs.

Café Arabe BAR
(☎0524 429728; www.cafearabe.com; 184 Rue el-Mouassine, Medina; ⊙10am-midnight) Gloat over souq purchases with cocktails on the roof at sunset or a glass of wine next to the Zen-*zellij* courtyard fountain. The food is mixed.

Shopping

Marrakesh is a shopper's paradise: its souqs are full of skilled artisans producing quality products in wood, leather, wool, metal, bone, brass and silver. The trick is to dive into the souqs and treat shopping as a game.

Ensemble Artisanal ARTS & CRAFTS
(Ave Mohammed V; ⊙8.30am-7.30pm) To get a feel for the quality of merchandise it is always good to start at this government-run spot in the Ville Nouvelle.

Cooperative Artisanale Femmes de Marrakesh ARTS & CRAFTS
(☎0524 378308; 67 Souq Kchachbia; ⊙9.30am-12.30pm & 2.30-6.30pm) A hidden treasure worth seeking in the souqs, with breezy

Marrakesh

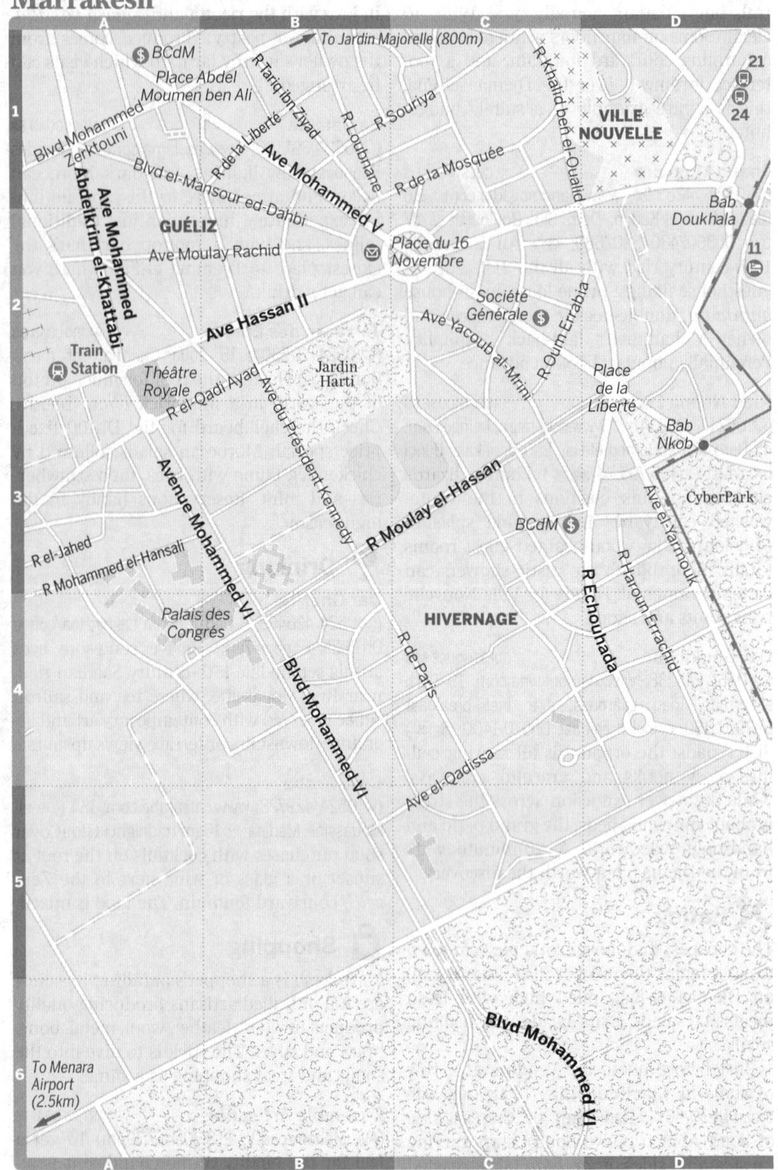

cotton clothing and household linens made by a Marrakesh women's cooperative, and a small annexe packed with varied items from nonprofits and women's cooperatives from across Morocco.

Information

Cybercafes ringing the Djemaa el-Fna charge Dh8 to Dh12 per hour; just follow signs reading 'c@fe'. There are plenty of ATMs along Rue de Bab Agnaou off the Djemaa el-Fna.

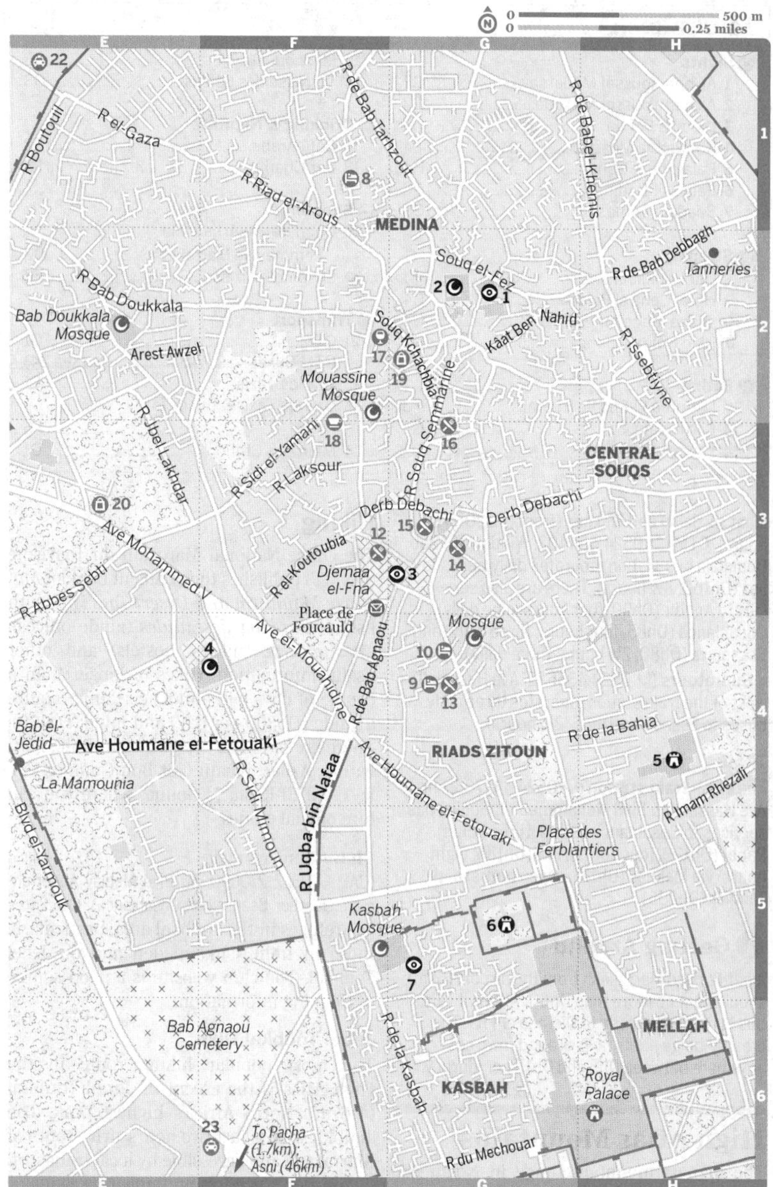

Main Post Office (☎0524 431963; Place du 16 Novembre; ⊙8.30am-2pm Mon-Sat)

Polyclinique du Sud (☎0524 447999; cnr Rue de Yougoslavie & Rue Ibn Aicha, Guéliz; ⊙24hr) Private hospital for serious cases and emergency dental care.

ℹ Getting There & Away

BUS

Most buses arrive and depart from the **main bus station** (☎0524 433933; Bab Doukkala), just outside the city walls. A number of companies run buses to Fez (from Dh130, 8½ hours, at

Marrakesh

Sights
1 Ali ben Youssef Medersa ... G2
2 Ali ben Youssef Mosque ... G2
3 Djemaa El-Fna ... G3
4 Koutoubia Mosque ... F4
5 Palais de la Bahia ... H4
6 Palais el-Badi ... G5
7 Saadian Tombs ... G5

Sleeping
8 Dar Soukaina ... F1
9 Hôtel Central Palace ... G4
10 Jnane Mogador ... G4
11 Riad Nejma Lounge ... D2

Eating
12 Djemma El-Fna Food Stalls ... F3
13 Earth Café ... G4
14 Le Salama ... G3
15 Mechoui Alley ... G3
16 Terrasse des Épices ... G3

Drinking & Nightlife
17 Café Arabe ... F2
18 Dar Cherifa ... F3

Shopping
19 Cooperative Artisanale Femmes de Marrakesh ... G2
20 Ensemble Artisanal ... E3

Transport
21 CTM ... D1
CTM Buses ... (see 24)
22 Grands Taxis ... E1
23 Grands Taxis & Buses for Asni ... F6
24 Main Bus Station ... D1

least six daily) and Meknès (from Dh120, six hours). **CTM** (☎0524 434402; Window 10, Bab Doukkala bus station) operates daily buses to Fez (Dh160, 8½ hours). There are also services to Agadir (Dh90, four hours, nine daily), Casablanca (Dh85, four hours, three daily) and Essaouira (Dh80, 2½ hours, three daily).

Supratours (☎0524 435525; Ave Hassan II), west of the train station, operates three daily buses to Essaouira (Dh65, 2½ hours).

TRAIN

The swish **train station** (☎0524 447768; cnr Ave Hassan II & Blvd Mohammed VI, Guéliz) has services to Casablanca (Dh90, three hours), Rabat (Dh120, four hours), Fez (Dh185, eight hours) via Meknès (Dh174, seven hours) and Tangier (Dh205).

Getting Around

A *petit taxi* to Marrakesh from the airport (6km) should cost no more than Dh60. Alternatively, bus 11 runs irregularly to Djemaa el-Fna. The creamy-beige *petits taxis* around town cost anywhere between Dh5 and Dh15 per journey.

High Atlas Mountains

The highest mountain range in North Africa, the Berbers call the High Atlas Idraren Draren (Mountain of Mountains) and it's easy to see why. Flat-roofed, earthen Berber villages cling tenaciously to the valley sides, while irrigated terraced gardens and walnut groves flourish below.

Hiking

The Office National Marocain du Tourisme (ONMT) publishes the excellent booklet *Morocco: Mountain and Desert Tourism,* with lists of *bureaux des guides* (guide offices), *gîtes d'étape* (hikers' hostels) and other useful information. Hikes of longer than a couple of days will almost certainly require a guide (Dh300 per day) and mule (Dh100). There are *bureaux des guides* in Imlil, Setti Fatma, Azilal, Tabant (Aït Bou Goumez Valley) and El-Kelaâ M'Gouna, where you can hire official guides.

Club Alpin Français HIKING
(CAF; ☎0522 270090; 50 Blvd Moulay Abderrahman, Quartier Beauséjour, Casablanca) Operates key refuges in the Toubkal area, particularly those in Imlil, Oukaïmeden and on Jebel Toubkal. The club website is a good source of trekking information.

Jebel Toubkal Hike

The most popular hiking route in the High Atlas is the ascent of **Jebel Toubkal** (4167m), North Africa's highest peak. The Toubkal area is just two hours' drive south of Marrakesh and accessible by local transport.

You don't need mountaineering skills or a guide to reach the summit, provided you follow the standard two-day route and don't do it in winter. You will, however, need good boots, warm clothing, a sleeping bag, food and water, and should be in good physical condition before you set out. It's not particularly steep, but it's a remorseless uphill trek all the way.

The starting point is the village of **Imlil**, where you can stock up on supplies. There's plenty of accommodation here – try **Café-Hotel Soleil** (tel/fax 0524 485622; d incl breakfast Dh220, without bathroom Dh170, per person without/with bathroom & half board Dh170/220) or **Dar Zaratoustra** (0524 485601; http://toubkal-maroc.voila.net/; d with half board Dh350-500; Mar-Oct).

The first day's walk (10km; about five hours) winds steeply through the villages of Aroumd and Sidi Chamharouch to the large **Toubkal Refuge** (0664 071838; dm CAF member/HI member/nonmember Dh46/69/92), at 2307m.

The ascent to the summit on the second day should take about four hours and the descent about two. It can be bitterly cold at the summit, even in summer.

Frequent local buses (Dh15, 1½ hours) and *grands taxis* (Dh30, one hour) leave south of Bab er-Rob in Marrakesh to Asni, where you change for the final 17km to Imlil (Dh15 to Dh20, one hour).

Other Hikes

In summer, it's quite possible to do an easy one- or two-day trek from the ski resort of **Oukaïmeden**, which also has a CAF refuge, southwest to Imlil or vice versa. You can get here by *grand taxi* from Marrakesh.

From **Tacheddirt** there are numerous hiking options. One is a pleasant two-day walk northeast to the village of **Setti Fatma** (also accessible from Marrakesh) via the village of **Timichi**, where there is a welcoming *gîte*. A longer circuit could take you south to **Amsouzerte** and back towards Imlil via **Lac d'Ifni**, Toubkal, **Tazaghart** (also with a refuge and rock climbing) and **Tizi Oussem**.

Aït Benhaddou

Aït Benhaddou, 32km from Ouarzazate, is one of the most exotic and best-preserved kasbahs in Morocco. It's regularly used as a film set, starring in everything from *Lawrence of Arabia* and *Gladiator* to *Game of Thrones*.

From Ouarzazate, take the main road towards Marrakesh as far as the signposted turn-off (22km); Aït Benhaddou is another 9km. *Grands taxis* run from outside Ouarzazate bus station when full (Dh20 per person).

Drâa Valley

A ribbon of Technicolor palmeraies (palm groves), earth-red kasbahs and Berber villages, the Drâa Valley is a special place. Eventually seeping out into the sands of the desert, it helped control the ancient trans-Saharan trade routes that built Marrakesh's wealth.

Zagora

The iconic 'Tombouktou, 52 jours' ('Timbuktu, 52 days') signpost was recently taken down in an inexplicable government beautification scheme, but Zagora's fame as a desert outpost is indelible. It feels very much like a border town, fighting back the encroaching desert with its lush palmeraie. Though modern and largely unappealing, the spectacular **Jebel Zagora**, rising up across the other side of the river Drâa, is worth climbing for the views.

Activities

Camel rides are practically obligatory in Zagora. Count on around Dh300 per day if you're camping; ask about water, bedding, toilets and how many other people will be sharing your campsite.

Caravane Dèsert et Montagne DESERT EXCURSIONS
(0524 846898; www.caravanedesertetmontagne.com; 112 Blvd Mohammed V)

Caravane Hamada Drâa DESERT EXCURSIONS
(0524 846930; www.hamadadraa.com)

Sleeping & Eating

Most hotels have their own restaurants. Moroccan fare with less flair can be had at cheap restaurants along Blvd Mohammed V.

Hôtel la Rose des Sables HOTEL $
(0524 847274; Ave Allal Ben Abdallah; s/d Dh80/150, without bathroom Dh60/90) Off-duty desert guides unwind in these basic, tidy rooms right off the main drag. You might be able to coax out stories of travellers over tasty tajine meals at the outdoor cafe (set menu Dh40 to Dh50).

Dar Raha GUESTHOUSE $
(0524 846993; www.darraha.com; Amezrou; s/d with half board Dh235/310) 'How thoughtful!' is the operative phrase here, with oasis-appropriate details such as local palm

mats, recycled wire lamps and thick straw *pisé* (earthen) walls eliminating the need for a pool or air-con. Enjoy home-cooked meals and check out the exhibition of local paintings and crafts.

Information

Banks with ATMs and normal banking hours are on Blvd Mohammed V, along with internet cafes.

Getting There & Away

The **CTM bus station** (☎0524 847327) is at the southwestern end of Blvd Mohammed V, and the main bus and *grand taxi* lot is at the northern end. CTM has a daily service to Marrakesh (Dh100) and Casablanca (Dh175) via Ouarzazate. Other companies also operate buses to Boumalne du Dadès (Dh75) and Erfoud (Dh85).

M'hamid

M'hamid's star attraction is **Erg Chigaga**, a mind-boggling 40km stretch of golden Saharan dunes. It's 56km away – a couple of hours by 4WD or several days by camel. A closer alternative is **Erg Lehoudi** (in bad need of rubbish collection). **Sahara Services** (☎0661 776766; www.saharaservices.info) and **Zbar Travel** (☎0668 517280; www.zbar-travel.com) offer tours – an overnight camel trek should start at about Dh400. M'Hamid Bali, the old town, is 3km away across the Oued Drâa, with a well-preserved kasbah.

If you're not sleeping with your camel in the dunes, **Dar Sidi Bounou** (☎0524 846330; www.darsidibounou.com; s/d with full board in tent/hut/r Dh330/420/540) is a desert dream. **Camping Hammada du Drâa** (☎0524 848080; campsites/Berber tents per person Dh15/50, per car Dh20) offers simpler fare.

There's a daily CTM bus to Zagora (Dh25, two hours), Ouarzazate (Dh70, seven hours) and Marrakesh (Dh120, 11 to 13 hours), plus an assortment of private buses, minibuses and *grands taxis*.

Merzouga & the Dunes

Morocco's greatest Saharan *erg* (sand sea) is **Erg Chebbi**. It's an impressive, drifting chain of sand dunes that deserves much more than the sunrise or sunset glimpse many visitors give it. The largest dunes are near the villages of Merzouga and Hassi Labied. At night, you only have to walk a little way into the sand, away from the light, to appreciate the immense clarity of the desert sky and the brilliance of its stars.

Some 50km south of Erfoud is **Merzouga**, a tiny village with Téléboutiques, general stores, a mechanic and, of course, a couple of carpet shops. It also has a reputation for some of the pushiest touts in Moroccoo.

Most hotels offer **excursions** into the dunes, which can range from Dh80 to Dh200 for a couple of hours' sunrise or sunset camel trek. Overnight trips usually include a bed in a Berber tent, dinner and breakfast, and range from Dh300 to Dh650 per person. Outings in a 4WD are more expensive – up to Dh1200 per day for a car taking up to five passengers.

Sleeping & Eating

Chez Julia GUESTHOUSE $
(☎0535 573182; s/d/tr/q Dh200/400/600/800) Pure charm in the heart of Merzouga, Chez Julia offers nine simply furnished rooms in soft, sun-washed colours, with immaculate white-tiled shared bathrooms. The

WORTH A TRIP

TODRA GORGE

The spectacular canyons of Todra Gorge, at the end of a lush valley thick with palmeraies and Berber villages, are one of the highlights of the south. A massive fault in the plateau dividing the High Atlas from Jebel Sarhro, with a crystal-clear river emerging from it, the gorge rises to 300m at its narrowest point. It's best in the morning, when the sun penetrates to the bottom of the gorge, turning the rock from rose pink to a deep ochre.

About a 30-minute walk beyond the main gorge is the Petite Gorge. This is the starting point of many pleasant day hikes, including one starting by the Auberge-Camping Le Festival, 2km after the Petite Gorge. A good accommodation option is **Dar Ayour** (☎0524 895271; www.darayour.com; Km 13, Gorges du Todra, Tinghir; rwithout/ with bathroom Dh100/150, r incl breakfast/half board Dh200/350).

Todra Gorge is near Tinerihr, accessible by bus from Marrakesh (Dh105, five daily) via Ouazazarte. *Grands taxis* run throughout the day to Todra Gorge (Dh8).

Moroccan ladies who run the place can cook up a storm of delicious meals.

Dar el Janoub GUESTHOUSE **$$**
(☎tel/fax 0535 577852; www.dareljanoub.com; d standard/large/ste per person Dh580/725/800; ❄≋) In Hassi Labied, 5km north of Merzouga, the architect here stuck to elemental building shapes, because when you're facing the dunes, why compete? For the price, you get great rooms with a million-dirham view, half board, a pool and pure poetry.

ℹ Getting There & Away

Most hotels are located at least 1km off the road at the base of the dunes, but all are accessible by car. Supratours has a daily service to Marrakesh (Dh185) and there are plentiful *grands taxis* to Rissani (and further transport).

UNDERSTAND MOROCCO

Morocco Today

Mohammed VI has ruled since 1999 and overseen small but reformist steps, including elections, and the Mudawanna, a legal code protecting women's rights to divorce and custody. The king has also forged closer ties with Europe and overseen a tourism boom, aided in great part by the arrival of European budget airlines. Morocco's human-rights record is one of the cleaner in North Africa and the Middle East, though repressive measures were revived after September 11 and the 2003 Casablanca bombings.

Clever politicking by Mohammed VI saw the sting drawn from the Arab Spring when revolutionary events overtook Tunisia and Egypt. The nascent 20 February protest movement was overtaken by the announcement of a new constitution in 2011, drafted without consultation but approved in a national referendum. Amazigh, the main Berber language, was granted official language status, although political power continues to be concentrated in the palace rather than in a move to a more constitutional monarchy.

History

Berbers & Romans

Morocco's first-known inhabitants were Near Eastern nomads who may have been distant cousins of the ancient Egyptians. Phoenicians appear to have arrived around 800 BC. When the Romans arrived in the 4th century BC, they called the expanse of Morocco and western Algeria 'Mauretania' and the indigenous people 'Berbers', meaning 'barbarians'.

In the 1st century AD, the Romans built up Volubilis into a city of 20,000 (mostly Berber) people, but emperor Caligula declared the end of Berber autonomy in North Africa in AD 40. However, Berber rebellions in the Rif and the Atlas ultimately succeeded through a campaign of near-constant harassment.

As Rome slipped into decline, the Berbers harried and hassled any army that dared to invade, to the point where the Berbers were free to do as they pleased.

Islamic Dynasties

In the second half of the 7th century, the soldiers of the Prophet Mohammed set forth from the Arabian Peninsula. Within a century, nearly all the Berber tribes of North Africa had embraced Islam, although local tribes developed their own brand of Islamic Shi'ism, which sparked rebellion against the eastern Arabs.

By 829, local elites had established an Idrissid state, with its capital at Fez, dominating Morocco. Thus commenced a cycle of rising and falling Islamic dynasties, which included the Almoravids (1062–1147), who built their capital at Marrakesh; the Almohads (1147–1269), famous for building the Koutoubia Mosque; the Merenids (1269–1465), known for their exquisite mosques and *madrassas* (Quranic schools), especially in Fez; the Saadians (1524–1659), responsible for the Palais el-Badi in Marrakesh; and the Alawites (1659–present), who left their greatest monuments in Meknès.

France took control in 1912, making its capital at Rabat and handing Spain a token zone in the north. Opposition from Berber mountain tribes continued to simmer away and moved into political channels with the development of the Istiqlal (independence) party. Sultan Mohammed V proved vocally supportive of movements opposing colonial rule and was exiled for his pains.

Morocco Since Independence

France allowed Mohammed V to return from exile in 1955, and Morocco successfully negotiated its independence from France and Spain in 1956.

When Mohammed V died in 1961, King Hassan II became the leader of the new nation. Hassan II consolidated power by cracking down on dissent and suspending parliament for a decade. With heavy borrowing and an ever-expanding bureaucracy, Morocco was deeply in debt by the 1970s.

In 1973 the phosphate industry in the Spanish Sahara started to boom. Morocco staked its claim to the area with the 350,000-strong Green March into Western Sahara in 1975. It settled the area with Moroccans while greatly unsettling indigenous Sahrawi people agitating for self-determination. The UN brokered a cease-fire in 1991, but the promised referendum, in which the Sahrawis could choose between independence and integration with Morocco, has yet to materialise, and Western Sahara's status remains undecided in international law.

However, the growing gap between the rich and the poor ensured that dissent against the regime was widespread. Protests against price rises in 1981 prompted a government crackdown, but sustained pressure from human-rights activists achieved unprecedented results in 1991, when Hassan II founded the Truth and Reconciliation Commission to investigate human-rights abuses that occurred during his own reign – a first for a king.

Culture

Culturally, Moroccans cast their eyes in many directions – to Europe, the economically dominant neighbour; to the east and the lands of Islam; and to their traditional Berber heartland. The result is an intoxicating blend of the modern and the traditional, the liberal and the conservative, hospitality and the need to make a dirham. Away from the tourist scrum, a Moroccan proverb tells the story – 'A guest is a gift from Allah'. The public domain may belong to men, but they're just as likely to invite you home to meet the family. If this happens, consider yourself truly privileged, but remember to keep your left hand firmly out of the communal dish.

In present-day Morocco, *jellabas* (flowing cloaks) cover Western suits, turbans jostle with baseball caps, European dance music competes with sinuous Algerian rai and mobile phones ring in the midst of perhaps the greatest of all Moroccan pastimes – the serious and exuberant art of conversation. An inherently social people, Moroccans have a heightened sense of mischief, love a good laugh and will take your decision to visit their country as an invitation to talk...and drink tea and perhaps buy a carpet, a very beautiful carpet, just for the pleasure of your eyes...

People

Morocco's population is of mixed Arab-Berber descent. The population is young, growing and increasingly urbanised. Nearly 60% of Moroccans live in cities and the median age is just 25 years and decreasing – two trends that present the country with clear social and economic challenges. Fundamentalism is discouraged but remains a presence – especially among the urban poor, who have enjoyed none of the benefits of economic growth. That said, the majority of Muslims do not favour such developments and the popularity of fundamentalism is not as great as Westerners imagine.

Emigration to France, Israel and the US has reduced Morocco's once-robust Jewish community to approximately 7000 from a high of around 300,000 in 1948. The Jewish communities that once inhabited the historic *mellahs* (Jewish quarters) of Fez, Marrakesh, Essaouira and Meknès have largely relocated to Casablanca.

Arts & Crafts

Architecture

Moroccan religious buildings are adorned with hand-carved detailing, gilded accents, chiselled mosaics and an array of other decorative flourishes. A mosque consists of a courtyard, an arcaded portico and a main prayer hall facing Mecca. Great examples include the 9th-century Kairaouine Mosque in Fez and the colossal Hassan II Mosque in Casablanca. While all but the latter are closed to non-Muslims, the *madrassas* that bejewel major Moroccan cities are open for visits.

Although religious architecture dominates, Casablanca in particular boasts local architectural features grafted onto whitewashed European edifices in a distinctive crossroads style that might be described as Islamic geometry meets art deco.

The street facades of the Moroccan riads (traditional courtyard houses; also called *dars*) usually conceal an inner courtyard that allows light to penetrate during the day and cool air to settle at night. Many classy guesthouses occupy beautifully renovated traditional riads.

Music

The most renowned Berber folk group is the Master Musicians of Jajouka, who famously inspired the Rolling Stones and collaborated with them on some truly experimental fusion. Joyously bluesy with a rhythm you can't refuse, Gnaoua music, which began among freed slaves in Marrakesh and Essaouira, may send you into a trance – and that's just what it's meant to do. To sample the best Gnaoua, head to Essaouira on the third weekend in June for the Gnaoua & World Music Festival.

Rai, originally from Algeria, is one of the strongest influences on Moroccan contemporary music, incorporating elements of jazz, hip-hop and rap. A popular artist is Cheb Mami, famous for vocals on Sting's 'Desert Rose'.

Food & Drink

Influenced by Berber, Arabic and Mediterranean traditions, Moroccan cuisine features a sublime use of spices and fresh produce.

It would be a culinary crime to skip breakfast in Morocco. Sidewalk cafes and kiosks put a local twist on a Continental breakfast, with Moroccan pancakes and doughnuts, French pastries, coffee and mint tea. Follow your nose into the souqs, where you'll find tangy olives and local *jiben* (fresh goat's or cow's milk cheeses) to be devoured with fresh *khoobz* (Moroccan-style pita bread baked in a wood-fired oven).

Lunch is traditionally the biggest meal of the day in Morocco. The most typical Moroccan dish is tajine, a meat-and-vegetable stew cooked slowly in an earthenware dish. Couscous, fluffy steamed semolina served with tender meat and vegetables, is another staple. Fish dishes also make an excellent choice in coastal areas, while *harira* is a thick soup made from lamb stock, lentils, chickpeas, onions, tomatoes, fresh herbs and spices. *Bastilla,* a speciality of Fez, includes poultry (chicken or pigeon), almonds, cinnamon, saffron and sugar, encased in layer upon layer of very fine pastry.

Vegetarians shouldn't have any problems – fresh fruit and vegetables are widely available, as are lentils and chickpeas. Salads are ubiquitous, particularly *salade marocaine* made from diced green peppers, tomatoes and onion. Ask for your couscous or tajine *sans viande* (without meat), or go for beans *(loubiya)* or pea-and-garlic soup *(bsara)*.

For dessert, Moroccan patisseries concoct excellent French and Moroccan sweets. Local sweets include flaky pastries rich with nuts and aromatic traces of orange-flower water. Another variation is a *bastilla,* with toasted almonds, cinnamon and cream.

Cafe culture is alive and well in Morocco, and mint tea – the legendary 'Moroccan whisky' – is made with Chinese gunpowder tea, fresh mint and copious amounts of sugar. Fruit juices, especially freshly squeezed orange juice, are the country's greatest bargain. It's not advisable to drink tap water in Morocco. Beer is easy to find in the Villes Nouvelles – local brands include Casablanca and Flag. Morocco also produces some surprisingly good wines from the Meknès area: try President Cabernet and Medallion Cabernet for reds, or the whites Coquillages and Sémillant Blanc.

Environment

Morocco's three ecological zones – coast, mountain and desert – host more than 40 different ecosystems and provide habitat for many endemic species, including the iconic and sociable Barbary macaque (also known as the Barbary ape). The pressure upon these ecosystems from ever-more-sprawling urban areas and the encroachment of industrialisation in Morocco's wilderness has ensured that 18 mammal and 11 bird species are considered endangered.

Pollution, desertification, overgrazing and deforestation are the major environmental issues facing Morocco. Despite plantation programs and the development of new national parks, less than 0.05% of Moroccan territory is protected, one-third of Morocco's ecosystems are disappearing, 10% of vertebrates are endangered and 25,000 hectares of forest are lost every year.

SURVIVAL GUIDE

Directory A–Z

ACCOMMODATION

Hotels vary dramatically, ranging from dingy dives to fancy five-star options (the latter mostly in larger cities). Cities that see many tourists also offer gorgeous guesthouses in the style of a riad (traditional courtyard house).

Expect to pay up to Dh400 for budget-style accommodation, Dh400 to Dh800 for midrange and over Dh800 for top end. Exceptions to this are Casablanca, Essaouira, Fez, Rabat and Tangier, where budget accommodation may cost up to Dh600, midrange Dh600 to Dh1200 and top end more than Dh1200. Places include a private bathroom unless otherwise stated. Prices given are for high season and include tax; always check the price you are quoted is TTC (all taxes included).

Advance reservations are highly recommended for most places, especially in summer.

ACTIVITIES

Camel Treks & Desert Safaris

Exploring the Moroccan Sahara by camel is one of the country's signature activities and one of the most rewarding wilderness experiences, whether done on an overnight excursion or a two-week trek. The most evocative stretches of Saharan sand are Erg Chigaga (the Drâa Valley) and Erg Chebbi (Merzouga).

Autumn (September to October) and winter (November to early March) are the only seasons worth considering. Prices hover around Dh350 to Dh450 per person per day but vary depending on the number of people involved and the length of the trek.

Hammams

Visiting a *hammam* (traditional bathhouse) is a ritual at the centre of Moroccan society. Every town has at least one public *hammam*, and the big cities have fancy spas – both are deep-cleaning and relaxing. A visit to a standard *hammam* usually costs Dh10, with a massage costing an extra Dh15 or so.

Hiking

Morocco is a superb destination for mountain lovers, offering a variety of year-round hiking possibilities. It's relatively straightforward to arrange guides, porters and mules for a more independent adventure. Jebel Toubkal (4167m), the highest peak in the High Atlas, attracts the lion's share of visitors, but great possibilities exist throughout the country, including in the Rif Mountains around Chefchaouen. The Dadès and Todra Gorges also offer good hiking opportunities. Spring and autumn are the best seasons for trekking.

EMBASSIES & CONSULATES

For details of all Moroccan embassies abroad and foreign embassies in Morocco, go to www.maec.gov.ma.

Many countries have representation in Rabat. Ireland has no embassy, but some consular services are provided by the Canadian embassy.

Belgian Embassy (☎0537 268060; info@ambabel-rabat.org.ma; 6 Ave de Marrakesh)

Canadian Embassy (☎0537 687400; fax 0537 687430; 13 Rue Jaafar as-Sadiq, Agdal)

French Embassy (☎0537 689700; www.ambafrance-ma.org; 3 Rue Sahnoun, Agdal) There is also a French Consulate-general (☎037 268181; Rue Alla Ben Abdallah, Rabat; ⊙visa applications 8.30-11.30am Mon-Fri, visa pick-up 1.30-3pm Mon-Fri). Consulates-General are also in Agadir, Casablanca, Tangier, Marrakesh and Fez.

German Embassy (☎0537 709662; www.amballemagne-rabat.ma; 7 Rue Madnine)

Italian Embassy (☎0537 706598; ambaciata@iambitalia.ma; 2 Rue Idriss el-Azhar)

Japanese Embassy (☎0537 631782; fax 0537 750078; 39 Ave Ahmed Balafrej, Souissi)

Mauritanian Embassy (☎0537 656678; ambassadeur@mauritanie.org.ma; 7 Rue Thami Lamdaouar, Soussi)

Dutch Embassy (☎0537 219600; nlgovrab@mtds.com; 40 Rue de Tunis)

Spanish Embassy (☎0537 633900; emb.rabat@mae.es; Rue Ain Khalouiya, Km 5.300, Rte des Zaers, Souissi) Consulates are also located in Agadir, Casablanca, Nador, Rabat, Tangier and Tetouan.

UK Embassy (☎0537 238600; www.britain.org.ma; 17 Blvd de la Tour Hassan)

US Embassy (☎0537 762265; www.usembassy.ma; 2 Ave de Marrakesh)

EMERGENCIES

Ambulance (☎15)

Fire (☎16)

Police (☎19)

FESTIVALS & EVENTS

Religious festivals are significant for Moroccans. Local *moussems* (saints days) are held all over the country throughout the year and some draw big crowds. The Fez Festival of World Sacred Music (p121) is always a favourite.

Gnaoua & World Music Festival (www.festival-gnaoua.co.ma; Essaouira) Held in June.

Moussem of Moulay Idriss II (Fez) September/October.

GAY & LESBIAN TRAVELLERS

Homosexual acts are officially illegal in Morocco. Discretion is the key and public displays of affection should be avoided (aggression towards gay travellers is not unheard of). This advice applies equally to heterosexual couples.

Marrakesh and Tangier are more gay-friendly, with 'gay' bars found here and there. Lesbians shouldn't encounter any problems.

It is also worth bearing in mind that the pressures of poverty mean some young men will consider having sex for money or gifts; and exploitative relationships can be an unpleasant dimension of the Moroccan gay scene.

INTERNET ACCESS

Internet access is widely available, efficient and cheap (Dh5 to Dh10 per hour) in internet cafes. One irritant for travellers is the widespread use of French or Arabic (non-qwerty) keyboards.

Most top-end and many midrange hotels offer wi-fi, and it's more or less standard in most riads and *maisons d'hôtes*.

MONEY

The Moroccan currency is the dirham (Dh), which is divided into 100 centimes. It's forbidden to take dirhams out of the country. The Spanish enclaves of Ceuta and Melilla use the euro.

ATMs *(guichets automatiques)* are widespread and generally take international bank cards. Major credit cards are widely accepted in the main tourist centres. Australian, Canadian and New Zealand dollars are not quoted in banks and are not usually accepted.

Tipping

Tipping and bargaining are integral parts of Moroccan life. Practically any service can warrant a tip, and a few dirham for a service willingly rendered can make your life a lot easier. Tipping between 5% and 10% of a restaurant bill is appropriate.

OPENING HOURS

Cafes 7am to 11pm.

Restaurants Noon to 3pm and 7pm to 11pm.

Shops 9am to 12.30pm and 2.30pm to 8pm Monday to Saturday (often closed longer from noon on Friday).

Tourist offices 8.30am to 12.30pm and 2.30pm to 6.30pm Monday to Thursday.

POST

Post offices are distinguished by the 'PTT' sign or the 'La Poste' logo. You can sometimes buy stamps at *tabacs*, the small tobacco and newspaper kiosks you see scattered about the main city centres.

The postal system is fairly reliable but not terribly fast. The parcel office, indicated by the sign *'colis postaux'*, is generally in a separate part of the post-office building. Take your parcel unwrapped for customs inspection. Some parcel offices sell boxes.

PUBLIC HOLIDAYS

All banks, post offices and most shops are shut on the main public holidays.

PRACTICALITIES

- **Newspapers** For a full list of Moroccan newspapers online, go to **onlinenewspapers.com.** (www.onlinenewspapers.com/morocco.htm)
- **Radio** Moroccan radio encompasses a handful of local AM and FM stations, the bulk of which broadcast in either Arabic or French. Midi 1 at 97.5 FM covers northern Morocco, Algeria and Tunisia, and plays reasonable contemporary music.
- **TV** Satellite dishes are everywhere in Morocco and pick up dozens of foreign stations. There are two government-owned stations, TVM and 2M, which broadcast in Arabic and French.
- **Electricity** Electric current is 220V/50Hz but older buildings may still use 110V. Moroccan sockets accept the European round two-pin plugs.
- **Languages** Moroccan Arabic (Darija), French and Berber.

New Year's Day 1 January

Independence Manifesto 11 January

Labour Day 1 May

Feast of the Throne 30 July

Allegiance of Oued-Eddahab 14 August

Anniversary of the King's and People's Revolution 20 August

Young People's Day 21 August

Anniversary of the Green March 6 November

Independence Day 18 November

In addition to secular holidays there are many national and local Islamic holidays and festivals, all tied to the lunar calendar.

Eïd al-Adha Marks the end of the Islamic year. Most things shut down for four or five days.

Eïd al-Fitr Held at the end of the month-long Ramadan fast, which is observed by most Muslims. The festivities last four or five days, during which Morocco grinds to a halt. Ramadan will most likely fall in summer when you read this.

Mawlid an-Nabi (Mouloud) Celebrates the birthday of the Prophet Mohammed.

SAFE TRAVEL

Plenty of *kif* (marijuana) is grown in the Rif Mountains, but possession is illegal and drug busts are common.

A few years ago the *brigade touristique* (tourist police) was set up in the principal tourist centres to clamp down on Morocco's notorious *faux guides* and hustlers. Anyone convicted of operating as an unofficial guide faces jail time and/or a huge fine. This has reduced but not eliminated the problem of *faux guides*. You'll still find plenty of these touts hanging around the entrances to medinas and train stations (and even on trains approaching Fez and Marrakesh), and at Tangier port. Remember that their main interest is the commission gained from certain hotels or on articles sold to you in the souqs.

If possible, avoid walking alone at night in the medinas of the big cities; knife-point muggings aren't unknown.

TELEPHONE

Privately run Téléboutiques can be found in every town and village on almost every corner. Public payphones are card operated, with *télécartes* (phonecards) sold in general stores and news kiosks.

All domestic phone calls in Morocco require a 10-digit number, which includes the four-digit area code. The country code is ☎212.

Morocco has three GSM mobile phone networks, Méditel, Maroc Telecom and Inwi, which cover 90% of the population. A local SIM card costs around Dh20; top-up scratch cards are sold everywhere.

TOURIST INFORMATION

The national tourism body, **Office National Marocain du Tourisme** (ONMT; www.visit-morocco.com), has offices in the main cities, with the head office in Rabat. These offices are often called Délégation Régionale du Tourisme. Regional offices, called Syndicat d'Initiative, are to be found in smaller towns. Most tourist offices inside Morocco offer little more than standard brochures and helpless smiles.

VISAS

Most visitors to Morocco do not require visas and are allowed to remain in the country for 90 days on entry. Exceptions to this include nationals of Israel, and most sub-Saharan African countries (including South Africa). Moroccan embassies have been known to insist that you get a visa from your country of origin. Should the standard 90-day stay be insufficient, it is possible (but difficult) to apply at the nearest police headquarters (Préfecture de Police) for an extension – it's simpler to leave (eg travel to the Spanish enclaves of Ceuta and Melilla) and come back a few days later. Your chances improve if you re-enter by a different route. The Spanish enclaves have the same visa requirements as mainland Spain.

Visas for Onward Travel

Algeria Although Algeria has now emerged from over a decade of civil war, the border with Morocco remains closed and visas are not being issued.

Mauritania Everyone, except nationals of Arab League countries and some African countries, needs a visa, which is valid for a one-month stay. These are issued in 24 hours at the Mauritanian embassy in Rabat (apply before noon). Visas cost Dh340, with two photos and a passport photocopy. An onward air ticket to Nouakchott is not required. Get to the embassy well before the 9am opening time, and be prepared to fight for your place in the queue.

WOMEN TRAVELLERS

Women can expect a certain level of sexual harassment when travelling in Morocco. It comes in the form of nonstop greetings, leering and other unwanted attention but is rarely dangerous. If possible, it's best to try and ignore this attention. Women can save themselves a great deal of grief by avoiding eye contact, dressing to cover their knees and shoulders, and refraining from walking around alone at night.

ℹ Getting There & Away

AIR

Morocco's two main international entry points are **Mohammed V international airport** (☎022 539040; www.onda.ma), 30km southeast of Casablanca, and Marrakesh's **Ménara Airport** (☎0524 447865). Other international airports are in Fez, Tangier and Agadir.

International Airlines in Morocco

Air Algérie (AH; ☎0522 314181; www.airalgerie.dz)

Air France (www.airfrance.com)

Alitalia (AZ; ☎0522 314181; www.alitalia.it)

British Airways (BA; ☎0522 229464; www.ba.com)

EasyJet (EZY; www.easyjet.com)

Iberia (IB; ☎0522 279600; www.iberia.com)

KLM-Royal Dutch Airlines (KL; ☎0522 203222; www.klm.com)

Lufthansa Airlines (LH; ☎0522 312371; www.lufthansa.com)

Royal Air Maroc (RAM; ☎0522 311122; www.royalairmaroc.com)

Ryanair (www.ryanair.com)

Tunis Air (TU; ☎0522 293452; www.tunisair.com.tn)

LAND

The Moroccan bus company **CTM** (☎in Casablanca 0522 458080; www.CTM.co.ma) operates buses from Casablanca and most other main cities to France, Belgium, Spain, Germany and Italy. It's part of the **Eurolines** (www.eurolines.com) consortium.

Algeria

The border with Algeria has been closed since 1994 and is not expected to open any time soon.

Mauritania

The trans-Saharan route via Mauritania is now the most popular route from North Africa into sub-Saharan Africa. This crosses the internationally disputed territory of Western Sahara, although the border itself is administered by Morocco.

The only border crossing between Morocco/Western Sahara and Mauritania is at Guegarat, north of Nouâdhibou. Crossing this border is straightforward and the road is entirely tarred to Nouakchott, except for the 3km no-man's-land that separates the two border posts. For more detailed information see p385.

SEA

Regular ferries run to Europe from several ports along Morocco's Mediterranean coast. The most trafficked is Tangier, from where there are boats to Algeciras (60 to 70 minutes) and Tarifa (35 minutes, five daily) in Spain, and Gibraltar. Ferries also run from Ceuta to Algeciras. Typical fares are around €35. Bringing a bicycle costs €8 to €15 extra, while a car adds €60 to €80. Children are half price.

Getting Around

AIR

Royal Air Maroc (RAM; ☎0890 000800; www.royalairmaroc.com) dominates the Moroccan airline industry, with Casablanca as its hub. For most routes, flying is an expensive and inconvenient option compared to road or rail.

BUS

A dense network of buses operates throughout Morocco, with many private companies competing for business alongside the comfortable and modern buses of the main national carrier, CTM (p140).

The ONCF (p141) train company runs buses through Supratours to widen its train network; for example, running connections from Marrekesh to Essaouira. Morocco's other bus companies are all privately owned and only operate regionally. It's best to book ahead for CTM and Supratours buses, which are slightly more expensive than those of other companies.

CAR & MOTORCYCLE

Taking your own vehicle to Morocco is straightforward. In addition to a vehicle registration document and an International Driving Permit (many foreign licences, including US and EU ones, are acceptable), a Green Card is required from the car's insurer. Not all insurers cover Morocco.

Renting a car in Morocco isn't cheap, with prices starting at Dh3500 per week or Dh500 per day for a basic car with unlimited mileage. International rental companies are well represented; booking in advance online secures the best deals.

In Morocco drive on the right-hand side. On a roundabout, give way to traffic entering from the right.

LOCAL TRANSPORT

Cities and bigger towns have local *petits taxis*. They are not permitted to go beyond the city limits, are licensed to carry up to three passengers and are usually metered. Fares increase by 50% after 8pm.

The old Mercedes vehicles belting along roads and gathered in great flocks near bus stations are *grands taxis* (shared taxis), linking towns to their nearest neighbours. *Grands taxis* take six cramped passengers and leave when full.

TRAIN

Morocco's train network is run by **ONCF** (www.oncf.org.ma). There are two lines that carry passengers: from Tangier in the north down to Marrakesh; and from Oujda in the northeast, also to Marrakesh, joining with the Tangier line at Sidi Kacem.

Trains are comfortable, fast and generally preferable to buses. There are different 1st- and 2nd-class fares, but 2nd class is usually more than adequate on any journey. Couchettes are available on the overnight trains between Marrakesh and Tangier. Children aged under four travel free. Those aged between four and 12 years get a reduction of 10% to 50%, depending on the service.

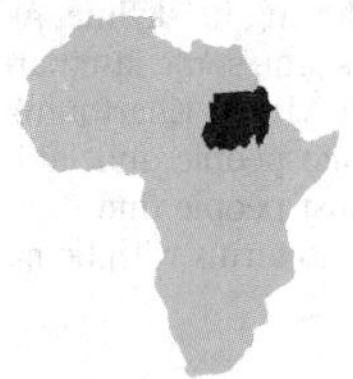

Sudan

Includes ➡

Best Ancient Sites

- Begrawiya pyramids (p151)
- Soleb Temple (p152)
- Jebel Barkal sites (p154)
- Kerma sites (p153)
- Nuri pyramids (p154)
- El Kurru (p154)

Best for Sudanese Culture

- Nile-side village life (p152)
- Halgt Zikr (p145)
- Nuba wrestlers (p146)
- Nuba Mountains (if safe; p157)

Why Go?

Wake at the break of day under the golden pyramids of god-like kings of old; traverse a searing desert to the place where two Niles become one and watch a million blood red fish swarm through gardens of coral. Whichever way you look at it, there's just no denying that among Sudan's sweeping hills of sand lie treasures the rest of the world are only just beginning to understand.

Until July 2011 Sudan was the biggest country in Africa, but now, with South Sudan having broken away to form a new nation, maps of Africa are being redrawn. This redefining of national boundaries is making for huge changes, geographically, politically, financially and culturally, for the Sudanese. But for a traveller some things never change; Sudanese hospitality remains second to none, and for most people, travelling through Sudan is such an eye-opening and rewarding experience that many come away saying that Sudan was their favourite country in Africa.

When to Go

Khartoum

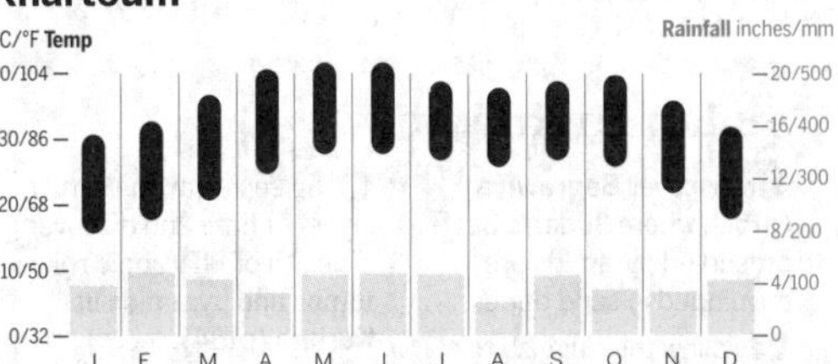

Nov–Feb Winter offers perfect temperatures and clear skies.

Sep–Oct Catch the camel races in Kassala.

Nov The European Film Festival is held in Khartoum.

KHARTOUM

POP 5,274,000 (GREATER KHARTOUM)

Built where the two Niles meet, Khartoum defies expectations. Rather than the run-down, undeveloped city many people imagine, Khartoum is a boisterous, modern, flashy city with an ever-increasing number of glass tower blocks altering its skyline. As well as an excellent museum, some fascinating souqs and Nile-side views, Khartoum's good facilities, hospitable people and laid-back vibe mean that most people find it an agreeable place to come to terms with being in Sudan.

Sudan Highlights

1. Discover **Begrawiya** (p151), where Sudan's best-preserved pyramids are enveloped in sand dunes.
2. Follow the sluggish Nile through searing desert past beautiful old ruins and remote sun-baked towns from **Wadi Halfa to Dongola** (p152).
3. Explore exotic markets and the Taka Mountains in **Kassala** (p155).
4. Sweep away the sandy layers of time and discover a wealth of Pharaonic ruins, tombs and pyramids in **Karima** (p154).
5. Be overawed by the mighty Egyptian temple of **Soleb** (p152) and look for crocodiles in the nearby Nile.
6. Relish the lush greenery of the mountains where Africa meets Arabia in the **Nuba Mountains** (but only if it's safe; p157).
7. Survey the world from the top of Kerma's **deffufa** (p153), centrepiece of one of the world's oldest towns.
8. Dive into a rainbow of colour on the pristine coral reefs of the Sudanese Red Sea near **Port Sudan** (p156).

Sights

★National Museum
MUSEUM

(Map p146; al-Nil St; admission S£2; ⏲9.30am-6.30pm Tue-Thu, Sat & Sun, 9am-midday & 3-6.30pm Fri) This museum, the best in the country, has some breathtaking exhibits. The ground floor covers the rise and fall of the kingdoms of Kerma, Kush and Meroe. There's some stunning royal statues and perfectly preserved 3500-year-old artefacts from Kerma. Upstairs are numerous medieval Christian frescos removed from the ruined churches of Old Dongola and elsewhere. Outside are some temples rescued, Abu Simbel–style, from the rising waters of Lake Nasser. Allow at least one and a half to two hours for a visit.

Ethnographical Museum
MUSEUM

(Map p148; al-Jamia St; ⏲8.30am-6pm Tue-Thu & Sat) FREE The Ethnographical Museum contains a small but fascinating collection of tribal artefacts. Displays are ordered by geographic region and illustrate how people adapt to each climatic area. It begins with what is now the tropics of South Sudan followed by the savannah regions south of Khartoum and finishes with the deserts of the north.

Natural History Museum
MUSEUM

(Map p148; al-Jamia St; admission S£2; ⏲8.30am-6pm Tue-Sun, closed noon-3pm Fri) The mostly unlabelled taxidermied animals here look happier than the handful of live crocodiles, monkeys and snakes in sorry cages outside.

Republican Palace Museum
MUSEUM

(Map p148; al-Jamia St; admission free; ⏲9am-1pm & 4-8pm Wed & Fri-Sun) A hall of heroes of sorts, with mementos such as presidential limos and General Gordon's piano. Hours are flexible!

White Nile Bridge
VIEWPOINT

(Map p146) The confluence of the Blue and White Niles, best seen from this bridge, is a languid high point of the world's longest river. You can actually see the different colours of each Nile flowing side by side before blending further downstream – although neither are blue or white! Don't attempt to take a photograph of the Nile from this bridge; numerous foreigners have been arrested for doing so.

Omdurman

This traditional Muslim city, founded by the Mahdi in the 1880s, is a big attraction

> **SET YOUR BUDGET**
>
> **Budget**
> - *Lokanda* bed US$4–6
> - Plate of *fuul* US$0.50
> - Cup of tea US$0.20
> - Four-hour bus ride US$8
>
> **Midrange**
> - Hotel room US$35–50
> - Two-course dinner US$10–15
> - Entry to historic site US$11
> - 1.5L bottled water US$0.80
>
> **Top End**
> - Hotel room US$100+
> - Two-course dinner US$20–30
> - 4WD rental US$170
> - Short taxi ride US$5

Omdurman Souq
MARKET

(Map p146) This famous souq – the largest in the country – is abuzz with noise, activity and colour, and a couple of hours exploration is bound to turn up all manner of surprises.

Camel Market
MARKET

(Off Map p146; Souq Moowaileh) On the far western edge of the city, this is spectacular, especially on Saturday, but there is no public transport (a taxi will cost at least S£75).

Mahdi's Tomb
MONUMENT

(Map p146; admission free; ⏲8am-5pm Fri) This rocket-topped tomb is worth making the effort to see. Respectifuly dressed foreigners are generally allowed inside. The original was destroyed on Kitchener's orders by General Gordon's nephew 'Monkey', who, somewhat unsportingly, threw the Mahdi's ashes into the Nile.

Khalifa's House Museum
MUSEUM

(Map p146; admission S£1; ⏲9am-1.30pm Tue-Thu, Sat & Sun) The Mahdi's successor lived across the street, and this 1887 museum showcases the history of the Mahdi era.

Hamed el-Nil Mosque
MOSQUE

(Map p146) Every Friday afternoon you can see the **Halgt Zikr**, where a colourful local troupe of whirling dervishes stirs up the dust in worship of Allah at this mosque. It starts at 4pm (5pm in winter). The atmosphere is colourful and laid-back. Note: not on in Ramadan.

Greater Khartoum

Bahri

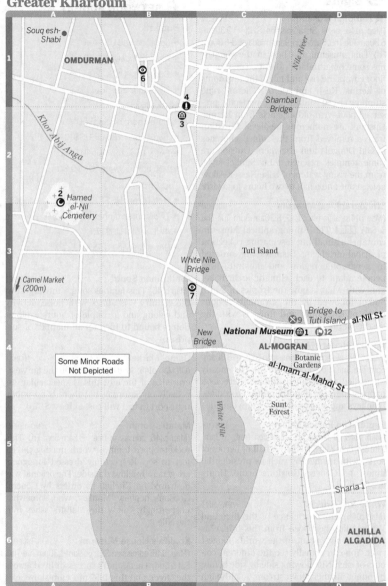

Nuba Wrestlers WRESTLING

(Map p146; Souq Seta; admission S£2) Traditional wrestlers go through their paces at 4pm on Fridays. Take a minibus from UN square to Omdurman, alight at Ghobba al-Hamed al-Nil.

Marin Water Sports Club CRUISE

(Map p148; ☎0912207565; al-Nil St; 10-/13-person boat per hr S£150/250) It's never going to be the same as a felucca ride along the Egyptian

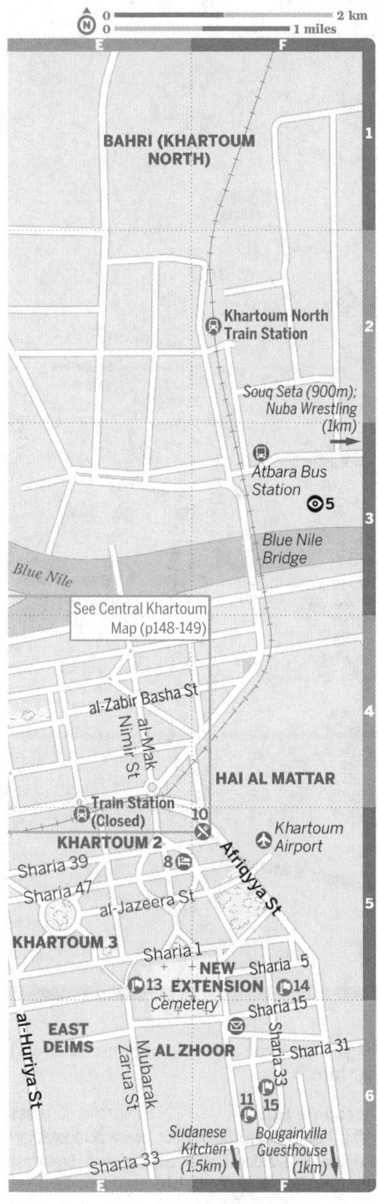

Nile; however, any Khartoum day is bound to feel better if you finish it off with a sunset cruise along the Blue Nile. This sailing club offers a variety of boats to choose from. Call and reserve in advance.

Greater Khartoum

Top Sights

1 National Museum D4

Sights

2 Hamed el-Nil Mosque A2
3 Khalifa's House Museum B2
4 Mahdi's Tomb B1
5 Nuba Wrestlers F3
6 Omdurman Souq B1
7 White Nile Bridge B3

Sleeping

8 Khartoum Youth Hostel E5

Eating

9 Askela D4
10 Tangerine F5

Information

11 Chadian Embassy F6
Dutch Embassy .... (see 8)
12 Egyptian Embassy D4
Eritrean Embassy .... (see 14)
13 Ethiopian Embassy E5
14 French Embassy F5
15 Saudi Arabian Embassy F6

Sleeping

Khartoum Youth Hostel HOSTEL $
(Map p146; 0912500322; info@sudaneseyha.net; Sharia 47; campsites S£35, dm S£70; P ✻) Far and away the best budget option in Khartoum. This is a slick and clean youth hostel run by helpful staff. Foreigners will normally be given a room containing just two beds. Good news for overlanders in their own vehicles – they allow camping in the gardens, and have safe parking and clean toilet blocks for your use.

Central Hotel HOTEL $
(Map p148; Abdul al-Munami Mhammad St; s/d S£75/85; ✻) It's not a big claim, but of the real bottom-end budget places in the city centre this is probably the best. Even so, it's still noisy and some of the bathrooms are like a disaster zone. If you're travelling alone it's worth splashing out on a double as you get a much bigger and brighter room.

Dubai Hotel HOTEL $$
(Map p148; 01837908001; Sayed Abdul Rahman St; d/tw S£117/195; ✻ @ ☎) One of the very few places in Khartoum that really feels as if it offers value for money – and it's in the rare midrange price category. The immaculate rooms are quiet, comfortable and spacious, and they combine a central location with cheery staff.

Central Khartoum

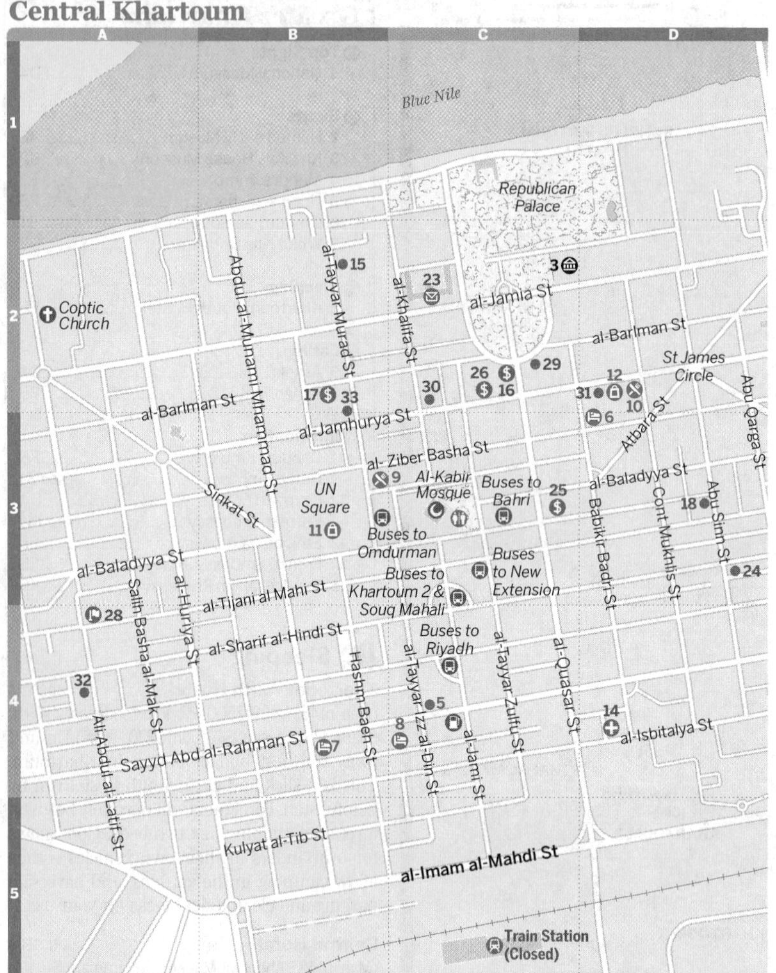

★Bougainvilla Guesthouse BOUTIQUE HOTEL **$$$**
(Off Map p146; ☎0183222104; www.bougainvillaguesthouse.net; Block 21, Riyadh; s without bathroom US$35-45 incl breakfast, s/d/tw US$55/77/77 incl breakfast; ❄@📶) Osman, the new owner of the Bougainvilla Guesthouse in the upscale Riyadh neighbourhood, has done fab things here. The stylish rooms have been totally renovated in the last two years and prices have actually been slashed by 50%. With its warm welcome, rooftop restaurant and bar, and staff who are on the ball with tourist information, it's easily the best place in town to stay. Staff can also help organise visas and car hire.

Acropole Hotel HISTORIC HOTEL **$$$**
(Map p148; ☎0183772860; www.acropolekhartoum.com; al-Ziber Basha St; s/d incl breakfast US$105/134; ❄@📶) This hotel, the first choice of journalists, reeks of history and intrigue. The Greek owners are very friendly and organise free city tours for guests on Fridays. Recent renovations to some of the rooms make it great value. Can help organise visas and tours.

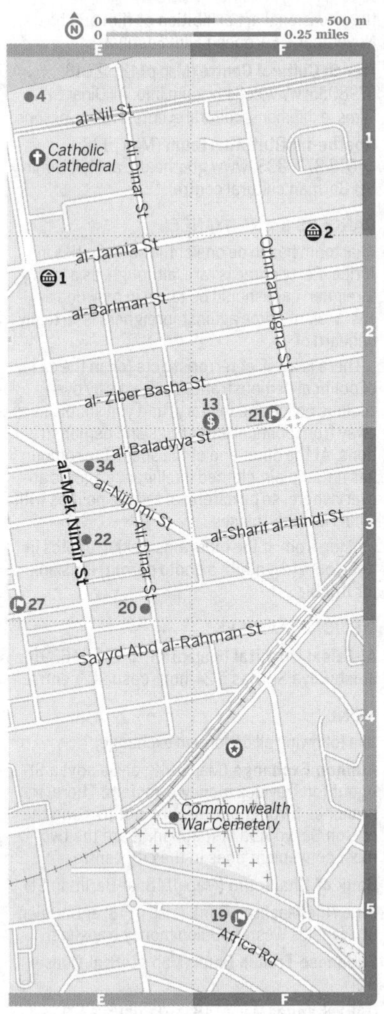

Central Khartoum

Sights

- 1 Ethnographical Museum E2
- 2 Natural History Museum F1
- 3 Republican Palace Museum C2

Activities, Courses & Tours

- 4 Marin Water Sports Club E1
- 5 Mashansharti Travel Agency C4

Sleeping

- 6 Acropole Hotel D3
- 7 Central Hotel B4
- 8 Dubai Hotel C4

Eating

- 9 Kh.T Restaurant B3
- 10 Papa Costa D2

Shopping

- 11 Al Waha Mall B3
- 12 Central Bookshop D2

Information

- 13 Alamon Exchange F2
- 14 Al-Faisal Hospital D4
- 15 Aliens Registration Office B2
- 16 Bank of Khartoum C2
- 17 Blue Nile Mashreg Bank B2
- 18 British Council D3
- British Embassy .... (see 21)
- 19 Canadan Embassy F5
- 20 French Cultural Centre E3
- 21 German Embassy F2
- 22 Goethe-Institut Khartoum E3
- 23 Main Post Office C2
- 24 Ministry of Tourism and Wildlife D3
- 25 Sudanese-French Bank C3
- 26 UAExchange C2
- 27 Ugandan Embassy E3
- 28 US Embassy A4

Transport

- 29 EgyptAir C2
- 30 Emirates C2
- 31 Ethiopian Airlines D2
- Gulf Air .... (see 33)
- 32 Kenya Airways A4
- 33 Lufthansa B2
- 34 Sudan Airways E3

Eating

The many informal, cheap joints south of Al-Kabir Mosque and around al-Tijani al Mahi St serve meals for S£2 to S£3, and plenty of larger restaurants throughout the city centre also serve kebabs, burgers and *shwarma* (a kebablike dish) for around S£3 to S£5. As a rule they're all pretty much of a muchness.

Sudanese Kitchen MIDDLE EASTERN $

(Off Map p146; ☎0905636000; Riyadh; mains S£5-10; ⏰9am-11pm) Khartoum has to be one of the few capitals in the world without a top-notch restaurant serving divine local food. The Sudanese Kitchen is far from fancy but is about as close to that lofty goal as Khartoum gets. Meals are served in 'huts' with mud walls and floors.

Kh.T Restaurant MIDDLE EASTERN $

(Map p148; UN Sq; mains S£5-16) The immensely popular Kh.T Restaurant is a canteenlike place serving lots of cheap kebabs and other Middle Eastern fast-food dishes.

Askela SUDANESE **$$**
(Map p146; al-Nil St; mains around S£30) A large riverside restaurant opposite the National Museum, with plenty of fish on the menu and wonderful views. It's also a great place for an evening drink.

Papa Costa INTERNATIONAL **$$**
(Map p148; ☎0155123260; cnr al-Jamhurya & Cont Mukhis; mains S£20-40; ⏰8.30am-midnight Mon-Thu, Sat & Sun, 11am-midnight Fri; ❄) Papa Costa was one of the original members of Khartoum's not insignificant Greek community. Back in the 1950s he set up a bakery in his home which over time has evolved into a family-run restaurant serving a broad range of international dishes such as pasta, pizzas and steaks. The food is actually only average but it's one of the few proper restaurants in the city centre. Hosts frequent live music and screens art-house films.

Tangerine INTERNATIONAL **$$$**
(Map p146; ☎0155663563; 39 St; mains S£50-75; ❄) This place, in the heart of the embassy district, touts itself as a 'boutique restaurant' and the setting is suitably classy. The food, an international mish-mash of flavours prepared by a German chef, is great for Khartoum (try the house masterpiece of a grilled prawn cake) but only so-so by international standards.

Shopping

Al Waha Mall SHOPPING CENTRE
(Map p148; UN Sq; 📶) This brand-new, glossy shopping mall half filled with flashy clothing shops and Western-style cafes is about the height of Khartoum entertainment and is always busy with local teenagers and excited families. There's a well-stocked supermarket in the basement.

Central Bookshop BOOKSHOP
(Map p148; al-Jamhurya St) Sells novels in English.

Orientation

Three cities sit at the confluence of the White and Blue Niles: Khartoum, Bahri (Khartoum North) and Omdurman, each separated by an arm of the river. You'll find everything you need in central Khartoum; continuing south, the city gets more upscale and international.

Information

CULTURAL CENTRES

British Council (Map p148; ☎0187028000; Abo Sin St; ⏰8.30am-4.30pm Sun-Thu) Hosts the occasional art exhibition or film and hosts November's European Film Festival.

French Cultural Centre (Map p148; ☎018 3798035; www.ccfkhartoum.info; Ali Dinar St) Films, exhibitions, cultural events, French lessons.

Goethe-Institut Khartoum (Map p148; ☎018 3777833; www.goethe.de; al-Mek Nimir St) German cultural centre.

DANGERS & ANNOYANCES

Khartoum has to be one of the safest cities in Africa. Petty crime is rare, although, as a 'rich' foreigner, care should be taken in crowded areas. Violent crime against foreigners is virtually unheard of.

There is a risk of terrorist acts (or, in the case of political demonstrations, attacks by overzealous police and military) and you should keep away from political gatherings and demonstrations. At the other end of the spectrum rumour has it that plain-clothed intelligence agents are everywhere, so be careful of talking politics with locals in public places.

Aside from at the museums, taking photos in Khartoum (even with a photo permit) is asking for trouble.

MEDICAL SERVICES

Al-Faisal Hospital (Map p148; ☎0183463914; al-Isbitalya St) Has a 24-hour casualty centre.

MONEY

The following all do foreign exchange.

Alamon Exchange (Map p148; al-Baladyya St) Agent for Travelex money transfers. There are branches throughout the city, but this and the one on Sayyd Abd al-Rahman St are the two most convenient ones in the city centre.

Bank of Khartoum (Map p148; al-Barlman St)

Blue Nile Mashreg Bank (Map p148; al-Barlman St) Handles Western Union money transfers.

Sudanese-French Bank (Map p148; al-Quasar St)

UAExchange (Map p148; al-Jamhurya St) Agents for Travelex money transfers. There are also other branches throughout the city.

POST

Main Post Office (Map p148; al-Khalifa St)

TRAVEL AGENCIES

There are a cluster of travel agencies selling plane tickets around the EgyptAir office on al-Barlman St.

Getting There & Away

AIR

Khartoum International Airport is virtually in the city centre but a new international airport, 40km south of Khartoum, was due to open in 2010. This was put back to 2013 but at the time of writing there was little sign of it opening soon. If and when it does open the old airport will be used for domestic flights only.

BUS

Most road transport departs from one of four bus stations.

Abu-Adam Bus Station For Dongola, Karima, Wadi Halfa and other points north use this new station to the south of the centre. A taxi from the city centre will cost a local S£50. A foreigner can expect to pay at least a third more

Atbara Bus Station In Bahri.

Mina al-barri Almost everything rolling south, east and west – including for Gedaref, Kassala and Port Sudan – goes from this modern and chaotic station near Souq Mahali in southern Khartoum. There's a S£1.50 entrance fee even if you're just reserving a ticket.

Souq esh-Shabi Further buses to the north, as well as El-Obeid, use this station in Omdurman.

Getting Around

Buses (S£1) and minibuses (S£1.50) cover most points in Khartoum and run early to very late.

Taxi prices (if they have no passengers the minibuses work like taxis and often cost less) are negotiable: expect to pay around S£10 to S£20 for journeys within the city centre and S£30 to S£50 to destinations within greater Khartoum. For shorter trips (except in central Khartoum) there are also cheaper motorised rickshaws.

You have more chance of building a snowman in the Sahara than persuading a taxi driver to take you the short distance from the airport to downtown for anything less than S£50.

AROUND KHARTOUM

Meroe Sites

The one sight that is seen by almost all of Sudan's very few visitors are the deeply romantic pyramids of Begrawiya, but there are a couple of other ancient sites, Naqa and Musawarat, on the way up from Khartoum, that are also well worth taking the time to see.

★Begrawiya MONUMENT

(Meroe Pyramids; admission S£50; ⏲6am-6pm) Seemingly lost under the folds of giant apricot-coloured dunes, this ancient royal cemetery, with its clusters of narrow pyramids blanketing the sandswept hills, is one of the most spectacular sights in Sudan – and the best thing is that you'll probably have the place largely to yourself. The Meroitic Pharaohs thrived from the 8th century BC until a combination of encroaching desert and marauding Abyssinians put an end to Begrawiya's use as a royal cemetery in AD 350. Some of the tombs' antechambers contain well-preserved hieroglyphics. There are two main groups of pyramids here seperated by several hundred metres of sandy desert. In total there are about 100 pyramids, or remains of pyramids.

Many of the pyramids are missing their tops thanks to a 19th-century Italian 'archaeologist' who thought treasure might be contained within. Rather than going about the laborious task of opening them properly he merely chopped the tops off and, somewhat to the surprise of many people, he did indeed find treasure.

On the opposite side of the road to the main pyramids are the **Noble Tombs**, a collection of several dozen far smaller pyramids. Entry is free. From these head straight west towards the Nile and you'll come across the **Royal City** (admission S£50), where the so-called Roman bath is the top attraction. In truth this site is very ramshakle and overgrown and probably only of interest to an archaeologist.

Naqa & Musawarat MONUMENT

(admission Naga S£50, Musawarat S£50; ⏲6am-6pm) These two Meroitic sites lie in an area of wild and remote desert 35km off the highway southeast of Shendi, and are about the same distance from each other.

Naqa consists of a large and well-preserved temple of Amun dating from the 1st century. Very close by is the Lion Temple. Dating from the same period, this temple is dedicated to the lion-headed god Apedemak and has wonderful exterior carvings depicting the temples creators, King Natakamani and Queen Amanitore. The exact purpose of the site remains unclear as it's located in an area that has never really been inhabited.

Musawarat is the largest Meroitic temple complex in Sudan. Like Naqa, its purpose remains a little unclear though it's believed to have served as a pilgrimage site. The enormous Great Enclosure consists of numerous tumbledown columns and walls carved with reliefs of the wild animals that once inhabited this region. Check out the former elephant stables and the marriage room with the engravings of newlyweds getting to know one another. A few hundred metres away is another large Lion Temple dating to the 3rd century BC.

To get to either of these sites you will need your own transport. The sites are signposted to the right (if coming from Khartoum) next to a Nile Petroleum station off the Khartoum–Atbara road. Follow the dirt tracks through the desert sticking close to the telegraph wires (keep these on your left). At the fork take the left trail for Musawarat and the right for Naqa.

Sleeping

Muzn Beach Resort HOTEL **$$**
(☎0912642566; dm S£100, d & tw S£200; ❄) Just a kilometre or so south of the pyramids on the main road, this new complex is part of a petrol station. Despite being almost new we wouldn't be at all surprised if it has fallen down in a few years – yes, it's that kind of place.

Meroe Tented Camp TENTED CAMP **$$$**
(☎0915124871; www.italtoursudan.com; s/tw with half-board S£817/920; ⊙Oct-Apr) If you want to catch the sunset over the Begrawiya pyramids, you can camp in the desert (head towards the mountains) or splash out here, close to the pyramids, which has comfy walk-in safari-style tents with exterior bathrooms. The food is good and sitting outside watching the stars rain down over you at night is almost perfect.

Getting There & Away

These ruins are easily visited from Khartoum. If you hire a car and driver (starting at about US$100 plus fuel), you can visit the Sixth Cataract (Sabalooka Falls) too. A pick-up truck in Shendi should cost around half that. Begrawiya is just 700m off the highway and easily reached by public transport: take an Atbara bus (S£35) from Bahri and ask to be let out at Al-Ahram (Pyramids). Coming back, flag down vehicles heading south; you'll probably have to change in Shendi. Note that while most tourists refer to the pyramids at Begrawiya as Meroe, if you were to tell a Sudanese person that you want to go to Meroe, you'll probably end up by the dam near Karima.

NORTHERN SUDAN

Wadi Halfa

POP 15,725

Wadi Halfa is where the ferry to Egypt docks. And that's really about all that can be said for the place!

The only real difference between the half-dozen or so rough *lokandas* (basic accommodation; dorm bed S£15) is in the names, snag the first bed you can find when the ferry is in town because they fill fast.

Most transport runs in line with the ferry. You can get off the boat and right onto a bus to Khartoum (S£120, 10 to 12 hours) or, better, make the journey in stages (to Arbi S£30). Nowadays the trains to Khartoum only carry freight.

Wadi Halfa to Dongola

Hundreds of historic sites and some striking desert and river scenery line this 400km stretch of the Nile, while the many villages offer a fascinating taste of Nubian life. For many this is the highlight of Sudan.

Buses and *bokasi* (minibuses) run fairly frequently between all these towns and Dongola and Wadi Halfa.

Abri

The first significant town on the stretch between Wadi Hald and Dongola is Abri (market day is Monday), the base for visiting **Sai Island** (admission S£50), 10km south. With a temple from Egypt's Middle Kingdom, a medieval church and an Ottoman fort among the many ruins, Sai Island is something of a synopsis of ancient Sudanese history. None of the sites are in good condition, but walking between them is fun. The fort is actually built on the foundations of a 1500 BC Egyptian town. The ground around the ruins is littered with millions of bits of broken pottery – you are literally walking on history! Little but some upright granite columns and a few walls remain of the medieval church, but physically it's probably the most striking site on the island. Most of the sites on the island are close to the river and the most enjoyable way to get between them is to hire a boat for a couple of hours. **Mr Shorbatjiy** (☎0122028966; half-day S£80) has a good boat and knows all the sites. He can also help organise a homestay on the island. More formal lodging is available at **El-Fager** (dm S£10), Abri's only *lokanda*, but it certainly can't be described as the nicest hotel we've ever seen.

Soleb

A little south of Abri, the wonderfully evocative Egyptian temple of **Soleb** (admission S£50) is the highlight of this part of Sudan. It's not just that this enormous temple is visually stunning, but getting to it is a right rollicking *Boys Own* adventure. This involves getting to the tiny east-coast village of Wawa, finding the boat man (S£50 return with waiting time) and puttering across an especially beautiful stretch of the Nile (if you fancied a swim then take note that we saw two impressively large and unfriendly-looking crocodiles sunning themselves on the sand-bank isle in the middle of the river). Once on the west bank walk through the palm groves and there, on the edge of fertility and desolation, sits the temple. It was built in the 14th century BC by Amenhotep III, the same Pharaoh who gave us Luxor in Egypt, and the design and carvings are similar.

Sesibi

South of Soleb, and on the west bank, are the remains of the Egyptian town of Sesibi. Founded in the 14th century BC by Akhenaten (who is known for having abandoned the classical Egyptian gods to worship the sun disc Aten). Today the site is pretty ramshackle but at sunset the remaining temple columns are wildly exotic. To get here head first for the east-coast village of Delgo where a car ferry (car and passengers S£20) crosses the river to the village of Kuka a couple of times a day. From Kuka it's a good 7km drive north to Sesibi. If you get stuck for the night the ferry man, **Mohamed Abdul Halim** (☎0128129641), can sort you out with a bed in his house. There is also a guest house, the **Tourist Motel** (☎0117 839202), not far from the temple. This seemed very pleasent from the outside, but sadly it was locked and the owner wasn't around so we were unable to verify anything more about it. If you want to stay then arrange it in advance.

Dongola

Famous for its palm groves, the relaxed little town of Dongola is full of character and boasts good amenities. The east-bank ruins

DON'T MISS

KERMA

The seemingly insignificant town of Kerma may have been largely left behind by the rest of the world today, but that wasn't always the case. This is one of the oldest inhabited towns in Africa and a place of immense historical importance. The area around Kerma has been occupied for at least 8000 to 10,000 years, but the town reached its peak around 1800 BC to 1600 BC when it was capital of the Kingdom of Kush and an important trade centre during Egypt's Middle Kingdom. It was at this time that Kerma's kings built two giant mudbrick temples, known as *deffufas*; the oldest, and arguably largest, mudbrick buildings on the continent.

The **western deffufa** (admission S£50, camera S£5; ⏲8.30am-sunset Tue-Sun) stood about 19m high and stretched 50m long. Nobody is really certain what it was used for but most agree it served a religious purpose. Today it has crumbled into an oddly appealing form and you can still climb to the top. Next to the *deffufa* is a **museum** (admission S£10; ⏲8.30am-sunset Tue-Sun) that contains interesting relics from the site. Although both these are technically closed on Monday, if you do turn up then someone will be sent to find the keys and open up. About 3km away is the smaller, **eastern deffufa** (at the time of writing it was closed to the public due to archaeolgical digs). This is thought to have been a royal cemetery. Around the kings' tombs archaeologists have discovered some 30,000 other graves. Many of the people buried in these graves appear to have been ritually sacrificed in order to accompany the king to the underworld. Archaeologists have also unearthed around 5000 cattle skulls encircling the human graves, a, which indicates just how important cattle were to the people who once lived here.

In addition to the two *deffufas* there are a number of other historic sites around the town including **Duki Gail**, a little-understood site containing the remains of a huge temple with 2m-thick walls. The site is closed to the public most of the time but between December and Februaury a French archaeologist is often to be found working here and he might give interested parties a quick tour.

Accommodation is limited to a couple of rough *lokandas* in Kerma village and Burgig village (which is closer to the western *deffufa*).

of the **Temple of Kawa**, which are almost totally buried under sand, are about 4km south of the bus station and are a little hard to find. Many people find the two-hour walk there along the banks of the Nile more of a highlight than the temple.

Most hotels and restaurants are clustered together on the main road, near the market. The best place to stay in town by far is the **Candaca Nubian House** (Nubian Guest House; ☎0915545337; https://sites.google.com/site/nubianhouse; campsites US$7, with breakfast dm US$10, tw US$40; P ❄ @), just a little way north of the centre. This brightly painted building is run by a knowledgable South Korean family and is basically the closest Sudan gets to a backpacker hotel. The rooms come in an array of sizes and styles and camping in the courtyard is also possible. In the town centre the **Al-Muallem** (☎0241824425; tw S£100) has smart and clean rooms and a cheery owner but they are sometimes reluctant to rent rooms to foreigners. Of the many *lakondas* the **Binna Tourist Hotel and Cafeteria** (☎0906478440; dm S£10, r S£50) is the most inviting.

Buses run to Kerma (S£10, one hour), Karima (S£25, 2½ hours) and Khartoum (S£60, six hours).

Karima

Karima itself is just a dusty Nile-side Nubian village. If it weren't for its extraordinary collection of ancient sites, which together have given the whole area Unesco World Heritage status, there would be little reason to stop here. As it is though, the majesty of Karima's past will probably remain with you for a long time.

Sights

Jebel Barkal, the table-topped mountain hanging on the town's south side, was sacred ground for the Egyptians at the time of the 18th-dynasty pharaohs. Both they and the Kushites believed that the mountain was home to the god Amun and if you look closely (and with a little imagination!) at the needle of rock sticking out of the mountain's southern side you can make out the shape of a cobra wearing a crown; the symbol of the king. At the base of the mountain are some well-preserved **pyramids** and the **Temple of Amun**. Buried into the belly of the mountain, and immediately below the needle of rock, is the fresco-decorated **Temple of Mut** (admission S£30), dedicated to the Egyptian sky goddess. There's a small **museum** (admission S£5; ⏲8.30am-3pm Sat-Thu) containing finds from around Jebel Barkal close to the Temple of Amun.

Across the river at **Nuri** (admission S£30; ⏲6am-sunset), there are some delightfully dilapidated pyramids – among the largest in Sudan – lost among a stormy sea of orange sand. Dating from around the 7th century BC, these are both the oldest and largest pyramids in Sudan. Take a minibus (S£2, 30 minutes) from Karima. The royal cemetery of **El Kurru** (☎0910983391; admission S£30), 20km south of Karima, contains the remains of dozens of tombs. Most have either faded away to virtually nothing, or the entrances have been buried under tonnes of sand. However, two tombs, cut into the rock and containing wonderfully preserved paintings, can still be entered. Dating to the 7th century BC, they were the final resting place of King Tanwetamani and his mother, Queen Qalhata. The tombs are kept locked and you might have to ask about the village for the guardian to come and open up. To get to El Kurru take a minibus (S£20, 30 minutes) from Karima. You must buy an entry ticket from the museum in Karima in advance.

Sleeping

Al Nasser HOTEL
(dm/tw S£15/30) A cleaner and greener *lokanda* than most.

Ahmed Mousa Homestay GUESTHOUSE
(☎0912585462; per person S£50) The best budget place to stay. Ahmed has a couple of clean rooms with fans set around a sandy, chicken-filled courtyard. The communal bathrooms are spotless. You can normally find him at the ticket office for the museum, where he works, otherwise call ahead for directions.

Nubian Rest-House LODGE
(☎0115545201, Khartoum 0231820368; www.italtoursudan.com; s/d with half-board S£868/1004) This lovely mudbrick Nubian-style structure is built around lush, flowering gardens at the foot of Jebel Barkal.

Getting There & Away

There are frequent buses to Dongola (S£40, 2½ hours) and Atbara (S£50, four hours), as well as less-regular ones to Khartoum (S£55, six hours) and Wadi Halfa (S£145, 10 hours).

WORTH A TRIP

OLD DONGOLA

If you're travelling in your own car between Dongola and Karima it's well worth making the short detour to beautiful, sandswept **Old Dongola** (admission S£30) with its faded Christian glories and massive Sufi saints' tombs.

The city was capital of the Christian kingdom of Makuria between the 7th and 14th centuries and at its peak it was home to dozens of churches. The churches were generally plain on the outside but the interiors were painted in beautiful frescos – some of which are now to be found in Khartoum's National Museum. Today little but scattered blocks, tumbledown walls and leaning columns remain of Old Dongola, but the setting is sublime and chances are you'll have the place to yourself.

A few hundred metres from the main Christian sites is a large Islamic cemetery containing several massive mudbrick, slightly pyramid-like Sufi saints' tombs.

To get to Old Dongola follow the Dongola–Khartoum road as far as the town of Ed-Debba, cross the Nile on the new bridge, turn west and follow the road for 20 minutes until you see the tombs. To get to Karima you needn't cross back over the Nile but can race along the new road on the northern side of the river.

Atbara

POP 107,903

Hot, dusty, noisy – and did we mention hot? Atbara is not a place that many people would wish to linger in. Fortunately, with Sudan's ever-improving transport infrastructure you're unlikely to need to spend longer than a night here. However it makes a useful overnight stop if you've come up from Khartoum, visited the pyramids at Begrawiya and are looking to continue onwards to Karima the next day.

Sleeping

Nile Hotel HOTEL $$
(☎0912994029; s/d S£60/80; ❄) This bright and friendly hotel is a bit of a hike north of the town centre (call for directions), but it has smart, clean rooms, with hot water in the shared showers. There's a pretty garden to kick back in and meals can be prepared.

Al-Asfia A Hotel HOTEL $$
(☎0912343910; r from S£130; ❄ 📶) Close to the railway lines on the southern edge of town, this is considered the best hotel in central Atbara and while most of the rooms are not bad you should avoid the roasting-hot ones up on the roof.

Getting There & Away

There are many buses to Khartoum (S£35, 4½ hours) and several through the desert to Port Sudan (S£65, six hours), plus some to Karima (S£50, four hours).

EASTERN SUDAN

Kassala

POP 419,000

Kassala, with its wonderful setting at the foot of the melting granite peaks of the **Taka Mountains**, is where half the tribes of northern Sudan seem to meet. Its huge souqs are an ethnic mosaic of colours, smells, noises and experiences. There are famous **camel races** annually in September or October.

At the base of the mountains is the **Khatmiyah Mosque**, centre of the Khatmiyah Sufi sect. It's a lovely mudbrick building and non-Muslims are quite welcome to take a peek about. Afterwards have a little scramble around the bizarre peaks of the Taka Mountains.

What makes the **Kassala Hotel** (☎091 5659190; dm S£15, r without bathroom S£50; ❄) stand out from the rest of the really cheap options is that it's been recently painted and tidied up – a rare event indeed in Sudan! The **El-Nada Tourism Hotel** (☎0119879607; tw S£90; ❄) has grotty and rather overpriced rooms, but it'll do as a standby option. The **Hipton Hotel** (☎0411822357; r S£120; ❄) is a longstanding favourite and, bar the odd roach crawling up the walls, it's still a decent place to stay.

Cheap eats abound around town, but clued-up locals insist that the **Lulua Restauant** (name in Arabic only; mains S£7-15) by the central *bokasi* stand is the bee's knees, and after tasting its delicious chicken tikka we'd be silly to argue. Don't miss the chance to try the brain-bending spicy Eritrean coffee, the aroma of which wafts through the streets of Kassala.

Minibuses (S£1) and taxis (S£15) shuttle from town to Souq esh-Shabi (about 6km), where the buses to Port Sudan (S£68, six hours) and Khartoum (SD£77, seven hours) arrive and depart.

Port Sudan

POP 489,275

Sudan's only major industrial port is the base for some of the world's most spectacular and undeveloped diving. Above the waves, watching ships unload in the port is about as exciting as it gets.

Sleeping & Eating

There are plenty of *lokandas* around the market, with facilities ranging from basic to bomb site.

The area around the local bus station teems with brightly lit, cheap restaurants and juice bars, giving it a fairground atmosphere at night. For something swankier try the clutch of restaurants along the waterfront, which spring to life in the evening and do a good range of meat and fish dishes for a few bucks.

Saba Hotel HOTEL $
(☎0311822252; tw with/without bathroom S£80/40; ❄) Probably the pick of the cheapies, it's pleased to accept foreign guests and has a range of rooms, from scrappy non-air-con twins with shared bathrooms up to really fairly comfortable en suite rooms.

Baashar Palace Hotel HOTEL $$
(☎0311823341; s/d from S£190/215; ❄) This is a sweet deal with spotless, quiet rooms guaranteeing a decent night's sleep. There's a pleasant courtyard garden and a juice bar, and the restaurant conjures up such exotics as curry.

Coral Port Sudan BUSINESS HOTEL $$$
(☎0311839800; www.coral-international.com; s/d incl breakfast from US$220/256; P❄@📶🏊) This fancy business hotel, which was formally the Mercure Hotel, is the place to go to pretend you're not in Sudan anymore.

Getting There & Away

Minibuses (S£5, 45 minutes) for Suakin leave from the city centre. The major bus companies serve Kassala (S£68, six hours), Atbara (S£65, six hours) and Khartoum (S£95, nine hours). Sudan Airways and the odd 'operating one minute, closed down the next' kind of airline link Port Sudan with Khartoum.

Suakin

Suakin was Sudan's only port before the construction of Port Sudan. Abandoned in the 1930s, it's now a melancholy ghost town, full of crumbling coral buildings, demonic cats said to be cursed, and circling kites and hawks with a devil's shrill call. The **ruins** (admission S£10; ⏲6am-6pm), connected to the mainland by a short causeway, are fascinating to explore. Suakin is best visited as a day trip from Port Sudan.

SOUTH OF KHARTOUM

Wadi Medani

POP 345,290

Love is in the air! Wadi Medani, a couple of hours south of Khartoum, is every Sudanese newlywed's favourite honeymoon destination. Though you might not choose it for your honeymoon, it certainly makes a pleasant night stop if you're looping between Kassala and El-Obeid or Khartoum. Buses head to Khartoum (S£22.50), Kassala (S£41 to S£53) and El-Obeid (S£53).

Continental Hotel HOTEL $
(☎0912362185; r S£90-130; ❄) In a gorgeous old colonial building overlooking the languid Nile. It has giant rooms and a foliage-filled garden.

Imperial Hotel HOTEL $$
(☎0511841501; s S£150-250, d S£180-300; P❄@📶) Set beside the Nile, this is excellent value and has enormous, cool and clean rooms, very helpful staff and a good restaurant serving more than the staples. However, it's quite far out of town.

Gedaref

The busy market and farming town of Gedaref lies just a couple of hours from the main border crossing into Ethiopia and, if you're heading to or from Ethiopia, you stand a good chance of spending a night here.

All accommodation is overpriced. There are several cheap and grotty places to stay around the central market area. The **Al-Motawakhil Hotel** (☎0441843232; s/d

OFF THE BEATEN TRACK

THE NUBA MOUNTAINS & EL-OBEID

Smack in the heart of the country, the beautifully green and (in places) forested Nuba Mountains are, in a sense, a gateway to sub-Saharan Africa. This Scotland-sized slab of fertile land is inhabited by the Nuba people, 60-some related tribes and subtribes with as many differences as similarities. During the autumn harvest, generally November to February, festivals (called Sebir) are held, which usually include wrestling and dancing.

The whole region feels like another country altogether from the sandy wastes of northern Sudan. That, of course, is the problem – the Nuba people long fought on the side of the Sudanese People's Liberation Army against the government. After the signing of the peace agreement, parts of the area opened up to intrepid travellers. But with the coming of independence for South Sudan, the Nuba once again found themselves in the firing line as conflict erupted between the Sudanese armed forces and rebels allied with groups in South Sudan. At the time of writing the Sudanese People's Liberation Movement–North controlled much of the countryside in and around the Nuba Mountains, and the Sudanese armed forces controlled the main towns. Numerous atrocities, including indiscriminate air raids, are reported to have been commited by both sides, there was a major refugee crisis, and the entire area was off limits to foreigners.

North of the Nuba Mountains, and still open to foreigners, is **El-Obeid**, a prosperous market centre. If you find your way out here then the **Shikan Museum** (admission free; ⊙8am-3pm) has some intriguing displays, including many ancient Nubian pieces. The nearby tan-and-red **El-Obeid Cathedral** is also worth a look.

S£200/300; ❄) is much plusher (note: we're not saying its plush, just plusher than the rest!) and the attached restaurant is probably the most pleasant place to eat in the town centre.

Buses run along the smooth road to Gallabat (the Sudanese border town with Ethiopia) for S£25; the journey takes two hours. Buses to Khartoum cost S£51, and take around 3½ hours.

UNDERSTAND SUDAN

Sudan Today

Sudan is entering new territory and its future has never been so unpredictable. Most Sudanese consider South Sudan's independence something of a disaster for the future of this now shrunken nation. The loss of the oil revenue since the south obtained independence has sent the Sudanese economy on a sharp downward spiral and the cost of basic daily goods has skyrocketed. While the conflict in Darfur has reduced in intensity (though it is by no means over) the security situation elsewhere has taken a serious turn for the worse. There are near-constant fears of renewed war with South Sudan over the oil-rich flashpoint region of Abyei, which is claimed by both countries and, since 2011, there has been serious conflict, stemming from the fact that provisions laid out for them in the 2005 Comprehensive Peace Agreement have never fully been implemented, in the Nuba Mountains and other parts of South Kordofan as well as Blue Nile state. With outside observers banned from the area it's very hard to get a clear sense of what is happening here, but many accounts speak of widespread aerial bombardment by Sudanese airforce planes and the specific targeting of civilians.

Add all these things together, throw in some Arab Spring inspiration and you get a recipe for disaster. Dissatisfaction with the Bashir government is growing by the day and street protests have taken place in Khartoum and a number of other major urban centres. Talk to people in the privacy of their own homes and many will say that the current government doesn't have long left to live.

Many outside observers agree that the Bashir government is starting to loose control. But what will come next nobody knows. One thing that is likely though is that Sudan will look increasingly towards the Arab Gulf States and China for financial and political support while its new neighbour, South Sudan, will be more under the influence of East Africa and the West.

History

Modern Sudan is situated on the site of the ancient civilisation of Nubia, which predates Pharaonic Egypt. For centuries sovereignty was shuttled back and forth between the Egyptians, indigenous empires such as Kush, and a succession of independent Christian kingdoms.

After the 14th century AD the Mamelukes (Turkish rulers in Egypt) breached the formidable Nubian defences and established the dominance of Islam. By the 16th century the kingdom of Funj had become a powerful Muslim state and Sennar, 200km south of present-day Khartoum, was one of the great cultural centres of the Islamic world.

Colonialism & Revolt

In 1821 the viceroy of Egypt, Mohammed Ali, conquered northern Sudan and opened the south to trade. Within a few decades British interests were also directed towards Sudan, aiming to control the Nile, contain French expansion from the west and draw the south into a British–East African federation. The European intrusion, and in particular the Christian missionary zeal that accompanied it, was resented by many Muslim Sudanese.

The revolution came in 1881, when one Mohammed Ahmed proclaimed himself to be the Mahdi – the person who, according to Muslim tradition, would rid the world of evil. Four years later he rid Khartoum of General Gordon, the British-appointed governor, and the Mahdists ruled Sudan until 1898, when they were defeated outside Omdurman by Lord Kitchener and his Anglo-Egyptian army. Sudan then effectively became a British colony.

Independence & Revolt

Sudan achieved independence in 1956, but in a forerunner of things to come, General Ibrahim Abboud, the deputy commander-in-chief of the Sudanese army, summarily dismissed the winners of the first post-independence elections and made himself president. Ever since, flirtations with democracy and military coups have been regular features of the Sudanese political landscape. So has war in the mostly non-Muslim south, which revolted after its demands for autonomy were rejected.

In 1969 Colonel Jaafar Nimeiri assumed power and held it for 16 years, surviving several coup attempts and making numerous twists and turns in policy to outflank opponents and keep aid donors happy. Most importantly, by signing the 1972 Addis Ababa Agreement to grant the southern provinces a measure of autonomy, he quelled the civil war for more than a decade.

...And More Revolt

In 1983 Nimeiri scrapped the autonomy accord and imposed sharia (Islamic law) over the whole country. Hostilities between north and south recommenced almost immediately. Army commander John Garang deserted to form the Sudanese People's Liberation Army (SPLA), which quickly took control of much of the south.

Nimeiri was deposed in 1985 and replaced first by a Transitional Military Council, then, after elections the next year, Sadiq al-Mahdi became prime minister. In July 1989 power was seized by the current president, Lieutenant General Omar Hassan Ahmad al-Bashir; however, Hassan al-Turabi, fundamentalist leader of the National Islamic Front (NIF), was widely seen as the man with real power.

The government's brand of belligerent fundamentalism, border disputes with half of its neighbours and possible complicity in a 1995 assassination attempt on Egypt's president, soon cost Sudan all of its regional friends.

1999: Infighting (& Revolt)

The year 1999 was something of a watershed in Sudanese politics: in December, just when the country's domestic and international situation seemed to be improving, President al-Bashir dissolved parliament, suspended the constitution and imposed a three-month state of emergency, all as part of an internal power struggle with Al-Turabi. The subsequent elections in December 2000 were boycotted by opposition parties, giving Al-Bashir an easy win, and in 2001 Al-Turabi and several members of his party were arrested after signing an agreement with the SPLA.

By 2002 things were looking up again – the economy had stabilised and a ceasefire was called after President al-Bashir and SPLA leader John Garang met in Nairobi – but it seems good news in Sudan is always followed by bad. In February 2003 rebels in the western Darfur region rose up against the government, which they accused of oppression and neglect. The army's heavy-handed response, assisted by pro-government Arab militias (the Janjaweed), escalated to what many have called genocide. The government's scorched-earth campaign is thought to have killed between 200,000 and 400,000 Sudanese and uprooted millions more. The Sudanese government say the real death toll is 10,000.

A New Sudan (& More War)

While Darfur spun out of control, peace crept forward in the south, and in January 2005 a deal was signed ending Africa's longest civil war. It included accords on sharing power and wealth (including equal distribution of oil export revenue), and six years of southern autonomy followed by a referendum on independence. In July 2005 the beloved Garang became the first vice-president in a power-sharing government, and president of the south, but he was killed less than a month later in a helicopter crash. Garang's number two, Salva Kiir, took his place.

In March 2009 an international arrest warrant was issued for Al-Bashir after the International Criminal Court accused him of war crimes and crimes against humanity in Darfur. However, both the African Union and the Arab League condemned the arrest warrant. Ironically the warrant was issued just as things were finally starting to calm down in Darfur, but violence was about to flare elsewhere.

In January 2011 the South Sudanese went to the polls and voted overwhelmingly for independence and in July 2011 Sudan found itself with a new neighbour, an independent South Sudan. Almost before the new flag was raised in Juba, capital of South Sudan, the new neighbours were at each other's throats over the oil-rich territory of Abyei, which both nations claimed as theirs. In April 2012 they came to the very brink of war over the issue. But the bad news didn't stop there, and rebellions have broken out in the Nuba Mountains and other parts of South Kordofan as well as in Blue Nile state.

Culture

Sudan's 26 million people are divided into many ethnic groups. Some 70% of Sudan's population is of Arab descent; much of the remainder of the population consists of Arabized ethnic groups such as the Nubians of the northern Nile valley and the sword-wielding Beja of the east. There is a significant nomadic population concentrated largely in the west and east. About 97% of the population is Muslim (Sunnis, mostly), but there are populations of Coptic Christians throughout the country. The people of the Nuba Mountains practise a mixture of Islam, Christianity and shamanistic beliefs.

Food & Drink

Sudanese food isn't particularly varied – the staples are *fuul* (stewed broad beans) and *ta'amiya,* known elsewhere as felafel. Outside the larger towns you'll find little else. That said, the food is generally fresh, tasty and healthy.

Meat dishes include *kibda* (liver), shish kebabs and *shwarma,* hunks of chicken or lamb sliced fresh from the classic roasting spit. Along the Nile you can find excellent fresh perch.

Tea is the favourite drink, served as *shai saada* (black, sometimes spiced), *shai bi-laban* (with milk) or *shai bi-nana* (with mint). Also common is *qahwa turkiya* (Turkish coffee) and *jebbana* (spiced coffee), served in distinctive clay or metal pots and spiked with cardamom, cinnamon or ginger. Local fruit juices are usually made with untreated water or ice, but even so they are generally too good to pass up!

Sharia law means that alcohol is hard to come by and people caught with it face 40 lashes.

SURVIVAL GUIDE

Directory A–Z

ACCOMMODATION

Many top-end hotels quote rates in US dollars (but accept payment in Sudanese pounds); all other hotels quote in Sudanese pounds. We have quoted prices in the currency the hotel uses.

The most basic places to stay are called *lokandas,* with beds in shared rooms or courtyards, though you can take all of the beds in a room if you want privacy. It's best to pack a sleep sheet if you will be using them. Women are often not welcome in *lokandas.*

All hotels outside Khartoum will request a copy of your travel permit and hotels everywhere will need a copy of your passport and visa.

ACTIVITIES

With many sharks and manta rays, and incredibly good visibility, Sudan's Red Sea dive sites are as good as Egypt's, but without the crowds. Most people use live-aboard operations based outside the country, but there are some captains

PRACTICALITIES

- **Electricity** 230V/50Hz and plugs usually have two round pins.
- **Languages** Arabic, English, Nubian, Fur, Beja and many others in the Nuba Mountains.
- **Newspapers** Several private, English-language daily newspapers, such as *Khartoum Monitor* and *Citizen*, but press freedom is limited.
- **Radio** Both the government-owned Omdurman Radio (95FM) and the BBC World Service (95FM) occasionally broadcast news in English.
- **TV** Satellite TV is so common that few people watch the four government-owned stations.
- **Weights & Measures** Sudan uses mostly imperial weights and measures, but distances are measured in kilometres.

in Port Sudan. One recommended operator is UK-based **Regal Dive** (☎ 0044 1353 659999; www.regal-diving.co.uk). For local operators try **Sudan Red Sea Resort** (☎ 0912465650; www.sudanredsearesort.com).

EMBASSIES & CONSULATES

Canadian Embassy (☎ 0156550500; Africa Rd)

British Embassy (☎ 0183777105; al-Baladyya St)

Central African Republic Embassy (CAR; ☎ 0922815860; off Medani Rd, El-Maamoura)

Chadian Embassy (☎ 0183471612; St 57, Amarat)

Dutch Embassy (☎ 0183471200; Sharia 47)

Egyptian Embassy (☎ 0183777646; al-Nil St)

Eritrean Embassy (☎ 0183483834; off Sharia 15, New Extension)

Ethiopian Embassy (☎ 0183471379)

French Embassy (☎ 0183471082; www.ambafrance-sd.org; off Sharia 15, New Extension)

German Embassy (☎ 0183777990; al-Baladyya St) At the time of research this embassy was closed after an angry mob destroyed it in protest to a perceived anti-Muslim film made in the US. (Yes, we wondered what relevance this had to the German embassy.) Rumour has it that a new embassy will be built elsewhere.

Saudi Embassy (☎ 0183472583; St 29, Amarat)

South Sudanese Embassy (☎ 0926289528; Al-Safa Rd, Riyadh) Expect huge queues and not much help.

Ugandan Embassy (☎ 0183797867; Abu Qarga St)

US Embassy (☎ 0187022000; http://sudan.usembassy.gov/; Ali Abdul al-Latif St)

HOLIDAYS

As well as the religious holidays, the principal public holidays in Sudanare **Independence Day** (1 January) and **Revolution Day** (30 June).

INTERNET ACCESS

Internet access is generally very good in Sudan – even in small towns connection speeds are decent and prices low. Most towns, even quite small ones, have an internet cafe (or perhaps internet cabin is a better description) or two and an increasing number of mid and top-end hotels have wifi.

MONEY

The official currency is the Sudanese pound (S£/SDG), which is divided into 100 piastres.

In the last couple of years the Sudanese pound has started to lose value against the US dollar at a steady rate and with inflation increasing a black market has sprung up. If you use it be very discreet. Hotels are good places to enquire. Khartoum has numerous private exchange offices which have better rates than the banks, and longer working hours. The rates offered by these offices is generally only a little lower than the black-market rate. Euros and US dollars are the easiest to change (outside Khartoum you'll be hard pressed to change anything else), though British pounds and most Middle Eastern currencies are widely accepted in Khartoum and Port Sudan. The only way to change Egyptian pounds and Ethiopian birr is on the black market, which is easy at the borders.

Money can be wired to Khartoum and Port Sudan (even from the US and UK, though this could always change because of sanctions) with Western Union and Travelex. Credit cards and travellers cheques are useless and there are no ATMs accepting foreign cards; bring all the money you might need in cash.

It's worth noting that due to international sanctions some online banking systems will block your account the moment you try and log in from Sudan. Paypal is also likely to do this (yes, we speak from experience!).

OPENING HOURS

Banking hours are 9am to 12.30pm, while most government, airline and similar offices are usually open until 3pm. Most local shops stay open late, but might close briefly between 1pm and 5pm. Few places open on Friday.

PHOTOGRAPHY

Photo permits are obligatory for foreigners and they form part of your travel permit. On the permit you must write down everything you want to photograph. Put historical sites, landscapes and tourist sites. Permits are issued by Khartoum's Ministry of Tourism & Wildlife (p162).

Photography along the northern Nile route is generally a breeze and people will be keen to pose for your camera. Anywhere else it can be something of a pain thanks to overzealous officials. Photography in Khartoum (away from recognised tourist attractions) is asking for trouble.

POST

Mail in and out of Sudan is unreliable.

SAFE TRAVEL

While there are still many no-go areas, the rest of Sudan is a very safe place – one of the safest in Africa, in fact. Crime is almost unheard of, but watch your wallet among crowds and lock your luggage in hotels. The Nuba mountains, Darfur and the borderlands with South Sudan are generally dangerous and out of bounds to foreign travellers.

TELEPHONE

Private telephone centres are found all over the country. Mobile-phone reception is excellent throughout the country and buying a SIM card is a quick, cheap and, for Sudan, easy process involving only a few photocopies of your passport and a couple of passport photos.

Sudan's country code is ☎249.

TOURS

There are very few local tour operators and of those that exist many are overpriced, disorganised and unreliable, and cannot be recommended wholeheartedly. However, in order to obtain a visa you will probably have to deal with one of them.

Italian Tourism Company (☎0183487961; www.italtoursudan.com; St 31, Amarat, Khartoum) This Italian-run agency is easily the most professional tour company in the country and is the one that virtually every overseas tour company offering trips to Sudan uses for on-ground organisation.

Lendi Travel (☎183794990; www.lenditravel.com; Eid Allah building, El Said Abdul Rahman St, Khartoum) Of the Sudanese-run tour companies, this one is probably the most reliable. It can supply cars and drivers, book hotels, help organise visas and it runs set tours around the country.

Mashansharti Travel Agency (☎Khartoum 0912253484, Wadi Halfa 09122380740; www.tour-sudan.com; 3rd floor, Sati Bldg, cnr Sayyd Abd al-Rahman St & al-Tayyar Izz al-Din St) In online forums and websites this agency goes under several names, including Sudan Tours & Travels, Glob Tours and the name of the owner, Midhat Mahir. In reality it's an unmarked office on the 3rd floor of a city-centre building. Midhat can provide good information for independent travellers, help obtain visas and travel permits and arrange ferry tickets to Egypt, and he has had some luck in arranging permits for travellers wishing to use the road between Sudan and Egypt. His brother, Mazar, runs a seperate office in Wadi Halfa. Where they fall down is in responding to emails.

VISAS & DOCUMENTS

Everyone, except Egyptians, needs a visa (if there is evidence of travel to Israel you will be denied) and getting one could be the worst part of your trip. Some embassies are easier to deal with than others and in all cases a transit visa (which gives you up to a fortnight to transit the country) is easier to get than a month-long tourist visa. Currently Cairo and Aswan (Egypt) remain the easiest places to get a visa; they are normally issued in a couple of days or even less in the case of Aswan. A tourist visa is very hard to get in Addis Ababa (Ethiopia), but transit visas are possible. In Europe the embassy in London is barely worth bothering with, but at the time of writing the embassy in Paris was issuing tourist visas within 48 hours; in the US it's a slow old process to say the least! Expect all this information to change constantly.

If you need a tourist visa rather than a transit visa, it helps to let an agent arrange it. Most of the time they will get you a counter visa: they arrange everything at the Ministry of Interior in Khartoum and you pick it up at the airport. This service is likely to cost around US$150 and, if you are lucky, can take as little as two days. The other option (used primarily by those crossing overland, since it costs more) is an invitation visa, in which you are sent a number that you give the embassy or consulate that *should* speed up the normal process. With either option, there is a good chance something will go wrong along the way, so get started as early as possible.

If the listed tour companies give you the run around, it's also worth trying some of the hotels in Khartoum. The Bougainvilla Guesthouse and Acropole Hotel are very helpful in this regard.

Registration

You have to register within three days of arrival in Khartoum, Port Sudan, Gallabat or Wadi Halfa. In Khartoum, go to the **Aliens Registration Office** (61 St, Al-Diyum East; ⏲8am-2.15pm); the process costs S£241. You need one photo and photocopies of your passport and visa (there's a photocopier in the building) and a letter from a sponsor in Sudan; your hotel will normally act as your sponsor and provide you with the required letter. Even cheap hotels should be able to do this although you might have to go and collect the required form from the office for them to fill in. If for some reason your hotel can't or won't do this then tour companies such as Mashansharti Travel Agency will complete all the registration formalities for you for S£60. If you're travelling with a tour company they will take care of this for you. If doing it all independently allow several hours and a headache.

There is also another office at the airport. Technically this office is only for emergency cases and shouldn't be relied on, but on Fridays, when the main office is closed, you can do it here.

If you registered on entry at a land border, you need to do it again in Khartoum, but you don't have to pay again. In many towns you will need to register with the police – this is free.

Travel Permits

The Sudanese authorities have always been renowned for their paranoia about foreigners nosing about their country, and travel permits were required for journeys to more sensitive areas outside Khartoum. Recently, however, the authorities have become even more paranoid and now any and all travel outside Khartoum requires a permit. Take one photo and a copy of your passport and visa to the **Ministry of Tourism and Wildlife** (☎0911121856; Al-Mashtal St, Riyadh; ⏰8am-4pm Sun-Thu) in the Riyadh area south of the city centre. A permit covering everywhere featured in this book (except the Nuba Mountains, which are out of bounds) can be issued on the spot. This permit is a combined travel and photograph permit. Carry dozens of photocopies of this permit along with copies of your passport and visa to give to police.

Visas for Onward Travel

Visas for the following neighbouring countries are available from embassies in Khartoum.

Egypt This consulate is not the most organised place – arrive early to beat the worst queues. You'll need two photos and US$20. The visa is ready the same day. It's easier to get a tourist visa on arrival (which most but not all nationalities can do), especially if you're flying.

Ethiopia One-month visas cost US$20 and require two photos. You can pick your visa up the same day.

Saudi Arabia Visa applications are handled by travel agencies (many of which surround the embassy), which can get you a transit visa in two days (perhaps one day if you go very early). You need a visa to a neighbouring country (normally Jordan), two photos, a letter of introduction from your embassy and US$100. Visas are not issued during the haj and nor are they issued to unmarried women under 40 unless they are accompanied by their husband or brother (and can prove it).

South Sudan Not the most helpful of embassies and more than a little vague about what is required in order to obtain a tourist visa! What you will need though is a hotel reservation/letter of invitation, S£180 and two passport photos. Visas take two days to issue.

Women Travellers

Contrary to expectations women travelling alone or in groups in Sudan are unlikely to face any major problems bar the odd cheap hotel refusing to rent you a room. What you will encounter though is general astonishment that you are here alone (although you've probably already had your fill of that when you told friends at home where you were planning on holidaying!). People (particulary families and Sudanese women) will constantly try and take you under their wing and there will be lots of invites to people's houses. You should dress conservatively – a headscarf will likely make you feel more comfortable but is by no means essential.

Getting There & Away

AIR

Khartoum is well connected to Africa and the world.

EgyptAir (☎0183780064; www.egyptair.com; New Abuella Bldg) Connections to Cairo.

Emirates (☎0156777777; www.emirates.com; Cnr Al-Jamburya St & Al-Khalifa St) Has flights worldwide via the Middle East.

Ethiopian Airlines (☎0183762088; www.ethiopianairlines.com; Al-Jamburya st) Connections to Addis Ababa.

Gulf Air (☎0183778503; al-Tayaar Murad St) Flights worldwide via the Middle East.

Kenya Airways (☎0183782579; www.kenya-airways.com; Ali Abdel al-Latif St) Services to Nairobi.

Lufthansa (☎0183771322; www.lufthansa.com; El Tayar Murad St) Flies to Germany. At the time of research there was talk of this office moving.

Sudan Airways (☎0187011000; 161 Obied Khatim St, Block 10, Riyadh; ⏰8am-6pm Sat-Thu, 9-11am Fri) Has frequent flights to North and East Africa and the Middle East, though its competitors usually have similar prices and better service. The address here is the headquarters. There are several other booking offices throughout the city.

LAND & SEA

Sudan shares borders with many countries, but there are few crossing options. The security situation along the border with South Sudan is highly volatile and though locals are taking boats down the White Nile between the two countries we've not heard of any travellers doing it and most people consider an overland crossing between Sudan and South Sudan too dangerous to attempt. Libya is also risky and while the Chadian border is technically open (but dangerous) there's no way a foreign traveller will be granted travel permits for Darfur.

Egypt

The roads between Sudan and Egypt have long been closed to overlanders, but the big rumour of the day is that the road between Wadi Halfa and Aswan is about to open for all (though the scheduled opening date has already been pushed back several times, so don't be surprised if it never actually happens).

More fun, and until the road opens your only option, is to take the weekly passenger ferry on Lake Nasser from Wadi Halfa to the port near Aswan in Egypt. It heads north at about 5pm on Wednesday, returning on Monday at 3pm (though expect severe delays and occasional cancelations). The journey takes around 17 hours plus immigration time, and costs S£350/212 in 1st/2nd class. There's also a port tax of S£21. First-class passengers share two-bunk cabins, whereas in 2nd class you fight for seats with hundreds of others. You can buy tickets in Wadi Halfa at the port and from the train station in Khartoum. With the recent unrest in Egypt ferry departures have become increasingly unreliable. If a ferry is cancelled you can hire a private boat, but this costs an impressive US$3000.

Vehicles go on the barge attached to the rear of the ferry, but you should arrive in Wadi Halfa in advance if you want to do this. **Mazar Mahir** (☎ 09122380740), the brother of Midhat Mahir of Khartoum-based tour company Mashansharti, has a good reputation for speeding people through the paperwork.

Eritrea

The crossing between Kassala and Teseney is open, but don't start celebrating just yet. Visas for Eritrea are increasingly hard to come by and the Eritrean side of the border area is closed to foreigners anyway so even if you do have a visa you're unlikely to be allowed to cross overland between the two countries.

Ethiopia

From Gedaref take a pick-up to the border town of Gallabat (S£25, two hours) and walk over the bridge to Metema, where buses go direct to Gonder or, if you miss the bus, you can reach Gonder by changing vehicles in Shihedi. Note that you cannot get Ethiopian visas on the border.

Saudi Arabia

Regular ferry services run between Suakin and Jeddah. Tickets (one way S£340) are available through travel agencies in Khartoum and Port Sudan.

ℹ Getting Around

AIR

Half a dozen airlines connect Khartoum to all large Sudanese cities.

Sudan Airways has the most flights and, along with **Marsland** (www.marsland-avi.com), the fewest problems with cancellations and overbookings; though neither company will win a reliability award.

LOCAL TRANSPORT

Sudan is undergoing a road-building frenzy and all significant towns northeast of El-Obeid are now linked by excellent paved roads. Fast comfortable buses have almost totally replaced most of the *bokasi* that formerly bounced over the desert between big northern towns. It's best to buy bus tickets a day in advance.

TRAIN

Sadly the last passenger trains recently ceased puff-puffing and the only trains now operating carry freight only.

Tunisia

216 / POP 10.67 MILLION

Includes ➡

Best Places to Eat

- Dar Slah (p170)
- Au Bon Vieux Temps (p171)
- Patisserie Segni (p175)
- Saffoud Abid (p181)
- Bougainvillea (p189)

Best Places to Stay

- La Chambre Bleue (p169)
- Dar Fatma (p171)
- Dar Gaïa (p189)
- Dar Nejma (p183)
- Camping Desert Club (p186)

Why Go?

It's but a slim wedge of North Africa's vast expanse, but Tunisia has enough history, cultural diversity and extremes of landscape to fill a country many times its size. With a sand-fringed, jasmine-scented coast, it's a destination usually equated with Mediterranean sun holidays. But get beyond the beaches and you'll find stunning Roman sites, forested hinterland, Saharan dunes and mountain oases, all of which can be experienced in a few days.

The country's tourist sector has struggled mightily since the historic Jasmine Revolution of 2011. Isolated incidents of instability grab international headlines, but it's essentially business as usual. Tunis, the capital, continues to offer an enthralling mix of tradition and modernity, Islamic serenity and seaside hedonism. Surprisingly, while much of the tourist industry founders, there's a number of new guesthouses and small hotels popping up throughout the country. Now, more than ever, Tunisians will welcome you with open arms.

When to Go

Tunis

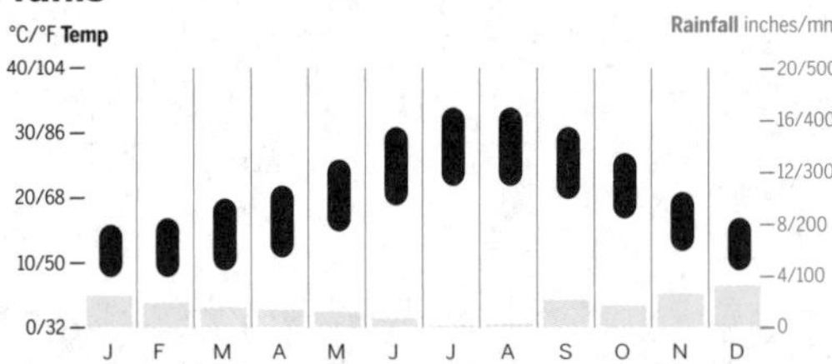

Mar–May Explore Roman ruins and hike the wildflower-strewn countryside.

Jun–Sep Balmy beach frolics and music festivals.

Nov–Jan The Saharan south's high season.

Tunisia Highlights

1. Kick back in gorgeous bougainvillea-clad village **Sidi Bou Saïd** (p171), with its nonstop views of the intensely blue Gulf of Tunis.
2. Take in the splendour of Roman Africa, the mysteries of Carthage and the elegance of Islamic decoration all in one museum at Tunis' **Bardo** (p167).
3. Find desert-island bliss on **Jerba** (p186), with date palms, white-sand beaches, evocative architecture and ancient cultural traditions.
4. Sip mint tea in the cool of an enchanting palmeraie in **Tozeur** (p182), a bustling southern oasis.
5. Slow down and experience traditional Tunisian life in **Le Kef** (p173), against a spectacular natural backdrop.

TUNIS

POP 1.29 MILLION

Tunis is a fabulous introduction to the wildly divergent layers that make up modern Tunisia. The medina's organic tangle of souqs, squares, mosques and shuttered town houses is surrounded by the straight, colonial lines of the Ville Nouvelle. 'French' Tunis centres on Ave Habib Bourguiba, a wide, tree-lined street made famous by the scenes of Jasmine Revolution protest; its crowds are now again made up of shoppers and cafe-goers. Apart from the medina, Tunis' main attractions are outside the city

Tunis

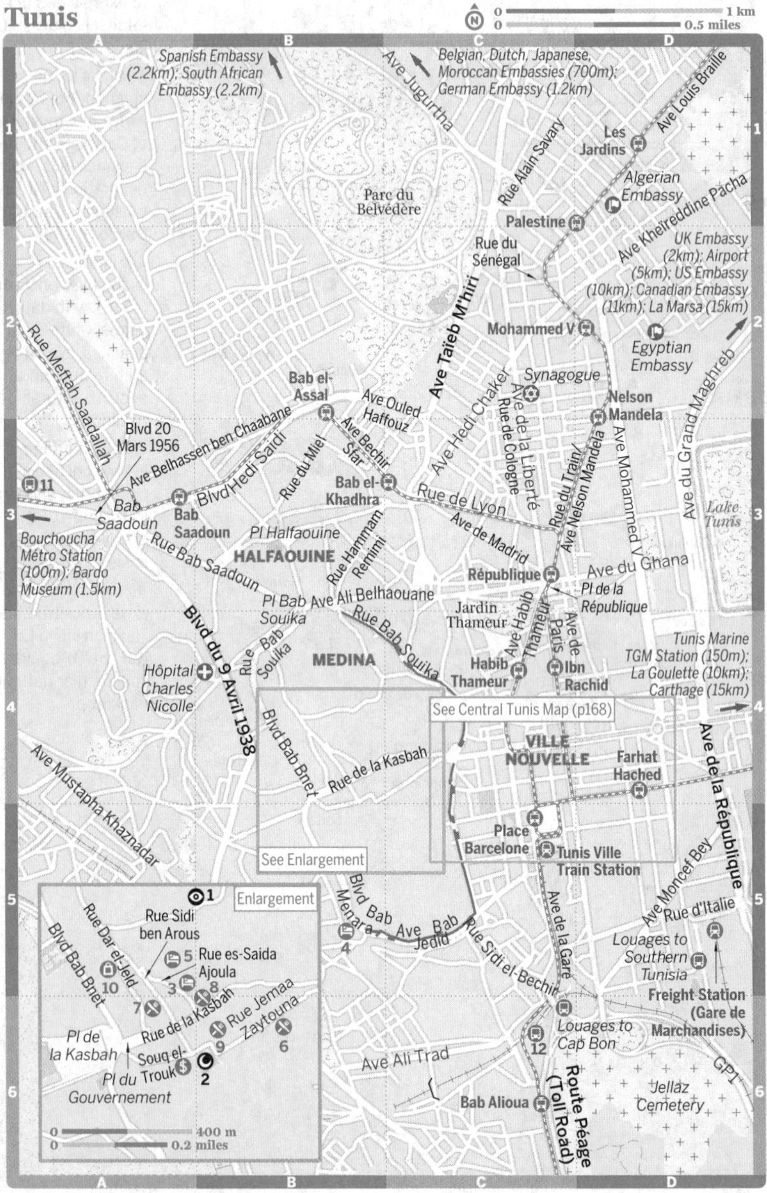

proper; they include the wonderful Bardo Museum. For beach outings, interesting shops and night-time fun, join the young and well-to-do in the gorgeous northern suburbs.

Sights & Activities

Tunis Medina NEIGHBOURHOOD

(Map p166) This sprawling maze of ancient streets and alleyways is a national treasure. It's home to numerous cave-like souqs selling everything from shoes to *shisha* (hookah) pipes, as well as lavishly tiled cafes, backstreets full of artisans at work, and residential areas punctuated by grand, brightly painted doorways. Historic palaces, mosques and *medersas* (Quranic schools) are scattered throughout. An atmospheric time to explore is early morning, when all is serene apart from the cafes and fragrant breakfast stalls. The main drag at any other time can be unbearably hot, crowded and noisy, but the crush soon dissipates a few streets either side. You'll also find a number of ancient *hammams* (traditional bathhouses; ask your hotel for a recommendation and opening hours).

Zaytouna Mosque MOSQUE

(Grande Mosquée; Map p166; admission TD4; ⏲non-Muslims 8am-1pm Thu & Sat-Tue) At the medina's heart lies this beautiful mosque, its forest of columns scrounged from Roman Carthage. Non-Muslims can only enter the courtyard, but it's still deeply impressive.

Tunis

Sights

1 Tunis Medina....A5
2 Zaytouna Mosque....B6

Sleeping

3 Auberge de Jeunesse....A5
4 Dar Lakhdar....B5
5 La Chambre Bleue....A5

Eating

6 Café Culturel El Ali....B6
7 Dar El Jeld....A6
8 Dar Slah....B6
9 Restaurant Mahdaoui....B6

Shopping

10 Boutique Brocante....A5

Transport

11 Northern Bus Station....A3
12 Southern Bus Station....C6

SET YOUR BUDGET

Budget

- Hotel room US$30
- *Brik*, salad and chips US$2.50
- Coffee US$0.60
- TGM trip US$0.30

Midrange

- Hotel room US$65
- Two-course dinner US$18
- Beer in bar US$2
- Short taxi ride US$1.25

Top End

- Hotel room US$160
- Two-course dinner US$40
- Glass of wine US$4
- Driver and car per day US$200

Bardo Museum MUSEUM

(Off Map p166; ☎71 513 650; admission TD12; ⏲9.30am-4.30pm mid-Sep–Apr, 9am-5pm May–mid-Sep Tue-Sun) The country's top museum has a magnificent, must-see collection that provides a vibrant vision of ancient North African life. The original, glorious Husseinite palace now connects with a stark and dramatic contemporary addition, doubling exhibition space. Highlights are a huge stash of incredibly well-preserved Roman mosaics, rare Phoenician artifacts and early Islamic ceramics. The Bardo is 4km northwest of the city centre. Take *métro léger* line 4 (TD0.5) to the Bardo stop, or a taxi (around TD5).

Carthage ARCHAEOLOGICAL SITE

This Punic and Roman site lies northeast of the city and is easily reached by the suburban train from Tunis Marine TGM station. Get off at Carthage Hannibal station and wander up to the top of **Byrsa Hill** for a fine view across the site. You'll have to use a bit of historical sixth sense, as the ruins are scant and scattered over a wide area, but they include impressive Roman baths, houses, cisterns, basilicas and streets. The **Carthage Museum** (www.patrimoinedetunisie.com.tn; Byrsa Hill; admission all sites TD9; ⏲7.30am-7pm May–mid-Sep, 8am-6pm Apr, 8.30am-5pm mid-Sep–Mar) backs up imaginings of the site's former glories with material finds, including such wonders as monumental statuary, mosaics and extraordinary everyday stuff, including razors

Central Tunis

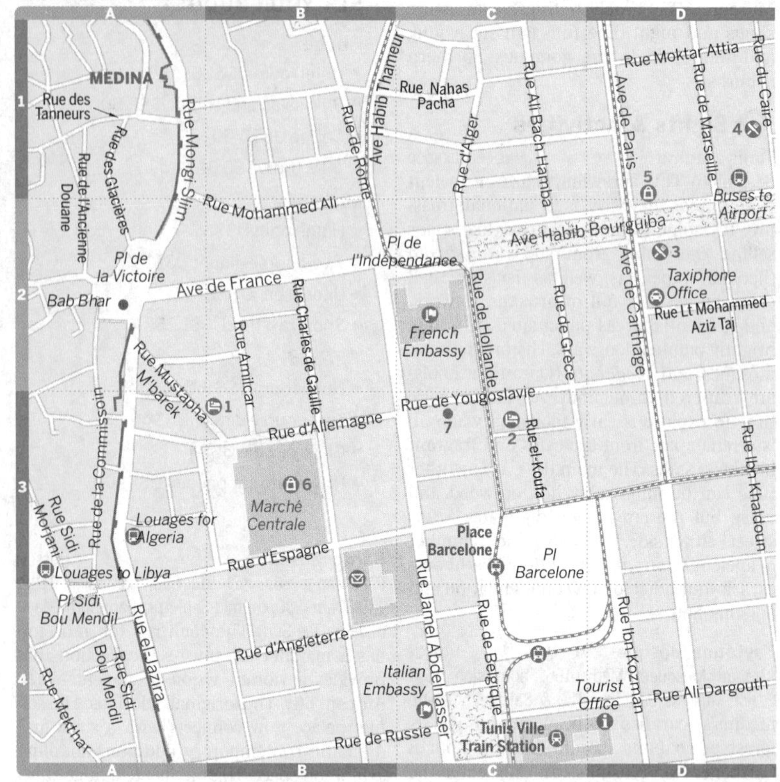

and kohl pots. The **Byrsa Quarter**, an excavated quarter of the Punic city, once home to 400,000 people and surrounded by 13m-high walls, is also in the grounds of the museum.

Sleeping

There are lots of rock-bottom budget places in and around the medina, most of which are unsuitable for women travelling alone.

Auberge de Jeunesse HOSTEL $
(Map p166; ☎71 574 884; www.hostelworld.com; 25 Rue Es-Saida Ajoula; dm/d TD8/20; 📶) Located in a wonderful 18th-century former palace in the medina, the rooms are basic – white walls and bunk beds upstairs, comfortable, if stuffy, doubles downstairs. But all are set around a pretty, tiled courtyard, the welcome is friendly and the position is priceless.

Grand Hôtel de France HOTEL $
(Map p168; ☎71 326 244; hotelfrancetunis@yahoo.fr; 8 Rue Mustapha M'barek; s without bathroom TD23, d TD53, AC extra; ❄) This colonial-era hotel has welcoming, English-speaking staff. Rooms are airy, high-ceilinged and light, with a faded 1930s elegance. Some have marble fireplaces and balconies – ask for one overlooking the leafy inner courtyard.

Dar Lakhdar HOTEL $
(Map p166; ☎71 565 175; Rue el-Marr; without bathroom s/d 25/35TD, without bathroom TD25/35; ❄) Near the Bab Jedid, in one of the traditional shopping streets that surround the medina, this is a great choice if you're looking for something ultralocal but also efficiently run. There's an airy internal courtyard and roof terrace with excellent views, and rooms are simple but spotless.

Hôtel Maison Dorée HOTEL $
(Map p168; ☎71 240 632; 3 Rue el-Koufa; s/d TD47/55, without bathroon TD37/45, AC extra; ❄) Maison Dorée has an old-fashioned formality, with shuttered balconies and comforting

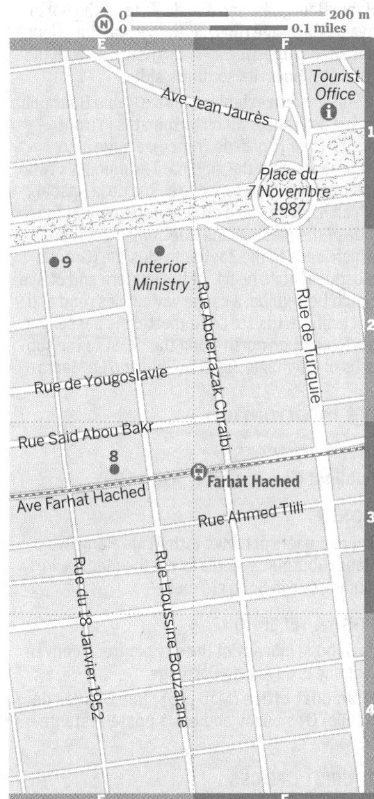

Central Tunis

Sleeping

1 Grand Hôtel de France B3
2 Hôtel Maison Dorée C3

Eating

3 Café de Paris Brasserie D2
4 Restaurant Pastacaza D1

Shopping

5 Mains des Femmes D1
6 Marché Centrale B3

Transport

7 Compagnie Tunisienne de Navigation C3
8 SNCM E3
9 Tunisair E2

1950s furniture in clean, good-sized rooms. There's a well-patronised restaurant and bar downstairs, but, like the lobby, they can get extremely smoky.

★La Chambre Bleue B&B $$
(Map p166; ☎22 579 602; www.lachambrebleue.net; 24 Rue du Divan; s/d TD100/140; wi-fi) La Chambre Bleue gives you medina digs with a cool, creative family as well as privacy, peace and space. The jewel-coloured guest room is vast and combines exquisite original architectural features (pretty painted ceiling, endless tile work) with contemporary boho furniture. The freshly made breakfasts include delicious local favourites. At time of writing, three self-contained apartments were being made ready in the 12th-century Hafsid stables downstairs.

Eating

You can buy addictively spicy tuna-filled chapattis (hot flat-bread parcel) in the medina for around TD1.5, or dine like a *bey* (king) in a traditional palace restaurant. Fresh ricotta is a Tunis speciality, along with *bombalouni* – freeform Sicilian-style doughnuts.

Restaurant Pastacaza TUNISIAN $
(Chez Abid Sfaxi; Map p168; ☎71 996 341; 4 Rue du Caire; dishes TD4-10; noon-10pm) Bright (perhaps too bright) Sfaxoise place that pulls Tunisian families with friendly service, and a good selection of standards and regional specialities, such as *riz au lapin* (rabbit rice).

Restaurant Mahdaoui TUNISIAN $
(Map p166; 2 Rue Jemaa Zaytouna; mains TD5-13; noon-3.30pm Mon-Sat) Central and cheap, with tables that fill a narrow alley by the Zaytouna Mosque. The simple menu offers Tunisian soul food: couscous, grilled fish, fried chicken, half-a-head of lamb.

Café de Paris Brasserie TUNISIAN $
(Map p168; ☎71 240 583; Ave Habib Bourguiba; mains TD4-15; noon-11pm Mon-Sat; air-con) This handy little diner serves up pizzas, pastas, couscous and French, Italian and Tunisian salads in gargantuan serves. It also serves alcohol, as does its (all-male) bar next door.

★Café Culturel El Ali TUNISIAN $$
(Map p166; ☎71 321 927; 45bis Rue Jemaa Zaytouna; mains TD13-15; 10am-9pm Mon-Sat) It is indeed a cultured hideaway, with atmospheric wood-beamed ceilings, a library, sofas and a rooftop terrace overlooking the Zaytouna Mosque. Charming staff serve up *citronnade* (fresh lemonade, TD4.5) with almonds or mint, fruit smoothies, mint tea and espresso. The midlevel dining room specialises in

vielle marmites (slow-cooked meat in terracotta) and other traditional meat dishes.

★ Dar Slah TUNISIAN **$$**

(Map p166; 145 Rue de la Kasbah; set menus TD17 & TD19; ⏲noon-3pm Mon-Sat; ❄) Dar Slah is calm and clean-lined despite its location on the medina's busiest thoroughfare. A daily changing multicourse menu is built around fresh seasonal ingredients and is a generous feast of traditional flavours.

Dar El Jeld TUNISIAN **$$$**

(Map p166; ☎71 560 916; 5-10 Rue Dar el-Jeld; mains TD25-35) A special experience from the moment you knock on the grand bee-yellow arched doorway – the magnificent dining room is in the covered central courtyard of an elaborate 18th-century mansion. Try dishes such as *lahma m'jamra* (stuffed lamb shoulder) or lighter options, like a cold seafood salad. A Tunis institution, but we do wish they'd take themselves less seriously.

Shopping

For perfume, leather goods, *chechias* (traditional red felt hats), *fouta* (cotton towels), cheap clothes and miles of glorious tat, head to the medina. Chain stores and the Monoprix and Carrefour supermarkets can be found on Ave Habib Bourguiba and the surrounding streets.

Marché Centrale MARKET

(central market; Map p168; Rue Charles de Gaulle; ⏲6am-3pm) Atmospheric covered market: stock up on fresh produce, olives, harissa and cheese.

Mains des Femmes HANDICRAFTS

(Map p168; 1st fl, 47 Ave Habib Bourguiba; ⏲9am-6.30pm Mon-Fri, to 5pm Sat) This nonprofit women's co-operative sells quality traditional handicrafts, including rugs, jewellery and clothing, all at fixed prices.

Boutique Brocante ANTIQUES

(Map p166; ☎55 343 618; 36 Rue Dar el-Jeld; ⏲10am-1pm & 3-6pm Mon-Sat) Fantastic hideyhole of affordable bric-a-brac, much of it dating to the early 20th century.

Orientation

The city's main thoroughfare, Ave Habib Bourguiba, runs west–east from Place de l'Indépendance to Lake Tunis. It is lined with cafes, restaurants, shops, theatres and banks. The main north–south thoroughfare of the Ville Nouvelle is Ave de Carthage to the south of Ave Habib Bourguiba and Ave de Paris to the north. Ave de Carthage runs south to Place Barcelone, hub of the *métro léger* (tram) network, with the train station on its southern side.

The western extension of Ave Habib Bourguiba is Ave de France, which terminates in front of Bab Bhar (Porte de France), a huge arch, beyond which is the medina. The medina's two main streets lead from here: Rue de la Kasbah, which leads to Place du Gouvernement at the far side of the medina; and Rue Jemaa Zaytouna, which leads to the Zaytouna Mosque (Grande Mosquée) at its heart. At the eastern end of Ave Habib Bourguiba, a causeway carries road and rail traffic across to La Goulette, the passenger port, and then north along the coast to the suburbs of Carthage, Sidi Bou Saïd and La Marsa.

Information

INTERNET ACCESS

Publinet (Rue de Grece; per hr TD2)

MONEY

There are lots of banks with ATMs along Ave Habib Bourguiba, and a few in the medina, including one in Souq el-Trouk.

POST & TELEPHONE

Taxiphone offices dot the city centre. A convenient one is on Ave de Carthage.

Main post office (Map p168; Rue Charles de Gaulle) Open daily and has a poste-restante service.

TOURIST OFFICES

Tourist office (☎71 341 077; 1 Ave Mohammed V) Has free maps of the medina, greater Tunis and Tunisia's road network. Staff speak English but their role doesn't seem to entail more than doling out glossy brochures. There's another branch at the train station, open the same hours.

Getting There & Away

AIR

The airport is 8km northeast of the city centre. Tunisair Express (p195), the domestic arm of Tunisair (p194), has inexpensive flights to Jerba, Tozeur and other regional cities. Book ahead for Jerba in summer.

BOAT

Ferries from Europe arrive at La Goulette. The cheapest way to reach the city from there is by TGM suburban train or by taxi, which will cost around TD5.

Boats sail from Tunis to Genoa, Naples, Civitavecchia (Rome), Palermo and Trapani in Italy. There are also frequent crossings to Marseilles.

WORTH A TRIP

SIDI BOU SAÏD

Thirty minutes up the TGM line, Sidi Bou Saïd has to be one of the prettiest spots in Tunisia, if not the whole of the Mediterranean. With cascading bougainvillea, bright-blue window grills, narrow, steep cobbled streets and jaw-dropping glimpses of azure coast, it's a tour-bus favourite, but it wears its popularity surprisingly well. Come for a swim at its little bayside beach, or take tea at one of the historic cafes.

There's a good choice of places to eat: **Au Bon Vieux Temps** (☎71 744 733; 56 Rue Hedi Zarrouk; mains TD18-32; ⏲noon-3pm & 7pm-midnight; ❄) is known for its excellent seafood and sophisticated takes on old standards, and both the ridiculously romantic terrace and the elegant dining room have amazing views. Tasty fish couscous can be had at the courtyard at cute cheapie **Le Chargui** (☎71 740 987; 39 Rue Habib Thameur; mains TD6-15; ⏲noon-midnight Apr-Oct, to 8pm Nov-Mar).

It's worth forking out to stay here: early mornings are sublime. Relaxed but stylish, **Dar Fatma** (☎71 981 284; www.darfatma.com; Rue Sidi Bou Taraa; r €120; ❄) is set at the top of the village, next to the small graveyard and eucalypt-clad slopes tumbling from the lighthouse to the sea. Its five rooms cleverly highlight the house's traditional architecture using a contemporary design aesthetic. Views from the roof terrace and its small plunge pool are breathtaking. Around the corner, friendly family-run **Hôtel Sidi Bou Fares** (☎71 740 091; 15 Rue Sidi Bou Fares; s/d/tr TD90/130/160; ❄) has small, prettily tiled, barrel-vaulted rooms with Goldilocks-style wooden beds set around a fig-shaded courtyard.

You can easily pop over to **Carthage**, **La Marsa** or **Gammarth** from here. All were once distinct villages and towns and each retains an individual appeal, not to mention stunning views, sea breezes and swimming spots.

BUS

The **southern bus station** (Gare Routière Sud de Bab el-Fellah; Map p166; ☎71 399 440, 71 399 391), for international buses, buses to the south and *louages* (shared taxis) for Cap Bon, is opposite the huge Jellaz Cemetery on *métro léger* line 1 to Bab Alioua station.

The **northern bus station** (Gare Routière Nord de Bab Saadoun; Map p166; ☎71 562 299, 71 563 653), for buses heading north, is reached by *métro léger* line 4 to Bouchoucha station. *Louages* from the north also arrive and leave from the northern bus station.

Société Nationale du Transport Rural et Interurbain (SNTRI; www.sntri.com.tn) has timetables and prices online.

LOUAGE

Tunis has a number of main *louage* stations. Cap Bon *louages* leave from opposite the southern bus station, and services to other southern destinations leave from the station at the eastern end of Rue El-Aid el-Jebbari, off Ave Moncef Bey. *Louages* to the north leave from the northern bus station.

The station on Place Sidi Bou Mendil in the medina serves Libya (Tripoli; around TD40, 20 hours); services to Algeria leave from nearby.

Prices are usually equivalent to bus fares.

TRAIN

Long-distance **Société Nationale des Chemins de Fer Tunisiens** (SNCFT; www.sncft.com.tn) trains run from the centrally located **Tunis Ville train station** (Map p168; ☎71 345 511; www.sncft.com.tn; Pl Barcelone). See the website for timetables and ticket prices.

Getting Around

TAXI

Private taxis are cheap and easy to find. It's hard to run up a fare of more than TD15, even out to the northern beach suburb of La Marsa. A short hop will cost less than TD2; a longer one, such as to the Bardo Museum, is around TD5. Higher night rates apply from 9pm to 5am. Always ensure that the driver turns on the meter and check the appropriate rate is being used.

Taxi drivers working from the official airport rank are particularly aggressive, and often charge exorbitant flat rates and luggage charges. They are also known to grab tourists' luggage without permission. Do not pay more than TD10 for a trip to the city (the actual fare should be more like TD5). Locals suggest avoiding the rank altogether and hailing a taxi outside the departures-area curb upstairs.

TRAIN

The Tunis-Goulette-Marsa (TGM) rail system connects central Tunis with the northern beachside suburbs of La Goulette, Carthage, Sidi Bou Saïd and La Marsa. Fares cost between TD0.5 and TD1.8; services run from 5am to midnight.

The suburban trains that run from the Tunis Ville station are rarely of use to travellers.

TRAM

The modern *métro léger* system has several routes. The useful lines are 1 for the southern bus and *louage* stations, 2 for Ave de la Liberté, and 3 and 4 for the northern bus and *louage* station. Line 4 also has a stop for the Bardo Museum. The main stations are Place Barcelone and Place de la République. Fares start at TD0.5.

NORTHERN TUNISIA

Northern Tunisia is a hilly, magnificently green region, little explored by foreign visitors. Trump the tour buses and have your fill of hazy valleys, deserted beaches, interesting towns and the extraordinary Roman cities of Dougga and Bulla Regia.

Tabarka

POP 15,600

Tabarka, a quiet coastal town with a tough old Genoese fort watching over a long curve of white sand, is locally known as 'music town', thanks to the music festivals that take place here. In July, the renowned jazz festival segues into the sounds of rai (Algerian protest pop fusion), then Latin and world beats. This midsummer action and excellent scuba-diving aside, Tabarka has always been a nicely old-fashioned local's resort, but in the current climate has become increasingly rundown. It does make a good base, however, for exploring the coast's remote beaches and hiking the surrounding cork forests.

Sleeping & Eating

Tabarka has a lot of accommodation, none of it compelling. The *zone touristique* is to the town's east; some of the resorts are pleasant, others are fast going to seed.

Prices drop by over half outside of July and August.

Hôtel Novelty HOTEL $

(78 670 176; 68 Ave Habib Bourguiba; s/d TD50/60;) Right near the *louage* and bus stations, this place seems depressing from the outside but has simply furnished, neat and clean rooms and an English-speaking owner.

Hôtel La Plage HOTEL $$

(78 670 039; 11 Ave 7 Novembre 1987; s/d TD50/70;) Clean, small and central, and some rooms have balconies overlooking the street.

Hôtel Les Mimosas HOTEL $$

(78 673 018; www.hotel-les-mimosas.com; Ave Habib Bourguiba; s/d TD88/120;) This hotel's big attraction is its garden bar and pool, with sweeping views across the town and along the coast. Rooms have a (presumably unintentional) high-camp '80s appeal, and staff are sweet.

Restaurant Khemir SEAFOOD $

(11 Ave Habib Bourguiba; mains TD8-15) Simple and reliable fish dinners come with wine or beer; what you miss out on in marina views, you make up for in terms of attitude-free service.

Getting There & Away

The office of **Société Régionale de Transport de Jendouba** (SRTJ; 84 Ave Habib Bourguiba, cnr Rue Mohammed Ali) is the main bus stop in town. It runs buses to Ain Draham (TD1.3, 45 minutes, half-hourly), Jendouba (TD3.5, 1¾ hours, 10 daily) and Le Kef (TD6.5, 3½ hours, twice daily).

SNTRI buses to Tunis (TD10.3, 3¼ hours, five daily) depart from the SRTJ stop. *Louages* leave from Ave Habib Bourguiba for Ain Draham (TD1.5), Jendouba (TD3.9) and Tunis (TD9).

Ain Draham

POP 8890

In the middle of the cork forest of the Kroumirie Mountains, you'll find the alpine village of Ain Draham. Its primary appeal lies in the hunting, hiking and horse-riding opportunities it affords and the welcome respite offered by cooler summertime temperatures. Situated at an altitude of around 900m, there's usually snow in winter. The road up from Tabarka is one of Tunisia's most beautiful.

Sleeping

Hôtel Beau Séjour HOTEL $

(78 656 112; hotelbeausejour@live.fr; s/d TD35/50;) This dusty relic of a hunting lodge, complete with wild-boar-trophy decor, is an experience unto itself. Rooms are pleasant, as is the management.

Résidence Le Pins HOTEL $

(78 656 200; Ave Habib Bourguiba; s/d TD43/70) It's a standard cheapie, but there's a friendly owner and sweeping views from the back rooms' balconies and roof terrace.

Royal Rihana Hôtel HOTEL $$

(78 655 391; www.royalrihana-hotel.com; s/d full board TD85/120;) This forest lodge has lots of amenities including an indoor pool

and large restaurant, and an atmospheric lounge. The 74 rooms are spotless and comfortable, if dated, and have good views. This is the only place that does organised hikes and activities in the Kroumirie Mountains. It's 2km south of the fountain roundabout along Ave Habib Bourguiba.

Getting There & Away

There are regular buses to Jendouba (TD2.5, one hour, hourly), Tabarka (TD1.3, 45 minutes, half-hourly), Le Kef (TD5.5, two hours, twice daily) and Tunis (TD11, four hours, four daily). Regular *louages* go to/from Tabarka and Jendouba.

You can get public transport to the Algerian border from here. A taxi to Babouch and the border post costs around TD1. You'll have to cross the border on foot and find transport on the other side.

Bulla Regia

Famed for its extraordinary underground villas, the Roman city of **Bulla Regia** (admission TD5, camera TD1; 8am-7pm Apr–mid-Sep, 8.30am-5.30pm mid-Sep–Mar), 7km northwest of Jendouba, offers a rare opportunity to walk into complete, superbly preserved Roman rooms – there's no need to guess at how things once looked from remnant waist-high walls.

To escape the summer heat, the ever-inventive Romans retreated below the surface, building elegant homes – complete with colonnaded courtyards – that echo the troglodytic Berber homes at Matmata. The name each villa is known by reflects the theme of the mosaics found inside. Some (but not all) of the best are now in the Bardo Museum. Especially lovely examples can be seen at the oldest (though simplest) structure, the House of Fishing, which dates from the 2nd century. The newer villas become increasingly more ostentacious. The star attraction is the House of Amphitrite, with its nude Venus and centaurs, and attendant cherubs riding dolphins (what's not to like?). For an informative guided tour, call **Amel Ayadi** (96 014 141; tours per hr from TD30), or ask for her at the ticket office.

Bulla Regia is approximately 160km west of Tunis and may be easily visited on a day trip from Tunis, Le Kef or Tabarka. Trains or buses to Jendouba are your best bet to and from Tunis, and there are also regular buses and *louages* to and from Le Kef and Tabarka. A taxi from Jendouba costs around TD4. Any bus travelling between Jendouba and Ain Draham can drop you off at the Bulla Regia turn-off, from where it's a 3km walk. Note, the site can get *very* hot.

Le Kef

POP 41,600

Le Kef (El Kef in Arabic, meaning 'rock') is topped by a story-book Byzantine kasbah. On the slope below is the medina, a hilltop of narrow cobbled streets and blue-shuttered buildings, both traditional and early colonial in style. Highlights include beautiful ancient Muslim, Christian and Jewish places of worship. You'll find this proud, well-kept city is also laid-back and friendly – a real gem.

Sights

Many of Le Kef's sights are free but their custodians will generally welcome a tip, particularly if they show you around.

Kasbah HISTORIC SITE

(8am-1pm & 2pm-dusk) Frequently used as a film location, this pine-scented fortress dominates the city from a spur running off Jebel Dyr. There are great views looking out across the rolling blue-green landscape dotted with trees. A stronghold of some sort has occupied this site since the 5th century BC. To get to the kasbah, follow the stone steps leading uphill through the old medina from Place de l'Indépendance.

★Zaouia of Sidi Boumakhlouf MAUSOLEUM

(96 254 798; call for admission) Below the kasbah sits this enchanting 17th-century Sufi mausoleum, with a brilliantly tiled interior and narrow tower. The guardian, gorgeous Madame Zemourda, is a descendant of one of the occupants; call and she will arrive to open the door and show you around. Just outside is a bewitchingly pretty, tree-shaded square and cafe; ask there if you don't have a phone.

Musée des Arts et Traditions Populaires MUSEUM

(admission TD4, camera TD1; 9.30am-4pm Tue-Sun mid-Sep–Mar, 9am-1pm & 4-7pm Tue-Sun Apr–mid-Sep) The road that flanks the kasbah leads to this well-laid-out museum, housed in a sprawling, ornate Sufi complex founded in 1784. The museum concentrates on the culture of the region's Berber nomads, and exhibits include Berber tents and silver jewellery.

Sleeping & Eating

Le Kef has a good selection of clean, comfortable accommodation options. There's little in the way of restaurants, but hotels and guest houses can usually provide dinner and there's also a string of convivial fast-food places with eat-in tables along Rue Mongi Slim. Male travellers will find the city's bars – it has the highest concentration of drinking holes in the country – entertaining.

Hôtel Medina HOTEL **$**
(☎78 204 183; 18 Rue Farhat Hached; s/d TD7/14) Super basic but clean enough, this little place has a great medina location and fine views from the rooms at the back and rooftop terrace. Just don't expect the shared bathrooms to be plush (or have toilet seats).

Résidence Vénus HOTEL **$**
(☎78 204 695; www.hotel-lespins.com; Rue Mouldi Khamessi; s/d TD30/40) This pleasant *pension* (guest house) has twittering canaries in the courtyard, great views from the rooftop and 20 rooms that are simple and clean. It's under the same management as Hôtel Les Pins and, if you ask nicely, they will let you use the pool there.

Dar Boumakhlouf B&B **$$$**
(☎78 201 467; www.dar-boumakhlouf.com; 13 Rue Kheireddine Becha; s/d €80/100;) Situated up in between the kasbah and the medina, position alone would make this a good choice, but it's also an opportunity to stay in a beautiful traditional home, with cultured and welcoming hosts. The owner is an excellent cook – breakfast includes a rare taste of Keffoise favourites, including the morish *abraj* (semolina biscuits) and *rfissa* (date crumble).

Restaurant Vénus TUNISIAN **$**
(Rue Farhat Hached; mains TD10-15; noon-3pm & 6-11pm Sat-Thu) Under the same management as Résidence Vénus, this is the only 'proper' restaurant in town, and is not a bad option. The dining room doubles as a bar, and the terrace, well, *is* a bar.

Information

The city centre, around Place de l'Indépendance, is a 10-minute walk uphill from the bus and *louage* station, or a cheap ride in a shared taxi. There are several banks scattered throughout Place de l'Indépendance, and a busy **post office** (Rue Hedi Chaker) and internet cafes located nearby.

Getting There & Away

There are SNTRI buses travelling to and from Tunis (TD9.2, 3¼ hours, hourly). To visit Dougga, take the Le Kef–Tunis bus and ask to be dropped off at the New Dougga turn-off (TD3.8, one hour).

Dougga

A Roman city with a view, **Dougga** (☎78 466 636; admission TD5, camera TD1; 8am-7pm Apr-mid-Sep, 8.30am-5.30pm mid-Sep–Mar) is set on a hillside surrounded by olive groves and overlooking fields of grain, with forested hills beyond. Built of tan stone, its mellow tones meld harmoniously with the dusty landscape of the Kalled Valley and Tebersouk Mountains.

One of the most magnificent Roman sights in Africa, Dougga's ancient remains are startlingly complete, giving a beguiling glimpse of how well-heeled Romans lived, flitting between the baths (including the fine **Thermes de Caracalla**), the imposing **Capitole** (the 3500-seat theatre) and various temples (21 have been identified). The city was built on the site of ancient Thugga, a Numidian settlement, which explains why the streets are so uncharacteristically tangled. The 2nd-century-BC Libyo-Punic **mausoleum** is the country's finest pre-Roman monument, and is startlingly adorned.

The site is located 110km southwest of Tunis and can easily be visited on a day trip from there or Le Kef – or en route between the two cities. Buses and *louages* stop at Tebersouk, about 8km northeast of Dougga. From Tebersouk's *louage* station, hiring an entire yellow-striped *louage* or a taxi to Dougga should cost about TD10 one way and TD15 to TD20 return (the driver will, with luck, return to pick you up at a prearranged time; note that some demand a lot more or set exorbitant per-person rates). If you're driving from Le Kef, turn at Nouvelle Dougga. The best time to visit is in the morning or late in the day; allow at least three hours and pack a picnic.

CENTRAL TUNISIA

Home to Kairouan, one of Islam's most holy cities, several of Tunisia's largest beach resorts, and El-Jem, its most impressive Roman monument, this region is hardly lacking in superlatives. Despite its great diversity, it's only a short commute to get from one site to the other.

Kairouan

POP 117,900

With its Grande Mosquée, the oldest in North Africa, the walled city of Kairouan is considered the fourth-holiest site of Islam. Unlike many of the cities and towns in the region that cultivate tourism as an industry, Kairouan seems able to absorb the day trippers and retain its conservative, low-key relationship to outsiders. Besides its religious significance, the medina is a beautiful place to wander, especially in the late afternoon when the shadows make the crumbling, white-washed, blue- and green-edged houses, hung with birdcages or marked by the hand of Fatima, a hauntingly lovely sight.

It was here that Arabs established their first base when they arrived from the east in AD 670 – Kairouan became so important in the Islamic hierarchy that seven visits now equal one visit to Mecca.

This is also the rug capital of the country: if you're in the market for a carpet, it's a good place to do your haggling. Watch out for carpet touts and people offering 'professional guide services'; if you want a guide to show you around, arrange one through the Syndicat d'initiative. These guys carry accreditation, with photos, and they know their stuff. They charge TD20 for a one-and-a-half to two-hour tour of all the major sites and speak Arabic and French; some also speak English, Spanish or German. Also go here to buy the admission ticket that covers all sights.

Sights

Grande Mosquée MOSQUE

(Rue Okba ibn Nafâa; 8am-2pm Sat-Thu, to noon Fri) This 9th-century mosque, with its buttressed walls, has a typically unadorned Aghlabid design. Impressions change once you step into the huge marble-paved courtyard, surrounded by an arched colonnade. Non-Muslims can't cross into the richly decorated prayer hall, but the doors are left open to allow a glimpse.

Zaouia Sidi Sahab MAUSOLEUM

(Ave Zama el Belaoui; 8am-6pm Mon-Thu, to 2pm Fri, to 4pm Sat & Sun) Northwest of the medina is this 17th-century place tiled in luminescent colours and known as the 'barber mosque', because it contains the mausoleum of one of the Prophet's companions, Abu Zama el-Belaoui, who used to carry around three hairs from the Prophet's beard.

Bir Barouta HISTORIC SITE

(9am-6pm Sat-Thu) Here a blinkered camel walks in a circle, drawing water from a holy well said to be connected to Mecca. Stagey, yes, but the well forms a large part of the city's foundation story, and is also an important spiritual ritual for many visitors.

Tapis-Sabra HISTORIC BUILDING

(8am-4pm) The 18th-century residence of the former *beys* of Kairouan is now a carpet shop. It's worth enduring the carpet spiel to see an exquisitely restored medina house and witness the women rug weavers at work.

Sleeping

Hôtel Sabra HOTEL $

(77 230 263; Pl des Martyrs; s/d TD15/30) This noisy, hot, hostel-like dump has the best location in Kairouan opposite the Bab ech Chouhada, and the views from the rooftop (where you may be able to sleep in summer) are breathtaking.

Hôtel la Kasbah LUXURY HOTEL $$$

(77 237 301; www.goldenyasmin.com; Ave Ibn el-Jazzar; s/d TD110/210; P @) Occupying the old kasbah in the northern section of the medina, this is the city's five-star hotel. Traditional elements like the colourful tiled walls and dark wood ornate ceilings spell luxury but service can be perfunctory. However, the pool is enormous: a relief in Kairouan's summer swelter.

Eating

Restaurant Sabra TUNISIAN $

(Ave de la République; mains TD7-10, set meal TD9) Serves good, filling staples in a pleasant little dining room. Staff are super friendly.

Restaurant Karawan TUNISIAN $

(Rue Soukina bint el-Hassan; set meals from TD10) Clean, friendly family-run place, with all the usual dishes; the tajines (omelettes) and *briks* (filled pastries) are particularly good.

Patisserie Segni PATISSERIE $

(Ave 7 Novembre) This patisserie is the best in town and bakes a staggering aray of the local speciality biscuit, the sticky date-filled *makroud*.

Information

All the major banks are on the streets south of Place des Martyrs, the main post office is southwest of Bab ech Chouhada.

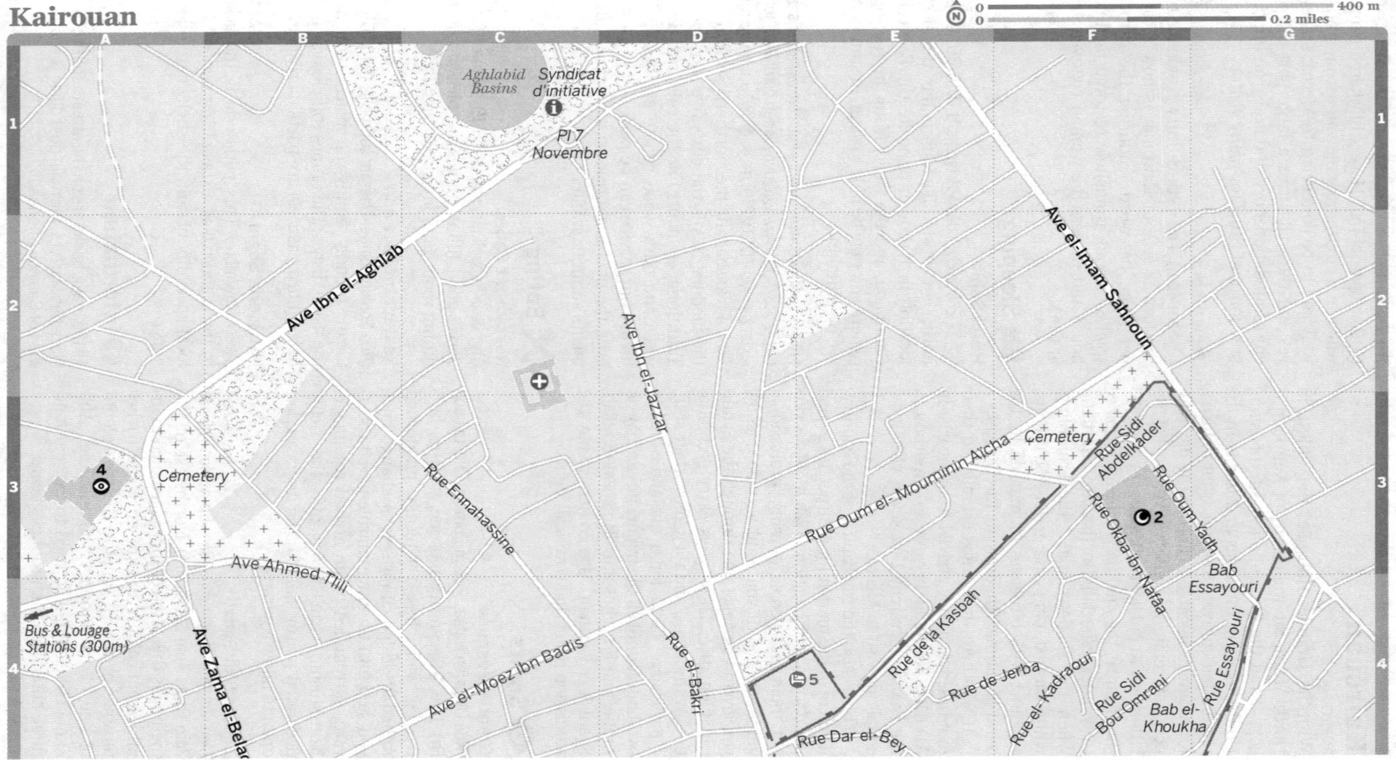
Kairouan
0
400 m
0
0.2 miles
Aghlabid Basins
Syndicat d'initiative
Pl 7 Novembre
Ave Ibn el-Aghlab
Ave Ibn el-Jazzar
Ave el-Imam Sahnoun
Cemetery
Rue Sidi Abdelkader
Rue Oum el-Mouminin Aïcha
Rue Oum Yadh
Rue Okba ibn Nafâa
2
Bab Essayouri
Rue Essay ouri
4
Cemetery
Rue Ennahassine
Ave Ahmed Tlili
Bus & Louage Stations (300m)
Ave Zama el-Belac
Ave el-Moez ibn Badis
Rue el-Bakri
5
Rue de la Kasbah
Rue de Jerba
Rue el-Kadraoui
Rue Sidi Bou-Omrani
Bab el-Khoukha
Rue Dar el-Bey

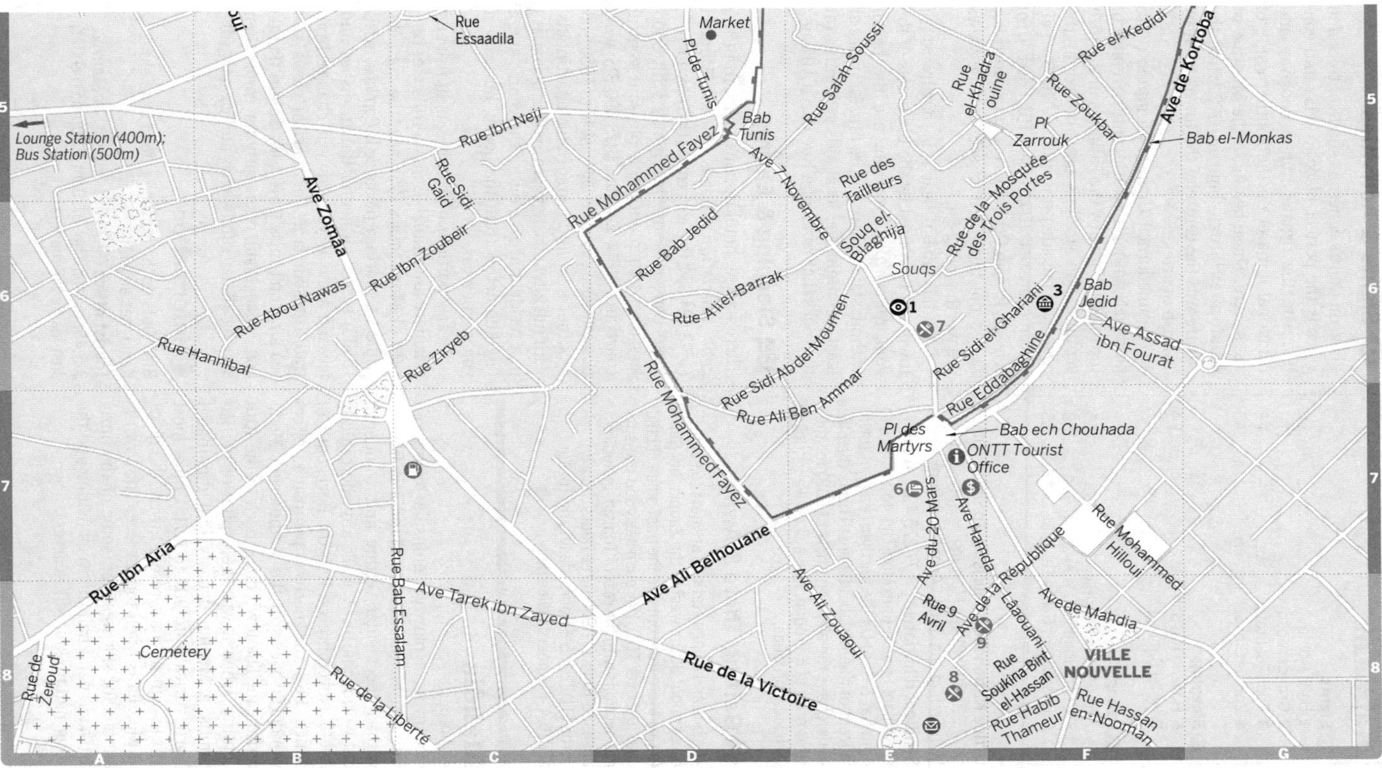
Rue Essaadila
Market
Pl de Tunis
Rue Salah Soussi
Rue el-Khadra ouine
Rue el-Kedidi
Ave de Kortoba
Rue Zoukbar
Pl Zarrouk
Bab el-Monkas
Lounge Station (400m); Bus Station (500m)
Rue Ibn Neji
Bab Tunis
Rue Mohammed Fayez
Ave 7 Novembre
Rue des Tailleurs
Rue de la Mosquée des Trois Portes
Ave Zomâa
Rue Sidi Gaid
Rue Bab Jedid
Souq el-Blaghjia
Souqs
Rue Ibn Zoubeir
Rue Abou Nawas
Rue Ali el-Barrak
Bab Jedid
Rue Sidi el-Ghariani
Ave Assad ibn Fourat
Rue Hannibal
Rue Ziryeb
Rue Sidi Abdel Moumen
Rue Ali Ben Ammar
Rue Eddabaghine
Pl des Martyrs
Bab ech Chouhada
ONTT Tourist Office
Ave du 20 Mars
Ave Hamda Lâaouani
Rue Mohammed Hilloui
Ave de la République
Ave Ali Belhouane
Rue Ibn Aria
Rue Bab Essalam
Ave Tarek ibn Zayed
Ave Ali Zouaoui
Rue 9 Avril
Ave de Mahdia
VILLE NOUVELLE
Cemetery
Rue de Zeroud
Rue de la Liberté
Rue de la Victoire
Rue Soukina Bint el-Hassan
Rue Habib Thameur
Rue Hassan en-Nooman

Kairouan

Sights

Sleeping

Eating

Office National du Tourisme Tunisien (ONTT; 77 231 897; Pl des Martyrs; 8am-6pm Mon-Thu, to 1pm Fri, to 4pm Sat & Sun)

Syndicat d'initiative (77 270 452; Ave Ibn el-Aghlab; 8am-6pm Mon-Thu, to 1pm Fri, to 4pm Sat & Sun) On the northern edge of town in front of the Aghlabid Basins. This is the place to purchase the all-in-one ticket (TD8) for the sites around Kairouan. Has a shop well stocked with local produce.

Getting There & Away

The bus and *louage* stations are next to each other about 300m west of the Zaouia Sidi Sahab (a taxi there from outside the post office should cost just over TD1). Kairouan has good transport connections with the rest of Tunisia, including buses to Tunis (TD9.4, three hours, hourly), Jerba (TD22.1, 6½ hours, daily) and Tozeur (TD16.4, 4½ hours, twice daily).

Mahdia

POP 46,000

Occupying a narrow peninsula jutting out into the Mediterranean, Mahdia is blessed with a spectacular setting and wonderful old-world charm. A walk anywhere along Ave 7 Novembre or Rue du Borj, both of which hug the narrow peninsula, offers wonderful views of the shimmering Mediterranean. The town dates back to the 10th century, when it was the capital of the Fatimids, a Muslim dynasty that dominated North Africa from 909 to 1171. Unlike most of the central coast resort towns, the heart of Mahdia is often tourist free. The town is famous for silk weaving (some of the burly artisans spend half the week fishing and the other half making silk scarves).

Sights & Activities

Place du Caire's generous shade of trees and vines is the perfect place to relax and contemplate the ornate arched doorway and octagonal minaret on the southern side of the square. These belong to the **Mosque of Mustapha Hamza**, built in 1772 when the square was the centre of the town's wealthy Turkish quarter.

The unadorned **Grande Mosquée** (Place Khadi en-Noamine) is a 20th-century replica of the mosque built by the Fatimids in the 10th century; non-Muslims are allowed in the courtyard outside prayer times. The **Borj el-Kebir** (admission TD4, camera TD1; 9am-7pm Jun-Sep, to 4pm Oct-May) is a large fortress; there's not much left to see, but the views are worth paying for.

Mahdia's main beach is northwest of town and is fronted by the big hotels of the *zone touristique* (you can use the beach without staying here). More fun, for males at least, is joining the local kids swimming off the rocks that run along Rue Cap d'Afrique.

Sleeping & Eating

There's a few hotel options apart from the *zone touristique* hotels. **Hôtel Médina** (73 694 664; Rue el-Kaem; r TD40) is set in a large converted medina house with spotless rooms surrounding a pleasant central courtyard. **Villa Zouila** (73 690 315; www.closetothelocals.com; 19 C96; apt from TD50) offers four neat and comfortable apartments, with full kitchens, terraces and barbecue. It's in a residential area out of the centre and a few kilometres from the beach, but easy if you've got a car.

Hearty portions of freshly caught fish and calamari are available at no-frills **Restaurant el-Moez** (mains TD5), near the markets, while **Le Meriem** (Route de la Corniche; mains TD5-15) serves authentic Italian dishes and ice-cold wine if you fancy a change from trad Tunisian fare. For magical views and sea air, don't miss **Café Sidi Salem** (Rue de Borj; 8am-11pm), open early for coffee then serving all-day sandwiches and casual grills.

Information

BIAT Outside the fortified gate of Skifa el-Kahla, has an ATM.

Tourist office (73 681 098; 8am-1pm & 3-5.45pm Mon-Thu, 8.30am-1.30pm Fri & Sat) Just inside the medina.

Getting There & Away

The bus and *louage* stations are about 1km southwest of the train station. There are *louages* to Sousse (TD4.1, one hour), El-Jem (TD2.6, 40 minutes), Monastir (TD2.8, 45 minutes), Sfax (TD5.8, 1½ hours), Kairouan (TD7.5, 1½ hours) and Tunis (TD11, three hours).

The **train station** (Ave Farhat Hached) is just west of the port. There is a daily service to Tunis (TD10.4, four hours). The Banlieue du Sahel line runs half-hourly to hourly trains to Monastir (TD1.9, 1½ hours) and Sousse (TD2.5, 1¾ hours).

El-Jem

POP 18,300

El-Jem's dramatic honey-coloured **Roman colosseum** (admission TD8, camera TD1; 7.30am-5.30pm) rises up from a low plateau halfway between Sousse and Sfax, dwarfing the tiny modern town around it. This sight is all you need to grasp the scope of Roman civilisation in Africa. Built 2000 years ago by olive-oil traders with money to burn, it's a confident culmination of a couple of centuries of engineering expertise. It included state-of-the-art features including a movable floor – all the better to showcase gladiatorial combat, executions and other forms of Roman popular culture. Steps reach up to the top balconies; a couple of millenia on, there are still olive trees as far as the eye can see.

The other treasure here is the beautiful archaeological **museum**, home to an outstanding mosaic collection. It may not be as big as that in the Bardo, but the mosaics' vividness and pristine condition definitely outdo those in the capital, plus some of them are in situ, in a street of excavated villas alongside the museum proper.

There's nowhere to stay, but you can eat well at **Restaurant Les Emirs** (Place du Coliseum; set menus TD13-20; noon-3pm, dinner Jul & Aug), just across from the colosseum entrance.

The *louage* station is 300m west of the train station along Ave Hedi Chaker. There are frequent departures to Mahdia (TD2.6, 40 minutes), Sousse (TD4.7, 40 minutes) and Sfax (TD4.7, 40 minutes). For Kairouan and Tunis, you'll need to change at Sousse. The last *louage* has usually left the station by 7pm and often well before. There are trains north to Sousse (TD4.5, one hour) and Tunis (TD10.4, three hours), and south to Sfax (TD4.5, one hour), but their timing isn't so convenient.

Sfax

POP 265,000

Locals from Sfax have the reputation of being hard-working, thrifty and, well, dull. In Tunisia this doesn't do you any favours – everyone will tell you to head straight down to Jerba. But the country's second-largest city is

BEACH LIFE: CAP BON & THE CENTRAL COAST

The golden-sand coast stretching from the tip of Cap Bon to the city of Sfax has drawn millions of European sun-seekers since the 1960s. While some resort strips could hardly be described as sensitively developed, Tunisia has at least been spared the high-rise towers that blight the Mediterranean elsewhere. And while the resorts do aim to be a world unto themselves, you're also never that far from Roman ruins, Berber villages or seldom-visited countryside.

With tourism numbers down in the years since the Jasmine Revolution, discounting is common and hotels are rarely crowded. There's also a number of small hotels and B&Bs, both in the backstreets of the popular resort towns and in the remoter coastal towns, that offer comfort and a more low-key experience.

Hammamet Yes, the resorts are huge and stretch for miles, but the town itself is relaxed and charming and has an increasing number of stylish B&Bs.

Nabeul This bustling, prosperous town of farmers and artisans does double duty as a laid-back beach destination.

Kélibia and El Haouaria Remote and largely untouristed, up here the stunning sandy beaches give way to rocky coves and pine forests.

Monastir The town's unloveliness is offset by a dramatic seaside ribat (fort) and the quirk of Bourghiba's mausoleum.

Sousse Loud, brash, crowded but beautiful, Boujaffar Beach is an enduring favourite.

Mahdia Scenic and historic, this town has handled resortification better than most.

definitely worth a look, if only to try delicious *ojja* (prawn stew with eggs and tomatoes) and to check out its busy, picturesque medina. Wandering the Ville Nouvelle too, has its rewards, with some of the best-preserved 20th-century architecture in Tunisia. It's concentrated around the Place de la République, Ave Hedi Chaker and Ave Habib Bourguiba

Sights

★ Sfax Medina NEIGHBOURHOOD
Surrounded by ancient crenulated walls that could have been filched from a child's toy castle, this tourist-tat-free zone hasn't been prettified for visitors. The main narrow thoroughfares bustle with everyday commerce, while away to the northeast and southwest wind quiet, twisting lanes. The main souq heading north is the celebrated **Souq des Etoffes**, which was used as the setting for the Cairo markets in the film *The English Patient*. Don't miss a glimpse of the **Grande Mosquée**, with its 9th-century minaret.

Dar Jellouli Museum of Popular Traditions HISTORIC BUILDING
(admission TD4, camera TD1; ⌚9.30am-4.30pm Tue-Sun) Dar Jellouli Museum is in a classic courtyard house, built by a wealthy mer-

Sfax

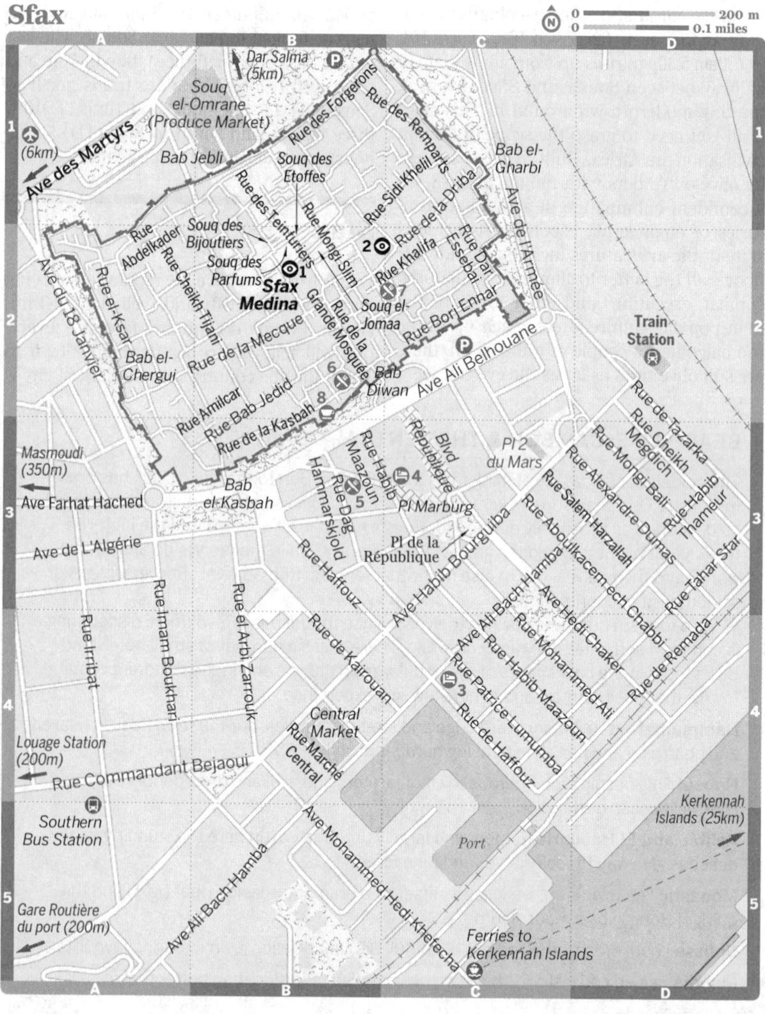

chant family in the 17th century, and is filled with beautiful carved-wood panels, rich tile decoration and ornate stuccowork. The displays include traditional costumes and jewellery, but the building is the star attraction.

Sleeping

Dar Salma B&B $$
(www.darsalma.com; off Route Gremda; s/d TD60/70) Out in a quiet residential neighbourhood, this is a truly special B&B in an elegant family home. The host, from an old Sfaxoise family, can walk you through the souqs and fresh markets of the medina. She's also an excellent cook – you'll be plied with homemade cakes and yogurt at breakfast and fabulous, inventive seafood dishes at dinner.

Hotel El Layeli HOTEL $$
(74 228 999; www.hotellayeli.com; Rue Bach Hamba; s/d 40/60;) This friendly, clean and comfortable place is in a good central street and many rooms have views over the port (though sadly, at time of writing, this was an aquatic rubbish tip). The air-con is super efficient and the breakfast spread is generous.

Hôtel Thyna HOTEL $$
(74 225 317; www.hotel-thyna.com; 37 Rue Habib Maazoun; s/d TD40/65;) Ideally located and excellent value. Rooms are perfectly comfortable and kept immaculate and there's a nice cafe on the 3rd floor.

Eating & Drinking

Restaurant Budaya TUNISIAN $
(Rue de la Kasbah; mains TD6-9; 7am-9pm Tue-Sun) Sfaxoises rich and poor head to this clean and air-conditioned place for fast and filling dishes like chicken ragu or couscous.

★ **Saffoud Abid** BARBECUE $
(Rue Khalifa; 2-course meal TD9; 8am-4pm Tue-Sun) A wonderfully authentic medina favourite where shoppers come for lamb *brochette* (kebab) lunches, the meat grilled to order in an ashy pit. Opposite, the (nameless) seafood place serves heaping plates of octopus stew, spaghetti marinara, salads and prawn *briks*.

Le Bagdad TUNISIAN $$
(74 223 856; 63 Ave Farhat Hached; mains TD12-22; noon-2pm & 7-11pm Tue-Sun) The decor has a formal vibe, but the service is friendly and the menu gives pride of place to traditional dishes such as *kamounia* (cumin-flavoured stew).

Masmoudi PATISSERIE
(www.masmoudi.com; 6 Ave Farhat Hached; 10am-6pm) This international chain is a local business made good. Come here for the top-notch presentation and huge selection (the local speciality is the *mlabes*, a fat orb of almond paste encased in silver-annointed icing).

Café Maure Diwan CAFE
(off Rue de la Kasbah; 7am-11pm) Cut into the medina wall between Bab Diwan and Bab el-Kasbah, this atmospheric cafe is a refuge from the heat and a relaxing spot to kill a few hours over *thé au pignons et menthe* (mint tea with pinenuts, TD1).

Sfax

Top Sights
1 Sfax Medina B2

Sights
2 Dar Jellouli Museum of Popular Traditions B2

Sleeping
3 Hotel El Layeli C4
4 Hôtel Thyna C3

Eating
5 Le Bagdad B3
6 Restaurant Budaya B2
7 Saffoud Abid C2

Drinking & Nightlife
8 Café Maure Diwan B2

Getting There & Away

Ferries to the rustic Kerkennah Islands (TD0.7, 11 daily) leave from the docks on Ave Mohammed Hedi Khefecha.

SNTRI buses leave from the Gare Routière du Port, southwest of the port, with regular buses to Tunis (TD14.9, five hours, 10 daily), Sousse (TD7.3, two hours, 12 daily), Douz (TD15.5, four to five hours, two daily), El-Jem (TD3.8, one hour, 12 daily), Jerba (TD13.6, four to five hours, one daily) and Tripoli (TD25, eight hours, two daily). Kairouan and Medenine are serviced by Soretras, which also runs additional services to Jerba.

The *louage* station is 300m west of Soretras' southern bus station on Rue Commandant Bejaoui. *Louages* run to all the same destinations as buses for around the same price, as well as to El-Jem (TD4, one hour) and Tripoli (TD36, eight hours).

The train station is at the eastern end of Ave Habib Bourguiba. There are four trains per day south to Gabès (2½ hours), and two services to Gafsa (three hours). At time of writing, trains were not running on to Tozeur. Heading north, there are five trains daily to El-Jem (one hour), three to Sousse (two hours) and eight to Tunis (three to 3½ hours).

SOUTHERN TUNISIA

The dunes of the Grand Erg Oriental, one of the Sahara's most expansive sand seas, spill into Tunisia's far south, and it's here you'll find desert landscapes that have enchanted travellers for centuries, their seeming emptiness the stuff of dreams, nightmares and much colonial musing. Life-giving palmeraies support a network of busy oasis towns, and produce an autumn harvest of the world's best dates. Beyond these, salt lakes shimmer in the sun like mirages and ruined Berber forts stare from scrubby hilltops. Back on the coast, the palm-dotted island of Jerba is an intriguing mix of ancient traditions, both Berber and Jewish, and beach-resort languor.

Tozeur

POP 35,500

Tozeur makes an excellent base for longer forays into the surrounding area, including the mesmerising Chott el-Jerid, Tunisia's largest salt lake, and the mountain oases to the north. Bounded on one side by an enormous palmeraie and with the desolate snow white expanse of salt on the other, the town feels at once far-flung and urban and lively. It's easy to spend a few days here occupied by the labyrinthine old quarter, Ouled el-Hadef, and the cool, winding paths of the palmeraie. The postrevolution drop in tourists has hit this town particularly hard, with many hotels shutting down in 2011–12. But a large range of accommodation still exists and prices can be highly negotiable (including day rates at five-star properties, where you'll have no trouble nabbing a sunlounger by the pool).

Sights & Activities

Excursions that can be made from Tozeur include a half-day trip via 4WD to **Ong Jemal**, a dramatic location used in both *Star Wars* and *The English Patient*; **Nefta**, with its exquisite sunken palmeraie; or the beautiful Berber villages of **Midès**, **Chebika** and **Tamerza**. Half-day trips cost from TD45.

Ouled el-Hadef NEIGHBOURHOOD
This 14th-century medina has a unique, striking architecture of pale brickwork arranged in relief patterns of endless, rhythmic variation; the easiest way in is from Ave de Kairouan. The families living here come outside to socialise come dusk – strolling at this time is quite special.

★ **Palmeraie** GARDENS
This enormous green space has over 200,000 date palms, as well as fig and pomegranate trees and canopied garden holdings. It's best explored by foot or bicycle (ask at your hotel for recommended bike hire). Calèches (horse-drawn carriages) can be found opposite the Hôtel Residence Karim and cost around TD6 per hour, though you are at the mercy of the driver as to the route taken, and the horses don't look like they are treated well.

Chak Wak Park MUSEUM
(palmeraie; admission TD15; ⏲ noon-midnight) This incongruous, trippy park is a testament to the liberal vision of the former mayor of Tozeur. Scattered around gorgeous grounds is what amounts to a 3D education on evolution, history and religion. Highlights include dinosaur-sized replicas of dinosaurs, a gallery of icons of the world's major religions and an excellent history of Hannibal and the Carthaginian wars. It's all tremendous fun and there's a particularly prettily situated restaurant, pizza place and cafe.

Sahara Lounge ADVENTURE SPORTS
(☎ 25 616 001; www.sahara-lounge.com; palmeraie; activities adult/child TD25/10; 👪) This 2-hectaure activity park is beautifully located and sensitively designed. Climbing walls and flying foxes are set out among the palms and there's also a range of family-friendly cultural programs.

Sleeping

Camping Les Beaux Rêves CAMPGROUND $
(☎ 76 453 331; http://beauxreves.koi29.com; Ave Abdulkacem Chebbi; tent/bungalow per person TD8/12) Small and a little rundown, this place is, however, pleasantly shaded by trees – you can even set up a hammock to sleep – and is in a convenient, if busy, location between the main drag and the palmeraie. The cabins make for a good alternative to a budget hotel.

Hôtel Residence Karim HOTEL $
(☎ 76 454 574; 150 Ave Abdulkacem Chebbi; s/d TD18/26; ❄) Offering excellent value, the Karim has bright and cheerful tiled rooms, shady courtyards and a rooftop terrace.

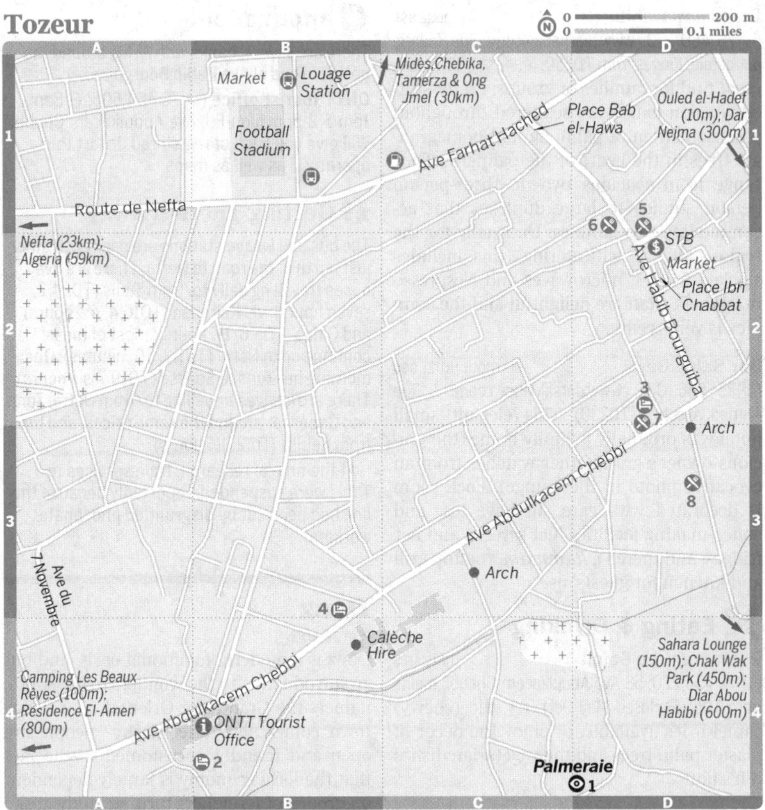

Residence el-Amen HOTEL **$**
(☎76 473 322; amentozeur@yahoo.fr; 10 Ave Taoufik el-Hakim; s/d TD25/40; ❄) The friendly el-Amen, on a side street off Ave Abdulkacem Chebbi, has cute little rooms. Rooftop rooms share a large terrace with excellent views.

Résidence L'Oued HOTEL **$$**
(☎76 463 036; www.residenceloued.com; Entrée Sahraoui; s/d TD40/60; P❄📶🏊) This small, professionally run hotel has a great setting on a lane facing the palmerie and has a pleasant pool area. Rooms are comfortable and well equipped, and there's a broad range of room types – all but the cheapest are super large.

★**Dar Nejma** BOUTIQUE HOTEL **$$$**
(☎74 598 837; www.darnejma-tozeur.com; Quartier Amaria, Ouled el-Hadef; ste TD200; 🚭❄📶🏊) This is a true destination hotel and one of the country's best places to stay. Secreted in a huge medina house, six stylish, private suites are set around an impossibly romantic, lushly planted pool area. There's a quiet, simple sort of luxury here, with date-wood furniture, glowing hand-mixed colour on the walls and individual terraces to lounge around.

Tozeur

Top Sights
1 Palmeraie ... D4

Sleeping
2 Résidence L'Oued ... B4
3 Dar Saida Beya ... D2
4 Hôtel Residence Karim ... B3

Eating
5 Patisserie el Qods ... D1
6 Restaurant de la République ... D1
7 Restaurant Le Soleil ... D2
8 Restaurant-Bar Le Petit Prince ... D3

Diar Abou Habibi LODGE $$$

(☎76 460 270; www.diarhabibi.com; Rue Toureg, palmeraie; lodges from TD350; P ❄ 📶) This is a great find for families or groups. Pretty, stilted wooden lodges are scattered throughout a dense garden of palm, fig and pomegranate trees in the heart of the palmerie. They range from spacious two- to three-person person studios to large duplexes that accommodate two families. Unusually for the region, all are self-catering (this includes stocked fridges, microwaves and Nespresso machines). Staff are delightful and the complex is very secure.

Dar Saida Beya BOUTIQUE HOTEL $$$

(☎25 566 066; www.darsaidabeya.com; 1 Rue Ahmed Ayech; d TD230) This elegant small hotel was originally a family home (the gracious owner's grandfather watches from an evocative photo in the lounge). Each room is decorated with care, all have tea- and coffee-making facilities, flat screens and bar fridges, and there's a *hammam*, rooftop grill and kitchen for guests' use.

Eating & Drinking

Restaurant Le Soleil TUNISIAN $

(☎76 454 220; 58 Ave Abdulkacem Chebbi; mains from TD5; ⏲closed May-Oct) Try the (chewy) camel if it's available, or enjoy the decor of plaster palm trees and the vegetarian dishes if it's not.

Restaurant de la République TUNISIAN $

(108 Ave Habib Bourguiba; mains TD6.5-12) Set back off the street, in an arcade next to the Mosque el-Ferdous, this is an ever-popular local place and great for kebabs or couscous and salad.

Restaurant-Bar Le Petit Prince TUNISIAN $$

(☎76 452 518; off Ave Abdulkacem Chebbi; mains TD14-25) Tunisian dishes, pasta and steaks are served in a palm-shaded courtyard. Wine and beer are available (there's a raucous local-boozers bar attached).

Patisserie el Qods PATISSERIE $

(Ave Habib Bourguiba) A handy and welcoming place to drop into for a quick sandwich, or something sweet and sticky, washed down with a fresh juice or good coffee (pastry and coffee TD1).

Café El Brak CAFE

(palmeraie) Tables are set in a pretty shaded garden; it's very relaxed and popular with couples and families.

Information

There are several banks with ATMs around the northern end of Ave Habib Bourguiba.

ONTT tourist office (☎76 454 503; ⏲8am-1pm & 2-5pm Mon-Fri; Ave Abdulkacem Chebbi) Will give you a list of registered desert tour operators, as well as maps.

Getting There & Away

The bus and *louage* stations are near each other just north of the road to Nefta. There are five buses travelling daily to/from Tunis (TD24.2, seven hours), via Kairouan (TD16.4, 4½ hours) and Gafsa (TD5.6, 1½ hours); most of these continue on to Nefta (TD1.3, 30 minutes). One morning bus runs to Sousse (TD19.7, six hours). There are *louages* travelling to/from Nefta, Tunis and Gabès for around the same prices, and to/from Kebili (TD7.2, 1½ hours).

At the time of research, train services to Tunis were suspended, reportedly because the line had been cut by disgruntled phosphate workers.

Douz

POP 28,000

Douz is a modern, functional oasis, and but an introduction to the wonders to the south, namely the Grand Erg Oriental. The sleepy town comes alive after dark – people are open and friendly, accustomed to the fact that the local economy is largely dependent on groups of foreigners turning giddy at the prospect of riding a camel. There are several hotels in the town centre that cater to independent travellers. Every Thursday, the souq is home to a colourful weekly market, where the last of Tunisia's nomadic camel herders come to trade. It's worth arranging to be here just to see it. The palmeraie, at the town's edge, is the largest in the country: more than 400,000 trees slice into the fierce sunlight.

Sights & Activities

Douz is the most convenient place to get a taste for the Sahara, though it's really only a taste. The desert proper starts 80km south of the *zone touristique*, so unless you're planning a longer excursion, you'll have to make do with the **great dune**. (It can't compare with the sand seas of the Grand Erg Oriental, but it's at least an introduction.) **Pegase** (☎75 470 793; Café de Dunes; ⏲8am-sunset) is a one-stop shop that seems to have

TOP TEN STAR WARS LOCATIONS

Tunisia's sensuous Saharan dunes set the scene in *The English Patient* and its impressive fortifications served as a Levantine backdrop for *Monty Python's Life of Brian*. But its most famous screen role was providing the otherworldly architecture and desertscapes that gave the *Star Wars* series such a powerful visual identity. If you want to walk in the steps of R2-D2, hotels and travel agencies in Tozeur or Douz can organise tours of various locations.

Sidi Driss Hotel (Matmata) The famous Sidi Driss was used for interior shots of the Lars family homestead in *Star Wars*. Bits of set are still in place here (and were used again in *The Phantom Menace* and *Attack of the Clones*). The dining room is where Luke tucked into a blue milkshake and went head to head over the harvest with his Uncle Owen. Note, there are better places to stay in town.

Ong Jemal (30km north of Tozeur) This was Darth Maul's lookout in *The Phantom Menace* and the location for his tussle with Qui-Gon Jinn, as well as lots of pod-race action. Its dunes were also used to dramatic effect in *The English Patient*.

Mos Espa (30km north of Tozeur) Near Ong Jemel, Mos Espa village is a construct in the middle of the desert used for the prequel films; its battered sets echo local Berber architecture.

Sidi Bouhlel (on the edge of Chott el-Jerid, east of Tozeur) Nicknamed Star Wars Canyon, this has seen Jawas parking their sand-crawlers, R2-D2 trundling plaintively along, Luke attacked by Tusken Raiders, and Ben and Luke overlooking Mos Eisley. Scenes from *The Phantom Menace* and *Attack of the Clones* were filmed here too.

Ksar Haddada (near Tataouine) A location for the Mos Espa slave quarters, Ksar Haddada has stunningly weird architecture, and is where Qui-Gon Jinn learned the truth about Anakin's parentage in *The Phantom Menace*. Though it's falling into ruin, some brightly painted doors from the set remain.

Ksar Ouled Soltane (near Tataouine) More slave quarters; these are perhaps the finest example of the curious moulded courtyard-centred buildings.

La Grande Dune (near Nefta) This stood in for the *Star Wars* Dune Sea, where C-3PO staggered past a Krayt dragon skeleton; if you're lucky, you might pick up some fibreglass bones.

Chott el-Jerid (east of Nefta and Tozeur) Here, in the first film, Luke contemplated two suns while standing soulfully at the edge of a crater, peering over these vast, dry salt flats. The landscape around its fringes doubled as Jundland Wastes populated by Krayt dragons and sand people.

Medenine (near Tataouine) Anakin Skywalker's *Phantom Menace* slave-quarters' home is off bustling Ave 7 Novembre.

Ajim (Jerba) Obi-Wan Kenobi's house exterior is about 3km out of town, while the freak-filled *Star Wars* cantina scene was filmed in the town centre (not, as many think, at the Sidi Driss).

a great dune monopoly, and offers camel rides at TD20 per hour.

Overnight treks are simple to organise; longer treks generally require 24 hours' notice (two- to three-week circuits are possible during the winter). The tourist office advises travellers to stay clear of the town's many unlicensed guides, as they are uninsured and unaccountable if problems arise. Officially recognised agencies include **Espace Libre** (☎75 470 620; www.libre-espace-voyages.com; Ave M'hemed Marzougui) and **Ghilane Travel Services** (☎75 470 692; www.ghilane.com; 38 Ave Taieb Mehiri)

The **Sahara Festival** usually takes place in November. This is very popular with Tunisians as well as travellers, and has displays of traditional desert sports, colourful parades and music.

Sleeping & Eating

★Camping Desert Club CAMPGROUND $
(☎75 470 575; campingdouz.skyrock.com; off Ave du 7 Novembre 1987; per person TD5, plus motorbike/car/campervan TD3/4/5) One of the best camping grounds in the country, not only because of its pretty setting among the date palms. Its excellent modern facilities and caring management make this special. If you're in a group, call ahead for a Berber tent. Three-course Italian or Tunisian menus (TD12) in the airy dining room are available to guests and nonguests, but need to be booked.

Hôtel 20 Mars HOTEL $
(☎75 470 269; hotel20mars@planet.tn; Rue 20 Mars; s/d TD25/30, without bathroom TD13/18; ❄) A justifiably popular traveller's option, with a helpful English-speaking manager who also organises tours and treks. Rooms are simple and on the small side, but an interior courtyard and terraces give the place real character.

Dar Souleiman B&B $$
(☎75 474 267; http://randomadairedouz.org; BP 104; r TD80-120;) Situated just out of town at the desert's edge, this guesthouse is built in the local low-slung style. Rooms are simple and pretty, as is the garden. The owners know the desert environment intimately and organise excursions.

Restaurant Les Palmier TUNISIAN $
(Ave Taeïb Mhiri; mains TD5-9) This bustling dining room serves up good local cuisine – soups, couscous, *briks*, salads – with a smile. You can also eat out the back under a shady trellis or on a cushioned floor.

Information

There are banks on Ave Taeïb Mhiri.

ONTT tourist office (☎75 470 351; Place des Martyrs; ⊙8am-1pm & 2-6pm Mon-Sat) Can give recommended prices for camel expeditions.

Publinet (cnr Rue 20 Mars & Rue el-Hounine; per hr TD2; ⊙8am-10pm) Has good internet connections.

Getting There & Away

There are regular local buses and *louages* running to Kebili (TD2.6, 30 minutes), Tozeur (TD8.2, two hours), Gabès (TD7, three hours) and Zaafrane (TD0.7, 20 minutes). SNTRI has two air-con services per day to Tunis (TD28.7, eight hours), Gabès (TD8.9, two hours) and Sfax (TD15.5, four hours).

Matmata

POP 1500

From above, the troglodytic pit homes that have made Matmata famous look like bomb craters. Home to around 500 people, the ingenious dwellings only come into focus up close and are a testament to humankind's urge to domesticate, even somewhere as inhospitable as here. More recently, the town has drawn its fame from playing the home planet of Luke Skywalker in *Star Wars*. It's not often you get the locals offering to show you outer space, but this little village brims with such delights.

The best place to stay is **Hôtel Marhala** (☎75 240 015; www.hotel-marhala-matmata.webs.com; s/d incl breakfast TD20/40, half board TD30/60), run by the Touring Club de Tunisie. It's everything you might hope a troglodytic hotel to be (there's even a dining-room cave and a bar with beer).

There are regular buses and *louages* to and from Gabès (TD2.6, 45 minutes) and Tunis (TD23.5, eight hours).

Jerba & Houmt Souq

The island of Jerba has an intoxicating mixture of sandy beaches, desert heat and wonderfully idiosyncratic architecture. Berber culture is dominant – as the women wrapped in cream-striped textiles, topped with straw hats attest – while a Jewish community, once integral to the island's ethnic make-up, retains a small presence. To the classically inclined, the mere mention of the island's name conjures images of Homer's Land of the Lotus Eaters, a place so seductive that it's impossible to leave; 'drugged by the legendary honeyed fruit' as they were, poor Ulysses had a lot of trouble prising his crew away. The visitors that flock to the luxury hotels along beautiful Sidi Mahres beach appear to understand. While the appeal of a beach resort speaks for itself, rest assured there's a whole lot more to discover here.

Houmt Souq is the island's capital, situated in the middle of the north coast. It's a charming small town, chock-a-block with outdoor cafes, shops and a handful of ancient *funduqs* (converted Ottoman-era camel caravan inns – also known as *caravansérail*), the town's architectural trademark.

Other places of note include the Jewish village of Erriadh (Hara Seghira/small ghetto); Midoun, the functional but pleasant big

WORTH A TRIP

TATAOUINE

While the name is evocative to *Star Wars* fans, the town of Tataouine is more a base for exploring the ruined hilltop *ksar* (fortified stronghold) than a destination in itself. The wonderful **Festival of the Ksour** in April uses the courtyards of the town for music, dance and other festivities.

The best sites are quite a way from town, but can be easily reached by chartering a taxi (around TD20 return), or, with luck, patience and a knack for timing, by taking local transport. Don't miss the beautiful **Ksar Ouled Soltane**, 22km southeast of Tataouine, where the *ghorfas* (ancient grain stores) rise a dizzying four storeys, reached by precarious dream-sequence staircases, and overlook desert-scrub hills.

Equally impressive are the ancient hilltop villages of **Chenini** and **Douiret**, which spill across and merge with the rocky ochre slopes southwest of Tataouine. To get the most out of your visit, it can be worth asking someone to show you around, as some of the features can be hard to find.

Visit one of the many patisseries selling local speciality, *corne de gazelle* (TD0.5) – a pastry case, shaped like a gazelle's horn, filled with chopped nuts and soaked in honey.

Buses and *louages* leave from the centre of town. SNTRI runs three daily air-con buses to Tunis (TD25, eight hours) that travel via Gabès (TD6.5, two hours), Sfax (TD12.6, four hours) and Sousse. Regular *louages* run to Tunis (TD23.5, eight hours) and Gabès (TD7, two hours).

You can reach Chenini, Douiret and sometimes Ksar Ouled Soltane via *camionnette* (pick-up; around TD5). These leave from near the Banque du Sud on Rue 2 Mars, though they serve the destinations only in the mornings – unless you start out early, you could get stuck there. Full or half-day tours from Jerba (4WD for four people TD100 to TD180) are easy to arrange at short notice.

town servicing the east coast; and the southern potters' town of Guellella.

The nicest, most accessible public beach is near the lighthouse on the east coast, just along from Club Med. It's scenic, clean and there's a *buvette* (kiosk) for drinks and casual seafood meals.

A causeway built in Roman times links the east of the island to the mainland. In addition, 24-hour car ferries ply between western Ajim (where Obi-Wan Kenobi had his house) and El-Jorf.

Sights & Activities

Houmt Souq Old Town NEIGHBOURHOOD
Jerba's traditional architecture is delightful and unlike any other in Tunisia. Domes dot the skyline and all is bathed in a dusty whitewash. Once a market town, always a market town; there's no escaping the carpets, jewellery, ceramics, *brocante* (bric-a-brac), ubiquitous leather goods and kaftans. Despite the tourist hustle, it's still highly atmospheric with plenty of pretty squares where you can watch it all go by.

Borj Ghazi Mustapha FORTRESS
(admission TD5, camera TD1; ⏲9.30am-4.30pm mid-Sep–Mar, 8am-5pm Apr–mid-Sep) This fairytale fort, on the beach 500m north of town, was first built in the 13th-century by the Aragonese. When the Ottomans captured it in 1560, they stacked the skulls of their Spanish victims into a tower, although this grim monument was dismantled last century.

★**El-Ghriba** JEWISH
(Erriadh; admission by donation; ⏲8am-6pm Sun-Thu, to 3pm Fri Oct-May, 9am-4pm Sun-Thu, to 3pm Fri Jun-Sep) The most important synagogue on Jerba and the oldest in North Africa is signposted 1km south of Erriadh, 7km south of Houmt Souq. Blank from the outside, the interior is an exquisite combination of glowing blue tilework and moodily dark wooden furniture. The inner sanctuary, with its elevated pulpit, is said to contain one of the oldest Torahs in the world. Bring ID for the security checks outside. The synagogue is a major place of pilgrimage in May.

Sleeping

Houmt Souq is known for its handful of good-value *funduqs*. There's also a growing number of equally reasonable B&Bs, both on the coast and in the fascinating palm-strewn interior.

Houmt Souq

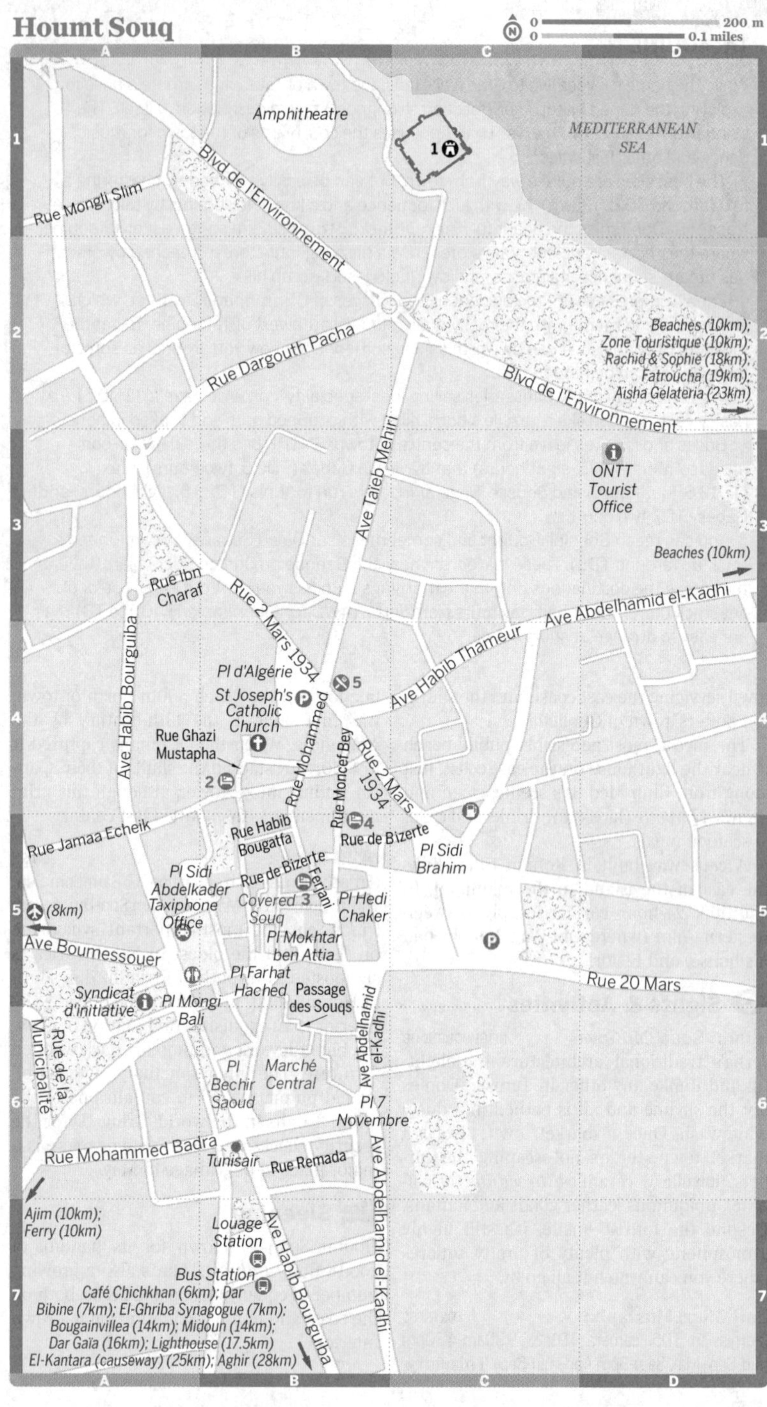
0 200 m
0 0.1 miles
Amphitheatre
MEDITERRANEAN SEA
Blvd de l'Environnement
Rue Mongli Slim
Rue Dargouth Pacha
Beaches (10km); Zone Touristique (10km); Rachid & Sophie (18km); Fatroucha (19km); Aisha Gelateria (23km)
Ave Taieb Mehiri
ONTT Tourist Office
Beaches (10km)
Rue Ibn Charaf
Rue 2 Mars 1934
Ave Abdelhamid el-Kadhi
Ave Habib Thameur
Pl d'Algérie
St Joseph's Catholic Church
Rue Ghazi Mustapha
Ave Habib Bourguiba
Rue Mohammed
Rue Moncef Bey
Rue Jamaa Echeik
Rue Habib Bougatfa
Rue de Bizerte
Pl Sidi Brahim
Pl Sidi Abdelkader
Taxiphone Office
Covered Souq
Ferjani
Pl Hedi Chaker
(8km)
Ave Boumessouer
Pl Mokhtar ben Attia
Pl Farhat Hached
Passage des Souqs
Syndicat d'initiative
Pl Mongi Bali
Rue 20 Mars
Rue de la Municipalité
Pl Bechir Saoud
Marché Central
Pl 7 Novembre
Rue Mohammed Badra
Tunisair
Rue Remada
Ajim (10km); Ferry (10km)
Louage Station
Bus Station
Café Chichkhan (6km); Dar Bibine (7km); El-Ghriba Synagogue (7km); Bougainvillea (14km); Midoun (14km); Dar Gaïa (16km); Lighthouse (17.5km) El-Kantara (causeway) (25km); Aghir (28km)

Houmt Souq

Sights

Sleeping

Eating

Hôtel Marhala HOTEL $

(☎75 650 146; Rue Moncef Bey, Houmt Souq; s/d TD19/32 ,without bathroom TD12/24) A converted *funduq* with barrel-vaulted rooms that have a spartan elegance. It's great fun, with good staff and bags of character.

Hôtel Erriadh HOTEL $

(☎75 650 756; www.erriadh.com; Rue Mohammed Ferjani, Houmt Souq; s/d TD28/45; ❄) A charmingly decorated *funduq* with tiles throughout. It's super traditional, but the welcome is warm.

★Dar Gaïa B&B $$

(http://dargaia.tingitingi.com; ste TD60-120; P ❄ 🛜 🏊 🐾) This peaceful *menzal* (Jerban farmhouse) sits in a large garden up a *piste* (sandy track) between the beach and Midoun, in the island's east. Carefully decorated rooms nestle around an inner courtyard and have all the contemporary comforts as well as authentic charm. There's a guest kitchen or dinner can be taken with the ever hospitable and interesting host family. They also own a great beachside apartment complex called Oxalá, complete with pet camel; it's perfect if you're looking for weekly self-catering accommodation

Hotel Arischa HOTEL $$

(☎75 650 384; www.hotelarischa.com; Rue Ghazi Mustapha, Houmt Souq; s/d TD47/72; ❄ 🛜 🏊) This *funduq* hotel's comfortable rooms are sweetly decorated and there's a good choice of configurations for those travelling in groups. The courtyard around the pool doubles as bar and restaurant, giving the place a rare conviviality. The restaurant is well patronised by locals as well as visitors, and while the service is friendly and efficient, the food is overpriced.

Dar Bibine BOUTIQUE HOTEL $$$

(7 Rue Abdel Wahab, Erriadh; s/d €95/120; ❄ 🛜 🏊) This small hotel, in a quiet backstreet, combines a super-chic European design aesthetic with the traditional lines of a Jerban village house. There's an ingenious use of space, with multiple nooks and crannies, rooftop terraces and courtyards to enjoy. Breakfasts are a gastronomic delight.

Eating

★Bougainvillea FAST FOOD $

(Rue November 7, Midoun; brik TD0.6-0.9, with salad TD1.5; ⏰9am-7.30pm Mon-Sat, to noon Sun) Tucked away in tiny street behind Midoun's Carrefour supermarket, this *brik* stall is totally no-frills but the wares are tasty and super fresh. Jerba is the place to taste-test the country's best *brik* (the Jewish community once dominated the corner frying business).

Essofra TUNISIAN $

(☎98 281 049; Ave Taïeb Mehiri, Houmt Souq; mains TD9-12; ⏰noon-3pm & 7-10pm) This place is a favourite with local families and has covered terrace tables as well as a large dining room. Try traditional island dishes such as stuffed calamari, Jerban rice or lamb cutlets. Great value in an expensive destination.

Rachid et Sophie TUNISIAN, FRENCH $$

(☎20 946 915; Blvd de l'Environnement, zone touristique; mains TD10-18; ⏰noon-10pm Tue-Sun) Casual place out on the road to Midoun that doles out French and Tunisian standards: zucchini fritters, slow-cooked lamb, steaks. The terrace is far from scenic, but it does get nicely lively. Take a taxi and ask for the Rond point du Rendezvous.

Fatroucha SEAFOOD $$$

(☎75 733 676; zone touristique; mains TD18-30) Considered a chic option, and a local favourite for a big night out, but the menu here is nothing to get excited about. However, the service is courteous, a very generous range of complimentary appetisers (tajine, Tunisian scotch eggs, potato croquettes) appears quickly, and there's live oud music. Plus the fish is fresh and perfectly cooked.

Aisha Gelateria ICE CREAM $

(zone touristique; ⏰10am-1am) The gelati (cups from TD1.5) here is the real deal. Squeezed between the Vincci Resorts Steakhouse and the Salsa Nightclub (near Rond point du Rendezvous), it can be easy to miss.

Café Chichkhan CAFE $

(Route de Houmt Souq) This huge cafe is beautifully decorated with swaths of kilms, tiled tables and old French radios and serves cakes and tea as well as coffee. Outside it's men-only, but inside you'll find happy mixed groups and couples.

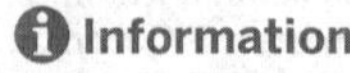

Information

There are ATMs and a Taxiphone on Ave Habib Bourguiba.

ONTT tourist office (☎75 650 016; Blvd de l'Environnement; ⌚8.30am-1pm & 3-5.45pm Mon-Thu, 8.30am-1.30pm Fri & Sat) Out on the beach road.

Post office (Ave Habib Bourguiba)

Syndicat d'initiative (☎75 650 915; Ave Habib Bourguiba; ⌚8am-2pm Nov-Mar, 8am-3pm Mon-Sat Apr-Oct) In the centre.

Getting There & Away

Tunisair (☎75 650 159; Ave Habib Bourguiba) has an office in Houmt Souq; the airport is to the northwest of the island.

The bus and *louage* stations are at the southern end of Ave Habib Bourguiba. There are buses to Gabès (TD6.4, 2½ hours), Sfax (TD13.6, four to five hours), Sousse (TD19.9, six hours) and Tunis (TD29.9, nine hours). *Louages* head to the same destinations for around the same prices, as well as to Tataouine (TD7.5, two hours) and Matmata (TD8.6, three hours)

UNDERSTAND TUNISIA

Tunisia Today

Tunisia, long considered North Africa's most liberal and stable nation, had kept a fairly low international profile until 2011. Its popular uprising, the poetically named Jasmine Revolution, fuelled a wave of popular dissent across the region and the Middle East, sparking the Arab Spring. It's put a country that was best known as a destination for summer getaways firmly in the headlines.

Tunisia's transition to democracy has not been an easy one, and the seeming lack of volition continues to damage an already limping economy and its all-important tourist industry. Along with, and perhaps because of, its current economic woes, the emergence of the hardline Islamist Salafist movement has become a major concern both within the country and internationally. The Salafis' capability for violence grabs headlines, but they are a small, if highly visible, minority.

While these might be anxious times for this fledgling democracy, most Tunisians continue to insist that the tolerant and secular values bequeathed to them by their first president still define who they are. The armoured trucks stationed on Ave Habib Bourghiba might signal instability, but life goes on much as it always did, with the surrounding cafe tables perpetually full and the young soldiers checking out the glamorously dressed women heading to global fashion retailer Zara. Tunisians across the country are quick to declare that anyone who thinks that this is a radical Islamist state in the making obviously does not understand their history or character, and would do well to remember that they took to the street for freedom and democracy once, and they are certainly willing to do it again.

History

Tunisia's long history is a rich and storied one, taking in the vicissitudes of a couple of millennia of foreign occupation while revealing a unique culture and resilient national identity.

Empires Strike Back

The Phoenicians set their sights on Tunisia around 800 BC, and their capital Carthage – today a suburb of Tunis – was the main power in the western Mediterranean by the 6th century BC. The burgeoning Roman Empire became uneasy with a nation of such mercantile genius and mercenary strength on its doorstep, and 128 years of conflict – including the three Punic Wars – ensued. The legendary general of Carthage, Hannibal, invaded Italy in 216 BC, but the Romans finally triumphed. They razed Carthage, re-creating it a hundred years later as a Roman city. Roman Tunisia boomed in the first centuries AD, as sights such as Dougga and El-Jem attest.

In the 7th century, Arabs arrived from the east, bringing Islam. Despite occasional Berber resistance, various Arab dynasties ruled Tunisia until the 16th century, leaving behind the strongest ongoing cultural impact of all of Tunisia's invaders. After fending off the Spanish Reconquistas, Tunisia became an outpost of the Ottoman Empire until France began its colonial push into the region in the 19th century.

Establishing their rule in 1881, the French spent the next 50 years attempting to reinvent Tunisia as an outpost of Europe.

Bourguiba & Ben

Tunisia was granted full independence from France and became a republic in 1956, a relatively peaceful process that saw exiled lawyer Habib Bourguiba returning to become the first president. He swore to eradicate poverty and separate politics from religion, while 'righting all the wrongs done to women'. Tunisia's economic savvy and famed tolerance dates to this period. Bourguiba gave Tunisia a secular state, championed women's rights, and introduced free education and heath care. As the years wore on, however, he wasn't too keen to give up power. Despite being declared president for life, his increasingly erratic and autocratic behaviour led to a bloodless coup in 1987. His successor, Zine el-Abidine Ben Ali, continued down a similar, if far less radical, road. Unfortunately, he too had an aversion to retirement. An appalling human-rights record and his zeal for feathering his extended family's nest was to prove his undoing.

The Jasmine Revolution & Democratic Beginnings

Even dedicated Maghreb watchers failed to predict the momentous events of early 2011, and the wide-reaching Arab Spring that was to follow, but few who visited the country in the few years before could help but notice that all was not well. High unemployment and a spiraling cost of living fuelled despair and discontent, particularly among the highly educated, outward-looking young. The government's petulant, paranoid censoring of the internet served only to irritate them further (while the uptake of social media tellingly outstripped the secret police's ability to monitor and control). Then the country's dirty laundry was aired to the world, when the infamous WikiLeaks release of US embassy cables told of the Ben Ali family's grossly lavish lifestyle in colourful, cinematic detail.

In this febrile climate, Mohamed Bouazizi, a street merchant in the poverty-stricken central town of Sidi Bouzid, self-immolated. His act, a protest against persistent police harassment and the dire lack of opportunity he faced, and his subsequent death, set the population in motion. For years willing to put up with a repressive and openly corrupt dictator in exchange for stability and prosperity, Tunisians could no longer stay silent. A new and potent combination of social media and a strong network of trade unions facilitated coordinated, countrywide street uprisings, and on 14 January, 2011, Ben Ali and his much-hated wife Leila Trabelsi ('the hairdresser') fled.

Daily life returned to normal in the following months as interim presidents came and went but the revolutionary elation was short-lived. Tunisia's economy was in worse shape than ever and ominous rumblings from a number of newly radicalised mosques began to be heard. In October 2011, Tunisians were finally able to vote in free elections – the country's first. With progressive, secular and left-wing parties divided and disorganised, Ennahda (a moderate Islamist group, said to be buoyed by Qatari cash) emerged as the winner. In a deal-sharing agreement with two centrist secular parties, Moncef Marzouki, a formerly exiled doctor and human-rights campaigner, became president. Despite pledging its committment to women's rights and Tunisia's secular laws, and disavowing religious extremism, the government's record to date has not been encouraging. With admittedly a hard task in front of them, they have been accused of everything from incompetence and corruption to covert collusion with the most violent elements of the Salafist movement.

The People of Tunisia

Almost 98% of Tunisia's population is Arab-Berber. Although Arabs and Berbers have mixed for 14 centuries, people living in the south of the country, along the fringe of the Sahara desert, claim a purely Berber heritage. Europeans and Jews make up the remaining 2% of the population. Islam is the official religion in Tunisia, and over 98% of the population are Sunni Muslims. Since the Jasmine Revolution increasing numbers of women wear the veil, though it's still far from universal.

Food & Drink

Tunisians love spicy food, and it's almost impossible to encounter a meal that doesn't involve harissa, a fiery chilli paste from Cap Bon or Jerba. Fresh produce is plentiful and salads form part of most meals. The most popular are *salade tunisienne,* a tomato, onions and cucumber mix, topped with tuna, and *salade mechuoia*, a smoky, room-temperature capsicum stew.

Couscous is ubiquitous and served with lamb kebabs, legumes and vegetables, or, Tunisian-style, with fish. Baguettes are a daily staple, along with *tabouna*, the traditional flat Berber bread strewn with dark nigella seeds. Traditional pastries combine Ottoman and Sicilian techniques and flavours, and are sold side by side with *pain au chocolate* and *gateaus*.

Street food here is an absolute treat. Tuck into *brik* (deep-fried, crispy pastry pockets filled with egg and meat, prawns or tuna), *lablabi* (chickpea soup) or huge sandwiches stuffed with tuna, egg, harissa and, often enough, fries.

Environment

It may be small, but Tunisia packs in a range of landscapes worthy of a continent, from its thickly forested northern mountains to crystallised salt lakes and endless dunes in the south. The Kroumirie and Tebersouk Mountains in the north are the easternmost extent of the High Atlas Mountains, and are covered with dense forests where there's a chance of glimpsing wild boars, jackals, mongooses and genets. The foothills dive down to the lavish, northern coastal plain.

Further south, the country's main mountain range is the rugged, dry central Dorsale, which runs from Kasserine in the west and peters out into Cap Bon in the east. Between these ranges lies the lush Medjerda Valley, once the Roman larder, watered by the country's only permanent river, Oued Medjerda. Olive trees cover the east coast, particularly around Sfax. South of the Dorsale, a high plain falls away to a series of huge, glittering *chotts* (salt lakes) and the silent *erg* (sand sea). The date palm is king here.

Tunisia's environmental headaches include a millennium of deforestation, regional desertification and endless forms of pollution: industrial pollution, sewage disposal and, depressingly, domestic litter. The tourist industry in Jerba has created huge problems with water supply, severely depleting artesian water levels and springs.

SURVIVAL GUIDE

Directory A–Z

ACCOMMODATION

Tunisia's *auberges de jeunesse* (youth hostels) can be good, and budget hotels outside the medina are often a better bet than the truly bottom-end places within, especially for women. When well run, usually by a family, cheapies can be delightful, with simple but highly atmospheric rooms. Tunisia has few campsites with good facilities, but you can sometimes pitch a tent with a landowner's permission.

Midrange options often have adequate facilites but can be disappointing service- and maintenance-wise, while top-end hotels, if far cheaper, rarely compare to four- or five-star hotels elsewhere. Coastal towns and Tozeur have a *zone touristique* where resorts are grouped together.

A promising development is the appearance of many new independently run guesthouses, B&Bs and small hotels. These often offer rates that are similar to or less than midrange hotels but give you genuine connections into local communities. Many are members of the Edhiafa organisation and Mille et Une Tunisie (p194) has a comprehensive listing.

EMBASSIES & CONSULATES

The following embassies and consulates are in Tunis. The Canadian embassy handles consular affairs for Australians.

Tunisia has embassies in Libya, Algeria, Egypt and Morocco.

Algerian Embassy (☎71 908 588; www.consalg.com.tn; 18 Rue de Niger)

Belgian Embassy (☎71 781 655; 47 Rue du 1er Juin, Belvédère)

British Embassy (☎71 108 700; ukintunisia.fco.gov.uk/en; Rue du Lac Windermere, Berges du Lac)

Canadian Embassy (☎70 010 393; Rue de la Feuille d'Erable, Berges du Lac II)

Dutch Embassy (☎71 155 300; 6-8 Rue de Meycen)

Egyptian Embassy (☎71 903 223; Rue de El Khames)

French Embassy (☎71 105 111; www.ambassadefrance-tn.org; 2 Place de l'Indépendance)

German Embassy (☎71 143 200; 1 Rue el-Hamra, Mutuelleville)

Italian Embassy (☎71 321 811; 37 Rue Jamel Abdelnasser)

Japanese Embassy (☎71 791 251; 9 Rue Apollo 11)

Moroccan Embassy (☎71 782 775; 39 Rue du 1er Juin, Mutuelleville)

South African Embassy (☎71 800 311; 7 Rue Achtart)

Spanish Embassy (☎71 782 217; 22 Rue Dr Ernest Conseil, Cité Jardin)

US Embassy (☎71 107 000; http://tunisia.usembassy.gov; Berges du Lac 1053)

FESTIVALS & EVENTS

Tabarka International Jazz Festival & Festival des Variétés Outdoor festival with international headliners in July and August.

Carthage International Festival (www.festival-carthage.com.tn) Big names in the Roman theatre in July and August.

Carthage International Film Festival (www.jccarthage.org) Cinema with an Arabic and African focus, held biennially in October.

Festival of the Sahara Camel racing, as well as music, parades and poetry in Douz in November.

INTERNET ACCESS

Publinet has offices in all the main towns. Most charge around TD2 per hour for access. Note they only have French keyboards and are often very crowded. Wi-fi is available in an increasing number of hotels.

MONEY

The unit of currency is the Tunisian dinar (TD), which is divided into 1000 millimes (mills). It's illegal to import or export dinars and they are not accepted in the duty-free shops at Tunis Airport.

You can re-exchange up to 30% of the amount you changed into dinar, up to a certain limit. You need bank receipts to prove you changed the money in the first place.

Major credit cards, such as Visa, American Express and MasterCard, are widely accepted at big shops, tourist hotels, car-rental agencies and banks. ATMs are common in major towns and resort areas.

POST

The Tunisian postal service is slow but reliable: allow a week to Europe and at least two weeks to North America, Asia and Oceania.

PUBLIC HOLIDAYS

As well as the religious holidays that vary by date, the principal public holidays in Tunisia are as follows:

New Year's Day 1 January

Independence Day 20 March

Youth Day 21 March

Martyrs' Day 9 April

Labour Day 1 May

Republic Day 25 July

PRACTICALITIES

Electricity 220V, European two-pin wall plugs

Languages Tunisian Arabic, Berber, French

Newspapers *Tunisia Live* (www.tunisia-live.net in English); *La Presse* (www.lapresse.tn), *Kapitalis* (www.kapitalis.com) and *Le Temps* (www.letemps.com.tn in French); *Al-Hourriah* (www.alhourriah.org in Arabic)

Radio Radio Tunis International, Mosaïque FM

TV Télévision Tunisienne 1, Tunisie 21, Hannibal TV, Nessma TV, Rai 1, Tunisie 21

Women's Day 13 August

Evacuation Day 15 October

SAFE TRAVEL

Postrevolutionary Tunisia is still an overwhelmingly safe place to travel, although it's wise to excercise caution. Most travellers' complaints continue to stem from sexual harassment and overly persistant touts or dishonest taxi drivers; the isolated incidents of violence by hardline Salafis have not targeted tourists. But it's wise to avoid any public demonstrations, especially so on Friday, the day of prayer. As always, keep an eye on your bag and pockets in crowded medinas and on public transport.

Emergencies:

Allo Docteur ☎71 780 000

Ambulance ☎190

Fire ☎198

Police ☎197

When travelling in the desert, it's wise to register with the local Garde Nationale office's Brigade de Tourisme.

Douz ☎75 470 319/75 470 554

Tataouine ☎75 870 077

Tozeur ☎76 454 392/76 452 194

TELEPHONE

There are lots of public telephones, known as Taxiphones. They accept 500-mill and TD1 coins. All public telephones can be used for international direct dialling. The Tunisian country code is ☎216. All Tunisian landlines use a two-digit area beginning with 7. Mobile phones begin with 2, 5, 9 or 4.

Mobile phones are ubiquitous and there are three national carriers: Tunisiana, Tunisie Telecom and Orange. You can buy local SIM cards and 3G keys at the airport or in offices in larger towns (you'll usually find at least one English-speaking staff member). Voice and data plans are extremely cheap and top-up cards are widely available.

TOURIST INFORMATION

The **Office National du Tourisme Tunisien** (ONTT) has an office in most towns. They usually have maps, silly glossy brochures and basic local information, but don't expect much more. Local websites that can be of use for preplanning are Tunisia Live (www.tunisia-live.net) and **Mille et Une Tunisie** (www.mille-et-une-tunisie.com).

VISAS

Nationals of most Western European countries and Canada can stay up to three months without a visa – just collect a stamp in your passport at the point of entry. Those from the US can stay for up to four months. Australians and South Africans can get a visa at the airport seven days costs TD10, a month TD35. Other nationalities, including Israelis, must apply before they arrive. It should take 14 to 21 days in person or via post, and the length of stay is up to the embassy.

Visa Extensions

Applications can be made at the **Interior Ministry** (Ave Habib Bourguiba) in Tunis and regional offices in Houmt Souq. They cost around TD10 per week (payable only in *timbres fiscales* – revenue stamps available from post offices) and take up to 10 days to issue. You'll need two photos, and may need bank receipts and a *facture* (receipt) from your hotel, for starters. It's a process to be avoided – far easier to leave the country and return instead.

Visas for Onward Travel

The Algerian and Libyan embassies in Tunis do not issue visas. If you want to visit either country from Tunisia, you should apply to the Algerian or Libyan representatives in your home country. Australians and New Zealanders can apply in London. It can be a lengthy process and you usually need an invitation, obtained from a citizen or through a travel agency.

WOMEN TRAVELLERS

Tunisian women enjoy freedoms that women in most Muslim societies don't, but that doesn't mean that sexual mores aren't still extremely conservative in all but the most privileged cosmopolitan circles. Foreign women, especially those travelling alone or without male companions, are seen as existing outside the protective family structure and this freedom is usually equated with promiscuity. Compounding the notion that all foreign women are up for it is the thriving beach gigolo scene (known as *beezness*).

All these factors mean that unwanted attention, from constant stares to actual sexual harassment, is par for the course. It's tiring at best, and can become very intimidating.

You will reduce your hassle quota if you completely ignore sexist remarks or come-ons, as passivity is equated with modesty. Any engagement, even an angry one, may be seen as an opportunity. Sunglasses are a good way of avoiding eye contact, and affecting a demure, downcast gaze will sometimes be discouragement enough. Dressing modestly – covering at least shoulders, upper arms and legs – can make a difference. Physical assault is rare, but it does happen. If someone does touch you, shouting '*Harem alek*' (Arabic for 'Shame on you') may be useful.

ℹ Getting There & Away

AIR

There are regular flights, both scheduled and chartered, from Tunisia to destinations all over Europe, Africa and the Middle East, but no direct flights to the Americas, Asia or Oceania. The main international airports are Tunis Carthage, Enfidha-Hammamet and Djerba–Zarzis. **Tunisair** (Map p168; ☎71 330 100; www.tunisair.com; 48 Ave Habib Bourguiba) flies to a number of European, African and Middle Eastern cities.

Other airlines flying to and from Tunisia include the following:

Air France (☎71 105 324; www.airfrance.com; 1 Rue d'Athènes, Tunis)

Alitalia (☎71 767 722; www.alitalia.com; Tunis-Carthage Airport)

British Airways (☎71 963 120; www.british-airways.com; Rue du Lac Turkana, Berges du Lac, Tunis)

Lufthansa (☎71 751 096; www.lufthansa.com; Tunis-Carthage Airport)

BOAT

The **Compagnie Tunisienne de Navigation** (CTN; Map p168; ☎71 322 802; www.ctn.com.tn) handles tickets for ferries to Genoa and Marseilles, as does its French partner **SNCM** (Société Nationale Maritime Corse Méditerranée; Map p168; ☎71 338 222; www.sncm.fr; 47 Ave Farhat Hached, Tunis). **Grandi Navi Veloci** (www.gnv.it; Résidence La Brise, Ave Habib Bourguiba, La Goulette) also sails to Genoa, Civitavecchia (Rome) and Palermo. All international ferries dock at La Goulette, in Tunis.

LAND

Algeria

All bus and train services between the two countries have been cancelled since the start of the Algerian civil war in 1993. *Louages* are the only form of public transport still operating. They leave from Place Sidi Bou Mendil in the Tunis medina to Annaba and Constantine, or you can walk across the border at Babouch, a taxi ride away from Ain Draham.

Libya

The only crossing point open to foreigners is at Ras al-Jedir, 33km east of Ben Guerdane. There are daily buses to Tripoli from the southern bus station in Tunis. The trip costs TD35 and takes from 12 to 16 hours. *Louages* (yellow with a white stripe) are faster, with regular services to Tripoli via Ras al-Jedir from many Tunisian towns.

Getting Around

AIR

Domestic flights to Jerba, Tozeur, Sfax, Gabes, Gafsa and Tabarka are operated by Tunisair subsidiary **Tunisair Express** (☎71 942 626; www.tunisairexpress.com.tn), formerly Sevenair.

BOAT

There is a 24-hour car ferry that plies the short hop between El-Jorf and Ajim on the island of Jerba. There are ferries from Sfax to the sleepy Kerkennah Islands.

BUSES & LOUAGES

The national bus company, **Société Nationale du Transport Rural et Interurbain** (SNTRI; www.sntri.com.tn), operates daily air-con buses from Tunis to just about every town in the country. Frequency for large towns can be up to half-hourly. The buses run pretty much to schedule, and they're fast, usually comfortable and inexpensive. Local buses – creaky and never air-conditioned – go to all but the most remote villages.

Louages (long-distance shared taxis) are colour-coded: a red stripe signifies long-distance, a blue stripe regional, and a yellow stripe local or rural. In most towns, the *louage* station is close to, or combined with, the bus station, enabling you to choose between them. Fares cost around the same as those for the equivalent bus service (working out at around TD5 per 100km), but *louages* depart when full rather than following a timetable. Don't leave catching your *louage* too late – most stop running by 7pm.

All towns have metered private yellow taxis. These can either be hired privately or operate on a collective basis – they collect four passengers for different destinations. You will sometimes need to insist the meter is used.

TRAIN

The **Société Nationale des Chemins de Fer Tunisiens** (SNCFT; www.sncft.com.tn) rail network isn't extensive, but it's efficient enough, cheap and comfortable. The best-serviced route is the north–south line from Tunis to Sousse and Sfax. Timetables and ticket prices can be found online.

West Africa

NIGEL PAVITT / GETTY IMAGES ©

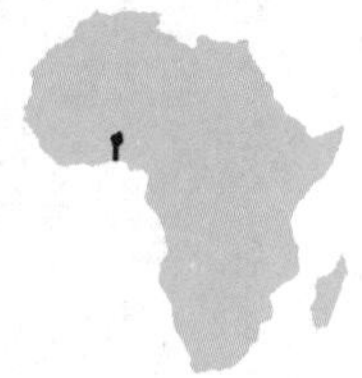

Benin

POP 9.6 MILLION

Includes ➡

Best Places to Eat

- Chez Delphano (p210)
- Saveurs d'Afrique (p209)
- L'Atelier (p201)
- Bab's Dock (p205)
- La Brèche (p212)

Best Places to Stay

- La Guesthouse (p200)
- Maison Rouge (p200)
- Auberge Le Jardin Secret – Chez Pascal (p208)
- Pendjari Lodge (p213)
- Hôtel Chez Théo (p210)

Why Go?

The birthplace of voodoo and a pivotal platform of the slave trade for nearly three centuries, Benin is steeped in a rich and complex history still very much in evidence across the country.

A visit to this small, club-shaped nation could therefore not be complete without exploring the Afro-Brazilian heritage of Ouidah, Abomey and Porto Novo, learning about spirits and fetishes.

But Benin will also wow visitors with its natural beauty, from the palm-fringed beach idyll of the Atlantic coast to the rugged scenery of the north. The Parc National de la Pendjari is one of the best wildlife parks in West Africa. Lions, cheetahs, leopards, elephants and hundreds of other species thrive here.

In fact, Benin is wonderfully tourist friendly. There are good roads, a wide range of accommodation options and ecotourism initiatives that offer travellers the chance to delve deeper into Beninese life. Now is an ideal time to go because the country sits on the cusp of discovery.

When to Go

Cotonou

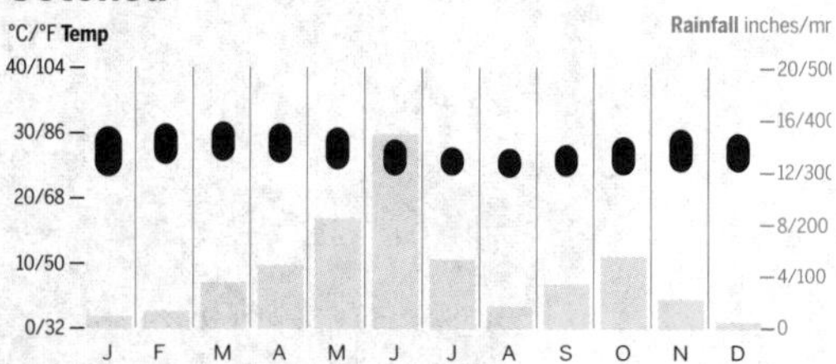

Nov–Feb Warm and dry weather. Prime wildlife watching. Harmattan can produce hazy skies.

Mar–May The hottest period, after the harmattan lifts. Clear skies and some rain in the south.

Jun–Oct Usually downright wet and humid; a dry spell mid-July to mid-September in the south.

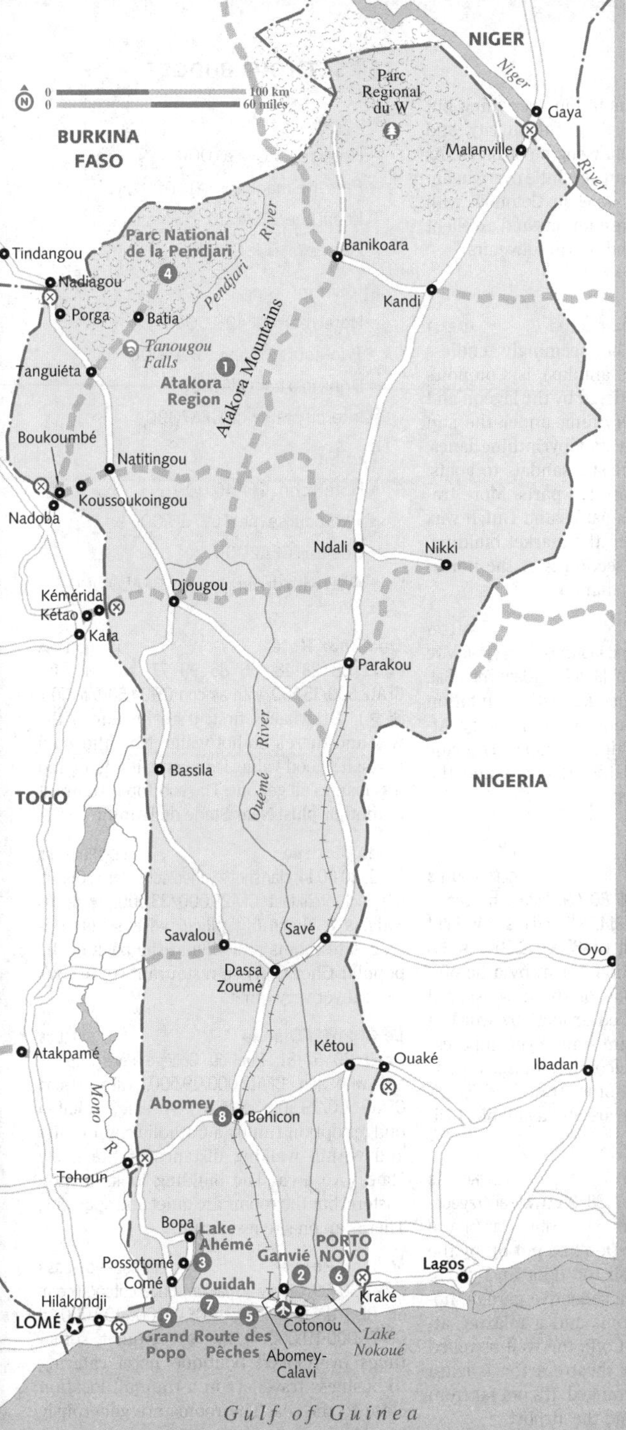

Benin Highlights

1. Exploring the rugged landscapes of the **Atakora Region** (p212) and be awed by the intriguing Somba country.
2. Spending a night at the lacustrine stilt village of **Ganvié** (p206).
3. Learning traditional fishing techniques on the shores of **Lake Ahémé** (p209).
4. Spotting lions, cheetahs, elephants and more in **Parc National de la Pendjari** (p213), West Africa's best wildlife park.
5. Spending an afternoon chilling out at **Route des Pêches** (p205), blessed with endless beaches.
6. Discovering **Porto Novo** (p205), Benin's mellow capital, with its Afro-Brazilian heritage.
7. Checking out **Ouidah** (p207), once a capital of the slave trade and now the centre of voodoo worship.
8. Visiting the ruined palaces of the kings of Dahomey in **Abomey** (p210).
9. Putting your bags down at lovely **Grand Popo** (p209) and relaxing on Benin's beautiful, palm-fringed coast.

COTONOU

POP 890,000

Cotonou is Benin's capital in everything but name: a vibrant, bustling, full-on city, and very much the economic engine of Benin. As a first port of call, it can be a little overwhelming, but life can be sweet in Cotonou, with good nightlife, great restaurants and excellent shopping (ideal for end-of-trip souvenirs).

Sights

Grand Marché de Dantokpa MARKET

(north of Jonquet) The seemingly endless Grand Marché du Dantokpa is Cotonou's throbbing heart, bordered by the lagoon and Blvd St Michel. Everything under the sun can be purchased in its labyrinthine lanes, from fish to soap, plastic sandals to goats, pirated DVDs to spare car parts. More traditional fare, such as batiks and Dutch wax cloth, can be found in the market building. The **fetish market** section is at the northern end of the larger market.

Fondation Zinsou GALLERY

(21 30 99 92; www.fondationzinsou.org; Haie Vive District; 8.30am-7pm Mon-Fri, 10am-7pm Sat, 2-7pm Sun) FREE This fantastic exhibition space seeks to promote contemporary African art among Beninese people. The chic boutique sells beautiful art books and the cafe offers wi-fi access.

Sleeping

★ **La Guesthouse** GUESTHOUSE $

(67 34 64 77, 99 36 80 09; laguesthousecotonou@gmail.com; Rue 214, Sikécodji; s/d without bathroom incl breakfast CFA8500/12,500; P) This adorable guesthouse, run by a helpful French couple, is one of those whispered secrets that are passed around by word of mouth. The rooms are simple yet impeccably clean and the welcoming lounge area is a good place to meet other travellers. Excellent meals (CFA4500) are also available. Brilliant value.

Ancrage de l'Océan GUESTHOUSE $

(90 04 58 17, 97 07 38 95; www.ancragedelocean.com; Fidjirossé; r with fan/air-con CFA10,500/15,500;) Don't be put off by the concrete facade; push the door and you're in another reality – a seductive garden, no-frills, but spruce rooms and a relaxing atmosphere. Edouard Coffi, the well-travelled owner and a former theatre actor, is extra nice. Meals can be arranged. It's not far from the Rte des Pêches and the airport.

SET YOUR BUDGET

Budget

- Hotel room CFA10,000
- *Pâte* in a *maquis* CFA1000
- Local beer CFA600
- *Zemi-john* ride CFA300

Midrange

- Hotel room CFA20,000
- Two-course dinner CFA4000
- Drink in a bar CFA1500
- Intercity bus ride CFA7000

Top End

- Hotel room CFA40,000
- Two-course meal CFA10,000
- Cocktail CFA2000
- 4WD with driver, per day CFA50,000

Qualimax Hotel HOTEL $$

(21 38 23 18, 66 85 99 77; s/d with fan CFA12,500/15,500, with air-con CFA14,500/18,500;) Drawbacks first: it's a bit out of the way and there's no hot water. Now the good news: it's good value, it's secure, it's quiet and it's clean as all get out. The rooftop restaurant is another plus. Near Stade de l'Amitié.

Chez Clarisse GUESTHOUSE $$

(21 30 60 14; clarishot@yahoo.com; Camp Guézo; s/d incl breakfast CFA28,000/33,000;) This is a charming place, with seven immaculate rooms in a villa at the back of the popular Chez Clarisse restaurant (p201). It's central yet very quiet.

Le Chant d'Oiseau HOTEL $$

(21 30 57 51; Rue du Collège Père Aupiais; s/d with fan CFA12,000/19,500, with air-con CFA19,500/29,500; @) A safe, reliable budget option run by a Catholic community and within walking distance of the lively Haie Vive area. The building looks a little austere, but the rooms are quiet and spacious. There's an on-site restaurant.

Maison Rouge BOUTIQUE HOTEL $$$

(21 30 09 01; www.maison-rouge-cotonou.com; off Blvd de la Marina; s CFA65,000-100,000, d CFA76,000-111,000; P) A quiet, sometimes overlooked boutique hotel catering to business travellers in a tranquil location close to the sea. The rooms are generously

sized and tastefully designed, and the communal areas are expertly decorated with arts and crafts. Other perks include a soothing plant-filled garden, a gym, a pool and a panoramic terrace with sea views. Evening meals are available by request. Rates include breakfast.

Hôtel du Lac HOTEL **$$$**
(☎21 33 19 19; www.hoteldulac-benin.com; r CFA41,000-45,000; P ❄ @ ᯤ ≋) A good-value choice on a breezy spot at the edge of the lagoon. Though the rooms show some signs of wear and tear, they are sunny, spacious and clean, and most have water views. The restaurant has a great panoramic terrace and the large swimming pool is popular at the weekend.

Azalai Hotel de la Plage HOTEL **$$$**
(www.azalaihotels.com; Blvd de la Marina; s CFA105,000-135,000, d CFA115,000-145,000; P ❄ @ ᯤ ≋) The ultramodern rooms at this waterfront hotel are arguably the best in the city – especially those with sea views – with sleek bathrooms and attractive decor. The list of facilities is prolific, with a restaurant, a bar, a swimming pool, a business centre and tennis courts. Rates include breakfast.

Novotel Orisha & Ibis Cotonou HOTEL **$$$**
(☎21 30 56 69; www.accorhotels.com; Blvd de la Marina; Novotel r CFA95,000, Ibis s/d CFA60,000/66,000; P ❄ @ ᯤ ≋) The Accor chain has two hotels on the same property. Both lack charm, but rooms are spotless and well equipped. If you want water views, opt for the Novotel Orisha. The beautiful swimming pool is a great perk.

Eating

Most places to stay have an on-site restaurant.

★**Maman Aimé** OPEN-AIR RESTAURANT **$**
(☎97 64 16 49; off Pl de Bulgarie; mains CFA1200; ⏲11.30am-10pm daily) This is a super atmospheric Beninese *maquis* (rustic open-air restaurant) with little more than a few wooden benches and tables under a corrugated-iron roof. Here you'll get a blob of *pâte* (starch staple, often made from millet, corn, plantains, manioc or yams) and a ladle of sauce for next to nothin'. And yes, you'll eat with your fingers. There's no signboard; it's in a *von* (alleyway) off Pl de Bulgarie.

Chez Maman Bénin AFRICAN **$**
(☎21 32 33 38; Rue 201A; meals CFA1000-3000; ⏲11.30am-11pm daily) This long-standing no-frills canteen off Blvd St Michel has a large selection of West African dishes scooped from steaming pots. There's no decor except for a couple of blaring TVs showing the latest football action.

Maquis du Port AFRICAN **$$**
(☎21 31 14 15; Blvd de la Marina; mains CFA2000-6000; ⏲lunch & dinner daily) Great-value local food. More an upmarket African eatery than a *maquis*, this hugely popular venture serves a good mix of local classics like *ndole* (a stew made of leaves and nuts), salads, braised fish and meat stews. It's in a multistorey building overlooking the fishing harbour.

Pili Pili AFRICAN **$$**
(☎21 31 29 32; Zongo; mains CFA2500-5000; ⏲lunch & dinner daily) This well-run eatery rates equally highly with Beninese and expats for its amazing West African food. Prices are very reasonable and the jugs of freshly squeezed pineapple juice at lunchtime are a refreshing godsend.

Chez Clarisse FRENCH **$$**
(☎21 30 60 14; Camp Guézo; mains CFA3000-4500; ⏲breakfast, lunch & dinner daily) This small French restaurant, in a pretty residential area next to the US embassy, is a perennial favourite that churns out excellent French specialities as well as pancakes and sandwiches.

Hai King CHINESE **$$**
(☎97 98 53 63; Carrefour de Cadjéhoun; mains CFA2500-5500; ⏲lunch & dinner daily) One of Cotonou's older Chinese restaurants, this has an atmospheric covered roof terrace overlooking the bustling Carrefour de Cadjéhoun, a row of red lanterns, a comprehensive menu and a complement of Chinese expat clientele – always a good sign.

★**L'Atelier** FRENCH **$$$**
(☎21 30 17 04; Cadjéhoun; mains CFA6000-12,000; ⏲lunch & dinner Mon-Sat) Considered by some connoisseurs to be one of the most refined restaurants in town, with excellent French and fusion cuisine, and an ambience that's as optimal for business lunches as it is for a romantic evening out.

Les Trois Mousquetaires FRENCH **$$$**
(☎21 31 61 22; Ave Dodds; mains CFA6000-12,000; ⏲lunch & dinner Mon-Sat) This fine establishment serves delicate French cuisine and features an extensive wine list. The old colonial dining room is the perfect setting for a sophisticated evening.

Cotonou

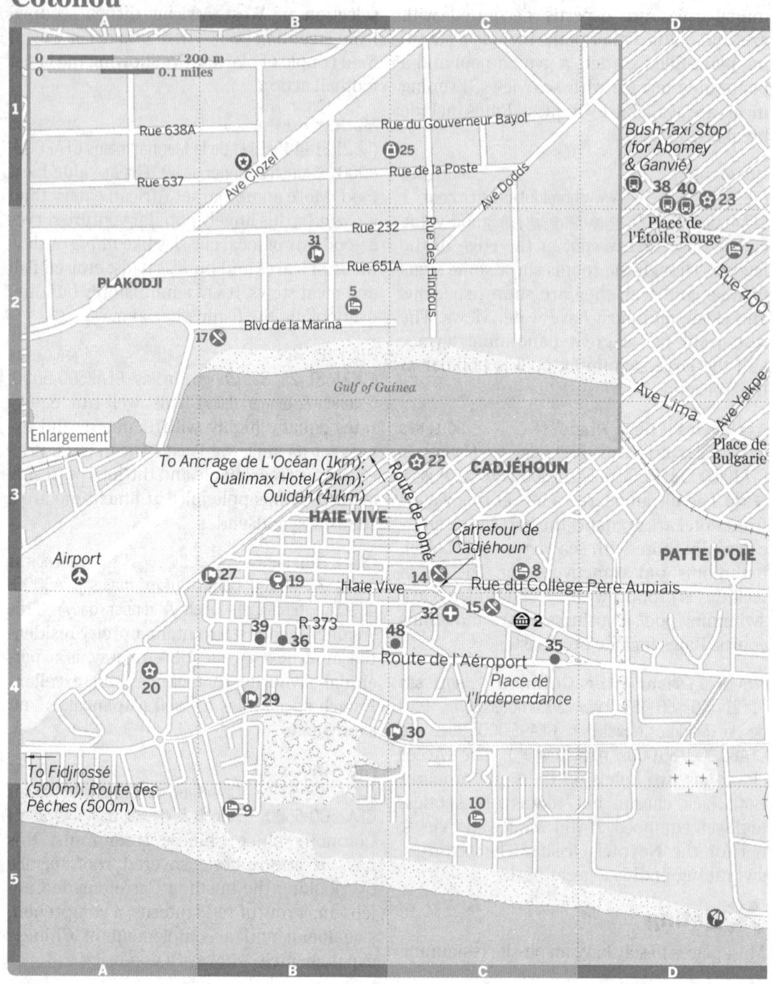

Drinking & Nightlife

Haie Vive is a lively, safe area by night, with many of the city's best bars and restaurants. There are also plenty of unpretentious bars and *buvettes* (small cafes that double as drinking places) in the Jonquet area and around Stade de l'Amitié.

★Jammin Bar BAR
(☎97 64 82 74; Fidjirossé; ⊙6pm-late Thu-Sat) This hip, convivial bar with an open-air terrace is a great spot to swill a beer or two before hitting the clubs. The crowd ranges from expats to well-heeled locals. Also serves good food.

Le Livingstone BAR
(☎21 30 27 58; Haie Vive; ⊙11am-late daily) One of the most atmospheric spots for a drink is the terrace of this pub in Haie Vive. There's also a tempting menu (meals CFA3400 to CFA6200), and darts.

The Sanctuary MUSIC
(Haie Vive; ⊙6pm-late Thu-Sat) This cool den hosts gigs from local bands, with an emphasis on rock 'n' blues. There's no cover charge, but a beer costs CFA3000.

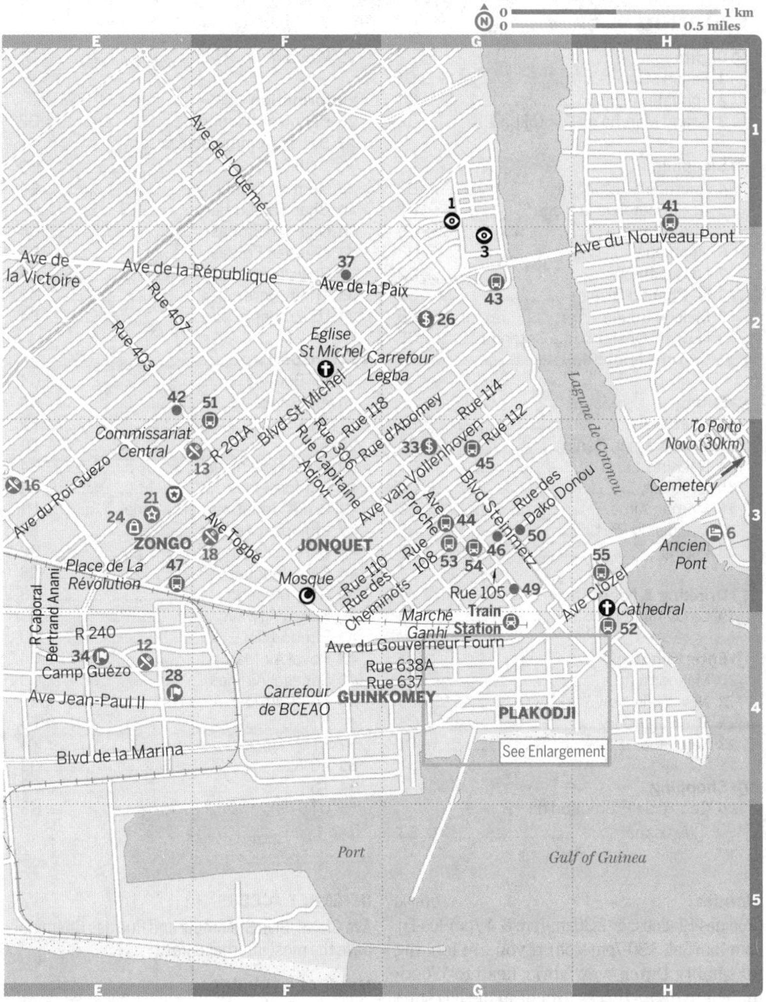

Yes Papa MUSIC

(leyespapa.blogspot.fr; Sikécodji; ⏲9pm-late Thu-Sat) This venture is famed for the quality of its live music sessions featuring reggae, jazz and African sounds. Near Pl de l'Étoile Rouge.

Makoomba CLUB

(Rte de l'Aéroport; ⏲from 10pm daily) A pulsating club near the airport. It plays African and Western tunes and doesn't really kick off before 1am.

New York, New York CLUB

(Blvd St Michel; ⏲daily) This Cotonou institution has been around for yonks and isn't showing signs of slowing down. If you want to rub shoulders with hip-gyrating Beninese dancing to African tunes, this is the place.

Shopping

Centre de Promotion de l'Artisanat HANDICRAFTS

(Blvd St Michel; ⏲9am-7pm) Here you'll find woodcarvings, bronzes, batiks, leather goods, jewellery and appliqué banners.

Cotonou

Sights
1 Fetish Market ... G1
2 Fondation Zinsou ... C4
3 Grand Marché de Dantokpa ... G2

Sleeping
4 Ancrage de L'Océan ... B2
5 Azalai Hotel de la Plage ... B2
Chez Clarisse ... (see 12)
6 Hôtel du Lac ... H3
7 La Guesthouse ... D2
8 Le Chant d'Oiseau ... C3
9 Maison Rouge ... B5
10 Novotel Orisha & Ibis Cotonou ... C5
11 Qualimax Hotel ... A1

Eating
12 Chez Clarisse ... E4
13 Chez Maman Bénin ... F3
14 Hai King ... C3
15 L'Atelier ... C4
16 Maman Aimé ... E3
17 Maquis du Port ... B2
18 Pili Pili ... F3

Drinking & Nightlife
19 Le Livingstone ... B3

Entertainment
20 Makoomba ... A4
21 New York, New York ... E3
22 The Sanctuary ... C3
23 Yes Papa ... D1

Shopping
24 Centre de Promotion de l'Artisanat ... E3
25 Woodin ... C1

Information
26 Banque Atlantique ... G2
27 British Community Liaison Officer ... B3
28 German Embassy ... E4
29 Ghanaian Embassy ... B4
30 Nigerian Embassy ... C4
31 Nigerian Embassy ... B2
32 Polyclinique les Cocotiers ... C4
33 Trinity Forex ... G3
34 US Embassy ... E4

Transport
35 Air Burkina ... C4
36 Air France ... B4
37 Asky ... F2
38 ATT ... D1
39 Brussels Airlines ... B4
40 Confort Lines ... D1
41 Cross Country International ... H1
42 Ethiopian Airlines ... E2
43 Gare du Dantokpa ... G2
44 Gare Jonquet ... G3
45 Gare Missébo ... G3
46 Kenya Airways ... G3
47 Rimbo-RTV ... E3
48 Royal Air Maroc ... C4
49 Senegal Airlines ... G3
50 South African Airways ... G3
51 STC ... F3
52 STIF ... H4
53 TCV ... G3
54 TSR ... G3
55 UTB ... H3

Woodin CLOTHING
(Rue des Hindous; ⏲8.30am-1pm & 4-7pm Tue-Fri, 9am-1pm Sat, 3.30-7pm Mon) If you are looking for quality Dutch wax fabric, head to Woodin, where *demi-pièces* (6m of material) start at CFA15,000.

Information

DANGERS & ANNOYANCES

The biggest danger in Cotonou is the traffic – the 80,000 reckless *zemi-johns* (taxi-motos) in particular. They're unavoidable, however, so always make sure that the driver agrees to drive slowly *(aller doucement)* before hopping on.

The Jonquet, the beach and the port area all have their fair share of undesirables: don't walk alone at night and watch your bag at traffic lights if you're on a *zem*.

INTERNET ACCESS

Ave Clozel, Blvd Steinmetz and Rue des Cheminots have the most internet cafes.

MEDICAL SERVICES

There are numerous pharmacies around town.

Polyclinique les Cocotiers (☎21 30 14 20; Rue 373, Cadjéhoun) A private clinic at Carrefour de Cadjéhoun; also has a dentist.

MONEY

All banks change cash. There are plenty of ATMs in Cotonou, most of which accept Visa.

Banque Atlantique (Blvd St Michel; ⏲8am-5pm Mon-Fri, 9am-12.30pm Sat) Has a MasterCard and Visa ATM, but it was not functioning at the time of research.

Trinity Forex (Bureau de Change Forex Bureau; ☎21 31 79 38; Ave van Vollenhoven; ⏲8am-6.30pm Mon-Fri, to 2pm Sat) Changes US dollars, euros, Swiss francs and British pounds.

STREET NAMES

Only major roads have names – small, unsealed alleyways are called *von* and directions given with reference to another main street or a landmark.

Getting There & Away

BUSH TAXI & BUS

Cotonou has a confusingly large number of stations for minibuses, buses and bush taxis. It's easiest to ask a taxi or a *zemi-john* to take you to the right one.

Gare Jonquet (Rue des Cheminots), just west of Blvd Steinmetz, services western destinations such as Grand Popo (CFA4000, two hours).

Bush taxis for Porto Novo (CFA500 to CFA700, 45 minutes) leave from **Gare du Dantokpa** (Ave de la Paix) at the new bridge; those to Calavi-Kpota (for Ganvié; CFA500, 25 minutes), Ouidah (CFA1000) and Abomey (CFA3000, two hours) leave north of Stade de l'Amitié. **Gare Missébo** (Ave van Vollenhoven) services Abomey (CFA2500).

For more-distant destinations, such as Natitingou, take the bus. The most reliable companies at the time of writing were **ATT** (☎95 95 34 18; Pl de l'Étoile Rouge) and **Confort Lines** (Pl de l'Étoile Rouge). Both have daily services for Natitingou (CFA8500).

There are also international services.

Getting Around

TO/FROM THE AIRPORT

The international airport is on the western fringe of town. A private taxi from the city centre to the airport costs around CFA3000, although drivers will demand double this amount *from* the airport. *Zemi-johns* will be happy to load you and your luggage for much less.

TAXI

A *zemi-john* will whiz you around town for CFA100 to CFA500, depending on the distance.

Fares in shared taxis are CFA150 to CFA400.

AROUND COTONOU

Route des Pêches

West of Cotonou, past the airport and all the way to Ouidah, is the sandy Rte des Pêches, a land of seemingly endless beaches and fishing villages, a world away from the big-smoke mayhem.

As you leave Cotonou behind, the suburb gives way to thatched huts and palm groves. Many expats and Beninese families rent little *paillotes* (huts) for the weekend around here. For those just passing by, there are many popular bars and restaurants along the route.

Sleeping & Eating

Tichani GUESTHOUSE $

(☎96 66 80 08, 97 88 65 60; www.tichani.com; off Rte des Pêches; r with fan/air-con incl breakfast 10,000/15,000;) This well-run guesthouse scores high points with its location – it's only 300m away from the beach in a peaceful area. The five sun-soaked rooms are neat and tidy, the flower-filled garden is a great spot to decompress and the views of the sea from the rooftop terrace are nothing short of charming. Meals can be arranged (from CFA3000).

★**Bab's Dock** EUROPEAN, BAR $$$

(☎97 97 01 00; off Rte des Pêches; mains CFA3000-7000; ⏰10am-7pm Sat, Sun & bank holidays) The hidden gem near the Rte des Pêches is this secluded retreat on the edge of the lagoon. Almost everything is made of local wood – the tables, the bar, the deck. You can swim in the shallow (but somewhat murky) waters of the lagoon, canoe and even sail or just relax in a hammock. Food is European in style but local in production. Bab's Dock is 11km from Cotonou. A secure car park is signposted from the route; from there, a boat takes you to the restaurant through thick mangrove. There's an admission fee (CFA2500) for the day, which covers the car park and boat trip.

Wado SEAFOOD $$

(☎97 68 53 18; Rte des Pêches; mains CFA3700-3900, seafood platters CFA25,000; ⏰lunch & dinner Sat & Sun) This eatery overlooking the beach has garnered high praise for its ultra-fresh fish and seafood platters.

THE SOUTH

Benin's south is an enticing but intriguing mix of heavenly shores and momentous history.

Porto Novo

POP 270,00

Nestling on the shores of Lake Nokoué, Porto Novo is Benin's unlikely capital. Its leafy streets, wonderful colonial architecture, unperturbed pace and interesting museums are in striking contrast to full-on Cotonou.

WORTH A TRIP

GANVIÉ

The main attraction near Cotonou (and one of Benin's highlights) is Ganvié, where 30,000 Tofinu people live in bamboo huts on stilts several kilometres out on Lake Nokoué. They live almost exclusively from fishing.

Despite the fact that the town has become a tourist magnet, it's a terrific place to explore and sample village life. Tip: rather than signing up for a tour, it's not a bad idea to overnight in Ganvié – thus you'll soak up the atmosphere and get a better understanding of the environment and traditional life of the community. Ganvié has a handful of guesthouses, including the friendly **Chez M** (☎95 42 04 68, 97 37 22 71; hotelcarrefourchezm@hotmail.fr; Ganvié; s CFA8500, d CFA10,500-12,500), which offers 22 rooms with bathrooms, standing fans and mosquito nets. The setting is lovely – the dining room overlooks the main stream and the floating market, right in the middle of the village. Meals (CFA4500) are available on request and various tours can be organised. Transfers from Calavi-Kpota cost CFA7500 return and must be booked in advance.

To get there, get a taxi from Pl de l'Étoile Rouge or Stade de l'Amitié to Calavi-Kpota (CFA500, 25 minutes). The embarkation point is 800m downhill (take a *zem*). If you opt for a tour, head to the **official counter** (⏲9am-5pm). Return fares to Ganvié in a regular/motorised *pirogue* are CFA6050/7050 per person, CFA4050/5050 each for two to four people. Prices include a circuit of the village with stop-offs. The trip takes about 2½ hours. You can also hire a guide.

The Portuguese named the city after Porto when they established a slave-trading post here in the 16th century.

Sights

Centre Songhai GARDENS
(☎20 24 68 81; www.songhai.org; Rte de Pobè; guided tours CFA500; ⏲guided tours at 8.30am, 10.30am, noon, 3.30pm & 5pm Mon-Sat) The Centre Songhai is a major research, teaching and production centre in sustainable farming. There are one-hour **guided tours** to visit the plantations and workshops. You can also buy the centre's produce – anything from fresh quail eggs to biscuits and preserves. Songhai is about 1km north of town. Every *zem* knows where it is.

Musée Ethnographique de Porto Novo MUSEUM
(☎20 21 25 54; Ave 6; admission CFA1000; ⏲9am-6pm, closed 1 May & 1 Jan) Housed in a pretty colonial building, this museum is well worth a gander. The top floor is organised thematically around birth, life and death, with everything from costumes to carved drums. Downstairs there's an impressive display of ceremonial masks.

Musée Honmé MUSEUM
(☎20 21 35 66; Rue Toffa; admission CFA1000; ⏲9am-6pm, to 5pm Sat & Sun) This establishment is housed in the walled compound of King Toffa, who signed the first treaty with the French in 1863. The site hasn't been well maintained and you'll need some imagination to make something out of the bare chambers, but François, the guide, puts on a good show.

Musée da Silva MUSEUM
(☎20 21 50 71; Ave Liotard; admission CFA2000; ⏲9am-6pm) This wonderfully eclectic museum is housed in a beautiful 1870 Afro-Brazilian house.

Sleeping & Eating

Centre Songhai HOTEL $
(☎20 24 68 81; www.songhai.org; Rte de Pobè; r with fan CFA5500-7500, with air-con CFA12,500-15,500, ste CFA30,000-50,000; P ❄ @ ≋) Built to accommodate its numerous visitors, the 70 rooms at Centre Songhai are spartan but clean. Fan rooms have a shower cubicle but shared toilets; the more-expensive air-con rooms have a private bathroom (with hot water) but are still very good value. The centre has two good restaurants: a cheap African *maquis* (mains CFA1200) and a more upmarket restaurant (mains CFA2500 to CFA3500). There's also an internet cafe (CFA250 per hour).

Le Palais BUNGALOW $$
(☎20 21 40 90; www.cthlepalais.com; Blvd Lagunaire; bungalows CFA30,000-41,800; P ❄ ≋) Poised on the edge of the lagoon, this is an unexpected oasis: well-furnished, comfy bungalows with all mod cons, neat garden,

good views and a restaurant-bar. Service is a bit lackadaisical, though.

Java Promo AFRICAN, FRENCH $

(☎66 96 68 78; Pl du Gouvernement; meals CFA1000-3500; ⏰breakfast, lunch & dinner daily) No one seems to remember a time before Java Promo. Hidden behind the aquamarine shutters of a crumbling colonial building and shielded from the sun by a big *paillote*, this is a popular haunt for an omelette at brekkie or rustic European meals for lunch.

JPN AFRICAN $

(mains CFA1500-2500; ⏰breakfast, lunch & dinner daily; wi-fi) Here the setting is the real draw, with an Eden-like garden replete with big trees, which puts you in the mood for a cold beer or a braised chicken as soon as you sit down. Free wi-fi. It's inside the Jardin des Plantes et de la Nature, right in the centre of town.

Information

Porto Novo has several banks with Visa ATMs and internet cafes.

Tourist Office (☎97 02 52 29; www.porto-novo.org; Pl Bayol; ⏰9am-1pm & 3-6pm Mon-Fri) Has a few brochures and can help with finding guides. Near the cathedral.

Getting There & Away

Plenty of minibuses and bush taxis leave for Cotonou (minibus/bush taxi CFA500/800, 45 minutes) from Carrefour Catchi and in front of Ouando mosque. To Abomey from Porto Novo is CFA3500. ATT buses that ply the Cotonou–Natitingou route also stop in front of Ouando mosque (CFA7500 for Natitingou).

For Nigeria, you can get a taxi to the border point in Kraké (CFA800, 30 minutes), but you'll have to change there to go on to Lagos.

Ouidah

POP 87,200

Some 42km west of Cotonou is Ouidah, a relaxed, relatively prosperous town and a must-see for anyone interested in voodoo or Benin's history of slavery. From the 17th to the late 19th century, captured countrymen from across West Africa left Ouidah for the Americas.

When voodoo has finished working its magic on you, there are sweeping expanses of golden-sand beaches to laze upon.

Sights

Route des Esclaves MEMORIAL

Once sold, slaves were taken from the fort to the beach down the 4km Rte des Esclaves. Lining the sandy track now are fetishes and monuments, such as the Monument of Repentance and the Tree of Forgetfulness. There is a poignant memorial on the beach, the **Point of No Return**, with bas-relief depicting slaves in chains. It's such a beautiful spot that it's hard to fathom that 12 million people were deported from this very shore.

Musée d'Histoire de Ouidah MUSEUM

(☎21 34 10 21; www.museeouidah.org; Rue van Vollenhoven; admission CFA1000; ⏰8am-12.30pm & 3-5pm Mon-Fri, 9am-5pm Sat & Sun) Ouidah's main site is its Musée d'Histoire de Ouidah, housed in the beautiful Fortaleza São João

WORTH A TRIP

ADJARA

Adjara, 9km northeast of Porto Novo on a back road to Nigeria, is a wonderful detour from Porto Novo. It's famous for its market, one of the most colourful in Benin. Held every fourth day, it's stocked with fetishes, *grigri* charms, unique blue and white tie-dyed cloth, some of the best pottery in Benin, *tamtams* and other musical instruments. You'll also see blacksmiths at work. Culture buffs will make a beeline for the small **Musée d'Adjara** (☎97 60 07 95; admission CFA1000; ⏰9am-6pm daily), which has a good display of African masks. The curator, Noël Agossou, will be happy to show you Adjara's highlights (CFA5000) and can also organise *pirogue* trips on a nearby river.

No visit to Adjara would be complete without having lunch at **Chez Houssou** (mains CFA1000; ⏰lunch daily). This unpretentious *maquis*, with no more than a couple of wooden benches, is famous for one thing and one thing only: *porc grillé sauce sang* (grilled pork cooked in a blood sauce). Houssou cuts morsels of pork, puts them in a mud-brick oven, and then serves them on a small plate – it can't get more authentic than that.

From Porto Novo, a *zem* ride shouldn't cost more than CFA900.

DON'T MISS

VOODOO DAY

Vodou (voodoo) got its current name in Haiti and Cuba, where the religions arrived with Fon and Ewe slaves from the Dahomey Kingdom and mixed with Catholicism. It means 'the hidden' or 'the mystery'. Traditional priests are consulted for their power to communicate with particular spirits and seek intercession with them. This communication is achieved through spirit possession and ritual that often involves a gift or 'sacrifice' of palm wine, chickens or goats.

Voodoo was formally recognised as a religion by the Beninese authorities in February 1996. Since then, 10 January, Voodoo Day, has been a bank holiday, with celebrations all over the country. Those in Ouidah, voodoo's historic centre, are among the best and most colourful, with endless singing, dancing, beating of drums and drinking.

Batista, a Portuguese fort built in 1721. It retraces the town's slave-trading history and explores the links between Benin, Brazil and the Caribbean.

Python Temple RELIGIOUS
(off Rue F Colombani; admission CFA1000, photos CFA5000; ⏲9am-6.30pm) Those interested in voodoo could visit the python temple, home to some 60 sleepy pythons. The guide explains some of the beliefs and ceremonies associated with the temple.

Sleeping & Eating

For a tasty meal, a hotel is your best bet. Otherwise, Rue F Colombani is peppered with food stalls and small *maquis*.

★Auberge Le Jardin Secret – Chez Pascal GUESTHOUSE $
(☎96 66 90 14; www.lejardinsecretouidah.net; near Radio Kpassé; r CFA10,000; P) An atmosphere of dreamlike tranquillity wafts over this well-organised guesthouse tucked away in a side *von* in a tranquil neighbourhood. The neatly tended garden has places to lounge, the six rooms, though not luxurious, are crisp and spruce, and there's an on-site restaurant (meals from CFA3500). Everything was built using natural materials. Bike rental is available. It's run by a Frenchman who travelled around West Africa by moped.

Le Jardin Brésilien Auberge de la Diaspora HOTEL $$
(☎94 56 96 73; www.bda2.com; Porte du Non Retour; r CFA8000-30,000; P ❄ 📶 🏊) Just off the beach near the Point of No Return, rooms here occupy two characterless, muscular buildings. Opt for the air-con rooms, which are spacious and meticulously clean. Avoid the fan rooms, which are overpriced and furnace-like. Also available is a cluster of modern, well-appointed bungalows. The real draws are the large pool and the restaurant (mains CFA4500 to CFA6500) slap bang on the beach.

Casa Del Papa RESORT $$$
(☎95 95 39 04; www.casadelpapa.com; Ouidah Plage; d incl breakfast CFA47,000-68,000; P ❄ 🏊) Squeezed between the ocean and the lagoon, Casa Del Papa is the closest thing to an exclusive resort you'll find on the coast. It features a host of facilities and amenities, including three pools, a volleyball court, two bars and a restaurant overlooking the beach. There are numerous activities on offer as well as excursions across the lagoon and to nearby villages. The hotel is 7km beyond the Point of No Return.

Côté Pêche SEAFOOD $$
(☎96 82 27 03, 97 46 43 79; Rte des Esclaves; mains CFA2500-3500; ⏲breakfast, lunch & dinner daily) Fish lovers, you'll find nirvana here: Côté Pêche has a wide assortment of fish delivered daily from the harbour, including barracuda and grouper. The menu also features meat dishes, pasta, salads and sandwiches. The owners have three rooms for rent (CFA6000). It's at the beginning of Rte des Esclaves.

Information

There are several internet cafes in town but only one bank (UBA) with an ATM (Visa only).

Tourist Office (☎21 19 35 11, 97 87 80 93; ouidah_tourisme@yahoo.fr; ⏲8.30am-6.30pm daily) Has various brochures and can arrange cultural tours. Ask for Modeste Zinsou. Near the post office.

Getting There & Away

From Carrefour Gbena, north of town, you can catch shared taxis to Cotonou (CFA1000, one hour), Grand Popo (CFA1500, one hour) and the Hilakondji border (CFA1500, 1½ hours).

Grand Popo

POP 10,000

Grand Popo is a wonderful spot to spend a few tranquil days. The village has plenty going on at the weekend when Cotonou residents come to decompress.

Sights & Activities

On the main road through the village, **Villa Karo** (☎94 20 31 20; www.villakaro.org; gallery 8am-noon & 4-6pm Mon-Fri, 8-11am Sat) has a small gallery with great exhibitions.

Run by two local guides, **GG Tours** (☎95 85 74 40) organises excursions on the Mono River or to the Bouche du Roy, where the river meets the ocean. Trips on the river last about two hours (CFA5000 per person). Trips to the Bouche du Roy cost CFA45,000 as you need a motorised boat; boats fit up to eight people and the trip lasts about six hours.

Sleeping & Eating

★ **Saveurs d'Afrique** BUNGALOW $
(☎97 89 28 19, 66 69 69 80; www.saveursdafrique.net; bungalows CFA15,500; P) Looking for a night at some place extra-special? Make a beeline for this lovely property, the pride and joy of affable Mathieu Yélomé, a young Beninese chef. The six units borrow from African traditional designs and are embellished with various artistic touches. Food is a big thing here; the range of daily specials (around CFA4500) on offer – mostly French-influenced dishes prepared with local ingredients – is well priced and filled with subtle flavours. Near the beach.

Lion Bar GUESTHOUSE $
(☎95 42 05 17; kabla_gildas@yahoo.fr; campsites per person CFA1500, r without bathroom CFA5000) Down a track from the main street, you'll easily find this reggae land by following Bob Marley's languorous beats. It's the hideout of choice for Cotonou's expat beatniks and oozes peace and love: cocktails flow at all hours of the day and night, rooms are spartan yet funky and the shared facilities surprisingly clean. Daily specials cost CFA2500. It's right on the beach and you're free to pitch your tent.

Auberge Victor's Place CAMPGROUND $
(☎97 04 91 02; campsites per person CFA1000, bungalows without bathroom s/d CFA5500/7500; P) Victor's Place boasts a spiffing beach frontage in a green location. Pitch your tent on the grassy plot or choose one of the three slightly threadbare bungalows. The real draws are the cool atmosphere and the wicked cocktails prepared by Victor, a friendly Rasta. You can hire a tent if you don't have your own. Overall, it's very simple, but there's plenty of heart.

Awalé Plage RESORT $$
(☎22 43 01 17; www.hotel-benin-awaleplage.com; Rte du Togo; campsites CFA6000, bungalows with fan/air-con CFA20,500/25,500; P) A great place to recharge the batteries, Awalé Plage's most notable features are its beachfront setting, its beautiful gardens awash with tropical trees, its large swimming pool and its well-maintained bungalows. There is an excellent beach bar and the on-site restaurant (mains CFA2000 to CFA6500) prepares delectable French-inspired dishes with a tropical twist. It's also a good bargain for campers.

Getting There & Away

From Cotonou, take a bush taxi from Gare Jonquet, Stade de l'Amitié or Pl de l'Étoile Rouge (CFA2500, two hours) and have it drop you off at the Grand Popo junction on the main coastal highway, 20km east of the Togo border crossing at Hilakondji. The beach and village are 3.5km off the main road and are easily accessible via *zemijohn* (CFA250).

Possotomé & Lake Ahémé

The fertile shores of Lake Ahémé are a wonderful place to spend a few days, particularly around Possotomé, the area's biggest village. It's even possible to swim in the lake.

Various trips and excursions are offered by local tour operators, including **Eco-Bénin** (www.ecobenin.org). Learn traditional fishing techniques, meet craftspeople at work or go on a fascinating two-hour botanic journey to hear about local plants and their medicinal properties. There are half a dozen thematic circuits to choose from (from two hours to day trips, CFA3500 to CFA12,000), all run by delightful local guides.

Sleeping & Eating

Gîte de Possotomé GUESTHOUSE $
(☎94 38 80 34, 67 19 58 37; www.ecobenin.org; s without bathroom CFA4500-6000, d CFA7000-8500, s/d with bathroom CFA9500/12,500; P) Embedded in a manicured tropical garden, this well-run venture has eight impeccable rooms with salubrious bathrooms. It's not on the lakeshore, but the congenial atmosphere

more than makes up for this. The ethos here is laid-back, ecological and activity-oriented – various tours can be arranged.

Camping de Possotomé – Chez Préfet CAMPGROUND $

(☎95 35 86 53; campsites per person CFA3000; P) How does watching the sun rise over Lake Ahémé sound? This campsite, on an idyllic spot on the sandy lakeshore, is basic (bucket showers and toilets) but very atmospheric. Prefet, the cook, will whisk up African wonders for sustenance (meals CFA3500).

Hôtel Chez Théo RESORT $$

(☎95 05 53 15, 96 44 47 88; www.chez-theo.com; r CFA15,000-20,000, bungalows CFA30,000; P ❄ ⓦ) In a stunning lakeside location, Chez Théo is guaranteed to help you switch to 'relax' mode. A path through a garden bursting with all sorts of exotic trees leads to a great bar-restaurant (mains from CFA3500) on a stilt platform with cracking views. Rooms are far from fancy but are kept scrupulously clean. Four bungalows, including two overwater units, were being built at the time of research. All kinds of tours can be organised.

Getting There & Away

Taxis that ply the Cotonou–Hilakondji (or Comé) route will generally drop you off at the Comé turn-off (CFA2000), from where the only option to Possotomé is a *zemi-john* (CFA1000).

Abomey

POP 125,000

If you're looking to immerse yourself in ancient Beninese history, one of the best places to start is Abomey. The name is mythical, and not without reason: Abomey, 144km northwest of Cotonou, was the capital of the fierce Dahomey Kingdom and a force colonial powers had to reckon with for centuries. Its winding lanes dotted with palaces and temples, Abomey is shrouded with a palpable historical aura and filled with character.

Sights

Musée Historique d'Abomey MUSEUM

(☎22 50 03 14; www.epa-prema.net/abomey; admission CFA2500; ⏲9am-4.30pm) Abomey's main and seriously impressive attraction (and a World Heritage Site), this sprawling museum is housed in two palaces, those of the ancient kings Ghézo and Glélé. The museum displays royal thrones and tapestries, human skulls that were once used as musical instruments, fetish items and Ghézo's throne, mounted on four real skulls of vanquished enemies.

The admission fee includes a guide (only French is spoken), who will take about an hour to show you around the courtyards, ceremonial rooms and burial chambers. The tour finishes at the Centre des Artisans, where you can buy appliqué banners.

DON'T MISS

THE ROUTE OF KINGS

The tourist office runs excellent cultural tours focusing on Abomey's rich architectural heritage. They last about two hours and cost CFA3000 per person (not including *zem* rental). There are some 10 sites to be seen, all of which have an air of faded majesty about their crumbling walls. Highlights include Palais Akaba, Place de Goho, Palais Ghézo, Palais de Glélé, Temple Hwemu, Temple Zéwa and Palais Agonglo – the best kept of Abomey's nine palaces.

Sleeping & Eating

A La Lune – Chez Monique GUESTHOUSE $

(☎22 50 01 68; north of Rond-Point de la Préfecture; r CFA7500-8500; P) You'll love the exotic garden, complete with antelopes, crocodiles, tortoises, monkeys, flower bushes and huge wood carvings. Accommodation-wise, it's a bit less overwhelming, with no-frills, yet spacious, rooms. The on-site restaurant is average; opt for a contemplative drink in the garden instead.

Auberge d'Abomey GUESTHOUSE $$

(☎95 82 80 28, 97 89 87 25; www.hotels-benin.com; Rond-Point de la Préfecture; s/d with fan CFA12,500/14,000, with air-con CFA17,000/20,000; ❄) This reliable option off the main roundabout is a small, rustic hotel with a colonial feel and just a handful of spare rooms. It gets high marks from travellers for its relaxing garden full of mango trees and its on-site restaurant (mains from CFA2500). Various excursions can be organised.

★**Chez Delphano** OPEN-AIR RESTAURANT $

(☎93 64 02 40; mains CFA800-1900; ⏲breakfast, lunch & dinner daily) This delightful *maquis* is a winner. Marguerite prepares exquisite Beninese cuisine in a jovial atmosphere. She also prepares *crêpes* in the morning, with freshly ground coffee and a mountain of fruit. Yum! Chez Delphano is north of Rond-Point de la Préfecture.

Information

You'll find banks and internet cafes in Bohicon, 9km east of Abomey.

Tourist Office (☎95 79 09 45, 94 14 67 30; Office du Tourisme d'Abomey; ⌚9am-1pm & 3-6pm Mon-Fri, 9am-4pm Sat) Has some interesting brochures and can provide information about Abomey's main sights. It also keeps a list of accredited guides (some of whom speak English) and can arrange guided tours. Ask for Gabin Djimassé, the knowledgeable director. It's near the Rond-Point de la Préfecture.

Getting There & Away

Plenty of bush taxis depart from Cotonou (CFA3000, three hours), sometimes with a connection at Bohicon. *Zemi-johns* (CFA800) frequently run between Abomey and Bohicon.

ATT and Confort Lines buses (between Cotonou and Natitingou) stop in Bohicon on the way.

THE NORTH

Northern Benin's arid, mountainous landscape is a world away from the south's beaches and lagoons but all the more attractive for it. It's all about the natural heritage, with one fantastic wildlife park and a mountain range. It is also ethnically more diverse than the south, and Islam is the main religion.

Natitingou

POP 75,600

Affectionately known as Nati, Natitingou is the most vibrant town in northern Benin and is a fabulous base for excursions to the nearby Atakora Mountains and the Parc National de la Pendjari.

Sights

Musée Régional de Natitingou MUSEUM
(☎23 02 00 53; Rte Inter-État; admission CFA1000; ⌚8am-12.30pm & 3.30-6.30pm Mon-Fri, 9am-noon & 4-6pm Sat & Sun) Housed in a colonial building built by slaves at the beginning of the 20th century, this museum gives an overview of life in Somba communities. The exhibition includes various musical instruments, jewellery, crowns and artefacts. Most interesting is the habitat room, which has models of the different types of *tata somba* (Somba houses).

Sleeping & Eating

Hôtel Bellevue BUNGALOW $
(☎90 92 33 69, 23 82 13 36; myriamsare13@hotmail.com; s/d with fan from CFA7500/8500, with air-con from CFA14,500/17,000; P ❄ @ ☺) Set in a rambling garden, the Bellevue is a charming collection of sweet bungalows and *paillotes*. Myriam, the formidable owner, runs a tight ship and rooms are simple yet spotless, as is the food in the restaurant (much of which comes from her vegie garden). Your host also makes jewellery, for sale at the reception. She had plans to retire at the time of writing.

Palais Somba BUNGALOW $
(☎96 27 29 51; s/d with fan CFA6500/8500, with air-con CFA12,500/16,500; ❄) 'Palace' might be pushing it a bit, but this venture is something special, blending African touches with European levels of comfort. All the bungalows, which are arranged around a leafy compound, are embellished with paintings made by a local artist. The garden is compact but easily one of the nicest in Nati. There's an on-site restaurant, with a limited selection of simple dishes. It's in a quiet area.

Hôtel de Bourgogne HOTEL $$
(☎23 82 22 40, 97 90 97 38; www.natitingou.org/bourgogne; Rte Inter-État; r with fan CFA14,000-18,000, with air-con from CFA18,000-25,000; P ❄ ☺) This efficiently run hotel is a safe bet. Although not the height of luxury, rooms are colourful, comfy, spacious and serviceable, with modern, clean beds, and the restaurant has a reputation for fine food, with an emphasis on meat dishes (mains from

THE SOMBA

Commonly referred to as the Somba, the Betamaribé people are concentrated to the southwest of Natitingou in the plains of Boukoumbé on the Togo border. What's most fascinating about the Betamaribé is their *tata somba* houses – fort-like huts with clay turrets and thatched spires. The ground floor of a house is mostly reserved for livestock. A stepladder leads from the kitchen to the roof terrace, where there are sleeping quarters and grain stores.

The Betamaribé's principal religion is animism – as seen in the rags and bottles they hang from the trees. Once famous for their nudity, they began wearing clothes in the 1970s.

CFA4800). Hot water is available in the more expensive rooms. One downside: the hotel is not shielded from the noise of the main road.

La Brèche AFRICAN $$
(☎96 90 07 66; mains CFA1700-3000; ⏰lunch & dinner daily) Highly original is this appealing eatery set in a *tata somba* house with superb views of Nati and the Atakora Mountains. Book ahead for the house specialities: *canard au tchouk* (duck cooked in *tchoukoutou* – sorghum beer – sauce) and *lapin au sodabe* (rabbit cooked in *sodabe* – moonshine – sauce). And be sure to try the delicious *salade peule* (tomatoes with local cheese).

Information

Internet cafes are easy to find around town. Ecobank, at the main junction, changes cash and has one ATM (Visa only).

For information about tours and excursions in the wider area, including the Atakora and the Parc National de la Pendjari, ask at your hotel or contact the Natitingou-based Bénin Aventure (p218), a highly recommended company run by excellent local guides.

Getting There & Away

From the *gare routière* in the centre, bush taxis and minibuses go to Tanguiéta (CFA1500, one hour), from where you can find services to the border with Burkina Faso and Ouagadougou (there aren't any direct services to Burkina Faso from Natitingou). For Koussoukoingou and Boukoumbé, it's easier to get there by *zem* (about CFA300).

Bus services linking Nati and Cotonou (CFA8500, eight hours) include ATT and Confort Lines and leave from the *gare routière* south of town. Services leave at 7am; book ahead or arrive early on the day.

WORTH A TRIP

KOTA FALLS

Fancy a refreshing dip? Consider heading to the **Kota Falls** (admission CFA300), 15km southeast of Natitingou, off the main highway. You can swim in the pool at the bottom of the falls or just sit down and read in the cool shade of the undergrowth. Pure bliss! Hire a *zem* (CFA5000 per day) to get there. Take note that it's possible to overnight near the falls – there's a cluster of surprisingly well-maintained bungalows (room CFA10,500).

The Atakora Region

About 30km west of Nati is the mountain village of **Koussoukoingou** (also known as Koussou-Kovangou), famous for its stunning location and breathtaking views of the Atakora range. Further west, 43km southwest of Natitingou, on the Togo border, **Boukombé** is the capital of Somba country, at the heart of the Atakora Mountains. The drive there is stunning, bumping along a red *piste* (rough track) past corn fields and huge baobab trees. Boukombé has a lively market every four days, when *tchoukoutou* (sorghum beer) gingerly flows.

Sights & Activities

Ecotourism association **Perle de l'Atakora** (Pearl of the Atakora; ☎97 44 28 61; www.ecobenin.org/koussoukoingou) offers guided walks around Koussoukoingou (CFA2500 to CFA3500 for 2½ to 3½ hours) taking in local sights such as the famous *tata* houses (fort-like huts with clay turrets and thatched spires). You can arrange to spend the night at a *tata* (CFA6000 per person including breakfast and dinner).

Sleeping & Eating

Ecolodge La Perle de l'Atakora GUESTHOUSE $
(☎67 46 78 01, 97 35 02 86; www.ecobenin.org; Koussoukoingou; r without bathroom CFA8000; P) We can't think of a better place for immersion in local culture. This modernish *tata* house features five rooms that are tidy, functional and well priced, and a well-scrubbed ablutions block. Hearty meals too. It's run by Ecobenin, which offers high-quality ecotours in the area. Bikes are also available.

Tata Touristique Koubetti Victor GUESTHOUSE $
(☎94 68 75 49, 97 35 29 24; www.tatabenin.wordpress.com; Boukombé; r without bathroom CFA5000; P 📶) This is a wonderfully laid-back Boukombé haven, with a leafy courtyard, a chilled-out ambience and tasty meals. Rooms occupy a large *tata* house. It's basic but clean and high on character. Joséphine and her daughter Valérie can organise village visits, cultural tours and dance classes. Pick-ups from Natitingou can also be arranged.

Getting There & Away

It's best to get to the Atakora with your own transport, but a few bush taxis do ply the dusty trail between Nati, Koussoukoingou and Boukoumbé (CFA2000, two hours), where you can cross into Togo. Otherwise, *zemi-johns* (about CFA5000, three hours) will take you, but be prepared for a dusty and tiring ride.

CROSSING INTO TOGO

If you cross into Togo from Boukombé, make sure you get your passport stamped at the *gendarmerie* (police station) at Boukoumbé as there is no border checkpoint.

Parc National de la Pendjari

Amid the majestic landscape of the Atakora's rugged cliffs and wooded savannah live lions, cheetahs, leopards, elephants, baboons, hippos, myriad birds and countless antelopes. The 275,000-hectare **Parc National de la Pendjari** (Pendjari National Park; www.pendjari.net; per person CFA10,000, per vehicle CFA3000; 6am-5pm), the main entrance of which is 100km north of Natitingou, is one of the best in West Africa. The best viewing time is near the end of the dry season, when animals start to hover around waterholes.

To maximise your chances of seeing animals, go for an accredited guide (graded as 'A' or 'B'). The list of accredited guides can be found on the park's website, at park entrances and in Nati's better hotels. It costs CFA10,000 for a 'A' guide and CFA8000 for a 'B' guide.

The main entrances to Pendjari are roughly 100km north of Natitingou, in Porga (near the border with Burkina Faso) and Batia (41km northeast of Tanguiéta, on a good track).

On the park's periphery, some 11km before Batia in Tanougou, you can take a dip in the lovely natural pools at the bottom of the **Tanougou Falls** (admission CFA1000).

Sleeping & Eating

Many visitors stay in Natitingou and make excursions from there, but you'll have a better chance of seeing animals if you stay at the park itself.

★ **Pendjari Lodge** LODGE $$
(in France 336 68 42 73 43; www.pendjari-lodge.com; tents CFA31,000; Nov-Jul; P) A lovely place in a beautiful setting on a small hill (views!), Pendjari Lodge mixes old-style safari ambience with nouveau bush chic. It sports a handful of luxury, semipermanent tents and a large dining area and lounge with wooden decks overlooking a valley. One quibble: the menu (mains from CFA4000) is a bit limited. No phone network, but wi-fi is available.

Hôtel de la Pendjari HOTEL $$
(23 82 11 24; www.hoteltatasomba.com; r with fan/air-con CFA21,000/26,000, bungalows without bathroom CFA15,000; Dec-May; P) Although it's starting to fray around the edges, this establishment offers spacious, utilitarian rooms with good bedding, and its location at the heart of the park is hard to beat. If you're watching your money, opt for the spartan bungalows. Electricity runs for a few hours a day only. There's an on-site restaurant (meals CFA6000), but service can be absent-minded.

Getting There & Away

Travellers without vehicles could try to team up with other parties at hotels in Natitingou. Most guides based in Natitingou can also organise vehicle rentals, and some of them have their own 4WDs. **Bénin Aventure** rents out 4WD vehicles for CFA75,000 per day (for up to four people), including a chauffeur guide (rated 'A' by the park) and fuel.

UNDERSTAND BENIN

Benin Today

The country is one of the more stable in the region, although things are not all that rosy. The current president, Yayi Boni, former head of the West African Development Bank, beat Adrien Houngbédji in a run-off in 2006. In his campaign, which he based around the slogan of 'change', he pledged to fight corruption and revive the country's economy.

It hasn't, however, been plain sailing: despite Boni's party winning a majority of seats in the parliamentary elections of 2007 and a number of local seats in the 2008 municipal elections, reforms have come about more slowly than hoped. Yayi Boni was re-elected in March 2011. In theory, the constitution limits presidents to two terms in office, but opposition parties fear that Boni may try to reform the constitution in order to stand for a third mandate in 2016.

History

More than 350 years ago the area now known as Benin was split into numerous principalities. Akaba of Abomey conquered his neighbouring ruler Dan and called the new kingdom Dan-Homey, later shortened to Dahomey by French colonisers. By 1727, Dahomey spread from Abomey down to Ouidah and Cotonou and into parts of modern Togo. The kingdoms of Nikki, Djougou and Parakou were still powerful in the north, as was the Kingdom of Toffa in Porto-Novo.

Each king pledged to leave his successor more land than he inherited, achieved by waging war with his neighbours. They grew rich by selling slaves to the European traders, notably the Portuguese, who established trading posts in Porto Novo, Ouidah and along the coast. For more than a century, an average of 10,000 slaves per year were shipped to the Americas. Southern Dahomey was dubbed the Slave Coast.

Following colonisation by the French, great progress was made in education, and many Dahomeyans were employed as government advisers throughout French West Africa.

Independence & Le Folklore

When Dahomey became independent in 1960, other former French colonies started deporting their Dahomeyan populations. Back home without work, they were the root of a highly unstable political situation. Three years after independence, following the example of neighbouring Togo, the Dahomeyan military staged a coup.

During the next decade Dahomey saw four military coups, nine changes of government and five changes of constitution: what the Dahomeyans called, in jest, *le folklore*.

Revolution

In 1972 a group of officers led by Lieutenant Colonel Mathieu Kérékou seized power in a coup, then embraced Marxist-Leninist ideology and aligned the country with superpowers such as China. To emphasise the break from the past, Kérékou changed the flag and renamed the country Benin. He informed his people of the change by radio on 13 November 1975.

The government established Marxist infrastructure, which included implementing collective farms. However, the economy became a shambles, and there were ethnic tensions between the president, a Natitingou-born northerner, and the Yoruba population in the south. There were six attempted coups in one year alone.

In December 1989, as a condition of French financial support, Kérékou ditched Marxism and held a conference to draft a new constitution. The delegates engineered a coup, forming a new cabinet under Nicéphore Soglo.

Soglo won the first free multiparty elections, held in March 1991, but his autocracy, nepotism and austere economic measures – following the devaluation of the CFA franc – came under fire. Kérékou was voted back into power in March 1996. Kérékou's second and final five-year term in office finished with the presidential elections in March 2006, bringing an end to his 33 years at the top.

People of Benin

There is an array of different ethnic groups within Benin's narrow borders, although three of them account for nearly 60% of the population: Fon, Adja and Yoruba. The Fon and Yoruba both migrated from Nigeria and occupy the southern and mideastern zones of Benin.

The Bariba and the Betamaribé, who make up 9% and 8% of the population respectively, live in the northern half of the country and have traditionally been very protective of their cultures and distant towards southern people.

The nomadic Fula (also called Fulani or Peul), found widely across West Africa, live primarily in the north and constitute 6% of the population.

Despite the underlying tensions between the southern and northern regions, the various groups live in relative harmony and have intermarried.

Religion

Some 40% of the population is Christian and 25% Muslim, but most people practise voodoo, whatever their religion. The practice mixed with Catholicism in the Americas, where the Dahomeyan slaves took it and from where their Afro-Brazilian descendants brought it back. Christian missionaries also won over Dahomeyans by fusing their creed with voodoo.

The Arts

Under the Dahomeyan kings, richly coloured appliqué banners were used to depict the rulers' past and present glories. With their bright, cloth-cut figures, the banners are still being made, particularly in Abomey.

Benin has a substantial Afro-Brazilian architectural heritage, best preserved in Porto Novo and Ouidah – there are plenty of hidden gems to seek out in the streets. The Lake Nokoué stilt villages, especially Ganvié, and the *tata somba* houses around Natitingou are remarkable examples of traditional architecture.

The *cire perdue* (lost wax) method used to make the famous Benin bronzes originates from Benin City, which lies in present-day Nigeria. However, the method spread west and the figures can be bought throughout Benin itself.

If you're into music, you'll love Angélique Kidjo, a major international star and Benin's most famous recording artist. Born in Ouidah in 1960 to a choreographer and a musician with Portuguese and English ancestry, Kidjo is a world musician in the true, boundary-busting sense of the phrase. Her music is inspired by the links between Africa and Latin America and the fusion of cultures. Check out www.kidjo.com for more information about her career. Other well-known Beninese artists include Gnonnas Pedro, Nel Oliver and Yelouassi Adolphe, and the bands Orchestre Poly-Rythmo and Disc Afrique.

Food & Drink

Beninese grub is unquestionably among the best in West Africa and is very similar to Togolese food, the main differences being the names: *fufu* is generally called *igname pilé,* and *djenkoumé* is called *pâte rouge,* for example. In southern Benin, fish is a highlight of local cuisine. It's usually barracuda, dorado or grouper, and is usually served grilled or fried.

The local beer, La Béninoise, is a passable drop. Mineral water and fruit juices are sold in all major towns. The adventurous could try the millet-based brew *tchoukoutou* or *sodabe* (moonshine).

Environment

Sandwiched between Nigeria and Togo, Benin is 700km long and 120km across in the south, widening to about 300km in the north. Most of the coastal plain is a sand bar that blocks the seaward flow of several rivers. As a result, there are lagoons a few kilometres inland all along the coast, which is being eroded by the strong ocean currents. Inland is a densely forested plateau and, in the far northwest, the Atakora Mountains.

Wildlife thrives in Parc National de la Pendjari, with elephants and several feline species.

Deforestation and desertification are major issues because of the logging of valuable wood, such as teak.

SURVIVAL GUIDE

Directory A–Z

ACCOMMODATION

Benin has accommodation to suit every budget – from beach resorts to guesthouses. Swanky hotels are confined to Cotonou and, to a lesser extent, Ouidah and Natitingou. Most have restaurants and bars, and offer wi-fi service and have air-con.

EMBASSIES & CONSULATES

The following offices are all in Cotonou.

British Community Liaison Officer (☎21 30 32 65; www.fco.gov.uk; Haie Vive) Officially, British nationals must deal with the British Deputy High Commission in Lagos (Nigeria). However, the Community Liaison Officer for the British community in Benin, based at the English International School, can be of some help.

French Embassy (☎21 36 55 33; www.ambafrance-bj.org; Ave Jean-Paul II)

German Embassy (☎21 31 29 67; www.cotonou.diplo.de; Ave Jean-Paul II)

Ghanaian Embassy (☎21 30 07 46; off Blvd de la Marina)

Nigerian Embassy (☎21 31 56 65; Blvd de la Marina)

Nigerien Embassy (☎21 31 56 65; off Blvd de la Marina)

US Embassy (☎21 30 06 50; cotonou.usembassy.gov; Rue Caporal Bernard Anani)

FOOD & DRINK

For more information on the gastronomy of Benin, see p215.

INTERNET ACCESS

- In towns and cities, complimentary wi-fi is available in almost every midrange and top-end hotel.
- Internet cafes are plentiful in towns and cities. Rates are CFA300 per hour. Connection speeds vary from pretty good to acceptable.

MONEY

- The currency in Benin is the West African CFA franc.
- The best foreign currency to carry is euros, easily exchanged at any bank, hotel or bureau de change.
- Travellers cheques cannot be exchanged in Benin.
- There are numerous Visa ATMs in every city; the only bank to accept MasterCard is Banque Atlantique (in Cotonou only), though its MasterCard ATMs were not functioning at the time of research.
- Credit cards are accepted at some upmarket hotels and shops. Some places levy a commission of about 5% for credit-card payment.

OPENING HOURS

Banks Open 8am to 12.30pm and 3pm to 6.30pm Monday to Friday, plus 9am to 1pm Saturday. Some banks are open through lunchtime.

Bars Normally serve from late morning until the last customers leave (late); nightclubs generally go from 10pm into the wee hours.

Restaurants Lunch is usually from 11.30am to 2.30pm, dinner 6.30pm to 10.30pm.

Shops & Businesses Open 8am to noon and 3pm to 7pm Monday to Saturday.

PUBLIC HOLIDAYS

Benin celebrates Muslim holidays.

New Year's Day 1 January
Vodoun 10 January
Easter Monday March/April
Labour Day 1 May
Ascension Thursday May
Pentecost Monday May
Independence Day 1 August
Assumption 15 August
Armed Forces Day 26 October
All Saints' Day 1 November
Christmas 25 December

SAFE TRAVEL

Cotonou has its fair share of traffic accidents and muggings, so be careful. In Ouidah, avoid the roads to and along the coast at any time of day.

Children, and sometimes also adults, will shout '*Yovo! Yovo!*' (meaning 'white person') ad nauseam. It's normally harmless, but tiresome.

The beaches along the coast are not safe for swimming because of strong currents. Stick to hotel swimming pools or the lagoon.

PRACTICALITIES

Electricity Supply is 220V and plugs are of the European two-round-pin variety. Network cuts are frequent.

Newspapers Cotonou's daily newspapers include *La Nation* and *Le Matinal*.

Radio The state-owned ORTB broadcasts on the radio in French and local languages.

Languages Include French, Fon, Yoruba, Dendi, Aja and Bariba. More than 50 languages are spoken in total.

TELEPHONE

- Benin's country code is 229.
- Phone numbers have eight digits. Landline numbers start with 21, mobile numbers with 9 or 6.
- Mobile-phone coverage is excellent and fairly cheap. Local networks include Moov and MTN.
- Depending on which mobile network you use at home, your phone may or may not work while in Cotonou – ask your mobile network provider. You can also bring your phone and buy a local SIM card (CFA1000). Top-up vouchers are readily available.

VISAS

Visas are required for all travellers except nationals of the Economic Community of West African States (Ecowas).

Local authorities have had a couple of U-turns on visa policies in recent years. At the time of writing, visas were not obtainable at the border or upon arrival at the airport. Be sure to get your visa from a Beninese embassy before travelling. Allow €50 for a one-month single-entry visa.

Note that at the time of research the Visa des Pays de l'Entente was not available in Benin.

Visas for Onward Travel

The following embassies deliver visas:

Burkina Faso No diplomatic representation in Benin – contact the French consulate.

Niger The embassy in Cotonou issues 30-day visas. They cost CFA22,500 and you'll need two photos. Allow three to four working days. You cannot get visas at the border.

Nigeria The Nigerian embassy only issues transit visas to travellers with a Nigerian embassy in their home country (there is no need to contact the embassy in your home country beforehand). You need two photos, along with photocopies of your passport and, if you have one, your ticket for onward travel from Nigeria. Fees vary according to nationality. Visas are normally issued on the same day.

Togo Seven-day visas (CFA10,000) are issued at the border. If crossing the border at Nadoba (coming from Boukombé), head to Kara where the Direction Régionale de la Documentation Nationale issues 30-day multiple-entry visas (CFA10,000, four photos).

WOMEN TRAVELLERS

Beninese men can be sleazy and women travellers will get a lot of unwanted attention. Particularly unnerving are military and other officials using their power to get more of your company than is strictly necessary. Always stay polite but firm and make sure you have a good 'husband story'.

Getting There & Away

You will need a yellow-fever vaccination certificate to come to Benin.

AIR

The **Aéroport International de Cotonou Cadjéhoun** (www.aeroport-cotonou.com) is Benin's main gateway.

The main international carriers are **Air France** (www.airfrance.com; Rte de l'Aéroport), **Royal Air Maroc** (☎21 30 86 04; www.royalairmaroc.com; Rte de l'Aéroport), **Brussels Airlines** (☎21 30 16 82; www.brusselsairlines.com; Rte de l'Aéroport) and **Ethiopian Airlines** (☎21 32 71 61; www.flyethiopian.com; Rue 403), which offer direct flights to France, Morocco, Belgium and Ethiopia respectively, and connecting flights to the rest of the world.

Other major airlines include **Asky** (☎21 32 54 18; www.flyasky.com; Ave de la Paix), which flies to major capitals in West and Central Africa via Lomé; **South African Airways** (www.flysaa.com; Ave Steinmetz), which flies to Johannesburg (South Africa); **Kenya Airways** (☎21 31 63 71; www.kenya-airways.com; Ave Steinmetz), which flies to Nairobi (Kenya) and Ouagadougou (Burkina Faso); **Air Burkina** (www.air-burkina.com; Rte de l'Aéroport), which serves Ouagadougou (Burkina Faso) and Abidjan (Côte d'Ivoire); and **Senegal Airlines** (☎21 31 76 51; www.senegalairlines.aero; Ave Steinmetz), which flies to Dakar (Senegal) and Abidjan (Côte d'Ivoire). All airlines have offices in Cotonou.

LAND

Burkina Faso

From Tanguiéta in north western Benin, you can find bush taxis to Nadiagou, on the Burkina side of the border north or Porga, from where you can find services to Ouagadougou. There's also a daily bus from Tanguiéta to Ouagadougou.

TCV (☎97 60 39 68; Rue 108) and **TSR** (☎97 88 17 94; Rue Proche) run bus services three times a week between Cotonou and Bobo Dioulasso via Ouagadougou (CFA18,000, 18 hours).

Niger

From Malanville in northeastern Benin, a *zemi-john* or shared taxi can take you across the Niger River to Gaya in Niger.

From Cotonou, **Rimbo-RTV** (☎95 23 24 82; Zongo) has daily services to Niamey (CFA22,000, 18 hours).

Nigeria

ABC Transport (☎66 56 45 15; Stade de l'Amitié) and **Cross Country International** (☎66 99 92 41; Ave du Nouveau Pont) both operate a daily Lagos–Accra bus service, which stops in Cotonou (CFA11,000 to CFA12,500, four hours). Add another CFA5000 for the *convoyeur* (the middleman who'll handle and facilitate formalities at the border).

There are no direct taxis to Lagos from Porto Novo, so you'll have to change at the Kraké–Seme border (CFA800, 30 minutes). Make sure you have some naira to pay for your journey on the other side.

Togo

Cotonou and Lomé are connected by frequent bush taxis (CFA5000, three hours), which regularly leave the Gare Jonquet in Cotonou for Lomé. Alternatively, pick up a taxi to the border point at Hilakondji and grab another taxi on the Togolese side of the border.

Various bus companies, including **STIF** (☎97 98 11 80; off Ave Clozel), **STC** (☎21 32 66 69; off Rue 303) and **UTB** (☎95 42 71 20; Ave Clozel), also regularly plough the Cotonou–Lomé–Accra–Abidjan route (CFA5000 for Lomé, four hours).

Other crossings are at Kétao–Ouaké, on the Kara–Djougou road, and between Nadoba in Togo and Boukoumbé in Benin along a good track. The latter crossing takes you through spectacular countryside but has little public transport except on Wednesday, Nadoba market day.

Getting Around

BUSH TAXI

Bush taxis, generally beaten-up old vehicles, cover outlying communities that large buses don't serve but also run between major towns and cities. There is sometimes a surcharge for luggage. Most leave from the *gares routières*; morning is the best time to find them.

BUS

- Buses are the most reliable and comfortable way to get around, especially between cities in southern Benin and Natitingou to the north.
- ATT and Confort Lines buses are better maintained and more reliable than those of other companies. They also have air-con.
- Buses almost always operate with guaranteed seating and fixed departure times; arrive early or book the day before to ensure you have a seat on your preferred service.

CAR & MOTORCYCLE

- Roads are in relatively good condition throughout Benin except the Cotonou–Bohicon road, which is appalling. It's scheduled to be resurfaced though.
- Hiring a car with a driver is a good option if you're short on time. Travel agencies and tour operators in Cotonou can organise 4WD rental for about 50,000 per day (with driver). For a regular vehicle, you'll pay about CFA20,000 per day. Fuel is extra.
- If you're driving, you need an International Driving Permit.
- A litre of petrol cost around CFA600 at the time of research. Petrol stations are easy to find throughout the country.

ZEMI-JOHNS

The omnipresence of *zems* (*zemi-johns;* motorbike taxis) has translated into the near disappearance of car taxis for short journeys. While they are by far the fastest and most convenient way of getting around, they are dangerous: most drive like lunatics and helmets are not available.

Zem drivers wear numbered yellow shirts in Cotonou (various colours in other towns). Hail them just as you would a taxi, and be sure to agree on a price before the journey. The typical fare costs from CFA150 to CFA250 for trips within a town. They are also an easy way to get to remote villages where public transport is infrequent.

TOURS

For tours around Benin and further afield, the following companies are recommended and can arrange English-speaking guides.

Bénin Aventure (☎ 97 50 23 74, 23 02 00 17; www.beninaventure.com; Hôtel de Bourgogne, Rte Inter-État) Organises guided, tailor-made trips around Benin in chauffeur-driven 4WDs.

Eco-Bénin (www.ecobenin.org) This small Beninese NGO promoting sustainable tourism runs activities in three sites across the country: Possotomé and Lake Ahémé, Koussoukoingou in the Somba country and Tanougou next to the Parc National de la Pendjari. The basis of its activities is guided tours exploring the culture and heritage of the area. It also organises vehicle rentals.

Double Sens (www.doublesens.fr) Another reputable tour operator with a strong ethic. Can arrange all kinds of tours, including village stays.

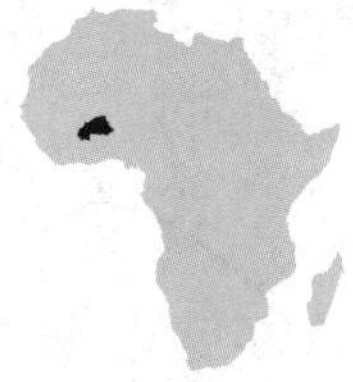

Burkina Faso

POP 17 MILLION

Includes ➡

Best Places to Eat

- La Canne d'Or (p227)
- Le Calypso (p230)
- Maquis Aboussouan (p223)
- Le Verdoyant (p223)
- Le Saint-Germain (p227)

Best Places to Stay

- Villa Bobo (p226)
- Le Pavillon Vert (p222)
- Le Calypso (p230)
- Les Jardins de Koulouba (p222)
- Campement de l'Éléphant (p233)

Why Go?

Burkina may not have many big-ticket attractions, yet it invariably wins the hearts of travellers for the warmth of its welcome. The Burkinabé are disarmingly charming and easygoing, and wherever you go you'll be greeted with a memorable *bonne arrivée* (welcome).

The country's other big draws are its enchanting landscapes – from atmospheric Sahelian plains, to rolling savannah and surprising geology – and the lively cultural scene. Ouagadougou and Bobo-Dioulasso, Burkina's two largest and gloriously named cities, are famous for their musical traditions and beautiful handicrafts. Throw in Fespaco, Africa's premier film festival, held in the capital every odd-numbered year, and there's enough to engage your mind and senses for a couple of weeks or so.

Tourism infrastructure is fairly limited, but there is a handful of gems, especially in Ouaga, Bobo and Banfora, as well as family-run, simple *campements* (guesthouses) in more remote areas.

When to Go

Ouagadougou

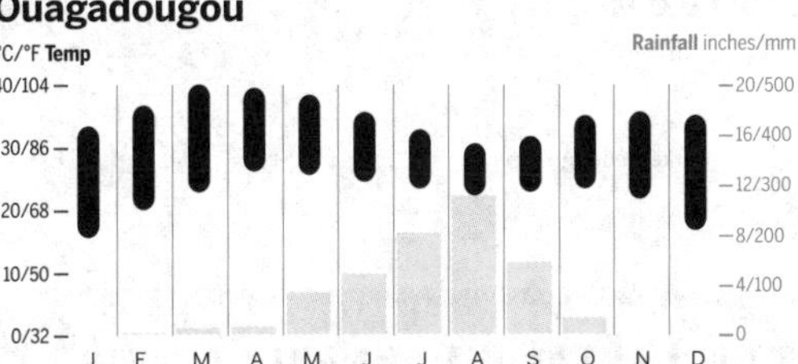

Jan–Feb Perfect wildlife-viewing time; dusty harmattan winds can produce hazy skies.

Apr–Sep Hot season (Apr/May) best avoided; rainy season (Jun–Sep) can be challenging for transport.

Oct–Dec A lovely time of year, with green landscapes and pleasant temperatures.

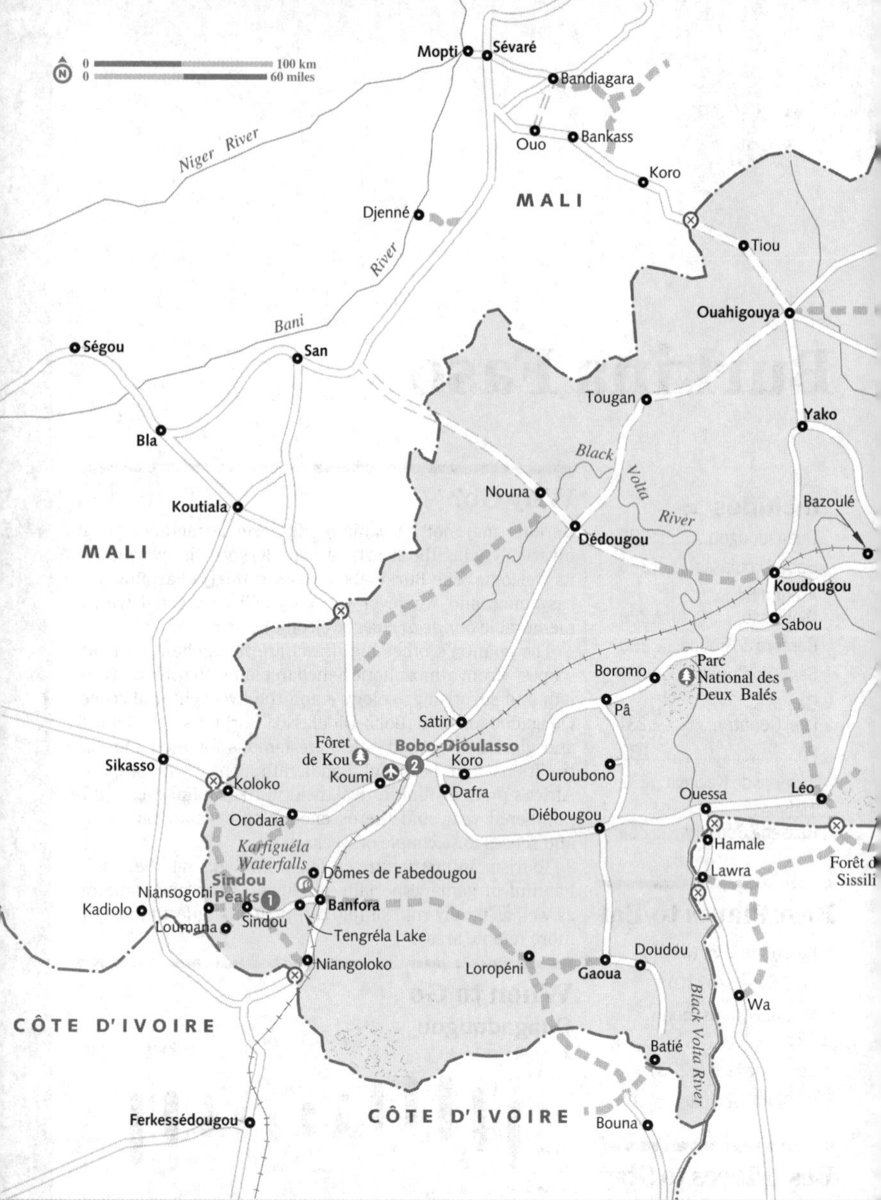

Burkina Faso Highlights

1. Wander amid otherworldly rock formations and Burkina's lush landscapes at the **Sindou Peaks** (p231)

2. Sip a few beers to the sound of Bobo-Dioulasso's fantastic **live music scene** (p228)

3. Come face to face with elephants at **Réserve de Nazinga** (p232)

4 Marvel over the meaning and originality of Kassena houses at Tiébélé's **Cour Royale** (p233)

5 Join in one of the fabulous Ouagadougou **art festivals** (p222)

OUAGADOUGOU

POP 1.4 MILLION

Ouaga, as it's affectionately dubbed, lacks standout sights and its architecture doesn't have much to turn your head, but it thrives as an eclectic arts hub, with dance and concert venues, live bands, theatre companies, a busy festival schedule and beautiful handicrafts.

Sights & Activities

Moro-Naba Palace PALACE
(Ave Moro-Naba) On Fridays at 7am the Moro-Naba of Ouagadougou – emperor of the Mossi and the most powerful traditional chief in Burkina Faso – presides over the Moro-Naba ceremony at the palace. It's a formal ritual that lasts only about 15 minutes. Travellers are welcome to attend, but photos are not permitted.

Musée de la Musique MUSEUM
(Ave d'Oubritenga; admission CFA1000; 9am-noon & 3-6pm Tue-Sat) You don't need to be into music to enjoy this excellent museum: the Burkinabé live and breathe music and a visit to the museum serves as a great introduction to Burkinabé culture. At the time of writing, the museum was about to relocate to shiny new premises on Ave d'Oubritenga.

Festivals & Events

Ouagadougou has one of the liveliest calendars of events in West Africa, with Fespaco definitely justifying you tailor your trip to match its dates.

★**Fespaco** FILM
(Festival Pan-Africain du Cinéma de Ouagadougou; www.fespaco.bf; Feb-Mar of odd-numbered years) Going strong since 1969, this world-renowned festival, held biennially, sees African films competing for the prestigious Étalon d'Or de Yennenga – Fespaco's equivalent of the Oscars.

Rock à Ouaga MUSIC
(Mar) A low-key festival featuring Burkina's most happening musicians, with international guest stars.

Jazz à Ouaga MUSIC
(www.jazz-ouaga.org; Apr-May) This is a well-established music festival that brings out the Afrobeat, soul and blues influence in jazz.

SIAO ARTS & CRAFTS
(Salon International de l'Artisanat de Ouagadougou; www.siao.bf; Oct of even-numbered years) Biennial trade fair of reference for the arts and crafts sector in Africa and a godsend for gem-hunting visitors.

Sleeping

★**Le Pavillon Vert** BACKPACKERS $
(50 31 06 11; www.hotel-pavillonvert.com; Ave de la Liberté; s/d with fan CFA12,500/13,500, with air-con CFA17,000/18,000, with fan & without bathroom CFA8000/8500;) The stalwart 'PV' is the best backpackers spot in Ouaga. It has competitive prices, a lively bar and restaurant, a gorgeous plant-filled garden and an assortment of well-kept rooms for all budgets. It's run by the same management as the excellent Couleurs d'Afrique (p225) travel agency.

Case d'Hôtes B&B $
(78 00 86 16, 50 31 03 61; www.case-hotes.com; off Ave de la Liberté; s/d with fan & without bathroom CFA10,000/13,500, with air-con & without bathroom CFA14,500/17,500;) Expect firm beds, crisp linen, artistic touches and spic-and-span bathrooms at this friendly guesthouse. Alain, the French owner, prepares great, jovial evening meals, which are served in a shady courtyard. Rates include breakfast.

Cocooning GUESTHOUSE $
(50 34 28 14; www.cocooning-faso.com; s/d/tr CFA8000/10,000/15,000, without bathroom CFA6500/8000/12,000) Cocooning's great selling point is its delightful owner, Dalila, a French-Algerian woman who fell in love with Burkina and never left. She runs an NGO to help destitute families and it is her welcome, grace and knowledge that make staying here special rather than the utilitarian rooms.

★**Les Jardins de Koulouba** GUESTHOUSE $$
(50 30 25 81; www.jardins-koulouba.fr; r with air-con CFA25,000, with fan & without bathroom CFA15,000;) Considering its chic decor, spacious rooms, fantastic location, pool and, as its name suggests, rather wonderful garden and patio, this lovely guesthouse wins the *palme d'or* for best value in Ouaga.

Villa Yiri Suma GUESTHOUSE $$
(50 30 54 82; www.yirisuma.com; 428 Ave du Petit Maurice Yameogo; d CFA21,000-28,000;) Yiri Suma is all about art. Lucien, the owner, is passionate about African art and likes nothing better than to share his passion with guests. The villa regularly houses exhibitions and cultural events, and the five spotless rooms enjoy their own contemporary decor and unique works.

Chez Giuliana GUESTHOUSE $$
(☎50 36 33 97; www.chezgiuliana.com; Rue Lamine Gueye, Quartier 1200 Logements; s/d CFA19,500/23,000, without bathroom CFA15,000/19,000; ❄ 📶) This bustling Italian guesthouse is a perennial favourite among aid workers: the welcome is as colourful as the rooms and the roof terrace is simply awesome for sundowners. It's about 3km outside the centre, near the Maternité Sainte Camille. Rates include breakfast.

Auberge Le Karité Bleu B&B $$$
(☎50 36 90 46; www.karitebleu.com; 214 Blvd de l'Onatel, Zone du Bois; d CFA30,000-43,000; ❄ 📶) In a residential neighbourhood, this adorable B&B offers eight spiffy rooms decorated according to different African styles (Dogon, Berber, Ashanti etc). The gorgeous terrace and Jacuzzi are lovely perks. It's about 2km west of the city centre. Prices include breakfast.

Hôtel Les Palmiers HOTEL $$$
(☎50 33 33 30; www.hotellespalmiers.net; Rue Joseph Badoua; d CFA32,000-41,000; ❄ 📶 🏊) Les Palmiers is an oasis blending African touches with European levels of comfort. The rooms are arranged around a leafy compound and embellished with local decorations. The garden, pool and terrace provide the finishing touches.

Eating

Marina Market MARKET $
(Ave Yennenga; ⏰8am-9pm Mon-Sat, 9am-8pm Sun) Great selection of groceries and long opening hours.

★**Maquis Aboussouan** AFRICAN $$
(☎50 34 27 20; Rue Simon Compaoré; mains CFA2500-5000; ⏰11am-11pm Tue-Sun; ❄) This upmarket *maquis* is the place to enjoy Burkinabé staples such as *poulet kedjenou* (slow-cooked chicken with peppers and tomatoes) or *attiéké* (grated cassava).

★**Le Verdoyant** PIZZERIA $$
(☎50 31 54 07; Ave Dimdolobsom; mains CFA4000-6000; ⏰noon-2.30pm & 6.30-11pm Thu-Tue) A favourite haunt of expats, the ultracentral Le Verdoyant is famous for its pasta, wood-fired pizzas and ice creams. Note that the mosquitoes are ferocious at night.

Kfête CAFE $$
(Institut Français, Ave de la Nation; mains CFA2000-5000; ⏰9am-6pm; 📶) The Institut Français' gorgeous restaurant is a lovely spot for lunch: sit in colourful raffia chairs under the modern *paillote* (straw awning) and tuck into bursting baguettes, juicy crêpes, or just sip a coffee to the sound of *chanson française*.

Cappuccino EUROPEAN $$
(Ave Kwame N'Krumah; mains CFA2000-6000; ⏰6am-1am; ❄ 📶) Long opening hours and a large menu catering to all tastes and all budgets (anything from pastries to copious salads and pizzas) make this brasserie one of Ouaga's popular eateries.

L'Eau Vive FRENCH $$
(Rue de l'Hôtel de Ville; mains CFA2000-7000; ⏰noon-2.30pm & 7-10pm; ❄) This Ouagadougou institution is run by an order of nuns and promises an air-conditioned haven from the clamour outside; there's also a garden dining area out the back. 'Ave Maria' is sung at 9.30pm every night.

Espace Gondwana FUSION $$$
(☎50 36 11 24; www.africartisanat.com; Rue du Dr Balla Moussa Traoré, Zone du Bois; mains CFA4000-9000; ⏰6-11pm; ❄ 📶) Espace Gondwana sports sensational decor, with four dining rooms richly adorned with masks and traditional furniture. The food impresses, too, with an imaginative menu that runs the gamut from frogs' legs and fish dishes to grilled meats and salads.

Drinking & Entertainment

Maquis dancing (simple open-air bars with blaring sound systems) are scattered all around Ouaga, but the most happening area is Gounghin, west of the centre.

★**Bar K** BAR
(Koulougou; ⏰noon-2am) Bar K is all about its vast roof terrace: order a cold beer or cocktail, sink into one of the sofas and enjoy the music under a canopy of stars and fairy lights.

De Niro BAR
(off Ave Houari Boumedienne; ⏰5pm-midnight Thu-Tue) This jazz bar is a gem: the music is great, the decor original (with fab photos, posters and two beautiful pool tables), the terrace breezy and the service super friendly.

Institut Français PERFORMING ARTS
(Ave de la Nation) The French cultural centre has one of the best line-ups of Burkinabé

Ouagadougou

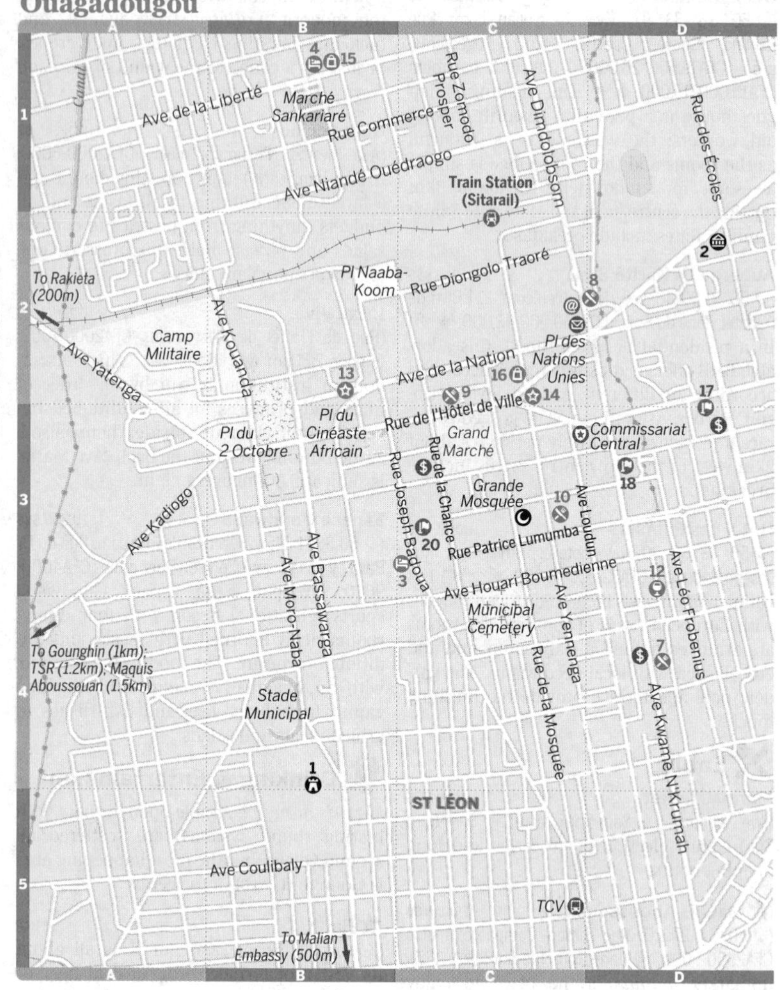

and West African musicians, theatre directors and visual artists.

Zaka LIVE MUSIC
(⏲10am-late) A pleasant watering hole by day and live-music venue by night (especially traditional music), with bands every night from 8pm.

Shopping

Nuances SOUVENIRS
(☎50 31 72 74; Ave Yennenga; ⏲8.30am-12.30pm & 3.30-7pm Mon-Sat, 10am-noon Sun) A gorgeous boutique, with a combination of eclectic African art, textiles, clothing and carvings.

Nimba Art JEWELLERY
(www.nimbaart.com; Ave de la Liberté; ⏲8am-7pm) A great boutique specialising in jewellery but also stocking woodcarvings and other souvenirs.

Village Artisanal de Ouaga SOUVENIRS
(☎50 37 14 83; Blvd Tengsoba, known as Blvd Circulaire; ⏲7am-7pm) A government-run cooperative with a wide range of crafts, ideal for souvenir shopping without the hard sell.

Ouagadougou

Sights

1 Moro-Naba Palace ... B4
2 Musée de la Musique ... D2

Sleeping

3 Hôtel Les Palmiers ... C3
4 Le Pavillon Vert ... B1
5 Les Jardins de Koulouba ... E3
6 Villa Yiri Suma ... E3

Eating

7 Cappuccino ... D4
Kfête ... (see 13)
8 Le Verdoyant ... D2
9 L'Eau Vive ... C2
10 Marina Market ... C3

Drinking & Nightlife

11 Bar K ... E3
12 De Niro ... D3

Entertainment

13 Institut Français ... B2
14 Zaka ... C2

Shopping

15 Nimba Art ... B1
16 Nuances ... C2

Information

17 Canadian Embassy ... D3
18 Dutch Embassy ... D3
19 French Embassy ... E2
20 German Embassy ... C3
21 Ghanaian Embassy ... E1
22 Ivorian Embassy ... F2

Transport

L'Agence Tourisme ... (see 3)

Information

Ouagadougou is one of the safer cities in the region, but avoid walking alone at night. Bag snatching is a problem: don't carry valuables.

There are numerous banks around town, most with ATM.

Centre Médical International (70 20 00 00, 50 30 66 07; Rue Nazi Boni; 24hr)

Commissariat Central (17; Ave Loudun)

Couleurs d'Afrique (www.couleurs-afrique.com; Ave de l'Olympisme, Gounghin) Run by Frenchman Guillaume Adeline, this well-established operator offers circuits in Burkina and neighbouring countries. Highly recommended.

Cyberposte (off Ave de la Nation; per hour CFA500; 8am-8pm Mon-Sat) Also offers printing and scanning services.

L'Agence Tourisme (www.agence-tourisme.com; Rue Joseph Badoua, Hôtel les Palmiers, Burkina Faso) Excellent tour operator, with many years' experience in Burkina and West Africa.

Visa extension (Service des Passeports; Ave Kadiogo; 8-11.30am & 3-5pm Mon-Fri) Visa extensions (two photos, CFA39,000 for six months) and Visa de l'Entente (p237). Both services take 72 hours.

Getting There & Away

Buses leave from the bus companies' depots. Every taxi knows where to find them. Routes include:

- **Bobo Dioulasso** (CFA7000, five hours, seven daily; operated by TCV, Rakiéta)

- **Banfora** (CFA8500, 6½ hours, six daily; operated by TCV, Rakiéta)
- **Gaoua** (CFA7000, four hours, five daily; operated by TSR, STAFF)
- **Pô** (CFA2500, 2½ hours, four daily; operated by Rakiéta)

For international services, see p237.

Getting Around

The taxi ride to the Aéroport International de Ouagadougou from the centre costs about CFA3000.

Shared taxis (beaten-up old green cars) cost a flat CFA300; flag them anywhere in town. They tend to follow set routes, often to/from the Grand Marché. Chartered taxis will cost a minimum of CFA1500; negotiate before you set off.

A good alternative if you happen to be in a street without much traffic or would like to be picked up at a certain time or place is **Allo Taxi** (☎50 34 34 35). Taxis must be booked and they run on the meter. They are more expensive than green taxis.

THE SOUTHWEST

Southwestern Burkina Faso ticks all the right boxes, with a heady mix of natural and cultural sights vying for your attention.

Bobo-Dioulasso

POP 490,000

Bobo, as it's widely known, may be Burkina Faso's second-largest city, but it has a small-town charm and its tree-lined streets exude a languid, semi-tropical atmosphere that makes it a favourite rest stop for travellers.

You'll have plenty to do during the day in and around the city, but save some energy for night-time to enjoy Bobo's thriving music scene and excellent restaurants.

Sights

Grande Mosquée MOSQUE

(admission CFA1000) Built in 1893, the Grande Mosquée is an outstanding example of Sahel-style mud architecture, with conical towers and wooden struts (which both support the structure and act as scaffolding during replastering). Visits take you inside the building and onto the roof terrace, where you'll get a different perspective of the towers.

Kibidwé NEIGHBOURHOOD

(admission CFA1000) Bobo's historical centre is a thriving neighbourhood. Little has changed over the centuries in terms of organisation: Muslims, *griots* (traditional caste of musicians or praise singers), blacksmiths and 'nobles' (farmers) still live in their respective quarters but happily trade services and drink at the same *chopolo* (millet beer) bars.

Guided tours are not official, but are unavoidable in practice – allow CFA2000 to CFA3000. They offer a great insight into local life, although the compulsory craft-shop stops are tedious.

Musée Communal Sogossira Sanon MUSEUM

(Place de la Nation; admission CFA1000; ⏲9am-12.30pm & 3-5.30pm Tue-Sat) A small museum that showcases masks, statues and ceremonial dress from all over Burkina Faso. There are full-scale examples of traditional buildings inside the grounds.

Sleeping

Campement Le Pacha HOTEL **$**

(☎76 61 16 01; lepachabo@yahoo.fr; Rue Malherbe; d with air-con CFA15,000, with fan & without bathroom CFA9500; ❄) For a Franco-Swiss venture, the unadorned rooms are a tad disappointing, but there's an attractive courtyard and a great garden restaurant famed for its wood-fired pizzas. Location is ace, too.

Villa Rose GUESTHOUSE **$**

(☎70 63 54 88, 20 98 54 16; www.villarosebobodioulasso.com; Koko; s/d with fan CFA9000/10,000, with air-con CFA15,000/17,000; ❄📶) This lovely guesthouse run by a Dutch-Burkinabé couple, Franca and Moctar, was about to move to a new location in the leafy neighbourhood of Koko, east of the centre, at the time of our visit. Thankfully, the friendly welcome will stay the same.

★ **Villa Bobo** B&B **$$**

(☎70 53 78 17, 20 98 20 03; www.villabobo.com; Koko; s/d/tr with fan CFA12,000/15,000/17,000, with air-con CFA17,000/20,000/22,000; ❄📶🏊) With its four zealously maintained rooms, prim bathrooms, atmospheric verandah, colourful garden and pool, Villa Bobo is a delight. Xavier, the French owner, speaks English and can arrange excursions in the area.

Entente Hôtel
HOTEL $$

(☎20 97 12 05; sopresbobo@yahoo.fr; Rue du Commerce; s/d with fan CFA9300/12,600 s/d/tr with air-con CFA12,300/20,600/27,900;) One of the few central establishments in Bobo, L'Entente has clean, tidy rooms. The fan rooms are rather small for the price, but there is plenty of space to hang out in the pleasant courtyard.

Les 2 Palmiers
HOTEL $$$

(☎20 97 27 59; www.hotelles2palmiers.com; off Rue Malherbe; d CFA34,500-39,500;) In a quiet street, this excellent option gets an A-plus for its spotless rooms embellished with African knick-knacks. The on-site restaurant is hailed as one of the best in Bobo.

Eating

As well as restaurants, there are lots of *maquis* in the centre that serve inexpensive food. Les Bambous (p228) also serves excellent pizzas.

Mandé
AFRICAN $

(Ave de la Révolution; mains CFA1000-4000; 7am-3pm & 6-11pm;) With an open-air terrace, great prices and a wide-ranging menu specialising in African dishes, Mandé is an excellent deal. If you just eat *riz sauce* (rice with sauce) or couscous and drink tamarind juice, you'll be well fed for around CFA1500.

Boulangerie Pâtisserie La Bonne Miche
BAKERY $

(Ave Ouédraogo; 6am-7pm) Excellent bread and pastries.

FÊTE DES MASQUES

In the Bobo-Dioulasso region, whenever there's a major funeral, it's accompanied by a late-night *fête des masques* (festival of masks).

Masked men dance to an orchestra of flutelike instruments and narrow drums beaten with curved canes. Each dancer, representing a different spirit, performs in turn, leaping, waving sticks and looking for evil spirits that might prevent the deceased from going to paradise.

As the celebrations go on, dancers become increasingly wild, performing acrobatic feats and waving their heads backwards and forwards until they catch someone and strike them. The victim, however, must not complain.

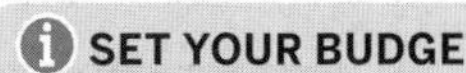

SET YOUR BUDGET

Budget

- Hotel room CFA10,000
- *Riz sauce* in a *maquis* CFA1000
- Brakina CFA650
- Shared taxi ride CFA300

Midrange

- Hotel room CFA18,000
- Pizza CFA4000
- Drink in a bar CFA1500
- Moped rental, per day CFA4000

Top End

- Hotel room CFA30,000
- Two-course meal CFA8000
- Glass of wine CFA3000
- 4WD with driver, per day CFA60,000

Marina Market
SUPERMARKET $

(Ave de la République; 8am-1pm & 3.30-9pm Mon-Sat, 9am-1pm Sun) Great range of grocery items, ideal for stocking up ahead of picnics and bus journeys.

L'Eau Vive
FRENCH $$

(Rue Delafosse; mains CFA2500-6000; noon-2.30pm & 6.30-10pm Mon-Sat) L'Eau Vive offers imaginative French cooking and a varied menu. It's the sister venue of the restaurant of the same name in Ouagadougou, and is also run by nuns.

★La Canne d'Or
FRENCH $$$

(☎20 98 15 96; Ave Philippe Zinda Kaboré; mains CFA4000-6000; 11.30am-2.30pm & 6.30-10pm Tue-Sun) This villa-style eatery, with its African decor and riot of fairy lights, serves French fare with an African twist. House faves include frogs' legs and a great grill selection (kebabs, steak, Nile perch etc). Service is stellar.

★Le Saint-Germain
FRENCH $$$

(Ave du Gouverneur Clozel; mains CFA6000-10,000; noon-3pm & 6.30-11pm;) Bobo's gourmet address is wrapped around an exotic garden and art gallery. The restaurant serves delicious spiced-up French cuisine; it also has one of the finest wine cellars in Burkina. All this class comes at a price: expect to pay an eye-watering CFA15,000 to CFA20,000 per person.

Bobo-Dioulasso

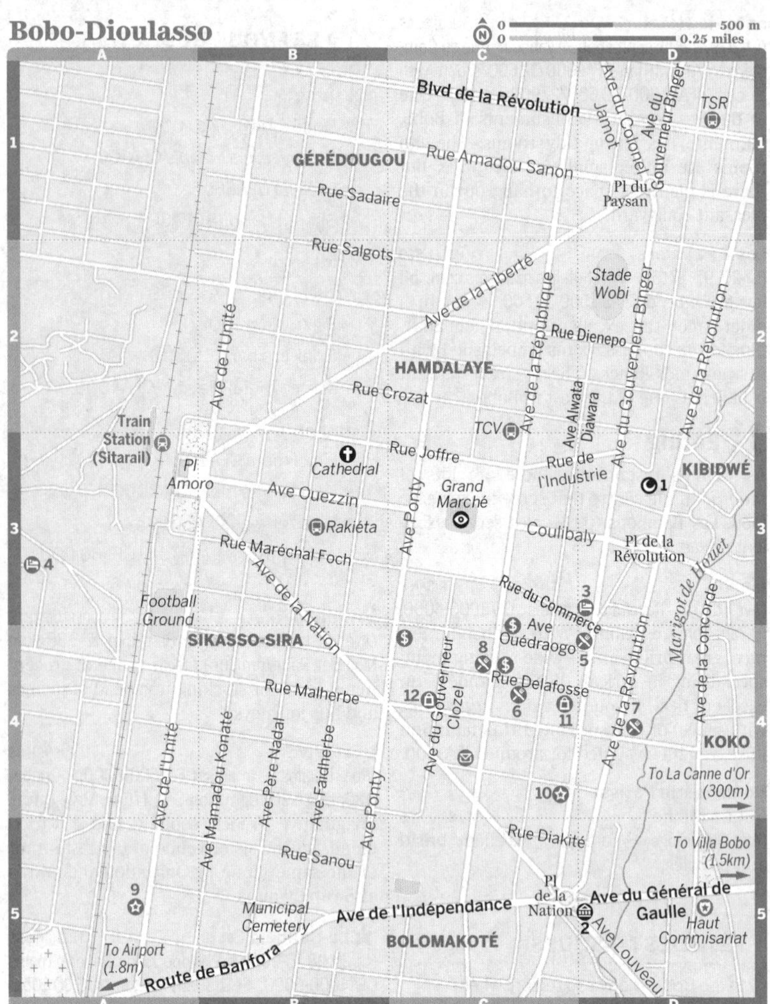

Drinking & Entertainment

Drinking in Bobo goes hand in hand with music, whether live or in the form of dancing. Admission (CFA500) is sometimes charged for live-music events. There is dancing at most *maquis* on Friday and Saturday nights, and from 4pm onwards on Sundays (known as *matinée*).

★Le Samanké LIVE MUSIC
(Koko; 10am-late) Bobo's best live-music venue, with an excellent sound system, a big stage, a fab garden and a fantastic program of Burkinabé and African artists (music mostly but also dance and theatre).

Tharkay CLUB
(Koko; 11am-late) Come and shake your stuff to *coupé-décalé* (Ivorian beats) and other Afro-beats at the funky Tharkay. The Sunday *matinée* is particularly popular.

Les Bambous LIVE MUSIC
(Ave du Gouverneur Binger; 6.30pm-late Tue-Sun) One of Bobo's long-standing music venues, with concerts every night. It also serves excellent pizzas (CFA3000 to CFA4000).

Bobo-Dioulasso

Sights

Sleeping

Eating

Entertainment

Shopping

Le Bois d'Ébène LIVE MUSIC

(Ave de l'Unité; noon-late) One of the best venues in town for live music. Concerts Thursday to Sunday.

Shopping

★ **Gafreh** ACCESSORIES

(www.gafreh.org; Rue Delafosse; 7am-7pm Mon-Sat) This brilliant initiative, a women's cooperative, recycles the millions of black sachets handed out with purchases across Burkina into chic handbags, wallets and other accessories.

Galerie Le Saint Germain ARTS & CRAFTS

(Ave du Gouverneur Clozel; 9am-7pm) This swish gallery showcases fantastic works by Burkinabé and other West African artists, including furniture and decorative objects.

Getting There & Away

Buses leave from the companies' depots. Routes include:

- **Ouaga** (CFA7000, five hours, seven daily; operated by TCV, Rakiéta)
- **Banfora** (CFA1500, 1½ hours, eight daily; operated by TCV, Rakiéta)
- **Gaoua** (CFA5000, 2½ hours, two daily; operated by TSR)

For international services, see p237.

Getting Around

Standard taxi fare is CFA300 for a shared cab ride in town.

Ismael Sawadogo (76 45 85 71) is a delightful and very reliable taxi driver (he is also a professional storyteller). He can arrange anything from early-morning pick-ups for bus services to day trips around Bobo.

Around Bobo-Dioulasso

The area around Bobo is rich in day trips, many of which are scenic excursions. Pack a picnic.

Kou & Koumi

About 18km west of Bobo-Dioulasso, the 115-hectare **Forêt de Kou** (admission CFA1000) is an unexpected gem: the reserve includes three completely different ecosystems – tropical rainforest, teak plantation and wooded savannah – that visitors can explore through a small network of paths. The rainforest in particular is delightful, remaining blissfully cool even during the midday heat.

A couple of kilometres before the forest, you'll pass a small drinking shack and a bathing area referred to as **La Guinguette** (admission CFA500). It's popular at weekends but generally quiet during the week.

Six kilometres south of Kou along a well-maintained dirt track, the village of **Koumi** (admission CFA1000, guiding fee CFA1000), on the Bobo-Orodara road, is well-known for its ochre adobe houses. Villagers run informative tours taking in animist beliefs, architecture and local life.

La Mare aux Poissons Sacrés & Koro

The sacred fish pond of **Dafra**, around 6km southeast of Bobo, is an important animist site: local people come here to solicit spirits by sacrificing chickens and feeding them to the fish. It is a fairly grisly sight, with chicken bones and feathers everywhere; the 30-minute walk from the nearest parking spot to the pond is truly stunning, however, with arresting rock formations and gorgeous savannah landscapes. A taxi there and back from Bobo-Dioulasso will cost around CFA10,000 (the track is atrocious).

You can easily follow on from Dafra to the village of **Koro** (admission CFA1000), 13km east of Bobo, off the main Ouagadougou road. Perched on the hillside, its houses – built amid rock formations – are unique in the area, and there are fine panoramic views over the countryside from the top of the village.

Banfora & Around

Banfora

POP 76,000

Banfora is a sleepy town in one of the most beautiful areas in Burkina Faso. It has delightful accommodation and eating options and therefore makes an ideal base for exploring the lush surrounding countryside. The town itself has a lively Sunday **market**, with plenty of goods from nearby Côte d'Ivoire.

Sleeping & Eating

★Le Calypso LODGE $
(☎70 74 14 83, 20 91 02 29; famille_houitte@yahoo.fr; Rte de Bobo-Dioulasso; r with fan/air-con CFA9500/16,000;) Le Calypso's lovely rooms combine traditional adobe architecture with modern comforts and impeccable cleanliness. The huts are arranged around a beautiful garden. It's about 1km outside of town on the road to Bobo.

Hôtel La Canne à Sucre HOTEL $$
(☎20 91 01 07; www.banfora.com; off Rue de la Poste; d with fan from CFA7500, with air-con from CFA18,900, 4-bed apt CFA49,000;) Beautiful rooms are kitted out with African woodcarvings and cloth and the leafy garden feels like heaven after a tiring day. The apartments are ideal for groups and have exclusive use of the pool.

The restaurant is the fanciest in town, perfect for a treat (mains CFA3000 to CFA5000).

★Le Calypso EUROPEAN, AFRICAN $$
(☎20 91 02 29; off Rue de la Poste; mains around CFA3000; ⏲11.30am-11pm;) Run by the same jovial Franco-Burkinabé family as Le Calypso hotel, this popular restaurant is a wonderful place for tasty slow-cooked fish, marinated steak and pizzas. The homemade juices are highly recommended.

McDonald BURGERS $$
(off Rue de la Préfecture; mains CFA1500-3000; ⏲11am-10pm Thu-Tue) This cool den off the main drag boasts an inviting covered terrace. It churns out a good range of satisfying dishes, including its famous *hamburger frites* (burger with fries).

Drinking & Entertainment

Le Mistral BAR
(⏲11am-midnight) The outdoor terrace bar is open every night and is a relaxed place for a beer, but what really draws the crowds to this place is the indoor (air-con) nightclub open Friday, Saturday and Sunday nights (CFA500; doors open at 9pm). The bar is located southeast of town on one of the new sealed roads.

Information

Banque Atlantique (Rte de la Côte d'Ivoire)
Ecobank (Rte de la Côte d'Ivoire)

Getting There & Away

Rakiéta (Rue de la Poste) and **TCV** (Rue de la Poste) have regular departures for Bobo-Dioulasso (CFA1500, 1½ hours, eight daily) and Ouaga (CFA8500, 6½ hours, six daily), and one daily service each to Bouaké in Côte d'Ivoire (CFA11,500, 10 hours).

The road to Gaoua is in bad condition and only serviced by *taxi-brousse* (bush taxi; CFA5000, four to five hours). Pick them up at the **Gare Routière** (bus station; Rte de Bobo-Dioulasso). Otherwise go by bus via Bobo.

Around Banfora

Just 7km west of Banfora, **Tengréla Lake** (admission CFA2000) is home to a variety of bird life and, if you're lucky, you'll see hippos (especially from January to April). The admission price includes a *pirogue* (traditional canoe) trip. Want to laze a few days away in the area? Park your backpack at **Campement Farafina** (☎76 45 75 15, 78 17 25 04; soloisa6@hotmail.com; Tengréla; r without bathroom CFA4000), a five-minute walk from the lake: facilities are very basic (bucket shower, mud huts without fan), but the owner, Solo, is an adept musician and a fantastic host.

Some 11km northwest of Banfora, the **Karfiguéla Waterfalls** (Cascades de Karfiguéla; admission CFA1000) are reached through a magnificent avenue of mango trees. You can take a dip in the lovely natural pools on the upper part of the waterfalls. About 3km north, off the N2 road to Bobo, the **Dômes de Fabedougou** (admission CFA1000), limestone formations sculpted over millennia by water and erosion into quirky domelike shapes, are another arresting sight.

On the road to the Dômes, the sugar factory **Société Nouvelle Sucrière de la Comoé** (Sosuco; ☎20 91 81 11; www.sn-sosuco.com;

off Rte de Bobo-Dioulasso; admission free) is one of Burkina's more unusual sights. It produces 35,000 tonnes of sugar a year from 4000 hectares of sugar cane. You can visit the factory and attend the spectacular sugar-cane fires from November to April. Ring the factory for details of the visits or ask your hotel.

You'll need wheels to explore the area; if you don't have your own, charter a taxi for the day. Taxi driver **Hema Dounbia** (☎76 40 44 47) comes warmly recommended.

Sénoufo Country

Sindou Peaks

One of Burkina Faso's most spectacular landscapes, the **Sindou Peaks** (Pics de Sindou; admission CFA1000, includes 45min guided walk) are a narrow, craggy chain featuring a fantastic array of tortuous cones sculpted by the elements.

Located about 50km west of Banfora, this geological fantasyland is ideal for hiking. Coming from Banfora, the main gateway is about 1km before the entrance to Sindou town. There's a little booth staffed by guides from the local tourism cooperative **Association Djiguiya** (☎76 08 46 60; www.djiguiya.org). Run by the brilliant Tiémoko Ouattara, it promotes responsible travel and offers a range of services to travellers: anything from half-day walks to multiday treks in Sénoufo country with sunrise breakfast in the peaks, moped and cycling tours, cultural activities and homestays.

The association runs the friendly **Campement Soutrala** (☎76 08 46 60; Sindou; r without bathroom CFA4000) in Sindou. Facilities are spartan (bucket showers, no electricity) and meals must be ordered two hours in advance (mains CFA800 to CFA2000), but it's a good base if you'd like to spend time in the area rather than visit on a day trip from Banfora.

There is a handful of *taxis-brousses* plying the dirt road (slated to be surfaced in 2013) between Sindou and Banfora every day. Consider chartering a taxi for the day (CFA25,000) to make it more expedient.

Niansogoni

Well off the beaten path – Niansogoni is 37km southwest of Sindou, near the border with Mali – this tiny settlement is a terrific place to experience local life. The scenery is gorgeous, with a series of limestone hills, cliffs and escarpmentlike formations that loom on the horizon. From Niansogoni, you can walk to an old village nestled in an alcove of the escarpment, where you can see old granaries and dwellings. The village dates back to the 14th century and was abandoned in 1980.

From Sindou, it's a long way along a dirt track to Niansogoni (no public transport). But the reward is sweet. The **Campement de Niansogoni** (☎76 48 06 59; traorichard@yahoo.fr; Niansogoni; r without bathroom CFA4000) offers simple yet well-maintained huts with thatched roofs in a glorious setting. Meals (and cold beer!) are available (CFA2000). The owner, Richard Traoré, is passionate about the region and can arrange all kinds of excursions.

Gaoua & Lobi Country

The small town of Gaoua (population 25,100) is a good base for exploring Lobi country, an area that's culturally distinct (see p232).

There are a couple of ATMs (Visa only) in town. For internet, head to the women-run **Association Pour la Promotion Féminine de Gaoua** (Gaoua; per hr CFA500; ⏲7.30am-8pm Mon-Sat) in the centre. It also sells local handicrafts such as shea-butter soap and creams, pottery and textiles (the shop is open 7.30am to 12.30pm and 3pm to 6pm Monday to Friday).

Sights

There's a vibrant Sunday **market**, but the town's unique selling point is its excellent ethnological museum, **Musée de Poni** (www.musee-gaoua.gov.bf; Gaoua; admission CFA2000; ⏲8am-12.30pm & 3-6pm Tue-Sun). There are full-scale reproductions of a Lobi and a Gan compound as well as a wide range of photographs and artefacts. The guides really know their stuff too; Loukmane Savadogo (☎76 93 12 55) is particularly recommended.

Sleeping & Eating

Maison Madeleine Père GUESTHOUSE $

(☎20 90 03 26; Gaoua; s/d CFA6000/8000) Run by nuns, this quiet establishment in a monastery southwest of the city centre has impeccable rooms in pretty grounds. The biggest downside is that it doesn't serve meals. To find it, ask in the centre: most people know it.

Hôtel Hala HOTEL $$
(☎20 90 01 21; www.hotelhala.com; Gaoua; s/d with fan CFA12,500/15,000, with air-con CFA23,000/27,500;) This is, all told, Gaoua's best option: service is glacial and the rooms are nothing to write home about, but the compound is very pleasant, it has a handy location between town and the bus station, and the wi-fi works. It also has the only decent restaurant in town, serving grilled meat and a few Lebanese specials (mains CFA2000 to CFA3000).

Le Flamboyant AFRICAN $
(Gaoua; mains CFA800-2000; 10am-10pm) One of the town's better *maquis*, right in the centre of town; expect the usual rice or *tô* (millet or sorghum-based *pâte*) with sauce.

Getting There & Around

The *gare routière* is 2km out of town. You'll find bus services to Bobo-Dioulasso (CFA5000, 2½ hours, two to three daily) and Ouagadougou (CFA7000, five daily, four hours). Direct services to Banfora are by *taxi-brousse* only (CFA5000, four hours); it's best to go to Bobo and find onward connections.

To get around Lobi country, charter a taxi in Gaoua (starting around CFA25,000, depending on how far you want to go).

THE SOUTH

The beauty of southern Burkina is a highlight of any Burkina itinerary; this area is also one of the most accessible. The gateway town of Pô is just a couple of hours from Ouaga (and 20 minutes from the Ghanaian border).

Pô

24,300

There isn't much of interest for travellers in Pô, but it makes a useful halt on journeys between Ouaga and southern sights or Ghana.

If you need to spend the night, the friendly **Hôtel Tiandora** (☎70 74 63 67, 50 40 34 39; r with fan/air-con CFA5000/7500;) has acceptable rooms at very reasonable prices. For sustenance, *maquis* **La Pyramide** (mains CFA500-2000; 11am-10pm) on the main street is an institution, with regal service and delicious daily specials (grilled chicken, couscous, macaroni etc).

Ecobank (7.30am-5.30pm Mon-Fri, 8am-1pm Sat) on the main drag has an ATM (Visa). Rakiéta runs four buses a day to and from Ouaga (CFA2500, 2½ hours).

Réserve de Nazinga

This 97,000-hectare wildlife **reserve** (☎50 41 36 17; admission CFA10,000, vehicle entry CFA1000, guiding fees CFA5000; 6am-6pm), about 40km southwest of Pô near the Ghanaian border, has become a highlight on many a wildlife lover's itinerary. The park has antelopes, monkeys, warthogs, crocodiles and plenty of birds, but elephants are the stars of the show. The best times to see them are December to April, although the chances of sightings are pretty good year-round.

There are some good accommodation options in Nazinga. At the heart of the reserve, **Ranch de Nazinga** (☎50 41 36 17; nazinga-ranch@yahoo.fr; Réserve de Nazinga; r CFA10,000, bungalows CFA16,000) has an exceptional location right by the reserve's biggest watering

LOBI TRADITIONS

Lobi traditions are some of the best preserved in West Africa. For travellers, the most obvious is the architecture of rural Lobi homes. The mudbrick compounds are rectangular and walls only have small slits for windows, for defensive purposes. In the old days, polygamous men built a bedroom for each of their wives.

The Lobi are also known for their cultural rituals. For example, the *dyoro* initiation rites, which take place every seven years, are still widely observed. As part of this important rite of passage, young men and women are tested on their stamina and skills; they also learn about sexual mores, the clan's history and the dos and don'ts of their culture.

Your best bet to explore Lobi heritage is to hire a guide in Gaoua (ask at Hôtel Hala). Visits will take in villages such as **Sansana** and **Doudou**, where you can admire different architectural styles and crafts (pottery, basket weaving, sculpture). Doudou is famed for its artisanal gold-mining, which is the prerogative of women, and its market (every five days).

hole. Accommodation is a little lacklustre, but the restaurant churns out tasty meals (mains CFA3000 to CFA4000) and the setting is unrivalled with animals regularly roaming among the bungalows.

Those in search of something a little more sophisticated should opt for **Campement de l'Éléphant** (70 17 34 34; www.nahourisafari.com; Réserve de Nazinga; d/f CFA25,000/35,000; Nov-May;), right on the edge of the reserve. Rooms are spacious and clean, but it is the pool that's the real draw, perfect to while away the hours between wildlife drives. The restaurant also gets the thumbs up from travellers for its impeccable French cuisine.

You will need your own vehicle to access the reserve and go on wildlife drives. The travel agencies in Ouagadougou (p225) are your best bet.

Tiébélé & Kassena Country

Set in the heart of the green and low-lying Kassena country, Tiébélé, 40km east of Pô on a dirt track, is famous for its *sukhala*, colourful windowless traditional houses. Decorated by women, who work with guineafowl feathers, in geometrical patterns of red, black and white, the houses offer an antidote to the monochrome mudbrick villages found elsewhere in Burkina Faso.

Association Pour le Développement de Tiébélé (70 02 78 26; www.tiebele-developpement.org; Tiébélé) is the best organisation to contact for local guides, be it to tour Kassena houses, visit local markets or organise treks in the area.

Sights & Activities

Cour Royale ARCHITECTURE
(Tiébélé; admission CFA2000; 8am-5.30pm) More than 450 people live in Tiébélé's royal court, a large compound of typical *sukhalas*. Children live with their grandparents in eight-shaped huts, couples in rectangular huts and single people in square ones. Painting is generally done in February or March, after the harvest. Each drawing (geometrical or illustrative) has a meaning (fertility, afterlife, wisdom etc).

Nahouri Peak HIKING
(admission CFA1000, local guide CFA500) This cone-shape karst is the tallest structure for miles around and the steep climb to its summit guarantees 360 degrees of uninterrupted savannah views. Guides from the Association pour le Développement de Tiébélé can organise sunrise and sunset climbs, a good option both for wow factor and clement temperatures.

Sleeping & Eating

Auberge Kunkolo GUESTHOUSE $
(76 53 44 55, 50 36 97 38; Tiébélé; d with fan & without bathroom CFA5000) This lovely guesthouse, with its impeccable Kassena-style huts and beautiful garden, is the best place to stay in the area. It's just 200m from the chief's compound in Tiébélé. Meals are also served.

Getting There & Around

There is one direct bus from Ouaga (bus station Ouagainter) to Tiébélé (and back) on Tuesdays, Fridays and Sundays (CFA3000, 3½ hours).

If you don't have your own vehicle, you can easily rent mopeds in Tiébélé for CFA4000 to CFA6000 per day.

UNDERSTAND BURKINA FASO

Burkina Faso Today

Burkina Faso stands out as a beacon of stability in a region rocked by insecurity. Despite widespread riots in 2011, the country managed to steer itself back on course and held peaceful municipal and legislative elections in December 2012. There are still rumblings about the state of the country – Burkina ranks 181st out of 187 countries on the UN's Human Development Index – and a president who has been in power for 25 years, but Burkinabés mostly just want to get on with things.

The economy has been steadily growing over the past decade, averaging more than 5% per year between 2000 and 2010. It remains overly reliant on cotton export, however, and a recent gold rush – which has seen a huge increase in illegal mining – has increased the country's exposure to market fluctuations. Socially, Burkina's biggest challenges are to improve access to education (the child literacy rate remains under 30%) and address chronic food insecurity.

THE SAHEL

Northern Burkina Faso is dominated by the desolate confines of the Sahel. It's certainly inhospitable at most times of the year, but it also features stupendously colourful markets, fascinating local cultures and traditions, and landscapes that are much less monotonous than you might imagine.

The deteriorating security situation in neighbouring Mali has severely affected tourism in the Sahel; more than 30,000 Malian refugees have settled in the area, leading the Burkinabé authorities and foreign governments to advise against travel to the region. It was unclear at the time of writing when the situation would improve, so check the latest travel advice before you set off.

History

The Mossi & the French

Little is known about Burkina Faso's early history, though archaelogical finds suggest the country was populated as far back as the Stone Age. Its modern history starts with the Mossi peoples (now almost half of Burkina Faso's population), who moved westward from settlements near the Niger River in the 13th century; they founded their first kingdom in what is now Ouagadougou. Three more Mossi states were subsequently established in other parts of the country, all paying homage to Ouagadougou, the strongest. The government of each of the Mossi states was highly organised, with ministers, courts and a cavalry known for its devastating attacks against the Muslim empires in Mali.

During the Scramble for Africa in the second half of the 19th century, the French exploited rivalries between the different Mossi kingdoms and established their sway over the region. At first the former Mossi states were assimilated into the Colonie du Haut Sénégal-Niger. Then, in 1919, the area was hived off for administrative expedience as a separate colony, Haute Volta (Upper Volta).

Independence & Thomas Sankara

World War II brought about profound changes in France's relationship with its colonies. The Mossi, like numerous other people in Africa, started challenging the colonial hegemony. The Upper Volta became a state in 1947, and in 1956 France agreed to give its colonies their own governments, with independence quickly following in 1960.

Following independence, dreams of freedom and prosperity quickly evaporated. Between 1960 and 1983, the country experienced six coups and counter-coups and the economy stagnated. Then, in 1983, Captain Thomas Sankara, an ambitious young left-wing military star, seized power.

Over the next four years 'Thom Sank' (as he was popularly known) recast the country. He changed its name to Burkina Faso (meaning 'Land of the Incorruptible'), restructured the economy to promote self-reliance in rural areas and tackled corruption with rare zeal. He was ahead of his time, promoting women's rights and standing up against Western paradigms on aid and development. But his authoritarian grip on power and his intolerance of those who didn't share his ideals were to be his downfall: in late 1987 a group of junior officers seized power and Sankara was killed.

The Compaoré Years

The new junta was headed by Captain Blaise Compaoré, Sankara's former friend and co-revolutionary. In late 1991 Compaoré was elected president. But as sole candidate, with low turnout and with the assassination of Clément Ouédraogo, the leading opposition figure, a couple of weeks later, his legitimacy remained weak.

In a bid to mark a clear break with Sankara, Compaoré immediately orchestrated a U-turn on the economy, overturning nationalisations and bringing the country back into the IMF fold. He has since been re-elected three times, in 1998, 2005 and 2010, each time with more than 80% of the vote. He is one of Africa's last 'big men' (long-serving, authoritarian leaders) and his democratic credentials will be tested in 2015: a 2000 constitutional amendment stipulates that a president may only run for two terms, although Compaoré craftily only introduced it after his victory in 2005.

People of Burkina Faso

Burkina Faso, which occupies an area about half the size of France, is extremely diverse, with its 17 million people scattered among some 60 ethnic groups. The largest of these is the Mossi, who are primarily concentrated in the central plateau area. Important groups in the south include the Bobo, Senoufo, Lobi and Gourounsi. In the Sahel areas of the north are the Hausa, Fulani, Bella and Tuareg. Around 75% of Burkinabés live in rural areas.

Religion

An old joke goes that 50% of Burkinabés are Muslim, 50% Christian and 100% animist. The figures for Islam and Christianity are about 60% and 23%, respectively, in reality, but most people do retain traditional beliefs.

The Arts

Burkina Faso has a vibrant contemporary arts and crafts scene (painting, sculpture, woodcarvings, bronze and brass work, and textiles). Artists' works are exhibited in Ouagadougou's galleries, cultural centres and collective workshops. And there's no shortage of artisans' stalls and craft shops, selling masks and leatherwork, in Ouagadougou and Bobo-Dioulasso.

The Burkinabés live and breathe music. It is the mainstay of traditional celebrations with *djembe* (drum), *balafon* (a kind of xylophone) and flutes the main instruments. Modern musicians draw on traditional influences from home and the rest of the continent, especially Mali, Congo and Côte d'Ivoire, as well as Jamaican reggae, jazz, rock and rap. You'll find numerous bars in Ouga and Bobo offering live music several nights a week.

Burkina Faso also has a thriving film industry that receives considerable stimulation from the biennial Fespaco film festival. Two Burkinabé film-makers who have won prizes and developed international reputations are Idrissa Ouédraogo, who won the 1990 Grand Prix at Cannes for *Tilä,* and Gaston Kaboré, whose film *Buud Yam* was the 1997 winner of the Étalon d'Or.

Food & Drink

Burkinabé food is largely influenced by Senegalese and Côte d'Ivoire cuisines. Sauces, especially *arachide* (groundnut) or *graine* (a hot sauce made with oil-palm nuts), are the mainstay and are always served with a starch – usually rice (it's called *riz sauce* or *riz gras*) or the Burkinabé staple, *tô,* a millet- or sorghum-based *pâte* (a pounded, doughlike substance). The Ivorian *attiéké* (grated cassava), *aloco* (plantain fried with chilli in palm oil) and *kedjenou* (simmered chicken or fish with vegetables) are also commonly found.

Grilled dishes of chicken, mutton, beef, guinea fowl, fish (especially Nile perch, known locally as *capitaine*) and agouti (a large rodent) also feature on the menu. In the Sahel, couscous (semolina grains) is widely available.

Castel, Flag, Brakina, Beaufort and So.b.bra are popular and palatable lagers. More adventurous – and potent – is *dolo* (millet beer). Locally produced juices include *bissap* (hibiscus), *gingembre* (ginger), tamarind and mango; soft drinks are available everywhere, too.

Environment

Landlocked Burkina Faso's terrain ranges from the harsh desert and semidesert of the north to the woodland and savannah of the green southwest. Around Banfora rainfall is heavier, and forests thrive alongside irrigated sugar-cane and rice fields; it's here that most of Burkina Faso's meagre 13% of arable land is found. The country's dominant feature, however, is the vast central laterite plateau of the Sahel, where hardy trees and bushes thrive.

Burkina's former name, Haute Volta (Upper Volta), referred to its three major rivers – the Black, White and Red Voltas, known today as the Mouhoun, Nakambé and Nazinon Rivers. All flow south into the world's second-largest artificial lake, Lake Volta, in Ghana.

SURVIVAL GUIDE

Directory A–Z

ACCOMMODATION

Ouagadougou, Bobo and Banfora have a good range of accommodation, including charming B&Bs. In more remote areas, *campements* (basic mud huts with bucket showers and no electricity) are usually the only option but can be very atmospheric.

PRACTICALITIES

- **Electricity** Supply is 220V and plugs are of the European two-round-pin variety.
- **Languages** French, Moré, Fulfudé and Dioula.
- **Newspapers & Magazines** International versions of French- and (a few) English-language publications are available in Ouagadougou and Bobo-Dioulasso.
- **Radio** BBC World Service is on 99.2FM in Ouagadougou. For a French-language service, tune in to RFI, 94FM.

EMBASSIES & CONSULATES

The following embassies are based in Ouagadougou. British citizens should contact the British High Commission (p332) in Accra, Ghana.

Beninese Embassy (☎50 38 49 96; 401 Rue Bagen Nini, near Ouagainter)

Canadian Embassy (☎50 31 18 94; www.canadainternational.gc.ca/burkinafaso; 316 Ave du Professeur Joseph Ki Zerbo) Also offers diplomatic help to Australian citizens.

Dutch Embassy (☎50 30 61 34; http://burkinafaso.nlambassade.org; 415 Ave Kwame N'Krumah)

French Embassy (☎50 49 66 66; www.ambafrance-bf.org; Ave du Trésor)

German Embassy (☎50 30 67 31; www.ouagadougou.diplo.de; Rue Joseph Badoua)

Ghanaian Embassy (☎50 30 76 35; embagna@fasonet.bf; Ave d'Oubritenga; ⌚8am-2pm)

Ivorian Embassy (☎50 31 82 28; cnr Ave Raoul Follereau & Blvd du Burkina Faso)

US Embassy (☎50 49 53 00; http://ouagadougou.usembassy.gov; Ouaga 2000)

INTERNET ACCESS

- Wi-fi is available in most midrange and top-end establishments in towns and cities.
- Internet cafes are plentiful in towns and cities (the post office is usually a good bet) but nonexistent in more remote areas.

MONEY

- The currency in Burkina Faso is the West African CFA franc.
- The best foreign currency to carry is euros, easily exchanged at any bank, hotel or bureau de change.
- Travellers cheques cannot be exchanged in Burkina.
- There are numerous Visa ATMs in every city; the only bank to accept MasterCard is Banque Atlantique (in Ouaga, Bobo and Banfora only).
- Payments by credit card are rarely accepted and subject to a 5% surcharge.

OPENING HOURS

Banks Typically open 8am to 11am and 3.30pm to 5pm Monday to Friday.

Bars Normally serve from late morning until the last customers leave (late); nightclubs generally open from 9pm into the wee hours.

Restaurants Lunch 11.30am to 2.30pm; dinner 6.30pm to 10.30pm.

Shops and businesses Usually 8am to noon and 3pm to 6pm Monday to Friday, and 9am to 1pm Saturday.

PUBLIC HOLIDAYS

Burkina Faso also celebrates Islamic holidays, whose dates change every year.

New Year's Day 1 January

Revolution Day 3 January

Women's Day 8 March

Easter Monday March/April

Labour Day 1 May

Ascension Day 40 days after Easter

National Day 5 August

Assumption 15 August

All Saints' Day 1 November

Republic Day 11 December

Christmas Day 25 December

SAFE TRAVEL

Burkina Faso is one of the safest countries in West Africa. Crime isn't unknown, particularly around big markets and *gares routières*, but it's usually confined to petty theft and pickpocketing.

TELEPHONE

- Burkina's country code is 226.
- Landline numbers start with 5, mobile numbers with 7.
- Mobile-phone coverage is excellent and cheap. Local networks include Telmob, Airtel and Telecel. International texts cost from CFA50 and calls from CFA75 per minute with pay-as-you-go credit (CFA500 for a SIM card).

VISAS

- Everyone except Ecowas nationals needs a visa.
- One-month visas are available at border crossings and the airport for CFA10,000 (bring two photos), but visa policies can change, so it is strongly recommended you get your visa from a Burkinabé embassy before travelling; allow €35/45 for a three-month single/multiple-entry visa.

Visas for Onward Travel

The Visa de l'Entente, valid in Côte d'Ivoire, Niger, Togo and Benin, is available at the Service des Passeports (p225) in Ouagadougou; bring two photos, your passport and CFA25,000. It takes 72 hours to process.

If you're only visiting a single country, the following embassies deliver visas:

Benin A three-month, single-entry visa costs CFA15,000. You need two photos and photocopies of your passport.

Côte d'Ivoire A three-month, single-entry visa costs €100 and requires one photo and a hotel confirmation. Check www.snedai.ci for details.

Ghana Three-month visas are issued within 48 hours for CFA17,500 and require four photos.

Getting There & Away

You will need a yellow-fever vaccination certificate to come to Burkina.

AIR

- The tiny Aéroport International de Ouagadougou is Burkina's main gateway.
- The main international carriers are **Air France** (www.airfrance.com) and **Royal Air Maroc** (www.royalairmaroc.com), which offer direct flights to France and Morocco and connecting flights to the rest of the world.
- **Air Burkina** (www.air-burkina.com), the national carrier, flies to Paris (France) as well as regional destinations including Accra (Ghana), Abidjan (Côte d'Ivoire), Bamako (Mali), Cotonou (Benin), Dakar (Senegal) and Lomé (Togo).

LAND

Burkina's land borders are open from 6am to 6pm. Crossings are generally hassle-free. The main border points are:

- Niangoloko for Côte d'Ivoire
- Tanguiéta for Benin
- Paga for Ghana
- Sinkasse for Togo
- Kantchari for Niger
- Koloko or Tiou for Mali

There are plenty of international bus services from Ouaga and Bobo. Routes include:

- **Kumasi, Ghana** (CFA10,000, 11 hours, one daily; operated by TCV)
- **Bamako, Mali** (CFA17,000, 17 hours, one daily; operated by TCV)
- **Bouaké & Abidjan, Côte d'Ivoire** (CFA17,000 & CFA27,000, 20 hours & 36 hours, one daily; operated by TCV, Rakiéta)
- **Cotonou, Benin** (CFA18,000, 24 hours, two weekly; operated by TCV, TSR)
- **Lomé, Togo** (CFA18,000, 24 hours, two weekly; operated by TCV, TSR)
- **Lagos, Nigeria** (CFA38,000, 36 hours, one weekly; operated by TCV)

Getting Around

BUS

- Buses are the most reliable and comfortable way to get around.
- TCV and Rakiéta buses are better maintained and more reliable than those of other companies. They also have air-con.
- Buses almost always operate with guaranteed seating and fixed departure times; arrive early or book the day before to ensure you have a seat on your preferred service.

BUSH TAXI

- Bush taxis *(taxis-brousses)*, generally beaten-up old vehicles, cover outlying communities that large buses don't serve.
- Most leave from the *gares routières*; morning is the best time to find them.

CAR & MOTORCYCLE

- Travel agencies in Ouagadougou can organise 4WD rental for about CFA60,000 per day (with driver).
- In rural areas, mopeds are ideal on unsealed roads and readily available for CFA4000 per day (not including fuel).

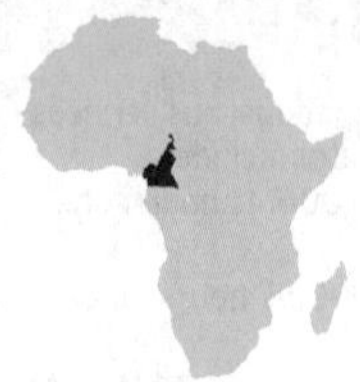

Cameroon

POP 20.1 MILLION

Includes ➡

Best Places to Eat

➡ La Fourchette (p248)
➡ Vegetarian Carnivore (p262)
➡ La Plazza (p259)
➡ La Paillote (p243)

Best Places to Stay

➡ Foyer du Marin (p245)
➡ Bird Watchers' Club (p251)
➡ Relais de la Porte Mayo (p259)
➡ Hotel Ilomba (p256)

Why Go?

Cameroon is Africa's throbbing heart, a crazed, sultry mosaic of active volcanoes, white-sand beaches, thick rainforest and magnificent parched landscapes broken up by the bizarre rock formations of the Sahel. With both Francophone and Anglophone regions, not to mention some 230 local languages, the country is a vast ethnic and linguistic jigsaw, yet one that, in contrast to so many of its neighbours, enjoys a great deal of stability.

With good infrastructure (think decent roads and functioning trains), travel is a lot easier here than in many parts of Africa. Still, you'll miss none of those indicators that you're in the middle of this fascinating continent: everyone seems to be carrying something on their heads, *makossa* music sets the rhythm, the street smells like roasting plantains and African bliss is just a piece of grilled fish and a sweating beer away.

When to Go

Yaoundé

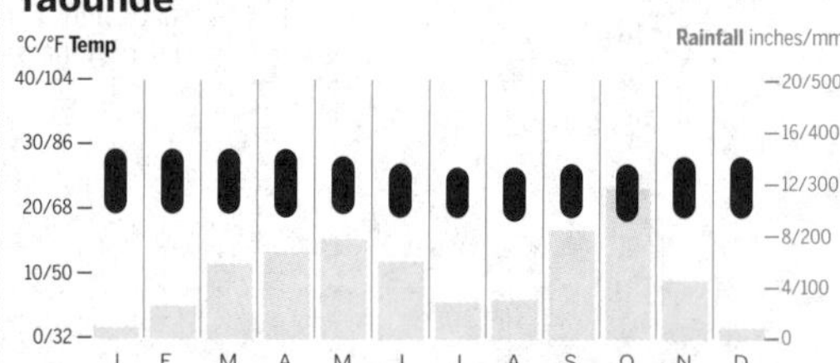

Nov–Feb It's dry but not too hot, though you can usually expect a harmattan haze.

Feb Join athletes running to the summit of Mt Cameroon in the Race of Hope.

Oct Cameroon's biggest festival, Tabaski, takes place, most impressively in Foumban.

YAOUNDÉ

POP 1.8 MILLION

Let's be brutally honest: West Africa is famous for many things, but pleasant cities – especially capitals – are not among them. Then Yaoundé comes along: green and spread over seven hills, though not exactly a garden city, it's planned, thoughtfully laid out and self-contained. While it is nowhere near as vibrant (or chaotic) as its coastal rival Douala, it enjoys a temperate climate, relatively clean and well-maintained streets and even boasts a host of 1970s government buildings in various exuberant styles that will keep architecture fans happy. Located in the centre of the country, Yaoundé makes a fine stop for getting a visa or before heading off into the rest of Cameroon.

Sights & Activities

Musée d'Art Camerounais MUSEUM

(Quartier Fébé; admission CFA1500; 3-6pm Thu, Sat & Sun) At the Benedictine monastery on Mt Fébé, north of the city centre, the Musée d'Art Camerounais has an impressive collection of masks, bronze- and woodwork and other examples of Cameroonian art. The chapel is also worth a look.

Mvog-Betsi Zoo ZOO

(Mvog-Betsi; admission CFA2000, camera CFA5000; 9am-6pm) This is one of the better zoos in West Africa, co-run by the **Cameroon Wildlife Aid Fund** (www.cwaf.org), with a sizeable collection of native primates, rescued from poachers and the bushmeat trade.

Sleeping

Ideal Hotel HOTEL $

(Map p242; 2266 9537, 2220 9852; idealhotel72@yahoo.fr; Carrefour Nlongkak; r CFA8000-10,000, apt CFA15,000; P) Rooms here are decent enough for the low price, though there's no hot water and rooms are fan cooled. Balconies in some make up for a general lack of light (plus you get Yaoundé smog for free). If you're visa hunting, this is well located for embassies.

Foyer International de l'Église Presbytérienne HOSTEL $

(Map p242; 9985 2376; off Rue Joseph Essono Balla; tents/dm/s/d CFA2000/5000/8000/10,000; P) This 100-year-old building has two fairly uninviting private rooms and two eight-bed dorms, all of which share the same very basic bathrooms. Campers can set up their own tents in the garden. From the main road, walk to the right of the water towers, and it's in the second brick house on your left.

SET YOUR BUDGET

Budget

- Hotel room CFA5000
- Two-course dinner CFA2000
- Coffee CFA500
- Local bus ride CFA1000

Midrange

- Hotel room CFA20,000
- Two-course dinner CFA6000
- Coffee CFA1000
- Short taxi ride CFA2000

Top End

- Hotel room CFA40,000
- Two-course dinner CFA10,000
- Coffee CFA1000
- Long taxi ride CFA5000

Tou'ngou Hotel HOTEL $$

(2220 1026; www.toungouhotel.com; Rue Onembele Nkou; s/d/ste incl breakfast CFA20,000/30,000/45,000; P) One of Yaoundé's better-value midrange hotels, the Tou'ngou is a smart and popular option. Staff can seem a little indifferent, but the rooms are comfortable and clean, the location is central and there's a good restaurant. It's best to book ahead.

Prestige Hotel HOTEL $$

(Map p242; 2222 6055, 2222 6039; www.grouprestigehotel.com; Ave Charles Atangana;) This sprawling and rather raucous hotel has good-value rooms and is handily located for buses to Douala. Rooms are on the small side, but they're clean and secure, with many enjoying balconies. There's a popular bar and restaurant on the site too, but also lots of traffic noise.

El Panaden Hotel HOTEL $$

(Map p244; 9858 7419; elpanaden@yahoo.fr; Pl de l'Indépendance; r CFA15,500-30,000;) This is an old travellers' favourite, with a good wanderer vibe going around. The generously sized and spotless rooms often come with balconies. A renovation was ongoing at the time of our last visit, and so prices may go up when it's complete.

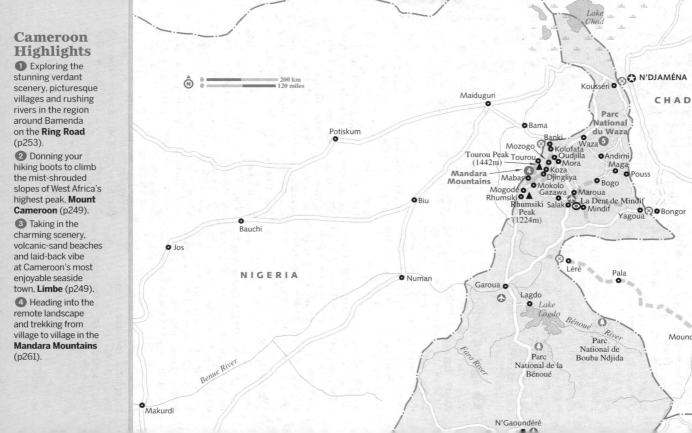

Cameroon Highlights

1. Exploring the stunning verdant scenery, picturesque villages and rushing rivers in the region around Bamenda on the **Ring Road** (p253).
2. Donning your hiking boots to climb the mist-shrouded slopes of West Africa's highest peak, **Mount Cameroon** (p249).
3. Taking in the charming scenery, volcanic-sand beaches and laid-back vibe at Cameroon's most enjoyable seaside town, **Limbe** (p249).
4. Heading into the remote landscape and trekking from village to village in the **Mandara Mountains** (p261).

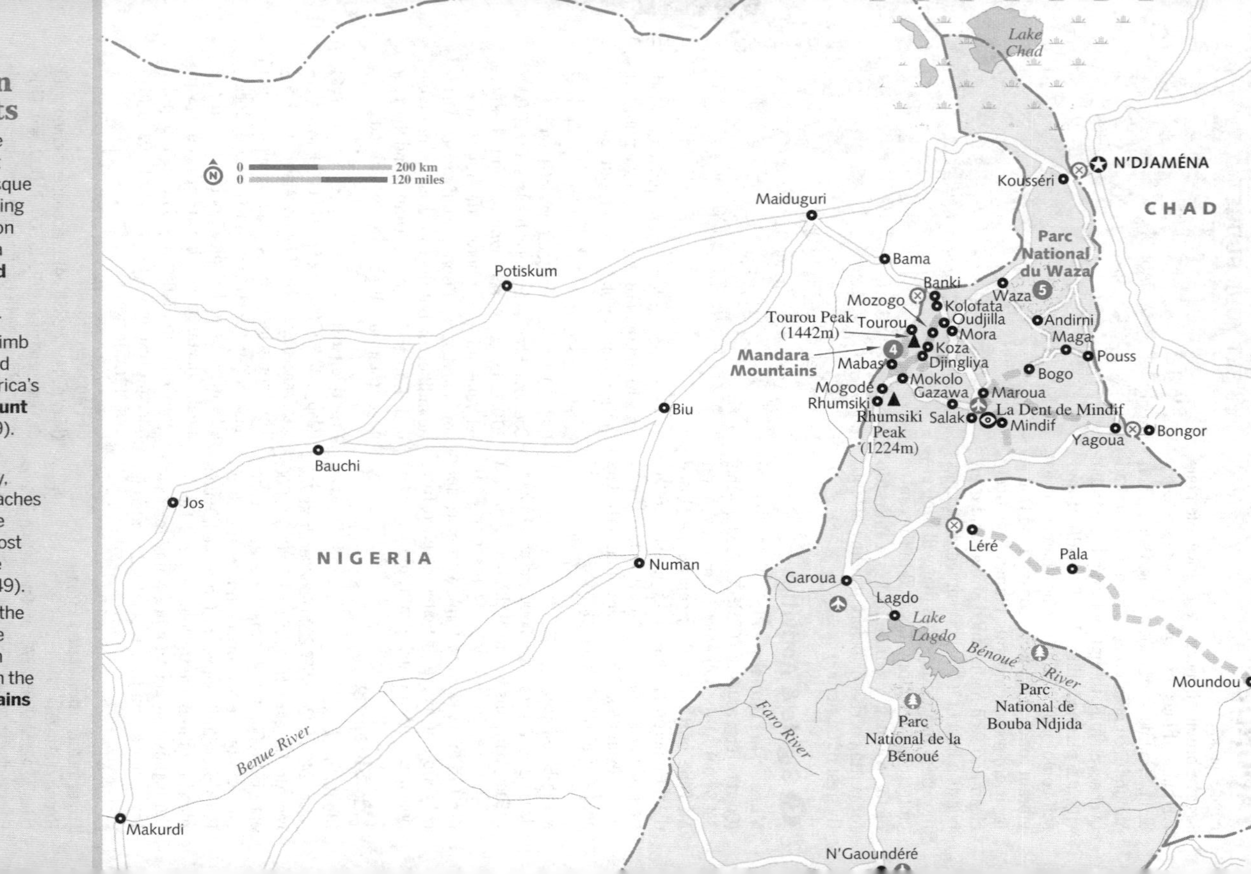

5 Watching elephants at the waterholes of the region's excellent **Parc National du Waza** (p261).

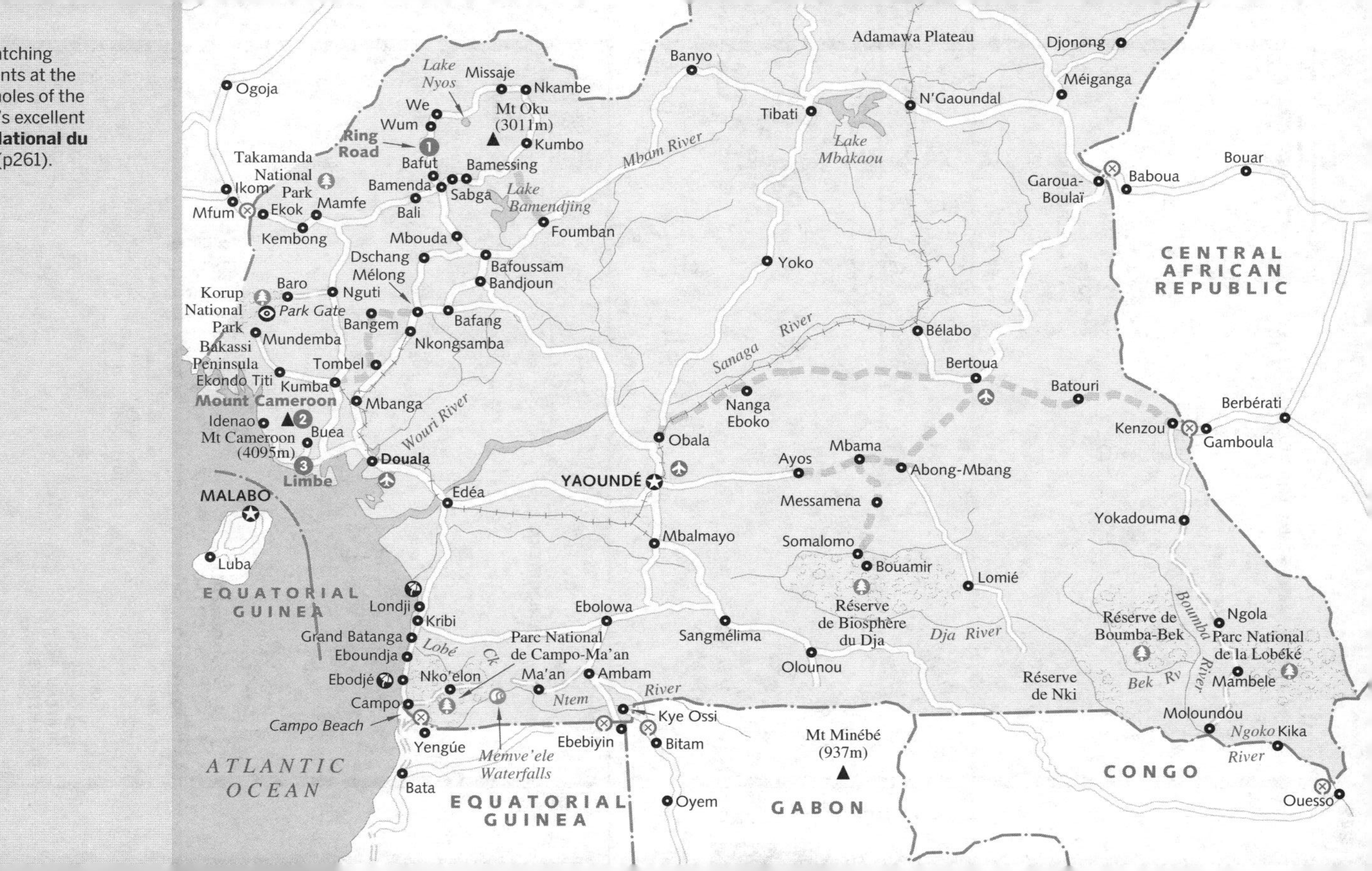

Yaoundé

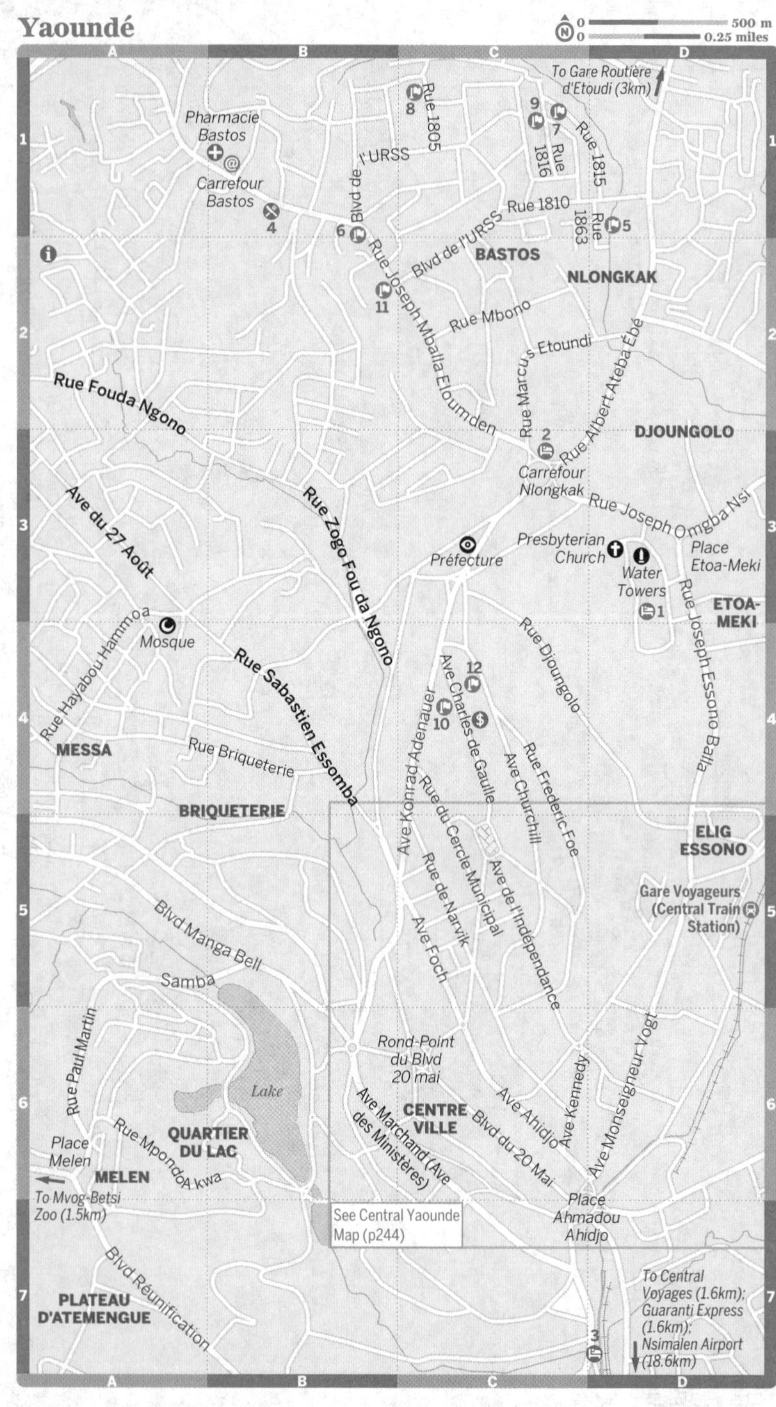

500 m
0.25 miles
To Gare Routière d'Etoudi (3km)
Pharmacie Bastos
Carrefour Bastos
Rue 1805
Blvd de l'URSS
Rue 1816
Rue 1815
Rue 1810
Rue 1863
BASTOS
NLONGKAK
Rue Joseph Mballa Eloumden
Rue Mbono
Rue Marcus Etoundi
Rue Albert Ateba Ébé
Rue Fouda Ngono
DJOUNGOLO
Carrefour Nlongkak
Rue Joseph Omgba Nsi
Ave du 27 Août
Rue Zogo Fou da Ngono
Préfecture
Presbyterian Church
Water Towers
Place Etoa-Meki
ETOA-MEKI
Rue Joseph Essono Balla
Mosque
Rue Hayabou Hammoa
Rue Sabastien Essomba
Rue Djoungolo
Ave Charles de Gaulle
Ave Konrad Adenauer
Rue Frederic Foe
Ave Churchill
MESSA
Rue Briqueterie
BRIQUETERIE
Rue du Cercle Municipal
Rue de Narvik
Ave de l'Indépendance
ELIG ESSONO
Gare Voyageurs (Central Train Station)
Ave Foch
Blvd Manga Bell
Samba
Rond-Point du Blvd 20 mai
Rue Paul Martin
Lake
Ave Kennedy
Ave Monseigneur Vogt
Ave Ahidjo
CENTRE VILLE
Blvd du 20 Mai
Ave Marchand (Ave des Ministères)
QUARTIER DU LAC
Place Melen
Rue Mpondo Akwa
MELEN
To Mvog-Betsi Zoo (1.5km)
See Central Yaounde Map (p244)
Place Ahmadou Ahidjo
Blvd Réunification
PLATEAU D'ATEMENGUE
To Central Voyages (1.6km); Guaranti Express (1.6km); Nsimalen Airport (18.6km)

Yaoundé

Sleeping
1 Foyer International de l'Église Presbytérienne D3
2 Ideal Hotel C3
3 Prestige Hotel D7

Eating
4 Istanbul B1

Information
5 Central African Republic Embassy D1
6 Chadian Embassy B1
7 Congolese Embassy C1
8 Equatorial Guinean Embassy C1
9 Gabonese Embassy C1
10 German Embassy C4
11 Nigerian Embassy B2
12 UK Embassy C4

Merina Hotel HOTEL $$$
(Map p244; 2222 2131; hotelmerina@cameroun-plus.com; Ave Ahidjo; s & d CFA37,000-42,000; P) Located right in the heart of the city, the smart Merina has a fancy orchid-strewn lobby, modern and comfortable rooms and good service. Other perks include a free airport-shuttle service and a small pool.

Eating

Around Carrefours Bastos and Nlongkak you can find grills serving *brochettes* (kebabs) throughout the day. On Pl de l'Indépendance, there are women grilling delicious fish, served with chilli or peanut sauce from CFA1000.

Le Sintra INTERNATIONAL $
(Map p244; Ave Kennedy; dishes CFA3000-5000; 6am-11pm Mon-Sat) A friendly welcome, a whiff of colonial atmosphere and a terrace made for people-watching in the heart of Yaoundé, La Sintra does a full breakfast menu, Italian and Cameroonian cuisine as well as delicious French dishes such as *crevettes à la provençale* (shrimps cooked in garlic).

Istanbul TURKISH $
(Map p242; Rue Joseph Mballa Eloumden; mains CFA4500; 8am-11pm) Fresh and well-prepared Turkish food is served up at this smart terrace restaurant (with an even smarter inside dining room complete with white tablecloths and silver service). Take away is available.

Patisserie Select Plus BAKERY $
(Map p244; Ave Monseigneur Vogt; baked goods CFA200-1500; breakfast, lunch & dinner) This excellent bakery sells a delicious line of freshly baked croissants, *beignets* (pastries) and sandwiches. Other treats include pizzas, burgers and coffee to go.

★ **La Paillote** CHINESE $$
(Rue Joseph Essono Balla; mains CFA3500-6000; noon-2pm & 7-10pm) This stylish Chinese restaurant has a charming shaded terrace and a smart dining room inside, both of which attract a loyal crowd of expats. The dishes are delicious and service is good.

Drinking & Nightlife

The best bars are in Carrefours Bastos and Nlongkak, most with open-air seating facing the street – great for people-watching. Solo female travellers might find the atmosphere uneasy in some bars once the sun dips.

Information

DANGERS & ANNOYANCES

Yaoundé is more relaxed than Douala, but muggings happen. Daytime is generally fine, but take taxis at night and be particularly wary around the Marché Central and tourist hotels.

INTERNET ACCESS

Your best bet is the smarter hotels and restaurants for a wireless connection.

Espresso House (Carrefour Bastos; 9am-11pm) Offers wi-fi for CFA1500 per hour.

MEDICAL SERVICES

Pharmacie Bastos (220 6555; Carrefour Bastos) Well-stocked pharmacy.

Polyclinique André Fouda (222 6612) For medical emergencies; in Elig-Essono, southeast of Carrefour Nlongkak.

MONEY

There are ATMs at most of the major banks. As always in Cameroon, travellers cheques are problematic to change in banks – try the banks around the cathedral.

Bicec Bank (Map p244; Ave Ahidjo) Has an ATM.

SCB (Map p244; near Pl Ahmadou Ahidjo) Money exchange and ATM.

POST

Central Post Office (Map p244; Pl Ahmadou Ahidjo; 7.30am-3.30pm Mon-Fri, to noon Sat)

Central Yaoundé

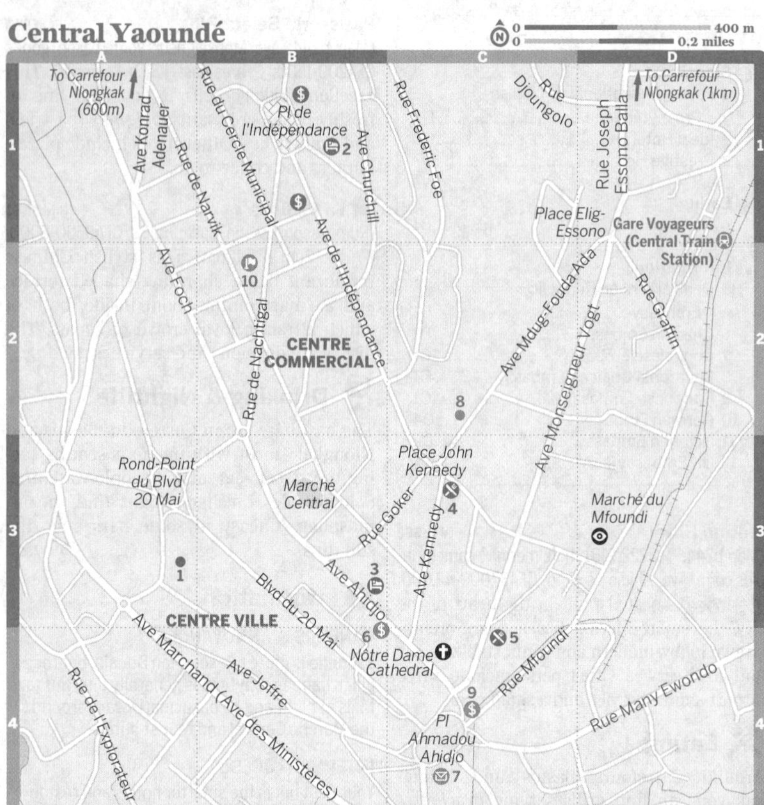

Central Yaoundé

Activities, Courses & Tours
1 Safar Tours A3

Sleeping
2 El Panaden Hotel B1
3 Merina Hotel B3

Eating
4 Le Sintra C3
5 Patisserie Select Plus C4

Information
6 Bicec Bank B4
7 Central Post Office C4
8 Ministry of Immigration C2
9 SCB C4
10 US Embassy B2

Getting There & Away

AIR

Yaoundé has an international airport, although far more international services go to and from Douala. Internal flights with Camair-Co connect Yaoundé to Douala (CFA31,100, 45 minutes), Garoua (CFA108,700, three hours) and Maroua (CFA121,100, three hours).

BUS

There are buses between Yaoundé and all major cities in Cameroon. Buses leave from their companies' offices, spread out on the outskirts of town. For Douala (CFA3000 to CFA6000, three to four hours), **Central Voyages** (Mvog-Mbi) and **Guaranti Express** (Quartier Nsam) are recommended. Guaranti Express is also recommended for Limbe (CFA5000, five hours), Bamenda (CFA5000, six hours), Bafoussam (CFA2500, three hours) and Kumba (CFA4000, four hours).

Otherwise, all agency and nonagency buses for Kribi, Bertoua, Batouri, Ebolowa, Limbe and

Buea depart from Blvd de l'Ocam, about 3km south of Pl Ahmadou Ahidjo (direct taxi drivers to Agences de Mvan).

Transport to Bafoussam, Bamenda and points north departs from Gare Routière d'Etoudi, 5km north of Centre Ville.

TRAIN

The most popular and convenient way to travel north from Yaoundé is by train, which runs all the way to N'Gaoundéré. Trains depart daily at 6.15pm and are scheduled to arrive in N'Gaoundéré at 6.30am the next day, although in practice delays on the line are common.

For seating, there's a choice of comfortable 1st-class couchettes (sleeping compartments; per person four-/two-bed cabin CFA25,000/28,000), 1st-class airline-style seats (CFA17,000) and crowded 2nd-class benches (CFA10,000). Seats in 1st and 2nd class are in open wagons, with no way to secure your bag. Even in couchettes, be alert for thieves.

The train has a restaurant car where you can buy passable meals (breakfast/dinner CFA1000/2500). If you're in 1st class, someone will come and take your order and deliver it to you. At every station stop, people will offer street food at the windows.

There are also two daily services between Yaoundé and Douala (1st/2nd class CFA6000/3000), though these are used much less frequently, as buses are cheaper, faster and more convenient.

Getting Around

Shared taxis and *moto-taxis* (motorbike taxis) are the only public-transport option. Fares are CFA200 per place for short- to medium-length rides. A private taxi to Nsimalen airport from central Yaoundé should cost CFA4000 to CFA6000 (40 minutes).

WESTERN CAMEROON

Imagine Africa: wormy red tracks and vegetation so intensely green you can almost taste the colour. This image comes alive in Western Cameroon. The country's economic heart intermittently beats in Douala, and from here it's a short hop to the haze and laze of beach towns like Limbe and the savannah-carpeted slopes of the Mountain of Thunder – Mt Cameroon. In the Anglophone northwest you can slip between sunburnt green hills while exploring a patchwork of secret societies, traditional chiefdoms and some of the country's best arts and crafts, particularly the wooden masks that are so often associated with Africa.

Douala

POP 2 MILLION

Sticky, icky and frenetic, Douala isn't as bad as some say, but it's not likely to be your first choice for a honeymoon, either. By any measure but political power this is Cameroon's main city: its primary air hub, biggest port and leading business centre, and the result is a chaotic hodgepodge. There are few charms, but you can set your finger here to gauge Cameroon's pulse.

Sights

Espace Doual'art MUSEUM
(Pl du Gouvernement; 9am-7pm Mon-Sat) FREE
Well worth dropping into if you're nearby, this contemporary-art space hosts changing displays of work from all over Cameroon and the rest of Africa. There's a little cafe here too, and it's a good place to gauge the city's small art scene.

Sleeping

Centre d'Accueil Missionaire HOSTEL $
(7707 1283, 3342 2797; aprocure@yahoo.fr; Rue Franqueville; s CFA10,000, without shower CFA8000, d/tr CFA14,000/18,000; P) Praise be to this Catholic mission, with its clean if basic rooms, pleasant verandah and lovely pool. A convenient laundry service and an excellent location seal the deal.

★ **Foyer du Marin** GUESTHOUSE $$
(9991 5448, 3342 2794; www.seemannsmission.org; Rue Gallieni; s/d/apt CFA22,000/25,000/30,000; P@) Definitely the best-value accommodation in Douala, the German Seaman's Mission is a literal oasis of tranquillity in the city centre. It's set in a gorgeous garden with a pool and terrific views towards the port, the rooms are comfortable and spacious and the restaurant serves up delicious poolside food all day long. The only complaint is the management's attitude towards tourists, who are generally made to feel like they're there under sufferance: the wireless password is only given to regular guests and front-desk staff can seem frosty. Book ahead.

Hotel Beausejour Mirabel HOTEL $$
(9978 9725, 3300 5996; resahotelbsejour@gmail.com; Rue Joffre; r from CFA30,000) Centrally located and with very friendly staff, the Beausejour was once quite a smart place, as evidenced by its impressive facade and former rooftop pool. It's fallen on less

Douala

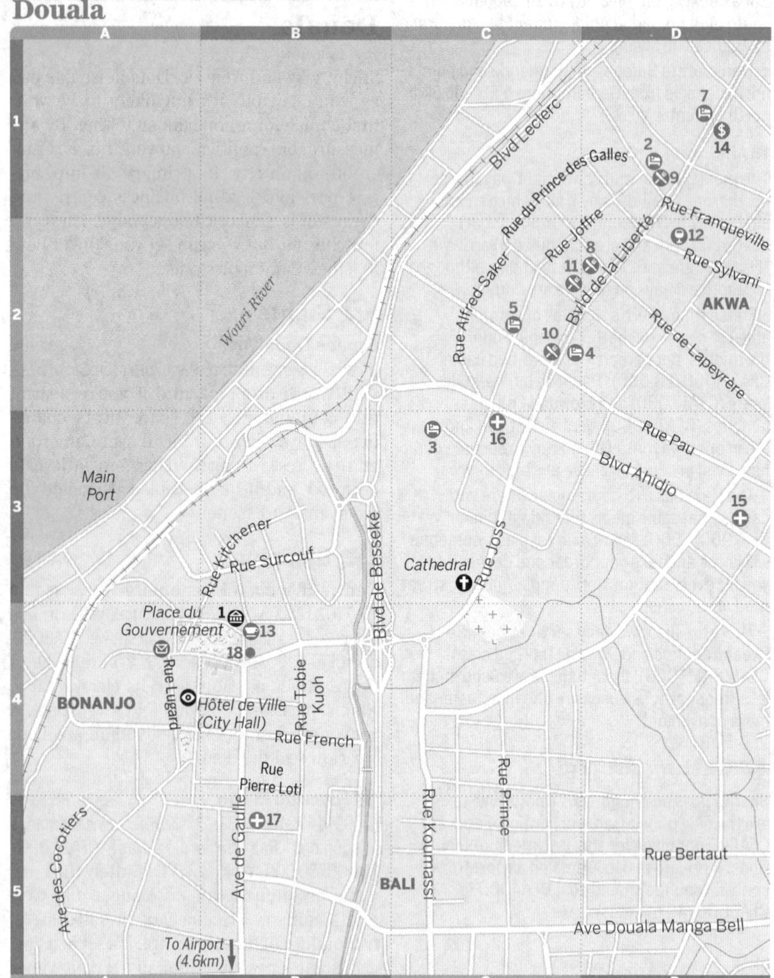

glamorous times, but the rooms have balconies and are clean and spacious, while downstairs there's wi-fi and a good on-site restaurant, making it one of Douala's best midrange options.

Hotel Majestic HOTEL **$$**

(☎9767 1332, 3342 8734; ngatcherv1@yahoo.fr; Blvd de la Liberté; r from CFA25,000; ❄📶) You can expect quite a bit of noise at this otherwise excellent-value hotel; as well as the traffic on Douala's main avenue outside, there's an incredibly loud music shop downstairs blaring out pop music all day. That said, rooms are clean and comfortable, each coming with fridge, TV and decent modern bathroom.

Hotel Hila HOTEL **$$**

(☎9975 0082; Blvd de l'Unité; s CFA17,000-20,000, d CFA25,000; ❄) Ideally located for the Yaoundé bus agencies, the Hila sits on a very busy road, so get a room at the back if you can. Rooms are a decent size and clean, if rather sterile. Many have balconies, all have hot water, and there's even a mosque on the 2nd floor.

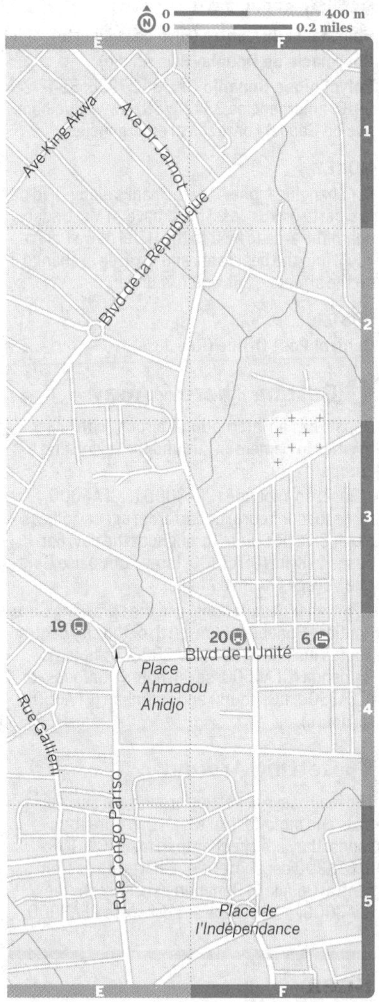

Douala

Sights
1 Espace Doual'art B4

Sleeping
2 Centre d'Accueil Missionaire D1
3 Foyer du Marin C3
4 Hotel Akwa Palace C2
5 Hotel Beausejour Mirabel C2
6 Hotel Hila F4
7 Hotel Majestic D1

Eating
8 Delices D2
Foyer du Marin .... (see 3)
9 La Fourchette D1
10 Méditerranée Restaurant C2
11 Saga African Restaurant C2

Drinking & Nightlife
12 American Graffiti D2
13 Café des Palabres B4

Information
14 Bicec Bank D1
15 Pharmacie de Douala D3
16 Pharmacie du Centre C3
17 Polyclinique Bonanjo B5

Transport
18 Air France B4
19 Centrale Voyages E4
20 Guaranti Express F4

Hotel Akwa Palace LUXURY HOTEL $$$
(3343 3916, 3342 2675; www.hotel-akwa-palace.com; Blvd de la Liberté; r CFA120,000-180,000; P ❄ @ ᯤ ≋) If money's not a concern then this is still the best choice in town, if for nothing else than its superb location in the heart of things. Rooms are plush and stylish, staff helpful, and the vast and normally empty swimming pool in the back garden is the best place to forget the chaos outside.

Eating

There are plenty of good restaurants along Blvd de la Liberté.

Delices BAKERY $
(Blvd de la Liberté; pastries from CFA500; 7am-10pm, to 3pm Sun) A great early-morning stop for pastries and a shot of coffee, this Douala institution has a good selection of baked goods as well as more filling toasted sandwiches.

Méditerranée Restaurant MEDITERRANEAN $$
(3342 3069; Blvd de la Liberté; mains CFA3000-6000; 8am-midnight) With an open terrace but still cleverly sheltered from the busy road, the Méditerranée is a perennially popular spot for expats to soak up the city. The menu is a good mix of Greek, Italian and Lebanese dishes, including wood-fired pizzas and changing daily specials.

Saga African Restaurant AFRICAN $$
(Blvd de la Liberté; mains CFA4000-7000; noon-11pm) Atmospheric and upmarket, the Saga offers an interesting mix of African dishes with some local classics, such as *ndole* (sauce made with bitter leaves similar to spinach and flavoured with smoked fish), plus pizza,

Chinese and pasta dishes. It's nicely decked out, with an open-air area at the front and a cool glass-fronted dining room behind.

Foyer du Marin EUROPEAN **$$**
(Rue Gallieni; mains CFA4000-8000; 8am-10pm) It's worth making a diversion for the nightly poolside grill at this hotel; great kebabs, steaks, chicken, seafood dishes and juicy German sausage are all well prepared and served up by the friendly staff. This is also a great drinking spot.

★**La Fourchette** INTERNATIONAL **$$$**
(3343 2611; Rue Franqueville; mains CFA7000-18,000; 10am-11pm Mon-Sat) An incredibly smart and tasteful option, La Fourchette's menu is out of this world if you're used to the more normal Cameroonian choice of chicken or fish. Here you'll find steak tartare, grilled zebu fillet, goat's cheese ravioli and stuffed crab, with prices to match. Service is charmingly formal, you should dress to impress and booking ahead is a good idea.

Drinking & Nightlife

Douala has a lively nightlife scene, though much of it can be inaccessible to visitors without local contacts. The areas of Bonapriso, Bonanjo and Akwa contain the most bars and clubs.

Café des Palabres CAFE
(Pl du Gouvernement; 7.30am-11pm Mon-Sat;) Housed inside a 1905 colonial German residence, this charming cafe on Bonanjo's main square has a great garden terrace perfect for an evening drink, as well as a cool interior with a full menu and an intellectual/alternative vibe. Literary types might like to know that this is the building identified as 'la Pagode' in Céline's *Journey to the End of the Night*.

American Graffiti BAR
(Rue Sylvani;) Pool bar, retro-diner and generally cool hang-out, this is the place to go drinking with a friendly and cool selection of Doualan youth. Try the delicious burgers, or your hand at pool on one of the two tables while downing a cool beer.

Information

DANGERS & ANNOYANCES

Muggings happen: if you'd rather be safe than sorry, it's recommended to take a taxi after dark. Leave valuables in a safe place, and be extra careful around nightspots.

MEDICAL SERVICES

Pharmacie du Centre (Blvd de la Liberté)
Pharmacie de Douala (Blvd Ahidjo)
Polyclinique Bonanjo (3342 7936, 3342 9910, emergencies 3342 1780; www.clibo.com; Ave de Gaulle) For medical emergencies.

MONEY

For changing money, try the banks along Blvd de la Liberté or Rue Joss; most have ATMs. Underneath the arcade next to the Hôtel Akwa Palace you'll find the best rates and tax-free exchange on the streets – but watch yourself.

POST

Central Post Office (Rue Joss)

Getting There & Away

Douala has an international airport with links to cities in Cameroon, around the region and to Europe.

Buses to Yaoundé (CFA3000 to CFA6000, three to four hours) depart from agency offices along Blvd de l'Unité throughout the day. For buses to Kribi (CFA2000, three hours) use Centrale Voyages on Blvd Ahidjo.

For other destinations, use the sprawling Gare Routière Bonabéri, 6km north of the city centre. Routes include Limbe (CFA2000, 1½ hours), Bamenda (CFA4500, seven hours), Bafoussam (CFA3500, five hours) and Foumban (CFA3500, six hours).

Getting Around

The main ways of getting around are shared taxis and *moto-taxi*, of which there are thousands; they are cheaper than taxis (CFA100 to CFA200 per short ride). Charter taxis from central Douala to Bonabéri generally charge CFA3000. A taxi to the airport costs CFA3000.

Buea

Basically built into the side of Mt Cameroon, Buea (pronounced boy-ah) has a hill station's coolness, especially compared to sticky Limbe. If you're going up the mountain, you're inevitably coming here.

Conveniently, **Express Exchange** (Molyko Rd) will exchange euros, US dollars and travellers cheques.

Sleeping

Presbyterian Mission GUESTHOUSE **$**
(3332 2336; Market Rd; campsites CFA1000, s/d CFA4000/6000, without bathroom CFA3000/5000; P) This church mission is set in attractive gardens and has comfy and

spotless rooms. There's a tidy communal sitting room and cooking facilities. It's up the hill from the police station.

Paramount Hotel HOTEL $
(☎3332 2341, 3332 2074; Molyko Rd; s/d/tr CFA7000/9000/11,000; P) The Paramount Hotel is one of the better places to sleep in Buea. The pretty rooms come with TV and are a nice respite from the mountain. To get here turn left off the main road and continue some way up the hill and you'll find the hotel on your right.

Hiking Mount Cameroon

Most hikes to the summit of West Africa's highest peak take two or three days, but it's no stroll in the park. The difficulty stems not only from its height (4095m), but from the fact that you start from near sea level, making a big change in altitude in a relatively short distance. November to April is the main climbing season, and although it's possible to climb the mountain year-round, you won't get much in the way of views during the rainy season. Warm clothes and waterproofs are a must. A popular ascent is a two-night, three-day hike via the Mann Spring route and descending via the Guinness Route.

Hikes are arranged in Buea through the **Mt Cameroon Ecotourism Organisation** (☎332 2038; mountceo@yahoo.uk; Buea Market; ⏲8am-5pm Mon-Fri, 7am-noon Sat & Sun). The organisation works closely with the 12 villages around the mountain, employing many villagers as guides and porters. All hikers pay a flat 'stakeholder fee' of CFA3000, which goes into a village development fund and is used for community projects, such as improving electricity and water supply. The organisation's office also has a small shop selling locally produced handicrafts.

Guides, well versed in the local flora and fauna, cost CFA6000 per day (maximum five hikers per guide); porters cost CFA5000. Establish a comfortable pace for yourself; some guides have a tendency – conscious or not – of rushing up the mountain. Equipment can be hired on a daily basis in Buea.

Limbe

Limbe is a charming place, blessed with a fabulous natural position between the rainforest-swathed foothills of Mt Cameroon and the dramatic Atlantic coastline. Popular with both foreign and Cameroonian tourists, this is a great spot to chill out on the beach for a few days before heading on elsewhere.

Sights & Activities

Limbe Wildlife Centre ZOO
(www.limbewildlife.org; admission CFA3000; ⏲9am-4.30pm) Many zoos in Africa are depressing places, but the Limbe Wildlife Centre is a shining exception. Jointly run by the Ministry of the Environment and the primate charity Pandrillus, it contains rescued chimpanzees, gorillas, drills and other primates, all housed in large enclosures, with lots of interesting information about local conservation issues. Staff are well informed, and are heavily involved in community education.

Botanical Gardens GARDENS
(admission CFA2000, camera CFA2000; ⏲8am-6pm) The second-oldest botanical gardens in Africa are the home of, among others, cinnamon, nutmeg, mango, ancient cycads and an unnamed tree locals describe as 'African Viagra'. There's a small visitor centre and an area with Commonwealth War Graves. Guides (CFA1000) aren't required but are recommended as labelling is minimal. Bring bug spray.

Beaches BEACH
The best of Limbe's beaches are north of town and known by their distance from Limbe. Mile 6 and Mile 11 beaches are popular, but our favourite is at the village of Batoké at Mile 8, from where the lava flows of one of Mt Cameroon's eruptions are still visible.

Bimbia Rainforest & Mangrove Trail WALKING
(☎7733 7014; bbcnaturetrail@yahoo.com) Located about an hour south of Limbe and running through the only coastal lowland rainforest remaining between Douala and Limbe. An experienced guide will take you on day tours through some rather lovely submerged woods, birdwatching areas and old slave-trading sites. You'll have to pay CFA5000 for the local development fee, which goes towards the village of Bimbia and mangrove preservation, CFA3000 for a guide, and CFA15,000 for a *taxi brousse* (bush taxi) from Limbe,

Limbe

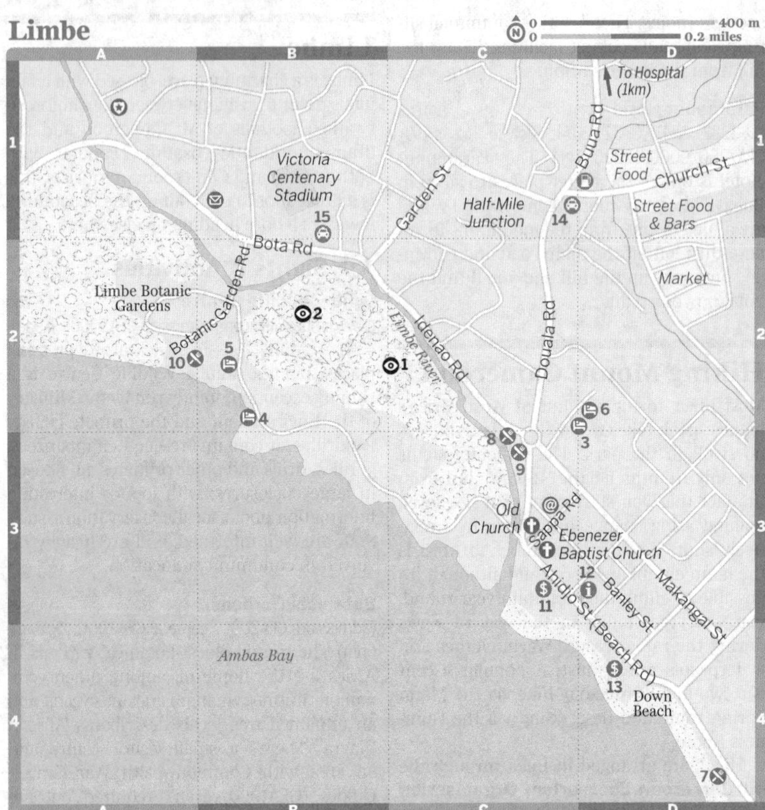

Limbe

Sights

1 Botanical Gardens ... C2
2 Limbe Botanic Gardens Visitors Centre ... B2

Sleeping

3 Bay Hotel ... D2
4 Bird Watchers' Club ... B2
5 Miramare Gardens Resort ... B2
6 Victoria Guest House ... D2

Eating

7 Grilled Fish Stalls ... D4
8 Le Moulin ... C3
9 Mt Cameroon Bakery ... C3
10 The Hot Spot ... A2

Information

11 Bicec Bank ... C3
12 Fako Tourist Board ... D3
13 SGBC Bank ... D4

Transport

14 Shared Taxis to Mile 4 Motor Park & Douala ... C1
15 Shared Taxis to Western Beaches ... B1

making this a trip best done in a group. To arrange tours talk to the guys who hang around the botanic gardens, arrange a trip through the Fako Tourist Board (p251) or contact Bimbia Rainforest and Mangrove Trail.

Sleeping

Victoria Guest House GUESTHOUSE $

(☎2281 6245; off Makangal St; r CFA9000, with air-con CFA12,000-16,000; P ❄) The best-value budget place in town, the Victoria has clean and well-maintained rooms on the hill above Limbe's main restaurant strip: follow the path up behind the King William Hotel. Nearly all rooms have air-con, but there are a couple of cheaper fan-cooled variants.

Bay Hotel HOTEL $

(☎7467 8084; off Makangal St; s/d/ste from CFA6000/10,000/15,000) If you're on a very tight budget then the Bay offers big, rather damp fan-cooled rooms with tiny bathrooms that, in some cases at least, come with wide verandahs. Unfortunately, they also tend to pick up the noise of the party people in the nearby bars.

★**Bird Watchers' Club** GUESTHOUSE $$

(☎9683 8188, 7573 4086; Limbe Botanical Gardens; r CFA15,000; P ❄) This charmingly secluded spot on a rocky promontory overlooks the sea. With just two rooms it's a good idea to call ahead and book. You'll be rewarded with spacious accommodation with double beds and mosquito nets and a great restaurant with superb sea views.

Hotel Seme Beach RESORT $$

(☎9496 5751, 7793 4552; www.semebeach.com; Mile 11, Rte d'Idenau, Bakingili; r incl breakfast CFA25,000-35,000, ste incl breakfast CFA50,000-100,000; P ❄ 📶 ≋) Not in Limbe itself, but 18km beyond along the coast, this is a good choice if you want to enjoy the beach and some creature comforts. The location is gorgeous, with full frontage onto the beach and views of Equatorial Guinea rising in the distance, while touches such as a freshwater swimming pool and a spa make for great relaxation. Service can be on the surly side, but otherwise this is a highly recommended place.

Miramare Gardens Resort HOTEL $$

(☎3333 2941, 3332 2332; miramare.breeze@facebook.com; Botanic Garden Rd; incl breakfast campsites CFA5000, s/d CFA15,000/20,000; P ❄ 📶 ≋) While this place has certainly seen better days, its location on a wave-kissed cliff backed by screaming jungle is unbeatable. Accommodation is in cute, if rather dark, *boukarous* (self-contained huts) that abut a restaurant and a decent-sized, though rather green, swimming pool. Book ahead, as this place remains Limbe's most popular choice.

Eating

The Hot Spot INTERNATIONAL $

(Limbe Botanical Gardens; mains CFA3000-4000; ⏲7.30am-11pm) With hands down the best location in town, overlooking the dramatic coastline and the Park Hotel Miramar, this place offers a fairly standard selection of meat grills, shrimps, fish and chicken dishes. The friendly staff, outdoor seating and views make it, though. On the dirt road to the hotels through the gardens take the middle path after the bridge.

Le Moulin INTERNATIONAL $

(Idenao Rd; mains CFA2000-3000; ⏲10am-10pm) Right on the roundabout in the thick of things, Le Moulin is the best eating option in the town centre. The menu encompasses *ndole,* chicken and beef dishes served up with fresh vegetables, plantains or rice. Service is friendly.

Mt Cameroon Bakery BAKERY $

(Idenao Rd; pastries from CFA500; ⏲6am-11pm) Limbe's best spot for breakfast if your hotel doesn't serve it. Here you'll find life's essentials such as fresh-baked pastries and coffee.

Grilled Fish Stalls SEAFOOD $

(Down Beach; dishes from CFA1000; ⏲7am-10pm) You'll find this cluster of open-air grills with attached seating where the fishing boats haul up on the beach. Soak up your beer with something from the sea that was probably happily unaware it would be your dinner a few minutes before you ordered it.

Information

The **Fako Tourist Board** (☎3333 2861; Banley St; ⏲7.30am-5pm Mon-Sat) can arrange local tours, hotels and bookings with the Mt Cameroon Ecotourism Organisation. Internet access is available at **Computer World** (Banley St; per hr CFA300; ⏲closed Sun). Ahidjo St has several ATMs.

Getting There & Away

The main motor park is Mile 4, about 6km out of town. Minibuses and *taxis brousses* leave approximately hourly to Buea (CFA800, 25 minutes) and Douala (CFA1500, 70 minutes). From Mile 2, there are buses to Yaoundé (CFA5000, five hours).

Ferries (☎9998 9491, info 7727 6211) travel every Monday and Thursday from Limbe to Calabar in Nigeria (1st/2nd class CFA35,000/45,000, four hours), departing at 2am and returning on Tuesday and Friday at 7am. Take your own food and water.

Ferries weren't going to Malabo in Equatorial Guinea at the time of research, although a new ferry service was being discussed in late 2012.

Bamenda

The capital of Northwest Province is a dusty sprawl that tumbles down a hill at an altitude of more than 1000m; you'll see some impressive views of the town as you descend the hill coming from Douala. With a decent range of hotels and restaurants, it's a good jumping-off point for exploring the Ring Road circuit. It's also a centre of political opposition to President Biya.

Sleeping

Baptist Mission Resthouse GUESTHOUSE **$**
(☎7545 8339; Finance Junction; dm/s/d CFA4000/9000/13,000, apt CFA50,000; P ᯤ) This compound on the main road into the town centre has a bunch of well-maintained rooms, all fan cooled and with mosquito nets and hot water, though some are a little on the small side and rather mildewy. There's a communal kitchen and it's secure and welcoming.

International Hotel HOTEL **$**
(☎7606 7018; off Commercial Ave; s/d CFA10,000/12,000; ❄) Right in the middle of town and convenient for buses, this budget place charges extra for hot water and air-con. Rooms are modern and clean and have decent bathrooms as well as balconies offering sweeping views over, er, 'scenic' Bamenda.

Ex-Serviceman's Rest House GUESTHOUSE **$**
(☎7727 6375; Hotel Rd; r CFA5000) This compound is intended for ex-soldiers, but if rooms are available they'll be happily rented out to travellers on a tight budget; expect very basic digs with running water. It's a decent deal, but solo female travellers may feel uncomfortable.

Hotel Mondial HOTEL **$$**
(☎7793 8378; off Hotel Rd; s/d/ste CFA14,500/16,000/22,000; P) Definitely one of Bamenda's smarter choices, the Mondial is a little more modern than its equivalents elsewhere, though bathrooms are in a poor state and the swimming pool sits forlorn and empty. The otherwise comfortable rooms come with hot water, balconies and satellite TV.

Eating

Dreamland Restaurant AFRICAN **$**
(Commercial Ave; mains CFA1500-3500; ⏲7am-11pm) Dreamland doesn't look like much from the outside, but inside it's a well set out establishment with a large menu. There's a daily lunchtime buffet (CFA3500 per person) and a choice of grills, salads, fish and soups the rest of the time.

Super Class Restaurant AFRICAN **$**
(near Finance Junction; mains CFA3000; ⏲7.30am-8pm) This cute little shack with red tablecloths and friendly service serves up simple Cameroonian fare such as fried chicken and plantains or meat grills with rice.

CTT Restaurant & Handicrafts Cooperative AFRICAN **$$**
(near Finance Junction, Upstation; mains CFA1000-9000; ⏲8am-9pm) The food here is a standard blend of Cameroonian and slightly better Western fare. The real drawcard is the surrounds, specifically a workshop of regional handicrafts, a shop with a superb collection of handcrafted souvenirs and great views of Bamenda below.

Information

The **tourist office** (☎336 1395) can provide basic maps and dates of local festivals. **Express Exchange** (City Chemist's Roundabout) changes travellers cheques as well as US dollars. **SGBC Bank** (Commercial Ave) has an ATM.

Bamenda

Sleeping
1 Baptist Mission Resthouse D1
2 Ex-Serviceman's Rest House C2
3 Hotel Mondial C2
4 International Hotel B1

Eating
5 CTT Restaurant & Handicrafts Cooperative D1
6 Dreamland Restaurant B1
7 Super Class Restaurant D1

Information
8 Express Exchange B1
9 SGBC Bank B2
10 Tourist Office B1

Transport
11 Bali Motor Park (Transport to Bali & Mamfe) A3
12 Nkwen Motor Park D1
13 Ntarikon Motor Park A1
14 Vatican Express & Agency Bus Offices to Bafoussam & Points South B1

Bamenda

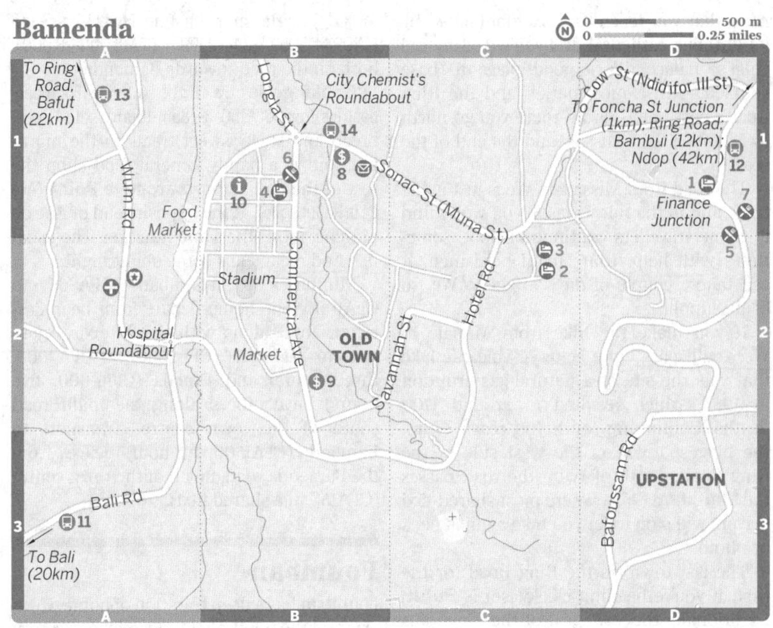

Getting There & Away

Most agency offices for destinations to the south are on Sonac St. Destinations include Yaoundé (CFA5000, six hours), Douala (CFA4500, seven hours) and Bafoussam (CFA1500, 90 minutes). Nkwen Motor Park has transport to the eastern stretch of the Ring Road, including Ndop (CFA1200, 90 minutes) and Kumbo (CFA3000, five hours). The west Ring Road is served by Ntarikon Motor Park, which runs minibuses to Wum (CFA3000, six hours). Shared taxis to the further motor parks shouldn't cost you any more than CFA150.

The Ring Road

The northwest highlands bear the pretty name 'Grassfields', an appellation too pleasant to really capture the look of this landscape. These aren't gentle fields; they're green and yellow valleys, tall grass, red earth and sharp mountains. Clouds of mist rise with wood smoke and dung smoke that mark the location of villages speckled on this deceptively inviting – but hard and rugged – terrain.

The 367km Ring Road runs a circle around the Grassfields, and if it were in better shape, it'd be one of Cameroon's great scenic drives. In fairness, it still can't be missed – but get your butt ready for some bumpy, red-earth roads. The pay-off? Mountains dolloped with lakes, cattle loping into the hills and one of the greatest concentrations of *fondoms* (traditional kingdoms) in Cameroon. Tourism is DIY here, with public transport extremely slow, crowded and irregular and very basic sleeping options in the few actual towns on the road. But a visit here is all about the journey itself: driving through tiny villages and enjoying the extraordinary and ever-changing scenery along the route.

Hiking, cycling and camping are all options, but always ask the permission of the local chief, and bring some gifts (whisky is a good idea). If you plan to drive this incredibly challenging road, hire a 4x4 and don't even think about it in the rainy season.

Transport links are reasonable but not particularly frequent, with minibuses usually leaving very early in the morning. Roads are poor throughout. Kumbo is the Ring Road's largest town, but apart from there, there's little infrastructure and nowhere to change money (stock up on CFA before leaving Bamenda). There are basic hotels in Ndop, Kumbo, Nkambe and Wum.

Starting from **Bamenda** and heading east, you pass **Sabga Hill**, which rises powerfully above Ndop, then **Bamessing**, with a handicraft centre and pottery workshop.

After that you reach **Kumbo**, dominated by its Catholic cathedral and *fon*'s (traditional chief's) palace. It's a good place to base yourself, with a nice market and the Ring Road's best hotels. From there you go north to Nkambe, then Missaje and the end of the road.

The road from Missaje to We is just a dirt track and in the rainy season you won't find it. Some travellers continue on foot, sometimes with help from Fulani herdsmen. It can take a couple of days to get to We, so bring supplies.

If you make the hike from Missaje to We, you'll pass **Lake Nyos**, a volcanic lake that was the site of a natural-gas eruption in 1986, which resulted in around 1700 deaths. Continuing south you reach **Wum**, the biggest town on the west side of the Ring Road. South of Wum the road passes the **Metchum Falls**, where most shared-taxi drivers will stop to let you take a quick peek or photo.

The last town on the Ring Road (or the first, if you're heading clockwise) is **Bafut**, traditionally the strongest of the kingdoms in this region. The **fon's palace** (admission CFA1000, camera CFA1500, museum CFA2000) is a highlight of the Ring Road and includes a tour of the compound where the *fon*'s large family lives.

Bafoussam

There's initially little to love about Bafoussam. The Bamiléké stronghold seems haphazardly built on agriculture money and a refined sense of chaos. But despite its heavy traffic and uninspiring appearance, the town is super friendly and has one of the best traditional palaces in the country. Make sure you check out the huge **chefferie** (Chief's Compound; www.museumcam.org; admission CFA2000; ⌚10am-5pm), about 15km south at Bandjoun.

Good value, with a decent bar to boot, the rooms at **Hotel Federal** (☎3344 1309; Rte de Foumban; r CFA10,000-12,000, with air-con CFA16,000) are neat and tidy. Although located in a blocky bomb-shelter chic building, the rooms in **Hotel du Centre** (☎7512 4025, 3344 2079; Carrefour Total; r CFA12,000-15,000) are open and fresh, many come with a balcony, and the toilets – bless them – have seats. It's well located (as the name suggests) and a useful landmark. For far better midrange accommodation head to **Hotel Altitel** (☎3344 5111; www.hotelaltitel.net; r CFA23,000-33,000; P❄📶) or the more distant **Hotel Le Saré** (☎9944 5059, 3344 2599; r CFA15,000-28,000), both on the road towards Bamenda.

Boulangerie La Paix (Rte de Foumban; pastries from CFA150; ⌚8am-10pm) sells good bread and sticky sweet treats in the morning, and is a handy general food shop the rest of the day. **Supermarché le Point** (Ave de la République), at the opposite end of Rue de Marché, fulfils the same function. The usual fish and meat stalls come out at night.

Minibuses to Foumban (CFA800 to CFA1000, one hour) depart from near Carrefour Total, along with shared taxis. Agencies to Yaoundé (CFA2500 to CFA3000, three hours) and Douala (CFA4000, five hours) have offices along the main road south of the town centre. Transport to Bamenda (CFA1500, 1½ hours) leaves from the Bamenda road, north of the town centre (CFA150 in a shared taxi).

Foumban

Foumban has a deep tradition of homegrown arts and the traditional monarchy centred on a sultan, who resides in a palace. The town is plopped architecturally and conceptually between West and North Africa, as if the Sahel and its sharp music, bright robes and Islam – this is the city with most Muslims in the south – were slowly creeping into the eastern corner of West Province.

There's a slow internet cafe east of the market. CPAC bank (south of the market) may change euros if you're lucky, but it's best to change money in Bafoussam.

Sights

The **Grand Marché** is a warren of narrow stalls and alleys, which are great fun to explore; the paths eventually lead to where the **Grande Mosquée** faces the palace.

Palais Royal PALACE

(Rue du Palais; admission CFA2000, camera CFA2000; ⌚9am-6pm) The must-see attraction of Foumban is the sultan's palace, currently home to the 19th sultan of the Bamoun dynasty. It has a fascinating and well-organised museum containing previous sultans' possessions and great historical insight into the region – assuming you know French. You'll find the palace opposite the market and main mosque, the minaret of which can be climbed as part of the palace tour.

Village des Artisans ARTS CENTRE
(Rue des Artisans) South of town, the Village des Artisans seems to produce more handicrafts than the rest of Cameroon combined.

Musée des Arts et Traditions Bamoun MUSEUM
(admission CFA1000; 9am-5pm) Close to the Village des Artisans, this museum houses a private collection of art and historical artefacts.

Festivals & Events

Every year at **Tabaski**, the Islamic holiday of Eid al-Adha, Foumban attracts thousands of pilgrims for an extraordinary blend of Muslim and traditional Bamoun ceremonies.

It all starts before sunrise with the call to prayer blasting from loudspeakers at the mosque. Thousands of men and boys, dressed in their finest, climb the hill to the Sacred Mountain and kneel in prayer. Around dawn the imam arrives, followed by the sultan in his white Cadillac. There are sunrise prayers, a sermon from the imam and a blessing from the sultan (on Eid al-Adha this is when the sheep is sacrificed). The sultan then gets on his horse surrounded by warriors in full regalia, and everyone follows him in an enormous parade to the palace, while the women and girls, so far absent from the proceedings, line the streets dressed all in white and ululate as the sultan passes.

After the parade there's a rest, and then horses race through town. There's another break until it gets dark, when the drumming and dancing start in front of the Palais Royal. Meanwhile (this is still Cameroon, after all) people pack the bars and clubs, and when these are full they set up speakers on the streets for heavy drinking and dancing until the sun comes up.

Sleeping & Eating

Bars, beer and grilled meat are abundant. Happy days.

Hotel Complexe Adi HOTEL $
(7607 9507, 9953 5515; Rue de l'Hotel Beau Regarde; r CFA6000) Look for the giant voodoo statue of a man studded by nails to find Adi's entrance. While the rooms here are clean, they're smallish and very basic (just a bed and a small bathroom), and the bar downstairs gets pretty loud. If there are no rooms available here, try the similar Hotel Beau Regard across the road.

★ **Hotel Pekassa de Karché** HOTEL $$
(3348 2935; hotelpekassadekarche@yahoo.fr; Rte de Bafoussam; s/d without air-con CFA10,000/15,000, d with air-con & balcony CFA25,000, ste CFA40,000; P ❄ @) This brand-new hotel is by far the best choice in Foumban. Just 200m from the royal palace, it makes for a pleasant change from the norm in Cameroonian hotels: smart, clean rooms with relatively tasteful decor, friendly staff and good security. There's a good on-site restaurant (mains CFA2500 to CFA4000) too.

Rifam Hotel HOTEL $$
(3348 2878; Rte de Bafoussam; r CFA10,000-25,000; P) Near the bus-agency offices, this hotel is one of Foumban's plushest. There's a big choice of rooms at various different prices, all of which have been recently repainted. There's also hot water, a TV set and plenty of space in each. A good restaurant downstairs makes up for the location, some way from the town centre.

Getting There & Away

There are a few direct buses to Yaoundé (CFA3500, five hours) and Douala (CFA3500, six hours); otherwise head for Bafoussam (CFA800 to CFA1000, one hour) and change there. Bus-agency offices are on the west side of town, about 3km from the Grande Marché (CFA150 in a shared taxi).

Transport between Foumban and Kumbo (CFA3000, around six hours) runs year-round, with journey times varying according to the rains. Although the road is very, very poor, it's easily one of the most beautiful in the country, skirting along the edge of the spectacular Mbam Massif.

SOUTHERN CAMEROON

Southern Cameroon is largely taken up by thick jungle, and there are few large towns or other population centres here. However, the coastline here is by far Cameroon's best: head to Kribi for great scenery and a relaxed vibe, and continue further down the coast to indulge in a spot of beach exploration and ecotourism in Parc National de Campo-Ma'an.

Kribi

Kribi is home to Cameroon's best beaches: the sand is fine, the water crystal clear, fresh fish is on the menu and cold beer on tap; there are times when Africa hugs you.

Most of Kribi's hotels, usually with their own beachfronts, start at the southern end of town, but camping isn't advised. The **Chutes de la Lobé**, 8km south of town (*moto-taxi* CFA500), are an impressive set of waterfalls that empty directly into the sea – it's a beautiful sight.

Sleeping

Kribi's main business is tourism and there's plenty of choice in where to stay. If you're visiting in the rainy season, ask for a discount.

Hotel Panoramique HOTEL **$**
(2346 1773, 9694 2575; hotel panoramique@yahoo.fr; Rue du Marché; r CFA6000-15,000;) This semi-sprawling compound feels like a down-at-heel villa evolved into low-rent flophouse. Some rooms are good value, but at the cheapest end you're in an ugly annexe with the dust and roaches.

★ **Hotel Ilomba** HOTEL **$$**
(9991 2923; www.hotelilomba.com; Rte de Campo; r CFA40,000, ste CFA120,000; P@) Some way out of Kribi, this is the loveliest hotel in the area. Rooms are in *boukarous* and all well furnished and tastefully decorated. It's also just a short walk to the Chutes de la Lobé and right on a beautiful stretch of beach, so it's a great place to base yourself for true relaxation.

New Hotel Coco Beach HOTEL **$$**
(9999 8790, 3346 1584; off Rte de Campo; r without/with sea view CFA20,000/30,000; P) There's not much new about the New Hotel Coco Beach, indeed its rooms have certainly seen better days, but they're clean and comfortable and some of them have fantastic sea views. The beach is just below the hotel and you can have breakfast as the waves splash just a short wander away – magic.

Les Gîtes de Kribi GUESTHOUSE **$$**
(7508 0845; www.kribiholidays.com; Rte de Campo; r CFA20,000, gîtes CFA45,000; P) Ideal for families, the *gîtes* (self-contained cottages) here are of varying sizes, but all are well equipped and have their own small kitchens. There are also normal rooms in the main building for those not *en famille*. Across the road there's a charming beach restaurant that serves up fresh fish in high season.

Auberge du Phare GUESTHOUSE **$$$**
(7564 0464; www.pharedekribi.cm; off Rte de Campo; r CFA28,000-50,000; P) Right on the seafront, this great place has classy blonde-wood accents, navy-blue sheets and nautical embellishments that give rooms some character, while the peeling courtyard, crystal pool and thatched bar are tropically indulgent.

Eating

All of the beach hotels have restaurants, and these are the nicest dining options in Kribi. Expect to pay from CFA3000 per meal; seafood obviously features heavily.

Fish Market SEAFOOD **$**
(meals from CFA1000; 10am-5pm Wed & Sat) This market at the marina grills the day's catch over coals. From crab and lobster to massive barracuda, you'd be hard-pressed to find a better and tastier selection of seafood anywhere in Cameroon.

Fish & Meat Stands FAST FOOD **$**
(meals from CFA1000; 10am-late) On Carrefour Kingué you'll find plenty of fish and meat stands lined up in front of the bars.

Getting There & Away

Bus agencies have offices on Rue du Marché in the town centre. Nonagency transport leaves from the main *gare routière* (bus station). Buses for Douala (CFA1800 to CFA2000, three hours) leave throughout the day, along with transport to Campo (CFA2000, three hours) and Yaoundé (CFA3000, 3½ hours).

Ebolowa

Ebolowa, capital of Ntem district, is a bustling place and a possible stopping point en route between Yaoundé and Equatorial Guinea or Gabon. Its main attraction is the artificial **Municipal Lake** in the centre of town.

The best accommodation is at **Hotel Porte Jaune** (2228 4339; Rte de Yaoundé; r CFA10,000-12,000) in the town centre, with some cheaper *auberges* (hostels) near the main roundabout, including **Hotel Âne Rouge** (2228 3438; Pl Ans 2000; r CFA5000).

During the dry season there's at least one vehicle daily along the rough road between Ebolowa and Kribi. There are also many buses daily to Yaoundé (CFA3000, three hours). Several vehicles depart in the morning for Ambam (CFA1000, one hour), from where you can find transport towards Ebebiyin (Equatorial Guinea) or Bitam (Gabon).

Campo & Ebodjé

Campo is the last town before the Equatorial Guinea border. Taking the road here is half the attraction – it's a hard but rewarding slog through immense rainforest past pygmy villages with views out to the ocean and fire-spouting petrol platforms shimmering in the west.

For travellers, Campo mainly serves as a jumping-off point for visiting Parc National de Campo Ma'an as well as the community-tourism project in nearby Ebodjé. There's scruffy accommodation, simple meals and very friendly faces at **Auberge Bon Course** (7451 1883; r CFA5000) at Bon Course Supermarché at the main junction in Campo.

Parc National de Campo-Ma'an, comprising 2608 sq km, protects rainforest, many plants and various animals, including buffalo, elephants and mandrills. The park is being developed by WWF as an ecotourism destination, with newly constructed canopy walks and river trips available.

Ebodjé, a small fishing village 25km north of Campo, is home to a **sea turtle conservation project** and ecotourism site run by **KUDU Cameroun** (3348 1648, 9622 0829). Visitors are taken out at night to spot egg-laying turtles, although there's no guarantee you'll see any – some tour groups encounter none, some as many as six. Even if you don't see any turtles, the beach is gorgeous, pristine and better than anything in Kribi.

The cost of a turtle walk (around CFA12,000 per person) includes accommodation in a local home, village development fee, meal and tour. A portion of fees help locals, many of whom have been trained as guides, and for between CFA5000 and CFA10,000 you can arrange trips up local rivers or cultural nights with traditional dancing and singing. Remember to bring your own water or filter, mosquito net and sleeping sheets.

There are daily minibuses between Campo and Kribi (CFA1500), which also stop at Ebodjé. *Moto-taxis* to Campo Beach (for Equatorial Guinea) cost CFA500. Taxis to Ebodjé from Campo cost CFA500. *Moto-taxis* to Ebodjé cost around CFA2000.

NORTHERN CAMEROON

The north of Cameroon is the fringe of the world's greatest dry zone. This is the Sahel, a red and ochre and yellow and brown rolling sea of dust, dirt and strange, utterly beautiful hills and pinnacles of rock, crisscrossed by the dry wind, the thin strides of Fulani people and the broad steps of their long-horned cattle.

N'Gaoundéré

N'Gaoundéré is the terminus of the railway line and beginning of the great bus and truck routes to the far north and Chad. The sense of adventure imparted upon reaching the Sahel is helped by the sight of government soldiers – there's a major training facility nearby – striding through the desert lanes with AK-47s strapped to their backs and extra banana clips taped to the stocks of their guns.

Some areas of N'Gaoundéré have a bad reputation for safety at night, including the area around the stadium and north of the cathedral. If in doubt, take a *moto-taxi*.

Sights

Palais du Lamido PALACE

(admission CFA2000, guide CFA1000, camera CFA1000; 9am-5pm) To enter the Palais du Lamido, the palace of the local Muslim ruler, you pass between three pillars stuffed with the remains of individuals who were buried alive to consecrate the site of the royal residence. One of Cameroon's more macabre foyers, yes, which leads into a complex of low-slung, heavily thatched roundhouses whose aesthetic feels more West African than Islamic. Some rooms are underwhelming, but if you come on a Friday or (especially) Sunday, when nobles pay their respects and thin, gorgeous desert music settles over the nearby square dominated by the Grande Mosquée, there's a palpable sense of being... well, somewhere else. Beware of black-painted areas within the compound – these sections are reserved for the *lamido*.

Sleeping

Nice Hotel HOTEL $

(7550 7523, 2225 1013; Rte de Garoua; r from CFA10,000; P) With spacious rooms, a peaceful, leafy setting, long cool corridors and TV in all rooms, the Nice is just that, and about as good as midrange options get in town, and surprisingly cheap. It's a very quick *moto-taxi* ride from the station.

Auberge de la Gare GUESTHOUSE $

(9980 3680, 2225 2217; r CFA8500; P) This pleasant enough spot in a N'Gaoundéré backstreet offers easy access to bus agencies

N'Gaoundéré

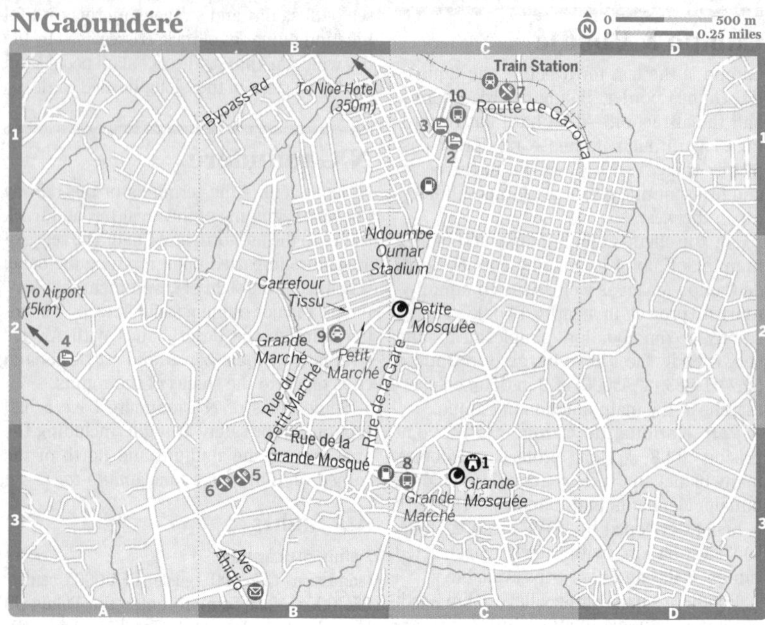

N'Gaoundéré

Sights

1 Palais du Lamido C3

Sleeping

2 Adamaoua Hotel C1
3 Auberge de la Gare C1
4 Hotel Pousada Style A2

Eating

5 La Plazza B3
6 Le Verger B3
7 Train Station Street Food C1

Transport

8 Gare Routière C3
Kawtal Voyages .... (see 8)
9 Taxi Stand B2
10 Touristique Express C1

and the train station. Rooms are tidy and simple, some with hot water, making it a good budget option There's a cute outdoor bar-restaurant with a thatched roof here too.

Hotel Pousada Style HOTEL $
(☎9985 4454, 2225 1703; r CFA5000-9000; P) A basic but friendly resthouse a short walk from the Catholic cathedral, the Pousada Style is divided into two wings. The one around the back is a little cheaper with smaller rooms, while those at the front are better, though still quite basic. All have mosquito nets, TV and bathrooms. Take a *moto-taxi* late at night in this area.

★ **Adamaoua Hotel** HOTEL $$
(☎9901 7566, 2225 1255; adamaouahotel@yahoo.fr; Rue de la Gare; r CFA15,000-25,000; P) This brand-new hotel is easily the best option in town: a short stroll from the station and next to the main bus companies, its sparkling fan-cooled modern rooms all have hot water, cable TV and plenty of African art on the lurid pink walls. Staff are friendly, there's a good on-site restaurant and even (yes, really!) wi-fi in the lobby.

Eating

The best street food is easily found at the row of shops, stalls and bars opposite the train station – worth the detour even if you don't have a train to catch.

The main market is the Petit Marché; the Grand Marché only sells vegetables.

Le Verger AFRICAN $
(Rue de la Grande Mosquée; mains CFA1500-3000; 6am-10pm) Tucked away in a courtyard off the main drag (look for the small sign), this green-painted restaurant serves up a range

of local dishes as well as the chicken and fish mains you find everywhere else. There's breezy outdoor seating as well as a more formal dining room with white tablecloths. Staff are charming.

★ **La Plazza** INTERNATIONAL **$$**
(Rue de la Grande Mosquée; mains from CFA3000-7000; ⏲10am-2pm & 7-11pm) Something of a N'Gaoundéré institution, this place has live music nightly and cold draught beer from the thatched bar. The Lebanese and pasta dishes are excellent, but don't miss the perennially popular Sunday buffet from noon (CFA6000). It's a little tricky to find as it's not on the street itself, but in a courtyard. Look for Ecobank and go through the gates to one side.

Getting There & Away

The airport, 5km outside the town, was being rebuilt at the time of research, so your only option for reaching N'Gaoundéré at present is overland.

The train station is at the eastern end of town. Trains to Yaoundé leave daily at around 7pm (CFA28,000 in 1st-class couchette, 12 hours), and you can reserve your seat a day in advance.

By bus, Touristique Express and Alliance Voyages are the best, with several buses daily to Garoua (CFA3500, five hours) and Maroua (CFA6000, eight hours). Kawtal Voyages operates a battered Garoua-Boulaï (CFA4000, 12 hours) service most days from the *gare routière* by the Grande Mosquée. Think twice before attempting this during the rains. Equally strenuous is the appalling road south to Foumban, run by Alliance Voyages (CFA11,000, around 15 hours).

Garoua

Garoua is a pleasant enough spot to spend the night or wait for a vehicle transfer, which is the extent of most people's plans here. You may need to make a stopover if you're overlanding into Chad; pay a visit to the **Chadian consulate** (☎2227 3128) for visas, a far better place to get a visa than the embassy in Yaoundé.

Near the port, **Auberge Hiala Village** (☎2227 2407; Rue Cicai; r CFA5000-8000; P ❄) has decent self-contained rooms, with a good bar and restaurant. **Super Restaurant** (Rte de Maroua; mains from CFA1000) is a breezy place, with decent food and juices.

Several bus agencies run daily to Maroua (CFA2500, 2½ hours), and N'Gaoundéré (CFA3500, five hours), while Camair.Co flies to Yaoundé and Douala.

Maroua

Red and brown streets of sand run like dry riverbeds between rounded beige buildings while a cast of Fulani and Chadians in robes of sky blue, electric purple and blood red populate the chaos. This is Maroua, Cameroon's northernmost major town and its best base for exploring the extreme North Province, particularly the Mandara Mountains, as well as a good place to plan border crossings into Nigeria and Chad.

Tours

Maroua has numerous tour operators that can arrange hiking in the Mandara Mountains and visits to Parc National du Waza.

Fagus Voyages GUIDED TOURS
(☎9986 1871, 9616 6070; www.fagusvoyages.ch) Swiss-owned company offering safaris to nearby national parks.

Jean-Luc Sini GUIDED TOURS
(☎7143 8603, 9985 5328; sinijeanluc@yahoo.fr) Runs sightseeing and trekking tours to the villages of the Mandara Mountains.

Safari Kirdi GUIDED TOURS
(☎9976 8395, 7764 4831) English-speaking Mr Dabala can arrange drivers, guides and safaris to the Mandara Mountains and national parks.

Sleeping

Relais Ferngo GUESTHOUSE **$**
(☎9452 8488, 2229 2153; off Blvd de Diarenga; r CFA6000; P ❄) By far the best budget choice in town: sleep in spacious, whitewashed *boukarous* in the shade of willowy neem trees and shower in the alfresco but walled-off bathrooms. There's a busy bar at the back and guides offering tours often hang out here.

Residence Walya GUESTHOUSE **$**
(☎9991 6523, 2229 2026; residencewalya@yahoo.fr; off Blvd de Diarenga; r CFA12,000; ❄ @ 🛜) This recently opened guesthouse in a pristine courtyard off a sandy side street offers excellent, bright and clean rooms. There's no hot water, but it's well located and friendly.

★ **Relais de la Porte Mayo** HOTEL **$$**
(☎9950 0149, 2229 2692; Pont Rouge; s/d/apt CFA15,000/18,00/19,500; P ❄ @) Streets ahead of anywhere else in town, it's frankly amazing that a place like this exists in a town like Maroua. French run, the Porte Mayo has bundles

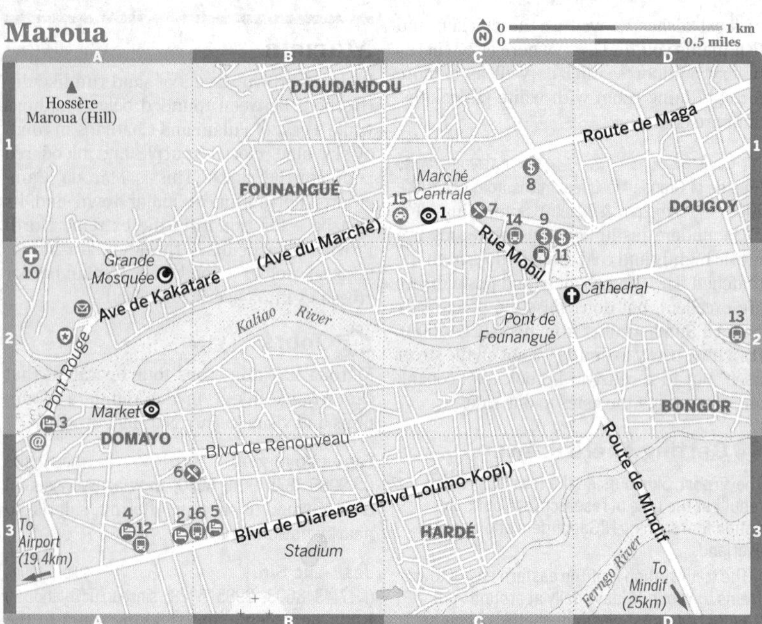

Maroua

Sights

1 Marché Centrale C1

Sleeping

2 Hotel Le Sahel A3
3 Relais de la Porte Mayo A2
4 Relais Ferngo A3
5 Residence Walya B3

Eating

6 Brochette and Grilled Fish Stalls A3
Relais de la Porte Mayo .... (see 3)
7 Restaurant Le Baobab C1

Information

8 Bicec Bank C1
9 CCA Bureau de Change C1
10 Meskine Hospital A2
11 SGBC Bank C1

Transport

12 Alliance Voyages A3
13 Gare Routière for Kousséri, Banki & Points North D2
14 Star Express C1
15 Taxi Stand C1
16 Touristique Express B3

of charm with its relaxed, modern-amenities-but-you're-still-in-the-Sahel kinda vibe, with roomy *boukarous,* an excellent restaurant-bar and friendly staff. A true oasis in the middle of dusty Maroua. Internet is by cable only.

Hotel Le Sahel HOTEL $$
(☎2215 3901, 2229 2960; Blvd de Diarenga; r CFA15,000-25,000, ste 50,000; P ❄ @ 📶) The cheapest rooms here will get you fairly dark and forlorn cells at the back of this otherwise impressive property, but they're still decent value and allow you the perks of the hotel such as the pool, courtyard bar and wi-fi. The rooms in the main building are far better, with balconies and both light and space in most.

Eating & Drinking

Maroua doesn't have many eating options, but there are plenty of bars, the liveliest of which are strung along Blvd de Renouveau. Several stalls on Blvd de Renouveau offer *brochettes* and grilled fish.

Restaurant Le Baobab AFRICAN $
(dishes CFA2000-4000; ⏰7am-11pm) This pleasant spot by the main market has outdoor seating under a thatched roof, a friendly atmosphere and good food, including a nightly buffet. Check what's available – the lunchtime menu can be limited.

Relais de la Porte Mayo FRENCH **$$**
(dishes CFA4000-8000; ⏲7am-11pm) For upscale dining, this is Maroua's best option, popular with the local French community. The restaurant has great French options, including a good-value daily set meal. Tables are scattered around outside in the charming garden.

Information

If your hotel doesn't have wi-fi try **Braouz** (internet per hr CFA750).

For medical emergencies, try Meskine Hospital, southwest of town off the Garoua road.

Maroua's banks can be reluctant to change even cash euros. If the main banks won't help, try CCA Bureau de Change next to SGBC Bank. The latter also has an ATM, as does **Bicec Bank** (Rte de Maga).

Getting There & Away

Flights with Camair.Co connect Maroua with Douala via Yaoundé (CFA115,000 to both cities) three times a week. The airport is 20km south of town along the Garoua road (CFA3000 in a chartered taxi, if you can find one).

Touristique Express and Alliance Voyages have several daily buses to Garoua (CFA2500, 2½ hours) and N'Gaoundéré (CFA6000, eight hours). You can book tickets for the N'Gaoundéré–Yaoundé train here at the same time. Several other bus agencies operate along the N'Gaoundéré route, with depots on the same road; Star Express in the town centre is also good.

Plentiful transport to Mokolo (CFA1000, 1½ hours) and less frequently to Rhumsiki (CFA2000, around three hours) departs from Carrefour Parrah in Djarangol at the southern end of town.

Transport to Kousséri for the Chad border (CFA3500, five hours) departs from the *gare routière* on Maroua's eastern edge. Minibuses to Banki for the Nigerian border (CFA2000, two hours) also depart from here.

Mandara Mountains

Basalt cliffs dot a volcanic plain, dust storms conceived on the Nigerian border sweep out of the sunset onto thorn trees, red rock cairns and herds of brindle cattle...and frankly, you wouldn't be half surprised to see a cowboy or a dragon or both pass across this awesome, evocative landscape. The Mandara Mountains run west from Maroua to the Nigerian border and have become very popular – justifiably so – with Africa hikers.

The villages that dot these ranges are as captivating as the vistas they are built on, including **Rhumsiki**, with its striking mountain scenery; **Djingliya** and **Koza**, set against steep terraced hillsides; **Tourou**, known for the calabash hats worn by local women; and **Maga**, with its domed houses made entirely of clay. **Mora** has a particularly notable weekly market. Hiking between villages is one of the best ways to appreciate the scenery and culture alike.

Rhumsiki is the main entrance point for visitors to the Mandara Mountains, and is the one place where there's a tangible feel of a tourist scene (although in Cameroon this is a relative term).

There's accommodation in Rhumsiki, Mokolo, Mora, Waza, Maga and a few other villages, but otherwise no infrastructure. If you're travelling independently, allow plenty of time and plan to be self-sufficient with food and water. Local minibuses usually set off around 6am. *Moto-taxis* are sometimes the only option for getting around.

For those with limited time, travel agencies in Maroua can organise visits, although it's just as easy to arrange things on the spot in Rhumsiki or Mokolo, which will ensure that more of the money you spend is pumped directly into the local economy. Expect to pay around CFA9000 per day, including guide, simple meals and accommodation.

Parc National du Waza

The most accessible of Cameroon's national parks, **Parc National du Waza** (admission CFA5000, vehicle CFA2000, camera CFA2000; ⏲6am-6pm 15 November-15 May) is also the best for viewing wildlife. While it can't compare with East African parks, you're likely to see elephants, hippos, giraffes, antelopes and – with luck – lions. Late March to April is the best time for viewing, as the animals congregate at water holes before the rains. Waza is also notable for its particularly rich birdlife. The park is closed during the rainy season.

A guide (CFA5000) is obligatory in each vehicle. Walking isn't permitted.

The park entrance is signposted and about 400m off the main highway. Unless you have your own vehicle, the best way to visit is to hire a vehicle in Maroua (about CFA30,000 per day plus petrol). A 4WD vehicle is recommended.

Accessing the park by public transport is difficult; any bus between Maroua and Kousséri should be able to drop you off at the park turn-off, but after that you'll be reliant

DON'T MISS

EATING WELL IN RHUMSIKI

In Rhumsiki make a beeline for **Vegetarian Carnivore** (mains CFA2500), at the entrance to the village. Here you'll be met by friendly, English-speaking Kodji, who runs one of Cameroon's most innovative and charming restaurants. All the produce comes from Rhumsiki (much of it from the kitchen garden behind the outdoor eating area) and is prepared to order whenever guests come. The freshly made bread is the restaurant's calling card, and the Cameroonian vegetable pizza is superb. As its name suggests, both carnivores and vegetarians are well catered for, and if you're tired, you can even take a nap in one of the hammocks strung up in the garden, or take a room (CFA2500) for the night.

on hitching a lift into the park itself, which is likely to involve a long wait.

Sleeping

Waza can easily be done as a day trip from Maroua if you start early (bring a packed lunch). Otherwise, there are a few places to stay near the park entrance.

There's (very) basic accommodation in Waza village, just north of the park entrance.

Centre d'Accueil de Waza LODGE $
(☎2229 2207; campsites per person CFA3000, r CFA8000) This simple place at the park entrance has accommodation in no-frills two-person *boukarous* with shared bathroom facilities. Meals can be arranged (CFA2000) and there is a small kitchen.

Campement de Waza LODGE $$
(☎2229 1646, in Maroua 2229 1646, in Waza 7765 7717; r CFA18,000; ❄) Perched on a hill amid smooth boulders are these *boukarous,* with views that stretch out to the scrub plains and some lizards thrown in gratis. The huts are comfy, staff helpful and the on-site restaurant good for sinking a beer post lion-spotting.

EASTERN CAMEROON

Cameroon's remote east is wild and untamed. Seldom visited by travellers, it's very much a destination for those with plenty of time and the stamina to back up an appetite for adventure. There's little infrastructure and travel throughout is slow and rugged, with dense green forest and red laterite earth roads. The rainforest national parks are the main attraction, along with routes into the Central African Republic and Congo.

Bertoua

The capital of East Province, Bertoua is a genuine boomtown, born of logging and mining. Here you'll find all the facilities lacking elsewhere in the region, including banks and sealed roads.

The town's best hotel is **Hotel Mansa** (☎2224 1650; Mokolo II; r CFA25,000-35,000; ❄≋), which comes complete with an artificial lake, satellite TV and a tennis court. It's definitely worth a splurge if you've been lost in the forest.

Buses to Yaoundé (CFA5000, seven hours), Bélabo (for the train; CFA1000, one hour) and Garoua-Boulaï leave from the *gare routière* near the market.

Garoua-Boulaï

If you're looking for a rough African frontier town, Garoua-Boulaï is it. On the Central African Republic border, it's a place of bars, trucks and prostitutes. The *auberges* aren't recommended, so try the **Mission Catholique** (dm for a donation, r about CFA5000) instead.

There's a bus to N'Gaoundéré (CFA4000, 12 hours, one daily) during the dry season and year-round service to Bertoua; both roads are just tolerable. The Central African Republic border crossing is on the edge of Garoua-Boulaï next to the motor park.

UNDERSTAND CAMEROON

Cameroon Today

Having re-elected presidential strongman Paul Biya in a contentious yet, broadly speaking, free election in 2011, Cameroon has sealed its reputation as a stable and peaceful country.

For most people though, corruption remains Cameroon's major issue. For example, the paperwork for opening a business can take an extremely long time to process, and many people feel that paying bribes is the only way to get government services. The international anticorruption organisation, Transparency International, consistently ranks Cameroon among the world's most corrupt countries. Until this is addressed and genuine political openness permitted, Cameroon will inevitably continue to limp along.

Yet the most spoken about person in the country is none other than the first lady, Chantal Biya, who has taken on the mantle of an African Princess Diana. Her love of haute couture, her famous 'banana' haircut and high-profile charity work mean she is a staple in the national press.

History

Parts of what is now Cameroon were divided and ceded between European countries throughout the colonial era until the modern boundaries were established in 1961, creating a part-Anglophone, part-Francophone nation.

Prawns for Starters

Portuguese explorers first sailed up the Wouri River in 1472, and named it Rio dos Camarões (River of Prawns). Soon after, Fulani pastoral nomads from what is now Nigeria began to migrate overland from the north, forcing the indigenous forest peoples southwards. The Fulani migration took on added urgency in the early 17th century as they fled Dutch, Portuguese and British slave-traders.

British influence was curtailed in 1884 when Germany signed a treaty with the chiefdoms of Douala and central Bamiléké Plateau. After WWI the German protectorate of Kamerun was carved up between France and Great Britain.

Local revolts in French-controlled Cameroon in the 1950s were suppressed, but the momentum throughout Africa for throwing off the shackles of colonial rule soon took hold. Self-government was granted in French Cameroon in 1958, quickly followed by independence on 1 January 1960.

Wily Ahidjo

Ahmadou Ahidjo, leader of one of the independence parties, became president of the newly independent state, a position he was to hold until his resignation in 1982. Ahidjo ensured his longevity through the cultivation of expedient alliances, brutal repression and wily regional favouritism.

In October 1961 a UN-sponsored referendum in British-mandated northwestern Cameroon split the country in two, with the area around Bamenda opting to join the federal state of Cameroon and the remainder joining Nigeria. In June 1972 the federal structure of two Cameroons was replaced by the centralised United Republic of Cameroon – a move that is resented to this day by Anglophone Cameroonians, who feel they have become second-class citizens.

The Biya Era

In 1982 Ahidjo's hand-picked successor, Paul Biya, distanced himself from his former mentor, but adopted many of Ahidjo's repressive measures, clamping down hard on calls for multiparty democracy. Diversions such as the national football team's stunning performance in the 1990 World Cup bought him time, but Biya was forced eventually to legalise 25 opposition parties. The first multiparty elections in 25 years were held in 1992 and saw the Cameroonian Democratic People's Movement, led by Biya, hang on to power with the support of minority parties. International observers alleged widespread vote-rigging and intimidation; such allegations were repeated in elections in 1999, 2004 and, most recently, 2011.

Culture

It's hard to pigeonhole more than 280 distinct ethnolinguistic groups divided by colonial languages, Christianity and Islam and an urban-rural split into one identity. The Cameroonian psyche is, ultimately, anything and everything African – diversity is the key.

There's a distinct cultural and political gap between the Francophone and Anglophone parts of Cameroon, albeit one felt predominantly by the Anglophone minority, who complain of discrimination in education (most universities lecture in French only) and in the workplace.

A few characteristics do seem shared across Cameroon's divides. Traditional social structures dominate life. Local chiefs (known as *fon* in the west or *lamido* in the north) wield considerable influence, and when travelling in places that don't receive many tourists, it's polite to announce your presence.

Many Cameroonians demonstrate a half-laconic, half-angry sense of frustration with the way their country is run. Many are aware that while Cameroon is doing well compared with its neighbours, it could be immeasurably better off if corruption didn't curtail so much potential. Mixed in with this frustration is a resignation ('such is life'), expressed as serenity in good times, but simmering rage in bad times.

Meanwhile, the arrival of Chinese immigrants in great numbers – especially visible in Yaoundé and Douala – is bringing an even richer dash of multiculturalism to this already incredibly multiethnic society.

Arts & Crafts

Cameroon has produced a few of the region's most celebrated artists: in literature, Mongo Beti deals with the legacies of colonialism; musically, Manu Dibango is the country's brightest star.

Woodcarving makes up a significant proportion of traditional arts and crafts. The northwestern highlands are known for their carved masks. These are often representations of animals, and it's believed that the wearers of the masks can transform themselves and take on the animal's characteristics and powers. Cameroon also has some highly detailed bronze- and brasswork, particularly in Tikar areas north and east of Foumban. The areas around Bali and Bamessing (both near Bamenda), and Foumban, are rich in high-quality clay, and some of Cameroon's finest ceramic work originates here.

Sport

Cameroon exploded onto the world's sporting consciousness at the 1990 World Cup when the national football team, the Indomitable Lions, became the first African side to reach the quarter-finals. Football is truly the national obsession. Every other Cameroonian male seems to own a copy of the team's strip; go into any bar and there'll be a match playing on the TV. When Cameroon narrowly failed to qualify for the 2006 World Cup, the country's grief was almost tangible. In contrast, when Cameroon qualified for the 2010 World Cup, the nation exploded into wild celebration. This qualification marked the sixth time Cameroon had entered the tournament, setting a record for any African nation.

Food & Drink

Cameroonian cuisine is more functional than flavourful. The staple dish is some variety of peppery sauce served with starch – usually rice, pasta or *fufu* (mashed yam, corn, plantain or couscous). One of the most popular sauces is *ndole,* made with bitter leaves similar to spinach and flavoured with smoked fish.

Grilled meat and fish are eaten in huge quantities. Beer is incredibly popular and widely available, even in the Muslim north.

A street snack of fish or *brochettes* (kebabs) will rarely cost more than CFA1500. In sit-down restaurants and business hotels outside of the major cities, expect to pay around CFA5000 to CFA7000 for a full meal; that can climb to CFA10,000 or more in Yaoundé and Douala.

Environment

Cameroon is geographically diverse. The south is a low-lying coastal plain covered by swaths of equatorial rainforest extending east towards the Congo Basin. Heading north, the sparsely populated Adamawa Plateau divides the country in two. To the plateau's north, the country begins to dry out into a rolling landscape dotted with rocky escarpments that are fringed to the west by the barren Mandara Mountains. That range represents the northern extent of a volcanic chain that forms a natural border with Nigeria down to the Atlantic coast, often punctuated with stunning crater lakes. One active volcano remains in Mt Cameroon, at 4095m the highest peak in West Africa.

There is a range of wildlife, although more exotic species are in remote areas. Lions prowl in Parc National du Waza in the north, and elephants stomp through the southern and eastern jungles. Of note are several rare primate species, including the Cross River gorilla, mainland drill, chimpanzees and Preuss' red colobus.

Bushmeat has traditionally been big business in Cameroon. While there have been crackdowns on the trade both here and abroad (African expats are some of the main consumers of bushmeat), it has not been entirely stamped out.

SURVIVAL GUIDE

Directory A–Z

ACCOMMODATION

Cameroon has a decent range of accommodation options, from simple *auberges* (hostels) and dorm beds in religious missions to luxury hotels. Expect to pay around CFA15,000 for a decent single room with bathroom and fan. Most hotels quote prices per room – genuine single and twin rooms are the exception rather than the norm.

In Cameroon, budget accommodation costs up to CFA15,000 for a double room, midrange from CFA15,000 to CFA30,000 and top end from CFA30,000. Rather than seasonal rates, most hotels in Kribi and Limbe generally charge more during holidays and weekends.

ACTIVITIES

Hiking is a big drawcard in Cameroon. The two most popular hiking regions are Mt Cameroon near the coast and the Mandara Mountains in the north. The Ring Road near Bamenda also offers great hiking possibilities, but you'll need to be self-sufficient here.

BUSINESS HOURS

Banks From 7.30am or 8am to 3.30pm Monday to Friday.

Businesses From 7.30am or 8am until 6pm or 6.30pm Monday to Friday, generally with a one- to two-hour break sometime between noon and 3pm. Most are also open from 8am to 1pm (sometimes later) on Saturday.

Government offices From 7.30am to 3.30pm Monday to Friday.

EMBASSIES & CONSULATES

A number of embassies and consulates are located in Yaoundé. Australians and New Zealanders should contact the Canadian High Commission in case of an emergency.

Canadian Embassy (☎2223 2311; Ave de l'Indépendance, Immeuble STC-TOM, Pl de l'Hôtel de Ville)

Central African Republic Embassy (Map p242; ☎2220 5155; Rue 1863, Bastos)

Chadian Embassy (Map p242; ☎2221 0624; Rue Joseph Mballa Eloumden, Bastos)

Congolese Embassy (Map p242; ☎2223 2458; Rue 1815, Bastos)

Equatorial Guinean Embassy (Map p242; ☎2221 0884; Rue 1805, Bastos)

French Embassy (☎2222 7900; Rue Joseph Atemengué, near Pl de la Réunification)

Gabonese Embassy (Map p242; ☎2220 2966; Rue 1816, Bastos)

German Embassy (Map p242; ☎2221 7292; Ave Charles de Gaulle, Centre Ville)

PRACTICALITIES

- **Electricity** Supply is 220V and plugs are of the European two-round-pin variety.
- **Languages** French throughout the country, English in the northwest and some 280 local languages.
- **Newspapers** The *Cameroon Tribune* is the government-owned bilingual daily. The thrice-weekly *Le Messager* (in French) is the main independent newspaper.
- **Radio & TV** Most broadcast programming is government run and in French, through Cameroon Radio-TV Corporation (CRTV). TVs at top-end hotels often have CNN or French news stations.

Nigerian Embassy (Map p242; ☎2223 4551; Rue Joseph Mballa Eloumden, Bastos)

UK Embassy (Map p242; ☎2222 0545; Ave Churchill, Centre Ville)

US Embassy (Map p244; ☎2220 1500; Ave Rosa Parks, Centre Ville)

EMERGENCIES

The number for all emergencies is ☎112, but it really only applies in big cities.

FESTIVALS & EVENTS

The biggest festival celebrated in Cameroon is Tabaski (p255), with most festivities taking place in Foumban.

Each February Cameroonian and international athletes gather for the **Race of Hope** to the summit of Mt Cameroon, attracting large crowds of spectators. Considerably faster than the leisurely hike most people opt for, winners usually finish in a staggering 4½ hours for men and 5½ hours for women. For more information contact Fako Tourist Board (p251) in Limbe or the **Fédération Camerounaise d'Athlétisme** (☎2222 4744) in Yaoundé.

INTERNET ACCESS

Internet access can be found in any town of a reasonable size. Connections range from decent to awful, and costs average CFA300 to CFA600 per hour.

MONEY

The unit of currency is the Central African Franc (CFA), which is pegged to the West African Franc. Cash is king in Cameroon, especially in remote regions where it's the only way to pay – bring plenty of euros. Banks regularly refuse to change travellers cheques, and charge around 5% commission when they do. Moneychangers on the street in Douala and Yaoundé will change money at good rates and without taxes or commission, but there's always an element of risk to such transactions.

Most towns now have at least one ATM, which is always tied to the Visa network. Banks won't generally offer cash advances on credit cards. If you get stuck, Western Union has branches throughout Cameroon for international money transfers.

Express Exchange moneychangers change travellers cheques and US dollars; there are branches in many towns across the country.

POST

International post is fairly reliable for letters, but international couriers should be preferred for packages – there are branches in all large towns.

PUBLIC HOLIDAYS

New Year's Day 1 January
Youth Day 11 February
Easter March/April
Labour Day 1 May
National Day 20 May
Assumption Day 15 August
Christmas Day 25 December

Islamic holidays are also observed throughout Cameroon; dates change yearly for these.

SAFE TRAVEL

The major cities, Douala and Yaoundé, both have reputations for petty crime, especially in the crowded central areas. The roads pose a greater risk, with plenty of badly maintained vehicles driven at punishing speeds.

Scams and official corruption are a way of life in Cameroon; keep your guard up and maintain a sense of humour. It's theoretically a legal requirement to carry your passport with you at all times. In practice the police rarely target travellers, however.

TELEPHONE

All Cameroonian telephone numbers have eight digits. Mobile numbers begin with 7, 8 or 9. There are no city area codes in Cameroon – all landline numbers begin with a 2 or 3. It's quite easy to buy a SIM card for an unlocked mobile phone to make local calls. MTN and Orange are the main national networks.

VISAS

Visas are required for all travellers and must be bought prior to arrival in the country. At Cameroonian embassies in neighbouring countries, visas are issued quickly for around US$60. Applications in Europe and the US will require a confirmed flight ticket, a hotel reservation and proof of funds for the trip (a copy of a recent bank statement should suffice).

Visa Extensions

You can obtain visa extensions at the **Ministry of Immigration** (Map p244; ☎222 2413; Ave Mdug-Fouda Ada) in Yaoundé, where one photo plus CFA15,000 is required.

Visas for Onward Travel

Visas available in Yaoundé for neighbouring African countries include the following:

Central African Republic A one-month visa costs FA55,000 and takes 48 hours to process.

Chad The embassy in Yaoundé is unhelpful and generally only issues visas to residents. The Garoua consulate is a far better place to try (CFA50,000).

Congo A 15-day visa costs CFA50,000, three months costs CFA100,000. An invitation is required and processing takes 48 hours.

Equatorial Guinea Does not generally issue visas to nonresidents or people with an Equatorial Guinea embassy in their home country.

Gabon A one-month visa costs CFA50,000; unlike at many Gabonese embassies, a hotel reservation is not required here.

Nigeria In Yaoundé a one-month visa costs CFA45,000 to CFA60,000 and takes 48 hours to process, and you'll need an invitation.

ℹ Getting There & Away

AIR

Both Yaoundé and Douala have international airports linking Cameroon to major cities in Africa and Europe. The national carrier of Cameroon is **Camair-Co** (www.camair-co.cm), which flies to Libreville, N'Djaména, Malabo, Brazzaville, Lagos, Cotonou, Kinshasa and Paris. There is a departure tax of CFA10,000 payable on all international flights.

LAND

Neighbouring countries' borders are open, but the border with Congo is sometimes closed, so check in advance.

Central African Republic

The standard, if rough, route is via Garoua-Boulaï, which straddles the border, and on to Bangui (via Bouar). An alternative is to travel to Kenzou, south of Batouri.

Chad

Travellers head to Kousséri in the north for the border near N'Djaména. Minibuses go to Kousséri from Maroua; some border officials have been known to rip travellers off.

Congo

This border is as remote as you can get, but possible to reach if it's the dry season. From Yokadouma, travel south to Sokamba, where you can catch a ferry (large enough for 4WDs) or *pirogue* (traditional canoe) across the Ngoko River to the Congolese port of Ouesso. From there, head for Pokola and the logging road to Brazzaville. If you come this way, consider visting Congo's Parc National Nouabalé-N'doki, one of the best parks in Central Africa, and relatively convenient to access from here.

Equatorial Guinea & Gabon

The main border crossings into Equatorial Guinea and Gabon are a few kilometres from each other, and are accessible from Ambam. The road splits here, with the easterly route heading for Bitam and Libreville (Gabon) and the westerly route heading for Ebebiyin and Bata (Equatorial Guinea).

The Cameroon–Equatorial Guinea border at Campo is normally closed.

Nigeria

The main crossing points are Ekok, west of Mamfe, where you cross to Mfum for shared taxis to Calabar (treacherous in the rainy season), and at Banki in the extreme north for crossings to Maiduguri.

SEA

Nigeria

A twice-weekly ferry sails from Limbe to Calabar on Monday and Thursday, and in the opposite direction every Tuesday and Friday. Boats are dangerous and not recommended.

Getting Around

AIR

Internal flights are operated by Camair-Co and connect Douala and Yaoundé to Maroua and Garoua. The hop between Yaoundé and Douala costs around CFA30,000 one way; from either city to Maroua or Garoua they will cost around CFA125,000 one way.

BUS

Agences de voyages (agency buses) run along all major and many minor routes in Cameroon. Prices are low and fixed, and on some bus lines you can even reserve a seat. From Yaoundé to Douala it costs anywhere between CFA3000 and CFA6000, depending on the class of bus you take: so called 'VIP' services have air-conditioning and aren't quite so cramped. However, some drivers are extremely reckless, and bus accidents occur all too frequently. *Taxis brousses* (bush taxis) are also popular, especially to some more remote destinations.

CAR

Driving in Cameroon is perfectly feasible, with decent roads and no police harassment. You can hire cars in all large towns, but there's more choice in Douala and Yaoundé. Car hire is very expensive, however, partly because you'll need a 4x4 for most itineraries, and this becomes essential in the rainy season. A couple of outfits in Douala include **Location Auto Joss** (☎9984 4404, 3342 8619; locationauto.joss@gmail.com; Rue Score, Bonapriso), and **Avis** (☎2230 2627) in the Hotel Akwa Palace.

TRAIN

Cameroon's rail system (Camrail) operates three main lines: Yaoundé to N'Gaoundéré, Yaoundé to Douala, and Douala to Kumba. In practice, only the first is of interest to travellers, as it's the main way to get between the southern and northern halves of the country.

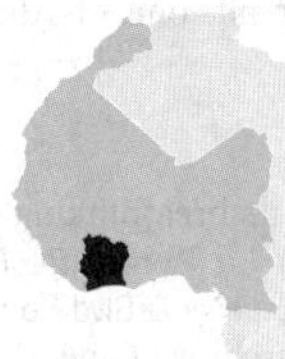

Côte d'Ivoire

☎225 / POP 21.9 MILLION

Includes ➡

Best Places to Eat

- Aboussouan (p273)
- Mille Maquis (p271)
- Des Gateaux et Du Pain (p273)

Best Places to Stay

- La Licorne (p271)
- Beneath the forest canopy, Parc National de Taï (p279)
- Le Wafou (p271)

Why Go?

Blighted by recent conflict but bejewelled by beaches and rainforests, it would be a shame to sidestep Cote d'Ivoire because of its baggage.

Cote d'Ivoire is a stunner, shingled with starfish-studded sands, and forest roads so orange they resemble strips of bronzing powder.

In the south, the Parc National de Taï hides secrets, species and nut-cracking chimps under the boughs of its trees, while the peaks and valleys of Man offer a highland climate, fresh air and local art.

The beach resorts of low-key Assinie and arty Grand Bassam were made for weekend retreats from Abidjan, the capital in all but name, where lagoons wind their way between skyscrapers and cathedral spires pierce the blue heavens.

When to Go

Abidjan

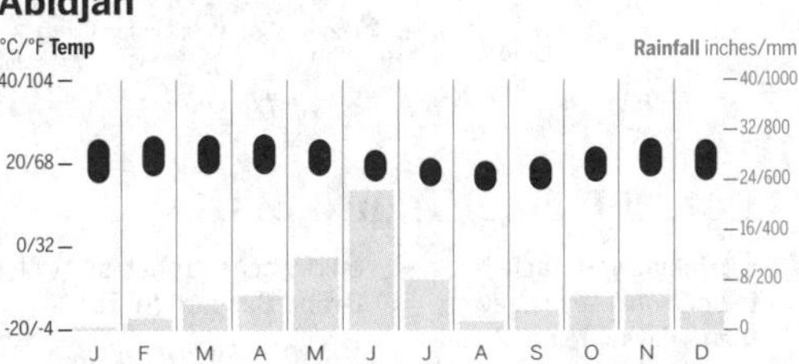

May–Jul Storms to rival those in Oct–Nov; be prepared for buckets of rain and lightning.

Jun–Oct Wet in the north but humid with bursts of rain in the south. Temperatures about 28°C.

Dec–Feb Prime beach season, with temperatures hitting 30°C and not a cloud in the sky.

ABIDJAN

POP 4.5 MILLION

Côte d'Ivoire's economic engine is strapped between lagoons and waterways, overlooking the crested waves of the Atlantic. At first glimpse, you wonder if these shiny scrapers can really be in West Africa.

Although Abidjan took a beating during the 2011 crisis, the engine rattled on, and new bars, bistros and hotels are opening regularly; this is, after all, one of Africa's sleekest party cities.

Sights

Abidjan gets props for its breathtaking skyline. It all started with **La Pyramide** (Map p274; cnr Ave Franchet d'Esperey & Blvd Botreau-Roussel), by the Italian architect Olivieri.

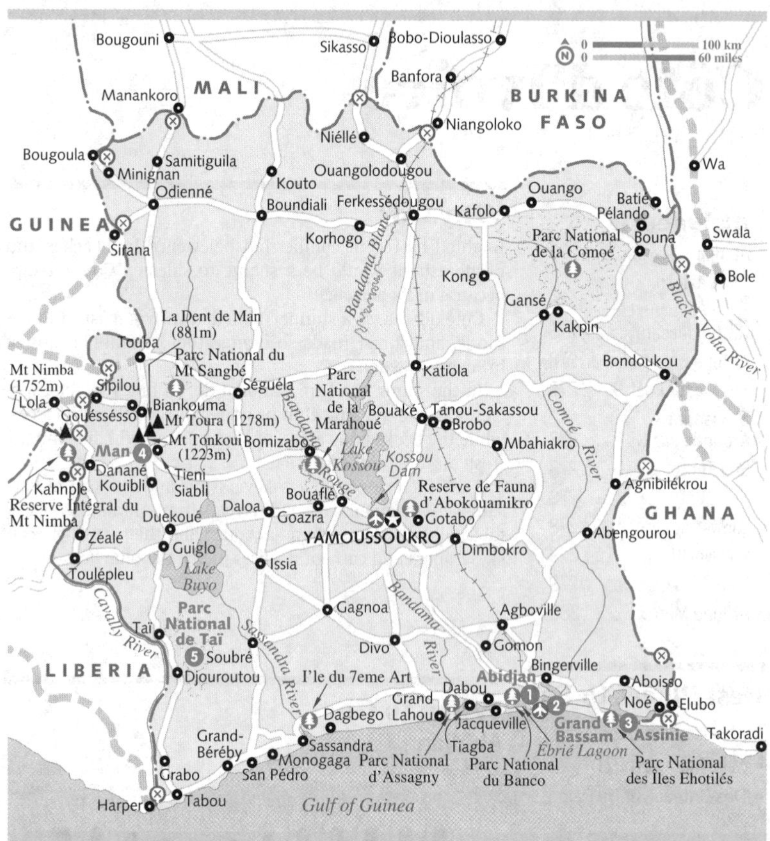

Côte d'Ivoire Highlights

1. Taking your taste buds to *poisson braisé* heaven then swaying to the sweet sounds of *coupé-decalé* in the shadow of the stunning skyline in **Abidjan** (p270).
2. Tapping into Côte d'Ivoire's artistic vibe, visiting galleries and the quirky beachfront bistros of **Grand Bassam** (p275).
3. Lazing in a *pirogue*, watching surfers slide to shore and tucking into fresh seafood under the stars of **Assinie** (p278).
4. Hiking to the point where three West African countries converge and feasting upon the green fields below, home to mask and jewellery makers, in **Man** (p279).
5. Exploring the dense **Parc National de Taï** (p279), home to a colony of nut-cracking chimps.

Cathedrale St Paul CHURCH
(Map p272; Blvd Angoulvant, Le Plateau; 8am-7pm) FREE Designed by the Italian Aldo Spiritom, the Cathedrale St Paul is a bold and innovative modern cathedral. The stained glasswork is as warm and rich as that inside the Yamoussoukro basilica.

Musée National MUSEUM
(Map p272; Blvd Nangul Abrogoua, Le Plateau; admission CFA2000; 9am-5pm Tue-Sat) This museum houses an interesting collection of traditional art and craftwork, including wooden statues and masks, pottery, ivory and bronze.

Sleeping

La Nouvelle Pergola HOTEL $
(21-753501; Blvd de Marseille/Rue Pierre et Marie Curie; d CFA30,000;) For reasonable rooms on a budget, La Nouvelle Pergola is an OK bet. There are over 130 rooms in this complex, which includes a pool and nightclub, and there's wi-fi and the usual creature comforts, although few of Côte d'Ivoire's charms.

Le Marly BUNGALOW $$
(21-258552; Blvd de Marseille, Zone 4; s/d/ste CFA40,000/50,000/60,000; P) Le Marly offers simple plantation-style huts in a pretty garden setting. At the end of a short track just off Blvd de Marseille.

Hotel Onomo HOTEL $$
(08-939377; Blvd de l'Aéroport Félix Houphouet Boigny; d from CFA51,000) Within spitting distance of the airport, the Onomo – a chain hotel present in several African cities – is a reliable bet regardless of whether you have an early flight to catch. The rooms are sleek and comfortable, with a nod to local style, and there's fast wi-fi, a good restaurant and midrange hotel service.

★**La Licorne** BOUTIQUE HOTEL $$
(Map p272; 22-410730; www.licogriff.com; Rue des Jardins, Deux Plateaux Vallons; r CFA55,000-70,000; P@) La Licorne, like its sister hotel Le Griffon around the corner, is a pretty boutique hotel run by a friendly French family. Rooms are individually decorated, and there's wi-fi, a bar, a hot tub, book exchange and a decent restaurant.

★**Le Wafou** BOUTIQUE HOTEL $$$
(21-256201; Blvd de Marseille, Zone 4; standard r/ste CFA55,000/125,000; P) If the Flintstones won the lottery and moved to West Africa, they'd live somewhere like this. Set in large grounds, Le Wafou's gorgeous bungalows take cues from traditional Dogon villages in neighbouring Mali. At night you can enjoy great food and wine poolside. A hit with kids, too.

Novotel HOTEL $$$
(20-318000; www.novotel.com; 10 Ave du Général de Gaulle; r from CFA70,000; P@) During the 2011 conflict, soldiers loyal to ex-leader Laurent Gbagbo stormed the Novotel, terrorising journalists sheltering inside. Don't let that dissuade you from staying here; there's a reason the Novotel was their place of choice, including smart rooms, four-star amenities and a large outdoor pool, all in the heart of Le Plateau. And great security.

Le Pullman HOTEL $$$
(Map p274; 20-302020; www.sofitel.com; Rue Abdoulaye Fadiga, Le Plateau; r from CFA115,000; P@) This is the best of the upmarket chain hotels. Plush rooms equipped with wi-fi and everything you could possibly need.

Eating

Don't miss **Mille Maquis** (Map p272), an energy-infused local strip of *maquis* (rustic open-air restaurants) offering fresh Ivorian dishes served with a side of banter, at Place de la République and at Treicheville's Maquis Rue 19. There are two useful supermarkets: **Cash Center** (Map p274) and **Hypermarché Sococé** (Map p272; Blvd Latrille).

SET YOUR BUDGET

Budget

- Basic hotel room CFA12,00
- Plate of *poisson braisé* CFA800
- Coffee from street vendor CFA200
- Shared taxi in Abidjan CFA300

Midrange

- Room with air-con CFA30,000
- Two-course meal CFA12,000
- Glass of wine CFA3000
- Private taxi hire, per hour CFA3500

Top End

- Hotel room with mod cons CFA60,000
- Meal for two with wine and dessert CFA50,000
- Cocktail in nightclub CFA5500
- 4x4 rental per day CFA65,000, plus petrol

Abidjan

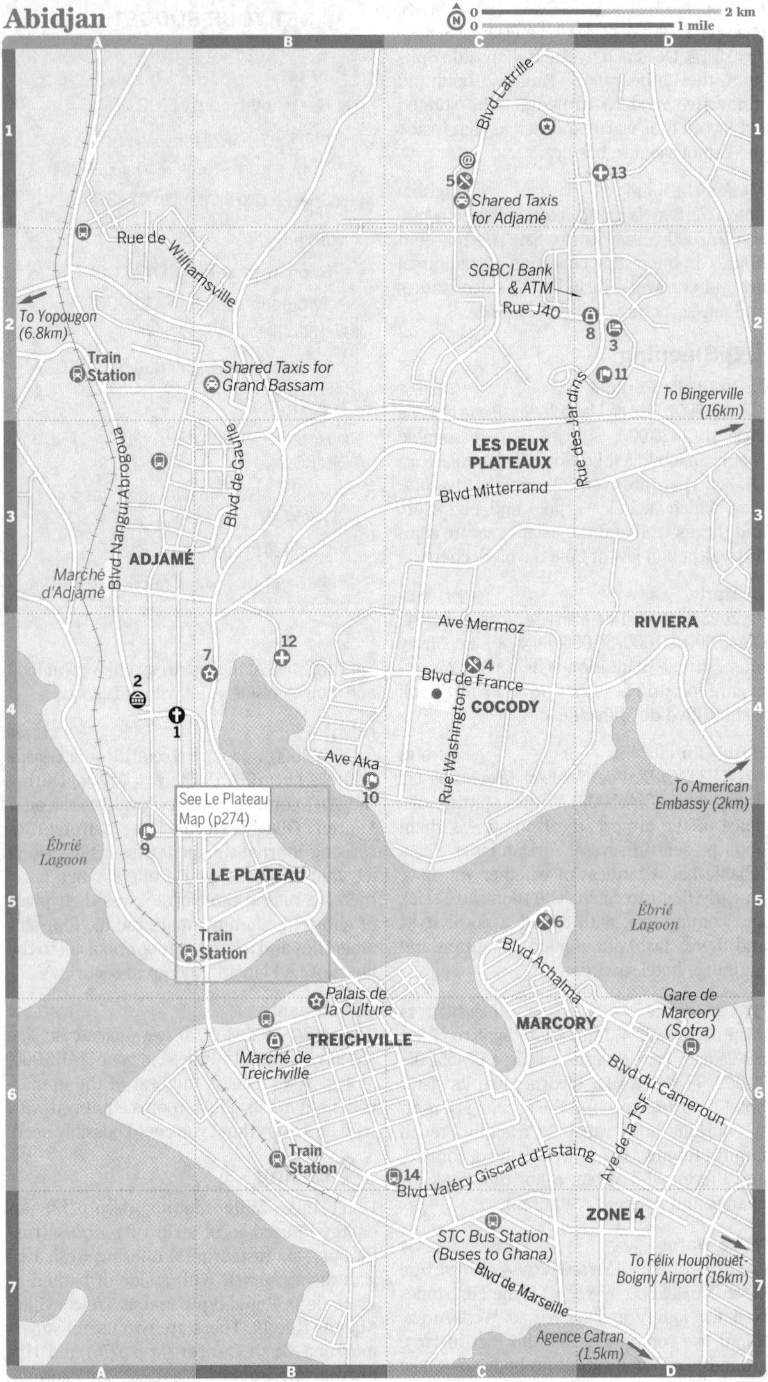

0 2 km
0 1 mile

A B C D
1 2 3 4 5 6 7

Blvd Latrille
5 Shared Taxis for Adjamé
13
Rue de Williamsville
SGBCI Bank & ATM
Rue J40
8
3
11
To Yopougon (6.8km)
Train Station
Shared Taxis for Grand Bassam
Rue des Jardins
To Bingerville (16km)
LES DEUX PLATEAUX
Blvd Nangui Abrogoua
Blvd de Gaulle
Blvd Mitterrand
ADJAMÉ
Marché d'Adjamé
Ave Mermoz
RIVIERA
12
7
4
Blvd de France
2
COCODY
1
Rue Washington
Ave Aka
10
To American Embassy (2km)
See Le Plateau Map (p274)
9
Ébrié Lagoon
LE PLATEAU
6
Ébrié Lagoon
Train Station
Blvd Achalma
Palais de la Culture
TREICHVILLE
MARCORY
Gare de Marcory (Sotra)
Marché de Treichville
Blvd du Cameroun
Ave de la TSF
Train Station
14
Blvd Valéry Giscard d'Estaing
ZONE 4
STC Bus Station (Buses to Ghana)
To Félix Houphouët-Boigny Airport (16km)
Blvd de Marseille
Agence Catran (1.5km)

Abidjan

Sights

1 Cathedrale St Paul....A4
2 Musée National....A4

Sleeping

3 La Licorne....D2

Eating

4 Allocodrome....C4
5 Hypermarché Sococé....C1
6 Mille Maquis....C5

Entertainment

7 La Mostra....B4

Shopping

Espace Latrille....(see 5)
8 Galerie d'Arts Pluriels....D2

Information

9 Burkinabé Embassy....A5
10 German Embassy....B4
11 Ghanaian Embassy....D2
12 PISAM....B4
13 Polyclinique des Deux Plateaux....D1

Transport

14 Gare de Bassam....C6

Allocodrome AFRICAN $
(Map p272; Rue Washington, Cocody; mains around CFA2000; dinner) *Brochettes* (kebabs), beer and beats: this fantastic outdoor spot, with dozens of vendors grilling meats, sizzles until late.

Urban Chic CAFE $
(Rue du Docteur Blanchard; mains from CFA4500;) Get past the sultry scarlet lounge seating and you'll find a great lunch and dinner menu, and an even better Saturday brunch one.

Le Nandjelet AFRICAN $
(opposite cemetery, Blockosso; mains from CFA2000; dinner) Tucked away in Blockosso, this enchanting local spot offers good, basic fare. Make a beeline for one of the outdoor tables on the edge of the lagoon – they offer a breathtaking panorama of the Abidjan skyline.

★ **Des Gateaux et Du Pain** BAKERY $
(22-415538; Rue des Jardins, Deux Plateaux; 7am-8pm Mon-Sat;) Around the corner from La Licorne and Le Griffon hotels, this patisserie does exactly what it says: great freshly baked breads, chocolate puddings and divine fruit-topped cakes.

★ **Aboussouan** AFRICAN $$
(21-241309; Blvd Giscard-D'Estaing, Treichville; mains from CFA8000; lunch & dinner Tue-Sat;) Take Côte d'Ivoire's best *maquis* dishes, ask top chefs to prepare them and add fine, innovative touches: that's Aboussouan. Foodie heaven, and there's an excellent wine list too.

Abidjan Cafe FRENCH $$
(Map p274; 20-224434; Rue Gourgas; mains from CFA7500; lunch & dinner Tue-Sat;) This Plateau dining hall has a good French menu featuring everything from local grilled fish to *fois gras* and *créme brûlèe* infused with Nutella.

Hippopotamus FRENCH $$
(Map p274; Ave Chardy, Plateau; mains from CFA5000; noon-11pm Mon-Sun;) French bistro chain Hippopotamus has swung its meaty hips onto the Abidjan restaurant scene: come for *steak frites,* cocktails and the best burgers in town.

Drinking & Nightlife

Parker Place BAR
(06-643381; Rue Paul Langevin, Zone 4; evening Tue-Sun) Abidjan's most famous reggae bar, Alpha Blondy and Tikin Jah Fakoly played here before they were famous. The bar is still going strong and welcomes live acts most Thursday, Friday and Saturday nights (there's usually a cover charge).

Le Bidule BAR
(cnr Blvd du 7 Decembre & Rue Paul Langevin, Zone 4) Expats and travellers congregate here on weekends. It's a drinking lounge with walls the colour of Ivorian soil.

L'Acoustic LIVE MUSIC
(Rue des Jardins, Deux Plateaux) L'Acoustic's stage has held the feet of everyone from hip female vocalists to jazz and big-band ensembles. The place attracts an arty, music crowd. There's also a kitchen for late-night dinners.

La Mostra CLUB
(48-378709) Inside the Cafe de Rome complex (which also includes a hotel and a casino), La Mostra is a mainstay on the Abidjan clubbing scene, which otherwise changes regularly. Mingle with models and party people; a night here doesn't run cheap.

Shopping

Galerie d'Arts Pluriels ARTS & CRAFTS
(Map p272; 22-411506; Rue des Jardins, Deux Plateaux) This fantastic art gallery and shop is run by an Ivorian art historian. You can view

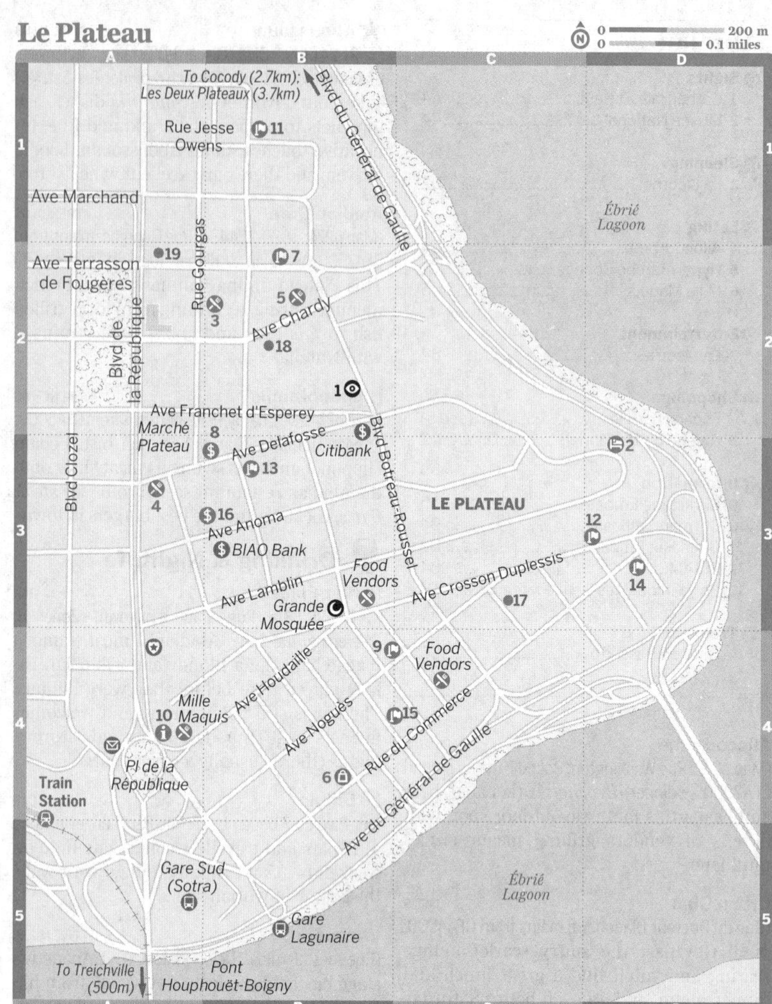

and buy paintings, sculptures and jewellery from all over the continent.

Espace Latrille DEPARTMENT STORE
(Map p272; Deux Plateaux) Contains a range of stores including the revered Hypermarché Sococé.

Woodin CLOTHING
(Map p274; ☎20-310565; Rue du Commerce, Le Plateau) This is part of a highly regarded West African group that sells quality wax-clothing. Great for gifts.

Information

INTERNET ACCESS

Most hotels, and a growing number of restaurants and bars, offer wi-fi.

Inkoo (☎21-247065; Cap Sud Centre Commercial & Gallerie Sococé, Deux Plateaux; 9am-8pm) Speedy connections, a printing centre, phone booths, faxes and scanners.

MEDICAL SERVICES

The US embassy publishes a list of recommended practitioners on its website (http://abidjan.usembassy.gov).

Le Plateau

Sights
1 La Pyramide B2

Sleeping
2 Le Pullman D3

Eating
3 Abidjan Cafe B2
4 Cash Center A3
5 Hippopotamus B2

Shopping
6 Woodin B4

Information
7 Belgian Embassy B2
8 Bicici Bank B3
9 Canadian Embassy B4
10 Côte d'Ivoire Tourisme A4
11 French Embassy B1
12 Guinean Embassy D3
13 Liberian Embassy B3
14 Malian Embassy D3
15 Senegalese Embassy C4
16 SGBCI Bank B3

Transport
17 Air France C3
Air Ivoire .... (see 10)
18 Ethiopian Airlines B2
Kenya Airways .... (see 19)
19 South African Airways A2

Polyclinique des Deux Plateaux (Map p272; ☎22-413320; Deux Plateaux)

PISAM (Polyclinique Internationale St Anne-Marie; ☎22-445132; off Blvd de la Corniche, Cocody) Recommended by UN staff. Has a 24-hour intensive-care unit.

MONEY

Euros and dollars can be changed at main branches of banks in Le Plateau. Most branches of SGBCI and Bicici have ATMs that accept Visa, MasterCard and Maestro.

Bicici Bank (Map p274; www.bibici.org; Ave Delafosse) Has an ATM.

SGBCI Bank (Map p274; www.sgbci.org; Ave Anoma) Good ATM option – accepts Visa, MasterCard and Maestro.

POST & TELEPHONE

For postal services, head to **La Poste** (Pl de la République; ⏰7.30am-noon & 2.30-4pm Mon-Fri), which also has a Western Union and poste restante. Mobile phone SIM cards are sold on the roadside all around town (from CFA2000). Inkoo has phone booths for local, national and international calls.

TOURIST INFORMATION

Côte d'Ivoire Tourisme (Map p274; ☎20-251610, 20-251600; Pl de la République, Le Plateau; ⏰7.30am-noon & 2.30-4pm Mon-Fri) There's a good map on the wall and the helpful staff will happily shower you with brochures.

TRAVEL AGENCIES

Agence Catran (☎21-759163; Blvd de Marseille, Zone 4)

Amak Agence (☎20-211755; www.amak-international.com; ground fl, Botreau Roussel Bldg, Le Plateau)

Getting There & Away

The shiny Félix Houphouët-Boigny International Airport takes all of the international air traffic. The main bus station is the chaotic Gare Routière d'Adjamé, some 4km north of Le Plateau. Most UTB and Sotra buses and bush taxis leave from here, and there's frequent transport to all major towns.

Bush taxis and minibuses for destinations east along the coast, such as Grand Bassam, Aboisso and Elubo at the Ghanaian border, leave primarily from the **Gare de Bassam** (Map p272; cnr Rue 38 & Blvd Valéry Giscard d'Estaing), south of Treichville.

Getting Around

Woro-woro (shared taxis) cost between CFA300 and CFA800, depending on the length of the journey. They vary in colour according to their allocated area. Those between Plateau, Adjamé, Marcory and Treichville, for example, are red, while those in Les Deux Plateaux and Cocody are yellow, and Yopougon's are blue.

A short hop in a cab from Le Plateau to Zone 4 costs around CFA2000. If you want to hire a taxi driver for a day, bank on anywhere between CFA15,000 and CFA30,000 depending on the strength of your negotiating skills (and the state of the economy).

THE EASTERN BEACHES

Grand Bassam

Arty and bathed in faded glory, beachside Bassam was Côte d'Ivoire's former French capital, until a yellow-fever epidemic broke out there, prompting the French to move their capital to Bingerville.

The city is laid out on a long spit of land with a quiet lagoon on one side and the turbulent Atlantic Ocean on the other. If you take a dip, watch the strong currents.

Sights

A walk through town will take you past the **colonial buildings** the city is known for; some have been restored, while others are slowly falling apart. The **Palais de Justice** (Blvd Treich-Laplene) should be your first stop. Built in 1910, it was in this building that members of Côte d'Ivoire's PDCI-RDA political group – that of Houphouët-Boigny – were arrested by the French authorities in 1949, in the struggle that preceded independence. The **Musée National du Costume** (Blvd Treich-Laplene; admission by donation), in the former governor's palace, has a nice little exhibit showing housing styles of various ethnic groups.

If you're in the market for an Ivorian painting, head to **Nick Amon's art gallery** (Blvd Treich-Laplene). One of Côte d'Ivoire's most respected contemporary artists, he'll greet you with paint-splattered clothing and a warm smile. His canvases start at around CFA50,000; profits go to an organisation that gives street kids art classes.

Augustin Édou runs a **horse-riding school** (Blvd Treich-Laplene). You can arrange riding trips (one/two hours for CFA13,000/20,000) along the coast at sunrise. Dugout-canoe trips to see traditional crab fishers, mangroves and birdlife can be arranged with local boatmen.

Sleeping & Eating

There are guesthouses spread all along Blvd Treich-Laplene, Bassam's main road.

COUPÉ-DECALÉ: CUT & RUN

Picture the scene: it's 2002 and you're at the swish l'Atlantic nightclub in Paris. Around you, tight-shirted Ivorian guys are knocking back Champagne, throwing euros into the air and grinding their hips on the dance floor.

Coupé-decalé is one of the most important music movements to hit Côte d'Ivoire. From the French verb *couper,* meaning to cheat, and *decaler,* to run away, the term loosely translates as 'cut and run'. It evolved as a comment on the shrewd but stylish Ivorian and Burkinabé guys – modern-day Robin Hoods, if you like – who fled to France at the height of the conflict in 2002, where they garnered big bucks and sent money home to their families.

They splashed the rest of their cash on the Paris club scene. It wasn't unusual for them to shower audiences with crisp notes. The late Douk Saga, one of the founders of the movement, was famous for wearing two designer suits to his shows. Halfway through, he'd strip provocatively and throw one into the crowd.

Soon this music genre took off in Côte d'Ivoire, becoming increasingly popular as the conflict raged on. With curfews in place and late-night venues closed, Ivorians started going dancing in the mornings. The more that normal life was suppressed, the more they wanted to break free from the shackles of war. *Coupé-decalé,* the who-gives-a-damn dance, allowed them to do exactly that.

Early *coupé-decalé* was characterised by repetitive vocals set to fast, jerky beats. Lyrics were either superficial, facetious or flippant – 'we don't know where we're going, but we're going anyway', sang DJ Jacab. As the trend has matured, *coupé-decalé* lyrics have become smarter, more socially aware and dripping with double and triple entendres. The movement is now a national source of pride and, above all, a comment on Ivorian society; despite years of conflict, misery and fear, Ivorians have never stopped dancing.

Today's *coupé-decalé* is cheeky, crazy and upbeat, and to fully appreciate it you should get yourself to an Abidjan dance floor. Tracks to seek out include Bablée's 'Sous Les Cocotiers', Kaysha's 'Faut Couper Decaler', 'Magic Ambiance' by Magic System, DJ Jacab's 'On Sait Pas Ou On Va', 'Guantanamo' by DJ Zidane and Douk Saga's 'Sagacité'. The latter spawned the Drogbacité dance craze, inspired by the footballer Didier Drogba. In 2006 DJ Lewis' hugely popular 'Grippe Aviaire' did for bird flu what early *coupé-decalé* did for the conflict – it replaced fear with joy.

Grand Bassam

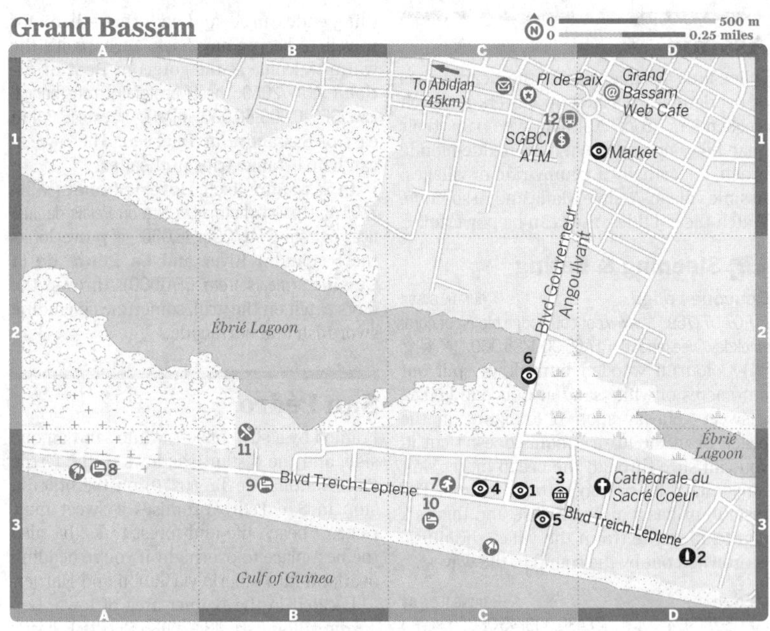

Grand Bassam

Sights

1 Mairie C3
2 Monument aux Morts D3
3 Musée National du Costume C3
4 Nick Amon's Art Gallery C3
5 Palais de Justice C3
6 Pont de la Victoire C2

Activities, Courses & Tours

7 Horse-riding School C3

Sleeping

8 Hôtel Boblin la Mer A3
9 La Madrague B3
10 Taverne la Bassamoise C3

Eating

11 La Playa B3

Transport

12 Gare Routière C1

Hôtel Boblin la Mer HOTEL $
(☎21-301418; Blvd Treich-Laplene; r with air-con CFA15,000-20,000; P ❄) Breezy and sun-washed, Boblin la Mer is easily the best value in Bassam. The rooms are decorated with masks and woodcarvings, and breakfast is served on the beach.

★ **La Madrague** HOTEL $$
(☎21-301564; Blvd Treich-Laplene; d CFA30,000) La Madrague taps into Grand Bassam's spirit, with its smart, lovingly decorated rooms. There's local art on the walls and Ivorian cloth swaddling the luxurious beds, and the humour of the owner is evident in the signs he hangs around the hotel.

Taverne la Bassamoise BUNGALOW $$
(☎21-301062; Blvd Treich-Laplene; r/bungalows incl breakfast CFA29,000/35,000; P ❄ ≋) It's worth a visit just to check out the courtyard – wooden monkeys and parrots hang from every branch of a colossal tree. Bungalows (a little shabby) are hidden underneath a canopy of bougainvillea.

La Playa AFRICAN $
(Blvd Treich-Laplene; dishes from CFA3000) A *maquis* that does a great line in upmarket versions of Senegalese and Ivorian dishes.

Getting There & Away

Shared taxis (CFA700, 40 minutes) leave from Abidjan's Gare de Bassam. In Bassam, the *gare routière* (bus station) is beside the Pl de Paix roundabout, north of the lagoon.

Assinie

Quiet little Assinie tugs at the heartstrings of overlanders, washed-up surfers and rich weekenders from Abidjan who run their quad bikes up and down its peroxide-blonde beach. It's actually a triumvirate of villages: Assinie village, Assinie Mafia and Assouindé. Watch the rip tides; they can be powerful.

Sleeping & Eating

Coucoue Lodge BUNGALOW $$
(07-077769; www.coucouelodge.blogspot.com; weekday/weekend d CFA65,000/85,000;) Colourful wooden bungalows spill out onto acres of white sand at Coucoue Lodge, a sweet getaway spot. If lounging on the beach or in the luxury rooms doesn't cut it, you can slice through the ocean on jet skis, rent inflatables or play a round of golf. The restaurant has a nice wine list, and there's a nightclub onsite (from the villas, the music is drowned out by the sound of the waves).

L'Eden BUNGALOW $$
(05-780934; s/d CFA30,000/45,000;) Laid-back L'Eden is one of Assinie's sweetest spots, sandwiched between the beach and Assinie Mafia. A good bet for a relaxed weekend away with friends, there's nice Ivorian fare on offer and cool, calm, clean, comfortable rooms.

Akwa Beach VILLA $$
(08 833 374; www.akwa-beach.com; d CFA45,000;) On the beach between Assinie and Assouindé, Akwa has sleek, comfortable rooms housed in modern whitewashed villas. There's a restaurant serving upscale French fare and a pool area with stylish beach furniture.

Getting There & Around

Coming from Grand Bassam or Abidjan, take a shared taxi to Samo (CFA2000, 45 minutes). From here you can pick up another car to Assouindé, 15 minutes away. Once there, the rest of the area is accessible by *pirogue* (traditional canoe) or shared taxi.

THE WEST COAST

Sassandra & Around

Sassandra, a low-key beach resort in the far-western corner of Côte d'Ivoire, may be a little dog-eared these days, but there's something endearing – and enduring – here, for travellers keep going back. Perhaps it's the warm welcome at the gorgeous **Best of Africa** (34-720606; best@bestofafrica.org; bungalows CFA40,000-60,000;) resort, 35km east of Sassandra at Dagbego. The owners can help arrange trips in the area.

In Sassandra itself, **Hôtel le Pollet** (34-720578; lepollet@hotmail.fr; Rte du Palais de Justice; r/ste CFA17,000/38,000;) overlooks the Sassandra River and **La Route de la Cuisine** (meals from CFA1000) throws the day's catch on the grill, sometimes including swordfish and barracuda.

San Pédro

Framed by a strip of soft, white sand on one side, and the distant shadows of the fertile Parc National de Taï (p279) on the other, a stop in San Pedro promises a sweet marriage of beach life and forest treks. It's also the best place to overnight if you're heading overland into Liberia via Tabou and Harper.

Located in the Balmer area of town, **Les Jardins d'Ivoire** (34-713186; Quartier Balmer; r CFA25,000;) has a pretty garden, swimming pool and clean, smart rooms. **Le Cannelle** (34-710539; r CFA25,000) is a little more lively and has rooms in the same price range.

UTB buses link San Pédro with Abidjan once daily (CFA5000). Shared taxis go west to the balmy **beaches** of Grand-Béréby (CFA2500) and east to Sassandra (CFA3000). For Harper, just across the Liberian border, you can take a shared taxi to Tabou (about CFA4000), then continue on by a combination of road and boat; it's not worth attempting in the rainy season.

THE CENTRE

Yamoussoukro

Yamoussoukro (or Yamkro, as it's affectionately dubbed) isn't exactly its country's cultural epicentre, but it is worth a stop here, if only to marvel at the oddity of the capital that was built on the site of former President Félix Houphouët-Boigny's ancestral village.

Sights

Yamoussoukro's spectacular **basilica** (Rte de Daloa; admission CFA2000; 8am-noon & 2-5.30pm Mon-Sat, 2-5pm Sun) will leave you

DON'T MISS

PARC NATIONAL DE TAÏ

There are many places in West Africa that could be dubbed one of the region's 'best-kept secrets', but perhaps none so as much as **Taï** (☎34-712353; www.parc-national-de-tai.org), a 5000-sq-km reserve of rainforest so dense that scientists are only just beginning to discover the wealth of flora and fauna that lies within.

Until about 2009, Taï was off limits due to the presence of militias, who set up camp beneath its birdsong-strung canopies. Now the only camp inside is an eco-camp, the year-round **Touraco Ecotel** (☎34-722299; www.parcnationaltai.com), which has a sprinkling of thatch-topped round huts and a restaurant on the edge of a forest clearing. It's early days; the camp was not yet complete at the time of research, but you can be among the first to discover Taï, taking forest hikes with local rangers, visiting the Hana River, Buya Lake and Mt Niénokoué, where you can stop at the primate research base famous for its nut-cracking chimps.

Taï is 213km from San Pédro; it's about a three-hour drive outside the rainy season. If you have your own vehicle, hit the road until you reach the village of Djouroutou, on the west side of the park. You can also reach Djouroutou via public transport, but it will take longer and you may have to change cars. In theory, there's a **shuttle** (☎34-722299) linking San Pedro to Tai, but you'll need to call ahead and make sure it's functioning before counting on it.

wide-eyed. It remains in tip-top shape, with English-speaking guides on duty. Don't forget to take your passport, which the guard holds until you leave. The **presidential palace**, where Houphouët-Boigny is now buried, can only be seen from afar. Sacred crocodiles live in the lake on its southern side and the keeper tosses them some meat around 5pm. In 2012, a veteran keeper was killed by one of the creatures during a photo op staged for UN peacekeepers.

The **tourist office** (☎30-640814; Ave Houphouët-Boigny; ⏰8am-noon & 3-6pm Mon-Fri) arranges Baoulé dancing performances in nearby villages.

Sleeping & Eating

You'll find *maquis* all over town, concentrated at the *gare routière* and by the lake. The French-owned **Bouclier de Brennus** behind SIB bank serves upmarket Gallic fare with occasional helpings of televised rugby.

Residence Berah HOTEL $
(☎30 64 17 80; r from CFA20,000; P ❄ 🛜 🏊) Over in *le quartier des millionaires* (yes, such a thing exists), Residence Berah isn't as swish as its address. But the rooms are clean and modern, with wi-fi and television, and there's a pool and restaurant.

Hôtel Président HOTEL $$$
(☎30-641582; Rte d'Abidjan; s/d/ste US$65/80/150; ❄ 🏊) Yamoussoukro's signature hotel, imposing but faded. Rooms are old but still swish, and there is an 18-hole golf course, as well as three restaurants (including a panoramic eatery on the 14th floor), four bars and a nightclub.

Getting There & Away

MTT and UTB, whose bus stations are south of town, run buses frequently to Abidjan (CFA4500), with the latter also going frequently to Bouaké (CFA3800) and once daily to Man (CFA5000) and San Pédro (CFA6000).

THE NORTH

Man

When you've had your fill of the sun and sand in the south, or the hot winds and dust in the north, head to the green, green peaks and valleys of Man. Here the air is cooler, the food lighter and the landscapes muddier: perfect hiking territory.

For local art, check out the **Tankari Gallery** and **Jacky Gallery** in the centre of town.

Hôtel Amointrin (☎33-792670; Rte du Lycé e Professionel; r standard/superior CFA14,000/16,000; ❄) is probably Man's smartest hotel; the rooms come with hot water and pretty views out over the mountains. The centrally located **Hôtel Leveneur** (☎33-791776; Rue de l'Hôtel Leveneur; r CFA12,000; ❄) has the dishevelled backpacker thing down pat, though we suspect it's not deliberate. Less crumpled, clean and with all mod cons is **Goulou Marie** (☎33-784010; Rte du Lycee; r with air-con from CFA10,000; ❄).

Man has a host of decent *maquis* – **Le Boss** and **Maquis Jardin Bis** (Rte du Lycée Professionnel) both do great *attiéké* (grated cassava; a slightly bitter couscouslike dish) and *brochettes*. The **Pâtisserie la Brioche** (Rue du Commerce; croissants CFA240) is a fine place for breakfast or morning coffee.

You can reach Abidjan by shared taxi (CFA8000) or UTB bus (CFA7000). Taxis for N'zérékoré in Guinea run via Sipilou.

Around Man

If you're considering scaling Mt Tonkoui, give **La Dent de Man** (Man's Tooth) a shot first. Northeast of town, this steep, molar-shaped mountain hits a height of 881m. Allow at least four hours for the round trip and bring snacks. The hike starts in the village of **Zobale**, 4km from Man.

At 1223m, **Mt Tonkoui** is the second-highest peak in Côte d'Ivoire. The views from the summit are breathtaking and extend to Liberia and Guinea, even during the dusty harmattan winds. The route begins about 18km from Man.

The area around Man is also famous for **La Cascade** (admission CFA300), 5km from town, a crashing waterfall that hydrates a bamboo forest. You walk a pretty paved path to reach it.

One of Man's most celebrated neighbours is **Silacoro**, about 110km north, which is famous for its stilt dancing.

UNDERSTAND CÔTE D'IVOIRE

Côte d'Ivoire Today

In November 2011 former President Laurent Gbagbo was extradited to The Hague, and charged with war crimes committed during a 2010–11 post-election conflict, in which Gbagbo had contested election results and refused to cede power to current leader Alassane Ouattara. This sparked months of violence that, according to Human Rights Watch, left 3000 people dead and 500,000 homeless. Gbagbo's trial was scheduled to begin in late 2012. Human-rights groups have alleged that atrocities, including the burning of inhabited homes and the hacking of limbs, were committed by both sides, and have called for allies of Ouattara to also be tried.

History

Côte d'Ivoire's troubles began in September 2002, when troops from the north gained control of much of the country. A truce was short-lived and fighting resumed, this time also over prime cocoa-growing areas. France sent in troops to maintain the ceasefire boundaries; meanwhile, Liberian tensions from that country's war began to spill over the border, which escalated the crisis in parts of western Côte d'Ivoire and foreshadowed future events.

In January 2003, Gbagbo and the leaders of the New Forces, a newly formed coalition of rebel groups, signed accords creating a 'government of national unity', with representatives of the rebels taking up places in a new cabinet. Curfews were lifted and French troops cleaned up the lawless western border, but the harmony was short-lived.

In March 2004 a peace deal was signed, and Guillaume Soro, formerly the secretary of the New Forces rebel coalition, was named prime minister. UN peacekeepers arrived, but on 4 November Gbagbo broke the ceasefire and bombed rebel strongholds, including Bouaké. Two days later, jets struck a French military base, killing nine French peacekeepers. In retaliation, the French destroyed much of the Ivorian air force's fleet. Government soldiers clashed with peacekeepers, while most French citizens fled, and dozens of Ivorians died.

Amid reports that Gbagbo was rebuilding his air force, a UN resolution backed his bid to stay in office until fair elections could be held. In April 2007 French peacekeepers began a staged pullback from the military buffer zone, to be replaced gradually by mixed brigades of government and rebel troops. Gbagbo declared the end of the war and the two sides moved to dismantle the military buffer zone.

In June that year a rocket attack on Prime Minister Soro's plane killed four of his aides, shaking the peace process further. Protests over rising food costs spread through the country in April 2008, causing Gbagbo to put the elections back to November. A month later, northern rebels began the long disarmament process. Just days before the planned elections, the government postponed them yet again, amid disorganised voter registration and uncertainty about the validity of identity cards.

Côte d'Ivoire began to embrace a wary peace and was looking to 2010 elections when tensions boiled over, sparking the conflict that has left the country in the state it is in today.

Culture

None of Côte d'Ivoire's conflicts have killed the population's *joie de vivre;* even in Abidjan, nightclubs remained open at the height of the fighting. Education and professional life are taken seriously in Abidjan and other large urban areas, and literature, art and creativity are valued; even in refugee camps on the Liberian border, you might come across book-club meetings and philosophical salons. In rural areas, family ties are deeply treasured and you'll meet many Ivorians who are supporting as many as 20 kin on their pay cheques.

Arts & Crafts

The definitive Ivorian craft is Korhogo cloth, a coarse cotton painted with geometrical designs and fantastical animals. Also prized are Dan masks from the Man region, and Senoufo wooden statues, masks and traditional musical instruments from the northeast.

Food & Drink

Côte d'Ivoire is blessed with a cuisine that's lighter and more flavoursome than that of its immediate coastal neighbours. There are three staples in Ivorian cooking: rice, *fufu* and *attiéké*. *Fufu* is a dough of boiled yam, cassava or plantain, pounded into a sticky paste. *Attiéké* is grated cassava and has a couscouslike texture. *Aloco,* a dish of ripe bananas fried with chilli in palm oil, is a popular street food. The most popular places to eat out are *maquis;* these are cheap, open-air restaurants, usually under thatch roofs, that grill meats each evening. *Poisson braisé,* a delicate dish of grilled fish with tomatoes and onions cooked in ginger, is a must to try.

The standard beer is Flag, but if you're after a premium lager, call for a locally brewed Tuborg or a Beaufort.

Environment

Côte d'Ivoire used to be covered in dense rainforest, but most of it was cleared during the agricultural boom, and what remains today is under attack from illegal logging. According to 2008 World Bank data, Côte d'Ivoire is still losing more than 3000 sq km of forested land per year.

Several peaks in the west rise more than 1000m, and a coastal lagoon with a unique ecosystem stretches 300km west from the Ghanaian border. The north is dry scrubland.

SURVIVAL GUIDE

 ## Directory A–Z

ACCOMMODATION

Abidjan is expensive and not always good value for money. Elsewhere in the country, you'll find better deals, but standards of comfort are generally lower.

ACTIVITIES

Several spots on the coast, most notably Assinie and Dagbego, have decent surfing. Côte d'Ivoire also has a lot to offer birdwatchers, particularly during the (European) winter migration season from December to March. For hiking, head to Man or the beautiful Parc National de Taï.

BOOKS

There is a wealth of books in French about the country's trials and tribulations. Guillaume Soro's autobiography, *Pourquoi Je Suis Devenu Rebelle* (Why I Became a Rebel), is a page-turner. *Le Peuple n'Aime pas le Peuple* (The People Don't Like the People), by Kouakou-Gbahi Kouakou, describes the conflict well.

EMERGENCIES

Fire (☎180)

Medicins Urgence (Private Company) (☎07-082626)

SOS Medecins (Private Company) (☎185)

EMBASSIES & CONSULATES

The following embassies are in Abidjan.

Belgian Embassy (☎20-210088, 20-219434; Ave Terrasson des Fougères 01, 4th fl, Immeuble Alliance) Also assists Dutch nationals.

Burkinabé Embassy (☎20-211501; Ave Terrasson de Fougères) There's also a consulate in Bouaké.

Canadian Embassy (☎20-300700; www.dfait-maeci.gc.ca/abid jan; 23 Ave Noguès,

PRACTICALITIES

- **Electricity** Voltage is 220V/50Hz and plugs have two round pins.
- **Languages** The main languages are French, Mande, Malinke, Dan, Senoufo, Baoulé, Agni and Dioula.
- **Newspapers** Among the nearly 20 daily newspapers, all in French, *Soirinfo*, *24 Heures* and *L'Intelligent d'Abidjan* steer an independent course. *Gbich!* is a satirical paper.
- **Radio** Jam (99.3FM) and Radio Nostalgie (101.1FM) play hit music. The BBC World Service broadcasts some programs in English on 94.3FM.

Immeuble Trade Centre) Also assists Australian nationals.

French Embassy (☎20-200404; www.consulfrance-abidjan.org; 17 Rue Lecoeur)

German Embassy (☎22-442030; 39 Blvd Hassan II)

Ghanaian Embassy (☎22-410288; Rue des Jardins, Deux Plateaux)

Guinean Embassy (☎20-222520; Ave Crosson Duplessis, 3rd fl, Immeuble Crosson Duplessis)

Liberian Embassy (☎20-324636; Ave Delafosse, Immeuble Taleb)

Malian Embassy (☎20-311570; Rue du Commerce, Maison du Mali)

Senegalese Embassy (☎20-332876; Immeuble Nabil, off Rue du Commerce)

FESTIVALS & EVENTS

Fête du Dipri Held in Gomon, northwest of Abidjan, in March or April. An all-night and all-the-next-day religious ceremony where people go into trances.

Fête de l'Abissa Held in Grand Bassam in October or November. A week-long ceremony honouring the dead.

HEALTH

Whether you're travelling by air or by land, you'll need a yellow-fever certificate to enter Côte d'Ivoire. If you don't have one, you'll be ushered behind a curtain for an on-the-spot jab when you arrive.

MONEY

Visa ATMs are widespread in Abidjan, Grand Bassam, Yamoussoukro and major towns. Most SGBCI branches have ATMs that accept Visa, MasterCard and sometimes Maestro. There are no banks in Assinie, but there is a branch of SGBCI (with an ATM) in Grand Bassam.

OPENING HOURS

Banks From 8am to 11.30am and 2.30pm until 4.30pm Monday to Friday.

Government offices From 7.30am to 5.30pm Monday to Friday, with breaks for lunch.

Shops From 8am to 6pm.

PUBLIC HOLIDAYS

New Year's Day 1 January

Labour Day 1 May

Independence Day 7 August

Fête de la Paix 15 November

Christmas 25 December

SAFE TRAVEL

Abidjan and other parts of the south were safe at the time of research, although pockets of tension remained. If you're heading north or to the border with Liberia, check with locals first and follow news reports: tensions flare sporadically.

Take care when walking at night; it's unwise to walk alone outside of well-populated areas. Also beware of riding in cars without a seat belt. The Atlantic has fierce currents and a ripping undertow and people drown every year – often strong, overly confident swimmers.

TELEPHONE

If you have a GSM mobile (cell) phone, you can buy SIM cards from CFA2500. Street stalls also sell top-up vouchers from CFA550. Calls generally cost between CFA25 and CFA150 per minute. The Orange network is reliable and accessible in most parts of the country, even some rural areas, although it can be expensive. The country code is 225.

VISAS

Everyone except nationals of Economic Community of West African States (Ecowas) countries must arrange a visa in advance.

Visas can be extended at **La Sureté Nationale** (Blvd de la République, Police de l'Air et des Frontières, Immeuble Douane; ⏰8am-noon & 3-5pm Mon-Fri) in Le Plateau in Abidjan.

Getting There & Away

AIR

Félix Houphouët-Boigny is Côte d'Ivoire's swish international airport, complete with wi-fi access.

Air France (AF; Map p274; ☎20-202424; www.airfrance.com; Rue Nogues, Immeuble Kharrat, Le Plateau)

Air Ivoire (VU; Map p274; ☎20-251561, 20-251400; www.airivoire.com; Pl de la République, Immeuble Le République)

Ethiopian Airlines (ET; Map p274; ☎20-215284; www.flyethiopian.com; Ave Chardy, Le Plateau)

Kenya Airways (KQ; Map p274; ☎20-320767; www.kenya-airways.com; Blvd de la République, Immeuble Jeceda, Le Plateau)

SN Brussels (SN; ☎27-232345; www.flysn.com) Off Blvd Valéry Giscard d'Estaing, Treichville.

South African Airways (SA; Map p274; ☎20-218280; www.flysaa.com; Blvd de la République, Immeuble Jeceda, Le Plateau)

LAND

Burkina Faso Passenger train services (36 hours, three times a week) run between Abidjan and Bobo-Dioulasso in Burkina Faso. Romantic in a gritty way, the Abidjan–Ouagadougou sleeper takes two days. Contact **Sitarail** (☎20-208000).

Ghana It will take you about three hours to reach the crossing at Noé from Abidjan. Note that the border shuts at 6pm promptly, accompanied by a fancy flag ceremony.

Guinea The most frequently travelled route to Guinea is between Man and N'zérékoré, either through Danané and Nzo or Biankouma and Sipilou. The Liberia–Guinea border closes at 6pm each day.

Liberia Minibuses and shared taxis make the quick hop from Danané to the border at Gbé-Nda. A bus takes this route from Abidjan to Monrovia (two days) several times a week. From Monrovia, plan on about three days to cross through Guinea and board a bus for Abidjan.

Mali Buses and shared taxis run from Abidjan, Yamoussoukro and Bouaké to Bamako, usually via Ferkessédougou, and Sikasso in Mali. The Mali–Côte d'Ivoire border closes at 6pm each day.

Getting Around

AIR

When it's running, Air Ivoire offers internal flights throughout the country, but prices can be high.

BUS

The country's large, relatively modern buses are around the same price and are significantly more comfortable than bush taxis or minibuses.

BUSH TAXI & MINIBUS

Shared taxis (ageing Peugeots or covered pick-ups, known as *bâchés*) and minibuses cover major towns and outlying communities not served by the large buses. They leave at all hours of the day, but only when full, so long waits may be required.

TRAIN

The romantically named *Bélier* and *Gazelle* trains link Abidjan with Ferkessédougou (CFA12,000, daily).

The Gambia

POP 1.8 MILLION

Includes ➡

Why Go?

The tiny sliver of Africa's smallest country is wedged into surrounding Senegal, and is seen as a splinter in its side, or the tongue that makes it speak, depending on who you talk to. For many, The Gambia is a country with beaches that invite visitors to laze and linger on package tours. But there's more than sun and surf.

Small fishing villages, nature reserves and historic slaving stations are all within easy reach of the clamorous Atlantic resorts. Star-studded ecolodges and small wildlife parks dot the inland like a green belt around the coast and The Gambia is a bird lovers' utopia: on a leisurely river cruise, you'll easily spot more than 100 species while your *pirogue* charts an unhurried course through mangrove-lined wetlands and lush gallery forests. You won't be able to resist wielding binoculars with the excellent network of guides.

Best Places to Stay

- Hibiscus House (p296)
- Ngala Lodge (p293)
- Mandina River Lodge (p296)

Best of Nature

- Abuko Nature Reserve (p296)
- Bijilo Forest Park (p289)
- Makasutu Culture Forest (p296)

When to Go

Banjul

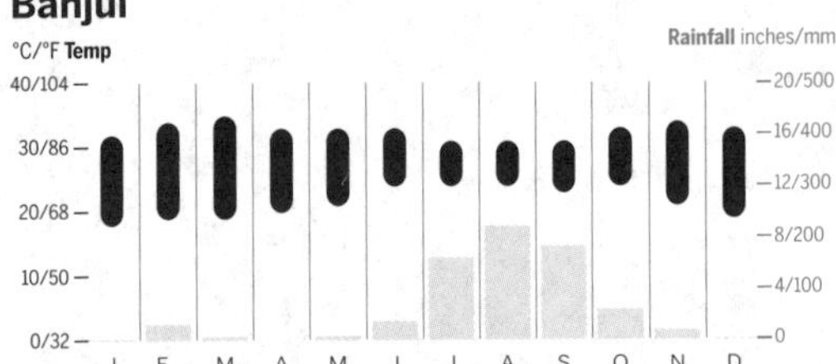

Nov–Feb The dry season and the best time to watch wildlife and birds.

Late Jun–Sep Rainy season. Many places close, but you'll avoid the crowds.

Oct & Mar–May Decent weather and ideal for bagging a shoulder-season discount.

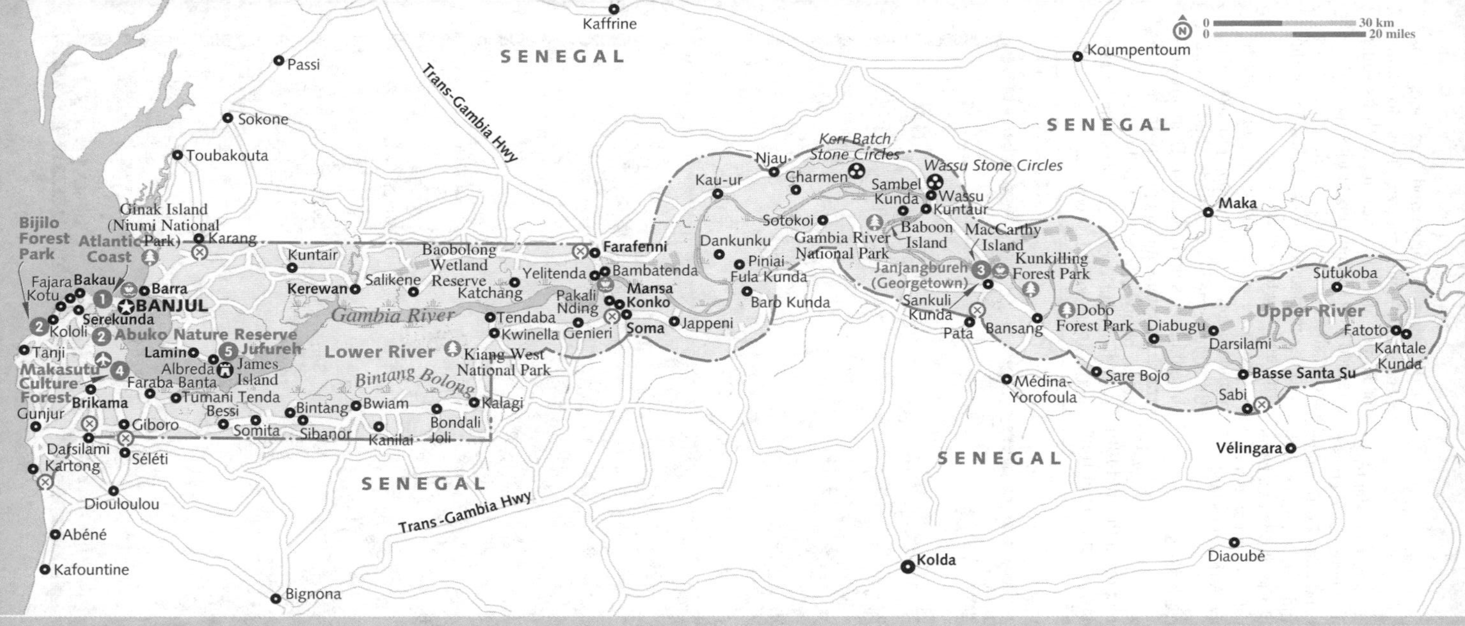

The Gambia Highlights

1 Indulging in fabulous food, then party the night away in the **Atlantic Coast resorts** (p288).

2 Being teased by monkeys on the 4.5km nature trail in **Bijilo Forest Park** (p289) and looking out for rare birds and giant crocodiles in tiny **Abuko Nature Reserve** (p296).

3 Following the call of the birds in the forest around **Janjangbureh (Georgetown)** (p298).

4 Touring the whole country, squeezed into 1000 hectares of abundant nature at **Makasutu Culture Forest** (p296).

5 Contemplating history at the slavery museum in the town to where Alex Haley traced his origins, **Jufureh** (p297).

BANJUL

POP 37,000

It's hard to imagine a more consistently ignored capital city. It sits on an island crossed by sand-blown streets and dotted with fading colonial structures. And yet, it tempts with a sense of history that the plush seaside resorts lack, and is home to a busy harbour and market that show urban Africa at its best.

Sights & Activities

★Albert Market MARKET

(Russell St) Since its creation in the mid-19th century the Albert Market, an area of frenzied buying, bartering and bargaining, has been Banjul's hub of activity. This cacophany of Banjul life is intoxicating, with its stalls stacked with shimmering fabrics, hair extensions, shoes, household and electrical wares and the myriad colours and flavours of the fruit and vegetable market.

Give yourself a good couple of hours to wander around – long enough to take in all the sights, smells and sounds – and get your haggling skills up to scratch. There are several drinks stalls and chop shops in the market to pacify shopped-out bellies. It's never calm here, but early in the morning or late in the afternoon is less crazed.

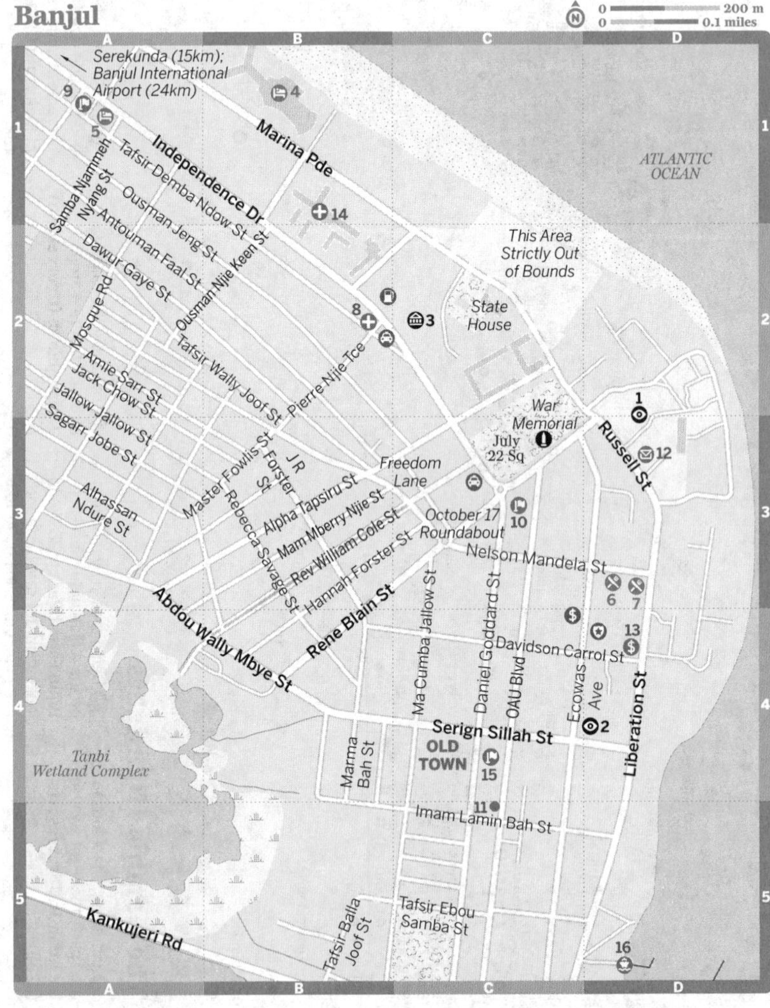

★ St Joseph's Adult Education & Skills Centre SCHOOL
(☎4228836; stjskills@qanet.com; Ecowas Ave; ⏱10am-2pm Mon-Thu, to noon Fri) Tucked away inside an ancient Portuguese building, this centre has provided training to disadvantaged women for the last 20 years. Visitors can take a free tour of sewing, crafts and tie-dye classes, and purchase reasonably priced items such as patchwork products, embroidered purses and cute children's clothes at the on-site boutique.

Arch 22 MONUMENT
(Independence Dr; admission D100; ⏱9am-11pm) This massive, 36m-high gateway, built to celebrate the military coup of 22 July 1994, grants excellent views. There's also a cafe and a small **museum** (☎4226244) that enlightens visitors about the coup d'état and often houses good exhibitions.

National Museum MUSEUM
(☎4226244; www.ncac.gm; Independence Dr; admission D50; ⏱9am-6pm Mon-Thu, to 5pm Fri-Sun) Well-presented, if slightly dusty, displays of historical and cultural artefacts, including musical instruments, agricultural tools and ethnographic items. There's an interesting archaeological section reconstructing some of the earliest periods of human habitation of the region, and a history floor with photographs that lead right up to the present.

Banjul

Top Sights
1 Albert Market D2
2 St Joseph's Adult Education & Skills Centre D4

Sights
3 National Museum C2

Sleeping
4 Laico Atlantic Hotel B1
5 Princess Diana Hotel A1

Eating
6 Ali Baba Snack Bar D3
7 King of Shawarma Café D3

Information
8 Banjul Pharmacy B2
Gamtel Internet Café .... (see 5)
9 German Embassy A1
10 Guinean Embassy C3
11 Immigration Office C5
12 Main Post Office D3
13 PHB Bank D4
14 Royal Victoria Teaching Hospital B1
15 Sierra Leonean Embassy C4

Transport
16 Ferries D5

SET YOUR BUDGET

Budget
- Hotel room D800
- Sandwich or *shwarma* (kebab) D150
- Soft drink D80
- Local bus ride D50

Midrange
- Hotel room D1500
- Two-course dinner D450
- Bottle of beer D90
- Short shared taxi ride D100

Top End
- Hotel room D3000
- Two-course dinner D700
- Glass of wine D100
- Private taxi ride D250

Old Town NEIGHBOURHOOD
West from the ferry terminal towards the wide Ma Cumba Jallow St (Dobson St) is a chaotic assembly of decrepit colonial buildings and Krio-style clapboard houses (steep-roofed structures with wrought-iron balconies and corrugated roofs). It's no coincidence they resemble the inner-city architecture of Freetown, Sierra Leone, as many of them still belong to families who came to Banjul from Freetown, some as early as the 1820s.

Sleeping

Not many tourists stay in Banjul, and the best hotels are along the coast.

Princess Diana Hotel HOTEL $
(☎4228715; 30 Independence Dr; r D900) This is slightly better than most Banjul dosshouses, simply because it has doors that lock plus occasional live music in the bar.

Denton Bridge Resort HOTEL $$
(☎7773777; s/d D1200/1500; wi-fi, air-con) Near Oyster Creek, this is a breezy, decent hotel with large rooms. It also functions as a watersports centre, *pirogue* (traditional canoe) landing and excursion point.

Laico Atlantic Hotel HOTEL $$$
(☎4228601; www.laicohotels.com; Marina Pde; s/d from D2500/3500; P❄@🛜🏊) This plush palace has all the makings of a classy hotel (good restaurants, massage centre, nightclub), modern swanky rooms, plus, it's within walking distance of the heart of Banjul.

Eating

Banjul's restaurant scene is a culinary desert and many eateries roll down the blinds before the evening has even started. Around Albert Market you can find several cheap chop shops where plates of rice and sauce start at about D40. The Laico Atlantic Hotel restaurant offers international fare if you are looking for a more high-end experience.

★**Nefertiti Bar & Restaurant** SEAFOOD $
(☎7776600; Marina Pde; meals D200-300; ⏲11am-11pm) Smack on the beach with a gorgeous view of the beach, this laid-back spot serves up local seafood and is a popular spot for drinks in the late afternoon and evening.

Ali Baba Snack Bar MIDDLE EASTERN $
(☎4224055; Nelson Mandela St; dishes around D150-200; ⏲9am-5pm) Banjul's main snack bar has a deserved reputation for tasty *shwarmas* (sliced, grilled meat and salad in pita bread) and felafel sandwiches.

King of Shawarma Café MIDDLE EASTERN $
(☎4229799; Nelson Mandela St; dishes D100-200; ⏲9am-5pm Mon-Sat) Friendly, fresh and happy to relax its opening hours, this place serves delicious meze and pressed fruit juice.

Information

Banjul Pharmacy (☎4227470; ⏲10am-8.30pm) Across the road from the hospital.

Gamtel Internet Café (Independence Dr; per hr D40; ⏲9am-midnight) Internet access and phone service.

Main Post Office (Russell St; ⏲8am-4pm Mon-Sat) Has telephone facilities next door.

PHB Bank (☎4428144; 11 Liberation St; ⏲8am-4pm Mon-Thu, to 1.30pm Fri) Has an ATM and changes money.

Royal Victoria Teaching Hospital (☎4228223; Independence Dr) The Gambia's main hospital has an emergency department, but facilities aren't great.

SAFE TRAVEL

The Barra ferry is rife with pickpockets, and tourists are easy prey at the ferry terminals and at Albert Market.

Getting There & Away

Banjul International Airport (BLJ; ☎4473117) is at Yundum, 24km from Banjul city centre and 16km from the Atlantic coast resorts. For more information about flights, see p301.

Ferries (☎4228205; Liberation St; passengers D15, cars D200-300) travel between Banjul and Barra, on the northern bank of the Gambia River. They are supposed to run every one to two hours from 7am to 9pm and take one hour, though delays and cancellations are frequent.

Gelli-gellis (minibuses) and shared taxis to Bakau (D12) and Serekunda (D15) leave from their respective taxi ranks near the National Museum. Note that you might have to pay a bit more for luggage. A private taxi to the coastal resorts will cost D200 to D400.

Getting Around

TO/FROM THE AIRPORT

A tourist taxi from Banjul International Airport to Banjul costs around D300 to D400. There is no airport bus.

SHARED TAXI

A short ride across Banjul city centre (known as a 'town trip') in a private taxi costs about D30 to D60.

SEREKUNDA & THE ATLANTIC COAST

POP 326,000

Chaotic, splitting-at-the-seams Serekunda is the nation's largest urban centre, and appears to consist of one big, bustling market. The nearby Atlantic Coast resorts of Bakau, Fajara, Kotu Strand and Kololi are where the sun 'n' sea tourists flock. If you can manage to dodge the persistent ganja peddlers and bumsters (touts), this is a great place to spend long days on the beach and late nights on the dance floor.

Sights & Activities

Botanic Gardens GARDENS
(☎7774482; Bakau; adult/child D65/free; ⏲8am-4pm) Bakau's botanic gardens were established in 1924 and offer shade, peace and good bird-spotting chances.

★**Kachikally Crocodile Pool** WILDLIFE RESERVE
(☎7782479; www.kachikally.com; off Salt Matty Rd, Bakau; admission D60; ⏲9am-dusk) One of Gambia's most popular tourist attractions is a sacred site for locals. As crocodiles represent the power of fertility in Gambia, women

who experience difficulties in conceiving often come here to pray and wash (any child called Kachikally tells of a successful prayer at the pool). The pool and its adjacent nature trail are home to 78 fully grown and several smaller Nile crocodiles that you can observe basking on the bank. If you dare, many are tame enough to be touched (your guide will point you in their direction). A small museum containing musical instruments and other cultural artefacts is also on the premises.

★**Bijilo Forest Park** WILDLIFE RESERVE
(☎9996343; Kololi; admission D30; ⏲8am-6pm) This small reserve and community forest is a lovely escape. A 4.5km walk takes you along a well-maintained series of trails that pass through lush vegetation, gallery forest, low bush and grass, towards the dunes. You'll see green vervet, red colobus and patas monkeys, though feeding by visitors has turned them into cheeky little things that might come close and even steal items. Try not to feed them, as this only encourages them further. Monitor lizards will likely come and stare you down, too. Birds are best watched on the coastal side. The more than 100 species that have been counted here include several types of bee-eater, grey hornbill, osprey, Caspian tern, francolin and wood dove.

Sakura Arts Studio ARTS CENTRE
(☎7017351; Latrikunda; ⏲10am-5pm) Art lovers should visit Njogu Touray's Sakura Arts Studio for a private view of the acclaimed painter's colourful works.

★**African Living Art Centre** ARTS CENTRE
(☎4495131; Garba Jahumpa Rd, Fajara; ⏲10am-7pm) A fairy-tale cross between an antique gallery, a cafe and an orchid garden, the African Living Art Centre is the hub of Gambia's arts scene. It hosts exhibitions, brings artists together, offers workshops and infuses Gambia's contemporary scene with life. You can arrange to meet artists here and talk to them about their work, and find out how to participate in creative exchanges. Or simply enjoy the shade of the garden setting and kick back with a cocktail at the loungy cafe.

Sportsfishing Centre FISHING
(☎7765765; Denton Bridge) The Sportsfishing Centre is the best place in Serekunda to arrange fishing and *pirogue* excursions. Various companies are based there, including **African Angler** (☎7721228; www.african-angling.co.uk; Denton Bridge), which runs fishing excursions, and the **Watersports Centre** (☎7773777; Denton Bridge), which can organise jet-skiing, parasailing, windsurfing or catamaran trips.

Tours

Gambia Experience GUIDED TOURS
(☎4461104; www.gambia.co.uk; Senegambia Beach Hotel, Kololi) Gambia's biggest tour operator. Does everything from charter flights and all-inclusive holidays to in-country tours.

Gambia River Excursions GUIDED TOURS
(☎4494360; www.gambia-river.com; Fajara) Also has a base at Janjangbureh Camp in Janjangbureh. Renowned for its bird-and-breakfast excursions.

Gambia Tours GUIDED TOURS
(☎4462602, 4462601; www.gambiatours.gm) Efficient, family-run enterprise.

★**Hidden Gambia** GUIDED TOURS
(☎Skype 0120-2884100; www.hiddengambia.com) Has a base at Bird Safari Camp in Janjangbureh and arranges trips from the coast. Great for tailor-made tours.

Tilly's Tours GUIDED TOURS
(☎9800215; www.tillystours.com; Senegambia Strip, Kololi) Small company with responsible tourism products.

Sleeping

At the time of research, **Coconut Residence** (☎4463377; www.coconutresidence.com; Badala Park Way), one of the best top-end options, was closed for refurbishment but is due to reopen in late 2013. Check the website for details and updates.

★**Fajara Guesthouse** GUESTHOUSE $
(☎4496122; fax 4494365; Fajara; s/d D800/1100; ❄@) This cosy place exudes family vibes with its leafy courtyard and welcoming lounge. There's hot water and self-caterers can use the kitchen.

★**Luigi's** HOTEL $
(☎4460280; www.luigis.gm; Palma Rima Rd, Kololi; s/d incl breakfast D800/900, apt from D2200; ❄@🛜≋) This impressive complex has three restaurants and attractive lodgings set around the pool and Jacuzzi. Despite this tropical growth rate, the place manages to keep its family feel.

Bakau Lodge LODGE $
(☎9901610; www.bakaulodge.com; Bakau market, Bakau; d from D700; ≋) This small place

Atlantic Coast Resort & Serekunda

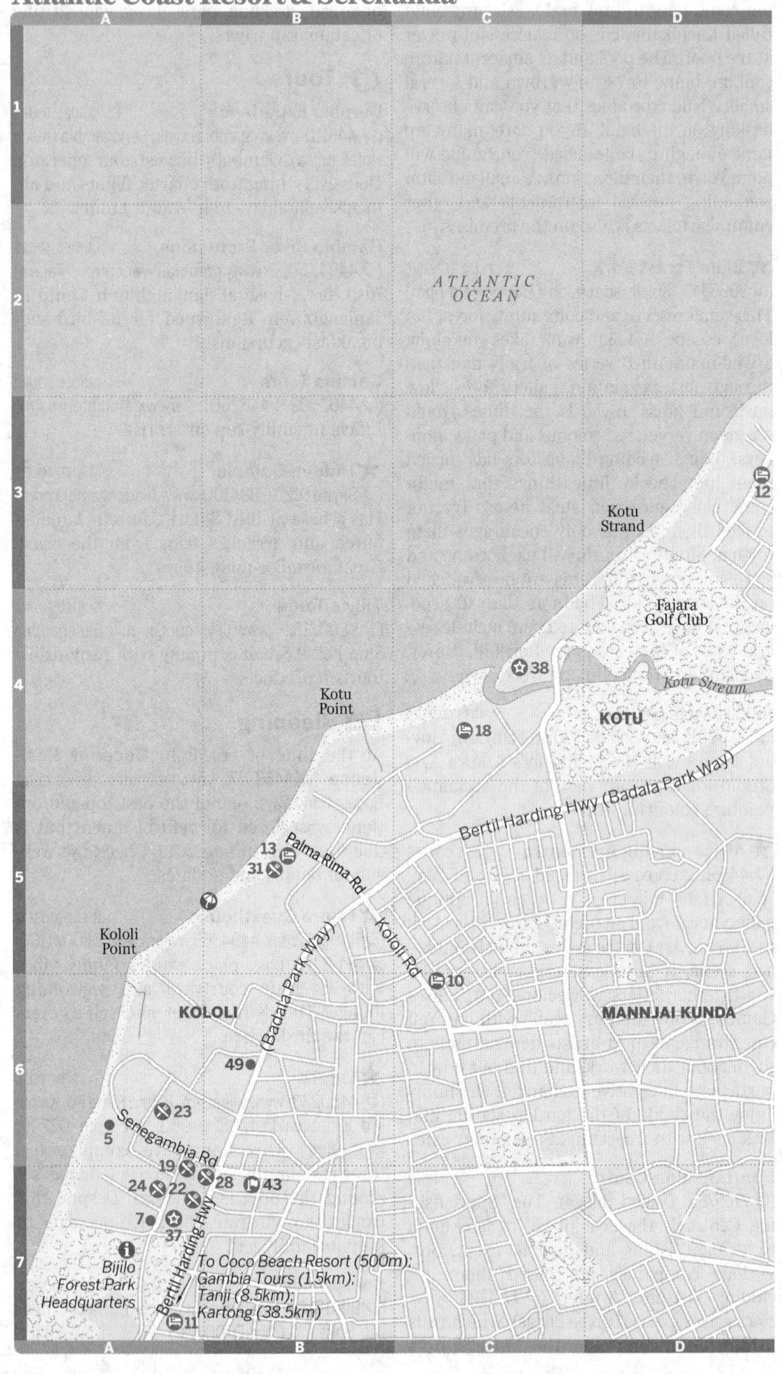

A
B
C
D
1
2
3
4
5
6
7
ATLANTIC OCEAN
Kotu Strand
12
Fajara Golf Club
38
Kotu Stream
Kotu Point
18
KOTU
Bertil Harding Hwy (Badala Park Way)
13
Palma Rima Rd
31
Kololi Point
(Badala Park Way)
Kololi Rd
10
KOLOLI
MANNJAI KUNDA
49
23
5
Senegambia Rd
19
28
43
24
22
7
37
Bijilo Forest Park Headquarters
Bertil Harding Hwy
To Coco Beach Resort (500m); Gambia Tours (1.5km); Tanji (8.5km); Kartong (38.5km)
11

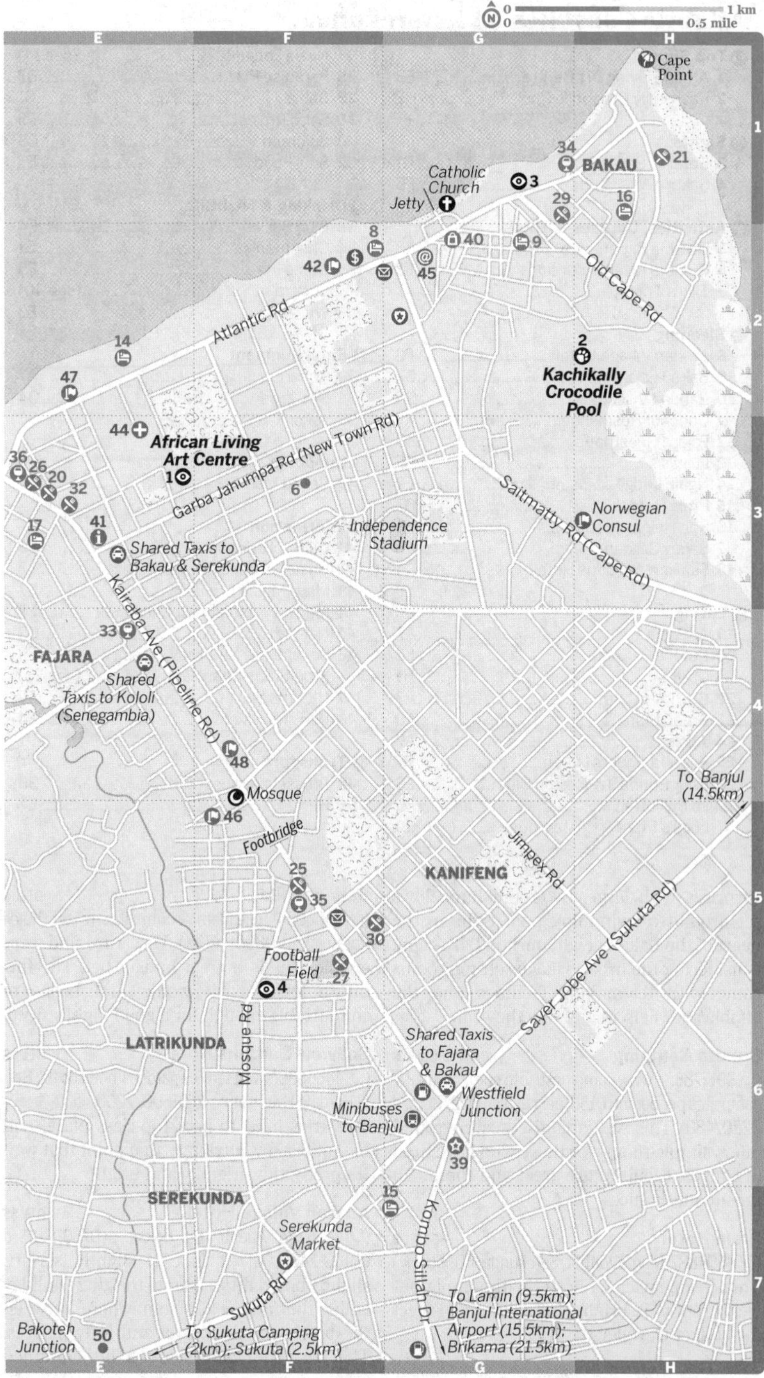

0 1 km
0 0.5 mile
E
F
G
H
Cape Point
BAKAU
34
21
Catholic Church
Jetty
3
29
16
8
40
9
42
45
Old Cape Rd
Atlantic Rd
14
2
Kachikally Crocodile Pool
47
44
African Living Art Centre
1
Garba Jahumpa Rd (New Town Rd)
36
26
20
32
6
Saitmatty Rd (Cape Rd)
Norwegian Consul
17
41
Independence Stadium
Shared Taxis to Bakau & Serekunda
Kairaba Ave (Pipeline Rd)
33
FAJARA
Shared Taxis to Kololi (Senegambia)
48
Mosque
46
To Banjul (14.5km)
Footbridge
Jimpex Rd
25
KANIFENG
35
30
Sayer Jobe Ave (Sukuta Rd)
Football Field
27
4
Shared Taxis to Fajara & Bakau
LATRIKUNDA
Mosque Rd
Westfield Junction
Minibuses to Banjul
39
15
SEREKUNDA
Kombo Sillah Dr
Serekunda Market
Sukuta Rd
To Lamin (9.5km); Banjul International Airport (15.5km); Brikama (21.5km)
Bakoteh Junction
50
To Sukuta Camping (2km); Sukuta (2.5km)
1
2
3
4
5
6
7

Atlantic Coast Resort & Serekunda

Top Sights
1 African Living Art Centre ... E3
2 Kachikally Crocodile Pool ... H2

Sights
3 Botanic Gardens ... G1
4 Sakura Arts Studio ... F5

Activities, Courses & Tours
5 Gambia Experience ... A6
6 Gambia River Excursions ... F3
7 Tilly's Tours ... A7

Sleeping
8 African Village Hotel ... F2
9 Bakau Lodge ... G2
10 Banana Ville ... C6
11 Coconut Residence ... A7
12 Fajara Guesthouse ... D3
13 Luigi's ... B5
14 Ngala Lodge ... E2
15 Praia Hotel ... G7
16 Roc Heights Lodge ... H1
17 Safari Garden ... E3
18 Seaview Gardens Hotel ... C4

Eating
19 Ali Baba's ... A7
20 Butcher's Shop ... E3
21 Calypso ... H1
22 Gaya Art Café ... A7
23 Green Mamba ... A6
24 Jojo's ... A7
25 Kairaba Supermarket ... F5
26 Keur Bouba J & Cotton Club ... E3
27 La Paillotte ... F5
Luigi's Pizza & Pasta House ... (see 13)
Ngala Lodge ... (see 14)
28 Paradiso Pizza ... B7
29 Saffie J ... G1
30 Solar Project ... F5
31 Solomon's Beach Bar ... B5
32 Soul Food ... E3

Drinking & Nightlife
33 Blue Bar ... E4
34 Chapman's ... G1
35 Come Inn ... F5
Sinatra's ... (see 40)
36 Weezo's ... E3

Entertainment
37 Aquarius ... A7
38 Destiny's ... C4
39 Jokor ... G6

Shopping
40 Bakau Market ... G2

Information
41 Cultural Encounters ... E3
42 Guinea-Bissau Embassy ... F2
43 Mauritanian Embassy ... B7
44 Medical Research Council ... E3
45 Net Bar ... G2
46 Senegalese Embassy ... F5
Stop Steps Pharmacy ... (see 25)
47 UK Embassy ... E2
48 US Embassy ... F4

Transport
49 Brussels Airlines ... B6
50 Hertz ... E7

surprises with large, two-room bungalows set around a swimming pool right in the heart of the Bakau neighbourhood. It's calm, considering the urban village setting, rooms come with tea-making facilities and the affable staff help in any way they can.

Sukuta Camping CAMPGROUND $
(☎9917786; www.campingsukuta.com; Sukuta; campsites per person D150, per car/van D22/30, s/d D280/480) This well-organised campground offers simple rooms for those who have tired of canvas. Facilities are great and there's an on-site mechanic.

Praia Hotel HOSTEL $
(☎4394887; Mame Jout St, Serekunda; r D550; ❄) This clean, spacious hostel with simple but clean rooms is bright, friendly and perfect for budget travellers.

Banana Ville HOTEL $
(☎9906054; njieadama@hotmail.com; off Kololi Rd, Kololi; d D800; ❄@) Very tiny and very simple, this is a great budget bet. The furniture looks a bit wonky, but beds are comfortable enough for a good night's sleep.

Seaview Gardens Hotel HOTEL $$
(☎4466660; www.seaviewgardens-hotel.co.uk; Bertil Harding Hwy, Kotu; s/d D1600/2200; ❄@🛜≋) This tries hard to be a top-class place, and has quite a few attributes that point that way. It's pretty, tidy, friendly and bright.

African Village Hotel HOTEL $$
(☎4495384; Atlantic Rd, Bakau; s D750-1700, d D1400-2400; @≋) Like a slightly scruffy, slightly bored little sister to the glitzy holiday clubs, this fills a gap somewhere between the bottom of the barrel and lofty palaces. The basic bungalows are a bit crammed

together, but the pool is great, the location practical and extra services like bicycle hire and exchange bureau welcome.

Safari Garden HOTEL $$
(☎4495887; www.safarigarden.com; Fajara; s/d D1300/1799; ❄@☎≋) The soul of this cute garden place with excellent food and service are managers Geri and Maurice, a couple so dedicated to the possibilities for ecotourism in Gambia that travellers tend to get drawn in. Rooms are bright with plenty of colourful bedspreads and an open, airy feel.

Roc Heights Lodge LODGE $$
(☎4495428; www.rocheightslodge.com; Samba Breku Rd, Bakau; s/d/apt D1800/2500/3500; ❄@☎) This three-storey villa sits in a quiet garden that makes the bustle of Bakau suddenly seem very far away. Self-catering apartments, with an appealing decor of wood-and-tile simplicity, come with fully equipped kitchens, bathtub, hairdryer, TV, telephone and plenty of space (though 'penthouse' is a slightly ambitious label).

★**Coco Ocean Resort & Spa** HOTEL $$$
(☎4466500; www.cocoocean.com; Bamboo Dr, Bijilo; d from D3500, ste from D4500; P❄@☎≋) With its full-service spa, and Moroccan architecture and endless chalk-white structures sprawling across vast tropical gardens, this is five-star pampering at its best. You won't get a feel for The Gambia hidden behind walls of bougainvillea, but for a dose of luxury you can't beat this place.

★**Ngala Lodge** LODGE $$$
(☎4494045; www.ngalalodge.com; 64 Atlantic Rd, Fajara; ste per person from D2200; ❄@≋) Now here's a hotel loved and fussed over by its owner. Even the simplest lodging in this red-brick palace is a large suite with its own Jacuzzi and hand-picked paintings. Our favourite was the Rolling Stones room, kind of a stylish shrine to one of owner Peter's passions. It's not one for families but is perfect for couples, and the penthouse with sky-gazer dome and sea view is ideal for honeymoons. Perfect down to the frosted glasses and thoughtfully chosen book collection, the Ngala has also one of the top restaurants in Gambia.

Eating

Serekunda and Bakau are best for street food and cheap eateries. For supermarkets head to Kairaba Ave, where there's plenty of choice, including the large and well-stocked **Kairaba Supermarket** (Kairaba Ave, Serekunda).

Solomon's Beach Bar SEAFOOD $
(☎4460716; Palma Rima Rd, Kololi; meals D200-300) At the northern end of Kololi beach, this cute round house serves excellent grilled fish in a youthful atmosphere. As light and sunny as the reggae classics on loop.

Saffie J AFRICAN $
(☎9937645; Old Cape Rd; snacks D200) This is the low-key approach to restaurant management: purchase a few cheap seats, paint them with the Gambian flag, put them on the roadside and erect a semblance of a fence around it. Now you can serve simple snacks with street views.

La Paillotte FRENCH $
(☎4375418; Serekunda; dishes D70-200; ⊙noon-4pm) The restaurant of the Alliance Franco-Gambienne does cheap, tasty meals of the day.

Soul Food AFRICAN $
(☎4497858; Kairaba Ave, Fajara; meals from D150) This is a place for generous portions of solid

BEACHES

Most beaches in this area are relatively safe for swimming, but currents can sometimes get strong. Care should be taken along the beach in Fajara, where there's a strong undertow. Always check conditions before plunging in.

The erosion that used to eat its way right up to the hotels has largely been reversed, so that the beaches of Kotu, Kololi and Cape Point are once again wide, sandy and beautiful. **Kotu** is particularly attractive, with sand and palm trees, beach bars and juice sellers on one side, and an area of lagoons a bit further north, where Kotu Stream cuts into the land (that's where birdwatchers head to).

Cape Point, at the northern tip of Bakau, has the calmest beaches. As this is a more residential area, you get less hassle from touts.

If the Atlantic Ocean or fending off bumsters doesn't appeal, all the major hotels have swimming pools. Most places allow access to nonguests if you buy a meal or a drink, or pay a fee.

meals. Think platters of rice dishes, mashed potatoes and rich sauces.

Solar Project AFRICAN $
(☎7053822; 18 Sainey Njie St, Faji Kunda; snacks D75-150; ⊙7am-midnight Mon-Sat) All of the omelettes, meatballs, cakes and dried fruit served here are cooked on the parabolic solar cookers; you can watch them being made in the backyard.

Ali Baba's MIDDLE EASTERN $
(☎9905978; Senegambia Strip, Kololi; meals around D200-300; ⊙9.30am-2am) Everyone knows Ali Baba's, so it's as much a useful meeting point as a commendable restaurant. A fast-food joint during the day, it serves dinner with a show in its breezy garden. There are frequent live concerts (mainly reggae), and important football matches on a big screen.

★ **Butcher's Shop** MOROCCAN $$
(☎4495069; www.thebutchersshop.gm; Kairaba Ave, Fajara; dishes D250-450; ⊙8am-11pm) Driss, the Moroccan celebrity chef (and TV star), knows how to grill a pepper steak to perfection, subtly blend a sauce until the spices sing in harmony and present a freshly pressed juice cocktail like a precious gift. It does a mean Sunday brunch from 10am to 4pm, and even at this self-service occasion, Driss makes sure everything runs smoothly.

★ **Gaya Art Café** INTERNATIONAL $$
(☎4464022; www.gaya-artcafe.com; Badala Park Way, Kololi; meals D400-600; ⊙noon-midnight Mon-Sat; 📶✍) Arty, veggie, healthy and organic, this is an unlikely addition to Senegambia's loud and boisterous food stations. The airy sculpture garden with its comfy armchairs is a great place to relax, the food absolutely fresh, the coffee made from freshly ground beans and the smoothies perfect for an energy boost after a walk around town.

Keur Bouba J & Cotton Club INTERNATIONAL $$
(☎4498249; Kairaba Ave, Fajara; mains D300-400; ⊙9am-6am) With two venues wrapped in one, this restaurant and music club only closes for three hours every night. That means morning coffee between its warm, red walls, a huge plate of rice for lunch, and à la carte dinners before enjoying live jazz or salsa.

Calypso INTERNATIONAL $$
(☎4496292; Chez Anne & Fode, Bakau; dishes from D300; ⊙9am-late) This cute, round beach bar serves delicious seafood, snacks and an African dish of the day between red-brick walls and attractive paintings, plus a full English breakfast.

Paradiso Pizza PIZZA $$
(☎4462177; Senegambia Strip, Kololi; pizzas from D350) No one argues with Paradiso's claim of serving the best pizza in town. Amid the host of indistinguishable eateries that line the Senegambia Strip, this is a real find. Sticking with the Italian theme, the espresso here has flavour.

Luigi's Pizza & Pasta House ITALIAN $$
(☎4460280; www.luigis.gm; Palma Rima Rd, Kololi; dishes from D350; ⊙6pm-midnight; ✍👪) A song of praise to Italy and its culinary achievements. The pasta is al dente, the pizzas are crisp and everything is cooked with the freshest ingredients.

Jojo's INTERNATIONAL $$
(☎7295711; Senegambia; dishes D400-600; ✍) Jojo's, with its earthy, minimalist ambience, sets out to rival established kitchens. The saltimbocca chicken is divine, and for vegetarians there's a great choice of salads.

Green Mamba ASIAN $$
(☎6662622; www.greenmambagarden.com; Senegambia; woks D500-600; ⊙7pm-midnight; ✍) This inspired restaurant is built around the concept of an Asian grill, meaning you have the rare treat of choosing the raw ingredients for your personalised stir-fry and watching them being cooked – unless you wish to relax over an original local fruit cocktail while the attentive staff bring your plate over. Spread across a large garden, tables grant a couple-enticing amount of privacy.

★ **Ngala Lodge** INTERNATIONAL $$$
(☎4494045; Atlantic Rd, Fajara; meals D700-1200) One of Gambia's most renowned restaurants, this has always been the top address for sumptuous and lovingly presented meals; service and sea-view setting are impeccable.

🍷 Drinking & Nightlife

Come Inn PUB
(☎4391464; Serekunda; ⊙10am-2am) For a good draught beer and a solid dose of local gossip, there's no better place than this German-style beer garden. It's popular with overlanders. Hearty international fare is useful to line the stomach with all that beer flowing freely.

Chapman's PUB

(☎4495252; Atlantic Rd, Bakau; ⏰11am-10pm Thu-Tue) Very popular, this pub is usually packed with a mixed crowd. Good, varied meals are washed down with pints of draught beer and good conversation.

Sinatra's BAR

(☎7781727; Atlantic Rd, Bakau) With a different program every day (movies on Monday, live music on Friday and Saturday, grill party on Sunday afternoon) and the fixed point of cheap draught beer to guide you through it all, this is a place you're unlikely to visit only once.

Blue Bar BAR

(☎9991539; Kairaba Ave, Fajara; ⏰11am-3am) This cheerful, dimly lit bar has an excellent selection of drinks to be sipped in the relaxed vibe and good company on the outdoor terrace.

Weezo's BAR

(☎4496918; Kairaba Ave, Fajara) Fajara's favourite Mexican diner undergoes a fascinating transformation around sunset, when the lights are dimmed, the tables readied for spontaneous dancing, and the sumptuous tortilla dishes replaced with one of the best cocktail menus on the coast.

Aquarius CLUB

(☎4460247; Bijilo Forest Park Rd, Senegambia Strip; ⏰10am-3am) A smart cafe during the day, Aquarius turns into a glittering dance floor at night. The drinks are expensive and the atmosphere is strictly party-vibe.

Destiny's CLUB

(Kotu Beach) This sparkling place is where parties go on until late, clothes are tight and tiny, and the beat is thumping. It's the nightlife version of a holiday beach club.

Jokor CLUB

(☎4375690; 13 Kombo Sillah Dr, near Westfield Junction) This open-air club is a raucous local affair, and makes a convincing claim to be the most entertaining club of all. It's open, and packed, every night, and there's a live band, usually *mbalax* (percussion-driven, Senegalese dance music) or reggae, on Friday and Saturday.

Shopping

A good place to pick up sculptures, batiks and souvenirs is **Bakau Market**.

FRESH FOOD ON THE FARM

Near Yundum, the **Gambia is Good Farm Yard** (☎9891560, 4494473; Alhagie Darboe; adult/child D30/20) is the public face of a socially engaged marketing company that has, since 2004, helped over 1000 poor (and mostly female) farmers sell the produce of their small agricultural farms. On a visit, you can learn about the farmers' horticultural techniques, attend cookery classes (minimum of four people, per person US$19) and taste an organic Gambian stew in the restaurant (US$9 including tour). Do phone before setting out so they can prepare for your visit. A return trip from the coastal resorts by taxi will cost around D80.

Information

INTERNET ACCESS

Wi-fi connections are becoming popular at restaurants and hotels, where they are typically free for guests. Connections are usually slow. Most internet cafes charge D30 per hour.

Net Bar (☎4498212; Atlantic Rd, Bakau; ⏰9am-midnight) Small snack bar outside.

MEDICAL SERVICES

Medical Research Council (MRC; ☎4495446; Fajara) If you find yourself with a potentially serious illness, head for this British-run clinic.

Stop Steps Pharmacy (☎4371344; Serekunda; ⏰9am-10pm Mon-Sat) Well stocked; has several branches.

SAFE TRAVEL

Crime rates in Serekunda are low. However, tourists (and especially women) will have to deal with the constant hustling by 'bumsters' or beach boys (see box, p301). Decline unwanted offers firmly – these guys are hard to shake off. Steer clear of the beaches after dark.

TOURIST INFORMATION

To find out about sustainable tourism options, drop into **Cultural Encounters** (☎4497675; www.asset-gambia.com; Fajara).

Getting There & Away

Bush taxis and *gelli-gellis* for most destinations in The Gambia leave from Westfield Junction and Tippa petrol station in Serekunda. Destinations include Brikama (D25, one hour), Soma (D100, five hours) and Gunjur (D30, 45 minutes). For journeys eastward, you're better off going to Barra and using the northbank road.

Getting Around

TO/FROM THE AIRPORT

A tourist taxi from Banjul International Airport to the coastal resorts costs around D12 to D15. Private taxis cost about D200 to D400.

TAXI

Shared taxis called *six-six* (a short hop costs D10) operate on several routes around the coastal resorts. They connect Bakau to Westfield Junction and Serekunda, passing through Sabina Junction near the Timbooktoo bookshop at Fajara. You can also get *six-six* from the traffic-lights junction in Fajara to Senegambia Strip in Kololi and from there to Bakau. Simply flag a taxi down, pay your fare and get off where you want.

You can also hire yellow or green taxis (they're more expensive) for trips around town. Rates are negotiable.

WESTERN GAMBIA

Abuko Nature Reserve

Abuko Nature Reserve (☎4375888; adult/child US$1.30/0.70; ⏰8am-6pm) is rare among African wildlife reserves: it's tiny, it's easy to reach, you don't need a car to go in, and it's well managed, with an amazing diversity of vegetation and animals. It is possibly the mightiest of Gambia's national parks.

More than 250 bird species have been recorded in Abuko's compact area, making it one of the region's best birdwatching haunts. Birds include sunbirds, green hylias, African goshawks, oriole warblers, yellowbills and leafloves. Abuko is also about the only place in Gambia where you can observe green and violet turacos, white-spotted flufftails, ahanta francolins and western bluebills. And among the 52 mammal species calling Abuko home are bushbucks, duikers, porcupines, bushbabies and ground squirrels, as well as three monkey types: the green or vervet, endangered western red colobus, and patas. The reserve is particularly famous for its Nile crocodiles and other slithering types such as pythons, puff adders, green mambas and forest cobras.

Be sure to pop into the reserve's Darwin Field Station and educational centre, packed with information on the animal species you'll encounter here. The animal orphanage here is a rehabilitation centre whose aim is to return injured or mistreated animals back to the wild. Many of the animals are baboons or monkeys that were previously kept as pets.

To get to Abuko, take a private taxi (D400 to D500) or a minibus headed for Brikama from Banjul or Serekunda (D15).

Makasutu Culture Forest & Ballabu Conservation Project

Like a snapshot of The Gambia, Makasutu Culture Forest bundles the country's array of landscapes into a dazzling 1000-hectare package. The setting is stunning, comprising palm groves, wetlands, mangroves and savannah plains, all inhabited by plenty of animals, including baboons, monitor lizards and hundreds of bird species.

A day in the forest includes a mangrove tour by *pirogue;* guided walks through a range of habitats, including a palm forest where you can watch palm sap being tapped; a visit to a crafts centre; and demonstrations of traditional dancing. The tours are well organised and run by excellent staff. This is a great day out, especially for families seeking a taste of nature away from the beaches and without the hassle of braving the roads upcountry.

If you feel like a treat, you can stay in the forest at the exclusive and very stunning eco-retreat **Mandina River Lodge** (☎9951547; www.mandinalodges.com; s/d withhalf board from D4000/7800; ❄✉), an elegant marriage of lavishness and respect for nature. It provides three types of lodge: in-the-jungle accommodation tucked away in the mangroves with roof terraces that beg you to perch for hours; solar-powered luxury lodges floating on the river; and stilt houses boasting open-air bathrooms and hammock- and day-bed filled terraces.

Phone or email beforehand to be picked up from Brikama in the morning and dropped off in the evening with the park's bus (D150 one way). A private taxi from Brikama costs around D200.

Tanji, Brufut & Around

Located just to the south of the Atlantic Coast resorts, **Brufut** has rapidly changed from a tranquil fishing village to a built-up tourist centre. Small and attractive **Hibiscus**

House (☎7982929; www.hibiscushousegambia.com; Brufut; s/d incl breakfast from D2800/3500; ❄≋) is tucked away at the end of a bougainvillea-lined road.

A short drive southward takes you to **Tanji**. Here, the charming **Tanji Village Museum** (☎9926618; tanje@dds.nl; adult/child D120/30; ⏲9am-5pm) presents Gambian nature and life scenes by recreating a traditional Mandinka village, where you can peer into huts and learn about the country's history and artisan crafts. The **Tanji River Bird Reserve** (☎9919219; admission D40; ⏲9am-6pm) is an area of dunes, lagoons and woodland, and contains Bijol Island, a protected breeding ground for the Caspian tern.

Tanji village, 3km south of the reserve office, has a couple of good lodgings. **Nyanya's Beach Lodge** (☎9808678; www.nyanyas-beach-lodge.com; s/d D500/600) has bright bungalows in a leafy garden on the bank of a Gambia River branch.

A little further south in **Tujering**, you can observe batik makers and weavers in the village. Put in a stop at the quirky and wonderful **Tunbung Arts Village** (☎9982102; www.tunbungartvillage.com; Tujering Village; admission free), a ragged assembly of skewed huts, wildly painted walls and random sculptures that peer out behind walls and from treetops. This is the creative universe of Etu Ndow, a renowned Gambian artist. It's fun to look at this piece of live art in progress, including the small museum displaying exhibits relating to local history. The arts centre also offers a few **rooms** (per person incl breakfast D350) in mud houses, decorated with bright colours and Ndow's whimsical style. Alternatively, **Bendula Bed & Breakfast** (☎7717481; www.bendula.com; s/d D570/850) offers a clutch of no-frills, colourful huts huddled on green terrain within walking distance of the beach.

The beautiful beaches of **Sanyang**, the next spot on the coast, are popular with tour groups from the Kombos. **Rainbow Beach Bar** (☎9726806; www.rainbow.gm; d from D500/700, mains from D200) has clean, thatched-roof bungalows, a generator and a chef who knows how to grill prawns properly, but it's best for relaxing with a beer with a view of the beach.

Gunjur

Ten kilometres south of Sanyang lies the tranquil fishing village of Gunjur, one of The Gambia's largest fishing centres. This place is all about fish, guts and nets, though the **Gunjur Environmental Protection and Development Group** (GEPADG; ☎8800986; gepadg.jilankanet.com) can introduce you to the ecological side of town, notably its community reserve and lagoon. Stay eco-friendly at the excellent **Footsteps Eco Lodge** (☎7411609; www.footstepsgambia.com; bungalows incl breakfast D2800; ❄@≋) and indulge in the great food. Five kilometres further south, **Balaba Nature Camp** (☎9919012; www.balabacamp.co.uk; Medina Salaam; r with half board D850) is much more basic but also environmentally committed.

LOWER GAMBIA RIVER

Jufureh & James Island

When Alex Haley, the American author of *Roots,* traced his origins to **Jufureh**, the tiny village quickly turned into a favourite tourist destination. There's little to see, though the small **slavery museum** (☎7710276; www.ncac.gm/juffureh.html; Jufureh; admission D50; ⏲10am-5pm Mon-Sat), which traces slavery in The Gambia and includes a replica slave ship, is worth a visit.

One of Gambia's most significant historical sights is **James Island**. It houses the remains of **Fort James** (1650s), an important British colonial trading post since 1661 and the departure point of vessels packed with ivory and gold as well as slave ships. Over subsequent decades, it was the site of numerous skirmishes. Variously held by British, French and Dutch traders, as well as a couple of privateers (pirates), it was completely destroyed at least three times before being finally abandoned in 1829.

The ruins of the fort are quite extensive, though badly neglected – the only intact room is a food store, which is often called the slave dungeon for dramatic effect. The biggest threat, though, is rapid coastal erosion, which literally pulls away the ground the ruins stand on.

The easiest way to visit Jufureh and James Island is with an organised tour. Otherwise, take the ferry to Barra and find a shared (D35) or hire taxi (return D400) or hop on a *pirogue* (from D600) from Albreda (the town next to Jufureh).

UPPER GAMBIA RIVER

Janjangbureh & Around

Janjangbureh (Georgetown) is a sleepy, former colonial administrative centre. It is situated on the northern edge of MacCarthy Island in the Gambia River, and is reached via ferry links from either bank. There is little in terms of infrastructure – no banks and no hospital. And persistent young kids in Janjangbureh haggle you more than the usual amount, so it's best to avoid loitering and head straight to a lodge or hut out of the town centre.

A walk around town does reveal a few **historic buildings**, including the old Commissioner's Quarter, a 200-year-old wooden house once inhabited by freed slaves, and the foundations of a colonial warehouse. The main reason to come here, however, is to stay in a local lodge and take advantage of the superb birdwatching opportunities. Some 2.5km west of Janjangbureh, near a patch of woodland, **Bird Safari Camp** (☎7336570, Skype 0120-2884100; www.bsc.gm; per person incl breakfast US$34; @❄) is the remotest of the accommodation available (not a problem if you come with a Hidden Gambia boat excursion), and fantastic if you're here for birdwatching. **Janjangbureh Camp** (☎9816944; www.gambia-river.com; per person D280) has quirky if dusty bungalows on a vast terrain between forest and water and is a good base for river trips.

Janjangbureh/MacCarthy Island can be reached by ferry (passenger/car D8/100) from either the southern or the northern bank of the river. Most bush taxis turn off the main road between Soma and Basse Santa Su to drop off passengers at the southern ferry ramp; request this when entering the taxi.

UNDERSTAND THE GAMBIA

The Gambia Today

After decades in power, Yahya Jammeh's leadership style has become increasingly authoritarian. Amnesty International, Reporters Without Borders and other human rights organisations have denounced what they say is a climate of fear felt by opposition voices and journalists. Jammeh also claims to have found cures for HIV/AIDS and asthma, which he administers in weekly TV shows. A 2009 televised declaration in which he threatened human rights activists with death heightened international concern.

In late 2011, The Gambia's presidential elections, in which Jammeh won another five-year term, were deemed corrupt by most of the international community and labelled 'not conducive for the conduct of free, fair and transparent polls' by the Economic Community of West African States (Ecowas).

In August 2012, Gambia again attracted international condemnation when Jammeh announced all death-row convicts would be executed – thought to be 40 or 45 people – by September 2012. After nine prisoners were killed by firing squad, Jammeh bowed to foreign pressure and halted the executions indefinitely.

History

Ancient stone circles and burial mounds indicate that this part of West Africa has been inhabited for at least 1500 years. The Empire of Ghana (5th to 11th centuries) extended its influence over the region, and by the 13th century the area had been absorbed into the Empire of Mali. By 1456 the first Portuguese navigators landed on James Island, turning it into a strategic trading point.

Built in 1651 by Baltic Germans, the James Island fort was claimed by the British in 1661 but changed hands several times. It was an important collection point for slaves until the abolition of slavery in 1807. New forts were built at Barra and Bathurst (now Banjul), to enforce compliance with the Abolition Act.

The British continued to extend their influence further upstream until the 1820s, when the territory was declared a British protectorate ruled from Sierra Leone. In 1886 Gambia became a Crown colony.

Gambia became self-governing in 1963, although it took two more years until real independence was achieved. Gambia became The Gambia, Bathurst became Banjul, and David Jawara, leader of the People's Progressive Party, became Prime Minister Dawda Jawara and converted to Islam, while the queen remained head of state.

High groundnut prices and the advent of package tourism led to something of a boom in the 1960s. Jawara consolidated his power, and became president when The Gambia became a fully fledged republic in 1970. The economic slump of the 1980s provoked social unrest. Two coups were hatched – but thwarted with Senegalese assistance. This cooperation led to the 1982 confederation of the two countries under the name of Senegambia, but the union had collapsed by 1989. Meanwhile, corruption increased, economic decline continued and popular discontent rose. In July 1994, Jawara was overthrown in a reportedly bloodless coup led by Lieutenant Yahya Jammeh. After a brief flirtation with military dictatorship, the 30-year-old Jammeh bowed to international pressure, inaugurated a second republic, turned civilian and won the 1996 election comfortably.

Culture

Holiday brochures like to describe Gambia as the 'Smiling Coast'. Hospitality certainly is part of Gambian culture, but it's more easily found upcountry, away from the large tourist centres.

Years of authoritarian rule have resulted in a climate of distrust. Conversations are often conducted with care, and few people will express their views on governmental politics openly – you never know who might be listening. Short-term travellers might not readily notice this. Yet being aware of the troubles the population faces will help you understand the country better and grant you an insight into the real Gambia that lies beyond the polished smiles and tourist hustling.

People

With around 115 people per square kilometre, The Gambia has one of the highest population densities in Africa. The strongest concentration of people is around the urbanised zones of the Atlantic Coast. Forty-five per cent of the population is under 14 years old.

The main ethnic groups are the Mandinka (comprising around 43%), the Wolof (about 15%) and the Fula (around 18%). Smaller groups include the Serer and Diola (also spelt Jola). About 90% of the population is Muslim. Christianity is most widespread among the Diola.

Arts & Crafts

The *kora,* Africa's most iconic instrument, was created in the region of Gambia and Guinea-Bissau after Malinké groups came here to settle from Mali. Famous *kora* players include Amadou Bansang Jobarteh, Jali Nyama Suso, Dembo Konte and Malamini Jobarteh.

In the 1960s, The Gambia was hugely influential in the development of modern West African music. Groups like the Afro-funky Super Eagles and singer Labah Sosse had a huge impact in The Gambia, Senegal and beyond. Today, it's locally brewed reggae and hip hop that get people moving. Even the president has been seen rubbing shoulders with the world's reggae greats, proud to hear his country nicknamed 'Little Jamaica'.

Banjul's national museum has a few good examples of traditional statues and carved masks on display. Leading contemporary artists Njogu Touray and Etu produce colourful works from mixed materials. Fabric printers such as Baboucar Fall and Toimbo Laurens push the art of batik in new creative directions.

Food & Drink

National dishes include *domodah* (rice with groundnut sauce) and *benachin* (rice cooked in tomato, fish and vegetable sauce). Vegetarians ought to try *niebbe,* spicy red beans that are served with bread on street corners.

The Gambia has great local juices, such as *bissap* (made from sorrel) and creamy *bouyi* (made from the fruits of the baobab tree). *Ataaya* (strong, syrupy green tea) is a great pick-me-up. For something more potent, try a cup of thick, yeasty palm wine or an ice-cold JulBrew beer.

Environment

At only 11,295 sq km, The Gambia is mainland Africa's smallest country. It's also the most absurdly shaped one. Its 300km-long territory is almost entirely surrounded by Senegal and dominated by the Gambia River that runs through it. The country is flat, and vegetation consists mainly of savannah woodlands, gallery forests and saline marshes. Six national parks and reserves protect 3.7% of the country's landmass. Some of the most interesting ones are Abuko, Kiang West and Gambia River. The Gambia boasts a few large mammals, such as hippos and reintroduced chimps, but most animal lovers are drawn to the hundreds of spectacular bird species that make The Gambia one of the best countries in West Africa for birdwatching. The main

PRACTICALITIES

- **Driving** Gambians drive on the right-hand side.
- **Electricity** 220V. Most plugs have three square pins (same as Britain); two round pins (same as continental Europe) are also in use.
- **Languages** English, Mandinka, Wolof, Pulaar (Fula).
- **Newspapers** *The Point* is a daily newspaper published in Bakau.

environmental issues are deforestation, overfishing and coastal erosion.

SURVIVAL GUIDE

 Directory A–Z

ACCOMMODATION

At the Atlantic Coast resorts of Bakau, Fajara, Kotu Strand and Kololi the choice of accommodation ranges from simple hostels to five-star hotels. Upcountry, your options are normally limited to basic guesthouses and hotels. All prices quoted are high-season rates (November to April). In low season, they may be 25% or even 50% lower.

ACTIVITIES

Beach-related activities such as swimming, water sports and fishing are popular around the coast. Upcountry, it's all about birdwatching tours around the national parks and *pirogue* excursions (see p289).

EMBASSIES & CONSULATES

German Embassy (4227783; 29 Independence Dr, Banjul; 8am-1pm, closed Tue)

Guinean Embassy (909964, 4226862; 78A Daniel Goddard St, top fl, Banjul; 9am-4pm Mon-Thu, 9am-1pm & 2.30-4pm Fri)

Guinea-Bissau Embassy (4226862; Atlantic Rd, Bakau; 9am-2pm Mon-Fri, to 1pm Sat)

Malian Embassy (26 Cherno Adama Bah St, Banjul)

Mauritanian Embassy (4491153; Badala Park Way, Kololi; 8am-4pm Mon-Fri)

Senegalese Embassy (4373752; off Kairaba Ave, Fajara; 8am-2pm & 2.30-5pm Mon-Thu, to 4pm Fri)

Sierra Leonean Embassy (4228206; 67 Daniel Goddard St, Banjul; 8.30am-4.30pm Mon-Thu, to 1.30pm Fri)

UK Embassy (4495134, 4495133; http://ukingambia.fco.gov.uk; 48 Atlantic Rd, Fajara; 8am-1pm Mon-Thu, to 12.30pm Fri)

US Embassy (4392856; http://banjul.usembassy.gov; 92 Kairaba Ave, Fajara; 8.30am-12.30pm)

Several European countries have honorary consuls, including Belgium (at the Kairaba Hotel, Kololi), Denmark, Sweden and Norway (Saitmatty Rd, Bakau).

EMERGENCIES

Ambulance (16)

Fire (18)

Police (17)

FESTIVALS & EVENTS

Held biannually, the one-week **Roots International Festival** (May-Jun) (formerly the Roots Homecoming Festival) features concerts by Gambian and diaspora artists, as well as seminars and lectures, held in various towns. The high point is the weekend in Jufureh, where local dance troupes and bands drown the village in music.

INTERNET ACCESS

It's easy to find a (sluggish) internet cafe along the coast. Upcountry, access is harder to find.

MONEY

The local currency, dalasi (D), fluctuates strongly. There aren't any official changing points at the border, just very persistent black-market changers. You'll be fine using CFA, though, until you get to the coast, where changing money is easier. Many hotels can recommend an informal changer, though the rates may be similar to those the banks propose. Many hotels will accept UK pounds sterling.

There are no ATMs upcountry, and you're best off changing all you need at the coast.

OPENING HOURS

Banks From 1pm to 4pm Monday to Thursday, with lunch break from 1pm to 2.30pm on Friday.

Government offices From 8am to 3pm or 4pm Monday to Thursday, 8am to 12.30pm on Friday.

Restaurants Lunch from 11am to 2.30pm, dinner from 6pm.

Shops and businesses From 8.30am to 1pm and 2.30pm to 5.30pm Monday to Thursday; from 8am until noon Friday and Saturday.

VACCINATION CERTIFICATES

A yellow-fever vaccination certificate is required of travellers coming from an infected area.

BEACH BOYS

A beach boy, also referred to as a *sai sai* or bumster, is a womaniser, a smooth operator, a charming hustler, a con man or a dodgy mixture of all of these. These guys are usually young, often good-looking men, who approach women (sometimes bluntly, sometimes with astonishing verbal skills) in towns, nightclubs, bars and particularly on beaches. While some of them are fairly harmless (just don't get your heart broken), others can pull some pretty sly jobs, involving sexual advances, tricking you out of money or downright stealing.

Use the same yardsticks you would at home before getting involved. It's best to ignore these guys completely. They might respond with verbal abuse, but it's all hot air.

PUBLIC HOLIDAYS

As well as religious holidays, there are a few public holidays observed in The Gambia:

1 January New Year's Day
18 February Independence Day
1 May Workers' Day
15 August Assumption

SAFE TRAVEL

Serious crime is fairly rare in The Gambia, though muggings and petty theft do occur, particularly around the tourist centres. Avoid walking around alone after dark. Kids will often hassle you for money or tours, but usually this is just a harmless annoyance. Beach boys are another matter.

TELEPHONE

The telephone country code is 220.

TOURIST INFORMATION

The **Gambia Tourism** (www.visitthegambia.gm) website has a wealth of information.

VISAS

Visas are not needed for nationals of the UK, Germany, Italy, Australia, Luxembourg, the Netherlands, and Scandinavian and Ecowas countries for stays of up to 90 days. For those needing one, visas are normally valid for one or three months and cost D1000 or 3000; you'll need to provide two photos. The **Immigration Office** (☎ 4228611; OAU Blvd, Banjul; ⏱ 8am-4pm) deals with visa extensions (D400). For onward travel, get your visa from the relevant embassy. Most embassies will deal with requests within 48 hours. You cannot buy visas on the borders with Senegal, but they will let you in to purchase one at the immigration office within 72 hours. If you are flying into the country, get your visa before you leave home.

ℹ Getting There & Away

AIR

Brussels Airlines (☎ 4466880; www.brusselsairlines.com; Badala Park Way, Kololi) is the only scheduled airline connecting Gambia and Europe. Most people arrive on charter flights with **Gambia Experience** (☎ in UK 0845 330 4567; www.gambia.co.uk). For inner-African flights, you'll usually have to go to Dakar first.

LAND

Minibuses and bush taxis run regularly between Barra and the border at Karang (D60), where Dakar-bound bush taxis and minibuses (D700, six hours) are normally waiting.

To get to southern Senegal (Casamance), minibuses and bush taxis leave from Serekunda petrol station (D200, five hours). Transport also goes from Brikama to Ziguinchor.

At the far-eastern tip of The Gambia, bush taxis run from Basse Santa Su to Vélingara (D70, 45 minutes; 27km), and from there bush taxis go to Tambacounda (D75, three hours).

ℹ Getting Around

BOAT

There are no scheduled passenger boats, but several tour operators (p289) offer excursions, including tailor-made trips upriver.

CAR & MOTORCYCLE

Reliable car-hire companies include **Hertz** (☎ 4390041; Boketh Total petrol station).

LOCAL TRANSPORT

The southbank road from the coast eastward is in a perennial state of construction; the northbank road is a good alternative option for journeys upcountry. It's best to cross on the ferry from Banjul to Barra on foot and get a *sept-place* (shared seven-seater) taxi to Kerewan, from where you can change for transport heading further east. *Sept-place* taxis are by no means a comfy way of travelling; however, they are infinitely better than the battered *gelli-gelli* minibuses. A few green, government-owned 'express' buses also ply the major roads. You can get on at Tippa petrol station in Serekunda – prepare for a slow, bouncy ride.

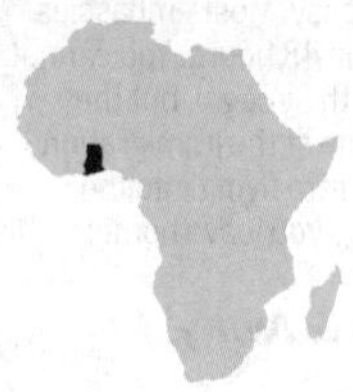

Ghana

POP 25 MILLION

Includes ➡

Best Places to Eat

- ➡ Buka (p309)
- ➡ El Gaucho (p324)
- ➡ Khana Khazana (p309)
- ➡ Okorye Tree (p320)
- ➡ Nik's Pizza (p324)

Best Places to Stay

- ➡ Lake Point Guesthouse (p325)
- ➡ Green Turtle Lodge (p321)
- ➡ Four Villages Inn (p323)
- ➡ Mountain Paradise (p314)
- ➡ Aylos Bay (p313)

Why Go?

Hailed as West Africa's golden child, Ghana deserves its place in the sun. One of Africa's great success stories, the country is reaping the benefits of a stable democracy in the form of fast-paced development. And it shows: Ghana is suffused with the most incredible energy.

With its welcoming beaches, gorgeous hinterland, rich culture, vibrant cities, diverse wildlife, easy transport and affable inhabitants, it's no wonder Ghana is sometimes labelled 'Africa for beginners'.

It's easy to come here for a week or a month, but no trip can be complete without a visit to Ghana's coastal forts, poignant reminders of a page of history that defined our modern world.

Travel north and you'll feel like you've arrived in a different country, with a different religion, geography and cultural practices. The beauty is that this diversity exists so harmoniously, a joy to experience and a wonder to behold in uncertain times.

When to Go

Accra

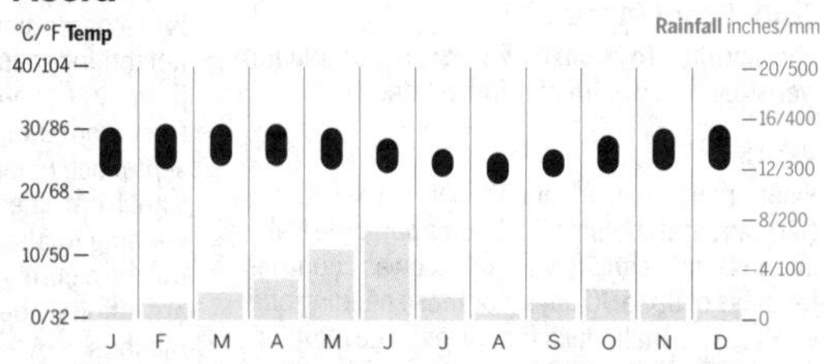

Apr–Jun The heaviest of the two rainy seasons (autumn can also be wet).

Nov–Mar The dry and easiest season to travel.

Dec–Apr Best for wildlife viewing, with good visibility and animals congregating at water holes.

ACCRA

POP 2.29 MILLION

Ghana's beating heart probably won't inspire love letters, but you might just grow to like it. The capital's hot, sticky streets are perfumed with sweat, fumes and yesterday's cooking oil. Like balloons waiting to be burst, clouds of dirty humidity linger above stalls selling mangoes, *banku* (fermented maize meal) and rice. The city's tendrils reach out towards the beach, the centre and the west, each one a different Ghanaian experience.

The city doesn't have any heavy-hitting sights like Cape Coast or Elmina, but it does have good shopping, excellent nightlife and definitely the best selection of eating options in Ghana.

SET YOUR BUDGET

Budget

- Dorm bed C10
- Fried rice in chop bar C2
- Star beer C3
- Accra–Tamale by bus C40

Midrange

- Hotel room with bathroom & air-con C80
- Pizza C15
- Drink in a bar C6
- Flight Accra–Tamale C100

Top End

- Room in a lodge US$100
- Two-course meal C30
- Cocktail C10
- 4WD with driver, per day US$110

Sights & Activities

Osu Castle (Map p306) is currently the seat of government and is off-limits to visitors, but at the time of research the government was scheduled to move to the brand-new **Flagstaff House** (Map p306) on Liberation Rd and for Osu Castle to open to the public.

Jamestown NEIGHBOURHOOD

(Map p306) Jamestown originated as a community that emerged around the 17th century British James Fort, merging with Accra as the city grew. These days, Jamestown is one of the poorer neighbourhoods of Accra but it remains vibrant. For a great view of the city and the busy and colourful fishing harbour (haze and pollution permitting), climb to the top of the whitewashed **lighthouse** (admission C5).

There are several boxing gyms in Jamestown that have nurtured a long line of local kids into champions. You'll see plenty of posters around.

Kwame Nkrumah Park MEMORIAL

(Map p310; High St; park & museum admission adult/child C6/1; 10am-5pm) It's all bronze statues and choreographed fountains at the Kwame Nkrumah park, dedicated in the early 1990s to Ghana's first president. The park **museum** houses a curious collection of Nkrumah's personal belongings, including his presidential desk, bookcase, jacket and student sofa, as well as numerous photos of him and various world leaders.

Independence Square MONUMENT

(Map p306) Independence Sq is a vast, empty expanse of concrete overlooked by spectator stands of Stalinesque grace. The square is dominated by an enormous McDonald's-like arch, beneath which the Eternal Flame of African Liberation, lit by Kwame Nkrumah, still flickers. It stands empty for most of the year, except for special commemorations. Super churches sometimes get the authorisation to preach here.

Across the street stands **Black Star Square** (Map p306), with an angular arch, crowned by a large black star, Ghana's national symbol. Note: taking photos is forbidden.

Makola Market MARKET

(Map p310; 8am-6pm) There is no front door or welcoming sign to the Makola Market. Before you know it, you've been sucked by the human undertow from the usual pavements clogged with vendors hawking food, secondhand clothes and shoes to the market itself. For new arrivals to Africa, it can be an intense experience, but it's a fun – though perhaps a slightly masochistic – Ghanaian initiation rite.

Labadi Beach BEACH

This is where Accra residents love to congregate and party at weekends. It does get extremely crowded, and the pumping music, food smells and heat can all become a bit too much, but there is no denying that this is typical Ghana-style partying. Labadi is about 8km east of Accra; to come here,

Ghana Highlights

❶ Tour the castles of **Cape Coast** (p315) and Elmina to learn about the history of slavery.

❷ Go hiking, climb waterfalls and swim in the former German Togoland, Ghana's Volta Region in **the east** (p313).

❸ Join the world's most inexpensive safari at **Mole National Park** (p327).

❹ Shop till you drop (and get very lost) in West Africa's biggest market, the exhilarating **Kejetia Market** (p321) in Kumasi.

❺ Sample Accra's lively nightlife and join **Nima Tours** (p308) for a behind-the-scenes look at what everyday life is like in the capital.

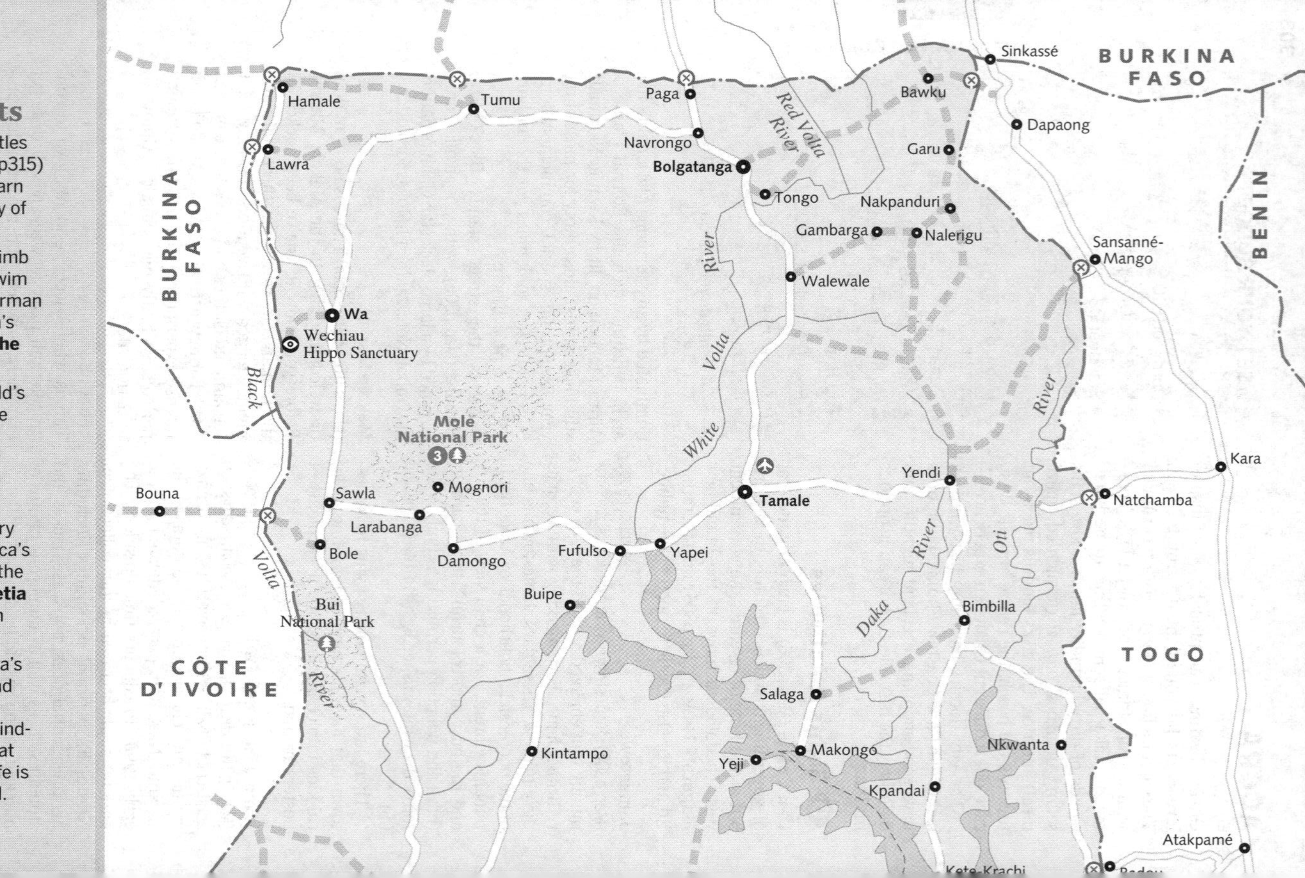

6 Surf, chill and hike for a few days around **Busua** (p320).

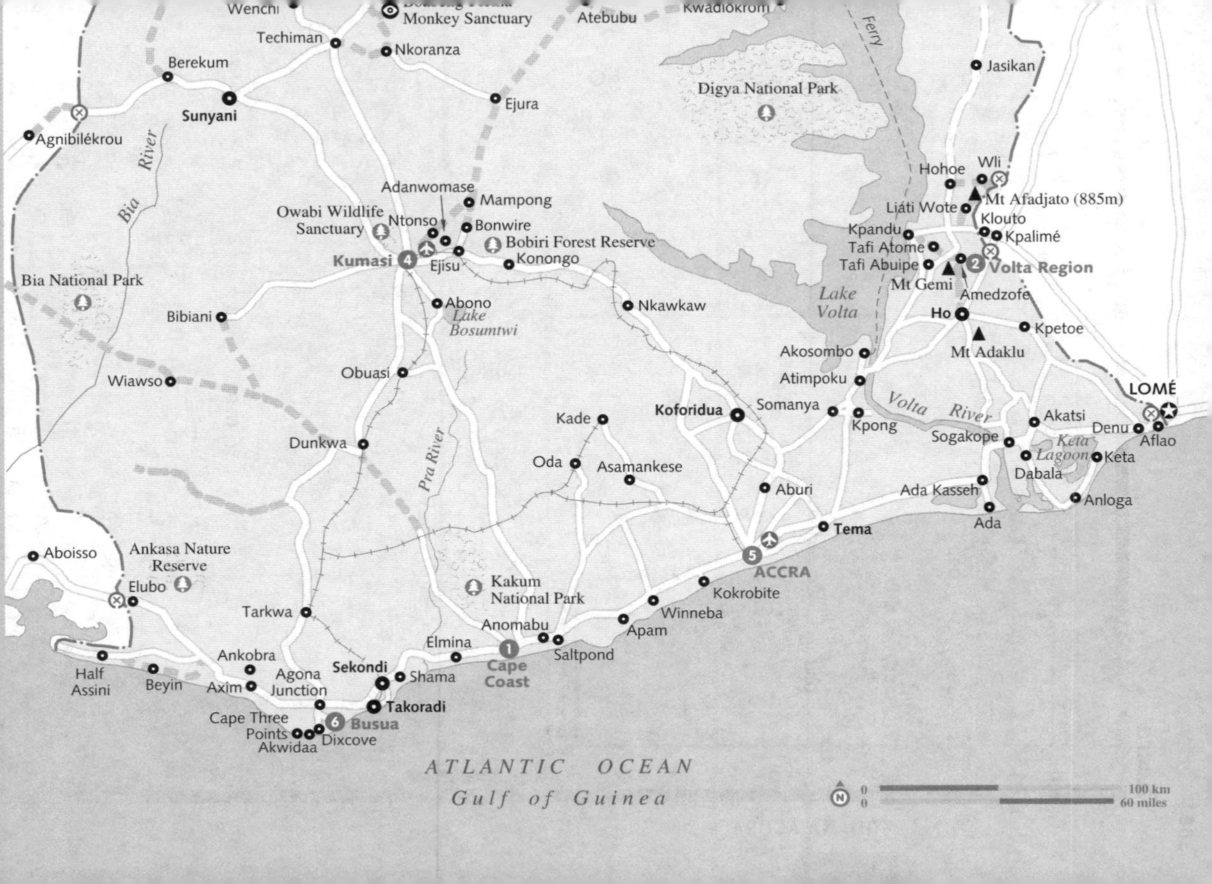

Wenchi
Monkey Sanctuary
Atebubu
Kwadiokrom
Techiman
Nkoranza
Berekum
Sunyani
Ejura
Agnibilékrou
Bia River
Digya National Park
Ferry
Jasikan
Hohoe
Wli
Mt Afadjato (885m)
Liati Wote
Klouto
Kpalimé
Kpandu
Tafi Atome
Tafi Abuipe
Mt Gemi
2 Volta Region
Amedzofe
Ho
Kpetoe
Mt Adaklu
Lake Volta
Adanwomase
Mampong
Owabi Wildlife Sanctuary
Ntonso
Bonwire
Bobiri Forest Reserve
Kumasi 4
Ejisu
Konongo
Nkawkaw
Bia National Park
Abono
Lake Bosumtwi
Bibiani
Obuasi
Wiawso
Akosombo
Atimpoku
Somanya
Kpong
Volta River
Koforidua
Kade
Oda
Asamankese
Dunkwa
Pra River
Aburi
Tema
5 ACCRA
Kokrobite
Winneba
Apam
Saltpond
Anomabu
1 Cape Coast
Kakum National Park
Elmina
Shama
Sekondi
Takoradi
6 Busua
Dixcove
Akwidaa
Cape Three Points
Agona Junction
Ankobra
Axim
Beyin
Half Assini
Elubo
Ankasa Nature Reserve
Aboisso
Tarkwa
LOMÉ
Aflao
Denu
Akatsi
Sogakope
Keta Lagoon
Keta
Dabala
Ada Kasseh
Ada
Anloga
ATLANTIC OCEAN
Gulf of Guinea
0 100 km
0 60 miles

Accra

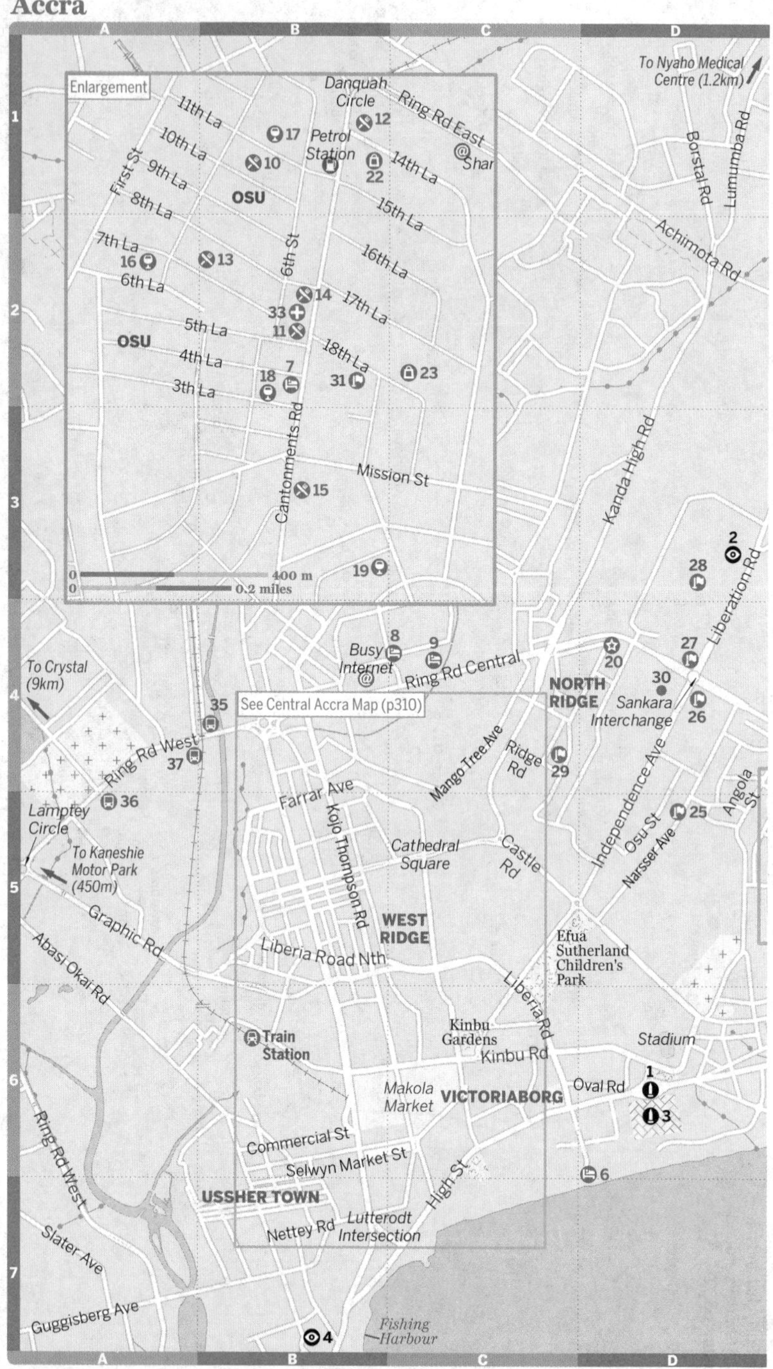

Enlargement
Danquah Circle
Ring Rd East
11th La
10th La
9th La
8th La
7th La
6th La
5th La
4th La
3th La
First St
6th St
14th La
15th La
16th La
17th La
18th La
OSU
Petrol Station
Shar
Cantonments Rd
Mission St
400 m
0.2 miles
To Nyaho Medical Centre (1.2km)
Borstal Rd
Lumumba Rd
Achimota Rd
Kanda High Rd
Liberation Rd
Busy Internet
Ring Rd Central
NORTH RIDGE
Sankara Interchange
To Crystal (9km)
See Central Accra Map (p310)
Ring Rd West
Mango Tree Ave
Ridge Rd
Farrar Ave
Independence Ave
Osu St
Narsser Ave
Angola St
Lamptey Circle
To Kaneshie Motor Park (450m)
Cathedral Square
Castle Rd
Kojo Thompson Rd
Graphic Rd
WEST RIDGE
Abasi Okai Rd
Liberia Road Nth
Efua Sutherland Children's Park
Liberia Rd
Train Station
Kinbu Gardens
Kinbu Rd
Stadium
Oval Rd
Makola Market
VICTORIABORG
Ring Rd West
Commercial St
Selwyn Market St
High St
USSHER TOWN
Lutterodt Intersection
Nettey Rd
Slater Ave
Guggisberg Ave
Fishing Harbour

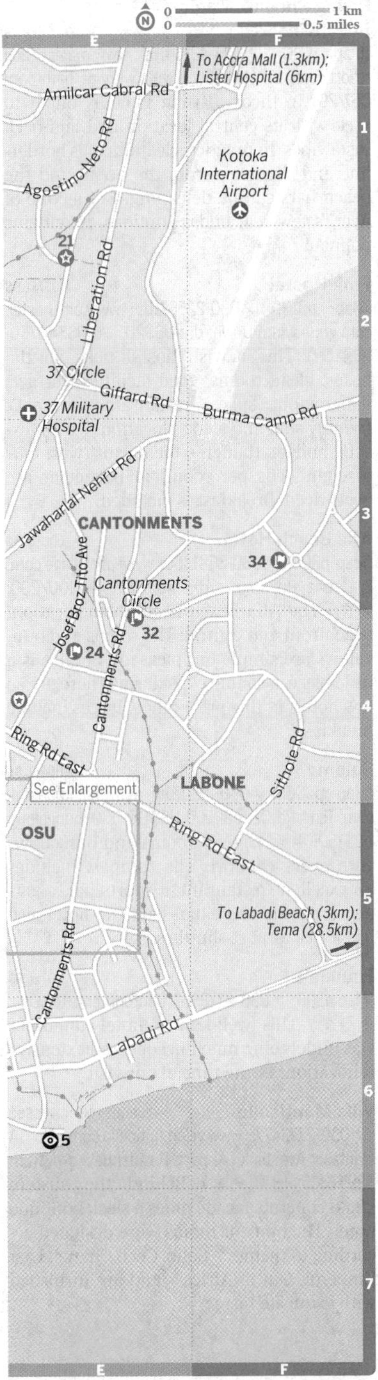

Accra

Sights

1 Black Star Square....D6
2 Flagstaff House....D3
3 Independence Square....D6
4 Jamestown....B7
5 Osu Castle....E6

Sleeping

6 Afia Beach Hotel....D6
7 Frankie's....B2
8 New Haven....C4
9 Paloma....C4

Eating

10 Buka....B1
11 Dynasty....B2
Frankie's....(see 7)
12 Koala Supermarket....B1
13 Mamma Mia's....B2
14 Monsoon....B2
15 Nourish Lab Smoothy's....B3
Paloma Restaurant....(see 9)

Drinking & Nightlife

16 Epo's Spot....A2
17 Firefly....B1
18 Republic Bar & Grill....B2
19 Ryan's Irish Pub....B3
The Lexington....(see 9)

Entertainment

20 +233....D4
21 Alliance Française....E2

Shopping

22 Global Mamas....B1
23 Vidya Books....C2

Information

24 Australian High Commission....E4
25 British High Commission....D5
26 Canadian High Commission....D4
27 Dutch Embassy....D4
28 French Embassy....D3
29 German Embassy....C4
30 Immigration Office....D4
31 Ivorian Embassy....B2
32 Togolese Embassy....E4
33 Trust Hospital....B2
34 US Embassy....F3

Transport

35 Neoplan Motor Park....B4
36 STC Ring Road....A5
37 VIP....A4

take a *tro-tro* (minibus) at Nkrumah Circle in Central Accra or along the Ring Rd.

National Museum MUSEUM
(Map p310; Barnes Rd; admission C7; ⏲9am-4.30pm Mon-Sun) Set in pleasant grounds, the national museum features excellent displays on various aspects of Ghanaian culture and history. The displays on local crafts, ceremonial objects and the slave trade are particularly noteworthy.

★ **Nima Tours** WALKING TOUR
(☎024-6270095; http://ghana-nima-tours.yolasite.com; Nima; per hr C5) Charles Sablah loves his neighbourhood. He also loves meeting new people, so he started welcoming couch-surfers in his home a few years ago. He showed them around Nima and what started as a standard friendly welcome has become a regular tour. Charles has done a lot of research to learn the history of the area and his enthusiasm and smile are infectious. He'll take you around the market, a primary school, local houses (all friends), bars and more. It's all tailored according to how long you have and what you'd like to do. A highly authentic and heartily recommended experience.

Sleeping

Accra has a good range of places to sleep, though prices are generally high.

New Haven HOTEL $
(Map p306; ☎030-2222053; newhavenhotel@yahoo.com; off Ring Rd Central, Asylum Down; s/d/tw C29/50/68) As far as budget places go in Accra, the New Haven is one of the best. Rooms are spacious and spotless, there is a pleasant courtyard and the location is excellent. The one problem is the extremely noisy generator used during power cuts (unfortunately still quite frequent).

Crystal GUESTHOUSE $
(☎030-2304634; www.crystalhostel.com; 27 Akorlu Cl, Darkuman; dm/s/d US$10/18.50/37;) The hosts go out of their way to make travellers welcome at this lovely budget set-up in the quiet suburb of Darkuman. Rooms have TV and fridge. There's a leafy communal lawn area and a rooftop terrace.

Rising Phoenix Magic Beach Resort BACKPACKERS $
(Map p310; ☎024-4315416; www.magicbeachresort.com; off High St; r with/without bathroom C57/29) In theory, Rising Phoenix ought to rock with its central location and laid-back rasta vibes. In practice, cleanliness is borderline and the noise from the ocean and the beach bars can be defeaning. But as one of Accra's few real budget options, it remains popular.

Pink Hostel HOSTEL $$
(Map p310; ☎030-2256710; www.pinkhostel.com.gh; Asylum Down; dm US$20, s/d US$40/50; @) This newish hostel ticks all the boxes: clean rooms, good facilities (terrace, hanging-out space, restaurant, internet), friendly staff and a good location. It's not exactly budget, though – the dorms (with four to eight beds per room) in particular are overpriced. Breakfast is included.

Afia Beach Hotel LODGE $$
(Map p306; ☎030-2681460; www.afiavillage.com; 2 Liberia Rd, Osu; s/d/f from US$85/100/200;) The Afia Beach is all about location: beachfront and central. The rooms and bungalows are simple but pleasant. Service is a little blasé, a shame considering there are so few hotels in this price range. Prices include breakfast.

Paloma HOTEL $$
(Map p306; ☎030-2231815; www.palomahotel.com; Ring Rd Central; s/d US$110/130, bungalows US$150; @) Cool rooms and bungalows with every comfort. The complex includes an excellent restaurant, a sports bar, a garden area and a cocktail bar. The hotel also has a free airport-shuttle service.

Frankie's HOTEL $$
(Map p306; ☎030-2773567; Cantonments Rd, Osu; @) This well-known hotel-cum-diner was undergoing much-needed and extensive renovations at the time of our visit.

Villa Monticello BOUTIQUE HOTEL $$$
(☎030-2773477; www.villamonticello.com; No 1A Mantaka Ave Link, Airport Residential; s/d from $295/345; @) Behind the austere khaki concrete facade hides a sleek boutique hotel. The opulent rooms were designed according to themes – Soho, Coco Chanel, Last Emperor, Out of Africa – and are furnished with exquisite taste.

Esther's Hotel BOUTIQUE HOTEL **$$$**
(030-2765751; www.esthers-hotel.com; No 4 Volta St, Airport Residential; s/d from $150/180;) Long one of Accra's fancier addresses, Esther's now looks a little frumpy in the face of Accra's swanky new establishments. It's still a lovely address, though, friendly and cosy. Prices include breakfast.

Eating

Accra has the best choice of restaurants in the country, and the food will seem like haute cuisine if you're returning to the city after time spent elsewhere in Ghana. Osu has the widest choice of restaurants (many cluster along the main street, Cantonments Rd, which is universally referred to as Oxford St), but if you're not fussy you'll find the ubiquitous chop bars everywhere around town.

You'll also find supermarkets, cafes and fast-food outlets at the Accra Mall (p311).

★**Khana Khazana** INDIAN **$**
(Map p310; www.khanakhazanaghana.getafrica online.com; Kojo Thompson Rd, Adabraka; mains around C10; 9am-10pm) Tucked behind a petrol station (Engen), this outdoor Indian restaurant is a gem – cheap, delicious and with long opening hours. One of the house specialities are the *dosas* (savory parcels made of rice flour normally eaten for breakfast). Sunday is *thali* (set meals) day.

Cuppa Cappuccino CAFE **$**
(off Volta St, Airport Residential; sandwiches C7-15; 8am-8pm Mon-Sat) This little cafe in the leafy Airport Residential Area is the king of sandwiches and juices. With its alfresco sitting area and fresh products, it's a top lunch choice.

Nourish Lab Smoothy's CAFE **$**
(Map p306; Cantonments Rd, Osu; smoothies C5, snacks from C4; 8am-11pm Mon-Sat, from 9am Sun;) Escape the heat at this air-conditioned smoothie bar. The staff will whip up anything you fancy while you sit back on the sofas, use the free wi-fi or watch MTV. Tasty pies, sandwiches and cakes too.

Koala Supermarket SUPERMARKET **$**
(Map p306; Cantonments Rd, Osu; 8.30am-9pm Mon-Sat, 11am-8pm Sun) An excellent, but expensive, range of products.

★**Buka** AFRICAN **$$**
(Map p306; 10th Lane, Osu; mains from C15-20; noon-9pm) Dig into mouth-watering Ghanaian, Nigerian, Togolese and Senegalese specials at hip Buka. The stylish 2nd-floor open-air dining room seals the deal. Come early for *fufu* (cooked and mashed cassava, plantain or yam).

Mamma Mia's PIZZERIA **$$**
(Map p306; 024-4264151; 7th Lane, Osu; mains C21-32; 6-10.30pm Tue-Fri, noon-10.30pm Sat & Sun) Expats swear by the pizza here and the pretty outdoor garden dining area makes everything taste better. Spaghetti and kid-friendly chicken fingers are also served.

Frankie's FAST FOOD **$$**
(Map p306; Cantonments Rd, Osu; mains C20-40; 24hr;) Stainless-steel tables, big-screen sports and a vast menu covering everything from hot dogs to meze. Though it feels a bit like the kind of diner you might find at a bowling alley, Frankie's is a crowd-pleaser.

Dynasty CHINESE **$$**
(Map p306; Cantonments Rd, Osu; mains C30-45; noon-3pm & 6-11pm Mon-Sat, noon-6pm Sun;) Accra's most central Chinese restaurant is also its plushest, with white tablecloths and easy-listening music; Sunday is dim sum day.

Paloma Restaurant AFRICAN **$$**
(Map p306; Ring Rd Central; mains C12-20; 6.30am-11pm;) With its string of outdoor terraces, charming staff and great African cuisine, this is a nice place to stop for lunch. In the evenings, the restaurant shows English Premier League football games.

Monsoon JAPANESE **$$$**
(Map p306; Cantonments Rd, Osu; mains C20-50; 6.30-11pm Mon-Sat;) Sushi, sashimi, teppanyaki – the food at this swanky Japanese establishment is delicious. The roof terrace is popular with expats for post-work drinks.

La Chaumière FRENCH **$$$**
(030-2772408; Liberation Rd; mains C35-50; 12.30-2.30pm & 6.30-10pm Mon-Fri, 6.30-10pm Sat;) Accra's swishest dining establishment with soft lighting, polished wooden floors, classical music and delicious French fusion gastronomy. La Chaumière is renowned for its steaks, but there is plenty of seafood on the menu too. Bookings essential.

Drinking & Entertainment

Accra's drinking scene is a moving target: new bars open every couple of months and the trend at the time of writing was for

Central Accra

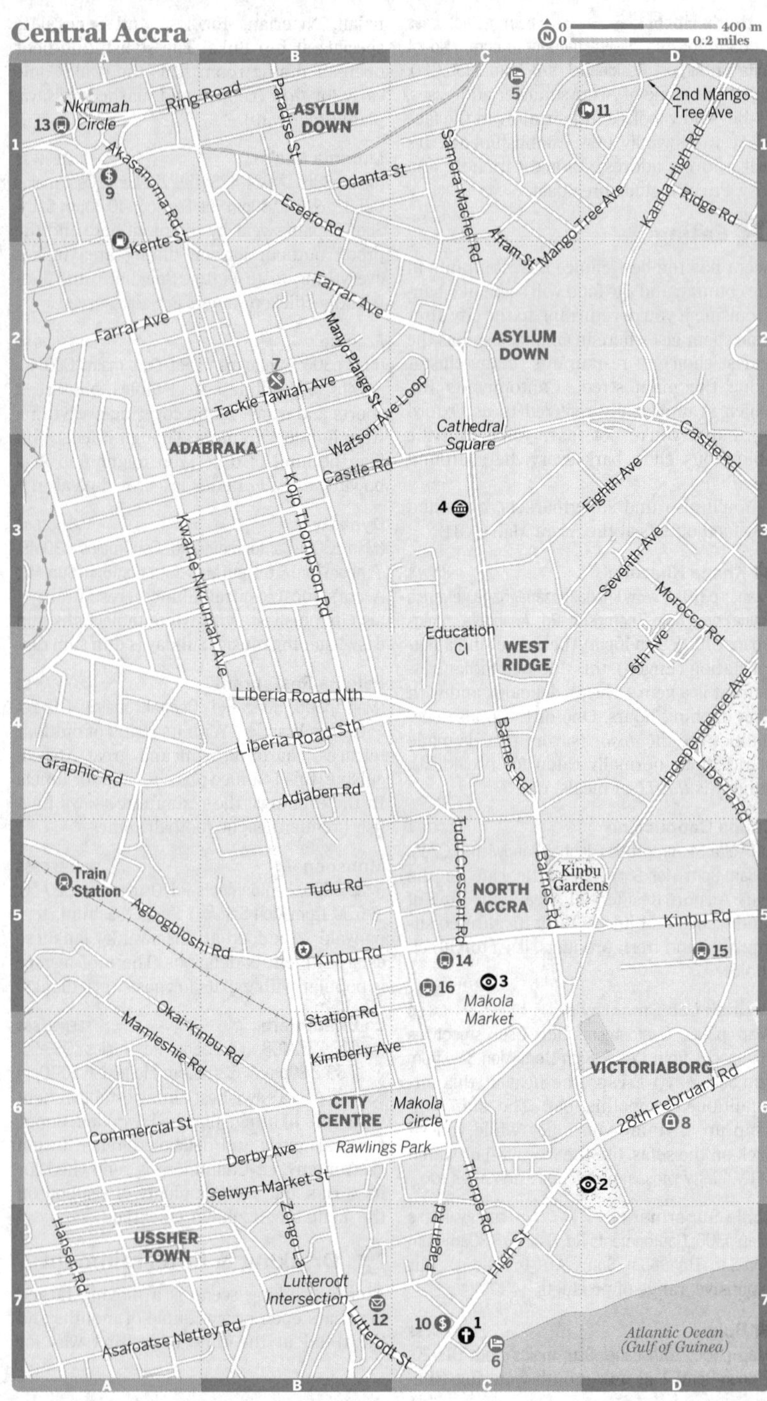

Central Accra

Sights
1 Holy Trinity Cathedral C7
2 Kwame Nkrumah Park D6
3 Makola Market C5
4 National Museum C3

Sleeping
5 Pink Hostel C1
6 Rising Phoenix Magic Beach Resort C7

Eating
7 Khana Khazana B2

Shopping
8 Centre for National Culture D6

Information
9 Barclays Bank A1
10 Barclays Bank Headquarters C7
11 Burkinabe Embassy D1
12 Main Post Office B7

Transport
13 Nkrumah Circle A1
14 STC Tudu C5
15 Tema Station D5
16 Tudu Station C5

super-sleek cocktail bars, not unlike those of Soho or Manhattan.

Epo's Spot BAR
(Map p306; off 7th Lane, Osu; 11am-late) Climb to the rooftop terrace of this low-slung building for cold drinks and good conversation. Epo's Spot is popular with Ghanaian couples who order simple dishes from the chop bar next door.

Republic Bar & Grill BAR
(Map p306; 3rd Lane, Osu; noon-midnight;) With its bright red walls, b&w photos, vintage postcards and outdoor wooden deck, this fab new bar wouldn't look out of place in Brooklyn. Here, it delights happening young Ghanaians and expats in equal measure.

The Lexington COCKTAIL BAR
(Map p306; www.thelexingtonaccra.com; Ring Rd Central, Paloma Hotel complex; 5pm-late Mon-Fri, 9am-late Sat & Sun) Entirely renovated and given a sleek new lounge-bar look, the Lexington is one of Accra's most happening spots, with karaoke, live music, sports nights, pub quiz and more. It also has an extensive menu, with tapas, bar snacks and mains, so you can make a night of it.

Ryan's Irish Pub PUB
(Map p306; behind Cantonments Rd, Osu; 11am-late) This Osu gastro pub is homely and welcoming. Ever true to its roots, there's beer on tap, footy on TV and a stash of board games.

Firefly LOUNGE BAR
(Map p306; 030-2777818; 11th Lane, Osu; 4pm-late) Accra's sleekest cocktail bar, where the capital's beautiful people come to see and be seen; dancing generally starts around 10pm on Friday and Saturday nights.

★+233 LIVE MUSIC
(Map p306; Ring Rd East, Ridge; 4.30pm-midnight) This 'Jazz Bar & Grill', as the strapline goes, is one of the best live music venues in Accra. Bands come from all over the continent and there is a great atmosphere.

Alliance Française LIVE MUSIC
(Map p306; www.afaccra.com; Liberation Link, Airport Residential Area) With several concerts a week (rock, jazz, reggae, hip-hop), exhibitions, and various cultural events, the cultural arm of the French embassy is a good bet whenever you're in town. Concerts generally cost C10 to C20.

Shopping

The **Accra Mall** (www.accramall.com; near Tetteh Quarshie Interchange; 10am-9pm Mon-Sat, noon-6pm Sun) has chain stores as well as supermarkets.

★Global Mamas FASHION
(Map p306; www.globalmamas.org; 14th Lane, Osu; 9am-8pm Mon-Sat, from 1pm Sun) This shop, which stocks pretty dresses, hats, tops, accessories (including lush scented shea butter), and kids clothes in colourful fabrics, is part of a bigger Fair Trade enterprise that is promoting sustainable income-generating activities for women.

Centre for National Culture MARKET
(Arts Centre; Map p310; 28th February Rd; 8am-6pm) A warren of stalls selling arts and crafts, known simply as the Arts Centre, this is the place to shop in Accra. The level of aggressive hassling may make you want to keep your cedis in your pocket, but if you have the patience and wherewithal, you can come away with good-quality handicrafts from all over Ghana.

Vidya Books BOOKS
(Map p306; 18th Lane, Osu; ⏲9.30am-6pm Mon-Fri, to 5.30pm Sat) Accra's most popular stop for new fiction and magazines.

Information

In addition to the following you can ask your embassy for a list of recommended doctors and specialists. Pharmacies are everywhere. You'll find dozens of banks and ATMs all over town.

Abacar Tours (☎024-9574691; 39 Bobo St, Tesano) Reputable operator run by a Franco-Ghanaian team, with plenty of options in Ghana and the possibility to extend into neighbouring Togo, Benin and Burkina Faso.

Barclays Bank Headquarters (Map p310; High St; ⏲8.30am-4.30pm Mon-Fri) Changes cash and travellers cheques (max US$250); ATM.

Busy Internet (Ring Rd Central; per hr C2.50; ⏲6am-11pm; wi-fi) Fast browsing, printing services and a laptop lounge.

Easy Track Ghana (☎027-665 7036; www.easytrackghana.com) Set up by two friends, an American and a Ghanaian, Easy Track has a strong focus on sustainable tourism and runs tours all over the country as well as in the rest of West Africa.

Immigration Office (Map p306; ☎021-2021667; off Independence Ave, North Ridge; ⏲8.30am-2pm Mon-Fri) Three-month visa extensions cost C40 and take two weeks to process. You will need a photo and a letter of application explaining the reasons for your extension request.

Lister Hospital (☎030-3409030; www.listerhospital.com.gh; Airport Hills, Cantonments) Ultra-modern 25-bed hospital. Has lab, pharmacy and emergency services.

SharpNet (Ring Rd East; per hr C2; ⏲24hr; wi-fi)

Time Out Accra (www.timeoutaccra.com; C15) A fantastic, glossy annual magazine with the low-down on what's hot and what's not in Accra. Great features on Ghana's cultural scene plus a section on day trips. Available in the capital's bookshops and large hotels.

Trust Hospital (Map p306; ☎030-2761974; www.thetrusthospital.com; Cantonments Rd, Osu) A private, slightly shabby-looking hospital that nevertheless has decent general practitioner and lab services.

Getting There & Away

AIR

Kotoka International Airport (www.ghanairports.com.gh), just 5km north of the ring road, is the main international gateway to the country. There are also domestic flights to Kumasi, Takoradi and Tamale.

BUS

The main **STC** (Map p306; ☎030-2252849; www.stcghana.com.gh; Ring Rd West) bus station and the **VIP** (Map p306; ☎020-8402080; Ring Rd West) bus station are on Ring Rd West. **STC** (Map p310) also has another depot in Tudu. For international services, see p334.

Services from Accra include:

- **Kumasi** (C18, 4½ hours, half-hourly, VIP station)
- **Cape Coast** (C9, two hours, three daily, STC Ring Rd station)
- **Takoradi** (C14, three hours, three daily, STC Ring Rd station)
- **Tamale** (C40, 11 hours, three daily, STC Ring Rd station)
- **Bolgatanga** (C44, 18 hours, three weekly, STC Ring Rd station)
- **Paga** (C46, 20 hours, three weekly, STC Ring Rd station)
- **Wa** (C42, 13 hours, two weekly, STC Ring Rd station)
- **Aflao** (C12, three hours, one daily, STC Tudu station)
- **Ho** (C6, three hours, one daily, STC Tudu station)
- **Hohoe** (C9, four hours, one daily, STC Tudu station)

TRO-TRO

Tro-tros (minibuses or pick-ups) leave from four main motor parks. Every taxi knows exactly which services leave from where.

Kaneshie Motor Park (Kaneshie): Cape Coast (C10, 2½ hours), Takoradi (C11, three hours) and other destinations to the west.

Neoplan Motor Park (Map p306; Ring Rd West): Kumasi (C12, four hours), Tamale and northern destinations.

Tema station (Map p310): Tema (C4, one hour), Ho (C8, three hours), Hohoe (C10, four hours).

Tudu station (Map p310): Aflao (C10, three hours), Akosombo (C4, 1¼ hours), Ho (C8, three hours), Hohoe (C9, four hours).

Getting Around

TO/FROM THE AIRPORT

It is essential that you allow plenty of time to get to the airport: even though it is relatively close to the city centre, it can only be accessed through one of Accra's most congested roads. A one-hour journey is common, two or three hours not unheard of.

A taxi from the airport to the centre should cost around C10.

TRO-TROS & TAXIS

Shared taxis and *tro-tros* travel on fixed runs from major landmarks or between major circles, such as Danquah Circle, 37 Circle and **Nkrumah Circle** (Map p310) (usually just called 'Circle'), the centre of Accra's public-transport universe. It can be quite daunting for newcomers, but Ghanaians are experts at navigating the system and will readily direct you or take you under their wing if they're travelling in the same direction.

- Major routes include Circle to Osu via Ring Rd; Circle to the main post office via Kwame Nkrumah Ave; Tudu station to Kokomlemle; 37 Circle to Osu; Makola Market to Osu; and Circle to the airport.
- Fares are usually very cheap, C0.2 to C0.40.
- *Tro-tros* run virtually 24 hours a day, with reduced frequency between midnight and 4am.
- Private taxis within the Ring Rd shouldn't cost more than C5.

THE EAST

The Volta region has to be Ghana's most underrated gem. The area is covered in lush, fertile farmland flanked by rocks, and mountains offering beautiful vistas. It is prime hiking territory and has great eco-tourism ventures.

Having your own car to explore the area really pays off here as the main points of interest are relatively scattered; *tro-tros* and charter taxis will get you everywhere – just not as quickly. Ho and Hohoe are the two main cities and transport hubs in the region, with regular buses and *tro-tros* to and from Accra (from Tudu station); allow three hours from Ho, four hours from Hohoe.

Akosombo

Built in the early 1960s to house construction workers involved in the completion of the hydroelectric dam of the same name, Akosombo is the site of the world's second-largest artificial lake (it was the largest until the Three Gorges Dam was completed in China).

Amazingly, you can visit the dam: the **Volta River Authority** (☎034-30220658) organises daily **tours** (per person C5; ⏲ on the hour, 10am-3pm), which explain its history and the essential role Akosombo plays in Ghana's economy. The agency also organises tours of the hydroelectric plant, although these must be booked in advance.

Sleeping & Eating

★ **Aylos Bay** LODGE $$
(☎024-3374443, 034-3020093; aylosbay@yahoo.com; Atimpoku; campsites C15, bungalows with fan/air-con C70/80; ❄) Set in lush green grounds right on the Volta River, Aylos Bay has lovely bungalows. The air-con waterside bungalows are well worth the extra C10. There's a gar-

GHANA READS

Ghana is one of the most interesting places to be in Africa right now, and there are tremendous books exploring the country's history.

- Ekow Eshun's *Black Gold of the Sun: Searching for Home in England and Africa* is an excellent account of the author's journey to reconcile his Ghanaian and British roots.
- *In My Father's Land*, by Star Nyanbiba Hammond, is part autobiography, part novel, inspired by the author's move from England to Ghana at the age of eight.
- Maya Angelou's *All God's Children Need Travelling Shoes* beautifully documents the author's emigration to Ghana.
- Albert van Dantzig's *Forts and Castles of Ghana* remains the definitive work on the early European coastal presence.
- *Kwame Nkrumah, The Father of African Nationalism* by David Birmingham is a comprehensive biography of the first African statesman; Nkrumah's own works give you an insight into the man and his beliefs.
- Paul Nugent's *Big Men, Small Boys and Politics in Ghana* is a good account of the Rawlings era.
- *My First Coup d'Etat: Memories from the Lost Decade of Africa* by the current president, John Dramani Mahama, chronicles his coming of age during the post-independence years.

den bar-restaurant and a beach, and you can rent canoes (C10). It's located just 500m from the Adomi Bridge on the Akosombo Rd.

Volta Hotel HOTEL **$$$**
(☎034-3020731; www.voltahotel; Akosombo; s/d/ste US$150/180/250; ❄@📶≋) Built on a hill overlooking the dam and the lake, it offers the most breathtaking panoramas. The interior looks a tad passé but the staff's professionalism and the spectacular setting are second to none. Rates include breakfast.

ℹ Getting There & Away

Akosombo is located about 7km north of the Accra–Ho road; the turn-off is at Atimpoku, just before the beautiful Adomi Bridge on the Volta River.

There are daily *tro-tros* from Accra to Akosombo (C4, 1½ hours). More likely, you'll have to change at Kpong (C4, one hour), a major transport hub on the Accra–Ho road, for onward travel to Atimpoku and Akosombo (C1, 30 minutes).

Amedzofe

Amedzofe's claim to fame is that, at 750m altitude, it is Ghana's highest settlement. The drive to the village, through the stunning Avatime Hills, is scenic and tortuous; it almost comes as a surprise when Amedzofe suddenly appears around a bend.

The village offers breathtaking vistas, a waterfall, forests, a cool climate and plenty of hiking opportunities. There's a fantastic community-run **visitor centre** (☎054-7297493; ⏲8am-6pm) where you can arrange hikes. Popular choices include a 45-minute walk to Amedzofe Falls (admission C5) – the last section is treacherous – and a 30-minute walk to the summit of Mt Gemi (611m; admission C5), one of the highest mountains in the area, where there is a 3.5m iron cross and stunning views.

You can stay at the **Abraerica** (☎054-7752361; www.abraericahospitalities.com; Amedzofe; s/d with fan C40/50, d/tw with air-con C65/75), a newly built hotel with squeaky-clean, slightly impersonal rooms but fabulous views. The nicest place to stay in the area, however, is **Biakpa Mountain Paradise** (☎024-4166226; www.mountainparadise-biakpa.com; Biakpa; campsites C9, s/d/f C25/40/50), a former government rest home converted into a lovely mountain hideaway near the village of Vane. It's a peaceful place, with a good restaurant, and staff can arrange hikes along the Kulugu River (C5) and bike rental (per hour C3).

For better or for worse, the (unsealed) road on which the guesthouse is located is about to become the main (sealed) Ho-Hohoe road. The traffic will definitely affect the site's tranquility but will also make it more accessible. At the moment, you can get as far as Vane by *tro-tro* but you then have to charter a taxi from Vane (C20).

There are *tro-tros* between Ho, Vane and Amedzofe (C3, one hour) except on Sunday. A private taxi between Ho and Amedzofe will cost C40.

Tafi Atome & Tafi Abuipe

These two small villages are worthy eco-tourism destinations in the region. **Tafi Atome** (admission C8) has long been known for its **Monkey Sanctuary**: the mona monkeys, revered by the villagers, are habituated and readily come to feed off the hand of visitors. Early in the morning and late in the afternoon, they can be seen roaming the village.

In **Tafi Abuipe** (admission C10), it is the village's kente weaving tradition that takes pride of place. You can visit the weaving room, tour the village and organise homestays (C7 per person per night). The kente in this part of Ghana is good value and with a bit of notice, villagers will produce any textile to any measurement and deliver it to where you're staying.

Tafi Atome and Tafi Abuipe lie a couple of kilometres west off the Ho-Hohoe road, not far off the village of Fume. If you don't have your own transport, you can charter a taxi from there for about C20.

Wli Falls

Ghana's tallest waterfalls, the Wli (pronounced 'vlee') falls stand amid an exquisite landscape of rolling hills, forests and bubbling streams.

It takes about 40 minutes to walk from the welcome centre to the lower waterfalls (C10) along an easy path. Much more challenging is the hike to the upper falls (C13), which takes about two hours and requires clambering in places. The falls are most impressive during the rainy season, when you can hear – and feel – the flow of water thundering down.

The excellent **Wli Water Heights Hotel** (☎020-9119152; wliheights@yahoo.com; r without/

with bathroom C40/55, d with air-con C80) is a beautiful spot just 500m from the falls. The garden is the perfect place to wind down after a day of trekking.

Wli is right on the border with Togo. Regular *tro-tros* and shared taxis make the scenic run between Wli and Hohoe (C2, 40 minutes). If you're heading for Togo, the Ghanaian border post is on the eastern side of Wli (turn left at the junction as you enter the village).

THE COAST

Kokrobite

It seems that Kokrobite has become victim of its own success. Endowed with a long stretch of white sand just 45 minutes from Accra, it is a favourite of backpackers, volunteers and Accra weekenders. But a number of travellers have complained about the pollution on the beach (used as the local toilet), robberies and the poor service at Kokrobite's main hotel, **Big Milly's Backyard** (☎0249 999330; www.bigmilly.com; camping C8, dm C12, d without bathroom & with fan C35, d/tr with bathroom & air-con C59/79; ❄ @). Still, it remains a good party spot (particularly on Friday and Saturday nights, with live music and barbecue) and a pleasant place to relax with a beer and the sound of the ocean for a couple of days.

Tro-tros (C1.25, 45 minutes) to Kokrobite go from the western end of Kaneshie motor park in Accra. A taxi from Accra will cost around C40.

Anomabu

Many travellers rate Anomabu's stunning beaches as second only to those further west, like Busua and Akwidaa. The sands and ribbons of low-key surf are certainly a big draw, but the village has its charms too. Former slave fort **Fort William** is now open to the public. It is in a bad state of repair, having served as a prison from 1962 to 2000, but fortkeeper Philip's **tours** (per person C5) are lively and fascinating.

The town also has a number of *posubans* (the shrines of the city's Asafo companies, ancient fraternities meant to defend the city); Posuban No 6, in the shape of a ship, is one of the largest. To find it, walk west from Fort William for about 50m towards the yellow house. When you see Posuban No 7 on your right, turn left down some steps, where you'll find Posuban No 6. Company No 3's *posuban*, which features a whale between two lions, is about 50m from the main road, opposite the Ebeneezer Hotel.

Anomabu Beach Resort (☎033-21291562; www.anomabo.com; campsites $15, huts with/without air-con US$45/75; ❄) is without a doubt the best place to stay here, and has attractive bungalows set within a sandy and shady grove of coconut palms. It tends to be very quiet during the week, and very busy at weekends and holidays when the restaurant puts on large barbecues. Wi-fi was in the works at the time of our visit.

You'll have no problem finding a *tro-tro* (C0.50, 15 minutes) to Cape Coast along the main road.

Cape Coast

POP 217,000

Forever haunted by the ghosts of the past, Cape Coast is one of the most culturally significant spots in Africa. This former European colonial capital, originally named Cabo Corso by the Portuguese, was once the largest slave-trading centre in West Africa. At the height of the slave trade it received a workforce from locations as far away as Niger and Burkina Faso, and slaves were kept locked up in the bowels of Cape Coast's imposing castle. From the shores of this seaside town, slaves were herded onto vessels like cattle, irrevocably altering the lives of generations to come.

Today, Cape Coast is an easygoing fishing town with an arty vibe, fanned by salty sea breezes and kissed by peeling waves. Crumbling colonial buildings still line the streets, while seabirds prowl the beaches and fishermen cast nets where slave ships once sailed. Many travellers use Cape Coast as a base to explore Kakum National Park, Anomabu and even Elmina.

Sights & Activities

You'll notice the ruins of Fort William, which dates from 1820 and now functions as a lighthouse, and Fort Victoria, originally built in 1702, on the town's hills, but you are advised not to venture to either because of muggings.

Cape Coast

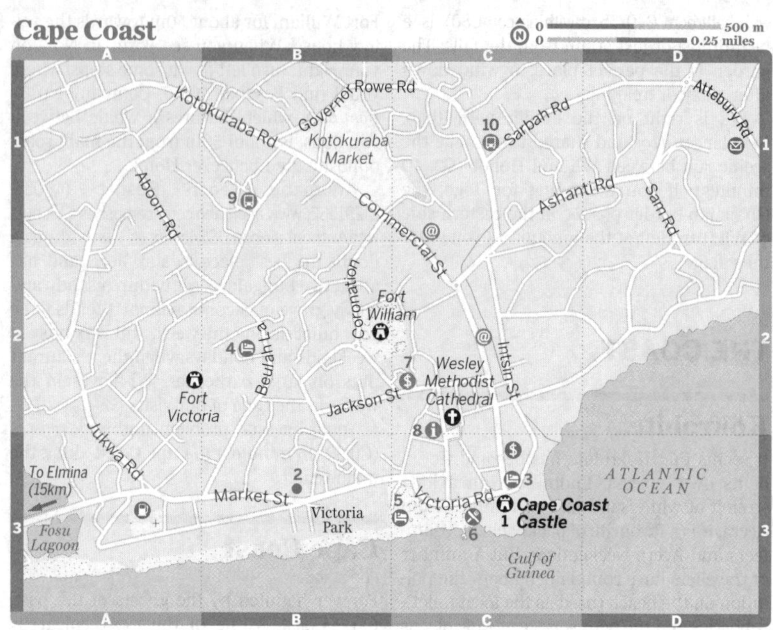

Cape Coast

Top Sights

1 Cape Coast Castle C3

Activities, Courses & Tours

2 Global Mamas B3

Sleeping

3 Baobab C3
4 Mighty Victory Hotel B2
5 Oasis Guest House C3

Eating

Baobab .... (see 3)
6 The Castle C3

Information

7 Coastal Foreign Exchange C2
8 Tourist Office C2

Transport

9 Kotokuraba Station B1
10 Tantri Bus Station C1

★ **Cape Coast Castle** CASTLE

(Victoria Rd; adult/student/child C11/7/2, camera fee C20; 9am-5pm) Cape Coast's imposing, whitewashed castle commands the heart of town, overlooking the sea. First converted into a castle by the Dutch in 1637 and expanded by the Swedes in 1652, the castle changed hands five times over the 13 tumultuous years that followed until, in 1664, it was captured by the British. During the two centuries of British occupation, it was the headquarters for the colonial administration until Accra was declared the new capital in 1877.

Now extensively restored, Cape Coast Castle deserves as much time as you can give it. Mountains of rusty cannonballs line the route walked by slaves, and castle staff conduct excellent tours of the grounds every hour or so (less frequently on Sunday). You'll be shown into the dark, damp dungeons, where slaves sat waiting for two to 12 weeks, all the while contemplating rumours that only hinted at their fate.

A visit to the condemned-slave cell (not for the claustrophobic) contrasts sharply with the incredible governor's bedroom, blessed with floor-to-ceiling windows and panoramic views of the ocean. There's also an excellent **museum** on the 1st floor, detailing the history of Ghana, the slave trade and Akan culture.

The castle buildings, constructed around a trapezoidal courtyard facing the sea, and the dungeons below, provide a horrifying insight into the workings of the slave trade.

Tours, which last about an hour, end with a passage through the Door of No Return.

★Global Mamas COURSE
(☎024-4973353; www.globalmamas.org; Market St) This fantastic outfit organises cooking courses (C34), batik courses (C48) and drumming and dancing courses (C22, minimum two people). All courses last three hours and can be organised at short notice (the day before); drumming courses cannot be held on Wednesday for taboo reasons.

Sleeping

Baobab GUESTHOUSE $
(☎054-0436130; www.baobab-children-foundation.de; Commercial St; s/d/tr/q without bathroom C18/25/35/40;) A lovely guesthouse with simple but well-kept rooms a stone's throw from Cape Coast Castle. All profits from the guesthouse go to the Baobab Children Foundation, which runs a school for disadvantaged children.

Oasis Guest House HOSTEL $
(☎024-3022594, 024-4089535; www.oasisbeach.net; seafront, Victoria Park; hut without/with bathroom C40/60, dm C12) Like a hip party spot, a night at Oasis is loud, hot and sweaty. Backpackers, volunteers and Cape Coast's beautiful people gravitate towards the beachfront bar, which does a good line in sandwiches, salads and cocktails. Staff are very friendly.

Sasakawa Guesthouse GUESTHOUSE $
(☎033-2136871; sasakawa@yahoo.com; University of Cape Coast, Newsite; s/d C50/60;) Originally built to accommodate Cape Coast University's visiting lecturers, this modern facility on the university's beautiful campus is now open to all. It is an absolute bargain, with wi-fi, satellite TV, air-con and breakfast all included in the price, and it's a great place to meet young Ghanaians. The campus is about 5km out of town, served by a constant stream of taxis.

Mighty Victory Hotel HOTEL $$
(☎033-2130135; http://mightyvictoryhotel.com; Aboom Cl; r with fan/air-con C40/75;) One of the best options in town: rooms are modern and cool, with crisp white sheets and hot running water. There's a good on-site restaurant, fast wi-fi in the reception area (per day C5) and helpful staff.

Kokodo Guesthouse GUESTHOUSE $$
(☎024-4673486; jcasmah@yahoo.co.uk; Residency Rd; r US$50-60;) This gorgeous, modern villa – formerly the house of Barclays Bank's manager – sits atop a bluff in a pretty garden. Rooms are spacious and airy, with gigantic beds. There is a wonderful restaurant lounge (mains C15). The only drawback is the location, on the outskirts of town.

Eating

As well as the options listed here, Oasis Guest House and the Kokodo Guesthouse restaurant are open to nonguests, and are definitely recommended.

Baobab VEGETARIAN $
(www.baobab-children-foundation.de; Commercial St; sandwiches C4.50, mains C6-7; 7am-8pm;) A tiny organic food bar with a wholesome touch, Baobab serves up great aubergine sarnies, soy lattes and refreshing pineapple or *bissap* juice (made from hibiscus and ginger).

The Castle AFRICAN $
(Victoria Rd; mains C6-15; 7am-11pm) Though not as impressive in size as its next-door neighbour (Cape Coast Castle), this wooden bar-restaurant is a charmer. The fare (a mix of Ghanaian and international dishes) is good, though not sensational.

Information

Barclays Bank (Commercial St; 8am-5pm Mon-Fri) Can change travellers cheques and cash; has an ATM.

Coastal Foreign Exchange (Jackson St; 8am-4.30pm Mon-Fri, 9am-1pm Sat) A good alternative to the perennially full Barclays for changing cash.

Cornell Internet (Commercial St; per hr C1; 7am-7pm)

Ocean View Internet (Commercial St; per hr C1; 7.30am-11pm) Printing, scanning, CD burning.

Tourist Office (King St; 8.30am-5pm Mon-Fri) On the 1st floor of Heritage House, a gorgeous colonial building; staff can help with practical information such as transport and directions but little else.

Getting There & Away

BUS

The STC bus station is near the Pedu junction, about 5km northwest of the town centre. Destinations include Accra (C5, three hours, twice daily), Takoradi (C4, one hour, twice daily) and Kumasi (C9, five hours, twice daily).

GHANA'S COASTAL FORTS

The chain of forts and castles (the terms are used interchangeably) along Ghana's coast is an extraordinary historical monument, unique in West Africa. Most of the forts were built during the 17th century by various European powers, including the British, Danes, Dutch, French, Germans, Portuguese and Swedes, who were vying for commercial dominance of the Gold Coast and the Gulf of Guinea. Competition was fierce and the forts changed hands like a game of musical chairs. By the end of the 18th century, there were 37 along the coastline.

The forts were concentrated along this reasonably short (around 500km) stretch of coast because access to the interior was relatively easy compared with the more swampy coastlines elsewhere along the West African coast, and because the rocky shore provided building materials. They were fortified not against the locals, with whom they traded equitably, but against attack from other European traders.

The forts were originally established as trading posts to store goods brought to the coast, such as gold, ivory and spices. Later, as the slave trade took over, they were expanded into prisons for storing slaves ready for shipping. Slaves were packed into dark, overcrowded and unsanitary dungeons for weeks or months at a time. Thousands died during their sequestration. If you tour any of the forts, you'll leave with a deep impression of just how brutally the captives were treated. When a ship arrived, they were shackled and led out of the forts to waiting boats through the Door of No Return.

Cape Coast Castle and St George's Castle at Elmina are both Unesco World Heritage Sites and must-sees. There are many smaller forts along the coast too, some of them not as well preserved, others not open to the public, but they all tell the same poignant story.

TRO-TROS

Shared taxis and *tro-tros* to local destinations such as Anomabu (C0.50, 15 minutes) and Elmina (C1.10, 15 minutes) leave from **Kotokuraba station** (Johnston Rd).

For *tro-tros* to Accra (C10, 2½ hours) and Kumasi (C12, four hours) head to **Tantri station** (cnr Sarbah & Residential Rds).

Ciodu Station (Jukwa Rd) serves destinations west of Cape Coast, such as Kakum National Park (C3.50, 30 minutes) and Takoradi (C3.50, one hour).

Kakum National Park

An easy day trip from Cape Coast, **Kakum National Park** (☎020-0420831, 033-2196146; admission C1; ⏰8.30am-3.30pm) is home to over 300 species of bird, 600 species of butterfly and 40 mammal species – on paper, that is. In practice, you'll be lucky if you see a monkey.

The park is famous for its **canopy walk** (adult/student C30/15), a series of viewing platforms linked by a string of bouncy suspension bridges 30m above the ground. The trouble is that it is being sold as an attraction rather than a national park, with steep admission fees, raucous noise on visits (which are always done in large groups, with no insistence from rangers to keep quiet) and, consequently, very little wildlife. The short **nature walks** (adult/student C15/7) offered from the visitor centre are hardly more authentic.

If you would like to see wildlife, you will need to venture further into the park and make special arrangements with a guide the day before.

The cafe at the visitor centre serves basic food, snacks and homemade ginger juice.

Kakum is easily accessible by public transport. From Cape Coast, take a *tro-tro* from Ciodu Station (C3.50, 30 minutes).

Elmina

POP 32,800

The enchanting town of Elmina lies on a narrow finger of land between the Atlantic Ocean and Benya Lagoon. Here, the air is salty and the architecture is a charming mix of colonial remnants, elderly *posubans*, and an imposing historical legacy in the shape of St George's Castle.

Sights & Activities

St George's Castle CASTLE

(Elmina Castle; adult/student/child C11/7/2, camera fee C20; ⏰9am-5pm) St George's Castle, a Unesco heritage site, was built by the Portuguese in 1482, and captured by the Dutch in 1637. From then until they ceded it to the British in 1872, it served as the African headquarters of the Dutch West India Company.

It was expanded when slaves replaced gold as the major object of commerce, and the storerooms were converted into dungeons. The informative tour (included in the entry fee) takes you to the grim dungeons, punishment cells, Door of No Return and the turret room where the British imprisoned the Ashanti king, Prempeh I, for four years. Later, soldiers of the Royal West African Frontier Force trained at the castle.

These days there are palm trees growing in the (dry) moat. The Portuguese church, converted into slave-auctioning rooms by the Protestant Dutch, houses a museum with simple but super-informative displays on the history and culture of Elmina.

Lagoon NEIGHBOURHOOD
The traditional name of Elmina is Anomansa, meaning inexhaustible supply of water. Watching the colourful *pirogues* pull in and out of the lagoon, breathing in the salty air and listening to the cacophony of shouts at the crowded Mpoben port is like having front-row theatre seats. The vast fish market is also fascinating to wander around, particularly when the day's fishing catch is being unloaded in the afternoon.

★**Ghana Ecotours** WALKING TOUR
(024-2176357; www.ghanaecotours.com; 1st fl, St George's Castle; 1-5 people C15) Run by the ebullient Felix, this sensational outfit offers highly informative walking tours (one hour) that retrace the city's history. Tours take in the local fish market, the town's *posuban*, colonial buildings, small alleyways and great panoramas.

Sleeping & Eating

★**Stumble Inn** LODGE $
(054-1462733; www.stumbleinnghana.com; dm C10, d C50) This little slice of heaven gets rave reviews from travellers, and rightly so: the spotless huts and dorm are homely (and eco-friendly, with solar panels and dry-composting toilets), the location right on the beach with gorgeous grounds is dreamy, the food is delicious and the staff are exquisite. It's located about 4km west of town, just before the Elmina Bay Resort.

Almond Tree Guesthouse B&B $$
(024-4281098; www.almond3.com; r C63-135;) It is Byron, Sonia and Michelle's warm welcome that makes this guesthouse so special. Originally from Jamaica, the family settled in Britain and then here. The rooms are impeccable and homely; some have shared facilities while others enjoy their own little balcony. Prices include breakfast.

Coconut Grove Beach Resort RESORT $$$
(033-2191213; www.coconutgrovehotelsghana.com; village d C100, resort d C260; @) This beach resort offers a variety of upmarket rooms as well as a pool, ball court and nine-hole golf course. Rooms in the resort's extension – called 'the village' – are good value. The resort is 3km west of Elmina.

Bridge House AFRICAN $
(mains C15; 11.30am-8pm;) With a terrace overlooking the fort and the lagoon, Bridge House is the nicest place to eat in town. The Black Star special is recommended. Portions are huge.

Getting There & Away

From the main taxi and *tro-tro* station (outside the Wesley Methodist Cathedral) you can get *tro-tros* to Takoradi (C3, one hour) or passenger taxis to Cape Coast (C1.10, 15 minutes).

Takoradi

POP 445,000

Takoradi was just a fishing village until it was chosen as Ghana's first deep-water seaport; since then it has prospered. Now feeding on Ghana's oil boom, Takoradi (or Taadi, as it's known) is growing larger by the day.

There isn't much for visitors here, but the town is an important transport hub so you're bound to go through it at some stage.

Sleeping & Eating

Amenla Hotel HOTEL $
(031-2022543; New John Sarbah Rd; d C35-40) A block from the STC station, a decent budget option, with plain rooms set around a pleasant courtyard.

Planter's Lodge LUXURY HOTEL $$$
(031-2199271; www.planterslodge.com; d from US$200; @) Originally built to accommodate British Royal Air Force flying officers, this exquisite compound is now a stylish

hideaway popular with oil magnates and the Takoradi jet set.

Bocadillos CAFE $
(6am-7pm Mon-Sat) Perfect for pastries and sandwiches.

North Sea AFRICAN $$
(Axim Rd; meals from C15-30; 7am-9pm) A kitsch restaurant serving the usual Ghanaian staples.

Getting There & Away

BUS

From the STC bus station, you'll find services to the following destinations:

- **Accra** (C11, four hours, three daily)
- **Kumasi** (C17, six hours, two daily)
- **Tema** (C12, five hours, two daily)
- **Tamale** (C33, 13 hours, one daily)
- **Bolgatanga** (C36, 16 hours, one daily)

TRO-TROS

Tro-tro stops are scattered around the main market roundabout. Everyone should be able to direct you. Destinations include Accra (C11, three hours), Kumasi (C13, five hours) and Agona Junction (C2, 40 minutes).

Busua

Some 30km west of Takoradi, the small village of Busua is a magnet for volunteers and backpackers, who love coming here to chill on the beach for a few days.

The surf here is some of the best in Ghana and there are some lovely excursions to do from the village. Make sure you contact local guide **Ebenezeer** (027-5283759, 029-3522188; per hr C5) if you want to explore the surroundings: not only does he know the area inside out, he's great company and always partial to a laugh.

Sights & Activities

★Butre VILLAGE
The stunning village of Butre is well worth the 3km walk from Busua. In fact, the walk itself is half the attraction: head east along the beach from Busua for about 2km then veer left along a path to go up a hill. The views of Butre when you reach the summit are a sight to behold, with the ruined Fort Batenstein nestled in palm trees on a bluff, Butre sandwiched between the ocean and the lagoon, and the ocean lapping a long, curvy beach beyond the lagoon.

Dixcove VILLAGE
Dixcove (or Dick's Cove, as it was once known) is a large, bustling fishing village, with a very different feel from Busua. Its natural harbour is deep enough for small ships to enter – one of the reasons the British chose to settle here, building **Fort Metal Cross** in 1696.

Dixcove is just 20 minutes' walk over the headland to the west of Busua. Locals warn against walking the track alone, however, so heed their advice and take a local guide with you.

Black Star Surf Shop SURFING
(026-1951360; www.blackstarsurfshop.com) This stalwart surfing establishment rents longboards, shortboards (per hour C15) and bodyboards (C6). They also run regular surfing lessons (C40, two hours).

Sleeping

Alaska Beach Club BACKPACKERS $
(020-7397311; huts with/without bathroom C50/25) Owned by an Alaskan with an eccentric sense of humour, the lovely Alaska offers an assortment of bungalows right on the beach. There is a large bar and restaurant too, complete with loud music and hammocks. All told, it offers the best value in town.

Busua Inn GUESTHOUSE $$
(020-7373579; www.busuainn.com; r with fan & cold water C55, r with air-con & hot water C110;) Busua's most charming midrange option. Owners Danielle and Olivier offer four clean, spacious and breezy rooms with sea views. There's a leafy terrace restaurant that backs onto the beach, serving good but overpriced French and West African dishes (mains C20 to C30) against a good wine list.

Busua Beach Resort RESORT $$$
(031-2093307; www.busuabeach.com; s/d/ste US$132/162/187; @) This plush resort has a slight corporate feel with its manicured lawns and impersonal bungalows. That said, you can't fault the service and facilities, so if you're after a little pampering you can be sure that the Busua Beach Resort will see you right. Rates include buffet breakfast.

Eating

The hotels listed here all serve food too. Being so close to the coast, the seafood is usually excellent and cheap, including lobster.

★**Okorye Tree** CAFE $

(mains C7-15; ⏲7am-9pm) Attached to the Black Star Surf Shop, the Okorye Tree does a roaring trade in pancakes and big burritos. Grab a table on the wooden deck, order a frozen margarita and watch the waves break.

Julian's AFRICAN $

(mains C4-8; ⏲8am-9pm) A cheerful and excellent local eatery that serves the usual fried rice and starch'n'sauce as well as very good thin-crust pizzas.

Information

There are no banking facilities in Busua (the nearest are in Agona or Takoradi. Internet (per hour C6) is available at the Busua Inn Resort.

Getting There & Away

Busua is about 12km from the main coastal road between Takoradi and Axim. To get there, get a *tro-tro* from Takoradi to Agona (C2, 40 minutes) and then a shared taxi to Busua (C1, 15 minutes).

To get to Akwidaa, you'll need to go back to Agona; from Akwidaa to Busua, however, you could stop at Dixcove and then walk from there.

Akwidaa & Cape Three Points

Akwidaa's unique selling point is its long, pristine white sandy beach, by far one of the best in Ghana. The village itself isn't as interesting as other settlements on the coast, but you can explore cocoa plantations and forests, organise canoe trips or visit the windswept Cape Three Points, Ghana's most southern point. The walk to the cape follows the local track for a while, which is monotonous landscape-wise but fascinating for local encounters (charcoal makers, *akpeteshie* – palm wine – distilleries etc).

By far and away the best place to stay in the area is **Green Turtle Lodge** (📱sms only after 5pm 026 4893566; www.greenturtlelodge.com; Akwidaa Beach; dm C12, d without/with bathroom C30/60). Built entirely from locally sourced, natural materials, the lodge has cute bungalows dotted all over a private stretch of beach. The bar plays laid-back tunes, the restaurant churns out chocolate-covered bananas and there's a stack of board games. The beach is a turtle nesting site and the staff organise nightly tours, as well as guided tours to all local attractions (C8 to C15). Magical.

Akwidaa is about 16km south of the Takoradi–Axim road. Take a *tro-tro* from Takoradi to Agona (C2, 40 minutes) and then a *tro-tro* from Agona to Akwidaa (C2, one hour). The driver can drop you off at the Green Turtle Lodge. *Tro-tros* stop in Dixcove on the way, handy if you want to get to Busua.

THE CENTRE

Kumasi

POP 1.98 MILLION

Once the capital of the rich and powerful Ashanti kingdom, Ghana's second city is still dripping with Ashanti traditions. Its heart, the huge Kejetia market, throbs like a traditional talking drum and its wares spill into the city so that no matter where you are in Kumasi, it sometimes feels like one enormous marketplace.

Kumasi has some interesting sights but the city's constant traffic congestion can be oppressive. Consider staying at Lake Bosumtwe, a gorgeous spot just one hour from Kumasi, and visiting Kumasi as a day trip.

If you're coming from Accra or Tamale, you might feel a pleasant drop in temperature.

Sights & Activities

★**Kejetia Market** MARKET

From afar, the Kejetia Market looks like an alien mothership landed in the centre of Kumasi. Closer up, the rusting tin roofs of this huge market (often cited as the largest in West Africa; there are 11,000 stalls and at least four times as many people working there) look like a circular shantytown. Inside, the throbbing Kejetia is quite disorienting but utterly captivating.

There are foodstuffs, secondhand shoes, clothes, plastic knick-knacks, glass beads, kente strips, Ashanti sandals, batik, bracelets and more.

Wandering around the market by yourself is absolutely fine: few tourists come here and shopkeepers will be pleasantly surprised to see you. Alternatively, go with a guide, who not only knows his or her way around but can also explain the more obscure trades and goods, and help you bargain and meet stallholders. Allow about C10 for a two-hour

Kumasi

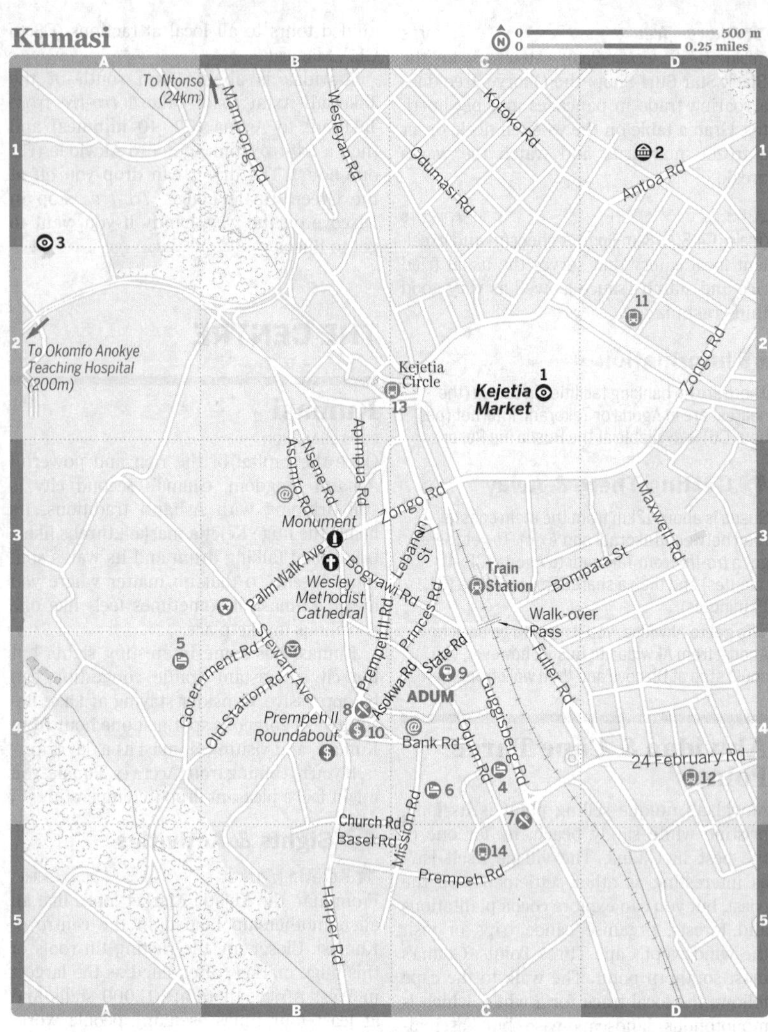

tour; contact the Ghana Tourist Authority or your hotel for recommendations.

Prempeh II Jubilee Museum MUSEUM
(National Cultural Centre; adult/student/child C5/4/1; ⏲8am-5pm Mon-Fri, 10am-4pm Sat & Sun) This museum may be small, but the personalised tour included with admission is a fascinating introduction to Ashanti culture and history. Among the displays are artefacts relating to the Ashanti king Prempeh II, including the king's war attire, ceremonial clothing, jewellery, protective amulets, personal equipment for bathing and dining, furniture, royal insignia and some fine brass weights for weighing gold.

Constructed to resemble an Ashanti chief's house, it has a courtyard in front and walls adorned with traditional carved symbols. Among the museum's intriguing photos is a rare one of the famous Golden Stool. The museum also contains the fake golden stool handed over to the British in 1900.

National Cultural Centre ARTS CENTRE
(⏲8.30am-5pm) The National Cultural Centre is set within peaceful, shaded grounds and includes craft workshops, where you

Kumasi

Top Sights
1 Kejetia Market C2

Sights
2 Manhyia Palace Museum D1
3 National Cultural Centre A1
Prempeh II Jubilee Museum .... (see 3)

Sleeping
4 Fosua Hotel C4
5 Kumasi Catering Rest House A4
6 Presbyterian Guesthouse C4

Eating
7 A-Life Supermarket C4
8 Vic Baboo's B4

Drinking & Nightlife
9 Eclipse C4

Information
10 Barclays Bank B4
Ghana Tourist Authority .... (see 3)

Transport
11 Alaba Station D2
12 Asafo Station D4
13 Kejetia Station C2
14 STC C5

can see brassworking, woodcarving, pottery making, batik cloth dyeing and kente cloth weaving, as well as a gallery and crafts shop.

Manhyia Palace Museum MUSEUM
(off Antoa Rd; adult/student C10/8; 9am-5pm) Manhyia Palace was built by the British in 1925 to receive Prempeh I when he returned from a quarter of a century of exile in the Seychelles to resume residence in Kumasi. It was used by the Ashanti kings until 1974; the current Asantehene now lives in a modern compound behind the museum.

On display is the original furniture and assorted royal memorabilia. During the festivities of Adae, which take place every 42 days, the Asantehene receives visitors; it's a fairly formal occasion but travellers are welcome.

Festivals & Events

The Ashanti calendar is divided into nine cycles of 42 days called Adae, which means 'resting place'. Within each Adae, there are two special days of worship, when a celebration is held and no work is done. The most important annual festival is the **Odwira festival**, which marks the last or ninth Adae. The festival features lots of drumming, horn blowing, food offerings and parades of elegantly dressed chiefs. Contact the tourist office for exact dates.

Sleeping

Accommodation in the budget and lower midrange categories is positively lacklustre in Kumasi.

Presbyterian Guesthouse GUESTHOUSE $
(032-2026966; Mission Rd; tw without bathroom C30, d with bathroom C50; P) Set in attractive green grounds, this two-storey guesthouse is the cheapest budget option in central Kumasi. The building and staff are rather austere and the bathrooms are only just clean. There's an on-site cafe, with meals from C2.50.

Ashanti Gold HOTEL $$
(032-2025875; www.ashantigoldhotel.com; s/d C40/65; ❄) This lemon-meringue building tucked behind the National Cultural Centre is a great midrange option, with friendly welcome, super-clean rooms and a certain charm with its ornamental fountain and kitsch furniture.

Fosua Hotel HOTEL $$
(032-2037382; Aseda House; s/d C50/60; ❄) Occupying the top floor of the Aseda Complex a block from the STC station, the rooms here are clean and comfortable. The place doesn't have much soul, but for the price and location it's as good as it gets in Kumasi.

Kumasi Catering Rest House GUESTHOUSE $$
(032-2026506; kcrhouse@yahoo.com; Government Rd; s/d/ste C65/80/125; ❄@) This charming guesthouse set within shady grounds a short walk from the centre gets top marks for its friendly service, huge and impeccable rooms and excellent on-site bar and restaurant (mains C10 toC15).

★ **Four Villages Inn** GUESTHOUSE $$
(032-2022682; www.fourvillages.com; Old Bekwai Rd; s/d US$80/90; ❄@) The Ghanaian-Canadian owners have pulled out all the stops at this impressive guesthouse. Each of

the four enormous air-conditioned rooms is decorated in a different style and there's a TV lounge and a tropical garden.

Chris and Charity are wonderful, knowledgeable hosts and can help you organise all manner of tours, including tip-top market tours with their local guide and excursions around Kumasi (C60 per person per day plus fuel). Prices include breakfast but exclude the 15% VAT.

Sir Max Hotel HOTEL $$
(032-2025222; sirmaxhotel@live.com; Ahodwo; d/tr US$80/100;) The rooms at Lebanese-run Sir Max are rather ordinary, but it's the facilities that really make the place: lovely pool, excellent travel agency, fab restaurant. Sir Max, it seems, does have it all.

Eating

Good Ghanaian chop houses (basic local-style restaurants) are dotted all over Kumasi.

Vic Baboo's INTERNATIONAL $
(Prempeh II Rd; mains C7-20; 11am-9.30pm;) Vic Baboo's is an institution among travellers and expats. With the biggest menu in town, this place is whatever you want it to be – Indian takeaway, decent burger joint, Lebanese deli or cocktail bar. It also has ice cream, cashew nuts and popcorn. Last orders are around 9pm.

A-Life Supermarket SUPERMARKET $
(Asafo Interchange; 8am-5pm Mon-Sat) A good range of snacks, ideal ahead of long bus journeys.

★ **Nik's Pizza** PIZZERIA $$
(off Old Bekwai Rd; pizza from C17; 2-9pm) New Image Kitchen, or Nik's as it's known, is a Kumasi gem. Friendly waiters serve excellent pizza (and only pizza) in a quiet, leafy garden setting. You're advised against walking here after dark because of the lack of street lighting. Go there with a taxi and keep his phone number to call him once you're finished. To find it: from Apino Plaza on the Old Bekwai Rd, turn left, and Nik's is signposted from there.

Chopsticks Restaurant CHINESE $$
(Old Bekwai Rd; mains C15-20; 11am-2.30pm & 6-10pm) Looking like the remains of a restaurant, Chopsticks is only a few outdoor tables with plastic chairs serving standard Chinese dishes and delicious large pizzas.

Moti Mahal Restaurant INDIAN $$$
(www.motimahalgh.com; Southern Bypass Rd; mains C17-30; noon-3pm & 7-11pm;) One of the most expensive restaurants in Kumasi, Moti Mahal is a formal place serving a large and excellent selection of Indian cuisine; because everything is a la carte (bread and rice must be ordered separately) the bill quickly adds up. Note too that prices do not include the 15% VAT, which can leave a sour note at the end of your meal...

★ **El Gaucho Restaurant** GRILL $$$
(Ahodwo; mains C17-40; 11am-10pm;) As the name suggests, Sir Max's restaurant prides itself in its grill: every kind of meat is thrown on the huge barbecue, including succulent (and pricey) T-bone steaks. El Gaucho also does an excellent line in Lebanese food (the owners are from Lebanon) and some fine pizzas.

Drinking & Nightlife

El Gaucho Restaurant and Nik's Pizza are some of the nicest bars in town (it's 'buy one drink and get one free' at El Gaucho on Tuesday).

Eclipse BAR
(Adum Rd; 11am-11pm) A friendly beer joint with an outdoor patio on the street; inside it's all diamond-shaped mirrors and big-screen sports.

Funkies BAR
(11am-11pm) Big outdoor space, English premiership football and blaring music are the staples at this low-key bar.

Information

There are half a dozen banks in the centre, all with ATMs and foreign exchange facilities. Pharmacies are dotted all over town.

Barclays Bank (Prempeh II Roundabout; 8.30am-4.30pm Mon-Fri) Changes travellers cheques; ATM.

Ghana Tourist Authority (National Cultural Centre; 7am-5pm Mon-Fri) In the National Cultural Centre complex. Staff can help arrange guided tours of the city and surrounding villages: their prices at the time of our visit were outrageous, though (about six times the going rate), so just get the information you need and arrange a guide through your hotel instead.

Okomfo Anokye Teaching Hospital (032-2022301; www.kathhsp.org; Bantama Rd) Kumasi's main public hospital with 700-plus beds.

State Internet Café (Asomfo Rd; per hr C1; 7.30am-8pm)

Unic Internet (Bank Rd; per hr C1; 8am-7pm)

Getting There & Away

AIR

Kumasi airport is on the northeastern outskirts of town, about 2km from the centre. **Fly 540 Africa** (www.fly540africa.com) and **Antrak Air** (www.antrakair.com) both offer regular flights to Accra (one way starts around US$25). A taxi from the centre to the airport costs about C10. Allow plenty of time because of the traffic.

BUS

You will find the following bus services:

- Accra (C17, four hours, half-hourly; operated by VIP)
- Cape Coast (C9, five hours, twice daily; operated by STC)
- Takoradi (C17, six hours, twice daily; operated by STC)
- Tamale (C25, eight hours, once daily; operated by STC)
- Ouagadougou (Burkina Faso; C36, 15 hours, three weekly; operated by STC)

TRO-TRO

There are three main motor parks in Kumasi, each with its allocated destinations:

Asafo station (Asafo): Cape Coast (C10, four hours), Accra (C10, four hours), Kunatase (C2, 45 minutes)

Alaba station (Alaba): Wa (C20, six hours), Tamale (C15, five hours)

Kejetia station (Kejetia Circle): for local *tro-tros* around Kumasi

Around Kumasi

The area around Kumasi is famed for its craft villages. Some have become quite touristy, but a couple of community-run initiatives are well worth a day trip.

The easiest way to visit these scattered villages is to hire a private taxi (about C70 for a full day).

Ntonso

Ntonso, 15km north of Kumasi, is the centre of adinkra cloth printing. Adinkra symbols represent concepts and aphorisms; they are traditionally printed on cotton fabric by using a natural brown dye and stamps carved out of calabash. You can see the whole process explained at **Ntonso's Craft Centre** (admission C3) and even create your own works; strips of fabric are sold for C10 and make a lovely keepsake.

Tro-tros travelling north from Kejetia station stop at Ntonso (C1).

Adanwomase

This kente-weaving and cocoa-growing village wins the Palme d'Or of eco-tourism in Ghana. Villagers here have put a huge amount of effort into developing fun, informative tours.

There are two visits on offer: a kente tour and a village tour (C5 each, or C7 combined). The kente tour takes you through the kente production process, from thread to finished product, and lets you try your hand at spinning and weaving. The village tour for its part takes you through the cocoa plantations, to local shrines and the local palace.

There are direct *tro-tros* (C1.10) from Kejetia station in Kumasi.

Lake Bosumtwe

With a depth of 86m, Lake Bosumtwe (also spelled Bosumtwi) is a crater lake that was formed from the impact of a huge meteorite. The lake is hugged by lush green hills in which you can hike, cycle and ride horses. Local hotels are your best bet to organise excursions. **The Green Ranch** (☎020 2917058; Lake Bosumtwe) offers horse-riding (per hour C30).

Located 38km southeast of Kumasi, the village of **Abono** is the gateway to Lake Bosumtwe; it is a popular weekend holiday spot for Kumasi residents, who come here to relax and swim (the water is bilharzia free). It's also a sacred site. The Ashanti people believe that their souls come here after death to bid farewell to the god Twi. Historically, dugout canoes and boats were forbidden on the lake, but the tide has turned and Bosumtwe becomes a haven for water-sport enthusiasts on the weekends.

Foreign visitors will be charged C2 upon arriving in Abono.

Sleeping & Eating

Lake Bosumtwe makes a great alternative to Kumasi for exploring Ashanti country: the accommodation is better value and the setting is, well, unrivalled. The downside is that there is less choice.

★ **Lake Point Guesthouse** LODGE $
(☎024-3452922; Lake Bosumtwe; dm/d/tr C10/38/46) This little piece of heaven sits right on the shore of Lake Bosumtwe, in a

secluded spot about 2km east of Abono. The bungalows, bright and charming, are scattered on the slopes of a beautiful garden. Stephen, the Ghanaian owner, is a delightful host and can help you organise excursions around the lake and Ashanti country. His restaurant is the best in the area, with a daily changing menu (mains C12 to C25) and, a rare thing in Ghana, desserts.

Rainbow Garden Village LODGE $$
(☎024-3230288; Lake Bosumtwe; dm/d/bungalows C15/50/65) The Rainbow used to be the place to stay in Bosumtwe, but the hotel is looking a little tired these days. The location, right on the lakeside, is as enchanting as ever, but the service and rooms need a new lease of life. It's located 4km west of Abono.

Getting There & Away

You can sometimes find *tro-tros* travelling directly between Kumasi and Abono, but it's more likely you'll need to go to Kunatase first (C2, 45 minutes) and then catch a shared taxi from there (C1, 15 minutes).

THE NORTH

Tamale

POP 538,000

If the northern region is Ghana's breadbasket, Tamale is its kitchen. If you can take the heat, you'll discover a town with some good food, charm and a whole lot of soul. (If you can't, don't panic: Mole National Park is generally cooler.)

Tamale's population is largely Muslim and there are several interesting **mosques** around town, notably on Bolgatanga Rd. The **National Culture Centre** (off Salaga Rd) is a lively place, with **craft shops** and regular dance and music performances.

Sleeping

TICCS Guesthouse GUESTHOUSE $
(☎037-2022914; www.ticcs.org/residence; s/d with fan C20/23, with air-con C27/30) Set in lovely grounds, this Christian guesthouse offers clean, simple rooms, serene surroundings and the great roof-terrace Jungle Bar. The full breakfast (fruit, porridge, bread, omelette, hot drink) is well worth the C8.

Catholic Guesthouse GUESTHOUSE $
(☎037-2022265; Gumbihini Rd; s/d with fan C21/36, with air-con C25/48; P ❄) Simple, air-conditioned rooms wrapped around a pretty courtyard.

African Dream Hotel GUESTHOUSE $$
(☎037-2091127; www.africandreamhotel.com; Bolgatanga Rd; r US$75-80; ❄ wifi) A dream indeed to find this boutique guesthouse 10km north of Tamale. The work of a Franco-Ghanaian-Swiss couple, African Dream offers gorgeous rooms in pretty landscaped grounds. Because the guesthouse is outside of town, Abu Prince offers pick-ups and drops from town and the airport. He can also arrange tours to Mole National Park and northern Ghana.

Eating & Drinking

Swad Fast Food INDIAN $
(Gumbihini Rd; mains C7-13; ⏰9am-10pm) The name might not be a winner, but this is one of the best places to grab a bite in Tamale. The speciality is Indian, but there are also such delights as French onion soup, red red (a Ghanaian dish with beans) and fish-finger sandwiches.

Sparkles CAFE $
(Culture Centre; mains C6-10; ⏰8am-8pm) A simple cafe serving good Ghanaian food alongside Western staples such as sandwiches. It's popular with local volunteers.

Jungle Bar BAR
(TICCS Guesthouse, Gumbihini Link Rd; ⏰4-9pm) The Jungle Bar, on the grounds of the TICCS Guesthouse, is on a leafy balcony with an all-wood bar, cable TV and comfy benches and is probably the nicest spot for a drink in Tamale. Also serves food.

Giddipass BAR
(Crest Restaurant, Salaga Rd; ⏰10am-10pm) Sit on the rooftop terrace and let an ice-cold beer and the sweet sounds of northern hiplife into your world at this decent drinking spot.

Information

Barclays (Salaga Rd; ⏰8.30am-5pm Mon-Fri) Changes cash and travellers cheques; ATM.

Stanbic (Salaga Rd; ⏰8.30am-4.30pm Mon-Fri) Changes cash; ATM.

Tamale Teaching Hospital (☎037-2022454; Salaga Rd) The main hospital in Northern Ghana, 2km southeast of town.

Vodaphone (internet per hr C1.40; ⏰9am-10pm; wifi) The fastest connection in town (still pretty slow at busy times); it's right next to the towering radio mast near the STC bus station.

Getting There & Away

Buses and *tro-tros* congregate around the Total petrol station and the radio mast in the centre of town. There are regular *tro-tros* to Bolgatanga (C6, three hours) and Wa (C15, six hours).

Air The airport is about 20km north of town; a private taxi there costs around C20. Antrak Air and Fly 540 Africa fly between Tamale and Accra from US$50 one way.

Bus STC buses go to Accra (C40, 12 hours, daily), Kumasi (C25, six hours, daily), Cape Coast and Takoradi (C33 to C35, 13 hours, twice a week). The daily Metro Mass bus to Mole National Park (C5, four to six hours) leaves in theory at 2.30pm (but in practice much later) from the bus station behind the Total petrol station. Buy a ticket in advance or arrive at the bus station well before the scheduled departure time to be sure of a seat.

Mole National Park

With its swaths of saffron-coloured savannah, **Mole National Park** (☎027-7564444, 024-4316777; www.molemotelgh.com; adult/student C10/5, car C4, driver C5) offers what must surely be the cheapest safaris in Africa. There are at least 300 species of bird and 94 species of mammal, including African elephants, kob antelopes, buffalos, baboons and warthogs.

The park organises walking and driving **safaris** (2hr safari per person C6; ⊙7.30am & 3.30pm). If you do not have your own vehicle, you can rent the park's for C100 for the two-hour safari; park rangers are happy to let you pool with other travellers.

The safaris are excellent and sightings of elephants are common from December to April. You're guaranteed to see other mammals year-round, however. Sturdy, covered footwear is a must; if you come without, the rangers will insist on lending you a pair of Wellington boots for a fee of C2.

Sleeping & Eating

Mole Motel HOTEL **$$**
(☎024-4316777, 027-7564444; www.molemotelgh.com; Mole National Park; dm C24, r without/with aircon C70/90, bungalows C105; ❄ 🏊) The park's only accommodation, Mole Motel is overpriced, with tired rooms and blasé service, but the location is stupendous (and the pool a godsend): at the top of an escarpment, with a viewing platform overlooking plains teeming with wildlife. There's also a reasonable restaurant, serving a mix of Ghanaian and international fare (mains from C12 to C18). The hotel gets very busy, so make sure you book well in advance.

Getting There & Away

A daily Metro Mass bus from Tamale (C5) arrives at the park motel around 7pm, if all goes well. The same bus overnights at the park, returning to Tamale the next day, leaving the park at around 4am.

A daily Metro Mass bus from Tamale to Wa (C8) passes through Larabanga around 9am or 10am; Mole Motel can arrange transport to Larabanga (C5).

CULTURE AT MOLE

As well as the fantastic wildlife, Mole has some cultural gems to offer. Larabanga, the nearest village to the national park on the Tamale–Wa road, is famous for its **mud-and-stick mosque**, reputedly the oldest of its kind in Ghana.

Travellers have reported a fair bit of hassle at Larabanga in the past. To avoid complications, make sure you go with a local guide (C5), which you can easily arrange at the park's visitor centre.

About 10km east of the visitor centre, the village of **Mognori** (canoe trip 1-5 people C25, village tour per person C8, cultural performance 1-4 people C30) has become a flourishing ecotourism venture. The village sits right on the edge of the national park and villagers offer canoe safaris on the river (there are monkeys, birds and crocodiles), village tours (where you can learn about shea-butter production and traditional medicine), and drumming and dancing performances. Homestays can also be arranged (C10 per person per night, C10 for breakfast and dinner).

Tours are informative and the village very pretty and it makes a nice change from the Mole Motel if you're there for a few days.

Bolgatanga

POP 66,685

Bolgatanga – usually shortened to Bolga – was once the southernmost point of the ancient trans-Saharan trading route, running through Burkina Faso to Mali.

Bolga doesn't have much in the way of sights, but the city is laid-back and a fine base to explore the surrounding area – and it's the last stop on the road to Burkina.

Tanga Tours (☎024-9874044; tangatoursgh@gmail.com; Black Star Hotel, Bazaar Rd) offers guided scooter/bike excursions in the region. The renowned **crafts market**, where you'll find some of the best selections of textiles, leatherwork, baskets and the famous Bolga straw hats, takes place every three days.

For internet, head to **Sirius Click Internet Café** (Black Star Hotel, Bazaar Rd; per hr C1; ⏰7.30am-9pm). Banks congregate around the main *tro-tro* station off Zuarungu Rd.

Sleeping & Eating

Nsamini Guesthouse GUESTHOUSE $
(☎027-7316606, 038-2023403; off Navrongo Rd; r without/with bathroom C16/20) A popular choice, this cute courtyard set-up is one of Bolga's best budget buys. Rooms are clean and Koffi, the affable owner, will make you feel at home. It's up a lane leading off the Navrongo Rd.

Sands Garden Hotel HOTEL $
(☎038-2023464; sandgardenshotel@yahoo.com; off Zuarungu Rd, behind Metro Mass station; r with fan/air-con C30/50) A very pleasant establishment, with simple but impeccable rooms and very friendly management. The courtyard restaurant (mains C7 to C15) is one of the more popular in town. Rates include breakfast.

Black Star Hotel HOTEL $
(☎038-2022346; Bazaar Rd; s/d without bathroom C28/36, with bathroom C40/48; ❄@) The prices say budget, but the hotel definitely feels midrange, with air-con throughout and good facilities including a bar and an internet cafe. Some of the ground-floor rooms feel a little claustrophobic; ask to see a couple before you choose.

Swad Fast Food INTERNATIONAL $
(off Navrongo Rd; mains C10; ⏰11am-9pm) The outdoor terrace is lovely, but if the heat is too much, you can always retreat to the air-con dining room. The menu is eclectic – Indian, Chinese, Ghanaian – but excellent overall.

PAGA'S CROCODILE PONDS

If you've ever dreamt of a *Crocodile Dundee* photo opportunity, make a beeline for **Paga's Crocodile Ponds** (adult/student C7/6, chicken to feed the croc C5). The ponds' reptiles, which are held sacred by the locals, are reputed to be the friendliest in Africa and, while we're not totally convinced, plenty of visitors do indeed safely pose with the crocs. Local women even do their laundry in the pond while kids frolic in the water. It is frankly disarming when you know how dangerous crocodiles can be.

Legend has it that this state of blissful cohabitation goes back to a pact the town's founders made with local crocodiles not to hurt each other.

There are two ponds to visit: Chief's Pond on the main road and Zenga Pond, about 500m east off the main road. Both are signposted.

Getting There & Away

Tro-tros to Tamale (C6, three hours) and Paga (C4, 40 minutes) leave from the motor park off Zuarungu Rd, past the police station.

The STC bus station is 500m south of the centre, on the road to Tamale. There are daily services to Kumasi (C30, eight hours) and Accra (C44, 12 hours).

THE NORTHWEST

This remote corner of Ghana is hard to reach and seldom visited for that reason.

Wa

The capital of the Upper Northwest region is basically an overgrown village. If you happen to overnight here (to visit Wechiau or break the journey between Bobo-Dioulasso and Kumasi), check out the town's mud-and-stick mosque.

The **Tegbeer Catholic Guesthouse** (☎039-2022375; r with shared bathroom & fan C30, s/d with bathroom & air-con C28/45; ❄), about 3km north of town, is an excellent option with clean, good rooms and a nice on-site bar-restaurant (mains C7). More upmarket is **Upland Hotel** (☎039-2022180; s/d C60/80), west of the town centre, which is popular with the town's businesspeople and has air-con and DSTV in the rooms. The restaurant serves international cuisine (mains C10).

There are regular *tro-tros* and buses to Wechiau (C2, one hour), Tamale (C15, six hours), Hamale (C6, three hours) and Kumasi (C20, six hours).

Wechiau Hippo Sanctuary

This much-hyped **hippo sanctuary** (www.ghanahippos.com; adult/student C7/5) on the Black Volta River was initiated by local village chiefs in 1999. Hippos can usually be seen from December to August; once the rainy season is under way, however, hippos disappear and the site becomes very hard to reach – probably not worth the considerable effort it takes to get to this remote corner of Ghana.

When you arrive, report at the community centre in Wechiau village, where you'll pay your fees and organise activities. Options include river safaris, birdwatching, village tours and nature walks. All activities cost C6 per person per hour.

Accessing Wechiau is no small feat, even if you have your own vehicle. The village is located about 50km southwest of Wa, about an hour's drive; the sanctuary is then a further 20km (of bad tracks) from Wechiau. *Tro-tros* run between Wa and Wechiau (C2, one hour); the community centre can then help you hire a bicycle/motorbike/*tro-tro* for C5/10/20 to cover the last leg of the journey.

Unless you have your own vehicle, you'll have to overnight at the sanctuary. There is a very basic guesthouse (rooms C10); meals are not available, so you'll need to bring all your food.

UNDERSTAND GHANA

Ghana Today

Ghana is regarded by international analysts as West Africa's golden child: one of the continent's most stable democracies and fastest-growing economies.

Since the country discovered oil off the coast in 2007, the economy has gone into overdrive. Signs of this newfound prosperity abound, especially around Takoradi, the epicentre of the oil industry, and Accra: cranes work around the clock on new real estate developments, traffic congestion is horrendous, smart phones are everywhere – it definitely feels more like South Africa than Guinea or the DRC.

This is way too simplistic a portrait of Ghana, however. If you're a middle-class young professional living in the leafy 'burbs of Accra, life is good. Chances are you have running water, power, street lights and a fair wage.

But in Accra's poorest suburbs or the rural parts of northern Ghana, development is a work in progress. People defecate in the open for lack of sanitation; school-aged children sell water sachets in the street and women still spend many hours fetching water at the village pump.

The 2012 presidential elections made much of the debate on universal education and sharing the profits of wealth. John Dramani Mahama (who succeeded John Atta Mills as leader of the NDC after he died in July 2012) won, although his victory was being challenged at the time of writing by opposition candidate Nana Akufo-Addo on the grounds of alleged rigging.

History

Present-day Ghana has been inhabited since 4000 BC, filled by successive waves of migrants from the north and east. By the 13th century several kingdoms had developed, growing rich from the country's massive gold deposits and gradually expanding south along the Volta River to the coast.

Power & Conflict

By the 16th century one of the kingdoms, the Ashanti, emerged as the dominant power, conquering tribes left, right and centre and taking control of trade routes to the coast. Its capital, Kumasi, became a sophisticated urban centre, with facilities and services equal to those in Europe at the time. And it wasn't long until the Europeans discovered this African kingdom. First the Portuguese came prospecting around the coast; the British, French, Dutch, Swedish and Danish soon followed. They all built forts by the sea and traded slaves, gold and other goods with the Ashanti.

But the slave trade was abolished in the 19th century, and with it went the Ashanti domination. By that time the British had taken over the Gold Coast, as the area had come to be known, and began muscling in on Ashanti turf. This sparked several wars between the two powers, culminating in the

British ransacking of Kumasi in 1874. The British then established a protectorate over Ashanti territory, which they expanded in 1901 to include areas to the north. The Gold Coast was now a British colony.

The Road to Independence

By the late 1920s the locals were itching for independence, and they set up political parties dedicated to this aim. However, parties like the United Gold Coast Convention (UGCC), formed in 1947, were too elitist and detached from those they were meant to represent – the ordinary workers. So the UGCC's secretary-general, Kwame Nkrumah, broke away in 1948 and formed the Conventional People's Party (CPP), which became an overnight success. Nkrumah was impatient for change and called for a national strike in 1949. The British, anxious about his popularity, jailed him. Despite this, the CPP won the elections of 1951. Nkrumah was released and he became prime minister.

Independence & the Nkrumah Years

When Ghana finally won its independence in March 1957, Nkrumah became the first president of an independent African nation. His speeches, which denounced imperialism and talked about a free, united Africa, made him the darling of the pan-African movement.

But back home Nkrumah was not popular among traditional chiefs and farmers, who were unimpressed with the idea of unity under his rule. Factionalism and regional interests created an opposition that Nkrumah tried to contain through repressive laws, and by turning Ghana into a one-party state.

Nkrumah, however, skilfully kept himself out of the fray and concentrated on building prestige projects, such as the Akosombo Dam and several universities and hospitals.

But things were starting to unravel. Nkrumah expanded his personal bodyguard into an entire regiment, while corruption and reckless spending drove the country into serious debt. Nkrumah, seemingly oblivious to his growing unpopularity, made the fatal mistake of going on a state visit to China in 1966. While he was away his regime was toppled in an army coup. Nkrumah died six years later in exile in Guinea.

Dr Kofi Busia headed a civilian government in 1969 but could do nothing to overcome corruption and debt problems. Colonel Acheampong replaced him in a 1972 coup, but few things changed under his tenure.

The Rawlings Years

By 1979 Ghana was suffering food shortages and people were out on the streets demonstrating against the army fat cats. Enter Jerry Rawlings, a good-looking, charismatic, half-Scottish air-force pilot, who kept cigarettes behind his ear and spoke the language of the people. Nicknamed 'Junior Jesus', Rawlings captured the public's imagination with his calls for corrupt military rulers to be confronted and held accountable for Ghana's problems. The military jailed him for his insubordination, but his fellow junior officers freed him after they staged an uprising. Rawlings' Armed Forces Revolutionary Council (AFRC) then handed over power to a civilian government (after a general election) and started a major 'house cleaning' operation – that is, executing and jailing senior officers.

The new president, Hilla Limann, was uneasy with Rawlings' huge popularity, and later accused him of trying to subvert constitutional rule. The AFRC toppled him in a coup in 1981, and this time Rawlings stayed in power for the next 15 years.

Although Rawlings never delivered his promised left-wing revolution, he improved the ailing economy after following the orders of the International Monetary Fund (IMF). During part of the 1980s, Ghana enjoyed Africa's highest economic growth rates.

The Democratic Era

By 1992 Rawlings was under worldwide pressure to introduce democracy, so he lifted the 10-year ban on political parties and called a general election. However, the hopelessly divided opposition couldn't get their act together, and Rawlings won the 1992 elections freely and fairly, with 60% of the vote. Still licking their wounds, the opposition withdrew from the following month's parliamentary elections, giving Rawlings' newly formed National Democratic Congress (NDC) an easy victory. In 1996 he repeated this triumph in elections that were again considered free and fair. At much the same time, the appointment of Ghanaian Kofi Annan as UN secretary-general boosted national morale.

After eight years of Rawlings and the NDC (the constitution barred Rawlings from standing for a third term in the 2000 presidential elections), his nominated successor and former vice-president, Professor John Atta Mills, lost to Dr John Kufuor, leader of the well-established New Patriotic Party (NPP). Some fun-loving members of Accra's growing middle class say his biggest legacy is the creation of the Accra Mall, a shiny shopping mall on the outskirts of town, complete with the country's first multiscreen cinema. Under the Kufuor administration, primary-school enrolment increased by 25% and many of Ghana's poor were granted access to free health care.

The 2008 election was widely regarded as a test of Ghana's ability to become a modern democracy. Atta Mills won by a slim margin and, despite the tensions with NPP competitor Nana Akufo-Addo, the election passed without serious violence.

People of Ghana

Ghana's population of 25 million makes it one of the most densely populated countries in West Africa. Of this, 44% are Akan, a grouping that includes the Ashanti (also called Asante), whose heartland is around Kumasi, and the Fanti, who fish the central coast and farm its hinterland. The Nzema, linguistically close to the Akan, fish and farm in the southwest. Distant migrants from present-day Nigeria, the Ga are the indigenous people of Accra and Tema. The southern Volta region is home to the Ewe.

In the north, the Dagomba heartland is around Tamale and Yendi. Prominent neighbours are the Gonja in the centre, Konkomba and Mamprusi in the far northeast, and, around Navrongo, the Kasena. The Sisala and Lobi inhabit the far northwest.

Religion

Ghana is a deeply religious country and respect for religion permeates pretty much every aspect of life, from hilarious sideboards ('Jesus Loves Fashion', 'If God Says Yes Snack Bar') to preachers on public transport and street corners, ubiquitous religious celebrations such as funerals, and the wholesale takeover of Ghana's airwaves by God (and his workers) on Sunday.

You'll come across churches of every imaginable Christian denomination; even the smallest village can have two or three different churches. About 70% of Ghanaians are Christian. Pentecostal and Charismatic denominations are particularly active, as are the mainline Protestant and Catholic churches. If you can bear the length (three to four hours), attending a service is an enlightening experience, whatever your creed.

Christianity was introduced by European missionaries, who were also the first educators, and the link between religion and education persists.

About 15% of the population is Muslim; the majority are in the north, though there are also substantial Muslim minorities in southern cities such as Accra and Kumasi.

Many Ghanaians also have traditional beliefs, notably in spirits and forms of gods who inhabit the natural world. Ancestor veneration is an important part of this tradition. Many people retain traditional beliefs alongside Christian or Muslim beliefs.

The Arts

Music

There's no doubt about it: Ghana's got rhythm. Whichever part of the country you visit, Ghana's soundtrack will be a constant travel companion. From the age of three or four children are taught to dance: it's not unusual to see little kids copying the hip-grinding and ass-shaking that characterises the average Ghanaian party.

Traditional music doesn't have the popular following that it has in countries such as Burkina. It tends to be reserved for special occasions and associated with royalty.

Contemporary music, on the other hand, is thriving. Highlife, a mellow mix of big-band jazz, Christian hymns, brass band and sailor sonnets, hit Ghana in the 1920s, and popular recordings include those by ET Mensah, Nana Ampadu and the Sweet Talks. Accra trumpeter ET Mensah formed his first band in the 1930s and went on to be crowned the King of Highlife, later performing with Louis Armstrong in Ghana.

WWII brought American swing to Ghana's shores, prompting the first complex fusion of Western and African music. Hiplife, a hybrid of rhythmic African lyrics poured over imported American hip-hop beats, has now been ruling Ghana since the early 1990s.

TEXTILES

Kente cloth, with its distinctive basketwork pattern in garish colours, is Ghana's signature cloth. Originally worn only by Ashanti royalty, it is still some of the most expensive material in Africa. The cloth can be single-, double- or triple-weaved and the colour and design of the cloth worn are still important indicators of status and clan allegiance.

Kente is woven on treadle looms, by men only, in long thin strips that are sewn together. Its intricate geometric patterns are full of symbolic meaning, while its orange-yellow hues indicate wealth.

Imported American hip-hop and Nigerian music closely compete for the number two spot after highlife. Gospel music is also big, as is reggae.

Arts & Crafts

Ghana has a rich artistic heritage. Objects are created not only for their aesthetic value but as symbols of ethnic identity or to commemorate historical or legendary events, to convey cultural values or to signify membership of a group.

The Akan people of the southern and central regions are famous for their cloth, goldwork, woodcarving, chiefs' insignia (such as swords, umbrella tops and linguist staffs), pottery and bead-making.

Around Bolgatanga in the north, fine basket weaving and leatherwork are traditional crafts. Drums and carved *oware* boards – the game of *oware* has various names throughout West Africa – are also specialities.

Food & Drink

Fiery sauces and oily soups are the mainstay of Ghanaian cuisine and are usually served with a starchy staple like rice, *fufu* (cooked and mashed cassava, plantain or yam) or *banku* (fermented maize meal).

About the most common dish you'll find is groundnut stew, a warming, spicy dish cooked with liquefied groundnut paste, ginger and either fish or meat. Palm-nut soup (fashioned from tomatoes, ginger, garlic and chilli pepper, as well as palm nut) takes its bright red colour from palm oil. Red-red is a delicous bean stew normally served with fried plantain.

Cold water is sold everywhere in plastic sachets (called 'pure water') for about C0.10. Fresh fruit juices are, oddly, rather hard to find. Beer, on the other hand, isn't: popular brands include Star, Club, Gulder and Guinness. For something stronger, look no further than *akpeteshie* (palm wine), the fiery local spirit made from palm wine.

SURVIVAL GUIDE

Directory A–Z

ACCOMMODATION

- If you're looking for a bargain, Ghana probably isn't it.
- Budget hotels don't often provide a top sheet, so pack a sleeping liner.
- Despite the high prevalence of malaria in Ghana, remarkably few hotels have mosquito nets; wear repellent and cull before you go to sleep.
- Rooms with bathrooms are generally called 'self-contained'.

EMBASSIES & CONSULATES

The following are all in Accra.

Australian High Commission (Map p306; ☎030-2216400; www.ghana.embassy.gov.au; 2 Second Rangoon Cl, Cantonments)

British High Commission (Map p306; ☎30-2213250; http://ukinghana.fco.gov.uk; 1 Osu Link)

Burkinabe Embassy (Map p310; ☎030-2221988; 2nd Mango Tree Ave, Asylum Down)

Canadian High Commission (Map p306; ☎030-2211521; www.canadainternational.gc.ca/ghana; 46 Independence Ave, Sankara Interchange)

Dutch Embassy (Map p306; ☎030-214350; www.ambaccra.nl; 89 Liberation Rd, Ako Adjei Interchange)

French Embassy (Map p306; ☎030-2214550; www.ambafrance-gh.org; 12th Lane, off Liberation Rd)

German Embassy (Map p306; ☎030-2211000; www.accra.diplo.de; 6 Ridge Rd, North Ridge)

Ivorian Embassy (Map p306; ☎030-774611; 18th Lane, Osu)

Togolese Embassy (Map p306; ☎030-777950; 4th Circular Rd)

US Embassy (Map p306; ☎030-2741000; http://ghana.usembassy.gov; 4th Circular Rd)

EMERGENCY

Call ☎193 for ambulance, ☎192 for fire and ☎191 for police.

ETIQUETTE

- Ghanaians are an affable lot and greetings are of paramount importance. You will always be welcomed, greeted and asked how you are and it is expected you do the same in return.
- Humour is entrenched in Ghanaian culture and always the best way to deal with tricky situations; for instance, when calls of 'Obroni' (meaning white person) become too much, it's fine to call back 'Bebeni' (meaning black person).
- In Muslim areas, remember not to pass food or shake hands with your left hand.
- The only way to call somebody or get their attention is by hissing or making a 'tsssss' sound; this is also how people will try to get your attention.

FESTIVALS & EVENTS

Ghana has many festivals and events, including the Fetu Afahye Festival (first Saturday of September) in Cape Coast, the Bakatue Festival (first Tuesday in July) in Elmina, the Fire Festival (dates vary according to the Muslim calendar) of the Dagomba people in Tamale and various year-round Akan celebrations in Kumasi. Panafest, an arts festival, is celebrated biennially in Cape Coast.

INTERNET ACCESS

You can get online pretty much anywhere in Ghana these days. Many hotels offer wi-fi, all mobile-phone networks have 3G and there are internet cafes in every town and city (connection costs C1 to C2.50 per hour).

MONEY

In 2007 four zeros were lopped off the value of the old Ghana cedi (divided into 100 pesewas), making it the highest-value currency in West Africa. For the most part, Ghanaians have adjusted, but you'll still hear people asking for C10,000 when they really want C1.

- The best currencies to bring are US dollars, UK pounds and euros, in that order.
- Barclays is the only bank to exchange travellers cheques; there is a maximum of US$250 per transaction.
- Foreign-exchange bureaus are dotted around most major towns: note that they give lower exchange rates for small USD denominations, so pack your $50 and $100 notes.
- There are ATMs virtually everywhere; almost every bank accepts Visa. Stanbic accepts Mastercard and Maestro.
- Midrange and top-end hotels tend to accept credit cards, but at a surcharge.

OPENING HOURS

Administrative buildings From 8am until 2pm or so. Embassies tend to keep similar hours.

Banks 8am-5pm Monday to Friday; some additionally run until noon on Saturday.

Markets 7am-5pm; in predominately Muslim areas, Friday is quieter; in Christian areas, it's Sunday.

Shops 9am-5pm or 6pm every day except Sunday, when only large stores open.

PUBLIC HOLIDAYS

New Year's Day 1 January
Independence Day 6 March
Good Friday March/April
Easter Monday March/April
Labour Day 1 May
May Bank Holiday 1st Monday in May
Africa Unity Day 25 May
Republic Day 1 July
Founders Day 21 September
Christmas Day 25 December
Boxing Day 26 December

Ghana also celebrates Muslim holidays, which change dates every year.

SAFE TRAVEL

Ghana has proved to be a stable and generally peaceful country. Take care of your valuables on beaches and avoid walking alone at night. If swimming, beware strong currents; ask locals before diving in.

PRACTICALITIES

- **Newspapers** Accra's best dailies are *Daily Graphic* (www.graphic.com.gh) and *Ghanaian Chronicle* (www.ghanaian-chronicle.com).
- **BBC World Service** Listened to widely; in Accra it's 101.3FM.
- **Radio** Local Ghanaian stations include the excellent Joy FM (news and music; 99.7FM), Choice FM (102.3) and Gold FM (90.5).
- **TV** Ghana's biggest TV stations are GTV, Metro TV and TV3. Satellite TV is increasingly available in midrange and upmarket hotels.
- **Electricity** 230V and three-pin British-style plugs are used. Power cuts remain frequent.
- **Languages** English, plus nine local languages.

TELEPHONE

- Ghana's country code is +233.
- Mobile (cell) phones are ubiquitous in Ghana and the network coverage is virtually universal and excellent value.
- If you have an unlocked phone, SIM cards (C5) can be picked up in shopping centres and communication centres.
- MTN, Vodafone, Tigo and Airtel are the main networks; all have 3G.
- International SMS costs about C0.1, international calls from C0.13 per minute.

TOURIST INFORMATION

As a rule, tourist information is pretty useless in Ghana, and staff working in tourist offices have little understanding of what travellers need.

NCRC (www.ncrc-ghana.org) The driving force behind Ghana's most successful community-tourism ventures and a good source of information on the topic.

No Worries Ghana (www.noworriesghana.com) Published by the North American Women's Association, this guide (both paper and electronic) is more targeted at people moving to rather than travelling to Ghana; nonetheless, the dozens of eating, drinking and entertainment listings as well as the information on shipping, transport and so on is very useful.

Touring Ghana (www.touringghana.com) Ghana's official tourism portal; worth a look for inspiration and general information.

VISAS

Visas are required by everyone except Economic Community of West African States (Ecowas) nationals. Though it's technically possible to pick up a visa upon arrival, they only get granted in rare cases, so it is highly advisable you get one ahead of travelling.

- Single-entry three-month visas (US$60/£50) and multiple-entry six-month visas (US$100/£70) are standard.
- You can get a visa extension at the immigration office (p312) in Accra near the Sankara Interchange.

Visas for Onward Travel

Most nationalities need a visa for onward travel throughout West Africa.

Burkina Faso The embassy issues visas for three months (C73), usually in 24 hours. You need three photos.

Côte d'Ivoire A three-month visa costs CFA65,000 and requires a hotel confirmation. See full list of requirements at www.snedai.com. The Visa de l'Entente, available in Burkina Faso, is a much more expedient and cheaper process.

Togo The embassy issues visas for one month on the same day. Alternatively, you can get a visa at the border at Aflao, but it's only valid for seven days and you'll need to extend it in Lomé.

VOLUNTEERING

Ghana is one of Africa's top volunteering spots, and you'll find literally hundreds of organisations that arrange short-term and long-term placements.

Many guesthouses listed in this book can help arrange short-term placements within their communities or local schools. The government-sponsored US Peace Corps and UK Voluntary Service Overseas are both active in Ghana.

Getting There & Away

You need a yellow-fever vaccination certificate to enter Ghana.

AIR

Kotoka International Airport in Accra is Ghana's international gateway and an increasingly important hub for regional African air travel.

- Every major European airline flies to Accra; Emirates now also flies daily to Dubai, opening a host of easy connections to Asia-Pacific. There are direct flights to the US east coast.
- You'll find plenty of direct flights to other parts of Africa, including South Africa, Kenya, Ethiopia, Egypt, Morocco and most neighbouring West African countries.

LAND

Ghana has land borders with Côte d'Ivoire to the west, Burkina Faso to the north and west, and Togo to the east. Crossing is generally straightforward. The main border crossings:

- With Côte d'Ivoire: Elubo, Sunyani-Agnibilékrou and Bole-Ferkessédougou
- With Burkina Faso: Paga and Hamale
- With Togo: Aflao and Wli

Border crossings are normally open 6am to 6pm, except Afloa, which shuts at 10pm.

Burkina Faso

- Direct STC buses run to Ouagadougou from Accra (C48 + CFA1000, 24 hours) and Kumasi three times a week.
- From Paga, there are frequent *tro-tros* to Bolgatanga (C4, 40 minutes); on the Burkina side, you'll find plenty of onward transport to Pô and Ouagadougou.
- There were rumours that a direct bus service between Kumasi and Bobo-Dioulasso via Wa would start running in 2013. Until then, you'll need to get a *tro-tro* from Wa to Hamale. On the Burkina side, you'll find transport to Diebougou and then Bobo-Dioulasso.

Côte d'Ivoire

- STC buses run daily between Accra and Abidjan (C39 + CFA1000, 12 hours).

➡ Otherwise you'll find *tro-tros* running between Takoradi and Elubo (three hours), from where you can cross into Côte d'Ivoire and find onward transport to Abidjan.

Togo

➡ The easiest way to cross into Togo is to catch a bus or a *tro-tro* to Aflao, pass the border on foot and catch a taxi on the other side to central Lomé.

➡ Overlanders may prefer to cross at the less hectic Wli border post near Hohoe.

Getting Around

AIR

➡ Antrak Air (p324) and Fly 540 Africa (p324) operate domestic flights in Ghana.

➡ There are several daily flights from Accra to Kumasi (45 minutes), Takoradi (35 minutes) and Tamale (1¼ hours). They tend to be relatively cheap and a huge time saver when travelling north.

BUS

➡ Buses are preferable to *tro-tros* for long journeys as they tend to be more comfortable and reliable.

➡ **STC** (http://beta.stcghana.com.gh) is Ghana's main long-haul bus company; its route network is extensive, it is fairly reliable and despite the sometimes unbearably loud music/film/radio, it's relatively comfortable (air-con).

➡ Other relevant bus companies for travellers include **VIP**, which runs half-hourly buses between Accra and Kumasi, and **Metro Mass** (www.metromass.com), which runs local services in various parts of the country.

➡ It's wise to book in advance as tickets get snapped up fast on the more popular routes.

➡ Services are usually less frequent on Sunday.

➡ There is always a charge for luggage. Theoretically, it should be per kilogram, but in practice, large rucksacks or suitcases just tend to be charged a flat C1.

CAR & MOTORCYCLE

➡ Driving is on the right in Ghana.

➡ Most main roads are in pretty good condition, though almost all secondary roads are unsealed.

➡ You will need an international driver's license.

➡ Hiring a car with a driver is a good option if you're short on time; travel agencies can usually arrange this. Depending on the distance, car and driver experience, factor in anything from US$70 to US$120 per day, plus fuel.

TAXIS

➡ Within towns and on some shorter routes between towns, shared taxis are the usual form of transport. They run on fixed routes, along which they stop to pick up and drop off passengers. Fares are generally very cheap (C0.30 to C0.50).

➡ Private taxis don't have meters and rates are negotiable. It's best to ask a local in advance for the average cost between two points.

➡ Taxis can be chartered for an agreed period of time, anything from one hour to a day, for a negotiable fee.

TRO-TRO

Tro-tro is a catch-all category that embraces any form of public transport that's not a bus or taxi. Generally they're minibuses.

➡ *Tro-tros* cover all major and many minor routes.

➡ They don't work to a set timetable but leave when full.

➡ Fares are set but may vary on the same route depending on the size and comfort (air-con) of the vehicle.

➡ There is generally an additional luggage fee.

➡ The area where *tro-tros* and buses congregate is called, interchangeably, lorry park, motor park or station.

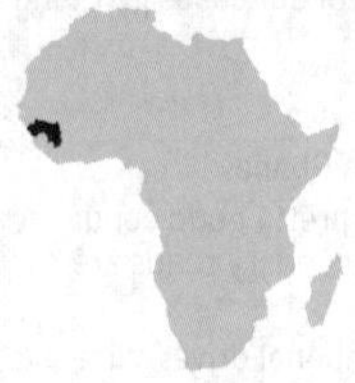

Guinea

Includes ➜

Fast Facts

- ➜ **Capital** Conakry
- ➜ **Population** 10.8 million
- ➜ **Languages** French, Malinke, Pulaar (Fula) and Susu
- ➜ **Area** 245,857 sq km
- ➜ **Currency** Guinean franc (GFr)
- ➜ **Visa requirements** 90-day visa and yellow-fever certificate required
- ➜ **Tourist information** www.ontguinee.org

Rugged Landscapes & Vibrant Beats

Imagine you're travelling on smooth highway, and then get tempted by a tiny, dusty turn-off into rugged terrain, where surprising beauty and treacherous vistas define the route. Guinea is that turn-off. This is a country blessed with amazing landscapes; from the mountain plateau Fouta Djalon to wide Sahelian lands and thick forests.

Overland drivers are drawn here by rugged tracks, and the challenge of steering their vehicles over rocks and washed-out paths. Nature lovers can lose themselves on long hikes past plunging waterfalls, proud hills and tiny villages, or track elephants through virgin rainforest. While Guinea is not famed for its beaches, those it does have are stunning, and often deserted.

Guinea Top Sights

- ➜ **Îles de Los** Stretch out on palm-fringed strands, sipping fresh coconut juice
- ➜ **Fouta Djalon** Ramble through the mountains and swim in the waterfalls of this majestic mountain plateau
- ➜ **Bossou** Come face to face with chattering chimps
- ➜ **Conakry** Hop through the capital's dubious dives, getting drunk on some of West Africa's best live music
- ➜ **Forêt Classée de Ziama** Track elephants in the virgin rainforest
- ➜ **Parc National du Haut Niger** Look for chimps and buffaloes in one of West Africa's last tropical dry-forest ecosystems
- ➜ **Kankan** Squeeze through narrow market streets and visit the beautiful Grand Mosquée in this lively university town

UNDERSTAND GUINEA

Guinea Today

Following the death in 2008 of president Lansana Conté, an army contingent under Captain Moussa Dadis Camara took power in a coup d'état. 'Dadis' promised that he'd quickly clean up the Guinean house, organise elections and return to the army barracks. His initial measures, such as cracking down on Guinean drug rings (Guinea is one of West Africa's hubs of the cocaine trade), and announcing anti-corruption measures and new mining deals (Guinea is hugely rich in natural resources, owning 30% of the world's bauxite resources), gained him many followers.

However, his announcement in 2009 that he would consider standing in the upcoming elections, and increasing violence committed by members of the army, provoked furious reactions. On 28 September 2009, army elements quashed a large demonstration with extreme violence. A UN commission denounced the events as a crime against humanity, and it is thought that over 150 people were killed. Two months later, 'Dadis' was shot (but not killed) following a dispute with his aide-de-camp Toumba Diakite.

After meeting in Ouagadougou in January 2010, 'Dadis', his vice-president Sekouba Konaté and Blaise Compaoré, president of Burkina Faso, produced a formal statement of 12 principles promising a return of Guinea to civilian rule within six months. A provisional government supervised the transition to civilian rule at the end of 2010.

After half a century in opposition, Alpha Conde, from the Malinke ethnic group, was declared winner in Guinea's first democratic election since independence from France in 1958. However, the vote kindled ethnic tensions. Conde's defeated rival, Cellou Dalein Diallo, is a member of the Fula ethnic group,

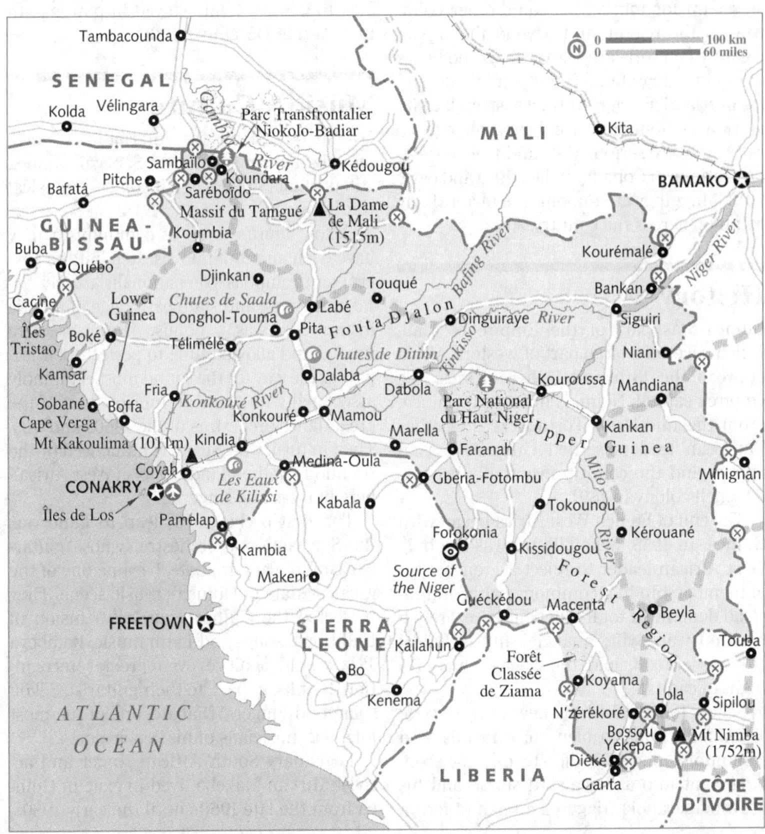

COUNTRY COVERAGE

At the time of research very few travellers were heading to Guinea, so we're providing historical and cultural information rather than reviews and listings. A good source of information for on-the-ground travel in Guinea is Lonely Planet's Thorn Tree on-line travel forum www.lonelyplanet.com/thorntree. Another source of good internet-based information is www.ontguinee.org.

to which 40% of Guineans belong. Diallo has consistently accused the president of marginalising his constituents, including many Fula.

Conde's Conakry residence suffered an armed attack in July 2011. The building was partially destroyed, but Conde was unharmed.

Travel here can be difficult. Guinea is not as set up for tourism as some other countries in the region, and beyond the capital creature comforts are scarce. Taxis and buses are poorly maintained and unreliable, and for overlanders, rugged tracks, steep laterite and washed-out paths can be a challenge.

There were serious riots and violent demonstrations in Conakry in late 2012 and early 2013. Muggings at gunpoint are increasingly common across the country.

History

Guinea was part of the Empire of Mali, which covered a large part of western Africa between the 13th and 15th centuries; the empire's capital, Niani, is in eastern Guinea. From the mid-1400s Portuguese and other European traders settled Guinea's coastal region, and the country eventually became a French colony in 1891.

The end of French West Africa began with Guinea. In 1958, Sekou Touré was the only West African leader to reject a French offer of membership in a commonwealth, and instead demanded total independence. French reaction was swift: financial and technical aid was cut off, and there was a massive flight of capital.

Sekou Touré called his new form of state a 'communocracy', a blend of Africanist and communist models. It didn't work; the economy went into a downward spiral, and his growing paranoia triggered a reign of terror. 'Conspiracies' were being sensed everywhere; thousands of supposed dissidents were imprisoned and executed. By the end of the 1960s over 250,000 Guineans lived in exile.

Towards the end of his presidency Touré changed many of his policies and tried to liberalise the economy. He died in March 1984.

Days after Touré's death, a military coup was staged by a group of colonels, including the barely known, barely educated Lansana Conté, who became president. He introduced austerity measures, and in 1991 bowed to pressure to introduce a multiparty political system. Initial hopes for a new era of freedom and prosperity were quickly dashed. Conté claimed victory in three highly disputed elections, and there were incidents of obstruction and imprisonment of opposition leaders. In 2007 demonstrations were violently quashed, though a few concessions (such as the nomination of a prime minister) were made. Severely ill and barely able to govern, Conté stayed in power until his death in December 2008.

Music & Culture

Overshadowed on the international stage by neighbouring Mali and Senegal, Guinea still packs a punch when it comes to musical tradition.

Sekou Touré's form of communism may have been an economic disaster, but the government's emphasis on nationalist *authenticité* in the arts, and state patronage of artistic institutions, was a bonus. Musicians were funded and allowed time to perfect their art, paving the way for the sound most commonly associated with Guinean music – that of the great dance orchestras of the 1960s and '70s. They, in turn, were strongly influenced by the traditions of the Mande *griots* (West Africa's hereditary praise singers).

The first orchestra to leap to fame was the Syli National Orchestra, whose guitarist, 'Grand' Papa Diabaté, became one of the greatest stars of Guinea's music scene. They perfected the Guinean rumba, a fusion of traditional songs and Latin music. Bembeya Jazz would achieve even greater recognition, thanks, in part, to their guitarist, Sékou 'Diamond Fingers' Diabaté, one of the most talented musicians of his generation.

Legendary South African singer and activist Miriam Makeba lived in exile in Guinea from the late 1960s until the early 1980s, recording with and performing alongside some of the top local musicians.

In the early 1980s, Guinea's dire economic situation had worsened and large orchestras became difficult to fund, forcing many artists to Abidjan, where 90% of all Guinean releases were recorded. The centre of the pop world soon shifted to Paris, where acclaimed Guinean vocalist and kora player Mory Kanté was based.

Alongside Kanté and Sekouba Diabaté, who joined Bembeya Jazz at the age of 19 before going solo in the 1990s, popular musicians today include Ba Cissoko (a band whose sound has been described as 'West Africa meets Jimi Hendrix'), and *kora* player and vocalist Djeli Moussa Diawara. Guinea also has a vibrant hip-hop scene, with many young artists using their music to lash out at Guinea's poor living conditions and political corruption. The best-known name in Guinean hip-hop is Bill de Sam.

Dance is also popular in Guinea. The dance group Les Ballets Africains today remains the 'prototype' of West African ballet troupes, while Circus Baobab mixes trapeze shows and acrobatics with their dance shows.

Camara Laye, author of *L'Enfant Noir*, is the country's best-known writer.

To pick up some typical arts and crafts, try the indigo and mud-cloth cooperatives in many towns.

When it comes to eating out, proper restaurants are rare outside Conakry, though most towns have a couple of basic eating houses serving *riz gras* (rice fried in oil and tomato paste and served with fried fish, meat or vegetables) or simple chicken and chips. In Fouta Djalon, creamy sauces made from meat and potato leaves (*haako putte*) or manioc leaves (*haako bantara*) are common.

Guinea's main ethnic groups are the Fula (about 40% of the population), Malinke (about 30%) and Susu (about 20%). Fifteen other groups, living mostly in the forest region, constitute the rest of the population. Susu predominantly inhabit the coastal region; Fula, the Fouta Djalon; and Malinke, the north and centre. The total population is about 9.8 million. About 85% of the population is Muslim (the Fouta Djalon being a centre of Islam), 8% are Christian and the remainder follow traditional animist religions (especially in the forest region and the Basse Côte).

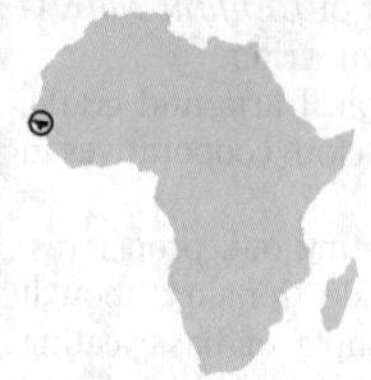

Guinea-Bissau

✆ 245 / POP 1.5 MILLION

Includes ➡

Best Places to Eat

- Oysters on Quinhámel beach (p347)
- Dom Bifana (p344)
- Adega do Loureiro (p343)
- Berca do Rio (p347)

Best Places to Stay

- Ponta Anchaca (p346)
- Kasa Afrikana (p346)
- Pensão Creola (p341)

Why Go?

For a country that consistently elicits frowns from heads of state and news reporters, Guinea-Bissau will pull a smile from even the most world-weary traveller. The jokes here, like the music, are loud but tender. The bowls of grilled oysters are served with a lime sauce spicy enough to give a kick, but not so strong as to mask the bitterness. The buildings are battered and the faded colonial houses bowed by sagging balconies, but you'll see beauty alongside the decay.

Here, bare silver trees spring up like antler horns between swathes of elephant grass, and cashew sellers tease each other with an unmistakably Latin spirit. Board a boat for the Bijagós, where you can watch hippos lumber through lagoons full of fish and spot turtles nesting.

Despite painful wars, coups and cocaine hauls, Guinea-Bissau buzzes with joy, even when daily life is tough and the future bleak. There must be magic in that cashew juice.

When to Go

Bissau

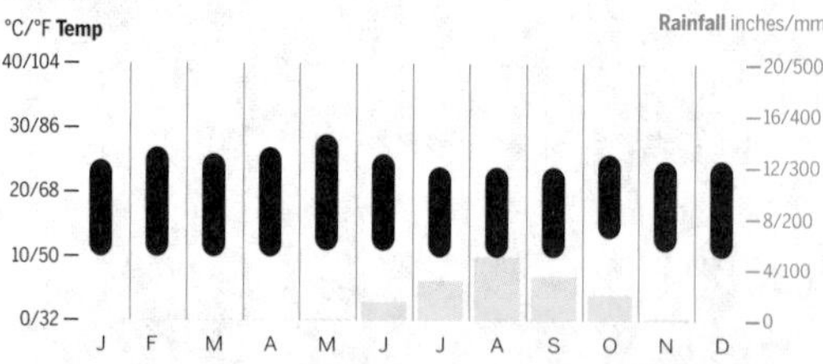

Dec–Feb The year's coolest months, when sea turtles emerge from their nests.

Mar–Jul Hot, humid and sweaty; travel with plenty of water and sunscreen.

Aug–Oct Batten down the hatches or dance in the rain; the rainwater will just keep fallin'.

BISSAU

POP 450,000

In the early evening, the fading sunlight lends the crumbling colonial facades of Bissau Velho (Old Bissau) a touch of old-age glamour. Dozens of generators set the town trembling, and ignite the lights of stylish bars and restaurants that form something of a modern, indoor city in startling contrast with the worn exterior.

Sights

Bissau Velho (Old Bissau), a stretch of narrow alleyways and derelict buildings, is 'guarded' by the **Fortaleza d'Amura** (off the southern end of Av Amílcar Cabral), an imposing fort that is not accessible to visitors. With its bombed-out roof and shrapnel-riddled neoclassical facade, the **former presidential palace** (Praça dos Heróis Nacionais) sends a powerful message about Guinea-Bissau's simmering conflicts. The rebuilt and brushed-up **Assembleia Ministério da Justiça**, by contrast, is an architectural expression of democratic hopes.

Festivals & Events

Carnaval CARNIVAL

Bissau and Bubaque's Carnaval is the country's biggest party. It takes place every year in February or early March during the week leading up to Ash Wednesday and the beginning of Lent. Music, masks, drinking and dancing are the order of the day.

Sleeping

Bissau has a mix of accommodation for most budgets.

Pensão Creola PENSION $

(☎6633031; www.pensaobissau.com; Ave Domingos Ramos; s/d from CFA15,000/18,000) Run by a knowledgeable Swiss-Guinean couple, this is Bissau's best budget stop. Rooms in the pretty colonial-style villa are ideal for groups, with two or three single beds and a shared bathroom. At the back of the house, single rooms with fans, showers and desks are housed in a wooden extension that backs onto the garden. There's 24-hour power, but, at the time of research, no wi-fi or air-con.

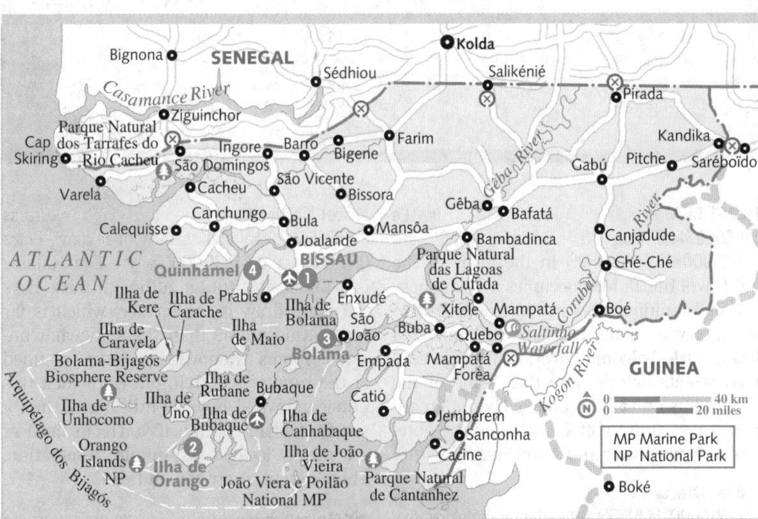

Guinea-Bissau Highlights

1. Dancing tango in cobbled streets by candlelight, after a dinner of *bacalau* (salted flakes of cod) and red wine at **Bissau Velho** (p341)
2. Locking eyes with hippos as they emerge from the warm saltwater lagoons of **Ilha de Orango** (p346)
3. Sitting on the steps of the abandoned town hall, with its crumbling Greek-style pillars, on the island of **Bolama** (p346)
4. Dipping oysters in hot lime sauce after a day in the water at **Quinhámel** (p347)

Bissau

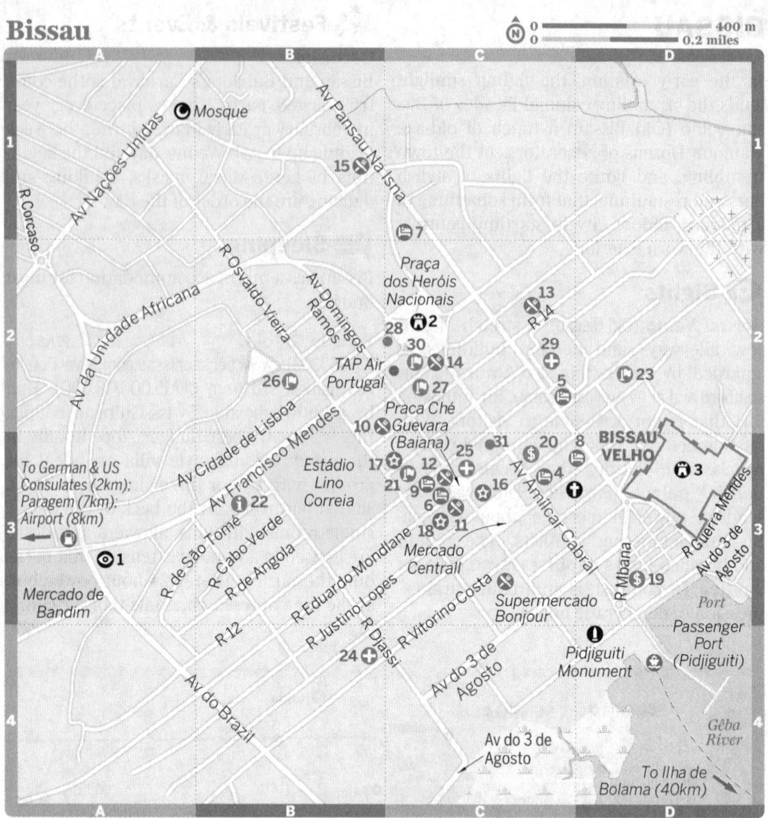

Hotel Ta Mar HOTEL $

(☎6606744; Rua 3, Bissao Velho; s/d CFA15,000/25,000; ❄📶) In the heart of the old town, the Ta Mar occupies a Portuguese colonial building. Gloomy corridors lead to small, basic rooms that are redeemed by lovely little balconies overlooking the cobbled streets below. Note that some of the bathrooms don't have doors. There's an adjacent restaurant/coffee shop, and the hotel has 24-hour power and, theoretically, wi-fi.

Hotel Diarama HOTEL $$

(☎6716000, 5651255; http://bissau-hoteldiarama.com; Ave Pansau Na Isna ; s/d CFA40,000/50,000; ❄📶) Popular with visiting NGO workers, the Diarama has modern, bright, clean rooms with 24-hour power, air-con, wi-fi and decent bathrooms. From here it's a five-minute walk to the old town, and you can hail a taxi outside the front door.

Hotel Kalliste HOTEL $$

(☎6765662; kallistebissau@hotmail.com; Praça Ché Guevara; d CFA35,000; ❄📶) The Kalliste is a Bissau institution, although these days the main draw is the terrace, which is far more atmospheric than the somewhat unloved rooms. Renovations were planned at the time of research, but until then this Corsican-owned hotel is little more than a scruffy fallback option if you're in need of a centrally located last-minute reservation. There's security, air-con and wi-fi.

★Coimbra Hotel BOUTIQUE HOTEL $$$

(☎3201490, 3213467; www.hotelcoimbra.net; Ave Amílcar Cabral; r from CFA76,000; ❄@📶) The Coimbra has smart, modern rooms decked out with African art and speakers. Climb the steps to the bougainvillea-fringed terrace or head downstairs into the main building, which houses a bar, piano room, chess tables and a spa. The restaurant does an excel-

Bissau

Sights

1 Assembleia Ministério da justiça ... A3
2 Former Presidential Palace ... C2
3 Fortaleza d'Amura ... D3

Sleeping

4 Coimbra Hotel ... C3
5 Hotel Diarama ... C2
6 Hotel Kalliste ... C3
7 Hotel Malaika ... C1
8 Hotel Ta Mar ... D3
9 Pensão Creola ... C3

Eating

10 Adega do Loureiro ... B2
11 Kalliste Restaurant ... C3
12 Morabeza ... C3
13 O Bistro ... C2
14 Pastelaria Imperia ... C2
15 Restaurant Samaritana ... B1

Entertainment

16 Centre Culturel Franco-Bissao-Guinéen ... C3
17 Insonias ... C3
18 X Club ... C3

Information

19 BAO ... D3
20 Ecobank ... C3
21 Guinean Embassy ... C3
22 IBAP Office ... B3
23 Jan van Maanen ... D2
24 Pharmacia Nur Din ... B4
25 Policlinica ... C3
26 Portuguese Embassy ... B2
27 Senegalese Embassy ... C2
28 Serviço de Estrangeiros ... C2
29 Simão Mendes ... C2
30 Spanish Embassy ... C2

Transport

31 TACV Cabo Verde Airlines ... C3

lent lunch and dinner buffet with a choice of wines, and the breakfast bar is easily the best in town. Call ahead for airport pick-up.

Hotel Malaika HOTEL $$$
(☎6710010, 3207474; http://hotelinbissau.blogspot.de; Ave Osvaldo Vieira; s/d from CFA80,000/100,000; ❄📶) Despite its African name, you could be anywhere in the world when you step into the chain hotel–like lobby of the Malaika. The rooms are smart, stylish and comfortable, with the usual creature comforts, and there's a bar and ATM downstairs.

Eating

Spicy local dishes, waters brimming with fresh fish and Portuguese culinary influences make Bissau a foodie's paradise.

Restaurant Samaritana AFRICAN $
(☎6131392; off Ave Pansau Na Isna; mains CFA2500) It's made from a cut-out container and buzzes with Guineans of all ranks and incomes eager to sample the reliably delicious meals.

Adega do Loureiro PORTUGUESE $
(Rua 5 de Julho; mains from CFA4000; ❄📶) There are wooden chairs, patterned tablecloths, terracotta ceiling tiles and carafes of red wine at this old-style Portuguese restaurant. The *bacalau* (salted flakes of cod) is salty and succulent, the pork chops are flavorsome and the little red pots of beans and rice are the perfect comfort food.

Morabeza INTERNATIONAL $
(Praça Ché Guevara; meals from CFA2000) Order fast food at the counter downstairs or climb the rickety stairs to the terrace, where you can eat *brochettes* (kebabs), pizza, steak and salads under a sky full of stars.

O Bistro FRENCH $
(☎3206000; Rua Eduardo Mondlane; mains CFA4000; ⏰noon-3pm & 7pm-late; ❄🍸) This Belgian-owned spot has all the right ingredients: excellent, reasonably priced mains including fresh catches, sautéed vegetables and *crepes au chocolat,* friendly service, a well-stocked bar and a warm ambience that transcends the air-con. Bring mosquito spray if you want the big table on the verandah.

Mamaputcha CAFE $
(Rua Eduardo Mondlane; meals from CFA2000) Scratched tables spill out onto the pavement outside Mamaputcha, owned by the sister of Super Mama Djombo bandleader Atchuchi. If you're after glamour, you won't find it here. But you will find warm bowls of fries begging to be dipped in mayonnaise and plates of *brochettes* marinated to perfection.

Kalliste Restaurant FRENCH $$
(☎6765662; Praça Ché Guevara; meals from CFA4000) If the potted plants lining Hotel Kalliste's terrace had ears, what stories they would tell...this central bar/restaurant buzzes at night, attracting everyone from tired UN lawyers to politicians, activists, conservation volunteers and mosquitoes. There's live music most evenings and the pizzas are pretty good.

Pastelaria Imperia BAKERY $$
(pastries from CFA500) Across the roundabout from the presidential palace, the *pastelaria* (cake shop) has the largest selection of cakes, pastries and ice cream in Bissau. Swing by here to pick up breakfast fodder, or head to the big covered terrace for mid-afternoon coffee and cake.

Dom Bifana EUROPEAN $$
(❄) Adjacent to Bissau's parliament building, this classy restaurant serves up more than just *bifanas* (Portuguese sandwiches). Expats and parliamentarians come for steak, finely grilled shrimp and divine desserts. There's a decent wine list and a tranquil atmosphere in the semialfresco dining room.

SET YOUR BUDGET

Budget

- Hotel room CFA15,000
- Rice, fish and spicy okra sauce CFA2000
- Imported Cristal beer CFA600
- Shared taxi ride in Bissau CFA350

Midrange

- Hotel room CFA35,000
- Bowl of grilled oysters for two CFA7000
- Gin and tonic in a bar CFA2500
- Private taxi ride in Bissau CFA1000

Top End

- Hotel room CFA76,000
- Steak in upmarket restaurant CFA7000
- Glass of wine CFA3000
- 4x4 with driver, per day outside Bissau CFA70,000

Drinking & Nightlife

X Club CLUB
(☎3213467; Rua Osualdo Vieira) At X (pronounced 'sheesh') Club, join the odd assembly of hard-working UN staff, shady businessmen and sparkling party folk on their glitzy trip through the night.

Insonias CLUB
Get lost among the plastic palm trees and plastic people at Insonias, a bizarrely decorated club popular with the NGO and UN crowd at weekends. Open until dawn.

Saboura CLUB
Guineans and expats head to Saboura (in Pilom) to dance until the sun comes up. The place is usually teeming on Thursday nights.

Centre Culturel Franco-Bissao-Guinéen PERFORMING ARTS
(☎3206816; Praça Ché Guevera; ⏲9am-10pm Mon-Fri; 📶) This bright, modern centre houses a library/workspace, an art gallery, a performance space and a small cafe. There are regular performances by dance and theatre groups and the centre hosts film screenings. The cafe does coffees, breakfast sandwiches and great-value mains for lunch. Specials include lasagne, baked fish and salads and prices start at around CFA2000. Wi-fi access is available for CFA2000 per day.

Shopping

Diagonally across from Ta Mar Restaurant is **Cabaz di Terra** (Ave Pansau Na Isna), which stocks gorgeous, fairly produced Guinean throws, handbags and jewellery. Part of the store is devoted to condiments such as honey, cashew juice and *fleur du sel*. At nearby **Bibas** (Ave Pansau Na Isna) you can flip through the racks of vintage and recycled dresses.

Bissau's main market is at **Bandim**, a five-minute cab ride in the direction of the airport. Here you can pick up everything from fresh cherry tomatoes to oysters to black-and-white cloth embroidered with the image of Amílcar Cabral.

Orientation

Bissau's main drag is the wide Ave Amílcar Cabral, running between the port and Praça dos Heróis Nacionais. On the northwestern edge of the centre is the Mercado de Bandim. From here, Ave de 14 Novembro leads northwest to the main *paragem* (bus and taxi park), the airport and all inland destinations.

WARNING

Although beautiful, Guinea-Bissau is unstable, and even periods of calm can be followed by violent flare-ups. Although attacks and coup attempts rarely wound civilians or visitors, human rights abuses have been documented. If the current situation looks calm, however, don't let the chronic instability dissuade you from visiting – people here will be thrilled to welcome you, and tourism could help get Guinea-Bissau on its feet again. Do note that shops, banks, businesses and, more rarely, borders may close during tense periods.

Information

INTERNET ACCESS

For wi-fi access, head to the terrace of the Hotel Kalliste (CFA2000 per day) or the Centre Culturel Franco-Bissao-Guinéen (p344; CFA2000 per day). Both places have accessible power sockets and will allow you to linger. Where the road to the airport meets Bairro Ajudda is **Lenox**, a sports cafe/performance space that has a small cybercafe inside.

MEDICAL SERVICES

Pharmacia Nur Din (Rua Vitorino Costa) A reasonably well-stocked pharmacy.

Policlinica (☎3207581; info@policlinica.bissau.com; Praça Ché Guevera) A better option for illnesses than a trip to the hospital.

Simão Mendes (☎3212861; Ave Pansau Na Isna) Bissau's main hospital; in a poor state.

MONEY

It's wise to travel with a supply of cash. At the time of research, there were only two ATMs in the country that accepted international Visa cards (MasterCard was not compatible); one is inside Hotel Malaika, the other across the road from Hotel Kalliste. Hotels do not take payment by credit or debit cards, although some, such as the Coimbra Hotel, accept wire transfers. To change money, either ask your hotel for an informal moneychanger or try Ecobank or Banco da Africa.

BAO (Banco da Africa Occidental; ☎3202418; Rua Gerra Mendes)

Ecobank (☎7253194; Ave Amílcar Cabral) Changes dollars and euros.

Getting There & Away

There are daily flights to Bissau with TACV Cabo Verde Airlines, TAP Air Portugal, Senegal Airlines and Royal Air Maroc.

Once in Bissau, you can get *sept-place* taxis (Peugeot 504s with 'seven seats') and *transporte misto* (literally 'mixed transport') buses to just about anywhere in the country at the *paragem* (bus park), about 4km (CFA1000 by taxi) west outside town.

Getting Around

The airport is 9km west of the town centre. A taxi to town should be around CFA3000.

Shared taxis – generally blue, well-worn Mercedes – are plentiful and ply all the main routes. Trips cost CFA350. Rates for longer routes vary and have to be negotiated.

Blue-yellow *toca-tocas* serve main city routes (for CFA100), including Ave de 14 Novembro towards the *paragem* and airport.

ARQUIPÉLAGO DOS BIJAGÓS

The Bijagós islands look like the perfect postcard from paradise. Protected by swift tides, treacherous sandbanks and the Unesco heritage fund, the Bijagós, a matriarchal people, eluded Portuguese control until the 1930s.

You need to bring either time or money, as transport to and between the islands is either difficult or pricey. Life swings to the rhythm of the tide – and mind the stingrays lurking in the waters.

Getting There & Away

Ilha de Bubaque is the gateway to the rest of the Bijagós, with the exception of Ilha de Bolama and the private resort islands.The former Greek island ferry **Expresso dos Bijagós** (☎6538739; Bissau Velho; tickets CFA3500-12,500) normally leaves Bissau port for Bubaque every Friday, returning from Bubaque on Sunday. Exact departure times depend on the tide but are between 9am and 3pm; posters advertise the exact time the evening before. On other days, your choice is between rough and risky *canoas* (motor canoe; per person CFA2500, six hours), private plane (from CFA250,000 per person) or speedboat (per four-seater boat CFA200,000 to CFA300,000, two hours).

The Expresso dos Bijagós also ferries passengers between Bissau and Bolama once a week but timings vary; ask around at the port for the latest departure times. If you miss the ferry, *canoas* operate three times per week, but be warned: one sank on this route in 2012, killing many of those on board. You can also reach Bolama by taking a *sept-place* to Buba (three hours), where you can overnight before hiring motorbikes for the journey (three hours, CFA15,000) along rough forest roads to the *pirogue* hopper at São João.

The 1950s cruise ship **Africa Queen** can take you island hopping for a week (from CFA700,000); ask at the port or your hotel for information. It's wise to exercise caution when contemplating taking any kind of boat from Bissau during heavy rains.

Ilha de Bolama

Geographically closer to Bissau than any other island in the Bijagós, eerily beautiful Bolama feels worlds away, both aesthetically and socially. The Portuguese capital of Guinea-Bissau until 1943, Bolama's shores are awash with crumbling relics that were abandoned after independence. Tree-lined boulevards are mapped out by lamp posts that no longer shine, and the colonial barracks have been recast as a hospital, now – like much of the island – in a dark and desolate state.

The former **town hall**, flanked by Greek-style pillars, was built in 1870; these days huge splinters hang like stalactites from its ceilings. The turrets of the once grandiose **Hotel Turismo** sit in an overgrown nest of lianas, 3m-tall weeds and snakes. It's worth walking out to Ofires Beach, an hour's stroll from the town, to see the spooky sweeping **staircase** of a beach hotel that no longer exists.

You can rent a breezy room at the **fishing training centre** (call Ivan Gomes for reservations 5286345; r incl breakfast CFA12,500) close to the port. There is electricity at the centre, but the rooms do not have fans. Alternatively, ask for directions to the smarter **Hotel Ga Djau** (r CFA13,000), a 15-minute walk from the market. The rooms do have fans, but the generator shuts off late at night.

Feisty **Lionessa** (meals CFA1000) serves up fresh fish and potatoes most evenings if you order in advance. Find her cafe about halfway up the main road, on the right-hand side if you're walking from the port.

Ilha de Bubaque

At the centre of the Bijagós, Bubaque is home to the archipelago's largest town, which serves as its major transport hub. If you can't make it to more remote islands, Bubaque makes a comfortable place to unwind and a good weekend getaway from Bissau. Its best beach is **Praia Bruce** on the southern tip.

There's an internet cafe, the research and information centre **Casa do Ambiente** (3207106) and a small **museum** (6115107; admission CFA1000; 10am-1pm & 4-7pm).

You can lay your head at pretty **Casa Dora** (6928836, 5967714, 6925836; susybubaque@gmail.com; s/d CFA10,000/15,000), housed in a colourful garden, or from November to May at **Le Calypso** (5949207, 6106436; calypso@gtelecom.gw; s/d CFA20,000/22,000), which has a pool and bar. At the top of Bubaque's game is **Kasa Afrikana** (5949213, 7243305; www.kasa-afrikana.com; per person from CFA40,000), a fishing lodge that hits the right ratio of charm to luxury, with comfortable rooms, a pool and on-site chef.

Orango Islands National Park

Ilha de Orango (Bijagós Archipelago; boat to Eticoga village from Bubaque) is the heart of Orango Islands National Park. The island is home to rare saltwater hippos, and is also the burial site of the Bijagós kings and queens. Pretty **Orango Parque Hotel** (6615127; laurent.durris@cbd-habitat.com; r incl full board CFA30,000) is run in association with the local community, and guides can take you **hippo spotting** (around CFA150,000). You can reach Orango by speedboat transfer from Ilha de Kere or by scheduled *pirogue* from Bubaque. For the latter, you'll need to have time and tides on your side.

Other Islands

The islands of Kere and Rubane are home to luxury fishing lodges. The latter's **Ponta Anchaca** (6056032, 6394352; www.pontaanchaca.com; r per day with half board from €100) is divine, with a pool, spa, masseuse and gorgeous wooden huts bedecked with four-poster beds and Jacuzzis under the stars. You can travel by speedboat from Bissau (€460 per boatload) or board a private plane from Senegal's Cap Skirring for €530. On **Kere** (http://bijagos-kere.fr) prices are slightly cheaper for a similar experience. Contact Manuel (5909531), the booking agent in Bissau, for more information. Trips can be arranged from there to Biombo and other islands.

On the idyllic island of João Vieira lies **João Viera e Poilão National Marine Park**, a nesting area for endangered sea turtles. The owner of the guesthouse Chez Claude can arrange speedboat pick-up from Bubaque (CFA200,000 per boatload). Close to Bubaque, the large island **Canhabaque** (one hour by *pirogue*) is a good place to experience village life in the Bijagós.

THE NORTHWEST

Quinhámel

Quinhámel, 35km west of Bissau, makes an interesting day or weekend trip. You can overnight at **Mar Azul** (☎6760990, 6656086; r incl lunch CFA40,000), where rooms overlook the pool, gardens and ocean. The restaurant serves grilled oysters served with a hot citrus sauce. About 2km away, nestled between the mangroves, is a local **beach** popular with families and young people at the weekends. The inspiring community project **Artissal** (☎6604078; artissal@gmail.com; ⏲9am-5pm) introduces visitors to the region's unique weaving traditions.

Transporte misto from Bissau costs CFA500; a private taxi is around CFA15,000 return.

Varela

The 45km road from São Domingos is rough, even in a good 4WD – and that's why the white-sand, windswept beaches of Varela remain deserted. There are plans to tarmac the road, but until that happens, Varela's charm lies in its remoteness.

Transporte misto leaves every afternoon from São Domingos (CFA3000) taking around four hours and returning the following morning. If you're driving by 4WD, plan on at least two hours. You can also come in from Senegal, via Kabrousse, but this route involves several hours' walk and arranging a *pirogue* with local fishermen in advance.

To reach the main **beach** from Fatima's place, turn right out of the gate and drive until you reach the end of the main road. Turn right again, and follow the long track for about five minutes until you hear the sound of the waves.

Chez Fatima GUESTHOUSE $
(Aparthotel Chez Helena; ☎5120036, 6640180; d/ste CFA15,000/20,000; P) Friendly owners Fatima and Franco offer nine brightly coloured huts in a pretty garden setting. The huts are lovingly decorated, with fans, mosquito nets and bathrooms. There's Italian food and fresh juices (they grow their own tomatoes and passion fruits) on hand in the restaurant. Call ahead for information on road conditions. The generator kicks in after dark.

THE NORTHEAST

Bafatá & Gabú

Bafatá ('the place where the rivers meet' in the Mandinga language), feels surprisingly hot and dry. Independence hero Amílcar Cabral was born here in 1924 and Unesco has transformed his childhood home into a **museum** that's open daily (ask for the *'casa rosa Amílcar Cabral'*).

You can sleep at the basic but clean **Hotel Maimuna Capé** (☎6648383; s/d CFA10,000/15,000; ❄) or try the yellow **Apartamento Imel** (r CFA5000) in the centre of town. **Ponto de Encontro** (☎6921690; Chez Celia; dishes around CFA3500), at the end of the main street, is run by a charming older Portuguese couple. Head there for hearty fare and a glimpse into Bafatá's past.

Transporte misto to Bissau (CFA1750, two hours) and Gabú (CFA800) departs from the petrol station area.

Gabú, once the capital of the eponymous 19th-century kingdom is mainly a stopover on the way to Guinea, or a base for excursions to the rocky lands of Boé (40km from Gabú). The best hotel in town is the **Boca-Branco** (☎7229065, 6744403; r from CFA24,000). There's also the central **Residencial Djaraama** (☎6938442; r/d without bathroom CFA15,000/20,000), or the simple **Hotel Baga Baga** ('Termite Mound' in Crioulo; s CFA15,000), near the entrance to town.

THE SOUTH

Buba

With its calm streets and pretty, tranquil lakes and lagoons, Buba comes as a surprise. You can bed down at the pleasant **Berca do Rio** (☎5208020, 6619700; r CFA12,000), a short walk from the lake, where Slow Food chef Abdon, who trained in Cotonou, serves up wonderful three-course meals with wine using innovative, local ingredients. He can also arrange picnics and *pirogue* trips through the mangroves.

Transporte misto run regularly along the asphalt road from Bissau to Buba (CFA3000, three hours).

Jemberem & Parque Natural de Cantanhez

The hardest-to-reach places are often the most beautiful, and so it goes with Jemberem. You'll need a 4WD, time and patience to get here, but if you do, you can stay at the clean and simple **U'Anan Camp** (☎6637263, 6060019; d/q CFA15,000/25,000) on the edge of **Parque Natural de Cantanhez**, which supports a fully fledged ecotourism project. The camp can arrange forest treks into the chimp- and elephant-inhabited park.

UNDERSTAND GUINEA-BISSAU

Guinea-Bissau Today

In 2012, President Malam Bacai Sanha died from illness, plunging the country into another bout of instability and adding another name to the long list of presidents who have failed to complete a full term in power. A coup d'etat ousted the prime minister and election frontrunner three months later and a transitional government was installed, headed by Manuel Serifo Nhamadjo, who was chosen by West African bloc Ecowas. Nhamadjo's time in power was shaken by coup attempts and attacks, and fresh elections were tentatively planned for 2013. At the time of research tensions were rising between the Balanta and other ethnic groups.

History

In around 1200, when a group of Malinké was led to present-day Guinea-Bissau by a general of Sunjata Keita, the region became an outpost of the Empire of Mali. In 1537, it became a state in its own right – the Kaabu Empire. Gabù became the capital of this small kingdom.

European Arrival & Colonisation

Portuguese navigators first reached the area around 1450, and established lucrative routes for trading slaves and goods. With the abolition of the slave trade in the 19th century, the Portuguese extended their influence beyond the coast towards the interior in order to continue extracting wealth.

Portuguese Guinea descended into one of the most repressive and exploitative colonial regimes in Africa, particularly accentuated when right-wing dictator António Salazar came to power in Portugal in 1926.

War of Liberation

By the early 1960s African colonies were rapidly winning independence, but Salazar refused to relinquish control. The result was a long and bloody war of liberation for Guinea-Bissau and Cape Verde, fought on Guinean soil. Many Guineans were recruited to fight for the Portuguese, essentially pitting brothers against brothers and neighbours against neighbours.

The father of independence was Amílcar Cabral, who in 1956 helped found the Partido Africano da Independência da Guiné e Cabo Verde (PAIGC). In 1961 the PAIGC started arming and mobilising peasants, and within five years controlled half of the country. Cabral was assassinated in Conakry in 1973, but independence had become inevitable. When Salazar's regime fell in 1974, the new Portuguese government recognised the fledgling nation.

Independence

Once in power, the PAIGC government faced staggering problems of poverty, lack of education and economic decline. In 1986 a coup attempt forced President João Vieira to privatise state enterprises.

Intractable poverty and growing corruption under Vieira culminated in national strikes in 1997, which spiralled into civil war. Vieira was killed in a 2009 coup and instability has been endemic ever since, fuelled by deep tensions between the government and the military, which includes ageing officers who fought in the war of independence. The squabble for profits from Bissau's main cash cow – not the humble cashew, but cocaine – is a symptom of these tensions.

Culture

Despite grinding poverty, a severely damaged infrastructure and wide religious and ethnic differences, Bissau-Guineans are generally united in their approach to the troubles in their country – although tensions have

SUPER MAMA DJOMBO

In the tiny, nigh-on-impossible to access village of Cobiana, a spirit rose to prominence during the independence era of the late 1960s and early 1970s. Her name was Mama Djombo, and she was said to protect the independence fighters as they waged a bloody battle against Portugal. A few years earlier, musician Ze Manel (then seven years old) and his compatriots created a band at their summer scout camp in Bissau. They named it Super Mama Djombo, after the forest spirit, and later shot to fame, accompanying independence figures to neighbouring countries, to Cuba and to Europe.

Today, the re-formed Super Mama Djombo is Bissau's most famous band, performing their woozy independence era harmonies throughout the region and as far afield as Iceland and Hong Kong. With tracks like 'Djan Djan', about the ship on which bandleader Atchutchi sailed to Senegal during the civil war, and 'Guine Cabral', their music contains the sad notes and the euphoria of the independence era – and then some. 'The people of Guinea-Bissau are like termite mounds,' Ze Manel told us, referring to the track 'Baga Baga'. 'Knock us down and we get right back up.'

brewed in recent years between the Balanta ethnic group and rivals. While many feel detached from the military-government chaos, its impact is felt on a daily basis, in everything from making banking transactions to the challenges of the decrepit healthcare system.

Politeness and sincerity are deeply respected in Guinea-Bissau. Among the citizens of neighbouring countries, Guineans are known as relentless partygoers, but people in Guinea-Bissau will tell you they just know how to let their hair down properly. There's a spirit of liberty, joy and acceptance in many situations.

People

Guinea-Bissau's 1.5 million inhabitants are divided among some 23 ethnic groups. The two largest are the Balanta (30%) in the coastal and central regions and the Fula (20%) in the east and south. Other groups include the Manjak, Papel, Fulup and the Mandinka. The offshore islands are mostly inhabited by the Bijagós people. In the last few years, tensions have been growing between the Balanta and other ethnic groups.

About 45% of the people are Muslims and 10% Christians. Animist beliefs remain strong along the coast and in the south.

Arts & Crafts

The Bijagós people are famous for their traditions of mask making and sculpture – you will see these come out in carnival season.

The traditional Guinean beat is *gumbé,* though contemporary music is mainly influenced by zouk from Cape Verde. Guinea-Bissau's classic band is Super Mama Djombo; Manecas Costa and Justino Delgado are two contemporary stars.

Food & Drink

Seafood is the highlight of Guinean cuisine, including shrimp, oysters and meaty *bica* (sea bream), best served sautéed with onion and lime. A national favourite is *chabeu:* deep-fried fish served in a thick palm-oil sauce with rice.

Local brews include palm wine and the very potent liquors *caña* (rum) and *cajeu* (cashew liquor). The best beers are the imported Portuguese brands.

Environment

Tiny Guinea-Bissau has an area of just over 36,000 sq km. The natural savannah woodlands have largely been replaced by cashew plantations.

In the Bijagós archipelago you find rare saltwater hippos, aquatic turtles, dolphins, manatees and sharks. The rainforests of the southeast are the most westerly home of Africa's chimpanzee population.

Among the main environmental issues are mangrove destruction, deforestation, soil erosion and overfishing. A number of areas are protected, including the Bolama-Bijagós Biosphere Reserve. For more information, contact **IBAP** (☎3207106; Rua São Tomé), the institute that oversees all the parks from Bissau.

SURVIVAL GUIDE

Directory A–Z

ACCOMMODATION

While Bissau has a range of accommodation to suit most budgets, conditions are generally more basic elsewhere in the country (the luxury fishing lodges of the Bijagós are an exception). National electricity is severely limited, forcing hoteliers to rely on expensive generator power.

ACTIVITIES

The waters around the Bijagós are renowned for their deep-sea fishing spots. Snorkelling is also possible, as is forest trekking.The national parks are fabulous for birdwatchers.

BUSINESS HOURS

Banks and government offices Usually 8am to noon and 2pm to 5pm Monday to Friday, although hours vary.

Shops From 8am or 9am until 6pm Monday to Saturday. Some close for lunch.

EMBASSIES & CONSULATES

All embassies and consulates are in Bissau. The consul for the UK and the Netherlands is **Jan van Maanen** (☎6622772; Rua Eduardo Mondlane, Supermercardo Mavegro, Bissau).

French Embassy (☎3201312; cnr Ave de 14 Novembro & Ave do Brazil)

German Embassy (☎3255020; escritorio-bissau@web.de; SITEC Bldg; ⏲9-11am Mon-Fri)

Guinean Embassy (☎3201231; Rua 12; ⏲8.30am-3pm Sat-Thu, to 1pm Fri) East of the central stadium.

Portuguese Embassy (☎3203379; Ave Cidade de Lisboa; ⏲8am-noon)

Senegalese Embassy (☎3212944; off Praça dos Heróis Nacionais; ⏲8am-noon)

Spanish Embassy (Praça dos Heróis Nacionais; ⏲8am-noon)

FESTIVALS & EVENTS

Guinea-Bissau's main event is Carnaval (p341). The biggest party happens in Bissau, but Bubaque has the more interesting masks and costumes.

HEALTH

A certificate with proof of yellow-fever vaccination is required for all travellers.

INTERNET ACCESS

Wi-fi is increasingly common in hotels and restaurants in Bissau. Roaming is possible on phones and iPads, but connections are generally slow. Don't count on internet access outside the capital.

MONEY

Some ATMs in the capital accept international visa cards. Try the Malaika Hotel or the ATM opposite the Kalliste Hotel.

The unit of currency is the West African CFA franc.

POST

The postal service is slow. You're better off posting mail home from Senegal or The Gambia.

PUBLIC HOLIDAYS

Islamic feasts, such as Eid al-Fitr (at the end of Ramadan) and Tabaski, are celebrated. Guinea-Bissau also celebrates a number of public holidays.

New Year's Day 1 January

Anniversary of the Death of Amílcar Cabral 20 January

Women's Day 8 March

Easter March/April

Labour Day 1 May

Pidjiguiti Day 3 August

Independence Day 24 September

Christmas Day 25 December

TELEPHONE

You can pick up an Orange or MTN SIM card for an unlocked phone, and buy top-up credit on the street. Service can be unreliable in remote areas, including the Arquipélago dos Bijagós.

VISAS

All visitors, except nationals of Ecowas countries (who must pay CFA1000 on entry), need visas before arrival. Visas can be valid for single or multiple entries and the price varies depending on the point of issue.

Visa Extensions

Extensions are easy to obtain at **Serviço de Estrangeiros** (Praça dos Heróis Nacionais, Bissau). For virtually all nationalities, 45-day visa extensions cost around CFA4000 and are ready the same day if you apply early.

Getting There & Away

AIR

Guinea-Bissau's international airport is on the outskirts of Bissau. The main airlines flying to Guinea-Bissau are TAP Air Portugal, Royal Air Maroc, Senegal Airlines and TACV Cabo Verde Airlines. Private planes can also be arranged.

TACV Cabo Verde Airlines (VR; ☎3206087; www.tacv.com; Ave Amílcar Cabral)

TAP Air Portugal (TP; ☎3201359; www.flytap.com; Praça dos Heróis Nacionais)

PRACTICALITIES

➡ **Radio** National radio and TV stations broadcast in Portuguese. Most interesting for travellers is Radio Mavegro FM (100.0MHz), which combines music with hourly news bulletins in English from the BBC.

➡ **Newspapers** Newspapers come and go quickly in Bissau. If you sit at one of the city's cafes or restaurants, a vendor will quickly offer you the latest options. If you can read Portuguese or Crioulo, it's worth checking out the Friday editions for the serialised fiction.

➡ **Electricity** Supply is 220V and plugs are of the European two-round-pin variety.

➡ **Language** Portuguese is the official language, though the tongue that unites Bissau-Guineans of diverse ethnic groups is the soft and rhythmic Crioulo. French is also fairly widely spoken.

LAND

Guinea

Transport for Guinea (plan on 24 to 48 hours to reach Conakry, depending on road/taxi conditions) leaves from Gabu and traverses a rough pass through the beautiful Fouta Djalon mountains via Labe. There is an alternative, tougher route via Quebo and Pitche.

Senegal

From Dakar, the cheapest, and most scenic, way to reach Bissau is by taking the biweekly overnight ferry to Ziguinchor (cabin beds from CFA18,000), collecting a visa from the consulate in Ziguinchor (issued on the spot; single entry CFA10,000) and travelling onwards by *sept place* (CFA3500 plus small luggage fee, four hours). There are also regular flights on Senegal Airlines.

Getting Around

BOAT

The main boat connection is the Expresso dos Bijagós (p345) that links Bissau to Ilha de Bubaque. *Canoas* (motor canoes) also go between individual islands.

SEPT PLACE & TRANSPORTE MISTO

Sept places are Peugeot 504 seven-seaters that link the main towns. More common and far less comfortable are large minibuses called *transporte misto* (literally 'mixed transport'). Mornings (before 8am) are the best time to get transport.

The main roads between Bissau and Bafatá, Gabú, São Domingos and Buba are all tar and generally in a good state. Stretches between Buba and Jemberem and São Domingos and Varela are unpaved and in bad condition.

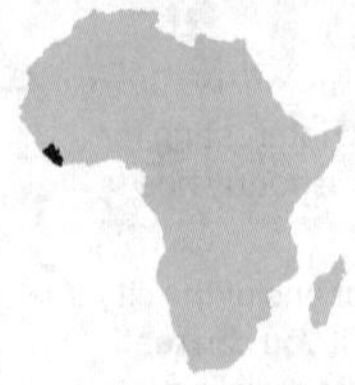

Liberia

231 / POP 4.1 MILLION

Includes ➡

Best Places to Eat

- Fresh seafood on Buchanan beach (p359)
- Ministry of Fruit (p355)
- Sharing a bowl of palm butter upcountry

Best Places to Stay

- Camping beneath Robertsport's cotton tree (p359)
- Mamba Point Hotel (p359)
- Libassa Eco-Lodge (p359)

Why Go?

It wasn't long ago that Liberians talked with obvious nostalgia of 'normal days'. Now, over a decade after the war has ended, 'normal days' are back in this gorgeous green land.

They can be seen in the Liberian designer who's launched a fashion store in Monrovia; the former refugee who runs a motorbike-taxi business; the Liberian surfer who's touring West Africa and the salesman investing in ecotourism.

You might be among his customers, leaning back in a string hammock on the edge of a forest singing with tropical birds. Or you might visit Monrovia, exploring the relics of Liberia's rich history and the American influence that still shapes it. Sapo National Park is one of the most stunning patches of rainforest left in West Africa, while the sands of pretty Robertsport are shingled with fishing canoes and huge granite gems.

Today's 'normal days' are the spark that will light your travels in Liberia.

When to Go

Monrovia

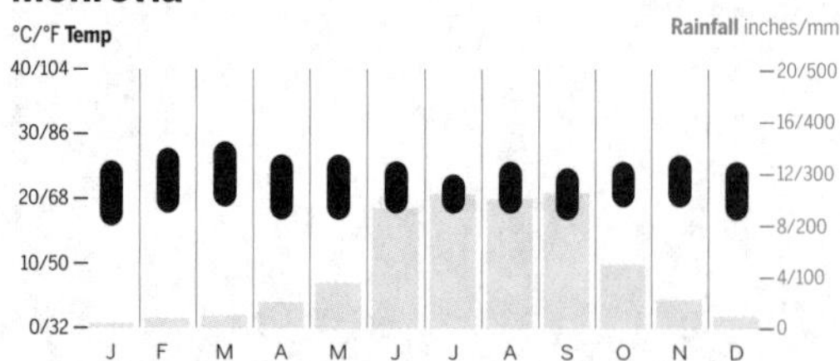

Jan–May This is the hot, dry season, so head to the beaches. The mercury can easily top 32°C.

Jun–Oct Spectacular storms and impressive surf, but country roads are impassable.

Oct–Dec A touch of harmattan breeze from the Sahel occasionally cools the air.

MONROVIA

POP 1.8 MILLION

Monrovia has been everything over the decades – a splendid African capital brimming with elegant stores and faces, a party city monitored by sheriffs wearing secondhand US police uniforms, a war zone marred by bullet holes and a broken-hearted city struggling to climb to its feet. Now aid workers are packing their bags, Liberians are returning from the US and Europe and the city is forging a fresh identity.

Walk along Broad St, Monrovia's main boulevard, and you'll hear the original beat of locally brewed hip-co and the gentle rhythm of Liberian English. You'll see the architectural ghosts of Monrovia's past and the uniformed schoolchildren of its future. You'll watch entrepreneurs climb into sleek, low-slung cars, market men sell coconuts from rusty wheelbarrows and models sashay

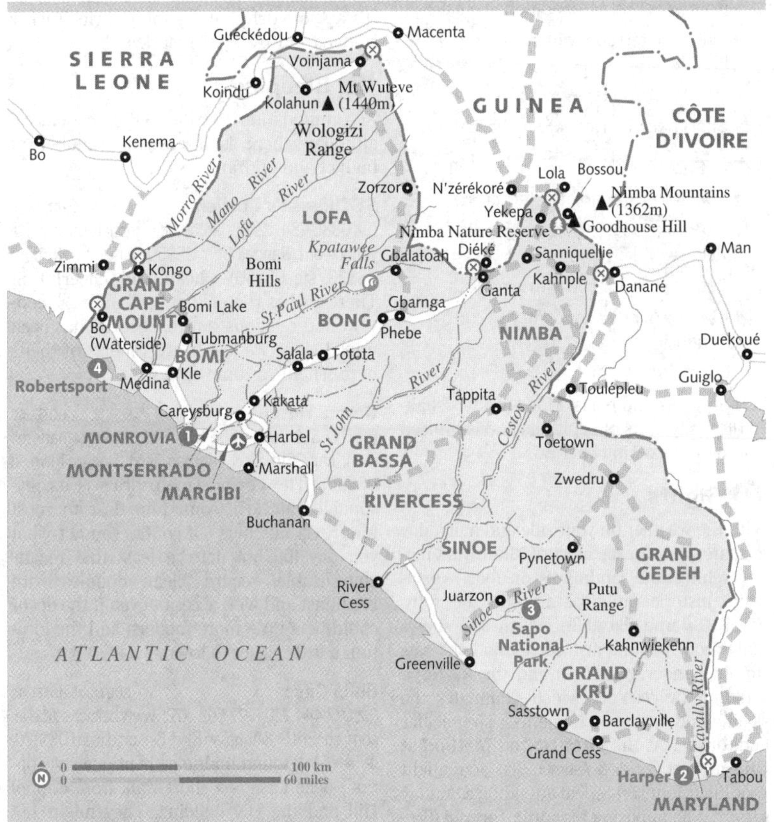

Liberia Highlights

1 Gaining a history lesson walking around the Liberian capital **Monrovia** (p353).

2 Hitting the long, bumpy road to **Harper** (p360), a town blessed with southern American architecture and an end-of-the-line feel.

3 Exploring the habitat of the endangered pygmy hippo, camping beneath the forest canopy and listening to the sounds of the rainforest at **Sapo National Park** (p360).

4 Riding the waves with Liberian surfers, running your hands through the phosphorescent swell and eating fresh lobster in the shade of the cotton tree in **Robertsport** (p359).

SET YOUR BUDGET

Budget

- Sachet of drinking water $0.10
- Bed in convent guesthouse $20
- Bowl of palm butter and rice $2
- Monrovia–Robertsport by bush taxi $3.50

Midrange

- Bottled cola in air-conditioned bar $2
- Simple hotel room with fan and wi-fi $65
- Lunch at Lebanese cafe $6
- Short hop in private Monrovia taxi $5

Top End

- Cocktail in upmarket hotel bar $6
- Centrally-located hotel room with air con and wi-fi $200
- Sushi dinner for two with wine $70
- 4x4 hire per day upcountry $120, plus petrol

in tight jeans and heels. Monrovia has shaken off many of its old epithets and is infused with a new, exciting energy.

Sights

With the weather on your side and half a day to spare, you can see most of Monrovia's major architectural landmarks on foot. Worthwhile historic buildings include the retro **Rivoli Cinema** (Broad St), which still shows Bollywood movies (just don't mind the rats running under your feet) and the **EJ Roye building** (Ashmun St), which dominates the skyline and was once home to a spectacular auditorium. At the **First United Methodist Church** (cnr Gurley & Ashmun Sts) you might spot Ellen Johnson-Sirleaf attending a Sunday service. The imposing **Masonic Temple** (Benson St) overlooks the city at the western end of Broad St, in the shadow of the abandoned **Hotel Ducor**; this was West Africa's finest hotel in the 1970s, where Idi Amin swam in the pool and Miriam Makeba sang in the bar.

Liberia National Museum MUSEUM
(077-232 682; Broad St; admission US$5; 9am-4pm Mon-Sat, 2-4pm Sun) The museum's collection was depleted during the war years, but renovations have created space for photo and art exhibitions as well as the ethnic and historical exhibits. Wander through the light-filled 2nd and 3rd floors, where you can see founding father Joseph Jenkins Roberts' dining table – a gift from England's Queen Victoria. The building was the former legislature.

Providence Island ISLAND
There isn't much to mark the spot where freed American slaves first disembarked, but the government has plans to turn Providence Island into a historical attraction. It's a short drive across the Gabriel Tucker bridge from Waterside Market.

Sleeping

Accommodation in Monrovia is expensive, although there is a growing number of budget and midrange beds.

St Theresa's Convent HOSTEL $
(0886-784 276; archdiocesanpastoralcenter@yahoo.com; Randall St; r US$30, without bathroom US$20, ste US$50) Cheap and cheerful St Theresa's has rooms that back onto the convent and religious centre. Security has been upped since we last heard reports of thefts here. There's a 10pm curfew.

Corina Hotel HOTEL $$
(077-514 708, 0886-514 708; www.corinahotel.com; cnr 26th St & Tubman Blvd, Congo Town; d US$65) The Corina's main draw is its reasonable ratecard, something lost to most Monrovia hoteliers. Of course you get what you pay for, but here at least that means comfortable, secure, clean doubles with breakfast and wi-fi access – even if the decor could be a little more modern and the location a little closer to town.

Bella Casa BOUTIQUE HOTEL $$
(077-444 110, 077-692 272; www.bellacasaliberia.com; cnr 3rd St & Tubman Blvd, Sinkor; d from US$120; P) A sound midrange boutique-style option, Bella Casa is a short walk from Capitol Hill and the UN building. They might not quite evoke dreams of Italy, but the rooms are comfortable and clean and come with air-con, desk and free wi-fi. The suites are large, with stylish bed linen and a more luxurious touch.

Cape Hotel HOTEL $$
(077-006 633; http://thecapehotelliberia.com; UN Dr, Mamba Point; d US$160; P) The Mamba Point Hotel's next-door neighbour may forever be in its shadow, but it is a more reasonably priced option and there's

an on-site terrace restaurant, friendly staff, parking and a pool. Ask for one of the renovated rooms, which are sleeker and more stylish than the rest.

★ Mamba Point Hotel LUXURY HOTEL **$$$**
(☎06-544 544, 06-440 000; mambapointhotel@yahoo.com; r/ste US$200/350; P ❄ 📶 🏊) Monrovia's finest hotel is an institution. It has 60-plus beautiful rooms, decked out with stylish furnishings and luxurious bathrooms (the suites are divine, with stunning sea views). There's an excellent terrace restaurant, adjacent sushi bar, casino and pool, and there are plans to add a spa, gym and cocktail bar.

Royal Hotel LUXURY HOTEL **$$$**
(☎077-777 788; royalhotelliberia@yahoo.com; cnr 15th St & Tubman Blvd; r/presidential ste US$200/800; P ❄ 📶) Recent renovations have turned the Royal into the most talked about hotel in town. The new complex holds 58 plush rooms (including two presidential suites), coffee shop, hair salon, art gallery, Asian fusion restaurant and rooftop cocktail bar.

Eating

Sweet Lips LIBERIAN **$**
(Newport St; meals US$1.50-2.50; ⏰11am-9pm Mon-Sat) This firm favourite is said to serve up the very best Liberian food in town – try the excellent *fufu* (puréed, fermented cassava) and palm butter.

Shark's Ice Cream ICE CREAM **$**
(Airfield, Sinkor; P ❄ 👪) Head here for American-dreamt, Liberia-made ice cream. There are usually a handful of flavours on offer, such as chocolate and passion fruit, although many regulars swear by the creamy vanilla. There's also a sandwich and burger menu, a popcorn machine, rides for toddlers and, upstairs, sports on the big screen.

Sajj House LEBANESE **$$**
(☎06-830 888; cnr Tubman Blvd & 18th St, Sinkor; mains US$5-10; ⏰9am-10pm; P 📶 🍸) Lebanese meze, cheese-and-spinach pies, sandwiches and pizzas are served beneath the awnings of a large, traditional Liberian garden hut. Popular with salsa-dancing expats on Friday nights, Sajj has a fully stocked bar, blender (try the frozen strawberry juice) and dessert menu, featuring chocolate crepes. The volume dial turns with the clock.

Evelyn's INTERNATIONAL **$$**
(☎0777-001 155, 0886-710 104; 80 Broad St; mains US$8-20; ⏰11am-8pm Mon-Sat; ❄ 📶) One of Monrovia's best lunch spots, Evelyn's offers up-market Liberian dishes (such as palm butter and rice; from US$8), American mains including sandwiches, and an all-you-can-eat lunch buffet on Wednesday. You can order sides of cassava fries, stuffed plantain and fried chicken, while for dessert there's papaya pie and cornbread muffins.

Bishoftu ETHIOPIAN **$$**
(☎0886-639 120; cnr 11th St & Payne Ave) For a change from Monrovia's plethora of American, Lebanese – and of course Liberian – restaurants, there's Ethiopian restaurant Bishoftu in Sinkor, which has an outdoor courtyard. The *injera* (flatbread) gets mixed reviews.

Embassy Suites LEBANESE, AMERICAN **$$**
(☎0886-985 985; www.embassysuiteslib.com; near US Embassy, Mamba Point) The friendly staff at Embassy Suites (also a good hotel) will bring over bowls of popcorn before you start your meal. On the menu is a mix of Lebanese and American dishes, including fresh salads, steaks and pizzas. There's live music most Saturdays.

Golden Beach INTERNATIONAL **$$**
(5th St, Sinkor; meals US$5-12; ⏰noon-late Mon-Sun; P 👪) Life in Liberia doesn't get better than this. Exhale, kick off your shoes and start your evening here, where tables sink into the sand and sunsets dip behind gin 'n' tonics. Nobody's in a hurry here, including the chefs, who prepare Liberian, European and Thai food.

★ Ministry of Fruit CAFE **$$**
(Cheeseman Ave & 17th St, Sinkor; meals from US$5; ⏰8am-9pm Mon-Fri, 10am-9pm Sat, 10am-2pm Sun; 📶 🍸) 🌿 Climb the red spiral staircase for Chris' freshly squeezed juices, coffee, sweet smoothies, great sandwiches and homemade banana bread. You can even sip on a root-beer float while you flick through the bookshelves or access the wi-fi. The Sunday brunch (US$5 to US$10) crowd is a mix of locals and expats – something that's reflected in the ethos, warm welcome and decor.

Blue House LIBERIAN **$$$**
(☎0880-888 884; Oldest Congo Town) A smart restaurant serving creative dishes made from local ingredients, a glam cocktail bar, and the occasional live jazz act, Blue House

Monrovia

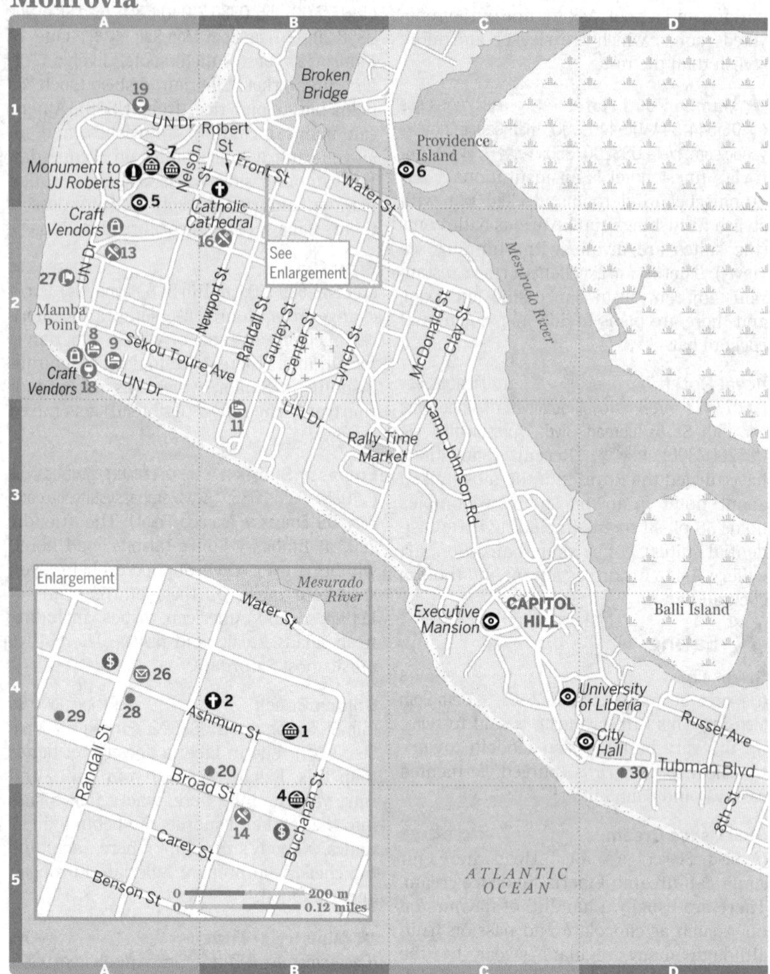

fits the bill for a date or special evening. In the furthest part of Congo Town, it's about a 20- to 30-minute drive from the city centre.

Drinking & Nightlife

Lila Brown's BAR

(UN Dr; 5pm-late Mon-Sun) Lila B's is a duplex bar nestled between the Mamba Point Hotel and the Atlantic. Downstairs, there's a food menu and a party vibe on weekend nights. Climb the wooden staircase for sea views, waiter service and relaxed tables shielded from rainy-season downpours by stylish shower curtains.

Tides BAR

(0777-666 444; UN Dr, near Swedish Embassy; 4pm-late Tue-Sun) Wicker armchairs and loveseats line the wide verandah at Tides, which looks out over the ocean. Inside, find the cocktail list scribbled on a blackboard (try the bissap margarita), a pool table and a long bar beneath a safari-lodge ceiling. The kitchen – which serves sandwiches, cassava fries and crispy fried plantain, known

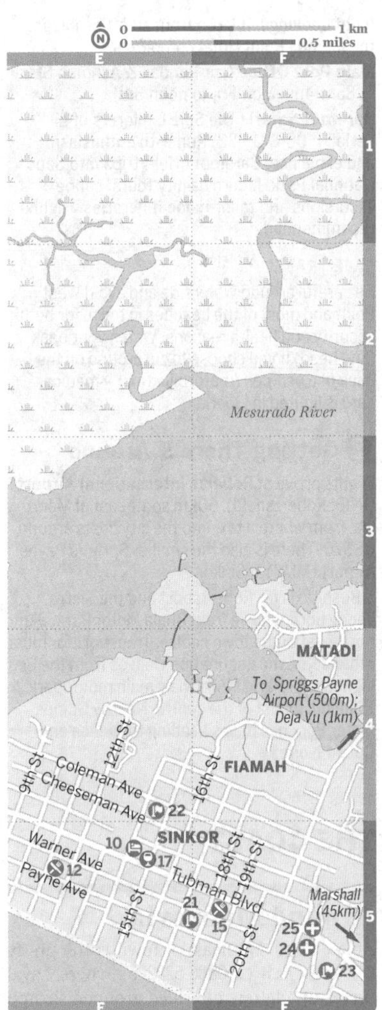

Monrovia

as *kelewele* – opens after 4.30pm. There are movie nights and special events.

JR's Beach Bar BAR
(Mamba Point beach; afternoons & evenings) Take any one of the beach tracks from Mamba Point Rd and you'll stumble upon JR's Beach Bar, Rasta Bar, Miami Beach or any of the other beach bars that are popping up here. Rasta Bar has a pool table.

Jamal's Boulevard Cafe BAR
(cnr 14th St & Tubman Blvd, Sinkor; 5pm-late Mon-Fri, 10am-late Sat & Sun; wi-fi) This Sinkor institution comes alive on weekend nights, and has drinks specials, karaoke, quiz nights and special events. There's also food, including good pizza (call ahead for delivery), and wi-fi. Sunday brunch includes the likes of mimosas and bloody Marys.

Deja Vu CLUB
(05-555 000; Airfield Short Cut, Sinkor; 10pm-4am Tue-Sat) Join the shimmering, moneyed party people at Liberia's sleekest club, which hosts DJs and regular special nights. No shorts or sandals for men.

Palm Spring Resort CASINO
(0880-606 060; www.liberiapalmspring.com; Tubman Blvd, Congo Town; wi-fi) Friday nights

at the Palm Spring Resort in Congo Town herald live music in the bar, before the mass exodus into the casino, where the younger generations of Liberia's political elite mingle with Russian croupiers, curious expats and elegant ladies of the night.

Shopping

For souvenirs, visit the Guinean craft vendors opposite Mamba Point Hotel or on the hilltop above the US Embassy, where you can strike a good bargain.

Kasawa (0886-698 005; www.kasawa.org; 1st St, Sinkor) is a fair-trade initiative that brings together clothing designers and producers from Robertsport, while **Jola House** (0880-652 933; Duport Rd, Paynesville) stocks fairly produced bags, place mats and cushions. **Afropolitan** (0880-514 514; cnr Benson & Newport Sts) has a colourful range of clothing, laptop bags, purses, souvenirs and jewellery.

German entrepreneur **Manfred** (0886-963 969) creates bottle openers and candlesticks from old war weapons and **Benjamin Somon** (077-027 751) makes chess sets from discarded AK-47 bullets. **Leslie Lumeh** (0886-430 483) sells his watercolour and acrylic paintings.

Orientation

The heart of town is around Benson and Randall Sts, and along Broad St, where you'll find most shops and businesses. Southwest of here at Mamba Point are hotels, restaurants and NGO offices. To the southeast is Sinkor, with more hotels, eateries and businesses. It leads into Congo Town, Elwa junction and Red Light Motor Park.

Information

Lucky Pharmacy (Tubman Blvd; 8.30am-late Mon-Sun) Right opposite JFK Hospital, this pharmacy is trusted by international organisations and has knowledgeable staff.

SOS Clinic (0886-841 673; Tubman Blvd, Congo Town) Head here in the first instance if you fall sick; this clinic is the best equipped in the country, trusted by expats. It's between the YWCA and Total Garage.

JFK Hospital (Tubman Blvd, Sinkor) Monrovia's main hospital is fine for basic needs (they can do malaria tests) but should be avoided for more serious matters, unless the hospital's annual flying surgeons are in town.

Karou Voyages (0886-517 454; Mamba Point Hotel, UN Dr) Good for continent-wide flight bookings. It's run from an office inside the Mamba Point Hotel complex.

Main Post Office (cnr Randall & Ashmun Sts; 8am-4pm Mon-Fri, to noon Sat)

Barefoot Safari (The Sole Explorers of Liberia; 06-841 582) Run with enthusiasm and expertise, Barefoot offers trips into Sapo National Park, Monrovia city tours, canoe excursions and tailor-made itineraries. Highly recommended.

SAFE TRAVEL

Be careful around Waterside and avoid West Point and most of the beaches in town, for both security and health reasons. Watch your back (and head) if you choose to zip around on the back of a *pen-pen* (motorbike taxi) – medical care is limited in Liberia.

Getting There & Around

Flights arrive at **Roberts International Airport** (ROB; Robertsfield), 60km southeast of Monrovia, from where a taxi into the city costs around US$70. There is also the smaller Spriggs Payne Airport (MLW) in Sinkor.

Bush taxis for Robertsport and the Sierra Leone border leave from Duala Motor Park, 9km northeast of the town centre. Transport for most other domestic destinations leaves from the Red Light Motor Park, Monrovia's main motor park, 15km northeast of the centre. Nearby Guinea Motor Park has buses heading to Guinea and Côte d'Ivoire.

THE COAST

Around Monrovia

About 15km southeast of town is the pretty **Silver Beach** (0886-522225), where Layal serves up platters of grilled grouper, shrimp and lobster against a Sunday backdrop of salsa dancing (US$10 by charter taxi). Another 2km further south is **Thinker's Beach**, popular with a party crowd on weekends. In the shadow of the now-skeletal Hotel Africa is **CeeCee Beach**, 40 minutes west of Monrovia. Soil erosion is claiming the restaurant, but you can still swim in a lagoon sheltered by rocks.

Just beyond Careysburg is the quirky **Wulki Farms** (0886-327 637), owned by a former minister in Charles Taylor's cabinet, where you can ride horses (US$10), visit the zoo and order steak in the restaurant.

Marshall

A short drive from Robertsfield International Airport and 45 minutes or so from Monrovia is the rural area surrounding Marshall, which makes for an easy weekend escape from the city. You can camp on the quiet beaches here (speak to the locals to find a good spot, and be mindful of security) or see **Monkey Island**, a small archipelago that's home to chimpanzees evacuated from a hepatitis research lab during the war. Call the animals' feeder Joseph (☎0886-537 942) for information on joining a food run. Just don't get too close; these chimps know how to throw mangoes.

Nearby is **Wolokor Cultural Village**, where you can watch performances from a talented cultural troupe. If you're passing **Harbel**, it's worth taking a detour into **Firestone Rubber Plantation**, the world's largest rubber plantation, which is leased from the government on a controversial 99-year plan. You can play a round at the 18-hole **golf course**.

★ **Libassa Eco-Lodge** LODGE $$
(☎05-940 930, 0888-555 563; www.libassa.com; day entry fee US$10, huts US$125, honeymoon ste US$250; P) With pretty, solar-powered huts (named after endangered Liberian species) on the edge of the forest, Libassa makes for a gorgeous weekend retreat near Marshall. Pack your swimsuit; there's a pool, a lagoon and a beach as well as a lunch buffet run by helpful staff. The 2km stretch of road beyond Kpan Town is rough and only accessible by 4WD (45 minutes from Monrovia).

RLJ Kendeja RESORT $$$
(☎from the US 240-744 7850, 0886-219 939; www.rljkendejaresort.com; r from US$205; P) This sleek, dreamy resort is spread across a beach in the environs of the airport. Interlinked walkways take you to the pool, the plush bar and restaurant, and the spa. Sunday brunch is a hit with expat NGO workers and there are romantic getaway deals.

Robertsport

Framed by gold-spun beaches, phosphorescent waves and a thick mane of forest, pretty Robertsport was just a fishing village a few years ago. Now, as you emerge from the rust-red roads and wind your way through the old town with its architecture in various states of undress (look out for the stunning scarlet ruins of the defunct Tubman Center of African Culture), you're greeted by surf lodges and body-boarding tourists.

Thankfully, the capital of Grand Cape Mount has largely retained its simple, paradise-found feel and you can still pitch your tent beneath the fabled **cotton tree** (☎Prince at Robertsport Community Works 0886-546 214; per person US$5). The lodges offer breakfast, lunch and dinner, or you can drive into the lively Grassfields part of town for Liberian food.

For the best **surf breaks**, wait for the rainy season and head to Fisherman's Point (good for beginners), Cotton Trees (along a shallow sand bar) or the more ambitious Cassava Point, which heaves towards the shiny granite rocks.

★ **Kwepunha Villas** GUESTHOUSE $
(☎0888-132 870; www.kwepunha.com; Fisherman's Beach, Robertsport; s/d US$25/35; P) Run by Californian surfers in conjunction with community initiatives, this blue-and-yellow beach house offers pleasant, breezy rooms with wooden four-poster beds. You can join grassroots-style surf retreats here, or book the rooms independently. The house is situated on Fisherman's Beach (a 15-minute walk from Nana's along the sand), where you can tuck into fish tacos and margaritas.

Nana's Lodge LODGE $$
(☎086-668 332; Cassava Beach; canvas/wooden bungalows for 2 from US$60/110; P) Robertsport's original ecolodge, Nana's has 11 bungalows overlooking the beach. The wooden huts are pricier than the canvas ones, but both styles of accommodation come with two comfortable double beds, fans and balconies. The sandy cantina down on the beach is a top sunset spot.

Buchanan

Liberia's second port hosts wild, beautiful **beaches** that are perfect for camping, plus an annual dumboy festival in January: two good reasons to make it here. You can sleep at the clean, reasonably comfortable **Teepro Lodge** (☎0880-961 568; Roberts St; r with net & fan US$25), next to the Buchanan Renewables site. The owners can advise on beach camping – it's advisable to hire an overnight security guard and watch the strong currents if you swim. In town, **Black**

and White is a nightclub that also serves food, and there are beach bars along the coastal strip.

Bush taxis ply the route from Monrovia (L$350, three hours) or you can charter a car (US$100 one way) or a 4WD (US$150 plus petrol per day) for the 125km to Buchanan, which is mostly paved.

NORTH OF MONROVIA

Gbarnga

Liberia's most prestigious seat of learning, the country's second city and capital of the county of Bong is home to **Cuttington University**, on the site of the old Africana Museum, which once had a 3000-piece collection. Gbarnga's historical significance runs deeper than that; it is the site of **Charles Taylor's farm** (on the outskirts of town), from where he masterminded rebel operations in Sierra Leone and Liberia. An hour outside of Gbarnga is **Kpatawee waterfall**, a pretty picnic and swimming spot.

You can sleep at the **Hill Top Hotel** (☎0886-423 702; r US$50), 5km from town on the Ganta Hwy, or **Paulma's Guesthouse** (☎0886-771 297; r US$25) nearby. By bush taxi, Gbarnga can be reached in about five hours from Monrovia (L$400).

Mount Nimba

When the heat gets too much in Monrovia, there's only one thing for it – head for higher climes. Beautiful Mt Nimba is Liberia's tallest peak, 1362m above sea level, and you can feasibly climb it if you have a few days on your hands.

The jumping-off point is the curious town of **Yekepa**, a 10-hour drive from Monrovia and a *Truman Show*-esque mining town owned by Arcelor Mittal. The road to Mt Nimba is paved for almost three-quarters of the way to the top; you can drive to the peak using a 4WD, and camp along the way if you have your own equipment, hiking along the peaks. Bring GPS and warm clothing as it can get misty and very cool at night. Accommodation in Yekepa is available at the **Noble House Motel** (☎077-285 158; r from US$12).

THE SOUTHEAST

Zwedru

Flanked by thick, lush rainforest that runs along the Côte d'Ivoire border, Zwedru is the capital of Grand Gedeh, one of Liberia's greenest counties. It's only 200km from Monrovia, but you'll need to allow at least 10 hours to get there by road, for the route is long, rough and bumpy. This is the hometown of Samuel Doe, who stole power in a bloody coup in 1980. His mark is still evident in Zwedru, where he installed pavements and was in the process of constructing a house on the edge of town when he was murdered. Many people in Grand Gedeh, particularly those who feel forgotten by the Monrovia administration, remain vocal supporters of Doe.

The best place to stay is the **Munnah Guesthouse** (☎0886-485 288; r from US$30), also used by NGOs working in the area's Ivorian refugee camps. The modern, airy rooms have fans. The other option is the more basic **Monjue Hotel** (☎0880-748 658), which can be noisy at weekends. **Florida restaurant**, on the main road that runs through town, is a popular meeting spot that serves cheap Liberian dishes and European mains.

Sapo National Park PARK
(scnlib2001@yahoo.com) FREE Sapo, Liberia's only national park, is a lush 1808-sq-km tract of rainforest containing some of West Africa's last remaining primary rainforest, as well as forest elephants, pygmy hippos, chimpanzees, antelopes and other wildlife, although these populations suffered greatly during the war. If you'd like to visit, your best bet is to go with a tour organised by the likes of Barefoot Safari (p358), as the park is not set up for independent travel. The park is in Sinoe Province. You'll need to allow at least a full day's travel to reach Sapo from Monrovia. Take a 4WD from Monrovia to Greenville, then head north to Juarzon and then southeast to Jalay's Town.

Harper

Reachable after two days on some of Liberia's worst roads, deliquescent, small-town Harper feels like the prize at the end of a long treasure hunt. The capital of the once-autonomous Maryland state, this gem is shingled with decaying ruins that hint at its former grandeur.

The drive from Monrovia to Harper can be broken up in Zwedru (10 hours), from where it's around five hours further south. It's inadvisable to attempt this route during the rainy season, even if you're travelling by 4WD.

Sights

In the early evenings, the soft light gives an eldritch feel to the shell of the **presidential mansion** of former president William Tubman, who was born in Harper, and the remnants of the **Morning Star Masonic Lodge**, built by Tubman, himself a Grand Master Freemason.

Cape Palmas Lighthouse is no longer functional but can be climbed for an outstanding panoramic view of the cape. It's on a UN base, so get permission first, and don't attempt to scale the small, slippery steps during the rainy season. Don't miss the stunning, palm-lined **beach** at nearby Fish Town (not to be confused with the larger town of the same name), but take care with the currents if you swim.

Sleeping

The town's best-established hotel is **Adina's Guest House** (☎0886-620 005; r US$25), which has several basic rooms with fans. If it's fully booked, as is often the case, you can try your luck at Tubman University campus 6.5km north of town or the Pastoral Centre of the Catholic archdiocese.

Eating & Drinking

Jade's LIBERIAN $

(cnr Water & Rushman Sts) Jade's (or Sweet Baby, as some locals lovingly call it) serves fish, chicken and rice for US$5 per helping, as well as sandwiches and pizzas if the delivery truck has brought supplies.

Sophie's LIBERIAN $

(Mechlin St) Sophie's offers good potato greens and cassava-leaf stew.

Bobby's CAFE $

(Maryland Ave) Bobby's tea shop does the best breakfasts in town: think beans, spaghetti, instant coffee and greasy egg baps.

Pak Bat ASIAN $

There's great south Asian food to be had at Pak Bat, the Pakistani UN peacekeepers' battalion, so long as you're prepared to pay US$3 and can pull off an NGO worker vibe.

Oceanview BAR

(Printey St) For beachside drinks, Oceanview can't be beaten.

UNDERSTAND LIBERIA

Liberia Today

Liberia's Nobel Peace Prize–winning president, Ellen Johnson-Sirleaf, won a second term in power in 2011, after rival party Congress for Democratic Change (CDC) – led by Winston Tubman and former AC Milan footballer George Weah – boycotted the second round of the violence-ridden vote, complaining of fraud. 'Ellen', as she is widely known, enjoys support from a loyal band of Liberians. Others criticise her for being a part of the old set of politicians and accuse her of failing to understand their woes.

Ellen also failed in 2010 to implement the findings of Liberia's Truth and Reconciliation Commission, a post-conflict justice organ that was modelled on South Africa's. The body's final report recommended that the president herself be barred from holding public office for 50 years, after she admitted partially bankrolling former leader Charles Taylor's rebellion that sparked the civil war.

Taylor was sentenced to 50 years behind bars by a UN-backed war-crimes tribunal in The Hague in 2011. Many Liberians expressed frustration that Taylor was tried not for his role in the painful Liberian conflict but for masterminding rebel operations during Sierra Leone's war.

Many middle-class Liberians are excited about the country's new dawn, but for others – particularly those outside Monrovia – the fresh coats of paint and eager investors in the capital do little to heal old wounds. Justice, they say, is still a way away.

History

The Love of Liberty

Liberia was ruled along ethnic lines until American abolitionists looking for a place to resettle freed slaves stepped off the boat at Monrovia's Providence Island in 1822. They saw themselves as part of a mission to bring civilisation and Christianity to Africa, but their numbers were soon depleted by tropical diseases and hostile indigenous residents.

The surviving settlers, known as Americo-Liberians, declared an independent republic in 1847, under the mantra 'The Love of Liberty Brought Us Here'. However, citizenship excluded indigenous peoples, and every president until 1980 was of American freed-slave ancestry. For nearly a century, Liberia foundered economically and politically while the indigenous population suffered under forced labour. They were not afforded the right to vote until 1963.

During William Tubman's presidency (1944–71) the tide began to turn. Foreign investment flowed into the country, and for several decades Liberia sustained sub-Saharan Africa's highest growth rate. Firestone and other American companies made major investments, and Tubman earned praise as the 'maker of modern Liberia'.

Yet the influx of new money exacerbated existing social inequalities, and hostilities between Americo-Liberians and the indigenous population worsened during the era of Tolbert, who succeeded Tubman. While the elite continued to live the high life, resentment among other Liberians quietly simmered.

Death in Pyjamas

Master-sergeant Samuel Doe crept into the presidential palace one night in 1980 and killed Tolbert, who was ready for bed in his pyjamas. For the first time, Liberia had a ruler who was not an Americo-Liberian, giving the indigenous population a taste of political power and an opportunity for vengeance. One of Doe's first moves was to order the execution of 13 of Tolbert's ministers on a beach in Monrovia. Ellen Johnson-Sirleaf, a member of Tolbert's cabinet, narrowly escaped.

The coup was widely condemned both regionally and internationally. While relations with neighbouring African states soon thawed, the post-coup flight of capital from the country, coupled with ongoing corruption, caused Liberia's economy to plummet.

Doe struggled to maintain power, but opposition forces began to gain strength and inter-tribal fighting broke out. On Christmas Eve 1989, Charles Taylor launched an invasion from Côte d'Ivoire. By mid-1990, Taylor's forces controlled most of the countryside. Doe was murdered in 1991, his death captured on a video tape that shows Prince Johnson – who came third in the 2012 presidential race – sipping a beer while shouting instructions to the killers.

Following a series of failed peace accords interspersed with factional fighting, the 1996 elections brought Charles Taylor to the presidency with a big majority. His election slogan was: 'He killed my ma, he killed my pa, I'll vote for him'.

In August 2003, with rebel groups controlling most of the country, and under heavy pressure from the international community (and from Johnson-Sirleaf), Charles Taylor went into exile in Nigeria. A transitional government was established, leading to elections in late 2005. Johnson-Sirleaf's winning candidature made her the first elected female president in Africa.

Culture

Liberia remains a country of exceptions. The old inequality hang-ups haven't gone away; you'll notice that Americo-Liberians and returning, educated Liberians often enjoy better treatment than those with indigenous roots. Various initiatives are under way to even things out, but the road to cultural equality is likely to be long.

Regardless of their roots, one thing all Liberians have in common is their devotion to family. Many people you meet will be supporting a dozen others. Religion is also important, with Christian families regularly attending revivals at churches.

The Liberian handshake (practised mostly by men) has Masonic origins and involves a snappy pull-back of the third finger, often accompanied by a wide grin.

People

The vast majority of Liberians are of indigenous origin, belonging to more than a dozen major tribal groups, including the Kpelle in the centre, the Bassa around Buchanan and the Mandingo (Mandinka) in the north. Americo-Liberians account for barely 5% of the total. There's also an economically powerful Lebanese community in Monrovia.

Close to half of the population are Christians and about 20% are Muslim, with the remainder following traditional religions.

Arts & Crafts

Liberia has long been famed for its masks, especially those of the Gio in the northeast, including the *gunyege* mask (which shelters a power-giving spirit), and the chimpanzee-like *kagle* mask. The Bassa around Buchanan are renowned for their *gela* masks, which often have elaborately carved coiffures, always with an odd number of plaits.

Food & Drink

Rice and spicy meat sauces or fish stews are popular Liberian dishes. Palm butter with fish and potato greens are two favourites. Other popular dishes include palava sauce (made with plato leaf, dried fish or meat and palm oil) and *jollof rice* (rice and vegetables with meat or fish). American food is popular in Monrovia. Club beer is the local brew.

Environment

Illegal logging both during and after the conflict has threatened a number of species in Liberia, including the forest elephant, hawk, pygmy hippo (nigh-on impossible to see), manatee and chimpanzee. Liberia's rainforests, which now cover about 40% of the country, comprise a critical part of the Guinean Forests of West Africa Hotspot, an exceptionally biodiverse area stretching across 11 countries in the region.

Liberia's low-lying coastal plain is intersected by marshes, creeks and tidal lagoons, and bisected by at least nine major rivers. Inland is a densely forested plateau rising to low mountains in the northeast. The highest point is Mt Nimba (1362m).

SURVIVAL GUIDE

Directory A–Z

ACCOMMODATION

Accommodation prices in Monrovia have been driven up by the presence of private companies and NGOs. You can expect to pay top dollar in the capital, with a few exceptions. Upcountry, both prices and standards are lower.

BOOKS

Journey Without Maps, Graham Greene's tale of adventuring across Liberia in the 1930s, is the Liberia classic. Less well-known but equally recommended is *Too Late to Turn Back*, written by Greene's cousin and travelling companion Barbara.

President Ellen Johnson-Sirleaf's autobiography, *This Child Will be Great*, explores pre- and postwar Liberia, including Johnson-Sirleaf's backing of Taylor's rebellion.

MOVIES

Pray the Devil Back to Hell is a 2008 documentary that focuses on Nobel Prize–winner Leymah Gbowee's efforts to bring the war to an end. *An Uncivil War* includes disturbing images of the conflict and America's alleged failure to help.

Shot in the years following the war, *Sliding Liberia* is a short surf documentary that beautifully captures post-conflict Liberia and a local surfer's effort to catch the waves, rather than go under.

EMBASSIES & CONSULATES

Canadians and Australians should contact their high commissions in Abidjan (Côte d'Ivoire) and Accra (Ghana), respectively.

Côte d'Ivoire Consulate (☎0886-519 138; Warner Ave btwn 17th & 18th Sts, Sinkor)

French Embassy (☎031-235 576; German Compound, Congo Town)

German Embassy (☎0886-438 365; Tubman Blvd, UNMIL Bldg, Congo Town)

Ghanian Embassy (☎077-016 920; cnr 15th St & Cheesman Ave, Sinkor)

Guinean Embassy (☎0886-573 049; Tubman Blvd btwn 23rd & 24th Sts, Sinkor)

Nigerian Embassy (☎0886-261 148; Tubman Blvd, Nigeria House, Congo Town)

Sierra Leonean Embassy (☎0886-427 404; Tubman Blvd, Congo Town)

UK Embassy (☎06-516 973; chalkleyroy@aol.com; UN Dr, Clara Town, Bushrod Island) Honorary consul, emergency assistance only; otherwise contact the British High Commission in Freetown, Sierra Leone.

US Embassy (☎077-054 826; http://monrovia.usembassy.gov/; UN Dr, Mamba Point)

HEALTH

You will need a valid yellow-fever vaccination certificate in order to enter Liberia. Malaria is endemic and prophylaxis is recommended. Typhoid is also relatively common, so take care to wash your hands before eating.

MONEY

Liberia has two units of currency; the Liberty dollar (L$, or LD) and the US dollar, which is accepted in most places. There are between 60 and 73 Liberty dollars to one US dollar. For small purchases such as newspapers, shared taxi rides and cheap meals, Liberians use Liberty dollars. For anything else, it's US dollars.

PRACTICALITIES

➡ **Electricity** Voltage is 110V. Plugs are a mixture of US-style (two flat pins) and European style. Grid power is gradually improving in Monrovia, although most hotels and apartment blocks still rely on fuel-heavy generators. Outside of the capital, it's generators all the way.

➡ **Language** Liberian English – which to the untrained ear sounds something like Caribbean-lilted English, with southern American undertones and missing consonents – is the main language. Upcountry, as many as 25 languages are spoken, including Bassa, Mende, Vai and Kpelle.

➡ **Newspapers** There are dozens of national newspapers; among the best-regarded are the *New Dawn*, the *Observer* and *Front Page Africa*.

If you have a Visa (not MasterCard) card, Ecobank's ATMs are reasonably reliable in Monrovia. Elsewhere, carry cash. Western Union and Moneygram operate in most towns.

OPENING HOURS

Banks Generally open 9am to 4pm Monday to Friday and 9am to noon on Saturday.

PUBLIC HOLIDAYS

New Year's Day 1 January
Armed Forces Day 11 February
Decoration Day Second Wednesday in March
JJ Roberts' Birthday 15 March
Fast & Prayer Day 11 April
National Unification Day 14 May
Independence Day 26 July
Flag Day 24 August
Liberian Thanksgiving Day First Thursday in November
Tubman Day 29 November
Christmas Day 25 December

SAFE TRAVEL

Liberia – notably the beaches in and around Monrovia – has some of the strongest rip currents in the world, and expat drownings transcend tropical diseases as one of the most common causes of death. Check with locals before you swim, never swim alone and learn how to negotiate rip tides before you dip your toes into the ocean. Poor sanitation facilities in many waterside communities mean that central Monrovia's beaches aren't the healthiest places to sunbathe or swim, but clean white sands await on the outskirts of town.

Otherwise, the biggest dangers are the roads. The security situation is stable, although it's wise not to walk in Monrovia after dark. Exercise caution if using motorbike taxis – medical care is limited – and don't be afraid to ask the driver to go slow. Electric shocks are common in badly wired buildings; wear shoes before plugging in appliances if you're worried.

TELEPHONE

The country code is 231.There are no area codes or landlines. You can call the US (but not Europe) cheaply from most mobile networks. You can pick up a Cellcom, Comium or Lonestar SIM card from booths on the street for US$5.

VISAS

Visas are required by all (except nationals of Ecowas countries), with costs varying depending on where they are procured. In the US a three-month single-entry visa for US citizens costs US$140. In a pinch, airport visas can be secured, but you must have a company apply to immigration ahead of time and someone must bring the visa to meet your plane at the airport.

Visa Extensions

Visas can be extended at the **Bureau of Immigration** (Broad St; ⏲ 9am-5pm Mon-Fri, to 3pm Sat) in Monrovia.

Visas for Onward Travel

Côte d'Ivoire Bring one passport photo and leave your passport between 9am and 1pm or 2pm and 3pm Monday to Friday. A one-month single-entry visa costs US$75 for all nationals. Processing usually takes five working days but can be done faster at no extra cost if you're in a hurry.

Guinea Bring two passport photos and leave your passport between 9.30am and 4pm Monday to Friday. One-month single-entry visas cost US$65 for citizens of the EU, Australia and New Zealand, or US$100 for US and Canadian nationals. Processing takes 24 hours.

Sierra Leone You'll need two passport photos and a photocopy of your passport to get a visa. Applications are accepted only between 10am and 2pm on Monday, Wednesday and Friday, and single-entry visas valid for up to three months cost US$100 for citizens of the EU, Canada, Australia and New Zealand. US citizens are charged US$131.

ℹ Getting There & Away

AIR

A number of airlines serve Monrovia.

Air France (www.airfrance.com; Broad St)

British Airways (www.ba.com; Royal Hotel, Tubman Blvd, Sinkor)

Brussels Airlines (www.brusselsairlines.com; Randall St)

Delta Air Lines (DL; www.delta.com)

Kenya Airways (KQ; ☎06-511 522, 06-556 693; www.kenya-airways.com; Broad St, KLM Bldg)

Royal Air Maroc (AT; ☎06-956 956, 06-951 951; www.royalairmaroc.com; Tubman Blvd)

LAND

Côte d'Ivoire

Border crossings with Côte d'Ivoire are just beyond Sanniquellie towards Danané, and east of Harper, towards Tabou.

From Harper, you must cross the Cavally River by ferry or canoe to reach the Ivorian border. Plan on two days if you want to reach Abidjan via San Pedro using public transport along this route.

Alternatively, daily bush taxis go from Monrovia to Ganta and Sanniquellie, from where you can continue in stages to Danané and Man (12 to 15 hours).

Guinea

For Guinea, the main crossing is just north of Ganta. From just north of Ganta's Public Market you can take a *moto-taxi* the 2km to the border and walk across. Once in Guinea, there are frequent taxis to N'zérékoré. From Sanniquellie's bush-taxi rank, known as the 'meat packing', there are irregular bush taxis via Yekepa to the Guinean town of Lola (US$6.50). A place in a shared taxi is the same price. A *moto-taxi* (if you can find one!) from Yekepa to the border should cost only US$0.50, after which there are Guinean vehicles to Lola. There is also a border crossing at Voinjama to Macenta via a bad road from Gbarnga (often impassable in the wet season).

Sierra Leone

Using a 4WD, you can reach Freetown in about 12 hours. The main Sierra Leone crossing is at Bo (Waterside). There are frequent daily bush taxis between Monrovia and the Bo (Waterside) border (three hours), from where it's easy to find onward transport to Kenema (about eight very rough hours further), and then on to Freetown.

Getting Around

BUSH TAXI & BUS

Bush taxis go daily from Monrovia to most destinations, including Buchanan, Gbarnga, Ganta, Sanniquellie and the Sierra Leone border, although distant routes are severely restricted during the rainy season. Minivans (called 'buses') also ply most major routes, although they're more crowded and dangerous than bush taxis.

CAR & MOTORCYCLE

Vehicle rental can be arranged through better hotels from about US$150 per day plus petrol for a 4WD. You can travel by private taxi in Monrovia for US$5 per short hop; contact the well-run and trusted network of Guinean taxi drivers, **Alpha** (☎0886-600 022), for more information, including on airport pick-ups. Motorbike taxis known as *pen-pens* ply the streets of Monrovia and other cities. In the capital they have a 10pm curfew for a reason; ride with caution.

Mali

☎ 223 / POP 14.5 MILLION

Includes ➡

Fast Facts

- **Capital** Bamako
- **Population** 15 million
- **Area** 1,240,140 sq km
- **Languages** French, Bambara, Fulfulde, Tamashek, Dogon and Songhai
- **Money** West African CFA franc; US$1 = CFA504.29, €1 = CFA656
- **Seasons** Hot (October to February), very hot (April to June), wet (July to August)
- **Tourist Information** www.le-mali.com/omatho/index.htm
- **Visa** One- to three-month visas available at Mali embassies; short-stay and transit visas may be issued at borders depending on security situation.

Rugged Land of Sahelian Sands & Lush Forests

Like an exquisite sandcastle formed in a harsh desert landscape, Mali is blessed by an extraordinary amount of beauty, wonders, talents and knowledge.

Yet for now, it's landscapes, monuments, mosques and music bars are off-limits, sealed from tourists by a conflict that is threatening the culture of this remarkable country.

The beating heart of Mali is Bamako, where Ngoni and Kora musicians play to crowds of dancing Malians from all ethnicities, while in the Dogon country, villages still cling to the cliffs as they did in ancient times.

Further west, Fula women strap silver jewellery to their ears and their belongings to donkeys, forming caravans worthy of beauty pageants as they make their way across the *hamada* (dry, dusty scrubland).

And in the northeast, the writings of ancient African civilizations remain locked in the beautiful libraries of Timbuktu.

Mali Top Sights

- **Dogon Country** Rose-coloured villages, big blue skies, sacred crocodiles and sandstone cliffs
- **Djenné** Stunning mud-brick town with a fairy-tale mosque overlooking a clamorous Monday market
- **Bamako** Spicy grilled fish, live music, sprawling markets and motorbikes purring along the banks of the Niger river
- **Timbuktu** Few places in the world hold a pursuit of knowledge so dear, with its ancient libraries, monuments and never-digitized texts on philosophy and astronomy
- **Segou** Acacia trees, shea butter, pottery and waterside griots
- **Niger River** Africa's third-longest river, bending and twisting on its way to the ancient Sahelian trading kingdoms

UNDERSTAND MALI

Mali Today

Mali's fall from grace in 2012 came as a surprise to many, although not to close watchers of former President Amadou Toumani Toure (commonly referred to as ATT) who was ousted in a coup in April 2012. A band of mutinous soldiers ousted the president and his cabinet in the run-up to elections in which ATT was not planning to stand, claiming the leader was not adequately supporting the under-equipped Malian army against an Tuareg rebellion in the northeast of the country.

Somewhat ironically, the coup only worsened the situation in the northeast, allowing Islamist groups to gain hold of the region. They in turn pushed out the Tuareg groups and went on to install sharia law in the ancient towns of Gao and Timbuktu, destroying ancient monuments, tombs and remnants of history. 700,000 civilians were forced to flee in 2012 and early 2013, winding up in refugee camps in neighbouring countries as French forces and Regional West African Ecowas (Economic Community of West African States) troops launched air raids and ground attacks, successfully pushing back the Islamists from many of their strongholds. French forces began to draw down in April 2013, but the majority of the displaced had not returned home at the time of research, and Jihadi attacks continued.

Visiting Mali was dangerous and strongly unrecommended at the time of research. Although there is some semblance of normality in the capital, Bamako, the risk of kidnapping and violence remains. Venturing further north or east than Mopti and Sevare should be done with extreme caution.

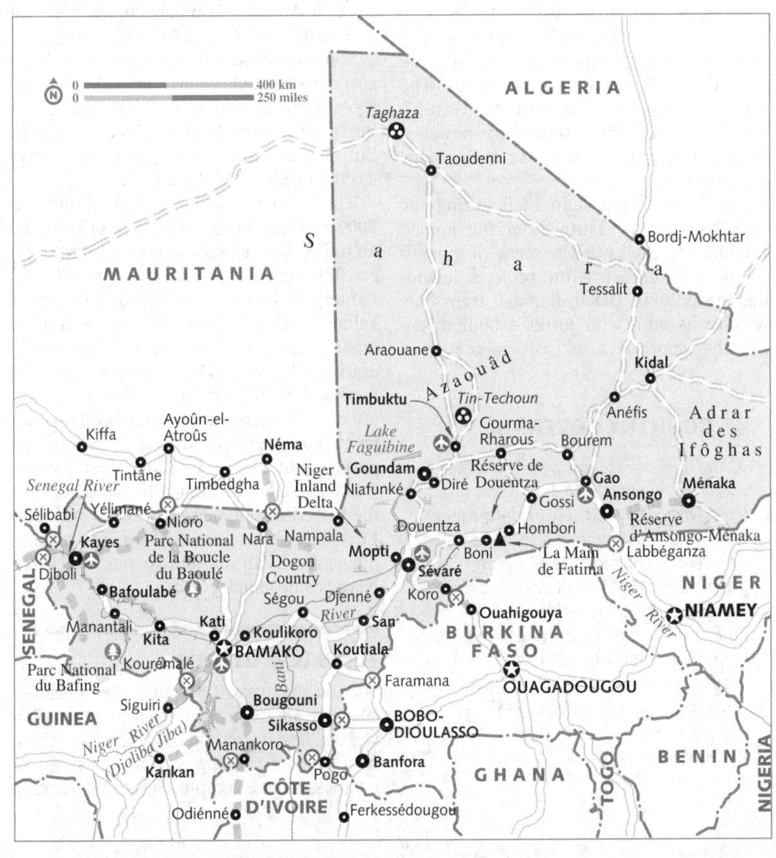

The instability is deeply felt by most Malians; many businesses have closed, tourism revenue has dropped dramatically; with the destruction of important sites in Gao and Timbuktu, many sadly feel that it is not only Mali's future that is under threat but its long-celebrated culture and history.

History

Early Empires

Rock art in the Sahara suggests that northern Mali has been inhabited since 10,000 BC, when the Sahara was fertile and rich in wildlife. By 300 BC, large organised settlements had developed, most notably near Djenné, one of West Africa's oldest cities. By the 6th century AD, the lucrative trans-Saharan trade in gold, salt and slaves had begun, facilitating the rise of West Africa's great empires.

From the 8th to the 16th centuries, Mali formed the centrepiece of the great empires of West African antiquity, most notably the empires of Ghana, Mali and Songhaï. The arrival of European ships along the West African coast from the 15th century, however, broke the monopoly on power of the Sahel kingdoms.

The French arrived in Mali during the mid-19th century. Throughout the French colonial era, Mali was the scene of a handful of major infrastructure projects, including the 1200km Dakar–Bamako train line, which was built with forced labour to enable the export of cheap cash crops, such as rice and cotton. But Mali remained the poor neighbour of Senegal and Côte d'Ivoire.

> **COUNTRY COVERAGE**
>
> At the time of research very few travellers were heading to Mali so we're providing historical and cultural information rather than reviews and listings. A good source of information for on-the-ground travel in Mali is Lonely Planet's Thorn Tree online travel forum www.lonelyplanet.com/thorntree. Other sources of good internet-based information are www.maliactu.net (local news in French) and blogs like Bridges from Bamako (http://bridgesfrombamako.com).

Independence

Mali became independent in 1960 (for a few months it was federated with Senegal), under the one-party rule of Mali's first president, Modibo Keïta. In 1968, Keïta was overthrown by army officers led by Moussa Traoré.

During the Cold War, Mali was firmly in the Soviet camp; food shortages were constant, especially during the devastating droughts of 1968–74 and 1980–85. One bright spot came in 1987 when Mali produced its first grain surplus.

The Tuareg rebellion began in 1990, and the following year a peaceful prodemocracy demonstration drew machine-gun fire from security forces. Three days of rioting followed, during which 150 people were killed. The unrest finally provoked the army, led by General Amadou Toumani Touré (General ATT as he was known), to seize control.

Touré established an interim transitional government and gained considerable respect when he resigned a year later, keeping his promise to hold multiparty elections. But he was rewarded for his patience and elected president in April 2002.

The Tuareg rebellion gained ground in 2007 and was bolstered in 2011 and 2012 by an influx of weapons and unemployed fighters following the Libyan civil war. Islamist fighters, including those linked to Al Qaeda, gained footing in the northeast soon after, ousting the main Mouvement pour le Libération d'Azawad (MNLA) Tuareg group and forcing 400,000 civilians to flee the region after harsh sharia law was imposed and ancient monuments destroyed. A transitional government, headed by Dioncounda Traore, was installed, but deemed too weak to handle the crisis alone. French forces and later ECOWAS troops launched air and ground offensives in an attempt to push back the Islamists in January 2013.

Arts & Culture

For the majority of Malians, life continues as usual, although the impact of the conflict weighs heavily on their minds. For those who eke out a living working in shops or businesses, the emphasis is on earning

AND THE BANDS PLAYED ON

The backdrop of the events of 2012 shook artists and musicians as well as politicians, interrupting album recordings and forcing Tuareg musicians to leave the country. The famous *ngoni* player Bassekou Kouyate, who also served as a griot to ousted President ATT was in the middle of recording an album when the coup hit. He finished the record, but the mark of the coup on it – and perhaps his future sales – is indelible.

Tinariwen, an intoxicating Tuareg group of former rebels from Kidal, were caught up in the crisis multiple times in 2012, with some of their members going missing and turning up in refugee camps in neighboring countries. Sadly the Festival in the Desert, usually held in January and organized by Tuareg musicians, has become another victim of the crisis. Amano Ag Issa, who recently toured the world with his Tuareg group Tartit, fled the country in the wake of the 2012 Tuareg rebellion. 'I was living quietly in my country, until the day that shook all our lives. Everything changed!' he told us. 'My Tuareg people were attacked and killed for no reason. That's what made me leave Mali. I had to go, we really didn't have much choice but to leave our homeland,' he said.

Fortunately, music is harder to destroy than the threatened ancient monuments and libraries of Timbuktu but the crisis has certainly silenced some musicians, restricting access to funding, electricity and inspiration. In the northeast, sharia law has meant that live bands and dancing venues have been silenced.

Outside of Mali, the music plays on, including bluesy stuff such as that from the late Ali Farka Touré. Other much-loved blues performers include many from Ali Farka's stable, among them Afel Bocoum, Ali Farka's son Vieux Farka Touré, Baba Salah and Lobi Traoré. Some scholars believe that the roots of American blues lie with the Malian slaves who worked on US plantations.

The breadth and depth of Mali's musical soundtrack is attributable not just to centuries of tradition but also to the policies of Mali's postindependence government. As elsewhere in West Africa, Mali's musicians were promoted as the cultural standard-bearers of the newly independent country and numerous state-sponsored 'orchestras' were founded. The legendary Rail Band de Bamako (actual employees of the Mali Railway Corporation) was one of the greatest, and one of its ex-members, the charismatic Salif Keita, has become a superstar in his own right. We have yet to see what kind of sounds the next, tense chapter in Mali's history will produce.

enough to take care of their (large) families on a day-to-day basis. But many have placed long-term plans on hold, as they simply can't predict what the future will bring.

In the northeast of the country, life has changed drastically. The imposition of sharia law has meant that many bars and restaurants have been closed. The majority of Malians are Muslim, but the strain of Islam that is followed is moderate and liberal – many enjoy dancing, drinking and being social butterflies. Now women must cover their heads, couples are stoned to death for having sex outside of marriage and live music is banned. For those who have not fled from the towns of Kidal, Gao and Timbuktu, life has become fairly miserable. For those in refugee camps in neighbouring countries, it's worse still.

Malians hold fast to tradition and politeness is respected. Malians find it rude to ask questions or stop someone in the street without first asking after their health and their families.

People

Mali's population is growing by almost 3% per year, which means that the number of Malians doubles every 20 years; 48% of Malians are under 15 years of age.

Concentrated in the centre and south of the country, the Bambara are Mali's largest ethnic group (33% of the population). Fulani (17%) pastoralists are found wherever there is grazing land for their livestock, particularly in the Niger inland delta. The lighter-skinned Tuareg (6%), traditionally nomadic pastoralists and traders, inhabit the fringes of the Sahara.

Between 80% and 90% of Malians are Muslim, and 2% are Christian. Animist beliefs often overlap with Islamic and Christian practices, especially in rural areas.

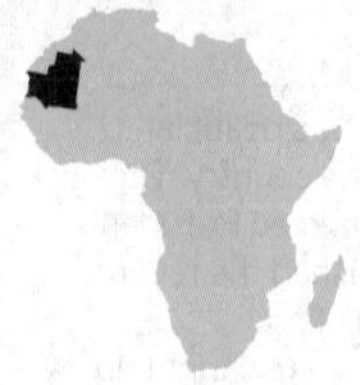

Mauritania

☎ 222 / POP 3.36 MILLION

Includes ➡

Best Places to Eat

- Restorante Galloufa (p377)
- Le Méditerranée (p374)
- Bla Bla Thé (p374)

Best Places to Stay

- Auberge Bab Sahara (p377)
- Auberge La Gueïla (p379)
- Maison d'Hôtes Jeloua (p373)
- Eco-lodge du Maure Bleu (p381)

Why Go?

If West Africa is a playground for overlanders, then Mauritania often seems to be little more than a transit between the better-known attractions of Marrakesh, Dakar or Bamako. That's a shame because Mauritania has some tremendous secrets to reveal.

Just as impressive as the cultural diversity is some of the continent's grandest scenery. The Adrar region offers epic sand dunes, eye-popping plateaus and Africa's biggest monolith. The Tagânt has similar charms, and both hide ancient (and World Heritage–listed) caravan towns – Chinguetti, Ouadâne and Oualâta. The World Heritage feast continues along the coast at Parc National du Banc d'Arguin, which attracts millions of migratory birds and is a renowned birdwatching site.

If you just breeze through, you'll miss out on a truly incredible country. No one in Mauritania is in a rush, and you shouldn't be either.

When to Go

Nouakchott

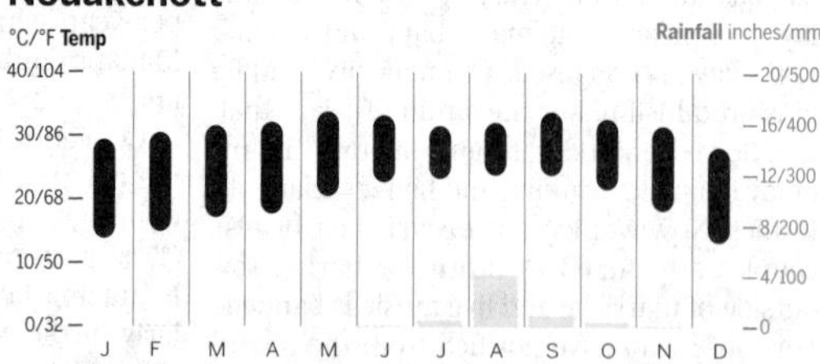

Nov–Mar The most pleasant months to visit the desert, although nights can be cold.

Jun–Aug The *rifi* (hot winds) send temperatures soaring to 45°C and above.

Jul–Sep The short rainy season in Nouakchott can be prone to flooding after downpour.

NOUAKCHOTT

POP 1 MILLION

Barely 50 years old, Nouakchott has to be simultaneously one of Africa's strangest and most unassuming capital cities. This is urban planning nomad style: a city simply plonked down 5km from the coast as if on an overnight caravan stop and left to grow by accident. Most travellers use it as a staging post before the Adrar, Parc National Banc d'Arguin or the next international border.

Although it's not a highlight of the country, Nouakchott is sleepily idiosyncratic and you could do worse than spend an afternoon at the gloriously frantic fish market (one of the busiest in West Africa), treat yourself to a comfy guesthouse or feast in a good restaurant. It's also laidback and amazingly safe – bliss after the rigours of the desert.

Sights & Activities

Major landmarks in the centre include the **Grande Mosquée** (Rue Mamadou Konaté), also

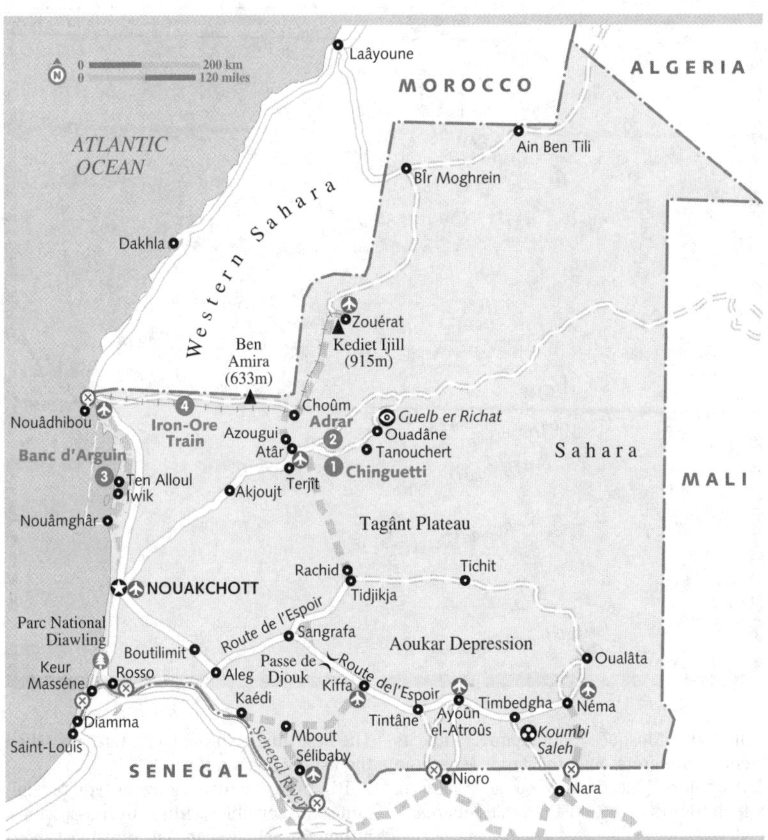

Mauritania Highlights

1. Wake up at the crack of dawn in order to catch a glorious sunrise from the labyrinthine lanes of the old city in **Chinguetti** (p379).
2. Experience the magic of the Sahara and sleep beneath the star-studded skies at the saffron dunes in the **Adrar** (p377).
3. Pack your binoculars and observe vast flocks of birds from a traditional *pirogue* in **Parc National du Banc d'Arguin** (p377).
4. Hop on the **iron-ore train** (p376) – one of the world's longest trains – and be ready for the most epic journey of your life!

Nouakchott

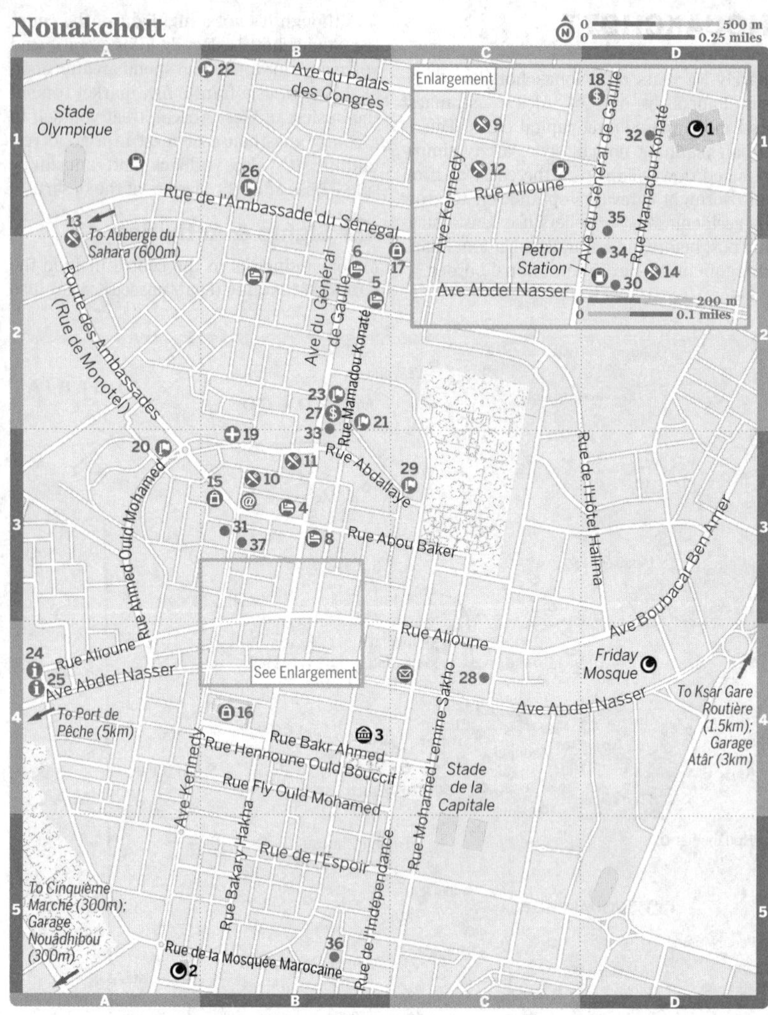

called the Mosquée Saoudienne, with its slender minarets, and the large **Mosquée Marocaine** (Rue de la Mosquée Marocaine), which towers over a bustling market area.

Port de Pêche MARKET

(Fish Market) The Port de Pêche is Nouakchott's star attraction. Both lively and colourful, you'll see hundreds of teams of mostly Wolof and Fula men dragging in heavy fishing nets. Small boys hurry back and forth with trays of fish, which they sort, gut, fillet and lay out on large trestles to dry. The best time is in the late afternoon, when the fishing boats return.

It's pretty safe as long as you're vigilant and sensible with your possessions, although people can be sensitive about photography. Take a taxi to get there from the centre.

Musée National MUSEUM

(Rue Mohamed el Habib; admission UM300; ⏲8am-3.30pm Mon-Fri) Moderately worthwhile for anyone with an interest in Moorish culture. On the 1st level is a prehistoric gallery with archaeological exhibits while

Nouakchott

Sights	**Information**
1 Grande Mosquée ... D1	18 Bureaux de Change ... D1
2 Mosquée Marocaine ... A5	19 Cabinet Médical Fabienne Sharif ... B3
3 Musée National ... B4	20 French Embassy ... A3
Sleeping	21 German Embassy ... B2
4 Auberge Menata ... B3	22 Malian Embassy ... B1
5 Hôtel Halima ... B2	23 Moroccan Embassy ... B2
6 Hôtel Tfeila ... B2	24 Parc National du Banc d'Arguin ... A4
7 Maison d'hôtes Jeloua ... B2	25 Parc National du Banc D'arguin headquarters ... A4
8 Maison d'hôtes la Bienvenue ... B3	26 Senegalese Embassy ... B1
Eating	27 Societe Generale ... B2
9 Café Tunisie ... C1	28 Sûreté ... C4
10 La Salamandre ... B3	29 US Embassy ... C3
11 Le Méditerranée ... B3	**Transport**
12 Le Prince ... C1	30 Air Algérie ... D2
13 Pizza Lina ... A2	31 Air France ... B3
14 Rimal ... D2	32 Mauritania Airlines ... D1
Entertainment	33 Regional Air – Rega Tours ... B2
Institut Français Mauritanie ... (see 20)	34 Royal Air Maroc ... D2
Shopping	35 Sénégal Airlines ... D1
15 Artisans Shops ... B3	36 Transport to Ayoûn el-Atroûs & Néma (4WDs) ... B5
16 Marché Capitale ... B4	37 Tunis Air ... B3
17 Zein Art ... C2	

the 2nd level is taken up with more recent ethnographic displays from Moorish society. The building is labelled as the Ministry of Culture.

Nouakchott beach SWIMMING

There are two decent beaches around 5km north of the centre, **Plage Pichot** and **Plage Sultan**. Both have small restaurants and shade, and are popular with the small expat community on weekends. Beware of undertows.

Sleeping

Nouakcott has a reasonable selection of accommodation. The big news is the construction of a five-star Rotana Hotel in the Ribat Al Bahar district, to open in late 2014.

Auberge du Sahara GUESTHOUSE $

(☎4764 1038; www.auberge-sahara.fr/; tent per person UM2000, dm UM2500, r UM6000-8000, parking UM1500; P ❄ wi-fi) Well-signed on the road to Nouâdhibou. Dorms and rooms are plain, but functional, and shared bathrooms are kept in good nick. Other pluses are the outdoor areas, a kitchen for guests' use and a rooftop terrace.

Auberge Menata GUESTHOUSE $

(☎4643 2730; auberge.menata@voila.fr; off Ave du Général de Gaulle; tent per person UM2000, dm UM3000, s/d with air-con UM5000/10,000, parking UM2000; P ❄ wi-fi) A centrally located and perennially popular haunt for backpackers and overlanders, the laidback Menata is a decent option. Good meals are available upon request or you can use the kitchen.

★ **Maison d'hôtes Jeloua** GUESTHOUSE $$

(☎3636 9450, 525 0914, 643 2730; maison.jeloua@voila.fr; r UM10,000-12,000, r without bathroom UM5000; P ❄ @ wi-fi) Run by the same people as the Auberge Menata, this is a lovely *maison d'hôtes* (B&B). It's charmingly decorated and the garden has its own restaurant. Deservedly popular.

Maison d'hôtes la Bienvenue GUESTHOUSE $$

(☎4525 1421; dominiqueidris@hotmail.com; Ave du Général de Gaulle; s/d UM12,000/14,000; ❄ wi-fi) Although it's on the main drag, this *auberge* (small hotel) is surprisingly peaceful and there's a pleasant leafy garden at the front, ideal for breakfast – the front of the hotel has been converted into the great (and fuschia-pink) Bla Bla Thé cafe. Rooms (all with bathrooms) are good value for the price tag.

SET YOUR BUDGET

Budget

- Hotel room UM2000
- Street food UM500
- Tea in nomad's tent Free
- Nouakchott taxi ride UM200

Midrange

- Hotel room UM14,000
- Pizza UM1500
- Coffee UM800

Top End

- Hotel room UM35,000
- Two-course meal UM3000
- Can of beer UM1200 (if available)
- 4WD with driver, per day UM30,000

Hôtel Halima HOTEL **$$$**
(☎4525 7921; www.hotel-halima.com; Rue de l'Hôtel Halima; s/d UM30,700/34,400; ❄) Sure, the well-run Halima doesn't claim the glitz of its top-end competitors but for the price it's a good bet in this bracket, with well-organised rooms, good facilities and a tough-to-beat location. Accepts credit cards.

Hôtel Tfeila HOTEL **$$$**
(☎4525 7400; www.hoteltfeila.com; Ave du Général de Gaulle; s from UM45,200, d from UM47,200; P❄📶🏊) Forget the blinding orange and yellow facade of this former Novotel; the interior shows money and a classy eye bonded with impeccable service. From swish rooms to free wi-fi, a good restaurant and a pool, this is by some degree Mauritania's best hotel.

Eating & Drinking

Unless otherwise stated, all restaurants are open for lunch and dinner every day. In principle, alcohol is available at higher-end places.

Rue Alioune between Ave Kennedy and Ave du Général de Gaulle is good for fast food, with most places open until 11pm or later – most have a Lebanese bent.

Le Prince FAST FOOD **$**
(Rue Alioune; mains UM500-1300) A bit grander than most fast-food joints, Le Prince claims to be Nouakchott's oldest restaurant. Plonk yourself on a wobbly chair in the room at the back and tuck into a plate of well-prepared *shwarma* (a kebab-like dish), sandwiches, salads and ice cream – all great value.

Café Tunisie CAFE **$**
(Ave Kennedy; set breakfast UM1000) Next to Tunis Air, this cafe is fine for coffee and smoking a water pipe, but comes into its own with fantastic breakfasts – freshly squeezed orange juice, bread, jam, pastries, yoghurt, coffee and a bottle of mineral water. A fine way to start the day.

Rimal INTERNATIONAL **$**
(☎4525 4832; Ave Abdel Nasser; mains about UM1000; ⏲closed lunch Sun) This place thoroughly lacks any pretensions but is all the better for it. The surroundings might have seen better days, but the service is fast and the food piping hot. There are good salads, chicken dishes and a variety of tasty fish straight from the Port de Pêche.

★**Bla Bla Thé** CAFE **$$**
(☎tel, info 3669 1073; www.facebook.com/blablathe; Ave du Général de Gaulle; mains from UM1400, juices UM800) A fresh and funky cafe inside Maison d'hôtes la Bienvenue.

Pizza Lina PIZZERIA **$$**
(☎4525 8662; Rte des Ambassades; mains UM1500-3500) A long-established player on the Nouakchott dining scene, Pizza Lina now faces stiff competition from the many similar places along this stretch of Rte des Ambassades. All the same, you'll find decent crispy pizzas and a selection of pasta and meat dishes.

★**Le Méditerranée** FRENCH **$$**
(☎3318 1240; off Ave du Général de Gaulle; mains from UM2000; ⏲closed Fri & lunch Sat) Good French and continental dishes, served up in a pleasant garden. Excellent service with a hint of sophistication rare in Nouakchott.

La Salamandre FRENCH **$$$**
(☎4524 2680; off Rte des Ambassades; mains UM2000-4000; ⏲Mon-Sat) La Salamandre enjoys a decent reputation for lip-smacking French cooking, but throws in a little Mexican and even Japanese for variety. The sleek setting, with lashings of bright colours splashed all over the walls, is another draw.

Entertainment

Pick up a copy of the excellent (French-language) monthly magazine *City Mag* (distributed free at many hotels) for listings of events, exhibitions and concerts.

Institut Français Mauritanie PERFORMING ARTS
(☎4529 9631; www.institutfrancais-mauritanie.com; next to French Embassy) Pick up a program for the Institut from many hotels; it's an excellent place for concerts by local musicians, films, talks, art exhibitions and dance lessons.

CIMAN LIVE MUSIC
(☎2500 1288; ciman.nkc@gmail.com) Conservatoire International de Musique et des Arts de Nouakchott (CIMAN) has regular classical and traditional music concerts.

Shopping

You'll find a bit of everything at **Marché Capitale** (Grand Marché; Ave Kennedy), including brass teapots, silver jewellery, traditional wooden boxes and colourful fabrics.

Zein Art ARTS & CRAFTS
(☎4651 7465; www.zeinart.com; ⊙3.30-7.30pm Mon-Wed, 10am-7.30pm Thu & Sat, closed Fri & Sun) A new gallery, curating the very best work from Mauritanian artists and craftsmen. Full of beautiful things to buy.

Artisans Shops JEWELLERY
(cnr Ave Kennedy & Rte des Ambassades) Check these places out for wooden boxes with silver inlay, daggers and jewellery.

Information

Bureaus de Change There are bureaus de change on Ave du Général de Gaulle and on Ave du Gamal Nasser, as well as in the Marché Capitale. CFA and Moroccan dirhams can be changed.

Cabinet Médical Fabienne Sharif (☎4525 1571) English-speaking doctor, recommended by expats.

Cyber Neja (off Ave Kennedy; per hr UM200; ⊙8am-midnight)

Main Post Office (Ave Abdel Nasser; ⊙8am-3pm Mon-Thu, to noon Fri) Postal services.

Societe Generale (Ave du Général de Gaulle) Two branches 100m apart; both have ATMs.

TOUR AGENCIES

Le Phare du Désert (☎4644 2421; www.desertmauritanie.com; info@desertmauritanie.com) Reliable tour operator around Mauritania by 4WD and camel, including the Adrar and Banc d'Arguin.

Getting There & Away

AIR

The major airlines have offices in Nouakchott.

Regional Air – Rega Tours (☎632 8735, 524 0422; Ave du Général de Gaulle; ⊙8am-5pm Mon-Thu, 8am-noon Fri) For purchasing domestic or international air tickets.

Air Algérie (☎4525 2059; www.airalgerie.dz; cnr Ave du Général de Gaulle & Ave Abdel Nasser)

Air France (☎4525 1808, 525 1802; www.airfrance.com; Ave Kennedy)

Mauritania Airlines (☎4524 4767; www.mai.mr; Rue Mamadou Konaté)

Royal Air Maroc (☎4525 3564; www.royalairmaroc.com; Ave du Général de Gaulle)

Sénégal Airlines (☎4525 6363; www.senegalairlines.aero; Ave du Général de Gaulle)

Tunis Air (☎4525 8762; www.tunisair.com.tr; Ave Kennedy)

BUSH TAXI

There are specific garages for Mauritania's different regions.

For Nouâdhibou (about UM5000, six hours), Garage Nouâdhibou is close to Cinquième Marché; for Rosso (about UM2000, 3½ hours), Garage Rosso is just over 5km south of the centre. For Atâr (UM4500, six hours), Garage Atâr is on the road to Atâr, about 3km north of the airport. Ksar Gare Routière (bus station; near the airport) serves destinations to the southeast including Kiffa, Ayoûn el-Atroûs and Néma. You should also be able to find bush taxis to Tidjikja from here.

Getting Around

A taxi ride within the centre costs around UM200. From the airport, the standard taxi fare to the centre is about UM1000, but it's cheaper to hail a taxi from the highway nearby (UM300).

THE ATLANTIC COAST

No tacky resorts. No pollution. This coastline is a rapturous place for tranquillity seekers and nature lovers. It's mostly occupied by the Parc National du Banc d'Arguin, something of a pilgrimage site for birdwatchers.

Nouâdhibou

POP 80,000

With the new tar road connecting the Moroccan border to Nouakchott, the fishing port of Nouâdhibou has lost much of its *raison d'être* for travellers, who prefer to dash to the capital or to the Adrar region. It's a good base, though, if you plan to visit Banc d'Arguin. The setting is also appealing: Nouâdhibou is on the Baie du Lévrier,

AN EPIC JOURNEY ON THE IRON-ORE TRAIN

Africa offers some pretty wild train trips, but the train ferrying iron ore from the mines at Zouérat to Nouâdhibou might just be the wildest. One of the longest trains in the world (typically a staggering 2.3km long), when it arrives at the 'station' in Nouâdhibou, a decrepit building in the open desert, a seemingly endless number of ore wagons pass before the passenger carriage at the rear finally appears. The lucky ones find a place on one of the two long benches (UM2500); the rest stand or sit on the floor. There are also a dozen 'berths' (UM3000) that are so worn out you can see the springs. It's brutally basic. It's also possible to clamber into the ore cars and travel for free. Impossibly dusty, it's only for the hardcore. Plastic sheets are essential to wrap your bags (and person), plus plenty of warm clothes, as the desert can get fearsomely cold at night, as well as food and drink.

The train leaves Nouâdhibou at around 2pm to 3pm daily. Most travellers get off at Choûm, 12 hours later, where bush taxis wait to take passengers to Atâr, three hours away. In the other direction, the train leaves Zouérat around midday and passes through Atâr at about 5.30pm.

in the middle of a narrow 35km-long peninsula.

Sights & Activities

Réserve Satellite du Cap Blanc WILDLIFE RESERVE
(admission UM2000; ⏲10am-5pm Tue-Sat) A small nature reserve with an excellent information centre, dedicated to the colony of endangered Mediterranean monk seals *(phoque moin)* that live here. Resembling elephant seals, these grey-skinned animals were hunted since the 15th century for their valuable skins and oil. The protected colony here of roughly 150 seals is one of the last on earth. The colony is at the foot of the cliffs; you have a reasonable chance of seeing them swimming offshore.

The reserve is near the lighthouse at the southern tip of Cap Blanc. To get there, cross the railtracks near the SNIM refinery on the edge of Nouâdhibou; the *piste* (track) is rough. Also near the lighthouse is the spectacular wreck of the *United Metlika*, a cargo ship beached on a wide sandy beach and looking all the world like the set of a Hollywood movie.

Sleeping

In the centre, you'll find a slew of cheap restaurants along Rue de la Galérie Mahfoud. They're nothing fancy, serving fish and *mafé* (groundnut-based stew) for around UM300 a plate.

Camping Chez Abba CAMPGROUND $
(☎4574 9896; fax 574 9887; Blvd Médian; tent per person UM1500, s/d UM2000/4000; P) A good overlanders' haunt, with plenty of space to park and pitch a tent, and a few decent rooms with their own bathrooms and hot water. Recommended.

Camping Baie du Lévrier HOSTEL $
(☎4574 6536, mobile 650 4356; Blvd Médian; s/d UM3000/5000; P) Also known as Chez Ali, this *auberge*-style place has a good location. Rooms are a bit cell-like, and bathroom facilities are shared, but there is a tent to relax in and cooking facilities.

Hôtel Al Jezira HOTEL $$
(☎4574 5317; Blvd Maritime; s/d incl breakfast UM13,000/15,000; P❄) Nouâdhibou isn't overrun with top-class accommodation, but this midrange hotel slightly north of the centre just about works out. Rates are slightly high for what's on offer, but the rooms are fair, and occasionally border on the comfy.

Hotel Sahel HOTEL $$$
(☎4574 3857; info@hotel-sahel.com; Rte de l'Aeroport; s/d from UM24,000/28,000; 📶) Top of the hotel spectrum as far as Nouâdhibou goes, the Sahel is a solidly comfortable business-class option.

Eating

Restaurant-Pâtisserie Pleine Lune CAFE $
(☎574 9860; off Blvd Médian; mains UM1000-1500) We like this place for its breakfasts – decent coffee and a good selection of pastries, but it's good at any time of day, with pizzas and sandwiches as quick fillers, or grilled fish and *brochettes* (kebabs) for something more substantial.

★ **Restorante Galloufa** SPANISH $$
(☎2216 8770; Rte de l'Aeroport; mains from UM1500; 📶) Excellent laid-back Spanish restaurant, with a heavy emphasis on seafood.

Information

There are several bureaus de change along the city's main drag, Blvd Médian, as well as two ATMs; most of the internet outlets along here also double as telephone offices.

Getting There & Away

Mauritania Airlines (☎4574 4291; Blvd Médian) flies four times a week to Nouakchott (UM20,000, one hour), and three times a week to Casablanca in Morocco.

There are plenty of minibuses and bush taxis from the *gare routière* to Nouakchott (UM5000, six hours). You can also get transport from here to Morocco (Western Sahara). Taxis go most days to Dakhla (UM11,500, eight hours). Arrive early – any later than 8am and you'll be facing a long wait for the vehicles to fill and go.

There is also a train that runs from Nouâdhibou to Choûm and Zouérat. The train 'station' is about 5km south of town.

Parc National du Banc d'Arguin

This World Heritage–listed **park** (www.mauritania.mr/pnba; per person per day UM1200) is an important stopover and breeding ground for multitudes of birds migrating between Europe and southern Africa, and as a result is one of the best birdwatching sites on the entire continent. It extends 200km north from Cape Timiris (155km north of Nouakchott) and 235km south of Nouâdhibou. The ideal way to approach the birds is by traditional fishing boat (UM15,000, plus UM3000 for the guide), best organised from the fishing village of **Iwik**.

Inside the park there are official **campsites** (per tent UM3000-6000) that are equipped with traditional tents. Meals can also be ordered. There's no public transport, so you'll need to hire a 4WD with a knowledgeable driver, either in Nouakchott or in Nouâdhibou, allowing a couple of days for the trip. Permits are issued either at the entrance gates or in Nouâdhibou at the **park office** (☎574 6744; Blvd Médian; ⏰8am-4pm Mon-Thu, to noon Fri). Both this office and the Nouakchott **Parc National du Banc D'arguin headquarters** (Map p372; ☎525 8514; Ave Abdel Nasser) sell a map and guide to the park, including GPS waypoints.

THE ADRAR

The Adrar is the undoubted jewel in Mauritania's crown. It's epic Saharan country, and shows the great desert in all its variety: the ancient Saharan towns of Chinguetti and Ouadâne, mighty sand dunes that look sculpted by an artist, vast rocky plateaus and mellow oases fringed with date palms. For desert lovers, the Adrar is a must.

Atâr

POP 25,000

With the grandiose Adrar on its doorstep, this secluded town in the middle of the desert is an excellent place in which to organise camel or 4WD forays into the dunefields.

A large *rond-point* (roundabout) marks the centre of Atâr and the market is just north of it. You'll find several bureaus de change, telephone offices and internet cafes on or around the main drag.

Activities

There are over a dozen agencies in Atâr that can arrange **camel rides** or **4WD tours**, so shop around. The main costs are the vehicle and driver, so trips are a lot cheaper if you're in a group. Count on paying up to UM21,000 per day for a Toyota Hilux plus petrol. Add about UM2000 per day per person for food. Camel trips start at UM12,000 per day with food and lodging.

Sleeping & Eating

★ **Auberge Bab Sahara** GUESTHOUSE $
(☎4647 3966; www.bab-sahara.com; tent per person UM2000, caravan/stone hut UM5000/8000; P❄) Off Rte de Azougui, Bab Sahara has been a little slice of overlanders' heaven for over 15 years. There's a selection of *tikits* (stone huts; with air-con), caravans and tents, plus a campsite in another compound and a mechanic's workshop. Meals are available on request. The Dutch-German couple who run it are great sources of local information and travel advice.

Auberge du Bonheur GUESTHOUSE $
(☎546 4537; fax 546 4347; tent/hut per person UM1500, r UM4000; ❄@) Those wanting a

BEN AMIRA

Big rocks don't come much more awesome than Ben Amira. Rising 633m out of the desert, it's Africa's biggest monolith, and in size is second only to Australia's Uluru (Ayers Rock). It's clearly visible from the train between Nouâdhibou and Zouérat, but if you have a 4WD it makes a brilliant one-night camping trip from Atâr.

There are actually two granite monoliths. Ben Amira is the largest, with slightly smaller Aïsha to the west. While Ben Amira is more massively spectacular, Aïsha holds a delightful surprise of her own. In December 1999, a symposium of 16 international sculptors was held here to celebrate the millennium, turning many of the boulders at the base of Aïsha into art. The natural shapes of the rocks were reinterpreted as animals, birds, faces and abstract creations. It's a wonderful spot, all the more so for being completely unheralded by its surroundings.

The monoliths are 4km north of the train track between Nouâdibhou and Choûm, at Km 395 (Ben Amira village sits next to the tracks here). The route is sand rather than gravel *piste*. Aïsha is 5km west of Ben Amira. To find the sculptures, head for the eastern side of Aïsha, where it appears to join a lower mound made of giant 'melted' rocks: the sculptures are here.

reliable base could do worse than this welcoming outfit, a five-minute stroll from the centre. It's nicely turned out, with simple but decent rooms, a large tent in the courtyard and everything kept scrubbed pretty clean.

Camping Inimi CAMPGROUND $
(☎2229 4127; camping.inimi@yahoo.fr; Rte de Nouakchott) Cheap but welcoming overlanders' option on the main road south from Atâr.

Auberge Andaloss GUESTHOUSE $
(☎2229 3592; aubtwe@gmail.com; r UM6000-7000) Simple, bright green guesthouse with lots of rooms and plenty of lounging space (the more expensive have air-con). Meals on request, and are even prepared for free if you buy your own ingredients.

Hotel Waha HOTEL $$
(☎4421 1692; hotelwaha@gmail.com; s/d UM12,000/15,000, dinner UM4000; wi-fi) Atâr's fanciest option, with two-dozen *tikit*-style rooms, all with air-con and fridge. Good facilities mainly aimed at tour groups.

Restaurant du Coin AFRICAN $
(market, off Rte de Chinguetti; meals UM300) From the *rond-point* head down the Chinguetti road for a block, then turn left. This place is on the right-hand corner, marked by a tiny sign. It's as down-at-heel as you can get, serving up great quantities of rice, fish and Senegalese *mafé*. It's always busy, and the food piping hot and delicious.

Restaurant Agadir AFRICAN $
(Rte de Chinguetti; mains UM500-700) Near the *rond-point*, this cheap and cheerful eatery rustles up some good couscous and tajines as well as sandwiches and lighter bites.

Getting There & Away

The main *gare routière*, in the heart of town, is where you can get vehicles for Nouakchott (UM3500, six hours) and Choûm (UM1500, three hours). Choûm transport is timed to meet the train heading to/from Nouâdhibou (see p376).

Vehicles for Chinguetti (car/4WD UM1500/2500, about two hours) leave once a day from near a shop a block north of Hotel Monod. Most days there is also transport to Ouadâne (bush taxi/4WD UM3000/4000, about four hours), leaving from a street north of the *rond-point* (ask for *'gare de Ouadâne'*). For Azougui (UM500, 20 minutes) and Terjît (UM1000, one hour), infrequent 4WDs leave from near the *rond-point*.

Terjît

We've never visited an oasis quite like Terjît. About 40km south of Atâr, a streak of palm groves is hemmed in by great red cliffs. At its head, two springs tumble out of the rocks. One is hot, the other cold, and they mix to form a natural swimming pool the perfect temperature for a dip. It's simply bliss. You pay UM1000 to enter the site.

The main spring has been taken over by **Auberge Oasis de Terjît** (☎644 8967, in Atâr 546 5020; tent/hut per person UM1500), where a mattress in a tent by the trickling stream is on offer. A meal costs about UM1500. The only other place to stay is the **Auberge des Caravanes** (☎4593 1381; r/tikit per person

UM1500, dinner UM1500, breakfast UM1000; P), a traveller-friendly place at the entrance of the village.

To get here by private car, drive 40km south of Atâr on the road to Nouakchott, then turn left at the checkpoint and follow a sandy track for 11km. By public transport, take anything headed towards Nouakchott and hitch a ride from the checkpoint.

Chinguetti

POP 4000

One of the more attractive of the ancient caravan towns in the Sahara, Chinguetti is shrouded with a palpable historic aura. It was once famous for its Islamic scholars, and was the ancient capital of the Moors; some of the buildings date from the 13th century. Chinguetti butts up against Erg Warane, Mauritania's biggest stretch of dunes, and is more than enough to meet traveller's expectations of the great Saharan sand ocean.

The highlight of any visit is a wander through the labyrinthine lanes of **Le Ksar** (Old Town). The principal attraction is the 16th-century stone mosque (no entry to non-Muslims). Also of great interest are the five old **libraries**, which house the fragile-as-dust ancient Islamic manuscripts of Chinguetti.

The best way to see the fascinating dunes around Chinguetti is by camel. Numerous *méharées* (camel trips) are available. Standard costs start from UM8000 per person per day for the camel, food and guide. Any reputable travel agency in Atâr or *auberge* owner can arrange **camel rides**. If you don't want to sweat it out, you can hire a 4WD and driver. They cost from UM17,000 per day, petrol not included.

Sleeping & Eating

Most places have shared bathroom unless otherwise stated. Breakfast and meals are available on request (about UM2000 per meal). The tourist industry has collapsed in recent years in Chinguetti, so many guesthouses are closed – all those listed are currently open for business.

Auberge des Caravanes GUESTHOUSE **$**
(540 0022; fax 546 4272; r per person UM2000) With its eye-catching, traditional architecture, it's hard to miss this place right in the centre of town. Rooms are pretty simple, and it can feel a bit impersonal, but it's adequate for the price.

★ **Auberge La Gueïla** GUESTHOUSE **$$**
(2205 5056; www.lagueila.com; s/d UM8000/12,800, dinner UM2800; wifi) A fabulous, newly built, French-run place, with six charming rooms, excellent food (to be taken in the courtyard garden), a library and even a massage room for real unwinding.

L'Eden de Chinguetti GUESTHOUSE **$$**
(2220 38844; mahmoudeden@yahoo.fr; r UM8000) This impressive *auberge* is a great place to stay. It's neat, well tended and embellished with well-chosen knick-knacks and a nice garden. The English-speaking owner is a mine of information. It's on the road to Atâr, not far from Auberge La Rose des Sables.

Getting There & Away

There is at least one vehicle a day to/from Atâr (car/4WD UM1500/2500, two hours) They leave from just behind the market. There are no bush taxis between Chinguetti and Ouadâne; you'll have to go back to Atâr.

Ouadâne

Sitting on the edge of the Adrar plateau, 120km northeast of Chinguetti, Ouadâne is one of the most enchanting semighost towns of the Sahara. As you arrive across the sands or plateau from Atâr or Chinguetti, the stone houses of **Le Ksar al Kiali** (Old Quarter; admission UM1000) seem to tumble down the cliff. The top of the hill is dominated by the minaret of the new mosque, which is a mere 200 years old, while at the western end, at the base of the town, is the 14th-century **old mosque**. In between, the crumbling structures seem to have been piled up higgledy-piggledy by some giant child playing with building blocks. Like Chinguetti, Ouadâne was a place of scholarship and is home to over 3000 manuscripts held in private **libraries**. Only 20 to 30 families still live in the old town.

Sleeping & Eating

All places to stay can prepare meals for their guests (about UM2000 for lunch or dinner) – try the *ksour,* a local thick pancake made of wheat. Most places are down on the plateau. Mellow **Auberge Vasque – Chez Zaid** (681 7669; tikit per person UM2000, r with bathroon & air-con UM10,000) is run by Zaida, a congenial lady who goes out of her way to make your stay a happy one. There are five *tikits* and a couple of nomads' tents. Rooms at **Auberge Warane** (☎4687 3508; r/tent per person UM1500) are a bit bunkerlike but the place is friendly enough. **Auberge Agoueidir – Chez Isselmou** (☎4525 0791; agoueidir@yahoo.fr; tikit/tent per person UM1200/2500, s/d UM5000/7000) is the grandest outfit, but was block-booked by oil workers when we visited.

Getting There & Away

Without your own vehicle, getting to Ouadâne isn't always straightforward. Atâr is the place to look for transport, and vehicles run between the two most days, usually in the morning (bush taxi/4WD UM3000/4000, about four hours). Direct transport between Ouadâne and Chinguetti runs next to never.

If driving you have two alternatives: the southerly Piste du Batha, which passes through sand dunes and requires a 4WD and guide, and the northerly Piste du Dhar Chinguetti along the plateau, which is in very good condition. The latter departs the Atâr–Chinguetti road 18km before Chinguetti.

Tanouchert

This charming oasis, approximately halfway between Chinguetti and Ouadâne, is a popular stop for 4WD trips and camel treks. Nestled around a freshwater source, it's complete with palm trees and surrounded by superb dune fields, miles from anywhere.

You'll need to hire a 4WD with driver to get to Tanouchert. Otherwise, if you do a camel trek from Chinguetti to Ouadâne, you'll probably spend a night here.

Sleeping & Eating

Oasis Tanouchert CAMPGROUND $
(Chez Chighaly; ☎4654 1885; Azougi; bed UM1500, breakfast/dinner UM800/1500) Unsophisticated (mattresses under palm-frond shelters) but welcoming. If there's a group, the host can organise a *méchoui* (nomads') feast.

THE ROAD TO MALI

The Rte de l'Espoir (Road to Hope) from Nouakchott to Néma (around 1100km) is now entirely tarred, giving a smooth (if still very long) trip to the border. Check trusted security sources before travelling towards the border.

The first major town on the road to the Malian border is **Kiffa** (population 30,000), an important regional trading centre and crossroads, where you can bunk down at **Auberge Le Phare du Désert** (☎644 2421; pharerim@yahoo.fr; tikit UM10,000; ❄) on the outskirts.

You could also break up your journey at lively **Ayoûn el-Atroûs**, which is a good place to spend your last ouguiyas before crossing into Mali. For accommodation, try the unpretentious **Hôtel Ayoûn** (☎515 1462; s/d UM5000/8000; ❄), which is in the centre, or **Auberge Saada Tenzah** (☎641 1052, 515 1337; r UM2500-6000), about 3km east of the centre on the road to Néma.

The tarred road ends at the town of **Néma**, the jumping-off point for Oualâta. You'll find several petrol pumps here, a couple of modest stores and a police station at which you can get your passport stamped. You can base yourself at **Complexe Touristique N'Gady** (☎513 0900; bungalow s/d UM7000/9000, r 12,000-15,000; P❄), a few kilometres west of the centre.

Oualâta

Possibly one of Mauritania's best-kept secrets, Oualâta is another ancient Saharan town high on atmosphere and personality. Dating from 1224, it used to be the last resting point for caravans heading for Timbuktu. It's about 100km north of Néma but is definitely worth the gruelling ride to get here.

Entering the town you'll be struck by the red **mudbrick houses** adorned with decorative paintings on the exterior and interior. There's a small museum and a **library**, which houses ancient Islamic manuscripts. There are also several rock paintings and archaeological sites in the vicinity. Various **camel trips** can be organised (ask your hosts).

Although you're miles from anywhere, you'll find about six guesthouses to rest your weary limbs, including **Auberge Tayib/Gamni – Auberge de l'Hotel de Ville** (r per person UM3000) and **Auberge Ksar Walata** (r per person UM5000), which features a lovely patio and attractive rooms. They all serve meals.

There are two dirt tracks between Néma and Oualâta (approximately 110km). Land Rovers ply the route between the two towns

(UM2000, 2½ hours) on an infrequent basis. Ask around in Néma market.

THE ROAD TO SENEGAL

Parc National Diawling

This little known national park is a sister to the Djoudj National Bird Sanctuary in Senegal on the opposite side of the border. It has important mangroves and an acacia forest, as well as large coastal dunes. Incredibly rich in birdlife, it's well-worth a detour if you have a 4WD. Facilities are almost completely undeveloped; the Eco-Lodge du Maure Bleu offers the best access as well as being involved with local communities to receive visitors.

Sleeping & Eating

★**Eco-Lodge du Maure Bleu** LODGE $$
(☎4412 0379; www.ecolodgemaurebleu.net; 2-bed tent UM12,500, meals UM1000-3500) A gorgeous off-grid tent-camp offering a surprising degree of comfort and home-cooked food, as well as arranging walking and *pirogue* (traditional canoe) tours in the national park.

UNDERSTAND MAURITANIA

Mauritania Today

The rule since 2008 of General Mohamed Ould Abdel Aziz has seen mixed fortunes for Mauritania. The economy has grown, in part due to mineral extraction, gas exploration and new factory fishing licences given to EU and Chinese fleets, but a prolonged drought in 2011 led to rocketing food prices and an increase in aid dependency for swathes of the population.

Mauritania's long border with Mali has also seen it receive large numbers of refugees, and the government has had to tread carefully to avoid being dragged into the Malian conflict. In October 2012, Aziz survived an 'accidental' shooting by one of his soldiers, the exact circumstances of which still remain unclear.

History

From the 3rd century AD, the Berbers established trading routes all over the Western Sahara, including Mauritania. In the 11th century, the Marrakesh-based Islamic Almoravids pushed south and, with the assistance of Mauritanian Berber leaders, destroyed the Empire of Ghana, which covered much of present-day Mauritania. That victory led to the spread of Islam throughout Mauritania and the Western Sahara. The descendants of the Almoravids were finally subjugated by Arabs in 1674.

As colonialism spread throughout Africa in the 19th century, France stationed troops in Mauritania, but it was not until 1904 that, having played one Moorish faction off against another, the French finally managed to make Mauritania a colonial territory. Independence was fairly easily achieved in 1960 because the French wanted to prevent the country from being absorbed by newly independent Morocco. Mokhtar Ould Daddah became Mauritania's first president.

Ould Daddah took a hard line, especially against the (mainly black African) southerners, who were treated like second-class citizens and compelled to fit the Moors' mould. Any opposition was brutally suppressed.

The issue of Western Sahara (Spanish Sahara) finally toppled the government. In 1975 the very sandy Spanish Sahara (a Spanish colony) was divided between Morocco and Mauritania. But the Polisario Front launched a guerrilla war to oust both beneficiaries from the area. Mauritania was incapable, militarily and economically, of fighting such a war. A bloodless coup took place in Mauritania in 1978, bringing in a new military government that renounced all territorial claims to the Western Sahara.

A series of coups ensued. Finally, Colonel Maaouya Sid' Ahmed Ould Taya came to power in 1984. For black Africans, this was even worse than being under Ould Daddah. Ethnic tensions culminated in bloody riots between the Moors and black Africans in 1989. More than 70,000 black Africans were expelled to Senegal, a country most had never known.

In 1991 Mauritania supported Iraq during the Gulf War, and aid dried up. To counter criticism, Taya introduced multiparty elections in 1992, which were boycotted by the opposition. Riots over the price of bread in 1995 worsened the political situation. Cosmetic elections were held in 2001, with Taya still holding the whip hand.

The 2000s have been marked by coups. In June 2005, Taya was toppled in a bloodless coup led by Colonel Ely Ould Mohamed Vall. Vall was largely popular and formulated a new constitution and voluntarily gave up power by holding elections in March 2007. Sidi Ould Cheikh Abdallahi was returned as Mauritania's first democratically elected president. He openly condemned the 'dark years' of the late 1980s, and sought rapprochement with the expelled black Moors – a move that angered the traditional elites and which led, in part, to his overthrow by General Mohamed Ould Abdel Aziz in a coup in August 2008. Despite international condemnation, his position was consolidated the following year in elections that saw Azis narrowly returned as president.

Culture

Mauritanian society is changing fast. Tourism development in the heart of the desert, the internet and mobile phones have played a crucial role in the last decade. But despite the profound social changes, the extended family, clan or tribe remains the cornerstone of society, especially with the Moors.

As in many Muslim countries, religion continues to mark the important events of life. Although slavery was declared illegal in 1980, it is still widespread and the caste system permeates society's mentality.

The iconic image of nomadic Moors sipping a cup of tea under a tent in the desert belongs to the past. Over the past three decades, drought has resulted in a mass exodus of traditionally nomadic Moors from the desert to Nouakchott.

Women are in a fairly disadvantaged position. Only a third as many women as men are literate and few are involved in commercial activities. Female genital mutilation and forced feeding of young brides are still practised in rural communities. However, Mauritanian women do have the right to divorce and exert it routinely.

People

Of Mauritania's estimated three million inhabitants, about 60% are Moors of Arab and Berber descent. The Moors of purely Arab descent, called 'Bidan', account for 40% of the population, and hold the levers of political power. The other major group is black Africans, ethnically split into two groups. The Haratin (black Moors), the descendants of people enslaved by the Moors, have assimilated the Moorish culture and speak Hassaniyya, an Arabic dialect. Black Mauritanians living in the south along the Senegal River constitute 40% of the total population and are mostly Fulani or the closely related Tukulor. These groups speak Pulaar (Fula). There are also Soninke and Wolof minorities.

More than 99% of the population are Sunni Muslims.

Arts & Crafts

Mauritania has a strong tradition of arts and craftwork, especially silverwork. Most prized are wooden chests with silver inlays, but there are also silver daggers, silver and amber jewellery, earthtone rugs of camel hair, and hand-dyed leatherwork, including colourful leather cushions and leather pipe pouches, camel saddles and sandals.

The traditional music of Mauritania is mostly Arabic in origin, although along its southern border there are influences from the Wolof, Tukulor and Bambara. One of the most popular Mauritanian musicians is Malouma. She has created what is called the 'Saharan blues' and is to Mauritania what Cesária Évora, is to Cape Verde.

There's some superb traditional architecture in the ancient Saharan towns in the Adrar as well as in Oualâta.

Food & Drink

The desert cuisine of the Moors is rather unmemorable and lacks variety. Dishes are generally bland and limited to rice, mutton, goat, camel or dried fish. With negligible agriculture, fruit and vegetables are imported, and hard to find outside Nouakchott. Mauritanian couscous, similar to the Moroccan variety, is delicious. A real treat is to attend a *méchoui* (traditional nomads' feast), where an entire lamb is roasted over a fire and stuffed with cooked rice.

The cuisine of southern Mauritania, essentially Senegalese, has more variety, spices and even a few vegetables. Look for rice with fish and *mafé* (a groundnut-based stew).

SLAVERY IN MAURITANIA

Mauritania has one of the most stratified caste systems in Africa. The system is based on lineage, occupation and access to power, but colour has become a major determinant of status, splitting the population into Bidan and Haratin – White and Black Moors. At the bottom of the social pile are slaves and ex-slaves.

Chattel slavery has long been apart of Mauritanian culture, with the owning of slaves a sign of social status. Incredibly, it was only in 1980 that the government finally declared slavery illegal. Despite this, the head of Mauritania's Human Rights Commission has said that antislavery laws are rarely enforced, despite tougher punishments legislated for in 2007. Estimates vary, but a 2010 UN special report on slavery suggests that upwards of 340,000 Mauritanians may still be enslaved. The Mauritanian antislavery organisation SOS-Esclaves ('SOS-Slaves'; www.sosesclaves.org) works with runaway slaves.

Mauritanian tea is also ubiquitous, invariably strong, sweet and endlessly decanted between tiny glasses to produce a frothy head. It's polite to accept the first three glasses offered. *Zrig* (unsweetened curdled goat or camel milk) often accompanies meals served in private homes. Alcohol is technically forbidden but is sometimes openly (and expensively) available in Nouakchott restaurants.

Environment

Mauritania is about twice the size of France. About 75%, including Nouakchott, is desert, with huge expanses of flat plains broken by occasional ridges, sand dunes and rocky plateaus, including the Adrar (about 500m high).

The highest peak is Kediet Ijill (915m) near Zouérat. Mauritania has some 700km of shoreline, including the Parc National du Banc d'Arguin, one of the world's major bird-breeding grounds and a Unesco World Heritage site. The south is mostly flat scrubland.

Major environmental issues are the usual suspects of desertification, overgrazing and pollution. Overfishing is another concern, with hundreds of tonnes of fish caught every day off the Mauritanian coastline.

SURVIVAL GUIDE

Directory A–Z

ACCOMMODATION

In general, you can expect to spend less than US$15 per person in budget places and up to US$50 for midrange. There's also a sprinkle of air-conditioned hotels meeting international standards in Nouakchott and, to a lesser extent, Nouâdhibou and Atâr. In the desert, you'll find numerous basic *auberges* or *campements*. They consist of a series of *tikits* (stone huts) or *khaimas* (tents) that come equipped with mattresses on the floor.

ACTIVITIES

Camel rides and 4WD expeditions in the desert are the most popular activities. For birdwatching, nothing can beat the Parc National du Banc d'Arguin, one of the world's greatest birdlife-viewing venues.

BUSINESS HOURS

Mauritania is a Muslim country, and for business purposes Mauritania adheres to the Monday to Friday working week. Friday is the main prayer day, so many businesses have an extended lunch break on Friday afternoon. Many shops are open every day.

Government offices, post offices & banks Usually open 8am to 4pm Monday to Thursday and 8am to 1pm on Friday.

CUSTOMS REGULATIONS

It is illegal to bring alcohol into the country.

EMBASSIES & CONSULATES

The majority of embassies and consulates have locations in Nouakchott.

French Embassy (☎4525 2337; Rue Ahmed Ould Mohamed)

German Embassy (☎4525 1729; Rue Abdallaye)

Malian Embassy (☎4525 4081, 525 4078)

Moroccan Embassy (☎4525 1411; Ave du Général de Gaulle)

Senegalese Embassy (☎4525 7290; Rue de l'Ambassade du Sénégal)

US Embassy (☎4525 2660; fax 525 1592; Rue Abdallaye)

INTERNET ACCESS

You can get online in any reasonably sized town, although outside Nouakchott connection speeds can often be wanting. Expect to pay around UM200 an hour.

MONEY

The unit of currency is the ouguiya (UM). There are a handful of ATMs in Nouakchott and Nouâdhibou accepting international bank cards, but take euros or US dollars as back-up. Credit cards are accepted only at top-end hotels and larger businesses.

PUBLIC HOLIDAYS

New Year's Day 1 January
National Reunification Day 26 February
Workers' Day 1 May
African Liberation Day 25 May
Army Day 10 July
Independence Day 28 November
Anniversary of the 1984 Coup 12 December

Mauritania also celebrates the usual Islamic holidays.

SAFE TRAVEL

Mauritania is generally one of the safest countries in Africa, particularly the capital and the main tourist region of the Adrar.

In 2008, the Paris–Dakar Rally was cancelled due to threats against the Mauritanian leg by Islamist groups. Although there have subsequently been a small number of incidents, these have been restricted to remote areas unvisited by foreigners. On the main roads, regular police checkpoints take note of all foreigners passing through for security. In the southeast, however, security problems in Mali have threatened to spill across the border. Coupled with periodic reports of banditry on the roads, travellers should take trusted advice before planning to travel in this region.

TELEPHONE

You can make international calls and send faxes at post offices. The innumerable privately run phone shops in the major cities and towns cost about the same and are open late. A GSM SIM card for the Mauritel, Chinguitell or Mattel networks costs around UM2000.

There are no telephone area codes.

VISAS

Visas are required for all except nationals of Arab League countries and some African countries. In countries where Mauritania has no diplomatic representation, including Australia, French embassies often issue visas. For overlanders heading south, Rabat (Morocco) is a good place for visas (US$45). Visas are no longer issued at the Morocco–Mauritania border.

One-month visa extensions can be obtained for UM5000 at the **Sûreté** (off Ave Abdel Nasser; ⌚8am-3pm Mon-Thu) in Nouakchott.

Visas for Onward Travel

In Nouakchott you can get visas for most neighbouring countries.

Mali

One-month visas are issued the same day (UM6500). You need two photos and a passport photocopy.

Morocco

Most nationalities do not require visas, and simply get an entry stamp valid for 90 days on arrival. Nationalities that do (mostly Africans, including Mauritanians) must pay UM8700 and provide two photos and passport photocopies and (according to whim) an air ticket.

Senegal

One-month visas (UM1500) are issued in 24 hours. You need to supply four photos plus passport photocopies.

WOMEN TRAVELLERS

Mauritania is a conservative Muslim country, but it is by no means the most extreme in this regard. Women might receive the odd bit of sexual harassment, but it's nothing in comparison with some North African countries. It's wise to dress modestly, covering the upper legs and arms and avoiding shorts or skimpy T-shirts.

Getting There & Away

AIR

Nouakchott, Nouâdhibou and Atâr have international airports. Nouakchott's airport handles most traffic.

The only direct flights from Europe are through Paris, with Air France.

Mauritania Airlines flies twice a week between Nouakchott and Dakar, six times to Bamako (three of which continue to Abidjan, Cotonou and Brazzaville). Senegal Airlines flies five times a week to Dakar. For other Saharan or

PRACTICALITIES

- **Electricity** Current is 220V AC, 50Hz and most electrical plugs are of the European two-pin type.
- **Languages** Hassaniya (Arabic), French, Fula, Soninké and Wolof.
- **TV** Mauritania's only TV station is TVM, with programs in Hassaniyya and French, but top-end hotels have satellite TV.
- **Newspapers** For the news (in French), pick up *Le Calame* or *Horizons*.

sub-Saharan countries, you'll have to change in Dakar or Abidjan.

Mauritania is well connected to North Africa. Royal Air Maroc operates between Casablanca and Nouakchott five times a week, while Tunis Air connects Tunis with Nouakchott (three times a week). Air Algérie flies to Algiers twice a week. Mauritania Airlines has four flights a week to Casablanca from Nouakchott, and twice weekly from Nouâdhibou.

LAND

Mali

All border information is subject to security advice as to the situation in Mali.

At the time of research, the most straightforward route to Mali was from Ayoûn el-Atroûs to Nioro. You can also cross at Néma, Timbedgha (both connecting with Nara in Mali) and Kiffa (connecting with Nioro in Mali).

From Nouakchott, you can catch bush taxis to Néma and Ayoûn el-Atroûs. From these places you can catch a bush taxi to Nara or Nioro. It's also possible to travel from Sélibaby to Kayes.

If crossing into Mali, have your passport stamped by police at the first town you reach after crossing the border. You must also clear customs, which is done in Néma or Ayoûn el-Atroûs.

Morocco

The trans-Sahara route via Mauritania is a very popular route from North Africa into sub-Saharan Africa. This crosses the internationally disputed territory of Western Sahara, although the border itself is administered by Morocco.

The only border crossing between Morocco/Western Sahara and Mauritania is north of Nouâdhibou. Crossing this border is straightforward and the road is entirely tarred to Nouakchott, except for the 3km no-man's land that separates the two border posts.

There are direct bush taxis heading north from Nouâdhibou to Dakhla (Western Sahara), but travelling in the opposite direction you'll need to change vehicles at the border. The 425km trip can easily be accomplished in a long day.

Senegal

The main border crossing for Senegal is at Rosso (by ferry), but it's also possible to cross by bridge at Diamma (Keur Masséne), west of Rosso. The latter is a much calmer experience (officials at Rosso often give travellers hassle) although road conditions make Diamma largely a dry-season option.

From Dakar to Nouakchott by public transport usually takes from 11 to 13 hours depending on the wait at the border. At Rosso, most travellers without vehicles cross by *pirogue* (UM200/CFA500, five minutes) as the ferry crosses only four times daily. The border is open 8.30am to noon and 3pm to 6pm.

Vehicles cost CFA5000 (foot passengers free). Customs fees are around UM1500 if you're entering Mauritania, CFA2000 for Senegal, but officials here are reported to be notoriously greedy, so keep your paperwork (and vehicle) in good order.

PAPERS PLEASE

Mauritania is a country in love with police roadblocks, and you'll frequently be asked to produce ID, especially when entering or leaving a town. This is usually a straightforward procedure and police are generally polite. Your details are registered, so to speed things up make your own form (*fiche* or *ordre de mission*) to hand over. List all the personal details from your passport (including visa number), occupation and destination. If you're driving, include your vehicle's make, colour and registration number. Make plenty of photocopies.

Getting Around

AIR

Mauritania Airlines flies daily from Nouakchott to Nouâdhibou (UM20,000, one hour), three times a week via Zouérat (UM39,000, three hours).

CAR & MOTORCYCLE

Mauritania's road network is mostly good, with tarred roads leading from the border with Western Sahara to Nouakchott, and on to the Senegalese and Malian borders at Rosso and Nioro respectively. The roads from the capital to Atâr and Tidjikja are also tarred. Elsewhere, *piste* is the order of the day, although great swathes of the country are little more than sandy tracks (at best). Police checkpoints abound; make your own form *(fiche)* to hand over. List all the personal details from your passport (including visa number), home address, occupation and parents' names, plus your vehicle's make, colour and registration number. Make plenty of photocopies.

Consider renting a 4WD and driver if you want to reach more remote parts of the country. The standard Toyota Hilux usually costs around UM21,000 per day for the vehicle, plus petrol.

MINIBUS & BUSH TAXI

Minibus routes stitch together the main towns and cities linked by tarmac roads. Where tarmac is replaced by *piste*, the bush taxi *(taxi brousse)* – often Mercedes 190s and Peugeot 504s – take over, along with pick-up trucks for the rougher routes.

TOURS

There are numerous travel agencies in Nouakchott that offer tours around the country, but it's not a bad idea to arrange a tour with a more regional-focused company – eg in Atâr for the Adrar or the Tagânt. If there are at least four travellers, prices should average around UM20,000 per person per day.

TRAIN

The Nouâdhibou–Zouérat train is certainly an epic adventure (see boxed text, p376). It's an iron-ore train with no passenger terminals, but it's become a passenger train for lack of better alternatives. The trip takes 16 to 18 hours, but most travellers get off at Choûm (close to Atâr), 12 hours from Nouâdhibou.

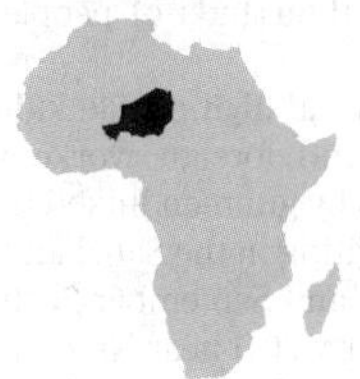

Niger

Includes ➡

Fast Facts

- **Capital** Niamey
- **Population** 16.3 million
- **Languages** French, Hausa, Djerma, Fulfulde, Tamashek
- **Area** 1,267,000 sq km
- **Currency** CFA franc
- **Visa requirements** A tourist visa is required, valid for three months
- **Tourist information** www.friendsofniger.org

Haunting Desertscapes & Ancient Cities

Niger only seems to make the news for negative reasons: its recent coup, the Tuareg Rebellion, a devastating famine. But visit this desert republic and you'll find a warm and generous Muslim population and superb tout-free travel through ancient caravan cities at the edge of the Sahara.

To the north, the stark splendour of the Aïr Mountains hides Neolithic rock art and stunning oasis towns. Within the expansive dunes of the Ténéré Desert you'll find dinosaur graveyards and deserted medieval settlements. Head south and the ancient trans-Saharan trade-route town of Agadez and the sultanate of Zinder are home to magnificent mazes of mudbrick architecture. For nature lovers, there's the fantastically diverse Parc Regional du W and herds of wild giraffes at Kouré.

The security situation meant that much of Niger was off limits to travellers at the time of writing. Attacks against foreigners have occurred across the Sahel, and the threat of kidnapping remains high.

Niger Top Sights

- **Agadez** Spiral up to the spiky summit of a majestic mud mosque for incredible views over the Sahara and beyond
- **Kouré** Wander in wonder with West Africa's last wild herd of giraffes
- **Zinder** Explore the Birni Quartier and soak up the brutal history at the sultan's palace in this fascinating Hausa city
- **Parc Regional du W** Come face to face with lions, crocodiles, monkeys and elephants in this incredibly diverse national park
- **Ténéré Desert** Dive into the deep end with an expedition to this sublime section of the Sahara
- **Aïr Mountains** Make tracks with camels through red sands and blue rocks in these mystical mountains

UNDERSTAND NIGER

Niger Today

A series of unpleasant events have defined Niger to the outside world in recent years. In 2007 the Tuareg in the north of the country began a rebellion against Niger's government, whom it accused of hoarding proceeds from the region's enormous mineral wealth and failing to meet conditions of previous ceasefires, in a conflict that has reignited at regular intervals since the early 20th century.

A year later Niger again made headlines around the world for less-than-positive reasons when in a landmark case an Economic Community of West African States (Ecowas) court found Niger guilty of failing to protect a young woman from the continued practice of slavery in the country. According to anti-slavery organisations, thousands of people still live in subjugation.

There have been several high-profile kidnappings of tourists and foreign workers over the past few years by gunmen linked to al-Qaeda factions operating in the Sahel and Sahara zone – in April and September 2010 near Arlit, and in January 2011 near Niamey. The Islamist takeover of northern Mali in 2012 created a security vacuum and opened up a safe haven for extremists and organised-crime groups in the Sahara desert. Tens of thousands of refugees flooded into the country.

The country's main export, uranium, is prone to price fluctuations and the industry has been hurt by the threat of terrorism and kidnapping. Niger began producing and refining oil in 2011 following a US$5 billion joint-venture deal with China.

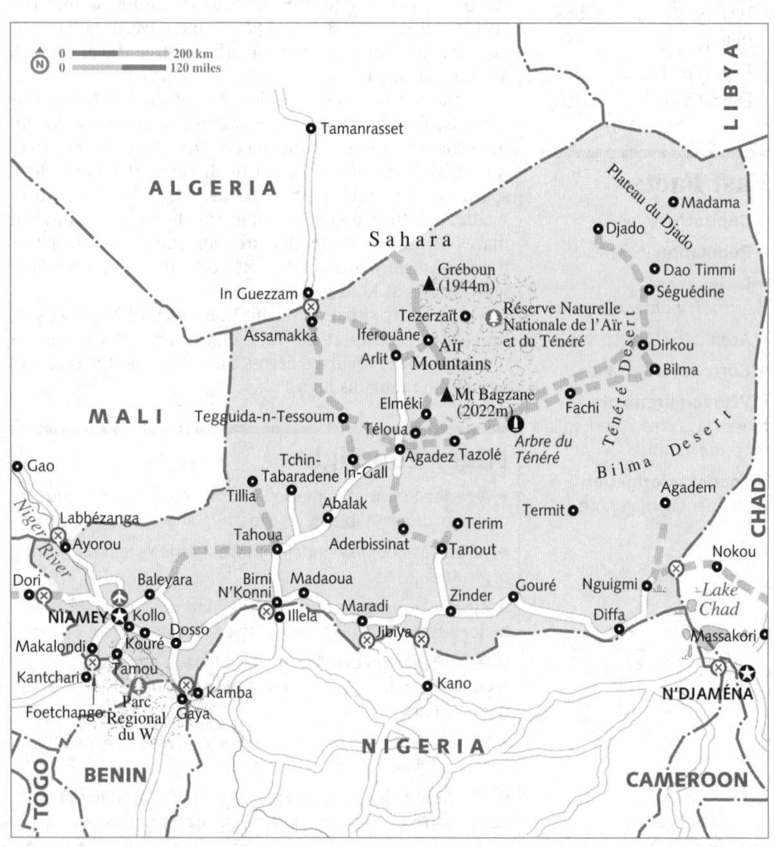

History

Before the Sahara started swallowing Niger around 2500 BC, it supported verdant grasslands, abundant wildlife and populations thriving on hunting and herding. Long after the desert pushed those populations southward, Niger became a fixture on the trans-Saharan trade route. Between the 10th and 18th centuries, West African empires, such as the Kanem-Borno, Mali and Songhaï, flourished in Niger, trafficking gold, salt and slaves.

The French strolled in late in the 1800s, meeting stronger-than-expected resistance. Decidedly unamused, they dispatched the punitive Voulet-Chanoîne expedition, destroying much of southern Niger in 1898–99. Although Tuareg revolts continued, culminating in Agadez's siege in 1916–17, the French had control.

French rule wasn't kind. They cultivated the power of traditional chiefs, whose abuses were encouraged as a means of control, and the enforced shift from subsistence farming to high-density cash crops compounded the Sahara's ongoing migration.

In 1958 France offered its West African colonies self-government in a French union or immediate independence. Countless votes disappeared, enabling France to claim that Niger wished to remain within its sphere of influence.

Maintaining close French ties, Niger's first president, Hamani Diori, ran a repressive one-party state. After surviving several coups, he was overthrown by Lieutenant Colonel Seyni Kountché after food stocks were discovered in ministerial homes during the Sahel drought of 1968–74. Kountché established a military ruling council.

Kountché hit the jackpot in 1968 when uranium was discovered near the town of Arlit. Mining incomes soon ballooned, leading to ambitious projects, including the 'uranium highway' between Agadez and Arlit. Yet not everyone was smiling: inflation skyrocketed and the poorest suffered more than ever.

The 1980s were unkind to all: uranium prices collapsed, the great 1983 drought killed thousands, and one-party politics hindered democracy. By the 1990s, Nigeriens were aware of political changes sweeping West Africa and mass demonstrations erupted, eventually forcing the government into multiparty elections in 1993. However, a military junta overthrew the elected president, Mahamane Ousmane, in 1996.

> **COUNTRY COVERAGE**
>
> At the time of research very few travellers were heading to Niger so we're providing historical and cultural information rather than reviews and listings. A good source of information for on-the-ground travel in Niger is Lonely Planet's Thorn Tree on-line travel forum www.lonelyplanet.com/thorntree. Other sources of good internet-based information are www.friendsofniger.org and http://voyageforum.com/forum/niger/.

In 1999, during widespread strikes and economic stagnation, president Mainassara (a 1996 coup leader) was assassinated and democracy re-established. Peaceful elections in 1999 and 2004 witnessed victory for Mamadou Tandja.

In 2009 Mamadou Tandja won a referendum allowing him to change the constitution to allow him to run for a third term. In the presidential elections that year Tandja won by a large margin, though Ecowas did not accept the result and suspended Niger's membership. The tables were turned on Tandja in February 2010 when a military coup in Niamey led to his arrest. A year-long military junta ended when veteran opposition leader Mahamadou Issoufou was declared winner of a presidential poll in March 2011.

Culture

Niger boasts the highest birth rate in the world: women have a staggering average of eight children each. The population is predicted to reach 21.4 million by 2025.

More than 90% of Nigeriens live in the south, which is dominated by Hausa and Songhaï-Djerma, making up 56% and 23% of Niger's populace respectively. The next largest groups are nomadic Fulani (8.5%) and Tuareg (8%), both in Niger's north, and Kanuri (4.3%), located between Zinder and Chad.

Nigeriens are predominantly Muslim (over 90%), with small percentages of Christian urban dwellers. Several rural populations still practise traditional animist religions. Due to the strong influence of Nigeria's Islamic community, some Muslims around the border town of Maradi call for sharia law.

Despite most Nigeriens being devoutly Muslim, the government is steadfastly secular and Islam adopts a more relaxed aura than in nations with similar demographics. Women don't cover their faces, alcohol is quietly consumed and some Tuareg, recognising the harshness of desert life, ignore Ramadan's fast.

While Islam plays the greatest role in daily life, shaping beliefs and thoughts, little is visible to visitors. The biggest exceptions are *salat* (prayer), when Niger grinds to a halt – buses even break journeys to partake.

Religion aside, survival occupies most people's days. Around 90% make their tenuous living from agriculture and livestock, many surviving on US$1 or less per day. Producing numerous children to help with burdening workloads is a necessity for many, a fact contributing to population growth. The fact of children being obliged to work has led to staggering adult illiteracy rates.

Niger's best-known artisans are Tuareg silversmiths, who produce necklaces, striking amulets, ornamental silver daggers and stylised silver crosses, each with intricate filigree designs representing areas boasting Tuareg populations. The most famous cross is the *croix d'Agadez*. To Tuareg, crosses are powerful talismans protecting against ill fortune.

Leatherwork by *artisans du cuir* is well regarded, particularly in Zinder, where traditional items – such as saddlebags, cushions and tasselled pouches – rank alongside attractive modernities like sandals and briefcases.

Beautifully unique to Niger are vibrant *kountas* (Djerma blankets), produced from bright cotton strips.

Food & Drink

Dates, yoghurt, rice and mutton are standard Tuareg fare, while *riz sauce* (rice with sauce) is omnipresent in Niger's south. Standard restaurant dishes include grilled fish (particularly capitaine, or Nile perch), chicken, and beef *brochettes* (kebabs). Couscous and ragout are also popular. Outside Niamey vegetarian options diminish.

Sitting for a cup of Tuareg tea is rewarding and thirst-quenching. For a wobble in your step, try Bière Niger. For a serious stagger, down some palm wine.

Environment

Three-quarters of Niger is desert, with the Sahara advancing 10km a year. The remaining quarter is Sahel, the semidesert zone south of the Sahara. Notable features include the Niger River (Africa's third-longest), which flows 300km through Niger's southwest; the Aïr Mountains, the dark volcanic formations of which rise over 2000m; and the Ténéré Desert's spectacularly sweeping sand dunes.

Desertification, Niger's greatest environmental problem, is primarily caused by overgrazing and deforestation. Quartz-rich soil also prevents topsoil from anchoring, causing erosion.

The southwest's dry savannah woodland hosts one of West Africa's better wildlife parks, Parc Regional du W.

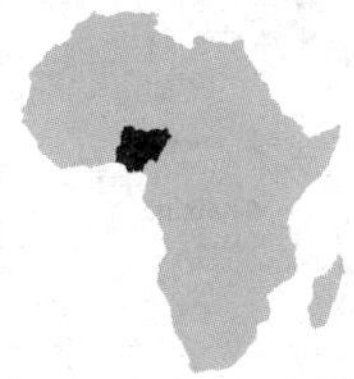

Nigeria

☎234 / POP 162 MILLION

Includes ➡

Best Places to Shake Your 'Yansh'

- New Afrika Shrine (p396)
- Elegushi Beach (p397)
- Likwid (p397)

Best Places to Worship Orishas

- Osun Sacred Grove (p402)
- Oòni's Palace (p402)
- Olumo Rock (p400)

Why Go?

Nigeria is a pulsating powerhouse: as the most populous nation on the continent it dominates the region economically and culturally, spreading the fruits of its rapid development throughout Africa with fury. Lagos, Nigeria's main city, is bursting at the seams: with burgeoning technology and telecommunications industries, posh restaurants and clubs, and an absolutely exploding music and arts scene, this megacity is the face of modern Africa.

In villages and towns outside Gidi (as Lagosians call their city), you may often feel as if you're a lone explorer getting a glimpse of the raw edges of the world. Immersing yourself in the deep and layered cultures, histories, and surroundings – from the ancient Muslim cities of the north to the river deltas, from Yoruba kingdoms and spiritual shrines to the legacy of tribal conflict and the slave ports, and among simply stunning natural environments – provides a worthy antidote to a sometimes exhausting journey.

When to Go

Lagos

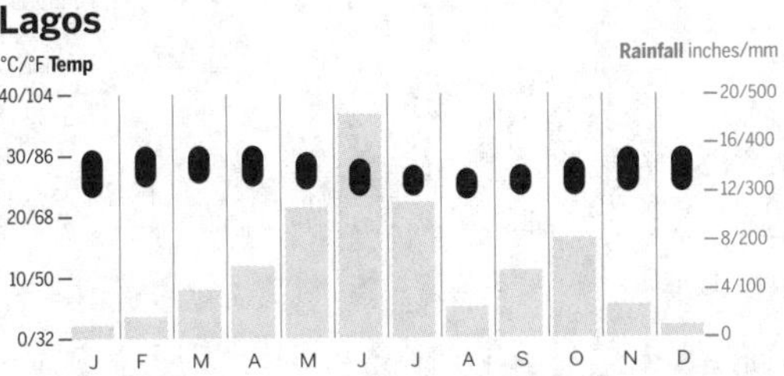

Oct–Jan Your best bet for dry weather.

Dec–Jan Lots of events and festivals; also the busiest (and most expensive) time of year.

Jun–Aug Nigeria's rainy season and usually quite wet, but not necessary to avoid.

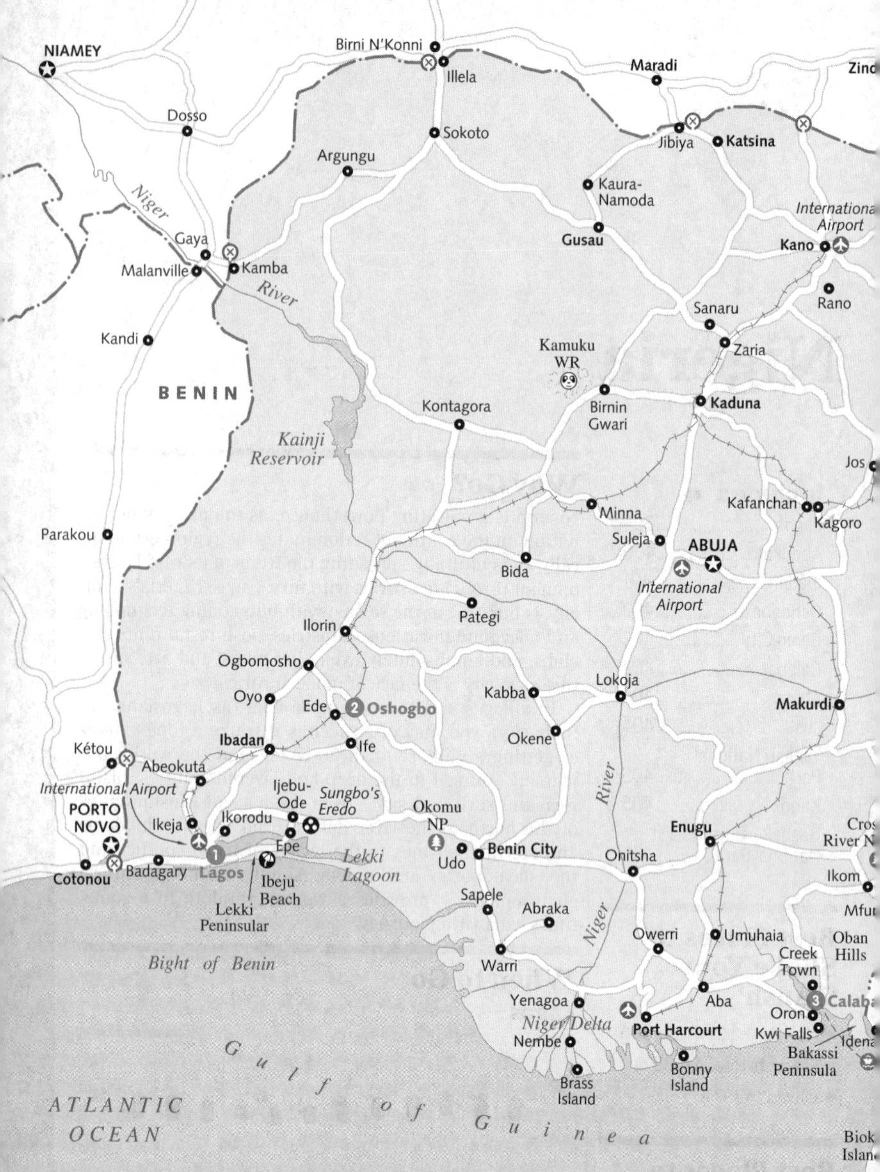

Nigeria Highlights

1 Joining the gold rush of **Lagos** (p394), the newly moneyed, fastest growing, and largest African city on the continent.

2 Learning about the traditional arts and ancient spiritual shrines in **Oshogbo** (p402), the centre of Yoruba culture.

3 Taking in colonial history and cutting-edge conservation in the easygoing old river port, **Calabar** (p402).

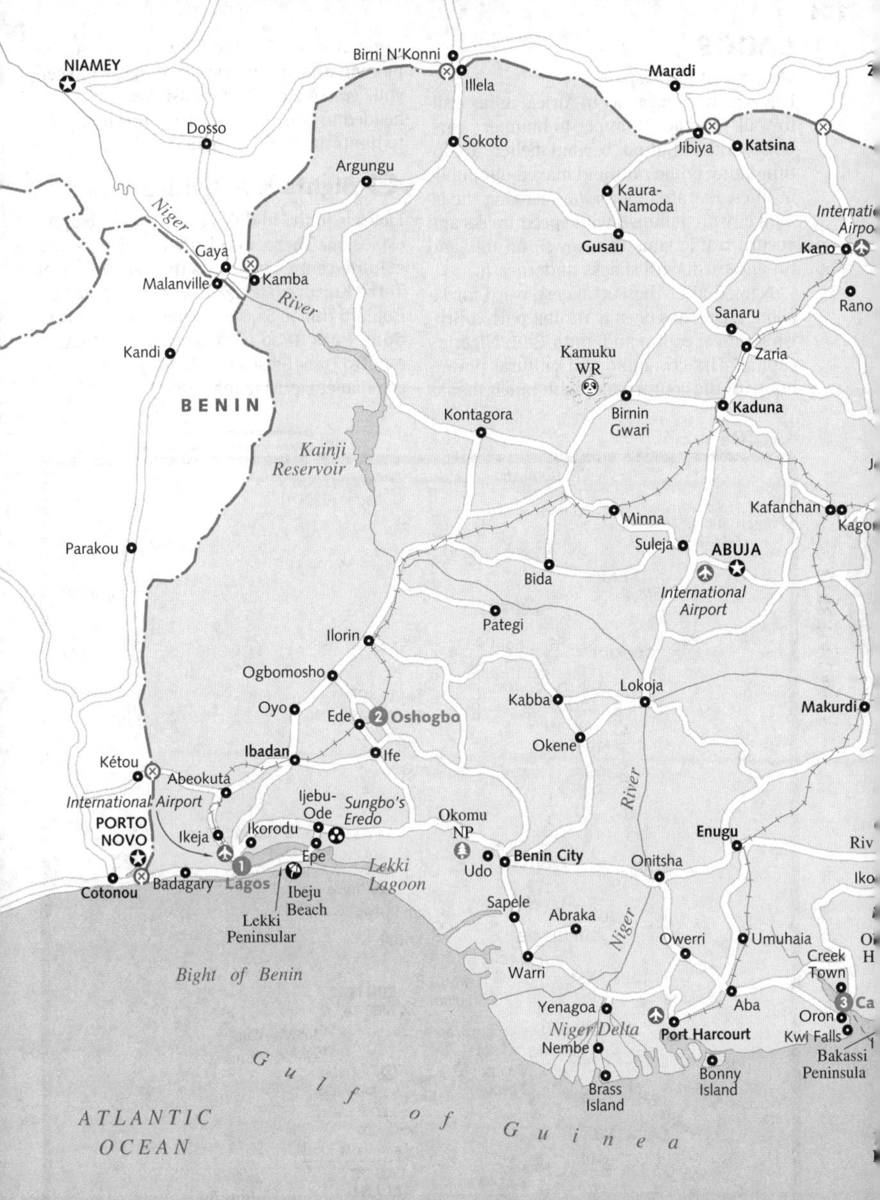

4 Heading into the real wilds to explore, **Gashaka-Gumti National Park** (p406), a newly reorganised mountain-meets-savannah national park.

LAGOS

☎01 / POP 25 MILLION

Lagos is the largest city in Africa; it has wall-to-wall people, bumper-to-bumper cars, noise and pollution beyond belief, an intimidating crime rate, and maxed-out public utilities. Elevated motorways ringing the island city are jammed with speed freaks and absurd traffic jams ('go-slows') on top, and tin-and-cardboard shacks underneath.

Named after the Portuguese word for lagoon, Lagos has been a Yoruba port, a British political centre and, until 1991, Nigeria's capital. The economic and cultural powerhouse of the country, and with much thanks to an absurd influx of oil money, it has an exploding arts and music scene that will keep your *yansh* engaged far past dawn. If you're headed to Nigeria, you'll have no choice but to jump right into the madness here.

Sights & Activities

Lagos is in the middle of an arts and culture explosion. There are plenty of galleries and cultural centres worth visiting, among them **Terra Kulture** (Map p400; www.terrakulture.com; Plot 1376 Tiamiyu Savage St, Victoria Island), **Freedom Park** (Map p398; www.freedomparklagos.com; Old Prison Ground, Broad St, Lagos Island), the colonial-era prison that now holds cultural

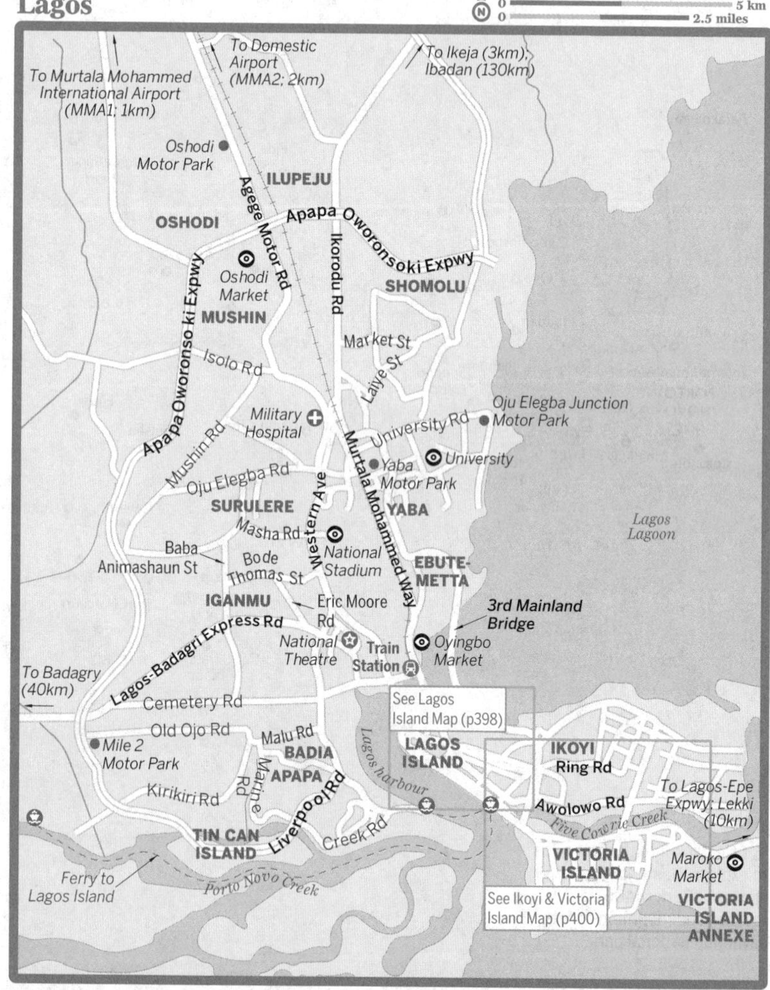

events, the **African Artists' Foundation** (Map p400; www.africanartists.org/; 54 Raymond Njoku St, Ikoyi), a contemporary arts gallery, and **Quintessence** (Map p400; ☎0803 3275401; Falomo Shopping Centre, Awolowo Rd, Ikoyi).

For markets try **Jankara Market** (Map p398; off Adeyinka Oyekan Ave), full of fabric, *juju* ingredients, and crafts. **Balogun Market** (Map p398; off Breadfruit St) sells fabric from across West Africa. **Lekki Market** (Elegushi Market; off Epe Expressway, Lekki) has the best selection of crafts from around Nigeria and West Africa.

On Lagos Island look out for examples of old Brazilian architecture in the distinctive houses built by former slaves and their descendants who returned from Brazil.

Also head to Lagos institution **Jazz Hole** (Map p400; Awolowo Rd), a bookshop, a record store and a lovely cafe.

★ **Kalakuta Republic Museum** MUSEUM

(Gbemisola St, Ikeja) Legendary musician Fela Kuti's former house and revolutionary headquarters is now a fascinating museum, with everything intact from Fela's bedroom to his underwear. Breathe deep and you may even catch a high.

★ **Nike Art Gallery** GALLERY

(☎0803 4096 656; www.nikeart.com; 2nd Roundabout, Epe Expressway, Lekki) FREE One of Nigeria's most important artists, Nike Davies-Okundaye, runs this enormous gallery full of contemporary and traditional Nigerian arts. Nike herself is practically an incarnation of love and beauty, which is reflected in this astonishing four-storey space. If you're lucky she'll be there and may grace you with a new Yoruba name. Cultural tours to other Yoruba towns can be arranged through the gallery.

Sleeping

It's hard to find a cheap place to rest your head in this surprisingly expensive city. While there are plenty of small midrange guesthouses with basic rooms, there is an absolute boom in high-end hotels.

Peerage Retreat HOTEL **$$**

(Map p400; ☎01 271 9650; peerageretreat@yahoo.com; 1 Olabode George St, Victoria Island; r N10,000; ❄) The best option for the money on the island, this family-run hotel is clean, friendly and well run. Given the deal, it fills up fast.

Hotel Victoria Palace HOTEL **$$**

(Map p400; ☎01 262 5901; victoriapalace@gmail.com; 1623 Sake Jojo St; s/d N12,500-14,000; P ❄) Basic rooms and a friendly staff, a good budget-ish choice on Victoria Island. The **Bombay Palace** (Map p400; Awolowo Rd; mains from N1200; ⏲noon-3pm & 6-10pm) on the top floor serves good Indian food.

Bogobiri House BOUTIQUE HOTEL **$$$**

(Map p400; ☎01 270 7436; www.bogobirilagos.com; 9 Maitama Sule St, Ikoyi; r incl breakfast from N30,000; ❄ @ ᯤ) This charming boutique hotel, beautifully decorated with paintings and sculptures by local artists, serves as the hub of the vibrant art and cultural scene. Its side-street location provides a calm escape from the Lagos buzz. The restaurant has some of the best Nigerian favourites in the city, and there is often excellent live music.

The Wheatbaker BOUTIQUE HOTEL **$$$**

(☎01 277 3560; www.legacyhotels.com; 4 Onitolo Rd, Ikoyi; r from N88,000; P ❄ @ ᯤ ≋) A luxury boutique hotel, The Wheatbaker ranks at the absolute top. Experience the secluded grounds and gorgeous pool at Sunday brunch to get a taste of the elite Lagos lifestyle.

Eating

Broad St and Campbell St in Lagos Island are good for chophouses and *suya* (Nigerian kebab); the better restaurants are in Ikoyi and Victoria Island. Some of the best places to eat are attached to hotels and cultural centres, such as Bogobiri, Terra Kulture and **Purple at The Blowfish** (☎014631298;

SET YOUR BUDGET

Budget

- Hotel room US$50
- Two-course dinner US$7
- Coffee US$1
- Local bus ride US$1

Midrange

- Hotel room US$150
- Two-course dinner US$25
- Beer in bar US$4
- Short taxi ride US$10

Top End

- Hotel room US$400
- Two-course dinner US$75
- Glass of wine US$11
- Longer taxi ride US$20

WARNING: BOKO HARAM

Since 2009, Boko Haram, a jihadist organisation based in the northeast of Nigeria, has waged a low-level war against Christian communities and the central government, killing thousands. Known for bombing churches and markets, assassinating police, and motorcycle drive-bys, the group, whose name means 'Western education is sinful' in Hausa, has made travel to northern Nigeria a dicey proposition.

Attacks are sporadic and have taken place in Adawama, Gombe, Yobe, Jigawa and Plateau States, occasionally in an outskirt of Abuja or Jos, with many incidents centred on Maiduguri, the capital of Borno State.

Boko Haram's goal is ostensibly to impose sharia law. But Nigerians in the south have other suspicions about their motivations. The 2010 death of northern-born President Yar'Adua ushered in the current president Goodluck Jonathan – a southern native – losing the north the seat of governmental power. Boko Haram's continued terrorism may be seen as angling for more resources and control.

While Lagosians will tell you flat out not to go north, the astounding sites there make it alluring to explore. Travellers should proceed with extreme caution: check the news reports and ask locals with specific knowledge before attempting to go.

www.theblowfishhotel.com; 17 Oju Olobun, Victoria Island).

Ikoyi Hotel Suya AFRICAN $
(Map p400; Kingsway Rd, Ikoyi Hotel, Ikoyi; suya from N100; 10am-10pm) Lagosians claim the best *suya* in town can be found at the stall outside the Ikoyi Hotel. Not just beef and goat, but chicken, liver and kidney, plus some great fiery *pepe* (pepper) to spice it all up.

Pizze-Riah PIZZA $$
(Map p400; 13 Musa Yardua St, Victoria Island) Brick-oven pizza in a lovely outdoor setting.

Bangkok Restaurant THAI $$
(Map p400; Muri Okunola St; 11am-11pm) With the best Thai food in Lagos, the Bangkok is a treat. The cooks and waitresses are all Thai, and offer you a broad menu of fragrantly spiced dishes. Portions are very generous, and if you can't finish your meal, they're used to sending people home with a doggie bag.

Cactus BAKERY $$
(Map p400; Maroko Rd; mains from N1200; 8am-10pm) This place labels itself primarily as a patisserie, but it also serves up proper meals throughout the day. Breakfasts of pancakes or bacon are good, as are the pizzas, and the club sandwiches with salad and chips are simply huge – excellent value at N1800.

Yellow Chilli AFRICAN $$
(Map p400; 27 Ojo Olubun Cl, Victoria Island; mains N1500-2500; 11am-10pm;) Well-presented Nigerian dishes in swish surroundings. It's carried off well, with tasty dishes in reasonable portions and good service – a great way to eat your way around the country without leaving your table.

Drinking & Nightlife

As they say in Lagos, what happens in Gidi stays in Gidi. In other words, Lagos' nightlife is legendary. Be prepared to stay up past dawn and arrive home sore. Note that what's hot is constantly changing. Ask around for the best nights out. Drink spots are best up until midnight when dance spots then heat up.

New Afrika Shrine LIVE MUSIC
(Adeleye St, Ikeja (mainland); cover charge N500; Thu-Sun 6pm-1am) Just by showing up you'll get a political education, a scandalising lesson in shakin' it, and a contact high. Though Fela Kuti's original Shrine was burnt down, this replacement run by his children is possibly the best show in town. Femi Kuti plays free on Thursday night and does a paid show on Sunday. Fela's most approximate reincarnation, the younger Seun Kuti, plays the last Saturday of the month. Snacks, ice cream, palm wine, and more are on offer. Smoking encouraged.

Bogobiri II/Nimbus BAR
(Map p400; Maitama Sule St, Ikoyi; 8am-11pm) Part of Bogobiri House (p395), this is a lovely place for a drink (and eat) – mellow in the day and happening at night. There's an attached art gallery with works from local artists, and at weekends there's usually live music.

Motherlan' LIVE MUSIC
(Opebi Rd, Ikeja; cover charge N1000; ⌚Thu-Sun) Owned by renowned musician Lagbaja, this is a big outdoor venue with lots of live music and a robust local following.

Likwid Lounge BAR
(Map p400; Samuel Manuwa St, Victoria Island) Starts late, gets good even later. Nigeria's elites, socialites and pop stars come here for the post-party partying. If you get the munchies, head across the street, outside the gate of 1004 Housing Estates, to Chopbox; it's always open.

Sip Lounge BAR
(Map p400; Akin Adesola St, Victoria Island) Another swank late-night drinking hole for the fancy-inclined.

Elegushi Beach BAR
Dancing bumper-to-bumper, bottles of the hard stuff, lots of ladies – the party does not get better than Elegushi Beach on a Sunday night. Go with a local; there have been robberies. Not for the faint of heart. During the day, pay a fee (N1000) to enjoy the semi-private beach.

Orientation

For the traveller, there are three main areas dividing Lagos: the mainland, a massive area of upper, middle, and working-class neighbourhoods along with innumerable business centres and some universities; Lagos Island, the heart of the city, including Ikoyi, an elite suburb, some embassies and top-end hotels; and Victoria Island (VI), an even smarter suburb facing the Atlantic Ocean with the bulk of the embassies and a number of top-end hotels. Beyond VI is the Lekki Penninsula. The islands are connected by elevated expressways and bridges constantly clogged with traffic.

Information

INTERNET ACCESS

Internet cafes are everywhere and cost upwards N200 per hour. Many upscale restaurants and cafes also have wi-fi. Have lunch at Bogobiri House (p395) for a fast connection. Satisfy your sweet tooth and wireless needs at the bakery-restaurant **Cafe Royale** (Map p400; No 267A, Etim Inyang Cres, Victoria Island; ⌚7am-10pm; ❄📶).

MEDICAL SERVICES

Healthplus Integrative Pharmacy (Map p400; ☎0802 802 5810; Unit 54, The Palms Shopping Centre, Lekki; ⌚8am-7pm Mon-Sat) With branches in Ikeja, Yabo and the airport.

St Nicholas Hospital (Map p398; ☎0802 290 8484; http://saintnicholashospital.com; 57 Campbell St) Has a 24-hour emergency clinic.

MONEY

ATMs are ubiquitous. GTB bank is the most reliable for foreign cards.

At money changers, high-denomination bills trade at a much better rate. Find them at Alade Market on the mainland, or outside Federal Palace and Eko Meridien hotels on Victoria Island.

SAFE TRAVEL

Contrary to popular perception, violent crime has decreased in recent years. Most crime against foreigners targets expats in expensive cars, and travellers are unlikely to encounter any serious problems. Still, never carry more money than is necessary and avoid flaunting valuables and walking outside at night – particularly

FELA KUTI: MUSIC IS THE WEAPON

The impact of Fela Anikulapo Kuti's music in Nigeria, and worldwide, cannot be overstated. Fela Kuti (1938–97) is Africa's musical genius, the creator of Afrobeat – a genre combining traditional African highlife, jazz, James Brown funk grooves and Latin rhythms into a unique mix that is wholly his own – and a revolutionary. Fela's politically inflammatory songs laid bare the corruption, violence and greed of the ruling regimes in his country and beyond. He was arrested over a hundred times by the Nigerian government, and ultimately 1000 soldiers invaded and destroyed the Kalakuta Republic – Fela's living and performing compound that he shared with his 27 wives – sending nearly all of the inhabitants to the hospital, or worse. Despite the death of his own mother due to the siege, Fela never stopped fighting the powers of imperialism, colonialism and racism with – as the legend himself put it – music as his weapon. Due to the recent re-release of his music worldwide and, interestingly, a Broadway musical based on his life, Fela's legacy is now enjoying renewed attention and a reinvigorated profile in Nigeria. The Lagos government even donated money to launch the new Kalakuta Museum (p395), and Felabration is celebrated each year around his birthday on 15 October.

Lagos Island

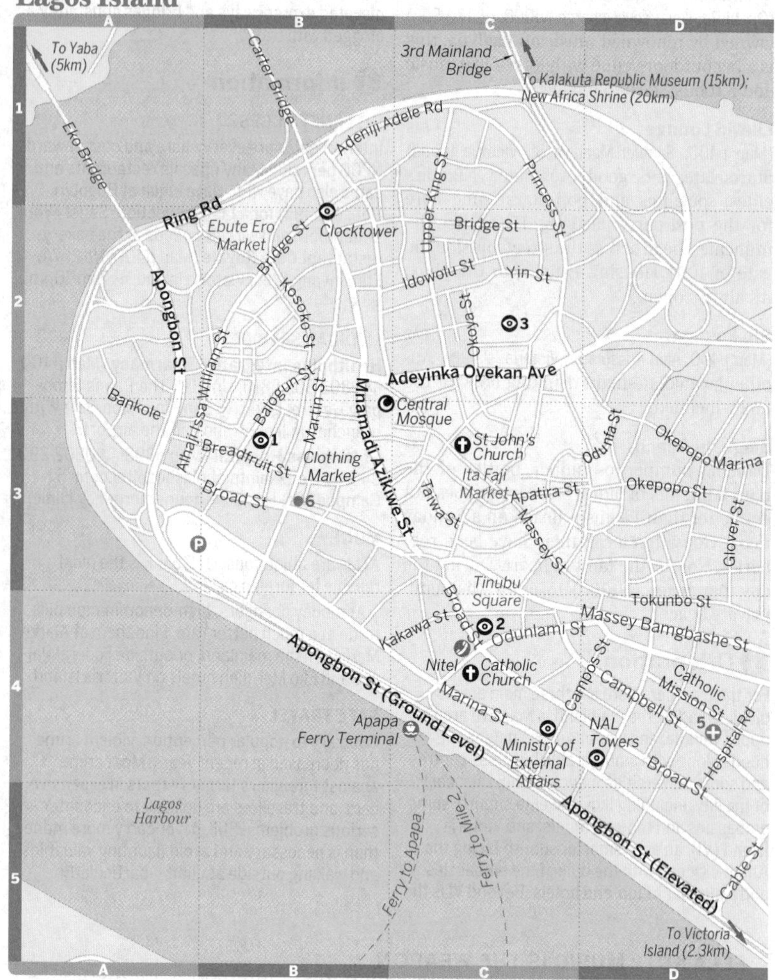

around hotels and restaurants frequented by foreigners.

🛈 Getting There & Away

Murtala Mohammed International Airport (MMA1) is the main gateway to Nigeria and is roughly 10km north of Lagos Island. The domestic terminal (MMA2) is 4km away; tickets can be bought on departure or from an agent. Though there are airline offices at the airport and in Lagos, it's best to use a travel agency that can sort your flights all-in-one.

Ojota Motor Park (with Ojota New Motor Park next door), 13km north of Lagos, is the city's main transport hub. Minibuses and bush taxis leaving to all destinations depart from here. Sample fares are Benin City (N3000, four hours), Ibadan (N1000, two hours), Oshogbo (N2500, three hours) and Abuja (N5000, 10 hours).

Mile-2 Motor Park serves destinations east of Lagos, including the Benin border at Seme (N800, 90 minutes). You'll also find a few minibuses going as far north as Ibadan from here.

ABC Transport (Map p400; ☎ 01 740 1010; www.abctransport.com) is a good intercity 'luxury' bus company, serving many major cities, as well as destinations in Benin, Ghana and Togo. The depot is at Jibowu Motor Park, but there's a useful **booking office** (☎ 01 740 1010; Awolowo

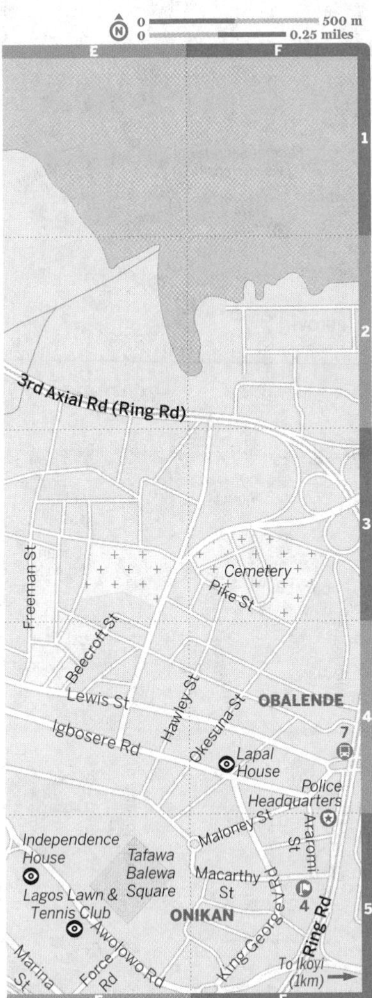

Lagos Island

Sights

1 Balogun Market ... B3
2 Freedom Park ... C4
3 Jankara Market ... C2

Information

4 Ghanaian High Commission ... F5
5 St Nicholas Hospital ... D4

Transport

6 Lufthansa ... B3
7 Obalende Motor Park ... F4

Rd, Block D, Falomo Shopping Centre) inside a shoe shop at Falomo Shopping Centre.

Aero Contractors (☎01 628 4140; www.acn.aero; airport desk)

Air France (Map p400; ☎01 461 0777; www.airfrance.com; Idejo Danmole St)

Arik Air (☎01 279 9999; www.arikair.com; Lagos Murtala Muhammed International Airport)

Cameroon Airlines (Map p400; ☎01 261 6270; Oko Awo Cl)

Ethiopian Airlines (Map p400; ☎01 774 4711; www.flyethiopian.com; 3 Idowu Tayor St, Victoria Island)

Ghana International Airlines (Map p400; ☎01 266 1808; www.fly-ghana.com; 130 Awolowo Rd, Ikoyi)

Kenya Airways (Map p400; ☎01 271 9433; www.kenya-airways.com; Badaru Abina St, Churchgate Tower)

KLM (Map p400; ☎0703 415 3801; www.klm.com; 1 Adeola Odeku St, Sapetro, Victoria Island)

Lufthansa (Map p398; ☎01 461 2222; www.lufthansa.com; Churchgate Tower, Victoria Island)

South African Airlines (Map p400; ☎01 270 0712; www.flysaa.com; 28c Adetukonbo Ademola St, Victoria Island)

Getting Around

Traffic in Lagos is legendary – and it's not getting any better – especially with occasional governmental edicts outlawing *okada*, small (and sometimes unsafe) motorcycles that are your best best for skirting the 'go-slow'.

A taxi costs from N4000 to reach Lagos Island. Always allow way more time than you think to get to the airport when catching a flight. There are no airport buses.

Arriving in Lagos can be complicated and you may be dropped at one of several motor parks – Oshodi, Yaba and Oju Elegba Junction are the likeliest candidates. Minibuses run from these to more central points, such as Obalende Motor Park on Lagos Island.

Yellow minibuses (*danfos;* fares N70 to N250 according to distance) serve points all over Lagos – prices increase when you cross a bridge from one part of Lagos to another. Yellow private taxis start at N500.

Keke Napep (motorised tricycles that can carry three passengers) are useful for short-distance travel and have replaced the services previously provided by *okada*.

A decent, cheap option to avoid traffic, the official city Bus Rapid Transit (BRT) buses have

Ikoyi & Victoria Island

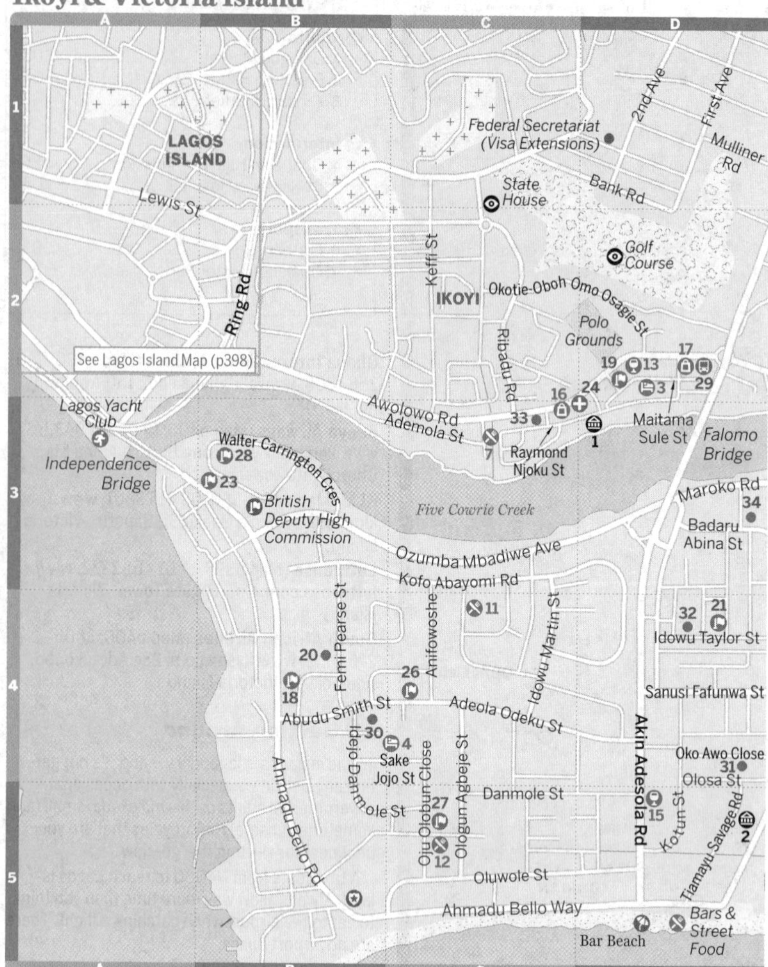

routes that stretch from Lagos Island to the mainland. Buy tickets (N70 to N150) at terminals scattered around Lagos. Boarding may require waiting on long queues.

SOUTHERN NIGERIA

Abeokuta

About 100km north of Lagos, Abeokuta is well known as the birthplace of many famous Nigerians, notably former president Obasanjo and Fela Kuti.

The founding site of Abeokuta, the famed **Olumo Rock** (admission N200) has a rich history and great spiritual significance. Hire a guide (dash around N500) and climb the rock. You'll see shrines, sacred trees, the elderly women of the god of thunder, tribal war-time hideouts, and ultimately, at the top, an astonishing view of the city.

To make the two-hour trip from Lagos take a bush taxi (N300) from Ojota Motor Park. You'll arrive at Kuto Motor Park, where you can hop on an *okada* (N100) or taxi.

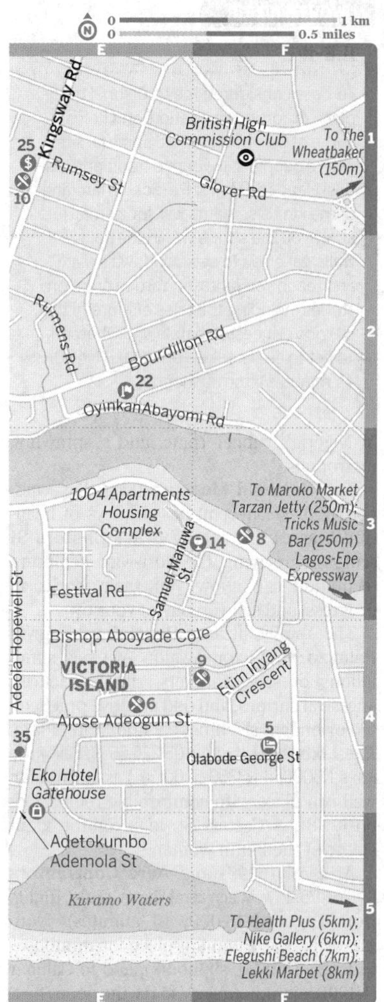

Ikoyi & Victoria Island

Sights

1 African Artists' Foundation ... D3
2 Terra Kulture ... D5

Sleeping

3 Bogobiri House ... D2
4 Hotel Victoria Palace ... C4
5 Peerage Retreat ... F4

Eating

6 Bangkok Restaurant ... E4
7 Bombay Palace ... C3
8 Cactus ... F3
9 Cafe Royale ... F4
10 Ikoyi Hotel Suya ... E1
11 Pizze-Riah ... C4
12 Yellow Chilli ... C5

Drinking & Nightlife

13 Bogobiri II/Nimbus ... D2
14 Likwid Lounge ... F3
15 Sip Lounge ... D5

Shopping

16 Jazz Hole ... C3
17 Quintessence ... D2

Information

18 Beninese Embassy ... B4
19 Burkinabé Embassy ... D2
20 Cameroonian Embassy ... B4
21 Canadian Embassy ... D4
22 French Embassy ... E2
23 German Embassy ... B3
24 Healthplus Integrative Pharmacy ... D3
25 Moneychangers ... E1
26 Nigerien Embassy ... C4
27 Togolese Embassy ... C5
28 US Embassy ... B3

Transport

29 ABC Transport ... D2
30 Air France ... B4
31 Cameroon Airlines ... D4
32 Ethiopian Airlines ... D4
33 Ghana International Airlines ... C3
34 Kenya Airways ... D3
KLM ... (see 34)
35 South African Airlines ... E4

Ibadan

02 / POP 2.7 MILLION

The word sprawling could have been invented to describe Ibadan. You're likely to pass through this major transport junction, but there's little to keep you here.

Hotels are generally shoddy and expensive. The best bet on the higher end is **Kakanfo Inn** (www.kakanfoinn.com; 1 Nihinlola St, Ring Rd, Ibadan; P ❄ @ 🛜 ≋), which has a decent Indian restaurant. A cheaper option is the **University of Ibadan Guest House** (012 273 9865; University of Ibadan Campus; P ❄ @). If you want something other than local chophouses, go to **Pancho Vino** (off Town Planning, Oluyole; pizzas around N1400; noon-3pm & 6-11pm) for pizzas and Lebanese food in clean, modern surroundings.

The Gbagi market has an enormous selection of fabric.

Iwo Rd is Ibadan's major motor park; minibuses run to all points from here, including Lagos (N500, 90 minutes), Abuja (N2000, eight hours) and points north. For Oshogbo (N300, 90 minutes), go to Gate Motor Park in the east of the city.

Oshogbo

This quiet city has been a traditional centre for Yoruba spirituality and, since the 1950s, the birthplace for much contemporary Nigerian art.

The best sight is the **Osun Sacred Grove** believed to be the dwelling of Osun, the Yoruba fertility goddess. In the late 1950s, Austrian-born artist Susanne Wenger, later accepted as a high Yoruba priestess, revived the neglected grove, filling it with her own and her many pupils' sculptures and shrines revering traditional deities.

For an extra fee, tour the groves with one of Susanne's adopted children (and traditional priests) Sangodare (0803 226 2188) or Doyin Faniyi (0803 226 2188). Also visit Susanne's remarkable house and the cooperative shop run by the artists of the **New Sacred Movement** (41A Ibokun Rd).

There's no reason to stay anywhere else but the divine **Nike Ambassador Guest House** (r N5000-7000) with lovely gardens (including giant tortoises and peacocks) and an incredibly friendly staff. They can take you to Nike's traditional Yoruba craft workshops for Nigerian youth as well as the village where local women make traditional black soap.

There are several contemporary art galleries where you can buy fantastic crafts including the **Nike Centre for Arts & Culture** (Old Ede Rd) and **Jimoh Buraimoh's African Heritage Gallery** (1 Buraimoh St).

Also wander through the Oja Oba Market across from the Oba's Palace – it's packed with stalls selling *juju* material.

Okefia Rd is the main motor park. Minibuses leave regularly for Ibadan (N500, 90 minutes) and Lagos (N700, three hours).

Benin City

052

Benin City, which served as the capital of the Benin Kingdom, starting in the 15th century, gave rise to one of the first African art forms to be accepted internationally – the Benin brasses. Today the city is the centre of Nigeria's rubber trade, and a sprawling metropolis.

The **National Museum** (King's Sq; admission N100; 9am-6pm) has displays of beautiful brasses. On nearby **Brass Casters St** sculptors reviving the 'lost-wax' sculpture technique can show you their works in progress, and sell you one of your own.

The totally bizarre **Revelation Tourist Palazzo** on Victor Awaido Ave has simulations of slave markets, ritual practices, ancestral shrines, and odd punitive practices.

For budget sleeping, try Edo Motel Plaza. The **Lixborr Hotel** (05 225 6699; Sakowpba Rd; s N3000, d N3250-5000;) is a popular, well-run place with comfortable rooms. Opposite Brass Casters St, look for the giant statue of the Benin woman.

Arik Air (p399) and **Aero Contractors** (764 7571; www.acn.aero) have daily flights from Lagos (N45,000, 40 minutes). Iyaro Motor Park is the main place for minibuses to Lagos (N1600, six hours), and to Calabar (N1900, eight hours). Also try the depot next to the Edo-Delta Hotel on Akpakpava Rd which serves most destinations.

WORTH A TRIP

ILE-IFE

Ile-Ife is considered the traditional birthplace of Yoruba civilisation, and holds some of the most revered spiritual sites where people still worship traditional deities. Head to **Òòni's Palace**, where one of the king's servants will, for a small fee, show you the shrine within the palace walls, take you to see Oduduwa's staff, and teach you fantastic Yoruba creation stories including the tales of Moremi the warrior-princess, Obatala and Obameri. To get to Ile-Ife, take a bush taxi (N400, 45 minutes) from Oshogbo.

Calabar

087 / POP 500,000

Tucked into Nigeria's southeastern corner, the capital of Cross River State has a rich history and is well worth a trip. Originally a cluster of Efik settlements, Calabar was once one of Nigeria's biggest slave ports, and later a major exporter of palm oil. A popular stopover for travellers heading to Cameroon, this tourist-friendly city has an amazing museum and two excellent primate-conservation centres.

Sights

Calabar Museum MUSEUM
(Court Rd; admission N100; 9am-6pm) Housed in the beautiful old British governor's building overlooking the river, the museum has a fascinating collection covering Calabar's days as the Efik kingdom, the slave and palm-oil trade, and the colonial period.

Drill Ranch WILDLIFE SANCTUARY
(0803 5921262; www.pandrillus.org; Nsefik Eyo Layout, off Atekong Rd; donations appreciated; 9am-5pm) Home to a colony of rescued drill monkeys and chimpanzees, the Drill Ranch is home to Pandrillus, one of Africa's most progressive primate-conservation bodies, which places emphasis on local education to combat poaching and the bushmeat trade. Spending time with Liza, Peter and Tunje at the Calabar headquarters is fascinating. The organisation can arrange trips to its excellent **Afi Mountain Drill Ranch** (community charge N250, guides N1000, per car/motorbike N500/250, campsites N2000, huts N6000) near Cross River National Park. This is one of Nigeria's highlights, with a rainforest-canopy walk and close primate encounters.

Cercopan WILDLIFE SANCTUARY
(www.cercopan.org; Mary Slessor Ave; donations appreciated; 9am-5pm) On the other side of town from the Drill Ranch, Cercopan in the Botanic Gardens works with smaller monkeys such as guenons and mangabeys. The **gardens** (www.irokofoundation.org) are worth visiting to learn about the amazing biodiversity of the area.

Sleeping & Eating

For traditional dishes (N500) and palm wine with the locals, head to Atimbo, on the way to Akpabuyo town. The swish hotel Le Chateau has fine upscale local meals (N3000).

Nsikak Sea Side Hotel HOTEL $
(45 Eden St; r N1000) At 59 years old, this hotel, smack in the middle of colonial Old Calabar, is a throwback to a different era. It's incredibly dilapidated, and the staff will be pleased to host foreigners (their clientele is nearly all Nigerian). There's no air-con, and the electricity only works when there's national power, but get the top room with a balcony overlooking the sea and you'll find yourself transported. A very local experience.

Nelbee Executive Guesthouse GUESTHOUSE $
(08 723 2684; Dan Achibong St; r from N3500; P ✻) Close to Watt Market is this handy budget option. Rooms are comfortable, the management is friendly, and there's a terrifically formal dining room.

Jacaranda Suites HOTEL $$
(08 723 9666; off Atimbo Rd; r from N12,000; P ✻ ≋) Lovely suites, a lively outdoor thatch-roof bar with secluded cabanas, and a restaurant serving Cross River specialities and grilled fish, Jacaranda is an easy choice for high-end sleeping and eating.

Marian Hotel HOTEL $$
(08 722 0233; Old Ikong Rd; r N7000-8000; P ✻) Well located, the Marian has had a lick of paint and a tidy-up since our last visit, and is all the better for it. Rooms are spacious, tidy and comfortable.

K's Court AFRICAN $
(74 Ndidan Usang Iso Rd; dishes from N300; 11am-late) An open-air chophouse and bar, this place gets going later in the day. It serves up fiery bowls of cow-leg soup with plantain, and once that's gone, pushes back the tables and cranks up the music to dance the weekend nights away.

Getting There & Away

Aero Contractors (www.acn.aero) and Arik Air (p399) fly daily to Lagos and Abuja (for around N55,000).

Fakoships (0806 9230753) sails every Wednesday and Friday around 7am to Limbe in Cameroon (N6000, seven hours).

The main motor park is tucked between Mary Slessor Ave and Goldie St. Sample minibus fares

WORTH A TRIP

CREEK TOWN

For a worthwhile day trip from Calabar, head to Creek Town by boat (N400) from the wharf on Marina Rd, leaving around 7am and noon, coming back at 4pm.

Once there, get in touch with **Itaeyo** (0803 741 2894), who will show you the prefab colonial buildings and artifacts, traditional architecture and the king's palace (bring booze as a gift for the king). Also learn about the legacy of missionary Mary Slessor, who ended the traditional practice of killing twins.

include Lagos (N3200, 10 hours) and Ikom (for Afi Mountain Drill Ranch; N700, three hours).

NORTHERN NIGERIA

Abuja

POP 2.5 MILLION

Nigeria's made-to-measure capital, Abuja was founded during the boom years of the 1970s. After the divisive Biafran war, the decision was made to move the capital from Lagos to the ethnically neutral centre of the country. Clean, quiet and with a good electricity supply, sometimes Abuja hardly feels like Nigeria at all. There's not much to do, but it's a good place to catch your breath and do some visa shopping.

Abuja tends to empty at weekends, with people leaving for more exciting destinations, so many hotels offer discounts for Friday and Saturday nights.

Good budget options include **African Safari Hotel** (☎09 234 1881; Plot 11, Benue Cres; r from N3000-7000; ❄@), which has Area 1 Shopping Centre nearby (good for street food), Browelf Hotel on Lagos Cres, and Dannic Hotel (which has a great restaurant).

For something more upscale, **The Nordic Villa** (☎0703 682 9922; http://thenordicvilla.com/; No 52, Mike Akhigbe Way; r from N19000) is a modern Scandinavian-style guesthouse with helpful staff, a calm atmosphere and good internet access.

The main draw at **Smi Msira Restaurant** (Moshood Abiola Way; dishes from N700) is being able to sit out in the pleasant leafy surroundings – something of a genuine beer garden.

For a splurge, hit the many restaurants at the Hilton and Sheraton hotels.

The airport is 40km west of Abuja (N3500 by taxi). Flights depart hourly for Lagos with several airlines (N54,000, one hour). There are also daily flights to Kano and Port Harcourt, as well as flights several times a week to Ibadan, Calabar and Maiduguri.

Jabi Motor Park (also called Utoka) is the main terminus for Abuja. Transport goes to all points from here; sample minibus fares include Kano (N1000, four hours), Jos (N800, three hours), Ibadan (N1500, eight hours) and Lagos (N2600, 10 hours).

Okadas have been banned in Abuja. Instead, there are plentiful green taxis (around N200 a drop).

TRAVELLING IN THE NORTH

Due to the activities of Boko Haram and the subsequent unstable security situation, we were unable to travel independently in Kano, Jos, Yankari, and Gashaki-Gumpti National Park to update this chapter. Research for this part of the country was done using local contacts, the internet and other sources.

Jos

☎073

The temperate climes of the Jos plateau are perhaps the oldest inhabited parts of Nigeria. The earliest known Nigerians, the Nok people, originated in the area, witnessed by the famed Nok terracottas. At 1200m above sea level, it's noticeably cooler than most other parts of the country – in colonial times it was a recommended holiday destination for British officers. A former tin-mining centre, Jos now sits astride one of Nigeria's major Christian–Muslim fault lines. With communal violence not unknown, it's essential to keep your ear to the ground before planning a visit.

The **Jos National Museum** (admission N50; ⏲8.30am-5.30pm) has a superb collection of pottery, including several Nok terracotta sculptures – at over 2500 years old, they're Africa's oldest figurative sculptures. On the same site, the **Museum of Traditional Nigerian Architecture** (⏲8.30am-5.30pm) FREE has full-scale reproductions of buildings from each of Nigeria's major regions.

Good meals can be found at **Old Airport Junction** (old airport junction near Nasco; meals from N500) – pull up a table and munch on grilled fish, Suya or masa (meals from N500). **Decency Restaurant** (Beach Rd; meals from N300) provides traditional Nigerian cuisine. Afrione/Net Café is a great meeting place and serves western and Mexican dishes, baked goods and ice creams.

The areas around Jos hold some spectacular landscapes. To the east, Shere Hills offer a prime view of the city below, good hiking and rock climbing.

Kurra Falls is a great place for camping, boating, hiking and rock climbing. The area includes several lakes, a cascading waterfall and many hills and rock formations. Having a local guide is useful for finding the way and security measures.

There is a daily flight between Jos and Lagos with Arik Air (p399). You can book in the mornings at Hill Station Hotel. The airport is 30km south of Jos (N1800 by taxi).

Head for Plateau Riders Motor Park at Tafawa Balewa St near Terminus to go anywhere in the country. Cars and buses run to Bauchi (N800, two hours), Kano (N1500, five hours) and Abuja (N1500, four hours)

The motor park opposite NTA also offers taxis to cities close to Jos.

Cocin Guesthouse GUESTHOUSE **$**
(07 345 2286; 6 Noad A St; dm N600, r N1400) One of two church missions on this street. Accommodation is clean, yet spartan, and bathroom facilities are shared, but it's hard to beat the price. Next door, **Tekan Guesthouse** (07 345 3036; 5 Noad St; dm N350, r N1000) has more of the same.

Les Rosiers B&B **$$**
(0803 357 5233; https://sites.google.com/site/lesrosiersjos/; 1 Rest House Rd; r from N9000; P) This bungalow B&B is a delightfully unexpected find with a couple of chalets amid pleasant gardens. The French-Nigerian hosts are a good source of information and can help organise hiking trips and further travel. Entrance is opposite the Plateau Hotel.

Yankari National Park

Yankari, 225km east of Jos, is Nigeria's best-known **national park** (admission N300, car N500, photo permit N1250) for observing wildlife. The park still holds reasonable numbers of buffaloes, waterbucks, bushbucks, hippos and plenty of baboons. The biggest draw is the 300-strong population of elephants – a few lions also survive there. The birdwatching is excellent.

The best time to see wildlife is from late December to late April, before the rains, when the thirsty animals congregate at the Gaji River. You're permitted to drive your own vehicle if you take a guide; otherwise, the park has a safari truck that takes two-hour tours (N300) at 7.30am and 3.30pm daily.

Yankari's other attraction is the **Wikki Warm Spring** (admission N200), near the park campground. The crystal-clear water is a constant 31°C, forming a lake 200m long and 10m wide. Bring your swimming gear – the spring is a real highlight and shouldn't be missed.

Set high above the spring, the **Wikki Camp** (campsites per person N600, bungalows from N9000;) has chalets for rent (from N9000) and a serene view over the lush area. There's a decent restaurant and bar.

You can get to the park gate at Mainamaji by minibus from Bauchi (N600, five hours). After paying the entrance fee (N300), you'll need to arrange transport to the camp – around N3000 in a taxi or N1000 by *okada*.

Kano

064 / POP 10 MILLION

Founded around 1400 years ago, Kano is the oldest city in West Africa and Nigeria's second largest. It was a major crossroads in the trans-Saharan trade routes and, from the Middle Ages, an important centre for Islamic scholarship.

But Kano is now at the forefront of the imposition of sharia law, with issues such as gender segregation of public transport cutting across community fault lines. Boko Haram have been active in the area. Kano has some fascinating sights, but proceed only with extreme caution.

Sights

With thousands of stalls in a 16-hectare area, **Kurmi Market** is one of the largest markets in Africa and is the city's main attraction. It's a centre for African crafts, including gold, bronze and silver work, and all types of fabric. Away from the throng are the **Kofar Dye Pits** (Kofar Mata Gate; 7am-7pm), where indigo cloth has been dyed for hundreds of years. Finished cloth is for sale, starting from around N1500 according to the design.

The **Gidan Makama Museum** (Emirs Palace Rd; admission N200; 8am-6pm) stands on the site of the original emir's palace (the modern one sits opposite) and is a wonderful example of traditional Hausa architecture. The museum has a fascinating photographic history of Kano, and displays on Nigerian Islam and traditional culture. The **Gidan Dan Hausa** (Dan Hausa Rd; admission N100; 8am-4pm Mon-Thu, to 1pm Fri) is another museum in a beautifully restored traditional house showcasing regional crafts and ceremonial costumes.

Festivals & Events

Held annually just after the end of Ramadan (exact dates vary), is the Kano Durbar – the biggest and best festival of its kind in Nigeria. It includes an exquisite cavalry procession featuring ornately dressed men and colourfully bedecked horses flanked by musicians. Finishing outside the emir's palace, there is drumming, singing and massed cavalry charges.

Sleeping

Ecwa Guesthouse GUESTHOUSE $
(☎06463 1410; 1 Mission Rd; r N1500-3500; ❄) This Christian mission guesthouse is a great budget option. The cheapest rooms are in the old block, are fan only, and some have shared facilities; the more expensive rooms in the new block have bathroom, TV and air-con. Alcohol is forbidden on site.

Prince Hotel HOTEL $$$
(☎06 498 4251; Tamandu Rd; r N16,200-21,000; P ❄ wi-fi) Professionally understated with a posh restaurant and bar, 24-hour power, wi-fi and a swimming pool, the Prince is a classy operation in a quiet part of town. Rooms are modern and exceedingly comfortable. The Calypso Restaurant is a popular meeting place for expats and journalists.

Eating & Drinking

Kano is the home of *suya,* so if you're looking for a quick 'meat-on-a-stick' eat, you'll be in heaven here.

The best 'food-is-ready' fare is found in Sabon Gari. Enugu Rd has plenty of **chophouses** (dishes from N250; ⊙8am-late), most doubling as bars.

Al-Amir AFRICAN $
(12B Club Rd; dishes N250-400; ⊙11am-10pm) If you want to eat like a local, head here. The 'special plate' has a bit of everything in a serving, but also try northern specialities like *miyan taushe* (pumpkin-seed soup) and *tuwo shunkafa* (pounded rice), washed down with a glass of *zobo* (hibiscus tea).

Fasania CHINESE $$
(Ahmadu Bello Way; mains N680-1100; ⊙noon-11pm) This Chinese restaurant has a better-than-average selection of dishes, all cooked and served efficiently. Alcohol is served.

Spice Food INDIAN $$
(Magasin Rumfa Rd; dishes from N550; ⊙noon-3.30pm & 6-11pm) If you've been craving some vegetarian food, this fantastic Indian restaurant will answer your prayers (meat dishes are also served) and the owner loves talking to backpackers.

Information

When in doubt, head to the Sabon Gari, a kind of foreigners area of the city.

Try the money changers at the craft stalls outside the Central Hotel; they'll also exchange West African CFA francs. The tourist office has a bureau de change.

Friends Internet (Murtala Mohammed Way; per hr N200) Also serves coffee, cakes and sandwiches.

Kano State Tourist Board (☎06 464 6309; Bompai Rd, Tourist Camp) A rarity in Nigeria – a working tourist office. Has pamphlets and can arrange guides to the Old City (N1500 per hour).

See & Sweet Bakery Cybercafé (Bompai Rd; per hr N250) Also a good place for a quick bite.

Getting There & Away

The airport is 8km northwest of Sabon Gari – N150 by *okada,* three times that in a taxi.

There are daily flights to Lagos (N20,000, 90 minutes) and Abuja (N15,000, one hour).

Overnight luxury buses to Lagos are found at the Sabon Gari and cost around N4000.

Kuka Motor Park is the motor park for the north and the Niger–Nigerian border. Naiwaba Motor Park serves points south and west. Sample fares and times: Zaria (N500, 90 minutes), Kaduna (N700, three hours), Maiduguri (N2000, six hours), Sokoto (N900, six hours) and Jos (N700, four hours).

Gashaka-Gumti National Park

Nigeria's largest national park, **Gashaka-Gumti** (admission N1000, vehicles N500) is also the remotest and least-explored part of the country. Its 6700-sq-km area contains rolling hills, savannah, montane forest – as wild and spectacular a corner of Africa as you could wish for. It also holds incredible diversity and is one of West Africa's most important primate habitats, as well as supporting lions, elephants, hippos and buffaloes.

The park is open year-round, although access is easiest during the dry season (December to March). The best way to visit is through the **Gashaka Primate Project** (www.ucl.ac.uk/gashaka), a UK-based conservation group that works with the park to protect the watershed and wildlife within. They have rooms for around N1500 a night, but you must bring your own food. It's important to get in touch with them first because you need to be prepared. There are also volunteer opportunities.

The park entrance is at Serti, 10 hours from Jos; from there head to the riverside park headquarters at **Gashaka** (campsites N200, chalets N300), or take an *okada* to Kwano (a further 12km), where the primate researchers are mainly based. Exploring with a guide, you can go chimp-tracking by foot (there are plentiful other monkeys to see too), or do a great two- or three-day hike to the mountains, via several Fulani villages. It's a truly magical place.

UNDERSTAND NIGERIA

Nigeria Today

After years of coups and military rule, Nigeria now has an elected leadership – international bodies declared President Goodluck Jonathan's 2011 victory as relatively free of violence and voter fraud. And Nigeria's explosive economic growth – due almost entirely to the influx of oil money – has ushered in a time of leaps in modernisation and development. But these advances haven't addressed entrenched government mismanagement, inaction and corruption. Images of barefoot children hawking fruit alongside slick SUVs are a reminder that new wealth doesn't often trickle down. While Lagos is awash in glitz, once outside major cities people often live as they did a hundred years ago.

In addition, President Goodluck Jonathan's government faces the challenge of stemming the jihadist-fueled violence of northern separatist group Boko Haram, who seek to overthrow the government and establish an Islamic state. The conflict has taken the lives of thousands in attacks that break along ethnic and religious fault lines.

History

Early Nigeria

Northern and southern Nigeria are essentially two different countries, and their histories reflect this disparity. The first recorded empire to flourish in this part of West Africa was Kanem-Borno around Lake Chad, which grew rich from the trans-Saharan trade routes. Islamic states based in the Hausa cities of Kano, Zaria and Nupe also flourished at this time.

Meanwhile, the southwest developed into a patchwork of small states, often dominated by the Yoruba. The Ijebu kingdom rose in the 10th century and constructed the mysterious earthworks at Sungbo's Eredo. Most famously the Benin kingdom became an important centre of trade and produced some of the finest metal artwork in Africa. In the southeast, the Igbo and other agrarian peoples never developed any centralised empires, instead forming loose confederations.

Colonial Era

The first contact between the Yoruba empires and the Europeans was made in the 15th century, when the Portuguese began trading in pepper and, later, slaves. In contrast, the northern Islamic states remained untouched by European influence until well into the 19th century.

In the early 19th century, the British took a lead in suppressing slavery along the Niger delta, leading to the annexation of Lagos port – a first colonial toehold. This led to further annexation to thwart the French, who were advancing their territory along the Niger River. By the beginning of the 20th century, British soldiers had advanced as far north as the cities of Kano and Sokoto, where Islamic revivalism had created a rapidly expanding caliphate.

Nigeria was divided in two – the southern, mainly Christian, colony and the northern Islamic protectorate. The British chose to rule indirectly through local kings and chiefs, exacerbating ethnic divisions for political expediency.

Military Misrule

These divisions came back to haunt Nigeria when independence came in October 1960. Politics split along ethnic lines, and in 1966 a group of Igbo army officers staged a coup. General Johnson Ironsi took over as head of state. Another coup quickly followed on its heels, along with massacres of Igbos, which in 1967 provoked civil war by secessionist Igbos.

The war dragged on for three years. Biafra was blockaded, and by the time its forces capitulated in 1970, up to a million Igbos had died, mainly from starvation.

An oil boom smoothed Nigeria's path to national reconciliation, but as the army jockeyed for political control, the next two decades were marked by a series of military coups, with only a brief democratic interlude in the early 1980s. When General Ibrahim Babangida offered elections in 1993, he annulled them when the result appeared to go against him, only to be toppled in a coup soon after by General Sani Abacha.

Abacha was ruthless, purging the army and locking up intellectuals, unionists and pro-democracy activists. His rule reached a nadir in 1995 with the judicial murder of the Ogoni activist Ken Saro-Wiwa, an act that led to Nigeria's expulsion from the Commonwealth.

Salvation finally came in June 1998, in what Nigerians called the 'coup from heaven'. Aged 54, and worth somewhere between US$2 billion and US$5 billion in stolen government money, Abacha died of a heart attack while in the company of two prostitutes. His successor immediately announced elections and, in February 1999, Olusegun Obasanjo, a former military leader, was returned as president.

Culture

With nearly 165 million people, Nigeria has a huge and expanding population. The main ethnic groups are the Yoruba (in the southwest), Hausa (north) and Igbo (southeast), each making up around a fifth of the population, followed by the northern Fulani (around 10%). It's thought that up to 250 languages are spoken in Nigeria.

Ordinary Nigerians struggle against systematic corruption through the natural entrepreneurship of one of Africa's better-educated populations.

American-style evangelical mega-churches have sprouted up everywhere, though in villages many traditional belief systems remain intact. The north is predominantly Muslim.

Chinua Achebe *(Things Fall Apart)* was probably Nigeria's most famous author; he died in March 2013. Equally acclaimed writers from Nigeria include the Nobel Laureate Wole Soyinka, Booker Prize–winner Ben Okri *(The Famished Road)* and Chimamanda Ngozi Adichie *(Half a Yellow Sun)*.

Some of Africa's best-known musicians have been Nigerian. Two styles have traditionally been dominant, Afrobeat and *juju*, with their respective masters being the late Fela Kuti and King Sunny Ade.

Food & Drink

Nigerians like their food ('chop') hot and starchy. The classic dish is a fiery pepper stew ('soup') with a little meat or fish and accompanied by starch – usually pounded yam or cassava (*garri*, *eba*, or the slightly sour *fufu*). Another popular dish is *jollof* – peppery rice cooked with palm oil and tomato. Cutlery isn't generally used – the yam or cassava is used to soak up the juices of the stew. As in most of Africa, you only eat with your right hand.

Environment

The north touches on the Sahel and is mostly savannah with low hills. Mountains are found only along the Cameroon border in the east, although there is a 1500m-high plateau around Jos in the centre of the country. The coast is an almost unbroken line of sandy beaches and lagoons running back to creeks and mangrove swamps and is very humid most of the year.

An underfunded national parks service does exist, but in practice very little land in Nigeria is effectively protected. The expanding population has contributed to widespread deforestation – 95% of the original forests have been logged. However, the oil industry has caused the greatest number of environmental problems: oil spills and gas flaring have damaged the fishing industry, with little of the industry's wealth trickling down to the local level.

SURVIVAL GUIDE

Directory A–Z

ACCOMMODATION

Hotels are of a fair standard throughout Nigeria, but they're expensive.

Lagos is particularly expensive; rooms are either very cheap and shoddy or very expensive – there's not much middle ground.

Watch and listen for the ubiquitous power cuts and the sound of generators striking up.

EMBASSIES & CONSULATES

Some embassies have yet to relocate from Lagos to Abuja.

Australian Embassy (☎09 461 2780; www.nigeria.embassy.gov.au; 48 Aguyi Ironsi St, 5th fl, Oakland Centre, Maitama, Abuja)

Beninese Embassy Abuja (☎09 413 8424; Yedseram St; 9am-4.30pm Mon-Fri); Lagos (Map p400; ☎01 261 4411; 4 Abudu Smith St, VI; 9am-11am Mon-Fri).

Burkinabé Embassy (Map p400; ☎01 268 1001; 15 Norman Williams St, Ikoyi, Lagos)

Cameroonian Embassy (☎01 261 2226; 5 Elsie Femi Pearse St, VI) Calabar (☎087-222782; 21 Ndidan Usang Iso Rd; 9am-3.30pm Mon-Fri);

Lagos (Map p400; ☎261 2226; 5 Femi Pearse St, VI; ⏰8am-11am Mon-Fri).

Canadian Embassy Abuja (☎09 413 9910; 15 Bobo St, Maitama); Lagos (Map p400; ☎01 262 2616; 4 Anifowoshe St, VI).

Dutch Embassy (☎01 261 3005; 24 Ozumba Mbadiwe Ave, VI, Lagos)

French Embassy (Map p400; ☎01 269 3430; 1 Oyinkan Abayomi Rd, Ikoyi, Lagos)

German Embassy (Map p400; ☎01 261 1011; 15 Walter Carrington Cres, VI, Lagos)

Ghanaian Embassy (☎01 263 0015; 23 King George V Rd, Lagos Island, Lagos)

Irish Embassy (☎09 413 1751; Plot 415 Negro Cres, off Aminu Kano, Maitama, Abuja)

Ivorian Embassy (☎01-261 0963; 5 Abudu Smith St, VI, Lagos)

Nigerien Embassy Abuja (☎01 413 6206; Pope John Paul II St; ⏰9am-3pm Mon-Fri); Kano (☎0806 548 1152; Airport Roundabout; ⏰9am-3pm Mon-Fri); Lagos (Map p400; ☎01 261 2300; 15 Adeola Odeku St, VI; ⏰9am-2.30pm Mon-Fri).

Spanish Embassy (☎01 261 5215; 21c Kofo Abayomi St, VI, Lagos)

Togolese Embassy (Map p400; ☎01 261 7449; Plot 976, Oju Olobun Cl, VI, Lagos)

UK Embassy Abuja (☎09 413 4559; www.ukinnigeria.fco.gov.uk; Aguyi Ironsi St, Dangote House, Maitama); Lagos (☎01 261 9531; 11 Walter Carrington Cres, VI).

US Embassy Abuja (☎09 461 4000; http://nigeria.usembassy.gov; Plot 1075, Diplomatic Dr, Central Business District); Lagos (Map p400; ☎01 261 0150; 2 Walter Carrington Cres, VI).

FESTIVALS & EVENTS

Thousands descend on Oshogbo in late August for the Osun Festival held in honour of the river goddess. Music, dancing and sacrifices form one of the centrepieces of the Yoruba cultural and spiritual year.

Calabar hosts a festival throughout December with concerts from national and international stars scheduled closer to Christmas. The highlight of the festival is the cultural masquerade carnival, when tens of thousand of costumed revellers descend on the city.

The Eyo Festival in Lagos is a large Yoruba masquerade organised to commemorate the life of a recently passed spiritual leader.

Around mid-February, the spectacular three-day Argungu Fishing and Cultural Festival in Argungu is held. Possibly the most interesting in the country, the festival has sadly been cancelled for the past few years due to politics.

Some of the most elaborate festivals are the celebrations in northern Nigeria (particularly in Kano, Zaria and Katsina) for two important Islamic holidays: the end of Ramadan, and Tabaski, 69 days later, which feature colourful processions of cavalry. Ramadan can be a tiring time to travel in the north – head for the Sabon Gari (foreigners' quarter) in each town, where food is served throughout the day.

The Igue (Ewere) Festival, held in Benin City, usually in the first half of December, has traditional dances, a mock battle and a procession to the palace to reaffirm loyalty to the *oba*. It marks the harvest of the first new yams of the season.

DASH

Used freely as both a noun and a verb, dash is a word you'll hear a lot in Nigeria. It can mean either a bribe or a tip. The most frequent form of dash you're likely to encounter is at police roadblocks. In large-scale corruption, money is referred to as 'chopped' (literally 'eaten'). Although you're actually unlikely to be asked for dash as a bribe, dashing someone who performs a service for you, such as a guide, is often appropriate.

INTERNET ACCESS

Decent connections are widespread in major towns, for around N200 per hour. Never use internet banking in a Nigerian cybercafe.

MONEY

The unit of currency is the naira (N). Bring higher-denomination dollars or pounds for the best exchange rate. ATMs are increasingly widespread and many are connected to international systems like Mastercard or Visa. GTB is the most reliable. Credit cards are accepted only a few places, and use them with caution. Notify your bank before you use your cards in Nigeria as fraud scams have made it a red-flag country for transactions.

There are money changers in each town and they are almost always Hausa.

Western Union branches are useless unless you have a Nigerian bank account.

OPENING HOURS

General business hours are from 8.30am to 5pm Monday to Friday. Sanitation days are held on the last Saturday of the month – traffic isn't allowed before 10am for street cleaning.

Banks 8am to 4pm weekdays, closed Saturday and Sunday.

Government offices 7.30am to 3.30pm Monday to Friday.

POST

Mail sent to or from Nigeria is notoriously slow. Worldwide postcards cost about N80. For parcels, use an international courier like DHL or FedEx, which have offices in most towns.

PUBLIC HOLIDAYS

New Year's Day 1 January
Easter March or April
May Day 1 May
National Day 1 October
Christmas 25 December
Boxing Day 26 December
Islamic holidays are observed in northern Nigeria.

SAFE TRAVEL

Lagos has a reputation for petty and violent crime, not always undeserved, although it's been on the decline in the past few years. As a traveller you're unlikely to have trouble with large-scale corruption and bribery. Police road-blocks are common, but fines and bribes are paid by the driver. Some caution should be exercised on the major highways into Lagos, where armed robbery is a problem at night.

Currently the most dangerous region is northern Nigeria, where Boko Haram, a militant jihadist organisation, wages a low-grade war against the federal government. Most Nigerians will tell you to avoid northern Nigeria altogether.

A previously troubled region of the country is the Niger delta. Recent amnesty agreements have quelled long-running grievances between the local population and the big oil companies.

Enugu has a reputation for kidnapping schemes, but they're more likely after wealthy oil execs rather than scruffy backpackers.

TELEPHONE

Nigeria is in love with the mobile phone, and cellular networks are more reliable than landlines. Having a local SIM card to use in a smart phone is extremely useful. The best service is Etisalat (SIMs cost N300), though MTN has the widest coverage. Street vendors everywhere sell top-up scratch cards.

Calls at roadside phone stands are quick and easy to make, costing around N20 per minute inside Nigeria, and around N60 for an international call. Most mobile numbers start with ☎080. The country code is ☎234.

VISAS

Everyone needs a visa to visit Nigeria, and applications can be quite a process. Many Nigerian embassies issue visas only to residents and nationals of the country in which the embassy is located, so it's essential to put things in motion well before your trip. Exact requirements vary, but as a rule of thumb, forms are required in triplicate, along with proof of funds to cover your stay, a round-trip air ticket, and possibly confirmed hotel reservations. You also need a letter of invitation from a resident of Nigeria or a business in the country. The cost of a 30-day visa is from US$70 to US$190, according to nationality.

If you're travelling overland to Nigeria, the embassy in Accra (Ghana) is consistently rated as the best place in West Africa to apply for a visa, as no letter of introduction is required. The embassy in Niamey (Niger) also claims to issue visas the same way.

Visa Extensions

Visas can reportedly be extended at the **Federal Secretariat** (Alagbon Cl, Ikoyi) in Lagos, but it's a byzantine process of endless forms, frustration and dash, with no clear sense of success.

Visas for Onward Travel

Benin One-month visas cost CFA15,000 (CFA, not naira), with two photos, and take 24 hours to issue. The embassy in Lagos carries an uninviting reputation, and unexpected extra fees are not unknown.

Cameroon A one-month single-entry visa costs CFA50,000 (CFA, not naira), with two photos, and is issued in a day. As well as Lagos and Abuja, there's a useful consulate in Calabar.

Chad Two photos and N5500 will get you a one-month single-entry visa, which you can pick up the next day.

Niger Best obtained in Abuja, a one-month single-entry visa costs N5300 with two photos, and is issued in 48 hours. The consulate in Kano (where the fee can also be paid in CFA) is also an excellent and speedy place to apply – take three photos.

PRACTICALITIES

Newspapers Privately owned English-language daily newspapers include the *Guardian, This Day, Punch* and *Vanguard*.
TV There are more than 30 national and state TV stations, broadcasting in English and all major local languages. South African satellite DSTV is hugely popular.
Electricity Supply is 220V. Plugs are square British three pin, but most hotels have European two-pin adaptors.
Languages English, Pidgin, Hausa, Yoruba, Igbo, Edo, Efik.

Getting There & Away

AIR

The vast majority of flights to Nigeria arrive in Lagos, although there are also international airports in Abuja, Port Harcourt and Kano. Airports are well organised and have official porters, but plenty of touts outside.

LAND

Benin

The main border crossing is on the Lagos to Cotonou (Benin) highway. Expect requests for bribes. There's a good direct Cotonou–Lagos bus service run by Nigerian bus company **ABC Transport** (☎01 326 1919, 01 879 3070; www.abctransport.com). An alternative border crossing is further north at Kétou on the Benin side.

Cameroon

There are two main border crossings. The northern border post is at Bama, 2½ hours from Maiduguri, across to Banki in Cameroon. A remote alternative crossing is at Ngala (Nigeria), which is used mainly for transiting to Chad.

The southern border crossing is at Mfum (Nigeria), near Ikom. The road infrastructure collapses pretty much as soon as you cross to Ekok (Cameroon), making this border problematic during the rainy season, so consider taking the Calabar–Limbe ferry instead during the wettest months.

Chad

Although there are no official border crossings between the two countries, it's possible to make a quick transit across Cameroon. In Nigeria, the border crossing into Cameroon is at Ngala. On the Cameroon side ask for a *laissez-passer* to allow you to make the two-hour traverse to the Chad border point at Kousséri.

Niger

There are four main entry points into Niger. The busiest is the Sokoto route, which crosses at Ilela (Nigeria). Minibuses and bush taxis run daily to the border, just past Ilela. Crossing to Birni N'Konni, you can get on a bus straight for Niamey. Travelling between Kano (Nigeria) and Zinder (Niger) is equally straightforward. The final option is between Katsina and Maradi.

From Niger, it's easiest to cross at Gaya. You'll probably have to hire a bush taxi to take you from the Nigerian side at Kamba on to Sokoto. Beware the potholes.

Note that there is heavy presence of security and more scrutiny because of Boko Haram, as it is believed that they have operations in Niger.

SEA

A ferry sails from Calabar to Limbe every Tuesday and Friday evening (N6000, five hours), returning on Monday and Thursday. It's an overnight trip in each direction. Your passport is collected on boarding and returned at immigration. Try to keep hold of your luggage – if it gets stowed in the hold, you'll be waiting hours to get it back.

Getting Around

AIR

Internal flights are a quick way of getting around Nigeria. Flights start at around N20,000. Most cities are linked by air to Lagos.

The most reliable domestic airlines with the best connections are Arik Air (p399) and Aero Contractors (p402).

CAR & MOTORCYCLE

Nigeria's road system is good. But the smooth, sealed roads allow Nigerians to exercise their latent talents as rally drivers and accident rates are high. The only real road rule is survival of the fittest.

Foreigners driving in Nigeria shouldn't get too much hassle at roadblocks, particularly if your vehicle has foreign plates. If you get asked for dash, a smile and some patience will often defuse the request. It's a legal requirement to wear a seatbelt; not doing so leaves you open to both official and 'unofficial' fines. Petrol stations are everywhere, but fuel shortages are common, causing huge queues and worsening the already terrible traffic. Diesel can sometimes be hard to come by, so keep your tank topped up.

LOCAL TRANSPORT

Each town has at least one motor park serving as the main transport depot full of minibuses and bush taxis.

Vehicles have signs on their roofs showing their destination, while touts shout out destinations. Minibuses don't run on any schedule but depart when full.

Bush taxis cost about 25% more, though true pricing is nearly impossible to ascertain.

MOTORCYCLE-TAXI

The quickest way to get around town is on the back of a motorcycle-taxi called an *okada* (*achaba* in the north). Because of their general lawlessness, the government has banned *okada* in a few of the major cities, badly affecting traffic and driving up the prices with drivers who are willing to flout the law.

TRAIN

There are still old rail lines in Nigeria, but no services are currently available. A project to relaunch the national railway service, starting in 2009, has stalled.

Senegal

POP 13.8 MILLION

Includes ➡

Best Places to Eat

- Chez Agnes (p431)
- Le Patio du Mar y Sol (p427)
- Cabane des Pêcheurs (p421)

Best Places to Stay

- Chez Valerie (p425)
- Lodge des Collines de Niassam (p427)
- La Maison Rose (p429)

Why Go?

One of West Africa's most stable countries is definitely not dull: the capital, Dakar, is a dizzying, street-hustler-rich introduction to the country. Perched on the tip of a peninsula, elegance meets chaos, noise, vibrant markets and glittering nightlife while nearby Île de Gorée and the beaches of Yoff and N'Gor tap to slow, lazy beats. In northern Senegal, the enigmatic capital of Saint-Louis, a Unesco World Heritage Site, tempts with colonial architecture and proximity to luscious national parks. Along the Petite Côte and Cap Skiring, wide strips of beaches beckon and the broad deltas of the Casamance River reveal hundreds of bird species, from the gleaming wings of tiny kingfishers to the proud poise of pink flamingos. Whether you want to mingle with the trendsetters of urban Africa or be alone with your thoughts and the sounds of nature, you'll find your place in Senegal.

When to Go

Dakar

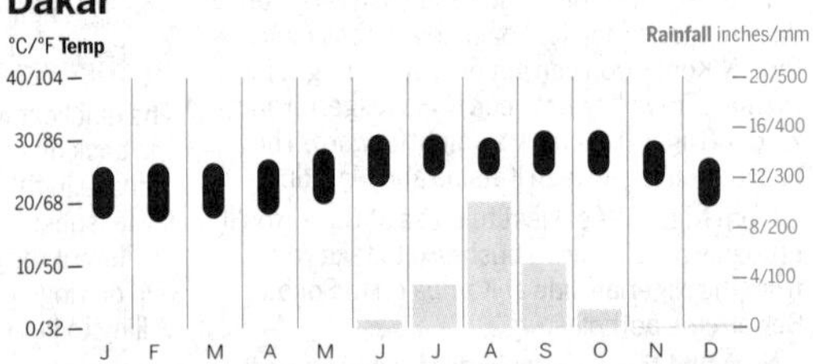

Nov–Feb Senegal's main tourist season is dry and cool.

Dec & Mar–Jun When most music festivals are on, including the Saint-Louis Jazz Festival (p429).

Jul–late Sep Rainy, humid season, but hotels reduce prices by up to 40%.

DAKAR

POP 2.9 MILLION

Once a tiny settlement in the south of the Cap Vert peninsula, Dakar now spreads almost across its entire triangle, and keeps growing. This is a city of contrasts, where horse-cart drivers chug over swish highways and gleaming SUVs squeeze through tiny sand roads, where elegant ladies dig skinny heels into dusty walkways and suit-clad businessmen kneel down for prayer in the middle of the street. A fascinating place – once you've learned how to beat its scamsters, hustlers and traders at their own game.

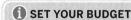

SET YOUR BUDGET

Budget

- Hotel room CFA25,000
- Sandwich or *shwarma* (kebab) CFA1000
- Soft drink CFA40
- Local bus ride CFA50

Midrange

- Hotel room CFA50,000
- Two-course dinner CFA6000
- Bottle of beer CFA50
- Short bush-taxi ride CFA500

Top End

- Hotel room CFA85000
- Two-course dinner CFA8000
- Glass of wine CFA100
- Short *sept-place* taxi ride CFA800

Sights

Place de l'Indépendance SQUARE

(Map p418) Dakar's central Place de l'Indépendance is the beating heart of the city. Symmetrically laid out and home to countless cars, crooks and 1960s concrete blocks, the square also contains majestic colonial buildings, including the Gouvernance (governor's office) and the Chambre de commerce (chamber of commerce).

Palais Présidentiel HISTORIC BUILDING

(Map p418; Ave Léopold Senghor) Surrounded by sumptuous gardens and guards in colonial-style uniforms, the presidential palace was originally built for the governors but now serves as the residence of the current sitting president. You can't go inside, but it's a popular spot to take photos of the stately 1907 structure and its regal guards.

Musée Théodore Monod MUSEUM

(Musée IFAN; Map p418; ☎33 823 9268; Pl de Soweto; adult/child CFA2300/200; ⏲9am-6pm Tue-Sun) The Musée Théodore Monod is one of the best museums in West Africa. The museum is a testament to African art and culture with over 9000 objects on display. Lively exhibits show masks and traditional dress across the region (including Mali, Guinea-Bissau, Benin and Nigeria) and provide an excellent overview of styles, without bombarding you with more than you can take in.

You can also see beautiful fabrics and carvings, drums, musical instruments and agricultural tools. A gallery behind the main building often houses excellent exhibitions of contemporary art.

Medina NEIGHBOURHOOD

A bustling popular quartier with tiny tailor's shops, a busy Marché Tilène and streets brimming with life, the Medina was built as a township for the local populace by the French during colonial days and is the birthplace of Senegalese superstar and current minister of culture Youssou N'Dour. Besides being a very real neighbourhood, where creative ideas and new trends grow between crammed, makeshift homes, it's also home to Dakar's 1664 **Grande Mosquée** (Map p416), impressive for its sheer size and landmark minaret.

★**Village des Arts** ARTS CENTRE

(Map p422; ☎33 835 7160; www.levillagedesarts.com; Rte de Yoff) An arts tour around Dakar is simply not complete with a visit to this famous art complex, where some of Senegal's most promising and established photographers, painters and sculptors create, shape and display their works in a large garden space. The on-site gallery shows a selection of their work and it's easy to grab a drink and chat to the friendly artists at the nearby restaurants.

Layen Mausoleum MONUMENT

(Map p422; Mbenguene & the beach; ⏲10am-6pm Sun-Thu) In Yoff village, take a look at the Layen Mausoleum, a shrine to the founder of the Layen Muslim brotherhood. Residents of Yoff are noted for their strong Islamic culture: smoking and drinking are not allowed and visitors should be appropriately dressed (meaning long skirts or trousers). It's right on the beach and its floors are made of sand.

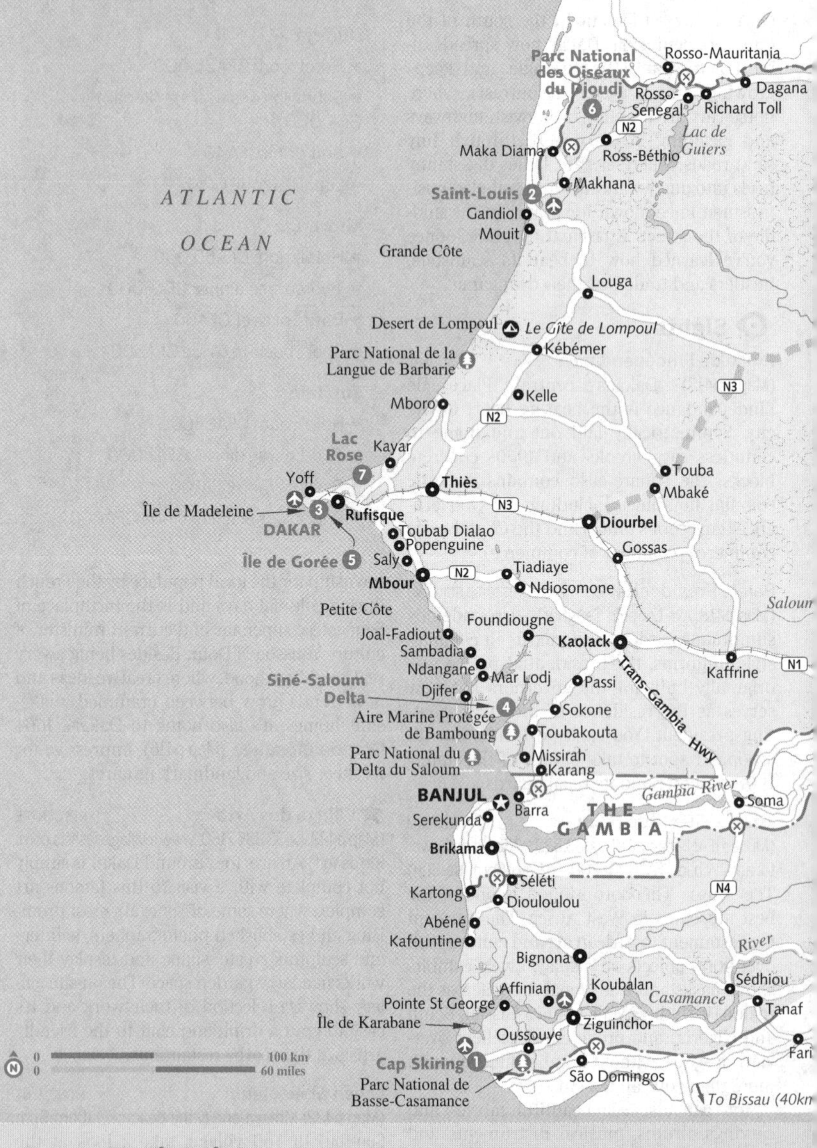

Senegal Highlights

1. Weaving your way via tiny villages to Senegal's best beaches on **Cap Skiring** (p435) and kicking back for a day of doing absolutely nothing.

2. Wandering in the footsteps of history in West Africa's first French settlement and Unesco World Heritage Site **Saint-Louis** (p429).

3. Spending sleepless nights touring the vibrant nightclubs, bars and concerts of **Dakar** (p421).

4. Winding through the mangroves of the **Siné-Saloum**

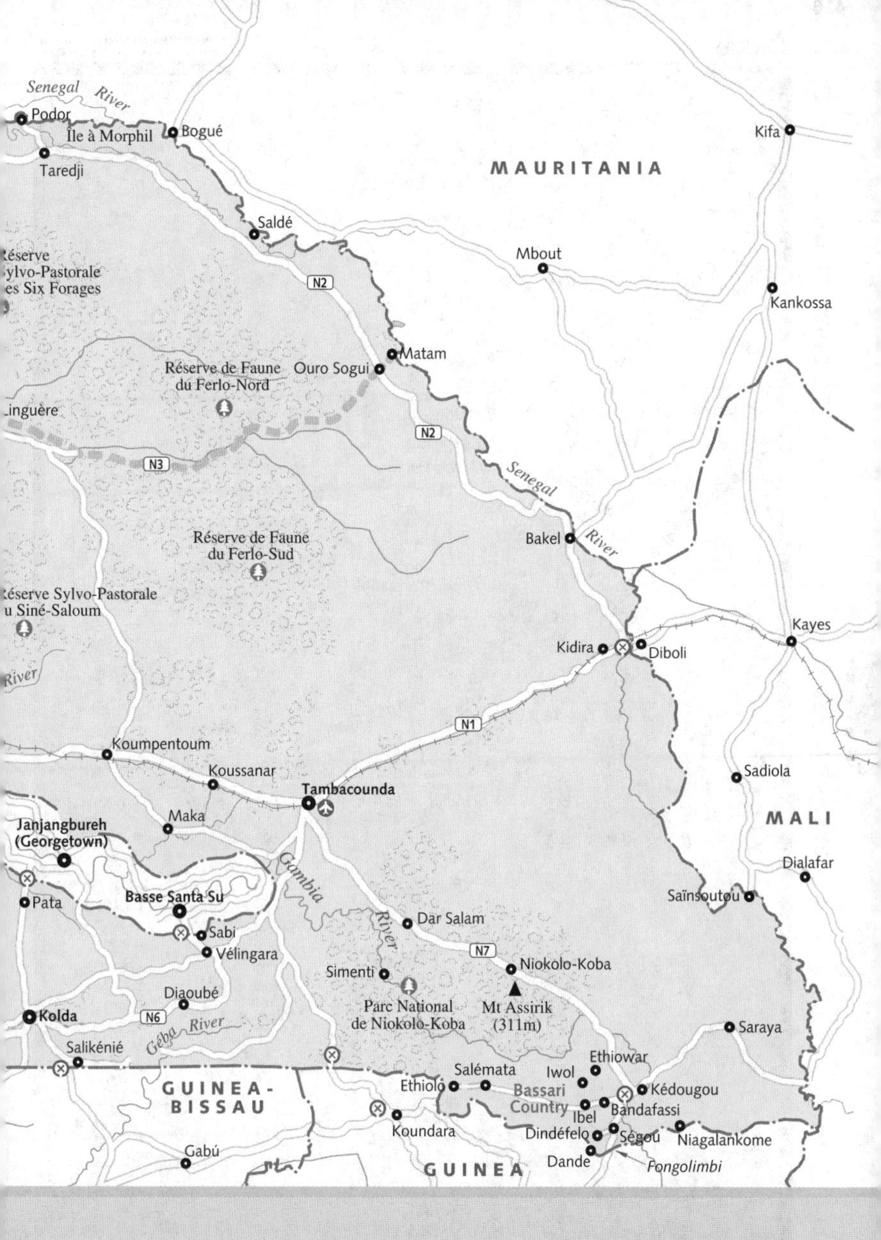

Delta (p426) in a *pirogue* (traditional canoe).

5 Contemplating history at **Maison des Esclaves** (p425) and breathing in the atmosphere of ancient peaceful **Île de Gorée** (p425).

6 Enjoying peaceful birdwatching at **Parc National des Oiseaux du Djoudj** (p432).

7 Floating on the salt-heavy **Lac Rose** (p426) and snap the otherworldly pics of the pink water contrasted with the bright blue sky.

Dakar

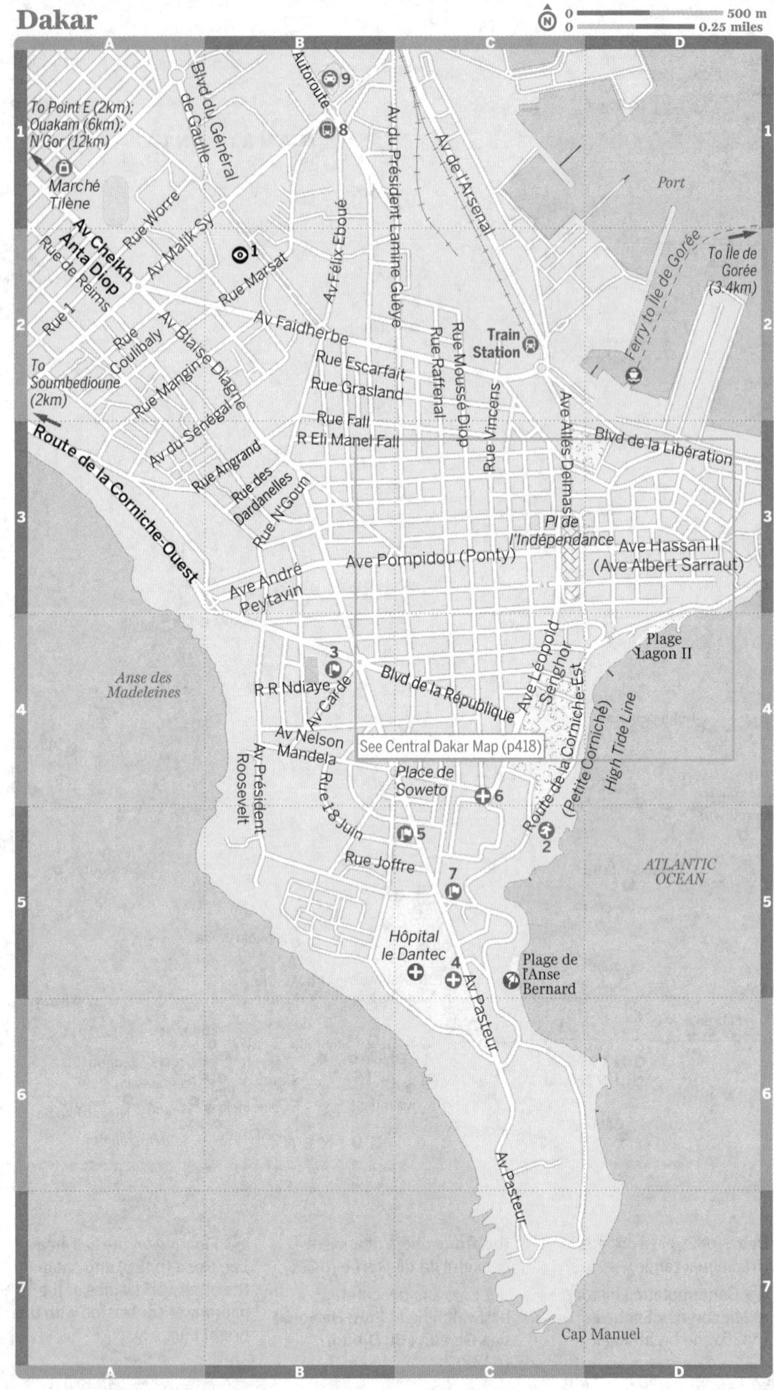

To Point E (2km); Ouakam (6km); N'Gor (12km)
Marché Tilène
Av Cheikh Anta Diop
Rue de Reims
Rue 1
Rue Worre
Av Malik Sy
Blvd du Général de Gaulle
Autoroute
Rue Marsat
Av Faidherbe
Rue Coulibaly
Av Blaise Diagne
Rue Mangin
To Soumbedioune (2km)
Av du Sénégal
Rue Angrand
Rue des Dardanelles
Rue N'Goun
Route de la Corniche-Ouest
Av Félix Eboué
Av du Président Lamine Guèye
Av de l'Arsenal
Port
To Île de Gorée (3.4km)
Ferry to Île de Gorée
Train Station
Rue Escarfait
Rue Grasland
Rue Fall
R Eli Manel Fall
Rue Raffenal
Rue Moussé Diop
Rue Vincens
Ave Allés Delmas
Blvd de la Libération
Pl de l'Indépendance
Ave Hassan II (Ave Albert Sarraut)
Ave Pompidou (Ponty)
Ave André Peytavin
Plage Lagon II
Anse des Madeleines
R R Ndiaye
Av Carde
Blvd de la République
Ave Léopold Senghor
Route de la Corniche-Est (Petite Corniche)
High Tide Line
Av Nelson Mandela
See Central Dakar Map (p418)
Av Président Roosevelt
Rue 18 Juin
Place de Soweto
Rue Joffre
ATLANTIC OCEAN
Hôpital le Dantec
Plage de l'Anse Bernard
Av Pasteur
Cap Manuel
500 m
0.25 miles

Dakar

Sights

1 Grande Mosquée B2

Activities, Courses & Tours

2 Océanium C5

Information

3 Canadian Embassy B4
4 Clinique de Cap C5
5 German Embassy C5
6 Hôpital Principal C4
7 UK Embassy C5

Transport

8 Car Mouride Bus Stop B1
9 Gare Routière Pompiers B1

Activities

Dakar's best beaches are found in the north of the peninsula. **Plage de N'Gor** (Map p422; admission CFA500) is often crowded; if so, you're better off catching the frequent *pirogues* (roughly CFA500 to CFA700 one way) to Île de N'Gor, which has two small beaches. In Yoff, **Plage de Virage** (Map p422) is good; **Plage de Yoff** (Map p422) is rubbish strewn in parts, but waves are strong enough for surfing. Dakar has decent waves and a growing surf scene. **Tribal Surf Shop** (Map p422; ☎33 820 5400; www.tribalsurfshop.net; Yoff Virage; ⏰10am-7pm) and **Pantcho Surf Trip** (Map p422; ☎77 534 6232; www.senegalsurf.com/pantchosurftrip; Plage de N'Gor) can point out additional surf spots, run courses and hire out boards.

Piscine Olympique SWIMMING
(Map p422; ☎33 869 0606; Tour de l'Œuf, Point E) The 50m pool of the Piscine Olympique is for serious swimmers.

Océanium WATERSPORTS
(Map p416; ☎33 822 2441; www.oceaniumdakar.org; Rte de la Corniche-Est; ⏰Mon-Sat) The environmental agency Océanium runs recommended kayak, diving and snorkeling excursions.

Sleeping

Dakar has a range of accommodation, from filthy doss houses to palatial hotels – although everything is expensive and the steadily increasing prices are only justified in a few places.

SenegalStyle Bed & Breakfast GUESTHOUSE $
(Map p422; ☎77 791 5469; SenegalStyle@gmail.com; Ouest Foire, Cite Africa; per person CFA32,000; 📶) Affable American-Senegalese owners who make you feel at home and happily arrange tours, ferry tickets, excursions, drumming lessons and more paired with snug, Africa-themed rooms a short walk from the beach make this of the best-value sleeps in town.

Keur Diame HOTEL, HOSTEL $
(Map p422; ☎33 855 8908; www.keurdiame-senegal.com; Parcelles Assainies; s/d incl breakfast CFA15,000/23,000; @📶) In a busy, local neighbourhood and close to Plage de Yoff, this friendly Swiss-owned hotel-hostel offers spotless rooms with mosquito nets and fans, plus a roof terrace.

Chez Nizar HOSTEL $
(Map p418; ☎77 319 1224; 25 Ave Pompidou; r CFA16,000) Nizar's basic rooms boast the charm of social housing, *but* this is essentially Dakar's backpacker hub and the cheapest digs in the city centre.

LES MAMELLES – DAKAR'S BREASTS

Mamelles means 'breasts', and you don't need a great amount of imagination to guess why the pair of sloping mounds that form Dakar's only two hills have been given that name. The pretty white 1864 **Mamelles lighthouse** (Map p422) graces the top of the first hill – a leisurely 25-minute walk up is rewarded with a sweeping view across the town and water.

The second hill is topped by the massive, North Korean–built **African Renaissance** (Map p422; admission CFA6500; ⏰10am-6pm) monument. Allegedly Africa's highest statue, at 49m high it's taller than New York City's Statue of Liberty and Rio de Janeiro's Christ the Redeemer and was unveiled in 2010 to commemorate Senegal's 50 years of independence from France. The Soviet-style bronze of a man, woman and child looking out to sea has been heavily criticised for its cost (over US$30 million), the un-African shapes of its figures and the scantily dressed female, which offers a partial view of her breast and thighs. You can walk around the base for free; the entry fee is for the interior of the monument. A small display explains its construction and an elevator whisks you up to the head of the male figure, boasting expansive views of Dakar.

Central Dakar

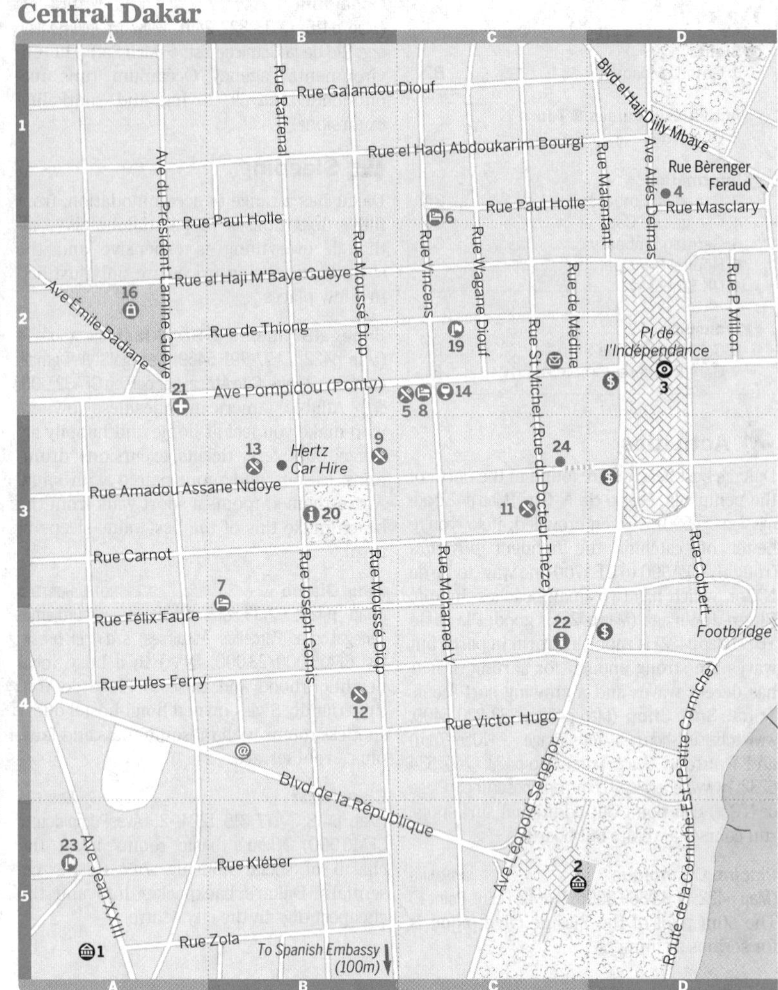

Hôtel du Phare HOTEL $
(Map p422; ☎33 860 3000; www.lesmamelles.com; Les Mamelles; s with/without bathroom CFA25,000/18,000, d CFA31,000/23,000; ❄@📶) This family-friendly, patio-adorned guesthouse has a handful of rooms with simple charm and a homely ambience.

★ **La Demeure** GUESTHOUSE $$
(Map p422; ☎33 820 7679; www.lademeure-guesthouse.com; Rte de Ngor; d CFA59,000-79,000; ❄📶🏊) Oozing laid-back elegance, this little guesthouse offers pleasant rooms (all with balconies) in a rambling, well-maintained house filled with a clutch of tasteful art collected by its engaging owner. It boasts a fantastic terrace and kitchen access in the afternoons and evenings.

La Brazzérade HOTEL $
(Map p422; ☎33 820 0683; www.labrazzerade.com; Plage de N'Gor; d/ste CFA30,000/50,000; ❄@📶) Known for its fabulous grill, this place has a hotel floor perched above the restaurant like a half-forgotten afterthought (or your little hideaway). The more expensive rooms have a small balcony and views over Île de N'Gor – an investment you should make.

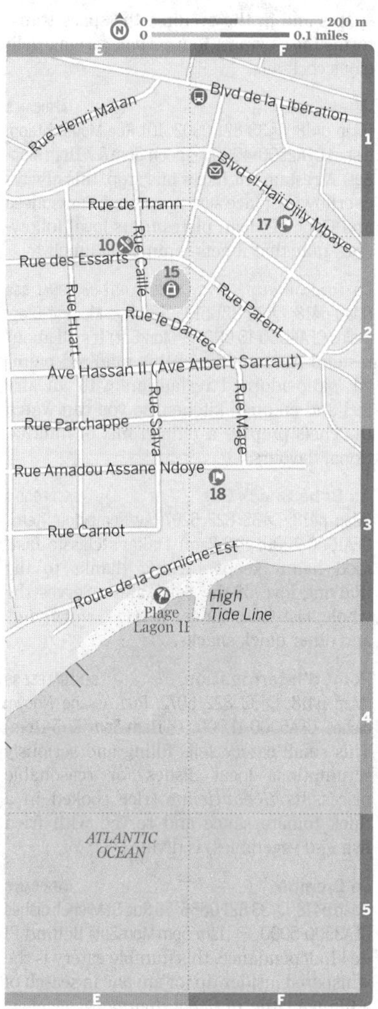

Central Dakar

Sights
1 Musée Théodore Monod....................A5
2 Palais Présidentiel..............................C5
3 Place de l'Indépendance....................D2

Activities, Courses & Tours
4 Sahel Découverte Bassari..................D1

Sleeping
5 Chez Nizar...C2
6 Hôtel Farid...C1
7 Hôtel Saint-Louis Sun........................B3

Eating
8 Ali Baba Snack Bar.............................C2
9 Chez Loutcha.......................................B3
10 Le Cozy...E2
11 Le Djembé...C3
12 Le Toukouleur.....................................B4
13 Point d'Interrogation..........................B3
Restaurant Farid.........................(see 6)

Drinking & Nightlife
14 Le Viking...C2

Shopping
15 Marché Kermel....................................E2
16 Marché Sandaga..................................A2

Information
17 Cape Verdean Embassy.......................F1
18 French Embassy..................................F3
19 Gambian Embassy...............................C2
20 Institut Français Léopold Sédar Senghor...B3
21 Pharmacie Guigon...............................A2
22 Senegal Tours......................................C4
23 US Embassy..A5

Transport
24 Senegal Airlines Agency.....................C3

Hôtel Saint-Louis Sun HOTEL $
(Map p418; ☎33 822 2570; htlstlouisun@orange.sn; Rue Félix Faure; s/d CFA25,000/33,000; ❄@) Rooms are pretty basic, but the central courtyard with huge palm trees turns the space into a calm oasis in the heart of Dakar.

Maison Abaka HOTEL $
(Map p422; ☎33 820 6486; www.maison-abaka.com; Plage de N'Gor; r from CFA38,000; ❄@📶🏊) This surfers' favourite has airy and lovingly decorated rooms located right behind the beach.

Hôtel Farid HOTEL $$
(Map p418; ☎33 821 6127; www.hotelfarid.com; 51 Rue Vincens; s/d from CFA41,000/45,000; ❄@📶) This small place with a fabulous Lebanese restaurant is by no means luxurious but is a safe and comfortable option in the city centre.

Ambre GUESTHOUSE $$
(Map p422; ☎33 820 6338; www.ambre.sn; Rte des Almadies; r from CFA52,000; ❄@📶🏊) Green, art adorned and beautifully designed, this small guesthouse is as friendly as a smile. A unique gem close to the city's best hotels and bars.

GETTING UNDER DAKAR'S SKIN

A brilliant way of getting to know Dakar and the rest of the country, its changeable moods and early-morning faces is by staying with a local family, sharing their lives for a few days and finding out what their world is really like. **Senegal Chez l'Habitant** (☎77 517 2666; www.senegalchezlhabitant.com) maintains a regularly updated register of families across Senegal who would like to open their houses to foreigners and puts you in touch with recommended families. The organisation checks the places it recommends and takes time to connect you with a home that fits your profile, from the most basic to the more luxurious stay.

Le Djoloff HOTEL **$$**
(Map p422; ☎33 889 3630; www.hoteldjoloff.com; 7 Rue Nani, Fann Hock; s/d/ste CFA55,000/70,000/130,000;) Designed to make you feel like Malian royalty, this place comes with a wide, wonderful roof terrace and a solid restaurant.

Radisson Blu HOTEL **$$$**
(Map p422; ☎33 869 3333; www.radissonblu.com; Rte de la Corniche-Ouest; d from CFA150,000;) As one of Dakar's most luxurious hotel, with a contemporary, business feel, this plush spot is a decadent place to enjoy all the standard upmarket trimmings.

Eating

Dakar's restaurant scene unites the scents and flavours of the world, though you need a healthy budget to eat out. If you're getting by on a few crumpled CFA notes a day, stop at the ubiquitous street stalls selling rice and sauce or one of the many *shwarma* places. The best-stocked supermarket is **Casino** (Map p422; ☎33 820 3361; Rte de N'Gor, in the Dakar City shopping complex; ⏲8am-8pm).

★**Le Cozy** INTERNATIONAL **$$$**
(Map p418; ☎33 823 0606; www.lecozy.com; Rue des Essarts; dishes CFA8000-14,000; ⏲noon-3pm & 7pm-midnight) Waltz through Le Cozy's heavy wooden doors and you're instantly swept off the market streets into a temple of refined cuisine. Presentation and service are as perfect as the swanky restaurant and bar spaces and in the evening, the space transforms into a smart lounge bar, serving delicious cocktails.

Chez Loutcha AFRICAN **$**
(Map p418; ☎33 821 0302; 101 Rue Moussé Diop; dishes CFA2500-4000; ⏲noon-3pm & 7-11pm Mon-Sat) A restaurant like a bus stop, this always overflowing place serves up huge Senegalese and Cape Verdean plates to its loyal followers – note that it gets rammed at lunch.

Le Toukouleur AFRICAN, INTERNATIONAL **$$$**
(Map p418; ☎33 821 5193; 122 Rue Moussé Diop; mains CFA6000-10,000; ⏲Mon-Sat) It's all about tasteful African chic in this mud-red painted, patio-adorned restaurant with an airy feel and an open kitchen, so you can watch the chefs prepare a refined mix of international flavours.

Ali Baba Snack Bar FAST FOOD **$**
(Map p418; ☎33 822 5297; Av Pompidou; items CFA1000-2000; ⏲8-2am) Dakar's classic fast-food haunt keeps turning thanks to the undying love of the Senegalese. Serves the whole fast-food range: kebabs, *shwarmas* and other quick snacks.

Point d'Interrogation SENEGALESE **$$**
(Map p418; ☎33 822 5072; Rue Assane Ndoye; dishes CFA5000-11,000; ⏲11am-3pm & 5-11pm) This small eatery sells filling and seriously scrumptious local dishes for reasonable prices. Its *tiéboutienne* (rice cooked in a thick tomato sauce and served with fried fish and vegetables) is divine.

Le Djembé AFRICAN **$**
(Map p418; ☎33 821 0666; 56 Rue St Michel; dishes CFA3500-5000; ⏲11am-5pm Mon-Sat) Behind Pl de l'Indépendance, this humble eatery is the whispered insider tip for anyone in search of a filling platter of *tiéboudienne*.

Restaurant Farid LEBANESE **$$**
(Map p418; ☎33 823 6123; 51 Rue Vincens; dishes CFA5800-14,000; ⏲noon-11pm;) Squeezed between grey inner-city walls, this little oasis serves the best Lebanese meze in town, plus quality grilled meat and fish.

Le Ngor SEAFOOD **$$**
(Map p422; ☎77 504 3006; Corniche des Almadies; dishes CFA5000-7500; ⏲11am-11pm Tue-Sat) At this quirky, seashell-adorned place, waves lap at your feet while you enjoy a perfectly grilled fish.

Le Récif des Almadies SEAFOOD $$
(Map p422; ☎33 820 1160; Pointe des Almadies; mains CFA5500-7800; ⊙noon-midnight Thu-Tue) Occupying a prime location right on the Pointe des Almadies with views across the Atlantic; the menu here is as big as a book and packed with seasonal dishes.

Sao Brasil ITALIAN $$
(Map p422; ☎33 820 0941; Rte de N'Gor, Station Shell; pizzas CFA6000; ⊙noon-4pm & 6.30pm-midnight;) Very confusingly named, this is one of Dakar's favourite restaurants (especially among the local expat community). Pizzas come with a huge diameter, a thin base and a large range of toppings.

★**Cabane des Pêcheurs** SEAFOOD $$
(Map p422; ☎33 820 7675; Plage de N'Gor; dishes CFA6000-10,000; ⊙11am-3pm & 7-11pm) Dakar's best fish restaurant serves you absolutely fresh treats, such as amberjack and dolphinfish, that you'll find hardly anywhere else in the city.

Drinking & Nightlife

There are bars to suit every taste in Dakar, but glam venues are mainly in the Les Almadies area. Live-music venues with dance floors are extremely popular, but nights on the dance floor start late – most places don't start to boogie before 1am. And always, always overdress. Bars are usually free, but cover charges at clubs and live-music venues are roughly CFA4000 to CFA12,000.

Le Viking PUB
(Map p418; ☎77 244 8056; 21 Ave Pompidou) At this old-style, beer-scented pub, the pints spill over and the guests are red-faced. Women will feel safer if they've come with a few friends.

INSTITUT FRANÇAIS LÉOPOLD SÉDAR SENGHOR

Dakar's **Institut Français Léopold Sédar Senghor** (Map p418; ☎33 823 0320; www.ifdakar.org; 89 Rue Joseph Gomis), a spacious arts centre occupying a whole city block, is one of the main hubs of cultural activity in Dakar. It features an open-air stage (a fantastic place to catch a live-music gig), a good cafe, and exhibition and cinema rooms, and also houses a couple of artists' workshops and shops in its vast garden.

DAKAR MARKETS

You need plenty of energy and a safe place to hide your purse for a Dakar market tour. **Marché Sandaga** (Map p418; cnr Ave Pompidou & Ave du Président Lamine Guèye) in the centre is the largest market, with rickety stalls that claim most of the area around Ave Pompidou. **Marché des HLM** (Map p422; Av CA Bamba) is stacked with dazzling African fabrics. **Marché Tilène** is chock-full of fruits, vegetables and tiny tailor shops. The **Village Artisanal Soumbédioune** (Map p422) is the most popular place for buying souvenirs such as wood carvings, metal work and batiks. Also in the town centre, the historical, covered **Marché Kermel** (Map p418) includes both souvenir and food stalls.

Le Patio BAR
(Map p422; ☎33 820 5823; Rte de N'Gor) Past the broad-shouldered bouncers and across the red carpet, this large outdoor place serves excellent cocktails within stumbling distance of the nightclubs.

New Africa BAR
(Map p422; ☎33 827 5371; 9794 Sacré Cœur III) This may be the only bar where there's no pressure to dress up and sparkle. The Friday salsa nights are fantastic.

Just 4 U LIVE MUSIC
(Map p422; ☎33 824 3250; www.just4udakar.com; Ave Cheikh Anta Diop; ⊙11am-3am) If you only have time for one live music venue, don't miss Just 4 U. The small stage of this outdoor restaurant has been graced by the greatest Senegalese and international stars, from jazz to rap to folk and reggae. There's a concert on every day, and you often get to catch the big names.

Pen'Art BLUES, JAZZ
(Map p422; ☎33 864 5131; Blvd du Sud) This cosy jazz club always impresses with good bands in a relaxed atmosphere.

Thiossane CLUB
(Map p422; Rue 10) Owned by Youssou N'Dour, one of Africa's most notable musicians and Senegal's tourism and culture minister, this legendary club is always packed and jamming to anything from *mbalax* to international beats.

Greater Dakar

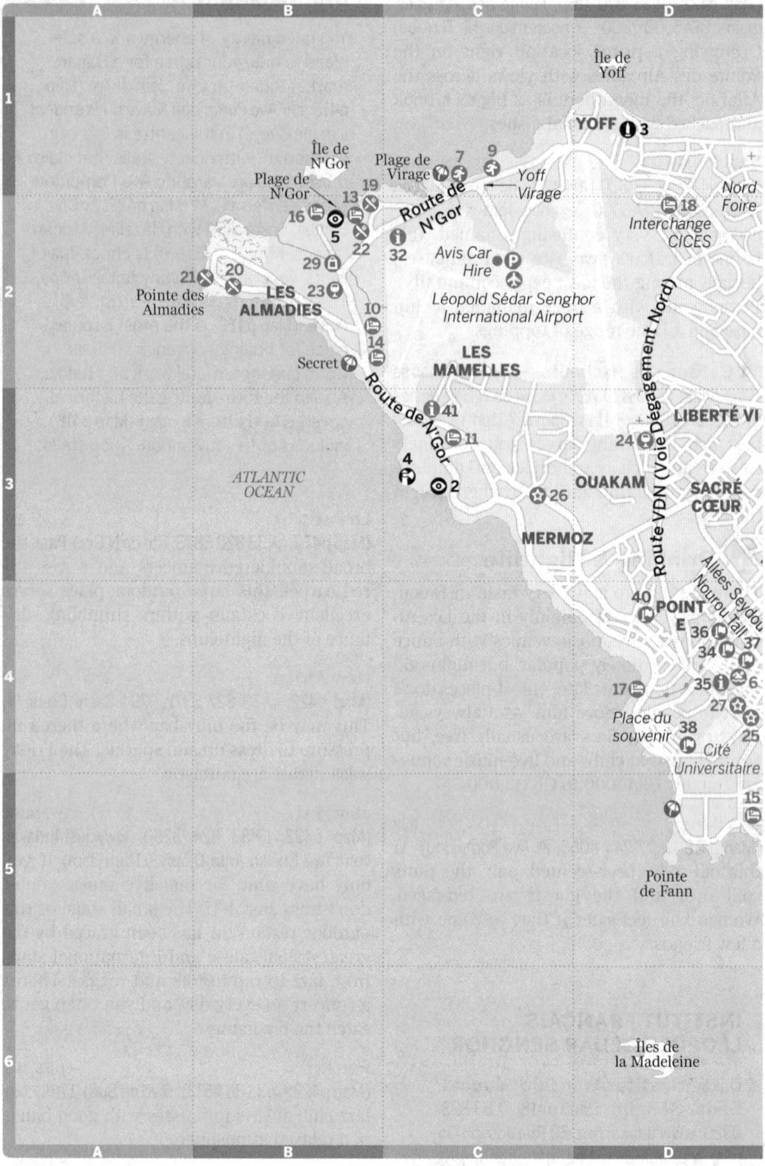

Le Balajo LIVE MUSIC
(Map p422; ☎33 864 51 00; Ave Cheikh Anta Diop; ⊙Thu-Sun) Excellent bar and venue for live music with mainly African bands.

Orientation

The expansive Pl de l'Indépendance is the city's heart. From here, major streets lead in all directions, including Ave Léopold Senghor and Ave Pompidou, which leads west to Marché Sandaga.

From here, Ave du Président Lamine Guèye goes north to Gare Routière Pompiers. The quickest route out of the centre is the coastal Rte de la Corniche-Ouest. To the north of the city centre lie the suburbs Point E, Fann, Mermoz and Ouakam, all of which have good bars and restaurants. The airport is 19km north of the town centre, and north of there are Les Almadies, Yoff and N'Gor, with Dakar's best beaches.

Information

CULTURAL CENTRES

British Council (Map p422; ☎33 869 2700; Rue AAB-68, Amitié Zone A&B) Has English magazines and occasional events.

Goethe Institut (Map p422; ☎33 869 8880; www.goethe.de/ins/sn/dak; cnr Rue de Diourbel & Piscine Olympique) The German cultural centre frequently hosts exhibitions and shows films.

INTERNET ACCESS

There are a few internet cafes, and wi-fi is spreading fast; it's offered free for customers in dozens of hotels and restaurants.

Espacetel Plus (☎33 822 9062; Blvd de la République; per hr CFA400; ⏰8am-midnight)

MEDIA

The exhaustive website www.au-senegal.com gives you an answer to almost any question about Senegal. Most parts of this French site are available in software-translated English.

The 221 section (CFA100) contains a cultural calendar, as well as interesting write-ups on music, arts and sports around the country.

MEDICAL SERVICES

Hospitals are understaffed and underequipped; for faster service try a private clinic. Pharmacies are plentiful in Dakar; most are open 8am to 8pm Monday to Saturday but rotate with 24-hour shifts.

Clinique de Cap (Map p416; ☎33 821 6146; www.cliniqueducap.com; Ave Pasteur) One of the biggest private medical clinics in Dakar.

Hôpital Principal (Map p416; ☎33 839 5050; www.hopitalprincipal.sn; 1 Ave Nelson Mandéla) Main hospital and emergency department.

Pharmacie Guigon (Map p418; ☎33 823 0333; 1 Ave du Président Lamine Guèye; ⏰8am-11pm Mon-Sat) One of the best-stocked options.

MONEY

ATM-equipped banks are never too far away in Dakar. Main branches are at Place de l'Indépendance.

POST & TELEPHONE

There are many small *télécentres* (call centres); post offices also have telephone facilities.

SAFE TRAVEL

Dakar's notorious street hustlers and hard-to-shake-off traders do a pretty good job at turning any walk around town into mild punishment, particularly for women. Stride purposefully on, and throw in a brief *bakhna* ('it's OK') and they'll eventually leave you alone. Many of them also

Greater Dakar

Top Sights
1 Village des Arts E2

Sights
2 African Renaissance Monument C3
3 Layen Mausoleum D1
4 Mamelles Lighthouse C3
5 Plage de N'Gor B2

Activities, Courses & Tours
Pantcho Surf Trip ......(see 16)
6 Piscine Olympique D4
7 Plage de Virage C1
8 Plage de Yoff E1
9 Tribal Surf Shop C1

Sleeping
10 Ambre B2
11 Hôtel du Phare C3
12 Keur Diame E1
13 La Brazzérade B2
14 La Demeure B2
15 Le Djoloff D5
16 Maison Abaka B2
17 Radisson Blu D4
18 SenegalStyle Bed & Breakfast D2

Eating
19 Cabane des Pêcheurs B2
20 Le Ngor B2
21 Le Récif des Almadies B2
22 Sao Brasil B2

Drinking & Nightlife
23 Le Patio B2
24 New Africa D3

Entertainment
25 Just 4 U D4
26 Le Balajo C3
27 Pen'Art D4
28 Thiossane E4

Shopping
29 Casino B2
30 Marché des HLM E4
31 Village Artisanal Soumbédioune E5

Information
32 ATG C2
33 British Council E4
34 Ghanian Embassy D4
35 Goethe Institut D4
Guinea-Bissau Embassy ......(see 34)
36 Guinean Embassy D4
37 Ivorian Embassy D4
38 Malian Embassy D4
39 Mauritanian Embassy E4
40 Moroccan Embassy D4
41 Nouvelles Frontières C3

double as pickpockets – be particularly vigilant at markets and in town.

Muggings – often at knifepoint or from passing scooters – are not uncommon. Avoid walking around after dark. Trouble spots include the Petite Corniche (behind the presidential palace), the Rte de la Corniche-Ouest and the beaches.

TRAVEL AGENCIES

ATG (Map p422; ☎33 869 7900; www.africa-travel-group.com; Rte de N'Gor; ⏰10am-6pm Mon-Fri, to 1pm Sat) Great for tours.

Nouvelles Frontières (Map p422; ☎33 859 4447; www.nfsenegal.com; Rte des Almadies, Lot 1 Mamelles Aviation; ⏰8.30am-6pm Mon-Fri, 9am-12.30pm Sat)

Senegal Tours (Map p418; ☎33 839 9900; www.senegal-tours.sn; 5 Pl de l'Indépendance; ⏰9am-6pm Mon-Fri, to noon Sat) Large tour operator that does ticketing and tours.

Getting There & Away

AIR

Léopold Sédar Senghor International Airport (p439) is in Yoff. Senegal Airlines (p440) flies to and from 15 destinations across Central and West Africa (including Cap Skiring and Ziguinchor in Senegal and Banjul in the Gambia), at the time of research, with plans to expand the network. It also operates a **ticket office downtown** (Map p418; ☎33 839 77 77; Rue Amadou Assane Ndoye/Rotunda Building; ⏰9am-6pm Mon-Fri, to noon Sat).

BOAT

Aline Sitoé Diatta Ferry Dakar-Ziguinchor Ticket Office (☎33 849 4893; 1 Blvd de la Libération; one way CFA16,000-31,000) The Aline Sitoé Diatta ferry travels between Dakar and Ziguinchor twice weekly in each direction, leaving Dakar every Tuesday and Friday at 8pm, arriving in Ziguinchor the next day at 10am. Note that you *cannot* buy tickets over the phone.

BUSH TAXI

Road transport for long-distance destinations leaves from Gare Routière Pompiers, off Ave Malik Sy (a taxi from Place de l'Indépendance should cost around CFA2000). Rates are fixed but change frequently with fluctuations in the cost of petrol. Main destinations include Mbour (CFA3000), Saint-Louis (CFA4900), Karang at the Gambian border (CFA5800), Tambacounda (CFA9800) and Ziguinchor (CFA12,000).

TRAIN

Dakar's train station is 500m north of Place de l'Indépendance. In the past there has been an unreliable line between Dakar and Bamako (Mali), but at the time of research it was not running.

Getting Around

Most car-hire agencies in Dakar (see map p422) are at the airport or in the city centre.

BUS

Dakar Dem Dikk (DDD; www.demdikk.com) buses are a pretty good way of travelling cheaply. There are several connections to the town centre. Fares cost beween CFA150 and CFA275. They're quite reliable and only crammed full during rush hour. Check the website for a detailed list of DDD routes.

More frequent but less user-friendly are the white Ndiaga Ndiaye minivans and the blue-yellow *cars rapides*, Dakar's battered, crammed and dangerously driven symbols of identity. Unless you know your way around, it's hard to find out where they are going. They stop randomly and suddenly – tap a coin on the roof to signal that you're getting off.

TAXI

Taxis are the easiest way of getting around town. Rates are entirely negotiable. A short hop costs from CFA600 upwards. Dakar centre to Point E is around CFA1700; it's up to CFA2700 from the centre to N'Gor and Yoff.

The official taxi rates for trips from Léopold Sédar Senghor International Airport are put up outside the airport. Don't pay more.

AROUND DAKAR

Île de Gorée

Ruled in succession by the Portuguese, Dutch, English and French, the historical, Unesco-designated Île de Gorée is enveloped by an almost eerie calm. There are no sealed roads and no cars on this island, just narrow alleyways with trailing bougainvilleas and colonial brick buildings with wrought-iron balconies – it's a living, visual masterpiece. But Gorée's calm is not so much romantic as meditative, as the ancient, elegant buildings bear witness to the island's role in the Atlantic slave trade.

You pay a tourist tax of CFA600 at the booth to the left of the ferry landing. If you need a guide, you can arrange it there, but the island is easily explored independently.

Sights & Activities

Gorée is an internationally famous symbol of the tragedy of the Atlantic slave trade. Though relatively few slaves were actually shipped from here, the island was a place where much of the trade was orchestrated. Many artists also live here and their work is displayed at various small art galleries around town.

★Maison des Esclaves MUSEUM
(Slave House; admission CFA600; ⏲10am-noon & 2.30-6.30pm Tue-Sun) Set in a former grand home, allegedly used as a departure point for slaves (see boxed text p426), this is one of the most important monuments to the slave trade and features the famous 'doorway to nowhere' opening directly to the sea.

IFAN Historical Museum MUSEUM
(☎33 822 2003; admission CFA600; ⏲10am-noon & 2.30-6pm Tue-Sat) Contains ancient island maps, photos and artefacts under low, white arcs. Note: when you walk upstairs you're greated by fabulous views of Dakar.

Castel HILL
Climb to the top of the Castel, the southern tip of the island, for great views, and seek out the cluster of tiny arts workshops filled with pieces by local artists.

Sleeping & Eating

Many Gorée residents keep a spare room for unexpected (and paying) visitors – just ask around and someone will know someone. Prices per person start at around CFA9000 per night.

For cheaper food options than the Hostellerie, check out any of the many eateries opposite the jetty.

★Chez Valerie GUESTHOUSE $
(☎33 821 8195; csaodakar@orange.sn; 7 Rue St Joseph; r CFA15,000-20,000; 📶) One of the prettiest and friendliest private options is Chez Valerie, an old Goréen house.

Hostellerie du Chevalier de Boufflers FRENCH $$
(☎33 822 5364; r from CFA18,000-23,000; 📶) Set in one of Gorée's classic elegant old homes, this place is mainly famous for its garden restaurant serving seafood-focused fare (meals CFA5000-7000) but also offers five tasteful rooms.

THE SLAVE HOUSE

Île de Gorée was an important trading station during the 18th and 19th centuries, and many merchants built houses in which they would live or work in the upper storey and store their human cargo on the lower floor.

La Maison des Esclaves (The Slave House; p425) is one of the last remaining 18th-century buildings of this type on Gorée. It was built in 1786 and renovated in 1990 with French assistance. With its famous 'doorway to nowhere' opening directly from the storeroom onto the sea, this building has enormous spiritual significance for some visitors, particularly African Americans whose ancestors were brought from Africa as slaves.

Walking around the dimly lit dungeons, you can begin to imagine the suffering of the people held here. It is this emotive illustration that really describes La Maison des Esclaves as a whole – its historical significance in the slave trade may not have been huge, but the island's symbolic role is immense.

The island's precise status as a slave-trading station is hotly debated. Of the 20 million slaves that were taken from Africa, the general belief is that only around 300 per year may have gone through Gorée (historians and academics dispute the exact number and some argue that no slaves passed through this specific house) and, even then, the famous doorway would not have been used – ships could not get near the dangerous rocks and the town had a jetty a short distance away.

But the number of slaves transported from here isn't what matters in the debate around Gorée. The island and museum stands as a melancholy reminder of the suffering the Atlantic slave trade inflicted on African people.

Getting There & Away

A **ferry** (☎33 849 7961, 24hr info line 77 628 1111) runs regularly from the wharf in Dakar to Gorée (CFA6000 return for nonresidents, 20 minutes).

Lac Rose

Also known as Lac Retba, this shallow lagoon surrounded by dunes is a popular day-trip destination for *dakarois* and tourists alike, all coming to enjoy the calm and catch the lake's magic trick – the subtle pink shimmer that sometimes colours its waves. The spectacle is caused by the water's high salt content, which is 10 times that of your regular ocean. It's a beautiful sight but can only be enjoyed when the light is right. Your best chance is in dry season, when the sun is high. But even if nature refuses to put on her show, a day out here is still enjoyable. You can swim in the lake, buoyed by the salt, or check out the small-scale salt-collecting industry on its shores. And up until the demise of the Dakar rally, Lac Rose is where the Sahara drivers would arrive and celebrate their victories or drown their woes.

Most hotels here are clustered near the Village Artisanal, a spot that's plagued by touts and hustlers. One of the cheapest is **Chez Salim** (☎33 836 2466; www.chez-salim.com; d CFA20,000; wi-fi), with well-maintained bungalows set in a garden, but the best place is **Chevaux du Lac** (☎77 630 0241; www.chevauxdulac.com; half board CFA22,000; horseback tours 1½/3hr CFA12,000/20,000; air-con, wi-fi) on the other end of the lake. It's friendly and welcoming and offers tours around the lake on horseback.

Trying to get here by public transport involves a journey by minibus, *car rapide* (CFA600) or DDD bus 11 to Keur Massar; from there it's a 5km walk to the lake. It's much easier to hire a private taxi (round trip with some waiting time costs around CFA18,000).

PETITE CÔTE & SINÉ-SALOUM DELTA

The 150km Petite Côte stretches south from Dakar and is one of Senegal's best beach areas. Where the Siné and Saloum Rivers meet the tidal waters of the Atlantic Ocean, the coast is broken into a stunning area of mangrove swamps, lagoons, forests and sand islands. It forms part of the magnificent 180-sq-km Siné-Saloum Delta.

Mbour & Saly

Eighty kilometres south of Dakar, Mbour is the main town on the Petite Côte and the region's most vibrant and important fishing centre. Nearby Saly, with its strip of big ocean-front hotels, is the heavier weight when it comes to tourism.

Mbour's busy, slightly nauseating fish market on the beach, where the catch is immediately gutted and dispatched, is a sight to behold. **Chez Martine La Suissesse** (☎33 957 3109; Mbour; d incl breakfast CFA12,000-18,000) is a mere 100m from the beach and offers simple, clean rooms. **Tama Lodge** (☎33 957 0040; www.tamalodge.com; Mbour; s/d from CFA35,000/48,000; @) has exquisitely designed bungalows, an eclectic art collection scattered around the property and a great restaurant, while the simple **New Blue Africa** (☎33 957 0993; Rte de Niakhniakhal, Mbour; s/d CFA35,000/42,000) sits on Mbour's finest dune. Perennially popular **Chez Paolo** (☎33 957 1310; Mbour; mains CFA3000-4500) is the local favourite and serves up super Senegalese dishes in modest digs.

If it's a beach holiday you're after, then Saly is the perfect corner for soaking up the sun and sipping cocktails. **Ferme de Saly & Les Amazones** (☎77 638 4790; www.farmsaly.com; Saly; d CFA20,000-36,000, apt CFA40,000-50,000) is a classic with overlanders, a place of sound sleep, good food and the generous company of host Jean-Paul. Nearer Saly village, **La Medina** (☎33 957 4993; Terrain de Football, Saly village; s/d CFA17,000/22,000; @) has good, clean rooms surrounding a leafy patio. For a splurge try the bright and classy bungalows with private, sunny terraces at **Espadon** (☎33 939 7099; www.espadon-hotel.com; Saly; s/d incl breakfast CFA72,000/120,000 ;) – the hotel restaurant (international fare) is stellar and there's a great wellness centre for relaxation. For a daytime dose of fresh seafood with a view of the beach hit **Les Tables du Marlin** (☎33 957 2477; Saly; mains CFA3000-8000; 10am-7pm), but the best food is dished up at **Le Patio du Mar y Sol** (☎33 957 0777; Saly; mains CFA5000-9000), where you can dine on luscious French fare, poolside with a chilled beverage.

Joal-Fadiout

The twin villages of Joal and Fadiout are located south of Mbour at the end of the tar road. Joal sits on the mainland, while Fadiout is on a small island made of clam and oyster shells (even the houses, streets and cemeteries!), reached by an impressive wooden bridge. It's dreamy to wander around the island's narrow alleys, admire the shell-world and pop into artisan workshops dotted around. Your best bets for lodging are on Joal, but it's an easy hop to the island. Culturally, the local citizens are proud of their tolerance – this is a place where Christians and Muslims live in harmony.

The tiny auberge **Le Thiouraye** (☎77 515 6064; Joal; s/d incl breakfast CFA12,000/14,000;) has basic riverside rooms and a menu composed by one of Senegal's top chefs. **Keur Seynabou** (☎33 957 6744; www.keurseynabou.com; Joal; r CFA35,000-40,000; @) sparkles with magazine-perfect lodgings overlooking a pool.

Minibuses go to/from Mbour (CFA800) and Palmarin (CFA1400). A *sept-place* taxi goes directly to Dakar most mornings (without changing at Mbour) for CFA3000.

Palmarin

Palmarin, with its soft lagoons, tall palm groves and labyrinthine creeks, is one of Senegal's most beautiful, and secret, spots.

There's a seductive choice of *campements* (guesthouses). The straw huts of **Yokam** (☎77 567 0113; Palmarin Facao; per person incl breakfast CFA9000) are cheap and lightweight, but the company is good. The red-mud structure of **Lodge de Diakhamor** (☎33 957 1256; Palmarin; s/d with half board CFA26,000/46,000; @) is a stylish redbrick place where *pirogue* excursions, horse riding, and bicycle and fishing trips are all included in the price. **Lodge des Collines de Niassam** (☎77 639 0639; www.niassam.com; Palmarin; per person with half board CFA59,000; @) is one of Senegal's most original *campements*. You can sleep in classy tree houses that cling to the mighty branches of baobabs, or sit on stilts in the river.

Palmarin is most easily reached by minibus from Mbour, via Joal-Fadiout and Sambadia (where you may have to change). The fare from Joal to Sambadia is CFA600 in a Ndiaga Ndiaye, and from Sambadia to Palmarin it's CFA450.

Ndangane & Mar Lodj

Siné-Saloum Delta's Ndangane is a thriving traveller centre along the coast from where you can take a *pirogue* to almost any point in the delta. Ndangane's cheapie is the lively

BIRDWATCHING & MORE IN PARC NATIONAL DU DELTA DU SALOUM

Covering over 76,000 hectares of mangrove-lined creeks, sandy islands, large sea areas and woodland, the **Parc National du Delta du Saloum** (admission CFA2000) is Senegal's second-largest national park. Beyond the mangrove swamps and a large marine section its main attraction is the fantastically varied landscape and the hundreds of bird species it attracts in the south. In the gallery forest and savannah woodlands of the Forêt de Fathala you might also spot wild boars and patas monkeys. You need a bit of luck to view the park's common duikers, bushbucks and red colobus monkeys – they're becoming very rare as human settlements, deforestation and hunting impact on the park, despite its protected status.

But if birds are your focus, Toubakouta offers enough bird life to have keen spotters stay here for days. It's mostly an area for sea birds and waders, though the nearby forest areas house some other species, including hornbills and sunbirds.

A good place to start a birdwatching tour is Diorom Boumag, an ancient seashell mound where giant baobabs have taken root, a 20-minute *pirogue* ride from Toubakouta. In their branches nestle numerous Senegalese parrots and rose-ringed parakeets. It's best to visit this place by *pirogue* in the late afternoon and move further along the river to arrive around dusk at the Reposoir des Oiseaux, where you can watch swarms of pelicans, cormorants, egrets and plenty of other species prepare noisily for the night.

The northern creeks and wetlands of the park can be explored on *pirogue* tours from Palmarin, Dionewar or Djifer. The Forêt de Fathala and the southern islands are best reached from Missirah.

Le Barracuda (Chez Mbacke; ☎33 949 9815; Ndangane; r per person CFA7000), with great views from the restaurant terrace. Brightly coloured **Auberge Bouffe** (☎33 949 9313; www.aubergebouffe.com; Ndangane; d CFA22,000; @ 🛜 ≋) has well-maintained rooms and plenty of character. Opposite, **Les Cordons Bleus** (☎33 949 9312; www.lescordonsbleus.com; Ndangane; s/d/tr CFA34,000/46,000/58,000; P ❄ @ 🛜 ≋) has the best rooms in town.

Mar Lodj island is a much calmer choice, especially if you bunk at **Le Bazouk** (☎77 633 4894; www.bazoukdusaloum.com; Mar Lodj; per person with half board CFA18,000), with its spacious bungalows scattered over a vast, sand-covered garden in which bougainvilleas lend shade and palm trees carry hammocks. **Essamaye** (☎77 555 3667; www.senegalia.com; Marfafako; per person with full board CFA22,000) on the other side of the island is a place like a hug from a loved one – highly recommended for family vibes and its impressive Casamance-style *case à l'impluvium* (large, round traditional house).

Take any bus between Kaolack and Mbour, and get off at Ndiosomone, from where bush taxis shuttle back and forth to Ndangane. For Mar Lodj, contact your *campement* for *pirogue* pick-up, or hire a boat at the **GIE des Piroguiers** (☎77 226 6168, 77 213 7497), the boat owners association at the jetty in Ndangane.

Toubakouta & Missirah

Toubakouta is a fantastically calm and pretty spot in the south of the Siné-Saloum Delta, and is one of the country's best places for birdwatching. In town, **Keur Youssou** (☎33 948 7728; www.keuryoussou.com; Toubakouta; s/d CFA7700/13,000; ❄) has beautifully furnished rooms and a relaxed ambience. **Keur Thierry** (☎77 439 8605; Toubakouta; d incl breakfast CFA14,000; ❄) has equally lovely rooms but the better kitchen and colder beers. **Hôtel Keur Saloum** (☎33 948 7715; www.keursaloum.com; Toubakouta; s/d incl breakfast CFA38,000/58,000; P ❄ @ 🛜 ≋) is the classiest place in town. A *pirogue* and donkey-cart ride away, **Keur Bamboung** (☎77 510 8013; www.oceanium.org; bungalows with half/full board CFA17,000/22,000) is the hub of the Marine Protected Area surrounding it. Things are simple and green, and the location is stunning. Phone to arrange pick-up from Toubakouta.

South of Toubakouta, Missirah is the point of entry to the Parc National du Delta du Saloum. The peaceful **Gîte de Bandiala** (☎33 948 7735; www.gite-bandiala.com; Missirah; per person with half/full board CFA16,900/23,200) sits right on its edge, has a water hole on site and organises tours through the Forêt de Fathala.

A private taxi from Toubakouta to Missirah costs around CFA6200.

NORTHERN SENEGAL

Saint-Louis

POP 172,000

With its crumbling colonial architecture, horse-drawn carts and peaceful ambience, West Africa's first French settlement has a unique historical charm – so much so it's been a Unesco World Heritage Site since 2000. The old town centre sits on an island in the Senegal River, but the city sprawls into Sor on the mainland, and onto the Langue de Barbarie, where you'll find the lively fishing community of Guet N'Dar.

The island is reached via the 500m-long Pont Faidherbe, a feat of 19th-century engineering.

Sights & Activities

Place Faidherbe SQUARE

With its statue of the French governor who led the colonial expansion eastwards and initiated many ambitious infrastructural projects, this square sits adjacent to several intact 19th-century houses, including the **Governor's Palace** and the 1837 **Rognât Casernes** on its north and south. Next to the governor's palace, you'll find a lovely 1828 **cathedral** (Rue de l'Eglise) with a neoclassical facade worth admiring. This central space is where Saint-Louis splits into its southern part (Sindoné) and northern part (Lodo); the former the old Christian town, the latter the original home to the Muslim population.

★**Pont Faidherbe** BRIDGE

(Senegal River) Transferred to Saint-Louis in 1897, the metal arches of this bridge designed by Gustav Eiffel and originally built to cross the Danube, the Pont Faidherbe is the city's most significant landmark. You'll cross its steel planks when driving into town; it links the mainland and island. The bridge is a grand piece of 19th-century engineering – 507m long with a noteworthy middle swing span that rotates to allow ships to steam up the Senegal River. The entire bridge was rehabilitated in stages between 2008 and 2012, with sections of the original bridge's crumbling metal spans replaced piece by piece with steel replicas of the original design.

IFAN Museum MUSEUM

(☎33 961 1050; Quai Henri Jay; adult/child CFA600/350; ⏲9am-noon & 3-6pm) This heritage, art and culture museum contains photos of famous Saint-Louis personalities, an informative history section (in French) and exhibits on local culture and topography including antique dolls and exhibits on local flora and fauna.

Grand Mosque RELIGIOUS, SPIRITUAL

(Ave Jean Mermoz) The Maghreb-style building of the Grand Mosque in the north was constructed in 1847 on order of the colonial administration to appease the growing Muslim population. The oddity of an attached clock tower betrays the designers' religious affiliation.

Les Ateliers Tësss ARTS CENTRE

(☎33 961 6860; www.tesss.net; Rue Khalifa Ababacar Sy; ⏲9am-1.30pm, 3-8pm Mon-Sat) Les Ateliers Tësss displays beautiful woven products (you can see the artisans at work).

Guet N'Dar VILLAGE

On the Langue de Barbarie, Guet N'Dar is a fantastically busy fishing town worth checking out to observe local culture. Come here to watch dozens of *pirogues* being launched in the morning, and fish being brought in, gutted and smoked on the shore in the afternoon.

Festivals & Events

Saint-Louis Jazz Festival FESTIVAL

(http://saintlouisjazz.net) The most internationally renowned festival in West Africa is held annually in early May and attracts jazz greats from around the world. The main event usually happens at the Quai des Arts or on an open-air stage in Place Faidherbe, and there are fringe events all over town.

Les Fanals FESTIVAL

Celebrated the last week of December around Christmas, this historic lantern procession has its roots in the *signares'* (p431) lantern-lit marches to midnight Mass. Today it evokes Saint-Louisian history and reaffirms the town's unique identity.

Sleeping

Hotel Dior & Camping Océan HOTEL $

(☎33 961 3118; www.hotel-dior-senegal.com; Hydrobase; campsites CFA6,000, s CFA25,000-33,000, d CFA32,000-37,000; @📶) With Mauritanian tents tucked away behind sand dunes, this overlander favourite feels like a desert

Saint-Louis

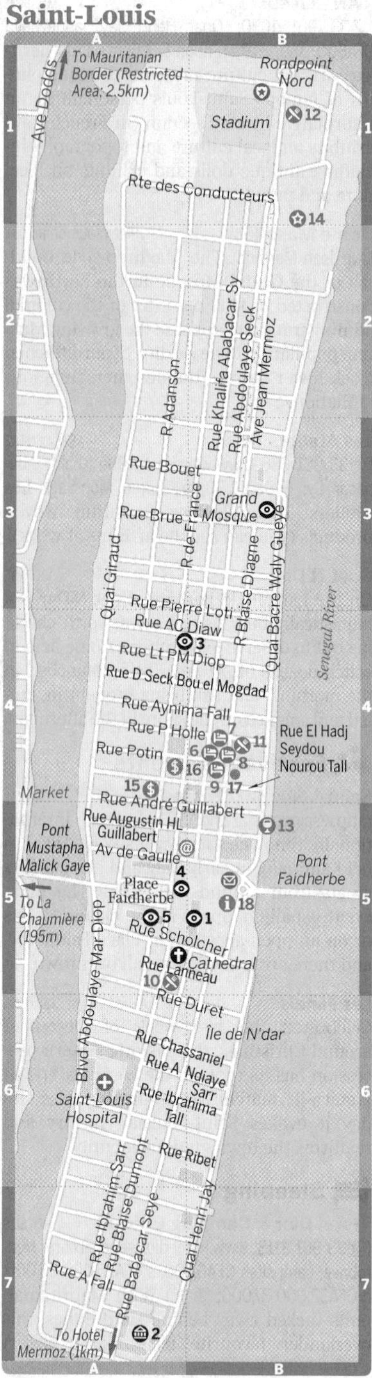

Saint-Louis

Sights

1 Governor's Palace B5
2 IFAN Museum A7
3 Les Ateliers Tësss A4
4 Place Faidherbe A5
5 Rognât Casernes A5

Sleeping

6 Auberge de la Vallée B4
7 Jamm B4
8 La Maison Rose B4
9 La Résidence B4

Eating

10 Chez Agnes A5
11 Layalina B4
12 Pointe Nord B1

Drinking & Nightlife

13 Flamingo B5

Entertainment

14 Quai des Arts B1

Information

15 BICIS A4
16 CBAO A4
17 Sahel Découverte B4
18 Syndicat d'Initiative B5

home. For more comfort, rent a bungalow with hot water and minibar.

Auberge de la Vallée HOTEL $
(☎33 961 4722; Ave Blaise Diagne; d/tr from CFA16,000/18,000; ❄@📶) A basic but friendly choice in the heart of the city, with bright, simple rooms and friendly staff.

★ **Hôtel Mermoz** BOUTIQUE HOTEL $$
(☎33 961 3668; www.hotelmermoz.com; Rte de l'Hydrobase; d CFA25,000-40,000, with sea view CFA40,000-55,000; P❄📶🏊) With huts and bungalows spaced out in a large, sandy garden, and all buildings connected by meandering paths, this place oozes character. It has free bikes for guests to use, and offers a range of seaside excursions and sports.

La Résidence HOTEL $$
(☎33 961 1260; www.hoteldelaresidence.com; Ave Blaise Diagne; s/d/ste from CFA35,000/42,000/50,000; ❄@📶) The Bancals, the old Saint-Louisian family that owns this classic place, have done a great job of evoking history. Each item and picture in the guest rooms has a meaningful link to Saint-Louis' colourful past.

Jamm GUESTHOUSE **$$**

(Chez Yves Lamour; ☎77 443 4765; www.jamm-saintlouis.com; Rue Paul Holle; s/d incl breakfast CFA55,000/62,000; ❄@📶) One of Saint-Louis' most beautifully restored houses offers four tiled and brick-walled rooms with ceilings high enough to impress even regular churchgoers. Every tiny decorative detail has been restored with care.

★**La Maison Rose** HOTEL **$$$**

(☎33 938 2222; www.lamaisonrose.net; Rue Blaise Diagne; d CFA67,000-85,000, ste CFA94,000-140,000; P❄📶; taxi) Old-time elegance meets contemporary luxuries in one of Saint-Louis' most famous old buildings: every room and suite here is unique, though they all exude a spirit of old-time comfort. The classic furniture and wonderful art works on display are all part of the extensive collections of the daughter of Senegal's former president, who owns the place. It's romantic, classy and oozes luxury.

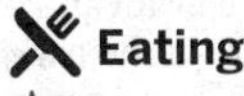

Eating

★**Chez Agnes** AFRICAN **$**

(Complexe Aldiana; ☎33 961 4044; Rue Duret; mains CFA2500-4000) In this pretty, tree-lined patio-restaurant, lovely Agnes serves portions of Senegalese rice and sauce that are so generous the word generosity itself ought to be redefined.

Pointe Nord AFRICAN, SEAFOOD **$$**

(☎33 961 8716; Ave Jean Mermoz; mains CFA3500-5500; ⊙11am-4pm & 7pm-midnight Mon-Sat) This laughter-filled greasy spoon is Saint-Louis' best place for grilled fish served Côte D'Ivoire–style, with *athieke* (cassava couscous) and *aloko* (fried plantains).

Layalina MIDDLE EASTERN **$$**

(☎33 961 8102; Rue Blaise Diagne; mains CFA5000-9,000) In the morning, hot croissants, cakes and pastries entice you to a lush breakfast in this Moroccan-style restaurant; later in the day, you can stop here for rich kebabs and other fast food, before relaxing into the cushions of the dimly lit teahouse for an elegant dinner.

Drinking & Nightlife

Flamingo BAR

(☎33 961 1118; Quai Bacre Waly Guèye; ⊙11am-2am) Any night out here starts at the pool-adorned riverside bar Flamingo. Always packed, it's Saint-Louis' best place for live music.

Le Papayer CLUB

(☎77 566 8382; Carrefour de l'Hydrobase; ⊙10am-5am) On Hydrobase, Le Papayer is the party place of choice.

Quai des Arts ARTS CENTRE

(☎33 961 5656; Ave Jean Mermoz) The biggest concerts in town (including the main acts of the jazz festival) happen at the vast Quai des Arts.

Orientation

The city of Saint-Louis straddles part of the Langue de Barbarie Peninsula, Île de N'Dar and the mainland. From the mainland you reach the island via the 500m-long Pont Faidherbe; Pont Mustapha Malick Gaye links the island to the peninsula, where the thriving fishing community of Guet N'Dar inhabits the areas of the old African quarter.

Information

Internet Cafe (Ave de Gaulle; per hr CFA500; ⊙8am-11pm) Decent terminals and several phone booths.

Sahel Découverte (☎33 961 4263; www.saheldecouverte.com; Rue Blaise Diagne) Quite simply the best address for exploring the northern region.

Syndicat d'Initiative (☎33 961 2455; www.saintlouisdusenegal-tourisme.com; Gouvernance; ⊙9am-noon & 2.30-5pm) A haven of regional information with excellent tours.

Getting There & Away

There are frequent *sept-place* taxis between Dakar and Saint-Louis (CFA4900, five hours,

SIGNARES

Founded in 1659, Saint-Louis was the first French settlement in Africa. A busy centre for the trade of goods and slaves, it had developed into a large and wealthy town by the 1790s, marked by the cosmopolitan culture of a large *métis* (mixed-race) community, which defines Saint-Louis' cultural make-up to this day. The *signares* (women of mixed race who married wealthy European merchants temporarily based in the city) are the most famous example of this. They were essentially bourgeois female entrepreneurs and formed a key part of the economic, social, cultural and political make up of Saint-Louis, controlled most of the river trade and supported local Catholic institutions.

264km). You'll be dropped off at the *gare routière* (bus station), 3.5km south of Saint-Louis. A taxi to the island costs CFA600.

Parc National des Oiseaux du Djoudj

With almost 300 species of bird, this 16,000-hectare **park** (☎33 968 8708; admission CFA2400, pirogue CFA3800, car CFA5200; ⏲7am-dusk Nov-Apr) is one of the most important bird sanctuaries in the world. Flamingos, pelicans and waders are most plentiful, and large numbers of migrating birds travel here in November. The park is best explored by *pirogue*. Boat trips can be arranged at the park entrance or at the hotels.

The main hotel is the large **Hôtel du Djoudj** (☎33 963 8702; www.hotel-djoudj.com; r CFA29,000, pirouge & bike hire half/full day CFA3000/6000; ⏲Nov-May; ❄📶🏊) near the park headquarters. It arranges *pirogue* rides around the park, and rents bikes.

The park is 25km off the main road, and there's no public transport. You can either negotiate a private taxi from Saint-Louis (around CFA28,000) or join an organised tour.

CENTRAL SENEGAL

Tambacounda

The junction town Tambacounda is all about dust, sizzling temperatures and lines of traffic heading in all directions. It's a jumping-off point for Mali, Guinea and Gambia and is a fine place to base yourself to visit the Parc National de Niokolo-Koba.

Bloc Gadec (☎77 531 8931; dm/r CFA3000/8000) is a friendly hostel in the centre of town with clean rooms and shared toilets. **Hôtel Niji** (☎33 981 1250; www.hotel-niji.com; s/d CFA18,500/22,000; P❄@🏊) has everything from simple bungalows to lush (but soulless) quarters. Try **Oasis Oriental Club** (☎33 981 1824; www.oasisoriental.com; Rte de Kaolack; s/d incl breakfast CFA27,500/34,500; P❄@🏊) for some comfort and service.

Relais du Rais (☎77 552 7096; dishes from CFA2500; ⏲noon-2.30pm & 6-11pm) serves filling plates of rice and sauce, and **Saveur Orientale** (☎77 322 5619; Garage Kothiary; pizzas CFA2500; ⏲11am-1am) is a step above the grubby usual in these parts and does good pizzas and snacks. **Chez Nanette** (sandwiches CFA1800-2200; ⏲8am-midnight), right outside Bloc Gadec, is a busy, rootsy drinking hole that offers snacks and sandwiches.

If you're travelling on to Mali, you get your *sept-place* taxi to Kidira (CFA6000, three hours) at Garage Kothiary on the eastern side of town. Vehicles to other destinations go from the larger *gare routière* near the market.

Parc National de Niokolo-Koba

Niokolo-Koba, at 900 sq km, is Senegal's largest national park. It's listed as a World Heritage Site in danger, as park resources barely suffice to adequately protect the remaining animals (including elephants, lions, warthogs, and various monkey and antelope species).

You can explore the park by 4WD, though sightings of the rare mammals are far from guaranteed. The best option is a river tour (CFA6500), where you'll most certainly spot hippos and crocodiles, combined with an exploration of Simenti, the centre of the park. The water hole nearby is a good viewing spot.

The park is officially open from 15 December to 30 April, as most areas are inaccessible during the wet months. The entrance fee (adult/child under 10 years CFA2000/free, vehicles CFA5000) gives you access for 24 hours. You get your obligatory guide (CFA8000) at the entrance gate.

To spend a night in the park, your best bets are to pitch a tent or stay in the rustic but tidy thatched huts of **Camp du Lion** (☎Park headquarters 33 981 2454; campsites CFA5000, s/d CFA9000/12,500).

You will need a vehicle to enter the park. It's best to hire a 4WD (CFA90,000 to CFA130,000) in Tambacounda. Enquire at the *gare routière,* at the hotels or at the **National Park Office** (☎33 981 2454; Tambacounda; ⏲8am-5pm). You won't save any money using public transport, as pick-up and drop-off from the park entrance and the tours will also add up to around CFA90,000.

CASAMANCE

With its lush tropical landscapes, watered by the graceful, winding Casamance River, and the unique culture of the Diola, this area seems far from Dakar and its surroundings, in every sense. That's what many locals feel as well, so strongly that separatist rebellions have troubled the region for years. Things have largely calmed down, but they've left a destabilising legacy of banditry that flares up regularly – check recent travel advisories and news before you go.

If the area is safe enough for visits, you'll discover a fascinating place. Between the sleepy capital, Ziguinchor, and the wide, sandy beaches of Cap Skiring, the banks of the Casamance River are dotted with tiny community *campements* that nestle between mangroves and lagoons.

WARNING

Since the 1980s, conflicts in Casamance have flared up regularly. The latest peace deal between the Movement of Democratic Forces in Casamance (MFDC) rebels and the Senegalese government was signed in 2004 and was largely adhered to. Still, there were occasional incidents of road blocks and armed street robberies, and in 2009 reports of violence, gun fire and attacks of military posts became more frequent. Whether the work of common criminals or rebels with a cause, it can render trips to Casamance dangerous. Check the situation carefully before setting out, never travel after dark and don't venture off into the bush without a guide.

Ziguinchor

POP 157,000

Ziguinchor is the largest town in southern Senegal, and the main access point for travel in the Casamance region. With its old houses, tree-lined streets and busy markets, this former colonial centre exudes real atmosphere. The city has no major sights per se but does boast some colourful historical buildings, including colonial beauty and central **post office** (Rue du Général de Gaulle) and the old **Conseil Régional** (regional council). The huge *case à impluvium* (large, round traditional house) of the **Alliance Franco-Sénégalaise** (☎33 991 2823; ⏱9.15am-noon & 3-7.15pm Mon-Sat), with its stunning South African–Casamançais decor, is a beauty worth admiring. At **Africa Batik** (☎77 653 4936), you can try your hand at making batiks.

For *pirogue* excursions, ask at your hotel or speak to the boat owners at the *pirogue* jetty near **Le Perroquet** (☎33 991 2329; perroquet@orange.sn; Rue du Commerce; s/d CFA12,000/14,000), Zig's favourite budget place where dozens of yellow-billed storks attract you with their noisy chatter as you enter the place. Invest in a 1st-floor room for the river views. Alteratively, the three log cabins on the croc farm **Ferme de Djibelor** (☎33 991 1701; s/d CFA17,000/23,000) are cosy and strangely reminiscent of ski chalets, until the lush gardens remind you where you are.

Humble outdoor eatery **Le Erobon** (☎991 2788; Rue du Commerce; mains CFA 3500-5500; ⏱10am-1am) boasts carefully spiced grilled fish served with a sea view. The ambience is wonderfully relaxed and often includes live music like a sole guitar player or a small local band. **Le Kassa** (☎33 991 1311; Rond-Point Jean-Paul II; mains CFA2800-4400; ⏱8am-2am), a patio-pretty place on the roundabout, offers an African-food-focused kitchen that stays open late, and there's live music on weekends. **L'Abondance** (Rue du Général de Gaulle; ⏱5pm-2am) is a small bar-cum-*dibiterie* (grilled-meat place) where you can round off a night out on the town with pork skewers, grilled lamb and cold beers. Lastly, **Le Bombolong** (☎33 938 8001; Rue du Commerce; cover CFA1800-3500) has the most raucous party for clubbers. There's also a small **Superette** (Rue Lemoine; ⏱9am-10pm), as well as a good **pâtisserie** (Rue Javelier; cakes CFA300-500) in the centre of town. **Diambone Voyages** (☎77 641 5132; www.diambonevoyages.com; Rue de France) offers flight bookings, tours, car hire and more. The **Aline Sitoé Diatta ferry** travels between Dakar and Ziguinchor twice weekly in each direction, leaving Dakar every Thursday and Sunday at 3pm, arriving in Dakar the next day at 6pm. Buy your ticket (CFA16,000 to CFA31,000 one way) in advance and in person at the port.

The *gare routière* is to the east of the city centre. There are frequent *sept-place* taxis to Dakar (CFA12,000, nine hours, 454km) and Cap Skiring (CFA1600). To get anywhere around town by private taxi costs CFA600.

Oussouye

Roughly halfway between Ziguinchor and Cap Skiring, relaxed Oussouye is the main town in the Basse Casamance. For the local Diola population, this town is of significance because it's home to an animist king who is often sought for advice.

Bikes can be hired and tours booked at **Casamance VTT** (Chez Benjamin; ☎33 993

Casamance

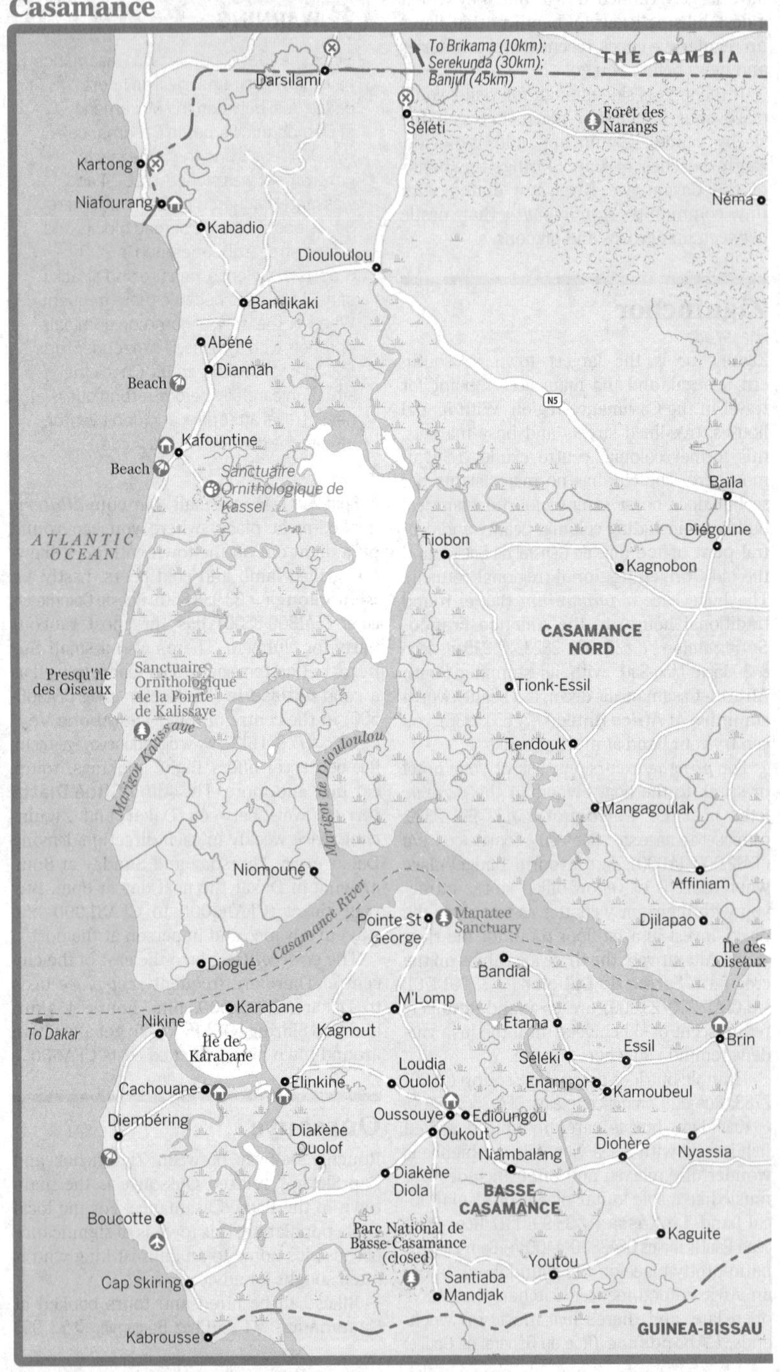

To Brikama (10km); Serekunda (30km); Banjul (45km)
THE GAMBIA
Darsilami
Séléti
Forêt des Narangs
Kartong
Niafourang
Kabadio
Néma
Diouloulou
Bandikaki
Abéné
Diannah
Beach
N5
Kafountine
Beach
Sanctuaire Ornithologique de Kassel
Baïla
Diégoune
Tiobon
Kagnobon
ATLANTIC OCEAN
CASAMANCE NORD
Presqu'île des Oiseaux
Sanctuaire Ornithologique de la Pointe de Kalissaye
Tionk-Essil
Marigot Kalissaye
Marigot de Diouloulou
Tendouk
Mangagoulak
Niomoune
Affiniam
Casamance River
Pointe St George
Manatee Sanctuary
Djilapao
Île des Oiseaux
Diogué
Bandial
Karabane
M'Lomp
To Dakar
Nikine
Kagnout
Etama
Brin
Île de Karabane
Essil
Séléki
Loudia Ouolof
Cachouane
Elinkine
Enampor
Kamoubeul
Diembéring
Oussouye
Edioungou
Oukout
Diakène Ouolof
Diohère
Nyassia
Niambalang
Diakène Diola
BASSE CASAMANCE
Boucotte
Parc National de Basse-Casamance (closed)
Kaguite
Youtou
Cap Skiring
Santiaba Mandjak
Kabrousse
GUINEA-BISSAU

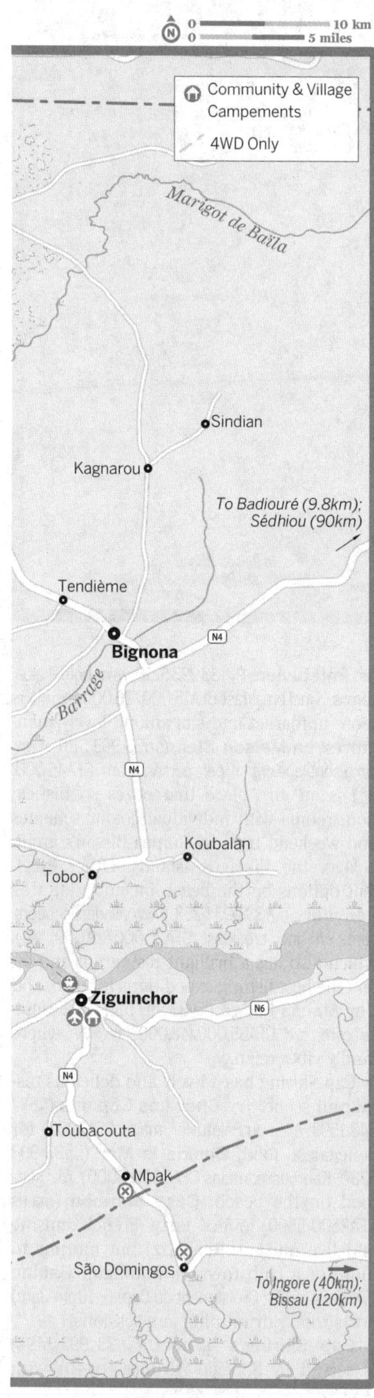

1004; www.casamancevtt.com; half-/full-day bike or kayak hire CFA8000/15,500; ⏲10am-5pm).

Campement Villageois d'Oussouye (☎33 993 0015; http://campement.oussouye.org; s/d CFA5500/6500) and **Campement Emanaye** (☎77 573 6334; emanaye@yahoo.fr; s/d CFA4800/7300) are striking two-storey mud dwellings, an architectural style typical of the region. **Aljowe** (Chez François; ☎77 517 0267; s/apt per person CFA6000/8000) has cute rooms and mini-apartments in a redbrick structure. **Le Kassa** (mains CFA3000) serves up tasty Senegalese dishes under the cool shade of a massive kapok tree.

All bush taxis between Ziguinchor and Cap Skiring pass through Oussouye (CFA1600).

Elinkine & Île de Karabane

Elinkine is a busy fishing village and jumping-off point for the peaceful Île de Karabane, a former French trading station (1836–1900). On the island, you can still see the Breton-style church, with dusty pews and crumbling statues and visit the dilapidated cemetery where settlers and sailors were laid to rest.

The simple but charming **Campement Villageois d'Elinkine** (☎77 376 9659; campementelinkine@free.fr; Elinkine; per person CFA9000) offers basic rooms and friendly service. **Campement Le Barracuda** (☎77 659 6001; Karabane; r with half/full board CFA7700/10,200) has a recommended fishing and excursions centre, and helpful management. **Hôtel Carabane** (☎77 569 0284; hotelcarabane@yahoo.fr; r with half/full board CFA16,500/25,000), in the former Catholic mission, is the most upmarket option on the isle.

For drinks and Senegalese dishes try **Africando** (☎77 533 3842; Île De Karabane; mains CFA2000-4000), nestled among the giant roots of a kapok tree.

Elinkine can be reached by minibus from Ziguinchor (CFA2400, two hours) or Oussouye (CFA700, one hour). For Karabane, take the public *pirogue* from Elinkine (CFA1550, five minutes, twice daily). Hiring a private *pirogue* costs around CFA17,000 one way.

Cap Skiring

The beaches at Cap Skiring are some of the finest in West Africa and, better still, they are usually empty. Most *campements* and hotels are on the beach, 1km from the village, at the end of a dirt track off the Ziguinchor road.

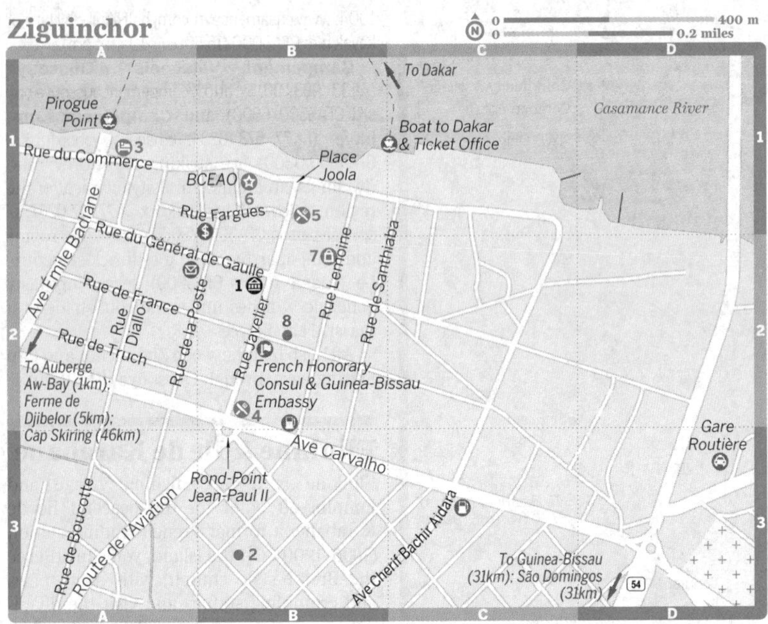

Ziguinchor

Sights
1 Conseil Régional B2

Activities, Courses & Tours
2 Africa Batik B3

Sleeping
3 Le Perroquet A1

Eating
4 Le Kassa B2
5 Pâtisserie B1

Entertainment
6 Le Bombolong B1

Shopping
7 Superette B2

Information
8 Diambone Voyages B2

Most hotels offer a mix of activities like kayaking, quad hire and fishing trips.

Le Paradise (☎33 993 5303; r CFA15,000; ❄) is the best of a row of cheap *campements*. In Cap Skiring village, the small **Auberge Le Palmier** (☎33 993 5109; d from CFA12,000; ❄) is a decent budget bet, while the riverside **Kaloa les Palétuviers** (☎33 993 5210; www.hotel-kaloa.com; s/d incl breakfast CFA15,000/26,000; ❄ 🏊) is more upmarket and sits among lovely mangroves. **La Maison Bleu** (☎33 993 5161; www.lamaisonbleue.org; r per person from CFA45,000; 📶) is an airy place that oozes sophistication, rooms with individual colour schemes and weekend trips to Guinea-Bissau's archipelago, the Bissagos Islands. Other excellent options on the beach include **Villa des Pêcheurs** (☎33 993 5253; www.villadespecheurs.com; s/d incl breakfast CFA25,000/29,000; ❄), which also has a brilliant restaurant and offers the best fishing expeditions in town, and tiny **Mansa Lodge** (☎33 993 5147; www.capsafari.com; s/d CFA35,000/48,000; ❄ 🏊), where family vibes reign.

Cap Skiring has a lively and delicious restaurant scene. Try **Chez Les Copains** (☎77 548 1593; Allée du Palétuvier; mains CFA3000) for Senegalese food, **Bar de la Mer** (☎33 993 5280; Kabrousse; mains CFA3000-5000) for seafood on the beach. **Casa Bambou** (mains CFA2500-5500) offers tasty French cuisine and live music (often jazz) but morphs to more of a club towards midnight. **Bakine** (☎33 641 5124; Croisement du Cap; ⏲10pm-3am) hosts rootsy drumming jam sessions.

Cap Skiring's airport (☎33 993 5194) is served by Senegal Airlines (p440) with flights to and from Dakar. Otherwise it's a *sept-place* taxi (CFA1600) from Ziguinchor.

UNDERSTAND SENEGAL

Senegal Today

Senegal's February 2012 presidential elections were controversial: the Senegalese constitution prohibited a president from serving more than two terms, but then-sitting President Wade amended the constitution in 2011 to enable him to run for a third term. Several youth opposition movements contested the amendment. However, former prime minister Micky Sall won, and Wade conceded the election to Sall. The smooth democratic transition was heralded by many foreign observers as a sign of peace and stability.

History

Senegal was part of several West African empires, including the Empire of Ghana (8th century), and the Djolof kingdom, in the area between the Senegal River and Dakar (13th and 14th centuries). In the early 16th century, Portuguese traders made contact with coastal kingdoms and became the first in a long line of 'interested' foreigners: soon the British, French and Dutch jostled for control of strategic points for the trade in slaves and goods. In 1659, the French built a trading station at Saint-Louis; the town later became the capital of French West Africa.

Dakar, home to tiny fishing villages, was chosen as capital of the Senegalese territory, and as early as 1848 Senegal had a deputy in the French parliament.

Independence

In the run-up to independence in 1960, Senegal joined French Sudan (present-day Mali) to form the Mali Federation. It lasted all of two months, and in August 1960, Senegal became a republic. Its first president, Léopold Sédar Senghor, a socialist and poet of international stature, commanded respect in Senegal and abroad. His economic management, however, didn't match his way with words. At the end of 1980, he voluntarily stepped down and was replaced by Abdou Diouf, who soon faced a string of mounting crises.

The early 1980s saw the start of an ongoing separatist rebellion in the southern region of Casamance. Seven years later a minor incident on the Mauritanian border led to riots and deportations in both countries, as well as a three-year suspension of diplomatic relations and hundreds of casualties. Tensions mounted in other parts of the country as a result of austerity measures.

The arrest of opposition leader Abdoulaye Wade in February 1994 only increased his huge popularity. In March 2000, Wade won in a free and fair presidential election, thanks to his hope-giving *sopi* (change) campaign. Diouf peacefully relinquished power. The following year, a new constitution was approved, allowing the formation of opposition parties and consolidating the prime minister's role.

In 2002 the country was shaken by a huge tragedy when the MS *Joola,* the ferry connecting Dakar and the Casamance capital, Ziguinchor, capsized due to dangerous overloading, leaving almost 2000 people dead.

In 2009 Wade declared in a very early announcement that he intended to stand as candidate at the 2012 elections. There wasn't much cheering; after promising initial measures, Wade's government has not been able to lead the country out of crisis. The steadily rising cost of living, increasing power cuts and widening gap between rich and poor provoke anger and despair among the population. The images of young Senegalese emigrants crossing to the Canary Islands in tiny boats have been beamed around the world. In 2009, 2011 and 2012, conflicts flared up again in Casamance, which had been calm since the peace deal in 2004.

Culture

'A man with a mouth is never lost' goes a popular Wolof saying, and indeed, conversation is the key to local culture, and the key to conversation is a great sense of humour. The Senegalese love talking and teasing, and the better you slide into the conversational game, the easier you'll get around.

Personal life stories in Senegal tend to be brewed from a mix of traditional values, global influences, Muslim faith and family integration. More than 90% of the population is Muslim, and many of them belong to one of the Sufi brotherhoods that dominate religious life in Senegal. The most important brotherhood is that of the Mourides, founded by Cheikh Amadou Bamba. The *marabouts* who lead these brotherhoods play a central role in social life and wield enormous political and economic power (possibly the power to make or break the country's leaders).

The dominant ethnic group is the Wolof (44% of the population), whose language is the country's lingua franca. Smaller groups include the Fula (around 23%); the Tukulor, a sub-branch of the Fula (10%); the Serer (14%); and the Diola (4%). Senegal's population is young: around 40% are under 14 years old. The greatest population density is found in the urban areas of Dakar.

Senegal has a vast music scene; names such as Youssou N'Dour and Baaba Maal are famous worldwide. The beat that moves the nation is *mbalax*. Created from a mixture of Cuban music (hugely popular in Senegal in the 1960s) and traditional, fiery *sabar* drumming, *mbalax* was made famous by Youssou N'Dour in the 1980s.

Hip-hop is also an exciting scene in Senegal, with leading names including Didier Awadi and Daara J. 'Urban folk', led by Carlou D, is on the rise.

Visual arts are also huge (and celebrated every two years during the Dak'Art Biennale). Leading artists include Soly Cissé, Souleymane Keita and Ndaary Lô. Moussa Sakho, Babacar Lô and Gora Mbengue are famous artists practising *sous-verre* (reverse-glass painting).

The doyen of Senegalese cinema is the late Ousmane Sembène, and there's a new generation producing exciting work.

Food & Drink

Senegal's national dish is *tiéboudienne* (rice cooked in a thick tomato sauce and served with fried fish and vegetables). Also typical are *yassa poulet* or *poisson yassa* (marinated and grilled chicken or fish) and *mafé* (peanut-based stew).

Local drinks include *bissap,* made from sorrel flowers, and *bouyi,* made from the fruits of the baobab. The best local beer is Flag.

Environment

Senegal consists mainly of flat plains, cut by three major rivers: the Senegal River in the north, which forms the border with Mauritania; the Gambia River; and the Casamance River in the south, watering the lush green lands of Casamance.

The national parks of the coastal regions, including the Siné-Saloum Delta, the Parc National de la Langue de Barbarie and the Parc National des Oiseaux du Djoudj, are noted for their spectacular birdlife. Parc National de Niokolo-Koba has some large mammals, though they're hard to spot.

Overfishing, deforestation, desertification, and coastal erosion, largely caused by uncontrolled illegal sand mining, are the main environmental issues the country faces. The dwindling of fish stocks also threatens the economy.

SURVIVAL GUIDE

Directory A–Z

ACCOMMODATION

Senegal has a very wide range of places to stay, from top-class hotels to dirty dosshouses. Dakar has the biggest choice, though you're hard-pushed to find a budget place there. Many rural areas, particularly the Casamance, have pleasant *campements*.

EMBASSIES & CONSULATES

If you need to find an embassy that is not listed here, check www.ausenegal.com/practique_en/ambassad.htm. Most embassies close late morning or early afternoon Monday to Friday, so set off early.

Canadian Embassy (Map p416; ☎33 889 4700; 45-47 Blvd de la République, Immeuble Sorano, 3rd fl, Plateau)

Cape Verdean Embassy (Map p418; ☎33 821 3936; 3 Blvd el Haji Djily Mbaye, Plateau)

Ivorian Embassy (Map p422; ☎33 869 0270; www.ambaci-dakar.org; Allées Seydou Nourou Tall, Point E)

French Embassy (Map p418; ☎33 839 5100; www.ambafrance-sn.org; 1 Rue Amadou Assane Ndoye, Dakar)

Gambian Embassy (Map p418; ☎33 821 7230; 11 Rue de Thiong)

German Embassy (Map p416; ☎33 889 4884; www.dakar.diplo.de; 20 Ave Pasteur)

Ghanaian Embassy (Map p422; ☎33 869 4053; Rue 6, Point E)

Guinea-Bissau Embassy Dakar (Map p422; ☎33 824 5922; Rue 6, Point E; ⏲8am-12.30pm Mon-Fri); Ziguinchor (☎33 991 1046; ⏲8am-2pm Mon-Fri)

Guinean Embassy (Map p422; ☎33 824 8606; Rue 7, Point E)

Malian Embassy (Map p422; ☎33 824 6252; 23 Rte de la Corniche-Ouest; ⏰9am-1pm Mon-Fri)
Mauritanian Embassy (Map p422; ☎33 823 5344; Fann Mermoz; ⏰8am-2pm Mon-Fri)
Moroccan Embassy (Map p422; ☎33 824 3836; Ave Cheikh Anta Diop, Mermoz)
Spanish Embassy (☎33 821 3081; 18-20 Ave Nelson Mandela)
UK Embassy (Map p416; ☎33 823 7392; 20 Rue du Dr Guillet) One block north of Hôpital le Dantec.
US Embassy (Map p418; ☎33 823 4296; Ave Jean XXIII)

EMERGENCIES

Fire (☎18)
Police (☎17)
SOS Medecin (☎33 889 1515)
SUMA Urgences (☎33 824 2418)

FESTIVALS & EVENTS

December, May and June are the best times for music and arts festivals, including the Saint-Louis Jazz Festival (p429), the **Dak'Art Biennale** (☎33 823 0918; www.dakart.org) and **Kaay Fecc** (☎33 824 5154; www.kaayfecc.com).

INTERNET ACCESS

Internet cafes are plentiful, and the number of wi-fi spaces is increasing almost daily (particularly in Dakar). Surfing costs from CFA400 to CFA500 per hour; wi-fi in hotel lobbies and bars is usually free with a purchase.

MONEY

The unit of currency is the West African CFA franc. Banks with ATMs are found in all larger towns across the country. Banks and exchange bureaux tend to offer similar rates; the currencies most easily changed are the euro and US dollars.

OPENING HOURS

Banks Usually close around 4pm; only a few open Saturday morning.
Business and government offices Open 8.30am to 1pm and 2.30pm to 5pm Monday to Friday.
Restaurants Offer lunch from noon to 2.30pm and dinner from 7pm onwards; many are closed on Sunday.

POST

Senegal's postal service is inexpensive though not entirely reliable.

PUBLIC HOLIDAYS

As well as Islamic religious holidays, Senegal celebrates a few principal public holidays.

New Year's Day 1 January
Independence Day 4 April

PRACTICALITIES

- **Languages** French, Wolof, Malinke, Pulaar (Fulfulde), Diola.
- **Electricity** 220V. Plugs have two round pins (same as continental Europe).
- **Newspapers** *Le Soleil* (www.lesoleil.sn) is the main daily newspaper.

Workers Day 1 May
Assumption 15 August

SAFE TRAVEL

There are two main dangers you may encounter in Senegal: civil unrest in Casamance and street crime in Dakar.

TELEPHONE

Good mobile-phone coverage means that most of the public *télécentres* have now closed. You'll still find them, but it's much easier to buy a SIM card. Top-up credit is available absolutely anywhere. Network coverage (especially for Orange) is excellent across the country.

The country code is ☎221. For directory assistance dial ☎1212.

TIME

Senegal is at GMT/UTC. There is no daylight-saving time.

VISAS

At the time of writing, visa requirements were in flux and Senegal now requires that visitors from nations that require entry visas from Senegalese citizens are required to obtain a visa for travel to Senegal. This includes citizens of the EU, EEA, Switzerland, Canada, USA and Australia. Tourist visas for one to three months cost between US$30 to US$80.

Visa Extensions

If you don't need a visa, just hop across the Gambian border and earn another three months on re-entry to Senegal.

Getting There & Away

AIR

Dakar's **Léopold Sédar Senghor International Airport** (DKR; ☎24hr info line 77 628 1010; www.aeroportdakar.com) is one of Africa's transport hubs, with links across Africa, Europe and America.

Major airlines servicing Senegal, many with offices in Dakar, are as follows:

Air France (AF; ☎33 839 7777; www.airfrance.fr)

Brussels Airlines (SN; ☎33 823 0460; www.brusselsairlines.com)

Ethiopian Airlines (ET; ☎33 823 5552; www.flyethiopian.com; 16 Ave Léopold Sédar Senghor)

Kenya Airways (www.kenya-airways.com)

Royal Air Maroc (AT; ☎33 849 4748; www.royalairmaroc.com)

Senegal Airlines (www.senegalairlines.aero) Senegal's national airline flies to Ziguinchor, Cap Skiring and various cities throughout West Africa and at the time of research it had just started nonstop flights to Paris via its partner airline Corsair. Check the website for details.

South African Airways (SA; ☎33 869 4000; www.flysaa.com)

TACV Cabo Verde Airlines (VR; ☎33 821 3968; www.flytacv.com)

TAP Portugal (TAP; www.flytap.com)

LAND

The Gambia

From Dakar there are *sept-place* taxis south to Karang (CFA6800, six hours) at the Gambian border, where you connect to Barra and then via ferry to Banjul.

From southern Senegal, *sept-place* taxis run regularly between Ziguinchor and Serekunda (CFA4900, five hours), and between Kafountine and Brikama (CFA3500, two hours).

In eastern Senegal, *sept-place* taxis go from Tambacounda to Vélingara (CFA1800, three hours), and from there to Basse Santa Su (CFA1400, 45 minutes, 27km).

Guinea

Most traffic is by *sept-place* from Diaoubé (Senegal), via Koundara (Guinea), where you may have to change; some go via Kédougou (Senegal). The very rough ride costs CFA22,000 and takes up to 48 hours.

Guinea-Bissau

Sept-place taxis leave every morning from Ziguinchor for Bissau (CFA6600, four hours, 147km), via the main border post at São Domingos, and Ingore. The road is sealed and in good condition.

Mali

Sept-place taxis leave regularly from Tambacounda to Kidira (CFA5500, three hours), where you cross the border to Diboli in Mali, from where long-distance buses run to Kayes and Bamako. If you're brave, you can do Dakar–Bamako by long-distance bus (CFA24,000); buses leave from Gare Routière Pompiers in Dakar.

The legendary Dakar–Bamako 'express' train was no longer running at the time of research.

Mauritania

Sept-place taxis run regularly from Dakar to the main border point at Rosso (CFA7000, six hours, 384km), a crowded, hasslesome place, where four daily ferries (CFA2500/3500 per passenger/car) cross to Rosso-Mauritania.

If you have your own wheels, you can cross at the Maka Diama dam, 97km southwest of Rosso and just north of Saint-Louis, where the border crossing is swift.

Getting Around

AIR

Senegal Airlines flies between Dakar, Ziguinchor and Cap Skiring.

LOCAL TRANSPORT

The quickest (though still uncomfortable) way of getting around the country is by *sept-place* taxi – battered Peugeots that negotiate even the most ragged routes. Slightly cheaper but infinitely less reliable are the minibuses (Ndiaga Ndiaye or *grand car*), carrying around 40 people. Vehicles leave from the *gare routière* when they're full, and they fill up quickest in the morning, before 8am.

Taxi prices are theoretically fixed, though they're steadily increasing as petrol prices rise. There's an extra, negotiable charge for luggage (10% to 20% of the bill).

Cars mourides (large buses, financed by the Mouride brotherhood) connect major towns in Senegal. Book ahead of travel. In Dakar, go to **Gare Routière Pompiers** (Map p416; ☎33 821 8585; off Ave Malick Sy), where most *sept-places* also go from. Arriving in Dakar, *sept-places* stop at Gare Routière Colobane.

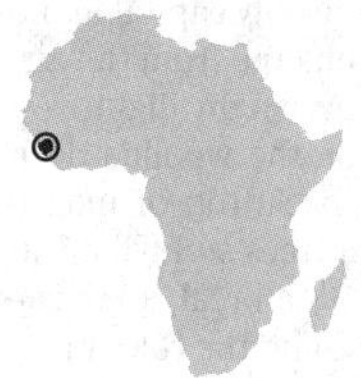

Sierra Leone

☎232 / POP 5.4 MILLION

Includes ➡

Best Places to Eat

- ➡ Seafood at Franco's (p449)
- ➡ Oasis (p446)
- ➡ Picnic at Turtle Islands (p451)

Best Places to Stay

- ➡ Tokeh Sands (p449)
- ➡ Tiwai Island (p451)
- ➡ Tribe Wanted (p449)

Why Go?

West Africa's secret beach destination rises from the soft waters of the Atlantic, dressed in sun-stained hues, rainforest green and the red, red roads of the north. Sierra Leone: the land so-named because it's shaped like a mountain lion. Sweet Salone, the locals say.

In Freetown, colourful stilted houses remember the days when freed slaves from the Caribbean were resettled upon these shores. Some landed on the peninsula, blanketed with sands as white and soft as cotton wool.

In the north, the Loma Mountains form the highest point west of Cameroon. Further east, streams cut national parks and mangrove swamp water swathes rainforest that shelter endangered species like the shy, waddling pygmy hippo.

The curtains have been drawn on the painful past, and it's time for a new act in Sierra Leone. Join the island-hoppers and sun-seekers, swim in the clear blue waters, explore the archipelagos and crack open fresh lobster in the shade of skinny palms and rope-strung hammocks.

When to Go

Freetown

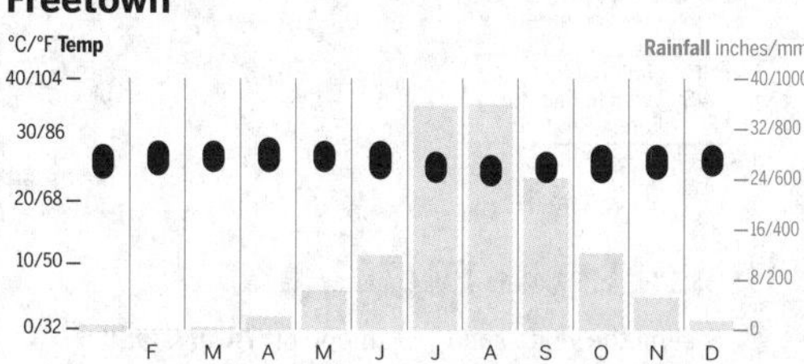

Nov–Jun The dry season is marked by mild, dusty harmattan winds from December until February.

April The average daytime temperature is 32°C.

Jun–Nov The rainy season sees spectacular storms and up to 3200mm of precipitation.

FREETOWN

022 / POP 1.1 MILLION

Strung between the mountains and the sea, Sierra Leone's capital is a cheeky, quicksilver capital bubbling with energy, colour and charm. One minute it's calm, offering up quiet beaches, friendly Krio chat and warm plates of soup and rice. The next it's frenzied and playing dirty, throwing you into the back of a shared taxi and hurtling you up and down its pretty little hills.

And it might just be the only capital in the world where when you emerge from the airport, blinking after an overnight flight, you find yourself standing on the wooden deck of a port flanked by a backdrop of mountains, beaches and palm trees so idyllic you wonder if it's real. Well it's all real, all of it – the chatter and the chaos and the colour and the dirt and the lush lobster dinners and the devastating war history – and those lovely white sands too.

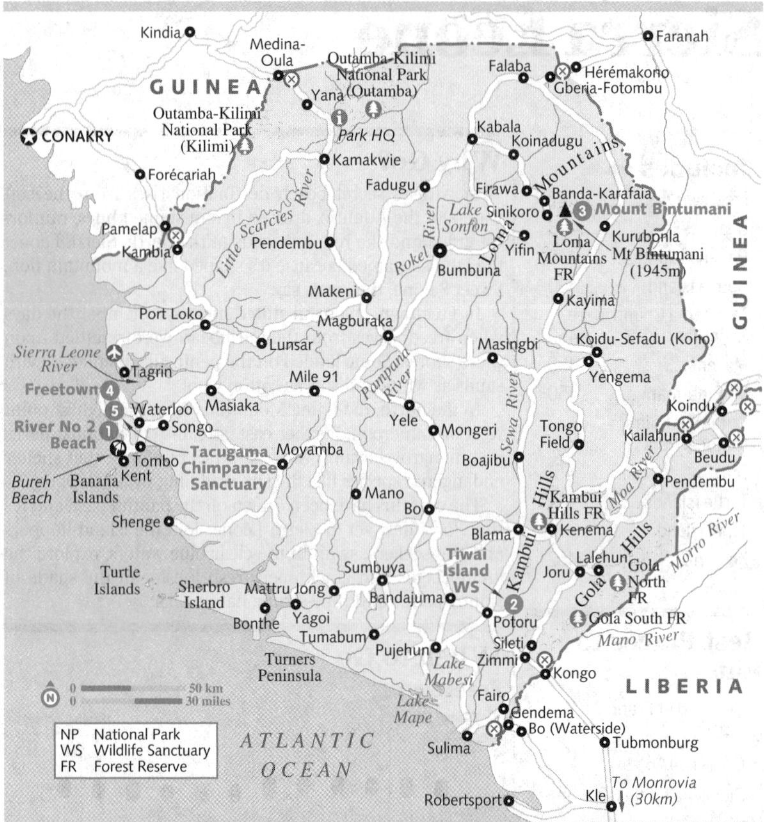

Sierra Leone Highlights

1. Feeling the white sand between your toes on **River No 2 Beach** (p448) and other Freetown beaches that line the stunning peninsula.
2. Tracking colobus monkeys and joining the search for the elusive pygmy hippo on **Tiwai Island** (p451).
3. Pushing through the cool mist as you scale, **Mt Bintumani** (p450) West Africa's highest peak this side of Cameroon.
4. Soaking up the spirit of **Freetown** (p442), the colourful, cheeky capital.
5. Sleeping in tree houses in **Tacugama Chimpanzee Sanctuary** (p450) while rescued chimps chatter in the rainforest below.

Sights & Activities

Cotton Tree GARDENS

(Map p446) Freetown's most famous landmark is the fat Cotton Tree in the centre of the old part of town. Nobody's sure if it can be quite that old, but some say the city's poor black settlers rested in its shadows when they landed in Freetown in 1787. Either way, the tree has witnessed a lot, including the invasion of a huge colony of chirpy bats that were kicked out by authorities in 2010 – rumour has it that one day the bats will return.

Sierra Leone National Museum MUSEUM

(Map p446; ☎223555; Siaka Stevens St; ⏲10.30am-4pm Mon-Fri) FREE The Sierra Leone National Museum has a small but fascinating collection of juju trinkets and historical artefacts, including Temne Guerrilla leader Bai Bureh's drum, clothes and sword.

State House HISTORIC BUILDING

(Map p446; Independence Ave) The State House, up on Tower Hill and overlooking the Downtown area, is an example of the area's old Krio architecture, which features brightly washed buildings and higgledy-piggledy window frames. This building incorporates the bastions and lion gate from Fort Thornton (built at the turn of the 19th century).

St John's Maroon Church CHURCH

(Map p446; Siaka Stevens St) Built around 1820, St John's Maroon Church is a squat white building with big windows. An example of the area's Krio architecture, it was built by returned slaves from Jamaica. It's located two blocks southwest of the Cotton Tree.

Old Boundary Cannons HISTORIC SITE

(Map p444) Over at the junction of Kissy Road – known locally as Up Gun community – you can see one of the three old boundary cannons that were used to mark the mapped-out limes of Freetown. It is believed to date back to about 1805.

King's Yard Gate HISTORIC SITE

(Map p446; Wallace Johnson St) The ancestors of nearly all present-day Krios passed through King's Yard Gate, atop Tower Hill in the strategic military Martello Tower, built in 1805. Here they awaited resettlement and medical care by the British. Now the site of Connaught Hospital, this is where the British brought rescued slaves to begin their new lives. Many of these new arrivals climbed the nearby Old Wharf Steps, sometimes erroneously called the Portuguese Steps.

SET YOUR BUDGET

Budget

- Simple room upcountry $6
- Rice and sauce lunch $2
- Bottle of Star beer $1.20
- Shared taxi ride $1

Midrange

- Hotel room with fan $15
- Sandwich in a cafe $5
- Glass of wine $4
- Private taxi hire, per hour $5

Top End

- Hotel room with air-con and TV $70
- Two-course meal in Freetown $25
- Cocktail in Freetown beach bar $6
- 4x4 hire, per day $120 plus petrol

National Railway Museum MUSEUM

(Map p444; Cline St; ⏲9.30am-5pm Mon-Sat) FREE Visitors to the National Railway Museum are rare, but the short tour around these restored engines and cars is fairly interesting. You don't have to be a rail fan to enjoy this Clinetown museum, where there's a surprising collection of restored locomotives, including one commissioned for the Queen of England in 1961.

Lumley Beach BEACH

With every patch of beachfront property purchased and many construction projects underway, it's not hard to imagine what Lumley Beach will look like in a few years, but for now development is pretty much limited to a few bamboo and thatch beer-shacks. Lifeguards and beach wardens are on duty and the public toilets and showers are kept clean, but the beach is not. Lumley Beach is the busiest beach on the peninsula, teeming with bars and lunch spots. If it's relaxation you're after, better to head out of town to River No 2 or one of the islands.

Bureh Beach Surf Club SURFING

If you want to catch some waves, Bureh Beach Surf Club – initially set up before the war by a Peace Corps volunteer – is now in the hands of Irish surfer Shane, who works with local surf legends to boost tourism through surf trips, lessons and board rentals.

Greater Freetown

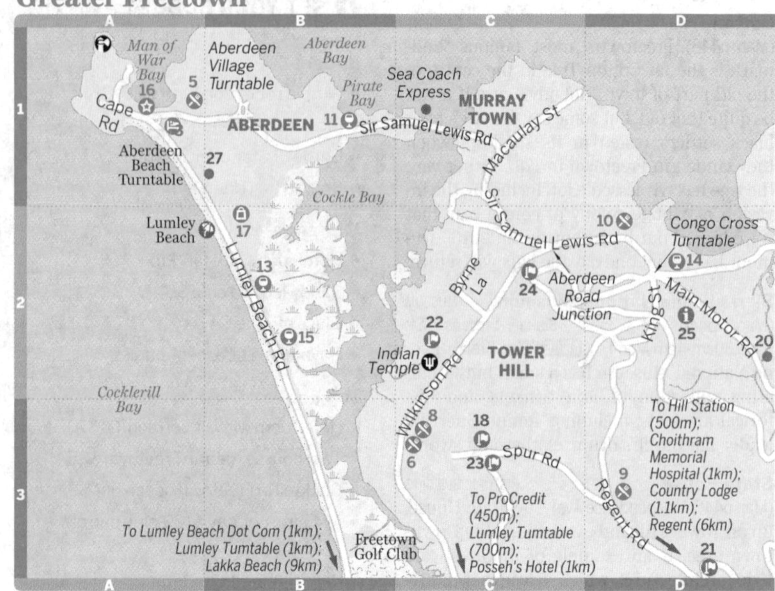

Sleeping

Freetown has a good mix of accommodation, with new options opening regularly.

Hotobah Lodge HOTEL $$
(Map p444; ☎076-241212; www.thehotobahlodge.com; 5 Boyle Lane, off Murray Town Rd; d/ste US$75/85; P ❄ wi-fi) A gem of a hotel that opened in 2013, Hotobah sits at Murray Town junction – on the main route into town from the west, dubbed 'Banana Wata' – and has smart, clean rooms with wi-fi and TVs (the generator is switched on in the evenings only). A friendly, great value place.

Family Kingdom HOTEL $$
(Map p444; ☎076-77794, 22236133; Lumley Beach Rd; P ❄ wi-fi) Don't mind the deer, they're tame, and part of the weird, wonderful family at this Lumley Beach hotel. The rooms here are upmarket and spacious, with 24-hour air-con and wi-fi, and you've good access to the eating and drinking spots that line the main beach drag.

Kona Lodge HOTEL $$
(Map p446; ☎076-611793; 32 King St; r from US$55; ❄ wi-fi) Favoured by NGO workers, Kona Lodge is a sound option for a good night's work and sleep: there's 24-hour power, reliable wi-fi and the rooms are clean and modern.

The Place RESORT $$$
(Map p446; ☎079-685494; 42 Rawdon St; P ❄ wi-fi pool) The Place has been transformed from a budget hotel to a luxury, boutique retreat. Renovations are expected to result in a sleek new pool and spa.

Country Lodge HOTEL $$$
(☎076-691000; www.countrylodgesl.com; Hill Station; r US$150-195, ste US$250-300; P ❄ @ wi-fi pool) Country Lodge is Freetown's most upmarket address, popular with the odd combination of glittering celebrities and suited development consultants. There's a lap-length pool, a gym, a tennis court and free wi-fi. The only downside to the fabulous hilltop location is reaching it – you'll need your own car or a private taxi.

Eating

You can find local chop houses serving *plasas* (pounded potato or cassava leaves cooked with palm oil) all over town around lunchtime.

Dee's Bazaar RESTAURANT $
(Map p446; cnr Liverpool & Siaka Stevens Sts) Both the name and the food beat the decor at this local *plasas* spot. The menu changes daily, according to what's on-hand, but you can ex-

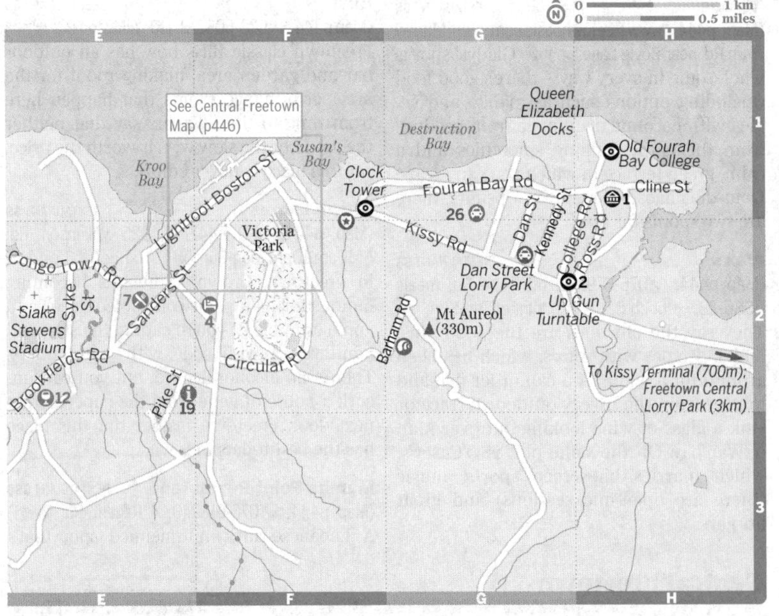

Greater Freetown

Sights
1 National Railway Museum H1
2 Old Boundary Cannons G2

Sleeping
3 Family Kingdom A1
4 Hotobah Lodge F2

Eating
5 Alex's A1
6 Bliss C3
7 Caribbean Restaurant E2
8 Crown Express C3
9 Mamba Point Restaurant D3
10 Oasis D2

Drinking & Nightlife
11 Atlantic B1
12 China House E2
13 O Bar B2
14 Plum Store D2
15 Roy's B2

Entertainment
16 Ace's A1

Shopping
17 Lumley Beach Arts & Crafts Market B2

Information
18 British High Commission C3
19 Conservation Society of Sierra Leone E2
20 DHL D2
21 German Embassy D3
22 Guinean Embassy C2
23 Liberian Embassy C3
24 Malian Consulate C2
25 Visit Sierra Leone D2

Transport
Diamond Hovercraft .... (see 16)
26 Poda-podas to Waterloo G1
27 UTAir B1

pect to fill up with cassava leaves or simple rice and fish for less than Le10,000.

Caribbean Restaurant CARIBBEAN $
(Map p444; ☎078-102813; Sanders St;) Krio goes back to its roots at this old but colourful Caribbean joint. There are great freshly squeezed juices to be had, as well as an all-you-can-eat Wednesday lunch buffet brimming with banana balls, jerked chicken and fried plantains. For dinner, you must book in advance.

★Oasis RESTAURANT **$$**

(Map p444; www.freetownoasis.com; 33 Murray Town Rd, near Boyle Lane;) Gladys' spot is wholesome in every way – there's good food (including options such as mango and vegies with coconut rice) made from produce from the garden, filling smoothies and a calm, green terrace in which you can escape from the chaos of Freetown. Upstairs, there are two rooms for rent.

Alex's RESTAURANT **$$**

(Map p444; 076-679272; off Cape Rd; meals US$6-28; lunch Sat & Sun, dinner Tue-Sun; P) They say the old ones are the good 'uns, and so it goes with Alex's, which has been around for a while. You can order fish and lobster from the breezy outdoor terrace or sink a glass of wine looking out over Man o' War bay. On the same plot is O'Casey's, which marries big-screen sports, music (there are open-mic sessions) and great burgers.

Bliss RESTAURANT **$$**

(Map p444; 078-609312; 110 Wilkinson Rd;) Freetown classic Bliss now has an outdoor bar and garden area, making room for the arts performance events that happen here from time to time. Expats say that neither the food nor the slow wi-fi is worth the price, yet this place is never empty.

Crown Express RESTAURANT **$$**

(Map p444; 077-447744; 125 Wilkinson Rd; 10am-10pm Mon-Sun;) A slice of London in Freetown, Crown Express is becoming famous for its hip, air-con-cooled decor and apple crumble. If you're eating, the staff will hand you a wi-fi code with your cutlery. There's no alcohol licence, but you can uncork a bottle of wine from the supermarket next door. Freetown insider tip: this place has the best toilets in town.

Mamba Point Restaurant RESTAURANT **$$$**

(Map p444; 076-618240; 4 Regent Rd;) A Lebanese-run, multimenued spot that's

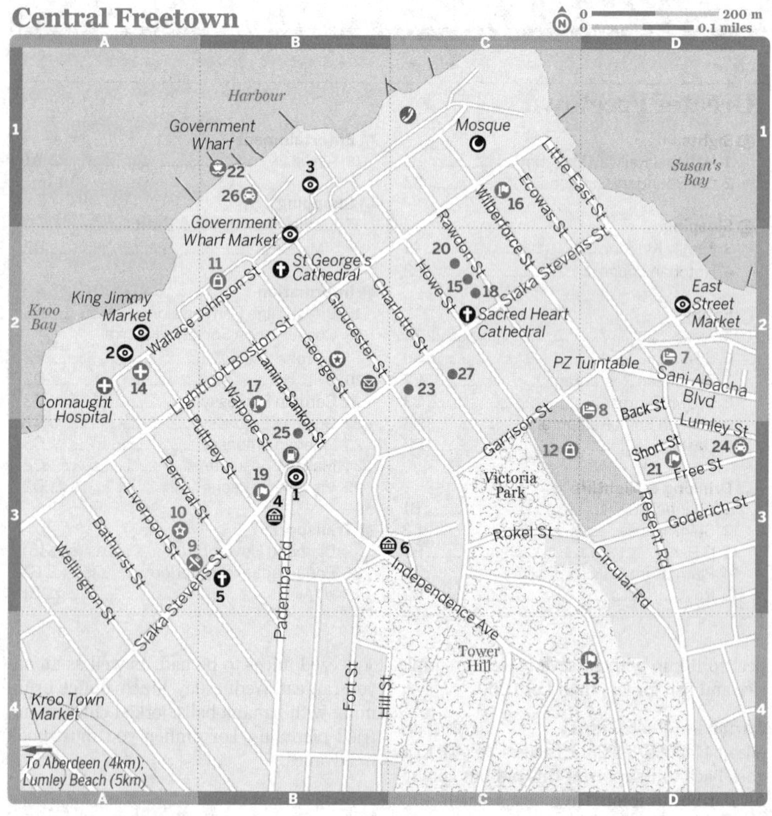

the sister restaurant of Monrovia's famous Mamba Point. The bar area is styled like a typical English gastropub, but it's the (expensive) sushi bar that's the main draw here. It's also a decent hotel.

Drinking & Nightlife

O Bar BAR
(Map p444; Lumley Beach; ⌚4pm-late Tue-Sun) You'll feel the strain on your wallet – and maybe your ears – at this swanky outdoor lounge that has banging music on the weekends. Popular with moneyed Sierra Leoneans and Lebanese, it also has an indoor club that's separated from the beach bar by the road.

Plum Store BAR
(Map p444) Cute Plum Store is shielded from the busy Congo Cross junction by greenery, making it an ideal spot for a quick drink on your way back from town.

Atlantic BAR
(Map p444; 63 Sir Samuel Lewis Rd) Toufic, the owner, will greet you with a weary grin at this old-time bar right on the water. Anything seems to go at the Atlantic – you can grind to Nigerian hip-hop, shoot some pool, catch a live band or chew on a sandwich.

Roy's BAR
(Map p444; ☎33405060) Watch the sun go down and the party people wake up on the deck at Roy's, a perfect sundowner's spot on Lumley Beach. It's hard to find a problem with this place – everyone from backpackers to ministerial employees seems to come here.

China House BAR
(Map p444; Youyi Building, cnr Main Motor & Brookfield Rds) Mingle with ministers at China House, strangely located in the compound of the ministerial building. There's live reggae music on Fridays, although you might want to watch who you elbow on your way to the bar.

Ace's CLUB
(Map p444; 74 Cape Rd; ⌚7pm-late) It's all smoke and mirrors at Ace's, a club that doesn't really get going until the wee small hours. Cultural groups occasionally interrupt the DJ sets here, soaring above the party people on trapezes. Out the back, there's an outdoor area, ping-pong and pool tables.

Balanta Music Academy DANCE
(Map p446) On the last Friday of every month, Balanta Music Academy opens its doors to the public for a great evening of student performers, attracting an artsy crowd – there's everything from African dance to a capella and big-band joy.

Shopping

Victoria Park Market MARKET
(Map p446; Garrison St) This is the place to find colourful local wax cloths and *gara* (thin tie-died or batik printed sheet).

Central Freetown

Sights
1 Cotton Tree B3
2 King's Yard Gate A2
3 Old Wharf Steps B1
4 Sierra Leone National Museum B3
5 St John's Maroon Church B3
6 State House C3

Sleeping
7 Kona Lodge D2
8 The Place D2

Eating
9 Dee's Bazaar A3

Entertainment
10 Balanta Music Academy A3

Shopping
11 Big Market B2
12 Victoria Park Market C3

Information
13 British Council D4
14 Central Pharmacy A2
15 DHL C2
16 Gambian High Commission C1
17 Ghanaian High Commission B2
18 Immigration Department C2
19 Nigerian Embassy B3
20 ProCredit C2
21 Senegalese Consulate D3

Transport
22 Allied Marine B1
23 Brussels Airlines C2
24 Bush Taxis for Conakry D3
25 Kenya Airways B3
26 Poda-podas to Hill Station Regent B1
27 Royal Air Maroc C2

Big Market MARKET

(Basket Market; Map p446; Wallace Johnson St; ⌚7am-7pm Mon-Sat) The top floor of the Big Market, also known as Basket Market, has a larger selection than markets in Lumley. What makes this the best place to shop for souvenirs is the traditional household goods on the ground floor.

Orientation

Central Freetown is set out on a grid pattern with Siaka Stevens St as the main thoroughfare. Budget hotels are clustered near PZ Turntable, which stays busy late into the night. Aberdeen and Lumley lie 30 minutes to an hour west, depending on traffic.

Information

CULTURAL CENTRES

British Council (Map p446; ☎224683; www.britishcouncil.org; Tower Hill; ⌚8.30am-4.30pm Mon-Thu, 8.30am-2pm Fri) Cultural Centre.

DANGERS & ANNOYANCES

Freetown has less crime than you'd imagine, but it still makes sense to be cautious and avoid walking alone late at night or leaving apartment doors unlocked. Walking on the beach alone, even during the day, is a bad idea.

By far the most dangerous creatures in Freetown are not the mosquitoes but the (admittedly cheap) motorbike taxis, which buzz far more loudly and swoop up and over the hills like there's no tomorrow. There might not be if you take one – do so at your peril and wear a helmet.

EMERGENCY

The emergency services (☎999) are unreliable in Sierra Leone.

INTERNET ACCESS

Most of the good hotels and some of the restaurants listed in the eating section offer access to wi-fi. Most expats get by with USB pay-as-you-go internet sticks. You can also pick up internet-ready SIM cards for smartphones and iPads.

MEDICAL SERVICES

Central Pharmacy (Map p446; ☎076-615503; 30 Wallace Johnson St) Reasonably well-stocked pharmacy.

Choitram Memorial Hospital (☎232598; Hill Station) Freetown's best hospital.

MONEY

Forex bureaus are found throughout the city. Rates at the airport's exchange bureau aren't too bad, but you'll do better in town.

ProCredit Central (Map p446; 11 Rawdon St) **Lumley** (157 Wilkinson Rd) Has Visa card-linked ATMs, as do most major banks and some of the hotels in the upper price-bracket.

POST

DHL Central (Map p446; ☎033-315299) Greater (Map p444; ☎236156; 30 Main Motor Rd)

Post Office (27 Siaka Stevens St)

TOURIST INFORMATION

Conservation Society of Sierra Leone (Map p444; ☎033-470043; cssl_03@yahoo.com; 2 Pike St; ⌚9am-5pm Mon-Fri) Very helpful for travellers to Sierra Leone's natural reserves, including the Turtle Islands.

TRAVEL AGENCIES

Visit Sierra Leone (Map p444; ☎076-877618; www.visitsierraleone.org; 28 Main Motor Rd) Brilliant one-stop shop for tours, information, transport, guides and historical knowledge.

Getting There & Away

From the main bus station, reasonably well-maintained buses operate to cities such as Bo, Kabala, Kenema, Koidu-Sefadu (Kono) and Makeni and Conakry (Guinea). Shared bush taxis head to the same destinations, stopping at villages and communities along the way. They leave from **Freetown Central Lorry Park** (Bai Bureh Rd), also known as Clay Factory, at Texaco Junction on the far east side of town. Taxis to Conakry park along Free St near Victoria Park Market.

For airlines serving Sierra Leone and overland options to Liberia, see Getting There & Away (p455).

Getting Around

Shared taxis and *poda-podas* (minibuses) cost Le1000 per short hop and run on fixed routes around town. You can also bargain for a charter taxi, which feels like the lap of luxury after being squashed into the back of a shared ride with four or five others. The motorbike taxis, known as *okadas*, as they are in Nigeria, can be downright reckless: ride with caution, or even better, don't ride at all.

AROUND FREETOWN

Beaches

Freetown's tongue stretches out along the coast, kissing beaches lined with tall, elegant palms and iced with sand that's white as snow.

River No 2 shot to fame after the Bounty chocolate bar ad was filmed here, and the sugary white sands don't disappoint. The

TO & FROM THE AIRPORT

Sierra Leone has something rare: a journey to and from the airport that is arguably more spectacular than the views you'll see from the air. Lungi International Airport is located across the Sierra Leone River on an island, and you have five options to reach it: choppers (when they're running), a slow ferry (ditto), hovercraft, speedboat and water taxis.

Lungi International Airport is inconveniently located across the Sierra Leone River from Freetown. The fastest way to town is by **UTAir** (Map p444; ☎033-807420; one way US$80) helicopter, followed by **Diamond Hovercraft** (Map p444; ☎076-614888). Both drop and depart at Aberdeen, but they don't meet every flight. **Sea Coach Express** (☎033-111118; one way US$40) runs slower, smaller boats to Aberdeen Bridge for every flight. **Allied Marine** (Map p446; ☎033-664545; one way US$40) uses buses and ferries to take you to Government Wharf in the city centre. Other companies also plan to enter the airport transport game.

The helicopters are by far the most expensive (in more than one way) option, with prices starting at US$80 for the five-minute ride, and there have been several crashes throughout the years. Then there's the hovercraft, which can be booked at the Visit Sierra Leone office for US$40 one-way. Speedboats arranged through Pelican or Sea Coach Express cost US$40 and the boats are well maintained with life-jackets for all. They run in coordination with the airport's flight schedule. The two-to-three-hour ferry was not running at the time of research, and there were several other water taxi companies beginning operations.

You can find a taxi from any of the landing sites, although you might want to book ahead if you're arriving early or late.

eponymous **River No 2 Guesthouse** is a community-run spot that has simple, clean rooms and red wooden tables sunk into the sand. The food – skewers of lime-soaked barracuda, or lobster and chips – is hearty and fresh. Boat trips can be arranged up the river to waterfalls, and down the peninsula to the Banana Islands.

Around the bend and cradled by the mountains behind is **Tokeh Beach** (you can walk here from River No 2, using a boat over the river at high tide), one of the most spectacular beaches on the peninsula, purportedly popular with European celebs before the war. **Tokeh Sands** (☎078-911111; r US$60-180), which has sleek, white rooms with 24-hour power and air-con, opened here in 2013. You can swim out to the old helipad nearby, or kick off your sandals and nap in one of the hammocks strung between the palms while you wait for the daily dinner menu – which features the likes of seared tiger prawns and homemade sorbet – to fall into your palms.

About 20km south of Freetown along the peninsula is **John Obey Beach**, home to the unusual ecotourism project **Tribe Wanted**. Guests stay in tents (US$50), hip beach bungalows (US$80) or smooth clay honeydomes (US$80) that look as if they were created in a pottery class. There are eco-toilets and showers open to the stars. Meals at the open beach 'chop house' are included, and you're expected to pitch in or get involved with the community projects to make the most of the experience.

Half an hour from Freetown is the Sierra Leone foodie institution **Franco's** (☎078-366366), sprawled on Sussex Beach (beside the lagoon). Run by an Italian–Sierra Leonean couple, this is a favourite spot for a long, wine-fuelled Sunday lunch. It's worth ordering in advance as food can take a while to prepare at busy times of the year.

Ask someone in York, an interesting Krio village, to show you the caves on **York Beach** where slaves supposedly stayed before being loaded onto ships. From here you can look across Whale Bay to deserted and tough-to-reach **Black Johnson Beach**. It may be possible to walk here in the dry season; otherwise get a boat in York or follow the unmarked mile-long dirt road (veer right at the first junction) that begins after the Whale River Bridge.

At the tip of the peninsula is **Kent**, with its ruined fort and frequent transport to the Banana Islands.

Thanks to a freshly paved road, shared transport now runs down the coast all the way to Tokeh (US$2) and onto Kent.

Banana Islands

Dublin (*doo-blin*), Ricketts and Mes-Meheux are the three bananas in this pretty archipelago, hanging from the southern tip of the peninsula like a ripe bunch of fruit. The islands were first settled by the Portuguese in the 17th century and were later inhabited by freed slaves from the Caribbean – the descendents of those who live here now.

★**Banana Island Guest House** (☎076-989906; www.bananaislandguesthouse-biya.org; r US$65-115) has cute, solar-powered bamboo-style chalets on Dublin Island. The owners can organise sea transport from Kent. The 25-minute crossing costs Le150,000 per boatload. There's also **Dalton's Banana Guest House** (☎076-570208; per person Le30,000), which is a cheaper accommodation option.

Alternatively, you can make your own way to the islands by shared boat; a seat on a regular transport boat will cost you just under US$2.

Bunce Island

The former slave-trading post of Bunce Island lies some 30km up the Sierra Leone River from the ocean. Slave traders began operations here around 1670, and before the British outlawed the industry in 1807 some 30,000 men, women and children were shipped off into exile by four British slave-trading companies. Among those who have been traced back to here are the Gullah families of South Carolina.

You can visit the island and fort by boat from Freetown's Kissy Terminal, where you can charter a small boat for US$100, reaching Bunce in about two hours. A speedboat (about US$300 per boatload) can do it in under an hour from Man o' War Bay.

Tacugama Chimpanzee Sanctuary

Up and over Sugar Loaf Mountain, Sri Lankan founder Bala created **Tacugama Chimpanzee Sanctuary** (☎076-611211; www.tacugama.com; adult/child US$10/3.50; ⊙tours by appointment 10.30am & 4pm), a leafy, waterfall-framed hideaway set up with the purpose of educating humans about one of our closest relatives. This excellent sanctuary remained operational throughout the war.

You can sleep here, bedding down in tree houses (from US$90) that overlook the sanctuary, or you can come for the day, watching rescued chimps lark around in enclosures or spotting those who have been released to a larger area in the mountains beyond. Ninety-minute tours of the sanctuary run by appointment at 10.30am and 4pm each day and you can follow walking trails around the area.

A short drive from Freetown in the Peninsula Mountains, Tacugama is off the Regent/Bathurst road. The last stretch of the route follows a rough, unpaved path through the rainforest that can only be reached by 4WD or on foot (20 minutes).

THE NORTH

Makeni

POP 105,000

Makeni mixes politics with football as the birthplace of both Ernest Bai Koroma and the Wusum Stars, Sierra Leone's oldest football club. It's a good base for exploring the northern highlands. Any of the city's hotels will be able to advise you on getting out into the countryside, including rock climbing and hiking.

Straight-talking Irish Sister Mary will welcome you into the fold at **St Joseph's School for the Deaf**, where you can sleep in one of the lovely, fan-blown rooms with high-ceilings and bathrooms (from Le129,000). You can also tour the well-run school, eat meals here, book in for a massage and take a look at the arts and crafts on sale.

Or you can head to the fancier **Wusum Hotel** (☎076-341079; wusum.hotel@yahoo.co.uk; 65 Teko Rd; s/d US$88/110, chalets US$117; P ❄ @ ≋), which is more of a luxury resort (with a pool and conference facilities) than just a place to lay your head.

About 45 minutes from Makeni is **Rogbonko Village** (☎08-8631079), where you can go back to basics, overnighting in a thatched guest hut and sampling local country food.

Bush taxis and *poda-podas* run to many destinations including Freetown (two hours).

Mt Bintumani

Also known as Loma Mansa, the breathy King of the Mountains, 1945m-high Mt Bintumani is West Africa's highest peak – until you hit Cameroon. The mountain range is rich in highland birds and mammal species, including duikers, colobus monkeys, buffaloes, leopards and snakes. Any climbing attempt should be taken seriously – you might want to stay away during the slippery rainy season and come prepared with a GPS and hiking and camping equipment.

The main climbing route winds up from the village of Sokurala via Kurubonla, about 180km from Kabala. You can also stay overnight in Yifin, or if you're coming from Makeni in the east, follow the dirt road all the way to Sinekoro. Neither village had a guesthouse at the time of research, but you can take an offering to the local chief and ask if you might rent sleeping space from a local family. You can also hire local porters if you have camping gear you'd like to safely lug to the top. There are two campsites located just before the mountain becomes steep.

It's well worth the four-to-five day adventure; the spectacular summit looks out over most of West Africa, veiled by soft cool mist.

Outamba-Kilimi National Park

About 300km north of Freetown, Outamba-Kilimi seems like something out of East Africa rather than a treasure of the west, with its rolling savannah, elephant watering holes and hippo-trodden rivers. There are nine species of primates here, and there have been leopard and pygmy hippo sightings.

Sadly much of the park facilities were destroyed during the war, but efforts are underway to rebuild. Until then, you can stay in huts on the outskirts of the park for a small fee, and guides (US$5) can be arranged to accompany you on the trails. Fifteen kilometres to the south, Kamakwie is the nearest town. You can hire motorbikes (from US$12) or 4WDs (which cost much more) from here to reach the reserve.

THE SOUTH

Bo

POP 245,000

Sierra Leone's second-largest city, Bo escaped the scars of the war and is in better shape than many other urban centres. Still, there isn't much to do besides sleep, eat, chat and wander – just don't stray too far as this is somewhat sketchy diamond territory too.

For low budgets, there's **Madame Woki's** in the centre of town, while the **Sahara Hotel** (☎033908929; New Gerihun Rd; r Le50,000 incl breakfast) has comfortable rooms.

Bush taxis to Freetown (four hours) depart frequently each morning from Maxwell Khobe Park near the centre. Abess buses (US$6) leave from Tikonko Rd around midnight. The quickest way to Kenema is usually to go out to Shell-Mingo on the highway and jump in a taxi there.

Turtle Islands

This beautiful, remote eight-island archipelago in Sierra Leone's southwest peninsula is made from soft white sand, thick shavings of palm fronds and the purest turquoise water. Tethered to a traditional way of life, the islands swing to their own rhythms. You can explore most of them with the exception of Hoong, which is a male-only island reserved for rites of passage.

The Conservation Society of Sierra Leone (p448) can arrange boats (US$600 per boatload) from Freetown and accommodation at a basic lodge, or you can talk to Visit Sierra Leone (p448) to arrange to take a speedboat down (US$300 per person) and camp on the shores.

Tiwai Island

'Big Island' in the Mende language, 12-sq-km **Tiwai Island** (☎076-755146; www.tiwaiisland.org; day-trip/overnight US$10/20) certainly packs a punch when it comes to its primate population. Set on the Moa River, the entire island is run as a conservation research project. There are more than 700 different plant species, 11 species of primates – including Diana monkeys and chimpanzees – 135 bird species, plus otters, sea turtles and the endangered, elusive pygmy hippopotamus.

From Bo or Kenema, the departure point for Tiwai is Poturu; from Freetown, head to Kambama (eight hours). Speedboats (US$10 per person including island entrance fee) carry you the short distance to the island, where you can stay overnight on canopied platforms (US$20 per person) and drift off to sleep, listening to the midnight chatter of the rainforest.

Guided forest walks cost between US$4 and US$6 per person, depending on the size of the group. Canoe tours cost US$10 per person.

Gola Forest Reserve

Part of the same tract of rainforest as Tiwai Island, the **Gola Forest Reserve** (☎076-420218) is home to an abundance of creatures great and small, from rare, intricately patterned butterflies to lost, lumbering forest elephants having a hard time locating the rest of their species (as in most parts of West Africa, their numbers are critically low). The reserve, which has been declared a national park, runs from Tiwai Island in the south (a short boat ride away) up to the rocky Malema hills in the north (an hour's drive from Kenema).

There's a simple, reasonably priced guesthouse at the southern tip in the village of Belebu, or you can rent camping equipment (US$25) and rough it in the rainforest. The park entrance fee is US$10, and the forest guides charge US$10 per day (plus a tip).

Kenema

POP 160,000

Unless you're caught up in the murky world of diamonds there isn't much to bring you to the red roads of Kenema, although the surrounding countryside is pretty and a visit to the area will give you an idea of what life is like upcountry. It's also a good stopping point on the way to the Gola Forest Reserve or Tiwai Island.

Ericsons (☎076-410722) has clean, spacious doubles, while **Capitol Hotel** (☎033-161616; 51 Hangha Rd; s/d/ste US$52/85/138; P ❄ ≋) has all the mod-cons and a central location.

Bush taxis to Bo (1½ hours), Potoru (three hours), Freetown (five hours) and the Liberian border depart from the bus station in the centre of town.

UNDERSTAND SIERRA LEONE

History

The North American slave trade was effectively launched from Freetown in 1560 and by the 18th century Portuguese and British trading settlements lined the coast. In the late 1700s, freed slaves from places such as Jamaica and Nova Scotia were brought to the new settlement of Freetown. Soon after, Britain abolished slavery and Sierra Leone became a British colony. Many subsequent settlers were liberated from slaving ships intercepted by the British navy and brought here. These people became known as Krios and assumed an English lifestyle together with an air of superiority.

But things didn't run smoothly in this brave new world. Black and white settlers dabbling in the slave trade, disease, rebellion and attacks by the French were all characteristics of 19th-century Sierra Leone. Most importantly, indigenous people were discriminated against by the British and Krios, and in 1898 a ferocious uprising by the Mende began, ostensibly in opposition to a hut tax.

Diamonds Are Forever

Independence came in 1961, but the 1960s and 1970s were characterised by coups (once there were three in one year, an all-African record), a shift of power to the indigenous Mende and Temne peoples, and the establishment of a one-party state (which lasted into the 1980s). By the early 1990s the country was saddled with a shambolic economy and rampant corruption. Then the civil war began.

It's entirely possible that buried in the depths of Foday Sankoh's Revolutionary United Front (RUF) was a desire to end the corruption and abuses of power committed by the ruling military-backed elites in Freetown, who had turned the country into a basket case. But any high ideals were quickly forgotten, replaced by a ferocious desire for Sierra Leone's diamond and goldfields, with looting, robbery, rape, mutilation and summary execution, all tools of the RUF's trade. While their troops plundered to make ends meet, Charles Taylor, the former president of Liberia, and the RUF's leaders enriched themselves from diamonds smuggled south.

The Sierra Leone government was pretty ineffective and tried using South African mercenaries against the RUF, who, bolstered by disaffected army elements and Liberian irregulars, were making gains across the country. In 1996 elections were held and Ahmad Tejan Kabbah was declared president, but a year later, after peace talks had brought some hope, the Armed Forces Revolutionary Council (AFRC) grabbed control of government and decided to share power with the RUF. By this time fractionalisation and desertion on both sides had led to an utter free-for-all, with the civilian population suffering atrocities at every turn.

Hopes & Fears

In March 1998 the Economic Community of West African States Monitoring Group (Ecomog), a Nigerian-led peacekeeping force, retook Freetown and reinstated Kabbah. Some sort of peace held until January 1999, when the RUF and AFRC launched 'Operation No Living Thing'. The ensuing carnage in and around Freetown killed 6000 people, mutilated many more (lopping a limb off was an RUF calling card) and prompted the government to sign the Lomé Peace Agreement. A massive UN peacekeeping mission (Unamsil) was deployed, but 10 months later it came under attack from the RUF. Three hundred UN troops were abducted, but as the RUF closed in on Freetown in mid-2000 the British government deployed 1000 paratroopers and an aircraft carrier to prevent a massacre and shift the balance of power back to Kabbah's government and UN forces. By February 2002 the RUF was disarmed and its leaders captured. Elections were held a few months later; Kabbah was re-elected and the RUF's political wing was soundly defeated.

Unamsil became the largest and most expensive peacekeeping mission in UN history up until that time, and also one of its most effective. The last of the 17,500 soldiers departed in 2005. Peace had won.

The road to justice, however, was just beginning. The Special Court for Sierra Leone, a UN-backed judicial body charged with investigating war crimes during the conflict, was set up in 2002 and headquartered in Freetown. It took 10 years for proceedings against more than 15 people to be completed; among them Issa Sesay, the RUF's senior military officer and commander, who received 52 years – the court's highest sentence – behind bars in Rwanda. The court's most famous convictee was Charles Taylor, the former president of next-door Liberia, who received a jail sentence of 50 years in 2012. His case was transferred to The Hague, amid fears it could spark a resurgence of unrest in Liberia and Sierra Leone. At the time of research Taylor was appealing his sentence.

Sierra Leone Today

Former insurance broker Ernest Bai Koroma won a second – and, according to the constitution, final – term in power in November 2012, with 59% of the votes cast. The poll, Sierra Leone's second since the post-conflict period began, passed largely without violence and was hailed as a marker of the peaceful postwar era. The country now has one of the fastest-growing economies in Africa, and the ongoing boost and interest in tourism is likely to continue to drive that.

Culture

The two largest of the 18 tribal groups, the Temnes of the north and Mendes of the south, each make up about one-third of the population. Krios, mostly living in Freetown, constitute about 1.5% of the population but a large percentage of the professional class.

About 75% of Sierra Leoneans are Muslim; most of the remaining are Christian, who live in the south. Sierra Leoneans are very tolerant and mixed marriages are common.

The Mendes and Temnes operate a system of secret societies responsible for maintaining culture and tradition. For example, if you see young girls with their faces painted white, you'll know that they're in the process of being initiated. They wear coloured beads when they have finished.

When Sierra Leoneans get together, talk always seems to turn to politics, development and corruption. The war did much to foster nationalism (everyone suffered together), but the elections showed that a significant north-south, Temne–Mende divide remains and it has become natural for the political parties to exploit it. Some people worry about how this will play out in coming years.

Handicrafts

Sierra Leone is known for its fabrics, especially country cloth, a coarse, naturally dyed cotton material, and *gara*, a thin tie-dyed or batik-printed sheet. Distinctive Temne basketry also makes a good souvenir.

Books

For a classic, there's Graham Greene's colonial-era *The Heart of the Matter*, set in Freetown. Aminatta Forna's *The Memory of Love* is a thrilling, poignant take on the effect of the conflict in Sierra Leone.

Food & Drink

Sierra Leone is known for its cuisine, and every town has at least one *cookery* (basic eating house) serving *chop* (meals). Rice is the staple and *plasas* (pounded potato or cassava leaves, cooked with palm oil and often fish or beef) is the most common sauce. Other typical dishes include okra sauce, groundnut stew and pepper soup. Street food, such as fried chicken, roasted corn, chicken kebabs and *fry fry* (simple sandwiches), is easy to find.

Star, the top-selling beer, is reasonable. *Poyo* (palm wine) is light and fruity, but getting used to the smell and the wildlife floating in your cup takes a while.

Environment

Sierra Leone's coast is lined with cracking beaches, mangrove swamps and many islands. The Freetown peninsula is one of the few places in West Africa where mountains rise near the sea. Inland are sweeping plains punctuated by random mountains, including Mt Bintumani (1945m), one of West Africa's highest peaks. About 30% of the country is forested and significant patches of primary rainforest remain in the south and east.

Outamba-Kilimi National Park (which still has elephants) in the north, and Tiwai Island (incredible for primates) in the south are worth a visit, but don't expect East African-style wildlife encounters.

SURVIVAL GUIDE

Directory A–Z

ACCOMMODATION

Freetown has a growing number of accommodation choices, although you may have to pay through the roof for 24-hour power, water and internet. Elsewhere in the country, choices are more limited, but you can still find some gems.

BUSINESS HOURS

Banks Usually Monday to Friday 8.30am to 4pm, with a select few also open Saturday 9am to 1pm.

General shops and offices 9am to 5.30pm Monday to Saturday, though some places close at 1pm on Saturday.

EMBASSIES & CONSULATES

Most embassies are located in Freetown.

British High Commission (Map p444; ☎232961; http://ukinsierraleone.fco.gov.uk; 6 Spur Rd) Assists French nationals.

Gambian High Commission (Map p446; ☎225191; 6 Wilberforce St)

German Embassy (Map p444; ☎231350; 3 Middle Hill Station)

Ghanaian High Commission (Map p446; ☎223461; 13 Walpole St)

Guinean Embassy (Map p444; ☎232496; 6 Carlton Carew Rd)

Liberian Embassy (Map p444; ☎230991; 2 Spur Rd)

Malian Consulate (Map p444; ☎033-422994; 40 Wilkinson Rd)

Nigerian Embassy (Map p446; ☎224229; 37 Siaka Stevens St)

Senegalese Consulate (Map p446; ☎030-230666; 7 Short St, 2nd fl)

US Embassy (☎076-515000; http://freetown.usembassy.gov; Leicester Rd)

FESTIVALS & EVENTS

Freetown's recently revived **Lantern Parade** is a procession of illuminated floats on 26 April, the night before Independence Day.

INTERNET ACCESS

Most of the good hotels, and some of the restaurants listed in the Eating section, offer access to wi-fi. Most expats get by with USB pay-as-you-go internet sticks. You can also pick up internet-ready SIM cards for smartphones and iPads.

MONEY

The most easily exchangeable currencies in Sierra Leone are US dollars, UK pounds and euros, in that order. Large denominations get the best rates. Forex bureaus (and street traders, though avoid them unless somebody you trust makes the introduction) invariably offer better rates than banks.

PRACTICALITIES

- **Electricity** i230V/50Hz. Plugs have three large pins, like the UK.
- **Newspapers** *Awoko* and *Concord Times* are the most respected newspapers, though the satirical *Peep* is more popular.
- **Magazines** *Newsweek* and *BBC Focus On Africa* are sold at supermarkets.
- **TV** Sierra Leone's two TV stations are the government-owned SLBS and the private ABC, both of whose most popular programming is Nigerian soap operas.
- **Radio** The BBC World Service is heard on 94.3FM and Voice of America on 102.4FM. SKYY (106.6FM) plays the most local music.
- **Languages** Include English, Krio, Mende and Temne.

You can rarely pay with a credit card in Sierra Leone, but some Rokel Commercial Bank branches give cash advances (up to US$2000) on Visa cards and ProCredit Bank has ATMs in Freetown that spit out up to US$100 per day for those with Visa credit and debit cards. Don't rely on them too heavily, as they sometimes don't work.

POST & TELEPHONE

Cell phone service is good and so popular that landlines are disappearing. SIM cards cost US$5.

Sierra Leone's regular post is semi-reliable if you send something from Freetown.

PUBLIC HOLIDAYS

Besides the Islamic and Christian holidays, Sierra Leone celebrates New Year's Day (1 January) and Independence Day (27 April).

SAFE TRAVEL

Sierra Leone is generally safe, although the biggest dangers are the roads and the tides, both of which can claim travellers who aren't vigilant about safety. Read up on rip tides before you travel, and be sure to wear a seatbelt whenever possible: driving safety standards aren't always the highest. Avoid walking on Freetown's beaches alone – you should be fine on the peninsula – and it's best to walk in a group at night. Motorbike taxis are not the safest way to travel, especially in Freetown and other places with smooth roads.

TOURIST INFORMATION

The **National Tourist Board** (www.welcometosierraleone.org) might be helpful, but the best source of pre-departure information is Visit Sierra Leone (p448).

VISAS

Everyone from outside Ecowas (Economic Community of West African States) countries needs a visa. Prices and rules vary widely by nationality of applicant and embassy of issuance, but generally you need a plane ticket and a letter of invitation (a hotel reservation should suffice), and your passport needs one year of validity, rather than the typical six months. The regulations are generally more relaxed in embassies of neighbouring countries.

Some people manage to get visas on arrival for an extra fee, but this is unofficial and you risk being turned away.

Visa Extensions

Visas can be easily extended for 30 days at the **Immigration Department** (Map p446; ☎223220; Rawdon St; ⏲10am-3.30pm Mon-Fri) in Freetown.

Getting There & Away

AIR

British Airways (☎076-541230; www.flybmi.com; 14 Wilberforce St) flies to London for around £700 return, while **Brussels Airlines** (☎076-333777; www.brusselsairlines.com; 30 Siaka Stevens St) serves its hub in Brussels.

Kenya Airways (☎076-536899; www.kenya-airways.com; 13 Lamina Sankoh St) flies from Nairobi for around US$1300 return and **Royal Air Maroc** (☎076-221015; www.royalairmaroc.com; 19 Charlotte St) flies from Casablanca for around £600.

For regional flights, Asky routes go via its hub in Lome and Arik Airlines flies to Dakar (and onwards to London).

> **DEPARTURE TAX**
>
> The airport departure tax is US$40, payable in dollars, pounds or leones.

LAND

Guinea

The main route to Guinea is via Pamelap. Bush taxis from Freetown to Conakry run regularly. The journey usually takes eight to 10 hours, depending on the season and the state of the roads.

From Kamakwie to Kindia (Guinea) there's little transport on the Sierra Leone side, where the road is quite bad. 4WDs usually leave Kamakwie every two or three days (US$10, eight to 10 hours). Alternatively, hire an *okada* to the border (they'll ask for US$20), where it's about a 1.5km walk to Medina-Oula in Guinea, which has plenty of transport.

The road from Kabala to Faranah (Guinea), is also in bad shape and only has 4WDs (US$13.50, four to eight hours, twice weekly). *Okada* drivers will take you to Faranah for US$50 in four hours or you could stop in Hérémakono to get a taxi.

Liberia

You can reach Liberia via the Mano River Bridge by Bo (Waterside), provided the raft ferry is running (otherwise you'll have to leave your car and take a pirogue, which is not recommended for safety reasons). Taxis (US$13.50) and sometimes *poda-podas* (US$12) depart from Bo and Kenema to the border post at Gendema (taking six to eight hours in the dry season and 10 to 12 hours in the wet), where you walk over to Liberia and continue in one of the frequent taxis to Monrovia. If you have your own 4WD, you can reach Monrovia in 10 to 12 hours from Freetown.

Getting Around

BOAT

Pam-pahs (large cargo and passenger boats) operate to several towns, most notably between Mattru Jong and Bonthe.

Speedboat hire costs from US$300 per day while slower *pam-pahs* (which hold up to 20 people) cost around US$165. In Freetown, inquire at Man o' War Bay, Government Wharf, Kissy Terminal and the Conservation Society of Sierra Leone.

CAR

Car hire is expensive (starting at around US$100 in Freetown, much more to head upcountry), but don't choose a company only on the price; ask about the terms too.

You could also just charter *(chatah)* a taxi. In Freetown you can usually negotiate an hourly rate of US$5 for one hour, and US$4 per hour for several hours.

LOCAL TRANSPORT

Bush taxis and *poda-podas* link most towns; except for departures to and from Freetown and between Bo and Kenema, you'll find that traffic is usually pretty sparse, especially on Sunday. Buses will usually cost a little less, but they are slower.

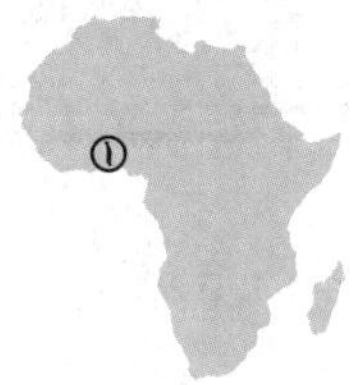

Togo

POP 6.9 MILLION

Includes ➡

Best Places to Eat

- Côté Jardin (p462)
- La Belle Époque (p462)
- Le Fermier (p465)
- Centre Grill (p466)

Best Places to Stay

- Hôtel Napoléon Lagune (p459)
- Côté Sud (p459)
- Le Geyser (p464)
- Coco Beach (p463)
- La Douceur (p466)

Why Go?

For those fond of travelling off the beaten track, Togo will prove a rewarding destination. It offers a great diversity of landscapes, from the lakes and palm-fringed beaches along the Atlantic coastline to the rolling forested hills in the centre. As you head further north, the landscape leaves its mantle of lush forest green for the light green and yellowy tinges of savannah land. The cherry on top is Lomé, the low-key yet elegant capital, with its large avenues, tasty restaurants and throbbing nightlife – not to mention the splendid beaches on its doorstep. Togo is also an excellent playground for hikers – there's no better ecofriendly way to experience the country's savage beauty than on foot.

Another highlight is the culture. Togo is a melting pot. The fortified compounds of Koutammakou are a reminder that the country's ethnically diverse population didn't always get along. Nowadays, however, voodoo, Muslim, Christian and traditional festivals crowd the calendar and are often colourful celebrations for all.

When to Go

Lomé

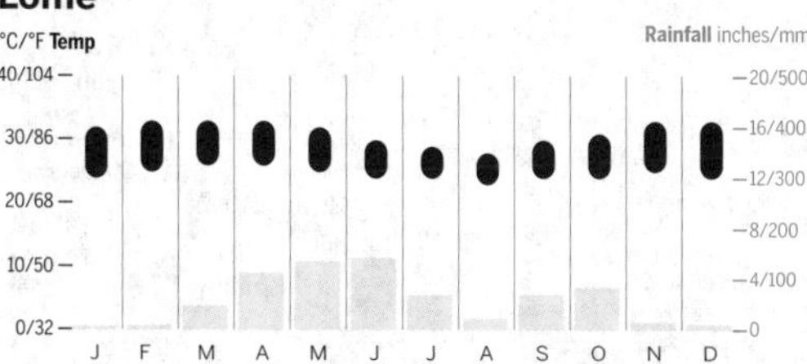

Nov–Feb The best time to visit, with pleasant temperatures. Perfect for outdoor activities.

Mid-Jul–mid-Sep There's a dry spell in the south, which makes transport less challenging.

Mar & Apr The hottest period throughout the country is best avoided.

Togo Highlights

1. Soaking up the the mellow vibes of **Lomé** (p459), the coastal capital.
2. Unwinding on blissful **Coco Beach** (p463).
3. Relaxing on the shores of **Lac Togo** (p463).
4. Hiking in lush forested hills and taking in the chilled vibe of **Kpalimé** (p464).
5. Tracking buffaloes and antelopes at **Parc Sarakawa** (p466), Togo's most underrated wildlife reserve.
6. Seeking out northern Togo's remote clay-and-straw fortresses, the *tata* compounds, around **Koutammakou** (p467).

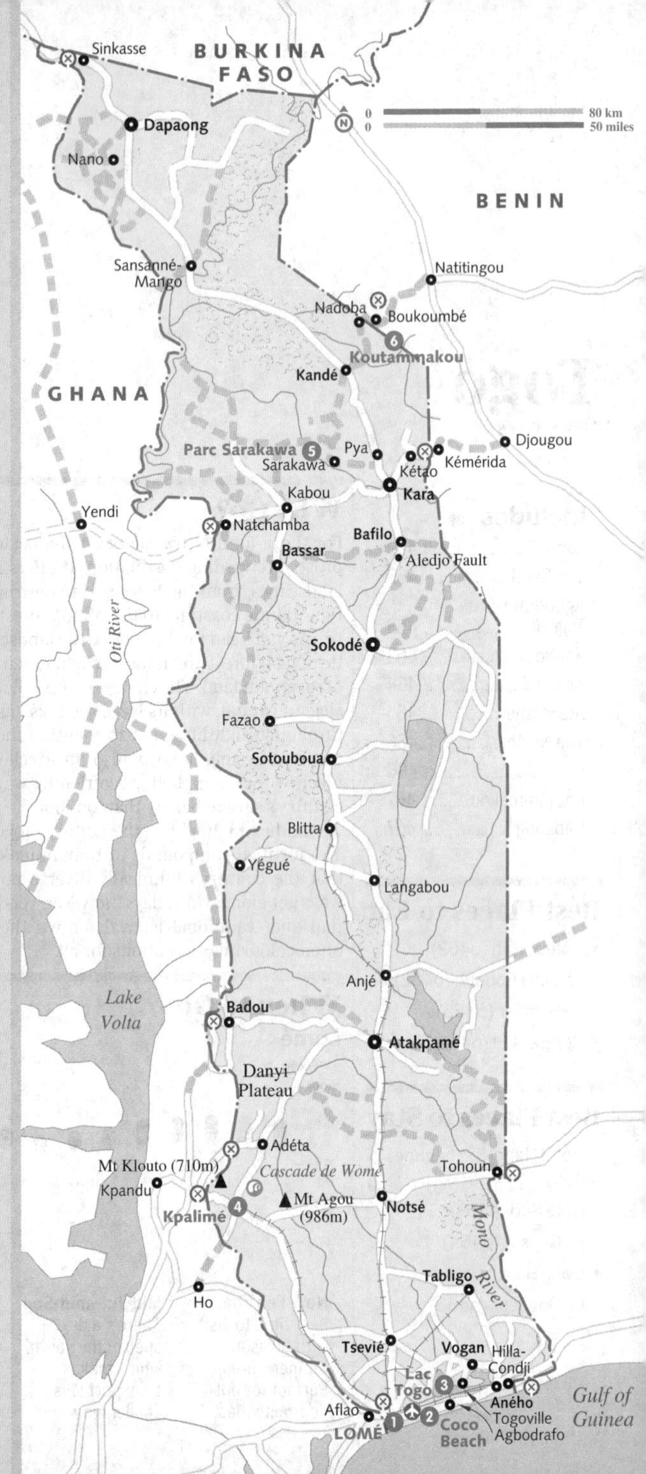

LOMÉ

POP 750,000

Togo's capital may be a shadow of its former self, when it was dubbed 'the pearl of West Africa', but it retains a charm and nonchalance that is unique among West African capitals. You'll probably appreciate its human scale and unexpected treats and gems: from tasty *maquis* (informal street-side eateries) to colourful markets and palm-fringed boulevards.

Sights

Marché des Féticheurs MARKET

(Fetish Market; ☎227 20 96; Quartier Akodessewa; admission & guide CFA3000, plus per camera/video CFA5000/10,000; ⏰8.30am-6pm daily) The Marché des Féticheurs, 4km northeast of the centre, stocks all the ingredients for traditional fetishes, from porcupine skin to serpent head. It's all a bit grisly but it's important to remember that a vast majority of Togolese retain animist beliefs and fetishes are an integral part of local culture. To get there charter a taxi (CFA1000) or a *taxi-moto* (motorbike taxi; CFA500).

Grand Marché MARKET

(Rue du Grand Marché; ⏰to 4pm Mon-Sat) The labyrinthine Grand Marché is Togo at its most colourful and entrepreneurial. You'll find anything at this market from Togolese football tops to cheap cosmetics.

Sleeping

Auberge Le Galion HOTEL $

(☎22 22 00 30; www.hotel-galion.com; 12 Rue des Camomilles, Kodjoviakopé; r with fan CFA7000-10,000, with air-con CFA13,000-17,000; ❄📶) This Swiss-owned hotel is the stalwart of budget accommodation in Lomé. The 24 rooms are basic but clean and the restaurant (mains CFA1800 to CFA4900) and bar are very popular, particularly for the live-music session on Friday night. The more expensive rooms have hot water. It's in a quiet residential area.

My Diana Guesthouse GUESTHOUSE $

(☎91 25 08 80; Rue des Jonquilles; r CFA6000-8000; ❄) A family affair, this lovely guesthouse is a simple but proudly maintained establishment. You'll have to pay more for air-con (CFA500 to CFA1000 per night, depending on electricity consumption) but considering you get use of the kitchen, garden terrace and TV lounge, it's a great bargain.

SET YOUR BUDGET

Budget

- Hotel room CFA10,000
- Sandwich CFA600
- Fruit juice CFA400
- *Moto-taxi* ride CFA300

Midrange

- Hotel room CFA20,000
- Two-course dinner CFA4000
- Drink in a bar CFA1000
- Intercity bus ride CFA7000

Top End

- Hotel room CFA40,000
- Two-course meal CFA10,000
- Cocktail CFA2000
- 4WD with driver, per day CFA50,000

Hôtel Belle-Vue HOTEL $$

(☎22 20 22 40; www.hotel-togo-bellevue.com; Kodjoviakopé; s CFA29,000-35,000, d CFA31,000-40,000; P❄@📶) In the leafy district of Kodjoviakopé, the Belle-Vue is a stylish option that won't break the bank. Rooms are spotless and elegantly decorated with African print curtains and dark-wood furniture. It is also home to one of Lomé's best restaurants, La Belle Époque, and has a great *paillote* (shaded seats) bar in a lush garden. A cool retreat.

★**Côté Sud** GUESTHOUSE $$

(☎91 93 45 50, 23 36 12 70; www.hotelcotesud.com; Rue Nima; r CFA23,000-30,000; ❄📶) Seeking a relaxing cocoon in Lomé with homely qualities? This champ of a guesthouse run by a French guy who fell in love with Togo has all the key ingredients, with five spacious, light and spick-and-span rooms, prim bathrooms and a small garden. The on-site restaurant (mains CFA3500 to CFA6000) is a winner – your host will treat you to tasty French dishes with an African twist.

★**Hôtel Napoléon Lagune** HOTEL $$

(☎22 27 07 32; www.napotogo.com; Rte 20 Bé; d CFA24,000-33,000; P❄📶🏊) Yes, the Napoléon Lagune is not in the centre, but its perch on a lively stretch of the Bé lagoon is outstanding. It offers a range of well-equipped if unspectacular rooms at reasonable prices. Good service, satellite TV, a plant-filled garden, a small pool and

Lomé

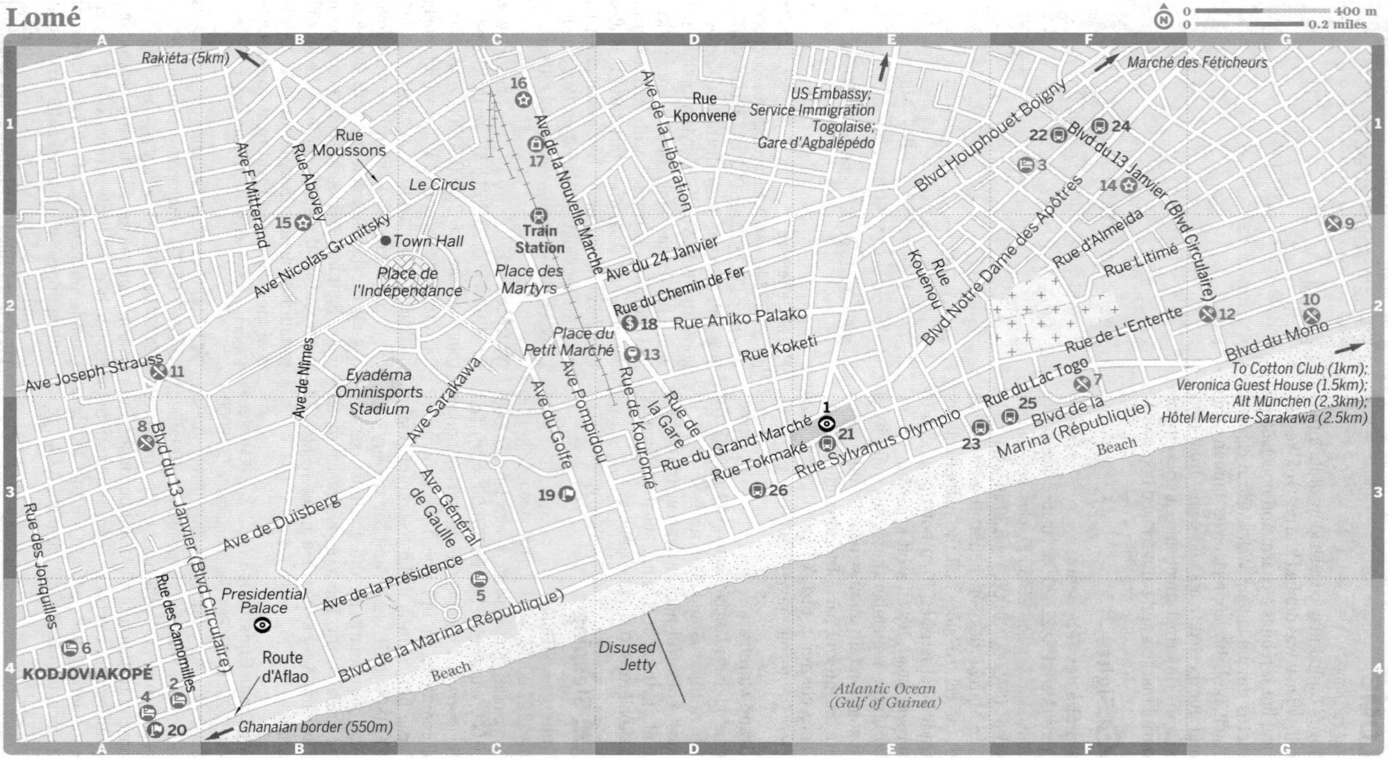

0 400 m
0 0.2 miles
Rakiéta (5km)
Marché des Féticheurs
US Embassy;
Service Immigration
Togolaise;
Gare d'Agbalépédo
Rue Kponvene
Ave de la Libération
Blvd Houphouet Boigny
Blvd du 13 Janvier (Blvd Circulaire)
Rue Moussons
Rue Abovey
Ave F Mitterand
Le Circus
Ave de la Nouvelle Marche
Train Station
Town Hall
Ave Nicolas Grunitsky
Place de l'Indépendance
Place des Martyrs
Ave du 24 Janvier
Rue du Chemin de Fer
Rue Aniko Palako
Rue Koketi
Rue Kouenou
Blvd Notre Dame des Apôtres
Rue d'Almeida
Rue Litimé
Rue de L'Entente
Blvd du Mono
To Cotton Club (1km);
Veronica Guest House (1.5km);
Alt München (2.3km);
Hôtel Mercure-Sarakawa (2.5km)
Place du Petit Marché
Ave Joseph Strauss
Ave de Nîmes
Eyadéma Ominisports Stadium
Ave Sarakawa
Ave du Golfe
Ave Pompidou
Rue de Kouromé
Rue de la Gare
Rue du Grand Marché
Rue Tokmaké
Rue Sylvanus Olympio
Rue du Lac Togo
Blvd de la Marina (République)
Beach
Rue des Jonquilles
Ave de Duisberg
Ave Général de Gaulle
Ave de la Présidence
Presidential Palace
Route d'Aflao
Rue des Camomilles
KODJOVIAKOPÉ
Disused Jetty
Atlantic Ocean
(Gulf of Guinea)
Ghanaian border (550m)

Lomé

Sights
1 Grand Marché E3

Sleeping
2 Auberge Le Galion A4
3 Côté Sud F1
4 Hôtel Belle-Vue A4
5 Hôtel Ibis-le Bénin C4
6 My Diana Guesthouse A4

Eating
7 Bena Grill F2
8 Big Metro A3
9 Côté Jardin G2
La Belle Époque .... (see 4)
10 Le Pêcheur G2
11 Lomé La Belle A2
12 Nopégali Plage G2

Drinking & Nightlife
13 Domino D2

Entertainment
14 Byblos F1
15 Le 54 .... B2
16 Le Rézo C1

Shopping
17 Village Artisanal C1

Information
18 Banque Atlantique D2
19 French Embassy C3
20 German Embassy A4

Transport
21 ABC E3
22 CTS F1
23 Gare de Cotonou E3
24 NTI F1
25 STIF F3
26 UTB D3

an excellent restaurant (mains CFA2500 to CFA6000) are among the other highlights.

Veronica Guest House GUESTHOUSE $$$
(☎22 22 69 07; www.veronicatogo.com; Blvd du Mono; d CFA36,000-51,000;) This charming 10-room hotel with professional staff, beautiful mahogany fittings and a pint-sized pool is a more Togolese alternative to the chain hotels. Although it is on the busy highway, the rooms have thick double glazing and views across the road to the beach. Meals are available (CFA10,000).

Hôtel Ibis-le Bénin HOTEL $$$
(☎22 21 24 85; www.ibishotel.com; Blvd de la Marina; d CFA56,000-60,000;) Travellers love the swimming pool here, not to mention the expansive shady grounds. The rooms in the motel-like building lack character, but it's tidy enough and renovation plans are under way. Rooms on the top floors have lovely sea views.

Hôtel Mercure-Sarakawa RESORT $$$
(☎22 27 65 90; www.accorhotels.com; Blvd du Mono; r with city view CFA112,000-116,000, with sea view CFA124,000-128,000;) Despite its concrete-bunker exterior, this is one of West Africa's most exclusive hotels, 3km east of the centre on the coastal road to Benin. The 164 rooms are comfortable, but the Sarakawa's main drawcard is its stunning Olympic-size swimming pool set in acres of coconut grove. Rates include breakfast.

Eating

Nopégali Plage AFRICAN $
(☎222 80 62; Blvd du 13 Janvier; mains CFA1500-2000; 8am-10pm daily) You'll find no cheaper place for a sit-down meal in the centre. It's very much a canteen, but a good one, with friendly service and copious African dishes prepared grandma-style.

Bena Grill STEAKHOUSE $$
(Marox; ☎22 21 50 87; Rue du Lac Togo; mains CFA2000-7000; breakfast, lunch & dinner daily) A nirvana for carnivores, this cheery restaurant in the market area is lauded for its top-quality meat dishes, including a sensational *côte porc grillée* (grilled pork rib). Also serves sandwiches, burgers and salads. It's next to the Marox supermarket.

Greenfield PIZZERIA, INTERNATIONAL $$
(☎22 21 21 55; Rue Akati; mains CFA2500-4400; lunch & dinner daily) It's a bit out of the action, but this great garden bar-restaurant, with a French owner, has an original decor, with colourful lanterns and funky colonial seats with retro faux-leather cushions. Foodwise, it features wood-fired pizzas (evenings only), meat grills, salads and pastas.

Lomé La Belle AFRICAN $$
(☎22 22 88 23; Blvd du 13 Janvier; mains CFA3000-5000; lunch & dinner daily) You'll find all the usual Togolese favourites served in hearty portions at this informal joint right in the centre. It has outdoor seating.

Big Metro AFRICAN $$
(Blvd du 13 Janvier; mains CFA1000-4500; ⌚ lunch & dinner daily) This little eatery with a pavement terrace is a great spot to catch local vibes and nosh on unpretentious yet tasty African staples. The braised fish (CFA4000) is superb. Unfortunately, it's set on a busy thoroughfare.

★ **Côté Jardin** INTERNATIONAL $$$
(Rue d'Assoli; mains CFA3000-7000; ⌚ lunch & dinner Tue-Sun) Hands-down the most atmospheric eatery in Lomé, Côté Jardin has an exotic pleasure garden replete with tropical plants and woodcarvings. The supremely relaxing surrounds and eclectic menu make this a winner. Dim lighting contributes to romantic dining.

Le Pêcheur SEAFOOD $$$
(☎91 59 63 50; Blvd du Mono; mains CFA4500-8000; ⌚ lunch Mon-Fri & dinner Mon-Sat) The name gives it away: this is a fantastic seafood place where you'll enjoy fish fillet *a la plancha* (cooked on a griddle) and skewered gambas. Well worth the splurge – if only it had an outdoor terrace!

★ **La Belle Époque** FRENCH $$$
(☎22 20 22 40; Hôtel Belle-Vue, Kodjoviakopé; mains CFA4500-14,000; ⌚ lunch & dinner daily) One of Lomé's finest tables, La Belle Époque, all crisp white table cloths and dimmed lighting, serves a refined French-inspired cuisine. You can also enjoy your meal in a verdant courtyard. Budget tip: ask for the 'Côté Paillotte' menu, with simpler dishes costing less than CFA5000.

Alt München FRENCH, GERMAN $$$
(☎22 27 63 21; Rte d'Aného; mains CFA5000-10,000; ⌚ lunch & dinner Thu-Tue) A well-regarded restaurant just east of Hôtel Mercure-Sarakawa, offering a good selection of French and Bavarian specialities, including *jarret de porc* (pork knuckle) and *fondue bourguignonne* (meat fondue). Fish dishes are also available.

Drinking & Entertainment

Cotton Club MUSIC
(☎90 04 45 70; Ave Augustino de Souza; ⌚ 6pm-late Tue-Sun) This jazz and blues lounge bar is polished, homely and welcoming. Snacks are available.

Domino BAR
(665 Rue de la Gare; ⌚ from 6pm) Den-like but cool and very popular, Domino houses Lomé's biggest selection of beers (50 or so) as well as a dozen whiskies.

Le Rézo JAZZ
(☎22 20 15 13; 21 Ave de la Nouvelle Marche; ⌚10am-1am) Inside, it's like a 1980s disco with its blacked-out windows, but Le Rézo is more contemporary than it looks, with giant screens showing Champions League football games, karaoke nights and live jazz on Thursday.

Byblos CLUB
(Blvd du 13 Janvier; admission around CFA5000; ⌚from 10pm Wed-Sun) This trendy nightclub is a favourite haunt of rich young Togolese.

Le 54 BAR
(☎22 20 62 20; Blvd du 13 Janvier; ⌚10am-midnight Thu-Sun) A nice blend of exhibition space, affordable craft and jewellery, and a vibrant restaurant-bar. There's great live music Thursday to Sunday, catering for all musical tastes.

Shopping

Village Artisanal SOUVENIRS
(☎221 68 07; Ave de la Nouvelle Marche; ⌚8am-5.30pm Mon-Sat) At this easy-going centre you'll see Togolese artisans weaving cloth, carving statues, making baskets and lampshades, sewing leather shoes and constructing cane chairs and tables – all for sale at reasonable fixed prices.

Information

INTERNET ACCESS

There are numerous internet cafes in Lomé. Expect to pay CFA300 per hour.

MONEY

All banks change cash. Banks with ATMs are easy to find in the centre; they accept Visa cards.

Banque Atlantique (☎22 20 88 92; Place du Petit Marché; ⌚8am-4pm Mon-Fri, 9am-2pm Sat) This is the only place that accepts MasterCard in Togo; also accepts Visa and has an ATM.

SAFE TRAVEL

There are pickpockets around the Rue de Grand Marché and along Rue du Commerce. Avoid walking on the beach alone, especially at night.

There is a very strong undertow along coastal waters, so if you'd like a swim, head for a pool, such as the ones available to nonguests at Hôtel Mercure-Sarakawa or Hôtel Ibis-le Bénin.

TELEPHONE

Local and international calls can be made from any of the multitude of private telephone agencies around the city.

Getting There & Away

BUS & BUSH TAXI

Rakiéta (☎90 29 88 04) runs a daily bus service between Lomé and Kara (CFA5600, 6½ hours). It leaves at 7.30am from its depot in Atikoumé. Book ahead or arrive early (6am) on the day. This service is a better option than bush taxis.

Bush taxis and minibuses travelling east to Aného (CFA1000, one hour), Lac Togo/Agbodrafo (CFA800, 45 minutes) and to Cotonou (in Benin; CFA5000, three hours) leave from **Gare de Cotonou** (Blvd de la Marina), just west of the STIF bus station.

Gare d'Agbalépédo (Quartier Agbalépédo), 10km north of central Lomé, serves all northern destinations. Services include Atakpamé (CFA3500, two hours), Dapaong (CFA8500, 10 hours) and Kara (CFA6200, five hours).

Minibuses to Kpalimé (CFA2000, two hours) leave from **Gare de Kpalimé** (Rue Moyama), 1.5km north of the centre on Rte de Kpalimé.

There are also international services (see p471), including to/from Ghana.

Getting Around

- To the airport (5km from central Lomé) the taxi fare is about CFA1500 (but count on CFA2000 from the airport into the city).
- Taxis are abundant and have no meters. Fares are CFA350 for a shared taxi (more after 6pm) and CFA1000 nonshared. A taxi by the hour should cost CFA2500 if you bargain well.
- Zippy little *taxi-motos* are also popular, if rather dangerous. You should be able to go anywhere in the centre for CFA300 to CFA500.

THE SOUTH

The area between Aného, Kpalimé and Atakpamé is one of the most alluring in West Africa, with a combination of superb beaches, a vast lake, forested hills and numerous waterfalls. If you could only see one place in Togo, this would surely be it.

Agbodrafo & Togoville

On the southern shores of **Lac Togo** (part of the inland lagoon that stretches all the way from Lomé to Aného), **Agbodrafo** is a popular weekend getaway for frazzled Lomé residents. Swimming in the lake – croc and bug free – is blissful. It is also a good place to find a *pirogue* (traditional canoe) to **Togoville**, which was the former seat of the Mlapa dynasty and Togo's historical centre of voodoo.

> WORTH A TRIP
>
> **COCO BEACH**
>
> Past the port and customs east of Lomé is another world – a mellow land of beachfront auberges where you can recharge the batteries. The best option on this part of the coast is **Hôtel Coco Beach** (☎22 71 49 37; www.hotel-togo-cocobeach.com; Coco Beach; s CFA31,000-39,000, d CFA33,000-62,000; P❄📶🏊), with boardwalks leading to a great restaurant (meals CFA5500 to CFA7000), a seafront bar, a pool and a private beach with deckchairs and *paillotes* (shaded seats) for hire. It's also the safest beach to swim from, thanks to a reef that blocks the strong undertow. Rooms are bright and comfortable but devoid of character.

Sleeping & Eating

Hôtel Le Lac RESORT $$$
(☎90 36 28 58; www.hotellelactogo.com; r weekdays/weekends CFA44,000/35,000; P❄🏊) East of Agbodrafo, this breezy resort-like venture on the shores of Lac Togo is a reliable choice. The renovated rooms are spacious, with private patios and sweeping lake views. There's a good restaurant (mains CFA2000 to CFA6000) overlooking the lake, a swimming pool and a small beach from where you can swim in the lake. *Pirogue* trips to Togoville (CFA3000) can easily be arranged.

Getting There & Away

From the Gare de Cotonou in Lomé, bush taxis frequently travel along the coastal road to Aného (CFA1000) via Agbodrafo.

Aného

POP 49,000

All that remains of Aného's days as colonial capital in the late 19th century are crumbling pastel buildings. Voodoo is strong here and most obvious at **Vogan's Friday market**, one of the biggest and most colourful in Togo, about 20km northwest of Aného; taxis

DON'T MISS

HIKING IN THE KPALIMÉ AREA

The heartiest walk is up Togo's highest peak, **Mt Agou** (986m), 20km southeast of Kpalimé. The path climbs between backyards, through cocoa and coffee plantations and luxuriant forests bristling with life. Small terraced mountain villages pepper the slopes and provide fabulous views of the area. On a clear day, you can see Lake Volta in Ghana. The walk takes four hours' return from the village of Nyogbo. The track can be hard to find so it's best to take a guide. Alternatively, there is a road to the top so you could walk one way and arrange a taxi for your walk back.

The area around **Mt Klouto** (710m), 12km northwest of Kpalimé, is another walking heaven, with forested hills, waterfalls and a myriad butterflies. Early morning is the best time to search for them.

It's best to go with a local guide. As well as showing you the way, a good guide will show you cool plants, unusual fruit and veg, and fill you up on local culture and history. Contact Adetop (p471), which can arrange guided butterfly walks and village stays, as well as treks in the area.

from Aného (CFA800, 30 minutes) leave from the junction on route to Lomé.

Festivals & Events

Aného plays host to the **Festival des Divinités Noires** (Festival of Black Divinities), which has been held in December each year since 2006. It celebrates voodoo – expect singing, dancing, beating of drums and parades.

Sleeping & Eating

Hôtel Oasis GUESTHOUSE $
(23 31 01 25; Rte de Lomé-Cotonou; d with fan/air-con CFA10,000/15,000; P ❄) An unbeatable location east of the bridge, looking across the lagoon and the beach to the sea. The terrace is a prime place for a sunset drink. Rooms are basic, though – you'll pay for the location.

La Becca Hôtel HOTEL $$
(23 31 05 13; Route de Lomé-Cotonou; r with fan CFA11,000-13,000, with air-con CFA15,000-21,000; ❄) The cheap and cheerful La Becca is a good budget option, with smallish, yet well-scrubbed, rooms. The air-con rooms are significantly better than the fan-cooled units.

Getting There & Away

From the *gare routière* (bus station), bush taxis and minibuses head to Lomé (CFA1000, one hour), as well as to the Beninese border and Cotonou (CFA2500, 2½ hours).

Kpalimé

POP 101,000

Kpalimé is only 120km from Lomé, but feels like another world. Hidden among the forested hills of the cocoa and coffee region, it offers some of Togo's best scenery and hiking. It's also a busy place thanks to its proximity to the Ghanaian border and important market (Tuesday and Saturday), where local farmers sell their products along with the usual bric-a-brac of plasticware and clothes.

Sleeping & Eating

Auberge Vakpo Guest House GUESTHOUSE $
(91 53 17 00, 24 42 56 64; www.vakpoguesthouse.com; Kpodzi; r with fan CFA8500-12,000, with air-con CFA9500-14,500; P ❄) A well-run little number with a quiet location near the Catholic church, Auberge Vakpo offers neat rooms with good bedding, meticulous bathrooms and a lovely pleasure garden complete with flower bushes, mural frescoes and sculptures. Meals are available for CFA3500.

Hôtel Chez Felicia HOTEL $
(90 10 97 77, 22 46 33 49; Rte de Missahoe; r with fan/air-con CFA7000/12,000; P ❄) Off the road to Klouto, the discreet Hôtel Chez Felicia is an excellent bargain. This low-slung building set in verdant surrounds shelters immaculate, bright rooms with back-friendly mattresses, crisply dressed beds and impeccable bathrooms. Meals are CFA2000 to CFA4000.

Le Geyser HOTEL $$
(24 41 04 67; www.hotellegeyser.com; r CFA14,000-19,000; P ❄) You'll find the tranquil Hôtel Le Geyser 2km from the centre on the road to Klouto, in a balmy garden setting. Rooms are well-tended, functional and airy, and the restaurant (mains

CFA2000 to CFA5000) serves good African and European dishes. A real hit is the pool.

Chez Fanny INN $$
(☎24 41 00 99; hotelchezfanny@yahoo.fr; Rte de Lomé; r CFA18,000; P ❄ ☎) This jolly good villa 2km south of town is a homey retreat. The eight rooms are huge and the patio is a lovely spot to relax, despite the fact it overlooks the busy Rte de Lomé. The restaurant (mains CFA2000 to CFA6000) is the best in town.

Hotel Agbeviade HOTEL $$
(☎24 41 05 11; agbeviade2003@yahoo.fr; Rte de Missahoé; r with fan CFA8500, with air-con CFA16,500-19,500; ❄) Off the road to Klouto, the Agbeviade is a safe choice, although the smallish air-con rooms are a bit disappointing for the price. The short menu concentrates on European dishes.

★Le Fermier AFRICAN, FRENCH $$
(☎90 02 98 30; mains CFA2000-4000; ⊙lunch & dinner daily) For excellent European and African food, try this low-roofed, intimate spot on the northwestern outskirts of town. You can't really go wrong – everything is pretty good – but if you want a recommendation, go for the *fufu* (pounded yam), served in a clay pot.

Chez Lazare FRENCH $$
(Rte de Missahoé; mains CFA1000-4000; ⊙lunch & dinner daily) Don't be put off by the unappealing concrete walls. Lazare cooks up excellent French specialities as well as pasta. How does a *côte de porc à la dijonnaise* (pork rib in mustard sauce) sound? The rooftop terrace is pleasant in the evening.

Drinking & Nightlife

Chez Fomen BAR
(Rue de Bakula; ⊙8am-late daily) This cheerful, easy-going bar is a fun place for a drink. It also shows regular football games and serves food.

Bar Alokpa BAR
(⊙9am-late daily) A popular bar on the main road, north of the centre.

Information

Banks with ATMs and internet cafes can be found in the centre.

Getting There & Away

The *gare routière* is in the heart of town, two blocks east of the Shell petrol station. The road between Kpalimé and Atakpamé is the worst in the country, which means few taxis from Kpalimé travel further north than Atakpamé (CFA2000, four hours) and you'll have to change there for services to Sokodé or Kara.

You can get minibuses direct to Lomé (CFA2000, two hours), to the Ghanaian border (CFA1000, 30 minutes) and to Ho in Ghana (CFA1500, 1½ hours).

Atakpamé

POP 85,000

Once the favourite residence of the German colonial administrators, Atakpamé today is a commercial centre. There are no sights, but it makes a pleasant enough stopover on long journeys.

Sleeping & Eating

Hôtel California HOTEL $
(☎23 35 85 44; Rte Internationale; r with fan & without bathroom CFA3000, r with air-con & bathroom CFA8000-10,000; ❄) Despite being at the back of the Total petrol station, this hotel-restaurant is a good surprise, with uncomplicated yet spotless rooms, salubrious bathrooms, excellent food (mains CFA1500 to CFA4000) and a friendly welcome. Opt

WORTH A TRIP

CASCADE DE WOMÉ

One great attraction in the Kpalimé area is the **Cascade de Womé** (Womé Falls; ☎99 01 01 12; www.akatamanso-togo.comli.com; Womé; admission CFA1000; ⊙8am-5pm daily), 12km from Kpalimé. Access to the falls is at the village of Womé. You have to pay CFA1000 to the Association Akatamanso at the entrance to the village (ask for a receipt). It's a further 4km to the picnic area near the falls. From the picnic area, it's a short but steep descent to the waterfalls through lush vegetation. You can swim beneath the falls – bliss!

From Kpalimé, a *moto-taxi* ride to the falls should cost around CFA3500 return, including waiting time.

for the air-con rooms, which are noticeably better than the fan-cooled units.

Le Sahélien AFRICAN $$
(☎440 12 44; Rte Internationale; mains CFA1500-4000; ⊙lunch & dinner daily) The downstairs *maquis* with its enormous grill and informal atmosphere does a brisk trade with the town's *moto-taxis*. Upstairs is more upmarket, and the roof terrace is a nice spot to catch the evening breeze. It also doubles as a hotel, but the rooms need a freshen-up.

Information

There are banks with ATMs as well as internet cafes in the centre.

Getting There & Away

Taxis and minibuses leave from the main *gare routière* south of the centre to Dapaong (CFA7500, eight hours), Kara (CFA4200, five hours), Kpalimé (CFA2000, four hours) and Lomé (CFA2800, two hours).

There's a secondary *gare routière* next to the market in the centre of town, from where taxis regularly go to Kpalimé (CFA2000).

THE NORTH

As you head north, Islam takes over from Christianity as the dominant religion. Most towns are short on sights, but for those with their own vehicle, or the determination to have a showdown with local bush taxis, fabulous highlights await in the castellated shapes of the Tamberma compounds in Koutammakou.

Kara

POP 109,000

Laid out by the Germans on a spacious scale, Kara is the relaxed capital of northern Togo and a good base for trips to Koutammakou. Because Eyadéma was from Pya, a Kabye village about 20km to the north, he pumped a lot of money into Kara and the region has remained a political stronghold of the Eyadéma clan.

Festivals & Events

The area is famous for the **Evala** coming-of-age festival in July. The main event is *la lutte* (wrestling), in which greased-up young men try to topple each other in a series of bouts.

Sleeping & Eating

★**La Douceur** INN $
(☎660 11 64; douceurkara@yahoo.fr; off Rue de Chaminade; r with fan CFA6000, with air-con CFA8000-12,000; ❄📶) Down a dirt track in the stadium's neighbourhood you'll find this cosy bird's nest in a proudly maintained and flowered little compound. Rooms are spotless with simple decor, the well-stocked bar serves the coldest beer in town and the *paillote* restaurant (mains CFA1500 to CFA4000) does great food.

Marie-Antoinette HOTEL, CAMPGROUND $
(☎26 60 16 07; http://ma.kara-tg.com; Rte Internationale; campsites per person CFA1500, s with fan CFA7500, d with fan CFA8500-9500, s with air-con CFA10,500-13,500, d with air-con 11,500-14,500; P❄📶) In a pretty house 3km south of Kara on Rte Internationale, Marie-Antoinette has rooms of varying size and shape. Opt for the dearer rooms, which are spacious and well organised, and come with bathrooms in good working order (hot water). Downside: the hotel is not shielded from the noise of the highway. The restaurant cooks up decent meals for CFA2500 and you can camp in the annexe across the street.

★**Centre Grill** AFRICAN, EUROPEAN $$
(Marox; ☎90 70 22 33; cnr Rte de Prison & Ave Eyadéma; mains CFA1300-3600; ⊙breakfast, lunch & dinner daily) An attractive place with its straw roof, wicker light shades and blackboard menus, Centre Grill serves divine Togolese food and good Western dishes. Try its *fufu sauce arachide* with grilled fish, or *pâte sorgho* (mashed sorghum), wash the lot down with a cold beer and polish it off with banana fritters. Great value.

WORTH A TRIP

PARC DE SARAKAWA

Unpretentious and relaxing, **Parc de Sarakawa** (☎90 55 49 21; hel228@hotmail.fr; adult/child CFA5000/2500; ⊙8am-5pm daily) is easily accessed from Kara as a day trip. While its terrestrial wildlife-watching can't compare with that in the better-known parks in West Africa, it spreads out over 1500 acres and is home to various species of antelope, buffalo, ostrich and zebra. Game drives (CFA5000) can be arranged at the gate. There are plans to build a lodge within the park.

Information

Banks with ATMs and internet cafes are easy to find in the centre.

Getting There & Away

From the main *gare routière*, about 2km south of the town centre, minibuses regularly head south to Atakpamé (CFA4300, four hours), Kandé (CFA1200) and Lomé (CFA4800, seven hours). Taxis heading north to Dapaong (CFA3600, four hours) are scarce and it's not unusual to have to wait half a day for one to fill up.

For buses heading to Lomé, **Rakiéta** (Rue du 23 Septembre) has a daily departure at 7.30am (CFA5600, six hours) from its depot.

To get to the border with Benin via Kétao (CFA600, 30 minutes), get a minibus or bush taxi from **Station du Grand Marché** (Ave Eyadéma), next to the market.

Koutammakou

Also known as Tamberma Valley after the people who live here, Koutammakou has a unique collection of fortress-like mud houses, founded in the 17th century by people fleeing the slave-grabbing forays of Benin's Dahomeyan kings. Listed as a World Heritage Site by Unesco in 2004, the area is one of the most scenic in the country, with stunning mountain landscapes and intense light.

You can visit Koutammakou as a day trip from Kara. To get there, turn eastward off the Kara–Dapaong highway in Kandé and follow the track in the direction of Nadoba, the area's main village. About 2km down the road, you'll have to pay CFA1500 at the Accueil et Billetterie office to enter the site.

The *piste* is in good condition and crosses the valley all the way to Boukoumbé and Natitingou in Benin. If you don't have your own transport, chartering a taxi/*moto-taxi* for the day will cost around CFA20,000/5000.

In Nadoba, guides will be happy to show you the valley's highlights.

TAMBERMA COMPOUNDS

A typical Tamberma compound, called a *tata*, consists of a series of towers connected by a thick wall with a single entrance chamber, used to trap an enemy so he can be showered with arrows. The castle-like nature of these extraordinary structures helped ward off invasions by neighbouring tribes and, in the late 19th century, the Germans. As in the *tata somba* in nearby Benin, life in a *tata* revolves around an elevated terrace of clay-covered logs, where the inhabitants cook, dry their millet and corn, and spend most of their leisure time.

Skilled builders (that's what Tamberma means), the Tamberma only use clay, wood and straw – and no tools. There may be a fetish shrine in front of the compound.

Dapaong

POP 31,800

This lively little town is a West African melting pot, with the Burkinabé and Ghanaian borders both within 30km. It sits in the middle of Togo's most arid landscape and gets the full force of the harmattan between November and February.

Sleeping & Eating

Hôtel Le Campement HOTEL $

(☎90 01 81 06; Rte de la Station de Lomé; r with fan/air-con CFA9600/14,800; P ❄) Dapaong's only midrange hotel, but overpriced. However, rooms are pleasant and spacious, and the overgrown garden that is filled with oversized sculptures is a cool place to laze around. The French bar-restaurant is expensive (mains from CFA3500), but the food is very tasty and the desserts are amazing.

Auberge Idriss GUESTHOUSE $

(☎27 70 83 49; off Rte Internationale; r with fan & without bathroom CFA4000, r with air-con & bathroom CFA13,000-15,000; P ❄) A tidy little guesthouse in a quiet neighbourhood 2km north of town. Rooms in the main building are spacious; those in the annexe have shared facilities but are cosier.

Getting There & Away

Taxis leave the station on Rte de Nasablé for Sinkasse on the Burkinabé border (CFA1200), from where transport heads to Ouagadougou.

From Station de Lomé on Rte Internationale, 2km south of the centre, bush taxis head to Kara (CFA3800, four hours) and Lomé (CFA8000, 12 hours).

UNDERSTAND TOGO

Togo Today

In March 2010, president Faure Gnassingbé was re-elected for a second term. Unlike in 2005, the process was largely trouble free, but opposition parties claimed that these presidential elections – Faure won 60% of the vote – were marred by serious irregularities. Politically, the situation has barely evolved in 30 years.

Economically, there are better perspectives. Severely damaged by two decades of political unrest, the economy is now picking up. International business and aid donors are returning to Togo and Lomé's port infrastructure is expanding. Landlocked countries, such as Niger and Burkina Faso, increasingly use Lomé's port over that of Cotonou.

History

The country was once on the fringes of several great empires and, when the Europeans arrived in the 16th century, this power vacuum allowed the slave-traders to use Togo as a conduit.

Following the abolition of slavery, Germany signed a treaty in Togoville with local king Mlapa. Togoland, as the Germans called their colony, underwent considerable economic development, but the Togolese didn't appreciate the Germans' brutal 'pacification' campaigns. When the Germans surrendered at Kamina – the Allies' first victory in WWI – the Togolese welcomed the British forces.

However, the League of Nations split Togoland between France and Britain – a controversial move that divided the populous Ewe. Following a 1956 plebiscite, British Togoland was incorporated into the Gold Coast (now Ghana). French Togoland gained full independence in 1960 under the country's first president, Sylvanus Olympio. But his presidency was short-lived. Olympio, an Ewe from the south who appeared to disregard the interests of northerners, was killed by Kabye soldiers in 1963. His replacement was then deposed by Kabye sergeant Gnassingbé Eyadéma. The new leader established a cult personality and became increasingly irrational following a 1974 assassination attempt.

In 1990, France began pressuring Eyadéma to adopt a multiparty system, but he resisted. The following year, after riots, strikes and the deaths of pro-democracy protestors, 28 bodies were dragged from a lagoon and dumped in front of the US embassy, drawing attention to the repression in Togo.

Eyadéma finally agreed to a conference in 1991, where delegates stripped him of his powers and installed an interim government. However, Eyadéma-supporting troops later reinstalled Eyadéma. Back in power, the general retaliated by postponing planned elections, which prompted strikes in 1992. The strikes paralysed the economy and led to violence, during which 250,000 southerners fled the country.

Eyadéma triumphed his way through ensuing elections throughout the 1990s – elections typically marred by international criticism, opposition boycotts and the killing of rival politicians. Amnesty International made allegations of human rights violations, such as executions and torture, and pressure on the president increased at the same rate that aid from international donors decreased.

Eyadéma finally left office the way many suspected he would – in a coffin. Following his death in February 2005, his son, Faure Gnassingbé, seized power in a military coup, then relented and held presidential elections, which he won. Some 500 people were killed in riots in Lomé, amid allegations the elections were fixed.

Faure's Rally of the Togolese People (RPT) party won legislative elections in 2007, the first to be deemed reasonably free and fair by international observers. Opposition parties also won seats in parliament, a political first. Following this milestone, the EU resumed relations with Togo, which had been suspended for 14 years, and dealings with international agencies such as the IMF and the World Bank have restarted.

People

With about 40 ethnic groups in a population of over six million people, Togo has one of Africa's more heterogeneous populations. The three largest groups are the southern Ewe and Mina, and the northern Kabye; the latter counts President Gnassingbé among its population and is concentrated around Kara.

Religion

Christianity and Islam are the main religions in Togo – in the south and north respectively. However, a majority of the population have voodoo beliefs, which are strongest in the southeast.

The Arts

Batik and wax printing is popular throughout Togo, but the most well-known textile is the Ewe kente cloth, which is less brilliantly coloured than the Ashanti version.

Music and dance play an important part in Togolese daily life. Today, traditional music has fused with contemporary West African, Caribbean and South American sounds, creating a hybrid that includes highlife, reggae and soukous. Togo's most famous singing export was Bella Bellow, who, before her death in 1973, ruled the local music scene, toured internationally and released a recording, *Album Souvenir*. Nowadays, King Mensah is Togo's best-known artist, at home and abroad.

The fortified Tamberma compounds in Koutammakou are some of the most striking structures in West Africa.

Food & Drink

Togolese dishes, some of the best in West Africa, are typically based, as in much of the region, on a starch staple such as *pâte* (a dough-like substance made of corn, manioc or yam) accompanied by sauce. Some Togolese specialities are *fufu* (cooked and puréed yam served with vegetables and meat), *djenkoumé* (a *pâte* made with cornflour cooked with spices and served with fried chicken) and *pintade* (guinea fowl).

Common snacks include: *aloko* (fried plantain), *koliko* (yam chips), *gaou* (bean-flour fritters) and *wagasi* (a mild cheese fried in hot spice). You'll also find fresh fruit everywhere you go.

Togo has its fair share of generic (Flag, Castel, Lager) and local brews. *Tchoukoutou* (fermented millet) is the preferred tipple in the north. Elsewhere, beware of *sodabe,* a terrifyingly potent moonshine distilled from palm wine.

Environment

Togo's coastline measures only 56km, but the country stretches inland for over 600km. The coast is tropical; further inland are rolling hills covered with forest, yielding to savannah plains in the north.

Wildlife is disappointing because larger mammals have largely been killed or scared off. The country's remaining mammals (monkeys, buffaloes and antelopes) are limited to the north; crocodiles and hippos are found in some rivers.

The coastline faces serious erosion and pollution problems.

SURVIVAL GUIDE

Directory A–Z

ACCOMMODATION

Togo has a fairly good range of accommodation options, from basic cubicle hotels to upmarket establishments with all mod cons. Unsurprisingly, Lomé has the widest range of hotels.

EMBASSIES & CONSULATES

British nationals should contact the **British High Commission** (302 213250; http://ukinghana.fco.gov.uk; 1 Osu Link) in Accra (Ghana).

French Embassy (22 23 46 00; www.ambafrance-tg.org; Ave du Golfe, Lagos)

German Embassy (22 23 32 32; www.lome.diplo.de; Blvd de la Marina, Lagos)

Ghanaian Embassy (22 21 31 94; Rue Moyama, Tokoin; 8am-2pm Mon-Fri)

US Embassy (22 61 54 70; http://togo.usembassy.gov; Blvd Eyadéma, Lagos)

INTERNET ACCESS

- In towns and cities, wi-fi is available at almost every midrange and top-end establishment.
- Internet cafes are easy to find in towns and cities but nonexistent in more remote areas.

MONEY

- The currency in Togo is the West African CFA franc.
- The best foreign currency to carry is euros, easily exchanged at any bank or hotel.
- Travellers cheques cannot be changed in Togo.
- You'll find Visa ATMs in major towns. Only Banque Atlantique in Lomé accepts MasterCard.
- Credit cards are accepted at a few upmarket hotels.

PRACTICALITIES

- **Electricity** Supply is 220V and plugs are of the European two-round-pin variety.
- **Languages** French, Ewé, Kabiyé.

OPENING HOURS

Administrative offices Open 7am to noon and 2.30pm to 5.30pm Monday to Friday.

Banks Open 7.45am to 4pm or 5pm Monday to Friday. Most banks are now open through lunchtime and on Saturday, too.

Restaurants Open for lunch and dinner daily, unless otherwise specified.

Shops Operate 7.30am to 12.30pm and 2.30pm to 6pm Monday to Saturday.

PUBLIC HOLIDAYS

Togo also celebrates Islamic holidays, which change dates every year.

New Year's Day 1 January
Meditation Day 13 January
Easter March/April
National Day 27 April
Labour Day 1 May
Ascension Day May
Pentecost May/June
Day of the Martyrs 21 June
Assumption Day 15 August
All Saints' Day 1 November
Christmas Day 25 December

SAFE TRAVEL

- Petty theft and muggings are common in Lomé, especially on the beach and near the Grand Marché. *Taxi-motos* in the city may be convenient, but they are dangerous.
- Driving in Togo is, to say the least, hair-raising: take care on the roads, particularly at night.
- The beaches along the coast are not safe for swimming because of strong currents.

TELEPHONE

Togo's country code is 228. Landline numbers start with 2, mobile numbers with 9. Make international calls at the private telephone agencies in every town.

Mobile phone coverage is excellent. Local networks include Togocel and Moov. Depending on which mobile network you use at home, your phone may or may not work in Togo – ask your mobile network provider. You can also bring your phone and buy a local SIM card. Top-up vouchers are easily available.

VISAS

Everyone except nationals of the Economic Community of West African States (Ecowas) countries needs a visa.

One-week extendable visas (CFA10,000) are issued at major border crossings with Ghana (Aflao/Lomé), Benin (Hilakondji) and Burkina Faso (Sinkasse), and upon arrival at the airport.

The **Service Immigration Togolaise** (☎ 250 78 56; Ave de la Chance, Service des Passeports; ⌚ 8am-4pm Mon-Fri), near the GTA building 8km north of central Lomé, issues 30-day visa extensions in one or two days. They're free when you extend the seven-day visa. Four photos are required.

Visas for Onward Travel

The Visa des Pays de l'Entente, valid in Côte d'Ivoire, Niger, Benin and Burkina Faso, is available at the Service Immigration Togolaise. Bring two photos, your passport and CFA15,500. It takes 24 hours to process, but note that the office is closed on weekends.

If you're visiting only a single country, the following embassies deliver visas:

Benin A two-week/one-month single-entry visa costs CFA10,000/15,000. You need two photos and photocopies of your passport. It takes one day to process.

Burkina Faso Contact the French consulate in Lomé.

Ghana One-month single-entry visas are issued within three days for CFA20,000 and require four photos and a photocopy of your yellow-fever vaccination certificate.

WOMEN TRAVELLERS

The Togolese are rather conservative when it comes to marriage: it is therefore incomprehensible to them that women past their 20s might not be married. This will lead to many questions, but it is generally harmless. To avoid attracting any more attention, dress conservatively.

ℹ Getting There & Away

AIR

Togo's international airport is 5km northeast of the centre of Lomé. A few major airlines operate in Togo and have offices in Lomé.

The main international carriers are Air France, Brussels Airlines, Royal Air Maroc and Ethiopian Airlines, which offer direct flights to France, Belgium, Morocco and Ethiopia respectively, and connecting flights to the rest of the world.

Other major airlines include Asky, which flies to major capitals in West and Central Africa, Air Burkina, with flights to Ouagadougou (Burkina Faso) and Air Côte d'Ivoire, which flies to Abidjan (Côte d'Ivoire).

- All airlines have offices in Lomé.

LAND

Benin

Bush taxis regularly ply the road between Gare de Cotonou in Lomé and Cotonou (Benin; CFA5000, three hours) via Hilakondji (CFA800, one hour), while **ABC** (☎90 07 69 56; Rue Olympos Sylvano) in Lomé has daily buses to Cotonou (CFA6000, three hours).

The main northern crossing is at Kétao (northeast of Kara). You can also cross at Tohoun (east of Notsé) or Nadoba (in Koutammakou country), arriving in Boukoumbé, but public transport is infrequent. Note that Beninese visas are not issued at the border.

Burkina Faso

The best way to get to Ouagadougou from Lomé is by bus, via Dapaong. **NTI** (☎90 19 80 92; Blvd du 13 Janvier), **CTS** (☎99 27 83 32; Blvd du 13 Janvier) and **TCV** (☎92 29 48 93; Ave Agustino de Souza) are reliable companies. NTI and CTS have three services weekly (CFA12,500) and TCV has two weekly (CFA15,000).

From Dapaong, you'll easily find a taxi to Sinkasse (CFA1500, 45 minutes), which straddles the border. From there it's CFA6000 to Ouagadougou by bus. The border is open from 6am to 6pm.

Ghana

From central Lomé it is only 2km – CFA500/1500 in a shared/chartered taxi or *taxi-moto* (CFA500) – to the chaotic border crossing (open 6am to 10pm) with Aflao in Ghana. From there, you can cross on foot to pick up minibuses to Accra.

STIF (☎99 42 72 72; off Blvd de la Marina) runs daily buses between Lomé and Abidjan via Accra (CFA6000, four hours), while **UTB** (☎99 45 46 34; Rue Sylvanus Olympo) offers three-weekly services between Lomé and Accra (CFA7000).

There are other crossings from Kpalimé to Ho and Klouto to Kpandu.

Getting Around

BUS

- Buses are the most reliable way to get around, especially for long-distance trips.
- Rakiéta buses were more reliable than those of other companies at the time of writing.
- Buses almost always operate with guaranteed seating and fixed departure times.

BUSH TAXI

Togo has an extensive network of dilapidated bush taxis, which can be anything from an old pick-up truck to a normal sedan car or nine- or 15- seat people carriers. Travel is often agonisingly slow; unfortunately, these bush taxis are generally the only way to get around. Fares are fixed-ish.

CAR

- If you're driving, you will need an International Driving Permit (IDP). Police checkpoints are common throughout the country but rarely nasty or obstructive.
- Petrol stations are plentiful in major towns. A litre of petrol cost CFA610 at the time of research.

LOCAL TRANSPORT

- You'll find taxis in most cities. *Taxi-motos*, also called *zemi-johns*, are everywhere. A journey across town costs about CFA200, and more in Lomé. They are also a handy way to get to remote locations in the bush.
- Chartering a taxi will generally cost CFA2000 to CFA3000 per hour.

TOURS

1001 Pistes (1001 'sandy tracks'; ☎90 27 52 03; www.1001pistes.com) Run by a French couple, 1001 Pistes offers excellent excursions across the country. These range from easy day walks from Lomé to several-day hikes and 4WD adventures with bivouacs to whale-watching outings along the Atlantic coast. They also offer guided mountain-bike tours in Lomé and elsewhere in the country.

Adetop (☎90 08 88 54, 24 41 08 17; www.adetop-togo.com; Rte de Klouto) A small NGO promoting sustainable tourism, Adetop is based in Kpalimé but runs activities throughout the country. Its main activities are guided tours exploring the culture and heritage of Togo, as well as hiking.

Central Africa

CAMILLA WATSON / GETTY IMAGES ©

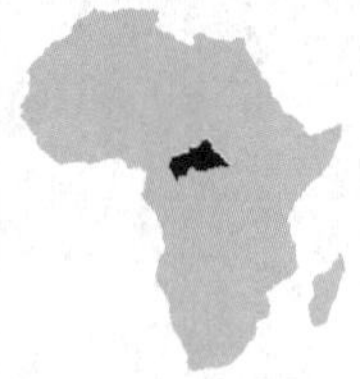

Central African Republic

Includes ➡

Fast Facts

- **Capital** Bangui
- **Population** 5.05 million
- **Languages** French (official), Sango (national)
- **Area** 622,984 sq km
- **Currency** Central African franc (CFA)
- **Visa requirements** Required by most visitors and should be obtained in advance. If there is no CAR embassy near you the French embassy will issue CAR visas.
- **Tourist information** www.centrafricaine.info

Jungle, Elephants & Lowland Gorillas

Central African Republic (CAR) is a country with staggering rare natural beauty and some of the world's most amazing wildlife. It's one of the best places in Africa for encounters with forest elephants and lowland gorillas, and the best place in the world, some say, to see butterflies. It's also one of the most impoverished and least developed countries on the continent.

For centuries CAR has endured rapacity from colonisers and then from its own leaders in collusion with former colonisers. Yet the people of this plundered nation are open and friendly; and their conversations are more full of hope than despair.

CAR is landlocked, its border crossings can be difficult and dangerous, and flights are expensive and infrequent. At the time of writing most of the country was not considered stable or safe enough to travel through. Whatever you do, check the situation with your embassy before attempting to visit.

Central African Republic Top Sights

- **Dzanga-Sangha Reserve** Get up close to lowland gorillas and elephants in this little-visited pocket of virgin rainforest
- **Bangui** Sip beer on the banks of the Oubangi River in the country's capital and largest city
- **Bayanga** Go out on a hunting trip with the BaAka (a pygmy tribe) from this village outside the Dzanga-Sangha Reserve

UNDERSTAND CENTRAL AFRICAN REPUBLIC

Central African Republic Today

General François Bozizé won some 60% of the vote in elections held in 2011, which the opposition denounced as fraudulent. Today the government still controls less than half the country.

History

Although stone tools provide evidence of human life from 6000 BC, the most notable ancients resided around present-day Bouar some 2500 years ago. Little is known about them, though it must have been a highly organised civilisation because it left behind about 70 groups of megaliths, some weighing three or four tonnes. The present cultures most likely arrived in the 15th century, probably fleeing Arab slave traders, but by the 18th century they, too, were sending their captives across the Sahara to markets in Egypt or down the Congo River to the Atlantic Ocean. This industry, which didn't completely end until 1912, decimated entire cultures and largely depopulated the eastern half of the country.

Colonial Days

France launched into CAR in 1885, finding a shattered society rich in agricultural potential and under the rule of Sudanese-born Sultan Rabah. France killed Rabah in 1900 and soon after consolidated its control of the country, which it divided into 17 parts that were offered to European companies in exchange for a fixed annual payment plus 15% of agricultural profits. Vast cotton, coffee and tobacco plantations were established and worked by an often brutally conscripted local population. They resisted for decades, but opposition was eventually broken through a combination of French military action, famine and severe smallpox epidemics.

The first signs of nationalism sprang up after WWII via Barthélemy Boganda's Mouvement d'Evolution Sociale de l'Afrique Noire. In 1960, a year after Boganda was killed in a suspicious plane crash, his party forced the French to grant independence.

Forty Years of Chaos

The leadership was taken over by David Dacko, who became the country's first president. Dacko's rule quickly became repressive and dictatorial and in 1966 he was overthrown by an army commander and close relative, Jean-Bédel Bokassa, kicking off 13 years of one of the most brutal regimes Africa has ever experienced. In one instance Bokassa

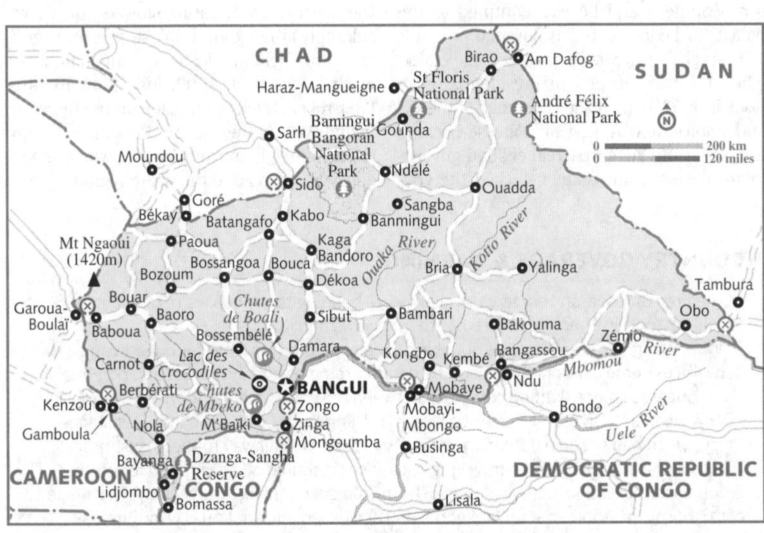

reportedly ordered the killing (some claim he participated) of schoolchildren who protested against expensive mandatory school uniforms made by a company owned by his wife.

France, coveting the uranium deposits at Bakouma and the abundant big-game hunting grounds near the Sudan border (personally sponsored by the former French president, Valéry Giscard d'Estaing), supported Bokassa and bailed out his floundering economy. Using the country's mineral resources as carrots, Bokassa also negotiated loans from South Africa and private US banks. He then squandered virtually all this money. His final fantasy was to have himself crowned 'emperor' of a renamed Central African Empire in 1977. Despite the worldwide derision, France helped to fund much of his coronation's price tag of more than US$20 million.

Such excess, together with the out-of-control violence, made Bokassa an embarrassment to his backers. In 1979 France abruptly cut off aid to the 'empire' and, while Bokassa was in Libya seeking still more funds, flew in former president David Dacko together with loads of French paratroopers. Dacko did no better this time around and was overthrown again in 1981 and replaced by André Kolingba, who in 1986 created a one-party state that was also widely seen as corrupt. At this point Bokassa popped up again but was promptly convicted of treason, murder and, for good measure, cannibalism, and sentenced to death. This was changed to life imprisonment and he was confined to the palace he'd constructed at Berengo.

Kolingba's 12 years of absolute rule ended when he was defeated in presidential elections in 1993, held at the insistence of the US and France, and Ange-Félix Patassé became the leader of CAR's first real civilian government. Patassé immediately stacked the government with fellow ethnic group members, which prompted a 1996 army mutiny, led by officers from a southern ethnic group. The capital became a war zone, although a peace deal signed the next year was backed up by an 800-strong African peacekeeping mission, later replaced by UN forces. Patassé's 1999 re-election was followed by riots over government mismanagement and corruption in 2000 and attempted coups in 2001 and 2002.

Former army chief of staff General François Bozizé, who led the 2002 coup attempt, didn't stop fighting after Libyan forces sent to protect the regime thwarted his initial bid on Bangui. The next year, when Patassé made the familiar African mistake of popping out of the shop (for a state visit to Niger), Bozizé marched into the capital and made himself president. Patassé scooted off to exile in Togo. The euphoria was short-lived, however, as little changed under the Bozizé regime. He made the usual promise to hold elections, but abandoned the second part of the promise, not to stand himself. Bozizé won the election in 2005, though Patassé was not allowed to run.

After Bozizé came to power the safety situation in Bangui improved dramatically, as did the economy, but not much changed elsewhere. Fighting continued upcountry, and by the end of 2006 rebel attacks in the northeast and northwest forced some 300,000 people to flee their villages. In June 2008, after most rebel groups signed a peace agreement with the government, fighting slowed down considerably although it didn't stop. A unity government, including leaders of the main rebel groups, kicked off 2009; just a few months later rebel attacks were back on the increase, including by the Lord's Resistance Army (LRA) of neighbouring Uganda, whose insurgency had spread to the wider region.

COUNTRY COVERAGE & WARNING

At the time of research very few travellers were heading to CAR so we're providing historical and cultural information rather than reviews and listings.

While Bangui was secure (but not at the time of writing), and the southwest can be visited with extreme caution, the rest of the country remains largely lawless and potentially very dangerous since fighting continues between the government and various rebels. In 2013 African and United States troops were tracking the murderous Lord's Resistance Army, which had set up a base in the east of the country. Highway robbery is common.

Check the situation before travelling here. A good source of information for on-the-ground travel in CAR is Lonely Planet's Thorn Tree online travel forum www.lonelyplanet.com/thorntree. Another source of good internet-based information is www.africas-eden.com/Central-African-Republic.asp.

DZANGA-SANGHA RESERVE

Hoots and laughter rattled through the forest, flashes of colour flitted in and out of the shade and then a pathetic gurgled bleat indicated that the hunt had been a success and the BaAka, otherwise known as pygmies, would be eating blue duiker (a type of forest antelope) that night. Just a few kilometres away, in Bai Dzanga, dozens and dozens of lumbering elephants frolic and play in the sunshine of this forest clearing. Moving shyly through the shadows slinks a family of western lowland gorillas.

Dzanga-Sangha National Park (www.dzanga-sangha.org) is even better than you dared hope Central Africa would be. This massive forest reserve, in the southwest corner of the Central African Republic, today sits at the heart of the newly created Unesco World Heritage–listed Sangha Trinational reserve. Neighbouring parks in the DRC and Cameroon make up the other two-thirds of this botanical hothouse, but of the three this would be the pick of the bunch. Sure the neighbouring parks might be a bit less disturbed by humans, but CAR's Dzanga-Sangha has huge concentrations of elephants. And then there are the chimpanzees and gorillas, both of which are found in impressive numbers; some of the gorillas are habituated to humans, meaning heart stopping close-up encounters. But a trip to Dzanga-Sangha is about more than just megafauna. It's about people as well and you can join the BaAka net hunting for forest antelopes or even spend days camping deep in the jungle with them.

This is the most organised and visitor friendly of the three parks, and has the best array of accommodation. You won't do much better than the South African–run **Sangha Lodge** (www.sanghalodge.com), where delicious food, a peaceful location and comfortable cottages will keep any jungle explorer happy. The park authorities can organise all activities, including hunting trips with the BaAka, but for a more intensive immersion contact **Louis Sarno** (akkaman11@yahoo.co.uk), an American and author of *Song from the Forest: My Life Among the Ba-Benjelle Pygmies*.

Despite a ceasefire agreement the New Seleka rebel alliance swept into capital Bangui in March 2013, ousting President François Bozizé, who fled to neighbouring Cameroon.

Culture

Half of Central Africans are Christian, 15% are Muslim and 35% have stuck wholly with traditional animistic convictions; these ancient customs still strongly influence most people's lives, regardless of their principal faith.

CAR encompasses over 80 ethnic groups, which can basically be grouped into riverine, grassland and forest cultures; the latter include the Aka people (pygmies, though they don't like that term; singular is MoAka, plural is BaAka). The Baya-Mandjia and Banda, originating in the western and central savannahs respectively, compose 75% of the population.

Some 70% of the population lives a rural existence, and subsistence agriculture remains the backbone of the economy. The same percentage lives on less than a dollar a day.

While rice and yam are sometimes available, Central Africans love their cassava, eating it at virtually every meal with a meat, fish or vegetable sauce. Koko, which is a little like eating grass (only it's pretty tasty), is another popular sauce ingredient. Bushmeat, particularly monkey, boa and antelope, is also common in markets and even on menus. Forest caterpillars are a popular treat during June. A dash of piment (hot sauce) is put on almost everything.

Palm wine is the most popular firewater in the south, while *bili-bili*, a sorghum-based alcohol, predominates in the north. Both are available in Bangui, but beer is king there.

Environment

CAR, just a tad smaller than France, is landlocked smack bang in the middle of the continent. The country is one immense plateau varying in height mostly between 600m and 700m, tapering down to 350m in the far southwest. The closest thing to a real mountain is Mt Ngaoui, which at 1420m is the highest point in the country.

Often associated with the tropical rainforest found in the southwest, CAR is mainly covered by savannahs interspersed with rivers. Poaching is a huge problem and logging is on the increase, threatening CAR's standing as one of the last great wildlife refuges.

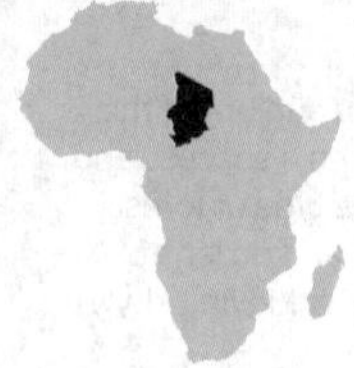

Chad

Includes ➡

Fast Facts

- ➡ **Capital** N'Djaména
- ➡ **Population** 10.9 million
- ➡ **Languages** French, Arabic and more than 120 local languages
- ➡ **Area** 1,284,000 sq km
- ➡ **Currency** Central African franc (CFA)
- ➡ **Visa requirements** Must be obtained before arrival from the nearest Chadian embassy or consulate

Dramatic Moonscapes & Oasis Towns

Wave goodbye to your comfort zone and say hello to Chad. Put simply, Chad is a place and an experience that you'll never forget! If Ghana and Gambia are Africa for beginners, Chad is Africa for the hard core.

Travel here is tough. Many of the roads are broken due to years of conflict and lack of maintenance. There are few comfortable hotels and there is plenty of bureaucracy and demands for *cadeaux* (gifts) to negotiate. Added to that, the summer heat is mind-melting, travel costs can be astronomical and the security situation remains unpredictable.

So why bother, you may ask? Well, we could list the sublime oases lost in the northern deserts, tell you about the stampeding herds of wildlife in the national parks or the deep blue lure of a boat trip on Lake Chad. But let's be honest about it, these things alone aren't why people come to Chad. Chad offers an opportunity to break emphatically with a comfortable Western world and come to a place that promises experiences, good and bad, that you'll be recalling forever.

Chad Top Sights

- ➡ **Zakouma National Park** Track herds of elephants and ogle dazzling birds in this sublime national park
- ➡ **Gaoui** Sigh over the beautiful painted houses of Gaoui, a fascinating village just minutes from N'Djaména
- ➡ **Sarh** See the green and pleasant side of sandy Chad and chill out along the Chari River
- ➡ **Guetè** Scan the horizon for egrets and hippos on Lake Chad, Africa's most mysterious lake
- ➡ **Bol** Get out on Lake Chad from this frontier market town
- ➡ **Ennedi** Marvel at dramatic desert scenery and rock formations

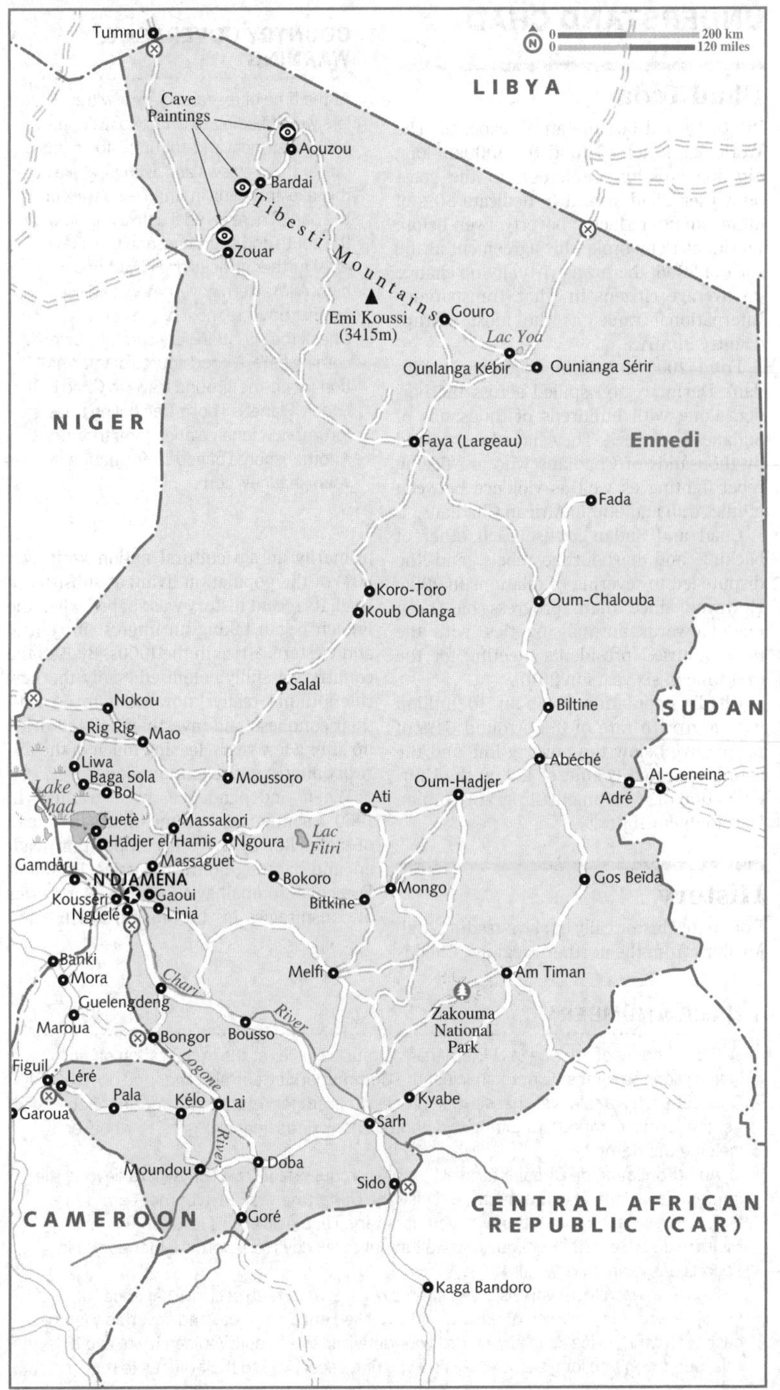

0 200 km
0 120 miles
LIBYA
Tummu
Cave Paintings
Aouzou
Bardai
Tibesti Mountains
Zouar
Emi Koussi (3415m)
Gouro
Lac Yoa
Ounianga Kébir
Ounianga Sérir
NIGER
Faya (Largeau)
Ennedi
Fada
Koro-Toro
Koub Olanga
Oum-Chalouba
Salal
Biltine
SUDAN
Nokou
Rig Rig
Mao
Liwa
Baga Sola
Bol
Lake Chad
Moussoro
Abéché
Al-Geneina
Adré
Oum-Hadjer
Ati
Guetè
Massakori
Hadjer el Hamis
Ngoura
Lac Fitri
Massaguet
Gamdâru
N'DJAMÉNA
Bokoro
Gos Beïda
Kousséri
Gaoui
Nguelé
Linia
Mongo
Bitkine
Banki
Mora
Melfi
Am Timan
Chari
Guelengdeng
Zakouma National Park
Maroua
Bousso
River
Bongor
Logone
Figuil
Léré
Pala
Kélo
Lai
Kyabe
Garoua
Sarh
River
Doba
Moundou
Sido
CENTRAL AFRICAN REPUBLIC (CAR)
CAMEROON
Goré
Kaga Bandoro

UNDERSTAND CHAD

Chad Today

In 2004 Chad became an oil exporter. The World Bank helped fund the 1000km-long pipeline crossing Cameroon to the coast only after Chad agreed to dedicate 80% of oil income to reducing poverty. Even before President Déby broke this agreement at the start of 2006, there was virtually no change for average citizens in what Transparency International ranks as the most corrupt country in Africa.

From 2003 unrest in neighbouring Sudan's Darfur region spilled across the border, along with hundreds of thousands of Sudanese refugees. They have been joined by thousands of Chadians who are fleeing rebel fighting as well as violence between ethnic Arab and ethnic African Chadians.

Chad and Sudan accuse each other of backing and harbouring rebels, and the dispute led to severing of relations in 2006. However, since then, progress has been made towards normalising ties, with the two countries' presidents meeting for the first time in six years in 2010.

Chad's population is about 10 million with a growth rate of 3%. Around 64% of people live below the poverty line and the country is rated 175 out of 182 on the United Nations Development Program Human Development Index.

COUNTRY COVERAGE & WARNING

At the time of research very few travellers were heading to Chad, so we're providing historical and cultural information rather than reviews and listings. Make no mistake, travelling in Chad is no walk in the park. There is rebel activity all across the south and southeast and the chances of further attacks on N'Djaména are high. All Western governments advise against travel to most of the country. Check the situation very carefully before coming here. A good source of information for on-the-ground travel in Chad is Lonely Planet's Thorn Tree online travel forum www.lonelyplanet.com/thorntree. Another source of good information is www.chadnow.com.

History

Dominated historically by slave-trading Arab Muslims from the northern regions, Chad is primarily an agricultural nation with over 80% of the population living at subsistence level. Its recent history was shaped when the French began taking an interest in central and western Africa in the 1900s. By 1913 the country was fully colonised: sadly the new rulers didn't really know what to do with their conquest, and investment all but dried up after a few years, leaving much of the territory almost entirely undeveloped.

When independence was granted in 1960, a southerner became Chad's first head of state. But by arresting opposition leaders and banning political parties, President François Tombalbaye provoked a series of conspiracies in the Muslim north – the

NAME & NUMBER

Within 72 hours of arriving in N'Djaména you must register at the immigration office, which is on the right side at the back of the Commissariat Central compound on Ave Félix Éboué. It's a relatively hassle-free process (except for returning to your hotel to get the forms stamped), requiring two photos and various financial 'gifts' to whoever is yielding the stamps.

An Autorisation de Circuler (Travel Permit) is required for travel anywhere beyond the immediate vicinity of N'Djaména. First visit the Department of Development and Tourism, which will type up a letter with your itinerary. Then deliver this letter to the nearby Ministre de la Securité Publique and wait about three days for approval. In theory this sounds easy – in theory...

Finally, in each town you visit, you should register with both *securité* (Agence National de Securité) – which needs a long form filled out, one photo and, invariably, some cash – and the police, who just record your details in their book. You can try to avoid this, but it won't be long before they find you and escort you to their offices to register.

ZAKOUMA NATIONAL PARK

Years of poaching and civil war ravaged local wildlife in this 305,000-hectare park, with elephant numbers falling from an estimated 4300 in 2002 to 454 in April 2011. However, the Chadian government with the help of the EU has restocked the park and begun to implement tough anti-poaching measures.

As a result, Zakouma is once again one of the best places in Central Africa to see large herds of elephants, as well as giraffes, wildebeests, lions and a wide variety of antelopes, primates, and weird and wonderful birdlife. The best time to come is March and April when the animals congregate around watering holes. June to October is to be avoided because of the rains.

Zakouma is 800km south of N'Djaména. Public transport is practically nonexistent so the most realistic option is to organise a trip through one of N'Djaména's travel agencies, such as the **Tchad Evasion Travel Agency** (www.tchadevasion.com). Expect a six-day round trip since it takes two just to reach the park.

Inside Zakouma, **Le Campement Hôtelier Tinga** (www.zakouma.com) has comfortable rooms and a good restaurant.

violent repression of which quickly escalated into full-blown guerrilla war.

For the next quarter of a century, Chadian politics was defined by armed struggles, shifting alliances, coups and private armies, overseen and often exacerbated by France and Libya, who took a keen interest in the area. In addition, the Sahel drought of the 1970s and early 1980s destroyed centuries-old patterns of existence and cultivation, causing large-scale migration to urban centres.

In 1975 Tombalbaye was assassinated, and succeeded by General Félix Malloum, a fellow southerner. Over US$1 million in cash was found in Tombalbaye's residence, along with plans to proclaim himself emperor.

The Government of National Unity was then formed by Malloumand Hissène Habré (a former northern rebel commander); it was a tenuous alliance between two men who shared little more than mutual distrust. The resulting internal power struggle in 1979 pitted north against south, and Muslim against Christian or animist, all colliding with destructive force in the capital, where thousands of civilians were massacred. Eventually Malloum fled the country, and Goukouni Oueddei – the son of a tribal chieftain from northwestern Chad and an arch-enemy of Habré – took over.

In 1980 Libyan forces supporting Oueddei briefly occupied N'Djaména. The French army drove them northwards, leaving Habré as the nominal ruler of Chad.

In 1990 Idriss Déby, a northern Muslim warlord in self-imposed exile in Sudan, swept back into Chad with a private army of 2000 soldiers and Libyan backing. Habré fled to Senegal leaving Déby with a clear run to N'Djaména and the presidency of his war-ravaged country, which Déby consolidated by winning the first-ever presidential elections in 1996. While this ballot was widely regarded as rigged, the parliamentary elections a year later were considered much fairer. In 1998 a new rebellion broke out in the north, led by the Movement for Democracy and Justice (MDJT) under Déby's former minister Youssouf Togoimï.

To nobody's surprise, Déby won the May 2001 presidential elections by a comfortable margin, although results from a quarter of the polling stations had to be cancelled because of irregularities.

Three weeks after a failed 2006 coup and one year after the constitutional two-term presidential limit was overturned, Déby won a presidential election boycotted by the opposition and most citizens. In the April 2011 presidential election, boycotted by the opposition, Déby was again declared winner.

The fact that Déby's government has not already fallen has much to do with the presence of the French. France maintains a huge military base on the edge of N'Djaména (due to be closed in 2013) and, while the French have never admitted to actual involvement in repelling the rebel attacks of 2006 and 2008, it was reported in the French media that in the 2008 attack France provided logistical support to the government, funnelled weapons to the government via Libya, offered to evacuate Déby to France and sent special forces in to fight the rebels.

Culture

The north is populated by people of Arab descent, as well as nomadic Peul-Fulani and Toubou people. Black Africans are in the majority in the south – the Sara are by far the biggest ethnic group (25% of the population) and have traditionally dominated business and the civil service. The difference between these two broad groups is profound – the Christian (35% of the population) or animist southerners are mostly peasant farmers, tilling fertile land, while the northern Muslims (54%) are desert-dwelling pastoralists.

Surprisingly, for such a subsistence economy, education is looked upon favourably and literacy stands at 48%. Freedom of speech is also fiercely, if somewhat vainly, defended – but as the security situation continues to deteriorate, so too does the media's room to move.

Most of the crafts you'll see in Chad are imported from Nigeria and Cameroon, though the leatherwork and pottery is usually made locally and many of the large wool rugs come from Abéché and other desert towns.

Food & Drink

The food in Chad is typical of the region: tiny street stalls dish up meals of rice, beans and soup or stew, while indoor restaurants offer omelettes, liver, salads, *brochettes* (kebabs), fish and *nachif* (minced meat in sauce). To drink you have the usual range of *sucreries* (soft drinks), including the local Top brand, and fresh *jus,* fruit concoctions with more resemblance to smoothies than normal juice – bear in mind they're usually made with local water and ice. Beer is the favoured poison in bars, with a choice of local brews, Gala and Chari, or Cameroonian Castel. Also popular is *bili-bili,* a millet beer; *cochette* is a low-alcohol version.

Congo

Includes ➡

Best Places for Wildlife

- Parc National Nouabalé-Ndoki (p491)
- Parc National d'Odzala (p491)
- Parc National Conkouati-Douli (p490)
- Lésio Louna Gorilla Reserve (p489)
- Lac Télé (p491)

Best Places for Adventure

- Lac Télé (p491)
- Brazzaville to Impfondo/Bangui boat ride (p489)
- Parc National Nouabalé-Ndoki (p491)
- Parc National Conkouati-Douli (p490)

Why Go?

A land of steamy jungles hiding half the world's lowland gorillas, masses of forest elephants, and hooting, swinging troops of chimpanzees; the Congo (not to be confused with the Democratic Republic of Congo across the Congo River) is on the cusp of becoming one of the finest ecotourism destinations in Africa. Parc National Nouabalé-Ndoki and Parc National d'Odzala are two of the most pristine forest reserves on the continent and between them they are arguably the highlight of the whole of Central Africa.

Despite this impressive resume the Congo remains an unknown quantity to most outsiders and currently recieves very few visitors. But for those ready to heed the call of the wild, and not afraid of adventure, the Congo awaits.

When to Go

Brazzaville

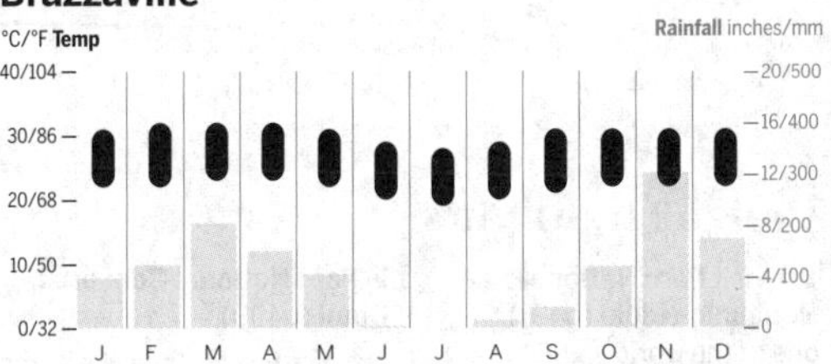

Jun–Dec The best overall time to travel in Congo .

Oct–Jan The easiest time to see wildlife in the northern forest parks.

Dec–Feb Sea turtles nest on beaches of Parc National Conkouati-Douli.

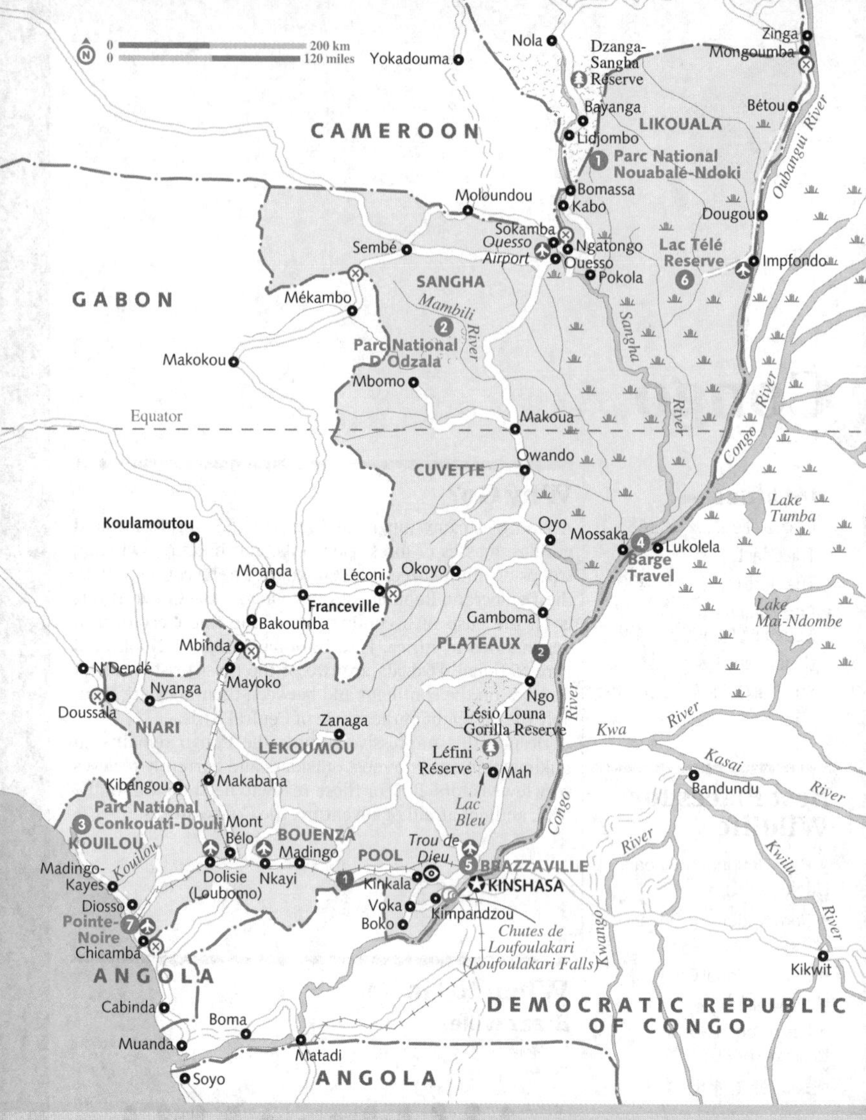

Congo Highlights

❶ Visit **Parc National Nouabalé-Ndoki** (p491), one of the world's great wildernesses.

❷ Let a guide lead you to a family of gorillas in **Parc National d'Odzala** (p491).

❸ Explore beach, savannah and jungle all on the same day in **Parc National Conkouati-Douli** (p490).

❹ Journey for the sake of the journey and travel by **barge** (p495).

❺ Relax in **Brazzaville** (p485), a big city with a small-town feel.

❻ Search for the legendary monster of the mysterious **Lac Télé** (p491).

❼ Munch seafood in the Congolese 'Riviera' of **Pointe-Noire** (p489).

BRAZZAVILLE

POP 1.28 MILLION (GREATER BRAZZAVILLE)

Founded in 1880 on the Stanley Pool (called Malebo Pool in the DRC) area of the Congo River, 'Brazza' has always been the junior partner economically with Kinshasa (DRC), which tempts and taunts from the other shore; though for travellers it's the more laid-back, and safer, town.

Low-key and unassuming, with most evidence of the war years washed away, Brazzaville has a lot of charm and many visitors claim that it's the most pleasant city in Central Africa.

SET YOUR BUDGET

Budget

- Hotel room US$20–35
- Two-course dinner US$10
- Beer US$1.20
- Seven-hour bus ride US$40

Midrange

- Hotel room US$50–80
- Two-course dinner US$15–20
- Short taxi ride US$5

Top End

- Hotel room US$80+
- Two-course dinner US$25–50
- Gorilla trekking permit US$400
- 4WD rental US$200–300

Sights

Brazza Memorial MEMORIAL
(Ave Cabral; admission free; 10.30am-10.30pm) The body of Pierre Savorgnan de Brazza, who founded the city, was returned to Congo in 2006 and interred in this gleaming memorial. Opening hours are a little flexible!

Basilique Sainte-Anne CHURCH
(Ave Orsii) This modernist 1949 building was the crowning achievement of French architect Roger Erell, who was known for fusing Western architectural ideas with local building techniques.

Marché Total MARKET
(Ave Matsoua) Brazza's biggest market, in Bacongo, sells everything from technological wonders to caterpillars and monkeys to Congolese fabrics and aphrodisiac charms.

Marché Touristique MARKET
(Marché Plateau Ex-Trésor; Ave de Gaulle; 8am-5pm Mon-Sat, to 1pm Sun) Sift through all the schlock here and you'll find some decent weavings and woodcarvings.

Ecole de Peinture de Poto-Poto GALLERY
(5567961; Ave de la Paix; 9am-6pm) Perhaps the best place to pick up a souvenir is from this association of painters; many of its members have exhibited in Europe and the USA.

Les Rapides RIVER
These wide and powerful rapids on the Congo River at the outskirts of the city are where the Congo River gets nasty. Take a minibus to Pont Djoué from next to Centre Culturel Français. Most people observe the rapids from the nearby bar **Site Touristique Les Rapides** (7am-11pm), but the best viewing is at the other end, down the sandy track after the bridge. The main rapids themselves are well out into the middle of the river and quite hard to see, but it's still impressive even from this distance. A taxi from the city centre costs around CFA2000.

Sleeping

Armée du Salut HOTEL $
(053074853; off Ave des Trois Martyrs; r with/without bathroom CFA10,000/5000; P) The spick-and-span Salvation Army has the cheapest beds in Brazza, in part because the mattresses are exceptionally thin. There's a 10.30pm curfew.

Hôtel M Domingo HOTEL $
(05213308; Ave de la Paix; r with fan CFA12,000, with air-con CFA14,000-18,000;) This ageing, no-nonsense place in Poto-Poto is popular due to its low prices and location, though electricity and water often cut out.

SIL Congo HOTEL $
(055218054; Ave Foch; s/d from CFA12,000/20,000) Rooms at this Christian missionary centre are often booked up by long-term renters, but if you can get one then the spacious, clean rooms (some of which have hot-water bathrooms) are some of the best value in the city. Check-in is between 9am and 3pm and curfew is at 10pm.

★ **Hôtel Hippocampe** HOTEL $$
(066686068; www.hippocampe.asia; Rue Behangle; r CFA28,000-38,000; P @) Congo's number-one travellers' meeting point has clean, comfortable and well-maintained rooms (though try to avoid the smaller,

Brazzaville

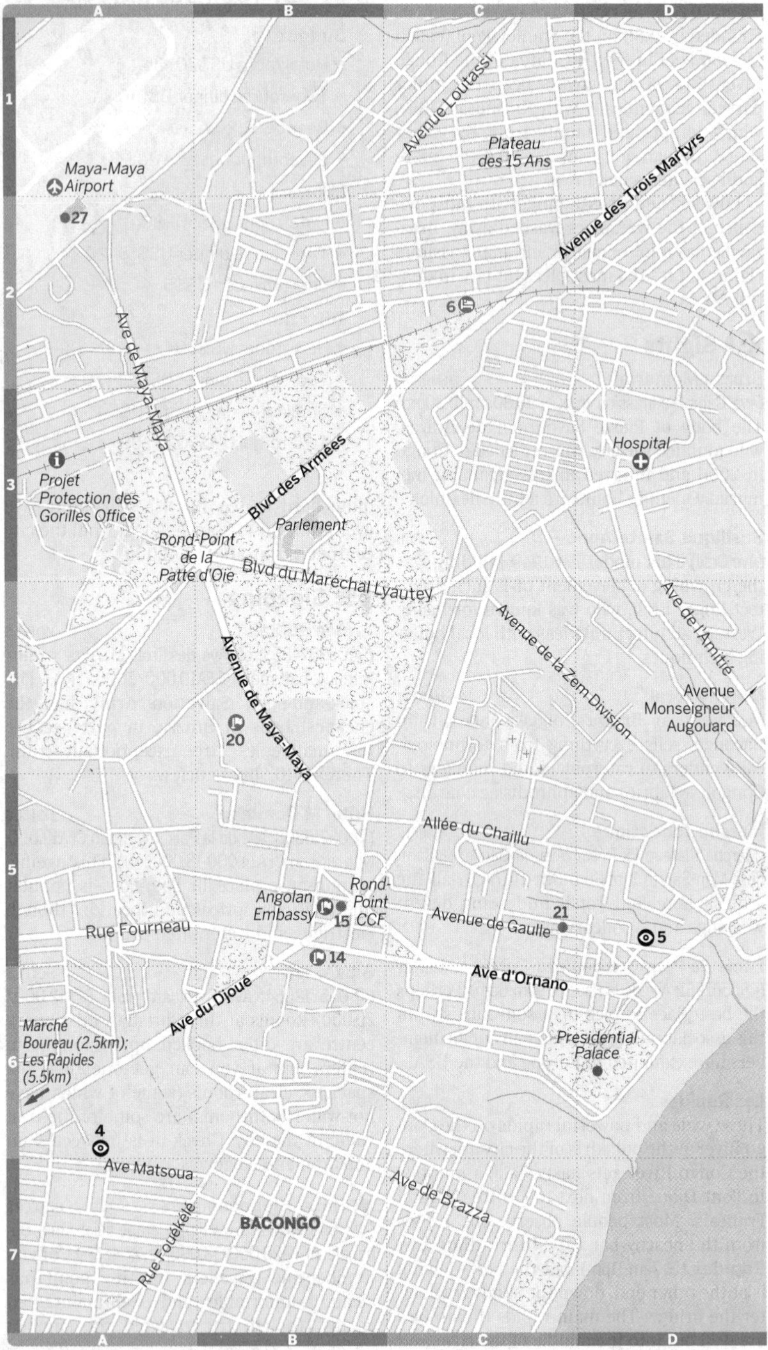

A B C D

1 2 3 4 5 6 7

Maya-Maya Airport
27
Avenue Loutassi
Plateau des 15 Ans
Avenue des Trois Martyrs
6
Ave de Maya-Maya
Hospital
Projet Protection des Gorilles Office
Blvd des Armées
Parlement
Rond-Point de la Patte d'Oie
Blvd du Maréchal Lyautey
Avenue de la Zem Division
Ave de l'Amitié
Avenue de Maya-Maya
Avenue Monseigneur Augouard
20
Allée du Chaillu
Rond-Point CCF
Angolan Embassy
15
21
Avenue de Gaulle
5
Rue Fourneau
14
Ave d'Ornano
Ave du Djoué
Marché Boureau (2.5km); Les Rapides (5.5km)
Presidential Palace
4
Ave Matsoua
Ave de Brazza
BACONGO
Rue Fouékélé

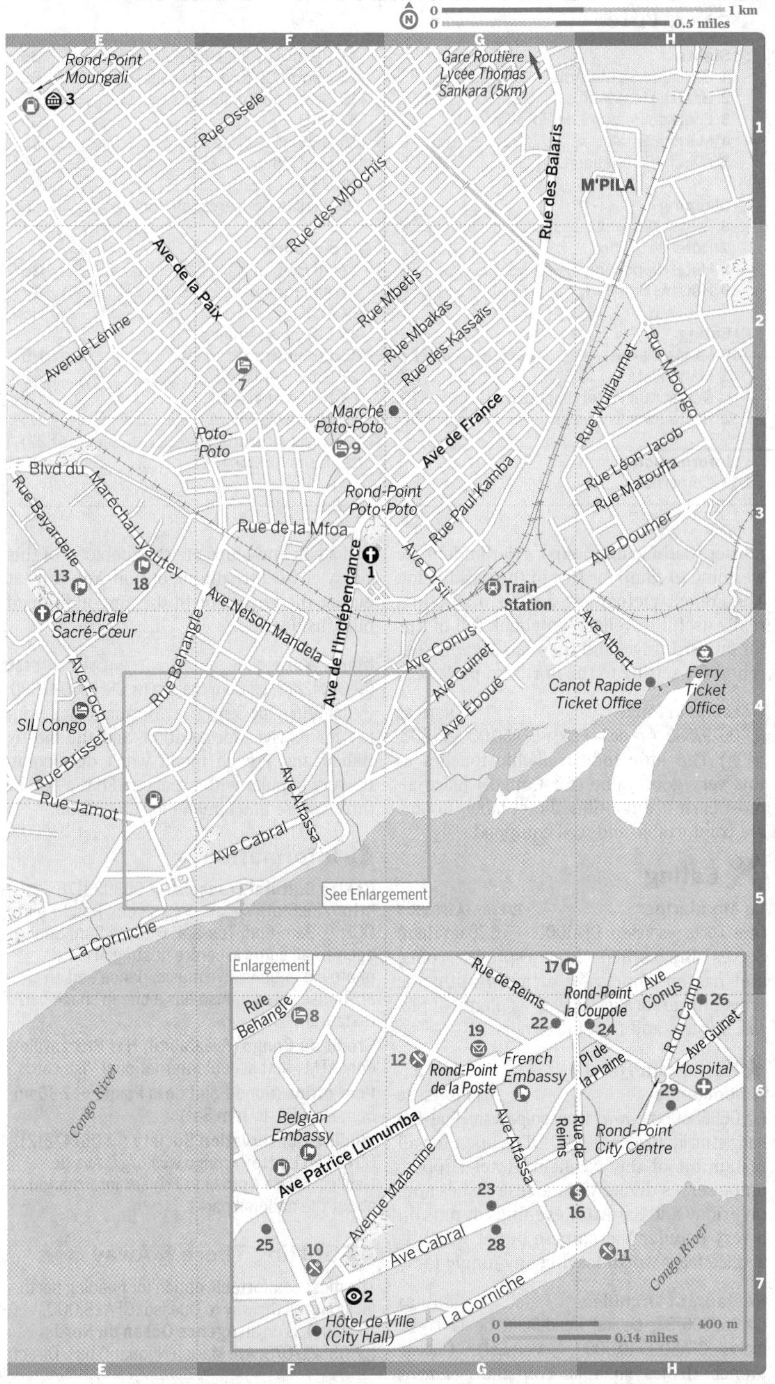

0 1 km
0 0.5 miles
Rond-Point Moungali
Gare Routière Lycée Thomas Sankara (5km)
Rue Ossele
Rue des Mbochis
Rue des Balaris
M'PILA
Ave de la Paix
Rue Mbetis
Rue Mbakas
Rue des Kassaïs
Avenue Lénine
Rue Mbongo
Rue Wuillaumet
Marché Poto-Poto
Ave de France
Poto-Poto
Blvd du Maréchal Lyautey
Rue Léon Jacob
Rue Matouffa
Rond-Point Poto-Poto
Rue Paul Kamba
Rue Bayardelle
Rue de la Mfoa
Ave Doumer
Ave de l'Indépendance
Ave Orsii
Train Station
Cathédrale Sacré-Cœur
Ave Nelson Mandela
Rue Behangle
Ave Albert
Ave Conus
Ave Guinet
Canot Rapide Ticket Office
Ferry Ticket Office
Ave Foch
SIL Congo
Ave Éboué
Rue Brisset
Ave Alfassa
Rue Jamot
Ave Cabral
See Enlargement
La Corniche
Congo River
Enlargement
Rue de Reims
Rond-Point la Coupole
Ave Conus
Rue Behangle
R du Camp
Ave Guinet
Rond-Point de la Poste
French Embassy
Pl de la Plaine
Hospital
Belgian Embassy
Rue de Reims
Rond-Point City Centre
Ave Patrice Lumumba
Avenue Malamine
Ave Alfassa
Ave Cabral
La Corniche
Hôtel de Ville (City Hall)
Congo River
0 400 m
0 0.14 miles
CONGO BRAZZAVILLE

Brazzaville

Sights
- 1 Basilique Sainte-Anne F3
- 2 Brazza Memorial F7
- 3 Ecole de Peinture de Poto-Poto E1
- 4 Marché Total A6
- 5 Marché Touristique D5

Sleeping
- 6 Armée du Salut C2
- 7 Hôtel de la Paix F2
- 8 Hôtel Hippocampe F6
- 9 Hôtel M Domingo F3

Eating
- 10 La Mandarine F7
- 11 Mami Wata H7
- Restaurant Hotel Hippocampe .... (see 8)
- 12 Restaurant Orchidée G6

Information
- 13 Cameroon E3
- 14 Central African Republic B5
- 15 Centre Culturel Français B5
- 16 Crédit du Congo H7
- 17 DRC G5
- 18 Gabon E3
- 19 Post Office G6
- 20 USA B4
- 21 Wildlife Conservation Society C5

Transport
- 22 Air Congo G6
- 23 Air France G7
- 24 EC Air H6
- 25 Ethiopian Airlines F7
- 26 Europcar H6
- 27 Gabon Airlines A2
- 28 Kenya Airways G7
- Mistral Aviation .... (see 27)
- Royal Air Maroc .... (see 27)
- 29 Trans Air Congo H6

noisier road-facing rooms). Overlanders are welcome to camp for free in the parking lot. The French/Vietnamese owners maintain a really useful travellers' notebook full of tips for onward travel and they can organise car rental for getting to the northern parks.

Hôtel de la Paix HOTEL **$$**
(☎06797580; Ave de la Paix; r CFA50,000-65,000; ❄📶) The little industrial-chic touches at this very good-value (for Congo!) place almost earn it a boutique hotel label. Rooms are comfortable and well equipped.

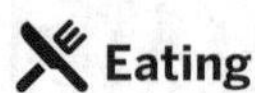

Eating

La Mandarine BAKERY, FAST FOOD **$**
(Ave Foch; espresso CFA1000; ⌚6.30am-11pm) Serves Brazzaville's best espresso coffee and has an impressive array of authentic croissants and cakes as well as plenty of pizzas, burgers and fruit juices.

★ **Restaurant Hotel Hippocampe** VIETNAMESE **$$**
(☎066686068; www.hippocampe.asia; Rue Behangle; mains CFA2500-7000) The open-for-all restaurant of the excellent Hotel Hippocampe serves divine Vietnamese dishes and, on Friday and Saturday evenings, it puts on a very popular Vietnamese buffet which is a spice feast worth leaving any jungle for.

Restaurant Orchidée FRENCH **$$**
(☎066606732; behind Rond-Point de la Poste; mains CFA8000-10,000; ⌚Mon-Sat) Classic French dishes such as *confit de canard* and steak and chips are the lifeblood of this classy city-centre dining option. You can eat out on the terrace or in the air-conditioned bliss inside.

Mami Wata INTERNATIONAL **$$$**
(☎05342879; La Corniche; mains CFA6500-11,500; ⌚11am-11pm Tue-Sun) The 'Mermaid' is a winner for its riverside location, and the mostly Italian and French menu won't disappoint. It's very popular with expats and has a decent three-course lunch menu for CFA13,500.

Information

Centre Culturel Français (☎053929176; http://institutfrancais-congo.com; Rond-Point CCF; ⌚9am-6pm Tue-Sat, 6-10pm Sun) Superb open-to-all cultural centre hosting art and photo exhibitions, live music, dance and an art-house cinema. Also has a cheap snack bar/restaurant.

Crédit du Congo (Ave Cabral) Has Brazzaville's only ATMs that accept international Visa cards.

Post office (Rond-Point de la Poste; ⌚7.30am-5pm Mon-Fri, to 1pm Sat)

Wildlife Conservation Society (☎057472121, 057227411; http://congo.wcs.org/; Ave de Gaulle; ⌚8am-4pm Mon-Fri) For information about the national parks.

Getting There & Away

The most comfortable option for heading north, including all the way to Ouesso (CFA28,000, 16 hours), is on an **Agence Ocean du Nord** (☎055217678; Ave Marien Ngouabi) bus. Direct buses to Ouesso leave on Monday, Wednesday and Friday at 8am. Buy tickets several days in advance. All other buses, taxis and trucks leave from Gare Routière Lycée Thomas Sankara further north.

For transport to points west of Brazzaville, like Kinkala and Boko, go to Marché Boureau. The road to Pointe-Noire is being upgraded and the journey is far easier, and safer, than it has ever been.

Getting Around

Taxis are everywhere in Brazzaville. They don't have meters, so expect to pay CFA500 for a short hop, CFA1000 across town, and CFA2000 to the airport and the northern bus stations. After 9pm or so, you're going to have to pay about CFA1000 to CFA2000 to get anywhere. Crowded minibuses (CFA150) are nearly as common as taxis.

AROUND BRAZZAVILLE

The **Lésio Louna Gorilla Reserve**, 140km north of Brazzaville, is a home for orphaned and confiscated gorillas. During a visit (CFA35,000 per person) you can see the babies in the nursery and watch the adults living wild on an island get fed. You can also swim or just enjoy the peace and quiet at lovely **Lac Bleu**. If you leave Brazzaville by 5am it can all be done as a long day trip. Make arrangements several days in advance with the **Projet Protection des Gorilles** (www.aspinallfoundation.org; 125 Rue Matsiona-Nzoulou; 8am-4pm Mon-Fri).

THE COAST

Pointe-Noire

POP 635,000

Congo's outlet to the sea is something of a resort town, though it's mostly expat oil workers rather than sun-loving tourists filling the seaside hotels and restaurants. **Rénatura Congo** (069449999; www.renatura.org; per person CFA10,000; 8am-6pm Mon-Fri, to noon Sat) is a turtle protection society that allows you to accompany its workers who free sea turtles from fishing nets.

Sleeping

The best budget lodging in the centre, and probably the whole city, is **Sueco** (222940555; Ave Moe Teli; s/d without bathroom CFA10,000/15,500, r with bathroom CFA18,000-30,000; P @), the Swedish Mission. Curfew is 11pm.

The **Migitel** (055743636; www.congo-hotel-migitel.com; Blvd de Gaulle; s/d/ste CFA45,000/50,000/60,000;) has plain but comfortable rooms at half the price you'd pay on the beach or elsewhere on Blvd de Gaulle. Set around a courtyard flower garden, but with a city-centre location, **Le Guest House** (055204010; www.leguesthouse.com; Blvd Général de Gaulle; r CFA42,000-55,000; P) has clean and comfortable rooms that are good value.

For something more upmarket again the **Elais Hotel** (222941251; www.hotelelais.com; Blvd Général de Gaulle; r CFA100,000-150,000; P @) is the new boy on the block and has cool modern rooms and great service. With attractive thatched-roof cottages overlooking a little lagoon and a private beach, **Malonda Lodge** (055575151; www.malondalodge.com; r incl breakfast from CFA84,000; P), 18km south of town, is the loveliest hotel in Congo.

Eating

Excellent barbecued fish and Congolese cuisine make **Restaurant Gaspard** (Blvd Moe Mokasso; dishes CFA3000; 9am-10.30pm) a must-do. It's a fair way out of the city centre.

Down by the beach the **Twiga Hotel Restaurant** (Av Docteur Jacques Bouity; mains CFA7000-15,000) has breezy ocean views and decent seafood – try the spicy pile of squid, prawns and lobster (CFA9500).

For something more down to earth don't miss the stalls that set up at the southern end of La Côte Sauvage every afternoon and evening. Locals flock to them for a sunset beer and plate of spicy fried fish (CFA2000).

Getting There & Around

Despite great improvements in the road and security situation most people still fly between Pointe-Noire and Brazzaville. There are at least six flights (CFA37,000 to CFA40,000) a day with various companies.

Buses (CFA17,000) to Brazza run daily and take a full day. The other option is the newly revamped railway. Smart Chinese-built trains (CFA15,000) clatter to Brazza on Monday and Friday and the trip takes up to 24 hours. Most taxi trips cost CFA500 to CFA1000, and it's CFA2000 to the airport.

Diosso & Around

On the edge of the village of Diosso, 25km north of Pointe-Noire, runaway erosion has created the colourful **Diosso Gorge**, which looks like a mini Badlands. Also in town, the **Musée Ma-Loango** (☎05336816; admission CFA2000; ⏰10am-5pm Sat & Sun, by appointment Mon-Fri) has good displays on Congolese culture, the Loango kingdom and slavery. Bush taxis run from Grande Marché in Pointe-Noire (CFA800, 45 minutes) or a taxi can be hired for a round trip for CFA10,000 to CFA15,000.

Parc National Conkouati-Douli

Congo's most diverse **national park** (☎05440034; admission CFA10,000, community fee CFA5000) stretches from the Atlantic Ocean through a band of coastal savannah up into jungle-clad mountains. Poaching problems (fed by demand for bushmeat in Pointe-Noire) mean the wildlife-watching has for a long time been somewhat limited, but recent investment in the park infrastructure and security means that the elephants, gorillas and buffalo that live here are becoming more common, and more easily seen.

The main activities are boat rides (CFA10,000 to CFA25,000 per person) up the Ngongo River; forest walks (CFA10,000); and, between November and February, watching sea turtles lay their eggs on the beach (CFA20,000). You can also help feed the island-dwelling chimpanzees (CFA50,000) being prepared for reintroduction to the forest.

Sleeping

Currently the only lodging is the very comfortable **Base Vie House** (campsites CFA10,000, 1-2 people/3-4 people CFA90,000/120,000) with full kitchen overlooking Conkouati Lagoon. However, at the time of writing new accommodation was about to open at Tchirila (prices unconfirmed), a wooden house situated way up in the forested hills in a region populated by chimpanzees and lowland gorillas, and **Loukani** (huts CFA15,000, campsites CFA7500), which has cabins and camping a few hundred metres away from a small lake in an area of savannah populated by herds of buffalo. In all cases you must bring all your own food and water.

Getting There & Away

Traffic is so sparse that hitching isn't an option. Goods trucks (seat in cabin/on top of load CFA6000/3000, eight to nine hours) head to Conkouati village from Pointe-Noire and back again four days a week. From Conkouati you will need to walk to Base-Vie or arrange a pick-up. A much more sensible idea is to hire a 4WD (around CFA200,000 per day) in Pointe-Noire or, better, from the park itself (CFA250,000). You will need to hire the jeep for the entire duration of your stay. No matter how you travel, you must call the park before visiting.

THE NORTH

Heading north of Brazzaville the road passes across the top of an unexpected high savannah plateau. It is not until you reach Makoua (or veer off east or west onto minor roads) that the road starts to tilt downwards and enter the dense rainforests of Congolese fame.

Owando

POP 24,000

Owando sits around the halfway point between Brazza and Ouesso and has a reasonable array of facilities. If you are making the trip north in stages it makes for a good overnight stop, although onward public transport is better from little Makoua, an hour up the road.

For accommodation try the **Hotel Daniels Club** (☎066515830; Av Marian Gouabi; r CFA35,000-60,000; P ❄), which, with its mirrored exterior and water fountains, certainly stands out. The rooms are comfortable and arranged around a quiet courtyard.

Agence Ocean du Nord (p488) has buses to Ouesso (CFA25,000) at around 2.30pm Monday, Wednesday and Friday. There are daily buses to Brazzaville (CFA10,000, 7am). Frequent share taxis run north to Makoua (CFA3000).

Makoua

POP 11,355

The small town of Makoua has a gentle country vibe. Its main claim to fame is that it sits smack on the equator.

The **Hotel la Fleur de Makoua** (r CFA25,000-30,000; P), which has the best

OFF THE BEATEN TRACK

LAKE TÉLÉ RESERVE

In a country like the Congo getting off the beaten tourist track is not difficult. But for those who really want to immerse themselves in the deepest of jungle adventures, a journey to the perfect circular form of Lake Télé, hidden away in the unimaginably remote northeast of Congo, is the kind of journey people write books about. It's not just that this lake is surrounded by swamp-forests that remain largely unexplored, and not just that are there an estimated 100,000 lowland gorillas inhabiting the area or indigenous groups living an almost completely traditional lifestyle, but if rumours are to be believed Lake Télé is also the home of the Mokèlé-mbèmbé, a large semiaquatic creature that many believers describe as being similar to a sauropod; a type of long-extinct dinosaur.

To get there you'll need firstly to take a not-very-regular flight from Brazza to the river town of Impfondo. Barges also float past Impfondo as they travel between Brazza and Bangui in CAR. From Impfondo a road of sorts runs to little Epéna after which nothing but unexplored swamp forest stands between you and your goal! If you're serious about visiting allow a lot of time and money, and contact the Wildlife Conservation Society (p488) in Brazzaville, which is working to establish a community reserve there.

rooms in town, is a new place on a side street next to the police station.

The road south to Brazzaville is surfaced all the way but a little north of Makoua the tarmac runs out and a muddy, red track (at the time of writing Chinese road crews were busy upgrading this section of road) runs through increasingly dense jungle to Ouesso. Buses (CFA15,000) bounce up to Ouesso Monday, Wednesday and Friday at around 4pm.

Parc National d'Odzala

One of the oldest national parks in Africa, the Parc National d'Odzala has had a turbulent past. Once celebrated for having around 20,000 gorillas, the population was decimated about a decade ago by several outbreaks of the ebola virus, which wiped out between 70% and 95% of the gorilla population.

Today the situation is much improved, gorilla numbers are growing and the park itself has received a much-needed boost with the arrival of **African Parks** (www.africanparks.org) and **Wilderness Safaris** (☎in South Africa + 27 11 807 1800; www.odzala-kokoua.com; 6-night all-inclusive package s/d US$9416/11,770), who between them have rejuvenated the park's infrastructure, stepped up antipoaching patrols and established two luxury tourist lodges (rumour has it that in the future Wilderness Safaris will also establish some budget accommodation). Currently, the only way to visit Odzala is on one of Wilderness Safari's exclusive fly-in safaris setting out from Brazza. Costs include all transport; accommodation; food; and activities, such as encounters with habituated gorilla families, jungle walks with local BaAka guides and *pirogue* (canoe) trips downriver in search of birds, elephants and other wildlife. If you want a comfortable safari to the wilds of Congo this is the way to go.

Ouesso

POP 28,179

Some 800km from Brazzaville, Ouesso (*way-so*) is the last city of the north. It's a rather lifeless town, but if you're heading to Parc National Nouabalé-Ndoki you'll probably spend some time here. Ouesso's one bank doesn't change money: enquire instead at the various Lebanese-run hardware shops.

The cottages at **Nianina Auberge** (☎05871906; Rue Ile Elapas; r CFA10,000-20,000; P ❄) are surprisingly colourful and cozy considering the brick exteriors. It's not the best hotel in town, but arguably the best value. For something altogether more luxurious head to **Espace Mbale** (☎055285920; r CFA35,000, cottage CFA45,000; P ❄) a little way south of town. The cheaper rooms here are a delight of whitewash and decorated bedspreads, and the more expensive wooden cottages have art on the wall, low-slung beds and stone-lined hot showers.

Parc National Nouabalé-Ndoki

A team from *National Geographic* magazine, who visited the fledgling **Parc National Nouabalé-Ndoki** (Nouabalé-Ndoki

BOATS TO DZANGA-SANGHA

If you're visiting Parc National Nouabalé-Ndoki then it's easy, and a lot of fun, to travel by boat between the park and Central African Republic's Dzanga-Sangha Reserve, from where you could continue up to Bangui by road. You can hire a speedboat from either park authority or from the Sangha Lodge (p477) in CAR for around CFA328,000. The alternative is to rent a very leaky *pirogue* (traditional canoe) with a small engine for which you'll pay half but take at least twice as long. Crossing the border on this route is memorable, but generally painless. Putter for hours along the stately brown Sangha River under the guard of what seems to be millions of big trees and then, quite suddenly, you come to a small clearing on the riverbank with a single wooden building staffed by a handful of soldiers, immigration officials and their families from the CAR. They'll merely ask a few questions, stamp your passport and send you on your way. Arrive like us during a massive thunderstorm, with bolts of lightning crashing into the river waters around you and the *pirogue* rapidly filling with water and you'll feel like an 18th-century explorer!

National Park; www.wcs-congo.org; park entry per day CFA20,000, village development fee per day CFA10,000) in the mid-1990s, called this northern corner of Congo the world's 'Last Eden', and they chose their words wisely.

The Parc National Nouabalé-Ndoki is truly the world before the chainsaw. This vast region of swampy forest is home to healthy populations of western lowland gorillas, forest elephants, chimpanzees and others.

So extraordinary is Nouabalé-Ndoki that in 2012 Unesco declared it a World Heritage Site, as a part of the much larger (750,000-hectare) Sangha Trinational Park, which covers both this park and neighbouring Dzangha-Sangha park in CAR and Lobéké park in Cameroon.

From the point of view of a visitor what makes this park so enthralling is the ease with which some of the creatures are seen. The forest is known for its natural clearings in which masses of elephants and gorillas gather.

Alongside these clearings viewing platforms have been constructed at Mbeli Bai (CFA97,500) and Wali Bai (CFA19,400) from which visitors can ogle the antics of Congolese megafauna. Mbeli is renowned for its elephants, gorillas and sitatunga antelopes, and Wali for its buffaloes. If you need to get even closer to the wildlife, then Nouabalé-Ndoki also has groups of habituated gorillas (CFA196,800 per person) at Mondika.

Children under 14 cannot visit the gorillas and those under 12 are not allowed at Mbeli Bai or Wali Bai. Everyone wishing to visit the gorillas at Mondika will need to provide a TB-negative test certificate.

Simple rooms at the park headquarters in Bomassa cost CFA32,800 per person including food. At Mondika camping in permanent tents cost CFA78,720/118,080 per single/double with food, and at Mbeli accommodation is in raised huts and also costs CFA78,720/118,080 including meals. Wali is just a short walk from Bomassa so you can base yourself there. Visiting Nouabalé-Ndoki is truly one of those 'once in a lifetime' kind of experiences and is as genuine a slice of raw, wild Africa as you will ever encounter, but don't expect much in the way of comfort. Bookings should be made with the **Wildlife Conservation Society** (WCS; rollabeg@yahoo.fr) as far in advance as possible (at least a month).

Getting There & Away

The easiest way to reach Bomassa is to charter a boat. The park charges CFA328,000 from Ouesso or Bayanga (CAR) for one to four people. You can also negotiate with private boat owners, though prices won't be much lower unless they paddle you rather than use a motor (which would be very, very slow – up to two days from Ouesso to Bomassa).

From Bomassa to Ndoki (the drop-off point for Mondika) WCS charges CFA78,720 for a jeep. You then have to wade through a swamp for 45 minutes and walk through dense jungle for two hours. This is almost as much a highlight as the gorillas themselves (though do try not to think about what sort of creepy-crawlies live in a Congolese swamp!). From Bomassa to Djeke (for Mbeli) a car is CFA65,600. This is also something of an adventure, with an hour or so spent in a *pirogue* paddling slowly through thick swamps. There's plenty of wildlife visible – sometimes too much, as we got chased by a hippo!

UNDERSTAND CONGO

Congo Today

With the civil war beginning to fade from memory Congo is finally at peace with itself for the first time in years. This has led to a surge of foreign investment in the country; the oil industry is booming, new roads are springing up, tourism is on the up and in 2010 the Congolese government even adopted a law for the promotion and protection of the BaAka, the first such law in Africa for these much abused peoples.

Of course it's not all good news. Corruption among officials and the oil industry is rife, and the economy's heavy reliance on oil revenues is said to substantially contribute to President Denis Sassou-Nguesso's ability to maintain tight control over the country. (He is currently under investigation in France for using millions of dollars of embezzled public funds to buy luxury homes and cars there.) Not surprisingly then, despite this oil wealth most Congolese remain desperately poor (over 70% of the population lives on less than US$2 a day) and are still somewhat sceptical about the future.

History

BaAka, arriving from the east, were most likely Congo's first inhabitants. Later several kingdoms of Bantu origin (the Kongo, Loango and Teke among them) arrived and opened trade links across the Congo River basin.

The Portuguese were the first Europeans to arrive on the banks of the Congo River, quickly establishing a slave-trade system with partnering coastal tribes. The French had an early presence here too, and it was Franco-Italian empire-builder Pierre Savorgnan de Brazza who led a major expedition inland in 1875, and then five years later charmed local rulers into putting their land on the river's west bank under French control.

French Rule

The French government made quick work of acquiring Congo's considerable natural resources such as ivory, tropical hardwoods and rubber, as well as raising hell with the local population who were used as forced labour. Because of human-rights scandals perpetrated by the companies running the region, the French were forced to take a greater role in overseeing things and by 1910, Congo (called Middle Congo) had been formally streamlined into French Equatorial Africa along with Chad, Gabon and CAR. Brazzaville was the capital.

Except for initiating construction of the Congo-Ocean Railway (1924–34), the French made few significant changes and locals revolted in protest in 1928.

Brazzaville had its moment in the sun during 1940–43 when it served as the symbolic capital of Free France. In 1944 genuine reforms such as the abolition of forced labour and the election of local councils were enacted, but ethnic integration was never a colonial priority. Tribal differences continued to fester, and with independence in 1960 the bubbling pot finally boiled over.

Africa's First Marxist State

Congo's first president, Fulbert Youlou, lasted just three tumultuous years before being deposed in a popular uprising that put Alphonse Massamba-Débat in power. Introducing a one-party state and treading a socialist path, he proved to be equally unpopular and was ousted in a 1968 military coup by Captain Marien Ngouabi. The next year Ngouabi formed the Congolese Worker's Party (PCT) and inaugurated the People's Republic of Congo, ushering in Africa's first Marxist-Leninist state. After Ngouabi was assassinated in 1977, the PCT appointed Joachim Yhombi-Opango as successor but, charged with 'deviation from party directives' and corruption, he was replaced in 1979 by vice president and defence minister Denis Sassou-Nguesso. Sassou's political survivalism proved to be superior to that of his predecessors (he's still in power today) and his pragmatism got results. Congo forged ties with both capitalist and communist countries and gradually moderated its political course. Following the downfall of the economy and the subsequent collapse of the Soviet Union, Sassou agreed to allow multiparty elections in 1992.

War & Peace

Sassou lost the election to former prime minister Pascal Lissouba, who had been exiled for complicity in the assassination of Ngouabi. Accusations that he rigged 1993's parliamentary elections sparked violent unrest between pro-government and opposition militias (both tribally based) until a 1994 ceasefire. Congo fell under full-scale civil war in 1997. Brazzaville was devastated (most of its citizens were forced to flee to the bush for many months) and Sassou's 'Cobra' militia, with the help of Angolan troops, put him back into power.

The coming years saw sporadic fighting, including more attacks on the capital; peace-agreement signings with some rebel groups; the approval of a new constitution in a national referendum; and Sassou winning another election (in which his main rivals, including Lissouba, were barred) in 2002. In 2003 the main rebel group, the 'Ninjas', finally agreed to a peace accord, but there was no follow through on disarmament and even after another peace deal in 2007 a few Ninjas continue their low-level insurgency in the Pool region, but today they're more interested in banditry than politics.

In the 2007 parliamentary elections, which were boycotted by the opposition, Sassou's allies won a strong majority. Then, in the presidential vote of 2009 Sassou took 79% of the vote. Both elections were widely criticised by international election observers as illegitimate.

Culture

Of Congo's 16 ethnic groups, the Kongo people predominate, making up nearly half the population. Other key groups include the Sangha (20%), Teke (17%), M'Bochi (12%) and BaAka (2%). Seventy percent of the population lives in Brazzaville, Pointe-Noire and along the railroad in between these two cities. In terms of faith, Congo is divided about half and half between Christian and animist, with a tiny Muslim minority. No matter the faith, belief in spirits and magic runs deep in Congolese society and many people consult traditional healers and various magic men for advice and medical treatment.

Food & Drink

Northern Congolese are meat eaters (very often bushmeat) while southern Congolese love their fish. Both eat their protein almost exclusively with cassava, though you will sometimes find yams or rice in restaurants.

SURVIVAL GUIDE

Directory A–Z

ACCOMMODATION

Outside Brazzaville and Pointe-Noire, accommodation options remain limited, but the situation is improving and better hotels are popping up in towns across the country. Prices are usually high regardless of whether you prefer budget, midrange or top-end accommodation.

EMBASSIES & CONSULATES

The following countries have diplomatic representation in Brazzaville. France, Belgium and Angola also have consulates in Pointe-Noire.

Angolan Embassy (☎055063217; Ave de Gaulle)

Belgian Embassy (☎0222813712; www.diplomatie.be/brazzaville; Ave Patrice Lumumba)

Cameroonian Embassy (☎069434747; Rue Bayardelle)

CARepublic Embassy (☎066318696; Rue Fourneau)

DRC Embassy (☎02813052; Ave de l'Indépendance)

French Embassy (☎066200303; www.ambafrance-cg.org; Ave Alfassa)

Gabon Embassy (Blvd du Maréchal Lyautey)

US Embassy (☎06122000; http://brazzaville.usembassy.gov; Ave de Maya-Maya)

MONEY

Euros are the best currency to bring, though you can change US dollars and British pounds in Brazzaville and Pointe-Noire. Banks willing to exchange money are rare outside these cities, but businesses owned by Lebanese and West Africans usually change money: rates vary widely so shop around. Make sure the bills are in pristine condition.

Crédit du Congo bank has ATMs in Brazzaville and Pointe-Noire that accept Visa, MasterCard and Plus cards, but don't rely on them always working.

POST & TELEPHONE

Landlines (starting with ☎281 – there are no proper area codes throughout the country) are appalling in Congo and you'll be lucky if they work. Most businesses use mobile phones.

The postal system is thoroughly unreliable.

SAFE TRAVEL

Travel in Congo is quite safe these days. Brazzaville and Pointe-Noire are typical African cities: trouble-free by day, but best traversed by taxi at night. Power cuts and fuel shortages are common. Be very discreet taking photos; you could easily end up in jail for several days.

VISAS

All visitors to Congo need a visa. You can buy a 15-day, single-entry visa (CFA20,000) on arrival at most borders, if you have a letter of introduction (a hotel reservation *should* suffice), but there will likely be hassles and additional 'fees' if you take this route. Visas from embassies in neighbouring nations are around CFA30,000 for one month.

Visas for Onward Travel

Angola Visas are only issued to residents of Congo. You'll need to post your passport back to your home country and obtain one there. Should this change the long list of requirements for any visa attempt includes a letter of invitation, legalised copy of an ID card, two photos, a letter explaining the reasons for your visit and a photocopy of the identity card of the person who invited you. Transit visas are equally problematic from the Brazzaville embassy or the consulate in Pointe-Nore. However, one glimmer of hope is that some people have sucessfully obtained transit visas from the consulate in Dolisie.

Cameroon Three-month, single-entry visas cost CFA5000, and require two photos, a photocopy of your passport and a hotel reservation. Takes 48 hours.

CAR One-month, single-entry visas require two photos, a photocopy of your passport, hotel reservation and CFA45,000. Takes 48 hours.

DRC Putting a dampener on many an overlander's plans, the embassy of DRC is now only issuing visas in Brazzaville to citizens and residents of Congo. The *only* way you will currently get a visa and be allowed to actually enter DRC is by sending your passport to the embassy in your home country and applying there.

Gabon Visas valid for a month cost CFA45,000. Bring a hotel reservation, a photocopy of your passport and two photos. Takes one day.

PRACTICALITIES

- **Electricity** 230V/50Hz. The plugs are two-pin continental-Europe style.
- **Languages** French (official), Lingala (north), Munukutuba (south).
- **Media** English-language news on the BBC World Service (92.6FM). All other print and broadcast media is in French.

Getting There & Away

AIR

All airlines have offices at the airports in Brazzaville and Pointe-Noire, but it's easier to use their offices in town (if they have one) or a travel agency. The following are just the bigger international airlines.

Air France (☎0222815135; www.airfrance.com; Ave Cabral) Flies direct to/from Europe to Brazzaville and Pointe-Noire.

Ethiopian Airlines (☎0810761; www.ethiopianairlines.com; Ave Foch)

Kenya Airways (☎055167796; www.kenya-airways.com; Ave Amilcar Cabral)

Royal Air Maroc (☎0222811010; www.royalairmaroc.com) This airline's office is at Maya-Maya Airport in Brazzaville.

LAND & RIVER

Angola

Crossing to Cabinda is possible on good roads, but check the situation carefully before trying it, especially if you are driving your own vehicle, as attacks by separatists are on the rise.

Cameroon

Travel to Cameroon is slow going, but possible in the dry season. The best way is to take a boat from Ouesso to Sokamba and continue through remote southwest Cameroon to Moloundou and Yokadouma. If you're driving, first head southeast of Ouesso to Ngombe, where there's a car ferry over the Sangha River, and then drive to Ngatongo, where another ferry will get you to Sokamba.

Central African Republic

Between June and December, when river levels are high enough, barges run up the Congo and Oubangui River from Brazzaville. Some go to Bangui (CAR) and Impfondo and others veer left at Mossaka taking the even wilder Sangha River to Ouesso. There are more or less weekly departures (Bangui/Impfondo CFA30,000/15,000), but no schedule; boats go when they're ready. Ideally the journey between Brazza and Impfondo can be done in five days downstream and nine upstream. Between Bangui and Brazza allow 10 days downstream and two weeks upstream. The boats used are creaky old multilevel boats that are virtual floating markets. There are hundreds of people packed on board and there's zero privacy or comfort but there is bucketloads of genuine adventure.

To find a boat start your search at the river port in Brazza or Bangui. In Brazza ask at the Di.Ge. Na.F office (the third building), which keeps a blackboard of boats that might be leaving soon. Take plenty of food and fresh water (although fish, fruit and bushmeat can be bought en route).

Gabon

Although it's possible to cross the border at Doussala or Mbinda north of Dolisie, most people heading to Gabon travel between Oyo and Franceville via Léconi (Gabon; it's not on the border, but take care of Gabonese immigration formalities here). There's no public transport along most of this route and few lorries, so it can take several days.

Getting Around

AIR

Trans Air Congo and Air Congo are the two most reliable airlines in Congo. There are also a few fly-by-night airlines flying to Dolisie, Impfondo, Nkayi and other remote towns. Except for the Pointe-Noire to Brazzaville route, flight schedules are rarely followed; cancellations are common. Travel agencies can often get seats when airlines say their planes are full.

EC Air (☎065090525; www.flyecair.com; Rond Point la Coupole, Brazzaville) This new Congolese airline is aiming to set new standards in Congolese aviation. It currently flies between Brazzaville and Pointe-Noire as well as to Paris.

Trans Air Congo (☎066262605; www.flytransaircongo.com; Ave Cabral, Brazzaville) Flies frequently between Brazzaville and Pointe-Noire (one way CFA24,700 to CFA40,000).

Air Congo (☎06710671; Ave Conus, Brazzaville) Flies frequently between Brazzaville and Pointe-Noire (one way CFA33,000 to CFA40,000) and occassionally from Brazza to Ouesso.

Mistral Aviation (☎055190747; airport) Flies from Brazzaville to Pointe-Noire as well as Dolisie and sometimes Ouesso.

LAND

Hwy 1 to Pointe-Noire has long been in such a bad state as to be almost impassable. Today upgrading work is ongoing and the journey time is dropping. Still, even with the improvements it still takes at least a day by bus. Hwy 2 north to Ouesso, however, is paved and in mostly good condition to just north of Makoua. Beyond here there are still some horribly rough spots, but reconstruction work is underway.

A few proper buses now run to the north, but it's still mostly bush taxis and lorries. **Europcar** (☎069692222; www.europcar.com; Rue du Camp, Brazzaville) offers expensive car and 4WD hire, but it's easier and about half the price to just charter a taxi with driver for travelling around Brazzaville. Or for cross-country travels you can go to Brazzaville's Marché Total to haggle with truck drivers parked on Ave Matsoua; the best price we found was CFA100,000 per day. The Hotel Hippocampe (p485) can also provide an excellent car and driver for a reasonable (for Congo at any rate) price.

RIVER

For information on the epic barge ride up the Congo and Oubangui River to the remote river port town of Impfondo (and onwards to Bangui in CAR) see p495.

TRAIN

Trains run twice a week between Brazzaville and Pointe-Noire (1st-/2nd-class CFA22,500/CFA14,000). Trains are supposed to run daily except Saturdays in both directions. At the time of writing though it was more like four times weekly in either direction (two day trains and two night trains). The train carriages themselves have recently been upgraded but sadly neither the track nor the engines were and it still takes 15 to 24 hours. Purchase tickets (1st-/2nd-class CFA22,500/14,000, 12 to 24 hours) the day before. First class gets you a seat, 2nd class is standing in the aisles.

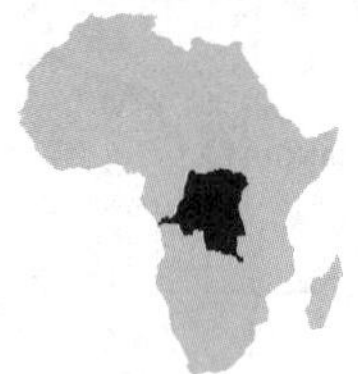

Democratic Republic of Congo

Includes ➡

Best for Wildlife

- ➡ Parc National des Virunga (p506)
- ➡ Parc National de Kahuzi-Biéga (p506)
- ➡ Okapi Wildlife Reserve (p508)
- ➡ Kundelunga National Park (p509)
- ➡ Lola Ya Bonobo Sanctuary (p505)

Best for Adventure

- ➡ Congo River by boat (p507)
- ➡ Overland Kinshasa to Lubumbashi (p514)
- ➡ Forest hikes with the pygmies (p508)
- ➡ Sleeping on the rim of Nyiragongo volcano (p505)
- ➡ Hiking the Rwenzori Mountains (p505)

Why Go?

As much a geographical concept as a fully fledged nation, the Democratic Republic of Congo (DRC; formerly Zaïre) has one of the saddest chapters in modern history: from the brazen political folly of King Leopold of Belgium to the hideously corrupt kleptocracy of maverick leader Mobutu Sese Seko and the blood-stained battlegrounds of Africa's first 'world war'.

But after a decades-long decline in which much of the country descended into anarchy, Africa's second-largest nation is, by and large, headed in the right direction. It still has a long way to go (militias continue to brutalise civilians in many areas), but new roads, enormous untapped mineral wealth and the world's largest UN peacekeeping force have bred optimism among its tormented but resilient population.

Carpeted by huge swaths of rain forest and punctuated by gushing rivers and smoking volcanoes, DRC is the ultimate African adventure. There is absolutely nothing soft nor easy about about it but for an African immersion you'll never forget, this is the place to be.

When to Go

Kinchasa

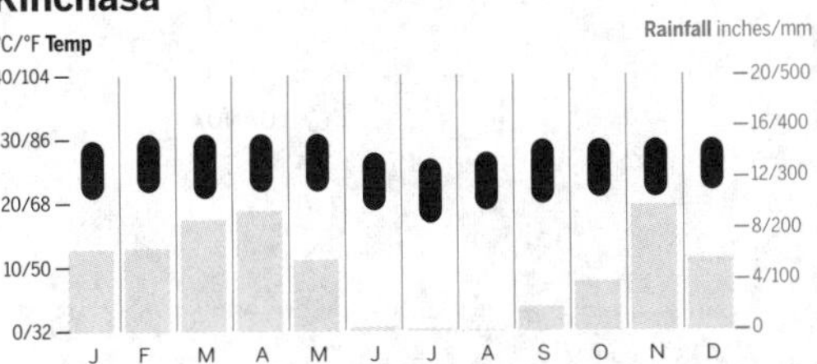

Dec–Mar Dry season for the north means slightly easier travel conditions.

Jan A good month to have the mountain gorillas totally to yourself.

Apr–Oct Dry season for the south and best time to attempt Kinshasa to Lubumbashi route.

Democratic Republic of Congo Highlights

1. Gaze into a volcano's liquid eye at **Nyiragongo** (p505).
2. Get up close and personal with gorillas at **Parc National des Virunga** (p506) and **Parc National de Kahuzi-Biéga** (p506).
3. Meet the bonobo, a rare, peace-loving relative of chimpanzees, at **Lola Ya Bonobo Sanctuary** (p505).
4. Take the legendary boat trip down the still-wild **Congo River** (p507).
5. Dance to the pulsating beat of **Kinshasa** (p500), DRC's megacity.
6. Cross the mighty jungle of the **Congo** (p514), the adventure of a lifetime.
7. Look for elusive okapis and learn the secrets of the Mbuti in **Okapi Wildlife Reserve** (p508).

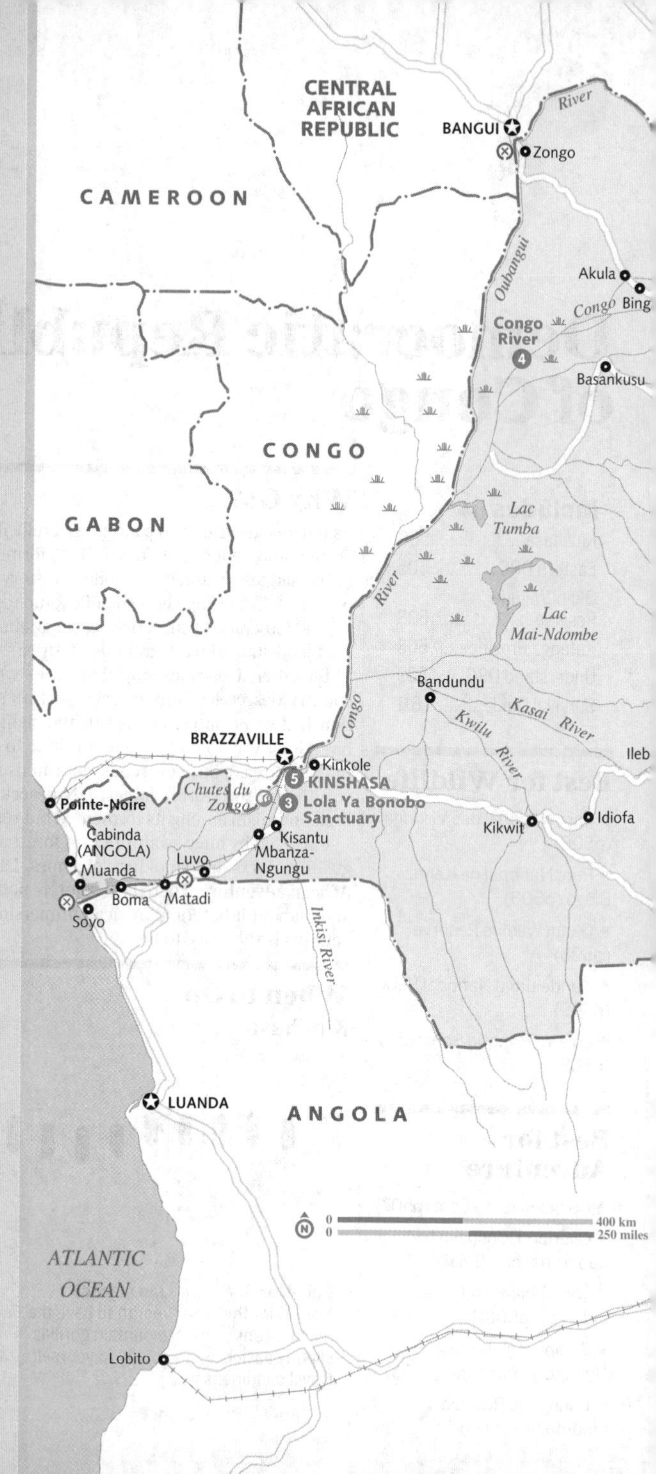

SUDAN
Obo
Juba
ongbo
Bangassou
Mobayi-Mbongo
Ndu
Gbadolite
Garamba National Park
Yei
Aba
Faradje
Niangara
Bondo
Arua
Aru
Isiro
Buta
Opaki Wildlife Reserve
7
Pakwach
Mahagi
Lisala
Bumba
Lake Albert
Bunia
Lulonga
River
River
Mambasa
Epulu
Komanda
UGANDA
Kisangani
Beni
Boyoma Falls
Kasindi
Butembo
Ubundu
Lake Edward (Lake Rwitanzige)
Tshuapa
Lubutu
Kayna-Bayonga
Ishasha
Parc National des Virunga
2
Rutshuru
Congo
Nyiragongo
1
Mount Nyiragongo (3470m)
Goma
RWANDA
River
River
Parc National de la Salonga
KIGALI
Parc National de Kahuzi-Biéga
2
Lake Kivu
Kalima
Bukavu
Kindu
The Congo
6
Kampene
Uvira
BUJUMBURA
BURUNDI
Kigoma
TANZANIA
Kananga
Kabalo
Kalemie
Tshikapa
Congo
Lake Tanganyika
Sankuru
River
River
Kamina
Mpulungu
Lake Mweru
Bukama
River
Parc National de Kundelungu
Luau
Dilolo
Kolwezi
Likasi
Lake Bangweulu
Lubumbashi
Kasumbalesa
Chingola
ZAMBIA
Kitwe
Ndola

KINSHASA

POP 7.2 MILLION

Once touted as Kin la Belle (beautiful Kinshasa), the chaotic capital has long since been redubbed as 'Kin la Poubelle' (Kinshasa the trashcan) by locals. Sprawling seemingly forever from the banks of the Congo River, 'Kin' has the same maniacal drivers, dismaying poverty, mounds of trash, belching black tailpipes and persistent street hawkers that you've seen in many other African cities, but here it's all bigger, faster and louder than you've probably experienced before.

Sights

Museé National MUSEUM
(Ave de la Montagne, Mont Ngaliema; admission US$10; 7.30am-3pm Mon-Fri) This amazing ethnographic archive comprising some 45,000 objects will shortly get a new home thanks to a US$10 million investment from South Korea. At the moment the staff will gladly show you around the warehouses where the collection is currently stored. The proposed new museum will be in the Lingwala area of the city, close to the Académie des Beaux-Arts and the Palais du Peuple.

Académie des Beaux-Arts GALLERY
(http://academiebeauxartskinshasa.blogspot.fr; Ave Mulélé-Pierre) This regarded art school has loads of sculpture around the grounds, and you can often see students and professors at work. Behind the back of the school is the **Museé National de Kinshasa.** At the time of writing it was closed due to a lack of funds but if it reopens it houses a small but impressive collection of Congolese masks.

Marché Central MARKET
It's worth losing yourself in this, one of the largest markets in Central Africa.

WARNING

Although rebel armies continue marauding around parts of the east (see p506 for important safety information on this area), these days most places in Democratic Republic of Congo are safe most of the time. But this is a country where anything can happen, from rebellion to riots to volcanic eruptions. It's imperative to get up-to-the-minute information before travelling here.

Marché du Art MARKET
(Ave Lubetu; 7am-6pm) In need of a souvenir? Desperate for a fetish? Searching for distinctive art? Then say hello to the vendors at the Marché du Art. Take note that the market has been moved a couple of times in the last few years and there was talk of it moving again in the next year or two (but nobody knew where).

Laurent Kabila's Tomb MONUMENT
This tomb of former President Laurent Kabila is worth seeing although reaching it involves passing through several layers of security – why a dead man needs so much security isn't totally clear!

Sleeping

Hôtel La Crèche HOTEL $
(0999494155; Ave Badjoko; r with fan CDF15,000, with air-con US$25-35;) Matonge's best-known hotel is rather rough, very noisy (especially on weekends) and the cheapest rooms are not meant to be occupied all night, if you know what we mean. It's a friendly and safe enough place though.

Procure Ste Anne HOTEL $$
(0125100073; propas-kin@micronet.cd; Ave Dumi; r incl breakfast US$60; P@) This quiet colonial-era compound offers Kinshasa's best value. Rooms are historic and immaculate and it's safe and quiet. Popular with foreigners looking to adopt a local child.

HG Hotel HOTEL $$
(0897717263; Ave Kasa-Vubu; r US$50-80, apt US$100, all incl breakfast;) This fairly new hotel offers the most salubrious lodgings in Matonge. The US$70 rooms, with their flat-screen TVs, hot-water bathrooms and fake-leather furnishings, are probably the pick of the bunch. As with all the hotels around here, night-time noise can be an issue.

Hotel Ixoras HOTEL $$
(0991061610; 7éme rue, Pl Commerciale, Limete; r incl breakfast US$80-100;) The grubby exterior and screeching of car tyres on the busy road outside would normally be enough to make you turn and run, but in Kinshasa this ageing place, with large and clean rooms, offers really good value – just make sure you don't get a room overlooking the road.

Hôtel Pacha 786 HOTEL $$
(0991088786; www.hotelpacha786.com; Ave du Tchad; r US$80-100;) Across the street from the landmark (and very overpriced)

Hôtel Memling, the rooms, set around a triangular terrace, are large and have bold furnishings that distinguish them from the normally staid competition at this price.

Hôtel Estoril Sol HOTEL **$$$**
(☎0810206209; estorilsolrdc@yahoo.fr; Ave Kabasele; r incl breakfast US$90-120; P ❄ @ 🛜) Pleasant courtyard gardens and a fading colonial style are the hallmarks of this lime green place on the edge of downtown. You can lounge and dine (Congolese, French and Portuguese cuisine) on the streetside terrace or in the shady backyard.

Hotel Invest de Presse RESORT **$$$**
(☎0998237477; www.hotelinvests.com; Ave Kabinda; s/d incl breakfast US$130/145, apt US$160-175; P ❄ @ 🛜 🏊) This resortlike place has small and colourful rooms set in large gardens with a swimming pool (nonguests US$10). Like so many places in town it's somewhat let down by the overly high prices and 'couldn't care less' attitude of the reception staff.

Eating

There are some good restaurants in Kinshasa, but prices are very high. Outside Gombé, most neighbourhoods have plenty of streetside vendors working deep into the night.

Downtown Kinshasa is flush with supermarkets selling expensive imported goods.

Restaurant Al-Dar LEBANESE **$**
(Blvd du 30 Juin; mains CDF4800-10,000; ⏲8am-10pm) There's a reason why this large, canteenlike Lebanese place is always full to bursting, and that reason is price. The food is classic Lebanese fast food and everyone from smart suited business people to hip hop–styled young locals and exhausted UN workers come to eat here.

Spice Restaurant & Lounge Bar INDIAN **$$**
(☎0818555005; cnr Ave Commerce & Ave des Travailleur; mains US$12-20; ⏲closed alternate Mondays) If you've a craving an authentic Indian curry this upmarket, but reasonably priced, restaurant and lounge bar will do very nicely indeed.

Extrême FRENCH, ITALIAN **$$$**
(☎0999925126; Ave de l'Equateur; mains US$18-25; ⏲12.30-10.30pm Tue-Sat & Mon lunch; ❄) A trendy French-run restaurant that also serves Italian dishes as well as Gallic flavours. The pizzas are wood-fired beauties. The rooftop terrace is virtually a jungle.

SET YOUR BUDGET

Budget

- Hotel room US$30
- Two-course dinner US$10
- Beer US$1.20
- Place on Kisangani-Kinshasa boat US$50

Midrange

- Hotel room US$60–100
- Two-course dinner US$15–20
- Short taxi ride US$5

Top End

- Hotel room US$100+
- Two-course dinner US$25–50
- Gorilla trekking permit US$400
- 4WD rental US$200–300

Super Aubaine CONGOLESE **$$$**
(☎0815085586; Ave du Haut Congo; mains US$20-45, all-day buffet US$30; ⏲noon-10pm; ❄) Takes Congolese cooking to the gourmet level with choices like grilled pigeon and crocodile in tomato sauce. The menu also features such environmentally sound delicacies as elephant! We said, 'Elephant? The animal with the big nose? Is that legal?', to which the waitress replied, 'Oh, don't worry, we only eat a bit of the elephant'. Quite.

Entertainment

Live bands rock the rooftop of **Hôtel La Crèche** (Ave Badjoko) most nights. Trust us, you don't want to visit Kinshasa's **zoo** (Ave du Commerce) for the animals, but Staff Benda Belili, a group of homeless paraplegic musicians now making waves on the world music scene, often perform there.

During our visit, **Black & White** (Ave Bousin), which spins music from all corners of the globe, had Kinshasa's favourite dance floor. Upstairs is a bar with a pool table. **Ibizabar** (Ave de la Nation; ⏲Mon-Sat) is a relaxing lounge with live jazz on weekends. Loud, brash and filled with ladies of the night, the **Fiesta Club** (www.thefiestaclub.com) is only for the most thick-skinned of tourists.

The **Centre Culturel Français** (☎0810 581512; www.institutfrancais-kinshasa.org/; Ave de la Gombé) is Kinshasa's premier arts venue and has an energetic calender of live music, art exhibitions and cultural events. It

Kinshasa

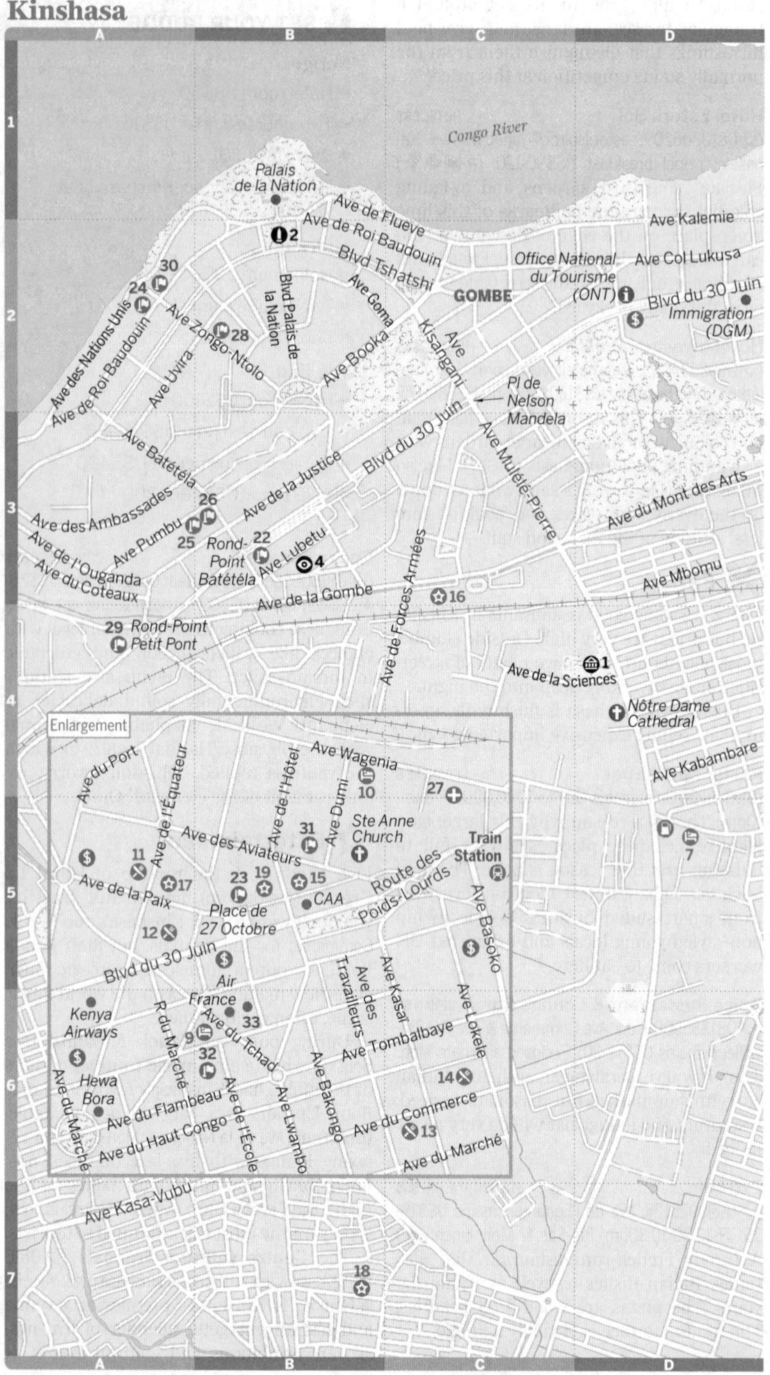

Congo River
Palais de la Nation
2
Ave de Flueve
Ave de Roi Baudouin
Blvd Tshatshi
Ave Goma
Blvd Palais de la Nation
30
24
Ave des Nations Unis
Ave de Roi Baudouin
Ave Zongo-Ntolo
28
Ave Uvira
Ave Booka
Ave Kisangani
GOMBE
Office National du Tourisme (ONT)
Ave Kalemie
Ave Col Lukusa
Blvd du 30 Juin
Immigration (DGM)
Pl de Nelson Mandela
Ave Batétéla
Blvd du 30 Juin
Ave de la Justice
Ave Mulélé-Pierre
26
Ave des Ambassades
Ave Pumbu
25
Rond-Point Batétéla
22
Ave Lubetu
4
Ave de l'Ouganda
Ave du Coteaux
Ave de la Gombe
Ave de Forces Armées
16
Ave du Mont des Arts
Ave Mbomu
29
Rond-Point Petit Pont
1
Ave de la Sciences
Nôtre Dame Cathedral
Enlargement
Ave du Port
Ave de l'Équateur
Ave de l'Hôtel
Ave Wagenia
10
27
Ave Dumi
Ste Anne Church
31
Ave des Aviateurs
Train Station
Ave Kabambare
7
11
17
23
19
15
Ave de la Paix
CAA
Route des Poids-Lourds
Place de 27 Octobre
12
Ave Basoko
Blvd du 30 Juin
Air France
33
Kenya Airways
R du Marché
9
Ave du Tchad
Ave des Travailleurs
Ave Kasaï
Ave Lokele
Ave Tombalbaye
32
Hewa Bora
Ave du Marché
Ave du Flambeau
Ave de l'École
Ave Lwambo
Ave Bakongo
14
Ave du Commerce
13
Ave du Haut Congo
Ave du Marché
Ave Kasa-Vubu
18

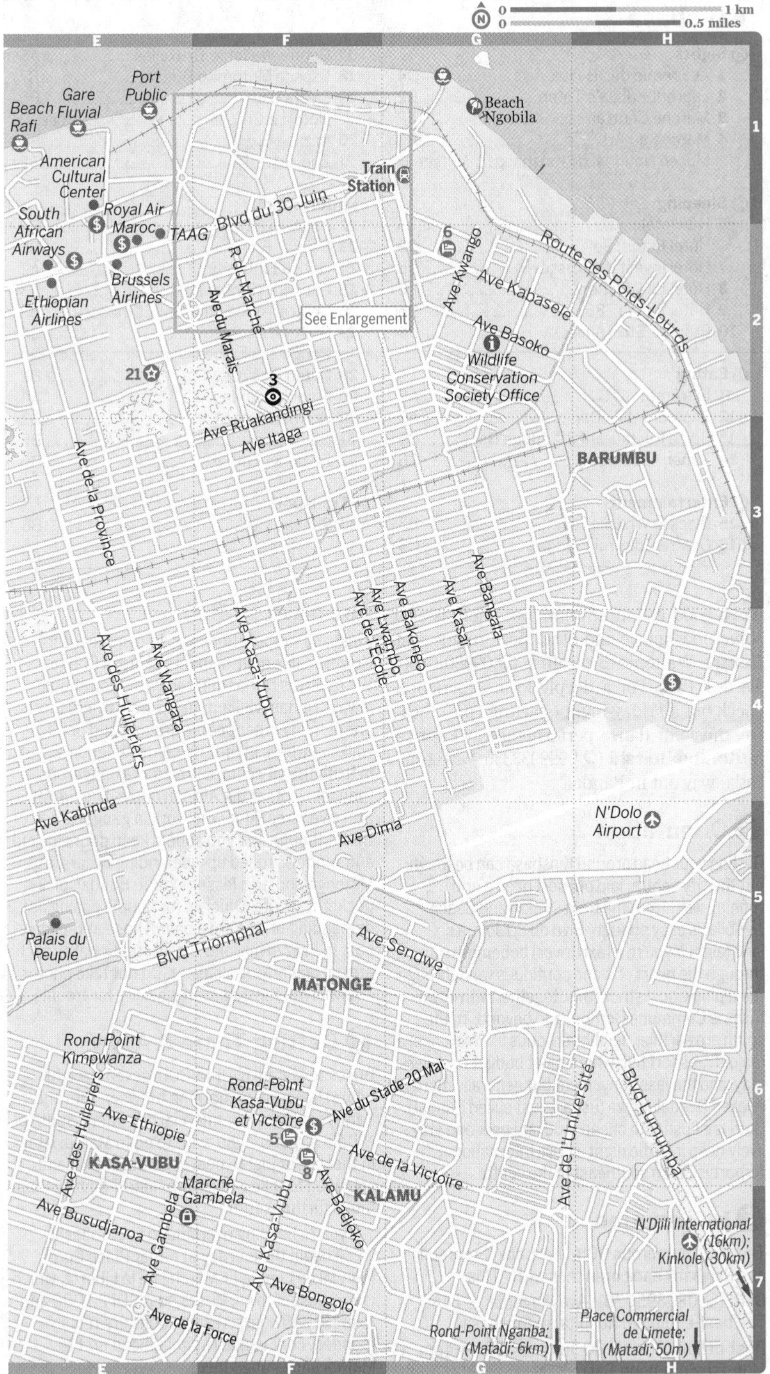

0 1 km
0 0.5 miles
E
F
G
H
1
2
3
4
5
6
7
Port Public
Gare Fluvial
Beach Rafi
Beach Ngobila
American Cultural Center
South African Airways
Royal Air Maroc
TAAG
Brussels Airlines
Ethiopian Airlines
Train Station
Blvd du 30 Juin
R du Marche
Ave du Marais
See Enlargement
6
Ave Kwango
Ave Kabasele
Route des Poids-Lourds
Ave Basoko
Wildlife Conservation Society Office
21
3
Ave Ruakandingi
Ave Itaga
BARUMBU
Ave de la Province
Ave Bangala
Ave Kasai
Ave Bakongo
Ave Lwambo
Ave de l'Ecole
Ave Kasa-Vubu
Ave Wangata
Ave des Huileriers
Ave Kabinda
Ave Dima
N'Dolo Airport
Palais du Peuple
Blvd Triomphal
Ave Sendwe
MATONGE
Rond-Point Kimpwanza
Rond-Point Kasa-Vubu et Victoire
Ave du Stade 20 Mai
5
8
Ave de la Victoire
Ave Ethiopie
Ave des Huileriers
KASA-VUBU
Marché Gambela
KALAMU
Ave Badjoko
Ave de l'Université
Blvd Lumumba
Ave Busudjanoa
Ave Gambela
Ave Kasa-Vubu
Ave Bongolo
Ave de la Force
N'Djili International (16km); Kinkole (30km)
Rond-Point Nganba; (Matadi; 6km)
Place Commercial de Limete; (Matadi; 50m)

Kinshasa

Sights
- 1 Académie des Beaux-Arts D4
- 2 Laurent Kabila's Tomb B2
- 3 Marché Central F2
- 4 Marché du Art B3
- Museé National de Kinshasa .... (see 1)

Sleeping
- 5 HG Hotel F6
- 6 Hôtel Estoril Sol G2
- 7 Hotel Invest de Presse D5
- 8 Hôtel La Crèche F6
- 9 Hôtel Pacha 786 .... B6
- 10 Procure Ste Anne B4

Eating
- 11 Extrême A5
- 12 Restaurant Al-Dar A5
- 13 Spice Restaurant & Lounge Bar C6
- 14 Super Aubaine C6

Entertainment
- 15 Black & White B5
- 16 Centre Culturel Français C3
- 17 Centre Wallonie-Bruxelles A5
- 18 Espace Mutombo Buitshi B7
- 19 Fiesta Club B5
- Hôtel La Crèche .... (see 8)
- 20 Ibizabar ....
- 21 Zoo E2

Information
- 22 Angolan Embassy B3
- 23 Belgian Embassy B5
- 24 British Embassy A2
- 25 Canadian Embassy A3
- 26 Central African Republic Embassy B3
- 27 CMK C4
- Congolese Embassy .... (see 22)
- 28 Dutch Embassy B2
- 29 French Embassy A4
- 30 German Embassy A2
- 31 US Embassy B5
- 32 Zambian Embassy B6

Transport
- 33 Renka B6

has a good restaurant-bar, too. There is also sometimes music and other performances at **Centre Wallonie-Bruxelles** (0998010800; Ave de la Paix). For a deeply local experience, check out a Friday-night (starting 7pm) theatre, music or dance performance at **Espace Mutombo Buitshi** (0999933336; Ave Lubumbashi) way out in Bandal.

Orientation

Getting your head around Kinshasa can be tough, but the city centre, laid out sort of on a grid running west from the train station and Beach Ngobila, is easy enough. Blvd du 30 Juin, a six-lane (eight if you're a taxi driver) behemoth runs through the heart of it and continues west through the diplomatic district (this, together with downtown, is Cummune Gombé) and beyond. To the south are earthier neighbourhoods like Matonge, a major transport hub where most budget travellers stay, and the less convenient but generally more relaxed Bandalungwa (usually just called Bandal). Both are flush with cheap food and beer and stay lively deep into the night. N'Djili International Airport is 20km southeast of the centre.

Information

There are numerous BCIA, Ecobank, Procredit and Rawbank bank branches with ATMs.

CMK (0898950301; Ave Wagenia; 24hr) The best-equipped hospital in Kinshasa.

Post office (Blvd du 30 Juin; 7.30am-4pm Mon-Fri, 8am-noon Sat)

SAFE TRAVEL

Kinshasa's reputation for crime proceeds it. However, like many aspects of life in Congo the reality is rather different. Yes, you should always remain vigilant, never walk where there aren't many other people around, and don't walk anywhere in the city centre after dark, but in truth the city centre is no more dangerous than many other big African cities. *Shegue* (aggressive street kids who work in gangs) are a threat though and you should keep doors locked and windows rolled up when riding in cars. In Matonge and, to a lesser extent, Bandal, pickpocketing is rife. Officials (or people posing as) demanding bribes are a pain. Those at the ferry port to Brazzaville and the international airport are particularly unpleasant. Do not take photos anywhere in Kinshasa – it's asking for trouble.

Getting There & Away

Buses to Matadi (CDF14,000, seven to eight hours) leave every morning between 7am and 8am from Place Commercial de Limete, south of N'Dolo Airport. If you want to go to Matadi later in the day, or just to nearer points like Kisantu, you need to take a taxi from Rond-Point Nganba, much further south.

If you're heading overland to Lubumbashi you'll begin the journey at either Place Commercial de Limete or Marché de la Liberté, which is well east of town. Buses cost CDF22,000 and take 13 to 15 hours; reservations are recommended. For Luanda (Angola) head first to Matadi and change there.

Flights shorter than Kisangani use the convenient domestic-only N'Dolo Airport (all airlines have ticket offices here), while for anything longer, you must head out to N'Djili International Airport.

Getting Around

Few taxis wear the official blue-and-yellow paint job, but it's easy to tell which vehicles are taking passengers. Drivers charge around CDF500 for a journey across the city centre. To charter a taxi, ask for 'express' and negotiate the price. Minibuses cost CDF400 and are always crowded.

Several international car-hire firms, including **Renka** (☎0815021957; Hôtel Memling, Ave du Tchad), have very small and cheap Chinese-made cars from US$59 a day or 4WD from US$145; however, it's probably safer and easier to just charter a taxi for the day for around US$75 to US$100.

A taxi from the city centre to N'Djili International Airport will take over an hour and cost an unfathomably expensive US$50 at an absolute minimum. Going from the airport into town they will ask for US$80 – this author has bought a car for the same price before! A shared taxi taken from outside the airport grounds can be found for CDF1000 to the *centre-ville* (town centre) or Matonge.

AROUND KINSHASA

Lola Ya Bonobo Sanctuary

Ninety minutes west of Kinshasa, just beyond the city's sprawl, this **sanctuary** (Paradise for Bonobos; www.friendsofbonobos.org; foreigners US$5; ⏲9.30am-4pm Tue-Sun) provides a home for orphaned bonobos. Bonobos were long thought to be chimpanzees, and it is only fairly recently that scientists have realised that they are a separate species altogether and one that is even more closely related to humans. Bonobos are known for being much more peaceful than chimpanzees and instead of fighting they prefer to have sex – make love not war! Trails lead around the large, forested enclosures, but the playful bonobos often hang out right at the front, especially in the morning. The sanctuary is 8km off the Matadi road: follow the signs for Chutes de Lakaya, which has a little beach and weekend-only restaurant. If you're patient, you can hitch the last 8km off the highway. A hire car with driver from Kinshasa will cost US$100, but in the wet season you'll need a 4WD, which is US$150 to US$200.

Kinkole

On Sundays and holidays Kinshasa's jetsetters descend to the little 'beach' town (you wouldn't really describe it as having a beach and you certainly wouldn't want to swim here) well east of Kinshasa, to drink beer, eat the country's best *liboké de poisson* (fish cooked in banana leaves) and listen to live music. The action starts around midday, but peaks after dark. Talk to boat operators here if you'd like a ride on the river. Taxis (CDF500, one hour) run from Marché de la Liberté in Kinshasa; the last ones return around 10.30pm on Sunday.

Chutes du Zongo

A popular trip for those who can afford 4WD hire (US$200), the gorgeous Zongo Falls are about 100km out of Kinshasa, the last half signed off the highway at Sona-Bata.

Kisantu

Kisantu, 100km out of Kinshasa, has many colonial-era relics, including the incongruously large **Cathèdrale Notre Dame de Sept Douleurs** and the 222-sq-km **Jardin Botanique de Kisantu** (admission CDF1000; ⏲8am-5pm), with trees from around the world. There's a small natural history museum, a cactus garden and a pleasant restaurant.

EASTERN DRC

Although the classic image of the DRC is that of a steaming untamed jungle, the part of the country that most travellers see is the very far east; an area of cloud-scraping volcanic mountains, lakes of lava and those lumbering giants, the mountain gorillas. All this is best experienced in the breathtaking **Parc National des Virunga**. Elsewhere the east does live up to the Congo clichés; there are vast stretches of dense tropical forest haunted by half-giraffe half-zebra okapis and riven with muddy rivers and muddier roads.

Goma

POP 450,000

Until the M23 rebel advance of late 2012 this dusty border town, home to a massive UN presence, hosted more travellers than any

TRAVEL IN THE EAST

The far east of DRC (in particular the provinces of North and South Kivu and Ituri) have born the brunt of the violence and insecurity that has wracked DRC for years. Despite a generally improving security situation over much of the country, the Kivus (which includes Goma, Bukavu and Virunga park) and Ituri (which corresponds roughly to the area between Kisangani and Virunga) continue to have a highly volatile security situation and numerous armed groups operate throughout the region. In April 2012 a group of soldiers defected from the national army and formed what has become known as the M23. By November 2012 they controlled large swaths of North Kivu including much of Parc National des Virunga. As the situation stands you should not visit eastern DRC and we were unable to conduct on-the-ground research anywhere in the east for this edition. The information contained here is based on a mixture of research from 2011 (Goma and Virunga) and a remote update using local contacts (all other areas).

Anyone wishing to travel to eastern DRC in the future should check the security situation very carefully first. The Virunga park website (www.visitvirunga.org) is useful, as is Lonely Planet's Thorn Tree online forum.

other place in DRC, though that's still very few. Mostly people popped over briefly to track mountain gorillas, climb Nyiragongo volcano, or, for the truly adventurous, trek the western slopes of the Rwenzori Mountains, all of which happens in **Parc National des Virunga** (☎0991715401; http://gorillacd.org; Blvd Kanya Mulanga; ⏲8am-4pm Mon-Fri), one of Africa's most diverse parks.

At the time of writing the park was pretty much closed to tourists: this includes gorilla tracking and Nyiragongo. The M23 rebels have, however, been leading gorilla-tracking trips that some travellers have taken advantage of. Partaking in such trips has to be one of the most irresponsible things a traveller could do – official park authorities cannot stress enough the risks these unauthorised trips pose to the gorillas. If that weren't enough, there is evidence to suggest that the money the M23 earns through these trips is used to purchase weapons – and this is a group whose leader is wanted by the International Criminal Court for war crimes and the use of child soldiers.

The national park website contains frequent updates as to the status of the park and whether or not it is open to tourists. It also includes a list of tour companies they have blacklisted due to working alongside the M23.

The city itself has no proper attractions, but you can witness the destruction caused by Nyiragongo's 2002 eruption at the **ruined cathedral** and the aptly named **Hôtel Volcano**, where the basement used to be the ground floor before 3m of lava engulfed the building. Northeast of the airport is a moonscape with several **lava vents** that sent the stream of lava straight through the city centre. **Lake Vert**, west of town, is a much older crater now filled with a greenish-tinged lake.

If price is your primary concern, head to **Guesthouse Shushu** (☎0991347578; Ave Grevilleas; r without bathroom US$15-20). Each room here contains a small double bed, chair and mosquito net. The shared showers are cold and would benefit from a decent scrub. **Stella Matutina Lodge** (☎0811510760; stellamatutina@yahoo.fr; Himbi; r incl breakfast US$65-100; P❄📶) is better than anything in the town centre, plus it has great gardens and sweeping lake views. The best value in town, however, is **La Brise Guesthouse** (☎0994403000; labriseguesthouse@yahoo.fr; Ave la Corniche; r US$30-50; ❄📶), which has large rooms, tight security, semireliable hot water and a quiet lakeside location (although the restaurant is insanely overpriced). In the evenings, Belgian-owned **Le Petit Bruxelles** (Ave du Rond Point; mains US$7-13; ⏲Mon-Sat) fires up its courtyard barbecue and serves tasty seared steaks and cold beer. The lunch menu is more limited, but the burgers are some of the best in town.

Road travel out of Goma to the rest of DRC is unsafe at the moment, but taking the boat to Bukavu is rarely a problem.

There are daily flights to Kinshasa and Kisangani.

Bukavu

POP 472,000

DRC's most attractive city, which crawls along a contorted shoreline at the southern tip of Lake Kivu, is the base for visiting the criminally undervisited **Parc National de Kahuzi-**

Biéga (English enquires 0971300881, French enquires 0822881012; http://kahuzibiega.wordpress.com; ICCN office, Ave Lumumba; 8am-4pm Mon-Fri), Virunga's little-known neighbour, where you can track habituated eastern lowland gorillas (Grauer's gorillas). It's often possible to get permits (US$400 per person) for same-day hiking. The starting point is at Tshivanga, 30km northwest of town. *Taxi-motos* (motorcycle taxis) there and back cost about US$20 to US$30, while hiring a jeep costs US$100. The park also has a chimpanzee orphanage (and is in the process of habituating wild groups of chimps to human presence) and some worthy hikes up the mountains (US$35 to US$100). You can camp in the park for US$50.

Floating in the middle of Lake Kivu, **Idjwi Island** is, at 340 sq km, the second-largest lake island in Africa. Little visited by tourists, it's a safe and low-key place to relax for a few days. Lodging is available in small guesthouses and boats run daily to the island from Bukavu.

There are only two rooms at the friendly little **Esperance Guest House** (0999941197; lhenkinbrant@hotmail.com; 8 Ave Pangi, Ibanda; d incl breakfast US$40;) and they both share a bathroom, but everything is kept polished and clean and a good dinner is available for US$10 extra. Call ahead. The smartest place in town is the resort-style **Orchids Safari Club** (0813126467; www.orchids-hotel.com; incl breakfast s US$125-180, d US$170-215;) where gorgeous rooms are set around even more gorgeous gardens and there are views over Lake Kivu that are, yes you guessed it, gorgeous.

CROSSING CONGO

The DRC is a unique travel destination and travelling here will give you a lifetime supply of unlikely tales about nights spent asleep on the rim of bubbling volcanic craters, encounters with massive gorillas, hunting forest antelopes or simply surviving the chaos of Kinshasa. But for the most unlikely story of all, and one that promises to be the biggest adventure you will ever set out on, you'll need to take the slow river barge ride from Kisangani to Kinshasa.

The classic path crosses east to west and requires a two-week, 1730km boat ride down the Congo River through still-untamed jungle. The reason most people prefer to go east to west is because going upriver from Kinshasa to Kisangani means at least a month – if not six weeks – on the boat! Assuming that the situation between the government and M23 and other rebel groups cools down then your journey will most likely start at Kasindi on the Ugandan border, near Beni. The road from here to Kisangani has been upgraded recently and is in better shape than it has been for years (note that this doesn't mean it's in good shape!). There are still some bandits and various rebel groups (it's often hard to know the difference) operating around here, so be careful if driving your own vehicle. Kisangani is where you catch the boat. You'll probably spend a lot of time in this legendary town; not because it's so appealing but because boats are still quite infrequent. There's usually one departure a week (around US$50, though prices aren't fixed). Bear in mind that, unlike the old days, there are no longer steamers with passenger cabins, although you can try to rent one from a crew member. You'll be living out on the deck of the barges (go early to find a space under a roof) with hundreds of other people, plus all their cargo and livestock. Villagers sell food from *pirogues* (traditional canoes) along the way, but this trip still requires careful preparation for cooking, water and shelter.

Travelling in reverse prices are about double. The best places to seek boats in Kinshasa are Gare Fluvial and Beach Rafi; boats docked at Port Public rarely take passengers, but it can't hurt to ask there too.

A typically quicker, but more hassle-filled, journey substitutes a train for a barge. From Kinshasa a sealed road runs southeast to Kikwit and transport is fairly easy to find. From Kikwit to Kananga things get decidely tougher. The road disintegrates into a rutted mess and only a few trucks are brave enough to battle on. Once in Kananga you might be in for a very long wait (we're talking days and weeks rather than hours!) as trains are very, very infrequent and when they do come it takes about another six days to Lubumbashi.

However you do it, just allow a lot of extra time and money. And after two days stuck on a river sandbank or sitting on the side of a muddy track just remember: this is what you came here for!

Several boats depart daily to Goma. Choices range from US$15 on the shadeless, grossly overcrowded deck of a ferry (eight to 10 hours) to US$50 for a *canot rapide* (speedboat; two to three hours). The road to Kisangani is so devastated that only motorcycles can manage it.

Okapi Wildlife Reserve

Created to protect prime habitat of its bizarre namesake mammal, this is one of the biggest (1,372,625 hectares) parks in DRC. In addition to the okapis there are 17 resident primate species here and a fairly healthy elephant population. Combine this with excellent guided forest hikes (ranging from a few hours to several days) led by the Mbuti and the result is one of the best places in Central Africa to get the real genuine jungle experience – at least that was the case until the middle of 2012. In June of that year a major attack on the park headquarters at Epulu and nearby villages by *mai-mai* (community) militia left six people (including park rangers) and 13 okapi dead, and hundreds of people were forced to flee the area. Whilst the park was closed to visitors at the time of research, as we go to press the latest news is that the security situation has improved enough to allow tourism activities to recommence. For the latest check out www.okapiconservation.org.

The road between Kisangani and Beni, which passes by the reserve, has been upgraded but there are still some horrendous sections. Allow at least a full day to travel from either Beni or Kisangani to Epulu – longer in the wet season.

Kisangani

POP 683,000

Kisangani was known in colonial times as Stanleyville and was immortalised as the unnamed city in VS Naipaul's classic novel *A Bend in the River*. Once a pleasant place and a major hub for travellers, Kisangani suffered as much as any town during the war years. The city was founded by its original namesake in 1883 because it's the last point ships can travel upriver from Kinshasa before being blocked by **Boyoma Falls**, a 100km stretch with seven major waterfalls. The final drop, just east of town, is a lovely spot, with a rocky stage and a jungle-clad backdrop, though the **Wagenia Fishers** (best seen on the south bank) are pushing it in their demands for US$30 to look at their famous scaffolds and conical fish traps. **Tshopo Falls**, 3km north of town by the dam and the old Skol Brewery, is far smaller, but still nice. There are sandy beaches and a bar-restaurant (popular at night) nearby.

Rooms are small, but copious plants and other quaint touches make **Les Chalets** (☎0998508407; Ave de l'Industrie; r incl breakfast from US$55; P ❄ @ ≋) Kisangani's best-value place to stay. **Guest House Saint Charles** (☎0998539701; Ave de l'Eglise; r US$30-50; P ❄ @) offers cheaper and fairly pleasing rooms. **Riviera Restaurant** (Ave Bondekwe; mains US$5-20; ⊙6am-late; ❄ ☎) part of the hotel of the same name, is fronted by a terrace, trees and colonial homes and is the most popular place to dine.

Almost everyone arrives from Kinshasa by air, but riverboats are sailing once again. Land transport departs from northeast of the central market. There are several jeeps and buses to Beni (US$45 to US$60, jeeps 12 to 15 hours, buses 16 to 20 hours) daily; most travel overnight to avoid hassles with the police.

KATANGA PROVINCE

Mineral rich, but all-too-often cash poor, Katanga, in the far southeast, is the mining capital of DRC. Milked for all it was worth during the Mobutu era, Katanga has weathered the recent storms better than most, and is one of the more stable parts of the country.

Lubumbashi

POP 1,400,000

Known to locals as L'shi or Lubum, this languid yet likeable city was known as Elizabethville during the Belgian colonial period. Founded in 1910 as a hub for the extraction industry, it suffered willful neglect during the Mobutu years, but briefly found a starring role as the legislative capital from 1999 to 2003.

Sleeping

Hotel Belle-Vue HOTEL $$

(☎0815056409; www.bellevuelubum.com; Rond Point de l'Elephant; s/d US$50/60; @) Set in one of the most striking colonial-era buildings in Lubumbashi, this will be a glamorous boutique hotel when DRC is stable, but for now it is affordable and atmospheric, if a little dilapidated.

Bougain Villa Guesthouse B&B $$$
(☎0811851985; www.bougainvillagh.com; 5859 Ave Lukonzolwa; r from US$145; ❄@📶) This South African–run B&B is a real home away from home in L'shi. Secure, comfortable and including the basics like air-con, clean linen and satellite TV. Definitely book ahead.

Greek Club INTERNATIONAL $$
(975 Ave Lilela Balanda; meals US$7-20) Officially known as the tongue-twisting Taverna Communaute Hellenique, but the Greek Club to you and I, this is the place to try Hellenic specialities as well as French and Chinese fare.

Planet Holly-Bum INTERNATIONAL $$
(3000 Ave Lubumba; meals US$8-25; ⏰11am-late) The comical name aside, this is one of the best restaurants in town, serving French, Belgian and Italian food.

Getting There & Away

Luano Airport is the main gateway to L'shi and Katanga province.

Korongo Airlines (p514) is considered the most reliable domestic airline and has daily flights to Kinshasa (from US$255 one way).

International connections include Kenya Airways to Nairobi, Ethiopian Airlines to Addis Ababa and South African Airways to Johannesburg. A taxi from the airport to downtown L'shi costs about US$10.

WORTH A TRIP

TRAVELLING AROUND KATANGA PROVINCE

Katanga has a few major attractions that are accessible to travellers with time and money. Best known is Kundelunga National Park, which is home to the Lofoi Falls, one of the most impressive in all of Africa. **Congo Star Safaris** (☎0812569577; www.congostarsafaris.com) operates two upmarket lodges in the Katanga area, including Kafubu River Lodge and Kiubo Falls Lodge, and can arrange a unique and memorable (if expensive) trip.

UNDERSTAND DEMOCRATIC REPUBLIC OF CONGO

Democratic Republic of Congo Today

DRC has turned a corner, but the challenges facing it remain huge. The war ended in 2003, but in the volatile east, the fighting didn't stop. Despite the presence of 19,000 UN blue-helmets (the world's largest peacekeeping mission), ill-disciplined government soldiers and a plethora of militias continue to terrorise the population, particularly in North and South Kivu provinces. In the biggest threat to the nation's stability since the official end of the civil war, in May 2012 the M23 rebel group began to advance across North Kivu and by November of the same year they had occupied the regional capital of Goma and threatened to march to Kinshasa.

It's likely we will never know exactly how many people have died during the recent wars in DRC. Figures range from 900,000 to 5.4 million. Taking into account the conflict, hunger, disease and disruption of health services the fighting has, and continues to, cause, most reports cite a figure of around three million conflict-related deaths since 2004, and millions more remain displaced.

And even if things are better than before, they're still not easy. Life expectancy is just 47 years for men and 51 for women and 71% of the population lives below the poverty line.

History

A Tragic Story

The first inhabitants of the steaming Congo River basin arrived as early as 8000 BC. Bantu people settled most of the Congo by 1000AD, bringing agriculture and iron-smelting, and Portuguese explorers took home the first stories from the region 500 years later. Trading goods such as ivory, cloth, pottery, ironware and slaves, the Portuguese made contact with a highly developed kingdom known as the Kongo that was ruled over by a patriarchal monarch and stretched as far south as the Kwanza River in Angola. Kongo royalty became enthusiastic allies, adopting Portuguese names, clothes and customs and converting to Christianity.

In the mid-19th century, Arab traders crossed East Africa to eastern Congo, taking back slaves and ivory. During the same era,

Dr David Livingstone opened up the African interior to European exploration.

In 1874 the *New York Herald* and the British *Daily Telegraph* newspapers sent Henry Morton Stanley (the man who had found Dr Livingstone in 1871) across Africa to trace the course of the Congo River. His epic 999-day journey cemented the Welsh-American explorer's place in history and piqued the interest of King Leopold II of Belgium. Devious, greedy and wholly ignorant of African affairs, Leopold had been eyeing the unclaimed African gateau for some time, but he was unable to convince the Belgian government to go along. To solve the problem he decided to acquire a colony of his own.

In 1878 Leopold commissioned Stanley to return to the Congo under the smokescreen of the International African Society, a supposed philanthropic organisation. Over the ensuing five years Stanley signed treaties with chiefs on Leopold's behalf, tricking them into handing over their land rights in return for paltry gifts. At the Berlin Conference called by Bismarck in 1884 to carve up Africa, Leopold, aware of a German desire to offset French and British colonial interests, managed to convince the famous Iron Chancellor to declare the Congo a free-trade area and cede it to him.

Philanthropy was the last thing on Leopold's mind as he set about fleecing his Congo Free State of its ivory, copper and rubber. Hideous crimes were committed against the Congolese by Leopold's rubber traders. These included raiding villages and taking women and children captive as an incentive for the men to bring back ever-greater supplies of rubber from the forest.

Independence

As Leopold's crimes gradually became public knowledge, the Belgian government realised enough was enough and took over in 1908. Thereafter, things improved. The new Belgians ended forced labour, built schools and roads, and nearly eradicated sleeping sickness. By the 1940s mining had made this Africa's richest country, though even up to the end of their reign, the Belgians largely excluded Congolese from roles in the government or economy, and very few Congolese had college educations.

Gathering pace in the 1950s under charismatic revolutionary Patrice Lumumba, the independence movement finally wrested control from the colonisers on 30 June 1960. Lumumba became prime minister of the new Republic of Congo, but tribalism and personal quests for power came to the front, and just a week later the army mutinied. By the end of the year, army chief Joseph Mobutu had seized power, Lumumba had been arrested (and would soon be assassinated) and Congo had split into four quasi-independent states. An aggressive intervention by UN and Belgian troops plus several mercenary armies put the country together again by 1965, though there were further small-scale rebellions in the following years.

Renaming himself Mobutu Sese Seko, and the country Zaïre, the new leader embarked on a campaign of 'Africanisation', with colonial city names changing and suits giving way to the *abacost* (a Congolese version of the Mao jacket); though Mobutu himself was no communist, allying the country firmly in the US camp.

He'd brought stability to Congo, but he also ruled with an iron fist, quashed opposition, and turned corruption and the squandering of state resources into an art form later named kleptocracy. It's estimated he pocketed US$5 billion during his rule.

Civil War

Throughout the 1970s and '80s Mobutu survived several coup attempts and repelled armed insurrections in various parts of the country. By the early 1990s he'd driven an economic collapse so epic in scale that most of the country had degenerated to, in the words of Tim Butcher (from his book *Blood River*), 'a feral state of lawlessness and brutality'. Not only did schools and hospitals cease to function, but highways were reclaimed by the jungle.

Backing the Hutu perpetrators of the 1994 Rwandan genocide who escaped into Zaïre, Mobutu enraged local Tutsis, who, supported enthusiastically by Rwandan and Ugandan troops, started a march across the country in 1996 and easily took Kinshasa in 1997. Mobutu died four months later of cancer in Morocco.

Soon after renaming the country the Democratic Republic of Congo, the new leader, Laurent Kabila, a one-time protege of Che Guevara, dashed any hopes of change by outlawing political opposition. Proving himself every bit as corrupt and repressive as Mobutu, he lost support at home and abroad, even from the same governments who propelled him to power.

The DRC's second war (aka 'Africa's World War') started in 1998 when Rwandan and Ugandan troops again entered the country. Kabila was saved by troops from Angola, Zimbabwe, Namibia and other countries, but much of DRC was now under the control of Rwanda and Uganda, and even they clashed at times, leading to the destruction of Kisangani. In 2010 a UN report into the killing of Hutus in DRC between 1993 and 2003 implicated Rwanda, Uganda, Burundi, Zimbabwe and Angola in what it described as 'crimes of genocide'.

A New Start

Laurent Kabila was shot by one of his bodyguards in January 2001, though the details of and motivations behind the assassination remain mysteries. He was succeeded by his 29-year-old son Joseph (largely raised in Tanzania), who, to the surprise of nearly everyone, proved a competent leader. Kabila the younger welcomed UN troops and presided over a peace agreement that in 2002 paved the way for a transitional government. He also oversaw a new constitution and heeded the advice of the World Bank and International Monetary Fund, setting the economy back on course. In 2006 Kabila won DRC's first legitimate elections in over 40 years. Though the elections were marred by incidents of violence, outside observers pronounced them free and fair.

In November 2011 Kabila won another round of presidential and parliamentary elections, but the vote was criticised by foreign observers and the opposition disputes the result.

In May 2012 a new rebel group was added to the two-dozen groups already operating in eastern DRC. The M23 rebels were made up of mainly Tutsi fighters who deserted from the Congolese army after saying they were mistreated and not paid enough, and that the military lacked vital resources. The UN has accused the group of being backed by Rwanda and Uganda.

Culture

Though DRC has more than 250 ethnic groups (and over 700 different languages and dialects), four tribes dominate. The Kongo, Luba, Mongo and Mangbetu-Azande groupings collectively make up 45% of the population.

Half the population practises Roman Catholicism, while 20% are Protestant and 10% Muslim. The remaining 20% follow traditional beliefs or a religion that merges Christianity with indigenous ideas, such as Kimbanguism. Founded by faith-healer Simon Kimbangu in 1921 (that same year Belgian authorities, fearing his popularity, sentenced him to life in prison), it now has three million adherents.

Environment

Encompassing 18 different ecoregions and blanketing the greater part of the Congo River basin, DRC is Africa's most biologically rich country. Savannahs cover much of the south and there's 37km of coast on the Atlantic, but tropical rain forests, home to all manner of creatures found nowhere else in the world, including bonobo and okapi, dominate the ecological scene.

The eastern border runs through a cornucopia of geological wonders, including Lake Tanganyika, the second-deepest lake in the world, and several other Great Rift Valley waters; the Rwenzori Mountains, which exceed 5000m; and several active volcanoes.

SURVIVAL GUIDE

Directory A–Z

ACCOMMODATION

Real budget accommodation is hard to come by, and where it does exist it's often grotty. At the US$20 to US$40 level you might get a fan or TV, but running water is still unlikely. Move into the US$50 to US$100 range and rooms will be much more comfortable, but no matter what you pay, your hotel will usually be much simpler than similarly priced properties back home.

EMBASSIES & CONSULATES

A great many countries have diplomatic representation in Kinshasa.

Angolan Embassy (☎0999906927; 4413 Blvd du 30 Juin)

Belgian Embassy (☎0817005900; www.diplomatie.be/kinshasafr; Pl du 27 Octobre)

British Embassy (☎0815566200; http://ukindrc.fco.gov.uk; Ave de Roi Baudouin)

Canadian Embassy (☎996021500; www.congo.gc.ca; 17 Ave Pumbu)

Central African Republic Embassy (11 Ave Pumbu)

Congolese Embassy (☎0999909544; Blvd du 30 Juin)

PRACTICALITIES

- **Electricity** 220V/50Hz; the European two-pin plug is the most common
- **Languages** French (official), Lingala, Swahili, Tshiluba
- **Radio** UN-funded Radio Okapi (103.5FM) is the best source of local news and culture. You can sometimes catch English-language programming on BBC World Service (92.6FM).

Dutch Embassy (☎0996050600; http://dr-congo.nlambassade.org; 11 Ave Zongo-Ntolo)
French Embassy (☎0815559999; www.ambafrance-cd.org; 1 Ave du Colonel Mondjiba)
German Embassy (☎0815561380; www.kinshasa.diplo.de; 82 Ave de Roi Baudouin)
US Embassy (☎0815560151; http://kinshasa.usembassy.gov; Ave des Aviateurs)
Zambian Embassy (☎0819999437; Ave de l'Ecole)

MONEY

The local currency, the Congolese franc (CDF), is worthless beyond the borders. CDF500 is currently the biggest bill available, which results in a massive bundle of banknotes when you change money; but DRC is unofficially undergoing dollarisation and US dollars are widely accepted for purchases of US$10 and up. In Goma, US dollars can be used for everything. It used to be that dollar bills needed to be pristine. That's no longer the case, but many merchants still won't accept dirty bills and nobody will take one with even a tiny tear. Learn to spot counterfeits, as there are many.

Money changers (the same people selling phonecards) work on nearly every block of every city. They all change US dollars, plus sometimes euros and local currency from nearby countries. Rates are invariably better than the banks.

Internationally linked ATMs are now common in Kinshasa (look for the prominent Visa and MasterCard signs; though note that the signs go up long before the service is actually available) and are also available (or a machine at the counter that works like an ATM) in several other major towns, including Goma, Matadi and Boma.

Credit cards (usually Visa *or* MasterCard) are accepted in many hotels, restaurants and upper-end shops, but fraud is a problem so cash is still best. In Kinshasa, **Rawbank** (Blvd 30 du Juin) cashes American Express travellers cheques in US dollars and euros with a 5% commission.

POST & TELEPHONE

Landlines are virtually extinct in DRC. In any town that has mobile-phone service, there are plenty of street hawkers who let people use their mobile phones: fees are about CDF150 per minute within Congo and CDF250 per minute international. If calling from outside DRC, drop the zero at the front of the number. SIM cards cost just US$1. The country code is ☎243 and the international access code is ☎00.

The postal system remains unreliable.

SAFE TRAVEL

There are still rebel armies and bandits (plus government soldiers, who are often just as dangerous) terrorising people in large swaths of the north and east. Areas that are particularly volatile include Ituri and North and South Kivu (of which Goma and Bukavu are the main towns) and the far northeast around Garamba National Park. See our Warning box (p500) for more.

Though the situation is improving, police and other officials, particularly those working for immigration (you're supposed to register with them every time you arrive in or depart from a town), frequently request money, though they rarely demand it. In all cases, calm and confident is your best play. Do all you can to avoid handing over your passport (present copies instead) since it might cost you to get it back.

Photography in towns and cities across DRC is a real pain and it's best not to bother. We have heard numerous tales of travellers arrested, and even jailed, for taking photos in Kinshasa and other towns. In the countryside things are generally easier but avoid taking photos within sight of police.

Finally, if everyone around you comes to a halt, follow suit. It's required by law during the raising and lowering of the national flag, which occurs daily around 7.30am and 6pm.

VISAS

All visitors need a visa, and they're not available on arrival. Getting a visa has recently become much harder. You must apply at the DRC embassy in your home country. Note that some embassies offer visas to anyone (including the embassy in Togo). However, a visa issued anywhere but your home country will not be accepted and you will be refused entry on arrival. If you're reading this halfway through a long trans-Africa trip then sorry, but you'll need to post your passport back home and apply there. The exact requirements vary from embassy to embassy but in general you will need proof of hotel booking, return plane tickets, a letter stating your reasons for travel and a legalised letter from a sponsor in DRC. Oh, and quite a lot of money as well! The only exception to these visa rules is if you're crossing from Uganda or Rwanda to Goma in order to visit Parc National des Virunga, in which case you can apply for a two-week visa valid only for Goma and the park via the national park website (www.visitvirunga.org). You must fill in the online form, pay US$50 and wait around a week.

Visas for Onward Travel

Angola Tourist visas are only issued to residents of DRC. You might be able to get a transit visa but even this was very hard to get at the time of research. Most people end up having to post their passports back to their home country and apply there. A letter of introduction is not needed for transit visas though. At the time of research some people (but not all) were getting transit visas via the consulate in Dolisie (Congo).

Central African Republic (CAR) A one-month, multiple-entry visa costs US$150 and requires two photos and a photocopy of your passport and DRC visa. You can wait three days or pay US$20 for same-day service.

Congo Bring a photo and US$80/120 for a 15-day/three-month visa. They're typically ready in two days, but you can pay an extra US$90/120 for same-day service.

Getting There & Away

AIR

Few airlines fly to Kinshasa, apparently due to mismanagement at the airport, so despite the hassles, some people use Brazzaville (Congo) as their gateway to DRC; although crossing between these two cities is not without its own share of problems. The only two options direct from Europe are nonstop from Paris with **Air France** (www.airfrance.com; Ave du Tchad, Hôtel Memling, Kinshasa) and from Brussels via Cameroon with **Brussels Airlines** (☎0996017000; http://congo.brusselsairlines.com; Blvd du 30 Juin, Kinshasha). **Ethiopian Airlines** (☎0817006585; www.ethiopianairlines.com; 9 Ave du Port), **Kenya Airways** (☎099 93 03; www.kenya-airways.com; 4 Ave du Marché) and **Royal Air Maroc** (☎0817252526; www.royalairmaroc.com; Blvd du 30 Juin) all link their respective capital cities to Kinshasa. Ethiopian Airlines and Kenya Airways fly to Lubumbashi.

LAND & RIVER

Whether you're heading to Goma or Bukavu, normally crossing from Rwanda couldn't be any easier (although at the time of research, with the M23 rebel advance, these borders were subject to closure at short notice). Transport from Kigali to the border towns of Gisenyi and Cyangugu is frequent, and from there you just walk into DRC and hire a *taxi-moto* to take you to your destination in town.

Various bus companies run from Bukavu to Bujumbura, Burundi, via the border at Gatumba.

The principal route to Uganda is from Beni to Kasindi, where you walk over the border and get another taxi to Kasese. Tour guides in Kisoro sometimes take clients across at Bunagana to

GOING TO LE BEACH

Travel between Kinshasa (the port is called Beach Ngobila, or just 'Beach') and Brazzaville ('Le Beach'; Congo) can be a real headache. It helps to travel in the afternoon and on weekends when the crowds are thinner. The easiest way across is a *canot rapide* (speedboat), which takes five minutes and costs US$25/CFA11,000. The overcrowded passenger ferries charge CDF10,000/CFA6500 and take 45 minutes. Boats sail 8.30am to 4pm Monday to Saturday, and there's also speedboat service until noon on Sunday. Boats usually don't run on holidays. Although these journey times make it look like you'll be done and dusted in an hour or so they don't take account of the extraordinary amount of general time wasting that takes place. In reality you need to allow at least a half-day to complete all formalities and cross the river – sometimes even longer.

On both sides officials will want to know exactly how many phones, cameras, computers and cash you have with you – declare everything otherwise kiss it goodbye. Various 'taxes' and additional 'fees' add at least CFA20,000 to your journey. There's no point being stubborn and trying to avoid these. Because of the lack of signs and the abundance of hustlers many people pay a fixer to get them through the process, but it's not really necessary; and some of those found on the street have their own cons going on, so be careful. If you arrange a fixer through a recognised tour company or better hotel you can expect to pay around US$70 for their services, but they will deal with all the 'problems'.

If you're driving, there are two car ferries daily, and you'll have to shell out about CFA25,000 for a car and driver, a whole lot more (up to several hundred US dollars) to various officials (including money to have your car disinfected on arrival in DRC!) and deal with an awful lot of hassle before boarding. Many overlanders were instead taking the Kinkala (Republic of Congo) to Kimpese (DRC) route via Boko, crossing the river at Luozi. The officials here are reportedly much more relaxed, but the road is awful and requires a decent 4WD in the dry season and in the wet season is close to impossible. Motorbikes travel free on this route and cars pay US$15.

LOCAL KNOWLEDGE

HOW TO CROSS DRC BY BICYCLE

There's no denying the fact that crossing DRC by land is a genuine adventure. The 'road' network in DRC is generally so dreadful that many overlanders travelling in their own vehicles find a car or jeep to actually be a hinderance. The way to go, everyone says, is by motorbike or bicycle.

In Kinshasa we met up with Balthazar Sieders, a traveller who'd just spent two months with a friend (George Symonds), cycling across DRC from Lubumbashi to Kinshasa. He gave us his top tips for anyone attempting the same journey by bike.

Follow the bianda trails *Bianda* is local slang for the human mules who transport up to 300kg of cargo between villages on old bicycles. They know better than anyone how to avoid the sandbanks and metre-deep truck tracks that make up most of the N1 (the Lubumbashi to Kinshasa road). Thanks to the *biandas* we were usually faster than the odd truck ploughing in the same direction.

Avoid cheap bicycle tubes Six weeks into our journey we realised that earlier puncture repairs to our tyres were starting to split apart our inner tubes and that trying to repair them was a losing battle. Twenty-eight patches later we ended up towing each other with a bamboo-pole construction for the remaining 400km to Kinshasa.

Learn some French By far our biggest psychological battle was having to bounce off the constant shouts and whistles that spread like wildfire every time we passed through a city or village. At times it felt like we were part of the Tour de France but it would have been more fun to have had the language ability to fully explain what in the world we were doing there.

Mission hospitable The churches in larger towns always sheltered us. In one we met a fascinating Indonesian priest called Jeff. He'd lived in the DRC since the mid-'90s, and was managing a banana plantation and fish farm.

see Parc National des Virunga's gorillas at Djomba. At the time of writing though this border was firmly closed due to rebel activity in DRC.

If you're driving to Angola, the easiest route is via Luvo where the road is better than that from Matadi (technically this border is at Ango-Ango, 3km from Matadi), but there's little traffic through either of these borders except for Luvo on Saturdays, so the best bet for those without wheels is Soyo, at the mouth of the Congo River, from where buses head to Luanda, though these are in short supply. Boats head there daily from Boma; however, once the road to Muanda is paved the service might shift there. For Cabinda take a taxi from Muanda to the border and then another to Cabinda city. Transport is frequent.

Few travellers cross to/from CAR, Tanzania (there are infrequent Kigoma–Kalemie cargo boats you can get a lift on) or Zambia (the crossing is at Kasumbalesa, south of Lubumbashi) because of the difficulties of moving on to other places in DRC.

Much of the border with South Sudan is generally considered unsafe. That said we have recieved reports recently from adventurous travellers heading to Garamba National Park in DRC and afterwards crossing into South Sudan via the Aba to Yei and on to Juba road. Problems along this route seem to be increasingly rare but check the latest on Lonely Planet's Thorn Tree forum first.

Getting Around

AIR

The combination of long distances and terrible roads means flying is often the best (and sometimes the only practical) way to reach many towns; airlines, usually flying small prop planes, reach every sizeable town from Muanda to Beni. DRC is not known for effective safety regulations, but airlines are starting to take safety, and even punctuality, a little more seriously. **CAA Congo** (☎ 0995903900; www.caacongo.com), formerly called Fly Congo, and prior to that Hewa Bora; an airline which ceased operations after a fatal accident in 2011, is the newest airline and is gaining a reputation as the best in the DRC. **Korongo Airlines** (☎ 081996030101; www.flykorongo.com) is another newly formed airline and also one of the more reliable. Both these airlines also link Lubumbashi to South Africa. Other more minor airlines include Tropic Air, which flies from Kinshasa to various places in Bas-Congo, and Kin Avia, which flies roughly the same routes. In most cases you can buy tickets a day or two before departure, and often even the same day. For most cities you can only buy tickets at N'Dolo Airport since travel agencies don't do business with the smaller airlines. Typical one-way fares from Kinshasa are US$260 to US$300 to Kisangani and US$290 to US$350 to Goma.

BOAT

River traffic on the Congo has restarted; see Crossing Congo (p507) for more.

BUS, CAR & MOTORCYCLE

Although there's still much work to be done, DRC is on a road-repair binge, which is making getting around the country easier for those who don't want to fly. Most roads remain dirt, however, so rainy-season travel is slow and difficult. Buses are available where the roads are good enough, but the fastest way to travel is in 4WDs.

TOUR COMPANIES

Getting around the DRC can be a slog. The transport network is virtually nonexistent, there are danger areas to be avoided and even getting a visa can give you a migrane. So no surprise then that some travellers find it easier to just let someone else organise everything for them. The following tour companies are highly recomended and can help with everythng from obtaining a visa to organising a full expedition down the Congo River.

Emmanuel Munganga Rufubya (☎0994 328077; www.gorillastracking.com) A one-man band, Emmanuel has a lot of experience and a vast network of contacts (though his speciality area is the east). You can expect a high degree of friendly, personal advice, but some of his drivers are unfamiliar with the roads outside of Goma and drive dangerously.

Go Congo (☎0811837010; www.gocongo.com) A Kinshasa-based tour company specalising in boat tours down the Congo River between Kisangani and Kinshasa. Also has a representative in Goma.

Kivu Travels (☎0995755643, in Belgium 495 58 68 07; www.kivutravel.com) A Belgian/Congolese company with a sound reputation and great connections throughout the east.

TRAIN

Every now and then a train runs from Lubumbashi to Kananga. The journey takes at least six days. From here you'll need to hitch a ride with trucks along the torn-up dirt road to Kikwit, but from there to Kinshasa it's a sealed road all the way.

Equatorial Guinea

Includes ➡

Fast Facts

- **Capital** Malabo
- **Population** 685,991
- **Languages** Spanish, French, Fang, Bubi
- **Area** 28,051 sq km
- **Currency** Central African franc (CFA)
- **Visa requirements** US visitors can get a visa at the point of entry. Other nationals must obtain a visa before travel.

Virgin Rain Forest & Glittering Oil Towns

Failed coups, danger money, bushmeat and buckets of oil – you could say Equatorial Guinea has something of a reputation. But mercenaries and crime writers aren't the only ones attracted to the country's beautiful black-and-white shores. This is the land of primates with painted faces, soft clouds of butterflies and insects so colourful they belong in the realm of fiction.

Though the country is dripping in oil wealth, many people's taps run dry. Poverty permeates ordinary life, making a trip to Malabo – alive with the flames of oil rigs and the buzz of rapid construction – at once hedonistic and heartbreaking.

Beyond Malabo, on Bioko Island, are volcanic views, fishing villages, rain forests full of endangered primates and shores of nesting sea turtles. On the mainland, white beaches, forest paths and junglescapes await.

But be prepared to hack and bribe and hold tight to bush taxis, and don't forget to pack all the patience you can fit in your bag – you'll be stopped often by the military and government officials wanting something.

Equatorial Guinea Top Sights

- **Bata** Watch the city grow vertically with oil money
- **Bioko Island** Go wide-eyed over the strange combination of dense rain forest, rare wildlife and oil platforms
- **Monte Allen National Park** Whisper during forest walks in search of gorillas, elephants and chimps
- **Cogo** Pierce the border by *pirogue* (canoe) at this southern frontier village
- **Isla Corisco** Tread softly on the squeaky-clean sand of this paradise isle
- **Malabo** Explore the architecture and nightlife of this bizarre oil town

UNDERSTAND EQUATORIAL GUINEA

Equatorial Guinea Today

The US imports up to 100,000 barrels of oil every day from Equatorial Guinea's shores. But though the country has a per-capita income of about US$50,000, profits have not trickled down to most of the population, who linger in appalling poverty while the government generates an oil revenue of about US$3 billion a year. According to anti-corruption-watchdog Transparency International, Equatorial Guinea is the 12th most corrupt country in the world. The group accuses President Obiang of using public money on fancy cars, sleek jets and luxury homes in Los Angeles. Obiang, Africa's longest-serving leader, is believed to be suffering from prostate cancer but shows no sign of releasing his grip; in 2009 he was voted in for another presidential term, in an election that banned EU monitors and some foreign media. Obiang won, as he predicted, 97% of the vote.

In November 2011 the government held a referendum proposing changes to the constitution which it claimed would facilitate

COUNTRY COVERAGE

At the time of research very few travellers were heading to Equatorial Guinea so we're providing historical and cultural information rather than reviews and listings. A good source of information for on-the-ground travel in Equatorial Guinea is Lonely Planet's ThornTree online travel forum www.lonelyplanet.com/thorntree. Another source of good internet-based information is http://equatorialguineaonline.com/.

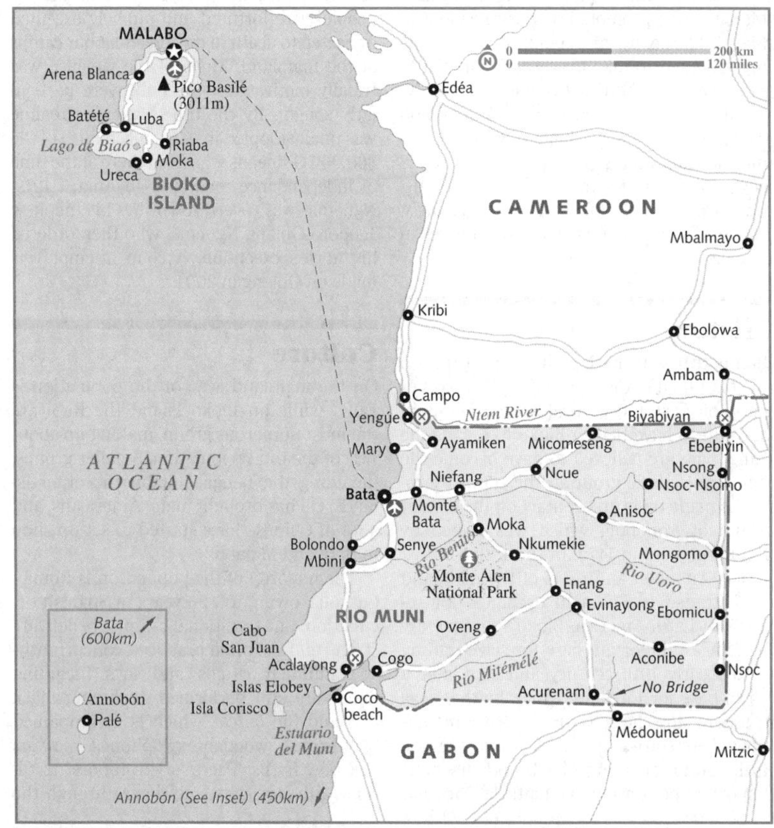

LIFE AT BLACK BEACH

Though it's not far from the warm waters of the Atlantic, the whitewashed prison at Playa Negra (Black Beach) is one of Africa's most notorious hellholes. It's here that South African mercenary Nick du Toit and fellow coup plotter Simon Mann were locked up for their roles in a 2004 attempted coup, an operation that aimed to overthrow President Obiang and install exiled opposition leader Severo Moro in his place. Oil rights were promised to the coup's financiers and plotters, among them Mark Thatcher, the son of former British prime minister Margaret Thatcher. But the coup attempt failed spectacularly: in March 2004 Mann, du Toit and 60 others were arrested when their Boeing jet landed in Harare, Zimbabwe, on a weapons-gathering stop. While du Toit was sent to Black Beach immediately, Mann served four years in jail in Zimbabwe before being extradited to Malabo in 2007, where he was handed a 34-year sentence. The same year, Amnesty International called a Black Beach term a 'slow, lingering death sentence'. President Obiang released Mann, du Toit and other accused prisoners in early 2009, citing good behaviour.

democratic reform. However, critics of the changes say that the reforms, which were endorsed by voters, will in fact cement Obiang's position.

Obiang's son, Teodoro Nguema Obiang Mangue, was promoted to vice president in May 2012, fueling speculation that he is being groomed to take his father's place. The same year he asked a US court to dismiss an attempt to seize around US$71 million worth of his assets, including a California mansion and a Gulfstream jet. The US government alleges they were obtained using corrupt funds taken from his country. Teodoro is also facing corruption charges in France.

History

Bantu tribes, including the Bubi, came to the mainland in the 12th century from other parts of West and Central Africa. The Bubi are said to have fled to Bioko to escape the Fang, who are believed to have become the dominant ethnic group in the 1600s. Europeans made their first contact on the distant island of Annobón, which was visited by the Portuguese in 1470. In the 18th century, Bioko, Annobón and parts of the mainland were traded to Spain in exchange for regions in Latin America. Bioko subsequently became an important base for slave-trading in the early 19th century and was later a naval base for England, which by then was trying to stop the slave trade. Cocoa plantations were started on the island in the late 19th century, making Malabo Spain's most important possession in equatorial Africa.

Equatorial Guinea attained independence in October 1968 under the presidency of Macias Nguema. Months later, relations with Spain deteriorated rapidly and Nguema's 10-year dictatorship began. Thousands of people were tortured and publicly executed or beaten to death in the forced-labour camps of the mainland. Much of the violence was tribally motivated – the Bubi were particularly sought. By the time Nguema's regime was finally toppled in 1979, only a third of the 300,000 Guineans who lived there at the time of independence remained. In August 1979, Nguema was overthrown by his nephew Teodoro Obiang Nguema, who then ordered his uncle's execution. A coup attempt was made on Obiang in 2004.

Culture

On the mainland 80% of the population is Fang, while on Bioko Island the Bubi are the most numerous group, making up about 15% of the total population. Smaller groups, including the Benga, inhabit the other islands. Oil has brought many Americans, and a lot of Chinese have started to set up shop in Bata and Malabo.

The majority of the population is Roman Catholic, owing to 400 years of Spanish occupation, but traditional animist beliefs are strong and are often practiced concurrently.

Traditional rituals and arts including dance are still performed, including mask arts and the *balélé*, which is accompanied by drums, wooden xylophones, *sanzas* and bow harps. There's a strong oral tradition, with stories passed down through the generations, often involving the same cast of famous characters such as the grumpy tortoise and the wily monkey.

Environment

Both Bioko Island and the mainland hide a wealth of wildlife, some of which is endangered. Rio Muni is home to a hefty wedge of Central African rain forest with gorillas, chimpanzees and forest elephants. It is unknown exactly how many large mammals remain. Large sections of the interior have been set aside as protected areas, including Monte Alen National Park, which covers much of the centre of Rio Muni and offers some amazing hikes. Logging is being more carefully controlled than in the past, but deforestation and the bushmeat trade are still big problems. Over the past decade, conservation staff have recorded the number of monkeys in meat markets; the tally had reached more than 20,000 by the end of March 2008, according to the Bioko Biodiversity Protection Program.

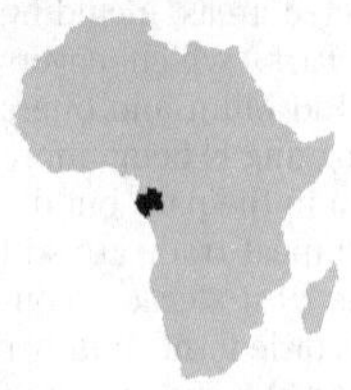

Gabon

POP 1,608,000

Includes ➡

Best Places to Eat

- Odika (p523)
- Garden Café (p523)
- Jacky Cochon (p523)
- DTH Traiteur (p530)

Best Places to Stay

- La Baie des Tortues (p528)
- Loango Lodge (p531)
- Ch20 (p532)
- L'Hôtellerie de l'Hôpital Albert Schweitzer (p530)
- Le Leet Dorian (p523)

Why Go?

Unlike many of its neighbours, this slab of equatorial Africa enjoys both peace and stability, while its superb wildlife makes it an increasingly popular place to safari away from the crowds of East Africa. With its seemingly endless rain forest now safeguarded by the 2003 decision to turn an incredible 10% of the country into protected national parkland, Gabon is Central Africa's most progressive and traveller-friendly destination, although the competition is admittedly not too fierce.

Despite being far ahead of its unstable, war-torn neighbours, tourism in Gabon remains DIY – you either put yourself in the hands of a travel agency, or negotiate the poor roads, infrequent transport and almost total lack of reliable infrastructure yourself. Outside cosmopolitan Libreville, the country's only real city, Gabon is an undiscovered wonderland of thick jungle, white-sand beaches, rushing rivers and ethereal landscapes. Bring either plenty of money or plenty of patience, but don't miss out on this Eden-like travel experience.

When to Go

Libreville

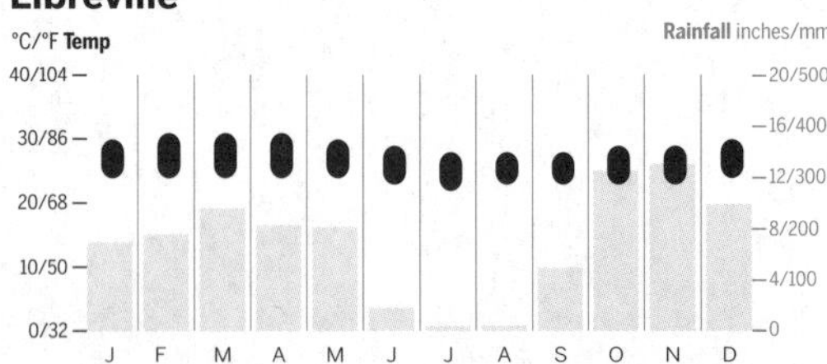

May–Sep The dry season makes overland transport faster and wildlife easier to see.

Jul–Sep Have a close encounter with a whale swimming off Gabon's coastline.

Nov–Jan Spot turtles coming ashore to lay their eggs on the beaches.

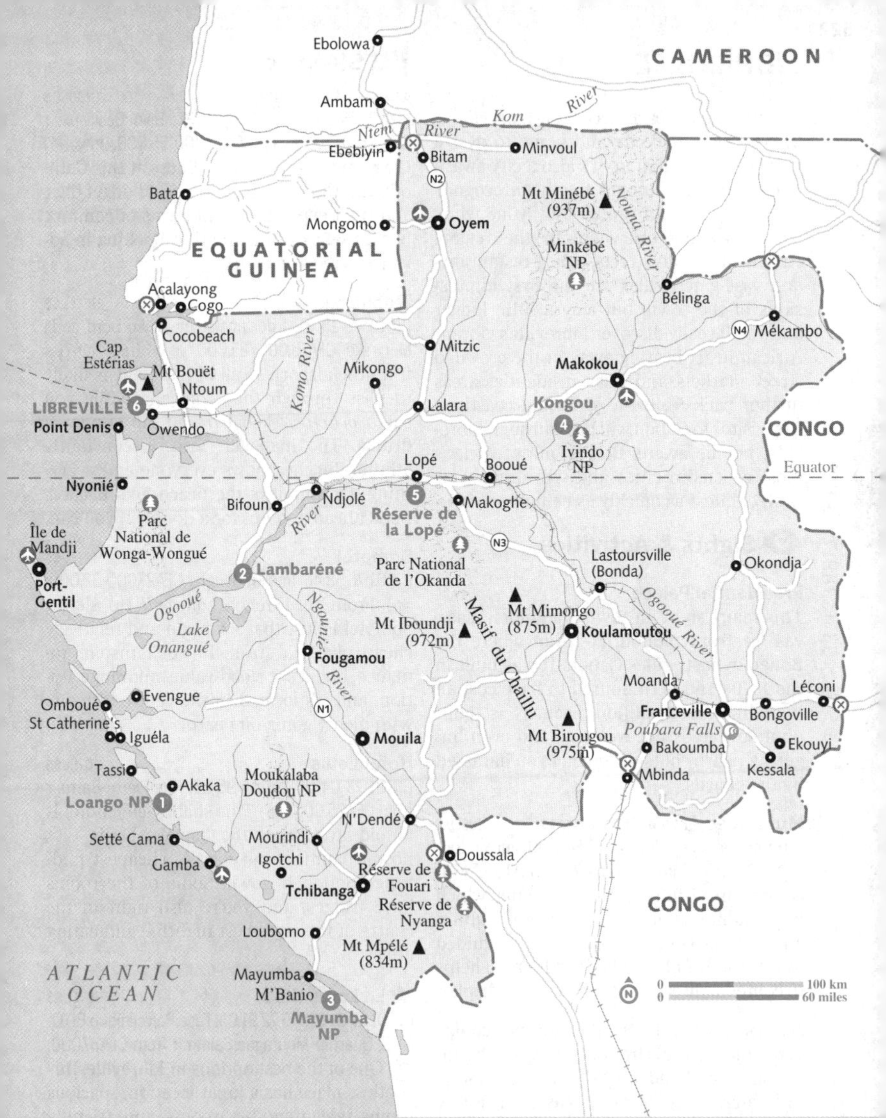

CAMEROON
Ebolowa
Ambam
Kom River
Ntem River
Ebebiyin
Bitam
Minvoul
N2
Bata
Mt Minébé (937m)
Nouna River
Mongomo
Oyem
EQUATORIAL GUINEA
Minkébé NP
Bélinga
Acalayong
Cogo
Cocobeach
Mékambo
N4
Mitzic
Cap Estérias
Mt Bouët
Komo River
Mikongo
Makokou
Ntoum
LIBREVILLE
Lalara
Kongou
Point Denis
Owendo
Ivindo NP
CONGO
Lopé
Booué
Equator
Nyonié
Ndjolé
Makoghe
Bifoun
Réserve de la Lopé
Parc National de Wonga-Wongué
River
N3
Île de Mandji
Port-Gentil
Lambaréné
Parc National de l'Okanda
Lastoursville (Bonda)
Okondja
Ngounié River
Ogooué
Masif du Chaillu
Mt Mimongo (875m)
Ogooué River
Lake Onangué
Mt Iboundji (972m)
Koulamoutou
Fougamou
Moanda
Léconi
Evengue
N1
Franceville
Bongoville
Omboué
St Catherine's
Iguéla
Mt Birougou (975m)
Poubara Falls
Mouila
Bakoumba
Ekouyi
Tassi
Akaka
Moukalaba Doudou NP
Mbinda
Kessala
Loango NP
N'Dendé
Setté Cama
Mourindi
Doussala
Gamba
Igotchi
Réserve de Fouari
Tchibanga
Réserve de Nyanga
CONGO
Loubomo
Mt Mpélé (834m)
ATLANTIC OCEAN
Mayumba
M'Banio
Mayumba NP
0 100 km
0 60 miles

Gabon Highlights

1. Gape at beaches full of elephants, buffaloes and surfing hippos at **Loango National Park** (p531).
2. Explore **Lambaréné** (p530), the charming and laid-back town made famous by the Nobel Prize–winning Albert Schweitzer.
3. Bodysurf the waves while watching humpback whales breach in the distance at **Mayumba National Park** (p532).
4. Head to Gabon's most spectacular falls at **Kongou** (p533) and take a trip by *pirogue* (traditional canoe) through the jungle.
5. Explore beautiful **Réserve de la Lopé** (p532), see wild elephants and enjoy spectacular scenery.
6. Kick back in the decidedly un-African city of **Libreville** (p522), eat well and take a day trip to Point Denis.

LIBREVILLE

POP 578,000

The muscular heart of Gabon, Libreville is Gabon's only real city and home to over a third of its population. It's also a city awash in oil money and almost totally unrecognisable as an African capital to anyone who's been travelling elsewhere in the region. Pavements, clean streets, smart restaurants and vast gated villas are the first impressions of the town, but stay a little longer and you'll easily discover Libreville's vibrant African heart beating away in the crowded street markets and busy residential areas further back from the gleaming coastline. Any visitor to Gabon will pass through Libreville, but be aware, this is one of Africa's most expensive cities and will drain your wallet almost as quickly as being on safari.

Sights & Activities

Presidential Palace PALACE

This main 'sight' in town – a golden glass, vast seafront monolith – from where the Bongo dynasty rules Gabon. It was built in the 1970s and is rumoured to have cost an incredible $250 million. Security is tight: photography is not welcome and even lingering nearby outside will get you harassed by the guards.

Musée des Arts et Traditions MUSEUM

(Au Bord de Mer; admission CFA1000, guided tour CFA2000; h8.30am-3.30pm Mon-Fri) More welcoming to visitors is this museum, which has exhibitions on tribal crafts and culture and a great collection of masks. A guided tour (usually only available in French) helps to contextualise a lot of the items on display.

Just as interesting are the **folk-art sculptures** on the waterfront across from the Intercontinental and, a nice walk south along the water, across from the casino. The row of **ministry buildings** with Soviet-inspired architecture on Blvd Triomphal is worth a wander through, as is the northern suburb of **Sablière**, the home of ministers and ambassadors. The city's most interesting market is at **Mont Bouet**.

On weekends most of Libreville heads to the beach; young people congregate in front of the Tropicana. You can use the pools at the Meridien and Intercontinental for a fee, or even better, head to Point Denis by boat for the day.

Sleeping

Maison Liebermann GUESTHOUSE $

(01 76 19 55, 06 95 03 37; Blvd Bessieux; r CFA9000-15,000, apt CFA20,000-35,000; P) Cleanliness is next to godliness at this Catholic guesthouse, Libreville's best budget digs. You can't expect much in terms of comfort, but it's safe, central and tidy. Booking in advance is recommended.

Tropicana HOTEL $$

(01 73 15 31; tropicana@inet.ga; Au Bord de la Mer; s/d CFA16,000/25,000;) Just across from the airport, so all of Libreville is likely to pass through the Tropicana while you eat *brochettes* (kebabs) and sip sundown drinks. The manager, Eric, is constantly aflutter, but he knows everyone and everything. On Sundays the beach gets packed. Book ahead and opt for a double if you can.

Somotel MOTEL $$

(01 76 58 46; Rue Mt Bouët; r CFA27,000-32,000;) From the French *sommeil* (to sleep), Somotel is just that – a clean and relatively cheap place to crash. It won't inspire romance but it's a good-value midrange option, and it's located in the centre of town, with plenty going on nearby.

Hotel Louis HOTEL $$

(01 73 04 00, 04 44 96 26; Rue Pierre Barro; r from CFA25,000;) This shabby-chic hotel is an old favourite in the Quartier Louis – it's no oil painting, but it's the cheapest midrange option in town. Some of the rooms have fridges, and you're also right in the centre of the city's best nightlife and eating area.

★**Le Lotus Bleu** HOTEL $$

(01 77 81 85, 05 72 91 03; Face Polyclinique BIYOGHE, Quartier Montagne Sainte; r from CFA37,000;) One of the best options in Libreville, this spotless place has a great location, spacious rooms, gleaming bathrooms and friendly service. There's wi-fi in the (more expensive) upstairs rooms only, but you can also access it in the lobby area at no extra charge.

Le Patio HOTEL $$

(01 73 47 16; www.lepatio-gabon.com; Rue Pierre Barro; d/tw CFA40,000/55,000, ste CFA65,000-90,000;) This hotel could easily be the best-value comfortable option in town: its rooms are spotless, its location is great and there's a charming courtyard that's a joy to relax in. So why are the staff so unwelcoming?

GABON LIBREVILLE

For these prices we'd expect some basic friendliness. If smiles at breakfast aren't a priority for you though, this is a great option.

Sunset Beach HOTEL **$$$**
(☎06 71 58 90, 07 18 25 70; www.sunsetlbv.wordpress.com; s/d CFA35,000/50,000; ❄ 📶) Sunset Beach overlooks the sea on a great stretch of beach as its name suggests, some 15km from the city centre. This is its main plus point – rooms are actually fairly mediocre (though they're better in the main building than the annex), and staff could be friendlier. It's convenient for the airport though, and taxis into town aren't expensive.

Hotel La Grande Muraille de Chine HOTEL **$$$**
(☎05 44 93 10, 06 25 24 86; hotelmuraille@yahoo.fr; Rue Ange M'ba; r/ste CFA40,000/58,000; ❄ 📶) Run by members of Libreville's ever-growing Chinese community, the 'Great Wall of China' is right in the centre of town and boasts a large Chinese restaurant to boot. Its rooms are spacious, with large double beds, tiled floors and brand-new bathrooms.

Similar prices, rooms and facilites can be had at the Star Hotel, run by the same management, around the corner.

★**Le Leet Dorian** BOUTIQUE HOTEL **$$$**
(☎01 72 55 46, 07 38 51 84; www.hoteldorian.ga; Quartier Montagne Sainte; r/ste CFA70,000/85,000; P ❄ @ 📶) Definitely the pick of Libreville's hotels, this gorgeous, design-conscious place has individually decorated rooms with Gabonese art on the walls, stylish touches and sleek bathrooms. There are also delicious breakfasts and DVD rentals to make you feel right at home. Of course the price tag isn't small, but it's still far cheaper and more charming than the city's large five-star hotels.

Le Meridien LUXURY HOTEL **$$$**
(☎01 79 32 00; www.lemeridienrendama.com; d from CFA116,000; P ❄ @ 📶 🏊) A full-service hotel with a health club and a beautiful pool with an ocean view. It's not particularly central, however, but if you can afford to stay here then the cost of a taxi into town isn't going to worry you.

Eating

You'll eat well in Libreville, but at a price. If you've been travelling elsewhere in Central Africa, the cost of eating here will astonish you – reckon on at least CFA10,000 for a decent restaurant meal.

SET YOUR BUDGET

Budget

- Hotel room CFA20,000
- Two-course dinner CFA10,000
- Coffee CFA2000
- Local bus ride CFA1000

Midrange

- Hotel room CFA40,000
- Two-course dinner CFA15,000
- Beer in bar CFA3000
- Short taxi ride CFA1000

Top End

- Hotel room CFA80,000
- Two-course dinner CFA20,000
- Glass of wine CFA4000
- Short taxi ride CFA1000

★**Garden Café** INTERNATIONAL **$$**
(Quartier Louis; mains CFA6500-9500) This self-styled 'brasserie des sports' has a funky diner feel and a mixed crowd of regulars. There's a fantastic menu (French cuisine with nods to African flavours), with daily specials and superb desserts – though it's very noisy and not always a great place for a conversation. This is also a good place to come for drinks.

★**Odika** AFRICAN **$$**
(☎01 73 69 20; Blvd Joseph Deemin; mains CFA6500-11,000) This superb terrace restaurant in the heart of the Quartier Louis has an enviable buzz any night of the week, with a mixed local and European crowd, tempting dishes such as beef *ndolé*, *colombo du porc* or seafood *brochettes*, local art on the walls, polished timber floors and fresh flowers. Reservations are a good idea at the weekends.

★**Jacky Cochon** STEAKHOUSE **$$**
(☎06 25 15 14; Blvd Léon Mba; mains CFA7500-14,000; ⏰6pm-midnight) It's beside a prison, the decor is Rasta chic and your food is fixed by a charmer of a long-dredded musician who's been rearing pigs for years. Pork heaven: try the various delicious pork main courses, but don't miss something from the selection of terrines and smoked hams or the excellent wine list.

Libreville

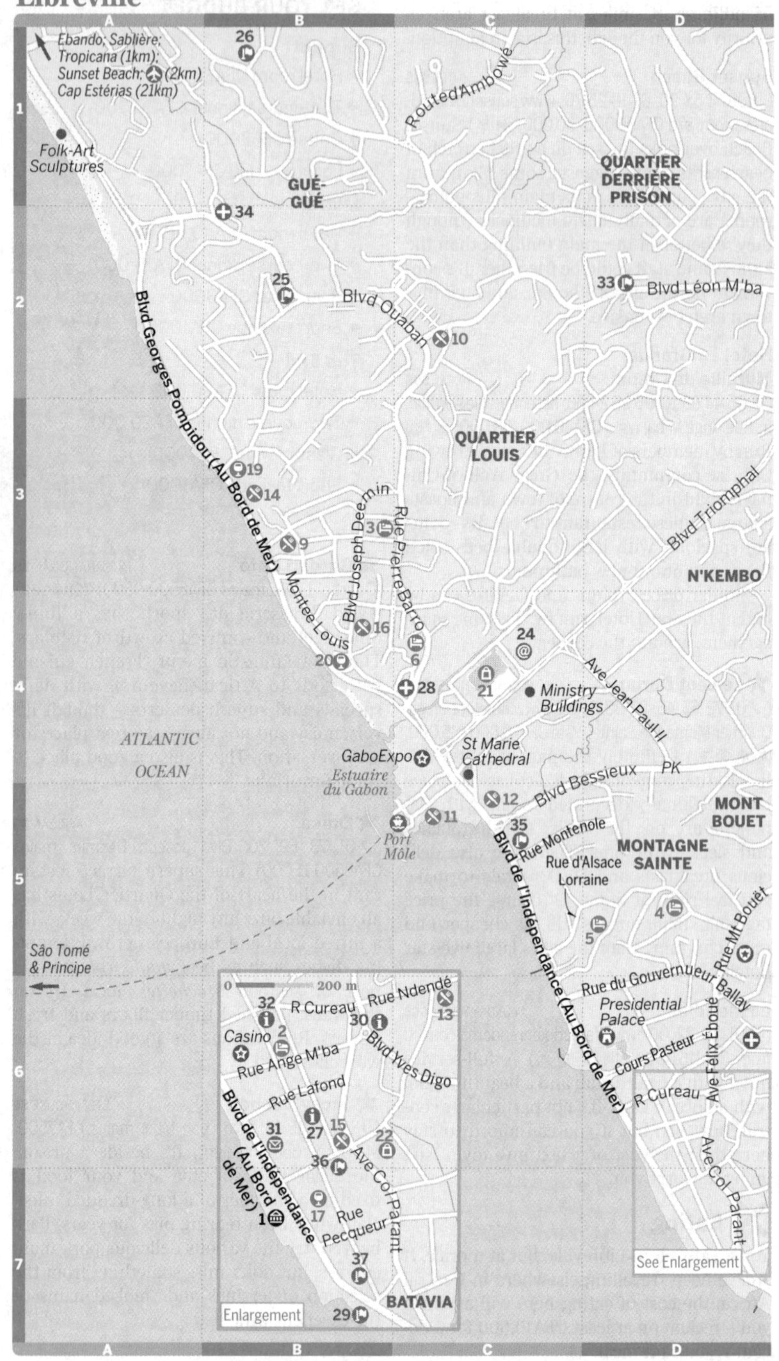

Ebando; Sablière; Tropicana (1km); Sunset Beach; (2km) Cap Estérias (21km)
Folk-Art Sculptures
GUÉ-GUÉ
Route d'Ambowé
QUARTIER DERRIÈRE PRISON
Blvd Léon M'ba
Blvd Ouaban
Blvd Georges Pompidou (Au Bord de Mer)
QUARTIER LOUIS
Blvd Joseph Deemin
Rue Pierre Barro
Montee Louis
Blvd Triomphal
N'KEMBO
Ave Jean Paul II
Ministry Buildings
ATLANTIC OCEAN
GaboExpo
Estuaire du Gabon
St Marie Cathedral
Blvd Bessieux
PK
MONT BOUET
Port Môle
Rue Montenole
MONTAGNE SAINTE
Rue d'Alsace Lorraine
Blvd de l'Indépendance (Au Bord de Mer)
Rue Mt Bouët
São Tomé & Principe
Rue du Gouverneur Ballay
Presidential Palace
Cours Pasteur
Ave Félix Éboué
R Cureau
Ave Col Parant
See Enlargement
Enlargement
0 200 m
R Cureau
Rue Ndendé
Casino
Rue Ange M'ba
Blvd Yves Digo
Rue Lafond
Ave Col Parant
Rue Pecqueur
BATAVIA

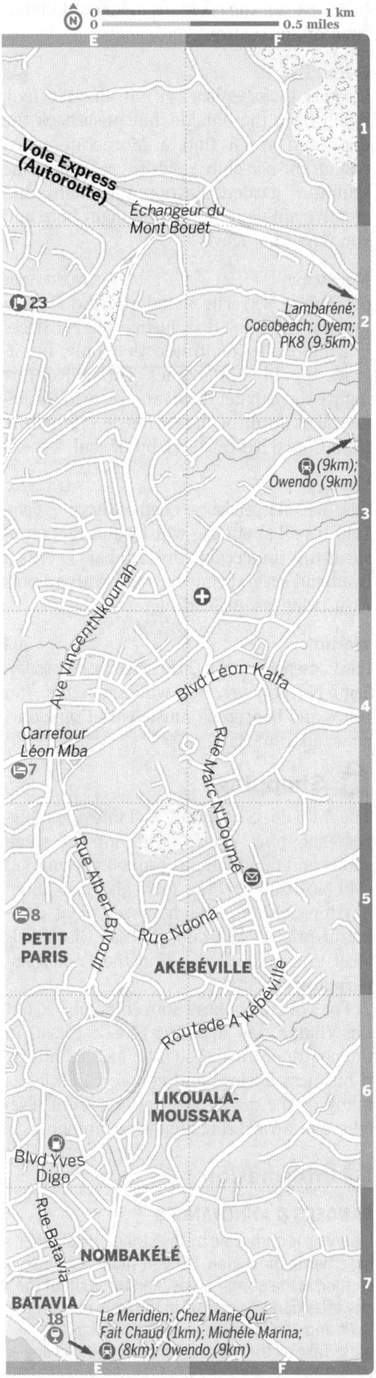

Libreville

Sights

1 Musée des Arts et Traditions.............B7

Sleeping

2 Hotel La Grande Muraille de Chine.............B6
3 Hotel Louis.............B3
4 Le Leet Dorian.............D5
5 Le Lotus Bleu.............D5
6 Le Patio.............C4
7 Maison Liebermann.............E4
8 Somotel.............E5

Eating

9 Garden Café.............B3
10 Jacky Cochon.............C2
11 La Dolce Vita.............C5
12 La Genoise.............C5
13 La Parisienne.............C6
14 Le Bateau Ivre.............B3
15 Le Pelisson.............B6
M'bolo.............(see 21)
16 Odika.............B4

Drinking & Nightlife

Butterfly.............(see 20)
17 Le Cactus.............B7
18 Lokua.............E7
19 No Stress.............B3
20 Warhol.............B4

Shopping

21 M'bolo.............C4
22 Village des Artisans.............B6

Information

23 Cameroon Embassy.............E2
24 Centre Culturel Français.............C4
25 Congolese Embassy.............B2
26 Equatorial Guinea Embassy.............B1
27 Eurafrique Voyages.............B6
28 Fondation Jeanne Ebori.............C4
29 French Embassy.............B7
30 Gabon Tour.............B6
31 Main Post Office.............B6
32 Mistral Voyages.............B6
33 Nigerian Embassy.............D2
34 Polyclinique El Rapha.............B2
35 São Tomé & Príncipe Embassy.............C5
36 South African Embassy.............B6
37 US Embassy.............B7

La Dolce Vita SEAFOOD **$$**

(Port Môle; mains from CFA6000; midday-3pm Mon-Sat, 6-10pm daily) Ocean views and fabulous seafood make this local institution in the bustling passenger port a Libreville favourite. Great specials, friendly staff and huge portions keep people returning.

Le Bateau Ivre EUROPEAN $$$
(☎01 44 34 87; Au Bord de la Mer; mains from CFA18,000; ⊙noon-4pm & 6-11pm Mon-Fri, 6-11pm Sat) The Bateau isn't drunken at all, in fact it's rather refined, with a huge glass window giving views over the open sea, a smart menu of sophisticated European gastronomy and a great wine list. This is another place for a blow-out meal – its silky white chairs attract the local Land Cruiser classes. Reservations are recommended for Friday and Saturday.

Chez Marie Qui Fait Chaud SEAFOOD $$$
(☎05 32 13 59; Quartier Batavia; set meal incl drinks CFA20,000; ⊙6-10pm Tue-Sun) Prices have gone up steeply at this Libreville institution of late, especially given that it's a taxi ride from the centre (all cab drivers know the place) and isn't particularly atmospheric. However, Marie's welcome is warm, and you'll eat very well indeed – dishes include fresh lobster and *poisson braisé* (a dish of grilled fish served with onions and tomatoes). Reservations are recommended.

There are clusters of street-food stands – among them *beignet* (doughnut) sellers known as *les bédoumeuses* – around Blvd Bessieux and on Ave John Paul II. For self-caterers, M'bolo is the (overpriced) French-style supermarket. Another money-saving alternative is to eat in one of the city's excellent bakeries. Try the traditional **Le Pelisson** (Ave Col Parant; pastries from CFA500; ⊙7am-8pm Mon-Sat) for breakfast, the smarter **La Parisienne** (Rue Ndendé; mains CFA1500-6000; ⊙7am-9pm Tue-Sat, to 2pm Sun) for excellent sandwiches, and **La Genoise** (Au Bord de la Mer; mains CFA2500-5000; ⊙6am-10pm) on the seafront, which has the widest range of pastries, sandwiches and dishes. All do good coffee as well.

Drinking & Nightlife

If you wanna get out and get down, hit the Quartier Louis where there is a host of great drinking spots and clubs, which rarely get going before midnight. Check out Blvd Joseph Deemin and the surrounding streets.

Le Cactus BAR
(Au Bord de la Mer; ⊙noon-midnight) Gabon's only real cactus-strewn landscape is in the extreme northeast; if you're not a brave soul heading that way you might want to hole up here instead. Top cocktails in an outdoor bar right on the seafront.

Butterfly BAR
(Quartier Louis; ⊙6pm-2am) It doesn't look much from the outside, but push back the door and you'll find a Moroccan-owned restaurant-bar-club with a fantastic sculpture garden, flavoured hookahs and creative ambience. Start the night here and you might not leave.

No Stress CONCERT VENUE
(Au Bord de Mer) The name and the Gothic-looking sign don't do it justice, but No Stress is a Libreville institution that pulls in Africa's top hip-hop names. On nonconcert nights you can get down and dirty to *coupé-decalé* (a form of dance music originating from Côte d'Ivoire) and a bit of soul.

Lokua LIVE MUSIC
(Blvd de l'Independence, Quartier Glass; ⊙6pm-1am) It's all about the whisky and roots music at this impeccably dressed bar. There's a live band several times a week with a Louis Armstrong–esque lead singer.

Warhol BAR
(Blvd Joseph Deemin, Quartier Louis; ⊙midday-2am) No pop art, but winking lights, fun tunes and big-screen music vids. Come one, come all, come late.

Shopping

The M'bolo compound is Libreville's biggest shopping centre, with lots of small shops and one Walmart-esque hypermarket (M'bolo itself) selling food and just about anything else you might need, all at exorbitant prices. Next door, M'bolo Disco sells local tunes. You'll also find the French supermarket Géant.

For your Gabonese souvenirs, check out the **Village des Artisans** (Ave Col Parant) in the centre of town. You'll be hassled a little if business is slow, and choose carefully as many of the goods are imports from elsewhere in Africa. Haggling is recommended.

Information

DANGERS & ANNOYANCES

Libreville is quite safe by the standards of other big cities in the region, but you should exercise caution in the poorer areas, and throughout the city after dark. Be careful in the back of shared taxis and don't wander onto the beach after dark. Take all the precautions you would in any big city and carry a copy of your passport with you at all times.

INTERNET ACCESS

There are few internet cafes in Libreville, but most hotels and smarter restaurants, bars and cafes offer a connection.

Centre Culturel Français (CCF; per hr CFA1000; ⏲10am-9pm Mon-Sat) This air-conditioned centre has internet access as well as cultural events, films, concerts and helpful staff.

MEDICAL SERVICES

Fondation Jeanne Ebori (☎01 73 20 12) Across from Port Môle in Quartier Louis. One of Libreville's biggest hospitals, with modern lab facilities and 300 beds.

Polyclinique El Rapha (☎01 44 70 00; Blvd Ouaban) The best hospital in Libreville.

MONEY

Banks in Libreville will change cash and travellers cheques, though all charge commission. Hotels also change at good rates, as do local merchants. There are ATMs (accepting Visa cards only) in town at some banks, M'bolo and top-end hotels.

POST

Main post office (La Grand Poste; Au Bord de Mer) Located in the heart of the city. Western Union is directly behind it.

TOURIST INFORMATION

Gabon Tour (☎01 72 85 04; Ave Félix Éboué; ⏲7.30am-3.30pm Mon-Fri) Has official info and some glossy brochures to hand. Staff seem initially baffled by tourists coming in, but warm up if you persist.

TRAVEL AGENTS

Ebando (☎06 25 09 17, 07 81 95 55; www.ebando.org; Rte des Pecheurs) Organises quirky ecotourism ventures. Located north of Libreville in the neighbourhood of La Sablière.

Eurafrique Voyages (☎01 76 27 87; www.gabon-destinationinsolite.com) An agency that has been running tours throughout Gabon since 1972, specialising in La Lopé.

Mistral Voyages (☎01 76 04 21; www.ecotourisme-gabon.com) This is one of the most consistently used travel agencies in Gabon, and also works in São Tomé. Owner Patrice knows everything about the country, and tour packages to almost anywhere in Gabon can be booked here.

ℹ Getting There & Away

AIR

Libreville has Gabon's only international airport (p537), and it's well connected to major African cities, to Europe and to towns in Gabon. Internally there are several domestic airlines flying from here primarily to Port Gentil, but also other towns and airstrips throughout the country. These include National Régionale Transport (**NRT**; ☎06 66 90 77, 07 37 22 55; Rue Ndendé) and **Allegiance Airways** (☎01 44 30 83; Airport). NRT flies to Port Gentil, Tchinbanga, Oyem, Mouila, Koulamoutou, Franceville and Makokou, while Allegiance flies to Port Gentil, Oyem, Mvengué and Gamba.

LOCAL TRANSPORT

All *taxis-brousses* (bush taxis) leave from PK8 (pronounced peek-a-weet), 8km out of Libreville. A taxi to this chaotic place will cost around CFA4000, and allow plenty of time to get there, as traffic can crawl. Overpacked minibuses, 4WDs, pick-ups and *clandos* (cars that act as long-distance taxis) can be found daily for most destinations; early morning is the best time to show up. You can pay extra for the remaining seats in a shared taxi if you want to leave quickly, or would prefer not to be crowded. From Libreville, you can catch local transport to Lambaréné (CFA7000, four hours), Cocobeach (CFA5000, two to three hours) and Oyem (CFA22,000, 11 hours).

TRAIN

Gabon's main transport artery is the Transgabonaise train line, run by Setrag, which begins at Owendo, 8km south of Libreville, and goes all the way to Franceville, deep in Gabon's interior. There are four trains a week in each direction, and tickets can be bought in the centre of Libreville at the **Setrag** (☎0170 8060; off Rue Lafond; ⏲8.30am-6pm Mon-Fri, to 1pm Sat) office.

It's a comfortable ride, but be prepared for delays and breakdowns, and bring warm clothing if you're travelling in 1st class, as the air-con can be brutal. There are no sleeping cars, so even if you're in 1st class you'll be sitting the entire way.

Trains run to Lopé (the town at the entrance to Réserve de la Lopé; CFA20,250/15,000 in 1st/2nd class, six to eight hours) and Franceville (CFA44,400/32,800 in 1st/2nd class, 12 hours). It's best to book at least 48 hours ahead, as trains are often full.

ℹ Getting Around

A cab from the airport into town costs CFA3000; expect to pay more after dark. The fancier hotels have airport shuttle buses. Shared taxis on predetermined routes cost CFA200. *Une course* (private hire of a shared cab) should be CFA1000 for a short hop, CFA2000 to CFA3000 for longer journeys, though rates differ depending on the mood of the driver and your bargaining skills. Be prepared for terrible traffic jams all over Libreville.

AROUND LIBREVILLE

Point Denis

Point Denis is Libreville's weekend bolt hole, a quick boat ride and yet a world away from the capital's traffic and crowds. The superb stretch of sand here runs for miles along the peninsula, backing onto the Pongara National Park, and lined with fancy weekend houses. There are several beachside hotels on Point Denis, and it's perfectly feasible to go there for the day by boat from Libreville. Stick to the beaten track and you'll find boutique hotels, lazy restaurants and watersports; walk to the Atlantic side of the point and you'll discover miles of empty white sand that is the nesting ground of sea turtles from November to January.

If you're doing a day trip to Point Denis, then bring your own food and drinks, otherwise you'll need to eat at one of the hotels here. If you plan to stay, then the **Assala Lodge** (☎03 16 80 69; www.assalalodge.com; r CFA55,000; ❄) is the best choice, with its superb stretch of beach, four-poster beds, wooden furniture and good restaurant. Further down the beach towards the national park is **La Maringa** (☎05 32 17 45, 07 31 11 04; r CFA40,000), where cute little timber chalets with wooden furniture and mosquito nets are spread out in the sandy yard and similar rooms are housed in a two-floor block a moment's stroll from the beach.

You can reach Point Denis from either Port Môle or Michèle Marina in Libreville. From Port Môle, **Navette Pointe Denis** (☎06 27 78 15, 05 33 28 66) has a departure at 10am and 3pm on Saturday and 9.30am and 10am on Sunday (CFA10,000 return), with return ferries at the end of both days. Alternatively, from Michèle Marina **Nauti Service** (☎05 31 80 80, 06 26 40 77) has departures at 9.30am and 4pm Tuesday to Friday, at 9.30am and 3.30pm Saturday and 9am and 11am on Sunday (CFA12,000 to CFA14,000 depending on where in Point Denis you want to be dropped off). However, there needs to a minimum of 10 people for the service to run, so during the week it's a good idea to call ahead and ensure boats will be running.

Pongara National Park

Perhaps the easiest place to get into the wild expanses of Gabon if you're only in the country for a few days, Pongara National Park is an expanse of forest, savannah and empty beaches that backs onto Point Denis.

Recently opened within the park is the very charming **La Baie des Tortues** (☎03 28 64 45, 06 22 50 00; www.baiedestortuesgabon.com; r all-incl per person CFA200,000), with an enviable location miles from anywhere right on the beach. The 10 thatched rooms here are all beautifully presented, each with double beds, beautiful bathrooms, rain showers and timber floors. There's an excellent restaurant and peacocks roam the beautiful grounds, backed by the rain forest into which there are daily excursions (included in the price, as is all food and transportation). You can also arrange to come here for a day from Libreville; the cost is CFA50,000 per person and includes lunch, drinks and return boat transfers.

Even more remote is the excellent **Pongara Lodge** (☎06 26 33 64, 03 19 26 88; www.pongara-lodge.com; r with full board incl transfers CFA200,000), further down the coastline and deeper into the national park. With just six bungalows, the look and feel is more rustic, while still being very comfortable and exclusive. As well as a gorgeous beach, there's plenty of scope for nature walks, fishing, and turtle- and whale-watching. The price includes return transfers from Libreville.

Cocobeach

Though it sounds like the stuff of honeymoon fantasies, Cocobeach won't have you getting down on one knee in a hurry. But if it's adventure you're after, this dusty little seaside town is a *pirogue* (CFA5000) trip away from Equatorial Guinea's Cogo, the gateway to handsome Isla Corisco (now we're talking). You can bed down for the night at the basic **Motel Esperance** (r from CFA10,000) down the road from the local Directeur Genérale de la Documentation (formerly Sedoc) branch (see p537), which will grant you an exit stamp in your passport. Get a visa beforehand – no easy task for Equatorial Guinea, as visas on arrival are not possible. There's a shady terrace at Chez Tante Mado on the main street if you want to fill up on reasonably priced food before leaving the country.

Shared taxis leave from PK8 in Libreville and cost CFA5000 for a space in a packed vehicle.

NORTHERN GABON

Oyem

POP 38,000

Oyem is a town of fat tree trunks, apricot-coloured lanes and pretty lakes. Though it's the heart of Fang culture, few travellers make it here due to its isolated location. But if you do take the road less travelled, you'll find a pleasant little lakeside town surrounded by forest villages. It's also a good spot to cross into Equatorial Guinea and Cameroon.

The best place to stay is undoubtedly the **Hotel Mvet Palace** (☎01 98 61 72; r from CFA15,000; ❄).

There are buses from Libreville (in addition to the *taxis-brousses*) that leave from PK8 (CFA12,000, around 11 hours) with a stop at Ndjolé. By plane from Libreville to Oyem costs around CFA70,000 one way and takes just under an hour.

Taxis-brousses leave from Oyem to Mongomo in Equatorial Guinea daily; you must already have a visa. It takes about 30 minutes to the border, where you can switch cabs on the EG side.

Minkébé National Park

Shingled with cacti and rock-dome *inselbergs* (isolated ranges and hills), Minkébé is one of Gabon's most inaccessible parks, the home of forest elephants, gorillas, cheetahs and isolated ethnic groups. Conservation programs are in place through the **WWF** (☎01 73 00 28), which is trying to boost the income of villagers through artistic endeavours.

Though travel here is tricky, it's not an impossibility. You can contact the WWF or head to **Bitam**, a little rubber town not far from the park. There, bed down at **Hotel des Voyageurs** (☎01 96 80 20; r CFA8000), where staff can help you get deeper into the region.

From Bitam you can also find shared-taxi rides to the Cameroon border (CFA2500 to river border, CFA2500 for the *pirogue* across). Don't forget to stop at immigration and get an exit stamp or you'll be turned back at the border checkpoint.

SOUTHERN GABON

Port-Gentil

POP 80,000

Your first thought after stepping off the boat in Port-Gentil is that it doesn't feel as welcoming or kind as its name suggests. Most travellers don't make it to Gabon's second city, named for former French administrator Émile Gentil, but if you do swing by you'll see Gabon's petroleum industry and economic engine up close – perhaps not a great reason to come, but it makes a change from wildlife-watching.

The centre of town is of course the port, and Gentil stretches northeastwards from there. There's a shortage of good budget accommodation; a midrange bet is the **Hirondelle** (☎01 55 17 82; r from CFA25,000; ❄), off Ave Savorgnan. It has bungalows and a tidy garden area. For a taste of Port-Gentil's high life, the **Hotel du Parc** (☎01 55 25 28; www.hotelduparc-pog.com; Nouveau Port; r from CFA60,000; ❄📶) is down by the new port. There's every comfort, including wi-fi and even a mini zoo.

CNI (p538) runs boats between Libreville and Gentil three times a week in both directions. The 14-hour one-way trip in 2nd class is CFA15,000, and cars cost CFA120,000 to CFA180,000 depending on their size. A far better option is the 45-minute flight, offered by all domestic airlines for around CFA60,000.

What does Johann Sebastian Bach circa 1724 have in common with Gabon's Bantu drummers? Until the 1990s, not a lot. But that was before Pierre Akendengué, one of Africa's most celebrated composers, holed up for one hundred days in a Paris studio and recorded 'Lambarena', a fabulously energetic track that sets traditional Gabonese drumming and singing to the pure notes of Bach's 'St John Passion'.

Akendengué – who has been both 1970s protest singer and cultural adviser to the late Omar Bongo since his first foray into music in the 1940s – recorded the track as a tribute to Dr Albert Schweitzer, founder of the eponymous, world-renowned hospital at Lambaréné.

The result is a beautiful, unlikely marriage, like coming across a violin concerto in the middle of the Réserve de la Lopé.

Lambaréné

POP 24,000

'Everyone has his Lambaréné', Nobel Prize-winner Albert Schweitzer said. This, then, is his, with its glossy lakes, fast-flowing rivers, thick green foliage and ingrained sweetness. The town is somehow kinder and gentler than the rest of Gabon, as if the profound humanitarian efforts of Schweitzer ('the greatest man in the world' said *Life* magazine in 1947) changed the character of the land. And his legacy is indeed felt everywhere, from the wonderful, still-operational hospital (which Schweitzer founded in 1924 to treat people with leprosy) to the volunteer-staffed lab that researches malaria and other tropical diseases.

The town is divided into three areas spanning the river, quite close to each other. The area near the bank has the Schweitzer hospital grounds; across the bridge is the island with the main markets, the river port, and Le Tribune, from where shared taxis leave; across another bridge is the Quartier Isaac, where you'll find nightlife, restaurants and most hotels. Short taxi rides around town vary from CFA300 to CFA800 depending on how many bridge crossings you make.

Sights & Activities

At the **hospital museum** (admission CFA500; 8.30am-1pm & 1.30-5.30pm Mon-Fri, 9am-6pm Sat & Sun), housed in the former hospital building (it moved to the new, current premises in 1981), you can see photos, paintings and the impeccably arranged house and artefacts of Schweitzer and his wife on a guided tour. There's also a small zoo, the animals of which include descendents of Schweitzer's beloved pelican Parzival. You're also able to see the graves of Schweitzer, his wife and colleagues.

Explore the many **lakes** by *pirogue*, arranged at the port in town, through the Ogooué Palace hotel. A long boat trip will cost around CFA40,000 but can be split with many people.

Sleeping & Eating

Do be sure to book accommodation ahead at weekends, as Lambaréné is a very popular weekend retreat from Libreville and on a Friday and Saturday night everything is normally full.

★L'Hôtellerie de l'Hôpital Albert Schweitzer GUESTHOUSE $
(07 14 16 62; Hospital Grounds; r with fan/air-con CFA15,000/20,000;) Right next to the hospital museum and the river, this is by far the most atmospheric and interesting accommodation in town. Sleek and smart rooms are housed in what used to be the hospital staff's quarters, and as a nice touch in each there's the biography of the room's previous inhabitant. Meals are available if you order ahead.

Mission Soeurs de l'Immaculée Conception GUESTHOUSE $
(01 58 10 73, 04 10 84 53; dm/r per person CFA5000/CFA8000;) This place won't, in the words of Schweitzer, 'let your soul have no Sunday'. It's staffed by adorable nuns who make you feel as if you've been spirited into *The Sound of Music*. The grounds are gorgeous, there's a kitchen available for use, and the fan-cooled rooms are clean and have mozzie nets.

Banana's MOTEL $
(01 58 12 28; Quartier Isaac; r with fan/air-con CFA15,000/20,000;) If you're looking for a simple place in the Quartier Isaac to lay your head and fill your belly, Banana's might be your Lambaréné. Rooms are clean but verging on the basic. It's opposite the Cecado Building on the Quartier Isaac's main drag.

Hotel Ogooué Palace LUXURY HOTEL $$$
(07 16 28 02; r/ste CFA50,000/150,000; P) Reopened in 2012 after a full renovation, this is definitely the place to stay for a weekend of pampering. Set on the tip of the island, with fabulous river views, the Ogooué Palace has modern, smart rooms with dark wood furniture, flat-screen TVs and posh bed linen. All 54 rooms have terraces and the gardens are a delight.

At night fish and *brochette* stands line the streets in the bustling Quartier Isaac, or you can try the low-key **La Pléiade** (Quartier Isaac; mains CFA5000-9000; noon-3pm & 7pm-midnight), on Quartier Isaac's main road, which has an interesting menu and does a good *soupe de poissons*. Continue further up the main road of Quartier Isaac, away from the island, and you'll find **DTH Traiteur** (mains CFA5000-12,000; 10am-11pm), an unexpectedly good find of a place with elaborate table decorations and excellent food from classic steaks to *brochette* of oysters. If you don't fancy the walk, take a CFA100 taxi and ask for 'le commissariat'.

Getting There & Away

If you beat the Libreville traffic, you can be in Lambaréné in four hours in a shared taxi (around CFA7000). A place in a shared taxi to Ndjolé, from where you pick up the Transgabonaise railway, costs CFA6000 and takes about three hours. Shared taxis leave from a place known as 'Le Tribune' on the island, a short distance from the port and the bridge to Quartier Isaac.

Loango National Park

The conservationist Mike Fay called Loango 'Africa's last Eden'. Here, warm streams criss-cross pockets of thick forest and salty savannah, while vast island-dotted lagoons and miles of white-sand beach provide habitat for all manner of creatures. It's perhaps best known for its mythic surfing hippos, but you'll also find the largest concentration and variety of whales and dolphins in its waters, elephants wandering the beaches and an assortment of rare land mammals cavorting in the savannah. If your pockets can take it, Loango is one of the best wildlife-watching destinations on the planet. Sadly, there's trouble in paradise: in 2010 Africa's Eden, which invested millions in the network of luxury camps within the park, withdrew its Gabon operations, citing long-standing problems with Gabon's civil-aviation authorities who refused to renew the license for Africa's Eden's own airline. The operation is now under new management, and travelers now arrive by boat from Port-Gentil.

★ **Loango Lodge** LODGE $$$

(07 79 22 07; www.loango-safari.com; r per person with full board €325;) This impressively remote and high-end lodge is the only show in town if you want to visit the northern end of the Loango National Park. Centred around the luxury Loango Lodge, it has no less than four other beautifully appointed satellite camps elsewhere in the park, meaning that your experience never gets samey.

Camps include St Catherine's on the beach; Akaka Forest camp where animals roam; Evengue ('gorilla island'), where gorilla rehabilitation is underway; and Tassi, in the savannah and coastal grasslands. Activities include whale-watching trips, savannah and lagoon tours, multiple-day gorilla odysseys and visits to Mission Sainte Anne, where Gustave Eiffel's prefab iron church is still in use. Note that on top of the daily rate, there's a flat €300 per person transfer charge for getting you here from Port-Gentil and back.

SURFING HIPPOS

Though it hardly seems credible – a fantasy that belongs in the realm of children's novels, unicorns and flying carpets – Gabon's surfing hippos have been making waves around the world since their hobby was outed by conservationist Mike Fay in the 1990s. Unlike human surfers, the two-ton creatures are hardly a picture of grace as they frolic among the waves, but surf they do: wading into the ocean and opening their legs to catch the swell. Despite the hype, however, it's extremely unlikely you'll see hippos partaking – after all, their name comes from the Greek for 'river horse' and in general they prefer fresh water to seawater. Still, who can blame them for seeking a bit of extra excitement?

Gamba & Setté Cama

Loango National Park can be entered from its southern end, and while the experience won't be written up in *Condé Nast Traveller* any time soon, it's a far better deal than coming from the north, and the experience can certainly compare to if not always equal that of a luxurious safari based at Loango Lodge. Gamba is the oil-town transport hub, with flights to and from both Libreville and Port Gentil, while Setté Cama is the tiny hamlet with the incomparable location on a spit of land between miles of stunning beach and an enormous lagoon packed full of wildlife.

Setté Cama is accessible from Gamba either by boat or 4WD transfer (each lasting around an hour), which, in turn, is best reached with one of Allegiance Airways' three flights a week from Libreville (one hour, CFA85,000 one way). It's a good idea to set up your transfers and accommodation in advance, as getting stuck in Gamba isn't the best way to experience the wildlife. If you do get stuck, then the best place to stay is the **Conseil Départmental** (r CFA12,500), the government hotel.

In Setté Cama itself, there are currently two functioning hotels. A third, Missala Lodge, closed in 2011, but there are rumours that the site will be redeveloped into a luxury ecolodge sometime in the future. Setté Cama itself is just a collection of fishers' houses; there are no shops, so bring anything you need with you from Gamba.

★**Ch2O** LODGE $$$
(Setté Cama Safari; ☎04 78 32 60, 07 57 15 31; Setté Cama; per person all inclusive from CFA97,000; ❄) This smart collection of six bungalows overlooks the gorgeous lagoon at Setté Cama and is the village's most comfortable accommodation option. The chalets are spacious and smart, with wooden floors, private bathrooms and small terraces with lagoon views. The price includes transfers, meals in the restaurant and guiding fees as well, making this a very reasonable deal for the quality.

Case Abietu GUESTHOUSE $$
(☎07 68 48 28, 07 35 91 81; gambareservation@yahoo.fr; Setté Cama; r per person all-incl from CFA65,000) This guesthouse (also known as the Case de Passage) offers six simple but comfortable fan-cooled bedrooms, a lounge, and a delightful terrace overlooking the lagoon, while the Atlantic beaches are a two-minute walk away. Villagers prepare traditional meals and act as ecoguides in daily park excursions, and the initiative pours money back into the local community.

This is definitely the best Loango safari option for those on a budget. While prices may look steep, they include transfers, meals, guiding, accommodation, transport within the park and park entrance fees, and the cost drops off steeply as soon as there's more than one of you.

Mayumba National Park

Closer to Congo than to Libreville, Mayumba feels like the edge of the earth. No wonder expats whisper about it – the **national park** (www.mayumbanationalpark.com) is the domain of barnacled whales and shy sea turtles, and the land, if you listen to the locals, is hushed by the spirits of ancestors.

At the time of writing Mayumba's airstrip was still not receiving scheduled flights, despite a full revamp. Check on the ground if they've restarted, but to get here otherwise, take one of the twice-weekly flights with NRT from Libreville to Tchibanga (CFA65,000 one way) and then hop on a *taxi-brousse* to Mayumba (CFA7,000, three hours) leaving the next morning around 6.30am from the Gare Routière.

It is possible to travel overland the entire way, but it's an extremely long and exhausting journey. People travelling by *taxi-brousse* from Libreville often break up the long travel with a stopover in Tchibanga. The park's excellent website has many details about navigating the long journey there, and there's plenty of hotel choice too.

Mbidia Koukou HOTEL $
(☎07 31 13 02, 07 38 87 83; r CFA15,000; ❄) With sea views, a great beach, comfortable rooms and a full restaurant, this place makes for a good base that doesn't break the bank.

Motel Mayeye Foutou MOTEL $
(☎07 28 35 38; r with fan/air-con CFA8500/12,500; ❄) A cheaper, though less charming, bet is this central place which is owned by the mayor. Rooms are clean and fan-cooled, but little else.

Safari Club HOTEL $$
(☎07 71 06 91; r from CFA25,000; ❄📺) Having just been renovated, this Kenyan-style beach lodge by the lagoon edge has expansive gardens, charming chalets and plenty of space to relax in after a hard day's fishing or safari.

EASTERN GABON

Réserve de la Lopé

Smack bang on the equator, Gabon's calling card doesn't disappoint. Undulating hills meet scrubby patches of savannah and enclaves of rain forest where elephants, buffaloes, gorillas and some of the biggest mandrill troupes in the world can be found. There are vehicle and foot safaris (from CFA5000) on offer and there's an ecomuseum near the park entrance.

The train from Libreville takes between six and eight hours, depending on whether it's an express or not. Lopé Hotel vehicles meet the train, which often arrives in the middle of the night. It's best to book in advance as Lopé is a tiny one-horse town with little or no tourist infrastructure, and not a good place to be stranded.

Made up of 30 cottages of varying sizes, the **Lopé Hotel** (☎04 20 63 27; hotellope@yahoo.fr; r CFA52,000-95,500; ❄📺) has a superb position overlooking a dramatic bend of the Ogooué River surrounded by dramatic hills and thick woods. It's a fairly formal place, and feels quite touristy, being on nearly all Gabon visitors' itineraries, but the accommodation is comfortable and service friendly.

The rooms range from comforable (if rather cramped) quarters in the lowest categories to huge free-standing cottages with great views. The focus here is on activities in and around the national park, which is adjacent to the property. Activities include forest and savannah wildlife-watching, climbing Mt Brazza, river trips and hiking to see ancient stone engravings. However, with a pool and lovely gardens to wander in, you can also spend your time relaxing in the grounds. Food is pretty decent, though prices add up fast – the best deals are usually full-board ones with activities included. Enquire at the Lopé Hotel office in Libreville for what's being offered.

Motel E. Mbeyi HOTEL **$$**
(☎04 17 98 32, 07 47 18 18; r CFA25,300; ❄) This catchily named place is run by the same management as the Lopé Hotel, but it's worlds away in style and price. Just a short walk from the train station, the accommodation is made up of pink painted units with clean, modern bathrooms, wrought-iron beds and freshly painted walls. There's also a cute thatched dining area and ecotours available.

Case de Passage GUESTHOUSE **$**
(☎07 69 65 96; r CFA15,000) If you're really on a budget, then the Case de Passage, run by a ranger on the edge of the park, is the only option. Ecotours are available as well by joining the Lopé Hotel groups, which means that you'll still have to pay standard safari fees. Accommodation is basic but clean.

Ivindo National Park

Langoué Bai, in the dense, tropical 3000-sq-metre **Ivindo National Park** (www.ivindo.org), is perhaps the pièce de résistance of all the Gabonese ecodestinations, presenting the rare opportunity to view forest animals undisturbed in their own environment. The Bai, a local word for a marshy clearing in the forest, serves as a source of minerals for the animals and acts as a magnet for large numbers of forest elephants, western lowland gorillas, sitatungas, buffaloes, monkeys and rare bird species. A Wildlife Conservation Society–built research station and ecocamp near the clearing allow visitors to easily view the wildlife.

All-inclusive stays at the stunning, ecologically friendly base camp, designed to reduce human impact on the environment (composting toilets, solar energy, no chemicals), are US$315 per night – but worth it.

Arrangements to get to the Bai must be made well in advance through travel agents in Libreville.

Makokou & Kongou Falls

Gabon's answer to Niagara is the gushing falls at Kongou, and Makokou – the small capital of the Ogooué-Ivindo region – is the gateway to the falls. **Fondation Internationale Gabon Eco-tourisme** (Figet; ☎07 90 55 13, 06 06 82 47; www.trusttheforest.org), an excellent environmental organisation, organises camping trips into the rainforest and to the falls, *pirogue* excursions and a long list of other activities, all at fairly reasonable prices. You can also negotiate a bed for the night.

The budget way to get here from Libreville is to take the train to Booué and then a *taxi-brousse* to Makokou. NRT flights between Libreville and Makokou's airstrip go on Wednesday and Friday (CFA70,000 one way). It's possible to then go on to Congo via Mékambo if you have a visa, but the road is terrible. Ask around for a *taxi-brousse*.

Franceville & Around

POP 56,000

Birthplace of the late Omar Bongo (check out the statue of him in town), Gabon's third city, Franceville, is quite literally the end of the line, as the impressive Transgabonaise railway line terminates here. There's nothing much to see in the town itself, but it's a good jumping-off point for the amazing scenery around the stunning Batéké Plateau.

On the Poto-Poto roundabout, **Bien et Bien** (☎06 21 65 72; r CFA12,000) is, well, *bien*. If luxury's calling you, the top-notch **Poubara Hotel** (☎07 84 91 72; hotel_poubara@hotmail.com; r from CFA55,000; ❄) has more amenities than anyone would ever need, including a beautiful pool and a popular Sunday brunch. Also along the main drag are some great places to eat, namely 5ème Dimension and Au Bord de la Mer.

East of Franceville the savannah rises up into the **Batéké Plateau**, a dry, cool and flat stretch of land that extends south and east into Congo, encompassing the spectacular **Cirque de Léconi**, a deep, circular, red-rock canyon of loose sand. This is some of the most impressive landscape in the country and locals say spirits lie within. Also in the area (but harder to find) are some spectacular green-and-white canyons. After trips into the canyons, you can bathe in the endlessly clear L'Eau Claire at Abouyi village, just five minutes from Léconi towards Franceville.

It's best to hire a guide in Franceville to visit the plateau or the Cirque de Léconi. Ask about at the hotels. Alternatively there are infrequent *taxis-brousses* to Léconi from Franceville, but a 4WD is necessary to get to the cirque. It's possible to camp overnight if you have your own equipment.

UNDERSTAND GABON

Gabon Today

After the death of his father, Ali Ben Bongo won the 2009 presidential election with just 42% of the vote. The dynastic succession was secure even though riots spread through Port-Gentil as rumours flew that France had helped propel Bongo to power. Less than a year later Bongo grabbed the world media's attention when he was revealed to have purchased a €105 million residence in Paris – perhaps not the best way to endear himself to the population of Gabon, who while well off by African standards, still largely struggle to get by and live in one-room huts.

One of Ali Ben Bongo's first decisions as president was to downsize the government, reducing the ministerial count to 30. Though opinion was divided over the president when he first stepped into his father's shoes, in office he has become increasingly popular, largely due to a lack of credible opposition. The boulevards of Libreville are lined with life-size posters of the president – and populist pledges such as ones to double the minimum wage, build new social housing and back changes to the justice system have all kept Ali Bongo's popularity high. It remains to be seen whether Gabon's immense oil wealth will start to trickle down to the man or woman on the street.

History

Of Petroglyphs & People

Gabon has been inhabited for at least 400,000 years. Some 1200 rock paintings made by iron-working cultures that razed the forest for agriculture, creating today's savannah, have been found in the area around Réserve de la Lopé. The earliest modern society, the forest-dwelling tribes, was displaced between the 16th and 18th centuries by migrating peoples from the north, principally the Fang, who came after settling in what is now Cameroon and Equatorial Guinea.

Contact with Europeans, starting with the arrival of the Portuguese in 1472, had a profound effect on tribal structures. British, Dutch and French ships traded for slaves, ivory and tropical woods. The coastal tribes established strong ties with these colonial powers, but the interior tribes defended their lands against European encroachment. To this day, animosity still lingers between the coastal tribes and the rest of the country.

The capital, Libreville, was established in 1849 for freed slaves, on an estuary popular with traders. In 1885 the Berlin Conference of European powers recognised French rights in Gabon, which became part of the French Congo and later French Equatorial Africa. The country became self-governing in 1958, and won independence in 1960 under President Léon M'Ba. After M'Ba died in a French hospital in 1967, his vice president, Albert Bernard Bongo, took power of the nation (changing his name to Omar when he adopted Islam in 1974).

The Omar Bongo Years

The newly independent nation got off to an extravagant start. As money rolled in from the sale of timber, manganese ore, iron ore, chrome, gold, diamonds and, finally, oil, Gabon's per-capita income soared higher than South Africa's. Relations with France remained tight throughout Bongo's rule – 'Gabon without France is like a car with no driver. France without Gabon is like a car with no fuel,' he said of the relationship with the former colonial power.

In 1976 Bongo's government announced a four-year, US$32-billion plan to create a modern transport system, encourage local industry and develop mineral deposits. Few of these projects ever took shape. The government did, however, spend vast sums hosting a summit of the Organization of African Unity in 1977 and (conservative estimates say) US$250 million on the presidential palace.

In 1990, after the country's first real political unrest, Bongo ended more than two

THE 'CONSERVATION COUP'

In the late 1990s Mike Fay, of *National Geographic* and the Wildlife Conservation Society, walked more than 3200km through Central Africa, documenting the stunning natural environment he passed through. The late President Omar Bongo, after seeing the photos of what became known as the 'Megatransect', did the unthinkable: in 2002 he created a 13-park network of protected lands that covered 11% of the country. Overnight Gabon leapt from having almost no land conserved to having the most in the world. Hailed as a 'conservation coup', it was a wise move for Bongo, who was looking for new sources of revenue. Wildlife organisations and ecotourist outfits subsequently rushed in to set up camps in the parks to support the fledgling conservation economy. It's just one of the measures lined up by the late president to ease the impact of rapidly decreasing oil supplies. However, there's still a long way to go before Gabon is recognised as the next Kenya: several foreign investors in ecotourism in Gabon have subsequently cut their losses and withdrawn from the country, citing terrible infrastructure, corruption and bureaucracy as reasons it's difficult to run profitable operations here.

decades of one-party rule by legalising the opposition (though subsequent elections were marred by fraud). He died, at the age of 73, in a Spanish hospital in 2009, officially of a heart attack though it's widely believed that he was suffering from cancer. Gabon initially denied the death of the man it couldn't bear to see gone, but two days after the news leaked from Paris, it was confirmed by Libreville. At the funeral in Libreville, France's President Sarkozy was jeered at – many Gabonese felt the relationship with Paris had gone too far.

Culture

In the early oil days, Gabon's new rich knocked back the champagne like it was going out of fashion. Though there's still a hefty gap between the country's rich and poor, even in remote villages you won't find the kind of poverty seen in parts of Congo and Equatorial Guinea, Gabon's poorer neighbours. In the clubs of Libreville, you'll see Gabonese hot shots splashing the cash and acting like the oil is endless. Oil wealth has brought a fairly good education system to Gabon; the World Bank estimates that 95% of young women can read and write, a rarity in Central Africa. Still, infant disease and human trafficking are issues, especially in rural areas.

People

Of the people living in Gabon today, the original forest-dwelling tribes survive only in the remote north of the country, barely keeping their culture intact. Most other people are descendants of the Bantu peoples, and the Fang are still the most numerous. There is also a sizeable French expat community in Libreville and Port-Gentil.

Missionary influence is palpable; over 50% of the country counts itself as Christian, though traditional animist beliefs are still strong and beliefs in superstition and witchcraft hold great power over much of the Gabonese population. Interestingly, both Presidents Bongo converted to Islam in the 1970s, when African nationalism was all the rage and friendship with Qaddafi was seen as desirable. As a result there are several mosques prominently located in Libreville, despite the Muslim segment of society as a whole being very small.

Arts & Crafts

Traditional masks, carvings and bieri (ancestral sculpture) using natural materials such as wood, raffia and feathers are found throughout Gabon. However, they're rarely sold in the markets as they are still used in religious ceremonies and activities. (Though you will find these kinds of items from neighbouring countries in the markets.) Fang masks are prized throughout the world and sold for big bucks at art auctions.

Dancing is a national pastime, and recent dance crazes include the Ivorian *coupé-decalé*, and the L'Oriengo, which originated as a dance for people handicapped by polio. Traditional tribal dance is still widely practiced and can be seen at cultural villages.

Hip-hop is big in Gabon, and there are plenty of home-grown groups playing on the radio. You'll also find recordings of the sacred music of the Bwiti, which uses, among other extraordinary instruments, harps played with the mouth, as well as brilliant, inspiring tribal group recordings.

Food & Drink

If you don't like *fufu*, don't sweat. The heat-inducing cassava staple is a long-time favourite in Gabon, but the cuisine is just as heavy in other Central and West African staples, such as fried plantains and rice and fish dishes. Okra, spinach and palm oil are widely eaten here, and in a country coated with such thick forest, the lure of bushmeat – notably bush hogs, antelopes, primates (including chimpanzees and to a lesser extent gorillas) and crocodiles – has been hard to shake. Beer is the drink of choice – most common among those available is Castel.

Environment

Gabon is a country of astonishing landscapes and biodiversity, much of which is still undiscovered and unexploited. Though almost 75% of the country is covered in dense tropical rain forest, this equatorial country is also full of endless white-sand beaches, savannahs, rushing rivers, hidden lagoons, rocky plateaus and canyons, cloud-tipped mountains and *inselbergs*, all of which are home to an amazing array of flora and fauna.

You're likely to come across gorillas, chimpanzees, mandrills, forest elephants, buffaloes, crocodiles, antelopes, hippos, humpback and killer whales, monkeys of all shapes and sizes, leopards, red river hogs, sea turtles and a rainbow of rare birds – to name just a few.

SURVIVAL GUIDE

Directory A–Z

ACCOMMODATION

Gabon is no bargain destination, and hotels will take the biggest bite out of your budget. Most towns have cheap and basic convent hotels – they're generally your best bet if you're pinching pennies. In remote villages, if you greet the chief and bring a small gift you'll likely be welcome to stay in a hut. Libreville and any form of national-park accommodation tends to be universally very expensive by African standards – there are some good exceptions in both cases, and we've noted these when they exist, but don't count on being able to find them everywhere. Most safaris in Gabon will cost even more than their East African equivalents.

ACTIVITIES

Gabon really isn't set up for the independent traveller and even the most determined go-it-aloners will actually have an easier time and be able to do far more if tours through travel agencies in Libreville are booked. Waiting can be involved, flights infrequent and roads terrible (especially in the rainy season), so start early in making plans for trips out to the national parks.

EMBASSIES & CONSULATES

There is no British or Canadian embassy in Gabon. In an emergency contact the British or Canadian high commissions in Yaoundé (p265). Countries with diplomatic representation in Libreville include the following:

Cameroon Embassy (☎01 73 28 00; Face Université)

Congo Embassy (☎01 73 00 62; Batterie IV)

Equatorial Guinea Embassy (☎01 73 25 23; Haut Gué-Gué)

French Embassy (☎01 79 70 00; Au Bord de Mer)

German Embassy (☎01 76 01 88; Immeuble 'Les Frangipaniers')

Nigerian Embassy (☎01 73 22 03; Blvd Léon M'ba)

São Tomé & Príncipe Embassy (☎01 72 15 27; Au Bord de Mer)

South African Embassy (☎01 79 11 50; Immeuble des Arcades)

US Embassy (☎01 45 71 00; Au Bord de Mer)

EMERGENCIES

Ambulance (☎1300)

Fire (☎18)

Police (☎177)

MONEY

A word of warning – money seems to fall out of your pockets in Gabon, and to get anywhere or do pretty much anything you'll be spending it like nobody's business. Cash is king here, so bring plenty with you, and certainly take more than you need everywhere you go outside of Libreville, as you won't be able to get more cash outside the capital.

ATMs in Libreville will only work with Visa cards, and credit cards are only accepted at top-end hotels. There is a national change shortage so ask for small notes wherever possible. US dollars are the preferred currency for exchange, but euros are also easy to change. It's not generally possible to change other currencies at a decent rate in Gabon.

OPENING HOURS

Shops and businesses open early and close for siesta between noon or 1pm and 3pm. Most shops are closed on Sundays, with some banks opening Saturday mornings but not afternoons.

PUBLIC HOLIDAYS

As well as religious holidays, the following are the principal public holidays in Gabon:

New Year's Day 1 January
Renovation Day 12 March
Labour Day 1 May
Independence Day 17 August
All Saints' Day 1 November

SAFE TRAVEL

Treat Libreville like any big city with its fair share of crime. Police can hassle you, so always carry your passport or a copy (and a copy of your visa).

The dreaded *fourous* (tiny insects) will leave red splotches, but won't hurt until a few days into the forest when infernal itchiness ensues. Insect repellent is a must, and calamine lotion will ease the itchiness. The terrible roads, crazy drunk drivers and huge trucks carrying unsecured loads of old-growth forest are probably the biggest dangers in the country.

TELEPHONE

Mobile phones are used more widely than landlines, although coverage can be very patchy outside of Libreville. You can buy a SIM card for an unlocked GSM phone cheaply and quickly in Libreville and other towns, and recharge cards are available pretty much everywhere. All Gabonese numbers, mobile and landline, have eight digits. There are no area codes. Landlines nationwide begin with ☎01, while numbers beginning with anything else are mobiles. The country code for Gabon is ☎241.

TOURIST INFORMATION

Travel agencies and conservation organisations tend to have the most up-to-date information on various parts of the country. There is a tourist office (p527) in Libreville, but the staff's English and their ability to help are both pretty limited.

VISAS

Visas are required by all travellers and must be obtained before arrival; they are not available at the airport or at border crossings. Getting a visa for Gabon can be both difficult and expensive. From countries outside Africa it can cost more than US$100. Unless you're flying straight to Libreville from Europe, it may be best to apply for one at the Gabonese embassy in a nearby African country, where it only takes a couple of days and costs around US$50. Most Gabonese embassies in Europe require certified proof of accommodation for the first few nights of your trip, as well as a return or onward plane ticket.

At the **Directeur Genérale de la Documentation** (☎01 76 24 24; PK5, Libreville; ⏲8am-3pm Mon-Fri), formerly known as Sedoc, you can obtain visa extensions.

Visas for Onward Travel

It's possible to get the following visas for nearby African countries in Libreville:

Cameroon Same-day processing; CFA51,000.
Congo Takes 24 hours; 15-day visa CFA30,000; three-month visa CFA70,000. A hotel reservation is required.
DRC Takes 24 hours; CFA50,000; only issued to residents of Gabon.
Equatorial Guinea Takes 72 hours; CFA80,000; only issued to residents of Gabon or people with no EG embassy in their home country.
São Tomé & Príncipe Takes 48 hours; CFA13,000.

WOMEN TRAVELLERS

Equality is on the up in Gabon, and it's a very safe place for a lone woman to travel by African standards, though lone female travellers may still be viewed as a curiosity outside Libreville and its environs. Though passive in many areas of life, the Gabonese are generally much more active about seeking coupledom than most Europeans and Americans, so you can expect a few come-ons. Bring a photo of a fictitious husband (Johnny Depp will do) if you're concerned about unwelcome advances.

PRACTICALITIES

- **Electricity** 220v AC, 50Hz (European-style two-round-pin plugs).
- **Languages** French (official), Fang, Mbere, Sira and dozens of other Bantu languages.
- **Media** *L'Union* is one of the biggest national papers. Radio France International broadcasts at 104FM.
- **Weights & Measures** Gabon uses the metric system.

Getting There & Away

AIR

Libreville Airport (www.adlgabon.com) is the only international airport in Gabon. There is no national airline, but Air France, Royal Air Maroc, Lufthansa and South African Airways regularly connect Libreville to Paris, Casablanca, Frankfurt and Johannesburg respectively.

To neighbouring countries, there are regular flights to Abidjan (Côte d'Ivoire), Addis Ababa (Ethiopia), Brazzaville (Congo), Cotonou (Benin), Dacca (Senegal), Douala (Cameroon), Kigali (Rwanda), Lagos (Nigeria), Lomé (Togo), Malabo (Equatorial Guinea), Pointe Noire (Congo) and São Tomé (São Tomé & Príncipe).

LAND

Cameroon

Travellers to and from Cameroon cross at the Ntem River between Bitam (Gabon) and Ambam (Cameroon). From the town of Ebolowa in Cameroon there's a regular bus service to Yaoundé and Douala. Visas can be purchased at the border.

Congo

The main crossing to Congo is between Leconi (the official, but not geographical border – don't leave here without getting your exit stamp) and Oyo. There's no public transport along most of this route and few cargo trucks, so it can take several days and involve more than a few police checkpoints. There's another crossing at N'Dendé (Gabon) and Doussala (Congo), from where you head to Loubomo to connect with the Pointe-Noire–Brazzaville railway.

Equatorial Guinea

Crossings can be made at Cocobeach (Gabon) by *pirogue* to Cogo and Acalayong (Equatorial Guinea), and via Oyem and Bitam (Gabon) to either Mongomo or Ebebiyin (Equatorial Guinea). Taxis leave daily from all towns and the ride to Bata is around four hours with the new roads. You must have a visa before travelling.

SEA

SEM (☎ 01 77 31 41) plies the seas between Port Môle and São Tomé (one way from CFA60,000, two days). There are occasional cargo ships to and from Cotonou (Benin), São Tomé & Príncipe and Cameroon. Expect long, uncomfortable journeys and schedules that shift without warning. Ask for details at the Maritime Express office at Port Môle in Libreville.

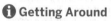

ℹ Getting Around

AIR

Air is by far the easiest way to move around in Gabon, as the roads are terrible, distances long and buses slow. However, flights aren't cheap or regular. Also be aware that it's perfectly common for flights to leave before their scheduled departure time, so take those two-hour check-ins seriously. Airlines flying internally in Gabon include Allegiance Airways (p527) and NRT (p527).

BOAT

There are passenger boats between Lambaréné and Port-Gentil (CFA13,000, about five hours) in both directions on Thursday and Sunday.

There are also three boats a week between Libreville and Port-Gentil (CFA15,000, 12 hours), and it's also possible to take cars on this (CFA120,000 to CFA180,000). Inquire at the **CNI** (Compagnie nationale de Navigation Intérieure et Internationale; ☎ 01 72 39 28, 07 07 39 45; Port Môle) office at Port Môle in Libreville.

CAR & MOTORCYCLE

Car hire is always more expensive than renting a vehicle with a driver, but **Europcar** (☎ 01 74 58 45), **Hertz** (☎ 01 73 20 11) and **Avis** (☎ 01 72 42 51) have offices at the airport. Driving in Gabon is perfectly feasible, but you'll need a 4WD and lots of patience in the rainy season.

TRAIN

Taking the Transgabonaise train line that crosses the country is a cheaper, faster and far more comfortable option than taking a *taxi-brousse*.

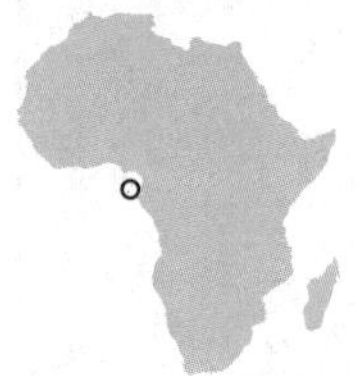

São Tomé & Príncipe

Includes ➡

Fast Facts

- **Capital** São Tomé
- **Population** 183,000
- **Languages** Portuguese, Portuguese-based Creole
- **Area** 1000 sq km
- **Visa requirements** Required by all
- **Tourist Information** www.saotomeislands.com

Beaches, Whales & Faded Colonial Splendour

If you adore quietude, take a trip to São Tomé & Príncipe, Africa's second-smallest country. These two tiny volcanic bumps anchored off the Gabonese coast easily win the hearts of foreigners with their Portuguese-Creole flavour and relaxed vibes, and it won't take too long before you're infected with the pervasive *leve leve* (which loosely means 'take it easy') mood.

The sublime laid-back tempo is enhanced by a wealth of natural attractions: miles of perfect palm-fringed beaches, huge swaths of emerald rain forest, soaring volcanic peaks and mellow fishing villages. The birdlife is excellent, and endemic plants (especially orchids) are plentiful. In season, turtle- and whale-watching opportunities abound.

This two-island nation has its cultural gems as well, with a surprising number of heritage buildings dating back to the colonial era, including impressive *roças* (plantation estates). Tourism is still low-key and is being developed in a carefully controlled, ecologically minded way. There are no tacky resorts, just a number of locally run, enticing, nature-oriented lodges and hotels.

São Tomé & Principe Top Sights

- **São Tomé town** Wander amid the faded colonial buildings of this charming capital town
- **Roça São João** Feast on gourmet eats and stay the night in this ethereal, rejuvenated plantation estate
- **Banana Beach** Dive into the crystal-clear waters of this deserted beach, one of many ringing the island of Príncipe
- **Praia Jalé** Witness the nesting sea turtles in this ecotourism haven, located at the southernmost point of São Tomé island
- **Ilhéu das Rolas** Straddle the equator and sun yourself on the divine white-sand beaches of this tiny islet off the south of São Tomé

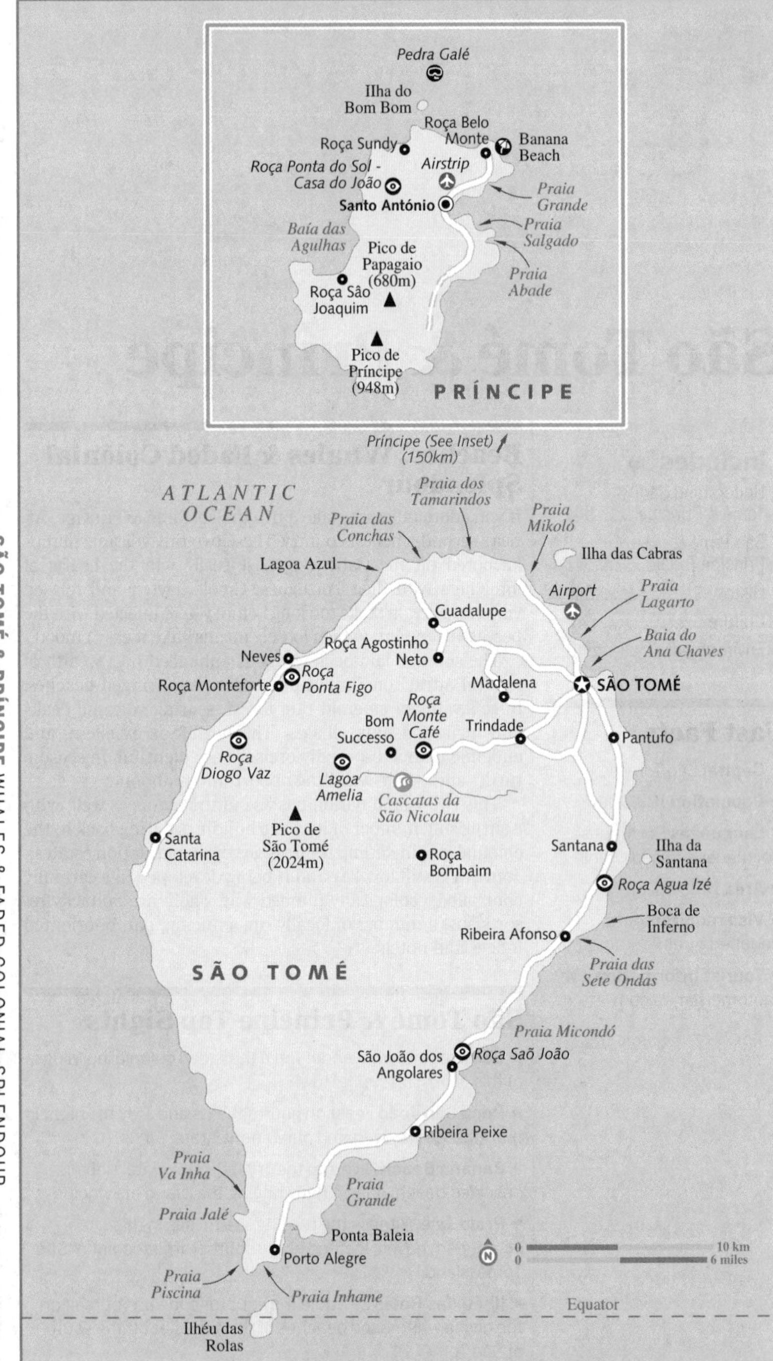
Pedra Galé
Ilha do Bom Bom
Roça Belo Monte
Banana Beach
Roça Sundy
Airstrip
Roça Ponta do Sol - Casa do João
Santo António
Praia Grande
Praia Salgado
Baía das Agulhas
Pico de Papagaio (680m)
Praia Abade
Roça São Joaquim
Pico de Príncipe (948m)
PRÍNCIPE
Príncipe (See Inset) (150km)
ATLANTIC OCEAN
Praia dos Tamarindos
Praia das Conchas
Praia Mikoló
Ilha das Cabras
Lagoa Azul
Airport
Praia Lagarto
Guadalupe
Baia do Ana Chaves
Roça Agostinho Neto
Neves
Roça Ponta Figo
Roça Monteforte
Madalena
SÃO TOMÉ
Roça Monte Café
Bom Successo
Trindade
Pantufo
Roça Diogo Vaz
Lagoa Amelia
Cascatas da São Nicolau
Santa Catarina
Pico de São Tomé (2024m)
Santana
Ilha da Santana
Roça Bombaim
Roça Agua Izé
Boca de Inferno
Ribeira Afonso
Praia das Sete Ondas
SÃO TOMÉ
Praia Micondó
Roça São João
São João dos Angolares
Ribeira Peixe
Praia Va Inha
Praia Grande
Praia Jalé
Ponta Baleia
Porto Alegre
0 10 km
0 6 miles
Praia Piscina
Praia Inhame
Equator
Ilhéu das Rolas

UNDERSTAND SÃO TOMÉ & PRINCIPE

São Tomé & Príncipe Today

Former strongman Manuel Pinto da Costa returned to power in presidential elections in 2011, two decades after losing office. Patrice Trovoada, the son of former president Miguel Trovada, was named prime minister after his Independent Democratic Action (ADI) party won parliamentary elections in August 2010.

History

Before being 'discovered' and colonised by the Portuguese during the late 15th century, the islands of São Tomé & Príncipe comprised rain forests dense with vegetation and birdlife, but, most likely, no people. The islands' volcanic soil proved good for cultivation, and, under Portuguese rule, by the mid-16th century the islands were the foremost sugar exporter, though the labour-intensive process required increasing numbers of slaves from Africa. When sugar prices fell and slave labour proved difficult to control, the islands increasingly looked towards the slave trade to bolster the economy, becoming an important weigh station for slave ships heading from Africa to Brazil. In the 19th century two new cash crops, coffee and cocoa, overtook the old sugar plantations. By the early 20th century São Tomé was one of the world's largest producer of cocoa.

In 1876 slavery was outlawed, but was simply replaced with a similar system of forced labour for low wages. Contract workers came from Mozambique, Cape Verde and other parts of the Portuguese empire. During these times there were frequent uprisings and revolts, often brutally ended by the Portuguese. In 1953 the Massacre of Batepá, in which many Africans were killed by Portuguese troops, sparked an independence movement in the country. Portugal held on, however, until the fall of its fascist government in 1974, after which it got out of its colonies in a hurry. São Tomé & Príncipe achieved independence on 12 July 1975, but the Portuguese exodus left the country with virtually no skilled labour, an illiteracy rate of 90%, only one doctor and many abandoned cocoa plantations.

Manuel Pinto da Costa ruled Sao Tome with an iron fist for 15 years after independence. The country remained aligned with Angola, Cuba and communist Eastern Europe until the demise of the Soviet Union, when São Toméans began demanding multiparty democracy. The first multiparty elections were held in early 1991, and led to the inauguration of the previously exiled Miguel Trovoada as the new president in April of that year.

Elections in 2001 brought Fradique de Menezes to power. De Menezes pledged to use revenues from increased tourism and exploitation of the country's newly discovered offshore oilfields to improve the standard of living and modernise the islands' infrastructure. Grand changes seemed imminent. But complications with extracting the oil, in addition to possible overestimations of the oil deposits, have delayed economic progress, and there is a palpable growing restlessness in the deeply indebted nation. A brief and bloodless coup attempt was peacefully resolved in 2003 while the president was out of the country. De Menezes was re-elected in 2006 in internationally observed, peaceful elections.

SÃO TOMÉ TOWN

São Tomé may be the country's economic, political and commercial hub, but rush hour in the capital lasts an unbearable five minutes! São Tomé town has a charming seafront setting, a budding arts scene, some excellent dining options, a collection of fading pastel colonial buildings and plenty of activities of its own and nearby, making it an ideal base from which to make day and overnight trips. **Cocoa Residence** (www.hotelcocoasaotome.st), in a tranquil setting not far from the seafront, is highly recommended.

COUNTRY COVERAGE

At the time of research very few travellers were heading to São Tomé & Príncipe so we're providing historical and cultural information rather than reviews and listings. A good source of information for on-the-ground travel in São Tomé & Príncipe is Lonely Planet's ThornTree online travel forum www.lonelyplanet.com/thorntree. Other sources of good internet-based information are www.saotome.st and www.africas-eden.com/Sao-Tome--Principe.asp.

GET ACTIVE IN SÃO TOMÉ

When it comes to activities, São Tomé really delivers.

➡ **Whale- and dolphin-watching** From July to September, don't miss the chance to snorkel with dolphins. The best spots include Ilha das Cabras and Lagoa Azul.

➡ **Birdwatching** São Tomé is a paradise for birdwatchers. It's home to 29 endemic species including the São Tomé sunbird and the elusive São Tomé Grosbeak.

➡ **Hiking** Northern São Tomé offers excellent hiking, from two-hour jaunts to a challenging two-day expedition to Pico de São Tomé, the island's highest point (2024m). Cross-island trips with overnights in plantation estates can be arranged through travel agents.

➡ **Diving** Just when you thought that nothing could be more beautiful than the primeval landscape, a trip below the ocean's surface reveals a scenic kingdom of plateaus and arches teeming with life. The owner of **Club Maxel** (☎904424; www.clubmaxel.st; Praia Lagarto) tells us that the best sites are around Ilha da Santana and Ilhéu das Rolas, where you'll find that the seascape is particularly dramatic. This reputable dive centre is staffed with qualified, English-speaking instructors. It's located on Praia Lagarto, but there's also an annexe at the Pestana Equador.

Culture

Leve leve is the name of the game in São Tomé. Island life is slow and there's no use in getting fussed about anything. This is as evident in daily life as it is in the islands' politics. During the 2006 elections, disruptions were rare. The few villages that protested did so by politely turning vote staff away from their polling stations, saying 'no water, no electricity, no votes, thank you'.

A recent influx of young repatriates from Portugal determined to make good happen here has brought a new energy to the islands.

Outside the capital most São Toméans still live simple island lives, with agriculture and fishing the main occupations. In the morning the boats come in and fish are distributed, the market bustles late morning, a siesta is taken to avoid the afternoon heat and then it's time to drink some imported boxes of *vinho*. In the evening people gather wherever there's a TV set and a generator, or a full deck of cards.

São Toméans are a mixed bunch of *mestiços*, mixed-blood descendants of Portuguese colonists and African slaves; Angolares, reputedly descendants of Angolan slaves who survived a 1540 shipwreck and now earn their livelihood fishing; Forros, descendants of freed slaves; Tongas, the children of *serviçais* (contract labourers from Angola, Mozambique and Cape Verde when slavery was 'abolished'); and Europeans, primarily Portuguese.

About 80% of São Toméans belong to the Roman Catholic Church, though traditional animist beliefs are still strong.

In addition to the traditional crafts of the island (including intricately carved wooden boxes, masks, and seed and shell jewellery), there is a budding arts scene drawing international attention revolving around the Teia D'Arte gallery, which has held several biennales and holds arts workshops.

When it comes to food, don't miss out on the *con-con*, fish grilled and served with baked breadfruit. Traditional stews, such as *calulu*, are made with more than 20 different plants and can take hours to prepare. Other dishes include fish or meat with beans, rice or plantains, and omelettes with endemic spices, some said to be aphrodisiacs. Palm wine, freshly gathered from the trees, is a local favourite.

Environment

The islands are of volcanic origin and almost 30% of the land is covered by high-altitude, virgin rain forest, referred to as the Obo, and filled with more than 700 species of flora and bird, some of which exist nowhere else in the world. In the interior are lakes, waterfalls and volcanic craters. Since São Tomé's forests were classified as the second most important in Africa in biological terms, they have received much attention, and conservation groups have started to set up protection programs and ecotourism outfits.

Outside the jungle the islands comprise varying beaches, including some nesting sea turtle grounds from October to December. Whales and dolphins can be observed from July to September.

East Africa

FRANCES LINZEE GORDON / GETTY IMAGES ©

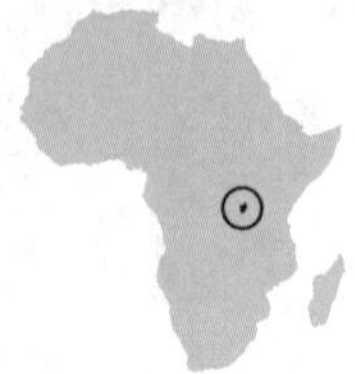

Burundi

POP 10.5 MILLION

Includes ➡

Best of Nature

- Saga Beach (p545)
- Chutes de la Karera (p549)
- Source du Nil (p549)

Best of Culture

- Les Tambourinaires drummers (p548)
- Bujumbura Central Market (p547)
- Musée National de Gitega (p549)

Why Go?

Tiny Burundi is an incongruous mix of soaring mountains, languid lakeside communities and a tragic past blighted by ethnic conflict.

When civil war broke out in 1993, the economy was shattered and the tourist industry succumbed to a quick death. Until now, many of the upcountry attractions, including the southernmost source of the Nile and waterfalls of Chutes de la Karera, had been off limits.

Now the word is out that the war is over, Burundi is receiving a trickle of travellers and the country is safer now than it has been for years. Its steamy capital, Bujumbura, has a lovely location on the shores of Lake Tanganyika, and just outside the city are some of the finest inland beaches on the continent. Burundians also have an irrepressible joie de vivre, and their smiles are as infectious as a rhythm laid down by a Les Tambourinaires drummer.

When to Go

Bujumbura

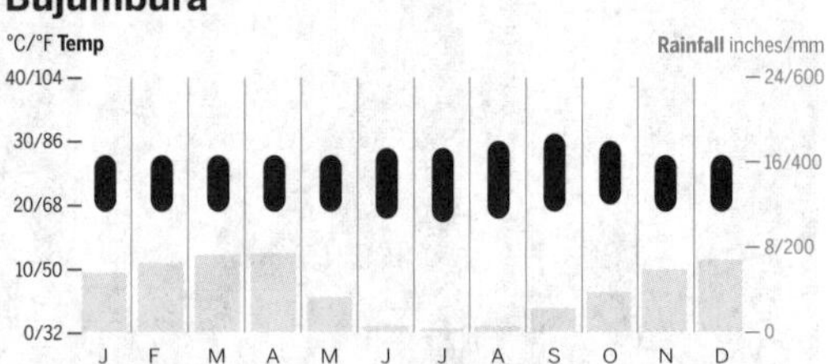

Year-round Altitude affects regional temperature. Bujumbura is warmer than elsewhere.

Oct–May Mild rainy season with a brief dry spell in December and January.

Jun & Aug Locals flock to Lake Tanganyika beaches during the 'long dry' season.

BUJUMBURA

POP 800,000

Burundi's capital has been frozen in time thanks to more than a decade of conflict; there has been almost no development since the 1980s, a stark contrast to the changes in Kigali (Rwanda) and Kampala (Uganda) to the north. Bujumbura retains much of its grandiose colonial town planning, with its wide boulevards and imposing public buildings, and continues to function as one of the most important ports on Lake Tanganyika.

'Buj' has earned a free-wheelin' reputation for its dining, drinking and dancing scene, but it isn't exactly the safest city in the region, so keep your wits about you, especially once the sun goes down.

Sights & Activities

★Saga Beach BEACH

(Plage des Cocotiers) Although it's got nothing on nearby Kenya and Tanzania, Burundi's inland beaches along the coast of Lake Tanganyika are white, powdery and surprisingly attractive. Saga Beach, which is the

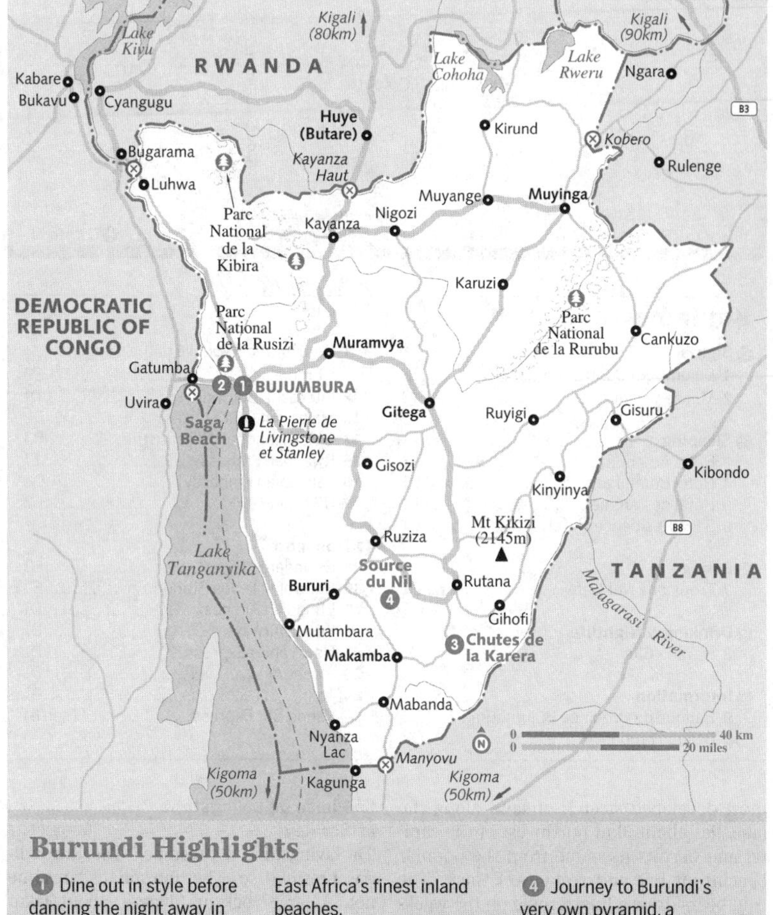

Burundi Highlights

1. Dine out in style before dancing the night away in **Bujumbura** (p545), where people love to live it up.
2. Throw down a towel on **Saga Beach** (p545), one of East Africa's finest inland beaches.
3. Take a cold shower under one of four waterfalls at **Chutes de la Karera** (p549).
4. Journey to Burundi's very own pyramid, a memorial marking a small stream in Kasumo, reputedly the southernmost **Source du Nil** (p549).

Bujumbura

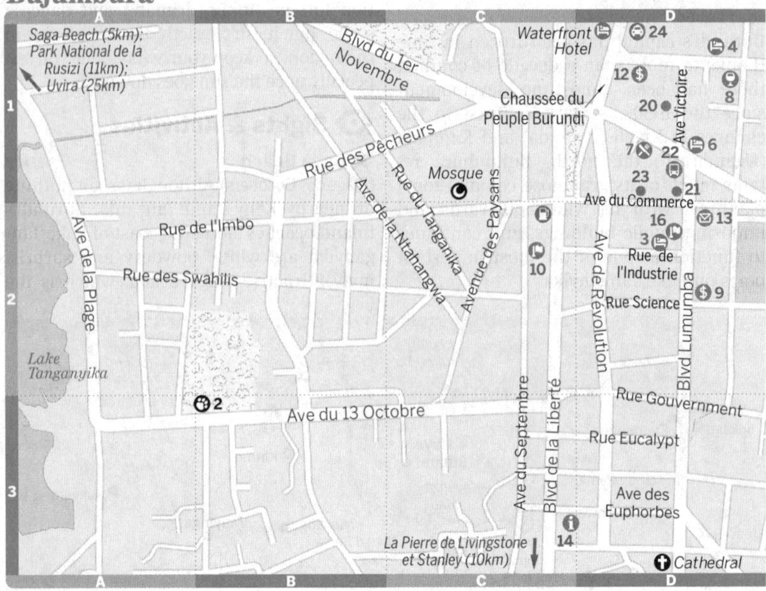

Bujumbura

Sights
1 Bujumbura Central Market....E2
2 Musée Vivant....B3

Sleeping
3 Hotel Amahoro....D2
4 Hotel Botanika....D1
5 Hôtel de l'Amitié....E1
6 Saga Residence Hotel....D1

Eating
7 Tropicana Net Cafe....D1

Drinking & Nightlife
8 Havana Club....D1

Information
9 Banque du Crédit de Bujumbura....D2
10 Belgian Embassy....C2
11 Democratic Republic of the Congo Embassy....E2
12 Interbank Burundi....D1
13 Main Post Office....D2
14 Office National du Tourisme....C3
15 Rwandan Embassy....E1
16 Tanzanian Embassy....D2
17 US Embassy....E2

Transport
18 Belvèdéré....E2
19 Central Ville bus Station....E2
20 Ethiopian Airlines....D1
21 Kenya Airways....D1
22 New Yahoo Express....D1
23 RwandAir....D1
24 Taxi....D1
Yahoo Car Express....(see 6)

most developed stretch of sand along the lake, lies about 5km northwest of the capital and derives its name from the popular beachfront bar and restaurant there. The cold beers draw a huge crowd on the weekends and the whole complex rocks on as a club by night.

La Pierre de Livingstone et Stanley HISTORIC SITE
'Dr Livingstone, I presume?' The Burundians presume so. The Tanzanians presume not. A large rock at Mugere, about 11km south of the capital, is alleged to mark the spot where the encounter between Livingstone and Stanley took place. Some graffiti

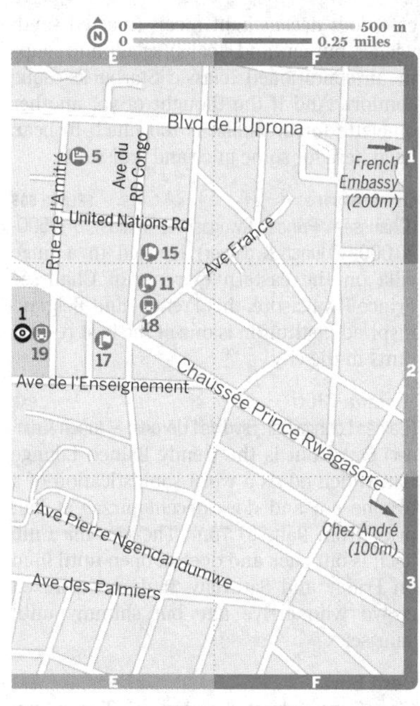

marks the date as 25 November 1871. Ujiji in Tanzania is the other contender.

Bujumbura Central Market MARKET
(Ave de l'Enseignement) This covered market is the largest in Burundi and is an interesting place to poke around in with its mazelike corridors and closet-sized stalls. The tiny fish that smell so bad when fresh are a local delicacy *(mukeke)* when dried.

Musée Vivant ZOO
(Ave du 13 Octobre; admission BFr5000; 7.30am-6.30pm) After years of neglect, this small zoo is attempting to regain the innovative 'living museum' reputation it enjoyed before things turned ugly during the civil war. We say 'attempting' because presently the animals are housed in fairly cramped and dirty cages.

Tours

Given the time restraints imposed by the three-day transit visa and lingering concerns over security, it can make sense to hire a local tour operator.

Burundi Access TOUR
(78283273; www.burundiaccess.com; Ave du Lac) is passionate about promoting Burundi to the world and can arrange everything from airport transfers to countrywide tours.

Sleeping

Hotel prices in Bujumbura shot up when the UN came to town and pickings are now slim at the budget end of the spectrum. If you have no pressing need to be in the city centre, consider staying at the beaches on Lake Tanganyika, 5km northwest of town.

Town Centre

★Hôtel de l'Amitié HOTEL $
(22226195; hotamitie@cbinf.com; Rue de l'Amitié; r incl breakfast US$25-50; P) One of the best budget places in town, particularly for couples as all rooms contain either twin or large double beds (although you will have to shell out for an additional breakfast). The free wi-fi and cheap(ish) laundry service are added bonuses, and thanks to a generator you'll still have power when the electricity cuts out.

Saga Residence Hotel HOTEL $
(22242225; Chaussée Prince Rwagasore; r US$25-45) Saga Residence is safe, secure and affordable with basic rooms in three price categories. Rooms have huge beds, cold-water showers and temperamental plumbing. The big drawback – at least for those trying to sleep – is the popular and extremely noisy bar.

Hotel Botanika BOUTIQUE HOTEL $$
(22226792; www.hotelbotanika.com; Blvd de l'Uprona; r incl breakfast US$90;) The seven-room Botanika is a charming retreat from the rigours of life in Burundi. The breakfast here is top-notch.

Hotel Amahoro HOTEL $$
(22247550; www.hotelamahoro.com; Rue de l'Industrie; s US$47, d & tw US$71-94, incl breakfast;

SET YOUR BUDGET

Budget
- Hotel room US$40
- Main meal US$4
- Local minibus US$0.20

Midrange
- Hotel room US$90
- Main meal US$7
- *Moto-taxi* (motorbike) US$1

Top End
- Hotel room US$200
- Main meal US$10
- Taxi US$3.50

LES TAMBOURINAIRES DRUMMERS

Les Tambourinaires du Burundi is the country's most famous troupe and has performed in cities such as Berlin and New York. Their recitals are a high-adrenalin mix of drumming and dancing that drowns the audience in waves of sound and movement. Unfortunately, without a national theatre or any other such venue, you'll have to be content with a smaller beachside performance or an impromptu practice session.

From around 4.30pm on Sunday, drummers run through a series of routines at Saga Beach. There is no charge but tips are appreciated and you'll be charged (BFr5000) if you take photos.

❄📶) One of the better midrange hotels in town, the Amahoro has established a name for itself as a comfortable, centrally located place to stay with a good range of amenities. More expensive rooms include air-con, but all have satellite TV, fridge and hot water in the bathroom.

Lake Tanganyika

Saga Beach Resort HOTEL **$$**
(☎75826514; sagaplage@yahoo.fr; r incl breakfast US$50-100; P❄📶) The Saga Beach Resort consists of the older Hotel Keza, which is set back from the beach with its block of comfortable if dated rooms, and the newer Hotel Urugo. Rooms here are right in the thick of the beach action and the only thing preventing beachgoers wandering onto your private deck is the stick fence that runs around the hotel complex. The bar and restaurant here are extremely popular on the weekends.

Hotel Club du Lac Tanganyika HOTEL **$$$**
(☎22250220; www.hotelclubdulac.com; s/d/ste US$160/200/250-450, incl breakfast; P❄📶🏊) Occupying a slice of prime lakeside real estate, the Hotel Club du Lac Tanganyika creates an excellent, resort-style ambience in a country where you'd least expect it. Its huge swimming pool (nonguests BFr6000) is its greatest draw.

Eating & Drinking

Tropicana Net Cafe AMERICAN **$**
(Chaussée Prince Rwagasore; mains BFr5000-9000; ⏲breakfast, lunch & dinner) This trendy internet cafe does decent light meals (toasted sandwiches, burgers and steaks), salads and soups in air-conditioned, classic Starbucks-esque comfort. And if the thought of yet another omelette for breakfast is too much to bear, head here for some juice and croissants.

Chez André FRENCH **$$$**
(Chaussée Prince Rwagasore; mains BFr7500-20,000; ⏲lunch & dinner) Housed in a huge villa on the eastern extreme of Chaussée Prince Rwagasore, this French- and Belgian-inspired institution is one of the best restaurants in the city.

Havana Club BAR
(Balneo Lounge Bar; Blvd de l'Uprona; ⏲lunch & dinner) Out front is the trendy Balneo Lounge Bar, which oozes a worn sophistication of a bygone era and does decent pizzas at half price from 9am to 7pm. The Havana Club itself is out back and doesn't open until 9pm on Friday and Saturday. It draws a mixed crowd who arrive late but shimmy until sunrise.

Bora Bora BAR
(Saga Plage; ⏲lunch & dinner; 📶) The white-washed weatherboards, palm-studded beach, blue-and-white nautical-inspired decor and a huge terrace-fronted villa make this the most popular of all the beachside bars with the expat community. The big draw here is the free pool and the chilled Caribbean vibe. On Saturday and Sunday nights the laid-back reggae and Cuban jazz give way to a mix of African and Western house and pop spun by a local DJ.

Information

DANGERS & ANNOYANCES

It is generally safe to wander about on foot during the day, though the streets empty at night – take a taxi once the sun goes down. The character of the city changes around 8pm, as *'les petits bandits'* move in. Street crime is prevalent in Bujumbura, and foreigners are especially vulnerable given their perceived wealth.

EMERGENCY

The official emergency number for police is ☎17, though it's unlikely anyone will answer should you call. It's best to make contact with your embassy in the event of an emergency.

INTERNET ACCESS

Internet cafes are plentiful within the city centre and cost between BFr10 and BFr40 per minute; many cafes offer free wi-fi.

MEDICAL SERVICES

In the event of a medical emergency, it is best to get out of the country to somewhere with better medical facilities, like Nairobi.

MONEY

Banque du Crédit de Bujumbura (Rue Science) Offers credit-card cash advances

Interbank Burundi (Blvd de l'Uprona) Offers credit-card cash advances and has an ATM that will accept foreign Visa and MasterCard. It can also arrange Western Union money transfers.

POST

Main post office (cnr Blvd Lumumba & Ave du Commerce; ⌚8am-noon & 2-4pm Mon-Fri, 8-11am Sat)

TOURIST INFORMATION

Office National du Tourisme (☎22224208; Ave des Euphorbes; ⌚7.30am-noon & 2-4pm Mon-Fri) Not many tourists in Burundi equals not much information in the tourist office.

Getting There & Away

International buses and minibuses leave from the Siyoni bus station at the Buyenzi Market, which is 2km north of the city centre, while those bound for Gitega leave from the Gare du North bus station, which is 5km north of the city centre.

Getting Around

Taxi fares range from BFr1000 for short hops in the centre to BFr5000 out to the beaches. Mototaxis (BFr1500) will also get you to the beaches if you're not scared of Bujumbura's racing traffic.

Minibuses to Gatumba can drop you off at Saga Beach and charge BFr300. These, along with minibuses to all places around Bujumbura (including out to Siyoni and Gare du North bus stations), can be caught at the **Central Ville bus station** at Bujumbura's Central Market.

AROUND BUJUMBURA

As Burundi is so small, it is feasible (some would say, advisable) to visit these sights during the day and return to Bujumbura before nightfall.

Gitega

Gitega is the second-largest town in Burundi and home to the **Musée National de Gitega** (☎402359; admission BFr3000; ⌚7.30am-3.30pm, closed Sat) which, although unlikely to enthrall you, is the best museum Burundi has to offer. The one-room hall has a dusty collection of traditional household items and musical instruments.

Minibuses (BFr5000) and shared taxis (BFr7000) from Bujumbura's Gare du North bus station make the run to Gitega throughout the day (two hours). Once in Gitega, the museum is a short walk or BFr500 bicycle-taxi hop out of town.

Chutes de la Karera

The **Chutes de la Karera** (admission incl guide BFr5000, vehicle BFr1000) is the collective name for the four beautiful waterfalls near Rutana. The prettiest is the cascade where you park your car. As you would expect, the falls are at their best during the wet season. They are 64km south of Gitega, but as there's no public transport, you'll have to charter a vehicle in Bujumbura to get here.

Source du Nil

This insignificant-looking little spring, 115km southeast of Bujumbura, high up on the slopes of Mt Kikizi (2145m), is supposedly the southernmost source of the Nile. The Ugandans dispute this, claiming the source as Jinja – where the Nile flows out of Lake Victoria. In Burundi the **Source du Nil** (Source of the Nile; admission BFr5000) is no more than a trickle and is marked by a small stone pyramid. You will need to arrange your own transport with a Bujumbura tour operator to get here.

UNDERSTAND BURUNDI

Burundi Today

Burundi remains one of the poorest countries in the world and according to the United Nations Development Programme, 84.5% of the population live in extreme poverty without adequate access to fresh water, medical care and electricity. Poor education, systemic corruption, a shaky economy and a soaring HIV/AIDs infection rates mean many face daily hardships in one form or another.

Since the 2010 elections, the political situation in Burundi remains tense. There have been no official talks between the government and opposition parties including the Hutu-led National Liberation Forces (NLF) who have since gone underground. In late 2012, the Murundi People's Front (FPM-

Abatabazi) became the sixth significant rebel group to launch an attack on government forces when armed insurgents crossed into Burundi from Democratic Republic of Congo (DRC; formerly Zaire), attacking soldiers and police in three northern communities.

However, beyond the disputed 2010 presidential elections, there is little common ideology to unite the various rebel groups and without unity it is questionable if any one rebel group can bring about meaningful political change. What remains to be seen is whether the regions' general volatility and current political impasse has the power to reverse the last decade's progress and push the country back into civil war.

History

A Fragile Independence

Burundi, like Rwanda, was colonised first by Germany and then Belgium, and as they did in its northern neighbour, the Europeans played on ethnic differences to divide and conquer the population. Power was traditionally concentrated in the hands of the minority Tutsi, though Hutus began to challenge this following independence in 1962. In the 1964 elections Tutsi leader Mwami Mwambutsa refused to appoint a Hutu prime minister, although Hutu candidates attracted the majority of votes. Hutu frustration soon boiled over, and Hutu military officers and political figures staged an attempted coup. Although it failed, Mwambutsa was exiled to Switzerland and was replaced by a Tutsi military junta.

A wholesale purge of Hutu from the army and bureaucracy followed, and in 1972 another large-scale Hutu revolt resulted in more than 1000 Tutsi being killed. The Tutsi military junta responded with the selective genocide of elite Hutu; after just three months, 200,000 Hutu had been killed and another 100,000 had fled into neighbouring countries.

In 1976 Jean-Baptiste Bagaza came to power in a bloodless coup, and three years later he formed the Union pour le Progrès National (Uprona). His so-called democratisation program was largely considered to be a failure, and in 1987 his cousin Major Pierre Buyoya toppled him in another coup.

The new regime attempted to address the causes of intertribal tensions by gradually bringing Hutu representatives back into positions of power. However, there was a renewed outbreak of ethnic violence in northern Burundi during the summer of 1988; thousands were massacred and many more fled into neighbouring Rwanda.

A Bloody Civil War

Buyoya finally bowed to international pressure, and multiparty elections were held in June 1993. These brought a Hutu-dominated government to power, led by Melchior Ndadaye, himself a Hutu. However, a dissident army faction, led by a Tutsi, Colonel Sylvestre Ningaba, staged yet another coup in late October the same year, and assassinated president Ndadaye. The coup eventually failed, though thousands were massacred, and almost half a million refugees fled across the border into Rwanda.

In April 1994 Cyprien Ntaryamira, the new Hutu president, was killed in the same plane crash that killed Rwanda's president and ignited the subsequent genocide over there. In Burundi, Sylvestre Ntibantunganya was immediately appointed interim president, though both Hutu militias and the Tutsi-dominated army went on the offensive. No war was actually declared, but at least 100,000 people were killed in clashes between mid-1994 and mid-1996.

In July 1996 former president Major Pierre Buyoya again carried out a successful coup, and took over as the country's president with the support of the army. However, fighting continued between Hutu rebels and the Tutsi-dominated government and Tutsi militia. Hundreds of thousands of political opponents, mostly Hutus, were herded into 'regroupment camps', and bombings, murders and other horrific activities continued throughout the country.

A Fragile Peace

At the end of 2002, the Forces for the Defence of Democracy (FDD), the largest rebel group, signed a peace deal. In April 2003 prominent Hutu Domitien Ndayizeye succeeded Buyoya as president, and a road map to elections was hammered out.

In 2004 the UN began operations in Burundi, sending more than 5000 troops to enforce the peace. Parliamentary elections were successfully held in 2005, and the former rebels, the FDD, emerged victorious. Pierre Nkurunziza, leader of the FDD, was sworn in as president in August. The 2010 elections were marred by violence and allegations of fraud and corruption. Despite international observers recognising the local elections as mainly free and fair, a growing mistrust of the incumbent's commitments to democracy saw all opposition withdraw their candidacy and Nkurunziza was re-elected unopposed.

As of 2011, the situation remains tense. Since the elections, there have been no official talks between the government and opposition parties including the Hutu-led National Liberation Forces (NLF) who have since gone underground. What remains to be seen is whether this political impasse has the power to reverse the last decade's progress and push the country back into chaos.

Culture

Burundi's population comprises 84% Hutu, 15% Tutsi and 1% Twa. Although the stormy relations between Hutu and Tutsi dominate the headlines, it is the Twa who have had the roughest deal, with their forests stripped by successive outsiders.

Burundi is more francophone than any other country in the region, and city dwellers take their siestas seriously. Out in the countryside, most of the people are engaged in farming. Coffee and tea are the main export crops.

Ivan Goldschmidt's *Na Wewe* (You Too), a gripping account of Burundi's bloody civil war, received a 2011 Academy Award nomination for best live action short film.

Economy

The UN's 2010 *Human Development Report* listed Burundi as the fourth-poorest country in the world. Civil wars, corruption, landlocked geography, poor education, AIDS and a lack of economic freedom have all but economically crippled the country and today it is largely dependent on foreign aid.

Burundi's largest industry is agriculture and its largest source of revenue is coffee.

Environment

Rwanda may be the 'land of a thousand hills', but Burundi isn't far behind. The north is a stunning landscape of dramatic peaks and deep valleys, best experienced on the bus between Bujumbura and Kigali (Rwanda). Many of the mountains are carved with gravity-defying terraces that plunge into deep valleys below, where farmers somehow eke out a living from the land. To the southwest, it levels out along the shores of lovely Lake Tanganyika. The capital, Bujumbura, is on the northern tip of this vast lake. Sadly, however, Burundi's tourist infrastructure is in tatters after the long war, and most of the national parks have been closed for more than a decade. Parc National de la Rusizi, just 15km north of Bujumbura, is the most accessible and the only one currently open.

SURVIVAL GUIDE

Directory A–Z

ACCOMMODATION

The choice of accommodation is reasonable in Bujumbura, but tends to be skewed upmarket due to the large foreign presence. Elsewhere in the country accommodation is fairly limited.

EMBASSIES & CONSULATES

Foreign embassies in Bujumbura include the following:

Belgian Embassy (☎22226781; www.diplomatie.be/bujumbura; Blvd de la Liberté)

DRC Embassy (☎22226916; Ave du RD Congo)

French Embassy (☎22222854; 60 Blvd de l'Uprona)

Rwandan Embassy (☎22226865; Ave du RD Congo)

Tanzanian Embassy (☎248636; Blvd Lumumba)

US Embassy (☎223454; Chaussée Prince Rwagasore)

FOOD

Brochettes (kebabs) and *frites* (fries) are a legacy of the Belgian colonial period, but there is also succulent fish from Lake Tanganyika and serious steaks. When it comes to drink, Burundi is blessed with a national brewery churning out

PRACTICALITIES

- **Electricity** 240V, 50 cycles and plugs are two-round-pin European variety.
- **Language** Kirundi and French are the official languages, with Swahili widely spoken along Lake Tanganyika.
- **Newspapers** The local press includes French-language *Le Renouveau*.
- **Radio** Government-controlled radio Burundi broadcasts in Kirundi, French, Swahili and English.

SATURDAY COMMUNITY WORK

From 8am to 10am every Saturday the country comes to a grinding halt. The reason? *Ibikorwa rusangi* – a time for obligatory community work. During these hours the populace is required to lend a hand on community projects for the greater good of their country. Shops, taxis, buses and restaurants are closed, and trash is gathered, grass cut and drains dug. One of the few exceptions is the international buses that have special dispensation to operate.

huge bottles of Primus, and coffee is the country's leading export.

MONEY

The unit of currency is the Burundi franc (BFr). Interbank in Bujumbura has an ATM (Visa and MasterCard) on the international network and cash advances on credit cards are possible at other major banks.There's an open black market in Bujumbura for changing money and you will find plenty of currency exchange bureaus (forex bureaus) around the Central Market and along Chaussée Prince Rwagasore. Travellers cheques are next to useless here.

OPENING HOURS

Businesses tend to open between 8.30am and 5.30pm Monday to Friday but close for a couple of hours at lunch. Some will also open on Saturday morning. Most eateries are open from 7am to about 9pm.

PUBLIC HOLIDAYS

Unity Day 5 February
Labour Day 1 May
Independence Day 1 July
Assumption 15 August
Victory of Uprona Day 18 September
Anniversary of Rwagasore's Assassination 13 October
Anniversary of Ndadaye's Assassination 21 October
All Saints' Day 1 November

SAFE TRAVEL

Burundi's civil war has ended, but the country is still far from stable. Consider restricting your visit to Bujumbura and making day trips from there to the countryside. The capital is safe by day though the streets empty at night – it is imperative to use a taxi or private vehicle once the sun goes down.

TELEPHONE

There are no telephone area codes within the country. The country code for Burundi is ☎257.

VISAS

One-month tourist visas cost US$90 and are available on arrival at the international airport in Bujumbura. For those arriving overland who haven't obtained a visa from an embassy elsewhere, your only option is to get a three-day transit visa (US$40) at the border and have it extended in Bujumbura.

Visa Extensions

Visa extensions are issued at the **Bureau de l'immigration** (near Police de l'Air et Frontières, Ngagara; ⊙7.30am-noon & 2-4pm Mon-Fri). Besides your passport, you need a photocopy of your passport ID page and the page containing your border-entry stamp, a passport-sized photo and US$70. If you apply for a visa extension in the morning, you can collect your passport that afternoon.

Visas for Onward Travel

Visas for Rwanda are issued at the border provided you have completed the online registration process. Visas for Tanzania can be issued to most nationalities at the border or obtained from the Tanzanian embassy in Bujumbura. Without a visa issued by the DRC embassy from *your* country of residence, it is next to impossible to cross into DRC from Burundi.

Getting There & Away

AIR

Bujumbura International Airport (BJM) is located about 12km north of the city centre. Thanks to the protracted war, very few international airlines still serve Burundi, and Air Burundi itself, the national airline, has suspended operations and now functions only as a travel agency.

Air Uganda (U7; www.air-uganda.com)
Ethiopian Airlines (ET; www.ethiopianairlines.com)
Kenya Airways (KQ; www.kenya-airways.com; Blvd Lumumba)
RwandAir (WB; www.rwandair.com; Ave du Commerce)

LAND

Burundi shares land borders with DRC, Rwanda and Tanzania.

Democratic Republic of Congo

The main crossing between Burundi and DRC is at Gatumba on the road between Bujumbura and Uvira (DRC), about 15km west of the capital. Unfortunately, this crossing is risky and the areas south of Bukavu are prone to lawlessness.

Rwanda

The main crossing point is between Kayanza (Burundi) and Huye (also known as Butare; Rwanda) on the main road linking Bujumbura and Kigali. The safest and quickest option for travel between Bujumbura and Kigali is to use one of the scheduled bus services (six hours, BFr12,000), which pass through Huye (four hours, BFr10,000). All buses depart at 7am and 10am daily from the Siyoni bus station, although some have booking offices in the centre of town.

An alternative route would be to travel to Cyangugu at the southern tip of Lake Kivu in Rwanda. This would involve a series of minibuses and shared taxis via Rugombo to the Luhwa border from where you reach Cyangugu via Bugarama and Kamembe.

Belvèderé (booking office Ave France)

Horizon Coaches

Kampala Coach

New Yahoo Express (booking office Chaussée Prince Rwagasore)

Yahoo Car Express (booking office Chaussée Prince Rwagasore)

Tanzania

For Kobero, the trip is done in stages via Ngara (Tanzania). There are daily buses between Mwanza (Tanzania) and Ngara, from where there is onward transport to the border. From Kigoma (Tanzania), take a bus to Nyakanazi (Tanzania) and get onward transport to Ngara from there.

For the Manyovu crossing: *dalla-dalla* (pick-up trucks or minibuses) leave Kigoma from behind Bero petrol station (BFr10,000, five hours). Once through the Tanzanian side of the border, you'll need to take one of the many waiting vehicles on to Makamba, where the Burundian immigration post is located. From there get another vehicle on to Bujumbura.

ℹ Getting Around

AIR

There are no internal domestic flights in Burundi.

ROAD

Travelling around the countryside is not as dangerous as it once was, though things change quickly in this part of the world.

Most major roads in Burundi are sealed and public transport is mainly by minibus. Destinations are displayed in the front window of minibuses, which depart when full. They depart throughout the day from the *gare routière* (bus station) in any town.

Djibouti

POP 906,000

Includes ➡

Best Places to Eat

- Restaurant-Café de la Gare (p559)
- Restaurant Saba (p559)
- Mukbassa Central – Chez Youssouf (p559)

Best Places to Stay

- Le Héron Auberge (p558)
- Sheraton Djibouti Hotel (p559)
- Campement Touristique d'Asboley (p561)
- Campement Touristique de Bankoualé (p562)
- Plage des Sables Blancs Campement (p563)

Why Go?

This tiny speck of a country packs a big punch. What it lacks in size, it more than makes up for in beauty, especially if you're a fan of geological oddities. Few countries in the world, with the possible exception of Iceland, offer such weird landscapes – think salt lakes, extinct volcanoes, sunken plains, limestone chimneys belching out puffs of steam, basaltic plateaus and majestic canyons. Outdoor adventure comes in many forms, with superb hiking, diving and kitesurfing – not to mention snorkelling alongside whale sharks in the Gulf of Tadjoura.

Barring Djibouti City, the country is refreshingly void of large-scale development. It's all about ecotravel, with some great sustainable stays in the hinterland that provide a fascinating glimpse into rural life.

Travelling independently around Djibouti may not come cheap, but despite the high cost of living you'll surely leave this little corner of Africa with new experiences and wonderful memories.

When to Go

Djibouti City

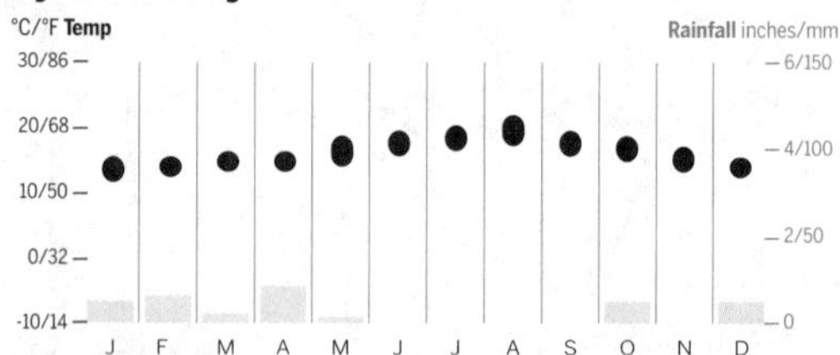

May–Sep You'll swelter under average daily temperatures of about 40°C.

Oct & Feb–Apr The shoulder seasons are not a bad time to visit, especially in the Goda Mountains.

Nov–Jan Ideal time to visit. Perfect for outdoor activities. Whale sharks make their annual appearance.

DJIBOUTI CITY

POP 600,000

Djibouti City is evolving at a fast pace, and there's a palpable sense of change in the air. Today's forward-looking city is vastly different from the battered French outpost to which it was reduced in the 1980s and 1990s. Yet under its veneer of urban bustle, the city remains a down-to-earth place, with jarring cultural and social combinations. Traditionally robed Afar tribesmen, stalwart GIs, sensuous Somali ladies and frazzled businessmen with the latest mobile phones stuck to their ears all jostle side by side.

Djibouti City boasts good infrastructure, including hotels, bars, clubs and restaurants.

Sights

Djibouti City is big on atmosphere but short on sights. The European Quarter, with its whitewashed houses and Moorish arcades, is a strange mix of Arab and European. To

Djibouti Highlights

1. Catch local vibes while wandering through the animated streets of **Djibouti City** (p555).
2. Dive or snorkel around **Moucha Island** (p560).
3. Get up close and personal with (harmless) **whale sharks** (p557).
4. Unwind on picture-perfect **Plage des Sables Blancs** (p563).
5. Descend to the lowest point on the African continent, 150m below sea level, at **Lac Assal** (p561).
6. Wander flabbergasted in a Martian landscape at **Lac Abbé** (p561).

the south lies the shambolic Pl Mahmoud Harbi (Pl Rimbaud), dominated by the minaret of the great Hamoudi mosque, Djibouti City's most prominent building.

The **cathedral** (Map p556; Blvd de la République) and the diminutive **Orthodox Church** (Église Éthiopienne Orthodoxe Tewahido St Gabriel du Soleil; Map p556) west of Blvd de la République, are also well worth a look.

The only decent beach is at the Kempinski, but there's an entrance fee of DFr3000 for nonguests.

Djibouti City

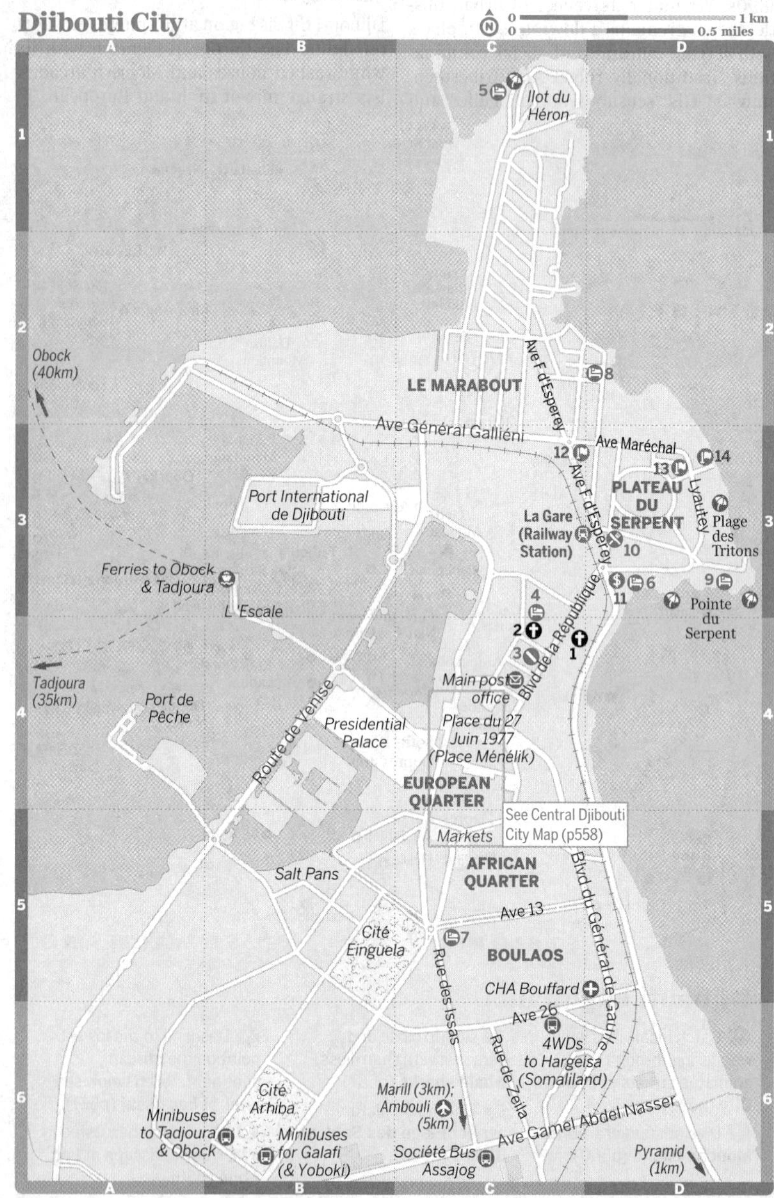

Activities

Diving

Most diving takes place off the islands of Maskali and Moucha in the Gulf of Tadjoura, which rewards divers with a host of scenic sites for all levels. Wreck enthusiasts will be spoiled, with a handful of atmospheric shipwrecks. Some excellent reef dives also beckon.

The weak point is the low visibility, which seldom exceeds 10m to 15m. Djibouti is diveable year-round but the best season for diving is from November to March.

You'll find two professional dive centres in Djibouti City, staffed with qualified instructors who speak English.

Dolphin DIVING

(Map p556; ☎21350313, 77825318; www.dolphin-services.com; Blvd de la République) Offers introductory dives, day trips to Moucha Island and the Bay of Ghoubbet (from DFr17,700), snorkelling trips and certification courses.

Le Lagon Bleu DIVING

(☎21250296, 21325555; www.djiboutidivers.com; Djibouti Palace Kempinski; ⏲closed Aug) The main office is based at Djibouti Palace Kempinski but the dive centre is on Moucha Island.

Whale Shark–Spotting

Snorkelling with whale sharks is possible in the Bay of Ghoubbet, at the western end of the Gulf of Tadjoura, from November to January. This spot is one of only a few places in the world where these giant yet gentle creatures appear regularly in near-shore waters, easily accessible to observers

This activity has exploded in recent years. Stick to Le Lagon Bleu or Dolphin; these two operators are more ecologically sensitive and follow protocols. Give the sharks a berth of at least 4m.

A full-day excursion costs from DFr14,000.

Kitesurfing

The combination of constant strong breezes, protected areas with calm water conditions and a lack of obstacles make Djibouti a world-class destination for kitesurfers. In the Bay of Ghoubbet, winds can reach 35 knots and blow about 300 days a year. For beginners, Île de la Tortue, near the international airport, is a hot favourite, with shallow waters and more manageable breezes.

Djibouti Kitesurf KITESURFING

(☎77828614, 21357233; www.djiboutikitesurf.com) Run by friendly Dante Kourallos, this outfit can arrange tuition and courses for

SET YOUR BUDGET

Budget

- Hotel room CFA10,000
- Sandwich CFA600
- Fruit juice CFA400
- *Moto-taxi* ride CFA300

Midrange

- Hotel room CFA20,000
- Two-course dinner CFA4000
- Drink in a bar CFA1000
- Intercity bus ride CFA7000

Top End

- Hotel room CFA40,000
- Two-course meal CFA10,000
- Cocktail CFA2000
- Four-wheel drive with driver, per day CFA50,000

Djibouti City

all levels, as well as a half-day 'discovery' session (DFr20,000).

Hiking

Hiking is popular in the Goda Mountains. In the cooler months, various hikes led by Afar nomads can also be arranged along ancient salt routes in western Djibouti. Duration varies from two-day hikes near Lac Assal to 10-day expeditions as far as Ethiopia.

Contact Agence Safar (p566) for further information.

Sleeping

Hôtel de Djibouti HOTEL $

(Map p556; ☎21356415; Ave 13; s/d DFr6300/8600; ❄📶) This place is located in the heart of the African Quarter and is appropriately colourful. Fight tooth and nail to get a room at the back of the hotel, otherwise the crazy road noise will make sleep a wishful dream. Keep your expectations in check, especially regarding the quality of the plumbing.

Auberge Sable Blanc HOTEL $

(Map p556; ☎21351163; d DFr7700; ❄) A short stagger west of Blvd de la République, this little modern construction is a discreet place with clean, if rather unloved, rooms and salubrious bathrooms.

★Le Héron Auberge HOTEL $$

(Map p556; ☎21324343; www.aubergeleheron.net; Rue de l'Imam Hassan Abdallah Mohamed; s/d incl breakfast DFr10,000/14,000; ❄📶) An attractive, secure compound in a residential area, Le Héron is Djibouti City's best-value hotel. Rooms: well appointed and clean as a whistle. Staff: competent and friendly. Location: on a peaceful street. A shuttle service is also available to drive you to the centre (by reservation). Book ahead.

Hotel Alia HOTEL $$

(Map p556; ☎21358222; Ave Maréchal Lyautey; s/d incl breakfast DFr16,800/18,800; ❄📶) Popular with expats, aid workers and businesspeople, this well-managed establishment gets kudos for its convenient location, immaculate rooms, squeaky-clean bathrooms and professional service. Some rooms upstairs

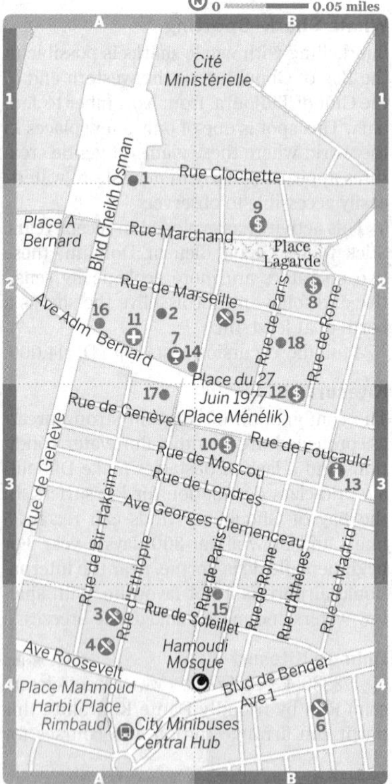

Central Djibouti City

Activities, Courses & Tours
1 Agence Le Goubet A1
2 ATTA/Globe Travel A2

Eating
3 Blue Nile A4
4 La Terrasse A4
5 Le Pizzaiolo B2
6 Mukbassa Central – Chez Youssouf B4

Drinking & Nightlife
7 L'Historil A2

Information
8 Bank of Africa B2
9 BCIMR B2
Dilip Corporation ....(see 10)
10 Mehta B3
11 Pôle Médical A2
12 Saba Islamic Bank B3
13 Tourist Office B3

Transport
14 Air France A2
15 Daallo B4
16 Ethiopian Airlines A2
FlyDubai ....(see 2)
17 Jubba Airways A3
Kenya Airways ....(see 2)
18 Yemenia B2

WORTH A TRIP

DECAN

Weary of the hustle and bustle of Djibouti City? Have a soft spot for endangered species? Make a beeline for **Decan** (21340119; www.decandjibouti.org; admission DFr1500-2000; 3.30-6.30pm Mon, Thu & Sat Oct-May, 4.30-6.30pm Mon, Thu & Sat Jun-Sep). This efficiently run wildlife refuge about 10km south of Djibouti City (on the road to Somaliland) makes for an easy two- to three-hour excursion from the capital.

Decan was set up as a rehabilitation centre for various species that have been orphaned or illegally caged for trafficking purposes. You'll see cheetahs, lions, hyenas, ostriches, turtles, Somali donkeys, caracals, squirrels, antelopes and porcupines. A dedicated birdwatching area was under construction at the time of writing.

The only practical option for getting here from Djibouti City is by taxi (DFr3000, including waiting time).

come with partial sea views. It's within walking distance of Pl du 27 Juin 1977.

★Sheraton Djibouti Hotel RESORT $$$
(Map p556; 21328000; www.sheraton.com/djibouti; Plateau du Serpent; s DFr29,000-40,000, d DFr35,000-45,000; P ❄ @ ☎ ≋) After an extensive renovation in 2012, the Sheraton now ranks as one of the best-value options in town, with nicely laid-out rooms (some with sensational sea views), enticing bathrooms and a prolific list of facilities, including two restaurants and a pool.

Djibouti Palace Kempinski RESORT $$$
(Map p556; 21325555; www.kempinski.com/djibouti; Îlot du Héron; s DFr98,000-113,000, d DFr110,000-125,000 incl breakfast; P ❄ @ ☎ ≋) You know exactly what you'll get at the swanky Kempinski: shiny-clean rooms and a host of top-notch facilities, including three restaurants. What you won't get is any indication that you are in Djibouti; but, as you flake out on the beach or do laps in the gleaming pool, you probably won't be that bothered.

Eating

La Terrasse ETHIOPIAN $
(Map p558; 21350227; Rue d'Ethiopie; mains DFr800-1500; dinner) This place has plenty of character and serves up good Ethiopian food as well as pasta and sandwiches at puny prices. It occupies a rooftop, with a moodily lit dining area and an open kitchen.

Blue Nile FAST FOOD $
(Map p558; Rue d'Ethiopie; DFr900-1800; breakfast, lunch & dinner Sat-Thu) Frills are sparse, but servings are anything but stingy in this super cheap Djiboutian restaurant. The menu runs the gamut from fish dishes and salads to pizzas and sandwiches.

★Restaurant Saba YEMENI, SEAFOOD $$
(Map p556; 21354244; Ave Maréchal Lyautey; mains DFr1000-3000; breakfast & lunch Sat-Thu, dinner daily) This Yemeni-run institution serves well-prepared fish and meat dishes without fuss. Some reliable choices are skewered fish, fillet of barracuda, camel steak and *poisson yemenite* (oven-baked fish). There are some good pastas and salads (from DFr800), as well as superb fruit juices.

★Mukbassa Central – Chez Youssouf YEMENI $$
(Map p558; 21351899; fish menu DFr2200; lunch Sat-Thu, dinner daily) In business for ages, this Djibouti City icon off Ave 1 is famous for one thing and one thing only: *poisson yemenite*. The colourful, wooden building feels a bit ramshackle, but that's part of the experience. Dessert (pancakes) is extra (DFr400).

Le Pizzaiolo PIZZERIA $$
(Map p558; 21354439; Rue d'Ethiopie; mains DFr1600-3100) Perfect crusts and well-chosen ingredients are two of the components that make Le Pizzaiolo the best pizza place in town. Pasta, salads and meat dishes are also available.

★Restaurant-Café de la Gare FRENCH $$$
(Map p556; 21351530; Ave F d'Esperey; mains DFr2500-3600; lunch & dinner Sat-Thu) Alfresco on a little pavement terrace or inside the pretty dining room decorated with earthy tones, dining at this cosy eatery is a treat. A true alchemist, the Senegalese chef here conjures up French-inspired specialities with an African twist. Highlights include fish fillet, king prawns and duck leg preserved in its own fat.

Drinking & Nightlife

There's no shortage of watering holes in Djibouti City, especially around Pl du 27 Juin 1977. Plenty of teahouses are also scattered around the town centre. Most clubs are on or around Rue d'Ethiopie, in the European Quarter.

L'Historil BAR

(Map p558; Pl du 27 Juin 1977) L'Historil has an appealing terrace that offers excellent people-watching opportunities. There's a restaurant upstairs.

Association de la Communauté Ethiopienne de Djibouti BAR

(Club Éthiopien; Map p556) Down-to-earth bar, with large outdoor courtyard west of Blvd de la République. It's a pleasant place to enjoy a very cheap beer (a bottle of St George costs only DFr350) and meet locals. Also serves food.

Information

INTERNET ACCESS

There's a slew of internet outlets in the town centre. They all offer fast connections; expect to pay around DFr200 per hour.

MEDICAL SERVICES

Pôle Médical (Map p558; ☎21352724; ⊙8am-noon & 4-7pm Sat-Thu) A well-equipped clinic off Pl du 27 Juin 1977.

MONEY

There are banks and two bureaus de change in the centre, as well as a few Visa-friendly ATMs (but only one ATM accepts MasterCard). Both the Djibouti Palace Kempenski and Sheraton Djibouti Hotel have an ATM.

Bank of Africa (Map p558; Pl Lagarde; ⊙7.30am-noon & 4.15-6pm Sun & Wed, 7.30am-noon Mon, Tue & Fri) Changes cash and has one ATM.

BCIMR (Map p558; Pl Lagarde; ⊙7.30-11.45am Sun-Thu) Changes cash and has ATMs.

BCIMR (Map p556; Ave F d'Esperey; ⊙7.45am-noon & 4-5.15pm Sun-Thu) Has ATMs.

Dilip Corporation (Map p558; Pl du 27 Juin 1977; ⊙8am-noon & 4-7.30pm Sat-Thu) Authorised bureau de change. Changes cash (no commission) and does cash advances on Visa and MasterCard for a 6% commission.

Mehta (Map p558; ☎21353719; Pl du 27 Juin 1977; ⊙7.30am-noon & 4-7.30pm Sun-Thu) Authorised bureau de change. Changes cash (no commission).

Saba Islamic Bank (Map p558; off Pl du 27 Juin 1977) Has one ATM, which accepts both Visa and MasterCard.

TELEPHONE

The most convenient places to make international or local calls are the various telephone outlets scattered around the city centre.

TOURIST INFORMATION

Tourist office (Map p558; ☎21352800; www.office-tourisme.dj; Rue de Foucauld; ⊙7am-1.30pm Sat-Thu, plus 4-6pm Sat, Mon & Wed) Mildly helpful.

Getting There & Away

BOAT

A ferry plies the Djibouti–Tadjoura and Djibouti–Obock routes two to three times a week (DFr1500 one way, two to three hours). It doesn't operate from mid-June to mid-September. Boats leave from L'Escale.

BUS

Minibuses leave from various departure points south of town. They connect Djibouti City to Tadjoura, Galafi (at the Ethiopian border) and Obock. Most minibuses leave early in the morning and only when they are full. Most journeys cost from DFr600 to DFr2000, depending on distance.

CAR

For 4WD rental (from DFr25,000 per day, with driver), contact the following outfits.

Marill (☎21329400; www.groupe-marill.com; Route de l'Aéroport)

Pyramid (☎21358203; www.pyramidrental.com; Route de Boulaos)

Getting Around

The central hub for city minibuses (DFr50) is on Pl Mahmoud Harbi. A taxi ride within the centre costs about DFr600 (DFr1000 to/from the airport).

AROUND DJIBOUTI

Moucha Island

It ain't Bora Bora, but this island, easily accessible from Djibouti City, is a welcome respite from the hustle and bustle of the capital, with uncrowded beaches and warm waters.

Activities

Moucha Island is an excellent underwater playground and a good place to learn to dive, with a couple of very safe dive sites that are less than 15 minutes away by boat. Snorkelling is also superb.

Le Lagon Bleu (p557) is a professional dive shop that offers introductory dives (from DFr10,000), single dive trips (from DFr8000, half day), snorkelling excursions (from DFr6000) and courses. Its day trips to Moucha Island (from DFr24,000 per person, including two dives and lunch) are very popular.

Sleeping & Eating

Lagon Bleu Village RESORT $$

(☎21250296; Moucha Island; d incl full board & transport from DFr17,000; ❄) This is a good place to take up a Robinson Crusoe lifestyle without sacrificing comfort, with 19 well-equipped bungalows, a restaurant and a diving centre. One grumble: air-con and electricity are on at night only.

Getting There & Away

ATTA/Globe Travel (Map p558; ☎353036, 250297; atta@intnet.dj; off Pl du 27 Juin 1977, Djibouti City) offers various packages that include transfers to/from Djibouti City, accommodation and meals. Day trips are also possible (from DFr8000, including lunch).

Lac Assal

Just over 100km west of the capital lies one of the most spectacular natural phenomena in Africa: Lac Assal. Situated 150m below sea level, this crater lake is encircled by dark, dormant volcanoes. It represents the lowest point on the African continent. The aquamarine water is ringed by a huge salt field, 60m in depth. The salt field has been mined by the Afar nomads for centuries, and they can still be seen loading up their camels for the long trek south to Ethiopia.

Getting There & Away

There's no public transport to Lac Assal. Most visitors come with tours or hire their own vehicles from the capital. A tour should set you back about DFr15,000.

Lac Abbé

You'll never forget your first glimpse of Lac Abbé. The scenery is sensational: the plain is dotted with hundreds of limestone chimneys, some standing as high as 50m, belching out puffs of steam. It is often described as 'a slice of moon on the crust of earth'.

Though desolate, it is not uninhabited. Numerous mineral-rich hot springs feed the farms of local nomads who graze their camels and goats here. The banks of the lake are also where flamingos gather at dawn.

The best plan is to arrive in the late afternoon, stay the night, and leave after sunrise the following morning.

Sleeping & Eating

★Campement Touristique d'Asboley HUT, BUNGALOW $

(☎77822291, 21357244; houmed_asboley@hotmail.fr; huts/bungalows with full board DFr8000/10,000) This *campement touristique* lies on a plateau that proffers stupendous views of the big chimneys. It comprises traditional Afar huts and three simple bungalows made of cement (true, they don't really blend in such a grandiose environment). Prices include a guided walk to the chimneys.

Getting There & Away

The only way of getting there is by hiring a 4WD with driver or by taking a tour. If you are (or can find) a party of four, the *campement touristique* can arrange all-inclusive packages for DFr17,700 per person a day – prices include transfers from Djibouti City, accommodation, meals and guided walks.

Goda Mountains

If you want to get away from it all, look no further. Northwest of the Gulf of Tadjoura, the Goda Mountains rise to a height of 1750m and are a spectacular natural oddity. This area shelters one of the rare specks of green on Djibouti's parched map, like a giant oasis. It's a real shock for some visitors, who find it inconceivable that the tiny settlements of **Dittilou**, **Day**, **Bankoualé** and **Randa** belong to the same country as the one they left on the burning plain just an hour before.

The area offers ample hiking opportunities. From canyons and valleys to waterfalls and peaks, the mountainscape is fantastic. All *campements touristiques* can organise guided nature walks, from one-hour jaunts to more challenging day hikes.

Sleeping & Eating

Campement Touristique de la Forêt du Day HUT $

(☎77829774; Day; huts with full board DFr8000) If you like peace, quiet and sigh-inducing views, you'll have few quibbles with this atmospheric *campement* near the Forêt du Day, at an altitude of 1400m. The traditional huts are welcoming and the ablution block is in good nick.

Campement Touristique de Dittilou HUT $
(☎27510871, 21354520, 77810488; Dittilou; huts with full board DFr8000) This venture has helpful and friendly management offering a series of well-designed *daboytas* (traditional huts) that are set against a lush and wonderfully peaceful landscape. The laid-back restaurant is chilled and the food is great.

★**Campement Touristique de Bankoualé** HUT $
(☎77814115; Bankoualé; huts with full board DFr8000) This ecofriendly camp (electricity is solar powered) is perched on a hillside and overlooks a deep gorge. Many huts are equipped with traditional Afar beds made of wood and goat skin, and the views of the valley are sensational. The ablution blocks are well scrubbed, and the food gets good reports.

Getting There & Away

The most convenient way to visit the area is on a tour or with a rental 4WD. Transport can also be organised by the *campements* if there's a group (usually a minimum of four people).

Tadjoura

POP 25,000

Nestled in the shadow of the green Goda Mountains with the bright-blue sea lapping at its doorstep, Tadjoura is a picturesque little place. There's little to do here besides stroll around and soak up the atmosphere, but it's a great place to spend a few hours.

Sleeping & Eating

Hôtel-Restaurant Le Golfe HOTEL $
(☎27424091, 27424153; http://hotel-restaurant-le-golfe-djibouti-tadjourah.e-monsite.com; bungalows incl breakfast DFr10,000; P ❄) Under French-Ethiopian management, this low-key but well-kept resort is situated in a relaxing waterfront setting about 1.5km from the town centre. The 11 units are not fancy but they're functional, and there's a good onsite restaurant (seafood!). No beach to speak of, but the owners can organise transfers to Plage des Sables Blancs.

Getting There & Away

Regular morning buses ply the route between Djibouti City and Tadjoura (DFr1500, three hours). A passenger ferry runs two to three times weekly between Djibouti City and Tadjoura (DFr1500 one way, two to three hours).

Obock

Obock exudes a kind of 'last frontier' feel, light years away from the hullabaloo of Djibouti City. This little town is something of a backwater, and survives primarily from its small fishing industry.

It has a couple of sights, including **Ras Bir lighthouse**, about 6km east of the town centre, and the eerily quiet **Cimetière Marin** (Marine Cemetery), on the western outskirts of town.

Sleeping & Eating

Campement Oubouky HUT $
(☎77816034; huts with full board DFr8000) Facilities are fairly run down at this *campement* about 5km east of the centre, but it's right on a blissfully quiet beach with excellent swimming and snorkelling. Lovers of seafood will enjoy the cooking here, and fishing trips can be organised. The owner, Abdou, also rents rooms in a villa in the centre of Obock.

Getting There & Away

A regular morning minibus service operates between Djibouti City and Obock (DFr2000, about 4½ hours).

There's a twice-weekly passenger-ferry service between Djibouti City and Obock (DFr1500 one way, two to three hours).

UNDERSTAND DJIBOUTI

Djibouti Today

Djibouti's stability and neutrality, combined with its strategic position, have brought lots of benefits. In an effort to combat piracy off the Somali coast, the Americans have reinforced their military presence – it's America's only Africa base. As if this wasn't enough, the Japanese set up a huge military base near the international airport in 2011. The total number of foreign soldiers on Djiboutian territory is estimated at 7000.

Foreign investors from Asia and the Gulf are increasingly active in Djibouti, and there are building projects springing up all over the capital. There are also plans to build a port in Tadjoura and to upgrade the road system throughout the country.

History

From Aksum to Islam

Around the 1st century AD, Djibouti made up part of the powerful Ethiopian kingdom of Aksum, which included modern-day Eritrea and even stretched across the Red Sea to parts of southern Arabia. It was during the Aksumite era, in the 4th century AD, that Christianity first appeared in the region.

As the empire of Aksum gradually fell into decline, a new influence arose that superseded the Christian religion in Djibouti: Islam. It was introduced to the region around AD 825 by Arab traders from southern Arabia.

European Ambitions

In the second half of the 19th century, European powers competed to grab new colonies in Africa. The French, seeking to counter the British presence in Yemen on the other side of the Bab al-Mandab Strait, made agreements with the Afar sultans of Obock and Tadjoura that gave them the right to settle in these areas. In 1888 construction of Djibouti City began on the southern shore of the Gulf of Tadjoura. French Somaliland (present-day Djibouti) began to take shape.

France and the emperor of landlocked Ethiopia then signed a pact designating Djibouti as the 'official outlet of Ethiopian commerce'. This led to the construction of the Addis Ababa–Djibouti City railway, which was of vital commercial importance until recently.

Throwing Off the French Yoke

As early as 1949 there were a number of anticolonial demonstrations led by the Issa Somalis, who were in favour of the reunification of the territories of Italian, British and French Somaliland. Meanwhile, the Afars were in favour of continued French rule.

Major riots ensued, especially after the 1967 referendum, which produced a vote in favour of continued French rule. After the referendum, the colony's name was changed from French Somaliland to the French Territory of the Afars and Issas.

In June 1977 the colony finally won its sovereignty from France. The country became the Republic of Djibouti.

DON'T MISS

PLAGE DES SABLES BLANCS

Plage des Sables Blancs, 7km east of Tadjoura, is tranquillity incarnate and a lovely place to sun yourself, with a good string of white sand and good facilities. Your biggest quandary here: a bout of snorkelling (or kayaking) or a snooze on the beach? You can lay your head at the **Plage des Sables Blancs Campement** (☎21354520; goubet@intnet.dj; Plage des Sables Blancs; beds with full board DFr11,500, r DFr25,000), which is right on the beach. Accommodation is simple (beds and mattresses only), or you can opt for a room with all mod cons in the recently built hotel at the western tip of the beach. The on-site restaurant serves up toothsome local dishes. One grumble: although it has only 10 rooms, the hotel feels a bit incongruous in such a scenic setting. You'll need your own wheels to get there.

Small Country, Adroit Leaders

Despite continuous clan rivalries between the two main ethnic groups, the Afars and Issas, who have been jostling for power since the 1970s, Djibouti has managed to exploit its strategic position.

When the Gulf War broke out in 1990, the country's president, Hassan Gouled Aptidon, while claiming to oppose the military build-up in the Gulf, simultaneously allowed France to increase its military presence in the country, as well as granting the Americans and Italians access to the naval port. During the war between Eritrea and Ethiopia in the 1990s, Ethiopia stopped using the ports of Massawa and Assab and diverted all its foreign trade through Djibouti.

In 2006 the first phase of the Doraleh Project, which consists of a large-capacity oil terminal about 8km east of the current seaport, was completed. Thanks to this mega-project, partly financed by Dubai Port International, Djibouti aims to be the 'Dubai of East Africa'.

However, relations with Eritrea (its northern neighbour) have deteriorated since 2008, following a brief fighting in the Ras Doumeira border area. At the time of writing, Djibouti had not managed to reestablish dialogue with Eritrea and the borders between the two countries remained closed.

People of Djibouti

Of Djibouti's estimated 900,000 inhabitants, about 35% are Afars and 60% are Issas. Both groups are Muslims. The rest of the population is divided between Arabs and Europeans. The south is predominantly Issa, while the north is mostly Afar. Ethnic tensions between Afars and Issas have always dogged Djibouti. These tensions came to a head in 1991, when Afar rebels launched a civil war in the north. A peace accord was brokered in 1994, but ethnic hostility has not completely waned.

Despite an increasing tendency towards a more sedentary lifestyle, most Djiboutians living in towns retain strong links with their nomadic past.

The Arts

Dance is arguably the highest form of culture in Djibouti, along with oral literature and poetry. Some dances celebrate major life events, such as birth, marriage or circumcision.

If you are looking for handicrafts, the traditional Afar and Somali knives and the very attractive Afar woven straw mats (known in Afar as *fiddima*) are among the finest products.

Food & Drink

Djibouti City is endowed with a plethora of tasty restaurants that will please most palates – a testimony to the French presence. You'll find excellent seafood, rice, pasta, local meat dishes such as stuffed kid or lamb, and other treats imported from France. In the countryside, choice is obviously more limited, with goat meat and rice as the main staples. Alcohol (wine and beer) is widely available in the capital.

TIME FOR QAT

One of the most striking features in Djibouti is the overwhelming presence of *qat*. The life of most Djiboutian males seems to revolve entirely around the consumption of this mild narcotic. Every day, *qat* consumers meet their circle of friends in the *mabraz* (*qat* den) to *brouter* (graze). Only 10% of women are thought to consume the plant regularly.

Environment

Djibouti's 23,000 sq km can be divided into three geographic regions: the coastal plains, which feature white, sandy beaches; the volcanic plateaus in the southern and central parts of the country; and the mountain ranges in the north, where the altitude reaches more than 2000m above sea level. Essentially the country is a vast wasteland, with the exception of pockets of forest and dense vegetation to the north.

Livestock rearing is the most important type of agriculture. As demand for scarce grazing land mounts, the forests of the north are increasingly coming under threat, including the fragile Forêt du Day.

SURVIVAL GUIDE

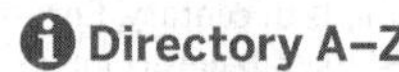

Directory A–Z

ACCOMMODATION

Most hotels are in the capital, with few options outside. Hotel categories are limited in range; most of them fit into the upper echelon and are expensive. At the lower end, the few budget hotels that exist tend to be pretty basic. There's a limited choice in between.

A rather popular option that is developing around the major attractions in the hinterland is the *campements touristiques*. These are traditional huts with shared showers and toilets. These quaint, low-key establishments are great places to meet locals and get an authentic cultural experience. They're also a good budget option, although there's no public transport to get to them.

Listings in this book quote full board when the accommodation rate includes three meals a day.

EMBASSIES & CONSULATES

Canadian Consulate (☎21355950; Pl Lagarde; ⏰8am-noon Sun-Thu)

Ethiopian Embassy (☎21350718; Ave Maréchal Lyautey; ⏰8am-noon Sat, 8am-12.30pm & 4.30-6pm Sun-Thu)

French Embassy (Map p556; ☎21350963; www.ambafrance-dj.org; Ave F d'Esperey; ⏰7am-1.30pm & 3-6pm Mon & Wed, 7am-1.30pm Sun, Tue & Thu)

Somaliland Bureau de Liaison (Somaliland Liaison Office; Map p556; ☎21358758; Ave Maréchal Lyautey; ⏰7.30am-1pm Sat-Thu)

US Embassy (Map p556; ☎21453000; http://djibouti.usembassy.gov; Lotissement Haramous)

INTERNET ACCESS

- Internet cafes are found only in Djibouti City.
- Wi-fi is widespread and free in most hotels in Djibouti City.

MAPS

The best map of the country is the 1:200,000 *Djibouti* map published in 1992 by the French Institut Géographique National (IGN).

MONEY

- The unit of currency is the Djibouti franc (DFr), which is divided into 100 centimes.
- You'll find a few ATMs in Djibouti City. All ATMs accept Visa. At the time of writing, only one ATM accepted MasterCard.
- Visa credit cards are accepted at some upmarket hotels and shops, and at some larger travel agencies. Some places levy a commission of about 5% for credit-card payment.
- There are several banks and a couple of authorised bureaus de change in the capital. Outside the capital, banking facilities are almost nonexistent.
- The euro and the US dollar are the favoured hard currencies. Travellers cheques are not useful; euros and dollars in cash and a Visa card are the way to go.

OPENING HOURS

Friday is the weekly holiday for offices and most shops.

Banks 7.30am–2.30pm and 4pm–6pm Sunday to Thursday.

Businesses 7.30am–1.30pm Sunday to Thursday; reopen 4pm–6pm.

Government offices 7.30am–1.30pm Sunday to Thursday.

Restaurants Breakfast from 6.30am, lunch 11.30am–1.30pm, dinner 6.30pm–9pm.

PUBLIC HOLIDAYS

Djibouti also celebrates Islamic holidays, which change dates every year.

New Year's Day 1 January

Labour Day 1 May

Independence Day 27 June

Christmas Day 25 December

SAFE TRAVEL

- Djibouti is a relatively safe country, and serious crime or hostility aimed specifically at travellers is very rare. However, the usual big-city precautions apply.
- Djibouti's security services are known for being sensitive and active. There is no reason why travellers should attract the attention of the police, but if it happens, remain polite and calm – it's usually pretty harmless.
- The area north of Godoria (up to the border with Eritrea) is off limits to travellers.

PRACTICALITIES

- **Electricity** Djibouti uses the 220V system, with two-round-pin plugs
- **Languages** Arabic, French, Afar, Somali
- **Media** Most widely read newspaper is La Nation (www.lanation.dj)

TELEPHONE

- The country code for Djibouti is ☎253.
- Phone numbers have 10 digits. Mobile numbers start with ☎77; landline numbers start with ☎21 or ☎27.
- International and local calls are best made from one of the numerous phone shops (look for the *cabine telephonique* signs).
- Mobile (cell) phone coverage is pretty good across Djibouti. Depending on which mobile network you use at home, your phone may or may not work while in Djibouti – ask your mobile network provider. You can also bring your phone and buy a local SIM card (DFr2000).
- The only mobile network is Djibouti Telecom.

TOURIST INFORMATION

The only tourist office in the country is in Djibouti City. Travel agencies are also reliable sources of travel information.

Information for travellers is hard to come by outside the country. In Europe, the most knowledgable organisation is the **Association Djibouti Espace Nomade** (ADEN; ☎01 48 51 71 56; aden@club-internet.fr; 64 Rue des Meuniers, Montreuil-sous-Bois, France).

VISAS

- All visitors, including French nationals, must have a visa to enter Djibouti. Tourist visas cost from US$30 to US$60 depending on where you apply, and are valid for one month. Visas can be obtained at the nearest Djibouti embassy (including Addis Ababa) or, where there is none, from the French embassy.
- Travellers from most Western countries can also obtain a single-entry tourist visa on arrival at the airport; it's issued on the spot. It costs DFr5000 for three days and DFr10,000 for one month. Payment can also be made in US dollars or in euros.
- You must have a valid visa to enter overland as none are available at borders. That said, we've heard from travellers coming from Somaliland that visas can also be purchased at the Loyaada border for DFr15,000 or the equivalent in US dollars.

Visas for Onward Travel

For Ethiopia, a one-month single-entry visa costs DFr3600 (DFr12,600 for US nationals). You need to supply two photos. It takes 24 hours to process.

For Somaliland, a two-week single-entry visa costs DFr5400. You need to supply one photo and it's issued on the spot.

Getting There & Away

You'll need a valid passport and a visa to enter Djibouti.

AIR

Djibouti has one international gateway for arrival by air, **Djibouti-Ambouli Airport** (☎341646), about 5km south of Djibouti City.

The following airlines fly to and from Djibouti, and have offices in Djibouti City.

Air France (Map p558; ☎21351010; www.airfrance.com; Pl du 27 Juin 1977)

Daallo (Map p558; ☎21353401; www.daallo.com; Rue de Paris)

Ethiopian Airlines (Map p558; ☎21351007; www.flyethiopian.com) Off Blvd Cheikh Osman.

FlyDubai (Map p558; ☎21350964; www.flydubai.com) Off Pl du 27 Juin 1977.

Jubba Airways (Map p558; ☎21356264; www.jubba-airways.com) Off Pl du 27 Juin 1977

Kenya Airways (Map p558; ☎21353036; www.kenya-airways.com; Pl Lagarde)

Turkish Airlines (☎21340110; www.turkishairlines.com)

Yemenia (Map p558; ☎21355427; www.yemenia.com; Rue de Paris)

LAND

Eritrea

The border with Eritrea was indefinitely closed at the time of writing, and travel overland between Djibouti and Eritrea was not possible.

Ethiopia

Bus

- There is a daily service between Djibouti City and Dire Dawa – a strenuous 10- to 12-hour ride on a gravel road. Take your first bus to the border town of Gelille, then another bus to Djibouti City.
- From Djibouti City, buses leave at dawn from Ave Gamel Abdel Nasser. The company is Société Bus Assajog. Buy your ticket (DFr3000) at least a day in advance.

Train

There are plans to resurrect the old Djibouti City–Addis Ababa train.

Somaliland

Four-wheel drives depart daily to Hargeisa and Borama from Ave 13. They usually leave around 3pm (it's wise to buy your ticket in the morning). The border crossing is at Loyaada; it costs from DFr6000 (back seat) to DFr9000 (front seat). Be warned: it's a taxing journey.

Getting Around

BOAT

A passenger boat operates between Djibouti City and Tadjoura and between Djibouti City and Obock.

CAR

- The Route de l'Unité, a good sealed road, covers the 240km from the capital around the Gulf de Tadjoura, as far as Obock.
- Off-road excursions into the interior are usually off limits to anything other than a 4WD.
- There are several car-hire agencies in Djibouti City. For a 4WD with driver expect to pay around DFr25,000 a day.

TOURS

The only way of getting to some of the country's principal attractions is by joining an excursion. They're expensive (from DFr15,000 per person), but the price includes food and accommodation.

Agence Le Goubet (Map p558; ☎21354520; valerie@riesgroup.dj; Blvd Cheik Osman) Can organise trips to Plage des Sables Blancs and make bookings in the *campements touristiques*. Also sells flight tickets. Ask for Valerie, who can get by in English.

Agence Safar (☎77814115; safar.djibouti@gmail.com) This outfit organises all kinds of customised tours throughout the country, including multiday guided treks and excursions to Lac Abbé and Lac Assal. Can also make bookings in the *campements touristiques*.

Dolphin (☎21350313, 77718034; dolphinexcursions.free.fr; Blvd de la République) This well-established operator can organise all kinds of tours throughout the country, on land and at sea.

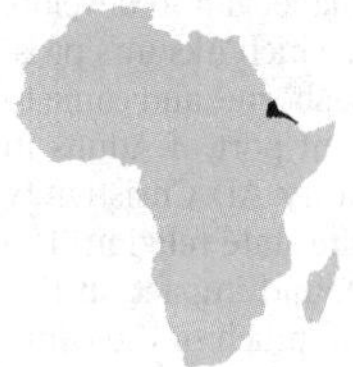

Eritrea

Includes ➡

Fast Facts

- **Capital** Asmara
- **Population** 6.09 million
- **Languages** Tigrinya, Arabic
- **Area** 124,320 sq km
- **Currency** Nakfa
- **Visa requirements** All foreign nationals require visas, from the Eritrean embassy or consulate before you leave your home country
- **Tourist information** www.asmera.nl

Nature, Culture & Adventure

Historically intriguing, culturally compelling and scenically magical, Eritrea is one of the most secretive countries in Africa. For those who have a hankering for off-the-beaten-track places, it offers challenges and excitement aplenty, with a unique blend of natural and cultural highlights.

Eritrea wows visitors with its awesome scenery, from the quintessentially Abyssinian landscapes – escarpments, plateaus and soaring peaks – to the deserted beaches of the Red Sea coast. Culturally, Eritrea is a melting pot. It might be a tiddler of a country by Africa's standards, but it hosts a kaleidoscopic range of ethnic groups. It also features a superb array of archaeological sites that tell volumes of history. The cherry on top is Asmara, Eritrea's utterly adorable capital and a whimsical art deco city.

Despite the tough political and economic landscape and the odd travel restrictions, this country remains one of the most inspiring destinations in Africa.

Eritrea Top Sights

- **Asmara** Discover the capital's dazzling collection of colonial architectural wonders
- **Massawa** Explore the alleyways and streets of this historic coastal town
- **Keren** Soak up the languid atmosphere of Eritrea's beguiling second city
- **Dahlak Archipelago** Sunbathe on sparkling beaches
- **Qohaito** Speculate on Eritrea's mysterious past at these enigmatic ruins
- **Dankalia** Travel to the ends of the earth and immerse yourself in Martian landscapes
- **Old Railway** Hop on Africa's most atmospheric train and be ready for the most scenic ride of your life

UNDERSTAND ERITREA

Eritrea Today

Today Eritrea is not exactly a wonderland. Freedom of press and speech is nonexistent. The state has taken control of all private companies, and the country has one of the most restrictive economies on the planet. Mass conscription has deprived many industries of manpower. The end result? Eritrea has won the less-than-enviable sobriquet of 'the North Korea of Africa'. Despite these harsh realities and the clampdown on civil liberties, Eritreans show an exceptional resilience and have not entirely lost hope in the future.

History

Around the 4th century BC, the powerful kingdom of Aksum, situated in Tigray, in the north of modern Ethiopia, began to develop. Much foreign trade – on which Aksum's prosperity depended – was seaborne, and came to be handled by the ancient port of Adulis in Eritrea. By the 4th century AD Christianity had become the Aksumite state religion. The new religion had a profound impact on Eritrea's culture, influencing much of the country's art and literature.

Islam, the arrival of which coincided with Christian Aksum's decline in the 7th century, was the other great influence on the region. Islam made the greatest inroads in the Dahlak Islands. Muslims traders also settled in nearby Massawa on the mainland.

The Turks first arrived in the Red Sea at the beginning of the 16th century. For the next 300 years (with a few short-lived intervals) the coast, including the port of Massawa, belonged to the Ottomans.

By the middle of the 19th century, new powers were casting covetous eyes over

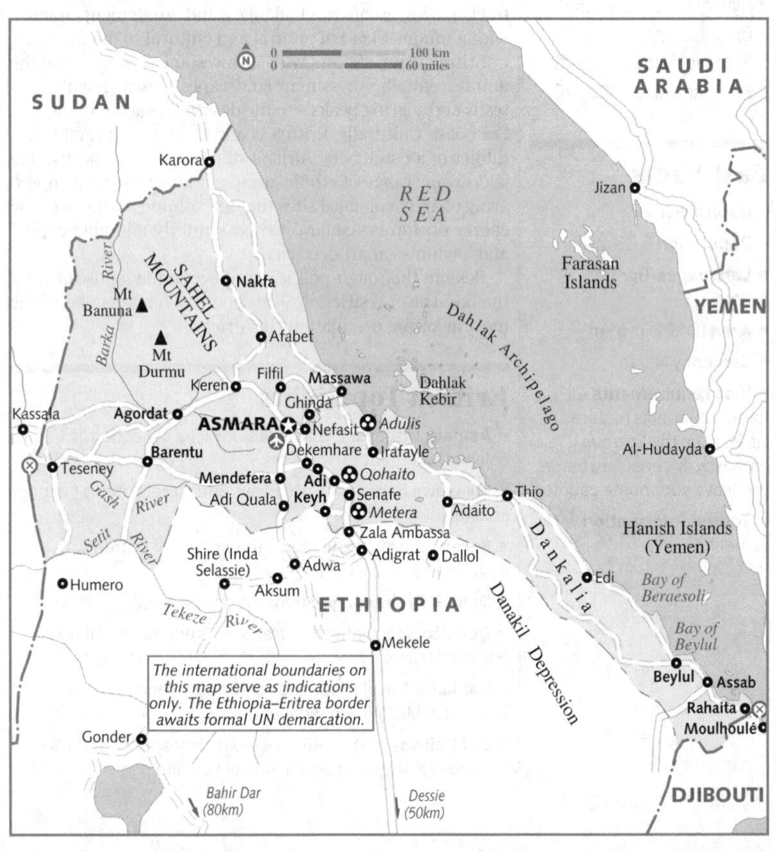

the region. The Egyptians took the western lowlands of modern-day Eritrea. When the Egyptian armies were defeated by the Ethiopian forces in 1875, another foreign power – Italy – stepped in. Italian colonisation started in 1869 near Assab.

Following the Battle of Adwa in 1896, when the Ethiopians resoundingly defeated the Italian armies, new international boundaries were drawn up: Ethiopia remained independent and Eritrea became, for the first time, a separate territory – and an Italian colony. Of all Italy's colonies (Eritrea, Libya and Italian Somaliland), Eritrea was considered the jewel in the crown, and much effort was put into industrialising the little country. By the end of the 1930s, Eritrea was one of the most highly industrialised colonies in Africa.

In 1940, with the outbreak of WWII, Italy declared war on Britain, and soon became embroiled in conflicts in what was then Anglo-Egyptian Sudan. The year 1941 marked a turning point: the British took the strategically important town of Keren before defeating the Italians in Asmara. The colony became administered by the British. At the end of WWII, the territory lost its strategic importance and in 1945 the British began a slow withdrawal.

In 1948 Eritrea's fate was pondered by a commission consisting of the UK, the USA, France and the Soviet Union. Unable to reach a decision, the commission passed the issue on to the UN's General Assembly. In 1950 the very contentious Resolution 390 A (V) was passed. Eritrea became Ethiopia's 14th province and disappeared from the map of Africa. Little by little, Ethiopia began to exert an ever-tighter hold over Eritrea, as both industry and political control were shifted to Ethiopia's capital, Addis Ababa. When, in the early 1960s, Ethiopia formally annexed Eritrea in violation of international law, Cold War politics ensured that both the US and the UN kept silent.

With no recourse to the international community, the frustration of the Eritrean people grew. In 1961 the fight for independence began. In 1978 the Eritreans were on the brink of winning back their country, but the Ethiopians benefitted from the logistical support of the Soviet Union. From 1988 the Eritrean People's Liberation Front (EPLF), the most important resistance movement, began to inflict major losses on the Ethiopian army. In 1990, amid some of the fiercest fighting of the war, the EPLF took the strategically important port of Massawa.

COUNTRY COVERAGE

At the time of research very few travellers were heading to Eritrea so we're providing historical and cultural information rather than reviews and listings. A good source of information for on-the-ground travel in Eritrea is Lonely Planet's Thorn Tree online travel forum www.lonelyplanet.com/thorntree. Other sources of good internet-based information are www.dehai.org and www.asmera.nl.

By a fortuitous turn of events, the Ethiopian dictator Mengistu was overthrown in 1991, his 140,000 troops fled Eritrea and a final confrontation in the capital was avoided. The EPLF walked into Asmara without having to fire a single bullet. Asmara was one of the very few Eritrean towns to survive the war undamaged.

In April 1993 the provisional government of Eritrea held a referendum on Eritrean independence. More than 99.81% of voters opted for full Eritrean sovereignty, and on 24 May 1993 independence was declared. Eritrea was back on the African map.

After the war, the little nation worked hard to rebuild its infrastructure, repair the economy and improve conditions for its people. Eritrea was also at pains to establish good international relations with, among others, Ethiopia, the Gulf States, Asia, the USA and Europe. However, this progress was seriously undermined in 1998, when war broke out with Ethiopia. In early May 1998 a number of Eritrean officials were killed near the border. On 12 May Eritrea upped the stakes by occupying the border town of Badme. Over the next month there was intense fighting between the two sides. In February 1999 a full-scale military conflict broke out that left tens of thousands dead on both sides before it finally ceased for good in mid-2000.

In December 2000 a formal peace settlement was signed in Algiers. In April 2001 a 25km-wide demilitarised strip, which ran the length of the internationally recognised border on the Eritrean side, was set up under supervision of the UN Mission in Ethiopia and Eritrea (UNMEE).

Since the guns fell silent there have been periods of extreme tension between the two nations that have seen forces massed on both sides of the border, and today the two armies continue to eye each other

ART (DECO) ATTACK IN ASMARA

One of the most entrancing cities in Africa, Asmara is a surprisingly slick city crammed with architectural gems harking back to the city's heyday as the 'Piccolo Roma' (small Rome). Isolated for nearly 30 years during its war with Ethiopia, Asmara has kept its heritage buildings almost intact. Wander the streets in the centre and you'll gaze upon a showcase of the art deco, international, cubist, expressionist, functionalist, futurist, rationalist and neoclassical architectural styles. Among the most outstanding buildings are the Opera House, the Ministry of Education, the Cinema Impero, the Municipality Building, the Cinema Roma and the Irga Building. But nothing can compare with the Fiat Tagliero Building. Built in 1938, it is designed to look like a plane (or a spaceship, or a bat). The central tower with its glass 'cockpit' is similar to many structures in Miami, USA.

The best way to see Asmara's built heritage is to walk around town. *Asmara – Africa's Secret Modernist City*, by Edward Denison, is the most comprehensive book on the subject.

suspiciously over the desert. For the moment a wary calm prevails, but everyone knows that the merest spark could reignite a war that neither country can afford.

Culture

Eritreans appear different in temperament from Ethiopians (which partly explains the bitter relations between the two countries). Years of invasion have created a siege mentality and a sense of isolation. Though impoverished, the nation has from the outset shown self-reliance, vigour and independence.

The contrast in lifestyle between Asmara and elsewhere is stark. No matter the state of the economy and rationing, Asmarans still take the *passeggiata* (evening promenade) very seriously – a legacy of the Italian era. Then there is the rest of Eritrea, where poverty is about the only prevalent excess.

In a country where people have lost faith in their government, the family remains one pillar of society on which Eritreans continue to depend. Religious occasions and public holidays are vigorously celebrated, as are more personal, family events, such as weddings.

Women enjoy far greater equality in Eritrea than in most other African countries. Eritrea's women comprised more than one-third of troops in both the recent wars against Ethiopia.

People of Eritrea

There are nine ethnic groups, each with their own language and customs, as well as a handful of Italians who live in Asmara. The most important group is the Tigrinya, who make up approximately 50% of the population, followed by the Tigré (30%), the Saho (5%) and the Afar (5%).

Approximately 35% of the population are nomadic or seminomadic. About one million Eritreans live abroad, mostly in Europe and the USA.

Environment

Eritrea has three main geographical zones: the eastern escarpment and coastal plains, the central highland region, and the western lowlands.

The eastern zone consists of desert or semidesert, with little arable land. The northern end of the East African Rift Valley opens into the infamous Dankalia region in the east, one of the hottest places on earth. The central highland region is more fertile, and it is intensively cultivated by farming communities. The western lowlands, lying between Keren and the Sudanese border, are watered by the Gash and Barka Rivers.

Several mountains exceed 2500m, with the highest peak, Amba Soira, reaching 3018m. Offshore lie 350 islands, including the Dahlak Archipelago, the largest in the Red Sea. Major Eritrean marine ecosystems include the coral reefs, sea-grass beds and mangrove forests.

Eritrea's birdlife is very rich. Of the 2600 species of birds in Africa, Eritrea hosts 560 to 660 species, including 18 endemic ones.

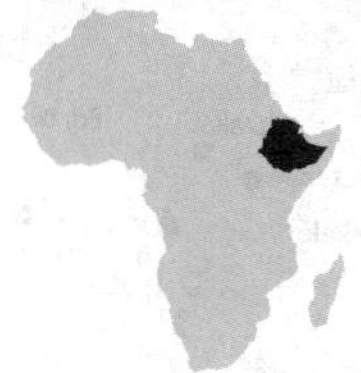

Ethiopia

POP 85 MILLION

Includes ➡

Best Places for Nature

- Simien Mountains National Park (p583)
- Nechisar National Park (p119)
- Abiata-Shala Lakes National Park (p587)
- Lake Ziway (p587)

Best Places for Culture

- Lalibela (p585)
- Rock-hewn churches of Tigray (p585)
- Lower Omo Valley (p588)
- Harar (p586)
- Aksum (p583)

Why Go?

Ethiopia is truly a world apart. Here there are over two millennia worth of ancient treasures scattered about, from the giant obelisks and hidden tombs of the legendary Queen of Sheba, to castles that would make Camelot jealous and the breathtaking rock-carved churches of Lalibela, the New Jerusalem.

Not to be outdone by human craftsmen, Mother Nature also let her creative juices flow here. East Africa's great Rift Valley has left some of its most memorable signatures in Ethiopia; milky brown lakes scar the south and deep canyons and steep peaks wrinkle the land...well, just about everywhere.

Though you can hit the highlights in a couple of weeks, it takes three or four for proper exploration. But no matter how long you stay, you'll probably wish for just a few more days.

When to Go

Addis Ababa

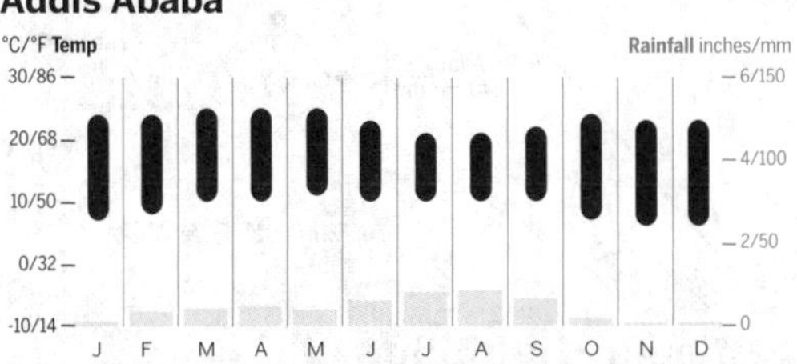

Jan Perfect weather and the festivals of Leddet and Timkat take place.

Mar–Apr Fasika (Orthodox Easter) brings huge crowds of pilgrims to Ethiopian churches.

Sep Everything is green after the rains and the colourful Meskel festival is celebrated.

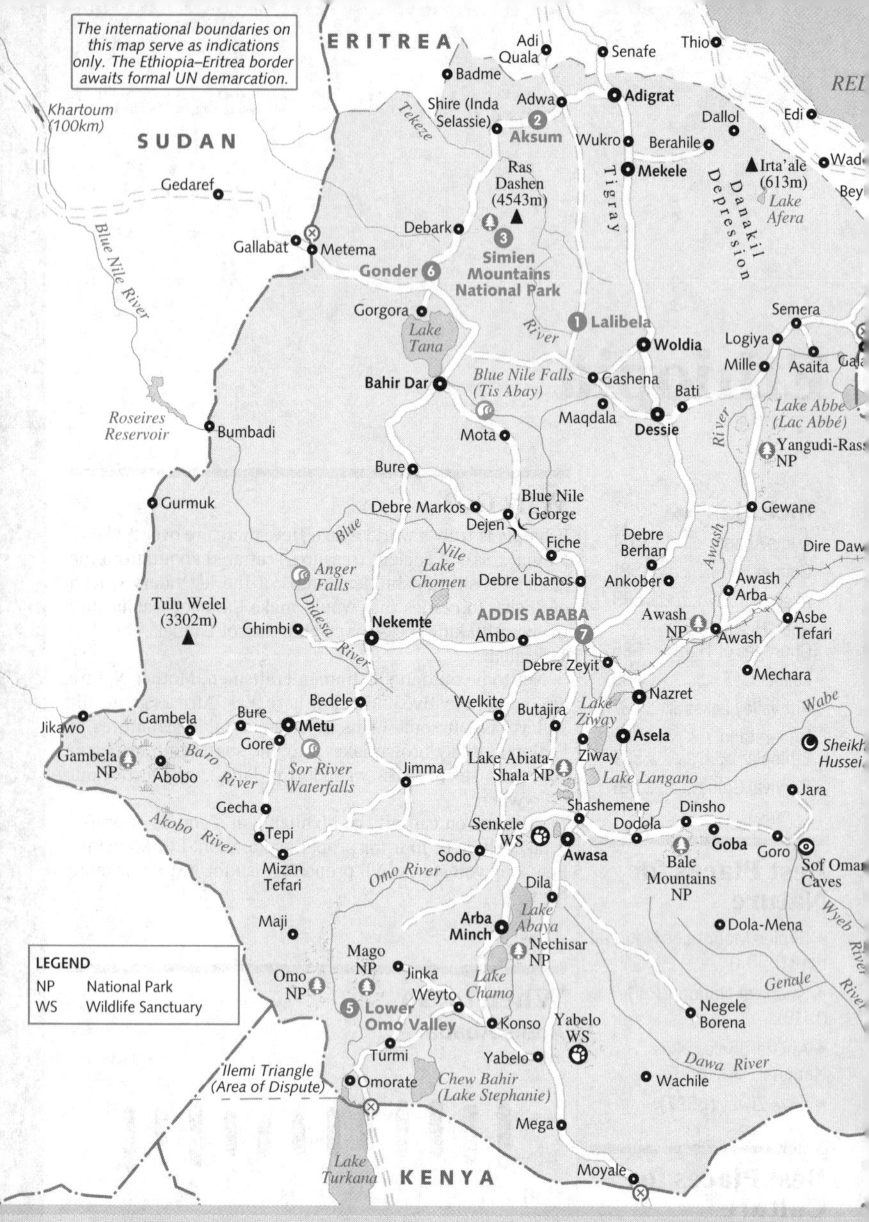

Ethiopia Highlights

1 Immerse yourself in Christianity's most raw and powerful form at the rock churches of **Lalibela** (p585).

2 Search for hidden treasure in the dank gloom of ancient tombs and ponder the mysteries of the stelae of **Aksum** (p583).

3 Lace up your boots to hike through the home of magnificent wildlife and unparalleled panoramas of Abyssinian abysses in the sublime **Simien Mountains National Park** (p583).

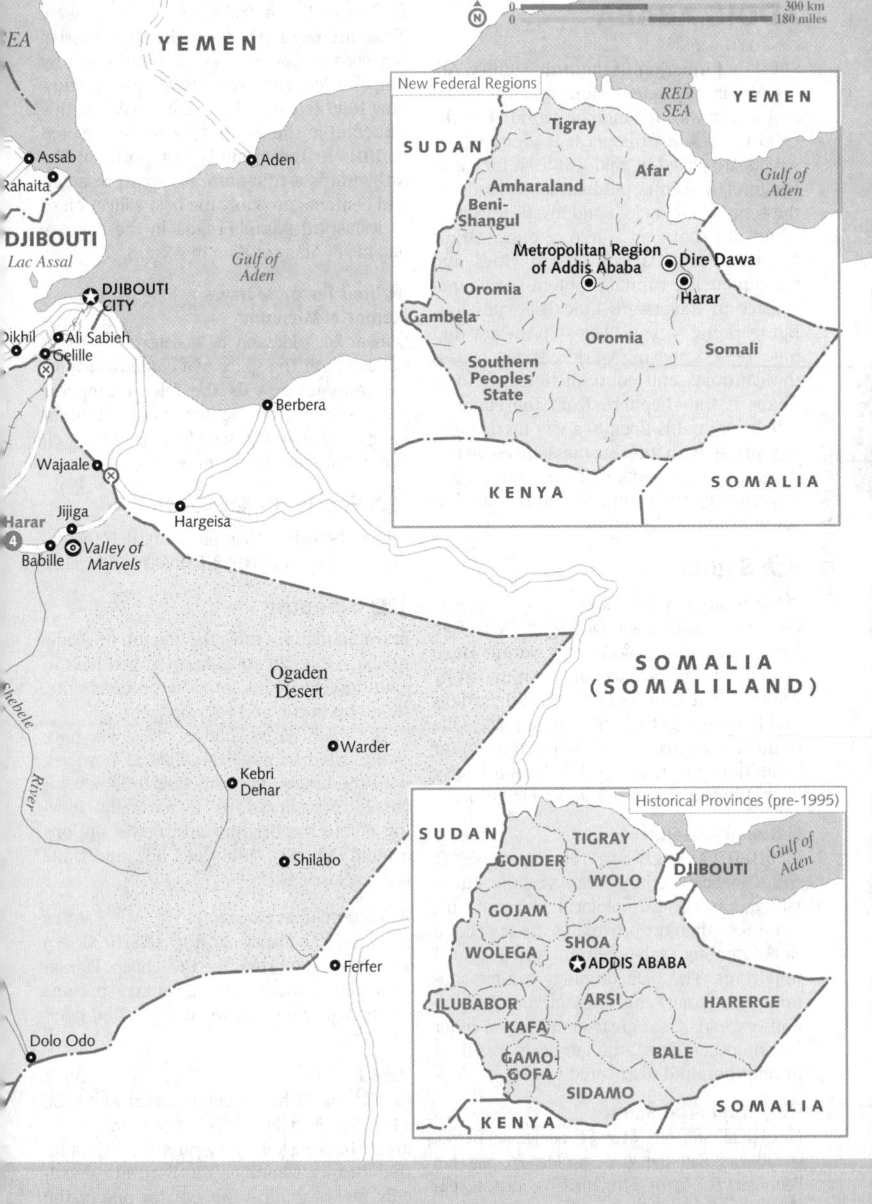

4 Explore the labyrinth of alleyways and shrines in the old walled city of **Harar** (p586).

5 Visit 'Africa's last great wilderness' and possibly the continent's most diverse and fascinating peoples in the **Lower Omo Valley** (p588).

6 Feel the thrill of Africa's 'Camelot' wreathed in legends and full of fascinating historical sites at **Gonder** (p581).

7 Get to know the superb museums, tasty restaurants and happening nightlife in the buzzing capital, **Addis Ababa** (p574).

ADDIS ABABA

POP 3.38 MILLION

Since its formation in the 19th century, Addis Ababa has acted like a magical portal and a gateway to another world. For the rural masses of Ethiopia it is a city whose streets are paved in gold – at least for some. For foreign visitors, Addis Ababa stands on the verge of an ancient and mystical world.

Yet for both of these groups, Addis Ababa, one of Africa's largest cities and the diplomatic capital, is often considered a place to traverse as quickly as possible. But by doing so, travellers skip the key that links these opposing worlds. If you bypass the contrasts and contradictions of Addis Ababa – the shepherd from the countryside bringing his flock to a city market, the city priest with the business investments, the glossy nightclubs with the country-girl prostitutes – then you risk failing to understand Ethiopia altogether.

Sights

★Ethnological Museum MUSEUM

(Algeria St; adult/student Birr50/30; ⏲8am-5pm Mon-Fri, 9am-5pm Sat & Sun) Set within Haile Selassie's former palace and surrounded by Addis Ababa University's beautiful gardens and fountains is this enthralling place. One of the finest museums in Africa, the vibrant exhibitions inside are well laid out and give a great insight into Ethiopia's rich cultures.

National Museum MUSEUM

(☎0111-117150; King George VI St; admission Birr10; ⏲8.30am-5pm) Although less visually stimulating than the Ethnological Museum, this is no less thought-provoking. Its collection ranks among sub-Saharan Africa's most important. The palaeontology exhibit contains two remarkable casts of your 3.2-million-year-old great-great-something-or-other grandmother, 'Lucy', the famously fossilised upright hominid discovered in 1974.

Holy Trinity Cathedral CHURCH

(☎0111-233518; off Niger St; admission Birr50; ⏲cathedral 8am-1pm & 2-6pm Mon-Fri, museum 8am-noon & 2-5pm) The massive ornate cathedral is Ethiopia's second-most important place of worship. It's also the final resting place of Emperor Haile Selassie and his wife. The entrance fee also includes admission to a small, but impressive, **museum** of ecclesiastical artefacts.

St George Cathedral CHURCH

(Fitawrari Gebeyehu St; museum Birr50; ⏲museum 9am-noon & 2-5pm Tue-Sun) Commissioned by Emperor Menelik to commemorate his stunning 1896 defeat of the Italians in Adwa, this cathedral in the Piazza area was completed in 1911. In the grounds just north of the cathedral is a **museum**. It's well presented and contains probably the best collection of ecclesiastical paraphernalia in the country outside St Mary of Zion in Aksum.

★'Red Terror' Martyrs Memorial Museum MUSEUM

(Meskal Sq; admission by donation; ⏲8.30am-6.30pm) Over the space of a couple of rooms the museum reveals the fall of Emperor Haile Selassie and the horrors of life under Mengistu's Derg regime. The museum is well laid out and incredibly moving.

Festivals & Events

Addis Ababa is a great place to catch the national festivals of Leddet, Timkat and Meskel.

Sleeping

Accommodation runs the gamut in Addis Ababa – you can snuggle up in bed next to giant insects or sink into a sumptuous suite. It's all up to you and your budget.

For many years, budget travellers have congregated around the Piazza; however, with the hotels there starting to look a bit creaky, travellers are increasingly moving out to the brighter and newer options around the more salubrious Bole and Haile Gebreselassie Rds.

Ankober Guest House HOTEL $

(☎0111-12350; Mundy St; d/tw US$20/30; 📶) The most salubrious of the cheap Piazza-area hotels, this place has smart, spacious rooms with polished wood floors and good showers.

Baro Hotel HOTEL $

(☎0111-551447; barohotel@ethionet.et; Mundy St; s from Birr170, d Birr225-330; P 📶) One of the great backpacker hang-outs of Ethiopia; the cheaper rooms at the Baro are decidedly low in quality, but opt for one of the more expensive options and you'll be the proud resident of a large and fairly well-maintained room.

Mr Martins Cozy Place HOTEL $

(☎0116-632611, 0910-884585; Mike Leyland St; d/ste Birr220/340; @) This colourful little German-run backpackers has gained a name for itself as one of the better-value cheapies in the city. All the rooms are impeccably clean, though a little poky, and there's a pleasant courtyard restaurant to hang out in and get acquainted with your fellow travellers. All rooms share clean common bathrooms.

Polaris Pension HOTEL $
(☎0920-224499; off Mike Leyland St; r from Birr200) Peach-pink rooms; inviting bathrooms (some with showers, some with bath tubs); art on the walls; cupboards for your gear; a TV; and a safe and quiet location. Oh yes, we like this one.

Holland House CAMPGROUND $
(☎0911-608088; wims_hollanhouse@ethionet.et; campsites Birr50, jeep Birr150, motorbike Birr70; @) Hidden in the maze of lanes to the east of the train station (look for the big yellow Shell signs) this camping ground, the sole overlanders' party in the city, is a cramped area normally overflowing with hardened road warriors talking about oil filters.

★**Itegue Taitu Hotel** HISTORIC HOTEL $$
(☎0111-560787; www.taituhotel.com; r Birr297-492, without bathroom Birr129-345; P) Built at the whim of Empress Taitu in 1907, this is the oldest hotel in Addis Ababa, and the main building, which has been tastefully renovated, is virtually a museum piece full of beautiful old furniture. The newer block contains a wide range of rooms, including some very jolly doubles. There's a lovely garden and plenty of other travellers to hang out with.

★**Stay Easy** BUSINESS HOTEL $$
(☎0116-616688; www.stayeasyaddis.com; off Haile Gebreselassie Rd; r US$40-50; P@) With its minimalist and utterly modern design, this business-class hotel is hands down the best place to stay in Addis Ababa. It has glittery art on the walls, high-quality mattresses, soundproofed rooms, flat-screen TVs with satellite channels, great service and a decent in-house restaurant.

La Source Guest House GUESTHOUSE $$
(☎0114-665510; lasourceguesthouse@gmail.com; Meskal Flower Rd; incl breakfast d US$25-35, tw US$35-40, ste US$45; @) Finally, Addis Ababa has produced a guest house that truly feels like it offers value for money. It's sparkling clean, with constant hot water, and it even has that rare thing – character – in abundance. All the rooms have loud and lovely African art and masks adorning the walls, rainbow-tinted bedspreads and furnishings made of bendy, twisted tree branches. The front-facing rooms can be very noisy.

Addis Regency Hotel HOTEL $$$
(☎0111-550000; www.addisregency.com; off Benin St; incl breakfast d US$75-95, tw US$90, ste US$150; P@) Friendly, immaculately well-kept, supremely comfortable, endless piping-hot water, a decent restaurant and a quiet side-street location put this place a cut above the competition.

Eating

Many of the more tourist-oriented Ethiopian restaurants offer a 'traditional experience': traditional food (called 'national food') in traditional surroundings with traditional music in the evening.

Many of the smarter restaurants add 15% tax and a 10% service charge to their bills; check before you order.

Raizel Café CAFE $
(Hailesilase St) This slick modern cafe speedily serves tasty cheese burgers, tuna melts, french fries and breakfast omelettes.

★**La Mandoline** FRENCH $$
(☎0116-629482; behind Bole Medanyalem Church, off Cameroon St; mains Birr55-80; closed Mon) This upper-crust French restaurant serving superb, and authentic, traditional French dishes might well get our vote as the best-value restaurant in the city. How traditional is the food? Try an excellent salad for a starter, a delicious steak with Roquefort cheese sauce for a main and a crème brûlée for dessert and you won't know you're not in La Belle France.

Itegue Taitu Hotel ETHIOPIAN $$
(☎0111-560787; www.taituhotel.com; mains Birr30-40, lunch buffet Birr59) If you've travelled overland to Addis Ababa, and eaten in a few cheap local restaurants, then reward yourself with the high-quality and utterly delicious Ethiopian fare served up in the refined and stately atmosphere of this old hotel's renovated dining room. Its bargain-priced lunchtime buffet (also available on Friday evenings) is immensely popular.

Elsa Restaurant ETHIOPIAN $$
(Mike Leyland St; mains Birr55-75, 1kg of meat Birr150; noon-10pm) This simple outdoor

Addis Ababa

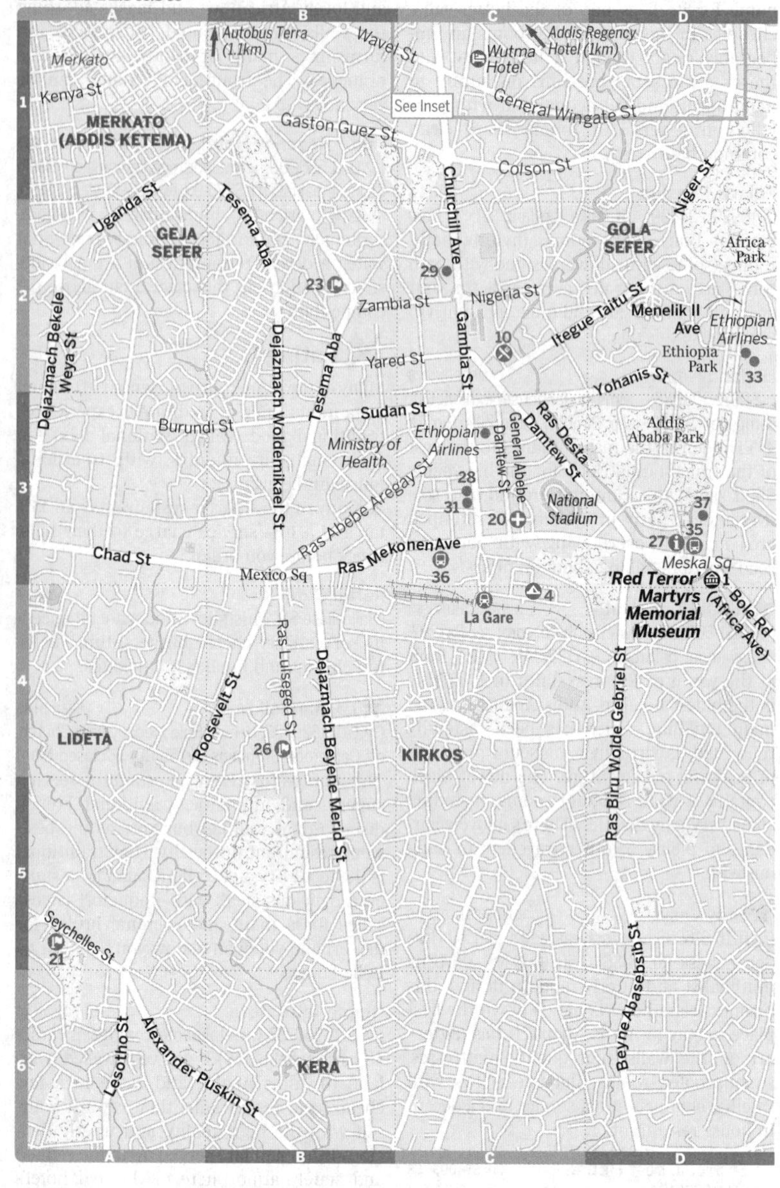

restaurant serves quality *yetsom beyaynetu* (variety of fasting foods), which is perfect for vegetarians, while *yedoro arosto* (roasted chicken) and *gored gored* (raw beef cubes with *awazi,* a kind of mustard and chilli sauce) assuage carnivorous cravings. Half the neighbourhood like to come here for an afternoon drink.

Shangri-la Restaurant ETHIOPIAN **$$**
(☎0116-632424; Cape Verde St; mains Birr50-70, 1kg of meat Birr160) Shangri-la has earned a

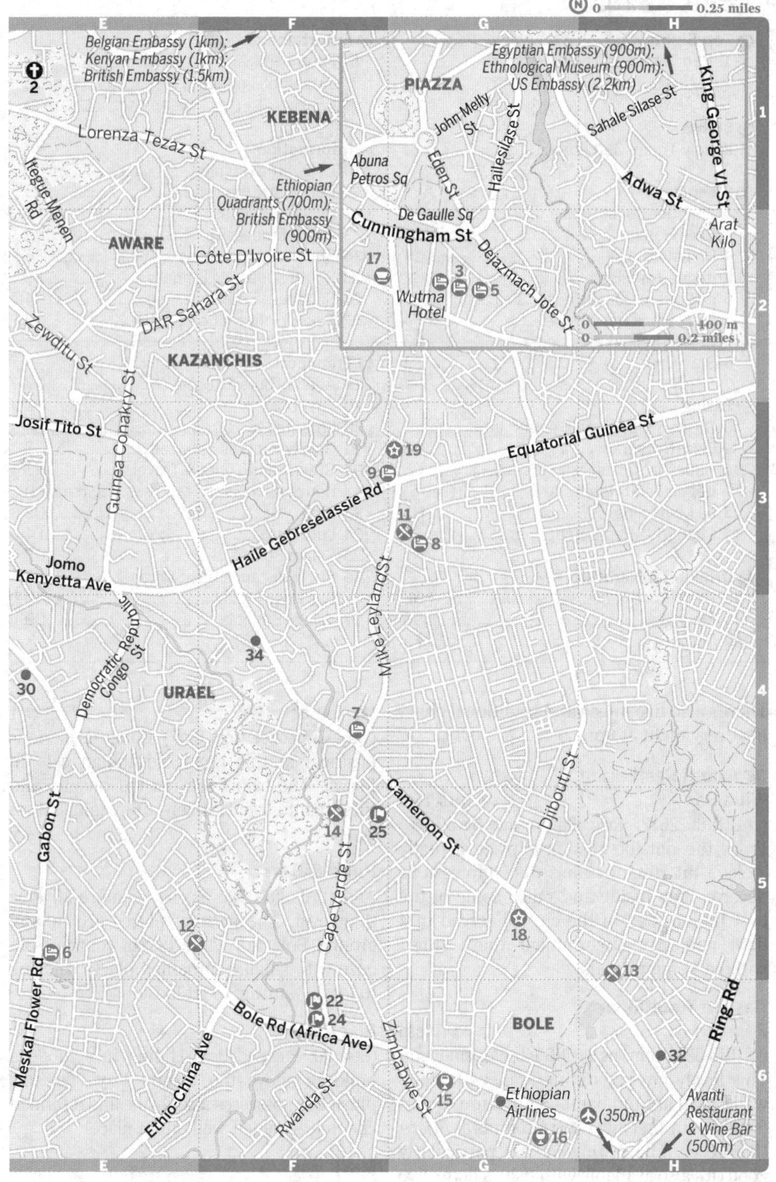

well-deserved reputation as an atmospheric place for great Ethiopian food, especially *tere sega* (raw meat; available Saturday only). Fasting food is the way to go on Wednesday and Friday.

Habesha Restaurant ETHIOPIAN **$$**
(0115-518358; Bole Rd; mains Birr60-80; lunch & dinner) For an Ethiopian meal that looks as good as it tastes, come to this fashionable Bole eatery where serving is an art form.

Addis Ababa

Top Sights
1 'Red Terror' Martyrs Memorial Museum ... D3

Sights
2 Holy Trinity Cathedral ... E1

Sleeping
3 Ankober Guest House ... G2
Baro Hotel ... (see 3)
4 Holland House ... C4
5 Itegue Taitu Hotel ... G2
6 La Source Guest House ... E5
7 Mr Martins Cozy Place ... F4
8 Polaris Pension ... G3
9 Stay Easy ... F3

Eating
10 Dashen Traditional Restaurant ... C2
11 Elsa Restaurant ... G3
12 Habesha Restaurant ... E5
Itegue Taitu Hotel ... (see 5)
13 La Mandoline ... H5
14 Shangri-la Restaurant ... F5

Drinking & Nightlife
15 Black Rose ... G6
16 Mask Bar ... G6
17 Tomoca ... F2

Entertainment
18 Farenheit ... G5
Jazzamba Lounge ... (see 5)
19 Topia Tej Bet ... G3

Information
20 Bethzatha Hospital ... C3
21 Canadian Embassy ... A5
22 Djibouti Embassy ... F6
23 Dutch Embassy ... B2
24 Somaliland Embassy ... F6
25 South Sudanese Embassy ... F5
26 Sudanese Embassy ... B4
27 Tourist Information Centre ... D3

Transport
28 Abeba Tours Ethiopia ... C3
29 EgyptAir ... C2
30 Emirates ... E4
31 Galaxy Express Services ... C3
32 Green Land Tours & Travels ... H6
Kenya Airways ... (see 33)
33 KLM ... D2
34 Lufthansa ... F4
35 Selam Buses ... D3
36 Short-distance Bus Station ... C3
Sky Buses ... (see 5)
37 Village Ethiopia ... D3

There's also live music and traditional dancing every night at 8pm.

★ Avanti Restaurant & Wine Bar ITALIAN $$$
(☎0111-8622632; Ring Rd; mains Birr80-120) From the outside this new place actually looks a bit rundown, but first impressions deceive. Step inside and relish some of the best Italian food in the city all served in a light and airy environment that's smart without being formal.

Dashen Traditional Restaurant ETHIOPIAN $$$
(☎0115-529746; mains Birr100-145; ⏰10am-10pm) This lovely low-key dining area, with stone walls, local art and bamboo furniture, is perfect for your first awkward attempts at *injera* (flatbread). The fasting food is particularly good (it's also available with fish). There's live music Wednesday to Sunday evenings.

Drinking & Entertainment

Cafes

Cafes and pastry shops are omnipresent and they are perfect for early-morning and afternoon pick-me-ups.

★ Tomoca CAFE
(Wavel St; coffee from Birr7) Coffee is serious business at this great old Italian cafe in Piazza. The beans are roasted on-site, and turned into what's likely the capital's best coffee.

Pubs & Bars

Addis Ababa's bar scene is more diverse than ever. The swanky places are in and around Bole Rd, while Piazza continues to ooze with smaller unnamed places catering to locals wanting to let loose.

Black Rose BAR
(Bole Rd; ⏰closed Mon) Hiding in a modern building above the Boston Day Spa, this plush bar possesses a cool vibe and a refined clientele – we felt well out of place!

Mask Bar BAR
(off Bole Rd) This tiny bar is as gaudy as it is cool. The crowd ranges from expats to well-heeled locals. It's well signposted off Bole Rd.

Tej Beats

If authentic experiences are what you're after, then there's no better place than a *tej bet* (a house to down the famed golden honey wine).

Topia Tej Bet
BAR

(off Haile Gebreselassie Rd; ⏲10am-10pm) Tucked up an alley behind the Axum Hotel, this is Addis Ababa's top *tej bet* and the only one to serve pure honey *tej* (honey wine).

Nightclubs

Addis Ababa's nightlife is slowly maturing, with modern clubs joining the circuit. Cover charges vary between Birr50 and Birr100 at most venues.

★Jazzamba Lounge
JAZZ

(Itegue Taitu Hotel; admission Birr50-80; ⏲8.30pm-1am) Back in the 1960s the jazz scene in Addis Ababa was booming, and Ethiopian jazz even had its own style and name: Ethiojazz. Then along came the Derg and away went the fun. Today the scene is making a slow recovery, the centre of which is Jazzamba Lounge, inside the creaky Itegue Taitu Hotel in Piazza. Every night there's a live jazz session that attracts renowned local and international artists including people like Samuel Yirga.

Farenheit
CLUB

(off Cameroon St) A reliably good club that's been around a while. It plays a wide range of music and mixes it up with DJs and live bands.

Information

DANGERS & ANNOYANCES

Violent crime is rare in Addis Ababa particularly where visitors are concerned. However, petty theft and confidence tricks are problematic. The Merkato (market) is the worst for this, as pickpockets abound, targeting *faranjis* (foreigners) and Ethiopians. Other spots requiring vigilance include Piazza, Meskal Sq, minibus stands and Churchill Ave.

Beware of distraction tactics (some involving someone enthusiastically grabbing your ankles, while others pilfer your pockets!). Another increasingly common scam involves someone 'accidentally' spitting on you; as they lean forward to wipe it off, your pockets get emptied.

EMERGENCY

Emergency 24-hour numbers:

Police (☎991)

Red Cross Ambulance Service (☎917)

MEDICAL SERVICES

Bethzatha Hospital (☎0115-514470; ⏲24hr) This quality private hospital, off Ras Mekonen Ave, is recommended by most embassies.

MONEY

You'll have no trouble finding a bank to change cash, and most larger Dashen Bank branches have ATMs that accept foreign Visa or MasterCard cards (but not Plus or Cirrus cards).

TOURIST INFORMATION

Tourist Information Centre (☎0115-512310; Meskal Sq; ⏲8.30am-12.30pm & 1.30-5.30pm) This helpful office does its best to provide information about the city and itineraries elsewhere.

Getting There & Away

AIR

Ethiopian Airlines (www.flyethiopian.com) is the only domestic carrier, and regularly serves almost a dozen Ethiopian destinations. It has branches on Bole Rd (☎0116-633163); Gambia St (☎0115-517000); Menelik II Ave (☎0115-511540); and in Piazza (☎0111-569247).

BUS

Journeys of less than 150km are served from the central **short-distance bus station** (Ras Mekonen Ave), while longer journeys depart from **Autobus Terra** (Central African Republic St), northwest of Merkato. Buses for the following destinations leave officially at 6.30am:

DESTINATION	FARE (BIRR)	DURATION
Aksum	308	2½ days
Arba Minch	148	12 hours
Awasa	80	6 hours
Bahir Dar via Dangala	165	12 hours
Bahir Dar via Mota	165	12 hours
Dire Dawa	150	11 hours
Gonder	216	2 days
Jinka	227	2 days
Lalibela	215	2 days
Moyale	226	1½ days

A couple of 'luxury buses' now fly down the country's highways and are proving immensely popular with both foreign visitors and locals. The best established is **Selam Buses** (☎0115-548800; www.selambus.com; Meskel Sq). Book tickets up to a week beforehand if possible. It has the following daily services (all departing at 5.30am) to: Bahir Dar (Birr290), Gonder (Birr375), Mekele (Birr400), Dessie (Birr205), Harar (Birr270), Dire Dawa (Birr265) and Jimma (Birr165).

Possibly even slicker (these puppies have reclining seats, air-con, onboard toilets and even free snacks and drinks!) are **Sky Buses** (☎0111-568080; Itegue Taitu Hotel), which also leave from Meskel Sq; the ticket office is handily inside the Itegue Taitu Hotel. It has buses to, among other places, Bahir Dar (Birr306.90, 12 hours), Gonder (Birr372.80, one day) and Harar (Birr278, 12 hours).

MINIBUS

As well as the normal buses, speedy (not always a good thing!) minibuses serve Bahir Dar and Gonder. There's no station per se, but commission agents patrol for customers near the Wutma Hotel in Piazza.

Getting Around

Bole International Airport is 5km southeast of the city centre. Blue city taxis to the airport for a local should cost around Birr80 to Birr100 from anywhere south of Meskal Sq to around Birr130 to Birr150 if leaving from Piazza; add Birr20 at night or early in the morning. As a foreigner you're likely to pay at least Birr100 more for either route. From the airport, prices are much higher and normally quoted in US dollars (though drivers accept Birr). Heading about halfway along Bole Rd will cost around US$20 and to Piazza around US$35.

There's an extensive network of efficient, cheap minibuses servicing Addis Ababa. Journeys cost around Birr1.30.

Taxis are everywhere. Journeys to 3km cost Birr40 to Birr50 (more at night), while medium/long journeys cost Birr80 to Birr100.

TOURS

Some recommended agencies in Addis Ababa include the following:

Abeba Tours Ethiopia (☎0115-159530; www.abebatoursethiopia.com; Ras Hotel, Gambia St)

Ethiopian Quadrants (☎0115-157990; www.ethiopianquadrants.com; near Adwa Bridge)

Galaxy Express Services (☎0115-510355; www.galaxyexpressethiopia.com; Gambia St)

Green Land Tours & Travels (☎0116-299252; www.greenlandethiopia.com; Cameroon St)

Village Ethiopia (☎0115-523497; www.village-ethiopia.net; National Hotel, Menelik II Ave)

NORTHERN ETHIOPIA

Bahir Dar

POP 180,000

Ethiopians like to describe Bahir Dar as being their Riviera and, with its wide streets shielded by palm trees and sweeping views across shimmering blue waters, it would be hard to argue.

It's a great place to spend a few days. Besides sights around town, you're on the doorstep of Lake Tana's mystical monasteries.

Sights & Activities

Though lounging lakeside and watching pelicans skirting the surface might be a relaxing pastime, you absolutely shouldn't miss a day spent exploring Lake Tana's treasure-filled **monasteries** (admission per church entry Birr100 (Birr150 for Tana Cherkos), video camera Birr100) lurking on 20 of its islands. Many date from the late 16th or early 17th centuries, though some may have been the site of pre-Christian shrines.

Boat operators abound and shifty commission agents lurk everywhere. Negotiated prices (for one to five people) range from Birr800 for a half-day trip to Birr2400 for 11 hours in a 25HP speedboat. Ensure your boat has life jackets and spare fuel.

The Blue Nile snakes out of Lake Tana's southern end, plummeting 30km later over the **Blue Nile Falls** (adult/student/child Birr30/20/free, video camera Birr50, mandatory guide 1-5/5+ people Birr60/120; ⏲7am-5.30pm). Named by locals Tis Abay, the once-mighty falls have now withered like an aged chain smoker, thanks to a hydroelectric project. Still, it's a pretty picnic spot with parrots, turacos, white-throated seedeaters and vervet monkeys. Buses (Birr13, one bumpy hour) access Tis Abay, the nearby village. The Ghion Hotel arranges tours.

Other interests include Bahir Dar's **market** and a massive **war memorial**, near the Blue Nile bridge (a few kilometres northeast of town), dedicated to those who died fighting the Derg.

Sleeping

Menen Hotel HOTEL $

(☎0582-263900; d Birr180-250, tw Birr300-400; P) A newish place near the bus station that offers clean rooms, fair value and good service. The lowest-priced rooms lack TVs and hot water.

Dib Anbessa Hotel HOTEL $$

(☎0582-201436; d/tw incl breakfast Birr300/400; P@) An older hotel with lots of carved wood giving it character. This doesn't extend into the rooms, but overlook the frayed carpets and you'll find that with their soft beds, satellite TV and balconies they offer fair value.

Ghion Hotel HOTEL **$$**
(☎0582-200111; campsites per tent Birr100, s Birr200-300, d Birr250-300; P@) Although the rooms are as tired and worn as your favourite pair of travel socks, there's no denying Ghion's beautiful lakeside setting. The gardens, full of flowers and paradise flycatchers, are gorgeous. Rooms aren't identical and you need to let staff know if you're interested in the cheaper, smellier ones. It's easily the most popular place for *faranjis* to rest their heads.

Kuriftu Resort & Spa RESORT **$$$**
(☎0920-959797; www.kurifturesortspa.com; s with half board incl 1 massage, manicure, pedicure US$132-139, d/tw/ste US$167/173/194; P@) There's lots of new luxe lodging going up in Bahir Dar, but this attractive spot will surely remain one of the best. Kuriftu's large, refined stone and wood cottages are filled with lovely furnishings and artistic touches. Be sure to request a lake-view room: they don't cost extra.

Eating & Drinking

Desset Resort EUROPEAN, ETHIOPIAN **$$**
(mains Birr28-85) This popular restaurant really makes the most of its long landscaped shoreline. Both the *habesha* (Ethiopian) and *faranji* dishes (try the roasted lamb) are quite good and the menu is bigger than normal.

Pelican Wine House WINE BAR
(noon-midnight Mon-Fri, 9am-midnight Sat & Sun) A chemistry degree from Bahir Dar University led owner Yordanos into a life of wine and she now makes her own honey, date, mango, apple and grape varieties (Birr17/34 for a small/large bottle). You can pair them with burgers and chips from her sister's kitchen. It's easy to find; head past the post office and then south 500m from the university gate.

Information

There are several banks and internet cafes, a small **tourist office** (☎0582-201686; 8.30am-12.30pm & 1.30-5.30pm Mon-Fri) and a telecommunications building. **Gamby Higher Clinic & Pharmacy** (☎0918-143195; 24hr), on the main drag, is the best medical facility.

DANGERS & ANNOYANCES

Women, accompanied by male companions or not, should not walk along the waterfront path that runs from the Ghion Hotel into town. We have received a large number of complaints regarding serious hassle from the sleazy men hanging out here.

Getting There & Around

Ethiopian Airlines (☎0582-200020) has two daily (some days three) flights to Addis Ababa (US$55, one hour) and a thrice-weekly flight to Lalibela (US$41, 35 minutes).

Two ordinary buses make the long trip to/from Addis Ababa (Birr100, 11 to 12 hours, 6am). Luxury Sky Bus (Birr307) has an office near the lake and uses Mango Park as its 6am departure point. The Selam (Birr290) ticket office is at the bus station, but the buses park in front of St George's Church and depart at 5.30am. The Post Bus (Birr216) departs at 5.30am from Bahir Dar three days a week. Minibuses travel at night (which makes them dangerous) and can do the trip in as little as seven hours.

Two buses travel to Gonder (Birr55, three hours) at 6am and minibuses (Birr65) go about hourly. There's nothing direct to Lalibela, but you can take one of about five morning minibuses (Birr100, three hours) or the 6am bus (Birr97, 3½ hours) to Woldia and get off at Gashena to catch a connection there.

Gonder

POP 227,100

It's not what Gonder is, but what Gonder was, that is so enthralling. The city lies in a bowl of hills filled with eucalyptus trees and tin-roofed houses, but rising above these and standing proud through the centuries are the walls of castles bathed in blood and painted in the pomp of royalty. Often called the Camelot of Africa, this description does the Royal City a disservice, for whereas Camelot is legend, Gonder is reality.

Sights

Royal Enclosure CASTLE
(adult/student Birr100/75, video camera Birr75; 8.30am-12.30pm & 1.30-6pm) The Gonder of yesteryear was a city of extreme brutality and immense wealth. Today the wealth and brutality are gone but the memories linger here in the form of impressive castles and high stone walls. Constructed piecemeal by successive emperors between the mid-17th and mid-18th centuries, the entire 70,000-sq-metre site was declared a Unesco World Heritage Site in 1979. Knowledgable, well-trained guides cost Birr100 and are well worth it.

Fasiladas' Bath HISTORIC SITE

(admission incl in Royal Enclosure ticket; ⏲8.30am-6pm) Around 2km northwest of the Royal Enclosure lies a shady, beautiful and historic spot attributed to Emperors Fasiladas (r 1632–67) and Iyasu I (r 1682–1706).

Empress Mentewab's Kuskuam Complex PALACE

(admission Birr50, video camera Birr75; ⏲8am-6pm) Melancholic, silent and little-visited, this complex, 3.5km northwest of the centre, was built in 1730 for the redoubtable Empress Mentewab upon her husband's death. Although less preserved than the Royal Enclosure, the complex offers an impressive mix of countryside views, each dramatically framed by its crumbling remnants.

Debre Berhan Selassie CHURCH

(admission Birr50, video camera Birr75; ⏲8am-12.30pm & 1.30-6pm) Another great sight, this church is an easy stroll 2km northeast of town. Despite its walls hosting the nation's most vibrant ecclesiastical artwork, it's the ceiling that captures most visitors' imaginations – rows and rows of winged cherubs smiling sweetly down at you.

Sleeping

L-Shape Hotel HOTEL $

(☎0918-787634; d Birr150-200, tw Birr300; P 📶) Rooms here are in better shape then the hallways would lead you to believe and the absence of *faranji* prices makes it highly recommended; especially if you score a room with a view.

Central Gonder Hotel HOTEL $

(☎0581-117020; d Birr288) Beyond a little wear and tear, the rooms, with satellite TV and some with good people-watching views, can't be faulted and the inflated *faranji* prices are definitely open to negotiation.

★**Lodge Fasil** HOTEL $$

(☎0581-110637; s/d & tw incl breakfast US$30/40; P @) A stone's throw from the Royal Enclosure's exit, this new place features many trees, eager staff and spotless rooms back away from traffic noise.

★**Lodge du Chateau** HOTEL $$$

(☎0918-152001; www.lodgeduchateau.com; dm/s/d & tw incl breakfast US$20/45/50; P @ 📶) Doing things their own way, this owner-managed spot next to the Royal Enclosure has the friendliest service in town, and an attention to detail. The rooms are nicely decorated and have good mattresses and the dining room-lounge is perched high to make the best of the valley views.

Eating

★**Habesha Kitfo** ETHIOPIAN $

(mains Birr30-65) Decked out with a woven mat floor, cow-hide stools and the odd live duck, this place drips with character and is the ideal spot to indulge in great Ethiopian food.

Four Sisters EUROPEAN, ETHIOPIAN $$

(mains Birr50-90) The food here is fine, but it's the ambience, with stone walls and Debre Berhan Selassie–inspired paintings plus nightly traditional music, that sets it apart. Special programs, such as learning how to make *tej* and *injera*, are available.

Information

Piazza marks the town centre and it hosts banks, internet cafes and the post office. For medical treatment head to **Ibex General Hospital** (☎0581-118273). Just east of Piazza is the very helpful **tourist information centre** (☎0581-110022; ⏲8.30am-12.30pm & 1.30-5.30pm Mon-Fri, 8.30am-12.30pm Sat).

Getting There & Away

Ethiopian Airlines (☎0581-117688) flies twice daily to Addis Ababa (US$65, one hour) and once to Lalibela (US$41, two hours) via Aksum (US$45, 40 minutes). Shared taxis to/from the airport cost Birr50 per person.

It's a rare traveller who heads direct to or from Addis Ababa, but it can be done in 13 to 14 hours with the luxury buses. Sky Bus (Birr373, 5am) departs from the Royal Enclosure entrance gate and the ticket office is nearby in the Genet Café. Selam (Birr375, 5.30am) departs from the Royal Enclosure exit gate and has a ticket office at Taye Hotel. The Post Bus (Birr283, 4.30am) has Gonder departures Monday, Wednesday and Friday, and Addis Ababa departures Sunday, Tuesday and Thursday. Ordinary Addis Ababa buses (Birr250, 5am) require an overnight stop along the way.

Shorter trips to Bahir Dar (Birr55 to Birr65, three hours) and Debark (Birr48, 2½ hours) are easiest by minibus. For Aksum, catch a connection in Shire (Birr120, 10 to 11 hours, 5.30am). There's nothing direct to Lalibela, but you can take the 5.30am bus (Birr85, four to five hours) or one of the minibuses (Birr160, four hours) headed to Woldia and get off in Gashena where you can easily catch a connection, as long as you don't arrive too late.

Simien Mountains National Park

No matter how you experience them, the Simien Mountains will leave you speechless. This massive table of rock, up to 4500m high and riven with gullies, offers easy but immensely rewarding hiking along the edge of a plateau that falls sheer to the plains far below. It's not just the scenery (and altitude) that will leave you speechless, but also the excitement of sitting among a group of 100 gelada monkeys or watching magnificent walia ibex joust on the rock ledges. Numerous trails allow walks ranging from a day to up to two weeks. Most people do the standard four- or five-day walk.

Camping equipment, guides, mandatory scouts, cooks, mules and mule-handlers are all easily arranged at **park headquarters** (☎0918-704211; admission per day Birr90, vehicle Birr20; ⏱8.30am-12.30pm & 1.30-5.30pm) in Debark. Note that park entrance fees include camping charges.

While in Debark, you can sleep and eat at the **Simien Park Hotel** (☎0581-170005; s/d/tw Birr200/250/300, s/d without bathroom Birr80/100; P).

Out on the mountain trails almost everyone camps at one of the designated camping areas although there are also simple huts. If camping on a mountain just ain't your thing, then treat yourself to the **Simien Park Lodge** (☎0582-310741; www.simiens.com; s & tw incl breakfast US$160-170).

Two morning buses and lots of minibuses run from Debark to Gonder (Birr48, 2½ hours). The only bus to Shire (for Aksum) is the Gonder service that passes through Debark around 8am, but it's often full. If you want to guarantee a seat, the national park office, your guide or hotel will reserve you a place by getting somebody in Gonder to ride in your seat between Gonder and Debark. They charge Birr300 to Birr350 for this service; arrange it a day in advance.

Aksum

POP 54,000

Aksum is a riddle waiting to be solved. Did the Queen of Sheba really call the town's dusty streets home? Does the very same Ark of the Covenant that Moses carried down from Mt Sinai reside in that small chapel? Are there actually secret hordes of treasure hidden inside undiscovered tombs? And just what exactly do those famous stelae signify?

This Unesco World Heritage Site is undoubtedly one of the most important and spectacular ancient sites in sub-Saharan Africa. Don't miss it.

Sights

One admission ticket (adult/student Birr50/25) covers all sights within the immediate vicinity of Aksum, except the St Mary of Zion Churches compound and the monasteries of Abba Pentalewon and Abba Liqanos. The ticket is good for three days and is sold at the Aksum Tourism Information Centre. All sights are open between 8am and 6pm though guards at smaller sites might vanish at lunchtime.

Stelae MONUMENT

Ancient Aksum stelae (obelisks) pepper the area, and looking down on a small specimen or staring up at a grand tower, you'll be bowled over. The **Northern stelae field** is the grandest, with over 120 stelae ranging from 1m to 33m. Beneath the rising monoliths are a series of tombs; it is estimated that 90% remain undiscovered, but the fantastic museum reveals a little of Aksum's glory.

St Mary of Zion Churches CHURCH

(admission Birr200, video camera Birr100; ⏱7.30am-12.30pm & 2.30-5.30pm Mon-Fri, 9am-noon & 2.30-5.30pm Sat & Sun) Immediately southwest of the Northern stelae field are the St Mary of Zion Churches, Ethiopia's holiest shrine. The rectangular old church was built on the site of a 4th-century Aksumite church by Emperor Fasiladas, Gonder's founder, in 1665. Nearby is a little museum (soon to be moved and expanded) containing a breathtaking haul of treasure, including an unsurpassed collection of former Ethiopian rulers' crowns and a dazzling display of gold and precious stones. The real reason for most people's visit, though, is to sneak a peek at the carefully guarded chapel said to contain the original Ark of the Covenant. Nobody is allowed to enter the chapel or see the Ark and foreigners are not even allowed to approach the fence surrounding the chapel.

Tombs of Kings Kaleb & Gebre Meskel MONUMENT

(general visit adult/student Br50/Br25; ⏱8am-5pm) On a small hill 1.8km northeast of the Northern stelae field, offering views of

Adwa's distant jagged mountains, are the monumental 6th-century tombs of Kings Kaleb and Gebre Meskel. En route, you will pass by **King Ezana's Inscription** (tip the guardian around Br3-5 for opening the hut), hiding in a timber shack. Dating back to the 4th century, it's the Ethiopian equivalent of the Rosetta Stone, a pillar inscribed in Sabaean, Greek and Ge'ez (the ancestor of Amharic).

Other important sites in the area include **King Bazen's tomb** (general visit adult/student Br50/Br25; 8am-5pm) and the remains of a 6th- or 7th-century **palace**, wrongly attributed to the Queen of Sheba.

Yeha HISTORIC SITE
(admission Birr50, video camera Birr100) Rewarding excursions outside of Aksum can be made to Yeha, considered to be the birthplace of Ethiopian civilisation. The site, 58km from Aksum, comprises a set of well-preserved ruins dating from the 8th to the 5th century BC.

Debre Damo Monastery MONASTERY
(admission Birr150, men only) With your own wheels, it's easy enough to push on after Yeha to the fantastical Debre Damo Monastery. Atop a sheer-sided *amba* (flat-topped mountain), this is one of the most fascinating, and least accessible, monasteries in the country. You might wonder how anybody first managed to climb the mountain walls in order to establish the monastery. The answer is that Abuna Aregawi, one of the Nine Saints (the group of wandering Syrian monks who helped establish Christianity in Ethiopia) and founder of the monastery, had a little helping hand in the form of a giant serpent that lowered its tail off the mountain and allowed Abuna Aregawi to clamber up. Fortunately you don't have to be a herpetologist to get there today; although you do have to like hauling yourself 20m up a very weathered-looking **leather rope** (Birr50; men only).

Festivals & Events

Festival of Maryam Zion RELIGIOUS
On 30 November thousands of pilgrims flood into Aksum to celebrate Mary. Expect a cornucopia of music and dance.

Sleeping

Abyssinia Hotel HOTEL $
(0347-751043; tw without bathroom Birr120, d Birr100) A clean and comfortable hotel that has yet to discover *faranji* pricing. One of the private bathrooms lacks hot water, as do the common showers, but the owner plans to rectify this.

★ **Africa Hotel** HOTEL $$
(0347-753700; www.africahotelaxum.com; s/d/tw/tr Birr175/200/250/300; P @ wifi) With an eager (too much sometimes) and engaged owner, this place offers a smooth stay and is easily the most popular budget guest house in town, so it's a good place to meet other travellers. The rooms are simple and bright and the bathrooms very clean.

Ark Hotel HOTEL $$
(0347-752676; s/d/tw Birr200/250/300; P) Very near the Africa Hotel, this place has essentially the same quality rooms, but minus the mostly *faranji* clientele.

Yeha Hotel HOTEL $$$
(0347-752377; www.yehahotelaxum.com; s/tw/ste US$57/76/102) Perched atop a bluff overlooking the stelae and the Mary of Zion Churches, this hotel has the most enviable location, and though it's too old to be able to claim the best rooms in town, all things considered it remains the best place to stay.

Eating

Ezana Café ETHIOPIAN $
(mains Birr13-25) An awesome breakfast spot with excellent *ful* (broad bean mash) and 'special *fata*' (bread *firfir* – torn-up injera – with yoghurt and egg). Complete your meal with a juice from No Name Juice House next door.

Atse Yohanes International Restaurant AMERICAN, ETHIOPIAN $$
(mains Birr45-75) The American half of the Ethio-Virginian couple who owns this pleasant spot has brought cinnamon rolls (high season only) and proper hamburgers to Aksum. This is also a great spot for Ethiopian food.

Information

On the two main streets you'll find several banks, health clinics and internet cafes, along with a post office, a telecommunications office and the very helpful **Aksum Tourism Information Centre** (0347-753924; www.aksumtourism.co; 7am-6pm).

Getting There & Away

Ethiopian Airlines (0347-752300) flies twice daily to Addis Ababa (US$80, one to three hours), sometimes direct and sometimes via Lalibela (US$46, 45 minutes) and Gonder (US$45, 40 minutes). Shared airport taxis cost Birr40. Almost every hotel provides airport pick-up.

For buses to Gonder and Debark (Simien Mountains), go to Shire (Birr23, 1½ hours) first. There are two morning buses to Mekele (Birr82, seven hours, 6am) which can drop you in Wukro (Birr65, six hours).

Aksum's travel agencies and numerous freelance agents rent vehicles (including driver and guide) for trips to Yeha, Debre Damo Monastery and the rock churches of Tigray. Birr1300 (excluding fuel) is a fair price for minibus trips of more than one day.

Rock-Hewn Churches of Tigray

Perched precariously atop huge rock needles among the sandy, semidesert wasteland of northern Tigray is a stash of ancient monasteries. Some of the 120-odd churches (plus a few invisible ones) found here may even predate those at Lalibela. It's one of the most other-worldly places in Ethiopia.

Sights

Most churches charge Birr100 for admission. A few should only charge Birr50, but usually demand Birr100. Expect all kinds of extra charges to be added onto your entrance fee. Patience and a positive attitude are essential for your enjoyment as it can take up to an hour to locate some priests.

Official guides from the **Gheralta Local Guide Association** (☎0914-616851; 1-3/4-6 people per day Birr250/350) are mandatory for Abuna Yemata Guh, but they can be hired for other places too. Their office is at the main junction in Megab.

Most churches are in groups or clusters. The Gheralta cluster, with the highest number of churches, and in the most mind-bending of settings, is considered the most important, while the Takatisfi cluster, only 3km east of the Mekele–Adigrat road, is the most accessible. Between Adigrat and Mekele there's a plethora of churches. Many are pretty inaccessible, meaning visiting some churches involves steep climbs or scrambling up almost sheer rock faces using toeholds.

Of those in the Gheralta cluster, don't miss easily accessible **Abraha Atsbeha**, **Abuna Gebre Mikael** with its beautiful scenery, and the most spectacularly sited of all the churches, **Abuna Yemata Guh**, which involves a heart-in-the-mouth climb up a sheer mountainside.

In the Takatisfi cluster, gorge your eyes on **Medhane Alem Kesho** and meet the friendly monk at **Petros and Paulos**.

Sleeping & Eating

The sandy village of Hawzien, where the following are located, is probably the best base.

Tourist Hotel HOTEL $$
(☎0346-670238; s/d Birr173/230, tw without bathroom Birr150; P) Rooms at this decent, family-run hotel almost look and feel brand new, though they aren't. Even the toilet seats remain attached.

★ **Gheralta Lodge** LODGE $$$
(☎0346-670344, Addis Ababa office 0116-632893; www.gheraltalodgetigrai.com; s/d & tw/tr incl breakfast from Birr600/1200/1400; P) In a word: fantastic. This lovely Italian-owned, African-themed lodge has great facilities and service and many guests declare it the best night of their trip to Ethiopia. Don't miss eating at the restaurant, which for Birr120 to Birr140 provides a set Italian-inspired menu that may be some of the finest food you eat in Ethiopia.

Getting There & Around

Many of the churches are in remote places, some 20km to 30km off the main road. A private 4WD is the easiest way of reaching them. However, if you're patient, exploration by public transport is possible.

There are minibuses from Adigrat to Wukro (Birr22, 1½ hours) and also from Mekele to Wukro (Birr15, one hour) and Hawzien (Birr33, 2½ hours) via Freweyni.

Lalibela

POP 15,000

With its buildings frozen in stone and its soul alive with the rites and awe of Christianity at its most ancient and unbending, stepping into Lalibela is like stepping into another time and another place. No matter what you've heard about Lalibela and its marvellous rock-hewn churches, nothing on earth can prepare you for the reality of seeing it for yourself.

Sights

Rock-Hewn Churches CHURCH
(admission for 5 days Birr350, video camera Birr300; ⊙6am-noon & 2-6pm) These churches

are remarkable for three main reasons: because many are not carved into the rock, but freed entirely from it; because the buildings are so refined; and because there are so many within such a small area. Descend into tunnels and pass priests and monks floating through the confines like clouds of incense, smell beeswax candles and hear chanting within the deep, cool recesses, only to find yourself standing in the sunlight, slack-jawed, staring up at a structure that defies reason.

Although visiting without a guide is possible – getting lost in the warren of tunnels is quite memorable and usually not permanent – you'll miss many of the amazing subtleties each church has to offer. The tourism office has licensed guides (Birr350 per day).

Sleeping

★Asheton Hotel HOTEL $
(0333-360030; d/tw Birr150/250; P) This classic budget-traveller haunt offers genuine value with old and cosy whitewashed rooms and a relaxing garden courtyard.

Selam Guest House PENSION $
(0333-3600374; d/tw Birr150/200) This very friendly four-room guesthouse has been around awhile, but the on-site owner makes sure it still has that new out-of-the-wrapper look. The rooms are plain and simple, but the calm, friendly vibe makes the price fair for Lalibela.

Alif Paradise Hotel HOTEL $$
(0333-360023; alparahotel@yahoo.com; old block d/tw US$10/15, new block d/tw US$25/35; P) Alif's pleasant new rooms are bright, tiled and clean with bathtubs and views. The older rooms, though dark and uninspiring, are still decent value. The restaurant makes a good choice for this part of town.

★Cliff Edge Hotel HOTEL $$$
(0333-360606; www.cliffedgehotel-lalibela.com; d/tw incl breakfast US$45/55; P) The rooms and the views from the balconies are just as good as its pricier neighbour Mountain View. They seem quick to discount, so always ask.

Eating

★Ben Abeba EUROPEAN, ETHIOPIAN $
(mains Birr35-69) Hands down the coolest restaurant in Ethiopia, this Ethio-Scottish-owned, Dali-esque jumble of walkways, platforms and fire pits is perched on the edge of the ridge for 360-degree views.

Unique Restaurant EUROPEAN, ETHIOPIAN $
(mains Birr35-58) This understated but cosy little restaurant, run by charming Sisco, serves the usual mix of national and *faranji* dishes and receives regular positive reviews from happy punters.

Mountain View Hotel EUROPEAN, ETHIOPIAN $$
(mains Birr85-109) When it comes down to the food, Mountain View isn't just tops in Lalibela, it's one of the best restaurants in Ethiopia. The diverse menu offers some Indian- and Jamaican-inspired dishes.

Getting There & Away

Ethiopian Airlines (0333-360046) flies twice daily to Addis Ababa (US$65, 45 minutes) and once daily to Gonder (US$41, two hours) and Aksum (US$46, 45 minutes). It's not currently possible to fly from Lalibela to Bahir Dar; though you can do it in the opposite direction thrice weekly.

Overland, the best approach is currently from Woldia via Gashena. There are two morning buses (Birr57, four hours) and usually four minibuses (Birr72) to/from Woldia, the last leaving about 2pm. A bus departs daily for Addis Ababa (Birr225, two days, 6am). The bus station is an inconvenient 2km out of town, and with no transport it's a long, hot and very sweaty walk. Call ahead and most hotels will collect you.

EASTERN ETHIOPIA

Harar

POP 108,200

Harar is a place apart. With 368 alleyways, countless mosques and shrines, coffee-scented streets, animated markets, crumbling walls and charming people all squished into just 1 sq km, it will make you feel like you've floated right out of the 21st century. It is the east's most memorable sight and shouldn't be missed. And, as if that wasn't enough, an other-worldly ritual takes place every night when men feed wild hyenas scraps of meat from their hands.

Sights & Activities

Harar's old **walled town** is a fascinating place that begs to be explored. Within the walls the city is a maze of narrow, twisting alleys and lanes, replete with historic buildings, including 82 small mosques, numerous shrines and tombs, as well as traditional Harari houses. Specific buildings to keep your eyes peeled for include the four main **gates**, Harar, Shoa, Buda and Fallana; the so-called Arthur Rimbaud's house (in reality it was probably never anything of the sort), which houses a **museum** (Arthur Rimbaud's House; admission Birr20; 8am-noon & 2-5pm Mon-Sat, 8am-noon Sun) dedicated to the poet; and **Ras Tafari's house**, containing the **Sherif Harar City Museum** (admission Bir30; 8.30am-noon & 2-5pm).

Hyena Feeding

As night falls (from around 7pm), two sets of hyena men set themselves up just outside the city walls.

The easiest way to see the show is to let your guide or hotel know so they can forewarn the hyena men. Watching costs Birr50. Most people go with a guide, but it's not required.

Sleeping

Tana Hotel HOTEL $
(0256-668482; New Town; d/tw Birr105/135; P) This large outfit up the hill on the Dire Dawa road is a solid budget choice in the new town. The odd cockroach or two aside, the rooms are clean, the staff friendly, and the water is more reliable than others in this price range.

★ **Rewda Guesthouse** GUESTHOUSE $$
(0256-662211; Old Town; d/tw without bathroom incl breakfast Birr350/700) This genuine Adare house percolates tradition and history into a comfy brew of warm welcome amid exotic decorations. Set in the heart of the old town down a nondescript side street, these four spotless bedrooms share two bathrooms.

Winta Hotel HOTEL $$
(0256-64267; d Birr500-700, tw Birr700; P) Currently Harar's best hotel by a big margin, rooms at Winta are comfortable, with satellite TV and minifridge. Since it has only eight rooms, reservations are wise. It's in the new town.

Eating

Hirut Restaurant EUROPEAN, ETHIOPIAN $
(0256-660419; New Town; mains Birr35-70; 11am-9pm) Decorated with traditional woven baskets and specialising in authentic local cuisine, this is the most atmospheric place in Harar to sink your teeth into a super-filling *kwanta firfir* (dried strips of beef rubbed in chilli, butter, salt and *berbere* – a famous Ethiopian spice).

Fresh Touch Restaurant EUROPEAN, ETHIOPIAN $$
(0915-740109; New Town; mains Birr35-121) Though we won't rave about this below-street-level place the way some visitors do, the *faranji* food (including pizzas and stir-fries) here is definitely better than average, which has made this a long-term favourite for locals and visitors alike.

Information

There are internet cafes and a bank near Harar Gate. The **tourist office** (0256-669300; 1st fl, Ras Makonnen's Palace; 8am-12.30pm & 2-5.30pm Mon-Thu, 8-11.30am & 2- 5pm Fri) is mildly useful. It's inside Ras Makonnen's Palace in the old town.

Getting There & Around

All transport leaves from the bus station near Harar Gate. Bountiful minibuses link to Dire Dawa (Birr21, one hour). Seven daily buses serve Jijiga (Birr40, 2½ to three hours). For Addis Ababa (nine to 10 hours), three normal buses (Birr180) leave around 6am from the bus station while Sky Bus (Birr275) and Selam (Birr270) depart at 5.30am from their ticket offices on opposite sides of Selassie Church.

SOUTHERN ETHIOPIA

Rift Valley Lakes

Africa's renowned Rift Valley cuts through the south, and hosts lakes, astounding birdlife and national parks.

South of Addis Ababa stretches a cluster of four Rift Valley lakes: **Lake Ziway**, **Lake Abiata**, **Lake Shala** and **Lake Langano**. While they're all known as havens for birdwatching, only Lake Langano has the double benefit of being safe for swimming (bilharzia- and crocodile-free). Lake Ziway sends twitchers into a twizzle of excitement – the place is crawling with feathered friends. There are also a couple of island monasteries here. The volcanic Lake Shala, part of **Lake Abiata-Shala National Park** (admission per 24hr Birr90, per vehicle Birr20, mandatory scout Birr70), is easily the most attractive, with trails leading to lookouts.

Awasa, southern Ethiopia's largest city, is 100km further south and sits on the shores of attractive **Lake Awasa**. With plenty of facilities, a great fish market and row boats to boot, Awasa is a great place to stop.

The wildest and most attractive of southern Ethiopia's lakes must be **Lake Abaya** and **Lake Chamo**. They are ringed by savannah plains, loaded with crocodiles and divided by the 'Bridge of God', which hosts Ethiopia's best safari opportunity, **Nechisar National Park** (admission Birr90, vehicle per 24hr Birr20, armed scouts per day Birr100), as well as the infamous **crocodile market**. To get up close and scary with the crocodiles hire a boat from **Rift Valley Boat Service Association** (0468-814080; Shecha; 1-6 people Birr770, mandatory guide Birr120; 7am-5.30pm). Scruffy Arba Minch is the best base for Lakes Abaya and Chamo and the Nechisar National Park.

Sleeping & Eating

Lake Langano

Lake Langano is a popular weekend escape. The prices below are for Sunday to Thursday. Add 15% to 30% at weekends.

Sabana Beach Resort LODGE $$$
(0461-191180; www.sabanalangano.com; incl breakfast s/d/tr US$59/71/91, f US$110-128; P) Occupying an elevated position with impressive views over the lake, Sabana sets the standard for Langano. Unlike most places in Ethiopia, the quality of the workmanship shows and the 25 cottages are as good as they are lovely.

Bishangari Lodge LODGE $$$
(0461-191276; www.bishangari.com; s bungalow incl breakfast US$78-98, tw bungalow US$137-162, s/tw hut without bathroom incl breakfast US$41/73; P) Hyped as Ethiopia's first ecolodge when it opened in 1997, Bishangari has nine beautiful *godjos* (bungalows), nestled privately along the lake's southeastern shore, and a monkey-friendly bar wrapped around a tree!

Awasa

Time Café HOTEL $
(0462-206331; d Birr230; P) The new rooms in back of this good restaurant score on all accounts: clean, comfy, good location and good value.

Hotel Pinna 1 HOTEL $$
(0462-210335; d/tw/f Birr280/395/420; P) An older property that, unusually for Ethiopia, is well maintained and up to date with wi-fi and satellite TV. Very good value.

Arba Minch

Zeweda Hotel HOTEL $
(0468-810364; Shecha; d Birr60; P) Simple and spartan (squat toilets and cold-water showers) but lacking mildewy odours, this small family-run spot is the first choice of many tour drivers. Even if they discover *faranji* pricing, it will probably still be worth considering.

Soma Lodge LODGE $$
(0911-737712; tw Birr600; P) Like giant, upturned onions, the beautifully crafted Sidamo huts here each have a small lounge, two bedrooms (with two beds and bathroom in each) and fantastic views over Nechisar National Park.

★ **Paradise Lodge** LODGE $$$
(0468-812914; www.paradiselodgeethiopia.com; campsite per tent with own/hired tent US$15/20, d/tw/f incl breakfast US$59/85/125; P) This upmarket lodge staring straight at the national park's 'Bridge of God' features comfortable Konso-inspired huts, all but a few with views, built from stone and wood.

Getting There & Away

Ethiopian Airlines flies between Addis Ababa and Arba Minch (US$57, one hour).

Buses connect Addis Ababa with Lake Ziway (Birr46, three hours), Awasa (Birr85, four to five hours) and Arba Minch (Birr147, nine hours).

Lower Omo Valley

If there's anything in southern Ethiopia that can rival the majesty of the north's historical circuit, it's the people of the Lower Omo Valley. Whether you're wandering through traditional Konso villages, watching Hamer people performing a Jumping of the Bulls ceremony or admiring the Mursi's mind-blowing lip plates, your visit to the Omo will stick with you for a lifetime.

A visit to the tribal villages is an extraordinary experience, but doesn't come without a catch. First, in high season masses of tourists pour into the most popular villages (ie the Mursi villages) every morning demanding photos (while the locals want ever larger sums of money). Second, a visit here cannot be described as cheap. Besides the cost of hiring a car, you are required to pay a village entrance fee of Birr100 to Birr150 per person, hire a local guide for another Birr100 to Birr200, and pay individuals for any photos you take. In the case of the Mursi people, you also need to pay for entry into **Mago National Park** (admission per person Birr100, per vehicle Birr30, tour agency fee Birr50, mandatory scout per day Birr80).

Jinka has decent facilities and most villages have some form of accommodation. In Jinka the **Goh Hotel** (☎0467-750033; d/tw Birr287/310, d without bathroom Birr81; P) attracts a wide cross-section of travellers. The rooms with bathroom are slightly aged and worn, but relatively bright and clean.

Most people visit this area as part of a tour from Addis Ababa, but it is possible to take a bus from Arba Minch to Jinka (Birr101, six hours) and hire transport (US$185 per day including driver) once there from the **Pioneers Guiding Association** (☎0467-751728) or the **New Vision Local Guide Association** (☎0916-712096; localtour.organizer@gmail.com). Both associations hire obligatory guides.

Several daily minibuses also leave Jinka for Konso (Birr70, 3½ hours), and one bus goes to Omorate (Birr100, 3½ hours) via Turmi (Birr70, 2½ hours) on Tuesday, Thursday and Saturday, returning the next day.

UNDERSTAND ETHIOPIA

Ethiopia Today

The year 2012 was one of great change in Ethiopia. On 20 August Meles Zenawi, who had led the country since the overthrow of the Derg regime in 1991, died. Zenawi had made economic growth and development his number-one priority and during his 21-year rule the country progressed out of all recognition to the Ethiopia Zenawi had inherited. Today, Hailemariam Desalegn stands at the helm as acting prime minister (elections are scheduled for 2015).

Just four days before the death of Meles Zenawi, the Patriarch of the Ethiopian Orthodox Church, Abune Paulos, also died. He was credited with modernising the Ethiopian Church.

Ethiopia has been developing at an astonishing rate. In the nine years leading up to 2013, economic growth has sometimes reached the giddy heights of 11%. Foreign investment has been tumbling into the country and the nation's infrastructure has been given a much-needed overhaul.

History

Ethiopia's human history dates back at least 4.4 million years, landing it squarely in East Africa's heralded cradle of humanity. Recorded history dates to 1500 BC, when a civilisation with Sabaean influences briefly blossomed at Yeha.

Kingdom of Aksum

This kingdom, ranking among the ancient world's most powerful, rose shortly after 400 BC. Its capital, Aksum, sat in a fertile area lying at an important commercial crossroads between Egypt, Sudan's gold fields and the Red Sea. At its height the kingdom extended well into Arabia.

Aksum grew on trade, exporting frankincense, grain, skins, apes and, particularly, ivory. In turn, exotic imports returned from Egypt, Arabia and India. Aksumite architecture was incredible, and impressive monuments still stand today.

The 4th century AD brought Christianity, which enveloped Aksum and shaped Ethiopia's future spiritual, cultural and intellectual life. Aksum itself flourished until the 7th century, when its trading empire was fatally isolated by the rise of Arabs and Islam in Arabia. Ethiopia soon sank into its 'dark ages', a period that has left few traces.

Early Dynasties

The Zagwe dynasty rose in Lalibela around 1137. Although only lasting until 1270, it produced arguably Ethiopia's greatest treasures: the rock-hewn churches of Lalibela. Yet, the period remains shrouded in mystery as there is no written evidence of it. The dynasty was overthrown by Yekuno Amlak, self-professed descendant of King Solomon and the Queen of Sheba. His 'Solomonic dynasty' would reign for 500 years.

Although Islam expanded into eastern Ethiopia during the 12th and 14th centuries, it wasn't until the late 15th century, when Ottoman Turks intervened, that hostilities erupted. After jihad was declared on the Christian highlands, Ethiopia experienced some of the worst bloodshed in its history. Only Portuguese intervention helped save the Christian empire.

Towards a United Empire

Filling the power vacuum that was created by the weakened Muslims, Oromo pastoralists and warriors migrated from what is now Kenya. For 200 years intermittent conflict raged. Two 17th-century emperors, Za-Dengel and Susenyos, converted to Catholicism to gain the military support of Portuguese Jesuits. The Muslim state wasn't immune to Oromo might either; Harar's old city walls were built in response to their conflicts.

In 1636 Emperor Fasiladas founded Ethiopia's first permanent capital since Lalibela. By the close of the 17th century, Gonder boasted magnificent palaces, beautiful gardens and extensive plantations. However, during the 18th century, assassination and intrigue became the order of the day. Gonder collapsed in the mid-19th century and Ethiopia disintegrated into a cluster of feuding fiefdoms.

The empire was eventually reunified by Kassa Haylu, who crowned himself Emperor Tewodros. But his lofty ambitions led him to cross the British, resulting in his death. His successor, Yohannes IV, fought to the throne with weapons gained by aiding the British during their Tewodros campaign. Later, Menelik II continued acquiring weaponry, using it to thrash the advancing Italians in 1896 and thus stave off colonisation. In 1936 Mussolini's troops overran Ethiopia. They occupied it until capitulating to British forces in 1941.

With the arrival of the British, Haile Selassie, the Ethiopian emperor at the time of Mussolini's invasion, reclaimed his throne and Ethiopia its independence, and the country started to modernise. The failure of an attempted coup against Selassie's autocratic rule did not prevent increased opposition to Selassie.

The Derg to Democracy

By 1973 a radical military group, known as the Derg, had emerged. They used the media with consummate skill to undermine and eventually depose Emperor Haile Selassie, before their leader, Colonel Mengistu Haile Mariam, declared Ethiopia a socialist state in 1974.

Despite internal tensions, external threats initially posed the Derg's biggest problem. Only state-of-the-art weaponry, gifted by the Soviet Union, allowed them to beat back an attempted invasion by Somalia in 1977. In Eritrea (which had been annexed by Ethiopia in 1962), however, the secessionists continued to thwart Ethiopian offensives.

The Ethiopia–Eritrea War

During the 1980s, numerous Ethiopian armed liberation movements arose. For years, with limited weaponry, they fought the Soviet-backed Derg's military might.

Mengistu lost Soviet backing after the Cold War, and the rebel Ethiopian and Eritrean coalition forces finally claimed victory in 1991. Eritrea was immediately granted independence, Mengistu's failed socialist policies were abandoned, and in 1995 the Federal Democratic Republic of Ethiopia was proclaimed. Elections followed, and the second republic's constitution was inaugurated. Meles Zenawi, as prime minister, formed a new government.

Despite having fought together against the Derg for over a decade, Meles Zenawi and Eritrea's President Isaias soon clashed. Bickering over Eritrea's exchange-rate system for its new currency led to Eritrea occupying the border town of Badme in 1998. Soon full-scale military conflict broke out, leaving tens of thousands dead on both sides before ceasing in mid-2000.

The New Century

In 2005 controversial elections were held, followed by heavy-handed government reprisals. Tensions with Eritrea continued and the two neighbours almost came to blows again in 2005.

Ethiopian troops entered Somalia in 2006 in support of the Somali government's fight against the Islamic milita who controlled Mogadishu. Officially Ethiopia withdrew its troops in early 2009, but by the middle of that year Ethiopia admitted that some of its forces had returned to Somalia. In late 2011 the Ethiopian military, working with the transitional government of Somalia, AU forces and the Kenyan military, officially re-entered Somalia as part of a concerted drive to destroy al-Shabaab, an al-Qaeda-affiliated Somali group.

The elections of 2010 saw Zenawi and the Ethiopian People's Revolutionary Democratic Front (EPRDF) returned to power. There was none of the violence that had marked the 2005 election, but international observers criticised the elections for falling short of international standards.

Culture

Ethiopians are nothing if not proud – and for good reason. To them, Ethiopia has stood out from all African nations and proved itself to be a unique world of its own – home to its own culture, language, script, calendar and history. Ethiopian Orthodox Christians and Muslims alike revel in the fact that Ethiopia was the only nation on the continent to successfully fight off colonisation.

The highlands have been dominated by a distinctive form of Christianity since the 4th century. Devout and keen to dispense centuries worth of Orthodox legends and tales dating back to Aksum and the Ark of the Covenant, these Christians, like all Ethiopians, still cling to their beliefs in magic and superstition.

Other than religion, agriculture and pastoralism fill the days of 83% of Ethiopians. Only 42.7% of Ethiopians are literate; only 82% of children attend primary school; and a mere 30% of boys and 23% of girls attend secondary school.

Food & Drink

Ethiopia's food is completely different from the rest of Africa. Plates, bowls and utensils are replaced by *injera,* a unique pancake of countrywide proportions. Atop its rubbery confines sits anything from *kai wat* (spicy meat stew) to colourful dollops of *gomen* (minced spinach) and *tere sega* (cubes of raw beef).

Whether it's *berbere* (a famous Ethiopian spice) joyfully bringing tears to your eyes, or an *injera's* slightly sour taste sending your tongue into convulsions, one thing's certain: Ethiopian fare provokes strong reactions and though you might not always enjoy it, you won't forget it!

Ethiopia is the original home of coffee, which is still ubiquitous throughout the country. Sip a macchiato made from a vintage Italian espresso machine, or sit down for a traditional coffee ceremony. Another beverage you must savour is *tej* (honey wine).

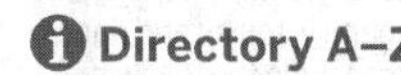

SURVIVAL GUIDE

Directory A–Z

ACCOMMODATION

Accommodation in Ethiopia continues to improve and most towns now have at least one hotel that won't make your toes curl in trepidation.

Budget options, with spartan rooms and shared toilets, dominate. Only larger centres provide midrange options, which are usually clean and quiet, but rundown. True top-end picks are limited to Addis Ababa and a few major tourist towns. Ethiopians call rooms with a double bed 'singles' and rooms with twin beds 'doubles'. We use typical Western interpretations in our reviews.

Outside of national parks there are few campsites. Some hotels allow camping, though it's not much cheaper than decent rooms.

EMBASSIES & CONSULATES

Embassies and consulates in Addis Ababa include the following:

Belgian Embassy (☎0116-623420; http://diplomatie.belgium.be/ethiopia; Fikremaryam Abatechan St)

British Embassy (☎0116-612354; http://ukinethiopia.fco.gov.uk; cnr Fikremaryam Abatechan & Comoros Sts)

Canadian Embassy (☎0113-170000; addis@international.gc.ca; Seychelles St) Also represents Australia.

Djiboutian Embassy (☎0116-613200) Off Bole Rd.

Dutch Embassy (☎0113-711100; http://ethiopia.nlembassy.org)

Egyptian Embassy (☎0111-550021; egyptian.emb@ethionet.et; Madagascar St)

French Embassy (☎0111-400000; www.ambafrance-et.org)

German Embassy (☎0111-235139; www.addis-abeba.diplo.de)

Italian Embassy (☎0111-235717; ambasciata.addisabeba@esteri.it)

Kenyan Embassy (☎0116-610033; kenigad@telecom.net.et; Fikremaryam Abatechan St)

Somaliland Embassy (☎0116-635921) Off Bole Rd.

South Sudanese Embassy (☎0116-620245) Off Cameroon St.

Sudanese Embassy (☎0115-516477; sudan.embassy@ethionet.et; Ras Lulseged St)

US Embassy (☎0111-306000; http://ethiopia.usembassy.gov; Entoto Ave)

FESTIVALS & EVENTS

Religious festivals, particularly Orthodox ones, are colourful events with pageantry, music and dancing. The most outstanding include the following:

Leddet (also known as Genna or Christmas) 6–7 January

Timkat (Epiphany, celebrating Christ's baptism) 19 January

Kiddus Yohannes (New Year's Day) 11 September

Meskel (Finding of the True Cross) 27 September

INTERNET ACCESS

Internet cafes are everywhere in Addis Ababa and other major towns and fairly easy to come by in smaller places that see few tourists.

In larger towns in-room wi-fi is increasingly common in many midrange and top-end hotels, and in budget hotels popular with foreign tourists.

MONEY

Ethiopia's currency is the birr. US dollars are the best currency to carry, both in cash and travellers cheques, though euros are gaining popularity. You'll have no trouble exchanging cash in most cities, but travellers cheques are more of a headache. Dashen Banks in all big towns have ATMs that accept international Visa cards and MasterCards.

Converting birr to US dollars or euros can only be done for people holding exchange receipts and onward air tickets from Ethiopia – overlanders need to budget accordingly.

PRACTICALITIES

➡ **Electricity** Supply is 220V. Sockets vary from European continental two-pin to South African/Indian-style with two circular metal pins above a large circular grounding pin.

➡ **Languages** Amharic is the national language. There are numerous regional languages, the most commonly spoken being Oromo, Tigrinya and Somali.

➡ **Newspapers** The government-owned *Ethiopian Herald* is the best-known newspaper in English.

➡ **Radio** Radio Ethiopia broadcasts in English from 3pm to 4pm and 7pm to 8pm weekdays. The BBC World Service can be received on radios with short-wave reception, though frequencies vary according to the time of day (try 9630, 11940 and 17640MHz).

OPENING HOURS

Banks, post offices and telecommunications offices Open at least 8.30am to 11am and 1.30pm to 3.30pm weekdays and 8.30am to 11am Saturdays.

Government offices Open 8.30am to 11am and 1.30pm to 3.30pm weekdays. Saturday mornings only.

Shops Open 8.30am to 1pm and 2pm to 5.30pm weekdays.

PUBLIC HOLIDAYS

Public holidays can be divided into three categories: national secular holidays, Christian Orthodox festivals and Islamic holidays.

National secular holidays include the following:

Victory of Adwa Commemoration Day 2 March

International Labour Day 1 May

Ethiopian Patriots' Victory Day (also known as 'Liberation Day') 5 May

Downfall of the Derg 28 May

POST & TELEPHONE

Ethiopia's postal system is reliable and reasonably efficient. Countless shops also operate as 'telecentres', connecting you anywhere worldwide for Birr15 to Birr25 per minute.

Mobile phones are as ubiqutious as anywhere else in Africa, but sadly the network is one of the worst in the continent and you shouldn't rely on local or foreign mobiles working outside large centres.

SAFE TRAVEL

Compared with many African countries, violent crime is rare; against travellers it's extremely rare. Petty theft is common in Addis Ababa, but is less common elsewhere.

At the time of writing the Ogaden region, as well as the areas around Moyale in the south, were experiencing a mix of rebel activity or tribal violence. Though you're highly unlikely to get caught up in it, do keep your ear to the ground for developments. In 2012 five foreign tourists were killed and four people kidnapped close to the Erte Ale volcano in the Danakil Depression. Tour companies are running trips here again, but you should always check the security situation beforehand.

In the annoyances department, Ethiopia has oodles of beggars, and travellers often resent being 'targeted'. Self-appointed guides can be annoying, but it's the money-demanding attitudes of some priests and church guardians that seem to cause the most agitation with visitors. Be polite but firm.

TIME

Time is expressed so sanely in Ethiopia that it blows travellers' minds! At sunrise it's 12 o'clock (6am our time) and after one hour of sunshine it's 1 o'clock. After two hours of sunshine? Yes, 2 o'clock. The sun sets at 12 o'clock (6pm our time) and after one hour of darkness it's...1 o'clock! When being quoted a time, always ask, *'Be habesha/faranji akotater no?'* (Is that Ethiopian/ foreigners' time?)

TOURIST INFORMATION

There's a helpful government tourist information office in Addis Ababa. Independent offices can be found in regional capitals. No national tourist office exists abroad.

VISAS

Nationals of most Western countries can obtain tourist visas on arrival at Bole International Airport. The process is painless and the one-month tourist visa costs only US$20, substantially less than that charged at some Ethiopian embassies abroad.

Be aware that visas are *not* available at any land border.

Visas for Onward Travel

Djibouti The embassy requires two photos, a hotel booking and return bus or plane ticket. Visas cost US$125 for a 48-hour turnaround and US$135 for 24 hours.

Kenya Three-month visas cost US$50 and require one photo. Apply in the morning and pick up the following afternoon. Visas are also easily obtained at the Moyale crossing and Nairobi's airport.

Somaliland Visas require US$40 and one passport photo. It's issued while you wait.

South Sudan South Sudan is a new country. It's not used to tourists, and when we passed by the embassy nobody appeared to know exactly what was required in order to get a tourist visa. But the essentials seemed to be proof of sufficient funds, a letter stating the purpose of your visit, a photo and US$100. In addition, you may be required to supply a letter from your home employer and they may ask you to attend an interview. Visas take 72 hours to issue.

Sudan Unless you're using the services of a registered Sudanese tour company, obtaining a tourist visa is mission impossible if ever there was one. All applications are sent to Khartoum for approval, so the process can take over a month to complete. However, don't go changing those plans just yet as there is one way in. Transit visas, allowing up to a fortnight in Sudan, are issued fairly easily. For this you require an onward visa for Egypt, a photo and, for most nationalities, US$100 cash. Americans have to pay US$200. It normally takes a day to issue.

ETHIOPIAN VISAS IN NAIROBI

Bad news for overlanders! Ethiopian visas are only being issued in Nairobi to Kenyan citizens or residents. Everyone else will need to apply elsewhere or fly into Addis Ababa.

Getting There & Away

AIR

Addis Ababa's Bole International Airport is the only international airport in Ethiopia. Airline offices in Addis Ababa include the following:

EgyptAir (MS; 0111-564493; www.egyptair.com; Churchill Ave)

Emirates (EK; 0115-181818; www.emirates.com; Dembel City Centre)

KLM (KL; 0115-525495; www.klm.com; Menelik II Ave)

Kenya Airways (KQ; 0115-525548; www.kenya-airways.com; Menelik II Ave)

Lufthansa (LH; 0111-551666; www.lufthansa.com; Cameroon St)

LAND

Djibouti

There are two current land routes: one via Dire Dawa and Gelille, and one via Awash and Galafi.

The Gelille route is best for those without vehicles as daily buses link Djibouti City and Dire Dawa. The journey takes 10 to 12 hours, though it involves changing buses at the border. In Djibouti City, try Société Bus Assajog. Buy your ticket (DFr3000) at least a day in advance to be sure of getting a seat departing at dawn from Ave Gamel Abdel Nasser. In Dire Dawa, buy your ticket the day of travel at the **Tibuuti Ee City** (0915-763203) office north of the 'old town' of Megala by Ashawa Market. Tickets cost Birr230 and buses depart around midnight from a spot north of this office.

Although further, the Awash/Galafi crossing is best for those driving, as it's entirely sealed.

Eritrea

The Eritrea–Ethiopia border remains closed.

Kenya

The most used crossing is at Moyale, 772km south of Addis Ababa. Daily Ethiopian buses link Addis Ababa and Moyale (Birr226, 1½ days), while Kenyan versions connect the border to Marsabit (KSh1000, 10 hours), from where transport continues on to Isiolo and then Nairobi. Banditry is an occasional issue in northern Kenya; check the latest before venturing this way.

Somaliland

Daily buses run between Jijiga and Wajaale at the border (Birr30, 1½ to two hours). After immigration procedures, you'll find taxis running frequently to Hargeisa (Birr120/US$7, two hours).

South Sudan

At the time of writing the border between Ethiopia and South Sudan at Jikawo was closed. There was talk of the border reopening and if this happens buses go from Gambela to the border town of Jikawo (Birr70, five hours). From there take a shared taxi to Adora (South Sudan).

Sudan

The only open Sudan crossing is Metema/Gallabat, 180km west of Gonder. In Gonder minibuses leave daily for Metema (Birr71, three hours). There's also a bus direct from Addis Ababa (Birr272, two days). From Gallabat there's plenty of transport to Khartoum.

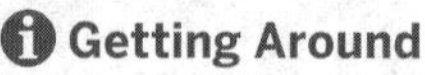

Getting Around

AIR

Ethiopian Airlines (p579) is the domestic carrier, regularly serving all major cities.

In Ethiopia standard rates always apply, whether buying tickets months or hours in advance.

BUS

A good network of buses slowly connects most towns. Recently a new breed of bus has taken to the roads of Ethiopia and these ones actually are pretty plush. The biggest company is **Selam Buses** (☎ 0115-548800; www.selambus.com), but **Sky Buses** (☎ 0111-568080; www.skybusethiopia.com) is fancier and the one to opt for if possible.

CAR & MOTORCYCLE

If you're bringing a 4WD or motorcycle, you'll need a *carnet de passage* (p1080), the vehicle's registration papers and proof of third-party insurance covering Ethiopia.

Hiring 4WDs (with mandatory driver) is costly (US$160 to US$180 per day) and primarily done through travel agencies.

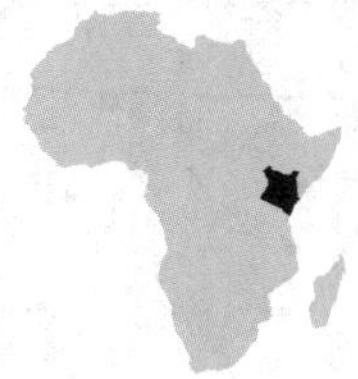

Kenya

POP 43 MILLION

Includes ➡

Best of Nature

- Masai Mara National Reserve (p612)
- Amboseli National Park (p623)
- Tsavo West and Tsavo East National Parks (p624)

Best of Culture

- Mombasa (p614)
- Maasai village stay (p613)
- Loyangalani (p611)
- Gede Ruins (p619)

Why Go?

Kenya is the Africa you always dreamed of: a land of vast savannah, immense herds of wildlife, and peoples with proud traditions rooted in the soil where human beings emerged. The Maasai, the Samburu, the Turkana, the Swahili, the Kikuyu: these are the peoples whose histories and daily struggles tell the story of a country and of a continent – the struggle to maintain traditions as the modern world crowds in, the daily fight for survival, the ancient tension between those who farm and those who roam.

Then, of course, there's the wildlife. From the Masai Mara to Tsavo, this is a country of vivid experiences – elephant families wallowing in swamps in the shadow of Mt Kilimanjaro, the massed millions of pink flamingos bathing in lake shallows, the landscape suddenly fallen silent and brought to attention by the arrival of an as-yet-unseen predator. There's nowhere better than Kenya to answer the call of the wild.

When to Go

Nairobi

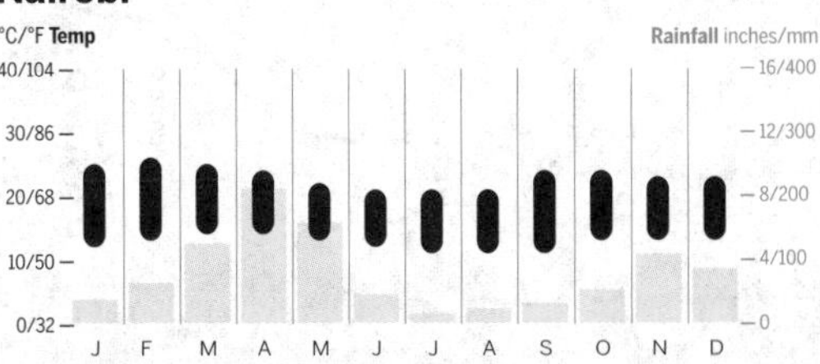

Jul–Oct The annual wildebeest migration arrives in the Masai Mara in all its epic glory.

Jan–Feb Hot, dry weather with high concentrations of wildlife in the major parks.

Nov–Mar Migratory birds present in their millions throughout the country.

Kenya Highlights

1. Experience the savannah, unmatched wildlife and the world's most fascinating traffic jam in the annual wildebeest migration at the **Masai Mara National Reserve** (p612).

2. Enjoy the tremendous hikes and jagged peaks that await on sacred **Mt Kenya** (p609); Kenya's highest and Africa's second-highest mountain.

3. Check out the elephants and Kilimanjaro, two of Kenya's most famous picture-postcard views, from **Amboseli National Park** (p623).

4. Explore the harsh conditions, unforgettable tribes and the sublime Lake Turkana, the

jade jewel at the end of a long quest, in **Loyangalani** (p611).

5 Visit the vibrant coastal city of **Mombasa** (p614), with its intriguing historic fort and a fragrant spice market.

NAIROBI

020 / POP 3.5 MILLION

Nairobi's reputation for crime is well known, but the alarming stories obscure a booming and cosmopolitan city with several attractions. Primary among these is the world's only national park on the cusp of a capital city, packed with free-roaming megafauna. There's also an elephant orphanage, a brilliant park, and fantastic restaurants and hotels. Keep your wits about you and you'll be more likely to leave with a lasting impression of Kenya's dynamism than tales of personal disaster.

History

When the East Africa railway arrived in the 1890s, a depot was established on the edge of a small stream known to the Maasai as *uaso nairobi* (cold water). Nairobi quickly developed into the administrative nerve centre of the Uganda Railway, and in 1901 the capital of the British Protectorate was moved here from Mombasa. Sadly, almost all of the colonial-era buildings were replaced by bland, modern office buildings following *uhuru* (independence) in 1963.

Sights

★Nairobi National Park WILDLIFE RESERVE
(2423423; www.kws.org/parks/parks_reserves/NANP.html; nonresident adult/child & student US$40/20) A visit to Nairobi National Park, a few kilometres from the city centre, features plentiful wildlife, including most of the plains animals (except elephants), against the bizarre backdrop of Nairobi skyscrapers. The 'Park Shuttle' is a Kenyan Wildlife Service (KWS) bus that leaves the main gate at 3pm Sunday for a 2½-hour tour of the park.

National Museum MUSEUM
(Map p600; www.museums.or.ke; Museum Hill Rd; adult/child KSh800/400, combined ticket with Snake Park KSh1200/600; 8.30am-5.30pm) Has a good range of cultural, geological and natural-history exhibits. Volunteer guides offer tours in English, Dutch and French; a donation is appropriate. The 1st floor also hosts the excellent **Gallery of Contemporary East African Art**.

National Archives ARCHIVES
(Map p602; 749341; Moi Ave; 8.30am-5pm Mon-Fri, to 1pm Sat) FREE The ground-floor atrium and gallery display an eclectic selection of contemporary art, historical photos, cultural artefacts, furniture and tribal objects.

David Sheldrick Wildlife Trust WILDLIFE ENCOUNTERS
(202 301 396; www.sheldrickwildlifetrust.org) Visit at 11am to see rescued baby elephants being fed.

Giraffe Centre WILDLIFE ENCOUNTERS
(www.giraffecenter.org; Koitobos Rd; adult/student & child KSh1000/500; 9am-5.30pm) Combines serious conservation of Rothschild's giraffes with enjoyable activities. Take mini-bus 24 or 126

Karen Blixen Museum MUSEUM
(www.museums.or.ke; Karen Rd; adult/child KSh800/400; 9.30am-6pm; Karen Metro Shuttle bus from City Hall, car) The farmhouse where Karen Blixen, author of *Out of Africa*, lived. Take the Karen Metro Shuttle bus from City Hall or visit by car.

Railway Museum MUSEUM
(Map p600; Station Rd; adult/child KSh400/100; 8am-5pm) Intriguing relics from the East Africa Railway.

Sleeping

★Kahama Hotel HOTEL $
(Map p600; 3742210; www.kahamahotels.co.ke; Murang'a Rd; s/d from KSh3100/3700;) Almost equidistant between the city centre and the National Museum, this is a terrific choice. Its catch cry is 'Economy with Style', with pleasant rooms, comfy beds and free wireless access.

Milimani Backpackers & Safari Centre BACKPACKERS $
(Map p600; 2724827; www.milimanibackpackers.com; Milimani Rd, Milimani; campsites KSh600, dm KSh750, s/d cabins KSh2200/2500, s/d cabins without bathroom KSh1500/2000;) Whether you camp out back, cosy up in the dorms or splurge on your own cabin, you'll end up huddled around the fire at night, swapping travel stories and dining on home-cooked meals with fellow travellers.

Wildebeest Camp BACKPACKERS $
(0734-770733; www.wildebeestcamp.com; 151 Mokoyeti Road West, Langata; campsites KSh1000, dm/s/d KSh1250/2500/3500, s/d garden tent from KSh3500/4500) This is an outstanding budget option, with ordinary camping, deluxe tents, dorm beds and budget rooms. Relaxed yet switched on, and the accommodation is spotless and great value.

Upper Hill Country Lodge HOTEL $$
(Map p600; ☎2881600; www.countrylodge.co.ke; Second Ngong Ave, Milimani; s/d from KSh11,400/15,600; P @) With a focus solely on affordable luxury for business travellers, the Country Lodge is one of the best-priced midrange options in Nairobi. Its minimalist yet stylish living quarters can compete with the best.

★**Norfolk Hotel** HOTEL $$$
(Map p600; ☎2265000; www.fairmont.com/norfolkhotel; Harry Thuku Rd; r from US$275; P ❄ ☎ ≋) Built in 1904, Nairobi's oldest hotel was *the* place to stay during colonial days, and still attracts plenty of guests who at least look like old-school settlers.

Palacina BOUTIQUE HOTEL $$$
(☎2715517; www.palacina.com; Kitale Lane; 1-/2-person ste US$270/409, penthouses US$690; P ☎ ≋) Possibly the first genuine boutique hotel in Kenya, this fabulous collection of stylish suites must be one of the country's top addresses for well-heeled sophisticates.

Nairobi Serena Hotel HOTEL $$$
(Map p600; ☎2822000; www.serenahotels.com; Procession Way, Central Park; s/d from US$290/320; P ❄ @ ≋) Has a fine sense of individuality, with international-class facilities displaying a touch of safari style.

Eating

★**Savanna: The Coffee Lounge** CAFE $
(Map p600; Museum Hill Rd; snacks from KSh180, mains KSh440-590; ⏲7am-8pm Mon-Sat, 9am-6pm Sun) Located inside the grounds of the National Museum. Decor is safari chic without being overdone, service is friendly and unobtrusive, and dishes include pies, wraps, samosas, sandwiches, burgers, pasta, soup and salads.

★**Beneve Coffee House** CAFE $
(Map p602; ☎217959; cnr Standard & Koinange Sts; dishes KSh50-150; ⏲Mon-Fri) A small self-service chop shop that has locals queuing outside in the mornings waiting for it to open.

★**Nairobi Java House** CAFE
(Map p602; ☎313565; www.nairobijava.com; Mama Ngina St; coffee KSh120-280; ⏲6.30am-10pm Mon-Fri, 7am- 9pm Sat, 8am-8pm Sun) This fantastic coffeehouse is rapidly turning itself into a major brand, and aficionados say the coffee is some of the best in Kenya.

SET YOUR BUDGET

Budget

- Basic hotel room US$5–10
- *Nyama choma* (barbecued meat) US$2
- Coffee US$1
- *Matatu* (minibus) ride US$1

Midrange

- Double room in midrange hotel US$50–200
- Two-course dinner US$8
- Beer in bar US$2
- Short taxi ride US$5

Top End

- Full board in safari lodge from US$200
- Independent safari with car rental US$75–100

Blue Nile Ethiopian Restaurant ETHIOPIAN $$
(Map p600; ☎0722-898138; Argwings Kodhek Rd, Hurlingham; mains KSh400-700) One of those rare places with a character all its own, Blue Nile's quirky lounge couldn't be mistaken for anywhere else, painted with stories from Ethiopian mythology.

Thorn Tree Café INTERNATIONAL $$
(Map p602; ☎228030; cnr Kimathi St & Kenyatta Ave, New Stanley Hotel; mains KSh950-1950; ⏲lunch & dinner) The Stanley's legendary cafe still serves as a popular meeting place for travellers, and caters to most tastes with a good mix of food. The original thorn-tree notice board in the courtyard inspired Lonely Planet's own online Thorn Tree community.

Tamarind Restaurant SEAFOOD $$$
(Map p602; ☎251811; www.tamarind.co.ke; Aga Khan Walk, off Harambee Ave; mains KSh1000-2500; ⏲lunch & dinner Mon-Sat) Kenya's most prestigious restaurant chain runs Nairobi's best seafood restaurant – you can dine on all manner of exotic dishes, and the lavish dining room is in a sumptuous modern Arabic-Moorish style.

Carnivore KENYAN $$$
(☎605933; www.carnivore.co.ke; off Langata Rd, Karen; vegie/meat buffet from KSh2530/2150; P) Love it or hate it, Carnivore is hands down

Nairobi

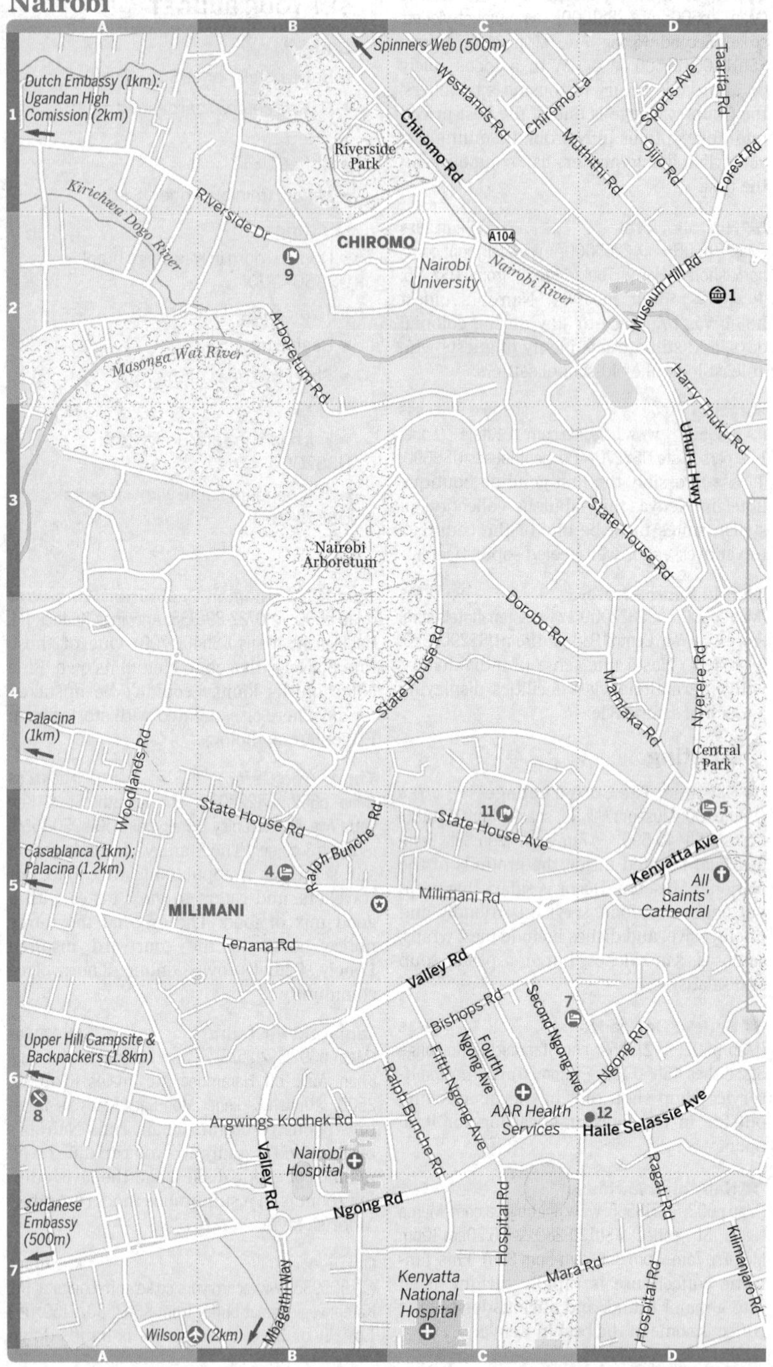

Spinners Web (500m)
Dutch Embassy (1km); Ugandan High Comission (2km)
Riverside Park
Westlands Rd
Chiromo Rd
Chiromo La
Muthithi Rd
Sports Ave
Ojijo Rd
Taarifa Rd
Forest Rd
Kirichwa Dogo River
Riverside Dr
9
CHIROMO
A104
Nairobi University
Nairobi River
Museum Hill Rd
1
Masonga Wai River
Arboretum Rd
Harry Thuku Rd
Uhuru Hwy
State House Rd
Nairobi Arboretum
Dorobo Rd
State House Rd
Mamlaka Rd
Nyerere Rd
Palacina (1km)
Woodlands Rd
Central Park
11
5
State House Rd
Ralph Bunche Rd
State House Ave
Casablanca (1km); Palacina (1.2km)
4
Kenyatta Ave
All Saints' Cathedral
Milimani Rd
MILIMANI
Lenana Rd
Valley Rd
Bishops Rd
Second Ngong Ave
7
Fourth Ngong Ave
Fifth Ngong Ave
Ralph Bunche Rd
Ngong Rd
Upper Hill Campsite & Backpackers (1.8km)
8
AAR Health Services
12
Haile Selassie Ave
Argwings Kodhek Rd
Valley Rd
Nairobi Hospital
Ragati Rd
Ngong Rd
Hospital Rd
Sudanese Embassy (500m)
Kilimanjaro Rd
Mara Rd
Mbagathi Way
Kenyatta National Hospital
Hospital Rd
Wilson (2km)
A
B
C
D
1
2
3
4
5
6
7

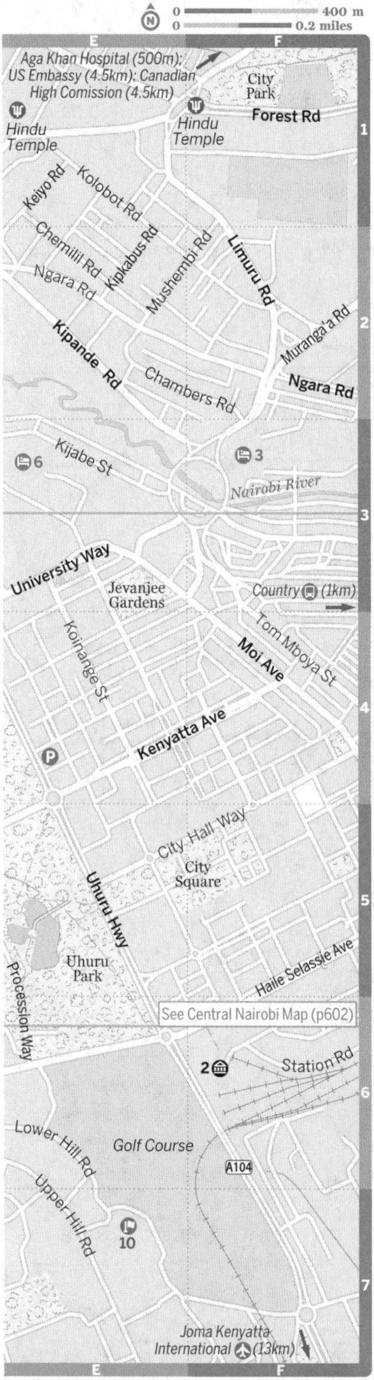

See Central Nairobi Map (p602)

Nairobi

Sights

1 National Museum....D2
2 Railway Museum....F6

Sleeping

3 Kahama Hotel....F3
4 Milimani Backpackers & Safari Centre....B5
5 Nairobi Serena Hotel....D5
6 Norfolk Hotel....E3
7 Upper Hill Country Lodge....C6

Eating

8 Blue Nile Ethiopian Restaurant....A6
Lord Delamere Terrace & Bar....(see 6)
Savanna: The Coffee Lounge....(see 1)

Information

9 Australian Embassy....B2
10 British Embassy....E7
11 Ethiopian Embassy....C5
12 Kenya National Library....D6

the most famous *nyama choma* (barbecued meat) restaurant in Kenya, beloved of tourists, expats and wealthier locals alike for the last 25 years. The restaurant is located in the well-to-do suburb of Karen, so it's best to take a taxi out here at night.

Lord Delamere Terrace & Bar INTERNATIONAL $$$
(Map p600; ☎216940; www.fairmont.com/NorfolkHotel; Harry Thuku Rd; mains KSh1450-2575) Since 1904, this popular rendezvous spot at the Norfolk Hotel has existed as the unofficial start and end point for East African safaris. Dishes include steaks, Lamu crab cakes, Indian Ocean lobster, crocodile kebabs and ostrich fillets.

Drinking & Nightlife

★ Simmers BAR
(Map p602; ☎217659; cnr Kenyatta Ave & Muindi Mbingu St; admission free; ⏱8am-1am) The atmosphere at this open-air nightclub is almost invariably amazing, with ever-enthusiastic crowds turning out to wind and grind the night away.

Casablanca BAR, LOUNGE
(☎2723173; Lenana Rd, Hurlingham; ⏱from 6pm) This Moroccan-style lounge bar was an instant hit with Nairobi's fastidious expat community, and you don't have to spend much time here to become a convert.

Central Nairobi

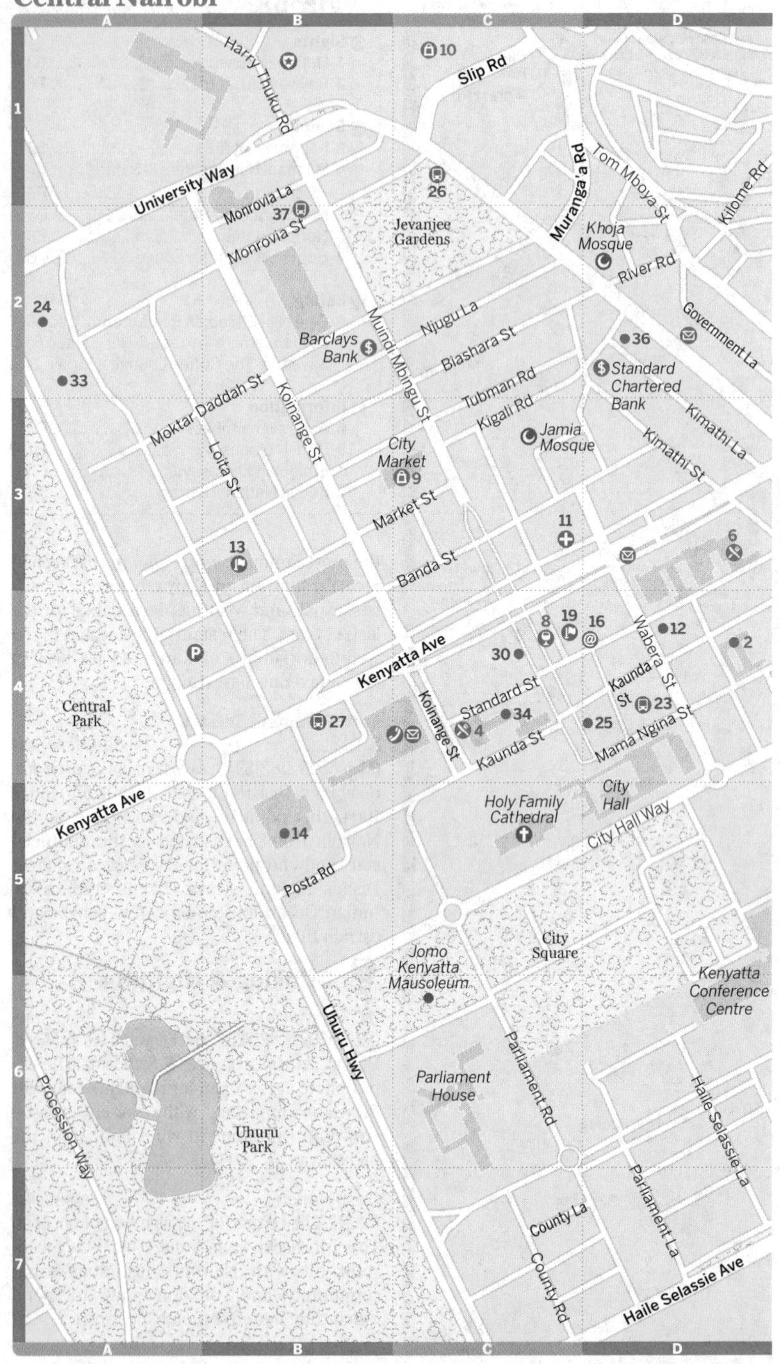

Kirinyaga Rd
Nairobi River
Keekorok Rd
Ngariama La
River Rd
44
Firestation La
22
Duruma Rd
Lagos Rd
39
Cross Rd
Cross La
Dubois La
Dubois Rd
Latema Rd
Timboroa Rd
Tom Mboya St
Tsavo La
Tsavo Rd
River Rd
Kumasi Rd
Duruma Rd
Accra Rd
Kamae La
20
Taveta Rd
Timboroa La
Barclays Bank
Cabral St
Government La
Gaberone La
Gaberone Rd
Matatus to Mtito Andei (50m); Matatus to Thika (200m)
Moi Ave
3
Sikh Temple
Munyu Rd
Sheikh Karume Rd
Luthuli Ave
40
15
29
Barclays Bank
1
Mfangano St
Sheikh Karume La
Machakos Country Bus Station (300m)
British Airways
32
7
Ronald Ngala St
Hakati Rd
17
35
42
28
Uyoma St
Racecourse Rd
38
18
Nairobi Cinema
Mfangano St
Mfangano La
Nkrumah La
Aga Khan Walk
Taifa Rd
Haile Selassie Ave
31
Exchange La
21
Harambee Ave
5
Tumbo Ave
41
Harambee La
Workshop Rd
Pate Bay Rd
Train Station
43
Station Rd
Ngaria Ave
0 200 m
0 0.1 miles

Central Nairobi

Sights
1 National Archives F4

Activities, Courses & Tours
2 Mountain Rock Safaris Resorts & Trekking Services D4
3 Sana Highlands Trekking Expeditions E3

Eating
4 Beneve Coffee House C4
5 Tamarind Restaurant F6
6 Thorn Tree Café D3

Drinking & Nightlife
7 Nairobi Java House E4
8 Simmers C4

Shopping
9 City Market C3
10 Maasai Market C1

Information
11 Acacia Medical Centre C3
AGX .... (see 13)
12 Bunson Travel D4
13 French Embassy B3
14 Immigration Office B5
Japan Information & Culture Centre .... (see 11)
15 KAM Pharmacy E3
16 Lucille Cyber Café D4
17 Spanish Embassy E4
18 Tanzanian Embassy E5
19 Uganda Consular C4

Transport
20 Adventure Upgrade Safaris E3
21 Air India F6
Airport Bus Departure Point .... (see 42)
22 Akamba E2
23 Akamba Booking Office D4
24 Avis A2
25 Budget D4
26 Bus & Matatu Stop C1
27 Bus & Matatu Stop (for Hurlingham & Milimani) B4
28 Bus Stop (for Langata, Karen & Airport) F4
Bus Stop (for Westlands) .... (see 26)
29 Buses to Kisii & Migori H3
30 Central Rent-a-Car C4
31 Easy Coach G6
32 Egypt Air E4
33 Emirates A2
34 Ethiopian Airlines C4
35 Glory Car Hire E4
36 Glory Car Hire D2
37 KBS Booking Office B2
38 KBS Bus Station H4
Kenya Airways .... (see 13)
KLM .... (see 13)
39 Main Bus & Matatu Area G2
40 Matatus to Naivasha, Nakuru, Nyahururu & Namanga H3
41 Matatus to Wilson Airport, Nairobi National Park, Langata & Karen G6
42 Metro Shuttle Bus Stand F4
43 Nairobi Train Station Booking Office G7
44 Scandinavia Express E2

Orientation

The compact city centre is in the area bounded by Uhuru Hwy, Haile Selassie Ave, Moi Ave and University Way. Kenyatta Ave divides this area in two; most of the important offices lie to the south, while hotels, the market and more offices are to the north. North of the city centre are Nairobi University, the National Museum and the expat-dominated suburb of Westlands. Jomo Kenyatta International Airport is southeast of central Nairobi; also south are Langata and Karen suburbs and Wilson Airport.

Information

DANGERS & ANNOYANCES

'Nairobbery', as it has been nicknamed by jaded residents and expats, is often regarded as the most dangerous city in Africa. But it's worth remembering that the majority of problems happen in the shanty towns, far from the main tourist zones.

The downtown area, bounded by Kenyatta Ave, Moi Ave, Haile Selassie Ave and Uhuru Hwy, is unthreatening and comparatively trouble-free as long as you use a bit of common sense. If you stay alert, walk with confidence, keep a hand on your wallet and avoid wearing anything too flashy, by day you should encounter nothing worse than a few persistent safari touts and the odd con artist. Once the shops in the CBD have shut, the streets empty rapidly. After sunset, mugging is a risk anywhere on the streets; you should always take a taxi, even if you're only going a few blocks.

Potential danger zones include the area around Latema and River Rds (east of Moi Ave), which is a hot spot for petty theft. Uhuru Park is a pleasant place during daylight hours, though it tends to accumulate all kinds of dodgy characters at night.

In the event that you are mugged, never, ever resist – simply give up your valuables and, more often than not, your assailant will flee the scene rapidly. Remember that a petty thief and a violent aggressor are very different kinds of people, so don't give your assailant any reason to do something rash.

EMERGENCY

Aga Khan Hospital (☎3662020; Third Parklands Ave; ⏲24hr) A reliable hospital with 24-hour emergency services.

Ambulance, Fire & Police (☎999) The national emergency number to call for fire, police and ambulance assistance, but don't rely on prompt arrival. For less-urgent police business, call ☎240000.

INTERNET ACCESS

There are hundreds of internet cafes in central Nairobi, most of them tucked away in anonymous office buildings. Connection speed is usually pretty good and rates are around KSh1 per minute.

AGX (Map p602; Loita St, Barclays Plaza; ⏲8am-6pm Mon-Fri, to 3pm Sat)

Lucille Cyber Café (Map p602; ground fl, Uganda House, Standard St; ⏲7am-8pm Mon-Fri, 9am-6pm Sat, 10am-4pm Sun)

MEDICAL SERVICES

See also the Aga Khan Hospital (above); try to avoid the Kenyatta National Hospital.

AAR Health Services (☎2715319; Williamson House, Fourth Ngong Ave)

Acacia Medical Centre (Map p602; ☎212200; info@acaciamed.co.ke; ICEA Bldg, Kenyatta Ave; ⏲7am-7pm Mon-Fri, 7am-5pm Sat, 8am-5pm Sun)

KAM Pharmacy (Map p602; ☎2251700; Executive Tower, IPS Bldg, Kimathi St; ⏲8.30am-6pm Mon-Fri, to 2pm Sat) Pharmacy, doctor's surgery and laboratory.

Nairobi Hospital (☎2846000; Ngong Rd; ⏲24hr)

MONEY

In the centre of Nairobi, Barclays branches with guarded ATMs include those located on Muindi Mbingu St, Mama Ngina St, and on the corner of Kenyatta and Moi Aves.

POST

Post office (☎243434; Kenyatta Ave; ⏲8am-6pm Mon-Fri, 9am-noon Sat)

TELEPHONE

Telkom Kenya (☎232000; Haile Selassie Ave; ⏲8am-6pm Mon-Fri, 9am-noon Sat)

TRAVEL AGENCIES

Bunson Travel (Map p602; ☎2248371; www.bunsontravel.com; Pan-African Insurance Bldg, Standard St) A good upmarket operator selling air tickets and safaris.

Uniglobe Let's Go Travel (☎4447151; www.uniglobeletsgotravel.com; ABC Pl, Waiyaki Way) Good for flights, safaris and pretty much anything else you might need.

GETTING THERE & AWAY

Air

Kenya Airways (www.kenyaairways.com), the country's principal international and domestic carrier, has a booking office in the city centre, though its website is efficient and reliable.

Bus

Most long-distance bus-company offices in Nairobi are in the River Rd area. Numerous companies do the run to Mombasa, leaving in the early morning or late in the evening; the trip takes eight to 10 hours. Buses leave from outside each company's office, and fares cost KSh400 to KSh700.

NATIONAL PARK ENTRY FEES

Kenya Wildlife Service (KWS; www.kws.org) is a government-run body that actively conserves and manages the country's parks, protected spaces and wildlife.

Nonresidents pay conservation fees ranging from $15/10 (adult/student or child) for sanctuaries to $25/15 for scenic parks like Hell's Gate, right up to $80/$40 for Amboseli and Nakuru. All fees cover visitors for a 24-hour period, but you cannot leave and reenter without paying twice. Resident park fees range from Ksh200–Ksh1000.

Admission to national parks in Kenya is in part converted to the 'Safari Card' system, for payment of entry and camping fees. The cards must be charged with credit in advance and can only be topped up at certain locations. Any credit left on the card once you finish your trip cannot be refunded.

The land-based parks and reserves charge KSh300 for vehicles with fewer than six seats and KSh1000 for vehicles seating six to 12. In addition to the public camping areas, special campsites cost US$25 per adult nonresident, plus a KSh7500 weekly reservation fee. Guides are available in most parks for US$30/KSh2500 per nonresident/resident per day.

CRAFTS & MARKETS

Some markets and shops worth checking out in Nairobi include **Maasai Market** (Map p110; ⌚Tue), off Slip Rd; **Spinners Web** (☎4440882; Waiyaki Way, Viking House); and **City Market** (Map p602; Muindi Mbingu St)

Akamba (p633) is the biggest private bus company in the country, with an extensive and reliable network. Buses serve Kakamega, Kisumu, Mombasa, Uganda and Tanzania, departing from Lagos Rd; there's a **booking office** (Map p602; ☎2365790; www.akambabus.com; Monrovia St) from where its international buses go to Uganda and Tanzania.

The government-owned **KBS** (Kenya Bus Service; ☎2341250) is another large operator. It's cheaper than Akamba, but the buses are much slower. The main depot is on Uyoma St, and there's a **booking office** (Map p602; ☎2341250; cnr Muindi Mbingu & Monrovia Sts) in the city centre.

Easy Coach (p633) is a reliable company serving western Kenyan destinations on the Kisumu/Kakamega route.

The **Machakos Country Bus Station** (Landhies Rd) is a disorganised place with buses running to Kakamega, Kisumu, Naivasha, Nanyuki, Nakuru and other destinations.

For typical fares and durations, see the boxed text below:

Matatu

Most *matatus* leave from the chaotic Latema, Accra, River and Cross Rds and fares are similar to the corresponding buses. Most companies are pretty much the same, although there are some that aim for higher standards than others. Mololine Prestige Shuttle, which operates along the Nairobi–Naivasha–Nakuru–Eldoret route, is one such company, with others set to follow its example on other routes. Departure points are shown on the Central Nairobi map.

Train

Nairobi train station has a small booking office, though don't bother trying to get in touch with it – you need to stop by in person to book tickets a few days in advance of your intended departure. For Mombasa (US$65/55 in 1st/2nd class, 14 to 16 hours), trains leave Nairobi at 7pm on Monday, Wednesday and Friday; arrive early.

GETTING AROUND

To/From Jomo Kenyatta International Airport

Kenya's main **international airport** (☎6611000) is 15km out of town, off the road to Mombasa. We recommend that you take a taxi (KSh1200 to KSh1500, but you'll need to bargain hard) to get to/from the airport, especially after dark.

A far cheaper way to get into town is by city bus 34 (KSh30), but a lot of travellers get robbed on the bus or when they get off. Always hold onto valuables and have small change ready for the fare. Buses run from 5.45am to 9.30pm weekdays, 6.20am to 9.30pm Saturdays and 7.15am to 9.30pm Sundays, though the last few evening services may not operate. Heading to the airport, the main departure point is along Moi Ave, right outside the Hotel Ambassadeur Nairobi. Thereafter, buses travel west along Kenyatta Ave.

To/From Wilson Airport

Wilson Airport (p632) is 6km south of the city centre on Langata Rd. To get to the airport for Airkenya services or charter flights, the cheapest option is bus or *matatu* 15, 31, 34, 125 or 126 from Moi Ave (KSh25). A taxi to the centre of town will cost you KSh750 to KSh1000 depending on the driver.

MAJOR MATATU ROUTES

TO	FARE (KSH)	DURATION (HR)	DEPARTURE POINT
Eldoret	700	6	Easy Coach Terminal
Kericho	650	3	Cross Rd
Kisumu	600-900	4	Cross Rd
Meru	550	3	Main Bus & Matatu Area
Naivasha	200-300	1½	cnr River Rd & Ronald Ngala St
Nakuru	400	3	cnr River Rd & Ronald Ngala St
Namanga	300-400	2	cnr River Rd & Ronald Ngala St
Nanyuki	400	3	Main Bus & Matatu Area
Narok	400	3	Cross Rd
Nyahururu	400	3½	cnr River Rd & Ronald Ngala St
Nyeri	350	2½	Latema Rd

Bus

The ordinary city buses are run by KBS, but hopefully you won't need to use them much. Forget about them if you're carrying luggage – you'll never get on. Most buses pass through the city centre, but the main KBS terminus is on Uyoma St, east of the centre.

Matatu

Nairobi's horde of *matatus* follow the same routes as buses and display the same route numbers. For Westlands, you can pick up number 23 on Moi Ave or Latema Rd. Number 46 to the Yaya Centre stops in front of the main post office, and numbers 125 and 126 to Langata leave from in front of the train station. As usual, you should keep an eye on your valuables on all *matatus*.

Taxi

Fares around town are negotiable but end up pretty standard. Any journey within the city centre area costs KSh400, from the city-centre to Milimani Rd costs KSh500, and for longer journeys such as Westlands or the Yaya Centre, fares range from KSh600 to KS700. From the city centre to Karen and Langata it is around KSh1000 (one way).

THE RIFT VALLEY

Lake Naivasha

☎050

Lake Naivasha has one of the largest settler and expat communities in Kenya, and half of Nairobi seems to decamp here at weekends. It can have a resort feel in high season, when it becomes Kenya's earthier version of St Tropez, with Tusker beer rather than champagne. With its shores fringed in papyrus and yellow-barked acacias, bulbous snorting hippos playing in the shallows, a cacophony of twittering birds and a gentle climate, there's no denying its appeal over the urban mayhem of Nairobi.

Sights & Activities

★Crescent Island WILDLIFE RESERVE
(☎2021030; www.crescentisland.co; adult/child US$25/12.50) This protruding rim of a collapsed volcanic crater forms an idyllic private sanctuary with giraffes, zebras, wildebeest, Thomson's and Grant's gazelles, elands, waterbucks and countless bird species (guide recommended; pay a tip). Combine a visit with a boat trip among the hippos; trips are cheaper here than from the hotels. You can do horse-back treks from neighbouring **Sanctuary Farm** (☎0722-761940; http://sanctuaryfarmkenya.com; Ksh 2000 per hour).

> DON'T MISS
>
> **ELMENTEITA WEAVERS**
>
> Visit this little **cooperative** (⌚8am-5pm) off Moi South Lake Rd and you'll see weavers producing hand-woven rugs, carpets and *kikoi*. Prices reflect the high quality. There's also a small pottery with tiles and pots painted with Kenyan birds and animals.

★Elsamere Conservation Centre WILDLIFE RESERVE
(☎2021055; www.elsamere.com; admission US$25; ⌚8am-6.30pm) The former home of the late Joy Adamson of *Born Free* fame. Now a conservation centre focused on lake ecology and environmental awareness programs, the site is open to the public and entry includes afternoon tea complete with a mountain of biscuits on the hippo-manicured lawns.

Crater Lake Game Sanctuary WILDLIFE RESERVE
(per person US$15, plus car KSh200) Surrounding a beautiful volcanic crater lake fringed with acacias, this small sanctuary has many trails, including one for hikers along the steep but diminutive crater rim.

Sleeping

★Carnelley's CAMPGROUND, HUT $
(☎0722-260749; www.campcarnelleys.com; Moi South Lake Rd; campsites Ksh600-800, dm Ksh800, d bandas Ksh8000-1000) Hip homestead Carnelley's features a lush lake setting, an imaginatively designed restaurant half open to the elements and a warm Kenyan/Irish welcome. Accommodation is either in your own tent, in pretty white plaster and timber *bandas* (thatched roof huts) or in dorm cottages. Healthy breakfasts and varied lunch and dinner options, including lake fish.

★Dea's Gardens GUESTHOUSE $$
(☎2021015; www.deasgardens.com; Moi South Lake Rd; per person with half board €70) On Moi South Lake Rd, 2km after the turning on the right, this charming guest house is run by the elegant Dea. The main house (with two rooms) is a gorgeous chalet of Swiss inspiration, while the two cottages in the lush grounds are large and comfortable. Meals are served in the main house.

DON'T MISS

HELL'S GATE NATIONAL PARK

Hell's Gate (☎050-2020284; adult/child & student US$25/15, bicycle KSh50, guide KSh500) is unique among Kenya's parks, as you are encouraged to walk or cycle unguided across its breadth. There's dramatic scenery, with looming cliffs, gorges and basalt columns. Lurking lions and leopards add to the excitement. Marking the eastern entrance to Hell's Gate Gorge is **Fischer's Tower**, one of the park's many popular rock-climbing sites. Lake Naivasha makes a convenient base for exploring the park, but camping here is recommended, and Ol Dubai and Naiberta campsites are the best (both $15). Access is by private car or even by bicycle.

Crater Lake Camp TENTED CAMP $$$
(☎2020613; www.craterlakecamp.com; campsites KSh500, s/d with full board US$187/280) The luxury tented camp is nestled among trees and overlooks the tiny jade-green crater lake.

Getting There & Away

Matatus (KSh100, one hour) run along Moi South Lake Rd between Naivasha town and Kongoni on the lake's western side, passing the turn-offs to Hell's Gate National Park and Carnelley's.

Nakuru

☎051 / POP 300,000

Kenya's fourth-largest centre feels like an overgrown country town, and has a relaxed atmosphere. It makes a pleasant base for a few days, and sits on the doorstep of the delightful Lake Nakuru National Park.

Buses, *matatus* and occasional Peugeots leave for Naivasha (KSh120, 1¼ hours), Nairobi (KSh200, three hours), Kitale (KSh350, 3½ hours) and Kisumu (KSh350, 3½ hours).

Sleeping & Eating

Carnation Hotel HOTEL $
(☎2215360; Mosque Rd; s/tw KSh1000/1550) The town's prettiest budget hotel, featuring rooms with colourful tiled floors and kitsch bed sheets.

Merica Hotel HOTEL $$
(☎2216013; www.mericagrouphotels.com; Kenyatta Ave; s/d US$80/125;) This contemporary tower hosts Nakuru's plushest rooms. Ride the glass elevators up through the sunlit atrium to well-appointed rooms large enough to host a wildebeest migration.

★ **Hygienic Butchery** KENYAN $
(Tom Mboya Rd; mains KSh180-250; ⊙lunch & dinner) Great name, great place. The Kenyan tradition of *nyama choma* is alive and well here. Sidle up to the counter, try a piece of tender mutton or beef and order half a kilo (per person) of whichever takes your fancy, along with chapattis or *ugali* (stiff, doughy maize).

Lake Nakuru National Park

This **park** (☎051-2217151; adult/child & student US$80/40) rivals Amboseli as Kenya's second-most-visited park. It's one of the best places in Kenya to see leopards, and white rhinos are commonly spotted at the lake's southern end. But the park's most famous attraction is the colony of pelicans and (occasionally) flamingos that ring the lake in thousands.

The main gate of the national park is 2km south of the centre of Nakuru. KWS smartcards are available here. In order to visit the national park, a taxi from Nakuru for a few hours should cost you around KSh2500, although note that you will most likely have to bargain hard for it.

Sleeping

★ **Wildlife Club of Kenya Guesthouse** HOSTEL $
(☎0710-579944; Nakuru town centre; per person without bathroom KSh1250) Like staying in a secluded cottage in the countryside, but instead of a garden full of bunny rabbits it's full of rhinos and buffaloes. There are six simple rooms here, as well as an equipped kitchen and a nicely appointed dining room.

Backpackers' Campsite CAMPGROUND $
(campsites US$25) Located just inside the main gate, this place has the park's best camping facilities. Baboons are particularly prevalent around here, so take care.

★ **Sarova Lion Hill Lodge** LODGE $$$
(☎in Nairobi 020-2315139; www.sarovahotels.com; s/d with full board US$366/486;) An upmarket lodge that offers 1st-class service and comfort from high up the lake's eastern slopes. There are fantastic views from the restaurant-bar as well as from the majority of rooms in the lodge.

Mt Kenya National Park

Africa's second-highest mountain, **Mt Kenya** (☎0722-279502; www.kws.go.ke; adult/child US$55/25, 3-day package adult/child US$150/70) attracts spry hikers, long, dramatic cloud cover and all the eccentricities of its mother continent in equal measure. Here, mere minutes from the equator, glaciers carve out the throne of Ngai, the old high god of the Kikuyu people. Mt Kenya's highest peaks, Batian (5199m) and Nelion (5188m), can only be reached by mountaineers with technical skills. However, Point Lenana (4985m), which is the park's third-highest peak, can be reached by hikers and is the usual goal for most mere mortals. The daily fees for the national park are charged upon entry, so you must estimate the length of your stay.

Activities

Hiking the Naro Moru Route

Although the least scenic, this is the most straightforward, popular route, and still a spectacular and very enjoyable trail. Allow a minimum of four days for the hike; it's possible in three if you arrange transport between Naro Moru and the Met Station Hut, but doing it this quickly risks serious altitude sickness.

Hiking the Sirimon Route

A popular alternative to Naro Moru, this route has more spectacular scenery, greater flexibility and a gentler rate of ascent, although it is still easy to climb too fast, so allow at least five days for the hike. It's well worth considering combining it with the Chogoria route for a six- to seven-day traverse that will really bring out the best of Mt Kenya.

Hiking the Chogoria Route

This route is justly famous for crossing some of the most spectacular and varied scenery on Mt Kenya, and is often combined with the Sirimon route (usually as the descent). The only disadvantage is the long distance between Chogoria village and the park gate. Allow at least five days for a hike here.

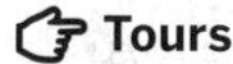

Tours

If you negotiate, a package hike may end up costing only a little more than organising each logistical element of the trip separately. Picking the right company is even more important here than on regular safari, as an unqualified or inexperienced guide could put you in real danger.

Mt Kenya National Park

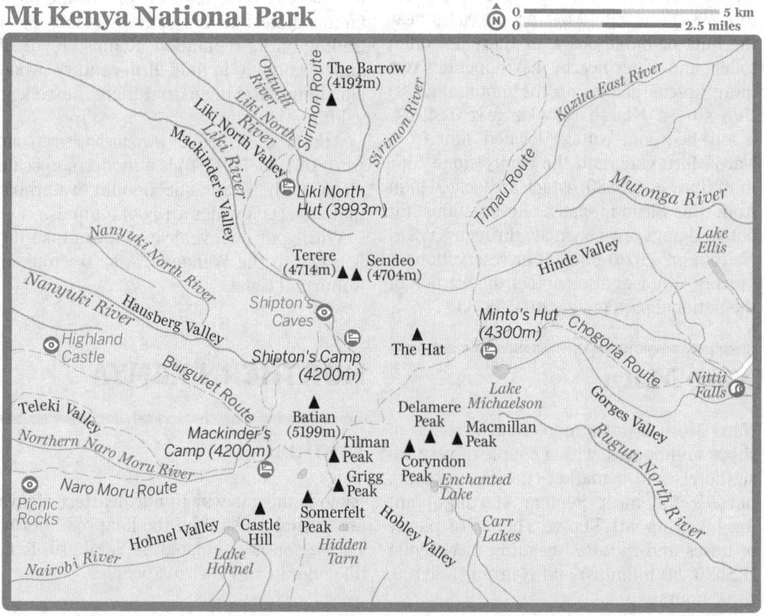

0 — 5 km
0 — 2.5 miles

The Barrow (4192m)
Ontulili River
Liki North River
Sirimon Route
Sirimon River
Kazita East River
Liki North Valley
Mackinder's Valley
Liki River
Liki North Hut (3993m)
Timau Route
Mutonga River
Lake Ellis
Nanyuki North River
Terere (4714m)
Sendeo (4704m)
Hinde Valley
Nanyuki River
Hausberg Valley
Shipton's Caves
Minto's Hut (4300m)
Chogoria Route
Highland Castle
Shipton's Camp (4200m)
The Hat
Nithi Falls
Burguret Route
Lake Michaelson
Gorges Valley
Teleki Valley
Batian (5199m)
Delamere Peak
Macmillan Peak
Northern Naro Moru River
Mackinder's Camp (4200m)
Tilman Peak
Coryndon Peak
Ruguti North River
Naro Moru Route
Grigg Peak
Enchanted Lake
Picnic Rocks
Somerfelt Peak
Castle Hill
Hobley Valley
Carr Lakes
Hohnel Valley
Hidden Tarn
Lake Hohnel
Nairobi River

GUIDES, COOKS & PORTERS

KWS issues vouchers to all registered guides and porters, who should also hold identity cards; they won't be allowed into the park without them. The cost of guides varies depending on their qualifications. You should expect to pay a minimum of US$20/18/15 per day for a guide/cook/porter. Agree on all costs before you depart. These fees don't include park entry fees and tips.

KG Mountain Expeditions (☎721604930; www.kenyaexpeditions.com; Naro Moru)

Mountain Rock Safaris Resorts & Trekking Services (Map p602; ☎020-242133, 0722-511752; www.mountainrockkenya.com; Suite 325, 4th fl, Jubilee Insurance House, Wabera St, Nairobi)

Naro Moru River Lodge (☎724082754; www.naromoruriverlodge.com; Naro Moru)

Sana Highlands Trekking Expeditions (Map p602; ☎020-227820; www.sanatrekking-kenya.com; Contrust Ho use, Moi Ave, Nairobi)

Sleeping

You can **camp** (adult/child US$10/5) anywhere on the mountain – the nightly fee is payable to KWS at any gate. Most people camp near the huts or bunkhouses, as there are often toilets and water nearby. KWS operates two more upscale lodges on the mountain: **Batian Guest House** (www.kws.go.ke; US$180), a four-bedroom cottage located 1km from Naro Moru gate; and the comfy stone **Sirimon Bandas** (US$80), which are located 9km from the Sirimon gates. Reservations for both lodgings must be made through KWS in Nairobi on ☎020-600800 or reservations@kws.org. You can also contact the warden of the national park on ☎020-3568763.

Naro Moru

☎062

Naro Moru is little more than a string of shops and houses, with a couple of very basic hotels and a market (there's no bank), but it's the most popular starting point for hikes up Mt Kenya. There are plenty of buses and *matatus* heading to Nanyuki (KSh80, 30 minutes) and Nairobi (KSh400, three hours).

★**Naro Moru River Lodge** (☎0724-082754; www.naromoruriverlodge.com; campsites/dm US$11/15, s with full board US$142-201, d & tw with full board US$204-309;) is a bit like a Swiss chalet, with a lovely collection of dark, cosy cottages and rooms embedded into a sloping hillside that overlooks the rushing Naro Moru River 3km from town.

Mountain Rock Lodge (☎62625, Nairobi 020-242133, 0722-511752; www.mountainrockkenya.com; campsites US$5, standard s/tw KSh3000/4000, superior s/tw KSh3500/5200) is one of the major bases for Mt Kenya climbers and the operator of Old Moses Hut and Shipton's Camp on the mountain. Rooms are serviceable enough but in need of refurbishment. It's located 9km north of Naro Moru.

Aberdare National Park

This **park** (☎061-2055024; adult/child US$50/25, smartcard required) protects a striking stretch of moorland, peaks and forest atop the western Kinangop Plateau, and the eastern outcrop of dense rain forest, known as the Salient. Wildlife sightings are dominated by elephants and buffaloes, but black rhinos, giant forest hogs, black servals and rare black leopards are also sometimes seen.

Treetops (☎Nairobi 020-4452095; www.aberdaresafarihotels.com; s/tw without bathroom with full board US$328/415) is one of the most famous hotels in Kenya, and has long been trading on its reputation. Rooms are small and decorated in mid-20th-century wood panelling/floral linens, but there is excellent wildlife-watching.

Ark (☎0737-799990; www.thearkkenya.com; s/d/tr US$180/210/288) is a modern, upscale place, with a fantastic floodlit waterhole that attracts a wider array of animals.

With your own vehicle, you can take the B5 Hwy to the Wanderis, Ark, Treetops or Ruhuruini Gates.

NORTHERN KENYA

Isiolo

☎064

Isiolo is the gateway to northeastern Kenya and a vital pit stop on the long road north. The region is populated by Samburu, Rendille, Boran and Turkana people.

Lots of bus companies serve Nairobi (KSh600, 4½ hours) with most buses leaving between 6am and 6.30am from the main road through town and also stopping at the *matatu* and bus stand just south of the market. Nightly buses creep north to Marsabit (KSh700, nine hours) and Moyale (KSh1600, 20 hours).

Bomen Hotel HOTEL $
(☎52389; bomenhotel.com; near the Mansile Hospital; s/tw/ste KSh900/1500/2500) A favourite home of NGO workers, this has the town's brightest and most comfortable rooms. There's a good restaurant too, serving fried tilapia, pepper steak and goulash.

Gaddisa Lodge LODGE $$
(☎0724-201115; www.gaddisa.com; campsites KSh400, s/tw KSh3000/4000) Around 3km northeast of town, this Dutch-run place has peaceful cottages overlooking the fringes of the northern savannah country.

Marsabit

☎069

The area surrounding Marsabit is actually a giant shield volcano, the surface of which is peppered with hundreds of cinder cones and volcanic craters, many flooded. Mt Marsabit's highest peak, Karantin (1707m), is a rewarding 5km hike from town through lush vegetation and moss-covered trees. The town has an interesting mixture of local tribespeople.

A bus now connects Marsabit to Moyale (KSh1000, 8½ hours). There's no designated stop – simply flag it down on the A2 Hwy as it comes through town around 5pm each day (en route from Nairobi). The same service heads south to Isiolo (KSh700, 8½ hours) at 9am.

JeyJey Centre HOTEL $
(☎0717-383883; A2 Hwy; s/tw without bathroom KSh400/600, r KSh750) This mudbrick castle bedecked in flowers is something of a travellers' centre. Basic rooms with mosquito nets surround a courtyard, and bathrooms (even shared ones) sport on-demand hot water. There's also an unattractive campsite (per person KSh250).

Loyangalani

Standing in utter contrast to the dour desert surrounding it, tiny Loyangalani assaults all your senses in a crazy explosion of clashing colours, feather head dresses and blood-red robes. Overlooking Lake Turkana and surrounded by small ridges of pillow lava, the sandy streets of this one-camel town are a meeting point of the great northern tribes, Turkana and Samburu, Gabbra and El Molo. It's easily the most exotic corner of Kenya and a fitting reward for the hard journey here.

Public transport is rare, which necessitates having your own private vehicle, preferably one with 4WD and high clearance.

★ **Palm Shade Camp** BANDA $
(☎0726-714768; campsites KSh500, s/tw bandas without bathroom KSh750/1500) Drop your tent on some grass beneath acacias and palms or crash in its tidy domed *rondavels* (round huts). The huts have simple wood beds with foam mattresses and unique walls with meshed cut-outs that let light and heavenly evening breezes in.

Lake Turkana

If you go to Loyangalani you can't help but visit Lake Turkana. Formerly known as Lake Rudolf, and nowadays often evocatively called the 'Jade Sea', vast Lake Turkana stretches all the way to Ethiopia. High salt levels render the sandy, volcanic area around the lake almost entirely barren, but its desolation and stark, surreal beauty contrast with the colourful tribespeople who inhabit the lake's shore.

South Island National Park WILDLIFE RESERVE
(adult/child US$20/10) Made a Unesco World Heritage Site in 1997, this is uninhabited apart from a large croc population, poisonous snakes and feral goats. To get there, you can hire a boat (per hour KSh2500) from Palm Shade Camp.

WESTERN KENYA

Kisumu

☎057

Set on the sloping shore of Lake Victoria's Winam Gulf, the town of Kisumu is the third-largest in Kenya. Declared a city during its centenary celebrations in 2001, it still doesn't feel like one; its relaxed atmosphere is a world away from the likes of Nairobi and Mombasa.

Sights & Activities

Kisumu Museum MUSEUM
(Nairobi Rd; admission KSh500; ⌚8am-6pm) Unlike many local museums, this one offers an interesting exploration of the historical and natural delights of the Lake Victoria region.

Main Market MARKET
(off Jomo Kenyatta Hwy) Kisumu has one of Kenya's most animated markets, now spilling out onto the surrounding roads.

Sleeping

New Victoria Hotel HOTEL $$
(☎2021067; Gor Mahia Rd; s without bathroom KSh900, s/tw/tr KSh1450/1950/2700) This Yemeni-run hotel has character in abundance and is something of a focal point for the town's small Arab population. Rooms have fans, mosquito nets and comfy foam mattresses.

Sooper Guest House BACKPACKERS
(☎0725-281733; kayamchatur@yahoo.com; Oginga Odinga Rd; s KSh1000-1200, d KSh1200-1400, tw/tr KSh1200/1600) Sooper has become the de facto backpackers in town and you have a good chance of meeting other travellers here.

Eating

The fact that Kisumu sits on Lake Victoria isn't lost on restaurants here: fish is abundant. If you want an authentic local fish fry, there is no better place than the dozens of smoky tin-shack restaurants sitting on the lake's shore at Railway Beach at the end of Oginga Odinga Rd.

Orientation

Kisumu is a fairly sprawling town, but everything you will need is within walking distance. Most shops, banks, cheap hotels and other facilities can be found around Oginga Odinga Rd, while the train station and ferry jetty are short walks from the end of New Station Rd.

Information

Abacus Cyber Cafe (Al-Imran Plaza, Oginga Odinga Rd; per hr KSh80; ⌚8am-8pm) Internet access.

Barclays Bank (Kampala St)

Police Station (Uhuru Rd)

Post office (Oginga Odinga Rd)

Getting There & Away

Akamba (off New Station Rd) Has its own depot in the town centre. Besides four daily buses to Nairobi (KSh1100 to KSh1350, seven hours) via Nakuru (KSh800, 4½ hours), there are also daily services to Kampala (KSh1500, seven hours).

Easy Coach (off Mosque Rd) Serves similar destinations, as well as Kakamega (KSh250, one hour), with some added comfort and cost. *Matatus* also travel to Kakamega (KSh200, 1½ hours).

Kakamega Forest Reserve

☎056

This small slab of virgin tropical rain forest is all that's left in Kenya of the once-mighty Guineo-Congolian rainforest. It boasts an extraordinary biodiversity, including 330 species of bird, seven different primate species and around 400 species of butterfly. Excellent official **guides** (per person for short/long walk KSh500/800), trained by the Kakamega Biodiversity Conservation and Tour Operators Association, can help you find birds and monkeys.

Udo's Bandas & Campsite BANDA $
(☎0727-415828; www.kws.go.ke; campsites US$15, bandas per person US$30) This is a tidy, well-maintained KWS-run campsite with simple *bandas*. Mosquito nets are provided, but bring your own sleeping bag and supplies.

★ **Rondo Retreat** GUESTHOUSE $$
(☎056-30268; www.rondoretreat.com; adult/child with full board KSh7400/5400) This has an idyllic setting in a former 1920s saw-miller's residence, about 3km east of Isecheno. Seven cottages, each with striking traditional fittings and large verandahs, sit in gorgeous gardens through which plenty of wildlife passes.

Masai Mara National Reserve

The world-renowned **Masai Mara** (adult/child US$80/45) is backed by the spectacular Siria Escarpment, watered by the Mara River and littered with an astonishing amount of wildlife. Its 1510 sq km of open rolling grasslands, the northern extension of the equally famous Serengeti Plains, is breathtaking at any time of year. However, the Mara reaches its pinnacle during the annual wildebeest migration in July and August, when literally millions of these ungainly beasts move north from the Serengeti seeking lusher grass before turning south again around October.

Sights & Activities

Wildlife Drives & Walks

Whether you're bouncing over the plains in pursuit of elusive elephant silhouettes or parked next to a pride of lions and listening to their bellowed breaths, wildlife drives are a highlight of a trip to the Mara.

Ballooning

If you can afford US$530 (per person including champagne breakfast), then balloon safaris are superb and worlds away from the minibus circuit. Trips can be arranged through top-end lodges.

Sleeping

★Riverside Camp HUT, CAMPGROUND $
(☎0720-218319; www.riversidecampmara.com; campsites KSh400 plus security fee KSh400, s/d KSh2250/4500) Run by Maasai, this camping ground has good facilities, like running water, hot showers and a kitchen area, complete with utensils. Trees provide shade for campers, while simple *bandas* provide shelter for the tentless. There is a bar, and if you call ahead, meals are available. Groups must pay for security.

★Aruba Mara Camp TENTED CAMP $
(☎0723-997524; www.aruba-safaris.com; Talek Gate; campsites KSh600, unpowered/powered tent per person KSh2000/8000) The tents are luxuriously appointed, but not overpowering, and have lots of privacy as well as memorable views over the Talek River.

Semadep CAMP, VILLAGE $$
(☎0721-817757; jplsemadep@gmail.com; campsite with full board $70, village stay with full board $45) Located 2km from Sekenani Gate, this camp and village stay offers a wonderful insight into Maasai life and culture. Owned and operated by local Maasai, it helps fund a local school and health clinic, which you can visit as part of your stay. Otherwise, you are immersed in Maasai life, learning how to milk cattle, fire bows and arrows, and light fires with sticks, grass and elephant dung. The hillside tented camp provides a better level of comfort, but adventurous travellers will find a couple of nights in the village itself even more rewarding: you sleep in a *manyatta* (mud hut) and will meet and interact with all generations in the village. Contact them direct for information on getting there: it's possible by *matatu* from Narok, though a taxi is easier.

Acacia Camp TENTED CAMP $$
(☎0726-089107; www.acaciacamp.com; Oloolaimutiek Gate; campsites US$8, s/tw tent US$36/54) Thatched roofs shelter closely spaced, spartan semipermanent tents in this quaint camping ground. There are numerous cooking areas, a bar, a campfire pit and a simple restaurant that serves meals for US$7 a pop.

★Basecamp Masai Mara LODGE $$$
(☎0733-333909; www.basecampexplorer.com; Talek Gate; s/d tent with full board US$290/500;) Solar panels provide power, organic waste is composted, dirty water is reused to water the grounds and local conservationists give informal lectures. The 16 individually designed permanent tents have thatched roofs, beautiful outdoor showers and large verandahs with day beds.

Mara Serena Safari Lodge LODGE $$$
(☎Nairobi 020-2842000; www.serenahotels.com; Masai Mara Reserve; s/d with full board US$445/595;) Built to resemble a futuristic Maasai village, Serena is the most colourful lodge in the reserve. Hip rooms, with vibrant curved walls and Juliet balconies, line a ridge and overlook the grassy plains below. Justifiably popular.

Information

Because most of the gates are located inside the reserve boundary, it is easy to enter the Masai Mara unknowingly. Wherever you enter, make sure you ask for a receipt: it is crucial for passage between the reserve's Narok and Transmara sections and for your eventual exit.

Getting There & Away

AIR

Airkenya (☎Nairobi 020-605745; www.airkenya.com) and Safarilink (p632) each have daily flights to Masai Mara. Return flights start at US$250.

MATATU, CAR & 4WD

Although it's possible to arrange wildlife drives independently, bear in mind that there are few savings in coming here without transport. That said, it is possible to access Talek and Sekenani Gates from Narok by *matatu* (KSh300 to KSh400). From Kisii, a *matatu* will get you as far as Kilkoris or Suna on the main A1 Hwy, but you will have problems after this.

For those who drive, the first 52km west of Narok on the B3 and C12 are smooth enough, but after the bitumen runs out you'll find that it gets

WORTH A TRIP

BOMBOLULU WORKSHOPS

The nonprofit **Bombolulu Workshops** (www.apdkbombolulu.org; admission nonresident KSh750; ⏲8am-6pm Mon-Sat, 10am-3pm Sun) produce crafts of a very high standard and give vocational training to hundreds of physically disabled people. Visit the workshops and showroom for free to buy jewellery and other crafts, or enter the cultural centre to tour mock-ups of traditional homesteads in the gardens; you can buy packets of seeds from the gardener. *Matatus* run here from Msanifu Kombo St, and Bamburi services in either direction also pass the centre.

pretty bumpy. The C13, which connects Oloololo Gate with Lolgorian out in the west, is very rough and rocky, and it's poorly signposted – a highway it's not.

Petrol is available (although expensive) at Mara Sarova, Mara Serena and Keekorok Lodges as well as in Talek village.

THE COAST

Mombasa

☎041 / POP 939,000

If your idea of Africa is roast meat, toasted maize, beer and cattle and farms and friendliness, those things are here. But it's all interwoven into the humid peel of plaster from Hindu warehouses, filigreed porches that lost their way in a Moroccan riad (traditional town house), spice markets that escaped India's Keralan coast, sailors chewing *miraa* (shoots chewed as a stimulant) next to boats bound for the Yemeni Hadramat and a giant coral castle built by invading Portuguese sailors.

Sights

Fort Jesus MUSEUM

(Map p615; adult/child KSh800/400; ⏲8am-6pm) Fort Jesus is Mombasa's most visited destination: a Unesco World Heritage Site and the anchor of the Old Town. The metre-thick walls, frescoed interiors, European graffiti, Arabic inscriptions and Swahili embellishment aren't just evocative – they're a record of the history of Mombasa writ in stone.

Old Town HISTORIC BUILDINGS

(Map p615) This doesn't have the medieval charm of Lamu or Zanzibar, but it's still an interesting area to wander around. The houses here are characteristic of coastal East African architecture, with ornately carved doors and window frames and fretwork balconies.

Sleeping

★**Mombasa Backpackers** BACKPACKERS $

(☎0701-561233; www.mombasabackpackers.com; Mwamba Dr 69, Nyali; dm/s/d KSh800/1200; ❄@🛜🏊) A huge white mansion surrounded by lush coconut gardens (with camping areas). The spacious rooms and dorms are well maintained and there's a decent swimming pool.

Glory Grand Hotel BUSINESS HOTEL $

(Map p616; ☎2228202; Kwa Shibu Rd; s/d from KSh2500/3500) The renovated Glory offers top-notch value for money. The rooms are cool, quiet and pleasantly furnished, and all up it's a great retreat from the noise and heat of the big city outside.

New Palm Tree Hotel HOTEL $

(Map p616; ☎311758; Nkrumah Rd; s/d incl breakfast KSh1600/2200) Rooms are set off a main building that has a terraced roof. While the

Mombasa

Sights
1 Fort Jesus ... D2
2 Old Town ... C2

Sleeping
Tamarind Village ... (see 4)

Eating
3 Jahazi Coffee House ... C2
4 Tamarind Restaurant ... D1

Shopping
Books First ... (see 5)
5 Nakumatt Supermarket ... A5

Information
6 AAR Health Services ... A2
7 Aga Khan Hospital ... B4
8 Fort Jesus Forex Bureau ... C2
9 Immigration Office ... D3
10 KWS Office ... D3
11 Mobasa Hospital ... D3
12 Standard Chartered Bank ... C2

amenities (like hot water) aren't always reliable, service is good and there's a sociable vibe.

★**Castle Royal Hotel** HISTORIC HOTEL $$
(Map p616; ☎2228780; Moi Ave; s/d US$95/130; ❄@📶) A creaky, old-fashioned place full of the ghosts of colonial days past, this charming institution offers great service, comfortable rooms with modern facilities and a primo (free) breakfast: coconut beans and *mandazi* (semisweet doughnuts), or bacon and croissants.

Tamarind Village RESORT $$
(Map p615; ☎ 474600; www.tamarind.co.ke; Silos Rd, Nyali; apt KSh9500-20,000; P❄@📶) Located in a modern (and quite elegantly executed) take on a Swahili castle overlooking the blue waters of the harbour, the Tamarind offers crisp, fully serviced apartments with satellite TV and palm-lined balconies.

Eating

★**Jahazi Coffee House** SWAHILI $
(Map p615; Ndia Kuu Rd; ⏲8am-8pm) Bringing a touch of cosmopolitan style to Mombasa Old Town, this stylish Swahili boutique

Mombasa

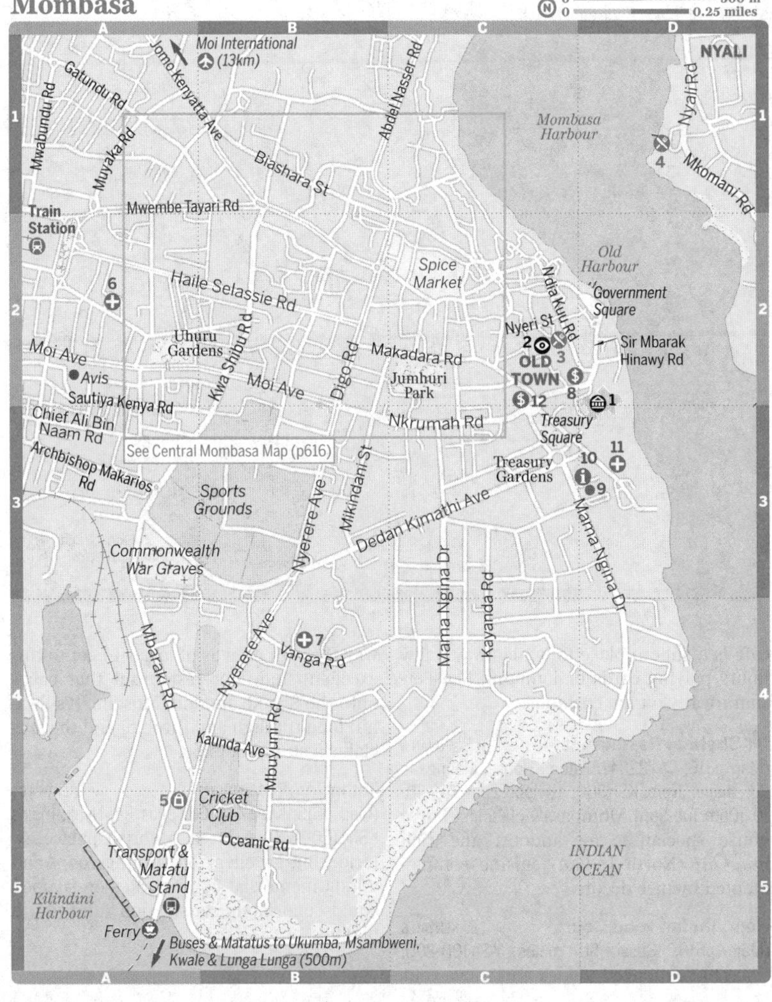

Central Mombasa

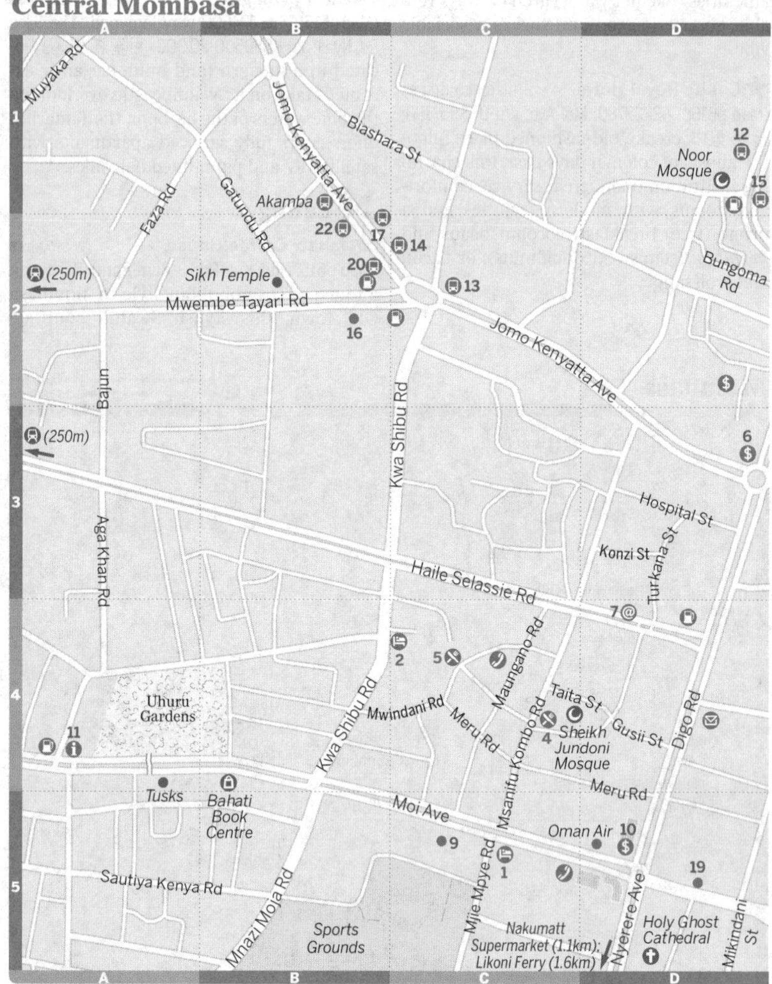

cafe is a superb place to while away a few hours playing cards or lounging like Persian royalty on the cushions.

★Shehnai Restaurant INDIAN $

(Map p616; ☎222847; Fatemi House, Maungano Rd; mains from KSh300; ⊙noon-2pm & 7.30-10.30pm Tue-Sun) Mombasa's classiest curry house specialises in tandoori and rich *mughlai* (North Indian) cuisine complemented by nice decor.

New Jundan Food Court KENYAN $

(Map p616; Gussi St; mains KSh100-200; ⊙lunch) You'll need to kick and shove your way through crowds of locals to get to this excellent 2nd-floor restaurant that backs onto the Sheikh Jundoni Mosque. It's Swahili food through and through and the special is a stunning pilau.

Tamarind Restaurant KENYAN $$

(Map p615; ☎ 474600; Silos Rd, Nyali; mains KSh1100-1800) A large, Moorish palace exterior, big jewellery box dining room and a long menu that concentrates on seafood equals enormous satisfaction (and yes, a big bill).

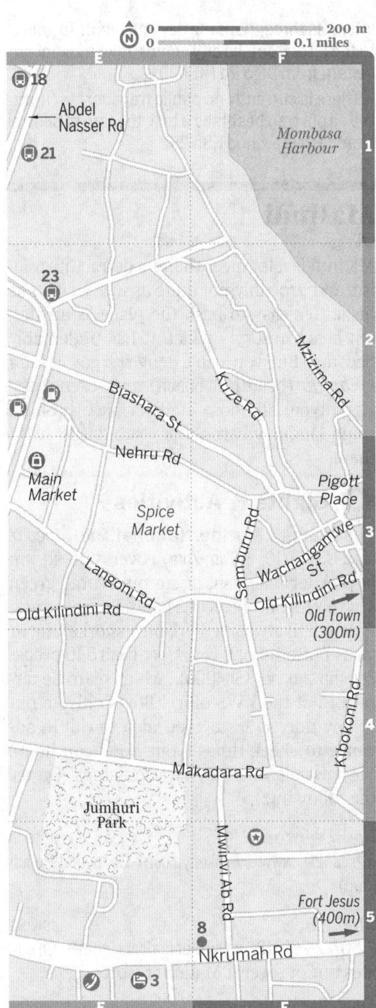

Central Mombasa

Sleeping

1	Castle Royal Hotel	C5
2	Glory Grand Hotel	C4
3	New Palm Tree Hotel	E5

Eating

4	New Jundan Food Court	C4
5	Shehnai Restaurant	C4

Information

6	Barclays Bank	D3
7	Blue Room Cyber Café	D4
8	Dial-A-Tour	F5
9	Fourways Travel	C5
10	Kenya Commercial Bank	D5
11	Mombasa & Coast Tourist Office	A4

Transport

12	Buses & Matatus to Malindi & Lamu	D1
13	Buses to Arusha & Moshi (Mwembe Tayari Health Centre)	C2
14	Buses to Dar es Salaam & Tanga	C2
	Busscar	(see 21)
15	Busstar	D1
16	Coastline Safaris	B2
17	Falcon	B2
18	Falcon	E1
19	Kenya Airways	D5
20	Matatus to Voi & Wundanyi	B2
21	Mombasa Raha	E1
22	Mombasa Raha	B2
23	TSS Express	E2

Information

DANGERS & ANNOYANCES

Mombasa is relatively safe compared to Nairobi, but the streets still clear pretty rapidly after dark, so it's a good idea to take taxis rather than walk around alone at night. You need to be more careful on the beaches north and south of town. The Likoni ferry is a bag-snatching hot spot.

EMERGENCY

AAR Health Services (Map p615; 312409; Lulu Centre, Machakos St, off Moi Ave; 24hr)

Police (222121, 999)

INTERNET ACCESS

Blue Room Cyber Café (Map p616; 224021; www.blueroomonline.com; Haile Selassie Rd; per min KSh2; 9am-10pm)

MEDICAL SERVICES

Aga Khan Hospital (Map p615; 2227710; www.agakhanhospitals.org; Vanga Rd)

MONEY

Barclays Bank (Map p616; 311660; Digo Rd)

Fort Jesus Forex Bureau (Map p615; 316717; Ndia Kuu Rd)

Kenya Commercial Bank (Map p616; 220978; Moi Ave)

Standard Chartered Bank (Map p615; 224614; Treasury Sq, Nkrumah Rd)

POST

Post office (227705; Digo Rd)

TELEPHONE

Post Global Services (☎230581; inglobal@africaonline.co.ke; Maungano Rd; ⏰7.30am-8pm)

Telkom Kenya (☎312811) Locations on Nkrumah Rd and Moi Ave.

TOURIST INFORMATION

KWS Office (Map p615; ☎312744/5; Nguua Court, Mama Ngina Dr; ⏰6am-6pm) Sells and charges smartcards.

Mombasa & Coast Tourist Office (Map p616; ☎225428; mcta@ikenya.com; Moi Ave; ⏰8am-4.30pm)

TRAVEL AGENCIES

Dial-A-Tour (Map p616; ☎221411; dialatour@ikenya.com; Oriental Bldg, Nkrumah Rd)

Fourways Travel (Map p616; ☎223344; Moi Ave)

VISA EXTENSIONS

Immigration Office (☎311745; Uhuru ni Kari Bldg, Mama Ngina Dr)

Getting There & Away

AIR

Daily flights are available with Kenya Airways between Nairobi and Mombasa's Moi International Airport (p632).

Airkenya (☎Nairobi 020-605745; www.airkenya.com) doesn't have a ticket office in Mombasa (you can book online), but it also flies between Nairobi and Mombasa once a day.

BUS & MATATU

Daytime services to Nairobi take at least six hours; overnight trips take eight to 10 hours and include a meal/smoking break about halfway. Fares vary from KSh800 to KSh1300. Most companies have at least four departures daily.

There are numerous daily *matatus* and small lorry-buses up the coast to Malindi, leaving from in front of the Noor Mosque on Abdel Nasser Rd. Buses take up to 2½ hours (KSh150), *matatus* about two hours (KSh180). You can also catch an 'express' *matatu* to Malindi (KSh200), which takes longer to fill up but is then supposedly nonstop all the way.

Tawakal, Falcon, Mombasa Raha and TSS Express have buses to Lamu, most leaving at around 7am (report 30 minutes early) from their offices on Abdel Nasser Rd. Buses take around seven hours to reach the Lamu ferry at Mokoke (KSh750 to KSh900), stopping in Malindi (KSh300 to KSh400).

Getting Around

The two Likoni ferries (per pedestrian/car free/KSh75 to KSh165) connect Mombasa Island with the southern mainland, running at frequent intervals throughout the day and night. To get to the jetty from the city centre, take a Likoni *matatu* from Digo Rd (KSh20).

There is currently no public transport to/from the airport, so best take a taxi; the fare to central Mombasa is around KSh750.

Malindi

☎042

Malindi is a lot nicer than its detractors realise, and probably not quite as nice as its fans insist. It's easy to bash the place as an Italian beach resort – which it has undeniably become. But you can't deny it's got a *bella spiaggia* (beautiful beach) and, excuse the stereotype, all those Italians have brought some high gastronomic standards with them.

Sights & Activities

The **Malindi Marine National Park** (adult/child US$15/10; ⏰7am-7pm) covers 213 sq km of powder blue fish, organ pipe coral, green sea turtles and beds of Thalassian sea grass.

You'll likely come here on a snorkelling or glass-bottom-boat **tour** (per boat, 5-10 people, 2hr trip around KSh4000), which can be arranged at the KWS office. Boats only go out at low tide, so it's a good idea to call in advance to check times (your hotel can help). Most hotels offer diving excursions. Or try the following:

Aqua Ventures BOAT TOUR
(☎32420; www.diveinkenya.com; Driftwood Beach Club)

Blue Fin DIVING
(☎0722-261242; www.bluefindiving.com) Operates out of several Malindi resorts.

Sleeping

Ozi's Guest House GUESTHOUSE $
(☎20218; ozi@swiftmalindi.com; Mama Ngina Rd; s/d KSh900/1800) Ozi's has long been popular with backpackers, likely because it perches on the attractive edge of Old Town.

★ **Scorpio Villas** RESORT $$
(☎20194; www.scorpio-villas.com; Mnarani Rd; s/d KSh4800/7600; ❄) The 40-odd rooms are whitewashed and art-bedecked and have wooden roof beams and four-posters. Throw in gardens heavy with foliage, a fantastic pool complex and a restaurant with excellent Italian food (four-course evening meal KSh1200) and it's hard to beat.

Jardin Lorna HOTEL $$

(☎30658; harry@swiftmalindi.com; Mtangani Rd; s/d KSh2500/5000, without bathroom KSh1500/3000; ❄ 🌊) Rooms are endearingly quirky with zebra rugs and local art punctuating the interior. Outside are peaceful gardens.

Driftwood Beach Club RESORT $$$

(☎20155; www.driftwoodclub.com; Mama Ngina Rd; s/d incl breakfast KSh10,560/15,070; ❄ 🌊) One of the best-known resorts in Malindi, Driftwood prides itself on an informal atmosphere and attracts a more independent clientele than many of its peers.

Eating

I Love Pizza ITALIAN $

(☎20672; nwright@africaonline.co.ke; Mama Ngina Rd; pizzas around KSh900, pastas around KSh400-600) We do too, and the pizza is done really well here – way better than you might expect this far from Naples.

Old Man & the Sea SEAFOOD $$

(☎31106; Mama Ngina Rd; mains KSh400-750, seafood KSh550-1100) The old man of Malindi's dining scene, this Old Man has been serving elegant, excellent cuisine using a combination of local ingredients and fresh recipes for years.

La Malindina ITALIAN $$$

(☎31449; www.malindina.com; Mtangani Rd; meals around KSh2000-2500; ⏲dinner only late Jul–mid-Apr) In the network of streets behind Lamu Rd is the very upmarket Italian restaurant La Malindina. It is open in high season only, and serves set meals; it's regarded by all and sundry as the best place in town to eat.

Information

Barclays Bank (☎20036; Lamu Rd)

Dollar Forex Bureau (☎30602; Lamu Rd)

Post office (Kenyatta Rd)

Standard Chartered Bank (☎20130; Stanchart Arcade, Lamu Rd)

Tourist office (☎20689; Malindi Complex, Lamu Rd; ⏲8am-12.30pm & 2-4.30pm Mon-Fri)

Getting There & Away

AIR

Airkenya (☎30646; Malindi Airport)

Kenya Airways (☎20237; Lamu Rd) Flies the route to Nairobi at least once a day.

Mombasa Air Safari (☎041-433061) Has daily flights to Mombasa and Lamu from June to September.

BUS & MATATU

There are numerous daily buses to Mombasa (KSh350, two hours). Companies such as Busstar, Busscar, TSS Express and Falcon have offices opposite the old market in the centre of Malindi. All have daily departures to Nairobi (KSh900 to KSh1200, 10 to 12 hours) at around 7am and/or 7pm, via Mombasa. *Matatus* to Watamu (KSh80, one hour) leave from the old market in town.

There are usually at least six buses a day to Lamu (KSh600). The journey takes at least four hours between Malindi and the jetty at Mokowe (on the mainland, near Lamu). From there, the ferry to Lamu from the mainland costs KSh80 (20 minutes); it's KSh200 for a speedboat.

Watamu

☎042

This small fishing village has evolved into a small expat colony, a string of high-end resorts and a good base for exploring a glut of ruins, national parks and ecosites that are within an easily accessible radius. The main attraction is 7km of pristine beach and a cosy scene that caters to peace, quiet and big-game fishing.

Sights & Activities

★Watamu Marine National Park WILDLIFE RESERVE

(adult/child & student US$15/10) The southern part of Malindi Marine National Park, this marine park includes some magnificent coral reefs and abundant fish life. It lies around 2km offshore from Watamu. To get to the park you'll need to hire a glass-bottomed boat, which is easy enough at the **KWS office** (☎32393), at the end of the coast road, where you pay the park fees. For marine-park trips, boat operators ask anything from KSh2500 to KSh3500 per person, excluding park fees; it's all negotiable.

★Gede Ruins ARCHAEOLOGICAL SITE

(adult/child KSh500/250; ⏲7am-6pm) Some 4km from Watamu, just off the main Malindi–Mombasa road, are the famous Gede ruins, one of the principal historical monuments on the coast. Hidden away in the forest is a vast complex of derelict houses, palaces and mosques, made all the more mysterious by the fact that there seem to be no records of Gede's existence in any historical texts.

Sleeping & Eating

Villa Veronika GUESTHOUSE $
(☎0728-155613; Beach Way Rd; r from Ksh800) Colourful walls, flowery murals and well-maintained rooms set around a shady courtyard garden make this cheapie hard to beat.

Turtle Bay Beach Club RESORT $$$
(☎32003; www.turtlebaykenya.com; s/d US$113/226;) This is easily one of the best top-end resorts in Watamu: an ecominded hotel that uses managed tree-cover to hide its environmental imprint, runs ecotourism ventures and contributes to local charities. On top of that, it's a pretty plush resort with beautiful marine-themed rooms.

Information

There are no banks here, but you can change money at foreign-exchange bureaus at the big hotels and **Tunda Tours** (☎32079; Beach Way Rd), which also has internet connection (KSh5 per minute).

Getting There & Around

There are *matatus* between Malindi and Watamu throughout the day (KSh80 to KSh100, one hour). All *matatus* pass the turn-off to the Gede ruins (KSh40). For Mombasa, the easiest option is to take a *matatu* to Gede and flag down a bus or *matatu*. A handful of motorised rickshaws ply the village and beach road; a ride to the KWS office should cost around KSh200. Bicycles can be hired from most hotels or guesthouses for around KSh100 per hour.

Lamu

☎042

Few would dispute that the Lamu archipelago forms the most evocative destination on the Kenyan coast. Lamu town itself has that excellent destination quality of immediately standing out as you approach it from the water. The shopfronts and mosques, faded under the relentless kiss of the salt wind, creep out from behind a forest of dhow masts. Then you take to the streets, or more accurately, the labyrinth: donkey-wide alleyways; robed children grinning from the alleys; women whispering by in full length *bui-bui* (black cover-all garment worn by Islamic women outside the home); cats casually ruling the rooftops; blue smoke from meat grilling over open fires; and the organic, biting scent of cured wood affixed to a town house made of stone and coral. Residents call Lamu 'Kiwa Ndeo' – the Vain Island – and, to be fair, there's plenty for it to be vain about.

In 2011 three tourists staying on islands neighbouring Lamu were kidnapped by Somali pirates. Since these serious but isolated events most Western governments have declared the island to be safe, but we would urge you to check the latest on the security situation in advance of a visit.

Sights & Activities

Lamu Museum MUSEUM
(Harambee Ave, Waterfront; adult/child KSh200/100) Housed in a very grand Swahili warehouse on the waterfront, the Lamu Museum is an excellent introduction to the culture and history of the island. It features displays on Swahili culture, the famous coastal carved doors, the Maulid Festival, Lamu's nautical history and the tribes who used to occupy this part of the coast in pre-Muslim days, including the Boni, who were legendary elephant-hunters.

Lamu Fort FORTRESS
(Main Sq) The bulky, atmospheric Lamu Fort squats on Lamu's main square like a weary intruder among the airy Swahili roofs. The building of this massive structure was begun by the Sultan of Paté in 1810 and completed in 1823. From 1910 right up to 1984 it was used as a prison, and it now houses the island's library; the highlight is scaling the ramparts for sweeping town views.

Donkey Sanctuary ANIMAL SANCTUARY
(☎633303; Harambee Ave ⏲9am-1pm Mon-Fri) FREE With around 3000 donkeys active on Lamu, *Equus asinus* is still the main form of transport here, and this sanctuary was established by the International Donkey Protection Trust of Sidmouth, UK, to improve the lot of the island's hard-working beasts of burden.

Sleeping

Yumbe House BOUTIQUE HOTEL $$$
(☎633101; lamuoldtown@africaonline.co.ke; r KSh2200) This coral castle has impressive carved-out rooms decorated with Swahili motifs, verandahs that are open to the stars and the breeze, and a ridiculously romantic top-floor suite.

★**Stone House Hotel** BOUTIQUE HOTEL $$$
(☎633544; www.stonehousehotellamu.com; s/d with breakfast from US$40) This Swahili mansion is set into a Fez-like alleyway and is notable for its fine, whitewashed walls and fantastic rooftop with a superb restaurant.

Lamu House BOUTIQUE HOTEL $$$
(☎633491; www.lamuhouse.com; Harambee Ave; s/d €190/235) This looks like an old Swahili villa, but it feels like a contemporarily decked-out boutique hotel, where they've blended the pale, breezy romance of the Greek islands into an African palace, with predictably awesome results.

Jambo House BOUTIQUE HOTEL $$$
(☎0713-411714; www.jambohouse.com; Harambee Ave; r from KSh2300; 📶) The new star on the Lamu hotel scene, this highly regarded budget hotel has small but immaculate rooms in terracotta colours with electric-blue bathrooms. There's a fantastic rooftop terrace and a breakfast to rave about.

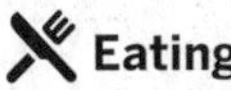

Eating

Olympic Restaurant AFRICAN $
(Harambee Ave; mains KSh250-700) The family that runs the Olympic makes you feel as if you've come home every time you enter, and their food, particularly the curries and biryani, is excellent.

★ **Mwana Arafa Restaurant Gardens** SEAFOOD $$
(Harambee Ave; meals KSh350-800) One of the more upmarket restaurants in Lamu, Mwana Arafa has a perfect combination of garden seating and views over the dhows bobbing about under the moonlight. Choose from barbecued giant prawns, grilled calamari, lobster or a seafood platter.

Bush Gardens Restaurant INTERNATIONAL $$
(☎633285; Harambee Ave; mains KSh180-800) The Bush Gardens is the template for a whole set of restaurants along the waterfront, offering breakfasts, seafood – excellent fish, top-value 'monster crab' and the inevitable lobster in Swahili sauce – and superb juices and shakes mixed up in panelled British pint mugs.

Drinking & Nightlife

Along the waterfront towards Shela village, the **Civil Servants' Club** (admission KSh100) is virtually the only reliable spot for a drink and a dance at weekends. It's small, loud, rowdy and great fun, though women travelling alone should run for cover.

ℹ Information

Immigration Office (☎633032) There's an office off Kenyatta Rd near the fort where you should be able to get visa extensions, although travellers are sometimes referred to Mombasa.

Kenya Commercial Bank (☎633327; Harambee Ave) The only bank on Lamu that has an ATM.

King Fadh Lamu District Hospital (☎633075) One of the most modern and well-equipped hospitals on the coast. It's south of the town centre.

Lamu Medical Clinic (☎633438; Kenyatta Rd; ⏲8am-9pm)

Lynx Infosystems (internet per min KSh2; ⏲8am-10pm) Temperamental connections over a Safaricom line – worth a look when the post office is closed. To find it, head west down the street next to the Khadi Star office and turn left at the end.

Post office (Harambee Ave) Postal services and cardphones.

Tourist Information Office (☎633132; lamu@tourism.go.ke; Harambee Ave; ⏲9am-1pm & 2-4pm)

ℹ Getting There & Away

AIR

Airkenya (☎633445; www.airkenya.com; Baraka House, Kenyatta Rd), **Fly540** (☎632054; www.fly540.com) and **Safarilink** (www.flysafarilink.com) offer daily afternoon flights between Lamu and Wilson Airport in Nairobi.

Kenya Airways has daily afternoon flights between Lamu and the domestic terminal at Nairobi's Jomo Kenyatta International Airport.

The airport servicing Lamu is on Manda Island and the ferry across the channel to Lamu costs KSh150. You will be met by 'guides' at the airport who will offer to carry your bags to the hotel of your choice for a small consideration (about KSh250).

BUS

There are booking offices for several bus companies such as TSS, Falcon and Zam Zam on Kenyatta Rd. The going rate for a trip to Mombasa (six hours) is KSh600 to KSh700 and to Malindi (four hours) it's KSh500; most buses leave between 7am and 8am, so you'll need to be at the jetty at 6.30am to catch the boat to the mainland. Book early.

ℹ Getting Around

There are ferries (KSh50) between Lamu and the bus station on the mainland (near Mokowe). Boats leave when the buses arrive at Mokowe; in the reverse direction, they leave at around 6.30am to meet the departing buses. Ferries between the airstrip on Manda Island and Lamu cost KSh150 and leave about half an hour before the flights leave. Expect to pay KSh200 for a custom trip if you miss either of these boats.

Between Lamu and Shela village there are plenty of motorised dhows in either direction through-

Lamu

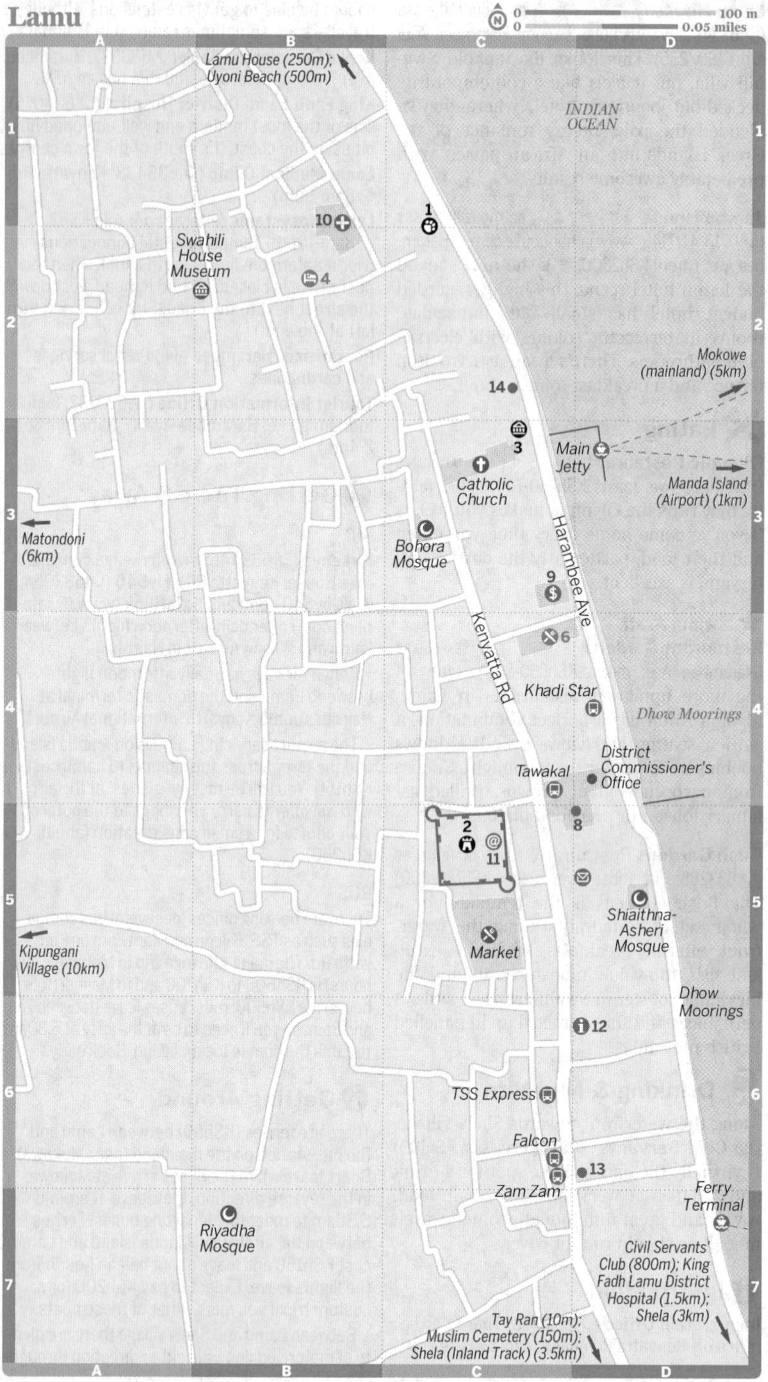

N
0 100 m
0 0.05 miles

Lamu House (250m); Uyoni Beach (500m)

INDIAN OCEAN

1

10

Swahili House Museum

4

Mokowe (mainland) (5km)

14

3

Main Jetty

Catholic Church

Manda Island (Airport) (1km)

Matondoni (6km)

Bohora Mosque

Harambee Ave

9

Kenyatta Rd

6

Khadi Star

Dhow Moorings

District Commissioner's Office

Tawakal

8

2

11

Shiaithna-Asheri Mosque

Market

Kipungani Village (10km)

Dhow Moorings

12

TSS Express

Falcon

13

Zam Zam

Ferry Terminal

Riyadha Mosque

Civil Servants' Club (800m); King Fadh Lamu District Hospital (1.5km); Shela (3km)

Tay Ran (10m); Muslim Cemetery (150m); Shela (Inland Track) (3.5km)

Lamu

Sights

1 Donkey Sanctuary ... C1
2 Lamu Fort ... C5
3 Lamu Museum ... C3

Sleeping

4 Stone House Hotel ... B2
5 Yumbe House ...

Eating

6 Bush Gardens Restaurant ... C4
7 Olympic Restaurant ...

Information

8 Immigration Office ... D5
9 Kenya Commercial Bank ... C3
10 Lamu Medical Clinic ... B1
11 Lynx Infosystems ... C5
12 Tourist Information Office ... D6

Transport

13 Airkenya ... D6
14 Kenya Airways ... C2

out the day until around sunset; these cost about KSh150 per person and leave when full.

Shela

Shela is sort of like Lamu put through a high-end wringer. It's cleaner and more medievally 'authentic' in spots, mainly because a lot of the houses have been lovingly done up by expats, who make up a sizeable chunk of the population. As a result, Shela feels somewhere between the East African coast and a swish Greek island, which you'll find either off-putting or appealing based on your travelling tastes.

To get to Shela, you can take a motorised dhow from the moorings at Lamu for KSh150 per person (or KSh250 to KSh300 for a solo ride). Alternatively, you can walk it in about 40 minutes.

Most people are here for the 12km-long sweep of sand where you're guaranteed an isolated spot to pitch your kit and catch some rays. But there is a violent current here and no lifeguards. Tourists drown every year, so don't swim out too far. Some backpackers camp in the long dunes behind the beach, but you risk a mugging if you do so.

★ **Stopover Guest House** GUESTHOUSE $
(☎0720-127222; s & d KSh4500-5000) The first place you come to on the waterfront is this simply beautiful guesthouse of pure white unfussy lines. Rooms are spacious, airy, bright and crisp, and a salt wind through your carved window-shutters is the best alarm clock we can think of.

Kijani House Hotel BOUTIQUE HOTEL $$$
(☎Nairobi 020-243700; www.kijani-lamu.com; s & d US$165-235; @ 🛜 ≋) This villa complex is enormous, yet the design is elegantly understated, achieving a sort of Zen or Swahili aesthetic even as it spoils you with luxuriant tropical gardens, the nicest pool in the Lamu area and palatially sized and decorated rooms.

Peponi Hotel HOTEL $$$
(☎Nairobi 020-2435033; www.peponi-lamu.com; s/d from US$230/280; ⊗closed May & Jun; ≋) If there were a capital of Shela, it would be located at this top-end resort, which has a grip on everything in this village, from tours to water sports to whatever else you can imagine.

★ **Stopover Restaurant** SEAFOOD $$
(☎633459; mains KSh350-1200) There are waterfront restaurants all over, but this has friendly staff and excellent grub (of the spicy Swahili seafood sort), which make it the clear cut above the competition.

SOUTHERN KENYA

Amboseli National Park

While it may lack the profusion of wildlife found at Masai Mara and Lake Nakuru, Kenya's third-most-popular park boasts one of the country's most spectacular backdrops, namely Mt Kilimanjaro. Africa's highest peak broods over the southern boundary of the park, and while cloud cover can render the mountain's massive bulk invisible for much of the day, you'll be rewarded with some stunning vistas when the weather clears. **Amboseli** (☎045-622251; www.kws.org/amboseli.html; adult/child & student US$80/40) is also prime elephant country, so add this park to your safari itinerary if you want to shoot some pics of these monolithic beasts.

Sights & Activities

Amboseli's permanent swamps of Enkongo Narok and Olokenya create a marshy belt across the middle of the park. These spots are the centre of activity for elephants, hippos, buffaloes and water birds, while the surrounding grasslands are home to grazing antelopes. Spotted hyenas are plentiful, and jackals, waterhogs, olive baboons and vervet monkeys all occur. Lions can still be found in Amboseli, although the once famous black-maned lions are no longer here. Black rhinos are also absent – the few that survived a sustained period of poaching were moved to Tsavo West National Park in 1995.

Sleeping & Eating

KWS Campsite CAMPGROUND $
(www.kws.org; campsites per adult/child US$25/20) Just inside the southern boundary of the park, with toilets, an unreliable water supply (bring your own) and a small bar selling warm beer and soft drinks.

★**Ol Tukai Lodge** LODGE $$$
(☎Nairobi 020-4445514; www.oltukailodge.com; d from US$370;) Lying at the heart of Amboseli on the edge of a dense acacia forest, Ol Tukai is a splendidly refined lodge with soaring *makuti* (thatched palm-leaf) roofs and tranquil gardens defined by towering trees.

Amboseli Serena Lodge LODGE $$$
(☎Nairobi 020-2842000; www.serenahotels.com; s/d US$270/370;) The poshest property in Amboseli, the Serena is comprised of fiery-red adobe cottages that overlook the wildlife-rich Enkongo Narok swamp, and are fringed by lush tropical gardens of blooming flowers and manicured shrubs.

Information

At 392 sq km, Amboseli is a small national park, though the landscape provides limited cover for wildlife. The vegetation here used to be much denser, but rising salinity, damage by elephants and irresponsible behaviour by safari vehicles has caused terrible erosion.

Getting There & Away

AIR

Airkenya (www.airkenya.com) has daily flights (from US$101) between Wilson Airport in Nairobi and Amboseli. You'll need to arrange with one of the lodges or a safari company for a vehicle to meet you at the airstrip.

CAR & 4WD

The usual approach to Amboseli is via Namanga. The road is sealed and in surprisingly good condition from Nairobi to Namanga. If you're heading to Tsavo, convoys leave from the turn-off near the Sopa Lodge at scheduled times – enquire at your lodge, as they change frequently.

Tsavo National Park

At nearly 21,000 sq km, Tsavo National Park is by far the largest national park in Kenya. For administrative and practical purposes, it has been split into the 9000-sq-km **Tsavo West National Park** (adult/child per day US$65/30) and the 11,747-sq-km **Tsavo East National Park** (adult/child per day US$65/30), divided by the Nairobi–Mombasa road (A109).

Tsavo West National Park

Tsavo West covers a huge variety of landscapes, from swamps, natural springs and rocky peaks to extinct volcanic cones and rolling plains. But for all of its diversity, Tsavo West is not a park where you will see animals constantly (although there are still some black rhinos here). Indeed, much of its appeal lies in its dramatic scenery and sense of space. If possible, come here with some time to spare – if you get off the beaten path here, you could have it all to yourself.

Sleeping

KWS Campsites CAMPGROUND $
(campsites per adult/child US$15/10) The public sites are at Komboyo, near the Mtito Andei Gate, and at Chyulu, just outside the Chyulu Gate. Facilities are basic, so make sure you're prepared to be self-sufficient. There are also some small independently run campsites along the shores of Lake Jipa.

★**Severin Safari Camp** TENTED CAMP $$$
(☎Nairobi 020-2684247; www.severinsafaricamp.com; tent with full board from US$215) This is a fantastic complex of thatched luxury tents with affable staff, Kilimanjaro views from the communal lounge area and nightly hippo visits.

Kilaguni Serena Lodge LODGE $$$
(☎045-622376; www.serenahotels.com; s/d US$225/320; @) The centrepiece here is a splendid bar and restaurant overlooking an illuminated waterhole. The extravagant suites are practically cottages in their own right, with chintzy living rooms and epic balconies.

Getting There & Away

The main access to Tsavo West is through the Mtito Andei gate on the Mombasa–Nairobi road in the north of the park. Although security is much improved, vehicles for Amboseli travel

EXPLORING TSAVO NATIONAL PARK

Both the Tsavo West and Tsavo East National Parks feature some excellent scenery, but the undergrowth here is considerably higher than in Amboseli or Masai Mara, so it takes a little more effort to spot the wildlife, particularly the big predators. The compensation for this is that the landscapes are some of the most dramatic in Kenya, the animals are that little bit wilder, and the parks receive few visitors compared to the hordes who descend on Amboseli and the Mara.

The northern half of Tsavo West is the most developed, with a number of excellent lodges, as well as several places where you can get out of your vehicle and walk. The landscape is also striking, and is largely comprised of volcanic hills and sweeping expanses of savannah. The southern part of the park, on the far side of the dirt road between Voi and Taveta on the Tanzanian border, is rarely visited.

Tsavo East is more remote, and most of the action here is concentrated along the Galana River – the north part of the park isn't truly secure due to the threat of banditry. The landscape here is drier, with rolling plains hugging the edge of the Yatta Escarpment, a vast prehistoric lava flow.

Camping at KWS campsites is US$15/10 per adult/child; as the two parks are administered separately, you have to pay separate entrance fees for each. Both use the smartcard system – you'll need enough credit for your entry fee and any camping charges for as long as you're staying. Smartcards can be bought and recharged at the Voi Gate to Tsavo East.

There's a small **visitor centre** (8am-5pm) FREE near the Mtito Andei Gate to Tsavo West, with interesting displays on conservation issues and some of the animals and birds in the park.

in armed convoys from Kilaguni Serena Lodge; check at the lodge for departure times.

Tsavo East National Park

Despite the fact that one of Kenya's largest rivers flows through the middle of the park, the landscape in Tsavo East is markedly flatter and drier than in Tsavo West. However, the contrast between the permanent greenery of the river and the endless grasses and thorn trees that characterise much of the park is visually arresting. In comparison to its more developed brother, Tsavo East doesn't see as many visitors, though it has an undeniable wild and primordial charm.

Sleeping & Eating

★Tsavo Mashariki Camp TENTED CAMP **$**
(0729-179443; www.masharikicamp.com; per person incl breakfast from KSh4500, with full board from KSh7000) The closest camp to Voi gate just outside the park, this charming Italian-run place has some fine tents made out of all-natural local materials; the family tent is brilliant. Best of all, the prices here put many other tented camps to shame.

Voi Safari Lodge LODGE **$$$**
(Mombasa 041-471861; www.safari-hotels.com; s/d high season US$140/200;) Just 4km from Voi Gate, Voi Safari is a long, low complex perched on the edge of an escarpment overlooking an incredible sweep of savannah.

Kilalinda LODGE **$$$**
(Nairobi 020-882598; www.privatewilderness.com; s/d high season US$400/650;) This very fine ecolodge was built without felling a single tree. The owners are spearheading a campaign to reintroduce wildlife to areas depleted by poachers in previous decades.

Getting There & Away

The main track through the park follows the Galana River from the Tsavo Gate to the Sala Gate. Most tourist safaris enter Tsavo East via the Sala Gate, where a good dirt road runs east for 110km to the coast. If you're coming from Nairobi, the Voi Gate (near the town of the same name) and the Manyani Gate (on the Nairobi–Mombasa road) are just as accessible.

UNDERSTAND KENYA

Kenya Today

At the time of writing, Kenya was holding its breath in advance of the 2013 election. The surprising stability with which the government of erstwhile foes – President Mwai Kibaki (who will be standing down after two terms) and Prime Minister Raila Odinga (a leading candidate for the presidency) – has ruled Kenya since being forced into a marriage of convenience has restored considerable faith in the country's democratic institutions.

Cynicism, however, remains understandably high among ordinary Kenyans when it comes to their notoriously corrupt and over-paid political class. More than that, the underlying suspicions between various tribal groupings, the resentment of the coastal region about perceived prejudice and unequal funding, poverty, and the increasing competition for scarce resources, which lay behind the postelection violence in 2007, remain unresolved.

Kenya's economy, however, is booming, and nothing can shake the country's confidence that it is on the up. There's just one problem: only a small percentage of Kenyans see the benefits of the growing prosperity. Unemployment sits at around 40%, a staggering 50% of Kenyans live below the poverty line and the prices of basic foodstuffs are soaring. By one estimate, Kenya would require an annual growth rate of 11% for the prosperity gains to even begin to trickle down to poorer sectors of society.

In October 2011, for the first time in its independent history, Kenya went to war. The spark for such a drastic move was a series of cross-border raids allegedly carried out by al-Shabaab, an al-Qaeda-affiliated Somali group accused of kidnapping foreign aid workers and tourists from inside Kenya. Aware that its lucrative tourism industry could be at risk, Kenya's military launched a large-scale invasion of Somalia, claiming that it was acting in self defence; most Western governments agreed.

A significant and cathartic moment in Kenyan history occurred at the high court in London in 2012: three elderly Kenyans gained the right to sue for damages for torture and sexual abuse allegedly inflicted by the British colonial administration in the 1950s.

History

The patchwork of ethnic groups, each with their own culture and language, that today exist side by side in modern Kenya are the result of waves of migration. These waves – some occurring as early as 2000 BC – came from every corner of Africa: Turkanas from Ethiopia; Kikuyu, Akamba and Meru from West Africa; and the Maasai, Luo and Samburu from the southern part of Sudan. Kenya, however, was occupied long before this: archaeological excavations around Lake Turkana in the 1970s revealed skulls thought to be around two million years old and those of the earliest human beings ever discovered.

By around the 8th century, Arabic, Indian, Persian and even Chinese merchants were arriving on the Kenyan coast, intent on trading skins, ivory, gold and spices. These new arrivals helped set up a string of commercial cities along the whole of the East African coast, intermarrying with local dynasties to found a prosperous new civilisation, part African, part Arabic, known as the Swahili.

By the 16th century, Europeans too had cottoned on to the potential of the East African coast, and most of the Swahili trading towns, including Mombasa and Lamu, were either sacked or occupied by the Portuguese. Two centuries of harsh military rule followed, punctuated by regular battles for control of the former Swahili empire. The Omani Arabs finally ousted the Portuguese in 1720, but it wasn't long before the coast came into the control of more European colonisers – the British, who used their battleships to protect their lucrative route to India and to suppress the hated slave trade.

Mau Mau Rebellion & Independence

Despite plenty of overt pressure on Kenya's colonial authorities, the real independence movement was underground. Groups from the Kikuyu, Maasai and Luo tribes vowed to kill Europeans and their African collaborators. The most famous of these movements was Mau Mau, formed in 1952 by the Kikuyu people, which aimed to drive the white settlers from Kenya forever. In true African fashion, the Mau Mau rebellion was a brutal war of attrition on white people, property and 'collaborators'. The various Mau Mau sects came together under the umbrella of the Kenya Land Freedom Army, led by

Dedan Kimathi, and staged frequent attacks against white farms and government outposts. By the time the rebels were defeated in 1956, the death toll stood at over 13,500 Africans (guerrillas, civilians and troops) and just over 100 Europeans.

In 1960 the British government officially announced its plan to transfer power to a democratically elected African government. Independence was scheduled for December 1963, accompanied by grants and loans of US$100 million to enable the Kenyan assembly to buy out European farmers in the highlands and restore the land to the tribes. The run-up to independence was surprisingly smooth, although the redistribution of land wasn't a great success. The immediate effect was to cause a significant decline in agricultural production, from which Kenya has never quite recovered.

Jomo Kenyatta became Kenya's first president on 12 December, ruling until his death in 1978. Under Kenyatta's presidency, Kenya developed into one of Africa's most stable and prosperous nations. But while Kenyatta is still seen as a success story, he was excessively biased in favour of his own tribe and became paranoid about dissent. Opponents of his regime who became too vocal for comfort frequently 'disappeared', and corruption soon became endemic at all levels of the power structure.

The 1980s & '90s

Kenyatta was succeeded in 1978 by his vice president, Daniel arap Moi, a member of the Kalenjin people, who became one of the most enduring 'Big Men' in Africa, ruling in virtual autocracy for nearly 25 years. In the process, he accrued an incredible personal fortune; today many believe him to be the richest man in Africa. Moi's regime was also characterised by nepotism, corruption, arrests of dissidents, censorship, the disbanding of tribal societies and the closure of universities.

Faced with a foreign debt of nearly US$9 billion and blanket suspension of foreign aid, Moi was pressured into holding multiparty elections in early 1992. Independent observers reported a litany of electoral inconsistencies, and about 2000 people were killed during ethnic clashes widely believed to have been triggered by KANU agitation. Nonetheless, Moi was overwhelmingly re-elected.

Preoccupied with internal problems, Kenya was quite unprepared for the events of 7 August 1998. Early in the morning massive blasts simultaneously ripped apart the American embassies in Nairobi and Dar es Salaam in Tanzania, killing more than 200 people. The effect on Kenyan tourism, and the economy as a whole, was devastating.

Further terrorist activity shook the country on 28 November 2002, when suicide bombers slammed an explosives-laden car into the lobby of the Paradise Hotel at Kikambala, near Mombasa. Moments before, missiles were fired at an Israeli passenger plane taking off from Mombasa's airport. Al-Qaeda subsequently claimed responsibility for both the 1998 and 2002 acts.

Culture

Many residents of Kenya are more aware of their tribal affiliation than of being 'Kenyan'; this lack of national cohesion undoubtedly presents the nation with some challenges, but is generally accompanied by an admirable live-and-let-live attitude. In fact, Kenyans generally approach life with great exuberance and warmth, which is evident on a crowded *matatu*, in a buzzing marketplace or in a bar.

Education is of primary concern to Kenyans. Literacy rates are around 85% and are considerably higher than in neighbouring countries. Although education isn't compulsory, the motivation to learn is huge, particularly now that it's free, and you'll see children in school uniform everywhere in Kenya, even in the most impoverished rural communities.

For all this, as Kenya gains a foothold in the 21st century it is grappling with ever-increasing poverty. Once categorised as a middle-income country, Kenya has become a low-income country, with the standard of living dropping drastically since the start of the new millennium.

People

Kenya's population is estimated at 41.7 million. The population growth rate, currently at around 2.75%, has slowed in the last few years due to the prevalence of HIV/AIDS, which affects 7% to 8% of adults according to the UN (with general life expectancy at 57 years).

Most Kenyans outside the coastal and eastern provinces are Christians of one sort or another, while most of those on the coast and in the eastern part of the country are Muslim. Muslims make up some 30% of the population. In the more remote tribal areas you'll find a mixture of Muslims, Christians and those who follow their ancestral tribal beliefs, such as animism, though this last group is in the minority.

Arts

Benga is the country's contemporary dance music, characterised by electric-guitar licks and bounding bass rhythms. Well-known exponents include DO Misiani and his group Shirati Jazz, and you should also look out for Globestyle, Victoria Kings and Ambira Boys.

Popular bands today are heavily influenced by *benga, soukous* (African rumba) and Western music, with lyrics often in Swahili. These include bands such as Them Mushrooms (now reinvented as Uyoya) and Safari Sound. For upbeat dance tunes, Ogopa DJs, Nameless, Redsan and Deux Vultures are recommended acts. Other names to look out for include Prezzo (Kenya's king of bling), Nonini (a controversial women-and-booze rapper), Nazizi (female MC from Necessary Noize) and Mercy Myra (Kenya's biggest female R&B artist).

Kenya best-known author is Ngugi wa Thiong'o. Ngugi's harrowing criticism of the Kenyan establishment landed him in jail for a year (described in *Detained: A Prison Writer's Diary*); his *Petals of Blood* is a powerful story of Mau Mau activism. Another important Kenyan writer is Meja Mwangi, who sticks more to social issues and urban dislocation but has a mischievous sense of humour, while Binyavanga Wainaina is one of Kenya's rising stars. Highly regarded female writers include Grace Ogot, Margaret Atieno Ogola, Marjorie Magoye and Hilary Ngweno. To stay up to date with the contemporary scene, look out for *Kwani* (http://kwani.org), Kenya's first literary journal; it hosts a literary festival that attracts a growing number of international names.

Food & Drink

Food isn't one of Kenya's highlights, and the best dining is usually in upmarket hotels or safari lodges. The one local speciality is *nyama choma* (barbecued or roast meat). You buy the meat (usually goat) by the kilogram; it's cooked over a charcoal pit and served in bite-sized pieces with a vegetable side dish.

Kenya grows some of the finest tea (chai) and coffee in the world, but getting a decent cup of either can be difficult. Chai is drunk in large quantities, but the tea, milk and sugar are usually boiled together and stewed for ages. In Nairobi there are a handful of excellent coffeehouses, and you can usually get good filter coffee at any of the big hotels. Soft drinks are available everywhere under the generic term of 'soda'.

The local beers are Tusker, White Cap and Pilsner (all manufactured by Kenya Breweries). *Pombe* is usually a fermented brew made with bananas or millet and sugar. It shouldn't do you any harm. Steer totally clear, however, of *chang'a*: in 2005, 48 people died from the effects of this dangerous brew; in some regions the drink is fermented with marijuana twigs, cactus mash, battery alkaline and formalin.

Environment

Kenya straddles the equator and covers an area of some 583,000 sq km, including around 13,600 sq km of Lake Victoria. The modern landscape was shaped by the Rift Valley, a gigantic crack in the earth's crust that runs from Lake Turkana to the Tanzania border, and the activity of titanic (but now extinct) volcanoes such as Mts Kenya, Elgon and Kilimanjaro (across the border in Tanzania). The Rift Valley floor features numerous 'soda' lakes, rich in sodium bicarbonate, created by the filtering of water through mineral-rich volcanic rock and subsequent evaporation.

Around 10% of Kenya's land area is protected by law, and the national parks and reserves here rate among the best in Africa. No trip to Kenya would be complete without going on safari. Kenya is a virtual microcosm of African environments and its biodiversity is extraordinary for the country's size. Iconic species such as lions, elephants, leopards and buffaloes are generally easy to see, but the biggest spectacle is the annual wildebeest migration that spills over from Tanzania's Serengeti Plains each year. Rhinos are very rare in Kenya, owing to a massive poaching problem. Lake Nakuru National Park almost guarantees sightings.

The variety of birds is extraordinary – some 1200 species – and a trip to Kenya has turned many a casual observer into a dedicated birder. Major reserves often support hundreds of bird species; interesting species include ostriches, vultures, colourful starlings and marabou storks. Wetlands support abundant flamingos, herons and pelicans, while the forests are home to hornbills, touracos, sunbirds, weavers and a host more.

Forest destruction continues on a large scale in Kenya – less than 3% of the country's original forest remains. Land grabbing, illegal logging, charcoal burning and agricultural encroachment all take their toll. The de-gazetting of protected forests is another contentious issue, sparking widespread protests and preservation campaigns. The main cause of this is untrammelled population growth; Kenya's population has doubled in the past 20 years. The predictable corollary is a vicious cycle of deforestation, land degradation and erosion, causing people to open up and destroy still more land.

Renewed poaching raids on elephants and rhinos have led to talk of abandoning some of the more remote parks and concentrating resources where they can achieve the best results. At the same time, community conservation projects are being encouraged, and many community-owned ranches are now being opened up as private wildlife reserves.

An increasing number of important wildlife conservation areas now exist on private land. Supporting these projects is a great way for travellers to directly contribute to local communities as well as assist Kenyan wildlife preservation.

PRACTICALITIES

- **Electricity** Kenya uses the 240V system, with UK-style square three-pin sockets. Bring a universal adaptor.
- **Languages** English, Swahili and 67 other languages.
- **Newspapers & Magazines** Major print media in Kenya include the *Daily Nation*, the *East African Standard*, the *East African*, and the *Weekly Review*.
- **Radio** KBC Radio broadcasts throughout the country on FM frequencies. Major towns also have local music and talkback stations. The BBC World Service is easily accessible.
- **TV** KBC and NTV are the main national stations; CNN, Sky and BBC are also widely available on satellite or cable (DSTV).
- **Video** Televisual equipment uses the standard European NTSC system.

SURVIVAL GUIDE

Directory A–Z

ACCOMMODATION

Kenya has a good range of accommodation, from basic cubicle hotels overlooking city bus stands to luxury tented camps hidden away in the national parks. There are also all kinds of campsites, budget tented camps, simple *bandas* (thatched-roof wooden huts) and cottages scattered around the parks and rural areas. You will find rates quoted in shillings, US dollars or euros.

ACTIVITIES

Diving & Snorkelling

The Malindi Marine National Park (p618) offers opportunities for snorkelling and scuba diving. October to March is the best time; silt affects visibility during June, July and August.

Hiking & Climbing

For proper mountain hiking, look no further than Mt Kenya (p609), the country's greatest high-altitude challenge.

Wildlife Safaris

Kenya is one of the greatest wildlife-watching destinations on earth and virtually every visitor to Kenya goes on safari at least once. There are seemingly endless safari operators to choose from, and it's worth spending some time to select a reliable one that matches your budget and itinerary. It's worth checking with the **Kenyan Association of Tour Operators** (KATO; ☎020-713348; www.katokenya.org) in Nairobi before making a booking.

CUSTOMS REGULATIONS

Export of products made from elephants, rhinos and sea turtles is prohibited. The collection of coral is also not allowed. Ostrich eggs will be confiscated unless you can prove you bought them from a certified ostrich farm.

The usual regulations apply to items you can bring into the country: 50 cigars, 200 cigarettes, 250g of pipe tobacco, 1L of alcohol and 250mL of perfume. Obscene publications are banned, which may extend to some lads' magazines.

EMBASSIES & CONSULATES

Following is a selection of countries that maintain diplomatic missions in Nairobi.

Australian Embassy (Map p600; ☎020-4277100; www.embassy.gov.au/ke.html; ICIPE House, Riverside Dr, Nairobi)

British Embassy (Map p600; ☎020-2844000; www.gov.uk/government/world/kenya; Upper Hill Rd, Nairobi)

Canadian Embassy (☎020-3663000; www.canadainternational.gc.ca/ kenya/index.aspx; Limuru Rd, Nairobi)

Dutch Embassy (020-4288000; http://kenia.nlembassy.org; Riverside Lane, Nairobi)

Ethiopian Embassy (Map p600; 020-2732050; State House Ave, Nairobi)

French Embassy (Map p602; 020-2778000; www.ambafrance-ke.org; Barclays Plaza, Loita St, Nairobi)

German Embassy (020-4262100; www.nairobi.diplo.de; 113 Riverside Dr, Nairobi)

South African Embassy (020-2827100; Roshanmaer Pl, Lenana Rd, Nairobi)

Spanish Embassy (Map p602; 020-342228; International House, Mama Ngina St, Nairobi)

Sudanese Embassy (020-720854; Kabernet Rd, off Ngong Rd, Nairobi)

Tanzanian Embassy (Map p602; 020-2311948; Reinsurance Plaza, Aga Khan Walk, Nairobi)

Ugandan High Commission (020-4445420; www.ugandahighcommission.co.ke; Riverside Paddocks, Nairobi) Uganda also has a consular section (Map p602; 020-311814; Uganda House, Kenyatta Ave, Nairobi).

USA (020-3636000; http://nairobi.usembassy.gov; United Nations Ave, Nairobi)

EMERGENCIES

The countrywide emergency number for ambulance, fire and police services is 999.

FESTIVALS & EVENTS

The major events around Kenya include the following:

Maulid Festival (www.lamu.org/maulid-celebration.html) Falling in March or April for the next few years, this annual celebration of the Prophet Mohammed's birthday is a huge event in Lamu town.

Tusker Safari Sevens (www.safarisevens.com) International rugby tournament held every June near Nairobi.

Kenya Music Festival (020-2712964) The country's longest-running music festival, held over 10 days in August in Nairobi.

Mombasa Carnival (zainab@africaonline.co.ke) November street festival, with music, dance and other events.

East African Safari Rally (www.eastafricansafarirally.com) Classic car rally now more than 50 years old, covering Kenya, Tanzania and Uganda using only pre-1971 vehicles. Held in December.

INTERNET ACCESS

Most towns have at least one internet cafe (and Nairobi has lots) where you can surf and access webmail accounts or instant-messenger programs and Skype. Rates are cheapest in Nairobi and Mombasa (as little as KSh1 per minute), rising to up to KSh20 per minute in rural areas and top-end hotels.

MAPS

Bookshops, especially the larger ones in Nairobi, are the best places to look for maps in Kenya. The *Tourist Map of Kenya* gives good detail, as does the *Kenya Route Map;* both cost around KSh250.

Macmillan publishes a series of maps to the wildlife parks (KSh250 each; three are available in Europe: *Amboseli, Masai Mara* and *Tsavo East and West*). Tourist Maps also publishes a national park series for roughly the same price. The maps by the KWS are similar.

MONEY

The unit of currency is the Kenyan shilling (KSh), which is made up of 100 cents. Notes in circulation are KSh1000, 500, 200, 100, 50 and 20, and there are also coins of KSh40, 20, 10, 5 and 1 in circulation.

The euro, US dollar and British pound are all easy to change throughout the country. Cash is easy and quick to exchange at banks and foreign-exchange bureaus; travellers cheques are not as widely accepted and often carry high commission charges.

Virtually all banks in Kenya have ATMs at most branches. Barclays Bank has the most reliable ATMs for international withdrawals, with ATMs in most major Kenyan towns supporting MasterCard, Visa, Plus and Cirrus international networks.

Credit cards are becoming increasingly popular, although connections fail with tedious regularity. Visa and MasterCard are now widely accepted, but it would be prudent to stick to upmarket hotels, restaurants and shopping centres to use them.

Tipping is not common practice among Kenyans, but most tourist guides and all safari drivers and cooks will expect a gratuity at the end of your tour or trip.

OPENING HOURS

Banks Banking hours are from 9am to 3pm Monday to Friday and from 9am to 11am on Saturday.

Government offices Open from 8am or 8.30am to 1pm and from 2pm to 5pm Monday to Friday.

Internet cafes Generally keep longer evening hours and may open on Sunday.

Post offices, shops and services Open roughly from 8am to 5pm Monday to Friday and 9am to noon on Saturday.

Restaurants As a rule cafes open at around 6am or 7am and close in the early evening, while more expensive ethnic restaurants will be open from 11am to 10pm daily, sometimes with a break between lunch and dinner.

POST

The Kenyan postal system is run by the government Postal Corporation of Kenya, now rebranded as the dynamic-sounding **Posta** (www.

posta.co.ke). Letters sent from Kenya rarely go astray, but can take up to two weeks to reach Australia or the USA. Incoming letters to Kenya can be sent care of poste restante to any town. Make sure your correspondents write your name in block capitals and also underline the surname. They take anywhere from four days to a week to reach the poste-restante service in Nairobi.

PUBLIC HOLIDAYS

Muslim festivals are significant events along the coast. Many eateries in the region close until after sundown during the Muslim fasting month of Ramadan.

Other public holidays in Kenya include the following:

New Year's Day 1 January
Good Friday and Easter Monday March/April
Labour Day 1 May
Mataranka (Self-Rule) Day 1 June
Moi Day 10 October
Kenyatta Day 20 October
Independence Day 12 December
Christmas Day 25 December
Boxing Day 26 December

SAFE TRAVEL

Banditry

Wars in Somalia, Sudan and Ethiopia have all affected stability and safety in northern and northeastern Kenya. However, tourists are rarely targeted and security has also improved considerably in previously high-risk areas, such as the Isiolo–Marsabit, Marsabit–Moyale and Malindi–Lamu routes. You should always check the situation locally before taking these roads, or travelling between Garsen and Garissa or Thika. The areas along the Sudanese and Ethiopian borders are risky, so enquire about the latest security situations if you're heading overland.

Crime

The country's biggest problem is crime, ranging from petty snatch theft and mugging to violent armed robbery, carjacking and corruption. As a visitor, you needn't feel paranoid, but always keep your wits about you, particularly at night.

Perhaps the best advice for when you're walking around cities and towns is not to carry anything valuable with you. Most hotels provide a safe or secure place for valuables, although you should be cautious of the security at some budget places.

Always take taxis after dark or along lonely dirt roads. In the event of a crime, you'll need a police report if you intend to make an insurance claim.

Scams

Nairobi is a scam hot spot, with 'friendly' approaches a daily, if not hourly, occurrence. You should always ignore any requests for money. Be sceptical of strangers who claim to recognise you in the street, and anyone who makes a big show of inviting you into the hospitality of their home probably has ulterior motives. The usual trick is to bestow some kind of gift upon the delighted traveller, who then becomes emotionally blackmailed into reciprocating to the order of several hundred shillings.

TELEPHONE

The Kenyan fixed-line phone system, run by **Telkom Kenya** (www.telkom.co.ke), is more or less functional, though theft of copper wire has rendered some landlines defunct. International call rates from Kenya are relatively expensive, though you can save serious cash by using voice-over-IP programs like Skype. Operator-assisted calls are charged at the standard peak rate, but are subject to a three-minute minimum. You can always dial direct using a phonecard. All phones should be able to receive incoming calls (the number is usually scrawled in the booth somewhere). The international dialling code for Kenya is ☎254. Kenyan phone numbers have an area code followed by a four- to seven-digit number.

More than two-thirds of all calls in Kenya are now made on mobile phones, and coverage is amazingly good in all but the furthest rural areas. Kenya uses the GSM 900 system, which is compatible with Europe and Australia but not with the North American GSM 1900 system. If you have a GSM phone, check with your service provider about using it in Kenya, and beware of high roaming charges. Remember that you will generally be charged for receiving calls abroad as well as for making them.

Alternatively, if your phone isn't locked into a network, an infinitely cheaper options is to pick up a prepaid starter pack from one of the Kenyan mobile-phone companies – the main players are **Safaricom** (www.safaricom.co.ke) and **Celtel** (www.ke.celtel.com). A SIM card costs about KSh100, and you can then buy top-up 'scratchcards' from shops and booths across the country. Cards come in denominations of KSh100 to KSh2000; an international SMS costs around KSh10, and voice charges vary according to tariff, time and destination of call.

With Telkom Kenya phonecards, any phone can now be used for prepaid calls; you just have to dial the **access number** (☎0844) and enter in the number and passcode on the card. There are booths selling the cards all over the country. Cards come in denominations of KSh200, KSh500, KSh1000 and KSh2000, and call charges are slightly more expensive than for standard lines.

TIME

Time in Kenya is GMT/UTC plus three hours year-round. You should also be aware of the concept of 'Swahili time', which perversely is six hours out of kilter with the rest of the world. Noon and midnight are 6 o'clock *(saa sitta)*

Swahili time, and 7am and 7pm are 1 o'clock *(saa moa)*. Just add or subtract six hours from whatever time you are told; Swahili doesn't distinguish between am and pm.

VISAS

Tourist visas can be obtained on arrival in Kenya at Nairobi's Jomo Kenyatta International Airport and at the country's land borders with Uganda and Tanzania. This applies to Europeans, Australians, New Zealanders, Americans and Canadians, although citizens from a few smaller Commonwealth countries are exempt. Visas cost US$50/€40/UK£30 and are valid for three months from the date of entry.

Under the East African partnership system, visiting Tanzania or Uganda and returning to Kenya does not invalidate a single-entry Kenyan visa, so there's no need to get a multiple-entry visa unless you plan to go further afield. Always check the latest entry requirements with embassies before travel.

Visa Extensions

Visas can be renewed at immigration offices during normal office hours, and extensions are usually issued on a same-day basis. Staff are generally friendly and helpful, but the process takes a while. You'll need two passport photos for a three-month extension, and prices tend to vary depending on the office and the whims of the immigration officials. Immigration offices are only open Monday to Friday; note that the smaller offices may sometimes refer travellers back to Nairobi or Mombasa for visa extensions.

Local immigration offices include the following:

Kisumu (Nyanza Bldg, cnr Jomo Kenyatta Hwy & Wuor Otiende Rd)

Lamu (☎042-633032; off Kenyatta Rd, Lamu)

Malindi (☎042-20149; Mama Ngina Rd, Malindi)

Mombasa (Map p615; ☎041-311745; Uhuru ni Kari Bldg, Mama Ngina Dr, Mombasa)

Nairobi (Map p602; ☎020-222022; Nyayo House, cnr Kenyatta Ave & Uhuru Hwy, Nairobi)

Visas for Onward Travel

Most embassies will want you to pay visa fees in US dollars, and most open for visa applications from 9am to noon, with visa pick-ups around 3pm or 4pm.

Three-month, single-entry visas can be obtained for South Sudan, Tanzania and Uganda, but the Ethiopian embassy was not issuing tourist visas at the time of writing, putting a major dent in the overland travel plans of many.

ℹ Getting There & Away

AIR

Most international flights to and from Nairobi are handled by **Jomo Kenyatta International Airport** (NBO; ☎020-825400; www.kenyaairports.co.ke), 15km southeast of the city. Some flights between Nairobi and Kilimanjaro International Airport or Mwanza in Tanzania, as well as many domestic flights, use **Wilson Airport** (WIL; ☎020-501941), which is 6km south of the city centre on Langata Rd. The other arrival point in the country is **Moi International Airport** (MBA; ☎041-433211) in Mombasa, 12km west of the city centre, but apart from flights to Zanzibar this is mainly used by charter airlines and domestic flights.

Kenya Airways is the main national carrier, and has a generally good safety record. The following airlines fly to and from Kenya:

African Express Airways (☎020-824333; www.africanexpress.co.ke; Wilson Airport)

Air India (Map p602; ☎020-340925; www.airindia.com)

Air Madagascar (☎020-225286; www.airmadagascar.mg)

Air Malawi (☎020-240965; www.airmalawi.net)

Air Mauritius (☎020-229166; www.airmauritius.com)

Airkenya (☎020-605745; www.airkenya.com)

British Airways (☎020-244430; www.britishairways.com)

Daallo Airlines (☎020-317318; www.daallo.com)

Egypt Air (Map p602; ☎020-226821; www.egyptair.com.eg)

Emirates (Map p602; ☎020-211187; www.emirates.com)

Ethiopian Airlines (Map p602; ☎020-330837; www.ethiopianairlines.com)

Gulf Air (☎020-241123; www.gulfairco.com)

Jetlink Express (☎020-244285; www.jetlink.co.ke)

Kenya Airways (☎020-6422560; www.kenya-airways.com)

KLM (Map p602; ☎020-3274747; www.klm.com)

Monarch (www.monarch.co.uk)

Precision Air (☎020-602561; www.precisionairtz.com)

Qatar Airways (www.qatarairways.com)

Rwandair (☎0733-740703; www.rwandair.com)

Safarilink (☎020-600777; www.flysafarilink.com) Kilimanjaro only.

SN Brussels Airlines (☎020-4443070; www.brusselsairlines. com)

South African Airways (☎020-229663; www.flysaa.com)

Swiss International Airlines (☎020-3744045; www.swiss.com)

LAND

Ethiopia

With ongoing problems in Sudan and Somalia, Ethiopia offers the only viable overland route into Kenya from the north. The security situation around the main entry point at Moyale is changeable – the border is usually open, but security problems often force its closure. Check the security situation carefully before attempting this crossing. If you're heading in the other direction, be aware that you may not be able to obtain an Ethiopian visa in Nairobi.

Tanzania

The main land borders between Kenya and Tanzania are at Namanga, Taveta, Isebania and Lunga Lunga, and can be reached by public transport. There is also a crossing from the Serengeti to the Masai Mara, which can only be undertaken with your own vehicle; you'll need the appropriate vehicle documentation (including insurance and entry permit).

Although all of the routes may be done in stages using a combination of buses and local *matatus*, there are six main land routes to/from Tanzania:

- Mombasa–Tanga/Dar es Salaam
- Mombasa–Arusha/Moshi
- Nairobi–Arusha/Moshi
- Nairobi–Dar es Salaam
- Serengeti–Masai Mara
- Nairobi–Mwanza

Following are the main bus companies serving Tanzania:

Akamba (Map p602; ☎0722-203753; www.akambabus.com; Lagos Rd, Nairobi)

Easy Coach (Map p602; ☎020-3210711; Haile Selassie Ave, Nairobi)

Riverside Shuttle (☎020-3229618; www.riverside-shuttle.com; Room 1, 3rd fl, Pan African Insurance House, Kenyatta Ave, Nairobi) Departure point Parkside Hotel, Monrovia St.

Uganda

Numerous bus companies run between Nairobi and Kampala. From Nairobi – and at the top end of the market – Easy Coach and Akamba have buses at least once daily, ranging from ordinary buses at around KSh1200 to full-blown 'luxury' services with drinks and movies, hovering around the KSh2400 mark.

Getting Around

AIR

Five domestic operators, including the national carrier Kenya Airways (☎020-6422560; www.kenya-airways.com), run scheduled flights within Kenya. Destinations served are predominantly around the coast and the popular southern national parks.

Book well in advance (essential during the tourist high season, June to September) with all these airlines. You should also remember to reconfirm return flights 72 hours before departure, especially when connecting with an international flight.

Airlines flying domestically:

Airkenya (☎Nairobi 020-3916000; www.airkenya.com) Amboseli, Diani, Lamu, Masai Mara, Malindi, Meru, Mombasa, Nanyuki and Samburu.

Fly540 (www.fly540.com) Eldoret, Kisumu, Kitale, Lamu, Lodwar, Malindi, Masai Mara and Mombasa.

Mombasa Air Safari (☎0734-400400; www.mombasaairsafari.com) Amboseli, Diani Beach, Lamu, Malindi, Masai Mara, Meru, Mombasa, Samburu and Tsavo West.

Safarilink (☎Nairobi 020-6000777; www.flysafarilink.com) Amboseli, Diani Beach, Kiwayu, Lamu, Lewa Downs, Masai Mara, Naivasha, Nanyuki, Samburu, Shaba and Tsavo West.

BUS

Kenya has an extensive network of long- and short-haul bus routes, with good coverage of the areas around Nairobi, the coast and the western regions. Buses offer varying levels of comfort, convenience and roadworthiness, but as a rule services are frequent, fast and often quite comfortable. The downside is the often diabolical condition of Kenya's roads.

CAR & MOTORCYCLE

There are numerous car-hire companies that can hire you anything from a small hatchback to Toyota Land Cruiser 4WDs, although hire rates are some of the highest in the world.

An International Driving Permit (IDP) is not necessary in Kenya, but can be useful.

Hire

Hiring a vehicle to tour Kenya (or at least the national parks) is expensive, but it does give you freedom and is sometimes the only way of getting to remote areas. A minimum age of between 23 and 25 years usually applies for hirers. Some companies prefer a licence with no endorsements (lost points) or criminal convictions, and most require you to have been driving for at least two years. You will also need acceptable ID, such as a passport. While hiring a driver may sound like a luxury, it can actually be a very good idea in Kenya for financial, practical and safety reasons.

Local and international hire companies:

Adventure Upgrade Safaris (Map p602; ☎0722-529228; www.adventureupgradesafaris.co.ke) An excellent local company.

Avis (Map p602; ☎020-2533610; www.avis.co.ke; Mombasa Rd, Nairobi)

Budget (Map p602; ☎020-223581; www.budget.co.ke; Mombasa Rd, Nairobi)

Central Rent-a-Car (Map p602; ☎020-2222888; www.carhirekenya.com; Ground Fl, 680 Hotel, Kenyatta Avenue, Nairobi)

Road Hazards

Driving practices in Kenya are appalling and all are carried out at break-neck speed. Kenyans habitually drive on the wrong side of the road in order to avoid potholes or animals – flashing your lights should be enough to persuade the driver to get back into their own lane. Never drive at night unless you absolutely have to, as very few cars have adequate headlights and the roads are full of pedestrians and cyclists.

HITCHING

Hitching is never entirely safe in any country in the world, and we don't recommend it. Travellers who decide to hitchhike should travel in pairs, and let someone know where they are planning to go.

LOCAL TRANSPORT

Boat

The only local boat service in regular use is the (often very crowded) Likoni ferry between the mainland and Mombasa island, which runs throughout the day and night and is free for foot passengers (vehicles pay a small toll).

Boda-Boda & Piki-Piki

Boda-bodas (bicycle) and *piki-piki* (motorcycle taxis) operate in smaller towns and cities such as Nakuru or Kisumu. There's a particular proliferation of *piki-pikis* on the coast. Helmets are a rarity, but it's an undeniably fun and flexible way to get around. A short ride should cost around KSh50 or so.

Matatu

Local *matatus* are the main means of getting around for local people, and any reasonably sized city or town will have plenty of services covering every major road and suburb. Fares start at KSh20 and may reach KSh100 for longer routes in Nairobi.

For inter-city transport, apart from in the remote northern areas, where you'll rely on occasional buses or paid lifts on trucks, you can almost always find a *matatu* going to the next town or further afield.

Matatus leave when full and the fares are fixed. It's unlikely you will be charged more than other passengers. Despite a briefly successful government drive to regulate the industry, *matatus* are once again notorious for dangerous driving, overcrowding and general shady business. Under no circumstances should you sit in the 'death seat' next to the *matatu* driver. Play it safe and sit in the middle seats away from the window. The upside: they're cheap as chips and offer a great way to meet local people.

Shared Taxi (Peugeot)

Shared Peugeot taxis are a good alternative to *matatus*. The vehicles are usually Peugeot 505 station wagons that take seven to nine passengers and leave when full. Peugeots take less time to reach their destinations than *matatus*, as they fill quicker and go from point to point without stopping, and so are slightly more expensive.

Taxi

You'll find taxis on virtually every corner in the larger cities, especially in Nairobi and Mombasa, where taking a taxi at night is virtually mandatory. Fares are invariably negotiable and start at around KSh250 for short journeys.

TRAIN

The Uganda Railway was once the main trade artery in East Africa, but these days the network has dwindled to two main routes, Nairobi–Kisumu (via Nakuru and Naivasha) and Nairobi–Mombasa.

There are three classes on Kenyan trains, but only 1st and 2nd class can be recommended. Fares for the night train between Nairobi and Mombasa are US$65 in 1st class, US$55 in 2nd class, including bed and breakfast. Note that passengers are divided by gender.

First class consists of two-berth compartments with a washbasin, wardrobe, drinking water and a drinks service. Second class consists of plainer, four-berth compartments with a washbasin and drinking water. No compartment can be locked from the outside, so don't leave any valuables lying around. You might want to padlock your rucksack to something during dinner and breakfast. Always lock your compartment from the inside before you go to sleep.

Passengers in 1st class on the Mombasa line are treated to a meal that typically consists of stews, curries or roast chicken served with rice and vegetables. Tea and coffee are included; sodas (soft drinks), bottled water and alcoholic drinks are not.

There are booking offices in Nairobi and Mombasa, and it's recommended that you show up in person rather than trying to call. You must book in advance for 1st and 2nd class. Two to three days is usually sufficient, but remember that these services run just three times weekly in either direction. Compartment and berth numbers are posted up about 30 minutes prior to departure.

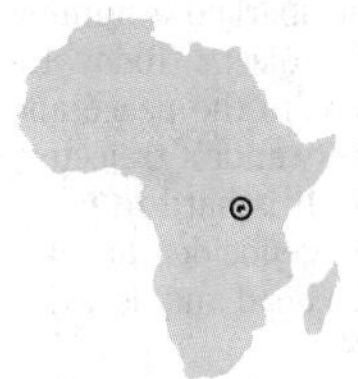

Rwanda

POP 11.5 MILLION

Includes ➡

Best of Nature

- ➡ Parc National des Volcans (p642)
- ➡ Nyungwe Forest National Park (p645)
- ➡ Lake Kivu (p644)

Best Museums

- ➡ National Museum of Rwanda (p644)
- ➡ Rukari Ancient History Museum (p645)
- ➡ Kigali Memorial Centre (p637)

Why Go?

Mention Rwanda to anyone with a small measure of geopolitical conscience, and they'll no doubt recall images of the horrific genocide that brutalised this tiny country in 1994 when, in the span of just three months, nearly one million Tutsis and moderate Hutus were systematically butchered. But since those dark days a miraculous transformation has been wrought and today the country is one of ethnic unity and relative political stability, and a new-found air of optimism pervades the country.

Tourism is once again a key contributor to the economy and the industry's brightest star is the chance to track rare mountain gorillas through bamboo forests in the shadow of the Virunga volcanoes. These conical mountains are shrouded in cloud and equatorial jungles and helped earn Rwanda the well-deserved moniker of 'Le Pays des Mille Collines' (Land of a Thousand Hills).

When to Go

Kigali

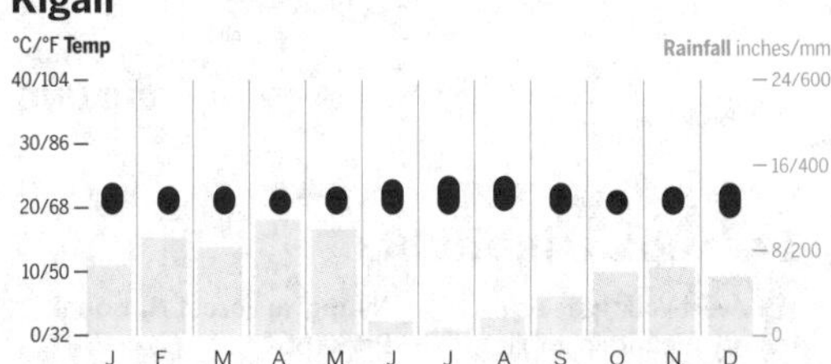

The long dry Trekking is more pleasant when rains ease between mid-May and September.

June Baby gorillas are named during the Kwita Izina ceremony.

The long rains Although often wet from mid-March to mid-May, travel is still possible.

KIGALI

POP 965,500

Founded in 1907 by German colonists, Kigali now spans several ridges and valleys, its winding boulevards and bustling streets climbing and falling over the hilly topography that characterises the city.

In recent years a massive amount of rehabilitation work has restored the city to its former graces, while increasing waves of foreign investment have sparked a number of ambitious building projects. Today Kigali exists as a testament to the peace and order that has defined Rwanda's trajectory for more than a decade. It is hard to imagine that during the 1994 genocide, the city's streets were littered with dead and decaying bodies.

Kigali Memorial Centre gives an insight into those dark days.

Rwanda Highlights

1. Avert your gaze as a mighty mountain gorilla ambles towards you in the **Parc National des Volcans** (p642).
2. Hike through steamy rain forests on the trail of colobus monkeys and chimpanzees in the **Nyungwe Forest National Park** (p645).
3. Kick back with a locally brewed Bralirwa in Kibuye or Gisenyi, on the sandy shores of **Lake Kivu** (p644).
4. Confront the horrors of the genocide at the haunting **Kigali Memorial Centre** (p637) on the outskirts of the capital.
5. Get educated at the **National Museum of Rwanda** (p644), one of East Africa's best ethnographic museums in Huye (Butare), Rwanda's intellectual capital.

Sights & Activities

★Kigali Memorial Centre MEMORIAL

(www.kigalimemorialcentre.org; 8am-4pm, closed public holidays) FREE In the span of 100 days, an estimated one million Tutsis and moderate Hutus were systematically butchered by the Interahamwe in one of the most savage genocides in history. This memorial honours the 250,000 people buried here in mass graves.

The informative audio tour (US$15) includes background on the divisive colonial experience in Rwanda and as the visit progresses, the exhibits become steadily more powerful as you are confronted with the crimes that took place here and moving video testimony from survivors.

The memorial concludes with sections on the refugee crisis in the aftermath of the genocide and the search for justice through the international tribunal in Arusha as well as the local *gacaca* courts (traditional tribunals headed by village elders).

Camp Kigali Memorial MEMORIAL

(Rue de l'Hopital; 7am-noon) The 10 stone columns here mark the spot where 10 Belgian UN peacekeepers were murdered on the first day of the genocide. Each stone column represents one of the soldiers and the horizontal cuts in it represent the soldier's age.

Museum of Natural History MUSEUM

(www.museum.gov.rw; adult/child incl guide RFr6000/3000; 8am-5pm) This small museum, off Ave de la Justice, houses a few simple exhibits (predominately captioned in German) on Rwanda's geology, fauna and flora. More interesting is the fact that this was the 1907 residence of explorer Richard Kandt and reputably the first building in Kigali.

Hotel des Mille Collines NOTABLE BUILDING

(Hotel Rwanda; 252-576530; www.millecollines.net; Ave de la République) This luxury hotel in the centre of Kigali was owned by the Belgian airline Sabena in 1994. At the time of the genocide, the hotel's European managers were evacuated, and control of the Mille Collines was given to Paul Rusesabagina. His heroic story of saving those he could is one of self-sacrifice in the most dire of situations and inspired the film *Hotel Rwanda*.

Rwanda Development Board City Tour TOUR

(RDB; 252-502350; www.rwandatourism.com; per person US$20; departs at 8am or 2pm daily) This three-hour tour includes the Kigali Memorial Centre, as well as a few other prominent buildings around town. It departs with a minimum of two people.

SET YOUR BUDGET

Budget

- Hotel room $35
- Main course $5
- Local minibus $0.40

Midrange

- Hotel room including breakfast $50
- Main course $10
- *Moto-taxi* (motorbike) $1.50

Top End

- Hotel room including breakfast from $150
- Main course $14
- Taxi $15

Sleeping

★Hôtel Isimbi HOTEL $

(252-75109; hotelisimbi@hotmail.com; Rue de Kalisimbi; s/d US$30/35) The most central of all the budget hotels, Isimbi is a good option for those who don't fancy walking up and down Kigali's endless hills. While the functional rooms here are somewhat lacking in atmosphere, they constitute a real bargain by Kigali standards and you may need to book ahead. If given a choice, opt for any room other than those that face the noisy street.

Procure d'Accueil Religieux HOSTEL $

(072-8527974; s incl breakfast RFr10,000, tw without bathroom RFr8000) This small lodging, off Blvd de l'OUA, can be found tucked behind the St Famille Church next to the Gemera petrol station, in the heart of town. The problem is it's nearly always full with volunteers who book out these spotlessly clean rooms for months at a time.

Motel Le Garni du Centre BOUTIQUE HOTEL $$

(252-572654; garni@rwanda1.com; Ave de la République; s/d incl breakfast US$100/135;) Kigali's first and only boutique hotel, this intimate and atmospheric little *auberge* (inn) is tucked away on a side road below Hotel des Mille Collines. Le Garni du Centre boasts individually decorated rooms that are built around an inviting swimming pool. The tariffs get cheaper with every night you stay.

Kigali

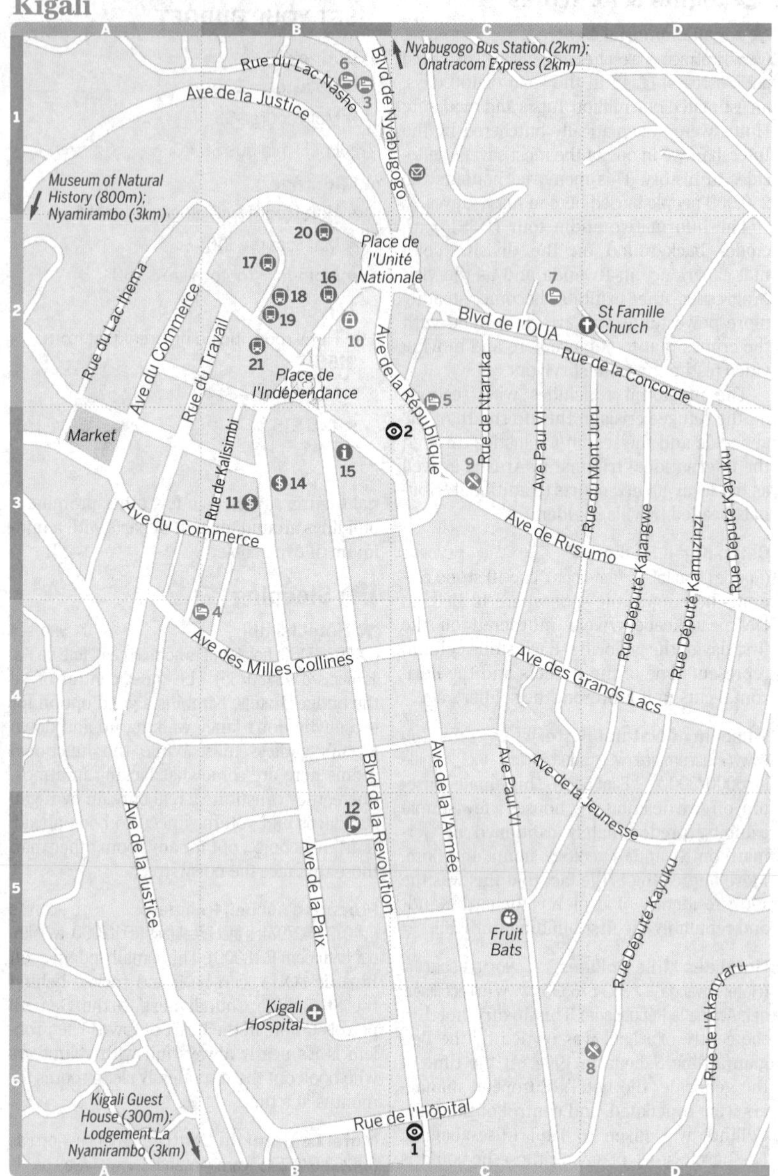

Dream Inn Hotel HOTEL $$
(☎252-503988; dreamapple333@yahoo.com; Blvd de Nyabugogo; d incl breakfast US$40-60; P 📶) Fair prices, spacious rooms and a handy central location means that this hotel is often full. The double beds are huge – large enough for a whole family of mountain gorillas.

Okapi Hotel HOTEL $$
(☎078-8359877; hotelokapi@hotmail.com; Rue du Lac Nasho; s US$30-60, d US$40-80, incl breakfast;

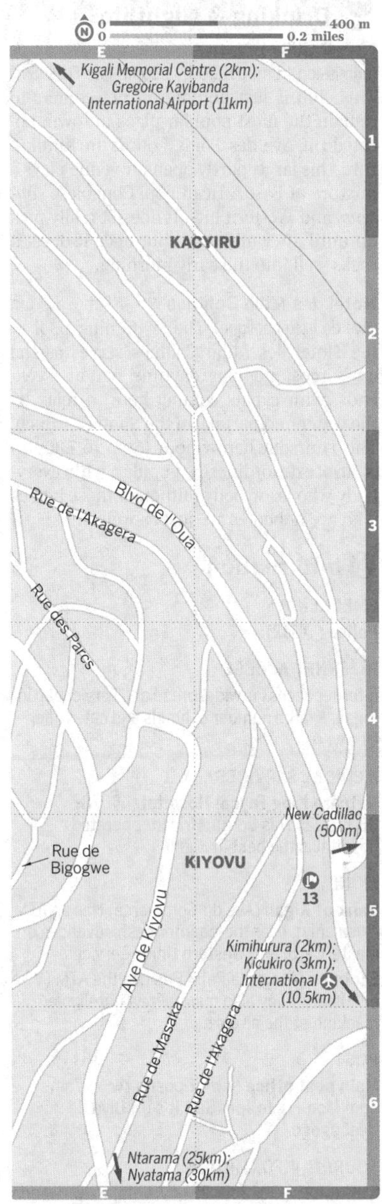

Kigali

Sights

1 Camp Kigali Memorial C6
2 Hotel des Mille Collines C3

Activities, Courses & Tours

RDB City Tour .... (see 15)

Sleeping

3 Dream Inn Hotel B1
4 Hôtel Isimbi B4
5 Motel Le Garni du Centre C2
6 Okapi Hotel B1
7 Procure d'Accueil Religieux C2

Eating

Bourbon Coffee Shop .... (see 10)
Nakumatt .... (see 10)
8 New Cactus D6
9 Shokola C3

Drinking & Nightlife

Hotel des Mille Collines .... (see 2)

Shopping

10 Union Trade Centre B2

Information

11 Bank of Kigali B3
12 Belgian Embassy B5
13 Canadian Embassy F5
14 Ecobank B3
15 RDB B3

Transport

Air Uganda .... (see 10)
16 Belvèdéré B2
Brussels Airline .... (see 2)
17 Capital B2
Ethiopian Airlines .... (see 10)
18 Horizon Express B2
19 Impala B2
International .... (see 19)
Kenya Airways .... (see 10)
20 New Yahoo Express B2
RwandAir .... (see 10)
Sotra Tours .... (see 17)
South African Airways .... (see 2)
Stella .... (see 17)
21 Virunga Express B2
Volcano Express .... (see 21)

P) A well-established midrange option that attracts a loyal following, the Okapi benefits from a decent location that's within easy walking distance of the city centre. The rooms come in four levels of comfort. The bottom category has tiny, cell-like rooms with shared bathrooms and at US$40 a double is a complete rip-off. The middle two categories are another thing entirely, with satellite TV, comfy beds and balconies with wide views.

Eating

Bourbon Coffee Shop AMERICAN $
(252-505307; Union Trade Centre, Ave de la Paix; mains RFr3500-5000; breakfast, lunch & dinner; wi-fi) If you don't like your morning blend served in a packet, head to this popular spot where locals and expats alike queue up for the real stuff. You can follow your frothy cappuccino with a burger, light meal or continental pastry. The free wi-fi is switched off during the lunchtime rush hour.

Nakumatt SUPERMARKET $
(Union Trade Centre, Place de l'Unite Nationale; 24hr) By far the best option for self-caterers, this huge supermarket in the Union Trade Centre has pretty much everything you'll need.

★ **Shokola** MEDITERRANEAN, MEXICAN $$
(Rue de Ntaruka; RFr3500-7000; lunch & dinner; wi-fi) Step inside a walled garden to find an oasis of tranquility that has become a firm favourite among expats in the relatively short time it's been open. Guests can sequester themselves beneath trees on comfy outdoor couches, in the book-lined drawing room or in one of the private Arabic-style tents in the garden. There is a hint of the Mediterranean about the menu, which ranges from delicately spiced Moroccan tagines to Turkish hummus. A Mexican-inspired buffet brunch (RFr7000) is served between 10am and 4pm every Sunday.

★ **New Cactus** ITALIAN $$
(252-572572; Rue Député Kayuku; mains RFr4400-7000; lunch & dinner; wi-fi) Outrageously popular with expats and well-to-do Rwandans alike, the New Cactus is set on a commanding ridge up in Kiyovu where you can soak up the sparkling lights of Kigali by night. It boasts a broad menu of French favourites, gourmet pizzas, rich fondues and a well-rounded wine list: spend a bit liberally here if you really want to live well.

Flamingo CHINESE $$
(252-586589; Kimihurura; mains RFr5000-7000; lunch & dinner; menu) Something of a Kigali institution, the Flamingo (now located in the leafy Kimihurura sector of town) remains the best Chinese restaurant in the country and has all the accoutrements you'd expect in a successful Asian restaurant – the ubiquitous red-and-black colour scheme, the compulsory bamboo water feature, and juices served with swizzle sticks.

Drinking & Nightlife

New Cadillac CLUB
(admission from RFr2000; 10pm-late Fri & Sat) This club is just holding off newcomers to remain the most popular place in town. Located off Ave des Poids Lourds in Kimikurure, this large, partly open-air venue plays a mixture of East African pop, Congolese *soukous* and Western hits. It doesn't really pick up until after midnight, but once it does, it rocks well into the early morning.

Hotel des Mille Collines BAR
(Ave de la République) The swimming pool at the Hotel des Mille Collines serves as the city's most popular daytime bar at weekends, with expats coming here to relax by the water and partake of the Sunday brunch. The Thursday happy hour (6pm to 7.30pm) is also extraordinarily popular with everybody who is anybody (although those bodies who are nobodies are just as welcome).

Information

EMERGENCY

Police (112)

INTERNET ACCESS

Internet access is widespread and very cheap in Kigali. A large number of hotels and cafes offer free wi-fi.

MEDICAL SERVICES

Netcare King Faycal Hospital (078-8309002) This South African–operated hospital is the best in Kigali.

MONEY

Bank of Kigali (Ave du Commerce) Has an ATM (Visa only), over-the-counter cash advances on MasterCard, and Western Union services.

Ecobank (Ave de la Paix) Besides the ATM (Visa only) here, they also maintain an unreliable machine at the airport.

POST

Main post office (www.i-posita.rw; 7am-5pm Mon-Fri, to 1pm Sat) It's off Blvd de Nyabugogo.

TOURIST INFORMATION

RDB (252-502350, 252-573396; www.rwandatourism.com; Blvd de la Revolution; 7am-5pm Mon-Fri, to noon Sat & Sun) Formerly known as ORTPN (pronounced *or*-ti-pen), the national tourism office has friendly staff who help promote tourism to the increasing streams of foreign visitors. Independent travellers can make reservations to track the mountain gorillas in Parc National des Volcans. There are rumours that this office will move as the great 'Kigali makeover' continues.

Getting There & Away

AIR

Gregoire Kayibanda International Airport (KGL) is located at Kanombe, which is 10km east of Kigali centre. **RwandAir** (WB; ☎252-503687; www.rwandair.com; Union Trade Centre, Ave de la Paix) has domestic flights to Gisenyi (US$150 return) and Kamembe (US$150 return).

BUS

Several bus companies operate services to major towns and most have offices in town as well as at the Nyabugogo bus terminal, about 2km north of the city centre in the valley. Nyabugogo is easily reached by minibuses heading down Blvd de Nyabugogo.

Belvèderé (Nyabugogo bus terminal & Ave de la Paix) Runs buses from 7.30am hourly to Gisenyi (RFr3100, three hours) via Musanze (Ruhengeri; RFr1800, 1½ hours).

Capital (Nyabugogo bus terminal & off Ave du Commerce) Hourly departures for Kibuye (Rfr2700, 2½ hours) via Gitarama (RFr900, one hour).

Horizon Express (Nyabugogo bus terminal & off Ave du Commerce) To Nyanza (RFr1800, 1¾ hours) and Huye (Butare; RFr2600, 2½ hours).

Impala (off Ave du Commerce) Runs buses west to Kibuye (RFr2700, 2½ hours) and Cyangugu (RFr5300, six hours).

International (Nyabugogo bus terminal & off Ave du Commerce) Heads east including Kayonza (RFr1500, 1½ hours) and Rusumo (RFr3000, three hours).

Sotra Tours (Nyabugogo bus terminal & off Ave du Commerce) To Nymata (RFr700, 45 minutes), Rusumo (RFr3000, three hours) and Huye (Butare; RFr2500, 2½ hours).

Stella (off Ave du Commerce) To Kayonza (RFr1500, 1½ hours) and Rusumo (RFr3000, three hours).

Virunga Express (Nyabugogo bus terminal & off Ave du Commerce) To Musanze (Ruhengeri; RFr1800, two hours) and Gisenyi (RFr3100, three hours).

Volcano Express (off Ave du Commerce) Reliable operator for Huye (Butare; RFr2600, 2½ hours) and Nyanza (RFr1800, 1¾ hours).

MINIBUS

Local minibuses depart from the Nyabugogo bus terminal for towns all around Rwanda, including Huye (Butare; RFr2400, two hours), Katuna (RFr1600, 1½ hours), Kibuye (RFr2000, two hours), Musanze (Ruhengeri; RFr2500, two hours) and Gisenyi (RFr3000, four hours). These minibuses leave when full throughout the day, except at weekends when they tend to dry up after 3pm.

Getting Around

A taxi/*moto-taxi* (informal moped taxi) costs RFr10,000/1500 to the airport but a KBS, International or Sotra Tours bus is cheaper (RFr250) and can be caught from outside the airport gates. In town you can catch one opposite the Bank of Kigali.

Minibuses advertise their destination in the front window and run to districts throughout the city. Fares are very cheap (from RFr100 to RFr300).

There are no metered taxis, but a fare within the city centre costs, on average, RFr3000 to RFr4000, and double that out to the suburbs or later at night. *Moto-taxi* can whisk you around the city for a negotiable price (usually less than RFr1000).

NORTHWESTERN RWANDA

The northwest of Rwanda is where the country really earns its nickname as the 'land of a thousand hills'. It's a beautiful region and the peaks culminate in the stunning Virunga volcanoes, forming a formidable natural border between Rwanda, Uganda and Democratic Republic of Congo (DRC; formerly Zaire).

Musanze (Ruhengeri)

POP 115,000

For most travellers, Musanze is the preferred staging post on their way to the magnificent Parc National des Volcans. Since gorilla trackers are required to check in at the park headquarters in nearby Kinigi at 7am on the day of the tracking, staying in Musanze is a much safer option than leaving from Kigali at the crack of dawn.

Sleeping

★ **Amahoro Guesthouse** GUESTHOUSE $
(☎078-5402928; www.amahoro-guesthouse.com; per person without bathroom RFr12,000, d RFr18,000; P) A little difficult to find as it doesn't have a sign, Amahoro Guesthouse is tucked behind a green gate in a house with a green roof. Although the rooms here have two or three beds in each, they are not dorms and each group is given their own room and share the common bathrooms.

WORTH A TRIP

NYAMATA & NTARAMA GENOCIDE MEMORIALS

During the genocide, victims fled to churches seeking refuge, only to find that some of the clergy was providing information to the Interahamwe. As a result of this lack of compassion, some of the most horrific massacres took place inside the holy sanctums of churches. Two of the most powerful genocide memorials are churches located on the outskirts of Kigali.

Nyamata, about 30km south of Kigali, is a deeply disturbing memorial where skulls and bones of the many victims are on display. While the visual remains of the deceased are a visceral sight, their inclusion here is to provide firm evidence to would-be genocide deniers.

The nearby church at Ntarama, about 25km south of Kigali, is more understated but no less powerful. The church has not been touched since the bodies were removed and there are many bits of clothing scraps still on the floor.

Both of these memorials can be visited on a day trip from Kigali. Sotra Tours (p641) runs buses every half hour to Nyamata (RFr700, 45 minutes) from Kigali and the memorial is a 1km walk from the Nyamata bus station. Ntarama can easily be reached from Nyamata by *moto-taxi* (motorcycle taxi; RFr1500).

This guesthouse is owned by local tour operator Amahoro Tours.

Hotel Muhabura HOTEL **$**
(☎078-8364774; muhabura12@yahoo.fr; Ave du 5 Juillet; s/d/apt RFr20,000/25,000/25,000; P @) Long-time favourite Muhabura was once the town's leading hotel and although it has been superseded by a whole slew of midrange options it straddles the niche between midrange and budget options nicely. The doubles and 'apartments' are particularly good value as they cost only a fraction more than the singles. Even if you're not staying here, stop by for dinner as the hotel arguably has the best restaurant in town.

Gorillas Volcanoes Hotel HOTEL **$$$**
(☎252-546700; www.hotelgorillas.com; Ave de la Paix; s/d/ste incl breakfast US$90/110/180) Part of the Gorilla group and one of the smartest hotels in Musanze town, this establishment caters mostly to package tours here to see the apes. Facilities include a restaurant-cum-bar and a massage/sauna room.

Getting There & Away

Numerous bus companies offer scheduled hourly services between Musanze and Kigali (RFr1800, two hours) and between Musanze and Gisenyi (RFr1200, 1½ hours). The two most reliable are **Belvèderé** (Ave du 5 Juillet) and **Virunga Express** (Ave du 5 Juillet). The latter also travels to Cyanika (RFr500, 45 minutes), on the Rwanda–Uganda border. Minibuses also travel these routes for much the same prices.

Parc National des Volcans

Volcanoes National Park, which runs along the border with DRC and Uganda, is home to the Rwandan section of the Virungas and comprises five volcanoes – the highest is Karisimbi (4507m).

Thanks to the pioneering work of American zoologist Dian Fossey and her team of dedicated rangers, the bamboo- and rainforest-covered slopes of these volcanoes are some of the last remaining sanctuaries of the endangered eastern mountain gorilla.

Sights & Activities

★**Gorilla Tracking** WILDLIFE ENCOUNTER
(per person US$750) An encounter with these charismatic creatures is the highlight of a trip to Africa for many visitors. However, make no mistake about it – gorilla tracking is no joy ride. The guides can generally find the gorillas within one to four hours of starting out, but this often involves a lot of strenuous effort scrambling through dense vegetation up steep, muddy hillsides, sometimes to more than 3000m.

There are 10 habituated gorilla groups in Parc National des Volcans. Visits to the gorillas are restricted to one hour, and flash photography is banned. While you are visiting the gorillas, do not eat, drink, smoke or go to the bathroom in their presence. If you have any potential airborne illness, do not go tracking as gorillas are extremely susceptible to human diseases.

Bookings for gorilla permits can be made through the RDB tourist office (p640) in Kigali or a Rwandan tour company. With demand exceeding supply you'll need to book well in advance if you want to be assured of a spot, especially during the peak seasons of December–January and July–August. Bookings are secured with a US$100 deposit (via bank transfer), and full payment must be made upon your arrival in Kigali.

You'll need to present yourself at 7am on the day that your permit is valid at the **park headquarters** (RDB; ☎078-8771633; ⊙6am-4pm) in Kinigi. It's worth emphasising that you will need to have your own transport arranged between park headquarters and assigned trail head and if you are late, your designated slot will be forfeited, and your money will not be refunded.

Golden Monkey Tracking WILDLIFE ENCOUNTER
(per person US$100) Endangered golden monkeys, which are a subspecies of the wider-spread blue monkey, are endemic to the Albertine Rift Valley and can only be seen in the Virungas. Guided golden monkey tracking is more like chimp-viewing than a gorilla encounter because you don't get as close to these elusive creatures as you do to the gorillas.

Sleeping

★ **Kinigi Guesthouse** HOTEL $
(☎078-8533606; kinigi2020@yahoo.fr; dm US$10, s/d incl breakfast from US$40/50; P 📶) Located very close to park headquarters in Kinigi village. All profits from this local lodge are ploughed back into the Association de Solidarité des Femmes Rwandaises, which assists vulnerable Rwandan women of all backgrounds and ages. Accommodation is in a small clutch of wooden bungalows that are set in lush gardens with views of the towering Virungas.

La Paillotte Gorilla Place HOTEL $
(☎078-5523561; www.lapaillottegorillaplace.com; s/d RFr15,000/20,000) Right in Kinigi village, not far from the market and bus stand, this small hotel has six clean rooms (with hot showers) set around a garden restaurant.

Mountain Gorilla View Lodge HOTEL $$$
(☎078-8305708; www.3bhotels.com; s/d with full board US$230/300; P) These 25 rock cottages with impressive views down the volcano range are more functional than comfortable and some may find the stone floors a little cold (ask the staff for a hot-water bottle). A cultural show featuring traditional dancers is held here at 4.30pm every evening during the high season.

Getting There & Away

The park headquarters is located near the village of Kinigi, approximately 12km north of Musanze. The condition of this road has been greatly improved over recent years and Virunga District Service runs buses every 30 minutes between Musanze and Kinigi (first departure 6am, RFr300, 35 minutes). From Kinigi it's a further 4km to the park headquarters (RFr700 to RFr1000 by *moto-taxi*).

It's also necessary to arrange transport from the park headquarters to the point where you start climbing up to where the gorillas are situated. Some solo travellers opt to hitch a ride with other tourists but there's always the chance you'll be refused.

If you want the assurance of your own wheels, it's best to join a group in Musanze. Two places to ask around at are **Amahoro Tours** (☎078-8687448; www.amahoro-tours.com) or Hotel Muhabura. The cost of hiring a vehicle and driver is US$80 at either of these places.

SOUTHWESTERN RWANDA

The endless mountains don't stop as you head south towards Burundi. Highlights here include the intellectual capital of Huye (Butare) and the magnificent primate-filled forest of Parc National de Nyungwe.

Huye (Butare)

POP 107,000

Huye (Butare) is one of the most distinguished towns in Rwanda, having served as the country's most prominent intellectual centre since the colonial era. In the early days of the 1994 genocide, Tutsis and moderate Hutus fled to Butare in the hope that its intellectual tradition would reign over the ensuing madness. For a short while Jean Baptiste-Habyarimana did manage to maintain peace and order in the town but he was quickly murdered and replaced by Colonel Tharchisse Muvunyi. Under his tenure, Butare was the site of horrific massacres that claimed the lives of nearly a quarter of a million people.

WORTH A TRIP

LAKE KIVU

Land-locked Rwanda may be a long way from the ocean, but that doesn't mean you can't have a beach holiday here. On the contrary, if you take another look at the map, you'll quickly realise that Rwanda's eastern border with Democratic Republic of Congo (DRC; formerly Zaire) runs the entire length of Lake Kivu – one of the Great Lakes in the Albertine Rift Valley.

The best places to take in the lake's charms are at either **Gisenyi** in the north or **Kibuye** further south. Gisenyi has the better beaches and much of the lake's frontage here is lined with landscaped villas, plush hotels and private clubs. In fact, the biggest obstacle to Gisenyi assuming full-on resort status is simply its ongoing image problem. The town is unfortunately remembered as the location of a major flashpoint during the Rwandan Civil War, the 1994 genocide and the First and Second Congo Wars. Indeed, sharing a border with DRC and the recent rebel problems there hasn't done wonders for the town's reputation.

Kibuye has not caught on as a tourist destination for sun and sand in the same way that Gisenyi has, but for our money – and there are plenty who will disagree – this is the better of the two with its stunning location, spread across a series of hills jutting into Lake Kivu.

Both Gisenyi and Kibuye have a good range of accommodation options. A clean, budget option in Gisenyi is **Centre d'Accueil de l'Église Presbytérienne** (☎078-5730113; eprcagisenyi@yahoo.fr; Ave du Marché; dm RFr2000-3000, s/d/tr RFr8000/10,000/12,000), and **Paradis Malahide** (☎078-8648650; parmalahide@yahoo.fr; Rubona Peninsula; s/d/tr incl breakfast RFr45,000/45,000/65,000), on the nearby Rubona Peninsula, has waterfront stone villas set amid tropical gardens. In Kibuye, our pick is **Hotel Centre Béthanie** (☎252-568235; eprbethanie@yahoo.com; s RFr20,000-35,000, d RFr28,000-45,000; P Wi-Fi) or **Hôme St Jean** (☎078-8823135; r incl breakfast RFr10,000-15,000, s/tw without bathroom RFr6000/8000; P), both with sensational views over the indented coast.

There are buses to both Kibuye (RFr2700, 2½ hours) and Gisenyi (RFr3100, three hours) from Kigali, the latter via Musanze (Ruhengeri; RFr1200, 1½ hours).

Sights

National Museum of Rwanda MUSEUM
(www.museum.gov.rw; Rue de Kigali; adult/child RFr6000/3000; 7am-7pm Mon-Fri, 8am-7pm Sat & Sun) This outstanding museum was given to the city as a gift from Belgium in 1989 to commemorate 25 years of independence. While the building itself is certainly one of the most beautiful structures in the city, the museum wins top marks for having one of the best ethnological and archaeological collections in the entire region.

National University of Rwanda GARDENS
This university is Rwanda's finest institution of learning, and strolling through its campus is a pleasant diversion, especially if you find yourself wandering in the leafy park, **Arboretum de Ruhande**.

Sleeping & Eating

Hotel Ineza HOTEL $
(☎078-8953533; r RFr5000-6000) The rooms aren't very big but they're bright and clean, so if you're a solo traveller and after something cheap, then look no further. It's off Rue de Kigali.

Hôtel des Beaux-Arts HOTEL $
(☎078-5316034; Ave du Commerce; s/d/tw incl breakfast RFr5000/8000/7000) Set a little way back from Ave du Commerce, this hotel has quite a bit of character for a cheapie. The hotel is attractively decorated with local products and there's a pleasant courtyard to unwind in.

Hotel Ibis HOTEL $$
(☎252-530335; campionibis@hotmail.com; Rue de Kigali; s RFr15,000-26,000, d RFr19,000-35,000; P Wi-Fi) The Ibis is one of the smartest, midrange hotels in town although it has a bewildering pricing structure – ask to see a few rooms before committing.

Getting There & Away

There are several bus companies, including Belvèdéré, Horizon, New Yahoo Car, Sotra Tours and Volcano Express, strung along Rue de Kigali. Most operate between Huye and Kigali (RFr2600, 2½ hours); some of these also have services to Nyamagabe (RFr600, 30 minutes), Nyanza (RFr700, 45 minutes), Cyangugu (RFr4000 to RFr5300, four hours) and Bujumbura (Burundi; RFr6000, four hours).

Nyungwe Forest National Park

Nyungwe Forest is Rwanda's most important area of biodiversity, and has been rated the highest priority for forest conservation in Africa. Nyungwe's strongest drawcard is the chance to track chimpanzees, which have been habituated over the years to human visits.

Sights & Activities

Chimpanzee Tracking WILDLIFE ENCOUNTER
(per person US$90) Chimpanzee habitation in Nyungwe forest is still very much a work in progress, and there are no guarantees that you'll come face-to-face with one in the wild. If you are lucky and happen to come across a group of chimps on the move, you need to be quick with your camera. Chimps have a tendency to quickly disappear in the underbrush, or climb up into the canopy and out of sight.

Currently there are two habituated groups. The **Uwinka group** is the largest, and usually found within 12km of the Uwinka Reception Centre, often off roads that are only drivable in sturdy 4WDs.

The second group, the **Cyamudongo group**, is named after the Cyamudongo forest, a protected annexe of Nyungwe Forest National Park located approximately 45 minutes west of Gisakura on the road out to Cyangungu. Again, you need to have your own 4WD in order to get to this tiny forest.

Colobus Monkey Tracking WILDLIFE ENCOUNTER
(per person US$70) A subspecies of the widespread black-and-white colobus, the Angolan colobus is an arboreal Old World monkey that is distinguished by its black fur and long, silky white locks of hair. While they may not be as charismatic as chimps, colobi are extremely social primates that form enormous group sizes – the semi-habituated troop in the Nyungwe forest numbers no less than 400 individuals and is by far the largest primate aggregation on the continent.

Sleeping & Eating

There is a **campsite** (per person US$30) at the Uwinka headquarters, occupying a ridge (2500m) overlooking the forest and offering impressive views in all directions.

A more sophisticated option for those without a tent can be found at the **Gisakura Guest House** (ORTPN Resthouse; ☎078-8675051; www.gisakuraguesthouse.com; s/d/tr without bathroom incl breakfast US$43/64/85), which offers accommodation in simple but functional rooms that share communal showers and toilets.

WORTH A TRIP

NYANZA (NYABISINDU)

In 1899, Mwami Musinga Yuhi V established Rwanda's first permanent royal capital in Nyanza. Today a large thatched hut, his traditional palace (well, actually a very good replica of it) and the first home built by his son and successor Mutara III Rudahigwa have been restored and form the **Rukari Ancient History Museum** (www.museum.gov.rw; adult/student RFr6000/3000; 8am-5pm).

After visiting Belgium and seeing the stately homes there, Mutara concluded his own home wasn't up to scratch and had a second, and altogether grander, palace built on nearby Rwesero Hill, although he died before its completion. Today, this new palace serves as the **Rwesero Art Museum** (www.museum.gov.rw; adult/student RFr6000/3000; 8am-5pm), housing mostly contemporary paintings and stylistic sculptures on themes dealing with the genocide, unity and brotherhood.

Keep hold of your ticket, as admission to one museum entitles you to entry to the other. Most people visit the Nyanza museums as a day trip from either Kigali or Huye (Butare). Volcano Express and Horizon have buses directly to Nyanza from either Kigali (RFr1800, 1¾ hours) or Huye (RFr700, 45 minutes). The museums are a further 2km from town and can be reached on foot or by *moto-taxi* (motocycle taxi; RFr400).

ℹ Information

The park headquarters is at the **Uwinka Reception Centre** (☎ tourist warden for bookings 078-8436763; kambogoi@yahoo.fr) on the Huye–Cyangugu road, although park fees can also be paid at the **Gisakura Booking Office** (☎ 078-8841079). It is prohibited to enter the park or walk on any of the park trails unguided. Ranger guides for trails 5km or less cost US$40 per person and trails between 5km and 10km cost US$50 per person.

ℹ Getting There & Away

Nyungwe Forest National Park lies between Huye and Cyangugu. Impala Express and Sotra Tours buses travel between Huye (Butare; RFr4000 to RFr5300, two hours, 90km) and Kamembe (for Cyangugu; one hour, 55km) throughout the day. Any one of these buses can drop you at either Uwinka Reception Centre or at the Gisakura Tea Plantation.

The trouble is that having arrived, your ability to move around the park is severely limited if you don't have a car.

Leaving can also be problematic as many of the passing buses are full and you may have to wait some time before one will stop.

UNDERSTAND RWANDA

Rwanda Today

Since coming to power in 2003, the Rwanda Patriotic Front (RPF) government has continued to make an impressive effort to promote reconciliation and restore trust between the Hutu and Tutsi communities. However, its ongoing involvement in DRC's affairs has come under increasing criticism and done much to tarnish Rwanda's international reputation.

In 2012 the UN released a report which accused the country of supporting the M23 rebels and ultimately led to the United States and the European Union suspending aid.

Within Rwanda opinions have become more polarised in recent years. Critics of Paul Kagame's government argue that there is a dark side to Rwanda: one in which dissenting journalists are silenced, outspoken CEOs are forced to leave the country at an hour's notice and all information is tightly controlled. Supporters of RPF say the fact that a million people have been removed from poverty between 2006 and 2011 speaks largely for itself and it holds Rwanda high, hailing it an economic model for the developing world.

History

Early Days

The original Rwandans, the Twa, were gradually displaced by bigger groups of migrating Hutu tribespeople from AD 1000. Later came the Tutsi from the north, arriving from the 16th century onwards. The authority of the Rwandan *mwami* (king) was far greater than that of his opposite number in Burundi, and the system of feudalism that developed here was unsurpassed in Africa outside Ethiopia. Tutsi overlordship was reinforced by ceremonial and religious observance.

European Meddling

The Germans took the country in 1890 and held it until 1916, when their garrisons surrendered to Belgian forces during WWI. During Belgian rule, the power and privileges of the Tutsi increased, as the new masters found it convenient to rule indirectly through the *mwami* and his princes.

However, in 1956 Mwami Rudahigwa called for independence from Belgium and the Belgians began to switch allegiance to the Hutu majority. The Tutsi favoured fast-track independence, while the Hutus wanted the introduction of democracy first.

Following the death of the *mwami* in 1959, armed clashes began between the two tribes, marking the start of an ethnic conflict that was to culminate in the 1994 genocide. Tutsi fled the country in numbers, resettling in neighbouring Uganda, Kenya and Tanzania.

Following independence in 1962, the Hutu majority came to power under Prime Minister Grégoire Kayibanda. The new government introduced quotas for Tutsis, limiting opportunities for education and work, and small groups of Tutsi exiles began to launch guerrilla raids from neighbouring Uganda.

In the round of bloodshed that followed, thousands more Tutsis were killed by Hutus and Hutu-sympathisers and tens of thousands fled to neighbouring countries.

A Simmering Conflict

The massacre of Hutus in Burundi in 1972 reignited the old hatreds in Rwanda and prompted the army commander, Major General Juvenal Habyarimana, to oust Kayibanda in 1973. Habyarimana made some progress towards healing the ethnic divisions during the early years of his regime, but before long it was business as usual.

In October 1990 the entire intertribal issue was savagely reopened when 5000 well-armed rebels of the RPF, a Tutsi military front, invaded Rwanda from their bases in western Uganda. Two days later, at Habyarimana's request, France, Belgium and Zaïre (as DRC was then known) flew in troops to assist the Rwandan army to repulse the rebels.

The RPF invaded again in 1991, this time better armed and prepared. By early 1992 the RPF was within 25km of Kigali. A ceasefire was cobbled together and the warring parties brought to the negotiating table. A peace accord between the government and the RPF was finally signed in August 1993.

The Genocide

In 1994 the conflict erupted again on an incomprehensible scale. An estimated 800,000 Rwandans were killed in just three months, mostly by Interahamwe militias – gangs of youths armed with machetes, guns and other weapons supplied by officials close to Habyarimana. Three million people fled to refugee camps in Tanzania, DRC and Uganda, and an estimated seven million of the country's nine million people were displaced.

The spark for the carnage was the death of Habyarimana and his Burundian counterpart, Cyprien Ntaryamira, on 6 April as their plane was shot down attempting to land in Kigali on their return from peace talks in Tanzania. It will probably never be known who fired the missile, but most observers believe it was Hutu extremists. Whoever was responsible, the event unleashed one of the 20th century's worst explosions of bloodletting. The massacres that followed were, according to political analysts, no spontaneous outburst of violence but a calculated 'final solution' by extremist elements of Habyarimana's government to rid the country of all Tutsi and the Hutu reformists. Rwandan army and Interahamwe death squads ranged over the countryside killing, looting and burning, and roadblocks were set up in every town and city.

The UN Assistance Mission for Rwanda (UNAMIR) was in Rwanda throughout the genocide, but was powerless to prevent the killing due to an ineffective mandate. The inter-national community's failure to intervene effectively to help the local population left Rwanda to face its fate. By the time UNAMIR was finally reinforced in July, it was too late. The genocide was already over and the RPF had taken power in Kigali.

The Aftermath

Hutu extremists and their allies fled into eastern DRC to regroup and launched cross-border raids into both Rwanda and Burundi from the refugee camps in the Goma and Uvira regions. Rwanda responded with raids into eastern DRC and support for Tutsi rebels north of Goma.

The Hutu fought alongside the Congolese army, and the entire situation turned ugly, as one million or so refugees were caught in the middle. But the RPF and their allies soon swept across DRC, installing Laurent Kabila in power and breaking the grip of the extremists on the camps. However, they soon decided Kabila was not such a reliable ally and became embroiled in Africa's biggest war to date, fighting over DRC's mineral wealth with nine other African states.

The **International Criminal Tribunal for Rwanda** (www.ictr.org) was established in Arusha (Tanzania) in November 1994 to bring to justice former government and military officials for acts of genocide. Several big fish have been sentenced in the past decade and in Rwanda the prisons are still overflowing with smaller fish.

The Road Ahead

Since coming to power the RPF government has continued to make an impressive effort to promote reconciliation and restore trust between the Hutu and Tutsi communities.

On 29 November 2009, Rwanda, although it lacks any British colonial ties, joined the Commonwealth but its ongoing involvement in the DRC's affairs have come under increasing criticism and done much to tarnish Rwanda's international reputation. In 2012 the UN released a report which accused the country of supporting the M23 rebels and ultimately led to the United States and the European Union suspending aid.

People of Rwanda

In the new Rwanda, ethnic identities are out. It is considered inappropriate to ask if someone is either Hutu or Tutsi; most people are keen to put ethnic divisions behind them and consider themselves simply Rwandan.

In Kigali people follow a Mediterranean pattern of starting early before breaking off for a siesta or a long and boozy lunch. Late dinners inevitably lead into drinking and socialising that sometimes doesn't wind down until the early morning.

The rhythm of rural life is very different and follows the sun. People work long hours from dawn until dusk, but also take a break during the hottest part of the day. However, it is a hard life for women in the countryside, who seem burdened with the lion's share of the work.

Despite the role some churches played in the genocide, faith remains an important rock in the lives of many Rwandan people, with Christianity firmly rooted as the dominant religion.

The Arts

Rwanda's most famous dancers are the Intore troupe. Their warriorlike displays are accompanied by a trancelike drumbeat similar to that of the famous Les Tambourinaires in Burundi.

The film *Hotel Rwanda* has put Rwanda back on the map for many moviegoers. Although it was shot in South Africa, it tells the story of Hotel des Mille Collines manager Paul Rusesabagina, played by Don Cheadle, turning his luxury hotel into a temporary haven for thousands fleeing the erupting genocide.

Gorillas in the Mist, starring Sigourney Weaver, is based on the autobiography of Dian Fossey and her work with the rare mountain gorillas in Parc National des Volcans. It's essential viewing for anyone wishing to track the gorillas.

SURVIVAL GUIDE

Directory A–Z

ACCOMMODATION

Generally, budget accommodation in Rwanda is more expensive than in neighbouring countries. Cheap hotels are essentially clean but they are often noisy, largely due to the fact that most have attached bars.

Top-end hotels and ecolodges are found mostly found in Kigali, Gisenyi and near Musanze (Ruhengeri) on the edge of Parc National des Volcans and are modern with professional service.

EMBASSIES & CONSULATES

Quite a number of embassies are now located on Blvd de l'Umuganda, across the valley in the Kacyiru suburb of Kigali.

Belgian Embassy (☎252-575553; www.diplomatie.be/kigali; Rue de Nyarugenge)

British High Commission (☎252-556000; http://ukinrwanda.fco.gov.uk; Blvd de l'Umuganda, Kacyiru)

Burundian Embassy (☎252-517529; Blvd de l'Umuganda, Kacyiru)

Canadian Embassy (☎252-573210; Rue de l'Akagera)

French Embassy (☎252-551800; http://ambafrance-rw.org; Rue du Député Kamuzinzi)

Kenyan Embassy (☎252-583332; Blvd de l'Umuganda, Kacyiru)

Tanzanian Embassy (☎252-505400; Telecom House, Blvd de l'Umuganda, Kacyiru)

Ugandan High Commision (☎252-503537; http://ugandaembassy.rw; KG 205 St, Nyarutarama Hill)

US Embassy (☎252-596400; http://rwanda.usembassy.gov; 2657 Ave de la Gendarmerie, Kacyiru)

FOOD & DRINK

In the rural areas of Rwanda, food is very similar to that in other East African countries. Popular meats include tilapia (Nile perch), goat, chicken and beef *brochettes* (kebabs), though the bulk of most meals are based on *ugali* (maize meal), *matoke* (mashed plantains) and so-called 'Irish potatoes'. In the cities, however, Rwanda's francophone roots are evident in the *plat du jour* (plate of the day), which is usually excellently prepared and presented continental Europe–inspired cuisine.

It is not recommended that you drink the tap water in Rwanda; bottled water is cheap and widely available. Soft drinks (sodas) and the local beers, Primus and Mulzig, are available everywhere, as is the local firewater, *konyagi*. A pleasant, nonalcoholic alternative is the purplish juice from the tree tomato (tamarillo), which is a sweet and tasty concoction that somewhat defies explanation – give it a try!

INTERNET ACCESS

Email and internet access in Rwanda has fast improved and is now widely available in Kigali, as well as on a more limited basis in smaller towns.

MONEY

Rwanda's unit of currency is the Rwandan franc (RFr). It's best to come to Rwanda with US dollars or euros in cash. US bank notes pre-2006 and travellers cheques are seldom accepted in Rwanda.

Banks in Kigali have a network of ATMs, but most are not yet wired up for international transactions (despite Visa signs at some). The notable exceptions are the Bank of Kigali and Ecobank, which both have ATMs that accept international Visa cards.

Bureaus de change, which are mostly in Kigali, offer slightly better exchange rates than banks.

OPENING HOURS

Banks Open between 8.30am and 4.30pm or 5.30pm (with no break for lunch); closed Saturday afternoons; some banks close early at 3.30pm.

Government offices and businesses Generally open between 8.30am and 4.30pm or 5.30pm, with a short break for lunch sometime between noon and 2pm.

Restaurants Local restaurant hours are 7am to 9pm, and international-type restaurants are open 11.30am to 2.30pm and 5.30pm to 10.30pm.

Shops Open between 8.30am and 4.30pm or 5.30pm; most shops do not break for lunch.

Umuganda Day From 8am to 11am on the last Saturday of every month, the whole country stops whatever it is doing and works for the public good, cleaning streets, repairing roads and building schools. Some tour operators may have dispensation to travel during these hours.

PUBLIC HOLIDAYS

New Year's Day 1 January
Democracy Day 8 January
Easter (Good Friday, Holy Saturday and Easter Monday) March/April
Labour Day 1 May
Ascension Thursday May
Whit Monday May
National Day 1 July
Peace & National Unity Day 5 July
Harvest Festival 1 August
Assumption 15 August
Culture Day 8 September
Kamarampaka Day 25 September
Armed Forces Day 26 October
All Saints' Day 1 November
Christmas Day 25 December

SAFE TRAVEL

Mention Rwanda to most people and they think of it as a highly dangerous place. However, the reality today is very different. Stability has returned to all parts of the country and Kigali is one of the safest cities in Africa.

That said, it is worth checking security conditions before entering Rwanda. There is always the remote possibility of problems spilling over from neighbouring DRC or Burundi.

Take care where you point your camera anywhere in the country, as most Rwandans are very sensitive about who or what you are snapping.

PRACTICALITIES

- **Electricity** 240V, 50 cycles, and are mainly two-pin plugs.
- **Language** The official languages are Kinyarwanda and English. French was dropped as an official language in favour of English in 2008.
- **Newspapers** The English-language *New Times* is published several times a week, plus the Ugandan *New Vision* and *Monitor* are also available.
- **Radio** Radio Rwanda is the government-run station, broadcasting in Kinyarwanda, French, Swahili and English.
- **TV** TV Rwandaise (TVR) is the state-owned broadcaster.

TELEPHONE

There are three main operators in Rwanda: MTN, Tigo and Rwandatel.

In 2009 all old six-digit numbers were extended by adding the prefix ☎252 to landline numbers, ☎078 and ☎072 to mobile numbers, and ☎55 to CDMA numbers. There are currently no area codes in Rwanda. The international country code is ☎250.

For calls within Rwanda, the easiest option is to use one of the street kiosks. International calls can be made from Kigali's main post office.

VISAS

Visas are required by everyone except nationals of Germany, South Africa, Sweden, the UK, the USA and other East African countries. Everyone else needs to apply for a visa in their country of residence (US$50, valid for 90 days and multiple entries).

If Rwanda isn't represented in your country, you need to register online at **Rwanda Immigration** (Ministère de l'Intérieur; ☎078-8152222; www.migration.gov.rw; Blvd de l'Umuganda, Kacyiru, Kigali; ⏲application submission 7-11.30am Mon-Wed & Fri, visa collection 1-4.30pm Mon-Wed & Fri, 1-3.30pm Thu) before

LEAVE YOUR PLASTIC BAGS AT HOME

In an effort to preserve the natural beauty of Rwanda, the government enforces a strict ban on plastic bags throughout the country. Police are particularly vigilant at border crossings, and you will be searched and possibly fined if contraband is found.

you travel. Present the letter they send you at the border along with the US$30 fee to obtain a single-entry, 30-day visa. It is no longer possible to obtain a visa on arrival without first obtaining one of these letters of entitlement.

Visa Extensions

Both tourist and transit visas can be extended in Kigali at Rwanda Immigration in the Kacyiru district, about 7km northeast of the city centre. Bring the appropriate form (available online), a passport-sized photo, your passport and a letter of introduction or a letter addressed to the Director of Immigration explaining why you require a visa extension. Extensions take five working days to issue and cost RFr30,000.

Visa for Onward Travel

Visas for Uganda and Tanzania can be issued to most nationalities at the border or obtained from their respective embassies in Kigali.

Burundian tourist visas are issued at their Kigali embassy and three-day transit visas at their border. These can be extended in Bujumbura.

To enter DRC from Rwanda you will need a visa issued in your country of residence (the DRC embassy in Kigali was issuing visas but these were not being accepted by border guards when we passed through) or obtain one with Parc National des Virunga, which was organising visas in 2012 on its website (www.visitvirunga.org). However, given the rise in rebel activity within the park and the suspension of gorilla trekking trips there, it is uncertain for how long this will continue.

Getting There & Away

AIR

Gregoire Kayibanda International Airport is located at Kanombe, 10km east of Kigali centre.

The following airlines have offices in Kigali:

Air Uganda (U7; 252-577928; www.air-uganda.com; Union Trade Centre, Ave de la Paix)

Brussels Airline (SN; 252-575290; www.brusselsairlines.com; Hotel des Mille Collines)

Ethiopian Airlines (ET; 252-570440; www.flyethiopian.com; Union Trade Centre, Ave de la Paix)

Kenya Airways (KQ; 252-501652; www.kenya-airways.com; Union Trade Centre, Ave de la Paix)

RwandAir (WB; 252-503687; www.rwandair.com; Union Trade Centre, Ave de la Paix) Has domestic flights to Gisenyi (US$177 return) and Kamembe (US$177 return).

South African Airways (SA; 252-577777; www.flysaa.com; Easy Travel, Hotel des Mille Collines)

LAND

Burundi

The main border crossing between Rwanda and Burundi is via Huye (Butare) and Kayanza, on the Kigali to Bujumbura road, which is sealed pretty much all the way. The border post is called Kayanza Haut, and Burundian transit visas are available on arrival. Bus companies Belvèderé (p641), Horizon Express (p641), **Kampala Coach** (www.kampalacoach.com; Nyabugogo bus terminal) and **New Yahoo Express**, off Ave du Commerce, all run buses between Kigali and Bujumbura (RFr6000, six hours).

There is also a direct road between Bujumbura and Cyangugu, There are no direct buses between the two, although a minibus from Bujumbura can take you to Rugombo (you may have to change in Cibitoke) from where you can catch onward transport to Cyangugu (one hour, RFr1500).

Democratic Republic of Congo

Assuming you have prearranged a visa, there are two main crossings between Rwanda and DRC, both on the shores of Lake Kivu. To the north is the crossing between Gisenyi and Goma, and this is considered the safest, although recent rebel activity near Goma means that this could easily change. Needless to say it is important to check security in the area prior to contemplating crossing here.

The southern border between Cyangugu and Bukavu (DRC) is also open for crossing, but the security situation around Bukavu is more volatile than Goma.

Tanzania

International, Sotra Tours (p641) and Stella (p641) buses along with daily minibuses go from Kigali to Rusumu (RFr3000, three hours), where you'll need to walk across the Kagera river bridge. Once across, there are pick-up taxis to the tiny town (and former refugee camp) of Benako (marked as Kasulo on some maps), about 20km southeast.

Alternatively, Kampala Coaches (p650) from Kigali reach Tanzania via Kampala (Uganda).

Uganda

There are two main crossing points for foreigners: between Kigali and Kabale (Uganda) via Gatuna (Katuna on the Ugandan side), and between Musanze (Ruhengeri) and Kisoro (Uganda) via Cyanika.

There are lots of minibuses between Kigali and the border at Gatuna (RFr1300, 1½ hours) throughout the day. There are also plenty of shared taxis (USh4000) and special hire taxis (USh20,000 for the whole car) travelling back and forth between Katuna and Kabale.

Minibuses link Musanze (Ruhengeri) to the border (RFr1000, 25km) from where onward transport can be arranged to Kisoro. There are also direct buses from Musanze to Kampala (Rfr8000, 12½ hours).

Those travelling direct between Kigali and Kampala can travel with either Horizon Express (p641) or Kampala Coach (p650; RFr6000 to RFr8000, six to nine hours).

Getting Around

AIR

RwandAir recently introduced domestic flights between Kigali and Gisenyi.

BUS & MINIBUS

Privately run buses cover the entire country and have scheduled departure times. Tickets are brought in advance from a ticket office which is usually (although not always) the point of departure. You will also find plenty of well-maintained, modern minibuses serving all the main routes.

CAR & MOTORCYCLE

Rwanda has a reasonable road system, for the most part due to its small size and a large dose of foreign assistance. The only major unsealed roads are those running alongside the shore of Lake Kivu and some smaller stretches around the country.

South Sudan

Includes ➡

Fast Facts

➡ **Capital** Juba (government considering moving the capital further north)

➡ **Population** 8.2 million

➡ **Languages** English, Arabic and numerous tribal languages – Arabic as an official language is being replaced entirely with English.

➡ **Area** 619,745 sq km

➡ **Currency** South Sudan Pound

➡ **Visa Requirements** Best obtained in Nairobi (Kenya), Kampala (Uganda), Washington (USA) or Brussels (Belgium)

The World's Newest Country

On 9 July 2011 Africa's largest country, Sudan, split into two and with that South Sudan, the world's newest country, was born.

The birthing process was a violent and bloody one. For decades the people of South Sudan have known little but war as they fought for independence from the north – and potential visitors should know that fighting between the new government and various rebel groups continues today in many parts of the country.

Today South Sudan is one of the poorest, least-developed and most little-known nations on the planet, but the very fact that fact that South Sudan remains such an unknown is the thing that is likely to attract the first intrepid visitors here. And once they arrive they will be amazed by a wealth of tribal groups and excited by national parks packed with vast numbers of large mammals.

South Sudan Top Sights

➡ **Boma National Park** This vast wilderness is home to huge quantities of wildlife including migrating herds of over a million antelope

➡ **Nimule National Park** Home to hippo, Uganda kob, elephants, buffalo and beautiful scenery

➡ **Bandingalo National Park** A paradise for giraffe, hippo and wild dog, this park also welcomes hundreds of thousands of migrating antelope

➡ **Tribes** Possibly no other corner of Africa has such a wide diversity of tribal peoples, many of whom continue to live a largely traditional lifestyle

➡ **Juba** The capital is a bustling boom town with busy markets and the grave of John Garang, the former leader of the South Sudan independence movement

➡ **Wau** The nation's second city is a tribal meeting point and homeland of the Dinka people

UNDERSTAND SOUTH SUDAN

South Sudan Today

The road to independence for South Sudan has been long and hard. Sudan, formally Africa's largest country, was an ethnic jigsaw comprising hundreds of tribes and languages, but broadly these could have be divided into a black African south and an Arab Islamic north. The people of what is now South Sudan had long complained of discrimination at the hands of the north Sudanese and it was this discrimination that was partially to blame for the fact that for 40 of the past 40 years Sudan had been at war with itself. The war left around two million dead, but with the hammering out of a peace agreement the people of South Sudan went to the polls and in January 2011 voted overwhelmingly for independence from north Sudan.

The independence honeymoon was shortlived. The new government faces a daunting task in building a stable state from almost nothing. On independence South Sudan was ranked one of the poorest, least developed nations on Earth. There are almost no surfaced roads, and outside the main towns virtually no hospitals or medical centres, few schools and little industry. Almost all South Sudanese survive by subsistence agriculture. Violence, or the threat of violence, has continued to grip the country. There's widespread tribal fighting (often over grazing land, water and cattle) that can result in heavy casualties, there are a number of armed rebel groups fighting the government in Juba and, perhaps most worryingly, South Sudan and its old foe Sudan have already come close to all-out war over disputed areas of the shared border (and the oil wealth that lies underneath).

It's not all bad though. South Sudan has oil, and Juba and other urban centres are

COUNTRY COVERAGE

At the time of research very few travellers were heading to South Sudan so we're providing historical and cultural information rather than reviews and listings. A good source of information for on-the-ground travel in South Sudan is Lonely Planet's Thorn Tree online travel forum www.lonelyplanet.com/thorntree. Privately run Juba Travel Guide (www.jubatravelguide.com) is an excellent source of practical travel information for this tourism frontier. Another source of good internet-based information is the Wildlife Conservation Society (www.wcs.org), which can give you a brief low down on some of the national parks in South Sudan. The government of South Sudan's website (www.goss-online.org) has a few pages dedicated to tourism and immigration rules.

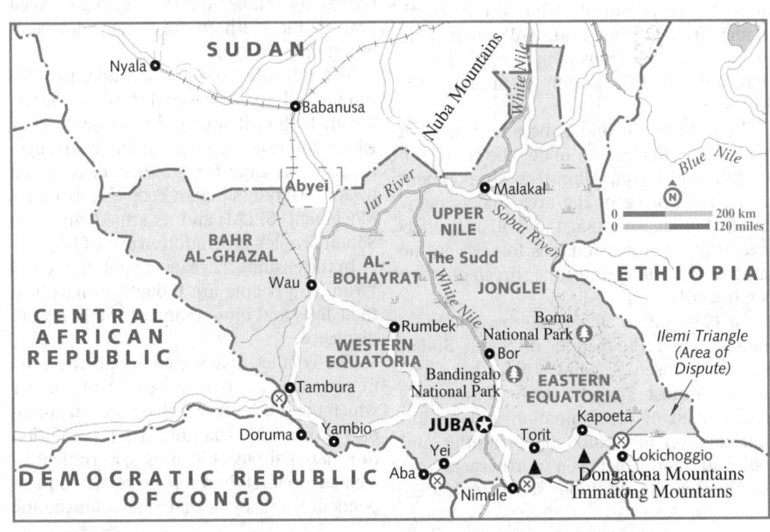

THE GREATEST (WILDLIFE) SHOW ON EARTH

So you've heard all about the wildebeest migration in Kenya and Tanzania and how it's been described as the greatest wildlife show on earth. Well, have you heard about South Sudan's own wildlife migration involving possibly even larger numbers of animals? When the **Wildlife Conservation Society** (WCS; www.wcs.org) conducted aerial surveys of what is now South Sudan in 2007, the last thing they expected to see was migrating herds of over a million white-eared kob, tiang antelope and Mongalla gazelle, but that's exactly what they found. In addition there are thought to be over 8000 elephants, 8900 buffalo and 2800 ostriches as well as lions, leopards, giraffe, hippos and numerous other species.

Looking at how big-buck-spending tourists flock to the national parks of neighbouring Kenya, the new government of South Sudan has not been slow to recognise the tourist goldmine these animals may represent, and it is now trying to promote wildlife-watching tourism. The focus of these efforts is Boma National Park. This huge park, abutting the Ethiopian border, is crawling in mega-fauna. A visit is a real wild adventure to a near-pristine African wilderness. Due to the limited tourist facilities in the park, and throughout rural South Sudan in general, the vast majority of the park's few visitors sign up to one of the trips organised by the couple of safari companies based in Juba.

now rapidly growing boomtowns full of investors from around the world. If South Sudan plays its cards right it could in the short term become a major regional centre and in the long term – well, the sky's the limit.

History

The history of South Sudan is of course very much tied up with that of its northern neighbour Sudan.

We know little of the history of early South Sudan. Around the 1500s Nilotic speakers such as the Dinka and Luo are thought to have moved down into what is now South Sudan from further north. Although there is evidence that transhumant cattle raisers have inhabited the region for around 5000 years.

In 1899 South Sudan became a part of Anglo-Egyptian Sudan under the control of Britain and Egypt. Almost no development at all took place in the area that is today South Sudan, although the British encouraged Christian missionaries to work in the area in order to counter the spread of Islam southwards.

In 1956 Sudan as a whole became independent and the people of South Sudan found themselves being ruled by Khartoum. Almost straight away southerners complained of discrimination and an unfair division of wealth, opportunities and political power between northerners and southerners. In addition, southern leaders accused Khartoum of trying to impose an Islamic and Arabic identity on the south and of reneging on promises to create a federal system.

In 1962 a rebellion originally launched by southern army officers seven years earlier turned into a full-scale civil war against Khartoum led by the Anya Nya guerrilla movement. In 1969 a group of socialist and communist Sudanese military officers led by Colonel Jaafar Muhammad Numeiri seized power in Khartoum. For the people of South Sudan the defining moment of Numeiri's 16 years in power came in 1972 when he signed the Addis Ababa agreement which granted the southern provinces a degree of autonomy.

The future looked bright when, in 1978, the first oil was discovered in South Sudan, but in 1983 civil war broke out again after Khartoum cancelled the autonomy arrangements. This time the southeners were led by John Garang's Sudan People's Liberation Movement (SPLM) and its armed wing, the Sudan People's Liberation Army (SPLA).

In the ensuing 22 years of fighting around 1.5 million people are thought to have lost their lives and more than four million were displaced.

The conflict finally ended with the 2005 Comprehensive Peace Agreement, under which the south was granted regional autonomy along with guaranteed representation in a national power-sharing government as well as a referendum for the south on independence. In July of that year John Garang was sworn in as first vice-president of Sudan, but then, just one month later, he was killed in a plane crash. Many southerners suspected foul play and demonstrations and fighting broke out again. John Garang was replaced by Salva Kiir Mayardiit.

Despite the establishment in Khartoum of a power-sharing government between Omar al-Bashir and Salva Kir, numerous deadly skirmishes occured. The oil-rich state of Abeyi, which sits on the frontier of Sudan and South Sudan is, and continues to be, a particular flash point.

Finally, in January 2011, 99% of southern Sudanese voted in the long-promised referendum to split from the rest of Sudan. In July of that year South Sudan became independent.

Culture

The population of South Sudan is around 8 million. There are numerous ethnic groups speaking around 60 languages. The main ethnic groups are the Dinka, who make up around 15% of the population, the Nuer (around 10%), the Bari and the Azande. Indigenous traditional beliefs are widespread and even though Christianity has made inroads it's still very much a minority religion that's often overlaid with traditional beliefs and customs.

Despite the potential oil wealth the vast majority of South Sudanese live a life of subsistance farming and cattle herding. For many tribes cattle are of huge cultural importance. They are the source of wealth and the key to marriage. A young boy is traditionally given an ox to care for by his father and he is even given a 'bull name', which often relates to the colour of his ox. Many tribes have a large vocabulary for cattle and their different colours. Cattle rustling is very common and clashes between tribal groups occur frequently.

Wildlife & Environment

South Sudan is made up of vast areas of savannah (including the biggest savannah ecosystem in Africa), swamps (the Sudd, a swamp the size of England, is the largest such habitat in Africa) and flood plains interspersed with areas of woodland.

The wildlife of South Sudan has fared the years of war remarkably well, but since the end of the war conservationists have faced a number of challenges in their bid to protect the nation's wildlife. Oil companies are looking for oil in a number of wildlife-rich areas and illegal hunting, farming and construction work is taking place in and around protected zones. A big potential threat is water diversion projects, which could have a dramatic impact on the annual flooding of the White Nile. Fortunately the government has realised the potential value of wildlife tourism and, working alongside international conservation bodies, appear to be serious in its efforts to conserve the environment.

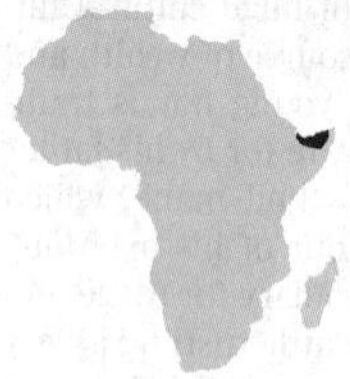

Somaliland

POP 3.5 MILLION

Includes ➡

Best Places to Eat

- ➡ Summer Time Restaurant (p659)
- ➡ Saba (p659)
- ➡ Kulan Art Cafe (p659)
- ➡ Shamaxle Restaurant (p663)

Best Places to Stay

- ➡ Ambassador Hotel Hargeisa (p658)
- ➡ Oriental Hotel (p658)
- ➡ City Plaza Hotel (p662)
- ➡ Maan-Soor Hotel (p658)

Why Go?

While Puntland and Somalia have been sliding towards the abyss and are absolute no-go zones for all Westerners, the self-proclaimed Republic of Somaliland has, like a phoenix, risen from the ashes by restoring law and order within its boundaries. It's slowly emerging as a potential destination for adventurous travellers, with plenty of wonderful surprises. Admire some exceptional rock paintings, feel the pulse of the fast-growing captal, walk along deserted beaches, visit bustling market towns and be awed by stunning landscapes – wherever you go, you'll feel like a pioneer. Its tourist infrastructure is still embryonic but it's this sense of pushing Africa's secret door ajar that makes Somaliland one of the most weirdly fascinating countries you could hope to visit right now. Even if you can't get a cold beer.

When to Go

Hargeisa

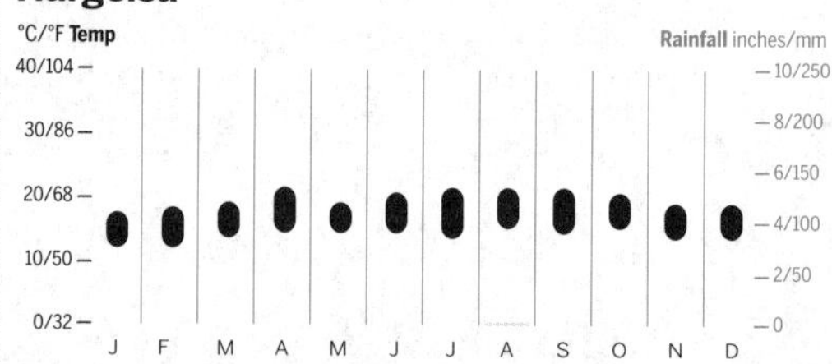

Dec–Mar Best weather: very few rains and cool temperatures.

Apr–Sep Rain in April, May and September makes travel tough. July and August are oppressively hot.

Oct & Nov Weather is mixed, but temperatures make shoulder season a good travel time.

HARGEISA

POP 1.2 MILLION

You'll never forget your first impression of Hargeisa. Sure, the capital of Somaliland still bears the scars of the civil war that destroyed the country in the past decades, but it's a city in transition. The streets are alive, the roads are busy, and the air thick with a very bearable cacophony of vehicle horns and calls to prayer. And it's surprising to see that Hargeisa has all the conveniences a traveller could hope for: good-value hotels with English-speaking staff, a couple of tasty restaurants, internet cafes, electronics stores, tea shops, markets, bus stations, taxis…but no alcohol, and absolutely no nightlife.

Hargeisa lacks standout sights but if you like your markets colourful and clamorous, and enjoy the feeling of being the only tourist wandering its streets, you might just find it appealing.

Sights

Let's be frank: the ambience and the sense of exploration are the pull here. Visually, Hargeisa is fairly underwhelming, with nothing much of interest except perhaps the city's war memorial – a Somali Air Force **MiG jet** (Independence Rd) – and the imposing **Jama Mosque** (Independence Rd).

Central Market MARKET

(off Independence Rd) Hargeisa's centrepiece, the expansive central market is a wonderful (and largely hassle-free) place to experience a typical Somali market. Its lanes hide everything from perfume to household objects, electronic goods, wind-up radios and clothes. The food vendors have some of the most fascinating displays – think pyramids of colourful fruits and vegetables.

Livestock Market MARKET

(daily) An essential part of the Hargeisa experience is the livestock market, which lies on the outskirts of town. It's a fascinating place to wander. Always ask permission before taking photographs.

Sleeping

Hadhwanaag HOTEL $

(521820; s/d US$10/15) As far as Hargeisa prices go, the Hadhwanaag is good value. The low-slung building occupies a leafy compound, a five-minute walk away from

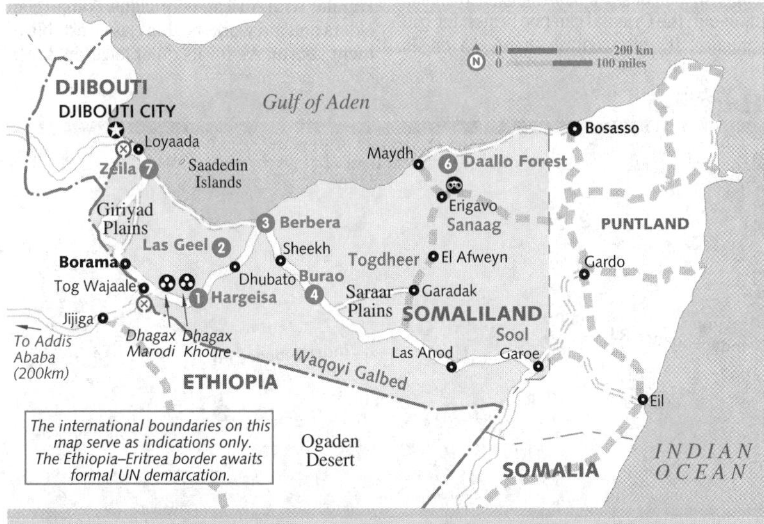

Somaliland Highlights

1. Dream of purchasing your own ship of the desert at the livestock market in **Hargeisa** (p657).
2. Visit one of the world's finest open-air galleries of prehistoric rock art at **Las Geel** (p660).
3. Nurse a soft drink, feast on fresh fish and relax on deserted beaches in **Berbera** (p661).
4. Immerse yourself in the bustling provincial town of **Burao** (p662).

SET YOUR BUDGET

Budget

- Hotel room US$15
- Breakfast US$1.50
- Somali tea US$0.50
- Shared taxi ride US$6

Midrange

- Hotel room US$30
- Bottle of water US$1
- Two-course meal US$3
- Day trip in a private vehicle US$80

Top End

- Hotel room US$50
- Dinner at a hotel restaurant US$6
- 4WD with driver, per day US$150

the main drag. The attention to detail could be sharper (you'll have to ask for a fan) but the rooms are acceptable.

★**Oriental Hotel** HOTEL $$
(☎514999; www.orientalhotelhargeisa.com; off Independence Rd; s/d incl breakfast US$15/30; wi-fi) The closest Hargeisa comes to a travellers hang-out, the Oriental can't be beaten for convenience. It's ultracentral, there's an on-site restaurant and it's nicely laid out, with the reception area opening onto the pleasant sun-filled patio. Rooms are kept clean and functional, with standing fans, hot shower and satellite TV. Service is a bit lackadaisical, though.

Imperial Hotel HOTEL $$
(☎520524; imperialhotelhargeisa@hotmail.com; off Independence Rd; s US$20-25, d US$30; wi-fi) The modernish Imperial Hotel is in a calm neighbourhood, but within walking distance of the centre. Expect well-appointed rooms, working fans, salubrious bathrooms and a restaurant in a shady courtyard at the back.

★**Ambassador Hotel Hargeisa** HOTEL $$$
(☎526666; www.ambassadorhotelhargeisa.com; Airport Rd; s/d incl breakfast US$53/95; P @ wi-fi) A reassuring choice. The squeaky-clean rooms are equipped with everything to ensure a comfortable stay, including satellite TV, glittering bathrooms and a restaurant. Its single drawback is its location away from the central buzz, about 4km from the centre, near the airport.

★**Maan-Soor Hotel** HOTEL $$$
(☎527000; www.maan-soor.com; off Jijiga Yer Rd; s US$35, d US$45-80, incl breakfast; P @ wi-fi) Popular with African politicians, Somali clan elders and aid workers, this classic establishment gets an A+ for its quiet location, green

Hargeisa

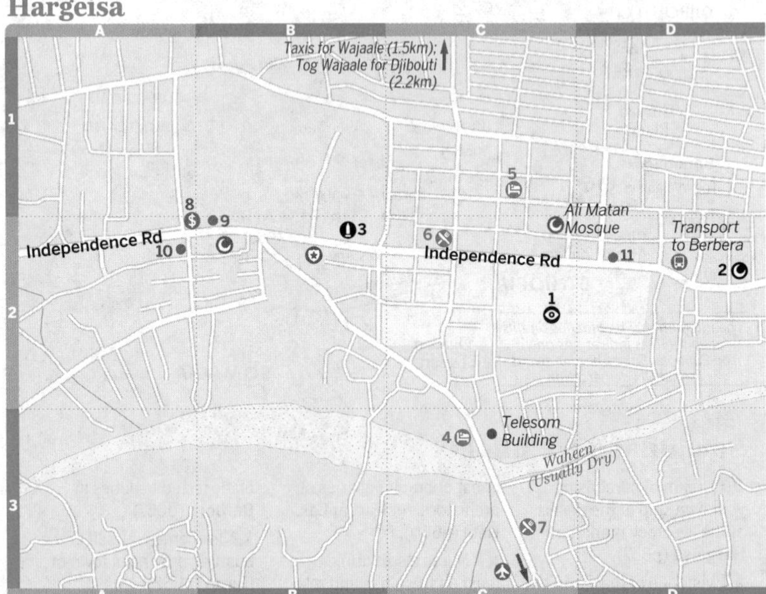

surrounds, well-furnished yet unspectacular rooms and good service. It offers a wide array of facilities (a restaurant, a business centre and a conference hall). Northwest of the centre.

Eating

Many hotels have an on-site restaurant open to nonguests.

Cadaani CAFETERIA $
(Independence Rd; mains US$1-3; breakfast, lunch & dinner) You can't miss this bustling cafeteria – look for the red-and-white building beside Telesom. It rustles up simple dishes, such as spaghetti and sandwiches.

★**Summer Time Restaurant** SOMALI $$
(Jijiga Yer Rd; mains US$2-6; breakfast & dinner) This trendy (for Hargeisa) outfit gets kudos for its expansive menu (written in English) that will satisfy even the pickiest eater. The leaf-dappled outdoor terrace is perfect for escaping sticky Hargeisa on a hot day. Northwest of the centre.

★**Saba** YEMENI $$
(Independence Rd; mains US$4-6; lunch & dinner) You'll leave this excellent restaurant, which specialises in Yemeni dishes, as full as an egg. The *mendi* (lamb) and *hanid* mutton or goat (meat slow-cooked in a beehive oven) are tasty and filling, but leave room for the Yemeni desserts – the *fatamus* (a concoction with banana) and the *fata timir* (a concoction with dates) are finger-licking. West of the centre.

★**Kulan Art Cafe** CAFETERIA $$
(Jijiga Yer Rd; mains US$2-5; breakfast & dinner) Ease into low gear sinking a fruit juice or a Somali tea at this atmospheric cafeteria owned by Kulan, a fashion designer whose shop is just across the street. It's genteel and civilised, and a popular hang-out for well-heeled diaspora Somalilanders. It serves burgers, pastas, kebabs and mouthwatering cakes.

Fish & Steak PIZZERIA $$
(mains US$3-6; breakfast, lunch & dinner) Belying its name, this venture is regarded as the best place in town for a fresh pizza. If pizzas aren't doing it for you, delve into Somali fish and meat dishes. It's in a street running parallel to Independence Rd.

Dalxiis Restaurant SOMALI $$
(mains US$3-5; breakfast & dinner) The Dalxiis is an enticing 'park restaurant', with a gardenlike setting. Get your fingers dirty experimenting with the wide range of Somali dishes, including *geel hanid* (roast camel), basmati rice, mutton and grilled fish.

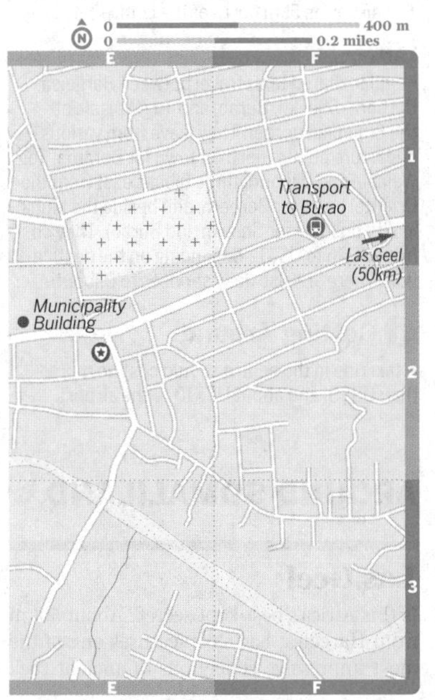

Hargeisa

Sights
1 Central Market C2
2 Jama Mosque D2
3 MiG Jet B2

Activities, Courses & Tours
Dalmar Tours .... (see 5)

Sleeping
4 Hadhwanaag C3
5 Oriental Hotel C1

Eating
6 Cadaani C2
7 Dalxiis Restaurant C3
Hadhwanaag .... (see 4)

Information
8 Dahabshiil A2

Transport
9 African Express Airways B2
10 Daallo Airlines A2
11 Jubba Airways D2

SAFE TRAVEL

Somaliland was safe at the time of writing, and our on-the-ground research included Hargeisa, Las Geel, Berbera, Borama, Zeila, Tog Wajaale, Sheekh, Burao, Erigavo and Maydh. Somaliland is not a destination for first-timers to Africa. Its tourist infrastructure is still embryonic, and despite what officials may claim, there's still an element of uncertainty regarding the security situation. The Somalilanders have established law and order in their separatist territory, but as long as their brothers from Puntland and southern Somalia don't settle for peace, there will be an element of risk – borders are not terrorist-proof.

Although security has improved considerably in previously high-risk areas such as Sanaag province, you should check the situation locally before heading there. All travel in the Sool region is currently unsafe due to conflict in Puntland, which claims this province.

Hadhwanaag SOMALI **$$**
(mains US$2-5) Hadhwanaag is a great place to sample Somali specialities like *loxox* (a pancakelike flat bread with butter and honey), fish dishes, mutton, chicken and roast beef.

Orientation

Shops, businesses and hotels are mostly on or around Independence Rd, which snakes for several kilometres from the western outskirts of town to the east. A fast-growing neighbourhood is on the northwestern edge of the centre, near Jijiga Yer Rd. Most streets don't have names; places are often identified by their proximity to landmarks.

Information

DANGERS & ANNOYANCES

You can explore the city on your own; an escort is not mandatory in the capital. That said, the usual precautions apply. Avoid walking alone at night, don't be ostentatious with valuables and beware of pickpockets in crowded areas.

Always ask permission before taking photographs.

INTERNET ACCESS

There's a profusion of internet cafes in the city centre (about US$0.50 per hour).

MEDICAL SERVICES

There are lots of pharmacies around town.

Edna Adan Hospital (☎4426922; www.ednahospital.org) Has excellent facilities. It's staffed by qualified, English-speaking doctors (mostly volunteers).

MONEY

Most transactions can be conducted using US dollars, but if you want to change money, head to one of the Dahabshiil branches around town. You'll also find plenty of foreign-exchange stalls near the central market. Most hotels also change money and don't take commission. One ATM had just been introduced at the time of writing but it didn't accept foreign cards – check while you're there.

POST & TELEPHONE

There's no post office in Hargeisa. You'll have to use courier services, such as DHL.

Making phone calls is easy and cheap. You can also bring your mobile phone and buy a local SIM card from Telesom or any other mobile phone company.

TOURIST INFORMATION

Hotel owners are the best sources for travel information and can also help with visa matters and escort and car rentals.

Getting There & Away

AIR

The airport is 5km north of the centre.

LAND

Regular shared taxis travel between Hargeisa, Berbera, Sheekh, Burao, and Tog Wajaale at the Ethiopian border. They leave from various departure points (north of town for Borama, Tog Wajaale and Djibouti; three blocks east from the Oriental Hotel for Berbera; and beside the Municipality building for Sheekh and Burao). They cost from US$6 to US$12 depending on the destination. There are also daily services to Djibouti.

Getting Around

A taxi ride in the centre should cost no more than US$3, and about US$10 to the airport.

AROUND SOMALILAND

Las Geel

Is this Africa's best-kept secret? About 50km from Hargeisa, Las Geel features one of the most impressive collections of ancient rock art on the African continent. The poignant paintings, the typical Somali landscape of dry plains covered in acacia shrub, the spectacular granite outcrops and the total lack of crowds make for an eerie ambience that is unforgettable.

This archaeological wonder was only brought to light in 2003, following research conducted by a French team of archaeologists.

Sights

Rock Art Paintings ARCHAEOLOGICAL SITE
(Las Geel; permit US$25; ⏲ dawn-dusk) Hundreds of magnificent neolithic rock art paintings adorn the walls of several interconnected shelters and overhangs on the eastern face of a massive granite outcrop. The paintings contain stylised polychromatic depictions of humans and various animals, notably cows, dogs and a few antelopes, goats and giraffes. The colours are mostly shades of red, ochre, yellow and white. Some paintings exceed 1m in length and their state of preservation is exceptional.

There's a small **museum** at the entrance of the site, immediately below the main rock shelters. It has panels in English.

Getting There & Away

Las Geel is about 50km from Hargeisa, along the road to Berbera (the turn-off is at Dhubato village and Las Geel is about 6km down the road).

There's no public transport to Las Geel. Most travellers visit the site on a half-day trip from Hargeisa or en route to Berbera. Your best bet is to arrange such a trip through your hotel. Hotels charge from US$80 to US$120 per vehicle, which usually includes the cost of the mandatory armed guard (it's wise to double-check, though). If you're travelling solo, try to share costs with other travellers.

Berbera

POP 35,000

The name alone sounds impossibly exotic, conjuring up images of tropical ports, spices and palm oil. The reality is a little more prosaic; today this shady town consists mostly of crumbling buildings and mud-and-thatch houses. There's great potential, though, with superb beaches and a relaxed atmosphere. It's a great place to chill out for a few days.

Sights

Berbera is one of those places where the real attraction is just the overall feel of the place and there actually aren't all that many

TRAVELLING AROUND SOMALILAND

Independent travel is possible in Somaliland, but there are restrictions. Local authorities take the safety of Westerners very seriously, to the point of being overprotective, following the belief that if foreigners were to encounter a 'problem', the diplomatic efforts of the country to gain international recognition would be ruined.

In principle, foreigners are required to travel accompanied by a member of the Special Protection Unit (SPU) outside Hargeisa, whether you travel on public transport or private car with driver. If you don't have a soldier with you, you'll be turned back at checkpoints. That said, this rule is ambiguous and erratically enforced. We were told that foreigners are permitted to travel without an SPU officer between Hargeisa, Berbera and Burao, and between Hargeisa and the Ethiopian and Djiboutian borders. However, prior to leaving Hargeisa, it's a good idea to meet the Police Commissioner Secretary at the Somaliland Police Force Headquarters (south of Independence Rd), who will either issue a waiver letter on the spot or give a call to the soldiers at checkpoints so that they let you through. In theory, you are allowed to use public transport between these towns. For all parts of the country east of Burao, you must have SPU protection and travel in a private vehicle.

All hotels can arrange SPU protection. It costs about US$20 per day for a soldier, plus food.

It also helps at checkpoints if you have an official form from the **Ministry of Commerce, Industry & Tourism** (☎440148, 4014801; south of Independence Rd; ⏲7am-noon Sat-Thu), in Hargeisa, that lists all the places you intend to visit in the country. For Las Geel and all travel east of Burao, this form is mandatory. Get there in the morning, fill in the form, fork out US$25 and it's issued on the spot. It's on a side street near Imperial Hotel.

VISITING LAS GEEL

You'll need a private vehicle (with driver) and an armed guard to get there, both easily arranged in Hargeisa. You'll also need a permit (US$25) from the Ministry of Commerce, Industry & Tourism (p661) – get there in the morning and it'll be issued on the spot. You'll have to present it to the guard at the entrance of the site.

'sights' to tick off. Having said that there is an array of pre-20th-century buildings dotted around the historic centre. You'll see a few remarkable examples of **mansions** dating back to the Ottoman era as well as venerable old mosques. Sadly, these fragile architectural beauties are gradually disintegrating due to a lack of funds.

You can also delve into the small **market** area and soak up the atmosphere. The tiny fishing harbour deserves a few photo snaps (but ask permission first).

Towards the commercial port, the **Ottoman Mosque**, with its balconied minaret, is worth a peek. To visit the port you must have permission from the Municipality and the harbourmaster.

Berbera is also bound by sweeping beaches, about 3km from the centre, including **Baathela Beach**, just in front of Maan-Soor Hotel. At dawn, dolphins can be seen frolicking in the bay.

Sleeping & Eating

Yaxye HOTEL $

(☎4410098, 740577; s with fan US$7-10, with air-con US$25, d with air-con US$25; ❄📶) The Yaxye feels a little more modern than its equivalents elsewhere in the centre. Rooms are simple but tidy and quite spacious considering the price. The upstairs rooms catch cool breezes and salty scents.

Al Madiina Hotel HOTEL $

(☎740254; r with fan US$3-6, with air-con US$30; ❄) Right in the centre, this venture doesn't feel the need for fancy touches and what you see is what you get, which in this case is a bed plonked in a threadbare room. A couple of rooms have private bathrooms.

Esco Hotel HOTEL $

(☎740121; r with fan & without bathroom US$7, with air-con & bathroom US$30; ❄📶) Fine in a pinch, the Esco has bare but acceptable rooms with furniture you would be happy to find at a flea market. Rooms vary in size, layout and plumbing quality so scope out a few before committing yourself.

Maan-Soor Hotel HOTEL $$$

(☎4244240; www.maan-soor.com; s/d incl breakfast US$50/60; P❄📶) This venture consists of a handful of square 'cottages' scattered around a large property just spitting distance from Baathela Beach. Rooms are impersonal but crisp and comfortable. Note that they don't face the sea. This hotel does struggle to find much personality beyond its slightly dour exterior. It's about 3km from the centre.

Al Xayaat Restaurant & Fish House SEAFOOD $$

(☎740224; mains US$3-5; ⏲breakfast, lunch & dinner) Lap up a reviving fruit juice and scoff a piece of grilled fish at this colourful eatery overlooking the bay and you'll leave with a smile on your face. While eating you'll be surrounded by a menagerie of cats, crows and seagulls expecting a titbit. Ali, the amiable owner, speaks good English.

Xeeb Soor SEAFOOD $$

(mains US$3-5; ⏲breakfast, lunch & dinner) Facing the bay, the Xeeb Soor enjoys outdoor seating. There are good rice dishes and a variety of tasty fishes straight from the fishing harbour.

Getting There & Away

Regular shared taxis travel between Hargeisa and Berbera (US$6, 150km) and between Burao and Berbera (US$4).

Burao

POP 200,000

The capital of Todgheer province and the second-largest city in the country, Burao feels a bit rougher around the edges than Berbera or Hargeisa, but that's part of the adventure. There's nothing of interest here, but you can soak up the atmosphere at the livestock market (and enjoy being the focus of attention).

Sleeping & Eating

★**City Plaza Hotel** HOTEL $$

(☎710658, 4315217; www.buraocityplazahotel.com; s/d US$21/23; P❄📶) The City Plaza is a low-slung compound of cottages scattered amid a leafy garden full of birdsong. Rooms are well appointed and cleaned with soldierly precision. Amenities include a restaurant (mains US$3 to US$5). It's in a quiet area, about 3km out of town along the road to Erigavo.

Deero Hotel & Restaurant HOTEL $$
(☎714499, 712299; s/d US$10/15; 📶) Central hotel and eatery featuring well-maintained rooms with good beds and a rooftop restaurant which trots out fish and meat dishes.

★**Shamaxle Restaurant** SOMALI $$
(⏲lunch & dinner) The location, in a leafy compound right by the Togdheer River, is top-notch. And the juicy lamb *hanid* will have your tastebuds leaping for joy.

Getting There & Away

Shared taxis leave for Hargeisa (US$12, 260km) via Berbera (120km).

UNDERSTAND SOMALILAND

Somaliland Today

Somaliland is eager to confirm its status as a functioning democracy. The second presidential elections took place in 2010, and municipal elections were held in late 2012 without trouble.

Somaliland has a fragile economy that is based on agriculture and pastoralism – it's compounded by the fact that the diplomatic isolation of the country and its nonrecognition restrict foreign investment and access to loans. Expat Somalilanders have started to invest massively in the capital in recent years. But what could really give a new impetus to the country is oil exploration; eastern Somaliland is said to be rich in oil resources.

History

Originally, Somalis probably hail from the southern Ethiopian highlands, and have been subject to a strong Arabic influence since the 7th century when the Somali coast formed part of the extensive Arab-controlled trans-Indian Ocean trading network.

In the 19th century much of the Ogaden Desert – ethnically a part of Somalia – was annexed by Ethiopia (an invasion that has been a source of bad blood ever since) and in 1888 the country was divided by European powers. The French got the area around Djibouti, Britain much of the north, while Italy took Puntland and the south. Sayid Maxamed Cabdulle Xasan (known affectionately as 'the Mad Mullah') fought the British for two decades, but it wasn't until 1960 that Somaliland, Puntland and southern Somalia were united.

Interclan tensions, radical socialism, rearmament by the USSR and the occasional (often disastrous) war with Ethiopia tore the country apart. Mohammed Siad Barre, Somalia's last recognised leader, fled to Nigeria in 1991 after the forces of General Aideed took Mogadishu. At the same time the Somali National Movement (SNM) declared independence for Somaliland. Puntland also broke away.

While fierce battles between warring factions plagued southern Somalia throughout the 1990s, Somaliland has remained largely peaceful and stable since 1991, thanks mainly to the predominance of a single clan (the Isaq). Somaliland has great oil and gas potential and voted for complete independence in 1997 before holding free presidential elections in 2003. However, Somaliland is not officially recognised as a separate state by the international community, the main reason being that the UN still hopes for a peace agreement covering all of Somalia. As well, its other neighbours are wary of an independent Somaliland, fearing a potential 'Balkanisation' of the Horn.

However, unlike the rest of Somalia, Somaliland has established law and order. Expat Somalilanders continue to try to influence diplomatic corps in Europe, East Africa and North America. Somaliland's leaders have nurtured good relations with Kenya, Ethiopia, France, the UK, Germany and Norway, and seem to be backed by the African Union.

In 2003 their efforts were partly ruined when 'terrorists' from Mogadishu illegally entered Somaliland and shot dead several aid workers with the aim of destabilising the fledgling country and causing it to lose its credibility on the international scene. As a result, local authorities tend to be overprotective of foreigners once they venture outside the capital. In October 2008 another group of terrorists from Mogadishu carried out suicide bombings in Hargeisa. The targets included the presidency, the Ethiopian Liaison Office and one UN office.

Culture

The clan structure is the main pillar of Somali culture, which partly explains why the ideal of a modern 'state' was hard to implement here. Somalis all hail from the same tribe, which is divided into six main clans and loads of subclans. This interclan rivalry has fuelled two decades of conflict.

Well over a million Somalis are scattered across Europe, North America and the Middle East; together they send hundreds of millions of dollars back to Somaliland each year.

All Somalis are Sunni Muslims and Islam is extremely important to the Somali sense of national identity. Most women wear headscarves, and arranged marriage is still the norm in rural areas.

Somalis have a tremendous oral (often poetic) tradition. Written Somali is a very young language (the Somali Latin script was established in 1973) and spelling variations, especially place names, are very common.

Food & Drink

Goat and camel meat are popular dishes in Somaliland. The standard breakfast throughout the country is fried liver with onions and *loxox*, a flat bread similar to the Ethiopian *injera* accompanied with honey, sugar and tea. Rice and noodles are also common staples.

Tea is the favourite drink. Goat or camel's milk is widespread. Alcohol is strictly prohibited and not available.

SURVIVAL GUIDE

Directory A–Z

ACCOMMODATION

Accommodation in Somaliland is generally good value compared to neighbouring countries. Hargeisa has the widest choice of available options.

In larger towns you can find at least one comfortable midrange option with reliable hot shower, air-con and wireless internet.

Upmarket hotels are confined to the capital.

All places to stay quote their prices in US dollars. Note that payment is by cash only.

EMBASSIES & CONSULATES

Ethiopian Liaison Office (south of Independence Rd; 8.30am-noon Mon-Thu & Sat) This is the only official foreign representation in Somaliland. It's not signed; it's on a backstreet not far from the Ministry of Finance.

INSURANCE

It's worth checking your insurance to ensure you're covered in case of emergency while travelling around Somaliland.

INTERNET ACCESS

Internet cafes can be found in all major towns.

An increasing number of hotels, including budget and midrange places, have complimentary wi-fi.

Connection speeds vary from pretty good to acceptable.

MONEY

Somaliland's currency is the Somaliland shilling (SlSh). There are bills of SlSh500 and SlSh1000.

Your best bet is to carry considerable amounts of US dollars (vastly preferable to euros) that can be exchanged for shillings in hotels, shops and bureaus de change; payment in US dollars is accepted everywhere. Bring a good stash of smaller denomination bills.

At the time of writing one ATM was being installed in Hargeisa, and there were plans to introduce more ATMs in the city. Don't get too excited, though – there's no guarantee that they will work with all foreign credit cards; check while in Hargeisa.

If you need to wire money, you'll find **Dahabshiil** (www.dahabshiil.com), **Western Union**

SOMALILAND LIAISON OFFICES

Somaliland Liaison Offices abroad include the following:

- **Djibouti** (21358758; Ave F d'Esperey, Djibouti City)
- **Ethiopia** (0116-635921; btwn Bole Rd & Cameroon St, Addis Ababa)
- **France** (0950815094, 0617677075; wakiil_sl_fr@hotmail.fr; 19 rue Augustin Thierry, 75019 Paris)
- **UK** (0207-7027064; contact@somaliland-mission.com; 319 Waterlily Business Centre, 10 Cleveland Way, London E1 4UF)
- **USA** (202-587-5743; www.somaliland.us; 1425 K Street, NW, Washington, DC 20005)

(www.westernunion.com) and **WorldRemit** (www.worldremit.com) offices in Hargeisa.

OPENING HOURS

Friday is the weekly holiday for offices and most shops.

Businesses Open from 7.30am to 1.30pm and 4pm to 6.30pm Saturday to Thursday.

Government offices Open 8am to 12.30pm and 4pm to 6pm Saturday to Thursday.

Restaurants Breakfast from 6.30am, lunch from 11.30am, dinner 6.30pm to 9pm.

PUBLIC HOLIDAYS

As well as major Islamic holidays, these are the principal public holidays in Somaliland:

Restoration of Somaliland Sovereignty 18–19 May

Independence Day 26 June

TELEPHONE

- The international dialling code for Somaliland is +2522.
- There are several private telephone companies in Somaliland including Telesom and Somtel.
- International telephone calls made from Somaliland are the cheapest in Africa (less than US$0.20 per minute).
- Mobile-phone coverage is good and being continuously expanded as new phone towers are built.
- Mobile-phone users can use their phones in Somaliland. If you have a GSM phone that is unlocked you can purchase a new SIM card for it from any Telesom or Somtel branch. This gives you a local number to call from and is much cheaper in the long run compared to global roaming.

VISAS

You will need a visa to enter Somaliland. Visas are not issued at the airport.

The most convenient place to get a visa is Addis Ababa in Ethiopia. They are issued while you wait through the Somaliland Liaison Office and cost US$40 for a one-month visa. Visas can also be obtained in Djibouti, the UK, the USA and France; visa fees cost about US$40, although requirements tend to vary arbitrarily from one Liaison Office to another (US$80 in the USA).

Another option is to go through a local sponsor, such as a hotel. Email them the (scanned) ID pages of your passport and allow least three days. They will email a visa certificate back to you as an attached document. Print it and present it upon arrival at the airport (or at any land border). Note that this is a certificate; the original visa should have been deposited at the immigration office at the airport (or at the border crossing, if you arrive by land) by your sponsor. In many cases your sponsor will be waiting for you at the airport with the original visa. If you plan to enter Somaliland at Tog Wajaale (from Ethiopia), ask your sponsor to send the original visa to the Somaliland border post (your sponsor will put it in an envelope and give it to a reputable taxi driver heading to Tog Wajaale). Hotels charge US$20 to US$50 for the service.

PRACTICALITIES

- **Electricity** 220V, 50Hz, with square three-pin sockets as used in the UK.
- **Language** Written Somali is a very young language. English is widely used in Somaliland.
- **Newspapers** Somaliland Times (www.somalilandtimes.net) is an independent weekly English newspaper.
- **TV** Horn Cable TV (www.hctv.tv) is the major private television station and has programs in English

Visas for Onward Travel

The Ethiopian Liaison Office (p664) can issue Ethiopian visas. You'll need two photos, US$20 and a letter from the **Immigration Department Office Headquarters** (north of Independence Rd; ⏰8am-noon Sat-Thy), though this letter is not always required by the Ethiopian officer. The whole process should take less than a day provided you arrive early in the morning.

ℹ Getting There & Away

AIR

Somaliland has two international gateways for arrival by air: Hargeisa Egal International Airport (HGA) and Berbera International Airport (BBO). Hargeisa is the busiest. Note that Hargeisa airport was closed for renovation at the time of writing – all international flights were landing at Berbera, from where passengers were bused to Hargeisa.

The most common routes are from Djibouti or Addis Ababa, Ethiopia. If you're coming from Australasia, your best bet is to fly to Dubai and find an onward connection to Djibouti (and on to Hargeisa) or to Berbera.

The following airlines fly to and from Hargeisa (or Berbera), and have offices in Hargeisa.

African Express Airways (☎523646; www.africanexpress.co.ke; Independence Rd)

Daallo Airlines (☎300063, 523003; www.daallo.com; Independence Rd)

Ethiopian Airlines (www.flyethiopian.com)

Jubba Airways (☎524022; www.jubba-airways.com; Independence Rd)

LAND

Djibouti

The land border between Somaliland and Djibouti is open. Shared taxis (usually 4WDs) ply the route on a daily basis from Hargeisa to Djibouti City – a strenuous 16- to 20-hour journey on a dirt road (about US$30; US$40 for the front seat). Taxis usually leave Hargeisa around 4pm so as to travel by night and avoid the scorching heat. They drive in convoy – a matter of survival in case of a breakdown in this desolate area. Bring food and plenty of water. The border crossing is at Loyaada.

Ethiopia

A significant proportion of visitors to Somaliland travel overland from Ethiopia. From Jijiga in eastern Ethiopia there's regular bus traffic to the border town of Tog Wajaale. In Tog Wajaale, take a shared taxi (about US$7, two hours) to Hargeisa, about 90km to the southeast. Ask to be dropped in front of your hotel. You can expect a couple of checkpoints, but no hassle

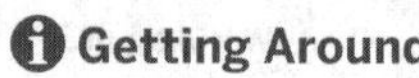

Getting Around

BUS

Medium-sized buses and crowded 4WDs service routes between Hargeisa and major settlements, including Berbera, Borama, Sheekh and Burao.

CAR

You can hire a taxi for about US$70 per day (fuel and escort are extra) or a 4WD with driver for about US$150. Hotels can help with logistics.

TOURS

There are a few tour operators in Hargeisa. Don't expect fully fledged outfits or Kenya-style safari companies, though – you'll be most likely dealing with a one-person operation or a freelance guide who will arrange car rental and SPU protection when required, and will accompany you to the Somaliland Police Force Headquarters and the Ministry of Commerce, Industry & Tourism.

Dalmar Tours (☎514999, 4129334; www.dalmartours.com; Oriental Hotel, Hargeisa) Based

THE CASE OF PUNTLAND & SOMALIA

Since 1991 the country that is still known as 'Somalia' has effectively been a patchwork state, with three countries stitched into one: Somalia in the south, Somaliland in the northwest on the Gulf of Aden, and Puntland perched in the northeast corner. The internal situation in each zone is radically different.

Forming the tip of the Horn of Africa, Puntland is the easternmost region of the continent. It broke away from Somalia and declared itself an autonomous state in 1998. It did reasonably well up until 2001, when President Colonel Yusuf refused to stand down after losing an election, a point he reinforced by waging a little war. But the central government was too weak and Puntland started to descend into violence and anarchy.

Puntland is now at odds with neighbouring Somaliland: there are territorial disputes over several border provinces, which translate into sporadic fighting, especially in the Sool, southern and eastern Sanaag regions, all of which currently lie in Somaliland, but are claimed by Puntland. The biggest issue is piracy, though; over the last few years, piracy has exploded in the waters off the coast of Puntland, and it's now the region's most profitable industry. Despite the presence of US and French warships in the area, dozens of vessels are hijacked each year by pirates operating from Puntland.

In southern Somalia, the law of the gun, kidnapping of foreigners, banditry, food shortages, fighting among rival factions, suicide bombings and a host of humanitarian crises have created a postapocalyptic feel for two decades. However, a turning point came in 2012 when the African Union mission (Amisom), based in Mogadishu since 2007, defeated the Islamist militias that controlled major cities, including Mogadishu and Kismayu. Islamist insurgents still exert control in southern Somalia's rural areas but have lost their once-powerful grip on the country. In September 2012, Hassan Cheikh Mohamud was elected president of Somalia by the Somali Federal Parliament in a democratic process backed by the UN. This largely trouble-free election was followed by the establishment of the first permanent, representative government in Somalia since 1991. In early January 2013 the newly elected president was received at the White House by Barack Obama.

Despite these few positive signs, Lonely Planet was not able to do on-the-ground research in southern Somalia and Puntland, which were an absolute no-go zone for Westerners at the time of writing.

> **DEPARTURE & ARRIVAL TAX**
>
> International departure tax is US$41, payable in cash. Arrival tax is US$33. You'll also have to change US$50 at Hargeisa airport.

at the Oriental Hotel, Dalmar is quite used to dealing with foreign visitors. Uses selected 4WDs with drivers and can organise day trips to Las Geel (US$125) and longer expeditions.

Nature Somaliland (☎4138813; abdi.jama@ymail.com) Specialises in birdwatching expeditions, but can also arrange all kinds of trips in the country.

Safari Somaliland Travel Tourism and Culture (☎4478201, 79152047; www.safarisomalilandtour.com) Friendly Mohamed Abdirizak works as a freelance guide and can help with logistics.

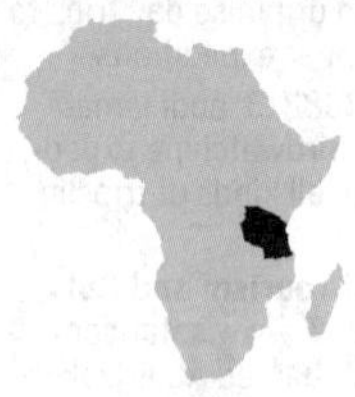

Tanzania

POP 23.5 MILLION

Includes ➡

Best of Nature

- ➡ Serengeti National Park (p700)
- ➡ Ngorongoro Crater (p700)
- ➡ Selous Game Reserve (p707)
- ➡ Ruaha National Park (p706)
- ➡ Mahale Mountains National Park (p705)

Best of Culture

- ➡ Arusha Cultural Tourism (p692)
- ➡ Usambara Mountains (p687)
- ➡ Zanzibar Archipelago (p676)
- ➡ Dar es Salaam Cultural Tourism (p676)
- ➡ Iringa Town (p705)

Why Go?

Tanzania is *the* land of safaris, with wildebeest stampeding across the plains, hippos jostling for space in rivers, elephants kicking up the dust and chimpanzees swinging through the treetops.

Tanzania's magical Indian Ocean coastline also entrances, with its tranquil islands, long beaches and sleepy villages steeped in centuries of Swahili culture. Coconut palms sway in the breeze, dhows glide by on the horizon, and colourful fish flit past spectacular corals in the turquoise waters.

More than anything, though, it is Tanzania's people that make a visit so memorable, with their characteristic warmth and politeness, and the dignity and beauty of their cultures. Chances are you will want to come back for more, to which most Tanzanians would say '*karibu tena*' (welcome again).

When to Go

Dodoma

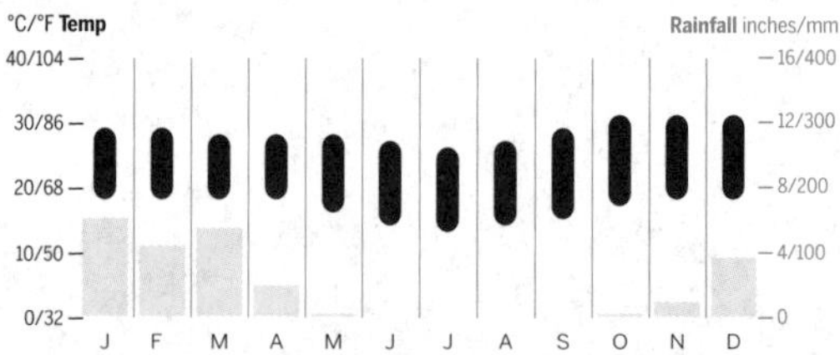

Mar–May Heavy rains bring green landscapes, lower prices, top-notch birding and muddy roads.

Jun–Aug The weather is cool and dry throughout, and wildlife watching is at its prime.

Sep–Oct The weather continues dry, and wildlife watching remains good, without the crowds.

DAR ES SALAAM

Dar es Salaam is Tanzania's major city and its capital in everything but name. Yet, despite its size, 'Dar' is a down-to-earth place, with a picturesque seaport, an intriguing mix of African, Arabic and Indian influences, and enough historic buildings, shops and restaurants to keep you busy for several days.

Sights & Activities

National Museum MUSEUM
(☎022-211 7508; Shaaban Robert St; adult/student Tsh6500/2600; ⏰9.30am-6pm) Dar's premier museum houses the famous fossil discoveries from Olduvai Gorge (only a copy is available for general viewing) and displays on the precolonial and colonial periods.

Village Museum MUSEUM
(☎022-270 0437; cnr New Bagamoyo Rd & Makaburi St; adult/student Tsh6500/2600; ⏰9.30am-6pm) The centrepiece of this open-air museum is a collection of authentically constructed dwellings illustrating traditional life in various parts of Tanzania. Traditional music and dance performances are held some afternoons. It's 10km north of the city centre; catch a Mwenge *dalla-dalla* (minibus) from New Posta transport stand (Tsh300, 45 minutes).

Tours

Afriroots CYCLING, WALKING
(☎0732-926350; www.afriroots.co.tz) Budget cycling, hiking and camping in and around Dar es Salaam.

Authentic Tanzania TRAVEL AGENCY
(☎0786-019965, 0784-972571; www.authentictanzania.com) Good-value southern circuit and southern coast itineraries.

Foxes African Safaris TRAVEL AGENCY
(☎in Tanzania 0784-237422, in UK 01452-862288; www.tanzaniasafaris.info)

Tent with a View TRAVEL AGENCY
(☎022-211 0507, 0713-323318; www.saadani.com)

Wild Things Safaris TRAVEL AGENCY
(☎0773-503502; www.wildthingsafaris.com)

Sleeping

It's cheaper to stay in the city centre and more convenient if you're relying on public transport. There's a range of pricier hotels on Msasani Peninsula.

SET YOUR BUDGET

Budget

- Double hotel room US$50
- Two-course dinner US$10
- Coffee US$2
- Bus Maputo–Inhambane US$20

Midrange

- Double hotel room US$50–150
- Two-course dinner US$10–20
- Beer US$2
- Car rental US$85 per day

Top End

- Double hotel room from US$150
- Two-course dinner US$20
- Glass of wine US$4
- Return flight Pemba–Ibo US$310

YWCA HOSTEL $
(☎0713-622707; Maktaba St; s/d from Tsh15,000/20,000) Just up from the post office in a central, noisy location, this is a good budget deal. Rooms have fan and clean shared bathrooms. The attached restaurant serves inexpensive lunches.

YMCA HOSTEL $
(☎022-213 5457, 0755-066643; Upanga Rd; r Tsh25,000) No-frills rooms in a small compound around the corner from the YWCA.

Econolodge HOTEL $
(☎022-211 6048/9; econolodge@raha.com; Band St; s/d/tr from Tsh22,000/30,000/40,000; ❄) Clean, bland rooms in an aesthetically unappealing high-rise on a tiny side street in the heart of Kisutu.

Safari Inn HOTEL $
(☎022-213 8101, 0784-303478; safari-inn@lycos.com; Band St; s/d with fan Tsh24,000/30,000, with air-con Tsh28,000/35,000; ❄@) A popular travellers' haunt in Kisutu, although there are no mosquito nets and no food.

Sleep Inn HOTEL $$
(☎022-212 7340/1, 0784-233455; www.sleepinnhoteltz.com; Jamhuri St; s/d US$55/65; ❄@📶) This good-value high-rise has a convenient location in the heart of the Asian Quarter and clean rooms with fan, air-con, refrigerator and small double bed.

Tanzania Highlights

1. Marvelling at nature's rhythms on the **Serengeti Plains** (p700)
2. Scaling the heights of **Mt Kilimanjaro** (p690) or hiking on its lower slopes
3. Watching an Indian Ocean moonrise, losing yourself in Zanzibar's Stone Town and exploring Pemba's hidden corners on the **Zanzibar Archipelago** (p676)
4. Browsing colourful markets, and spotting elephants amid Ruaha National Park's baobabs in the **Southern Highlands** (p140)
5. Enjoying the rolling hill panoramas, hiking and local culture of northeastern Tanzania's **Usambara Mountains** (p687)
6. Discovering Swahili culture, and boating past grunting hippos in **southeastern Tanzania** (p707)
7. Seeing chimpanzees up close, and exploring Lake Tanganyika's shoreline in **western Tanzania** (p704)

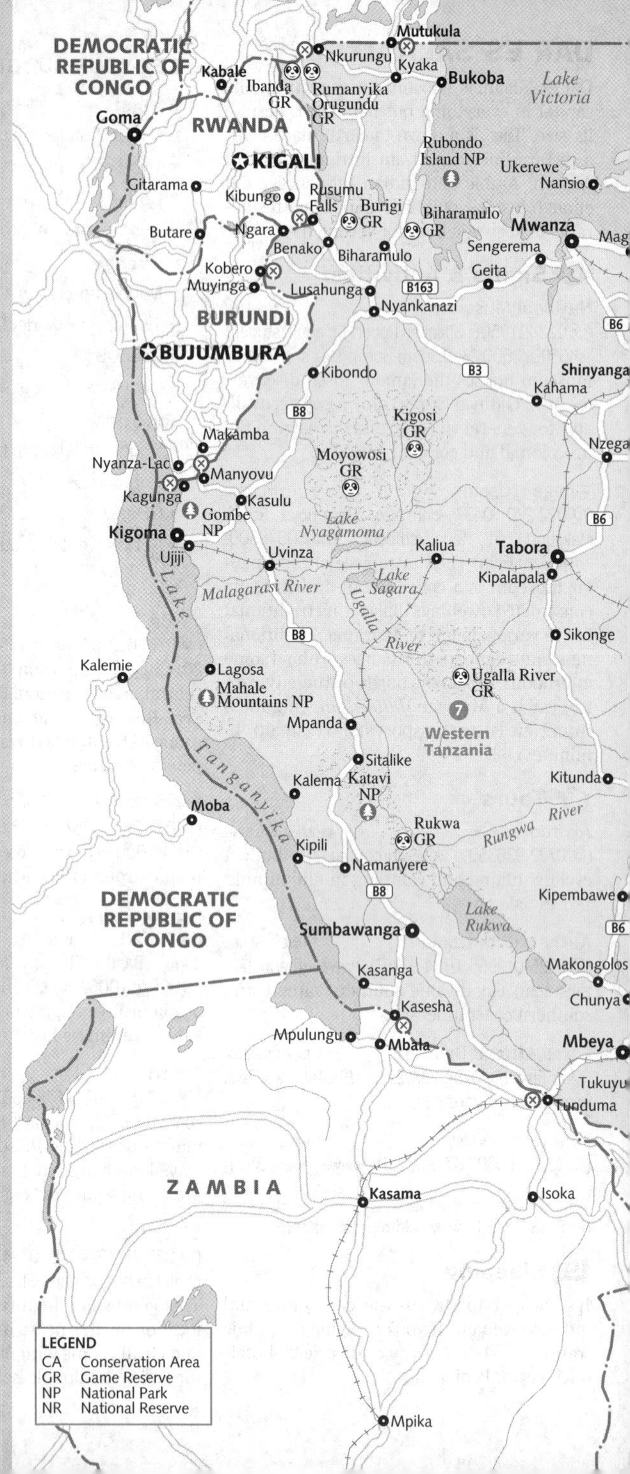

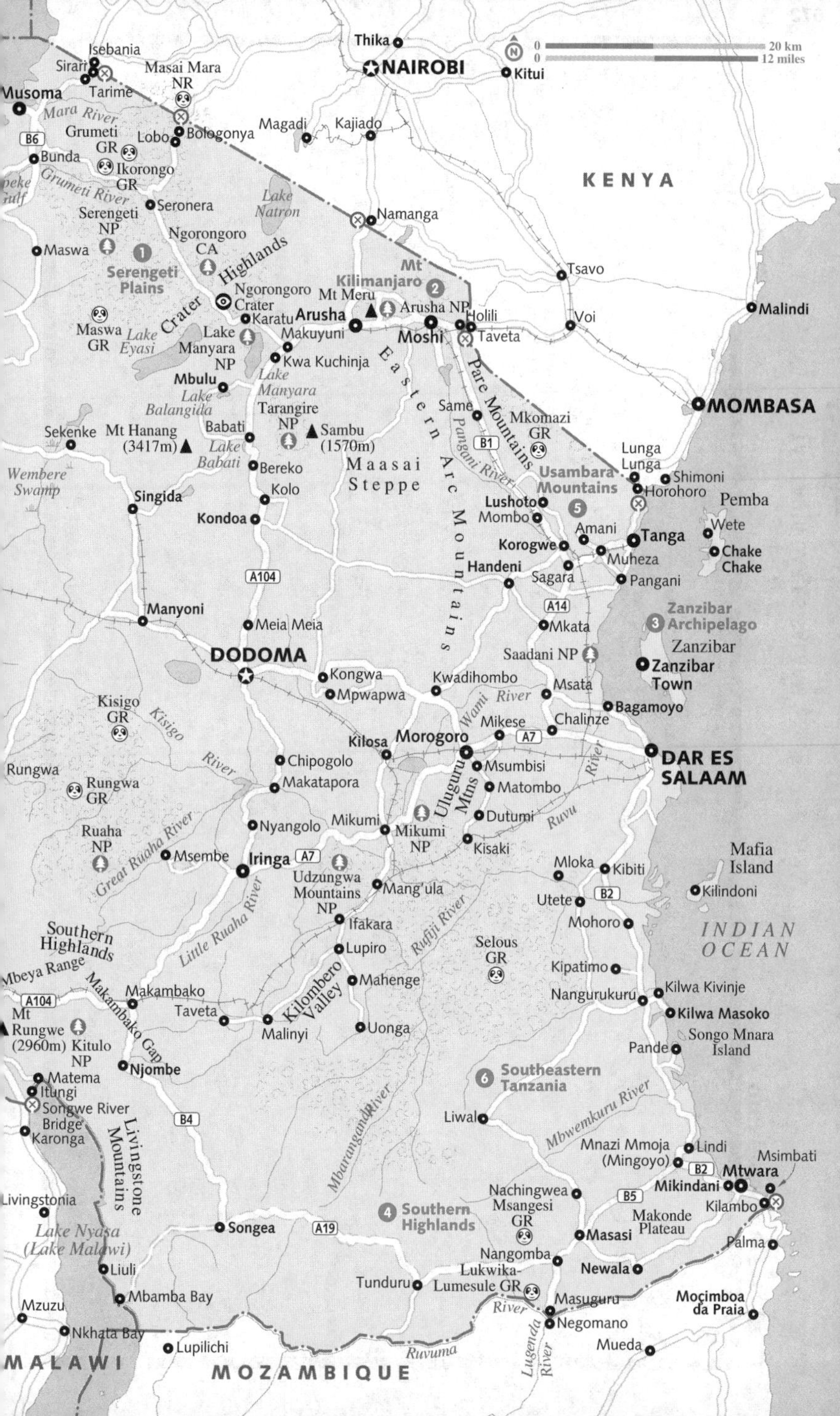

NAIROBI
Thika
Kitui
KENYA
Isebania
Sirari
Tarime
Musoma
Masai Mara NR
Mara River
Grumeti GR
Ikorongo GR
Lobo
Bologonya
Magadi
Kajiado
Bunda
Grumeti River
Seronera
Serengeti NP
Lake Natron
Namanga
Maswa
Ngorongoro CA
Serengeti Plains
Crater Highlands
Ngorongoro Crater
Karatu
Mt Kilimanjaro
Mt Meru
Arusha NP
Arusha
Moshi
Holili
Taveta
Tsavo
Voi
Malindi
MOMBASA
Maswa GR
Lake Eyasi
Lake Manyara NP
Makuyuni
Kwa Kuchinja
Eastern Arc Mountains
Pare Mountains
Mbulu
Lake Manyara
Lake Balangida
Tarangire NP
Same
Mkomazi GR
Sekenke
Mt Hanang (3417m)
Babati
Lake Babati
Sambu (1570m)
Pangani River
B1
Lunga Lunga
Shimoni
Horohoro
Wembere Swamp
Bereko
Maasai Steppe
Usambara Mountains
Pemba
Singida
Kolo
Lushoto
Mombo
Kondoa
Amani
Tanga
Wete
Korogwe
Muheza
Chake Chake
Handeni
Sagara
Pangani
A104
A14
Zanzibar Archipelago
Manyoni
Meia Meia
Mkata
Zanzibar
DODOMA
Saadani NP
Zanzibar Town
Kongwa
Kwadihombo
Msata
Mpwapwa
Wami River
Bagamoyo
Kisigo GR
Kisigo River
Mikese
Chalinze
Kilosa
Morogoro
A7
DAR ES SALAAM
Rungwa
Chipogolo
Msumbisi
Rungwa GR
Makatapora
Uluguru Mtns
Matombo
Dutumi
Ruvu River
Nyangolo
Mikumi
Mikumi NP
Ruaha NP
Great Ruaha River
Msembe
Iringa
Kisaki
Mafia Island
Mloka
Kibiti
Udzungwa Mountains NP
Mang'ula
Utete
B2
Kilindoni
Little Ruaha River
Ifakara
Rufiji River
Mohoro
INDIAN OCEAN
Southern Highlands
Selous GR
Lupiro
Mbeya Range
Makambako Gap
Mahenge
Kipatimo
Kilombero Valley
Kilwa Kivinje
Makambako
Nangurukuru
Kilwa Masoko
Mt Rungwe (2960m)
Kitulo NP
Taveta
Malinyi
Uonga
Songo Mnara Island
Pande
Njombe
Matema
Itungi
Southeastern Tanzania
Songwe River Bridge
Karonga
Livingstone Mountains
B4
Mbarangandu River
Liwale
Mbwemkuru River
Mnazi Mmoja (Mingoyo)
Lindi
Msimbati
Mtwara
Mikindani
Nachingwea
Msangesi GR
B5
Kilambo
Livingstonia
Southern Highlands
Makonde Plateau
Songea
A19
Masasi
Lake Nyasa (Lake Malawi)
Nangomba
Palma
Liuli
Lukwika-Lumesule GR
Newala
Tunduru
Mbamba Bay
Masuguru
Mocimboa da Praia
Mzuzu
River
Negomano
Nkhata Bay
Lupilichi
Ruvuma
Lugenda River
Mueda
MALAWI
MOZAMBIQUE
20 km
12 miles

Central Dar es Salaam

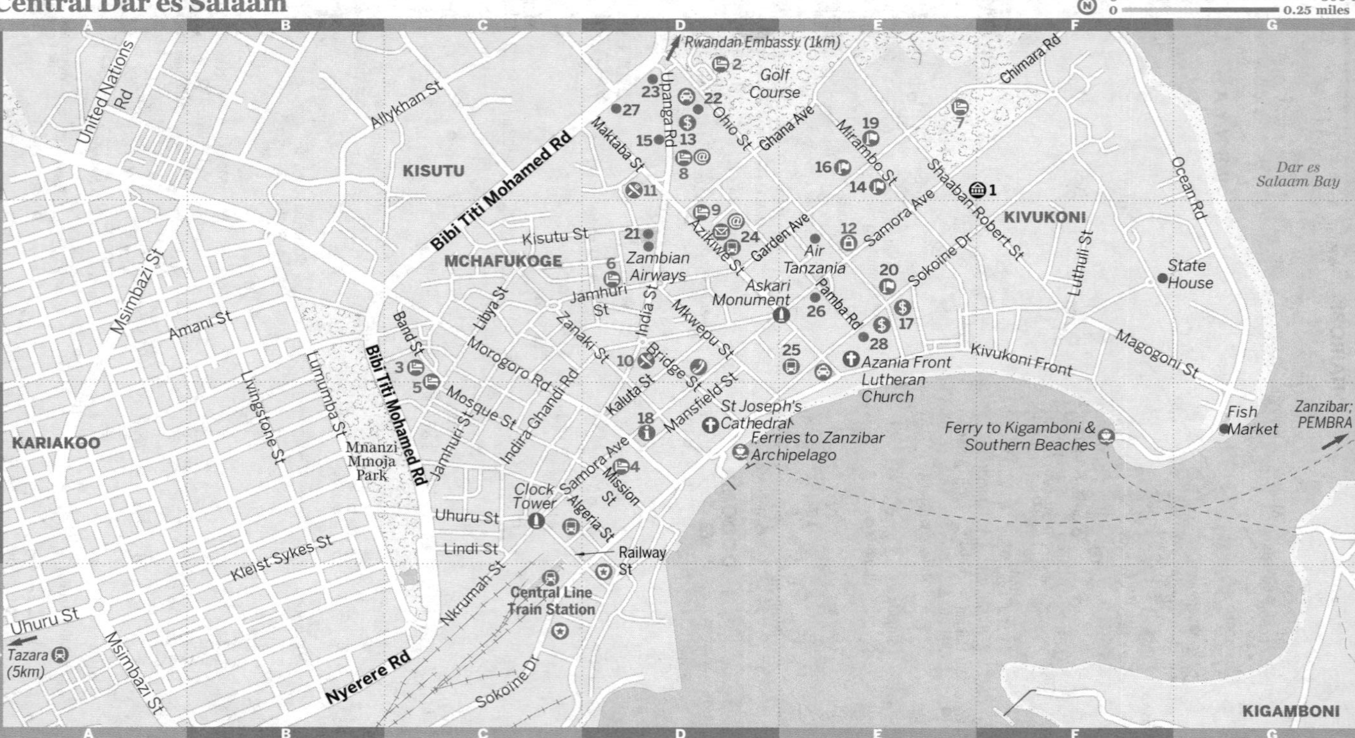

Central Dar es Salaam

Palm Beach Hotel HOTEL $$
(022-212 2931; www.pbhtz.com; Ali Hassan Mwinyi Rd; s/d/tr US$95/120/130;) This Dar es Salaam institution with bright-blue art deco architecture has spacious, good-value rooms and a restaurant.

Dar es Salaam Serena Hotel HOTEL $$$
(022-211 2416; www.serenahotels.com/serenadaressalaam; Ohio St; r from US$240;) Spacious, well-appointed rooms and expansive gardens.

Southern Sun HOTEL $$$
(022-213 7575; www.southernsun.com; Garden Ave; r from US$211;) Modern rooms and the standard amenities.

Harbour View Suites BUSINESS HOTEL $$$
(0784-564848; www.harbourview-suites.com; Samora Ave; r from US$160;) Well-equipped, centrally located business travellers' studio apartments. Underneath is JM Mall shopping centre, with an ATM and supermarket.

Eating

There's an array of eateries at both Msasani Slipway and Seacliff Village, both north of town on the Msasani Peninsula. In town, try the following.

YMCA TANZANIAN $
(022-213 5457; Upanga Rd; meals about Tsh3000; lunch & dinner) The YMCA canteen serves filling, inexpensive local food.

Patel Brotherhood INDIAN $
(Patel Samaj, off Maktaba St; evening entry fee Tsh1500, meals Tsh5000-7000; lunch & dinner;) This large compound is a favourite evening spot for local Indian families, with veg and nonveg meals.

Village Supermarket SUPERMARKET $
(Seacliff Village, Toure Dr) For self-catering.

Al Basha LEBANESE $$
(022-212 6888; Bridge St; meals Tsh8000-9500; breakfast, lunch & dinner) Tasty hummus and other Lebanese dishes, plus burgers and subs.

Kibo Bar EUROPEAN $$$
(022-211 2416; Serena Hotel, Ohio St; meals Tsh11,000-15,000; noon-11.30pm) Design-your-own sandwich station on weekdays, and pub fare at all hours at this upmarket sports bar.

Drinking & Nightlife

Waterfront Beach Bar BAR
(Msasani Slipway) Sundowners with sunset views.

Coco Beach BAR

(Sat & Sun) This beach – on the eastern edge of Msasani Peninsula, bordering Toure Drive – is packed with inexpensive beer and snacks.

Shopping

Wonder Workshop ARTS & CRAFTS

(022-266 6383; www.wonderwelders.org; Karume Rd, Msasani) At this workshop, disabled artists create jewellery, sculptures and other crafts from old glass and other recycled materials.

Mwenge Carvers' Market ARTS & CRAFTS

(Sam Nujoma Rd; 8am-6pm) Browse among the stalls and watch carvers at work. Take the Mwenge *dalla-dalla* from New Posta transport stand to the end of the route, from where it's five minutes on foot down the small street to the left.

A Novel Idea BOOKS

(022-260 1088; cnr Ohio St & Samora Ave, Seacliff Village) Dar es Salaam's best bookshop, with classics, modern fiction, travel guides, Africa titles, maps and more.

Orientation

The congested centre, with banks, shops and street vendors, runs along Samora Ave from the clock tower to the Askari Monument. Northwest around India and Jamhuri Sts is chock-a-block with Indian traders; northeast are shady, tree-lined streets. North along the coast is upper-middle-class Upanga, then the diplomatic areas of Oyster Bay and Msasani.

Information

DANGERS & ANNOYANCES

Dar es Salaam is considered safer than many other cities in the region, though it has its share of muggings and thefts, and the usual precautions must be taken. Watch out for pickpocketing at crowded markets and bus stations, and for bag snatching through vehicle windows.

At night, always take a taxi rather than a *dalla-dalla* or walking, and always only use taxis from reliable hotels. Avoid hailing taxis cruising the streets, and never get in a taxi that has a 'friend' of the driver or anyone else already in it.

EMERGENCY

Central Police Station (Sokoine Dr) Near Central Line train station.

IMMIGRATION OFFICE

Ministry of Home Affairs (022-285 0575/6; www.moha.go.tz; Uhamiaji House, Loliondo St; visa applications 8am-noon Mon-Fri, visa collections until 2pm) About 3.5km from the city centre off Kilwa Rd.

INTERNET ACCESS

Post Office Internet Café (Maktaba St; per hr Tsh1500; 8am-7pm Mon-Fri, 9am-3pm Sat)

Serena Hotel Business Centre (Serena Hotel, Ohio St; per 10min Tsh1000; 7am-8pm Mon-Fri, 8.30am-4pm Sat, 9am-1pm Sun)

MEDICAL SERVICES

IST Clinic (022-260 1307, 022-260 1308, 24hr emergency 0754-783393; www.istclinic.com; Ruvu Rd; 8am-6pm Mon-Fri, to noon Sat) Western-run clinic with a doctor always on call.

MONEY

Most bureaus de change are in the city centre on or near Samora Ave. There are ATMs all over the city, including:

Galaxy Forex Bureau (Airport; 6am-11pm) Cash.

Serena Forex Bureau (Serena Hotel, Ohio St; 8am-8pm Mon-Sat, 10am-1pm Sun & public holidays) Cash and travellers cheques (receipts required).

Barclays Bank (Ohio St) Accepts Visa and MasterCard; opposite Serena Hotel.

Stanbic Bank (Sukari House, cnr Ohio St & Sokoine Dr) Accepts Visa, MasterCard, Cirrus and Maestro.

POST

Main Post Office (Maktaba St; 8am-4.30pm Mon-Fri, 9am-noon Sat)

TOURIST INFORMATION

Tanzania Tourist Board Information Centre (022-212 0373; www.tanzaniatouristboard.com; Samora Ave; 8am-4pm Mon-Fri, 8.30am-12.30pm Sat) Just west of Zanaki St, with free tourist maps and brochures and city information.

TRAVEL AGENCIES

Coastal Travels (022-211 7959, 022-211 7960; safari@coastal.cc; Upanga Rd) Especially good for travel to Zanzibar and the parks.

Getting There & Away

AIR

Julius Nyerere International Airport has two terminals. Most regularly scheduled domestic flights and all international flights depart from Terminal Two ('new' terminal). Most flights on small planes (including most Zanzibar flights) depart from Terminal One (the 'old' terminal), 700m further down the road.

Air Uganda (022-213 3322; www.airuganda.com; 1st Fl, JM Mall, Samora Ave)

British Airways (☎022-211 3820; Serena Hotel, Ohio St)

Coastal Aviation (☎022-211 7959/60, 022-284 3293; aviation@coastal.cc; Upanga Rd) Flights to many parks and major towns, including Arusha, Dar es Salaam, Dodoma, Lake Manyara National Park, Mwanza, Pemba, Ruaha National Park, Selous Game Reserve, Serengeti National Park, Tanga, Tarangire National Park and Zanzibar.

Egyptair (☎022-213 6665/3; Ohio St) At Serena Hotel.

Emirates Airlines (☎022-211 6100; Haidery Plaza, cnr Kisutu & India Sts)

Ethiopian Airlines (☎022-211 7063; Ohio St) Opposite Serena Hotel.

Fastjet (☎0685-680533; www.fastjet.com; airport)

Kenya Airways (☎022-211 9376/7; Upanga Rd) With KLM.

KLM (☎022-213 9790/1; Upanga Rd)

Linhas Aéreas de Moçambique (☎022-213 4600; 1st fl, JM Mall, Samora Ave) At **Fast-Track Travel** (www.fasttracktanzania.com).

Precision Air (☎022-213 0800, 022-212 1718; cnr Samora Ave & Pamba Rd) In partnership with Kenya Airways. Connections between Nairobi and Mombasa in Kenya; and Entebbe and various cities in Tanzania.

South African Airways (☎022-211 7044; cnr Bibi Titi Mohamed & Ali Hassan Mwinyi Rds)

Swiss International Airlines (☎022-211 8870; Sokoine Dr)

Tropical Air (☎022-284 2333, 0773-511679; Terminal One, Airport)

ZanAir (☎022-284 3297, 024-223 3670; Terminal One, Airport)

BOAT

The main passenger routes are between Dar es Salaam, Zanzibar and Pemba.

There are several 'fast' ferry trips (on *Kilimanjaro I, II* and *III* and *Seabus*) daily between Dar es Salaam and Zanzibar, departing at about 7am, 10am, 1pm and 4pm. All take about two hours and cost US$35/40 regular/VIP (VIP gets you a seat in the air-con hold). There are also several slow ferries, including *Flying Horse*, which departs daily at 12.30pm (one-way US$25, four hours).

Departures from Zanzibar are daily at about 7am, 9.30am, 12.30pm, 3.30pm (all 'fast' ferries) and 10pm (arriving before dawn the next day). Buy your tickets at the tall, blue-glass 'Azam Marine/Coastal Fast Ferries' building diagonally opposite St Joseph's Cathedral.

BUS

Except as noted, all buses depart from and arrive at the main bus station at Ubungo, 8km west of the city centre on Morogoro Rd (Tsh300 in a *dalla-dalla* from New Posta or Old Posta transport stands, or from Tsh10,000 in a taxi). It's a sprawling place with the usual bus-station hustle, so keep an eye on your luggage and your wallet, and try to avoid arriving at night. Buses to Mtwara and other points south leave from Ubungo, but it's better to catch them at the Sudan Market area of Temeke, about 5km southwest of the city centre, off Nelson Mandela Rd.

Dar Express (Libya St, Kisutu) Daily buses to Arusha (Tsh30,000 to Tsh35,000) depart every 30 to 60 minutes from 6am to 10am from Ubungo bus station.

TRAIN

Tazara train station (☎022-286 5187, 0713-225292; cnr Nyerere & Nelson Mandela Rds; ⏱ticket office 7.30am-12.30pm & 2-4.30pm Mon-Fri, 9am-12.30pm Sat), for trains to Mbeya and Kapiri Mposhi (Zambia), is 6km southwest from the city centre (Tsh10,000 to Tsh15,000 in a taxi). *Dalla-dallas* depart from the New and Old Posta transport stands, and are marked Vigunguti, U/Ndege or Buguruni.

Central Line train station (☎022-211 7833; cnr Railway St & Sokoine Dr), for trains to Kigoma (the Mwanza line is currently closed), is just southwest of the ferry terminal.

ℹ Getting Around

TO/FROM THE AIRPORT

Julius Nyerere International Airport is 12km from the city centre. *Dalla-dallas* (marked U/Ndege) go to the airport from New Posta transport stand (one hour-plus, and no room for luggage). Taxis to central Dar es Salaam cost from Tsh25,000 (from Tsh35,000 to Msasani Peninsula).

PUBLIC TRANSPORT

Dalla-dallas go almost everywhere in the city for Tsh200 to Tsh500. City-centre terminals include the following:

New Posta Transport Stand (Maktaba St) At the main post office.

Old Posta Transport Stand (Sokoine Dr) Down from Azania Front Lutheran Church.

TAXI

Short rides within the city centre cost from Tsh4000. Fares from the city centre to Msasani Peninsula start at Tsh10,000.

For a reliable taxi driver, contact **Jumanne Mastoka** (☎0784-339735; mjumanne@yahoo.com). Never get into a taxi that has others in it, and always use taxis affiliated with reliable hotels and known by other drivers at the stand.

CULTURAL TOURISM IN DAR ES SALAAM

Investours (www.investours.com; adult/student US$50/35) offers tours to Mwenge Carvers Market that give visitors the chance to meet locals and invest in their business ideas. Following the tour, fees are pooled and given to an investor of the visitors' choice as an interest-free microloan to help them expand their business. This is an excellent way to get to know the 'real' Dar es Salaam while benefiting the local community.

The locally run Afriroots (p669) offers a range of bicycle and walking tours in and around Dar es Salaam that are ideal for getting acquainted with local life.

AROUND DAR ES SALAAM

Dar Beaches

The coastline south of Dar es Salaam gets more attractive the further south you go, and makes for an easy getaway. The budget places begin just south of Kigamboni, which is opposite Kivukoni Front and reached in a few minutes by ferry.

Mikadi Beach (0754-370269; www.mikadibeach.com; campsite per person Tsh10,000, d with/without bathroom Tsh60,000/40,000;), 2km from the dock, and **Kipepeo Beach & Village** (0754-276178; www.kipepeovillage.com; campsite per person US$8, s/d bandas US$20/28, cottages US$65/85), 8km south of the ferry dock, are both backpacker friendly. Kipepeo also has some midrange cottages.

Getting There & Away

The Kigamboni ferry (per person/vehicle Tsh100/1000, five minutes) runs frequently between the eastern end of Dar's Kivukoni Front and Kigamboni village. Once across, catch a *bajaji* (tuk-tuk) to Kipepeo/Mikadi for Tsh3500/1500.

ZANZIBAR ARCHIPELAGO

The 'spice islands' of Zanzibar (Unguja) and Pemba have an almost legendary allure and offer a complete change of pace from the Tanzanian mainland. Zanzibar gets most of the attention, with its historic Stone Town and its beautiful palm-fringed beaches. Pemba, by contrast, is seldom visited and laidback, with a largely undiscovered culture and challenging diving.

Yet, there is another side to life on the archipelago. Overdevelopment is suffocating the coast and mass tourism makes Zanzibar's allure ever more elusive. While the magic remains, you'll have to work harder to find it.

History

From around the 8th century, Shirazi traders from Persia established settlements in the archipelago. Then between the 12th and 15th centuries, Zanzibar became a powerful city-state, exporting slaves, gold, ivory and wood, and importing spices, glassware and textiles. In the early 16th century Zanzibar came under Portuguese control. Omani Arabs in the mid-16th century routed the Portuguese and by the 19th century had become so prosperous that in the 1840s the sultan of Oman relocated his court from the Persian Gulf.

In 1862, Zanzibar became independent from Oman, although Omani sultans continued to rule under a British protectorate. On 10 December 1963 Zanzibar gained independence and in 1964, Abeid Karume signed a declaration of unity with Tanganyika (as mainland Tanzania was then known), forming a fragile union that soon became known as the United Republic of Tanzania.

Zanzibar

Zanzibar's main attraction is Stone Town, where ancient Persia mixes with the old Omani sultanate and India's Goa coast, and quaint shops and bazaars line the winding, cobbled streets. Another of the island's drawcards is its spectacular sea, edged by fine, white-sand beaches, whitewashed coral-rag houses and waving palms.

Zanzibar Town

Sights

If Zanzibar Town is the archipelago's heart, **Stone Town** is its soul, and a historic wonder in itself, with a jumble of cobbled alleyways where it's easy to spend days wandering around. Each twist and turn of the narrow streets brings something new. Arabic-style houses with their recessed inner courtyards rub shoulders with Indian-influenced buildings designed with ornate balconies and latticework, and bustling oriental bazaars alternate with lively street-side vending stalls.

Zanzibar National Museum of History & Culture MUSEUM
(Map p680; Mizingani Rd; adult/child US$4/1; ⏲9am-6pm) Housed in the imposing Beit el-Ajaib (House of Wonders), this museum has exhibits on Swahili civilisation, the history of Stone Town and a *mtepe* (a traditional Swahili sailing vessel made without nails).

Beit el-Sahel MUSEUM
(Map p680; Palace Museum; Mizingani Rd; adult/child US$4/1; ⏲9am-6pm) The former sultan's palace is now a museum devoted to the era of the Zanzibar sultanate.

Anglican Cathedral CHURCH
(Map p680; admission Tsh5000; ⏲8am-6pm Mon-Sat, noon-6pm Sun) Constructed in the 1870s, Stone Town's cathedral was built on the site of an old slave market. Today only some holding cells remain.

Darajani Market MARKET
(Map p680; Creek Rd; ⏲predawn–mid-afternoon) This colourful, chaotic market is at its best in the morning, before the heat and the crowds.

Activities

One Ocean/The Zanzibar Dive Centre DIVING
(Map p680; ☎024-223 8374; www.zanzibaroneocean.com; off Shangani St) For diving and snorkelling, contact this PADI five-star centre with branches in Matemwe and elsewhere around the island. Caters all divers.

Tours

All the following can help with island excursions, and plane and ferry tickets.

Eco + Culture Tours CULTURAL TOUR
(Map p680; ☎024-223 3731, 0755-873066; www.ecoculture-zanzibar.org; Hurumzi St) Culturally friendly tours and excursions.

Gallery Tours & Safaris GUIDED TOUR
(Map p680; ☎024-223 2088; www.gallerytours.net) Top-of-the line tours and dhow cruises.

Madeira Tours & Safaris GUIDED TOUR
(Map p680; ☎024-223 0406, 0777-415997; www.zanzibarmadeira.com; Baghani St) All price ranges.

Sama Tours GUIDED TOUR
(Map p680; ☎024-223 3543; www.samatours.com; Hurumzi St) Reliable and reasonably priced.

Tropical Tours GUIDED TOUR
(☎0777-413454; www.tropicaltoursandsafari.com; Kenyatta Rd) Budget tours.

Zan Tours GUIDED TOUR
(☎024-223 3116, 024-223 3042; www.zantours.com; Migombani St) Upmarket tours.

Sleeping

Hotel Kiponda HOTEL $
(Map p680; ☎024-223 3052; www.kiponda.com; Nyumba ya Moto St; s/d/tr from US$30/50/65) The long-standing Kiponda has spotless, good-value rooms, most with private bathroom, in an atmospheric building tucked away in a small lane near the waterfront.

Garden Lodge GUESTHOUSE $
(Map p680; ☎024-223 3298; gardenlodge@zanlink.com; Kaunda Rd; s/d/tr US$30/40/60) This family-run place opposite the High Court has good-value rooms (the upstairs ones are brighter and more spacious) with hot water, ceiling fans and Zanzibari beds.

Warere Town House HOTEL $
(Map 678; ☎0782-234564; www.warere.com; s/d/tr from US$35/55/65; ❄) Good-value rooms (some with small balconies and all with hot water) plus a rooftop breakfast terrace and a trim gravel-grass entry area planted with bougainvillea.

Malindi Guest House HOTEL $
(Map 678; ☎024-223 0165; www.malindiguesthouse.com; Funguni Rd; s/d US$50/60, without bathroom US$30/45; ❄) Whitewashed walls, well-maintained rooms with fan or air-con, and a small rooftop restaurant. Reconfirm your room rates when booking.

Pyramid Hotel HOTEL $
(Map p680; ☎024-223 3000; www.pyramidhotel.co.tz; s/d from US$25/35; ❄@) Pyramid has a mix of rooms of varying size and standard, most with private bathroom, and all with Zanzibari beds and fan, plus a rooftop breakfast terrace.

Flamingo Guest House GUESTHOUSE $
(Map p680; ☎024-223 2850; www.flamingoguesthouse.com; Mkunazini St; s/d US$17/34, without bathroom US$14/28) Flamingo is no frills but cheap and fine, with straightforward rooms with fans around a courtyard, plus a rooftop sitting/breakfast area.

Jambo Guest House GUESTHOUSE $
(Map p680; ☎024-223 3779; info@jamboguest.com; s/d/tr without bathroom US$30/40/60; ❄@)

Zanzibar

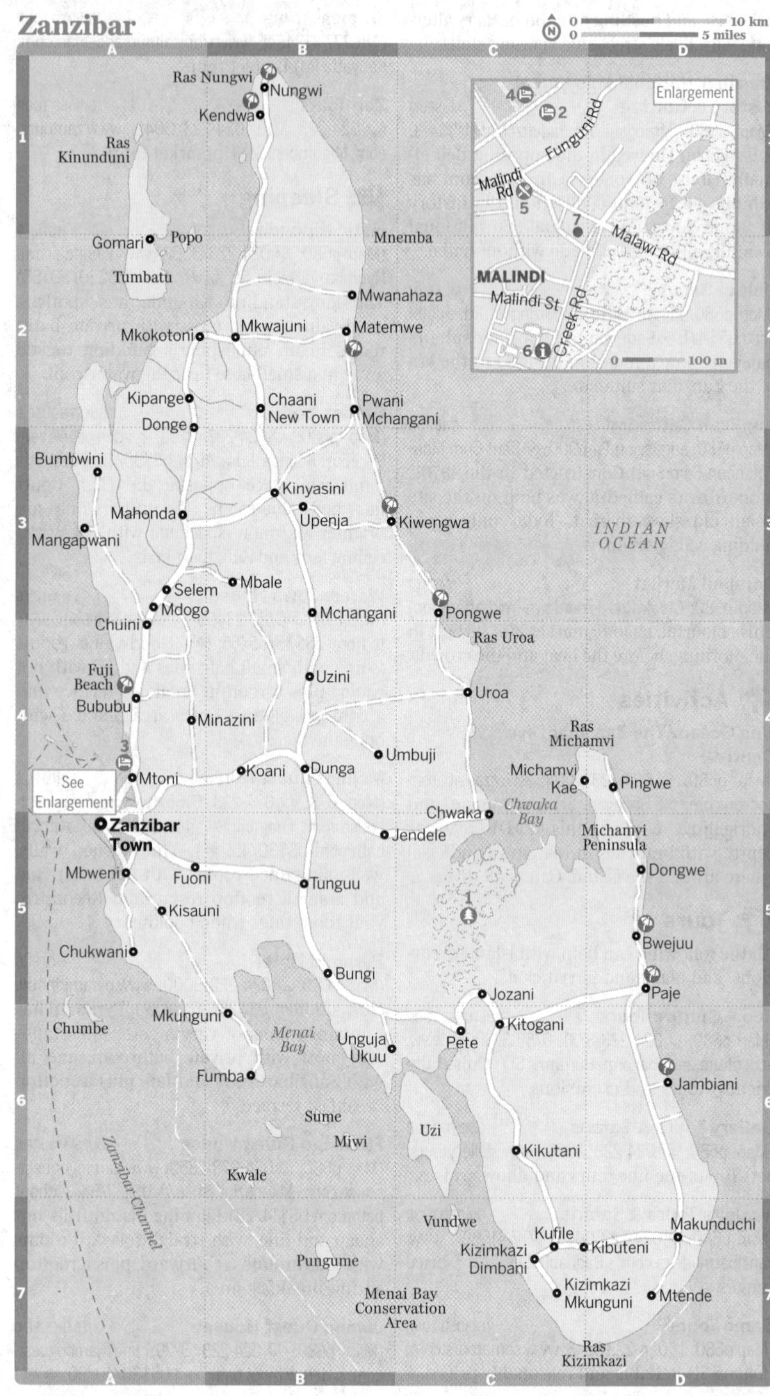

Ras Nungwi
Nungwi
Kendwa
Ras Kinunduni
Gomari
Popo
Tumbatu
Mnemba
Mwanahaza
Mkokotoni
Mkwajuni
Matemwe
Kipange
Donge
Chaani New Town
Pwani Mchangani
Bumbwini
Kinyasini
Upenja
Kiwengwa
Mahonda
Mangapwani
INDIAN OCEAN
Selem
Mbale
Mdogo
Chuini
Mchangani
Pongwe
Ras Uroa
Fuji Beach
Bububu
Uzini
Uroa
Minazini
Ras Michamvi
Umbuji
Mtoni
Koani
Dunga
Michamvi Kae
Pingwe
See Enlargement
Chwaka
Chwaka Bay
Jendele
Zanzibar Town
Michamvi Peninsula
Mbweni
Fuoni
Tunguu
Dongwe
Kisauni
Bwejuu
Chukwani
Bungi
Paje
Jozani
Mkunguni
Kitogani
Chumbe
Menai Bay
Unguja Ukuu
Pete
Fumba
Jambiani
Sume
Miwi
Uzi
Kikutani
Kwale
Zanzibar Channel
Vundwe
Makunduchi
Kufile
Kibuteni
Kizimkazi Dimbani
Pungume
Kizimkazi Mkunguni
Mtende
Menai Bay Conservation Area
Ras Kizimkazi
Enlargement
Funguni Rd
Malindi Rd
Malawi Rd
MALINDI
Malindi St
Creek Rd
0 10 km
0 5 miles
0 100 m

Zanzibar

Sights
1 Jozani-Chwaka Bay National Park.....C5

Sleeping
2 Malindi Guest House.....C1
3 Mtoni Marine Centre.....A4
4 Warere Town House.....C1

Eating
5 Passing Show.....C1

Information
6 Tourist Information Office.....C2

Transport
7 Traffic Police Office.....C1

Popular with backpackers, Jambo has free tea and coffee, clean rooms and decent breakfasts.

Haven Guest House GUESTHOUSE $
(Map p680; ☎024-223 5677/8; s/d US$20/40) Straightforward, no-frills rooms and a convenient location between Soko Muhogo St and Vuga Rd.

Tembo House Hotel HOTEL $$
(Map p680; ☎024-223 3005; www.tembohotel.com; s/d/tw/tr from US$105/125/125/160; ❄@📶🏊) A prime waterfront location, efficient management, a breakfast buffet and good-value rooms make this a long-standing favourite.

Dhow Palace HOTEL $$
(Map p680; ☎024-223 3012, 0777-878088; www.dhowpalace-hotel.com; s/d from US$80/110; ⏰Jun-Mar; ❄@🏊) The staid and attractive Dhow Palace has old Zanzibari decor, an airy foyer and well-appointed rooms.

Chavda Hotel HOTEL $$
(Map p680; ☎024-223 2115; www.chavdahotel.co.tz; Baghani St; s/d/tw from US$100/120/130; ❄) Reliable, quiet Chavda has a range of bland, carpeted rooms with TV and minibar. The rooftop bar-restaurant is open during high season only.

Abuso Inn HOTEL $$
(Map p680; ☎024-223 5886, 0777-425565; abusoinn@gmail.com; Shangani St; s/d/tr/f US$55/75/90/100; ❄📶) This family-run place has spotless, mostly spacious rooms with large windows and wooden floors.

Beyt al-Chai BOUTIQUE HOTEL $$
(Map p680; ☎0774-444111; www.stonetowninn.com; Kelele Sq; s/d from US$195/230) This converted teahouse is an atmospheric choice, with five individually designed rooms. Splurge on one of the top-floor Sultan suites.

★ **Mtoni Marine Centre** LODGE $$
(Map p680; ☎024-225 0140; www.mtoni.com; Bububu Rd; s/d from US$85/110; ❄@📶🏊) Mtoni offers spacious 'club rooms' and more luxurious 'palm court' sea-view rooms. There's a small beach, large gardens, a 25m infinity pool, a waterside bar and a restaurant. It's 3km north of town.

Kisiwa House BOUTIQUE HOTEL $$$
(Map p680; ☎024-223 5654; www.kisiwahouse.com; r US$180-240; 📶) Formerly Baghani House Hotel, this chic spot is full of character, with carved wood decor, steep staircases and period-style furnishings.

Seyyidda Hotel & Spa BOUTIQUE HOTEL $$$
(Map p680; ☎024-223 8352; www.theseyyidazanzibar.com; r US$170-290; ❄@📶) All rooms in this 17-room boutique hotel have satellite TV, some have sea views and some have balconies. There's also a rooftop terrace restaurant.

Eating

During the low season and Ramadan, many restaurants close or operate reduced hours.

New Radha Food House VEGETARIAN $
(Map p680; ☎024-223 4808; thalis Tsh10,000; ⏰8am-9.30pm; 🌶) This little place, tucked away on the small side street just before the Shangani tunnel, has a strictly vegetarian menu featuring thalis, lassis, homemade yoghurt and other dishes from the subcontinent.

Forodhani Gardens TANZANIAN $
(Map p680; meals Tsh3000-10,000; ⏰dinner; 🌶) These waterside gardens are the place to go in the evening, with piles of grilled fish and meat, chips, snacks and more, all served on a paper plate or rolled into a piece of newspaper and eaten while sitting on benches or on the lawn. Bargaining is expected.

Stone Town Café CAFE $
(Map p680; Kenyatta Rd; meals Tsh8000-15,000; ⏰8am-6pm Mon-Sat) Enjoy all-day breakfasts, milkshakes, freshly baked cakes, vegie wraps and good coffee on a small streetside terrace.

Stone Town

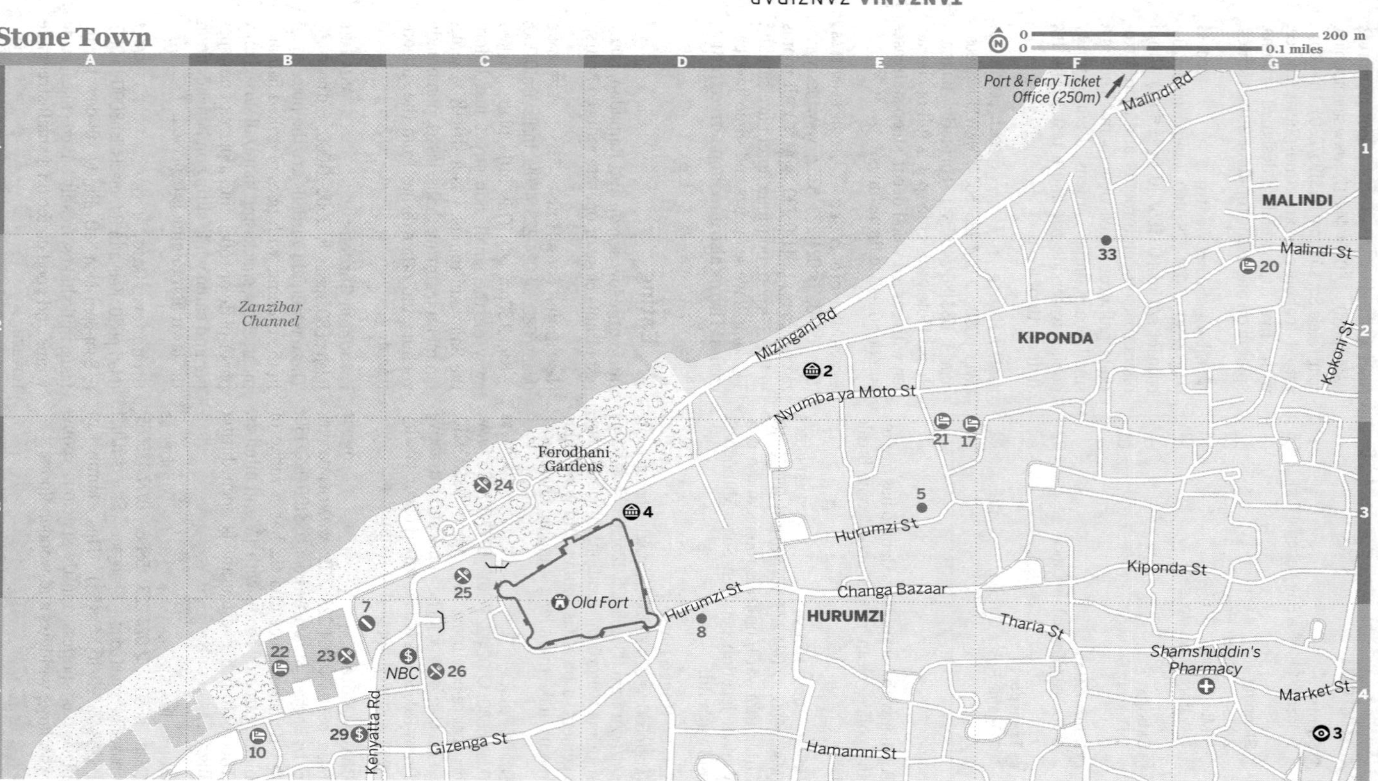
0 200 m
0 0.1 miles
Port & Ferry Ticket Office (250m)
Malindi Rd
MALINDI
Malindi St
Kokoni St
KIPONDA
Mizingani Rd
Nyumba ya Moto St
Zanzibar Channel
Forodhani Gardens
Old Fort
Hurumzi St
Changa Bazaar
HURUMZI
Tharia St
Kiponda St
Shamshuddin's Pharmacy
Market St
Hamamni St
Gizenga St
Kenyatta Rd
NBC
2
4
5
7
8
10
17
20
21
22
23
24
25
26
29
33
3

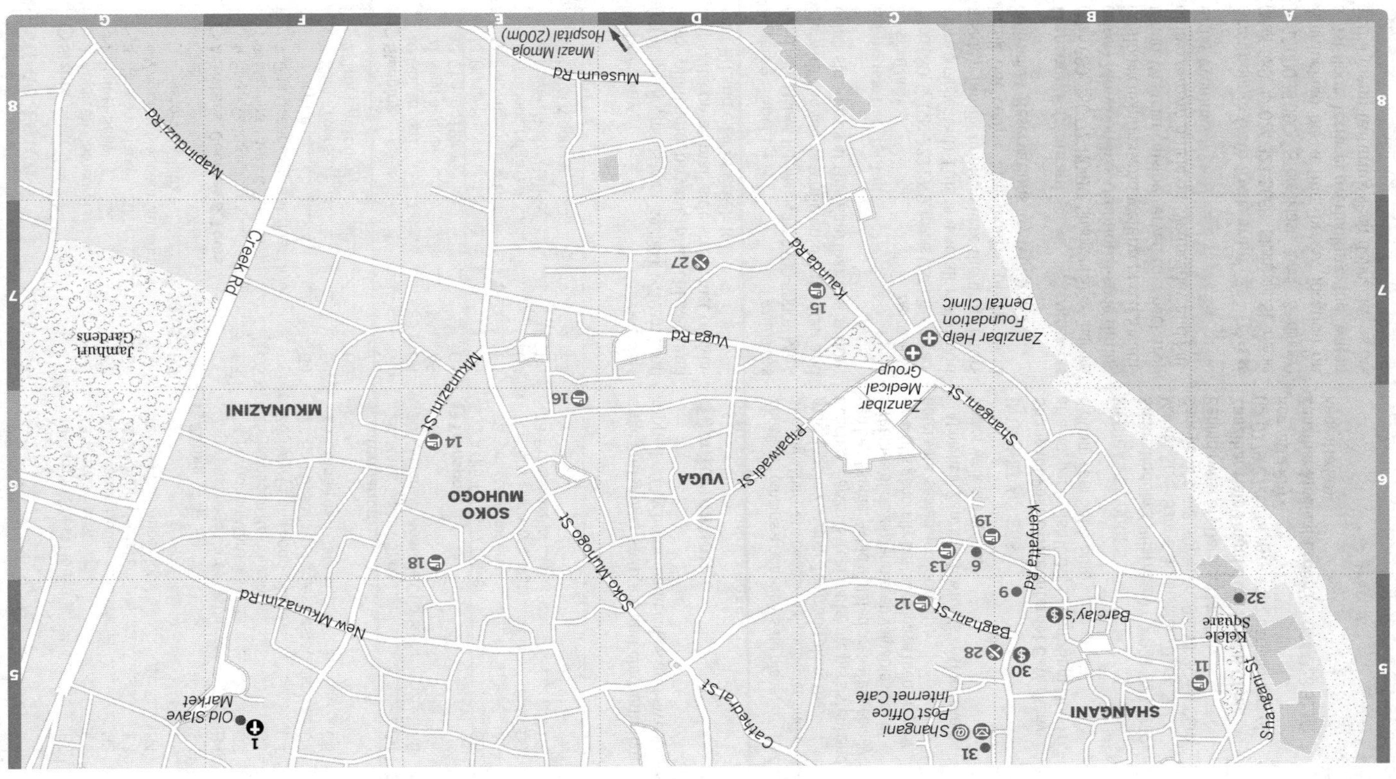
A
B
C
D
E
F
G
5
6
7
8
1
Old Slave Market
New Mkunazini Rd
Creek Rd
Jamhuri Gardens
Mapinduzi Rd
MKUNAZINI
SOKO MUHOGO
18
14
Mkunazini St
Soko Muhogo St
16
VUGA
Cathedral St
Pipalwadi St
Vuga Rd
27
Museum Rd
Mnazi Mmoja Hospital (200m)
15
Kaunda Rd
Zanzibar Medical Group
Zanzibar Help Foundation Dental Clinic
Shangani St
31
Shangani Post Office Internet Café
28
30
Baghani St
12
13
6
19
9
Kenyatta Rd
Barclay's
SHANGANI
11
Kelele Square
32
Shangani St

Stone Town

Sights

1 Anglican Cathedral F5
2 Beit el-Sahel E2
3 Darajani Market G4
4 Zanzibar National Museum of History & Culture D3

Activities, Courses & Tours

5 Eco + Culture Tours E3
6 Madeira Tours & Safaris C6
7 One Ocean/The Zanzibar Dive Centre B4
8 Sama Tours D4
9 Tropical Tours B5

Sleeping

10 Abuso Inn B4
11 Beyt al-Chai A5
12 Chavda Hotel C5
13 Dhow Palace C6
14 Flamingo Guest House E6
15 Garden Lodge C7
16 Haven Guest House E6
17 Hotel Kiponda E3
18 Jambo Guest House E6
19 Kisiwa House C6
20 Pyramid Hotel G2
21 Seyyidda Hotel & Spa E3
22 Tembo House Hotel B4

Eating

23 Archipelago Café-Restaurant B4
24 Forodhani Gardens C3
25 Monsoon Restaurant C3
26 New Radha Food House C4
27 Sambusa Two Tables Restaurant D7
28 Stone Town Café C5

Information

29 Maka T-Shirt Shop B4
30 Queens Bureau de Change B5

Transport

31 Asko Tours & Travel C5
32 Coastal Aviation A5
Kenya Airways .... (see 33)
33 Precision Air F2

Al-Shabany ZANZIBARI $
(off Malawi Rd; meals from Tsh3500; 10am-2pm) Tasty pilau and biryani, plus chicken and chips. It's on a small side street just off Malawi Rd and east of Creek Rd.

Passing Show ZANZIBARI $
(Map 678; Malawi Rd; meals Tsh2500-5000) Mingle with the locals while enjoying pilau and other standards at this Zanzibar institution.

Sambusa Two Tables Restaurant ZANZIBARI $$
(Map 680; 024-223 1979; meals US$15; by advance arrangement) This is a small restaurant inside a family home, where the proprietors bring out course after course of the local delicacies. Reservations are required.

Monsoon Restaurant ZANZIBARI $$
(Map 680; 0777-410410; Shangani St; lunch & dinner) Monsoon has traditional-style dining on floor cushions, and well-prepared Swahili and Western cuisine served to a backdrop of live *taarab* music on Wednesday and Saturday evenings.

Archipelago Café-Restaurant CAFE $$
(Map 680; 024-223 5668; Shangani St; meals Tsh12,000-15,000; breakfast, lunch & dinner) Archipelago has a fine, breezy location on a 1st-floor terrace overlooking the water, and a menu featuring such delicacies as orange and ginger snapper, and chicken pilau, topped off by homemade cakes and sweets.

Information

DANGERS & ANNOYANCES

Zanzibar remains a relatively safe place, although there are occasional robberies and muggings in Zanzibar Town and along the beaches. *Papasi* (street touts) are persistent and can be irksome. Avoid isolated areas, especially stretches of beach, and keep valuables out of view (it's generally better to leave them in your hotel safe, sealed and locked).

At night in Zanzibar Town, it's best to take a taxi or walk in a group.

INTERNET ACCESS

Shangani Post Office Internet Café (Kenyatta Rd; per hr Tsh1000; 8am-8pm Mon-Fri, 8.30am-7pm Sat & Sun)

MEDICAL SERVICES

Shamshuddin's Pharmacy (024-223 1262; Market St; 9am-8.30pm Mon-Thu & Sat, 9am-noon & 4-8.30pm Fri, 9am-1.30pm Sun) Behind (west of) Darajani Market.

Zanzibar Help Foundation Dental Clinic (0779-272600; www.zanzibarhelp.org; off Kenyatta Rd)

Zanzibar Medical Group (024-223 3134; Kenyatta Rd)

MONEY

There are several ATMs in Stone Town (though none elsewhere); all accept Visa and MasterCard. There are also many bureaus de change in Stone Town (most open until about 8pm daily) where you can change cash, but not travellers cheques.

Barclays (Kenyatta Rd) ATM.

CRDB (New Mkunazini Rd, Mkunazini) ATM.

Maka T-Shirt Shop (Map 680; Kenyatta Rd) Changes cash.

NBC (Shangani St) ATM.

Queens Bureau de Change (Map 680; Kenyatta Rd) Changes cash.

POST

Shangani Post Office (Kenyatta Rd; ⌚8am-4.30pm Mon-Fri, to 12.30pm Sat)

TOURIST INFORMATION

Tourist Information Office (Map 678; Creek Rd; ⌚8am-5pm)

Getting There & Away

AIR

Daily flights with Coastal Aviation and ZanAir connect Zanzibar with Dar es Salaam (US$75), Arusha (US$235), Tanga (US$140), Pemba (US$100), Selous Game Reserve and the northern parks.

Airline offices in Zanzibar Town include:

Coastal Aviation (Map 680; ☎024-223 3489, 0777-232747; www.coastal.cc; Kelele Sq) At the airport, with a booking agent next to Zanzibar Serena Inn.

Kenya Airways (Map 680; ☎024-223 4520/1; www.kenya-airways.com; Room 8, Ground fl, Muzamil Centre, Mlandege St)

Precision Air (Map 680; ☎024-223 4520/1, 0787-888417; www.precisionairtz.com; Room 8, Ground fl, Muzamil Centre, Mlandege St) With Kenya Airways.

ZanAir (☎024-223 3670; www.zanair.com; airport)

BOAT

Tickets for Dar es Salaam ferries are sold at the port (the ticket office is to the right when entering the main port gate), or with less hassle through local tour operators. The departure and arrivals areas for the ferry are a few hundred metres down from the port gate along Mizingani Rd. Foreigners are not permitted on dhows between Dar es Salaam and Zanzibar.

Getting Around

TO/FROM THE AIRPORT

The airport is 7km southeast of Zanzibar Town (Tsh15,000 in a taxi). *Dalla-dalla* 505 does this route (Tsh500, 30 minutes), departing from opposite Mnazi Mmoja hospital.

CAR & MOTORCYCLE

For car, moped or motorcycle hire, you'll need an International Driving Permit, a licence from Kenya, Uganda or South Africa, or a Zanzibar permit. Zanzibar permits can be obtained on the spot at the **traffic police office** (Map 678; cnr Malawi & Creek Rds) or through any tour company.

Daily rental rates average from about US$25 for a moped or motorcycle, and US$50 to US$60 for a Suzuki 4WD. Hires can be arranged through **Asko Tours & Travel** (Map 680; ☎024-223 0712; askotour@hotmail.com; Kenyatta Rd) or other tour companies. Full payment is usually required at the time of delivery, but don't pay any advance deposits.

DALLA-DALLA

Dalla-dallas piled with people and produce link all major towns on the island, leaving from Creek Rd opposite Darajani Market. None of the routes cost more than Tsh3000, and all take plenty of time (eg about two hours from Zanzibar Town to Jambiani).

ROUTE NO	DESTINATION
116	Nungwi
118	Matemwe
309	Jambiani
324	Bwejuu
326	Kizimkazi
505	Airport ('U/Ndege')

For Kendwa, have *dalla-dalla* 116 drop you at the Kendwa turn-off, from where it's a 2km walk to the beach.

PRIVATE MINIBUS

Private minivans run daily to Nungwi and to Paje, Bwejuu and Jambiani on the east coast. Book through any travel agency the day before you want to travel, and the vans will pick you up at your hotel in Stone Town between 8am and 9am. Travel takes 1½ to two hours to any of the destinations, and costs a negotiable Tsh6000 to Tsh10,000 per person. Don't pay for the return trip in advance. Most drivers only go to hotels where they'll get a commission.

TAXI

Taxis don't have meters. Town trips cost from Tsh4000, more at night.

Around Zanzibar

Beaches

Zanzibar has superb beaches, with the best along the island's east coast and to the north. The east-coast beaches are protected by coral reefs offshore and have fine, white coral sand, although at low tide the sea recedes a long way and swimming isn't possible.

NUNGWI

Traditional and modern collide at Nungwi, a large dhow-building centre that has also become one of Zanzibar's major tourist destinations, despite having only the thinnest sliver of sand (and sometimes no beach at all).

Sleeping

Safina Bungalows GUESTHOUSE $
(☎0777-415726; kihorinungwi@hotmail.com; s/d/tr from US$30/50/70) This decent budget choice has simple bungalows around a tiny garden, just in from the beach in the centre of Nungwi.

Baraka Beach Bungalows BUNGALOW $
(☎0777-415569, 0777-422910; http://barakabungalow.atspace.com; s/d US$30/45) Baraka has no-frills stone-and-thatch cottages around a tiny garden, and a restaurant.

Nungwi Guest House GUESTHOUSE $
(☎0772-263322; http://nungwiguesthouse.tripod.com; d/tr US$35/40) In the village centre, has simple rooms with shared bathroom around a small garden courtyard; all with fans.

Jambo Brothers Bungalows BUNGALOW $
(☎0773-109343, 0777-492355; jambobungalows@yahoo.com; s/d without bathroom US$20/30) Rooms here are basic, but among Nungwi's cheapest.

Union Beach Bungalows BUNGALOW $
(☎0777-432908, 0776-583412; http://unionbungalow.atspace.com; s/d from US$40/50; ❄) No-frills bungalows plus rooms in a two-storey block, some with air-con and fridge. Meals are available.

Mnarani Beach Cottages LODGE $$
(☎024-224 0494, 0777-415551; www.lighthousezanzibar.com; east Nungwi; s US$78-90, d US$140-200, tr US$180-225, all prices include half board; ❄@🛜🏊) On a low rise overlooking the sea, quiet Mnarani has small, spotless cottages, family rooms and a honeymoon cottage.

Smiles Beach Hotel HOTEL $$
(☎024-224 0472; www.smilesbeachhotel.com; s/d/tr US$90/120/150; ❄🛜) At the quieter edge of west Nungwi, Smiles has well-appointed rooms in two-storey tile-roofed blocks overlooking a manicured lawn and a small patch of beach.

Nungwi Inn Hotel HOTEL $$
(☎024-224 0091; www.nungwiinnhotel.co.tz; s/d US$55/75; ❄) Located towards the southern end of the main hotel strip, Nungwi Inn has small whitewashed cottages scattered around scruffy but spacious grounds and a restaurant.

Amaan Bungalows HOTEL $$
(☎024-224 0024, 024-224 0026; www.amaanbungalows.com; s US$70-150, d US$80-160; ❄@) At the centre of the action with various levels of accommodation, including sea-view rooms, plus a restaurant and a bar.

KENDWA

About 3km southwest of Nungwi along the coast is Kendwa, known for its long, wide stretch of sand, its full-moon parties and its seemingly nonstop hotel development.

Scuba Do (www.scuba-do-zanzibar.com) offers a full range of PADI courses.

Sleeping

Sunset Bungalows BUNGALOW $$
(☎0777-414647; www.sunsetkendwa.com; s US$45-75, d US$60-98; ❄) Sunset has a mix of rooms on the beach and on the cliff, all with bathroom with hot water. There's a restaurant-bar with evening beach bonfires.

Kendwa Rocks BUNGALOW $$
(☎0777-415475; www.kendwarocks.com; s/d bandas without bathroom from US$30/45, s/d beach bungalows from US$55/65; ❄) Kendwa Rocks has no-frills beach *bandas* (thatched-roof huts) sharing toilets, nicer self-contained bungalows on the sand, cool stone garden cottages and suites and rooms on the clifftop. Full-moon parties are an institution.

PAJE

Paje, on the southeastern coast, is a wide, white beach with a cluster of places to stay and a party atmosphere, though it's quieter than Nungwi. It's also Zanzibar's main kitesurfing centre.

Sleeping

Kitete Beach Bungalows HOTEL $$
(☎024-224 0226; www.kitetebeach.com; s/d main house US$40/60, new wing from US$50/80) Basic rooms with cold-water showers in the original cottage building in Paje centre, and newer, nicer rooms next door in double-storey bungalows.

Paradise Beach Bungalows BUNGALOW $$
(☎024-223 1387; http://paradisebeachbungalows.web.fc2.com; s/d US$60/70) This quiet, Japanese-run place at Paje's northern edge has rooms with two large beds and a restaurant.

Paje by Night LODGE $$
(☎0777-460710; www.pajebynight.net; s/d from US$60/75; ⊙Jun–mid-Apr; ❄@📶≋) This chilled place, known for its noisy bar and party vibe, has a crowded mix of rooms, a restaurant and a pizza oven.

BWEJUU

The large village of Bwejuu lies about 3km north of Paje on a long, palm-shaded beach. It's very spread out, and quieter than both Paje and Nungwi.

Sleeping

Evergreen Bungalows Bwejuu BUNGALOW $$
(☎024-224 0273; www.evergreen-bungalows.com; r US$70-90) Spiffy two-storey beach bungalows, plus single-storey 'garden cottages', a restaurant and a dive centre.

Twisted Palms Lodge BUNGALOW $$
(☎0776-130275; www.twistedpalms.zanzibarone.com; s/d on hill US$35/45, on beach US$50/60) Five, clean, bright cottages up on a hill just behind the road, plus several more on the beach, and a restaurant.

JAMBIANI

This sunbaked and somnolent village is stretched out over more than 1km, facing turquoise seas dotted with *ngalawa* (outrigger canoes) moored just offshore.

Sleeping

Kimte Beach Inn BUNGALOW $
(☎0778-832824; www.kimtebeachinn.com; dm US$20, s/d from US$25/50) At Jambiani's southern end, this quiet place has simple rooms on the land side of the road, a restaurant and evening bonfires.

Blue Oyster Hotel HOTEL $$
(☎024-224 0163, 0787-233610; www.zanzibar.de; s/d/tr from US$90/103/156) The German-run Blue Oyster has pleasant, spotless, good-value rooms (some around a small inner courtyard, others beachfront) and a restaurant.

Red Monkey Lodge BUNGALOW $$
(☎0777-713366; www.redmonkeylodge.com; s/d US$72/104) At Jambiani's far southern end, Red Monkey has nine bungalow-style, sea-facing rooms, a chill-out area, a restaurant, diving and kitesurfing.

Casa del Mar Hotel Jambiani HOTEL $$
(☎024-224 0400; www.casa-delmar-zanzibar.com; d downstairs/upstairs US$100/110; ≋) This small beachside place has 14 rooms in two crowded but pleasant double-storey blocks (the upper-storey rooms have lofts) in a small, enclosed beachside garden.

Jozani Forest

Now protected as part of the **Jozani-Chwaka Bay National Park** (Map p678; adult/child US$8/4; ⊙7.30am-5.30pm), Jozani is the largest area of mature forest left on Zanzibar, and is known in particular for its population of the rare red colobus monkey. There's a short nature trail and a tiny cafe. The colobuses are best seen early mornings and late evenings. Jozani can be reached via bus 309 or 310, or with an organised tour from Zanzibar Town.

Pemba

About 50km north of Unguja lies hilly, verdant Pemba, Zanzibar's 'other' island. It's seldom visited by tourists but has some idyllic offshore islets and an intriguing culture.

Sleeping & Eating

Pemba Island Hotel HOTEL $
(☎0777-490041; pembaislandhotel@yahoo.com; Wesha Rd, Chake Chake; s/d/tw US$40/60/80; ❄📶) This reliable place has clean rooms with cable TV and hot water, plus a rooftop restaurant.

Le Tavern HOTEL $
(☎0777-429057; Main Rd, Chake Chake; s/d US$20/30, s without bathroom US$6) Centrally located, reasonably clean and with a restaurant upstairs, these are Pemba's cheapest rooms. There's no hot water.

Ocean Panorama Hotel HOTEL $
(☎0773-545418; www.zanzibaroceanpanorama.com; Mkoani; dm/s/tw/tr US$20/35/50/75; @) The welcoming Ocean Panorama has bright, clean rooms with decks and Zanzibari beds, plus local info and excursions. Head left when exiting the port and walk 700m up the hill.

Sharook Guest House GUESTHOUSE $
(☎0777-431012; www.pembaliving.com; Wete; s/d US$30/50) Prices have risen at this small guesthouse while maintenance has lagged, but it remains Wete's homiest and most popular with travellers.

Information

Barclays Bank (Misufuni St, Chake Chake) ATM.

Getting There & Away

AIR

Coastal Aviation, Flightlink, Tropical and Zan Air fly daily between Dar es Salaam, Zanzibar and Pemba (Chake Chake) for about US$100/140 from Pemba to Zanzibar/Dar es Salaam. Coastal and Tropical also fly between Chake Chake and Tanga (US$100).

BOAT

Sea Bus (the most reliable), *Sea Gull* and *Sepideh* (least reliable) sail several times weekly to highly variable schedules between Zanzibar and Pemba for about US$40/45 economy/1st class (about three hours). Enquire locally about current conditions and seaworthiness before booking. Tickets for all companies can be booked commission-free at various businesses in Chake Chake, Wete and Mkoani.

Once in Mkoani, there are buses to Chake Chake and on to Wete.

NORTHEASTERN TANZANIA

Bagamoyo

Bagamoyo was the capital of German East Africa from 1887 to 1891, when the capital was transferred to Dar es Salaam. Since then, the town has been in a long decline, although its history, sleepy charm and nearby beaches make it an agreeable excursion from Dar es Salaam. Don't miss walking around the old town (after paying the Tsh2000 fee at the Caravan Serai Museum near the town entrance) and visiting the **Catholic Museum** (☎023-244 0010; adult/student Tsh2000/500; ⏰10am-5pm) and the **Kaole Ruins** (adult/student Tsh2000/500; ⏰8am-4pm Mon-Fri, to 5pm Sat & Sun), 5km south of Bagamoyo, with the remains of one of East Africa's oldest mosques. With pleasant cottages set around expansive beachside grounds, a restaurant and a children's play area, **Travellers Lodge** (☎023-244 0077, 0754-855485; www.travellers-lodge.com; campsite per person US$12, s/d cottages from US$55/75; ❄) is a fine all-round accommodation choice.

Getting There & Away

Dalla-dallas go throughout the day from Mwenge (north of Dar es Salaam along the New Bagamoyo road, and accessed via *dalla-dalla* from New Posta) to Bagamoyo (Tsh2000, two hours).

Tanga

Tanga seaport has a sleepy, semicolonial atmosphere, and makes a convenient stop en route to or from Mombasa in Kenya. About 50km south is historic **Pangani town**, with lovely beaches to the north and south.

Sleeping & Eating

Panori Hotel HOTEL $
(☎027-264 6044; Ras Kazone; s/d/tw/tr Tsh30,000/45,000/45,000/60,000; ❄) The reliable Panori is 3km from the centre, with clean rooms and a restaurant.

Ocean Breeze Hotel HOTEL $
(☎027-264 4445; cnr Tower & Market Sts; r with fan/air-con Tsh17,000/25,000; ❄) Just east of the market, this budget hotel has reasonable rooms, though not all have nets.

Capricorn Beach Cottages BOUTIQUE HOTEL $$
(☎0784-632529; www.capricornbeachcottages.com; s/d US$75/114; @ 📶) A classy, lovely place 31km south of Pangani, with three spacious self-catering cottages in baobab-studded gardens.

Peponi Holiday Resort LODGE $$
(☎0784-202962; www.peponiresort.com; campsite per person US$5, s/d bandas with half board US$75/95; @ 🏊) Backpacker- and family-friendly Peponi has camping, *bandas* and a restaurant in beachside gardens 30km south of Tanga. Take a Pangani bus to the turn-off, from where it's a two-minute walk.

Patwas Restaurant INDIAN $
(Mkwakwani Rd; meals from Tsh3500; ⏰8am-8pm Mon-Sat) Fresh juices and local-style meals just south of the market.

Information

Tatona (☎0768-971166; www.tangatourism.com; ⏲8.30am-5pm) Tourist information; just off Independence Ave, diagonally up from Exim Bank.

Getting There & Away

To/from Dar es Salaam, Raha Leo goes daily from 6.30am in each direction (Tsh12,000 to Tsh15,000, five hours).

To Arusha, there are at least three departures daily between about 6am and 11am (Tsh14,000, seven hours). To Lushoto (Tsh6000, three to four hours), there's a direct bus departing by 7am, or take any Arusha bus and transfer at Mombo junction.

To Pangani (Tsh2500, 1½ hours), there are small buses throughout the day along the coastal road.

Usambara Mountains

With their wide vistas, cool climate, winding paths and picturesque villages, the Usambaras are one of northeastern Tanzania's highlights. It's easily possible to spend at least a week here hiking from village to village, or relaxing in one spot and exploring with day walks.

Lushoto

Lushoto is a leafy highland town nestled in a fertile valley at about 1200m. It's the centre of the western Usambaras and makes a fine base for hikes into the surrounding hills.

Sleeping & Eating

St Eugene's Hostel GUESTHOUSE $
(Montessori Centre; ☎027-264 0055, 0784-523710; www.st-eugenes-hostel.com; s/tw/tr/ste US$25/45/54/60) Spacious, good-value rooms and meals. Profits go to support work with local children. It's on the main road about 3.5km before Lushoto.

Tumaini Hostel HOSTEL $
(☎027-264 0094; tumaini@elct-ned.org; Main Rd; d/ste Tsh25,000/35,000, s/d without bathroom Tsh15,000/20,000) Simple twin-bedded rooms and hot-water showers in the town centre, with a good restaurant next door.

Lawn's Hotel HOTEL $$
(☎027-264 0005, 0784-420252; www.lawnshotel.com; campsite per person US$10, s/d from US$40/50; @) Vine-covered buildings surrounded by extensive gardens; spacious, musty rooms with dark-wood floors and fireplaces; a restaurant; and hot-water showers for campers.

Information

MONEY

There's no ATM.

National Microfinance Bank (Main Rd; ⏲8am-3pm Mon-Fri) Changes cash only.

TOURIST INFORMATION

All of the following organise hikes:

Friends of Usambara Society (www.usambaratravels.com) Down the small road running next to the bank.

Tayodea (youthall2000@yahoo.com) On the small hill behind the bus station.

Tupande (www.tupande-usambara.org) In the southwestern corner of the bus station.

Getting There & Away

Daily buses travel from Lushoto to Tanga (Tsh6000, four hours), Dar es Salaam (Tsh12,000, six to seven hours) and Arusha (Tsh12,000 to Tsh14,000, six hours), with most departures from 6.30am.

NORTHERN TANZANIA

Moshi

Moshi, a bustling town at the foot of Mt Kilimanjaro, is home of the Chagga people and the centre of one of Tanzania's major coffee-growing regions. Most visitors use the town as a starting point for climbing Mt Kilimanjaro. It's also generally a less expensive place to stay than Arusha.

Tours

The following Moshi-based companies focus on Kilimanjaro treks and day hikes on the mountain's lower slopes.

Ahsante Tours GUIDED TOUR
(☎027-275 0248; www.ahsantetours.com; Karanga Dr)

Kessy Brothers Tours & Travel GUIDED TOUR
(☎027-275 1185; www.kessybrotherstours.com; Chagga St)

Moshi Expeditions & Mountaineering GUIDED TOUR
(MEM Tours; ☎027-275 4234; www.memtours.com; Kaunda St)

Moshi

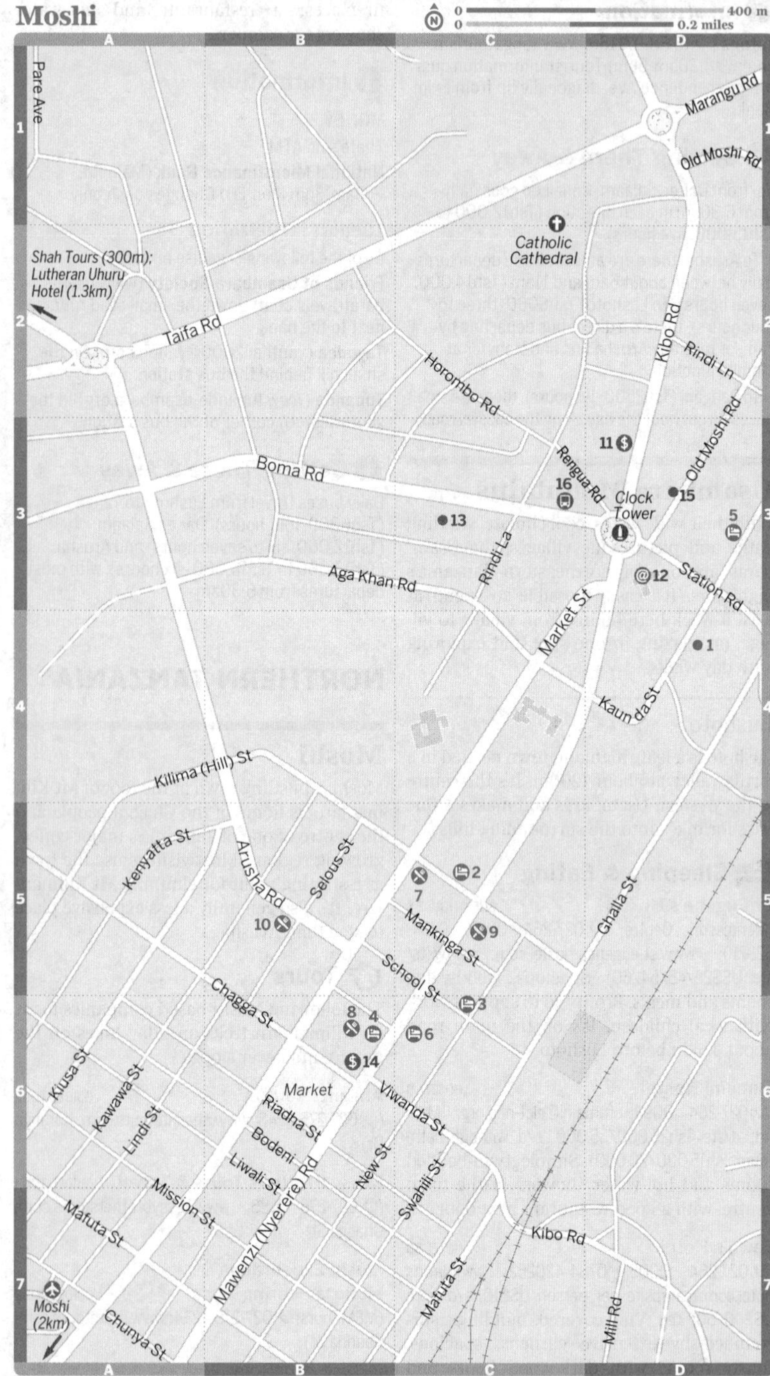
0
400 m
0
0.2 miles
A
B
C
D
1
2
3
4
5
6
7
Pare Ave
Marangu Rd
Old Moshi Rd
Catholic Cathedral
Shah Tours (300m); Lutheran Uhuru Hotel (1.3km)
Taifa Rd
Kibo Rd
Rindi Ln
Horombo Rd
Old Moshi Rd
11
Rengua Rd
16
15
Clock Tower
5
Boma Rd
13
Rindi La
12
Aga Khan Rd
Station Rd
Market St
1
Kaun da St
Kilima (Hill) St
Kenyatta St
Arusha Rd
Selous St
7
2
Mankinga St
9
10
Ghalla St
School St
3
Chagga St
8
4
6
14
Market
Viwanda St
Kiusa St
Kawawa St
Lindi St
Riadha St
Bodeni
Liwali St
New St
Swahili St
Mission St
Mafuta St
Mawenzi (Nyerere) Rd
Kibo Rd
Mafuta St
Mill Rd
Moshi (2km)
Chunya St

Moshi

Activities, Courses & Tours

1 Moshi Expeditions & Mountaineering ... D4

Sleeping

2 AA Hill Street Accommodation ... C5
3 Buffalo Hotel ... C6
4 Haria Hotel ... B6
5 Kilimanjaro Crane Hotel ... D3
6 Kindoroko Hotel ... C6

Eating

7 Coffee Shop ... C5
8 Kilimanjaro Coffee Lounge ... B6
9 Milan's ... C5
10 Union Café ... B5

Information

11 Classic Bureau de Change ... D3
12 EasyCom ... D3
13 Immigration Office ... C3
14 Trast Bureau de Change ... B6

Transport

15 Precision Air ... D3
16 Riverside ... C3

Shah Tours GUIDED TOUR
(027-275 2370, 027-275 2998; www.kilimanjaro-shah.com; Sekou Toure Rd)

Summit Expeditions & Nomadic Experience GUIDED TOUR
(027-275 3233; www.nomadicexperience.com)

Zara Tanzania Adventures GUIDED TOUR
(027-275 0233; www.zaratours.com; Springlands Hotel, Tembo Rd, Pasua Neighbourhood)

Sleeping

Hibiscus B&B $
(0768-146589; www.thehibiscusmoshi.com; off Taifa Rd; dm/s/tw US$17/20/40;) This cosy B&B has six spotless, impeccably decorated rooms, all with fan and most with private bathroom, plus a delightful garden and meals on request. Highly recommended. It's in a quiet residential area about 2km from the town centre; take the first right when coming from the Marangu road roundabout.

AA Hill Street Accommodation GUESTHOUSE $
(0754-461469; sajjad_omar@hotmail.com; Kilima St; s/d/tr Tsh20,000/30,000/40,000) Clean, quiet and pleasant rooms with fans, in a convenient location a short walk from the bus station. Alcohol is not allowed on the premises and unmarried couples cannot share a room. There's no breakfast.

Buffalo Hotel HOTEL $
(027-275 2775; New St; r with/without bathroom from Tsh35,000/20,000;) The popular Buffalo Hotel has straightforward double and twin rooms (the cheapest with fan; others with air-con) with cable TV.

Haria Hotel HOTEL $
(0763-019395; Mawenzi Rd; dm Tsh10,000, tw with/without bathroom Tsh30,000/20,000;) Bright, large no-frills rooms with fans make this place a good-value choice. There's a rooftop bar-restaurant. Breakfast costs Tsh3500.

Kindoroko Hotel HOTEL $
(027-275 4054; www.kindorokohotels.com; Mawenzi Rd; s/d/f US$25/35/50; @) This busy place has small rooms featuring cable TV and hot water, and a rooftop bar with Kilimanjaro views.

Lutheran Uhuru Hotel LODGE $$
(0753-037216; www.uhuruhotel.org; Sekou Toure Rd; s/d from US$40/50; @) This alcohol-free place has spotless, good-value, wheelchair-accessible rooms in leafy, expansive grounds, a good restaurant and Kili views. It's 3km northwest of the town centre.

Kilimanjaro Crane Hotel HOTEL $$
(027-275 1114; www.kilimanjarocranehotelsandsafaris.com; Kaunda St; s/d from US$40/50; @) This ageing midranger has a whiff of character, rooms with cable TV and large beds backing a small garden and Kili views from the rooftop.

Ameg Lodge LODGE $$
(027-275 0175, 0754-058268; www.ameglodge.com; off Lema Rd; s/tw from US$60/98; @) Comfortable, spacious rooms in detached cottages – all with TV, small porches and fans – set around a large, grassy compound, plus Moshi's best gym and a restaurant. It's about 4km northwest of the town centre.

Eating

Milan's INDIAN $
(Mankiga St; meals Tsh4000-8000; lunch & dinner;) This colourful all-vegetarian spot is recommended for its low prices and delicious Indian cuisine.

Coffee Shop CAFE $
(Kilima St; meals Tsh4000-10,000; breakfast, lunch & dinner Mon-Fri, breakfast & lunch Sat) Garden seating, good coffee and homemade

breads, cakes, yoghurt, breakfast and low-priced light meals. Proceeds go to a church project.

Kilimanjaro Coffee Lounge CAFE $
(Chagga St; meals Tsh5000-10,000; breakfast & dinner Mon-Sat, lunch daily;) Perpetually packed with travellers, this Western-style coffee shop is a good homesickness antidote should you need one.

Union Café CAFE $$
(Arusha Rd; meals Tsh7000-15,000; breakfast, lunch & dinner;) A stylish shop with pizzas, pastas, sandwiches and great coffee.

Information

IMMIGRATION

Immigration Office (Boma Rd; 7.30am-3.30pm Mon-Fri)

INTERNET ACCESS

EasyCom (Ground fl, Kahawa House, clock-tower roundabout; per hr Tsh1000; 7.30am-8pm) International dialling from Tsh200 per minute.

MONEY

Classic Bureau de Change (Kibo Rd; 8am-4pm)

Trast Bureau de Change (Chagga St; 9am-5pm Mon-Sat, 9am-2pm Sun)

Getting There & Away

AIR

Most flights to Moshi land at Kilimanjaro International Airport (KIA), 50km west of town (from Tsh35,000 in a taxi). **Precision Air** (0787-800820; www.precisionairtz.com; Old Moshi Rd) has daily flights to Dar es Salaam, Mwanza and Nairobi. **Fastjet** (0685-680533; www.fastjet.com) flies daily to Dar es Salaam and Mwanza.

BUS

Buses and minibuses run throughout the day to Arusha (Tsh2500, 1½ hours) and Marangu (Tsh1500, 1½ hours). To Dar es Salaam (seven to eight hours) try Dar Express, with several luxury buses (Tsh30,000) between 7am and 10.30am from their office near the clock tower. Dar Express' 7am bus sometimes arrives early enough for you to catch the afternoon ferry to Zanzibar, but don't count on it.

Dar Express, departing 6am, is also the best company to Mwanza (Tsh38,000, 12 to 13 hours). For Tanga (Tsh12,000 to Tsh15,000, five to six hours), try Simba Line from 6.30am.

There are taxi stands at the bus station and clock-tower roundabout.

Marangu

This small town on the slopes of Kilimanjaro makes a convenient overnight stop if you're trekking the Marangu route. It's also a pleasant place in its own right, with an agreeable highland atmosphere, and cool, leafy surroundings.

Sleeping & Eating

Coffee Tree Campsite CAMPGROUND $
(0754-691433; kilimanjaro@iwayafrica.com; campsite per person US$8, rondavels/chalets per person US$12/15) This place has expansive, trim grounds, hot-water showers, tents for hire, double *rondavels* (traditional huts) and four- to five-person chalets. There's no food.

Babylon Lodge LODGE $$
(027-275 6355; www.babylonlodge.com; campsite per person US$5, s/d/tr US$40/60/80) Friendly Babylon has simple, clean, twin and double-bedded rooms clustered around small, attractive gardens and a tiny lawn for camping. It's 700m east of the main junction.

Marangu Hotel LODGE $$$
(0754-886092; www.maranguhotel.com; campsite per person US$10, s/d/tr with half board US$100/150/200; @) This long-standing hotel has pleasant rooms in expansive grounds, lovely gardens, a restaurant and a campground with hot-water showers.

Information

CRDB (Main junction) ATM.

NBC (Main junction) ATM.

Getting There & Away

Minibuses run throughout the day between Marangu's main junction ('Marangu Mtoni') and Moshi (Tsh2000, 1½ hours).

Mt Kilimanjaro

At 5896m, Mt Kilimanjaro is Africa's highest peak and one of the continent's most magnificent sights. From cultivated farmlands on the lower levels, the mountain rises through lush rainforest, alpine meadows and a barren lunar landscape to the twin summits of Kibo and Mawenzi.

A hike up 'Kili' lures hundreds of hikers each year. It's even more attractive, because with the right preparation you can walk all the way to the summit without ropes or technical climbing experience. However, the climb

EXPERT ADVICE ON CLIMBING MT KILIMANJARO

How many times have you climbed Kilimanjaro to Uhuru Peak? I could say easily 500-plus times. But I still enjoy every time. It's a magical mountain, with its vegetation, forest and moorland. A truly beautiful mountain. The mountain has given me everything. My livelihood has been the mountain, and everything I can think of, the mountain has provided me.

What advice would you have for someone climbing the mountain for the first time? The most important advice is to practise, and to know what you are getting into. It is a huge mountain, it's not a hill, and climbing it is not a walkabout. You have to be able to run or walk that distance beforehand. People often arrive with not enough knowledge of proper drinking, eating and preparing themselves. You need stamina, but also knowledge and determination. All together, these add up to success. To do well, you must understand what could happen, and then properly prepare yourself. Climbers must be willing to pace themselves, to have the courage to know what they are getting into and then prepare themselves appropriately: take it easy, drink, eat and sleep. It is not the peak itself, but the journey to get there.

What about the environmental situation on Mt Kilimanjaro? I will have to speak only briefly here, as it is a large and sensitive issue. My wish is that all of us who enjoy the spirit of the mountain could do more. The mountain is fragile. Indigenous plants are disappearing. Also, the waterbed is drying off due to erosion and impact. I wish every one of us could take this more seriously. If you think of the numbers – about 45,000 visitors, multiplied by four (porters, guides etc) – this is the number of people on the mountain each year. We are not doing enough. The mountain is cleaner now than it was because of the efforts of many. But, human waste especially is a problem, with contamination of water sources. And trash – where is it going? We need to think what is happening. There is lots of involvement around the foothills with tree planting and re-establishing the forest. We need more people to be involved in putting back into the forest.

What can travellers do to contribute? They can start to think about the general impact on the mountain, choosing companies that invest in the mountain, companies with a 'leave no trace' policy. Also, allowing law-makers to enforce existing laws, including the one limiting the number of climbers on certain routes at any one time. Just asking the trekking companies questions shows that travellers take these issues seriously. While on the mountain, trekkers can point out to companies that claim to follow a 'leave no trace' policy any problems they may notice with trash removal or other issues.

What is your favourite thing about the mountain? So many things! Just to be on the mountain with its different vegetation zones – forest, moorland, alpine desert. Just to see the nature itself high up in the alpine area, when no one is around, to see the glacier field. There is no way I can describe it.

Marangu's Simon Mtuy is World Record Holder for the fastest unsupported ascent and descent of Mt Kilimanjaro (9 hours, 22 minutes)

is a serious venture and should only be undertaken with the right preparation.

Trekking Routes

There are six main routes to the summit. Of these, the **Marangu Route** is the easiest and the most popular. It is typically sold as a five-day, four-night return package, although at least one extra night is recommended to help acclimatisation.

Other routes usually take six or seven days. The popular **Machame Route** has a gradual ascent before approaching the summit via the top section of the Mweka Route. Beware of operators who try to sell an 'economy' version of the Machame Route, which switches near the top to the challenging **Umbwe Route**, summiting via the often ice-and-snow-covered Western Breach. The **Rongai Route** starts near the Kenyan border and goes up the northern side of the mountain. It's possible to do this in five days, but it's better done in six.

Information

Mt Kilimanjaro can be climbed at any time of year, with the best times from late June to October, and from late December to February.

Bring a full range of waterproof cold-weather clothing and gear, including a good-quality sleeping bag. Waterproof everything.

Apart from a small shop at Marangu Gate selling a limited range of chocolate bars and tinned items, there are no shops inside the park. You can buy beer and sodas at high prices at huts on the Marangu Route.

COSTS

No-frills five-day/four-night treks up the Marangu Route start at about US$1200, including park fees, and no-frills six-day budget treks on the Machame Route start at around US$1500. Better-quality six-day trips on the Marangu and Machame Routes start at about US$1600.

Whatever you pay for your trek, remember that at least US$525 of this goes to park fees for a five-day Marangu Route climb, and more for longer treks (US$745 for a seven-day Machame Route climb). The rest of the money covers food, tents (if required), guides, porters and transport to and from the start of the trek.

Most of the better companies provide dining tents, reasonable cuisine and various other extras to both make the experience more enjoyable and maximise your chances of getting to the top. If you choose a really cheap trip you risk having inadequate meals, mediocre guides, few comforts and problems with hut bookings and park fees. Also remember that an environmentally responsible trek usually costs more.

PARK FEES

Park entry is US$60 per adult per day (not per 24-hour period) and there is a rescue fee of US$20 per person per trip.

Huts on the Marangu Route cost US$50 per person per night; camping is US$50 per person per night.

Guide and porter fees (but not tips) are handled directly by the trekking companies. For anyone paying directly at the gate, all entry, hut, camping and other park fees must be paid with Visa or MasterCard and your PIN.

TIPPING

Most guides and porters depend on tips as their major source of income. As a guideline, plan on tipping about 10% of the total amount you've paid for the trek, divided up among the guides and porters. Common tips for satisfactory service are US$10 to US$15 per group per day for the guide, US$8 to US$10 per group per day for the cook and US$5 to US$10 per group per day for each porter.

GUIDES & PORTERS

Guides, and at least one porter (for the guide), are obligatory and are provided by your trekking company. You can carry your own gear on the Marangu Route, although porters are generally used, but one or two porters per trekker are essential on all other routes.

All guides must be registered with the national park authorities. If in doubt, check that your guide's permit is up to date. On Kili, the guide's job is to show you the way and that's it. Only the best guides, working for reputable companies, will be able to tell you about wildlife, flowers or other features on the mountain.

Porters will carry bags weighing up to 15kg (not including their own food and clothing, which they strap to the outside of your bag); your bags will be weighed before you set off.

While most guides, including those working for the budget companies, are dedicated, professional, properly trained and genuinely concerned with making your trip safe and successful, there are exceptions. If you're a hardy traveller you might not worry about basic meals and substandard tents, but you should be concerned about incompetent guides and dishonest porters. Although it doesn't happen often, some guides leave the last hut deliberately late on the summit day to avoid going all the way to the top. Going with a reputable company, preferably one who hires full-time guides (most don't), is one way to prevent bad experiences. Also, insist on meeting the guide before signing up for a trip, familiarise yourself with all aspects of the route, and when on the mountain have morning and evening briefings so you know what to expect each day. The night before summiting talk to other climbers to be sure your departure time seems realistic (though note that not everyone leaves at the same time). If it doesn't, get an explanation from your guide. Should problems arise, be polite but firm with your guide.

Arusha

The fast-growing town of Arusha, sprawling in the shadow of Mt Meru, is the gateway to Tanzania's northern safari circuit. The surrounding lush countryside is dotted with coffee, wheat and maize estates tended by the Arusha and Meru people.

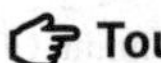

Tours

The following are safari and trekking operators.

Access2Tanzania TREKKING, SAFARIS
(☎0732-979903; www.access2tanzania.com)

Base Camp Tanzania TREKKING, SAFARIS
(☎027-250 0393, 0784-186422; www.basecamptanzania.com)

Hoopoe Safaris TREKKING, SAFARIS
(☎027-250 7011; www.hoopoe.com; India St) Upper midrange.

IntoAfrica TREKKING, SAFARIS
(☎in UK 114-255 5610; www.intoafrica.co.uk)

Roy Safaris TREKKING, SAFARIS
(☎027-250 2115, 027-250 8010; www.roysafaris.com; Serengeti Rd) A highly regarded company offering budget and semiluxury camping safaris in the northern circuit, as well as competitively priced luxury lodge safaris and Kilimanjaro and Meru treks. Known for its high-quality vehicles and value for money.

Safari Makers TREKKING, SAFARIS
(☎0732-979195; www.safarimakers.com)

Wayo Africa TREKKING, SAFARIS
(☎0784-203000; www.wayoafrica.com)

Sleeping

City Centre West

The best budget area is Kaloleni neighbourhood, north of Stadium St and east of Colonel Middleton Rd (a 10-minute walk from the bus stand), whose dusty streets host many cheap guesthouses and local restaurants and bars.

★Hotel Flamingo GUESTHOUSE $
(☎0754-260309; flamingoarusha@yahoo.com; Kikuyu St; s/d US$25/35) This low-key place has sparse but clean rooms. There's a little lounge, breakfast is reasonable and the staff is friendly.

Raha Leo GUESTHOUSE $
(☎0753-600002; Stadium St; s/tw without bathroom Tsh15,000/20,000, d with bathroom Tsh25,000) Undistinguished although adequate rooms around an open-air lounge. With hot-water and cable TV it's one of the better value places in town.

Kitundu Guesthouse GUESTHOUSE $
(☎027-250 9065; Levolosi Rd; r with/without bathroom Tsh25,000/15,000) A decent, reliable choice. Although it's pricier than some similar and even better guesthouses around here, the others don't offer Mt Meru views.

Arusha Backpackers BACKPACKERS $
(☎0773-377795; www.arushabackpackers.co.tz; Sokoine Rd; dm/s/d without bathroom US$10/12/20; @) Popular despite the cell-like shared bathroom and mosquito-net-less rooms, many of which lack windows and cost more than quieter properly sized self-contained rooms elsewhere.

CULTURAL TOURISM PROGRAMMES

Numerous villages outside Arusha have organised Cultural Tourism Programmes that offer an alternative to the safari scene. They range in length from a few hours to a few days, usually centre on light hikes and village activities, and offer an opportunity to experience Tanzania at the local level while supporting local employment.

Fees start from about Tsh25,000/60,000 per person for a half-/full-day program with lunch, and prices drop with bigger groups. Book tours through Arusha's Tanzania Tourist Board (TTB) Tourist Information Centre (p697).

Clock Tower & Eastern Arusha

Most of the following are in the green and quieter eastern part of town, while several are in the thick of things around the clock tower.

Spices & Herbs GUESTHOUSE $
(axum_spices@hotmail.com; Simeon Rd; s/d/tw US$40/50/50; @) The 19 rooms behind this popular Ethiopian restaurant are simple but warm, with woven grass mats and wooden wardrobes adding character. A fine budget choice.

Ujamaa Hostel HOSTEL $
(☎0753-960570; www.ujamaahostel.com; Fire Rd; dm with half board plus laundry US$18) Focusing on volunteers, but open to all, Ujamaa is the most communal spot to lay your head in Arusha. Besides the clean dorms with shelves, lockable draws and hot-water bathrooms, there's a lounge, travel advice and garden.

Centre House Hostel GUESTHOUSE $
(☎0754-089928; Kanisa Rd; dm/d Tsh15,000/40,000; @) On the grounds of a Catholic high school, this no-frills place – with dorms, doubles and hot water – is popular with long-term volunteers. Meals can be arranged. The gate shuts at 11pm.

Outpost Lodge LODGE **$$**
(☎0754-318523; www.outposttanzania.net; Serengeti Rd; s/d/tw/tr US$57/74/74/87; @ 🛜 🏊) The rooms are nothing special, albeit with attractive stone floors, but the lush grounds and communal poolside restaurant-lounge with fresh-squeezed juices more than compensate.

Le Jacaranda GUESTHOUSE **$$**
(☎027-254 4624; www.chez.com/jacaranda; s/d/tr US$50/55/75; @ 🛜) This French-owned place off Nyerere Rd has a variety of spacious rooms whose frumpiness is mostly hidden by the African themed art. There's a garden with minigolf and a restaurant.

Arusha

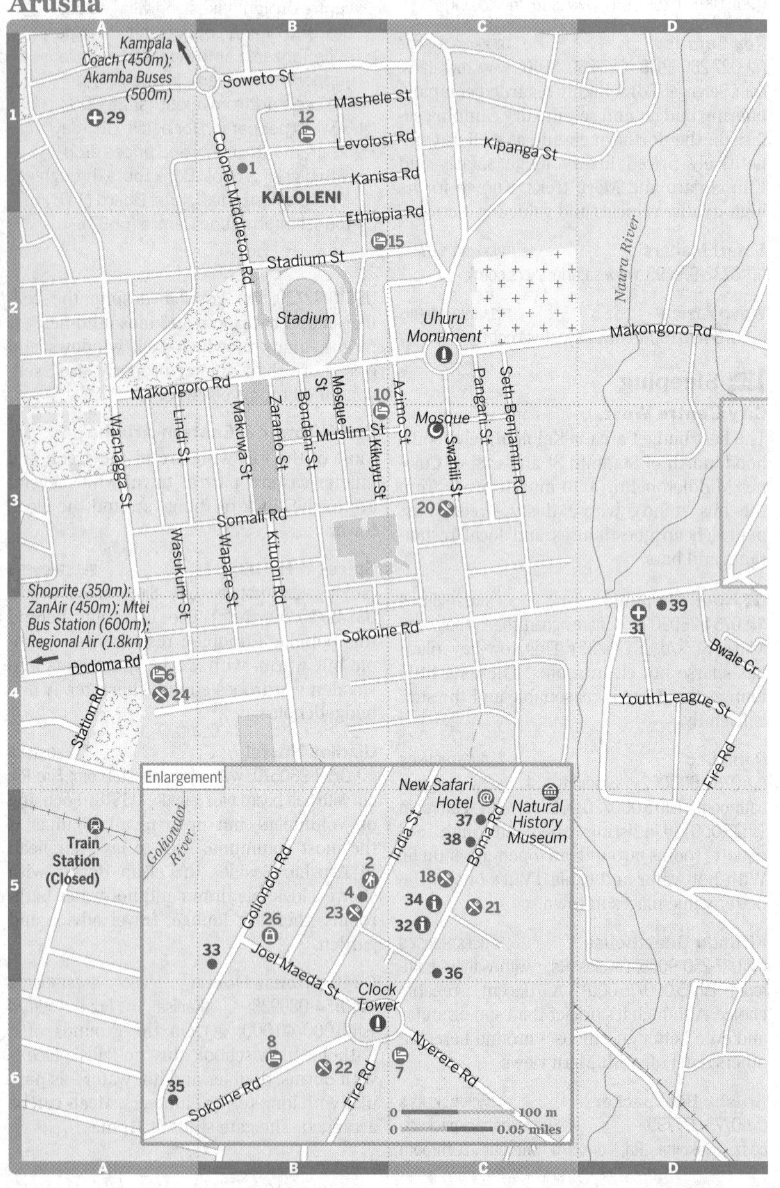

Impala Hotel HOTEL **$$**

(☎027-254 3082; www.impalahotel.com; Simeon Rd; s/d/tr US$90/110/155; ❄@🛜≋) Filling a gap between the small family-run guesthouses and big luxury hotels, the nothing-special Impala offers OK rooms (ask for one of the newer ones), a bureau de change and a restaurant.

Arusha Naaz Hotel HOTEL **$$**

(☎027-257 2087; www.arushanaaz.net; Sokoine Rd; s/d/tr from US$45/60/75; ❄🛜) Naaz is short on atmosphere, but otherwise good value, with comfortable 1st-floor rooms in a convenient location by the clock tower. Rooms vary, so check out a few.

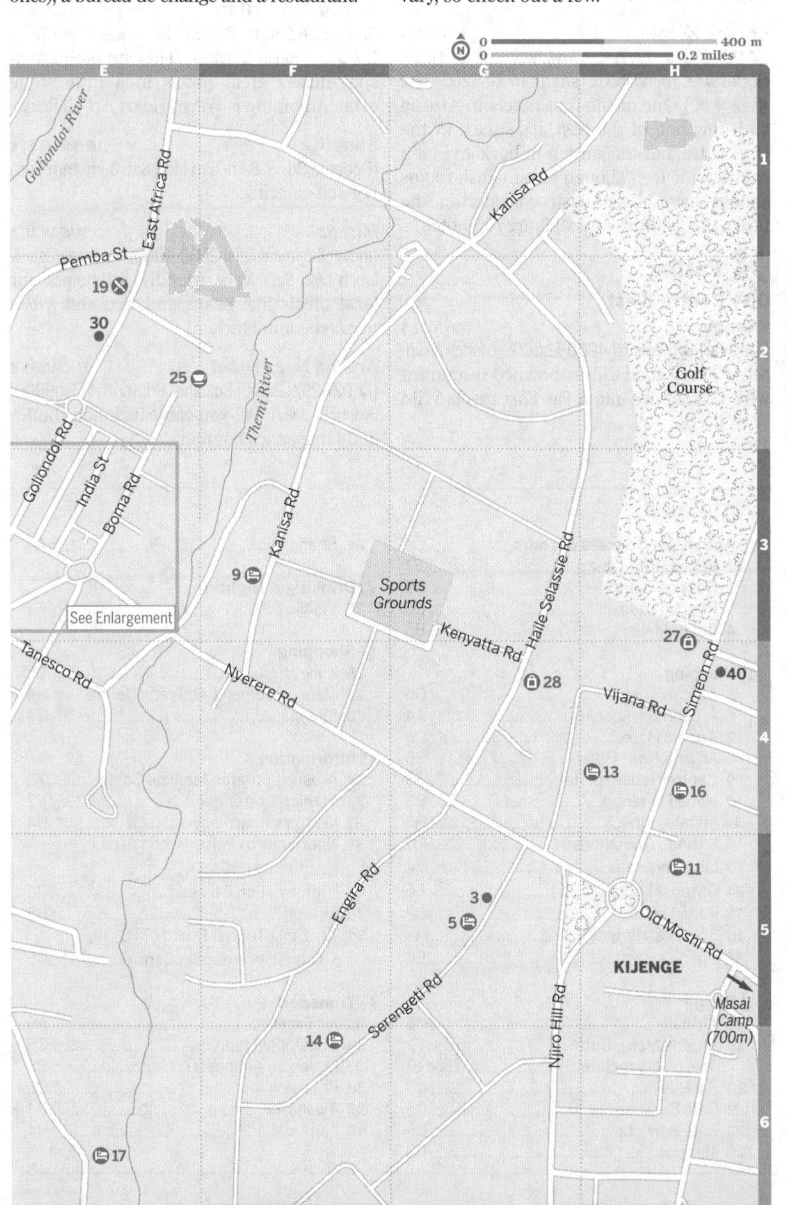

African Tulip HOTEL $$$
(☎0783-714104; www.theafricantulip.com; Serengeti Rd; s/d/tr/ste US$190/230/300/310; ❄@📶🏊) On a green, quiet side street, this lovely place successfully merges an African safari theme with a genteel ambience. The large rooms have all the mod cons.

Arusha Hotel HOTEL $$$
(☎027-250 7777; www.thearushahotel.com; clock-tower roundabout; s/d from US$260/320; ❄@📶🏊) One of the first hotels in Arusha and now one of the best, it's smack in the city centre, but the garden in back gives it a countryside feel. Though the smallish rooms should have more flash considering the price, the facilities and staff are top-notch.

Eating

City Centre West

Shanghai CHINESE $
(Sokoine Rd; meals Tsh4000-12,000; ⏰lunch & dinner; 🖊) Very good Chinese-owned restaurant with fast service and a Far East meets Wild West decor.

Big Bite INDIAN $$
(Swahili St; meals Tsh8000-12,000; ⏰lunch & dinner Wed-Mon; 🖊) One of the oldest and most reliable Indian restaurants in Arusha. Don't let the modest premises fool you.

Clock Tower Area

Arusha Masai Café PIZZERIA $
(☎0755-765640; Pemba St; meals Tsh7000-15,000; ⏰lunch & dinner) This simple garden spot makes great pizzas in a little stone oven. Adjoining is Warm Heart Art Gallery.

Shoprite SUPERMARKET $
(Dodoma Rd; ⏰8am-7pm Mon-Sat, 8am-4pm Sun) For self-catering.

Mirapot TANZANIAN $
(India St; meals Tsh2500-4000; ⏰breakfast & lunch Mon-Sat) Very friendly little spot for local meals like beans and rice and *kuku nazi* (coconut chicken).

Arusha Naaz Hotel TANZANIAN $
(☎027-257 2087; Sokoine Rd; buffet Tsh9000; ⏰lunch daily) All-you-can-eat lunch buffet and large snack counter.

Arusha

Activities, Courses & Tours
1 Base Camp Tanzania B1
2 Hoopoe Safaris B5
3 Roy Safaris G5
4 Safari Makers B5

Sleeping
5 African Tulip G5
6 Arusha Backpackers A4
7 Arusha Hotel C6
8 Arusha Naaz Hotel B6
9 Centre House Hostel F3
10 Hotel Flamingo B3
11 Impala Hotel H5
12 Kitundu Guesthouse B1
13 Le Jacaranda H4
14 Outpost Lodge F6
15 Raha Leo B2
16 Spices & Herbs H4
17 Ujamaa Hostel E6

Eating
18 Africafé C5
19 Arusha Masai Café E2
Arusha Naaz Hotel .... (see 8)
20 Big Bite C3
21 Café Bamboo C5
22 Café Barrista B6
23 Mirapot B5
24 Shanghai A4

Drinking & Nightlife
25 Via Via E2

Shopping
26 Kase B5
27 Maasai Women Fair Trade Centre H4
28 Shanga G4

Information
29 Arusha Lutheran Medical Centre A1
30 Immigration Office E2
31 Moona's Pharmacy D4
32 Ngorongoro Conservation Area Authority (NCAA) Information Office C5
33 Skylink B5
34 Tanzania Tourist Board (TTB) Tourist Information Centre C5

Transport
35 Air Excel A6
36 Coastal Aviation C5
37 Ethiopian Airlines C5
38 Precision Air C5
39 RwandAir D4
40 ZanAir H4

Café Barrista CAFE $

(Sokoine Rd; meals Tsh3000-8000; ⏲breakfast & lunch; 📶✍) Sandwiches, salads and pastries, plus an internet cafe.

Café Bamboo INTERNATIONAL $

(Boma Rd; meals Tsh6000-12,000; ⏲breakfast, lunch & dinner; ✍) Bamboo has a big menu of light Tanzanian and European meals, plus some less-successful Asian options.

Africafé CAFE $$

(Boma Rd; meals Tsh7500-18,000; ⏲breakfast, lunch & dinner) European cafe vibes, and prices. The menu is heavy on sandwiches and there's a bakery.

Drinking & Nightlife

Via Via CAFE

(Boma Rd; meals Tsh7000-18,000; ⏲lunch & dinner Mon-Sat) Cultured and laid-back with the best soundtrack of any restaurant in Arusha, this place behind the Natural History Museum has coffee, salads and sandwiches plus more substantial meals like pastas and grilled fish, a bar and live music.

Shopping

The clock-tower area, mainly Boma Rd and Joel Maeda St, is lined with craft vendors. Hard bargaining is required.

Shanga HANDICRAFTS

(www.shanga.org; Dodoma Rd) 🍃 Jewellery and other products made from recycled materials by disabled workers.

Maasai Women Fair Trade Centre HANDICRAFTS

(www.maasaiwomentanzania.org; Simeon Rd) This shop raises money for education and other projects with is sale of high-quality beadwork and several other crafts.

Kase BOOKS

(Boma Rd) National park books and maps.

Orientation

Central Arusha is divided by the small Naura River valley. To the west are the bus stations, the main market and many budget hotels. To the east are airline offices, craft shops, midrange and upmarket hotels, and other tourist facilities; many are clustered around the clock-tower roundabout (a 20-minute walk from the central bus stand) where Sokoine and Old Moshi Rds meet.

Information

DANGERS & ANNOYANCES

Arusha is the worst place in Tanzania for street touts. Their main haunts are the bus stations and Boma Rd, but they'll find you just about anywhere. Ensure that any tour company you sign up with is properly registered; get recommendations from other travellers and check the current blacklist at the Tourist Information Centre on Boma Rd.

At night, take a taxi if you go out. It's not safe to walk after dusk. Even during the daytime, try to avoid carrying a bag or anything that could tempt a thief.

IMMIGRATION

Immigration Office (East Africa Rd; ⏲7.30am-3.30pm Mon-Fri) Near the Makongoro Rd junction; visa extensions are usually processed while you wait.

INTERNET ACCESS

Café Barrista (Sokoine Rd; per hr Tsh2000; ⏲7am-6pm Mon-Sat, 7am-2pm Sun)

New Safari Hotel (Boma Rd; per hr Tsh3000; ⏲24hr)

MEDICAL SERVICES

Arusha Lutheran Medical Centre (☎027-250 254 8030; www.selianlh.habari.co.tz) Off Old Moshi Rd; lab tests and a doctor on call 24 hours.

Moona's Pharmacy (☎0754-309052; Sokoine Rd; ⏲8.45am-5.30pm Mon-Fri, to 2pm Sat) Well-stocked pharmacy, west of NBC bank.

MONEY

There are many ATMs. Bureaus de change are clustered along Joel Maeda St, India St and Sokoine Rd near the clock tower. Sanya Bureau de Change, with several locations along Sokoine Rd, is open until 8pm Sundays and public holidays.

TOURIST INFORMATION

Ngorongoro Conservation Area Authority (NCAA) Information Office (☎027-254 4625; Boma Rd) Booklets on Ngorongoro and a relief map of the Ngorongoro Conservation Area.

Tanzania National Parks Headquarters (Tanapa; ☎027-250 3471; www.tanzaniaparks.com; Dodoma Rd) About 5km west of town.

Tanzania Tourist Board (TTB) Tourist Information Centre (☎027-250 3842/3; www.tanzaniatouristboard.com; Boma Rd; ⏲8am-4pm Mon-Fri, 8.30am-1pm Sat) Information on Arusha and northern circuit parks and Cultural Tourism Programme tour bookings. Also keeps a 'blacklist' of tour operators and a list of registered tour companies.

TRAVEL AGENCIES

Skylink (☎0754-465321; www.skylinktanzania.com; Goliondoi Rd) Domestic and international flight bookings.

Getting There & Away

AIR

There are daily flights to Dar es Salaam and Zanzibar (Coastal Aviation, Precision Air, Regional Air, ZanAir), Nairobi (Precision Air), Serengeti National Park (Air Excel, Coastal Aviation, Regional Air), Mwanza (Precision Air), Lake Manyara National Park (Air Excel, Coastal Aviation, Regional Air) and Tarangire National Park (Coastal).

Most flights use Kilimanjaro International Airport (KIA), 45km east of town. Small planes leave from Arusha airport, 8km west of town along Dodoma Rd.

Air Excel (☎0754-211227; www.airexcelonline.com; 2nd fl, Subzali (Exim Bank) Bldg, Goliondoi Rd) Diagonally opposite Standard Chartered Bank.

Coastal Aviation (☎027-250 0343, 0752-059650; www.coastal.cc; Arusha Airport)

Ethiopian Airlines (☎027-250 4231; www.ethiopianairlines.com; Boma Rd)

Fastjet (☎0685-680533; www.fastjet.com; Blue Plaza, 2nd fl, India St)

Precision Air (☎0784-471202; www.precisionairtz.com; Boma Rd) Also handles Kenya Airways bookings.

Regional Air Services (☎027-250 4477, 027-250 2541, 0784-285753; www.regionaltanzania.com)

RwandAir (☎0732-978558; www.rwandair.com; Swahili St)

ZanAir (☎027-254 8877; www.zanair.com; Summit Centre, Dodoma Rd)

BUS

Arusha has two bus stations: the central bus stand near the market, and Makao Mapya bus stand (aka Dar Express bus stand) to the northwest for luxury buses to Dar es Salaam. The central bus station is intimidatingly chaotic in the morning and both are popular haunts for flycatchers and touts. To get your bearings, duck into the lobbies of one of the hotels across the street. To avoid the bus stations altogether, most buses first stop on the edge of town, where taxis will be waiting.

When leaving Arusha, book your ticket the day before, so that in the morning you can get straight on your bus with your luggage. For predawn buses, take a taxi to the station and ask the driver to drop you directly at your bus.

Dar es Salaam

Dar Express has five luxury (Tsh30,000) and three full luxury (Tsh35,000) buses departing Makao Mapya bus stand between 5.50am and 9am (eight to 10 hours). Kilimanjaro Express has four buses daily from its own stand on Colonel Middleton Rd.

The last departure of the day to Dar es Salaam is the non-air-conditioned Akamba.

Lushoto

Chikito and Fasaha (Tsh12,000 to Tsh14,000, six hours) depart daily from 6am.

Moshi

Buses and minibuses run throughout the day between Arusha and Moshi (about Tsh2500, 1½ hours) or, better, take an Arusha–Nairobi shuttle (US$10).

Mwanza

Most buses to Mwanza (Tsh30,000 to Tsh40,000, 12 hours) leave the central bus stand (some use Makao Mapya) from 6am.

Tanga

Frey's and other lines go from the central bus stand between 6am and noon (Tsh14,000, seven hours).

Arusha National Park

Although it's one of Tanzania's smallest national parks, Arusha is one of its most beautiful and topographically varied. Its main features are Ngurdoto Crater, the Momela Lakes and majestic Mt Meru.

Sleeping & Eating

The park has three **public campsites** (campsite per adult/child US$30/5).

Kiboko Lodge LODGE $$
(☎0784-652260; www.wfkibokolodge.com; s/d with half board from US$73/126) The spacious and attractive stone cottages at this non-profit, charity-run lodge have fireplaces, hot water and safes, and the thatched-roof lounge is almost homey. It's 5km down a 4WD-only road east of Ngongongare Gate.

Meru View Lodge LODGE $$
(☎0784-419232; www.meru-view-lodge.de; s/d/tr US$90/130/180; @ 🛜 🏊) This unassuming place has a mix of large and small (all priced the same) cottages set in quiet grounds just 1km south of Ngongongare Gate. The small rooms feel like children's playhouses, but the others are fine.

Information

Entry costs US$35/10 per adult/child per 24-hour period. The main park entrance is at **Ngongongare Gate** (⏰6.30am-6.30pm). **Momella Gate** (⏰6.30am-6.30pm), 12km further north near **park headquarters** (☎027-255 3995; arusha@tanzaniaparks.com), is the place to make campsite or resthouse reservations for Mt Meru.

Getting There & Away

Daily buses go between Arusha and Ngare Nanyuki village (6km north of Momella Gate) via Ngongongare Gate (Tsh3500, 1½ hours). A taxi direct from Arusha costs from Tsh45,000.

Tarangire National Park

Between August and October, the baobab-studded Tarangire National Park has one of the highest concentrations of wildlife of any Tanzanian park, and is especially known for its elephants.

Sleeping

There's a **public campsite** (campsite per adult/child US$30/5) just inside the park with cold-water showers.

Tarangire Safari Lodge TENTED CAMP **$$$**
(☎027-254 4752; www.tarangiresafarilodge.com; s/d with full board US$220/360;) This large lodge has a prime location on a bluff overlooking the Tarangire River, about 10km inside the park gate. Accommodation is in closely spaced tents or thatched bungalows.

Information

Entry costs US$35/10 per adult/child per 24 hours. The **entry gate** (tnp@tanzaniaparks.com; 6am-6.30pm) is near Tarangire's northern tip.

Getting There & Away

Tarangire is 130km (an easy two-hour drive) from Arusha via Makuyuni (the last place for petrol and supplies). It is often included as part of multinight packages continuing on to the Serengeti or Ngorongoro Crater.

Lake Manyara National Park

Among the attractions of the often underrated Lake Manyara National Park are superb birdlife, elusive tree-climbing lions and abundant hippos. The gateway village is Mto wa Mbu, where there are also many accommodation options.

You can arrange budget cultural walks and cycling outside the park through Mto wa Mbu's **Cultural Tourism Programme** (☎0784-606654; mtoculturalprogramme@hotmail.com; 8am-6.30pm) at the Red Banana Café on the main road.

Sleeping & Eating

There are several **public campsites** (per adult/child US$30/5) with cold-water showers and nine **park bandas** (per adult/child US$20/10) with hot water and a cooking area near the park gate.

Njake Jambo Lodge & Campsite BACKPACKERS **$$**
(☎027-250 5553; www.njake.com; Arusha–Karatu Rd; campsite per person US$7, s/d/tw US$60/90/90;) A base for independent travellers and large overland trucks, Jambo has a shaded and well-maintained grassy camping area, plus rooms in double-storey chalet blocks. It's in Mto wa Mbu.

Kirurumu Manyara Lodge TENTED CAMP **$$$**
(☎027-250 7011; www.kirurumu.net; s/d with half board US$179/290) A genteel, unpretentious ambience, bush setting and memorable cuisine are the hallmarks of this highly regarded camp. It's outside the park, and about 6km off the main road.

Information

Entry costs US$35/10 per adult/child per 24 hours. The **entry gate** (lake.manyara@tanzaniaparks.com; 6am-6pm) is at the park's northern tip just west of Mto wa Mbu village.

There's an ATM in Mto wa Mbu.

Getting There & Away

BUS

Buses and *dalla-dallas* run frequently from Arusha (Tsh5000 to Tsh6000, two hours) and Karatu (Tsh2000, one hour) to Mto wa Mbu.

CAR

Arrange car hire (US$150 including fuel and driver) into the park through the Cultural Tourism Programme office or Jambo campsite.

Ngorongoro Conservation Area

The world-renowned Ngorongoro Crater is just one part of a much larger area of interrelated ecosystems, including Olduvai (Oldupai) Gorge, alkaline lakes and the Crater Highlands – a string of volcanoes and collapsed volcanoes (calderas).

Ngorongoro Crater

At 19km wide, Ngorongoro is one of the largest unbroken calderas in the world that isn't a lake. Within its steep, unbroken walls an incredible natural drama plays out as lions, elephants, buffaloes, ostriches and plains herbivores graze and stalk their way around the grasslands, swamps and acacia woodland on the crater floor. Chances are good that you'll also see the critically endangered black rhino, and for many people this is one of the crater's main draws.

Sleeping & Eating

The only public campsite is crowded **Simba A** (campsite per person per adult/child US$30/10), with crater views if there's no cloud cover. It's also possible to stay in or near Karatu village, which is 14km before Ngorongoro's Lodoare Gate and has an ATM.

Vera Inn GUESTHOUSE $
(0754-578145; Milano Rd, Bwani, Karatu; s/d Tsh25,000/35,000) One of the best guesthouses in Karatu, Vera Inn has small but spotless rooms with hot-water showers and cable TV.

Rhino Lodge LODGE $$
(0762-359055; www.ngorongoro.cc; s/d with full board US$135/240;) Up on the crater rim, but without a crater view, this small, friendly lodge, run in collaboration with the Maasai community, is the cheapest place in the conservation area. The 24 rooms may be too rustic for some, but it's good for the price.

Octagon Safari Lodge & Irish Bar LODGE $$
(027-253 4525; www.octagonlodge.com; per person US$60; @) This Irish-Tanzanian owned lodge is tops in Karatu, with lush grounds, cosy cottages and a restaurant-bar.

Ngorongoro Camp & Lodge BACKPACKERS $$
(Ngorongoro Safari Resort; 027-253 4287; www.ngorongorocampandlodge.net; Arusha Rd, Karatu; campsite per person US$8, s/d/tr US$87/140/160; @) This place is always busy with overland trucks. Camping facilities are good and the rooms are too, albeit overpriced.

Ndutu Safari Lodge LODGE $$$
(027-253 7015; www.ndutu.com; s/d with full board US$287/474) This relaxed and rustic place has a lovely setting near the Serengeti border, and is well-placed for observing enormous wildebeest herds during the rainy season.

Information

Entry costs US$50/10 per adult/child per 24 hours, plus US$40/10,000 per foreign-/Tanzanian-registered vehicle per day, plus a crater descent fee of US$200 per vehicle to descend into the crater (maximum stay six hours).

All fees are paid at **Lodoare Gate** (027-253 7031; 6am-6pm), on the Arusha road, or at Naabi Hill Gate on the Serengeti border. Payment is by Visa or MasterCard only.

The crater descent road opens at 6am, and closes at 4pm; all vehicles must exit the crater area before 6pm.

Ngorongoro Conservation Area Authority (NCAA) has its **headquarters** (027-253 7006; www.ngorongorocrater.org; 8am-4pm) at Park Village at Ngorongoro Crater, where there's also a sporadically functioning NBC ATM.

Getting There & Around

If you aren't travelling on an organised safari, vehicles can be hired in Karatu for about US$160 per day including fuel. Buses go daily between Karatu and Arusha (Tsh5000, three hours).

Serengeti National Park

The Serengeti, which covers 14,763 sq km and is contiguous with Masai Mara National Reserve in Kenya, is easily Tanzania's most famous national park. Wildebeest, of which there are over one million, are among the most prominent residents roaming its vast plains, and their annual migration is the Serengeti's biggest drawcard.

Sleeping

There are nine **public campsites** (per adult/child US$30/5).

Twiga Resthouse GUESTHOUSE $$
(028-262 1510; serengeti_tourism@yahoo.com; Central Serengeti; per person US$30) Simple but decent rooms with electricity, hot showers and a kitchen.

Robanda Safari Camp TENTED CAMP $$
(0754-324193; www.moivaro.com; s with full board US$70-195, d with full board US$140-290) This small budget camp on the plains near Robanda village just outside Ikoma Gate has 10 no-frills tents, some with private bathroom.

Serengeti Stop-Over CAMPGROUND $$
(028-262 2273; www.serengetistopover.com; campsite/banda per person US$10/35) Just 1km from Ndabaka Gate along the Mwanza-

Musoma road, this place has camping with hot showers and a cooking area, 14 simple (and overpriced) *rondavels* and a restaurant-bar. Vehicle rental is usually available, and day trips are feasible.

Wayo Green Camp TENTED CAMP $$$
(☎0784-203000; www.wayoafrica.com; per person all-inclusive from US$300) These 'private mobile camps' combine the best aspects of both tented camps and budget camping safari and are a good way to get a deep bush experience in the Serengeti.

Seronera Wildlife Lodge LODGE $$$
(☎027-254 4595; www.hotelsandlodges-tanzania.com; s/d with full board US$355/610; @) With fantastic common areas built on and around the boulders (home to many rock hyrax), this large, crowded place has an ideal location. Rooms and service, however, are overdue for improvement.

Information

Entry costs US$50/10 per adult/child per 24 hours.

The **Serengeti Visitor Centre** (☎0732-985761; serengeti_tourism@yahoo.com; 8am-5pm) at Seronera has an excellent self-guided walk through the Serengeti's history and ecosystems.

Access from Arusha is via **Naabi Hill Gate** (6am-6pm), from where it's 45km further to Seronera, in central Serengeti. **Ndabaka Gate** (6am-6pm), for the western corridor, is 140km northeast of Mwanza and 145km from Seronera. Last entry at these gates is 4pm.

Wildlife concentrations are greatest between December and June, although the Serengeti is rewarding at any time of year. For the wildebeest migration, it's best to be based near Seronera or in the southeastern part of the park from about December to April. The famous crossing of the Grumeti River, in the park's Western Corridor, usually takes place somewhere between May and July. Northern Serengeti is a good base between August and October.

Getting There & Around

Air Excel, Coastal Aviation and Regional Air fly daily from Arusha to the park's seven airstrips (US$150 to US$225 per person one-way). Coastal's flight continues to Mwanza.

Most travellers visit the Serengeti with an organised safari or with their own vehicle.

LAKE VICTORIA

Mwanza

Mwanza is the economic centre of the Lake Victoria region and a jumping-off point for the western Serengeti. The surrounding area is the heartland of the Sukuma, Tanzania's largest tribe.

Tours

For Serengeti safaris, try the following:

Fortes Africa SAFARIS
(☎028-250 0561; www.fortes-africa.com; Station Rd)

Kiroyera Tours SAFARIS
(☎0784-568276; www.kiroyeratours.com; Uhuru St) Also does Rubondo Island excursions.

Masumin Tours & Safaris SAFARIS
(☎028-250 0192; www.masumintours.com; Kenyatta Rd)

Sleeping

Christmas Tree Hotel HOTEL $
(☎028-250 2001; off Karuta St; r Tsh18,000-20,000) The best hotel in the city centre in this price range, Christmas Tree has small but clean rooms with good beds, TV and hot water.

Midland Hotel HOTEL $
(☎028-254 1509; Rwagasore Rd; r Tsh40,000-120,000;) This eye-catching blue tower has noisy albeit well-equipped rooms, a rooftop bar, a breakfast buffet and occasional discounts.

Mwanza Yacht Club CAMPGROUND $
(☎0784-510441; Capri Point; campsite per person Tsh10,000) Mwanza's stop on the overlander's trail has basic facilities, but a lakeside location and good food.

Kishamapanda Guesthouse GUESTHOUSE $
(Kishamapanda St; s/d Tsh10,000/12,000) This tidy little place down a tiny alley is a good shoestring choice. The rooms, with shared bathroom, have ceiling fans and there are Western sit toilets.

Treehouse B&B $$
(☎0756-682829; www.streetwise-africa.org/treehouse; s without bathroom US$30, s/d/f from US$60/70/120; @) Ideal for socially conscious travellers, this homey place with clean, comfortable rooms gives much of its

Mwanza

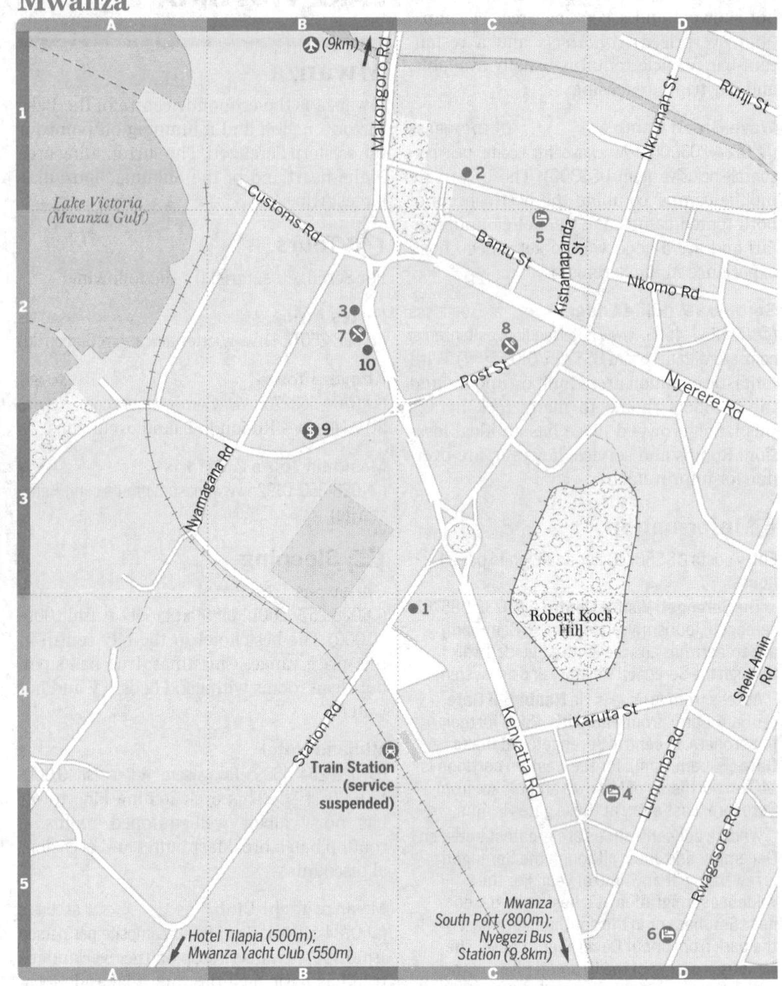

earnings to support the affiliated Streetwise Africa charity. It's in the Isamilo area and difficult to find, so call ahead.

Hotel Tilapia HOTEL $$
(028-250 0517; www.hoteltilapia.com; Capri Point; s/d/ste US$90/110/140;) The ever-popular Tilapia has a variety of dated but decent rooms, many with lake views, and a restaurant.

Eating

Kuleana Pizzeria INTERNATIONAL $
(028-256 0566; Post St; meals Tsh4000-10,000; breakfast, lunch & dinner;) Simple vegetarian meals (pizzas, omelettes, sandwiches and breads) and a mix of locals and expats.

Diners INDIAN $$
(Kenyatta Rd; meals Tsh5000-20,000; lunch & dinner;) This odd time-warp serves some of Mwanza's best Indian food, with Chinese decor and menu items that are

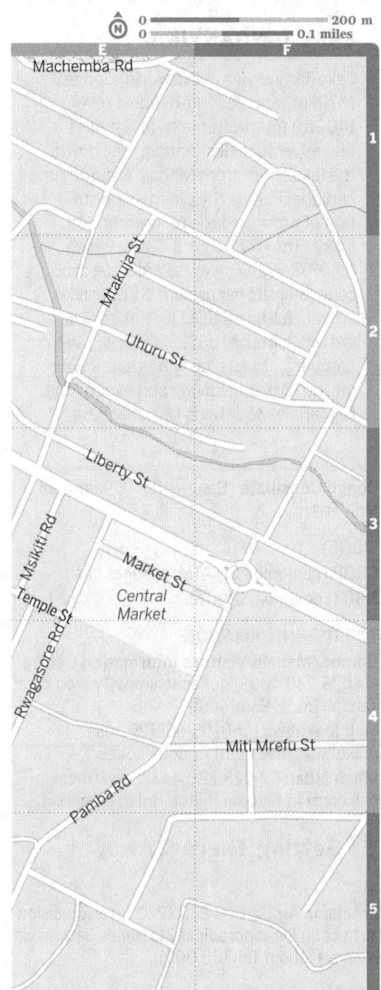

holdovers from its previous incarnation as Szechuan.

Information

MONEY

All the major banks are here with ATMs.

DBK Bureau de Change (Post St) Inside Serengeti Services travel agency; changes cash and travellers cheques.

Mwanza

Activities, Courses & Tours
1 Fortes Africa C4
2 Kiroyera Tours C1
3 Masumin Tours & Safaris B2

Sleeping
4 Christmas Tree Hotel D5
5 Kishamapanda Guesthouse C2
6 Midland Hotel D5

Eating
7 Diners B2
8 Kuleana Pizzeria C2

Information
9 DBK Bureau de Change B3

Transport
10 Precision Air B2

Getting There & Away

AIR

Precision Air (028-250 0819; www.precisionairtz.com; Kenyatta Rd) and **Fastjet** (www.fastjet.com) fly daily to Dar es Salaam (Tsh161,000 one-way). Precision also flies to and from Kilimanjaro International Airport and **Coastal Aviation** (0875-502000; www.coastal.cc; airport) flies to Arusha via Serengeti National Park (about US$180) and to Kigali (US$500).

BOAT

There's thrice-weekly passenger-ferry service between Bukoba and Mwanza on the MV *Victoria* (1st class/2nd-class sleeping/2nd-class sitting/3rd class Tsh35,000/25,600/20,600/15,600, nine hours).

BUS

Nyegezi bus stand, 10km south of town, handles buses to all points east, south and west including Dar es Salaam (Tsh40,000, 14 hours; try Mohammed Trans), Arusha (Tsh30,000, 12 hours), Bukoba (Tsh20,000, seven hours) and Kigoma (Tsh25,000 to Tsh30,000, 10 to 12 hours; try Golden Inter-City).

Buses towards the Kenya border depart from Buzuruga bus stand in Nyakato, 4km east of the centre.

Buy tickets at the bus booking offices at the old city centre bus terminal.

Bukoba

Bukoba, home of the Haya, has a waterside setting and convenient connections to nearby Uganda. Contact **Kiroyera Tours** (0784-568276; www.kiroyeratours.com; Shore Rd) for excursions, tourist information and bus ticket bookings. **ELCT Bukoba Hotel** (0754-415404; www.elctbukobahotel.com; Aerodrome Rd; s/tw/ste Tsh30,000/35,000/50,000; @) has comfortable rooms and pleasant grounds. **Kiroyera Campsite** (0784-568276; www.kiroyeratours.com; Shore Rd; campsite/banda per person US$5/15) is a great backpackers' spot on the beach with meals and three Haya *msonge* (grass huts) with beds and electricity.

LAKE TANGANYIKA

Lake Tanganyika is the world's longest (670km) and second-deepest (over 1400m) freshwater lake, and makes a fine adventure destination. Well down the lake shore from Mahale Mountains National Park is the old mission station of Kipili, and the recommended **Lake Shore Lodge & Campsite** (0763-993166; www.safaritourtanzania.com; campsite per person US$12, bandas s/d with full board US$130/190, chalets s/d with full board US$395/610;), with camping, chalets, cosy *bandas*, kayaking, quad biking, diving and excursions to Mahale Mountains National Park.

LAKE TANGANYIKA

Kigoma

The scrappy but agreeable town of Kigoma is the major Tanzanian port on Lake Tanganyika. It's also the end of the line for the Central Line train, and a starting point for visits to Gombe and Mahale Mountains National Parks.

Sleeping & Eating

Aqua Lodge GUESTHOUSE $
(0764-980788; Katonga Rd; s/d Tsh10,000/15,000;) This basic church-run place has large, good-value rooms (some with fans) on the beach, but no food.

Poyongo Lodge GUESTHOUSE $
(Ujiji Rd; r Tsh15,000) By virtue of being one of the newest hotels in the Mwanga neighbourhood (near the bus stand) Poyongo is one of the best.

Kigoma Hilltop Hotel HOTEL $$
(028-280 4437; www.mbalimbali.com; s/d from US$90/120;) Comfortable double and twin cottages here sit atop an escarpment overlooking the lake.

Sun City TANZANIAN $
(Lumumba St; Tsh2500-5000; breakfast, lunch & dinner) Inexpensive local meals.

Information

CONSULATES

Burundian Consulate (028-280 2865; 9am-3pm Mon-Fri)

Congo Consulate (Bangwe Rd; 9am-4pm Mon-Fri)

MONEY

CRDB (Lumumba St) ATM; changes cash.

NBC (Lumumba St) ATM.

TOURIST INFORMATION

Gombe/Mahale Visitors Information Centre (028-280 4009; gonapachimps@yahoo.com; Tanapa Rd; 9am-4pm)

Maji Makubwa (0755-662129; majimakubwa@mac.com) At Aqua Lodge.

Mbali Mbali (028-280 4437; www.mbalimbali.com) At Kigoma Hilltop Hotel; upmarket.

Getting There & Away

AIR

Precision Air (028-280 4720; www.precisionairtz.com) flies sporadically to Dar es Salaam via Mwanza (about Tsh300,000).

BOAT

The venerable MV *Liemba* sails between Kigoma and Mpulungu (Zambia) from the main port area.

Cargo ferries to Burundi and DRC, many of which also take passengers, depart from Ami port near the train station.

Small, motorised lake 'taxis' for Gombe National Park stop at Kibirizi village, 2km north of Kigoma.

BUS

All buses depart from behind Bero petrol station. Ticket offices, however, are scattered around the Mwanga area just to the west.

Buses go daily to Mwanza (Tsh25,000 to Tsh30,000, 10 to 12 hours) and thrice weekly to Bukoba (Tsh30,000, 13 to 15 hours).

Gombe National Park

In 1960 British researcher Jane Goodall arrived at Gombe to begin a study of wild chimpanzees, which is still ongoing, making it the longest-ever study of a wild animal population. Gombe's 100-plus chimps are well habituated and, with a few days' visit plus some sweaty steep climbing, sightings are highly likely.

Sleeping & Eating

Tanapa Resthouse GUESTHOUSE $
(r/campsite per person US$20/20) Next to the visitor centre at Kasekela, with six simple rooms, two overflow facilities with rooms of lesser quality and toilets out back, and a kitchen.

Information

Entry costs US$100/20 per adult/child per 24 hours.Children under 16 are not permitted to enter the forest. Guides cost US$10 per five-person group per trek.

Getting There & Away

Tanapa boats travel several times weekly to Kigoma and take visitors free if space is available. A lake taxi to the park (Tsh4000, 2½ to three hours) departs from Kibirizi Monday to Saturday around 2pm. Alternatively, charter a boat with local fishermen (hard bargaining required) or more safely and comfortably with one of the established companies.

Mahale Mountains National Park

Mahale Mountains National Park is primarily a chimpanzee sanctuary, but also offers white-sand beaches backed by lushly forested mountains.

Sleeping

Mango Tree Bandas BUNGALOW $$
(*bandas* per person US$30) Basic but decent park-run *bandas* somewhat back from the beach in the forest. Bring your own food.

Kungwe Beach Lodge TENTED CAMP $$$
(☎0713-620154, 0732-978879; www.mbalimbali.com; s/d all-inclusive US$775/1300; ⏲mid-May–mid-Feb; 📶) A lovely place with 10 spacious double tents and a comfy dining area and lounge. The price includes chimp tracking.

Information

Entry costs US$80/30 per adult/child. Children under seven years aren't permitted to enter the forest. Guides cost US$20 per six-person group.

Park headquarters (www.mahalepark.org), where fees are paid, are at Bilenge in the park's northwestern corner, 10 minutes by boat south of the airstrip and 20 minutes north of Kasiha and the park *bandas*.

Getting There & Away

AIR

Safari Airlink (www.flysal.com) and **Zantas Air** (www.zantasair.com) fly to Mahale from Dar es Salaam and Arusha, respectively (about US$930/825 from Dar es Salaam/Arusha).

BOAT

The MV *Liemba* stops at Lagosa (Mugambo) to the north of the park, about 10 hours from Kigoma. Email park headquarters in advance for a pick-up to Bilenge (about US$50 per boat, two hours, plus US$50 per boat from Bilenge to the park *bandas*).

SOUTHERN HIGHLANDS

Iringa

With its bluff-top setting, jacaranda-lined streets and highland feel, Iringa makes an agreeable stop if you're travelling along the Dar es Salaam–Mbeya highway.

Sights & Activities

Neema Crafts CRAFT WORKSHOP
(☎0786-431274; www.neemacrafts.com; Hakimu St; ⏲8.30am-6.30pm Mon-Sat) This vocational training centre for deaf and disabled people has workshop tours, crafts for sale and a good cafe.

Sleeping

Rivervalley Campsite CAMPGROUND $
(Riverside Campsite; ☎026-270 1988, 0782-507017; www.rivervalleycampsites.com; campsite per person US$6, d tented bandas/cottages US$40/50) A lovely riverside setting, shaded camping, tents, cottages, hot-water showers and buffet-style meals make this a popular choice. It's 13km northeast of Iringa (Tsh15,000 in a taxi); take a *dalla-dalla* heading towards Ilula to the turn-off (Tsh1000), from where it's 1.5km further down an unpaved track.

Iringa Lutheran Centre GUESTHOUSE $
(☎026-270 0722, 0755-517445; www.iringalutherancentre.com; Kawawa Rd; s/d/tr US$25/45/55) Clean, quiet, pleasant rooms with bathrooms and hot water, and a restaurant. It's 700m southeast of the main road.

Neema Umaki Guest House GUESTHOUSE $
(☎026-270 2499, 0786-431274; www.neemacrafts.com; Hakimu St; dm/s/d/f Tsh18,000/25,000/45,000/65,000; @ 📶) 🍃 At Neema Crafts Centre, this centrally located guesthouse has an array of rooms and can arrange homestays. Profits support the craft centre.

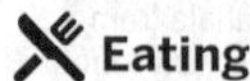

Eating

Hasty Tasty Too AFRICAN, EUROPEAN $
(☎026-270 2061; Uhuru Ave; meals from Tsh3500; ⏲7.30am-8pm Mon-Sat, 10am-2pm Sun) This Iringa classic has breakfasts, yoghurt, shakes and main dishes.

Information

MONEY

CRDB (Uhuru Ave) ATM.
Barclays (Uhuru Ave) ATM.

TOURIST INFORMATION

Iringa Info (☎026-270 1988; infoiringa@gmail.com; Uhuru Ave; ⏲9am-5pm Mon-Fri, 9am-3pm Sat) For Ruaha safaris, car rentals and excursions. Also has a cafe and bookstore.

Getting There & Away

Arriving in Iringa, you'll likely be dropped at the main Ipogoro bus station, 3km from town below the escarpment (Tsh5000 in a taxi from town).

To Dar es Salaam, Super Feo and others go daily from 7am onwards (Tsh20,000, 7½ hours); book in advance at the bus offices at the town bus station.

To Mbeya, Chaula Express departs daily at 7am (Tsh15,000, four to five hours) from the town bus station.

Ruaha National Park

Lovely, baobab-studded, elephant-packed Ruaha is Tanzania's largest national park, and the core of an extended ecosystem covering about 40,000 sq km. At its heart is the Great Ruaha River and a network of 'sand rivers'.

Sleeping & Eating

Inside the Park

There are several **public campsites** (campsite per adult/child US$30/5) plus the nice **new park bandas** (per person US$50) with bedding and basic meals. Book through Iringa Info in Iringa.

Ruaha River Lodge LODGE $$$
(☎0784-237422; www.tanzaniasafaris.info; s/d with full board & wildlife drives US$405/650) This unpretentious, beautifully situated 28-room lodge has stone cottages overlooking the river and a treetop-level bar-terrace.

Outside the Park

Tungamalenga Camp GUESTHOUSE $
(☎026-278 2196; Tungamalenga Rd; campsite per person US$10, r per person with breakfast/full board US$35/60) About 35km from the park gate, this place has a crowded garden for camping, small rooms and a restaurant. Vehicle rental with advance arrangement only.

Information

Entry costs US$20/5 per adult/child per 24 hours, payable with Visa or MasterCard.

Getting There & Away

Iringa Info in Iringa offers safaris from US$250 per vehicle per day. Organise fly-in safaris from Dar es Salaam or Zanzibar with Coastal Travels.

Mbeya

The thriving town of Mbeya is an important transit point en route to or from Zambia and Malawi. There's not much to the town itself, but the surrounding area offers hiking and excursions.

Sleeping & Eating

Karibuni Centre HOSTEL $
(☎025-250 3035, 025-250 4178; www.mec-tanzania.ch; campsite per person Tsh5000, s/d Tsh18,000/30,000) This quiet, mission-run place has a small space to pitch a tent, straightforward rooms and a restaurant. It's 3km southwest of the town centre; take a taxi from the bus station (Tsh3000).

New Millennium Inn GUESTHOUSE $
(☎025-250 0599; Mbalizi Rd; r Tsh18,000-20,000) Directly opposite the bus station, New Mil-

lennium is noisy but convenient for early departures.

Utengule Country Hotel LODGE **$$**
(025-256 0100, 0753-020901; www.riftvalley-zanzibar.com; campsite per person US$10, s/d/ste/f from US$85/125/180/170;) Set on a working coffee plantation in the hills 20km west of Mbeya, Utengule has camping and pleasant rooms. Follow the Tunduma road 12km to Mbalizi and the signposted right-hand turn-off, from where it's 8.5km further.

Information

Gazelle Safaris (025-250 2482, 0784-666600; www.gazellesafaris.com; Jacaranda Rd) Excursions, car rental and flight bookings.

Getting There & Away

To Dar es Salaam (Tsh30000 to Tsh35,000, 12 to 14 hours), Sumry and several others depart daily from 6am.

To the Malawi border (Tsh5000, two to 2½ hours; take the Kyela bus), there are several Coastal buses daily.

TRAIN

Book tickets at least several days in advance at **Tazara train station** (8am-noon & 2-5pm Mon-Fri, 10am-1pm Sat), 4km west of town (Tsh6000 in a taxi).

Mbamba Bay

The relaxing outpost of Mbamba Bay is the southernmost Tanzanian port on Lake Nyasa. **St Benadetta Guest House** (www.chipolestagnes.org/mbambabay.htm; r Tsh12,000) has simple, clean rooms and meals.

Entering or leaving Tanzania, stop at the immigration office/police station near the boat landing for passport formalities.

Songea

The sprawling, attractive town of Songea is a useful stop for travellers heading to and from Lichinga (Mozambique).

OK Hotels 92 (026-260 2640; d Tsh15,000-18,000) has small, decent rooms uphill from the bus stand, near the Lutheran church.

Getting There & Away

To and from Mbeya, try Super Feo (Tsh18,000, eight hours). For Mbamba Bay, a direct vehicle departs daily by 7am (Tsh9000, six to eight hours), or go via Mbinga. Transport to Mozambique departs from 'Majengo C' area. Drivers: head west 18km from Songea along the Mbinga road to the signposted turn-off, from where it's 120km further to the border.

SOUTHEASTERN TANZANIA

Selous Game Reserve

With an area of approximately 45,000 sq km, the Selous is one of Africa's largest wildlife reserves, although only the northernmost section is open for tourism.

Sleeping

There are two **public campsites** (per adult/child US$20/5).

Selous Mbega Camp TENTED CAMP **$$**
(022-265 0250, 0784-624664; www.selous-mbega-camp.com; campsite per person US$10, s/d with full board US$140/200, s/d 'backpackers' special' with full board US$90/130) This laid-back budget choice just outside Mtemere Gate has a small camping ground (bring your own food), pleasant twin-bedded tents and a 'backpackers' special' for those arriving by public bus at Mloka.

Ndoto Kidogo BUNGALOW **$$**
(0787-521808, 0782-416861; www.ndoto-kidogo-lodge.com; campsite per person US$10, per person with full board backpackers/bungalows US$60/140) Near Mloka village, with bungalows, camping and a backpackers' block.

Information

Entry costs US$50/30 per adult/child, plus US$30 per vehicle per day.Many camps close during the March to May rains.The entry point from Dar es Salaam is **Mtemere Gate** (6am-6pm).

Getting There & Away

BUS

Daily buses leave Dar es Salaam's Temeke bus stand (Sudan Market area) to Mloka village, about 10km east of Mtemere Gate (Tsh10,000, seven to nine hours). From Mloka, arrange advance pick-ups with the camps.

TRAIN

Tazara trains stop at Kisaki, Kinyanguru, Fuga and/or Matambwe (near Matambwe Gate), from where you can arrange advance pick-up with the lodges.

Mtwara & Mikindani

The sprawling town of Mtwara, a laid-back, likable place, is a good staging point on the overland journey to Mozambique. About 11km away is the tiny Swahili town of Mikindani, with a long history, coconut groves and a picturesque bay.

Sleeping & Eating

Drive-In Garden & Cliff Bar GUESTHOUSE $
(☎0784-503007; Shangani, Mtwara; campsite per person Tsh5000, r Tsh20,000) A tiny camping area, budget rooms and meals. Breakfast costs extra. Go left at the Shangani junction for 1.2km.

Ten Degrees South Lodge LODGE $
(ECO2; ☎0784-855833; www.tendegreessouth.com; Mikindani; r with/without bathroom Tsh75,000/30,000) A budget travellers' base, with bay views and meals.

Southern Cross Hotel HOTEL $$
(Msemo; ☎023-233 3206; www.msemoproject.com; Shangani, Mtwara; r US$80-100) Sea-facing rooms and a good restaurant in Mtwara's Shangani neighbourhood.

Information

There are ATMs in Mtwara, but none in Mikindani.

Getting There & Away

Daily buses go to and from Dar es Salaam's Temeke/Sudan Market area (Tsh22,000, eight hours).

Frequent minibuses (Tsh500) connect Mtwara and Mikindani.

To Mozambique (Kilambo border), daily pick-ups go from the 'kwa Mbulu' section of Mtwara's market (Tsh4000, one hour).

Masasi

This scruffy district centre is a potentially useful stop for self-drivers to and from Mozambique via Unity Bridge. There's an NBC ATM on the main road. **Holiday Hotel** (Tunduru Rd; r Tsh30,000-40,000) has clean, straightforward rooms with fan, diagonally opposite the bus stand.

UNDERSTAND TANZANIA

Tanzania Today

The 2005 presidential elections were won in a landslide by CCM's Jakaya Kikwete, Tanzania's charismatic former foreign minister. In the 2010 national elections, Kikwete again won, although with a considerably smaller majority (62% of the vote).

More significant is the future of multiparty politics in Tanzania, which seems to have taken several steps backwards in recent years with the entrenchment of the CCM and splintering of the opposition. However, despite this – and ongoing political tensions on the Zanzibar Archipelago notwithstanding – Tanzania as a whole remains reasonably well integrated, with comparatively high levels of religious and ethnic tolerance, particularly on the mainland. Tanzanians have earned a name for themselves in the region for their moderation and balance, and most observers consider it highly unlikely the country will disintegrate into the tribal conflicts that have plagued some of its neighbours.

History

Tanzania's history begins with the dawn of humanity. Hominid (humanlike) footprints unearthed near Olduvai Gorge show that our earliest ancestors were roaming the Tanzanian plains and surrounding areas over three million years ago.

Seafaring merchants from the Mediterranean and Asia came looking for gold, spices and ivory, and intermarried with local families. They formed a civilisation known as the Swahili, with a common language (Swahili) and a chain of prosperous cities stretching from Mozambique to Somalia. The Arabic kingdom of Oman eventually gained control of the Swahili coast, installing its sultan on

Zanzibar and growing rich on the profits of the slaving expeditions that penetrated far into the country's interior.

Dr Livingstone, I Presume?

The first Europeans to arrive in East Africa were the Portuguese, who clashed with the Omanis for control of the lucrative trade routes to India. Later came British, Dutch and American merchant adventurers. By the 19th century, European explorers were setting out from Zanzibar into the unknown African interior. While searching for the source of the Nile, Dr David Livingstone became so famously lost that a special expedition headed by Henry Stanley was sent out to find him. Stanley caught up with Livingstone near modern-day Kigoma after a journey of more than a year, whereupon he allegedly uttered the famous words: 'Dr Livingstone, I presume?'

British efforts to suppress the slave trade ultimately led to the downfall of the Omani Empire. But it was Germany that first colonised what was then known as Tanganyika. Following WWI, the League of Nations mandated Tanganyika to Britain.

Independence

In 1959 Britain agreed to growing demands for the establishment of internal self-government. On 9 December 1961, Tanganyika became independent and on 9 December 1962 it was established as a republic, with Julius Nyerere as president.

On the Zanzibar Archipelago, which had been a British protectorate since 1890, the main push for independence came from the radical Afro-Shirazi Party (ASP), but when independence was granted in December 1963, two British-favoured minority parties formed the first government. Within a month, a Ugandan immigrant named John Okello initiated a violent revolution that toppled the government and the sultan, and led to the massacre or expulsion of most of the islands' Arab population. The sultan was replaced by the Zanzibar Revolutionary Council headed by Abeid Karume.

On 26 April 1964, Nyerere signed an act of union with Karume, creating the United Republic of Tanganyika (renamed the United Republic of Tanzania the following October). The union was resented by many Zanzibaris from the outset. In 1972 Karume was assassinated. Shortly thereafter, in an effort to subdue the ongoing unrest, Nyerere authorised the formation of a one-party state and combined his ruling Tanganyika African National Union (TANU) party and the ASP into Chama Cha Mapinduzi (CCM; Party of the Revolution). CCM's dominance of Tanzanian politics endures to this day.

The Socialist Experiment

The Arusha Declaration of 1967 committed Tanzania to a policy of socialism and self-reliance. The policy's cornerstone was the *ujamaa* (familyhood) village: an agricultural collective run along traditional African lines, whereby basic goods and tools were held in common and shared among members, while each individual was obliged to work on the land.

After an initial period of euphoric idealism, resentment at forced resettlement programs and other harsh measures grew, and the economy rapidly declined – precipitated in part by steeply rising oil prices and sharp drops in the value of coffee and sisal exports.

Democracy at Last

In 1985 Nyerere resigned, handing over power to Ali Hassan Mwinyi. Mwinyi tried to distance himself from Nyerere and his policies, and instituted an economic recovery program. The fall of European communism in the early 1990s and pressure from Western donor nations accelerated the move towards multiparty politics, and in 1992 the constitution was amended to legalise opposition parties.

The first elections were held in 1995 in an atmosphere of chaos, and the voting for the Zanzibari presidency was denounced for its dishonesty. In the ensuing uproar, foreign development assistance was suspended and most expatriates working on the islands left.

Similar problems have plagued successive elections, and tensions continue to simmer.

Culture

Tanzanians place a premium on politeness and courtesy. Greetings are essential; don't launch straight into a question without first enquiring as to the wellbeing of your listeners and their families. Children greet their elders with a respectful *shikamoo* (literally, 'I hold your feet'), and strangers are frequently addressed as *dada* (sister), *mama* (for an older woman), *kaka* (brother) or *ndugu* (relative or comrade).

People

Most Tanzanians are of Bantu origin, with the largest groups including the Sukuma (around Mwanza and southern Lake Victoria), Makonde (southeastern Tanzania), Haya (around Bukoba) and Chagga (around Mt Kilimanjaro). The Maasai are of Nilo-Hamitic or Nilotic origin.

About one million people live on the Zanzibar Archipelago, with about one-third of these on Pemba. Small but economically significant Asian (primarily from the subcontinent) and Arabic populations are concentrated in major cities and along the coast.

Between 35% and 40% of Tanzanians are Muslim and between 40% and 45% are Christian, with the remainder following traditional religions. There are also communities of Hindus, Sikhs and Ismailis.

Arts & Crafts

Shaaban Robert (1909–62) is considered Tanzania's national poet, and was almost single-handedly responsible for the development of a modern Swahili prose style. Zanzibari Muhammed Said Abdulla is regarded as the founder of Swahili popular literature. A widely acclaimed contemporary writer is Zanzibari Abdulrazak Gurnah, whose *Desertion* was short-listed for the Commonwealth Writers' Prize in 2006.

The single greatest influence on Tanzania's modern music scene has been the Congolese bands that began playing in Dar es Salaam in the early 1960s. These include Orchestra Super Matimila, which was propelled to fame by the late Congolese-born, Dar es Salaam–based Remmy Ongala.

Tanzania's best-known school of painting is Tingatinga, developed by the self-taught artist Edward Saidi Tingatinga. Tingatinga paintings feature brightly coloured animal motifs set against a monochrome background.

Tanzania's Makonde are known throughout East Africa for their beautiful and highly stylised woodcarvings.

Food & Drink

Tanzania's unofficial national dish is *ugali* (stiff and doughy maize) Other favourites include *mishikaki* (marinated meat kebabs) and – along the coast – *mkate wa ufuta* (sesame bread).

In major towns, eateries range from local food stalls to Western-style restaurants. Smaller towns may only have *hoteli* (small, informal restaurants) and *mama lishe* (informal food stands where the resident 'mama' does the cooking) serving chicken, beef or fish with rice or another staple.

Bottled water and soft drinks are widely sold; avoid drinking tap water. Beers include the local Safari and Kilimanjaro labels. Finding one cold can be a challenge.

Environment

Tanzania (943,000 sq km) is bordered to the east by the Indian Ocean and to the west by the deep lakes of the Western Rift Valley. Much of the mainland consists of a central highland plateau nestled between the east and west branches of the geological fault known as the Great Rift Valley. In the northwest is the enormous, shallow Lake Victoria basin. Off the coast is the Zanzibar Archipelago.

Tanzania's wild animal population includes all the 'classic' African mammals. Particularly notable are the country's large elephant populations, its big cats (especially lions, which are regularly seen in Serengeti National Park and Ngorongoro Crater) and its large herds of wildebeest, buffalo and zebra. Tanzania also is home to over 1000 bird species, including many endemics.

National Parks & Reserves

Tanzania's 'northern circuit' (Serengeti, Lake Manyara, Tarangire, Arusha and Kilimanjaro National Parks, plus the Ngorongoro Conservation Area) is easily accessible and known for the high concentration, diversity and accessibility of its wildlife. In the relatively less developed 'southern circuit' (including Ruaha and Mikumi National Parks and the Selous Game Reserve) the wildlife is just as impressive, although it's often spread over larger areas.

SURVIVAL GUIDE

Directory A–Z

ACCOMMODATION

July, August and the Christmas and New Year holidays are high season; many hotels also levy a peak-season surcharge on top of regular high-season rates from late December through early January.

Carrying a tent can save you some money in and around the northern parks, although camping in the parks themselves will cost at least US$30 per person per night. Camping isn't permitted on Zanzibar.

National parks have 'public' or 'ordinary' campsites with basic facilities (generally pit toilets and sometimes a water source).

ACTIVITIES

The Zanzibar Archipelago is the best diving and snorkelling destination. For hiking head to the Usambara Mountains around Lushoto, plus Mt Kilimanjaro and Mt Meru (in Arusha National Park). All hiking requires local guides. Be aware of the dangers of acute mountain sickness (AMS), especially on Kilimanjaro. In extreme cases it can be fatal.

Wildlife watching is a country highlight, from the world-famous Serengeti and Ngorongoro Crater to chimpanzee tracking in Mahale Mountains and Gombe National Parks.

CHILDREN

Parks and reserves are free for children under five years of age. Some wildlife lodges are restricted for children, so enquire when booking.

Always specifically ask for children's discounts if booking a safari through a tour operator.

Mosquito nets are best brought from home.

CUSTOMS REGULATIONS

Exporting seashells, coral, ivory and turtle shells is illegal.

EMBASSIES & CONSULATES

Embassies and consulates in Dar es Salaam include the following:

Australian Embassy (www.embassy.gov.au) Contact the Canadian embassy.

British High Commission (☎022-229 0000; http://ukintanzania.fco.gov.uk; Umoja House, cnr Mirambo St & Garden Ave)

Burundian Embassy (☎022-212 7008; Lugalo St, Upanga) Just up from the Italian embassy, and opposite the army compound.

Canadian High Commission (☎022-216 3300; www.dfait-maeci.gc.ca/tanzania; Umoja House, cnr Mirambo St & Garden Ave)

Congolese Embassy (435 Maliki Rd, Upanga)

Kenyan High Commisssion (☎022-266 8285/6; www.kenyahighcomtz.org; cnr Ali Hassan Mwinyi Rd & Kaunda Dr, Oyster Bay)

Malawian High Commission (☎022-213 6951; 1st fl, Zambia House, cnr Ohio St & Sokoine Dr)

Mozambique High Commission (☎022-211 6502; 25 Garden Ave)

TANZANIA'S PARKS

Tanzania's parks are managed by the **Tanzania National Parks Authority** (Tanapa; www.tanzaniaparks.com). For the northern parks and Ngorongoro Crater, payment is by Visa or MasterCard only (with your PIN). A similar electronic payment system is being introduced in the southern parks and Selous Game Reserve as well, so for them, bring both cash and card.

Rwandan Embassy (☎022-212 0703, 022-213 0119; www.tanzania.embassy.gov.rw; 32 Ali Hassan Mwinyi Rd, Upanga)

Ugandan Embassy (☎022-266 7009; 25 Msasani Rd, near Oyster Bay Primary School)

US Embassy (☎022-229 4000; http://tanzania.usembassy.gov; Old Bagamoyo & Kawawa Rds)

Zambian High Commission (☎022-212 5529; Ground fl, Zambia House, cnr Ohio St & Sokoine Dr)

MONEY

Tanzania's currency is the Tanzanian shilling (Tsh). There are bills of Tsh10,000, Tsh5000, Tsh1000 and Tsh500, and coins of Tsh200, Tsh100 and Tsh50.

ATMs are widespread in major towns; most accept Visa and MasterCard only.

Visa (some parks also take Mastercard) is required for paying entry fees at many national parks.

Credit cards are not widely accepted for direct payment; if so, it's usually with a commission.

Old-style US bills (pre-2004) are not accepted anywhere.

Travellers cheques are changeable in major cities only, and only with original purchase receipts.

On hikes and safaris, it's common practice to tip drivers, guides, porters and other staff for good service.

OPENING HOURS

Bureaus de change 8am to 5pm Monday to Friday, 9am to noon Saturday

Shops and offices 8.30am to noon and 2pm to 5pm Monday to Friday. Along the coast, many shops also close Friday afternoons for mosque services.

PUBLIC HOLIDAYS

New Year's Day 1 January

Zanzibar Revolution Day 12 January

Easter March/April

> **PRACTICALITIES**
>
> - **Electricity** 220-250V AC, 50 Hz. Use British-style three-square-pin or two-round-pin plug adaptors.
> - **Language** Swahili
> - **Newspapers** *Guardian* and *Daily News* (dailies); *Business Times*, *Financial Times* and *East African* (weeklies)
> - **Radio** The government-aligned Radio Tanzania broadcasts in English and Swahili

Union Day 26 April
Labour Day 1 May
Saba Saba (Peasants' Day) 7 July
Nane Nane (Farmers' Day) 8 August
Independence Day 9 December
Christmas Day 25 December
Boxing Day 26 December

Islamic holidays are also celebrated as public holidays.

SAFE TRAVEL

Tanzania is in general a safe, hassle-free country, but you'll need to take the usual precautions. Avoid isolated areas, especially isolated stretches of beach, and in cities and tourist areas take taxis at night. When using public transport, don't accept drinks or food from someone you don't know, and be sceptical of anyone who comes up to you on the street asking you whether you remember them from the airport, your hotel or wherever.

Especially in Arusha, Moshi and Zanzibar, touts and flycatchers can be extremely persistent. Be very wary of anyone who approaches you on the street, at the bus station or in your hotel offering safari deals, and never pay for a safari or trek in advance until you've thoroughly researched the company.

TELEPHONE

- Tanzania's country code is ☎255.
- To make an international call, first dial ☎000.
- Area codes (given with each number) must be used whenever dialling long distance or from a mobile phone.

TOURIST INFORMATION

Tanzania Tourist Board (TTB; www.tanzaniatouristboard.com) is the official tourism entity.

VISAS

Almost everyone needs a visa (US$50 for most nationalities, US$100 for citizens of the USA and Ireland for a single-entry visa valid for up to three months; cash only). Single-entry visas are currently issued at Dar es Salaam and Kilimanjaro airports and at most border crossings, but not on the Mozambican border.

Visa Extensions

One month is the normal visa validity and three months the maximum. For extensions within the three-month limit, there are immigration offices in all major towns; the process is free and straightforward.

Visas for Onward Travel

Burundi

Three-month single-entry visas cost US$50 plus two photos, and are issued in 24 hours. The consulate in Kigoma issues one-month single-entry visas for US$40 plus two photos within 24 hours.

Congo

Three-month single-entry visas cost US$150 plus two photos and a letter of invitation from someone in Congo. Allow plenty of time for issuing. The consulate in Kigoma is much easier, issuing single-entry visas for US$50 (US$30 for Tanzania residents) plus two photos within two days or less.

Mozambique

One-month single-entry visas cost US$40 (US$55 for express service) plus two photos and are issued within three days.

Rwanda

Three-month single-entry visas cost US$60 plus two photos, and are issued within 48 hours. Citizens of the USA, UK, Germany, South Africa, Canada and various other countries do not require visas. See p649 for more information on getting a visa for Rwanda.

Uganda

Three-month single-entry visas cost US$30 plus two photos and are issued the same day.

Zambia

One-month single-entry visas cost from Tsh25,000 to Tsh125,000, depending on nationality, plus two photos, and are issued the next day.

Getting There & Away

ENTERING THE COUNTRY

Visas are available at most major points of entry, and must be paid for in US dollars cash.

Yellow-fever vaccination is required if you are arriving from an endemic area (including many of Tanzania's neighbours).

AIR

Airlines

Air Tanzania, the national airline, is currently not operating any flights. Regional carriers include the following (all servicing Dar es Salaam, except as noted).

Air Uganda (www.air-uganda.com)

Coastal Aviation (www.coastal.cc) Dar es Salaam to Moçimboa da Praia (Mozambique); Mwanza to Kigali (Rwanda).

Kenya Airways (www.kenya-airways.com)

Precision Air (www.precisionairtz.com) In partnership with Kenya Airways; also serves JRO.

Airports

Julius Nyerere International Airport (DAR) Dar es Salaam.

Kilimanjaro International Airport (JRO) Between Arusha and Moshi.

Kigoma Airport Regional flights.

Mtwara Airport (MYW) Regional flights.

Mwanza Airport (MWZ) Regional fights.

Zanzibar International Airport (ZNZ) International and regional flights.

LAND

Buses cross Tanzania's borders with Kenya, Uganda, Rwanda and Burundi. For crossings with other countries, you'll need to take one vehicle to the border and board a different vehicle on the other side.

To enter Tanzania with your own vehicle you'll need:

- the vehicle's registration papers
- your driving licence
- temporary import permit (Tsh20,000 for one month, purchased at the border)
- third-party insurance (Tsh50,000 for one year, purchased at the border or at the local insurance headquarters in the nearest large town)
- one-time fuel levy (Tsh5000)

Burundi

There are border crossings at Kobero Bridge between Ngara (Tanzania) and Muyinga (Burundi), and at Manyovu, north of Kigoma.

For Kobero Bridge, Zuberly and Nyehunge lines go daily from Mwanza to Ngara (Tsh16,000, seven to eight hours), and shared-taxis run from Nyakanazi to Ngara (Tsh9,000, 1½ hours). From Ngara, there is onward transport to the Tanzanian border town of Kabanga.

For Manyovu, Burugo Travel (office at Kigoma's Bero bus stand) goes between Kigoma and Bujumbura (Tsh13,000, five hours) twice weekly. Otherwise, take a *dalla-dalla* from Kigoma to Manyovu (Tsh4000, one hour), walk through immigration and find onward transport.

Kenya

Border crossings are at Namanga (open 24 hours) on the Arusha–Nairobi highway; Horohoro, north of Tanga; Holili (open 6am to 8pm), east of Moshi; Loitokitok (Kenya), northeast of Moshi; and Sirari, northeast of Musoma.

Daily buses go between Tanga and Mombasa (Tsh15,000, four to five hours).

For Nairobi, Kampala Coach, Dar Express and Akamba go daily from Dar to Nairobi (Tsh45,000 to Tsh55,000, 16 to 17 hours) via Moshi and Arusha (Tsh22,000, five hours from Arusha to Nairobi).

However, the best option between Moshi or Arusha and Nairobi is the shuttle buses, departing daily from Arusha and Nairobi at 8am and 2pm (five hours) and from Moshi (seven hours) at 6am and 11am. The nonresident rate is US$25/30 one-way from Arusha/Moshi, but with a little prodding it's usually possible to get the resident price (Tsh25,000/30,000). Try the following companies. Pick-ups and drop-offs are at their offices and centrally located hotels; confirm locations when booking.

Jamii Arusha (☎0757-756110; www.jamiitours.com; old Mezza Luna Hotel, Simeon Rd); Moshi (☎0755-763836; Kilimanjaro Crane Hotel, Kaunda St); Nairobi (☎0734-868686; Parkside Hotel, Monrovia St)

Rainbow Arusha (☎0754-204025; www.rainbowcarhire.com; New Safari Hotel, Boma Rd); Moshi (☎0784-204025; THB House, Boma Rd); Nairobi (☎0712-508922; Parkside Hotel, Monrovia St)

Riverside Arusha (☎027-250 2639; www.riverside-shuttle.com; Sokoine Rd); Moshi (☎027-275 0093; THB House, Boma Rd); Nairobi (☎254-20-229618; Lagos House, Monrovia St)

Raqib Coach's daily bus from Moshi to Mombasa travels via Voi (Tsh15,000, four hours) in Kenya. *Dalla-dallas* go frequently between Moshi and the Holili border (Tsh1500, one hour). At the border, hire a motorbike (Tsh1000) or bicycle to cross 3km of no-man's land to the Kenyan immigration post at Taveta. From Taveta, minibuses go to Voi, where there's onward transport to Nairobi and Mombasa.

Akamba passes Kisii on its daily runs between Mwanza and Nairobi (Tsh36,000, 14 to 15 hours, 1pm). Batco buses go daily from Mwanza to the Sirari–Isebania border crossing (Tsh10,000, four to five hours), from where there's Kenyan transport to Kisii.

Malawi

The border crossing is at Songwe River Bridge (7am to 7pm Tanzanian time, 6am to 6pm Malawi time).

From Mbeya, minibuses go daily to the border (Tsh5000, two hours), where there's a 300m walk to the Malawian side, and minibuses to Karonga. Look for buses going to Kyela (these detour to the border) and verify that your vehicle is really going all the way to the border, and not just to Tukuyu (40km north) or Ibanda (7km before the border). There are no cross-border vehicles from Mbeya into Malawi, although touts at Mbeya bus station may try to convince you otherwise.

Mozambique

For all crossings, arrange your Mozambique (or Tanzania) visa in advance.

Crossings are at Kilambo ('Namoto' or Namiranga), south of Mtwara; Mtambaswala/Negomano (open 8.30am to 5pm in Tanzania, 7.30am to 4pm in Mozambique) Unity Bridge, 115km southwest of Masasi; and Mtomoni Unity Bridge 2, 120km south of Songea.

Pick-ups depart Mtwara daily to Kilambo (Tsh4000, one hour) and the Rovuma River, which is crossed via dugout canoe (Tsh3000, 10 minutes to one hour-plus). Once across, pick-ups go to the Mozambique border post (4km further) and Moçimboa da Praia (Mtc250, two hours).

The Negomano border is best for drivers (4WD essential). From Masasi, go about 35km southwest along the Tunduru road to Nangomba village, from where a 68km track leads to Masuguru village and, 10km further, to Mtambaswala. On the other side, there's a 160km dirt road to Mueda (Mozambique).

Further west, there's a daily vehicle from Songea's Majengo C to Mitomoni village and the Unity 2 bridge (Tsh10,000, three to four hours). Once across, get Mozambique transport to Lichinga (Tsh25,000, five hours).

Rwanda

The border crossing is at Rusumu Falls southwest of Bukoba (Tanzania).

Golden Inter-City connects Mwanza to Kigali daily (Tsh25,000, 12 hours).

Uganda

The main border crossing is Mutukula (Tanzania), northwest of Bukoba.

Kampala Coach and Akamba go daily from Arusha to Kampala (Tsh60,000, 20 hours) via Nairobi, and daily buses go from Bukoba to Kampala (Tsh10,000, five to six hours). Akamba also goes thrice weekly between Mwanza and Kampala (Tsh38,000, 16 hours).

Zambia

The main border crossing is at Tunduma (open 7.30am to 6pm Tanzania time, 6.30am to 5pm Zambia time), southwest of Mbeya.

Minibuses go daily between Mbeya and Tunduma (Tsh3500, two hours), where you walk across the border for Zambian transport to Lusaka (US$20, 18 hours).

The **Tanzania-Zambia train line** (www.tazarasite.com) links Dar es Salaam with Kapiri Mposhi in Zambia twice weekly via Mbeya and Tunduma (1st/2nd/economy class Tsh75,000/60,000/45,000, about 40 hours for 'express'). Visas are available at both borders.

SEA & LAKE

There's a US$5 port tax for travel on all boats and ferries.

Burundi

Lake taxis go sporadically from Kibirizi (north of Kigoma) to Bujumbura, but are not recommended. It's better to take the afternoon lake taxi to Kagunga (on the border, where there's a simple guesthouse), then a motorcycle-taxi to Nyanza-Lac (Burundi) and then a minibus to Bujumbura.

Democratic Republic of Congo (DRC)

Cargo boats go several times monthly from Kigoma's Ami port to Kalemie (US$20, deck class only, seven hours) or Uvira. The MV *Liemba* also sometimes travels to Kalemie during its off week. Check with the Congolese consulate in Kigoma about sailing days and times.

Kenya

Cargo boats sail sporadically between Mwanza and Kisumu and are usually willing to take passengers. Enquire at the Mwanza South Port.

Malawi

The MV *Songea* sails weekly between Mbamba Bay and Nkhata Bay (1st/economy class US$12/5, four to five hours).

Uganda

It's straightforward to arrange passage between Mwanza and Kampala's Port Bell on cargo ships (about US$20, 16 hours). On the Ugandan side, get a letter of permission from the train station director (free); ask for the managing director's office, on the 2nd floor of the building next to Kampala's train station. In Mwanza, check in with the immigration officer at the South Port.

Zambia

The venerable MV *Liemba* has been plying the waters of Lake Tanganyika for the better part of a century on one of Africa's classic adventure journeys. It connects Kigoma (departing Wednesday afternoon) with Mpulungu in Zambia every other week (1st/2nd/economy class US$95/85/65, US dollars cash only, 40 hours). Stops include Lagosa (for Mahale Mountains National Park) and Kipili. Food is available on board, but bring some supplements and drinking water. **Booking** (☎028-280 2811 for enquiries) early is advisable. There's a dock at Kigoma, but at many smaller stops you'll need to disembark in the middle of the lake, exiting from a door in the side of the *Liemba* into small boats that take you to shore.

Getting Around

AIR

Domestic services include:

Air Excel (☎027-254 8429, 027-250 1597; www.airexcelonline.com) To Dar es Salaam, Zanzibar and northern parks.

Fastjet (☎0685-680533; www.fastjet.com) To Kilimanjaro, Dar es Salaam and Mwanza.

Precision Air (☎022-216 8000, 022-213 0800, 0784-402002, 0787-888407; www.precision-airtz.com) Dar es Salaam, Kigoma, Kilimanjaro, Mtwara, Mwanza and Zanzibar.

Safari Airlink (☎0777-723274; www.safariaviation.info) Dar es Salaam, southern and western parks.

Tropical Air (☎024-223 2511, 0777-412278; www.tropicalair.co.tz) Zanzibar, Dar es Salaam and Tanga.

ZanAir (☎024-223 3670/8; www.zanair.com) Arusha, Dar es Salaam, Zanzibar and many parks.

Zantas Air (☎022-213 0476, 0773-786016; www.zantasair.com) Arusha, Kigoma and western parks.

BUS & MINIBUS

On major long-distance routes, there's a choice of express and ordinary buses. Some express buses have toilets and air-conditioning; the nicest ones are called 'luxury' buses.

For popular routes, book in advance. Each bus line has its own booking office, at or near the bus station. Buy your tickets at the office and not from the touts; there's no luggage fee.

For shorter trips away from the main routes, the choice is often between 30-seater buses ('Coastals', 'Coasters' or *thelathini*) and *dalla-dallas*. Both options come complete with chickens on the roof, bags of produce under the seats and no leg room. Shared taxis are rare. Like ordinary buses, *dalla-dallas* and shared taxis leave when full, and are the least safe transport option.

CAR & MOTORCYCLE

Unless you have your own vehicle and are familiar with driving in East Africa, it's relatively unusual for travellers to tour mainland Tanzania by car. On Zanzibar, however, it's easy to hire a car or motorcycle for touring, and self-drive is permitted.

On the mainland you'll need your home driving licence or an International Driving Permit (IDP) together with your home licence. On Zanzibar you'll need an IDP plus your home licence, or a permit from Zanzibar, Kenya, Uganda or South Africa.

Daily rates for 4WD (necessary away from major towns) average US$80 to US$200 per day plus insurance, fuel, driver (usually required) and 20% value added tax.

Except as posted, the speed limit is 80km per hour.

There's a seat-belt law for drivers and front-seat passengers (Tsh30,000 penalty).

Motorcycles aren't permitted in national parks.

HITCHING

Hitching is prohibited inside national parks, and is usually fruitless around them. In remote areas, hitching a lift with truck drivers may be your only option. Expect to pay about the same or a bit less than the bus fare for the same route, with a place in the cab costing about twice that for a place on top of the load. For more information see p1081.

LOCAL TRANSPORT

Dalla-Dalla

Local routes are serviced by poorly maintained and overcrowded *dalla-dallas* (minibuses) and, in rural areas, pick-up trucks or old 4WDs. Prices average Tsh300 for town runs. Accidents are frequent.

Taxi

Taxis can be hired in all major towns. None have meters. Fares for short town trips start at Tsh3000. Only use taxis from reliable hotels or established taxi stands. Avoid hailing taxis cruising the streets, and never get in a taxi that has a 'friend' of the driver or anyone else already in it.

TRAIN

Tazara (☎022-286 5137, 022-286 0340, 022-286 0344, 0713-225292; www.tazarasite.com) links Dar es Salaam with Kapiri Mposhi in Zambia via Mbeya and Tunduma (Tsh35,000/29,800/22,000 for 1st/2nd/economy class express, 40 hours).

The run-down Central Line (p675) links Dar es Salaam with Tabora and Kigoma (Tsh60,600/19,100 1st/economy, approximately 40 hours), with branches from Tabora to Mpanda and Dodoma to Singida. Service to/from Mwanza has been suspended.

On both lines, breakdowns and long delays are common. Food is available.

Classes

Tazara has three classes: 1st class (four-bed compartments), 2nd-class sitting, and economy class (benches, usually very crowded). Some trains also have 2nd-class sleeping (six-bed compartments). Men and women can only travel together in the sleeping sections by booking the entire compartment. At night, secure your window with a stick, and don't leave your luggage unattended.

Central Line has only 1st class (four-bed compartments) and economy.

Reservations

Book tickets for 1st and 2nd class at least several days in advance.

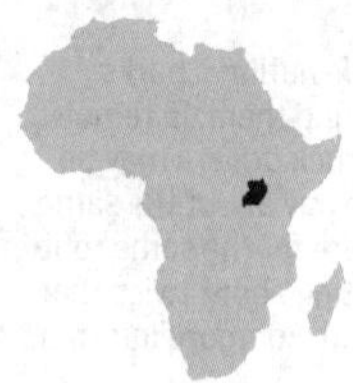

Uganda

POP 34.6 MILLION

Includes ➡

Best of Nature

- ➡ Bwindi Impenetrable National Park (p735)
- ➡ Source of the Nile, Jinja (p727)
- ➡ Murchison Falls National Park (p739)
- ➡ Ziwa Rhino Sanctuary (p738)

Best of Culture

- ➡ Sipi Falls coffee tours (p730)
- ➡ Twa (Batwa) people forest walks (p737)
- ➡ Kampala cycling tour (p717)

Why Go?

Emerging from the shadows of a dark history, a new dawn of tourism has risen in Uganda, polishing a glint back on the 'pearl of Africa'. Travellers are streaming in to explore what is basically the best of everything the continent has to offer.

For a relatively small country, there's a lot that's big about the place. It's home to the tallest mountain range in Africa, the world's longest river and the continent's largest lake. And with half the remaining mountain gorillas residing here, and the Big Five to be ticked off, wildlife watching is huge.

Although anti-gay sentiments have cast a shadow on the otherwise positive tourism picture, and tensions continue to simmer with the Karamojong in the northeast, Uganda remains one of the safest destinations in Africa. Other than watching out for the odd hippo at your campsite, there's no more to worry about here than in most other countries.

When to Go

Kampala

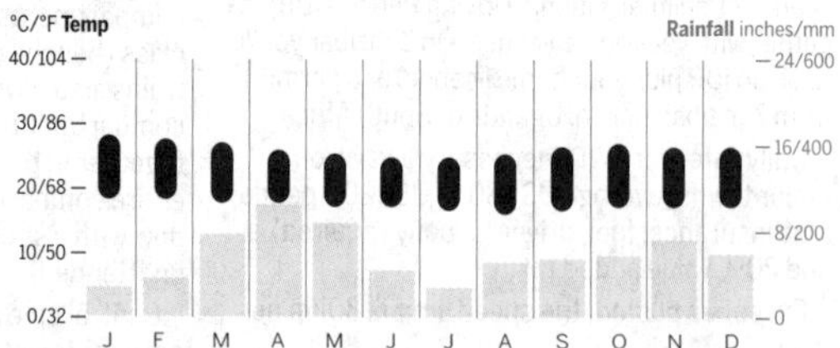

Jun–Sep The best bet weather-wise, with minimal rainfall and not too hot.

Jan–Feb Also great weather; the perfect time to climb the Rwenzoris or Mt Elgon.

Oct–Nov Can be a little rainy but, with fewer travellers, gorilla permits are much easier to obtain.

KAMPALA

☎ 0414 / POP 1.5 MILLION

Kampala makes a good introduction to Uganda. It's a dynamic city with few of the hassles of its eastern neighbour, Nairobi, and some worthy attractions to keep you occupied. It's safe to walk around virtually everywhere in the daytime, and downtown doesn't shut down until well into the evening. Mix in the excellent international restaurants and a thumping nightlife and there's enough going on to stop you from just touching down and rushing off.

Sights

Kasubi Tombs MAUSOLEUM

(Map p720; ww.kasubitombs.org; adult/child incl guide USh10,000/1000; 8am-6pm) The Unesco World Heritage–listed tombs, a huge reed and bark cloth mausoleum for the previous four kings of the Baganda people, was an amazing site until it burned down in March 2010. Fortunately, it's in the process of being rebuilt. Take a minibus to Kasubi trading centre; from there it's 500m uphill.

Uganda Museum MUSEUM

(Map p720; Kira Rd; adult/child USh3000/1500; 10am-5.30pm) One of East Africa's best museums with ethnographic exhibits (get the lowdown on banana beer here) and a hands-on display of traditional musical instruments.

Buganda Parliament BUILDING

(Map p720; Kabakanjagala Rd; admission incl guide USh10,000; 8am-5pm) A great place to learn about the history and culture of the Buganda Kingdom. Guided tours take you inside the parliament building, and provide interesting stories and details about the 56 different clans.

Mengo Palace PALACE

(Map p720; Twekobe; admission incl guide USh10,000) Built in 1922 this former home of the Buganda king has remained empty since 1966 when the then prime minister Milton Obote ordered a dramatic attack to oust King Mutesa II. The adjacent site became a notorious underground prison and torture-execution chamber built by Idi Amin in the 1970s.

Tours

Coffee Safari SAFARI

(Map p722; ☎ 0772-505619; www.1000cupscoffee.com; per person US$100; 7.30am Fri) You can trace back your coffee from the cup to the farm with this safari run by 1000 Cups Coffee House. Book before noon on Thursday.

Uganda Bicycle CYCLING

(☎ 0787-016688; www.ugandabicycle.com; per person USh100,000) Popular cycling tours explore some less visited parts on the outskirts of Kampala. Tours depart daily, meeting at Cassia Lodge at 8am.

SET YOUR BUDGET

Budget

- Double room with shared bathroom US$20
- Plate of *matoke* (mashed platains) and beans US$0.90
- Beer (500mL) US$0.75–1.25
- Car rental (self-drive) per day from US$55

Midrange

- Hotel double room from US$65
- Two-course dinner US$15
- Short taxi ride US$6
- Car rental (with driver) from US$80

Top End

- Hotel double room US$150
- Two-course dinner US$25
- Glass of wine US$5

Sleeping

Budget lodging fills up fast, so reservations are advised if you're arriving late in the day.

Red Chilli Hideaway BACKPACKERS $

(☎ 0414-223903; www.redchillihideaway.com; campsite per person US$5, dm US$8, d from US$30, s/d without bathroom from US$15/20, cottages from US$50; P @) One of Kampala's most popular backpackers, Red Chilli is always packed out with young travellers for its dorms, cottages, kitchen facilities, free internet and budget tours into the national parks. There are plans to move to a new site in Butabika, a few kilometres from its current spot.

Backpackers Hostel BACKPACKERS $

(Map p720; ☎ 0772-430587; www.backpackers.co.ug; Natete Rd, Lunguja; campsite per person USh12,000, dm USh16,000-18,000, s/d USh45,000/60,000, without bathroom USh26,000/48,000; P @) Kampala's original budget hostel is still

Uganda Highlights

1 Jaunting through the jungle to marvel at mountain gorillas in **Bwindi Impenetrable National Park** (p735)

2 Taking on some of the world's best white water near Jinja on the wild waters of the **Nile River** (p727)

3 Checking out the world's most powerful waterfall on a wildlife-watching cruise at **Murchison Falls** (p739)

4 Chilling out at beautiful **Lake Bunyonyi** (p737)

5 Exploring unvarnished Africa at its wild and colourful best in **Kidepo Valley National Park** (p740)

6 Tackling the ice-capped, evocatively named 'Mountains of the Moon', the **Rwenzori Mountains** (p733)

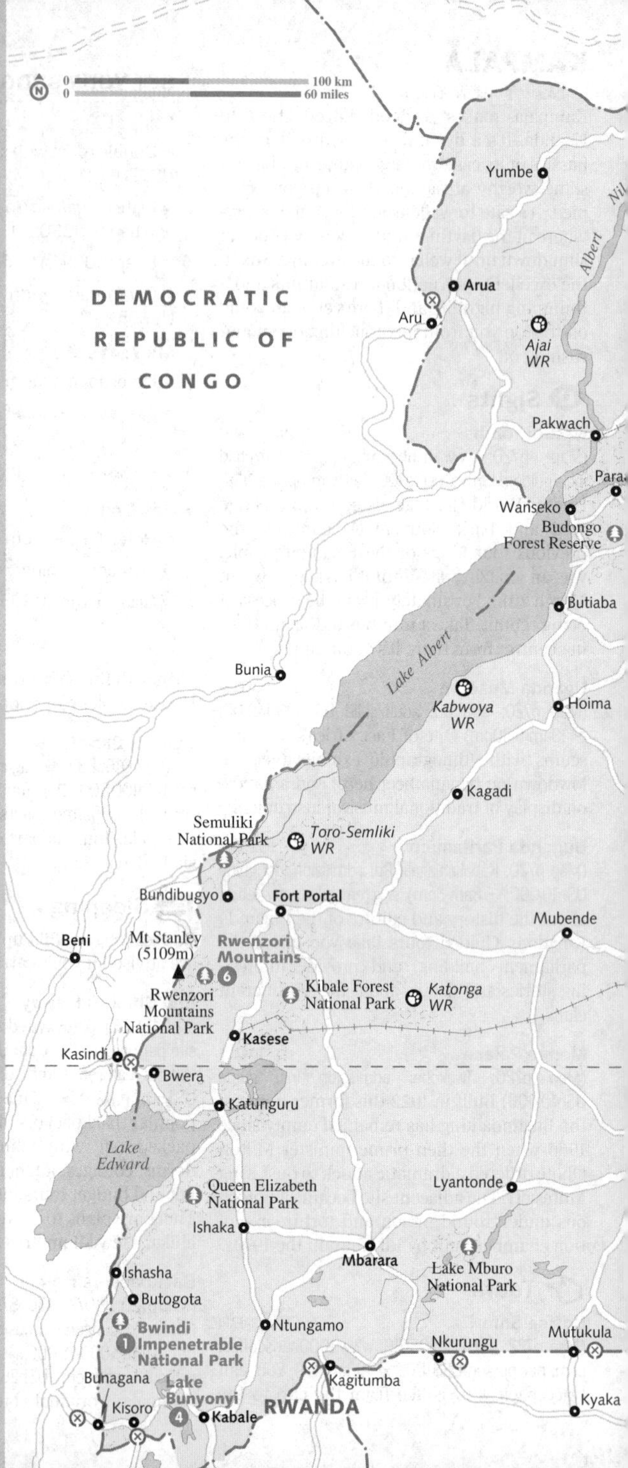

SUDAN
Mt Kinyeti (3187m)
Kidepo Valley National Park
Moyo
Nimule
Karenga
Kaabong
Rom
Koputh
KENYA
Atiak
Kitgum
Acholibur
Kotido
Gulu
Patongo
Waiwer
Bokora-Matheniko WR
Moroto
Ogur
Murchison Falls
Karuma
Aloi
Lira
Murchison Falls National Park
Nile River
Pian-Upe WR
Masindi
Soroti
Namasale
Kumi
Sipi Falls
Lake Kyoga
Ziwa Rhino Sanctuary
Mt Elgon National Park
Suam
Mt Elgon (4321m)
Bale
Mbale
Kiboga
Victoria Nile
Luwero
Tororo
Malaba
Busunju
Iganga
Nairobi (300km)
Busia
Jinja
KAMPALA
Port Bell
Lake Wamala
Mpanga Forest Reserve
Entebbe
Equator
Mabamba Swamp
Bulago Island
Kkome Island
Kisumu
Ngamba Island
Bukakata
Masaka
Kalangala
Buggala Island
Ssese Islands
LAKE VICTORIA
KENYA
TANZANIA

Kampala

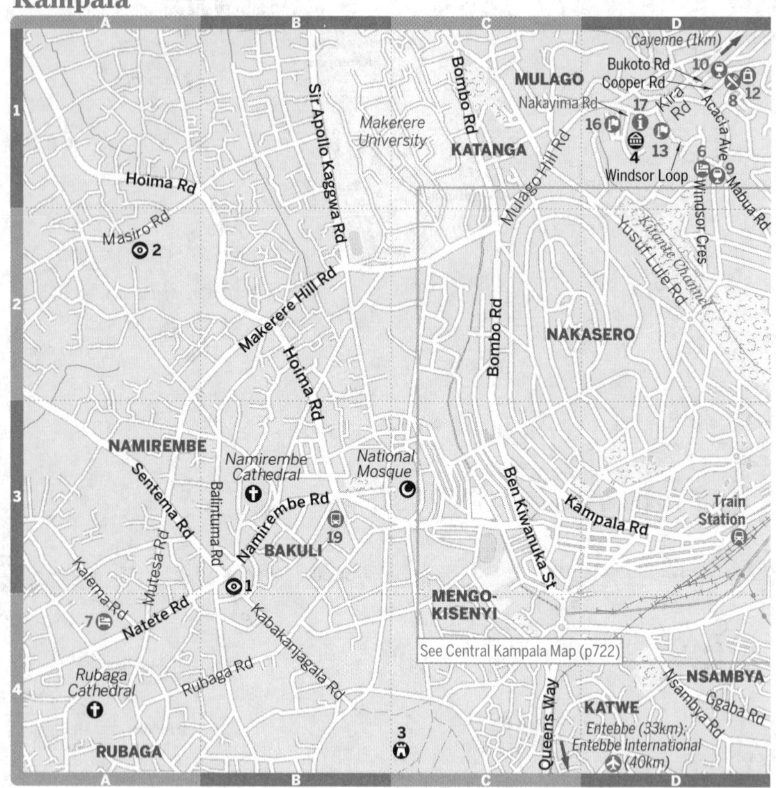

going strong. The facilities are good and the bar draws a mix of travellers and expats. Take a Natete/Wakaliga minibus (USh1000 uphill, but only USh500 return!) from the new taxi park.

Aponye Hotel HOTEL $

(Map p722; ☎0414-349239; www.aponyehotel.com; 17 William St; s USh40,000, d USh45,000-60,000; P ❄ @ ⓦ) One of the best-value places in downtown Kampala, this shiny glass tower offers high standards at midrange prices.

Tourist Hotel HOTEL $

(Map p722; ☎0414-251471; www.touristhotel.net; Dastur St; s/d from USh63,000/92,000; @ ⓦ) Overlooking the lively Nakasero Market, this hotel has rooms fitted with keycard entry, satellite TV and telephones.

Athina Club House GUESTHOUSE $$

(Map p720; ☎0414-341428; maryroussos@yahoo.com; 30 Windsor Cres; s/d incl breakfast US$60/65) The Cypriot-owned Athina boasts a great location in the well-heeled suburb of Kololo and is one of the city's few genuinely decent midrange options.

Villa Kololo BOUTIQUE HOTEL $$

(Map p722; ☎0414-500533; info@villakololo.com; 31 Acacia Ave; r incl breakfast from US$120; ⓦ) Tastefully decorated with a blend of North African and Rajasthani motifs, rooms have decadent touches such as four-poster beds and spa baths.

Emin Pasha Hotel LUXURY HOTEL $$$

(Map p722; ☎0414-236977; www.eminpasha.com; 27 Akii Bua Rd; s/d incl breakfast from US$260/290; P ❄ @ ⓦ ≋) This beautiful boutique hotel fills an old colonial property. The 20 rooms

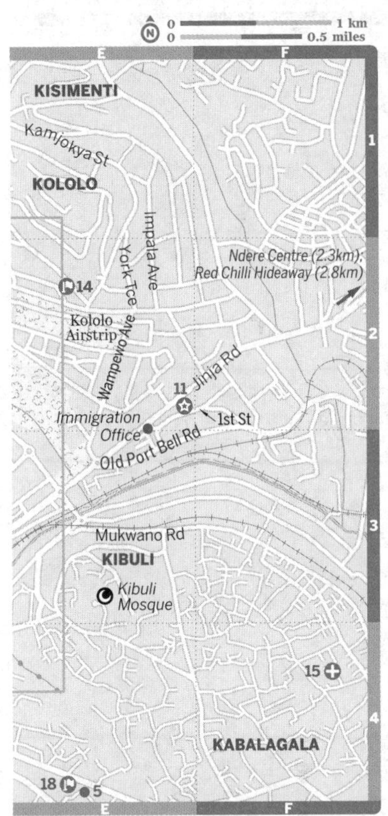

Kampala

Sights

1 Buganda Parliament ... B3
2 Kasubi Tombs ... A2
3 Mengo Palace ... C4
4 Uganda Museum ... D1

Activities, Courses & Tours

5 Great Lakes Safaris ... E4
Matoke Tours ... (see 10)

Sleeping

6 Athina Club House ... D1
7 Backpackers Hostel ... A4

Eating

8 Crocodile Café & Bar ... D1

Drinking & Nightlife

9 Bubbles O'Learys ... D1
10 Iguana ... D1

Entertainment

11 Ange Noir ... E2

Shopping

12 Banana Boat ... D1

Information

13 British Embassy ... D1
14 DRC Embassy ... E2
15 International Hospital Kampala ... F4
16 Rwandan Embassy ... D1
17 Uganda Wildlife Authority ... D1
18 US Embassy ... E4

Transport

19 Jaguar Executive Coaches ... B3

are the best in the city, blending atmosphere and luxury.

Eating

Kampala is packed with quality restaurants, and the international population brings considerable variety to the dining scene.

Mama Ashanti AFRICAN $
(Map p722; 20 Kyadondo Rd; mains USh11,000-20,000; 9am-11pm Mon-Sat) Specialises in delicious and authentic West African dishes. Tables are set in a lovely garden.

Crocodile Café & Bar CAFE $
(Map p720; 0414-254593; www.thecrocodile-kampala.com; Cooper Rd; sandwiches & salads USh6000-14,000, mains USh10,000-20,000; 9am-11pm Mon-Sat) A Kampala classic, this atmospheric cafe-bar manages to pull off something of an old Parisian vibe.

Masala Chaat House INDIAN $
(Map p722; 0414-236487; 3 Dewinton Rd; mains USh8000-12,000; 9.30am-10pm;) A winning combination of authentic Indian food and affordable prices has kept this local institution going strong.

Antonio's UGANDAN $
(Map p722; Kampala Rd; mains USh3500-7500; 6.30am-4.30pm) A pretty good greasy spoon serving Ugandan, Kenyan and Western favourites.

Mediterraneo ITALIAN $$
(Map p722; 0414-500533; 31 Acacia Ave; mains USh20,000-59,000; 10.30am-10.30pm;) Classy open-air Italian restaurant in atmospheric surrounds of raised polished-wood decking. The Italian chef does authentic thin-crust pizzas and handmade pastas.

Central Kampala

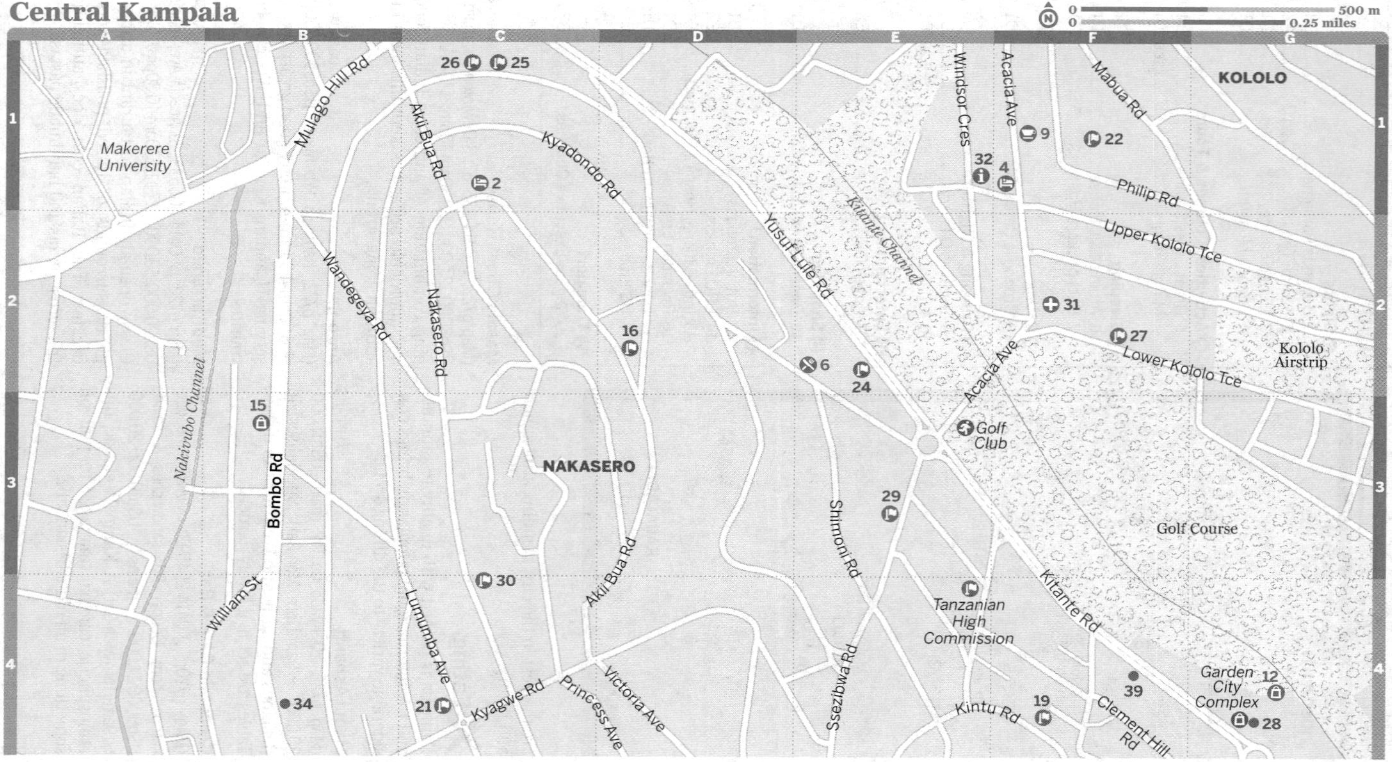
0 500 m
0 0.25 miles
A
B
C
D
E
F
G
1
2
3
4
KOLOLO
NAKASERO
Makerere University
Mulago Hill Rd
Akii Bua Rd
Kyadondo Rd
Yusuf Lule Rd
Kitante Channel
Windsor Cres
Acacia Ave
Mabua Rd
Philip Rd
Upper Kololo Tce
Lower Kololo Tce
Kololo Airstrip
Wandegeya Rd
Nakasero Rd
Nakivubo Channel
Bombo Rd
William St
Lumumba Ave
Kyagwe Rd
Princess Ave
Victoria Ave
Shimoni Rd
Ssezibwa Rd
Golf Club
Golf Course
Tanzanian High Commission
Kitante Rd
Kintu Rd
Clement Hill Rd
Garden City Complex
2
4
6
9
12
15
16
19
21
22
24
25
26
27
28
29
30
31
32
34
39

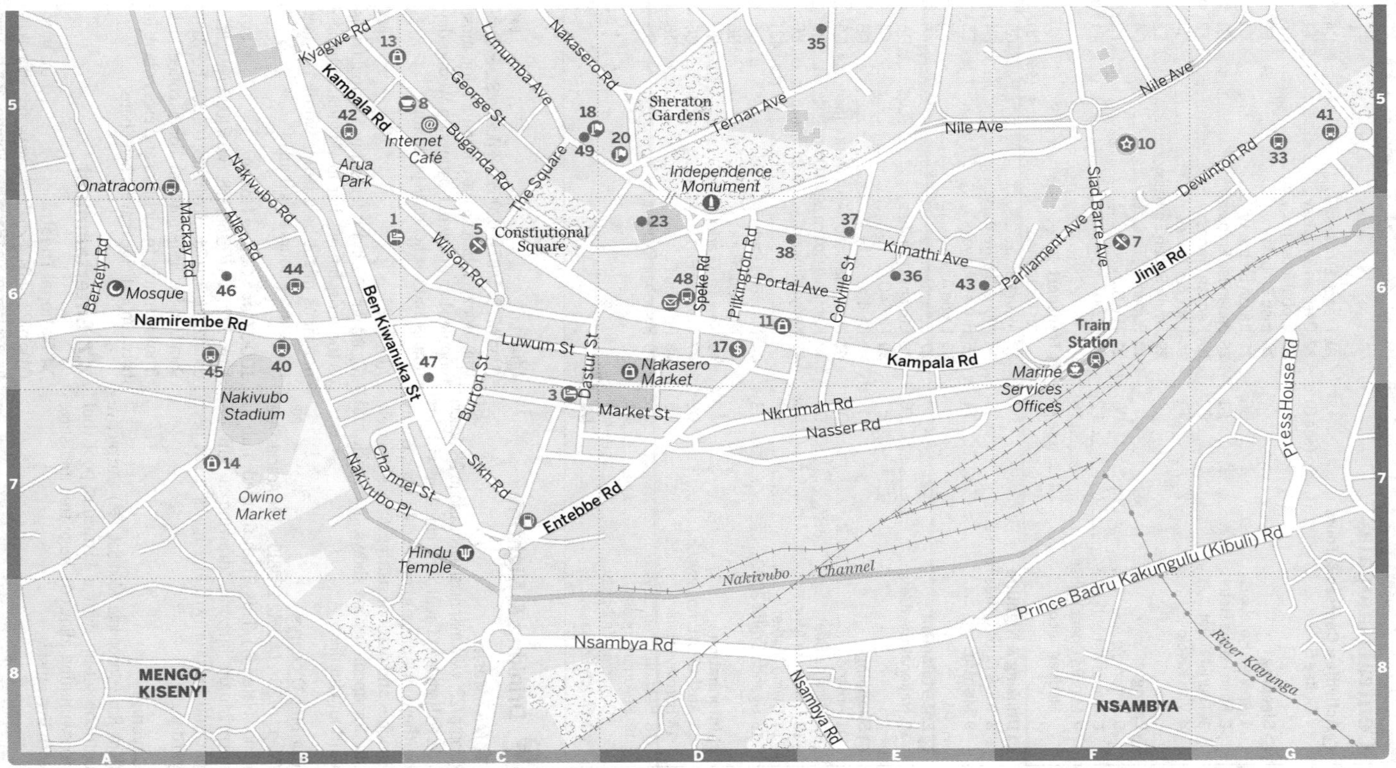

A
B
C
D
E
F
G
5
6
7
8
Kyagwe Rd
Kampala Rd
George St
Lumumba Ave
Nakasero Rd
Sheraton Gardens
Ternan Ave
Nile Ave
Internet Café
Buganda Rd
The Square
Arua Park
Independence Monument
Onatracom
Nakivubo Rd
Mackay Rd
Allen Rd
Wilson Rd
Constitutional Square
Berkely Rd
Mosque
Namirembe Rd
Ben Kiwanuka St
Speke Rd
Pilkington Rd
Portal Ave
Colville St
Kimathi Ave
Parliament Ave
Siad Barre Ave
Dewinton Rd
Jinja Rd
Luwum St
Dastur St
Nakasero Market
Kampala Rd
Train Station
Marine Services Offices
Nakivubo Stadium
Burton St
Market St
Nkrumah Rd
Nasser Rd
PressHouse Rd
Channel St
Nakivubo Pl
Sikh Rd
Owino Market
Entebbe Rd
Hindu Temple
Nakivubo Channel
Prince Badru Kakungulu (Kibuli) Rd
Nsambya Rd
River Kayunga
MENGO-KISENYI
NSAMBYA

Central Kampala

Activities, Courses & Tours

Coffee Safari ....(see 8)

Sleeping

1 Aponye Hotel B6
2 Emin Pasha Hotel C1
3 Tourist Hotel C7
4 Villa Kololo F1

Eating

5 Antonio's C6
6 Mama Ashanti E2
7 Masala Chaat House F6
Mediterraneo ....(see 4)

Drinking & Nightlife

8 1000 Cups Coffee House C5
9 MishMash F1

Entertainment

10 National Theatre F5

Shopping

11 Aristoc D6
12 Banana Boat G4
13 Exposure Africa B5
14 Owino Market B7
15 Uganda Crafts 2000 .... B3

Information

16 Australian Embassy D2
17 Barclays Bank D6
18 Belgium Embassy C5
19 Burundi Embassy F4
Canadian Embassy ....(see 43)
20 Dutch Embassy D5
21 French Embassy C4
22 German Embassy F1
23 Global Interlink D6
24 Irish Embassy E2
25 Italian Embassy C1
26 Japanese Embassy C1
27 Kenyan Embassy F2
28 Let's Go Travel G4
29 South Sudan Embassy E3
30 Sudanese Embassy C4
31 The Surgery F2
32 Tourism Uganda E1

Transport

Air Uganda ....(see 43)
33 Akamba G5
34 Alpha Car Rentals B4
35 British Airways E5
36 Eagle Air E6
37 Emirates E6
38 Ethiopian Airlines D6
39 Fly540 .... F4
40 Kalita B6
41 Kampala Coach Arua Park Office G5
42 Kampala Coach Main Office B5
43 Kenya Airways E6
KLM ....(see 43)
44 Main Bus Park B6
45 New Bus Park B6
46 New Taxi Park B6
47 Old Taxi Park C6
48 Post Bus D6
49 Rwandair Express C5

Drinking & Nightlife

★MishMash CAFE
(Map p722; www.mishmashuganda.com; 28 Acacia Ave; ⏲11am-late) Great new cafe-bar with art on the walls, proper coffee, cold beer, comfy couches and outdoor seating. Check the website for upcoming art shows, live music and outdoor cinema.

Bubbles O'Learys PUB
(Map p720; ☎0312-263815; 19 Acacia Ave; ⏲noon-late; 📶) This Irish-themed pub is surprisingly buzzing, drawing a fun expat and local crowd, and has a great beer garden.

Cayenne BAR
(Kira Rd; ⏲noon-late Mon-Sat; 📶) Attractive outdoor set-up with a luxurious pool (but no swimming allowed), huge tree and stage with live music.

Iguana BAR
(Map p720; ☎0777-020658; 8 Bukoto St; ⏲5pm-late) Boozy Iguana is a contender for most popular bar in town. Upstairs on Wednesday nights and weekends is pumping.

Al's Bar BAR
(Ggaba Rd; ⏲24hr) A legend in Kampala, this is the most famous bar in Uganda, although notorious might be a better word! The fact it's open 24 hours says it all.

1000 Cups Coffee House CAFE
Map 722; ☎0775-667858; www.1000cupscoffee.com; 18 Buganda Rd; spiced coffee USh3000; ⏲8am-9pm Mon-Sat, 8am-7pm Sun) For a coffee kick from Kentucky to Vietnam and everywhere in between, caffeine cravers head here.

Entertainment

★National Theatre LIVE MUSIC
(Map p722; ☎0414-254567; www.ugandanationalculturalcentre.org; Siad Barre Ave) Popular for its free

weeknight outdoor events. Grab a beer and a chair for informal open-stage jam on Monday evenings, infectious Afro-fusion grooves on Tuesdays, underground hip-hop on Wednesdays or comedy night on Thursdays.

Ange Noir CLUB

(Map p720; 1st St; ⌚Thu-Sun) The 'black angel' is pronounced locally as 'Angenoa', a pretty fair rendition of the French, and is the most popular club for dancing. Everyone knows it, but it's not signposted on the main road

Ndere Centre DANCE

(☎0414-597704; www.ndere.com; Kisaasi Rd; adult/child USh10,000/5000) The place for traditional dance and music, with the Ndere Troupe's high-energy show taking place every Sunday from 6pm to 9pm. It also offers traditional drumming and dance classes from USh20,000 per hour.

Shopping

Banana Boat ARTS & CRAFTS

(Map p722; www.bananaboat.co.ug; Kitante Rd; ⌚9.30am-7pm Mon-Sat, 10am-4pm Sun) Sophisticated craft shop with local items such as excellent batiks plus items from all over Africa. Also in **Kisimenti** (Map p720; Cooper Rd).

Uganda Crafts 2000 ARTS & CRAFTS

(www.ugandacrafts2000ltd.org; Bombo Rd) A non-profit shop selling a wide variety of crafts, including goods made from leather, wood and cane.

Exposure Africa ARTS & CRAFTS

(Map p722; 13 Buganda Rd) The largest of the city's craft 'villages', stocking woodcarvings, drums, sandals, batiks, basketry, beaded jewellery and *'mzungu'* (white person) T-shirts.

Aristoc BOOKS

(Map p722; 23 Kampala Rd; ⌚8.30am-5.30pm Mon-Fri, 9am-4.30pm Sat) Overflowing with books and maps about Uganda, East Africa and beyond. Also has a branch in Garden City.

Owino Market MARKET

(Map p722) Sprawling around Nakivubo Stadium, Owino has everything from traditional medicines to TVs, but it's most famous for its secondhand clothing.

Orientation

The city centre is on Nakasero Hill. Towards the bottom is a chaotic mix of shops, markets, bus stations, taxi parks and out-of-control traffic. The more orderly, upper end has office blocks and good restaurants. Old Kampala lies west of the centre, around Kampala Hill. East of the centre is exclusive Kololo, with international restaurants and bars. South lies Kabalagala, home to some of the city's wildest bars.

Information

DANGERS & ANNOYANCES

Kampala is a very hassle-free city and safe as far as Africa's capitals go. Follow the ordinary big-city precautions. Take care in and around the taxi parks, bus parks and market, as pickpockets operate there.

EMERGENCY

Police and ambulance (☎999) You can also dial ☎112 from mobile phones.

MEDICAL SERVICES

International Hospital Kampala (Map p720; ☎0772-200400; St Barnabus Rd; ⌚24hr) This should be your destination if you're suffering from serious trauma.

The Surgery (Map p722; ☎0752-756003, 0414-256003; www.thesurgeryuganda.org; 2 Acacia

BWINDI GORILLA PERMITS

With demand for gorilla permits exceeding supply for most of the year, if you haven't prearranged a gorilla permit, this should be your number one priority upon arrival in Kampala.

During the 'low seasons' of April to May and October to November (the rainiest months), you may be able to confirm a space a week or two in advance of your trip. During the rest of the year it's not unheard of for permits to be booked up months in advance. If nothing is available that fits your schedule, check at the backpacker places in Kampala and Jinja, where the safari companies advertise excess permits they want to sell. It's no problem to buy these, even when someone else's name is on them. Cancellations and no-shows are rare, but you can get on the list at the park office: it's first-come, first-served.

At the time of research Uganda Wildlife Authority (UWA; ☎0414-355000; www.ugandawildlife.org; 7 Kira Rd)) were offering discount permits during the low season months for US$350. The permits were for tracking newly habituated groups of gorillas, so it remains to be seen whether this initiative is a promotional or permanent move.

Ave; ⌚8am-6pm Mon-Sat, emergency 24hr) Highly respected clinic run by Dr Dick Stockley, an expat British GP. Stocks self-test malaria kits.

MONEY

Stanbic (17 Hannington Rd, Crested Towers Bldg) and **Barclays Bank** (Mpa p722; Kampala Rd) are the most useful banks in Kampala. Both accept international cards, but Stanbic is the only bank that takes MasterCard. There are plenty of ATMs about town.

POST & TELEPHONE

Main Post Office (Map p722; Kampala Rd; ⌚8am-6pm Mon-Fri, 9am-2pm Sat) Offers postal and telecom services. Poste restante service is at counter 14.

TOURIST INFORMATION

The best sources of information are Backpackers Hostel and Red Chilli Hideaway, where staff know what's going on in most of the country. The free listings magazine, the *Eye*, is available from selected hotels and restaurants.

Tourism Uganda (Map p722; ☎0414-342196; www.visituganda.com; 42 Windsor Cres; ⌚8.30am-5pm Mon-Fri, 9am-1pm Sat) Staff will try to answer your questions, but are frequently unable to.

Uganda Wildlife Authority (Map p720; UWA; ☎0414-355000; www.ugandawildlife.org; 7 Kira Rd) National park reservations and information.

TRAVEL AGENCIES

The following are reliable places to buy plane tickets.

Global Interlink (Map p722; ☎0414-235233; www.global-interlink.org; Grand Imperial Hotel) Hidden away in the mall behind the hotel.

Let's Go Travel (Map p722; ☎0414-346667; www.ugandaletsgotravel.com; Kitante Rd, Garden City) Part of the Uniglobe empire and also a representative for STA Travel.

Getting There & Away

Most bus companies use the main bus park (aka old bus park), but there are also many departures from the more pleasant new bus park; both are just off Namirembe Rd near Nakivubo Stadium.

Kampala has two chaotic parks for minibuses which serve destinations inside and outside the city. The old taxi park is the busier of the two and serves towns in eastern Uganda; the nearby new taxi park services western and northern destinations.

Post Buses take a little longer, but are safer than normal buses. They depart around 7.30am Monday to Saturday from Kampala's main post office. Information and day-before reservations are in the building next to the post office, or turn up around 7am.

Getting Around

The international airport is at Entebbe, 40km from Kampala. A private taxi (called a 'special-hire taxi') there costs about USh60,000. Or take a minibus between Kampala (from either taxi park) and Entebbe (USh2500, 45 minutes), and a special-hire to the airport for USh10,000. The cheapest and most direct option to the airport is the green bus (USh2500, one hour) from Nasser Rd (off Nkrumah Rd) in central Kampala, which departs hourly from 8am to 6pm; it's not overly reliable so leave plenty of time.

The ubiquitous white and blue minibuses fan out from the city centre to virtually every point in Kampala. You just have to ask around to find the right one. Most pass down Kampala Rd.

Special-hire taxis are unmetered, and most are unmarked to avoid licensing and taxes: parked cars with open doors or a driver sitting behind the wheel are probably special-hires. A standard short-distance fare is around USh5000.

Boda-bodas (motorcycle taxis), by far the fastest but definitely not the safest way to get around, charge USh1500 in the city centre and USh3000 from the centre to the UWA compound.

AROUND KAMPALA

Entebbe

POP 76,500

Sights & Activities

★Ngamba Island Chimpanzee Sanctuary WILDLIFE REFUGE
(☎bookings 0772-502155; www.ngambaisland.org; 24 Lugard Ave; day trip US$88, s/d with full board US$296/400) 'Chimp Island', 23km from Entebbe, is home to over 40 orphaned or rescued chimpanzees who are unable to return to the wild. Humans are confined to about one of the 40 hectares while the chimps wander freely through the rest, emerging from the forest twice a day for feeding at 11am and 2pm. There are also options for an overnight experience, a one-hour forest walk (US$400 per person) with the chimps, who'll climb all over you, and the caregiver experience (US$200 per person).

Uganda Wildlife Education Centre ZOO
(☎0414-322169; www.uweczoo.org; 56-57 Johnstone St; adult/child USh30,000/15000; ⌚9am-6.30pm) Most of the animals here, including rhinos, chimps and shoebill storks, were once injured or recovered from poachers and traffickers.

Beaches BEACH
Entebbe has several inviting beaches on the shores of Lake Victoria; however, swimming is a no-no due to risks of bilharzia.

Sleeping & Eating

Entebbe Backpackers BACKPACKERS $
(☎0414-320432; www.entebbebackpackers.com; 33/35 Church Rd; campsite per person from USh8000, dm USh14,000, s/d from USh20,000/25,000;) Popular, colourful, spick-and-span backpackers. It's often full, so book ahead.

Uganda Wildlife Education Centre HUT $
(☎0414-322169; www.uwec.ug; 56-57 Johnstone St; campsites US$10, dm US$10, r without bathroom US$20, bandas US$35) The choices here are very smart for the price, and the nightly lions' roars and hyenas' howls are free.

Airport Guesthouse GUESTHOUSE $$
(☎0414-370932; www.gorillatours.com; 17 Mugula Rd; s/d/tr incl breakfast US$45/55/75; @) A great balance between style and homeliness, with comfy beds and verandahs looking out to a peaceful garden.

Boma GUESTHOUSE $$
(☎0772-467929; www.boma.co.ug; 20A Julia Sebutinde Rd; s/d/tr incl breakfast US$100/130/180; @) Entebbe's answer to the upmarket B&B, this luxurious guesthouse has grown to 12 rooms, but hasn't lost its intimate atmosphere.

Anna's Corner CAFE $
(1 Station Rd; coffee USh5000, pizzas USh14,000-20,000;) Pleasant garden cafe with the best coffee in town, decent pizza and internet access.

Getting There & Away

Minibuses come from both taxi parks in Kampala (USh2500, one hour) throughout the day. A special-hire from the airport to Kampala will cost from USh80,000.

EASTERN UGANDA

Jinja & Around

POP 87,400

Famous as the source of the Nile River, Jinja has emerged as the adrenaline capital of East Africa. Here you can get your fix of white-water rafting, kayaking and bungee jumping. The town has a lush location and is the major market centre for eastern Uganda.

Many people bypass Jinja proper altogether and spend their time at **Bujagali Falls** (admission USh2000), 7km north, where most rafting trips start and a small backpacker community thrives.

Sleeping & Eating

Jinja

Explorers Backpackers BACKPACKERS $
(☎0434-120236; www.raftafrica.com; 41 Wilson Ave; campsites US$5, dm/d US$7/25; @) Jinja's original backpacker pad is a mellower alternative to the party scene at Bujagali Falls.

ADRENALINE CAPITAL OF EAST AFRICA

The upper stretch of the Nile is a long, rollicking string of class 4 and 5 rapids, and for many travellers a river trip is the highlight of their visit to Uganda. The two main operators are **Adrift** (☎0312-237438; www.adrift.ug) and **Nile River Explorers** (NRE; ☎0434-120236; www.raftafrica.com), both professionally run outfits. There are many options, but the typical half-/full-/two-day trips cost US$115/125/250. Both companies also have jet-boat rides (US$75 for 30 minutes). Both offer free transport from Kampala and a night of free lodging. **Kayak the Nile** (☎0772-880322; www.kayakthenile.com) is another thrilling way to ride the rapids.

Other ways of getting out on the water are to party on **sunset booze cruises** (☎0434-120236) or take the peaceful two-hour cruise on the **Africa Queen** (☎0776-237438), a steam-powered boat.

Exhilarating choices on terra firma include a 44m plunge with **Nile High Bungee** (☎0772-286433; www.adrift.ug; US$65), a variety of rides with **Explorers Mountain Biking** (☎0772-422373; www.raftafrica.com; from US$30), a slow look at the countryside with **Nile Horseback Safaris** (☎0774-101196; www.nilehorsebacksafaris.com; from USh90,000) and a circuit on a quad bike with **All Terrain Adventures** (☎0772-377185; www.atadventures.com/ata/index.html; from USh85,000).

Jinja

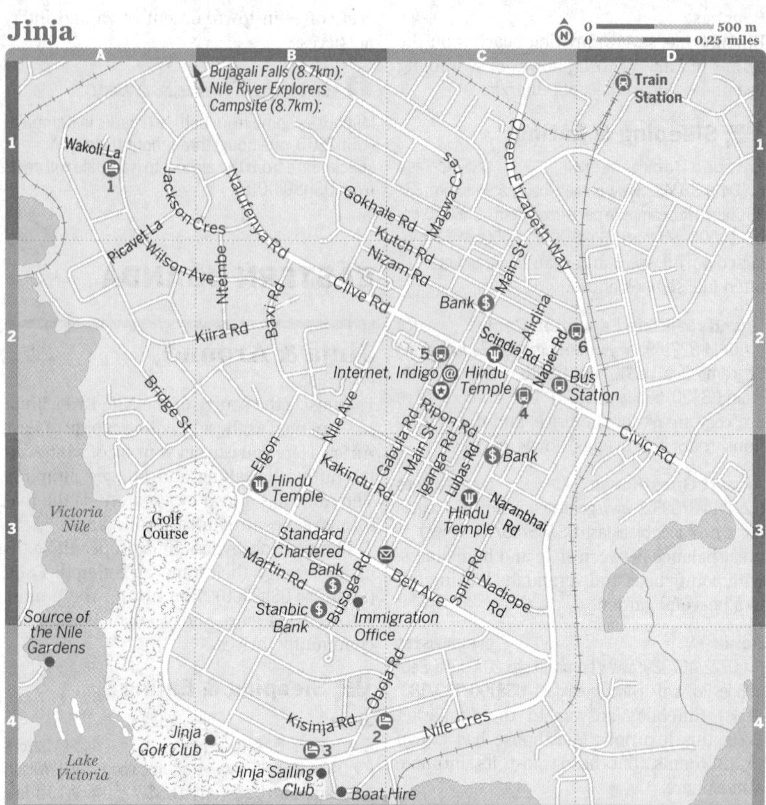

Surjio's BOUTIQUE HOTEL **$$**
(☎0772-500400; www.surjios.com; 24 Kisinja Rd; s/d incl breakfast US$65/110; 📶) A top midrange choice away from town near the edge of the water. It does tasty wood-fired pizzas.

Gately on Nile BOUTIQUE HOTEL **$$**
(☎0434-122400; www.gately-on-nile.com; 34 Kisinja Rd; annexe incl breakfast s/d US$60/80, house s/d US$100/140, cottages s/d US$120/160; @📶) Set in a grand old colonial house with sumptuous grounds. Plus, the restaurant attached is one of Jinja's best.

Around Jinja

Nile River Explorers Campsite BACKPACKERS **$**
(☎0782-320552; www.raftafrica.com/site/accommodation.html; campsites US$5, dm/r US$7/25; @📶) Nile River Explorers runs this rocking cliffside place at Bujagali, always full with overland trucks and backpackers.

Hairy Lemon HUT **$$**
(☎0772-828338; www.hairylemonuganda.com; campsites US$22, dm US$26, bandas s/d/q with full board from US$48/84/120) Seemingly in the middle of nowhere, on a small island 30km out of Jinja, the Hairy Lemon is a peaceful and beautiful getaway.

Nile Porch LODGE **$$**
(☎0782-321541; www.nileporch.com; safari tents s/d/tr incl breakfast US$75/95/120, cottages US$120; @🏊) Luxurious tents superbly set on a cliff above the river. Its Black Lantern Restaurant is Bujagali's best.

★ **Wildwaters Lodge** LODGE **$$$**
(☎0772-237400; www.wild-uganda.com; s/d with full board US$550/700; @📶🏊) One of the best luxury hotels in the country, Wildwaters lives up to its name by overlooking a raging stretch of the Nile from its stunning island location.

Jinja

Activities, Courses & Tours

Nile River Explorers .... (see 1)

Sleeping

1 Explorers Backpackers A1
2 Gately on Nile B4
3 Surjio's B4

Transport

4 Night-time Taxi Stage for Bujagali C2
5 Night-time Taxi Stage for Kampala C2
6 Taxi Park D2

Getting There & Away

Buses and minibuses frequently travel to Kampala (USh5000, two hours), Mbale (USh10,000, three hours) and Busia (USh10,000, two hours) on the Kenyan border. Taxis also head towards Bujagali and Kampala. Minibuses to Budondo pass near Bujagali (USh500, 30 minutes), but can take a while to fill up. *Boda-boda* rides to and from Jinja should cost about USh3000 and special-hires USh10,000, though prices go up late at night.

Mbale

POP 89,000

A bustling provincial city, Mbale is a place you'll pass through if planning an assault on Mt Elgon or en route to Sipi Falls. It has a scenic mountainous backdrop, but otherwise is your typical African town. You can arrange your Mt Elgon expedition at the **national park headquarters** (☎0454-433170; www.ugandawildlife.org/national-parks/mt-elgon-national-park; 19 Masaba Rd; ⊙8am-6pm Mon-Fri, 8am-3pm Sat & Sun).

The Indian-owned **New Mt Elgon View Hotel** (☎0772-445562; 5 Cathedral Ave; s/d without bathroom from USh15,000/20,000, annexe r USh75,000) offers clean, good-value rooms and has **Nurali's Café** (☎0772-445562; 5 Cathedral Ave; mains USh7500-14,000; ⊙7am-late) serving Indian and local dishes downstairs.

Minibuses run to Jinja (USh10,000, three hours), Kampala (USh13,000, four hours) and Soroti (USh5000, two hours). Buses are less frequent and there's an occasional Post Bus. For Sipi Falls (USh7000, one hour) and Budadari (USh4000, 45 minutes), head to the Kumi Rd taxi park, preferably in the morning.

Mt Elgon National Park

Mt Elgon is a good alternative to climbing the Rwenzoris since it offers lower elevation, a milder climate and much more reasonable prices. Also, it's arguably a more scenic climb than the former. It's the second-tallest mountain in Uganda (after Mt Stanley) and the eighth-tallest in Africa. An extinct volcano, it's peppered with cliffs, caves, gorges and waterfalls, and the views from the higher reaches stretch halfway across Uganda.

There are regular, if infrequent, minibuses from Mbale to Budadari (USh3000, 45 minutes).

Hiking

Climbing the highest peak, **Wagagai** (4321m), is nontechnical and relatively easy if you're in good shape, but don't ignore the possibility of altitude sickness. The best times to hike are June to August and December to March; however, the seasons are unpredictable and it can rain any time.

Five trails lead up the mountain. The **Sasa Trail**, starting near Budadari, is the easiest to reach and thus the most popular, but also the toughest. The **Sipi Trail** is a good return route since it lets you chill out at Sipi Falls after your trip to the top. The difficult-to-reach **Piswa Trail**, starting at Kapkwata, has a relatively gentle ascent. Piswa is the best wildlife-watching route and also spends the most time in the otherworldly moorland in the caldera. Most trips take four to six days.

The best place to organise a hike is the park headquarters in Mbale. It costs US$90 per person per day, which covers park entry fees and mandatory ranger-guides. Camping fees are USh15,000 per night and the campgrounds along the trails are good. Gear can be hired at Budadari only; either from the park or Rose's Last Chance. Also, Sipi River Lodge can organise hikes here.

Sleeping

Rose's Last Chance GUESTHOUSE $

(☎0772-623206; mananarose@gmail.com; campsites incl breakfast USh10,000, dm USh15,000, s/d with full board USh22,000/44,000) For many people, a night at Rose's Last Chance, near the trailhead in Budadari, is part of the Mt Elgon experience. The dining room has good vibes and bedrooms are cosy.

Forest Exploration Centre GUESTHOUSE $
(campsites USh15,000, dm USh15,000, s/d USh30,000/50,000) This lovely spot is right at the Sipi trailhead and has a little restaurant.

Kapkwata Guesthouse GUESTHOUSE $
(campsites per tent USh15,000, r USh35,000) This simple place serves the Piswa trailhead. Bring your own food.

Sipi Falls

Sipi Falls, in the foothills of Mt Elgon, is arguably the most beautiful waterfall in all of Uganda. There are three levels, and though the upper two are stunning, it's the 95m main drop that attracts the crowds. The views of the wide plains disappearing into the distance below are spectacular.

It's best to take a guide for walks along area trails. Figure on about USh6000 to USh10,000 to get to the bottom of the main drop and USh15,000 to USh20,000 for the four-hour, 8km walk to all three.

Grassroots **coffee tours** (per person approx USh25,000) take you through the whole process: from picking the coffee berries to deshelling them and grinding them with a traditional mortar and pestle. Abseiling and climbing can be arranged through **Rob's Rolling Rock** (☎0776-963078; www.rollingrock-sipifalls.wordpress.com).

Minibuses from Mbale to Kapchorwa will drop you right at your lodge of choice in Sipi (USh5000, one hour).

Sleeping & Eating

Moses' Campsite GUESTHOUSE $
(☎0752-208302; campsites USh6000, bandas per person USh12,000) Sipi's original backpacker destination has good views of the falls from its wonderful rickety terrace.

Crow's Nest GUESTHOUSE $
(☎0772-687924; thecrowsnets@yahoo.com; campsites USh6500, dm USh13,000, cabins USh31,000) Scandinavian-style cabins with views of all three waterfalls from their terraces. It can arrange cultural walks (USh15,000) that cover everything from throwing spears to learning how to ward off evil spirits.

Sipi River Lodge LODGE $$
(☎0751-796109; www.sipiriverlodge.com; dm US$50, banda s/d with full board US$85/105, cottage d/q with full board US$170/290; @) A tranquil setting among a lovely flower garden and bubbling river. The cottages are the best pick here.

SOUTHWESTERN UGANDA

Fort Portal

POP 46,300

There may be no fort, but this city on the edge of the Crater Lakes, Kibale Forest and Rwenzori Mountains is definitely a portal to places. With a whole holiday's worth of spots to explore around town and all the services travellers need available downtown, many travellers spend some time here.

Sights & Activities

Fort Portal's attractions are pretty minor. Looking down on the city from its highest hill, **Tooro Palace** is the someday-to-be home of King Oyo, who ascended the throne in 1995 at age three. You can't go inside, but there's usually someone around who, for USh5000, will explain the ceremonies that take place here. Eventually King Oyo will join the previous three kings at the modest, brick **Karambi Royal Tombs** (Kasese Rd; admission USh5000; ⏰8am-6pm). Learn all about local flora and organic farming techniques at **Tooro Botanical Garden** (☎0752-500630; www.toorobotanicalgardens.org; Kampala Rd, Km2; tours USh5000; ⏰8am-5pm).

Kabarole Tours (☎0483-422183; www.kabaroletours.com; 1 Moledina St; ⏰8am-6pm Mon-Sat, 10am-4pm Sun) can take you anywhere in Uganda but focuses on its little corner of the country. It also hires mountain bikes, as does **CA Bikes Uganda** (☎0382-280357; www.cabikesuganda.com).

Sleeping

In Town

Continental Hotel HOTEL $
(☎0772-484842; Lugard Rd; s without bathroom USh15,000, r incl breakfast USh25,000) Good shoestring choice in central location, with TV and hot water.

Golf Course View Guesthouse GUESTHOUSE $$
(☎0772-485602; golfcourse71@gmail.com; Rwenzori Rd; s/d incl breakfast from USh30,000/60,000) Well-priced, spacious rooms, with restaurant or kitchen guests are free to use.

Around Fort Portal

Many stay in the leafy, peaceful suburb of Boma, 3km north of town, with good mountain views and Fort Portal's best lodging.

Y.E.S. Hostel BACKPACKERS $
(☎0772-780350; www.caroladamsministry.com/yes_hostel.html; Lower Kakiiza Rd; campsites USh7000, dm USh10,000, s/d USh15,000/20,000; @ 📶) Popular with backpackers, with simply but remarkably tidy rooms, large kitchen and solar hot-water showers.

Ruwenzori View Guesthouse GUESTHOUSE $$
(☎0483-422102; www.ruwenzoriview.com; Lower Kakiiza Rd; s/d incl breakfast USh74,000/99,000, without bathroom USh45,000/70,000; 📶) This blissful little guesthouse run by an Anglo-Dutch couple is as homey as it gets in Uganda. Rooms have their own patios overlooking the garden.

Mountains of the Moon Hotel HOTEL $$
(☎0483-423200; www.mountainsofthemoon.co.ug; Nyaika Ave; s/d incl full breakfast from US$85/110; @ 📶 🏊) Prices are high at this colonial-era gem, but so are the standards.

★ **Kyaninga Lodge** LODGE $$$
(☎0772-999750; www.kyaningalodge.com; s/d with full board US$270/390; 📶 🏊) Eight beautifully designed thatched-roof log cottages soar high upon stilts looking over Kyaninga Lake. It's 12km northeast of Fort Portal.

Eating

The best dining options are the home-cooked dinners served around the family table at **Ruwenzori View Guesthouse** (per person USh22,000; ⏰8pm). Most safari traffic passing through town dines at the **Gardens** (☎0772-694482; Lugard Rd; mains USh2700-8800), while **Gluepot Bar & Pizzeria** (☎0701-367711; www.gluepotpizzeria.com; Kaboyo Rd; pizzas USh8000-21,000; ⏰8.30am-midnight Tue-Sun) is a good spot for a beer and thin-crust pizza.

Getting There & Away

Kalita Transport has the most daily buses to Kampala (USh15,000, four hours), but you can also get there with Link Coaches, whose buses tend to be more comfortable. There's also a Post Bus, which departs from the post office.

Both bus companies also go to Kasese (USh5000, 1½ hours). Kalita has two early-morning buses to Kabale (USh20,000, eight hours), via Katunguru (USh8000, 1½ hours), the entrance to Queen Elizabeth National Park.

The easiest way to Hoima (USh25,000, six hours), from where connections are frequent to Masindi, is the 7am coaster that goes every other day from in front of the Bata shoe store.

There are also fairly regular departures from the taxi park to Ntoroko (USh5000, three hours) and Bundibugyo (USh7000, three hours), often in the back of pick-up trucks.

Minibuses and shared taxis to Kamwenge (for Kibale Forest National Park; USh8000, 45 minutes) and Rwaihamba (for Lake Nkuruba; USh4000, 30 minutes) leave from the intersection near where the main road crosses the river.

The Crater Lakes

The picturesque Crater Lakes south of Fort Portal are great places to settle in for a few days to explore the footpaths or cycle the seldom-used roads. The common wisdom is that the lakes are bilharzia-free, but some locals suggest otherwise. There's fantastic birdlife and plenty of primates.

LAKE NYINAMBUGA

Emblazoned on Uganda's USh20,000 note, picturesque Lake Nyinambuga is home to the luxurious **Ndali Lodge** (☎0772-221309; www.ndalilodge.com; s/d with full board US$240/340; @ 🏊) with its stunning location on a ridge above the lake.

LAKE NKURUBA

Arguably the most beautiful crater lake, Nkuruba, 25km south of Fort Portal, is one of the few still surrounded entirely by forest. Many monkeys, including black-and-white colobuses, frolic here.

Lake Nkuruba Nature Reserve Community Campsite (☎0773-266067; www.lakenkuruba.com; campsites USh6000, tent hire USh6000, dm USh16,000, lakeside cottages USh36,000, bandas USh50,000), as the blue and yellow sign at the entrance gate says, is Nkuruba's original. It has great views and easy access to the lake, plus all funds go towards health and education programs. Be sure you're at the right place as the unrecommendable camp next door may try to entice you into walking up their drive instead.

Minibuses and shared taxis from Fort Portal to Rwaihamba pass Nkuruba (USh4000, 45 minutes). A special-hire will set you back about USh30,000, and a *boda-boda* USh15,000.

LAKE NYINABULITWA

Another tranquil lake, the midsized 'Mother of Lakes' is home to the attractive **Nyinabulitwa Country Resort** (☎0712-984929; www.nyinabulitwaresort.com; campsites incl breakfast US$15, s US$70-80, d US$120-140, tr US$180-210), an intimate place on the lake's south shore. It does boat trips around the lake and can deliver you to a treehouse for primate-watching and birdwatching. It's 20km from Fort Portal, 1.5km off the road to Kibale Forest National Park, just before Rweetera Trading Centre.

LAKE NYABIKERE

The lovely 'Lake of Frogs' lies along the road to Kibale (12km northwest of Kanyanchu visitor centre) and is a great lake to explore. **CVK Lakeside Resort** (0772-906549; info@kibaleforestcvklakesideresort.com; campsites per tent US$10, dm excl breakfast USh20,000, s USh35,000, r USh70,000;) is fairly basic, but the prices are fair. Take any minibus (USh3000) heading south from Fort Portal.

LAKE KASENDA

Want to really get away from it all? Get to **Ruigo Planet Beach** (0701-370674; campsites USh10,000, s/d/tr incl breakfast USh20,000/50,000/100,000), where visitors are very rare due to its isolation. Rooms are decent, but there's no actual beach. It's 35km south of Fort Portal and overloaded trucks trundle to Kasenda trading centre (USh5000, two to three hours), 2km before the lodge.

Kibale Forest National Park

This **national park** (0483-425335; adult/child US$35/20; 8am-5pm) is believed to have the highest density of primates in Africa, including rare red colobus and L'Hoest's monkey. But it's the chimpanzees who are the stars, with three groups habituated to human contact. Despite it being the most expensive place in Uganda for **chimp tracking** (per person incl park permit US$150; 8am & 2pm), it provides the best chance of seeing them and walking is relatively easy; reservations are recommended. Children 12 and under aren't permitted. Regular trackers get just one hour with the playful primates, but those on the **Chimpanzee Habituation Experience** (1/2/3 days US$220/440/660; Feb-Jun & Sep-Nov) can spend the whole day with them. To do this you must spend the night before at Kanyanchu. Nature walks are also available.

Kibale also has a great birdlist (over 375 species), which birdwatchers will want to combine with nearby **Bigodi Wetland Sanctuary** (0772-886865; www.bigodi-tourism.org; 7.30am-5pm), 6km south of the park. It's home to around 200 species of birds, as well as butterflies and eight different species of primates, including grey-cheeked mangabey.

Any shared taxis (USh6000, 45 minutes) between Fort Portal and Kamwenge can drop you there.

Sleeping & Eating

Sebitoli Forest Camp LODGE $

(0782-761512; campsites USh15,000, s/d USh30,000/40,000) In the northern end of the park, this budget lodge has a relaxing location surrounded by trees with black-and-white colobus monkeys.

★ **Chimps' Nest** LODGE $$

(0774-669107; www.chimpsnest.com; campsites US$5, dm US$8, cottages incl breakfast s/d US$60/80, treehouse s/d US$120/150; P @) This stunning place borders Kibale Forest and Magombe Swamp, so there's lots of wildlife around. All the choices are wonderful, but especially the amazing treehouse. It's 4km off the highway from Nkingo.

Primate Lodge LODGE $$

(0414-267153; www.ugandalodges.com; campsites incl breakfast USh15,000, treehouse USh50,000, cottages s/d with full board US$110/150, safari tents s/d with full board US$190/330) Just inside the park at Kanyanchu near the visitor centre, Primate Lodge is a mix of lovely stone cottages and safari tents.

Getting There & Away

Minibuses from Fort Portal to Kamwenge pass the Kanyanchu visitor centre (USh7000, one hour), 35km southeast of Fort Portal.

Semuliki National Park

The Semliki Valley is a little corner of Democratic Republic of Congo (DRC, formerly Zaïre) poking into Uganda. Here the steaming jungle of the Ituri Forest collides with the higher plateau that crosses East Africa. Most people visit the **national park** (0382-276424; adult/child US$25/15) for the beautiful and bizarre **hot springs** (guided walk per person US$15) near Sempaya Gate, but the two trails cutting through the forest to the border-forming Semliki River are fun and also very rewarding for birders.

The simple **Bumaga Campsite** (campsites USh15,000, r USh30,000) is a grassy campsite on the edge of the forest, 2km past the springs. Arrange accommodation at the UWA office at the Sempaya Gate.

The park is just 52km from Fort Portal, but plan on two hours to reach it by car in the dry season. Minibuses and pick-ups between Fort Portal and Bundibugyo pass the park (USh10,000, three hours) and if you leave early you should be able to make it a day trip.

Toro-Semliki Wildlife Reserve

The **Toro-Semliki Wildlife Reserve** (☎0772-649880; adult/child US$25/15) is the oldest protected natural area in Uganda, having first been set aside in 1926.

Wildlife is recovering after decades of poaching and you may encounter waterbuck, reedbuck, bushbuck, buffalo, leopard, elephants and hyenas. A number of lions have also recently returned.

Likely the best wildlife experience in the park is the morning **chimp tracking** (per person US$30). The hiking is more difficult than in Kibale and you're a little less likely to encounter chimps, but, when you do, the thinner forest means your views are superior. These are rare 'dry-habitat chimps' that spend considerable time in the savannah and so walk upright more often than the others.

Rangers also lead **nature walks** (per person US$15) to scenic spots, and a **Lake Albert boat trip** (the lodge charges US$180 for a half-day), usually revealing hippos, crocodiles and shoebill storks.

There's a simple **UWA Camp** (campsites USh15,000, bandas per person USh20,000) on Lake Albert at Ntoroko and also camping at the headquarters near Karugutu. **Semliki Safari Lodge** (☎0414-251182; www.wildplacesafrica.com; s/d all-inclusive US$570/810;) provides luxury tents.

The headquarters is 27km from Fort Portal. Minibuses and pick-ups from Fort Portal to Ntoroko (USh10,000, three hours) pass by.

Kasese

POP 67,000

Kasese is the uninspiring base for climbing the Rwenzoris, otherwise there's no reason to stop here.

White House Hotel (☎0782-536263; whitehse_hotel@yahoo.co.uk; 46 Henry Bwambale Rd; s/d without bathroom USh15,000/28,000, r USh35,000;) is the pick of the cheaper lodges. Otherwise head a few kilometres outside town for more upmarket choices such as **Rwenzori the Gardens** (☎0772-466461; www.rwenzori-hotel.webs.com; Bukonjo Rd; r/cottage/ste incl breakfast from USh50,000/70,000/100,000;) or **Hotel Margherita** (☎0483-444015; www.hotel-margherita.com; s/d/ste/apt incl breakfast from US$70/95/140/190;).

The quickest connection to Kampala (USh20,000, five hours) is via Fort Portal (USh4000, one hour).

For Queen Elizabeth National Park catch any Mbarara-bound vehicle and ask for the national park entrance (USh3000, one hour), which is signposted on the left just before the village of Katunguru.

Rwenzori Mountains National Park

The fabled, mist-covered 'Mountains of the Moon', the World Heritage–listed Rwenzoris feature many peaks permanently covered by snow and glaciers. Hiking here is tough, and the mountains have a well-deserved reputation for being very wet, but unlike at Mt Kilimanjaro or Mt Kenya, you're likely to have the trails all to yourself. Mt Stanley (5109m) is Africa's third-highest mountain.

Hiking

There are two routes up into the mountains. The **Kitembe route** has recently opened up through **Rwenzori Trekking Services** (RTS; ☎0774-199022; www.rwenzoritrekking.com), part of Backpackers Hostel in Kampala. Standards are high and their equipment is good quality. Three-/six-day hikes cost US$240/630 per person with a group of three or more, while nine-day summits of Margherita and Alexandra Peaks start at US$1030. Rates include everything (including porters) other than the park entry fee (US$30 per day).

Otherwise the classic six-day Central Circuit starts at Nyakalengija and is controlled by **Rwenzori Mountaineering Services** (RMS; ☎in Kampala 0772-523208, in Kasese 0772-572810; www.rwenzorimountaineeringservices.com; UWA compound), which doesn't have a stellar reputation. Check all the gear carefully before setting out and don't let your guide pressure you to move faster than you are comfortable with. The US$600 cost (US$780 if you want to summit Margherita Peak, the highest peak on Mt Stanley) covers everything, other than equipment.

The driest times to hike are from late December to mid-March and from mid-June to mid-August, though you may have the enjoyment of snow in the wet seasons. Both companies hire climbing and cold-weather gear.

Sleeping

Rwenzori Trekkers Hostel BACKPACKERS $
(Rwenzori Backpackers; ☎0774-199022; www.backpackers.co.ug/rwenzoribackpack.html; campsites USh7000, dm USh15,000, s/d USh20,000/35,000; P) Run by Backpackers Hostel in Kampala, this peaceful place is in restored miners' housing in Kilembe.

Ruboni Community Campsite HUT $
(☎0752-503445; www.rubonicamp.com; campsites US$3, r without bathroom per person US$20, bandas per person US$25) At the base of the hill just outside the park boundary, this campsite has an attractive setting and comfortable lodging; all profits go to the community.

Getting There & Away

Minibuses run from Kasese to Ibanda (USh4000, one hour); from there take a *boda-boda* to Nyakalengija (USh4000). For Kilembe (USh2000, 30 minutes) go to the Shell petrol station on Kilembe Rd. A special taxi-hire costs USh10,000 from Kasese.

Queen Elizabeth National Park

The 1978-sq-km **Queen Elizabeth National Park** (☎0782-387805; www.queenelizabethnationalpark.com; adult/child US$35/20; ⏲booking office 6.30am-7pm, park gates 7am-7pm) is one of the most popular in Uganda. Though the wildlife populations remain lower than the top Tanzanian and Kenyan parks, few reserves in the world can boast such a high biodiversity rating, best exemplified by the amazing 610 bird species (more than found in all of Great Britain). It has 96 species of mammals, including healthy numbers of hippos, elephants, lions and leopard as well as chimps and hyenas.

Besides **wildlife drives** (ranger-guides US$20), the park is well worth a visit for a **Kazinga Channel boat trip** (2hr trips US$25; ⏲9am, 11am, 3pm & 5pm) to see the thousands of hippos plus other animals, and a walk through beautiful **Kyambura (Chambura) Gorge** (☎0702-228292; per person US$50; ⏲8am & 2pm), a little Eden brimming with primates, including one difficult-to-find habituated troop of chimpanzees. The remote **Ishasha** sector, in the far south of the park, is famous for its tree-climbing lions.

Sleeping & Eating

Mweya Peninsula

Mweya is a great base because many animals roam through here (be careful at night) and you can also watch wildlife along the river down below.

Mweya Campgrounds CAMPGROUND $
(campsites per person USh15,000) Rustic facilities, but three superb campsites across the park. Book at the visitor centre in Mweya before setting up your tent.

Mweya Hostel HOSTEL $$
(☎0414-373050; s/d/f without bathroom & incl breakfast USh57,000/84,000/252,500) Basic, but a reasonably reliable option for finding a cheap bed.

Mweya Safari Lodge LODGE $$$
(☎0312-260260; www.mweyalodge.com; s US$135, d US$240-280, ste US$305, cottages US$520-775; ❄@📶≋) This large, sophisticated outfit has excellent views over Lake Edward and the Kazinga Channel. Its restaurant is stunning.

Elsewhere

Simba Safari Camp LODGE $
(☎0701-426368; www.ugandalodges.com; Bwera Rd; campsites USh10,000, dm US$10, s/d/tr incl breakfast US$45/60/90, cottages US$125; 📶) Just outside the park on the edge of its northern border, Simba is the most social option that's popular with backpackers and convenient for game drives.

Ishasha Camp CAMPGROUND $
(☎0200-901560; campsites USh15,000, bandas USh40,000) This basic and blissfully remote set-up is small, so beds fill fast. Local meals are available from USh10,000.

★ **Kyambura Game Lodge** LODGE $$$
(☎0414-322789; www.kyamburalodge.com; Kyambura; s/d incl breakfast low season US$90/150, high season US$130/220; ≋) Fantastic value for money, Kyambura offers panoramic views, where you've a good chance to see elephants, and rooms that strike the perfect balance between deluxe and safari.

Getting There & Away

The majority of people visit the park either as part of an organised tour or by renting their own car. Otherwise there's a direct bus to Katunguru (USh25,000, eight hours) from Kampala's main bus park at 9am. Regular minibuses between Kasese (USh4000, one hour) and Mbarara (USh10,000, three hours) stop at Katunguru.

DON'T MISS

GORILLA TRACKING

Hanging out with mountain gorillas is a genuine once-in-a-lifetime experience and one of the most thrilling wildlife encounters in the world – and Bwindi Impenetrable National Park is one of the best places to see them.

There are theoretically 64 daily permits available to track gorillas in Bwindi. Permits cost US$500 and are booked through the Uganda Wildlife Authority (UWA) office in Kampala.

Trips leave (from the park office nearest the group you'll be tracking) at 8.30am daily, but you should report to park headquarters by 7.45am.

Once you finally join a tracking group, the chances of finding the gorillas are almost guaranteed. But, since the terrain in Bwindi Impenetrable National Park is mountainous and heavily forested, it can take anywhere from 30 minutes to five hours to reach them. Walking sticks or a porter are a very good idea.

Of the 28 gorilla groups living in Bwindi (varying from families of five to 27), nine have been habituated to be visited by tourists, with permits issued for different parts of the park. **Buhoma** is the most popular due to it having the most permits and best tourist facilities. **Nkuringo** in the southwest is also stunning, while permits are also available to **Ruhija** and **Rushaga**.

Once in the park, you can either hitch or arrange a special-hire taxi in Katunguru.

The Ishasha sector is 100km from Mweya in the far south of the park. From Ishasha, you can head south for Butogota and Bwindi Impenetrable National Park in about two hours in the dry season.

If you don't have your own vehicle you can get special-hires from Katunguru. Count on paying US$50/70 for a half-/full day, including fuel and drivers' admission.

Red Chilli Hideaway (p717) and Great Lakes Safaris (p747) are the best budget providers.

Bwindi Impenetrable National Park

Home to almost half of the world's surviving mountain gorillas, the World Heritage-listed **Bwindi Impenetrable National Park** (☎0486-424121; adult/child US$35/25; ⏱park office 7.45am-5pm) is one of Africa's most famous. Set over 331 sq km of improbably steep mountain rainforest, the park is home to an estimated 360 gorillas: undoubtedly Uganda's biggest tourist drawcard. See p725 for more information on permits.

The Impenetrable Forest, as it's also known, has an incredible biodiversity of flora and fauna. Its 120 species of mammal is more than any of Uganda's other national parks, though sightings are less common because of the dense forest. For birdwatchers it's one of the most exciting destinations in the country, with almost 360 species.

The headquarters is at Buhoma on the northern edge of the park.

Activities

It's not all about gorillas in Bwindi with **forest walks** (per person US$10) and a variety of excellent community walks including the **Batwa Experience** (☎0392-888700; www.batwaexperience.com; US$70) to meet the Twa (Batwa) and learn how they lived in the forest.

Sleeping & Eating

Bwindi has more beds than gorilla permits, but prices are higher than elsewhere in Uganda.

Buhoma

Buhoma Community Rest Camp LODGE $
(☎0772-384965; www.buhomacommunity.com; campsites US$10, dm US$20, r US$60, without bathroom US$50) Enjoying a beautiful setting near the park headquarters, this community-run lodge has *bandas* (huts) and safari tents spread out on a hill heading down the valley. Meals available.

Buhoma Lodge LODGE $$$
(☎0414-321479; www.ugandaexclusivecamps/buhoma.html) Spacious rooms have a rustic touch mixed with polished-wood floors and plenty of natural light, private porch and fantastic views of Bwindi's forest.

Elsewhere

★**Nkuringo Gorilla Campsite** LODGE $$
(☎0754-805580; www.gorillacamp.com; Nkuringo; camp incl tent s/d US$30/45, s/d without bathroom US$67/84, cottages with full board s/d US$210/290; 📶) A wonderful nature-based set-up in Nkuringo with views looking out to the misty

Virungas, this is one of the best places to stay in Bwindi. Its atmospheric restaurant is alit by paraffin lanterns.

Nshongi Camp HUT $
(☎0774-231913; www.nshongicamp.altervista.org; Rushaga; camsites USh10,000, bandas with full board per person USh85,000) Delightful simple mud-brick *bandas* among a lovely garden and forest. It's a short walk to the Rushaga trailhead.

Ruhija Gorilla Friends Resort & Campsite GUESTHOUSE $
(☎0772-480885; bitarihorobert@gmail.com; Ruhija; campsites per person with/without tent US$10/7, s/d without bathroom from US$15/30) Good budget choice, where you can pitch a tent, use one of theirs, or go for a room or tented room. Proceeds go to the community.

Getting There & Away

BUHOMA

Getting to Buhoma can be complicated. The first step is Butogota. There are trucks between Kabale and Butogota (USh15,000, four to six hours) on Tuesday and Friday. Otherwise, take a Kihihi-bound vehicle as far as Kanyantorogo (USh10,000, three hours) and catch another vehicle to Butogota (USh2000, one hour).

The fastest way from Kampala is by bus to Kihihi (USh35,000, 10 hours) and then a pick-up or shared taxi (USh5000, 1½ hours) to Buhoma.

Taxis from Butogota and Buhoma (USh2000, one hour) are infrequent, except on Thursday and Saturday. Special-hires will be USh50,000 and *boda-bodas* half that.

If you're coming from Queen Elizabeth, Butogota is best accessed from Ishasha (three hours), but is problematic if you don't have your own car, in which case special-hire is the most realistic option, costing around USh180,000.

NKURINGO

From Kabale there's a truck departing Tuesday and Saturday afternoon (USh8000, four hours). Otherwise try a *boda-boda* (USh35,000, 2½ hours) or special-hire (one-way/return USh180,000/120,000, 2½ hours).

From Kisoro a truck travels to Nkuringo (USh8000, three hours) on Monday and Thursday. It leaves Nkuringo around 8am and returns about 3pm. A special-hire costs around USh100,000/150,000 one-way/return. A *boda-boda* driver will charge you USh30,000, but it's a long, bottom-shaking ride.

You can also just walk. **Nkuringo Walking Safaris** (☎0774-805580; www.nkuringowalkingsafaris.com; per 2 people from US$70) will lead you there with a three-hour paddle across Lake Mutanda and a 19km hike through the countryside.

RUSHAGA

Located 54km from Kabale, Rushaga can be reached via a special-hire taxi (USh100,000/160,000 one-way/return from Kabale) and takes two hours, while a *boda-boda* is around USh30,000 one-way.

Otherwise it's 32km from Kisoro, and costs USh60,000/90,000 one-way/return by special-hire taxi (one hour) or USh15,000 by *boda-boda* one-way. Trucks (USh3500, two hours) depart in the afternoon on Monday and Thursday, and 10am on Friday.

RUHIJA

Ruhija is about 50km (up to two hours) from Buhoma Gate, and 52km from Kasese. A special-hire will cost about USh140,000 return. If you're chancing your luck with public transport there are pick-up trucks that leave Kabale on Tuesday, Wednesday and Thursday.

Kabale

POP 44,000

While Uganda's highest (2000m) town is nothing to write home about, it's the gateway to Lake Bunyonyi, the top spot for serious rest and relaxation in Uganda, and a good staging post for trips to Bwindi Impenetrable National Park.

Sleeping & Eating

With beautiful Lake Bunyonyi just a short hop away, few travellers stay in Kabale very long.

You can eat well at Home of Edirisa and Kabale Backpackers (Amagara Guesthouse, which have a mix of local and international favourites in the USh3000 to USh10,000 range.

Home of Edirisa BACKPACKERS $
(☎0752-558222; www.edirisa.org; Muhumuza Rd; dm USh7000, d USh25,000, s/d without bathroom USh10,000/20,000; @ 📶) It's a hostel, museum, restaurant, cultural centre, fair-trade craft shop and a great place to hang out.

Kabale Backpackers BACKPACKERS $
(Amagara Guesthouse; ☎0772-959667; Muhumuza Rd; s incl breakfast USh17,000, r USh22,000-32,000; @) The people behind Byoona Amagara on Lake Bunyonyi also run this little spot with simple, meticulously clean rooms.

Cepha's Inn BOUTIQUE HOTEL $$
(☎0486-422097; www.cephasinn.com; Archer Rd; s/d/ ste USh50,000/90,000/150,000; @ 🏊) Fills two colourful buildings on the hill above town and offers good value.

Getting There & Away

There are frequent buses to Kampala (USh25,000, eight hours), most picking up passengers by the Skyblue Motel at the main junction. The Post Bus departs around 7am.

It's easiest to find rides to Kisoro (USh10,000, two hours) in front of the Highland Hotel on the northwest side of town. Horizon and Gateway buses depart for Fort Portal (USh25,000, eight hours), via Queen Elizabeth National Park (USh20,000, seven hours) and Kasese, at 7pm.

Lake Bunyonyi

Lake Bunyonyi (Place of Many Little Birds) is undoubtedly the loveliest lake in Uganda. Its contorted shore encircles 29 islands, and the steep surrounding hillsides are intensively terraced.

The guesthouses offer a variety of walking and boat trips, the most intriguing being Home of Edirisa's three-day **canoe trekking** (0752-558222; www.edirisa.org; half-/1-/2-/3-day trek per person US$35/65/105/135).

Sleeping & Eating

★ Byoona Amagara LODGE **$**

(0752-652788; www.lakebunyonyi.net; Itambira Island; campsites USh9000, dm USh14,000-18,000, geodome per person USh25,000-33,000, cabins per person USh33,000, cottages USh150,000; @) Byoona Amagara bills itself as a backpacker's paradise, and it's hard to disagree. Rooms are built of natural materials and very reasonably priced, with the open-faced geodome hut the best choice. The dugout canoe is free *to* the island.

Bunyonyi Overland Resort BACKPACKERS **$**

(0486-426016; www.bunyonyioverland.com; camp US$6, s/d from US$20/25; @) More attractive than most backpacker pads, but the vibe (and surfeit of overland trucks) is the same.

Arcadia Cottages LODGE **$$**

(0782-424232; www.arcadiacottages.net; campsites per tent USh30,000, cottages incl breakfast s/d USh142,000/182,000) Set high above the lake, Arcadia has some intoxicating views over dozens of islands *way* down below.

Getting There & Away

Many pick-ups (USh2000) and shared taxis (USh2500) travel the 9km to the lake from Kabale's main market on Monday and Friday. Transport is rare on other days, so you'll probably have to choose between a special-hire (USh20,000) and a *boda-boda* (USh6000).

Kisoro

POP 13,000

While Kisoro itself may not be much to look at – a gritty town with a frontier atmosphere – its verdant surrounds are undeniably beautiful. On a clear day the backdrop of the Virunga chain of volcanoes is stunning. Kisoro serves as a popular base for tourists, here primarily for nearby Mgahinga Gorilla National Park. The scenic **Lake Mutanda** lies just north of Kisoro and makes for a relaxing spot to hang out for a day.

Sleeping & Eating

Hotel Virunga BACKPACKERS **$**

(0486-430109; campsites USh14,000, s/d without bathroom USh20,000/30,000, r Ush50,000) Kisoro's busiest backpacker place, with a buzzing little restaurant that rocks on as a bar.

Travellers Rest Hotel HOTEL **$$**

(0772-533029; www.gorillatours.com/gorilla-tours/travellers-rest-hotel-kisoro.html; Mahuabura Rd; s/d/tr incl breakfast US$65/75/95, ste US$85; @) Through various little touches, this otherwise simple hotel, which Dian Fossey called her 'second home', has become a lovely little oasis.

Coffee Masters CAFE

(Bunagana Rd; coffee USh2000, mains USh3000-5000; 7am-10pm) Locally grown coffees, fruit smoothies and simple meals.

Getting There & Away

Several bus companies make the long run to Kampala (USh30,000 to USh35,000, eight to 10 hours). Minibuses to Kabale (USh10,000, two hours are frequent. See p746 for full details

The Rwandan border south of Kisoro at Cyanika is open 7am to 7pm and it's a pretty simple and quick trip to Musanze (Ruhengeri).

Mgahinga Gorilla National Park

Although it's the smallest of Uganda's national parks at just 34 sq km, with the towering Virunga volcanoes providing a dramatic backdrop, **Mgahinga Gorilla National Park** (0486-430098; adult/child US$35/20) punches above its weight.

Activities

There's **gorilla tracking** (☎0414-680793; Main St, Kisoro; incl park entrance fee US$500) here, though not all the time because the habituated family sometimes ducks over the mountains into Rwanda or DRC. Make your reservations by calling the park office in Kisoro no more than two weeks in advance and then pay at the park on the day of your trip. Permits for one or two people are often available with just a few days' wait.

Mgahinga is also popular for **golden-monkey tracking** (per person US$20) , almost as fun as hanging out with the big boys. There's also challenging but rewarding **volcano treks** (incl park fee & guide US$60) through the otherworldly Afro-alpine moorland atop the volcanoes, or the **Batwa Trail** (incl guide US$80) forest tours led by Twa people.

Sleeping & Eating

Amajambere Iwacu Community Campground CAMPGROUND $
(☎0382-278464; campsites USh10,000, dm USh15,000, bandas USh60,000, without bathroom USh45,000) A friendly place with a variety of rooms and a nice verandah for soaking up choice views of the Virungas. It's just outside the park gate. Proceeds fund school projects in the area.

Getting There & Away

There's no public transport along the rough 14km track between Kisoro and the park; and traffic is too light to rely on hitching if you must get there early in the morning.
Taking a *boda-boda*/special-hire costs about USh15,000/40,000.

Ssese Islands

If you're looking for a place to slow it right down, Ssese's lush archipelago of 84 islands along Lake Victoria's northwestern shore boasts some stunning white-sand beaches. There's not much to do here other than grab a good book and relax. There are canoes for hire, but swimming is unadvisable due to risks of bilharzia.

The only proper town is Kalangala, on Buggala Island, above Lutoboka Bay where the ferry lands and most of the resorts sit. There's no ATM.

Sleeping & Eating

Mirembe Resort GUESTHOUSE $
(☎0392-772703; www.miremberesort.com; campsites per tent USh15,000, safari tents per person USh20,000, s/d/tr USh65,000/90,000/135,000; @) The last resort on Lutoboka Bay is very peaceful with a variety of rooms and bonfires on the beach.

Islands Club GUESTHOUSE $
(☎0772-641376; sseseclub@yahoo.com; s/d incl breakfast USh50,000/100,000) Wooden bungalows on a blinding stretch of white sand. Its spiced, fried tilapia (fish) is delicious.

Banda Island Resort GUESTHOUSE $
(☎0772-222777; banda.island@gmail.com; Banda Island; dm USh50,000, r USh150,000) Once legendary among backpackers; few people head to Banda Island anymore now that it's so much easier to get to Buggala, but Banda is much more peaceful, which is what an island escape should be.

Getting There & Away

The new **EarthWise** (www.earthwise.com) ferry service from Port Bell in Kampala makes getting to Ssese a lot easier. Boats from Kampala depart Port Bell at 8am, arriving at Kalangala on Buggala Island at noon. Departure times from Buggala are at 1.30pm, arriving at Port Bell by 6pm. Fares are USh30,000/70,000 for economy/1st class.

Otherwise the MV *Kalangala* ferry (2nd-/1st-class seats USh10,000/14,000, vehicles USh50,000) from Nakiwogo, near Entebbe, departs from the mainland at 2pm daily and leaves the island at 8am.

Boats to Banda Island (USh35,000, 3¼ hours) leave daily from Kasenyi (halfway between Entebbe and Kampala) at 1pm, stopping via Kitobo Island. Otherwise there's a direct boat on Tuesday at noon (USh20,000). There's also a weekly boat on Friday to Bukasa Island (USh10,000, four hours).

From the west, a free car ferry links Bukakata (36km east of Masaka) on the mainland with Luku on Buggala Island. Shared taxis run from Kalangala to Luku (USh5000, one hour).

NORTHERN UGANDA

Ziwa Rhino Sanctuary

The Big Five is back. This private **reserve** (☎0772-713410; www.rhinofund.org; adult/child US$30/15; ⏲7.30am-5pm), halfway between

Kampala and Murchison Falls National Park, holds half a dozen southern white rhinos and after a drive into the bush (vehicle hire US$20 if needed), guides will walk you near them. There's both budget **accommodation** (camping per tent US$5, r US$15, cottages incl breakfast US$40) and the upmarket **Amuka Lodge** (www.amukalodgeuganda.com; bandas with full board per person US$180;).

All buses from Kampala heading to Gulu or Masindi pass nearby. Get off at Nakitoma (USh13,000, three hours) and take a *boda-boda* for USh7000.

Murchison Falls National Park

Uganda's largest **national park** (0392-881348; adult/child US$35/20; 7am-7pm) is one of its very best. Animals are in plentiful supply and it's home to the raging Murchison Falls, a sight to behold. The falls were once described as the most spectacular thing to happen to the Nile along its 6700km length; here the 50m-wide river is squeezed through a 6m gap and it shoots through this narrow gorge with explosive force.

It suffered drastic poaching during Uganda's dark years, but its recovery has been successful.

Activities

A must at Murchison is the **launch trip** (US$25) to the base of the falls. The three-hour ride from Paraa goes mornings and afternoons and passes hippos, crocodiles, buffaloes and birds galore, plus usually elephants, too. It's possible to be dropped at the base of the falls for a spectacular **hike to the top** (per person US$10), which must be arranged the day before.

Wildlife drives (ranger-guides US$20, vehicle hire US$160-300) in the Buligi area provide good sightings of elephants, giraffes, lions, leopards and spotted hyenas.

There's also **chimpanzee tracking** (low/high season $55/65) of a habituated community at **Kaniyo Pabidi** on the main park road, 29km north of Masindi. Two lucky visitors are allowed to spend a whole day for US$150 per person. Note that trekkers must be over 15 years. Book through Great Lakes Safaris (p747).

Sleeping & Eating

★ **Red Chilli Rest Camp** BACKPACKERS $
(0772-509150; www.redchillihideaway.com; campsites per person USh10,000, tent hire USh5000, d/q safari tents USh35,000/70,000, tw bandas without bathroom USh45,000, tw/q bandas USh70,000/120,000) The popular Red Chilli

Murchison Falls National Park

0 — 20 km
0 — 10 miles

LEGEND
FR Forest Reserve
WR Wildlife Reserve

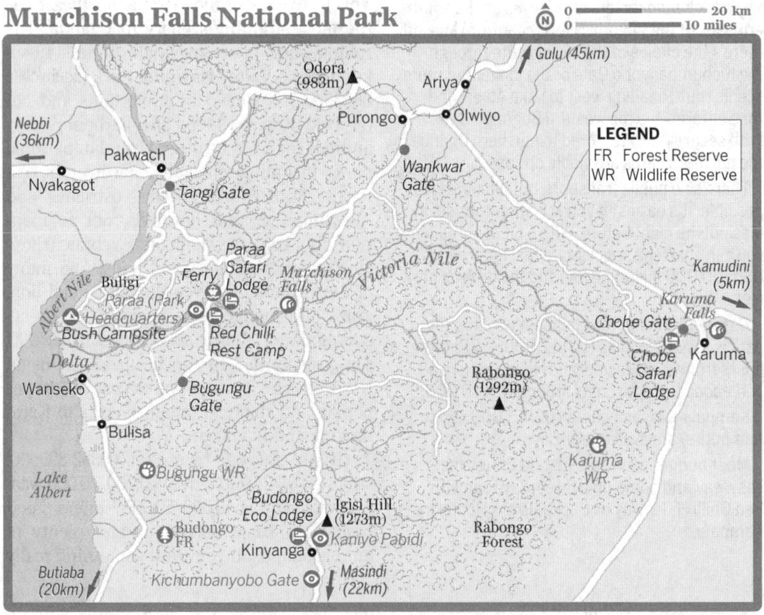

team from Kampala brings the best budget option to Murchison. The rooms here are great value, particularly the *bandas*.

Bush Campsite BUSHCAMP **$**
(per person US$40) Adventurous souls can have an unforgettable night in the wild, sleeping out at Delta Point overlooking Lake Albert.

Budongo Eco Lodge LODGE **$$**
(☎0414-267153; www.ugandalodges.com/budongo; dm/s/d/tr incl breakfast US$20/60/100/115) The only lodge in Kaniyo Pabidi, with comfortable cabins, surrounded by forest, that have hot water, solar power and eco-toilets.

Paraa Safari Lodge LODGE **$$**
(☎0312-260260; www.paraalodge.com; s/d/ste with full board US$165/265/335; @) On the northern bank of the river, this hotel-style lodge has a great location and excellent facilities, including a swim-up bar.

Chobe Safari Lodge LODGE **$$$**
(☎0312-259390; www.chobelodgeuganda.com; s/d/ste incl full board US$180/325/380; @) Isolated on the far eastern reaches of the park, a few kilometres from the Chobe Gate with a gorgeous river location that's teeming with honking hippos.

ℹ Getting There & Away

The park headquarters is at Paraa, on the southern bank of the Victoria Nile. By car from Masindi there's the choice of the direct route through the Kichumbanyobo Gate or the longer but more scenic route heading west to Lake Albert and then entering via the western Bugungu Gate. With security now restored to northern Uganda, the northern gates are viable options.

There's no public transport, but hitching is possible. It's easiest if you ask other tourists in Masindi the night before. With a bit of bargaining you can charter a special-hire taxi for around USh200,000 including fuel and the driver's park fees.

Besides hitching, the cheapest way into the park is to get to Bulisa (USh12,000, 2½ to three hours from both Masindi and Hoima) where a *boda-boda* to Paraa costs around USh40,000.

Kampala–Masindi buses (USh13,000, 3½ to four hours) are available all day.

Most budget travellers just do things the easy way and come on a three-day tour with Red Chilli Hideaway or Backpackers Hostel in Kampala.

Gulu

POP 142,000

Unless you're here volunteering or en route to Kidepo Valley National Park, there's no reason to visit Gulu. It's the largest town in northern Uganda and one of the hardest hit during the Lord's Resistance Army (LRA) conflict. Today it's a city on the rise and there's no shortage of *mzungu* NGO workers about.

Happy Nest Hotel (☎0782-791038; Corona-tion Rd; s/d without bathroom USh28,000/33,000) is a good budget choice, while the **Bomah Hotel** (☎0471-432479; bomahhotelltd@yahoo.com; Eden Rd; s/d/ste incl breakfast from USh82,000/182,000/502,000; @) is the most upmarket. **Coffee Hut** (Awich Rd; coffee USh4200;) buzzes with latte-sipping laptop users.

Frequent buses and minibuses run to Kampala (USh20,000, five hours) all day. Those heading to Kidepo can get a bus to Kitgum (USh10,000, three hours).

For Masindi it's quickest to take a minibus to Kigumba (USh10,000, 2½ hours), and transfer to Masindi (USh5000, 1½ hours).

Kidepo Valley National Park

This lost valley in the extreme northeast has the most stunning scenery in Uganda. The rolling, short-grass savannah of the 1442-sq-km **Kidepo Valley National Park** (adult/child US$35/20) is ringed by mountains and cut by rocky ridges. Kidepo also harbours many animals found in no other Ugandan national park, including cheetahs, aardwolves, caracals, Rothschild's giraffes, ostriches and Abyssinian ground hornbills, not to mention the copious elephants, zebras (these lack manes), buffaloes and lions. And many of these, including even the occasional lion, graze and lounge right near the park's accommodation. **Game drives** (per km USh4000, plus guide fee US$20) can be arranged using UWA vehicles. **Nature walks** cost US$10 per person and staff can organise visits to Karamojong and Ik villages.

UWA's **Apoka Hostel** (☎0392-899500; campsites USh15,000, s/d USh60,000/70,000, without bathroom USh40,000/50,000) offers good *bandas*, a basic restaurant and plenty of animal sounds. If you want something really special, stay at **Apoka Safari Lodge** (☎0414-251182; www.wildplacesafrica.com; s/d with full board & game drives US$450/810; P ❄) which features outdoor bathtubs. The **Nga'Moru Wilderness Camp** (☎0754-500555; brentait@gmail.com; s/d with full board US$150/300) has luxury camping at a peaceful spot on the park's border.

In Kitgum, on the northern route to the park, **Fugly's** (☎0757-760760; dm USh50,000, s USh80,000-150,000, d USh160,000-180,000) is the best place to stay, but **Acholi Pride** (☎0772-687793; r incl breakfast 26,000, with shared bathroom USh13,000) is cheaper.

Getting There & Away

NORTHERN ROUTE

The shortest, safest and easiest route, and currently the only one to consider if you're driving. The first leg is on one of the frequent buses to Kitgum (from Gulu/Kampala USh10,000/25,000, three/eight hours), where UWA has a small office.

Up until around noon, trucks head east from Kitgum to Karenga (USh25,000, three to five hours), 24km from the park's headquarters and lodging area. In Karenga you might get lucky and be able to hitch a ride, or arrange to be picked up by the UWA vehicle for a pricey USh4000 per kilometre; but you'll probably need a *boda-boda* (USh30,000).

EASTERN ROUTE

One for adventure travellers only, this journey takes you through the wilds of Karamojaland where many of the cattle-herding Karamojong people still wear traditional dress (similar to the Maasai) and AK-47s are as common as walking sticks.

Groups of Karamojong still sometimes ambush vehicles. Incidents, however, are pretty rare and the situation seems to be improving so travelling by public means is possible. Still, it's of paramount importance to enquire about security before setting out, and again at every stop.

Begin by heading to Kotido where the **UWA office** (☎0777-478856; ⏰7am-8pm Mon-Fri & most weekends) can give you onward travel advice. Gateway has daily buses to Kotido (USh35,000, 15 hours), departing from Kampala's new bus park at 5.30am. From Kotido there are frequent trucks and pick-ups to Kaabong (USh6500, two to three hours). Then jump on the less frequent trucks to Karenga (USh8000, two to three hours) and try for a special-hire or a *boda-boda* (USh30,000) to the park from there.

UNDERSTAND UGANDA

Uganda Today

President Museveni won his fourth election in 2011 with 68.4% of the vote, to make it 25 years in power. The main challenger was opposition leader, Kizza Besigye, who was also the runner-up in 2001 and 2006. During the campaigns, Besigye had been imprisoned and accused of everything from treason to rape, and subsequently cleared of all charges.

Although the Lord's Resistance Army (LRA) hasn't threatened Uganda since 2007, many northern Ugandans remain too terrified to return to their homes. In October 2011, it was announced that around 100 US troops would be deployed in Uganda to help train local military forces to tackle the LRA in the Central African Republic (where LRS leader Joseph Kony is believed to be hiding), the DRC and Sudan.

Uganda made international headlines from 2009 to 2012 with its controversial bill proposing the death penalty and life sentences for homosexual behaviour. The bill was drafted and presented to parliament by a right-wing MP, and proposed the death sentence to those convicted of 'aggravated homosexuality'. This would have included homosexuals convicted of rape, sex with a minor or knowingly spreading HIV. It would also have included those deemed 'serial offenders', a ruling which remains vague. The bill was strongly condemned by the international community. Although rejected on the occasions it has been debated in parliament (on the basis that homosexuality is already criminalised in Uganda), the bill has been shelved rather than defeated outright. In Februrary 2012 Bahati announced his intention to rewrite the bill to remove the death penalty. A life prison sentence would remain under the proposed legislation.

History

Uganda experienced two great waves of migration. The first brought the Bantu-speaking peoples from further west in Africa, and the second, the Nilotic people from Sudan and Ethiopia. These broad families are still geographically split today: the Bantu in the centre and south of the country and the Nilotic peoples in the north.

Until the 19th century, landlocked Uganda saw few outsiders compared with its neighbours. Despite fertile lands and surplus harvests, trading links with the great Indian Ocean ports were limited. Firm contacts were finally made with Arab traders and early European explorers in the mid-19th century.

The British Arrive

After the Treaty of Berlin in 1890, when Europeans carved up Africa, Uganda, Kenya and Zanzibar were declared British Protectorates. The Brits ruled indirectly, giving the traditional kingdoms a considerable degree of autonomy, but favoured the Baganda (the name of the people of the Buganda Kingdom) people for their civil service.

Other tribal groups, unable to make inroads into the Baganda-dominated colonial administration or commercial sector, were forced to seek alternative avenues for advancement. The Acholi and Lango people from the north soon became dominant in the military. Thus were planted the seeds for the intertribal conflicts that were to tear Uganda apart following independence.

Independence Time

By the mid-1950s a Lango schoolteacher, Dr Milton Obote, had cobbled together a loose coalition that led Uganda to independence in 1962, on the promise that the Baganda would have autonomy. The *kabaka* (king), Edward Mutesa II, became the new nation's president, and Milton Obote became prime minister.

It was not the ideal time for Uganda to get to grips with independence. Civil wars were raging in neighbouring Sudan, Zaïre and Rwanda, and refugees poured into the country. It soon became obvious that Obote had no intention of sharing power. In 1966, he arrested several cabinet ministers and ordered his army chief of staff, Idi Amin, to storm the *kabaka's* palace. Obote became president, the Bugandan monarchy (and all others) was abolished and Idi Amin's star was on the rise.

Enter Idi Amin

Idi Amin staged a coup in January 1971, and so began Uganda's first reign of terror. All political activities were suspended and the army was empowered to shoot on sight anyone suspected of opposition to the regime.

Over the next eight years an estimated 300,000 Ugandans lost their lives, often in horrifying ways. Amin's main targets were the educated classes; the Acholi and Lango people of Obote; and the 70,000-strong Asian community, which in 1972 was given 90 days to leave the country.

Meanwhile, the economy collapsed, infrastructure crumbled, prolific wildlife was slaughtered by soldiers and the tourism industry evaporated. The stream of refugees fleeing the country became a flood, inflation hit 1000% and the treasury ran out of money to pay the soldiers.

By the end of 1978 Amin had invaded Tanzania – ostensibly to teach that country a lesson for supporting anti-Amin dissidents – as a diversion from problems at home. However, the Tanzanians, with the help of exiled Ugandans, soundly defeated Amin and pushed on into the heart of Uganda in early 1979. Amin eventually ended up in Saudi Arabia where he died in 2003, never having faced justice.

Obote Rides Again

The rejoicing in Uganda after Amin's downfall was short-lived. The 12,000 Tanzanian soldiers who remained in Uganda, supposedly to assist with the country's reconstruction and to maintain law and order, turned on the Ugandans as soon as their pay dried up. Once again the country slid into chaos and gangs of armed bandits roamed the cities, killing and looting.

Yusufu Lule and Godfrey Binaisa came and went as leaders before Obote returned from exile in Tanzania. He swept to victory in an election that was widely reported to be rigged. Obote continued a policy of tribal favouritism, replacing many southerners in military and civil-service positions with his northern Lango and Acholi supporters, and the prisons began to fill again. Reports of atrocities leaked out of the country and several mass graves were discovered. In mid-1985 Obote was overthrown in a coup staged by the army under the leadership of Tito Okello.

A New Beginning

Okello, who turned out not to be much different from his predecessors, had many enemies, including Yoweri Museveni, who built a guerrilla army in western Uganda. Museveni's National Resistance Army (NRA) was different to the armies of Amin and Obote – new recruits, many of them orphans, were taught to be servants of the people, not oppressors, and discipline was tough. By January 1986 it was clear that Okello's days were numbered. The NRA launched an all-out offensive and easily took Kampala since most of Okello's troops chose to loot the capital rather than fight.

Museveni was a pragmatic leader. He appointed a number of arch-conservatives to his cabinet, and made an effort to avoid the tribal nepotism that had divided the country. The economy improved, and aid and investment returned. Political parties were banned to avoid a polarisation along tribal lines. Prosperity followed stability, and this was helped by Museveni's bold decision to invite Asians back. He also restored the monarchies. In 1996 he agreed to elections, which he won overwhelmingly. He was easily re-elected in 2001.

The darkness didn't end for northern Uganda, however, due to the Lord's Resistance Army (LRA). Its leader, Joseph Kony, grew increasingly delusional and paranoid during the 1990s and shifted his focus from attacking soldiers to attacking civilians in his attempt to found a government based on the biblical Ten Commandments. His tactics included torture, mutilation (slicing off lips, noses and ears), rape, and abducting children to use as soldiers and sex slaves. Eventually more than one million northerners fled their homes to refugee camps and tens of thousands of children became 'night commuters', walking from their villages each evening to sleep in schools and churches or on the streets of large towns. According to a 2007 UN report, government forces committed their own atrocities, too, during their half-hearted fight against the LRA.

Culture

Despite the years of terror and bloodshed, Ugandans are a remarkably positive and spirited people. They are very polite and friendly, and will often greet strangers.

Agriculture remains the single most important component of the Ugandan economy, and it employs 75% of the workforce. Coffee, sugar, cotton, tea and fish are the main export crops. Crops grown for local consumption include maize, millet, rice, cassava, potatoes and beans.

Eighty-five percent of the population is Christian, split about evenly between Catholics and Protestants. Muslims, mostly northerners, comprise about 12%. The Abayudaya are a small but devout group of native Ugandans living around Mbale who practise Judaism.

People

Uganda is made up of a complex and diverse range of people. Lake Kyoga forms the northern boundary for the Bantu-speaking tribes, such as the Baganda (17%), Banyankole (9.5%), Basoga (8.5%) and Bagisu (4.6%). In the north are the Lango (6%) near Lake Kyoga and the Acholi (4.7%) towards the Sudanese border, who speak Nilotic languages. To the east are the cattle-herding Iteso (6.4%) and Karamojong (2%), both related to the Maasai and also speaking Nilotic languages. About 4000 Batwa pygmies live in the forests of the southwest. Non-Africans, including a sizeable community of Asians, comprise about 1% of the population.

Food & Drink

Local food is much the same as elsewhere in the region, except in Uganda *ugali* (a food staple usually made from maize flour) is called *posho,* and is far less popular than *matoke* (mashed plantains). Rice, cassava and potatoes are also common starches. One uniquely Ugandan food is the *rolex,* a chapatti rolled around an omelette.

Popular local beers include the light Bell and stronger Nile Special. Waragi is the local hard stuff, a little like gin, so it's best with a splash of tonic.

Environment

Uganda is small by African standards (it's of a similar area to Great Britain) but it packs in everything from semidesert in the north to the snow-covered Rwenzori Mountains, the highest mountain range in Africa, in the southwest. Mt Stanley, its highest peak, tops out at 5109m. The southern half of the country is very lush. The tropical heat is tempered by the altitude, which averages more than 1000m in much of the country even higher in the cooler southwest.

Uganda can't compete with Kenya or Tanzania for sheer density of wildlife, but with 500-plus species of mammal and 1041 species of bird, it has amazing diversity. Mountain gorillas (almost half the world's remaining population lives in Uganda) are the stars of Uganda's national parks, but Big Five viewing can also be very good.

Uganda has environmental problems, most ominously rampant population growth. Also, oil drilling and exploration along Lake Albert have the potential to threaten Queen Elizabeth and Murchison Falls National Parks.

SURVIVAL GUIDE

Directory A–Z

ACCOMMODATION

Outside Kampala, single/double rooms without bathroom are available from around USh15,000/20,000, while rooms with bathroom usually start at USh20,000/25,000. For another USh5000 to USh10,000, breakfast will be included. Modern, more comfortable rooms can be found from USh50,000 to USh70,000. Top-end hotels and lodges start at around US$150 and can go much higher.

Almost every popular destination in Uganda has campsites available, so it's worth carrying a tent if you're on a budget. There are luxury lodges and tented camps with outlandish prices in most of the national parks, and simple campsites and basic *bandas* (huts) in all.

ACTIVITIES

The white-water rafting at Jinja is world class and other fun activities, such as bungee jumping and horseback riding, have emerged in the area.

Hiking Uganda's mountains is another pull. The hard-core head for the Rwenzoris, one of the toughest climbs in Africa, but for something less taxing (on the wallet and legs) try Mt Elgon. Both are gorgeous and lack the crowds of Mt Kilimanjaro and Mt Kenya.

Gorilla tracking is one of the major drawcards in Uganda and most people consider the US$500 price tag worth it, but cheaper chimpanzee tracking is also awe-inspiring. Walking safaris, available in most national parks, can be a real rush when you get near big wildlife. And, with 1041 species recorded (almost half the total in Africa), Uganda is an amazing birding destination.

Most national parks charge US$35 (US$20 for children aged five to 15) and admission is valid for 24 hours. For locally registered vehicles entry is USh10,000/20,000/30,000 per motorcycle/car/4WD; if you're coming in with a foreign registered vehicle, prices are expensive (US$30/50/150 per motorcycle/car/4WD). Nature walks cost US$10 per person and rangers for wildlife-watching drives are US$20.

Finally, many popular towns and parks have community projects, such as village walks and cooking tours, available. These can be fascinating insights into the culture around you and also provide important funding for schools and health clinics. Contact **Uganda Community Tourism Association** (UCOTA; ☎0414-501866; www.ucota.or.ug; 3rd fl Aqua House, Ggaba Rd, Kansanga) or **Pearls of Uganda** (www.pearlsofuganda.org) for more information.

EMBASSIES & CONSULATES

The following embassies are in Kamapala.

Australian Embassy (Map p722; ☎0312-515865; 15 Akii Bua Rd)

Belgium Embassy (Map p722; ☎0414-349559; www.diplomatie.be/kampala; Lumumba Ave, Rwenzori House)

British Embassy (Map p720; ☎0312-312000; http://ukinuganda.fco.gov.uk; Windsor Loop, Kamwokya)

Burundi Embassy (Map p722; ☎0414-235850; 12a York Tce)

Canadian Embassy (Map p722; ☎0414-258141; kampala@canadaconsulate.ca; 14 Parliament Ave)

DRC Embassy (Map p720; ☎0414-250099; 20 Philip Rd, Kololo)

Dutch Embassy (Map p722; ☎0414-346000; Lumumba Ave, Rwenzori Courts)

French Embassy (Map p722; ☎0414-304500; 16 Lumumba Ave)

German Embassy (Map p722; ☎0414-501111; www.kampala.diplo.de; 15 Philip Rd, Kololo)

Irish Embassy (Map p722; ☎0417-713000; 25 Yusuf Lule Rd, Nakasero)

Italian Embassy (Map p722; ☎0414-341786; www.ambkampala.esteri.it; 11 Lourdel Rd, Nakasero)

Japanese Embassy (Map p722; ☎0414-349542; www.ug.emb-japan.go.jp; 8 Kyadondo Rd)

Kenyan Embassy (Map p722; ☎0414-258235; www.kenyamission.or.ug; 4 Lower Kololo Tce)

Rwandan Embassy (Map p720; ☎0414-344045; 2 Nakayima Rd, Kamwokya; ⏰9.30am-noon Mon-Fri)

South Sudan Embassy (Map p722; ☎0414-230272; 2 Ssezibwa Rd)

Sudanese Embassy (Map p722; ☎0414-230001; 21 Nakasero Rd)

Tanzanian Embassy (☎0414-256272; 6 Kagera Rd)

US Embassy (Map p720; ☎0414-259791; http://kampala.usembassy.gov; Ggaba Rd, Nsambya)

EMERGENCIES

In addition to the following number, you can also dial ☎112 from mobile phones.

Police or ambulance (☎999)

INTERNET ACCESS

Internet cafes charge around USh2000 per hour and are ubiquitous in Kampala, and wi-fi hotspots are becoming more common. Elsewhere in the country, even most small towns have access for about the same price, albeit usually pretty slow.

Laptop users can easily get online by purchasing a wireless USB internet for around US$30, with the best operators being MTN and Orange.

MAPS

The Uganda maps by ITMB (1:800,000) and Nelles (1:700,000) will get you where you need to go. Only the latter is available in Uganda.

Being both beautiful and useful, *Uganda Maps'* national park maps, available in Kampala, are a great buy if you're heading to any of the popular parks.

MONEY

The Ugandan shilling (USh) is a relatively stable currency. Most tour operators and many hotels quote in US dollars, but you can pay with shillings.

The biggest banks (Barclays, Stanbic and Standard Chartered) have ATMs that accept international cards. Even many remote small towns will have at least one of these banks, though try not to let your cash run out as the system sometimes goes down and machines can run dry. You'll also notice tents and benches outside ATMs, which tells you how long the lines can get.

Credit cards (mostly Visa) are fairly widely accepted by businesses that deal with tourists, though commissions can be as high as 10%.

US dollars (post 2006) are the most useful hard currency, though euros and UK pounds sterling are also widely accepted. Bureaus de change offer slightly better rates than banks plus much faster service and longer hours; however, they're rare outside Kampala.

OPENING HOURS

Banks Most close at 1pm and don't do business on Saturday.

Businesses and government offices Generally open between 8.30am and 5pm, often with a short lunch break. Saturday hours, usually closing around 1pm, are increasingly common.

Restaurants Local restaurants open 7am to 9pm or 10pm, while international-type restaurants are often open from 11.30am to 2.30pm and 5.30pm to 10.30pm.

POST

Kampala's post office is slow but reliable, while there's a chance things will go missing at provincial branches.

PUBLIC HOLIDAYS

As well as religious holidays, the principal public holidays in Uganda are:

New Year's Day 1 January
Liberation Day 26 January
International Women's Day 8 March
Labour Day 1 May
Martyrs' Day 3 June
Heroes' Day 9 June
Independence Day 9 October

SAFE TRAVEL

Except for the far northeast, Uganda is a very safe destination; and even these areas see only sporadic confrontations. Also, although the ongoing conflict in eastern DRC rarely affects Uganda, cross-border incidents have happened in the past, so keep an ear to the ground for information.

Homosexuality is illegal in Uganda and in theory can result in a sentence of up to 14 years in prison. A controversial bill drafted (but not passed) in 2009 proposed the death penalty, receiving international condemnation from governments and human-rights groups. It's important GLBT travellers remain discreet.

While *boda-bodas* (motorcycle taxis) are perfect for getting through heavy traffic, they are also notorious for their high rate of accidents. Try to find a driver with a helmet you can borrow, and insist they drive slowly. *Boda-bodas* are best avoided at night.

TELEPHONE

- Telephone connections, both domestic and international, are pretty good.
- SIM cards for mobile phones cost around USh2000.
- Local calls can be made from a payphone; a person with a phone sitting at a little table along the street.
- The country code for Uganda is ☎256. To make an international call from Uganda, dial ☎000 or, on a mobile, the + button.

PRACTICALITIES

- **Electricity** 240V/ 50Hz, and British three-pin plugs are used.
- **Languages** English (official), Luganda and Swahili most widely understood
- **Newspapers** Local newspapers include the government-owned daily *New Vision* and the more independent *Daily Monitor*
- **Radio & TV** The state-run UBC and the private WBS are the main stations available on broadcast TV, but most hotels and bars have satellite TV for international news and sport; BBC World Service broadcasts on 101.3MHz and the phenomenally popular Capital FM can be found at 91.3MHz.

VISAS

Most non-African passport holders visiting Uganda require visas. These are available upon arrival at the airport or border; no photos are needed. A yellow-fever certificate is required if you are arriving from an affected area, but is rarely requested.

Single-entry tourist visas valid for up to 90 days (but unless you ask for 90, you'll probably be given 30 or 60 days) cost US$50. At the time of research, multiple-entry visas weren't available on arrival, but it was possible for embassies abroad to issue them (US$100 for six months).

Visa Extensions

Two-month extensions are free at immigration offices in large towns. Bring a copy of your passport and plane ticket, plus a letter explaining why you want to stay and when you will be leaving.

Visas for Onward Travel

Burundi A one-month single-entry visa costs US$90, requires two passport photos and takes two days to process. They're also issued at land borders and the airport.

DRC One-month single-entry visa costs US$60, requires two passport photos and takes one week to process. You can also get a seven-day visa at the border for US$50.

Kenya A single-entry visa costs US$50 and one passport photo is required. It will be ready the next day between 11am and 12.30pm. It's easier to get it on arrival.

Rwanda Visas cost USh110,000 (for those who need them; see p649 for details), require one passport photo and will take around 72 hours to process. They're also available on arrival at the airport and at borders.

South Sudan Single/multiple entry visas cost US$80/100 and you'll need two passport photos. They take one to two days to process. Visas were available at the border at time of research, but this often changes, so arrange one before you leave.

Tanzania Visas are valid for three months, require two passport photos and take 24 hours to issue. Costs vary according to your country of origin. Single-entry visas are also available on entry.

Getting There & Away

AIR

Entebbe International Airport, 40km south of Kampala, is Uganda's only aerial gateway. It's well connected to Uganda's near neighbours, but usually Nairobi is used as the gateway to East Africa and flights are almost always cheaper and more frequent there.

The main airlines serving Uganda (all with offices in central Kampala):

Air Uganda (Map p722; ☎0414-258262; www.air-uganda.com; Parliament Ave)

British Airways (Map p722; ☎0414-257414; www.britishairways.com; Centre Court, Plot 4 Ternan Ave, Nakasero)

Emirates (Map p722; ☎0414-770444; www.emirates.com; Kimathi Ave)

Ethiopian Airlines (Map p722; ☎0414-345577; www.flyethiopian.com; Kimathi Ave)

Fly540 (Map p722; ☎0414-346915; www.fly540.com; Kitante Rd)

Kenya Airways (Map p722; ☎0312-360000; www.kenya-airways.com; Parliament Ave)

KLM (Map p722; ☎0414-338006; www.klm.com)

Rwandair Express (Map p722; ☎0414-344851; www.rwandair.com; Lumumba Ave, Garden City)

LAND

Democratic Republic of Congo (DRC)

Because of the various rebels wreaking havoc just over Uganda's border, don't cross to DRC without checking the security situation *very* carefully. Except for quick hits from Kisoro to see mountain gorillas in Parc National des Virunga at Djomba, the only possible crossing at the time of research was the well-travelled border at Kasindi between Kasese and Beni, from where it's easy to carry on to Kisangani.

Kenya

There are many direct Nairobi–Kampala buses, most stopping in Jinja, and the journey takes about 12 hours. In recent years, some night buses have been robbed, so it's best to travel during the day. The two best companies, with good air-con buses and reliable service, are **Kampala Coach** (Map p722; ☎0784-573867; www.kampalacoach.com; Jinja Rd, Kampala) and **Akamba** (☎0414-250412; www.akambabus.com; 28 Dewinton Rd, Kampala). Other companies like **Kalita** (Map p722; ☎0772-522471; Namirembe Rd, Kampala) use older, rattletrap buses but charge as little as USh45,000.

Most buses use the busy crossing at Busia, though a few go the longer route through Malaba. To do the journey in stages, frequent minibuses link Jinja to Busia (USh7000, 2½ hours), and again from Busia to Kisumu.

Hikers in either the Ugandan or Kenyan national parks on Mt Elgon have the option of walking over the border.

Rwanda

The busiest crossing is between Kabale and Kigali via Katuna (Gatuna on the Rwandan side), and it can take over an hour to get through immigration. From Kabale there are shared taxis (USh3500, 30 minutes) to the border and a few minibuses each morning (except Sunday) direct to Kigali. On the Rwandan side, minibuses travel to Kigali (RFr1300, two hours) all day.

Another seldom-used but very convenient border is Cyanika, between Kisoro and Musanze; travel time is 1½ hours. The road on the Ugandan side is very rough and there's no public transport, so take a special-hire (USh50,000) or *boda-boda* (USh7000). Transport on the Rwandan side is frequent.

There are also many companies with direct Kampala–Kigali buses (USh25,000 to USh40,000, seven to eight hours). Akamba or **Jaguar Executive Coaches** (Map p720; ☎0782-417512; Namirembe Rd, Kampala) are the most comfortable option.

South Sudan

Most Kampala–Juba buses travel via Gulu (where they pick up more passengers), crossing at Nimule. All leave in the wee morning hours from Arua Park in Kampala, and most charge about USh80,000, though the big, modern air-con buses of Kampala Coach are definitely worth the extra cash on this rough 15- to 20-hour journey.

Arranging permission to travel by land between South Sudan and Sudan is nearly impossible, so Juba is effectively a dead end.

Tanzania

The principal direct route into Tanzania follows the western side of Lake Victoria from Masaka to Bukoba via Mutukula. It's about six hours by bus from Kampala. Several companies, departing from both of Kampala's bus parks, travel this route and charge USH17,000 to USh20,000. Very little transport uses the Nkurungu border due to bad roads.

EarthWise (p738) was aiming to run a ferry service from Kampala to Mwanaza in the future. In the meantime, intrepid travellers can book passage on the MV *Umoja* cargo ferry that goes from Kampala's Port Bell (USh45,000,16 to 17 hours).

Getting Around

AIR

At the time of research **Air Uganda** (p746) had announced plans to introduce domestic flights; check its website for details.

Otherwise **Eagle Air** (Map p722; ☎0414-344292; www.flyeagleuganda.com; 11 Portal Ave, Kampala) and **Kampala Aeroclub** (Map p722; ☎077-706107; www.flyuganda.com) have chartered flights to some northern towns and also Kihihi, convenient for Bwindi Impenetrable National Park.

BUS & MINIBUS

Uganda is the land of shared minibuses (called taxis or occasionally *matatus*), and except for long distances, these are the most common vehicles between towns. They're usually jam-packed and the drivers are often maniacs, so crash stories are regular features in the newspapers. Out-of-the-way destinations use saloon-car shared taxis rather than minibuses, and when the roads are really bad pretty much your only choice is sitting atop the assorted cargo in the backs of cargo trucks.

Except for very short distances, you're better off in a standard bus or half-sized 'coaster'. Fares are similar to minibuses (usually a little less), they're safer in a crash and they travel faster due to less-frequent stops.

In addition to the normal private buses, there are Post Buses delivering mail and people between Uganda's main post offices and most large towns. They're slower but safer and sometimes cheaper.

CAR

Roads are good between most major centres in the southern part of the country, but the north lags behind in this regard and here you'll almost always need a 4WD once you get off the sealed roads. With a good driver, 2WDs can handle many of the south's dirt roads.

Due to high taxes and bad roads, car-rental prices are high. Add fuel costs and there'll be some real sticker shock. **Road Trip Uganda** (p747) has good deals on Toyota RAV4s, inclusive of camping equipment. **Alpha Car Rentals** (Map p722; ☎0772-411232; www.alpharentals.co.ug; 3/5 Bombo Rd, EMKA House, Kampala) is a low-priced local outfit, or you could just negotiate with special-hire taxi drivers.

LOCAL TRANSPORT

Kampala has a local minibus network, as well as 'special-hire' taxis for private trips. Elsewhere you'll have to rely solely on motorbike taxis, known as *boda-bodas*. Tell drivers to slow down if you feel uncomfortable.

TOURS

The following are excellent for budget and mid-range trips.

Amagara Tours (☎0752-197826; www.amagaratours.com; Kabale) Budget packages for all the national parks in the southwest.

Backpackers Hostel (☎0772-430587; www.backpackers.co.ug; Natete Rd, Lunguja)

Great Lakes Safaris (Map p720; ☎0414-267153; www.safari-uganda.com; Gaba Rd, Suzie House, Kampala) Mixes cultural encounters with wildlife-watching.

Matoke Tours (Map p720; ☎0782-374667; www.travel-uganda.net; 8 Bukoto St, Kampala) Quality Dutch-based company that is one of the few going to Kidepo Valley National Park.

Red Chilli Hideaway (☎0414-223903; www.redchillihideaway.com; 17 Gangaram Rd, Kampala) In Kampala. Also offers good budget safaris.

Road Trip Uganda (☎0773-363012; www.roadtripuganda.com; Grace Musoke Rd, Bukuto) Self-drive tours in fully equipped RAV4s, including tents, cooking equipment and iPod speakers.

Southern Africa

TAI POWER SEEFF / GETTY IMAGES ©

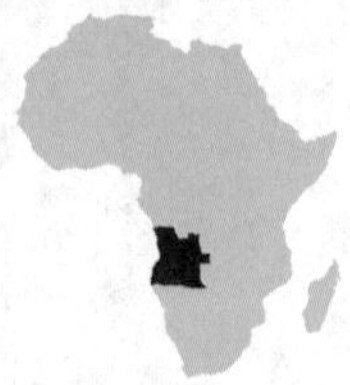

Angola

Includes ➡

Fast Facts

- **Capital** Luanda
- **Population** 18,056,000
- **Languages** Portuguese and various Bantu languages
- **Area** 1,246,700 sq km
- **Currency** Kwanza
- **Visa requirements** 30-day visas must be obtained in advance
- **Tourist information** www.angolamarket.com

Oil, Diamonds & Unspoilt Coastline

Angola is an eye-opener – in more ways than one. Scarred painfully by years of debilitating warfare and practically untouched by foreign visitors since the early 1970s, the country remains remote, with few observers privy to its geographic highlights and vast cultural riches.

Despite advancements in infrastructure and a dramatically improved security situation, travel in Angola remains the preserve of adventurers, or those on flexible budgets. But with the transport network gradually recovering and wildlife being shipped in to repopulate decimated national parks, the signs of recovery are more than just a mirage.

For outsiders, the attractions are manifold. Chill out on expansive beaches, sample the solitude in virgin wildlife parks or sift through the ruins of Portuguese colonialism. From Luanda to Lubango the nuances are startling.

Angola Top Sights

- **Lubango** Almost untouched by the war, breezy Lubango offers cascading waterfalls, spectacular volcanic fissures and a vibrant small-city ambience
- **Parque Nacional da Kissama** One of Africa's largest, emptiest and most surreal wildlife parks
- **Benguela** Chill out on the blissfully empty beaches of Angola's most laid-back town
- **Luanda** Expansive beaches, expensive bars and tatty overcrowded townships, Luanda is a kaleidoscopic vision of Angola at the sharp end
- **Miradouro de Lua** A spectacular lookout over a canyon of moonlike cliffs that cascade dramatically into the Atlantic Ocean

UNDERSTAND ANGOLA

Angola Today

Since 2002 Angola has entered a period of peace and regeneration unprecedented in its history. With the 85,000-strong Unita army reintegrated into the national forces and old animosities ceremoniously brushed underneath the carpet, the biggest obstacles to war and instability have been temporarily neutralised.

But the country still faces massive challenges before it can right four decades of economic and political disarray. Corruption is the most pressing problem. In 2004 Human Rights Watch, an independent lobby group, estimated that US$4 billion of Angola's undeclared oil revenue had gone missing since the late 1990s. Voices inside the International Monetary Fund(IMF) were raised and supervisors were sent to investigate. Their conclusion: either the president, José Eduardo dos Santos, was employing a very creative team of accountants or something, somewhere, was clearly not adding up.

It is these financial anomalies that have prevented the lion's share of Angola's new peace time economy from trickling down to the majority of the poorest classes. While skyscrapers reach new heights in Luanda and oil-obsessed government ministries forge investment deals with China and India, poverty in the countryside remains rampant and widespread.

The Popular Movement for the Liberation of Angola (MPLA) won a landslide victory in parliamentary elections held in September 2008, the first such polls to be held in the country for 16 years.

Long-awaited presidential elections were expected to be held in 2009, but were delayed, and in January 2010 parliament approved a new constitution abolishing direct elections for the president.

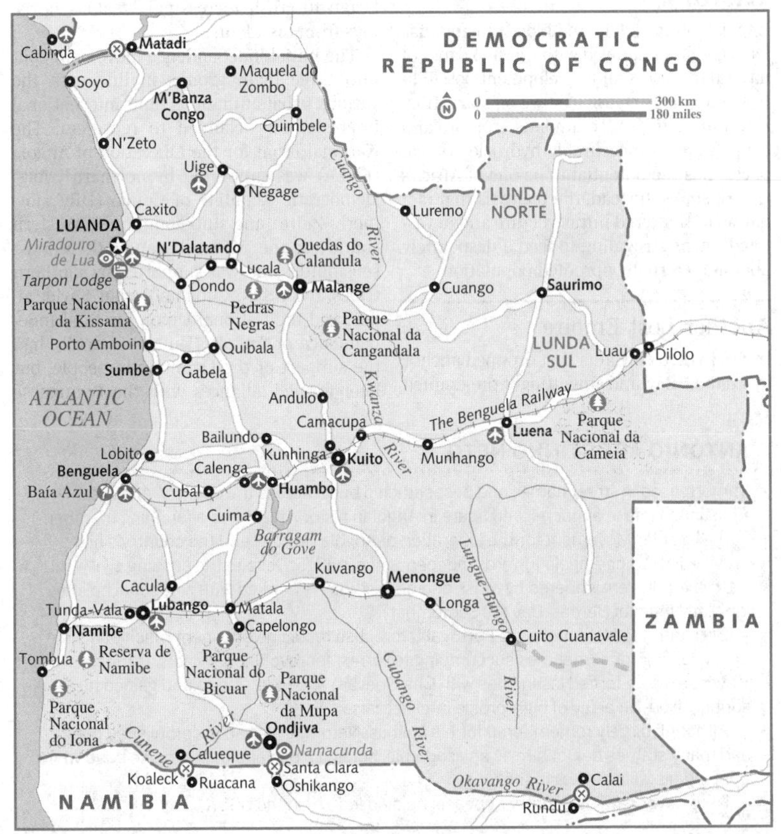

COUNTRY COVERAGE

At the time of research very few travellers were heading to Angola so we're providing historical and cultural information rather than reviews and listings. A good source of information for on-the-ground travel in Angola is Lonely Planet's Thorn Tree online travel forum www.lonelyplanet.com/thorntree. Another source of good internet-based information is www.angola-today.com.

The presidency is now automatically filled by the top-ranking candidate of the party winning the parliamentary election. The MPLA won the 2012 election comfortably, guaranteeing dos Santos another five-year term in office.

History

Angola's often violent and bloody history has left a country endowed with a vast expanse of natural resources and development possibilities perennially trying to stave off starvation. A terrain rich in oil, diamonds, iron ore and copper, plus a measurable hydroelectric capacity, has the potential to be one of Africa's richest states. Instead, the reality is that of a nation of shattered infrastructure and devastated towns struggling to feed a desperately poor and eternally uprooted population.

Another Lost Empire

In 1483 Vasco da Gama first dropped anchor in Luanda Bay and unwittingly pre-empted the start of a conflict that, save for a few intermittent lulls in the fighting, continued for over half a millennium. The land now known as Angola was, at the time, inhabited by a number of small tribes living in loosely defined kingdoms that lacked the organisation and administrative cohesiveness of 15th-century Europe. But despite a natural curiosity borne out of years of seafaring exploration, the Portuguese had no real desire to settle on this malaria-ridden African shoreline. Post-1500, the more fertile and less threatening lands of Brazil held a far greater attraction for colonial farmers and businessmen. For the next 300 years Portugal's African colonies had only two real functions: a strategic base on the route around the Cape of Good Hope, and a collecting centre for one of the largest forced human migrations in history.

Not surprisingly, slavery did little to endear the colonials to the Angolan people. Clashes first began after WWII and were inflamed in 1961 when colonial authorities began to crush increasingly zealous uprisings from dissidents.

The initial independence movement split into three main groups in line with the various tribal affiliations (and international interests) they claimed to represent. The National Front for the Liberation of Angola (FNLA) was supported by northern tribes, Democratic Republic of Congo (DRC; formerly Zaïre) and anti-communist Western countries; the MPLA began with Marxist sensibilities and was supported by southern tribes, the USSR, Cuba and other Soviet allies; and the National Union for Total Independence of Angola (Unita) originally had the support of the Ovimbundu people, but later formed alliances with the Portuguese

ANTÓNIO AGOSTINHO NETO

Immortalised in street names and bespectacled busts across the country, António Agostinho Neto ia a much-loved figure in Angolan history. Neto was a founding member of the Popular Movement for the Liberation of Angola (MPLA) and the country's first president, leading Angola towards independence in 1975. Despite the ensuing civil war, Neto is fondly remembered by most, and his birthday is marked with a national holiday, labelled National Heroes' Day (17 September).

Born in 1922, Neto moved to Portugal to practise medicine but spent much of his time avoiding (or sometimes succumbing to) arrest for revolutionary acts. During his 15-year exile he forged lasting ties with Che Guevara and Fidel Castro and gained huge support from an array of high-profile intellectuals.

Although largely remembered for his politics, Neto was also an accomplished poet and many statues depict him as an academic, holding a pen and paper in one hand while gripping his Kalashnikov in the other.

Neto never saw his country at peace; he died in 1979 in the USSR.

right wing, the USA and apartheid South Africa.

In 1975 the Portuguese finally granted independence to Angola, following the overthrow of the fascist Salazar government at home. But the colonial withdrawal – a mad scramble involving one of the biggest airlifts in history – was legendary in its ineptitude, converting central Luanda into a ghost town and robbing the country of its qualified human resources and administrative structure.

Angola in 1975 possessed all the essential ingredients for an impending civil war: a weak, uneven infrastructure, low levels of health and education, two feuding sets of tribally based elites and the inviting prospect of a large slice of unused government oil revenue up for grabs. As the Moscow-backed MPLA party stepped into a dangerous power vacuum, a combination of new outside factors were thrown into an already crowded arena: US communist paranoia, Cuba's ambiguous aim to promote 'world revolution', South African security obsessions and the woefully inadequate process of decolonisation. The stage was set.

Angola's second major war was a long, protracted affair dominated by foreign intervention. Indeed, for the next 15 years the wishes and desires of the Angolan people were consistently undermined as foreign governments and Western business interests continued to fight among themselves over a damaged and increasingly beleaguered country.

War & Peace

In 1991, prompted by the end of the Cold War, a ceasefire agreement was set in place by Cuba, the USA and Angola. But the accord broke down the following year after Unita, having lost a general election (seen by the UN as largely free and fair), returned to war with a new-found ferocity, claiming the poll was rigged. Almost 200,000 people died between May and October 1993 as Unita took war to the provincial cities, destroying most of the road, rail and communications network.

A revamped 'Lusaka Accord' signed in 1994 was consistently violated by both the governing MPLA and Unita, and the discovery of new diamond areas and oilfields allowed both sides to re-arm. UN sanctions against Unita diamonds caused Unita's cash supply to shrivel, and its control of the countryside gradually crumbled. Increasing military defeats drove a desperate Unita deeper into the hinterland, and its leader Jonas Savimbi – hunted and on the run – was finally killed in a government operation on 22 February 2002.

A new peace accord was signed on 4 April 2002.

LUBANGO

Surrounded by mountains and nestled in a cool central valley, Lubango, a peaceful city of 200,000 inhabitants, seems a different world from the capital. Relatively unscathed by the 40-year conflict that tore the heart of communities elsewhere, the order and tranquility of Lubango's central core has more in common with Namibia than with many other Angolan towns. You'll encounter a handful of adventurous overlanders here, some quirky cafes and some of the country's most charming hotels.

One of the best ways to get a bird's eye view of Lubango is to rent a taxi and motor up to the *Cristo Rei*, a statue of Jesus (a mini version of Rio's Cristo Redentor) that overlooks the city. Alternatively you could hike the 5km up from town.

Casper Lodge (www.casperlodge.com), set in lush gardens around a cool pool, is a popular choice.

Culture

Angola's cornucopia of ethnic groups is dominated by the Ovimbundu, Kimbundu and Bakongo. Local tribal traditions remain strong, though Portuguese has evolved as the national language of choice, particularly among the young. Due in part to its volatile history, much of Angola's cultural legacy has been exported abroad through slavery and emigration, where it has re-emerged in elements of modern Brazilian culture, such as the samba, carnival, Afro-American religion and the combative martial art, capoeira.

Badly damaged by the long-standing tribal conflicts that set neighbour against neighbour throughout the 1980s and '90s, Angolan culture has remained defiantly intact in a country divided by complex ethnic loyalties and 42 different indigenous languages. At the forefront of this colourful artistic patchwork is Angolan music, a rich and varied collection of offshoots and subgenres, with styles such as *kizombe,* samba, *zouk* and *rebita* manifesting themselves in countless dances and romantic songs.

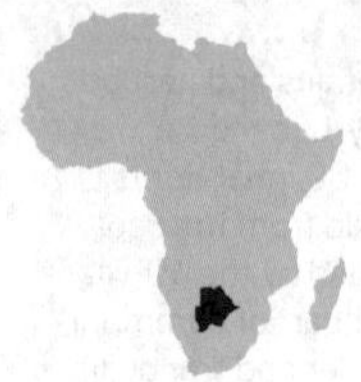

Botswana

POP 2.02 MILLION

Includes ➡

Best for Wildlife-Watching

- Moremi Game Reserve (p768)
- Chobe National Park (p762)
- Makgadikgadi Pans National Park (p761)
- Central Kalahari Game Reserve (p773)
- Tuli Block (p760)

Best of the Outdoors

- *Mokoro* trip, Okavango Delta (p771)
- Tsodilo Hills (p773)
- Camping, anywhere

Why Go?

Blessed with some of the greatest wildlife spectacles on earth, Botswana is one of the great safari destinations in Africa. There are more elephants in Botswana than in any other country on earth, the big cats roam free, and there's everything from endangered African wild dogs to aquatic antelopes, from rhinos making a comeback to abundant birdlife at every turn.

This is also the land of the Okavango Delta and the Kalahari Desert, at once iconic African landscapes and vast stretches of wilderness. Put these landscapes together with the wildlife that inhabits them and it's difficult to escape the conclusion that this is wild Africa at its best.

Botswana may rank among Africa's most exclusive destinations – accommodation prices at most lodges are once-in-a-lifetime propositions – but self-drive expeditions are also possible. Whichever way you visit, Botswana is a truly extraordinary place.

When to Go

Gaborone

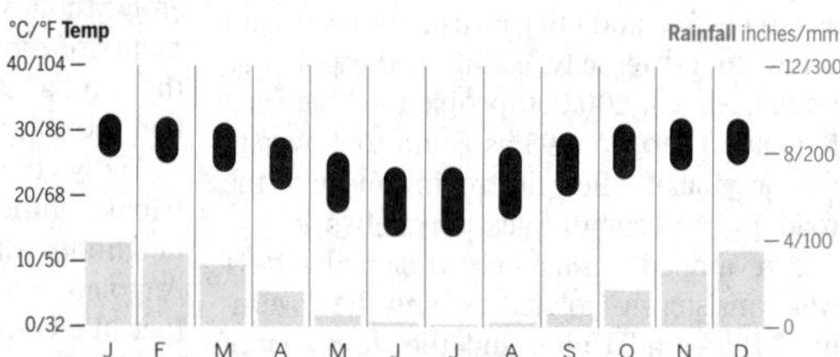

May–Aug Dry season, with fine weather and wildlife concentrations around waterholes.

Sep & Oct Extremely hot temperatures and good dry-season wildlife-watching.

Dec–Apr The rainy season; many tracks are impassable but tourist numbers are fewer.

GABORONE

POP 231,626

Botswana's small capital may be the country's largest city, but it's a pretty low-key place. There aren't many reasons to come here – it's a world of government ministries, shopping malls and a seemingly endless urban sprawl, which is why most travellers either fly to Maun or cross overland elsewhere. If you do find yourself here, 'Gabs' has a handful of decent restaurants and good hotels.

Sights & Activities

Gaborone Game Reserve WILDLIFE RESERVE
(☎318 4492; adult/child/vehicle P10/5/10; ⏲6.30am-6.30pm) This reserve, 1km east of Broadhurst, is accessible only by private vehicle (no bikes or motorcycles), and is home to a variety of grazers and browsers.

National Museum & Art Gallery MUSEUM
(Map p759; ☎397 4616; 331 Independence Ave; ⏲9am-6pm Tue-Fri, to 5pm Sat & Sun) FREE If you come with expectations reasonably lowered, you may enjoy this small but diverse museum. It's a good way to kill an afternoon, especially if you're into taxidermy. The ethnographic displays are interesting too.

Tours

Garcin Safaris GUIDED TOUR
(☎393 8190; www.garcinsafaris.com; 1-/2-day tours €126/402) Tours of the city, including a *No. 1 Ladies' Detective Agency*-focused jaunt.

Africa Insight GUIDED TOUR
(☎7265 4323; www.africainsight.com; half-/full-day tours P495/860) *No. 1 Ladies' Detective Agency* tours endorsed by the author himself.

Sleeping

Mokolodi Backpackers BACKPACKERS $
(☎7716 8685; admin@backpackers.co.bw; campsites/dm/s P95/165/220, chalets P370-525; @ 🏊) This excellent place around 10km south of the city centre is the only place with a real backpacker vibe around Gaborone. It has attractive chalets and good campsites and dorms. It's handy for the Mokolodi Game Reserve, 1km away.

Brackendene Lodge HOTEL $$
(Map p759; ☎391 2886; www.brackendenelodge.com; Tati Rd; r from P250, s/d incl breakfast P420/458; ❄ 📶) One of the better-value hotels in town. Rooms are simple but large and kitted out with TVs and air-con. It's quiet, but you're within walking distance of the Mall.

SET YOUR BUDGET

Budget

- Campsite for two US$50
- Two-course dinner US$8-10
- Maun-Kasane bus US$12

Midrange

- Hotel room US$100
- Two-course dinner US$20
- Maun-Kasane domestic flight US$50

Top End

- Luxury lodge US$250 to US$4500
- Two-course dinner USUS25
- Helicopter ride US$110 per person

★**Metcourt Inn** HOTEL $$
(☎363 7907; www.peermont.com; r from P720; ❄ 📶) Located within the Grand Palm Hotel complex and part of the reliable Peermont suite of hotels, this affordable business hotel has classy rooms with a hint of Afro-chic in the decor.

Eating

Cafe Dijo CAFE $
(☎315 0575; Kgale View Shopping Mall, Old Lobatse Rd; mains P62; ⏲7am-4pm Mon-Fri, 9am-1pm Sat; 📶) Next door to Kalahari Quilts in the Kgale View Shopping Mall, this classy but casual place is one of our favourite haunts in Gabs. Lunch specials include pepper steak pie, chicken tandoori wraps and light Thai-inflected dishes.

★**Courtyard Restaurant** AFRICAN, INTERNATIONAL $$
(☎392 2487; www.botswanacraft.bw; Western Bypass, off Airport Rd; mains P55-85; ⏲8am-4pm) In the garden area out the back of Botswanacraft, this tranquil spot serves up imaginative African cooking (including impala stew) with other local staples.

Bull & Bush Pub INTERNATIONAL $$
(Map p758; ☎397 5070; www.bullandbush.net; mains P85-110; ⏲noon-10.30pm Mon-Fri, to 11.30pm Sat & Sun) This long-standing Gaborone institution is deservedly popular with expats, tourists and locals alike. Though there's something on the menu for everyone, the Bull & Bush is renowned for its thick steaks and cold beers.

Botswana Highlights

1. Enjoy the ultimate safari in **Moremi Game Reserve** (p768), with some of the best wildlife-watching on earth.
2. Glide gently through the vast unspoiled wilderness of the **Okavango Delta** (p765) in a *mokoro* (dug-out canoe).
3. Get up close and personal with Africa's largest elephant herds in **Chobe National Park** (p762).
4. At the **Central Kalahari Game Reserve** (p773) look for black-maned lions in the heart of the Kalahari Desert.
5. Watch the wildlife gather by the banks of the Boteti River in **Makgadikgadi Pans National Park** (p761).
6. Leave behind the crowds and search for ancient rock art in the soulful and beautiful **Tsodilo Hills** (p773).

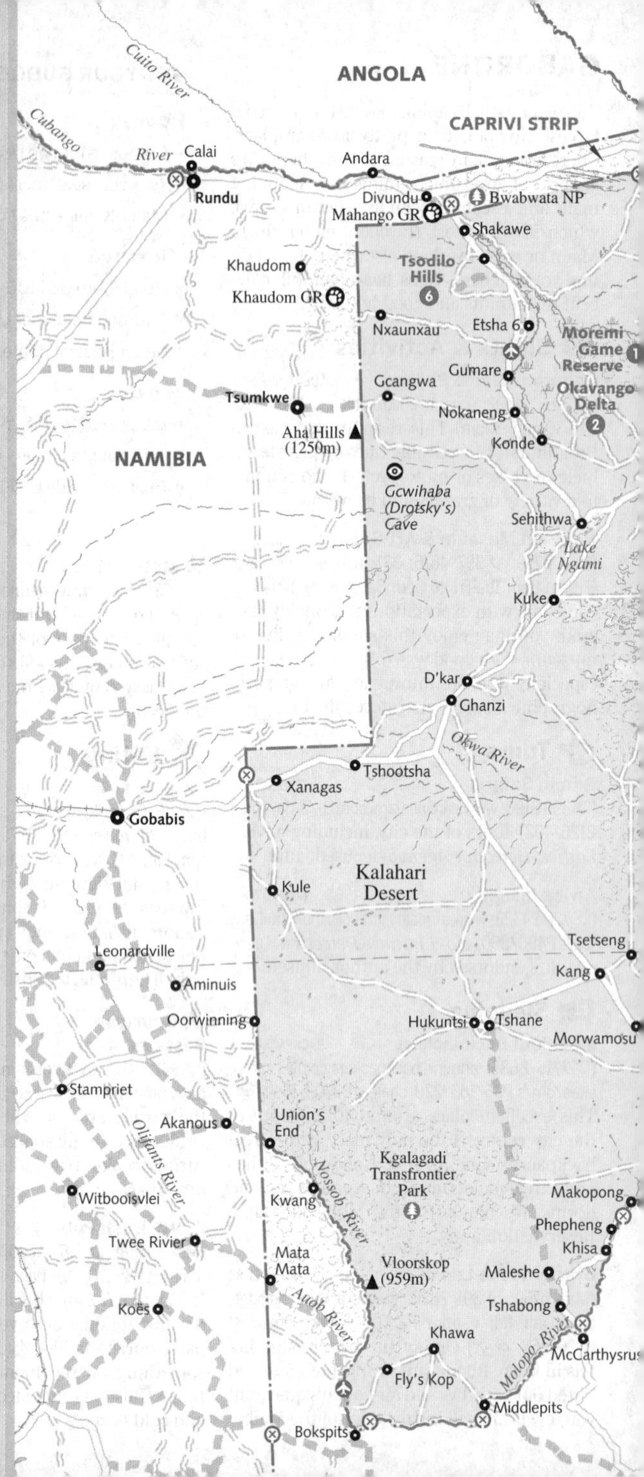

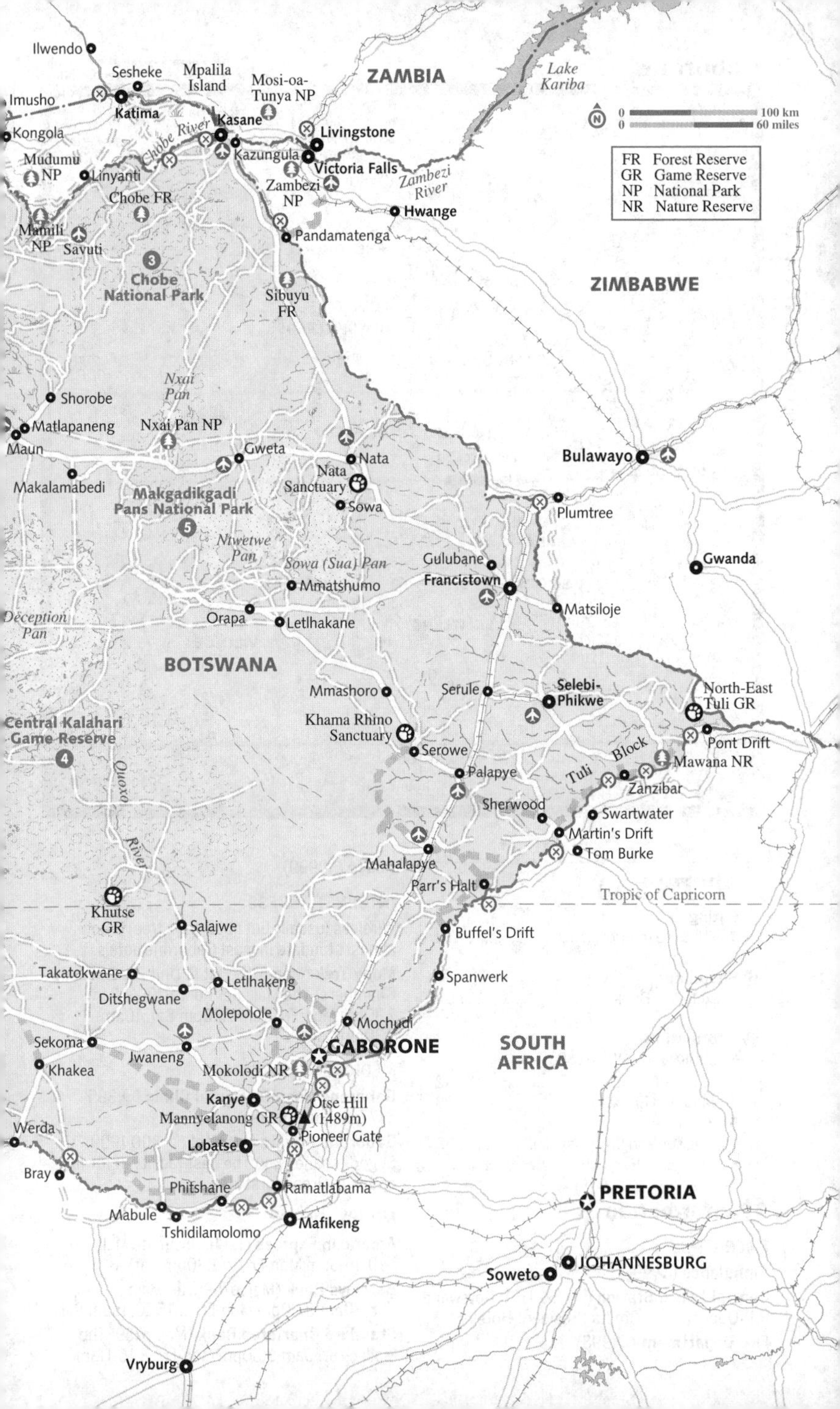

ZAMBIA
ZIMBABWE
BOTSWANA
SOUTH AFRICA
Lake Kariba
0 100 km
0 60 miles
FR Forest Reserve
GR Game Reserve
NP National Park
NR Nature Reserve
Ilwendo
Sesheke
Mpalila Island
Mosi-oa-Tunya NP
Imusho
Katima
Kasane
Kongola
Chobe River
Livingstone
Kazungula
Victoria Falls
Mudumu NP
Linyanti
Zambezi NP
Zambezi River
Chobe FR
Hwange
Mamili NP
Savuti
Pandamatenga
Chobe National Park
Sibuyu FR
Nxai Pan
Shorobe
Matlapaneng
Nxai Pan NP
Maun
Gweta
Nata
Makalamabedi
Nata Sanctuary
Bulawayo
Makgadikgadi Pans National Park
Sowa
Plumtree
Ntwetwe Pan
Sowa (Sua) Pan
Gulubane
Gwanda
Mmatshumo
Francistown
Matsiloje
Deception Pan
Orapa
Letlhakane
Mmashoro
Serule
Selebi-Phikwe
North-East Tuli GR
Central Kalahari Game Reserve
Khama Rhino Sanctuary
Pont Drift
Serowe
Tuli Block
Mawana NR
Quoxo River
Palapye
Zanzibar
Sherwood
Swartwater
Martin's Drift
Mahalapye
Tom Burke
Parr's Halt
Tropic of Capricorn
Khutse GR
Salajwe
Buffel's Drift
Takatokwane
Letlhakeng
Spanwerk
Ditshegwane
Molepolole
Mochudi
Sekoma
GABORONE
Jwaneng
Khakea
Mokolodi NR
Kanye
Otse Hill (1489m)
Mannyelanong GR
Werda
Pioneer Gate
Lobatse
Bray
Phitshane
Ramatlabama
PRETORIA
Mabule
Tshidilamolomo
Mafikeng
JOHANNESBURG
Soweto
Vryburg

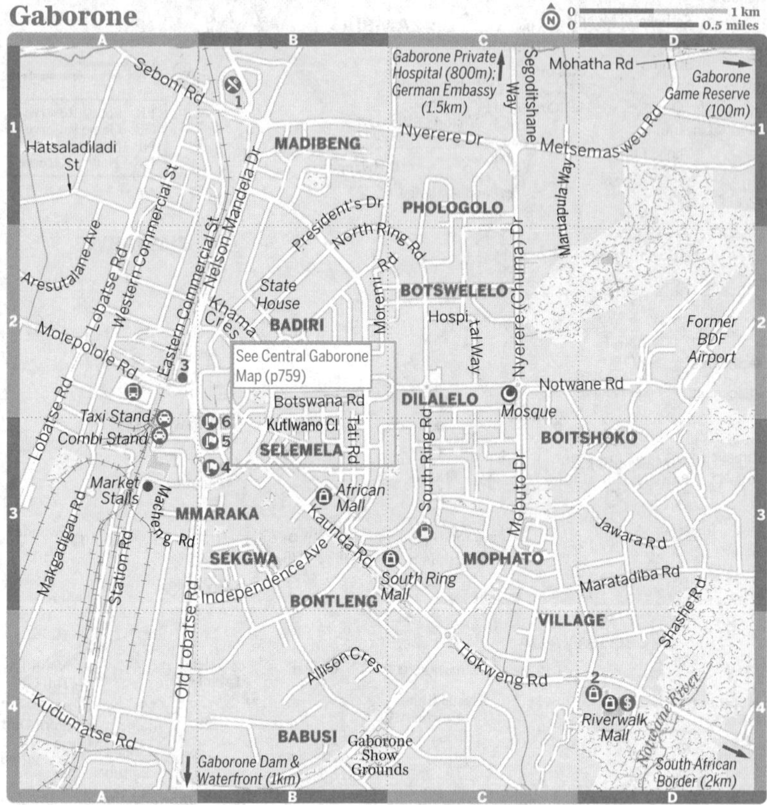

Gaborone

Eating
1 Bull & Bush Pub B1

Shopping
2 Exclusive Books D4

Information
3 Immigration Office & Passport Control A2
4 Namibian Embassy B3
5 US Embassy B3
6 Zimbabwean Embassy B3

Information

EMERGENCY

Ambulance (☎997)

Central Police Station (☎355 1161; Botswana Rd) Opposite the Cresta President Hotel.

Fire Department (☎998)

Police (☎999)

INTERNET ACCESS

Wireless (usually but not always free) is now almost standard in most Gaborone hotels.

Moby Trek (Map p759; 1st fl, Unit 24, Embassy Chambers, The Mall; per hour P10; ⏰8am-7.30pm Mon-Fri, 9am-7.30pm Sat, 10am-7.30pm Sun)

MEDICAL SERVICES

Gaborone Hospital Dental Clinic (☎395 3777; Segoditshane Way)

Gaborone Private Hospital (☎300 1999; Segoditshane Way) The best facility in town; opposite Broadhurst Mall.

MONEY

American Express (1st fl, Riverside Mall; ⏰9am-5pm Mon-Fri, to 1.30pm Sat)

Barclays Bank (Map p759; The Mall; ⏰8.30am-3.30pm Mon-Fri, 8.15-10.45am Sat)

Standard Chartered Bank (Map p759; The Mall; ⏰8.30am-3.30pm Mon-Fri, 8.15-11am

Central Gaborone

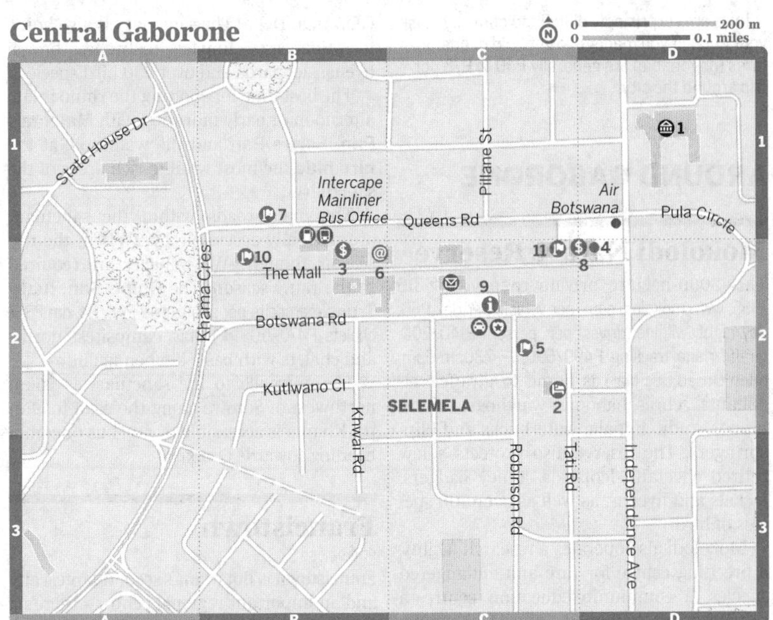

Sat) Major branches of Standard Chartered Bank have foreign-exchange facilities and ATMs, and offer cash advances.

TOURIST INFORMATION

Department of Wildlife & National Parks (DWNP; ☎381 0774; www.mewt.gov.bw/DWNP) One of two accommodation booking offices (the other is in Maun) for all national parks and reserves run by the DWNP.

Tourist office (Map p759; ☎395 9455; www.botswanatourism.co.bw; Botswana Rd; 7.30am-6pm Mon-Fri, 8am-1pm Sat) Moderately useful collection of brochures; next to the Cresta President Hotel.

Central Gaborone

Sights

1 National Museum & Art Gallery D1

Sleeping

2 Brackendene Lodge C2

Information

3 Barclays Bank B2
4 Botswana Tourism Board D2
5 French Embassy C2
6 Moby Trek B2
7 South African Embassy B1
8 Standard Chartered Bank D2
9 Tourist Office C2
10 UK Embassy B2
11 Zambian Embassy C2

Getting There & Away

From **Sir Seretse Khama International Airport** (GBE; ☎391 4401), 14km from the city centre, Air Botswana (p779) operates international services to Harare, Johannesburg and Lusaka, as well as domestic services to and from Francistown (from P680), Maun (from P882) and Kasane (from P1050).

Intercity buses and minibuses to Ghanzi (P130, 11 hours) and Francistown (P60, six hours) depart from the main bus terminal. To reach Maun or Kasane, change in Francistown. The Intercape Mainliner to Johannesburg (SAR240, 6½ hours) runs from the petrol station beside the Mall. Tickets can be booked online or at the **Intercape Mainliner Office** (☎397 4294; www.intercape.co.za); buses are very popular and should be booked a week or more in advance.

Getting Around

White combis (minibuses) circulate according to set routes and cost P5. They pick up and drop off only at designated lay-bys marked 'bus/taxi stop'. The main city loop passes all the main shopping centres except the new Riverwalk Mall and the Kgale Centre Mall, which are on the Tlokweng and Kgale routes, respectively.

Taxis are surprisingly difficult to come by – ask your hotel. If you manage to get hold of one, fares (negotiable) are generally P40 to P75 per trip around the city.

AROUND GABORONE

Mokolodi Nature Reserve

This 3000-hectare private **reserve** (☎316 1955; www.mokolodi.com; per vehicle per day P60, day/night wildlife drives per person P140/200, giraffe/rhino tracking P490/590; ⊙7.30am-6pm, often closed Dec-Mar) is home to giraffes, elephants, zebras, baboons, warthogs, rhinos, hippos, kudu, impala, waterbucks and klipspringers. The reserve also protects a few retired cheetahs, leopards, honey badgers, jackals and hyenas, as well as over 300 species of bird.

Mokolodi also operates a research facility, a breeding centre for rare and endangered species, a community-education centre, a sanctuary for orphaned, injured or confiscated birds and animals and is the base for **Cheetah Conservation Botswana** (www.cheetahbotswana.com). Among the activities on offer are rhino and giraffe tracking.

The reserve often closes during the rainy season (December to March). Visitors are permitted to drive their own vehicles around the reserve (4WD only in the rainy season). There are **campsites** (per adult/child P120/60).

The entrance to the reserve is 12km south of Gaborone.

EASTERN BOTSWANA

Khama Rhino Sanctuary

With the rhino all but disappeared from Botswana, the residents of Serowe banded together in the early 1990s to establish the 4300-hectare **Khama Rhino Sanctuary** (☎463 0713; www.khamarhinosanctuary.org.bw; adult/child P52/26, vehicle under/over 5 tonnes P63/190; ⊙7am-7pm). Today the sanctuary protects 40 white and four black rhinos; the sanctuary was not originally set up for black rhinos but when one wandered across the border from Zimbabwe it was the start of a beautiful relationship. Some rhinos have been released into the wild, especially in the Okavango Delta. The sanctuary is also home to wildebeests, impalas, ostriches, brown hyenas, leopards and over 230 bird species.

The best time for spotting the rhino is late afternoon or early morning, with **Malema's Pan**, **Serwe Pan** and the waterhole at the **bird hide** the most wildlife-rich areas of the sanctuary.

The main roads within the sanctuary are normally accessible by 2WD in the dry season, though 4WD vehicles are required in the rainy season. The **Rhino Sanctuary Trust** (campsite per adult/child P68/34, dm P317, chalets P470-710;) has campsites, dorms and chalets with basic kitchen facilities.

The entrance to the sanctuary is 26km northwest of Serowe along the road to Orapa. Khama is accessible by any bus or combi heading towards Orapa.

Francistown

POP 98,963

Francistown is Botswana's second-largest city and an important regional centre – there's a fair chance you'll overnight here if you're on way north coming from South Africa. There are banks and plenty of supermarkets.

The best place to stay is **Woodlands Stop Over** (☎244 0131; www.woodlandscampingbots.com; campsite per person P83, s/d chalets P330/475, r from P685;), 10km north of town off the road to Maun. In town, **Grand Lodge** (☎241 2300; Haskins St; s/d P275/350;) is an excellent budget option. For meals, try **Thorn Tree** (Village Mall, St Patrick St; mains P35-60; ⊙6am-3pm Mon-Sat;).

Air Botswana (p779) flies between Francistown and Gaborone (P680). From the main bus terminal, located between the train line and Blue Jacket Plaza, buses and combis connect Francistown with Gaborone (P60, six hours), Maun (P89.90, five hours), Kasane (P106, seven hours), Nata (P41, two hours), Bulawayo (Zimbabwe; P60, two hours) and Harare (Zimbabwe; P160, six hours).

Tuli Block

Tucked into the nation's right side pocket, the Tuli Block is one of Botswana's best-kept secrets. This 10km- to 20km-wide swath of freehold farmland extends over 300km along the northern bank of the Limpopo River and is made up of a series of private properties, many of which have a conservation bent. Wildlife is a big attraction here, but so too is the landscape, which is unlike anywhere else in Botswana with its moonscapes of muddy oranges and browns and *kopjes* (small hills) overlooked by deep blue sky. Elephants, hippos, kudu, wildebeests and impala as well as small numbers of lions, cheetahs, leopards and hyenas circle each other among rocks and *kopjes* scattered with artefacts from the Stone Age onwards. More than 350 species of bird have also been recorded in the reserve.

The northern reaches of the Block make up the Northern Tuli Game Reserve. In the longer term, there are plans to extend the reserve's boundaries south.

Sleeping

★Wild at Tuli TENTED CAMP **$$$**
(☎ 7211 3688; www.wildattuli.com; Kwa-Tuli Game Reserve; per person self-catering/full board P595/960) This fabulous camp on an island in a branch of the Limpopo River is run by respected conservationists Judi Gounaris and Dr Helena Fitchat, and they bring a winning combination of warmth and conservation knowledge to the experience. Meals are home-cooked, the tents are extremely comfortable and wildlife drives on the 5000-hectare property are also included in the price. They'll even let you sleep in one of the hides overlooking a waterhole.

Mashatu Game Reserve TENTED CAMP **$$$**
(☎ in South Africa 011-442 2267; www.mashatu.com; s/d chalet US$660/880, luxury tent US$480/640; ❄ 🏊) One of the largest private wildlife reserves in Southern Africa, renowned for its big cats and frighteningly large elephant population. Accommodation is in enormous luxury suites decorated with impeccable taste in the main camp, while the tents are also beautifully turned out. The game reserve is close to the Pont Drift border post.

Getting There & Away

Unless you're flying in on a charter, you'll need your own vehicle to reach the Tuli Block. If you're coming from South Africa, approach via the border posts of Platjan or Pont Drift. From elsewhere in Botswana, the lodges can be accessed from the west via the paved road from Bobonong.

Makgadikgadi Pans & Nxai Pan National Parks

The elemental power of Botswana's landscapes are nowhere more obvious than in the country's north. Within striking distance of the water-drowned terrain of the Okavango Delta, Chobe River and Linyanti Marshes lies Makgadikgadi, the largest network of salt pans in the world. Here the country takes on a different hue, forsaking the blues and greens of the delta for the burnished oranges, shimmering whites and golden grasslands of this northern manifestation of the Kalahari Desert. It's as much an emptiness as a place, a land larger than Switzerland, mesmerising in scope and in beauty.

Two protected areas – Makgadikgadi Pans National Park and Nxai Pan National Park, separated only by the asphalted A3 – protect large tracts of saltpans, palm forests, grasslands and savannah. Although they enclose only a fraction of the pan networks, the parks provide a convenient focal point for visiting; the horizonless pans of Nxai Pan have gained a reputation for cheetah sightings while the return of waters to the Boteti River in the west of Makgadikgadi has led to a wildlife bonanza of wildebeest, zebra and antelope species pursued by lions. But there are also some fabulous areas outside park boundaries, with iconic stands of baobab trees and beguiling landscapes.

Sights

Nata Bird Sanctuary WILDLIFE RESERVE
(☎ 7154 4342; admission P55; ⏰ 7am-7pm) This 230-sq-km community-run wildlife sanctuary sits at the northeastern end of Sowa Pan. The sanctuary's principal draw is the large population of water birds. Over 165 species of bird have been recorded here and when the Nata River flows in the rainy season, the sanctuary sttracts tens of thousands of white and pink-backed pelicans, and greater and lesser flamingos. In the dry season (May to October), it's possible to drive around the sanctuary in a 2WD with high clearance. There's a basic **campsite** (☎ 7154 4342; campsite per person/vehicle P35/15). The entrance to the sanctuary is 15km southeast of Nata.

Kubu Island LANDMARK
(www.kubuisland.com) Along the southwestern edge of Sowa Pan is a ghostly, baobab-laden rock known as Kubu Island, entirely surrounded by a sea of salt. In Setswana, *kubu* means 'hippopotamus' (in ancient times this was a real island on a real lake inhabited by hippos). It's not only the name that evokes a more fertile past – the fossilised bird-shit of water birds that once perched here still

adorns the boulders. There's a community-run **campsite** (☎7549 4669; www.kubuisland.com; Lekhubu; campsite per adult/child P100/50).

Access to Kubu Island (GPS: S 20°53.460', E 25°49.318') involves negotiating a maze of grassy islets and salty bays. Drivers will need a 4WD and a compass or GPS equipment; some GPS programs spell it as 'Lekhubu'.

Sleeping

In addition to the campsites, there are places to stay in Gweta, the closest town to the park gates and roughly midway between Maun and Nata.

Khumaga Campsite CAMPGROUND $
(www.sklcamps.com; S 20°27.311', E 24°30.968'; campsite per adult/child US$50/25) The Khumaga campsite sits high above the bank of the Boteti in Makgadikgadi Pans National Park and is an attractive site with good shade, *braai* (barbecue) pits and an excellent ablutions block with flush toilets and (usually) hot showers.

South Camp CAMPGROUND $
(www.xomaesites.com; S 19°56.159', E 24°46.598'; campsite per adult/child P226/113) Around 37km from the park gate along a sandy track in Nxai Pan National Park, South Camp has 10 sites clustered quite close together behind some trees at the edge of one of the pans. There's a good ablutions block.

Planet Baobab LODGE, CAMPGROUND $$
(☎in South Africa 011-447 1605; www.unchartedafrica.com; campsite per adult/child P68/45, d tents P450, s/d/q huts from P1010/1120/1760;) About 4km east of Gweta, this inventive lodge has campsites, *rondavels* (traditional round huts) and chalets, and a funky, laid-back vibe. It has an excellent range of activities and creative pan excursions.

Gweta Lodge LODGE $$
(☎621 2220; www.gwetalodge.com; d safari tents P350, s/d/f P390/525/795;) A friendly place with a campsite, good rooms, a swimming pool and pan-based activities on offer.

NORTHERN BOTSWANA

Chobe National Park

Chobe National Park is one of the great wildlife destinations of Africa. Famed for its massive elephants and enormous elephant population, Chobe, which encompasses nearly 11,000 sq km, is itself the size of a small country and is an important epicentre of Botswana's safari industry.

Of the two major wildlife-watching areas of the park, Chobe Riverfront supports the largest wildlife concentration in the park. It's also the most accessible and lies within easy striking distance of the gateway town of Kasane. Soulful Savuti, which can be reached from Maun or Kasane, is almost the riverfront's match when it comes to wildlife.

Chobe Riverfront

The Chobe Riverfront rarely disappoints with arguably Botswana's densest concentration of wildlife. Although animals are present along the riverfront year-round, the density of wildlife can be overwhelming during the dry season, especially during September and October. Whether you cruise along the river in a motorboat, or drive along the banks in a 4WD, you're almost guaranteed an up-close encounter with some of the largest elephant herds (and some of the largest elephants) on the continent.

Spend even a couple of hours here and you'll likely see elephants, giraffes, hippos, lions and possibly the more elusive cheetahs and leopards along the banks.

If you don't have your own wheels, any of the hotels and lodges in Kasane can help you organise a wildlife drive or boat cruise along the riverfront. Two- to three-hour cruises and wildlife drives typically cost around P200, though you will also have to pay separate park fees.

Ihaha Campsite CAMPGROUND $
(kwalatesafari@gmail.com; S 17°50.487', E 24°52.754'; campsite per adult/child P260/130) Ihaha campsite is the only camping ground for self-drivers along the Chobe Riverfront – staying here gives you the run of the park. The trees need more time to mature and shade can be in short supply at some of the sites. But the location is excellent – it's by the water's edge about 27km from the Northern Gate.

Chobe Game Lodge LODGE $$$
(☎625 0340, 625 1761; www.chobegamelodge.com; River Rd; per person Jan-Apr US$476, s/d May-Dec US$1113/1712;) This highly praised safari lodge has individually decorated rooms that are elegant yet soothing, and some have views of the Chobe River and Namibian flood plains. The lodge is about 9km west of the Northern Gate.

CHOBE AT A GLANCE

Gateway towns Kasane (for Chobe Riverfront) or Maun (Savuti).

Wildlife Chobe has tens of thousands of elephants and some of the largest elephant herds in Africa. Savuti is good for predators. Watch also for roan antelopes and the rare oribi antelopes.

Birdlife Over 440 species of bird have been recorded here.

When to go The best time to visit Chobe is during the dry season (April to October), when wildlife congregates around permanent water sources. Try to avoid January to March, as getting around can be difficult during the rains (although this is peak season for flying into Savuti).

Getting there Under optimum conditions, it's a four- to six-hour drive from Kasane to Savuti. The road is passable by 2WD as far as Kachikau, but after it turns south into the Chobe Forest Reserve the road deteriorates into parallel sand ruts that require high-clearance 4WD. Coming from Maun, you'll need 4WD to proceed north of Shorobe.

Moving around Unless you've joined a mobile safari, you'll need your own 4WD vehicle. Game trails are clearly marked.

Budget Safaris Most lodges and many camps in Kasane offer two- to three-hour wildlife drives or boat safaris to Chobe Riverfront for around P200 per person.

Savuti

Savuti, in the southwestern corner of Chobe National Park, is awash with distinctly African colours and vistas. With the exception of rhinos, you'll find all of Africa's most charismatic megafauna in residence here or passing through, and the return of waters to the Savuti Channel has only added to this area's considerable appeal.

Sights

The rocky monoliths that rise up from the Savuti sand make a perfect habitat for leopards; **Leopard Rock** is the first you come to if you're driving from Maun or Moremi Game Reserve. A 1.6km-long sandy track encircles the rock. The **Savuti Marshes**, in Savuti's southern reaches, are rich in wildlife, while **Gobabis Hill** is home to several sets of 4000-year-old rock paintings of San origin; it's also a known haunt of lions and leopards. The western edge of Gobabis Hill is guarded by a fine **baobab**, which is visible from the main track.

Sleeping

Savuti Campsite CAMPGROUND $
(www.sklcamps.com; S 18°34.014', E 24°03.905'; campsite per adult/child US$50/20) One of the best camping grounds in northern Botswana, with five of the seven sites overlooking the river – sites one to four could do with a little more shade but are otherwise lovely, while Paradise camp is our pick. The ablutions block has sit-down flush toilets, *braai* pits and (usually hot) showers.

Camp Savuti TENTED CAMP $$$
(www.sklcamps.com; s/d May-Dec with full board US$500/700, rates vary rest of year) These beautifully appointed canvas tents overlook the Savuti Channel. Prices are a touch below the longer-established camps but the quality is pretty much on a par.

Savute Elephant Camp LODGE $$$
(686 0302; www.savuteelephantcamp.com; s/d May-Dec full board US$1856/2650) The premier camp in Savuti is made up of 12 lavishly appointed East African–style linen tents on raised wooden platforms, complete with antique-replica furniture.

Kasane & Kazungula

Kasane lies in a riverine woodland at the meeting point of four countries (Botswana, Zambia, Namibia and Zimbabwe) and the confluence of two major rivers, the Chobe and the Zambezi. It's also the northern gateway to Chobe National Park, and Botswana's jumping-off point for excursions to Victoria Falls. About 12km east of Kasane is the tiny settlement of Kazungula, which serves as the border crossing between Botswana and Zimbabwe, and the landing for the Kazungula ferry, which connects Botswana and Zambia.

Kasane & Around

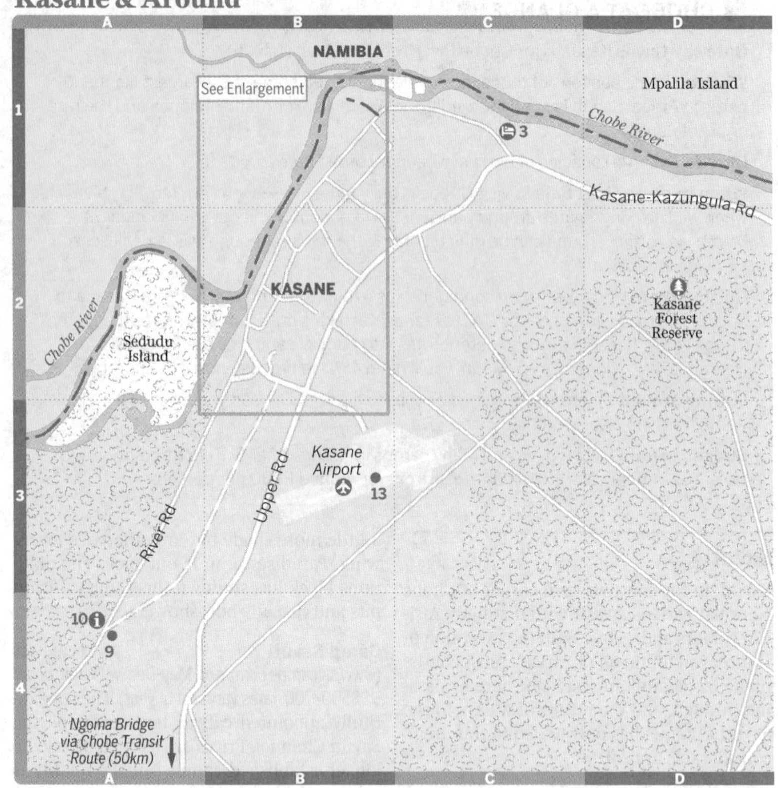

Sleeping & Eating

★Senyati Safari Camp CAMPGROUND, CHALET **$$**
(☎7188 1306; www.senyatisafaricamp.com; off Kazungula-Nata Rd; campsite per adult/child from P115/63, s/d/f chalets P400/520/690; ❄☒) Off the main highway south of Kasungula, this wonderful spot has comfy chalets and some of northern Botswana's best campsites, each with their own ablutions block. The bar and some of the chalets overlook a waterhole where elephants congregate in large numbers.

Old House GUESTHOUSE **$$**
(☎625 2562; www.oldhousekasane.com; President Ave; r P550-900; ❄☒☒) Close to the centre and with an intimate feel, the Old House has lovely rooms adjacent to a quiet garden by the riverbank. The bar-restaurant is one of Kasane's best and the rooms are stylish and comfortable without being overdone.

Toro Safari Lodge LODGE, CAMPGROUND **$$**
(☎625 2694; www.torolodge.co.bw; campsite per person P81, chalets from P671, apt P1003; ❄@☒) Down a side road off the main Kasane–Kazungula road, this excellent place has campsites beneath maturing trees, comfortable chalets (some with river view) and attractive grounds that run along the riverbank.

Thebe River Camping LODGE, CAMPGROUND **$$**
(☎625 0314; www.theberiversafaris.com; Kasane-Kazungula Rd; campsite per person P93, tent P396, tw/f P690/1000; ☒) Perched alongside the Chobe River, this leafy backpacker lodge is one of the more budget-friendly options in Kasane. Well-groomed campsites are located near *braai* pits and a modern ablutions block with steamy showers and flush toilets.

Chobe Safari Lodge LODGE **$$$**
(☎625 0336; www.chobesafarilodge.com; President Ave; campsite per adult/child P75/60, r P975-1175; ❄☒) One of the more affordable upmarket

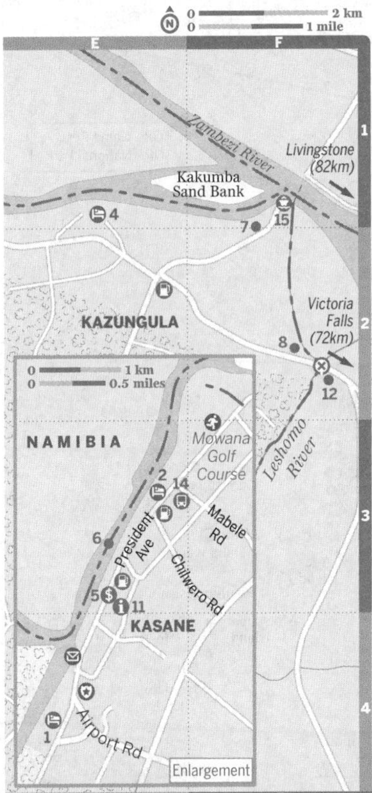

Kasane & Around

Sleeping

1	Chobe Safari Lodge	E4
2	Old House	E3
3	Thebe River Camping	C1
4	Toro Safari Lodge	E1

Information

5	Barclays Bank	E3
6	Botswana Immigration	E3
7	Botswana Immigration (for Kazungula Ferry to Zambia)	F1
8	Botswana Immigration (for Zimbabwe)	F2
	Cape to Cairo Bureau de Change & Internet	(see 5)
9	Chobe NP Entrance	A4
10	Department of Wildlife & National Parks	A4
11	Tourist Office	E3
12	Zimbabwe Immigration	F2

Transport

13	Air Botswana	B3
14	Bus Terminal	E3
15	Kazungula Ferry	F1

lodges in Kasane, Chobe Safari is excellent value. Understated but comfortable rooms are priced according to size and location.

Information

Be sure to stock up on US dollars (post-1996) if you're heading to Zimbabwe.

Barclays Bank (Hunters' Africa Mall, off President Ave; 8.30am-3.30pm Mon-Fri, 8.15-10.45am Sat)

Cape to Cairo Bureau de Change & Internet (Hunters' Africa Mall, off President Ave; 8.30am-5pm Mon-Fri, to 4.30pm Sat) Charges 3% commission on cash, 4% on travellers cheques.

DWNP (625 0235; Sedudu Gate) This is the place to pay for your park permit and get information on visiting Chobe National Park.

Tourist office (625 0555; Hunters' Africa Mall, off President Ave; 7.30am-6pm Mon-Fri, 9am-2pm Sat) Plenty of brochures for lodges and safari companies. Generally helpful, although you're better off visiting the park gate for information on Chobe National Park.

Getting There & Away

Air Botswana connects Kasane's airport to Maun (from P369) and Gaborone (from P105).

Combis heading to Francistown (P106, seven hours), Maun (P96, six hours) and Nata (P88, five hours) run when full from the Shell petrol station bus terminal on Mabele Rd. Most lodges and camps run day trips to Livingstone/Victoria Falls (from P1250).

Okavango Delta

The stirring counterpoint to the Kalahari Desert that consumes so much of the country, the Okavango Delta, the up-to-18,000-sq-km expansion and expiration of the Okavango River, is Southern Africa's massive outpouring of fertility. Indeed, the contrast the Okavango presents with the rest of Botswana is one of her most beguiling aspects: here, in the heart of the thirst lands, is one of the world's largest inland river deltas, an unceasing web of water, rushing, standing, flooding and dying.

The Okavango's fly-in luxury lodges make a strong claim to be Africa's most exclusive

Okavango Delta

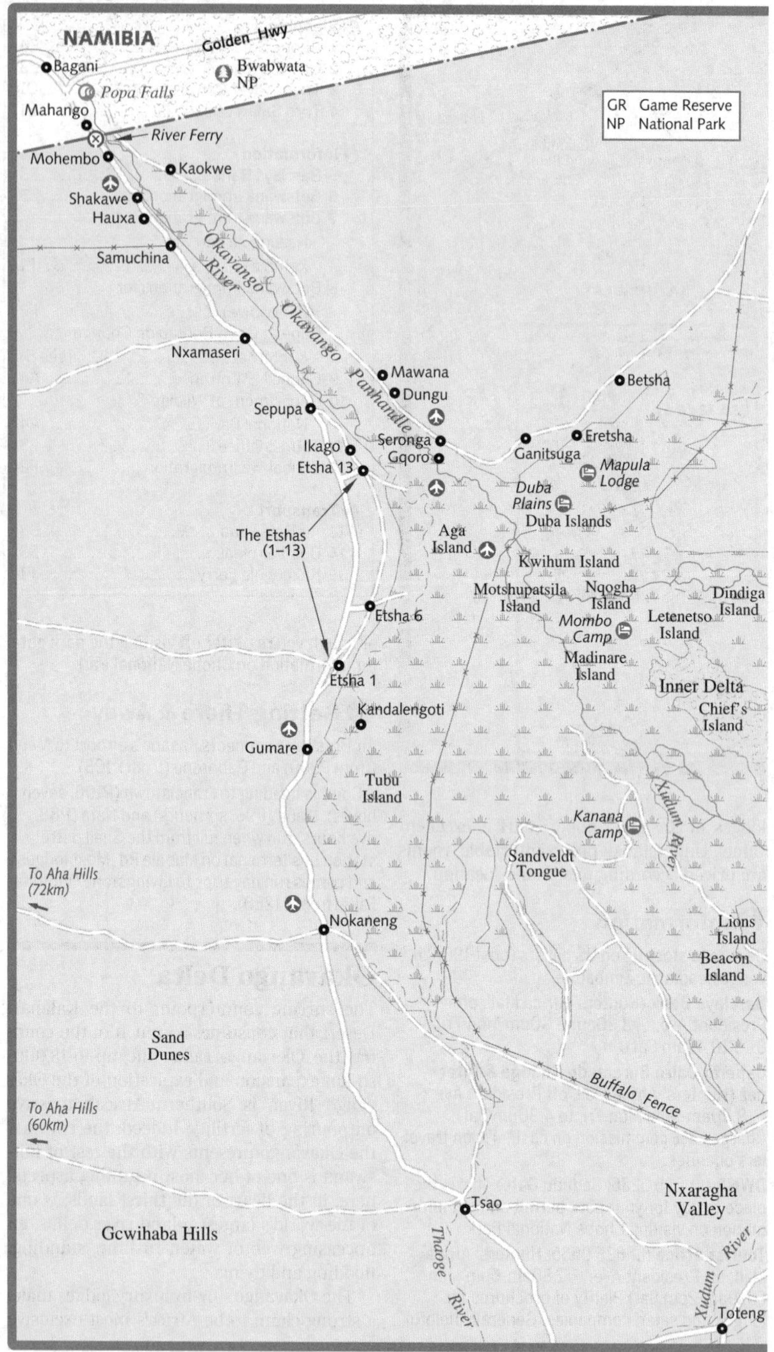
NAMIBIA
Golden Hwy
Bagani
Bwabwata NP
Popa Falls
Mahango
River Ferry
GR Game Reserve
NP National Park
Mohembo
Kaokwe
Shakawe
Hauxa
Samuchina
Okavango River
Okavango Panhandle
Nxamaseri
Mawana
Dungu
Betsha
Sepupa
Seronga
Gqoro
Ganitsuga
Eretsha
Ikago
Etsha 13
Mapula Lodge
Duba Plains
Duba Islands
The Etshas (1–13)
Aga Island
Kwihum Island
Motshupatsila Island
Nqogha Island
Dindiga Island
Etsha 6
Mombo Camp
Letenetso Island
Madinare Island
Etsha 1
Inner Delta
Kandalengoti
Chief's Island
Gumare
Tubu Island
Xudum River
Kanana Camp
Sandveldt Tongue
To Aha Hills (72km)
Nokaneng
Lions Island
Beacon Island
Sand Dunes
Buffalo Fence
To Aha Hills (60km)
Tsao
Nxaragha Valley
Gcwihaba Hills
Thaoge River
Xudum River
Toteng

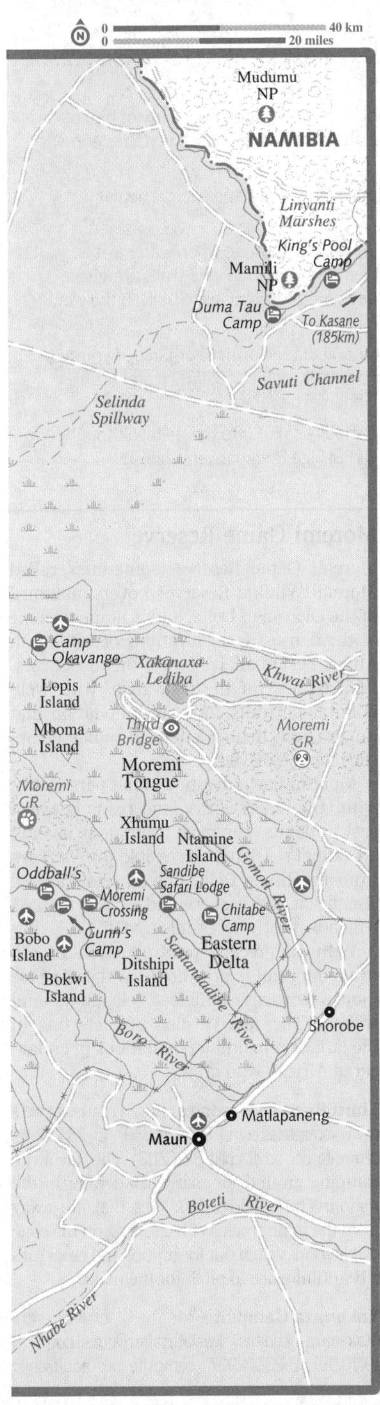

safaris destinations. Fork out a fortune for nights spent deep in the inner delta and you're unlikely to regret it. But for those on a small budget it's possible to gain a delta foothold through a combination of mobile safaris from Maun and self-driving to the campsites of the Moremi Game Reserve.

Eastern Delta

The Eastern Delta includes the wetlands between the southern boundary of Moremi Game Reserve and the buffalo fence that crosses the Boro and Santandadibe Rivers, north of Matlapaneng. If you're short of time and/or money, this part of the Okavango Delta remains an affordable and accessible option. From Maun, it is easy to arrange a day trip on a *mokoro* or a two- or three-night *mokoro* trip combined with bush camping.

Sandibe Safari Lodge LODGE **$$$**
(☎in South Africa 011-809 4300; www.andbeyondafrica.com; per person low/high season US$570/1145;) Understated elegance is the theme at this riverine forest retreat, which consists of eight ochre-washed chalets surrounded by thick bush and towering trees.

Chitabe Camp TENTED CAMP **$$$**
(☎in South Africa 011-807 1800; www.wilderness-safaris.com; s/d low season US$1123/1736, high season US$1588/2666;) Near the Santandadibe River, at the southern edge of Moremi Game Reserve, Chitabe is an island oasis (only accessible by boat or plane). Accommodation is in East African–style en suite luxury tents, which are built on wooden decks.

Inner Delta

Welcome to the heart of the Okavango, a world inaccessible by roads and inhabited by some of the richest wildlife concentrations on earth. Although budget trips are possible in some areas, the quintessential delta experience is staying in one of the fly-in luxury lodges – if you're going to make a splash with your money in Botswana, make it here.

Roughly defined, the Inner Delta occupies the areas west of Chief's Island and between Chief's Island and the base of the Okavango Panhandle. *Mokoro* trips through the Inner Delta are almost invariably arranged with licensed polers affiliated with specific lodges, and operate roughly between June and December, depending on water levels.

OKAVANGO DELTA AT A GLANCE

Gateway Town Maun

Wildlife A full complement of herbivores inhabit the delta (including plenty of hippos and elephants), as do large populations of predators, including lions, cheetahs, leopards, African wild dogs and hyenas.

Birdlife A world-class birding destination. The Okavango Panhandle in particular is known for its birdwatching.

When to go The best time to visit the delta is July to September, when water levels are high and the weather is dry. Tracks can get extremely muddy, and trails are often washed out during and after the rains. Mosquitoes are prevalent, especially in the wet season (November to March).

Moving around Unless you're staying at an upmarket lodge or have organised your visit on a mobile safari from Maun, you'll need your own fully equipped 4WD to get around. Boat trips are also an essential part of the Okavango experience.

Budget safaris Maun is the best place to join a mobile safari into the delta, although don't arrive in town without a reservation. Try Old Bridge Backpackers (p769).

Oddball's TENTED CAMP $$$
(☎686 1154; www.oddballscamp.com; tents low/high season US$240/340) For years, Oddball's was a well-regarded budget lodge and although it's still way below lodge prices elsewhere in the delta, we reckon they're asking too much considering you're still in budget dome tents.

Moremi Crossing TENTED CAMP $$$
(☎686 0023; www.moremicrossing.com; per person low season US$321, s/d high season US$567/892;) This well-priced collection of lovely chalets flanks a simply gorgeous (and enormous) thatched dining and bar area that overlooks a long flood plain where you can often see wandering giraffes and elephants. The camp is one of the delta's more environmentally sustainable.

Gunn's Camp TENTED CAMP $$$
(☎686 0023; www.gunns-camp.com; per person low season US$371, s/d high season US$672/1102) Gunn's is a beautiful option for those wanting the amenities of a high-end safari – expertly cooked meals, attentive service and wonderful views over its island location in the delta – with a more rugged sense of place. The elegant tented rooms are as comfy as you'll find anywhere.

Eagle Island Camp TENTED CAMP $$$
(☎686 0302; www.orient-express.com; per person high season from US$900) Widely considered to be one of the most beautiful camps in the delta, Eagle Island occupies a stunning concession deep in the waters. You'll be shacked up in silk-soft luxury tents, and helicopter safaris are part of your stay.

Moremi Game Reserve

Moremi Game Reserve (sometimes called Moremi Wildlife Reserve), covers one-third of the Okavango Delta, and is home to some of the densest concentrations of wildlife in Africa. Best of all, it's one of the most accessible corners of the Okavango, with well-maintained trails and accommodation that ranges from luxury lodges to public campsites for self-drivers.

Moremi has a distinctly dual personality, with large areas of dry land rising between vast wetlands. The most prominent 'islands' are Chief's Island, accessible by *mokoro* from the Inner Delta lodges, and Moremi Tongue at the eastern end of the reserve, which is mostly accessible by 4WD.

With the recent reintroduction of the rhino, Moremi is now home to the Big Five (lions, leopards, buffaloes, elephants and rhinos). The reserve also protects one of the largest remaining populations of endangered African wild dogs.

Third Bridge Campsite CAMPGROUND $
(www.xomaesites.com; S 19°14.340', E 23°21.276'; campsite per adult/child P226/113) The favourite camping ground for many self-drivers in the region, Third Bridge has sites that are away from the main track. With a setting on the edge of a lagoon (watch out for hippos and crocs), it's a beautiful place to pitch for the night.

Xakanaxa Campsite CAMPGROUND $
(Xakanaxa Lediba; kwalatesafari@gmail.com; S 19°10.991', E 23°24.937'; campsite per adult/child

P260/130) Another favourite Moremi camping ground, Xakanaxa occupies a narrow strip of land surrounded by marshes and lagoons. It's no coincidence that many upmarket lodges are located nearby – the wildlife in the area can be prolific.

Sango Safari Camp TENTED CAMP **$$$**
(☎683 0230; www.sangosafaricamp.com; per person low/high season US$295/540, without park fees & wildlife drives US$235/425) Sango's is somewhat less pretentious than some other Moremi camps but nonetheless maintains an air of quiet exclusivity. Hand-crafted furnishings are a nice touch while wildlife drives generally go where other lodges don't.

Xakanaxa Camp TENTED CAMP **$$$**
(☎in South Africa 011-463 3999; www.xakanaxacamp.com; per person low season US$531, s/d high season from US$1301/1786) This camp, of longer standing than most, offers a pleasant mix of delta and savannah habitat, and teems with huge herds of elephants and other wildlife. They're very good at providing the luxury safari experience here.

Mombo Camp TENTED CAMP **$$$**
(☎686 0086; www.wilderness-safaris.com; s/d low season US$2230/3430, high season US$3026/4862;) Ask anyone in Botswana for the country's most exclusive camp and they're likely to nominate Mombo, on the northwest corner of Chief's Island. The surrounding delta scenery is some of the finest in the Okavango and the wildlife-watching is almost unrivalled.

Maun

POP 65,693

As the main gateway to the Okavango Delta, Maun (mau-*uu*nn) is Botswana's primary tourism hub. With good accommodation and a reliably mad mix of bush pilots, tourists, campers, volunteers and luxury safari-philes, it's a decent enough base for a day or two. The town itself has little going for it – it's strung out over a number of kilometres with not much of a discernible centre – but some of the hotels and camps have lovely riverside vantage points.

Tours

African Secrets WILDLIFE TOUR
(☎686 0300; www.africansecrets.net; Mathiba I St, Matlapaneng) This excellent operation is run out of the Island Safari Lodge.

Audi Camp Safaris WILDLIFE TOUR
(☎686 0599; www.okavangocamp.com; Shorobe Rd, Matlapaneng) Well-run safaris into the delta and further afield out of the popular Audi Camp.

Crocodile Camp Safaris WILDLIFE TOUR
(☎686 0222; www.crocodilecamp.com; Shorobe Rd, Matlapaneng) This budget operator is at the Crocodile Camp.

Nxuma Adventure Safaris WILDLIFE TOUR
(☎7646 2829; nxumu@hotmail.com) *Mokoro* and other boat trips in the Okavango, as well as San-guided walks; ask for Oscar.

Okavango River Lodge WILDLIFE TOUR
(☎686 3707; www.okavango-river-lodge.com; Shorobe Rd, Matlapaneng) Reliable safaris run out of the Okavango River Lodge.

Old Bridge Backpackers WILDLIFE TOUR
(☎686 2406; www.maun-backpackers.com; Shorobe Rd, Matlapaneng) This experienced budget operation is run from the Old Bridge Backpackers and we're yet to hear a bad word about them.

BORDER CROSSINGS: KASANE & CHOBE

Namibia The **Ngoma Bridge–Kasane Gate** (6am-6pm) lies 57km west of Kasane and is handy for Namibia's Caprivi Strip. Apart from searches for fresh meat, fresh fruit and dairy products when entering Botswana, this crossing is relatively hassle-free.

Zambia The **Kazungula– Mambova Gate** (6am-8pm) requires a river crossing by ferry. For crossing into Zambia, we recommend hiring a local fixer (agree a fee up front, never hand over money until all formalities are completed, and get your fixer's mobile phone number and check that it works). All fees into Zambia are paid in kwacha apart from visa fee and road-toll fee.

Zimbabwe The surprisingly quiet **Kazungula–Victoria Falls Gate** (6am-6pm) is generally hassle-free. Those on day excursions to/from Victoria Falls will encounter few difficulties, while self-drivers can expect around two hours.

Maun

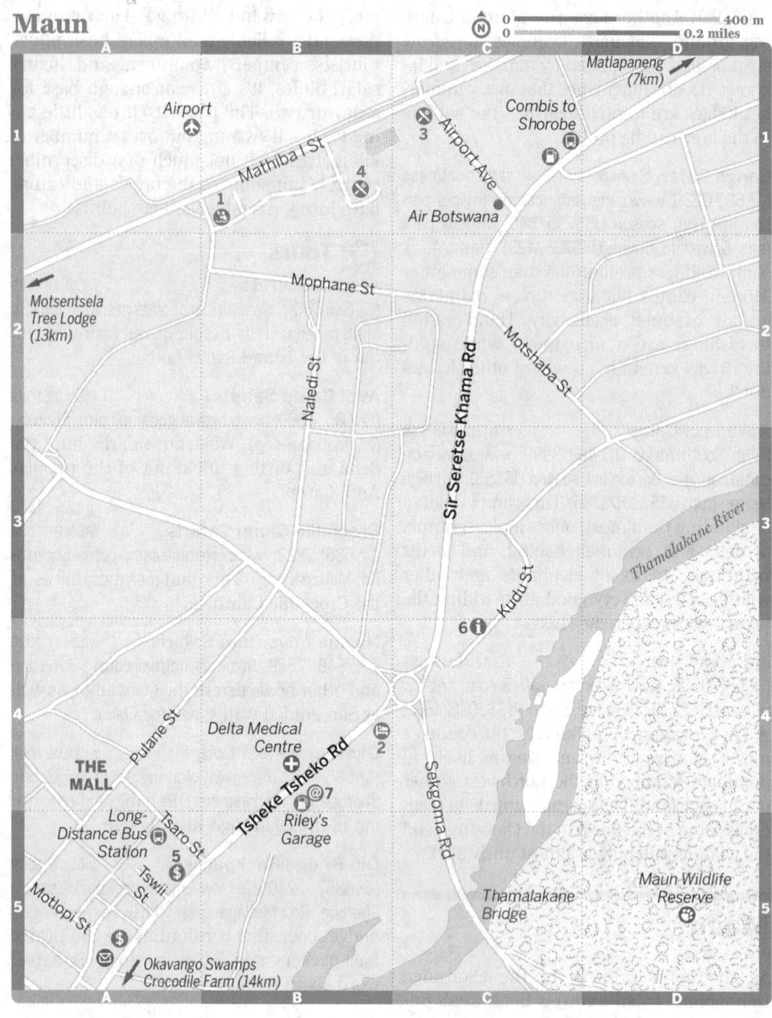

Sleeping

★Old Bridge Backpackers CAMPGROUND $
(☎686 2406; www.maun-backpackers.com; Hippo Pools, Old Matlapaneng Bridge; campsite per person P60, dm P155, s/d tents without bathroom P225/348, d tents with bathroom P505; @) One of the great boltholes on Southern African overland trails, 'The Bridge', as it's known, has a great bar-at-the-end-of-the-world kind of vibe. Accommodation ranges from dorms by the riverbank to well-appointed campsites and some more private tents to retreat to at day's end. In short, this is a place that understands travellers and doesn't make them pay over the odds for it.

Okavango River Lodge CAMPGROUND, CHALET $
(☎686 3707; www.okavango-river-lodge.com; Matlapaneng; campsite per person P70, s/d/f chalets P250/330/400, s/d tents P150/280) This down-to-earth spot off Shorobe Rd has a lovely setting on the riverbank. The owners are friendly and unpretentious and pride themselves on giving travellers useful (and inde-

Maun

Activities, Courses & Tours

1 Okavango Kopano Mokoro Community Trust ... B1

Sleeping

2 Cresta Riley's Hotel ... B4

Eating

3 Bon Arrivee ... C1
4 Hilary's ... B1

Information

5 Barclays Bank ... A5
6 Department of Wildlife & National Parks ... C4
7 Open Door Bureau de Change ... B4
Tourist Office ... (see 1)

pendent) information on trips through the delta.

Crocodile Camp CAMPGROUND, CHALET $
(☎7560 6864; www.crocodilecamp.com; Matlapaneng; campsite per person P60, chalets per person incl breakfast P400;) 'Croc Camp' occupies a superb spot right on the river and is a quieter place than others. Off Shorobe Rd, the camping ground is excellent and secure while there are also thatched riverside chalets with bathrooms.

Audi Camp CAMPGROUND $$
(☎686 0599; www.okavangocamp.com; Matlapaneng; campsite per person from P60, s/d tents without bathroom from P140/170, with bathroom P540/640; @) Off Shorobe Rd, Audi Camp is a fantastic camping ground that's become increasingly popular with families, although independent overlanders will feel utterly welcome as well.

Island Safari Lodge CAMPGROUND, CHALET $$
(☎686 0300; www.africansecrets.net; Matlapaneng; campsite per person P60, s/d P375/580, chalets P870;) One of the original lodges in Maun, Island Safari Lodge is also still one of its best with a range of accommodation that nicely spans different budgets. The campsites have ablutions blocks and there is access to the lodge's pool, restaurant and bar.

Discovery Bed & Breakfast B&B $$
(☎7244 8298; www.discoverybedandbreakfast.com; Matlapaneng; s/d from P275/425;) Dutch-run Discovery does a cool job of creating an African-village vibe in the midst of Maun – it strives for and achieves 'affordable accommodation with a traditional touch'.

Cresta Riley's Hotel HOTEL $$$
(☎686 0204; www.crestahotels.com; Tsheke Tsheko Rd; s/d P1039/1444;) Riley's is the only hotel or lodge in central Maun. It offers comfortable rooms in a convenient setting

THE MOKORO EXPERIENCE

One of the best (and also cheapest) ways to experience the Okavango Delta is to glide across the waters in a *mokoro* (plural *mekoro*), a shallow-draft dugout canoe traditionally hewn from an ebony or a sausage-tree log. With encouragement from several international conservation groups, however, the Batswana (people of Botswana) have now begun to construct more *mekoro* from fibreglass.

A *mokoro* may appear precarious at first, but it is amazingly stable and ideally suited to the shallow delta waters. It can accommodate two passengers and some limited luggage, and is propelled by a poler who stands at the back of the canoe with a *ngashi*, a long pole made from the mogonono tree.

The quality of a *mokoro* trip often depends on the passengers' enthusiasm, the meshing of personalities and the skill of the poler. Most polers (but not all) speak at least some English and can identify plants, birds and animals, and explain the cultures and myths of the delta inhabitants. Polers are often shy and lack confidence, so you may have to ask a lot of questions to get the information.

How much you enjoy your trip will depend partly on your expectations. If you come in the spirit of immersing yourself in nature and slowing down to the pace of life here on the delta, you won't leave disappointed. It's important to stress, however, that you should not expect to see too much wildlife. From the *mokoro*, you'll certainly spot plenty of hippos and crocs, and antelopes and elephants are frequently sighted during hikes. However, the main attraction of a *mokoro* trip is the peace and serenity you'll feel as you glide along the shallow waters of the delta.

BOOKING A MOKORO TRIP

A day trip from Maun into the Eastern Delta usually includes a two- to three-hour return drive in a 4WD to the departure point, two to three hours in a *mokoro* (perhaps longer each day on a two- or three-day trip), and two to three hours hiking. At the start of a *mokoro* trip, ask the poler what he has in mind, and agree to the length of time spent per day in the *mokoro*, out hiking, and relaxing at the campsite – bear in mind that travelling by *mokoro* is tiring for the poler.

One of the most refreshing things about booking *mokoro* trips is the absence of touts wandering the streets of Maun. That's because all polers operating *mokoro* trips out of Maun are represented by the **Okavango Kopano Mokoro Community Trust** (☎686 4806; off Mathiba 1 St; ⏰8am-5pm Mon-Fri, to noon Sat). This trust sets daily rates for the polers (P180 per poler per day, plus a P55 daily membership fee for the trust) by which all safari operators have to abide.

In terms of pricing, catering is an important distinction. 'Self-catering' means you must bring your own food as well as cooking, sleeping and camping equipment. This option is a good way to shave a bit off the price, though most travellers prefer catered trips. It's also easier to get a lower price if you're booking as part of a group or are planning a multiday tour.

Finally, a few other things to remember:

- Ask the booking agency if you're expected to provide food for the poler (usually you're not, but polers appreciate any leftover cooked or uncooked food).
- Bring good walking shoes and long trousers for hiking, a hat, and plenty of sunscreen and water.
- Water from the delta (despite its unpleasant colour) can be drunk if boiled or purified.
- Most campsites are natural, so take out all litter and burn toilet paper.
- Bring warm clothes for the evening between May and September.
- Wildlife can be dangerous, so make sure to never swim anywhere without checking with the poler first.

in leafy grounds – just don't expect a lodge/wilderness experience.

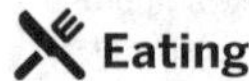

Eating

Motsana Arts Cafe CAFE $
(www.motsana.com; Shorobe Rd, Matlapaneng; meals P45-60; ⏰8am-8pm; 📶) Housed in an innovative new arts complex northeast of town on the road to Shorobe, this cool, casual and sophisticated cafe serves up burgers, salads, paninis, cajun chicken with avocado and all-day breakfasts, with free wi-fi thrown in.

Hilary's INTERNATIONAL $$
(meals from P50; ⏰8am-4pm Mon-Fri, 8.30am-noon Sat; 🌿) Just off Mathiba I St, this homy place offers a choice of wonderfully earthy meals, including homemade bread, baked potatoes, soups and sandwiches. It's ideal for vegetarians and anyone sick of greasy sausages and soggy chips.

Bon Arrivee INTERNATIONAL $$
(Mathiba I St; meals P60-120; ⏰8am-10pm) They lay on the pilot puns and flight-deck jokes very thick at this airport-themed place, which sits, of course, right across from the airport. The food is good – lots of pasta, steak and seafood – but don't come here an hour before your flight expecting a quick turnaround.

Information

Barclays Bank (Tsheke Tsheko Rd; ⏰8.30am-3.30pm Mon-Fri, 8.15-10.45am Sat)

Delta Medical Centre (☎686 1411; www.deltamedicalcentre.org; Tsheke Tsheko Rd) The best medical facility in Maun with 24-hour emergency service.

DWNP (☎686 1265; Kudu St; ⏰7.30am-4.30pm Mon-Fri, 7.30am-12.45pm & 1.45-4.30pm Sat, 7.30am-12.45pm Sun) To pay national park entry fees and book park campsites not in private hands; it's in a separate compound behind the main department building and well signposted.

Open Door Bureau de Change (Tsheke Tsheko Rd; internet per hour P30; ⏲7.30am-6pm Mon-Fri, 8am-4pm Sat, 9am-4pm Sun)

Tourist office (☎686 1056; off Mathiba I St; ⏲7.30am-6pm Mon-Fri, 9am-2pm Sat)

Getting There & Away

Air Botswana (p779) has flights between Maun and Gaborone (from P882) and Kasane (from P369). Flights into the delta are typically arranged by lodges through local air-charter companies.

The bus station for long-distance buses and combis is southwest of the centre. For Gaborone, you'll need to change in Ghanzi or Francistown. Destinations by bus or combi include Francistown (P89.90, five hours), Ghanzi (P63, five hours) and Kasane P96, six hours).

Getting Around

Combis marked 'Maun Route 1' or 'Sedie Route 1' travel every few minutes during daylight hours between the station in town and a stop near Crocodile Camp in Matlapaneng. The standard fare for all local trips is P5.

THE KALAHARI

The parched alter ego of the Okavango Delta, the Kalahari is a primeval landscape. The Tswana call this the Kgalagadi: Land of Thirst. And this is indeed dry, parched country. By some accounts, the Kalahari has the largest volume of sand of any desert on earth.

In addition to the Central Kalahari Game Reserve, **Khutse Game Reserve** and **Kgalagadi Transfrontier Park** are other important Kalahari parks.

Central Kalahari Game Reserve

The dry heart of the dry south of a dry continent, the Central Kalahari Game Reserve (CKGR) is epic in scale and, at all times, awe-inspiring. If remoteness, desert silences and the sound of lions roaring in the night are your thing, this could become one of your favourite places in Africa.

Covering 52,000 sq km (about the size of Denmark), this is one of Africa's largest protected areas. The CKGR is perhaps best known for **Deception Valley**, the site of Mark and Delia Owens' 1974 to 1981 brown hyena and lion study, which is described in their book *Cry of the Kalahari*. Three similar fossil valleys – the **Okwa**, the **Quoxo (Meratswe)** and the **Passarge** – also bring topographical relief to the virtually featureless expanses, although the rivers ceased flowing more than 16,000 years ago.

Kori Campsite CAMPGROUND $
(☎381 0774; dwnp@gov.bw; campsite per person P30) The four campsites known as Kori sit on the hill that rises gently from the western shoreline of Deception Valley. There's plenty of shade and some sites have partial views of the valley.

Piper Pan Campsite CAMPGROUND $
(☎395 3360; www.bigfoottours.co.bw; campsite per adult/child P200/100) Slightly removed from the main circuit in the heart of the reserve, Piper Pan has a wonderfully remote feel and wildlife-watching is good.

Motopi Campsite CAMPGROUND $
(☎395 3360; www.bigfoottours.co.bw; campsite per adult/child P200/100) In the northwestern cor-

WORTH A TRIP

TSODILO HILLS

The Unesco World Heritage–listed Tsodilo Hills rise abruptly from a rippled, oceanlike expanse of desert northwest of Maun and west of the Okavango Panhandle. They are threaded with myth, legend and spiritual significance for the San people, who believe this was the site of Creation. More than 4000 ancient rock paintings and carvings have been discovered at well over 200 sites. The majority of these are attributed to ancestors of today's San people. The hills can be explored along any of five walking trails. Although there are some signposts, most trails require a guide (expect to pay around P50 to P60 for a two- to three-hour hike, or P100 per day) which can be arranged at the Main (Rhino) Camp.

The hills are well signposted off the Sehitwa–Shakawe road with the Tsodilo Hills, along a good gravel track. The turn-off is just south of Nxamasere village. It's around 35km from the main road to the entrance to the site.

CENTRAL KALAHARI GAME RESERVE AT A GLANCE

Gateway towns Ghanzi, Rakops and (at a stretch) Maun

Wildlife In the heart of the park, gemsbok, springbok and bat-eared foxes are common, as are lions, leopards, cheetahs, jackals and brown hyenas.

When to go The park is most easily accessible during the dry season (May to September) when tracks are sandy but easily negotiated by 4WD vehicles. During the rainy season, tracks can be muddy and nearly impassable for inexperienced drivers; watch also for grass seeds clogging engines and searing temperatures in October.

Moving around Unless you're staying at an upmarket lodge or have organised your visit on a mobile safari from Maun, you'll need your own fully equipped 4WD to get around.

Budget safaris As always, Maun is the best place to join a mobile safari into the CKGR.

ner of the reserve, these three campsites are nicely isolated from the rest of the reserve. Nearby Motopi Pan is great for wildlife.

Tau Pan Camp LODGE $$$
(686 1449; www.kwando.co.bw; s/d from US$620/880;) The first camp to be opened within the CKGR, this solar-powered luxury lodge overlooks magnificent Tau Pan from a rugged sand ridge. Wildlife drives and San-led bushwalks are the order of the day and the lodge maintains a strong eco sensibility throughout.

UNDERSTAND BOTSWANA

Botswana Today

By any standards, Botswana's recent history is a lesson to other African countries. Instead of suffering from Africa's oft-seen resource curse, Botswana has used the ongoing windfall from its diamond mines to build a stable and for the most part egalitarian country, one whose economic growth rates have, for decades, been among the highest on earth. This is a place where things work, where education, health and environmental protection are government priorities – even when faced with one of the most serious challenges faced by Africa in the 20th century, HIV/AIDS, the government broke new ground in making antiretroviral treatment available to all.

For all such promising news, Botswana is far from perfect. The government's treatment of the indigenous San people remains a serious concern among human rights activists. In the economic sphere, the country's dependence on diamonds is also a major concern; diamond production is expected to peak and then decline over the next 20 years. The dependence on diamonds makes the economy vulnerable to a fluctuating world economy – when world demand contracted in 2009, so, too, did Botswana's economy (by almost 5%) for the first time in living memory. Impressive growth rates have since returned but the episode remains an important cautionary tale for the government.

History

Pre-Colonial History

Archaeological evidence and rock art found in the Tsodilo Hills suggests the San took shelter in caves throughout the region from around 17,000 BC.

Perhaps the most significant development in Botswana's history was the evolution of the three main branches of the Tswana tribe during the 14th century. It's a King Lear–ish tale of family discord, where three brothers – Kwena, Ngwaketse and Ngwato – broke away from their father, Chief Malope, to establish their own followings in Molepolole, Kanye and Serowe, respectively. These fractures probably occurred in response to drought and expanding populations eager to strike out in search of new pastures and arable land.

Colonial History

From the 1820s the Boers began their Great Trek across the Vaal River; 20,000 Boers crossed into Tswana and Zulu territory and established themselves as though the lands were unclaimed and uninhabited. At the Sand River Convention of 1852, Britain recognised the Transvaal's independence. The Boers informed the undoubtedly surprised Batswana (people of Botswana) that they were now subjects of the South African Republic.

Prominent Tswana leaders Sechele I and Mosielele refused to accept white rule and incurred the wrath of the Boers. By 1877 the British had annexed the Transvaal and launched the first Boer War. In 1882, Boers again moved into Tswana lands and subdued the town of Mafikeng, threatening the British route between the Cape and suspected mineral wealth in Zimbabwe. In 1885, thanks to petitions from John Mackenzie (a friend of the Christian Chief Khama III of Shoshong), lands north of the Molopo River became the British Crown Colony of Bechuanaland, attached to the Cape Colony. The area north became the British Protectorate of Bechuanaland.

A new threat to the Tswana chiefs' power base came from Cecil Rhodes and his British South Africa Company (BSAC). By 1894 the British had all but agreed to allow him to control the country. An unhappy delegation of Tswana chiefs – Bathoen, Khama III and Sebele – accompanied by a sympathetic missionary, WC Willoughby, sailed to England to appeal for continued government control (far less intrusive than Rhodes' proposed rule). Public pressure mounted and the British government was forced to concede.

In 1923, Chief Khama III died and was succeeded by his son Sekgoma, who died only two years later. The heir to the throne, four-year-old Seretse Khama, wasn't ready for the job of ruling the largest Tswana chiefdom, so his 21-year-old uncle, Tshekedi Khama, became clan regent.

After WWII, Seretse Khama went to study in England where he met and married an Englishwoman. Tshekedi Khama was furious at this breach of tribal custom, and apartheid-era South African authorities were none too happy either. The British government blocked Seretse's chieftaincy and he was exiled to England. Bitterness continued until 1956 when Seretse Khama renounced his right to power and returned with his wife to Botswana to serve as a minor official.

Nationalism & Independence

The first signs of nationalist thinking among the Tswana occurred in the late 1940s, and over time it became apparent that Britain was preparing to release its grip on Bechuanaland. In 1962, Seretse Khama and Kanye farmer Quett Masire formed the moderate Bechuanaland Democratic Party (BDP).

The BDP formulated a schedule for independence, drawing on support from local chiefs and traditional Batswana. They promoted the transfer of the capital into the country (from Mafikeng to Gaborone), drafted a new nonracial constitution and set up a countdown to independence to allow a peaceful transfer of power. General elections were held in 1965 and Seretse Khama was elected president. On 30 September 1966, the Republic of Botswana gained independence.

Sir Seretse Khama – he was knighted shortly after independence – adopted a neutral stance (until near the end of his presidency) towards South Africa and Rhodesia (on each of which Botswana was economically dependent). Nevertheless, Khama refused to exchange ambassadors with South Africa and, in international circles, officially disapproved of apartheid.

Botswana was transformed by the discovery of diamonds near Orapa in 1967. The mining concession was given to De Beers, with Botswana taking 75% of the profits. For 40 years the BDP managed the country's diamond windfall relatively wisely. Diamond dollars were ploughed into infrastructure, education and health. Private businesses were allowed to grow and foreign investment was welcomed. From 1966 to 2005, Botswana's economy grew faster than any other in the world.

After the death of Khama in 1980, Dr Ketumile Masire took the helm. His popular presidency ended in March 1998, when president Festus Mogae assumed control of Botswana. He was succeeded in April 2008 by Ian Khama, son of Sir Seretse Khama.

People of Botswana

All citizens of Botswana – regardless of colour, ancestry or tribal affiliation – are known as Batswana (plural) or Motswana (singular). Almost everyone, including members of non-Tswana tribes, communicates via the lingua franca of Tswana, a native language, rather than the official language of English. Alongside language, education has played an important role in building a unified country, and the government proudly claims that its commitment of over 30% of its budget to education is the highest per capita in the world.

The three major tribal groupings are the ethnic Tswana (80% of Botswana's population claims Tswana heritage), the Bakalanga (11%) and the indigenous San (3%).

Arts & Crafts

Botswana is most famous for the basketry produced in the northwestern regions of the Okavango Delta by Wayeyi and Mbukushu women. In the watery environs of the delta the baskets serve as watertight containers for grains, seeds and even beer. All the baskets are made from the leaf fibre of the real fan palm (*mokolane*) and colours are derived from soaking the fibres in natural plant dyes. Traditional San crafts include ostrich-eggshell jewellery, leather aprons and bags, and strands of seeds and nuts (some of which may be not be imported into some countries).

Literature

Botswana's most famous modern literary figure was South African–born Bessie Head (1937–86). Her most widely read work is *Serowe – Village of the Rain Wind*. Since the 1980s Setswana novel writing has enjoyed something of a revival with the publication in English of novels like Andrew Sesinyi's *Love on the Rocks* (1983) and Gaele Sobott-Mogwe's haunting collection of short stories, *Colour Me Blue* (1995). Other novels that lend insight into contemporary Batswana life are *Jamestown Blues* (1997) and *Place of Reeds* (2005) by Caitlin Davies, who was married to a Motswana and lived in Botswana for 12 years. Unity Dow, Botswana's first female High Court judge, has also authored four books to date, all of them dealing with contemporary social issues in the country; we recommend *Far and Beyon'* (2002).

Gaborone may once have been one of the world's lesser known capitals, but Alexander McCall Smith's runaway international success *No. 1 Ladies' Detective Agency* has changed that forever. Based around the exploits of the Motswana Mma Precious Ramotswe, Botswana's first female detective, the book spawned a whole series of novels (13 at last count, plus two novellas for younger readers; see his website for more www.alexandermccallsmith.co.uk) with names like *Morality for Beautiful Girls*, *The Kalahari Typing School for Men* and *The Double Comfort Safari Club*. This is crime -writing without a hard edge, a delightfully whimsical and almost gentle series of tales that seems to fit perfectly within Botswana's relatively peaceful society.

The author was born in Rhodesia (now Zimbabwe) in 1948 and went on to become a leading international expert in medical law. Before turning his hand to crime fiction, he wrote a number of children's books (among them *The White Hippo* and *Akimbo and the Lion*). He lectured at the University of Botswana from 1981 to 1984, but it was not until 1999 that his *No. 1 Ladies' Detective Agency* was published, changing his life forever and putting Botswana on the literary map. Although he lives in Scotland, he has sponsored a number of projects in Botswana, including the No.1 Ladies' Opera House. And if you're a fan of the series, don't miss one of the themed tours of Gaborone (p755).

Environment

With an area of 582,000 sq km, landlocked Botswana extends more than 1100km from north to south and 960km from east to west. The Kalahari Desert covers up to 85% of the country, in the central and southwestern areas – but despite the name, it's semidesert and can be surprisingly lush in places.

Because the Okavango Delta and the Chobe River provide an incongruous water supply, nearly all Southern African mammal species, including such rarities as pukus, red lechwe, sitatungas and African wild dogs, are present in Moremi Wildlife Reserve, parts of Chobe National Park and the Linyanti Marshes (at the northwestern corner of Chobe).

National Parks

Park fees were slated for a significant rise at the time of writing – don't be surprised if they're significantly above those listed here by the time you arrive.

Although there are exceptions (such as the Chobe Riverfront section of Chobe National Park) and it maybe possible on rare occasions to get park rangers to bend the rules, no one is allowed into a national park or reserve without an accommodation booking.

The gates for each DWNP park are open from 6am to 6.30pm (1 April to 30 September) and from 5.30am to 7pm (1 October to 31 March). All visitors must be out of the park, or settled into their campsite, outside of these hours.

SURVIVAL GUIDE

Directory A–Z

ACCOMMODATION

Botswana has fabulously sited campsites for self-drivers (the closest the country comes to budget accommodation) and top-end lodges where prices can be eye-wateringly high. In between, you will find some midrange options in the major towns, but elsewhere there's very little for the midrange (and nothing for the noncamping budget) traveller other than mobile safaris.

Seasons

While most budget and midrange options tend to have a standard room price, many top-end places change their prices according to season. High season is usually from June to November (and may also apply to Christmas, New Year and Easter, depending on the lodge), low season corresponds to the rains (December to March or April) and the shoulder is a short April and May window. The only exception is the Kalahari, where June to November is generally (but not always) considered to be low season.

Campsites

Just about everywhere of interest, including all major national parks, has a campsite. Once the domain of the Department of Wildlife and National Parks (DWNP), most of the campsites are now privately run. All campsites must be booked in advance and they fill up fast in busy periods, such as during South African school holidays; booking details are covered for each campsite throughout this chapter.

ACTIVITIES

Apart from wildlife-viewing and 4WD safaris, some safaris include a hiking component, while other possibilities include elephant or horseback safaris in the Okavango, quad biking on the Makgadikgadi Pans, fishing in the Okavango Panhandle, or scenic flights from Maun.

Travelling around the channels of the Okavango Delta in a *mokoro* (dugout canoe) is a wonderful experience that is not to be missed. The *mokoro* is poled along the waterways by a skilled poler, much like an African gondola.

EMBASSIES & CONSULATES

British Embassy (Map p759; ☎395 2841; www.ukinbotswana.fco.gov.uk/en/; Queens Rd, Gaborone; ⏲8am-12.30pm & 1.30-4.30pm Mon-Thu, to 1pm Fri)

French Embassy (Map p759; ☎397 3863; www.ambafrance-bw.org; 761 Robinson Rd, Gaborone; ⏲8am-4pm Mon-Fri)

German Embassy (☎395 3143; www.gaborone.diplo.de; Segoditshane Way, 3rd fl, Professional House, Broadhurst Mall, Gaborone; ⏲9am-noon Mon-Fri)

Namibian Embassy (Map p758; ☎390 2181; nhc.gabs@info.bw; Plot 186, Morara Close, Gaborone; ⏲7.30am-1pm & 2-4.30pm Mon-Fri)

South African Embassy (Map p759; ☎390 4800; 29 Queens Rd, Gaborone; ⏲8am-12.45pm & 1.30-4.30pm Mon-Fri)

US Embassy (Map p758; ☎355 3982; Embassy Dr, Gaborone; ⏲2-4:30pm Tue & Thu)

Zambian Embassy (Map p759; ☎395 1951; Plot No 1118 Queens Rd, the Mall, Gaborone; ⏲8.30am-12.30pm & 2-4.30pm Mon-Fri)

Zimbabwean Embassy (Map p758; ☎391 4495; www.zimgaborone.gov.zw; Plot 8850, Orapa Close, Government Enclave, Gaborone; ⏲8am-1pm & 2-4.30pm Mon-Fri)

> **PRACTICALITIES**
>
> - **Electricity** Two types of plugs are used; the South African type, with three round pins, and the UK type, with three square pins. Current is 220/240V, 50Hz.
> - **Languages** Tswana, English
> - **Radio** Yarona (106.6FM) and GABZFM (96.2FM) broadcast around Gaborone. RB2 (103FM) is the commercial network of Radio Botswana.

MAPS

The best paper map of Botswana is the *Botswana* (1:1,000,000) map published by **Tracks4Africa** (www.tracks4africa.co.za). Updated every couple of years using detailed traveller feedback, the map is printed on tear-free, waterproof paper and includes distances and estimated travel times. Used in conjunction with their unrivalled GPS maps, it's far and away the best mapping product on the market. Even so, be aware that, particularly in the Okavango Delta, last year's trails may this year be underwater depending on water levels, so these maps should never be a substitute for expert local knowledge.

MONEY

Botswana's unit of currency is the pula (P), which is divided into 100 thebe. 'Pula' means 'rain' – a valuable commodity in this desert land.

Full banking services are available only in major towns, although ATMs are sprouting up all over the country. Most credit cards are accepted at hotels and restaurants, and cash advances are available at major banks (but not through ATMs).

OPENING HOURS

Reviews in this chapter won't list business hours unless they differ significantly from the following standards. The whole country practically closes down on Sunday.

Banks Barclays 8.30am to 3.30pm Monday to Friday, 8.15am to 10.45am Saturday; Standard Chartered Bank 8.30am to 3.30pm Monday to Friday, 8.15am to 11am Saturday

National parks 6am to 6.30pm April to September, 5.30am to 7pm October to March

Post offices 9am to 5pm Monday to Friday, 9am to noon Saturday, or 7.30am to noon, and 2pm to 4.30pm Monday to Friday, 7.30am to 12.30pm Saturday

Restaurants 11am to 11pm Monday to Saturday; some also open the same hours on Sunday

PUBLIC HOLIDAYS

As well as religious holidays listed in the Africa Directory, the following are the principal public holidays in Botswana:

New Year's Day 1 January

Day after New Year's Day 2 January

Labour Day 1 May

Ascension Day April or May (40 days after Easter)

Sir Seretse Khama Day 1 July

President's Day 3rd Friday of July

Botswana/Independence Day 30 September

Day after Independence Day 1 October

TELEPHONE

Botswana has two main mobile (cell) phone networks, **Mascom Wireless** (www.mascom.bw) and **Orange Botswana** (www.orange.co.bw), of which Mascom is by far the largest provider. Both providers have dealers where you can buy phones, SIM cards and top up your credit in most large and medium-sized towns. The coverage map for these two providers is improving with each passing year, but there's simply no mobile coverage across large swaths of the country (including much of the Kalahari and Okavango Delta). The main highway system is generally covered.

> **CHANGING MONEY AT THE BORDER**
>
> A word of warning: if you're changing money at or near border posts and not doing so through the banks, be aware that local businesses (sometimes bureaus de change, sometimes just shops with a sideline in currencies so that arriving travellers can pay their customs duties) usually have abysmal rates. Change the minimum that you're likely to need and change the rest at a bank or bureau de change in the nearest large town.

There are no internal area codes in Botswana. The country code is ☎267 and the international access code is ☎00.

TOURIST INFORMATION

The Department of Tourism, rebranded in the public sphere as **Botswana Tourism** (www.botswanatourism.co.bw) has an excellent website and a growing portfolio of tourist offices around the country; we list some of these throughout this chapter. These tourist offices don't always have their finger on the pulse, but they can be an extremely useful source of brochures from local hotels, tour operators and other tourist services.

For information on national parks, you're better off contacting the Department of Wildlife and National Parks (p759). Another useful resource is the **Regional Tourism Organisation of Southern Africa** (☎ in South Africa 011-315 2420; www.retosa.co.za), which promotes tourism throughout Southern Africa, including Botswana.

VISAS

Most visitors can obtain tourist visas at the international airports and borders (and the nearest police stations in lieu of an immigration official at remote border crossings). Visas on arrival are valid for 30 days – and possibly up to 90 days if requested at the time of entry – and are available for free to passport holders from most Commonwealth countries (but not Ghana, India, Nigeria, Pakistan and Sri Lanka), all EU countries, the USA, and countries in the Southern African Customs Union (SACU), ie South Africa, Namibia, Lesotho and Swaziland. If you hold a passport from any other country, apply for a 30-day tourist visa at an overseas Botswanan embassy or consulate.

Getting There & Away

ENTERING THE COUNTRY

Entering Botswana is usually straightforward provided you are carrying a valid passport. Visas are available on arrival for most nationalities and are issued in no time.

If you're crossing into the country overland and in your own (or rented) vehicle, expect to endure (sometimes quite cursory) searches for fresh meat, fresh fruit and dairy products, most of which will be confiscated if found. For vehicles rented in South Africa, Namibia or another regional country, you will need to show a letter from the owner that you have permission to drive the car into Botswana, in addition to all other registration documents.

At border crossings, arriving travellers are often requested to clean their shoes – even those packed away in their luggage – in a disinfectant dip to prevent them carrying foot-and-mouth disease into the country. Vehicles must also pass through a pit filled with the same disinfectant.

RENTING A 4WD IN SOUTH AFRICA

Renting in South Africa is almost invariably cheaper and more reliable than doing so in Botswana, even accounting for the extra distance you'll need to drive just to get into Botswana. While you could rent from one of the mainstream car-rental agencies, there are some specialist 4WD operators that can set you up perfectly for almost any self-drive expedition into Botswana. You may be able to arrange to pick up the vehicle within Botswana itself, but this will, of course, cost extra.

On our most recent research trip we used a 4WD Land Rover Defender camper from **Explorer Safaris** (www.explorersafaris.co.za). All of their vehicles are two years old or less and are fitted with a fold-out camper, rooftop tent, gas cookers, a fridge and all necessary camping equipment. Rates start at ZAR995 and go up to ZAR1575 per day, depending on the vehicle and the duration of the rental period, plus petrol and insurance. Booked in conjunction with **Drive Botswana** (☎ in Palapye 492 3416; www.drivebotswana.com).

Other South African companies that rent 4WDs with camping equipment include: **Around About Cars** (www.aroundaboutcars.com), **Britz** (www.britz.co.za) and **Buffalo Campers** (www.buffalo.co.za).

At all border posts you must pay P120 (a combination of road levy and third-party insurance) if you're driving your own vehicle. Hassles from officialdom are rare.

AIR

Botswana has three main airports, in Gaborone, Maun and Kasane.

The national carrier is **Air Botswana** (BP; ☎ 390 5500; www.airbotswana.co.bw), which flies routes within Southern Africa. Air Botswana has offices in **Gaborone** (☎ 368 0900; Matstitam Rd; ⊙ 9.30am-5pm Mon-Fri, 8.30-11.30am Sat), **Francistown** (☎ 241 2393; Francis Ave), **Maun** (☎ 686 0391), **Kasane** (☎ 625 0161) and Victoria Falls (Zimbabwe). It's generally cheaper to book Air Botswana tickets online than it is through one of their offices.

The only scheduled international flights into Botswana come from Jo'burg and Cape Town (South Africa), Victoria Falls and Harare (Zimbabwe), Lusaka (Zambia) and Windhoek (Namibia). Airlines flying into the country include **South African Airways** (☎ in Gaborone 397 2397; www.flysaa.com) and **Air Namibia** (☎ in Maun 686 0391; www.airnamibia.com).

LAND

Overland travel to or from Botswana is usually straightforward as most travellers either arrive by private vehicle or by **Intercape Mainliner** (☎ 397 4294, in South Africa ☎ 021-380 4400; www.intercape.co.za) from South Africa.

The main border crossings into Botswana are as follows:

- From South Africa (14 crossings) – Martin's Drift (from Northern Transvaal), Tlokweng, Pioneer Gate and Ramatlabama (from Mafikeng).
- From Namibia (five) – Mamuno, Mohembo and Ngoma Bridge.
- From Zimbabwe (three) – Kazungula and Ramokgweban/Plumtree.
- From Zambia (one) – Kazungula River Ferry.

Getting Around

AIR

Air Botswana operates scheduled domestic flights between Gaborone, Francistown, Maun and Kasane.

CAR & MOTORCYCLE

The best way to travel around Botswana is to hire a vehicle. With your own car you can avoid public transport and organised tours. Remember, however, that distances are long and we generally recommend that you rent a vehicle outside the country (preferably South Africa) where the range of choice is greater and prices are generally lower.

Botswana's main roads are generally decent, but most of your driving will be off-road. When driving anywhere, look out for donkeys and cattle. Main highways are thick with livestock, plus other (larger) animals like elephants and kudu (if you hit one of these you're really screwed).

Your home driving licence is valid for six months in Botswana, but if it isn't written in English you must provide a certified translation. In any case, it is advisable to obtain an International Driving Permit (IDP). Your national automobile association can issue this and it is valid for 12 months.

LOCAL TRANSPORT

Public transport in Botswana is confined to main roads between major population centres. Although cheap and reliable, it is of little use to the traveller as most of Botswana's tourist attractions are off the beaten track.

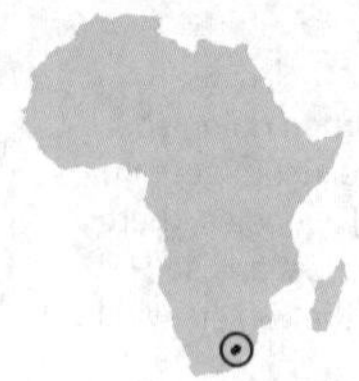

Lesotho

POP 1.8 MILLION

Includes ➡

Best Things to Do

- Ramabanta (p785)
- Thaba-Bosiu (p784)
- Quthing (p787)

Best Places to Stay

- Malealea Lodge (p786)
- Maliba Mountain Lodge (p790)
- Semonkong Lodge (p786)

Why Go?

Lesotho (le-*soo*-too) is a vastly underrated travel destination. It's beautiful, culturally rich, safe, cheap and easily accessible from Durban and Johannesburg. The hiking and trekking – often on a famed Basotho pony – is world class and and the national parks' infrastructure continues to improve, and getting around is reasonably easy.

The 1000m-high 'lowlands' are the scene of low-key Lesotho life, with good craft shopping around Teyateyaneng and Maseru. But be sure to head to the valleys and mountains, where streams traverse an ancient dinosaur playground.

Lesotho came into being during the early 19th century, when the *difaqane* (forced migration) and Boer incursions into the hinterlands were at their height. Under the leadership of the legendary king, Moshoeshoe the Great, the Basotho people sought sanctuary and strategic advantage in the forbidding terrain of the Drakensberg and Maluti ranges.

When to Go

Maseru

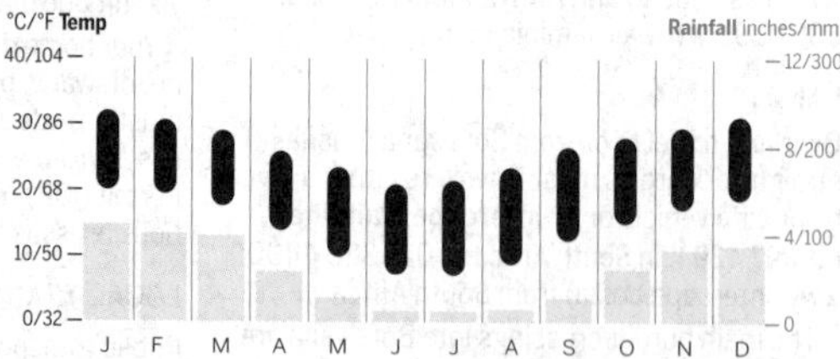

Sep Celebrate Lesotho culture at the renowned Morija Arts & Cultural Festival.

Dec–Jan Feel the full force of Maletsunyane, the magnificent waterfall near Semonkong.

Year-Round Experience year-round contrasting temperatures in the highlands and lowlands.

MASERU

POP 430,000 (MASERU DISTRICT)

Ever-expanding, bustling Maseru has a modest array of modern amenities and few sights, but it's a useful place to stock up on supplies before heading into the highlands.

Sights

Many sights in Lesotho, including Thaba-Bosiu and craft shops in and around Teyateyaneng, are easily accessible from the capital.

Catholic Cathedral CHURCH

The impressive Catholic cathedral, near the Circle at the end of Kingsway, is Maseru's main landmark.

Sleeping

Maseru Backpackers & Conference Centre BACKPACKERS $

(☎2232 5166; www.maserubackpackers.com; Airport Rd; per person r M140) The best budget choice, which is run by a British NGO, has sparse, clean backpackers' dorms, twins and doubles. It's 3km from the city centre, but accessible by public transport.

Black Swan B&B GUESTHOUSE $$

(☎2231 7700; www.blackswan.co.ls; 770 Manong Rd, New Europa; s/d M450/650;) The Black Swan makes a smart little refuge in a quiet suburb. Well-kept rooms, lap pool and small gym are a nice touch.

Lesotho Sun HOTEL $$$

(☎2224 3000; www.suninternational.com; r M1505; @) The moderately radiant Sun is a punter's paradise perched on a hill. It boasts the ubiquitous casino and offers a modern motel experience.

Eating & Drinking

Self-caterers should head to the well-stocked supermarket **Shoprite** in the Sefika Mall and **LNDC Centre**.

Good Times Cafe DINER $

(Kingsway, Level 1, LNDC Centre; mains M25-60; breakfast, lunch & dinner) Lesotho's rich, famous, young and beautiful gather here with a small expat community for a diner-style menu.

Regal INDIAN $$

(☎2231 3930; Kingsway, Level 1, Basotho Hat; mains M45-85; lunch & dinner;) Regal serves surprisingly delicious British-style Indian food at the smartest restaurant in town. It's a boon for vegetarians.

SET YOUR BUDGET

Budget

- Hotel room less than M400 (double)
- Two-course dinner M60
- Coffee M10–18
- Local bus ride from M10

Midrange

- Hotel room M400–1000 (double)
- Two-course dinner M120
- Beer in bar M10
- Taxi ride Around M5 per kilometre

Top End

- Hotel room more than M1000 (double)
- Two-course dinner from M180
- Glass of wine M20
- Overnight horse trek M380

Information

The top-end hotels will change currency (at poor rates). The main banks are all on Kingsway.

Nedbank (Kingsway) Does foreign-exchange transactions Monday to Friday.

Post office (cnr Kingsway & Palace Rd) Maseru's main post office.

Standard Bank (Kingsway) Has an ATM.

Tourist information office (☎2231 2427; Maseru Bridge Border Post; 8am-5pm Mon-Fri, 8.30am-1pm Sat) Managed by the Lesotho Tourism Development Corporation, the office at Maseru Bridge Border Post has information on all of Lesotho's major tourist areas, plus maps and transport tips.

DANGERS & ANNOYANCES

Maseru is fairly safe but muggings and crime are on the increase; always take a taxi at night, when the city and streets are deserted.

Getting There & Away

The hectic bus and minibus taxi departure points are in and around the Pitso Ground (and nearby streets) to the northeast of the Circle. To avoid feeling overwhelmed by the throngs of people and buses, check first with the tourist office for specific departure points.

The **Shoprite Money Market** kiosk in the LNDC Centre sells bus tickets, including those for Greyhound and Intercape.

Lesotho Highlights

1. Experiencing a unique lodge-village experience at **Semonkong** (p786), **Malealea** (p786), **Roma** (p785) or **Ramabanta** (p785).
2. Hiking the challenging wilderness hikes of the northern highlands and absorbing the awesome vistas from **Sani Pass** and **Sani Top** (p787).
3. Revelling in the nature and hikes (and luxury lodge) of the underrated wilderness of **Ts'ehlanyane National Park** (p790).
4. Hiking from Semonkong in the beautiful Thaba Putsoa mountains to the **Ketane Falls** (p786).
5. Climbing **Thaba-Bosiu** (p784) a place of pilgrimage outside Maseru.
6. Stomping for dinosaur prints in **Quthing** (p787).

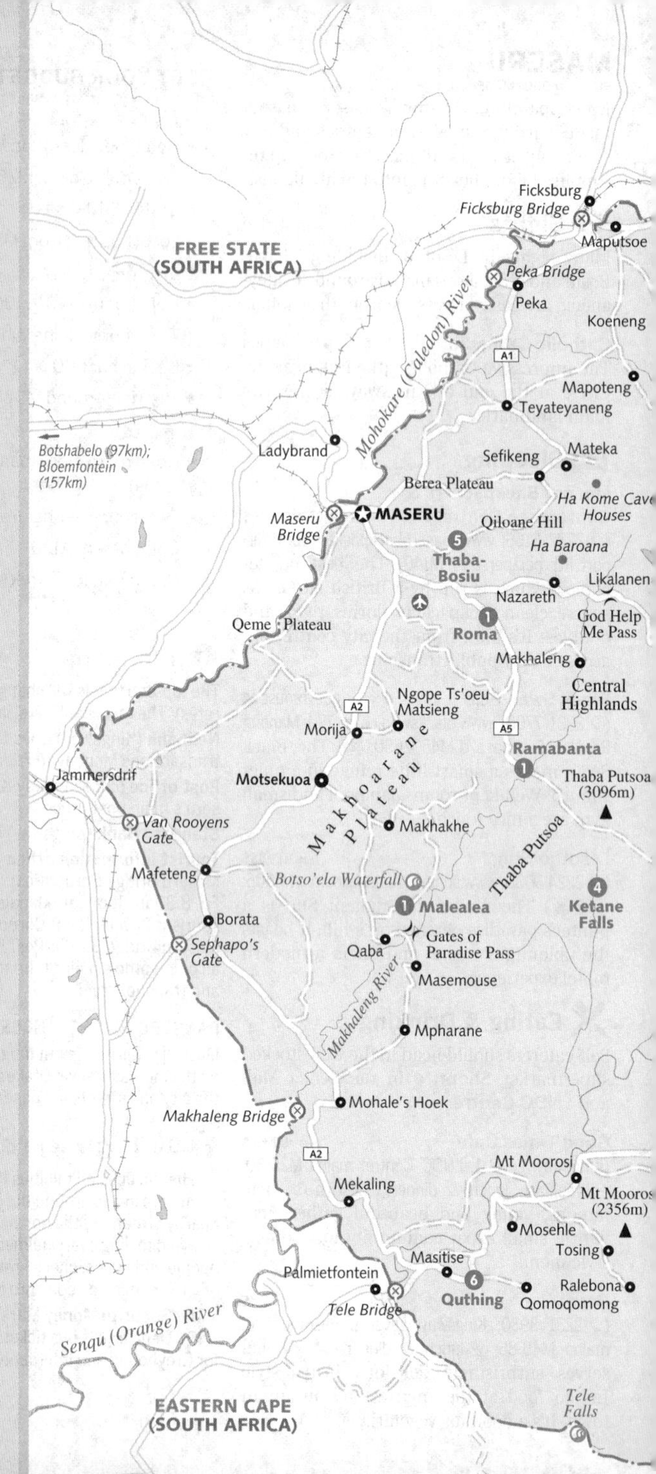

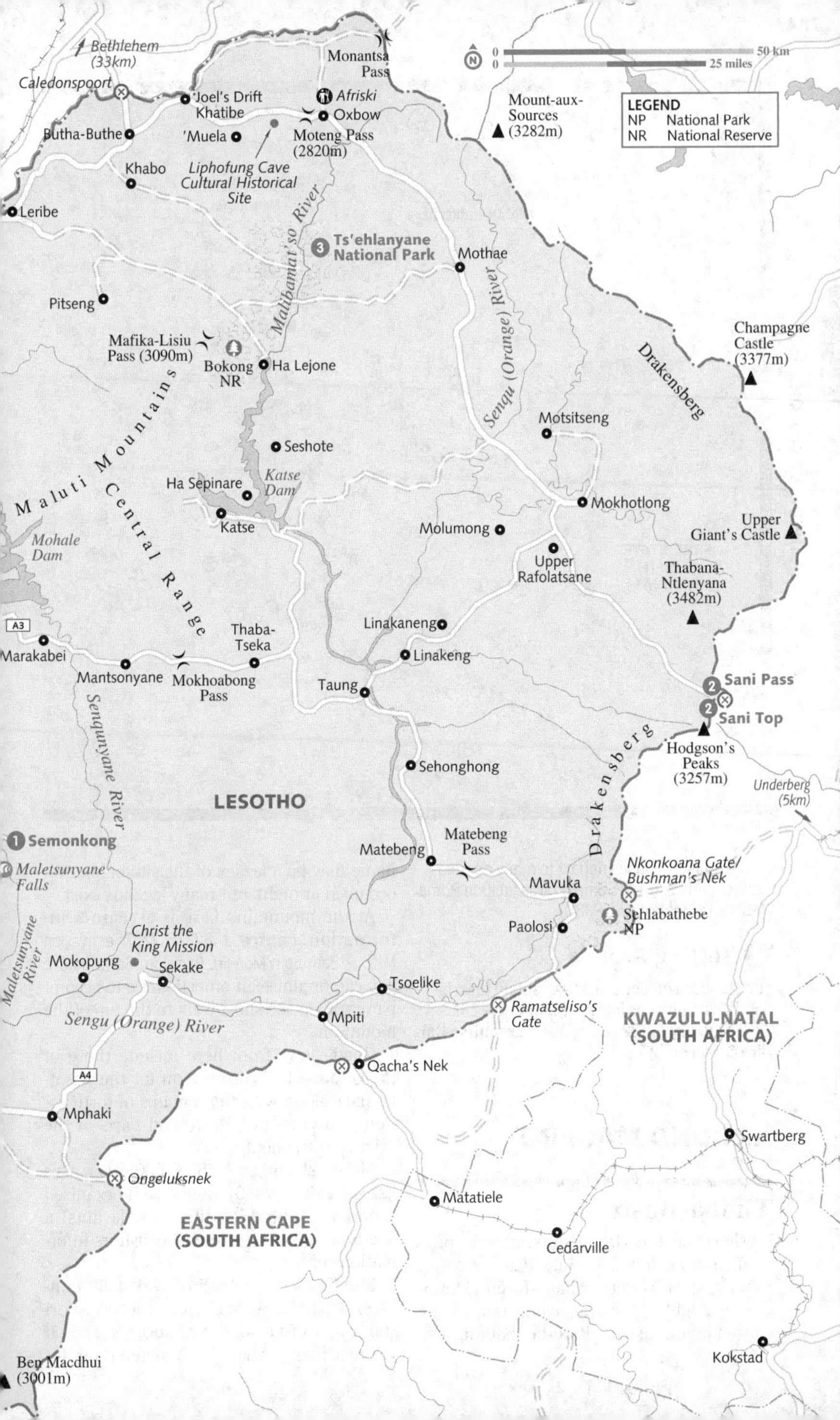

Bethlehem (33km)
Caledonspoort
Monantsa Pass
0 50 km
0 25 miles
LEGEND
NP National Park
NR National Reserve
Joel's Drift
Khatibe
Afriski
Oxbow
Mount-aux-Sources (3282m)
Butha-Buthe
'Muela
Moteng Pass (2820m)
Khabo
Liphofung Cave Cultural Historical Site
Leribe
Malibamat'so River
3 Ts'ehlanyane National Park
Mothae
Sengu (Orange) River
Pitseng
Champagne Castle (3377m)
Drakensberg
Mafika-Lisiu Pass (3090m)
Bokong NR
Ha Lejone
Maluti Mountains
Motsitseng
Seshote
Central Range
Katse Dam
Ha Sepinare
Katse
Mokhotlong
Mohale Dam
Molumong
Upper Giant's Castle
Upper Rafolatsane
Thabana-Ntlenyana (3482m)
A3
Marakabei
Thaba-Tseka
Linakaneng
Linakeng
Mantsonyane
Mokhoabong Pass
Taung
2 Sani Pass
2 Sani Top
Hodgson's Peaks (3257m)
Senqunyane River
Sehonghong
LESOTHO
Underberg (5km)
1 Semonkong
Maletsunyane Falls
Matebeng
Matebeng Pass
Drakensberg
Nkonkoana Gate/ Bushman's Nek
Mavuka
Sehlabathebe NP
Paolosi
Christ the King Mission
Maletsunyane River
Mokopung
Sekake
Tsoelike
Ramatseliso's Gate
Sengu (Orange) River
Mpiti
KWAZULU-NATAL (SOUTH AFRICA)
A4
Qacha's Nek
Mphaki
Swartberg
Ongeluksnek
Matatiele
EASTERN CAPE (SOUTH AFRICA)
Cedarville
Kokstad
Ben Macdhui (3001m)

Maseru

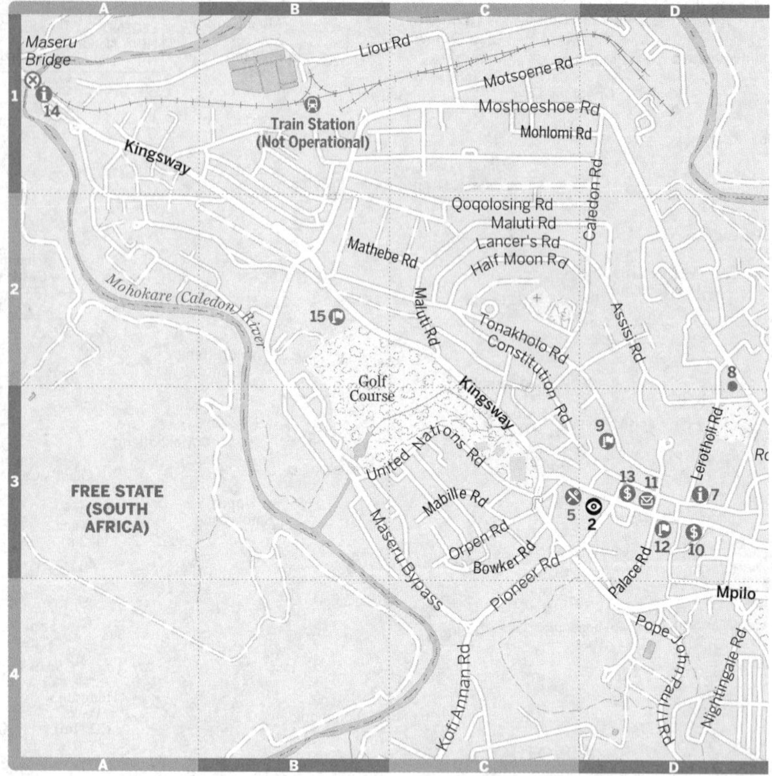

From Maseru, buses depart to many destinations within Lesotho. Sample fares include Roma (M18) and Mokhotlong (M80).

Getting Around

The standard minibus taxi fare around town is M4. Taxi companies include **Planet** (2231 7777), **Luxury** (2232 6211) and **Executive Car Hire & Travel** (2231 4460).

AROUND MASERU

Thaba-Bosiu

Moshoeshoe the Great's mountain stronghold, first occupied in July 1824, is about 16km east of Maseru. Thaba-Bosiu (Mountain at Night) played a pivotal role in the consolidation of the Basotho nation. The name may be a legacy of the site being first occupied at night, but many legends exist.

At the mountain's base is a **visitors information centre** (2835 7207; admission M10; 8am-5pm Mon-Fri, 9am-1pm Sat), where you can organise an official guide to accompany you on the short walk to the top of the mountain.

Good views from here include those of the **Qiloane Hill** (inspiration for the Basotho hat), along with the remains of fortifications, Moshoeshoe's grave and parts of the original settlement.

Mmelesi Lodge (5250 0006; www.mmelesilodge.co.ls; r M400) offers well-organised *rondavels* (round, traditional-style huts) a few hundred metres from the visitors information centre.

Minibuses to Thaba-Bosiu (M10, 30 minutes) depart from Maseru at the transport stand at **Sefika Mall transport stand**. If you're driving, take the Mafeteng Rd for

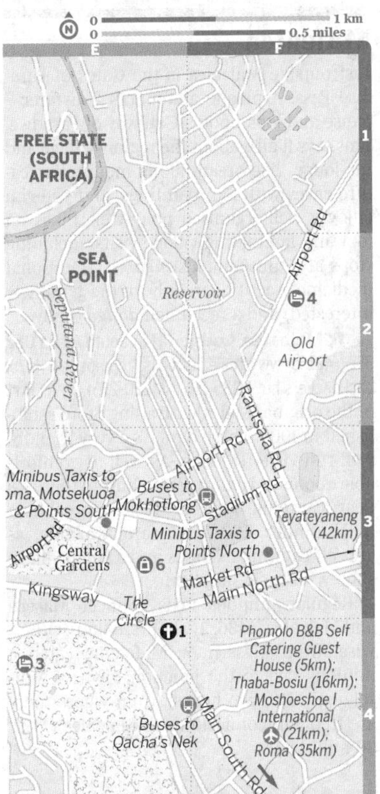

Maseru

Sights

1 Catholic Cathedral E4
2 LNDC Centre D3

Sleeping

3 Lesotho Sun E4
4 Maseru Backpackers & Conference Centre F2

Eating

Good Times Cafe .... (see 2)
LNDC Centre .... (see 2)
5 Regal C3

Shopping

6 Shoprite/Sefika Mall E3

Information

7 Department of Land, Surveys & Physical Planning D3
8 Director of Immigration & Passport Services D2
9 Irish Embassy D3
10 Nedbank D3
11 Post Office D3
Shoprite Money Market .... (see 2)
12 South African High Commission D3
13 Standard Bank D3
14 Tourist Information Office A1
15 US Embassy B2

about 13km and turn left at the Roma turn-off; ask for directions.

SOUTHERN LESOTHO

Roma & Around

Getting to Roma is half the fun, as it is reached through a spectacular gorge south of Maseru. After that there's not a lot to do, but this university town features attractive sandstone buildings. Roma Trading Post Guest House can point you in the right direction for activities.

A charming fifth-generation trading post operated since 1903 by the Thorn family, the **Roma Trading Post Guest House** (2234 0202, 082-773 2180; www.tradingpost.co.za; campsites per person M75, dm M125, r per person M175, s with half board M375;) includes garden rooms, *rondavels* and the original sandstone homestead set in a lush garden. Pony trekking, hiking, 4WD trails and even *minwane* (dinosaur footprints) are nearby attractions.

About 40km further along and owned by the same crew is **Ramabanta Guest House** (2234 0267; tradingpost@leo.co.ls; campsites per person M100, dm per person M150, rondavel with half board per person M440), which has 'to die for' views.

Minibus taxis run throughout the day to/from Maseru (M18, 30 minutes).

Morija

Morija is a tiny town with a big history. **Morija Museum & Archives** (2236 0308; www.morijafestival.wordpress.com; admission M10; 8am-5pm Mon-Sat, noon-5pm Sun), the best museum in Lesotho, has Basotho ethnographic exhibits. It also hosts the annual Morija Arts & Cultural Festival.

Morija Guest House (6306 5093; www.morijaguesthouses.com; r per person without bathroom M210-245) offers a range of excellent

ℹ TRANSPORT

There are three main transport stands to the northeast of the main roundabout: behind Sefi ka Mall (also called new taxi rank) for minibus taxis to Roma (M12), and points south including Motsekuoa (M13, for Malealea); just off Main North Rd near Pitso Ground for minibus taxis to points north; and, about a block away from here, reached via the same turn-off, for large Lesotho Freight Service buses to points south and north. Lesotho Freight Service buses to Mokhotlong (M80) depart from Stadium Rd behind Pitso Ground, while those to Qacha's Nek (M100) depart from next to St James Primary and High Schools on Main Rd South.

sleeping options – with views to match. **Lindy's B&B** (☎5885 5309; www.lindysbnb.co.ls; room in modern house per person M180, room in historic home per person M220) is another appealing option.

Minibus taxis run throughout the day between Maseru and Morija (M13, 45 minutes, 40km).

Semonkong

This place, in the lofty Thaba Putsoa range, is as beautiful as its name. The Maletsunyane Falls are a 90-minute walk from Semonkong (Place of Smoke). They are more than 200m high and are at their most spectacular in summer. For a thrilling descent, Semonkong Lodge offers abseiling (per person in a group of one/two/three or more M850/750/700).

The remote 122m-high **Ketane Falls** are an exciting day trip (30km one way) from Semonkong, or a four-day return horse ride from Malealea Lodge.

Semonkong Lodge (☎266 2700 6037, 6202 1021; www.placeofsmoke.co.ls; campsites per person M60, dm/s/d M100/395/660, rondavels s/d M465/720) is a model of community tourism and is an enchanting place. It has an excellent restaurant, and offers village tours, a pub crawl on donkey-back, hiking and pony trekking.

Buses between Maseru and Semonkong (M110) leave from both places in the morning, and arrive in the late afternoon.

Malealea

Just outside Malealea is the Gates of Paradise Pass. A plaque announces 'Wayfarer – pause and look upon a Gateway of Paradise'. This says it all – about the region, village and the lodge. The breathtaking mountains feature caves with San paintings, and you can enjoy a well-organised pony trek, hikes on foot and fascinating village visits, including stops at a museum, a *sangoma* (traditional medicine practitioner; only for the genuinely interested) and a reclaimed *donga* (gully).

★**Malealea Lodge** (☎in South Africa 082 552 4215; www.malealea.co.ls; campsites M75, backpackers hut M135-155, r M220-275) was part of the original Malealea Trading Store established in 1905. These days it's a very friendly, well-run visitors' lodge. As well as comfortable rooms – *rondavels* or huts – there's a neat camping ground. Meals (breakfast/lunch/dinner E60/70/95) are available, as are self-catering facilities and a small village shop with basic supplies.

Regular minibus taxis connect Maseru and Malealea (M36, 2½ hours, 83km). Otherwise, from Maseru or Mafeteng, catch a minibus taxi to the junction town of Motsekuoa (M13, two hours), from where there are frequent connections to Malealea (M22, 30 minutes).

CRAFTY DAY TRIP FROM MASERU

Referred to as 'TY', Teyateyaneng (Place of Quick Sands) has been developed as the craft centre of Lesotho. Tapestry workshops include **Helang Basali Crafts** (⏲8am-5pm) at St Agnes Mission, about 2km before Teyateyaneng; Setsoto Design, near Blue Mountain Inn; and Hatooa Mose Mosali, diagonally opposite Elelloang Basali Weavers, which is 100m before Agnes Mission. **Leribe Craft Centre** (☎2240 0323; ⏲8am-4.30pm Mon-Fri, 9.30am-1pm Sat) in Leribe also sells a range of high-quality mohair goods. To get to both places, minibus taxis run throughout the day from Maseru (from the bus stop just off Main North Rd near Pitso Ground). The Maseru-Teyateyaneng leg takes around 45 minutes (M14) while for Leribe (M25, 1.5 hours) you might need to change buses at Maputsoe.

Quthing

Quthing, the southernmost town in Lesotho, is often known as Moyeni (Place of the Wind). It was established in 1877, abandoned three years later and then rebuilt at the present site.

About 1.5km off the highway, 5km west of Quthing, is the intriguing **Masitise Cave House Museum** (☎5879 4167; admission by donation), built into a San rock shelter in 1866 by Reverend Ellenberger. Ask for the key from the local pastor in the house next to the church. There are San paintings nearby.

Between Quthing and Masitise there is a striking **twin-spired sandstone church**, part of the Villa Maria Mission.

Quthing's other claim to fame is a proliferation of **dinosaur footprints**. The most easily accessible are just off the main road to Mt Moorosi; watch for the small, pink building to your left. These footprints are believed to be 180 million years old.

At Qomoqomong, 10km from Quthing, there's a good gallery of **San paintings**; ask at the General Dealers store about a guide for the 20-minute walk to the paintings.

Fuleng Guest House (☎2275 0260; r per person M280-350), in Upper Quthing, offers excellent-value rooms, plus a friendly local experience. **Moorosi Chalets** (☎in South Africa 082 552 4215; www.moorosichalets.com; campsites M60, rondavel per person M175-225, hut without bathroom per person M150, self-catering house per person M150) is part of a community program that has awesome activities, ranging from village stays to fishing. It is located 6km from Mt Moorosi village; take the turnoff to Ha Moqalo 2km out of the village towards Qacha's Nek.

Minibus taxis run daily between Quthing and Maseru (M65, 3½ hours) and Qacha's Nek (M75, three hours).

EASTERN LESOTHO

Qacha's Nek

This pleasant town was founded in 1888 as a mission station near the pass (1980m) of the same name. It has an attractive church, colonial-era sandstone buildings and California redwood trees.

Hotel Nthatuoa (☎2295 0260; incl breakfast s M320-460, d M400-550) has simple rooms.

Minibus taxis go from Qacha's Nek to Maseru via Quthing (M110, six hours). A daily bus runs between Maseru and Qacha's Nek (M110, nine hours); another between Qacha's Nek and Sehlabathebe National Park departs Qacha's Nek around noon (M35, five hours).

Sani Top

Sani Top sits atop steep Sani Pass, the only dependable (albeit winding) road into Lesotho through the uKhahlamba-Drakensberg mountain range in KwaZulu-Natal. It offers stupendous views on clear days and unlimited hiking possibilities.

From the Sani Top Chalet at the top of the pass there are several day walks, including a long and arduous trek to Thabana-Ntlenyana (3482m), the highest peak in Southern Africa. A guide is advisable.

Hodgson's Peaks (3257m) is a much easier hike 6km south, from where you can see into Sehlabathebe National Park and KwaZulu-Natal.

Other hikes in this area are outlined in the excellent *A Backpackers' Guide to Lesotho* by Russell Suchet, available through the Morija Museum or Sani Lodge at Sani Pass.

At 2874m, **Sani Top Chalet** (☎in South Africa 033-702 1158; www.sanitopchalet.co.za; campsites per person M80, dm M150, rondavel s/d M650/1000) stakes a peculiar claim to the highest drinking hole in Southern Africa. Booze trivia aside, cosy *rondavels* and excellent meals reward those who make the steep ascent. Backpackers doss down the road. In winter, the snow is sometimes deep enough for skiing; pony trekking can be arranged with advance notice.

A minibus taxi runs daily from Mokhotlong via Sani Top down to Underberg (South Africa) and back (five hours). From Butha-Buthe (north) taxis cost M53. If you're driving, you'll need a 4WD to go on the pass. The border crossings are open 6am to 6pm daily. Note: allow enough time at either end and check the border times – they do change.

Mokhotlong

Mokhotlong (Place of the Bald Ibis) is 270km from Maseru and is the first major town north of Sani Pass. It has an appealing

Wild West feel to it thanks to the locals – sporting Basotho blankets – on their horses.

Sleeping

Molumong Guesthouse & Backpackers BACKPACKERS $
(in South Africa 033-394 3072; www.molumonglodge.com; campsites per person M80, s/d M150/300) This is a rustic lodge and former colonial trading post, about 15km southwest of Mokhotlong. It's a basic (electricity-free) self-catering stay. Pony trekking is a feature.

St James Lodge LODGE $
(071-672 6801, in South Africa 033-326 1601; www.stjameslodgeco.za; r per person M100-200) This working mission is a humble yet somehow stylish place to say (note: it's self catering). Pony trekking and scenic walks are available. It's 12km south of Mokhotlong on the road to Thaba-Tseka.

Senqu Hotel HOTEL $
(2292 0330; s M260-320, d M320-380) This is 2.5km from the buses on the western end of town.

Grow HOSTEL $
(2292 0205; dm R90) A Lesotho-registered development office with basic dorms and a simple kitchen.

Getting There & Away

Public transport runs to/from Butha-Buthe (M55, six hours), Maseru (M90, eight hours), Linakaneng (for Molumong Guesthouse & Backpackers; M35) and Sani Top (M75).

UNDERSTAND LESOTHO

Lesotho Today

Lesotho ranks among the region's poorer countries, and has few natural resources. During the last century, Lesotho's main export was labour – approximately 60% of males worked outside the country, mainly in mining in South Africa. In the late 1990s the restructuring of the South African gold-mining industry, mechanisation and the closure of mines resulted in massive job losses. Meanwhile, the Lesotho economy – which was under transformation due to the rapid growth of the textile industry – collapsed.

Many hope that economic initiatives, such as the Economic Partnership Agreement (EPA), signed with the EU in 2007 to create free trade zones, will help revive the local business sector.

Meanwhile, the spectre of HIV/AIDS is high but has stabilised in recent years. The infection rate (adult prevalence) is estimated at 24%.

In June 2012 Thomas Thabane, a former foreign minister and leader of the ABC (All Basotho Convention), the biggest opposition party, was appointed prime minister. He heads a coalition government along with two opposition parties, the Lesotho Congress for Democracy (LCD) and the Basotho National Party (BNP).

History

Neighbouring South Africa has always cast a long shadow over Lesotho, fuelling a perpetual struggle for a separate identity on an ever-diminishing patch of territory.

The first inhabitants of the mountainous region that makes up present-day Lesotho were the hunter-gatherer people known as the Khoisan. They have left many examples of their rock art in the river valleys. Lesotho was settled by the Sotho peoples in the 16th century.

Moshoeshoe the Great

King Moshoeshoe (pronounced 'mo-shwe-shwe' or 'mo-shesh') is the father figure of Lesotho's history. In about 1820, while a local chief of a small village, he led his villagers to Butha-Buthe, a mountain stronghold, where they survived the first battles of the *difaqane*, caused by the violent expansion of the nearby Zulu state. The loosely organised southern Sotho society managed to survive due largely to the adept political and diplomatic abilities of the king. In 1824 Moshoeshoe moved his people to Thaba-Bosiu, a mountaintop that was even easier to defend.

From Thaba-Bosiu, Moshoeshoe played a patient game of placating the stronger local rulers and granting protection, as well as land and cattle, to refugees. These people were to form Basutholand; at the time of Moshoeshoe's death in 1870, Basutoland had a population of more than 150,000.

As the *difaqane* receded a new threat arose. The Voortrekkers had crossed the Senqu (Orange) River in the 1830s and established the Orange Free State. By 1843 Moshoeshoe was sufficiently concerned by their numbers to ally himself with the British Cape Colony government. The British Resident in Basutoland decided that Moshoeshoe was becoming too powerful and engineered an unsuccessful attack on his kingdom.

Treaties with the British helped define the borders of Basutoland but the Boers pressed their claims on the land, leading to wars between the Orange Free State and the Basotho people in 1858 and 1865; Moshoeshoe was forced to sign away much of his western lowlands.

The Road to Independence

In 1868 the British government annexed Basutoland and handed it to the Cape Colony to run in 1871. After a period of instability, the British government again took direct control of Basutoland in 1884, although it gave authority to local leaders.

Lesotho's existence is attributable to a quirk of history and fortuitous timing. In the 1880s locals resented direct British rule as it was seen as an infringement on Basutoland's freedom and sovereignty. Ironically, British occupation secured the future independence of Lesotho: at the precise moment when the Union of South Africa was created, Basutoland was a British Protectorate and was not included in the Union.

In 1910 the advisory Basutoland National Council was formed from members nominated by the chiefs. In the mid-1950s the council requested internal self-government from the British; by 1960 a new constitution was in place and elections were held for a legislative council. The main contenders were the Basutoland Congress Party (BCP; similar to South Africa's African National Congress) and the conservative Basutoland National Party (BNP) headed by Chief Leabua Jonathan.

The BCP won the 1960 elections, then paved the way for full independence from Britain (achieved in 1966). However, at the elections in 1965 the BCP lost to the BNP and Chief Jonathan became the first prime minister of the new Kingdom of Lesotho, which allied itself with the apartheid regime across the border.

Big Brother

Stripping King Moshoeshoe II of the few powers that the new constitution had left him did not endear Jonathan's government to the people and the BCP won the 1970 election. After his defeat, Jonathan suspended the constitution, expelled the king and banned all opposition political parties. Jonathan changed tack, distancing himself from South Africa and calling for the return of land in the Orange Free State that had been stolen from the original Basutholand. He also offered refuge to ANC guerrillas and flirted with Cuba. South Africa closed Lesotho's borders, strangling the country.

Jonathan was deposed in 1986 and the king was restored as head of state. Eventually agitation for democratic reform rose again. In 1990 King Moshoeshoe II was deposed by the army in favour of his son, Prince Mohato Bereng Seeisa (Letsie III). Elections in 1993 resulted in the return of the BCP.

In 1995 Letsie III abdicated in favour of his father, Moshoeshoe II was reinstated and calm was restored after a year of unrest. Less than a year later he was killed when his 4WD plunged over a cliff in the Maluti Mountains. Letsie III became king for the second time.

A split in the BCP resulted in the breakaway Lesotho Congress for Democracy (LCD) taking power. The 1998 elections saw accusations of widespread cheating by the LCD, which won by a landslide. Major tensions arose between the public service and the government; the military was also split over the result.

Following months of protests, the government appeared to be losing control. In late September 1998 it called on the Southern African Development Community (SADC) treaty partners – Botswana, South Africa and Zimbabwe – to help restore order. Troops, mainly South African, invaded the kingdom. Rebel elements of the Lesotho army put up strong resistance and there was heavy fighting in Maseru.

The government agreed to call new elections, but the political situation remained tense with the spectre of South African intervention never far away. Political wrangling delayed the elections until May 2002. The LCD won again and Prime Minister Mosisili began a second – and peaceful – five-year term.

The 2007 elections were highly controversial. A newly formed All Basotho Convention (ABC) party accused the LCD party of manipulating the allocation of seats. National strikes followed and several ministers were allegedly attacked by gunmen. There was an assassination attempt on ABC's

HIGHLAND PARKS & RESERVES

Lesotho is blessed with some of the most remote and spectacular national parks and reserves in Southern Africa. Sure, they might lack lions and elephants, but they pack a punch when it comes to nature and beauty. Lesotho Northern Parks handles all accommodation bookings for the following parks (except Maliba Mountain Lodge).

Bokong Nature Reserve

The bearded vulture, the ice rat and the Vaal rhebok are just some of the denizens of this reserve, at the top of the 3090m Mafika-Lisiu Pass, near the Bokong River. There are a number of day walks, a visitors centre and an overnight camping ground. Guides (per person M30) and pony trekking (per day M180) can be arranged.

Sehlabathebe National Park

Lesotho's first national park, proclaimed in 1970, is isolated, rugged and beautiful. Getting here is a worthwhile adventure, especially if you're looking for wilderness, seclusion and fishing. Hiking and horse riding from Sani Top or the Drakensberg are the main ways to explore the waterfalls and surrounds.

You'll need to bring all your food, and be well prepared for the elements (summer sees frequent thick mists, winter nights are cold and snow is also possible).

A daily bus connects Qacha's Nek and Sehlabathebe, departing from Qacha's Nek at around noon and Sehlabathebe at 5.30am (M40, five hours). The bus terminates in Mavuka village, near the park gate. From here, it's about 12km further on foot to the lodge. If you're driving, you can arrange to leave your vehicle at the police station in Paolosi village while you're in the park.

Ts'ehlanyane National Park

Deep in the rugged Maluti Mountains, this 5600-hectare **national park** (admission per person/vehicle M40/10, campsite from M50) protects a beautiful, high-altitude, 5600-hectare patch of rugged wilderness. Excellent day walks, a challenging 39km hiking trail to Bokong Nature Reserve, and pony trekking (per half-/full day M300/350) are on offer.

Lesotho's smartest accommodation, **Maliba Mountain Lodge** (☎ in South Africa 031-266 1344; www.maliba-lodge.com; d with full board from M1720) is also here.

leader, Tom Thabane, and many people were detained and tortured. In May 2012, Thomas Thabane's All Basotho Convention, a coalition government, ousted Pakalitha Mosisili who had ruled for 14 years.

Culture

Traditional Basotho culture is central to the lives of many local people. It focuses on a belief in the power of ancestral spirits. The community chief is respected and revered, and family is an important social unit. Music plays a vital part in locals' lives.

Cattle occupy an important role in traditional culture; ownership indicates wealth and status. Shepherds, once revered, are today among the poorest males. The Basotho blanket, worn proudly by many in rural areas, reflects one's status in the community, according to the quality, material and design of the blanket itself.

Most Basotho in rural communities live in *rondavels,* round huts with mud walls (often decorated) and thatched roofs.

Poverty and death are ever present in Lesotho. Life for many people is incredibly harsh, and most try to eke out a living on the land or through subsistence agriculture, especially livestock. Education is not compulsory.

The citizens of Lesotho are known as the Basotho people. Most are southern Sotho and most speak Sesotho (Southern Sotho).

Around 80% of the population is Christian (mainly Roman Catholic, Anglican and Episcopal). The remaining 20% live by traditional Basotho beliefs. There are churches throughout the country, many of which were (and continue to be) built by missionaries.

Food & Drink

You won't be writing home about the food in Lesotho. Staples include maize (often in the form of *mealie pap,* a type of maize porridge), as well as some vegetables and pulses. Maseru boasts a decent selection of restaurants serving a range of local and foreign foods, but outside the capital, you'll usually have to take what you're given.

Environment

Lesotho's western border is formed by the Mohokare (Caledon) River. The eastern border is the rugged Drakensberg Range, and high country defines much of the southern border. All of Lesotho is over 1000m in altitude, with peaks reaching 3000m in the centre and east of the country.

This high, corrugated and often freezing kingdom is a tough environment at the best of times. Serious erosion (*dongas,* or gullies) exists in Lesotho due to the pressures of modern farming techniques and overgrazing.

There are also environmental concerns about the controversial Lesotho Highlands Water Project, which provides water and electricity to South Africa.

SURVIVAL GUIDE

Directory A–Z

ACCOMMODATION

Accommodation prices and standards are on par with the country's rocky passes – high and occasionally a little rough, although there is a range of comfort standards. The only five-star accommodation can be found in international-style hotels in Maseru and a smart lodge in Ts'ehlanyane National Park. The rest of the country offers lodges of all standards, B&Bs, rough-and-tumble hotels and very basic Agricultural Training Centres.

ACTIVITIES

The main options in Lesotho are hiking and pony trekking. All of the trading post lodges run fabulous trips for those who wish to do it on two or four legs.

BOOKS

An interesting history book on Lesotho is *A Short History of Lesotho* by Stephen Gill. Poignant Basotho accounts include *Singing Away the Hunger* by Mpho Matsepo Nthunya et al, and *Shepherd Boy of the Maloti* by Thabo Makoa.

CLIMATE

Come prepared. The climate in Lesotho is notoriously changeable: temperatures can plummet to near 0°C (even during summer – late November to March), rivers flood (most of Lesotho's rain falls between October and April) and thick fogs can delay you. During the dry season, water can be scarce. If hiking, bring your own food, sleeping bag, rain wear, sunscreen, warm clothing, a torch and water-purification tablets. Winter is from June to September.

EMBASSIES & CONSULATES

Lesotho has diplomatic representation in South Africa (Pretoria and Johannesburg). A number of countries have representation in Maseru:

French Consulate (☎2232 5722; www.french-embassy.com/lesotho.html; Alliance Française, cnr Kingsway & Pioneer Rd)

Irish Embassy (☎2231 4068; www.embassyofireland.org.ls; Tonakholo Rd)

Dutch Consulate (☎2231 2114; www.dutchembassy.co.za; c/o Lancer's Inn)

South African High Commission (☎2231 5758; www.dfa.gov.za; cnr Kingsway & Old School Rd)

US Embassy (☎2231 2666; maseru.usembassy.gov; 254 Kingsway Rd)

EMERGENCY

Ambulance (☎2231 2501)

Fire (☎115)

Police (☎2231 9900)

HOLIDAYS

As well as the Christian religious holidays, these are principal public holidays in Lesotho:

New Year's Day 1 January

Moshoeshoe Day 11 March

Independence Day 4 October

Boxing Day 26 December

INTERNET ACCESS

At the time of research internet access was available in Maseru only.

MAPS

The **Department of Land, Surveys & Physical Planning** (☎2232 2376; Lerotholi Rd; ⏲9am-3pm Mon-Fri) sells good topographic maps. The tourist office has free maps of Maseru city.

PRACTICALITIES

Electricity Lesotho's electricity is generated at 220V; appliances have three round pins as used in South Africa.

Languages Southern Sotho (Sesotho), English

Population 1.8 million

Time GMT/UTC +2

ACTIVITIES ON HIGH

Pony Trekking

Lesotho's tough and sure-footed little Basotho ponies can take you to some remote and awesome places in the highlands. The main pony centres are Semonkong Lodge, Malealea Lodge and Ramabanta Guest House. In some cases, the villagers provide the ponies and act as guides, contributing significantly to the local village economy.

Walking

Lesotho's high country offers some of the most spectacular walking in southern Africa, especially in the rugged mountains in the south and east (the Drakensberg Range), the national parks and in and around the lodges. For details on walks see *A Backpackers Guide to Lesotho*, by Russell Suchet, available locally and in South Africa.

When camping in or near a village, always ask permission from the village chief, and offer to pay a small fee.

MONEY

The unit of currency is the loti (plural: maloti; symbol: M), made up of 100 lisente. The loti is fixed at the value of the South African rand; rands are accepted everywhere in Lesotho, but maloti are not accepted back in South Africa. The only currency-exchange banks (including Nedbank and Standard Bank) are in Maseru and Maseru has the only ATMs.

OPENING HOURS

Government offices 8am to 12.45pm, 2pm to 4.30pm

Post offices 8am to 4.30pm weekdays, 8am to noon Saturday

Shops Generally 8am to 5pm weekdays (8.30am to 1pm Wednesday) and 8am to 1pm Saturday

SAFE TRAVEL

Keep off high ground during electrical storms and avoid camping in the open. In the highlands, school children and herd boys may request 'Sweets! Sweets!'; responding to this encourages begging.

TELEPHONE

The telephone system works reasonably well where there is access – it is limited in the highlands. Lesotho's area codes are already incorporated into their numbers. Lesotho's country code is ☎266; to call Lesotho from South Africa, dial the prefix ☎09 266. The international access code is ☎00. To call South Africa from anywhere in Lesotho, dial ☎00 27 and then the South African area code and phone number. Note: ☎082 and ☎083 numbers generally denote South African mobile phone numbers, so dial ☎00 82 and the number.

Mobile-phone signals are extremely rare in the highlands and can be picked up on a few mountain passes only. They should not be relied upon.

VISAS

Citizens of most Western European countries, the USA and most Commonwealth countries are granted an entry permit (free) at the border or airport. The standard stay permitted is between 14 and 28 days and is renewable by leaving and re-entering the country or by application to the **Director of Immigration & Passport Services** (☎2232 3771, 2232 1110; PO Box 363, Maseru 100).

Visa requirements change, so first check with an embassy. Pretoria is the place to obtain visas for other African countries. Vaccination certificates are required if you've recently been in a yellow-fever area.

ℹ Getting There & Away

AIR

Lesotho's Moshoeshoe I International Airport is 21km from Maseru. **South African Airways** (SAA; ☎2663 10662; www.flysaa.com; Maseru Bookcentre, Kingsway Rd) flies daily between Maseru and Johannesburg for around R2000 one way. The airport departure tax is M50.

LAND

All Lesotho's borders are with South Africa. Most people enter via Maseru Bridge (open 24 hours). Other main border crossings include Ficksburg Bridge (open 24 hours), Makhaleng Bridge (open 8am to 4pm) and Sani Pass (open 6am to 6pm, but ask around, as times change), however, these often have long queues.

Intercape (www.intercape.co.za; LNCD Centre) offers bus services to a changing timetable between Bloemfontein and Maseru (from M550, 1¾ hours). After your passport is stamped you need to catch a car taxi (called a four-by-one) from the Lesotho border to the Maseru taxi rank.

Via minibus taxi, daily minibuses run between Bloemfontein and Maseru (two hours).

Another option is to head from Bloemfontein to Botshabelo (one hour) from where you can catch a connection to Maseru (1½ hours), though direct services may be available. Other useful connections include a daily minibus taxi between Mokhotlong (Lesotho) and Underberg (South Africa) via Sani Pass; and several minibus taxis daily between Qacha's Nek (Lesotho) and Matatiele (South Africa).

There are at least three buses weekly between Johannesburg and Maseru (six to seven hours), and daily minibus taxis between both Johannesburg and Ladybrand (16km from the Maseru Bridge border crossing) and Maseru. Leaving Maseru, you'll need to go to the South Africa side of Maseru Bridge to catch the bus.

Getting Around

A good network of slow, no-frills buses and faster minibus taxis access many towns. These leave when full; no reservations are necessary. You'll be quoted long-distance fares on the buses but it's best to just buy a ticket to the next major town, as you might be stuck waiting for the bus to fill up again while other buses leave before yours.

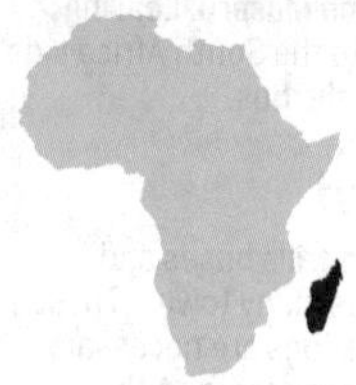

Madagascar

POP 19.6 MILLION

Includes ➡

Best Places to Eat

➡ La Varangue (p799)
➡ Le Bateau Ivre (p811)
➡ Surprise Betsileo (p803)
➡ Le Melville (p810)
➡ Le Pousse-Pousse (p801)

Best Places to Stay

➡ Bakuba (p806)
➡ Chez Sika (p815)
➡ Relais de la Reine (p804)
➡ Le Grand Bleu (p809)
➡ Hôtel Sakamanga (p797)

Why Go?

Lemurs, baobabs, rain forest, beaches, desert, trekking and diving: Madagascar is a dream destination for lovers of nature and the outdoors. The world's fourth-largest island is also a relatively easy destination: hassle-free, with good tourism infrastructure (but poor roads), sensational national parks, a plethora of activities and divine food. The drawcard for many travellers is the country's incredible natural diversity – you can go from rain forest to desert or high altitude in just 300kms – and unique wildlife: 5% of all known animal and plant species are endemic to Madagascar. Less well known but just as fascinating is Malagasy culture, in which ancestors and their spirits play a central role, and death is only the beginning of the (permanent) afterlife. The hardest thing will be to choose what to do: Madagascar is vast and unless you have unlimited time and/or money, you'll have to spend them wisely.

When to Go

Antananarivo

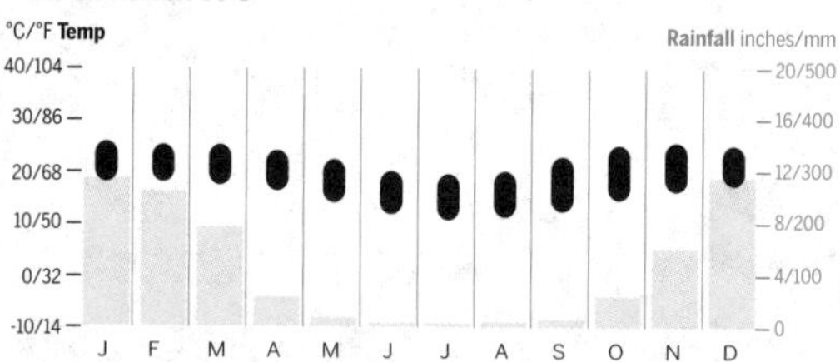

Jan–Mar Cyclone season on the east coast, rainy season everywhere.

Jul–Sep High season for tourism; book ahead. Balmy temperatures by day but cool at night.

Oct–Nov The best time to visit, with warm temperatures and the beauty of spring.

Madagascar Highlights

1 Scale Madagascar's second-highest mountain, Pic Boby, in spectacular **Parc National d'Andringitra** (p805).

2 Snorkel, dive and paddle at **Anakao** (p807) on Madagascar's Great Reef.

3 Take a dip in the natural swimming pools after a day's trek in **Parc National de l'Isalo** (p804).

4 Snorkel and dive to your heart's content around the island of **Nosy Be** (p807).

5 Go whale-watching off **Île Sainte Marie** (p813).

6 Trek along **Les Trois Baies** (p810), Madagascar's starkly beautiful northern edge.

7 Spend an afternoon in the spiritual home of Malagasy identity, the royal hill of **Ambohimanga** (p797).

8 Listen to the wail of the indri, one of Madagascar's most endangered lemurs, at **Parc National d'Andasibe** (p810).

ANTANANARIVO

POP 1.2 MILLION

Tana, as the capital is universally known, is all about eating, shopping, history and day trips. The town centre itself, with its pollution and dreadful traffic, puts off many travellers from staying, but bypassing the capital altogether would be a mistake: Tana has been the home of Malagasy power for three centuries and there is a huge amount of history and culture to discover by visiting its sacred hills.

Sights & Activities

Rova PALACE

(Haute-Ville) The *rova* (fortified palace) is the imposing structure that crowns the highest hill of Tana. The palace was designed for Queen Ranavalona I by a Scottish missionary named James Cameron. The outer structure, built in 1867 for Ranavalona II, was made of stone, with a wooden roof and interior. A number of monarchs are buried there.

Gutted in a fire in 1995, it is still under restoration and was not officially open to the public at the time of writing. However, it was possible to enter the grounds by paying Ar5000 to the gatekeeper and coming in with one of the freelance guides hanging about (Ar5000).

Musée Andafivaratra MUSEUM

(Haute-Ville; admission Ar5000; 9am-5pm) Housed in a magnificent pink baroque palace in the Haute-Ville, this museum is filled with furniture, portraits and memorabilia from the time of the Merina monarchs.

Ortana CULTURAL TOUR

(020 22 270 51; www.tourisme-antananarivo.com; Escalier Ravanalona I) This is the best place to go to if you would like a guide to visit historical sites around Tana such as the Rova, Musée Andafivaratra and Ambohimanga. Most guides are knowledgable and many speak English and/or Italian as well as French.

SET YOUR BUDGET

Budget

- Double room without bathroom Ar30,000
- Meal in hotel Ar3000
- Large THB beer Ar2500
- Taxi-brousse Tana-Tuléar Ar45,000

Midrange

- Double room with bathroom Ar60,000
- Pizza Ar10,000
- *Rhum arrangé* Ar3000
- Private vehicle (not 4WD) on RN7 Ar100,000 per day

Top End

- Plush bungalow Ar100,000
- Two-course meal in restaurant Ar25,000
- Bottle of wine Ar15,000
- Tana-Tuléar flight €187

Sleeping

Prices in Tana are usually higher than elsewhere in the country.

Hôtel Moonlight HOTEL $

(020 22 268 70; hasinaherizo@yahoo.fr; Rue Rainandriamapandry; s/d/tr without bathroom Ar23,000/29,000/34,000) This budget stalwart is an excellent option in a lively part of town with cool internet cafes and restaurants. Rooms have brightly coloured walls, parquet floors and clean bathrooms (some rooms have showers but all share toilets). There are two large communal terraces where you can watch the world go by.

Hôtel Tana-Jacaranda GUESTHOUSE $$

(020 22 562 39; www.tana-jacaranda.com; 24 Rue Rainitsarovy; d without/with bathroom Ar39,000/50,000; @) Rooms at this super-friendly family-run hotel are dark but quiet and clean. There is a tip-top dining room with fabulous views of the Rova and the Haute-Ville, piping-hot water in the showers, good wi-fi, a guest computer and multilingual, wonderfully helpful staff.

Merina Lodge GUESTHOUSE $$

(020 24 522 33; merinalodge@wanadoo.mg; off Rue Andrianary Ratianarivo; d/tr Ar54,000/81,000) This peaceful guesthouse has five simple but proudly maintained rooms with wooden floors, bright bedspreads and clean bathrooms. Its trump cards are the tranquil terrace – an unexpected find for such a central location – and friendly staff.

DON'T MISS

AMBOHIMANGA

Ambohimanga ('blue hill' or 'beautiful hill') was the original capital of the Merina royal family. Even after the seat of government was shifted to Antananarivo for political reasons, Ambohimanga remained a sacred site, and was off limits to foreigners for many years.

Poised atop the hill is Ambohimanga's **Rova** (admission Ar7000; ⏲9am-5pm), the fortress-palace of the all-powerful Merina king Andrianampoinimerina. The fortress was constructed using cement made from sand, shells and egg whites – 16 million eggs were required to build the outer wall alone.

Inside the compound stands the blackened wood hut (1788) that was King Andrianampoinimerina's **palace**. The original was thatched, but French engineer Jean Laborde replaced the grass roof with more durable wooden tiles in the 19th century.

Next door to King Andrianampoinimerina's hut, in a striking style contrast, is the elegant **summer palace** of Queen Ranavalona I (r 1828–1861), constructed in 1870 by Laborde (who was thought to be Ranavalona's lover). It's been beautifully restored and has original European-style furniture inside.

Ambohimanga is still revered amongst many Malagasies as a sacred site, and you will see offerings (zebu horns, blood, sweets, honey and small change) at various shrines around the compound.

Make sure you take a guide to go round the Rova to learn about the site's historical and cultural significance. Guides are available by the entrance where you pay your admission. Otherwise, contact the local tourism promotion office **OSCAR** (☎020 26 300 46), which organises guided circuits in the compound and surrounding area.

Ambohimanga is 21km north of Antananarivo and easily visited as a day trip. *Taxis-brousses* (bush-taxis) leave throughout the day from Ambodivona (Ar700, one hour). From the village, you'll need to walk 1km up the hill to the Rova.

Hôtel Saint-Germain HOTEL **$$**
(☎033 25 882 62; www.hotelstgermain.e-monsite.com; Rue Ravelontsalama, Ambatomena; d Ar45,000; 📶) This attractive pale-blue building is an excellent budget-friendly choice. Rooms are pocket-size but bright and spotless. There is a convivial bar/breakfast room downstairs, and the friendly management will happily recommend restaurants nearby.

★ **Hôtel Sakamanga** BOUTIQUE HOTEL **$$$**
(☎020 22 358 09; www.sakamanga.com; Lalana Andrianary Ratianarivo; d Ar50,000-135,000; ❄@📶) A perennial favourite, with a friendly atmosphere, varied rooms, character-filled decor and beyond-comprehensive services. The intriguingly mazy layout leads to a garden and cafe-bar-library, with enough artefacts in the corridors to open a museum. Reserve well in advance, as it is almost always full.

Résidence Lapasoa BOUTIQUE HOTEL **$$$**
(☎020 22 611 40; www.lapasoa.com; 15 Rue de la Réunion; d/ste Ar121,500/162,000; ❄@📶) The exquisite Lapasoa offers a modern twist on colonial decor: there are polished wood floors, beautiful wooden furniture (including stunning four-poster beds), colourful fabrics, and light flooding in from skylights and big windows. The top-floor rooms, with their high, sloped ceilings, are the loveliest.

Eating

Tana excels at eating; you'll find some of the country's finest restaurants in the capital, and although they're slightly more expensive than in the rest of the country, they remain great value.

Saka Express CAFE **$**
(www.sakamanga.com; Rue Andrianary Ratianarivo; mains Ar5000-10,000; ⏲7am-10pm) This snack cafeteria and takeaway outlet is the best place in town for lunch on the go. There are pizzas, kebabs and sandwiches, all bursting at the seams with fillings. There are a few tables inside, which fill quickly at lunchtime.

Shoprite SUPERMARKET **$**
(Ave Andrianampoinimerina; ⏲8.30am-7.30pm Mon-Sat, to 3pm Sun) Well-stocked supermarket.

Central Antananarivo

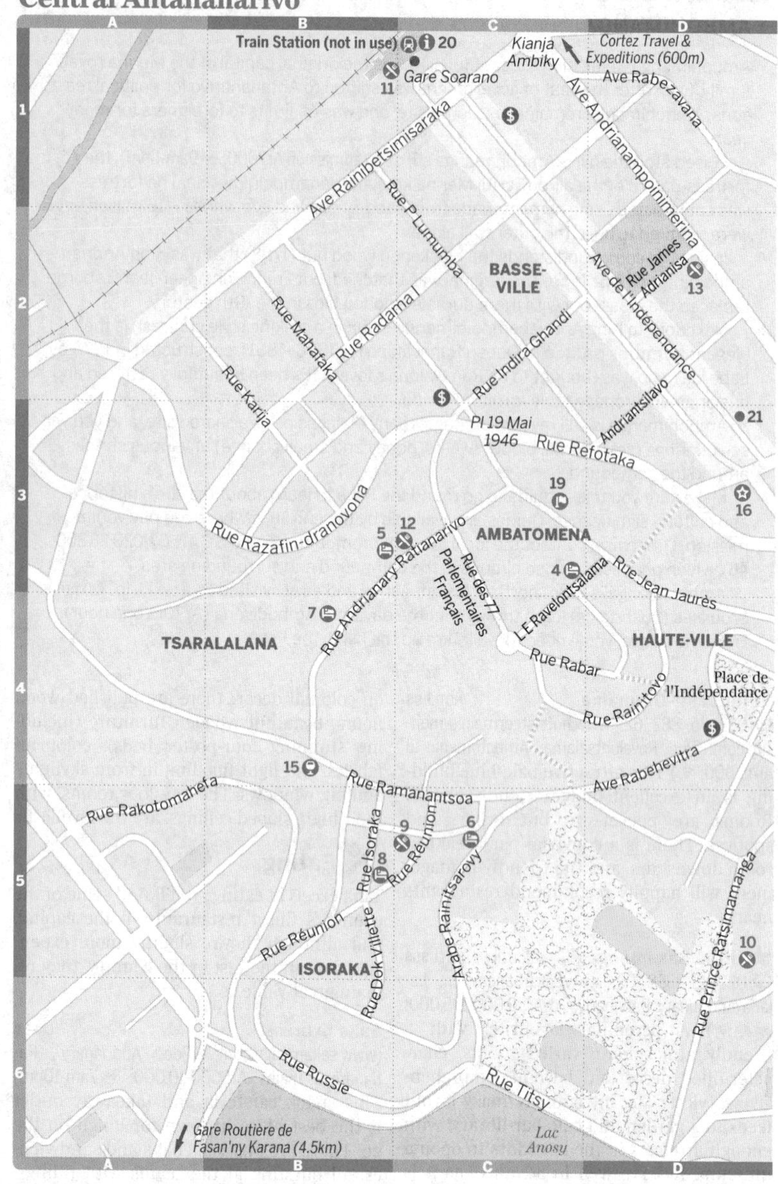

Le Saka FUSION $$

(☎020 22 358 09; Hôtel Sakamanga, Rue Andrianary Ratianarivo; mains Ar11,00-18,000; ⏲11.30am-3pm & 6.30-11pm) Striking the perfect balance between gastro French and straightforward local cooking, Le Saka is a Tana institution. The restaurant is housed in a gorgeous wooden house full of old black-and-white photos and local artwork. The chef whips up some mighty desserts using Malagasy chocolate.

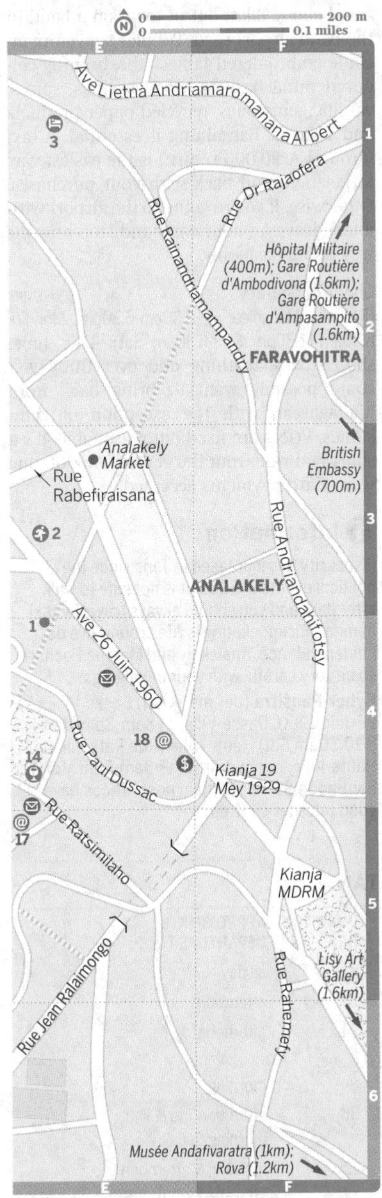

Central Antananarivo

Activities, Courses & Tours
1 Ortana E4
2 Tany Mena Tours E3

Sleeping
3 Hôtel Moonlight E1
4 Hôtel Saint-Germain C3
5 Hôtel Sakamanga B3
6 Hôtel Tana-Jacaranda C5
7 Merina Lodge B4
8 Résidence Lapasoa B5

Eating
9 Chez Sucett's C5
10 La Varangue D5
11 Le Café de la Gare B1
Le Saka .... (see 5)
12 Saka Express C3
13 Shoprite D2

Drinking & Nightlife
14 Buffet du Jardin E4
15 Manson B4

Entertainment
16 Hôtel Le Glacier D3

Information
17 Cyber-Paositra E5
18 Cyber-Paositra E4
19 French Embassy C3
20 Office National de Tourisme C1

Transport
21 Air Madagascar D3

Chez Sucett's CREOLE **$$**
(23 Rue Raveloary; mains Ar10,000-15,000; ⏲ noon-2.30pm & 6.30-10pm) The dining room looks a little dim from the outside, but inside the atmosphere is jovial, with tables of budget-conscious travellers and locals in the know tucking into Sucett's Malagasy and Creole (a blend of Asian, African and European influences) dishes.

★ **La Varangue** INTERNATIONAL **$$$**
(☎ 020 22 273 97; www.tana-hotel.com; 17 Rue Prince Ratsimamanga; mains Ar21,000-35,000; ⏲ 11.30am-2.30pm & 6.30-11pm Mon-Sat) Tana's gourmet address par excellence, La Varangue serves an elaborate melange of French gastronomy and Malagasy flavours. The chef is a chocolate specialist, so make sure you leave space for dessert. The wine list is one of the best in the country. Booking essential.

Le Café de la Gare INTERNATIONAL **$$$**
(www.cafetana.com; Gare Soarano; mains Ar16,000-19,000; ⏲ 11am-11pm; 📶) The fabulous Café de la Gare is the flagship of the beautifully renovated Soarano train station. The food is

stupendous, with well-executed international staples such as prawn curry, zebu burger, pan-fried fish etc. On Sunday, brunch is served between 11am and 3pm.

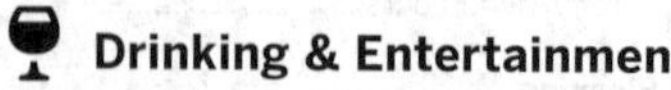

Drinking & Entertainment

Most nightclubs in Tana are packed with prostitutes, so unaccompanied guys can expect a bit of unsolicited attention.

Manson BAR
(Rue Ramanantsoa; ⏲5am-late) Manson wouldn't look out of place in Paris or London, so it should come as no surprise that this is the venue of choice for Tana's expat community. We like the graffiti decor outside, and the music inside is pretty good.

Buffet du Jardin BAR
(Place de l'Indépendance; ⏲24hr) This longstanding snack stop and bar is a favourite with taxi drivers; the terrace is a nice, low-key place for a beer.

Hôtel Le Glacier LIVE MUSIC
(Ave 26 Juin 1960; admission Ar3000; ⏲6pm-2am) The slightly disreputable bar has cabaret, bands and traditional music performances every night of the week; it's always full and the atmosphere is good.

Shopping

Marché Artisanal de La Digue SOUVENIRS
(La Digue; ⏲9am-5.30pm) The most popular place to pick up souvenirs is this market located about 12km out of town on a bend in the Ivato airport road. Popular souvenirs include embroidered tablecloths, brightly coloured raffia baskets, woodcarvings, spices, vanilla, gemstones, recycled paper products and T-shirts. Bargaining is essential. A taxi (around Ar20,000 return) is the easiest way to get here and back with your purchases. Otherwise, if you're going to the airport with a taxi, leave an hour early and stop on your way there. Cash only.

Lisy Art Gallery SOUVENIRS
(Rte du Mausolée; ⏲8.30am-6.30pm Mon-Fri, 8.30am-12.30pm & 2-6.30pm Sat) This huge shop stocks anything and everything you could possibly want to bring back from Madagascar, with the exception of gemstones. Prices are fixed but reasonable. It's a short taxi ride from the centre (Ar5000 one way). Card payments accepted.

Information

Insecurity has increased in Tana since the political events of 2009. It is not safe to walk after dark and you should always travel by taxi at night. Pickpocketing is rife around Ave de l'Indépendance, Analakely and Marché Pochart, so be very careful with your belongings.

Cyber-Paositra (per min Ar30) Basse-Ville (Ave 26 Juin 1960, Basse-Ville; ⏲8am-3pm Mon-Fri, 8-10.30am Sat) Haute-Ville (Rue Ratsimilaho, Haute-Ville; per min Ar50; ⏲8am-5pm Mon-Fri, 8am-noon Sat) Both main post offices have good internet centres.

TAXI-BROUSSE DEPARTURES FROM TANA

DESTINATION	TAXI-BROUSSE STATION	PRICE	DURATION HRS	APPROXIMATE DEPARTURE TIME
Antsirabe	Fasan'ny Karana	Ar17,000	3	all day
Ambanja	Ambodivona	Ar50,000	16	afternoon
Diego Suarez	Ambodivona	Ar65,000	24	afternoon
Fianarantsoa	Fasan'ny Karana	Ar23,000	8	morning
Fort Dauphin	Fasan'ny Karana	Ar85,000	36	afternoon Tue & Thu, morning Sat
Majunga	Ambodivona	Ar32,000	12	morning & afternoon
Manakara	Fasan'ny Karana	Ar37,000	13	afternoon
Miandrivazo	Fasan'ny Karana	Ar24,000	9	afternoon
Moramanga	Ampasampito	Ar5000	2	all day
Morondava	Fasan'ny Karana	Ar45,000	16	afternoon
Tamatave	Ambodivona/ Ampasampito	Ar20,000	10	morning & afternoon
Tuléar	Fasan'ny Karana	Ar45,000	18	afternoon

Hôpital Militaire (☎020 22 397 51; Rue Moss, Soavinandriana) The best-equipped hospital in the country.

Office National de Tourisme (www.madagascar-tourisme.com; Gare Soarano; ⏲9am-5pm Mon-Sat) Limited amounts of countrywide information.

Getting There & Away

AIR

Antananarivo's international airport (p820) is located in Ivato, a small town 19km north of Tana. It has international as well as domestic (p821) flights.

TAXI-BROUSSE

For morning departures, turn up early (6am); for afternoon departures, come around 2pm. It may take up to four hours for some vehicles to fill.

There are three main *taxi-brousse* stations (*gares routières*).

Gare Routière d'Ambodivona (northern *taxi-brousse* station; Ambodivona) About 2km northeast of the city centre. A taxi to/from the centre costs Ar3000.

Gare Routière d'Ampasampito (eastern *taxi-brousse* station; Ampasampito) About 3.5km northeast of the centre. A taxi to/from the centre will cost Ar6000.

Gare Routière de Fasan'ny Karana (southern *taxi-brousse* station; Anosibe) About 4km southwest of Lac Anosy. A taxi to/from the centre costs Ar8000.

Getting Around

TO/FROM THE AIRPORT

A taxi to/from the city centre costs Ar30,000, Ar40,000 at night. A much cheaper but slower alternative is **Navette Adema** (☎034 07 063 02; ⏲5am- 9pm), a shuttle service running between the airport and selected hotels in the town centre, with a terminus at Gare Soarana (Ar10,000, one hour).

TAXI

Tana's cream-coloured taxis are plentiful and cheap, even at night. Fares are negotiable: a journey in town should cost Ar3000 to Ar5000 during the day, or Ar5000 to Ar7000 at night. Always agree on a price before leaving. You may pay a different rate for the same journey if it is downhill or uphill!

CENTRAL HIGHLANDS

The *hauts plateaux* is a vast area of rolling hills interspersed with terraced valleys of rice paddies, the picture of rural tranquillity. It's a very scenic region, easily reached from Antananarivo, and features some of the country's most interesting and attractive towns.

Antsirabe

POP 215,000

Antsirabe makes an excellent base for excursions into the surrounding countryside. Its origins as a 19th-century spa town are reflected in elegant facades and wide boulevards.

Sights & Activities

Sabotsy Market MARKET

This sprawling open-air market in the town centre, with distinct areas of jewellery, clothing, food and more, will keep you occupied for hours either shopping or simply absorbing the spectacle. Saturday is the main day, but there is action all week long.

Sleeping

★**Chez Billy** GUESTHOUSE $

(☎020 44 484 88; www.chez-billy.net84.net; Antsenakely; d/tr/q Ar16,000/24,000/31,000; @ 📶) This eclectic melange of guest house, music bar, internet cafe, and restaurant inspires a hostel-like conviviality among the crossroads clientele. It's the best budget option in town so act quickly: the eight rooms go fast.

Trianon INN $$

(☎020 44 051 40; hotel.letrianon@gmail.com; Ave Foch; s/d/tr Ar50,000/60,000/70,000; 📶) This charming throwback to the colonial era, a nicely renovated French chateau, oozes atmosphere, from its old airline posters to its uniformed staff. The classy restaurant and terrace strike just the right note.

Résidence Camélia GUESTHOUSE $$$

(☎020 44 488 44; www.laresidencecamelia.com; Ave de l'Indépendance; d Ar70,000-126,000) A very genteel and well-done guesthouse with a tranquil shady garden and fresh, uplifting rooms. The charming restaurant, with its vaulted ceiling and winter fireplace, is a noteworthy bargain (mains from Ar10,000).

Eating

Shoprite SUPERMARKET $

(Antsenakely) Well-stocked supermarket.

★**Le Pousse-Pousse** MALAGASY $$

(Antsenakely; mains Ar8500-12,000; ⏲11.30am-1.30am Thu-Tue) This charming place, where

Antsirabe

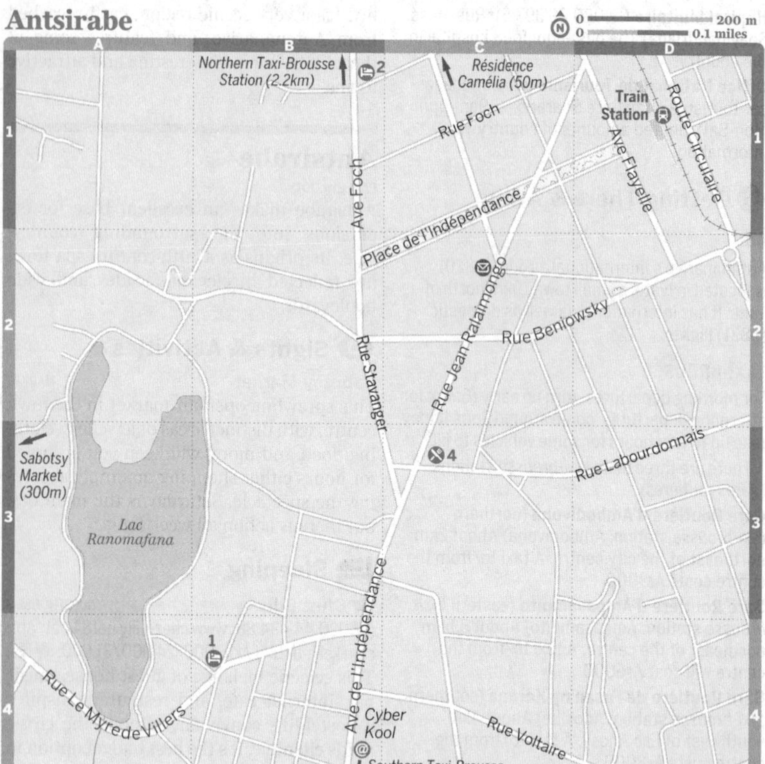

Antsirabe

Sleeping

1 Chez Billy B4
2 Trianon B1

Eating

3 Le Pousse-Pousse B4
4 Shoprite C3

you eat inside a *pousse-pousse* (rickshaw), is known for its cheeseburgers and occasional live music.

Information

There are numerous ATMs at the banks.

BNI-CA (Rue Ralaimongo) ATM takes both MasterCard and Visa.

Cyber Kool (Rue Ralaimongo; per min Ar30; 8am-midnight)

Getting There & Away

Taxis-brousses to Antananarivo (Ar8000, four hours) leave from the northern *taxi-brousse* station, about 5km north of town, behind the Jovenna petrol station.

Taxis-brousses for Ambositra (Ar5000, three hours) and Fianarantsoa (Ar15,000, six hours) leave from the southern *taxi-brousse* station.

Fianarantsoa

POP 193,000

Madagascar's second-largest city, Fianarantsoa (Fi-a-nar-ant-soo, or Fianar for short) is like a mild version of Tana. Surrounded by hills, it is both a regional commercial, administrative and religious center, and a major transit point. Tourists typically come here to spend the night on their way to Ranomafana or Isalo. The Haute-Ville is the most picturesque part of town.

Tours

Maison des Guides HIKING
(034 03 123 01, 032 02 728 97; coeurmalgache@hotmail.com; 8am-5pm) In an old railway car in front of the train station, this cooperative of local guides is your best choice for arranging a local tour of the surrounding area.

Sleeping & Eating

Hôtel Arinofy GUESTHOUSE $
(020 75 506 38; hotel_arinofy@yahoo.fr; camping Ar12,000, d/tr Ar23,000/40,000) This friendly guest house in a peaceful enclave has well-kept grounds, a professional uniformed staff, and a pleasant ambiance. There is also a campsite.

★**Tsara Guest House** GUESTHOUSE $$
(020 75 502 06; www.tsaraguest.com; Rue Philibert Tsiranana; d Ar48,000-175,000) This exceptionally stylish place with a beautiful garden was once a church. The cheaper rooms have shared bathroom but are spotless; hot water and valley views are available as prices go up.

Hôtel Cotsoyannis HOTEL $$
(020 75 514 72; cotso@malagasy.com; 4 Rue Printsy Ramaharo; d from Ar51,000;) 'Le Cotso' has a garden courtyard and rustic, attractive rooms that are good value for money. The cozy restaurant is a great place, with a log fire and good pizzas and crêpes (mains from Ar7500).

★**Surprise Betsileo** ITALIAN $$
(034 01 998 04; www.lasurprisebetsileo.com; mains from Ar12,000; lunch & dinner) The Italian owner has elegantly restored a 19th-century colonial villa and converted it into a sophisticated restaurant offering an interesting melange of Italian and Malagasy cooking. Book ahead.

Getting There & Away

Frequent *taxis-brousses* connect Fianarantsoa with Ambositra (Ar7000, three hours), Antsirabe (Ar14,000, six hours) and Antananarivo (Ar18,000, eight to nine hours).

Minibuses also go daily to Ambalavao (Ar2000, two hours), Ranohira (Ar9000, seven hours) and on to Tuléar (Ar25,000, 11 hours).

If you're heading east there are multiple vehicles between Fianarantsoa and Ranomafana (Ar4000, two hours).

Parc National de Ranomafana

This 43,549-hectare park is a superb tract of rain forest that offers great birdwatching and lemur-spotting. The park was created to protect the rare golden bamboo lemur.

The village of Ranomafana is the gateway to the park, with good amenities, but no banking facilities. Cards are not accepted anywhere.

Sleeping & Eating

Rianala Gîte HOSTEL $
(033 14 905 69, 034 06 298 45; edm@moov.mg; dm Ar10,000, campsite Ar3000) Right near the park entrance, this hostel feels immersed in the forest. Rooms are clean and come with blankets and hot water, and there is a nice porch to sit on. There is also a restaurant, which you'll need unless you bring your own food.

Cristo LODGE $$$
(034 12 353 97; http://cristohotel.cabanova.fr/page1.html; d Ar90,000, bungalow Ar70,000) Perched on a gorgeous bend in the Namorona River, this lodge has the best views of any property in the area. An attractive restaurant with open fire is another draw, as are the amiable owners.

Hôtel Domaine Nature LODGE $$$
(020 75 750 25; desmada@malagasy.com; d/ste Ar62,000/136,000;) Airy hillside bungalows with platform beds and space heaters are surrounded by jungle and the sound of rushing water; you look out into the canopy. A brand-new glass restaurant (mains Ar12,000) and super pool add creature comforts.

Information

Park visitors pay an entry fee (1/2 days Ar25,000/37,000) and a guide fee (2/3/4 hours Ar15,000/35,000/35,000, full day Ar60,000). Guides are mandatory and arranged at the **MNP Office** (located on a dirt road a half-mile northeast of the Ranomafana town centre), where they will assist you in working out an itinerary.

Getting There & Away

Taxis-brousses go daily from Ranomafana to Fianarantsoa (Ar5000, 1½ hours) and Manakara.

Ambalavao

POP 35,000

Set amid beautiful mountainous countryside with numerous boulderlike peaks, Ambalavao is like a charming French village reduced through years of neglect to a Wild West outpost. Some people find it beautiful. Others find it haunting. Everyone finds it interesting.

Sights

Réserve d'Anja WILDLIFE RESERVE

(admission Ar7000, guide fee per 2hr Ar8000) This small (37 hectare) reserve, about 7km from Ambalavao, encompasses three mountain-sized boulders ('the three sisters') ringed at the base by a narrow forest full of ring-tailed lemurs. You reach the lemurs after negotiating a cave, such that it feels like a private world beyond, with some fabulous views along the way.

To come here, take a *taxi-brousse* south and ask the driver to drop you off at the park office.

Fabrique de Papier Antaimoro ARTS CENTRE

(020 75 340 01; 7.30-11.30am & 1-5pm) This is where Ambalavao's signature paper comes from. It is made from the bark of a local bush, which has flowers pressed into it. Cards, envelopes and picture frames are all for sale.

Zebu Market MARKET

Ambalavao hosts the largest zebu market in the country every Wednesday and Thursday morning, with tough, wizened herdsmen walking from as far away as Tuléar to sell their cattle. Located about a mile south of town on the RN7, it starts well before dawn.

Sleeping & Eating

★ **Résidence du Betsileo** HOTEL $$

(033 02 863 89; residencedubetsileo@gmail.com; d/tr Ar34,000/44,000) This charming bargain is the best place to stay – and eat – in town. Located in a renovated store right on the main street, it has great views out back, and a nice patio restaurant (mains Ar7000 to Ar10,000) too. Choose the off-street rooms.

Hôtel aux Bougainvillées HOTEL $$

(020 75 340 01; ragon@wanadoo.mg; d/tr/q Ar45,000/60,000/85,000) Draped in its colourful namesake plant, this hotel has character. The rooms are comfortable and clean, but only the more expensive have hot water and private bathrooms. There's a decent restaurant (mains Ar10,000), which is popular with tour groups at lunch.

Getting There & Away

Ambalavao lies 56km south of Fianarantsoa. The town has direct *taxi-brousse* connections with Fianar (Ar3000, 1½ hours) and Ihosy (Ar5000, two hours). For destinations further north, you'll have to go to Fianar first.

SOUTHERN MADAGASCAR

Parc National de l'Isalo

Isalo is like a museum dedicated to the art of the desert canyon: canyons full of yellow savannah grass, bone-dry canyons, sculpted buttes, white-washed canyons, vertical rock walls, and best of all, deep canyon floors with streams, lush vegetation, and pools for swimming, all of which you'll be able to explore along some of the park's numerous trails.

The park is served by the small town of Ranohira, which contains the park office and a handful of hotels and restaurants; the better resorts are further out along the park's southern border.

Sleeping & Eating

Chez Alice BUNGALOW $

(032 04 042 22, 032 02 055 68; camping Ar6000, paillotte Ar25,000, d/tr/q bungalows Ar35,000/45,000/55,000) This convivial budget gem is conveniently located near the centre of Ranohira. Run by the irrepressible Alice, it has bungalows of various types and prices, with the *paillottes* (adobe huts) being the best deal. The restaurant is a super place to hang out, and the food (mains Ar6500) ain't bad either.

★ **Le Relais de la Reine** BOUTIQUE HOTEL $$$

(020 22 336 23; www.lerelaisdelareine.com; d €80, bungalows €70, mains from €10; @) Beautifully designed, Le Relais sits among canyons with a stately elegance. The gracious family that owns it understands the nature of hospitality from entry to exit. The spa and equestrian centre are added perks.

DON'T MISS

PARC NATIONAL D'ANDRINGITRA & THE TSARANORO VALLEY

Andringitra is the greatest national park south of Tana, and perhaps in Madagascar. It encompasses a majestic central mountain range with two gorgeous valleys, the Namoly and the Tsaranoro, on either side, forming a paradise for walkers and climbers. There are spectacular views in all directions, 100km of well-developed hiking trails, excellent accomodation, river swimming and three extraordinary peaks, including Pic Boby (Imarivolanitra), at 2658m the second-highest peak in the country.

The main **MNP office** (☎020 75 340 81; www.parcs-madagascar.com) is in the Namoly Valley, about three hours' drive from Ambalavao. Here you can hire guides, porters, cooks and equipment. Food can be arranged too, if you call one day ahead.

Entrance permits for 1/2 days are Ar10,000/15,000. Guide fees start at Ar15,000 and cooks/porters about half that, with prices dependent on how long you want to hike. Temperatures fall below zero at night in winter, so come prepared.

If you're not camping, **Camp Catta** (☎020 75 923 58; Parc National d'Andringitra; bungalows without/with bathroom Ar48,000/60,000) is the place to stay, with a breathtaking location at the foot of the massif and quality food and lodging.

If you don't have your own transport, *taxis-brousses* run between Ambalavao and Namoly Tuesday or Thursday. Otherwise Camp Catta can organise transfers.

Information

Arrange your mandatory guide at the **MNP Office** (☎033 13 172 58; Ranohira; ⏲7am-5pm). Entry fees for 1/2 days are Ar25,000/37,000. Guide fees are Ar20,000 to Ar30,000 per circuit, depending on whether you go by foot or car.

There are no banks in Ranohira.

Getting There & Away

For points north, you may be lucky enough to find a *taxi-brousse* travelling between Tuléar and Antananarivo with an empty seat. Each morning one or two *taxis-brousses* connect Ranohira directly with Ihosy, 91km to the east (Ar20,000, two hours), from where there are more options.

The Great Reef

A great reef stretches over 450km along the southwestern coast of Madagascar, making it the fifth-largest coral reef in the world. It is the main attraction in the region, yet no one knows what to call it!

Tuléar (Toliara)

POP 136,000

Tuléar is mostly used as a transit point. It has a bit of Antsirabe about it, with a sea of *pousses-pousses* bouncing down dusty lanes, crumbling relics of the colonial past and a raffish tropical ambience.

Sights

★ **Arboretum d'Antsokay** GARDENS
(www.antsokayarboretum.org; admission Ar10,000) Essentially a distillation of Madagascar's southern spiny forest in one place, the arboretum is a collection of 900 species of plants. Established by a Swiss botanist and conservationist in 1980, it is also a model for how much larger parks should be run, even though it is only 40 hectares. There is a classy interpretation centre, a small museum and self-guided tours in English.

The arboretum lies about 12km southeast, just a few hundred metres from the RN7, so it's a good stop as you arrive by car. Otherwise take a taxi.

Sleeping

Chez Lala HOTEL $
(☎020 94 434 17; Ave de France; d without/with bathroom Ar15,000/21,000; ❄📶) Tuléar's best budget option. The cozy rooms in the tropical courtyard are smaller than those in the parquet-tiled main block, but they are all great value. A TV lounge, great espresso, loads of info and free wi-fi help clinch the deal.

Serena Hôtel HOTEL $
(☎020 94 411 73; www.serenatulear.com; Blvd Tsiranana; d/tr Ar47,500/72,500; ❄📶) The 'African tribal chic' style elevates this hotel above the pack. Take your morning espresso in the glassed-in restaurant, the perfect place to

Tuléar (Toliara)

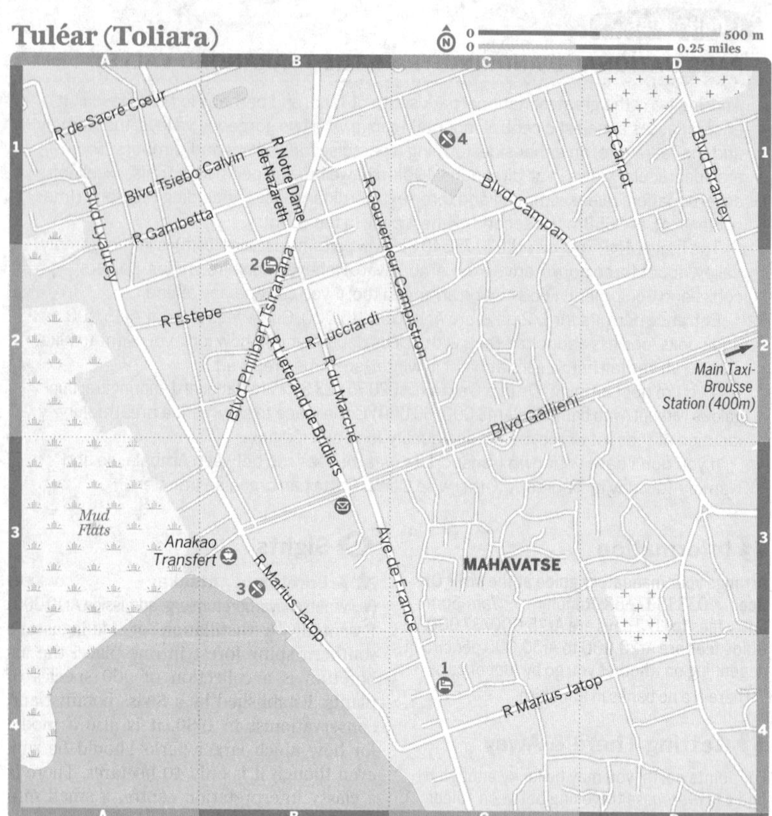

Tuléar (Toliara)

Sleeping

1 Chez Lala C4
2 Serena Hôtel B2

Eating

3 Bo Beach B3
4 Corto Maltese C1

watch the *pousse-pousse* carts gliding past below.

★ Bakuba GUESTHOUSE $$$
(☎03 464 927 82; www.bakubaconcept.com; r/ste €80/120) It would be more accurate to describe this place as a work of art that you stay in rather than an arty guest house. The work of Bruno Decorte, a Frenchman who has spent much of his life in Africa, Bakuba has three unique rooms, with features such as a wall of water, a dugout canoe-turned-bathtub and lamps made of gourds. It's located 14km southeast of the centre, on the shore, on the way to the airport.

Eating

Bo Beach BURGERS $
(mains Ar6000-15,000; ⏲7.30am-late; 📶) This lively sports bar and expat hang-out with its own private beach is the place to come for breezy waterfront dining, with enough beer, burgers, pizza and kebabs to displace the memory of all that rice you've been eating.

Corto Maltese INTERNATIONAL $$
(cnr Rue Gambetta & Blvd Campan; mains Ar10,000-18,000; ⏲lunch & dinner Mon-Fri) Generally considered the best restaurant in Tuléar, yet moderately priced, this creative bistro offers an eclectic menu including steaks. Nice outdoor seating too.

Information

There are plenty of banks and ATMs in Tuléar, including a BNI-CA, which accepts MasterCard (the rest take Visa).

Cyber Paositra (Blvd Gallieni; per min Ar30; ⌚8am-8pm Mon-Sat) Best for internet.

Getting There & Around

AIR

Air Madagascar flies from Tuléar to Tana, Morondava and Fort Dauphin. A taxi from the airport into town is Ar15,000.

BOAT

Anakao Transfert (☎020 94 924 16; anakao transfert@moov.mg; Ar50,000 each way) departs from the tourist port for Anakao every day at 9am. This is the best and safest option.

TAXI-BROUSSE

Taxis-brousses leave the main station very early every day for Antananarivo (Ar45,000), arriving a day later. Destinations and fares along the way include Isalo/Ranohira (Ar20,000), Ambalavao (Ar26,000), Fianarantsoa (Ar30,000), Ambositra (Ar36,000) and Antsirabe (Ar40,000).

Anakao

Anakao is the best overall tourist destination on the Great Reef. It is blessed with an entrancing semicircle of white-sand beach, a slice of turquoise water and a laid-back ambience. There is a plethora of activities (from snorkelling and diving to kitsurfing and quad-biking) and excellent accommodation to boot.

There are no banking facilities in Anakao. Access to Anakao is via boat transfer from Tuléar.

★ **Auberge Peter Pan** BOUTIQUE HOTEL $
(☎020 94 921 40; www.peterpanhotel.com; d bungalow Ar25,000-40,000) The young Italian owners have crafted a funky selection of warmly eclectic bungalows. The dynamic bar is a fusion of revolutionary and hip. And all of this on a beautiful beach. But apart from understanding the science of cool, these boys know how to cook (mains from Ar13,000). Booking essential.

Anakao Ocean Lodge LODGE $$$
(☎020 94 921 76; www.anakaooceanlodge.com; d bungalow €130) This is the premier resort on the Great Reef. The bungalows are beautiful; the smiling uniformed staff is always there when you need them; the food (menu €16) is a work of art and the whole place breathes effortless refinement.

NORTHERN MADAGASCAR

From Nosy Be's gorgeous shores to the windy coastline of the Bay of Diego Suarez, northern Madagascar is the perfect destination for active types, with diving and hiking the main attractions.

Nosy Be

Despite being Madagascar's number-one beach destination, Nosy Be remains relatively low-key. The climate is sunny year-round, and it is paradise for water-based activities. Diving and snorkelling are the island's top draws, but there is plenty to explore above water too.

Hell-Ville and Ambatoloaka are the two main towns. The latter has a seedy reputation but Hell-Ville is a pleasant place, with good facilities, including banks and internet.

Sights & Activities

★ **Réserve Naturelle Intégrale de Lokobe** WILDLIFE RESERVE
This gorgeous reserve protects most of Nosy Be's remaining endemic vegetation. You'll spot lemurs as well as boa constrictors, owls, chameleons and many wonderful plants.

You will need a guide to visit Lokobe. The best is **Jean Robert** (☎032 02 513 85). As well as knowing the reserve intimately and being a mine of information on all things fauna and flora, Jean is a real character. He organises lovely day trips for Ar80,000 per person including lunch and transport to the reserve by taxi and *pirogue* (traditional canoe).

★ **Nosy Komba & Nosy Tanikely** ISLAND
These two islands off Nosy Be make a fabulous day trip. Nosy Komba offers some wonderful walking opportunities while Tanikely is one of the best snorkelling spots in the country (turtles almost guaranteed). **Madavoile** (☎020 86 065 55; www.madavoile.com; Ambatoloaka) arranges trips (Ar90,000 per person including a picnic lunch).

Tropical Diving DIVING
(☎032 49 462 51; www.tropical-diving.com; Hôtel Coco Plage, Ambatoloaka) Offers a good range of PADI-CMAS courses and a variety of diving excursions to nearby islands.

Nosy Be Island

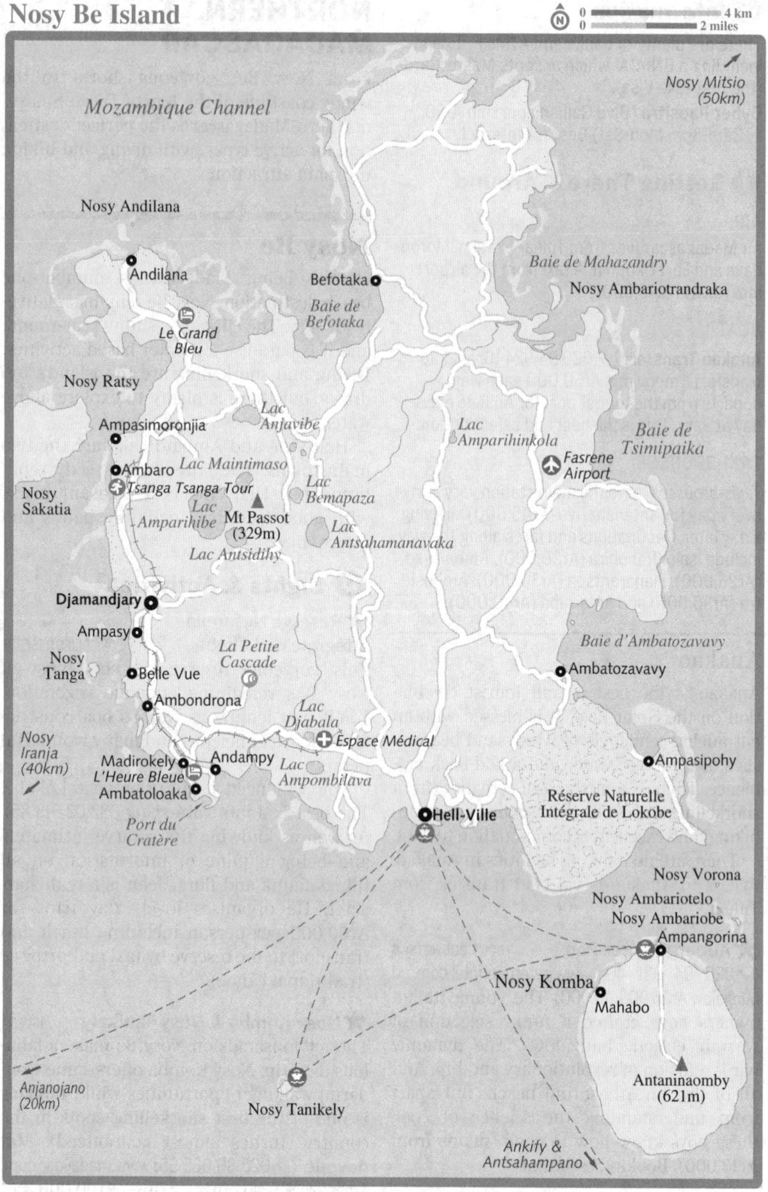

Tsanga Tsanga Tour DRIVING TOUR

(☎033 14 334 20; isoal@moov.mg; Ambaro) This outfit offers quad-bike tours of the island. Popular routes include a circuit around the crater lakes, remote beaches in the north and cocoa plantations to the south. Allow €60/100 for a half/full day.

Sleeping & Eating

Accommodation in Nosy Be is the priciest in Madagascar.

Hôtel Plantation HOTEL $$
(☎032 07 934 45; plantation_b@yahoo.fr; Rue Fortin, Hell-Ville; r Ar35,000-65,000;) In a beautiful old colonial mansion, this is a charming little place. Ask to see a few rooms before you settle as the cheaper ones can be a little dark, while the nicest have beautiful parquet floors and sea-facing balconies. The restaurant serves good food.

★**Le Grand Bleu** GUESTHOUSE $$$
(☎020 86 920 23; www.legrandbleunosybe.com; Andilana; bungalows €30-65;) On a hill overlooking the sea, Le Grand Bleu's star attraction is the dazzling infinity pool (with infinity views). The bungalows are very pretty, each with its own terrace and hammock. Half-board deals are available.

Les Bungalows d'Ambonara GUESTHOUSE $$$
(☎020 86 613 67; www.nosy-beholidays. com; off Route de l'Ouest, Hell-Ville; bungalows Ar75,000;) The bungalows are scattered in a luxuriant garden, with a small green pool sitting in the middle of it all like an emerald in its case. The whole place has been beautifully decorated using local materials. Owner Jean-Michel also runs an exquisite restaurant on-site (mains Ar16,000 to Ar18,000, closed Monday); his *rhums arrangés* (flavoured rums) are divine.

L'Heure Bleue BOUTIQUE HOTEL $$$
(☎020 86 060 20; www.heurebleue.com; Madirokely; bungalows €100;) On a hill overlooking the beach of Madirokely, this gorgeous hotel has a terrace with great views and a sensational saltwater pool just above the sea. The bungalows are made of polished wood and have dreamy balconies with ocean views.

Information

You'll find several banks in Hell-Ville (all with ATM) and one ATM in Ambatoloaka.

Espace Médical (☎020 86 925 99; Rte de l'Ouest; ⊙24hr) About halfway between Hell-Ville and Ambatoloaka. French, Italian and some English spoken.

Kelly Services (Gallerie Ankoay, Blvd du Général de Gaulle, Hell-Ville; per min Ar80; ⊙7am-10pm) Internet.

Getting There & Away

Air There are daily flights between Nosy Be's Fasrene Airport and Tana.

Boat Speedboats shuttle between the mainland port of Ankify, from where you'll find *taxis-brousses* for Diego Suarez (Ar30,000, five hours) and Hell-Ville on Nosy Be (Ar10,000, 30 minutes, 5.30am to 4pm). They work like *taxis-brousses* and leave when full.

Getting Around

To/from the airport The airport is on the island's east side, about 12km from Hell-Ville. Taxi fare from to Hell-Ville is around Ar30,000 or Ar40,000 to Ambatoloaka and Andilana.

Motorcycle Traffic is light and the roads are good so Nosy Be is the ideal place to rent motorbikes. You'll find plenty of rental places in Ambatoloaka (per day Ar20,000).

Taxi You'll find plenty of collective taxis between Hell-Ville and Ambatoloaka (Ar2000, 20 minutes) but very few elsewhere.

Diego Suarez (Antsiranana)

POP 75,000

With its wide streets, old colonial-era buildings and genteel air, Diego is a lovely base from which to explore Madagascar's northern region. It is a slow-moving place where nearly everything shuts between noon and 3pm.

Diego is located inside the immense Baie de Diego Suarez, the world's second-largest bay after Rio de Janeiro in Brazil.

Tours

À La Découverte de Diego Suarez WALKING TOUR
These themed, self-guided walking tours of Diego Suarez take in the main historical and architectural highlights of the city. Each itinerary (1½ to two hours) has a dedicated leaflet (Ar3000), complete with map, photos and detailed explanation about each highlight of the itinerary. Leaflets are available from the tourist office.

Diego Raid DRIVING TOUR
(☎032 40 001 75; www.diegoraid.com; Rue Colbert; tours per day Ar270,000-460,000) This operator organises highly recommended quad-bike excursions to areas such as Les Trois Baies. As well as taking in the main sights, the trips tend to leave the tarmac well behind and take the scenic route instead.

Sleeping

★**Le Jardin Exotique** BOUTIQUE HOTEL $$
(☎020 82 219 33; http://jardinexotique.hotel-diegosuarez.com; Rue Louis Brunet; r Ar65,000-75,000;) Rooms at this quirky boutique place all come with parquet floors, four-

WORTH A TRIP

LES TROIS BAIES

On the eastern side of the peninsula of the Bay of Diego Suarez is a series of beautiful bays with stunning beaches. The area is named after three majestic coves: Baie de Sakalava (Sakalava Bay), Baie des Pigeons (Pigeons Bay) and Baie des Dunes (Sand Dunes Bay). It's a wild, harsh but starkly beautiful environment, with not a village in sight, strong winds from April to November, and baking heat from December to March.

The walk from Baie de Sakalava (the southernmost of the three bays) to the village of Ramena via Baie des Pigeons and Baie des Dunes has become a popular excursion. It takes roughly half a day to walk from one end to the other, more if you include stops for swimming and/or a picnic. Tour operators in Diego can organise day trips with transport, guide and picnic.

poster beds, mosquito nets, bold and creative paint jobs and Italian showers in the bathrooms. The rooftop terrace has awesome views over the bay of Diego Suarez.

La Belle Aventure GUESTHOUSE $$
(☎032 44 153 83; www.labellaventure-diego.com; 13 Rue Freppel; d Ar55,000-85,000; ❄📶) The Beautiful Adventure is in a great neighbourhood of Diego: quiet, yet close to the centre, and with good views of the bay. Everything is bright, fresh and impeccable. Gilles and Elisabeth, the hosts, will bend over backwards to ensure you have a good time.

Allamanda Hôtel BOUTIQUE HOTEL $$$
(☎020 82 210 33; www.hotels-diego.com; Rue Richelieu; d from Ar216,000; ❄@📶🏊) Just steps from the sea, the Allamanda has all the luxuries you would expect from a top-end hotel. Rooms are spacious and elegantly decked out in nautical-themed decor.

Eating

Balafomanga INTERNATIONAL $$
(18 Rue Louis Brunet; mains Ar12,000-15,000; ⏰noon-2.30pm & 6.30-10pm Mon-Sat) The Balafomanga offers a bit of everything and it's all done well. It's a funky dining environment, with Chinese lanterns and multicoloured walls and tablecloths, and charming staff.

La Bodega FUSION $$
(cnr Rue Colbert & Rue Flacourt; mains Ar15,000-18,000; ⏰noon-3pm & 6-11pm Mon-Sat) Blending Spanish, French and Malagasy influences, this colourful place serves delicious fusion cuisine (and amazing rum cocktails). It's always busy and has a great atmosphere.

★**Le Melville** FRENCH $$$
(☎032 05 606 99; Allamanda Hôtel, Rue Richelieu; mains Ar15,000-23,000; ⏰7am-10.30pm) Right by the sea, with a fabulous deck, the atmosphere at Melville is romantic and sophisticated and the food divine: the fat zebu steak with vanilla mash is sumptuous, and seafood-lovers will be spoiled for choice.

Information

There are plenty of banks, all with ATMs and money-changing facilities.

Housseini.com (Ave Tollendal; internet per hr Ar1700; ⏰8am-9pm Mon-Sat, 3-8.30pm Sun)

Pharmacie de l'Espérance (Rue Colbert)

Tourist Office (www.office-tourisme-diego-suarez.com; Place Foch; ⏰8am-noon & 3-6pm Mon-Fri, 8.30-11.30am Sat)

Getting There & Away

Air Air Madagascar has daily flights to Tana; the airport is 6km south of town.

Taxi-brousse There are services to Tana (Ar50,000, 24 hours), Ankify (Ar30,000, five hours) and Ramena (Ar2000, one hour).

EASTERN MADAGASCAR

The RN2 twists spectacularly down the mountainsides between Tana and the coast to Tamatave, passing one of the country's great rain-forest reserves en route.

Parc National Andasibe-Mantadia

This national park comprises two separate parks, the northern Parc National de Mantadia (16,000 hectares) and the much smaller but more visited **Parc National d'Andasibe** (810 hectares).

The parks were created primarily to protect the indri, Madagascar's largest lemur, whose unforgettable wail can be heard emanating from the misty forest throughout the day, most commonly in the early morning.

A number of trails criss-cross the parks, all of them relatively easygoing. Night walks are also available.

Sleeping & Eating

Hôtel Les Orchidées HOTEL $

(☎020 56 832 05; d Ar30,000-40,000) Once you get past the rough exterior, Les Orchidées feels like a charming cabin, with cozy rooms upstairs. The great surprise is the large brick annex out back that triples its size. Food available (mains Ar7000).

Mikalo BUNGALOW $$

(☎020 56 832 08; new bungalows d Ar94,000) This hotel has a showpiece roadside restaurant (menu Ar19,000) offering the usual suspects – zebu, seafood, pasta – that gets high marks for design. The rooms are more hit and miss: opt for the new wooden bungalows in the forest.

Andasibe Hotel LODGE $$$

(☎034 143 2627; d Ar175,000, half board Ar45,000; 🏊) This lodge has the best double rooms around, with split-levels, bold Asian styling, and knock-out views across a verdant rice paddy. The restaurant (mains from Ar14,000) has equally creative French cuisine, and there's a nice pool deck. Located on a jungle lake, it offers many activities, and rents bikes so you can get around on your own.

Information

The **MNP office** (⊙6am-4pm) has a helpful interpretation centre. Entrance permits cost Ar25,000/37,000 for 1/2 days and are valid for both national parks.

Guiding fees vary depending on the walk.

Getting There & Away

From Tana, the best way to reach Andasibe is to take a *taxi-brousse* to Moramanga first, then another to Andasibe. Ask the driver to drop you at your hotel.

When leaving Andasibe, you either have to return to Moramanga first, or wait for a *taxi-brousse* on the RN2.

Tamatave (Toamasina)

POP 240,000

The emphasis in Tamatave, Madagascar's main port, is on commerce rather than tourism. For visitors, it's a good place to break the journey between Île Sainte Marie and the remote northeast corner of the country, and to visit the nearby Canal des Pangalanes.

Activities

Canal des Pangalanes BOAT TOUR

Touring the canals in a *pirogue* is high on most visitors' lists of things to do. A day trip provides a fascinating glimpse of life in the riverside villages. **Calypso Tours** (☎032 40 247 78; Hôtel Eden, Blvd Joffre) organises excursions from Tamatave (Ar70,000 per person).

Sleeping

Hôtel Eden HOTEL $

(☎020 53 312 90; calypsotour@netcourrier.com; Blvd Joffre; r without/with bathroom Ar16,000/25,000) This popular backpackers' hotel is a good budget choice, with a mix of shared and private bathrooms and helpful staff.

Génération Hôtel HOTEL $$

(☎020 57 220 22; www.hotel-generation.com; Blvd Joffre; d Ar65,000; ❄) A slightly cluttered but genial hotel, it is greatly helped by a resident group of local mining-company employees, who rate it highly. The attached restaurant reportedly serves good food too.

Le Palais des Isles GUESTHOUSE $$$

(☎020 53 314 33; tsarisland@moov.mg; d/f Ar120,000/150,000) This colonial mansion remade as a guesthouse is a white architectural gem from the 1930s. It has two floors with a huge wrap-around balcony, and three nice rooms with good mattresses.

Eating

★**Le Bateau Ivre** INTERNATIONAL $$

(Blvd Ratsimilaho; mains Ar9000-18,000; ⊙lunch & dinner; 📶) Tamatave's Cotton Club is a sprawling beachfront enterprise, with views of the port's commercial dock, and a

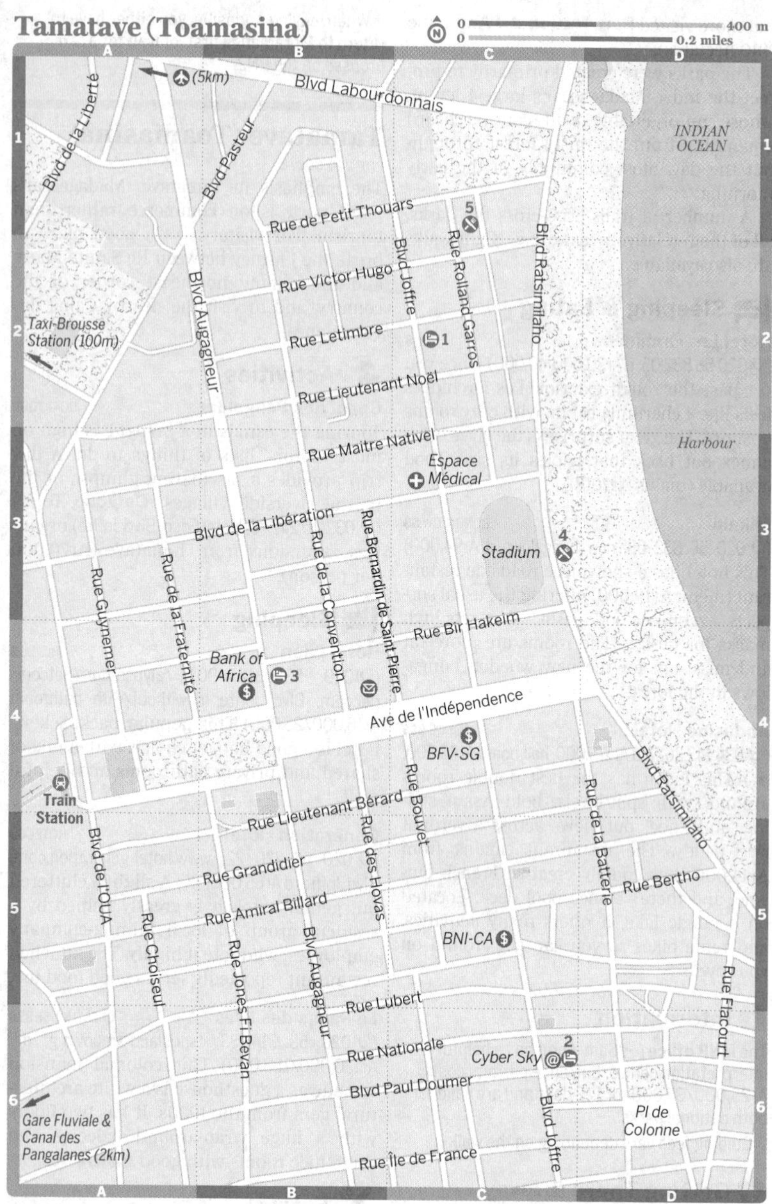

permanent festive mood. It serves excellent seafood, pizzas, burgers and creative drinks.

Piment Banane FRENCH **$$**
(Rue de l'Ourd; mains from Ar10,000; ⏲ lunch & dinner Mon-Sat; 📶) Exceptional is how to describe this welcome addition to the city, from the stylish decor to the creative cuisine to the extensive wine list, all of which has garnered rave reviews.

Tamatave (Toamasina)

Activities, Courses & Tours
Calypso Tours (see 2)

Sleeping
1 Génération Hôtel C2
2 Hôtel Eden C6
3 Le Palais des Isles B4

Eating
4 Le Bateau Ivre C3
5 Piment Banane C1

Information

There are plenty of banks in Tamatave.

Cyber Sky (upstairs next to Hôtel Eden, Blvd Joffre; per min Ar30; 8am-8pm Mon-Sat)

Espace Médical (020 53 315 66; Blvd de la Libération; 24hr)

Getting There & Away

Air There are daily flights with Air Madagascar to Tana and Île Sainte Marie.

Taxi-brousse Regular services to Tana (Ar15,000, seven hours) and Soanierana-Ivongo (Ar8000, four hours) for Île Ste-Marie.

Île Sainte Marie (Nosy Boraha)

The best thing about Île Sainte Marie is that it contains all the ingredients for a great vacation and great travel. This is a very long (57km), thin, lush and relatively flat tropical island surrounded by beaches and reef, spotted with thatched villages; the port of Ambodifotatra is the only sizeable town.

Some key dates: July to September is whale-watching season, peak season on the island, and December to March is cyclone season.

Sights & Activities

Most activities on the island – from quad excursions to whale-watching – tend to be organised by hotels.

Cimetière des Pirates CEMETERY
(Ambodifotatra; admission Ar2000) This is a fascinating spot from which to contemplate the history of the island. The scenic cemetery overlooks the Baie de Forbans, which, as a quick look at the map will tell you, was the perfect pirate hang-out. Most of the gravestones are actually of missionaries, but you can clearly see the skull and crossbones on the grave of one young English pirate. Access is via an isolated foot track, which crosses several tidal creeks and slippery logs about 10 minutes south of the causeway in Ambodifotatra.

Île aux Nattes ISLAND
This is a classic tropical island, with curving white beaches and overhanging palms, a turquoise sea, a gentle breeze and a lush green interior. While only a brief *pirogue* ride (Ar5000 return) from the tip of Saint Marie, or a mere walk at low tide, there's a palpable sense of isolation and adventure. Numerous sand pathways (beware the crab holes!) open the way for exploration without the possibility of getting too lost in an area only 2km across.

A WHALE OF A TIME

Every year several hundred humpback whales make their way from the Antarctic northward to the warmer Malagasy waters, where they spend the winter months breeding and birthing. En route they swim past Île Sainte Marie, where they are often sighted between July and mid-September.

Humpbacks are renowned for breaching (jumping) and singing, which are presumed to be related to mating patterns.

During humpback season you can go on 'whale safaris' around the island for about €40 for a half-day trip. Enquire at the dive centres and shuttle-boat companies, as hotels without their own boats often arrange trips through them.

The business is informally regulated by **Cétamada** (033 65 656 56; www.cetamada.org), a Madagascar conservation organisation that promotes responsible whale watching. Participating hotels agree to respect a code of approach, assure security protocols on board, and have a qualified guide. You can help by hiring a boat with a Cétamada sticker on it.

Île Sainte Marie (Nosy Boraha)

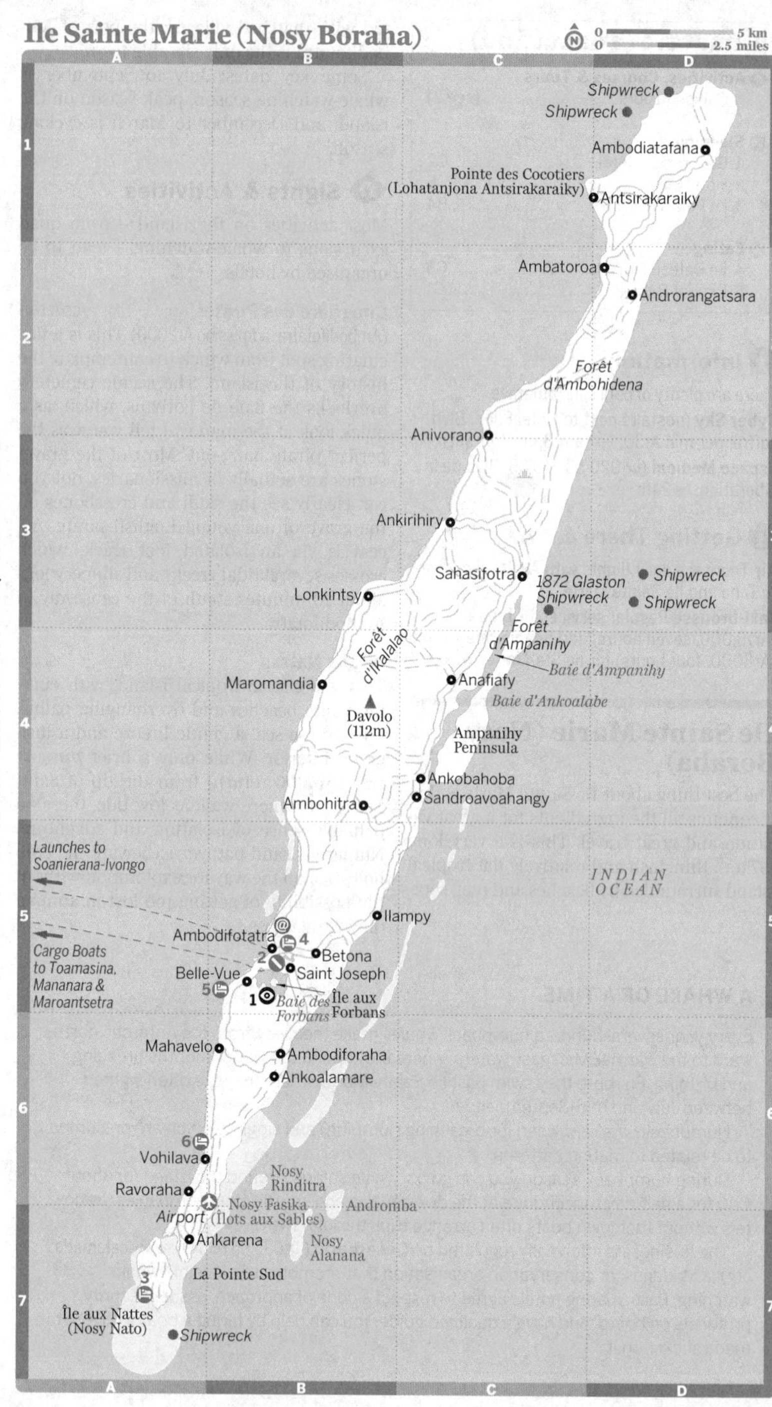

Ile Sainte Marie (Nosy Boraha)

Sights

Activities, Courses & Tours

Sleeping

Il Balenottero DIVING
(☎020 57 400 36; www.il-balenottero.com; Ambodifotatra) A large operation with five boats. Also offers whale-watching, yacht cruises and fishing trips.

AT-SM Agency TOUR
(☎032 40 084 43; atsm11@live.fr) If you are looking to put together any type of itinerary on the island, the best person to call is Orpheu ('or-*fay*'), the former head of the island's tourism office, who now runs his own agency. He's a dynamic young gentleman who speaks fluent English, makes things happen, and knows everyone.

Sleeping & Eating

★Chez Sika BUNGALOW $
(☎032 04 607 74; azafadysica@yahoo.fr; Île aux Nattes; d/f Ar30,000/50,000) Wow. If you are looking for inexpensive accommodation, look no further: Chez Sika on tiny Île aux Nattes outperforms places two or three times its cost. The hotel is like an open park beneath the palms, with an absolutely gorgeous location on a fringing reef. Only breakfast is served, but there is a kitchen for guests (and plenty of other hotels nearby).

Hôtel Freddy HOTEL $$
(☎020 57 907 03; Rue Belgique, Ambodifotatra; d without/with bathroom Ar30,000/40,000) This brand-new midrange hotel, conveniently located in the town centre, does all the basics right. Rooms are clean and sizeable with hot water, a shared balcony and lots of light.

Libertalia BUNGALOW $$$
(☎020 57 903 03; www.lelibertalia.com; d Ar94,000) The setting is unique, with a small private island connected to a lovely beach, and a great swimming dock. A sophisticated kitchen, with large breakfasts, lively staff, and special touches like a band and dancing, are all part of the winning formula.

★Princesse Bora Lodge & Spa LUXURY HOTEL $$$
(☎020 57 040 03; www.princessebora.com; d with half board per person low/high/whale-watching season Ar230,000/270,000/310,000; ❄@≋) One of Madagascar's top resorts, this luxury lodge offers everything you could hope for (idyllic setting, gourmet restaurant, unique bungalows) and more (extraordinary spa, fabulous wine cellar with private label, tropical nursery etc).

Information

The island's only banks (with ATMs) are in Ambodifotatra.

Alex Papurus (Ave Angleterre, Ambodifotatra; internet per min Ar50)

Getting There & Away

AIR

Daily flights are available with Air Madagascar from Île Sainte Marie to Tana and Tamatave.

BOAT

There are regular shuttle boats between Ambodifotatra and Soaniera-Ivongo on the mainland. The **Melissa Express** is the fastest (Ar70,000 one way).

Getting Around

TO/FROM THE AIRPORT

The airport is located at the southern tip of the island, 13km south of Ambodifotatra. Hotel transfer prices range from Ar2000 to Ar40,000 one way, depending on distance. If you can find one, *taxis-brousses* usually charge Ar5000 between the airport and Ambodifotatra. A private taxi costs Ar20,000.

MOTORCYCLE

Motorcycles and scooters are a great way to explore the island. Rental outfits can be found in Ambodifotatra.

UNDERSTAND MADAGASCAR

Madagascar Today

Madagascar has been in the throes of a political crisis since Andry Rajoelina came to power following violent uprisings in March

2009; his predecessor, Marc Ravalomanana, handed power to the army and fled to South Africa.

The international community decided that Rajoelina's accession to power was unconstitutional and refused to recognise his High Transitional Authority (HAT) as a legitimate government; all international aid funding, which represented about 50% of the government's public funding, was withheld.

In August 2010, Marc Ravalomanana was condemned, in absentia, to forced labour for life for the deaths of 30 protesters during the uprisings of February 2009 (the presidential guards had fired on the crowd without warning).

HAT's self-imposed deadline of running elections within 24 months came and went. After much hand-wringing and negotiating between rival stakeholders, it looked like, at the time of going to press, elections were finally going to take place by late 2013.

Madagascar has suffered greatly from the political crisis, and Malagasy are keen to turn the page and start a new chapter of their history.

History

Archaeological evidence suggests that Madagascar was uninhabited until about 2000 years ago, when the first Indo-Malayan settlers arrived in coast-hugging craft that skirted the Indian Ocean. They brought traditions with them, such as planting rice in terraced paddies, Southeast Asian food crops, and linguistic and musical roots that were buried in the subcontinent. The migration accelerated in the 9th century, when the powerful Hindu-Sumatran empire of Srivijaya controlled much of the maritime trade in the Indian Ocean.

European Arrival & Colonisation

Portuguese sailors named the island Ilha de São Lourenço, but like subsequent British, Dutch and French fleets they failed to establish a base here. European and North American buccaneers had notably more success, making Madagascar (and especially Île Sainte Marie) their base in the Indian Ocean during the 17th century.

Powerful Malagasy kingdoms developed with the growth of trade with European merchants. Most powerful of all were the Merina of the central highlands, whose chief, Ramboasalama, acquired the weaponry to subdue neighbouring tribes. His son Radama became king in 1810 and, sniffing the winds of fortune, entered diplomatic relations with the British in 1817 and allowed hundreds of Christian missionaries to enter the Merina court. However, his widow and successor, Ranavalona I, nicknamed 'The Bloodthirsty', passionately disliked all things *vahaza* (foreign); she persecuted the missionaries and ordered the execution of tens of thousands of her Malagasy subjects using barbarous and ingenious methods.

In 1890 the British handed Madagascar over to the French in exchange for Zanzibar. The French captured Antananarivo in 1895 and turned the island into an official colony in 1897. The French suppressed the Malagasy language; however, they constructed roads, expanded the education network and abolished slavery. Resentment of the French colonial presence grew in all levels of society, and Nationalist movements had developed by the 1920s. Strikes and demonstrations culminated in a revolt in 1947, which the French suppressed after killing an estimated 80,000 people and sending the rebel leaders into exile.

Nationalism & Independence

By 1958 the Malagasy had voted in a referendum to become an autonomous republic within the French community of overseas nations. Philibert Tsiranana became Madagascar's first president, and allowed the French to keep control of most of Madagascar's trade and industry. Tsiranana was forced to resign in 1972 and was succeeded by army general Gabriel Ramantsoa.

The socialist Ramantsoa made friends with China and the USSR, closed down the French military bases and collectivised the farming system, which led to an exodus of French farmers. The economy took a nosedive and Ramantsoa was forced to resign. His successor, Richard Ratsimandrava, lasted just one week before being assassinated by rebel army officers. They were almost immediately routed by Ramantsoa loyalists, and a new government headed by Admiral Didier Ratsiraka came to power.

The Ratsiraka years were characterised by more socialist reforms, but a debt crisis in the early 1980s forced him to abandon the reforms and obey the International Monetary Fund. In 1989 Ratsiraka was dubiously 'elected' to his third seven-year term, sparking riots that left six people dead. People were still demanding his resignation by 1991, and the ensuing demonstrations brought the economy to a standstill. In 1992 the Malagasy voted in a referendum to limit the presidential powers. General elections were held that year, and Professor Albert Zafy thrashed Ratsiraka, ending his 17 years in power.

Years of communist-style dictatorship and economic mismanagement made it hard for Zafy to ignite the economy and gain the trust of the people. He was eventually impeached for abuse of constitutional powers. Elections were called in 1996 and Ratsiraka surprised everyone by scraping by with a victory.

Ravalomanana

In the first round of the 2001 general election, Marc Ravalomanana, a dairy businessman, claimed victory, but Ratsiraka refused to accept the vote.

Ravalomanana and his supporters mounted mass protests and a general strike at the beginning of 2002. A month later Ravalomanana went ahead and declared himself president anyway, sparking off clashes between rival supporters that nearly brought Madagascar to civil war. Bridges were bombed, and Ratsiraka's supporters blockaded Antananarivo, cutting off its fuel and food supply for weeks.

The Supreme Court held a recount of the votes and declared Ravalomanana the winner. When the US recognised Ravalomanana as the rightful president, Ratsiraka fled in exile to Paris. Ravalomanana's 'I Love Madagascar' party sealed its popularity at parliamentary elections in December 2002. The new president set about reforming the country's ruined economy, and announced salary increases for politicians in an effort to stamp out corruption. His government generally made the right noises to the World Bank, which, along with France and the US, pledged a total of US$2.3 billion in aid.

Under his leadership, main roads were repaired and maintained, and tourism was promoted by the declaration of new national parks. But it was Ravalomanana's business drive that eventually brought about his demise: in July 2008 he signed a 99-year lease with Korean company Daewoo Logistics for 13,000 sq km of land for maize cultivation, half of all arable land on the island. The deal caused consternation (and was later rescinded) in a country where land customarily belongs to ancestors. What had been simmering discontent grew to a boil and led to the 2009 coup.

People of Madagascar

The Malagasy people are officially divided into 18 ethnic groups, whose boundaries are roughly based on old kingdoms. The main groups are Merina (27%), Betsimisaraka (15%), Betsileo (12%), Tsimihety (7%), Sakalava (6%), Antaisaka (5%) and Antandroy (5%), with a number of smaller groups making up the remainder. Also important is the distinction between Merina highlanders and so-called *côtiers* (literally, those from the coast, but referring to non-Merina in general).

Malagasy is the main language although there are huge variations across the island. French remains an official language too, and is widely spoken.

Religion & Beliefs

About half the Malagasy belong to the Roman Catholic and Protestant churches (a small proportion, around 7%, is Muslim), but all still attach tremendous importance to traditional beliefs, which are rooted in reverence for one's ancestors and their spirits.

Death is seen as the transition between temporary life on earth and the afterlife, which is permanent. This explains why tombs are sometimes much grander than homes. At *famadihana* (literally, 'the turning of the bones') exhumation ceremonies, people may line up for a photograph with the shroud-wrapped bodies of dead family members laid out neatly in the foreground. There's also a complex system of *fady* (taboos) that must be respected.

Malagasy also invoke spirits for prosperity and fertility and you'll see offerings and ribbons placed on sacred sites and shrines. Time and dates have an influence on Malagasy lifestyle. One example of this is seen in the belief in *vintana* (destiny), which determines the most auspicious date for activities and celebrations.

The Arts

Textiles have always played a huge part in Malagasy society, with some types of cloth even being imbued, it is believed, with supernatural powers. The Merina used cocoons collected from the wild silkworm to make highly valued textiles called *lamba mena* (red silk). Worn by the aristocracy in life and death, *lamba mena* were also used in burial and reburial ceremonies.

Hira gasy are popular music, dancing and storytelling spectacles held in the central highlands of Madagascar. Brightly clad troupes of 25 performers compete for prizes for the best costumes or the most exciting spectacle. An important part of *hira gasy* is *kabary*, in which a performer delivers an oratory using allegory, double entendre, metaphor and simile.

Hira gasy has long been used to deliver important information or raise awareness of certain topics (health, politics, environmental issues, respecting family values etc). Unfortunately, unless you have fluent Malagasy, you're unlikely to agree with the proverb that says: 'While listening to a *kabary* well spoken, one fails to notice the fleas that bite one'. All the same, it is a cultural event well worth seeing.

Food & Drink

You won't go hungry in Madagascar – eating is a real joy and prices are extremely cheap by Western standards. Rice is the staple and is often accompanied by a stew made from beef, fish, chicken, duck or vegetables. Favourite dishes include *romazava* (beef-and-vegetable stew) and *ravitoto* (pork stew with manioc), with *mi sao* (fried noodles with vegetables or meat) or a satisfying *soupe chinoise* (clear noodle soup with fish, chicken or vegetables) the most usual alternatives. Restaurants normally also serve excellent French cuisine, from simple zebu *steack frites* (steak and chips), to *foie gras* (goose liver pâté) and *magret de canard* (duck breast). Western staples such as pizza and pasta are easy to find too. Green peppercorn- or vanilla-flavoured sauces are common.

Seafood fans are in for a treat – every menu in coastal areas features cheap lobster, prawns or squid dishes together with a fish of the day.

The most popular local-brand beers are Three Horses Beer (known as THB) and Gold, but the alcoholic speciality is *rhums arrangé* – rum flavoured with fruits or spices. A taste of Malagasy wine is something you probably won't want to repeat, but imported French and South African wines are served in better restaurants.

Environment

Madagascar split from the African land mass around 165 million years ago and has been in its present position for about 100 million years. It is this isolation that has resulted in such high endemicity levels.

This unique wildlife is today one of the biggest tourist drawcards and a pressing global conservation issue. Over the last thousand years many large animals, including giant lemurs, have been hunted to extinction.

Madagascar is also struggling with deforestation for domestic fuel, and illegal logging of precious woods such as rosewood and ebony.

The country's outstanding national parks are a lifeline for the country's biodiversity. They also support local communities: 50% of park admission fees are returned to villagers to build wells and small dams, buy vegetable seeds, help with tree nurseries and build schools.

SURVIVAL GUIDE

Directory A–Z

ACCOMMODATION

- Accommodation comes in many guises in Madagascar, from camping to bungalows and luxury resorts.
- Madagascar's winter months (July to September) are the busiest; it's a good idea to book ahead at this time of year.
- Few hotels have official low/high season prices, although many offer discounts at quiet periods, notably during the rainy season.
- Hot water and a decent blanket or two are luxuries worth paying for if you're staying in

the highlands, especially in winter since hotels don't have central heating.

ACTIVITIES

Madagascar is an excellent destination for sport activities. Just make sure you pick a reliable operator: always check their certifications, affiliations and the equipment you'll be using.

Divers, note that there is no hyperbaric chamber in Madagascar; the closest one is on the French island of La Réunion.

CUSTOM REGULATIONS

Precious stones and woods must come with an export certificate; if the retailer doesn't provide it to you, enquire at the customs desk at the airport.

EMBASSIES & CONSULATES

Canadian citizens should contact the Canadian High Commission in Pretoria, South Africa. The **Australian High Commission** (☎+230 202 0160; www.mauritius.embassy.gov.au; Mauritius) in Mauritius has consular responsibility for Madagascar. The following are all located in the capital.

British Embassy (☎020 22 330 53; Tour Zital Ankorondrano, Rue Ravoninahitriniarivo, Ankorondrano)

Dutch Embassy (☎020 22 682 31; rad.ned@dts.mg; Immeuble Galaxy, Andraharo)

French Embassy (☎020 22 398 98; www.ambafrance-mada.org; 3 Rue Jean Jaurès, Ambatomena)

German Embassy (☎020 22 238 02; www.antananarivo.diplo.de; 101 Rue Pasteur Rabeony, Ambodiroatra)

South African Embassy (☎020 22 433 50; antananarivo.consular@foreign.gov.za; Rue Ravoninahitriniarivo, Ankorondrano)

US Embassy (☎020 23 480 00; www.antananarivo.usembassy.gov; Point Liberty, Andranoro, Antehiroka)

EMERGENCIES

Call ☎18 for fire and ☎17 for police.

INTERNET ACCESS

- Internet cafes can now be found in all major towns and cities.
- An increasing number of hotels, including budget and midrange, have complimentary wi-fi.
- Connection can be very slow.
- Prices range from Ar30 to Ar100 per minute.

MONEY

Madagascar changed its currency from the Malagasy franc (FMG) to the ariary (Ar) in 2005. But despite having had a few years to get used to the new currency, many Malagasies still count in FMG (one ariary is worth five FMG), particularly in rural areas.

- Euros, followed by US dollars, are the easiest currencies to exchange; €100 or US$100 notes are generally refused.
- You'll find ATMs in all major towns and cities; withdrawals are capped at Ar300,000.
- All ATMs accept Visa. ATMs from Crédit Agricole (BNI-CA) also accept MasterCard.
- Credit cards are accepted in some upmarket hotels and shops but are subject to a surcharge.
- All banks in Tana exchange travellers cheques; outside of the capital, the BFV-SG is your best bet.
- Banking facilities are sparse outside of cities – don't get caught short.

PRACTICALITIES

- **Electricity** Electricity is 220V AC (use European two-round-pin plugs).
- **Languages** Malagasy, French.
- **Media** The main French-language newspapers include *Midi Madagasikara*, *Madagsacar Tribune* and *L'Express de Madagascar*.
- **Time** Madagascar is three hours ahead of GMT; there is no daylight saving.

OPENING HOURS

Businesses 8am to 4pm Monday to Friday (Tana), 7.30am to 11.30am & 2pm to 4.30pm Monday to Friday (rest of the country)

Restaurants Lunch 11.30am to 2.30pm and dinner 6.30pm to 9.30pm

Bars 5pm to 11pm

Shops 9am to noon and 2.30pm to 6pm Monday to Friday, 9am to noon Saturday

POST

The postal service should only be used for postcards and letters.

PUBLIC HOLIDAYS

New Year's Day 1 January

Insurrection Day 29 March – celebrates the rebellion against the French in 1947

Easter Monday March/April

Labour Day 1 May

Anniversary Day 8 May

African Unity Day 25 May

Ascension Thursday May/June – occurs 40 days after Easter

Pentecost Monday May/June – occurs 51 days after Easter

National Day 26 June – Independence Day
Assumption 15 August
All Saints' Day 1 November
Christmas Day 25 December

SAFE TRAVEL

- **Crime** Insecurity has increased in Tana since the political crisis started; always travel by taxi at night and watch out for pickpockets, especially around Ave de l'Indépendance.
- **Natural disasters** Cyclone season runs from December to March; the east coast is the most affected but cyclones can also hit the west coast. Heed local warnings.
- **Robbery** There has been a spate of robberies on vehicles and *taxis-brousses* travelling at night along the RN2, RN6 and RN34. The police have responded by increasing their presence on the road but the advice should always be to avoid travelling at night, particularly in private vehicles.

TELEPHONE

- The country code for Madagascar is +261.
- Landline numbers start with 02; mobiles with 03.
- Mobile (cell) phone coverage is pretty good across Madagascar, but a number of remote areas only have coverage from one network instead of the three available (Telma, Airtel and Orange).
- SIM cards are very cheap (Ar500 to Ar2000) and can be bought pretty much anywhere in the country, as can credit.
- A national/international SMS costs around Ar120/340, national calls Ar350 to Ar400 per minute, and international calls Ar870 to Ar4000 per minute.

TOURIST INFORMATION

Madagascar's **tourist offices** (www.madagascar-tourisme.com) range from useless to incredibly helpful. They will generally be able to provide listings of hotels and restaurants in the area and, in the best cases, help you organise excursions or find a guide.

VISAS

- All visitors must have a visa to enter Madagascar.
- Travellers will need to provide a return plane ticket, have a passport valid for at least six months after the intended date of return, and one free page in their passport for the visa stamps.
- Visas of up to 90 days can be purchased at the airport upon arrival; 30-day visas are free, 60-day visas cost €45 and 90-day visas cost €70.
- Longer or different types of visas must be arranged before travel – note that applications can take a long time to be processed.

Visas for Onward Travel

Visas for travel to South Africa are available from its embassy in Antananarivo.

YELLOW-FEVER VACCINATION CERTIFICATE

If you have just arrived from a country where yellow fever is present, you will be asked for a yellow-fever certificate upon arrival at immigration. This includes transit destinations.

Getting There & Away

AIR

Intercontinental flights arrive at Ivato airport, 19km north of the Antananarivo city centre. Air Madagascar is the national carrier and is relatively efficient.

Because there isn't much competition, tickets can be expensive: expect to pay €800 to €1500 for a return ticket from Europe (where there are more options), at least €1700 from North America and at least €2000 from Australia.

The following airlines fly to and from Madagascar:

Air Austral (www.airaustral.com)
Air France (www.airfrance.com)
Air Madagascar (www.airmadagascar.mg)
Air Mauritius (www.airmauritius.com)
Corsair (www.corsairfly.com)
Kenya Airways (www.kenya-airways.com)
South African Airways (www.flysaa.com)

TOURS

Adventure Associates (www.adventureassociates.com; Australia) Runs tours to Madagascar, combined with Réunion.

Comptoir de Madagascar (www.comptoirdemadagascar.com; France) General interest tours.

Cortez Travel & Expeditions (www.air-mad.com; USA) Well-established operator with an agency in the US and one in Madagascar.

Madagaskar Travel (www.madagaskar-travel.de; Germany) General and specialist fauna and flora tours.

Rainbow Tours (www.rainbow tours.co.uk; UK) Specialist and general-interest guided trips to Madagascar; highly recommended by travellers.

Terre Malgache (www.terre-malgache.com; France) A wide range of tours to Madagascar.

Getting Around

AIR

Flying within Madagascar can be a huge time-saver considering the distances and state of the roads. Unfortunately most domestic routes are between Tana and the provinces, with few direct routes between provinces. **Air Madagascar** (☎020-22 222 22; www.airmadagascar.mg; 31 Ave de l'Indépendance) is the only airline to provide domestic flights.

- Cancellations and delays occur but the airline is generally reliable.
- Tickets are expensive (one way €125 to €187) but generally exchangeable.
- You can pay for tickets by credit card or in ariary, euros or US dollars at the head office in Antananarivo and Air Madagascar offices in larger towns.
- Certain routes such as Morondava–Tuléar and flights to/from Sambava are regularly booked months in advance.

AIR PENNY SAVER

Domestic flights are about 30% cheaper when bought in Madagascar compared to when purchased abroad. If your itinerary is flexible, this is a great way to save money. But bear in mind that flights on popular routes are booked far in advance and that it is difficult to get tickets at short notice.

Air Madagascar also offers a 50% discount on domestic flights to travellers who flew the airline to Madagascar. (The discount doesn't apply to taxes, so the final saving is about 30% of the final fare.)

BOAT

On the northeast coast, cargo boats (sometimes called *boutres*) are the primary means of transport. Overloaded cargo boats, including passenger ferries, have capsized with significant loss of life. Always check for lifejackets and don't get in if the seas are rough or if the boat is overcrowded.

Boat travel on the east coast is generally unsafe during the rainy season between May and September and doesn't run during the cyclone season, December to March.

CAR & MOTORCYCLE

- Due to the often difficult driving conditions, most rental agencies make hiring a driver compulsory with their vehicles.
- Prices for a car and driver are typically Ar80,000 to Ar100,000 per day, depending on the vehicle. Prices for a 4WD are Ar150,000 to Ar240,000 per day. Some drivers will charge by the road surface, dirt or paved, regardless of the car. Prices also decrease with long-term rentals of 10 days or so. This is negotiable, but a 10-day 4WD rental typically ranges from Ar130,000 to Ar200,000 per day.
- Of Madagascar's approximately 50,000km of roads, less than 20% are paved, and many of those are riddled with potholes the size of an elephant.
- Routes in many areas are impassable or very difficult during the rainy season.
- The designation route nationale (RN) is no guarantee of quality.
- Driving in Madagascar is on the right-hand side.
- Police checkpoints are frequent (mind the traffic spikes on the ground) – always slow down and make sure you have your passport and the vehicle's documents handy.

Car Hire

If you insist on driving yourself, read the following:

- You must have an International Driving Licence.
- You must be age 23 or over and have had your licence for at least a year.
- Fuel shortages are frequent, even in Tana, so stock up. For longer trips and travel in remote areas, take extra fuel with you.

Charter Taxi

An alternative to hiring a car and driver (difficult in areas where there is little tourism) is chartering a taxi or a *taxi-brousse*.

Motorcycles

- Motorcycles can be hired by the half or full day at various places in Madagascar, including Tuléar, Nosy Be and Île Ste Marie.
- Chinese motorbikes are increasingly replacing the well-known Japanese brands.
- Wearing a helmet is compulsory; they should be provided in the rental.

LOCAL TRANSPORT

The colourful *pousse-pousse* (rickshaw) is a popular way to get around in some cities. Fares vary between Ar500 and Ar2000 for a ride, depending on distance. When it's raining and at night, prices increase.

The good news is that *taxis-brousses* are cheap and go everywhere. The bad news is that they are slow, uncomfortable, erratic and sometimes unsafe.

- *Taxis-brousses* leave when full, which can take an hour or a day.
- Fares for all trips are set by the government and are based on distance, duration and route conditions. Ask to see the list of official fares.
- Specific seats can be booked, but you'll have to book at least the day before at the *taxi-brousse* station.
- Luggage goes on the roof under a tarpaulin and is tightly roped in.
- Never buy your ticket from a tout – always get it at the *taxi-brousse* station or from the driver if in doubt. In any case, get a receipt.
- General safety advice is not to travel after dark, but on longer routes it simply can't be helped. On some routes where highway robbery is on the increase, *taxis-brousses* are required to travel in convoys at night.

TOURS

Madagascar's many tour operators can organise anything from a three-week discovery trip with car and driver to smaller excursions (mountain-bike excursions, treks, wildlife-viewing trips and cultural and historic tours) to fit in your holidays.

All have English-speaking guides and/or drivers. Following is a non-exhaustive list of reliable operators.

Boogie Pilgrim (020 22 530 70; www.boogiepilgrim-madagascar.com) Adventurous ecotours and camps in several places in Madagascar. English- and German-speaking.

Cortez Travel & Expeditions (020 22 219 74; www.air-mad.com) US-Malagasy agency offering a wide range of itineraries for individuals and groups.

Espace Mada (020 22 262 97; www.madagascar-circuits.com) Vehicles, guides and 4WD excursions.

Mad Cameleon (020 22 630 86; www.madcameleon.com) Tours focusing on western and southern Madagascar.

Madamax (020 22 351 01; www.madamax.com) Specialist in adventure-packed holidays; rock-climbing and river trips are its forte.

Malagasy Tours (020 22 356 07; www.malagasy-tours.com) A reliable, upmarket operator offering tours in all areas of the country.

Ortour (032 07 704 64; www.ortour.com) All kinds of tours, including excellent trekking or birdwatching tours and budget/luxury options on the standards.

Tany Mena Tours (020 22 326 27; www.tanymenatours.com) Specialises in sustainable tourism, as well as taking in the country's main sights. All circuits have a heavy emphasis on cultural experiences, with village visits and specialist Malagasy guides (archaeologist, anthropologist etc).

Malawi

Includes ➡

Best Places to Eat

- Latitude 13° (p826)
- Buchanan's Grill (p827)
- Casa Mia (p837)
- Kaya Mawa (p834)

Best Places to Stay

- Kaya Mawa (p834)
- Mumbo Camp (p836)
- Mkulumadzi Lodge (p843)
- Latitude 13° (p826)

Why Go?

Malawi has been historically overlooked in the table of epic safari destinations. That was until Majete Wildlife Reserve was thoroughly restocked and a lion reintroduction program began there in 2012. The country now has its 'Big Five' again, added to which are new world-class boutique hotels and luxury safari lodges; it's easy to see then why travel editors are salivating over Africa's next *big* destination.

Slicing through the landscape in a trough formed by the Great Rift Valley is Lake Malawi; a shimmering mass of glittering water swarming with colorful cichlid fish. Whether it's diving, snorkelling, kayaking or chilling on its desert islands, the lake is unforgettable.

In Malawi's deep south are the dramatic peaks of Mt Mulanje and Zomba Plateau; both are a trekker's dream, with mist-cowled forests. Head further north and you'll witness the otherworldly beauty of Nyika Plateau, its grasslands reminiscent of the Scottish Highlands. In short, there's something for everyone here.-

When to Go

Lilongwe

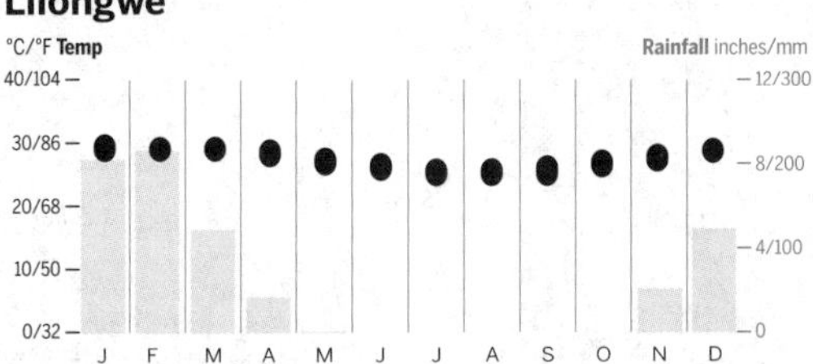

Nov–Apr Malawi's single wet season.

May–Oct Dry season, the best time to visit.

Oct & Nov Great for wildlife-viewing, but temperatures can be uncomfortably hot.

Malawi Highlights

1 Glide over glassy waters of **Lake Malawi** (p835) by kayak, or head beneath the turquoise surface to discover a world of brilliantly coloured fish.

2 Visit the first of Malawi's reintroduced lions, staying at gorgeous **Mkulumadzi Lodge** (p843) in Majete Wildlife Reserve.

3 Scramble up twisted peaks, sleep in mountain huts and soak up the astounding views of **Mt Mulanje** (p840).

4 Spot hippos and crocs on the Shire River in **Liwonde National Park** (p841), or get up close to elephants on foot.

5 Escape to dreamy beaches, Malawi's finest boutique hotel, and explore traditional villages and the magnificent cathedral on **Likoma Island** (p834).

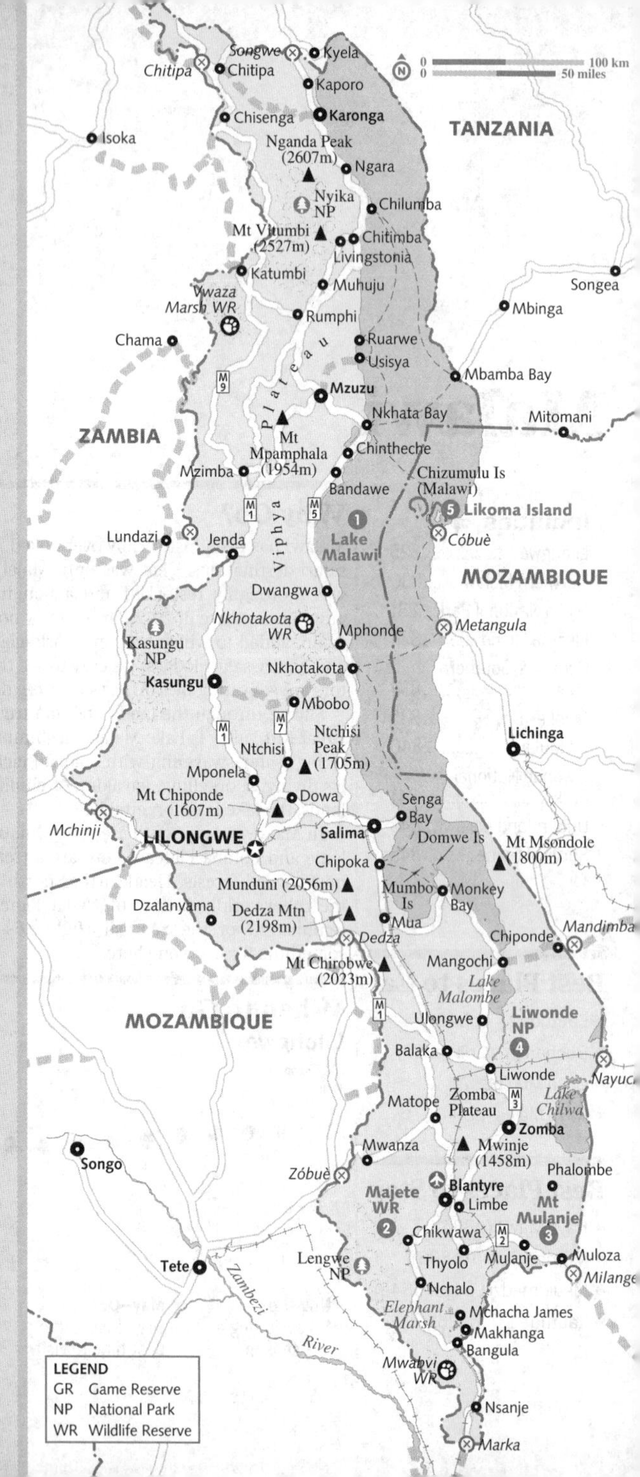

LILONGWE

POP 781,000

Admittedly Lilongwe is initially a little underwhelming, but give Malawi's capital a few days and the place really grows on you: a trip to the bustling city market is an eye-opener with African music pulsing over the animated faces of hawkers and gleaming fruit; while a visit to the tobacco auction floors is a great photo opportunity. Within easy reach of the city too are cool forest reserves and a famed pottery workshop at Dedza.

Lilongwe has two centres, some 3km apart: blandly bureaucratic City Centre (Capital City) and lively Old Town with its guest houses, malls and market.

Sights & Activities

Main Market MARKET

(Malangalanga Rd, Old Town) You'll find everything from bicycle parts to live chickens, vegetables, dustbins, underwear…the list goes on. Pickpockets operate.

Lilongwe Nature Sanctuary PARK

In between City Centre and Old Town lies the sanctuary. Taking pride of place within its 180-hectare expanse is the **Lilongwe Wildlife Centre** (01-757120; www.lilongwewildlife.org; Kenyatta Rd; admission MK1500; 8am-4pm Mon-Fri, to noon Sat), an animal rescue and educational facility.

Tours

Ulendo Travel Group ADVENTURE TOUR

(01-794555; www.ulendo.net; 441 Chilanga Dr, Area 10) An excellent one-stop travel shop for accommodation, booking flights, car hire and expertly tailored tours and safaris in Malawi. The reliable, specialist staff are what really sell them. It has recently moved to a great location in Area 10.

Wilderness Safaris ADVENTURE TOUR

(01-771393, 01-771153; www.wilderness-safaris.com; Bisnowaty Complex, Kenyatta Rd) Specializing in safari trips to their high-luxe lodges in Liwonde and Nyika National Parks, Wilderness is the country's top safari operator.

Land & Lake Safaris ADVENTURE TOUR

(01-757120; www.landlake.net; 84 Laws Ave, Area 3) Tours for all budgets in both Malawi and Zambia. For example, a four-day trip to South Luangwa National Park will cost US$590, and a five-day trip to Victoria Falls is US$1115.

SET YOUR BUDGET

Budget

- Camping or basic room US$2–20
- *Chambo* (fish) and chips US$7
- Four-hour bus ride US$9

Midrange

- Hotel room US$20–50
- Two-course dinner US$15
- Entry per person to safari parks US$10

Top End

- Hotel room US$50+
- Two-course dinner US$20–30
- 4WD rental US$145

Sleeping

Mabuya Camp HOSTEL, CAMPGROUND $

(01-754978; www.mabuyacamp.com; Livingstone Rd; campsites per person US$4, dm US$6, d & tw US$18, chalet d $45; P @) Lilongwe's liveliest backpacker spot has dorms and a double in the main house, and chalets and camping pitches in the garden; its rooms sharing clean showers are set in thatched *rondavels* (traditional thatched huts).

There's also a bar, its menu featuring salads and sandwiches. It's 15 minutes' walk from the centre of Old Town.

Mufasa Lodge GUESTHOUSE $

(0999 071665; www.mufasamalawi.com; Lister Rd, Area 3; dm from US$8, s/d US$21/33; P @) Mufasa sits in a leafy road, has clean singles, decent dorms and spacious doubles and twins. There are storage lockers, laundry service and tourist info. Continental breakfast is included and there's a well-stocked bar.

Kiboko Town Hotel GUESTHOUSE $$

(01-751226; www.kiboko-safaris.com; Mandala Rd; s/d incl breakfast from US$59/69; @) In central Old Town, Kiboko has pleasant rooms with four-posters, fresh linen, mozzie nets and DSTV. There's also a funky adjoining cafe. Come evening the bar is a real traveller magnet.

Sanctuary Lodge LODGE $$$

(01-775200; www.thesanctuarylodge.net; Youth Dr; campsites per adult/child US$9/6, s/d incl breakfast from US$135/160; P @) Sanctuary has well-appointed *rondavels*

Lilongwe

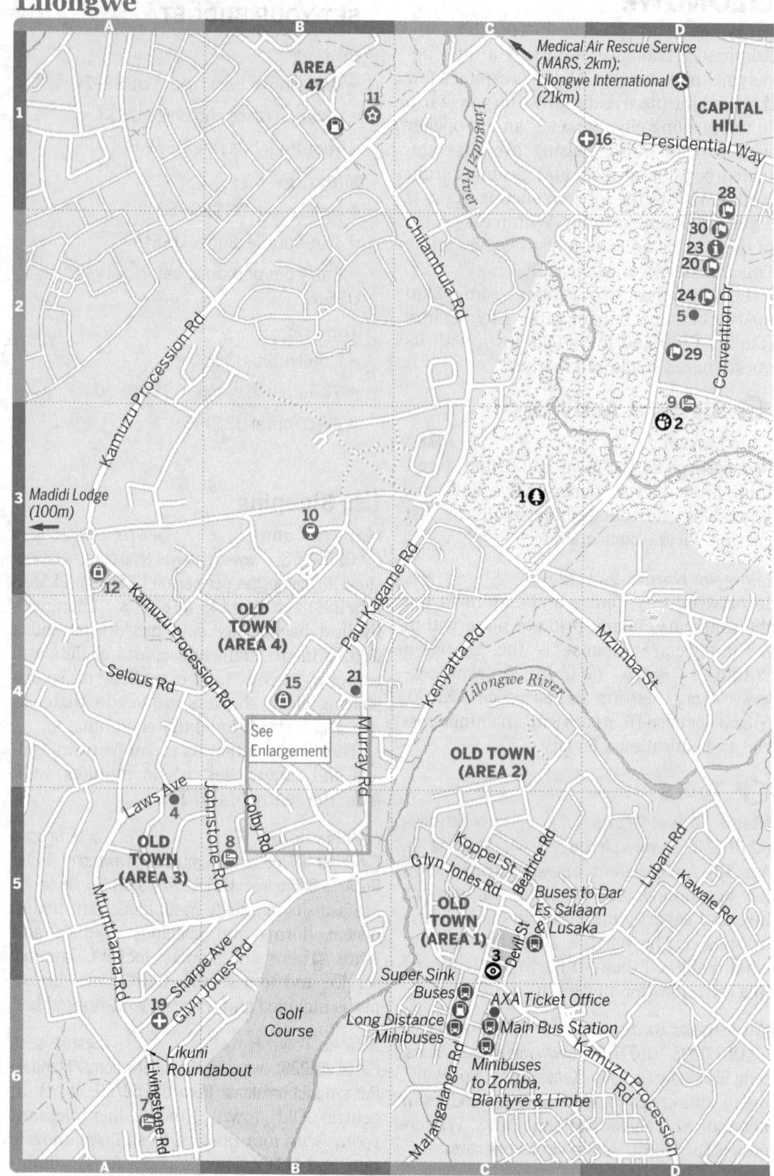

with tiled floors, step-in showers, wicker chairs and African-chic decor. Add to this the leafy setting and an equally charming restaurant.

★ **Latitude 13°** BOUTIQUE HOTEL **$$$**
(☎0996 403159; www.thelatitudehotels.com; 60/43 Mphonongo Rd; suites s US$170-220, d US$220-270; P ⊖ ❄ @ 🛜) Lilongwe's only boutique hotel is an oasis of chic, its walls

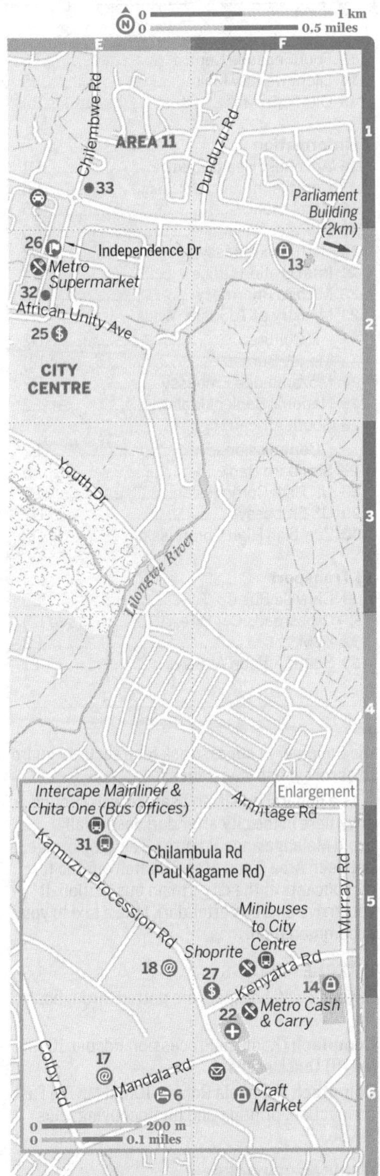

peppered with pop art and bespoke art installations. Sumptuous rooms have buffed cement floors, four-posters and plunge baths. Its restaurant serves the best food in the country. The hotel will organise airport transfers.

Eating

Mamma Mia ITALIAN $

(Old Town Mall; mains from MK1400; lunch & dinner;) Mamma's has a wide-ranging menu featuring antipasti, salads, paninis and homemade pasta. The pizza dough is mouthwatering.

Buchanan's Grill STEAKHOUSE $

(Four Seasons Centre, Presidential Way; mains MK1500-2300; lunch & dinner Mon-Sat) Eat in the old-world restaurant (with a stylish sports bar attached), or outside beside an ornamental pool. It's a carnivore-friendly menu with rump, sirloin and fillet steaks.

Ama Khofi CAFE $

(Four Seasons Centre, Presidential Way; mains MK2300; 7.30am-5pm Mon-Sat, 9am-5pm Sun;) Delightful Parisian-style cafe with wrought-iron chairs and pretty gardens. A menu of carrot cakes, ice cream, salads and main courses.

★**Don Brioni's Bistro** BISTRO $

(Mandala Rd; mains from MK2500; lunch & dinner;) Burgers, steaks, T-bone, spare ribs... this delicious expat magnet has check-cloth tables bathed in low-lit ambience. Take a pew in the dining room or outside on a candlelit terrace. Recommended.

Drinking & Nightlife

Chameleon Bar BAR, LIVE MUSIC

(Four Seasons Centre, Presidential Way; 11am-midnight Mon-Sat, to 10pm Sun;) An effervescent cocktail bar opposite Buchanan's Grill in a leafy compound, Chameleon puts on live music, DJ nights and poetry readings.

Harry's Bar BAR

(6pm-late) This lively wood shack dishes up a bubbling atmosphere and live jazz in the garden. A Lilongwe institution, situated off Paul Kagame Rd.

Chez Ntemba NIGHTCLUB

(Area 47; 6pm-late) Live acts (with a distinctly African flavour) and disco magnetizes locals and *mzungu* (white foreigners) in a fleshpot of sweaty bodies. Great fun.

Shopping

Malls

★**Four Seasons Centre** MALL

(Presidential Way;) An oasis of fine dining and upscale shopping.

Lilongwe

Sights
1 Lilongwe Nature Sanctuary C3
2 Lilongwe Wildlife Centre D3
3 Main Market C5

Activities, Courses & Tours
4 Land & Lake Safaris A5
5 Wilderness Safaris D2

Sleeping
6 Kiboko Town Hotel E6
7 Mabuya Camp A6
8 Mufasa Lodge B5
9 Sanctuary Lodge D2

Eating
Ama Khofi ..... (see 13)
Buchanan's Grill ..... (see 13)
Don Brioni's Bistro ..... (see 6)
Mamma Mia ..... (see 15)

Drinking & Nightlife
Chameleon Bar ..... (see 13)
10 Harry's Bar B3

Entertainment
11 Chez Ntemba B1

Shopping
12 Crossroads Complex A3
13 Four Seasons Centre F2
14 Lilongwe City Mall F5
15 Old Town Mall B4

Information
16 Adventist Health Centre D1
17 Comptech E6
18 Comptech E5
19 Dr Peter Kalungwe A6
20 German Embassy D2
21 Immigration Office B4
22 Michiru Pharmacy F6
23 Ministry of Tourism, Wildlife & Culture D2
Money Bureau ..... (see 12)
24 Mozambique Embassy D2
25 National Bank of Malawi E2
26 South African High Commission E2
27 Standard Bank F5
28 UK High Commission D1
29 US Embassy D2
30 Zambian High Commission D2

Transport
31 Chiwale Bus Co E5
Crossroads Car Hire ..... (see 12)
32 KLM E2
33 South African Airways E1

Lilongwe City Mall MALL
(Kenyatta Rd) The newest and best mall for fast-food joints, supermarkets and a central location.

Crossroads Complex MALL
(Mchinji Roundabout) This houses banks, a swanky hotel, Crossroads Car Hire (p849) and supermarket.

Old Town Mall MALL
(off Chilambula Rd) This small mall has a couple of bookshops and craft stores as well as Mamma Mia restaurant.

Markets

The city's main market is by the bus station. There's also a craft market outside the Old Town post office.

Information

DANGERS & ANNOYANCES

Avoid Lilongwe Nature Sanctuary after dark when hyenas appear on the road. Also there have been isolated cases of muggings around the Sanctuary Lodge, so ask for a security guard to escort you to your cabana.

As a general rule it isn't safe to walk around anywhere in the city after dark; especially avoid Malangalanga Rd, Area 3 and the bridge between Area 2 and Area 3. Watch out too for pickpockets at the city's main bus station. If you arrive on a bus after dark take a taxi to your accommodation.

INTERNET ACCESS

Skyband wi-fi hot spots are dotted throughout the city.

Comptech (Kamuzu Procession Rd; per 10min MK75) Quick access.

Comptech (Mandala Rd; per 10min MK75) Fast connection, printing and photocopying, plus Skype.

MEDICAL SERVICES

Adventist Health Centre (☎01-775680; Presidential Way) Good for consultations, plus eye and dental problems.

Michiru Pharmacy (☎01-754294; Kamuzu Procession Rd, Nico Shopping Centre; ⏰8am-5pm Mon-Fri, to 1pm Sat & Sun) Sells antibiotics and malaria pills (MK8000 for six tablets).

Dr Peter Kalungwe (☎01-750404, 0999 969548) Available for private consultations.

MONEY

Money Bureau (☎01-750659; Nico Shopping Centre, Kamuzu Procession Rd, Old Town) Has good rates, quick service and doesn't charge commission.

National Bank of Malawi (African Unity Ave, City Centre) You can change money here, get a cash advance on your Visa card and there's a 24-hour ATM that accepts Visa, MasterCard.

Standard Bank (Kamuzu Procession Rd, Old Town) Offers the same facilities as National Bank of Malawi but the ATM also accepts Maestro.

POST

Post Office (Kamuzu Procession Rd, Old Town; ⏲7.30am-noon & 1-5pm Mon-Fri) Another office, with the same opening hours, is located next to the City Centre Shopping Centre.

TOURIST INFORMATION

Immigration Office (☎01-754297; Murray Rd)

Ministry of Tourism, Wildlife & Culture (☎01-755499; Tourism House just off Convention Dr; ⏲7.30am-5pm Mon-Fri, 8-10am Sat) Information and advice is minimal here.

Getting There & Away

AIR

Airlines with offices in Lilongwe:

Air Malawi (☎01-700811; www.flyairmalawi.com; Kamazu International Airport)

KLM (☎01-774227; www.klm.com; Independence Dr)

South African Airways (☎01-772242, 01-770307; www.flysaa.com; Sunbird Capital Hotel, Chilembwe Rd)

Ulendo Airlink (☎01-794555; www.ulendo.net; 441 Chilanga Dr, Area 10) Ulendo Airlink flies to a number of safari parks in Malawi as well as Likoma Island.

BUS

AXA City Trouper and commuter buses leave from the main bus station where you'll find their ticket office.

AXA executive coaches depart from outside the City Centre Peoples Supermarket. An executive ticket between the two cities costs MK6000.

Destinations from the main bus station:

Mzuzu (MK3500, five hours, two or three daily)
Blantyre (MK2000, four hours, three daily)
Kasungu (MK1500, two hours, two daily)
Nkhotakota (MK3500, three hours, two daily)
Nkhata Bay (MK900, five hours, one daily)
Salima (MK390, one hour, two daily)
Dedza (MK1300, one hour).

Super Sink buses depart for Mzuzu (MK2000, six hours) and Songwe (MK5000) from the Engen petrol station next to the main bus station between 7am and 8am.

Long-distance minibuses depart from behind the bus station to nearby destinations such as Zomba (MK2500, four to five hours), Dedza (MK1000, 45 minutes to one hour), the Zambian border (MK1500, two hours), Nchitsi (MK1200, 2½ hours), Mangochi (MK2500, 4½ hours), Limbe (MK1900, three to four hours) and Nkhotakota (MK1800, three hours).

Intercape Mainline (p847) has modern buses and leaves from the Total petrol station in Old Town on Tuesday, Wednesday, Saturday and Sunday at 6am, arriving in Johannesburg at 6am the following day (one way MK29,500). Chiwale Bus Co (p847) leaves for Jo'burg at 6am on Saturday from the same location (one way MK21,000).

Zambia–Botswana Coach (☎0999 405340; Devil St) leaves Wednesday and Saturday at 6am, arriving in Lusaka at 5pm (MK9500). Kob's Coach leaves the same days, same price, at 6am. The Tarqwa coach departs from Devil St at 7pm on Saturday, Sunday and Tuesday for the 27-hour journey to Dar es Salaam (MK14,000) continuing on to Nairobi.

Getting Around

TO/FROM THE AIRPORT

Kamazu International Airport is 21km north of the city. A taxi from the airport into town costs MK8000. There's no airport bus.

BUS

From Old Town, local minibuses (marked Area 12) leave from either the bus rank near the market or next to Shoprite. They then head north up Kenyatta Rd to reach City Centre.

TAXI

Find taxis at the main hotels. There's a rank on Presidential Way, just north of City Centre Shopping Centre. Taxis also congregate outside Shoprite in Old Town. The fare between Old Town and City Centre is about MK2500. Short journeys within City Centre or Old Town cost around MK1500.

Particularly reliable is driver **Charlie Kandoje** (☎0999 935281, 0888 853373) who can take you around the city for as little as MK6500.

NORTHERN MALAWI

Remote northern Malawi sees ravishing highlands meet hippo-filled swamps, and vast mountains loom over pristine beaches straight out of a dream (desert islands Robinson Crusoe would have relished). It's Malawi's most sparsely populated region, and the first area many see after making the journey down from East Africa.

Karonga

POP 47,000

Dusty little Karonga is the first place you'll come across if you're making the journey down from Tanzania, and it suffices for an overnight stay: check emails, stock up on cash and have a close encounter with a 100-million-year-old dinosaur.

Karonga has the proud title of Malawi's 'fossil district', with well-preserved remains of dinosaurs and ancient people. Its most famous discovery is the *Malawisaurus* (Malawi lizard), a fossilized dino skeleton found 45km south of the town: go to the **Culture and Museum Centre Karonga** (CMCK; ☎01-362579; www.palaeo.net/cmck; ⏲8am-5pm Mon-Sat, 2-5pm Sun).

If you do decide to stay in town, opt for **Sumuka Inn** (☎0999 444816; r MK8500-12,500, stes from MK15,000) or **Safari Lodge Annex** (☎01-362340; r MK4500-6500).

Except for the **Mbande Cafe** (⏲8am-5pm Mon-Sat, 2-5pm Sun), eating options are slim. There are a couple of banks, while internet is at the museum.

Super Sink Buses leave at 8pm for Lilongwe. Alternatively head to Mzuzu (MK1600, four hours) from where AXA City Trouper buses also leave for Lilongwe and Blantyre. Minibuses go to numerous destinations, including Songwe (MK1200, 45 minutes) and Mzuzu (MK1600, four hours). Taxis to the Tanzanian border go from the main bus station and cost MK1200.

If you've got a 4WD you can cross into northern Zambia via Chitipa in northern Malawi – it's four hours' drive. After going through customs it's another 80km or further four hours' drive to the Zambian border post at Nakonde.

Livingstonia

Mountaintop Livingstonia feels otherworldly, its tree-lined main street graced with colonial-style buildings and smartly attired folk who look as if they're all headed to church.

After two failed attempts at establishing missions at Cape Maclear and Bandawe, the Free Church of Scotland moved its mission 900m above the lake to the village of Khondowe. Called Livingstonia after Dr David Livingstone, the mission was built in 1884 under the direction of missionary Dr Robert Laws, who lived in the Stone House.

Sights & Activities

The fascinating **museum** (admission MK250, photos MK100; ⏲7.30am-5pm) in the Stone House (the original home of Dr Laws) tells the story of the first missionaries in Malawi. The nearby **mission church**, dating from 1894, has a beautiful stained-glass window featuring Livingstone with his two companions. There are heartwarming services here every Sunday.

About 4km from town, the impressive **Manchewe Falls** thunders 125m into the valley below. Follow a small path behind the falls and there's a cave where, as the story goes, local people hid from slave traders. Allow an hour for descending and 1½ hours to get back up.

Sleeping

Stone House GUESTHOUSE $
(☎01-368223; campsites per person MK900, r MK1500-2000;) This atmospheric granite house was built in the early 20th century and its rooms are still redolent with history; cozy rugs, shadowy hardwood floors, and a twee lounge which might have been transplanted from an Edinburgh tearoom.

★ **Lukwe Permaculture Camp** CAMPING, ECOLODGE $
(☎0999 792311, 0999 434985; www.lukwe.com; campsites US$5, tent hire US$6, s/d cabins US$12/20;) Ten kilometres from Chitimba – above the zigzag hairpins, or an hour's walk (about 5km) east (downhill) from Livingstonia – Lukwe has extraordinary views from its funky timber verandah. The cafe serves delectable grub while the four super-clean chalets are set in leafy terraced gardens, and enjoy mozzie nets and balconies.

Mushroom Farm LODGE $
(☎0999 652485; www.themushroomfarmmalawi.com; campsites per person US$5, tent hire US$6, s/d US$16.50/23.50, cob chalets s/d US$33/41;) This permaculture camping ground perched on the mountainside is

worth the arduous journey for the astonishing views. Three chalets offer simple accommodation – best is the cob cottage.

Wake up in the morning to mist drifting up the mountain, Miles Davis on the speakers and owner Mick dishing up amazing food. If you've got the energy you can abseil and rock climb (US$40).

Shopping

The excellent Craft Coffee Shop sells carvings as well as its locally produced coffee (all proceeds go to the hospital and mission).

Getting There & Away

From the main north–south road between Karonga and Mzuzu, the road to Livingstonia turns off at Chitimba, forcing its way up the escarpment in a series of lethal hairpins, with an unpaved surface. Don't attempt this killer of a road in anything but a 4WD and *never* in rain. Alternatively, ask Mick at Mushroom Farm (p830) to collect you (US$50 each way for four people) from Chitimba (at the base of the mountain), or walk the 2½-hour, 15km trip up the mountain.

Another (more preferable) way to reach Livingstonia is to take the dirt road from Rumphi. A third option is to walk to Livingstonia from the Nyika Plateau which can be done through Chelinda Camp (p831).

Nyika National Park

Burnished amber by the afternoon sun, Nyika's highland grass flickers with zebra stripes and glittering boulders that look like set dressing from *Star Trek*. Towering 2500m above sea level, 3200-sq-km Nyika National Park is enigmatic; one moment its rolling grasslands remind you of the Yorkshire Dales, then an antelope leaps across your bonnet and you remember you're in Africa.

There are plenty of zebras, bushbucks, roan antelopes and elephants here and you may also spot elands, warthogs, klipspringers, jackals, duikers, hyenas and over 100 leopards. After the wet season the landscape bursts in a blaze of wildflowers.

Take a wildlife drive, explore by mountain bike, or ramble through the hills by foot. Log fires are provided in the chalets and rooms, but bring a warm sleeping bag if you're camping; it can get surprisingly cold at night, especially from June to August. Lions should have been reintroduced by the time you read this.

Activities

For trekking advice contact **Wilderness Safaris** (☎01-771393; www.wilderness-safaris.com) which runs Nyika's concession and can avail you with *obligatory* guides and porters. The only set route on Nyika goes from Chelinda to Livingstonia; it's a hugely spectacular three-day walk.

Day wildlife drives start from Chelinda Camp or Lodge at 8am every morning. The most exciting drives, however, are by night, with a 40% chance of sighting leopards.

Wildlife-viewing is good year-round, although in July and August the cold weather means the animals move to lower areas. Birdwatching is particularly good between October and April.

Nyika's network of dirt roads is ideal for mountain biking. You can base yourself at Chelinda and go for day rides (bike/guide per day US$40/40, kids half price) or camp out overnight (for which you'll need to hire a guide).

Sleeping & Eating

Self-caterers should stock up in Rumphi. There's a small shop at Chelinda but provisions are often basic and supplies sporadic.

Camping Ground CAMPSITE $
(campsites per person US$15) Set 2km from the main Chelinda Camp, this site is in a secluded spot with vistas of the rolling hills. The camping ground has permanent security, clean toilets, hot showers, endless firewood, and shelters for cooking and eating.

Chelinda Camp CHALET $$$
(☎01-771393; www.wilderness-safaris.com; Nyika National Park; chalets US$160; P) Nestled beside a lake, Chelinda Camp is insanely picturesque, with unfussy bungalows with decent self-catering facilities, cozy sitting rooms and stone fireplaces. Reception and an inviting restaurant are just a few yards away.

★ **Chelinda Lodge** LODGE $$$
(☎01-771393; www.wilderness-safaris.com; Nyika National Park; chalets US$450; P @) Located 1km from Chelinda Camp and sitting on a hillside is upscale Chelinda Lodge. Its main building crackles with a fiery hearth casting its glow on glittering chandeliers and lush wildlife photography.

No less enchanting are the Swiss-style chalets with roaring fires, wood floors and clawed baths.

Getting There & Away

Thazima Gate is 54km from Rumphi; once inside the park it's another 60-odd kilometres (about two hours' drive) to Chelinda Camp. Petrol is available at Chelinda but it's limited, so fill up before you enter the park. Entry by car into Nyika is US$10 per person and US$3 per vehicle.

Charter flights from Lilongwe to Nyika are now operating through Ulendo Airlink (p825), and cost US$500 each way per person.

Vwaza Marsh Wildlife Reserve

Despite being assailed by poachers, Vwaza boasts a population of around 2000 buffaloes and 300 elephants. The park's main focus is Lake Kazuni. Just sitting around Vwaza's main camp will bring plenty of animal sightings, as it looks over the lake, and on most days you'll see crocodiles lying out in the sun, hippos popping out of the water and a steady parade of animals coming down to the lake to drink.

The best time of year to visit is in the dry season (the rainy season's high grass restricts visibility). The park costs US$10 entry fee per person and US$3 per vehicle.

Activities

There are no park vehicles at present to take you on a wildlife drive; however, guide **Godwin** (0994 418625) can accompany you in your own vehicle (US$10 per trip for 1½ hours). Alternatively, a walking safari costs US$10 per trip.

Sleeping

Lake Kazuni Safari Camp BUSH CAMP $$
(0884 462518; huts US$40; P) The camp's basic en suite cabanas are perfectly positioned on the lakeshore – local feral residents are so plentiful it feels as if you've just stepped into the pages of a kid's illustrated story.

The National Parks skeleton staff can cook you dinner in the camp's kitchen if you stock up on food beforehand in nearby Rumphi.

Getting There & Away

If you're travelling by public transport, first get to Rumphi (reached from Mzuzu by minibus for MK1000). From Rumphi there are plenty of *matolas* (pick-ups) travelling to and from the Kazuni area and you should be able to get a lift to the main gate for around MK1000.

By car, head west from Rumphi. Turn left after 10km (Vwaza Marsh Wildlife Reserve is signposted) and continue for about 20km. Where the road swings left over a bridge, go straight on to reach the park gate and camp after 1km.

Mzuzu

POP 120,000

Dusty Mzuzu is northern Malawi's largest town and serves as the transport hub for the region. There are banks, shops, a post office, supermarkets, pharmacies, petrol stations and ATMs; especially useful if you've just entered Malawi from the north.

Internet access is available at **City Cyber** (per 10min MK100; 8am-5pm Mon-Fri, to 4pm Sat) and **Postdotnet** (Boardman Rd; per 30min MK300; 8am-5pm Mon-Fri, to 12.30pm Sat), both on Boardman Rd.

Sleeping

★**Mzoozoozoo** HOSTEL $
(0888 864493; campsites MK500, dm MK1400, r MK3800; P @ wi-fi) This backpackers' haven has a lovely garden and colourful rooms. A friendly vibe, art-spattered walls and warm management, plus terrific comfort food (steaks, chicken) may extend your travel plans by a night.

Mimosa Court Hotel HOTEL $$$
(01-312833, 01-312609; off Orton Chewa Ave; s/d MK12,700/14,500; P) Mimosa is clean and friendly and has a decent restaurant and bar. Rooms are large, scrupulously clean and well catered for with mozzie net, DSTV, bureau and fan.

Sunbird Mzuzu Hotel HOTEL $$$
(01-332622; www.sunbirdmalawi.com; s/d from US$160/180; P ❄ @ wi-fi) A plush hotel set in imposing grounds, it has huge rooms with DSTV, and views of a golf course. The service is efficient and there's also a cozy cafe with wi-fi for laptops.

Eating

★**A1 Restaurant** INDIAN $
(St Denis Rd; mains around MK1000; 11.45am-2pm & 6-10pm; ❄ wi-fi) Superfresh A1 has DSTV and a menu featuring North Indian cuisine, with classic dishes like rogan josh. The chicken korma is tasty too.

Greenvee Restaurant INDIAN, MALAWIAN $
(0888 899666; St Denis Rd; mains from MK800; 6am-10pm) With its red check-cloth tables,

airy interior and breezy verandah, Greenvee is a nice spot to people watch between tucking into *nshima* (maize porridge) or curries.

Getting There & Away

AXA City Trouper buses go to Lilongwe at 7am and 5pm (MK3500, five hours), as well as Karonga (MK1500, four hours), leaving at 6.30am and 10am; while local buses (MK700, five hours) leave at 6.30am and go via Rumphi (MK1000) and Chitimba (MK540).

Minibuses go to Nkhata Bay (MK850, one to two hours), Karonga (MK2000, three to four hours), Chitimba (MK1700, two hours), Rumphi (MK1000, one hour) and the Tanzanian border (MK2500, four hours).

National Bus Company has daily departures to Lilongwe (MK2250), Blantyre (MK3000) and Salima (MK3000).

The Taqwa (p848) bus travels between Mzuzu and Nairobi daily (MK24,000), calling at Songwe for the border (MK5000), Mbeya (MK7000) and Dar es Salaam (MK13,000) – report at 11.30pm for a midnight departure. The bus crosses the border at first light, goes through Mbeya in the morning, gets to Dar Es Salaam at around 10pm and leaves for Nairobi the next morning.

KM Bus Services (☎0888 639363) leaves from the forecourt of Mbacheda Guesthouse at 7pm on Friday, going to Harare (MK1700) and Jo'burg (MK23000).

Nkhata Bay

With its fishing boats, vivid market and guest houses perched on cliffs overlooking the glittering lake, pretty Nkhata Bay feels distinctly Caribbean. There are also loads of activities to enjoy before you hammock flop, be it snorkelling, diving, fish-eagle feeding, kayaking or forest walks.

Activities

On the southern side of Nkhata Bay, Chikale Beach is a popular spot for swimming and lazing on the sand. Snorkelling equipment is free for guests at most of the lodges.

Monkey Business (☎0999 437247; blondieleap@hotmail.com; Butterfly Space) and **Chimango Tours** (☎09 99268595; Mayoka Village) can organise kayaking excursions from anything from half a day to a few days down the coast. A full day costs US$40.

Both companies offer trips out on the lake to feed fish eagles (US$15).

Aqua Africa Diving (☎01-852284, 0999 921418; www.aquaafrica.co.uk) Casual dives for certified divers cost US$50, and full PADI four-day beginner courses cost US$375 (including all materials) at this reliable Western-run outfit.

Sleeping

Strung along the coast from the town centre, most lodges are secreted in small bays. All are reached via a road that climbs up and down a hill between bays.

★**Butterfly Space** GUESTHOUSE $
(☎0999 265065; www.butterfly-space.com; campsites per person MK750, dm MK1500, chalet with/without bathroom MK4000/2500; P@) Socially committed Butterfly is a backpacker's oasis; *palapa*-style lounge, beachfront bar, private beach, internet cafe, media centre, self-catering block and a restaurant serving tasty meals. Rooms in A-frame cabanas are basic but very clean.

Mayoka Village LODGE $$
(☎01-994025, 0999 268595; www.mayokavillage.com; dm US$8, s/d chalet US$20/40, without bathroom US$15/28; P@) Boutique-style Mayoka cascades down a cliff in a series of beautiful bamboo and stone chalets. All rooms are finished with tasteful furniture, fans and some with wrap-around verandahs. There's also a great waterfront bar.

Aqua Africa LODGE $$
(☎01-352284, 0999 921418; www.aqua-africa.co.uk; r US$35-80; @) Cozy en suite rooms with stone floors, private balconies and huge beds. The Dive Deck Cafe, complete with wicker loungers and viewing deck, has an excellent menu, while staff are friendly.

Eating

★**Kaya Papaya** THAI, MALAWIAN $
(mains from MK900; 7am-late, food served to 9pm;) With its shadowy interior, there's more than a touch of Afro-chic here. The Thai-accented menu has zesty salads, pizza and Malawian fare like butterfish with *nshima*.

Mayoka Village INTERNATIONAL $
(mains from MK950; 7am-3pm & 6-8.30pm;) Infused with African tunes and the lake's lapping waves, this alfresco lounge bar is a great place to enjoy organic salads, breakfasts, hamburgers, baguette sandwiches and stir-fries.

Information

There's nowhere to change money but there are two **ATMs** (next to FMB bank; 24hr) at the top of the hill (accepting Visa but not MasterCard) as you enter town. Internet access is available at Aqua Africa (p833) and **L-Net Internet Cafe** (per 30min MK250; 7am-5pm Mon-Fri, 8am-12.30pm Sat & Sun).

DANGERS & ANNOYANCES

Travellers have been robbed walking to and from Chikale Beach at night. Travel as a group or with a hotel guard.

Getting There & Away

All buses and minibuses go from the bus stand on the main road. AXA buses run to Mzuzu (MK800, two hours) and minibuses run to Nkhotakota (MK1000, five hours), Chintheche (MK600, one hour) and Mzuzu (MK700, one to two hours). To reach Lilongwe the quickest option is to go to Mzuzu and transfer bus.

Many come or go on the Ilala ferry which arrives at 1am on Sunday then heads for Ruarwe and Usiya at 7am.

Likoma Island

The 17-sq-km Likoma is a dream of turquoise waters and desert-island bliss, boasting outstanding views to nearby Mozambique. About 6000 people make their home here, and the island's relative isolation from the rest of Malawi has allowed the locals to maintain their reserved culture. It's absolutely worth the effort to get here.

Sights

Cathedral of St Peter CHURCH

The huge Anglican cathedral built by missionaries between 1903 and 1905 should not be missed. Climb the tower for spectacular views.

Activities

Swimming is best enjoyed off the southern beaches, and thanks to myriad tropical fish the snorkelling is amazing. Kaya Mawa runs three-day open-water PADI scuba-diving courses (US$315), while the island's compact size is perfect for walking or mountain biking; hire bikes from Mango Drift for US$10 per day.

Sleeping

★**Mango Drift** HOSTEL $$

(0999 746122; www.mangodrift.com; campsites per person US$6, dm US$8, chalets with/without bathroom US$30/70;) Mango has gorgeous stone cabanas with seriously 'boutique' genes. The shared toilets and shower block are immaculate, dorms are spacious, while double en suite cabanas are a few yards up the hill. Chill out in the bar, scuba dive or just flop on the beach shaded by mango trees. Tempted?

★**Kaya Mawa** BOUTIQUE HOTEL $$$

(0999 318359; www.kayamawa.com; per person chalets with full board US$375-435;) Lapped by turquoise water, Kaya Mawa has cliffside chalets cleverly moulded around the landscape – think plunge baths, scattered hibiscus petals on snow white linen, and a crescent of sugar-fine sand.

Candlelit dinner is set on the beach, staff are almost elfin in their discretion, and the food is sublime. It's only when you leave that you truly appreciate how special it is.

Getting There & Away

Ulendo Airlink (p829) provides charter flights to Likoma (one way from US$210 to US$320 per person).

The Ilala ferry stops at Likoma Island twice a week, usually for three to four hours. Heading south, the ferry then sails to Metangula on the Mozambican mainland. Local dhows also sail to Cóbuè for MK500 and for a little extra can pick you up or drop you off from Mango Drift on Likoma.

The main Mozambique border crossing to the east (where you can also get visas on arrival) is Cóbuè, a short ride over the water from Likoma Island. Local boats will take you there for US$3 and you pay US$82 for a visa. By the cathedral in the market there's an immigration office to fill in your exit pass. Right beside the office are the boatmen.

CENTRAL & SOUTHERN MALAWI

This is the most developed and densely populated part of Malawi, home to the country's commercial capital and two of its major industries – sugar and tea. Visitors are drawn by the chance to scale mountains and watch wildlife in an incredibly beautiful and diverse landscape.

Monkey Bay

Sultry Monkey Bay is enchanting: languid locals, a gas station, a few shops and a couple of magic beachside traveller joints where you can snorkel or flop in the sun. Conveniently the Ilala ferry stops at Monkey Bay's quaint harbour. There's a Peoples supermarket nearby and one ATM which sometimes works.

Sleeping

Venice Beach Backpackers HOSTEL $
(08 4416541; campsites per person MK800, dm MK2000, r MK4000; P @ wifi) This beachside backpacker joint is 1.5km from the main road. Kayak (MK55,000), dive, spear fish, play beach volleyball or chill at the reggae bar. There are dorms and doubles as well as plenty of hammocks. There are also a couple of chalets next to the main building.

Mufasa Rustic Camp CAMPGROUND, CABANAS $
(0993 080057; campsite per person MK850, dm MK2250, s/d MK5250/6750; P) Set 400m from the main harbour, Mufasa has its own beach. Rooms are basic bamboo affairs, but the bar is more appealing with lounging cushions and wicker swing chairs. Snorkel and boat trips for around MK3500. Please be wary of swimming to the inlet next to the camp's beach – a traveller was mauled by a croc here.

Getting There & Away

From Lilongwe, AXA buses go to Monkey Bay, usually via Mua and the southern lakeshore (MK1800, four hours). You're probably better off going by minibus to Salima (MK1500, one hour), from where you might find a minibus or *matola* going direct to Monkey Bay.

From Blantyre take the bus headed via Liwonde (MK2500, five to six hours), or go by minibus (MK2500, four to five hours). You might have to change at Mangochi.

From Monkey Bay, a *matola* ride to Cape Maclear should cost MK600.

Cape Maclear

A stretch of powder-fine sand bookended by mountains and lapped by dazzling water, Cape Maclear is peppered with desert islands and crayon-coloured boats. On shore, women wash clothes while fishermen spread out nets to dry. And there are bags of things to do, be it kayaking, sailing, snorkelling, walking or diving.

There are also plenty of sleeping options here, from reed huts and tents on the beach to upmarket lodges.

Sights & Activities

Much of the area around Cape Maclear, including several offshore islands, is part of **Lake Malawi National Park** (per person/car US$5/1), designated a Unesco World Heritage site back in 1986. The park headquarters are just inside the gate where you'll also find a **visitor centre**, which doubles up as a small **museum and aquarium** (7.30am-noon & 1-5pm Mon-Sat, 10am-noon & 1-4pm Sun).

Guides registered with the Cape Maclear Tour Guides Association can organise a number of half- and full-day trips involving snorkelling. For example, trips to Thumbi Island will cost around US$45 per person. Many places also rent snorkelling gear (rates start at about US$10).

Otter Point, around 1km from the National Park headquarters, is a small peninsula that is popular with snorkellers and more so with fish.

For diving, go to **Frogman Scuba** (09 99942661; www.kayakafrica.co.za) or **Danforth Yachting** (09 99960077, 09 99960770; www.danforthyachting.com; sunset cruise per person US$50). Both offer PADI open-water courses for around US$375, as well as casual dives for experienced divers.

Sleeping

★ **Kayak Africa** CAMPING $
(www.kayakafrica.net) On beautiful, deserted Domwe Island, Kayak Africa's **Domwe Island Adventure Camp** (in South Africa 0027-21-783 1955; www.kayakafrica.co.za; camp tents US$25, safari tents s/d US$75/120) offers rustic self-catering accommodation, with furnished safari tents sharing ecoshowers and toilets; as well as a bar and a beautiful dining area set among boulders.

Fat Monkeys GUESTHOUSE $$
(09 99948501; campsite per person US$3, vehicle US$6, dm US$10, s/d US$55/75; P @ wifi) Monkeys has tasty salads, pizza and excellent *chambo* (a bream-like fish). The dorms and rooms are clean and cool with fans, while pitches are shaded. Come evening the bar is lively.

Mgoza Lodge LODGE $$
(09 95632105; www.mgozalodge.com; dm MK1500, chalets US$55; P @ wifi) Mgoza has bags of charm with spacious chalets with

MALAWI'S LAKE OF STARS

Since 2004, Lake Malawi's sandy shores have been regularly rocking to international DJs and local pop acts. Organised by a British club promoter, the three-day **Malawi Lake of Stars festival** (www.lakeofstars.org) is held every September/October at different locations around the lake – think miniature Glastonbury but with heat and flip-flops. Acts range from Malawian reggae superstars to English folk musicians and globally celebrated DJs.

huge beds, and billowing step-in mozzie nets. There's also an inviting restaurant with an upstairs viewing deck for sundowners.

Gecko Lounge LODGE $$$
(☎01-599188, 09 99787322; www.geckolounge.net; s/d US$80/90, chalet d/tr US$110/120; P @ wi-fi) Gecko sports chalets with kitchenettes and self-catering facilities. There are bunk beds too for families, and fridges, fans, tiled floors and mozzie nets, as well as plenty of hammocks and swing chairs outside.

The thatch- and wicker-accented restaurant is worth a mention for its tasty pizza and burgers.

★**Mumbo Camp** BUSH CAMP $$$
(☎09 99942661, in South Africa 0027-21-783 1955; www.kayakafrica.co.za; adult/child with full board US$290/145, family tent with full board US$725) This desert-island eco-boutique campsite has delicious walk-in tents with astounding views.

Some get to the island by kayak from the Kayak Africa reception in Cape Maclear, while camp staff bring along your stuff in a separate boat.

Indulge in that 'castaway' feeling exploring the island while serenaded by fish eagles; kayak, snorkel, or take a scuba lesson. Impossibly romantic.

Eating & Drinking

Thomas's Grocery Restaurant and Bar MALAWIAN $
(dishes from MK1000) This simple joint sells toiletries, and dishes up chicken curry, *chambo*, catfish and chips. Authentic.

★**Mgoza Restaurant** INTERNATIONAL $
(mains MK1300; P wi-fi veg) Mgoza has shaded palapa shelters in a garden facing the lake, or you can eat in the friendly bar. The restaurant serves up great full English breakfasts, healthy fruit smoothies and perhaps the best homemade hamburgers in Malawi.

Boma/Hiccups Pub INTERNATIONAL, BAR $$
(dishes MK1500; ⏰noon-late; ❄ wi-fi veg) A great place for dinner and a cool *Green* (Carlsberg); feast on salads, Hungarian goulash, veggie lasagna, steak and chips or *chambo*. A projector screens live sport. Stylish.

Getting There & Away

By public transport, first get to Monkey Bay, from where a *matola* should cost MK400. If you're driving from Mangochi, the dirt road to Cape Maclear (signposted) turns west off the main road, about 5km before Monkey Bay.

From Cape Maclear, if you're heading for Senga Bay, ask around about chartering a boat. It will cost around US$300. *Matola* leave for Monkey Bay from around 6am and take about an hour. From there you can get onward transport.

Blantyre

POP 728,000

Blantyre is Malawi's second-largest city, and is more appealing than Lilongwe thanks to its compact size, national museum and diverse choice of restaurants, tour operators and decent accommodation. It also makes for a useful springboard when exploring areas such as Mulanje and the Lower Shire Valley. Attached to the city's eastern side is Limbe.

Sights & Activities

Blantyre's magnificent red-brick **CCAP Church**, built in the late 19th century, is an impressive feat of arches and towers topped with a grand basilica dome.

Mandala House (☎01-871932; Mackie Rd; ⏰8.30am-4.30pm Mon-Fri, to 1pm Sat) is the oldest building standing in Malawi (built in 1882). Inside is the inviting Mandala Cafe, the eclectic **La Galleria Gallery** (⏰9am-5.30pm Mon-Sun) and **Society of Malawi Library & Archive** (⏰9am-noon Mon-Fri & 6-7.30pm Thu), which contains journals, books and photographs dating as far back as the 19th century.

If you're feeling active head to **Blantyre Sports Club** (☎01-821172, 01-835095; cnr Victoria Ave & Independence Dr; daily membership MK2000) where, besides squash, tennis, golf and gym facilities, there's a great restaurant.

Tours

Jambo Africa TRAVEL AGENCY
(☎01-835356; www.jambo-africa.com; SS Rent A Car building, Glyn Jones Rd) One-stop shop for travel tickets, car hire, accommodation and package trips to safari parks.

Responsible Safari Company ADVENTURE TOUR
(☎01-602407; 0999 306635; www.responsiblesafaricompany.com; The Barn, behind Mandala House, Blantyre) Three-day trips to Lake Malawi and Mt Mulanje and specialized tours of southern or northern Malawi.

Wilderness Safaris ADVENTURE TOUR
(☎01-820955; www.wilderness-safaris.com; Protea Hotel Ryalls, 2 Hanover Ave)

Sleeping

Kabula Lodge LODGE $
(☎01-821216; www.kabulalodge.co.mw; off Michiru Rd, Kabula Hill; incl breakfast dm/s/d without bathroom US$10/15/30, r with bathroom US$40; @) Kabula enjoys scenic mountain views and rooms with wrought-iron beds, DSTV and fans.

Doogles GUESTHOUSE, CAMPGROUND $$
(☎01-621128, 0999 186512; www.dooglеslodge.com; Mulomba Pl; campsites MK1250, dm MK2000, chalets with/without bathroom US$35/25; P @) With its centerpiece pool, bar and lush gardens, Doogles is near the bus station. It has superfresh rooms, clean dorms and chalets, and you can pitch your tent.

House Five GUESTHOUSE $$$
(☎0888 901762; www.housefivemw.com; Kabula Hill Rd; s/d incl breakfast US$100/120; P) This hillside accommodation sits in a lush garden and brims with charm, from its outdoor bistro to its friendly staff. Rooms excel, with parquet floors and old-world furniture.

Sunbird Mount Soche Hotel HOTEL $$$
(☎01-820071; www.sunbirdmalawi.com; Glyn Jones Rd; s/d US$185/210; P @) Lovely rooms in the centre of town; think thick carpets, DSTV and dark wood furniture. There's an internet cafe as well as Pablo's Lounge, The Sportsman's Bar and Picasso's Brazzerie.

Protea Hotel Ryalls HOTEL $$$
(☎01-820955; ryalls@proteamalawi.com; 2 Hanover Ave; s/d US$215/245; P @) With its elegant restaurant, pool, gym and bar, this remains the businessman's choice. Rooms deserve the four-star rating with stylish fittings, huge beds and sumptuous decor. There's also a Wilderness Safaris office.

Eating

Hong Kong Restaurant CHINESE $
(☎01-820859; Robins Rd; mains MK1000; noon-2pm & 6-10pm Tue-Sun;) This pagoda-style building has a wooden red ceiling festooned in lanterns, and walls dancing with dragon murals. Oriental fare rendered with flair.

Mandala Cafe CAFE $
(Mandala House, Mackie Rd; mains MK1200; 8.30am-4.30pm Mon-Fri, 8.30am-12.30pm Sat;) Sit on the stone terrace or inside at this chilled cafe within the old house. Regulars love the Italian cuisine, fillet steak, freshly brewed coffee and homemade cakes of the day.

★ **21 Grill on Hanover** STEAKHOUSE $
(☎01-820955; Protea Hotel Ryalls, 2 Hanover Ave; mains around MK3000; noon-2pm & 6.30-10pm;) Fit for a senator, this restaurant sports a granite-topped bar and comfy Chesterfields. Tuck into a flame-grilled steak or the signature '21 spare ribs dipped in bourbon sauce'.

★ **Casa Mia** INTERNATIONAL $$$
(☎01-915559; casamia@africa-online.net; Kabula Hill Rd; mains MK2500-5000; P) Feast within Casa Mia's wine-stacked interior on a menu of grilled *chambo*, smoked salmon and risotto. Stylish.

Drinking & Entertainment

Sportsman's Bar BAR
(Sunbird Mount Soche Hotel, Glyn Jones Rd) Catering to a sophisticated market, its tranquil surrounds are appealing and is favoured by local businessmen.

Cine City Cinema CINEMA
(☎01-912873; Chichiri Shopping Mall, Kamuzu Hwy; closed Tue) Big-name films shown daily at 5.30pm and 8.30pm. It's in the basement of the Chichiri Shopping Mall, underneath Game supermarket.

Information

INTERNET ACCESS

Tusa Internet Café (off Livingstone Ave; per min MK6) High-speed internet.

Blantyre City Centre

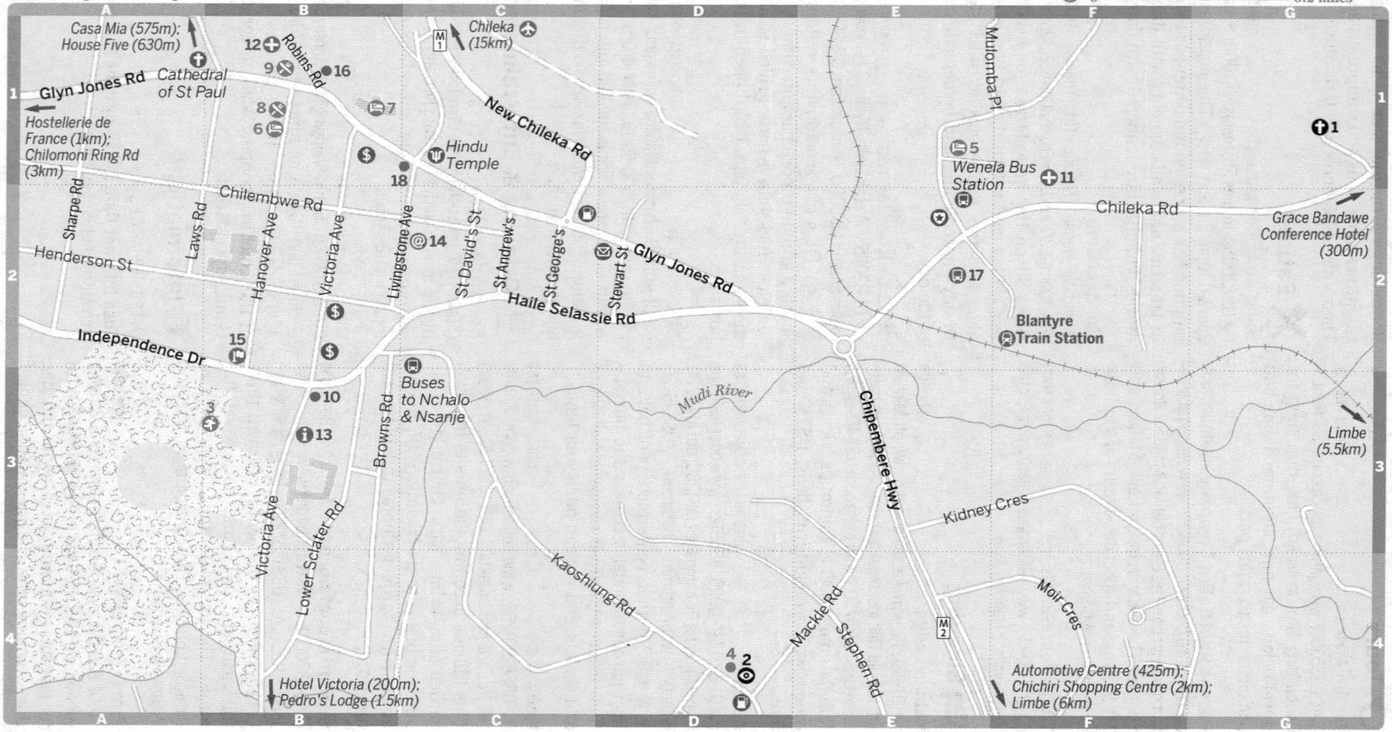

Blantyre City Centre

MEDICAL SERVICES

Mwaiwathu Private Hospital (01-822999, 01-834989; Chileka Rd; 24hr) For private medical consultations (US$10; all drugs and treatment are extra).

Seventh Day Adventist Clinic (01-820399; Robins Rd) For medical or dental problems, this clinic charges US$10 for consultations and US$10 for a malaria test.

MONEY

There are a couple of branches of the National Bank of Malawi and one branch of Standard Bank on Victoria Ave. They all change cash and travellers cheques and have 24-hour ATMs.

POST

Main Post Office (Glyn Jones Rd; 7.30am-5pm) Has poste restante.

TOURIST INFORMATION

Immigration Office (Government Complex, Victoria Ave) For visa extensions.

Tourist Office (Regional Tourism officer 08 88304362; 2nd fl, Government Complex, Victoria Ave; 7.30am-5pm Mon-Fri) A few leaflets and maps of Malawi.

Getting There & Away

AIR

Blantyre's Chileka Airport is about 15km north of the city centre.

Airline offices in Blantyre include the following:

Air Malawi (01-820811; Robins Rd; 7.30am-4.30pm Mon-Fri, 8am-noon Sat)

British Airways (01-820811; www.britishairways.com; Livingstone Towers, Glyn Jones Rd)

KLM & Kenya Airways (01-824524; Protea Hotel Ryalls, 2 Hanover Ave)

South African Airways (01-820627; Livingstone Towers, Glyn Jones Rd).

BUS & MINIBUS

Blantyre's main bus station for long-distance buses is **Wenela Bus Station** (Mulomba Pl), east of the centre. National Bus Company and AXA City Trouper buses run from here to the following:

Karonga (MK5500, 14 hours, change at Mzuzu)
Lilongwe (MK1800, four hours)
Mzuzu (MK4000, nine to 10 hours)
Monkey Bay (MK1800, five to six hours) via Zomba (MK750, 1½ to two hours) and Mangochi (MK1500, four to five hours)
Mulanje (MK1000, 1½ hours)

AXA Executive coaches depart from the **Automotive Centre** (Ginnery Corner) and call at the Chichiri Shopping Mall and the car park outside Blantyre Lodge (near the main bus station) before departing twice daily to Lilongwe (MK1800, four hours).

Long-distance minibuses go from the bus station in Limbe to Zomba (MK1000, one hour), Mulanje (MK1500, 1¼ hours), Mangochi (MK2000) and the border at Muloza (MK2200, 1½ hours).

Long-distance minibuses to the Lower Shire including Nchalo (MK1000, two hours) and Nsanje (MK2000, four hours) leave from the City Bus Station near Victoria Ave in Blantyre, between 8am and 5pm.

The car park next to Blantyre Lodge is the pick-up and drop-off point for **Intercape** (0999 403398) buses going to Jo'burg on Tuesday, Thursday, Saturday and Sunday (MK27,000, 25 hours). **KJ Transway** (01-914017, 01-877738) leaves for Lilongwe every morning at 7.30am (MK2000).

Getting Around

TO/FROM THE AIRPORT

A taxi from the airport to the city costs around MK8000. Frequent local buses between the City Bus Station and Chileka Township pass the airport gate. The fare is MK800.

BUS

Blantyre is a compact city, so it's unlikely you'll need to use public transport to get around, apart from the minibuses that shuttle along Chipembere Hwy between Wanela Bus Station and Limbe's bus station.

TAXI

You can find private-hire taxis at the Sunbird Mount Soche Hotel or at bus stations. A taxi across the city centre costs around MK800; between the centre and the main bus station costs from MK1000; and from Blantyre to Limbe costs around MK2000.

Mt Mulanje

A huge hulk of twisted granite rising from the surrounding plains, Mt Mulanje towers over 3000m high. The mountain is covered in dense green valleys, while its rivers drop from cliffs in dazzling waterfalls. Thanks to the prevalent mist, locals call it the 'Island in the Sky'.

Activities

For hikers, Mulanje is a big mountain with notoriously unpredictable weather; even during the dry season, it's not uncommon to get rain, cold winds and thick mists, which make it easy to get lost. Between May and August, periods of low cloud and drizzle can last several days and temperatures drop below freezing.

There are about six main hiking routes up and down Mulanje. The three main ascent routes go from Likhubula: the Chambe Plateau Path (also called the Skyline Path), the Chapaluka Path and the Lichenya Path. Other routes, more often used for the descent, are Thuchila Hut to Lukulezi Mission, Sombani Hut to Fort Lister Gap and Minunu Hut to Lujeri Tea Estate.

Sleeping

At the foot of Mt Mulanje is Mulanje town, which has several places to stay. At the village of Likhubula, about 15km from Mulanje town, are a couple more options.

On the mountain there are several **forestry huts** (campsites per adult/child MK400/200, huts per adult/child MK700/350) equipped with benches, open fires and plenty of wood. Bring your own food, cooking gear, candles, sleeping bag and stove. A caretaker chops wood, lights fires and brings water, for which a small tip should be paid.

CCAP Guesthouse GUESTHOUSE $
(Likhubula; campsite US$4, chalets per person US$8) At the CCAP Mission, after the reserve gates, with cosy rooms, self-catering chalets and camping.

Likhubula Forest Lodge LODGE $$
(☎0999 220560, 01-467737; campsite per person US$6, s/d without bathroom incl breakfast US$25/31, s/d incl breakfast US$31/37, whole lodge US$240; P @) This lovely colonial house has a homely kitchen, five clean rooms (two en suites) a communal lounge with rocking chairs, and nightly fire crackling.

Information

Hiking on Mt Mulanje is controlled by the **Likhubula Forestry Office** (PO Box 50, Mulanje; 7.30am-noon & 1-5pm), where hikers need to register, at the small village of Likhubula, about 15km from Mulanje town. Entry fees are MK100 per person, vehicle entry is MK200 and the forestry office car park costs MK100 a day.

Also good for information is the **Mulanje Infocentre** (☎01-466466, 01-466506; infomulanje@malawi.net; Phalombe Rd, Chitakale Trading Centre). It carries a good selection of books and maps and also rents out sleeping bags (MK500 per day) and tents (MK700 per day). It can also arrange mountain guides and porters.

Getting There & Away

AXA buses go between Mulanje town and Blantyre (MK850, 90 minutes). The dirt road to Likhubula turns off the main sealed Blantyre–Mulanje road at Chitikale, 2km west of the centre of Mulanje town; follow the signpost to Phalombe. If you're coming from Blantyre on the bus, ask to be dropped at Chitikale. From here, irregular *matola* run to Likhubula (MK300). Alternatively, you can walk (10km, two to three hours).

Zomba

POP 96,000

With its decrepit red-brick church and colonial buildings, Zomba feels like a lost chapter of the British Empire. The capital of Malawi from 1891 until the mid-1970s, today's town is home to tree-lined streets and an easy charm. East of the main road is the commercial centre, where you'll find a lively market, banks and a couple of decent eateries.

Carpeted in pine, rising nearly 1800m, the Zomba Plateau is beguilingly pretty. As you ascend the snaking road past wildflowers and roadside strawberry vendors, it almost feels like alpine France. This highland paradise, criss-crossed by streams, lakes and tumbling waterfalls, is home to leopards, bushbucks and birds like the mountain wagtail and Bertram's weaver.

The plateau can be covered on foot or by car (4WD on the backroads), and myriad winding trails cross the mountain. There's no bus up here, so you'll have to hitch or take a taxi (around MK8000).

Sleeping

Ku Chawe Trout Farm CAMPGROUND $
(campsites per person MK600, chalets per person MK2000, 4-bed self-contained chalets MK7000; P) This idyllic campsite has barbecue facilities, onsite toilets and showers. Alternatively, experience the Camp Crystal-meets-Norman Bates chalet on the hill, with its creaky verandah (complete with rocking chair!), bunk beds, en suite and kitchenette.

★ **Annie's Lodge** LODGE $$
(☎01-527002; Livingstone Rd; s/d from MK8250/9400; P ❄ @ ☎) Secreted in the foothills, Annie's has welcoming brick chalets with green roofs, surrounded by palm trees and flowers. Rooms are carpeted, clean and welcoming with DSTV and aircon. The executive rooms are housed in a new wing and sit at the top of the plot with great views. There's a bar and restaurant too.

★ **Ku Chawe Inn** HOTEL $$$
(☎01-514237, 01-773388; s/d US$125/160, hilltop rooms s/d US$185/210; ⊖ ❄ @ ☎) Set in gardens dripping with honeysuckle, upscale Ku Chawe boasts amazing views of the distant plain. Its red-brick exterior rooms have verandahs, appealing decor and cozy stone fireplaces. There are two restaurants dishing up terrific international fare. You can also mountain bike and trek, or ride horses with **Zomba Plateau Stables** (☎0888 714445, 0888 714443; maggieparsons@iwayafrica.com; per person per hour US$35).

Getting There & Away

AXA buses run to/from Zomba and Lilongwe (MK2000, five to six hours), Blantyre (MK750, 1½ to two hours) and Liwonde (MK650, one hour). Minibuses go every hour or so to Limbe (MK1000, one hour) and also leave to Lilongwe (MK2000, four to five hours) and Liwonde (MK700, 45 minutes).

Liwonde

Straddling the Shire River, diminutive Liwonde is one of the gateways to Liwonde National Park. To the east you'll find the main bus stations, the market, supermarkets and the train station. West of the river are several tourist lodges.

Shire Camp GUESTHOUSE $
(☎0888 909236, 0999 210532; campsite per person MK500, chalet incl breakfast MK3500; P) Shire Camp has clean cabanas with fans and hot-water bathrooms. The campsite has a basic ablutions block. Shire Camp can also take you on a river safari (US$25 per person) into Liwonde National Park. On the river's north bank; take the dirt road on the right just before the National Bank.

Getting There & Away

Lakeshore AXA buses pass by Liwonde on their way up to Mangochi but most drop off passengers at the turn-off and not in the town itself, so you're better of using a minibus; they run regularly from Zomba (MK250, 45 minutes), Limbe (MK500, three hours) and Mangochi (MK450, two hours). You can also get a minibus to the Mozambique border at Nayuchi (MK850, 2½ to three hours).

Liwonde National Park

Liwonde National Park has some 545 elephants, 1900 hippos, 500 water buffaloes and 1800 crocs. It's set in dry savannah and forest over 584 sq km, and you can walk, drive and putter along the Shire River to make the best of it.

The Shire River dominates the park and is prime hippo- and croc-spotting territory. Waterbucks are also common, while sable and roan antelopes, zebras and elands populate the flood plains in the east. Night drives may reveal bushbabies, jackals and spotted hyenas. The main event though is the elephants, and you'll get very close indeed.

Activities

Mvuu Camp's night drives (US$30 per person) take you past crocs, elephants and hippos; finishing in a romantic sundowner by the Shire River. Dawn walks (US$20 per person) are magical as you wander the savannah with a guide. Finally, you can take a boat safari (US$30 per person) which will take you past hippos and elephants.

Bushman's Baobabs offers wildlife drives, village walks, boat trips and kayaking excursions for around US$25 per person.

Tours

Njobvu Cultural Village CULTURAL TOUR
(☎0888 623530, through Mvuu Camp reception 01-542135; www.njobvuvillage.com; r per person US$16, all-inclusive US$50) Stay in a traditional Malawian village, sleeping in mud-brick huts and taking part in villagers' daily lives, visiting traditional doctors and the village school, and eating traditional food like *nshima*. All proceeds go directly to the community.

Sleeping

Bushman's Baobabs LODGE $$
(☎0888 838159, 0995 453324; www.bushmans-baobabs.com; per person campsites/dm/tents US$7.50/15/45, per person tented chalets US$60; P@) Comfortable rooms in the main house, as well as en suite walk-in safari tents. There's also a pool and large viewing deck. The nearby camping ground has plenty of pitches, a dorm and a bar and restaurant. Bushman's offers wildlife drives, village walks, boat trips and kayaking excursions for around US$25 per person.

★**Mvuu Camp** LODGE $$$
(☎01-771393, 01-771153; www.wilderness-safaris.com; campsite per person US$15, all-inclusive chalets per person US$260; @) Mvuu Camp sits on the Shire River, comprising a scattering of chalets with cozy interiors beside the open-plan, thatched restaurant. Dinner is communal and the food hearty. There's also a campsite with spotless ablution blocks and self-catering facilities. Magical.

Nearby is its more upscale sister, **Mvuu Wilderness Lodge** (☎01-771393, 01-771153; all-inclusive chalets per person US$445;).

Getting There & Away

The main park gate is 6km east of Liwonde town. There's no public transport beyond here. From the gate to Mvuu Camp is 28km along the park track (closed in the wet season), and a 4WD or high-clearance vehicle is recommended for this route.

Another way in for vehicles is via the dirt road from Ulongwe, a village between Liwonde town and Mangochi. This leads for 14km through local villages to the western boundary. A few kilometres inside the park is a car park and boat jetty, where the boat from Mvuu Camp will come and collect you.

Alternatively, catch any bus between Liwonde town and Mangochi and get off at Ulongwe, where local boys can take you by bicycle to the park gate.

Majete Wildlife Reserve

The **Majete Wildlife Reserve** (www.majete.org; adult/child MK2000/1000, vehicle MK200, maps MK100) is a rugged wilderness of hilly *miombo* woodland hugging the west bank of the Shire River. With Majete's lion reintroduction program, and the establishment of the sumptuous Mkulumadzi Lodge, this massively upgraded reserve makes for an exciting destination.

There are over 3000 animals in Majete (most translocated from other parks), including hyenas, sable, nyalas, bushbuck, impalas, serval, antelopes, black rhinos, buffaloes, elephants, hippos, civets, zebras and leopards.

Sights & Activities

Mkulumadzi Lodge (p843) has a 7000-hectare slice of the 70,000-hectare park, and is bursting with animals. There are 250km of tracks in the park, and you'll need a high-clearance car to get around – especially during the wet season.

If you'd rather your activities were organised there is plenty on offer, including bush walks (per person US20), wildlife drives (per person US$25), and night wildlife drives (US$35). You can also opt to have a scout join you in your own car (US$15). Boat rides past hippos on the Shire River (US$20) are also possible.

Sleeping

Community Campsite CAMPGROUND $
(campsites s/d US$10/15, tent hire US$25; P) Enabling visitors on a budget to stay in Majete, this camping ground has shady places to pitch and park, or you can sleep on a stilted deck under the stars. There's also drinkable water, clean ablution blocks, hot showers and cooking facilities. You do need to bring

your own food though. To get here turn left just before the heritage centre.

★**Mkulumadzi Lodge** LODGE $$$
(☎01-794491; www.mkulumadzi.com; per person all-inclusive midseason/high US$337/378; P ❄ @ ☰ ≋) This romantic lodge has a high thatched ceiling strung with contemporary lights, driftwood art installations and a kidney-shaped pool. Chalets look out onto the Shire River with step-in rain showers, widescreen views and sunken baths.

The camp offers morning walks to a hide close to the river (well situated for spotting black rhinos taking a dawn drink) and night drives to see hippos rising from the bank. All game drives are included, as is food and drink. If you're getting here by bus, free transfers are available from Chikwawa village.

Getting There & Away

Majete lies west of the Shire River, some 70km southwest of Blantyre. Follow the road to Chikwawa; from there signs will direct you to the reserve. By public transport, the nearest you can get is Chikwawa.

UNDERSTAND MALAWI

Malawi Today

Malawi is urbanising rapidly, its 16.3 million population growing at an unsustainable 2.8% a year, making it one of the highest population densities in Africa. Natural resources struggle to support the burgeoning population, and schools, hospitals and other social institutions are overflowing. About 85% of people live in rural areas and are engaged in subsistence farming or fishing, or working on commercial farms and plantations.

April 2012 saw vital fresh blood pumped into Malawi's corrupt political system in the form of new president – women's rights activist and former vice-president, Dr Joyce Banda. The next year was remarkable not least for Joyce Banda and Madonna's flaming row over the singer's assertions in the press that she was building schools in Malawi. Banda retorted that she was actually only contributing to the construction of classrooms.

Meanwhile in 2013 the Malawian economy was not responding well to austerity measures laid out by the International Monetary Fund(IMF) on which the Malawi's vital funding depended. Bloomberg reported that the kwacha was now the worst-performing currency in Africa. To make matters worse Banda's brave move to devalue the kwacha, had a massive impact on the cost of fuel and other commodities, which skyrocketed. The result? January and February 2013 saw mass protests, with civil servants and teachers going on strike demanding a 67% pay rise.

Blantyre pupils also protested in support of their teachers in their own independently organized rallies. The strike was called off only when Banda's government conceded to a 61% salary increase. The question now looms large: will Joyce Banda lose the next election if she closely adheres to the strict public spending measures the IMF are demanding of her, or can she somehow pull off her balancing act between reform and keeping the population calm?

History

Since the first millennium, the Bantu people had been migrating from Central Africa into the area now called Malawi, but migration to the area stepped up with the arrival of the Tumbuka and Phoka, who settled around the highlands of Nyika and Viphya during the 17th century, and the Maravi, who established a large and powerful kingdom in the south.

The early 19th century brought with it two significant migrations. The Yao invaded southern Malawi from western Mozambique, displacing the Maravi, while groups of Zulu migrated northward to settle in central and northern Malawi. This century also saw the escalation of the East African slave trade.

Enter the British

The most famous explorer to reach this area was Dr David Livingstone. He reached Lake Malawi in September 1859, naming it Lake Nyasa. His death in 1873 inspired a legion of missionaries to come to Africa, bringing the more 'civilised' principles of commerce and Christianity.

The early missionaries blazed the way for various adventurers and pioneer traders and it wasn't long before European settlers began to arrive in their droves. In 1889 Britain allowed Cecil Rhodes' British South Africa Company to administer the Shire Highlands, and in 1891 the British Central Africa (BCA) Protectorate was extended to include land along the western side of the lake. In 1907 the BCA Protectorate became the colony of Nyasaland.

Colonial rule brought with it an end to slave traders and intertribal conflicts, but it also brought a whole new set of problems. As more European settlers arrived, land was increasingly taken away from the locals and Africans were forced to pay taxes to the administration.

Transition & Independence

Not surprisingly, this created opposition to colonial rule and in the 1950s the Nyasaland African Congress (NAC) party, led by Dr Hastings Kamuzu Banda, pushed for independence. This came, after considerable struggle, in 1964, and Nyasaland became the independent country of Malawi. Two years later Malawi became a republic and Banda was made president, eventually declaring himself 'president for life' in 1971. He ruled for over 20 years before his downfall and died three years later. Many achievements were made during his presidency but these were overshadowed by his stringent rule: banning of foreign press, imposition of dress codes and vendettas waged against any group regarded as a threat.

In June 1993, Banda agreed to a referendum that resulted in the introduction of a multiparty political system; at Malawi's first full multiparty election in May 1994, the victor was the United Democratic Front (UDF), led by Bakili Muluzi. On becoming president, Muluzi closed political prisons, permitted freedom of speech and print, and instituted several economic reforms. Muluzi was re-elected in May 1999. Muluzi was followed by Bingu wa Mutharika in 2004; who quit the UDF, established his own party and began eight years of rule that delivered the country to its knees by the time he died in 2012.

Culture

Fact: Malawians are among the friendliest people in Africa – they avoid conflict and often use humour to diffuse tension. And while they're laid-back and patient, Malawians are quite conservative; women tend to dress modestly and respectable ladies are not seen in bars unaccompanied.

Malawi remains one of the world's poorest countries, with a per-capita Gross National Product (GNP) of less than US$250. Nearly half the population is chronically malnourished and life expectancy is only 43 years, due in large part to the HIV/AIDS infection rate in Malawi, which runs at almost 12%.

Malawi's main ethnic groups are Chewa, dominant in the centre and south; Yao in the south; and Tumbuka in the north. Other groups include the Ngoni (also spelt Angoni), inhabiting parts of the central and northern provinces; the Chipoka (or Phoka) in the central area; the Lambya; the Ngonde (also called the Nyakyusa) in the northern region; and the Tonga, mostly along the lakeshore.

There are small populations of Asian and European people living mainly in the cities and involved in commerce, farming (mainly tea plantations) or tourism.

Music & Dance

Traditional music and dance in Malawi are closely linked and form an important social function, beyond entertainment.

Modern home-grown contemporary music is growing in Malawi, due largely to influential and popular musicians such as Lucius Banda, who performs soft 'Malawian-style' reggae, and the late Evison Matafale. Look out too for the Black Missionaries and Billy Kaunda. Also for the new world music star, The Very Best.

Food & Drink

Markets and bus stations have food stalls where you can get tea with milk for around MK70 and a bread cake or deep-fried cassava for MK50, or a simple meal of beans or meat and *nshima* (maize porridge) for about MK150.

Local restaurants in small towns provide simple meals for around MK250. In cities and larger towns, cheap restaurants serve traditional food as well as chicken or fish with rice or chips for around MK600.

Most midrange hotels and restaurants serve European-style food, such as steak, chicken or fish, which is served with vegetables and chips or rice – usually around the MK1200 mark.

In Blantyre and Lilongwe you can find restaurants serving Ethiopian, Indian, Korean, Chinese and Portuguese food. Main courses range from around MK1400 to MK1600. More elaborate French and Italian cuisine is also available, and you'll also find several steakhouses. At most top-end estab-

MUST READS: THE BOY WHO HARNESSED THE WIND

When the drought of 2001 brought famine, and terrible floods dessicated his parents' crops, 14-year-old William Kamkwamba was forced from school. Self-educating at his old primary school, one book about electricity generation through windmills grabbed him.

A lightbulb moment flashed. William picked around for scrap and painstakingly began his creation; a four-bladed windmill. Soon neighbours were coming to see him to charge their phones on his windmill.

When news of William's invention spread, people from across the globe offered to help him. He was shortly reenrolled in college and travelling to America to visit wind farms, and has since been mentoring kids on how to create their own independent electricity sources. The book *The Boy Who Harnessed the Wind* (William Kamkwamba and Bryan Mealer) is his amazing story.

lishments, main courses start from about MK2500.

Traditional beer of the region is made from maize. Malawi's local lager is called Kuche Kuche but most travellers (and many Malawians) prefer the beer produced by Carlsberg at its Blantyre brewery.

Environment

The Land

Pint-sized, landlocked Malawi is no larger than the US state of Pennsylvania. It's wedged between Zambia, Tanzania and Mozambique, measuring roughly 900km long and between 80km and 150km wide, with an area of 118,484 sq km.

Lying in a trough formed by the Rift Valley, Lake Malawi makes up over 75% of Malawi's eastern boundary. Beyond the lake, escarpments rise to high rolling plateaus covering much of the country.

Wildlife & National Parks

Malawi has five national parks. These are (from north to south) Nyika, Kasungu, Lake Malawi (around Cape Maclear), Liwonde and Lengwe. There are also four wildlife reserves – Vwaza Marsh, Nkhotakota, Mwabvi and Majete – making 16.4% of Malawi's land protected. In 2012 Malawi began reintroducing lions at Majete Wildlife Reserve, finally giving the country its 'Big Five' stamp.

Many head for Liwonde National Park, noted for its herds of elephants and myriad hippos. Along with Majete, it's the only park in the country where you might see rhinos. Elephants are also regularly seen in Nkhotakota Wildlife Reserve, Majete and Nyika National Park. Nearby Vwaza Marsh is known for its hippos, elephants, buffaloes and waterbucks, but it's currently in poor shape due to poor management.

Lake Malawi has more freshwater fish species than any other body of water in the world (over 600, of which more than 350 are endemic). The largest family of fish in the lake is the Cichlidae (cichlids).

For birdwatchers, Malawi has over 600 species, while birds rarely spotted elsewhere in Southern Africa are easily seen here including the African skimmer, Böhm's bee-eater and the wattled crane.

SURVIVAL GUIDE

Directory A–Z

ACCOMMODATION

Camping costs around US$5 to US$10 and usually involves hot showers and power points. You'll also find backpacker hostels all over the country, charging US$5 to US$10 for a dorm, about US$10 to US$20 per person for a double or triple with shared facilities, and around US$30 for a room with bathroom. Ordinary guest houses are less inspiring.

Midrange hotels and lodges start from about US$30 up to US$80 for a double, including taxes, usually with private bathroom and breakfast, sometimes with air-con.

Top-end hotels range from US$100 to US$250 for a double room, with all the mod cons, plus hotel facilities such as swimming pools, tennis courts and boutiques. The price normally includes taxes and breakfast. Then there are the exclusive beach hotels and safari lodges, which charge anything from US$100 to US$450 per person per night.

PRACTICALITIES

- **Electricity** 220–240V; British three-pronged square plug BS-1363
- **Languages** English, Chichewa
- **Newspapers** Malawi's main newspapers are the *Daily Times*, the *Malawi News* and the *Nation*. Watch out too for the *Eye*, a quarterly directory of the best things to see and do.
- **TV** Consists mostly of imported programs, news and regional music videos. DSTV is available in most midrange and top-end hotels.

ACTIVITIES

Lake Malawi is one of the best freshwater diving areas in the world. Scuba, snorkel and learn to dive at Nkhata Bay, Cape Maclear and Likoma Island. Kayaking is available at Cape Maclear and Nkhata Bay.

The main areas for hiking are Nyika, Mulanje and Zomba. Mulanje is Malawi's main rock-climbing area.

The main area for horse riding is the Zomba Plateau, while Nyika's hilly landscape and good network of dirt tracks are also great for mountain biking.

EMBASSIES & CONSULATES

The following countries have diplomatic representation in Malawi.

British High Commission (☎01-772400; off Kenyatta Rd, City Centre, Lilongwe)

German Embassy (☎01-772555; Convention Dr, City Centre, Lilongwe)

Mozambican Embassy (☎01-774100; Convention Dr, City Centre, Lilongwe)

South African Embassy (☎01-773722; sahe@malawi.net; Kang'ombe Bldg, City Centre, Lilongwe)

US Embassy (☎01-773166; Convention Dr, City Centre, Lilongwe)

Zambian Embassy (☎01-772590; Convention Dr, City Centre, Lilongwe)

MONEY

Malawi's unit of currency is the Malawi kwacha (MK). This is divided into 100 tambala (t).

Bank notes include MK200, MK100, MK50, MK20, MK10 and MK5. Coins include MK1, 50t, 20t, 10t, 5t and 1t.

At big hotels that quote in US dollars you can pay in hard currency or kwacha at the prevailing exchange rate.

Standard Bank and National Bank ATMs are the best bet for foreigners wishing to draw money from their home account. Standard Bank accepts foreign Visa, MasterCard, Cirrus and Maestro cards. National Bank ATMs only take Visa cards.

You can use Visa cards at many large hotels and top-end restaurants, though there may be a surcharge of around 5%.

OPENING HOURS

Banks 8am to 3.30pm Monday to Friday

Offices 8am to 5pm Monday to Friday

Post and telephone offices 7.30am to 5pm Monday to Friday

Restaurants Breakfast 7am to 10am, lunch noon to 2pm, dinner 6pm to 9.30pm

Shops 8am to 5pm Monday to Friday and Saturday morning. In smaller towns, shops and stalls are open most days but keep informal hours.

POST

Some letters get from Lilongwe to London in three days, others take three weeks. Post offices in Blantyre and Lilongwe have poste restante services.

Airmail parcels now cost about MK2000 plus MK500 per kilo to send items outside Africa. Surface mail is cheaper.

PUBLIC HOLIDAYS

New Year's Day 1 January

John Chilembwe Day 15 January

Martyrs' Day 3 March

Easter March/April – Good Friday, Holy Saturday and Easter Monday

Labour Day 1 May

Freedom Day 14 June

Republic Day 6 July

Mother's Day Second Monday in October

National Tree Planting Day Second Monday in December

Christmas Day 25 December

Boxing Day 26 December

SAFE TRAVEL

Reports of travellers being robbed in Lilongwe, Blantyre and the resorts of Cape Maclear and Nkhata Bay have increased. However, incidents are still rare compared with other countries, and violence is not the norm.

Potential dangers while at Lake Malawi include encountering a hippo or crocodile, but for travellers the chances of being attacked are extremely remote.

TELEPHONE

Telephone calls within Malawi cost around MK50 per minute. Calls to mobiles within Malawi cost around MK70 per minute.

Mobile phone coverage is extensive. Mobile phone prefixes are ☎0888 or ☎0999 and the major network is Airtel. SIM cards are readily available for around MK1500 and include a small amount of airtime. You can buy top-up cards from supermarkets, internet cafes and petrol stations.

The international code for Malawi if you're dialling from abroad is ☎265. Malawi does not have area codes, but all landline numbers begin with ☎01, so whatever number you dial within the country will have eight digits. Numbers starting with ☎7 are on the Lilongwe exchange; those starting with ☎8 are in Blantyre; ☎5 is around Zomba; ☎4 is the south; and ☎3 is the north.

TOURIST INFORMATION

There are limited tourist information offices in Blantyre and Lilongwe. Outside Malawi, tourism promotion is handled by the excellent UK-based **Malawi Tourism** (☎0115-982 1903; www.malawitourism.com).

VISAS

Visas are not required by citizens of Commonwealth countries, the USA and most European nations. On entering the country you'll be granted a 30-day entry stamp, which can easily be extended at immigration offices in Blantyre or Lilongwe; however, the next month requires a fee of MK5000.

Getting There & Away

AIR

Kamuzu International Airport (LLW; ☎01-700766), 19km north of Lilongwe city centre, handles the majority of international flights. Flights from South Africa, Kenya, Zambia and Tanzania also land in Blantyre at **Chileka International Airport** (BLZ; ☎01-694244). The country's national carrier is Air Malawi. Ulendo Airlink (p825) operate domestic flights.

Airlines Flying To/From Malawi

Air Malawi (☎01-820811, 01-773680; www.airmalawi.com) Has a decent regional network, with flights heading to Dar es Salaam, Jo'burg, Nairobi, Lusaka and Harare from Blantyre and Lilongwe.

South African Airways (☎01-620617, 01-772242; www.flysaa.com) Flies twice weekly between Blantyre and Jo'burg, and five times weekly between Lilongwe and Jo'burg (with connections to Durban, Cape Town etc).

Kenya Airways (☎01-774227, 01-774624, 01-774524; www.kenya-airways.com) Flies four times a week to/from Nairobi and six times a week to/from Lusaka.

Ethiopian Airways (☎01-771002, 01-771308; www.flyethiopian.com) Flies four times a week from Addis Ababa.

BOAT

If you're heading to Mozambique, the Lake Malawi ferry Ilala (p848) stops at Metangula on the Mozambican mainland. If you're planning a visit you must get a visa in advance and make sure to get your passport stamped at Malawian immigration on Likoma Island or in Nkhata Bay. Another way to get to the Mozambican lakeshore is to take a dhow (local sailing boat) from Likoma Island to Cóbuè.

LAND

Mozambique

For the south, take a minibus to the Mozambican border crossing at Zóbuè (*zob*-way; MK500) and then a minibus to Tete (US$6), from where buses go to Beira and Maputo. You could also get a Blantyre–Harare bus to drop you at Tete and then get a bus to Beira or Maputo.

For central Mozambique, there are several buses per day from Blantyre to Nsanje (MK850), or all the way to the Malawian border at Marka (*ma*-ra-ka; MK900). It's a few kilometres between the border crossings – walk or take a bicycle taxi – and you can change money on the Mozambique side. From here pick-ups go to Mutarara and Vila de Sena.

There are three border crossings from Malawi into northern Mozambique: Muloza, from where you can reach Mocuba in Mozambique, and Nayuchi and Chiponde, both of which lead to Cuamba in Mozambique.

Regular buses run from Blantyre, via Mulanje, to Muloza (MK750). From here, you walk 1km to the Mozambican border crossing at Melosa, from where it's another few kilometres into Milange. From Milange there's usually a *chapa* (pick-up or converted minibus) or truck about every other day in the dry season to Mocuba, where you can find transport on to Quelimane or Nampula.

Further north, minibuses and *matolas* run a few times per day between Mangochi and the border crossing at Chiponde (MK800). It's then 7km to the Mozambican border crossing at Mandimba, and the best way to get there is by bicycle taxi (US$2). Mandimba has a couple of *pensãos* (pensions), and there's at least one vehicle daily, usually a truck, between here and Cuamba (US$10).

The third option is to go by minibus or passenger train from Liwonde to the border at Nayuchi (MK850). You can then take a *chapa* from the Mozambican side of the border to Cuamba.

A freight train *sometimes* departs from Limbe on Wednesday at 7am, travelling via Balaka and Liwonde to the border at Nayuchi. From Nayuchi (where there are money changers) you can walk to Entre Lagos, and then get a *chapa* to Cuamba. That said, this is an unreliable mode of transport and you're better off taking the bus.

South Africa

Intercape Mainline (☎0999 403398; www.intercape.co.za) operates a service between Lilongwe and Jo'burg for US$78, leaving at 6am; as does **Chiwale Bus Co** (☎0999 034014) from the same location outside the petrol station on

Paul Kagame Rd (in Old Town). From Blantyre, try Ingwe Coach (p839), departing from the car park outside Blantyre Lodge.

Tanzania

To get to Dar es Salaam, there are five **Taqwa** (☎0999 334538) buses per week (US$50) departing from Devil St in Lilongwe. These buses also pick up and drop off in Mzuzu (US$30), leaving at midnight and arriving in Dar es Salaam around 10pm the next day. Mbeya (Tanzania) is handy for going between northern Malawi and southern Tanzania.

Buses and minibuses run between Mzuzu and Karonga (MK2000, three to four hours), from where you can get a taxi to the Songwe border crossing (MK1200). It's 200m across the bridge to the Tanzanian border crossing.

Once on the Tanzanian side of the border, minibuses travel to Kyela (7km) and on to Mbeya, where you will need to overnight before continuing on the next morning to Dar es Salaam. You can change money with the bicycle-taxi operators.

Zambia

There are four direct buses per week (two on Tuesday and two on Friday) between Lilongwe and Lusaka (MK6000), departing from Devil St – the journey takes at least 12 hours. Regular minibuses run between Lilongwe and Mchinji (MK400). From here, it's 12km to the border. Local shared taxis shuttle between Mchinji and the border post for around MK200 per person, or MK1000 for the whole car.

From the Zambian side of the border crossing, shared taxis run to Chipata (US$2), which is about 30km west of the border.

Getting Around

AIR

Air Malawi (p847) only operates regular domestic flights between Lilongwe and Blantyre (MK43,000 one way). Ulendo Airlink (p825) flies twin-prop planes to various domestic safari parks as well as Likoma Island (from US$210 to US$320).

BOAT

The **Ilala ferry** (☎01-587311; ilala@malawi.net) chugs passengers and cargo up and down Lake Malawi once a week in each direction. Travelling between Monkey Bay in the south and Chilumba in the north, it makes 12 stops at lakeside villages and towns in between. The whole trip, from one end of the line to the other, takes about three days. The official schedules are detailed here (only selected ports are shown).

NORTHBOUND

PORT	ARRIVAL	DEPARTURE
Monkey Bay	-	10am (Fri)
Chipoka	1pm	4pm (Fri)
Nkhotakota	midnight	2am (Sat)
Metangula	6am	8am (Sat)
Likoma Island	1.30pm	6pm (Sat)
Nkhata Bay	1am	5am (Sun)
Ruarwe	10.15am	11.15am (Sun)
Chilumba	5pm (Sun)	-

SOUTHBOUND

PORT	ARRIVAL	DEPARTURE
Chilumba	-	1am (Mon)
Ruarwe	6.45am	8am (Mon)
Nkhata Bay	12.45pm	8pm (Mon)
Likoma Island	3.15am	6.15am (Tue)
Metangula	noon	2pm (Tue)
Nkhotakota	5.30pm	7.30pm (Tue)
Chipoka	3.30am	7.30am (Wed)
Monkey Bay	10.30am (Wed)	-

The *Ilala* has three classes. Cabin class was once luxurious and the cabins are still in reasonable condition. The spacious 1st-class deck is most popular with travellers, due largely to the sociable bar. Economy covers the entire lower deck and is dark and crowded, and engine fumes permeate from below.

Reservations are usually required for cabin class. For other classes, tickets are sold only when the boat is sighted.

Sample Routes & Fares

All of the following sample fares are from Nkhata Bay. See table below.

BUS & MINIBUS

Malawi's main bus company is **AXA Coach Services** (☎01-876000; agma@agmaholdings.net). AXA operates three different classes. Coaches are the best and the most expensive. It's a luxury nonstop service with air-con, toilet, comfortable reclining seats, snacks and fresh coffee. Servic-

FERRY CLASSES FROM CHILUMBA

DESTINATION	CABIN	1ST CLASS	ECONOMY
Nkhotakota	MK14,900	MK6,820	MK1,190
Ruarwe	MK12,500	MK3,000	MK1,140
Monkey Bay	MK28,240	MK16,110	MK2,710

es operate between Blantyre and Lilongwe twice a day from special departure points in each city (not the main bus stations).

AXA Luxury Coach and City Trouper services are the next in line. These buses have air-con and reclining seats as well as TVs, but don't have toilets. They ply the route between Blantyre and Karonga, stopping at all the main towns with limited stops elsewhere.

Lastly there are the country commuter buses, handy for backpackers as they cover the lakeshore route. If you're headed for Mzuzu another alternative is the comfortable Super Sink Bus between Lilongwe and Mzuzu.

There are also local minibus services which operate on a fill-up-and-go basis.

In rural areas, the frequency of buses and minibuses drops dramatically, and said 'bus' is often a truck or pick-up, with people just piled in the back. In Malawi this is called a *matola*.

CAR & MOTORCYCLE

The majority of main routes are sealed roads, though the roads along less major routes are potholed, making driving slow and dangerous. Secondary roads are usually graded dirt. Rural routes are often impassable after heavy rain, sometimes for weeks.

Avis (☎ in Blantyre 01-692368, in Lilongwe 01-756105, in Lilongwe 01-756103) Has offices at Lilongwe and Blantyre airports and at some large hotels.

Crossroads Car Hire (☎ 01-750333; Mchinji Roundabout, Crossroads Complex, Lilongwe; 2WD/4WD with fully comprehensive insurance per day US$100/149; ⏲ 9am-5pm Mon-Fri) Has solid 4WD vehicles, and fully comprehensive insurance.

Mozambique

Includes ➡

Best of Nature

- Gorongosa National Park (p862)
- Chimanimani Mountains (p862)
- Quirimbas Archipelago (p867)
- Lake Niassa (p866)

Best of Culture

- Mozambique Island p864)
- Ibo Island (p867)
- Maputo (p851)
- Inhambane (p859)

Why Go?

Mozambique beckons with its coastline and swaying palms, its traditions, its cultures, its vibe and - most of all - its adventure. This enigmatic southeast African country is well off most travellers' maps, but it has much to offer those who venture here: long, dune-fringed beaches, turquoise waters abounding in shoals of colourful fish, well-preserved corals, remote archipelagos in the north, pounding surf in the south, graceful dhows with billowing sails, colonial-style architecture, pulsating nightlife, vast tracts of bush populated with elephants, lions and birds galore, and an endlessly fascinating cultural mix. Discovering these attractions is not always easy, but it is unfailingly rewarding. Bring along some patience, a tolerance for long bus rides and a sense of adventure and jump in for the journey of a lifetime.

When to Go

Maputo

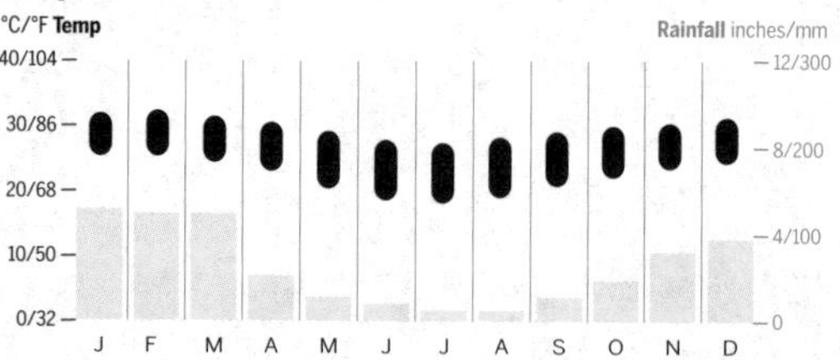

Dec–Apr Heavy rains bring muddy roads and flooding, especially during Feb and March.

May–Oct Cooler, dry and an ideal time to visit. In August, book ahead for the southern coastal resorts.

Nov Mostly dry, with increasing temperatures, but without the holiday crowds.

MAPUTO

☎21 / POP 1.59 MILLION

With its Mediterranean-style architecture, flame-tree-lined avenues, sidewalk cafes and waterside setting, Maputo is easily one of Africa's most attractive capitals. *Galabiyya*-garbed men gather in doorways to chat, while colourfully clad women hawk seafood and spices at the massive Municipal Market and banana vendors loll on their carts in the shade. There are museums, shops and markets galore – don't miss spending time here before heading north.

SET YOUR BUDGET

Budget

- Double room <US$50 per night
- Two-course dinner <US$10
- Coffee US$1.50

Midrange

- Double room US$50–150 per night
- Two-course dinner US$10–20
- Beer US$2

Top End

- Hotel room >US$150 per night
- Two-course dinner >US$20
- Glass of wine US$4

Sights & Activities

National Art Museum MUSEUM
(Museu Nacional de Arte; ☎21-320264; artemus@tvcabo.co.mz; 1233 Avenida Ho Chi Minh; admission Mtc20, Sun free; 11am-6pm Tue-Fri, 2-6pm Sat & Sun) Don't miss this small but intriguing collection of paintings and sculptures by Mozambique's finest contemporary artists.

Núcleo de Arte ARTS CENTRE
(☎21-492523, 21-499840; www.nucleodarte.com; 194 Rua da Argélia; 10am-8pm) This long-standing artists' cooperative features the work of up-and-coming artists. Watch the artists at work, or relax in the adjoining cafe.

Train Station HISTORIC BUILDING
(Caminho dos Ferros de Moçambique, CFM; Praça dos Trabalhadores) The landmark train station was designed by an associate of Gustav Eiffel (of Tower fame). A railway museum is opening 'soon' at the end of the platforms.

National Money Museum MUSEUM
(Museu Nacional da Moeda; Praça 25 de Junho; admission Mtc20; 11am-5pm Tue-Fri, 9am-3.30pm Sat, 2-5pm Sun) Housed in a restored 1860 building in the oldest part of town, with exhibits of local currency, ranging from early barter tokens to modern-day bills.

Fort FORTRESS
(Fortaleza; Praça 25 de Junho; 9am-5pm) FREE The 19th-century fort houses a small museum and Ngungunhane's carved wood coffin.

Praça da Independência PLAZA
On this wide plaza check out the spired **Cathedral of Nossa Senhora da Conceição**, neoclassical **City Hall** (Conselho Municipal) and the **Iron House** (Casa de Ferro).

Municipal Market MARKET
(Mercado Municipal; Avenida 25 de Setembro; from about 8am) Here, stalls overflow with fruits, vegetables and spices.

Sleeping

Maputo's backpackers' hostels don't have signs, just house numbers.

Base Backpackers BACKPACKERS $
(☎21-302723, 82-452 6860; thebasebp@tvcabo.co.mz; 545 Avenida Patrice Lumumba; dm/d Mtc350/900; @) Small but popular and often full, with a central location, kitchen, backyard bar, terrace and *braai* (barbecue) area overlooking the port in the distance. Via public transport from Junta, take a 'Museu' *chapa* (minivan) to the final Museu stop, from where it's a short walk.

Fatima's Place BACKPACKERS $
(☎82-185 1577; www.mozambiquebackpackers.com; 1317 Avenida Mao Tse Tung; dm Mtc500, s/d without bathroom Mtc1000/1500, s/d Mtc1250/1800) In the upper part of town, this long-standing place has an outdoor kitchen-bar, small courtyard and a mix of rooms.

Hoyo-Hoyo Residencial HOTEL $$
(☎21-490701, 82-300 9950; www.hoyohoyo.odline.com; 837 Avenida Francisco Magumbwe; s/d Mtc2000/2400) In the upper part of town, with good-value, no-frills rooms, familial ambience and a good restaurant.

Residencial Palmeiras BOUTIQUE HOTEL $$
(☎21-300199, 82-306 9200; www.palmeiras-guesthouse.com; 948 Avenida Patrice Lumumba;

Mozambique Highlights

1 Discover enchanting **Mozambique Island** (p864), with its time-warp atmosphere and cobbled streets.

2 Get to know **Maputo** (p851), with its lively sidewalk cafes and many museums.

3 Explore the **Quirimbas Archipelago** (p867), including magical Ibo, with its silversmiths, fort and crumbling mansions.

4 Relax along the ruggedly beautiful shoreline of **Lake Niassa** (p866).

5 Watch wildlife and enjoy fine birding at **Gorongosa National Park** (p862).

6 Hike in the lush **Chimanimani Mountains** (p862).

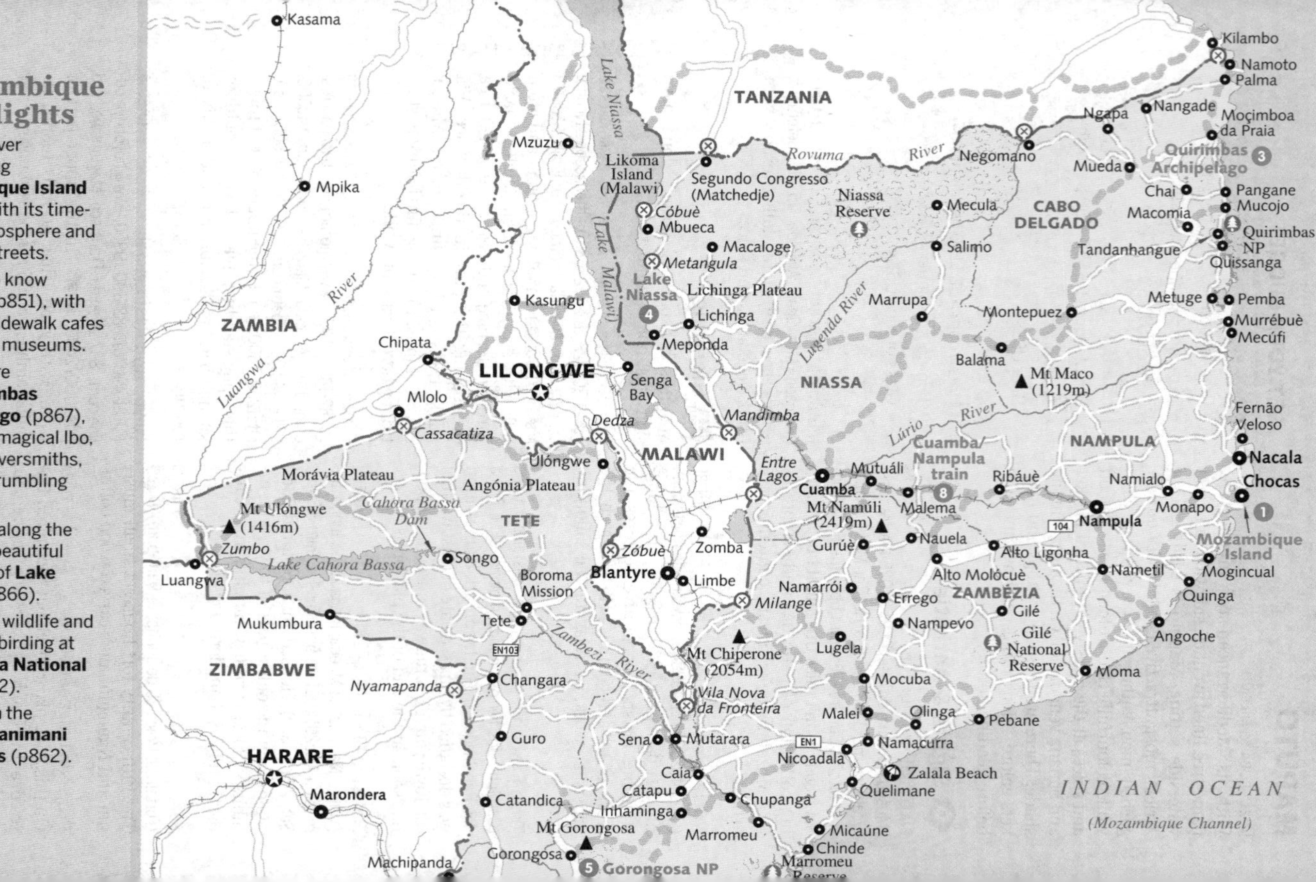

7 Wander historic **Inhambane** (p859) town's quiet streets before relaxing on beautiful nearby beaches.

8 Travel by **train** (p865) between Cuamba and Nampula, with its glimpses into rural life.

9 Sail and snorkel around the islands of the **Bazaruto Archipelago** (p861).

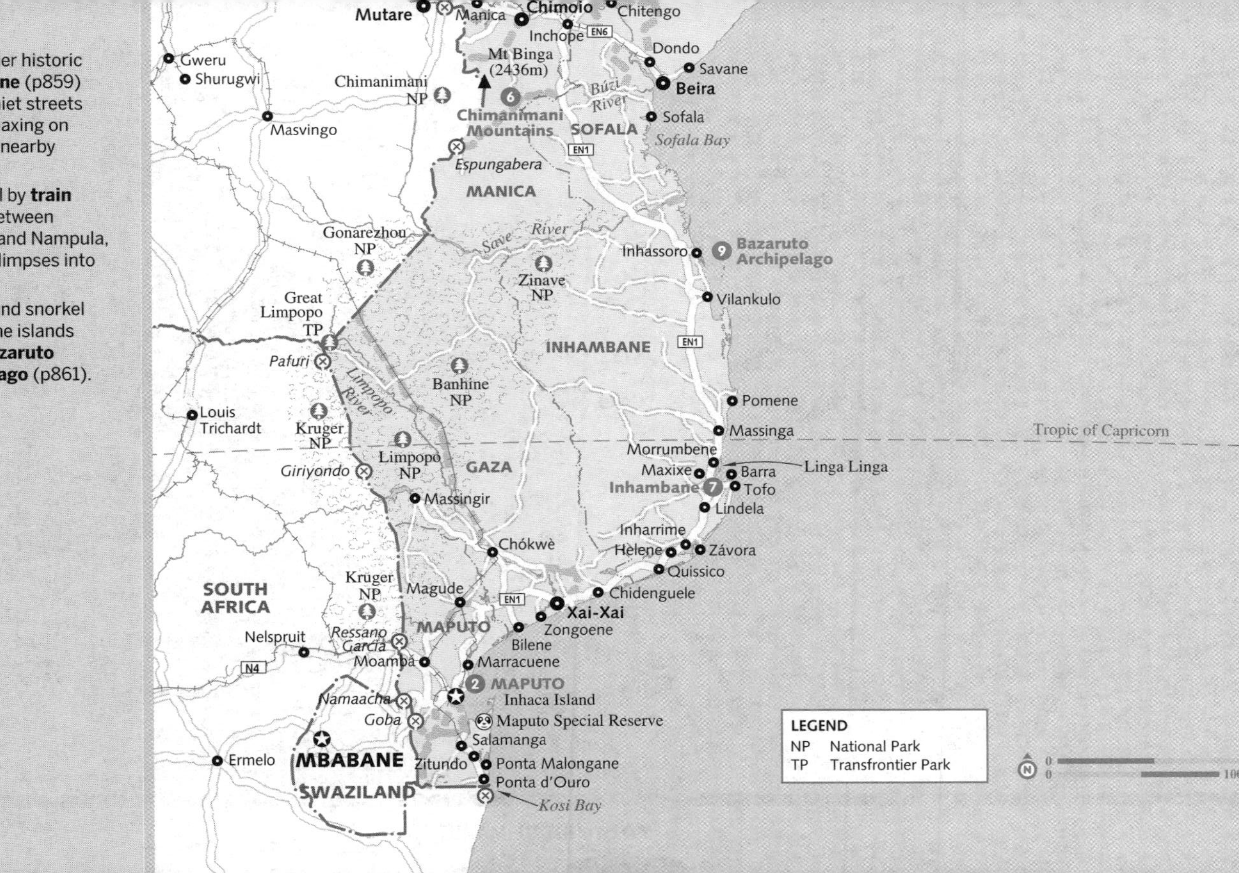

Central Maputo

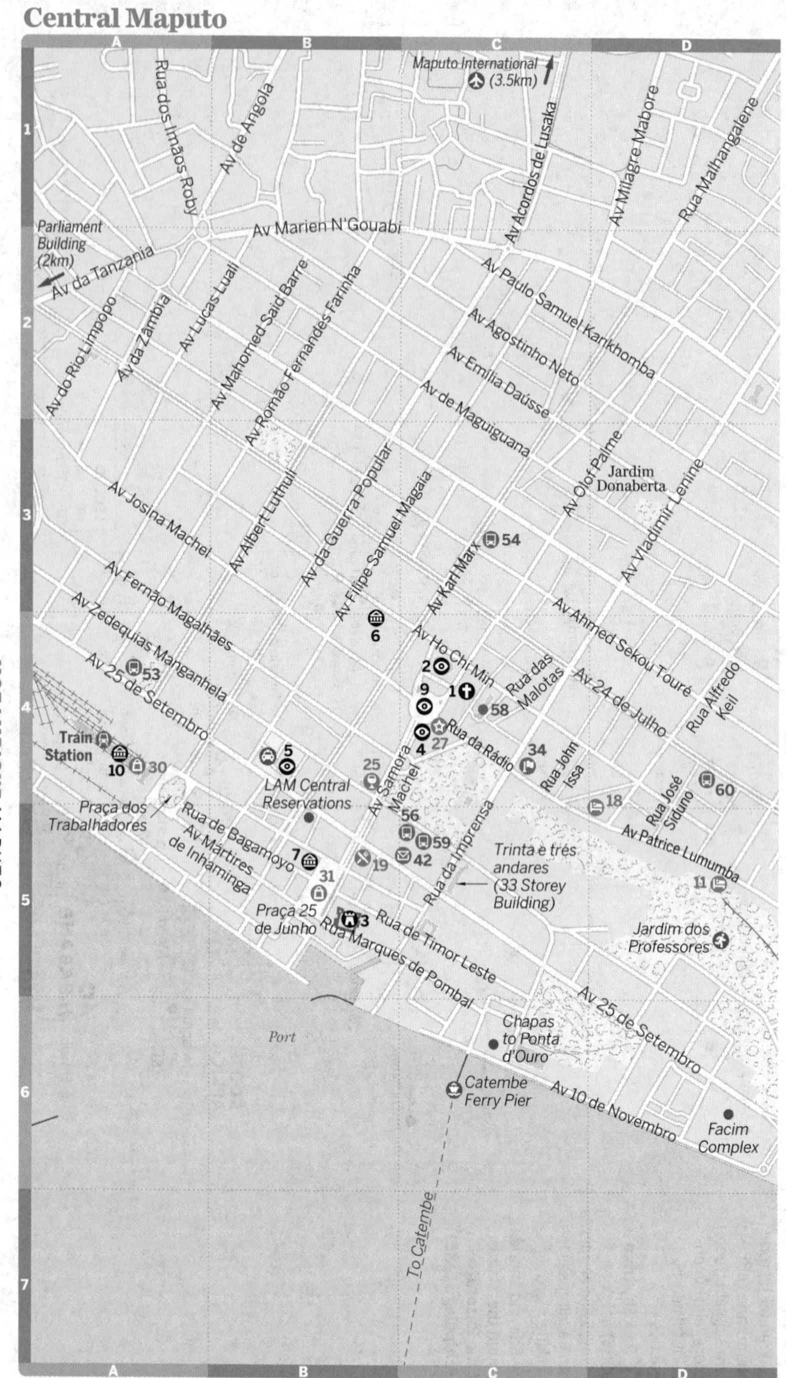

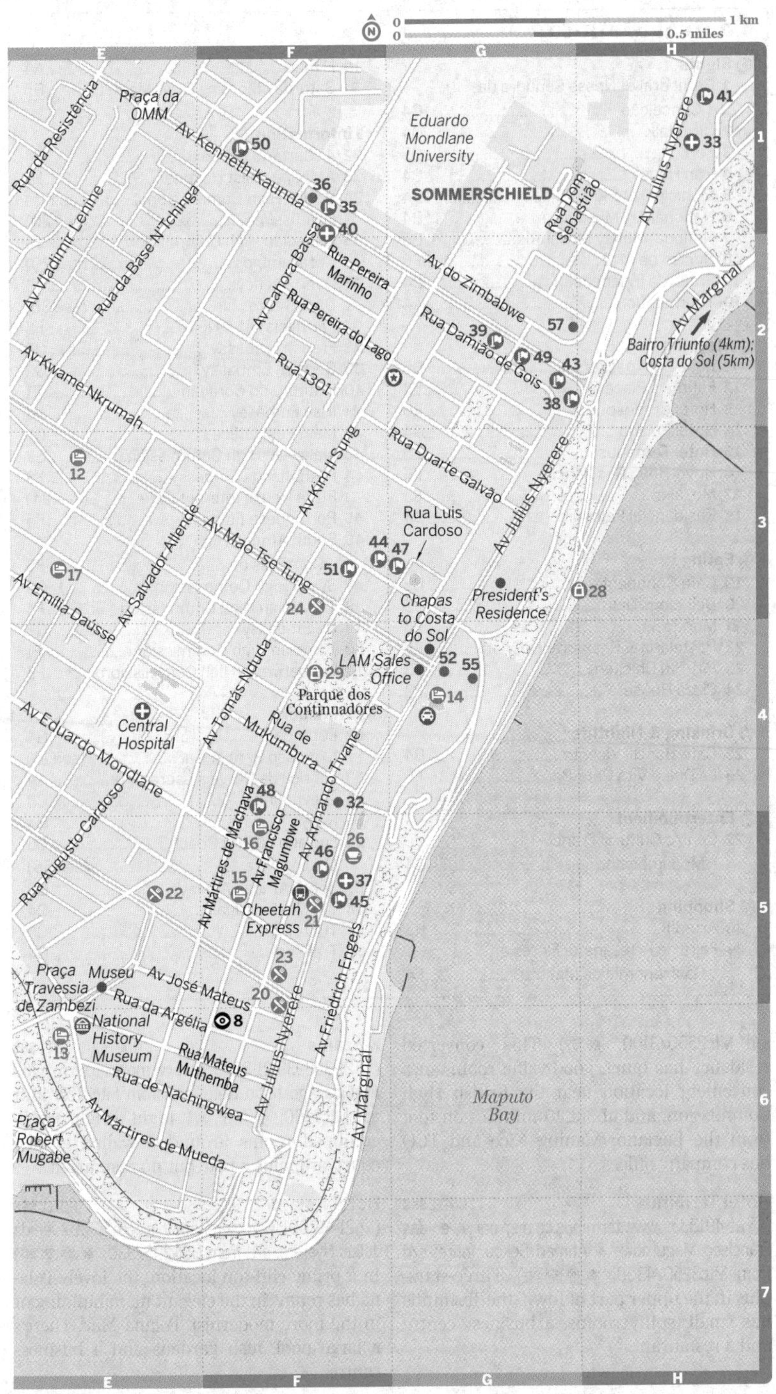
0
1 km
0
0.5 miles
E
F
G
H
1
2
3
4
5
6
7
Praça da OMM
Av Kenneth Kaunda
Rua da Resistência
Av Vladimir Lenine
Rua da Base N'Tchinga
Eduardo Mondlane University
SOMMERSCHIELD
Rua Dom Sebastião
Av Julius Nyerere
Av Cahora Bassa
Rua Pereira Marinho
Rua Pereira do Lago
Av do Zimbabwe
Rua Damião de Gois
Av Marginal
Bairro Triunfo (4km); Costa do Sol (5km)
Av Kwame Nkrumah
Rua 1301
Av Kim Il Sung
Rua Duarte Galvão
Rua Luis Cardoso
Av Salvador Allende
Av Mao Tse Tung
Av Emília Daússe
Chapas to Costa do Sol
President's Residence
LAM Sales Office
Parque dos Continuadores
Central Hospital
Av Tomás Nduda
Rua de Mukumbura
Av Eduardo Mondlane
Av Armando Tivane
Rua Augusto Cardoso
Av Mártires de Machava
Av Francisco Magumbwe
Cheetah Express
Av Friedrich Engels
Praça Travessia de Zambezi
Museu
Av José Mateus
Rua da Argélia
National History Museum
Rua Mateus Muthemba
Rua de Nachingwea
Av Mártires de Mueda
Praça Robert Mugabe
Maputo Bay
MOZAMBIQUE MAPUTO
8
12
13
14
15
16
17
20
21
22
23
24
26
28
29
32
33
35
36
37
38
39
40
41
43
44
45
46
47
48
49
50
51
52
55
57

Central Maputo

Sights

1	Cathedral of Nossa Senhora da Conceição	C4
2	City Hall	C4
3	Fort	B5
4	Iron House	C4
5	Municipal Market	B4
6	National Art Museum	B4
7	National Money Museum	B5
8	Núcleo de Arte	F6
9	Praça da Independência	C4
10	Train Station	A4

Sleeping

11	Base Backpackers	D5
12	Fatima's Place	E3
13	Hotel Cardoso	E6
14	Hotel Polana	G4
15	Hotel Terminus	F5
16	Hoyo-Hoyo Residencial	F5
17	Mozaika	E3
18	Residencial Palmeiras	D4

Eating

19	Café Continental	B5
20	Deli-cious Deli	F5
21	Mundo's	F5
22	Pastelaria & Restaurante Cristál	E5
23	Piri-Piri Chicken	F5
24	Pizza House	F3

Drinking & Nightlife

25	Café-Bar Gil Vicente	B4
26	La Dolce Vita Café-Bar	F5

Entertainment

27	Centro Cultural Franco-Moçambicano	C4

Shopping

28	Artedif	H3
29	Feira de Artesanato, Flôres e Gastronomia de Maputo	F4
30	Himbe	A4
31	Saturday Morning Craft Market	B5

Information

32	4° Cartário Notarial	F4
33	AMI Specialist Hospital	H1
34	British High Commission	C4
	Cafetíssimo	(see 20)
35	Canadian High Commission	F1
	Cotacambios	(see 20)
36	Dana Agency	F1
	Dana Tours	(see 36)
37	Farmácia Dia e Noite	F5
38	French Embassy	G2
39	German Embassy	G2
40	Instituto do Coração	F1
41	Irish Embassy	H1
42	Main Post Office	C5
43	Malawian High Commission	G2
44	Netherlands Embassy	F3
	Pizza House Internet Café	(see 24)
45	Portuguese Embassy	F5
46	South African High Commission	F5
47	Swazi High Commission	G3
48	Tanzanian High Commission	F4
49	US Embassy	G2
50	Zambian High Commission	F1
51	Zimbabwean High Commission	F3

Transport

52	Europcar	G4
	Expresso Rent-A-Car	(see 13)
53	Fábrica de Cerveja Laurentina	A4
54	Greyhound	C3
55	Kenya Airways	G4
56	Luciano Luxury Coach	C5
	Maning Nice	(see 56)
57	South African Airways	G2
58	TAP Air Portugal	C4
59	TCO	C5
60	Translux	D4

s/d Mtc2500/3100;) This converted residence has quiet, good-value rooms in a convenient location near the British High Commission, and about 10 minutes on foot from the Luciano, Maning Nice and TCO bus company offices.

Hotel Terminus HOTEL $$$

(21-491333; www.terminus.co.mz; cnr Avenidas Francisco Magumbwe & Ahmed Sekou Touré; s/d from Mtc3250/4300;) Three-stars-plus in the upper part of town, the Terminus has small, spiffy rooms, a business centre and a restaurant.

Mozaika BOUTIQUE HOTEL $$$

(21-303939, 21-303965; www.mozaika.co.mz; 769 Avenida Agostinho Neto; s/d from Mtc3125/4610, apt Mtc7900;) Eight bright, well-equipped rooms around a walled garden courtyard, plus a bar (but no restaurant).

Hotel Polana HOTEL $$$

(21-491001; www.serenahotels.com; 1380 Avenida Julius Nyerere; s/d from US$295/330;) In a prime cliff-top location, the lovely Polana has rooms in the elegant main building or in the more modernist 'Polana Mar'. There's a large pool, lush gardens and a business centre.

Hotel Cardoso HOTEL $$$
(☎21-491071; www.hotelcardoso.co.mz; 707 Avenida Mártires de Mueda; s/d from US$240/260; ❄@📶🏊) Opposite the Natural History Museum, with good service, well-appointed rooms and views over the water and port area.

Eating

Café Continental CAFE $
(cnr Avenidas 25 de Setembro & Samora Machel; light meals Mtc150-200; ⏱6am-10pm) A Maputo landmark, the Café Continental has lots of atmosphere, delicious pastries and light meals.

Pizza House CAFE $
(☎21-485257; 601/607 Avenida Mao Tse Tung; pizzas & light meals Mtc170-270; ⏱6.30am-10.30pm; ❄) Popular with locals and expats, with sandwiches, burgers, grilled chicken and local fare.

Piri-Piri Chicken FAST FOOD $$
(Avenida 24 de Julho; meals from Mtc200; ⏱11am-midnight) A Maputo classic, with grilled chicken (with or without hot pepper sauce), spicy shrimp curry, cold beers and local vibe.

Pastelaria & Restaurante Cristál CAFE, EUROPEAN $$
(☎82-281 5180, 84-302 3560; restaurantecristal@hotmail.com; 554 Avenida 24 de Julho; meals from Mtc300; ⏱6.30am-11pm) At the Pastelaria & Restaurante Cristál you'll find delicious pastries and breads, indoor and streetside seating and a popular restaurant.

Fish Market SEAFOOD $$
(Mercado da Peixe; off Avenida Marginal) Buy your fish fresh from this local market, then wait while it's cooked. The turn-off is opposite Clube Marítimo.

Restaurante Costa do Sol SEAFOOD $$
(☎21-450038, 21-450115; Avenida Marginal; meals Mtc350-500; ⏱noon-11pm; P) Another Maputo classic, this art-deco seafood restaurant on the beach draws the crowds on weekend afternoons.

Mundo's BURGERS, PUB $$
(☎21-494080; www.mundosmaputo.com; cnr Avenidas Julius Nyerere & Eduardo Mondlane; meals Mtc350-500; ⏱8am-midnight; 📶👪) Mundo's serves burritos, burgers, pizzas, all-day breakfasts, wraps and desserts.

Self-Catering

Deli-cious Deli DELI $
(Ground fl, Polana Shopping Centre, cnr Avenidas Julius Nyerere & 24 de Julho) Fresh breads, cheeses and sliced meats.

Supermares SUPERMARKET $
(Avenida Marginal, Costa do Sol; ⏱9am-7pm Mon-Sat, to 1pm Sun) A large mall with a Shoprite.

Drinking & Nightlife

Café-Bar Gil Vicente BAR
(43 Avenida Samora Machel) A popular place with a constantly changing array of musical groups.

La Dolce Vita Café-Bar CAFE
(822 Julius Nyerere; ⏱10am-late Tue-Sun) Live music on Thursdays.

Coconuts Live LOUNGE, DISCOTHEQUE
(Complexo Mini-Golfe, Avenida Marginal; disco Mtc250, lounge free; ⏱disco Fri & Sat, lounge Wed-Sun) A disco and chill-out lounge.

Entertainment

For upcoming events check with Centro-Cultural Franco-Moçambicano and the Living in Maputo pages on **Club of Mozambique** (www.clubofmozambique.com).

Centro Cultural Franco-Moçambicano CULTURAL CENTRE
(☎21-314590; www.ccfmoz.com; Praça da Independência) Art exhibitions, music and dance performances, films and theatre.

Shopping

Artedif ARTS & CRAFTS
(☎21-495510; Avenida Marginal; ⏱9am-3.30pm) 🍃 A cooperative of people with disabilities, selling carvings and basketry.

Saturday Morning Craft Market ARTS & CRAFTS
(Praça 25 de Junho; ⏱about 8am-1pm Sat) This weekly craft market has woodcarvings, batiks and more.

Feira de Artesanato, Flôres e Gastronomia de Maputo ARTS & CRAFTS
(Avenida Mártires da Machava, Parque dos Continuadores; ⏱9am-5pm) Paintings, batiks and carvings.

Himbe ARTS & CRAFTS
(Train Station, Praça dos Trabalhadores) Crafts made by local women.

DOCUMENT CHECKS

Carry a notarised copy of your passport (photo and Mozambique visa pages) when out and about, rather than the original. If you get stopped, insist on going to the nearest *esquadrão* (police station), and try to avoid handing over your actual passport.

Documents can be notarised at some embassies, and at **4° Cartário Notarial** (Avenida Armando Tivane; ⌚7.30am to 3pm Mon-Fri), off Avenida Julius Nyerere.

Orientation

Many businesses, the train station, banks and some hotels are in the low-lying baixa, on or near Avenida 25 de Setembro, while embassies and many more hotels are about a 20-minute walk uphill from here in the city's more staid upper section. At the northern end of the seaside Avenida Marginal, 7km from the centre, are Bairro Triunfo and Costa do Sol, with a small beach (not good for swimming) and several places to sleep and eat.

Information

DANGERS & ANNOYANCES

Walking around central Maputo during daytime hours is generally safe, and most tourists visit the city without mishap. However, be vigilant when out and about and avoid isolating situations. Also avoid the access roads leading down from Avenida Friedrich Engels to Avenida Marginal, and Av Marginal between Praça Robert Mugabe and the Southern Sun hotel.

INTERNET ACCESS

Cafetíssimo (3rd fl, Polana Shopping Centre, cnr Avenidas Julius Nyerere & 24 de Julho; ⌚8.30am-9pm Mon-Sat; ☏) Wi-fi.

Pizza House Internet Café (Avenida Mao Tse Tung; per hour Mtc60; ⌚8am-10pm; ☏) Upstairs at Pizza House.

MEDICAL SERVICES

AMI Specialist Hospital (Maputo Trauma Centre; ☎82-000 1999, 82-000 2999, 82-302 0999; 2986 Avenida Julius Nyerere; ⌚24hr) Western standards and facilities.

Farmácia Dia e Noite (☎82-832 3250, 84-505 8238; 764 Avenida Julius Nyerere; ⌚24hr) Opposite the South African High Commission.

Instituto do Coração (☎21-416347, 82-327 4800, 82-305 3097; 1111 Avenida Kenneth Kaunda; ⌚24hr) Treats all ailments (not just cardiac issues).

MONEY

There are 24-hour ATMs all over town, including at the airport.

Cotacambios Airport (Main terminal; ⌚open for international arrivals and departures); City (Ground fl, Polana Shopping Centre, cnr Avenida Julius Nyerere & Mao Tse Tung; ⌚9am-9pm Mon-Sat, 10am-8pm Sun)

POST

Main post office (CTT; Avenida 25 de Setembro; ⌚8am-6pm Mon-Sat, 9am-noon Sun)

TRAVEL AGENCIES

Dana Agency (☎21-484300; travel@dana.co.mz; Ground fl, 1170 Avenida Kenneth Kaunda) Domestic and international flight bookings.

Dana Tours (☎21-495514; info@danatours.net; 1st fl, 1170 Avenida Kenneth Kaunda) Destinations in Mozambique, Swaziland and South Africa.

Getting There & Away

AIR

Kenya Airways (p872) and **LAM** (☎84-147, 82-147; www.lam.co.mz) have regular flights to Maputo. **South African Airways** (☎21-488970/3, 84-389 9287; www.flysaa.com; Avenida do Zimbabwe, Sommerschield) is located near the South African High Commissioner's residence. **TAP Air Portugal** (☎21-3039279; www.flytap.com; 114 Rua da Sé) can be found at Hotel Pestana Rovuma.

BUS

For Upcountry Travel

Maputo's main long-distance bus depot is **'Junta'** (Avenida de Moçambique), 7km from the centre (Mtc300 in a taxi). Most departures are between 2.30am and 6am.

TCO (☎82-956 0600, 82-891 3020; Avenida Zedequias Manganhela) and **Maning Nice** (☎82-706 2820; Avenida Zedequias Manganhela; ⌚8am-5pm) have their less-chaotic ticket offices and arrival/departure point in the baixa.

TCO runs services to Xai-Xai (Mtc280, four hours), Maxixe (Mtc475, 6½ hours), Massinga (Mtc550, eight hours), Pambara Junction (for Vilankulo; Mtc700, nine hours) and Beira (Mtc1780, 16 hours); departure days vary.

For Nelspruit take a Cheetah Express (p873) bus, next to Mundo's Restaurant.

Arrange private minivan transport to Inhambane (about Mtc700) through Residencial Palmeiras (p851). Fatima's Place (p851) has a daily shuttle to Tofo (Mtc700).

Maning Nice runs to Nampula (Mtc2500, 31 hours) twice weekly, with connections to Pemba.

Other transport terminals are **Benfica** (Avenida de Moçambique), where you can take *chapas* to Marracuene, and **Fábrica de Cerveja Laurentina** ('Feroviario'; cnr Avenidas 25 de Setembro & Albert Luthuli), from where *chapas* run to Swaziland and South Africa.

For Johannesburg

Greyhound (21-302771; www.greyhound.co.za; cnr Avenidas Karl Marx & Eduardo Mondlane) At Cotur Travel & Tours.

Luciano Luxury Coach (21-752711, 84-860 2100, 82-769 9830; 273 Avenida Zedequias Manganhela; 8am-5pm for ticketing) Behind the main post office.

Translux (21-303825, 21-303829; www.translux.co.za; 1249 Avenida 24 de Julho) At Simara Travel & Tours.

Getting Around

TO/FROM THE AIRPORT

Maputo International Airport is 6km northwest of the city centre (Mtc400 to Mtc500 in a taxi).

BUS & CHAPA

Chapas go everywhere; town trips average Mtc5. For Junta, take a 'Jardim' *chapa*. From Junta into town, take a 'Museu' *chapa*. For Costa do Sol, take a *chapa* from the corner of Avenidas Mao Tse Tung and Julius Nyerere.

CAR

Rental agencies:

Europcar (82-300 2410, 21-497338; www.europcar.co.mz; 1418 Avenida Julius Nyerere) Next to Hotel Polana and at the airport.

Expresso Rent-A-Car (21-493619; timisay@tropical.co.mz) At Hotel Cardoso; 2WD vehicles only; unlimited kilometre packages.

Sixt (21-465250, 82-300 5180; www.sixt.com; Airport)

TAXI & TUK-TUK

There is a taxi rank at Hotel Polana. Taxis also park at the Municipal Market and on Av Julius Nyerere in front of Mundo's restaurant. Town trips start at Mtc100. From central Maputo to Costa do Sol costs Mtc300. From Junta to anywhere in the city centre costs Mtc350 to Mtc400.

Tuk-tuks (town trips from Mtc50) have stands opposite Hotel Cardoso, and on Av Julius Nyerere, just up from the South African High Commission.

THE SOUTHERN COAST

Fantastic beaches, heaped plates of prawns, good tourism infrastructure, and easy road and air access make the southern coast Mozambique's most popular destination and an easy introduction to the country.

Inhambane

293

Sleepy, charming Inhambane is one of Mozambique's oldest settlements, and well worth a stroll before heading to the beach at nearby Tofo.

Sleeping & Eating

Pensão Pachiça BACKPACKERS $

(293-20565, 84-412 5297, 84-389 5217; www.barralighthouse.com; Rua 3 de Fevereiro; dm/s/d Mtc400/900/1500) This waterfront backpackers has dorms and doubles, a restaurant-bar and a rooftop terrace. Go left from the ferry jetty for about 300m.

Casa do Capitão HOTEL $$$

(293-214089; www.hotelcasadocapitao.com; s/d from Mtc4800/6750;) Luxurious, bay-facing rooms, fantastic views and a restaurant.

TakeAway Sazaria CAFE $

(Avenida da Independência; meals from Mtc80; 8am-5pm Mon-Fri) Inexpensive soups, *pregos* (thin steak sandwiches) and sandwiches to eat in or take away.

Getting There & Away

Small motorised passenger boats (Mtc10, 25 minutes) operate from sunrise to sundown between Inhambane and Maxixe.

Buses to Maputo (Mtc500, seven hours) and *chapas* to Tofo (Mtc15, one hour) depart from behind the market. For northbound transport, go to Maxixe.

Tofo

293

Tofo has long been legendary on the Southern Africa holidaymakers' circuit, with its azure waters, sweeping white sands, rolling breakers and party atmosphere.

The closest ATMs and banks are in Inhambane. There is also an ATM in Barra.

Activities

Diversity Scuba DIVING

(293-29002; www.diversityscuba.com; town centre)

Liquid Adventures DIVING
(☎84-060 9218; www.divingtofo.com) Behind Tofo OnLine in the town centre.

Peri-Peri Divers DIVING
(www.peri-peridivers.com) At Albatroz Lodge.

Sleeping

Fatima's Nest BACKPACKERS $
(☎82-185 1575; www.mozambiquebackpackers.com; campsite per person Mtc250, dm Mtc400, s/d Mtc1000/1600) Camping, dorm beds, basic bungalows and rooms on low dunes overlooking the beach. There's also a kitchen, a bar, pool table and evening beach bonfires.

Bamboozi Beach Lodge BACKPACKERS $
(☎293-29040; www.barraresorts.com; campsites per person US$16, dm US$17, d hut US$36) Dorm beds and basic reed huts (bring your own towels and linens) behind the dunes, plus reed 'chalets' with bathrooms. It's 3km north of town along the beach road.

Casa Azul GUESTHOUSE $$
(☎82-821 5921; www.casa-azul-tofo.com; s US$72-108, d US$80-150) This converted colonial-era house on the beach is bright and cheery, with pleasant rooms, creative bathrooms and meals.

Aquático Ocean Annex PENSION $$
(☎82-857 2850; www.aquaticolodge.com; tr Mtc1700; ❄) Four attached, self-catering rooms, each with one double and one twin bed, directly on the beach. There are no meals.

Albatroz Lodge LODGE $$$
(☎293-29005; www.albatrozlodge.com; 4-/6-/8-person chalets Mtc3800/4600/5850) Large, rustic, thatched self-catering cottages on the bluff overlooking the beach.

Eating

Tofo Tofo AFRICAN $
(meals from Mtc150) Snacks, local food and groceries.

Casa de Comer FUSION $$
(☎293-29004; meals Mtc300-450; ⏲9am-10pm Wed-Mon; ✍) Mozambican/French fusion cuisine, including vegetarian dishes, in the town centre.

Dino's Beach Bar CAFE $$
(www.dinosbeachbar.com; meals from Mtc200; ⏲10am-late Thu-Tue) On the beach just past Fatima's Nest, with pizzas, sandwiches and more.

Getting There & Away

Chapas to Inhambane depart from about 5am, and there's sometimes a direct bus to Maputo at 4.30am (Mtc500, 7½ hours).

Maxixe

☎293

Maxixe is the place to get off the bus and onto the boat if you're heading to Inhambane, across the bay. **Stop** (☎293-30025, 82-125 2010; stopmaxixe96@hotmail.com; d/tw/ste Mtc1500/1500/1800; ❄), at the jetty, has rooms, meals (from Mtc225), and a pool.

Buses to Maputo (Mtc475, 6½ hours) depart from the bus stand by the Tribunal from 6am. *Chapas* to Vilankulo (Mtc180, 3½ hours) leave from Praça 25 de Setembro, a few blocks north.

Vilankulo

☎293

Vilankulo is the finishing (or starting) point of Mozambique's southern tourism circuit, the gateway for visiting the Bazaruto Archipelago.

Activities

Diving

Big Blue DIVING
(www.bigbluevilankulo.com) About 2km north of the Dona Ana Hotel, next to Aguia Negra.

Odyssea Dive DIVING
(www.odysseadive.com) Next to Baobab Beach Backpackers.

Dhow Safaris

Sailaway BOAT TOUR
(☎293-82385, 82-387 6350; www.sailaway.co.za) On the road paralleling the beach road, about 400m south of the Dona Ana Hotel.

Kite Surfing

Kite Surfing Centre KITE SURFING
(www.kitesurfingcentre.com) On the beach north of town.

Kite Surfing Vilankulo KITE SURFING
(www.kitesurfingvilankulo.com) At Casa Rex.

Sleeping

Complexo Turístico Josef e Tina BUNGALOW $
(☎82-789 7879; www.joseftina.com; campsites per person Mtc200, chalet r Mtc800) Basic reed huts in a large garden, plus a few no-frills rooms.

Baobab Beach Backpackers BACKPACKERS $
(☎82-731 5420; www.baobabbeach.net; campsite per person Mtc200, dm Mtc270, d bungalow Mtc1400) A chilled vibe and straightforward bungalows.

Zombie Cucumber Backpackers BACKPACKERS $
(☎84-686 9870, 82-804 9410; www.zombiecucumber.com; dm Mtc350, chalet d Mtc1500;) Comfy hammocks, a garden, bar and meals on order.

Palmeiras Lodge LODGE $$$
(☎293-82050, 84-380 2842; www.palmeiras-lodge.net; s/d from Mtc2700/4320) Whitewashed cottages in green grounds, and a restaurant.

Casa Rex BOUTIQUE HOTEL $$$
(☎293-82048; www.casa-rex.com; s from US$140, d US$220-360, f US$360;) A lovely, upmarket getaway in peaceful, manicured gardens.

Eating

Taurus Supermarket SUPERMARKET $
(Avenida Eduardo Mondlane; closed Sun) For self-catering.

Café Moçambicano CAFE $
(Avenida Eduardo Mondlane; pastries from Mtc15) Pastries, bread, yoghurt and a bakery.

Café Zambeziana CAFE $
(light meals from Mtc120) Inexpensive grilled chicken and barbecue sandwiches.

Complexo Âncora SEAFOOD, PIZZERIA $$
(☎293-82444; meals Mtc200-350; 7am-10pm Wed-Mon) Pizzas and continental fare.

Kilimanjaro Café CAFE $$
(breakfast Mtc140-280, sandwiches & light meals Mtc200-300; 7.30am-6pm Mon-Sat;) Salads, sandwiches, pizza, pasta and smoothies.

Information

Tourist Information Office (www.vilankulo.com; Rua da OMM; 8am-3.30pm Mon-Fri, 9am-1pm Sat)

Getting There & Away

Buses to Maputo (Mtc750, 10 hours) depart by 4.30am from near the old market. Buses to Beira (Mtc550, 10 hours) depart at 4am from the main transport stand at the new market. To Chimoio, take a Beira bus to Inchope junction (Mtc550 from Vilankulo), then a minibus from there.

Bazaruto Archipelago

The Bazaruto Archipelago – much of which is a **national marine park** (Parque Nacional de Bazaruto; adult/child Mtc200/100) – is a diver's paradise and a quintessential Indian Ocean retreat, with turquoise and jade waters, pristine coral reefs and white sand dunes.

There is no budget accommodation on the islands. Instead, try arranging an island dhow cruise or visiting in the off season for special deals.

If cost is no object, try the intimate **Benguerra Lodge** (☎in South Africa 011-452 0641; www.benguerra.co.za; r per person with full board from US$575;) or **Azura at Gabriel's** (☎in South Africa 0767-050599; www.azura-retreats.com; r per person with full board US$575-875;).

CENTRAL MOZAMBIQUE

Central Mozambique doesn't draw the tourist crowds, but it's a convenient transit zone for travel to/from Malawi and Zimbabwe. Among its attractions are lovely Gorongosa National Park, hill landscapes and hiking.

Beira

☎23 / POP 546,000

Beira, Mozambique's busiest port, is as famed for its steamed crabs and prawns as for its tawdry nightlife. A decent beach (at Makuti, 5km out of town) and a few well-preserved colonial buildings are the major attractions. It's primarily of interest as a transport hub.

Sleeping

Rio Savane CAMPGROUND $
(☎23-323555, 82-596 2560; campsite per person Mtc300) About 40km north of town on the Savane River, with camping, reed huts and self-catering chalets. Take the Dondo road past the airport to the signposted turn-off. Continue 35km to the estuary, where there's secure parking and a boat (until 5pm) to the camp.

Hotel Miramar HOTEL $
(☎23-322283; http://miramar.no.sapo.pt/; Rua Vilas Boas Truão; s/d Mtc800/1600;) The Miramar offers reasonably priced, no-frills rooms – some with private bathroom, most with TV – near

GORONGOSA NATIONAL PARK

Once one of southern Africa's premier wildlife areas, **Gorongosa National Park** (Parque Nacional de Gorongosa; ☎82-308 2252; www.gorongosa.net; adult/child/vehicle per day US$20/10/45; ⏰6am-6pm Apr-Dec) is on the rebound. It's worth visiting as much for its modest but improving wildlife-watching opportunities as for its lovely panoramas. **Girassol Gorongosa Lodge** (☎82-308 2252; www.gorongosa.net; campsite per person Mtc320, s/d tent Mtc1480/2100, s/d room from Mtc2600/3500; ❄ ≋), at Chitengo park headquarters, has comfortable *rondavels* (round, traditional-style huts). **Gorongosa Adventures Campsite** (☎82-957 1436; http://gorongosa-adventures.blogspot.com) 🍃, 9km outside the main gate and 500m off the park access road, offers camping, permanent tents, self-catering facilities and walks and birding on Mt Gorongosa.

Head 43km north from Inchope to Nota village, then 17km east to the park gate, or take a *chapa* (minivan) to Vila Gorongosa (25km further north) and arrange a pick-up from there in advance with the lodges or park staff.

the water (no beach), but inconvenient for the rest of town.

Jardim das Velas HOTEL $$
(☎23-312209; jardimdasvelas@gmail.com; 282 Avenida das FPLM, Makuti Beach; d/f Mtc3325/3850; ❄) Well-equipped doubles just back from the beach near the lighthouse, plus several family rooms. Very popular. There are no meals.

VIP Inn Beira HOTEL $$$
(☎23-340100, 82-305 4753; www.viphotels.com; 172 Rua Luís Inácio; s/d from Mtc4100/4400; ❄ 📶) Comfortable rooms in the heart of the baixa.

Eating

Café Riviera CAFE $
(Praça do Município; light meals from Mtc150; ⏰7.30am-9pm) Plump, pink sofas inside, and outdoor tables overlooking the praça for watching the passing scene.

Shoprite SUPERMARKET $
(cnr Avenidas Armando Tivane & Samora Machel) For self-catering.

Clube Náutico SEAFOOD $$
(☎23-311720; Avenida das FPLM; meals from Mtc200, plus per person entry Mtc20; ⏰lunch & dinner) Seafood grills by the beach.

Getting There & Away

Buses to Quelimane (Mtc650, 10 hours) and Vilankulo (Mtc550, seven to eight hours) depart from the main transport hub in the Praça do Maquinino area, between Avenidas Daniel Napatima and Samora Machel.

TCO (☎82-304 8163; tcobeira@tdm.co.mz; 28 Rua dos Irmãos Roby) services to Maputo (Mtc1780, 15–16 hours), Nampula (Mtc1900, 16–17 hours) and Tete (Mtc890, seven hours) depart from the TCO office in Bairro dos Pioneiros, 1km north of the centre, and just off Avenida Samora Machel.

To Chimoio (Mtc200, three hours), minibuses go throughout the day from the main transport stand.

Chimoio

☎251

Chimoio sits on the edge of scenic country near the **Chimanimani Mountains**, which offer wonderful hiking. You'll need to be self-sufficient and go with a guide; the recommended **Mozambique EcoTours** (www.mozecotours.com) 🍃 can help you sort out the logistics.

Sleeping & Eating

Pink Papaya BACKPACKERS $
(☎82-555 7310; http://pinkpapaya.atspace.com; cnr Ruas Pigivide & 3 de Fevereiro; dm Mtc400, s/d/q Mtc800/1000/2000; P) Friendly and helpful, with rooms and dorms (no camping). With the bus stand to your right and train station to your left, walk straight, then take the fourth right into Rua 3 de Fevereiro; continue one block to Rua Pigivide.

Hotel-Residencial Castelo Branco HOTEL $$$
(☎251-23934, 82-522 5960; Rua Sussundenga; s/d Mtc3800/4200; P ❄ 📶) A pleasant business travellers' hotel, just off Praça dos Heróis.

La Plaza CONTINENTAL $
(☎251-23716, 82-601 4980; Praça da OMM; meals from Mtc150; ⏰lunch & dinner Mon-Sat) Pizzas and Portuguese food.

Shoprite SUPERMARKET $
(N6) For self-catering.

Getting There & Away

Buses depart at 4am from the train station to Tete (Mtc400, seven hours) and Maputo (Mtc1200, 14 hours). For Vilankulo, take the Maputo bus to Pambara junction. *Chapas* to Beira (Mtc200, three hours) and the Machipanda border run throughout the day.

Tete

☎252 / POP 50,000

Tete's reputation as one of the hottest places in Mozambique discourages visitors, but it's a useful transport hub. Pass the time sipping a cold drink at a riverside bar. About 150km northwest is **Cahora Bassa** dam and lake, a prime angling destination.

Hotel Sundowner (☎82-306 1589; N103; r Mtc1000; ❄) near the river has cheap rooms and meals. **Hotel Zambeze** (☎252-23101, 252-24000; Avenida Eduardo Mondlane; s/d Mtc4500/5500; ❄) is pricey but central, with a restaurant. Rooms at **Prédios Univendas** (☎252-23198, 252-22670, 252-23199; Avenida Julius Nyerere; s/d without bathroom Mtc1300/1550, s/d from Mtc1550/1750; ❄) are simple, clean and spacious.

Getting There & Away

Chapas for Zóbuè (Mtc150, two hours) run from the far side of the bridge (to the left). Transport to Changara (Mtc100) and Zimbabwe departs from along Av 25 de Junho. Transport to Chimoio (Mtc400, seven hours) departs from Prédio Emose near Univendas.

Quelimane

☎24

Compact Quelimane is convenient for a break on the journey north. Nearby is long, wide **Zalala beach**.

Hotel 1 de Julho (☎24-213067; cnr Avenidas Samora Machel & Filipe Samuel Magaia; tw without bathroom Mtc1000, with bathroom & air-con Mtc1500; ❄), near the old cathedral, has no-frills rooms and meals. The popular **Hotel Flamingo** (☎24-215602, 82-552 7810; www.hotelflamingoquelimane.com; cnr Avenidas Kwame Nkrumah & 1 de Julho; s Mtc2000-3200, d Mtc2500-3800; ❄ 📶 🏊) has midrange rooms and a restaurant.

Estilo China (Bar Refeba, cnr Avenida Marginal & Rua Kwame Nkrumah; meals Mtc190-350), just back from the river, has Chinese food, seafood and meat grills and views.

Getting There & Away

Mecula buses to Nampula (Mtc480, 10 hours) and *chapas* to Mocuba (Mtc200, three hours, for Milange on the Malawi border) depart from the northern end of Avenida Eduardo Mondlane ('Romoza'). *Chapas* to Zalala (Mtc25, one hour) leave from the central market.

NORTHERN MOZAMBIQUE

Northern Mozambique is one of the continent's last wild frontiers, offering adventure travel and island luxury. Other highlights include magical, time-warped Mozambique Island, stunning beaches and the unspoilt Swahili culture of the Quirimbas Archipelago.

Nampula

☎26

Nampula, a crowded city with a hard edge, is the jumping-off point for visiting Mozambique Island.

Sights

National Ethnography Museum MUSEUM
(Museu Nacional de Etnografia; Avenida Eduardo Mondlane; admission Mtc100; ⏲9am-5pm Tue-Fri, 2-5pm Sat & Sun) Displays on local life and culture.

Sleeping

Ruby Nampula BACKPACKERS $
(☎82-717 9923; claudilhas@hotmail.com; Rua Daniel Napatima; dm/d Mtc700/1600; 📶) Spotless, good-value rooms and dormitories, a self-catering kitchen, a small bar and travel info, especially for Mozambique Island. It's one block from the museum.

Residencial da Universidade Pedagógica HOSTEL $
(☎82-833 7434; 840 Avenida 25 de Setembro; s/d/tw Mtc1400/2000/2400) Next to Hotel Milénio, with simple, good-value rooms and breakfast.

Hotel Milénio HOTEL $$
(☎26-218877, 26-218989; hotelmilenio@tdm.co.mz; 842 Avenida 25 de Setembro; tw/d/ste Mtc3200/3200/4500;) Large, modern rooms convenient to the Mecula bus garage.

Residencial Expresso HOTEL $$
(☎26-2188089; 574 Avenida da Independência; tw Mtc2200-2500;) Spotless, twin-bedded rooms with fridge and TV.

Villa Sands BOUTIQUE HOTEL $$
(☎82-744 7178; www.villasands.com; d Mtc3200-3700, ste Mtc4500;) This sleek boutique hotel overlooks the water on the northwestern side of the island. The upstairs rooms have their own pool, and there's a restaurant and a rooftop terrace.

Eating

Supermercado Ideal SUPERMARKET $
(326 Avenida Eduardo Mondlane) In the Hotel Girassol building.

Copacabana CONTINENTAL $$
(Rua Macombre; meals Mtc200-350; 7am-9pm Mon-Fri, to 11pm Sat & Sun) Pizzas, plus seafood and meat grills and outdoor seating behind the museum.

Getting There & Away

To reach Mozambique Island (Mtc140, three to four hours), get a *chapa* from the Padaria Nampula transport stand east of the train station between 7am and 10am. Be sure it's going direct, otherwise you'll need to change at Monapo.

To Pemba (Mtc350, seven to eight hours) or Quelimane (Mtc480, 11 hours), **Grupo Mecula** (☎26-213772; grupomecula@teledata.mz; Rua da Moma) runs services from the Mecula garage, off Avenida 25 de Setembro, or **Maning Nice** (☎82-706 2820; Avenida do Trabalho) runs from the Padaria Nampula transport stand.

For Beira (Mtc1900, 16 hours) and Maputo (Mtc2500, 30 hours), book with **TCO** (☎82-509 2180, 84-601 6861), next to Galp Fabião petrol station on Av da Independência, just east of Av Paulo Samuel Kankhomba. Departures are from 'Antiga Gorongosa', 2km from town along Av do Trabalho.

Trains to Cuamba (2nd/economy class Mtc350/140, 10 to 12 hours) leave daily (except Monday) at 5am. Buy tickets the day before between 2pm and 5pm. Second-class is only available every second day.

Mozambique Island

☎26

Tiny reed houses and pastel-coloured colonial mansions rub shoulders among the palm trees on tiny Mozambique Island (Ilha de Moçambique), the former capital of Portuguese East Africa. It's haunting, magical and a must-see.

The island is attached to the mainland by a 3.5km causeway. *Chapas* and buses arrive at the southern tip of the island, from where it's a short walk north through the *makuti* (reed) town to the old colonial stone town.

Sights

Wander through *makuti* town as it is awakening, with cocks crowing and children playing in the narrow streets. After a breakfast of spicy *bhajias* (fried Indian-style vegetable pancakes) from the food market, walk into the stone town as the museums open.

The **Palace & Chapel of São Paulo** (Palácio de São Paulo; ☎26-610081; adult/child Mtc100/50; 8am-4.30pm) has been impeccably restored, with opulent furniture, tapestries and sinister portraits of colonial grandees. Adjoining are a **Maritime Museum** and the **Museum of Sacred Art**, which are both included in the entry price. Behind the palace is the **Church of the Misericórdia**, still in active use.

The massive Portuguese **Fort of São Sebastião** (per adult/child Mtc100/50; 8am-4.30pm) is best visited in the late afternoon, when it's bathed in golden light.

Dominating the island's southern tip is the whitewashed **Church of Santo António**, overlooking fishermen repairing their nets on the sand.

Sleeping

Casa Branca GUESTHOUSE $
(☎26-610076, 82-454 3290; http://ilhamocambique.com.sapo.pt; Rua dos Combatentes; r without bathroom Mtc1100, with minifridge & bathroom Mtc1600) Simple, spotless rooms (one with bathroom), plus sea views, breakfast and a kitchen.

Mooxeleliya GUESTHOUSE $
(☎26-610076, 82-454 3290; http://ilhamocambique.com.sapo.pt; d with/without air-con

Mtc1500/1000, f Mtc2000) Large, high-ceilinged rooms, darker family rooms, breakfast and a small kitchen. It's near the Church of the Misericórdia.

Patio dos Quintalinhos GUESTHOUSE $
(Casa de Gabriele; ☎26-610090, 82-419 7610; www.patiodosquintalinhos.com; Rua do Celeiro; s/d without bathroom US$26/30, d/q from US$42/64, ste US$64; P@☎❄) Opposite the green mosque, with a handful of creatively designed rooms around a small courtyard, a rooftop terrace and help with excursions

Ruby Backpacker BACKPACKERS $
(☎84-398 5862; ruby@themozambiqueisland.com; Travessa da Sé; dm Mtc500, d Mtc1100; @☎) In a renovated 400-year-old house, with dorm beds, twins and doubles, kitchen, rooftop terrace and lots of travel help. From the 'arcade' street, take the first left after passing the Missanga craft shop (to your right), and then take the next left.

Casa de Yasmin GUESTHOUSE $
(☎26-610073, 82-676 8850; Rua dos Combatentes; r Mtc750-1500, ste Mtc2000; ❄) Near the cinema at the island's northern end, with small, clean rooms and no food.

Amakuthini GUESTHOUSE $
(Casa de Luís; ☎82-436 7570, 82-540 7622; dm Mtc350, s/d without bathroom Mtc600/800) Quite basic, but welcoming, and the only accommodation in crowded *makuti* town. It's near the green mosque.

Casuarina Camping CAMPGROUND $
(☎84-616 8764; casuarina.camping@gmail.com; campsite per person Mtc200, d with/without bathroom from Mtc1000/800; ☎) On the mainland opposite Mozambique Island. Boasts beachside camping, bungalows and a pizza oven.

O Escondidinho HOTEL $$
(☎26-610078; www.escondidinho.net; Avenida dos Heróis; s Mtc1400-2700, d Mtc1600-2900, extra bed Mtc650; ❄) Spacious, high-ceilinged rooms, some with bathrooms, plus a good restaurant.

Eating

O Paladar AFRICAN $
(meals Mtc250; ⊙lunch & dinner Thu-Tue) At the eastern corner of the old market, with local meals. Place your order in the morning.

Café-Bar Âncora d'Ouro CAFE $$
(☎26-610006; meals about Mtc350; ⊙8am-11pm Thu-Tue) Opposite the Church of the Misericórdia, with soups, muffins, sandwiches and ice cream.

Relíquias FUSION $$
(☎82-525 2318; Avenida da República; meals Mtc260-600; ⊙10am-10pm Tue-Sun) Delicious prawn curry and other meals, and views of the water.

Getting There & Away

All departures are from the bridge. Direct *tanzaniano chapas* to Nampula (Mtc120, three hours) leave between 3am and 5am; ask your hotel to arrange a pick-up. To Pemba, take the 4am *tanzaniano* to Namialo, and (with luck) connect there with a through bus from Nampula.

Cuamba

☎271

Lively Cuamba is a convenient stop en route to/from Malawi. It's also the starting or finishing point of the Cuamba–Nampula railway, one of southern Africa's classic **train** journeys. The slow (10-hour) journey takes you past magnificent landscapes and isolated villages, offering glimpses into local rural life. In Cuamba's town centre, and just a 10-minute walk from the train and bus stations, is **Pensão Saõ Miguel** (☎271-62701; r without bathroom Mtc500, r with fan/air-con Mtc800/1000; ❄), with small, clean rooms and a restaurant.

Transport leaves from Maçaniqueira market south of the railroad tracks. Trains to Nampula (2nd/economy class Mtc350/140, 10 to 12 hours) depart at 5am daily except Monday.

Lichinga

☎271 / ELEV 1300M

This low-key town with jacarandas and pine groves is a hub for travel to/from Lake Niassa and Malawi.

Sleeping & Eating

Ponto Final HOTEL $
(☎271-20912, 82-304 3632; Rua Filipe Samuel Magaia; s without bathroom Mtc800, d Mtc1200) Budget accommodation and a restaurant.

DON'T MISS

NKWICHI LODGE

Nkwichi Lodge (www.mandawilderness.org; s/d with full board in chalet US$395/640, in private house US$450/700) is a wonderful waterside retreat 15km south of Cóbuè, with handcrafted chalets, bush walks, boating, squeaky white sands and snorkelling. It's well worth a splurge.

Residencial 2+1 HOTEL **$$**
(82-381 1070; angelina.rosario.guita@gmail.com; Avenida Samora Machel; s/d Mtc1500/1800) Clean, efficient and central, with a restaurant.

Hotel Girassol Lichinga HOTEL **$$$**
(271-21280; www.girassolhoteis.co.mz; Rua Filipe Samuel Magaia; s/d Mtc3750/4200;) Large rooms, satellite TV and a restaurant.

Getting There & Away

Transport departs early from next to the market, including to Cuamba (Mtc500, seven hours), Metangula (Mtc150, 2½ hours) and the Rovuma River (Mtc500, six hours).

Lake Niassa

The tranquil Mozambican side of Lake Niassa (Lake Malawi) sees a small but steady stream of adventure travellers. Most pass through the tiny lakeside village of Cóbuè, which is the main jumping-off point if you're travelling to/from Malawi via Likoma Island (Malawi), about 10km offshore.

Sleeping & Eating

Khango Beach BUNGALOW **$**
(00-265-856 7885, 99-962 0916, in Malawi 88-856 7885; r without bathroom per person Mtc250; P) Reed bungalows on the sand in Cóbuè, plus meals on order.

Getting There & Away

Daily *chapas* connect Metangula and Lichinga (Mtc150, 2½ hours), and Metangula and Cóbuè (Mtc170, four hours). Local boats go daily between Likoma Island (Malawi) and Cóbuè. Mozambique visas are issued in Cóbuè.

Pemba

272

Sunny Pemba's centre of action is **Wimbi (Wimbe) beach**, 5km down the coast. About 7km further south is **Murrébuè** beach, which is ideal for kitesurfing.

Activities

CI Divers DIVING
(272-20102; www.cidivers.co.za; Complexo Náutilus, Avenida Marginal, Wimbi beach) PADI open-water certification, equipment rental and boat charters.

Sleeping

Pemba Dive & Bushcamp CAMPGROUND, BUNGALOW **$**
(Nacole Jardim; 82-661 1530; www.pembadivecamp.com; campsite per person US$10, dm US$20, d/q chalet US$100/160) Camping, chalets and a beachside bar and *braai* area. It's out of town (Mtc400 in a taxi), behind the airport on the bay.

Pemba Magic Lodge CAMPGROUND **$**
(Russell's Place; 82-686 2730, 82-527 7048; pembamagic@gmail.com; campsite per person US$10, dm/d US$20/65;) About 3.5km beyond Complexo Náutilus along the beach road extension, with camping (but no self-catering), chalets, a bar-restaurant and on-again/off-again security.

Hotel Cabo Delgado HOTEL **$**
(272-21552; cnr Avenidas 25 de Setembro & Eduardo Mondlane; s/d Mtc700/1000) Very faded, but central. There's no food.

Residencial Reggio Emilia GUESTHOUSE **$$**
(272-21297, 82-888 0800; www.wix.com/akeelz/Residencial-Reggio-Emilia; 8696 Avenida Marginal; r Mtc3000, 4-person self-catering chalet Mtc7000; P) Simple, clean rooms and self-catering chalets in green, quiet grounds, and (soon) a restaurant.

Pieter's Place GUESTHOUSE **$$**
(272-20102, 82-682 2700; cidivers@teledata.mz; Avenida Marginal; s/d from US$45/60) Along the extension of the Wimbi beach road with three small, airy rooms in the shaded grounds of a private residence, and a restaurant (closed Monday). Breakfast costs extra.

Kauri Resort HOTEL $$
(272-20936, 82-151 4222; www.kauriresort.com; r Mtc3000-4000;) On the extension of Wimbi beach, with small, clean, modern rooms and a restaurant (note though, this is closed on Monday).

Eating

Pastelaria Flor d'Avenida CAFE $
(272-20514; Avenida Eduardo Mondlane; meals Mtc180-220; 7am-9pm Mon-Sat) An informal eatery in the town centre.

Restaurante Rema AFRICAN $
(Avenida Marginal; meals from Mtc170) Inexpensive local meals.

Pemba Dolphin SEAFOOD $$
(272-20937; Avenida Marginal; pizzas Mtc150-250, seafood grills Mtc250-550; from 7am) Seafood grills and pizzas on the beach.

Shopping

Artes Maconde ARTS & CRAFTS
(artesmaconde@yahoo.com) At Pemba Beach Hotel and next to CI Divers at Complexo Náutilus.

Information

Kaskazini (272-20371, 82-309 6990; www.kaskazini.com; Pemba Beach Hotel, Avenida Marginal, Wimbi beach; 8am-3pm Mon-Fri, 8.30am-noon Sat) Tourist information, flight bookings and excursions.

Getting There & Away

Grupo Mecula (272-20821; grupomecula@teledata.mz; Rua Josina Machel) has daily buses to Nampula (Mtc350, seven hours) and Moçimboa da Praia (Mtc270, seven hours) departing at 4.45am from the Grupo Mecula office about 1.5km from the centre behind Osman's supermarket.

For Mozambique Island, continue to Nampula, and then get onward transport from there the next day.

Getting Around

To Wimbi beach, take a taxi from near Mcel (Mtc200).

Safi Rentals (82-380 8630; www.pembarentacar.com) has reliable car rentals for reasonable prices.

Quirimbas Archipelago

Ancient wooden sailing dhows take fishers around the remote and beautiful Quirimbas Archipelago, including sleepy **Ibo**, with its crumbling colonial mansions and centuries of history. Many of the islands are part of **Quirimbas National Park** (Parque Nacional das Quirimbas; adult/child Mtc200/100).

Sleeping & Eating

Tikidiri HOSTEL $
(82-590 3944; Airfield road; campsite per person Mtc100, s/d Mtc150/300) About 2km from the dhow port, with no-frills stone-and-thatch bungalows with nets, bucket baths and local-style meals.

Karibuni HOSTEL $
(Campsite do Janine; 82-703 2200; campsite per person Mtc120, r Mtc400-800) Next to Ibo Island Lodge with dark, no-frills rooms and a tiny space to pitch your tent. There's no food.

Panela Africana Guesthouse & Restaurant GUESTHOUSE $
(African Pot; 82-535 3113; sstephanec@hotmail.com; d US$30-40, meals Mtc250-350, set menu Mtc500; restaurant noon-3pm & 6pm-late) Mozambican/French fusion cuisine and a few rooms in the family house.

Miti Miwiri GUESTHOUSE $$
(26-960530, 82-543 8564; www.mitimiwiri.com; d/tr/f US$65/75/80, 3-course dinner about Mtc500; @) A lovely, atmospheric place in a restored house with a walled garden and good meals. Breakfast costs extra.

Ibo Island Lodge LODGE $$$
(www.iboisland.co.za; s/d with full board US$460/720;) Ibo's most upmarket option.

Getting There & Away

Kaskazini in Pemba arranges charter flights (US$310 return) and speedboat-vehicle transfers (US$270 one way for up to four people).

A *chapa* departs daily by 4.30am from Pemba's Paquitequete fish market to Quissanga and on to Tandanhangue village (Mtc200, five to six hours), from where public dhows go to Ibo (Mtc50 without motor, one to six hours) at high tide. There's parking at Gringo's (James') Place, next to Tandanhangue port.

Moçimboa Da Praia

272

This bustling port town is the last major stop between Pemba and the Tanzanian border. **Pensão-Residencial Magid** (272-81099; Avenida Samora Machel; r Mtc500), downhill from the transport stand, has no-frills rooms. **Hotel Chez Natalie** (272-81092, 82-439 6080; natalie.bockel@gmail.com; campsite per person Mtc300, d without bathroom Mtc800, 4-person chalets with/without internet & hot water Mtc2200/2000; @), 2.5km from town on the estuary, has spacious chalets and camping. **Restaurante Estrelha** (Avenida Samora Machel; meals from Mtc150) has meals.

Getting There & Away

Pick-ups to the Rovuma ('Namoto') border via Palma depart from the top of town between 2.30am and 3.30am (Mtc250, two hours). The Mecula bus to Pemba (Mtc270, seven hours) departs at 4.30am.

UNDERSTAND MOZAMBIQUE

Mozambique Today

After almost two decades of war, peace accords in 1992, followed by multiparty elections in 1994, brought a long-elusive stability to Mozambique. Thanks to this stability, plus a series of relatively smooth political transitions over the past decade and a half, Mozambique has won donor funding and acclaim as a successful example of postwar reconciliation and democracy-building in Africa. Recent major coal and natural gas finds in the north of the country have further polished Mozambique's star. Yet, many challenges remain, including widespread corruption, rising organised crime and opposition party Renamo's ongoing struggles to prove itself as a viable political party.

History

From Bantu-speaking farmers and fishers to Arabic traders, Goan merchants and adventuring Europeans, Mozambique has long been a crossroads of cultures.

Early Times

While Europeans were still struggling in the Dark Ages, the light of the ancient world had already fallen on Mozambique. From the 9th century AD, Mozambique's coast was part of a chain of civilised merchant kingdoms, visited by ships from as far afield as India, Arabia and Persia. Following the monsoon winds, they came to buy slaves, ivory, gold and spices. Muslim merchants intermarried with African families, and set up trading posts along the coast.

Sailing onto this scene came the first Europeans – Portuguese explorers such as Vasco da Gama. These 15th-century buccaneers pursued their trade interests with raids on coastal towns, and constructed forts to protect themselves from their English and Dutch rivals. In the 17th century, the Mozambican interior was divided into huge agricultural estates, nominally under the Portuguese crown but in fact run as private fiefdoms with their own slave armies.

In the late 19th century, Portugal and other European powers began a political arm-wrestle for Africa. Britain began to eye Mozambique, and Portugal reacted by strengthening its previously lax colonial control. The country was so wild, however, that the government had to lease large areas of land to private firms, which soon became notorious for the abuses they inflicted on their workers.

Resistance

Resistance was kindled, and the independence movement erupted into life after the 'Mueda Massacre' in 1960, in which peacefully protesting villagers were gunned down by Portuguese troops.

In 1962 the Front for the Liberation of Mozambique (Frelimo) was formed, led by the charismatic Eduardo Mondlane. Mondlane was assassinated in 1969 and succeeded by Frelimo's military commander, Samora Machel. Frelimo decided early on a policy of violent resistance. Finally, after bitter struggle, the independent People's Republic of Mozambique was proclaimed on 25 June 1975, with Frelimo as the ruling party and Samora Machel as president.

The Portuguese pulled out virtually overnight – after sabotaging vehicles and pouring concrete down wells – and left Mozambique in chaos with few skilled professionals and virtually no infrastructure. Mozambique's new government threw itself into a policy of radical social change. Ties were established with European communist powers, cooperative farms replaced private land, and companies were nationalised. Mass literacy programs and health initiatives were launched. For a while, the future looked rosy, and Mozambique was feted in left-wing Western circles as a successful communist state.

Civil War

By 1983 the country was almost bankrupt. The roots of the crisis were both economic and political. Concerned by the government's support for resistance movements such as the African National Congress (ANC), the white-minority-ruled countries of Rhodesia and South Africa deliberately 'destabilised' their neighbour with the creation of a manufactured guerrilla movement known as the Mozambique National Resistance (Renamo).

Renamo was made up of mercenaries, co-opted soldiers and disaffected Mozambicans, and funded by the South African military and a motley collection of Western interests. Renamo had no desire to govern – its only ideology was to paralyse the country. Roads, bridges, railways, schools and clinics were destroyed. Villagers were rounded up, anyone with skills was shot, and atrocities were committed on a massive scale.

By the late 1980s, change was sweeping through the region. The USSR's collapse altered the political balance in the West, and new, more liberal policies in South Africa restricted Renamo support. Samora Machel died under questionable circumstances in 1986 and was succeeded by the more moderate Joaquim Chissano. Frelimo switched from a Marxist ideology to a market economy, and Renamo began a slow evolution into a genuine opposition party. A formal peace agreement was signed in October 1992.

Peace

In October 1994 Mozambique held its first democratic elections. Frelimo won, but narrowly, with Renamo netting almost half the votes. The 1999 election produced similar results, this time followed by rioting and discord. Since then, things have settled down.

In December 2004 prominent businessman and long-time Frelimo insider Armando Guebuza was elected with a solid majority to succeed Chissano, who had earlier announced his intent to step down. Since taking the reins, Guebuza has pursued a more hard-line approach than Chissano, and tensions between Frelimo and Renamo have sharpened. Frelimo has also increased its dominance of political life, and an easy re-election for Guebuza followed in 2009.

There have been some isolated incidences of political unrest in the early lead-up to the 2014 elections. Yet, throughout its long history, Mozambique has shown a remarkable ability to rebound in the face of adversity, and most observers count the country among the continent's bright spots.

People of Mozambique

There are 16 main tribes in Mozambique, including the Makua and Makonde in the north and the Shangaan in the south. Although Mozambique is relatively free of tribal rivalries, there has long been an undercurrent of north–south difference, with geographically remote and independent-minded northerners often feeling neglected by the upwardly mobile denizens of powerhouse Maputo.

Once suppressed under the Marxist regime, religion now flourishes and most villages have a church, a mosque, or both. About 60% of Mozambicans are Christians, about 20% are Muslims (mostly in the north and along old trading routes), with the remainder following traditional animist beliefs.

The Arts

Mozambique has a superb dance tradition, and experiencing its rhythms and moves is not to be missed. Along the northern coast, watch for the Arab-influenced *tufo,* and for the masked *mapiko* dancing of the Makonde.

Marrabenta is Mozambique's national music, and features a light, upbeat guitar-driven style and distinctive beat. New-generation groups to watch out for include Kapa Dêch and Mabulu, which fuses *marrabenta* rhythms with hip hop.

Among the most famous musical traditions are the Chopi *timbila* (marimba) orchestras, which are best seen around Quissico, north of Xai-Xai.

The late José Craveirinha (1922–2003) is Mozambique's greatest poet, and his work, including *Poem of a Future Citizen,* is recognised worldwide. The best-known contemporary author is Mia Couto, whose works include *Voices Made Night* and *Every Man is a Race.*

Mozambique's most famous painter is Malangatana, whose art is exhibited around the world. Makonde carving traditions flourish in the north.

Food & Drink

Along the coast, tuck into a plate of giant *camarões* (prawns) or *lagosta* (crayfish), washed down with a cold Dois M (2M, Mozambique's favourite lager). Elsewhere the options include *xima* (maize porridge), *frango grelhado* (grilled chicken) and *matapa* (peanut and cassava-leaf stew). Freshly baked rolls are available everywhere.

Larger towns have restaurants, and many have sidewalk cafes where you can enjoy a light meal while watching the passing scene. For cheap local-style fast food, try the *barracas* (stalls) at markets, which offer plates of *xima* and sauce for about US$2.

Major towns have supermarkets for self-catering.

Environment

A wide coastal plain rises to mountains and plateaus on the borders with Zimbabwe, Zambia and Malawi. Three of Africa's major rivers (the Zambezi, the Limpopo and the Rovuma) flow through Mozambique.

Mozambique has six national parks: Banhine and Zinave parks are not yet set up for tourism. The others include Gorongosa (which is easy to reach and has rebounding wildlife populations), Limpopo (part of the Great Limpopo Transfrontier park, which also includes South Africa's Kruger), Bazaruto (famed for its corals and dugongs) and Quirimbas (encompassing northern offshore and coastal areas, and known for its diving).

Wildlife reserves include Niassa Reserve and Maputo Special Reserve; for hiking head to Chimanimani National Reserve.

SURVIVAL GUIDE

Directory A–Z

ACCOMMODATION

There are many campsites along the southern coast.

The cheapest hotels (called *pensões*) start at around Mtc350. Backpacker places, found especially in the south, are better value; dorm beds average Mtc400.

When quoting prices, many establishments distinguish between a *duplo* (twin beds) and a *casal* (double bed).

Around Christmas, Easter and during August, the southern coast fills up and peak pricing applies; advance bookings are recommended.

Except as noted, listings include continental breakfast and private bathroom.

ACTIVITIES

There are diving and snorkelling operators all along the coast, notably in Tofo, Vilankulo (for the Bazaruto Archipelago), Pemba and the Quirimbas Archipelago.

For kitesurfing, contact **Pirate Kites** (www.murrebue.com).

The main wildlife-watching destination is Gorongosa National Park.

CHILDREN

The beaches are ideal for visiting with young children. Many resorts also have swimming pools and most offer children's discounts.

In beach areas, be aware of the risk of hookworm infestation in populated areas (wearing beach shoes helps avoid this), as well as the risk of bilharzia in lakes. Other things to watch out for: sea urchins at the beach (beach shoes are a good idea for children and adults) and thorns in the bush.

For malaria protection, bring mosquito nets from home for your children and ensure that they sleep under them. Also bring mosquito repellent from home, and check with your doctor regarding the use of malaria prophylactics. Long-sleeved shirts and trousers are the best protection at dawn and dusk.

EMBASSIES & CONSULATES

The closest Australian representation is in South Africa. The following are all in Maputo.

British High Commission (82-313 8580; http://ukinmozambique.fco.gov.uk; 310 Avenida Vladimir Lenine)

Canadian High Commission (21-492623; www.canadainternational.gc.ca/mozambique; 1138 Avenida Kenneth Kaunda)

Dutch Embassy (21-484200; http://mozambique.nlembassy.org; 324 Avenida Kwame Nkrumah)

French Embassy (21-484600; www.ambafrance-mz.org; 2361 Avenida Julius Nyerere)

German Embassy (21-482700; www.maputo.diplo.de; 506 Rua Damião de Gois)

Irish Embassy (21-491440; maputoembassy@dfa.ie; 3332 Avenida Julius Nyerere)

Malawian High Commission (21-492676; 75 Avenida Kenneth Kaundam)

Portuguese Embassy (☎21-490316; www.embpormaputo.org.mz; 720 Avenida Julius Nyerere)

South African High Commission (☎21-243000; www.dfa.gov.za/foreign/sa_abroad/sam.htm; 41 Avenida Eduardo Mondlane)

Swazi High Commission (☎21-491601; swazi-moz@teledata.mz; 1271 Rua Luís Pasteur)

Tanzanian High Commission (☎21-491051, 21-490110/3; ujamaa@zebra.uem.mz; 852 Avenida Mártires de Machava)

US Embassy (☎21-492797; http://maputo.usembassy.gov; 193 Avenida Kenneth Kaunda)

Zambian High Commission (☎21-492452; 1286 Avenida Kenneth Kaunda)

Zimbabwean High Commission (☎21-490404, 21-486499; 1657 Avenida Mártires de Machava)

EMERGENCIES

There are no nationwide emergency numbers, and even city-based fire and police numbers rarely work. If you are in trouble, try seeking help from your hotel or embassy.

MONEY

Mozambique's currency is the metical (plural meticais, pronounced 'meticaish'), abbreviated here as Mtc. Note denominations include Mtc20, Mtc50, Mtc100, Mtc200, Mtc500 and Mtc1000, and coins include Mtc1, Mtc2, Mtc5 and Mtc10.

Visa card withdrawal from ATMs is the best way of accessing money. All larger and many smaller towns have ATMs for accessing cash meticais. Most (including Barclays, BCI and Standard Bank) accept Visa card only; Millennium BIM machines also accept MasterCard.

Carry a standby mixture of US dollars (or South African rand, especially in the south) and meticais (including a good supply of small denomination notes, as nobody ever has change) for times when an ATM is not available or not working.

Except for Millennium BIM, most banks don't charge commission for changing cash.

Travellers cheques can only be exchanged with difficulty (try BCI) and with a high commission plus original purchase receipts.

PUBLIC HOLIDAYS

New Year's Day 1 January
Mozambican Heroes' Day 3 February
Women's Day 7 April
International Workers' Day 1 May
Independence Day 25 June
Lusaka Agreement/Victory Day 7 September
Revolution Day 25 September
Peace & Reconciliation Day 4 October
Christmas/Family Day 25 December

PRACTICALITIES

- **Electricity** Electricity is 220V to 240V AC, 50Hz, usually accessed with South African–style three-round-pin plugs or two-round-pin plugs.
- **Languages** Portuguese, plus Changana, Nyanja, Makhuwa and other African languages
- **Newspapers** *Notícias* and *Diário de Moçambique* (dailies); *Savana* (weekly). Mozambique News Agency (AIM) website www.poptel.org.uk/mozambique-news (English-language news)
- **TV** TVM (www.tvm.co.mz; state run), RTK (commercial), RTPI (Portuguese TV)

SAFE TRAVEL

Mozambique is generally safe, but there are some areas and situations where caution is warranted.

Thefts and robberies are the main risks: watch your pockets in markets, avoid isolating situations, and don't carry a bag or otherwise give a potential thief reason to think you have anything of value.

More likely are simple hassles, such as underpaid authorities in search of bribes. You're required to carry your passport or (better) a notarised copy at all times. If stopped by the police, remain polite, but don't surrender your documents; insist on going to the nearest *esquadrão* (police station) instead.

If you are asked to pay a *multa* (fine) for a trumped-up charge, playing the game a bit (asking to speak to the supervisor or *chefe*, and requesting a receipt) helps to counteract some of the more blatant attempts, as does insisting on going to the nearest *esquadrão*.

TELEPHONE

Do not use an initial zero; seven-digit mobile numbers listed with zero at the outset are in South Africa, and must be preceded by the South Africa country code (☎27) when dialling.

Top-up cards and SIM-card starter packs are widely available; registration is necessary.

Telephone Codes

Country code ☎258
International dialling code ☎00
Landline area codes Included with all numbers in this chapter; must be used whenever dialling long distance. As with mobile numbers, there is no initial zero.

OPENING HOURS

Banks 8am to 3pm Monday to Friday

Foreign exchange bureaus (*casas de câmbio*) 8.30am to 5pm Monday to Friday, 8.30am to noon Saturday

Government offices 7.30am to 3.30pm Monday to Friday

Shopping 8am to noon and 2pm to 6pm Monday to Friday, 8am to 1pm Saturday

VISAS

Visas are required by all visitors except citizens of South Africa, Swaziland, Zambia, Tanzania, Botswana, Malawi, Mauritius and Zimbabwe.

Single-entry visas (only) are available at most land and air entry points (but not anywhere along the Tanzania border) for Mtc2085 (or the US dollar equivalent) for one month.

No matter where you get your visa, your passport must be valid for at least six months from the dates of intended travel, and have at least three blank pages.

Visas can be extended at the *migração* (immigration office) in all provincial capitals provided you haven't exceeded the three-month maximum stay, at a cost of Mtc2085 for one month. Processing takes up to one week.

Getting There & Away

AIR

Coastal Aviation (safari@coastal.co.tz) Dar es Salaam to Moçimboa da Praia, with connections to Pemba and the Quirimbas Archipelago.

Federal Air (www.fedair.com) Johannesburg to Vilankulo via Kruger Mpumalanga International Airport.

Kenya Airways (☎21-495483; www.kenya-airways.com; 33/659 Avenida Barnabé Thawé, Maputo) Nairobi to Maputo.

Linhas Aéreas de Moçambique (LAM; www.lam.co.mz) Domestic routes plus flights between Johannesburg, Maputo, Vilankulo and Beira; Dar es Salaam, Pemba and Nampula; Lisbon (Portugal) and Maputo.

SAAirlink (www.flyairlink.com) Johannesburg to Beira, Nampula and Pemba; Durban to Maputo.

South African Airways (www.flysaa.com) Johannesburg to Maputo

TAP Air Portugal (www.flytap.com) Lisbon to Maputo.

LAND

All overland travellers must pay an immigration tax of US$2 or the local currency equivalent. Most borders are open from 6am to 6pm.

Malawi

Main Border Crossings

- Zóbuè – On the Tete Corridor route linking Blantyre (Malawi) and Harare (Zimbabwe); the busiest crossing
- Dedza – 85km southwest of Lilongwe
- Melosa (Milange) – 120km southeast of Blantyre
- Mandimba – Northwest of Cuamba

To/From Blantyre

Via Zóbuè: vehicles depart Blantyre for the border via Mwanza, connecting in Zóbuè (Mozambique) with chapas to Tete (Mtc150, 1½ hours Zóbuè to Tete).

Crossing via Melosa (Milange) is convenient for Quelimane and Mozambique Island. Buses depart Blantyre via Mulanje (Malawi) to the border. Once across, daily vehicles service Mocuba, then Quelimane and Nampula.

Mandimba is the crossing for Cuamba and northern Mozambique. Malawian transport goes frequently to Mangochi, where you can get minibuses to Namwera, and on to the border at Chiponde. In Mozambique *moto-taxis* (motorcycle taxis) bridge the 1.5km of no man's land (Mtc50), and then vehicles take you to Mandimba town, and on to Cuamba and Lichinga.

To/From Lilongwe

From the Dedza border post, 85km southeast of Lilongwe, *chapas* run along the sealed route to Tete via Ulongwé. Otherwise, go in stages via Moatize. Arrange your Mozambique visa in advance.

South Africa

Border Crossings

- Lebombo/Ressano Garcia – Northwest of Maputo; open 6am to 10pm
- Kosi Bay/Ponta d'Ouro – 11km south of Ponta d'Ouro; open 8am to 4pm
- Pafuri – 11km east of Kruger Park's Pafuri Camp; open 6am to 5.30pm
- Giriyondo – 95km from Kruger's Phalaborwa Gate; open 8am to 4pm October to March, to 3pm April to September

To/From Johannesburg & Nelspruit

Large 'luxury' buses go daily between Johannesburg and Maputo (US$40 to US$50 one way, nine to 10 hours) via Lebombo–Ressano Garcia. If possible, organise your Mozambique visa in advance if travelling by bus. Most companies will take you without one, but if lines at the border are long the bus may not wait. If you get stuck, take a *chapa* the remaining 90km to Maputo. Companies include the following:

- Cheetah Express (☎84-444 3024, 21-486 3222; Av Eduardo Mondlane, Maputo) Daily between Maputo and Nelspruit (Mtc1100 one way).
- Greyhound (☎in South Africa 083-915 9000; www.greyhound.co.za)
- Luciano Luxury Coach (☎84-860 2100, in South Africa 083-993 4897)
- Translux (☎in South Africa 011-774 3333; www.translux.co.za)

To/From Kruger National Park

Neither of the borders between Mozambique and South Africa's Kruger park is accessible via public transport, and both require a 4WD on the Mozambique side. You'll need to pay entry fees for Kruger and for Limpopo park (Mtc200/100 per adult/child). The Giriyondo crossing requires proof of payment of one night's lodging within the Great Limpopo Transfrontier Park (ie, either in Limpopo National Park or South Africa's Kruger park).

Other Routes

Between Durban and Maputo, Luciano Luxury Coach (p873) has buses via Namaacha and Big Bend in Swaziland (Mtc1110, nine hours) twice weekly.

For Ponta d'Ouro, there's at least one daily *chapa* between the border and Maputo via Ponta d'Ouro (Mtc50 from border to Ponta d'Ouro) and Catembe town, a short ferry ride from Maputo. Coming from South Africa, you can leave your vehicle at the border and arrange a pick-up in advance with Ponta d'Ouro hotels (US$10 to US$15 per person).

Swaziland

Border Crossings

- Lomahasha/Namaacha – In Swaziland's extreme northeastern corner; open 7am to 8pm
- Goba/Mhlumeni – Southwest of Maputo; open 7am to 8pm

To/From Manzini

It's fastest to take a *chapa* between Maputo and Namaacha (Mtc70, 1½ hours), walk across the border, and get Swaziland transport (US$6, three hours to Manzini).

The quieter Goba border is good for drivers.

Tanzania

Border Crossings

For all Mozambique–Tanzania posts, it's essential to arrange your Mozambique (or Tanzania) visa in advance.

- Kilambo ('Namoto' or Namiranga) – 130km north of Moçimboa da Praia
- Mtambaswala/Negomano – Unity Bridge, 115km southwest of Masasi (Tanzania), 200km northwest of Mueda; open 7.30am to 4pm in Mozambique, 8.30am to 5pm in Tanzania; best for drivers (4WD essential)
- Mtomoni/Segundo Congresso – Unity Bridge 2; 120km south of Songea (Tanzania); road links (and public transport) north to Songea and south to Lichinga.

To/From Moçimboa da Prai

Pick-ups depart Mtwara (Tanzania) daily from 6am to Kilambo, and on to the Rovuma River, crossed via dugout canoe. Once across, pick-ups go to the Mozambique border post (4km further) and on to Moçimboa da Praia (Mtc250, two hours).

Zambia

Border Crossings

Cassacatiza is the main crossing, 290km northwest of Tete; it's open 7am to 5pm.

To/From Katete

Chapas go daily from Tete to Matema, from where there's sporadic transport to the border, and then daily vehicles to Katete (Zambia), and on to Lusaka or Chipata.

Zimbabwe

Border Crossings

Following are the main border crossings:

Nyamapanda – On the Tete Corridor, linking Harare with Tete and Lilongwe (Malawi)

Machipanda – On the Beira Corridor linking Harare with the sea

To/From Harare

Chapas go from Tete to Changara and on to Nyamapanda, for vehicles to Harare.

From Chimoio *chapas* go to Manica and the Machipanda border. Take a taxi to Mutare for Zimbabwe transport.

LAKE

Malawi

The *Ilala* ferry is currently grounded for repairs; contact **Malawi Lake Services** (☎in Malawi 1-587221; ilala@malawi.net) for an update. Meanwhile, the journey between Cóbuè and Likoma Island (Malawi) is done by local fishing boats (about US$7 one way).

ℹ Getting Around

AIR

LAM (☎21-468000, 84-147, 82-147; www.lam.co.mz) The national airline, with flights linking Maputo with Inhambane, Vilankulo, Beira, Chimoio, Quelimane, Tete, Nampula, Lichinga and Pemba.

CAR & MOTORCYCLE

A South African or international drivers licence is required to drive in Mozambique.

Driving on the beach, driving without a seatbelt (all vehicle occupants), driving while using a mobile phone, driving without carrying two red hazard triangles and a reflector vest, and turning without indicating are all illegal.

Speed limits (100km/h on main roads, 80km/h on approaches to towns and 60km/h or less when passing through towns) are enforced by radar.

Avoid night driving.

HITCHING

Hitching is never entirely safe, and we don't recommend it. Travellers who hitch should understand that they are taking a small but potentially serious risk. However, despite the potential dangers, hitching is often the only transport option in rural areas. Modest payment is expected.

LOCAL TRANSPORT

Machibombos (buses) are the best option for getting around on main routes. Elsewhere, overcrowded, wildly careening *chapas* (minivans) connect smaller towns daily. Take a bus if there's a choice.

Main companies include **TCO** (☎82-956 0600, 82-891 3020; Avenida Zedequias Manganhela), **Maning Nice** (☎82-706 2820; Avenida Zedequias Manganhela; ⏰8am-5pm), **Nagi Trans** (☎84-955 1669, 84-265 7082, 86-318 4004; Avenida do Trabalho) and **Grupo Mecula** (☎26-213772; grupomecula@teledata.mz; Rua da Moma).

'Express' services are slightly more expensive, but faster and more comfortable.

All transport leaves early (between 3am and 6am), and punctually.

Namibia

☎264 / POP 2.2 MILLION

Includes ➡

Best Wildlife Watching

- Etosha National Park (p890)
- Waterberg Plateau (p893)
- Namib-Naukluft Park (p887)
- Khaudum National Park (p895)
- Dorob National Park (p888)

Best of the Outdoors

- Swakopmund (p883)
- Fish River Canyon (p883)
- Damaraland (p889)
- Kaokoveld (p890)
- The Skeleton Coast (p888)

Why Go?

A journey through Southern Africa reveals its otherworldly nature when you cross the border into the vast reaches of Namibia. The combination of space and landscape ensures that a trip through this country is one of the great road adventures of the region. Natural wonders such as the mighty gash in the earth at Fish River Canyon and Etosha National Park enthrall, but it's the lonely roads cutting through swirling desert sands that will stay with you. Here, sand dunes in the world's oldest desert, the Namib, meet the crashing rollers along the wild Atlantic Coast and among this is a German legacy evident in the cuisine, art nouveau architecture and festivals.

Namibia is also the headquarters of adventure activities in Southern Africa, so whether you're a dreamer or love hearing the crunch of earth under your boots, travel in the country will sear itself in your mind long after the desert vistas fade.

When to Go

Windhoek

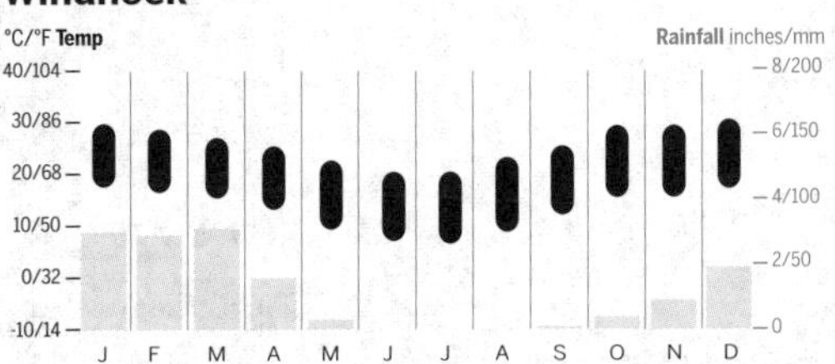

May–Oct Best time for wildlife viewing; animals congregate around remaining waterholes.

Jun–Aug Coastal town such as Swakopmund are subject to miserable sandstorm conditions.

Nov–Apr The off-season as the wet gets into full swing – downpours from January to April.

Namibia Highlights

1. Get off the beaten track (and the tarred road) in the true African wilderness of the **Skeleton Coast** (p888) and **Kaokoveld** (p890).
2. Hike through one of Africa's greatest natural wonders at the **Fish River Canyon** (p896).
3. Crouch by a waterhole in one of the world's premier wildlife venues in **Etosha National Park** (p890).
4. Hike to the top of **Waterberg Plateau** (p893) for breathtaking views, while keeping an eye out for rare sable and roan.
5. Watch the sun rise from the top of the fiery coloured dunes of **Sossusvlei** (p887).
6. Get your adrenaline fix at Namibia's extreme-sports capital of **Swakopmund** (p883).

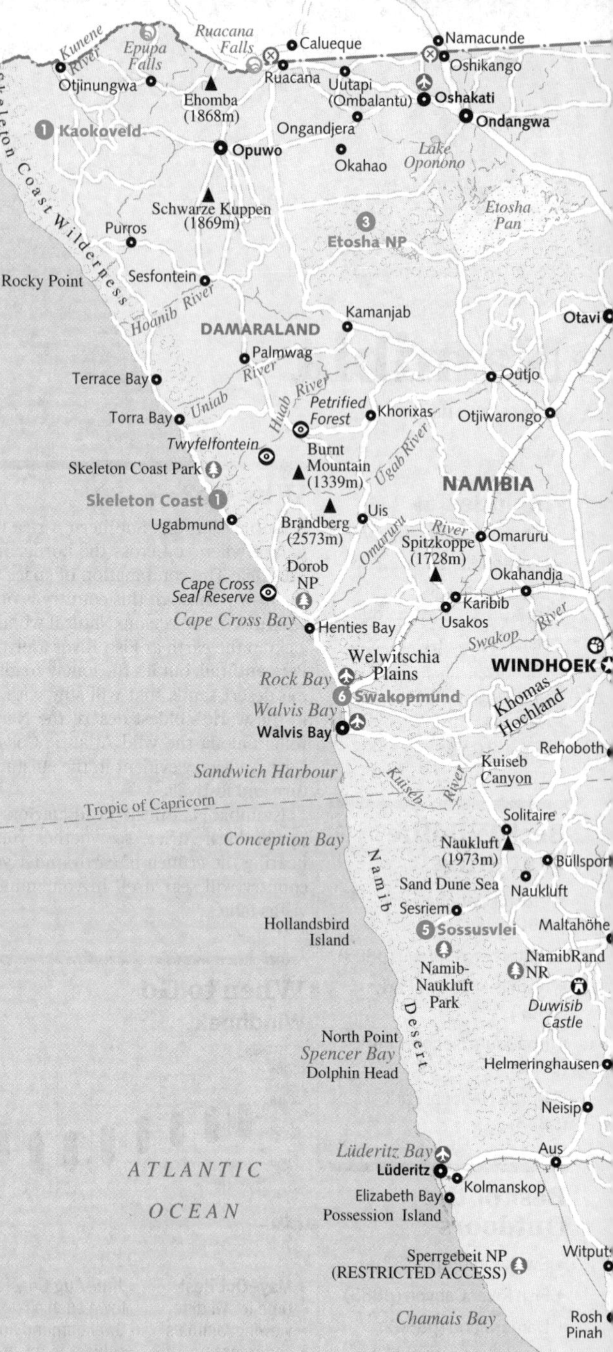

ANGOLA
Cubango River
Cuito River
Calai
Rundu
Andara
Divundu
Mahango GR
Bwabwata NP
Shakawe
Caprivi Strip
Kongola
Mudumu NP
Katima Mulilo
Kasane
Ngoma Bridge
Linyanti
Mamili NP
Chobe NP
Savuti
Mangetti
Khaudum NP
Tsumeb
Grootfontein
Tsumkwe
Aha Hills (1250m)
Konde
Maun
Nxai Pan
Nxai Pan NP
Waterberg Plateau
Okakarara
Eiseb River
NAMIBIA
Sehithwa
Lake Ngami
Kuke
Deception Pan
Okanuwa
Otjosondu
Labora
Epukiro River
Ghanzi
Rietfontein
Okwa River
BOTSWANA
Daan Viljoen Game Park
Buitepos/ Mamuno
Xanagas
Omitara
Seeis
Gobabis
Quoxo River
Kalahari Desert
Dorbabis
Bergland
Khutse GR
Leonardville
Aminuis
Kang
Salajwe
Oorwinning
Takatokwane
Tshane
Hukuntsi
Kalkrand Recreation Resort & Game Park
Stampriet
Sekoma
Union's End
Akanou
Mariental
Gochas
Voigtsgrund
Olifants River
Nossob River
Kwang
Witbooisvlei
Twee Rivier
Mata Mata
Vloorskop (959m)
Auob River
Katzies
Koës
Garinais
Khawa
Molopo River
McCarthysrus
Fly's Kop
Keetmanshoop
Bethanie
Rietfontein
Middlepits
Bokspits
Goageb
Seeheim
GR Game Reserve
NP National Park
NR Nature Reserve
Tsaraxaibis
Gondwana Cañon Park
SOUTH AFRICA
0 100 km
0 60 miles
Fish River Canyon
Ai/Ais
Upington
Richtersveld Transfrontier Park
Warmbad
Orange River
Vaal River
Kimberley
Noordoewer
Onseepkans
Vioolsdrif
Goodhouse

WINDHOEK

061 / POP 240,000

Central Windhoek is a surprisingly modern, well-groomed city where office workers lounge around Zoo Park at lunchtime, tourists funnel through Post St Mall admiring African curios and taxis whizz around honking at potential customers. In fact, first impressions confirm that the city wouldn't look out of place in the West. Of course, that's only part of the story and a trip into Katutura, the once ramshackle township on the outskirts of the city, now just another outer suburb, gives insight into the reality of most people's lives within the boundaries of the capital. Windhoek makes a great place to begin or break a journey through Namibia and Southern Africa. The accommodation choices, food variety, cultural sights, shopping and African urban buzz give it an edge not found anywhere else in Namibia.

Sights

National Museum of Namibia MUSEUM

(Robert Mugabe Ave; 9am-6pm Mon-Fri, 3-6pm Sat & Sun) FREE The whitewashed ramparts of Windhoek's oldest surviving building date from the early 1890s. The building houses the historical section of the State Museum, and exhibits focus mainly on Namibia's independence struggle.

Owela Museum MUSEUM

(State Museum; 4 Robert Mugabe Ave; 9am-6pm Mon-Fri, 3-6pm Sat & Sun) FREE The other half of the National Museum of Namibia, about 600m from the main building. Exhibits focus on Namibia's natural and cultural history and it has been popular with readers. Note, it sometimes closes early.

Christuskirche CHURCH

(Fidel Castro St) FREE Windhoek's best recognised landmark, this German Lutheran church stands on a traffic island and lords it over the city centre. The unusual building was constructed from local sandstone in 1907 in conflicting neo-Gothic and art nouveau styles. To view the interior, pick up the key during business hours from the nearby church office on Peter Müller St.

National Art Gallery GALLERY

(cnr Robert Mugabe Ave & John Meinert St; Mon-Fri/Sat free/N$20; 8am-5pm Tue-Fri, 9am-2pm Sat) Features work by local artists in various mediums, some of which is for sale. It also houses a permanent collection of works reflecting Namibia's history and nature.

Sleeping

Cardboard Box Backpackers BACKPACKERS $

(228994; www.cardboardbox.com.na; 15 Johann Albrecht St; campsites/dm N$70/95, r from N$300; @) Centred on a dreamy swimming pool that fronts a fully stocked bar, backpackers have a tough time leaving this oasis of affordable luxury, though no one seems to be bothered in the slightest.

Chameleon Backpackers Lodge & Guesthouse BACKPACKERS $

(244347; www.chameleonbackpackers.com; 5-7 Voight St; campsites N$80, dm/r incl breakfast from N$120/300; @) A popular and well equipped budget guesthouse that caters to a quieter crowd, offering luxurious African-chic rooms with private bathrooms and spic-and-span dorms at shoestring prices.

★ **Guesthouse Tamboti** GUESTHOUSE $$

(235515; www.guesthouse-tamboti.com; 9 Kerby St; s/d from N$415/620; @) Tamboti is very well priced, and has a great vibe. The rooms here are spacious and well set up – it's situated on a small hill just above the city centre. Book ahead as it's popular.

Hotel-Pension Steiner HOTEL $$

(222898; www.natron.net/tour/steiner/main.html; 11 Wecke St; s/d from N$540/850;) Although it has an excellent city centre location just a few minutes' walk from Independence Ave, this small hotel is sheltered from the hustle and bustle of the street scene.

Hotel Heinitzburg HOTEL $$$

(249597; www.heinitzburg.com; 22 Heinitzburg St; s/d from N$1530/2200; @) This is Windhoek's most royal B&B option – quite literally – as it's located inside Heinitzburg Castle, which was commissioned in 1914 by Count von Schwerin for his fiancée, Margarethe von Heinitz.

Eating

Paul's INTERNATIONAL $

(307176; Old Breweries Complex, Craft Market Inner Courtyard, cnr Garten & Tal Sts; mains N$30-60; 8am-5pm Mon-Fri, to 2pm Sat) Mixing brasserie, coffee shop and patisserie is this impressive eatery at the heart of Windhoek's craft market. It's a quirky mix – as are the menu options, which include tapas, salads, fresh baked rolls and more substantial meals.

La Marmite WEST AFRICAN $$
(☎240306; 383 Independence Ave; mains N$100; ⏲lunch & dinner) This humble West African eatery deserves its long-garnered popularity. Here you can sample wonderful North and West African cuisine, including Algerian, Senegalese, Ivorian, Cameroonian (try the curry) and Nigerian dishes.

Sardinia's Restaurant ITALIAN $$
(39 Independence Ave; dishes N$60-100; ⏲lunch & dinner) An energetic restaurant that is a focal point for dining along the main drag. It churns out first-class pizzas and an impressive array of pasta dishes. And it doesn't stop there: chicken and beef dishes and salads are also offered.

Gourmet INTERNATIONAL $$
(☎232360; www.thegourmet-restaurant.com; Kaiserkrone Centre, Post St Mall; mains N$70-180; ⏲breakfast, lunch & dinner Mon-Sat) Tucked away in a nondescript courtyard just off Post St Mall, this alfresco bistro has one of the most comprehensive menus you'll see.

Drinking

Wine Bar WINE BAR
(☎226514; www.thewinebarshop.com; 3 Garten St; ⏲4-10.30pm Mon-Thu, to 11.30pm Fri, 5-10.30pm Sat) Wine Bar occupies a historic mansion on a quiet side street, and strives to satiate your palate with one of the city's best wine selections, paired with Mediterranean-style tapas.

Café Balalaika BAR
(☎223479; Zoo Park, Independence Ave) This spot, cafe by day, bar by night, features a terrace with the capital's largest rubber tree. Live music and karaoke feature as does a cool bar scene with some great beer on tap.

Entertainment

National Theatre of Namibia THEATRE
(☎234633; www.ntn.org.na; Robert Mugabe Ave) Located south of the National Art Gallery, the National Theatre stages infrequent theatre presentations; for information see the *Namibian* newspaper.

Playhouse Theatre THEATRE
(☎402253; www.playhouse.99fm.com.na; Old South-West Brewery Bldg, 48 Tal St) A delightfully integrated club staging live African and European music and theatre productions.

SET YOUR BUDGET

Budget

- Dorm bed N$100
- Two-course dinner N$60
- Beer in a hostel N$10
- Minibus ride N$15

Midrange

- Hotel room N$600
- Two-course dinner N$150
- Beer in a bar N$15
- Taxi ride N$50

Top End

- Luxury lodge N$1200
- Two-course dinner N$400
- Beer in a hotel N$30
- 4WD hire per day N$120

Information

DANGERS & ANNOYANCES

Central Windhoek is actually quite relaxed and hassle free. As long as you stay alert, walk with confidence, keep a hand on your wallet and avoid wearing anything too flashy,you should encounter nothing worse than a few persistent touts and the odd con artist. As a precaution, always travel by taxi at night, even in the wealthy suburbs.

INTERNET ACCESS

Virtually all hotels and hostels offer cheap and reliable internet access, with wi-fi increasingly becoming the norm. If you're out and about, internet cafes can be found fairly easily, especially in shopping malls.

MEDICAL SERVICES

Rhino Park Private Hospital (☎225434; Sauer St) Provides excellent care and service, but patients must pay up front.

Mediclinic Windhoek (☎222687; Heliodoor St, Eros; ⏲24hr) Emergency centre and a range of medical services.

MONEY

Major banks and bureaux de change are concentrated around Independence Ave and all will change foreign currency and travellers cheques, and give credit card cash advances. First National Bank (FNB) and Standard Bank ATM systems handle Visa and MasterCard.

Central Windhoek

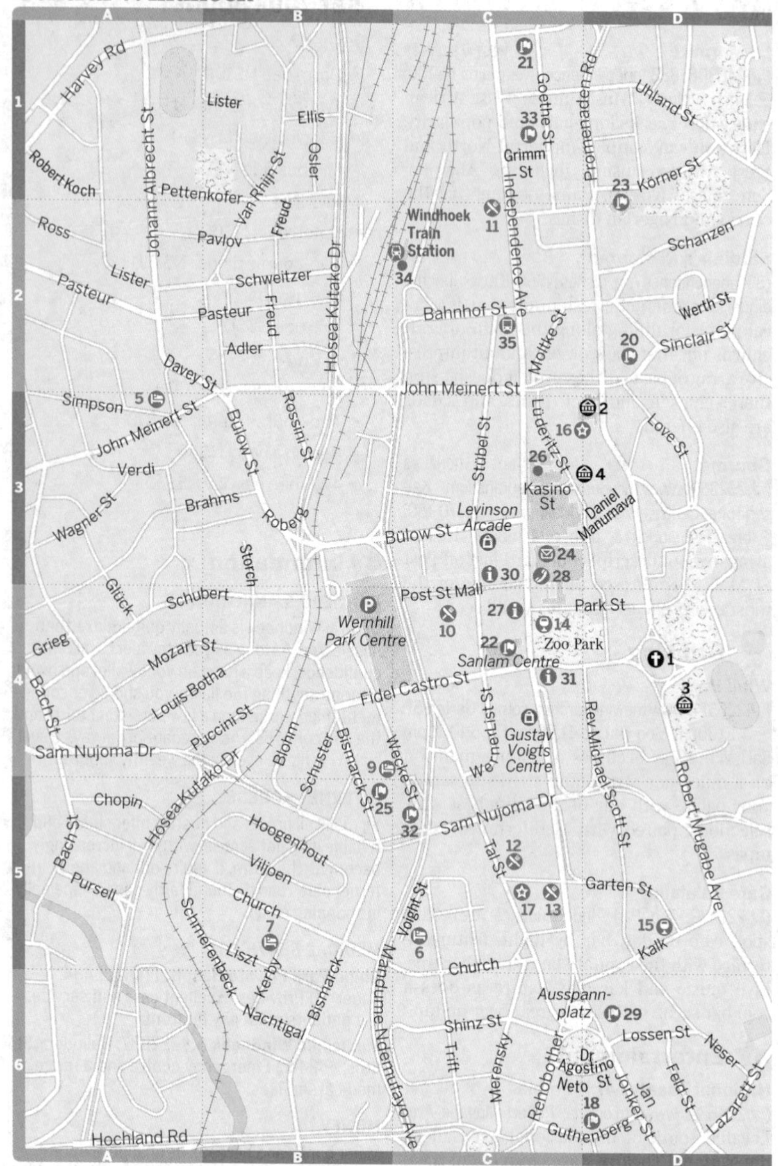

POST & TELEPHONE

The modern **Main Post Office** (Independence Ave) can readily handle overseas post. It also has telephone boxes in the lobby, and is located next door to the **Telecommunications Office** (Independence Ave), where you can make international calls and send or receive faxes.

TOURIST INFORMATION

Namibia Wildlife Resorts (NWR; ☎285 7200; www.nwr.com.na; Independence Ave) Books national park accommodation and hikes.

Central Windhoek

Sights

1 Christuskirche D4
2 National Art Gallery D3
3 National Museum of Namibia D4
4 Owela Museum D3

Sleeping

5 Cardboard Box Backpackers A3
6 Chameleon Backpackers Lodge & Guesthouse C5
7 Guesthouse Tamboti B5
8 Hotel Heinitzburg E5
9 Hotel-Pension Steiner B4

Eating

10 Gourmet C4
11 La Marmite C2
12 Paul's C5
13 Sardinia's Restaurant C5

Drinking & Nightlife

14 Café Balalaika C4
15 Wine Bar D5

Entertainment

16 National Theatre of Namibia C3
17 Playhouse Theatre C5

Information

18 Angolan Embassy D6
19 Botswanan Embassy F2
20 British High Commission D2
Cardboard Box Travel Shop .... (see 5)
Chameleon Safaris .... (see 6)
21 French Embassy C1
22 German Embassy C4
23 Kenyan High Commission D1
24 Main Post Office C3
25 Malawian Embassy B5
26 Ministry of Home Affairs C3
27 Namibia Wildlife Resorts C4
28 Telecommunications Office C3
29 US Embassy D6
30 Windhoek Information & Publicity Office (Branch Office) C3
31 Windhoek Information & Publicity Office (Main Office) C4
32 Zambian High Commission C5
33 Zimbabwean Embassy C1

Transport

34 Booking Office C2
35 Long-Distance Bus Terminal C2

Windhoek Information & Publicity Office (Main Office) (☎290 2596, 290 2092; www.cityofwindhoek.org.na; Independence Ave; ⏲7.30am-4.30pm) The friendly staff at this office answer questions and distribute local publications and leaflets, including *What's On in Windhoek* and useful city maps. There's

ANYONE FOR ZEBRA?

A legendary Windhoek institution that is something of an obligatory stop for foreign visitors, **Joe's Beer House** (☎232457; www.joesbeerhouse.com; 160 Nelson Mandela Ave; mains N$60-120; ⊙4.30pm-late Mon-Thu, 11am-late Fri-Sun) is where you can indulge (albeit with a little guilt...) in flame-broiled fillets of all those amazing animals you've seen on safari! Seriously. We're talking huge cuts of zebra tenderloin, ostrich skewers, peppered springbok steak, oryx medallions, crocodile on a hotplate and the house speciality, sliced and marinated kudu.

another **branch** (Post St Mall; ⊙7.30am-noon & 1-4.30pm) in the Post St Mall that is open the same hours but closes from noon to 1pm.

TRAVEL AGENCIES

Cardboard Box Travel Shop (☎256580; www.namibian.org; Johann Albrecht St) Attached to the backpacker hostel (p878) of the same name, this recommended travel agency can arrange both budget and upmarket bookings all over the country.

Chameleon Safaris (☎247668; www.chameleonsafaris.com; Voight St) Attached to a backpacker hostel (p878) of the same name, this travel agency is recommended for all types of safaris around the country.

Getting There & Away

AIR

Chief Hosea Kutako International Airport (WDH; ☎299 6602; www.airports.com.na), which is about 40km east of the city centre, serves most international flights into and out of Windhoek. **Air Namibia** (☎299 6333; www.airnamibia.com.na) operates flights daily between Windhoek and Cape Town and Johannesburg (South Africa), as well as daily flights to/from Frankfurt (Germany). Several airlines also offer international services to/from Maun (Botswana) and Victoria Falls (Zimbabwe).

Eros Airport (ERS; ☎299 6500), immediately south of the city centre, serves most domestic flights into and out of Windhoek. Air Namibia offers around three weekly flights to/from Katima Mulilo, Rundu and Swakopmund/WalvisBay.

Other airlines with flights into and out of Windhoek include **TAAG Angola** (☎226625; www.taag.com.br), Lufthansa Airlines and South African Airways.

Lufthansa Airlines (☎415 3747; www.lufthansa.com)

South African Airways (☎273340; www.flysaa.com)

BUS

From the main **long-distance bus terminal** (cnr Independence Ave & Bahnhof Sts) the Intercape Mainliner runs to/from Cape Town (N$800; 22 hours) and Johannesburg (N$650; 25 hrs), Victoria Falls (Zimbabwe; N$650, 22 hours) and Swakopmund (N$280, four hours), serving a variety of local destinations along the way. Tickets can be purchased either though your accommodation, from the **Intercape Mainliner** (www.intercape.co.za) office or the internet. Given the popularity of these routes, advance reservations are recommended.

Local combis (minibuses) leave when full from the **Rhino Park petrol station**, Katutura (get there very early in the morning) and can get you to most urban centres in central and southern Namibia. For northern destinations such as Tsumeb, Grootfontein and Rundu you need to go to the local minibus station opposite the hospital on Independence Ave, Katutura.

CAR & MOTORCYCLE

Windhoek is the crossroads of Namibia – the point where the main north–south route (B1) and east–west routes (B2 and B6) cross – and all approaches to the city are extremely scenic, passing through beautiful desert hills. Roads are clearly signposted and those travelling between northern and southern Namibia can avoid the city centre by taking the Western Bypass.

TRAIN

Windhoek Train Station has a **booking office** (☎298 2175; ⊙7.30am-4pm Mon-Fri), where you can reserve seats on any of the country's public rail lines. Routes are varied, and include overnight trains to Keetmanshoop, Tsumeb and Swakopmund, though irregular schedules, lengthy travel times and far better bus connections make train travel of little interest for the vast majority of foreign travellers.

Getting Around

Collective taxis from the main ranks at **Wernhill Park Centre** follow set routes to Khomasdal and Katutura, and if your destination is along the way, you'll pay around N$5 to N$15. With taxis from the main bus terminals or by radio dispatch, fares are either metered or are calculated on a per kilometre basis, but you may be able to negotiate a set fare per journey. Plan on N$50 to anywhere around the city.

If you're arriving at Hosea Kutako International Airport, it's a long drive into the city, so you can expect to pay anywhere from N$270 to N$300 depending on your destination. In the city there are always reliable taxis that hang around the tourist office (p881) on Independence Ave.

CENTRAL NAMIBIA

Central Namibia is defined by the barren and desolate landscapes of the Namib Desert. The Nama word *namib*, which inspired the name of the entire country, rather prosaically means 'vast dry plain'. Although travellers to Namibia are often surprised by the lushness of the Kalahari, the soaring sand dunes of the Namib rarely disappoint.

Omaruru

Omaruru has a growing reputation as an arts and crafts centre and in recent years has become home to the **Artist's Trail**, an annual arts event involving painters, musicians, sculptors and jewellers. It runs for three days in September and you can pick up a free copy of the programme of events around town.

Sights

Kristall Kellerei Winery WINERY
(☎570083; http://kristallkellerei.wordpress.com/; PO Box 83; ⏲8am-4.30pm Mon-Fri, to 12.30pm Sat) One of only three wineries in Namibia, this is a lovely spot to come for lunch. Apart from schnapps the winery produces colombard, a white wine, and Paradise Flycatcher, a red blend of ruby cabernet, cabernet sauvignon and tinta barocca.

Sleeping

Central Hotel Omaruru HOTEL **$$**
(☎570030; Wilhelm Zeraua St; s/d from N$300/400; ❄ ≋) This place is the town's focal point for eating and drinking and has *rondavels* (round, traditional-style and often thatched huts) in the huge garden. Here they are simple concrete setups with small beds, clean linen and good bathrooms.

Getting There & Away

The paved C33 passes through Omaruru and provides the quickest route between Swakopmund and Etosha.

Swakopmund

☎064 / POP 45,000

It can be an eerie feeling entering Swakop, especially out of tourist season when the city, sandwiched between Atlantic rollers and the Namib Desert, feels like a surreal colonial remnant. The people of Swakopmund are a quirky mix of German–Namibian residents and overseas German tourists, who feel right at home with the town's pervasive *Gemütlichkeit*, a distinctively German appreciation of comfort and hospitality. One thing Swakopmund isn't is boring. It's Namibia's most popular holiday destination, and there are myriad attractions for enjoying the great climate including surfing, fishing, lolling around on the beach. It is also the adventure sports capital of Namibia.

Sights

Swakopmund is Namibia's main beach resort but, even in summer, the water is never warmer than around 15°C (the Benguela current sweeps upwards from Antarctica). Swimming in the sea is best in the lee of the **Mole** sea wall.

At the lagoon at the Swakop River mouth, you can watch ducks, flamingos, pelicans, cormorants, gulls, waders and other birds. North of town you can stroll along miles and miles of deserted beaches stretching towards the Skeleton Coast. The best surfing is at **Nordstrand** or 'Thick Lip' near Vineta Point.

National Marine Aquarium AQUARIUM
(Strand St) This waterfront aquarium provides an excellent introduction to the cold offshore world in the south Atlantic Ocean. The place was getting a revamp at the time of research.

Activities

Swakopmund is one of the top destinations in Southern Africa for extreme sports enthusiasts. Although filling your days with adrenaline-soaked activities is certainly not cheap, there are few places in the world where you can climb up, race down and soar over towering sand dunes.

Most activity operators don't have offices in town, which means that you need to arrange all of your activities through either your accommodation provider or Namib-i (p886), the tourist information centre.

Sand boarding

Sand boarding with **Alter Action** (☎402737; www.alter-action.info; lie down/stand up US$40/55) is certain to increase your heart rate while going easy on your wallet. If you have any experience snowboarding or surfing, it's highly recommended that you have a go at the stand-up option.

Swakopmund

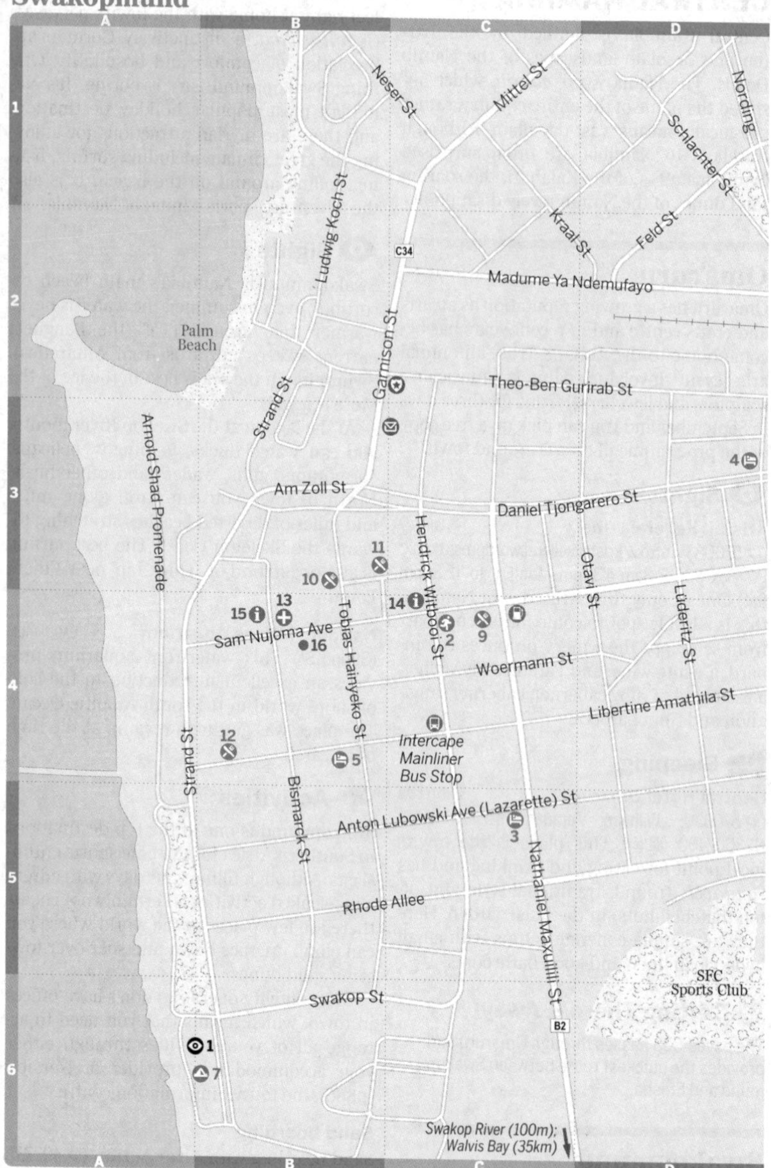

Scenic Flights

One of the most reputable light-plane operators in Namibia **Pleasure Flights** (☎404500; www.pleasureflights.com.na; prices variable) has been offering scenic aerial cruises for 20 years. Package prices do vary.

Skydiving

Ground Rush Adventures (☎402841; www.skydiveswakop.com.na; tandem jumps N$1950, handycam/professional video N$450/850) provides skydiving. In Swakopmund it's sweetened by the outstanding dune and ocean backdrop.

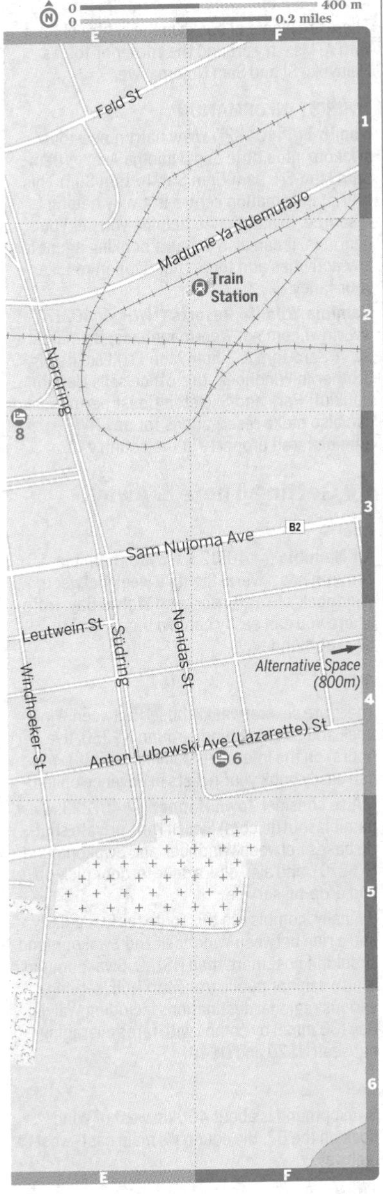

Swakopmund

Sights

1 National Marine Aquarium B6

Activities, Courses & Tours

2 Pleasure Flights C4

Sleeping

3 Desert Sky Backpackers C5
4 Dunedin Star Guest House D3
5 Hotel-Pension d'Avignon B4
6 Sam's Giardino Hotel F4
7 Tiger Reef Campsite B6
8 Villa Wiese E3

Eating

9 Fish Deli C4
10 Garden Cafe B3
11 Swakopmund Brauhaus B3
12 Tug B4

Information

13 Bismarck Medical Centre B4
14 Namib-i C4
15 Namibia Wildlife Resorts B4
Swakopmund Internet Cafe .... (see 11)

Transport

16 Air Namibia B4

Sleeping

Tiger Reef Campsite CAMPGROUND $
(☎081 380 6014; campsites N$200, plus per person N$75) This campsite sits right on the sand at the beach front, sheltered from the wind by lovely tamarisk trees. It's convenient to the city centre.

Desert Sky Backpackers BACKPACKERS $
(☎402339; Anton Lubowski Ave (Lazarette) St; campsites per person N$70, dm/r N$80/200; @) This centrally located backpackers' haunt is an excellent place to drop anchor in Swakopmund.

Villa Wiese B&B $$
(☎407105; www.villawiese.com; cnr Theo-Ben Gurirab Ave & Windhoeker St; dm N$120, s/d N$450/550; @) Villa Wiese and the nearby **Dunedin Star** (☎407105; www.dunedinstar.com; cnr Daniel Tjongarero and Windhoeker Sts) are friendly and funky guest lodges occupying historic colonial mansions, complete with vaulted ceilings, rock gardens and period furniture.

Hotel-Pension d'Avignon GUESTHOUSE $$
(☎405821; www.natron.net/tour/davignon/main.html; 25 Libertine Amathila St; s/d incl breakfast N$320/520;) A great option close to town that won't break the budget, d'Avignon is a smart, well-run guesthouse that has been recommended by travellers.

Sam's Giardino Hotel HOTEL $$$
(☎403210; www.giardinonamibia.com; 89 Anton Lubowski Ave (Lazarette) St; s/d from N$650/1200;) A slice of central Europe in the desert, Sam's Giardino Hotel mixes Swiss and Italian hospitality and architecture, while emphasising fine wines, fine cigars and relaxation in the rose garden.

Eating

Garden Cafe CAFE $$
(Tobias Hainyeko St; mains N$40-80; ⊙8am-6pm Mon-Fri, to 3pm Sat & Sun) Garden Cafe has changing specials and freshly prepared cafe food including salads, wraps and burgers (desserts are yummy too).

Fish Deli SEAFOOD $$
(☎462979; 29 Sam Nujoma Ave; dishes N$70-90; ⊙8.30am-5pm Mon, Tue, Thu & Fri, to 2pm Wed, 9am-1pm Sat) Recommended by locals as the best place for a seafood meal in town. It's a simple but clean setup inside and importantly the fish comes straight from the water to your plate – no frozen stuff.

Swakopmund Brauhaus GERMAN $$
(www.swakopmundbrauhaus.com; 22 Sam Nujoma Ave; mains N$75-100; ⊙closed Sun) This excellent restaurant and boutique brewery offers one of Swakopmund's most sought-after commodities, namely authentic German-style beer.

Tug SEAFOOD $$$
(☎402356; www.the-tug.com; mains N$80-140; ⊙lunch Sat-Sun, dinner daily) Housed in the beached tugboat *Danie Hugo* near the jetty, the Tug is something of an obligatory destination for any diner in Swakopmund.

Information

EMERGENCY

Ambulance (☎081 124 0019)

Fire Brigade (☎after-hours pager 405544, day 402411)

Police (☎10111, 402431)

INTERNET ACCESS

Swakopmund Internet Cafe (Shop 1, Atlanta Cinema Building, Nedbank Arcade; per 30min N$20; ⊙closed Sun morning) Down the mall opposite the Garden Cafe.

MEDICAL SERVICES

Bismarck Medical Centre (☎405000; cnr Bismarck St & Sam Nujoma Ave) For doctors' visits, see this recommended centre.

MONEY

There are plenty of banks in the centre of town with ATMs – try around the corner of Tobias Hainyeko St and Sam Nujoma Ave.

TOURIST INFORMATION

Namib-i (☎404827; www.natron.net/tour/swakop/infoe.htm; Sam Nujoma Ave; ⊙8am-5pm Mon-Fri, 9am-5pm Sat, to 1pm Sun) This tourist information centre is a very helpful resource. In addition to helping you get your bearings, it can also act as a booking agent for any activities and tours that happen to take your fancy.

Namibia Wildlife Resorts (NWR; ☎402172; www.nwr.com.na; Woermannhaus, Bismarck St; ⊙8am-1pm & 2-5pm Mon-Fri) Like its big brother in Windhoek, this office sells Namib-Naukluft Park and Skeleton Coast permits, and can also make reservations for any NWR–administered property in the country.

Getting There & Away

AIR

Air Namibia (☎405123; www.airnamibia.com.na) has several flights a week between Windhoek's Eros Airport and Walvis Bay, from where you can easily catch a bus or taxi to Swakopmund.

BUS

There are several weekly buses between Windhoek and Swakopmund (around N$230, five hours) on the Intercape Mainliner (p882). You can easily book your tickets in advance online.

Also consider **Town Hopper** (☎407223; www.namibiashuttle.com), which runs private shuttle buses between Windhoek and Swakopmund (N$270), and also offers door-to-door pick-up and drop-off service.

Finally, combis run this route fairly regularly, and a ride between Windhoek and Swakopmund shouldn't cost more than N$120. Swakopmund is also a minor public transport hub, serving various regional destinations including Walvis Bay (30 mins) by combi, with fares averaging between N$20 and N$40.

CAR

Swakopmund is about 400km west of Windhoek on the B2, the country's main east–west highway.

TRAIN

TransNamib (☎061-298 1111; www.transnamib.com.na) operates night trains (from N$100), although they're not very convenient or popular, especially given the ease of bus travel.

Namib-Naukluft Park

☎063

This is the Namibia of picture books and movies, and it does not disappoint. The park is best known for Sossusvlei, a huge, ephemeral pan set amid celebrated towering red dunes that leave you speechless at first glance. The dunes are part of the Namib Desert, which stretches more than 2000km along the coast from Oliphants River in South Africa all the way to southern Angola. The Naukluft portion of the park is not as well known, but the craggy peaks here are almost as impressive as the dunes themselves.

Campsites should be booked in advance at the NWR office in Windhoek (p880) or Swakopmund (p886). Permits for Sesriem-Sossusvlei and Naukluft hikes must be booked in the office in Windhoek.

There is no public transport to the area; you will either need to have your own vehicle or be part of an organised tour.

Sesriem & Sossusvlei

Despite being Namibia's number one attraction, Sossusvlei still manages to feel isolated. Hiking through the dunes, part of the 32,000 sq km sea of sand that covers much of western Namibia, is a sombre experience. The dunes, which reach as high as 325m, are part of one of the oldest and driest ecosystems on earth. The landscape here is constantly changing: colours shift with the light, and wind forever alters the dunes' shape. If you can, visit Sossusvlei at sunrise when the colours are particularly breathtaking.

Sesriem is the gateway to Sossusvlei. Here you can pick up the park permit that is needed to get to Sossusvlei. There is also a small food shop, a camping ground and the lodge. If you want to view the dunes at sunrise, you must stay at the camping ground or the lodge, and drive the 65km from Sesriem to Sossusvlei (on a sealed road). The park gate opens at sunrise and closes at sunset.

On the way from Sesriem, you'll pass Dune 45, the most accessible of the red dunes along the Sossusvlei road. It's a good place to take a photo (or 20) and is marked with a sign on the left side of the road driving towards Sossusvlei.

Unless you have a 4WD vehicle, you will have to park at the 2WD car park before you reach Sossusvlei. At the car park, either hike the last 4km into the pan or take one of the shuttles (N$100 round trip).

Sesriem Camp Site CAMPGROUND **$$**
(☎061-285 7200; www.nwr.com.na/sesriem_campsite.html; campsites per person N$130) This is one of only two accommodation sites inside the park gates – staying here guarantees that you will be able to arrive at Sossusvlei in time for sunrise. Given its popularity, you must book in advance at NWR and arrive before sunset or the camp staff will reassign your site on a stand-by basis; anyone who was unable to book a site in Windhoek may get in on this nightly lottery.

Sossus Dune Lodge LODGE **$$$**
(☎061-285 7200; www.nwr.com.na/sossus_dune_lodge.html; s/d chalet with half board N$2400/4600; ❄) If money is no object, then splash out at this ultra-exclusive place that is administered by NWR and situated inside the park gates. Constructed entirely of local materials, the lodge consists of elevated bungalows that run along a curving promenade and face out towards the silent desert plains.

Naukluft Mountains

The Naukluft Mountains, which rise steeply from the gravel plains of the central Namib, are characterised by a high plateau bounded by gorges, caves and springs cut deeply from dolomite formations. The Tsondab, Tsams and Tsauchab rivers all rise in the massif, and the relative abundance of water creates an ideal habitat for mountain zebras, kudu, leopards, springboks and klipspringers. In addition to wildlife watching, the Naukluft is home to a couple of challenging treks and unofficial campsites that open up this largely inaccessible terrain.

The lovely **Waterkloof Trail** is a 17km anticlockwise loop that takes about seven hours to complete, and begins at the Naukluft (Koedoesrus) campsite, located 2km west of the park headquarters.

The 11km **Olive Trail**, named for the wild olives that grow alongside it, begins at the car park 4km northeast of the park headquarters. The walk runs clockwise around the triangular loop and takes four to five hours.

Off-road enthusiasts can now exercise their machines on the national park's 73km

Naukluft 4WD Trail. It begins near the start of the Olive Trail and follows a loop near the northeastern corner of the Naukluft area. Book through the NWR office in Windhoek; the route (including accommodation) costs N$220 per vehicle plus an additional N$80 per person per day.

The Naukluft is best reached via the C24 from Rehoboth and the D1206 from Rietoog; petrol is available at Büllsport and Rietoog. From Sesriem, 103km away, the nearest access is via the dip-ridden D854.

NORTHWESTERN NAMIBIA

For 4WD explorers, Namibia is synonymous with the Skeleton Coast, a formidable desert coastline engulfed by icy breakers. Seemingly endless stretches of foggy beach are punctuated by rusting shipwrecks and flanked by wandering dunes. As you move inland, the sinister fogs give way to the wondrous desert wildernesses of Damaraland and Kaokoveld. The former is sparsely populated by the Damara people, and is known for its unique geological features; the latter is known as one of the last great wilderness areas in Southern Africa, as well as the home of the oft-photographed Himba people.

Skeleton Coast

The term Skeleton Coast is derived from the treacherous nature of the coast – a foggy region with rocky and sandy coastal shallows – which has long been a graveyard for unwary ships and their crews. Early Portuguese sailors called it *As Areias do Inferno* (The Sands of Hell), as once a ship washed ashore, the fate of the crew was sealed.

This protected area stretches from Sandwich Harbour, south of Swakopmund, to the Kunene River, taking in around 2 million hectares of dunes and gravel plains to form one of the world's most inhospitable waterless areas.

Dorob National Park

In December 2010 the previously named National West Coast Tourist Recreation Area was expanded in size, declared a national park and renamed Dorob National Park. Dorob now extends beyond the Swakop River and down to Sandwich Harbour in the south, while its northern border is the Ugab River.

Entry fees and a whole stack of regulations are supposed to apply to Dorob National Park, but information on this is confusing. At the time of research no fees were payable for ducking in and out of the park. Don't assume that this is still the case though; check with the nearest tourist office or NWR before you head into the park.

Cape Cross Seal Reserve WILDLIFE RESERVE
(per person/car N$40/10; ⌚10am-5pm) Most visitors head here where the seal population has grown large and fat by taking advantage of the rich concentration of fish in the cold Benguela current. The sight of more than 100,000 seals basking on the beach and frolicking in the surf is impressive.

Skeleton Coast Park

At Ugabmund, 110km north of Cape Cross, the salt road passes through the entry gate to the Skeleton Coast Park where rolling fogs and dusty sandstorms encapsulate its eerie, remote and wild feel. The zone south of the Hoanib River is open to individual travellers, but you need a permit, which costs N$80 per person and N$10 per vehicle per day. These are available through the NWR office (p880) in Windhoek. Accommodation is available only at Terrace Bay and Torra Bay (the latter is open only in December and January), both of which must be booked at NWR concurrently with your permit. To stay in either camp, you must pass the Ugabmund entrance before 3pm and/or Springbokwater entrance before 5pm.

No day visits to the park are allowed, but you can obtain a transit permit to pass between Ugabmund and Springbokwater, which can be purchased at the gates. To transit the park, you must pass the entry gate before 1pm and exit through the other gate before 3pm the same day. Note that transit permits aren't valid for Torra Bay or Terrace Bay.

SKELETON COAST WILDERNESS AREA

The Skeleton Coast Wilderness Area, stretching between the Hoanib and Kunene Rivers, makes up the northern third of the Skeleton Coast and is a part of the Skeleton Coast Park. This section of coastline is among the most remote and inaccessible areas in Namibia, though it's here in the wilderness that you can truly live out your Skeleton Coast fantasies. Since the entire area is a private concession, you're going to have to part with some serious cash to visit. Up until late 2012, the sole accommodation here was at the Skeleton Coast Wilderness Camp, which was accessible only by charter flight. That camp was closed after being gutted by a fire, but it's rumoured that a new luxury operation, the Hoanib Skeleton Coast Camp, will open for business in the region in the near future.

Damaraland

The territory between the Skeleton Coast and Namibia's central plateau has traditionally been known as Damaraland, after the people who make up much of its population. Although it's not an officially protected area, its wild open spaces are home to many desert-adapted species, including giraffes, zebras, lions, elephants and rhinos. In addition to its sense of freedom, the region is rich in both natural and cultural attractions, including Brandberg, Namibia's highest massif, and the rock engravings of Twyfelfontein.

Spitzkoppe

☎064

The 1728m **Spitzkoppe** (Groot Spitzkoppe village; per person/car N$50/20; ⏲sunrise-sunset) is one of Namibia's most instantly recognisable landmarks, rising like a mirage above the dusty plains of southern Damaraland.

Spitzkoppe Rest Camp (☎530879; http://www.natron.net/nacobta/spitzkoppe/main.html; Groot Spitzkoppe village; campsites per person N$45, bungalows from N$120) is an excellent community-run camp. The site was taken over by a private investor in mid-2012, who has pledged to upgrade the facilities while ensuring the local community continues to benefit from the enterprise.

Under normal dry conditions, a 2WD is sufficient to reach the mountain. Turn northwest off the B2 onto the D1918 towards Henties Bay. After 18km, turn north onto the D3716.

Brandberg

☎064

The Brandberg (Fire Mountain) is named for the effect created by the setting sun on its western face, which causes the granite massif to resemble a burning slag heap. Its summit, Königstein, is Namibia's highest peak at 2573m.

Its best-known attraction, the gallery of rock art in **Tsisab Ravine**, features the **White Lady of the Brandberg**. The Brandberg is a conservancy and the entry fee for admission is N$50 per person and N$20 per car. Note that this includes being allocated a compulsory guide – you cannot just walk around these fragile treasures by yourself. It's good to tip the guide afterwards if you're happy with their service.

Brandberg White Lady Lodge LODGE **$$**
(☎684004; www.brandbergwllodge.com; campsites per person N$80, twin luxury tents N$545, s/tw with half board N$775/1330) Here campers can pitch a tent along the riverine valley, all the while taking advantage of the lodge's upmarket facilities, while lovers of creature comforts can choose from rustic bungalows and chalets. From the C35 (Uis to Khorixas section), take the D2359 for 27km, following signs for the lodge.

Twyfelfontein

Twyfelfontein, or Doubtful Spring, at the head of the grassy Aba Huab Valley, is one of the most extensive rock-art galleries on the African continent. To date more than 2500 engravings have been discovered, and Twyfelfontein became a national monument in 1952. In 2007 Twyfelfontein was declared a Unesco World Heritage Site, the first such distinction in the whole of Namibia.

Sights

Rock Engravings ROCK ART
(per person/car N$50/20; ⏲sunrise-sunset) Twyfelfontein's rock engravings were probably the work of ancient San hunters, and were made by cutting through the hard patina covering the local sandstone. Guides are compulsory; note that tips are their only source of income.

Sleeping

Twyfelfontein Country Lodge LODGE **$$$**
(www.twyfelfonteinlodge.com; s/d from N$1324/1860; ❄@🏊) Over the hill from Twyfelfontein, this architectural wonder is embedded in the red rock. The lodge boasts stylish rooms, an immense and airy elevated dining room, and a good variety of excursions throughout Damaraland.

Camp Kipwe LODGE **$$$**
(☎687211, 232009; www.kipwe.com; r with half board per person N$1800; 🏊) Kipwe is languidly

draped over stunning landscape in very unobtrusive, large *rondavels* with thatched roofs that blend in beautifully with their surrounds. The lodge also runs nature drives (N$540) and excursions to the rock art.

Kaokoveld

☎065

The northwest corner of the country represents Namibia at its most primeval. The Kaokoveld is a vast repository of desert mountains that is crossed only by sandy tracks laid down by the South African Defence Force (SAFDF). It is one of the least developed regions of the country and is often described as one of the last true wildernesses in Southern Africa. It is also home to the Himba, a group of nomadic pastoralists native to Kaokoveld, who are famous for covering their skin with a traditional mixture of ochre butter and herbs to protect themselves from the sun.

Even if you're undaunted by extreme 4WD exploration, you must make careful preparations for any trip off the Sesfontein–Opuwo and the Ruacana–Opuwo–Epupa Falls routes. To summarise, you will need a robust 4WD vehicle, plenty of time and enough supplies to see you through the journey. It's also useful to take a guide who knows the region, and to travel in a convoy of at least two vehicles.

Opuwo

☎065

In the Herero language, Opuwo means the end, which is a fitting name for this dusty collection of concrete commercial buildings ringed by traditional *rondavels* and huts. While first impressions are unlikely to be very positive, a visit to Opuwo is truly one of the highlights of Namibia, particularly for anyone interested in interacting with the Himba people. As the unofficial capital of Himbaland, Opuwo serves as a convenient jumping-off point for excursions into the nearby villages, and there is a good assortment of lodges and campsites in the area to choose from.

Sights & Activities

Meeting Himba people and learning about them and their culture through village visits is the main activity in the area. You can either join an organised tour through your accommodation, stop by the Kaoko Information Centre (p890) or find an independent guide in Opuwo.

Sleeping

Ohakane Lodge LODGE **$$**
(☎273031, 081 295 9024; ohakane@iway.na; s/d N$520/900;) This well established and centrally located lodge sits along the main drag in Opuwo, and has fairly standard but fully modernised rooms.

Opuwo Country Hotel HOTEL **$$$**
(☎061-374 750; campsites per person N$100, s/d from N$920/1320;) This enormous thatched building elegantly lords over the town below. Accommodation is in bungalows facing out across the valley towards the Angolan foothills, though most of your time here will be spent soaking your cares away in the infinity pool.

Information

At **Kaoko Information Centre** (☎273420, 081 284 3681; www.kaokoinformationcenter.com; 8am-6pm) KK and Kemuu, the friendly guys at the centre (look for the tiny, tiny yellow shack), can arrange visits to Himba villages, in addition to providing useful information for your trip through the Kaokoveld region.

Getting There & Away

The marvellously paved C41 runs from Outjo to Opuwo, which makes Himbaland accessible even to 2WD vehicles. Although there is a temptation to speed along this long and lonely highway, keep your lead foot off the pedal north of the veterinary control fence as herds of cattle commonly stray across the road. If you're heading deeper into the Kaokoveld, be advised that Opuwo is the last opportunity to buy petrol before Kamanjab, Ruacana or Sesfontein.

Etosha National Park

Covering an area of more than 20,000 sq km, Etosha National Park ranks as one of the world's greatest wildlife-viewing venues. Its name, which means Great White Place of Dry Water, is inspired by the vast greenish-white Etosha Pan, an immense, flat, saline desert covering more than 5000 sq km, which for a few days each year, is converted by the rains into a shallow lagoon teeming with flamingos and pelicans. However, it's the surrounding bush and grasslands that provide a habitat for

RESPECTING THE LOCAL CULTURE

Throughout Opuwo, you will see Himba people in traditional attire wherever you go – they will be walking the streets, shopping in the stores and even waiting in line behind you at the supermarket! However tempting it might be, please do not sneak a quick picture of them as no one appreciates having a camera unwillingly waved in front of their face.

If you would like to have free reign with your camera, visiting a traditional village – if done in the proper fashion – can yield some truly amazing shots. Needless to say, a guide who speaks both English and the Himba language is essential to the experience.

Before arriving in the village, spend some time shopping for gifts – entering a village with food items will garner a warm welcome from the villagers, who will subsequently be more willing to tolerate photography. At the end of your time in the village, buying small bracelets and trinkets direct from the craftspeople is also a greatly appreciated gesture.

Finally, don't be afraid to ask lots of questions with the aid of your translator, and spend some time interacting with the Himba rather than just photographing them. Showing respect and admiration helps the Himba reinforce their belief that their tradition and way of life is something worth preserving.

Etosha's diverse wildlife. Although it may look barren, the landscape surrounding the pan is home to 114 mammal species, as well as 340 bird species, 16 reptile and amphibian species, one fish species and countless insects.

Sleeping

Advance booking for the NWR-run camps listed below is wise. Although it is sometimes possible to reserve a space at either of the park gates, it's best to contact the NWR office (p880) in Windhoek well in advance of your visit.

Okaukuejo Rest Camp LODGE, CAMPGROUND **$$**
(285 7200; http://www.nwr.com.na/okaukuejo_camp.html; campsites N$200, plus per person N$110, s/d from N$1020/1840, chalets from N$1100/2000; P) Pronounced 'o-ka-kui-yo', this is the site of the Etosha Research Station and functions as the official park headquarters and main visitor centre. The Okaukuejo water hole is probably Etosha's best rhino-viewing venue, particularly between 8pm and 10pm, though you're almost guaranteed to spot zebras, wildebeest, jackals and even elephants virtually any time of the day.

Halali Rest Camp LODGE, CAMPGROUND **$$**
(285 7200; www.nwr.com.na/halali_camp.html; campsites N$200, plus per person N$100, s/d from N$800/1400, chalets from N$1000/1700;) Etosha's middle camp, Halali, nestles between several incongruous dolomite outcrops. The best feature of Halali is its floodlit water hole, which is a 10-minute walk from the rest camp and sheltered by a glen of trees with huge boulders strewn about. There is a very well-serviced campsite here, in addition to a fine collection of luxury chalets that make for a wonderfully relaxed night of sleep despite being deep in the African bush.

Namutoni Rest Camp LODGE, CAMPGROUND **$$**
(285 7200; http://www.nwr.com.na/namutoni_camp.html; campsites N$200, plus per person N$110, s/d from N$850/1500, chalets from N$1000/1800;) Etosha's easternmost camp is defined by its landmark whitewashed German fort, a colonial relic that casts a surreal shadow over the rest of the camp. The floodlit King Nehale water hole is filled with reed beds and some extremely vociferous frogs. Namutoni also offers an immaculate campsite (the only campsite in the park with grass) in addition to a few luxury chalets on the edge of the bush.

Onkoshi Camp LODGE **$$$**
(285 7200; http://www.nwr.com.na/onkoshi_camp.html; per person with half board incl transfers from Namutoni N$2000;) Although it requires some serious purchasing power, the Onkoshi Camp at Etosha National Park is a shining crown jewel of NWR's Premier Collection. Upon arrival in Namutoni, you will be chauffeured to a secluded peninsula on the rim of the pan, and then given the keys to one of only 15 thatch and canvas chalets that rest on elevated wooden decks

Etosha National Park

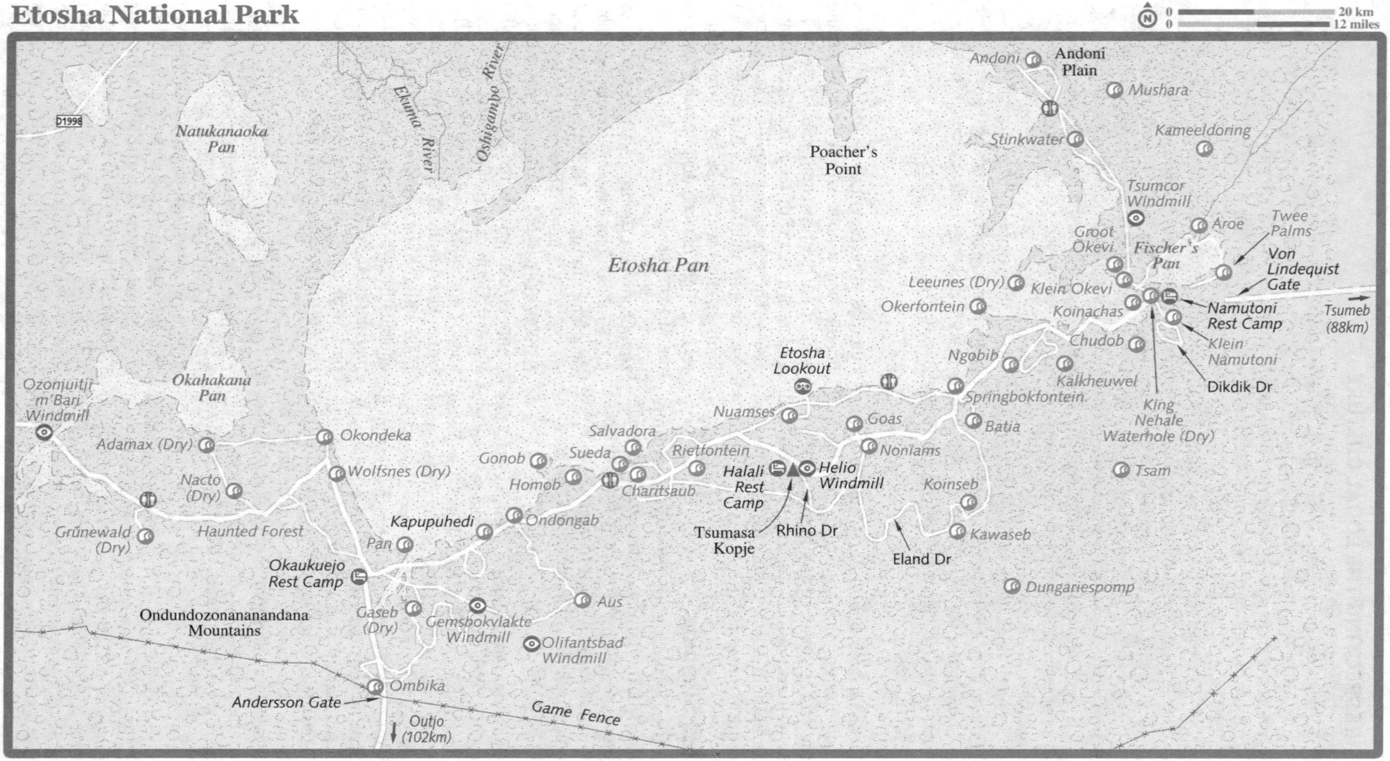

0 20 km
0 12 miles

Andoni
Andoni Plain
Mushara
Stinkwater
Kameeldoring
Poacher's Point
Natukanaoka Pan
D1998
Ekuma River
Oshigambo River
Tsumcor Windmill
Aroe
Twee Palms
Groot Okevi
Fischer's Pan
Von Lindequist Gate
Etosha Pan
Leeunes (Dry)
Klein Okevi
Okerfontein
Koinachas
Namutoni Rest Camp
Tsumeb (88km)
Chudob
Klein Namutoni
Ngobib
Kalkheuwel
Dikdik Dr
Etosha Lookout
Springbokfontein
King Nehale Waterhole (Dry)
Ozonjuitji m'Bari Windmill
Okahakana Pan
Nuamses
Goas
Batia
Salvadora
Okondeka
Adamax (Dry)
Rietfontein
Nonlams
Gonob
Sueda
Wolfsnes (Dry)
Halali Rest Camp
Helio Windmill
Tsam
Homob
Charitsaub
Koinseb
Nacto (Dry)
Ondongab
Kapupuhedi
Tsumasa Kopje
Rhino Dr
Kawaseb
Grünewald (Dry)
Haunted Forest
Pan
Eland Dr
Okaukuejo Rest Camp
Dungariespomp
Aus
Ondundozonananandana Mountains
Gaseb (Dry)
Gemsbokvlakte Windmill
Olifantsbad Windmill
Ombika
Andersson Gate
Game Fence
Outjo (102km)

and occupy exclusive locations well beyond the standard tourist route. Room prices include activities, entrance fees and transfers from Namutoni.

Information

Only the eastern two-thirds of Etosha are open to the general public (unless you are staying at the new **Dolomite Camp** (☎285 7200; http://www.nwr.com.na/dolomite_camp.html; s/d with half board from N$1250/2300; ❄ ≋) – an exclusive lodge recently opened in this part of the park). The western third is reserved exclusively for tour operators. Etosha's three main entry gates are Von Lindequist (Namutoni), west of Tsumeb; King Nehale, southeast of Ondangwa; and Andersson (Okaukuejo), north of Outjo.

Visitors are encouraged to check in at either Von Lindequist Gate or Andersson Gate (King Nehale Gate is frequently closed), where you must purchase a permit costing N$80 per person plus N$10 per vehicle per day. The permits are then to be presented at your reserved rest camp, where you pay any outstanding camping or accommodation fees.

Getting There & Away

There's no public transport into and around the park, which means that you must visit either in a private vehicle or as part of an organised tour.

Tsumeb

☎067

Tsumeb is one Namibian town worth a poke around, especially if you are trying to get a feel for the country's urban side. The streets are very pleasant to wander, made more so by the many shady trees, it's reasonably compact and there's usually a smile or two drifting your way on the busy streets.

Sights & Activities

Tsumeb Mining Museum MUSEUM
(☎220447; cnr Main St & 8th Rd; adult/child N$30/5; ⏲9am-5pm Mon-Fri, to noon Sat) Tsumeb's history is housed in a 1915 colonial building that once served as both a school and a hospital for German troops. In addition to outstanding mineral displays (you've never seen anything like psittacinite!), the museum also houses mining machinery, stuffed birds and Himba and Herero artefacts and weapons.

Sleeping & Eating

Mousebird Backpackers & Safaris BACKPACKERS $
(☎221777; 533 Pendukeni Iivula-Ithana St (4th St); campsites per person N$90, dm/tw N$120/380; @) Tsumeb's long-standing backpacker spot continues to stay true to its roots, offering economical accommodation without sacrificing personality or character – there's a really good feel to this place. The best twin rooms share a bathroom inside the house although the twin outside does have its own bathroom.

Travel North Namibia Guesthouse GUESTHOUSE $$
(☎220728; http://natron.net/tnn/index.htm; Sam Nujoma Dr; s/d N$365/480; ❄@wi-fi) This budget guesthouse is a wonderful spot if you're counting your Nam dollars. It's a fantastically friendly place delivering decent, good value accommodation. Rooms are a bit old-fashioned but it's well kept and well run.

Information

Travel North Namibia Tourist Office
(☎220728; 1551 Sam Nujoma Dr; wi-fi) This friendly office provides nationwide information, arranges accommodation, transport, car hire and Etosha bookings, and has internet access.

Getting There & Away

BUS

Intercape Mainliner (p882) buses make the trip between Windhoek and Tsumeb (from N$310, 5½ hours, twice weekly). Book your tickets in advance online as this service continues on to Victoria Falls (Zimbabwe) and fills up quickly.

Combis also run up and down the B1 with fairly regular frequency, and a ride between Windhoek and Tsumeb shouldn't cost more than N$220. If you're continuing on to Etosha National Park, be advised that there is no public transport serving this route.

CAR

Tsumeb is an easy day's drive from Windhoek along paved roads, and serves as the jumping-off point for Namutoni and the Von Lindequist Gate of Etosha National Park. The paved route continues north as far as the park gate.

Waterberg Plateau Park

Wild **Waterberg** (per person per day N$80, per vehicle N$10) is highly recommended – there is nothing quite like it in Namibia. It takes in a 50km-long, 16km-wide sandstone plateau, looming 150m above the desert plains. It doesn't have the traditional big wildlife attractions, such as lions or elephants, but what it does have is animals that are rarely seen. Even here however, you have to be lucky because they are skittish and the bush is very thick. The park protects these rare and threatened species, which include sable and roan antelopes, and white and black rhinos. Most animals here have been introduced, and after breeding successfully some are moved to other parks.

Activities

Waterberg Wilderness Trail HIKING
(per person N$220) From April to November, the four-day guided tour operates every Thursday. The walks, which are led by armed guides, need a minimum of two people. They begin at 2pm on Thursday from the visitors centre and end there early on Sunday afternoon. They must be pre-booked through NWR (p880) in Windhoek. There's no set route and the itinerary is left to the whims of the guide.

Waterberg Unguided Hiking Trail HIKING
(per person N$100) A four-day, 42km unguided hike around a figure-eight track begins at 9am every Wednesday from April to November. Groups are limited to between three and 10 people. Book through NWR (p880) in Windhoek.

Sleeping

The Waterberg Camp should be booked in advance through NWR (p880) in Windhoek, although walk-ins are accepted, subject to availability. The Waterberg Wilderness Lodge is privately owned and accepts walk-ins, though advanced reservations are recommended given its popularity.

Waterberg Camp LODGE $$
(285 7200; http://www.nwr.com.na/waterberg_camp.html; campsite N$100, s/d N$650/1000, s/d chalet from N$800/1300;) At Waterberg, campers can pitch a tent in any number of scattered sites around *braai* (barbecue) pits and picnic tables. Campsites benefit from space, views of the plateau and the plains beyond and well-kept amenities. If you're looking for a bit of bush luxury, try one of the well-designed chalets.

Waterberg Wilderness Lodge LODGE $$$
(687018; www.waterberg-wilderness.com; campsite N$120, s/d incl half board from N$1070/2100;) Despite its former life as a cattle farm, the property has been painstakingly transformed by the Rust family through repopulating game animals and allowing nature to return to its pregrazed state. The main lodge rests in a sun-drenched meadow at the end of a valley, where you'll find red sandstone chalets adorned with rich hardwood furniture.

Information

Waterberg Plateau Park is accessible by private vehicle, though visitors must explore the plateau either on foot, or as part of an official game drive, which is conducted by NWR.

Getting There & Away

Waterberg Plateau Park is only accessible by private car – motorcycles are not permitted anywhere within the park boundaries. From Otjiwarongo it's about 90km to the park gate via the B1, C22 and the gravel D512. While this route is passable to 2WD vehicles, go slow in the final stretches as the road can be in bad shape after summer (the rainy season). An alternative route is the D2512, which runs between Waterberg and Grootfontein – this route is OK during winter but can be terrible during the rainy season when it requires a high-clearance 4WD.

NORTHEASTERN NAMIBIA

Known as the Land of Rivers, northeastern Namibia is bounded by the Kunene and Okavango rivers along the Angolan border, and in the east by the Zambezi and the Kwando/Mashe/Linyanti/Chobe river systems. Although Windhoek may be the capital, northeastern Namibia, which is the country's most densely populated region, is undeniably its cultural heartland.

Rundu

Rundu, a sultry tropical outpost on the bluffs above the Okavango River, is a major centre of activity for Namibia's growing Angolan community. Although the town has little of specific interest for tourists, the area is home to a number of wonderful lodges where you can laze along the riverside and spot crocs and hippos doing pretty much the same.

Sights & Activities

Take a stroll around the large **covered market**, which is one of Africa's most sophisticated informal sales outlets. From July to September, don't miss the fresh papayas, sold straight from the trees. Alternatively, head for the **Khemo Open Market**, where you can shop for both African staples and Kavango handicrafts.

Situated on the banks of the Okavango, about 20km from Rundu's town centre, is the N'Kwazi Lodge. The lodge's owners, Valerie and Weynand Peyper, are active in the local community and have rebuilt a preschool that was previously washed away in the 2009 floods. They also have many other ongoing projects including supporting orphans in the area. You can visit the preschool and also local villages (N$50 for a village walk).

Sleeping & Eating

★N'Kwazi Lodge LODGE $
(☎081 242 4897; www.nkwazilodge.com; campsites/r per person N$120/420) Situated on the banks of the Okavango, about 20km from Rundu's town centre, is this tranquil and good-value riverside retreat. The lodge represents incredibly good value with no surcharge for singles and a justifiably famous buffet dinner for N$175 at night.

Sarasungu River Lodge LODGE $$
(☎255161; www.sarasunguriverlodge.com; campsites per person N$70, s/d/tr N$530/750/1000;) Sarasunga River Lodge is a very laid-back place, situated in a secluded riverine clearing 4km from Randu's town centre. It has attractive thatched chalets that surround a landscaped pool and a decent-sized grassed camping area with basic amenities and beautiful sunsets.

Getting There & Away

Several weekly Intercape Mainliner (p906) buses make the seven-hour trip between Windhoek and Rundu (fares from N$380). Book your tickets in advance online as this service continues on to Victoria Falls (Zimbabwe) and fills up quickly.

Combis connect Windhoek and Rundu with fairly regular frequency, and a ride shouldn't cost more than N$250. From Rundu, routes fan out to various towns and cities in the north, with fares costing less than N$40 a ride. Both buses and combis depart and drop-off at the Engen petrol station.

Khaudum National Park

☎066

Exploring the largely undeveloped 384,000-hectare Khaudum National Park is an intense wilderness challenge guaranteed not to disappoint. Meandering sand tracks lure you through pristine bush and across *omiramba* (fossil river valleys), which run parallel to the east–west Kalahari dunes. With virtually no signage, and navigation largely based on GPS coordinates and topographic maps, few tourists make the effort to extend their safari experience beyond the confines of Etosha.

In order to explore the reserve by private 4WD vehicle, you will have to be completely self-sufficient, as petrol and supplies are only available in towns along the Caprivi Strip. Water is available inside the reserve, though it must be boiled or treated prior to drinking. As a bare minimum, you will need a GPS unit, a proper topographic map and compass, as well as lots of common sense and genuine confidence and experience in driving a 4WD.

Wildlife viewing is best from June to October when herds congregate around the water holes and along the *omiramba*. November to April is the richest time to visit for birdwatchers, though you will have to be prepared for a difficult slog through muddy tracks.

NWR used to administer two official campsites in the park, but after one too many episodes of elephants gone wild, it decided to close up shop. These two sites have been neglected for a long time – if you are planning to stay at either one, keep your expectations low. Rumours of impending development in Khaudum persist, but to date that's all they are.

Sikereti Camp is located in a shady grove of terminalia trees, though full appreciation of this place requires sensitivity to its subtle charms, namely isolation and silence.

Khaudum Camp overlooks an ephemeral water hole, and is somewhat akin to the Kalahari in miniature.

From the north, take the sandy track from Katere on the B8 (signposted Khaudum), 120km east of Rundu. After 45km you'll reach the Cwibadom Omuramba, where you should turn east into the park.

From the south, you can reach Sikereti Camp via Tsumkwe. From Tsumkwe, it's 20km to Groote Döbe and another 15km from there to the Dorslandboom turning. It's then 25km north to Sikereti Camp.

Katima Mulilo

066

Out on a limb at the eastern end of the Caprivi Strip lies remote Katima Mulilo, which is as far from Windhoek (1200km) as you can get in Namibia. Once known for the elephants that marched through the village streets, Katima is devoid of wildlife these days – apart from the hippos and crocodiles in the Zambezi – though it continues to thrive as a border town and minor commercial centre.

Located behind the petrol station, **Mukusi Cabins** (253255; mukusi@mweb.com.na; Engen petrol station; campsites N$80, s/d from N$460/640;) has a good range of accommodation, from simple rooms with fans to small but comfortable air-con cabins.

Caprivi River Lodge (252288; www.capriviriverlodge.com; s N$415-1075, d N$620-1375;) offers options to suit travellers of all budgets, from rustic cabins with shared bathrooms to luxurious chalets facing the Zambezi River.

Several weekly Intercape Mainliner (p882) buses make the 16-hour run between Windhoek and Katima Mulilo. Book your tickets (fares from N$460) in advance online as this service continues on to Victoria Falls (Zimbabwe) and fills up quickly.

Combis connect Windhoek and Katima with fairly regular frequency, and the 12- to 14-hour ride shouldn't cost more than N$230. From Katima, routes fan out to various towns and cities in the north, with fares costing less than N$40 a ride.

SOUTHERN NAMIBIA

If you're beginning a regional odyssey in South Africa, one of the best ways to approach Namibia is from South Africa's vast Northern Cape, crossing the border into the infinite, desert-rich south of the country. The landscape is tinged with a lunar feel from the scattered rocky debris, and is marked from the irrepressible movement of the oldest sand dunes on the planet. Although the tourist trail in Namibia firmly swings north towards Etosha National Park, the deserts of southern Namibia sparkle beneath the sun – quite literally – as they're filled with millions of carats of diamonds.

Your first sight of Fish River Canyon will, more than any place in Namibia, leave you with feelings of awe and grandeur – it is Mother Earth at its very finest. One of the largest canyons in the world, it's also one of the most spectacular sights in the whole of Africa.

Fish River Canyon

063

Nowhere else in Africa will you find anything quite like Fish River Canyon. The canyon measures 160km in length and up to 27km in width, and the dramatic inner canyon reaches a depth of 550m. Although these figures by themselves are impressive, it's difficult to get a sense of perspective without actually witnessing the colossal scope of the canyon. In order to do this, you will need to embark on a monumental five-day hike that traverses half the length of the canyon, and ultimately tests the limits of your physical and mental endurance.

Fish River Canyon is part of the **|Ai-|Ais/Richtersveld Transfrontier Park**. Straddling southern Namibia and South Africa (and measuring 6045 sq km) it boasts one of the most species-rich, arid zones in the world. It also encompasses Richtersveld National Park and the Senqu (Orange) River valley in South Africa.

Sights

Hikers' Viewpoint VIEWPOINT

From Hobas (the main northern access point to the canyon), it's 10km on a gravel road to this viewpoint at the start of a hiking route. Just around the corner is a good overview of the northern part of the canyon. The viewpoint takes in the sharp river bend known as Hell's Corner.

Main Viewpoint VIEWPOINT

This viewpoint, a few kilometres south of the Hikers' Viewpoint, has probably the best (and most photographed) overall canyon view. It also takes in the sharp river bend known as Hell's Corner.

Hot Springs SPRING

(adult/child N$80/free; 9am-9pm) These springs at |Ai-|Ais (Nama for scalding hot) are beneath the towering peaks at the southern end of Fish River Canyon. Although the 60°C springs have probably been known to the San for thousands of years, the legend goes that they were 'discovered' by a nomadic Nama shepherd rounding up stray sheep. They're rich in chloride, fluoride and sulphur, and are reputedly therapeutic for sufferers of rheumatism or nervous disorders. The hot water is piped to a series of baths and Jacuzzis as well as an outdoor swimming pool.

Activities

Fish River Hiking Trail HIKING

(per person N$250) The five-day hike from Hobas to |Ai-|Ais is Namibia's most popular long-distance walk - and with good reason. The magical 85km route, which follows the sandy riverbed past a series of ephemeral pools, begins at Hikers' Viewpoint and ends at the hot-spring resort of Ai-Ais.

Due to flash flooding and heat in summer months, the route is open only from 15 April to 15 September. Groups of three to 30 people may begin the hike every day of the season, though you will have to book in advance as the trail is extremely popular. Reservations can be made at the NWR office (p880) in Windhoek.

Sleeping

Accommodation inside the national park must be prebooked through the NWR office (p880) in Windhoek.

Hobas Camp Site CAMPGROUND $

(campsites N$125;) Administered by NWR, this pleasant and well-shaded camping ground near the park's northern end is about 10km from the main viewpoints.

/Ai /Ais Hot Springs Spa RESORT $$

(http://www.nwrnamibia.com/ai-ais.htm; campsites N$125, mountain-/river-view d N$900/1100;) Administered by NWR, amenities include washing blocks, *braai* pits and use of the resort facilities, including the hot springs (p896).

Fish River Lodge LODGE $$$

(683005; www.fishriverlodge-namibia.com; s/d N$1500/2250) With twenty chalets located on the western rim of the canyon, this is a magical spot to enjoy the landscape. Activities include a five-night canyon hike (75km, April to September) or a day hike for the less ambitious; both are in a private concession so there is no need to book through NWR.

FIRST IMPRESSIONS – FISH RIVER CANYON

The canyon, seen most clearly in the morning, is stark, very beautiful and seemingly carved into the Earth by a master builder – it flaunts an other worldliness. The exposed rock and lack of plantlife is quite startling. Its rounded edges and sharp corners create a symphony in stone of gigantic and imposing proportions. If you have a viewpoint to yourself it's a perfect place to reflect on this country's unique landscape, harsh environment and immense horizons.

Information

The main access points for Fish River Canyon are at Hobas, near the northern end of the park, and |Ai-|Ais, near the southern end. Both are administered by NWR. Accommodation must be booked in advance through the Windhoek office. Daily park permits, N$80 per person plus N$10 per vehicle, are valid for both Hobas and |Ai-|Ais.

The **Hobas Information Centre** (7.30am-noon & 2-5pm) at the northern end of the park is also the check-in point for the five-day canyon hike. Packaged snacks and cool drinks are available here, but little else.

Getting There & Away

There's no public transport to Hobas or |Ai-|Ais, and you'll really need a private vehicle to get around. The drive in from Grünau to Hobas is on a decent gravel road.

Lüderitz

063

Before travelling to Lüderitz, pause for a moment to study the country map and appreciate the fact that the town is sandwiched between the barren Namib Desert and the windswept south Atlantic coast. As if Lüderitz's unique geographical setting wasn't impressive enough, its surreal German art nouveau architecture will seal the deal. Something of a colonial relic scarcely touched by the 21st century, Lüderitz might

Lüderitz

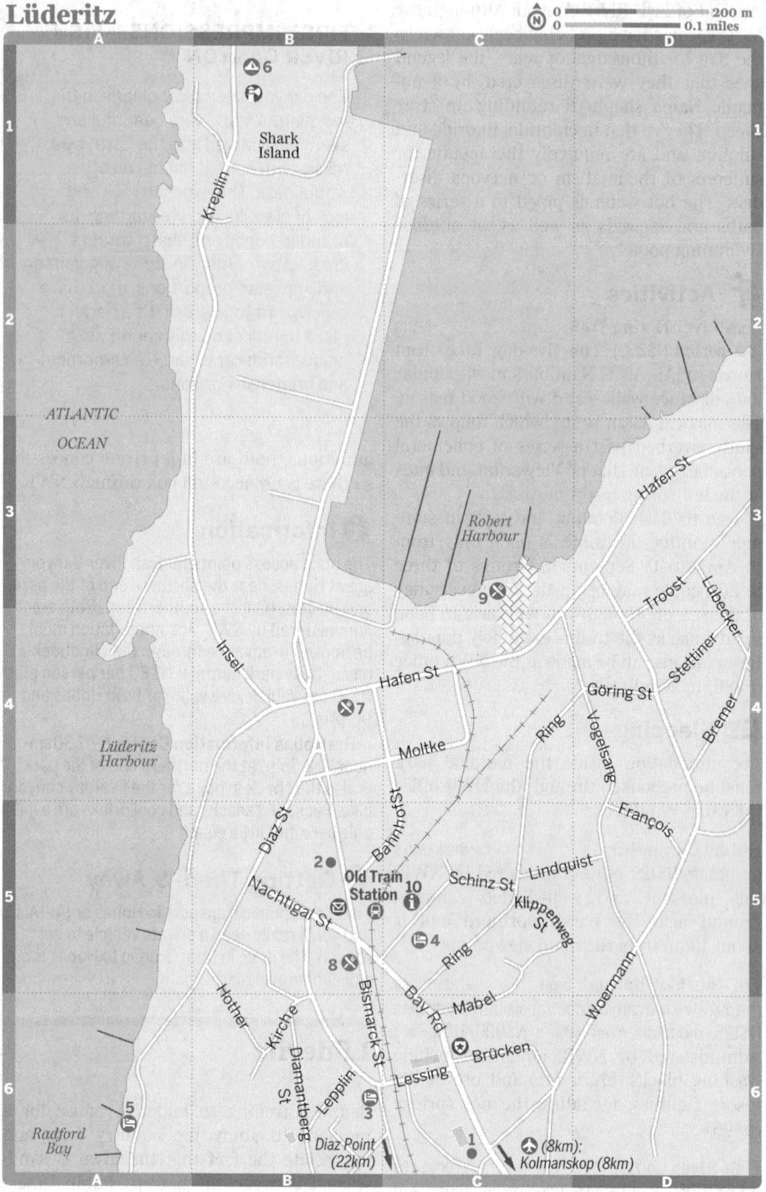

recall a Bavarian *dorfchen* (small village), with churches, bakeries and cafes.

Sights

Lüderitz is chock-a-block with colonial buildings including Lutheran churches and historic early C20th houses – every view reveals something interesting. The curiously intriguing architecture, which mixes German imperial and art nouveau styles, makes this bizarre little harbour-side town appear even more otherworldly.

Lüderitz

Activities, Courses & Tours

Sleeping

Eating

Information

Lüderitz Peninsula PENINSULA

This peninsula, much of which lies outside the Sperrgebiet Forbidden Zone (p900), makes an interesting half-day excursion from town.

Tours

With the exception of the Kolmanskop ghost town (p900), allow at least five days to plan any excursion into the Sperrgebiet, as tour companies require time to fill out all the relevant paperwork and acquire all of the necessary permits. The following tour companies are recommended.

Coastways Tours Lüderitz DRIVING TOUR

(202002; www.coastways.com.na) Highly reputable company runs multiday self-catering 4WD trips deep into the Sperrgebiet.

Lüderitz Safaris & Tours ADVENTURE TOUR

(202719; ludsaf@africaonline.com.na; Bismarck St; daily) Provides useful tourist info, organises visitor permits for Kolmanskop ghost town, books seats on the schooner *Sedina* (per person N$330), which sails past the Cape fur seal sanctuary at Diaz Point and the penguin colony on Halifax Island.

Sleeping

Shark Island Campsite CAMPGROUND $

(http://www.nwrnamibia.com/shark-island.htm; campsites per person N$100, 6-person bungalows per person N$220, lighthouse per person N$220) This is a beautifully situated but aggravatingly windy locale.

Lüderitz Backpackers Lodge BACKPACKERS $

(202000, 174513; www.namibweb.com/backpackers.htm; 7 Schinz St; campsites N$70, dm/d/f N$100/250/380) Housed in a historic colonial mansion, this friendly place is the only true backpacker spot in town – the vibe is congenial and low-key, and the friendly management is helpful in sorting out your onward travels.

Krabbenhoft une Lampe APARTMENT $$

(202674, 081 127 7131; http://klguesthouse.com/; 25 Bismarck St; twin-bed apt N$500) One of the more unusual sleeping options in town, the Krabbenhoft is a converted carpet factory that now offers a number of self-catering flats upstairs from a furniture shop and Avis car rental office.

Lüderitz Nest Hotel HOTEL $$$

(204000; www.nesthotel.com; 820 Diaz St; s/d N$930/1500;) Lüderitz's oldest upmarket hotel occupies a jutting peninsula in the southwest corner of town, complete with its own private beach.

Eating

Diaz Coffee Shop CAFE $

(cnr Bismarck & Nachtigal Sts; snacks & meals N$25-45; breakfast & lunch) The cappuccinos are strong and the pastries are sweet, and the ambience wouldn't be out of place at all in Munich.

Bistro D'Cafe BISTRO $$

(Hafen St; mains N$60-90; breakfast, lunch & dinner, closed Sun;) This cosy little restaurant has a simple setup with the emphasis on lovingly prepared food not aesthetics. The presentation of the food is delightful and everything is cooked fresh – love and time are the two most important ingredients in the food.

Ritzi's Seafood Restaurant SEAFOOD $$

(202818; Waterfront; mains N$80; breakfast, lunch & dinner, closed Mon breakfast, Sun) Occupying a choice location in the waterfront complex, Ritzi's is the town's top spot for amazing seafood matched with equally amazing sunset views.

Information

Lüderitz Safaris & Tours (202719; ludsaf@africaonline.com.na; Bismarck St; daily) A great information service with very knowledgeable staff; it sells curios, books, stamps and phonecards.

Namibia Wildlife Resorts (NWR; ☎202752; Schinz St; ⏲7.30am-1pm & 2-4pm Mon-Fri) This local office can help with national park information.

Getting There & Away

AIR

Air Namibia travels about three times a week between Windhoek and Lüderitz. The airport is 8km southeast of town.

BUS

Somewhat irregular combis connect Lüderitz to Keetmanshoop, with fares averaging around N$200. Buses depart from the southern edge of town at informal bus stops along Bismarck St.

CAR & MOTORCYCLE

Lüderitz and the scenery en route are worth the 334km trip from Keetmanshoop via the tarred B4.

Sperrgebiet National Park

Although it's been off-limits to the public for most of the last century, in 2008 the Namibian government inaugurated the Sperrgebiet. Known worldwide as the source of Namibia's exclusive diamonds, the Sperrgebiet, meaning Forbidden Area, could one day become the gem of Namibia's protected spaces. Geographically speaking, the park encompasses the northern tip of the Succulent Karoo Biome, an area of 26,000 sq km of dunes and mountains that appear dramatically stark, but represent one of 25 outstanding global 'hot spots' of unique biodiversity.

Sights

Kolmanskop Ghost Town HISTORIC TOWN

(admission N$55) Given that permits can be arranged from Namdeb with relative ease, the most popular excursion from Lüderitz is the ghost town of Kolmanskop. Named after an early Afrikaner trekker Jani Kolman, whose ox-wagon became bogged in the sand here, Kolmanskop was originally constructed as the Consolidated Diamond Mines headquarters. Today, Kolmanskop has been partially restored as a tourist attraction, and the sight of decrepit buildings being invaded by dunes is simply too surreal to describe.

You can turn up at any time, and you're not required to arrive as part of an organised tour, though you do need to purchase a permit in advance through either the NWR office (p900) in Lüderitz or a local tour operator.

Sleeping

There are no tourist lodges within the national park and bush camping is strictly forbidden. While it is likely that some form of accommodation will be constructed in the years to come, your best option in the meantime is to base yourself in Lüderitz.

Information

The **Forbidden Zone** was established in 1908 following the discovery of diamonds near Lüderitz. Although mining operations were localised along the coast, a huge swathe of southern Namibia was sectioned off in the interest of security.

The tight restrictions on access have helped to keep much of the area in a pristine condition. At the time of research, it appeared that disagreement between internal government departments was holding back further development and access for tourists in the park. Hopefully, once this has been resolved, more of this unique area will be open to visitors.

Getting There & Away

Do not attempt to access the Sperrgebiet in a private vehicle as you will be inviting a whole mess of trouble. The only exception to this is Kolmanskop, which can be accessed if you have the necessary permits.

UNDERSTAND NAMIBIA

Namibia Today

Namibia is presently one of the better performing democracies in Africa, and scores comparatively well in world development indicators assessed by the World Bank. Although affected by the global recession in 2008-09, its mineral deposits have ensured its economy rebounded as uranium and diamond prices recovered in 2010. In 2011, the government announced it had discovered an estimated 11 billion barrels of offshore oil reserves. With inflation topping 7% in late 2012, living costs are on the increase for most Namibians. Worryingly, food prices are part of the core reason for the increase.

Although Namibia is in relatively good shape compared to the region and for that matter the continent, poverty and disease are still enormous challenges for the government. Namibia also has one of the most unequal income distributions in the world.

History

Pre-Colonial Period

The first agriculturalists and iron workers of definite Bantu-speaking origin in Southern Africa belonged to the Gokomere culture. They settled in the temperate savannah and cooler uplands of Zimbabwe around 300-400 AD and were the first occupants of the Great Zimbabwe site, in the southeastern part of modern-day Zimbabwe, where a well sheltered valley presented an obvious place to settle. Cattle ranching became the mainstay of the community and earlier hunting and gathering San groups either retreated to the west or were enslaved or absorbed.

At the same time the San communities were also coming under pressure from the Khoikhoi people (the ancestors of the Nama), who probably entered the region from the south. The Khoikhoi were loosely organised into tribes and raised livestock. They gradually displaced the San, becoming the dominant group in the region until around 1500.

During the 16th century, the Herero arrived in Namibia from the Zambezi Valley and occupied the north and west of the country. As ambitious pastoralists, they inevitably came into conflict with the Khoikhoi over the best grazing lands and water sources. Eventually, given their superior strength and numbers, nearly all the indigenous Namibian groups submitted to the Herero.

By the late 19th century, a new Bantu group, the Owambo, settled in the north along the Okavango and Kunene rivers.

Colonial Period

Because Namibia has one of the world's most barren and inhospitable coastlines, it was largely ignored by European nations until relatively recently. The first European visitors were Portuguese mariners seeking a route to the Indies in the late 15th century, but they confined their activities to erecting stone crosses at certain points as navigational aids.

It wasn't until the last-minute scramble for colonies towards the end of the 19th century that Namibia was annexed by Germany (except for the enclave of Walvis Bay, which was taken in 1878 by the British for the Cape Colony). In 1904 the Herero launched a rebellion and, later that year, were joined by the Nama, but the rebellions were brutally suppressed.

The Owambo in the north were luckier and managed to avoid conquest until after the start of WWI, when they were overrun by Portuguese forces fighting on the side of the Allies. Soon after, the German colony abruptly came to an end when its forces surrendered to a South African expeditionary army also fighting on behalf of the Allies.

At the end of WWI, South Africa was given a mandate to rule the territory (then known as South West Africa) by the League of Nations. Following WWII, the mandate was renewed by the UN, who refused to sanction the annexation of the country by South Africa.

Undeterred, the South African government tightened its grip on the territory, and in 1949 it granted parliamentary representation to the white population. The bulk of southern Namibia's viable farmland was parcelled into some 6000 farms owned by white settlers, while indigenous families were confined by law to their 'reserves' (mainly in the east and the far north) and urban workplaces.

Nationalism & the Struggle for Independence

Forced labour had been the lot of most Namibians since the German annexation. This was one of the main factors that led to mass demonstrations and the development of nationalism in the late 1950s. Around this time, a number of political parties were formed and strikes organised. By 1960 most of these parties had merged to form the South-West African People's Organization (Swapo), which took the issue of South African occupation to the International Court of Justice.

The outcome was inconclusive, but in 1966 the United Nations (UN) General Assembly voted to terminate South Africa's mandate and set up a Council for South West Africa (in 1973 renamed the Commission for Namibia) to administer the territory. At the same time, Swapo launched its campaign of guerrilla warfare. The South African government reacted by firing on demonstrators and arresting thousands of activists.

In 1975 the Democratic Turnhalle Alliance (DTA) was officially established. Formed from a combination of white political interests and ethnic parties, it turned out to be a toothless debating chamber, which spent much of its time in litigation with the South African government over the scope of its responsibility.

The DTA was dissolved in 1983 after it had indicated it would accommodate members of Swapo. It was replaced by the Multiparty Conference, which had even less success and quickly disappeared. And so control of Namibia passed back to the South African-appointed administrator-general.

The failure of these attempts to set up an internal government did not deter South Africa from maintaining its grip on Namibia. It refused to negotiate on a UN-supervised program for Namibian independence until the estimated 19,000 Cuban troops were removed from neighbouring Angola. In response, Swapo intensified its guerrilla campaign.

In the end, however, it was neither the activities of Swapo alone nor the international sanctions that forced the South Africans to the negotiating table. The white Namibian population itself was growing tired of the war and the South African economy was suffering, making sustaining the war financially difficult.

The stage was finally set for negotiations on the country's future. Under the watch of the UN, the USA and the USSR, a deal was struck between Cuba, Angola, South Africa and Swapo, in which Cuban troops would be removed from Angola and South African troops from Namibia. This would be followed by UN-monitored elections held in November 1989 on the basis of universal suffrage. Swapo collected a clear majority of the votes but an insufficient number to give it the sole mandate to write the new constitution.

Independence

Following negotiations between the various parties, a constitution was adopted in February 1990. Independence was granted the following month under the presidency of the Swapo leader, Sam Nujoma. Initially, his policies focused on programs of reconstruction and national reconciliation to heal the wounds left by 25 years of armed struggle. In 1999, however, Nujoma had nearly served out his second (and constitutionally, his last) five-year term, and alarm bells sounded among watchdog groups when he changed the constitution to allow himself a third five-year term, which he won with nearly 77% of the vote. In 2004 he announced that he would finally be stepping down in favour of his chosen successor, Hifikepunye Pohamba. Since Pohamba took power, Namibia has profited considerably from the extraction and processing of minerals for export. Rich alluvial diamond deposits alongside uranium and other metal reserves put the country's budget into surplus in 2007 for the first time since independence.

People of Namibia

On a national level, Namibia is still struggling to attain a cohesive identity. History weighs heavy on generations who grew up during the struggle for independence. As a result, some formidable tensions endure between various social and racial groups. Although most travellers will be greeted with great warmth and curiosity, some people may experience unpleasant racism or apparently unwarranted hostility (this is not confined to black/white relations but can affect travellers of all ethnicities as Namibia's ethnic groups are extremely varied).

Most Namibians still live in homesteads in rural areas and lead typical village lives. Villages tend to be family and clan based and are presided over by an elected *elenga* (headman). The *elenga* is responsible for local affairs, everything from settling disputes to determining how communal lands are managed. He in turn reports to a senior headman, who represents a larger district comprised of several dozen villages. This system functions alongside Namibia's regional government bodies and enables traditional lifestyles to flourish side by side with the country's modern civic system.

Namibia's population in 2012 was estimated at 2,166,000 people, with an annual population growth rate of 0.82%. This figure takes into account the effects of excess mortality due to AIDS, which became the leading cause of death in Namibia in 1996. At approximately two people per square kilometre Namibia has one of Africa's lowest population densities.The population comprises 11 major ethnic groups: the majority of people are Owambo (50%), with the other ethnic groups each making up a relatively small percentage of the population: Kavango (9%), Herero/Himba (7%), Damara (7%), Caprivian (4%), Nama (5%), Afrikaner and German (6%), Baster (6.5%), San (1%) and Tswana (0.5%).

THE HIMBA

Even if you've never heard of the Himba prior to visiting Namibia, you'll quickly become enamoured with them. An ethnic group numbering not more than 50,000 people, the Himba are a seminomadic pastoral people that are closely related to the Herero, yet continue to live much as they have for generations.

The women in particular are famous for smearing themselves with a fragrant mixture of ochre, butter and bush herbs, which dyes their skin a burnt-orange hue, and serves as a natural sun block and insect repellent. As if this wasn't striking enough, they also use the mixture to cover their braided hair, which has an effect similar to dreadlocks. And of course, it is also worth mentioning that they tend to shun Western clothes, preferring to walk around bare-breasted, with little more than a pleated-animal skin covering their unmentionables.

The Arts

With its harsh environment and historically disparate and poor population, Namibia does not have a formal legacy of art and architecture. What it does have in abundance is a wealth of material arts: carvings, basketry, tapestry, beadwork and textile weaving.

There are some excellent festivals dedicated to the arts – for one of Namibia's newest, most exciting arts events head to Omaruru in September for the Artist's Trail (p883).

Food & Drink

Traditional Namibian food consists of a few staples, the most common of which is *oshifima*, a doughlike paste made from millet, and usually served with a stew of vegetables or meat. As a foreigner you'll rarely find such dishes on the menu, however, as most Namibian restaurants serve a variation on European-style foods, such as Italian or French, alongside an abundance of seafood dishes.

Environment

Despite its harsh climate, Namibia has some of the world's grandest national parks, ranging from world-famous wildlife-oriented Etosha National Park to the immense Namib-Naukluft Park, which protects vast dune fields, desert plains, wild mountains and unique flora. There are also the smaller reserves of the Caprivi region, the renowned Skeleton Coast Park and the awe-inspiring Fish River Canyon, which ranks among Africa's most spectacular sights.

Facilities in Namibian national parks are operated by the semiprivate NWR. Bookings may be made up to 12 months in advance, and fees must be paid by credit card before the bookings will be confirmed. Camping fees are good for up to four people; each additional person up to eight people will be charged extra. In addition, parks charge a daily admission fee per person and per vehicle, payable when you enter the park. Booking ahead is always advised for national parks. While you may be able to pick up accommodation at the last minute by just turning up at the park gates, it isn't recommended (especially for Etosha and Sossusvlei).

SURVIVAL GUIDE

Directory A–Z

ACCOMMODATION

Namibia is well equipped for travellers wanting accommodation of all price ranges – you can find backpacker accommodation in most places, camping areas throughout the country, midrange hotels and a healthy smattering of posh safari lodges. Quality is extremely high, and even budget lodges usually provide internet access, a pool, a bar and laundry facilities. Many hotels also serve meals and run travel centres.

The accommodation prices we list throughout this chapter are high season rates.

ACTIVITIES

Namibia is an outdoor enthusiast's dream. There are endless opportunities for hiking and camping. Swakopmund is the adrenalin capital of the country with everything from skydiving to sand boarding.

EMBASSIES & CONSULATES

All of the following representations are in Windhoek:

PRACTICALITIES

Electricity 220V to 240V AC, 50Hz and uses South African–style two- or three-round-pin plugs

Languages English, German, Afrikaans, Damara/Nama, Herero/Himba, Ovambo

News For English-language news, see www.namibianews.com

Radio The Namibian Broadcasting Corporation (NBC) operates a dozen or so radio stations in nine languages

Angolan Embassy (☎227535; 3 Dr Agostino Neto St; ⏰9am-3pm)

Botswanan Embassy (☎221941; 101 Nelson Mandela Ave; ⏰8am-1pm & 2-5pm)

British High Commission (☎274800; 116 Robert Mugabe Ave; ⏰8am-1pm & 2-5pm Mon-Thu, 8am-noon Fri)

French Embassy (☎276700; 1 Goethe St; ⏰9am-noon, afternoons by appointment Mon-Thu, 9am-noon Fri)

German Embassy (☎273100; 6th fl, Sanlam Centre, 154 Independence Ave; ⏰9am-noon Mon-Fri, plus 2-4pm Wed)

Kenyan High Commission (☎226836; 5th fl, Kenya House, 134 Robert Mugabe Ave; ⏰8.30am-1pm & 2-4.30pm Mon-Thu, to 3pm Fri)

Malawian Embassy (☎061-221391; 56 Bismarck St, Windhoek West; ⏰8am-noon & 2-5pm Mon-Fri)

South African High Commission (☎205 7111; cnr Jan Jonker St & Nelson Mandela Dr, Klein Windhoek; ⏰8.15am-12.15pm)

US Embassy (☎295 8500; 14 Lossen St; ⏰8.30am-noon Mon-Thu)

Zambian High Commission (☎237610; 22 Sam Nujoma Dr, cnr Mandume Ndemufeyo Ave; ⏰9am-1pm & 2-4pm)

Zimbabwean Embassy (☎228134; Gamsberg Bldg, cnr Independence Ave & Grimm St; ⏰8.30am-1pm & 2-4.45pm Mon-Thu, 8.30am-2pm Fri)

INTERNET ACCESS

Internet access is available at backpacker hostels, internet cafes and hotels in larger towns, and also at several tourist offices and remote lodges. Wi-fi is becoming far more common.

MAPS

Shell Roadmap – Namibia or *InfoMap Namibia* are the best reference for remote routes. *InfoMap* contains GPS coordinates and both companies produce maps of remote areas such as Namibia's far northwest and the Caprivi Strip.

MONEY

The Namibian dollar (N$) is divided into 100 cents, and is pegged to the South African rand, which is also legal tender in Namibia, at a rate of 1:1. This can be confusing, given that there are three sets of coins and notes in use, all with different sizes: old South African, new South African and Namibian. Namibian notes come in denominations of N$10, N$20, N$50, N$100 and N$200, and coins in values of 5, 10, 20 and 50 cents, and N$1 and N$5.

OPENING HOURS

Shopping 8am or 9am to 5pm or 6pm Monday to Friday, 9am to 1pm or 5pm Saturday; late-night shopping to 9pm Thursday or Friday

Eating Breakfast 8am to 10am, lunch 11am to 3pm, dinner 6pm to 10pm; some places open all day 8am to 10pm Monday to Saturday

Drinking & Entertainment 5pm to close (between midnight and 3am) Monday to Saturday

POST

Overseas airmail is normally faster than domestic post, and is limited only by the time it takes an article to reach Windhoek (which can be slow in the outer areas).

PUBLIC HOLIDAYS

Resort areas are busiest over both Namibian and South African school holidays, which normally occur from mid-December to mid-January, around Easter, from late July to early August and for two weeks in mid-October.

New Year's Day 1 January

Independence Day 21 March

Good Friday March or April

Easter Sunday March or April

Easter Monday March or April

Ascension Day April or May (40 days after Easter)

Workers' Day 1 May

Cassinga Day 4 May

Africa Day 25 May

Heroes' Day 26 August

Human Rights' Day 10 December

Christmas Day 25 December

Family/Boxing Day 26 December

SAFE TRAVEL

Theft isn't particularly rife, but take care walking alone at night, conceal your valuables in Windhoek and other towns around the country, and don't leave anything in sight inside a vehicle. Take the same precautions at campsites in towns – although there's no problem at campsites in national parks (not from humans anyway; just watch out for the monkeys).

East of Lüderitz, do not enter the prohibited diamond area, mainly south of the road to Keetmanshoop; well-armed patrols can be overly zealous.

TELEPHONE

Namibian area dialling codes all have three digits that begin with ☎06. When phoning from abroad, first dial the country code ☎264, followed by the area code without the leading zero.

Phonecards are sold at post offices and retail shops.

VISAS

Nationals of many countries, including Australia, the EU, USA and most Commonwealth countries do not need a visa to visit Namibia. Citizens of most Eastern European countries do require visas.

Visa Extensions

Tourists are granted an initial 90 days, which may be extended at the **Ministry of Home Affairs** (☎061-292 2111; www.mha.gov.na; cnr Kasino St & Independence Ave; ⏲8am-1pm Mon-Fri). For the best results, be there when the office opens at 8am, and submit your application at the 3rd floor offices (as opposed to the desk on the ground floor).

Visas for Onward Travel

Visas for the following neighbouring countries can be obtained in Windhoek, unless otherwise stated.

Angola Travellers should apply for a visa in their home country or attempt to secure an overland visa from the Angolan consulate in Oshakati, northern Namibia. Visas cost US$100 for 30 days. You will need a letter of invitation from somebody in Angola as well as a copy of their ID.

Botswana Visas on arrival are valid for 30 days and are available for free to passport holders from most Commonwealth countries (but not Ghana, India, Nigeria, Pakistan and Sri Lanka), all EU countries, the USA, South Africa, Namibia, Lesotho and Swaziland.

South Africa No visa is required by citizens of most Commonwealth countries (including Australia and the UK), most Western European countries, Japan and the USA; they'll be issued with a free entry permit on arrival, valid for a stay of up to 90 days. If you aren't entitled to an entry permit, you'll need to get a visa (also free) before you arrive.

Zambia Tourist visas are available at major borders, but it's important to note that you should have a Zambian visa before arrival if travelling by train or boat from Tanzania. Visas cost US$50 for single entry (up to one month) and US$80 for double entry (up to three months).

ℹ Getting There & Away

AIR

Most international flights into Namibia arrive at Windhoek's Chief Hosea Kutako International Airport, 42km east of the capital. Shorter-haul international flights may also use Windhoek's in-town Eros airport, although this airport mainly serves internal flights and light aircraft.

The main carrier is **Air Namibia** (www.airnamibia.com.na), which flies routes within Southern Africa as well as to Frankfurt. Most international airlines stop at Johannesburg or Cape Town in South Africa, where you'll typically switch to a **South African Airways** (www.flysaa.com) flight for your final leg to Windhoek.

Book well in advance for flights from the following neighbouring countries:

Botswana Air Namibia runs several flights a week between Windhoek and Maun.

Zimbabwe Air Namibia flies to Victoria Falls a few times a week.

Zambia You will need to transit through Jo'burg for flights to Lusaka or Livingstone.

LAND

To bring a foreign-registered vehicle into Namibia, you must purchase a N$160 road-use tax certificate at the border.

Angola

There are three border crossings between Namibia and Angola: at Ruacana–Calueque, Oshikango–Namacunde and Nkurenkuru–Cuangar (the crossing at Rundu). Travellers need an Angolan visa permitting overland entry, which is best obtained at the Angolan consulate in Oshakati. At Ruacana Falls, you can briefly enter the border area without a visa; just sign in at the border post.

Botswana

The most commonly used crossing is at Buitepos/Mamuno, between Windhoek and Ghanzi, although the border post at Mohembo/Mahango is also popular. The only other real option is the crossing at Ngoma Bridge across the Chobe River. The Mpalila Island/Kasane border is only available to guests who have booked accommodation at upmarket lodges on the island.

Drivers crossing the border at Mahango must secure an entry permit for Mahango Game Reserve. This is free if you're transiting, or US$3 per person per day plus US$3 per vehicle per day if you want to drive around the reserve (which is possible in a 2WD).

By Bus

The public transport options between Botswana and Namibia are few and far between. **Monnakgotla Transport** (☎067-350 0419; www.monnakgotla.co.bw) is your best bet – it runs a twice weekly service between Windhoek and

Gaborone on Friday and Sunday. The cost is N$440 one way.

South Africa

The **Intercape Mainliner** (☎ in South Africa 0861-287 287; www.intercape.co.za) service runs between Windhoek and Cape Town. Students and seniors receive a 15% discount. Bus tickets can be easily booked by phone or via the internet.

If you're driving, there are border crossings at Noordoewer, Vellorsdrif, Ariamsvlei and Klein Menasse–Aroab.

Zambia

A kilometre-long bridge (open from 7am to 6pm) spans the Zambezi between Katima Mulilo and Wenela, providing easy access to Livingstone and other destinations in Zambia. If you're heading to the falls, the road is now tarred all the way to Livingstone and is accessible by 2WD vehicle, even in the rainy season.

By Bus

The Intercape Mainliner (p906) service also runs between Windhoek and Livingstone.

Zimbabwe

There's no direct border crossing between Namibia and Zimbabwe. To get there you must take the Chobe National Park transit route from Ngoma Bridge through northern Botswana to Kasane/Kazungula, and from there to Victoria Falls.

Getting Around

AIR

Air Namibia (p882) has an extensive network of local flights operating out of Eros Airport. There are six flights per week to Rundu, Katima Mulilo and Ondangwa; and flights three times per week to Lüderitz and Oranjemund and daily to Walvis Bay.

CAR & MOTORCYCLE

The easiest way to get around Namibia is by road, and an excellent system of sealed roads runs the length of the country from the South African border at Noordoewer to Ngoma Bridge on the Botswanan border and Ruacana on the Angolan border in the northwest. Similarly, sealed spur roads connect the main north–south routes to Buitepos, Lüderitz, Swakopmund and Walvis Bay. Elsewhere, towns and most sites of interest are accessible on good gravel roads. C-numbered highways are well maintained and passable to all vehicles, and D-numbered roads, although a bit rougher, are mostly (but not always) passable to 2WD vehicles. In Kaokoveld, however, most D-numbered roads can only be negotiated with a 4WD.

For a compact car, the least-expensive hire companies charge US$45 to US$65 per day (the longer the hire period, the lower the daily rate) with unlimited kilometres. Hiring a 4WD vehicle opens up remote parts of the country, but it can get expensive at an average of US$85 to US$120 per day. Most companies include insurance and unlimited kilometres in their standard rates, but some require a minimum hire period before they allow unlimited kilometres.

It's cheaper to rent a car in South Africa and drive it into Namibia, but you need permission from the hire agency and paperwork to cross the borders. Drivers entering Namibia in a foreign-registered vehicle must pay a N$160 road tax at the border.

Avis (www.avis.com) Offices in Windhoek, Swakopmund, Tsumeb and Walvis Bay, as well as Chief Hosea Kutako International Airport.

Budget (www.budget.co.za) A big agency with offices in Windhoek and Walvis Bay, as well as Hosea Kutako International Airport.

HITCHING

Hitching is possible in Namibia, but it's illegal in national parks, and main highways see relatively little traffic. It's reasonably safe and fairly common, although hitching is never entirely safe and we don't recommend it. Travellers who hitch should understand that they are taking a small but potentially serious risk. Truck drivers generally expect to be paid per 100km, so agree on a price before climbing in. Your best options for lifts are Windhoek backpackers lodges, where you can post notices about rides.

LOCAL TRANSPORT

Namibia's bus services aren't extensive. Luxury services are limited to the **Intercape Mainliner** (☎ 061-227847; www.intercape.co.za), which has scheduled services from Windhoek to Swakopmund, Walvis Bay, Grootfontein, Rundu and Katima Mulilo. You're allowed only two items of baggage, which must not exceed a total of 30kg. Fares include meals.

There are also local combis, which depart when full and follow main routes around the country. From Windhoek's Rhino Park petrol station, they depart for dozens of destinations.

TOURS

Namibia's public transport system will get you to population centres, but not the sites most visitors want to see: the Skeleton Coast, Damaraland, Kaokoveld, Kunene River, Fish River Canyon, Sossusvlei, the Naukluft and so on. Therefore, even those who'd normally spurn organised tours may want to consider joining an inexpensive participation safari, or a more luxurious option.

As well as the following list, two recommended travel agencies in Windhoek are Cardboard Box Travel Shop (p882) and Chameleon Safaris (p882).

Kaokohimba Safaris (☎065-695106; www.kaoko-namibia.com) Kaokohimba organises cultural tours through Kaokoland and Damaraland and wildlife-viewing trips in Etosha National Park.

Turnstone Tours (☎403123; www.turnstone-tours.com) Turnstone runs 4WD camping tours around Swakopmund, including Sandwich Harbour and Damaraland.

Wild Dog Safaris (☎061-257642; www.wilddog-safaris.com) This friendly operation runs Northern Namibia Adventures and Southern Swings, and Etosha or Sossusvlei circuits, as well as longer participation camping safaris and accommodated excursions.

TRAINS

TransNamib (☎061-298 2032; www.transnamib.com.na) connects some major towns, but trains are extremely slow – as one reader remarked, moving 'at the pace of an energetic donkey cart'. In addition, passenger and freight cars are mixed on the same train, and trains tend to stop at every post, which means that rail travel isn't popular and services are rarely fully booked.

South Africa

☎27 / POP 49 MILLION

Includes ➡

Best Places to Eat

- Bistrot Bizerca (p915)
- Halfway House (p950)
- Narina Trogon (p940)
- Market (p931)
- Deli Street Café (p925)

Best Places to Stay

- 12 Decades Hotel (p937)
- Bulungula Lodge (p926)
- Hobbit Boutique Hotel (p936)
- Inkosana Lodge (p935)
- Palace of the Lost City (p948)

Why Go?

When Archbishop Desmond Tutu called South Africa the 'Rainbow Nation', he described the very essence of what makes this country extraordinary. The blend of cultures that his oft-used moniker referred to is instantly evident, but the country's diversity stretches far beyond its people.

You can sleep under the stars in russet-hued deserts or hike to craggy, sometimes snowcapped peaks. The *rondavels* (round, traditional-style and often thatched huts) which dot the hills of Zululand and the Wild Coast provide a bucolic antidote to the gritty bustle of large cities such as Johannesburg and Durban. Wildlife ranges from life-changing safari walks to up-close encounters with waddling penguins.

Variety continues in the cuisine, with the delicate (West Coast seafood), the hearty (Karoo meat feasts), the fragrant (Cape Malay stews) and the spicy (a Durban curry) all represented. And southwest sits Cape Town, where gourmands sip, surf and sunbathe in beautiful surrounds.

When to Go

Cape Town

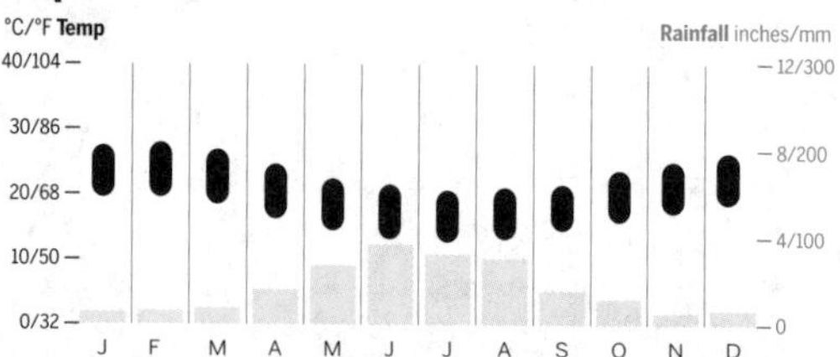

Apr–Aug Low season; ideal wildlife-watching conditions; whales on Western Cape coast.

Sep–Nov Spring flowers bloom; ideal weather for KwaZulu-Natal beaches and Karoo exploration.

Dec–Feb Coastal accommodation fills up; busy, vibrant time to be in the Cape.

CAPE TOWN

☎021 / POP 3.1 MILLION

Prepare to fall in love, as South Africa's 'Mother City' is an old pro at capturing people's hearts. And who wouldn't swoon at the sight of magnificent Table Mountain, its summit draped with cascading clouds, its flanks coated with unique flora and vineyards, its base fringed by golden beaches? Few cities can boast such a wonderful national park at its heart.

From the brightly painted facades of the Bo-Kaap to striking street art and the Afro-chic decor of countless guesthouses, this is one good-looking metropolis.

Above all, it's a multicultural city where nearly everyone has a fascinating, sometimes heartbreaking, story to tell. When the time comes to leave, you may find your heart breaking too.

SET YOUR BUDGET

Budget

- Dorm bed R120
- Cafe lunch R60
- Beer from store R8
- Local bus ride R5

Midrange

- Hotel room R850
- Two-course dinner R120
- Beer in bar R20
- Short taxi ride R50

Top End

- Hotel room R2000
- Two-course dinner R180
- Glass of wine R25
- Daily car hire R200

Sights & Activities

City Bowl

District Six Museum MUSEUM
(Map p916; ☎021-466 7200; www.districtsix.co.za; 25A Buitenkant St, City Bowl; adult/child R30/5, walking tour per person R120; ⊙9am-2pm Mon, 9am-4pm Tue-Sat) This emotionally moving museum tells the story of District Six, a once multicultural neighbourhood that was destroyed by forced evictions in the 1960s and 1970s. Most township tours stop here.

Long Street NEIGHBOURHOOD
(Map p916; City Bowl; Castle) Whether you come to browse the secondhand bookshops and streetwear boutiques, or to party at the bars and clubs, a stroll along Long St is an essential element of a Cape Town visit.

Gardens & Around

Table Mountain National Park PARK
(☎021-712 2337; www.sanparks.org/parks/table_mountain) This park stretches from flat-topped Table Mountain to Cape Point. For the vast majority of visitors the main attraction is the 1086m-high mountain itself, the top of which can easily be accessed by the **Table Mountain Aerial Cableway** (Map p912; ☎021-424 8181; www.tablemountain.net; Tafelberg Rd; 1-way/return adult R105/205, child R53/100; ⊙8.30am-7pm Feb-Nov, 8am-10pm Dec & Jan), which runs every 10/20 minutes in high/low season.

Operating hours change monthly and the cable car doesn't operate when it's dangerously windy. Look out for the 'tablecloth' – a dense cloud that will obscure the fabulous views. The best visibility and conditions are generally early in the morning or in the evening.

Green Point & Waterfront

Robben Island & Nelson Mandela Gateway LANDMARK
(☎021-413 4220; www.robben-island.org.za; adult/child R230/120; ⊙ferries depart at 9am, 11am, 1pm & 3pm, weather permitting; Waterfront) Used as a prison from the early days of the Vereenigde Oost-Indische Companie (VOC; Dutch East India Company) right up until 1996, this Unesco World Heritage Site is preserved as a memorial to those, such as Nelson Mandela, who were incarcerated here.

A visit to Robben Island is highly recommended but is not without its drawbacks. In peak times tickets often sell out days beforehand. Reserve well in advance via the web, or book a ticket in conjunction with a township tour. The packed guided tour allows two hours on the island (plus a 30-minute boat ride in both directions). A former inmate will lead you around the prison. Tours also include a 45-minute bus ride around the island.

Tours depart from the **Nelson Mandela Gateway** (Map p912; admission free; ⊙9am-8.30pm) beside the clock tower at the Waterfront. There's a worthwhile **museum** here, too.

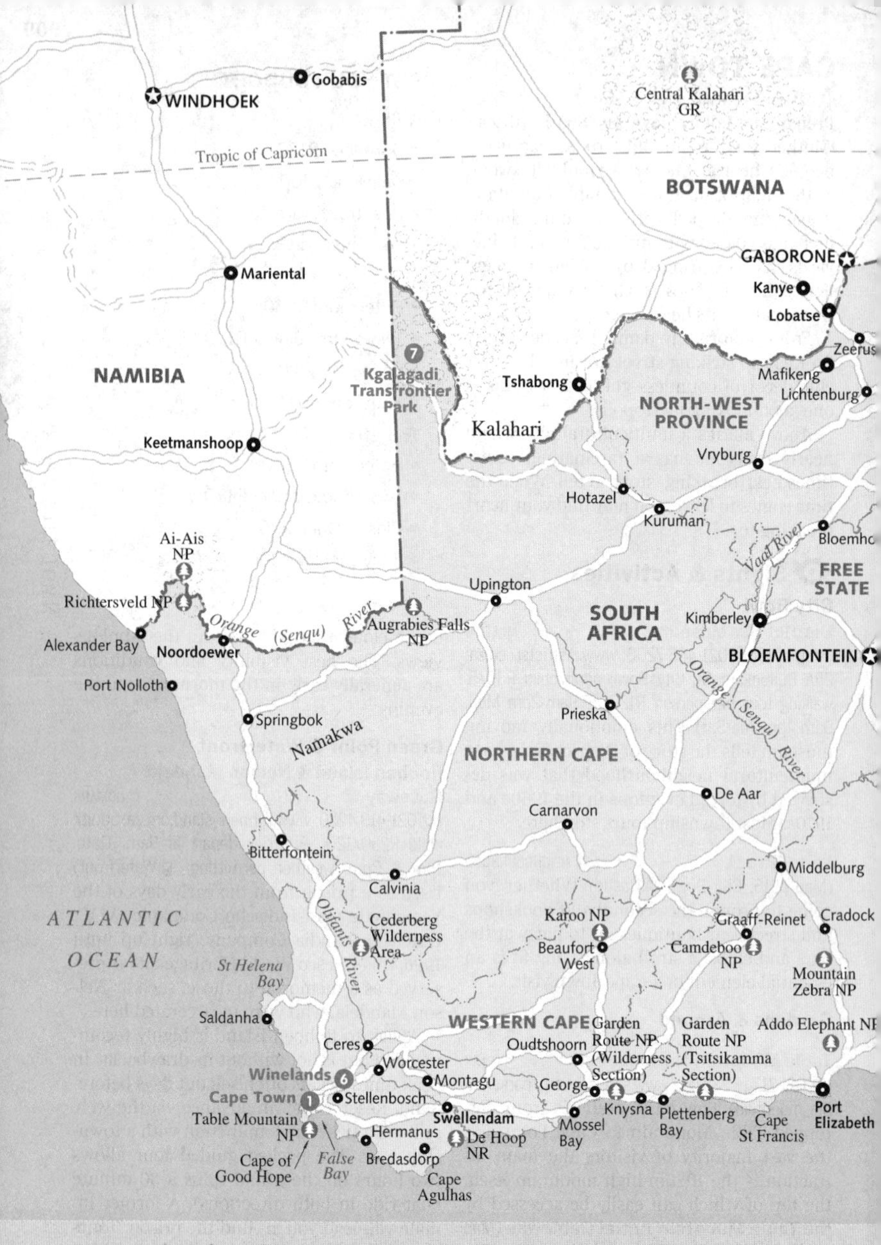

South Africa Highlights

1. Tackling Table Mountain, paddling with penguins or just lazing on Atlantic beaches in **Cape Town** (p909).

2. Joining rangers at **Kruger National Park** (p948) on a safari of the most involving kind – on foot.

3. Hiking past waterfalls and San rock art towards mountain peaks in the **uKhahlamba-Drakensberg** (p934).

4. Brushing up on recent history and learning about township life in **Soweto** (p944).

5. Choosing between a hammock and the beach at a

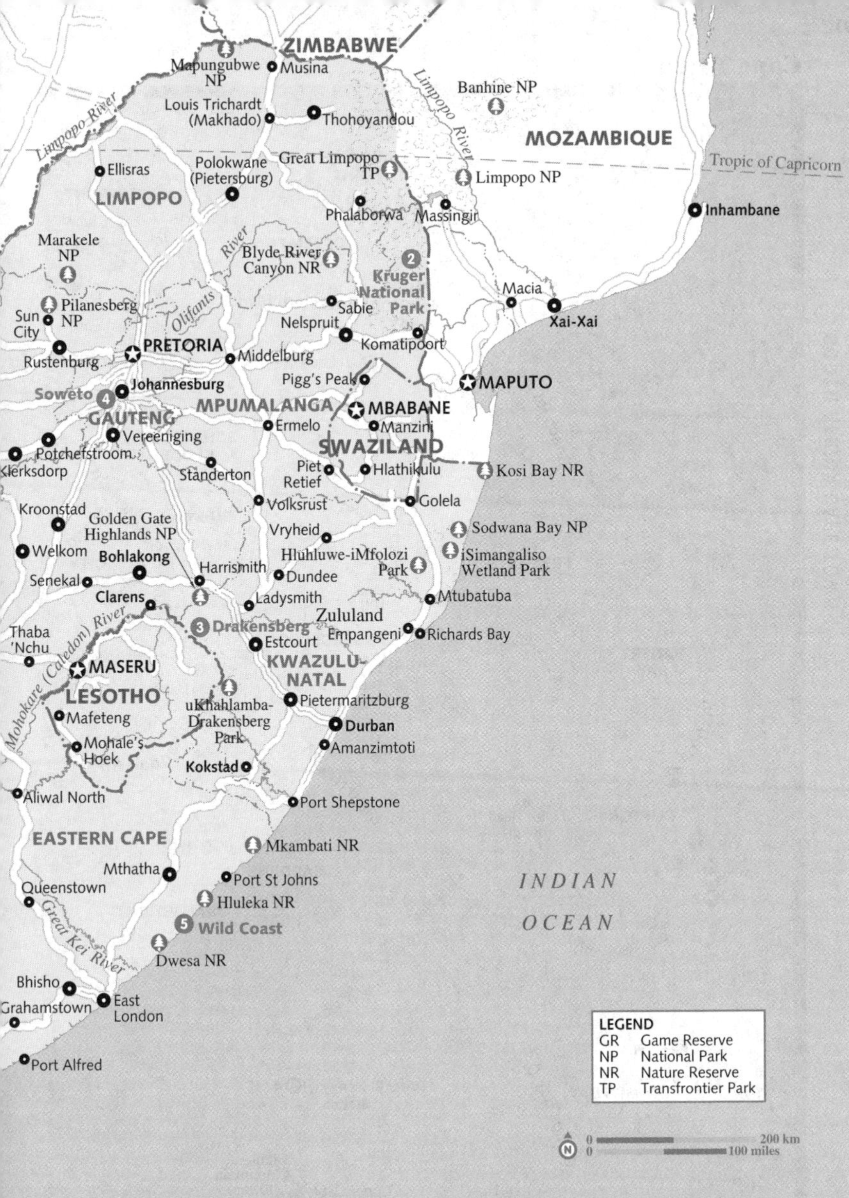

laid-back hostel along the **Wild Coast** (p926).

6 Sipping on world-class wines and enjoying posh nosh in the magnificent Cape Dutch surrounds of the **Winelands** (p920).

7 Watching a black-maned lion nap under a thorn tree in the crimson Kalahari wonderland of **Kgalagadi Transfrontier Park** (p951).

Cape Town

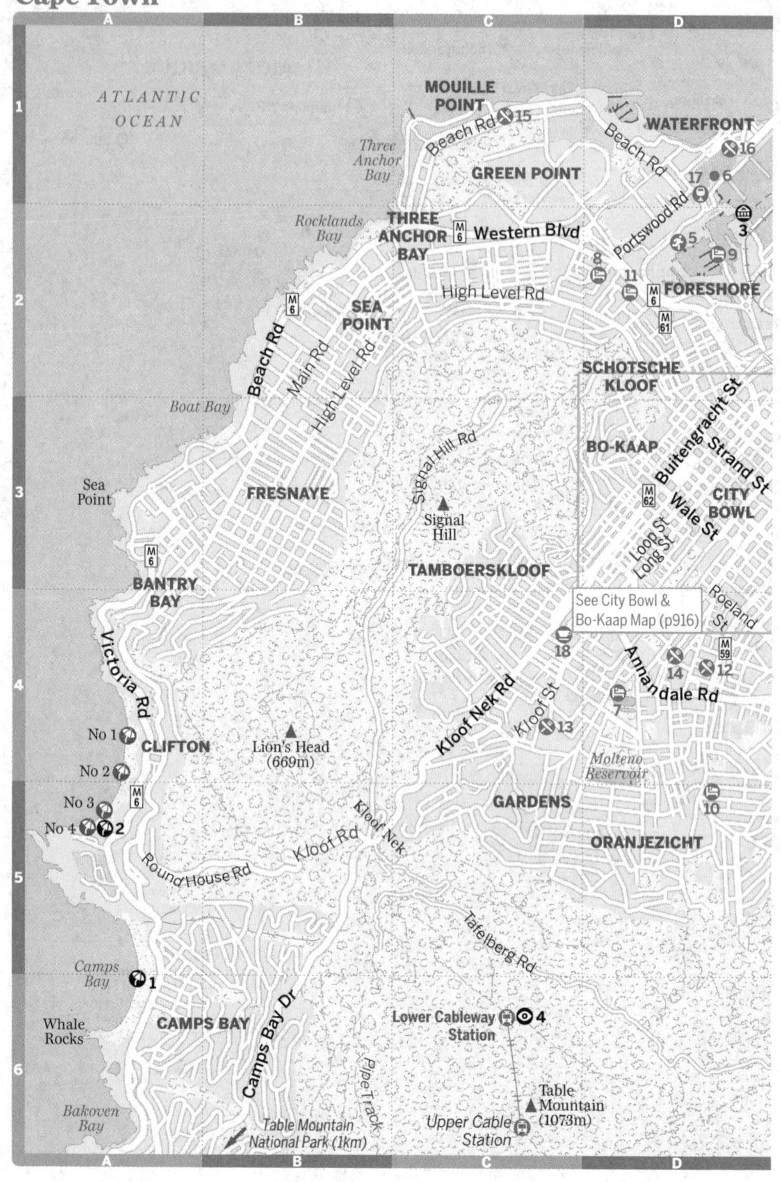

Victoria & Alfred (V&A) Waterfront WATERFRONT (www.waterfront.co.za; ⌚9am-9pm) Commonly referred to as just the Waterfront, this tourist-orientated precinct offers masses of shops, restaurants, bars, cinemas and other attractions, including cruises of the harbour.

Atlantic Coast

Cape Town's Atlantic Coast is all about spectacular scenery and soft-sand beaches. The

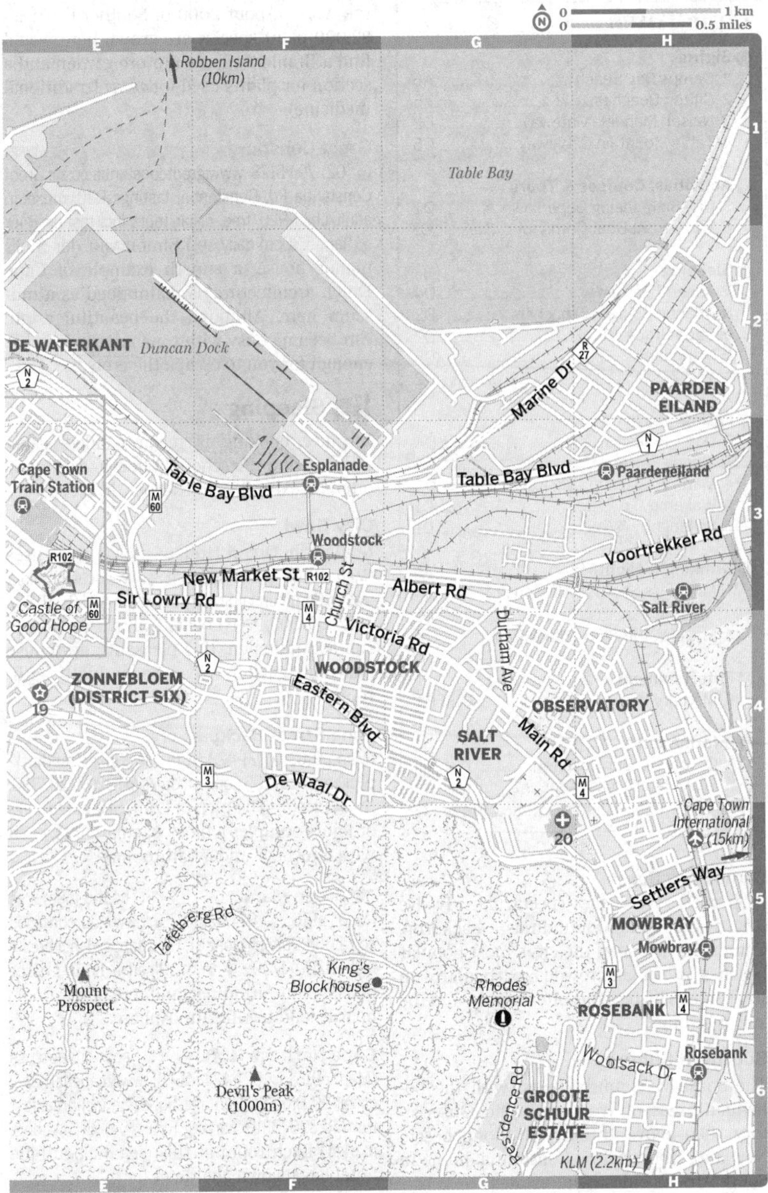

water at them all – flowing straight from the Antarctic – is freezing.

Clifton Beaches BEACHES

(Map p912) Almost always sheltered from the wind, Clifton's four linked beaches are Cape Town's top sunbathing spots. Local lore has it that No 1 and No 2 beaches are for models and confirmed narcissists, No 3 is the gay beach, and No 4 is for families.

Cape Town

Sights

1 Camps Bay Beach ... A6
2 Clifton Beaches ... A5
3 Nelson Mandela Gateway ... D2
4 Table Mountain Cableway ... C6

Activities, Courses & Tours

5 City Sightseeing Cape Town ... D2
6 Waterfront Boat Company ... D1

Sleeping

7 Ashanti Gardens ... D4
8 Atlantic Point Backpackers ... D2
9 Cape Grace ... D2
10 Mannabay ... D5
11 Villa Zest ... D2

Eating

12 Dog's Bollocks ... D4
13 Manna Epicure ... C4
14 Maria's ... D4
15 Wakame ... C1
16 Willoughby & Co ... D1

Drinking & Nightlife

17 Mitchell's Scottish Ale House & Brewery ... D1
18 Power & the Glory/Black Ram ... C4

Entertainment

19 Mercury Live & Lounge ... E4

Information

20 Groote Schuur Hospital ... G5
V&A Waterfront Visitor Information Centre ... (see 17)

Camps Bay Beach BEACH

(Map p912) With the spectacular Twelve Apostles of Table Mountain as a backdrop, Camps Bay is one of the city's most popular beaches. It can get crowded, particularly on weekends. The beach is often windy, and the surf is strong.

Southern Suburbs

The Southern Suburbs begin with the bohemian areas of Woodstock and Observatory then move through to Rondebosch, Newlands and wealthy Constantia, home to South Africa's oldest wine estates.

Kirstenbosch Botanical Gardens GARDENS

(021-799 8782; www.sanbi.org/gardens/kirstenbosch; Rhodes Dr, Newlands; adult/child R42/10; 8am-7pm Sep-Mar, 8am-6pm Apr-Aug, conservatory 9am-5pm) Location and unique flora combine to make this 36-hectare botanical garden among the most beautiful in the world. About 9000 of Southern Africa's 22,000 plant species are grown here. You'll find a Braille trail, a sculpture garden and a section for plants used for *muti* (traditional medicine).

Groot Constantia WINERY

(021-794 5128; www.grootconstantia.co.za; Groot Constantia Rd, Constantia; tastings R30, museum adult/child R20/free, cellar tours incl tasting R40; 9am-5.30pm daily; P) Simon van der Stel's manor house, a superb example of Cape Dutch architecture, is maintained as a museum here. Although the beautiful estate can become busy with tour groups, it is big enough for you to escape the crowds.

Sleeping

Advance booking is recommended, especially during the school holidays. Parking is often an extra R30 to R70 per day.

City Bowl

Scalabrini Guest House HOSTEL $

(Map p916; 021-465 6433; www.scalabrini.org.za; 47 Commercial St, City Bowl; dm/s/d/tw R180/350/500/500;) Located above a charity-run soup kitchen, this pleasant guesthouse has immaculately clean rooms with bathrooms.

Long Street Backpackers HOSTEL $

(Map p916; 021-423 0615; www.longstreetbackpackers.co.za; 209 Long St; dm/s/d R120/220/330; ; Bloem) The pick of Long St's backpacker joints occupies a block of small flats, each with four beds and a bathroom.

★ **Dutch Manor** BOUTIQUE HOTEL $$

(Map p916; 021-422 4767; www.dutchmanor.co.za; 158 Buitengracht St, Bo-Kaap; s/d incl breakfast R1200/1700; ; Bloem) Four-poster beds, giant armoires and creaking floorboards lend terrific atmosphere.

Cape Heritage Hotel BOUTIQUE HOTEL $$

(Map p916; 021-424 4646; www.capeheritage.co.za; 90 Bree St, Heritage Sq; d/ste incl breakfast from R2390/3310, parking R55; P@; Longmarket) Each room at this elegant boutique hotel has its own character.

Grand Daddy Hotel BOUTIQUE HOTEL $$

(Map p916; 021-424 7247; www.granddaddy.co.za; 38 Long St, City Bowl; r or trailer incl breakfast from R1800, parking per day R30; P@; Castle) The star attraction is the rooftop trailer park comprising vintage Airstream trailers.

HIKING TABLE MOUNTAIN

There are hundreds of hiking trails, but remember that the mountain is more than 1000m high, conditions can become treacherous quickly and it's easy to get lost. Tell someone where you're going and never hike alone. **Venture Forth** (☎021-554 3225, 086 110 6548; www.ventureforth.co.za; 4 Drummond Rd, West Beach), among other companies, offers a range of hikes on Table Mountain.

Overnight hikes include the two-day/one-night, 33.8km **Cape of Good Hope Trail** and the five-day, four-night, 80km **Hoerikwaggo Trail** running from Cape Point to the upper cable-car station. The former has to be booked and includes accommodation; the latter can be done freely.

Taj Cape Town LUXURY HOTEL $$$
(Map p916; ☎021-819 2000; www.tajhotels.com; Wale St; s/d/ste incl breakfast R5000/5200/10,000; P ❄ @ ≋; 🚌Dorp) Chic contemporary-styled rooms, many offering views of Table Mountain. Service and facilities are top grade.

Gardens & Around

Backpack HOSTEL $$
(Map p916; ☎021-423 4530; www.backpackers.co.za; 74 New Church St, Tamboerskloof; dm/s/d without bathroom R180/500/750, s/d R600/900, parking per day R20; P @ ≋; 🚌Buitensingel) This boutique backpackers offers pleasant dorms and charmingly decorated private rooms.

Ashanti Gardens HOSTEL $
(Map p912; ☎021-423 8721; www.ashanti.co.za; 11 Hof St, Gardens; dm/s/d without bathroom R160/350/500, d R700; P @ ≋; 🚌Government Avenue) You can camp on the lawn (R80 per person) and there are excellent self-catering rooms with bathrooms. There's a lively bar and deck.

★**Mannabay** BOUTIQUE HOTEL $$
(Map p912; ☎021-461 1094; www.mannabay.com; 1 Denholm Rd, Oranjezicht; r/ste incl breakfast from R1425/4000; P ❄ @ ≋) This gorgeous luxury property offers great views and seven guest rooms, each uniquely decorated.

Green Point & Waterfront

Atlantic Point Backpackers HOSTEL $$
(Map p912; ☎021-433 1663; www.atlanticpoint.co.za; 2 Cavalcade Rd, Green Point; dm/d without bathroom from R145/550, d R700; P @) Rates at this imaginatively designed place include a basic breakfast, wi-fi and parking.

Villa Zest BOUTIQUE HOTEL $$
(Map p912; ☎021-433 1246; www.villazest.co.za; 2 Braemar Rd, Green Point; s/d/ste incl breakfast R1790/1990/2390; P ❄ @ ≋) A quirkily decorated boutique hotel with seven guest rooms.

Cape Grace LUXURY HOTEL $$$
(Map p912; ☎021-410 7100; www.capegrace.com; West Quay Road, Waterfront; s/d/ste incl breakfast from R5290/5450/12,155; P ❄ @ ≋; 🚌Breakwater) A lovely luxury hotel with a winning combination of antiques and hand-painted decor.

Eating

City Bowl & Around

Long St has many great places to eat, plus fantastic street life. Head to the Bo-Kaap to sample authentic Cape Malay dishes.

Jason Bakery BAKERY, CAFE $
(Map p916; ☎021-424 5644; www.jasonbakery.com; 185 Bree St; mains R50; ⏲7am-3.30pm Mon-Fri, 8am-2pm Sat; 🚌Bloem) This popular cafe makes splendid breakfasts and sandwiches and serves decent coffee, craft beers and MCC (Methode Cap Classique or wine made in the traditional Champagne method) bubbles.

★**Bistrot Bizerca** FRENCH $$
(Map p916; ☎021-423 8888; www.bizerca.com; 98 Shortmarket St, Heritage Sq; mains R110-150; ⏲lunch & dinner Mon-Fri, dinner Sat; P; 🚌Longmarket) The atmosphere is contemporary and relaxed, and the expertly prepared food is bursting with flavour.

Africa Café AFRICAN $$
(Map p916; ☎021-422 0221; www.africacafe.co.za; 108 Shortmarket St; set banquets R245; ⏲cafe

CRUISES

If only to take in the panoramic view of Table Mountain from the water, a cruise into Table Bay should not be missed. **Waterfront Boat Company** (Map p912; ☎021-418 5806; www.waterfrontboats.co.za; Quay 5, Shop 5) offers a variety of cruises, including highly recommended 1½-hour sunset cruises (R200).

City Bowl & Bo-Kaap

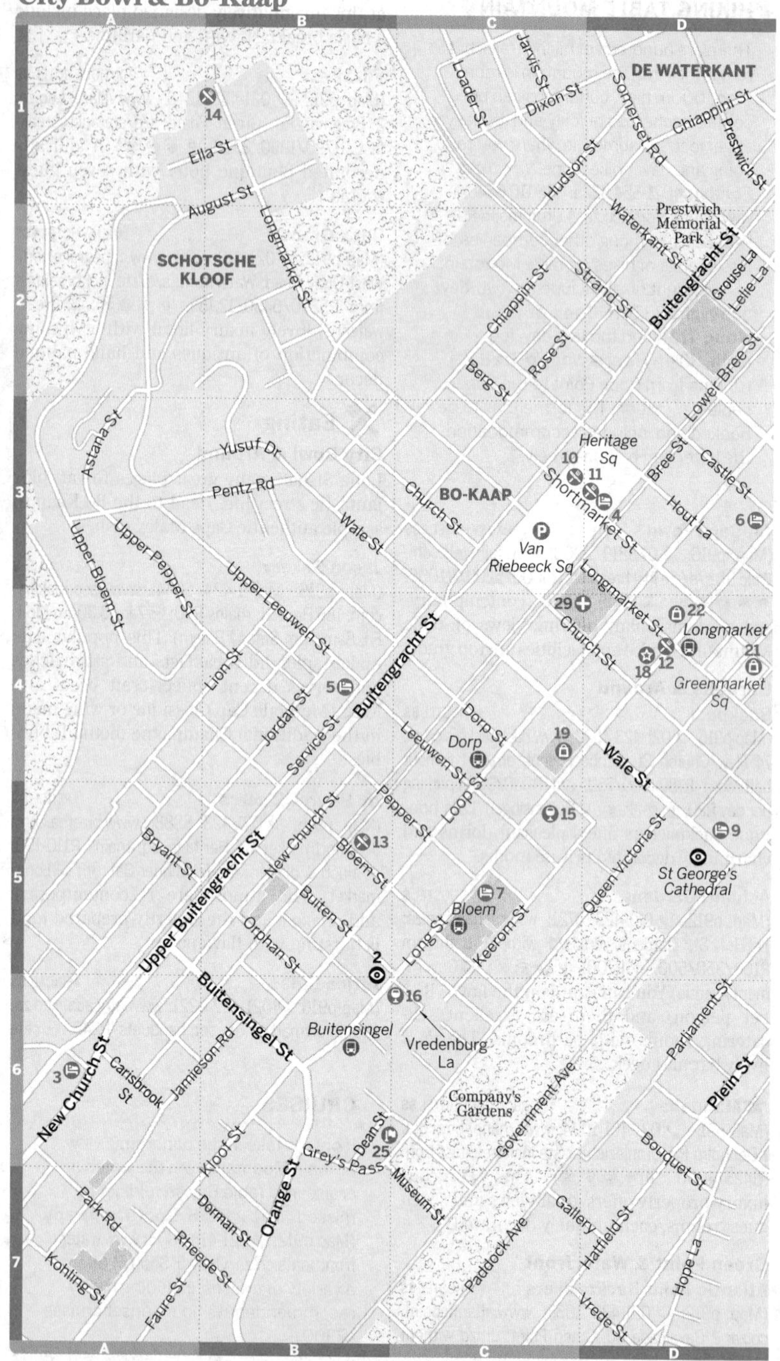

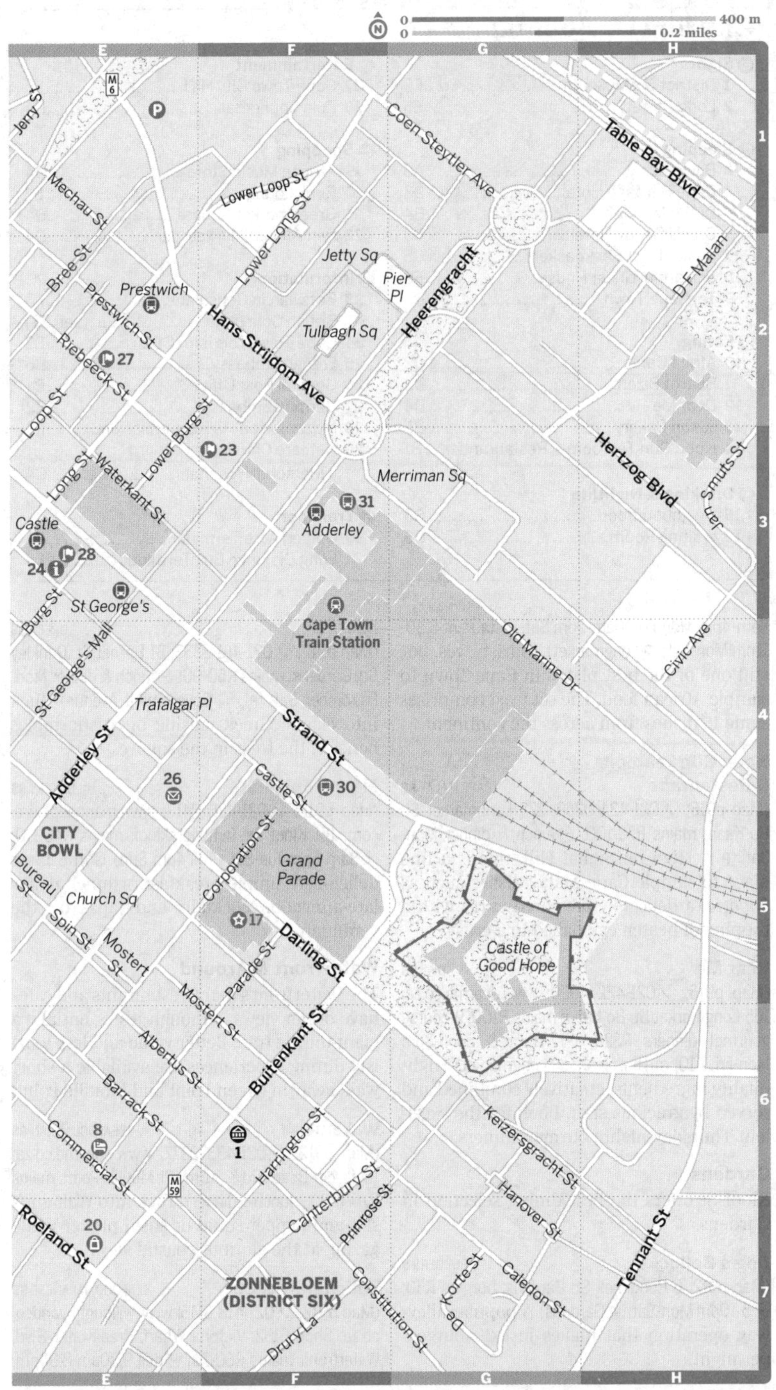

0
400 m
0
0.2 miles
E
F
G
H
Jerry St
Mechau St
Bree St
Prestwich
Prestwich St
Riebeeck St
27
Loop St
Lower Loop St
Lower Long St
Hans Strijdom Ave
Lower Burg St
23
Long St
Waterkant St
Castle
28
24
Burg St
St George's
St George's Mall
Trafalgar Pl
Adderley St
26
CITY
BOWL
Bureau St
Church Sq
Spin St
Mostert St
Mostert St
Albertus St
Barrack St
8
Commercial St
Roeland St
20
Coen Steytler Ave
Table Bay Blvd
Jetty Sq
Pier Pl
Tulbagh Sq
Heerengracht
D F Malan
Merriman Sq
Hertzog Blvd
Jan Smuts St
31
Adderley
Cape Town
Train Station
Old Marine Dr
Civic Ave
Strand St
Castle St
30
Corporation St
Grand
Parade
17
Darling St
Parade St
Buitenkant St
Castle of
Good Hope
1
Harrington St
Canterbury St
Primrose St
Keizersgracht St
Hanover St
Tennant St
De Korte St
Caledon St
Constitution St
ZONNEBLOEM
(DISTRICT SIX)
Drury La
1
2
3
4
5
6
7

City Bowl & Bo-Kaap

Sights
1 District Six Museum ... F6
2 Long Street ... B5

Sleeping
3 Backpack ... A6
4 Cape Heritage Hotel ... D3
5 Dutch Manor ... B4
6 Grand Daddy Hotel ... D3
7 Long Street Backpackers ... C5
8 Scalabrini Guest House ... E6
9 Taj Cape Town ... D5

Eating
10 Africa Café ... C3
11 Bistrot Bizerca ... D3
12 Dear Me ... D4
13 Jason Bakery ... B5
14 Noon Gun Tearoom & Restaurant ... B1

Drinking & Nightlife
15 Neighbourhood ... C5
16 Waiting Room ... C6

Entertainment
17 Cape Town City Hall ... F5
18 Zula Sound Bar ... D4

Shopping
19 African Music Store ... C4
20 Book Lounge ... E7
21 Greenmarket Square ... D4
22 Pan African Market ... D4

Information
23 Botswanan Consulate ... F3
British Consulate ... (see 23)
24 Cape Town Tourism (CBD) ... E3
25 French Embassy ... B6
26 General Post Office ... E4
27 German Embassy ... E2
28 Mozambican High Commission ... E3
29 Netcare Christiaan Barnard Memorial Hospital ... C4

Transport
30 Golden Acre Terminal ... F4
31 Long Distance Bus Terminus ... F3

8am-4pm Mon-Fri, 10am-2pm Sat, restaurant 6.30-11pm Mon-Sat; Longmarket) Touristy, yes, but still one of the best places in Cape Town to sample African food. The set feast comprises some 15 dishes from across the continent.

Noon Gun Tearoom & Restaurant CAPE MALAY $$
(Map p916; 021-424 0259; 273 Longmarket St, Bo-Kaap; mains R70-100; lunch & dinner Mon-Sat; P) High on Signal Hill, this is a fine place to sample Cape Malay dishes such as *bobotie* (a delicately flavoured curry with a topping of beaten egg baked to a crust).

Dear Me DELI $$
(Map p916; 021-422 4920; www.dearme.co.za; 165 Longmarket St, Bo Kaap; mains R100, 9-course gourmet dinners R320; 7-11am & noon-3pm Mon-Fri, 7-10pm Thu; ; Longmarket) High-quality ingredients, creatively combined and served by gracious staff. Book for the excellent Thursday-night gourmet dinners.

Gardens

Kloof St offers the best dining selection in Gardens.

Dog's Bollocks BURGERS $
(Map p912; 6 Roodehek St, Gardens; burgers R50; 5-10pm Mon-Sat; Gardens) A popular alleyway operation that makes just 30 burgers per night.

Maria's GREEK $$
(Map p912; 021-461 3333; 31 Barnet St, Dunkley Sq, Gardens; mains R50-90; lunch & dinner Mon-Fri, dinner Sat; P; Government Avenue) Tuck into classic Greek cuisine on rustic tables beneath the trees in the square.

Manna Epicure BAKERY $$
(Map p912; 021-426 2413; www.mannaepicure.com; 151 Kloof St, Tamboerskloof; mains R40-110; 8am-5pm Tue-Sat, until 4pm Sun) Come for a deliciously simple breakfast or lunch or for late-afternoon cocktails and tapas on the verandah.

Waterfront & Around

The Waterfront's many restaurants and cafes have ocean views, although it's essentially a giant tourist trap. Better value and less touristy dining experiences are available a short walk away in Green Point and Mouille Point.

Wakame SEAFOOD, ASIAN $$
(Map p912; 021-433 2377; www.wakame.co.za; 1st flr, cnr Beach Rd & Surrey Pl, Mouille Point; mains R70-120; lunch & dinner) Tuck into Wakame's salt-and-pepper squid or sushi platter while gazing at the glorious coastal view.

Willoughby & Co SEAFOOD, JAPANESE $$
(Map p912; 021-418 6115; www.willoughbyandco.co.za; Shop 6132, Victoria Wharf, Breakwater Blvd, Waterfront; mains R60-70; deli 9.30am-8.30pm,

restaurant noon-10.30pm; P; Waterfront) Huge servings of sushi are the standout on the good-value menu at this casual eatery-cum-fishmongers.

Drinking & Nightlife

Head out on a Friday or Saturday night to Long St, De Waterkant or Camps Bay.

Waiting Room BAR
(Map p916; 021-422 4536; 273 Long St; cover Fri & Sat R20; 6pm-2am Mon-Sat; Bloem) This hip bar has retro furniture, DJs spinning funky tunes and a roof deck for admiring the city lights.

Neighbourhood BAR
(Map p916; 021-424 7260; www.goodinthehood.co.za; 163 Long St; noon-late Mon-Sat; Dorp) A relaxed bar and casual restaurant styled after British gastropubs.

Power & the Glory/Black Ram CAFE, BAR
(Map p912; 021-422 2108; 13B Kloof Nek Rd, Tamboerskloof; cafe 8am-10pm, bar 5pm-late Mon-Sat) The coffee and food are good but it's the cosy bar with its range of local craft beers that packs the hipsters in.

Mitchell's Scottish Ale House & Brewery PUB
(Map p912; 021-418 5074; www.mitchellsbreweries.co.za; East Pier Rd, Waterfront; 10am-2am; Breakwater) This unpretentious and perpetually packed pub serves Mitchell's beers, brewed at the country's oldest microbrewery in Knysna.

Entertainment

Cape Town City Hall MUSIC
(Map p916; www.cityhallsessions.co.za; Darling St, City Bowl; St George's) One of several venues where the **Cape Philharmonic Orchestra** (www.cpo.org.za) performs. Local choirs also take advantage of the auditorium's acoustics.

Mercury Live & Lounge LIVE MUSIC, DJ
(Map p912; www.mercuryl.co.za; 43 De Villiers St, District Six; cover R30-50) A young, studenty crowd frequents Cape Town's premier rock venue, host to top South African bands and overseas acts.

Zula Sound Bar LIVE MUSIC, COMEDY
(Map p916; 021-424 2442; www.zulabar.co.za; 98 Long St, City Bowl; cover from R30; Longmarket) There's a cafe, bar and a range of performance spaces here. The line-up includes local bands, DJs and comedy.

SURFING

The **Cape Peninsula** has superb surfing possibilities, catering for all abilities. In general, the best surf is along the Atlantic side, while **Muizenberg** is the top spot for novices and the only place that rents out boards and wetsuits.

Shopping

Great buys include local township-produced items, such as beadwork dolls, toys made from recycled tin cans and wire sculptures.

Central markets include **Pan African Market** (Map p916; www.panafrican.co.za; 76 Long St, City Bowl; 8.30am-5.30pm Mon-Fri, 8.30am-3.30pm Sat in summer; 9am-5pm Mon-Fri, 9am-3pm Sat winter; Longmarket) and **Greenmarket Sq** (Map p916; cnr Shortmarket & Burg Sts; 9am-5pm), which is in a great area for galleries and shops.

Music lovers should head straight for Long St's **African Music Store** (Map p916; 021-426 0857; www.africanmusicstore.co.za; 134 Long St; Dorp).

For books, head to the **Book Lounge** (Map p916; 021-462 2425; www.booklounge.co.za; 71 Roeland St, The Fringe; 9.30am-7.30pm Mon-Fri, 8.30am-6pm Sat, 10am-4pm Sun), close to the District Six Museum.

Information

DANGERS & ANNOYANCES

Cape Town's relaxed vibe can instil a false sense of security. Thefts are most likely to happen when visitors do something foolish such as leaving their gear on a beach while they go swimming.

Paranoia is not required, but common sense is. There is tremendous poverty on the peninsula and the 'informal redistribution of wealth' is fairly common. The townships on the Cape Flats have an appalling crime rate; visit only with a trustworthy guide or on a tour.

While the city centre is generally safe to walk around, always listen to local advice on where to avoid.

Swimming at any of the Cape beaches is potentially hazardous, especially for those inexperienced in surf. Check for warning signs and only swim in patrolled areas.

INTERNET ACCESS

Cape Town is one of Africa's most wired cities. Most hotels and hostels offer internet facilities and you'll seldom have to hunt far for a wi-fi network or internet cafe.

MEDICAL SERVICES

Groote Schuur Hospital (Map p912; ☎021-404 9111; www.westerncape.gov.za/your_gov/5972; Main Rd, Observatory)

Netcare Christiaan Barnard Memorial Hospital (Map p916; ☎021-480 6111; www.netcare.co.za; 181 Longmarket St, City Bowl)

MONEY

Money can be changed at the airport and there are ATMs all over town.

POST

General Post Office (Map p916; www.postoffice.co.za; Parliament St, City Bowl; ⌚8am-4.30pm Mon-Fri, 8am-noon Sat)

TOURIST INFORMATION

At the head office of **Cape Town Tourism** (Map p916; ☎021-487 6800; www.capetown.travel; Pinnacle Bldg, cnr Castle & Burg Sts; ⌚8am-5.30pm Mon-Fri, 8.30am-2pm Sat, 9am-1pm Sun), advisers can book accommodation, tours and car hire.

Other Cape Town Tourism branches are at **Kirstenbosch Visitor Information Centre** (☎021-762 0687; www.capetown.travel; Rhodes Dr, Kirstenbosch Botanical Gardens, Main Entrance, Newlands; ⌚8am-5pm) and the **V&A Waterfront Visitor Information Centre** (Map p912; ☎021-408 7600; www.capetown.travel; Dock Rd, V&A Waterfront; ⌚9am-6pm).

Getting There & Away

Cape Town International Airport (☎021-937 1200; www.acsa.co.za) is 20km east of the city centre.

Apart from **South African Airways** (SAA; ☎0861 359 722; www.flysaa.com), two budget airlines, **Kulula** (☎0861 585 852; www.kulula.com) and **Mango** (☎021-815 4100, 086 100 1234; www.flymango.com), connect Cape Town with the major South African cities. During the summer, you could pick up a one-way flight to Durban for a little over R1000; to Jo'burg for less than R900.

Buses arrive and depart from the **bus terminus** (Map p916; cnr Adderley St & Old Marine Dr) next to Cape Town's **Central Train Station** (☎021-449 2991; cnr Adderley & Strand Sts). You'll find their booking offices here too.

All trains, including the recommended tourist- and premier-class services of **Shosholoza Meyl** (☎086-000 8888; www.shosholozameyl.co.za) to destinations including Jo'burg, leave from the main train station.

Getting Around

MyCiTi (☎086 010 3089, 0800 656 463; www.capetown.gov.za/myciti) buses run every 20 minutes between the airport and the Civic Centre station (adult/child R57/28.10). You cannot pay in cash; you need to buy a myconnect card and load it with credit at the ticket office, MyCiTi stations and selected retailers. MyCiTi buses also operate routes within the city including services between Gardens and the Waterfront via the City Bowl.

Backpacker Bus (☎021-424 1184, 021-439 7600; www.backpackerbus.co.za) picks up from hostels and hotels in the city and offers airport transfers from R180 per person.

Golden Arrow (☎0800 656 463; www.gabs.co.za) buses run from the **Golden Acre Terminal** (Map p916; Grand Pde) and are most useful for getting along the Atlantic Coast from the city centre to Hout Bay. A tourist-friendly alternative is the hop-on hop-off **City Sightseeing Cape Town** (Map p912; ☎021-511 6000; www.city-sightseeing.com; adult/child R120/60).

Minibus taxis cover most of the city with an informal network of routes, and are a cheap way of getting around.

A cross between a taxi and a shared taxi, **Rikkis** (☎0861 745 547; www.rikkis.co.za) offer shared rides around the city for R15 to R30. There is a degree of meandering as passengers are dropped off.

Consider taking a nonshared taxi at night or if you're in a group. Rates are about R10 per km. Call **Marine Taxi** (☎0861 434 0434, 021-913 6813; www.marinetaxis.co.za) or **Excite Taxis** (☎021-448 4444; www.excitetaxis.co.za).

Metrorail (☎0800 656 463; www.capemetrorail.co.za) commuter trains are a handy way to get around, although there are few trains after 6.30pm. Trains operate but are less frequent on weekends.

AROUND CAPE TOWN

Winelands

The Boland, stretching inland and upwards from Cape Town, isn't South Africa's only wine-growing region, but it's certainly the most famous. Its name means Upland, a reference to the dramatic mountain ranges that shoot up to more than 1500m, on whose fertile slopes the vineyards form a patchwork. Lively student town Stellenbosch offers the most activities.

Stellenbosch

☎021 / POP 220,000

South Africa's second-oldest European settlement, established in 1679, Stellenbosch wears many faces. At times it's a rowdy joint for Stellenbosch University students; at others it's a stately monument to colonial architectural splendour. But mostly it's just plain busy, as Capetonians and tourists descend on its museums, markets, quality hotels and varied eating and nightlife options.

There are too many good wineries to list all of them; it's best to stop on a whim or pick up a brochure from **Stellenbosch Tourism** (☎021-883 3584; www.stellenboschtourism.co.za; 36 Market St; ⏰8am-5pm Mon-Fri, 9am-2pm Sat & Sun). We do, however, recommend **Villiera** (☎021-865 2002; www.villiera.com; tastings free; ⏰9am-5pm Mon-Fri, 9am-3pm Sat), which produces excellent MCC wines and offers wildlife drives. The long-established **Easy Rider Wine Tours** (☎021-886 4651; www.winetour.co.za; 12 Market St) offers good-value day trips (R400, including lunch and tastings).

Sleeping & Eating

★ Banghoek Place BACKPACKERS $
(☎021-887 0048; www.banghoek.co.za; 193 Banghoek Rd; dm/r R150/450; @ ≋) A stylish suburban hostel with satellite TV, a pool table and plenty of tours on offer.

Ikhaya Backpackers BACKPACKERS $
(☎021-883 8550; www.stellenboschbackpackers.co.za; 56 Bird St; dm/d without bathroom from R100/310; @) Rooms in this centrally located hostel are in converted apartments, each with their own kitchen and bathroom.

Stellenbosch Hotel HOTEL $$
(☎021-887 3644; www.stellenboschhotel.co.za; 162 Dorp St, cnr Andringa St; s/d incl breakfast from R835/1040; ❄ @) A comfortable, country-style hotel with a variety of rooms. Some have self-catering facilities.

★ Apprentice@Institute of Culinary Arts FUSION $$
(☎021-887 8985; www.icachef.co.za; Oude Hoek Centre, Andringa St; mains R55-130; ⏰breakfast & lunch Sun & Mon, breakfast, lunch & dinner Tue-Sat) A small, inspired menu and excellent service are staples at this restaurant operated by culinary students.

Brampton Wine Studio MEDITERRANEAN $$
(☎021-883 9097; www.brampton.co.za; 11 Church St; mains R40-80; ⏰10am-7pm Mon-Sat) Munch on gourmet pizzas and sip shiraz at this pavement cafe doubling as Brampton winery's tasting room.

Getting There & Away

Long-distance bus services charge high prices for the short sector to Cape Town. The cheapest operator (R125, one hour) is **City to City** (☎011-774 3333, 0861 589 282; www.translux.co.za). The **Baz Bus** (☎0861-229 287; www.bazbus.com) picks up from hostels (R160, 30 minutes).

Metrorail (☎0800 656 463; www.metrorail.co.za) trains run to/from Cape Town (1st/economy class R13/7.50, about one hour). To be safe, travel in the middle of the day.

THE GARDEN ROUTE

The Garden Route is one of South Africa's most internationally renowned destinations, and with good reason. Within a few hundred kilometres, the range of topography, vegetation and outdoor activities is breathtaking. Roughly encompassing the coastline from Mossel Bay in the west to just beyond Plettenberg Bay in the east, it caters to all kinds of travellers, regardless of budget.

You can hike and cycle in old-growth forests, commune with elephants, monkeys and birds, chill out on superb beaches or canoe in lagoons. Knysna and Plettenberg Bay are the most common bases.

Places are described in this section from west to east. Most travellers visit Oudtshoorn while traversing the Garden Route so, although this town is technically in the Little Karoo, we've included it here.

Oudtshoorn

☎044 / POP 85,000

That Oudtshoorn bills itself as the ostrich capital of the world is no overstatement. The birds have been bred hereabouts since the 1860s, and fortunes were made from the fashion for ostrich feathers.

The town still turns a pretty penny from breeding the birds for meat and leather. The ostriches also pay their way with tourists – you can buy ostrich eggs, feathers and *biltong* (dried and salted meat) all over town. But more importantly, Oudtshoorn is a great base for exploring the **Karoo** and the **Garden Route**.

Sights & Activities

Devey Glinister's superb **Meerkat Adventures** (☎084 772 9678; www.meerkatadventures.co.za; per person R550; ⏰sunrise on sunny days) offer the chance to see up close how these

WORTH A TRIP

THE CEDERBERG

Bizarre sandstone formations, San rock art and craggy mountains all make the desolate **Cederberg Wilderness Area** a must-see.

Hiking trails crisscross a 240-sq-km area, with the Maltese Cross and the Wolfberg Cracks and Arch the most popular hikes. Arrange hiking permits at **Dwarsrivier Farm**, where you'll find **accommodation** (☎027-482 2825; www.cederbergwine.com/sanddrif; campsites R140, 4-person cottage from R680) and nearby, a stellar **winery**, an **astronomical observatory** and rock art at the **Stadsaal Caves**.

The Cederberg range is 200km north of Cape Town, accessible from Citrusdal, Clanwilliam and the N7. Public transport into the mountains is nonexistent.

highly intelligent creatures communicate and live. No children under 10 are admitted.

If you're heading north to the **Cango Caves** (☎044-272 7410; www.cango-caves.co.za; adult/child R75/35; ⊙9am-4pm) or Cango Ostrich Farm, carry on driving and take the gravel **Swartberg Pass** to Prince Albert, a delightful town for a lunch stop. Return via the **Meiringspoort Pass**, with its waterfall.

Sleeping & Eating

★**Backpackers Paradise** BACKPACKERS $
(☎044-272 3436; www.backpackersparadise.net; 148 Baron van Rheede St; campsite per person R60, dm/r/d R110/290/360; @≋) This lively hostel offers free ostrich-egg breakfasts, discounts to local attractions and arranges activities.

Karoo Soul Travel Lodge BACKPACKERS $
(☎044-272 0330; www.karoosoul.com; 170 Langenhoven Rd; campsite per person R60, dm/d R120/380, d with shared bathroom R320; @≋) There are comfortable rooms in the gracious old house and garden cottages with bathrooms (R420), all with luxury linens.

La Pension GUESTHOUSE $$
(☎044-279 2445; www.lapension.co.za; 169 Church St; s/d incl breakfast R650/940; ❄@≋) Spacious, stylish rooms and superb bathrooms, plus a good-sized pool, a sauna and a large garden.

★**Jemima's** SOUTH AFRICAN $$$
(☎044-272 0808; www.jemimas.com; 94 Baron van Rheede St; mains R95-180; ⊙lunch & dinner) A small menu specialising in traditional Cape fare.

Kalinka FUSION $$$
(☎044-279 2596; www.kalinka.co.za; 93 Baron van Rheede St; mains R85-170; ⊙dinner Tue-Sun) A long-standing favourite with an imaginative, upmarket menu.

Getting There & Away

Buses stop in the Riverside Centre off Voortrekker St.

The **Baz Bus** (☎0861 229 287; www.bazbus.com) stops at George, from where you can arrange a transfer to Oudtshoorn with Backpackers Paradise (R60).

Knysna

☎044 / POP 54,000

Perched on the edge of a serene lagoon and surrounded by forests, Knysna (*ny*-znah) has a sylvan setting, a gay-friendly vibe, good places to stay, eat and drink, and a wide range of activities, making it the major stop on the Garden Route. But if you're after something quiet and undeveloped, you should look elsewhere, particularly in high season.

Regulated by **South Africa National Parks** (SANParks; ☎044-302 5600; www.sanparks.org/parks/garden_route; Thesen Island), although much of it is privately owned, Knysna Lagoon (13 sq km) opens up between two sandstone cliffs, known as the Heads. A cruise is a good way to appreciate the lagoon – the **Featherbed Company** (☎044-382 1693; www.featherbed.co.za; Remembrance Dr, off Waterfront Dr) has several vessels, including the **John Benn** (adult/child R130/60; ⊙departs 12.30pm & 5pm winter, 12.30pm & 6pm summer).

Emzini Tours (☎044-382 1087; www.emzinitours.co.za; adult/child R350/100) visits a number of community projects as well as the Rastafarian community on their recommended township tours.

Sleeping & Eating

Island Vibe BACKPACKERS $
(☎044-382 1728; www.islandvibe.co.za; 67 Main Rd; dm/d R120/385, d with shared bathroom; @≋) A funky backpackers with excellent commu-

nal areas, nicely decorated rooms and free internet.

★Brenton Cottages CHALET $$
(☎044-381 0082; www.brentononsea.net; 242 CR Swart Dr, Brenton-on-Sea; 2-person cabin R890, 6-person cottage R1940; ❄) These well-equipped cottages and cabins are a short walk from a magnificent beach.

Inyathi Guest Lodge GUESTHOUSE $$
(☎044-382 7768; www.inyathiguestlodge.co.za; 52 Main Rd; s/d from R500/800) Accommodation in this imaginatively designed guesthouse is in decorated timber lodges.

★East Head Café CAFE $$
(☎044-384 0933; www.eastheadcafe.co.za; 25 George Rex Dr, Eastern Head; mains R45-110; ⏲breakfast & lunch; ✎) Wild oysters and a good range of vegetarian dishes, served on a deck overlooking the lagoon and ocean.

Sirocco INTERNATIONAL $$
(☎044-382 4874; www.sirocco.co.za; Main Rd, Thesen Island; mains R50-130; ⏲lunch & dinner) Dine on steaks and seafood or sample wood-fired pizzas and beers from local brewery, Mitchell's, in the outdoor bar.

ℹ Getting There & Away

Translux (www.translux.co.za) and **Intercape** (www.intercape.co.za) stop at the old train station at the Waterfront. **Greyhound** (www.greyhound.co.za) stops at the **Engen petrol station** (Main St). **Baz Bus** (www.bazbus.com) drops at all the hostels. For short journeys, you're better off taking a minibus taxi.

Plettenberg Bay

☎044 / POP 34,000

With its mountains, white sand and crystal-blue water, 'Plett' is one of the country's top local tourist spots. As a result, things can get very busy and are somewhat overpriced, but the town retains a relaxed, friendly atmosphere and does have good-value hostels.

Surf lessons are available with the **Garden Route Surf Academy** (☎082 436 6410; www.gardenroutesurfacademy.com; 2hr-group lesson incl equipment R350), which caters to all abilities.

Sleeping & Eating

★Nothando Backpackers Hostel BACKPACKERS $
(☎044-533 0220; www.nothando.com; 5 Wilder St; dm/d R160/500, d with shared bathroom R420) This award-winning place has a great bar area, yet you can still find peace and quiet in the large grounds.

Periwinkle Guest Lodge GUESTHOUSE $$
(☎044-533 1345; www.periwinkle.co.za; 75 Beachy Head Dr; d incl breakfast R2230) Beachfront Periwinkle offers individually decorated rooms with great views in the town's western suburbs.

★Ristorante Enrico SEAFOOD $$
(☎044 535 9818; www.enricorestaurant.co.za; Main Beach, , Keurboomstrand; mains R70-120; ⏲lunch & dinner) Readers recommend this seafood restaurant with awesome beach views.

Garden Route National Park – Tsitsikamma Section

The **Tsitsikamma section** (adult/child R120/60) of the **Garden Route National Park** protects 82km of coast between Plettenberg Bay and Humansdorp, including an area 5km out to sea. Located at the foot of the Tsitsikamma Range and cut by rivers that have carved deep ravines into the ancient forests, it's a spectacular area to walk through. Several short day walks give you a taste of the coastline.

Storms River Mouth Rest Camp (☎in Pretoria 012-428 9111; www.sanparks.org; campsite R270, forest hut R465, family cottage R1405) offers forest huts, chalets, cottages and 'oceanettes'; all except the forest huts have kitchens, bedding and bathrooms.

The main information centre is at Storms River Mouth Rest Camp, 68km from Plettenberg Bay and 8km from the N2. The camp, which is open 24 hours, is 2km inside the park from the gate.

Greyhound (p960), Intercape (p943) and Translux buses run along the N2, and the Baz Bus stops at Nature's Valley.

Storms River

☎042

Storms River is an odd little hamlet outside the national park with tree-shaded lanes, a few places to stay and an outdoor centre.

Fair Trade–accredited **Storms River Adventures** (☎042-2811836; www.stormsriver.com; Darnell St) arrange a variety of activities, including a tree-canopy slide (R450).

DON'T MISS

OTTER TRAIL

This 42km **hike** (☎012-426 5111; www.sanparks.org; per person R925) is one of South Africa's finest, hugging the coastline from Storms River Mouth to Nature's Valley. The five-day, four-night walk involves fording rivers, and gives access to some superb stretches of coast. Book through SANParks (p956) in Knysa. The trail is usually booked up one year ahead, but there are often cancellations, so it's always worth trying.

The world's highest bungee jump (216m) is at the **Bloukrans River Bridge** (☎042-281 1458; www.faceadrenalin.com; bungee jump R750, bridge walk R100; ⏰9am-5pm), 21km west of Storms River.

If you're after a post-bungee rest, try **Dijembe Backpackers** (☎042-281 1842; www.dijembebackpackers.com; cnr Formosa & Assegai Sts; campsites/dm/s/d R75/120/250/350; @ 📶), or **Armagh Country Lodge & Spa** (☎042-281 1512; www.thearmagh.com; 24 Fynbos Ave; s/d R850/1190; 📶 🏊), which also has one of the town's best restaurants.

The Baz Bus (p923) stops at Storms River; otherwise buses and minibus taxis could drop you at Bloukrans River Bridge or Tsitsikamma Lodge, 5km away on the N2.

SUNSHINE COAST

The Sunshine Coast – the stretch of shoreline between the Garden Route and the Wild Coast – is best known for the surfing mecca of Jeffrey's Bay. We have also included the mystical mountain hamlet of Hogsback in this section because, although it's not actually on the coastline, it's often visited from East London.

Jeffrey's Bay

☎042 / POP 25,000

Once just a sleepy seaside town, 'J-Bay' is now one of the world's top surfing destinations. Boardies from all over the planet flock here to ride waves such as the famous Supertubes, once described as 'the most perfect wave in the world'. June to September are the best months for experienced surfers, but novices can learn year-round. The biggest surf crowd comes to town every July for the Billabong Pro championship.

A number of operators offer surfing lessons. **Wavecrest Surf School** (☎073 509 0400; www.wavecrestsurfschool.co.za; Shop 6, Drommedaris St; 2hr lesson incl board & wetsuit R200) is a highly recommended, long-running operation.

Sleeping & Eating

Island Vibe BACKPACKERS $
(☎042-293 1625; www.islandvibe.co.za; 10 Dageraad St; campsite R80, dm from R120, d with/without bathroom R460/340; @ 📶) The most popular backpackers in town is 500m south of the centre. The bar can become raucous at night.

Beach Music GUESTHOUSE $
(☎042-293 2291; www.beachmusic.co.za; 33 Flame Cres; s/d from R200/300; 📶) The airy lounge has superb ocean views; some rooms share a kitchenette.

African Perfection B&B $$
(☎042-293 1401; www.africanperfection.co.za; 20 Pepper St; s/d incl breakfast from R600/1400, self-catering from R600/880; ❄ @ 📶) Every room has a private balcony offering stunning sea views. Smart budget accommodation is also available (dm from R350).

Die Walskipper SEAFOOD $$
(☎042-292 0005; www.walskipper.co.za; Clapton Beach, Marina Martinique; mains R95; ⏰lunch & dinner Tue-Sat, lunch Sun) Just metres from the sea, this alfresco restaurant specialises in seafood, plus crocodile and ostrich steaks.

Getting There & Away

The **Baz Bus** (☎0861 229 287; www.bazbus.com) stops daily at hostels in both directions.

Long-distance buses arrive at and depart from the Caltex petrol station on Saint Francis St.

Port Elizabeth

☎041 / POP 1.5 MILLION

Downtown 'PE', like many South African city centres, is mostly run-down and full of fast-food chains and cheap stores. The more upmarket shops, bars and restaurants are found in suburban shopping centres such as the Boardwalk.

The **South End Museum** (☎041-582 3325; www.southendmuseum.co.za; cnr Walmer Blvd & Humewood Rd, South End; ⏰9am-4pm Mon-Fri, 10am-3pm Sat & Sun) FREE is a worthy stop, looking at the city's forced removals during apartheid, when non-whites were evicted from designated white areas. The city also has some of the Eastern Cape's best bathing and surfing **beaches**.

Sleeping & Eating

Lungile Backpackers BACKPACKERS $
(041-582 2042; www.lungilebackpackers.co.za; 12 La Roche Dr, Humewood; campsites/dm R80/120, d with/without bathroom R385/310;) A well-managed operation minutes from the beachfront. The entertainment area rocks most nights.

Algoa Bay B&B B&B $$
(041-582 5134; www.algoabay.com; 13 Ferndale Rd, Humewood; s/d incl breakfast R550/900;) Rooms are tastefully furnished and have flat-screen TVs; top-floor rooms have views of King's Beach.

Deli Street Café SANDWICHES, SOUTH AFRICAN $$
(041-582 2157; delistreetcafe@gmail.com; Stanley on Bain Centre, Stanley St, Richmond Hill; mains R60, sandwiches R45; 7.30am-10pm;) Sitting on Stanley St, PE's snazzy eating district, this place serves light lunches in an airy space. Nearby, **Fushin** (041-811 7874; www.fushin.co.za; Shop 5, Stanley on Bain,, 15 Stanley St; mains R70-100; noon-10pm) offers pan-Asian cuisine. At both you can opt for tables out on the street.

Getting There & Away

South African Airways (SAA; 041-507 1111; www.flysaa.com) and **Kulula** (0861 585 852; www.kulula.com) have daily flights to Jo'burg (from R1150, 1¾ hours), Durban (from R1160, 1¼ hours) and Cape Town (from R1160, 1¼ hours).

Port Elizabeth has regular bus connections to the major South African cities, including:

Cape Town (R330, 12 hours)
Durban (R430, 14 hours)
East London (R225, five hours)

Baz Bus (0861 229 287; www.bazbus.com) picks up from hostels in PE.

Shosholoza Meyl (086 000 8888; www.shosholozameyl.co.za) runs services to Jo'burg (R420, 20 hours) via Bloemfontein.

Hogsback

045 / POP 1500

There's something about Hogsback, improbably located 1300m up in the beautiful Amathole Mountains, that makes you half expect to meet a hobbit.

Hogsback's artistic community, organic food and mind-boggling views of mountains and forested valleys in all directions, make it an ecodestination par excellence. There are some great walks, bike rides and drives in the area, but be prepared for inclement weather – rainy, and misty days can occur year-round and winter temperatures drop below freezing at night.

★**Away with the Fairies** (045-962 1031; www.awaywiththefairies.co.za; Ambleside Close; campsites/dm R70/120, d with/without bathroom R350/290;) is a delightful backpackers with terrific views. Alternatively **Edge Mountain Retreat** (045-962 1159, 082-603 5246; www.theedge-hogsback.co.za; Bluff End; cottage from R495;) has tastefully decorated cottages and a highly recommended restaurant.

The easiest way to get to Hogsback without a car is by shuttle bus from **Sugarshack Backpackers** (043-722 8240; www.sugarshack.co.za; Eastern Esplanade;) in East London or Buccaneer's Backpackers (p925) in Chintsa.

East London

043 / POP 980,000

East London is the country's only river port, situated on a spectacular bay that curves round to huge sand hills. Queenstown Park is pretty, and the beaches and surf are excellent, but there's not a lot to keep you here. It's largely a transport hub for the Wild and Sunshine Coasts.

WORTH A TRIP

BUCCANEERS BACKPACKERS

Chintsa (also spelt Cintsa) comprises two pretty villages, Chintsa East and Chintsa West, and an unspoilt stretch of white-sand beach. It's the best place on this part of the coast to hang out for a while. **Buccaneers Backpackers** (043-734 3012; www.cintsa.com; Chintsa West; campsites/dm/d incl breakfast R55/110/395;) is an excellent 'backpacker resort' offering loads of activities. Sleeping options include comfortable dorms, contemporary rooms and cottages with their own bathrooms (R1200 for four people).

Sleeping & Eating

John Bailie Guest Lodge GUESTHOUSE $
(043-735 1058; www.johnbailieguestlodge.co.za; 9 John Bailie Rd, Bunkers Hill; s/d from R350/400;) A family-run guesthouse near the golf course.

Hampton Court Guest Lodge HOTEL $$
(043-722 7924; www.hampton-court.co.za; 2 Marine Tce; s/d incl breakfast from R700/900;) A good, centrally located option with ocean views from some rooms.

Grazia Fine Food & Wine MEDITERRANEAN $$
(043-722 2009; www.graziafinefood.co.za; Upper Esplanade; mains R80-150; noon-10.30pm) A stylish spot offering largely Italian cuisine. Reservations recommended.

Getting There & Away

Translux (0861-589 282; www.translux.co.za), **City to City** (0861 589 282; www.translux.co.za), **Greyhound** (043-743 9284; www.greyhound.co.za) and **Intercape** (0861 287 287; www.intercape.co.za) all stop at the **Windmill Park Roadhouse** (cnr Moore St & Marine Tce). Destinations include **Durban** (R350, nine to 10 hours), **Cape Town** (R440, 16 hours) and **Jo'burg/Pretoria** (R350, 14 hours).

Baz Bus (0861 229 287; www.bazbus.com) picks up from hostels in East London.

WILD COAST

With its green rolling hills, rugged cliffs plunging into the sea, remote sandy beaches and a history of shipwrecks, the Wild Coast is a place for adventure and intrigue. Stretching for 350km from East London to Port Edward, the area is dotted with tiny Xhosa (amaXhosa) settlements and the occasional holiday resort or backpacker hostel.

You may hear some people refer to the area as the 'Transkei', the apartheid-era homeland that once covered this part of the country.

Coffee Bay

047 / POP 600

This once remote hamlet is today a backpackers playground, with two busy hostels and a couple of hotels. The village itself is fairly scruffy, but the surrounding scenery is dramatic, with a beautiful kilometre-long beach backed by towering cliffs.

OFF THE BEATEN TRACK

BULUNGULA LODGE

★ **Bulungula** (047-577 8900; www.bulungula.com; campsites per person R70, dm/safari tent R130/300, d without bathroom R330) has legendary status on the Wild Coast for its stunning location, community-based activities and ecofriendly ethos. It's 40% owned by the Xhosa community who run all the tours. There's an overall mellow vibe and beach parties take place well away from the main camp. All meals are offered; self-caterers should shop before they arrive.

Bulungula is around two hours from Coffee Bay. If you're driving, contact Bulungula in advance to get directions. Pick-ups are available from Mthatha (R70).

A minibus taxi from Mthatha to Coffee Bay costs R25 (one hour). The backpacker hostels meet the Baz Bus at the Shell Ultra City, 4km south of Mthatha.

Sleeping

Bomvu Paradise BACKPACKERS $
(047-575 2073; www.bomvubackpackers.com; No 19 Lower Nenga; campsites/dm R80/120, d with/without bathroom R350/280) A soulful place with organic food, yoga classes and drumming sessions.

Ocean View Hotel HOTEL $$
(047-575 2005; www.oceanview.co.za; s/d full board R850/1500;) Good-quality, chalet-style rooms, with a deck overlooking the ocean.

Port St Johns

047 / POP 2100

Laid-back Port St Johns has long been a magnet for hippy types. This idyllic little town on the coast at the mouth of the Umzimvubu River has tropical vegetation, dramatic cliffs, great beaches and no stress. Many travellers succumb to 'Pondo Fever' and stay for months.

Sleeping

Amapondo Backpackers BACKPACKERS $
(047-564 1344; www.amapondo.co.za; Second Beach Rd; campsites R80, dm/d without bathroom R120/350;) A mellow place with simple

rooms, awesome views of Second Beach and a lively bar.

Lodge on the Beach LODGE $$
(☎047-564 1276; www.lodgeonthebeach.co.za; Second Beach; r from R450) Each of the three rooms has its own deck overlooking Second Beach and an individual bathroom in the hallway.

Getting There & Away

Most backpacker places will pick you up from the Shell Ultra City, 4km south of Mthatha (where the Baz Bus stops), but it's essential to book ahead. There are also regular minibus taxis to Port St Johns from here (R40, two hours).

KWAZULU-NATAL

Rough and ready, smart and sophisticated, rural and rustic, KwaZulu-Natal is as eclectic as its cultures, people and landscapes. It has its metropolitan heart in the port of Durban and the nearby historic capital, Pietermaritzburg. The beaches along this coast attract visitors wishing to soak up the sand, surf and sun, and to the north is Zululand, home to some of Africa's most evocative traditional settlements. The region also boasts alluring national parks and isolated, wild coastal reserves. The province's border in the far west, the uKhahlamba-Drakensberg Park, features awesome peaks and excellent hiking.

Durban

☎031 / POP 3.5 MILLION

Durban is sometimes passed over for her 'cooler' Capetonian cousin, but there's a lot more to fun-loving Durbs than meets the eye. After a major makeover, South Africa's third-largest city features a revamped beachfront, stylish cafes and wonderful cultural offerings. The downtown area throbs to a distinctly African beat.

While the beachfront remains a city trademark for daytime activities, restaurants and accommodation are largely clustered in the safer suburbs.

Home to the largest concentration of people of Indian descent outside India, Durban also boasts the sights, sounds and scents of the subcontinent.

THE SIGNS THEY ARE A-CHANGIN'

In 2007–08 Durban's municipal council controversially renamed many of the city's streets to reflect a 'new' South Africa; debate still rages over the changes. Many streets are now labelled twice, the old moniker scored through with a red line.

We have provided the new street names, along with the former names, which many people still use.

Sights & Activities

The beachfront has experienced a resurgence, thanks to a massive revamp before the 2010 FIFA World Cup. Both the beaches and new promenade extend from the mouth of the Umgeni River to uShaka Marine World, a stretch known as the Golden Mile, although it's actually 6km long.

City Hall NOTABLE BUILDING
(Anton Lembede St/Smith St, City Centre) Dominating the city centre is the opulent 1910 Edwardian neo-baroque City Hall. Upstairs is the **Durban Art Gallery** (☎031-311 2264; ⌚8.30am-4pm Mon-Sat, 11am-4pm Sun) FREE, housing an outstanding collection of contemporary South African works, especially Zulu arts and crafts.

uShaka Marine World AMUSEMENT PARK
(☎031-328 8000; www.ushakamarineworld.co.za; uShaka Beach, the Point; Wet'n'Wild or Sea World adult/child R125/95, combo ticket for both parks R165/125; ⌚9am-5pm) uShaka Marine World boasts one of the largest aquariums in the world, a seal stadium, a dolphinarium and enough water rides to make you seasick.

Moses Mabhida Stadium STADIUM
(☎031-582 8222; www.mmstadium.com; 44 Isaiah Ntshangase Rd/Walter Gilbert, Stamford Hill; SkyCar adult/child R55/30, Adventure Walk per person R90, Big Swing per person R595; ⌚SkyCar 9am-6pm, Adventure Walk 10am, 1pm & 4pm Sat & Sun, Big Swing 9am to 5pm) There are numerous ways to explore Durban's 2010 FIFA World Cup stadium: head atop the arch in a **SkyCar**, puff up on foot on a 550-step **Adventure Walk** or plunge off the 106m arch on the **Big Swing**.

Sun Coast Casino CASINO
(☎031-328 3000; www.suncoastcasino.co.za; Suncoast Blvd, OR Tambo Pde/Marine Pde, Stamford Hill) The glitzy, art deco–style casino also features cinemas and some well attended restaurants.

Central Durban

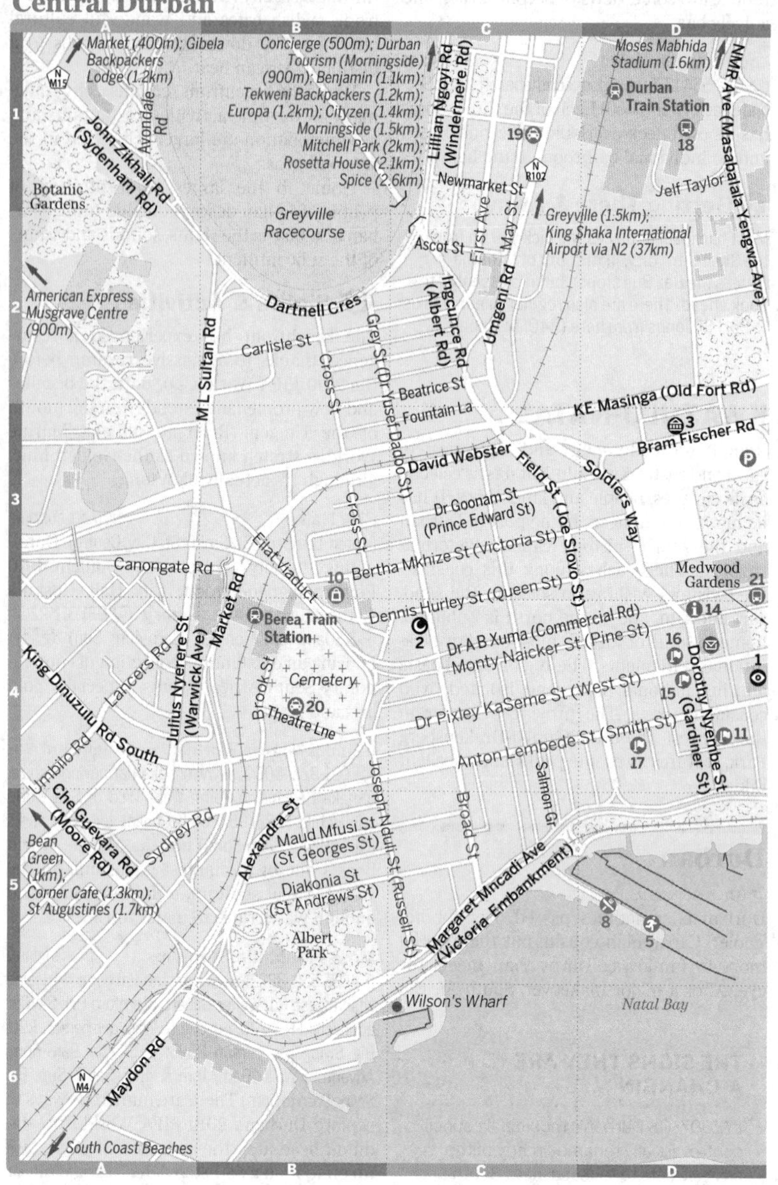

KwaMuhle Museum MUSEUM
(☎031-311 2233; 130 Bram Fischer Rd/Ordnance Rd, City Centre; ⊙8.30am-4pm Mon-Sat, 11am-4pm Sun) **FREE** The former Bantu Administration headquarters now houses powerful displays on the 'Durban System', the blueprint of apartheid policy

Juma Mosque MOSQUE
(☎031-306 0026; cnr Dennis Hurley/Queen & Dr Yusuf Dadoo/Grey Sts, City Centre; ⊙9am-4pm Mon-

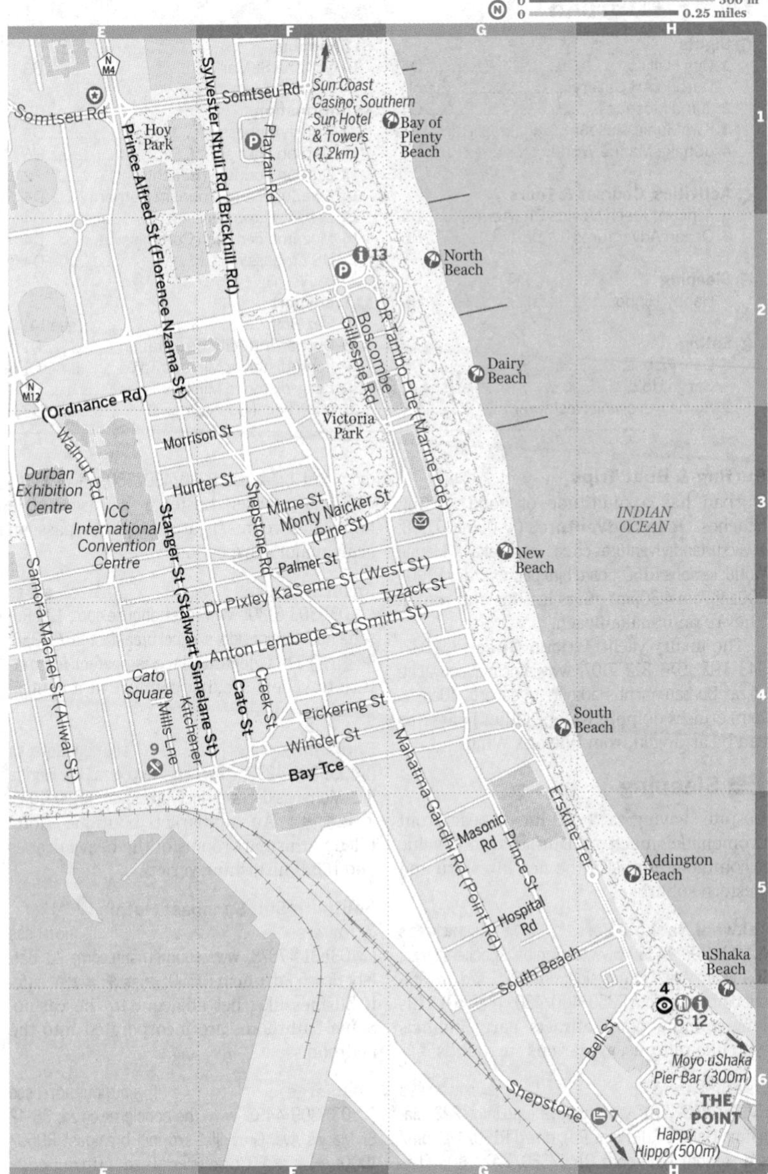

Fri, 9-11am Sat) Largest mosque in the southern hemisphere; call for a guided tour.

Victoria St Market MARKET
(☎031-306 4021; www.victoriastreetmarket.co.za; 151-55 Bertha Mkhize St/Victoria St, City Centre; ⊙6am-6pm Mon-Fri, 8am-2pm Sat & Sun) The hub of the Indian community offers a typically rip-roaring subcontinental shopping experience. Most shops run by Muslims close between noon and 2pm on Friday.

Central Durban

Sights
1 City Hall ... D4
Durban Art Gallery ... (see 1)
2 Juma Mosque ... C4
3 KwaMuhle Museum ... D3
4 uShaka Marine World ... H6

Activities, Courses & Tours
5 African Queen Marine Charters ... D5
6 Ocean Adventures ... H6

Sleeping
7 Happy Hippo ... H6

Eating
8 Cafe Fish ... D5
Cargo Hold ... (see 4)
9 Roma Revolving Restaurant ... E4

Shopping
10 Victoria St Market ... B3

Information
11 British Embassy ... D4
12 Durban Tourism ... H6
13 Durban Tourism (Beachfront) ... F2
14 KwaZulu-Natal Tourism Authority ... D4
15 Lesotho Embassy ... D4
16 Mozambican High Commission ... D4
17 US Embassy ... D4

Transport
Baz Bus ... (see 14)
18 Durban Intercity Bus Station ... D1
19 Long-distance Minibus Taxis ... C1
20 Long-distance Minibus Taxis ... B4
21 Main Local Bus Terminal ... D3

Surfing & Boat Trips

Durban has a multitude of good surfing beaches. **Ocean Adventures** (086-100 1138; www.surfandadventures.co.za; uShaka Marine World; lessons R150, board hire per hour/day R100/200; 7am-4.30pm) offers lessons and rental. They're on uShaka Beach.

The luxury yacht **African Queen** (032-943 1118, 076 812 7107; www.africanqueenyacht.co.za; Durban Yacht Harbour; departs 10am & 1pm) cruises dolphin waters. Other boat trips can be arranged from Wilson's Wharf.

Sleeping

Despite having a hotel-lined beachfront promenade, much of Durban's good-value accommodation is in the northwestern and western suburbs.

Tekweni Backpackers BACKPACKERS $
(031-303 1433; www.tekwenibackpackers.co.za; 169 Ninth Ave, Morningside; dm R125, s/d/tr without bathroom from R350/400/480;) This long-running place attracts party animals who like raucous, gregarious surrounds.

Happy Hippo BACKPACKERS $
(031-368 7181; www.happy-hippo.info; 222 Mahatma Gandhi Rd (Point Rd); dm/d R150/470, dm/s/d without bathroom R140/330/370;) This warehouse-style accommodation is close to the beach, but in the dodgy part of town. Rooms can be noisy.

★Gibela Backpackers Lodge BACKPACKERS $$
(031-303 6291; www.gibelabackpackers.co.za; 119 Ninth Ave, Morningside; dm/s/d without bathroom incl breakfast R220/430/580;) This 'flashpacker' hostel in a Tuscan-style home has rooms neat enough to pass an army major's inspection.

Rosetta House B&B $$
(031-303 6180; www.rosettahouse.com; 126 Rosetta Rd, Morningside; s/d incl breakfast R675/950;) This elegant place is perfect for mature travellers seeking comfort in a central location.

Benjamin BOUTIQUE HOTEL $$
(031-303 4233; www.benjamin.co.za; 141 Florida Rd, Morningside; s/d incl breakfast R850/1075;) An upmarket boutique hotel filled with smart rooms of the heavy drapes and floral furnishing variety.

Southern Sun Suncoast Hotel & Towers HOTEL $$$
(031-314 7878; www.southernsun.com; 20 Battery Beach Rd; r from R1550;) A safe, if businesslike, bet adjacent to the casino. Some bathrooms are incorporated into the bedrooms.

Concierge BOUTIQUE HOTEL $$$
(031-309 4453; www.the-concierge.co.za; 36-42 St Mary's Ave, Greyville; s/d incl breakfast R950/1500;) Concierge is a cutting-edge sleeping option that offers smallish, well-designed rooms.

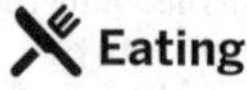

Eating

Takeaway places around Victoria St Market sell Indian snacks including *bunny chow,* a half or quarter loaf of bread hollowed out and filled with curry.

★Market INTERNATIONAL $$
(☎031-309 8581; www.marketrestaurant.co.za; 40 Gladys Mazibuko Rd/Marriott Rd, Greyville; mains R60-140; ⏰breakfast & lunch Mon, breakfast, lunch & dinner Tue-Sat) Delectable breakfasts, casual lunches and more formal dinners. Produce is locally sourced, free range and organic, where possible.

Cargo Hold SEAFOOD $$
(☎031-328 8065; uShaka Marine World, the Point; mains R75-150; ⏰lunch & dinner) This high-quality fish restaurant shares a glass wall with a shark aquarium.

Corner Cafe CAFE $$
(197 Brand Rd, Glenwood; mains R30-70; ⏰6am-5pm Mon-Fri, 8am-3pm Sat) A warehouse-style cafe serving up home-baked pies and breads, great cakes and foods with a low carbon footprint.

Cafe Fish SEAFOOD $$
(☎031-305 5062; 31 Yacht Mole, Margaret Mncadi Ave/Victoria Embankment, City Centre; mains R45-150; ⏰lunch & dinner) The seafood dishes here are as appealing as the ocean views.

Roma Revolving Restaurant INTERNATIONAL $$
(☎031-337 6707; www.roma.co.za; 32nd fl, John Ross House, Margaret Mncadi Ave/Victoria Embankment, City Centre; mains R70-150; ⏰lunch Fri-Sat & dinner Mon-Sat; ❄) Stunning city views and generous helpings of largely Italian cuisine.

★Spice FUSION $$
(☎031-303 6375; 362 Lilian Ngoyi Rd/Windermere Rd, Morningside; mains R130-150; ⏰lunch & dinner Tue-Sat, lunch Sun) A foodie favourite, offering South African and Indian fusion dishes.

Drinking & Nightlife

Moyo uShaka Pier Bar BAR
(☎031-332 0662; www.moyo.co.za; uShaka Marine World, the Point; drinks R45-55; ⏰11am-late) Perched on a pier in front of uShaka Marine World, this is Durban's top spot for a sundowner.

Bean Green CAFE
(147 Helen Joseph Rd/Davenport Rd, Bulwer; ⏰8am-5pm Mon-Thu, 9am-1pm Sat; 📶) This barely larger than a hole-in-the wall, award-winning roaster serves single origin beans.

Billy the Bum's CLUB
(www.billythebums.co.za; 504 Lilian Ngoyi Rd/Windermere Rd, Morningside) This reliably raucous suburban cocktail bar has DJs on Friday and Saturday.

☆ Entertainment

KwaZulu-Natal Philharmonic Orchestra CLASSICAL MUSIC
(☎031-369 9438; www.kznpo.co.za) The KwaZulu-Natal Philharmonic Orchestra has weekly performances in the City Hall in spring. It also performs a concert series in the Botanic Gardens.

Rainbow Restaurant & Jazz Club JAZZ
(☎031-702 9161; www.therainbow.co.za; 23 Stanfield Lane, Pinetown) In Pinetown, 8km west of the centre, Rainbow is considered the centre of the jazz scene.

Information

INTERNET ACCESS

Cityzen (161 Gordon Rd, Morningside; per hr R20; ⏰8am-midnight)

Europa (☎031-312 1099; 167 Florida Rd, Morningside) cafe offers wi-fi access.

MEDICAL SERVICES

St Augustines (☎031-268 5000; 107 Chelmsford Rd, Berea)

MONEY

There are banks with ATMs and change facilities across the city.

American Express Musgrave Centre (☎031-202 8733; 151 Musgrave Rd, FNB House, Musgrave)

TOURIST INFORMATION

Durban Tourism (www.durbanexperience.co.za) Can help with accommodation and arranges tours of Durban and beyond. Useful offices at uShaka Marine World (☎031-337 8099; the Point), Morningside (☎031-322 4164; 90 Florida Rd; ⏰8am-4.30pm Mon-Fri) and the beachfront (☎031-322 4205; Old Pavilion Site, OR Tambo Pde/Marine Pde; ⏰8am-5pm).

KwaZulu-Natal Tourism Authority (KZN Tourism; ☎031-366 7500; www.zulu.org.za; ground fl, Tourist Junction Bldg, 160 Monty Naicker St/Pine St, City Centre)

Getting There & Away

King Shaka International Airport (☎032-436 6585; www.kingshakainternational.co.za) is 40km north of the city, served by **South African Airways** (SAA; www.flysaa.com), **Mango** (www.flymango.com) and **Kulula** (www.kulula.com).

The **Baz Bus** (☎0861 229 287; www.bazbus.com) picks up and drops off at Durban's hostels.

Long-distance buses leave from the bus stations near the Durban Train Station. Destinations include the following:

Cape Town (R590, 22 to 26 hours)
Jo'burg (R230, seven hours)
Pietermaritzburg (R185, two hours)

Some long-distance minibus taxis leave from the streets opposite the Umgeni Rd entrance to the Durban Train Station. Others, running mainly to the South Coast and the Wild Coast, leave from around the Berea Train Station. Be alert in and around the minibus taxi ranks.

Even hardy travellers report feeling unsafe on the local inner-city and suburban trains, but tourist-class, long-distance **Shosholoza Meyl** (☎031-361 7167; www.shosholozameyl.co.za) services are recommended.

Getting Around

The **King Shaka Airport Shuttle Bus** (☎031-465 5573; www.airportbustransport.co.za; ⏲5am-10pm) runs hourly via Umhlanga Rocks. Tickets to Durban start at R80. Some hostels run their own shuttle services. A taxi should cost about R400.

The **Durban People Mover** (☎031-309 5942; http://www.durban.gov.za/City_Services/ethekwini_transport_authority/Pages/People_Mover.aspx; ⏲5am-10pm) operates several routes within the city. Hop-on, hop-off day passes are R15 and can be purchased on the bus. Single-leg tickets cost R4.

SOUTH COAST DIVING

The highlight of the coastal strip south of Durban is the **Aliwal Shoal** – touted as one of the world's 10 best dive sites. Today the shoal's ledges, caves and pinnacles are home to wrecks, rays, turtles, 'raggies' (ragged-tooth sharks), tropical fish and soft corals.

Numerous operators along the South Coast offer day dives and four-day courses (R2800 to R3500). Always speak to other travellers about their experiences, as safety standards vary.

Recommended operators include **2nd Breath** (☎039-317 2326; www.2ndbreath.co.za; cnr Bank St & Berea Rd, Margate) and **Aliwal Dive Centre** (☎039-973 2233; www.aliwalshoal.co.za; 2 Moodie St, Umkomaas).

STATION SAFETY

For safety reasons, it's best to enter Durban Train Station from NMR Ave (Masabalala Yengwa Ave), not Umgeni Rd.

The main bus terminal and information centre for inner-city and metropolitan buses is on Dr AB Xuma (Commercial Rd).

A taxi between the beach and Florida Rd, Morningside, costs about R50.

Zululand

Dominated by the Zulu tribal group, President Zuma's birthplace offers a fascinating historical and contemporary insight into one of the country's most enigmatic, and best-known, cultures. Intense poverty, and all the social problems that come with it, is still commonplace.

Eshowe

☎035 / POP 15,000

Situated around a beautiful indigenous forest and surrounded by green rolling hills, Eshowe has a rural, rough-and-tumble atmosphere, but the suburbs are leafy and quiet. It is well placed for exploring the wider region and offers decent attractions and accommodation options.

Sights & Activities

Fort Nongqayi Museum Village MUSEUM
(www.eshowemuseums.org.za; Nongqayi Rd; adult/child R25/5; ⏲7.30am-4pm Mon-Fri, 9am-4pm Sat & Sun) The village is based around a fort built by the British in 1883. Admission includes access to attractions including the Zululand Historical Museum.

Dlinza Forest Reserve NATURE RESERVE
(www.visitzululand.co.za/Activities_Dlinza.php; ⏲6am-5pm Sep-Apr, 7am-5pm May-Aug) FREE There is prolific birdlife here, as well as walking trails and the 125m-long **Dlinza Forest Aerial Boardwalk** (☎035-474 4029; www.visitzululand.co.za/Activities_Dlinza.php; adult/child R25/5; ⏲6am-5pm Sep-Apr, 7am-5pm May-Aug).

Sleeping

Eshowe Guesthouse B&B $$
(☎035-474 2362; www.eshoweguide.co.za/accomodation/eshowe_guesthouse; 3 Oftebro St; s/d

OFF THE BEATEN TRACK

ZULU SITES

Three spots for learning about Zulu history and culture:

Ondini (High Place; 035-870 2050; www.heritagekzn.co.za; adult/child R20/10; 8am-4pm Mon-Fri, 9am-4pm Sat & Sun) The former Zulu capital includes archaeological digs and the superb **KwaZulu Cultural-Historical Museum** (included in Ondini admission; 8am-4pm Mon-Fri, 9am-4pm Sat & Sun). It's just south of Ulundi.

Emakhosini Ophathe Heritage Park FREE Also known as the Valley of the Kings, the park comprises a number of historical sites and a **multimedia information centre** (035-450 0916; www.heritagekzn.co.za; adult/child R20/10; 8am-4pm Mon-Fri, 9am-4pm Sat & Sun). It's southwest of Ulundi.

Shakaland (035-460 0912; www.shakaland.com; Nandi Experience R275; display 11am & noon) This slightly Disney-fied cultural village includes a Zulu dance performance. It's 14km north of Eshowe.

R450/600;) Rooms are spotless, stylish and spacious and the guesthouse backs onto the bird-filled Dlinza Forest.

Getting There & Away

Minibus taxis connect to Empangeni (R40, one hour), the best place to catch taxis deeper into Zululand, and Durban (R70, 1½ hours).

KwaZulu-Natal Reserves

HLUHLUWE-IMFOLOZI PARK

035

Hluhluwe-iMfolozi Park (035-550 8476; www.kznwildlife.com; adult/child R110/55; 5am-7pm Nov-Feb, 6am-6pm Mar-Oct) covers 960 sq km and has plenty of wildlife including lions, elephants, rhinos (black and white), leopards and African wild dogs.

In summer (wet season) it's beautifully lush and animals range widely. Winter (dry season) visits can also be very rewarding, especially when animals congregate at water sources.

One of iMfolozi's main attractions is its (seasonal) trail system. The **Base Trail** (3 nights & 4 days R3592) is, as the name suggests, at a base camp. On the **Primitive Trail** (3 nights & 4 days R2220, 4 nights & 5 days R2685), you carry equipment, and help prepare the food (provided), and hikers must sit up in 1½-hour watches during the night.

The signature resort on the Hluhluwe side, with stupendous views, is **Hilltop Camp** (035-562 0848; 2-person rondavel/chalet R640/1280). Morning and night **wildlife drives** (adult/child R300/150) from here are very popular. Its sedate bush lodges offer more peace and quiet.

The main entrance, Memorial Gate, is 15km west of the N2, about 50km north of Mtubatuba.

ISIMANGALISO WETLAND PARK

035

This Unesco World Heritage Site stretches for 200 glorious kilometres from the Mozambican border to Maphelana, at the southern end of Lake St Lucia. With the Indian Ocean on one side, and a series of lakes on the other, the 3280-sq-km park protects five distinct ecosystems, featuring everything from offshore reefs and dolphins to woodlands and zebras.

St Lucia and **Sodwana Bay** are the main service centres for the park, both offering accommodation, limited eateries and a wealth of ecotour operators.

Activities on offer include birdwatching, boat tours, canoeing, deep-sea fishing, hiking, horse riding, turtle tours, wildlife watching, whale-watching (in season) and in Sodwana Bay, superlative diving.

Sleeping

Ezemvelo KZN Wildlife (in Pietermaritzburg 033-845 1000; www.kznwildlife.com) offers camping and self-catering accommodation throughout the park.

Hornbill House B&B **$$**
(035-590 1162; www.hornbillhouse.com; 43 Hornbill St; s/d incl breakfast R550/900;) This homey B&B in St Lucia has a small pool and offers eco-trips.

Sodwana Bay Lodge LODGE **$$**
(035-571 6015; www.sodwanabaylodge.co.za; s/d with half board R860/1560) This resort has

slightly dated rooms and offers various dive packages.

Getting There & Away

Driving is the best way to reach the park, though minibus taxis connect Durban to Mtubatuba, 25km from St Lucia. From here you can catch a connecting minibus taxi to St Lucia.

For Sodwana Bay, drivers should turn off the N2 at Hluhluwe Village and continue about 20km to the park. Minibus taxis ply this route.

Pietermaritzburg

033 / POP 457,000

Pietermaritzburg's grand historic buildings house museums and refurbished hotels. The large Zulu population, Indian community and student population make it a vibrant place.

One of the city's finest sights is the **Tatham Art Gallery** (033-392 2800; www.tatham.org.za; Chief Albert Luthuli St/Commercial Rd; admission free; 10am-5pm Tue-Sun), housed in the beautiful Old Supreme Court. The **Msunduzi Museum** (033-394 6834; www.voortrekkermuseum.co.za; 351 Langalibalele St; adult/student R8/5; 9am-4pm Mon-Fri, to 1pm Sat) incorporates Voortrekker, Zulu and Indian displays.

Sleeping & Eating

Sleepy Hollow Adventure Backpackers BACKPACKERS $
(082 455 8325, 033-342 1758; www.sleepyhollowbackpackers.com; 78 Leinster Rd, Scottsville; campsite R90, dm/d/family R130/330/495) A rambling 1940s abode in the heart of the student precinct. Rafting and cycling are on offer.

Heritage Guest House GUESTHOUSE $$
(033-394 4364; 45 Miller St; s/d incl breakfast R475/650, family ste R1200;) Six small units surround a pretty garden and pool. There's an excellent restaurant, open to nonguests.

Rosehurst INTERNATIONAL $$
(239 Boom St; mains R60-75; 8.30am-4.30pm Mon-Fri, to 2pm Sat) A quintessential English garden serving fresh and tasty salads, sandwiches and excellent breakfasts.

Getting There & Away

SAAirlink (033-3869 2861; www.flyairlink.com) flies to Jo'burg daily (from R1300). The airport is 4km south of the city centre.

Most bus companies are in Burger St. **Translux** (0861 589 282; www.translux.co.za) and **City to City** (0861 589 282; www.translux.co.za), are based at the train station.

NUD Express (033-701 2750, 079 696 7108; www.underbergexpress.co.za) offers a daily service to Durban's King Shaka International Airport (R350) and Durban Central (R250). **Baz Bus** (0861 229 287; www.bazbus.com) picks up from hostels in Pietermaritzburg.

THE DRAKENSBERG

If any landscape lives up to its airbrushed, publicity-shot alter ego, it is the jagged tabletop peaks of the Drakensberg range, which forms the boundary between South Africa and Lesotho and offers some of the country's most awe-inspiring landscapes.

Within the area is the World Heritage–listed **uKhahlamba-Drakensberg Park**, a vast 2430-sq-km sweep of basalt summits and buttresses.

In general, you must book all **Ezemvelo KZN Wildlife** (033-845 1000, 031-304 4934; www.kznwildlife.com) accommodation in advance.

Royal Natal National Park

036

Spanning out from some of the range's loftiest summits, the 8000-hectare **Royal Natal National Park** (036-438 6310; www.kznwildlife.com; adult/child R30/20; 5am-7pm summer, 6am-6pm winter) has a presence that far outstrips its relatively meagre size, with many of the surrounding peaks rising as high into the air as the park stretches across. With some of the Drakensberg's most dramatic and accessible scenery, the park is crowned by the sublime **Amphitheatre**, an 8km wall of cliff and canyon. Here the **Tugela Falls** (eight to nine hours return for fit hikers) drop 850m in five stages.

The park's **visitor centre** (8am-4.30pm) is about 1km in from the main gate. There's also a shop selling basic provisions.

The park is renowned for its excellent day walks, including the Tugela Falls, which takes in the Amphitheatre. The hike involves climbing chain ladders; avoid cloudy days in summer.

Accommodation at the park's main camp, **Thendele** (033-845 1000; www.kznwildlife.com; 2-person chalet R875-995, 4-person chalet

R1525-1735), includes two-bed chalets. You can camp at beautiful **Mahai** (campsites per person R90) or rustic **Rugged Glen Nature Reserve** (campsites per person R90). There are also several places outside the park, including **Amphitheatre Backpackers** (☎036-438 6675; www.amphibackpackers.co.za; campsites per person from R75, dm R125, d R280-520; P 📶 🏊), 21km north of Bergville.

Central Drakensberg

☎036

Crowned with some of the Drakensberg's most formidable peaks, the central 'Berg is a big hit with hikers and climbers. But with dramatic scenery aplenty, the region is just as popular with those who prefer to admire mountains from a safe distance.

A beautifully photogenic area in the shadow of the ramparts of Cathedral Peak, the **Cathedral Peak Nature Reserve** (☎036-488 8000; www.kznwildlife.com; adult/child R30/15; ⏱6am-6pm) has myriad hiking trails and offers guides.

Boasting the Monk's Cowl and Champagne Castle peaks, **Monk's Cowl** (☎036-468 1103; www.kznwildlife.com; adult/child R35/18; ⏱6am-6pm) is another superb spot for hiking and climbing. Overnight hiking (adult/child R40/20) can be booked at the **park office** (☎036-468 1103; campsites 2-person minimum R190).

★**Inkosana Lodge** (☎036-468 1202; www.inkosana.co.za; campsites R100, dm/d without bathroom R150/450, 2-person thatched rondavel with/without bathroom R600/450; P 🏊) is one of Africa's best backpackers hostels, with pristine rooms, a pool and excellent hiking advice.

Southern Drakensberg Wilderness Areas

Best accessed from the pleasant towns of Himeville and Underberg, the southern 'Berg boasts one of the region's highlights: the journey up to Lesotho over the Sani Pass. It is renowned as a serious hiking area, offering great walks, including the fabulous Giant's Cup Trail.

Kamberg Nature Reserve (☎033-267 7251; www.kznwildlife.com; adult/child R30/15, rock-art walks per person R50, documentaries R20; ⏱5am-7pm Oct-Mar, 6am-6pm Apr-Sep) has a rock-art centre run by the local community. From there you can join a 3.5km guided walk to the impressive **Game Pass Shelter**, known as the 'Rosetta Stone' of San rock art.

The drive up the **Sani Pass** is a spectacular ride around hairpin bends into the kingdom of Lesotho. At 2865m, this is the highest pass in the country, and the vistas (on a clear day!) are magical. There are hikes in almost every direction, and inexpensive horse rides are available. You need a passport to cross into Lesotho. The border is open daily from 6am to 6pm, but check beforehand; times alter.

At the bottom of the pass you can sleep at the **Sani Lodge** (☎033-702 0330; www.sanilodge.co.za; campsites R70, dm/d without bathroom R110/320, 2-bed rondavel R400, self-catering cottage per person from R230), which offers a range of tours and activities, plus transfers from Himeville or Underberg.

The **Giant's Cup Trail** (68km, five days and five nights), running from Sani Pass to Bushman's Nek, is one of the nation's great walks. Early booking through **Ezemvelo KZN Wildlife** (☎033-845 1000; www.kznwildlife.com) is advisable.

ℹ DOING THE 'BERG

It's not easy to cover the whole of Drakensberg. There is no single road linking all the main areas of interest – you have to exit and re-enter each region of the park. You are better off basing yourself in one spot and exploring the immediate area, otherwise you'll end up spending most of your time behind a wheel driving between hikes and sites.

Each section of the park essentially operates as its own self-contained reserve, with entry fees payable each time you enter. Allow at least an hour to drive from one section to the next.

ℹ Information

Central Drakensberg Information Centre (☎036-488 1207; www.cdic.co.za; ⏱8.30am-5pm) Based in the Thokozisa complex, 13km outside Winterton on Rte 600.

Southern Berg Tourism (☎033-701 1471; www.drakensberg.org; Old Main Rd, Clocktower Centre, Underberg; ⏱8am-4pm Mon-Fri, 9am-1pm Sat & Sun) Has the useful *Southern Drakensberg Pocket Guide*.

Getting There & Around

Long-distance buses stop at Estcourt and Ladysmith, where you can catch minibus taxis into the Drakensberg.

NUD Express (033-701 2750, 079-696 7018; www.underbergexpress.co.za) links Underberg with Durban (R200) and Pietermaritzburg; you must book in advance.

The **Baz Bus** (0861 1229 287; www.bazbus.com) services a couple of hostels in the area, but to explore in any great depth, a car is strongly recommended.

FREE STATE

In this rural province, farmers in floppy hats and overalls drive rusty *bakkies* (pick-up or utility trucks) full of sheep down empty roads, and brightly painted Sotho houses (thatch-roofed *rondavels*) languish by vast fields of sunflowers. The Free State may not boast many not-to-be-missed attractions, but it has a subtle country charm that's easy to fall for.

In this conservative bastion, the colour divide remains stark, but while the province is a long way from racial nirvana, progress is happening.

Bloemfontein

051 / POP 645,000

Both the state capital and South Africa's judicial capital, 'Bloem' is a spunky university town. When school's in session, nightlife is raging. There's no real reason to go out of your way to visit, but it has a few interesting sights if you do pass through.

The **Anglo-Boer War Museum** (051-447 3447; www.anglo-boer.co.za; Monument Rd; adult/child R10/5; 8am-4.30pm Mon-Fri, 10am-5pm Sat, 11am-5pm Sun) has some interesting displays, including photos from concentration camps. In front is the **National Women's Monument**, commemorating the 26,000 women and children who died in British concentration camps during the Anglo-Boer War.

Sleeping & Eating

Odessa Guesthouse GUESTHOUSE $
(084 966 0200; 4 Gannie Viljoen St; s/d from R320/440;) Readers give this guesthouse rave reviews for its friendly hosts.

★**Hobbit Boutique Hotel** BOUTIQUE HOTEL $$
(051-447 0663; www.hobbit.co.za; 19 President Steyn Ave, Westdene; r incl breakfast from R950;) Inspired by JRR Tolkien, who was born in Bloem, the charming, old-world Hobbit comprises two 1921 houses.

Urban Hotel HOTEL $$
(051-444 3142; www.urbanhotel.co.za; cnr Parfitt Ave & Henry St; r R750;) Slightly better value than midrange competitors and with an excellent location a short walk from Loch Logan.

Avanti INTERNATIONAL $$
(051-447 4198; www.avantirestaurant.co.za; 53 2nd Ave, Westdene; mains R60-130; breakfast, lunch & dinner Mon-Sat, breakfast & lunch Sun) This popular spot has an extensive SA wine list and the usual Bloem offerings including pizza, pasta, steaks and seafood.

Drinking & Entertainment

Second Ave, particularly around Kellner St, competes for the nightlife scene with the **Loch Logan Waterfront** (051-448 3607; www.lochlogan.co.za), which also has a cinema. **Mystic Boer** (www.diemysticboer.co.za; 84 Kellner St;) is a long-standing favourite with live music.

Getting There & Away

South African Airways (086 160 6606; www.flysaa.com) and **Mango** (086 100 1234; www.flymango.com) fly to Bloem from Cape Town, Jo'burg or Durban.

Long-distance buses leave from the tourist centre on Park Rd. Destinations include **Cape Town** (R475, 12½ hours) and **Jo'burg/Pretoria** (R275, 5½ hours)

Minibus taxis leave from opposite the train station and head to Maseru, Lesotho (R80, three hours).

Shosholoza Meyl (0860 008 888, 011-774 4555; www.shosholozameyl.co.za) trains run three times weekly to/from Jo'burg, Port Elizabeth and East London.

GAUTENG

Fast, booming and a cabaret of contradictions, Gauteng (how-teng) remains the pulse of the South African nation.

Jo'burg is the country's largest and most happening city, where gold was discovered in the late 19th century and where fortunes are still made and lost. The wealth divide here is stark and it can be difficult to reconcile the glistening wealth with the sprawling townships.

The political centre of Pretoria, a short drive north, is decidedly less urbane but somewhat grander with its stately buildings and jacaranda-lined streets.

Johannesburg

011 / POP 5.7 MILLION

Jo'burg, also known as Jozi, is a rapidly developing city at the forefront of South Africa's development. The city centre is smartening up and Newtown, with its theatres, restaurants, museums and jazz clubs, is a lively cultural hub.

A thriving, black, middle class has risen from the ashes of apartheid, both in the suburbs and in the famous township of **Soweto**. However, the wealth divide remains stark. The affluenza of Rosebank and Sandton breeds discontent in desperately poor, neighbouring townships such as Alexandra.

Still, Jo'burg is a friendly, unstuffy city and there's a lot to see, from sobering reminders of the country's recent past at the Apartheid Museum to the progressive streets of Melville.

Sights & Activities

Sights aside, the energy generated by the hawkers, hair-braiders and pungent street food gives the city centre an urban atmosphere that you won't find in the northern suburbs, and that alone makes it worth a visit.

Rejuvenation has made Newtown the most appealing section of the downtown area.

Constitution Hill MUSEUM
(Map p942; 011-381 3100; www.constitutionhill.org.za; Kotze St; tours adult/child R50/20; 9am-5pm Mon-Fri, to 3pm Sat) Tours explore various exhibits within the ramparts of the **Old Fort**, largely focusing on **Number Four**, the notorious apartheid prison that once held Nelson Mandela, the **Women's Gaol** and the **Constitutional Court**.

Museum Africa MUSEUM
(Map p942; 011-833 5624; www.gauteng.net/attractions/entry/museum_africa; Old Market Bldg, 121 Bree St, Newtown; 9am-5pm Tue-Sun) FREE Overlooking **Mary Fitzgerald Sq**, this has several excellent exhibitions, covering diverse aspects of South Africa.

WORTH A TRIP

APARTHEID MUSEUM

This must-see **museum** (Map p938; 011-309 4700; www.apartheidmuseum.org; cnr Gold Reef Rd & Northern Parkway, Ormonde; adult/child R60/45; 9am-5pm Tue-Sun) illustrates the rise and fall of South Africa's era of segregation and oppression. The museum uses film, text, audio and live accounts to provide a chilling insight into the architecture and implementation of the apartheid system, as well as inspiring accounts of the struggle towards democracy. It's invaluable in understanding the inequalities and tensions that still exist today.

Sleeping

Backpackers Ritz BACKPACKERS $
(Map p938; 011-325 7125; www.backpackers-ritz.co.za; 1A North Rd, Dunkeld West; dm/s/d without bathroom R125/250/375; P @) Rooms are decent and there are excellent shared facilities, a vibrant social scene and beautiful views.

Sunbury House GUESTHOUSE $
(Map p938; 011-726 1114; www.sunburyhouse.com; 24 Sunbury Ave, Melville; s/d incl breakfast from R250/315; P @) The best-value budget accommodation in Melville has a variety of rooms with quirky furniture and bright colour schemes.

Joburg Backpackers BACKPACKERS $
(Map p938; 011-888 4742; www.joburgbackpackers.com; 14 Umgwezi Rd, Emmerentia; dm R110, r with/without bathroom R440/330, fR660; P @) This new hostel in the leafy suburbs has well-appointed rooms and a relaxed country feel.

★**12 Decades Hotel** BOUTIQUE HOTEL $$
(Map p938; 011-026 5601; www.12decadeshotel.co.za; 7th floor, Main Street Life Bldg, 286 Fox St, Maboneng; s/d from R620/820; P @) This terrific concept hotel, in the heart of the Maboneng precinct, has rooms inspired by eras in the city's history.

★**Motel Mipichi** BOUTIQUE HOTEL $$
(Map p938; 011-726 8844; www.motelmipichi.co.za; 35 4th Ave, Melville; s/d incl breakfast from R520/780; P @) A minimalist delight, with

Johannesburg

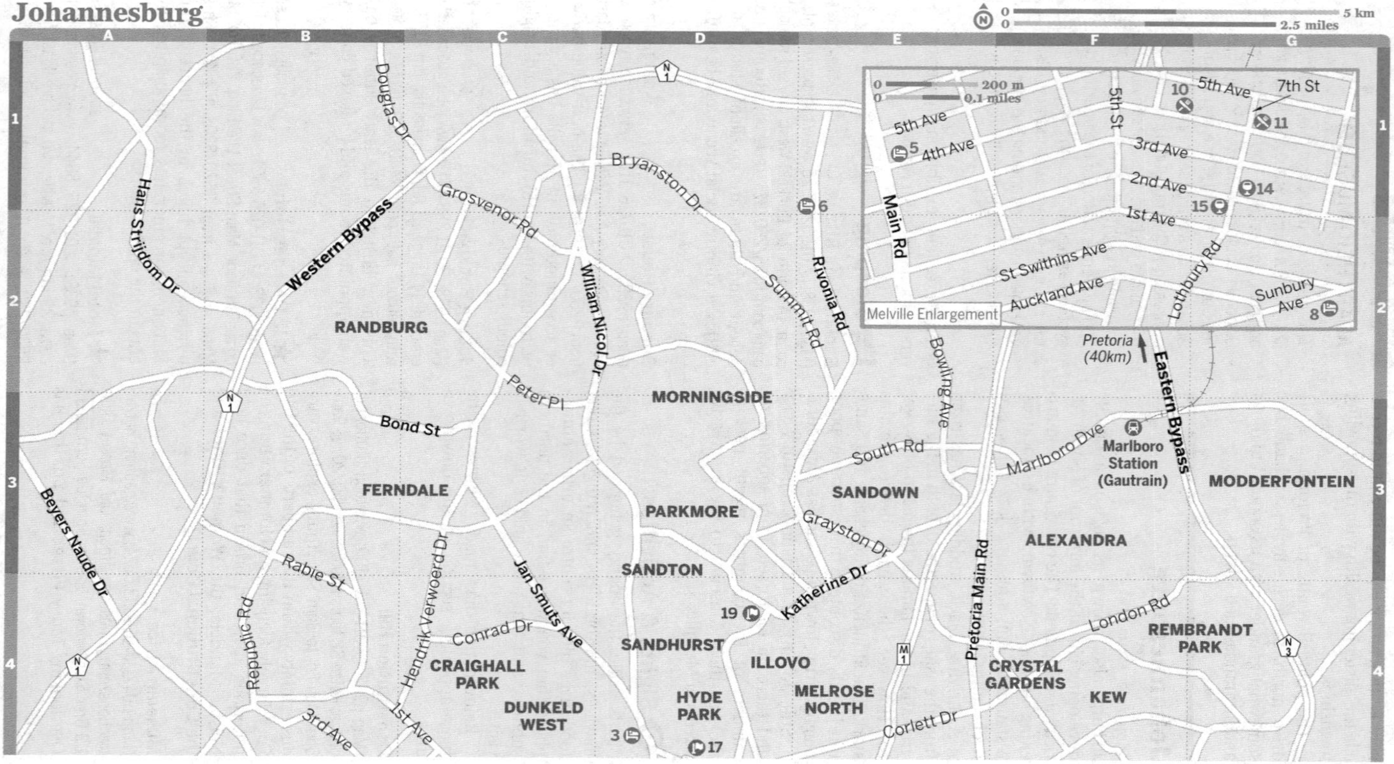

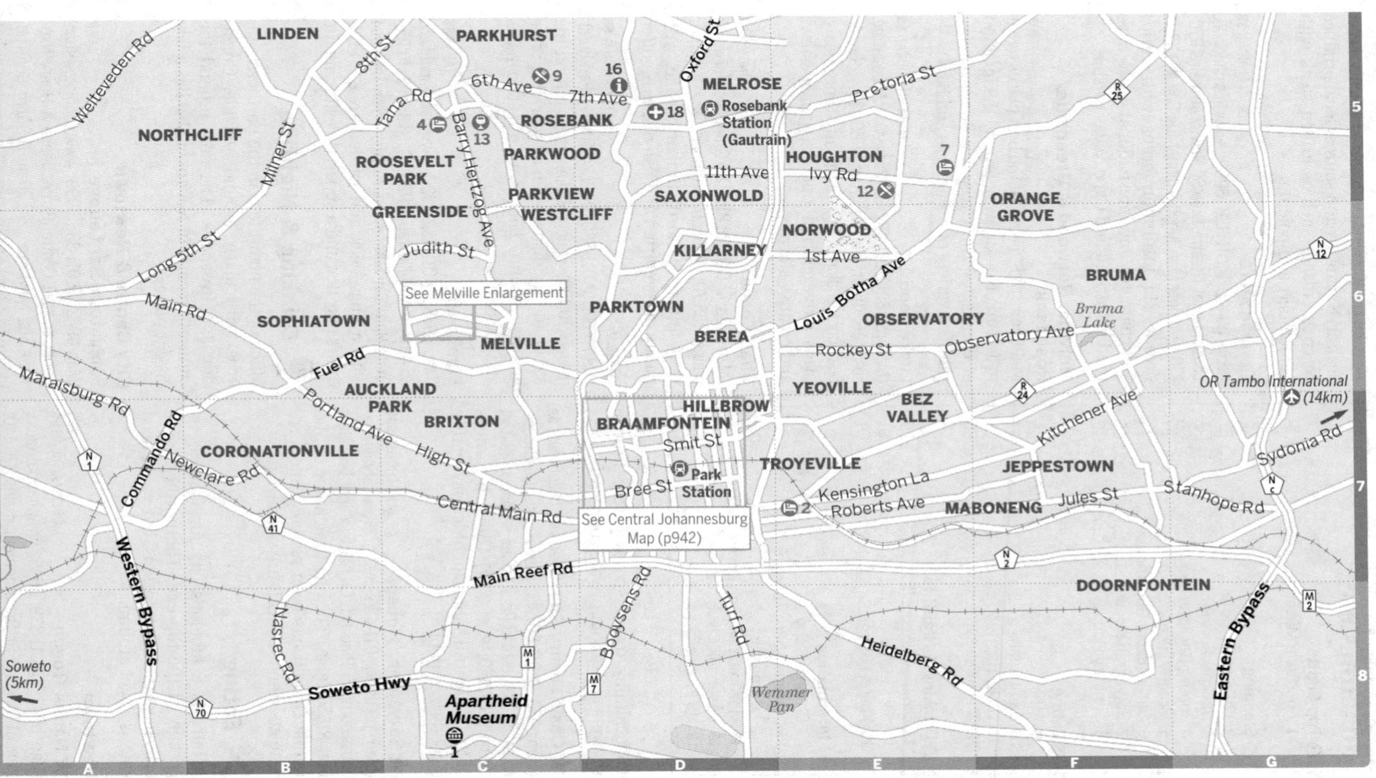
LINDEN
PARKHURST
Welteveden Rd
8th St
6th Ave
9
16
7th Ave
Oxford St
MELROSE
Pretoria St
Tana Rd
4
Barry Hertzog Ave
13
ROSEBANK
18
Rosebank Station (Gautrain)
NORTHCLIFF
Milner St
ROOSEVELT PARK
PARKWOOD
11th Ave
HOUGHTON
Ivy Rd
7
12
PARKVIEW
SAXONWOLD
GREENSIDE
WESTCLIFF
ORANGE GROVE
NORWOOD
KILLARNEY
1st Ave
Long 5th St
Judith St
BRUMA
Louis Botha Ave
See Melville Enlargement
PARKTOWN
Main Rd
SOPHIATOWN
OBSERVATORY
Bruma Lake
BEREA
MELVILLE
Rockey St
Observatory Ave
Fuel Rd
Maraisburg Rd
AUCKLAND PARK
YEOVILLE
OR Tambo International (14km)
HILLBROW
BEZ VALLEY
Portland Ave
BRIXTON
BRAAMFONTEIN
Kitchener Ave
Commando Rd
Smit St
CORONATIONVILLE
High St
Sydonia Rd
Newclare Rd
Park Station
TROYEVILLE
JEPPESTOWN
Kensington La
Bree St
Stanhope Rd
Jules St
2
Roberts Ave
MABONENG
Central Main Rd
See Central Johannesburg Map (p942)
Western Bypass
Main Reef Rd
DOORNFONTEIN
Boysens Rd
Turf Rd
Nasrec Rd
Heidelberg Rd
Eastern Bypass
Soweto (5km)
Soweto Hwy
Apartheid Museum
1
Wemmer Pan

Johannesburg

Top Sights
1 Apartheid Museum C8

Sleeping
2 12 Decades Hotel E7
3 Backpackers Ritz D4
4 Joburg Backpackers C5
5 Motel Mipichi E1
6 Oasis Luxury Guesthouse E1
7 Satyagraha House E5
8 Sunbury House G2

Eating
9 Attic C5
10 Bambanani F1
11 Lucky Bean G1
12 ShahiKhana E5

Drinking & Nightlife
13 Gin C5
14 Six G1
15 XaiXai Lounge G1

Information
Chroma Copy .... (see 12)
16 Johannesburg Tourism Company D5
17 Mozambican High Commission D4
18 Rosebank Clinic D5
19 US Embassy D4

four calming rooms sporting walk-through showers and adjoin private courtyards.

★**Oasis Luxury Guesthouse** GUESTHOUSE $$
(Map p938; 011-807 4351; www.oasisguesthouse.co.za; 29 Homestead Rd, Rivonia; s/d incl breakfast from R950/1150;) The lush gardens at this delightful suburban hideaway feature a good-sized pool.

★**Satyagraha House** GUESTHOUSE $$$
(Map p938; 011-485 5928; www.satyagraha-house.com; 15 Pine Rd, Orchards; r incl breakfast from R1650;) The one-time home of Mahatma Gandhi has been restored into a serene guesthouse. Meals are vegetarian.

Eating

Jo'burg is a fabulous city for foodies, especially at the top end. The northern suburbs have the most options, but you'll need wheels to get around.

Newtown

★**Narina Trogon** MODERN AFRICAN $$
(Map p942; 011-339 6645; www.narinatrogon.com; 81 De Korte St, Braamfontein; mains R70-140; breakfast & lunch Mon, breakfast, lunch & dinner Tue-Sat) Narina Trogon sources local produce to create dishes such as grilled steak with camembert and polenta.

Gramadoela's MODERN AFRICAN $$
(Map p942; 011-838 6960; www.gramadoelas.co.za; Market Theatre, Bree St, Newtown; mains R70-130; dinner Mon, lunch & dinner Tue-Sat;) This decades-old institution brims with curios and character, and international celebs have tried its African and Cape Malay cuisine.

Melville, Norwood & Greenside/ Rosebank

Melville's 7th St is one of the best places to eat in Jo'burg. Not far away, around the junction of Gleneagles and Greenway Rds in Greenside, is a variety of restaurants and bars.

Lucky Bean MODERN AFRICAN $$
(Map p938; 011-482 5572; www.luckybeantree.co.za; 16 7th St, Melville; mains R60-130; breakfast, lunch & dinner;) Light any-time meals, loads of vegetarian options, gamey stews and creative starters.

ShahiKhana INDIAN $$
(Map p938; 011-728 8157; 80 Grant Ave, Norwood; mains R55-70; lunch & dinner;) Super tasty and fiery North Indian cuisine, with plenty of vegetarian and fish dishes on offer.

Attic INTERNATIONAL $$
(Map p938; 011-880 6102; 24 4th Ave, Parkhurst; mains R70-130; lunch & dinner) Sit out on the street and try dishes such as sparkling wine and pea risotto. There's an attached tapas and cocktail bar.

Bambanani TAPAS $$
(Map p938; 011-482 2900; www.bambanani.biz; 85 4th Ave, Melville; tapas R25-30; 8am-8pm Tue-Fri, to 9pm Sat-Sun;) A family-friendly spot with a huge deck and garden area, a children's play den and a superlative kids' menu.

Drinking & Nightlife

Much of the nightlife is in the northern suburbs, particularly around Melville, Greenside and Rosebank. The area around the cultural precinct in Newtown also has a few decent places.

City Centre & Newtown

Sophiatown Bar Lounge BAR
(Map p942; 011-836 5999; www.sophiatownbarlounge.co.za; 1 Central Pl, cnr Jeppe & Henry Nxumalo Sts, Newtown; 8.30am-11.30pm Sun-Thu, to 2am Fri & Sat) Sophiatown's township spirit

is celebrated here, with live music on Friday and Saturday nights.

Carfax CLUB
(Map p942; ☎011-834 9187; 39 Pim St, Newtown; cover R70; ⏰9pm-late) Local and international DJs play house and hip hop at this popular converted factory space.

Melville

Six COCKTAIL BAR
(Map p938; ☎011-482 8306; 7th St, Melville) Fabulous artwork, iconic reggae and unobtrusive soul and house music.

XaiXai Lounge PUB
(Map p938; ☎011-482 6990; Shop 7, Melville Gardens, 7th St, Melville) Air your grievances loudly and proudly in this left-leaning Mozambican pub.

Greenside/Rosebank

Gin COCKTAIL BAR
(Map p938; ☎011-486 2404; 12 Gleneagles Rd, Greenside) House and hip hop keep the crowd happy at this bar, part shabby Caribbean shack, part gallery.

☆ Entertainment

Bassline LIVE MUSIC
(Map p942; ☎011-838 9145; www.bassline.co.za; 10 Henry Nxumalo St, Newtown; cover R60-170; ⏰6pm-late) The most respected live-music venue in Jo'burg, covering the full musical gamut.

Kippies Jazz International JAZZ
(Map p942; ☎011-833 3316; Margaret Mcingana St, Newtown; ⏰Thu-Sat) Once known as the 'sad man of jazz', Kippies Moeketsi would have a smile on his face if he could see what the city authorities have done to his classic jazz haunt.

Market Theatre THEATRE
(Map p942; ☎011-832 1641; www.markettheatre.co.za; Margaret Mcingana St, Newtown) Has three live theatre venues as well as galleries and a cafe.

ℹ Information

DANGERS & ANNOYANCES

Pay careful attention to your personal security in Jo'burg. Daylight muggings in the city centre and other inner suburbs, notably Hillbrow, do happen, and you must be on your guard. We've also heard of incidents in the underpasses leading out of Park Station. Don't walk around central Jo'burg at night – if you arrive after dark and don't have a car, catch a taxi.

Crime is a problem, but it is important to put things in perspective: remember that most travellers come and go without incident and that much of the crime afflicts parts of the city you would have little reason to stray into. It's when using ATMs that you're most vulnerable. Listen to local advice and remain aware of what's going on around you.

EMERGENCY

AIDS Line (☎0800 012 322)
Fire (☎10111)
Police (Map p942; ☎10111; Main Rd, Headquarters)
Rape Crisis Line (☎011-806 1888)

INTERNET ACCESS

Chroma Copy (Map p938; ☎011-483 2320; per hr R30; ⏰8.30am-6pm Mon-Thu, to 5pm Fri, to 1pm Sat)

MEDICAL SERVICES

Rosebank Clinic (Map p938; ☎011-328 0500; 14 Sturdee Ave, Rosebank; ⏰7am-10pm)

MONEY

There are banks with ATMs and change facilities at every commercial centre. **American Express** (www.americanexpress.co.za; Sandton City, OR Tambo International Airport) and **Rennies Travel** (www.renniestravel.com) have branches at the airport and in major malls.

POST

Main post office (Map p942; ☎011-336 1361; www.postoffice.co.za; Jeppe St; ⏰8.30am-4.30pm Mon-Fri, to noon Sat)

TOURIST INFORMATION

Gauteng Tourism Authority (Map p942; ☎011-085 2500; www.gauteng.net; 124 Main St; ⏰8am-5pm Mon-Fri)

Johannesburg Tourism Company (Map p938; ☎011-214 0700; www.joburgtourism.com; Ground fl, Grosvenor Cnr, 195 Jan Smuts Ave, Parktown North; ⏰8am-5pm Mon-Fri)

ℹ Getting There & Away

AIR

South Africa's major international and domestic airport is **OR Tambo International Airport** (Ortia; ☎011-921 6262; www.airports.co.za).

All flights with South African Airways and its subsidiaries can be booked through **SAA** (☎0861 606 606; www.flyairlink.com), which has offices in the airport's domestic and international terminals.

No-frills airlines **Kulula** (☎0861 585 852; www.kulula.com) and **Mango** (☎086 100 1234; www.flymango.com) offer better domestic rates.

Central Johannesburg

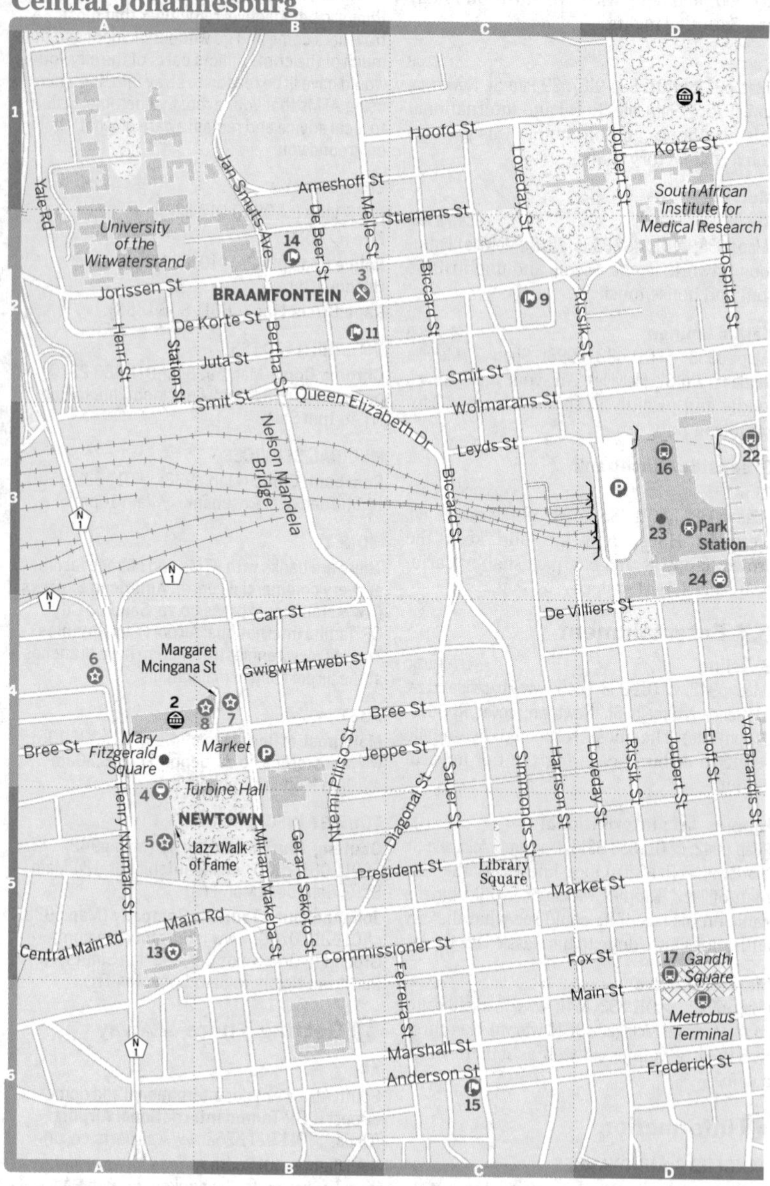

BUS

The main long-distance bus lines depart from and arrive at the Park Station transit centre. Here you will also find the booking offices for the major operators.

Except for **City to City** (☎ 011-774 333, 0861 589 282; www.translux.co.uk) buses, which start in Jo'burg, all services not heading north commence in Pretoria.

Cape Town (R550, 19 hours)

Durban (R300, eight hours)

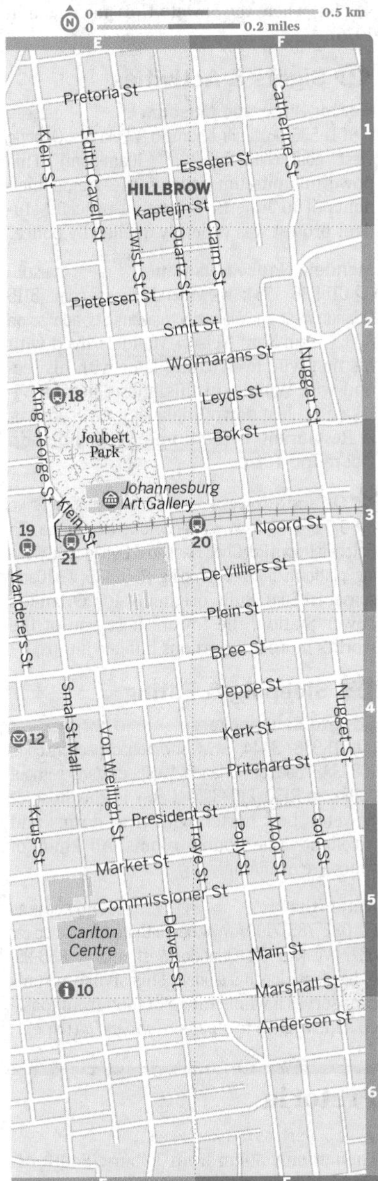

Central Johannesburg

Sights
1 Constitution Hill D1
2 Museum Africa A4

Eating
Gramadoela's .... (see 8)
3 Narina Trogon B2

Drinking & Nightlife
4 Sophiatown Bar Lounge A5

Entertainment
5 Bassline A5
6 Carfax A4
7 Kippies Jazz International B4
8 Market Theatre B4

Information
9 Botswanan Embassy C2
10 Gauteng Tourism Authority E5
11 Lesotho Embassy B2
12 Main Post Office E4
13 Police A5
14 Swazi Embassy B2
15 Zimbabwean Embassy C6

Transport
16 Long-distance Buses Booking Offices D3
17 Metropolitan Bus Services D5
18 Minibus Taxis to Bulawayo, Zimbabwe E2
19 Minibus Taxis to Durban E3
20 Minibus Taxis to Lesotho, Bloemfontein, Free State F3
21 Minibus Taxis to Pretoria E3
22 Minibus Taxis to Upington, Kimberley & Cape Town D3
23 Shosholoza Meyl D3
24 Taxis D3

Bloemfontein (R225, six hours)
Nelspruit (R255, five hours)
Kimberley (R250, 6½ hours)
Port Elizabeth (R350, 16 hours)

Baz Bus (☎ 0861 229 287;www.bazbus.com) picks up from hostels in Jo'burg.

Intercape (☎ 0861 287 287; www.intercape.co.za) operates a number of international bus services leaving from the Park Station complex for Botswana, Mozambique and Zimbabwe.

MINIBUS TAXI

Most minibus taxis use the road-transport interchange in Park Station, over the train tracks between the Metro Concourse and Wanderers St. Because of the risk of mugging, it is not a good idea to go searching for a taxi while carrying your luggage.

You can also find minibus taxis going towards Cape Town and the Northern Cape on Wanderers St; Bulawayo taxis at the northern end of King George St; Pretoria, Lesotho and Free State destinations on Noord St; and Durban taxis near the corner of Wanderers and Noord Sts. Take extreme care waiting in these areas; you should ideally be accompanied by a local.

TRAIN

Shosholoza Meyl (Map p942; ☎0860 008 888; www.shosholozameyl.co.za; Park Station) offers services to Cape Town, Durban and Port Elizabeth, among others.

Getting Around

OR Tambo International Airport is about 25km east of central Jo'burg. The 24-hour **Airport Shuttle** (☎0861 748 8853; www.airportshuttle.co.za) charges R370 for most destinations in Jo'burg; book a day in advance if possible. Most accommodation will collect you from the airport; most hostels do so for free.

The **Gautrain** (www.gautrain.co.za) connects the airport with Sandton (R115) and Park Station (R125).

Taxis operate meters (if the meter works). It's wise to ask a local the likely price and agree on a fare at the outset. From Park Station, a taxi to Rosebank should cost around R100.

Metropolitan Bus Services (Metrobus; Map p942; ☎0860 562 874; Gandhi Sq) runs services throughout Greater Jo'burg. Fares work on a zone system, ranging from Zone 1 (R7.90) to Zone 8 (R19.30).

If you take a minibus taxi into central Jo'burg, be sure to get off before it reaches the end of the route and avoid the taxi rank – it's a mugging zone. Fares differ depending on routes, but R5 will get you around the inner suburbs and city centre, and R9 will get you almost anywhere.

The Metro system is not recommended as it has a reputation for violent crime

Soweto

☎011

The 'South West Townships' have evolved from an area of forced habitation to an address of pride and social prestige. Travellers come to witness welcoming township life and to visit the excellent museums. A stroll down laid-back Vilakazi St offers an insight into modern African sensibilities, while Soccer City and the Soweto Bungee provide quality, concrete experiences in a place of great political abstraction.

Soweto is by far the most visited township in the country, so don't feel that visiting as a tourist is either unsafe or inappropriate. Most visitors still come on a tour, but the infrastructure is now such that a self-guided tour is not out of the question. If you choose to do this, heed local advice and stick to the area around Vilakazi St and Hector Pieterson Sq (where the Soweto Uprising began in 1976).

Sights & Activities

Hector Pieterson Museum MUSEUM
(☎011-536 0611; cnr Khumalo & Pela Sts, Orlando West; adult/child R30/10; ⏰10am-5pm) This powerful museum follows the tragic incidents of 16 June 1976, when a peaceful student protest was violently quelled by police.

Mandela House Museum MUSEUM
(☎011-936 7754; www.mandelahouse.com; 8115 Orlando West, cnr Vilakazi & Ngakane Sts; admission R60; ⏰9am-5pm) Nelson Mandela lived with his first wife Evelyn, and later with his second wife Winnie, in this house, just off Vilakazi St. Just down Vilakazi St, by Sakhumzi Restaurant, is the **home of Archbishop Desmond Tutu**.

★**Orlando Towers** BUNGEE JUMPING
(☎071 674-4343; www.orlandotowers.co.za; cnr Old Potchefstroom Rd/Chris Hani Rd & Dynamo St; viewing platform/bungee jumping R60/480; ⏰10am-sunset Fri-Sun) Built originally for Orlando's Power Station, the towers host one of the world's more incongruous bungee jumps.

Sleeping & Eating

Soweto Backpackers BACKPACKERS $
(☎011-936 3444; www.sowetobackpackers.com; 10823A Poe St, Orlando West; dm/s/d without bathroom R130/210/325) Lebo is the host of Soweto's best hostel, with neat dorms and excellent-value double rooms. All kinds of tours are available.

Nambitha SOUTH AFRICAN $$
(☎082 785 7190; www.nambitharestaurant.co.za; 6877 Vilakazi St, Orlando West; mains R50-95; ⏰breakfast, lunch & dinner) This stylish restaurant serves a whole range of food from toasted sandwiches to steaks to *mogodu* (tripe).

Pretoria

☎012 / POP 1.65 MILLION

Though only 50km from Jo'burg, South Africa's administrative centre is slower and more old-fashioned than its rough and tumble sister city, and many travellers feel safer here. It's also a handsome place, home to gracious old buildings, including the stately Union Buildings, and leafy suburbs. The wide streets are lined with a purple haze of jacarandas in October and November.

Culturally, Pretoria feels more like an Afrikaner-dominated country town than a capital city, and its bars and restaurants are less cosmopolitan than Jo'burg's. It was once at the heart of the apartheid regime, and its very name was a symbol of oppression, but today it's home to a growing number of black civil servants and foreign embassy workers, who are infusing the city with a new sense of multiculturalism.

Sights & Activities

Voortrekker Monument & Nature Reserve MONUMENT
(012-326 6770; www.voortrekkermon.org.za; Eeufees Rd; adult/child R45/25; 8am-6pm Sep-Apr, to 5pm May-Aug) This is a place of pilgrimage for many Afrikaners, built to honour the journey of the Voortrekkers (the original Afrikaner settlers of the Transvaal and the Orange Free State who migrated from the Cape Colony in the 1830s). There's a great panoramic view from the roof.

Freedom Park MONUMENT
(012-336 4000, 0800 470 740; www.freedompark.co.za; cnr Koch St & 7th Ave, Salvokop; adult/child R45/25; 8am-4.30pm, tours 9am, noon & 3pm) Freedom Park is a legacy of the Mandela government and honours all fallen South Africans in all major conflicts.

Church Square SQUARE
A statue of Paul Kruger takes pride of place in Church Sq, which is lined with imposing public buildings.

Sleeping

Backpackers are well served in Hatfield, and along with Arcadia and Brooklyn, this is the best place to look for midrange options.

1322 Backpackers International BACKPACKERS $
(012-362 3905; www.1322backpackers.com; 1322 Arcadia St, Hatfield; dm/s/d without bathroom from R135/195/305; P @) A friendly hostel with comfortable dorm beds, a guesthouse-standard double, and log cabins in the garden.

★Crane's Nest Guesthouse GUESTHOUSE $$
(012-460 7223; www.cranesnest.co.za; 212 Boshoff St, New Muckleneuk; s/d R675/880; P @) Our favourite place to stay in Pretoria has easy access to the bird sanctuary across the road and hotel-style touches like minibars.

★Manhattan Hotel HOTEL $$
(012-392 0000; www.manhattanhotel.co.za; 247 Scheiding St, City Centre; s/d from R920/1070; P) Five-star service, extensive dining options and shuttles to Gautrain stations. The area is not ideal for an evening amble.

That's It GUESTHOUSE $$
(012-344 3404; www.thatsit.co.za; 5 Brecher St, Clydesdale; s/d incl breakfast R495/690; P @) Professionally run and competitively priced. The plain-ish rooms face a sofa-filled *lapa* (entertainment area).

Hotel 224 HOTEL $$
(012-440 5281; www.hotel224.com; cnr Schoeman/Francis Baard & Leyds Sts, Arcadia; s/d incl breakfast R650/755; P) A smart, serviceable option if you need to be close to the city.

Eating

The best eateries are in Hatfield, Brooklyn and New Muckleneuk.

Café Riche PUB $
(012-328 3173; www.caferiche.co.za; 2 Church St, City Centre; mains R35-70; 6am-6pm) This historical bistro is popular with tourists and visiting dignitaries.

★Kream INTERNATIONAL $$
(012-346 4642; www.kream.co.za; 570 Fehrsen St, Brooklyn Bridge; mains R80-160; noon-late Mon-Sat, lunch Sun;) An uber-trendy menu featuring exotic starters and the usual grilled suspects for main course.

Blue Crane SOUTH AFRICAN $$
(012-460 7615; www.bluecranerestaurant.co.za; 156 Melk St, New Muckleneuk; mains R40-80; breakfast & lunch daily, dinner Tue-Sat;) Offering Afrikaner dishes as well as steak and seafood, this restaurant overlooks a lake that is the breeding site for its namesake.

Hombaze AFRICAN $$
(012-342 7753; www.hombazeafricacuisine.co.za; Eastwood Village Centre, cnr Eastwood & Pretorius Sts, Arcadia; mains R45-90; breakfast, lunch & dinner;) This small franchise serves African staples. Lots of meaty dishes and fried sides plus one of the longest vegetarian menus in the city.

Drinking & Nightlife

Hatfield is the best place for a night out. Hatfield Sq is a university student stronghold after dark.

Pretoria

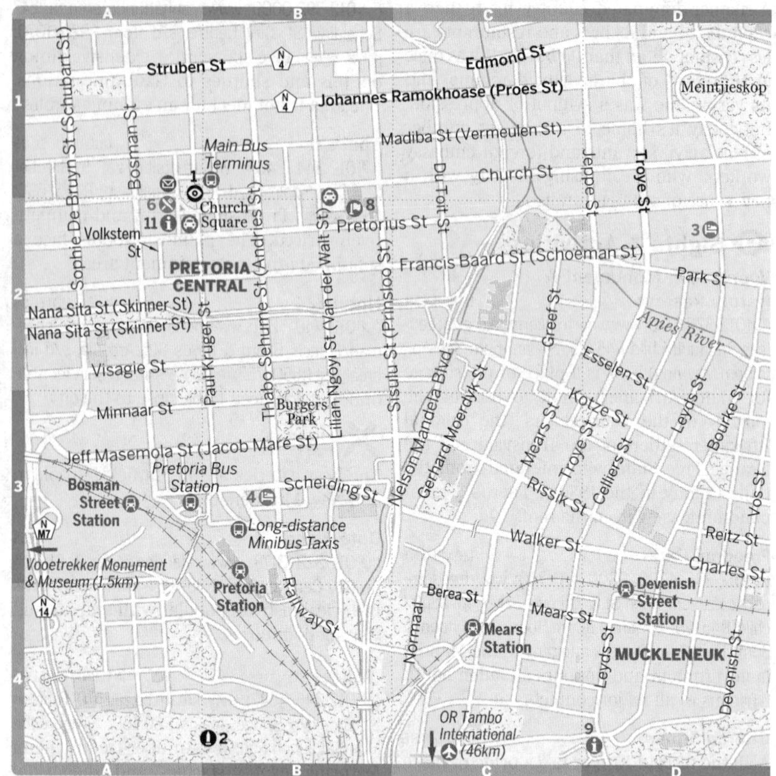

TriBeCa Lounge COCKTAIL BAR

(012-460 3068; Veale St, Brooklyn Sq, Brooklyn) The perfect place to chill out with a latte or to sip an exquisite cocktail.

Information

DANGERS & ANNOYANCES

Although Pretoria is safer and more relaxed than Jo'burg, crime is a problem, particularly in the city centre and Sunnyside. Avoid the centre after dark and be on guard at the weekend when there are fewer people about.

INTERNET ACCESS

Most accommodation offers internet facilities and wi-fi; **4 in Love Internet Café** (012-362 5358; 1077 Burnett St; per hr R10; 9am-7pm Mon-Fri, 9am-6pm Sat, 10am-5pm Sun) is a cheaper alternative.

MEDICAL SERVICES

Tshwane District Hospital (012-354 5958; Dr Savage Rd)

MONEY

There are banks with ATMs and change facilities across town.

American Express (012-346 2599; Brooklyn Mall, Brooklyn; 9am-5pm)

POST

Main post office (www.postoffice.co.za; Church Sq; 8.30am-4.30pm Mon-Fri, 8am-noon Sat)

TOURIST INFORMATION

South African National Parks (SANParks; 012-428 9111; www.sanparks.org; 643 Leyds St, Muckleneuk; offices 7.45am-3.45pm Mon-Fri, call centre 7.30am-5pm Mon-Fri, 8am-1pm Sat)

Tourist Information Centre (012-358 1430; www.tshwanetourism.com; Old Nederlandsche Bank Bldg, Church Sq; 7.30am-4pm Mon-Fri) Fairly unhelpful; better off asking your hotel for advice.

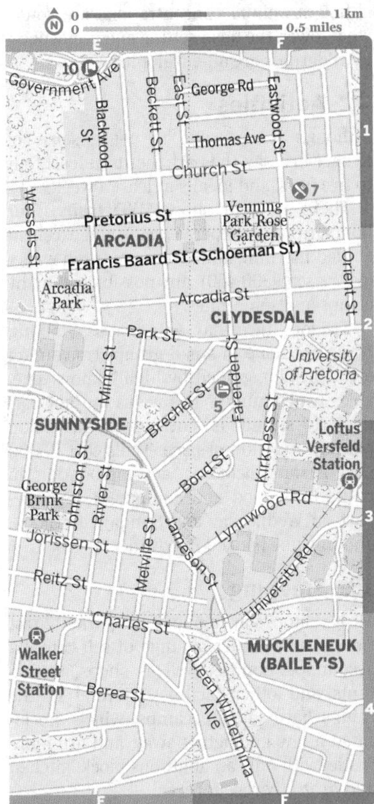

Pretoria

Sights

1	Church Square	A1
2	Freedom Park	B4

Sleeping

3	Hotel 224	D2
4	Manhattan Hotel	B3
5	That's It	F2

Eating

6	Café Riche	A2
7	Hombaze	F1

Information

8	Lesotho High Commission	B2
9	South African National Parks	D4
10	Swazi High Commission	E1
11	Tourist Information Centre	A2

Getting There & Away

Most interprovincial and international bus services commence in Pretoria, unless they are heading north. **Translux** (0861 589 282; www.translux.co.za), **Greyhound** (083 915 9000; www.greyhound.co.za) and **Intercape** (0861 287 287; www.intercape.co.za) fares from Pretoria are identical to those from Jo'burg. If you only want to go between the two cities, it will cost about R150.

The **Baz Bus** (0861 229 287; www.bazbus.com) picks up and drops off at Pretoria hostels.

Minibus taxis leave from the main terminal by the train station and travel to a host of destinations including Jo'burg (R45).

Because of the high incidence of crime, we don't recommend taking the metro between Pretoria and Jo'burg; take the **Gautrain** (0800 4288 7246; www.gautrain.co.za) instead (R46 to R52).

Shosholoza Meyl (0860 008 888; www.shoholoza meyl.co.za) has economy class services to Nelspruit, Komatipoort, Polokwane and Musina.

Getting Around

Get You There Transfers (012-346 3175; www.getyoutheretransfers.co.za) operates shuttles between Jo'burg's OR Tambo International Airport and Pretoria for about R400; the same price as a taxi. If you call ahead, most hostels, and many hotels, offer free pick-up. The Gautrain links the airport and Pretoria (R135).

There's an extensive network of local buses. Fares range from R5 to R10, depending on the distance.

There are taxi ranks on the corner of Church and Lilian Ngoyi (Van der Walt) Sts, and on the corner of Pretorius and Paul Kruger Sts.

Sun City

014

A popular destination in the nearby North-West Province for Gauteng weekenders, **Sun City** (014-557 1580; www.suncity.co.za; admission R60; 24hr) is South Africa's answer to Vegas. Disneyland collides with ancient Egypt at this gambling-centric resort, filled with gilded statues of lions and monkeys, 1200 hotel rooms and countless clinking slot machines.

The best part of Sun City is **Lost City**, which is entered over a bridge flanked by life-sized fake elephants, and includes **Valley of the Waves** (Sun City , North-West Province; adult/child R120/70, overnight guests free; 9am-6pm Sep-Apr, 10am-5pm May-Aug), a water park with an artificial beach. It's good, kitsch fun.

If you've got cash to spend, **Palace of the Lost City** (s/d incl breakfast from R5200/5460;) is one of the world's most luxurious hotels, but if Sun City's accommodation is too expensive (and you have your own transport), consider staying at **Pilanesberg National Park** (014-555 1600; www.parksnorthwest.co.za/pilanesberg; adult/pensioner & child R65/20, vehicle R20, map R20; 5.30am-7pm Nov-Feb, 6am-6.30pm Mar, Apr, Sep & Oct, 6.30am-6pm May-Aug, last entry an hour before gates close) or Rustenburg and visiting on a day trip.

From Jo'burg it's less than a three-hour drive to Sun City. **Ingelosi Shuttles** (014-552 3260; www.ingelositours.co.za; Welcome Centre, Sun City) runs shuttles to and from Jo'burg, Pretoria and OR Tambo International Airport (R400).

MPUMALANGA

Unassuming Mpumalanga (Place of the Rising Sun) adheres to a quieter pace of life. This inland province is where the plateaus of the highveld begin their spectacular tumble onto the lowveld plains at the dramatic **Drakensberg Escarpment**. Many travellers zip through on their way to Kruger National Park, but it's well worth setting aside a few days to explore the historical towns, roaring waterfalls and superlative hiking trails.

Kruger National Park

Kruger is one of South Africa's national symbols, and for many visitors, the park is *the* must-see wildlife destination in the country. Little wonder: in an area the size of Wales, enough elephants wander around to populate a city, giraffes nibble on acacia trees, hippos wallow in the rivers, leopards prowl through the night and a multitude of birds sing, fly and roost.

The park has an extensive network of sealed roads and comfortable camps, but if you prefer to keep it rough, there are also 4WD tracks, and mountain-bike and hiking trails. Even when you stick to the tarmac, the sounds and scents of the bush are never more than a few metres away.

Southern Kruger is the most popular section of the park, with the highest animal concentrations and the easiest access. Kruger is at its best in the far north. Here, although animal concentrations are somewhat lower, the bush setting and atmospheric wilderness are all-enveloping.

Activities

Although it's possible to get a sense of Kruger in a day, the park merits at least four to five days, and ideally at least a week.

There are four short **4WD trails** (four hours; from R500 per vehicle), and excellent guided morning and afternoon **bush walks** (per person R300-460) are possible at many camps and some gates.

Kruger's three-day **wilderness walking trails** are done in small groups (maximum eight people), guided by highly knowledgeable, armed guides. The walks are not particularly strenuous, covering about 20km per day at a modest pace. Trails cost R3900 per person, including accommodation in rustic huts, food and equipment; they depart on Wednesday and Sunday afternoon, and must be booked in advance.

Sleeping

Most visitors stay in one of the park's 12 rest camps, which offer a range of self-catering accommodation, as well as shops, restaurants and other facilities. Several of the camps have satellite camps, which are located a few kilometres away, and are more rustic, with only an ablutions block, kitchen and *braai* (barbecue) area.

Huts (2 people from around R410) are the cheapest option, with shared ablutions and communal cooking facilities; **bungalows** (2 people from around R865) range from simple to luxurious; **cottages** (up to 4 people around R1590) usually have a living area.

Some camps also offer **safari tents** (from R435), all of which are furnished and have a refrigerator and fan.

For those with tents or caravans, **camping** (per campsite for 1 to 2 people R200, per additional adult/child up to 6 maximum R62/31) is available at many rest camps.

There are also five **bushveld camps** (cottages for up to 4 people R1320-1910) – smaller, more remote clusters of self-catering cottages without shops or restaurants – and two **bush lodges** (lodges for 4/8 people R2465/5100), which are set in the middle of the wilderness and must be booked in their entirety by a single group.

At the opposite end of the spectrum, there's luxurious accommodation in the private reserves bordering Kruger to the west.

You could also stay outside the park and visit on day trips.

Information

Accommodation can be booked through **South African National Parks** (SANParks; ☎012-428 9111; www.sanparks.org) and **Lowveld Tourism** (www.lowveldtourism.com), which has offices in Nelspruit and Cape Town. Except in high season and on weekends, bookings are advisable but not essential.

Day or overnight entry to the park costs R204/102 per adult/child. Bicycles and motorcycles are not permitted to enter the park.

During school holidays you can stay in the park for a maximum of 10 days, and at any one rest camp for five days (10 days if you're camping). Visitor numbers are restricted, so arrive early in the high season if you don't have a booking. Opening times for the nine entry gates vary slightly with the season.

Getting There & Around

South African Airways (☎0861 359 722; www.flysaa.com) has daily flights linking Jo'burg (R950 to 1720) with Kruger Mpumalanga International Airport (MQP) near Nelspruit, Kruger Park Gateway Airport in Phalaborwa and Hoedspruit Eastgate Airport. There are also direct flights to MQP from Cape Town (R2540) and Durban (R2100).

Nelspruit is the most convenient large town near Kruger, and is well served by buses and minibus taxis to and from Jo'burg. Numbi Gate is about 50km away, and Malelane Gate about 65km away. Phalaborwa, right on the edge of the park, is a handy gateway for northern and central Kruger.

Most visitors drive themselves around the park, and this is the best way to experience Kruger. **Avis** (☎in Johannesburg 011-923 3600, in Skukuza 013-735 5651; www.avis.co.za) has a branch at Skukuza Rest Camp, and there is car rental from the Nelspruit, Hoedspruit and Phalaborwa airports.

Nelspruit

☎013 / POP 235,000

Nelspruit is Mpumalanga's largest town and provincial capital, sprawling along the Crocodile River Valley in the steamy, subtropical lowveld. There are some decent shopping malls and good accommodation and restaurants, making it a reasonable stopover on your way elsewhere.

> **CHANGING NAMES**
>
> Nelspruit has officially changed its name to Mbombela. The new moniker is scarcely used, but you might see it on the occasional map.

Sleeping & Eating

Funky Monkey Backpackers BACKPACKERS **$**
(☎013-744 1310; www.funkymonkeys.co.za; 102 Van Wijk St; campsites per person R80, dm R130, s/d without bathroom R200/380; @) A little out of town, the city's best hostel is a well-run place in a spacious house.

★**Utopia in Africa** GUESTHOUSE **$$**
(☎013-745 7714; www.utopiainafrica.co.za; 6 Daleen St; s/d incl breakfast from R675/990;) Rooms come with balconies overlooking the nearby nature reserve.

★**Jock & Java** PUB **$$**
(☎013-755 4969; www.jockandjava.co.za; Ferreira St; mains R60-110, breakfast R30; breakfast, lunch & dinner Mon-Sat;) A rambling pub and separate tearoom set in large lawns.

Getting There & Away

There are daily buses to Jo'burg/Pretoria and Maputo (Mozambique). Minibus taxis leave from Nelspruit Plaza to destinations including Graskop and Jo'burg. There are daily flights to Jo'burg.

City Bug (☎086 133 4433; www.citybug.co.za) operates a twice-weekly shuttle to Durban (R590), and a daily shuttle to OR Tambo International Airport (R370 per person).

Blyde River Canyon

The Blyde River's spectacular canyon is nearly 30km long and one of South Africa's most impressive natural features. Much of it is rimmed by the 260-sq-km **Blyde River Canyon Nature Reserve** (☎021-424 1037; www.mtpa.co.za; per person/car R25/5), which snakes north from Graskop, following the escarpment and meeting the Blyde River as it carves its way down to the lowveld. Most visitors drive along the edge of the canyon, with stops at the many wonderful viewpoints, but if you have the time, it's well worth exploring on foot.

God's Window and **Wonder View** (on Rte 534) are two of the finest viewpoints. The Blyde River Canyon starts north of here, near **Bourke's Luck Potholes** (on Rte 532), bizarre cylindrical holes carved into the rock by whirlpools.

Forever Blyde Canyon (0861 226 966; www.foreverblydecanyon.co.za; campsites per person R120, 2-/4-person self-catering chalets R725/1040, 2-/4-person deluxe chalets from R820/1550;) is a rambling resort with a range of accommodation and hiking trails.

Graskop

013 / POP 2000 / ELEV 1450M

A useful base for exploring the Blyde River Canyon, compact little Graskop is one of the area's most appealing towns.

★**Graskop Valley View Backpackers** (013-767 1112; www.yebo-afrika.nl; 47 De Lange St; campsite per person R70, dm R100, tw R240-290;) has a variety of rooms, plus tent sites and adventure tours on offer.

Graskop Hotel (013-767 1244; www.graskophotel.co.za; cnr Hoof & Louis Trichardt Sts; s/d incl breakfast R550/800;) has stylish rooms and country cottages with dollhouse-like furniture.

The minibus taxi stand (Hoof St) is at the southern end of town, with daily departures.

NORTHERN CAPE

Covering nearly a third of the country, the vast and sparsely populated Northern Cape is South Africa's last great frontier. This is a land of stark contrasts, where the red sands of the Kalahari drift towards the Atlantic Coast, and the plains of the Upper Karoo collide with sun-scorched Namakwa's lunar landscape, famous for its spring wildflowers. Lions stalk prey across crimson plains in remote Kgalagadi Transfrontier Park at dawn; in the evening, big orange-ball sunsets set the stage for bright starry nights.

Kimberley

053 / POP 171,000

An old diamond town with a chequered past, Kimberley is the capital of the Northern Cape and worth a few days' pause. Step inside one of the atmospheric old pubs with their dark smoky interiors and you'll feel you've been transported to the rough-and-ready diamond heyday of the late 19th century.

Sights & Activities

Big Hole Complex MUSEUM

(053-830 4426; www.thebighole.co.za; West Circular Rd; adult/child R75/45; 8am-5pm, tours on the hour Mon-Fri, weekends 9am, 11am, 1pm & 3pm) Hour-long tours of the world's largest hand-dug hole start with a film on Kimberley's mining legacy, followed by a visit to the viewing platform, jutting out over the 800m chasm. The coolest part of the tour is the simulated mining experience and partial reconstruction of Kimberley's 1880s mining camp.

Wildebeest Kuil Rock Art Centre ARCHAEOLOGICAL SITE

(053-833 7069; www.wildebeestkuil.itgo.com; Rte 31; adult/child R20/10; 9am-4pm Mon-Fri, 10am-4pm Sat & Sun) On a site owned by the !Xun and Khwe San people, this small sacred hill has 400-plus rock engravings. Guided tours are available.

The centre is 16km northwest of town, en route to Barkly West.

Sleeping & Eating

Ekhaya Guest House GUESTHOUSE $

(053-874 3795; ekhayag@telkomsa.net; cnr Hulana & Montshiwa Sts, Galeshewe; s R360, d from R440;) The thatched cottages at this township guesthouse are comfortable and stylish. Rooms are a notch above backpacker standards. Breakfast costs R65.

★**Kimberley Club** BOUTIQUE HOTEL $$

(053-832 4224; www.kimberleyclub.co.za; 72 Du Toitspan Rd; s/d from R945/1225;) Founded as a private club in 1881, the reputedly haunted hotel exudes history and rooms are period elegant. There's a good restaurant too. Breakfast costs R85.

★**Halfway House** PUB $$

(053-831 6324; www.halfwayhousehotel.co.za; 229 Du Toitspan Rd; mains R70; lunch & dinner) The interiors of this 1872 watering hole are beautifully historic and locals flock in to chomp pub grub.

Getting There & Away

There are regular flights to Jo'burg and Cape Town with **SA Express** (0861 729 227; www.flyexpress.aero).

The main bus lines serve Jo'burg/Pretoria and Cape Town.

Shosholoza Meyl (www.shosholozameyl.co.za) has regular trains to Jo'burg and Cape Town.

Upington

☎054 / POP 53,000

On the banks of the Senqu (Orange) River, orderly and prosperous Upington is a good place to catch your breath at either end of a long Kalahari slog. In the side streets, lazy river views and rows of date palms create a calm and quiet atmosphere, perfect for an afternoon stroll (if the heat is not too stifling).

Sleeping

Die Eiland Holiday Resort CAMPGROUND, CHALETS **$$**
(☎054-334 0287; www.kharahais.gov.za/eiland.html; campsites from R105, chalets from R660;) Upington's best budget option offers huts, bungalows and shaded camping spots alongside the river.

★ **Le Must River Residence** BOUTIQUE HOTEL **$$**
(☎054-332 3971; www.lemustupington.com; 14 Budler St; s/d incl breakfast from R890/1180;) This elegant riverside getaway has African-themed rooms. **Le Must's River Manor** (s/d from R495/730) boasts the same professional service.

Getting There & Away

SA Express (☎0861 729 227; www.flyexpress.aero)operates daily flights to/from Cape Town and Jo'burg.

Intercape (☎0861 287 287; www.intercape.co.za; Lutz St) buses leave from Lutz St. Destinations include Cape Town (R560, 12 hours), Jo'burg/Pretoria (R750, 11¼ hours) and Windhoek (Namibia; R550, 12 hours).

Kgalagadi Transfrontier Park

A long, hot road leads between crimson dunes from Upington to the magical **Kgalagadi Transfrontier Park** (☎054-561 2000; www.sanparks.org/parks/kgalagadi; adult/child R204/102), one of the world's last great, unspoilt ecosystems. The Kgalagadi is a wild land of harsh extremes and frequent droughts, where shifting red and white sands meet thorn trees and dry riverbeds.

Visitors are restricted to four gravel/sand roads, unless you pre-book one of the **4WD trails**.

The best time to visit is in June and July, when the days are coolest (below freezing at night) and the animals have been drawn to the bores along the dry riverbeds.

Inside the park there are three rest camps and seven luxury wilderness camps. All can be booked through **South African National Parks** (SANParks; ☎012-428 9111; www.sanparks.org). All rest camps have **campsites** (1-2 people R220, extra adult/child R68/34) with shared ablution facilities. The camps also have a range of huts, bungalows and cottages. The wilderness camps, though much more expensive, give you the opportunity to really get off the beaten path.

Twee Rivieren Gate is 270km northwest of Upington on the tarred Rte 360.

NAMAKWA FLOWERS

Outside of flower season there's little to see or do in the **Namakwa** region, although the desolate landscape is alluring. When the flowers bloom though, in August and September, the region comes into its own and accommodation fills up.

Springbok has some appealing accommodation options, but a better spot to sleep among the flowers is the **Namaqua National Park** (☎027-672 1948; www.sanparks.org/parks/namaqua; admission R48; 8am-5pm). There are coastal **campsites** (from R75) and the **Skilpad Rest Camp** (self-catering chalets from R650) in the park. A temporary tented **beach camp** (per person incl brunch, high tea & dinner from R2105) operates from mid-August to mid-September – book well in advance.

The park is about 70km southwest of Springbok – you'll need your own transport to reach it.

UNDERSTAND SOUTH AFRICA

South Africa Today

Two decades after the end of apartheid, life in South Africa remains dominated by social inequality. Seeing first-world wealth alongside African poverty is confronting for first-time visitors. Yet projects aiming to empower inhabitants of the townships and former homelands abound, making South Africa an uplifting and intriguing place.

South Africa is grappling with both apartheid's legacy and pan-African problems. Economic refugees continue arriving from neighbouring countries, intensifying pressure on infrastructure and competition for jobs.

Also reflecting pan-African issues, South Africa has the world's largest population of people with HIV/Aids. Educational efforts face numerous taboos; *sangomas* (traditional healers) preach superstitious lore and, every day, funerals commemorate supposed tuberculosis victims.

South Africa's record on gender issues exemplifies the country's contradictions. Its constitution is the world's most progressive, promoting the rights of women and gay people (same-sex marriage is legal) among others. Yet street-level reality is far harsher, with one of the world's highest reported incidences of rape, including 'corrective' rape of lesbians.

Crime and corruption will be hot topics at the 2014 elections, when Helen Zille is likely to shrink the gap between her opposition Democratic Alliance party, which already governs the Western Cape, and the African National Congress (ANC), the ruling party of South Africa.

History

South Africa's history extends back to around 40,000 BC when the San people first settled Southern Africa. By AD 500, Bantu-speaking peoples had arrived from West Africa's Niger Delta.

Competing colonial European powers began settling here in small numbers from the 17th century, mostly in the Cape. Widespread colonial settlement of South Africa began in the 19th century.

The British annexed the Cape in 1806 and when they abolished slavery in 1833, the Boers (Dutch-Afrikaner farmers) considered it an intolerable interference in their affairs. Dissatisfied with British rule, they trekked off into the interior in search of freedom. This became known as the Great Trek.

The Great Trek coincided with the *difaqane* (forced migration of the Zulu people) and the Boers mistakenly believed that what they found – deserted pasture lands, disorganised bands of refugees and tales of brutality – was the normal state of affairs. This gave rise to the Afrikaner myths that these Voortrekkers (pioneers) moved into unoccupied territory or arrived at much the same time as black Africans.

The Boers came into this chaos in search of new lands, and the British were not far behind them. The Zulu were eventually defeated, but relations between the Boers and the British remained tense – particularly after the formation of the Boer republics of the Orange Free State and the Transvaal.

Diamonds were discovered in 1867 at Kimberley, followed by the discovery of gold in 1886 on the Witwatersrand, the area around Jo'burg. The Boer republics were flooded with British business and immigrant labourers, which created resentment among Afrikaner farmers.

Wars ensued and while the Boers were victorious in the First Anglo-Boer War (known by Afrikaners as the War of Independence), the Second Anglo-Boer War (1899–1902) ended with the defeat of the Boer republics and the imposition of British rule. Britain had pursued a scorched-earth policy to combat Boer guerrillas, destroying homes, crops and livestock.

Independence & Apartheid

In 1910 the Union of South Africa was created, giving political control to the whites. Inevitably, this prompted black resistance, and political organisations were formed. Despite the moderate tone of these early resistance groups, the government reacted by intensifying repression.

The Afrikaner National Party won the election in 1948 and began to brutally enforce laws excluding nonwhites from having any political or economic power. The suppression of black resistance ranged from the Sharpeville massacre of 1960 and the shooting of high-school students in Soweto in 1976, to the forcible evacuation and bulldozing of entire urban areas, and the systematic torture – even murder – of political activists such as Steve Biko.

One of the most important organisations to oppose the racist legislation was the African National Congress (ANC). As it became obvious that the white rulers were unwilling to undertake even the most cosmetic reforms, some ANC members took to guerrilla warfare. In the early 1960s, many ANC leaders were arrested, charged with treason and imprisoned, the most famous being Nelson Mandela.

Apartheid was entrenched even further during the early 1970s by the creation of the so-called black homelands. These were, in theory, 'independent' countries. With the creation of the homelands, all black people within white-designated South Africa were deemed foreign guest-workers and were without political rights. Any black person without a residence pass could be 'deported' to a homeland.

The international community finally began to oppose the apartheid regime and the UN imposed economic and political sanctions. The government made some concessions, which included the establishment of a farcical new parliament of whites, 'coloureds' (people of mixed race) and Indians – but no black people.

The 'reforms' did nothing to ease sanctions. After the 1989 elections the new president, FW de Klerk, instituted a program that was aimed not only at dismantling the apartheid system, but also at introducing democracy. The release of political prisoners in February 1990 (including Nelson Mandela), the repeal of the Group Areas Act (which set up the homelands), and the signing of a peace accord with the ANC and other opposition groups all opened the way for hard-fought negotiations on the path to majority rule.

The Post-Apartheid Era

The country's first democratic elections took place in 1994, with the ANC winning 62.7% of the vote; 66.7% would have enabled it to rewrite the interim constitution. The National Party won 20.4% of the vote, enough to guarantee representation in cabinet. Nelson Mandela was made president of the 'new' South Africa.

In 1999 South Africa held its second democratic elections. The National Party lost two-thirds of its seats, losing official opposition status to the Democratic Party. Thabo Mbeki, who had taken over the ANC leadership from Mandela in 1997, became president.

While Mbeki was viewed with less affection by the ANC grassroots than the beloved 'Madiba' (Mandela), he was a shrewd politician, leading the ANC to a decisive victory in the 2004 elections.

However, Mbeki's effective denial of the AIDS crisis invited global criticism, and his failure to condemn the forced reclamation of white-owned farms in Zimbabwe unnerved both South African landowners and foreign investors.

In 2005, Mbeki dismissed his deputy president Jacob Zuma in the wake of corruption charges against Zuma, setting off a ruthless internal ANC power struggle. In September 2008, Mbeki was asked to step down as president in an unprecedented move by the party.

Corruption charges were dropped and the ANC won the 2009 election, with Jacob Zuma declared president. Zuma has strong grassroots popularity, but he has attracted considerable domestic and international criticism for weak leadership and failure to fulfil promises to create jobs and alleviate poverty.

Culture

The National Psyche

South African society has become more homogeneous in the almost 20 years since the country's first democratic elections. There's still a long way to go, perhaps even a generation or two, and there are flare-ups that increase racial tension, such as the hate-speech perpetrated by the likes of Julius Malema and the vast disparity between rich and poor.

While crime continues to undermine South Africa's reputation as a tourism destination, it's important to keep it in perspective. South Africa is one of the most inspiring and hope-filled places on the continent. Visiting provides a rare chance to experience a nation that is rebuilding itself after profound change. As a backdrop to all this is the magnificent natural scenery, and the remarkably deep bond that most South Africans feel for their land.

The People

During the apartheid era, the government attempted to categorise everyone into one of four major groups. The classifications – black (at various times also called African, native and Bantu), coloured, Asian or white – were often arbitrary and highly contentious. They were used to regulate where and how people could live and work, and became the basis for institutionalised inequality and intolerance.

While the apartheid-era classification terms continue to be used, there are dozens of subgroups that are even more subjective and less clearly defined.

Most of the 'coloured' population, descended from mixed ancestors as diverse as Afrikaners and Khoisan peoples, live in the Northern and Western Capes. A major subgroup is the Cape Malays, who are mostly Muslim and can trace their roots back to India, Indonesia and parts of East Africa. Most South Africans of Indian descent live in KwaZulu-Natal.

Rural provinces such as Limpopo and the Free State are the Afrikaner heartlands. People of British descent are concentrated in KwaZulu-Natal and the Western and Eastern Capes.

The Zulu have maintained the highest-profile ethnic identity and about 24% of South Africans speak Zulu as a first language. The second-largest group, the Xhosa, has been influential in politics (numerous figures in the apartheid struggle, including Mandela, were Xhosa). About 18% of the population uses Xhosa as a first language. Other major groups include the Basotho, the Setswana, and the distinct Ndebele and Venda peoples.

Gauteng is the most densely populated and urbanised province. At the other end of the scale is rural and underdeveloped Limpopo, where more than 30% of adults are illiterate.

Millions of immigrants from across the continent make their way to South Africa to take advantage of its powerhouse economy. This causes resentment among some South Africans who accuse the outsiders of taking jobs and housing.

Food & Drink

Before the end of apartheid, the Africans had their *mealie pap* (maize porridge), the Afrikaners their *biltong* (dried strips of salted meat), and the Indians and Cape Malays their curries. Today, culinary barriers are falling and a simmering *potjie* (pot) of culinary influences awaits the visiting gastronome.

Perhaps more than anything else, it's the *braai* (barbecue) – an Afrikaner institution that has broken across race lines – that defines South African cuisine.

The Afrikaner history of trekking led to them developing portable food. Staples include rusks (hard biscuits) for dunking, and *boerewors*, a well-seasoned sausage that can also be found dried *(droëwors)*.

The most famous example of Cape cuisine, a fusion of Malay and Dutch influences, is *bobotie* (curried mince pie topped with savoury egg custard, served on a bed of yellow rice).

Since it made its debut in 1659, South African wine has aged to perfection, and is both of a high standard and reasonably priced. However, beer is the national beverage. South Africa is home to the world's second largest brewer, SAB Miller and craft beer has taken off in a big way, with around 50 boutique breweries across the country.

Environment

The Land

South Africa occupies more than 1.23 million sq km – five times the size of the UK – and is Africa's ninth-largest and fifth-most populous country. On three sides, it's edged by a windswept and beautiful coastline, winding down the Atlantic seaboard in the west, and up into the warmer Indian Ocean waters to the east.

Much of the country consists of the highveld, a vast plateau averaging 1500m in height. To the east is the lowveld, while to the northwest is the low-lying Kalahari basin. The dramatic Drakensberg Escarpment marks the point where the highveld plummets down towards the eastern lowlands.

Wildlife

South Africa boasts some of the most accessible wildlife viewing on the continent; you have a good chance of seeing the Big Five (rhinos, buffaloes, elephants, leopards and lions). The chance to spot the big cats and great herd animals is one of the region's prime attractions.

The best time for wildlife watching is the cooler, dry winter months (June to September), when foliage is less dense and animals congregate at water holes. Summer (late November to March) is rainy and hot, with the animals more widely dispersed and often difficult to see, although the landscape is beautifully verdant.

South Africa's 800-plus bird species include the world's largest bird (ostrich), the heaviest flying bird (Kori bustard) and the smallest raptor (pygmy falcon). Birdwatching is good year-round, with spring (September to November) and summer the best.

WATER

Tap water is generally safe in the cities. However, in rural areas (or anywhere that local conditions indicate that water sources may be contaminated), stick to bottled water and purify stream water.

Environmental Issues

South Africa is the world's third-most biologically diverse country. It's also one of Africa's most urbanised, with more than 50% of the population living in towns and cities. Major challenges for the government include managing increasing urbanisation and population growth, while protecting the environment.

Land degradation is one of the most serious problems, with about 25% of South Africa's land considered to be severely degraded. In former homeland areas, years of overgrazing and overcropping have resulted in massive soil depletion. This, plus poor overall conditions, is pushing people to the cities, further increasing urban pressures.

South Africa receives an average of only 500mm of rainfall annually, and droughts are common. To meet demand, all major South African rivers have been dammed or modified.

National Parks & Reserves

South Africa has close to 600 national parks and reserves, many featuring wildlife, while others are primarily wilderness sanctuaries or hiking areas.

Oversight bodies include the following:

CapeNature (☎021-426 0723; www.capenature.org.za) Western Cape.

Ezemvelo KZN Wildlife (☎033-845 1000; www.kznwildlife.com) KwaZulu-Natal.

South African National Parks (SANParks; ☎012-426 5000; www.sanparks.org) Oversees most larger wildlife parks, except for those in KwaZulu-Natal.

All South African national parks charge a daily entry (conservation) fee, though amounts vary. One way to save is to purchase a **Wild Card** (www.wildcard.co.za) online. The version of the card for foreign tourists, which is valid for a year, gives unlimited entry into any of the parks and reserves in the Wild Card system. If you're planning more than five days in one of the more expensive parks such as Kruger, it's worth buying.

South Africa is also party to several transfrontier parks joining conservation areas across international borders, and private wildlife reserves abound. In total, less than 8% of South African land has been given protected status, though the government aims to increase this to more than 10%.

SURVIVAL GUIDE

Directory A–Z

ACCOMMODATION

South Africa offers a range of good-value accommodation that is generally of a high standard. Rates quoted in this chapter are for high season, with a private bathroom. Exceptions are noted in listings.

Rates rise steeply during school holidays, when minimum stays are imposed and advance bookings are essential. You can get excellent deals during the winter low season – the best time for wildlife-watching.

Budget options include campsites, backpacker hostels, self-catering cottages and community-run offerings such as homestays. The midrange category is particularly good value and includes guesthouses, B&Bs and many self-catering options in national parks.

South Africa boasts some of Africa's best wildlife lodges, as well as superb guesthouses and hotels. Prices at this level are similar to, or slightly less than, those in Europe or North America.

ACTIVITIES

Thanks to South Africa's diverse terrain and favourable climate, almost anything is possible. Good facilities and instruction mean that most activities are accessible to all, whatever your experience level.

Diving

Conditions Visibility tends to be highest along the KwaZulu-Natal shoreline from May to September. Along the Atlantic seaboard, the water is cold year-round, but at its most diveable, with better visibility, between November and January/February.

Costs Expect to pay around R3000 for a three- or four-day open-water certification course and upwards of R300 per day for equipment rental.

Equipment With the exception of Sodwana Bay during the warmer months (when a 3mm wetsuit will suffice), you'll need at least a 5mm wetsuit for many sites, and a dry suit in the south and west.

PRACTICALITIES

Languages English, isiZulu, isiXhosa, Afrikaans, Sesotho sa Leboa, Setswana, Sesotho, Xitsonga, siSwati, Tsivenda, isiNdebele

Newspapers *Mail & Guardian* (www.mg.co.za) is a national weekly newspaper; the *Sowetan* (www.sowetanlive.co.za) is a national daily.

Radio SAFM radio broadcasts in 11 languages; BBC World Service is available on some FM and AM stations.

Hiking

South Africa has an excellent system of well-marked trails, with something for every ability.

Accommodation Some trails have accommodation, from camping to simple huts with electricity and running water; all must be booked well in advance.

Regulations Many trails require hikers to be in a group of at least three or four.

Resources Ezemvelo KZN Wildlife controls most trails in KwaZulu-Natal. Elsewhere, most trails are administered by SANParks (www.sanparks.org) or the various forest region authorities. For information on hiking clubs, contact **Hiking South Africa** (☎083 535 4538; www.hiking-south-africa.info).

Seasons Hiking is possible year-round; the best time is March to October.

Surfing

The best time of the year for surfing the southern and eastern coasts is autumn and early winter (from about April to July). New boards start from R3000. Resources:

Wavescape (www.wavescape.co.za)

Zig Zag (www.zigzag.co.za) South Africa's main surf magazine.

EMBASSIES & CONSULATES

Most countries have their main embassy in Pretoria, with an office or consulate in Cape Town (which becomes the official embassy during Cape Town's parliamentary sessions).

Most open for visa services and consular matters weekdays, between about 9am and noon.

For more listings, see www.dfa.gov.za/consular/index.html.

Australian High Commission (☎012-423 6000; www.southafrica.embassy.gov.au; 292 Orient St, Arcadia, Pretoria)

Botswanan High Commission (www.botswanaconsulate.co.za) Pretoria (☎012-430 9640; www.mofaic.gov.bw; 24 Amos St, Colbyn); Cape Town (Map p916; ☎021-421 1045; www.mofaic.gov.bw; 7 Coen Steyler Ave, 13th fl, Metropolitan Life Bldg, City Bowl); Jo'burg (Map p942; ☎011-403 3748; 122 De Korte St, 2nd fl, Future Bank Bldg, Braamfontein)

British High Commission (www.ukinsouthafrica.fco.gov.uk) Pretoria (☎012-421 7500; 255 Hill St, Arcadia, consular section 256 Glyn St, Hatfield); Cape Town (Map p916; ☎021-405 2400; 8 Riebeeck St, 15th fl, Norton Rose Hse, City Bowl); Durban (☎031-572 7259; 86 Armstrong Rd, FWJK Court, La Lucia Ridge)

Canadian High Commission (☎012-422 3000; www.canadainternational.gc.ca/southafrica-afriquedusud; 1103 Arcadia St, Pretoria)

Dutch Embassy (www.dutchembassy.co.za) Pretoria (☎012-425 4500; 210 Queen Wilhelmina Ave, New Muckleneuk); Cape Town (☎021-421 5660; 100 Strand St, City Bowl)

French Embassy (www.ambafrance-rsa.org) Pretoria (☎012-425 1600; 250 Melk St, New Muckleneuk); Cape Town (Map p916; ☎021-423 1575; www.consulfrance-lecap.org; 78 Queen Victoria St, Gardens); Jo'burg (☎011-778 5600; 191 Jan Smuts Ave, Rosebank)

German Embassy (www.southafrica.diplo.de) Pretoria (☎012-427 8900; www.pretoria.diplo.de; 180 Blackwood St, Arcadia); Cape Town (Map p916; ☎021-405 3000; 22 Riebeeck St, 19th fl, Triangle House, City Bowl)

Irish Embassy (☎012-452 1000; www.embassyofireland.org.za; 570 Fehrsen St, 2nd fl, Parkdev Bldg, Brooklyn Bridge Office Park, Brooklyn, Pretoria)

Lesotho High Commission (www.foreign.gov.ls) Pretoria (☎012-460 7648; 391 Anderson St, Menlo Park; Durban (☎031-307 2168; 2nd fl, Westguard House, cnr Dr Pixley KaSeme/West St & Dorothy Nyembe/Gardiner St); Jo'burg (Map p942; ☎011-339 3653; 76 Juta St, Indent House, Braamfontein)

Mozambican High Commission (www.embamoc.co.za) Pretoria (☎012-401 0300; www.minec.gov.mz; 529 Edmond St, Arcadia); Cape Town (Map p916; ☎021-426 2944; www.minec.gov.mz; 8 Burg St, 11th fl, Pinnacle Bldg, City Bowl); Durban (☎031-304 0200; 320 Dr Pixley KaSeme/West St, Room 520); Jo'burg (Map p938; ☎011-336 1819; 18 Hurlingham Rd, Illovo); Nelspruit (☎013-752 7396; 43 Brown St)

Namibian High Commission (☎012-481 9100; www.namibia.org.za; 197 Blackwood St, Arcadia, Pretoria)

New Zealand High Commission (☎012-435 9000; www.nzembassy.com/south-africa; 125 Middel St, New Muckleneuk, Pretoria)

Swazi High Commission (www.swazihighcom.co.za) Pretoria (☎012-344 1910; 715 Government Ave, Arcadia); Jo'burg (Map p942; ☎011-403 7372, 011-403 2036; 23 Jorissen St, 6th fl, Braamfontein Centre)

US Embassy Cape Town (☎021-702 7300; southafrica.usembassy.gov; 2 Reddam Ave, Westlake); Pretoria (☎012-431 4000; south africa.usembassy.gov; 877 Pretorius St, Arcadia); Durban (☎031-304 4737; 333 Smith St, 29th fl, Durban Bay House); Jo'burg (Map p938; ☎011-644 8000; 1 River St, Killarney)

Zimbabwean High Commission (www.zimfa.gov.zw) Pretoria (☎012-342 5125; 798 Merton St, Arcadia); Jo'burg (Map p942; ☎011-838 2156; admin@zimbabweconsulate.co.za; 20 Anderson St, 17th fl)

INTERNET ACCESS

Internet access is widely available, with costs averaging R30 to R40 per hour. Many accommodation options, cafes and eateries have wi-fi, and branches of PostNet normally have a few terminals.

MONEY

South Africa's currency is the rand (R), which is divided into 100 cents. The coins are five, 10, 20 and 50 cents, and R1, R2 and R5. The notes are R10, R20, R50, R100 and R200.

Foreign currencies The best currencies to bring are US dollars, euros or British pounds in a mixture of cash and travellers cheques, plus a Visa or MasterCard for withdrawing money from ATMs.

ATMs ATMs are widespread, both in the cities and beyond, but stash some cash if visiting rural areas and be wary of scams.

Credit cards Credit cards are widely accepted, especially MasterCard and Visa. Because South Africa has a reputation for scams, many banks abroad automatically prevent transactions in the country. Inform your bank of your travel plans, particularly if you plan to use a credit card here.

Moneychangers The Thomas Cook agent in South Africa is the **Rennies Travel** (www.renniestravel.co.za) chain of travel agencies.

OPENING HOURS

Banks 9am to 3.30pm Monday to Friday, 9am to 11am Saturday; many foreign exchange bureaus have longer hours

Businesses and shops 8.30am to 5pm Monday to Friday, 8.30am to 1pm Saturday; many supermarkets open later and on Sundays

Cafes 7am to 5pm

Government offices 8am to 4.30pm Monday to Friday

Restaurants 11.30am to 3pm and 7pm to 10pm

Exceptions are noted in specific listings.

PUBLIC HOLIDAYS

New Year's Day 1 January
Human Rights Day 21 March
Good Friday March/April
Family Day March/April (Easter Monday)
Freedom Day 27 April
Workers' Day 1 May
Youth Day 16 June
National Women's Day 9 August
Heritage Day 24 September
Day of Reconciliation 16 December
Christmas Day 25 December
Day of Goodwill 26 December

TELEPHONE

South Africa's country code is ☎27. The three-digit area codes must be dialled for all numbers, even for local calls.

Local calls Cost R0.47 per minute

Long-distance calls Cost about R0.90 per minute.

Phonecards Are widely available.

International calls Cheaper between 8pm and 8am Monday to Friday and on weekends.

International reverse charge calls Dial ☎10903.

SIM cards Cheap and widely available. You need ID and proof of South African address (an acommodation receipt) to buy and register a SIM card.

TOURIST INFORMATION

The main government tourism organisation is **South African Tourism** (☎011-895 3000, 083 123 6789; www.southafrica.net), which has a helpful website.

Virtually every town has a tourism office. Some of these are private entities surviving on commissions.

Eastern Cape Tourism Board (☎043-701 9600; www.ectourism.co.za)

Free State Tourism Board (☎051-447 1362; www.dteea.fs.gov.za)

Gauteng Tourism Authority (☎011-639 1600; www.gauteng.net)

KwaZulu-Natal Tourism Authority (☎031-366 7500; www.kzn.org.za)

Limpopo Tourism Board (☎015-290 7300, 0860 730 730; www.golimpopo.com)

TIPPING

Wages are low, and tipping is expected; around 10% to 15% is usual.

The usual tip for a car guard or petrol-station attendant is R2 to R5.

Northern Cape Tourism Authority (☎053-832 2657; www.northerncape.org.za)

Mpumalanga Tourism Authority (☎013-759 5300; www.mpumalanga.com)

North-West Province Parks & Tourism Board (☎018-397 1500, 0861 111 866; www.tourism northwest.co.za)

Western Cape Tourism Board (☎021-426 5639; www.thewesterncape.co.za)

TRAVELLERS WITH DISABILITIES

South Africa is one of Africa's best destinations for disabled travellers, with an ever-expanding network of facilities. A helpful initial contact is the **National Council for Persons with Physical Disabilities in South Africa** (☎011-726 8040; www.ncppdsa.co.za).

SAN Parks (p956) has a detailed overview of accommodation and trail accessibility for the mobility impaired at all its parks.

VISAS

- Travellers from most Commonwealth countries (including Australia and the UK), most Western European countries, Japan and the USA are issued with a free 90-day visitor's permit on arrival.
- Your passport must be valid for at least 30 days after the end of your visit.
- If you aren't entitled to an entry permit, you'll need to get a visa (R425 or equivalent) before you arrive.
- Visas aren't issued at the borders.
- For more information, visit the **Department of Home Affairs** (www.home-affairs.gov.za).

VISAS FOR ONWARD TRAVEL

- Many nationalities don't require a visa to enter Lesotho, Swaziland, Namibia and Botswana for limited time periods.
- For Mozambique, it's cheaper to pick up a visa on the border than using the same-day service available at consular offices.
- Zimbabwe visas should be available at the border for most nationalities, although given the country's volatility, it may be worth applying at the High Commission in Pretoria (p957).
- Allow between three and 14 days for visas to be issued – check with each country's consulate.

Getting There & Away

AIR

Airports

The major air hub for South Africa, and for the surrounding region, is Jo'burg's **OR Tambo International Airport** (ORTIA; ☎011-921 6911; www.airports.co.za).

The other principal international airports are **Cape Town International Airport** (CPT; ☎021-937 1200; www.airports.co.za) and Durban's **King Shaka International Airport** (☎032-436 6585; www.kingshakainternational.co.za).

Airlines

National airline **South African Airways** (☎0861 359 722; www.flysaa.com) has an excellent route network and safety record.

Some other international carriers flying to and from Jo'burg (except as noted):

Air France (☎010-205 0100; www.airfrance.co.za)

British Airways (www.britishairways.com) Also serves Cape Town.

Emirates (☎086 136 4728; www.emirates.com) Also serves Cape Town and Durban.

Kenya Airways (www.kenya-airways.com/za)

KLM (☎0860 247 747; www.klm.com) Also serves Cape Town.

Lufthansa (☎0861 842 538; www.lufthansa.com) Also serves Cape Town.

Qantas (www.qantas.com.au)

Singapore Airlines (www.singaporeair.com) Also serves Cape Town.

Virgin Atlantic (☎011-340 3400; www.virgin-atlantic.com) Also serves Cape Town.

LAND

Botswana

Intercape (☎0861 287 287; www.intercape.co.za) runs daily between Pretoria and Gaborone (from R240, eight hours), while minibuses run between Jo'burg and Gaborone via Mafikeng (North-West Province). You can also pick up minibuses over the border from Mafikeng to Lobatse (1½ hours) and Gabarone (2½ hours).

Another route from Jo'burg is to Palapye via Grobler's Bridge/ Martin's Drift (eight hours).

Lesotho

Minibus taxis connect Jo'burg and Maseru, but it's quicker and easier to catch a bus to Bloemfontein, then continue by minibus taxi to Maseru (three hours), changing in Botshabelo (Mtabelo) or Ladybrand.

Long-distance minibus taxis leave Maseru from the rank at the Maseru Bridge crossing. There are also minibus taxis connecting Mokhotlong to Underberg (KwaZulu-Natal) via Sani Pass

SAFE TRAVEL

Crime is the national obsession and, apart from car accidents, it's the major risk that you'll face in South Africa. However, try to keep things in perspective, and remember that despite the statistics and newspaper headlines, the majority of travellers visit the country without incident.

The risks are highest in Jo'burg, followed by some townships and other urban centres.

Basic Safety Precautions

- If arriving at OR Tambo International Airport (Jo'burg), keep valuables in your hand luggage and/or vacuum-wrap your baggage.
- One of the greatest dangers during muggings or carjackings is that your assailants will assume you are armed and that you'll kill them if you get a chance. Stay calm and don't resist or give them any reason to think you will fight back.
- Avoid deserted areas day and night, and especially avoid the commercial business district areas of larger cities at night and weekends.
- If you're going to visit a township, go with a trusted guide or on a tour.

and from Qacha's Nek (Lesotho) to Matatiele (Eastern Cape).

The easiest entry points for car and motorcycle are on the northern and western sides of the country.

Mozambique

Buses operate between Jo'burg/Pretoria and Maputo via Nelspruit and Komatipoor, or the route can be tackled in minibus taxis.

Taxis run between Maputo and the Namaacha/Lomahasha post on the Swazi border (1¾ hours); some continue to Manzini (3¼ hours).

You can travel from Jo'burg/Pretoria on a domestic Shosholoza Meyl train to Komatipoort, then cross the border on foot and continue to Maputo on a Caminhos de Ferro do Moçambique (CFM) train.

Namibia

Intercape runs between Cape Town and Windhoek (from R680, 21 hours) via Springbok on Tuesday, Thursday, Friday and Sunday.

Swaziland

A daily shuttle runs between Jo'burg and Mbabane (Swaziland).

Minibus taxis routes:

Jo'burg To/from Manzini (four hours) via Mbabane.

Durban To/from Manzini (eight hours).

Manzini To/from Maputo (3¼ hours).

Zimbabwe

Greyhound and Intercape services operate daily buses between Jo'burg and Harare (16½ hours, R600), and between Jo'burg and Bulawayo (14 hours, R440), via Pretoria and Limpopo.

Minibus taxis run south from Beitbridge to Musina and beyond.

Getting Around

AIR

National airline **South African Airways** (☎0861 359 722; www.flysaa.com), along with its subsidiaries, **SAAirlink** (☎011-961 1700; www.saairlink.co.za) and **SA Express** (☎0861 729 227; www.flyexpress.aero), is the main domestic carrier, with an extensive network of routes.

Domestic fares aren't cheap; one way to save is to book online months ahead. Other domestic carriers:

Comair (☎0860 435 922; www.comair.co.za) Operates British Airways flights in Southern Africa. Flights link Cape Town, Durban, Jo'burg and Port Elizabeth.

Kulula.com (☎0861 585 852; www.kulula.com) No-frills flights linking Jo'burg, Cape Town, Durban, George, East London and Port Elizabeth.

Mango (☎0861 001 234; www.flymango.com) No-frills flights linking Jo'burg, Cape Town, Durban, Port Elizabeth and Bloemfontein.

BUS

A good network of buses, of varying reliability and comfort, links the major cities.

Classes There are no class tiers on the bus lines. Major companies generally offer a 'luxury' service, with features like air-con, a toilet and films.

Discounts The major bus lines offer student, backpacker and senior-citizen discounts. Enquire about travel passes if you'll be taking several bus journeys.

Fares Roughly calculated by distance, although short runs are disproportionately expensive. Prices rise during school holidays.

BAZ BUS

A convenient alternative to standard bus lines, **Baz Bus** (☎0861-229 287; www.bazbus.com) caters almost exclusively to backpackers and travellers. It offers hop-on, hop-off fares and door-to-door service between Cape Town and Jo'burg via the Garden Route, Port Elizabeth, Durban and Northern Drakensberg.

Baz Bus drops off and picks up at hostels, and has transfer arrangements with those off its route.

Point-to-point fares are more expensive than major bus lines, but hop-on/hop-off fares can work out economically.

Sample one-way hop-on, hop-off fares to Cape Town: from Jo'burg/Pretoria R2900; from Durban R2430; from Port Elizabeth R1250.

Safety Apart from where noted, the lines listed in this chapter are generally safe. Many long-distance services run through the night – take care of valuables and consider sitting near the front of the bus.

Ticket purchase For the main lines, purchase tickets at least 24 hours in advance, and as far in advance as possible during peak periods. Tickets can be bought through bus offices, Computicket (www.computicket.co.za) and Shoprite/Checkers supermarkets.

Bus Lines Extensive networks and comfortable buses are offered by **Intercape** (☎0861 287 287; www.intercape.co.za), **Greyhound** (☎0839 159 000; www.greyhound.co.za) and **Translux** (☎0861 589 282; www.translux.co.za).

City to City (☎011-774 3333, 0861-589 282; www.translux.co.za), in partnership with Translux, operates a no-frills service along the routes that once carried people between the apartheid-era homelands.

SA Roadlink (☎011-333 2223; www.saroadlink.co.za) has a smaller network than the others, but prices are reasonable – generally just above City to City fares.

CAR & MOTORCYCLE

South Africa is ideal for driving. If you're in a group, it's also often the most economical way to get around. Most major roads are in excellent condition. Cars drive on the left-hand side of the road, and you can use your driving licence from your home country if it is in English (or you have a certified translation) and it carries your photo.

Fuel

Petrol costs around R12 per litre. There is no self-service; an attendant will fill up your tank, clean your windscreen and ask if your oil or water needs checking. Along main routes there are plenty of petrol stations, many open 24 hours.

Hire

Car rental rates start below R200 per day, including insurance and 200km free per day (unlimited mileage in some cases), while 4WD rental starts at around R900 per day. Car-rental companies accept major credit cards; most do not accept debit cards.

As well as the companies below, check the budget domestic airlines and backpacker hostels; many can arrange good deals.

Argus (www.arguscarhire.co.za) Online consolidator.

Around About Cars (www.aroundaboutcars.com) Recommended budget agent operating nationwide.

Europcar (www.europcar.co.za)

First (www.firstcarrental.co.za)

Road Hazards

South Africa has a horrific road-accident record, with an annual death toll of more than 10,000. The N1 between Cape Town and Beaufort West is considered the most dangerous stretch of road in the country.

The main hazards are your fellow motorists, particularly minibus taxi drivers, who often operate on little sleep. Animals and pedestrians on the roads are another hazard, especially in rural areas such as the Wild Coast.

LOCAL TRANSPORT

Bus

Cape Town, Jo'burg, Pretoria and several other urban areas have city bus systems. Fares are cheap and routes are extensive.Note that services usually stop running early in the evening, and there aren't many buses on weekends.

Minibus Taxi

Minibus taxis run almost everywhere – within cities, to the suburbs and to neighbouring towns. In smaller towns, these may be the only public transport.

- They leave when full
- 'Full' in South Africa isn't as packed as in many African countries.
- Most minibus taxis don't carry luggage on the roof and stowing backpacks can be a hassle.
- In a few areas, notably Cape Town, they're a handy and popular way to get around during daylight hours.

Security

- Overall, taking minibus taxi is not recommended.
- Driving standards and vehicle conditions are poor; accidents are frequent.
- Minibus taxi stops are often unsafe.
- Don't ride at night; seek local advice on lines and areas to avoid.

Train

South Africa's **Shosholoza Meyl** (☎0860 008 888, 011-774 4555; www.shosholozameyl.co.za) offers regular services connecting major cities.

Classes

Premier class A luxurious experience, offering a more affordable alternative to the Blue Train.

Tourist class Recommended: a safe, albeit sometimes slow, way to travel. On overnight journeys, tourist-class fares include a sleeping berth (with a small charge for bedding). Meals and drinks are available.

Economy class Does not have sleeping compartments and is not a comfortable or secure option for overnight travel.

Tickets

All fares quoted in this chapter are for tourist class. Tickets must be booked at least 24 hours in advance (you can book up to three months in advance).

Bookings can be done at train stations, through the website or by phone. If booking by phone you must pay in person at a station or deposit the money in Shosholoza Meyl's bank account and send proof of payment.

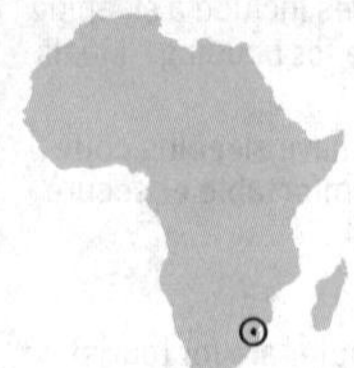

Swaziland

Includes ➡

Best Places to Stay

- Malandela's B&B (p967)
- Mkhaya Game Reserve (p968)
- Mlilwane Wildlife Sanctuary (p966)
- Bulembu (p969)

Best Wildlife Experiences

- Mkhaya Game Reserve (p968)
- Hlane Royal National Park (p968)

Why Go?

In short: big things come in small packages. The intriguing kingdom of Swaziland is diminutive, but boasts a huge checklist for any visitor. Wildlife watching? Adrenalin-boosting activities like rafting and mountain biking? Lively and colourful local culture? Tick. Tick. Tick. Plus there are superb walking trails, stunning mountain and flatland scenery, and excellent, high-quality handicrafts.

Presiding over this is King Mswati III, the last remaining absolute monarch in Africa. The monarchy has its critics but, combined with the Swazis' distinguished history of resistance to the Boers, the British and the Zulus, it has fostered a strong sense of national pride. This is exemplified in its national festivals: the Incwala ceremony and the Umhlanga (Reed) dance.

An excellent road system makes Swaziland a pleasure to navigate. Many make a flying visit on their way to Kruger National Park, but it's worth lingering here if you can.

When to Go

Mbabane

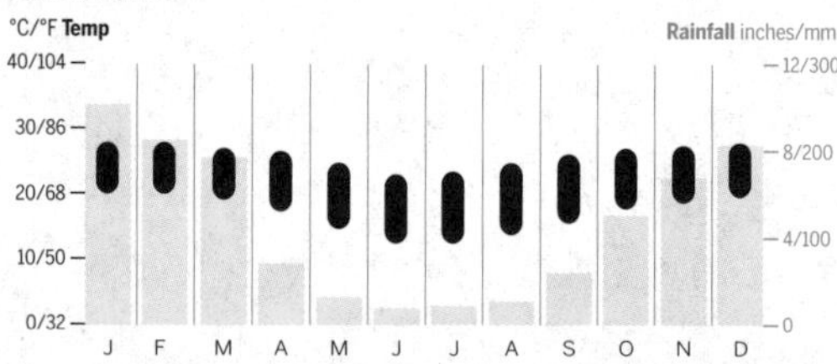

Jan–Apr Full rivers and lush vegetation for photography and adventuring (though it's hot).

Feb–Mar Buganu season – enjoy home-brew marula palm wine in rural Swaziland.

May–Sep Cooler days and winter foliage make for wonderful wildlife viewing in the lowveld.

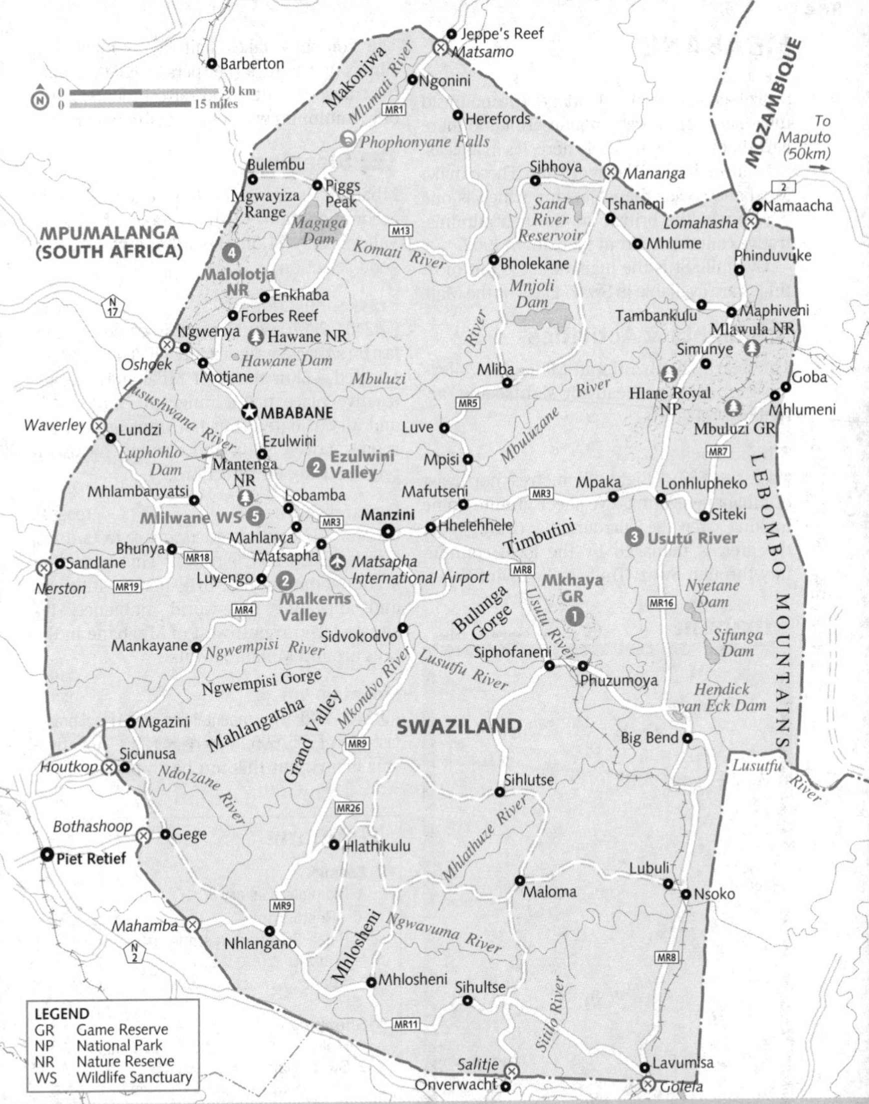

Swaziland Highlights

1. Spot black rhinos in the wild in **Mkhaya Game Reserve** (p968), one of Africa's great wildlife experiences.

2. Revel in a royal experience in the regal heartland of Swaziland and splurge on some handicrafts in the **Ezulwini and Malkerns Valleys** (p965).

3. Shoot the rapids or drift down the **Usutu River** (p966) through stunning gorges on a white-water rafting trip.

4. Hike in **Malolotja Nature Reserve** (p970), a tantalising area of genuine, unspoilt wilderness.

5. Cycle or meander in the **Mlilwane Wildlife Sanctuary** (p966) and relax in its bargain lodges.

MBABANE

POP 60,200

Swaziland's capital, Mbabane (pronounced mba-baa-nee), is pretty nondescript and there isn't that much to see or do here. It's in a pleasant setting in the Dlangeni Hills. These make Mbabane cooler than Manzini, which is one reason why the British moved their administrative centre here from Manzini in 1902.

Gwamile St is the main street is but most things are available in Swazi Plaza or the Mall.

Sights & Activities

The nearby Ezulwini and Malkerns Valleys are the places to head for sightseeing, activities and crafts.

Sibebe Rock ROCK

(admission E30) Eight kilometres northeast of Mbabane is a massive sheer granite dome hulking over the surrounding countryside; the area is managed by the local community through Swazi Trails in Ezulwini Valley.

The company takes half-day nontechnical climbs up the rock (per person E580, including transport, entry and refreshments; guide only, minimum two people, per person E295).

Sleeping

Mbabane is a bit short on decent budget accommodation; Ezulwini or Malkerns Valleys (only 14km and 18km away) have a good selection.

Brackenhill Lodge GUESTHOUSE $$

(☎2404 2887; www.brackenhillswazi.com; Mountain Dr; s/d incl breakfast from E640/840; P) Located 4.5km north of Mbabane, this attractive place has a range of comfortable and airy, if dated (but not unpleasantly so) rooms. Lovely staff, and evening meals on request. Ring for directions.

Foresters Arms LODGE $$

(☎2467 4177; www.forestersarms.co.za; s/d incl breakfast E620/960; P) This charming accommodation has British-style interiors and appealing olde-world ambience. It's situated 27km southwest of Mbabane in the hills around Mhlambanyatsi.

Mountain Inn INN $$

(☎2404 2781; www.mountaininn.sz; s/d incl breakfast from E795/696; P) It's not five-star luxury, but this inn has a pleasant and

Mbabane

Eating

1 Indingilizi Gallery & Restaurant B2
Plaza Tandoori Restaurant ..... (see 3)
Shoprite ..... (see 3)
Spar ..... (see 2)

Shopping

2 Mall A3
3 Swazi Plaza A4

Information

First National Bank ..... (see 3)
Nedbank ..... (see 3)
South African High Commission ..... (see 2)
Standard Bank & ATM ..... (see 3)
4 Tourist Information Office A4
5 Tourist Information Office A4
6 US Embassy B3

Transport

7 Bus Station A3
Minibus & Nonshared Taxi Rank ..... (see 7)

homey ambiance, a pool, a library, a restaurant and panoramas.

Kapola Boutique Hotel BOUTIQUE HOTEL $$
(☎2404 0906; www.safarinow.com/go/KapolaBoutiqueHotel; s/d incl breakfast E800/1100) About 5km from Mbabane, this recently built hotel boasts plush, stylish decor in its eight rooms. A major downside is that it's on and exposed to the busy and noisy MR3 (on the downhill route, or the Mbabane-Ezulwini Valley direction). Note: you'll need to do a loop on the MR3 if you miss it.

Eating

For self-catering, there are the **Shoprite** (Swazi Plaza) and **Spar** (The Mall) supermarkets.

Indingilizi Gallery & Restaurant CAFE $$
(☎2404 6213; www.africanoriginal.com; 112 Dzeliwe St; light meals E40-80; ⊙8am-5pm Mon-Fri, 8.30am-1pm Sat) This longstanding place – a gallery with a small outdoor cafe – offers snacks and light lunches.

Ramblas INTERNATIONAL $$
(mains E40-100; ⊙8am-late Mon-Sat; P) The top choice in Mbabane for good cuisine and a buzzing audience, located within the Serendipity Health complex; you'll need to drive here. It's worth the trip for a massive menu including great salads and meat dishes.

Plaza Tandoori Restaurant INDIAN $
(Swazi Plaza; mains E45-80; ⊙lunch & dinner) As well as great-value Indian curries, the usual grills and burgers add a touch of the international.

Information

Internet access is available in a few places in town, including the Mall. Banks with ATMs include First National Bank, Nedbank and Standard Bank; these are in Swazi Plaza.

Mbabane Clinic (☎2404 2423; St Michael's Rd, Mbabane) Medical services.

Post Office (Msunduza St)

Tourist Information Office (☎2404 2531; www.welcometoswaziland.com; Sozisa Rd, Shop 2, Cooper Centre; ⊙8am-4.45pm Mon-Thu, to 4pm Fri, 9am-1pm Sat) Operated by the Swaziland Tourism Authority, this office provides free maps and brochures on hotels, restaurants and entertainment. These include the tourist bible *What's Happening in Swaziland* and the smaller *What's on in Swaziland.*

DANGERS & ANNOYANCES

Mbabane can be unsafe at night, so don't walk around by yourself. Take precautions in the streets even during the day – muggings are on the increase.

> **SET YOUR BUDGET**
>
> **Budget**
> - Campsite up to E60
> - Two-course dinner E80
> - Mbabane-Malkerns Valley bus ride E11
>
> **Midrange**
> - Hotel room up to E700 (double)
> - Two-course dinner up to E200
> - Mbabane-airport taxi ride E80
>
> **Top End**
> - Luxury wildlife experience E3320 (double)
> - Two-course dinner E250
> - White-water rafting trip E750

Getting There & Away

Minibus taxis to South Africa (mostly northbound) leave from the minibus taxi park near Swazi Plaza, where you'll also find buses and minibus taxis to destinations within Swaziland.

Vehicles heading towards Manzini (E15, 35 minutes) and points east pass through the Ezulwini Valley though most take the highways, bypassing the valley itself. There are several minibus taxis daily to Piggs Peak (E25, one hour), Ngwenya and the Oshoek border post (E10, 50 minutes), and Malkerns Valley (E10.50, 45 minutes).

Nonshared taxis to the Ezulwini Valley cost from E70, more to the far end of the valley (from E100), and still more at night. To Matsapha International Airport, expect to pay from E150.

Getting Around

Nonshared taxis congregate near the bus station by Swazi Plaza.

AROUND SWAZILAND

Ezulwini & Malkerns Valleys

The pretty valleys of Ezulwini and Malkerns begin just outside Mbabane and extend eastwards, incorporating the royal domain of Lobamba village, 18km away. The area

GO WILD!

Wildlife Drives

For wildlife drives, the Big Game Parks reserves organise good-value tours. Mkhaya offers Land Rover day trips (per person E475, minimum two people, includes lunch). These trips must be pre-booked through **Big Game Parks** (☎2528 3943/4; www.biggameparks.org). Set arrival and departure times are 10am and 4pm. Hlane has a two-hour sunrise/sunset drive (per person E190, minimum two people). Mlilwane offers a shorter wildlife drive (per person E165, minimum two people). Check the website for the latest activities on offer, as these do change.

White-Water Rafting & Caving

One of Swaziland's highlights is white-water rafting on the Great Usutu River. In sections, you'll encounter Grade IV rapids, which aren't for the faint-hearted, although even first timers with a sense of adventure should handle the day easily.

Swazi Trails (☎2416 2180; www.swazitrails.co.sz) offers full-/half-day trips for E900/750 per person, including lunch and transport, minimum two people. Trips run from the Ezulwini Valley.

For an off-the-scale challenge rating, the company's adventure caving trips offer a rare window into the elite world of cave exploration. The vast Gobholo Cave is 98% unexplored. You can choose between the 8.30am departure (E595) or 4.30pm dinner trip (E695; it includes a hot-spring soak, pizza and beer).

boasts good accommodation, craft shopping and activities.

Sights & Activities

The beautiful and tranquil **Mlilwane Wildlife Sanctuary** (☎2528 3943; www.biggameparks.org; admission E35; ⏲6.30am-5.30pm summer, 6am-6pm winter) was created in the 1950s by conservationist Ted Reilly.

While it doesn't have the drama or vastness of some South African parks, it's easily accessible and worth a visit. Its terrain is dominated by the precipitous Nyonyane (Little Bird) peak. There are some fine walks in the area. Animals include zebras, giraffes, warthogs, antelopes, crocodiles, hippos and a variety of birds, including black eagles.

Activities include horse rides (one to three hours costs E135, fully catered overnight trips E1190), mountain biking (E105 per person per hour) and game walks (E75 per person per hour).

Sleeping

Within the Sanctuary

Book the following through the **Big Game Parks office** (☎2528 3943/4; www.biggameparks.org).

Sondzela Backpackers (IYHF) Lodge BACKPACKERS $$
(☎2528 3117; www.biggameparks.org; campsites per person E75, dm E100, s/d without bathroom E190/260, rondavel s/d E190/290;) Nestled in Mlilwane Wildlife Sanctuary, this has one of the best backpackers' settings in Southern Africa. A shuttle bus goes between Malandela's B&B in Malkerns Valley and the backpackers. Ring ahead to check for time.

Mlilwane Wildlife Sanctuary Main Camp CAMPSITE, HUTS $$
(☎2528 3943/4; www.biggameparks.org; campsites per person E84, huts s/d E400/570; P) This homey camp is set in a scenic wooded location 3.5km from Mlilwane's entry gate, complete with simple thatched huts – including traditional beehive huts, restaurant and great pool.

Outside the Sanctuary

Legends Backpackers Lodge BACKPACKERS $
(☎2416 1870; www.legends.co.sz; campsites per person E50, dm E100, d without bathroom E300; P) This mellow place offers a straightforward stay in one of the most central locations, in Ezulwini Valley's bushland, behind the Gables Shopping Centre. The lodge's sister company Swazi Trails offers a range of fabulous activities.

Lidwala Backpacker Lodge BACKPACKERS $
(☎2550 4951; www.lidwala.co.sz; camping spot R80, dm & safari tents per person E120, d E330; P@) This comfortable spot is set in a lovely garden with a pool. Rooms are a typical dorm-style, backpacker set-up, with

a laid-back friendly feel. Also offers safari tents. Located on the MR103 between Gables Shopping Centre and Royal Swazi Hotel.

★Malandela's B&B B&B $$
(☎2528 3339, 2528 3448; www.malandelas.com; s/d incl breakfast E400/550;) Along the MR27, Malandela's has fabulously creative and stylish rooms with a touch of ethnic Africa. Reservations are advised; it's understandably popular.

Mantenga Nature Reserve HUTS $
(☎2416 1151, 2416 1178; www.sntc.org.za; beehives E100, cottages incl breakfast per person E700) These cottages provide soft 'safari' adventure: these appealing rooms are set in lush bushland. Visitors don't pay entry to the nature reserve. There's a good on-site restaurant.

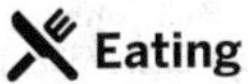

Eating

Khazimula's Restaurant ITALIAN $
(mains E50-80; ⏲10am-10pm Tue-Sun; P) This modest little place has a lovely outlook over the trees and is said to serve the best pizza in Swaziland. It's located in the Mantenga Craft Centre.

Malandela's Restaurant INTERNATIONAL $$
(mains E50-90; ⏲lunch & dinner Mon-Sun; P) Part of the Malandela's complex, this is one of the best restaurants in the region. A bar serves pub grub as well.

Lihawu Restaurant FUSION $$$
(www.lihawu.co.sz; Royal Villas; mains E78-120; ⏲breakfast, lunch & dinner; P) Within the swish Royal Villas resort nestles Swaziland's most elegant restaurant that serves Afro-fusion cuisine; a *lihawu* is the traditional shield made from cow hide. It attracts beautiful people – local politicians and business people – and serves beautiful cuisine.

Calabash GERMAN $$$
(mains E110-180; ⏲lunch & dinner) German and Austrian-Swiss cuisine are the incongruous highlights at this long-standing and dated, but smart, place.

☆ Entertainment

House on Fire MUSIC
(☎2528 2001; www.house-on-fire.com) Part of the Malandela's complex, House on Fire is a fantastically decorated cultural and entertainment space. It hosts everything from African theatre, music and films to raves. Since 2007, it has hosted the annual Bush Fire Festival, featuring music, poetry, theatre and any wacky thing you can think of.

Shopping

The best crafts are to be found at the **Ezulwini Craft Market**, in a slightly obscured location opposite the Zeemans Filling Station on the corner of MR103 and Mpumalanga Loop Rd (look for the blue tin roofs).

Information

Ezulwini Tourist Information Office (☎2416 2180; www.swazi.travel; Mantenga Craft Centre, Ezulwini Valley) Privately run by Swazi Trails, this office supplies tourist information and runs activities galore.

WORTH A TRIP

LOBAMBA & AROUND

Lobamba is the heart of Swaziland's Royal Valley – a position it has held since the early days of the Swazi monarchy. You can see the monarchy in action at the **Royal Kraal** in Lobamba during the Incwala ceremony and the Umhlanga (Reed) dance.

The **National Museum** (adult/child E25/15; ⏲8am-4.30pm Mon-Fri, 10am-4pm Sat & Sun) has some interesting displays on Swazi culture and a traditional beehive village. The ticket price also allows you to enter the **memorial to King Sobhuza II**, the most revered of Swazi kings.

Near the museum is the **parliament**, which is sometimes open to visitors.

All Out Africa (p969) runs a fascinating half-day cultural tour through Lobamba, including an unscripted 'what you see is what you get' wander through the local village (per person E250; no minimum numbers).

Not far from Lobamba is the **Mantenga Nature Reserve** (admission E150; ⏲8am-6pm), where you can visit a 'living' Swazi cultural village, and see a traditional *sibhaca* dance and the Mantega Falls.

Malandela's Tourist Information & Internet Cafe (per hr E45; ⏲8am-5pm Mon-Sat, 9am-5pm Sun)

Medi-Sun Clinic (☎2416 2800; Ezulwini Valley) Medical services.

Getting There & Away

During the day you could get on a Manzini-bound minibus, but make sure the driver knows that you want to alight in Ezulwini Valley, as many aren't keen on stopping.

Nonshared taxis from Mbabane cost E80 to E130, depending on how far down the valley you go.

If you're driving from either Mbabane or Manzini, take the Ezulwini Valley/Lobamba exit off the highway (this puts you on the MR103).

Manzini

POP 55,000

Manzini is the country's commercial and industrial centre. Central Manzini isn't large, but it feels like a different country from easygoing rural Swaziland. A hint of menace pervades; be careful both at day and night as muggings are common.

Manzini's main drawcard is its colourful **market** (cnr Mhlakuvane & Mancishane Sts; ⏲closed Sun). The upper section is packed with handicrafts.

Woza Nawe Tours (☎7642 6780; www.swaziculturaltours.com), headed by local Swazi Myxo Mdluli, runs village visits (day tour E1150) and overnight stays (adult/child E1250/625) to Kaphunga, 55km southeast of Manzini. The fee includes transport, meals and a guide. Guests join in on whatever activities are going on in the village – including cooking, planting, and harvesting.

George Hotel (☎2505 2260; www.tgh.sz; cnr Ngwane & du Toit Sts; s/d incl breakfast from E680/890; ❄🏊) is Manzini's fanciest, and priciest, hotel.

Manzini's elegant choice for dining, **Gil Vincente Restaurant** (Ngwane St, Mkhaya Centre; mains R70-100; ⏲lunch & dinner Tue-Sun) has smart decor and international cuisine and is located down from George Hotel.

The main bus and minibus taxi park is at the northern end of Louw St, where you can also find some nonshared taxis. A nonshared taxi to Matsapha International Airport costs around E80. A minibus-taxi trip to Mbabane costs E15 (35 minutes). Minibus taxis to Mozambique leave from the car park next to KFC up the hill.

Mkhaya Game Reserve

This top-notch **private reserve** (☎2528 3943; www.biggameparks.org), off the Manzini–Big Bend road near the hamlet of Phuzumoya, was established in 1979 to save the pure Nguni breed of cattle from extinction. Its focus expanded to antelopes, elephants, and white and black rhinos. The reserve's name comes from the *mkhaya* (knob-thorn) tree, which abounds here.

You can't visit or stay in the reserve without booking in advance, and even then you can't drive in alone; you'll be met at Phuzumoya at a specified pick-up time, usually 10am or 4pm. While day tours can be arranged, it's ideal to stay for at least one night.

Stone Camp (☎2528 3943; www.biggameparks.org; s/d with full board E2210/3320) has a smart, slightly colonial feel; it's well worth the layover. Accommodation is in rustic and luxurious semi-open stone and thatch cottages (a proper loo with a view!). The price includes wildlife drives, walking safaris, park entry and meals; it's excellent value compared to many of the private reserves near Kruger National Park in South Africa.

Hlane Royal National Park

With white rhinos, antelope species, elephants and lions, **Hlane Royal National Park** (☎2528 3943; www.biggameparks.org; admission E35; ⏲6am-6pm) offers wonderfully low-key wildlife-watching. There are guided walking trails (E155 per person), two-hour wildlife day drives (per person E235, minimum two), a cultural village tour (per person E70, minimum four) and mountain-bike rentals (per two hours E175).

Ndlovu Camp (campsites per person E40, rondavel s/d from E295/410, 8-person cottages per person E220) is a pleasant and rustic fenced-off camp, with no electricity, a communal area and a restaurant. Book for both through the **Big Game Parks office** (☎2528 3943/4; www.biggameparks.org).

Minibus taxis from Simunye will drop you at the entrance to Hlane (E5; 7km from Simunye).

OFF THE BEATEN TRACK

Several excellent community-owned tourism projects operate in Swaziland. **Shewula Mountain Camp** (☎7603 1931, 7605 1160; www.shewulacamp.com; dm/r E100/260), a camp northeast of Simunye in the Lebombo Mountains, is 36km by dirt road from Simunye. You can camp or stay in basic *rondavels* (round, traditional-style huts), with shared ablutions and self-catering facilities. The newer **Mahamba Gorge Lodge** (☎7617 9880, 2237 0100; Mahamba; s/d E285/400), near Nhlangano, has clean, modern stone chalets and wonderful guided walks (per person E50) through the nearby gorge, where there are nesting eagles. **Ngwempisi Hiking Trail** (☎7625 6004) is a community-run 33km trail with the atmospheric Khopho Hut (also known as Rock Lodge). It's located 30km south of the Malkerns Valley in the Ntfungula Hills that are on the Mankayane–Vlelzizweni road. Ezulwini Tourist Information Office (p967) and **All Out Africa** (☎2550 4951; www.alloutafrica.com) also take bookings as a community service on their behalf.

Mlawula Nature Reserve

This tranquil **reserve** (☎2383 8885; www.sntc.org.sz; adult/child E25/12; ⏲6am-6pm), where the lowveld plains meet the Lebombo Mountains, boasts antelopes, hyenas and crocodiles, plus rewarding birdwatching. You can bring your own mountain bike. Walking is a highlight, too, with hikes from two to nine hours in length.

The accommodation highlight is **Magadzavane** (s/d incl breakfast E450/700, s/d without breakfast E399/600), a great option that offers 20 new chalets situated in the southern part of the reserve, set up high with magnificent vistas. At the basic **Siphiso camping ground** (campsites per person E60) you can pitch your own tent. The self-catering **Mapelepele Cottage** (up to 7 people, per person E150, minimum E500) is equipped with a gas stove and fridge.

Piggs Peak

The small, gritty town of Piggs Peak is the centre of Swaziland's logging industry. Sadly, much of the forested area of pine plantations were destroyed by forest fires in 2007. The town was named after a prospector who found gold here in 1884.

As well as its scenery, including the **Phophonyane Falls** about 8km north of town, this area is known for its handicrafts. Check these out at the Peak Craft Centre where you'll find **Likhweti Kraft** (☎437 3127), a branch of **Tintsaba Crafts** (☎437 1260; www.tintsaba.com), which sells sisal baskets, jewellery and many other Swazi crafts. There are also numerous craft vendors along the road up from Mbabane.

Bulembu

An interesting detour from Piggs Peak is to wind your way 20km through scenic plantation country to the historic and very pretty town of Bulembu, a former asbestos mining centre and later a ghost town. The town's current investors run a community tourism project (based on Christian principles) to bring the town back to life, including renovating many corrugated iron houses and art deco buildings. The longest (now unused) cableway in the world extends from the old mine to Barberton, 20km away. These days, timber production, honey and tourism are the main source of employment. Warning: asbestos (chrysotile) dumps exist around the village.

The stretch of dirt road running west from Piggs Peak to Bulembu can be boggy when wet. The road to Barberton (Mpumalanga) has recently been paved.

Sleeping

Phophonyane Falls Ecolodge & Nature Reserve ECOLODGE
(☎2431 3429; www.phophonyane.co.sz; safari tent d incl breakfast from 1360, d beehive incl breakfast from R2040, cottage d incl breakfast from E1780; 🏊) This stunning hideaway, run by keen conservationists, lies northeast of Piggs Peak on a river in its own nature reserve of lush indigenous forest. There's a network of walking trails around the river and waterfall. Accommodation is in comfortable cottages (with a self-catering option), stylish beehives

RHINO WARS

In 1965 white rhinos were re-established in the kingdom after an absence of 70 years. That was the easy part. Since then there has been an ongoing battle to protect them from poachers. At the forefront of this battle has been conservationist Ted Reilly and a band of dedicated hand-picked rangers.

This defence wasn't easy, especially as the poachers had received hefty financial backing from crime syndicates supplying rhino horn to the lucrative Asian market. Poaching escalated in the late 1980s, and there were determined efforts to change rhino-poaching laws in Swaziland. Rhinos were dehorned and confined to enclosures for their own protection. After Hlane Royal National Park was attacked in January 1992 by poachers with AK47s, the rangers armed themselves. With the rhinos dehorned at Hlane, the poachers shifted to Mkhaya Game Reserve.

In April 1992 there was a shoot-out between rangers and poachers at Mkhaya, and some poachers were captured. Another shoot-out occurred at Big Bend, in which two poachers were killed while selling their freshly poached horns. While the Swazi courts deliberated over action against the rangers, another rhino, the majestic bull Mthondvo, was killed for his horn in 1992. The young king, Mswati III, intervened, and the poaching of rhinos came to a halt. The rangers, however, still wait with their rifles at the ready. You can help: your presence at any one of the big wildlife parks assists in rhino conservation.

In 1996 the Taiwanese government donated money to purchase six black rhinos; a gesture of good faith that was welcomed with open arms.

or luxury safari tents overlooking cascades. Excellent meals are available in the stylish dining area (mains from E50; open for breakfast, lunch and dinner). Day visitors to the reserve are charged E30/20 per adult/child, lodge residents E20/10. The lodge is about 14km north of Piggs Peak. Follow the signposts off the main road – you will cross a bridge over the waterfall and turn right 500m on.

Bulembu Lodge LODGE
(☎7602 1593; www.bulembu.org; per person from E456) The Bulembu Lodge is in the former general manager's residence or stylish directors' cottages, all renovated.

ℹ Getting There & Away

The minibus taxi stand is next to the market at the top end of the main street, with several vehicles daily to Bulembu (E15, 30 minutes) and Mbabane (E20, one hour).

Malolotja Nature Reserve

This beautiful middleveld/highveld nature **reserve** (☎2444 1744, 7613 3990; adult/child E28/14; ⏲6am-6pm) is a true wilderness area, rugged and for the most part unspoiled. The terrain ranges from mountainous and high-altitude grassland to forest and lower-lying bushveld, all with streams and cut by three rivers, including the Komati River.

It's an excellent walking destination, and an ornithologist's paradise, with over 280 species of birds. Wildflowers and rare plants are added attractions; several are found only in this part of Africa.

Basic brochures outlining the hiking trails are available for free at the restaurant/reception. These days, many visit the park for the **Malolotja Canopy Tour** (☎7613 3990; www.malolotjacanopytour.com; per person R450; ⏲7am-4pm summer, 8am-3pm winter). You can 'slide' your way across Malalotja's stunning, lush tree canopy on 11 slides (12 platforms).

Accommodation consists of **camping** (per person at main camp/on trails E70/50), either at the well-equipped (but infrequently used) main site, with ablutions and *braai* (barbecue) area, or along the overnight trails (no facilities). Self-catering wooden **cabins** (per person E250, minimum E400, children half-price) sleep a maximum of five people. Reservations are made through **Hawane Resort** (☎2444 1744; www.hawane.co.sz; dm E115, chalet s/d incl breakfast E550/840; @☒).

The entrance gate for Malolotja is about 35km northwest of Mbabane, along the Piggs Peak road (MR1); minibus taxis will drop you here (E15, 45 minutes).

UNDERSTAND SWAZILAND

Swaziland Today

King Mswati III continues his role as absolute monarch and comes under attack, especially in the foreign press, for his autocratic status, lax spending habits and polygamous practices. Following his predecessor's style, Mswati III dissolved parliament in 1992 and Swaziland was again governed by a traditional tribal assembly, the Liqoqo. Since then, democratic reform has begun with the drafting – albeit restrictive – of a constitution. Despite the increasing agitation for faster change, even his staunchest Swazi critics don't seem to want to do away with him altogether, calling for a constitutional king in a democratic system of government.

Recent pressure on national finances has seen unpopular salary freezes in most sectors of government, so it is likely that civil service unions will play an increasing powerful role in local politics.

Swaziland has one of the world's highest HIV infection rates, although in recent years it has stabilised; around 26% of the adult population is HIV positive and the average life expectancy is currently 37 years. Figures vary widely, but it's predicted that tens of thousands of children have lost either one or both parents to the disease.

History

In eastern Swaziland archaeologists have discovered human remains dating back 110,000 years, but the ancestors of the modern Swazi people arrived relatively recently.

During the great Bantu migrations into Southern Africa, one group, the Nguni, moved down the east coast. A clan settled near what is now Maputo in Mozambique, and a dynasty was founded by the Dlamini family. In the mid-18th century, increasing pressure from other Nguni clans forced King Ngwane III to lead his people south to what is now southern Swaziland. The next king, Sobhuza I, withdrew under pressure from the Zulus to the Ezulwini Valley, which today remains the centre of Swazi royalty and ritual. When King Sobhuza I died in 1839, Swaziland was twice its present size. Trouble with the Zulu continued, although the next king, Mswazi (or Mswati), managed to unify the whole kingdom. By the time he died in 1868, the Swazi nation was secure. Mswazi's subjects called themselves Swazis, meaning 'people of Mswazi', and the name stuck.

European Interference

The arrival of increasing numbers of Europeans from the mid-19th century brought new problems. Mswazi's successor, Mbandzeni, inherited a kingdom rife with European carpetbaggers – hunters, traders, missionaries and farmers, many of whom leased large expanses of land.

The Pretoria Convention of 1881 guaranteed Swaziland's 'independence' but also defined its borders, and Swaziland lost large chunks of territory. 'Independence' meant that both the British and the Boers administered their various interests in Swaziland: the result was chaos. The Boer administration collapsed with the 1899–1902 Anglo-Boer War, and the British took control of Swaziland as a protectorate.

During this time, King Sobhuza II was only a young child, but Labotsibeni, his mother, acted as regent until her son took over in 1921. Labotsibeni encouraged Swazis to buy back their land, and many sought work in the Witwatersrand mines (near Johannesburg) to raise money.

Independence

In 1960 King Sobhuza II proposed the creation of a legislative council, composed of elected Europeans, and a national council formed in accordance with Swazi culture. The Mbokodvo (Grindstone) National Movement pledged to maintain traditional Swazi culture but also to eschew racial discrimination. When the British agreed to elections in 1964, Mbokodvo won a majority and, at the next elections in 1967, won all the seats. Swaziland became independent on 6 September 1968.

The country's constitution was largely the work of the British. In 1973 the king suspended it on the grounds that it did not accord with Swazi culture. He also dissolved all political parties. Four years later the parliament reconvened under a new constitution that vested all power in the king. Sobhuza II, at that time the world's longest-reigning monarch, died in 1982. In keeping with Swazi tradition, a strictly enforced 75-day period of mourning was announced by

Dzeliwe (Great She-Elephant), the most senior of his hundred wives. Only commerce essential to the life of the nation was allowed.

Choosing a successor wasn't easy – Sobhuza II had fathered more than 600 children, thereby creating hundreds of potential kings. Prince Makhosetive, born in 1968, was finally chosen and crowned King Mswati III in 1986.

Culture

Swazis have an extremely strong sense of identity and pride. Social and cultural cohesion is maintained by a system of age-related royal regiments. Boys graduate from regiment to regiment as they grow older. This minimises the potentially divisive differences between clans, while emphasising loyalty to the king and nation.

The nonconfrontational, good-humoured and religious Swazis dislike embarrassment of any kind. Although there is widespread dissatisfaction with the lack of progress in their country's current socioeconomic climate, they tend to dislike outsiders meddling in internal political and social affairs and cultural practices. Despite constant controversy around the king, he represents the symbolic head of the Swazi family and, as such, he is generally highly regarded – disrespect for him can be interpreted as a lack of respect for the identity of the Swazi themselves.

As in other parts of Africa, the extended family is integral to a person's life. While polygamy is permitted and exists, it is not always practised. Traditional marriage allows for the husband to take a number of wives, although many Swazis also follow Western marriage conventions, rejecting polygamy but permitting divorce.

Many people in rural areas continue to live in the traditional beehive huts in homestead arrangements.

Schooling is not compulsory, though the recent roll-out of free primary-school education is believed to have helped counteract the impact of the increased numbers of orphans due to the HIV/Aids epidemic.

Swaziland's People

Almost all people are Swazi (although there are about 70 distinct subgroups). The rest are Zulu, Tsonga-Shangaan and European. The dominant clan is the Dlamini – it's the equivalent of having the name 'Smith' in anglophone countries, and you'll meet your fair share of them all over the country.

Around 70% of the population is Zionist (a mix of Christianity and traditional indigenous worship), with Roman Catholics, Anglicans and Methodists making up the balance. Muslim, Baha'i and Jewish faiths have small followings, too.

Arts & Crafts

Swaziland's handicrafts include jewellery, pottery, weapons and implements. Woven grass wares, such as *liqhaga* (grass-ware 'bottles') and mats, are popular, as are wooden items, ranging from bowls to *knobkerries* (wooden club carved from a branch with a large knob at one end).

Dance and music are an integral part of Swazi cultural festivals. The *sibhaca* is a vigorous foot-stamping dance performed by males.

Food & Drink

Swaziland isn't a gourmet's paradise, but you won't eat too badly. Tourist areas of the Malkerns and Ezulwini Valleys feature good international dishes and seafood. In more remote areas, African staples, such as stew and pap (also known as *mealie meal*), are common.

Environment

Swaziland has a wide range of ecological zones, from montane forest in the northwest to savannah scrub in the east. Western Swaziland is highveld, consisting mainly of short, sharp mountains; the centre and east of the country are plains, where plantations of sugar cane dominate the landscape. Further east, the harsh Lebombo Mountains form the border with Mozambique.

Conservation can come from the most unlikely sources. The monarchy reserved some areas for hunting; these preserve the remnants of indigenous flora (including 14% of the recorded plant life in southern Africa) and reintroduced animals (including elephants, warthogs, rhinos and lions) in parks such as Hlane Royal National Park, Mlilwane Wildlife Sanctuary and Mkhaya Game Reserve (these fall under the banner of 'Big Game Parks').

Swaziland has about a third of the non-marine mammal species in Southern Africa.

Environmental issues include overgrazing of cattle, soil erosion, illegal hunting and the loss of certain indigenous plants sought for natural medicines.

SURVIVAL GUIDE

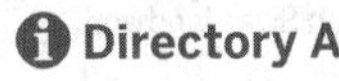

Directory A–Z

ACCOMMODATION

Many of the country's hotels and lodges are geared towards South African tourists and are pricey, but there are some good B&B-style options. Nearly all designated campsites in Swaziland are in national parks and reserves. If you intend to camp in rural areas, always ask permission from the local people first.

ACTIVITIES

Swaziland's wildlife reserves offer some excellent walking, mountain biking and birdwatching. In the rainy season, white-water rafting is at its best.

EMBASSIES & CONSULATES

American Embassy (☎2404 6441; http://mbabane.usembassy.gov; Central Bank Bldg, Mahlokohla St, Mbabane) Be sure to check its opening hours; hours for visas are limited.

Mozambican High Commission (☎2404 1296; Princess Drive Rd, Highlands View)

South African High Commission (☎2404 4651; www.dfa.gov.za; Dr Sishayi Rd, 2nd fl, the New Mall)

FESTIVALS & EVENTS

Colourful ceremonies (and traditional dress, which is still commonly worn) underline the Swazis' unique identity.

Ask at the tourist office in Mbabane for exact dates of the following festivals. Photography is not permitted at the Incwala ceremony but is at the Umhlanga dance.

Incwala ceremony Held sometime between late December and early January. Swaziland's most sacred ceremony, celebrating the New Year and the first fruits of the harvest in rituals of thanksgiving, prayer, atonement and reverence for the king. As part of the festivities, the king grants his people the right to consume his harvest, and rains are expected to follow the ceremony.

Umhlanga (Reed Dance) A great spectacle in August or September, performed by unmarried girls who collect reeds for the repair and maintenance of the royal palace. It is something like a week-long debutante ball for marriageable young Swazi women and is a showcase of potential wives for the king. On the sixth day they perform the reed dance and carry the reeds they have collected to the queen mother. Princesses wear red feathers in their hair.

> **PRACTICALITIES**
>
> **Electricity** Plugs have three large round pins, as used in South Africa.
>
> **Languages** English, Swati
>
> **Newspapers** *Times of Swaziland* and *Swazi Observer* are the country's English-language daily newspapers
>
> **Radio** Radio Swaziland broadcasts in English at 91.6 MHz (Mbabane) and 93.6 MHz (Manzini) and in Swazi at 88.5 MHz (Mbabane) and 105.2 MHz (Manzini)
>
> **TV** Swazi TV, a public broadcaster

Buganu Festival Another 'first fruits' festival, this takes place in February and celebrates the Marula fruit. The women gather the fruit and ferment a brew (known as *buganu*; it packs a punch). Locals – mainly males – gather to drink and celebrate.

HEALTH

Malaria is a minor summer risk in the northeast near Mozambique, with the country hoping to be declared malaria free by 2015. Bilharzia is present – be aware of the symptoms. Tuberculosis (TB) is widespread and care should be taken in sharing confined spaces with infected persons.

INTERNET ACCESS

Internet facilities are found in Mbabane and a couple of places in the Ezulwini and Malkerns Valleys. Internet costs around E30 per hour. Wi-fi is available in many of the less remote lodges and backpackers.

MAPS

The main tourist information office hands out a free map of Swaziland.

MONEY

The unit of currency is the lilangeni; the plural is emalangeni (E). It is tied in value to the South African rand. Rands are accepted everywhere and there's no need to change them. Emalangeni are difficult to change for other currencies outside Swaziland.

Most ATMs accept international credit or debit cards. The most convenient are at banks in Swazi Plaza and Mbabane, and inside the Royal Swazi Hotel's casino in the Ezulwini Valley.

The normal practice for tipping in rural parts of Swaziland is to round up a bill. In smarter tourist establishments, 5% to 10% is usual.

OPENING HOURS

Banks 8.30am to 3.30pm Monday to Friday (some also open 8.30am to 11am Saturday)

Offices 8am to 5pm Monday to Friday
Shops 8am to 7pm Monday to Friday
Restaurants & Cafes Hours vary from 8am to midnight depending on outlet

PUBLIC HOLIDAYS

As well as religious holidays, the principal public holidays in Swaziland are the following:

New Year's Day 1 January
King Mswati III's Birthday 19 April
National Flag Day 25 April
King Sobhuza II's Birthday 22 July
Umhlanga (Reed Dance Day) August/September
Somhlolo (Independence Day) 6 September
Incwala Day December/January (dates vary each year)

TELEPHONE

Swaziland has a reasonable telephone network. The international country code is 268 and the international access code is 00; there are no area codes. Swazi mobile SIM cards are available, as are public phone cards.

TOURIST INFORMATION

Swaziland's main tourist information office is in Mbabane. Privately run by Swazi Trails, the Ezulwini Tourist Information Office also supplies excellent tourist information and organises activities, as does Malandela's Tourist Information & Internet Cafe (p968). The websites of **Swaziland National Trust** (www.sntc.org.sz) and Big Game Parks (p966) offer some parks' information.

VISAS

Most nationalities don't need a visa to visit Swaziland. Those who do can obtain them in advance from the **Swaziland High Commission** (☎ in South Africa 012-344 1910; 715 Government Avenue, Arcadia) in Pretoria. Anyone staying for more than 30 days must apply for an extension of stay. If staying for longer than 60 days, you must apply for a temporary residence permit from the **Chief Immigration Officer** (☎ 2404 2941; PO Box 372, Mbabane), whose offices are in the Ministry of Home Affairs.

Visas for Onward Travel

Visas for Mozambique are available at the borders, but it's cheaper to arrange them in advance at the Mozambican high commission in Mbabane or Nelspruit (South Africa). Allow 24 hours.

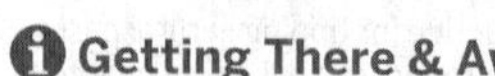

Getting There & Away

AIR

Swaziland's main airport is Matsapha International Airport, northwest of Manzini. (Schedules and tickets often refer to the airport as Manzini.) **Swaziland Airlink** (☎ 2518 6155; www.flyswaziland.com) flies daily between Swaziland and Johannesburg.

> **DEPARTURE TAX**
>
> A departure tax (E50) is levied at Matsapha International Airport.

LAND

Bus & Minibus Taxi

Generally speaking, Manzini has the main international transport rank for transport to Jo'burg, Durban and Mozambique. Less frequent departures are in Mbabane for the northern destinations of Gauteng and Mpumalanga (South Africa).

Mozambique

Swaziland shares two border crossings with Mozambique: Lomahasha–Namaacha (open 7am to 10pm) in the extreme northeast of the country, and Goba–Mhlumeni (open 24 hours). Check border times as these can change. Minibuses between Maputo (Mozambique)and Manzini depart throughout the day as soon as seats are filled. They travel via the Goba–Mhlumeni border (E90, 3½ hours). Extra charges for large luggage.

South Africa

The main border crossings with South Africa are Josefsdal–Bulembu (open 8am to 4pm); Oshoek–Ngwenya (open 7am to midnight); Houtkop–Sicunusa (open 8am to 6pm); Mahamba (open 7am to 10pm); and Golela–Lavumisa (open 7am to 10pm).

A daily luxury shuttle service, **TransMagnific** (☎ 2404 9977; www.goswaziland.co.sz), runs daily between Jo'burg and Swaziland (E500).

Minibus taxis run daily between Jo'burg (Park Station), Mbabane and Manzini (four hours) and between Manzini and Durban (eight hours). On many routes, you'll need to change minibuses at the border. Most long-distance taxis leave early in the morning.

Getting Around

BUS & MINIBUS TAXI

There are a few infrequent (but cheap) domestic buses, most of which set off from and terminate at the main stop in the centre of Mbabane. Generally you'll find minibus taxis are the best public transport, although they often run shorter routes. There are also nonshared (private hire) taxis in some of the larger towns.

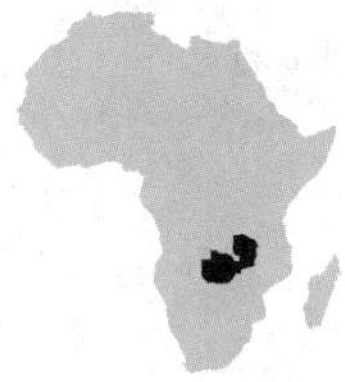

Zambia

POP 13 MILLION

Includes ➡

Best Places to Stay

- KaingU Safari Lodge (p989)
- Flatdogs Camp (p984)
- Chongwe River Camp (p985)
- Stanley Safari Lodge (p987)
- Kapishya Hot Springs Lodge (p991)

Best Off the Beaten Path

- Shiwa Ng'andu (p990)
- Lake Bangweulu (p990)
- Chimfunshi Wildlife Orphanage (p992)
- Lake Tanganyika (p991)

Why Go?

Get out into the bush where animals, both predators and prey, wander through unfenced camps, where nighttime means swapping stories around the fire, where one day you can canoe down a wide, placid river and the next raft through the raging rapids near world-famous Victoria Falls, and where the human footprint is nowhere to be seen. The rewards of travelling in Zambia are those of exploring remote, mesmerising wilderness as full of an astonishing diversity of wildlife as any part of Southern Africa.

Though Zambia is landlocked, three great rivers, the Kafue, the Luangwa and the Zambezi, flow through the country, defining both its geography and the rhythms of life for many of its people. For the independent traveller, however, Zambia is a logistical challenge, due to its sheer size, dilapidated road network and upmarket facilities. For those who do venture here, the relative lack of crowds means an even more satisfying journey.

When to Go

Lusaka

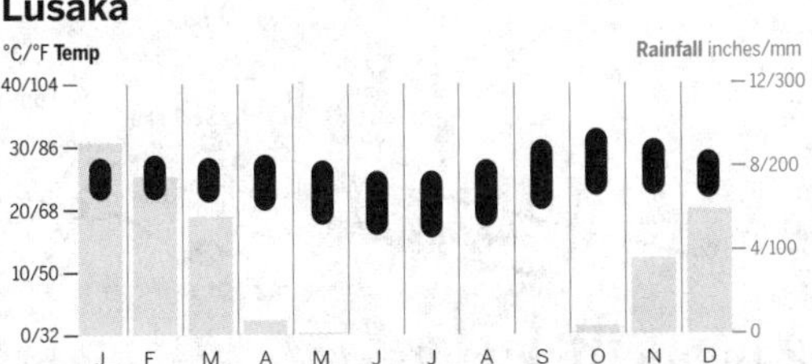

Late-May–early Oct The dry season, prime wildlife viewing time, but October can be brutally hot.

Jun–Aug Generally dry, though temperatures are cooler and it can get downright frosty at night.

Dec–Apr Rainy season; landscape is vibrant though wildlife difficult to spot; many lodges closed.

Zambia Highlights

1 Bushwalking like a detective following the tracks of wild animals in **South Luangwa National Park** (p983)

2 Paddling a canoe down the **Zambezi River** (p984) past pods of hippos, menacing-looking crocs and thirsty elephants.

3 Rafting, bungee jumping or getting your adrenalin going in any one of the adventures available at **Victoria Falls** (p986).

4 Spotting leopards in **Kafue National Park** (p989), a behemoth wilderness area

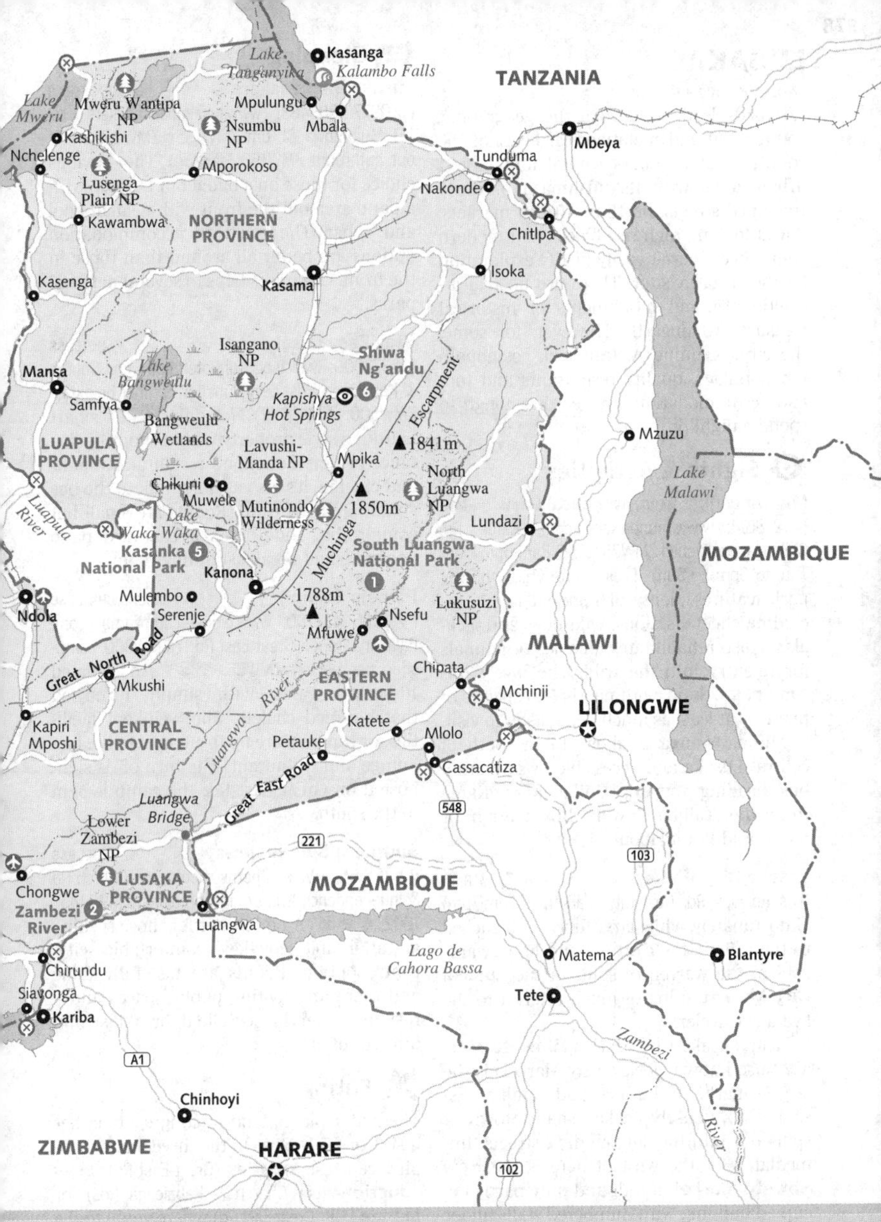

where wildlife dreams unfold amid stunning landscapes.

5 Spying on the elusive, semi-aquatic sitatungas from a tree-hide in **Kasanka National Park** (p990).

6 Taking a step back in time and a leap to another continent at **Shiwa Ng'andu** (p990), a remarkably well-preserved English manor estate.

7 Kicking back at **Lake Kariba** (p985), and watching a storm roll in over the jagged peaks of Zimbabwe across the waters.

LUSAKA

☎0211 / POP 1.4 MILLION

All roads lead to Lusaka, the geographic, commercial and metaphorical heart of the country. But Zambia's capital and largest urban zone, with its mishmash of dusty tree-lined streets, bustling African markets, Soviet-looking high-rise blocks and modern commerce, doesn't easily justify exploration by the casual visitor. There are no real attractions, grand monuments or historical treasures to unearth. However, for some, the city's genuine African feel, cosmopolitan populace, quality restaurants and top-end accommodation, are reason enough to spend a night or two.

Sights & Activities

Munda Wanga Environmental Park ZOO

(☎278614; www.mundawanga.com; Kafue Rd, Chilanga; adult/child ZMW25/15; ⏲8am-5pm Mon-Thu, to 6pm Fri-Sun) This somewhat shabby park features plenty of regional fauna, including cheetahs, lions, wild dogs and jackals; it also rehabilitates all sorts of animals for re-entry into the wild. The lovely **botanical gardens**, with nearly 500 species of plants is at least as much of a reason to visit.

Munda Wanga is about 16km south of central Lusaka and accessible by any minibus heading towards Chilanga or Kafue from the Kalima Towers Bus Station or South End Roundabout.

Lusaka City Market MARKET

(Los Angeles Rd, New City Market; ⏲7am-7pm) Unfortunately, while large, lively and packed to the rafters, the clothing and housewares sold in the warren of stalls of the **Lusaka City Market** aren't of much interest to the average traveler.

Near Lusaka City Market, **Soweto Market** (also known as New City Market) is the largest market in Lusaka (and Zambia). Essentially a densely packed shanty town, it spills out into the surrounding streets. Immediately to the west of here is the **New Soweto Market**, a dull and only partly occupied building with numbered stalls under a covered roof.

National Museum MUSEUM

(Nasser Rd; adult/child ZMW20/12; ⏲9am-4.30pm) The downstairs galleries display contemporary Zambian paintings and sculpture, while upstairs has a hodgepodge of cultural, ethnographic and archaeological artifacts.

Sleeping

Lusaka Backpackers BACKPACKERS $

(☎0977 805483; www.lusakabackpackers.com; 161 Mulombwa Cl; dm ZMW75, r ZMW250, without bathroom ZMW150; @🛜🏊) The obvious choice for those on a budget in Lusaka, with a patio area out the front with a small pool and a bar. The backyard accommodation options are better all around than those in the front. Organises trips to several national parks.

Stay Easy Lusaka HOTEL $$

(☎372000; www.tsogosunhotels.com; cnr Church & Kabalenga Rds, Levy Junction ; r incl breakfast ZMW500; ❄@🛜🏊) Not only is this smart boutique-style property within shouting distance of Levy Junction's restaurants, banks and cinema, it's also a short walk to the bus station and Cairo Rd. Rooms are small but comfortable and there's a backyard patio pool area and breakfast dining room.

Pioneer Camp CAMPGROUND, CHALET $$

(☎0966 432700; www.pioneercampzambia.com; Palabana Rd, off Great East Rd; r ZMW300, campsites per person ZMW35; 🛜🏊) An isolated 10-hectare camp with simply furnished thatch-roofed chalets. The well-kept facilities for campers are up front, next to the bar, lounge and restaurant. The turn-off is signposted on Great East Rd; the camp is 5km to the south.

Southern Sun Ridgeway HOTEL $$$

(☎251666; www.southernsun.com; cnr Church Rd & Independence Ave; s/d incl breakfast ZMW1445/1602; ❄🛜🏊) A no-brainer for those seeking an affordable, low-key, comfortable, city-centre option. Rooms are tastefully done and there are inviting public spaces and a restaurant serving excellent breakfast and dinner buffets.

Eating

The better places tend to congregate either inside or fairly close to the three main shopping centres: **Arcades** (Great East Rd), **Levy Junction** (cnr Church & Kabalenga Rds) or **Manda Hill** (Great East Rd) where you'll find a handful of quality independent restaurants and a wide range of mostly South African fast-food options. All three have massive and modern grocery stores as well.

Design House Cafe INTERNATIONAL, ORGANIC $$

(Leopards Hill Rd, Sugarbush Farm; mains ZMW35-60; ⏲8am-5pm Tue-Sat, 9am-4pm Sun) An idyllic cafe worth every kwacha of the journey out there.

Chill out at one of the picnic tables munching on pastries, salads, sandwiches and meat dishes. Past the turn-off for Kilimanjaro Lodge, on the same premises as the shop Jackal & Hide, also highly recommended.

Chicago's STEAKHOUSE $$
(Manda Hill Shopping Centre, Great East Rd; mains ZMW45-115; ⏲lunch & dinner) This theme restaurant with a large menu specialising in steaks and seafood is a nighttime haunt of Lusaka's young and fashionable.

Rhapsody's INTERNATIONAL $$$
(Arcades Shopping Centre, Great East Rd; mains ZMW55-110; ✎) This contemporary and stylish restaurant has huge eating areas, inside and outside, and the international-style menu does everything from steaks to Thai chicken, salads and even nasi goreng.

Drinking & Nightlife

Bars and restaurants aren't allowed to sell alcohol after 11pm, nightclubs after 2am; it's prohibited everywhere on Sundays.

Lusaka nightclubs play international house music on Friday and Saturday nights and the pub at the **InterContinental Hotel** (☎250000; www.ichotelsgroup.com; Haile Selassie Ave; 📶) and **O'Hagan's** (Woodlands Shopping Mall, Shop No 15) are good for watching English Premier League and rugby on the telly. Most of the hotels, from hostels to top-end places, have their own bars.

Levy Junction (p978) and **Manda Hill** (Great East Rd) Shopping Centres have stylish and state-of-the-art Fresh View Cinemas and Ster-Kinekor is at **Arcades** (Great East Rd; tickets from ZMW16).

Polo Grill BAR
(2374 Nangwenya Rd; ⏲8am-midnight) A large, open-air bar, under an enormous thatched roof overlooking a well-kept polo field (occasionally there's a match) – where you can knock back a few Mosis.

Shopping

Sunday Market MARKET
(Arcades Shopping Centre, Great East Rd; ⏲9am-6pm Sun) This weekly market in the parking lot at the Arcades Shopping Centre features Lusaka's best range of handicrafts.

Jackal & Hide ACCESSORIES
(www.jackalandhide.net; Leopards Hill Rd) For extremely high quality leather goods, head to this spot on Sugarbush Farm east of Kabulonga, around 15km from the city centre.

SET YOUR BUDGET

Budget

- Dorm room ZMW50
- Dinner ZMW25
- Three hour bus ZMW70

Midrange

- Hotel Room ZMW400
- Two course dinner ZMW75
- Business class bus Lusaka to Livingston ZMW115

Top End

- Bushcamp in national park per person US$500
- Dinner ZMW160
- Flight Lusaka to Mfuwe ZMW1300

It shares a location with the highly recommended Design House Cafe.

Information

DANGERS & ANNOYANCES

As in most African cities, pickpockets take advantage of crowds, so be alert in the markets and bus stations and along the busy streets immediately west of Cairo Rd. At night, most streets are dark and often empty, so even if you're on a tight budget, take a taxi.

EMERGENCY

Ambulance (☎992)
Police (☎991; Church Rd)

INTERNET ACCESS

Wireless internet is available at many cafes, restaurants and hotels. Look for the 'I Spot' sign. All three of the large malls have internet cafes and there are a couple along Cairo Rd.

I-Zone Internet (Arcades Shopping Centre, Great East Rd; per 30min ZMW6; ⏲9am-9pm)

MEDICAL SERVICES

Good options include the private clinics **Care for Business** (☎256731; Addis Ababa Rd) and **Corpmed** (☎222612; Cairo Rd; ⏲24hr), behind Barclays Bank. For evacuations, both clinics work with **Specialty Emergency Services** (☎273302; www.ses-zambia.com).

MONEY

Banks (Barclays Bank, FNB, Indo-Zambian Bank, Standard Chartered Bank and Zanaco) with ATMs and bureaux de change are located in

Lusaka

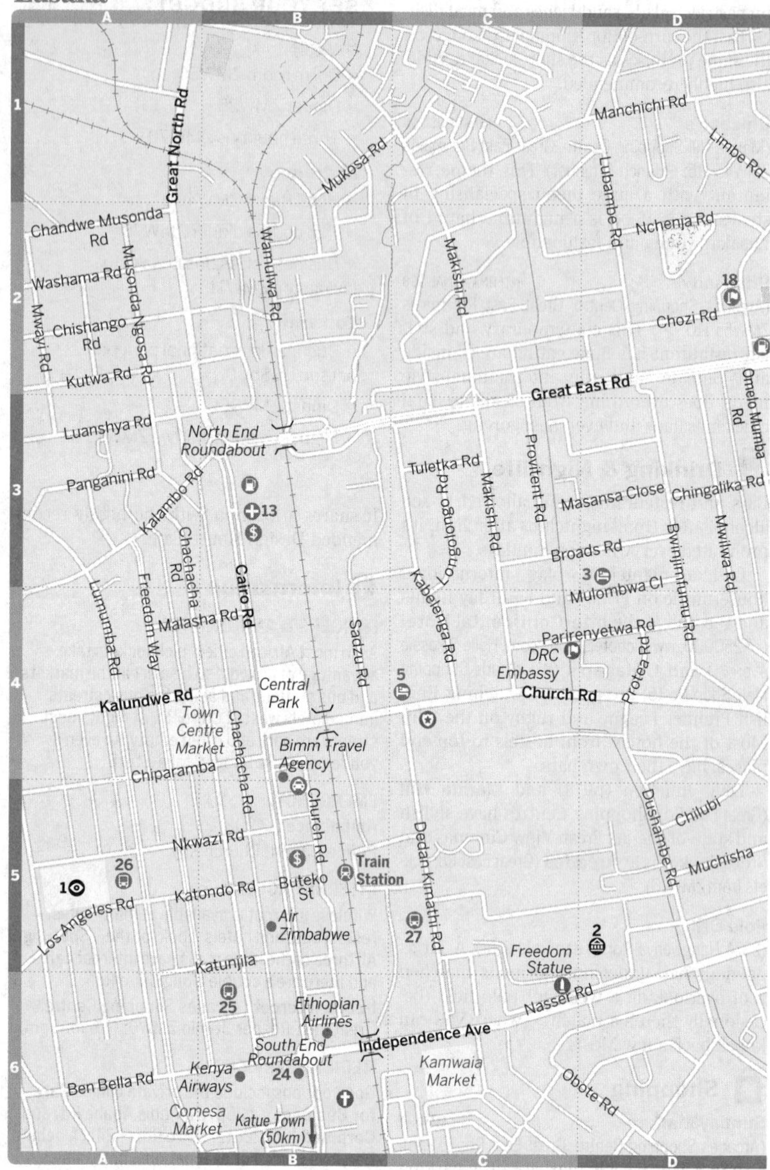

Arcades, Levy Junction and Manda Hill shopping centres, along Cairo Rd and elsewhere in Lusaka.

TRAVEL AGENCIES

Bush Buzz (☎256992; www.bush-buzz.com) This agency is especially popular for trips to the Kafue and Lower Zambezi national parks.

Voyagers (☎253064; www.voyagerszambia.com; Suez Rd) Perhaps the most popular agency in Zambia, it arranges flights, hotel reservations and car hire.

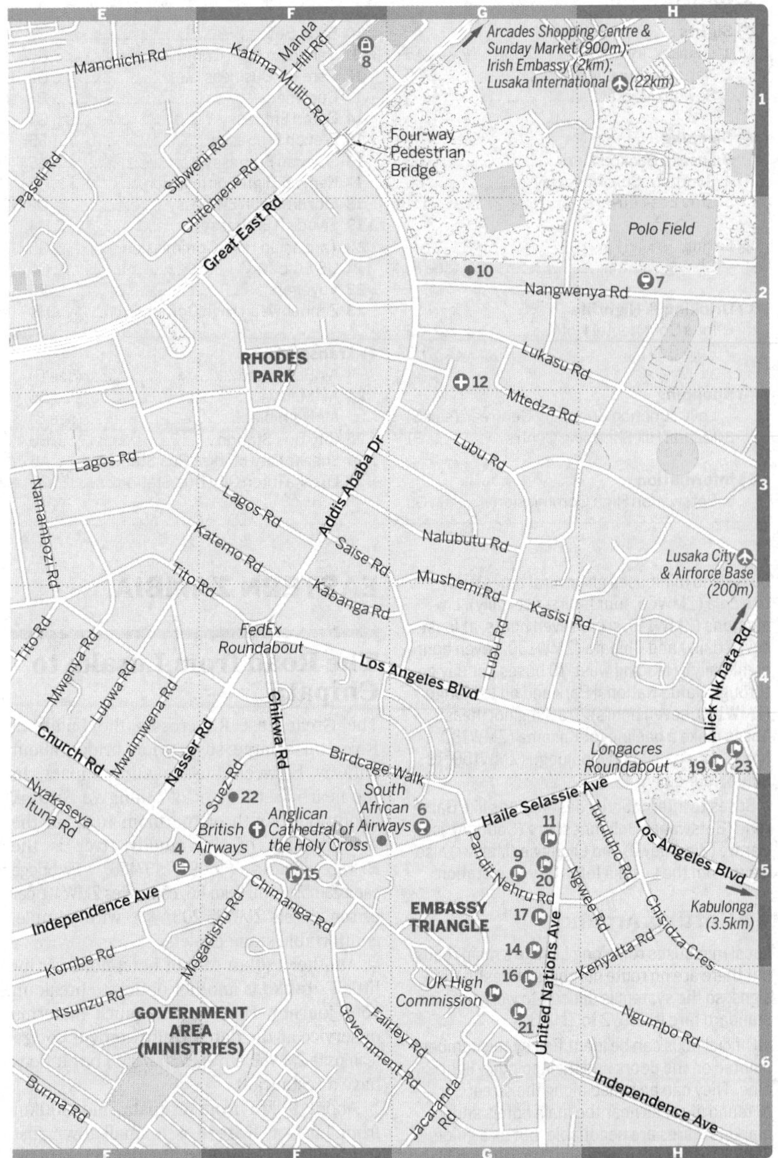

Getting There & Away

BUS & MINIBUS

Bus and minibus services to surrounding towns, such as Siavonga (ZMW70, three to five daily) and Chirundu (ZMW30, five to seven daily), leave from either **Lusaka City Market Bus Station** (Lumumba Rd) or the **City Bus Station** (Kulima Towers Bus Station; off Chachacha Rd), also called the Kulima Towers Station.

All long-distance public buses (and a few private ones) use the **Lusaka Inter-City Bus Station** (Dedan Kimathi Rd). From this terminal,

Lusaka

Sights
1 Lusaka City Market A5
2 National Museum D5
Soweto Market .... (see 1)

Sleeping
3 Lusaka Backpackers D3
4 Southern Sun Ridgeway E5
5 Stay Easy Lusaka C4

Eating
Chicago's .... (see 8)

Drinking & Nightlife
6 InterContinental Hotel G5
7 Polo Grill H2

Shopping
Levy Junction Shopping Centre ... (see 5)
8 Manda Hill Shopping Centre F1

Information
9 Botswanan High Commission G5
10 Bush Buzz G2
11 Canadian High Commission G5
12 Care for Business G2
13 Corpmed B3
14 Dutch Embassy G5
15 French Embassy F5
16 German Embassy G6
17 Kenyan High Commission G5
18 Mozambican Embassy D2
19 Swedish Embassy H4
20 Tanzanian High Commission G5
21 US Embassy G6
22 Voyagers F5
23 Zimbabwean High Commission H4

Transport
Air Botswana .... (see 6)
24 Air Malawi B6
Air Namibia .... (see 8)
25 City Bus Station B6
26 Lusaka City Market Bus Station A5
27 Lusaka Inter-City Bus Station C5

buses and minibuses go several times a day to Ndola (ZMW65, four hours, five daily), Livingstone (ZMW115, six to seven hours, at least seven daily) and Chipata (ZMW130, seven hours, eight daily). Heading west, 10 buses per day go through Kafue National Park and on to Mongu (ZMW160, seven hours). Tracking northeast, buses make a beeline for Kasama (ZMW130, 14 hours, four daily) and Mpulungu (ZMW150, 18 hours, four daily).

Buses to international destinations like Gaborone (Botswana), Johannesburg (South Africa), Harare (Zimbabwe) and Lilongwe (Malawi) also leave from the Lusaka Inter-City Bus Station.

Getting Around

Local minibuses run along Lusaka's main roads, but there are no route numbers or destination signs, so the system is difficult to work out. The standard fare is ZMW2 to ZMW3.

Official taxis can be identified by the numbers painted on the doors and their colour – light blue. They can be hailed along the street or found at ranks near the main hotels and markets. Fares are negotiable, but as a guide, ZMW30 will get you between Cairo Rd and Manda Hill Shopping Centre during the day. Taxis to and from the airport to central Lusaka cost anywhere from ZMW110 to ZMW150.

EASTERN ZAMBIA

The Road from Lusaka to Chipata

The Great East Rd crosses the Luangwa River on a large suspension bridge about halfway between Lusaka and Chipata. In the nearby settlement of **Luangwa Bridge**, about 3km south of the main road on the western side of the muddy river is the **Bridge Camp** (0977 197456; www.bridgecampzambia.com; Feira Rd; campsites ZMW40, per person chalets ZMW85-205;) with simple, comfortable stone chalets.

Another 180km east of here, nondescript little **Petauke** is another option to break up your journey. Don't expect much in terms of service at the dated **Chimwemwe Lodge** (campsite ZMW50, s/d ZMW300/350) but it does have a restaurant.

About 90km from Chipata and 500km from Lusaka, **Katete** is a small town just south of the Great East Road. On the main road, 4km west of Katete, **Tikondane Community Centre** (0216-252122; tikoeducation@gmail.com; dm ZMW30, campsites per person ZMW25, s/d from ZMW60/75), next to St Francis Hospital, is a grassroots initiative that works with local villages on educational, agricultural and health care initiatives. If you're interested in experiencing village life consider a stay at the friendly Community Centre's Guest House. The rooms are small and simple; meals (ZK30,000) are provided and internet access is available.

Chipata

0216

The primary commercial and urban centre in this district, Chipata is a traffic-clogged town in a valley surrounded by a fertile agricultural region. For travellers it's simply a stop on the way to South Luangwa National Park or Malawi only 30km away. There are a few decent accommodation options, petrol stations, banks with ATMs and a large Spar Supermarket to stock up on food and other supplies.

Sleeping

Mama Rula's CAMPGROUND, HOTEL $$

(0977 790226; www.mamarulas.com; campsites per person ZMW35, s/d incl breakfast ZMW248/315; @) This leafy compound around 4km out of Chipata along the road to Mfuwe has simply furnished rooms and a large grassy campground, excellent food (t-bone steak ZMW90) and a lantern-lit *lapa* (outside entertaining area) with a fire pit.

Deans Hill View Lodge CAMPGROUND, LODGE $

(221673; www.deanshillview.com; campsites per person ZMW25, r without bathroom per person ZMW50) Perched at the top of a hill with great views of the valley, this small lodge has simple rooms with shared bathrooms, and camping on a nice big sloping garden.

Getting There & Away

Of the handful of bus companies offering services to Lusaka, **Johabie** (ZMW130, seven hours, 5am, 6am, 8am & 2pm) is easily the most recommended.

Minibuses to Mfuwe (ZMW150, 3½ hours), the gateway to South Luangwa National Park, leave inconveniently at 11pm. A taxi (ZMW450) is a more comfortable option.

Minibuses also go to the Malawi border, as do taxis which should cost around ZMW80 (30 minutes).

South Luangwa National Park

0216

For scenery, variety of animals, accessibility and choice of accommodation, **South Luangwa** (admission per Zambian-registered vehicle/non-Zambian-registered vehicle/person ZMW15/US$15/US$25; 6am-6pm) is the best park in Zambia and one of the most majestic in Africa. Impalas, pukus and buffaloes wander on the wide, open plains; leopards, of which there are many, hunt in the dense woodlands; herds of elephants wade through the marshes; and hippos munch serenely on Nile cabbage in the Luangwa River.

The focal point is **Mfuwe**, a village with shops, a petrol station and a market. About 1.8km further on is **Mfuwe Gate**, the main entrance to the park, where a bridge crosses the Luangwa River and several lodges, camps and campsites are situated. Most of the park is inaccessible between November and April (especially February and March), so many lodges close at this time.

Activities

All lodges and camps run excellent day and night **wildlife drives** (all year) and most offer **walking safaris** (June to November). These activities are included in the rates charged by the upmarket places, while the less-expensive lodges and camps can organise activities at short notice. A three-hour morning or evening wildlife drive normally costs around ZMW210, and the evening drive in particular offers the chance to spot an elusive leopard.

Sleeping & Eating

All of the lodges and camps deep in the park are all-inclusive and at the very top end in terms of price (none are reviewed below). Some companies offer walking safaris for a few days from one bushcamp to the next. Most travellers will end up choosing from the places just outside the park boundary. These range from budget camping to top-end lodges, and you don't pay admission fees until you actually enter the park. Note that some lodges/camps open only in the high season (April to November), but those in and around Mfuwe are open all year (substantial discounts are available in the wet season).

All the lodges/camps and camping grounds provide meals – from simple snacks to creative haute cuisine at the top-end places. Flatdogs Camp probably has the best food of the 'drop in' lodge restaurants.

Croc Valley CAMPGROUND $
(☎246074; www.crocvalley.com; r without bathroom ZMW78, safari tents from ZMW180, campsites per person ZMW52;) This sprawling compound is set under a tangle of trees lining the riverbank. The campground is popular with independent travelers; 'backpacker rooms' with shared bathrooms are a good deal and safari tents of varying levels of luxury and cost are available. There's a big bar and restaurant with nightly three-course meals for those paying full board, not to mention plenty of shaded chill-out spots. Wildlife drives (ZMW208) and walking safaris (ZMW260) can be arranged.

Wildlife Camp CAMPGROUND $
(☎246026; www.wildlifecamp-zambia.com; safari tents/chalets ZMW211/317, campsites ZMW52;) This spacious, secluded spot about 5km southwest of Mfuwe village is popular with both overland groups and independent travellers. There are nine simple stone-and-thatch chalets, five airy tented ones and a big, open area for campers with its own bar and pool area. A restaurant serves up standard international fare (mains ZMW80). Wildlife drives and walks are available in the park and in the area round the camp.

Kawaza Village HUT $$
(www.kawazavillage.co.uk; day visits ZMW181, s with full board ZMW362) This enterprise run by the local Kunda people gives tourists the opportunity to visit a real rural Zambian village while helping the local community. Four rondavel huts (each sleeps two) are reserved for visitors, who are encouraged to take part in village life through activities such as learning how to cook *nshima* (maize porridge), attending local church services or visiting local schools. Traditional meals are provided and evenings are filled with dancing, drumming and storytelling around the fire. Transfers can be arranged from camps around Mfuwe village.

Flatdogs Camp TENTED CAMP $$
(☎246038; www.flatdogscamp.com; safari tents from ZMW240, chalets ZMW405; @) This large, leafy riverfront property is one of the best of the midrange options. Safari tents of varying features are at the end of snaking pathways and groups can consider the 'tree house' or one of the enormous two-storey chalets. The bar is a welcoming spot and the restaurant is open to nonguests. Wildlife drives and walking safaris are offered at affordable rates and all-inclusive packages are available.

Mfuwe Lodge BUSHCAMP $$$
(☎245041; www.bushcampcompany.com; per person per night all-inclusive US$450; year-round;) Laid out along an enviable stretch of a well-trafficked oxbow lagoon only 2km from the Mfuwe Gate, this lodge, one of the largest, is also certainly one of the nicest and best run. The 18 separate cottages are imaginatively designed and you have front-row seats to a parade of wildlife from the back porch of the suites, or from the huge outdoor deck with a restaurant, bar and swimmming pool. The base for its own six bushcamps in the southern section of the park, it's also the site of the recommended Bush-Spa with its beautifully designed Balinese-style spa built over a hippo pond.

Getting There & Away

Most people reach South Luangwa by air. Mfuwe airport is about 20km southeast of Mfuwe Gate and served by **Proflight** (☎0211-271032; www.proflight-zambia.com), with several daily flights from Lusaka (ranges from ZMW810 to ZMW1500 one way). **Bush & Lake Aviation** (www.bla.mw) and **Nyassa Air Taxi** (www.nyassa.mw) fly from Lilongwe in Malawi to Mfuwe. Almost every lodge meets clients at the airport. Otherwise, a taxi to locations near Mfuwe Gate should cost around ZMW80.

To get to Mfuwe Gate and the surrounding camps from Chipata, you should have a 4WD high-clearance vehicle. Work to improve this road has been ongoing for years and in the dry season the drive takes about three hours. In the wet season, however, the drive can take significantly longer (or be impassable), so seek advice before setting off.

Several crowded minibuses leave from the BP station in Mfuwe village for Chipata (around ZMW150, 3½ hours). Unfortunately, they depart around 7.30pm, meaning a late-night arrival. A shared taxi (around ZMW450 for the entire taxi) is a more convenient alternative.

SOUTHEASTERN ZAMBIA

Lower Zambezi Valley

One of the country's premier wildlife-viewing areas includes the Chiawa Game

Management Area (GMA) as well as the Lower Zambezi National Park, covering 4200 sq km along the northwestern bank of the Zambezi River. Several smaller rivers flow through the park itself, which is centered around a beautiful flood plain alongside the Zambezi, dotted with acacias and other large trees, and flanked by a steep escarpment on the northern side, covered with thick *miombo* woodland.

One of the best ways to see the Lower Zambezi is by canoe safari. Drifting silently past the riverbank you can get surprisingly close to birds and animals without disturbing them. Nothing beats getting eye-to-eye with a drinking buffalo, or watching dainty bushbuck tiptoe towards the river's edge. Excitement comes as you negotiate a herd of grunting hippos or hear a sudden 'plop' as a croc you hadn't even noticed slips into the water nearby.

The best time for tiger fishing (strictly catch and release) is September to December but still possible other months.

The main entrance is at Chongwe Gate along the southwestern boundary, though there are gates along the northern and eastern boundaries for hardy travellers.

Sleeping

There is a line of lodges running through the Chiawa GMA before the Chongwe Gate, a few in the park itself (all at the very the top end in terms of price) and one to the east of the park boundary (only really accessible to self-drivers).

Kiambi Safari CAMPGROUND **$$**
(0977 186106; www.kiambi.co.za; campsites per person ZMW52, chalets per person with full board from ZMW420;) This well-run operation at the confluence of the Zambezi and Kafue Rivers has a smattering of different, relatively affordable accommodation options including wood-floored tented chalets, spacious air-con chalets, well-equipped self-catering cottages and a campground with a fire pit, swimming pool and separate bar.

★**Chongwe River Camp** TENTED CAMP **$$$**
(0211-286 808; www.chongwe.com; s/d all-inclusive US$900/1400; Apr-Nov;) Right on the Chongwe River that marks the boundary between the national park and the GMA, this camp has an enviable position with plenty of game around the camp but without the park fees. Tented chalets, well spaced along the edge of the river, have plush bedding, shaded verandahs and charming open-air bathrooms.

Mvuu Lodge CAMPGROUND **$$$**
(in South Africa 012-660 5369; www.mvuulodge.com; campsites per person ZMW115, safari tents per person from ZMW1155) A large, leafy property with an informal vibe, Mvuu is built on the edge of the tree-lined riverbank. Comfortable elevated safari tents with balconies are on either side of a casual lounge and dining area. Each site in the campground, the furthest one into the GMA, has its own outdoor stone shower and toilet, fire pit, concrete cooking table and sink.

Getting There & Away

There's no public transport to Chongwe Gate, nor anything to the eastern and northern boundaries. Most people visit the park on an organised tour, and/or stay at a lodge that offers wildlife drives and boat rides as part of the deal. The lodges also arrange transfers from Lusaka – generally a minivan to Chirundu and then boat to the lodge (rates and travel times vary depending on the distance from Chirundu).

Siavonga

0211

Siavonga, the main town and resort along the Zambian side of Lake Kariba, has a location to be envied. Set among hills and verdant greenery, just a few kilometres from the massive Kariba Dam, views of the lake pop up from many vantage points, especially from the lodges. Built up primarily in the 1960s and '70s, it can at times appear as if no architects, builders or designers have visited since. But for those seeking down time at the closest 'beach vacation' to Lusaka, you can kick back or experience water activities available such as canoeing through Zambezi Gorge, as well as a civilised sunset cruise to the dam wall. Just don't even think of putting your big toe in the water – crocs lurk around the lakeshore.

A great change of pace from all those crack-of-dawn safari wake-up calls is **Eagles Rest** (0211-511168; www.eaglesrestresort.com; campsites per person ZMW50, s/d incl breakfast ZMW400/550;), a laid-back beachfront resort with a pool and the only campsite in town. Large, spacious chalets overlook the lake and everything from wake-boarding, tubing, fishing, canoeing and more can be arranged.

SOUTHWESTERN ZAMBIA

Livingstone

☎0213

The historic town of Livingstone, 11km away from the falls, has taken on the role of a backpacking mecca. It attracts travelers not only to experience the falls, but to tackle the thrilling adventure scene. The town is not much to look at, but it is a safe, lively place with some fantastic restaurants. Those looking for a more scenic and luxurious experience can treat themselves to the natural setting along the Zambezi River at any number of plush lodges with river and wildlife views.

Sights & Activities

While of course it's the spectacular sight of Victoria Falls that lures travellers to the region, the astonishing number of activities on offer here is the reason they hang around. From white-water rafting and bungee jumping to chopper rides over the falls or walking with rhinos, Vic Falls is well and truly established as one of the world's premier adventure destinations. To get the best value out of your time here, look into packages that combine various adrenaline-filled leaps, slides and swings for around US$125.

★Victoria Falls World Heritage National Monument Site WATERFALL

(admission ZMW103.5; ⏲6am-6pm) Taking its place alongside the Pyramids and the Serengeti, Victoria Falls – the 'smoke that thunders' – is one of Africa's original blockbusters. And although Zimbabwe and Zambia share it, Victoria Falls is a place all of its own. A magnet for tourists of all descriptions – backpackers, tour groups, thrill seekers, families, honeymooners – Vic Falls is one of Earth's great spectacles. View it directly as a raging mile-long curtain of water, in all its glory from a helicopter ride or peek precariously over its edge from **Devil's Pool**; the sheer power and force of the falls is something that simply does not disappoint.

Whether you're here purely to take in the sight of a natural wonder of the world, or for a serious hit of adrenaline via rafting or bungee jumping into the Zambezi, Victoria Falls is a place you're sure to tick off numerous items from that bucket list.

Victoria Falls is the largest, most beautiful and most majestic waterfall on the planet, and is the Seventh Natural Wonder of the World as well as being a Unesco World Heritage Site. A trip to Southern Africa would not be complete without visiting this unforgettable place.

Just to give you an idea, one million litres of water that fall – per second – down a 108m drop along a 1.7km wide strip in the Zambezi Gorge is the awesome sight before you.Victoria Falls is to be seen, heard, tasted and touched: it is a treat that few other places in the world can offer, a Must See Before You Die spot.

★Livingstone Island VIEWPOINT

One the most thrilling experiences at Vic Falls is the hair-raising journey to Livingstone Island, where you can bathe in Devil's Pool – nature's ultimate infinity pool, set directly on the edge of the raging falls. You can leap into the pool and then poke your head over the edge to get an extraordinary view of the 100m drop.

The island is accessed via boat, and prices include either breakfast (ZMW333), lunch (ZMW615) or high tea (ZMW486). When the water is low, you're able to access it by walking or swimming across, but a guide is compulsory. Access to the island is closed from around March to May when the water levels are too high.

Mosi-oa-Tunya Game Park WILDLIFE SANCTUARY

(admission US$10; ⏲6am-6pm) Upriver from the falls, and only 3km southwest of Livingstone, is a tiny **wildlife sanctuary**, with rhinos, zebras, giraffes, buffalo, elephants and antelopes.

Livingstone Museum MUSEUM

(Mosi-oa-Tunya Rd; admission ZMW25; ⏲9am-4.30pm) This stately museum contains a collection of David Livingstone memorabilia and historic maps dating back to 1690.

Sleeping

Staying in town means being able to walk to the bars and restaurants; the riverfront allows relaxation in seclusion along gorgeous stretches of the Zambezi, and sometimes views to the top of the falls. Downriver, where the Zambezi River opens up more, you can view wildlife without even leaving your hotel.

Town Centre

★Jollyboys Backpackers BACKPACKERS $

(☎324229; www.backpackzambia.com; 34 Kanyanta Rd; campsite/dm/r ZMW40/50/205; @🛜🏊) Wildly popular with independent travellers,

Jollyboys has a sunken lounge, excellent coffee, sparkling pool, cheap restaurant/bar and clean bright rooms; a quieter guesthouse is nearby to suit couples and families.

Fawlty Towers BACKPACKERS, LODGE **$$**
(☎323432; www.adventure-africa.com; 216 Mosi-oa-Tunya Rd; campsite/dm/tr ZMW40/76/215, d with/without bathroom ZMW307/205;) Once a backpacker institution, now a guesthouse full of upmarket touches: free internet and wi-fi, shady lawns, a great pool and some of the nicest, and most spacious, dorms that we've seen.

ZigZag GUESTHOUSE **$$**
(☎322814; www.zigzagzambia.com; off Mosi-oa-Tunya Rd; s/d ZMW280/410;) Don't be deceived by the motel-meets-caravan-park exterior, the rooms here are more boutique B&B with loving touches throughout, a swimming pool and a great restaurant.

Olga's Guesthouse GUESTHOUSE **$$**
(☎324160; www.olgasproject.com; cnr Mosi-oa-Tunya & Nakatindi Rds; s/d/f ZMW256/358/460;) If you need a lie down after gorging yourself at its restaurant, Olga's has it covered. Clean, spacious rooms with cool tiled floors, teak furniture and slick bathrooms are just a few feet away.

Zambezi Riverfront

Jungle Junction Bovu Island LODGE, CAMPGROUND **$**
(☎323708, 0978 725282; www.junglejunction.info; campsite per person ZMW50, hut per person ZMW128-179;) For hippos, hammocks and harmony: an island in the middle of the Zambezi for travellers who simply want to hang out and lounge beneath palm trees, or go fishing. Meals cost US$7 to US$12.

Zambezi Sun RESORT **$**
(☎321122; www.suninternational.com; s/d incl breakfast from ZMW2355/2,510, f ZMW2550;) Only a 10-minute walk from the falls and within the perimeters of the national park, this sprawling resort has North African kasbah-inspired rooms.

★**Stanley Safari Lodge** LODGE **$$$**
(☎in South Africa 27-72-170 8879; www.stanleysafaris.com; per person with full board & activities from ZMW2203;) Intimate and indulgent, Stanley is a 10km drive from the falls in a peaceful forested spot. Rooms are as plush as could be expected and the open-air suites come with a private plunge pool.

David Livingstone LODGE **$$$**
(☎324601; www.thedavidlivingstone.com; River Side Dr, Mosi-oa-Tunya National Park; s/d incl breakfast & activities ZMW1745/2675;) Located within the national park, this luxury hotel, the newest in Livingstone, has rooms with river views (as well as a riverfront infinity pool) and stand-alone bathtubs looking out to the water.

Zambezi Waterfront LODGE **$$$**
(☎320606; www.safpar.net/waterfront.html; campsite per person ZMW50, s/d tent per person ZMW155/200, s/d incl breakfast from ZMW640/920;) This waterfront lodge has a rustic wilderness charm with luxury tents and riverside chalets, not to mention a riverside open-air beer garden.

Eating & Drinking

★**Cafe Zambezi** AFRICAN **$$**
(☎0978 978578; 217 Mosi-oa-Tunya Rd; mains ZMW30-48; ⊗9am-midnight;) This favourite has a sunny outdoor courtyard and a broad menu covering everything from *mopane* caterpillars to wood-fired pizzas.

★**Olga's Italian Corner** ITALIAN **$$**
(www.olgasproject.con; cnr Mosi-oa-Tunya & Nakatindi Rds; pizza & pasta from ZMW40; ⊗7am-10pm;) Olga's does authentic wood-fired thin crust pizzas, as well as delicious homemade pasta classics.

ZigZag CAFE **$$**
(off Mosi-oa-Tunya Rd; mains from ZMW25; ⊗7am-9pm;) ZigZag has a drool-inducing menu of homemade muffins, fresh fruit smoothies and a changing small menu of comfort food.

Information

Barclays Bank (cnr Mosi-oa-Tunya Rd & Akapelwa St)
Computer Centre (216 Mosi-oa-Tunya Rd; internet per hr US$2; ⊗8am-8pm)
Livingstone General Hospital (☎0213-321475; Akapelwa St)
Police (☎0213-320116; Maramba Rd)
Standard Chartered Bank (Mosi-oa-Tunya Rd)
Tourist Centre (☎0213-321404; www.zambiatourism.com; Mosi-oa-Tunya Rd; ⊗8am-5pm Mon-Fri)

DANGERS & ANNOYANCES

Don't walk from town to the falls as there have been a number of muggings along this stretch of road. Take a minivan for under ZMW5 or a blue taxi for ZMW40.

Livingstone

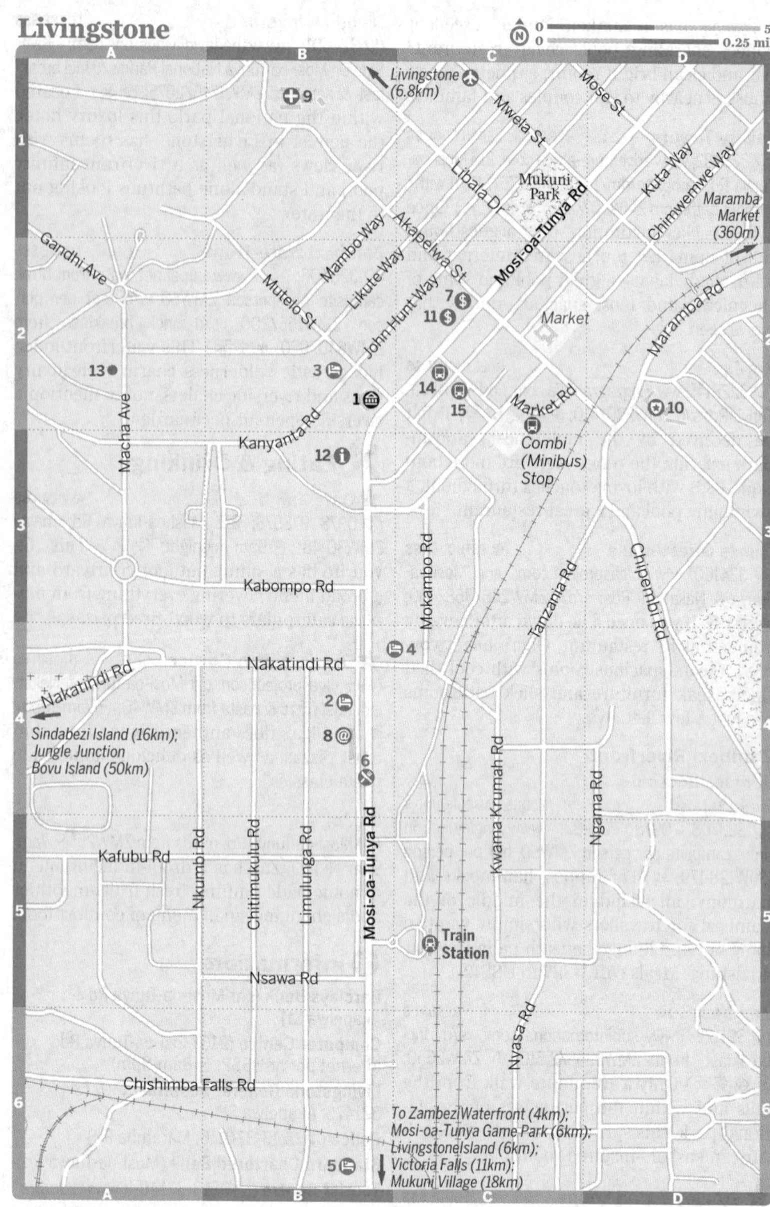

Getting There & Away

AIR

South African Airways (☎ 0212-612207; www.flysaa.com) and **British Airways** (www.britishairways.com) have daily flights to and from Johannesburg. The cheapest economy fare starts at around US$400 return. **Proflight Zambia** (☎ 0211-845944; www.proflight-zambia.com) flies daily from Livingstone to Lusaka.

BUS & MINIBUS

Mazhandu Family Bus (☎ 0975 805064) has seven daily buses to Lusaka (ZMW80 to

Livingstone

Sights
1 Livingstone Museum B2

Sleeping
2 Fawlty Towers B4
3 Jollyboys Backpackers B2
4 Olga's Guesthouse C4
5 ZigZag B6

Eating
6 Cafe Zambezi B4
Olga's Italian Corner .... (see 4)
ZigZag .... (see 5)

Information
7 Barclays Bank C2
8 Computer Centre B4
9 Livingstone General Hospital B1
10 Police D2
11 Standard Chartered Bank C2
12 Tourist Centre B3

Transport
13 Hemingways A2
14 Mazhandu Family Bus Services C2
15 Shalom Bus C2

ZMW115, seven hours); **Shalom Bus** (☎0977 747013; Mutelo St) has eight a day (ZMW75). Mazhandu Family also has buses to Sesheke (ZMW60, two hours) leaving at 5am and 2pm.

Combis (minibuses) to the Botswana border at Kazungula depart when they are full from Mingongo bus station and cost ZMW30. Shared taxis can be taken from the taxi rank by Shoprite and cost ZMW40.

TRAIN

The *Zambezi Express* leaves Livingstone for Lusaka (15 hours), via Choma, on Tuesday and Friday at 8pm. Book at the **train station** (☎320001).

Getting Around

TO/FROM THE AIRPORT

Livingstone Airport is 6km northwest from town, ZMW50 by taxi.

CAR & MOTORCYCLE

Hemingways (☎320996; www.hemingwayszambia.com; Mosi-oa-Tunya Rd) has new Toyota Hi-Lux campers, fully kitted.

COMBIS & TAXIS

Combis run regularly along Mosi-oa-Tunya Rd to the Victoria Falls Zambian border (ZMW5, 15 minutes). Blue taxis cost ZMW40.

WESTERN ZAMBIA

Kafue National Park

This stunning **park** (park fee per person per day ZMW105; self-drivers pay another ZMW79 per vehicle per day; ⏱6am-6pm) is about 200km west of Lusaka and is a real highlight of Zambia. Covering more than 22,500 sq km (nearly the size of Belgium), it's the largest park in the country and one of the biggest in the world. This is the only major park in Zambia that's easily accessible by car, with a handful of camps just off the highway that runs between Lusaka and Mongu, dividing it into northern and southern sectors. (You don't pay the park fee of ZMW105 per person per day if in transit).

To the far north is Kafue's top highlight, the **Busanga Plains**, a vast tract of Serengeti-style grassland, covered by huge herds of near-endemic red lechwes and more solitary grazers such as roan antelopes and oribis. (Note that this area is accessible only between mid-July and November.)

Sleeping

The following are all open year-round.

Mayukuyuku CAMPGROUND, BUSHCAMP $$
(www.kafuecamps.com; campsites per person ZMW78, with full board ZMW802) A rustic bushcamp, small and personal, in a gorgeous spot on the river with a well-landscaped camping area and four tastefully furnished thatch-roofed safari tents. Mayukuyuku is accessible by 2WD and is only 5km off the main highway on decent gravel.

★**Mukambi Safari Lodge** CHALET $$$
(☎0974 424013; www.mukambi.com; per person with full board ZMW1422; 📶🏊) Easily the most accessible of the Kafue lodges, Mukambi makes for a great base to explore the park. Tastefully designed *rondavels* (round, traditional-style huts) are set back from the riverfront, the pool is ideal for relaxing between morning and afternoon activities and the beautifully designed dining area has a 2nd-floor lounge, a great spot for contemplating sunsets.

★**KaingU Safari Lodge** CAMPGROUND, CHALET $$$
(☎in Lusaka 0211-256992; www.kaingu-lodge.com; campsites per person ZMW127, with full board & 2 activities ZMW1905; 📶) Experienced African travellers especially will love this remote camp set on a magical stretch of the Kafue River.

The four tastefully furnished Meru-style tents with large decks overlook the river. There are also three campsites, each with its own well-kept thatch bathroom and *braai* (barbecue) facilities. Contact KaingU for driving directions from the Lusaka–Mongu highway.

Mongu

☎0217

The largest town in Barotseland and the capital of the Western Province, Mongu is on high ground overlooking the flat and seemingly endless Liuwa Plain. Around the **harbour** is a fascinating settlement of reed-and-thatch buildings, where local fishermen sell their catch, and passenger boats take people to outlying villages.

Mongu really comes alive once a year when thousands of people flock here for the **Kuomboka ceremony** in March or early April. This colourful ceremony takes place when the king of the Lozi people is transported on a decorated river barge from his dry-season palace out on the plains to **Limulunga**, his wet-season palace on higher ground about 15km to the north; you'll also find a museum here containing exhibits about the Lozi people and the Kuomboka ceremony.

Next to the church in Mongu, **Greenview Guesthouse** (☎221029; www.limagarden.com; Limulunga Rd; campsites per person ZMW25, r from ZMW225; ❄) has good-value chalets and grassy grounds with views of the flood plains. To find it, head up the road to Limulunga and keep an eye out for the sign on the left.

Juldan and Shalom are the most recommended of the bus companies servicing the Lusaka to Mongu route (ZMW150, eight hours).

NORTHERN ZAMBIA

Kasanka National Park

One of Zambia's least known wilderness areas and a real highlight of a visit to this part of the country is the privately managed **Kasanka National Park** (www.kasanka.com; admission US$10; ⏲6am-6pm). At just 390 sq km, it's pretty small compared with most African parks, doesn't have a huge range of facilities and sees very few visitors, and this is what makes it special. You'll discover great tracts of *miombo* woodland, evergreen thicket, open grassland and rivers fringed with emerald forest, all by yourself.

Kasanka is perhaps most famous for its swampland though, and this is the terrain to see the park's shy and retiring star, the sitatunga, a semi-aquatic antelope distinguished by its long splayed hooves and oily coat. Night time brings out jackals, civets and porcupines, and during the months of November and December, this park is home to more than eight million migratory fruit bats – the biggest mammal gathering anywhere in the world – which can blanket the sky for several minutes at dusk.

Wasa Lodge (☎873 76 2067957; www.kasanka.com; per person self-catering chalets ZMW267, with full board incl all activities ZMW1920), which looks out over the lake of the same name, doubles as the park headquarters. Accommodation consists of thatched bungalows in two sizes; larger chalets are airy and cool with wide balconies and lovely stone showers. For relaxing, there's stone benches on the lakeshore, a small hide in the trees and the deck of the large bar and dining area.

Samfya

Perched on the western shore of Lake Bangweulu, about 10km east of the main road between Mansa and Serenje, you'll find Samfya. This small trading centre and lake-transport hub is small enough to get to know people and large enough to have rest houses, restaurants and bars. Just outside town is the majestic, sandy **Cabana Beach** – it may look inviting but the water is full of crocs.

Bangweulu Bay Lodge (☎in Lusaka 0211-266927; www.bangweulubaylodge.com; r per person US$150-180), located on the shores of the lake offers three smart guest chalets with views over the beach and blue waters beyond. Activities on tap include hobie cat sailing, boat trips and wildlife spotting in the area.

Samfya is served by minibuses from Serenje (ZMW70, four to five hours). Buses between Lusaka (ZMW120, 10 hours) go via Serenje.

Shiwa Ng'andu

☎0214

The vast estate of **Shiwa Ng'andu** (www.shiwangandu.com; tours US$20; ⏲9-11am Mon-Sat, closed to nonguests Sun) was established in the 1920s by British aristocrat Stewart Gore-Brown. At its heart is **Shiwa House**, a splendid English-style mansion as described in *The Africa House* by Christina Lamb.

Kapishya Hot Springs is about 20km west of Shiwa House, but still on the Shiwa Ng'andu estate. The setting is marvellous – a blue-green lagoon surrounded by palms – and the springs are bathwater hot. It is possible to stay next to the springs at **Kapishya Lodge** (0211-229261; www.shiwasafaris.com; campsite/chalet per person US $10/60, d incl breakfast and dinner per person US $110;), and rather grand accommodation is also available at **Shiwa House** (0211-229261; www.shiwasafaris.com; d per person with full board from US$350) itself.

To reach Shiwa House, head along the highway by bus/car from Mpika for 90km towards Chiosso. Look for the signpost to the west, from where a 20km dirt road leads to the house. Kapishya Hot Springs and the Lodge are a further 20km along this track. There's no public transport along this last section, but there are vehicle transfers from the Great North Road turn-off.

Kasama

0214

Kasama is the capital of the Northern Province and is the cultural centre of the Bemba people. With its wide leafy streets and handsome old tin-roofed colonial houses, it is the most appealing of the northern towns.

The deservedly popular family-run **Thorn Tree Guesthouse** (0214-221615; www.thorntreesafaris.com; 612 Zambia Rd; s/d ZMW230/290, f from ZMW350;) has rooms in the main house, and a three-room cottage (ZMW410). As well as the bar and a restaurant, the family runs a safari company that organises tours.

Mbala

0214

Mbala is a small town perched on the edge of the Great Rift Valley, from where the road drops over 1000m in less than 40km down to Mpulungu and Lake Tanganyika. Today the only reason to visit is the **Moto Moto Museum** (admission ZMW15; 9am-4.45pm), a fascinating collection of artefacts of the Bemba people or as a stop-off point for Kalambo Falls.

The most atmospheric, welcoming place to stay in Mbala is **Lake Chila Lodge** (0977 795241; lakechilalodge@yahoo.com; Lake Chila; r ZMW150), on the lake shores 2km from town.

All buses/minibuses travelling between Mpulungu and Kasama stop in Mbala.

Kalambo Falls

About 40km northwest of Mbala, along the border between Zambia and Tanzania, is the 221m-high **Kalambo Falls** (adult/child/car US$15/7/15). Kalambo is the second-highest single-drop waterfall in Africa. From spectacular viewpoints near the top of the falls, you can see the Kalambo River plummeting off a steep V-shaped cliff cut into the Rift Valley escarpment down into a deep valley, which then winds towards Lake Tanganyika. The **campsite** (campsites US$10) here has stunning views out over the Rift Valley though facilities are basic (there's only a long-drop toilet). The best way for travellers without a car to get here is from Mpulungu. One option is a thrice-weekly taxi boat that serves villages along the lakeshore east of Mpulungu.

Mpulungu

0214

Resting at the foot of mighty Lake Tanganyika, Mpulungu is a crossroads between eastern, central and southern Africa. As Zambia's only international port, it's the terminal for the ferry across the lake to Tanzania. Although it's always very hot, the presence of crocs should be enough to deter you from taking a dip in the lake.

Nkupi Lodge (455166; nkupilodge@hotmail.com; campsites per person ZMW40, dm ZMW75, rondavels from ZMW125), a short walk out of town near the lake, with a shady campsite and spacious *rondavels*, is the best place for independent travellers. There's also a self-catering kitchen and a bar, or food can be prepared. provided you give plenty of notice.

Most buses' and minibuses' schedules tie in with the Lake Tanganyika ferry. Long-distance buses link Mpulungu with Lusaka (ZMW150, 16 hours) via Kasama (ZMW40, three hours) and Mpika (ZMW100, six hours). Minibuses also depart from near the BP petrol station in Mpulungu for Mbala (ZMW15, 40 minutes).

THE COPPERBELT

Ndola & Kitwe

0212

These two towns lie at the heart of the industrial Copperbelt region and, although they're not tourist attractions in themselves, you might find yourself passing through on the way to Chimfunshi Wildlife Orphanage.

From Lusaka fast buses head to Ndola (ZMW65, four hours, 10 daily) and on to Kitwe (ZMW70, five hours). Slow 'ordinary' trains to Ndola and Kitwe, via Kapiri Mposhi, depart twice weekly.

Dazi Lodge LODGE $$
(0955 460487; Pamo Ave; r ZMW200-350;) This sparkling clean place in Kitwe has a wonderful kitschy air about it, as well as two bars, a swimming pool and a well-regarded restaurant.

★**Mukwa Lodge** LODGE $$$
(224266; www.mukwalodge.co.zm; 26 Mpezeni Ave; s/d incl breakfast ZMW585/690;) In Kitwe, this lodge has gorgeous, beautifully furnished rooms with stone floors. The bathrooms are as good as you'll find in Zambia.

New Savoy Hotel HOTEL $$$
(611097; savoy@zamnet.zm; Buteko Ave; r incl breakfast ZMW500-1100;) Ndola's best is a bit of a hulking concrete block from the outside; inside it's old-fashioned with a bit of charm.

Chimfunshi Wildlife Orphanage

On a farm 70km northwest of Chingola is this impressive **chimpanzee sanctuary** (www.chimfunshi.org.za; day visit adult/child project area ZMW50/25; 9am-3pm), home to around 120 adult and young chimps confiscated from poachers and traders in neighbouring Democratic Republic of Congo and other parts of Africa. It's the largest of its kind in the world. This is not a natural wildlife experience, but it's still fascinating to observe the chimps as they feed, play and socialise.

Visiting the sanctuary provides much-needed income and your entry fees go directly into helping it remain financially viable. Do not come, though, if you're sick in any way; the chimps can easily die of a disease like the flu. It is possible to stay overnight at the **campsite** (per person ZMW75) or in the **self-catering cottage** (adult/child ZMW150/75) at the education centre.

To get here by car, there is a new road that starts about 55km from Chingola and is well signposted. It's about 20km off the main road straight to the project area. If you contact the project in advance, staff can arrange a one-way transfer for ZMW100 to coincide with a supply run. Although buses between Chingola and Solwezi can drop passengers at the turn-off, it is generally easier to visit Chimfunshi with a private vehicle.

UNDERSTAND ZAMBIA

Zambia Today

In September 2011, Michael Sata, nicknamed 'King Cobra', and his party, the Patriotic Front (PF), won the national election, becoming only the fifth president in Zambia's post-independence history. There's an undercurrent of worry in the country that Sata's rhetoric and some of his decisions augur a move towards a more centralised economy and a less democratic government. But some of his populist tendencies – such as a significant increase of the minimum wage – can be interpreted as a sincere focus on redirecting the country's wealth to the poor majority.

One of the more pressing issues facing Zambia today is the impact of Chinese investment in the mining sector. Conflict over workers' rights and pay has sporadically spilled over into violence between workers and Chinese management, and tensions over the business practices and benefits of China's influence continue to weigh on the government.

Almost half of all Zambians live in urban centres, crowding into housing compounds; most unskilled city labourers work six to seven days per week, with their families sometimes living on less than US$1 per day. Still, a small middle class and expats frequent high-end shops and cinemas in Lusaka's malls, while in rural Zambia, life hasn't changed much – subsistence farmers still eke out a living and traditional religions mixed with Christian beliefs and village hierarchies are the mainstays of life.

History

Zambia was originally inhabited by hunter-gatherer Khoisan people. About 2000 years ago Bantu people migrated from the Congo basin and gradually displaced them. From the 14th century more immigrants came from the Congo and, by the 16th century, various dispersed groups consolidated into powerful tribes and nations, with specific territories and dynastic rulers.

The Colonial Era

The first Europeans to arrive were Portuguese explorers in the late 18th century, following routes established many centuries earlier by Swahili-Arab slave traders. The celebrated British explorer David Livingstone travelled up the Zambezi in the early 1850s in search of a route to the interior of Africa. In 1855 he reached the awesome waterfall that he promptly named Victoria Falls.

Livingstone's work and writings inspired missionaries to come to the area north of the Zambezi, and close on their heels came explorers, hunters and prospectors searching for whatever riches the country had to offer. In 1890 the area became known as Northern Rhodesia and was administered by the British South Africa Company, owned by empire-builder Cecil John Rhodes.

At around the same time, vast deposits of copper were discovered in the area now called the Copperbelt. Although the indigenous people had mined there for centuries, large European-style opencast pits were now being dug. The main sources of labour were the Africans who had to earn money to pay the new 'hut tax'; in any case, most were driven from their land by the European settlers.

In 1924 the colony was put under direct British control, and in 1935, the capital was moved to Lusaka. To make them less dependent on colonial rule, settlers soon pushed for closer ties with Southern Rhodesia and Nyasaland (Malawi), but various interruptions (such as WWII) meant the Federation of Rhodesia and Nyasaland did not come about until 1953.

Resistance & Independence

Meanwhile, African nationalism was becoming a greater force in the region. The United National Independence Party (UNIP) was founded in the late 1950s by Dr Kenneth Kaunda, who spoke out against the federation. Northern Rhodesia became independent in 1964, changing its name to Zambia. Kaunda became president and remained so for the next 27 years, largely because in 1972 he declared UNIP the only legal party and himself the sole presidential candidate.

Over the years, however, government corruption and mismanagement, coupled with civil wars in neighbouring states, left Zambia's economy in dire straits, and violent street protests were quickly transformed into a general demand for multiparty politics. Full elections were held in October 1991, and Kaunda and UNIP were resoundingly defeated by Frederick Chiluba and the Movement for Multiparty Democracy (MMD). Kaunda bowed out gracefully, and Chiluba became president.

With backing from the International Monetary Fund (IMF) and the World Bank, financial controls were liberalised to attract investors. But austerity measures were also introduced – and these were tough for the average Zambian. Food prices soared, inflation was rampant and state industries were privatised or simply closed, leaving many thousands of people out of work.

By the mid-1990s, the lack of visible change gave Kaunda the confidence to re-enter the political arena. He attracted strong support but withdrew from the November 1996 elections in protest at MMD irregularities. Chiluba won a landslide victory and remained in firm control. There was much speculation that the elections were rigged. However, most Zambians accepted the result, in the hope that at least the country would remain peaceful.

The 21st Century

Chiluba, unable to run for a third presidential term in December 2001, anointed his former vice-president, Levy Mwanawasa, as his successor. Mwanawasa only just beat a coalition of opposition parties, amid allegations of vote rigging. Mwanawasa stripped his predecessor of immunity from prosecution though Chiluba was eventually cleared of embezzlement charges by Zambia's High Court in August 2009.

Zambia's economy experienced strong growth in the early part of the 21st century, however it plummetted for a time when the price of minerals such as copper fell during the global economic slump of 2008/09. There has been large foreign investment in the mines (especially from China), and South African-owned businesses are multiplying in towns across the country, as there is finally a local demand for their businesses.

People

The population of Zambia is made up of between 70 and 80 different ethnic groups. The final count varies according to your definition of ethnicity, but the Zambian government officially recognises 73 groups in the country. The Bemba are the largest, followed by speakers of Tonga and Nyanja. The Lozi, who make up roughly 6% of the population, have their own distinct nation called Barotseland, which takes up a significant part of Zambia's Western Province and the vast Zambezi flood plain.

Around 75% of Zambians are Christians, the majority members of one of the hundreds of Protestant churches; in addition, there are some Catholics and those who follow homegrown Christian denominations, including large branches of the African Zion churches. Many of these people also follow traditional animist-based belief systems. There is also a significant Muslim population.

The vast majority (99%) of Zambians are indigenous Africans. The final 1% are people of Indian or European origin (mostly involved in business, commerce, farming and the tourist industry). These are Zambian citizens; many white and Asian families have lived here for generations – although race relations are still sometimes a little strained.

Relative newcomers to the country include South African businesspeople and Zimbabwean farmers who lost their land thanks to Robert Mugabe. There are also many Europeans and North Americans, some (such as mining consultants) living in Zambia for decades, others (such as aid workers) stay for only a few years before moving on.

Environment

Landlocked Zambia is one of Africa's most eccentric legacies of colonialism. Shaped like a contorted figure of eight, its borders do not correspond to any tribal or linguistic area. And Zambia is huge. At some 752,000 sq km, it's about the size of France, England and the Republic of Ireland combined.

The diversity of animal species in Zambia is huge. The rivers, including the Luangwa, the Kafue and the mighty Zambezi, support large populations of hippos and crocs, and the associated grasslands provide plenty of fodder for herds of zebras, impalas and pukus (antelopes common in Zambia, but not elsewhere), which in turn attract predators, so most parks contain lions, leopards, hyenas and cheetahs. The other two big drawcards – buffaloes and elephants – are also found in huge herds in the main national parks. Bird lovers will love Zambia, where about 750 species have been recorded.

Zambia boasts 20 national parks and reserves, and 34 game-management areas (GMAs). After decades of poaching, clearing and generally bad management, many are difficult to reach and others don't contain much wildlife. Since 1990, however, with the help of international donors, several of Zambia's parks have been rehabilitated and the wildlife protected by projects that also aim to give local people some benefit from conservation measures. Zambia's parks are well known for walking safaris, and some are considered to rival the best in Southern Africa.

SURVIVAL GUIDE

ℹ Directory A–Z

ACCOMMODATION

We list accommodation prices for the high (dry) season – ie April/May to October/November, based on 'international rates'. Some lodges/camps close in the wet season (November to April); if they're open, discounts of up to 50% are common.

In this book, we have defined the price categories for accommodation (per person) as follows: budget up to ZMW250, midrange between ZMW250 and ZMW500 and top end upwards of ZMW500.

However, it should be noted that the accommodation in the national parks is skewed towards the very high top end, that is, on average around ZMW2000 per person.

Most cities and larger towns have campsites where you can pitch your tent, but most are way out in the suburbs. Camping is also possible at privately run campsites just outside national park boundaries (you don't pay admission fees until you want to visit the park).

ACTIVITIES

Companies in Livingstone (and Victoria Falls town in Zimbabwe) offer a bewildering array of activities, such as white-water rafting in the gorge below the falls or river boarding and canoeing on the quieter waters above the falls. Those with plenty of nerve and money can try bungee jumping or abseiling, or take a ride in a microlight or helicopter.

Canoeing, either for a few hours or a few days, is a great way to explore the Zambezi River and can be arranged at lodges in the Lower Zambezi Valley and Siavonga. Fishing along the Zambezi, and at several lakes in northern Zambia, is also popular.

Most national parks, such as Kafue, Kasanka, Lower Zambezi and South Luangwa have activities for visitors, with wildlife drives and walks the

PRACTICALITIES

Electricity Supply is 220V to 240V/50Hz and plugs are of the British three-prong variety.

Languages English, Bemba, Lozi, Nyanja and Tonga

Money Zambian kwacha; US$1 = ZMW5.37, €1 = ZMW7

Newspapers The *Daily Times* (www.times.co.zm) and *Daily Mail* (www.daily-mail.co.zm) are dull, government-controlled rags. The columnists at the independent *Post* (www.postzambia.com) continually needle the government.

Radio Both of the Zambian National Broadcasting Corporation (ZNBC) radio stations can be heard nationwide; they play Western and African music, as well as news and chat shows in English. MUVI TV is independently owned while ZNBC also runs the solitary government-controlled TV station, but anyone who can afford it will subscribe to South African satellite TV. BBC World Service can be heard in Lusaka (88.2FM) and Kitwe (89.1FM); Radio France Internationale (RFI; 100.4FM) can also be heard in Lusaka.

Television PAL system

Time GMT/UTC +2

main focus and the main drawcard for visitors to Zambia.

EMBASSIES & CONSULATES

The following countries have embassies or high commissions in Lusaka. The British High Commission looks after the interests of Aussies and Kiwis. Most consulates are open from 8.30am to 5pm Monday to Thursday and from 8.30am to 12.30pm Friday.

Botswanan High Commission (☎0211-250555; 5201 Pandit Nehru Rd, Lusaka)

British High Commission (☎0211-423200; http://ukinzambia.fco.gov.uk/en; 5210 Independence Ave, Lusaka)

Canadian High Commission (☎0211-250833; 5119 United Nations Ave, Lusaka)

DRC Embassy (☎0211-235679; 1124 Parirenyetwa Rd, Lusaka)

Dutch Embassy (☎0211-253819; 5208 United Nations Ave, Lusaka)

French Embassy (☎0211-251322; 74 Independence Ave, Cathedral Hill)

German Embassy (☎0211-250644; 5209 United Nations Ave, Lusaka)

Irish Embassy (☎0211-291298; 6663 Katima Mulilo Rd, Lusaka)

Kenyan High Commission (☎0211-250722; 5207 United Nations Ave, Lusaka)

Malawian High Comission (☎0211-265768; 31 Bishops Rd, Kabulonga)

Mozambican Embassy (☎0211-220333; 9592 Kacha Rd, off Paseli Rd, Northmead)

Namibian High Comission (☎0211-260407; 30B Mutende Rd, Woodlands)

South African High Comission (☎0211-260999; 26D Cheetah Rd, Kabulonga)

Swedish Embassy (☎0211-251711; Haile Selassie Ave, Lusaka)

Tanzanian High Commission (☎0211-253323; 5200 United Nations Ave, Lusaka)

US Embassy (☎0211-357000; www.zambia.usembassy.gov; Kabulonga Rd, Ibex Hill)

Zimbabwean High Commission (☎0211-254006; 11058 Haile Selassie Ave, Lusaka)

FOOD

The staple diet for Zambians is unquestionably *nshima*, a thick, doughy maize porridge that's bland but filling. It's eaten with your hands and always accompanied by beans or vegetables and a hot relish, and sometimes meat or fish.

Although food is generally not a highlight of travel in Zambia, lodges and camps in and around the national parks usually offer the highest standards of culinary options.

Generally a budget meal is under ZMW30, midrange is between ZMW30 and ZMW70 and top end is upwards of ZMW70.

INTERNET ACCESS

There are internet centres in Lusaka, Livingstone and the bigger towns. Access at internet centres is cheap – about ZMW0.12 to ZMW0.20 per minute. Wi-fi is becoming more common.

MONEY

The unit of currency is the Zambian kwacha. President Sata passed legislation in 2012 that revalued Zambia's currency and prohibits any other currency from being accepted as a form of payment. Prices are sometimes quoted in US$, but you'll pay in local currency. Three zeros were removed from every bank note denomination eg ZMK90,000 is now ZMW90. Every single bank and ATM changed over to the new system on 1 January 2013.

In the cities and larger towns, you can easily change cash (no commission; photo ID required) and withdraw it (kwacha) from ATMs at branches of the major banks.

Visa is the most readily recognised credit card; a surcharge of 4% to 7% may be added to your bill.

PUBLIC HOLIDAYS

During the following public holidays, most businesses and government offices are closed:

New Year's Day 1 January
Youth Day Second Monday in March
Easter March/April – Good Friday, Saturday & Easter Monday
Labour/Workers' Day 1 May
Africa (Freedom) Day 25 May
Heroes' Day First Monday in July
Unity Day First Tuesday in July
Farmers' Day First Monday in August
Independence Day 24 October
Christmas Day 25 December
Boxing Day 26 December

SAFE TRAVEL

Generally, Zambia is very safe, though in the cities and tourist areas there is always a chance of being targeted by muggers or con artists. As always, you can reduce the risk considerably by being sensible.

TELEPHONE

Every landline in Zambia uses the area code system; you only have to dial it if you are calling outside of your area code. Remember to drop the zero if you are dialling from outside of Zambia.

Almost all telecommunication services are provided by Zamtel. Public phones use tokens for domestic calls, which last three minutes. Phone booths operated by Zamtel use phone cards (ZMW5, ZMW10, ZMW20 or ZMW50) available from post offices and grocery shops. These phone cards can be used for international calls but it's often easier to find a 'phone shop' or 'fax bureau', from where all international calls cost about ZMW12 per minute.

If you're calling Zambia from another country, the country code is 260, but drop the initial zero of the area code. The international access code is 00.

Mobile Phones

MTN and Airtel offer mobile (cell) phone networks. If you own a GSM phone, you can buy a SIM card for only around ZMW3 without a problem (easy to do at Lusaka airport) and then purchase credits in whatever denominations – from the same company as your SIM.

Numbers starting with 09--, that is plus another two numbers, eg 0977 are mobile phone numbers.

VISAS

Tourist visas are available at major borders, airports and ports, but it's important to note that you should have a Zambian visa *before* arrival if travelling by train or boat from Tanzania.

All foreign visitors – other than SADC passport holders, who are issued visas free of charge – pay US$50 for single entry (up to one month) and US$80 for double entry (up to three months). Applications for multiple-entry visas (US$80) must be made in advance at a Zambian embassy or high commission. If staying less than 24 hours, for example visiting Livingstone from Zimbabwe, you pay only US$20.

Payment can be made in US dollars, and sometimes UK pounds, although other currencies such as euros, South African rand, Botswanan pula or Namibian dollars, may be accepted at borders, but don't count on it.

Visas for Onward Travel

It's always best to visit any embassy or high commission in Lusaka between 9am and noon from Monday to Friday.

Visas for Zimbabwe, Malawi, Tanzania and Botswana are easy to obtain on arrival at the borders of these countries for most visitors. However, if you're travelling by train or boat to Tanzania, check with the Tanzanian high commission in Lusaka about whether you need a visa beforehand. If so, three-month visas cost about US$50 (depending on your nationality). For Namibia, most nationalities do not require a visa and are granted 90 days upon arrival. For Mozambique, single-entry visas (only) are available at most major land and air entry points for US$69 for one month.

Getting There & Away

AIR

Zambia's main international airport is in Lusaka, though several international airlines fly to the airport at Livingstone (for Victoria Falls).

The departure tax for all international flights is ZMW156. This tax is often included in the price of your airline ticket, but if not must be paid at the airport (in Zambian kwacha only).

The country is increasingly well-connected with direct flights to destinations outside Africa. **British Airways** (www.britishairways.com) has thrice-weekly flights from London, **KLM/Air France** (www.klm.com) from Amsterdam and **Emirates** (www.emirates.com) from Dubai.

South African Airways (www.flysaa.com) has daily direct flights from New York City to Johannesburg. From here there are regular flights to Lusaka, Ndola and Livingstone.

Zambia is also well connected with Southern Africa. **Zambezi Airlines** (☎ 0211-250342; www.flyzambezi.com) flies to regional destinations such as Johannesburg and to Dar es Salaam in Tanzania.

Air Malawi (☎ 0211-228120; www.flyairmalawi.com; COMESA Centre, Zone B, ground fl, Ben Bella Rd) connects Lusaka with Lilongwe and Blantyre, while **Air Zimbabwe** (www.airzimbabwe.com) flies to Harare. **Air Botswana** (☎ 0211-255024; www.airbotswana.co.bw; Intercontinental Hotel), **Air Namibia** (☎ 0211-258370; www.airnamibia.co.na; Manda Hill Shopping Centre) and **Kenya Airways** (☎ 0211-228886; www.kenya-airways.com; 3rd fl, Maanu Centre, Chikwa Rd) fly to other regional destinations.

LAND

Zambia's main borders are open from 6am to 6pm, except for those at Victoria Falls (closes at 8pm) and Chirundu (closes at 7pm).

Botswana

The pontoon ferry (ZMW40 for foot passengers, ZMW30 an ordinary Zambian registered vehicle) across the Zambezi at Kazungula is 65km west of Livingstone and 11km south of the main road between Livingstone and Sesheke. There are one or two buses (ZMW20, 35 minutes) here daily from Livingstone, departing from Nakatindi Rd in the morning.

Note that US dollars and other currencies are not accepted at the Botswanan border post

A quicker and more comfortable (but more expensive) way to reach Botswana from Zambia is to cross from Livingstone to Victoria Falls (in Zimbabwe), from where shuttle buses head to Kasane.

Buses to Gaborone, via Kasane and Francistown, leave several days a week from Lusaka.

Malawi

Direct buses between Lusaka and Lilongwe are infrequent and slow, so it makes sense to do this trip in stages. From Chipata regular minibuses and shared taxis go to the Malawi border crossing, 30km to the east (ZMW20). Once you've passed through Zambian customs, it's a few minutes' walk to the Malawian entry post. From the border post you can catch a shared taxi to nearby Mchinji (MK300) before getting a minibus all the way to Lilongwe.

Mozambique

There is no public transport between Zambia and Mozambique and the only common border leads to a remote part of Mozambique. Most travellers, therefore, choose to visit Mozambique from Lilongwe in Malawi.

Namibia

You can cross the border into Namibia from Zambia with your own vehicle or on public transport. Alternatively, cross from Livingstone to Victoria Falls (in Zimbabwe) and travel onwards from there.

There are bus services to Sesheke, the Zambian border town, from Lusaka and Livingstone; it's 200km west of the latter.

From the Namibian side, it's a 5km walk to Katima Mulilo, from where minibuses depart for other parts of Namibia.

South Africa

There is no border between Zambia and South Africa, but several buses travel daily between Johannesburg and Lusaka via Harare and Masvingo in Zimbabwe. Make sure you have a Zimbabwean visa and a yellow fever certificate for entering South Africa.

Tanzania

Although travelling by bus to the Tanzanian border is quicker, (services run from Lusaka to Nakonde (ZMW140, 15 hours, 3pm) and on to Dar es Salaam. the train is a better alternative.

The Tazara railway company usually runs two international trains per week in each direction between Kapiri Mposhi (207km north of Lusaka) and Dar es Salaam. The 'express train' leaves Kapiri Mposhi at approximately 3pm on Tuesdays and Fridays. The journey time can be anywhere between two and five days. The fares on the express train are ZMW238/200 in 1st/2nd class (both are sleeping compartments). A discount of 50% is possible with a student card.

Zimbabwe

There are three easy crossings: at Chirundu, along the road between Lusaka and Harare; between Siavonga (Zambia) and Kariba (Zimbabwe), about 50km upstream from Chirundu; and easiest and most common of all, between Livingstone (Zambia) and Victoria Falls town (Zimbabwe). Plenty of buses travel every day between Lusaka and Harare, via Chirundu.

ℹ Getting Around

AIR

The main domestic airports are at Lusaka, Livingstone, Ndola, Kitwe, Mfuwe, Kasama and Kasaba Bay, though dozens of minor air strips, most notably those in the Lower Zambezi National Park (Proflight flies here regularly) and North Luangwa National Park, cater for chartered planes.

Proflight (www.proflight-zambia.com) is the only domestic airline offering regularly scheduled flights connecting Lusaka to Chipata, Livingstone (for Victoria Falls), Lower Zambezi (Jeki and Royal airstrips), Mfuwe (for South Luangwa National Park), Ndola (also flies direct from here to Kasama) and Solwezi.

There are plenty of charter-flight companies (Proflight also does charters) catering primarily for guests staying at upmarket lodges/camps in national parks.

The departure tax for domestic flights is ZMW58. As of recently, Proflight tickets include this tax in the price, but for other flights it must be paid at the airport in Zambian kwacha.

BUS & MINIBUS

Distances are long, buses are often slow and many roads are full of potholes, so travelling around Zambia by bus or minibus can exhaust the hardiest of travellers, even those who do like a good butt massage.

All main routes are served by ordinary public buses, which run on a fill-up-and-go basis or have fixed departures (these are called 'time buses'). 'Express buses' are faster – often terrifyingly so – and stop less often, but cost about 15% more. In addition, several private companies run comfortable European-style express buses along the major routes. Many routes are also served by minibuses, which only leave when full. In remote areas the only public transport is often a truck or pick-up.

CAR & MOTORCYCLE

Cars can be hired from international and Zambian-owned companies in Lusaka, Livingstone, Kitwe and Ndola, but renting is expensive. For example, **Europcar/Voyagers** (☎ 0212-620314; www.europcarzambia.com) charges from ZMW365 per day for the smallest vehicle, plus ZMW2 per kilometre, and this doesn't even include 16% VAT, petrol or insurance. Other companies, such as **Hemingways** (☎ 0213-320996; www.hemingwayszambia.com) and **4x4 Hire Africa** (☎ in South Africa 721-791 3904; www.4x4hire.co.za) rent out vehicles, unequipped or fully decked out with everything you would need for a trip to the bush (including roof-top tents!), with prices starting at about ZMW680 per day.

Most companies insist that drivers are at least 23 years old and have held a licence for at least five years. You can drive in Zambia using your driving licence from home as long as it's in English.

While most main stretches of sealed road are OK, beware of potholes. Most gravel roads are pretty good, though they also suffer from potholes. If you're travelling outside of the main routes between urban centres, you'll need a 4WD.

TOURS

Tours and safaris around Zambia invariably focus on the national parks. Since many of these parks are hard to visit without a 4WD vehicle, joining a tour might be your only option. Most Zambian tour operators are based in Lusaka and Livingstone.

TRAIN

The Tazara trains between Kapiri Mposhi and Dar es Salaam in Tanzania can also be used for travel to/from northern Zambia. While the Lusaka–Kitwe service does stop at Kapiri Mposhi, the Lusaka–Kitwe and Tazara trains are not timed to connect with each other, and the domestic and international train station are 2km apart.

Zambia's only other railway services are the 'ordinary trains' between Lusaka and Kitwe, via Kapiri Mposhi and Ndola, and the 'express trains' between Lusaka and Livingstone.

Domestic trains are unreliable and slow, so buses are always better. Conditions on domestic trains generally range from slightly dilapidated to ready-for-scrap. Most compartments have no lights or locks, so take a torch and something to secure the door at night.

Tickets for all classes on domestic trains (but not the Tazara service) can be bought up to 30 days in advance.

Zimbabwe

Includes ➡

Best Places to Eat

- Amanzi (p1003)
- Garwe (p1003)
- 26 on Park (p1013)

Best Places to Stay

- Camp Amalinda (p1014)
- Jacana Gardens Guest Lodge (p1001)
- National Parks Lodges Mana Pools (p1008)

Why Go?

After a decade of political ruin, violence and economic disaster, finally some good news is coming out of Zimbabwe – tourism is back. Visitors are returning in numbers not seen since the turmoil began to spot the Big Five strut their stuff around spectacular parks, discover World Heritage–listed archaeological sites and stand in awe of a natural wonder of the world: Victoria Falls.

A journey here will take you through an attractive patchwork of landscapes, from central highveld, balancing boulders and flaming *msasa* trees, to laid-back towns, lush Eastern Highland mountains and a network of lifeblood rivers up north. Along the way you'll receive a friendly welcome from locals, famous for their politeness and resilience in the face of hardship.

While there may be a long way to go, sure signs of recovery continue in Zimbabwe, giving hope to this embattled nation that a new dawn will soon rise.

When to Go

Harare

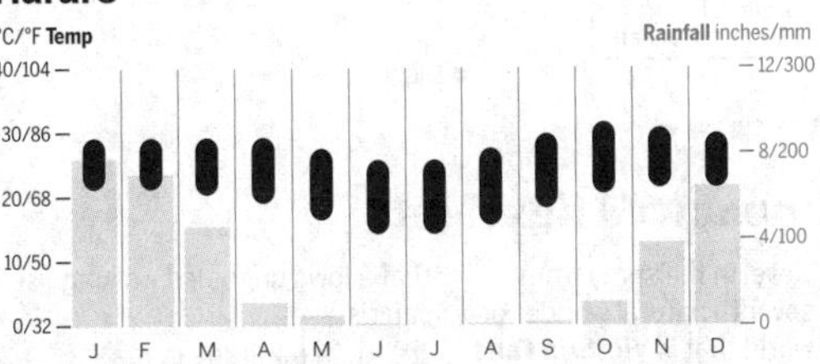

Apr–Oct Best time seasonally, with sunny days and spectacular Victoria Falls views.

Nov–Apr Sporadic rain and dramatic afternoon electrical storms.

Jul–Sep Prime wildlife-viewing, white-water rafting and canoeing the Zambezi.

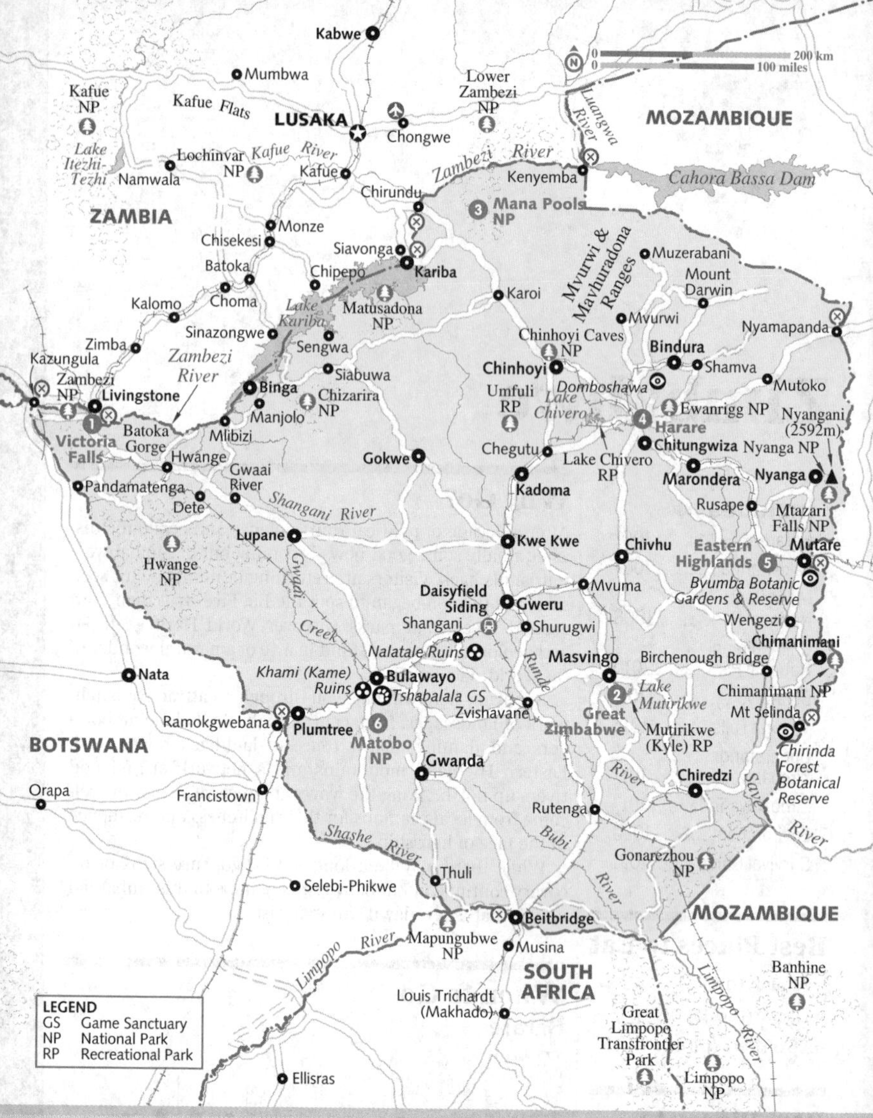

Zimbabwe Highlights

1 Revel in the spray from the seventh natural wonder of the world that is **Victoria Falls** (p1015).

2 Explore the atmospheric 11th-century stone ruins of **Great Zimbabwe** (p1010).

3 Visit **Mana Pools** (p1008), Africa's only park (with lions) that allows unguided walking safaris.

4 Shop for crafts in the capital city and don't miss HIFA – **Harare's International Festival of the Arts** (p1001).

5 Exchange arid highveld for cool, lush mountain air in the **Eastern Highlands** (p1008).

6 Find the spiritual heart of Zimbabwe, packed with balancing rocks and birdlife in **Matobo National Park** (p1014).

HARARE

☎04 / POP 1.8 MILLION

More attractive than most other South African capitals, Harare gets a bad rap and unjustly so. It's safe and laid back, and its wide avenues lined with dusty red earth, indigenous plants and blooming jacarandas give it a lovely African summertime feel. While it's tempting to rush off to your safari, hang around in Harare to sample its fine dining, museums, craft markets and hip bars.

Sights

National Gallery of Zimbabwe GALLERY

(Map p1004; ☎704666; cnr Julius Nyerere Way & Park Lane; admission US$1; ⊙9am-5pm Tue-Sun) Monthly exhibits here mix contemporary local and African art. You'll find paintings, photography, stone sculptures, masks and carvings.

National Heroes' Acre MONUMENT

(Map p1002; ☎277965; 107 Rotten Row; museum admission US$10; ⊙8am-4.30pm) The grandiose obelisk of Heroes' Acre, overlooking the town, is straight outta Pyongyang, yet lies just 7km from Harare. Designed with the assistance of North Korea, it serves as a war memorial to the forces who died during the Second Chimurenga.

Wild is Life WILDLIFE SANCTUARY

(☎0779 949821; www.wildislife.com; adult/teenager US$70/50; ⊙3.30-6.30pm) Sip on champagne while getting a hands-on experience with the injured, rescued or orphaned animals. Near the airport, book well in advance and children under 12 are not permitted.

National Archives of Zimbabwe MUSEUM

(Map p1002; Ruth Taylor Rd; admission US$1; ⊙8.30am-4pm Mon-Fri) Founded in 1935, this building is a repository for the history of Rhodesia and modern Zimbabwe: artefacts, photos, accounts of early explorers and settlers, and a display about the Second Chimurenga.

Festivals & Events

HIFA – Harare International Festival of Arts MUSIC

(☎300119; www.hifa.co.zw) *The* annual event, brings international acts alongside Zimbabwean artists. Performances include Afrobeat, funk, jazz, soul, opera, classical music, theatre and dance.The annual event, held over six days around late April or early May, brings international acts to produce a crammed timetable alongside Zimbabwean artists. Performances include Afrobeat,funk, jazz, soul, opera, classical music, theatre and dance. If you're in the region, don't miss it.

SET YOUR BUDGET

Budget

- Hotel room/dorm US$50/10
- Dinner US$10
- Coffee US$1
- Local bus ride US$1

Midrange

- Hotel room US$50–150
- Two-course dinner US$15
- Beer in bar US$3
- Short taxi ride US$5

Top End

- Hotel room US$150–300
- Two-course dinner US$25–40
- Glass of wine US$5
- Taxi day-hire US$50–100

Sleeping

★It's a Small World Backpackers Lodge BACKPACKERS $

(Map p1002; ☎335176; www.smallworldlodge.com; 25 Ridge Rd, Avondale; campsites US$5, dm from US$11, s/d without bathroom from $15/30, d from $40;) Single-handedly flying the flag for backpackers in Harare, this old faithful knows what backpackers want – clean affordable rooms, communal kitchen, wi-fi, a sociable low-key bar and a safe neighbourhood location

★Jacana Gardens Guest Lodge B&B $$

(Map p1002; ☎0779 715297; www.jacana-gardens.com; 14 Jacana Dr, Borrowdale; s/d incl breakfast US$95/130;) This guesthouse is as boutique as they come yet the best value in town. Renowned architect, Mick Pearce, designed the award-winning house with natural light pouring into open spaces. Other clinchers are free wi-fi, an alluring pool and trees full of birdlife.

Amanzi Lodges LODGE $$$

(Map p1002; ☎499257, 480880; www.amanzi.co.zw; 1 Masasa Lane, Kambanji; s/d US$185/280;) Set over a tropical garden, the 12 luxury lodges here are each individually

Harare

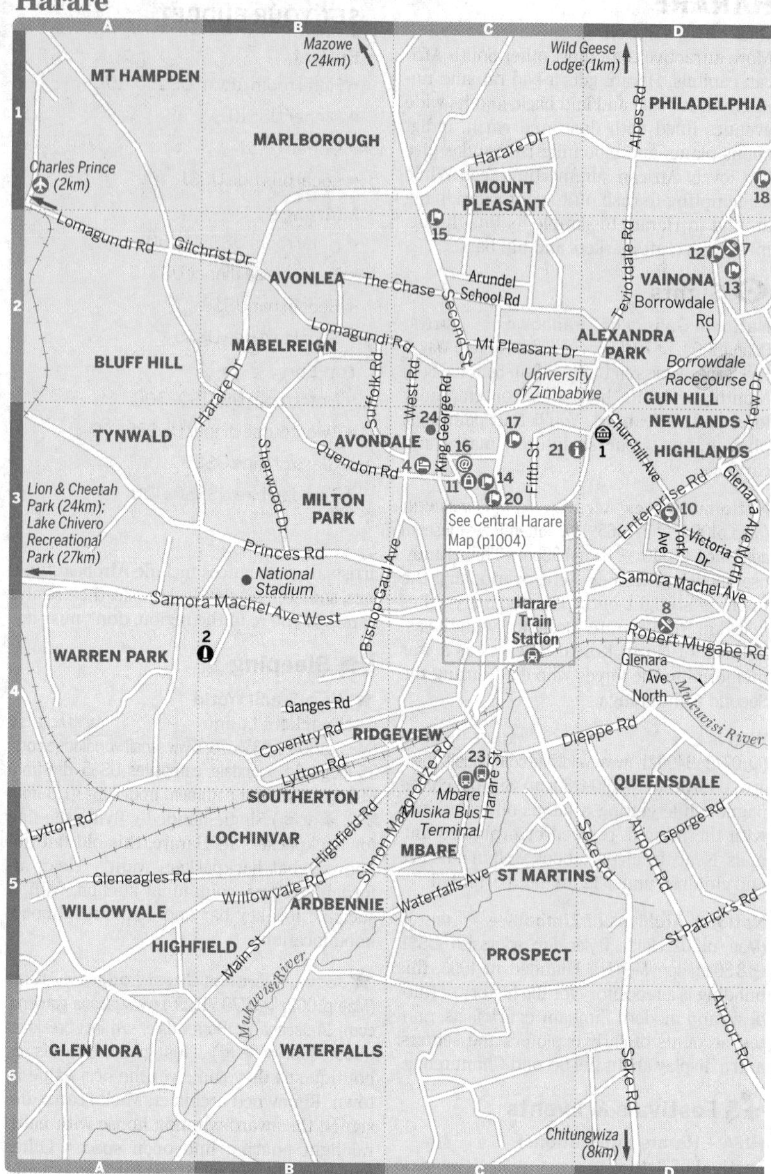

styled after different African countries, with results ranging from stunning to gaudy. Also recommended:

Bronte (Map p1004; ☎796631; www.brontehotel.com; 132 Baines Ave; s/d from US$125/155; ❄📶🏊) Its peaceful gardens and colonial-style rooms are popular with NGOs.

Meikles (Map p1004; ☎795655; www.meikles.com; cnr Jason Moyo Ave & Third St; r incl breakfast US$275; ❄📶🏊) Bit dated but still the fanciest hotel in town.

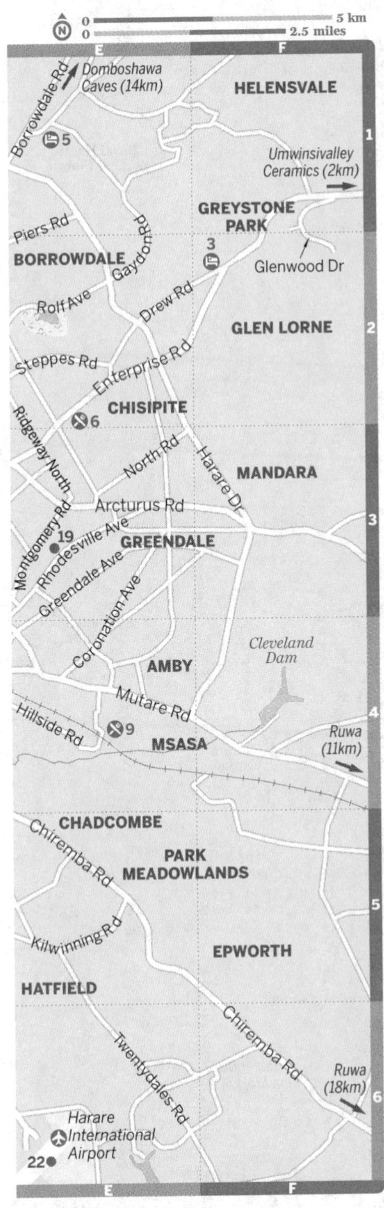

Harare

Sights
1 National Archives of Zimbabwe......... D3
2 National Heroes' Acre......... B4

Sleeping
3 Amanzi Lodges......... F2
4 It's a Small World Backpackers Lodge......... C3
5 Jacana Gardens Guest Lodge......... E1

Eating
6 Amanzi......... E2
7 Butchers Kitchen......... D2
Chang Thai......... (see 9)
8 Garwe......... D4
9 Shop Café......... E4

Drinking & Nightlife
10 Red Bar......... D3

Shopping
11 Avondale Flea Market......... C3

Information
12 Australian Embassy......... D2
13 Australian High Commission......... D2
14 Botswanan Embassy......... C3
15 British Embassy......... C2
16 Internet Cafe......... C3
17 Malawian High Commission......... C3
18 Namibian Embassy......... D1
19 Nyati Travel......... E3
20 South African Embassy......... C3
21 Zimbabwe Parks & Wildlife Central Reservations Office......... C3

Transport
22 Europcar......... E6
23 Pioneer Bus......... C4
24 South African Airways......... C3

Eating

★Garwe AFRICAN **$$**

(Map p1002; 18637 Donald McDonald Rd, Eastlea; mains US$8-20; noon-9pm Mon-Sat, to 4pm Sun;) Highly recommended by locals, this restaurant has traditional Zimbabwean cuisine served around a large roaring fire under a thatched roof.

★Amanzi FUSION **$$$**

(Map p1002; 497768; www.amanzi.co.zw; 158 Enterprise Rd, Highlands; mains US$15-25; noon-2.30pm & 6.30-9.30pm) Don some nice threads as Amanzi is a class act and still *the* special night out. It serves delicious international food with a great vibe. The outdoor patio is ridiculously atmospheric with a garden waterfall and crackling fire brazier. Bookings essential.

Central Harare

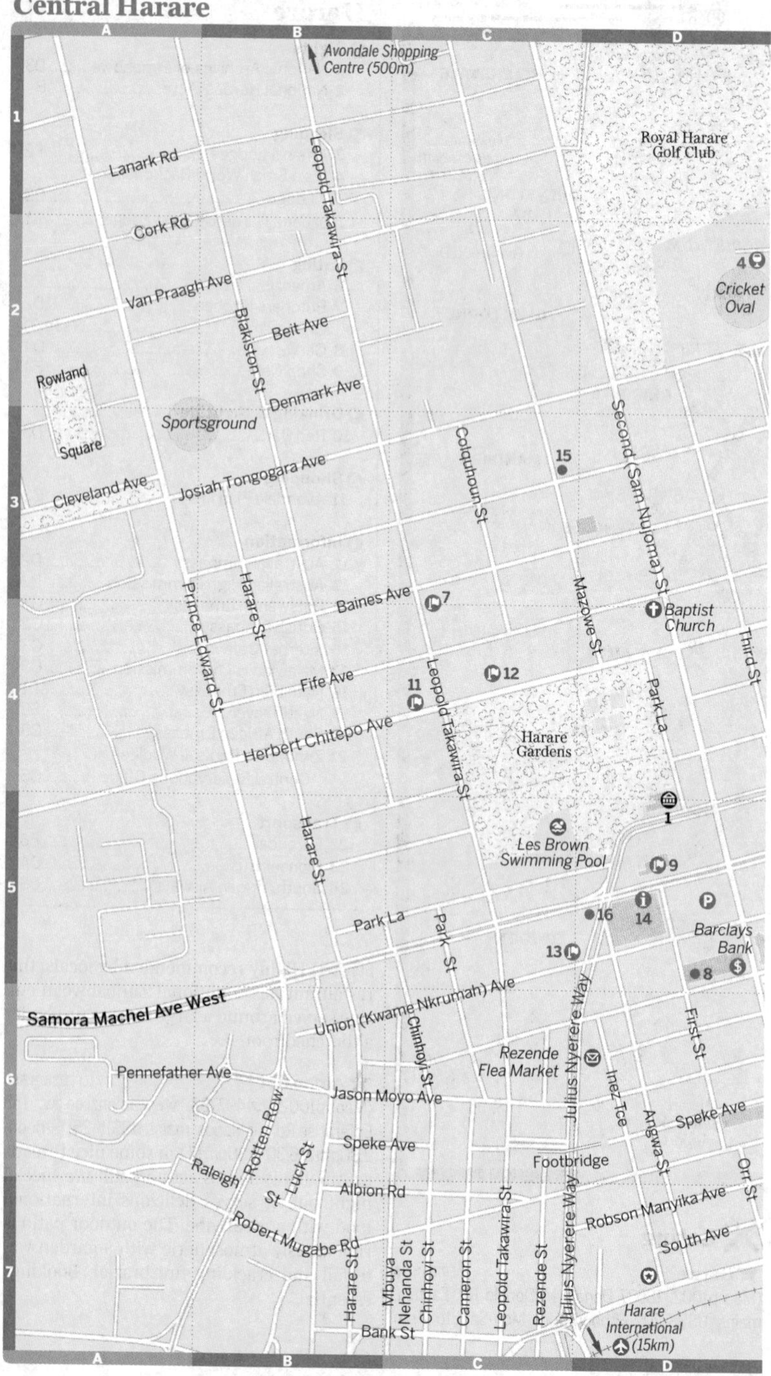
Avondale Shopping Centre (500m)
Royal Harare Golf Club
Lanark Rd
Cork Rd
Van Praagh Ave
Leopold Takawira St
Blakiston St
Beit Ave
Denmark Ave
Rowland Square
Sportsground
Cricket Oval
Cleveland Ave
Josiah Tongogara Ave
Colquhoun St
Second (Sam Nujoma) St
Baines Ave
Prince Edward St
Harare St
Mazowe St
Baptist Church
Third St
Fife Ave
Park La
Herbert Chitepo Ave
Harare Gardens
Les Brown Swimming Pool
Park St
Barclays Bank
Samora Machel Ave West
Union (Kwame Nkrumah) Ave
Julius Nyerere Way
First St
Pennefather Ave
Rezende Flea Market
Inez Tce
Jason Moyo Ave
Chinhoyi St
Rotten Row
Speke Ave
Angwa St
Footbridge
Raleigh St
Luck St
Albion Rd
Orr St
Robson Manyika Ave
Robert Mugabe Rd
South Ave
Mbuya Nehanda St
Cameron St
Rezende St
Bank St
Harare International (15km)

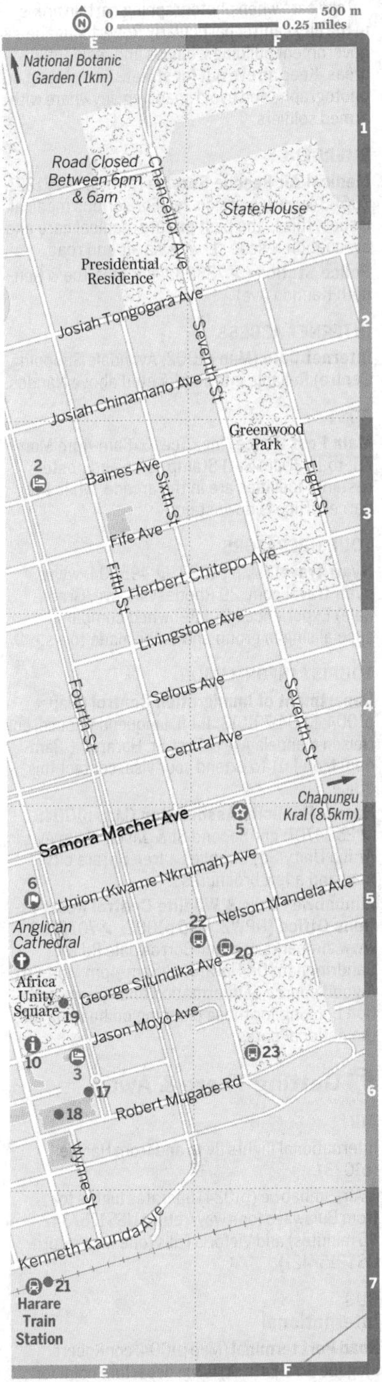

Central Harare

Sights
1 National Gallery of Zimbabwe D5

Sleeping
2 Bronte..E3
3 Meikles E6

Drinking & Nightlife
4 Maiden Public House D2

Entertainment
5 Book Café..F5

Information
6 Belgian Embassy.............................. E5
7 Canadian Embassy C3
8 Department of Immigration Control.............................. D5
9 French Embassy D5
10 Harare Publicity Association E6
11 Mozambican Embassy...................... C4
12 US Embassy C4
13 Zambian Embassy C5
14 Zimbabwe Tourism Authority............ D5

Transport
15 Air Botswana C3
16 Air Malawi....................................... D5
Air Namibia..............................(see 15)
17 Air Zimbabwe E6
18 Air Zimbabwe E6
19 Avis E6
20 Bravo Coaches F5
Greyhound.............................. (see 23)
21 Harare Train Station E7
Munorurama .... (see 23)
22 Pathfinder..F5
23 Road Port Terminal F6
Tenda Luxury .... (see 23)
Zupco..................................... (see 23)

Butchers Kitchen STEAKHOUSE $$$
(Map p1002; Sam Levy's Village; steak from US$20; 8am-5pm Mon, Tue, Thu, Sat & Sun, to 9pm Wed & Fri) Enticing aromas from charcoal-grilled meats thicken the air at this winning combo of buzzing restaurant, butcher and deli.

Also recommended:

Shop Cafe (Map p1002; 1 Harrow Rd, Doon Estate, Msasa; buffet US$10; 9am-3pm Tue-Sat;) A vegetarian cafe with buffets Tuesdays to Fridays.

Chang Thai (Map p1002; 1 Harrow Rd, Doon Estate; mains US$7-15) Some of the most authentic curries you'll find outside of Bangkok.

Drinking & Nightlife

Never walk to or from any of these (or any other) spots after dark; take a taxi.

Red Bar BAR
(Map p1002; www.redbar.co.zw; Enterprise Rd; closed Mon & Tue) The best place for Zimbabwe's hip, mixed-race crowd. DJs play pumping tunes and the decor is industrial minimalist. Watch for pickpockets.

Maiden Public House PUB
(Map p1004; 700037; Harare Sports Club; 9am-11pm) Looking out to Harare's international cricket ground, this cheerful pub is the ultimate spot to watch a match live or on the TV.

★**Book Café** LIVE MUSIC
(Map p1004; 139 Samora Machel Ave; 10am-late Mon-Sat) This no-frills place on the corner of Samora Machel and Sixth St is the place for live music, with a changing roster of bands and genres every night except Sunday.

Shopping

★**Patrick Mavros** JEWELLERY
(0772 414414, 860131; www.patrickmavros.com; 8am-5pm Mon-Fri, to 1pm Sat) His clients may include Bruce Springsteen and Kate Middleton, but Patrick Mavros' stunning silver jewellery is surprisingly affordable. To get here, follow the signpost to the studio and gallery at the end of Haslemere Lane, 1km off the Umwinsidale Rd.

Kikis ARTS & CRAFTS, HOMEWARES
(0774 125363; esther@iwayafrica.com) Displayed in a homely loungeroom, Kikis has stunning furniture, handpainted porcelain and Shona wooden stools. A few doors down from Patrick Mavros.

Avondale Flea Market MARKET
(Map p1002; Avondale Shopping Centre, King George Rd) This daily flea market predominantly sells clothing but it's also worth a browse for local music, crafts and second-hand books.

Information

DANGERS & ANNOYANCES

Harare is generally a safe city, but you'll need to be careful as robberies occasionally occur. Take a cab in the evening and watch bag snatchers and pickpocketing in markets, parks and bus stations. When driving, always keep your windows up and your bags in the boot or, if not possible, safely wedged under your feet.

Take care when photographing certain areas in the city centre, particularly Robert Mugabe's government buildings, offices and residential areas. Keep an eye out for street signs stating no photography and avoid snapping anywhere with armed soldiers.

EMERGENCY

Medical Air Rescue Service (MARS; 771221, 706034; www.mars.co.zw) For serious medical issues, this is the best private medical care and evacuation rescue service via air and road.

Police Station (733033; cnr Inez Tce & Kenneth Kaunda Ave)

INTERNET ACCESS

Internet Cafe (Map p1002; Avondale Shopping Centre) Reliable internet located above Nandos.

POST

Main Post Office (Inez Tce; 8am-4pm Mon-Fri, to 11.30am Sat) Stamp sales and poste-restante facilities are in the arcade, while the parcel office is downstairs.

TOUR OPERATORS

Nyati Travel (Map p1002; 495804; www.nyati-travel.com; 29 Rhodesville Ave, Greendale) Experienced Dutch-owned company specialising in group and tailor-made tours.

TOURIST INFORMATION

Department of Immigration Control (Map p1004; 04-791913; 1st fl, Linquenda House, cnr Nelson Mandela Ave & First St, Harare; 8am-4pm Mon-Fri) To extend your visa, contact this office.

Harare Publicity Association (Map p1004; 2504701; cnr Second St & Jason Moyo Ave, Africa Unity Sq) Supplies a free Harare city map and a few brochures.

Zimbabwe Parks & Wildlife Central Reservations Office (NPWZ; Map p1002; 7076259; www.zimparks.org; cnr Borrowdale Rd & Sandringham Dr, Harare; 8am-4pm Mon-Fri) A good source of information and accommodation booking for those planning on heading into the national parks.

Getting There & Away

AIR

International flights fly to and from Harare (p1023).

Air Zimbabwe (p1024) operates flights to/from Bulawayo (one way/return US$176/342, 45 minutes) and Victoria Falls (one way/return US$215/421).

BUS

International

Road Port terminal (Map p1004; cnr Robert Mugabe Rd & Fifth St) is the departure point for companies servicing international destinations p1023.

Domestic

The best way of getting to/from Harare is via its growing fleet of luxury buses. Otherwise you'll need to brave the chaotic **Mbare Musika bus terminal** (Ardbennie Rd) for local 'chicken' buses. There are no schedules, and buses depart when full. Careful of pickpockets here. The other option popular with intrepid travellers are combis (minibuses), which are inexpensive but have a poor safety record.

TRAIN

The **train station** (Map p1004; ☎78604416; cnr Kenneth Kaunda Ave & Second St) has departures to Bulawayo (sleeper US$12, nine hours) on Tuesday, Friday and Sunday at 8pm, and Mutare (US$7, 8½ hours) at 9.30pm on Wednesday, Friday and Sunday. Call ahead to confirm departure dates.

Getting Around

TO/FROM THE AIRPORT

All international and domestic airlines use Harare International Airport, 15km southeast of the city centre.

CAR

Car-rental companies in Harare include **Avis** (Map p1004; ☎796409; www.avis.co.zw; Third St) and **Europcar** (Map p1002; ☎575592; www.europcar.co.zw; Harare International Airport), yet mileage makes it pricey once outside Harare. Both have branches at the airport.

TAXI

Airport taxis cost US$25 to US$30 to town. Official services include **Rixi Taxi** (☎753080), **AA Taxi** (☎704222) and **AI Taxi** (☎703334). Count on around US$50 for a day hire touring Harare.

NORTHERN ZIMBABWE

Often overlooked by independent travellers without their own transport, the major attractions in this part of the country are Lake Kariba and Mana Pools National Park.

Lake Kariba

Lake Kariba is the nation's Riviera where it's all about houseboats, beer, fishing and amazing sunsets. It's one of the world's largest man-made lakes, covering an area of over 5000 sq km and holding 180 billion tonnes of water. Adjoining the Matusadona National Park means it's home to plenty of wildlife, including the Big Five.

It's a five-hour bus journey from Harare and also provides a good alternative route into Zambia, as well as Victoria Falls if you have a double-entry visa.

Try to avoid the summer months (October to December), when the humidity is stifling. Also take precautions for mosquitoes, as malaria is present. There's no swimming in the lake due to big crocs and reported bilharzia.

BUSES FROM HARARE

DESTINATION	COMPANY	FARE (US$)	SCHEDULE	TIME (HR)
Bulawayo	Pathfinder	30-40	departs 7.30am	5½
Bulawayo	Bravo	25-35	departs 2pm	5½
Bulawayo	Citylink	30-35	departs 7.30am & 2pm	5½
Bulawayo	local buses from Mbare terminal	15	times vary	5½
Hwange	Pathfinder	60	7.30am	9½
Kariba	local buses	12	times vary	5-6
Masvingo (for Great Zimbabwe)	local buses from Mbare	8-12	from 6.30am to early afternoon	3½
Mutare (for Eastern Highlands)	local buses from Mbare	8	times vary	4
Mutare (for Eastern Highlands)	combis outside Road Port Terminal	5-8	regularly	4
Victoria Falls	Pathfinder	60-80	departs 7.30am	12
Victoria Falls	Citylink	55	7.30am	12

A good source of information covering the region is **Wild Zambezi** (www.wildzambezi.com), which provides a comprehensive listing of houseboats, accommodation and activities in the area.

Kariba Town

061 / POP 27,500

The small sprawling lakeside settlement of Kariba is spread out along the steep lakeshore. There are lovely lake views and elephants often come through town.

Activities

There's no better way to experience the peacefulness and beauty of Lake Kariba than by renting a houseboat, which is best arranged in Kariba town. It allows you to have the whole lake to yourself, to get close to the wildlife of the adjoining Matusadona National Park and to enjoy stellar sunsets with cold drinks.

The best option for budget travellers is to hire through Warthogs Bush Camp a houseboat, which sleeps six and costs US$150 per night. Otherwise get in touch with **Rhino Rendezvous** (04-490124, 0772-220831; www.houseboatsonkariba.com) and **Marineland Harbour** (2845; www.marineland.co.zw).

Sleeping

★**Warthogs Bush Camp** LODGE $
(0775-068406; www.warthogs.co.zw; Kariba; campsite per person US$5, tented camps s/d US$10/15, lodges d US$40, 6-person chalet US$70;) On the lake, this bush camp is the only place catering to budget travellers. It provides basic but atmospheric accommodation, and has a 24-hour bar, great staff and houseboats for hire. You'll see plenty of animal visitors.

Getting There & Away

Taxis are the best way to get to Zambia (via Kariba border), 10km from Kariba. Expect to pay US$5 to US$7 for the 10 minute trip. Local buses run to Harare daily (US$12, five hours).

Kariba Ferries (p1024) offers a ferry service between Kariba and Mlibizi (adult/child including meals US$160/80, sedan US$120, 4WD US$180), departing 9am and arriving 7am the next day.

Mana Pools National Park

This magnificent 2200-sq-km **national park** (63513, 63512; admission adult/child US$30/15; 6am-6pm) is a Unesco World Heritage Site, and its magic stems from its remoteness and pervading sense of the wild and natural. This is one park in Zimbabwe where you're guaranteed to see plenty of hippos, crocs, zebras and elephants, and *almost* guaranteed to see lions, and possibly painted dogs.

What sets Mana Pools apart from just about any other park in the world is that it's all unfenced, so there can be elephants strolling by while you have your breakfast. You're also allowed to walk around without a guide, but be aware this is about personal responsibility: wild animals are incredibly dangerous – and fast. Hence walking with a guide is highly advised.

Sleeping

★**National Parks Lodges** CAMPGROUND $$
(706077; national-parks@gta.gov.zw; campsite per person US$20, lodges from US$100) Well-equipped lodges and campsites along the Zambezi River with prime animal-viewing. Lodges book out during July to October, so you'll need to make reservations well in advance through the Harare office.

Chikwenya Safari Lodge LODGE $$$
(0772 470065; www.chikwenyasafaris.com; s/d with full board & activities US$475/750; Apr-Dec;) Tented rooms are nestled into the bush and huge gauze windows look out across the mouth of the Sapi River to acacia floodplains, the Zambezi River and Chikwenya Island, with the Zambian escarpment as the awesome backdrop.

Getting There & Away

The park is only accessible via 4WD, so it's limited to self-drive or those on all-inclusive packages. Wet season (November to April) is best avoided, as dirt roads turn to sludge and no assisting car service is available. If self-driving, you need to register at the gate before 3pm. Charter flights are the other option to get here.

EASTERN HIGHLANDS

This narrow strip of mountain country that makes up Manicaland isn't the Africa that normally crops up in armchair travellers' fantasies. It's a land of mountains, national parks, pine forests, botanical gardens, rivers, dams and secluded getaways.

Mutare

020 / POP 188,750

Zimbabwe's third-largest city, Mutare has a relaxed atmosphere and is a handy gateway to the Eastern Highlands or Mozambique.

Sleeping & Eating

Ann Bruce Backpackers BACKPACKERS $
(0772 249089; annbruce@zol.co.zw; cnr Fourth St & Sixth Ave; dm/s/d US$15/15/30;) Homely feel with garden gazebo and a mix of dorms and private rooms. Ann is a great source of info for the Eastern Highlands.

Green Coucal CAFE $$
(111 Second St; 8am-5pm Mon-Sat;) Run by an Irishman and his wife with excellent coffee, hearty fare and an inviting garden and open-air deck.

Getting There & Away

Regular 'local' and express buses head to Harare (US$6 to US$8, four hours). Pathfinder was due to start operating buses here too.

Regular combis (US$1) head to the Mozambique border (6am to 8pm), 8km from Mutare. A taxi will cost US$10.

Bvumba Mountains

020

Sights & Activities

Just 28km southeast of Mutare, the Bvumba (pronounced Vumba) Mountains are characterised by cool, forested highlands, deep misty valleys and English gardens.

Twitchers can do a two-hour birdlife walk with the lodge **Seldomseen Farm** (68482, 0714-516743; per person per hour US$5), with around 250 birds spotted in the area.

Sleeping & Eating

★It's a Small World Lodge Vumba GUESTHOUSE $
(0912-612319; www.smallworldlodge.com; Lot 1 Cloudlands Arusha Estate; d from US$40, cottages weekday/weekend US$50/90) An attractive guesthouse set in a colonial-style holiday home with an English garden and outlooks to the valley. Rooms are large and comfy and bikes are available for hire.

> **MIDDLE ZAMBEZI CANOE SAFARIS**
>
> Adventurers describe canoe trips down this awesome wilderness route as one of the best things they've done in Africa. The trip is normally done in stages: Kariba to Chirundu (three days), Chirundu to Mana Pools National Park (three to four days) and Mana Pools to Kanyemba (four to five days). Any combination is possible, but if you can do only one, the Chirundu to Mana Pools offers the best scenery and diversity of wildlife. **Natureways Safaris** (0772 335038; www.natureways.com; Stand 473, Andora Harbour, Kariba) is a reliable operator that runs trips here.

Tony's Coffee House DESSERTS $$
(Bvumba Rd; coffee from US$5, slice of cake US$9-12; 10am-5pm Wed-Sun) Ten bucks is expensive for a slice of cake but Tony's can justify it. The white-chocolate cheese cake with edible flowers is divine.

Getting There & Away

Combis and taxis from Mutare (US$2 to US$3) depart when full, but getting back is trickier. Your lodge should be able to assist in arranging transport, otherwise hitching is an option.

Nyanga National Park

029

The 47,000-hectare **Nyanga National Park** (0773 500398, 8274; www.nyangapark.com; admission US$10; 6am-6pm) is a geographically and scenically distinct enclave in the Eastern Highlands. Nyanga is famous not for its wildlife but for its verdant, mountainous scenery, crystal-clear streams and waterfalls.

The **main gate** is a few kilometres from Nyanga town, close to the Rhodes Hotel. The **Nyanga Tourist Association** (0712-218440) is housed in Pine Tree Inn, Juliasdale, and has good local info and maps.

Sights & Activities

World's View (admission US$4) is perched atop the Troutbeck Massif with broad views of northern Zimbabwe. It's 11km up a winding, steep road from Troutbeck – follow the signposts.

The flat-topped and myth-shrouded **Nyangani** (2592m) is Zimbabwe's highest mountain. From the car park 14km east of Nyanga Dam, the climb to the summit takes two to three hours.

It's also famous for **Mutarazi Falls**, Zim's highest waterfall. Falling from a height of 479m, it outrumps Vic Falls by 300m, and is number two in Africa. It's at its peak from February to May.

Sleeping

National Park Lodge CAMPGROUND $
(☎8274, 0773 500398; campsite per person US$8, d from US$80) Set over three different locations within Nyanga. Choose from self-catering lodges and campsites at Rhodes Dam near the main gate, Udu Dam on the western side of the park, or Mare Dam, 10km from the main gate.

Getting There & Away

Regular combis run the 106km leg between Nyanga and Mutare for US$4.

Chimanimani

☎2700

Chimanimani village, 150km south of Mutare, is enclosed by green hills on three sides, and opens on the fourth side to the dramatic wall of the Chimanimani Mountains.

There's a **Chimanimani Tourist Association** (touristassociationchimanimani@gmail.com) in town; otherwise the website for the Frog & Fern lodge has good info.

Sleeping & Eating

★**Frog & Fern** LODGE $
(☎0774-659789; www.thefrogandfern.com; campsite US$15, r US$40-50; @) *Rondavels* (round, traditional huts)or stone cabins, all with cooking facilities, fireplaces and garden views. The owners are an excellent source of info.

Msasa Café CAFE $
(mains US$10; ⊙8am-5pm Mon-Sat) Best spot in the village for eating out. Serves a wide variety of meals; try the *sadza* (maize meal porridge), chicken and gravy.

Chimanimani National Park

With its pristine wilderness, Chimanimani National Park is a hiker's paradise and shares a border with Mozambique.

For hiking in **Chimanimani National Park** (admission US$10; ⊙6am-6pm), 19km from Chimanimani village, you must sign in and pay park fees at Mutekeswane Base Camp. The road ends here and the park is then only accessible on foot. Mountain biking is also popular.

Sleeping & Eating

Camping is free in the park, but you're better off either camping at **Mutekeswane Base Camp** (campsite per person US$8) or staying in the **mountain hut** (per person US$8), which at an elevation of 1630m is a long and steep half-day walk from the base camp. It's a bit grubby but has running water and cooking facilities.

THE MIDLANDS & SOUTHEASTERN ZIMBABWE

Geographically, the Midlands are known as the highveld, while the warmer, lower-lying southeast is the lowveld.

Great Zimbabwe

The greatest medieval city in sub-Saharan Africa, the World Heritage Listed **Great Zimbabwe** (adult/child US$15/8, guide $US3; ⊙6am-6pm) is one of the nation's most treasured sights. So much so, that it was named after it. This mysterious medieval city provides evidence that ancient Africa reached a level of civilisation not suspected by earlier scholars. As a religious and political capital, this city of 10,000 to 20,000 dominated a realm that stretched across eastern Zimbabwe and into modern-day Botswana, Mozambique and South Africa. The name is believed to come from one of two possible Shona origins: *dzimba dza mabwe* (great stone houses) or *dzimba woye* (esteemed houses).

The site is easily explored by yourself, but for more info, maps and the best routes, duck into the information centre at the site's checkpoint to pick up one of the booklets. For more in-depth detail you can arrange a two-hour guided tour (about US$12 per person) at the checkpoint.

The best time to explore is at dawn and dusk. Allow at least three hours.

Sights

The site is divided into several major ruins with three main areas: the Hill Complex, the Valley and the Great Enclosure.

Most likely the first of the Great Zimbabwe structures to be completed, the **Hill Complex** is a maze of enclosures with spectacular views over the ruins. These ruins were a series of royal and ritual enclosures and at the top is the most salient feature, the Western Enclosure. It can be reached by two paths: the Ancient Path and the Modern Path, both signposted near the start.

The **Great Enclosure**, thought to have served as a royal compound, is the structure most identified with Great Zimbabwe. Nearly 100m wide and 255m in circumference, it's the largest ancient structure in sub-Saharan Africa. The mortarless walls rise 11m and, in places, are 5m thick. The greatest source of speculation is the 10m-high **Conical Tower**, a solid and ceremonial structure that perhaps had phallic significance for fertility.

Leading north from the Conical Tower is the narrow 70m-long **Parallel Passage**. The outside wall of the Parallel Passage, perhaps the most architecturally advanced structure in Great Zimbabwe, is 6m thick at the base and 4m thick at the top, with each course of stone tapering to add stability to the 11m-high wall. This stretch is capped by three rings of decorative chevron patterns.

The **Valley** is a series of 13th-century walls and *daga* (traditional round house) platforms. The area is a significant architectural area that yielded metal tools as well as some of the soapstone bird carvings that are the national symbol of Zimbabwe.

Sleeping & Eating

Great Zimbabwe Campground & Lodges CAMPGROUND $
(☎0773 456622; campsite/dm/rondavel per person US$5/5/15, r/ste US$30/50) Inside the main gate, the dorms, lodges, campsite and *rondavels* are spread out over a stretch of around 500m. *Rondavels* are spacious with shared bathroom blocks but, like the campsite, can feel a bit isolated. Suite lodges provide a more comfortable option.

Great Zimbabwe Hotel HOTEL $$$
(☎039 262274; r from US$140) Overpriced for the mediocre rooms but a convenient location close to the ruins.

GET TO KNOW THE RUINS

Head to the **Great Zimbabwe Museum** (⏲9am-5pm) FREE before you start exploring the site to prep yourself and gain some insight through the informative displays here. It's located a short walk from the entry, across from the kiosk.

Getting There & Away

Combis run frequently between Masvingo and Great Zimbabwe (US$2, 30 minutes) from outside the Technical College and drop off at the Great Zimbabwe Hotel entrance. Walk through the grounds to reach the Great Zimbabwe main gate, about 800m.

WESTERN ZIMBABWE

With three of the country's major attractions – Victoria Falls and Hwange and Matobo National Parks – western Zimbabwe is an excellent place to spend your time in Zimbabwe.

Bulawayo

09 / POP 1 MILLION

Wide tree-lined avenues, parks and charming colonial architecture make Bulawayo, Zimbabwe's second city, an attractive one. It's also a popular base for trips to the nearby Khami Ruins and Matobo National Park.

Sights & Activities

National Art Gallery GALLERY
(☎70721; www.nationalgallerybyo.com; cnr Main St & Leopold Takawira Ave; admission US$5; ⏲9am-5pm Tue-Sat) Set in a beautiful 100-year-old classical Edwardian building, the National Art Gallery has temporary and permanent exhibitions of contemporary Zimbabwean sculpture and paintings, as well as a shop, studio and cafe.

Natural History Museum MUSEUM
(Centenary Park; adult/child US$10/5; ⏲8am-5pm) Explore the country's natural, anthropological and geological history, set over three floors at Zimbabwe's largest and best museum.

Sleeping

Burke's Paradise BACKPACKERS $
(☎246481; www.burkes-paradise.com; 11 Inverleith Dr, Burnside; campsite per person/dm/d

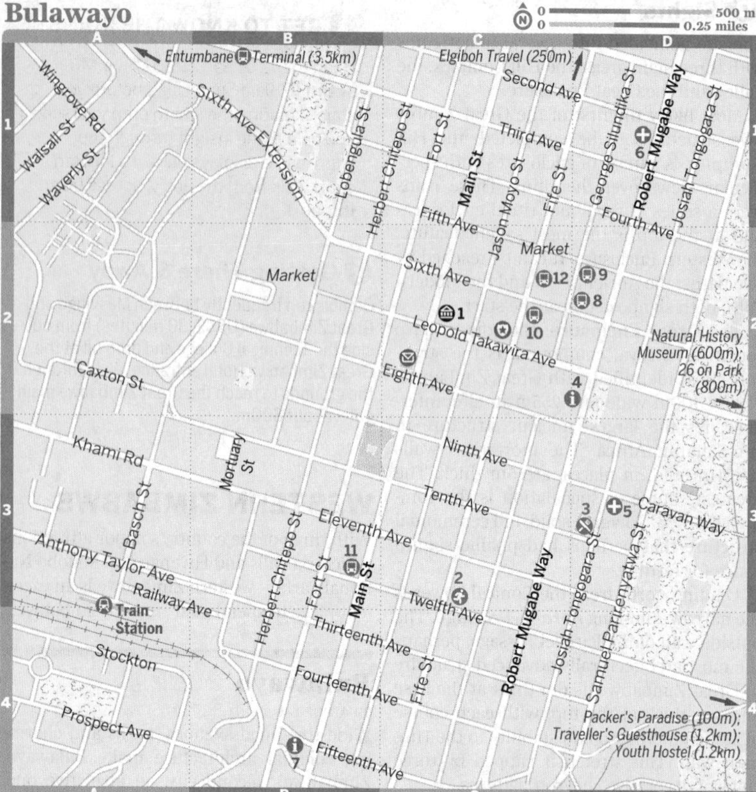

Bulawayo

Sights

1 National Art Gallery C2

Activities, Courses & Tours

2 Mike's Bike Shop C3

Eating

3 Dickies D3

Information

4 Bulawayo & District Publicity Association D2
5 Galen House Casualty D3
6 Medical Air Rescue Service D1
7 National Parks & Wildlife Zimbabwe B4

Transport

8 Bravo Tours D2
9 Eagle Liner D2
10 Greyhound C2
11 Intercape B3
12 Pathfinder C2

US$5/10/15) Set on 15 acres of bushland in the outskirts of town, Burke's caters primarily to the overland crowd, but is a good choice for independent travellers too.

★ **Traveller's Guest House** GUESTHOUSE $$$
(☎246059; www.travellerszim.net; 2 Banff Rd, Hillside; s/d US$47/65;) Charm oozes from this guesthouse where recently renovated rooms come with blondewood floors, stainless-steel bathroom fittings and African art.

Also recommended:

Packer's Paradise (☎251110; 1 Oak Ave; campsites per person US$10, dm US$15, s/d without bathroom US$40/50; @) Pricey dorms but decent private rooms and a homely kitchen.

Eating

Dickies AFRICAN $
(Tenth Ave; mains from US$5) Try a traditional Zimbabwean meal at this bright and cheery eatery.

★**26 on Park** INTERNATIONAL $$
(www.26onpark.com; 26 Park Rd; mains US$11-17; ⏰breakfast, lunch & dinner; 📶) Housed in a colonial building with sprawling lawns. Well-trained chefs serve up great dishes, and the cocktail bar is a lively spot for a drink.

Information

DANGERS & ANNOYANCES

As with most African cities, avoid walking at night and call a cab.

EMERGENCY

Main Police Station (☎72516; cnr Leopold Takawira Ave & Fife St)

Medical Air Rescue Service (MARS; ☎60351; 42 Robert Mugabe Way) For ambulance services

MEDICAL SERVICES

Galen House Casualty (☎881051; galen@gatorzw.co.uk; cnr Josiah Tongogara St & Ninth Ave) Privately run clinic; better than the central hospital.

POST

Main Post Office (☎62535; Main St)

TOUR OPERATORS & TRAVEL AGENCIES

African Wanderer (☎72736; www.african-wanderer.com) Offers fully qualified and passionate guides.

Elgiboh Travel (☎886497; www.elgibohtravel.com; 71 Fife St) Runs tours to Matobo (half day/full day US$75/100 excluding entry fees) and Khami Ruins.

TOURIST INFORMATION

Bulawayo & District Publicity Association (☎60867; www.bulawayopublicity.com; btwn Eighth & Leopold Takawira Aves; ⏰8.30am-4.45pm Mon-Fri, to noon Sat) In the City Hall car park, this is an excellent source of information on accommodation, transport, tours and activities in Bulawayo and around.

National Parks & Wildlife Zimbabwe (☎63646-7; 15th Ave, btwn Fort & Main Sts; ⏰8am-4pm Mon-Fri) Takes accommodation bookings for Matobo National Park.

Getting There & Away

BUS

Numerous buses operate between Bulawayo and South Africa (p1023).

To Harare

Luxury buses do trips to Harare in six hours:

Bravo Tours (☎0772-873438; www.bravotours.co.zw) Departs 7.30am; 1st/2nd class US$35/25.

Pathfinder (☎2936907-8; www.pathfinderlx.com) Daily departure at 7.30am and 2pm; US$30.

To Victoria Falls

Pathfinder (1.30pm, US$30) and Bravo Tours (10am, US$15) run daily luxury buses to Vic Falls in six hours. Pathfinder stops en route at Hwange Safari Lodge, around 5km from the Hwange main camp entrance, departing at around 11am.

TRAIN

To Harare

The train departs for Harare three times a week (sleeper US$12, nine hours).

To Victoria Falls

A nightly train from Bulawayo to Victoria Falls leaves at 7.30pm (1st class, $15) and arrives around 9.30am.

Getting Around

Mike's Bike Shop (☎0775-195174; Twelfth Ave; per day US$15) rents mountain bikes, ideal for getting around the city. Leave a US$300 security deposit or ID.

A taxi or combi is the best way to reach the outer limits, and taxi anywhere at night. Try **Proline Taxis** (☎886686); agree on a price before setting out.

WORTH A TRIP

KHAMI RUINS

Just 22km from Bulawayo, the Unesco World Heritage listed **Khami Ruins** (Kame, Kami; admission US$10; ⏰gates close at 4.30pm) may not have the grandeur of Great Zimbabwe, but it's an impressive archaeological site. The second largest stone monument built in Zimbabwe, Khami was developed between 1450 and 1650 (after Great Zimbabwe) and is spread over a 2km site in a peaceful natural setting overlooking the Khami Dam.

Matobo National Park

Home to some of the most majestic granite scenery in the world, the **Matobo National Park** (Matopos; admission US$15, car US$10; ⏰main gate 24hr, game park 6am-6pm) is one of the unsung highlights of Zimbabwe. Another of Zimbabwe's Unesco World Heritage Sites, the stunning and otherworldly landscape of balancing rocks, *kopjes* – giant boulders unfeasibly teetering on top of one another – makes it easy to understand why Matobo is considered the spiritual home of Zimbabwe.

The national park is essentially separated into two sections – the recreational park and the wildlife park.

Sights & Activities

World's View (Malindidzimu Hill) HISTORIC SITE

(adult/child US$10/5) One of Zimbabwe's most breathtaking sites, the aptly named World's View takes in epic 360-degree views of the park. The peacefulness up here is immense, taking on a spiritual quality that makes it clear why it's so sacred to the Nbebele people. It's also the burial spot of Rhodesia's founder, Cecil Rhodes whose somewhat controversial **grave** sits between two boulders. Downhill from Rhodes' grave is the **Shangani River Memorial**.

The entry fee also gains you access to the Pomongwe and Nswatugi rock art caves.

Rock Art Caves ARCHAEOLOGICAL SITE

Around the 425-sq-km park are 3000 officially registered rock-art sites, including one of the best collections in the world of San paintings (estimated to be anywhere from 6000 to 10,000 years old). **White Rhino Shelter**, **Bambata Cave**, and **Pomongwe Cave** have some fine examples.

Game Drive DRIVING TOUR

The wildlife park at Matobo National Park is a good spot to try your luck at spying both black and white rhino. It also has a high density of leopards, but you'll be very lucky to spot one. Guides can be arranged at the park if you have your own vehicle; otherwise sign up for a tour.

Sleeping & Eating

Farmhouse GUESTHOUSE $$

(☎60867; cozim@coz.co.zw; campsite US$10, cottage per person incl breakfast US$55, all-inclusive US$120) Just outside the park on the private Granite Ridge Lodge. Thatched-roof cottages are quaintly decked out, and you'll find a deep plunge pool and a resident zebra.

★ **Camp Amalinda** LODGE $$$

(☎243954; www.campamalinda.com; per person US$255;) Tucked away in the granite of the Matobo Hills, 10 thatched chalets are carved into the boulders, where they blend seamlessly, with bulging rocks an in-room feature. Each room is unique, some with clawfoot outdoor baths. End the day with a sundowner at the lagoon-style pool and bar.

Getting There & Away

Just 33km from Bulawayo, Matobo can be done as a day trip (p1013), although it's recommended to stay at least one night in this beautiful area. If you don't have transfers prearranged by your accommodation, take a taxi (around $US40).

Hwange National Park

One of the 10 largest national parks in Africa, and at 14,651 sq km the largest in Zimbabwe, **Hwange** (entry fee national-parks accommodation guests US$20, per day nonguests US$20; main gate 6am-6pm) ('Wang-ee') has a ridiculous amount of wildlife. Some 400 species of birds and 107 types of animals can be found in the park, including lions, giraffes, leopards, cheetahs, hyenas and painted dogs. But the elephants are what really defines Hwange, as it's home to around 40,000 tuskers, one of the world's largest populations.

The best time for wildlife viewing is July to October, when animals congregate around the 60 water holes or 'pans' (most of which are artificially filled) and the forest is stripped of its greenery.

The park is situated on the road from Bulawayo to Vic Falls, making it the most accessible and convenient park for many visitors. Access is possible in any sturdy vehicle between May and October, but you'll need a 4WD during the wet season. Consult a ranger (at any of the three camps) about road conditions before heading off too far into the park.

Maps and information about the park are available at the rangers' offices at the Hwange Main Camp, Sinamatella Camp and Robins Camp.

Sights & Activities

If you stay at Hwange Main Camp, you can book guided safaris in vehicles or walks (US$10 to $45) at the main office. At Sinamatella and Robins camps the only options available are guided walks with the national parks rangers (US$10 per person) – so for excursions further afield you'll need your own vehicle.

Sleeping

Hwange Main Camp CAMPGROUND $

(☎018-371; campsites per person US$15, chalet/cottage/lodge US$35/60/75; office 6am-6pm)

At the main park entrance, this attractive camp offers most services – safari vehicles, grocery shop, petrol station and restaurant. Accommodation ranges from self-catering lodges, cottages with communal kitchen, chalets (without bathroom) and campsites. Also has grazing wildlife and all the sounds of predators at night.

There's also decent national park lodges at Sinamatella and Robins Camp (same prices as Hwange Main Camp).

Ivory Safari Lodge LODGE $$
(☎09-64868; www.ivorysafarilodge.com; campsite per person US$15, per person with full board US$255) Take in the views of thirsty wildlife congregating at the water hole from your treehouse suite at this intimate lodge, just outside the park's border in Sikumi forest. The stilted huts with bathtubs overlooking the water hole are superb. There are also cheaper safari tents (without bathroom) and bush camping. It's located down a sandy track 1km off the Bulawayo–Vic Falls road.

Hwange Safari Lodge LODGE $$
(☎018-750; s/d incl breakfast US$81/137 ;) Clean motel-style rooms overlook a distant waterhole popular with wildlife. The lodge can arrange game drives (US$35) even if you're not staying here – a good way of getting to Hwange Main Camp if you've come by bus.

Getting There & Away

The park is between Bulawayo and Victoria Falls, 300km and 180km respectively.

The Pathfinder bus stops at Hwange Safari Lodge at 10am when coming from Vic Falls or 5pm when leaving Bulawayo. You'll need to arrange transport from here to the Main Camp, approximately 10km.

Victoria Falls

☎013

Tucked away in the far northwest of the country, the tourist town of Victoria Falls is home to the world-famous falls – one of the seven natural wonders of the world.

The lively town was built specifically for tourism, and has the best infrastructure in Zimbabwe, boasting quality accommodation, restaurants and shopping.

While for a few years during the turmoil it felt like a resort in off-season, there's no mistake about it now – Vic Falls has officially reopened for business.

Sights

★**Victoria Falls National Park** WATERFALL
(admission US$30; 6am-6pm) This is what you're here for, the mighty Victoria Falls. The 1km-long viewing path stretches along the top of the gorge, with various vantage points opening up to extraordinary front-on panoramas of the powerful curtain of water. One of the most dramatic spots is the westernmost point known as **Cataract View**. Another track leads to the aptly named **Danger Point**, where a sheer, unfenced 100m drop-off will rattle your nerves. From there, you can follow a side track for a view of the **Victoria Falls Bridge**.

Hire a raincoat and umbrella just inside the gates if you go from April to June, or you may as well walk in your swimsuit – you will get soaked!

Zambezi National Park WILDLIFE RESERVE
(admission US$15; 6am-6.30pm) Consisting of 40km of Zambezi River frontage and wildlife-rich mopane forest and savannah, Zambezi National Park is home to sable antelopes, giraffes, elephants and an occasional lion.

Activities

It's not just the falls that lures tourists to Vic Falls: it's also famous for **white-water rafting** (July to mid-February) on world-class grade-5 rapids, and **bungee jumping** from Victoria Falls' iconic bridge. More leisurely pursuits are **helicopter joy flights** over the falls or a **sunset cruise** along the Zambezi.

Activities are around US$125 and are booked through **Shearwater** (☎13-44471; www.shearwatervictoriafalls.com; Parkway Dr), **Wild Horizons** (☎13-42013, 0712 213721; www.wildhorizons.co.za; 310 Parkway Dr) or Backpackers Bazaar (p1017).

Sleeping

Shoestrings Backpackers BACKPACKERS $
(☎40167; 12 West Dr; campsite per person US$6, dm/d US$9/35;) Popular for overlanders and independent travellers, with a fun bar at night. Can book activities too.

Victoria Falls Restcamp & Lodges CAMPGROUND, LODGE $
(☎40509; www.vicfallsrestcamp.com; cnr Parkway & West Dr; campsite/dm/fitted dome tents US$10/11/20, s/d chalets without bathroom US$25/34, cottages US$67;) No-frills

Victoria Falls

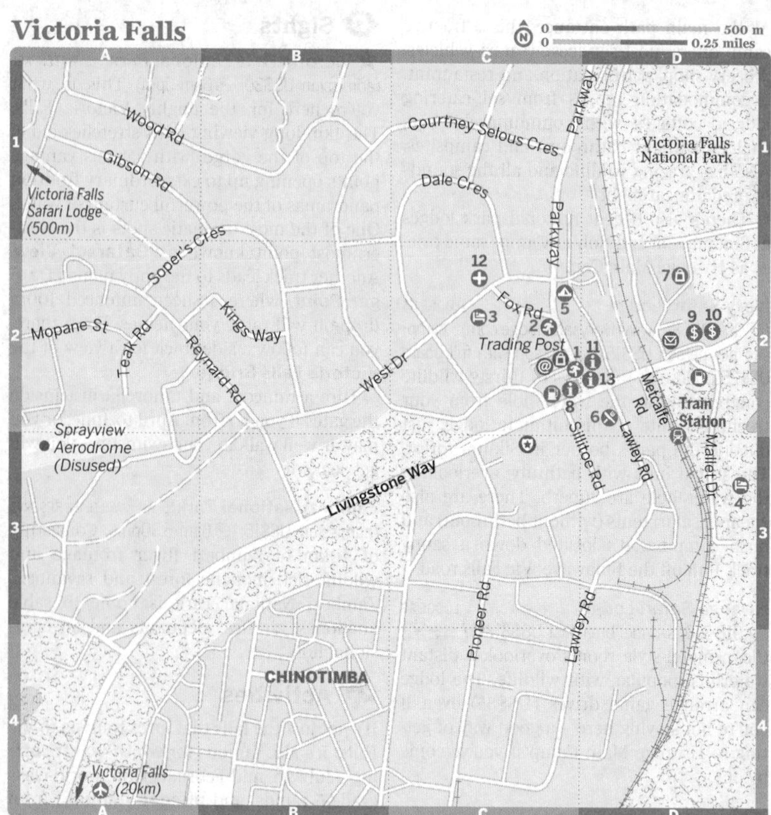

lodge-style budget accommodation and tented camps. Has a lovely pool.

★Victoria Falls Hotel LUXURY HOTEL $$$
(☎44751; www.victoria-falls-hotels.net; 2 Mallet Dr; s/d incl breakfast from US$312/336; ❄📶🏊) This famous 1904 hotel oozes colonial elegance, with lawns looking out to the gorge and bridge. High tea here is an institution.

Elephant Camp LUXURY LODGE $$$
(www.theelephantcamp.com; s/d full board US$350/700; @📶🏊) Luxurious 'tents' with classic lodge feel on a private wildlife reserve.

Eating & Drinking

In Da Belly Restaurant AFRICAN, INTERNATIONAL $
(☎332077; Parkway, Victoria Falls Restcamp & Lodges; meals US$5-15; ⏰7am-9.30pm) Relaxed open-air eatery with menu of warthog schnitzel, crocodile curry and impala burgers.

Mama Africa AFRICAN $$
(☎41725; www.mamaafricaeatinghouse.com; meals US$5-8; ⏰10am-10pm) Long-time tourist haunt specialises in local dishes, with live music and traditional dance.

★Stanley's Terrace RESTAURANT $$
(Mallet Dr, Victoria Falls Hotel; high tea for 2 people US$30; ⏰high tea 3-6pm; 📶) Brims with English colonial ambience. High tea here is served to a postcard-perfect backdrop of the gardens and Vic Falls Bridge.

Shoestrings Backpackers BAR
(12 West Dr) Raucous bar that's as popular with locals as it is with backpackers.

Shopping

★Elephant's Walk Shopping & Artist Village SHOPPING CENTRE
(☎0772 254552; www.elephantswalk.com; Adam Stander Dr) This boutique shopping village is

a must for those in the market for quality Zimbabwean and African craft.

Information

Backpackers Bazaar (013-45828; www.backpackersbazaarvicfalls.com; off Parkway; 8am-5pm Mon-Fri, 9am-4pm Sat & Sun) Definitive place for all tourist info and bookings.

Barclays Bank (off Livingstone Way)

Econet (Park Way; per 30min/1hr US$1/2; 8am-5pm Mon-Fri, to 1pm Sat & Sun)

Medical Air Rescue Service (MARS; 44764)

Victoria Falls Surgery (43356; West Dr)

Getting There & Away

AIR

For cheap flights check out www.flightsite.co.za or www.travelstart.co.za.

South African Airways (011-808678; www.flysaa.com) and **British Airways** (www.britishairways.com) fly every day to Johannesburg from around US$320 return.

BUS

Pathfinder has a daily service to Bulawayo (US$30, six hours) en route to Harare (US$60, 12 hours), stopping outside Hwange National Park on the way. Bravo Tours also plies the route for cheaper prices. Otherwise combis (US$20) and local buses (US$15) head to Bulawayo.

From Bulawayo, you can connect to Johannesburg with Intercaper Greyhound at 4pm.

To Botswana, shared taxis run from Vic Falls to Kazungula; they can get a bit erratic in the afternoon and leave when full (US$10 per person)

TRAIN

The overnight Mosi-oa-Tunya train leaves daily at 7pm for Bulawayo (US$12, 12 hours); 1st-class is the only way to go. Make reservations at the **ticket office** (44392; 7-10am & 2.30-6.45pm Mon-Fri, 9-10am & 4.30-6.45pm Sat & Sun) inside the train station.

Getting Around

Victoria Falls Airport is located 20km southeast of town, and is easily accessible by taxi (US$30). The town itself is easily navigable on foot; be very careful of roaming wildlife at night.

A taxi across the bridge to the Zambia border will cost around $US5, from where onward transport awaits.

UNDERSTAND ZIMBABWE

Zimbabwe Today

Zimbabwe continues to dip in and out of international headlines, often creating an unclear but daunting vibe for prospective visitors. Tourists have never been the targets for internal politics and violence, but always check with your embassy or consulate for the latest travel advice. And, somehow, despite the immense hardship for everyday Zimbabweans, crime still remains relatively low.

Despite general improvements, Zimbabwe faced an uncertain future leading into the 2013 elections. With a history of vote rigging and violence, observers around the world were holding their breath as reports of land grabs and voter intimidation continue, albeit on a much lower scale. Meanwhile the *Guardian* reported on a watchdog that accused Mugabe of pilfering some US$2 billion of much-needed revenue from the nation's lucrative diamond mines. And leaving the country's future even murkier was the likely end of its power-sharing government, which had provided much-needed political buoyancy.

VISAS FOR ZIM & ZAM

You will need a visa to cross sides between Zimbabwe and Zambia, even if just for the day. These are available at the border posts, open from around 7am to 10pm. Note that you can't get multi-entry visas at these crossings; in most cases you need to apply at the embassy in your home country before travelling.

Crossing into Zambia, a day visit costs US$20 for 24 hours, a single-entry visa costs US$50 and double entry is US$80.

Unfortunately, Zimbabwe's great gains since independence – life expectancy, education, health – have all been reversed since 1998 (due to gross mismanagement, corruption, and HIV/AIDS). Certainly, many Zimbabweans experience major difficulties in their day-to-day lives. The standard of living for residents has fallen dramatically over the past decade. Today, there's still a day-to-day struggle in some areas with weeks of no electricity and limited water.

Dollarisation at the beginning of 2009 solved many problems for those with access to cash. Diaspora funding has always buoyed the economy, which avoided collapse for years longer than it should have. It is estimated that 60% of Zimbabweans have someone from the diaspora sending them money. Those who do not – and are in rural areas – remain dangerously below the poverty line.

History

The Shona Kingdoms & the Portuguese

In the 11th century, the city of Great Zimbabwe was wealthy and powerful from trading gold and ivory to Swahili traders for glass, porcelain and cloth from Asia. However, by the 15th century, its influence was in decline because of overpopulation, overgrazing, political fragmentation and uprisings.

During this twilight period, Shona dynasties fractured into autonomous states. In the 16th century Portuguese traders arrived in search of riches and golden cities in the vast empire of Mwene Mutapa (or 'Monomatapa' to the Europeans). They hoped to find King Solomon's mines and the mysterious land of Ophir.

A new alliance of Shona was formed – the Rozwi State – which covered over half of present-day Zimbabwe, until 1834 when Ndebele raiders (Those Who Carry Long Shields), under the command of Mzilikazi, invaded from what is now South Africa. They assassinated the Rozwi leader. Upon reaching the Matobo Hills, Mzilikazi established a Ndebele state. After Mzilikazi's death in 1870, his son, Lobengula, ascended the throne and relocated the Ndebele capital to Bulawayo.

Lobengula soon came face to face with the British South African Company (BSAC). In 1888 Cecil Rhodes, the founder of the company, coerced him into signing the Rudd Concession, which granted foreigners mineral rights in exchange for 10,000 rifles, 100,000 rounds of ammunition, a gunboat and £100 each month.

But a series of misunderstandings followed. Lobengula sent a group of Ndebele raiders to Fort Victoria (near Masvingo) to stop Shona interference between the British and the Ndebele. The British mistook this as aggression and launched an attack on Matabeleland. Lobengula's *kraals* (hut villages) were destroyed and Bulawayo was burned. A peace offering of gold sent by Lobengula to the BSAC was commandeered by company employees. Ignorant of this gesture, the British sent the Shangani River Patrol to track down the missing king and finish him off. In the end, Lobengula died in exile of smallpox.

Without their king, the Ndebele continued to resist the BSAC and foreign rule. In the early 1890s they allied themselves with the Shona, and guerrilla warfare broke out against the BSAC in the Matobo Hills. When Rhodes suggested a negotiated settlement, the Ndebele, with their depleted numbers, couldn't refuse.

Meanwhile, finding little gold, the colonists appropriated farmlands on the Mashonaland Plateau. By 1895 the new country was being called Rhodesia, after its heavy-handed founder, and a white legislature was set up. European immigration began in earnest: by 1904 there were some 12,000 settlers in the country, and seven years later the figure had doubled.

Beginnings of Nationalism

Conflicts between black and white in Zimbabwe came into sharp focus after the 1922 referendum in which the whites chose to become a self-governing colony rather than join the Union of South Africa. In 1930 white supremacy was legislated in the form of the Land Apportionment Act.

Poor wages and conditions eventually led to a rebellion, and by the time Southern Rhodesia, Northern Rhodesia and Nyasaland were federated in 1953, mining and industrial concerns favoured a more racially mixed middle class as a counterweight to the radical elements in the labour force.

Two African parties soon emerged – the Zimbabwe African People's Union (ZAPU) under Joshua Nkomo, and the Zimbabwe African National Union (ZANU).

Ian Smith & the War for Independence

In 1964 Ian Smith took over the Rhodesian presidency and began pressing for independence. The British prime minister, Harold Wilson, argued for conditions to be met before Britain would agree: guarantee of racial equality, course towards majority rule, and majority desire for independence. Smith realised the whites in Rhodesia would never agree, so in 1965 he made a Unilateral Declaration of Independence.

Independence

On 10 September 1979, delegations met at Lancaster House, London, to draw up a constitution favourable to both the Patriotic Front (an alliance between ZANU and ZAPU) of Nkomo and Robert Mugabe, and the Zimbabwe-Rhodesian government of Abel Muzorewa and Smith. Mugabe, who wanted ultimate power, initially refused to make any concessions, but after 14 weeks the Lancaster House Agreement was reached. It guaranteed whites (then 3% of the population) 20 of the 100 parliamentary seats.

Soon after, the economy soared, wages increased, and basic social programs – notably education and healthcare – were initiated. However, the initial euphoria, unity and optimism quickly faded: a resurgence of rivalry between ZANU (run mostly by Shona people) and ZAPU (mostly by Ndebele) escalated into armed conflict, and Nkomo was accused of plotting against the government. Guerrilla activity resumed in ZAPU areas of Matabeleland, and Mugabe (elected prime minister in 1980) deployed the North Korean–trained Fifth Brigade in early 1983 to quell the disturbances. Villagers were gunned down and prominent members of ZAPU were eliminated in order to root out 'dissidents'. The result was massacres in which tens of thousands of civilians, sometimes entire villages, were slaughtered. A world that was eager to revere Mr Mugabe closed its eyes. The eyes of Zimbabweans were forced shut.

Nkomo, meanwhile, fled to England until Mugabe (realising the strife threatened to erupt into civil war) publicly relented and guaranteed his safe return. Talks resulted in a ZAPU–ZANU confederation (called ZANU-PF). Zimbabwe's one-party state had begun.

Life as the Opposition

In 1999 thousands attended a Zimbabwe Congress of Trade Unions (ZCTU) rally to launch the Movement for Democratic Change (MDC). Morgan Tsvangirai, the secretary general, stated he would lead a social democratic party fighting for workers' interests. The arrival of the MDC brought waves of new hope and real opportunity for the end of Mugabe's era.

Mugabe responded to the threat of defeat with waves of violence, voter intimidation, and a chaotic and destructive land reform program that saw many white farmers evicted from their land. He claimed the next three elections.

In February 2009, Morgan Tsvangirai signed a coalition deal with ZANU-PF, a mutual promise to restore the rule of law and to 'ensure security of tenure to all land holders'. Nonetheless, the violence and evictions continued. At the time of writing, MDC was in government with Mugabe's party, but largely impotent, and leading into the 2013 elections, Tsvangirai conceded the two-party government was unlikely to continue.

People & Culture

People

No matter what their race, Zimbabweans have a stoicism about them. In Zimbabwe, the Southern African expression to 'make a plan' can be defined as: 'If it's broke, fix it. If you can't fix it, live with it, or change your life' (overnight if need be). This kind of mental strength and generosity, combined with a deep love of Zimbabwe, are the keys to their survival.

About 65% of the population lives in rural areas, while around 40% of the population is under 18 years old. The average life expectancy is about 40 years. Most Zimbabweans are of Bantu origin; 9.8 million belong to various Shona groups and about 2.3 million are Ndebele.

Religion

The majority of Zimbabweans are Christian, although traditional spiritual beliefs and customs are still practised, especially in rural areas, where merciless economic times have led to an increase in faith (and fraud).

Literature

Zimbabwe has produced some fine literature. The most contemporary, *Mukiwa* (A White Boy in Africa) and its sequel, *When a Crocodile Eats the Sun,* by Peter Godwin, are engrossing memoirs. Likewise, *Don't Let's Go to the Dogs Tonight – An African Childhood,* by Alexandra Fuller, is about nature and loss, and the unbreakable bond some people have with Africa.

Since independence, Zimbabwean literature has focused on the struggle to build a new society. *Harvest of Thorns,* by Shimmer Chinodya, on the Second War for Independence, won the 1992 Commonwealth Prize for Literature. Another internationally renowned writer, Chenjerai Hove, wrote the war-inspired *Bones,* the tragic *Shadows* and the humorous *Shebeen Tales.*

The country's most famous female writer is the late Yvonne Vera, known for her courageous writing on challenging issues: rape, incest and gender inequality. She won the Commonwealth Prize in 1997 for *Under the Tongue,* and the Macmillan book prize for her acclaimed 2002 novel, *The Stone Virgins.*

Food & Drink

The staple for locals is *sadza,* a white maize meal made into either porridge or something resembling mashed potato, which is eaten with your fingers with tomato-based relishes, meat and/or gravy.

The tap water in Zimbabwe is not safe to drink, but bottled mineral water, fruit juices and soft drinks are widely available.

Tea and coffee are grown in the Eastern Highlands. Cafes and restaurants in the cities serve espresso coffee from either local or imported beans.

The beer you will more commonly see is lager. The domestically brewed lagers – Zambezi and Castle – are really good.

Environment

Landlocked Zimbabwe is roughly three times the size of England. It lies within both Tropics and consists of highveld and middle-veld plateaus, 900m to 1700m above sea level.

Wildlife

The Big Five and most of the animals highlighted in the Wildlife guide (p1058) are found in Zimbabwe. The number of elephants is almost at plague proportions, with Hwange having the more than any other park in the world.

There are hundreds of bird species found all over the country, including vultures, storks and herons, and Matobo National Park is home to one-third of the world's eagle species.

National Parks

Many of Zimbabwe's national parks are – or contain – Unesco World Heritage Listed Sites. Close to 20% of Zimbabwe's surface area is protected – or semiprotected – in the form of national parks, privately protected wildlife parks, nature conservancies and recreational parks.

Park entry fees range from US$5 to US$30 per day. Never enter without paying the fee (which constitutes a permit), as national parks are zealously guarded against poaching.

There are different rates for vehicles – none are free – and an average entry fee for a four-seater vehicle is US$5. Go to www.zimparks.com for the latest figures.

Environmental Issues

Zimbabwe is dry for at least nine months of the year and many areas suffer from long-term drought. Poaching, hunting and the destruction of the land has caused serious stress on flora, fauna and the land. Lakes and rivers have also been overfished. This then impacts on those whose lives depend on a properly functioning environment.

To learn more about Zimbabwe's ecological problems, visit **Wildlife & Environment Zimbabwe** (www.zimwild.org).

SURVIVAL GUIDE

Directory A–Z

ACCOMMODATION

Zimbabwe generally has a good standard of accommodation that will suit most traveller's needs, whether it's cheap dorms or luxury lodges. Camping is another option and a tent is handy for national parks.

The upmarket lodges in the parks are stunning. Most are in the the middle of the action, allowing you to enjoy wildlife from your room. Prices are expensive, but rates usually include activities, food and alcohol.

The national parks also have affordable lodges run by the Zimbabwe Parks & Wildlife Management Authority (www.zimparks.org), with a good choice of lodges and campsites. The main office (p1006) in Harare is the best place to book.

ACTIVITIES

Victoria Falls is the epicentre of activities in Southern Africa. The adventurous can get their adrenalin pumping with white-water rafting, helicopter rides, gorge swings and bungee jumping. There and elsewhere, it's all about natural features in Zimbabwe: river cruises, hiking in the Eastern Highlands, wildlife viewing in national parks, canoeing safaris on the Zambezi River or houseboating on Lake Kariba.

CHILDREN

Zimbabwe is a great place to travel with kids. Wildlife spotting in the national parks and a range of kid-friendly activities in Vic Falls such as canoeing and elephant rides are likely to be the most popular choices. Take note, however, that some lodges in the parks have age limits for safety reasons, so be sure to confirm before booking.

EMBASSIES & CONSULATES

The following embassies and high commissions are based in Harare.

For any embassies or websites not listed here, go to www.embassiesabroad.com/embassies-in/Zimbabwe to find addresses and contact details.

Australian Embassy (Map p1002; ☎04-870566; www.zimbabwe.embassy.gov.au; 1 Green Close, Borrowdale; ⏰8am-5pm Mon-Thu, to 1.30pm Fri)

Belgian Embassy (Map p1004; ☎04-700112, 04-700943; www.diplomatie.be/harare; 5th fl, Tanganyika House, 23 Third St/Union Ave)

Botswanan Embassy (Map p1002; ☎04-794645; www.embassiesabroad.com/embassies-of/Botswana; 22 Phillips Ave; ⏰visas 8am-12.30pm Mon, Wed & Fri)

British Embassy (Map p1002; ☎04-772990; www.britishembassy.gov.uk/zimb; cnr Norfolk Rd & Second St Extension)

Canadian Embassy (Map p1004; ☎04-252181; www.harare.gc.ca; 45 Baines Ave)

French Embassy (Map p1004; ☎04-703216; www.ambafrance-zw.org; First Bank Bldg, 74-76 Samora Machel Ave, Greendale)

Malawian High Commission (Map p1002; ☎04-798584; malahigh@africaonline.co.zw; 9/11 Duthie Rd, Alexandra Park; ⏰visas 9am-noon Mon-Thu)

Mozambican Embassy (Map p1004; ☎04-253871; 152 Herbert Chitepo Ave; ⏰visas 8am-noon Mon-Fri)

Namibian Embassy (Map p1002; ☎04-885841; 69 Borrowdale Rd)

South African Embassy (Map p1002; ☎04-753147; dhacon@mweb.co.zw; 7 Elcombe Ave)

US Embassy (Map p1004; ☎04-250593, 04-250594; www.usembassy.state.gov/zimbabwe; Arax House, 172 Herbert Chitepo Ave)

Zambian Embassy (Map p1004; ☎04-773777; zambians@africaonline.com; 6th fl, Zambia House, 48 Kwame Nkrumah Ave (Union Ave); ⏰9am-1pm)

GAY & LESBIAN TRAVELLERS

Homosexual activity for men is illegal and officially punishable by up to five years in jail (though penalties are invariably not nearly as severe); lesbianism is not illegal.

Contact **Gays & Lesbians of Zimbabwe** (☎04-741736, 04-740614; www.galz.co.zw; 35 Colenbrander Rd, Milton Park, Harare) for

PRACTICALITIES

Languages The official language of Zimbabwe is English. It's used in government, legal and business proceedings, but is the first language for only about 2% of the population. Most Zimbabweans speak Shona or Ndebele.

Newspapers The government's control over media has resulted in much self-censorship and bland press. The only surviving dailies (the *Herald* and the *Standard*) are both state-run. Friday's *Independent* and *The Zimbabwean*, which is produced out of London, offer the week's only dose of propaganda-free political reporting.

TV & Radio The government controls all TV and radio, though most hotels and many lodges have great DSTV satellite TV.

information about gay and lesbian clubs and meeting places in Zimbabwe.

INTERNET ACCESS

There are internet centres in all the main cities and towns for around US$2 per hour.

Wi-fi access is pretty prevalent these days but slow; you can find it in many hotels and cafes in the bigger cities for around $2 to $3 an hour.

Another option is mobile internet using USB prepaid internet on your phone or laptop. Econet and Telecel both have branches at Harare's airport and in town. The USB dongle costs around US$50, but connections are patchy at best.

LANGUAGE

The official language of Zimbabwe is English. It's used in government, legal and business proceedings, but is the first language for only about 2% of the population. Most Zimbabweans speak Shona (mainly in the north and east) or Ndebele (in the centre and west). Another dialect, Chilapalapa, is a pidgin version of Ndebele, English, Shona and Afrikaans, and isn't overly laden with niceties, so most people prefer you sticking to English.

MONEY

Since 2009, US dollars are the most commonly used currency in Zimbabwe, while the rand is used to a lesser extent. Change for cash is a big problem, so have plenty of small notes.

ATMs

There are ATMs aplenty across ZImbabwe, but the larger towns are the most reliable. Barclays, Standard Charter and Stanbic are the main banks and accept MasterCard, Visa and Cirrus.

OPENING HOURS

Shops and restaurants are generally open from 8am to 1pm and 2pm to 5pm Monday to Friday, and 8am to noon on Saturday. Most restaurants open on Sunday but shops and government buildings are mostly closed.

POST

Sending letters and postcards by surface mail to Europe and the UK costs US$0.80; it costs US$1.10 to the rest of the world.

PUBLIC HOLIDAYS

During the following public holidays, most government offices and other businesses are closed.

New Year's Day 1 January
Independence Day 18 April
Workers' Day 1 May
Africa Day 25 May
Heroes' Day 11 August
Defence Forces' Day 12 August
National Unity Day 22 December
Boxing Day 26 December

SAFE TRAVEL

Zimbabwe is nowhere near as dangerous as foreign media makes out, but crime is on the rise. Although the number of incidents and degree of violence are a far cry from that in South Africa, it is a reality. Don't walk around at night, and drivers should take the following precautions: lock all doors, lock all valuables in the boot, keep windows up and avoid stopping at traffic lights at night where safe to do so.

TELEPHONE

If calling from overseas, the country code for Zimbabwe is ☎263, but drop the initial zero for area codes. The international access code from within Zimbabwe is ☎00. The first two digits of mobile-phone numbers are ☎07.

Easily the best option for making calls is to arrange a prepaid SIM card on arrival for your mobile phone, which are cheap and easy to arrange. Econet and Telecel are the main operators, and have branches throughout the main towns, as well as Harare airport. Be aware that your phone needs to be unlocked to activate the SIM. Credit, or 'airtime', is widely available from street vendors.

TOURIST INFORMATION

The **Zimbabwe Tourism Authority** (Map p1004; ☎758712; www.zimbabwetourism.net; 55 Samora Machel Ave; ⏲8am-5pm Mon-Fri) has general tourist info. There are associations in Harare, Bulawayo, Victoria Falls, Kariba, Masvingo and Nyanga.

VISAS

With a few exceptions, visas are required by nationals of all countries. They can be obtained at your point of entry. Single-/double-entry visas cost US$30/45 (and can be issued upon arrival) and multiple-entry visas (valid for six months) cost US$55, but are only issued at Zimbabwean diplomatic missions. British and Irish citizens pay US$55/70 for single/double entry.

For visa extensions, contact the Department of Immigration Control (p1006).

Vaccination for yellow fever is not required for entry to Zimbabwe unless you have recently been to an infected area. However, for all sorts of reasons, get a jab before you come to Southern Africa and carry a certificate to prove it.

Visas for Onward Travel

Harare is one of the best places in Southern Africa to pick up visas for regional countries. Requirements constantly change, but nearly all require a fee (US dollars) and two passport-sized photos.

Visas for Zambia, Namibia, Malawi and Botswana are easy to obtain on arrival in those countries for most visitors, so no need to obtain them in advance. In theory South Africa is easy too, though such are the queues at Harare's South African Embassy each day that it's best to get one in advance.

Getting There & Away

AIR

A sure sign that Zimbabwe is back on the tourist radar is the return of international airlines such as Emirates and KLM to Harare.

International flights link to Johannesburg from (one way/return US$230/442, 1¾ hours), Gaborone (US$265/432, two hours), Windhoek (US$425/592, two hours), Maputo (US$468/767, 1½ hours), Lilongwe and Blantyre (US$395/582, 1½ hours), Lusaka (US$450/295 50 minutes), Dar es Salaam (US$1154/1888, 2½ hours) and Nairobi (US$1070/1274, 3½ hours).

International flights also arrive in Vic Falls from Johannesburg (US$340/750) and Windhoek (US$300/650).

Airlines with services to/from Zimbabwe:

Air Botswana (Map p1004; ☎04-707131, 04-793228, 04-793229; www.airbotswana.co.bw; Travel Plaza, Harare)

Air Malawi (Map p1004; ☎04-752563; www.airmalawi.com; 9th fl, Throgmorton House, cnr Julius Nyerere Way & Samora Machel)

Air Namibia (Map p1004; ☎0779 758869, 0736-688568, in Victoria Falls 1345825; www.airnamibia.com.na; Joina City, Harare)

Air Zimbabwe (Map p1004; ☎04-253751, 04-253752; Eastgate Centre)

South African Airways (Map p1002; ☎04-794511, 04-794512; 1st fl, Pa Sangano, 20 King George Rd, Avondale)

BORDER CROSSINGS

Travelling to neighbouring Southern African countries is fairly hassle-free, with visas on arrival issued to many nationalities (but be sure to check before you leave).

Botswana

The most popular border crossing into Botswana is from Kazungula (6am to 6pm), which links Vic Falls to Chobe National Park. The other crossing is at Plumtree, 94km from Bulawayo, heading to Francistown in Botswana. The border posts at Plumtree and Kazungula are open 6am to 6pm.

The following run buses from Harare (Road Port Terminal) to Francistown:

Zupco (Map p1004; ☎0772 666530, 750571; Road Port Terminal, Harare) Departs 6.30am Tuesday, Thursday and Friday (US$15).

PCJ Coaches Departs every day at 6pm (US$60).

Malawi

The most direct route between Malawi and Zimbabwe is via Mozambique's Tete Corridor. You'll need a transit visa for Mozambique if travelling through Mozambique to Malawi, which you can arrange in Harare. Alternatively you'll have to fork out extra for a visa at the border; enquire with the Mozambique embassy before setting out.

Harare (Road Port Terminal) to Blantyre:

Zupco (p1023) Departs Tuesday, Thursday and Sunday at 7.30am (US$25, 12 hours).

Munorurama (Map p1004; ☎0772 361296; Road Port Terminal, Harare) Departs daily at 8am (US$25).

Mozambique

There are two border crossings (open 6am to 8pm) into Mozambique. Easily the most popular is from Mutare, which links it up to Beira. The other is at Nyamapanda, northeast from Harare, used to get to Malawi.

South Africa

Beitbridge is the somewhat infamous border crossing into South Africa. It's open 24 hours, but is always fairly hectic.

Numerous luxury and semi-luxury buses ply the route from Harare or Bulawayo to Johannesburg (16 to 17 hours).

Harare buses depart from the Road Port Terminal:

Greyhound (Map p1004; ☎720801; Road Port Terminal) Departs 8pm Monday to Saturday, and 1pm on Sundays (US$52).

Pioneer (Map p1002; ☎795863, 790531; Road Port Terminal) Departs at 1pm and 7pm (US$42).

Buses from Bulawayo:

Intercape (☎27-21-3804400; www.intercape.co.za; Main St) Departs 4pm (US$55).

Citiliner (www.citiliner.co.za; Sixth Ave) Departs 2pm (US$42).

Greyhound (www.greyhound.co.za; Sixth Ave) Departs 4pm (US$50).

Eagle Liner (www.eagleliner.co.za; 5th Ave, George Silundika) Departs 2.30pm (US$40).

Trains are once again running between Zimbabwe and South Africa. Rovos Rail operates its train from Pretoria to Victoria Falls travelling through Zimbabwe via Bulawayo. This trip is a three-day, two-night journey each way.

Zambia

There are three border crossings into Zambia, with Victoria Falls (open 6am to 10pm) by far the most popular. You can also cross via Kariba and Chirundu (Zambia), which is open 6am to 6pm.

From Harare:

Zupco (p1023) Two daily buses depart for Lusaka (US$15, nine hours) at 7.30am and a slower bus at 7.30pm.

Tenda Luxury (Map p1004; ☎0773-817602; Road Port Terminal, Harare) Departs at 6.30pm (US$20, 15 hours).

Tenda also has a bus to Lusaka departing from Mutare (US$28) at 10am.

Getting Around

AIR

Air Zimbabwe (Map p1004; ☎04-253751, at airport 04-575111; www.airzimbabwe.aero; cnr Speke Ave & Third St) has one flight per day between Harare and Bulawayo (one way/return US$176/342, 45 minutes) and Harare and Victoria Falls (one way/return US$215/421). There's a domestic departure tax of US$10.

The only way by air from Harare or Vic Falls to Kariba is to charter, which is very expensive. The following can arrange charter flights, which will seat four to six people to Kariba, Mana Pools and Matusadona National Park from Harare or Vic Falls:

HAC (Halsteds Aviation Corporation; ☎0778 750086; www.flyhac.com)

Altair Charters (☎0772-515852; giles@altaircharters.com)

BumiAir (☎04-307087; www.bumihills.com) In Matusadona.

BOAT

Kariba Ferries (☎04-614162, 0772 236330; www.karibaferries.com; Andora Harbour, Kariba) runs a ferry service between Kariba at the eastern end of the lake and Mlibizi at the western end.

BUS

Express or 'luxury' buses operate according to published timetables. However, check carefully, as most bus companies have *both* local ('chicken buses' for locals) and luxury coaches. For example, Pioneer and Zupco have both luxury and chicken buses. For more information on buses starting from Harare, see p1007.

Pathfinder (Map p1004; ☎0778 888880, 36907; www.pathfinderlx.com; cnr 115 Nelson Mandela Ave & 5th St, Harare) This luxury '7-star' (it claims to have wi-fi) bus service has started up a daily service linking Harare to Vic Falls, Bulawayo and even Hwange. It has plans for services to Mutare and Kariba.

Bravo (Map p1004; ☎0772 873438; www.bravotours.co.zw; 88 George Sulindka Ave) Plies the Harare–Bulawayo–Vic Falls route.

CAR & MOTORCYCLE

Driving Licence

All foreigners can use their driving licence from their home country for up to 90 days in Zimbabwe as long as it's written in English. However, given the growing possibility of police trying to elicit bribes, it's best to ensure you also have an international driving licence.

Fuel

At the time of writing fuel was freely available, at a cost of around US$1.60 per litre for petrol and US$1.40 per litre for diesel.

Hire

- The minimum driving age required by rental companies varies, but is usually between 23 and 25 years. The maximum age is normally about 65 years.
- It's important to note that most collision damage waiver (CDW) insurance policies do not cover 2WD vehicles travelling on rough roads in national parks.
- Be sure you have all the relevant papers and your car is fitted with the legally required fire extinguisher, warning triangles and reflectors.
- Due to the high costs of car rental in Zimbabwe, many DIY travellers arrange a 4WD in South Africa and drive on through the border.

LOCAL TRANSPORT

Taxis are safe and can be booked through your hotel. Most are metered, charging around $2.50 for 1km at the time of writing. Taxis in cities travel within a 40km radius of the city. Most reliable taxis are booked through hotel front desks. Always take a taxi at night.

TRAIN

Connecting Harare, Bulawayo, Mutare and Victoria Falls, all major train services travel at night. The most popular route is from Vic Falls to Bulawayo. Definitely opt for 1st-class, which is cheap and comfortable and gets you a sleeping compartment.

Understand Africa

Africa Today

Disease, poverty, corruption and conflict continue to stalk the continent but recent headlines out of Africa are increasingly positive. Long-running dictators have been toppled across North Africa, while in 2011 the continent gained its newest nation, South Sudan. Sustained economic growth for scores of nations is bringing concrete benefits to millions of average Africans, including dramatic falls in child mortality.

Best in Print

Searching for Transwonderland (Noo Saro-Wira) Wry, insightful account of Africa's most populous country, Nigeria.

Shadow of the Sun (Ryszard Kapuścinski) Illuminating stories from a veteran foreign correspondent.

Dark Star Safari (Paul Theroux) The master traveller charts a Cairo to Cape Town journey.

Africa: a Beginners Guide (Tom Young) A great introduction to the continent and its politics, which examines the arguments from all sides.

Disgrace (JM Coetzee) Booker Prize–winner about post-apartheid South Africa.

Best on Film

Tsotsi (2005) Oscar-winning gangster drama set in Soweto.

The Constant Gardener (2005) Based on John le Carre's thriller set in Kenya.

Hotel Rwanda (2004) True story of heroism during the Rwandan genocide.

Best Websites

All Africa (allafrica.com) News from across the continent.

Africa Research Institute (www.africaresearchinstitute.org) Reports from a London-based think tank.

The Africa Guide (www.africaguide.com) All-purpose, all-Africa site.

After the Arab Spring

Euphoria accompanied the Arab Spring of 2011 and the ousting of long-term leaders in Egypt, Libya and Tunisia. But the hard realities of government and politics hit home in 2012. A two-part referendum in Egypt in late 2012 over the new constitution brought thousand of protesters back onto Cairo's streets and left the country, according to the *Economist*, 'ever more starkly divided' than before 2011. Meanwhile, in Libya US Ambassador Chris Stevens and three other American diplomats were killed in September 2012, a brutal reminder that the country is still dangerously unstable.

France Goes into Mali

The demise of Colonel Qaddafi's regime has sent dangerous ripples across the region. Mali was regarded to be a model of African democracy until a military coup in March 2012. Tuareg rebels and al-Qaeda allies, some of whom who had fought for Qaddafi, took the opportunity to declare the independence of 'Azawad state' in the north, an area of the Sahara as big as Spain. In January 2013 France deployed troops to its former colony, following an appeal from the Malian government, to help counter this threat from Islamist rebels. This was swiftly followed by a hostage crisis at a gas facility in the Algerian desert.

There was more bad news for West Africa in October 2012 when the International Maritime Bureau announced that piracy in the region had reached dangerous proportions. The problem is particularly acute in the waters off Nigeria.

East African Promise

On the other side of the continent, international efforts to combat piracy began to bear fruit as attacks by Somali pirates dropped sharply. The US also officially recognised Somalia's government, bringing the pariah state back out of the cold after 20 years and paving the way for international aid.

There was more good news, of sorts, when the *Economist* declared Kabira, the Nairobi shanty town often described as Africa's biggest slum, 'a thriving economic machine' that was possibly the 'most entrepreneurial place on the planet'. Economic growth here was mirrored across the continent and has resulted in dramatic improvements in other areas, such as child mortality; in the five years to 2010, Senegal cut its under-five mortality rate from 12.1 per cent to 7.2 per cent. Rates also tumbled in Rwanda and Kenya.

Trouble in Congo

Demand for oil and other scarce resources, particularly by China and the US, lies behind the recovery of economies such as Angola, Nigeria and Chad. However the scramble for control of the spoils of this trade continues to plague Africa. Conflict in the resource-rich Democratic Republic of Congo rumbles on with the rebel M23 group gaining the advantage in the eastern part of the country in late 2012.

Strife in South Africa

The continent's superpower remains South Africa, a member of the emerging global economies known as BRICS (standing for Brazil, Russia, Indonesia, China and South Africa). Bitter memories of the country's apartheid years were rekindled when police opened fire on striking platinum miners in August 2012, killing 34 of them. The incident highlighted persistent deep economic divisions in South African society.

President Jacob Zuma weathered the storm, comfortably securing re-election to lead the African National Congress, the essential stepping stone to a second term as the nation's president in 2014. South Africa has been on tenterhooks, though, as its most famous citizen, 94-year-old Nelson Mandela, has been in and out of hospital three times since December 2012 for treatment for his declining health.

Meanwhile in neighbouring Zimbabwe, elections in 2013 became possible when rival political leaders President Robert Mugabe and Prime Minister Morgan Tsvangirai reached a deal over a new constitution, which was approved in a referendum in March of 2013.

POPULATION: **1,032,532,974 (2011)**

LIFE EXPECTANCY: **54**

AREA: **30,221,532 SQ KM**

GDP PER CAPITA: **US$1189 (2010)**

if Africa were 100 people

95 would not have HIV
5 would have HIV

belief systems

(% of population)

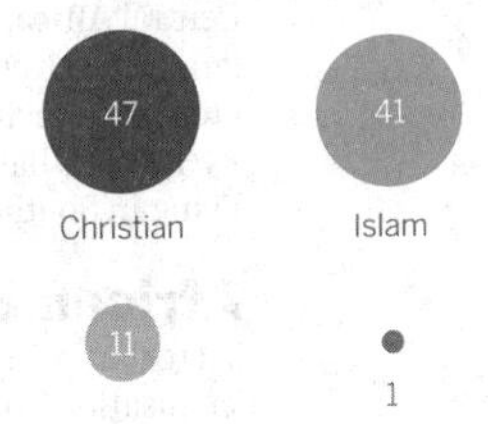

population per sq km

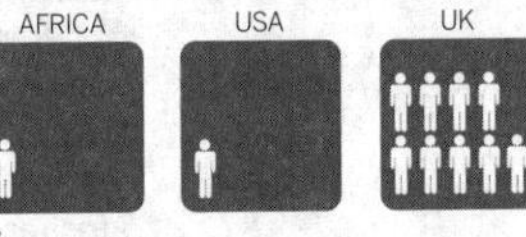

History

African history is a vast and epic tale. The continent has seen pretty much everything – from proto-bacteria and dinosaurs to the colonial 'scramble for Africa' and the Arab Spring that ousted long-time leaders in North Africa. The first humans walked out of the continent about 100,000 years ago to eventually populate the globe. Since then, African empires have come and gone as have European explorers and colonialists. What follows is a gallop through the pivotal events in the continent's past. For further details read the history sections of each country chapter.

To find out more information on the history of Africa try the following books: *Africa – A Biography of the Continent* by John Reader, *The Scramble for Africa* by Thomas Pakenham and *The State of Africa* by Martin Meredith.

Human Origins & Migrations

Around five to 10 million years ago, a special kind of ape called *Australopithecines* branched off (or rather let go of the branch) and walked on two legs down a separate evolutionary track. This radical move led to the development of various hairy, dim-witted hominids (early men) – *Homo habilis* around 2.4 million years ago, *Homo erectus* some 1.8 million years ago and finally *Homo sapiens* (modern humans) around 200,000 years ago. Around 50,000 years later, somewhere in Tanzania or Ethiopia, a woman was born who has become known as 'mitochondrial Eve'. All humans today descend from her: at a deep genetic level, we're all Africans.

The first moves away from the nomadic hunter-gatherer way of life came between 14,000 BC and 9500 BC, when rainfall was high and the Sahara and North Africa became verdant. By 2500 BC the rains began to fail and the sandy barrier between North and West Africa became the Sahara we know today. People began to move southwest into the rainforests of Central Africa, most notably a group of people speaking the same family of languages. Known as the Bantu, the group's population grew as it discovered iron-smelting technology and developed new agricultural techniques. By 100 BC, Bantu peoples had reached East Africa; by AD 300 they were living in Southern Africa, and the age of the African empires had begun.

African Empires Through the Ages

Victorian missionaries liked to think they were bringing the beacon of 'civilisation' to the 'backward' Africa, but the truth is that Africans were

TIMELINE

200,000 years ago

The first 'humans' *(Homo sapiens)* begin to definitively diverge from other similar species (such as *Homo erectus*, which persists for millennia), marking Africa as the birthplace of humanity.

From 5000 BC

The Sahara begins the millennia-long process of becoming a desert. The drying climate prompts people to settle around waterholes, to rely on agriculture and to move south.

DOUG PEARSON / GETTY IMAGES ©

Camel driver, Sahara

developing various commercial empires and complex urban societies while Europeans were still running after wildlife with clubs.

Pyramids of Power

Arguably the greatest of the African empires was the first: ancient Egypt. Formed through an amalgamation of already organised states in the Nile Delta around 3100 BC, Egypt achieved an amazing degree of cultural and social sophistication. The Pharaohs, kings imbued with the power of gods, sat at the top of a highly stratified social hierarchy. The annual flooding of the Nile kept the lands of the Pharaohs fertile and fed their legions of slaves and artisans, who in turn worked to produce some of the most amazing public buildings ever constructed. Many of these, like the Pyramids of Giza, are still standing today. Ancient Egypt was eventually overrun by the Nubian Empire, then by the Assyrians, Persians, Alexander the Great and finally the Romans.

Phoenician & Roman North Africa

Established in Tunisia by the Phoenicians (seafaring people with their origins in Tyre in what is now Lebanon) the city-state of Carthage filled the power vacuum left by the decline of ancient Egypt. By the 6th century BC, Carthage was an empire in its own right and controlled much of the Mediterranean sea trade. Back on land, scholars were busy inventing the Phoenician alphabet, from which Greek, Hebrew and Latin are all thought to derive. It all came to an abrupt end with the arrival of the Romans, who razed Carthage and enslaved its population in 146 BC.

The Romans built some of Africa's most beautiful ancient cities in what are now Libya, Algeria and Morocco, and African-born Septimius Severus (r AD 193–211), went on to become Emperor of Rome. But the Romans, like the Carthaginians before them and the Byzantines who came after, had their control over Africa effectively restricted to the Mediterranean coastal strip. This was swept away by the Arabs who arrived in North Africa, bearing Islam, around AD 670.

The Kingdom of Sheba

Aksum was the first truly African indigenous state – no conquerors from elsewhere arrived to start this legendary kingdom, which controlled much of Sudan and southern Arabia at the height of its powers between AD 100 and 940. Aksum's heart was the hilly, fertile landscape of northern Ethiopia. The Aksumites traded with Egypt, the eastern Mediterranean and Arabia, developed a written language, produced gold coins and built imposing stone buildings. In the 4th century AD, the Aksumite king converted to Christianity, founding the Ethiopian Orthodox church.

3100 BC

Lower Egypt in the Nile's Delta, and Upper Egypt, upstream of the Delta, are unified under Pharaoh Menes. Over the next 3000 years a great African civilization flourishes.

146 BC

The city-state of Carthage (in modern-day Tunisia) is destroyed by the Romans. Its people are sold into slavery and the site is symbolically sprinkled with salt and damned forever.

100 BC

The Bantu people arrive in East Africa from the west and northwest. By the 11th century they had reached Southern Africa.

4th century AD

Christianity is embraced by the East African kingdom of Aksum (in present-day Ethiopia). Three centuries later the trading empire is isolated by the rise of Arabs and Islam in Arabia.

Legend has it that Ethiopia was the home of the fabled Queen of Sheba and the last resting place of the mysterious Ark of the Covenant.

Swahili Sultans

As early as the 7th century AD, the coastal areas of modern-day Tanzania, Kenya and Mozambique were home to a chain of vibrant, well-organised city-states, whose inhabitants lived in stone houses, wore fine silks and decorated their gravestones with artisanal ceramics and glass. Merchants from as far afield as China and India came to the East African coast, then set off again, their holds groaning with trade goods, spices, slaves and exotic beasts. The rulers of these city-states were the Swahili sultans – kings and queens who kept a hold on their domains via their control over magical objects and knowledge of secret religious ceremonies. The Swahili sultans were eventually defeated by Portuguese and Omani conquerors, but the rich cultural melting pot they presided over gave rise to the Swahili language, a fusion of African, Arabic and Portuguese words that still thrives.

Golden Kingdoms

The area centred on present-day Mali was home to a hugely wealthy series of West African empires that flourished over the course of more than 800 years. The Empire of Ghana lasted from the 4th to 11th centuries, and was followed by the fabulously wealthy Empire of Mali (around AD 1250 to 1500), which once stretched all the way from the coast of Senegal to Niger.

The Songhaï Empire (AD 1000–1591), with its capital at Gao in modern-day Mali, was the last of Africa's golden empires, which, at their peak covered areas larger than Western Europe. Their wealth was founded on the salt from Saharan mines, which was traded ounce for ounce with West African gold. Organised systems of government and Islamic centres of scholarship – the most famous of which was Timbuktu – flourished in the kingdoms of West Africa, but conversely, it was Islam that led to their downfall when the forces of Morocco invaded in 1591.

PRECOLONIAL

Respected African-American scholar Henry Louis Gates Jr has spent a lifetime refuting perceptions of Africa's precolonial backwardness. The result is the compelling *Wonders of the African World* (1999).

The Age of the Explorers

By the 15th century, with gold and tales of limitless wealth making their way across the Sahara and Mediterranean, European royalty became obsessed with Africa.

The Portuguese were first off the block, building a fortified trading post, the earliest European structure in sub-Saharan Africa, along today's Ghanaian coast. By the end of the century their ships had rounded Southern Africa. In the early 16th century, French, British and Dutch ships had joined the Portuguese along the coast, building forts as they

670

Islam sweeps across North Africa, where it remains the dominant religion today. A century later the religion had spread down the East African coast.

8th century

In search of spices, Arabic, Indian, Persian and Chinese merchants begin arriving along what is now the Kenyan coast. The Swahili trading centres of East Africa start to prosper.

9th century

Islam reaches the Sahel via trans-Saharan camel caravans, almost 250 years after it swept across North Africa; it would later become the predominant religion of West Africa.

Around AD 1000

The city of Timbuktu is founded as a seasonal encampment for Tuareg nomads; by the 15th century it had become a centre of Islamic scholarship and home to 100,000 people.

THE CONTINUING IMPACT OF SLAVERY

One of the least thoroughly digested of Africa's many traumas was the slave trade. What is striking is how deep in the continent's subconscious this terrible episode has been buried. Some academics estimate that, had it not been for the slave trade, Africa's mid-19th-century population would have been double its 25 million figure. Yet, with the exception of the Swahili coast's old markets, Ghana's castles and Senegal's Goree Island, one rarely stumbles upon its traces.

The complicity of African rulers of the day may explain a reluctance to engage with the issue. As Senegalese president Abdoulaye Wade, whose ancestors were slave owners, told African delegates campaigning for reparations: 'If one can claim reparations for slavery, the slaves of my ancestors or their descendants can also claim money from me.' The other complicating factor may be awareness of the time it took many African states to outlaw slavery – Emperor Haile Selassie of Ethiopia for example, only set about it in the 1920s – and embarrassment at the knowledge that it still quietly persists in countries such as Sudan, Mauritania and Niger.

went. But unlike the Carthaginians and Romans, the European powers were never content with mere coastal footholds.

Victorian heroes such as Richard Burton and John Speke captured the public imagination with their hair-raising tales from the East African interior, while Mungo Park and the formidable Mary Wesley battled their way through fever-ridden swamps, and avoided charging animals while 'discovering' various parts of West Africa.

The European Slave Trade

There has always been slavery in Africa (slaves were common by-products of intertribal warfare, and the Arabs and Shirazis who dominated the East African coast took slaves by the thousands). But the slave trade took on a whole new dimension after the European arrival. The Portuguese in West Africa, the Dutch in South Africa and other Europeans who came after them saw how African slavery worked and, with one eye on their huge American sugar plantations, saw the potential for slavery to fuel agricultural production. They were helped by opportunistic African leaders who used slavery and other trade with Europeans as a means to expand their own power.

The extravagant, gold-laden pilgrimage to Mecca by Mali's King Kankan Musa in AD 1324 is often credited with sparking Europe's interest in Africa and its riches.

Exact figures are impossible to establish, but from the end of the 15th century until around 1870, when the slave trade was fully abolished, up to 20 million Africans were enslaved. Perhaps half died en route to the Americas; millions of others perished in slaving raids. The trans-Atlantic slave trade gave European powers a huge economic boost, while the loss

1137–1270

Ethiopia's Zaghwe dynasty builds Lalibela's rock-hewn churches. The dynasty was overthrown by Yekuno Amlak, a self-professed descendant of King Solomon and the Queen of Sheba.

1498

Portuguese explorer Vasco da Gama lands at Mozambique Island. Over the next 200 years, the Portuguese establish trading enclaves along the coast and several settlements in the interior.

1650s

The Dutch East India Company sets up a permanent supply station at Cape Town and the French set up a permanent trading post at Saint-Louis in modern Senegal.

1869

Opening of the Suez Canal. Discovery of the world's largest diamond deposits in Kimberley and gold in the Transvaal around the same time helps keep Cape Town as Africa's premier port.

of farmers and tradespeople, as well as the general chaos, made Africa an easy target for colonialism.

The slave trade was not all in one direction; slaves were also brought to Africa from Asia, in particular by the Dutch in South Africa.

To understand the horrors of the European slave trade and its ultimate abolition, look no further than Adam Hochschild's definitive 2006 book, *Bury the Chains*.

Colonial Africa

Throughout the 19th century, the region-by-region conquest of the continent by European powers gathered pace and became known as the 'Scramble for Africa'. This was formalised at the Berlin Conference of 1884–5, when Europe's governments divided Africa between them. That Africans had no say in the matter, and that Europeans had never set foot in many of the territories claimed, scarcely seemed to register. France and Britain got the biggest swathes, with Germany, Portugal, Italy, Spain and Belgium picking up the rest. The resulting boundaries, determined more by colonial expediency than the complex realities on the ground, remain largely in place today.

Forced labour, heavy taxation, and vengeful violence for any insurrection were all commonplace in colonial Africa. African territories were essentially organised to extract cheap cash crops and natural resources for use by the colonial powers. To facilitate easy administration, tribal differences and rivalries were exploited to the full, and industrial development, social welfare and education were rarely policy priorities. The effects of the colonial years, which in some cases only ended a few decades ago, continue to leave their mark on the continent.

Africa for the Africans

When Ethiopian rebel forces rolled into Addis Ababa in 1991 they were navigating with photocopies of the Addis Ababa map found in Lonely Planet's *Africa on a Shoestring!*

African independence movements existed throughout the colonial period, but organised political resistance gained momentum in the 1950s and '60s. Soldiers who had fought in both world wars on behalf of their colonial masters joined forces with African intellectuals who had gained their education through missionary schools and universities; their catchcry became 'Africa for the Africans'.

Many African countries became independent in the 1960s – some peacefully, others only after years of bloodshed and struggle. The Organisation of African Unity was established with 32 members in 1963 to promote solidarity and act as a collective voice for the continent. By the 1970s most African countries had become masters of their own destinies, at least on paper.

It is impossible to overstate the euphoria that gripped Africa in the postindependence period. The speeches of bright young leaders like Kwame Nkrumah (Ghana), Jomo Kenyatta (Kenya) and Patrice Lumumba (Congo) had Africans across the continent dreaming of a new African dawn. For the most part, they were disappointed. Most African countries were woefully unprepared for independence, ruled over by an ill-equipped political class. The situation worsened when fledgling African nations be-

1884–5

The Berlin Conference gives France almost one-third of the continent (mostly in West and Central Africa), while Britain gets Ghana, Nigeria and much of Southern and East Africa.

1931

Apart from Liberia (which became independent in 1847) and Ethiopia (which was never colonised save for an Italian occupation during WWII), South Africa becomes Africa's first independent country.

1960

Seventeen African countries gain independence from European colonial rule. Most are former French colonies, but include Congo (from Belgium), Somalia (from Italy and Britain) and Nigeria (from Britain).

1975

End of Portuguese rule in Angola and Mozambique; both countries align themselves with the Soviet Union, intensifying the Cold War between the superpowers on the continent.

CHINA IN AFRICA

Despite there being an American president with a Kenyan father and expectations that the US will source a quarter of its oil from Africa by 2015, Africa's bond with the US is arguably not the one that matters. The key relationship is becoming one with China, an economic behemoth hungry for Africa's minerals, oils and timbers.

Chinese trade with Africa dates back to the 15th century when Admiral Zheng He's fleet arrived on the continent's east coast. Some 60,000 Chinese joined the South African gold rush at the end of the 19th century, while Chairman Mao sent tens of thousands more workers to assist with the glorious revolutions planned across the continent in the 1960s and '70s. In recent decades, though, the scale of Chinese economic involvement in Africa has gone off the scale. Today, more than 900 Chinese companies operate on African soil and nearly a million Chinese live on the continent.

Beijing's readiness to provide much-needed infrastructure, which Western aid doesn't cover and local governments cannot afford, is already having a transformative impact. Such largesse holds out the potential of a Pax Sinica, as African nation states are finally linked together by modern infrastructure. Others warn that Beijing's relationship with Africa often bears a depressing resemblance to those of the colonial era, despite all the talk of fresh paradigms. It's a complex topic: for analysis and thoughts beyond the headlines read the blog China in Africa (www.chinaafricarealstory.com) by Professor Deborah Brautigam, author of *The Dragon's Gift: the Real Story of China in Africa*.

came pawns in the Cold War machinations of the US and USSR, and factors such as drought, economic collapse and ethnic resentment led many to spiral down into a mire of corruption, violence and civil war.

21st-Century Africa

The first decade in the 21st century is holding out hope for the continent. The Human Security Report Project (www.hsrgroup.org) found that between 1999 and 2006 the number of state-based armed conflicts dropped by 46%, while those between rebel groups fell by 54%. The annual number of deaths in battle actually diminished by two-thirds between 2002 and 2006.

Oil discoveries and lessening conflict resulted in more than 30 African countries growing economically at a rate of 4% or more in 2006 and 2007. Also in 2007, the G8 countries pledged $25 billion aid for Africa and promised to eliminate the outstanding debts of the poorest countries. However, by the end of the decade, shrinking remittances from the diaspora, cuts in exports and falls in tourism earnings had taken a measurable toll. Above all, the global economic crisis threatens to dry up the generosity of industrialised nations.

Zambian economist Dambisa Moyo's book *Dead Aid* (2009) denounced Western aid to Africa as patronising and counterproductive. Her view counters that of US economist Jeffrey Sachs, who has argued strongly for the role of aid in raising many African countries out of poverty.

1990

Nelson Mandela is released after almost three decades in prison. Four years later he is voted South Africa's president after multiracial elections.

2001

The African Union is established as successor to the Organisation of African Unity. All 54 African nations, except Morocco, are members; its secretariat is based in Addis Ababa.

CHRIS PAYLE / GETTY IMAGES ©

➡ Nelson Mandela

2011

The 'Arab Spring' series of popular uprisings sees long-time leaders Zine el-Abidine Ben Ali in Tunisia, Hosni Mubarak in Egypt and Colonel Muammar Qaddafi in Libya ousted from power.

The Culture

An estimated one billion people live in Africa, speaking well over 2000 different languages. Together, they make up the most culturally and ethnically diverse group of people on the planet. Many parts of Africa are also home to significant Asian, European and Middle Eastern populations.

For an exhaustive list of UN socio-economic data (ranging from literacy and life expectancy to income and infant mortality) for African countries, visit the website of the UN Development Programme (http://hdr.undp.org/en/countries).

Such is the continent's diversity that it is difficult to speak of Africa as a whole without descending into meaningless generalisations. Life for a villager in remote Central African Republic has little to do with the daily experience of an affluent Moroccan in Casablanca; the latter's daily life will likely have far more in common with that of Europeans than with most of his or her fellow Africans.

That said, for the overwhelming majority of African societies, life has changed beyond recognition in the last 100 years. Colonialism, globalisation, technological advances and foreign influences have all been factors in this social revolution.

Urbanisation

The key change in African daily life, however, has been the move to the cities. By some estimates, Africa's rate of urbanisation is the fastest in the world and the population of urban centres is growing at twice the rate of rural areas. At the beginning of the 20th century, around 5% of Africans lived in cities. Now, over a third of the continent's one billion population is urbanised with the figure set to rise to over half by 2030 according to a UN report in 2010.

The reasons for this epochal demographic shift are legion: growing populations due to improved health care, environmental degradation leading to shrinking grazing and agricultural land, and poor rural infrastructure are among the most important.

Unfortunately, urban population growth has far outpaced job creation; unemployment in many African cities is rife. One UN study found that in 38 African countries more than 50% of the urban population lives in slums. At the same time, many African cities have a growing and increasingly influential and sophisticated middle class.

Thanks to urbanisation, a whole generation of Africans is growing up with no connection to the countryside and its lores and traditions, and in many cases urbanisation has led to the breakdown of traditional social values such as respect for elders, and the loosening of family structures. Urbanisation has also caused critical labour shortages in rural areas, and has accelerated the spread of HIV.

In spite of these daunting challenges, rural life remains a pillar of African society, a place where the continent's historical memory survives. Family bonds are still much stronger than in many First World societies, with the concepts of community and shared responsibility deeply rooted.

WHY AFRICA SUFFERS FROM AIDS

In November 2012, Unaid's annual report headlined some very welcome news: between 2005 and 2011 the number of people dying from AIDS-related causes in sub-Saharan Africa had dropped from 18 million to 1.2 million. The number of new HIV infections had also dipped dramatically by 25% over the previous decade to a total of 1.8 million in 2011. That's the good news. The fact is that sub-Saharan Africa still has 23.5 million people living with HIV, or 69% of the global total.

There are many reasons why HIV/AIDS has taken such a hold in Africa. Collective denial of the problem, migration in search of work and to escape wars and famine, a general lack of adequate health care and prevention programs, and social and cultural factors – in particular the low status of women in many African societies – are all believed to have played a role in the rapid spread of the disease.

The personal, social and economic costs associated with the disease are devastating. HIV/AIDS predominantly hits the most productive members of society – young adults. This has a huge impact on family income, food production and local economies in general, and large parts of Africa face the loss of a significant proportion of entire generations. Employers, schools, factories and hospitals have to train other staff to replace those at the workplace who become too ill to work, setting economic and social development back by decades. The numbers of HIV/AIDS orphans (the UN estimates 11 million, with one in four Zambian children said to be without both parents) is at once an enduring human tragedy and a massive societal problem.

Antiretroviral drug treatments, available in the West to increase the life span of AIDS sufferers and reduce the risk of HIV-infected women passing the infection on to their unborn babies, are still out of the reach of most Africans; according to the World Health Organization (WHO), Brazil has managed to halve AIDS deaths by making such drugs free. Although things are improving, fewer than two out of every 10 Africans who need antiretroviral treatment are receiving it.

For all its international prominence, HIV/AIDS is by no means Africa's only killer: WHO reports that malaria kills an African child every minute with the Democratic Republic of Congo and Nigeria accounting for 40% of the worldwide total of deaths from the infection.

These values retain a deep hold over many Africans, even those who long ago left for the cities.

Sport

Football

Football (soccer) is the most popular of Africa's sports, and you'll never have to go far before you find someone kicking a ball (or a bundle of plastic bags tied together with string) around on a dusty patch of ground.

West African and North African countries are Africa's footballing powerhouses. Ever since Cameroon stormed to the quarter finals of the 1990 World Cup finals in Italy, West Africa has been touted as an emerging world power in the sport. Cameroon built on its success by winning the football gold medal at the 2000 Sydney Olympics. But apart from Senegal reaching the World Cup quarter finals in 2002, and Ghana's team winning the 2009 U-20 World Cup in Cairo, further success has proved elusive.

At the 2010 World Cup in South Africa, the host team was knocked out in the first round; of the other five African nations in the tournament only Ghana made it beyond round one into the quarter finals.

The African Cup of Nations also stirs great passions across the continent. Almost two years of qualifying rounds culminate in the 16 best teams playing for the crown of Africa's champions. North African sides (Tunisia in 2004, and Egypt in 2006, 2008 and 2010) have dominated the event in recent years, but in 2012 Zambia took the trophy. In January

2013 the tournament switched to being held every odd numbered year so as not to clash with the World Cup.

But the success or otherwise of national teams is only part of the story. West African footballers in particular have enjoyed phenomenal success in European leagues, in the process becoming the focal point for the aspirations of a generation of West African youngsters dreaming of becoming the next Samuel Eto'o (Cameroon and Anzhi Makhachkala, and currently one of the world's highest paid players), Didier Drogba (Côte d'Ivoire, Chelsea and since 2012 Shanghai Shenhua) or Emmanuel Adebayor (Togo and Tottenham Hotspur). And it's not just the kids: every weekend from September to May, Africans crowd around communal TV sets to follow the fortunes of teams in Spain, Italy, the UK and France, especially those games involving African players. There is a sense that the success of Africans in Europe is something in which they can all share with pride, something which reflects well on the continent as a whole.

Other Sports

Other popular sports in Africa include marathon running (at which Kenya and Ethiopia dominate the world) and boxing. Basketball is becoming increasingly popular with the arrival of American TV channels. In South Africa rugby is massively popular and had benefited from development programs across the colour divide. South African fans adore their beloved 'Boks', ranked third in the world after New Zealand and Australia after the Rugby World Cup in 2011. Cricket is also widely played, particularly in Southern Africa.

INTERNET ACCESS

In March 2011, Google's charitable foundation awarded five grants totalling US$5 million to African projects in support of improving internet access and to enable African countries to participate in and contribute to the global internet.

Media

Although no one doubts the potential of mass media such as newspapers, radio stations or TV to be a tool for development in Africa, the media industry on the continent is beset by many problems. Access is one, as many people still live in rural areas, with little or no infrastructure. Many corrupt governments also ruthlessly suppress all but state-controlled media.

A good barometer of press freedom in the region is to be found in the annual Press Freedom Index compiled by Reporters Without Borders (www.rsf.org), which ranks 179 countries according to the freedoms enjoyed by the independent media. In 2011–12, Eritrea came in last, while Sudan (170th), Egypt (166th), Somalia (164th) and Equatorial Guinea also fared badly. Cape Verde (9th), Namibia (joint 20th with Belgium) and Mali (25th) all performed well – and above both the UK (28th) and Australia (30th).

At the same time, many Africans feel that much reporting on the continent by the international media paints an unfair portrait of Africa as a hopeless case, beset by war, famine and corruption.

Internet

In 2012, Internet World Stats reported that Africa has around 167 million internet users (or 15.6% of the population, less than half the global average). The real figures, however, are probably considerably higher, as many Africans get online via shared PCs in internet cafes or schools.

Africans are now using the internet to bypass the often unreliable reporting of the state-funded media, while groups such as rural women, who have in the past been denied access to information on health care and human rights, are empowered by their access to online education resources. Many such grass-roots cyber-education projects are still in their infancy, but exciting times are ahead.

The power of the internet, in particular social media, came strongly to the fore in the Arab Spring uprisings across North Africa. Some repressive African governments have since taken precautionary measures to further censor and control internet usage; in May 2012, Ethiopia passed a law making it illegal to use Skype and other voice over internet protocols, punishable by up to 15 years in jail.

Newspapers & Magazines

Unesco reports that 38% of African adults are illiterate, a fact which severely limits the usefulness of print media as an information tool across the continent. This said, there is no shortage of newspapers and current-affairs mags available, including the monthly *New African* (www.newafricanmagazine.com) and *Africa Today* (www.africatoday.com).

The *East African* (www.theeastafrican.co.ke) is good for an overview of what's happening in Kenya, Tanzania and Uganda. South Africa's weekly newspaper the *Mail & Guardian* (http://mg.co.za) is highly respected and has a good selection of features on the continent. If you're in West Africa and your French is well oiled, *Jeune Afrique* (www.jeuneafrique.com) is a highly regarded weekly news magazine.

For links to a range of websites and local newspapers for most countries in Africa, as well as a handful of pan-African sites, head to www.world-newspapers.com/africa.

Radio

Radio remains by far the most popular medium of communication in Africa, with even the most remote rural villagers gathering around a crackling radio to listen to the latest news and music. Innovative projects such as the charity Farm Radio International (www.farmradio.org) supports rural radio broadcasters in 39 African countries.

For continental coverage, however, locals and travellers tune into international broadcasters; most have dedicated Africa slots. As well as the trusty BBC World Service (www.bbc.co.uk/worldservice), Voice of America (www.voanews.com) and Radio France Internationale (www.rfi.fr) are perennial favourites. If you'd rather hear African news from Africans, try Channel Africa (www.channelafrica.co.za), the international radio service of the South African Broadcasting Corporation.

TV

TV ownership in Africa is much lower than elsewhere in the world and televisions mostly remain luxury items, unavailable to most of Africa's poorer inhabitants. Walk around many African towns and villages after dark, however, and you're likely to come across the dim blue glow of a TV set, often set in a doorway so that an audience of 20 or 30 can gather around it to watch the latest episode of a local soap or a football match.

A sign of some African nations' growing affluence is that in January 2013, Digital TV Research reported that about 14 million homes in sub-Saharan Africa receive digital TV. They also forecast that digital TV penetration across this area of Africa will rocket to 95.5% by 2018 – with household numbers quadrupling to 49.0 million.

Religion

Most Africans are deeply religious, with religious values informing every aspect of their daily life. Generally speaking, a majority of the population in North Africa, West and Central Africa close to the Sahara, together with much of the East African coast, is Islamic; East and southern Africa, and the rest of the continent, is predominantly Christian.

Accurate figures are hard to come by, but roughly 40% of Africans are Muslim and 40% Christian (including a burgeoning evangelical Christian movement), leaving around 20% who follow traditional African beliefs. These figures should be taken with a pinch of salt, however, as

News Websites

AllAfrica.com (allafrica.com)

A24 (www.a24media.com)

Reuters Africa (www.reuters.com/places/africa)

Afrol News (www.afrol.com)

BBC (www.bbc.co.uk/news/world/africa)

IRINNews (www.irinnews.org/IRIN-Africa.aspx)

West Africa News (www.westafricanews.com)

Media Foundation for West Africa (www.mediafound.org)

To find out how to listen to the BBC World Service in Africa, visit www.bbc.co.uk/worldservice/programmeguide and type in the country where you are. In most countries you'll be given a range of locations from which to choose.

RELIGION AFRICAN-STYLE

Africa's traditional religions are generally animist, believing that objects such as trees, caves or ritual objects such as gourds or drums are endowed with spiritual powers. Thus a certain natural object may be sacred because it represents, is home to, or simply *is* a spirit or deity. Several traditional religions accept the existence of a supreme being or creator, alongside spirits and deities.

Most African religions centre on ancestor veneration, the idea that the dead remain influential after passing from the physical into the spiritual world. Ancestors must therefore be honoured in order to ensure that they intervene positively with other spiritual beings on behalf of their relatives on earth.

The practice of traditional medicine is closely intertwined with traditional religion. Practitioners (often derogatorily referred to as 'witch doctors' by foreigners) use divining implements such as bones, prayers, chanting and dance to facilitate communication with the spirit world. Patients are cured with the use of herbal preparations or by exorcist-style interventions to drive out evil spirits that have inhabited the body. Not all magical practitioners are benign – some are suspected of being paid to place curses on people, causing bad luck, sickness or even death.

Although traditional religious practices can be a force for social good within a community, and herbalists are often very skilled in their craft, there's a flip side: some religious practitioners discourage their patients from seeking conventional medical help at hospitals or clinics, and someone who considers themselves cursed will very often give up the will to live entirely. In some parts of Southern and East Africa, killings occasionally take place, in which children or adults are abducted and murdered in order to gain body parts for use in magic rituals. Albinos in Tanzania and Burundi have come under particular threat in recent years.

many Africans see no contradiction at all in combining their traditional beliefs with Islam or Christianity.

Hindus and Sikhs are found in places where immigrants arrived from Asia during the colonial era, particularly in East African countries such as Kenya, Tanzania and Uganda. Jewish communities, some centuries old, are found mainly in North and Southern Africa.

Women in Africa

Women form the bedrock of African society, especially in rural areas where they bear the burden of child-rearing and most agricultural work. Their task is made more difficult by the HIV/AIDS epidemic and the absence of men who move to the cities as migrant industrial workers.

Moolade, the powerful 2004 film by the Senegalese director Ousmane Sembène, is one of the few mass-release artistic endeavours to tackle head-on the taboo issue of female genital mutilation.

In some countries sexual equality is enshrined in law. African women made history in 2005 when a legal protocol came into force that specifically protects women's human rights in the 17 countries that ratified it. These countries have pledged to amend their laws to uphold a raft of women's rights, including the right to property after divorce, the right to abortions after rape or abuse, and the right to equal pay in the workplace, among many others.

The reality is, however, somewhat different, and in many places women are treated as second-class citizens. Families sometimes deny girls schooling, although education is valued highly by most Africans. More serious still are reports of female infanticide, forced marriages, female genital mutilation and honour killings.

Female genital mutilation (FGM), often euphemistically termed 'female circumcision' or 'genital alteration', is widely practised in West and North Africa. The term covers a wide range of procedures, from a small, mainly symbolic, cut, to sewing up a girl's vagina to leave just a tiny hole or the total removal of the external genitalia (known as infibulation).

Although outsiders often believe that FGM is associated with Islam, it actually predates the religion and has far more to do with longstanding cultural traditions than religious doctrine. The World Health Organization estimates that three million African girls are at risk from the procedure annually. In Egypt, Sudan, Somalia, Ethiopia and Mali, around 95% of young girls undergo FGM.

Arts

Traditional African art and craft consist of ceremonial masks, figures related to ancestral worship, fetishes (which protect against certain spirits), weapons, furnishings and everyday utensils. All kinds of materials are used (including bronze casting in some regions) and great skill can also be seen in the production of textiles, basketry and leatherwork. Contemporary African artists often use traditional as well as modern media to express themselves, with many now making an impact on the international art scene. Nowhere is this more evident than with African music.

Gogo Mama: A Journey into the Lives of Twelve African Women, by Sally Sara, includes illuminating chapters on a Liberian former child soldier, a Zanzibari diva, and a HIV/AIDS-fighting grandmother in South Africa.

Traditional Decorative Arts & Crafts

The creation of many African arts and crafts is often the preserve of distinct castes of blacksmiths and weavers who rely almost exclusively on locally found or produced materials. Tourism has, however, greatly affected African art and craft, with considerable effort now going into producing objects for sale rather than traditional use. Some art forms, such as the Tingatinga paintings of Tanzania, evolved entirely out of demand from tourists. Although it causes a departure from art's role in traditional society, tourism can ensure artisans remain employed in their

FEMALE GENITAL MUTILATION – AN INTERVIEW

In January 2009, Lonely Planet author Anthony Ham interviewed Menidiou Kodio who, along with his wife Maryam Dougnon, works in Mali's Dogon Country to end the practice of female genital mutilation.

What proportion of young girls undergo female genital mutilation (FGM)? In some traditional Dogon villages, it is every girl.

What made you start this work? We do it because we have six daughters.

Do you meet much resistance when trying to stop the practice? It is very difficult to convert people, so when I visit a village I organise a free concert and the lyrics of the songs speak against FGM, and then I make a speech. I tell people that I respect traditional culture, but that not everything in tradition is good. As one of my songs says, 'You don't have to listen to everything that the Ana Sara [Europeans] say and you shouldn't change all of your traditions for them. But in this case, we should listen to them.'

What reasons do you give for stopping the practice? First we explain to them that their daughters run a very high risk of contracting HIV, because the knife use[d] in some places is 40 years old. Tetanus is another risk. Then we tell them that it is a very risky procedure and that if the girls lose too much blood, they can die. We also tell them that childbirth is more difficult for a woman who has been cut. And finally we tell them that they are cutting the bodies of their daughters, the bodies that God gave to them.

And do people listen? Many people don't. Many men also still believe that it is bad to marry a woman who has not been cut, because they worry that the woman will be stronger than him. But some people are starting to listen and some villages have promised to stop the practice. The truth is, we won't know whether they have kept their promise until 15 years from now, when these girls start to have children.

What will it take for this practice to end? FGM will continue until all the old people, especially the old women, have died.

traditional professions, and many pieces retain their power precisely because they still carry meaning for Africa's peoples.

West Africa has arguably Africa's most extraordinary artistic tradition. The mask traditions of Côte d'Ivoire, Mali and elsewhere are world famous, and Picasso, Matisse and others found inspiration in its radical approach to the human form. Nigeria and Benin have long been associated with fine bronze sculptures and carvings, and the Ashanti people of Ghana are renowned for fine textiles and gold sculptures. In Central Africa, Congo is another renowned centre for masks and sculpture.

In North Africa, ancient Arabic and Islamic traditions have produced some beautiful artworks (ceramics and carpets are particularly refined), as well as some phenomenal architecture; in the Sahara, Tuareg silver jewellery is unique and beautiful.

Throughout East and Southern Africa the Makonde people of Mozambique and the Shona of Zimbabwe produce excellent and widely copied sculptures.

Modern & Contemporary Arts

The art world has its eye on Africa. In March 2011 a painting by South African artist Irma Stern (1894–1966) sold for US$4.94 million at auction in London. Some contemporary African artists such as Ghanaian sculptor El Anatsui, Kenyan ceramicist Magdalene Odunodo and Nigerian sculptor Ben Enwonwu are also securing six-figure sums at auction for their works.

The African Arts Trust (www.theafricanartstrust.org) was set up in 2011 to enable artists initially in Bostwana, Ethiopia, Kenya, Malawi, Mozambique, Uganda, Tanzania, Zambia and Zimbabwe to buy materials, create works, travel and study.

In recent years, recycled art has become popular, with artists from South Africa to West Africa producing sculpture and textiles created entirely from discarded objects such as tin cans and bottle tops.

ART SCENE

There's a thriving art scene in South Africa – read more about it about it at the website Artthrob (www.artthrob.co.za) and the magazine *ArtSouthAfrica* (www.artsouthafrica.com).

Literature

Sub-Saharan Africa's rich, multilayered literary history was almost entirely oral. Folk tales, poems, proverbs, myths, historical tales and (most importantly) ethnic traditions were passed down through generations by word of mouth. Some societies have specific keepers of history and storytelling, such as the *griots* of West Africa, and in many cases stories are sung or tales performed in a form of theatre. As a result, little of Africa's rich literary history was known to the outside world until relatively recently.

Twentieth and 21st century African literature has been greatly influenced by colonial education and Western trends. Some African authors have nonetheless made an effort to employ traditional structures and folk tales in their work; others write of the contemporary hardships faced by Africans and their fight to shake off the shackles of colonialism, using Western-influenced narrative methods (and penning their works in English, French or Portuguese).

Nigerian authors are prominent on the English-speaking African literature scene and some, like Amos Tutuola, adapt African folklore into their own works. Penned by Tutuola, *The Palm-Wine Drunkard* is a rather grisly tale of a man who enters the spirit world in order to find his palm-wine supplier! Dylan Thomas described the novel as 'brief, thronged, grisly and bewitching' and a 'nightmare of indescribable adventures'.

In March 2013 Chinua Achebe, hailed by Nobel Laureate Nadine Gordimer as 'the father of African Literature', died. His most famous novel is *Things Fall Apart* is a deeply symbolic tale about a man's rise and fall at the time colonialism arrived in Africa. Another Nigerian writer,

CONTEMPORARY NOVELS BY AFRICAN WRITERS

- *The Memory of Love* by Aminatta Forna (2010) is a tragic love story set in Freetown in 1969 and the present day that captures the horror of the conflict that engulfed Sierra Leone.
- *Zoo City* by South African writer Lauren Beukes (2010) is a dystopian fantasy thriller set in a near-future Johannesburg that won the 2011 Arthur C Clarke award.
- *Lyrics Alley* by Leila Aboulela (2010) is set in mid-1950s northern Sudan, Egypt and the UK and examines the clash between traditional and modern cultures in a time of political upheaval.
- *The Hairdresser of Harare* by Tendai Huchu (2010) is a sometimes comic novel about the daily realities of life in Zimbabwe and what it takes to run a hair salon.
- *Broken Glass* by Alain Mabanckou (2009) is a witty, culturally savvy novel set in a bar in the Congo where the narrator tells the stories of his fellow drinkers and himself.

Ben Okri, found worldwide fame with his novels *The Famished Road* and *Starbook*, which draw heavily on folk traditions.

South Africa has also produced many famous writers including Nobel Prize winners JM Coetzee and Nadine Gordimer, André Brink, Alan Paton and Man Booker–prize nominated Damon Galgut.

Cinema

Senegalese director Ousmane Sembène (1923–2007) is often called the 'father of African film'; his 1966 movie *La Noire de...* was the first movie released by a sub-Saharan African director. His final film *Moolade* won awards at Cannes and the premier African film festival FESPACO. Predating Sembène is Egyptian film-maker Youssef Chahine who made the musical melodrama *Cairo Station* in 1958.

Sarah Maldoror filmed *Sambizanga* in Congo in the early 1970s, although the movie is set in Angola. *Chronicle of the Year of Embers* won the coveted Palme d'Or at Cannes in 1975 for Algerian director Mohammed Lakhdar-Hamina. Mauritanian director Abderrahmane Sissako's *Waiting for Happiness* gained international attention in 2002.

The continent's most technically accomplished film makers gather in South Africa – local talent Neill Blomkamp's sci-fi thriller *District 10* was an international hit in 2009. Several major Hollywood productions have been shot at Cape Town Film Studios, including the Cape Town–set thriller *Safe House* (2012).

NOLLYWOOD

Nigeria's 'Nollywood' film industry is the second most prolific in the world (after India), pumping out up to 200 videos for the home market every month.

Food & Drink

Whether it's a group of Kenyans gathering in a *nyama choma* (barbecued meat) shop to consume hunks of grilled meat washed down with cold lager, or Ghanaians dipping balls of *fufu* (pounded yam or cassava with a dough-like consistency) into a steaming communal bowl of stew, there are two things all Africans have in common – they love to eat and it's almost always a social event. Folk tales and traditions from all over the continent feature stories about cooking and consuming food, a process that is the focus of almost all social and family activities. African food is generally bold and colourful, with its rich, earthy textures and strong, spicy undertones showing influences from Arab traders, European colonists and Asian slaves.

Staples & Specialities

Each region has its own key staples. In East and southern Africa, the base for many local meals is a stiff dough made from maize flour, called – among other things – *ugali, sadza, pap* and *nshima*. In West Africa millet

TASTES LIKE CHICKEN...

In many parts of Africa you'll find the locals chomping with gusto on some unusual foods. If you're brave in heart and stomach, why not try some of these more adventurous snacks:

Giant rat The agouti, a ratlike rodent about the size of a rabbit, frequently turns up in West African stews. Avoid this one though – it's under threat in the wild. Instead try a skewer of baby grasscutters (cane rats) roasted over coals and served up in West African markets.

Land snails Described as having a texture like 'stubborn rubber', giant land snails are eaten in parts of Nigeria.

Mopane worms These are actually not worms but caterpillars – the emperor moth's green and blue larvae, which make their home in the mopane trees of southern Africa. These protein-rich critters are boiled and then dried in the sun before being eaten.

is also common, and served in a similar way, while staples nearer the coast are root crops such as yam or cassava (*manioc* in French), served as a near-solid glob called *fufu*. In North Africa, bread forms a major part of the meal, while all over Africa rice is an alternative to the local specialities. In some countries, plantain (green banana) is also common, either fried, cooked solid or pounded into *fufu*. A sauce of meat, fish, beans or vegetables is then added to the carbo base. If you're eating local-style, you grab a portion of bread or dough or pancake (with your right hand, please!), dip it in the communal pot of sauce and sit back, beaming contentedly, to eat it.

Drinks

Tea and coffee are the standard drinks, and countries seem to follow the flavours of their former colonisers. In (formerly British) East Africa, tea and coffee tends to be weak, grey and milky. In much of (formerly French) West Africa, tea is usually served black, while the coffee from roadside stalls contains enough sugar and sweetened condensed milk to keep you fully charged for hours. In North Africa and some Sahel countries (the Sahel is a semi-arid region, which stretches from Mauritania, Gambia and Senegal to Chad), mint tea and strong Arab-style coffee are the local hot beverages of choice. Other variations include chai or coffee spiced up with lemongrass or cardamom in East Africa, or flavoured with a woody leaf called *kinkiliba* in West Africa.

International soft drinks are widely available, while many countries have their own brands that are cheaper and just as good (although often owned by the big multinationals, too). You can also get locally made soft drinks and fruit juices, sold in plastic bags, or frozen into 'ice-sticks', but avoid these if you're worried about your stomach, as the water they're made from is usually unpurified. Alcohol allegedly kills the bugs...

In bars, you can buy local or imported beer in bottles. Excellent wines and liqueurs, from South Africa or further afield, may be available in more upmarket establishments. Traditional beer is made from millet or maize, and drunk from huge communal pots with great ceremony at special events, and with less pomp in everyday situations.

West Africa's most popular brew is palm wine. The tree is tapped and the sap comes out mildly fermented. In other parts of the continent, alcohol is made using bananas, pineapples or other fruit, sometimes fermented overnight. This homemade alcohol is often outrageously strong, can lead to blindness or mental illness, and is often illegal in some places. You have been warned!

Habits & Customs

In Islamic countries, food is always eaten, passed and touched with the right hand only (the left hand is reserved for washing your bottom, and the two are understandably kept separate). Water in a basin is usually brought to wash your hands before you start eating – hold your hands out and allow the person who brings it to pour it over, then shake your hands dry. It's also customary in some parts of Africa for women and men to eat separately, with the women eating second after they've served the food. In some countries, lunch, rather than dinner, is the main meal of the day, and everything stops for a couple of hours while a hot meal is cooked and prepared.

Where to Eat & Drink

Food Stalls & Street Food

Most African towns have a shacklike stall or 10 serving up cheap local staples. Furniture is usually limited to a rough bench and a couple of upturned boxes, and hygiene is rarely a prime concern. However, this is the place to save money and meet the locals. Seek out these no-frills joints at bus stations or markets. Lighter snacks include nuts sold in twists of newspaper, hardboiled eggs (popular for long bus journeys), meat kebabs, or, in some places, more exotic fare like fried caterpillars or baobab fruits. Street food rarely involves plates or knives – it's served on a stick, wrapped in paper, or in a plastic bag.

African Cookbooks

The Africa Cookbook: Tastes of a Continent, Jessica Harris

A Flavour of West Africa (Festivals & Food), Ali Brownlie Bojang

The African Kitchen, Josie Stow and Jan Baldwin

Cafes & Restaurants

For something more comfortable, most towns have cheap cafes and restaurants where you can buy traditional meals, as well as smarter restaurants with facilities such as tablecloths, waiters and menus. If you're eating in cheaper places, you can expect to be served the same food as the locals, but more upmarket, tourist-oriented establishments serve up more familiar fare, from the ubiquitous chicken and chips, to pizzas, pasta dishes and toasted sandwiches.

Colonial influences remain important: you can expect croissants for breakfast in Madagascar, and Portuguese custard tarts in the bakeries of Mozambique. Africa also has its share of world-class dining, with the best restaurants brilliantly fusing African culinary traditions with those of the rest of the world. Less impressively, even smaller towns are now succumbing to the fast-food craze, with greasy burger and chicken joints springing up frequently.

CELEBRATING WITH FOOD

In much of Africa, a celebration, be it a wedding, coming-of-age ceremony or even a funeral, is an excuse to stuff yourself until your eyes pop out and you beg for mercy. In nonIslamic countries, this eating-fest could well be accompanied by a lot of drinking, followed mostly by falling down. Celebration food of course varies widely from country to country, but vegetarians beware – many feasts involve goats, sheep, cows or chickens being slaughtered and added to the pot.

If you're lucky enough to be invited to a celebration while you're in Africa, it's polite to bring something (litre bottles of fizzy drink often go down well), and be prepared for a lot of hanging around – nothing happens in a hurry. The accepted wisdom is that it's considered very rude to refuse any food you're offered, but in practice it's probably perfectly acceptable to decline something politely if you really don't want to eat it, as long as you eat something else with gusto!

Troth Wells' *New Internationalist Food Book* is more than just a recipe book – it tells vignettes from a whole host of countries and puts food at the heart of Africans' daily struggle for survival.

Vegetarians & Vegans

Many Africans may think a meal is incomplete unless half of it once lived and breathed, but across Africa many cheap restaurants serve rice and beans and other meals suitable for vegans simply because it's all the locals can afford. For vegetarians, eggs are usually easy to find – expect to eat an awful lot of egg and chips – and, for pescetarians, fish is available nearer the coast. Be aware that in many places chicken is usually not regarded as meat, while even the simplest vegetable sauce may have a bit of animal fat thrown in. Expect to meet with bemusement when you announce that you don't eat meat – the idea of voluntarily giving up something that's seen as an aspirational luxury is hard to understand for many people.

African Music

They don't call Africa the Motherland for nothing. The continent has a musical history that stretches back further than any other, a history as vast and varied as its range of rhythms, melodies and overlapping sources and influences. Here, music – traditional and contemporary – is as vital to communication and storytelling as the written word. It is the lifeblood of communities, the solace of the nomad, the entertainment of choice.

It can be a political tool – perceived as a threat (France and South Africa are full of exiled African artists; in December 2012 Islamist extremists banned secular music in Mali's north) or a campaign winner (African leaders are forever trying to cash in on popular musicians, many of whom have their own record labels and charitable foundations). Its biggest acts are treated as celebrities, followed wherever they go. Oh, and despite the world music boom, some are relatively unknown in the West. If in doubt, ask a local.

Africa Hit Music TV (www.africahit.com) is the first internet TV station that plays African music videos 24/7. Each month it features thousands of music videos from a host of artists and genres.

Artists who are popular in the West, such as Mali's Oumou Sangaré or Senegal's Baaba Maal, work in a double market, making different mixes of the same songs for home and abroad, or recording cassette-only albums for local consumption. (Their home-town performances are wildly different, too: most start late and run all night.) Cassettes, rather than CDs, proliferate across Africa, and government pledges to address the gargantuan problem of cassette piracy have so far remained precisely that. Still, if you're looking for a gig or club *sans* tourists, ask a cassette-stall holder. They might send you to a hotel or a dingy club in the suburbs, but it will be an experience.

Cross Cultural Influences

Without African music there would be no blues, reggae or – some say – rock, let alone Brazilian samba, Puerto Rican salsa, Trinidadian soca or any of a wide array of genres with roots in Africa's timeless sounds. And it works both ways: colonialism saw European instruments such as saxophone, trumpet and guitars integrated into traditional patterns. Independence ushered in a golden era; a swath of dance bands in 1970s Mali and Guinea spawned West African superstars such as Salif Keita and Mory Kante. Electric guitars fuelled Congolese rumba and soukous and innumerable other African genres (including Swahili rumba). Ghana's guitar-based high-life (urban dance music) blended with American hip-hop to become hip-life; current faves include Tic Tac, Sarkodie and prank-rap duo FOKN Bois. Jazz, soul and even classical music helped form the Afrobeat of late Nigerian legend Fela Kuti (which carries on through his sons, Femi and Seun, and a host of others today).

Online Resources

Afropop Worldwide (www.afropop.org)

The African Music Encyclopedia (www.africanmusic.org)

AfricMusic (www.africmusic.com)

Sterns Music (www.sternsmusic.com)

Music of North Africa

There is no pan-African music. The Motherland is simply way too big for that. But there are distinct musical trends too important to ignore. Looking north: in Algeria it's the oft-controversial trad-rock genre, *rai* (think Khaled, Messaoud Bellemou, the late grand dame Cheikha Rimitti), and the street-style pop known as *chaabi* (Arabic for 'popular'). Many of Algeria's Paris-based musicians are performing at home again: check out rocker Rachid Taha and folk chanteuse Souad Massi. In Egypt the stern presence of late diva Oum Kalthoum, the Arab world's greatest 20th-century singer, is everywhere; scratch the surface for a thrumming industry that includes pop stars Amr Diab and Samira Said, along with the 'Voice of Egypt' Mohammed Mounir and composer and pianist Omar Khairat.

There is also *chaabi* in Egypt and Morocco, along with the Arabic techno pop called *al-jil* and a wealth of other influences. The Berber shepherdess blues of Cherifa, the Maghreb's very own Aretha, have made her a singer-sheika (or popular artist) to be reckoned with. The pentatonic healing music of the Gnaoua – chants, side drums, metal castanets, the throbbing *guimbri*-lute (long-necked lute) – hijacks Essaouira each June during the huge Gnaoua World Music Festival; celebrity faces spotted in the thronging 20,000-strong crowd have included Mick Jagger and Robert Plant.

There's nomad desert blues in exile to be had, from Tuareg guitar bands such as Tinariwen to the so-called 'Jimi Hendrix of Niger' (well, each country's got to have one) Omara 'Bombino' Moctar. In the Côte D'Ivoire, Abidjan remains a hugely influential centre for music production (if you can make it here, you'll probably make it in Paris), while the percussive, melodious and totally vacuous *coupé-décale* dance music sound fills stadiums. Seek out the likes of reggae legend Alpha Blondy and fusionist Dobet Gnahoré – the latter in charisma and vocal power not unlike Beninese diva Angélique Kidjo.

PROTESTORS

Sout el Horreya (I'm Not Turning Around; search www.youtube.com) by Amir Eid and Hany Adel became the anthem for anti-government protestors in Egypt's Tahrir Square and beyond in November 2011.

TEN AFRICAN ALBUMS

- Ali Farka Touré, *Savane* (World Circuit) – Desert blues from the late, great Malian guitar maestro.
- Toumani Diabaté, T*he Mande Variations* (World Circuit) – Visionary instrumentals from the Malian kora player.
- Khaled, *Khaled* (Barclay/Universal) – In which Khaled shows why he's the king of *rai*.
- Miriam Makeba, *Best of Miriam Makeba and the Skylarks* (BMG) – Vintage stuff from the South African diva and her backing group.
- Fela Kuti, *The Black President* (Universal) – Nigeria's Afrobeat hero gives his all.
- Salif Keita, *Soro* (Sterns) – *Mande* music and world beats from a West African superstar.
- Bassekou Kouyate and Ngoni Ba, *I Speak Fula* (Out Here) – Power-packed *ngoni* riffs from a burgeoning big name.
- Cesaria Evora, *Miss Perfumado* (Lusafrica) – Classic *morna* (Creole-language form of blues) from the late Cape Verdean treasure.
- Staff Benda Bilili, *Bouger Le Monde!* (Crammed) – Band of mostly disabled polio victims recapture their early musical charm.
- Spoek Mathambo, *Father Creeper* (Sub Pop) – Visionary stuff from Soweto-based Afro-futurist singer-rapper-producer.

BASSEKOU KOUYATÉ

The gloriously upbeat music of Malian *ngoni* ace Bassekou Kouyaté and his band Ngoni Ba has become political, out of necessity. One of Africa's richest musical heartlands, Mali today is riven by conflict, an adverse state of affairs that has served to unite artists from Mali's different musical cultures: '*Jama ko* means a big gathering of people,' says Kouyaté of his third album *Jama ko*, the follow up to the Grammy-nominated *I Speak Fula*.

'There are over 90% Muslims in Mali, but our form of Islam has nothing to do with a radical form of Sharia: that is not our culture. We have been singing praise songs for the Prophet for hundreds of years. If the Islamists stop people music making they will rip the heart out of Mali.'

A call for unity, peace and tolerance in a time of crisis, *Jama ko* was recorded in March 2012 in Mali's capital Bamako, at the same time as the government was being overthrown half a mile away. The coup changed the mood of the country overnight.

'We were getting on with recording when we heard gunfire and went out to see what was going on. To our surprise we were told it was a coup d'etat. We struggled to finish the recording in good time.'

Meanwhile the situation in Mali's north was getting progressively worse. Bassekou plugged in his wah-wah pedal, ramped up his amp and let loose. 'Don't wear me out,' sings Amy Sacko, the group's main vocalist, in French, as Kouyaté wigs out on *ngoni* – an ancestor of the banjo – behind her.

'*Jama ko* shows how Mali's traditional instruments can lean towards rock and roll and hold their own with modern instruments and technology,' says Kouyaté. 'Musicians have a special role to play when affairs are generally disorderly in the country,' he adds. 'Now this role is more special, more urgent, than ever.'

Music of West Africa

Across West Africa the haunting vocals of the *griots* and *jalis*, the region's oral-historians-cum-minstrels, are ubiquitous. In Mali, the *jelimuso* (female *griot*) Babani Koné rules, though *jalis* in the country's north are currently out of work because of Islamic extremism; in Mauritania *griot* Veirouz Mint Seymali is poised to fill the formidable shoes of her late mother, the iconic Dimi Mint Abba.

Mali's Arabic-flavoured *wassoulou* rhythms have their most famous champion in songbird Oumou Sangaré, just as the 21-string kora, one of the traditional instruments of *griot* and *jali*, is closely linked to Toumani Diabaté. Others are making their mark: Guinea's electric *kora* master Ba Cissoko is pushing the envelope. *I Speak Fula*, the 2009 album by *ngoni*-player Bassekou Kouyaté, was nominated for a Grammy.

The mighty Youssou N'Dour kickstarted Senegal's pervasive *mbalax* rhythms when he mixed traditional percussion with plugged-in salsa, reggae and funk – though today it's Wolof-language rap groups that really appeal to the kids (there's a natural rap vibe to the country's ancient rhythmic poetry, *tasso*). Elsewhere, militant artists such as Côte d'Ivoire reggae star Tiken Jah Fakoly, former Sudanese child soldier-turned-rapper Emmanuel Jal, and Somalia's 'Dusty Foot Philosopher', rapper and poet K'Naan are telling it like it is.

With the passing of Ali Farka Touré in 2006, his son Vieux Farka Touré is – along with redoubtable Bambara blues guitarist Boubacar Traore et al – continuing the Malian guitar blues legacy. Guitar heroes abound throughout Africa: the Congo's Diblo Dibala, Malagasy originator Jaojoby and South African axeman Louis Mhlanga among them.

In the islands of Cape Verde they're singing the wistful, Creole-language blues known as *morna*, as delivered by a slew of talent including Lura and Mayra Andrade. Over in Cameroon they're whooping it

Benda Bilili!, by French film directors Florent de la Tullaye and Renaud Barret, is the inspirational 2010 feature film about Staff Benda Bilili, the group of paraplegic street musicians from Kinshasa, capital of the war-torn Democratic Republic of Congo.

Look out for a regional culture and music strand on new channel TV10 in Rwanda, courtesy of Eric Soul, the DJ-presenter son of Rwandan cultural icon Cecile Kayirebwa.

KINSHASA COOL: STAFF BENDA BILILI

Trilby tilted backwards, suit jacket flapping, Ricky Likabu comes fanging onstage in his shiny silver wheelchair, then spins around so quickly he draws sparks. Three similarly wheelchairbound musicians power on after him, waving towels above their heads as if they are prizefighters. As former street kid Roger Landu rocks out on a single-string guitar he made from a condensed milk can, and an all-acoustic rhythm section gets into some groove-laden rumba-funk, one-legged 'hype man' Djunana Tanga throws his crutches aside and starts boogying and body popping on the floor. 'I was born a strong man,' sings sixtysomething Likabu, as a frontline that includes cofounder Coco Ngambali strum guitars and contribute high-pitched harmonies. 'But polio crippled me/ Look at me today/ I have become the man with the canes.'

This group of Congolese buskers turned world-music darlings, whose unofficial mantra is that handicaps exist in the mind and not the legs, delivers their show with flair and *joie de vivre*. Staff Benda Bilili (which means 'look beyond appearances') is an unlikely global success story: comprising five middle-aged polio victims and three able-bodied musicians including resident sex symbol Landu, it has garnered international awards and popular praise for its live shows. The band's members no longer live and rehearse around the grounds of the zoo in Kinshasa, the desperately poor capital of the Democratic Republic of Congo. They used to sleep rough on cardboard or wedged into unsanitary living quarters with hundreds of other people; their lives have changed dramatically. They have mattresses. Houses. Land. Cars. Likabu has traded in his pimped-up tricycle, which he'd pedal with his hands while being pushed along, for a motorised quadbike. His three children are well dressed and go to school.

'We are still the same,' he says in French. 'It is just that now people recognise us in the street.'

Way before the release of *Tres Tres Fort*, when Staff was a sprawling collective of nearly 20 people, Likabu knew they'd make it somehow. 'We're incredibly persevering people,' says the former cigarette seller. 'Here, you have to be very strong-willed to survive.' The band has so many disabled members simply because no other Kinshasa musicians wanted to work with them. 'We were always told that we couldn't make music,' Likabu says. 'They said we would be late for work. So I decided to create my own band,' he adds with a shrug.

The band's second album, 2012's *Bouger le Monde*, won praise from rock and world critics alike. Having toured everywhere from Amsterdam to Sydney, in September 2012 Staff Benda Bilili played London's Royal Albert Hall as part of the BBC Proms.

'We have become ambassadors for handicapped people everywhere, but we just happen to be handicapped. What matters is that our music is strong.' A pause. 'Very, very strong,' he says with a grin.

up to the guitar-based *bikutsi* and the brass-heavy sound of *makossa* (a Cameroonian fusion of Highlife and soul) while the polyphonic voices of that country's pygmies have struck a chord with the Western world.

Sauti za Busara (Sounds of Wisdom; www.busaramusic.org) Swahili Music Festival in Stonetown, Zanzibar, is one of East Africa's finest annual events: a four-days-in-February extravaganza of music, theatre and dance before a horizon dotted with dhow boats.

Music of East Africa

In the often musically overlooked East Africa, *bongo flava* (that's Swahili rap and hip-hop) is thriving; as is *taarab*, Arab- and Indian-influenced music of Zanzibar and the Tanzanian-Kenyan coastal strip.

Hip-hop hybrids are creating musical revivals in countries such as Tanzania, Kenya, Angola and Guinea; Rwanda is nodding along to female hip-hop acts such as Knowless and Allioni.

Ethiopian jazz is enjoying an international renaissance thanks to the likes of Mulatu 'Daddy from Addy' Astatke and pianist and rising star Samuel Yirga. Mozambique sways to the sound of *marrabenta* – Ghorwane is a roots-based urban dance band and a national institution – and the marimba (African xylophone) style known as *timbila*.

Music of Southern Africa

Down in Zimbabwe they're listening to the *tuku* (swinging, rootsy, self-styled) music of Oliver Mutukudzi or, in secret, the *chimurenga* (struggle) music as created by their self-exiled Lion, Thomas Mapfumo.

In South Africa, where the ever-popular *kwaito* rules supreme (think slowed-down, rapped-over house music), the country's giant recording industry continues to rival that of Europe and America, embracing everything from the Zulu *iscathimiya* call-and-response singing as popularised by Ladysmith Black Mambazo, to jazz, funk, gospel, reggae, soul, pop, rap, Afrofuturism and all points in between.

Once exiled artists such as Hugh Masekela and Abdullah Ibrahim have returned to South Africa to inspire a new generation of artists who include the likes of R&B soulstress Simphiwe Dana and Afro-fusion popsters Freshlyground.

KigaliUp! (www.kigaliup.tumblr.com) is a two-day music festival that takes place during the second week of July in Kigali, Rwanda and features a range of African styles from traditional music to hip-hop.

Environment

Africa is the oldest and most enduring land mass in the world. When you stand on African soil, 97% of what's under your feet has been in place for more than 300 million years. Atop this foundation sits an astonishing breadth of landscapes, from the world's biggest desert to some of the largest rivers, lakes and tracts of rainforests on the planet, not to mention stirring mountains and the iconic savannah that tells you that you could only be in Africa. Inhabiting these epic landscapes is the world's largest collection of wildlife, extraordinary for its diversity. For these and many more reasons, Africa's natural world will take centre stage wherever you go.

Africa: Atlas of Our Changing Environment (2008), from the United Nations Environment Programme (UNEP), is the definitive study of Africa's environment, with country statistics and before-and-after satellite photos. Available from Earthprint (www.earthprint.com).

Land

Africa is the world's second-largest continent, after Asia, covering 30 million sq km and accounting for 23% of the total land area on earth. From the most northerly point, Cap Blanc (Ra's al Abyad) in Tunisia, to the most southerly point, Cape Agulhas in South Africa, is a distance of approximately 8000km. The distance between Cape Verde, the westernmost point in Africa, and Raas Xaafuun in Somalia, the continent's most easterly point, is 7440km. Such are the specs of this vast continent when taken as a whole. But zoom in a little closer and that's when the story really gets interesting.

Mountains & the Great Rift Valley

East and Southern Africa is where the continent really soars. It's here that you find the great mountain ranges of the Drakensberg in South Africa and Rwenzori (the fabled Mountains of the Moon) that straddle the borders of Uganda and Democratic Republic of Congo (DRC), as well as classic, stand-alone, dormant volcanoes such as Mt Kenya (5199m) and Mt Kilimanjaro (5895m), Africa's highest peak. And then there's Ethiopia, Africa's highest country, which lies on a plateau between 2000m and 3000m above sea level – in the space of a few hundred kilometres, the country rises to the Simien Mountains and Ras Dashen (4543m), then drops to 120m below sea level in the Danakil Depression.

North and West Africa also have plenty of topographical drama to call their own. In the far northwest of the continent, the Atlas Mountains of Morocco – formed by the collision of the African and Eurasian tectonic plates – run like a spine across the land, scaling the heights of Jebel Toubkal (4167m), North Africa's highest peak. In West Africa, Mt Cameroon (4095m) is the highest point, while other notable high-altitude landmarks include the Fouta Djalon plateau of Guinea and the massifs of the Aïr (Niger) and Hoggar (Algeria) in the Sahara.

The African earth deep beneath your feet is being slowly pulled apart by the action of hot currents, resulting in a gap, or rift. This action over thousands of years has formed what's known as the Great Rift Valley, which begins in Syria and winds over 5000km before it peters out in southern Mozambique. The valley is flanked in many places by sheer escarpments and towering cliffs, the most dramatic of which can be seen in Ethiopia, Kenya, and along DRC's border with Uganda and Rwanda. The valley's floor contains the legendary wildlife-watching habitats of the Serengeti and Masai Mara in Tanzania and Kenya, alkaline lakes such as Bogoria and Turkana, and some of Africa's largest freshwater lakes.

Deserts

Deserts and arid lands cover 60% of Africa. Much of this is the Sahara, the world's largest desert at over 9 million sq km, which is comparable in size to the continental United States. The Sahara occupies 11 countries, including more than half of Mauritania, Mali and Chad, 80% of Niger and Algeria and 95% of Libya. Contrary to popular misconceptions, sand covers just 20% of the Sahara's surface and just one-ninth of the Sahara rises as sand dunes. More typical of the Sahara are the vast gravel plains and plateaus such as the Tanezrouft of northeastern Mali and southwestern Algeria. The Sahara's other signature landform is the desert massif, barren mountain ranges of sandstone, basalt and granite such as the Hoggar (or Ahaggar) Mountains in Algeria, Aïr Mountains in Niger and Mali's Adrar des Iforas. By one estimate, the Sahara is home to 1400 plant species, 50 mammal species of and 18 bird species.

Another little-known fact about the Sahara is that this is the youngest desert on earth. As recently as 8000 years ago, the Sahara was a fertile land, made up of savannah grasslands, forests and lakes watered by relatively regular rainfall, and home to abundant wildlife. Around 7000 years ago, rains became less frequent and by 400 BC, the Sahara was the desert we know today, albeit on a smaller scale.

If the Sahara is a relatively recent phenomenon, the Namib Desert in Namibia is one of the world's oldest – a staggering 55 million years old. It was created (and is sustained) by cold-air convection that sucks the moisture from the land and creates an arid landscape of rolling sand dunes with its own unique ecosystem. Even larger than the Namib, the Kalahari Desert spans Botswana, Namibia and South Africa and is around the size of France and Germany combined.

Forests

African forests include dry tropical forests in eastern and Southern Africa, humid tropical rainforests in western and central regions, montane forests and subtropical forests in northern Africa, as well as mangroves in the coastal zones.

Despite the myth of the African 'jungle', Africa actually has one of the lowest percentages of rainforest cover in the world – just one-fifth of Africa is covered by forests, with over 90% of what's left found in the Congo basin. Not surprisingly, the countries of Central Africa have the highest proportion of their territory covered by forest – Gabon (84.5%), Congo (65.6%), DRC (58.9%) and Equatorial Guinea (58.2%) – although Guinea-Bissau (73.7%) is a rare West African exception.

The rainforest of the Congo Basin and Madagascar supports the greatest and most specialised biodiversity on the continent: 80% to 90% of species found in these biomes are endemic. The Congo Basin is also one of the last havens for gorilla, chimpanzee and other endangered primates.

GEOLOGISTS

Geologists believe that if the process that created the rift continues, the Horn of Africa may one day break away from the African mainland and become an island, just as Madagascar did in the distant past.

African Climbs

Mt Kenya, Kenya

Mt Kilimanjaro, Tanzania

Mt Cameroon, Cameroon

Simien Mountains, Ethiopia

Drakensberg Mountains, South Africa

Beyond their biodiversity mantle, however, forests are essential to the livelihood of many communities, providing food, fuel, livelihood, medicine and spiritual well-being.

Desert Beauties

- *Namib Desert, Namibia*
- *Adar, Mauritania*
- *Kalahari Desert, Botswana*
- *M'hamid, Morocco*
- *Grand Erg Oriental, Tunisia*

Savannah

The savannah is a quintessentially African landform, covering an estimated two-thirds of the African land mass. Savannah is usually located in a broad swath surrounding tropical rainforest and its sweeping plains are home to some of the richest concentrations of wildlife on earth, especially in East Africa. The term itself refers to a grasslands ecosystem. While trees may be (and usually are) present, such trees do not, under the strict definition of the term, form a closed canopy, while wet and dry seasons (the latter often with regenerating and/or devastating wildfires) are also typical of Africa's savannahs. The Serengeti is probably the continent's most famous savannah region.

Water

Rivers

Africa's waterways are more than stunning natural phenomena. They also serve as the lifeblood for millions of Africans who rely on them for transport, fishing, irrigation and water supplies. The Nile (6650km) and Congo (4700km) Rivers dominate Africa's hydrology, but it's the Niger River (4100km), Africa's third-longest, that is the focus of most environmental concern.

The Niger's volume has fallen by 55% since the 1980s because of climate change, drought, pollution and population growth. Fish stocks have fallen, water hyacinth is a recurring problem and the growth of sand bars has made navigation increasingly difficult. Given that an estimated 110 million people live in the Niger's basin, problems for the Niger could cause a catastrophic ripple well beyond the river's shoreline. In 2008 the alarming signs of a river in distress prompted nine West African countries to agree on a US$8 billion, 20-year rescue plan to save the river.

River Trips

- *White-water rafting, Zambezi River, Zimbabwe*
- *Cruising on the Nile, Egypt*
- *Canoe excursions, Okavango Delta, Botswana*
- *Travelling along the Congo River*

Lakes & Wetlands

Africa has its share of famous lakes. Lake Victoria, which lies across parts of Uganda, Tanzania and Kenya, is Africa's largest freshwater lake (and the second largest by area in the world after North America's Lake Superior). Lake Tanganyika, with a depth of 1471m, is the world's second-deepest lake after Lake Baikal in Russia, while Lake Malawi, which borders Malawi, Mozambique and Tanzania, is reportedly home to more fish species (over 1000) than any other lake on earth.

Less a lake than the world's largest inland delta, the Okavango Delta is home to a stunning array of wildlife, with over 2000 plant and 450 bird species. The delta's 130,000-strong elephant population is believed to be close to capacity, with increasing conflict between elephants and farmers around the delta's boundaries.

Coastal Africa

Along the coast of East Africa and the Red Sea, warm currents provide perfect conditions for coral growth, resulting in spectacular underwater coral reefs. Off the west coast, the Benguela current, which shadows Angola, Namibia and South Africa, consists predominantly of nutrient-rich cold water. Whales, sharks and turtles are common all along the African coastline – South Africa and Madagascar in particular are whale-watching hotspots.

Coral reefs are the most biologically diverse marine ecosystems on earth, rivalled only by tropical rainforests on land. Corals grow over geo-

SHRINKING LAKE CHAD

Lake Chad straddles the borders of Chad, Niger, Nigeria and Cameroon; its waters support the lives of 30 million people. Once the sixth-largest lake in the world and Africa's second-largest wetland, supporting a rich variety of wildlife, Lake Chad has shrunk by 95% since the 1960s because of over-extraction by the ever-expanding local population. Falling rainfall and the lake's notoriously shallow average depth (which makes it very prone to evaporation) have also taken their toll.

Various proposals to replenish the lake by diverting neighbouring rivers have been put forward, but the cost and environmental impact of such a plan mean the project remains on the shelf for the time being.

logic time – that is, over millennia rather than the decades that mammals live – and have been in existence for about 200 million years. The delicately balanced marine environment of the coral reef relies on the interaction of hard and soft corals, sponges, fish, turtles, dolphins and other life forms.

Coral reefs also rely on mangroves, the salt-tolerant trees with submerged roots that form a nursery and breeding ground for birds and most of the marine life that migrates to the reef. Mangroves trap and produce nutrients for food and habitat, stabilise the shoreline, and filter pollutants from the land base.

Diving Wonders

Dahab, Red Sea Coast, Egypt

Aliwal Shoal, South Africa

Ifaty, Madagascar

Zanzibar, Tanzania

Bazaruto Archipelago, Mozambique

Biodiversity

African wildlife accounts for almost a third of global biodiversity and its statistics alone tell the story – a quarter of the world's 4700 mammal species are found in Africa, as are a fifth of the world's bird species and more fish species than on any other continent. Discoveries in the 1990s in Madagascar alone increased the numbers of the world's known amphibian and reptile species by 25% and 18% respectively.

The continent is home to eight of the world's 34 biodiversity hotspots, as defined by Conservation International. To qualify, a region must contain at least 1500 species of vascular plants (more than 0.5% of world's total) and have lost at least 70% of its original habitat. Three of these touch on South Africa (where 34% of terrestrial ecosystems and 82% of river ecosystems are considered threatened), with others in West Africa, Madagascar, the Horn of Africa, the coastal forests of East Africa and the Great Rift Valley.

2050

In 1950 there were, on average, 13.5 hectares of land for every person in Africa. By 2050, that figure will have shrunk to 1.5 hectares.

National Parks

Africa's protected areas range from world-class national parks in eastern and Southern Africa to barely discernible wildlife reserves in West Africa.

Southern African countries lead the way in protected area cover, with Zambia and Botswana the only two countries in Africa having put aside more than 30% of their territory for conservation (36% and 31% respectively). In eastern Africa, Tanzania wins the stakes, with 27% of its surface area registered as protected, against just 12% and 10% in Kenya and Uganda. West Africa is a mixed bag, with countries like Guinea-Bissau, Benin and Senegal all scoring around 25%, while many of their neighbours hover around the 10% mark. All in all, 11.5% of sub-Saharan Africa is protected, but the proportion is much lower in North Africa (4%), which has very few national parks.

Africa has numerous examples of transfrontier national parks that stand out as shining examples of neighbourly cooperation. There are more than a dozen of these spread around the continent; among the ones you're most likely to encounter are the Park Régional du W, which spans Niger, Benin and Burkina Faso; the Masai Mara, which encompasses Kenya's Masai Mara National Reserve and Tanzania's Serengeti National Park; and the Great Limpopo Transfrontier Park, which links South Africa's Kruger and Mozambique's Limpopo National Parks.

Environmental Challenges

Africa is the second-most populous continent after Asia and population growth, although slowing, is still the highest in the world. This, along with poor natural resource management and the increasing effects of climate change, are putting tremendous pressure on the environment.

Africa only accounts for 3% of carbon credits on the market while CO2 emissions per head in Africa are four times lower than the world average.

Climate change

Africa, like everywhere else in the world, is grappling with climate change. The irony for the continent is that it has historically contributed little to the greenhouse gas emissions responsible for global warming.

Impacts

Whatever part Africa played in global warming, the effects are likely to be significant. The last report of the Intergovernmental Panel on Climate Change (IPCC) estimated that Africa would experience temperature increases of 1.5°C to 4°C (more than the global average), which will in turn disrupt rainfall patterns. Although forecast models still produce mixed results, it is thought that northern and Southern Africa will become drier, while equatorial parts of the continent will turn wetter and East Africa more unpredictable.

The impact of this climatic upheaval will be broad-ranging, from disruption to agricultural yields and cropping systems to reduced water availability, changes in ecosystem boundaries and an increase in extreme weather events (such as cyclones, drought and flooding).

In 2008 the then UN Secretary-General's Special Adviser on Conflict, Jan Egeland, described West Africa's Sahel region as the world's 'ground zero' for vulnerable communities struggling to adapt to climate change.

Mitigating and adapting

This need not be a doomsday scenario however; while profound changes are unavoidable, policymakers have been working hard on developing climate change mitigation and adaptation strategies.

On the mitigation side, Africa not being a great GHG emitter, efforts have focused on promoting a 'greener' growth on the continent, with emphasis on preventing deforestation (which globally accounts for 20% of greenhouse gas emissions) by paying for the carbon sink potential of forests, and renewable energy. Africa has substantial resources in wind,

GREEN HEROES

Along with the dozens of well-known conservation organisations, there are many Africans fighting the environment's corner at the grassroots level.

The **Goldman Environmental Prize** is an annual award that honours these green heroes on each continent. The prize has been dubbed the 'green Nobel' and many of its recipients have become role models for a generation. Among the most famous African winners are Kenyan Green Belt Movement founder and Nobel Peace Prize laureate **Wangari Maathai** (1940–2011), Nigerian oil campaigner **Ken Saro-Wiwa** (1941–1995), who was hanged by a military court for his defence of the rights of the Ogoni people in the Niger Delta; and founder of the NGO Brainforest and activist **Marc Ona-Essangui**, from Gabon, whose advocacy led to a change in the country's environmental legislation.

Other winners may not be as well known but they are just as deserving, their work focusing on anything from poaching to conservation and sustainable development. The prize is awarded in April every year; profiles of all laureates can be found on the Goldman Foundation's website (www.goldmanprize.org).

KILIMANJARO'S MELTING ICE CAP

Glittering white, like a mirage behind its veil of cloud, Mt Kilimanjaro's perfect white cap of ice is one of Africa's most iconic images. It has also become a *cause célèbre* in the debate over global warming. According to the UN, Kilimanjaro's glaciers have shrunk by 80% since the early 20th century and the mountain has lost over a third of its ice in the last 20 years alone. The causes are complex and not solely attributable to rising temperatures, with deforestation also to blame – the upper limit of the mountain's forests has descended significantly and overall forest cover has, thanks to fire, decreased by 15% since 1976. Whatever is to blame, some estimates suggest that Kilimanjaro's ice could disappear completely by 2025.

solar, geothermal and hydro power, yet only a fraction of that potential is being used. Development experts are particularly keen to use solar and micro-hydro power to provide 'off-grid' electricity to remote communities.

As for climate change adaptation, the answer lies in development. More than ever, experts agree that priority must be given to improving food security and drought resilience through better water resource management and agricultural practices: only 5% of Africa's arable land is irrigated for example. Disaster preparedness is also becoming increasingly relevant.

Deforestation

African forests are under threat: thousands of hectares are being chopped not only for timber, but also for firewood and charcoal, and to be cleared for agriculture.

A 2009 report by international forest-policy group the Rights and Resources Initiative (www.rightsandresources.org) found that African forests are disappearing at a rate four times faster than forests anywhere else in the world. The reason, according to the study, is that less than 2% of the continent's forests are under the control of local communities – over half of the rainforests of the Congo basin are already under commercial-logging leases – compared to around a third in Latin America and Asia.

East and Central Africa have the most to lose and the signs there aren't good – Burundi is losing around 5% of its forest cover every year, with massive deforestation issues in Congo, Central African Republic, Cameroon, Kenya, Tanzania and Zambia. West Africa is faring little better. Over 90% of West Africa's original forest has been lost, while Nigeria and Ghana in particular are losing forest cover at an alarming rate.

Internationally, these figures raise concern over the effect such large-scale deforestation has on global warming. At a local level, soil erosion (with its devastating impact on agriculture), loss of biodiversity and an increase in the amount of wildlife hunted for bushmeat as new roads and accompanying settlements penetrate the forests, rank among the major side effects.

Water scarcity

Africa has enormous water resources; the trouble is that they are unevenly distributed and often hard to access: the amount of groundwater stored in aquifers is thought to be 100 times the volume available in surface water. This spatial and temporal inequality is what causes scarcity. The continent also faces quality issues: pollution and increased salinity due to over-extraction of coastal aquifers are growing concerns.

African governments also have a poor track record in water resource management. Urban utilities lose 20% to 50% of the water they produce through leaks in their networks and few irrigation systems use modern,

GREEN ENERGY

The year 2012 was a bumper one for green energy in Africa: Morocco and Ghana each started work on the construction of large-scale solar power plants and South Africa approved 28 renewable energy projects worth $5.4 billion.

Forty million metric tonnes of Saharan sand reaches the Amazon annually, replenishing mineral nutrients depleted by tropical rains. Half of this dust comes from the Bodele Depression on the Niger–Chad border.

GREENING NIGER

Forests are considered to be an important buffer against desertification. Take, for example, the case of Niger, which has lost a third of its meagre forest cover since 1990.

Although just 1% of Niger is now forested, it's not all bad news. Satellite images show that three of Niger's southern provinces (especially around Tahoua) now have between 10 and 20 times more trees than they did in the 1970s.

According to UNEP, this is 'a human and environmental success story at a scale not seen before in the Sahel'. The secret to the success has been giving farmers the primary role in regenerating the land.

Faced with arid soil that made agriculture almost impossible, farmers constructed terraces and rock bunds to stem erosion, trap rainfall and enable the planting of trees. Trees planted by the farmers now serve as windbreaks against the desert and, for the first time in a generation, agriculture (millet, sorghum and vegetables) is almost possible year-round, thanks to improved water catchments and soil quality. This has made local populations more resistant to recurrent droughts.

efficient drip-irrigation technology. In Egypt for example, irrigated agriculture uses 90% of the country's water. And in Libya, vast amounts of non-renewable 'fossil' water (from deep aquifers) are piped over hundreds of kilometres along the Great Manmande River to irrigate desert parcels along the coast.

Learning to Share

One of the unique features of Africa's waterscape is its transboundary nature: 90% of the continent's surface water resources are shared; in some cases, more than 10 countries depend on the same river basin (for example, the Nile or the Niger River).

This has historically been a source of tension between riparian countries, particularly those along the Nile. A 2012 report from global agricultural research partnership CGIAR (formerly Consultative Group on International Agricultural Research) concluded that there was enough water in the Nile to go around – it just had to be better managed to ensure that small-holders as well as large-scale infrastructure projects such as dams and irrigation got access to the precious resource. This, the report argued, was key to poverty alleviation in the region.

Desertification

As forest cover diminishes, all too often the desert moves in. Desertification is one of the most serious forms of land degradation and it's one to which the countries of the West African Sahel and North Africa are particularly vulnerable. Desertification has reached critical levels in Niger, Chad, Mali and Mauritania, each of which some believe could be entirely consumed by the Sahara within a generation; up to 80% of Morocco is also considered to have a high risk of desertification. The Sahara's southward march is by no means a uniform process (and some scientists even doubt its existence), but the Sahel in particular remains critically vulnerable to short-term fluctuations in rainfall.

Desertification is also a problem for countries beyond the Sahelian danger zone: a high to moderate risk of desertification exists in numerous West African countries, as well as Botswana, Namibia, DRC, Central African Republic, Kenya, Ethiopia, Sudan and Somalia.

The major causes of desertification are easy to identify – drought, deforestation, overgrazing and agricultural practices (such as cash crops, which require intensive farming) that have led to the over-exploitation of fragile soils on the desert margin – and are the result of both human

DOCUMENTARIES

Perfect armchair-travel fodder, the BBC's *Wild Africa* series, available on DVD, consists of six stunningly filmed documentaries entitled *Jungle, Coasts, Mountains, Deserts, Savannahs* and *Rivers & Lakes*.

activity and climatic variation. But one of the most significant causes in West Africa is the use of deliberately lit fires. Such fires are sometimes necessary for maintaining soil quality, regenerating savannah grasslands and ecosystems, enabling livestock production and as a form of pest control. But when the interval between fires is insufficient to allow the land to recover, the soil becomes exposed to wind and heavy rains and can be unravelled beyond the point of recovery.

Sahara: A Natural History, by Marq de Villiers and Sheila Hirtle, covers the natural and human history of the Sahara like no other recent book, and the lively text makes it a pleasure to read.

Community-Based Conservation

While the history of environmental protection in Africa is one that often saw Africans evicted from their land to make way for national parks, the future lies in community-based conservation. This local, as opposed to large-scale, approach is based on the tenet that in order for the African environment to be protected, ordinary Africans must have the primary stake in its preservation.

There are dozens of community-run initiatives across the continent, from conservation areas to lodges and tour companies; look them up during your travels and support their efforts.

Africa's Wildlife

Africa is home to more than 1100 mammal species and some 2400 bird species, and throughout the continent, wildlife brings drama and life to the beauty of the African wilds. Your first sight of elephants in the wild, chimpanzees high in the forest canopy, or a lion or cheetah on the hunt will rank among the most unforgettable experiences of your trip. Many national parks and reserves across Africa provide refuges for wildlife under threat from changing land use and wars – but even here poaching is a persistent problem and one that conservationists report is getting worse. For more on safaris and the continent's best national parks and reserves see the planning feature on p35.

Internet Resources

Sahara Conservation Fund (www.saharaconservation.org)

African Conservation Foundation (www.africanconservation.org)

Elephant Spotting

Serengeti National Park, Tanzania

Masai Mara National Reserve, Kenya

Kruger National Park, South Africa

Chobe National Park, Botswana

Etosha National Park, Namibia

Elephants

The African elephant, the largest living land animal, is for many travellers the continent's most charismatic mammal. Elephants are plentiful in many areas of Africa but their survival is not assured.

In 1989 when the trade in ivory was banned under the Convention for International Trade in Endangered Species (CITES), elephant population numbers began to climb again from dangerously low levels. However, illegal poaching continues to feed demand in Asia, particularly in China. In September 2012, the *New York Times* reported that Africa was, once again, 'in the midst of an epic elephant slaughter'. In 2011 poaching levels in Africa were at their highest since detailed records started being kept in 2002. In the same year, a record-breaking 38.8 tons (equaling the tusks from more than 4000 dead elephants) was seized worldwide.

The WWF notes that most countries do not have adequate capacity to protect and manage their herds and, if conservation action is not forthcoming, elephants may become locally extinct in some parts of Africa within 50 years.

Primates

They may not be part of the 'Big Five', but the chance to see Africa's primates in their natural environment is alone worth the trip. Our obvious kinship with these always engaging animals has spawned various forms of 'primate tourism', whereby troops of monkeys or apes are habituated to human presence so visitors can observe them in their natural habitat.

Central Africa's rainforests are particularly rich in primate species, although West and East Africa also have considerable populations. Although gorillas and chimpanzees get most of the attention (and rightfully so), you'll also come across colobus monkeys, mangabeys, drills, beautiful and strikingly marked guenons and forest baboons, among others.

WILDLIFE-WATCHING – THE BASICS

- Most animals are naturally wary of people, so to minimise their distress (or aggression) keep as quiet as possible, avoid sudden movements and wear subdued colours when in the field.
- Avoid direct eye contact, particularly with primates, as this is seen as a challenge and may provoke aggressive behaviour.
- Good binoculars are an invaluable aid to observing wildlife at a distance and are essential for birdwatching.
- When on foot, stay downwind of animals wherever possible – they'll smell you long before they see or hear you.
- Never get out of your vehicle unless it's safe to do so.
- Always obey park regulations, including traffic speed limits; thousands of animals are needlessly killed on African roads every year.
- Follow your guide's instructions at all times – it may mean the difference between life and death on a walking safari.
- Never get between a mother and her calves or cubs.
- Exercise care when boating or swimming, and be particularly aware of the dangers posed by crocodiles and hippos.
- Never feed wild animals – it encourages scavenging, may adversely affect their health and can cause animals to become aggressive towards each other and humans.

Gorillas

The last refuges in Central Africa of the world's largest living primate have too often occupied war zones. In the Democratic Republic of Congo (DRC), the gorilla's forest habitat has often come under the control of rebel armies; in the first half of 2007, seven gorillas were shot in DRC's Parc National des Virunga. Poaching, the Ebola and Marburg viruses and even the trade in bushmeat have all contributed to the vulnerability of gorillas. The most endangered subspecies is the Cross River gorilla living in the highland forests of Cameroon and Nigeria and numbering no more than 300.

It's not all bad news. In November 2012, the Ugandan Wildlife Authority announced that the world's population of critically endangered mountain gorillas has risen to a total of 880 (400 in the Bwindi Impenetrable National Park, and 480 in the Virunga Masiff), which is up from the estimate of 786 animals in 2010. Across the other side of Africa, a staggering 125,000 western lowland gorillas were discovered in 2008 in the swamps of northern Congo, almost doubling previous projections; the WWF puts the current population at 100,000.

Gorilla Spotting

- *Bwindi Impenetrable National Park, Ugangda*
- *Parc National des Volcans, Rwanda*
- *Dzanga-Sangha Reserve, Central African Republic*
- *Parc National Nouabalé-Ndoki, Congo*
- *Takamanda National Park, Cameroon*

Chimpanzees & Other Primates

Chimpanzees are the animal world's closest living relative to humans, with whom they share 99% of their genetic make-up. You'll find these sometimes playful, sometimes cranky creatures throughout Africa and they're usually more accessible (and cheaper to see) than gorillas.

Tanzania is terrific for chimp tracking, especially the Mahale Mountains and Gombe Stream National Parks. Every bit as good is Uganda's Kibale Forest National Park, home to Africa's highest density of primates, and Murchison Falls National Park. In Rwanda, the Parc National de Nyungwe is the best place for chimpanzees, and you may also see colobus monkeys. Ethiopia's Simien Mountains National Park is home to a small population of gelada baboons.

MADAGASCAR – A WORLD APART

In any discussion of African wildlife, Madagascar rates a separate mention for its unique treasure trove of endemic wildlife that has remained virtually unchanged since the island split from the mainland 165 million years ago. Most of Madagascar's wildlife exists nowhere else on earth, including 98% of its land mammals, 92% of its reptiles, and 41% of bird species. Most famous are its lemurs, a group of primates that have followed a separate evolutionary path. Lemurs have adapted to nearly every feeding niche, and range in size from tiny pygmy mouse lemurs (at 85g, the world's smallest primate) to the 2.5kg ring-tailed lemur. Perhaps the most curious, however, is the indri, which looks like a cross between a koala and a giant panda, and has a voice like a police siren. The best wildlife-watching in Madagascar is to be found at Réserve Spécial d'Analamazaotra, Parc National de l'Isalo and Parc National de Ranomafana.

In Central Africa, you'll find the primate-rich national parks of Gabon, including Réserve de la Lopé, home to some of the world's largest mandrill troupes, and Ivindo National Park.

Sierra Leone's Tiwai Island Wildlife Sanctuary probably offers the best primate-viewing in West Africa. Other highlights include chimpanzees in Côte d'Ivoire's Parc National de Taï and Guinea-Bissau's Parque Nacional do Catanhez. For other primate species, Nigeria's Gashaka-Gumti National Park, Cameroon's Parc National de Campo-Ma'an and Ghana's Kakum National Park are excellent.

Cats

Some of Africa's most memorable wildlife-watching moments come from the great cats – lions, leopards and cheetahs – hunting prey, although these can be among the most elusive of Africa's megafauna. Spotting one of the smaller cat species, such as the caracal, serval, African wild cat or sand cat of the Sahara, is even more difficult.

Lions

Despite having been anointed as the 'king of the jungle', lions inhabit not forests but the savannah. Probably the easiest to spot of the big cats, lions are found predominantly in East Africa and parts of Southern Africa, with isolated populations dotted around West Africa. In Kenya, Masai Mara National Reserve, Amboseli National Park and Hell's Gate National Park offer the best chances for sighting lions. In Tanzania, it's Serengeti National Park, Ngorongoro Conservation Area and Lake Manyara National Park. Uganda's Murchison Falls National Park and Toro-Semliki Wildlife Reserve are also possibilities. Elsewhere, you might encounter lions in South Africa, Botswana, Zambia, Malawi and Namibia.

Leopards

Leopards are present throughout sub-Saharan Africa and, unlike lions, are at home in most African landscapes, from the semidesert to tropical rainforest. In addition to places where lions are found, leopards can be spotted in East Africa in Kenya's Lake Nakuru and Tsavo West National Parks. In southern Africa, try Zambia's South Luangwa National Park, South Africa's Kruger National Park, Malawi's Nyika National Park and Namibia's Namib-Naukluft National Park. In West Africa, leopards are found in Niger's Parc Regional du W.

Cheetahs

The fastest land animal on earth (it can reach speeds of 75km/h in the first two seconds of its pursuit and at full speed may reach 115km/h), the cheetah in full flight is one of the most thrilling sights in the African wild. They inhabit mostly open country, from the savannah to the desert, and they're most easily spotted in the major national parks of Kenya, Tanzania, Namibia, South Africa and Zambia. A small number of cheetahs are also believed to survive in the Sahara.

Hoofed Animals

Africa has the most diverse range of hoofed animals (also known as ungulates) on earth and, given their numbers, they're often the easiest of all large mammals to spot. Counted within their ranks are numerous signature African species such as the hippo, rhino, giraffe, wildebeest, zebra and numerous antelope species.

Rhinoceros

Rhinos rank among Africa's most endangered large mammals. These inoffensive vegetarians are armed with impressive horns that have made them the target of both white hunters and poachers – rhino numbers plummeted to the brink of extinction during the 20th century.

There are two species of rhino, black and white, both of which are predominantly found in savannah regions. White rhinos aren't white at all – the name comes from the Dutch word *wijd*, which means wide and refers to the white rhino's wide lip (the black rhino has a pointed lip).

The survival of the white rhino is an environmental-conservation success story, having been brought back from the brink of extinction in South Africa through captive breeding. As a result, it is now off the endangered list. Black rhinos are thought to now number around 3600, with small but encouraging gains made in recent years. The West African black rhino was declared extinct in 2006.

Hippopotamus

Hippos, the third-heaviest land mammal on earth (after the elephant and white rhino), are found throughout sub-Saharan Africa, with the largest numbers in Tanzania, Zambia and Botswana. They're usually seen wallowing in shallow water in lakes, ponds and rivers, although the wave-surfing hippos in Gabon's Loango National Park are international celebrities. They're also one of the most dangerous animals in Africa, thanks to their aggression towards humans and propensity for attacking boats.

Zebras & Giraffes

Zebras (of which Burchell's zebra is the most widespread) and giraffes may be found in small populations elsewhere, but they are especially plentiful in the open and lightly wooded savannah of East Africa, where you'll see them in most of the major national parks and reserves. Africa's most remarkable giraffes are perhaps those of Kouré in Niger, which are making a stirring comeback after coming close to extinction.

Wildebeest

The annual migration of more than a million wildebeest, the largest single movement of herd animals on earth, is one of the grandest wildlife spectacles you could imagine. It all takes place in Kenya's Masai Mara National Reserve and Tanzania's Serengeti National Park from June to October.

Antelope

Antelope range from the tiny, knee-high dik-dik and duiker, through to the graceful gazelle, impala and springbok, to giants such as the buffalo, eland and kudu. Many of these will be seen on a typical East or Southern African safari.

Rhino Spotting

Ngorongoro Crater, Tanzania

Liwonde National Park, Malawi

Ziwa Rhino Sanctuary, Uganda

Etosha National Park, Namibia

Khama Rhino Sanctuary, Botswana

West Africa also has its share of antelope species, including bushbucks, reedbucks, waterbucks, kobs, roans, elands, oribis and various gazelles and duikers. The Sahel-dwelling dama gazelle is the largest gazelle species in Africa, but is now close to extinction, and the red-fronted gazelle may still survive in Mali's remote far east. Buffalos in West Africa inhabit forest regions, and are smaller and redder than the East African version.

Wildlife Books

Field Guide to African Mammals, Jonathan Kingdon

Cats of Africa, Luke Hunter

Secrets of the Savanna, Mark and Delia Owens

Birds

Even if you're not into birdwatching, Africa's abundant and incredibly varied birdlife could turn you into an avid birder. In most sub-Saharan countries, you're likely to see hundreds of different species without looking too hard, and a bit of preparation – there are some excellent field guides – before you set out can greatly enhance your visit. Birds reach their highest profusion in the Congo rainforests, but are easier to see in habitats such as rainforest, savannah and wetland. Several bird families, such as the ostrich, secretary bird, touracos, shoebill, hamerkop and mousebird are unique to Africa. Apart from endemic species, hundreds more species flood into the continent on migration during the northern winter.

Bird Spotting

Any of East Africa's major national parks are good for birdwatching. Kenya has recorded 1200 bird species and, in particular, Kakamega Forest Reserve, Lake Naivasha and the flamingos of Lake Nakuru National Park stand out. Tanzania, with over 1000 species, isn't far behind – Lake Manyara National Park is a good choice. Southern Ethiopia is also prime birding country, especially the Rift Valley Lakes and Bale Mountains National Park.

In Southern Africa, Malawi's Nyika National Park, Liwonde National Park and Vwaza Marsh Wildlife Reserve are prime birders' destinations. Madagascar, too, has plenty of interest, especially in Parc National Ranomafana and Réserve Spécial d'Analamazaotra, as does Namibia at Swakopmund and Etosha National Park. Elsewhere, Botswana's Okavango Delta and Zimbabwe's Hwange National Park won't disappoint.

West Africa lies along one of the busiest bird migratory routes between Europe and Africa, and more than 1000 species have been recorded in the region. Tiny Gambia has a devoted following in the birding community. Good places include Abuko Nature Reserve, Tanji Bird Reserve and Kiang West National Park. Senegal also offers excellent birding, particularly in Parc National des Oiseaux du Djoudj and Parc National de la Langue de Barbarie; both are famous for vast pelican and flamingo flocks. Sierra Leone is also good; most notably, Outamba-Kilimi National Park supports more than 250 species, including the spectacular great blue turaco.

Survival Guide

Directory A–Z

Pan-continental information of a practical nature is briefly outlined in this Africa Directory.

Accommodation

In many rural areas you'll find budget homestays only, while in certain national parks there's little available besides expensive luxury lodges.

Prices provided in reviews are given for accommodation with a private bathroom, unless otherwise stated. If you're staying somewhere for a few nights, or at a quiet time, consider asking for discounts.

Camping

A tent usually saves you money, and can be vital in some national parks or wilderness areas. However, it's not essential for travel in Africa, as many campsites have simple cabins, with or without bedding and cooking utensils. Official campsites, of varying quality and security, allow you to pitch a tent, as do most backpackers' hostels.

Be cautious about 'wild camping' – you may be trespassing on private land or putting yourself at risk from attack by animals. In rural areas, if there's no campsite, you're usually better off pitching your tent near a village. Seek permission from the village chief first, and you'll probably be treated as an honoured guest and really get under the skin of Africa.

Homestays

In rural areas you can sometimes arrange informal 'homestays' simply by politely asking for somewhere to bed down and get a dish of local food, in return for a payment. Do not get carried away with bargaining – pay a fair fee, normally the cost of a cheap hotel.

Hostels

Lodges and hostels aimed squarely at backpackers line the popular routes from Nairobi to Cape Town, although elsewhere in Africa they're less common. Most have beds in a dorm, as well as double or twin rooms. Backpackers' hostels are good places to get information on stuff to do or onward transport, and they also offer a range of cheap safaris and tours. A potential downside is that you'll be surrounded by fellow travellers, rather than the Africans you came to meet.

Hotels

Africa's hotels range from no-frills establishments to sky's-the-limit dens of luxury. Under the 'hotel' category you could also be bedding down at a guesthouse, B&B,

LATEST TRAVEL ADVICE

Lonely Planet's website (lonelyplanet.com) contains information on what's new, and any new safety reports, as well as reports from other travellers recounting their experiences while on the road.

Most governments have travel advisory services detailing terrorism updates, potential pitfalls and areas to avoid. Remember, however, that most government travel advisories can overstate the risks somewhat, and you should read carefully through the reports to see when actual incidents occurred.

Australian Department of Foreign Affairs & Trade (☎1300 139 281; www.smartraveller.gov.au)

French Ministère des Affaires Étrangères Européennes (www.diplomatie.gouv.fr/en)

British Foreign & Commonwealth Office (☎0845-850 2829; www.fco.gov.uk)

US Department of State (☎202-647-4000; www.travel.state.gov)

rest house, *pensao* (in Mozambique) or *campement* (in West Africa). The latter is a simple rural hotel, often with a campsite attached. In West Africa (especially Burkina Faso), B&Bs can go by the names of '*chambres d'hôtes*' or '*maisons d'hôtes*'. A cheap local hotel in East Africa is called a *gesti* or lodgings, while *hoteli* is Swahili for basic eating place.

In cheaper local hotels, it's rare to get a private bathroom and you can forget air-conditioning. Other 'extras' like a fan or mosquito net usually increase the price. Africa has a huge choice of midrange hotels, and standards can be high, especially in privately run (as opposed to government-run) places.

Children

Approached sensibly, many families find an African holiday a rewarding and thrilling experience. While some posh hotels and camps ban kids under a certain age, some higher-end safari lodges run special wildlife-watching programs for kids, and babysitting services are pretty widely available in midrange and top-end hotels.

On the whole, Africans adore children, and wherever your kids go they will be assured of a warm reception and a host of instant new friends.

Outside the main cities, you can pretty safely assume that disposable nappies won't be available, so bring everything you need with you. Child car seats, high chairs in restaurants and cots in hotels are rare except in top-end hotels in tourist areas.

Courses

Africa doesn't have a whole lot of courses to plan your trip around, but West Africa in particular has a range of intriguing possibilities, from learning the *kora* (21-string harp/lute from West Africa) from master musician Toumani Diabaté in Mali to Fon-language classes in Benin, to surf classes in Senegal, drumming and dancing classes in Ghana, or percussion and cooking courses in Burkina Faso. You can also learn to cook local dishes in popular tourist cities such as Marrakesh and Cape Town.

BOOK YOUR STAY ONLINE

For more accommodation reviews by Lonely Planet authors, check out http://hotels.lonelyplanet.com. You'll find independent reviews, as well as recommendations on the best places to stay. Best of all, you can book online.

Customs Regulations

- At some borders you may have your bag searched, but serious searches are rare.
- Anything made from an endangered animal is likely to land you in trouble. You'll also need a permit from the Ministry of Antiquities or a similar office in the relevant country if you are exporting valuable cultural artefacts (no, not that 'ebony' hippo carving you bought on the beach with the shoe polish that comes off on your hands). It usually applies to artefacts that are more than 100 years old.
- Some countries limit the local currency you can take in or out, although a small amount (say, US$20 worth) is unlikely to be a problem. You can carry CFA francs between countries in the CFA zones.
- A few countries have restrictive exchange regulations, and occasionally you may need to fill in a declaration form with details of your dollars or other 'hard' currencies.

Electricity

Most countries use a 220/240V current, but some mix 110V and 240V. Some (eg Liberia) still use mostly 110V. Generally, in English-speaking countries, sockets are the British type. In Francophone parts of Africa they're the Continental European two-pin variety. South Africa has yet another system. In some countries you'll find whatever people can get hold of.

While the below plugs are the most common among African countries, major destinations including Botswana, Lesotho, Namibia, South Africa and Swaziland use a three-pin plug (two small pins and one larger pin). If possible, purchase plug adaptors before travelling.

Beware: power cuts and surges are part of life in many African countries.

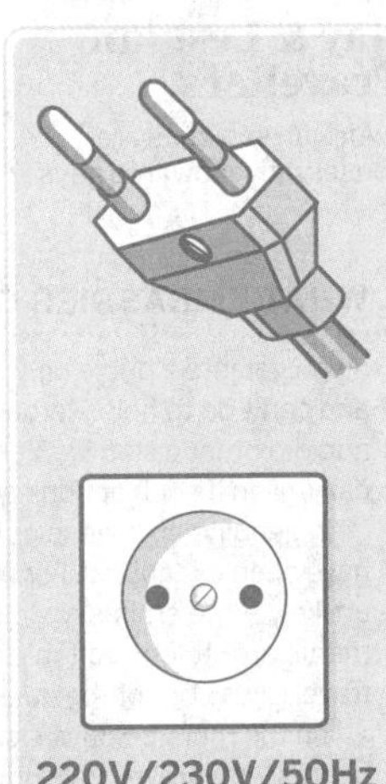

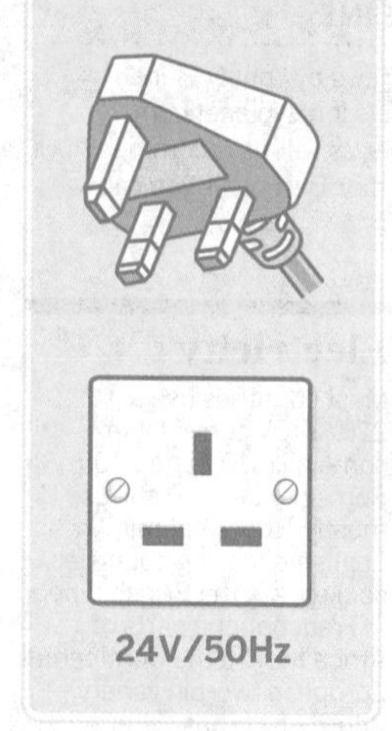

Embassies & Consulates

In this guide, the term 'embassy' often includes consulates and high commissions; for practical purposes they're pretty much the same thing.

It's easy to find an embassy of an African country in your own country (to obtain visas before you go) on the web.

Gay & Lesbian Travellers

- African societies are conservative towards gays and lesbians; same-sex relationships are a cultural taboo, and there are very few openly gay communities. Officially, homosexuality (male, female or both) is illegal in many African countries, even attracting the death penalty in Mauritania, Nigeria, Sudan and a few other areas.
- Although prosecutions rarely occur, discretion is key and public displays of affection should generally be avoided, advice which applies to both homosexual and heterosexual couples.
- Cape Town is Africa's most gay-friendly city, with a lively club scene and a welcoming vibe.
- Useful general web links include **Global Gayz** (www.globalgayz.com) and **Afriboyz** (www.afriboyz.com/Homosexuality-in-Africa.html).

Insurance

Travel insurance to cover theft and illness is essential. Although having your camera stolen by monkeys or your music player eaten by a goat can be a problem, the medical cover is by far the most important aspect because hospitals in Africa are not free, and the good ones aren't cheap. Simply getting to a hospital can be expensive, so ensure you're covered for ambulances (land and air) and flights home.

Some insurance policies forbid unscheduled boat or plane rides, or exclude dangerous activities such as white-water rafting, canoeing, or even hiking. Others also don't cover people in countries subject to foreign office warnings. Others are more sensible and understand the realities of travel in Africa. Ask your travel agent or search on the web, but shop around and read the small print to make sure you're fully covered.

Internet Access

- There are cybercafes in most capitals and major towns.
- Many hotels and hostels also offer internet access; midrange and top-end hotels increasingly offer wi-fi access for those carrying their own laptops.
- Expect to pay anything from US$1 to US$5 per hour, although wi-fi access is often free.
- Although things are improving, many connections are excruciatingly slow, with ancient PCs that are prone to crash (tip: write emails first in a word-processing program, then copy them across when you're ready to go online). Uploading photos

WHAT EMBASSIES CAN & CAN'T DO FOR YOU

If you get into trouble on your travels, it's important to realise what your embassy can and can't do to help. Remember that you're bound by the laws of the country you are in, and diplomatic staff won't be sympathetic if you're jailed after committing a crime locally, even if such actions are legal at home.

In genuine emergencies you might get some assistance, but only if other channels have been exhausted. For example, to get home urgently, a free ticket is exceedingly unlikely – the embassy would expect you to have insurance. If all your money and documents are stolen, staff might assist with getting a new passport, but a loan for onward travel is way out of the question.

On the more positive side, some embassies (especially US embassies) have notice boards with 'travel advisories' about security or local epidemics. If you're heading for remote or potentially volatile areas, it might be worth registering with your embassy, and 'checking in' when you come back.

to your blog site or emailing attachments can prove arduous, not to mention expensive.

Legal Matters

The buying, selling, possession and use of all recreational drugs is illegal in every country in Africa.

Maps

Buy Michelin maps of Africa (No 741 *North & West*, No 745 *North-East* and No 746 *Central & South*) before you leave home. Expect a few discrepancies, particularly with regard to roads, as rough tracks get upgraded and smooth highways become potholed disasters. For these and other African maps in the UK, try **Stanfords** (www.stanfords.co.uk). In France, **IGN** (www.ign.fr) sells its sheet maps at stores in Paris.

Money

This guide quotes prices in local currencies in those countries where the currency and inflation are stable. For everywhere else, prices are quoted in US dollars. However, it's important to remember that prices invariably increase – whatever prices are quoted, they should always be regarded as guidelines, not guaranteed costs.

ATMs

➡ In many (but by no means all) African countries you can draw local cash as you go with a credit or debit card. Visa is the most widely accepted card. Charges can be low and exchange rates are usually good, but check with your home bank or card provider before leaving.

➡ Although ATM numbers are on the rise, most are still located in capitals and major towns, plus there are usually daily withdrawal limits. What's more, due to dodgy phone lines, they frequently malfunction, so you'll still need a pile of hard cash as backup.

➡ Always keep your wits about you when drawing money out, as ATMs are often targeted by thieves. Try to visit them in busy areas during daylight hours, and stash your money securely before you move away.

Black Market

In countries with controlled exchange rates, you can get more local money for your hard currency by dealing with unofficial moneychangers on the so-called black market, instead of going to a bank or bureau. This helps with costs, but it's illegal and sometimes dangerous – think twice before you do it.

However, you may have to resort to unofficial methods if you're stuck with no local cash when banks and exchange offices are closed. Hotels or tour companies may help, although rates are lousy. Try shops selling imported items. Be discreet though: 'The banks are closed, do you know anyone who can help?' is better than a blunt 'D'you wanna change money?'.

Even in countries with free exchange rates (and therefore no black market), moneychangers often lurk at borders where there's no bank. Although illegal, they operate in full view of customs officers, so trouble from this angle is unlikely.

There's more chance of trouble from the moneychangers themselves, so make sure you know the exchange rates, and count all local cash carefully, *before* you hand over your money. Watch out for old or folded notes. A calculator ensures you don't miss a zero or two on the transaction. And beware of 'Quick, it's the police' tricks, where you're panicked into handing over money too soon. Use common sense and you'll have no problem, but it's best to change only small amounts to cover what you'll need until you reach a reliable bank or exchange office.

Credit Cards

➡ Credit or debit cards are handy for expensive items such as tours and flights, but most agents add a hefty 10% surcharge. It's therefore usually cheaper to use your card to draw cash from an ATM, if one is available.

➡ If there's no ATM, another option is to withdraw money from a local bank using your card, but be warned – this also incurs a charge of around 5%, and can be an all-day process, so go early.

➡ Before leaving home, check with your own bank to see which banks in Africa accept your card (and find out about charges). Cards with the Visa logo are most

EMERGENCIES

Generally speaking, emergency services in most African countries are not what you'd be used to at home. For example, if you're robbed or attacked, don't count on the police to respond quickly (or at all) when you dial an emergency number. However, you'll have to visit the police to report the offence – otherwise your insurance won't be valid – so expect an all-day form-filling process. Likewise, if you're sick or injured, don't waste time phoning an ambulance – get a taxi straight to a hospital or clinic. And if you want a private medical service or an English-speaking doctor, ask for directions at an embassy or a top-end hotel.

THE FINE ART OF BARGAINING

In many parts of Africa items are often worth whatever the seller can get. Once you get the hang of bargaining, it's all part of the fun. Hagglers are rarely trying to rip you off, so there's no point getting all hot and bothered about it. Decide what price you're prepared to pay and if you can't get it, simply decline politely and move on.

The following tips will help you hone your bargaining skills, but try to keep a sense of proportion – have you just wasted half an hour of your time arguing over a price difference that is worth a packet of chewing gum back home? By the same token, paying the first price asked may make it that much more difficult for the next person who comes along.

Everyday Goods

Market traders selling basic items such as fruit and vegetables may raise their prices when they see a wealthy foreigner (that's you), so some minor bargaining could be called for, as long as you know the price that locals pay. But away from cities or tourist areas, many sellers will quote you the local price.

After a couple of days in a new country (when you'll inevitably pay too much a few times), you'll soon learn the standard prices for basic items. But don't forget that these can change from place to place – a soft drink in a remote village can cost significantly more than what you'll pay in a city.

Souvenirs

At craft and curio stalls, where items are specifically for tourists, bargaining is very much expected. Some vendors may ask a price four (or more) times higher than what they're prepared to accept. You decide what you want to pay, and your first offer might be half this or even less. The vendor may feign outrage, while you plead abject poverty. Then the vendor's price starts to drop, and you make better offers until you arrive at a mutually agreeable price.

And Finally...

Something to remember when bargaining is your own self-respect. Souvenir sellers normally give as good as they get, but if their 'final' price is close to what you're prepared to pay, consider accepting it. You'll avoid stress, and most locals need that money more than you do.

readily recognised, although MasterCard is accepted in many places.

- Whatever card you use, don't rely totally on plastic, as computer or telephone breakdowns can leave you stranded. Always have cash or (less helpful) travellers cheques too.
- To avoid credit-card fraud, always make sure that you watch the transaction closely and destroy any additional transaction slips that are produced, whether innocently or otherwise.

Currencies

Whether you're carrying cash or travellers cheques, or both, give some thought to the currency you take before you leave home. This will depend on the countries you visit.

Wherever you go, remember to carry a mix of large and small denominations. In many countries US$100 bills get you better rates, but note that the US changed the design of the US$100 bill in the mid-1990s and old-style US$100 notes, and sometimes other denominations, are not accepted at many places that don't have a light machine for checking watermarks; they'll often ask for the dollars with the 'big head'. Smaller denominations (cash or travellers cheques) can be handy if you need to change money to last just a few days before leaving a country.

East and southern Africa

By far the most readily recognised international currency is the US dollar (US$). Also accepted are euros (€), UK pounds (UK£) and South African rand (R). Currencies from other European countries or Canadian dollars may occasionally be accepted, but don't count on it.

West and Central Africa

Many countries in these regions use a common currency called the Communauté Financière Africaine franc (usually shortened to CFA – pronounced 'say-eff-aah' in French), and here the euro is much more readily recognised by banks and bureaus. US dollars or other currencies are often not accepted at all. There are actually two CFA zones: the West

African (or Banque Centrale des Etats de l'Afrique de l'Ouest) zone, which includes Benin, Burkina Faso, Côte d'Ivoire, Guinea-Bissau, Mali, Niger, Senegal and Togo; and the Central African (or Banque des Etats de l'Afrique Centrale) zone, which includes Chad, Cameroon, Central African Republic, Congo, Gabon and Equatorial Guinea.

The CFA is pegged at exactly 655.957 to one euro. If you're changing cash euros into CFA that's usually the rate you'll get (although there will be charges for travellers cheques); however, some out-of-the-way places may offer a little less.

Technically, you should be able to exchange West African CFA for Central Africa CFA and vice versa at a rate of one-to-one, but in reality you'll pay a bit over or under the odds, depending on the rates – and especially if you're dealing with traders at remote border posts a very long way from the nearest bank.

In nonCFA West African countries, the handiest currencies for travellers are euros and US dollars.

North Africa Euros and US dollars are most common; UK pounds are also accepted in some places.

Money Changers

You can exchange your hard cash or travellers cheques into local currency at banks or foreign-exchange bureaus in cities and tourist areas. For cash, bureaus normally offer the best rates, low (or no) charges and the fastest service, but what you get for travellers cheques can be pitiful – if they're accepted at all. Travellers cheques are more readily accepted at banks, but while rates may be OK, the charges can be as high as 10% or 20% – plus you'll often spend a lot of time queuing.

Travellers Cheques

- Never make travellers cheques your sole source of money.
- The pros are that they're secure – ATMs sometimes don't work and cash, unlike travellers cheques, cannot usually be replaced if lost.
- The cons are that many countries don't accept travellers cheques, and in those that do it's rare to find a bank that will change them outside major cities, commissions can be prohibitive and they're often a pain to deal with.
- When exchanging travellers cheques, most banks also check the purchase receipt (the paper you're supposed to keep separate) and your passport, so make sure you have these with you.
- You can sometimes pay for items such as safaris and activities directly with travellers cheques, but most operators add a surcharge – usually 10%, but sometimes up to 20%, because that's what banks charge them.

Opening Hours

- This guide does not list main opening hours for every place listed unless it has 'unusual' habits – such as a restaurant that opens for lunchtime only, or a bar that doesn't serve drinks until midnight.
- Tourist offices, shops and travel agencies tend to open from around 8am or 9am to around 4pm or 5pm, Monday to Friday, and sometimes on Saturday mornings as well. Embassies are generally open to the public during the morning – so that's when you need to apply for visas. In Islamic countries, most offices (including banks and shops) close on Fridays, but may open on Saturdays and/or Sundays.
- Smaller shops and market stalls rarely keep strict business hours. When there are customers around, the shopkeepers are behind their counters ready to serve, and when everyone is asleep in the heat of afternoon, they're snoring round the back. In most cities, many shops and supermarkets stay open until late in the evening and on Saturdays too, although only the largest are open on Sundays.
- In East and southern Africa, shops and offices close for an hour or so around noon. In North, West and Central Africa, the noon break can be two to four hours long, and businesses may stay open until 7pm or 8pm, sometimes later. Places like phone and internet cafes keep much longer hours.
- Banks in most countries are open from Monday to Friday from 8am or 9am to around 2pm or 3pm. Some banks will even shut at noon.
- In Islamic countries, many businesses shut up shop at lunchtime and don't reopen during the Islamic fasting period of Ramadan.
- Most cafes and smaller restaurants offer lunch from around noon to 2pm (for locals it's the main meal of the day) and dinner in the evening from around 5pm to 7pm. Larger restaurants catering for more affluent locals and tourists keep the same lunch hours, but open later in the evening, usually from around 7pm to 10pm or later. Many restaurants open all day.

Photography

A simple point-and-shoot is fine for mementos of people, landscapes, market scenes and so on, but for better-quality shots, especially of animals, you'll need a zoom lens, and maybe an SLR camera with changeable lenses. It's also worth taking a couple of spare batteries with you and charging them whenever you have a reliable electricity source for those times when you're travelling in remote areas. For the same reasons, take extra memory cards and a cleaning kit. Africa's extremes of climate, especially heat, humidity and very fine sand can also take their toll on your camera, so always take appropriate precautions; changing lenses in a dust-laden wind is, for example, a recipe for disaster.

Other useful photographic accessories might include a small flash, a cable or remote shutter release and a tripod. Absolutely essential is a good padded bag, containing at least one desiccation sac, and sealed to protect your camera from dust and humidity. Avoid leaving your camera on the floor of buses or cars, as the jolting could well destroy the delicate inner workings of the lens.

Many internet cafes now offer to put your pictures on CD for you – a good idea is to get the CD copied at the same time, perhaps posting one home, to avoid the risks of files corrupting or the disc being damaged. Count on taking more photos than you expect to.

For more advice, Lonely Planet's *Guide to Travel Photography* is an excellent resource, full of helpful tips for photography while on the road. For more specific advice, Lonely Planet also publishes *Wildlife Photography* and *People Photography*.

Post

If you do want to send a letter, parcel or postcard, it's always better doing this from a capital city. From some countries, the service is remarkably quick (just two or three days to Europe, a week to the USA or Australia). From others it really earns the snail-mail tag, but it's still more reliable than sending stuff from really remote areas.

You can use the poste-restante service at any post office where mail is held for collection. Letters should be addressed clearly with surname underlined and in capitals, to '(Your Name), Poste Restante, General Post Office, Lusaka, Zambia', for example. In French-speaking countries, send it to 'Poste Restante, PTT', then the name of the city.

To collect mail, you need your passport, and to pay about US$0.50 per item. Letters sometimes take a few weeks to arrive, so have them sent to a town where you'll be for a while, or will be passing through more than once – although in some places mail is only held for a month, then returned to the sender.

The price, quality and speed for parcel post varies massively from place to place; courier companies can sometimes be more reliable than government postal services and not always a lot more expensive.

Public Holidays

The main holidays are Christmas and Easter in the largely Christian countries, while in Muslim countries the main events are Eid al-Moulid, the birthday of the Prophet Mohammed; Eid-al-Fitr, marking the end of Ramadan; and Eid al-Adha (also called Eid al-Haj, Eid al-Kebir or Tabaski), which commemorates Abraham's readiness to sacrifice his son on God's command, and coincides with the end of the pilgrimage to Mecca. Spellings may vary from country to country. Since the Islamic year has 354 or 355 days, these holidays fall about 11 days earlier each year in the Western calendar. During public holidays you can expect most businesses (apart from hotels, restaurants and tourist attractions) to close.

To check the dates of Islamic holidays, go to www.bbc.co.uk/religion/tools/calendar/faith.shtml?muslim.

Safe Travel

It's worth remembering that the overwhelming majority of travellers to Africa return home without encountering any of the following problems. That said, be aware of potential problems and keep your wits about you.

Crime

The vast majority of Africans are decent, hard-working people who want from you only respect and the chance to make an honest living; given the extreme poverty levels, robbery rates are incredibly low. Even so, you need to be alert on the streets of some cities. Nairobi (Kenya) is often called 'Nairobbery', Lagos (Nigeria) is not for the faint-hearted, while Dakar (Senegal), Abidjan (Côte D'Ivoire) and parts of Johannesburg (South Africa) all have edgy reputations. Snatch-theft and pickpocketing are the most common crimes, but violent muggings can occur, so it pays to heed the warnings in country chapters and the following dos and don'ts:

- Don't make yourself a target on the streets. Carry as little as possible.
- Don't wear jewellery or watches, however cheap. Strolling with a camera or iPod is asking for trouble.
- Don't walk the backstreets, or even some main streets, at night. Take a taxi.
- Do use a separate wallet for day-to-day purchases. Keep the bulk of your cash hidden under loose-fitting clothing.
- Do walk purposefully and confidently. Never look like you are lost (even if you are!).
- Do be discreet with your possessions, especially in dorms. Keep your gear in your bag.

SURVIVING SCAMS

Dud Sounds

You buy CDs from the market, but back at the hotel you open the box and it's got a blank CD inside, or music by a different artist. The solution: always listen to the CDs first.

Phone Home

You give your address to a local kid who says he wants to write. He asks for your phone number too, and you think 'no harm in that'. Until the folks back home start getting collect calls in the middle of the night. And when it's the kid's big brother making false ransom demands to your worried ma and pa, things can get serious. Stick to addresses, and even then be circumspect.

Police & Thieves

Local drug salesmen are often in cahoots with the police, who then apprehend you and conveniently find you 'in possession', or just tell you they've seen you talking to a known dealer. Large bribes will be required to avoid arrest or imprisonment. To complicate things further, many con artists pose as policemen to extort money. Insist on being taken to the police station, and get written receipts for any fines you pay.

Take a Tour

A tout offers to sell you a tour such as a safari or a visit to a local attraction, and says he can do it cheaper if you buy onward travel with him too. You cough up for bus/ferry/plane tickets, plus another tour in your next destination, only to find yourself several days later with your cash gone and your reservations nonexistent. Best to pay only small amounts in advance, and deal with recommended companies or touts only.

Welcome, Friend

You're invited to stay for free in someone's house, if you buy meals and drinks for a few days. Sounds good, but your new friend's appetite for food and beer makes the deal more expensive than staying at a hotel. More seriously, while you're out entertaining, someone else will be back at the house of your 'friend' going through your bag. This scam is only likely in tourist zones – in remote or rural areas you'll more often than not come across genuine hospitality.

Scams

The main annoyance you'll come across in Africa is the various hustlers, touts, con men and scam merchants who always see tourists as easy prey. Although these guys are not necessarily dangerous, some awareness and suitable precautions are advisable, and should help you deal with them without getting stung.

War Zones

Going to a war zone as a tourist is, to put it bluntly, bloody stupid. Unless you're there to help out with a recognised aid agency and are qualified to do so, you'll be no help to anyone, and you'll quite likely get yourself kidnapped or killed.

Telephone

In most capital cities and major towns, phone connections are good. Thanks to satellite technology, it's often easier to make an international call than to dial someone 20km up the road. Rates vary from country to country, ranging from US$5 to US$15 for a three-minute call to Europe, the USA or Australia. Many cybercafes now offer dirt-cheap internet-connected phone calls, but the quality of the line depends on the quality of the internet connection – if it's a dial-up connection as opposed to ADSL, it's unlikely to be worth the effort.

Bureaus

To call long distance or even locally, you're usually better off at a public-phone bureau than a booth in the street. In each city, there's normally a bureau at the main post office, plus numerous privately run bureaus where rates can be cheaper and the service faster. At most bureaus you can also send or receive faxes.

Mobile Phones

Mobile (cell) phones are almost universal in Africa, with connection rates, call rates and coverage becoming better at a galloping rate, although you're unlikely to have coverage in remote rural areas. You can buy local SIM cards just about everywhere where there's mobile coverage. Some local companies also offer rates for international calls that work out cheaper than using landlines.

To check whether your phone will work in the African countries you plan to visit, contact your network provider. Ask about charges as well – and don't forget that if anyone rings you while you're overseas, the bulk of the cost goes on *your* bill.

Phonecards

In some countries you can buy phonecards that let you dial a local number, enter a PIN, and then make cheap international calls. You can also buy scratchcards to top up mobile phones, and phonecards to use in public booths instead of coins.

Time

Africa is covered by four time zones, from UTC (formerly GMT) in the west to UTC +3 in the east. Crossing from Chad to Sudan there's a two-hour difference, but elsewhere it's one hour or none at all. At borders where there's a one-hour time difference (eg Malawi–Tanzania), some have their opening and closing hours coordinated to avoid problems, but others don't – try to plan your travels at these crossings to avoid getting caught in no-man's land after you've been stamped out of one side, only to discover that the other side is already closed.

Toilets

There are two types of toilet in Africa: the Western style, with a bowl and seat (common in most midrange or top-end hotels and restaurants); and the African style, a hole in the floor that you squat over. You might even find a combination of the two, with a Western-style toilet bowl propped over a hole in the floor. Standards vary tremendously, from pristine to those that leave little to the imagination as to the health or otherwise of the previous occupant. In our experience, a non-contact hole in the ground is better than a filthy bowl any day.

In rural areas, squat toilets are built over a deep hole in the ground and called 'long-drops'; the crap just fades away naturally, as long as the hole isn't filled with too much other material (such as tampons – these should be disposed of separately). Toilet paper is OK – although you'll need to carry your own. In Muslim countries, a jug of water or hosepipe arrangement is provided for the same task - use your left hand to wipe, then use the water to wash your hand. This is why it's a breach of etiquette in many countries to shake hands or pass food with the left hand.

Some travellers complain that African toilets are difficult to use, but it only takes a little practice to accomplish a comfortable squatting technique, and you'll soon become adept at assuming the position in one swift move, while nimbly hoiking your trouser hems up at the same time so they don't touch the floor.

Tourist Information

Much of Africa isn't geared for tourism, and decent tourist offices are rare. Some countries have a tourist-information office in the capital, but apart from a few tatty leaflets and vague advice from the remarkably little-travelled staff, you're unlikely to get much. Tour companies, hotels and hostels are often better sources of information.

Travellers with Disabilities

There are more people with disabilities per head of population in Africa than in the West, but wheelchair facilities are virtually nonexistent. Don't expect things like wheelchair ramps, signs in Braille, or any other facilities that are available in tourist areas in other parts of the world. Most travellers with disabilities find travel much easier with the assistance of an able-bodied companion, or with an organised tour through an operator that specialises in arranging travel for those with disabilities. Safaris in South Africa and diving holidays in Egypt are both easily arranged with companies like these.

A final factor to remember, which goes some way to making up for the lack of facilities, is the friendliness and accommodating attitude of the African people. In the majority of situations, they will be more than happy to help if you explain to them exactly what you need.

Before setting out for Africa, travellers with disabilities should consider contacting any of the following organisations, which may be able to help you with advice and assistance:

Access-able Travel Source (☎303-232 2979; www.access-able.com; PO Box 1796, Wheatridge, CO, USA) Has lists of tour operators offering tours for travellers with disabilities.

Accessible Travel & Leisure (☎01452-729739; www.accessibletravel.co.uk) UK travel agent; encourages disabled people to travel independently.

Disability Online (www.disabilityonline.com) A large database of links and resources for disabled travellers.

Endeavour Safaris (www.endeavour-safaris.com) Focuses on southern Africa.

Epic Enabled (www.epic-enabled.com) Trips in southern Africa for people with disabilities.

Mobility International (541-343 1284; www.miusa.org; 132 E Broadway, suite 343, Eugene, USA) Advises disabled travelers on mobility issues and runs an educational exchange program.

Royal Association for Disability & Rehabilitation (RADAR; 020-7250 3222; www.radar.org.uk; 250 City Rd, 12 City Forum, London, UK, EC1V 8AF)

Society for Accessible Travel & Hospitality (SATH; 212-447-7284; www.sath.org; 347 Fifth Ave at 34th St, New York, USA; 9am-5pm; M34 to 5th Ave, M1 to 34th St, S 6 to 33rd St) An excellent resource, which gives advice on how to travel with a wheelchair, kidney disease, sight impairment or deafness.

Tourism for All (0845 124 9971; www.tourismforall.org.uk; 7A Pixel Mill, 44 Appleby Rd, Kendal, Cumbria, UK)

Visas

For a short trip through Africa you might get all your visas before you leave home. For a longer trip, it's easier to get them as you go along. Most countries have an embassy in each neighbouring country, but not all, so careful planning is required. Some visas are valid from when they are issued, so you may have to enter the country pretty soon after getting them. On other visas you say when you plan to enter the country and arrive within a month of that date. Sometimes it's convenient (and relatively cheap) to get several visas in one place – South Africa or Kenya, for example.

Prices vary widely, but you can expect to pay US$10 to US$50 for standard one-month single-entry visas, and up to US$200 for three-month multiple-entry visas. If you want to stay longer, extensions are usually available for an extra fee.

Rules vary for different nationalities: for example, British and Aussie citizens don't need advance visas for some southern African countries; French citizens don't need them in much of West Africa; Americans need them nearly everywhere. The price of a visa also varies according to nationality (lucky Irish-passport holders seem to be able to get free visas in dozens of countries!), and where you buy it. In some of Africa's more, ahem, *informal* countries, you'll also be factoring in the mood/corruption level of the person you're buying it from.

Most visas are issued in 24 or 48 hours – and it always helps to go to embassies in the morning – but occasionally the process can take a week or longer (such as for Sudan or Angola). You may have to show you have enough funds to cover the visit, or prove that you intend to leave the country rather than settle down and build a hut somewhere. (This could be an air ticket home, or a letter from your employer stating you're expected to return to work on a specified date.) For most visas you also need two or three passport photos, so take what you'll need, although you can get new supplies from photo booths in most capitals. Some embassies ask for a photocopy of your passport data page, so it's always worth carrying a few spare copies.

A final note: if you have Israeli stamps in your passport, they may prove problematic when you enter Algeria, Libya and Sudan. Israeli border officials may stamp a piece of paper, which you can then remove, but if you're travelling overland your Egyptian entry-point can still be a giveaway.

Regulations can change, so it's always worth checking before you enter the country. For general details see lonelyplanet.com, which also has links to other visa sites.

EXTRA VISA REQUIREMENTS

A few countries demand a *note verbale* (letter of recommendation) from your own embassy before they issue a visa. This is generally no problem as your embassy will be aware of this, but be prepared to fork out yet more cash. It'll say: 'This letter is to introduce Mr/Ms [name], carrying [British/French] passport No [1234]. He/she is a tourist travelling to [Chad]. Please issue him/her with a tourist visa. All assistance you can give would be most appreciated.' Or: 'Par la présente, nous attestons que Mr/Ms [Name] est titulaire de passport [Britannique/Française] No [1234]. Il doit se rendre au [Tchad] pour faire le tourism. Toute assistance que pourrait lui être accordée serait appréciée.'

Australians travelling in Africa have only 10 of their own embassies or consulates on the entire continent, so it's handy to obtain a letter of introduction from the Passports section of the Department of Foreign Affairs & Trade before you leave home.

Some countries have other arcane requirements. For Libya, you'll only get a visa if you have a prior booking with a Libyan tour operator, and a paper confirming this in Arabic.

Regional Visas

WEST AFRICA

If you're travelling in West Africa, ask about a Visa des Pays de l'Entente, a multicountry visa that covers travel in Benin, Burkina Faso, Côte d'Ivoire, Niger and Togo. Before you rush off to your nearest West African embassy to ask for this visa, be aware that it's presently only obtainable within Burkina Faso, Côte d'Ivoire and Niger, which means that first you must obtain a visa for these countries and, once there, apply at the immigration or visa extension office in the capital city. To get the Visa des Pays de l'Entente, which is valid for two months, you'll need to take along CFA25,000 and two passport photos. It can take up to three days for the visa to be issued.

The Visa des Pays de l'Entente is only valid for one entry into each country, which makes it ideal for overlanders, but less so for those who plan to visit countries more than once. To further complicate matters, Benin and Togo border guards have been known to refuse to recognise the visa.

EAST AFRICA

For several years there's been talk about an East African tourist visa covering Tanzania, Kenya and Uganda; to our knowledge this has yet to come into practice. However, a single-entry visa for Kenya, Tanzania or Uganda allows you to visit either of the other two countries (assuming you've met their visa requirements and have been issued a visa) and then return to the original country without having to apply for a second visa.

Volunteering

There are very few openings for ad-hoc volunteer work in Africa. Unless you've got some expertise, and are prepared to stay for at least a year, you're unlikely to be much use anyway. What Africa needs is people with skills. Just 'wanting to help' isn't enough. In fact, your presence may be disruptive for local staff and management, prevent locals from gaining employment, or cause a drain on resources.

For formal volunteer work, which must be arranged in your home country, organisations such as Voluntary Service Overseas (VSO; in the UK) and the Peace Corps (in the US) have programs throughout Africa where people, usually with genuine training (eg teachers, health workers, environmentalists), do two-year stints. Similar schemes for 'gap-year' students (between school and university) tend to be for shorter periods, and focus on community-building projects, teaching or scientific research. Almost all these projects require an additional financial donation, which may be raised by sponsorship and fundraising in your home country.

If you've got a genuine interest in volunteering in Africa, the following websites can provide more information:

Australian Volunteers International (www.australianvolunteers.com)

Coordinating Committee for International Voluntary Service (ccivs.org/)

Earthwatch (www.earthwatch.org)

Frontier (www.frontier.ac.uk)

Global Volunteers (www.globalvolunteers.org)

Idealist (www.idealist.org)

International Volunteer Programs Association (www.volunteerinternational.org)

Intervol (www.intervol.org.uk)

Lattitude (www.lattitude.org.uk)

Peace Corps (www.peacecorps.gov)

Project Trust (www.projecttrust.org.uk) Schoolteaching near Maun.

Raleigh (www.raleighinternational.org)

Voluntary Service Overseas (VSO; www.vso.org.uk)

Working Abroad (www.workingabroad.com)

Worldwide Experience (www.worldwideexperience.com)

Worldwide Volunteering (www.wwv.org.uk)

Women Travellers

It's no use pretending otherwise – women travelling in Africa (alone or with other women) will occasionally encounter specific problems, most often harassment from men. North Africa can be particularly tiresome from this perspective, although Libya is generally better than Tunisia or Egypt. And in places where an attack or mugging is a real possibility, women are seen as easy targets, so it pays to keep away from these areas (talk to people on the ground to get the latest situation).

But don't panic! On a day-to-day basis, compared to many places, travel in Africa is relatively safe and unthreatening, and you'll meet friendliness and generosity – not to mention pure old-fashioned gallantry – far more often than hostility or predatory behaviour. Many men are simply genuinely curious as to why on earth a woman is out travelling the world rather than staying at home with the babies, so keep an open mind and try not to be too hostile in the face of endless questions. Remember also that half of the authors who worked on this book are women and many of them travelled alone and lived to tell the tale.

Having said that, when it comes to evening entertainment, Africa is a conservative society and in many countries 'respectable' women don't go to bars, clubs or restaurants without a male companion. However dis-

PHOTOS FROM HOME

Female backpackers may be regarded with a mixture of bewilderment and suspicion in places unused to tourists, especially if alone. You should be at home rearing families or tending the crops, not engaged in frivolous pastimes like travel, the thoughts sometimes go. To show you do have a home life, you could carry photographs of family or friends, or even a mythical husband (unless you've got a real one, of course). Photos of yourself at work sometimes do the same trick.

tasteful this may be to post-feminist Westerners, acting as if this isn't the reality may lead to trouble.

Meeting and talking with local women can be problematic. It may require being invited into a home, although since many women have received little education, unless you have learnt some of the local language, communication could be tricky. However, this is changing to some extent because a surprising number of girls go to school while boys are sent away to work. This means that many of the staff in tourist offices, hotels or government departments are educated women, and this can be as good a place as any to try and strike up a conversation. In rural areas, a good starting point might be teachers at local schools, or staff at health centres.

Some expatriates you meet may be appalled at the idea of a female travelling alone and will do their best to discourage you with horror stories, often of dubious accuracy. Others will have a far more realistic attitude. When you are on the road, the best advice on what can and can't be undertaken safely will come from local women. Use your common sense and things should go well. It's also worth remembering that, as a solo female traveller, you might be best to pay a little extra for midrange hotels where the surroundings may make you feel more comfortable – many of the cheapest hotels in African towns rent rooms by the hour.

Sexual Harassment

Unwanted interest from male 'admirers' is an inevitable aspect of travel in Africa, especially for lone women. This is always unpleasant, but it's worth remembering that although you may encounter a lewd border official, or a persistent suitor who won't go away, real harm or rape is very unlikely. If you're alone in an uneasy situation, act cold or uninterested, rather than threatened. Stick your nose in a book, or invent an imaginary husband who will be arriving shortly. If none of this works and you can't shake off a hanger-on, going to the nearest public place, such as the lobby of a hotel, usually works well, or you could try asking for help from local women in a public place. If the problem still persists, asking the receptionist to call the police usually frightens them off.

Part of the reason for the interest is that local women rarely travel long distances alone, and a single foreign female is an unusual sight. And, thanks to imported TV and Hollywood films (and the behaviour of some tourists), Western women are frequently viewed as 'easy'.

What you wear may greatly influence how you're treated. African women dress conservatively, in traditional or Western clothes, so when a visitor wears something different from the norm, she will draw attention. In the minds of some men this is provocative. In general, look at what other women are wearing and follow suit. Keep your upper arms, midriff and legs covered.

Sanitary Protection

You can buy tampons and pads in most cities and major towns from pharmacies or supermarkets. Prices are about the same as in Europe (from where they're imported), but you seldom have choice of type or brand. They're rarely found in shops away from the main towns, so you might want to bring supplies if you're spending a lot of time in remote areas.

Work

It's hard for outsiders to find work in most African countries, as high unemployment means a huge number of local people chase every job vacancy. You will also need a work permit, and these are usually hard to get as priority is rightly given to qualified locals over travellers. You're unlikely to see many jobs advertised, so the best way to find out about them is by asking around among the expatriate community.

Transport in Africa

GETTING THERE & AWAY

Getting yourself into Africa can be as simple as booking a direct-flight ticket from a major European hub, or as adventurous as hitching a lift on a car ferry then jumping onto a cargo truck. However you choose to do it, it pays to do advance research to make sure you don't blow unnecessary bucks or time. Flights and tours can be booked online at www.lonelyplanet.com/travel_services.

Air

Airports & Airlines

The bulk of air traffic with Africa is to and from Europe, but there are a handful of direct flights between Africa and North and South America, the Middle East and Asia. Many North American travellers pass through a European 'hub' en route to Africa. For Australasian travellers it's often cheaper to pass through a Middle Eastern and/or Asian hub before arriving.

Wherever you're coming from, the main thing to remember is that flying into one of Africa's main hubs is going to be your cheapest option; once you're there the national carriers of the various countries can easily transport you to other destinations across Africa. These extra flights are known as 'add-ons' and are often best booked in conjunction with your main international ticket through a decent travel agent at home (tip: flights with add-ons or multiple stops are still almost always best booked with a real live reservations agent rather than through a website).

The main gateway into East Africa is Nairobi (Kenya), although Dar es Salaam (Tanzania) is also busy. Johannesburg (South Africa) is the southern African hub offering the most options (flights arrive from the Americas, Asia and Australasia as well as Europe) and the biggest bargains; also look out for cheap deals into Cape Town (South Africa). In West Africa, Dakar (Senegal), Accra (Ghana) and Lagos (Nigeria) are the busiest gateways. In North Africa, flying into Casablanca (Morocco) or Cairo (Egypt) is the cheapest option. If you're travelling from Europe, Tunis (Tunisia) is often the cheapest African city in which to arrive. However, it's surrounded by Algeria and Libya, which can make for tricky onward overland travel.

Tickets

Wild climatic variations across Africa, and differing holiday seasons in the northern and southern hemispheres, mean that it's tricky to pin down the cheapest times to fly to Africa – get the low-down on costs from a travel agent well in advance. Using mile-wide brushstrokes, it could be argued that flying from June to September or around Christmas (a 'peak season' that can last from November to March if you're coming from Australasia) is going to hit your budget hardest.

If you're planning a big trip, consider open-jaw tickets, which allow you to fly into one city, then out of another, and can save you cash, time and hassle. All manner of combinations are available, enabling some great overland journeys:

> **ONE WAY, NO WAY**
>
> One-way tickets to Africa are rarely a good idea. For the most part, immigration regulations forbid (or at least discourage) entry to people with one-way tickets; you need to show that you have a ticket out of Africa, although this seems a little perverse considering you can get a ferry to Africa and travel overland through the continent before picking up a one-way flight back home (these tickets tend to cost about half of the usual return fare).

think about a ticket into Cairo, Nairobi or Dakar and out of Cape Town. Even if you're not travelling so far, it can be helpful – flying into Dakar and out of Bamako, for example.

Stopovers are another handy way of flitting around the continent. Many flights to Africa stop at least once before arriving at the main destination, and on some tickets (but not always those at the cheapest end of the spectrum) you'll have the chance to get off; on some happy occasions taking advantage of these stopovers can effectively save the cost of an internal flight. For example, a Kenya Airways flight from London to Addis Ababa (Ethiopia) goes via Nairobi, allowing you to explore Kenya first. If you're coming from North America or Australia, a stopover in Europe can be handy if you need to pick up an obscure visa in Paris.

Jumping on a charter flight can sometimes save you a bundle if you're travelling from or via Europe, especially if you pick something up at the last minute. The main drawback is that short-date returns are common, but there is sometimes some flexibility.

It's not rocket science, but take your time, shop around, double-check all restrictions and date- or route-change penalties on your ticket, look out for credit-card surcharges and book well in advance. A couple of hours on the internet should give you an idea of the most useful travel agents; talk to as many as possible. Remember that although websites are great for straightforward return tickets, they cannot tell you about little add-ons and short cuts or custom-build itineraries from a cluster of domestic and regional flights.

If you're under 26 or a student you'll occasionally be able to turn up some juicy deals. There are many specialist student travel agents, but many 'normal' travel agents offer student fares, just as student travel agents can serve older travellers. Travel agents that recognise the **International Student Identity Card** (ISIC; www.isic.org) scheme are another possibility – the contact details of thousands of agents are available on its website.

MASTER THE SAHARA

Chris Scott's **Sahara Overland** (www.sahara-overland.com) is an excellent place to start planning any trans-African routes, and his books *Sahara Overland* and *Adventure Motorcycling Handbook* are highly recommended reading. *Sahara Handbook*, by Simon Glen, is also worth reading although it dates back to 1990. All these books will give you a better background than we can do here.

INTERCONTINENTAL (RTW) TICKETS

On the cheapest round-the-world (RTW) tickets Nairobi and Johannesburg are the usual stops, but stopping in these major hubs will cut down your options once you leave the continent. If you want more stops within Africa, look at the Global Explorer or oneworld Explorer RTW tickets offered by **oneworld alliance** (www.oneworldalliance.com). Coming from Europe with British Airways and Air France can get you to a variety of interesting African destinations, but flights within Africa are limited.

The trick with RTW tickets is to decide where you want to go first and then talk to a travel agent, who will know the best deals, cunning little routes and the pitfalls of the various packages. If you're departing from the UK, you could also try the handy interactive route planner at www.roundtheworldflights.com.

Land

Africa's only land border divides Israel and Egypt in the Sinai – the continuing troubles in Israel and the Palestinian Territories mean that the direct route via Rafah is often closed to foreigners, so make your way via the Eilat–Taba border crossing on the Gulf of Aqaba. However, note that if your passport has an Israeli stamp in it you won't get into countries such as Libya; if this is going to be a problem, take the (car and passenger) ferry from Jordan.

Sea

Egypt

There are daily ferries between Nuweiba in Sinai (Egypt) and Aqaba (Jordan), which is a stone's throw from Eilat (Israel). There are also four sailings per week from Port Said to Iskenderun in Turkey.

Morocco

Two main companies sail the Spain to Morocco route: **Acciona Trasmediterránea** (www.trasmediterranea.es) and **FRS** (www.frs.es). The main routes run to Melilla (one of Spain's North African enclaves) from Almería and Málaga; to Nador from Almería; to Tangier from Gibraltar, Tarifa and Algeciras; and to Ceuta (another Spanish enclave on the Moroccan coast) from Algeciras. All routes usually take vehicles as well as passengers, and most services increase in frequency during the summer months, when other routes are sometimes added.

Longer-haul ferries that operate as part of the **Cemar** (www.cemar.it) network also sail to Tangier from Genoa (Italy) and Sète (France).

Tunisia & Algeria

Compagnie Tunisienne de Navigation (CTN; Map p168; ☎71 322 802; www.ctn.com.tn) runs ferries from Marseille (France) and Genoa (Italy) to Tunis (Tunisia). A host of other companies also offer services from Italy to Tunis (Genoa is a year-round departure point; summer services leave from La Spezia, Napoli and Trapani).

For Algeria, **Acciona Trasmediterránea** (www.trasmediterranea.es) runs ferries from Almería in southern Spain to Ghazaouet (Algeria), and you might also find services to Oran (Algeria) from Almería or southern France.

GETTING AROUND

Air

Africa's internal air network is comprehensive; certainly, flying over the Sahara, Democratic Republic of Congo (DRC) and the often difficult Chad and South Sudan can be a good idea. Always check flight details carefully (many tickets are flexible), but be prepared for delays and cancellations especially when travelling on state-owned enterprises. Don't expect to be put up in a four-star hotel should your flight get canned.

If you're serious about taking a few African flights, consider sorting it out when booking your main ticket. Any half-decent travel agent should be able to book a host of 'add-on' African flights and possibly find fares that allow a little flexibility. These add-ons are often sold at a discount overseas, so forward planning can save you a small fortune.

Airlines with extensive African networks from their hub cities include:

Ethiopian Airlines (www.flyethiopian.com; Addis Ababa)

Kenya Airways (www.kenya-airways.com; Nairobi)

Royal Air Maroc (www.royalairmaroc.com; Casablanca)

South African Airways (www.flysaa.com; Johannesburg)

Afriqiyah (www.afriqiyah.aero; Tripoli)

Senegal Airlines (www.senegalairlines.aero)

Interair (www.interair.co.za)

Air Passes

Air passes are something of a misnomer. All products purporting to be Africa air passes are just cheapo deals on domestic and transcontinental flights available to travellers flying into Africa with certain airlines. These schemes operate on a tailor-made basis – routes are usually divided into price bands or sectors and you pick 'n' mix to make an itinerary.

Most schemes are fairly limited and usually dictate that your flights include an arrival or departure at one or two hubs. However, if you're planning to take a few African flights, some 'air pass' schemes offer great value in the long run – the best offer savings of well over 50% on domestic and continental fares.

The 'Africa Airpass' scheme run by **Star Alliance** (www.staralliance.com) allows flights to 30 destinations across Africa if you fly in on a member carrier. **Skyteam** (www.skyteam.com) also have a 'Go Africa' pass that allows a minimum of three, and a maximum of 16, flights across the continent, with fully flexible dates

Bicycle

Cycling around Africa is predictably tough but rewarding. Long, hot, gruelling journeys are pretty standard, but you'll be in constant close contact with the peoples and environments of the continent and will get to visit small towns and villages that most people just shoot through. In general, the more remote the areas, the better the experience, but you've got to be fully prepared. A tent is standard issue, but remember to ask the village headman where you can pitch a tent when camping near settlements in rural areas.

Touring bikes aren't the best choice for Africa, a continent not exactly blessed with smooth tarmac roads. Adapted mountain bikes are your best bet – their smaller 660mm (26in) wheel rims are less likely to be misshaped by rough roads than the 700mm rims of touring bikes, and mountain-bike frames are better suited to the rigours of

BRINGING YOUR BIKE

You could cycle all the way into Africa or you could save your legs for Africa's rough roads and stick your wheels in the hold of a plane. There are two ways of doing this: you could partially dismantle your bike and stuff it into a large box, or just simply wheel your bike to the check-in desk, where it should be treated as a piece of baggage (although you might need to take the pedals off, turn the handlebars sideways and wrap it in cardboard and/or foam). Don't lose too much sleep about the feather touch of baggage handlers – if your bike doesn't stand up to air travel, it won't last long in Africa.

Some airlines don't include sports equipment in the baggage allowance; others may charge around US$50 extra because your bike is not standard luggage size; others, however, will take it without hassles.

BORDER CROSSINGS

There are a lot of borders in Africa, and a whole lot more border posts. Sometimes the process is quick and straightforward, but at other times it can take several hours to get through the queues at immigration or customs desks (even assuming that your visas and paperwork are in order), not to mention possible checks of medical certificates, or a detailed search of your luggage. At all times remember that patience and politeness will see you through. Getting shirty with a person in uniform is one sure-fire way for 'discrepancies' to be discovered, and delays to be even longer.

Country chapters in this guide list the main border-crossing points – usually those on more-frequented roads and transit routes. Smaller or less formal border crossings are often used by locals, but may not be able to process your papers, may have little public transport and could involve a long and pointless detour.

There's usually a border post on each side of the border crossing (ie one belonging to each country). Sometimes the border posts are just 100m apart, such as at the Namanga crossing between Kenya and Tanzania; sometimes they can be 100km apart, with a 'no-man's land' in between, such as those on the route between Algeria and Niger. If you're catching a bus 'to the border', check exactly how far it goes. Does it take you just to the first border post, from where you have to walk or take a taxi to the second one? Or does the bus go across the border all the way to the second border post, before you have to change to onward transport?

Although they're rare, it's also worth watching out for new border crossings. For example, the 'Unity Bridge' over the Rovuma River opened in 2010 becoming the main border crossing between Tanzania and Mozambique.

African travel. Multipurpose hybrid tyres with knobbles on their edges for off-road routes and a smooth central band for on-road cruising are useful in Africa, but your tyre choices (along with the types of components, number of spares and the like) should depend on the terrain you want to tackle.

You may encounter the odd antelope or zebra while cycling, but motorists are more of a threat to cyclists than rampaging wildlife. Cyclists lie just below donkeys on the transport food chain, so if you hear a vehicle coming up from behind, be prepared to bail out onto the verges. That said, many of Africa's roads are fairly quiet. Be very cautious about cycling in busy towns and cities.

The heat can be a killer so carry at least 4L of water and don't discount the possibility of taking a bus, truck or boat across some sections (bikes can easily be transported).

The **International Bicycle Fund** (IBF; www.ibike.org/africaguide) has a handy guide to cycling in Africa by country, although information for some countries is limited and out of date.

Boat

Lakes Malawi, Tanganyika, Kariba and Victoria in southern and East Africa all have ferries operating on them. There are even more fantastic river journeys to be had along the Niger, Congo and Nile. Boat trips may also be possible on the Senegal, Gambia and Zambezi Rivers.

On simple riverboats you'll be sat on mountains of cargo, the bows of the craft sitting just above the water line, but on some major river routes large ferries and barges are used. Generally speaking, 3rd class on all ferries is crammed with people, goods and livestock, making it hot and uncomfortable. Happily there's usually a better way: at a price, cabins (semiluxurious and otherwise) with bar and restaurant access can be yours.

The most important coastal ferry service is that between Dar es Salaam and Zanzibar. There are also some services along the West African coast, especially in Sierra Leone and Guinea-Bissau. There are also ferries between Limbe (Cameroon) and Calabar (Nigeria).

A more romantic alternative is to travel by small Arabic-style dhow sailing vessels that ply the Indian Ocean coast. The easiest place to organise this is in Mozambique, where you can sail to and around the Quirimbas Archipelago. Similar to dhows are feluccas, the ancient sailing boats of the Nile.

Pirogues (traditional canoes) and *pinasses* (motorised canoes) are staples of travel on remote waterways where the small, diesel-powered (and often unreliable) pontoon-style car ferries are not available. They're especially common in the rivers of West Africa. Not many ferries or boats take vehicles, but you can get a motorbike onto some.

Seafaring travellers might be able to hitch a lift on cargo boats down the West African

ROAD TIPS

- Watch out for kamikaze cyclists, pedestrians and livestock – and massive potholes.
- Night-time road travel isn't recommended because daytime hazards won't be illuminated.
- Driving skills are generally nerve-shatteringly poor, especially in rural areas; moderate your speed.
- Tree branches placed in the roadway signal a stopped vehicle or other problem ahead.
- Reckless overtaking on blind bends, hills and other areas with poor visibility is standard operating procedure; head-on collisions are common.
- Keep your fuel tank full and carry a jerry can. Fuel sold on the roadside is unreliable (it's often diluted), and some types of fuel (including diesel) aren't always available in remote areas.
- Expect frequent stops at checkpoints; police, customs and border officials will want to see all your documentation. The time taken at these checkpoints is one of the biggest variables of African overland travel. Sometimes it can take two minutes, sometimes hours.
- Mechanical knowledge and a collection of spares are essential. A winch and a set of planks can get you out of muddy trouble in the rainy season.
- Most trips off the beaten track require a 4WD.
- Motorcycles generally aren't permitted in national parks.

coast, up the east coast of Madagascar and on the Red Sea, but this will take some work.

A word of warning: travelling by boat can sometimes be hazardous. For the most part you can forget about safety regulations, lifeboats or life-jackets, and overloading is very common. To make matters worse, on some ferries the 3rd-class passengers are effectively jammed into the hold with little opportunity for escape.

Car & Motorcycle

Exploring Africa with your own wheels takes some doing, but is a wonderful way to see the continent. The easiest way to enter Africa with your own car or motorcycle is to cross from southern Europe to Morocco or Tunisia aboard a car ferry and then take it from there. The obvious main barrier to travelling this way is the Sahara, but it can be crossed with careful planning.

At the time of writing, most trans-Saharan routes were off limits to travellers due to simmering rebellion and banditry, although the Western Sahara route (from Morocco to Mauritania via Dakhla) was considered safe, while the Route du Hoggar (from Algeria to Niger) remains open if not always recommended. Other potential barriers to getting around Africa by car or motorcycle include the cost of hiring a barge to transport your vehicle from Egypt into Sudan; and either war or the nonexistent roads of the DRC (or both). For a multitude of other options and inspiring tales from those who've made overland trips present, future and past, check out the website of the **Africa Overland Network** (www.africa-overland.net) or, for motorcyclists, **Horizons Unlimited** (www.horizonsunlimited.com).

If you're keen to begin in East or South Africa, it can be expensive to ship your vehicle all the way to Mombasa or Cape Town – it may work out cheaper to fly there and purchase something once you arrive. South Africa in particular is a pretty easy place to purchase a car – either from a dealership or from a fellow traveller who has finished with it. Handily, cars registered in South Africa don't need a carnet de passage for travel around southern Africa, but you will need to have an international driving licence, your home licence, vehicle insurance and registration, and you will have to get a new set of plates made. The **AA of South Africa** (www.aa.co.za) offers vehicle check-ups, insurance and travel advice.

Travelling around Africa by motorcycle is popular among hard-core motorcyclists, but road conditions vary greatly. Remember also that many drivers (particularly truck drivers) are either unaccustomed or disinclined to taking two-wheeled transport into consideration. Motorcyclists, especially those with newer model bikes, should also, where possible, be self-sufficient in parts.

Carnets

A *carnet de passage* (sometimes known as a *triptyque*) is required for many countries in Africa, with the notable exceptions of Morocco, Algeria and Tunisia. A *carnet* guarantees that if you take a vehicle into a country, but don't take it out again, then the organisation that issued the *carnet* will accept responsibility for payment of import duties (up to 150% of its value). *Carnets* can only be issued by national motoring organisations; they're only issued if it's certain that if ever duties arose you, would reimburse them. This means you have to deposit a bond with a bank or insure yourself against the potential collection of import duties before getting a *carnet*.

You don't need to prearrange a *carnet* for many West and Southern African countries (most Southern African countries will issue a Temporary Import Permit at the border, which you must buy), but if you're driving through Africa, you're going to need a *carnet*, which sadly doesn't exempt you from the bureaucratic shenanigans encountered at numerous borders. If you're starting in South Africa, you can get one from **AA of South Africa** (www.aa.co.za) pretty easily. In the UK, try the **RAC** (www.rac.co.uk).

Also consider the following:

- Motoring organisations' insurance companies can be a little paranoid in their designation of 'war zones' in Africa so watch out; none will insure against the risks of war, thus denying you a *carnet*.
- If you intend to sell the vehicle at some point, arrangements have to be made with the customs people in the country in which you plan to sell the car for the *carnet* entry to be cancelled.
- If you abandon a vehicle in the Algerian desert, you'll be up for import duties that are twice the value of your car when it was new.

Hire

Hiring a vehicle is usually only an option to travellers aged over 25 years. For the most part, vehicle hire is a fairly expensive option (2WD vehicles commonly cost over US$75 a day in sub-Saharan Africa; you're looking at over US$100 a day for a 4WD) and rental can come with high insurance excesses and bundles of strings.

On a brighter note, car hire in South Africa can be a real bargain (if you hire for a longer period, it can be less than US$30 a day), especially if booked from overseas; have a look on internet sites such as **Travelocity** (www.travelocity.com), **Expedia** (www.expedia.com) and **Holiday Autos** (www.holidayautos.com). Some vehicles can then be taken into Namibia, Mozambique and Botswana. Also consider hiring a car for exploring southern Morocco and taking a 4WD (possibly with driver) to explore Kenya's wildlife parks at your leisure. In some places, it's not possible to rent a car without a local driver being part of the deal.

Insurance

Legislation covering third-party insurance varies considerably from one country to another – in some places it isn't even compulsory. Where it is, you generally have to buy insurance at the border (a process fraught with corruption), but the liability limits on these policies are often absurdly low by Western standards; this means if you have any bad accidents, you'll be in deep shit, so it's a smart plan to insure yourself before heading out. If you're starting from the UK, one company highly recommended for insurance policies and for detailed information on *carnets* is **Campbell Irvine** (☎020-7937 6981; www.campbellirvine.com).

Hitching

Hitching is never entirely safe in any country, and we don't recommend it. But in some parts of Africa, there is often simply no other option than grabbing lifts on trucks, 4WDs, lorries or whatever vehicle happens to come down the road first. Whatever vehicle you jump on to, you'll generally have to pay. In more developed countries, such as Ghana, Kenya, Morocco, South Africa, Tunisia and Zimbabwe, where there are plenty of private cars on the road, it may be possible to hitch for free.

Travellers who decide to hitch should understand that they are taking a small but potentially serious risk. People who do choose to hitch will be safer if they travel in pairs. Remember that sticking out your thumb in many African countries is an obscene gesture; wave your hand vertically up and down instead.

Local Transport

Bus

This is the way to go where there's a good network of sealed roads. International bus services are pretty common across the continent, and in the wealthier African states you may get a choice between

OVERLANDING ON THE CHEAP

Because most people prefer to travel north to south, overland truck companies sometimes drive empty trucks back from South Africa's Cape Town, Victoria Falls and Harare, and will sometimes transport travellers back up to Arusha (Tanzania) or Nairobi (Kenya) for negotiable knock-down prices, with a pleasant two-day stop by Lake Malawi sometimes thrown in. Ask around in backpacker hang-outs in the departure towns for tips on when these trucks may be leaving.

BUS SURVIVAL TIPS

- Bus station touts are there to drum up business and work on commission; they're occasionally a pain but they can be very helpful.
- When using bush taxis keep your options open; hold on to your money until departure.
- Sitting on a camping mat or towel can ease the pain of African roads.
- Drinking more means peeing more – balance hydration with bladder control.
- When travelling on dirt roads use a scarf to keep dust from your nose and mouth.
- That baby may look cute – but let it onto your lap and it WILL pee...
- Carry your passport at all times – getting through roadblocks without it can be expensive and complicated.
- Try to book your bus or minibus ticket in advance.
- Addressing questions to the driver directly is a social no-no – the conductor is the social hub of the journey, while the driver is the quiet achiever.
- If you have a choice as to your seat (more likely on buses), opt for what will be the shady side.

'luxury' air-con buses, with movies (the trashy Hollywood/Bollywood variety) on tap, and rough old European rejects with nonfunctioning air-con and questionable engineering. In some countries you just get the latter. Out in the sticks, where there are very few or no sealed roads, ancient buses tend to be very crowded with people, livestock and goods; these buses tend to stop frequently, either for passengers or because something is broken.

Minibus

Small minibuses take up the slack in many African transport systems. All too often they are driven at breakneck speed and crammed with close to 30 people when they were designed for 18 (there's always room for one more), with a tout or conductor leaning out the side door. The front seat is the most comfortable, but thanks to the high number of head-on collisions in Africa, this seat is called the 'death seat': how many old bus-drivers have you seen? (If you do see one, be sure to choose his bus!) These minibuses are known by different names across the continent (*matatus* in Kenya, *dalla-dallas* in Tanzania, *tro-tros* in Ghana, *poda-podas* in Sierra Leone), names that are, confusingly, fairly interchangeable for shared taxis and bush taxis. Minibuses usually only leave when very full (a process that may take hours), and will stop frequently en route to pick up and set down passengers. Minibuses are also the favourite prey of roadblock police, who are not averse to unloading every passenger while they enter into lengthy discussions about paperwork and 'fines' that may need paying.

Shared Taxi

Shared taxis are usually Peugeot 504s or 505s or old spacious Mercedes saloons (common in North Africa). They should definitely be considered, where available (which is not everywhere). Your average shared taxi is certainly quicker, more comfortable (if a little crowded) and less of a palaver than taking a bus or minibus, although many shared taxis are driven by lunatic speed freaks. They cost a little more than the corresponding bus fare, but in most cases once the vehicle has filled up (usually with nine to 12 people, packed in like sardines) it heads more or less directly to the destination, without constant stops for passengers. You should expect to pay an additional fee for your baggage in West Africa, but usually not elsewhere. Motorcycle taxis can also be convenient, if dangerous.

'Bush taxi' is something of a catch-all term and is used slightly differently across the continent. Basically, a bush taxi is any multiperson mode of public transport that isn't a bus.

Tours

Overland truck tours did much to open up cheap travel in Africa, blazing trails where no tourist had boldly gone before. Today there are a huge number of overland trucks chugging around East and Southern Africa (Arusha in Tanzania and Nairobi in Kenya are common starting points), but fewer range across West Africa. There are a number of trucks heading all the way from London or Istanbul to Cape Town, a trip that can last seven months.

Truck tours don't suit everyone, but a truck and its staff can take away many of the hassles of travelling in Africa (something you'll appreciate if you're crossing through tricky areas such as

Nigeria, Chad and Sudan), and if you get on well with your fellow travellers it can be a real laugh.

There are, of course, downsides: you don't always get time to explore a place in depth, and sightseeing can end up being a terrible rush; cliquey and racist attitudes can mean it's much harder to meet locals or even other travellers; getting stuck with a bunch of drunken morons or anal retentive types for weeks on end might send you crazy; many campsites won't let overland trucks in; if you're used to travelling independently, having to leave decisions to someone else can be very hard; some trucks take up to 30 passengers; and group chores and vehicle security can be a pain. Remember also that once you've committed money to the communal food kitty, you won't get it back, even if you want to leave the tour before the end.

Whatever you decide, go through company brochures with a fine-tooth comb and always ask what you're required to do (on most tours you'll have to do the washing up at least), how many people are on the truck (loads of people equals cheaper prices) and how much flexibility there is. It's probably best to start with a shorter trip to see how truck life suits you before you commit to a six-month trip.

The truck tour business is dominated by British companies, but they often have representatives in North America and Australasia (check out the websites for more information).

Acacia Expeditions (☎020-7706 4700; www.acacia-africa.com) Concentrates on East and Southern Africa.

African Trails (☎01524-419909; www.africantrails.co.uk) Truck tours through much of Africa, including West and North Africa.

Dragoman (☎01728-885103; www.dragoman.com) West Africa, plus the Cairo to Cape Town route.

Keystone Journeys (www.keystonejourneys.com)

Oasis Overland (☎01963-363400; www.oasisoverland.com) Runs overland truck tours through Africa and the Middle East.

Train

Where available, travelling by train is a wonderful way to get around Africa. Even the shortest rail journey can be a classic experience, full of cultural exchange, amazing landscapes and crazy stations where all kinds of food, drinks and goods are hawked at train windows. Train travel is safer and usually more comfortable than travelling by road, although outside Southern and North Africa the trains are often very slow. Long delays aren't uncommon. Second-class fares weigh in about the same as, or less than, the corresponding bus fare.

More expensive (but still negligible by Western standards) are sleeping compartments and 1st- or 2nd-class carriages, which take the strain out of long journeys and occasionally allow you to travel in style – some high-class train carriages are like little wood-panelled museums of colonialism. It's worth noting that in many countries male and female passengers can only sleep in the same compartment if they buy the tickets for the whole compartment (four or six bunks), and even then you might be asked for evidence that you're married!

The flip side of train travel is that security and sanitation facilities on trains can be poor, especially in 3rd class, which, although novel and entertaining at first, soon becomes simply crowded and uncomfortable. Keep an eye on your baggage at all times and lock carriage doors and windows at night.

Truck

In many out-of-the-way places, trucks are the only reliable form of transport. They may primarily carry goods, but drivers are always keen to supplement their income, so there's usually room for paying passengers. Most folks are stuck up on top of the cargo, but a few more expensive spots are often available in the cab.

Sitting high and exposed on top of a truck chugging through the African landscape can be a great experience; just take heavy precautions against the sun, wrap up against dust and bring a carry mat or similar to cushion yourself against uncomfortable cargo – you could find yourself sitting on top of a car engine for hours on end! Also, remember that trucks are even slower than buses.

On many routes you'll be able to wave down a truck, but lifts can often be arranged the night before departure at the 'truck park' – a compound or dust patch that you'll find in almost every African town of note. 'Fares' are pretty much fixed – expect to pay a little less than an equivalent bus fare, and make sure you agree on the price before climbing aboard. If the journey is going to take more than one night or one day, bring your own food and water.

Health

As long as you stay up to date with your vaccinations and take some basic preventive measures, you'd have to be pretty unlucky to succumb to most of the health hazards covered in this chapter. Africa certainly has an impressive selection of tropical diseases on offer, but you're much more likely to get a bout of diarrhoea (in fact, you should bank on it), a cold or an infected mosquito bite than an exotic disease such as Rift Valley or West Nile fever. When it comes to injuries (as opposed to illness), the most likely reason for needing medical help in Africa is as a result of road accidents – vehicles are rarely well maintained, the roads are potholed and poorly lit, and drink driving is common.

Before You Go

- Get a check-up from your dentist and from your doctor if you have any regular medication or chronic illness, eg high blood pressure and asthma.
- Organise spare contact lenses and glasses (and take your optical prescription with you)
- Assemble a first-aid and medical kit
- Arrange necessary vaccinations. Don't leave this until the last minute. Many vaccines don't take effect until two weeks after you've been immunised, so visit a doctor four to eight weeks before departure. Ask your doctor for an International Certificate of Vaccination (otherwise known as the yellow booklet), which will list all the vaccinations you've received. This is mandatory for the African countries that require proof of yellow fever vaccination upon entry, but it's a good idea to carry it anyway wherever you travel.
- Become a member of the **International Association for Medical Advice to Travellers** (IAMAT; www.iamat.org), which lists trusted English-speaking doctors.
- If you'll be spending time in remote areas, you might like to do a first-aid course (contact the Red Cross or St John's Ambulance) or attend a remote medicine first-aid course, such as that offered by the **Royal Geographical Society** (www.wildernessmedicaltraining.co.uk) or the **American Red Cross** (www.redcross.org).
- Bring medications in their original containers, clearly labelled.
- A signed and dated letter from your physician describing all medical conditions and medications, including generic names, is also a good idea.
- If carrying syringes or needles, be sure to have a physician's letter documenting their medical necessity.

Insurance

Find out in advance whether your insurance plan will make payments directly to providers or will reimburse you later for overseas health expenditures (in many countries doctors expect payment in cash). It's vital to ensure that your travel insurance will cover the emergency transport to get you to a hospital in a major city, to better medical facilities elsewhere in Africa, or all the way home, by air and with a medical attendant if necessary. Not all insurance covers this, so check the contract carefully. If you need medical help, your insurance company might be able to help locate the nearest hospital or clinic, or you can ask at your hotel. In an emergency, contact your embassy or consulate.

Recommended Vaccinations

The **World Health Organization** (www.who.int/ith) recommends that all travellers be covered for diphtheria, tetanus, measles, mumps, rubella and polio, as well as for hepatitis B, regardless of their destination. Planning to travel is a great time to ensure that all routine vaccination cover is complete. The consequences of these particular diseases can be severe, and outbreaks do occur.

According to the **Centers for Disease Control and Prevention** (www.cdc.gov/travel), the following vaccinations are recommended for all parts of Africa: hepatitis A, hepatitis B, meningococcal meningitis, rabies and typhoid, and boosters for tetanus, diphtheria and measles. A yellow-fever vaccination is not necessarily recommended for all parts of Africa, although the certificate is an entry requirement for a number of countries.

Medical Checklist

Consider packing.

- Acetaminophen (paracetamol) or aspirin
- Acetazolamide (Diamox) for altitude sickness (prescription only)
- Adhesive or paper tape
- Anti-inflammatory drugs (eg ibuprofen)
- Antibacterial ointment (eg Bactroban) for cuts and abrasions (prescription only)
- Antibiotics (prescription only), eg ciprofloxacin (Ciproxin) or norfloxacin (Utinor)
- Antidiarrhoeal drugs (eg loperamide)
- Antihistamines (for hay fever and allergic reactions)
- Antimalaria pills
- Bandages, gauze, gauze rolls
- DEET-containing insect repellent for the skin
- Iodine tablets (for water purification)
- Oral rehydration salts
- Permethrin-containing insect spray for clothing, tents and bed nets
- Pocket knife
- Scissors, safety pins, tweezers
- Sterile needles, syringes and fluids if travelling to remote areas
- Steroid cream or hydrocortisone cream (for allergic rashes)
- Sunblock
- Thermometer

If you are travelling through a malarial area – particularly an area in which falciparum malaria predominates – consider taking a self-diagnostic kit that can identify malaria in the blood from a finger prick.

Websites

There is a wealth of travel health advice online; the Lonely Planet website at www.lonelyplanet.com is a good place to start. The World Health Organization publishes a superb book called *International Travel and Health*, revised annually and available online at no cost at www.who.int/ith. Other websites of general interest are MD Travel Health at www.mdtravelhealth.com, which provides complete travel health recommendations for every country, updated daily, also at no cost; the Centers for Disease Control and Prevention at www.cdc.gov; and Fit for Travel at www.fitfortravel.scot.nhs.uk, which has up-to-date information about outbreaks and is very user-friendly.

It's also a good idea to consult your government's travel health website before departure, if one is available:

Australia (www.smartraveller.gov.au/tips/travelwell.html)

Canada (www.phac-aspc.gc.ca/index-eng.php)

UK (www.nhs.uk/nhsengland/Healthcareabroad/pages/Healthcareabroad.aspx)

USA (www.nc.cdc.gov/travel)

Further Reading

- *A Comprehensive Guide to Wilderness and Travel Medicine* by Eric A Weiss (1998)
- *How to Stay Healthy Abroad* by Richard Dawood (2002)
- Lonely Planet's *Healthy Travel Africa* by Isabelle Young & Tony Gherardin (2008)
- Lonely Planet's *Travel with Children* by Brigitte Barta et al (2009)
- *The Essential Guide to Travel Health* by Jane Wilson-Howarth (2009)
- *Travel in Health* by Graham Fry (1994)

In Africa

Availability & Cost of Health Care

Health care in Africa is varied: it can be excellent in the major cities, which generally have well-trained doctors and nurses, but it is often patchy off the beaten track.

Most drugs can be purchased over the counter throughout Africa, without a prescription. Many drugs for sale within Africa might be ineffective – they might be counterfeit or might not have been stored under the right conditions. The most common examples of counterfeit drugs are malaria tablets and expensive antibiotics, such as ciprofloxacin. Most drugs are available in capital cities, but in remote villages you will be lucky to find a couple of paracetamol tablets. It is strongly recommended that all drugs for chronic diseases be brought with you from home. Also, the availability and efficacy of condoms cannot be relied upon – bring all the contraception you'll need. Condoms bought in Africa might not be of the same quality as in Europe, North America or Australia, and they might have been stored in too hot an environment. Keep all condoms as cool as you can.

There is a high risk of contracting HIV from infected blood if you receive a blood transfusion in Africa. The **BloodCare Foundation** (www.bloodcare.org.uk) is a useful source of safe, screened blood, which can be transported to any part of the world within 24 hours.

The cost of health care might seem very cheap compared to first-world countries, but good care and drugs might be not be available. Evacuation to good medical care (within Africa or to your own country) can be very expensive indeed. Unfortunately, adequate – let alone good – health care is available only to very few residents of Africa.

Infectious Diseases

CHOLERA

Cholera is usually only a problem during natural or artificial disasters, eg war, floods or earthquakes, although small outbreaks can also occur at other times. Travellers are rarely affected.

Spread through Contaminated drinking water.

Symptoms and effects Profuse watery diarrhoea, which causes collapse if fluids are not replaced quickly.

Prevention and treatment Most cases could be avoided by close attention to good drinking water and by avoiding potentially contaminated food. Treatment is by fluid replacement (orally or via a drip), but sometimes antibiotics are needed. Self-treatment is not advised.

DENGUE FEVER (BREAK-BONE FEVER)

Present Sudan, Cameroon, Democratic Republic of Congo (DRC), Senegal, Burkina Faso, Guinea, Ethiopia, Djibouti, Somalia, Madagascar, Mozambique and South Africa.

Spread through Mosquito bites.

Symptoms & effects A feverish illness with headache and muscle pains similar to those experienced with a bad, prolonged attack of influenza. There might be a rash.

Prevention and treatment Mosquito bites should be avoided whenever possible. Self-treatment: paracetamol and rest.

In rare cases in Africa this becomes Severe Dengue Fever, with worsening symptoms including vomiting, rapid breathing and abdominal pain. Seek medical help, as this can be fatal.

DIPHTHERIA

Present Throughout Africa.

Spread through Close respiratory contact.

Symptoms and effects Usually causes a temperature and a severe sore throat. Sometimes a membrane forms across the throat, and a tracheostomy is needed to prevent suffocation.

Prevention and treatment Vaccination is recommended for all travellers, particularly those likely to be in close contact with the local population in infected areas. More important for long stays than for short-term trips. The vaccine is given as an injection alone or with tetanus, and lasts 10 years. Self-treatment: none.

FILARIASIS

Present Most parts of West, Central, East and southern Africa, and in Sudan in North Africa.

Spread through Mosquito bites, then tiny worms migrating in the lymphatic system.

Symptoms and effects Can include localised itching and swelling of the legs and or genitalia.

Prevention and treatment Avoid mosquito bites. Treatment is available, but self-treatments are not.

HEPATITIS A

Present Throughout Africa.

Spread through Contaminated food (particularly shellfish) and water.

Symptoms and effects Jaundice and, although it is rarely fatal, it can cause prolonged lethargy and delayed recovery. If you've had hepatitis A, you shouldn't drink alcohol for up to six months afterwards, but once you've recovered, there won't be any long-term problems. The first symptoms include dark urine and a yellow colour to the whites of the eyes. Sometimes a fever and abdominal pain might be present.

Prevention and treatment Hepatitis A vaccine (Avaxim, VAQTA, Havrix) is given as an injection: a single dose will give protection for up to a year, and a booster after a year gives 10-year protection. Hepatitis A and typhoid vaccines can also be given as a single-dose vaccine, hepatyrix or viatim. Self-treatment: none.

HEPATITIS B

Present Thoughout Africa.

Spread through Infected blood, contaminated needles and sexual intercourse. It can also be spread from an infected mother to the baby during childbirth.

Symptoms and effects Attacks the liver, causing jaundice and occasionally liver failure. Most people recover completely, but some people might be chronic carriers of the virus, which could lead eventually to cirrhosis or liver cancer.

Prevention and treatment Those visiting high-risk areas for long periods or at social or occupational risk should be immunised. Many countries now give hepatitis B as part of the routine childhood vaccination. It is given singly or can be given at the same time as hepatitis A. A course will give protection for at least five years. It can be given over four weeks or six months. Self-treatment: none.

HIV

Present Throughout Africa.

Spread through Infected blood and blood products, by sexual intercourse with an infected partner, and from an infected mother to her baby during childbirth and breastfeeding. It can be spread through 'blood to blood' contacts, such as with contaminated instruments during medical, dental, acupuncture and other body-piercing procedures, and through sharing used intravenous needles.

Prevention and treatment At present there is no cure;

medication that might keep the disease under control is available, but many countries in Africa do not have access to it for their own citizens, let alone for travellers. If you think you might have put yourself at risk of HIV infection, a blood test is necessary; a three-month gap after the exposure and before testing is required to allow antibodies to appear in the blood. Self-treatment: none.

LEISHMANIASIS

Present North Africa.

Spread through Bite of an infected sandfly.

Symptoms and effects Can cause a slowly growing skin lump or ulcer (the cutaneous form) and sometimes develop into a serious life-threatening fever with anaemia and weight loss. Dogs can also be carriers of Leishmaniasis.

Prevention and treatment Sandfly and dog bites should be avoided whenever possible. Self-treatment: none.

LEPTOSPIROSIS

Present West and southern Africa; in Chad, Congo and DRC in Central Africa; in Algeria, Morocco and Sudan in North Africa; and in Ethiopia and Somalia in East Africa.

Spread through The excreta of infected rodents, especially rats.

Symptoms and effects A fever, sometimes jaundice, hepatitus and renal failure.

Prevention and treatment It is unusual for travellers to be affected unless living in poor sanitary conditions. Self-treatment: none.

MALARIA

Present Endemic in Central, East, West and southern Africa; slight risk in North Africa (except for Sudan, where the risk is significant). The risk of malarial transmission at altitudes higher than 2000m is rare.

Spread through The bite of the female Anopheles mosquito. There are several types of malaria; falciparum malaria is the most dangerous type and the predominant form in Africa. Infection rates vary with season and climate, so check out the situation before departure. Unlike most other diseases regularly encountered by travellers, there is no vaccination against malaria (yet). However, several different drugs are used to prevent malaria, and new ones are in the pipeline. Up-to-date advice from a travel health clinic is essential, as some medication is more suitable for some travellers than others. The pattern of drug-resistant malaria is changing rapidly, so what was advised several years ago might no longer be the case.

Symptoms and effects The early stages include headaches, fevers, generalised aches and pains, and malaise, which could be mistaken for flu. Other symptoms can include abdominal pain, diarrhoea and a cough.

Prevention and treatment Anyone who develops a fever in a malarial area should assume malarial infection until a blood test proves negative, even if you have been taking antimalarial medication. If not treated, the next stage could develop within 24 hours (particularly if falciparum malaria is the parasite): jaundice, then reduced consciousness and coma (also known as cerebral malaria) followed by death. Treatment in hospital is essential, though the death rate might still be as high as 10% even in the best intensive-care facilities.

Many travellers are under the impression that malaria is a mild illness, that treatment is always easy and successful, and that taking antimalarial drugs causes more illness through side effects than actually getting malaria. In Africa, this is unfortunately not true. Side effects depend on the drug being taken. Doxycycline can cause heartburn and indigestion; mefloquine (Larium) can cause anxiety attacks, insomnia and nightmares,

Malarial Risk in Africa

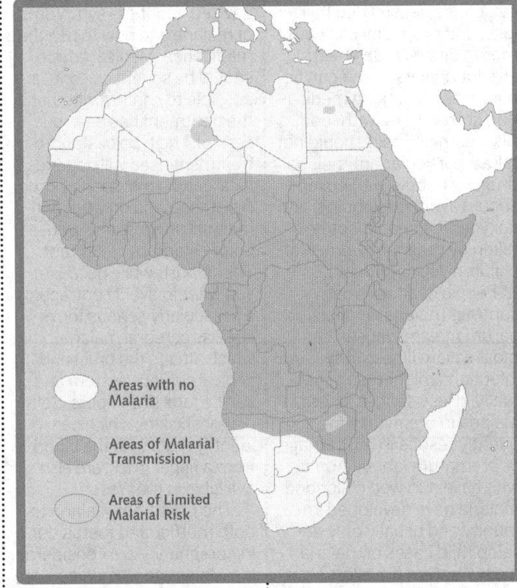

and (rarely) severe psychiatric disorders; chloroquine can cause nausea and hair loss; and proguanil can cause mouth ulcers. Side effects are not universal, and can be minimised by taking medication correctly, eg with food. Also, some people should not take a particular antimalarial drug, eg people with epilepsy should avoid mefloquine, and doxycycline should not be taken by pregnant women or children younger than 12.

People of all ages can contract malaria, and falciparum malaria causes the most severe illness. Repeated infections might result eventually in less serious illness. Malaria in pregnancy frequently results in miscarriage or premature labour. Adults who have survived childhood malaria have developed immunity and usually only develop mild cases of malaria; most Western travellers have no immunity at all. Immunity wanes after 18 months of nonexposure, so even if you have had malaria in the past and used to live in a malaria-prone area, you might no longer be immune. One million children die annually from malaria in Africa.

If you decide that you really do not wish to take antimalarial drugs, you must understand the risks, and be obsessive about avoiding mosquito bites. Use nets and insect repellent, and report any fever or flulike symptoms to a doctor as soon as possible. Some people advocate homeopathic preparations against malaria, such as Demal200, but as yet there is no conclusive evidence that they are effective, and many homeopaths do not recommend their use.

If you are planning a journey through a malarial area, particularly where falciparum malaria predominates, consider taking stand-by treatment. Emergency stand-by treatment should be seen as emergency treatment aimed at saving the patient's life and not as routine self-medication. It should be advised only if you will be remote from medical facilities and have been advised about the symptoms of malaria and how to use the medication. Medical advice should be sought as soon as possible to confirm whether the treatment has been successful. The type of stand-by treatment used will depend on local conditions, such as drug resistance, and on what antimalarial drugs are being used before stand-by treatment. This is worthwhile because you want to avoid contracting a particularly serious form such as cerebral malaria, which affects the brain and central nervous system and can be fatal in 24 hours. Self-diagnostic kits, which can identify malaria in the blood from a finger prick, are also available in the West.

The risks from malaria to both mother and foetus during pregnancy are considerable. Unless good medical care can be absolutely guaranteed, travel throughout Africa when pregnant – particularly to malarial areas – should be discouraged unless essential. Self-treatment: see stand-by treatment if you are more than 24 hours away from medical help.

MENINGOCOCCAL MENINGITIS

Present Central, West and East Africa; only in Sudan in North Africa; and only in Namibia, Malawi, Mozambique and Zambia in southern Africa.

Spread through Close respiratory contact and is more likely in crowded situations, such as dormitories, buses and clubs. Infection is uncommon in travellers. Vaccination is recommended for long stays and especially towards the end of the dry season, which is normally from June to November.

Symptoms and effects Fever, severe headache, neck stiffness and a red rash.

Prevention and treatment Immediate medical treatment is necessary. The ACWY vaccine is recommended for all travellers in sub-Saharan Africa. This vaccine is different from the meningococcal meningitis C vaccine given to children and adolescents in some countries, and it is safe to be given both types of vaccine. Self-treatment: none.

POLIOMYELITIS

Present Throughout Africa.

Spread through Contaminated food and water.

Symptoms and effects Polio can be carried asymptomatically (ie showing no symptoms) and can cause a transient fever. In rare cases it causes weakness or paralysis of one or more muscles, which might be permanent.

Prevention and treatment It is one of the vaccines given in childhood and should be boosted every 10 years, either orally (a drop on the tongue) or as an injection. Self-treatment: none.

RABIES

Present Throughout Africa.

Spread through The bites or licks of an infected animal on broken skin.

Symptoms and effects It is always fatal once the clinical symptoms start (which might be up to several months after an infected bite), so postbite vaccination should be given as soon as possible.

Prevention and treatment Avoid contact with animals, particularly dogs. Postbite vaccination (whether or not you've been vaccinated before the bite) prevents the virus from spreading to the central nervous system. Animal handlers should be vaccinated, as should those travelling to remote areas where a reliable source of postbite vaccine is not available within 24 hours. Three preventive injections are needed over a month. If you have not been vaccinated you will need a course of five injections starting 24 hours or as soon as possible after the injury. If you have been vac-

THE ANTIMALARIAL A TO D

A Awareness of the risk. No medication is totally effective, but protection of up to 95% is achievable with most drugs, as long as other measures are taken.

B Bites – avoid at all costs. Sleep in a screened room, use a mosquito spray or coils, sleep under a permethrin-impregnated net at night. Cover up at night with long trousers and long sleeves, preferably with permethrin-treated clothing. Apply appropriate repellent to all areas of exposed skin in the evenings.

C Chemical prevention (ie antimalarial drugs) is usually needed in malarial areas. Expert advice is needed as resistance patterns can change, and new drugs are in development. Not all antimalarial drugs are suitable for everyone, particularly for children, pregnant women or people with depression or epilepsy. Most antimalarial drugs need to be started at least a week in advance and continued for four weeks after the last possible exposure to malaria.

D Diagnosis. If you have a fever or flulike illness within a year of travel to a malarial area, malaria is a possibility, and immediate medical attention is necessary.

cinated, you will need fewer postbite injections, and have more time to seek medical help. Self-treatment: none.

BILHARZIA (SCHISTOSOMIASIS)

Present Throughout Africa with possible exception of Morocco, Algeria and Libya.

Spread through Flukes (minute worms) that are carried by a species of freshwater snail. The flukes are carried inside the snail, which sheds them into slow-moving or still water. The parasites penetrate human skin during paddling or swimming and then migrate to the bladder or bowel. They are passed out via stool or urine and could contaminate fresh water, where the cycle starts again.

Symptoms and effects There might be no symptoms. There might be a transient fever and rash, and advanced cases might have blood in the stool or in the urine.

Prevention and treatment Avoid paddling or swimming in freshwater lakes or slow-running rivers anywhere. A blood test can detect antibodies if you might have been exposed, and treatment is then possible in specialist travel or infectious disease clinics. If left untreated the infection could cause kidney failure or permanent bowel damage. It is not possible for you to infect others. Self-treatment: none.

TUBERCULOSIS (TB)

Present Throughout Africa.

Spread through Close respiratory contact and occasionally through infected milk or milk products.

Symptoms and effects Can be asymptomatic, only being picked up on a routine chest X-ray. Alternatively, it can cause a cough, weight loss or fever, sometimes months or even years after exposure.

Prevention and treatment BCG vaccination is recommended for those likely to be mixing closely with the local population. It is more important for long stays than for short-term stays. Inoculation with the BCG vaccine is not available in all countries. It is given routinely to many children in developing countries. In some countries, for example the UK, it is given to babies if they will be travelling with their families to areas with a high-risk of TB, and to previously unvaccinated school-age children if they live in areas of higher TB risk (eg multiethnic immigrant populations). The BCG gives a moderate degree of protection against TB. It causes a small permanent scar at the site of injection, and is usually given in a specialised chest clinic. It is a live vaccine and should not be given to pregnant women or immunocompromised individuals. Self-treatment: none.

TYPHOID

Present Throughout Africa.

Spread through Food or water contaminated by infected human faeces.

Symptoms and effects Starts usually with a fever or a pink rash on the abdomen. Sometimes septicaemia (blood poisoning) can occur.

Prevention and treatment A typhoid vaccine (typhim Vi, typherix) will give protection for three years. In some countries, the oral vaccine Vivotif is also available. Antibiotics are usually given as treatment, and death is rare unless septicaemia occurs. Self-treatment: none.

YELLOW FEVER

Present West Africa, parts of Central and Eastern Africa. Travellers should carry a certificate as evidence of vaccination if they have recently been in an infected country, to avoid any possible difficulties with immigration. For a full list of these countries visit the Centers for Disease Control and

Prevention website (www.cdc.gov/travel.htm). There is always the possibility that a traveller without a legally required, up-to-date certificate will be vaccinated and detained in isolation at the port of arrival for up to 10 days or possibly repatriated.

Spread through Infected mosquitoes.

Symptoms and effects Range from a flulike illness to severe hepatitis (liver inflammation), jaundice and death.

Prevention and treatment The yellow fever vaccination must be given at a designated clinic and is valid for 10 years. It is a live vaccine and must not be given to immunocompromised or pregnant travellers. Self-treatment: none.

Travellers' Diarrhoea

Present Throughout Africa. Although it's not inevitable that you will get diarrhoea, it's certainly very likely. Diarrhoea is the most common travel-related illness – figures suggest that at least half of all travellers to Africa will get diarrhoea at some stage.

Spread through Sometimes caused by dietary changes, such as increased spices or oils.

Symptoms and effects A few loose stools don't require treatment, but if you start having more than four or five stools a day, you should start taking an antibiotic (usually a quinoline drug, such as ciprofloxacin or norfloxacin) and an antidiarrheal agent (such as loperamide) if you are not within easy reach of a toilet.

Prevention and treatment To help prevent diarrhoea, avoid tap water unless you're sure it's safe to drink. You should also only eat fresh fruits or vegetables if cooked or peeled, and be wary of dairy products that might contain unpasteurised milk. Although freshly cooked food can often be a safe option, plates or serving utensils might be dirty, so you should be highly selective when eating food from street vendors (make sure that cooked food is piping hot all the way through).

If you develop diarrhoea, be sure to drink plenty of fluids, preferably an oral rehydration solution containing water, and salt and sugar. If diarrhoea is bloody, persists for more than 72 hours or is accompanied by fever, shaking chills or severe abdominal pain, you should seek medical attention.

AMOEBIC DYSENTERY & GIARDIASIS

Present Throughout Africa

Spread through Eating contaminated food and water

Symptoms and effects Amoebic dysentry causes blood and mucus in the faeces. It can be relatively mild and tends to come on gradually. Giardiasis usually appears a week or more after you have been exposed to the offending parasite. It causes only a short-lived bout of typical travellers' diarrhoea, but it can also cause persistent diarrhoea.

Prevention and treatment Seek medical advice as soon as possible if you think you have either illness as they won't clear up without treatment (which is with specific antibiotics).

Environmental Hazards

HEAT EXHAUSTION

Causes Occurs following heavy sweating and excessive fluid loss with inadequate replacement of fluids and salt, and is particularly common in hot climates when taking unaccustomed exercise before full acclimatisation.

Symptoms and effects Headache, dizziness and tiredness.

Prevention Dehydration is already happening by the time you feel thirsty – aim to drink sufficient water to produce pale, diluted urine.

Treatment Fluid replacement with water and/or fruit juice, and cooling by cold water and fans. The treat-

Yellow Fever Risk in Africa

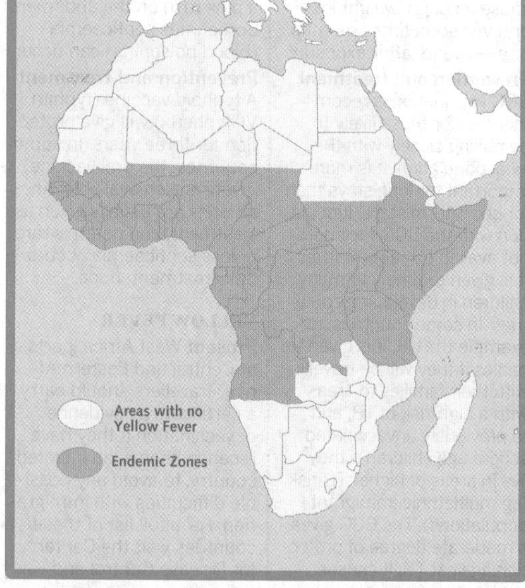

MANDATORY YELLOW FEVER VACCINATION

The following list is a guide only. Please check with your doctor and the embassy of the country to which you are travelling for the most recent requirements.

Central Africa Mandatory in Central African Republic (CAR), Congo, DRC, Equatorial Guinea and Gabon, and recommended in Chad.

East Africa Mandatory in Rwanda and Uganda; it is advised for Burundi, Ethiopia, Kenya, Somalia and Tanzania.

North Africa Not mandatory for any areas of North Africa, but Algeria, Libya and Tunisia require evidence of yellow fever vaccination if entering from an infected country. It is recommended for travellers to Sudan, and might be given to unvaccinated travellers leaving the country.

Southern Africa Not mandatory for entry into any countries of southern Africa, although it is necessary if entering from an infected country.

West Africa Mandatory in Benin, Burkina Faso, Cameroon, Côte d'Ivoire, Ghana, Liberia, Mali, Niger, São Tomé & Príncipe and Togo, and recommended for The Gambia, Guinea, Guinea-Bissau, Mauritania, Nigeria, Senegal and Sierra Leone.

ment of the salt loss component consists of consuming salty fluids, as in soup, and adding a little more table salt to foods than usual.

HEATSTROKE

Causes Heat exhaustion is a precursor to the much more serious condition of heatstroke.

Symptoms and effects Damage to the sweating mechanism, with an excessive rise in body temperature; irrational and hyperactive behaviour; and eventually loss of consciousness and death.

Treatment Rapid cooling by spraying the body with water and fanning is ideal. Emergency fluid and electrolyte replacement is often also required by intravenous drip.

INSECT BITES & STINGS

Mosquitoes might not always carry malaria or dengue fever, but they (and other insects) can cause irritation and infected bites. To avoid these, take the same precautions you would for avoiding malaria. Use DEET-based insect repellents, although these are not the only effective repellents. Excellent clothing treatments are also available; mosquitoes that land on treated clothing will die.

Bee and wasp stings cause real problems only to those who have a severe allergy to the stings (anaphylaxis.) If you are one of these people, make sure you carry an 'epipen' – an adrenalin (epinephrine) injection, which you can give yourself. This could save your life.

Sandflies are found around the Mediterranean beaches. They usually only cause a nasty itchy bite but can carry a rare skin disorder called cutaneous Leishmaniasis. Prevention of bites with DEET-based repellents is sensible.

Scorpions are frequently found in arid climates. They can cause a painful sting that is sometimes life-threatening. If stung by a scorpion, take a painkiller. Medical treatment should be sought if collapse occurs.

Bed bugs are often found in hostels and cheap hotels. They lead to very itchy, lumpy bites. Spraying the mattress with crawling insect killer after changing bedding will get rid of them.

Scabies is also frequently found in cheap accommodation. These tiny mites live in the skin, particularly between the fingers. They cause an intensely itchy rash. The itch is easily treated with malathion and permethrin lotion from a pharmacy; other members of the household also need treating to avoid spreading scabies, even if they do not show any symptoms.

SNAKE BITES

Basically, avoid getting bitten! Do not walk barefoot, or stick your hand into holes or cracks. However, 50% of those bitten by venomous snakes are not actually injected with poison (envenomed). If bitten by a snake, do not panic. Immobilise the bitten limb with a splint (such as a stick) and apply a bandage over the site, with firm pressure – similar to bandaging a sprain. Do not apply a tourniquet, or cut or suck the bite. Get the victim to medical help as soon as possible, where antivenom can be given if needed.

WATER

- Except in South Africa, never drink tap water unless it has been boiled, filtered or chemically disinfected (such as with iodine tablets)
- Never drink from streams, rivers and lakes.
- Avoid drinking from pumps and wells – some do bring pure water to the surface, but the presence of animals can still contaminate supplies.

Language

Africa's myriad ethnic groups speak several hundred local languages, many subdivided into numerous distinct dialects. The people of Nigeria, for example, speak around 500 languages and dialects according to the Ethnologue report, while even tiny Guinea-Bissau has around 20 languages. Consequently, common languages are essential, and several are used. These may be the language of the largest group in a particular area or country, such as Hausa, or a language that has spread beyond its original geographical boundaries due to trade, such as Swahili. The former colonial languages (English, French and Portuguese) also serve as common languages and have official status in many African countries. In some areas, the common tongue is a creole – a combination of African and European languages.

This chapter provides the basics in several European and African languages that you'll find most useful when travelling across the continent, as they are either in official use or spoken as regional lingua francas. See also the relevant destination chapter for a list of languages spoken in each country.

AMHARIC

Amharic is Ethiopia's national language, and it is also widely spoken in Eritrea.

If you read our pronunciation guides as if they were English, you'll be understood. The apostrophe (') before a vowel indicates a glottal stop, which sounds the pause in the middle of 'uh-oh'. Amharic's 'glottalised' consonants (ch', k', p', s' and t' in our pronunciation guides), are pronounced by tightening and releasing the vocal cords, a bit like combining the sound with the glottal stop. Note also that the sound r is trilled.

Amharic word endings vary according to the gender of people you're speaking to, which is indicated in this chapter where relevant by the abbreviations 'm' (for speaking to a male) and 'f' (for addressing a female).

Arabic numerals (ie those used in English) are commonly used in writing. Amharic words are used to refer to numbers in speech.

WANT MORE?

For in-depth language information and handy phrases, check out Lonely Planet's *Africa Phrasebook*. You'll find it at **shop.lonelyplanet.com**, or you can buy Lonely Planet's iPhone phrasebooks at the Apple App Store.

Hello.	ሰላም	suh·lam
Goodbye.	ደህና ሁን	duh·na hun (m)
	ደህና ሁኚ	duh·na hun·yee (f)
Yes.	አዎ	'a·wo
No.	አይደለም·	'ai·duh·luhm
Please.	እባክህ	'i·ba·kih (m)
	እባክሽ	'i·ba·kish·(f)
Thank you.	አመሰግናለሁ·	'a·muh·suh·gi·na·luh·hu
Sorry.	ይቅር	yi·k'ir·ta
Help!	እርዳታ	'ir·da·ta
	እርዳታ!	'ir·da·ta

Do you speak English?
እንግሊዘኛ ትችላለህ/ ትችያለሽ? — 'in·glee·zuh·nya ti·chi·la·luh·hi/ ti·chia·luhsh (m/f)

I don't understand.
አልገባኝም — 'al·guh·bany·mi

How much is it?
ዋጋው ስንት ነው? — wa·gow sint nuhw

Where are the toilets?
ሽንት ቤት የት ነው? — shint bet yuht nuhw

1	አንድ	and
2	ሁለት	hu·luht
3	ሶስት	sost
4	አራት	'ar·at
5	አምስት	'am·mist
6	ስድስት	si·dist
7	ሰባት	suh·bat
8	ስምንት	si·mint
9	ዘጠኝ	zuh·t'uhny
10	አስር	a·sir

AFRIKAANS

Afrikaans is one of the official languages of South Africa. It has about six million speakers and is also spoken in Botswana, Malawi, Namibia and Zambia.

Read our coloured pronunciation guides as if they were English and you'll be understood. The stressed syllables are in italics. Note that kh is pronounced as the 'ch' in the Scottish *loch* and r is trilled.

Hello.	*Hallo.*	ha·*loh*
Goodbye.	*Totsiens.*	tot·*seens*
Yes.	*Ja.*	yaa
No.	*Nee.*	ney
Please.	*Asseblief.*	a·si·*bleef*
Thank you.	*Dankie.*	*dang*·kee
Sorry.	*Jammer.*	*ya*·min
Help!	*Help!*	help

Do you speak English?
Praat jy Engels? praat yay *eng*·ils

I don't understand.
Ek verstaan nie. ek vir·*staan* nee

How much is it?
Hoeveel kos dit? *hu*·fil kos dit

Where are the toilets?
Waar is die toilette? vaar is dee toy·*le*·ti

1	*een*	eyn
2	*twee*	twey
3	*drie*	dree
4	*vier*	feer
5	*vyf*	fayf
6	*ses*	ses
7	*sewe*	see·vi
8	*agt*	akht
9	*nege*	*ney*·khi
10	*tien*	teen

ARABIC

The following phrases are in MSA (Modern Standard Arabic), which is the official language of the Arab world, used in schools, administration and the media. Note, though, that there are significant differences between MSA and the colloquial Arabic from different countries. Egyptian, Gulf, Levantine, Moroccan and Tunisian Arabic are the most common spoken varieties, sometimes mutually unintelligible and with no official written form.

Arabic is written from right to left in Arabic script. Read our coloured pronunciation guides as if they were English and you should be understood. Note that a is pronounced as in 'act', aa as the 'a' in 'father', aw as in 'law', ay as in 'say', ee as in 'see', i as in 'hit', oo as in 'zoo', u as in 'put', gh is a throaty sound, r is rolled, dh is pronounced as in 'that', th as in 'thin' and kh as the 'ch' in the Scottish *loch*. The apostrophe (') indicates the glottal stop (like the pause in the middle of 'uh-oh'). The stressed syllables are indicated with italics. Masculine and feminine options are indicated with 'm' and 'f' respectively.

Basics

Hello.	السلام عليكم.	as·sa·*laa*·mu 'a·*lay*·kum
Goodbye.	إلى اللقاء.	*'i*·laa al·li·*kaa'*
Yes.	نعم.	*na*·'am
No.	لا.	laa
Excuse me.	عفواً.	*'af*·wan
Sorry.	آسف.	*'aa*·sif (m)
	آسفة.	*'aa*·si·fa (f)
Please.	لو سمحتَ.	law sa·*maḥ*·ta (m)
	لو سمحتِ.	law sa·*maḥ*·ti (f)
Thank you.	شكراً.	*shuk*·ran

What's your name?
ما اسمكَ؟ maa *'is*·mu·ka (m)
ما اسمكِ؟ maa *'is*·mu·ki (f)

My name is ...
اسمي ... *'is*·mee ...

Do you speak English?
هل تتكلمُ/ hal ta·ta·*kal*·la·mu/
تتكلمينَ ta·ta·kal·la·*mee*·na
الإنجليزية؟ al·'inj·lee·*zee*·ya (m/f)

I don't understand.
أنا لا أفهم. *'a*·naa laa *'af*·ham

Accommodation

Where's a ...?	أين أجد ...؟	'ay·na 'a·ji·du ...
campsite	مخيم	mu·khay·yam
guesthouse	بيت للضيوف	bayt li·du·yoof
hotel	فندق	fun·duk
youth hostel	فندق شباب	fun·duk sha·baab

Do you have a ... room?	هل عندكم غرفةٌ ...؟	hal 'in·da·kum ghur·fa·tun ...
single	بسرير منفردٍ	bi·sa·ree·rin mun·fa·rid
double	بسرير مزدوَّج	bi·sa·ree·rin muz·daw·waj

How much is it per ...?	كم ثمنه لِـ ...؟	kam tha·ma·nu·hu li ...
night	ليلةٍ واحدة	lay·la·tin waa·hid
person	شخصٍ واحدة	shakh·sin waa·hid

Eating & Drinking

What would you recommend?
ماذا توصي؟ maa·dhaa too·see (m)
ماذا توصينَ؟ maa·dhaa too·see·na (f)

What's the local speciality?
ما الوجبة الخاصّة لهذه المنطقة؟ maa al·waj·ba·tul khaa·sa li·haa·dhi·hil man·ta·ka

Do you have vegetarian food?
هل لديكم طعامٌ نباتيّ؟ hal la·day·ku·mu ta·'aa·mun na·baa·tee

I'd like the ..., please.	أريد ...، لو سمحتَ.	'u·ree·du ... law sa·mah·ta
bill	الحساب	hi·saab
menu	قائمة الطعام	kaa·'i·ma·tu at·ta·'aam

beer	بيرة	bee·ra
bottle	زجاجة	zu·jaa·ja
breakfast	فطور	fu·toor
cafe	مقهىً	mak·han
coffee	قهوة	kah·wa
cold	بارد	baa·rid (m)
	باردة	baa·ri·da (f)
cup	فنجان	fin·jaan
dinner	عشاء	'a·shaa'
drink	مشروب	mash·roob
fish	سمك	sa·mak
food	طعام	ta·'aam
fork	شوكة	shaw·ka
fruit	فاكهة	faa·ki·ha
glass	كأس	ka's
hot	حار	haar (m)
	حارة	haa·ra (f)
juice	عصير	'a·see·ru
knife	سكين	sik·keen
lunch	غداء	gha·daa'
market	سوق	sook
meat	لحم	lahm
milk	حليب	ha·leeb
mineral water	مياه معدنية	mi·yaah ma'·da·nee·ya
plate	صحن	sahn
restaurant	مطعمٌ	mat·'am
spoon	ملعقة	mal·'a·ka
vegetable	خضراوات	khud·raa·waat
water	ماء	maa'
wine	نبيذ	na·beedh

Emergencies

Help!	ساعدني!	saa·'i·du·nee (m)
	ساعديني!	saa·'i·dee·nee (f)
Go away!	اتركني!	'it·ruk·nee (m)
	اتركيني!	'it·ru·kee·nee (f)

Call ...!	اتّصلْ بـ ...!	'it·ta·sil bi ... (m)
	اتّصلي بـ ...!	'it·ta·si·lee bi ... (f)
a doctor	طبيبٍ	ta·beeb
the police	الشرطة	ash·shur·ta

Numbers – Arabic

1	١	واحد	waa·hid
2	٢	اثنان	'ith·naan
3	٣	ثلاثة	tha·laa·tha
4	٤	أربعة	'ar·ba·'a
5	٥	خمسة	kham·sa
6	٦	ستة	sit·ta
7	٧	سبعة	sab·'a
8	٨	ثمانية	tha·maa·ni·ya
9	٩	تسعة	tis·'a
10	١٠	عشرة	'a·sha·ra

Note that Arabic numerals, unlike letters, are written from left to right.

Where are the toilets?

أينَ دورات المياه؟ *'ay*·na daw·*raa*·tul mee·*yaah*

I'm lost.

أنا ضائع. 'a·naa *daa*·'i' (m)

أنا ضائعة. 'a·naa *daa*·'i·'a (f)

I'm sick.

أنا مريض. 'a·naa ma·*reed*

Shopping & Services

I'm looking for ...

أبحثُ عن ... *'ab*·ha·thu 'an ...

Can I look at it?

هل يمكنني أن hal yum·*ki*·nu·nee 'an

أراه؟ 'a·*raa*·hu

Do you have any others?

هل عندك غيره؟ hal *'in*·da·kum *ghay*·ru·hu

How much is it?

كم سعره؟ kam *si'*·ru·hu

That's too expensive.

هذا غالٍ جدًّا. *haa*·dhaa *ghaa*·lin *jid*·dan

Where's an ATM?

أينَ جهاز الصرافة؟ *'ay*·na ji·*haaz* as·sar·*raa*·fa

Time & Dates

What time is it?

كم الساعة الآن؟ kam as·*saa*·'a·tul 'aan

It's (two) o'clock.

الساعة(الثانية). as·*saa*·'a tu (ath·*thaa*·nee·ya)

morning	صباح	sa·*baah*
afternoon	بعد الظهر	*ba'*·da adh·*dhuh*·ri
evening	مساء	ma·*saa'*

yesterday	أمس	*'am*·si
today	اليوم	al·*yawm*
tomorrow	غداً	*gha*·dan

Transport & Directions

Is this the ...	هل هذا الـ ...	hal *haa*·dhaa al ...
to (Dubai)?	إلى (دبي)؟	*'i*·laa (*du*·ba·yee)
boat	سفينة	sa·fee·na
bus	باص	baas
plane	طائرة	*taa*·'i·ra
train	قطار	ki·*taar*

What time's	في أيّ ساعةِ	fee *'ay*·yee *saa*·'a·tin
the ... bus?	يغادرُ الباص	yu·*ghaa*·di·ru al·*baas*
	الـ ...؟	al ...
first	أوّل	*'aw*·wal
last	آخر	*'aa*·khir

One ... ticket,	تذكرة ...	*tadh*·ka·ra·tu ...
please.	واحدة, لو سمحت.	*waa*·hi·da law sa·*mah*·ta
one-way	ذهاب فقط	dha·*haa*·bu *fa*·kat
return	ذهاب	dha·*haa*·bu
	وإياب	wa·'ee·*yaab*

How much is it to ...?

كم الأجرة إلى ...؟ kam al·*'uj*·ra·ti *'i*·laa ...

Please take me to ...

أوصلني عند ... 'aw·*sal*·nee 'ind ...

لو سمحتَ. law sa·*mah*·ta

Where's the (market)?

أين الـ (سوق)؟ *'ay*·na al (sook)

What's the address?

ما هو العنوان؟ maa *hu*·wa al·'un·*waan*

FRENCH

The sounds used in spoken French can almost all be found in English. There are a couple of exceptions: nasal vowels (represented in our pronunciation guides by o or u followed by an almost inaudible nasal consonant sound m, n or ng), the 'funny' *u* (ew in our guides) and the deep-in-the-throat *r*. Bearing these few points in mind and reading our pronunciation guides below as if they were English, you won't have problems being understood. Note that syllables are for the most part equally stressed in French.

Masculine and feminine forms of words are provided in the following phrases where relevant, indicated with 'm' and 'f' respectively.

Basics

Hello.	*Bonjour.*	bon·zhoor
Goodbye.	*Au revoir.*	o·rer·vwa
Excuse me.	*Excusez-moi.*	ek·skew·zay·mwa
Sorry.	*Pardon.*	par·don
Yes.	*Oui.*	wee
No.	*Non.*	non
Please.	*S'il vous plaît.*	seel voo play
Thank you.	*Merci.*	mair·see
You're welcome.	*De rien.*	der ree·en

How are you?
Comment allez-vous? ko·mon ta·lay·voo

Fine, and you?
Bien, merci. Et vous? byun mair·see ay voo

My name is ...
Je m'appelle ... zher ma·pel ...

What's your name?
Comment vous appelez-vous? ko·mon voo·za·play voo

Do you speak English?
Parlez-vous anglais? par·lay·voo ong·glay

I don't understand.
Je ne comprends pas. zher ner kom·pron pa

Accommodation

campsite	*camping*	kom·peeng
guesthouse	*pension*	pon·syon
hotel	*hôtel*	o·tel
youth hostel	*auberge de jeunesse*	o·berzh der zher·nes
a ... room	*une chambre ...*	ewn shom·brer ...
double	*avec un grand lit*	a·vek un gron lee
single	*à un lit*	a un lee

How much is it per night/person?
Quel est le prix par nuit/personne? kel ay ler pree par nwee/per·son

Is breakfast included?
Est-ce que le petit déjeuner est inclus? es·ker ler per·tee day·zher·nay ayt en·klew

Eating & Drinking

Can I see the menu, please?
Est-ce que je peux voir la carte, s'il vous plaît? es·ker zher per vwar la kart seel voo play

What would you recommend?
Qu'est-ce que vous conseillez? kes·ker voo kon·say·yay

I'm a vegetarian.
Je suis végétarien/végétarienne. (m/f) zher swee vay·zhay·ta·ryun/vay·zhay·ta·ryen

I don't eat ...
Je ne mange pas ... zher ner monzh pa ...

Cheers!
Santé! son·tay

Please bring the bill.
Apportez-moi l'addition, s'il vous plaît. a·por·tay·mwa la·dee·syon seel voo play

Numbers – French

1	*un*	un
2	*deux*	der
3	*trois*	trwa
4	*quatre*	ka·trer
5	*cinq*	sungk
6	*six*	sees
7	*sept*	set
8	*huit*	weet
9	*neuf*	nerf
10	*dix*	dees

beer	*bière*	bee·yair
bottle	*bouteille*	boo·tay
bread	*pain*	pun
breakfast	*petit déjeuner*	per·tee day·zher·nay
cheese	*fromage*	fro·mazh
coffee	*café*	ka·fay
cold	*froid*	frwa
dinner	*dîner*	dee·nay
dish	*plat*	pla
egg	*œuf*	erf
food	*nourriture*	noo·ree·tewr
fork	*fourchette*	foor·shet
glass	*verre*	vair
grocery store	*épicerie*	ay·pees·ree
hot	*chaud*	sho
(orange) juice	*jus (d'orange)*	zhew (do·ronzh)
knife	*couteau*	koo·to
local speciality	*spécialité locale*	spay·sya·lee·tay lo·kal
lunch	*déjeuner*	day·zher·nay
main course	*plat principal*	pla prun·see·pal
market	*marché*	mar·shay
milk	*lait*	lay
plate	*assiette*	a·syet
red wine	*vin rouge*	vun roozh
rice	*riz*	ree
salt	*sel*	sel
spoon	*cuillère*	kwee·yair
sugar	*sucre*	sew·krer
tea	*thé*	tay
vegetable	*légume*	lay·gewm
(mineral) water	*eau (minérale)*	o (mee·nay·ral)
white wine	*vin blanc*	vun blong
with/without	*avec/sans*	a·vek/son

Emergencies

Help!
Au secours! o skoor

I'm lost.
Je suis perdu/perdue. zhe swee·pair·dew (m/f)

Leave me alone!
Fichez-moi la paix! fee·shay·mwa la pay

Call a doctor.
Appelez un médecin. a·play un mayd·sun

Call the police.
Appelez la police. a·play la po·lees

I'm ill.
Je suis malade. zher swee ma·lad

Where are the toilets?
Où sont les toilettes? oo son lay twa·let

Shopping & Services

I'd like to buy ...
Je voudrais acheter ... zher voo·dray ash·tay ...

Can I look at it?
Est-ce que je peux le voir? es·ker zher per ler vwar

How much is it?
C'est combien? say kom·byun

It's too expensive.
C'est trop cher. say tro shair

Can you lower the price?
Vous pouvez baisser le prix? voo poo·vay bay·say ler pree

ATM	*guichet automatique de banque*	gee·shay o·to·ma·teek der bonk
internet cafe	*cybercafé*	see·bair·ka·fay
post office	*bureau de poste*	bew·ro der post
tourist office	*office de tourisme*	o·fees der too·rees·mer

Time & Dates

What time is it?
Quelle heure est-il? kel er ay til

It's (eight) o'clock.
Il est (huit) heures. il ay (weet) er

It's half past (10).
Il est (dix) heures et demie. il ay (deez) er ay day·mee

morning	*matin*	ma·tun
afternoon	*après-midi*	a·pray·mee·dee
evening	*soir*	swar
yesterday	*hier*	yair
today	*aujourd'hui*	o·zhoor·dwee
tomorrow	*demain*	der·mun

Transport & Directions

boat	*bateau*	ba·to
bus	*bus*	bews
plane	*avion*	a·vyon
train	*train*	trun

a ... ticket	*un billet ...*	un bee·yay ...
one-way	*simple*	sum·pler
return	*aller et retour*	a·lay ay rer·toor

I want to go to ...
Je voudrais aller à ... zher voo·dray a·lay a ...

At what time does it leave/arrive?
À quelle heure est-ce qu'il part/arrive? a kel er es kil par/a·reev

Does it stop at ...?
Est-ce qu'il s'arrête à ...? es·kil sa·ret a ...

Can you tell me when we get to ...?
Pouvez-vous me dire quand nous arrivons à ...? poo·vay·voo mer deer kon noo za·ree·von a ...

I want to get off here.
Je veux descendre ici. zher ver day·son·drer ee·see

Where's ...?
Où est ...? oo ay ...

What's the address?
Quelle est l'adresse? kel ay la·dres

Can you show me (on the map)?
Pouvez-vous m'indiquer (sur la carte)? poo·vay·voo mun·dee·kay (sewr la kart)

HAUSA

Hausa is spoken by around 40 million people. Most native speakers live in northern Nigeria and southern Niger. It's also spoken in parts of Benin, Burkina Faso, Cameroon, Côte d'Ivoire and Ghana.

Hausa's glottalised consonants (b', d', k', ts' and y'), indicated here by an apostrophe after the letter, are produced by tightening and releasing the space between the vocal cords; for the sounds b' and d', instead of breathing out, you breathe in. The apostrophe before a vowel indicates a glottal stop (like the pause in 'uh-oh').

Hello.	*Sannu.*	san·nu
Goodbye.	*Sai wani lokaci.*	say wa·ni law·ka·chee

Yes.	*I.*	ee
No.	*A'a.*	a'a
Please.	*Don Allah.*	don al·laa
Thank you.	*Na gode.*	naa gaw·dey
Sorry.	*Yi hak'uri.*	yi ha·k'u·ree
Help!	*Taimake ni!*	tai·ma·kyey ni

Do you speak English?
Kana/Kina jin turanci? (m/f) — ka·naa/ki·naa jin too·ran·chee

I don't understand.
Ban gane ba. — ban gaa·ney ba

How much is it?
Kud'insa nawa ne? — ku·d'in·sa na·wa ney

Where are the toilets?
Ina ban d'aki yake? — i·naa ban d'aa·kee yak·yey

1	*d'aya*	d'a·ya
2	*biyu*	bi·yu
3	*uku*	u·ku
4	*hud'u*	hu·d'u
5	*biyar*	bi·yar
6	*shida*	shi·da
7	*bakwai*	bak·wai
8	*takwas*	tak·was
9	*tara*	ta·ra
10	*goma*	gaw·ma

MALAGASY

Malagasy has around 18 million speakers and is the official language of Madagascar.

The pronunciation of Malagasy words is not always obvious from their written form. Unstressed syllables can be dropped and words pronounced in different ways depending on where they fall in a sentence. If you read our pronunciation guides as if they were English, you'll be understood. Note that dz is pronounced as the 'ds' in 'adds'. The stressed syllables are indicated with italics.

Hello.	*Manao ahoana.*	maa·*now* *aa*·hon
Goodbye.	*Veloma.*	ve·*lum*
Yes./No.	*Eny./Tsia.*	e·ni/*tsi*·aa
Please.	*Azafady.*	aa·zaa·*faad*
Thank you.	*Misaotra.*	mi·*sotr*
Sorry.	*Miala tsiny.*	mi·*aa*·laa tsin
Help!	*Vonjeo!*	vun·dze·u

Do you speak English?
Miteny angilisy ve ianao? — mi·*ten* aan·gi·*lis* ve *i*·aa·now

I don't understand.
Tsy azoko. — tsi *aa*·zuk

How much is it?
Ohatrinona? — o·*trin*

Where are the toilets?
Aiza ny trano fivoahana? — *ai*·zaa ni *traa*·nu fi·vu·*aa*·haan

1	*isa/iray*	*i*·saa/*i*·rai
2	*roa*	ru
3	*telo*	tel
4	*efatra*	e·faatr
5	*dimy*	dim
6	*enina*	e·nin
7	*fito*	fit
8	*valo*	vaal
9	*sivy*	siv
10	*folo*	ful

PORTUGUESE

Most sounds in Portuguese are also found in English. The exceptions are the nasal vowels (represented in our pronunciation guides by ng after the vowel), which are pronounced as if you're trying to make the sound through your nose; and the strongly rolled *r* (represented by rr in our pronunciation guides). Also note that the symbol zh sounds like the 's' in 'pleasure'. The stressed syllables are indicated with italics.

Masculine and feminine forms of words are provided in the following phrases where relevant, indicated with 'm' and 'f' respectively.

Basics

Hello.	*Olá.*	o·*laa*
Goodbye.	*Adeus.*	a·de·*oosh*
Excuse me.	*Faz favor.*	faash fa·*vor*
Sorry.	*Desculpe.*	desh·*kool*·pe
Yes./No.	*Sim./Não.*	seeng/nowng
Please.	*Por favor.*	poor fa·*vor*
Thank you.	*Obrigado.* *Obrigada.*	o·bree·*gaa*·doo (m) o·bree·*gaa*·da (f)
You're welcome.	*De nada.*	de *naa*·da

How are you?
Como está? — *ko*·moo shtaa

Fine, and you?
Bem, e você? — beng e vo·*se*

What's your name?
Qual é o seu nome? — kwaal e oo se·oo *no*·me

My name is ...
O meu nome é ... oo *me*·oo *no*·me e ...

Do you speak English?
Fala inglês? *faa*·la eeng·*glesh*

I don't understand.
Não entendo. nowng eng·*teng*·doo

Accommodation

campsite	*parque de campismo*	*paar*·ke de kang·*peezh*·moo
guesthouse	*casa de hóspedes*	*kaa*·za de *osh*·pe·desh
hotel	*hotel*	o·*tel*
youth hostel	*pousada de juventude*	poh·*zaa*·da de zhoo·veng·*too*·de

Do you have a single/double room?
Tem um quarto de solteiro/casal? teng oong *kwaar*·too de sol·*tay*·roo/ka·*zal*

How much is it per night/person?
Quanto custa por noite/pessoa? *kwang*·too *koosh*·ta poor *noy*·te/pe·*so*·a

Is breakfast included?
Inclui o pequeno almoço? eeng·*kloo*·ee oo pe·*ke*·noo aal·*mo*·soo

Eating & Drinking

I'd like (the menu).
Queria (um menu). ke·*ree*·a (oong me·*noo*)

What would you recommend?
O que é que recomenda? oo ke e ke rre·koo·*meng*·da

I don't eat ...
Eu não como ... e·oo nowng *ko*·moo ...

Cheers!
Saúde! sa·*oo*·de

Please bring the bill.
Pode-me trazer a conta. *po*·de·me tra·*zer* a *kong*·ta

beer	*cerveja*	ser·*ve*·zha
bottle	*garrafa*	ga·*rraa*·fa
bread	*pão*	powng
breakfast	*pequeno almoço*	pe·*ke*·noo aal·*mo*·soo
cheese	*queijo*	*kay*·zhoo
coffee	*café*	ka·*fe*
cold	*frio*	*free*·oo
dinner	*jantar*	zhang·*taar*
egg	*ovo*	*o*·voo
food	*comida*	koo·*mee*·da
fork	*garfo*	*gar*·foo

Numbers – Portuguese

1	*um*	oong
2	*dois*	doysh
3	*três*	tresh
4	*quatro*	*kwaa*·troo
5	*cinco*	*seeng*·koo
6	*seis*	saysh
7	*sete*	*se*·te
8	*oito*	*oy*·too
9	*nove*	*no*·ve
10	*dez*	desh

fruit	*fruta*	*froo*·ta
glass	*copo*	*ko*·poo
hot (warm)	*quente*	*keng*·te
juice	*sumo*	*soo*·moo
knife	*faca*	*faa*·ka
lunch	*almoço*	aal·*mo*·soo
main course	*prato principal*	*praa*·too preeng·see·*paal*
market	*mercado*	mer·*kaa*·doo
milk	*leite*	*lay*·te
plate	*prato*	*praa*·too
red wine	*vinho tinto*	*vee*·nyoo *teeng*·too
restaurant	*restaurante*	rresh·tow·*rang*·te
rice	*arroz*	a·*rrosh*
salt	*sal*	saal
spicy	*picante*	pee·*kang*·te
spoon	*colher*	koo·*lyer*
sugar	*açúcar*	a·*soo*·kar
tea	*chá*	shaa
vegetable	*hortaliça*	or·ta·*lee*·sa
vegetarian food	*comida vegetariana*	koo·*mee*·da ve·zhe·ta·ree·*aa*·na
(mineral) water	*água (mineral)*	*aa*·gwa (mee·ne·*raal*)
white wine	*vinho branco*	*vee*·nyoo *brang*·koo
with/without	*com/sem*	kong/seng

Emergencies

Help!	*Socorro!*	soo·*ko*·rroo
Go away!	*Vá-se embora!*	*vaa*·se eng·*bo*·ra

Call ...!	*Chame ...!*	*shaa*·me ...
a doctor	*um médico*	oong *me*·dee·koo
the police	*a polícia*	a poo·*lee*·sya

I'm lost.

Estou perdido.	shtoh per·*dee*·doo (m)
Estou perdida.	shtoh per·*dee*·da (f)

I'm ill.

Estou doente.	shtoh doo·*eng*·te

Where is the toilet?

Onde é a casa de banho?	*ong*·de e a *kaa*·za de *ba*·nyoo

Shopping & Services

I'd like to buy ...

Queria comprar ...	ke·*ree*·a kong·*praar* ...

Can I look at it?

Posso ver?	*po*·soo ver

How much is it?

Quanto custa?	*kwang*·too *koosh*·ta

It's too expensive.

Está muito caro.	shtaa *mweeng*·too *kaa*·roo

Can you lower the price?

Pode baixar o preço?	*po*·de bai·*shaar* oo *pre*·soo

ATM	*caixa automático*	*kai*·sha ow·too·*maa*·tee·koo
internet cafe	*café da internet*	ka·*fe* da eeng·ter·*ne*·te
post office	*correio*	koo·*rray*·oo
tourist office	*escritório de turismo*	shkree·*to*·ryoo de too·*reezh*·moo

Time & Dates

What time is it?

Que horas são?	kee *o*·rash sowng

It's (10) o'clock.

São (dez) horas.	sowng (desh) *o*·rash

Half past (10).

(Dez) e meia.	(desh) e *may*·a

morning	*manhã*	ma·*nyang*
afternoon	*tarde*	*taar*·de
evening	*noite*	*noy*·te

yesterday	*ontem*	*ong*·teng
today	*hoje*	*o*·zhe
tomorrow	*amanhã*	aa·ma·*nyang*

Transport & Directions

boat	*barco*	*baar*·koo
bus	*autocarro*	ow·to·*kaa*·roo
plane	*avião*	a·vee·*owng*
train	*comboio*	kong·*boy*·oo
... ticket	*um bilhete de ...*	oong bee·*lye*·te de ...
one-way	*ida*	*ee*·da
return	*ida e volta*	*ee*·da ee *vol*·ta

I want to go to ...

Queria ir a ...	ke·*ree*·a eer a ...

What time does it leave/arrive?

A que horas sai/chega?	a ke *o*·rash sai/*she*·ga

Does it stop at ...?

Pára em ...?	*paa*·ra eng ...

Please tell me when we get to ...

Por favor avise-me quando chegarmos a ...	poor fa·*vor* a·*vee*·ze·me *kwang*·doo she·*gaar*·moosh a ...

Please stop here.

Por favor pare aqui.	poor fa·*vor* *paa*·re a·*kee*

Where's (the station)?

Onde é (a estação)?	*ong*·de e (a shta·*sowng*)

What's the address?

Qual é o endereço?	kwaal e oo eng·de·*re*·soo

Can you show me (on the map)?

Pode-me mostrar (no mapa)?	*po*·de·me moosh·*traar* (noo *maa*·pa)

SHONA

Shona is spoken by about 11 million people. The vast majority of its speakers are in Zimbabwe, but it's also used in the southern African countries of Mozambique, Botswana and Zambia.

Shona's glottalised consonants, represented as b' and d' in our pronunciation guides, are made by tightening and releasing the space between the vocal cords when you pronounce them. Both sounds are 'implosive', meaning that instead of breathing out to make the sound, you breathe in. Note also that the r is trilled.

Yes.	*Hongu.*	ho·ngoo
No.	*Kwete.*	kwe·te
Please.	*-wo.*	-wo
Thank you.	*Mazviita.*	maa·zvee·ta
Sorry.	*Ndapota.*	nd'aa·po·ta

Do you speak English?

Munotaura chiNgezi here?	moo·no·taa·oo·raa chee·nge·zee he·re

I don't understand.

Handinzvisisi.	haa·ndee·nzvee·see·see

How much is it?

Inoita marii?	ee·o·ee·taa maa·ree·ee

Where are the toilets?
Zvimbudzi zviri kupi? zvee·mboo·dzee zvee·ree koo·pee

Could you help me, please?
Mungandibatsirawo here? moo·ngaa·ndee·b'aa·tsee·raa·wo he·re

1	*-mwe*	-mwe
2	*-viri*	-vee·ree
3	*-tatu*	-taa·too
4	*-na*	-naa
5	*-shanu*	-shaa·noo
6	*-tanhatu*	-taa·nhaa·too
7	*-nomwe*	-no·mwe
8	*-sere*	-se·re
9	*-pfumbamwe*	-pfoo·mbaa·mwe
10	*gumi*	goo·mee

SWAHILI

Swahili, the national language of Tanzania and Kenya, is also the key language of communication in the East African region. Although the number of speakers of Swahili throughout East Africa is estimated to be over 50 million, it's the mother tongue of only about 5 million people.

Most sounds in Swahili have equivalents in English. In our pronunciation guides, dh should be read as the 'th' in 'this'. Note also that in Swahili the sound ng can be found at the start of words, and that Swahili speakers make only a slight distinction between the sounds r and l – instead of the hard 'r', try pronouncing a light 'd'. The stressed syllables are indicated with italics.

Hello. (general)	*Habari?*	ha·*ba*·ree
Goodbye.	*Tutaonana.*	too·ta·oh·*na*·na
Yes.	*Ndiyo.*	n·*dee*·yoh
No.	*Hapana.*	ha·*pa*·na
Please.	*Tafadhali.*	ta·fa·*dha*·lee
Thank you.	*Asante.*	a·*san*·tay
Sorry.	*Pole.*	*poh*·lay
Help!	*Saidia!*	sa·ee·*dee*·a

Do you speak English?
Unasema Kiingereza? oo·na·*say*·ma kee·een·gay·*ray*·za

I don't understand.
Sielewi. see·ay·*lay*·wee

How much is it?
Ni bei gani? ni bay *ga*·nee

Where's the toilet?
Choo kiko wapi? choh *kee*·koh *wa*·pee

1	*moja*	*moh*·ja
2	*mbili*	m·*bee*·lee
3	*tatu*	*ta*·too
4	*nne*	*n*·nay
5	*tano*	*ta*·noh
6	*sita*	*see*·ta
7	*saba*	*sa*·ba
8	*nane*	*na*·nay
9	*tisa*	*tee*·sa
10	*kumi*	*koo*·mee

WOLOF

Wolof is the lingua franca of Senegal and Gambia, where it's spoken by about eight million people. It's also spoken in the neighbouring countries of Mauritania, Mali and Guinea.

Note that in our pronunciation guides, the stressed syllables are in italics. Also, uh is pronounced as the 'a' in 'ago', kh as the 'ch' in the Scottish *loch* and r is trilled.

Hello.	*Salaam aleekum.*	sa·*laam* a·*ley*·kum
Goodbye.	*Mangi dem.*	*maan*·gee dem
Yes.	*Waaw.*	waaw
No.	*Déédéet.*	*dey*·deyt
Please.	*Bu la neexee.*	boo la *ney*·khey
Thank you.	*Jërejëf.*	*je*·re·jef
Sorry.	*Baal ma.*	baal ma
Help!	*Wóoy!*	wohy

Do you speak English?
Ndax dégg nga angale? ndakh deg nguh *an*·ga·ley

I don't understand.
Dégguma. *deg*·goo·ma

How much is it?
Ñaata lay jar? *nyaa*·ta lai jar

Where are the toilets?
Ana wanag wi? a·na *wa*·nak wee

1	*benn*	ben
2	*ñaar*	nyaar
3	*ñett*	nyet
4	*ñeent*	nyeynt
5	*juróom*	*joo*·rohm
6	*juróom benn*	*joo*·rohm ben
7	*juróom ñaar*	*joo*·rohm nyaar
8	*juróom ñett*	*joo*·rohm nyet
9	*juróom ñeent*	*joo*·rohm nyeynt
10	*fukk*	fuk

XHOSA

Xhosa is the most widely distributed indigenous language in South Africa. About six and a half million people speak Xhosa.

In our pronunciation guides, the apostrophe after the consonant (eg k') indicates that the sound is 'spat out' (in Xhosa, only in case of b' the air is sucked in), a bit like combining it with the sound heard in the middle of 'uh-oh'. Xhosa has a series of 'click' sounds as well; they are not distinguished in the following phrases.

Hello.	*Molo.*	*maw*·law
Goodbye.	*Usale ngoxolo.*	u·*saa*·le ngaw·*kaw*·law
Yes.	*Ewe.*	e·*we*
No.	*Hayi.*	haa·*yee*
Please.	*Cela.*	*ke*·laa
Thank you.	*Enkosi.*	e·*nk'aw*·see
Sorry.	*Uxolo.*	u·*aw*·law
Help!	*Uncedo!*	u·*ne*·daw

Do you speak English?
Uyasithetha isingesi? u·yaa·see·*te*·taa ee·see·*nge*·see

I don't understand.
Andiqondi. aa·ndee·*kaw*·ndee

How much is it?
Yimalini? yee·*maa*·li·nee

Where are the toilets?
Ziphi itoylethi? zee·*pee* ee·*taw*·yee·le·tee

In Xhosa, numbers borrowed from English are commonly used and will be understood.

1	*wani*	*waa*·nee
2	*thu*	tu
3	*thri*	tree
4	*fo*	faw
5	*fayifu*	*faa*·yee·fu
6	*siksi*	*seek'*·see
7	*seveni*	se·*ve*·nee
8	*eyithi*	e·*yee*·tee
9	*nayini*	*naa*·yee·nee
10	*teni*	*t'e*·nee

YORUBA

Yoruba is spoken by around 25 million people. It is primarily used as a first language in southwestern Nigeria. There are also Yoruba speakers in Benin, eastern Togo and in Sierra Leone.

Yoruba's nasal vowels, indicated in our pronunciation guides with ng after the vowel, are pronounced as if you're trying to force the sound through the nose.

Hello.	*Pẹlẹ́ ọ.*	kpe·le o
Goodbye.	*Ó dàbọ̀.*	oh da·bo
Yes.	*Bẹ́ẹ̀ni.*	be·e·ni
No.	*Bẹ́ẹ̀kọ́.*	be·e·ko
Please.	*Jọ̀wọ́.*	jo·wo
Thank you.	*Ọṣẹ́.*	oh·shay
Sorry.	*Má bìínú.*	ma bi·i·nu
Help!	*Ẹ ràn mí lọ́wọ́ ọ!*	e rang mi lo·wo o

Do you speak English?
Ṣé ọ ń ṣọ gẹ̀ẹ́sì? shay o n so ge·e·si

I don't understand.
Ẹmi kọ̀ gbọ́. ay·mi koh gbo

How much is it?
Ẹ̀lọ́ ni? ay·loh ni

Where are the toilets?
Ibọ ni ilẹ́ ìgbọ̀nṣẹ̀ wà? i·boh ni i·lay i·gbong·se wa

1	*ọ̀kan*	o·kang
2	*ẹ̀jì*	ay·ji
3	*ẹ̀ta*	e·ta
4	*ẹ̀rin*	e·ring
5	*àrun*	a·rung
6	*ẹ̀fà*	e·fa
7	*ẹ̀jẹ*	ay·jay
8	*ẹ̀jọ*	e·jo
9	*ẹ̀ṣan*	e·sang
10	*ẹ̀wá*	e·wa

ZULU

About 10 million Africans speak Zulu as a first language, most of them in South Africa. It is also spoken in Lesotho and Swaziland.

In our pronunciation guides, b' indicates that the air is sucked in when you pronounce this sound (in Zulu, some other consonants are 'spat out'), a bit like combining it with the sound in the middle of 'uh-oh'. Note also that hl is pronounced as in the Welsh *llewellyn* and dl is like hl but with the vocal cords vibrating. Xhosa has a series of 'click' sounds as well; they are not distinguished in this section.

Hello.
Sawubona. (sg) saa·wu·*b'aw*·naa
Sanibonani. (pl) saa·nee·b'aw·*naa*·nee

Goodbye. (if leaving)
Sala kahle. (sg) saa·laa *gaa*·hle
Salani kahle. (pl) saa·laa·nee *gaa*·hle

Goodbye. (if staying)

Hamba kahle. (sg)	haa·mbaa *gaa*·hle
Hambani kahle. (pl)	haa·mbaa·nee *gaa*·hle

Yes./No.	*Yebo./Cha.*	*ye*·b'aw/kaa
Thank you.	*Ngiyabonga.*	ngee·yaa·*b'aw*·ngaa
Sorry.	*Uxolo.*	u·*kaw*·law

Do you speak English?

Uyasikhuluma isiNgisi? u·yaa·see·ku·lu·maa ee·see·ngee·see

I don't understand.

Angizwa. aa·*ngee*·zwaa

How much is it?

Yimalini? yee·maa·lee·nee

Where are the toilets?

Ziphi izindlu zangasese? zee·pee ee·*zee*·ndlu zaa·ngaa·*se*·se

Could you help me, please?

Ake ungisize/ ningisize. (sg/pl) aa·ge u·ngee·*see*·ze/ nee·ngee·*see*·ze

In Zulu, numbers borrowed from English are commonly used and will be understood.

1	*uwani*	u·*waa*·nee
2	*uthu*	u·*tu*
3	*uthri*	u·*three*
4	*ufo*	u·*faw*
5	*ufayifi*	u·*faa*·yee·fee
6	*usiksi*	u·*seek*·see
7	*usevene*	u·se·*ve*·nee
8	*u-eyithi*	u·e·yeet
9	*unayini*	u·*naa*·yee·nee
10	*utheni*	u·*the*·nee

Behind the Scenes

SEND US YOUR FEEDBACK

We love to hear from travellers – your comments keep us on our toes and help make our books better. Our well-travelled team reads every word on what you loved or loathed about this book. Although we cannot reply individually to postal submissions, we always guarantee that your feedback goes straight to the appropriate authors, in time for the next edition. Each person who sends us information is thanked in the next edition – the most useful submissions are rewarded with a selection of digital PDF chapters.

Visit **lonelyplanet.com/contact** to submit your updates and suggestions or to ask for help. Our award-winning website also features inspirational travel stories, news and discussions.

Note: We may edit, reproduce and incorporate your comments in Lonely Planet products such as guidebooks, websites and digital products, so let us know if you don't want your comments reproduced or your name acknowledged. For a copy of our privacy policy visit lonelyplanet.com/privacy.

OUR READERS

Many thanks to the travellers who used the last edition and wrote to us with helpful hints, useful advice and interesting anecdotes:
Abel Castro, Adelle Fischer, Doerte Bieler, Eric Moyet, Georg Caspary, John Brömstrup, John McCabe, Jonathan Harris, Krishna Gagne, Leire Orduna, Leon Liebenberg, Luke Aldred, Mats Bleikelia, Mike Custance, Paula Boer, Richard Cogswell, Samuel Folkard, Simon Barker, Stef Russell, Thomas Sollacher

AUTHOR THANKS

Simon Richmond

Thanks to Will Gourlay for getting the ball rolling and for Glenn van der Knijff for so ably picking it up and running with it. Also kudos to a superb group of fellow authors who did the hard work on the ground across Africa.

Kate Armstrong

A special thanks to the Raw family and Katie McCarthy for their kindness and ongoing help and to fellow writer, Tom Spurling, for doing the groundwork in Lesotho. Huge thanks to Simon Richmond, Glenn van der Knijff, Will Gourlay, David Carroll and fellow authors.

Stuart Butler

Having covered half-a-dozen countries for this book I have a huge cast of great and good to thank, but I will start with once again thanking my wife, Heather, young son, Jake, and my daughter Grace, who was born as I finished writing up my chapters. Thank you to my various travel companions on the road, Toby Adamson, Harry Gobat, Ben Clift, John Gray and Adrian Savio. Among many in Ethiopia I must thank Abayneh Temesgen, Blen Mandefro, Kate Bradlow, Yasmin Abdulwassie, Tania O'Connor, Cheru Alemu and Shemels. In the sticky forests of the DRC, Republic of Congo and CAR huge thanks to Eric de Lamotte, Olivier in Brazzaville, Balthazar Sieders, Cai Tjeenk Willink, Nick Ray, Eva Luef, Rod Cassidy and family, Michel, Louis Sarno, Louis-Philippe Lévesque, Richard Tshombe, Paul T Telfer, Emma Powell, Charlotte Hill, Emmanuel Munganga, Thomas Breuer, Sylvie Van Malderen and the Italian road builder in the portacabin who gave me a bed for the night and a meal when I got stranded in the forest! At the opposite end of the climatic spectrum thank you to the good people of Sudan and South Sudan and in particular to Musaab Hamid Ahmed, Hany Ajeeb, Midhat Mahir, Rosemary Behan, Thomas of Bahr el Jebel Safaris and Jessica Mottl. Finally, elsewhere in eastern Africa thank you to Charlotte Bourke, Julia Mut, Jeni Stow and Susan Nijiru.

Jean-Bernard Carillet

A huge thanks to everyone who made this trip a pure joy, including Arno, Gautier, Dominique, Julien, Myriam, Najiib, Nigel, Mohammed, Ramadan, Adam, Masso, Baragoïta, the two Houmeds, Dimbio, Nicolas and his team, Vicente and all the travellers I met while on the road. At Lonely Planet, a big thanks to Will, Glenn, Annelies, Brigitte and the carto team for their support. I'm also grateful to Simon Richmond, coordinating author *extraordinaire*. And finally, once again a *gros bisou* to Christine and Eva.

Paul Clammer

There are always too many friends in Morocco to acknowledge, but particular thanks this time to Kerstin Brand in Marrakesh, Robert Johnstone in Fez and Alia Radman for being a hostess for Eid. In Mauritania, big thanks to Melissa Nielson Andersson and Natsuko Sawaya, Cora at Bab Sahara, and to my driver in the Adrar, Jid Moma.

Lucy Corne

Thanks to my mum and dad for first introducing me to this wonderful country and to my husband, Shawn, for finding an excuse to keep us here. Thanks to Kate Armstrong for her KZN tips and to Elmar Neethling and Ed Salomons for all the Durban and Drakensberg insights, to Gary Pnematicatos for bringing me up to speed on Cape Town's nightlife and to my boys for being the best travel companions ever. At Lonely Planet I'd like to say *enkosi* to Simon, Glenn, David, Lucy and Brigitte for their help and support.

Emilie Filou

Thanks to all the travellers, tourism professionals and friends who chipped in with recommendations, shared a meal or a *taxi-brousse* ride and were part of the journey – simply too many to name here. And thank you to my husband Adolfo for putting up with this crazy life.

Mary Fitzpatrick

Many thanks to all those who helped me with this update, especially to Rick, Christopher, Dominic and Gabriel for their company, patience and good humour.

Michael Grosberg

Thanks to all those who welcomed me with open arms and shared their insight, experience and knowledge of Zambia: Amy Waldman, Oli Dreike, Andy Hogg, Jess and Ade Salmon, Alec Cole and Emma Wood, Tyrone McKeith, Linda van Heerden, Greg Heltzer, Riccardo Garbaccio, Meegan Treen, Natalie Clark, Adrian Penny, Lynda and Rick Schulz, Glenn Evans, Sheila Donnelly, Ian Stevenson (who let me 'co-spot' on an anti-poaching flight over the Lower Zambezi), Mindy Roberts, Nathalie Zanoli and Samrat Datta.

Anthony Ham

Andy Raggett was an invaluable source of information at all stages of the journey. Thanks also to Mike Romeo, Will Gourlay, Alan Murphy, Glyn Maude, Keitumetse Ngaka, Olefile Sebogiso, Nick Jacobsen, Monika Schiess and to Jan and Cleo in Khutse. Special thanks to Jan and Ron, and to my three girls Marina, Carlota and Valentina: *Os quiero con todo mi corazon*.

Trent Holden

For Uganda thanks to Tim Bewer, Anne-Marie Weeden, Robert Brierley, Debbie Willis, Cam McLeay, UWA, Jimmy, Jason, Miha, Fred, and John Hunwick. In Zimbabwe and Vic Falls, I'm indebted to Joy in Vic Falls, and Kim in Livingstone, plus Sally Wynn, Choice Mushunje, Gordon Adams, Ann Bruce, Jane High, Val from Bulawayo, and a big sing out to the Seremwe brothers (James and George). Finally huge thanks to the production team, particularly David Carroll, Will Gourlay and Glenn van der Knijff. Lots of love to my family and friends.

Jessica Lee

My heartfelt thanks to the people of Egypt who always make travelling in Egypt such a joy. I'd like to especially give a huge *alfa shuk* to Hoda Afifi, Hossam Moussa, Dan and Reham Southern-Tawfik and Salama Abd Rabbo.

Nana Luckham

At Lonely Planet, my thanks go to Will Gourlay, Brigitte Ellemor, Glenn van der Knijff, Simon Richmond, Adrian Persoglia and Bruce Evans. Thanks also to Patrick Smith, Reuben Swift and Yaa Yeboah.

Tom Masters

A huge debt of thanks to Rosemary Masters, who came to Africa for the first time in her sixties and proved to be an amazing travelling companion, never losing her sense of humour despite illness, bad weather and lots of long journeys. Enormous thanks also to Niall Cowley, whose company and high spirits in Cameroon were unforgettable, whether driving down the worst roads I've ever been on, befriending the mayor of Kumba, or surviving a night in a hotel in Wum without first eating fish from a plastic bag. Grids!

Alan Murphy

A big thanks to my travel companion and friend Smitzy for his patience, advice and adventurous spirit (and for not getting further traffic infringements). In Namibia there are too many to thank but special mention to Almuth Styles in Swakopmund whose assistance was much appreciated. Lastly, thanks to the numerous CEs at LP that I worked with.

Anja Mutić

Obrigada, Hoji, for coming along for the ride and making it more fun. A huge thanks to Samira and her crowd in Mindelo, who made me fall in love with the city. Special thanks go to Cristiano and Larissa on Boa Vista, Kate on Santo Antão and Patti for being a great connector. Finally, to my always-laughing mum and the inspiring memory of my father.

Caroline Sieg

Thanks to everyone who took the time to share their tips with me and for the countless, friendly conversations at waterside bars across The Gambia and Senegal. And a very special *merci* to Gilles in Dakar for some sensational nights out on the town.

Helena Smith

Helena Smith would like to thank all the warm and open people she met in Kenya. Especially Violet and Jonathan in Mombasa; Elias who helped for hours when she got lost in Nyali; driver Leonard for being cool under the pressure of traffic and storms; the Maasai people of Ewangan village for their unforgettable welcome, particularly James, Shinka, Taiyio, Oloiboni, John Tubula, Mpoe, Kaitikei, Charles and Geoffrey; plus Dea, Lisa, Linda and Christine in Naivasha. Also to Bahati, who was more fun to travel with than was strictly necessary.

Dean Starnes

It would be wrong not to acknowledge the legacy of work from previous editions, the assistance from my fellow authors and the hard work by the team at Lonely Planet. The company of my wife, Debbie Starnes, vastly improved long trips and thanks to the starry African nights we returned home with a baby on board. As always, thanks to my Mum and Dad for their unfailing support.

Kate Thomas

A big *obrigada* to everyone who helped out in the *terra sabi* (delicious land) of Guinea-Bissau. Especially Matt Boslego, Holly Pickett (for her company on the tough road to Varela), Brian King, Ze Manel, Amelia 'Betty' Gomes, Aicha and Bassiro Djalo, the Mama Djombos and the extended Djalo-King clan. Thanks to Lassana Cassama, Gorka Gamarra and, on the island of Bolama, to Felipa and to Queba Dabo for such a warm welcome. In lovely Liberia, special thanks to Othello Garblah, Saad Karim (for his company and couch), Saki Golafale, taximan Alpha, Chawki Bsaibes, Jamal and all the wonderful people I've known in six years' worth of time and trips to a country that I consider home. In Sierra Leone, Fid Thompson's help was invaluable. Thank you Fid! Shout-outs also to Koumba Jalloh, Aminata Seye, Nelson Gbarpor and Faty Serif. On the road in Côte d'Ivoire, thanks to Hortense and Franck, Amie 'Rainbow', David Diallo and Tessa, for fun had on our foodie tours of Abidjan.

Richard Waters

My special thanks to Rob and Lindsay McConaghy and their excellent team who provided specialist advice every step of the way; Chris Badger, Zane, and Emma and Chris; Gaye Russell, Kate Webb and my Malawian pal Gareth Watson for keeping me company. Thanks also to James Lightfoot for his valuable help. Finally my gratitude to the people of Malawi who remain in adversity among the most decent I've ever met.

Donna Wheeler

Much gratitude to my Tunisian and Algerian hosts and friends, along with many strangers, for great generosity with your time and knowledge. Special mention goes to, in Tunisia, Marouane and Sondos, Amel and Patrick, Amel, Tarek, Salma, Raaba, Zouheir and Erika, Isabelle and, last but not least, Vittorio, and to Ahcicene, Loute and Sami in Algeria. To my family, Joe, Rumer and Biba Guario, thank you for again putting up with the absences and obsessions with such good grace.

Vanessa Wruble

Many thanks to my excellent research assistant David Idagu, the amazingly generous Lemi Ghariokwu, Rikki Stein (and Captain!), Yeni, Femi, and Seun Kuti (and Osaro, Shigogo, Patches and Vibes), Obi Asika, Osahon Akpata, Azu Nwagbogu and AAF, Chike Nwagbogu Nike Davies-Okundaye, Robin Campbell, everyone at Pandrillus, Glenna Gordon, Ruth McDowall, Raphael Ayukotang, Vincent Taibi (in absentia), Lost In Lagos, and the dude who took me to the pharmacy.

ACKNOWLEDGMENTS

Climate map data adapted from Peel MC, Finlayson BL & McMahon TA (2007) 'Updated World Map of the Köppen-Geiger Climate Classification', *Hydrology and Earth System Sciences*, 11, 163344.

Cover photograph: Burchell's zebras, Etosha National Park, Namibia, Steve Coleman/Getty Images.

THIS BOOK

This 13th edition of Lonely Planet's *Africa* guidebook was researched and written by Simon Richmond (coordinating author), Kate Armstrong, Stuart Butler, Jean-Bernard Carillet, Paul Clammer, Lucy Corne, Emilie Filou, Mary Fitzpatrick, Michael Grosberg, Anthony Ham, Trent Holden, Jessica Lee, Nana Luckham, Tom Masters, Alan Murphy, Anja Mutić, Nick Ray, Caroline Sieg, Helena Smith, Dean Starnes, Kate Thomas, Richard Waters, Donna Wheeler and Vanessa Wruble, and Jane Cornwell wrote the African Music chapter. The previous edition was coordinated by Anthony Ham.

This guidebook was commissioned in Lonely Planet's Melbourne office, and produced by the following:

Commissioning Editors William Gourlay, Glenn van der Knijff

Coordinating Editor Tasmin Waby

Senior Cartographer Jennifer Johnston

Coordinating Layout Designer Jacqui Saunders

Managing Editors Brigitte Ellemor, Bruce Evans

Managing Layout Designers Chris Girdler, Jane Hart

Managing Cartographer Adrian Persoglia

Assisting Editors Penny Cordner, Victoria Harrison, Briohny Hooper, Kate James, Anne Mulvaney, Charlotte Orr, Gabrielle Stefanos, Jeanette Wall, Kate Whitfield, Amanda Williamson, Simon Williamson

Assisting Cartographers Valeska Canas, Xavier Di Toro, Julie Dodkins

Cover Research Naomi Parker

Internal Image Research Kylie McLaughlin

Language Content Branislava Vladisavljevic

Thanks to Anita Banh, Nigel Chin, Katie Connolly, Laura Crawford, Ryan Evans, Larissa Frost, Martin Heng, Genesys India, Jouve India, Bella Li, Darren O'Connell, Trent Paton, Wibowo Rusli, Dianne Schallmeiner, Kerrianne Southway, Geoff Stringer, Gerard Walker, Wendy Wright

Index

C

D

E

Map Pages **000**
Photo Pages **000**

Map Pages **000**
Photo Pages **000**

Map Pages **000**
Photo Pages **000**

N

Q

R

S

T

U

V

W

X

Y

Z

Map Legend

Sights
- Beach
- Buddhist
- Castle
- Christian
- Hindu
- Islamic
- Jewish
- Monument
- Museum/Gallery
- Ruin
- Winery/Vineyard
- Zoo
- Other Sight

Activities, Courses & Tours
- Diving/Snorkelling
- Canoeing/Kayaking
- Skiing
- Surfing
- Swimming/Pool
- Walking
- Windsurfing
- Other Activity/ Course/Tour

Sleeping
- Sleeping
- Camping

Eating
- Eating

Drinking
- Drinking
- Cafe

Entertainment
- Entertainment

Shopping
- Shopping

Information
- Bank
- Embassy/ Consulate
- Hospital/Medical
- Internet
- Police
- Post Office
- Telephone
- Toilet
- Tourist Information
- Other Information

Transport
- Airport
- Border Crossing
- Bus
- Cable Car/ Funicular
- Cycling
- Ferry
- Monorail
- Parking
- Petrol Station
- Taxi
- Train/Railway
- Tram
- Underground Train Station
- Other Transport

Routes
- Tollway
- Freeway
- Primary
- Secondary
- Tertiary
- Lane
- Unsealed Road
- Plaza/Mall
- Steps
- Tunnel
- Pedestrian Overpass
- Walking Tour
- Walking Tour Detour
- Path

Geographic
- Hut/Shelter
- Lighthouse
- Lookout
- Mountain/Volcano
- Oasis
- Park
- Pass
- Picnic Area
- Waterfall

Population
- Capital (National)
- Capital (State/Province)
- City/Large Town
- Town/Village

Boundaries
- International
- State/Province
- Disputed
- Regional/Suburb
- Marine Park
- Cliff
- Wall

Hydrography
- River, Creek
- Intermittent River
- Swamp/Mangrove
- Reef
- Canal
- Water
- Dry/Salt/ Intermittent Lake
- Glacier

Areas
- Beach/Desert
- Cemetery (Christian)
- Cemetery (Other)
- Park/Forest
- Sportsground
- Sight (Building)
- Top Sight (Building)

Dean Starnes

Burundi, Rwanda Dean first backpacked Africa in 2004 and has since returned multiple times, coauthoring the *Ethiopia* (4th edition), *Kenya* (8th edition) and *East Africa* (9th edition) guides. No stranger to off-the-map travel, he has also coauthored guides to Papua New Guinea, Kyrgyzstan and Mongolia. When he's not writing for Lonely Planet, Dean lives in New Zealand with his wife, their new baby and his wife's cat (the cat's not thrilled about that arrangement). His website, www.deanstarnes.com, features photography and stories about his wayfaring ways.

Kate Thomas Côte d'Ivoire, Guinea-Bissau, Liberia, Mali, Sierra Leone After Kate's first trip to Liberia in 2007, she was so taken by the destination that she left her job on the foreign desk of a national newspaper and moved there for two years. Since then she's combined travel writing with reporting on Africa, covering the fall-out from conflicts in Mali and Libya, and exploring rainforests, cities and lonely islands. While researching this book, she ate oysters on the beaches of Guinea-Bissau and experienced music and dancing, thirsty taxi rides through walls of heat, hungry political debate and popped tyres. After six years in the region, Kate is now mostly based in the seaside city of Dakar.

Richard Waters

Malawi Richard is an award-winning travel journalist and regularly works for publications including the *Independent*, *Sunday Times*, *Wanderlust* and *National Geographic Traveller*. He lives with his fiancé and two children in the Cotswolds.

Donna Wheeler

Algeria, Tunisia Donna was the coordinating author of Lonely Planet's last *Tunisia* guide. She has a long-term fascination with French history and decolonisation, not to mention a thing for Roman mosaics and Hafsid columns, beaches and palmeraies. Donna has written on French, Italian and Australian destinations for Lonely Planet and also publishes on contemporary art, architecture and design, history and food in a range of publications; she is also a creative consultant and travel experience planner.

Vanessa Wruble

Nigeria When not writing for Lonely Planet, Vanessa runs Okayafrica, a website and lifestyle company started by the legendary hip-hop band The Roots, which showcases new African music, art and culture. She has previously been a freelance writer, a humanitarian-aid worker, a TV correspondent and producer, an interactive artist and, of course, a world traveller. She holds two (somewhat useless) master's degrees (Psychology and Interactive Media), and dreams of living on a tropical beach. You'll currently find her in Brooklyn.

Contributing Authors

Jane Cornwell is an Australian-born, UK-based journalist, author and broadcaster who wrote the African Music chapter. After graduating with a master's degree in anthropology, she left for London. She currently writes about arts, books and music – most notably world music – for a range of UK and antipodean publications, including the *Times*, *Evening Standard* and the *Australian* newspaper. She regularly travels about the planet interviewing world musicians.

Nick Ray

Nick Ray wrote the Lubumbashi section of Democratic Republic of Congo. A Londoner of sorts, Nick comes from Watford, the sort of town that makes you want to travel. He lives in Cambodia with his wife Kulikar and his young children Julian and Belle. He has written for countless Lonely Planet guidebooks, including Lonely Planet's *East Africa* and *Zambia, Mozambique & Malawi*, plus the *Cambodia, Vietnam* and *Laos* books.

Jessica Lee

Egypt After backpacking extensively around Africa, Asia and Latin America, Jess moved to Egypt in 2007 and ended up living there for five years, leading adventure tours around the country before swapping to write full-time. Having climbed Mt Sinai more than 50 times, being hit by a bus in Cairo, and witnessing 2011's incredible political upheavals firsthand, she still never tires of the land of the pharaohs and considers it her second home.

Nana Luckham

Angola, Central African Republic, Chad, Equatorial Guinea, Guinea, Niger, São Tomé & Príncipe Born in Tanzania to a Ghanaian mother and an English father, Nana started life criss-crossing Africa by plane and bumping along the roughest of roads. After working as an editor in London and a UN press officer in New York, she became a full-time travel writer, and has hauled her backpack all over Africa researching guidebooks to destinations such as Algeria, Kenya, South Africa, Malawi, Ghana and Benin.

Tom Masters

Cameroon, Gabon Tom is a Berlin-based writer and photographer whose work has taken him to some of the strangest and most challenging countries on earth. Having covered Liberia, Niger and Algeria for the last edition of this book, Tom was very happy to head to the equator for the relative ease of Cameroon and Gabon this time round, even inviting his mother along to enjoy some safari time in the Loango National Park. Tom can be found online at www.tommasters.net.

Alan Murphy

Namibia Alan remembers falling under Southern Africa's ambient spell after bouncing around in the rear of a bakkie on the way from Johannesburg airport in 1999. Since then he has been back numerous times for Lonely Planet and travelled widely throughout the region, including this trip to Namibia. This was Alan's third time visiting Namibia, a country custom-built for road trips with landscapes that never cease to inspire. Alan lives with his wife in the Yarra Valley outside Melbourne, which he wishes was just a touch closer to Melbourne airport.

Anja Mutić

Cape Verde Croatian-born, New York–based Anja swayed to the infectious rhythms of Cape Verdean music long before she ever visited the archipelago. For this book, she spent several weeks braving prop planes, scary volcano climbs and rough ocean crossings to find the islands' best-kept secrets. She left the country charmed with the *morabeza* (hospitality) of its people and finally understood *sodade*, the bittersweet longing that Cesária Évora sang about. Anja is online at www.everthenomad.com.

Caroline Sieg

The Gambia, Senegal Caroline Sieg is a half-Swiss, half-American writer, editor and digital content manager based in Berlin. Her relationship with Africa began when she first visited Senegal years ago and fell in love with *mbalax* music and the architecture of Saint-Louis – she was delighted to return, wear her travel writer's cap and cover it for Lonely Plannet.

Helena Smith

Kenya Helena lived in Malawi as a kid, and was very happy to return to Africa to update the Kenya chapter of this book. When not travelling, she lives in London and blogs about food and her community at eathackney.com.

Paul Clammer

Mauritania, Morocco Paul has contributed to more than 25 Lonely Planet guidebooks, including several editions of *Morocco*, where he's also worked as a tour guide. He arrived in Nouakchott, for his second stint as Mauritania author, just days before the accidental shooting of the president, though these events are in no way connected. Find him at paulclammer.com, or on Twitter as @paulclammer.

Lucy Corne

South Africa Since she first visited South Africa in 2002, Lucy has been hooked and has returned on six occasions, spending time in more than 200 towns across the country. For this book she had the not-so-unpleasant tasks of 'researching' Wild Coast beaches, reacquainting herself with the Kruger, exploring culinary Cape Town and delving into some Drakensberg hikes. Lucy currently lives in Cape Town where she writes on travel and beer: www.lucycorne.com.

Emilie Filou

Burkina Faso, Ghana, Madagascar Emilie first travelled to Africa aged eight to visit her grandparents who had taken up a late career opportunity in Mali. More visits ensued, including an epic family holiday in Togo and Benin, the highlight of which was the beautiful and amusingly named Grand Popo ('big poo' in French – simply hilarious when you're aged 10). Emilie is now a freelance journalist specialising in business and development issues in Africa. Emilie also wrote the Environment chapter. Her website is www.emiliefilou.com; she tweets at @EmilieFilou.

Mary Fitzpatrick

Mozambique, Tanzania A travel writer for more than 15 years, Mary has lived, worked and travelled extensively in both Mozambique and Tanzania, and speaks Portuguese and Swahili. In addition to authoring many Lonely Planet Africa titles, Mary also writes for various newspapers and magazines, focussing on Africa. She is currently based in Tanzania.

Michael Grosberg

Zambia With a valuable philosophy degree in hand and business experience on a small Pacific island, Michael moved to Durban, South Africa, where he wrote about political violence and helped train newly elected government officials. He also found time to travel all over Southern Africa, including forays into Zambia. Later, during his years in graduate school and teaching in New York City, he fantasised about returning to the region, which he has been fortunate to do on numerous Lonely Planet assignments and for other publications.

Anthony Ham

Botswana, Libya Anthony has been travelling around Africa for more than a decade. A writer and photographer, his past Lonely Planet guidebooks include *Kenya*, *Botswana & Namibia*, *Africa*, *Libya* and three previous editions of *West Africa*. Anthony has written and photographed for magazines and newspapers around the world, among them *Travel Africa* and *Africa Geographic*. When he's not in Africa, Anthony divides his time between Madrid and Melbourne, where he lives with his wife and two daughters.

Trent Holden

Uganda, Zimbabwe As a regular visitor to Africa, Trent rates Uganda and Zimbabwe as his two favourites on the continent. His passion extends beyond the obvious appeal of amazing wildlife encounters with mountain gorillas and the Big Five, to its varied landscapes, world-class adventure sports and its good-natured people. Trent has worked on 15 books for Lonely Planet, and currently resides in Melbourne, Australia. When not travelling he works as a freelance editor, and writes about music and food.

OUR STORY

A beat-up old car, a few dollars in the pocket and a sense of adventure. In 1972 that's all Tony and Maureen Wheeler needed for the trip of a lifetime – across Europe and Asia overland to Australia. It took several months, and at the end – broke but inspired – they sat at their kitchen table writing and stapling together their first travel guide, *Across Asia on the Cheap*. Within a week they'd sold 1500 copies. Lonely Planet was born.

Today, Lonely Planet has offices in Melbourne, London and Oakland, with more than 600 staff and writers. We share Tony's belief that 'a great guidebook should do three things: inform, educate and amuse'.

OUR WRITERS

Simon Richmond

Coordinating Author Simon has been hooked on Africa since first visiting in 2001 to coordinate Lonely Planet's *South Africa, Lesotho & Swaziland* guide and the Cape Town city guide. He's returned for every edition since. Other travels in Africa include *Morocco*. Coordinating this guide has inspired him to boot a Cape-to-Cairo overland adventure swiftly up his bucket list of travel must-dos. An award-winning writer and photographer Simon has written scores of titles for Lonely Planet and other publishers as well as contributing features to magazines and newspapers around the world. Follow his travels at simonrichmond.com.

Kate Armstrong

Lesotho, Swaziland Kate was bitten by the Africa bug when she lived and worked in Mozambique, and returns to Southern Africa regularly. For this edition she danced her way through Swaziland, got her car bogged (more than once) and enjoyed hanging out for a day with some black rhinos. When she's not eating, hiking and talking her way around parts of Africa, Europe and South America, she's a freelance writer for newspapers and magazines around the world, from wherever she's living at the time. For more of Kate's adventures, see www.katearmstrong.com.au

Stuart Butler

Congo, Democratic Republic of Congo, Ethiopia, South Sudan, Sudan With £200 in his pocket and three months to spare, Stuart, who hails from southwest England, first hit Africa after hitching his way across Europe to Morocco in the early '90s. As soon as he arrived he was smitten, and he has since returned numerous times, travelling through every region of the continent and more than half the countries. The highlight of researching this book? A canoe ride down a jungle river between Congo and the Central African Republic! When not in Africa, Stuart lives on the beautiful beaches of southwest France with his wife and young son.

Jean-Bernard Carillet

Benin, Djibouti, Eritrea, Somaliland, Togo A Paris-based journalist and photographer, Jean-Bernard has travelled the breadth and length of Africa for more than two decades and has been thoroughly enlightened by 23 of its amazing countries. Highlights while researching for this edition included investigating voodoo culture in Benin, exploring the far-flung provinces of Somaliland, diving in Djibouti and visiting traditional villages in Togo. Jean-Bernard's wanderlust has taken him to six continents, inspiring numerous articles and some 30 guidebooks, including Lonely Planet's *West Africa* and *Ethiopia, Djibouti & Somaliland*.

OVER PAGE MORE WRITERS

Published by Lonely Planet Publications Pty Ltd
ABN 36 005 607 983
13th edition – Nov 2013
ISBN 978 1 74179 896 8

10 9 8 7 6 5 4 3 2 1
Printed in Singapore

TELL ME YOU'RE MINE

By Elisabeth Norebäck

Tell Me You're Mine